International Encyclopedia of the SOCIAL SCIENCES

Volumes 5 and 6
Complete and Unabridged

International Encyclopedia of the SOCIAL SCIENCES

DAVID L. SILLS EDITOR

VOLUME 5

The Macmillan Company & The Free Press, New York
COLLIER-MACMILLAN PUBLISHERS, LONDON

E

[CONTINUED]

ELECTRONS

I
THE FUNCTIONS OF ELECTIONS

Elections may be regarded as one procedure for aggregating preferences of a particular kind.

Liberal democratic theories attribute special authority to the amalgamation of the expressed preferences of individuals through recognized procedures. They reject the idea that social choice can be made by some sort of group mind or interpersonal entity built out of individuals but different from them in kind. They also reject the idea that social choice is a mere illusion, that is, the notion that what appears to be a choice between alternatives is really no more than the consequence of the interplay of various forces.

But it has been argued, in the attack on welfare economics (Arrow 1951; Little 1950), that the preference schedules of individuals cannot be amalgamated without paradox except on one of two conditions: either through the operation of a market or through the compliance of individual participants with decisions by a recognized authority. Liberal theories would certainly accept the idea that in certain cases to be defined social choice is made and should be made through the market or by relying on authority. But they postulate also that there are and should be public decisions in which citizens make an explicit choice between alternative courses of public action. This can be done in practice only through forms of procedure generally accepted as binding within the political society.

Voting is one of these procedures but not the only one. It is relevant to quote an authority on the practice of the Dominican order in the Middle Ages (Galbraith 1925, p. 33) to the effect that choice might be made by vote, by explicit agreement after negotiation, or "as if by the inspiration of God." Certainly one finds everywhere, even in the most developed societies, choice by bargaining between factions and choice by acclamation, and there may be other procedures as well. It appears, however, that in "liberal" societies voting is held in reserve as a procedure possessing special authority within the group, organization, or state. Conversely, elections are by no means the only occasion for procedure by vote. Voting on propositions is of great practical importance in many different social and political situations, and it raises similar problems of formal analysis (Black 1958).

Voting in nationwide elections has a position of special importance in Western democracies. Its authority is strengthened because similar procedures are used for social choice in many institutions, large and small, public and private, throughout the society. (It is not greatly weakened by the existence of formal paradoxes of voting, even though these anomalies are of some tactical importance to groups seeking victory for their own interests.) This predominance has led to the export of voting in elections to countries where voting procedure has not historically possessed the same social authority as in the West: countries of the Soviet bloc on the one hand and developing countries on the other. This may give rise to situations in which the procedure exists but the element of choice does not.

Definition of elections

Thus, it is not always easy to answer the question, What is a *real* election?—and it may be useful to attempt a formal definition. What follows is based on English usage of political terms and may not have general validity, but it will serve to indicate important points for discussion.

One requires, first, the concept of recognized positions or roles ("offices") which confer certain powers and duties within an organization. Individuals may be assigned to office either by choice or by a method independent of choice, such as a rule of inheritance, or seniority, or regulated trial by competition. Next, a general concept is needed, such as "to choose a man for a job" or perhaps "to decide between candidates for a job." Within this concept, one must distinguish among "electing," "appointing," and "co-opting" a man. In English each word has overtones of political evaluation. "Election" (provided it is "free") would be deemed "democratic" and therefore good, but for certain positions only. "Appointment" would be regarded as "patronage" that tends to increase the power of the patron, except insofar as it is hedged by rules specifying the field of "qualified" candidates. "Co-option" smacks of oligarchy, the self-perpetuation of a ruling group, unless similarly regulated.

On this basis election might be defined as *a form of procedure, recognized by the rules of an organization, whereby all or some of the members of the organization choose a smaller number of persons or one person to hold office of authority in the organization.*

This definition raises a number of points. (1) It attempts to embrace both formal procedure and social significance—both "rules" and "choice." Ideally, both elements should be present in an election. To mark a ballot paper and drop it in a ballot box is not "electing" unless the actor "chooses" in some socially significant sense. But equally a choice is not a "vote in an election" unless the chooser conforms to the specified legal procedure. J. L. Austin made the same point (1961; 1962) when he said that "I vote for Mr. A" is not a statement but a verbal act or performative utterance and that the same act can be achieved without words where this is the proper procedure. Nevertheless, it may be convenient to use the word "election" for something that falls short of such completeness; for instance, where procedure is followed but no choice is present, or where there is a sig-

nificant element of choice without close conformity to a socially recognized procedure (Akzin 1960).

(2) The rather loose word "organization" is chosen here deliberately. The word "election" is not used only for "state" elections to a hierarchy of public bodies. Indeed, it could be maintained that state elections are effective only where electoral procedure is regarded as a usual procedure throughout the society and is therefore written into the rules of all sorts of nonpublic bodies, such as business companies, trade unions, free churches, sports clubs, and so on. Nor would it do to replace "an organization" by "a society." This might imply that a voter can choose only within his society, whereas multiple membership of overlapping organizations is characteristic of complex societies, and one man may be a voter in many different capacities and under different rule systems.

(3) Two phrases in the definition—"the rules of an organization" and "the members of an organization choose"—refer to fundamental conceptual problems in social science. All that need be said here is that ordinary language about elections deals with persons acting within systems of ethical norms and legal procedures. It is possible to reject this language, as would happen if either economic determinism or behaviorism were strictly applied in social science. Such studies might have substantial predictive value in relation to electoral behavior, but they would leave unanswered some fundamental questions about what men think they are doing when they participate in elections.

(4) The word "office" implies a position designated by the same system of rules that determines the electoral procedure. The general problem is that in all social systems persons must somehow be linked to offices; election is one of many different procedures used to ensure legal succession to office in different organizations and societies.

(5) It remains to distinguish election from appointment or co-option. There are ambiguities in usage here. For instance, fellows of a college would use the word "elect" both for choosing a master and for choosing a junior colleague; critics of the college system might accept the former usage but would describe the latter as "co-option." Political advantage may be drawn from these ambiguities at various levels of political debate; in England, at least, "election" is a good word, "patronage" is a bad word, and "co-option" lies in between. This usage suggests the following distinctions:

(*a*) In an election the choosers are a relatively numerous body. Choice by one voter would, of course, be an appointment. But how many choosers are needed to make an election?

(*b*) There is a question of proportion as well as of absolute number. If ten choosers voted to fill one office, one might call it election; if they filled 100 offices, one would tend to call it appointment (or even patronage). But once again there is no sharp point of division.

(*c*) There is a question of the relationship between the choosers and the office to be filled. A person co-opted would be a colleague; a person appointed would be a subordinate, even though he might exercise great discretionary power; a person elected would hold an office of authority, which might include authority over those who elected him.

(*d*) It may be said that when electing, the voters act independently of one another and more or less at the same time, whereas an appointing body acts in consultation, with each member sharing in the deliberation and expressing his point of view in turn until a conclusion is reached (Akzin 1960). This is a very important problem in the study of political development, but it seems to be a distinction between voters and councilors, rather than between election and appointment. Deliberative procedure in council is very widespread in human societies at all stages; under some circumstances (which have nowhere been seriously studied) the device of voting is used to bring issues to a conclusion. But election does not inevitably entail voting; in certain societies the proper procedure for election is by council, in others by acclamation, and in yet others by voting.

Historical development

Elections first took a central place in politics in the Greek city-states of the eastern Mediterranean in the fifth and sixth centuries B.C. There has been no systematic study of elections in societies independent of this Western tradition; certainly, traces are to be found elsewhere, but it does not seem that elections have played a central part in other societies. In the following discussion it has been assumed that electoral procedures can usefully be studied historically in terms of the diffusion of a social pattern from a single source and its modification in a great variety of situations. Further, it is assumed that these procedures correspond functionally to certain general social needs, which are particularly marked in literate, technological, and mobile societies; hence they have periodically reappeared, after setbacks, in new forms in new corners of Western society. Finally, it is assumed that where these procedures meet no social needs they may be retained as forms but are filled with a new content.

The heroic age.   The poems of Homer reflect a state of society in which rule was by kings whose position was conspicuously unlike that of the "Oriental despots" of the river valley civilizations with which they came in contact. The evidence of the mythological and epic narratives is difficult to use, but it suggests a situation roughly parallel to cases found in mobile African societies where the king, although drawn from a royal lineage, emerges as leader by a process which may include competition, conciliar election, and acclamation by the people. Clearly the leader of the war coalition, Agamemnon, had attained his precarious eminence among other kings by a process of this kind. Analogies can be drawn from Tacitus' account of the Germans and from the world of Teutonic, Scandinavian, and Icelandic epics.

The Greek democracies.   The epic period of tribal mobility was succeeded by one of peasant agriculture tempered by growing commercial activity and emigration to colonies overseas. From this situation emerged the strife between the well-born and the people, which affected Greek ideas and practice about political institutions almost everywhere. Where this strife was intense, Greek elections assumed new forms, either through a complete popular victory or through attempts at compromise.

We are primarily concerned not with voting on measures in popular assemblies but with the choice of persons to fill offices of authority. Two points are of general importance. First, in voting on propositions in the assembly of the citizens the rule was apparently that of individual voting by show of hands ($\chi\epsilon\iota\rho\sigma\tau\sigma\nu\epsilon\hat{\iota}\nu$). Use was also made of written votes (in the procedure of ostracism) and of ballots in the form of pebbles ($\psi\hat{\eta}\phi\sigma\iota$)—hence, psephology. There was at times a leader of the assembly who held his informal position (for example, Pericles, Cleon, Demosthenes) because of fairly stable majority support. But holders of certain legally recognized offices (in particular, archons and generals) were elected by nonlocal constituencies known as tribes ($\phi\nu\lambda\acute{a}\iota$), which were held to have been instituted deliberately so as to cut across local divisions of interest within Attica. The number of voters in each tribe must have differed a good deal.

Second, the principle of election was accepted somewhat grudgingly in Athenian democratic theory; it infringed the principle of equality among citizens, and it was dangerous because it opened the way to power for ambitious, attractive, and well-trained young men of the old families (for example, Alcibiades) and equally for ambitious men of the people who were prepared to perpetuate their electoral victory by force (the common pattern of Greek "tyranny"). The orthodox principle was that citizens should hold offices of authority in rotation, the order to be determined by lot; this was the practice for the Council of 500 and its monthly committees, which maintained continuity in the control of public business, and also for the selection of juries (methods of "balloting" for juries are described in great detail by Aristotle, *Politeia athenaiōn*, chapters 63–66). Similar institutions were common in early English and American practice, and rotation in office is still quite usual in small voluntary societies. But there has been no modern discussion of the relation between the principles of rotation in office and that of election by vote. It is notable, however, that in general the Athenians used voting for elections to offices requiring special skills, such as military leadership, whereas in Western countries voting is now used to fill offices of a representative character, for which the Athenians used the lot; offices requiring special skills are now generally filled by appointment from a field determined by specified professional qualifications.

The Roman republic. Even under the republic the Romans never accepted the principle of "one man, one vote." Decision in legislation and in the choice of the principal officials was by a plurality of "centuries" or by a plurality of "tribes": within each of these constituencies one man, one vote prevailed, but the units varied in size. It was tactically important that each of them had some local basis, but locality was not decisive in their composition.

The medieval church. The tradition of ancient elections was preserved in the church rather than in the state. It continued unbroken in the Roman Catholic church, but many national and nonconformist churches also developed the use of elections as the basis of a legitimate claim to hold office. (It is an interesting coincidence that "election" has in Protestant theology a different meaning: that of the granting of spiritual grace to God's elect.)

The most ancient and continuous tradition has been that of the election of superiors (popes, bishops, deans, priors, and so on) by a relatively small electorate consisting of those next in rank. Up to a point the procedure is deliberative, tending toward a conclusion by "sense of the meeting." But there are also ancient and complex rules about voting procedures. These rights of election were defended, strongly but not always with success, against hierarchical and secular attempts to substitute appointment.

There is an undercurrent (almost Athenian in tone) emphasizing the electoral rights of the many against the few. In Presbyterian terms, the congregation will defend the position of the elders in appointing a minister insofar as that position is endangered by the lay patron, but it claims the right to confirm or to upset the verdict of the elders. Dissent sometimes accepts the authority of a charismatic leader; but it often tends toward the equal sovereignty of all true believers, which may be shown either by election or by rotation in office.

Feudalism. The position of the feudal emperor, king, or overlord was deemed to be limited by law and custom and to some extent by the consent of his vassals.

The relation between king and lord and between lord and man was in principle one of consent leading to binding mutual obligation. The vassal chose to do homage, the lord chose whether or not to accept it. It was not a long step from this to an elected emperor and (in a few instances) an elected king. The social situation greatly limited the application of the principles of consent and election in practice; but the idea of a binding legal right of succession to office emerged slowly, along with the growth of other notions of private and heritable property.

In principle, the king was independent insofar as he could "live of his own." But this was a limited independence in a period of quite rapid change, and in many cases its boundaries were obscure. Hence the need for consultation, first with a feudal council, then with assemblies "representing" others besides immediate vassals. These assemblies were the basis of the parliamentary tradition in Europe. They embodied two principles not yet wholly obsolete:

(*a*) The separate representation of "estates," which might be more or less numerous; for instance, great lords, great clergy, lesser lords, lesser clergy, burghers, peasants.

(*b*) The representation of local communities but not of individuals. The classic case is that of the English House of Commons, based on two knights from every shire and two burgesses from every burgh. Apart from the great men of the realm, the "units of account" in government were shires and burghs, not individuals. The choice of representatives by communities was a matter for each community, within the general law of the land. Elections thus established themselves in national government but without any national enactment about electoral procedure.

The seventeenth and eighteenth centuries. In most of Europe the assemblies of estates were displaced by autocratic, modernizing monarchies. For the diffusion of elections the only important survival was in England (the parliaments of Scotland and Sweden survived but had little or no influence outside their own countries) and in colonial assemblies based on the English model. During the struggle for survival certain basic principles of consent, franchise, and representation were hammered out; although these principles were never fully applied in practice, they were recognized as the ideological basis of a system of democratic elections. The classic statements are those of English popular leaders in the 1640s and 1650s: their language recalls both that of nonconformist congregations and that of Athenian democracy. The principle, in brief, is that all governments owe their just powers to the consent of the governed and that in numerous societies this consent may be expressed by representatives freely elected on a basis of universal adult suffrage.

This principle can readily be elaborated in institutional form, for example, by the extension of the suffrage, the equalization of constituencies, proportional representation, the elimination of intimidation and corruption, and so on. These elaborations in turn lead to political situations which illustrate ambiguities in the principle; for instance, as regards the relation between elected and electors, is there a difference between a "representative" and a "delegate"? [See REPRESENTATION.]

Parties in elections. By far the most important of these new problems is that of parties as intermediaries between voter and assembly. Clear recognition of this situation came first in American presidential elections, but it spread rapidly with the extension of the franchise in large states in the nineteenth century. By the last quarter of that century, parties and elections had become interdependent. Electoral parties were no longer limited to national politics; trade unions and large cooperative societies are obvious examples. But national elections are henceforth intelligible *only* in terms of parties; the traditional principles demand the scrutiny of procedure within parties, since they control the first stage of national elections. [See PARTIES, POLITICAL.]

Plebiscitary democracy and "unfree" elections. The predominance of parties has led to a change in the character of national elections, even in countries where electoral procedure is in constant use at subnational levels. The choice of a man to hold office as a member of an assembly has given place to a national vote between different "packages" consisting of leadership, party, and program. The election is a choice of government or even of regime,

and voting procedure is called on to bear new strains. In stable democracies the strains are mitigated because there is an understood difference between governmental structure ("government") and government in power ("regime"), and the former is not questioned by electors. But where this distinction is not drawn the strain may prove too great for the electoral system to bear, and the element of choice is removed (or greatly reduced) by various devices. The oldest of these are plebiscitary democracy, which dates from the time of Napoleon I, and the exercise of influence on elections by officials of the government in power, without blatant breach of legality. The *reductio ad absurdum* of these trends appears in "elections" such as those of East Germany, where a vote of 99.9 per cent was recorded in favor of the government in 1964. Such a result could only be due to fraud, or pressure, or both. However, the fact that the regime deems elections necessary seems to pay tribute to the immense strength of the tradition that elections confer legitimacy. [See DEMOCRACY.]

The functions of elections

This brief historical summary illustrates the persistence and adaptability of the use of electoral procedure as a means of legitimating the assignment of a person to an office of authority. It may be said that electoral procedure is functionally analogous to procedure in a marriage ceremony: "Do you take this man (or woman) to be your lawfully wedded husband (or wife)?" "I do" (Austin 1962). The point in time at which "I do" is said is not psychologically a moment of choice or decision—that came earlier; it is the point at which an individual preference becomes a social commitment. The words and acts are "performative"; if correctly said and done in the right context, they establish new social relationships of a binding character.

Such acts are generally associated with ritual which underlies the multiple relationships linking them to a complex system of behavior and belief. To continue the analogy with marriage ceremonies, there is a possible range of ritual complexity from ostentation to extreme simplicity—but even in marriage by registration in an advanced secular society, some elements of ritual are present. There is the same wide range in electoral ritual—for example the election of a pope and that of the directors of a manufacturing company; but in both cases there is a procedure which has binding effect if properly followed.

Thus, it is possible to speak of elections in general as a "ritual of choice"; the binding character of elections derives from the participation of an individual as chooser in a social act, and legitimate authority is thus conferred on the person chosen. But such a generalization tells one little about the position of elections in any given society.

Men are called by different kinds of elections to different offices in different societies. The historical sketch given above notes only a limited range of cases, but it may be sufficient to indicate that it is rash to talk of *the* function of elections. This may be illustrated by the British case. A British general election serves to choose a governing party and thus a government. But (on the one hand) that government, though powerful, has not a monopoly of legitimate authority in the political system. This authority is shared by many others—those professionally qualified by education and experience, the leaders of organized interests, property owners of various kinds, and so on. On the other hand, the electoral system serves many other functions besides choice of a government; the party organization based on it serves as a market place and reconciler of interests, a ladder for the political careers of national and local officials, a forum of national discussion, and so on. It would be quite amiss to assume at once that the same functions were filled by elections in Athens, or in the medieval church, or even in other industrial societies today.

Argument about the merits of different electoral systems is generally based on assessments of their efficiency in relation to one or more of their many possible functions. The political literature of England in the nineteenth and twentieth centuries contains a rich store of such arguments; and this has been added to in the process of "decolonization," since "free elections" were assumed to be a necessary step toward independence in most of Britain's dependent territories. This is, therefore, a convenient testing ground for theories about the nature of political argument, and in particular about the relation of ideology to rationality on one flank and to self-interest on the other.

A. H. Birch (1964) has shown how contemporary debate about elections in Britain draws in arguments from various historical stages, a mixture which can be logically justified only if one assumes that elections in England serve many functions that are not necessarily compatible with one another. If one had to ground the defense of elections on a single maxim it would doubtless be that of the Puritan revolution: "There are no laws that in their strictness and vigour of justice any man is bound to that are not made by those whom he doth consent to." Parallels for this maxim could be found in many other political cultures. The doctrine or ideology is one of great and continuing power: but it remains empty until expressed in terms of institutions and interests, and its simplicity is then obscured and complicated by arguments drawn from other streams of political doctrine.

There has been no general study of choice as an element in the legitimation of authority. Such a study would present great difficulties. It is safe to guess that where choice is an element in determining authority in simpler societies it is entangled with other factors such as seniority, lineage, and personal ascendancy. Isolating one factor would distort the situation. In complex societies elections appear in many different contexts, private and public, and electoral procedure often survives as a ritual although the element of choice is absent; so that it would be difficult, perhaps unwise, to take the forms of electoral procedure as a guide in unraveling the complexities of modern political structure.

It would be of value, nevertheless, if pilot studies could be made of the place of elections in one or two cases of simple and complex societies. Very little work has been done on the legitimation of authority in contemporary societies; it seems probable that the part played by elections is relatively small even in established democracies, if elections are considered separately as a single factor. An attempt to isolate this factor might therefore break down; but it could hardly fail to sharpen our perception of the problem, which is of central importance in political science and is now within the grasp of empirical inquiry.

W. J. M. MACKENZIE

[*See also* AUTHORITY; CONSTITUTIONS AND CONSTITUTIONALISM; DEMOCRACY; GOVERNMENT; LEGITIMACY; MAJORITY RULE; REPRESENTATION.]

BIBLIOGRAPHY

The bibliography for this article is combined with the bibliography of the article that follows.

II
ELECTORAL SYSTEMS

Elections are institutionalized procedures for the choosing of officeholders by some or all of the recognized members of an organization. Whether the organization is a club, a company, a party, or a territorial polity, an electoral institution can be described in a series of dimensions: the scope and structure of the organizational unit; the tasks and the authority of the offices to be filled; the types and levels of membership in the organization and the qualifications for participation in the choice of officers; the criteria, if any, used in differentiating the numerical weight of the choice of each qualified member; the extent and character of the subdivisions instituted within the organizations for purposes of such choice; the procedures for the setting of the alternatives of choice; the procedures used in eliciting and registering choices among these alternatives; and the methods used in translating the aggregated choices of members into authoritative collective decisions on the attribution of the given offices.

A club might recognize as qualified electors only a few senior members and require these to vote by a show of hands or by acclamation. This practice would contrast on a number of dimensions with the elaborate procedures of some joint-stock companies: all shareholders have the right to participate, but the weight of their votes is a function of the number of shares they hold; their preferences are expressed under elaborate provisions of secrecy, and their votes are aggregated through strict rules of accountability. A systematic discussion of all such dimensions of variation, even for just the major types of organizations, would take us far afield. In this article the discussion will center on one distinct type of organization: the territorially defined units of the nation-state—the self-governing local community and the overarching unitary, or federal body politic.

The histories of the known political systems present a bewildering variety of electoral arrangements (Braunias 1932; Meyer 1901). Any attempt to account for these variations through the construction of a basic model of strategic options and structural restraints must start out from an analysis of the histories of changes in each of six dimensions of the local and the national electoral system.

(1) The qualifications for franchise: how does a subject of the territory acquire political citizenship rights?

(2) The weighting of influence: how many votes are formally attributed to each elector and on what grounds? what is done to ensure differentiation or equality in the actual influence of each vote?

(3) The standardization of the voting procedures and the protection of the freedom to choose: what is done to ensure uniform and accountable practices of electoral administration, and what provisions are made to equalize the immediate cost of all alternatives for the elector?

(4) The territorial levels of choice: how is the territory divided for purposes of election, and how many levels of electoral aggregation are distinguished?

(5) The stages of electoral choice: how are the alternatives set for the electors? to what extent are the alternatives set in advance, and to what extent is the range still open for the electors?

(6) The procedures of calculation: how are the votes aggregated, and how are the aggregated distributions translated into authoritative collective decisions on territorial representation?

One man, one vote, one value

The Western developments toward equalitarian electoral democracy may conveniently be analyzed against an "ideal-type" model of five successive phases.

(1) An early, prerevolutionary phase was characterized by marked provincial and local variations in franchise practices but implicit or explicit recognition of membership in some corporate estate (the nobility, the clergy, the city corporations of merchants and artisans, or, in some cases, the freehold peasantry) as a condition of political citizenship (Hintze [1941] 1962; Lousse 1943; Palmer 1959).

(2) In the wake of the American and French revolutions, there was a period of increasing standardization of franchise rules; the strict regulation of access to the political arena under a régime censitaire was accompanied by formal equality of influence among the citizens allowed to vote under the given property or income criteria (Meyer 1901; Williamson 1960).

(3) In the first phase of mass mobilization the suffrage was greatly extended, but formal inequalities of influence persisted, under arrangements for multiple votes or for differential ratios of votes to representatives.

(4) In the next phase, manhood suffrage, all significant social and economic criteria of qualification for men over a given age were abolished. Although there were now no formal inequalities of voting rights within constituency electorates, marked differences in the weight of votes across the constituencies still existed (Zwager 1958).

(5) Finally, in the current phase, one of continued democratization, steps were taken toward the maximization of universal and equal citizenship rights by (a) extension of the suffrage to women, to younger age groups (down to 21 or even 18), and to short-term residents (reductions in "quarantine" periods) and (b) further equalization of voter–representative ratios throughout the national or federal territory.

Only three of the nation-states of the West passed through these five stages in anything like a regular sequence: England, Belgium, and Sweden. The step-by-step evolution characteristic of these countries contrasts violently with the abrupt and revolutionary changes in France (Bendix 1964; Rokkan 1961).

In England (Seymour 1915) the process took more than one hundred years, from the Reform Act of 1832 to the abolition of multiple votes in 1948. In Sweden (Verney 1957) the system of estate representation was abolished in 1866, but the extreme inequalities of electoral influence were maintained until 1921. The Belgians (Gilissen 1958) passed from the phase of estate representation into a *régime censitaire* as soon as they had achieved independence in 1831 and went through an intriguing phase of multiple voting from 1893 to 1917: all men over 25 were enfranchised, but additional votes were granted not only on *censitaire* criteria but also in recognition of educational achievement (*principe capacitaire*) and of responsibility for the maintenance of a family.

By contrast, in France (Bastid 1948; Charnay 1965) the transition from the first to the fourth stage took a mere four years: the Law of January 1789 maintained a system of indirect elections within the recognized corporations of nobles, clergy, and the *tiers état*; the constitution of 1791 stipulated a tax-paying criterion and introduced the concept of the *citoyen actif*; and the constitution of 1793 went straight to the stage of manhood suffrage, the only remaining qualification being a six-month minimum residence in the canton. This sudden thrust toward maximal mass democracy proved very short-lived: the Terror intervened, and for decades France was torn between traditionalist attempts to restrict the suffrage to a narrow stratum of owners and high officials and radical–plebiscitarian pressures for universal and equal elections. The period from 1815 to 1848 was one of classic *régime censitaire*: the property qualifications limited the franchise to less than 100,000 out of 7 million adult males before 1830 and to roughly 240,000 in 1848. The Revolution of 1848 brought on the next sudden thrust toward maximal democracy: the first modern mass election took place on Easter day that year, and 84 per cent of the 9,360,000 electors went to the polling stations.

The electoral histories of the rest of Europe fall at various points between these two models. In northwest Europe the Dutch went through the same sequence as the British and the Swedes, while Denmark and Norway came closer to the French model. The Dutch passed from estate representation to *régime censitaire* in 1848 but did not go through any phase of plural voting before they opted for manhood suffrage during World War I (Geismann 1964). Denmark, the most absolutist

of the Nordic polities, went through a brief period of estate representation after 1831 and then moved straight into a system of nationwide elections under a very extensive manhood suffrage in 1849: the result, again as in France, was a half century of constitutional struggle between an oligarchic elite and a coalition of urban radicals and the mobilizing peasantry. Under the impact of the struggle for independence, the dependent "colonial" territories of the north all proceeded rapidly to maximal suffrage. Norway gave the vote to close to half her adult males on establishing her own parliament in 1814 and proceeded to full manhood suffrage during the conflict over union with Sweden in the 1890s. Finland stuck to the inherited Swedish system of four estates until 1906 and then all of a sudden passed from the first to the fifth phase of the model: not only all men but also all women were given the vote, and the process of mass mobilization had gone so far under the restrictive estate system that the turnout at the first election under universal suffrage reached the record height of 70.7 per cent. Developments in the third of the Nordic "colonies" were less spectacular: Iceland saw the re-establishment of its parliament in 1874 and then passed through two successive phases of *régime censitaire* before the stage of near-universal suffrage for men and women was reached in 1915 (as in most other countries of the north, paupers receiving public assistance were kept out in the first round; the Icelanders did not admit them until 1934).

The German territories were torn among several competing models of the representative polity: the traditional notions of election through established estates; the *altliberale* ideology of unified national representation under a property or income suffrage; the Napoleonic ideas of plebiscitarian mass democracy; and the Roman Catholic models of functional representation within the corporate state, the *Ständestaat*. This electoral schizophrenia found a number of intriguing expressions. In Prussia and the Bismarckian Reich, two sharply contrasted systems of elections coexisted for half a century. In Prussia the "lower orders" had been given the right to vote in the wake of the Revolution of 1848, but the weight of their votes was infinitesimal in the three-class system introduced to protect the interests of the landowners and the officials. By contrast, the Reichstag was elected on strict criteria of equal suffrage for all men: this principle had been laid down, after much debate, by the German National Assembly in Frankfurt in 1848 but was not enforced until 1867, when Bismarck saw the importance of general elections as a source of legitimacy for the new Reich. The Hapsburg empire went through a much longer and more tortuous process of democratization: first, estate representation; from 1861, corporate-interest representation under a system of four *curiae*; in 1896, an extraordinary attempt to stave off equalitarian democracy, by adding a fifth *curia*, for the citizens so far without representation; and finally, in 1907, a unified system of national representation and enforcement of "one man, one vote, one value."

By the end of World War I the great majority of European and European-settled polities had opted for manhood suffrage, many of them even for universal suffrage for women as well. Suffrage for women (Kraditor 1965) came first in the settler nations (Wyoming, 1890, all of the United States, 1920; New Zealand, 1893; South Australia, 1895) and in Scandinavia (Finland, 1906; Norway, 1910 to 1913; Denmark, 1915; Sweden, 1918 to 1921). The British proceeded by steps: restricted suffrage for women in 1918; full suffrage, on a par with men, in 1928. The "Roman" countries took longer to recognize the rights of women: France, Belgium, and Italy waited until the end of World War II before they admitted all women to political citizenship, and Switzerland has still, after 120 years of smoothly functioning manhood democracy, to reach agreement on the enfranchisement of her women.

With the victory over the Axis powers in World War II and the subsequent dismantling of colonial empires, the principle of "one man, one vote" gained ground throughout the world, even in countries at the lowest level of literacy and without a trace of the traditions of pluralist competition, which had been essential for the growth of effective party oppositions in the West. In an increasing number of newly independent states the enforcement of equal and universal rights of political citizenship was no longer seen as a means for the channeling of legitimate claims against the power holders but was regarded simply as an element in a strategy of national unification and the control of dissidence. Really serious struggles over the old cry of "one man, one vote, one value" only occurred in the ethnically most divided polities, e.g., South Africa, Rhodesia, and the United States.

Resistance to electoral equalitarianism has generally tended to be stronger at the level of local government than at the national or federal level. Payment of local property taxes remained in many cases a criterion of local franchise long after the abolition of *régime censitaire* at the national level. Residence requirements, too, were retained much longer for local than for national elections. In fact, in recent years the increased flow of labor from the backward to the economically advanced countries is bringing about extensive disfranchisement even at the national level. In the earlier phase the migrant workers within the one national territory were kept locally disfranchised; today vast numbers of immigrants are denied political rights in their host countries because of the high barriers against citizenship. "One man, one vote, one value" may be upheld as a principle within a population of settled territorial citizens, but it breaks down at the cross-national level.

Standardization of electoral practices

The extension of the franchise to the economically and culturally dependent strata of each national society increased the pressures for a standardization of electoral practices. Before elections could be established as essential instruments of legitimation, local variations in the arrangements for the elicitation and recording of choices had to be minimized. The electoral returns constituted claims to legitimate representation that had to be established through procedures acceptable to all, or at least to the dominant, competitors for office and power. The history of the democratization of the suffrage was paralleled in country after country by a history of increasing standardization of administrative procedures in all phases of the electoral process: the establishment of registers; the determination of voting rights; the maintenance of order at the polling stations; the casting of the vote; the recording of the act in the register; the counting of choices; the calculation of outcomes.

Of all the issues facing the national administrations in the early phases of suffrage extension, one was of particular importance for the functioning of the electoral system: the measures taken to insure the independence of the individual electoral decision (Rokkan 1961).

The defenders of the estate traditions and the *régime censitaire* had argued that economically and culturally dependent subjects could not be expected to form independent political judgments and therefore the vote should be given only to citizens likely to withstand social or economic pressures and able to take public responsibility for their choices on election day.

Liberal advocates of an extended suffrage, such as John Stuart Mill, were placed in a dilemma. They knew that the new voters could easily be swayed by their social superiors or their economic masters, yet they were convinced that the vote ought to be open, that each voter ought to be prepared to defend his decision in his day-to-day environments. This moralist argument for the old tradition of open voting soon had to yield to another imperative: the safeguarding of the integrative and legitimizing functions of the electoral ritual. To generate legitimacy, elections had to be dignified and without any tinge of violence. The maintenance of the system of open voting under the conditions of mass elections could lead only to alienation, corruption, and disrespect for the institutions of the nation.

The result was a widespread movement to ensure the secrecy of the act of voting. To qualify as "democratic," elections had to be not only universal and equal but also secret. The French were the first to introduce this principle. The electoral law establishing the States General in 1789 retained open oral voting at the level of the general electorate but called for secret ballots in the colleges of delegates. The electoral law establishing the first legislative assembly in 1791 introduced secrecy at all levels of the electorate, but very little was done to ensure regular enforcement. There was a great deal of opposition to the principle; the Jacobins, in particular, wanted open voting to control dissidence. The constitution of 1793 left it to the voters themselves to decide whether to vote openly or in secret. Subsequent laws reintroduced the principle of secrecy for all voters, but electoral administration remained at a low level of standardization throughout the nineteenth century. The *isoloir* and the standard envelope for the ballot were introduced by law in 1913, but even these highly detailed provisions left leeway for a variety of abuses and manipulations, particularly in the south, in Corsica, and in the overseas *départements* (Charnay 1965).

The extension of the suffrage to vast numbers of illiterates made it impossible to stick to a strict rule of secrecy. In the economically and culturally backward areas of the national hinterland particularly, it proved easy to control the votes of the lower classes even under strict rules of secrecy. The secret ballot expressed an essential feature of literate urban society: it introduced an element of anonymity, specificity, and abstraction in the system of political interchange.

Significantly, the countries that retained the old tradition of open and oral voting longest were all heavily dominated by landed interests: Denmark did not abolish it until 1901; Iceland, until 1906; Prussia, until the collapse of the Reich in 1918; and Hungary retained it even into the 1930s. By contrast, Belgium, Switzerland, and Sweden had opted for secrecy even under the *régime censitaire*, and the English had only waited five years after the Reform Act of 1867 to introduce the Ballot Act,

which ensured the freedom of the voters from intimidation and bribery. In the settler nations overseas, the principle of secrecy was recognized quite early but there were marked local variations in enforcement. One of the Australian states developed an effective procedure of secret voting as early as 1856, and this innovation, the "Australian ballot," (Wigmore 1889) spread very rapidly through the United States during the 1880s and 1890s. The open recognition of legitimate partisanship made secrecy less important in the United States than in Europe. Most states allow primary elections within each party, and participation in these cannot easily be hidden from the public.

In all these countries the underlying purpose of the introduction of the ballot system was to take the act of voting out of the regular give and take of day-to-day life and enhance its dignity and ritual significance by isolating it from the sordid pressures and temptations of an unequal and divided society. Most histories of electoral arrangements emphasize the importance of secrecy, as a device to protect the economically dependent from the sanctions of their superiors. This was the essence of the Chartists' early demands in England, and it has traditionally been a basic concern of working-class movements. What has often been overlooked is that the provisions for secrecy could as easily cut the voter off from his peers as from his superiors. In fact, the secrecy provisions fulfill two distinct functions: first, they make it possible for the voter to keep his decision private and avoid sanctions from those he does not want to know; second, they make it impossible for the voter to prove how he voted to those he does want to know. The very rigorous rules set up in country after country for the invalidation of all irregularly marked ballots was directed to this second point. They were devised to ensure that the citizen could no longer treat his vote as a commodity for sale. He might well be bribed, but the price per vote clearly would decrease as soon as it proved impossible to check whether it was actually delivered. The salient point here is that by ensuring the complete anonymity of the ballots it became possible not only to reduce bribery of the economically dependent by their superiors but also to reduce the pressures toward conformity and solidarity within the working class.

With the secret ballot, a personal choice was placed before the worker that made him, at least temporarily, independent of his immediate environment: was he primarily a worker or primarily a citizen of the broader local or national community? Secret voting made it possible for the inarticulate rank and file to escape the pressures of their organizations, and at the same time it put the onus of political visibility on the activists within the working-class movement. The established national "system" opened up channels for the expression of secret loyalties, while forcing "deviants" to declare themselves openly. Some socialist parties tried to turn the tables by establishing intimate organizational ties with the trade unions and imposing political levies on their members, irrespective of their actual preferences. The controversy over "contracting in" versus "contracting out" in the British labor movement can be interpreted as the counterpart of the controversy over open versus secret voting in the total system. The Labour party wanted to put the onus of visibility on its own "deviants," the trade union members who did not want to vote for the party (contracting out), while the Conservatives and Liberals wanted the inarticulate masses to stay out of political commitments and to put the onus of visibility on the socialist militants (contracting in).

The introduction of mass elections in the developing countries of Africa and Asia during the final phases of decolonization raised a number of technical issues (MacKenzie & Robinson 1965; Maquet 1959; Smith 1960). In some British territories a system of separate ballot boxes for each candidate or party was introduced. These were marked by distinguishing symbols (a lion, an elephant, etc.) and the illiterate voters were asked to drop their ballot paper into the box of their choice. There were elaborate rules for the stamping of official identification marks on the ballot papers and for the screening of the ballot boxes from the eyes of the officials, but this procedure still left a wide margin for interference with the choice of individual voters. In other British colonies with high rates of illiteracy the voters had to mark off on the ballot the candidates of their choice. This often made it essential to allow election officials to accept "whispering votes" from voters who could not read the names on the ballot. The French colonies and their successor states adopted the system of separate party ballots and the *isoloir* for the placing of the chosen list in the official envelope. This simplified procedures (although it wasted a lot of paper) but still left a great deal of leeway for the exertion of social pressure. Even if the village chieftains or the political agents could not see what the voter did inside the *isoloir*, they could either observe him when he chose his party ballot from the separate piles placed at the polling station or, what was more common, prevail upon him to show them afterward the ballots he had not used, as proof

that he had voted as instructed. There was nothing new about this, of course. The experiences in the developing countries simply confirmed what had been known about voting in the backward rural areas of Europe for decades. Any attempt to uphold strict rules of secrecy in societies at low levels of economic differentiation is bound to run into difficulties. Relationships are too diffuse and the possibilities of observation too many to allow individuals to escape from control through the isolation of particular acts from their daily contexts.

From votes to seats

The emergence of mass electorates produced a great literature of political engineering, not just on the organization of party work and the waging of campaigns but also on the territorial structuring of constituencies and on the strategic pros and cons of alternative procedures of translating the registered distributions of votes into legitimate decisions on representation. Of the extraordinary tangle of issues debated in this literature, only two interconnected issues will be discussed here: the delimitation of units of aggregation, and the procedures for the allocation of seats within each unit. Basically, the bitter debates over the two issues reflect fears and resentments generated through changes in the equilibrium of political power under the impact of mass democracy: the influx of new voters altered the character of the system and a great variety of stratagems were tried out to bring it back into equilibrium.

Varieties of majority systems. The early systems of electoral representation all rested on some kind of majority principle. The will of a part of the electorate was taken to express the will of the whole, and all the participants were taken to be bound in law and conscience by the decision reached through this procedure.

Three distinct varieties of majoritarian decision-making procedure established themselves during the early phases of electoral development. The first of these stipulated *one* round of election, with decisions by simple plurality. The second and the third both stipulated *several* rounds and required absolute majorities in the first round. They differed, however, in their requirements for the final and decisive round. The second allowed an open field of candidacies and simple plurality; the third restricted the competition to the two foremost candidates and retained the absolute-majority requirement to the very end.

The first of the three procedures had been established in England since the Middle Ages and had been used to ensure the election of "two knights from every shire and two burgesses from every borough" to the House of Commons. It also became the standard method in the United States and soon spread to the other English-settled nations overseas. The method was originally used in two-member constituencies, but it met with general acceptance even when applied in single-member units.

The method of repeated ballots had a long tradition in the Roman Catholic church (Moulin 1953) and was formally instituted in the French *ordonnance* calling for elections to the States General in 1789. This stipulated three successive ballots —the first two open, the final one restricted to just twice as many candidates as there were seats left to fill. Three-ballot systems of this type prevailed throughout the *régime censitaire*. This method was clearly best suited to elections restricted to the economically independent classes, with leisure enough to travel to electoral sessions and spend the day or more required to get through all the balloting. The Revolution of 1848 swept away this system and introduced single-ballot mass elections. The old habit of repeated ballots persisted, however. Only four years after the revolution, Napoleon III devised a system of two-ballot elections suited to the new situation of manhood suffrage. He broke with the old tradition on a point of fundamental importance: he allowed an open field of candidacies even at the second ballot and required simple plurality only. This was an astute strategic move; in the half-free elections of the Empire, it allowed the officials maximal freedom of maneuver against the opposition. Interestingly, there was no return to the principle of second-ballot absolute majority in the Third, Fourth, or Fifth Republic: none of the parties or *groupements* wanted to be faced with the cruel yes-or-no alternatives of the two-way fight.

Other polities on the European continent stuck to the old rule of absolute majority and restricted last-ballot candidacies. This was the system upheld in the German Reich down to its defeat in 1918; it was, also, used in Switzerland until 1900 and in Austria, Italy, and the Netherlands until the end of World War I.

These majoritarian electoral methods came under heavy attacks in the later phases of democratization. The extension of the suffrage made possible the organization of strong lower-class parties but the electoral systems, inherited from the ages of estate representation and *régime censitaire*, set high barriers against the entry of such parties into national politics. The German rule of absolute majority set the highest barrier. A lower-class party had to reach the 50 per cent mark or go without

representation. The French and the Anglo–American systems also set high barriers against rising movements of the hitherto disfranchised, but the initial levels were not frozen at 50 per cent; the height of the barriers varied with the strategies of established, *censitaire*, parties. The essential difference between the French and the Anglo–American systems was that the one made for much greater local variations in such counterstrategies than the other: the first-ballot results offered a basis for bargaining among the established parties, and the coalition strategies would of necessity vary from constituency to constituency. The height of the barrier against new entrants depended essentially on the willingness of the established parties to enter into alliances. This was not always exclusively a matter of immediate payoffs but of trust and the openness of communication channels.

Origins of proportional representation. Karl Braunias (1932) distinguished two phases in the spread of proportional representation: the "minority protection" phase, before World War I; and the "antisocialist" phase, in the years immediately after the armistice. It was no accident that the earliest moves toward proportional representation (PR) came in the most ethnically heterogeneous European countries: Denmark in 1855; the Swiss cantons in 1891; Belgium in 1899; Moravia in 1905; Finland in 1906. In linguistically and religiously divided societies majority elections could clearly threaten the continued existence of the political system. The introduction of some element of minority representation came to be seen as an essential step in a strategy of territorial consolidation.

As the pressures mounted for extensions of the suffrage, demands for proportionality were also heard in the culturally more homogeneous nation-states. In most cases the victory of the new principle of representation came about through a convergence of pressures from below and from above. The rising working class wanted to lower the thresholds of representation in order to gain access to the legislatures, and the most threatened of the old established parties demanded PR to protect their position against the new waves of mobilized voters created by universal suffrage. In Belgium the introduction of graduated manhood suffrage in 1893 brought about an increasing polarization between the Labor party and the Catholics and threatened the continued existence of the Liberals. The introduction of PR restored some equilibrium to the system (Gilissen 1958).

The history of the struggles over electoral procedures in Sweden and Norway tells us a great deal about the consequences of the lowering of one threshold for the bargaining over the level of the next. In Sweden, Liberals and Social Democrats fought a long fight for universal and equal suffrage and at first also advocated PR, to ensure easier access to the legislature. The remarkable success of their mobilization efforts made them change their strategy, however, and from 1904 onward they advocated majority elections in single-member constituencies (Verney 1957). This aroused fears among the farmers and the urban conservatives, who, to protect their own interests, made the introduction of PR a condition for acceptance of manhood suffrage. Accordingly, the two barriers fell together. It became easier to enter the electorate and easier to gain representation. In Norway (Rokkan & Hjellum 1966) there was a longer lag between waves of mobilization. The franchise was much wider from the outset, and the first wave of peasant mobilization brought down the old regime as early as 1884. As a result, the suffrage had been extended well before the final mobilization of the rural proletariat and the industrial workers, under the impact of rapid economic change. The victorious radical–agrarian "left" felt no need to lower the threshold of representation and, in fact, helped to raise it through the introduction of a two-ballot system of the French type in 1906. There is little doubt that this contributed greatly to the radicalization and alienation of the Norwegian Labor party, which in 1915 gained 32 per cent of all the votes cast but which was given barely 15 per cent of the seats. The "left" did not agree to lower the threshold until 1921; the decisive motive was clearly not just a sense of equalitarian justice but the fear of rapid decline, with further Labor advances across the majority threshold.

In all these cases the high threshold might have been maintained if the parties of the property-owning classes had been able to make common cause against the rising working-class movements. But the inheritance of hostility and distrust was too strong. The Belgian Liberals could not face the possibility of a merger with the Catholics, and the cleavages between the rural and the urban interests went too deep in the Nordic countries to make it possible to build up any joint antisocialist front. By contrast, the higher level of industrialization and the progressive merger of rural and urban interests in Britain made it possible to withstand the demand for a change in the system of representation: the Labour party was seriously underrepresented only during a brief initial period, and the Conservatives were able to establish broad enough alliances in the counties and the suburbs to keep their votes well above the critical point.

Threshold strategies under PR.   PR systems differ markedly in their threshold levels, however, and the struggles over these details of electoral engineering tell us a great deal about the dynamics of multiparty systems.

The variant most frequently introduced in continental Europe was the one invented by the Belgian professor Victor d'Hondt (1878; 1882): the method of the "largest average." This method favors the largest party and, in fact, lowers the threshold very little in constituencies electing few members and choosing among few competing party lists. If the total number of votes cast is designated as V, the total number of mandates as M, and the total number of parties as P, the threshold formula for the d'Hondt procedure will read

$$T = \frac{V - 1}{M + P - 1}.$$

This means that the smallest number of votes (T) required for representation will be a function not only of the size of the constituency and its share of seats but also of the number of parties. A fragmented party system lowers the threshold but, by implication, also increases the overrepresentation of the largest of the parties (particularly if $P > M$, since the votes for a number of the small parties must of necessity go unrepresented).

Thus, the debates and bargains over electoral arrangements in a great number of PR countries have centered on the questions, Should there be some gentle overrepresentation of the largest party? and Should the threshold for the first seat be set high enough to discourage new parties and splinter movements? These concerns have been particularly prominent in the Scandinavian countries: the typical constellation there has been one party, Labor, in the range just below the 50 per cent mark; three or four parties, all nonsocialist, in the 5–20 per cent range; and one or two very small parties, with only minimal chances of representation. In such constellations the d'Hondt procedure would give the largest party more seats than its votes justified. In fact it often gave the Labor parties clear majorities in parliament without majorities among the voters. This overrepresentation was essentially achieved at the expense of the very smallest of the parties, such as the Communist, but often hurt the efforts of the one-seat parties to gain additional representation. A variety of remedies were suggested. The Danes retained the high d'Hondt threshold but ensured greater proportionality among the already represented parties through a two-level procedure: any underrepresentation produced at the constituency level was corrected through the allocation of additional seats at the regional level. In Sweden and in Norway the nonsocialist parties opted for another strategy: they found it impossible to join forces under one single list, but they were anxious to increase their representation through provisions for electoral cartels. In Sweden such cartels were allowed after 1921 and cost the Social Democrats a substantial number of seats. The system placed the Agrarians in a very difficult position. To avoid underrepresentation, they were tempted to join in cartels with the other nonsocialist parties; but to advance the interests of the farmers they found it best to support the Social Democratic government. In the end the provisions for cartels were abolished and the Sainte-Laguë method (1910) of calculation was introduced.

By a curious coincidence this alternative was adopted in all the three Scandinavian countries during 1952 and 1953. The Norwegian Labor party had gained a majority in parliament in 1945 and by 1947 had abolished the cartels. As a result, the party received 45.7 per cent of the votes but 56.7 per cent of the seats in the 1949 election. This caused a great deal of recrimination, and the party finally accepted the new method of allocation in 1952. A similar lowering of threshold was also brought about in Denmark, through provisions in the constitution of 1953.

The Sainte-Laguë method was once described as a "miracle formula" by the leader of the Swedish Agrarian party. In the typical Scandinavian situation it had a threefold effect: it strengthened the middle-sized nonsocialist parties by reducing the overrepresentation of the Social Democrats; it was nevertheless of strategic advantage to the governing parties because it reduced the pay-offs of mergers within the opposition; and finally, it helped all the established parties by discouraging splinters and new parties. How could all this be achieved in one formula? To explain this, we have to go into some technicalities of electoral mathematics (Janson 1961; Rokkan & Hjellum 1966).

Two procedures were frequently suggested as alternatives to d'Hondt in the discussions in the Scandinavian countries: the method of the "greatest remainder" and the Sainte-Laguë system of successive division by odd integers.

The method of the "greatest remainder" lowers the threshold of representation to a minimum: the threshold formula is $T = V/(MP)$. This is a direct invitation to party fragmentation, since the threshold decreases rapidly with increases in the number of parties. The simple Sainte-Laguë formula does not go quite that far. The threshold formula is $(V - 1)/(2M + P - 2)$. Its crucial contribution is the progressive increase in the cost of new seats. The greater the number of seats already won by a party in a given constituency, the more votes it will take to add yet another. The d'Hondt formula makes no distinction between first and later seats. The total votes cast for each party are divided successively by $1, 2, 3, \cdots$. The Sainte-Laguë method is to divide by $1, 3, 5, \cdots$. Thus, if the first seat costs each party 1,000 votes, the second seat will cost the party $(1,000 \cdot 3)/2 = 1,500$ votes and the third seat $(1,000 \cdot 5)/3 = 1,667$ votes, and so on. This is definitely the optimal formula for small parties: it is easy to gain representation but hard to reach a majority in parliament. At the same time, it discourages mergers and cartels. Two parties polling just beyond the threshold for their first seats will, in fact, lose out if they merge.

This procedure appealed both to the nonsocialist parties, typically at the one-seat level in most constituencies, and to the governing Social Democrats. The nonsocialists were anxious to reduce the "government bonus" built into the d'Hondt procedure, and the Social Democrats wanted to make sure that their opponents did not find it profitable to merge into one broad competitive party.

But this was not all. The electoral strategists went even further to ensure the perpetuation of the established party constellations. They wanted lower thresholds, but they wanted them set just below the typical voting levels of the smallest of the established parties. If the threshold were to be set much lower, it would increase the chances of even smaller, "antisystem" parties and encourage splinter movements. The solution proved very simple: the first divisor was set, not at 1, but at 1.4. In the example already used, this would mean that the first seat would cost 1,400 votes as against 1,500 for the second and 1,667 for the third. It cost more to gain entry, but once a party was in, the steps toward further representation were no longer so steep.

This formula fitted the established power constellations as closely as any procedure at this level of simplicity could ever be expected to. It had all the appearance of a universal rule, but in fact it was essentially designed to stabilize the party system at the point of equilibrium reached by the early 1950s.

Developments in the late 1950s and the early 1960s showed that even this formula would not protect the system against change. The Social

Democrats began to regret that they had given up so much of their "government bonus." Their parliamentary majorities had become very small and highly vulnerable, and they were reluctant to contemplate long-term alliances with one of the opposition parties. In Sweden the Royal Commission on Constitutional Reform proposed in 1963 a two-tier system of representation. They wanted to use the Sainte-Laguë procedure at the level of the old constituencies and the d'Hondt procedure to elect regional members at large. This was a deliberate attempt to bring back into a system some measure of overrepresentation for the largest party. The motive was explicitly stated to be the need for some stabilization of the majority basis for the cabinet. This proposal is still under debate, and there is no basis for any final prediction of the outcome of the complex bargaining currently under way. Similar discussions got under way in Norway in the wake of the defeat of the Labor party in the election of 1961. Some Labor strategists have guardedly suggested a return to d'Hondt or even a switch to simple majority elections of the British type, while their rivals in the nonsocialist camp have put forth a diametrically opposed solution: the lowering of the Sainte-Laguë threshold to 1.3 or even 1.2. Paradoxically, the old Labor party, once the champion of PR, now wants to increase the threshold of representation, while their opponents, once the defenders of the old majority threshold, now advocate a radical lowering. Their aim is clearly to encourage the Left Socialist splinters from Labor, but this gain can be bought only at the cost of all future mergers of the nonsocialist parties (Rokkan & Hjellum 1966).

PR without party lists. By 1920 PR systems of one sort or another had won out throughout Europe. Even the French gave up their two-ballot, single-member procedure from 1917 to 1927 and introduced a curious mixture of d'Hondt proportionality and majoritarianism. These systems all required the voter to elect several representatives at the same time and to choose among a number of lists of candidates. These lists were normally set up by competing political parties. The voters might have some influence on the fate of individual candidates on such lists, but it was nearly impossible to elect anyone not appearing on the initial lists. The Continental PR was a product of party bargaining. The parties wanted to survive and saw that they rated the best chances under a system that would allow them not only to control nominations but also to gain representation even when in minority.

In the Anglo-Saxon countries this type of PR never caught on. There were strong party organizations, but there was also a strong tradition of direct territorial representation through individual representatives. The early English advocates of proportionality were profoundly indifferent to the survival of organized parties; they wanted to equalize the influence of individual voters. The great innovation of these electoral reformers was the introduction of a procedure for the aggregation of individual rank-order choices. The election was not to be decided through the counting of so many choices for X and so many for Y but through the comparison of schedules of preference. The possibilities of such aggregations of rank orders had been analyzed with great ingenuity by Charles de Borda and the Marquis de Condorcet in the eighteenth century (Black 1958; Ross 1955), but these theoretical discussions had been confined to decision making in committees and assemblies. The French method of repeated ballots, in fact, developed out of decision-making situations in assemblies and entailed a rank ordering of preferences; the voters for the candidates at the bottom had to decide on their next-order preferences. The Australian system of the "alternative vote" is another approximation; the voter indicates his second and third choices, as well as his first, and knows that these lower preferences will be brought into the count if his first preference should not receive enough support. These methods, however, aim at the maximizing of support behind each candidate. First preferences count to the end, even when there are many more than needed to elect the given candidate. The great strength of the movement for the "single transferable vote" lay precisely in the insistence on the effective use of all the preference schedules, not only the ones given to the candidates with the smallest followings but also of those "wasted" through overconcentration on a single candidate.

This required the setting of a quota—the smallest number of preferences required for election. The inventors of the system, a Dane, Andrae (1855), and an Englishman, Hare (1857), set it at Votes ÷ Seats, but this was quickly shown to be too high. H. R. Droop (1868) had no difficulty in demonstrating that the correct quota would be [Votes ÷ (Seats + 1)] + 1. This would be just enough to beat competitors for the last of the seats.

Once the quota had been set, the procedure was in itself straightforward, if time consuming. The wasted first preferences at the top of the poll were treated just like the wasted ones at the bottom— the lower preferences were entered when the first ones could no longer help. There was one difference. At the bottom all the first preferences were wasted and had to be examined for lower preferences, while at the top it was impossible to say which ones were wasted—which ones were in the quota and which ones were beyond. The solution was to work out proportional shares of lower preferences. If an elected candidate had received 10,000 first preferences but needed only 9,000, the below-quota candidates would get $(10,000 - 9,000) \div 10,000 = \frac{1}{10}$ of the second preferences given each of them by those 10,000 voters (Lakeman & Lambert 1955).

The Andrae variant of this system was used in the election of some of the members of the Danish Rigsraad from 1855 to 1866 and in the electoral colleges for the Upper House from 1866 to 1915, but the method has otherwise found acceptance only in Britain and the British-settled areas: Tasmania since 1907, the two Irelands since 1920 (quickly abolished in Northern Ireland), Malta since 1921, New South Wales since 1932, and the Australian Senate since 1949. The "single transferable vote" was ardently advocated by British Liberals but never gained much of a foothold in England. Most Conservatives were against it, and the Labour party found it less and less interesting as they grew in strength. There was a strong move toward proportionalism in 1931. Labour promoted an "alternative-vote" bill and was supported by the Liberals in the House of Commons, but the government fell and the law was never enacted (Butler 1953).

On the European continent there has always been a great deal of resistance to the dominance of the organized parties in the determination of the lists of candidates, and a variety of devices has been invented to ensure some measure of voter influence on the fate of individual candidates. Denmark was the only country on the Continent to go as far as to opt for PR without party lists. Under the current system they provide three levels of electoral aggregation. At the level of the nomination district the voters choose among individual candidates; at the level of the constituency their votes are aggregated by party to determine the allocation of direct seats; while at the level of the region there is a further round of aggregation to decide the attribution of additional seats designed to maximize proportionality (Pedersen 1966). Another multilevel solution has been devised in the German Federal Republic. There the voters are allowed two votes, one for a simple plurality election in single-member constituencies, the other for a PR election among party lists. A high degree of candidate orientation can also be achieved in a single-level PR system. The Finnish system provides the most interesting example. The parties do not present multicandidate lists or indicate a preferred order among them but submit a number of separate candidacies. The voters then choose individual candidates only, but the votes are aggregated by party within each constituency to determine the allocation of seats.

Single-member versus multimember constituencies. On the Continent the conflict between the majority principle and the proportionality principle was, at the same time, a conflict over conceptions of the territoriality of elections. Majority elections were typically tied to single-member constituencies and posited close interaction between the elected representative and the entire local electorate. Proportional elections were held in larger constituencies and posited interaction between organized parties and functionally defined core sectors of the population. The Single Transferable Vote made little sense in single-member constituencies but offered an alternative to party dominance in multimember units. The voter was free to establish his own list of candidates and did not have to abide by any party nominations. Thomas Hare (1857) and John Stuart Mill went so far as to propose that all of Britain be turned into one single constituency, but this clearly would make for enormously laborious computations of transfers. The Government of Ireland Act of 1920 stipulated constituencies of three to eight members each, and most advocates of the Hare system now give five seats as the ideal (O'Leary 1961; Ross 1959).

PR-list systems have allowed wide variations in the size of constituencies. Several countries have, in fact, made the entire national territory one constituency. This was the system of the Weimar Republic, and it is still the system in use in the Netherlands; it has also been used in Israel since 1949. This does not necessarily mean that the same set of candidates is presented throughout the national territory. There may be primary constituencies for the presentation of local party lists, but the fate of these lists is not determined within that constituency alone but by the success of the party in the total national territory. The electoral arrangements in Denmark and in the German Federal Republic are of this type. Some of the seats are allocated directly by constituency (in Denmark by the Sainte-Laguë formula, in Germany by plurality); others are allocated on the basis of the nationwide result, to ensure proportionality.

Such large constituencies obviously favor the formation of splinter parties: direct PR thresholds are functions of both the number of seats and the number of parties. To guard against party fragmentation, many systems have introduced higher barriers, either on the basis of the percentage share of the total national vote or on the basis of the number of direct seats already won. Danish law requires as a condition for the allocation of "proportionalized seats" that the party has (*a*) gained one direct seat or (*b*) received 2 per cent or more of the vote across the nation or (*c*) received in two of the three regions a total number of votes higher than the average regional cost of direct seats. The German threshold is 5 per cent of the federal vote or three direct seats.

Cross-constituency equality. The demand for equality of representation was at first met at the constituency level only. "One man, one vote, one value" was enforced within the local unit of aggregation but not throughout the national territory. There were everywhere highly vocal movements for the equalization of electoral districts, but these demands met with greater resistance than the claims for equality of influence within each unit. Under the inherited systems of estate representation, elections were taken to express the will, not of individual citizens, but of the corporate units of the nation. A shire or borough might have declined in population or in number of enfranchised citizens, but it still constituted a unit of government worthy of representation on a par with larger units. Even after the Reform Act of 1832 in England, differences between the lowest and the highest numbers of constituents per representative were of the order of 1 to 60. The radical redistribution carried out in 1885 brought the ratio down to 1 to 7, but further progress was slow. Even after the reorganization of 1948 there are still constituencies with electorates only one-third the size of the largest in the country.

Great variations in the ratios of representatives to electorates was the rule throughout Europe and the West until well into the twentieth century. On the European continent the early systems of representation generally gave great advantages to the cities; the centers of commerce and industry were still small in population but had major stakes in the building of the nations. The continuing growth of the national economies brought about changes in this urban–rural balance. As the populations of the cities grew and the franchise was widened, the rural areas gradually gained in their electorate–representative ratios and became heavily overrepresented. This inequality of representation proved highly resistant to protest movements. The more conservative voters in the cities had found important allies in the countryside and preferred to stay underrepresented at home as long as their allies could help them in their fight against urban

radicals (Cotteret et al. 1960; David & Eisenberg 1961–1962; De Grazia 1963).

In some countries this urban–rural conflict was reinforced through conflicts between the central districts and the peripheries. The constituencies farthest away from the capital and the economically most advanced areas of the nation claimed a right to numerical overrepresentation to offset the difficulties of communication with the decision makers and the officials at the center. In Denmark the constitution of 1953 even goes so far as to stipulate that constituencies be allotted seats based not only on their population but also on the size of their territories. A representative speaks not just for a given number of citizens but also for a unit of physical territory. Even in the most "proportionalized" of democracies, the electoral arrangements still reflect tensions between three conceptions of representation: the numerical, the functional, and the territorial.

Priorities for comparative research

The development in so many countries of standardized arrangements for the conduct of elections at several levels of the polity sets a wide variety of challenging tasks for comparative social research. The comparative studies carried out thus far leave great gaps in our knowledge. It is, in fact, much easier to pinpoint lacunae and lost opportunities than to describe positive achievements.

Given the crucial importance of the organization of legitimate elections in the development of the mass democracies of the twentieth century, it is indeed astounding to discover how little serious effort has been invested in the comparative study of the wealth of information available. There is no dearth of literature, but exceedingly little of it stands up to scrutiny in the light of current standards of social science methodology. The great bulk of the items bear on technicalities and controversies within a single national or regional tradition, and the few wider-ranging ones tend to take the form of vehement polemics against competing systems, even when couched in the terms of academic discourse.

The polemical writers tend to fall into two categories: the violent majoritarians or the impassioned single-vote proportionalists. It is hard to trace any distinctive school of list-system proportionalists. The party lists have certainly had their defenders, but these have tended to be pragmatic and contextual in their argumentation and have not been inclined to advertise their solutions as panaceas for all countries of the world.

The majoritarians have been particularly articulate in the three European countries with the un-happiest records of mass politics: Germany, Italy, and France. In all these deeply divided countries there has been widespread nostalgia for the simplicity of the Anglo-Saxon system of plurality elections. A great number of publicists had hoped for the development of unified national political cultures that would foster the kind of trust in territorial representatives they could observe in England and had somehow come to the conclusion that this could be brought about through straightforward electoral engineering.

In its academic guise this argument was developed into a scheme of purportedly universal propositions about the consequences of electoral systems for the health of the body politic (Hermens 1941; 1951). This proved a very difficult enterprise. A great deal of information for a wide range of countries was processed, but the results were meager. The universal propositions gave way to complex statements about concrete sequences of change, and a bewildering multiplicity of conditioning variables had to be brought into the analysis. It turned out to be simply impossible to formulate any single-variable statements about the political consequences of plurality as opposed to those of PR. A variety of contextual conditions had to be brought into the analysis: the character of the national cleavage system; the cultural conditions for the legitimation of representatives; the burdens of government and the leeway for legislative versus executive action (Duverger 1950; 1951; Epstein 1964; Grumm 1958).

This did not reduce appreciably the ardor of the majoritarians. They stuck to their guns in discussing the three major countries of the western European continent, but they admitted that PR might not hurt the functioning of democracy in the smaller nations (Unkelbach 1956). A good case could be made for plurality elections in Germany, within a reasoned analysis of the strategic options for the one country (Sternberger 1964; Scheuch & Wildenmann 1965), but the academic enterprise broke down as soon as attempts were made to argue this move for all full-suffrage democracies, whatever their structure and whatever their experiences in consensus building.

In Anglo-Saxon circles the polemics *against* plurality elections have not been quite as vehement. Advocates of PR could not blame the inherited electoral system for major national disasters, such as Fascism in Italy, National Socialism in Germany, the 1940 debacle in France. The single-vote proportionalists (Lakeman & Lambert 1955; Ross 1955) do have something in common with the

majoritarians. They tend to express the same naive belief in the possibilities of electoral engineering, and they show little awareness of the cultural and the organizational conditions for the acceptance of different systems of representation.

The majoritarian–proportionalist polemic has recently been given a new dimension through the discussion of the consequences of electoral arrangements for the achievement and/or survival of democracy in the developing countries. A leading analyst of the conditions of economic growth, W. Arthur Lewis, has formulated a strong indictment of the Anglo–French majority systems which the new African states inherited from their colonial masters. He argues that the Anglo–French systems had been developed and had found widespread acceptance in "class societies" and cannot work in the same way in the African "plural" societies—territorial polities seeking to integrate within their boundaries populations historically hostile to each other.

The surest way to kill the idea of democracy in a plural society is to adopt the Anglo-American electoral system of first-past-the-post. . . . First-past-the-post does not even require 51 per cent of the votes in each constituency to give one party all the votes. If there are three parties it can be done theoretically, with only 34 per cent; or if there are four parties, with only 26 per cent. Governments can get away with this in secure democracies without destroying faith. But if you belong to a minority in a new state, and are being asked to accept parliamentary democracy, you can hardly build much faith in the system if you win 30 per cent of those votes and get only 20 per cent of the seats, or even no seats at all. If minorities are to accept Parliament, they must be adequately represented in Parliament. (Lewis 1965, pp. 71–72)

These, of course, are exactly the arguments used in the "plural societies" of Europe for the introduction of PR. The entrenched linguistic, religious, or ethnic minorities had no faith in the majority representatives and threatened to disrupt the system. The introduction of PR was essentially part of a strategy of national integration—an alternative to monopolization of influence or civil war. But the extent of minority entrenchment varied greatly from country to country, and the pressures for proportionalization were nowhere exactly the same. This is a high-priority area for comparative research. To bring about some understanding of the great variations in electoral arrangements both in the West and in the postcolonial polities, it will be essential to study the crucial decisions on the suffrage, on privacy versus secrecy, on plurality versus PR, in the context of the process of nation building (Bendix 1964; Rokkan 1961; 1966*b*).

Electoral systems have not changed *in vacuo*. They function within culturally given contexts of legitimacy, and they are changed under the strains of critical "growing pains" in the development of the over-all constellations of national institutions. The comparative study of electoral developments can contribute a great deal to the understanding of processes and strategies of national integration, but the contributions will be meager and unreliable as long as the principal motivation for new research is a concern with the pros and cons of different schemes of electoral engineering.

The conditions for a real advance in comparative electoral research are present. An increasing number of dispassionate analyses of national electoral histories have been forthcoming in recent years, and steps are being taken to facilitate the conduct of statistical investigations through the development of "data archives" for computer analyses of time-series records (Rokkan 1966*a*; Rokkan & Meyriat 1967). What has been lacking so far has been an international forum for the advancement of detailed comparative studies. A beginning has been made, however, and it is hoped that the next decades will see a breakthrough in the comparative study of electoral systems.

STEIN ROKKAN

[*See also* LEGISLATION; PARTIES, POLITICAL; REPRESENTATION, *article on* REPRESENTATIONAL SYSTEMS; VOTING.]

BIBLIOGRAPHY

THEORIES AND CONCEPTS

AKZIN, B. 1960 Election and Appointment. *American Political Science Review* 54:705–713.

ARROW, KENNETH J. (1951) 1963 *Social Choice and Individual Values.* 2d ed. New York: Wiley.

AUSTIN, JOHN L. 1961 Performative Utterances. Pages 220–239 in John L. Austin, *Philosophical Papers.* Oxford Univ. Press.

AUSTIN, JOHN L. 1962 *How to Do Things With Words.* Oxford: Clarendon.

BIRCH, ANTHONY H. 1964 *Representative and Responsible Government.* London: Allen & Unwin.

BLACK, DUNCAN 1958 *The Theory of Committees and Elections.* Cambridge Univ. Press.

BUCHANAN, JAMES M.; and TULLOCK, GORDON 1962 *The Calculus of Consent: Logical Foundations of Constitutional Democracy.* Ann Arbor: Univ. of Michigan Press.

DAHL, ROBERT A. 1956 *A Preface to Democratic Theory.* Univ. of Chicago Press.

LEIBHOLZ, GERHARD (1929) 1960 *Das Wesen der Repräsentation und der Gestaltswandel der Demokratie im 20. Jahrhundert.* 2d ed. Berlin: Gruyter.

LITTLE, IAN M. D. (1950) 1957 *A Critique of Welfare Economics.* 2d ed. Oxford: Clarendon.

RIKER, WILLIAM H. 1961 Voting and the Summation of Preferences: An Interpretive–Bibliographical Review of Selected Developments During the Last Decade. *American Political Science Review* 55:900–911.

ROSS, JAMES F. S. 1955 *Elections and Electors: Studies in Democratic Representation.* London: Eyre & Spottiswoode.

HISTORICAL DEVELOPMENTS

ARISTOTLE *Aristotle's Politics* and *Athenian Constitution.* Edited and translated by John Warrington. New York: Dutton, 1959.

BARKER, ERNEST 1913 *Dominican Order and Convocation: A Study of the Growth of Representation in the Church During the Thirteenth Century.* Oxford: Clarendon.

CLARKE, MAUDE V. (1936) 1964 *Medieval Representation and Consent: A Study of Early Parliaments in England and Ireland, With Special Reference to the Modus tenendi parliamentum.* New York: Russell.

EHRENBERG, VICTOR (1932) 1964 *The Greek State.* Rev. ed. New York: Barnes & Noble. → First published as *Der griechische und der hellenische Staat.*

GALBRAITH, GEORGINA R. (COLE-BAKER) 1925 *The Constitution of the Dominican Order: 1216–1360.* Manchester Univ. Press.

GLOTZ, GUSTAVE (1928) 1950 *The Greek City and Its Institutions.* London: Routledge. → First published as *La cité grecque.*

GREENIDGE, ABEL H. (1896) 1920 *A Handbook of Greek Constitutional History.* London and New York: Macmillan.

GREENIDGE, ABEL H. (1901) 1930 *Roman Public Life.* New York: Macmillan.

HINTZE, OTTO (1902–1932)1962 *Staat und Verfassung: Gesammelte Abhandlungen zur allgemeinen Verfassungsgeschichte.* 2d enl. ed. Göttingen (Germany): Vandenhoeck & Ruprecht.

LOUSSE, ÉMILE 1943 *La société d'ancien régime: Organisation et représentation corporatives.* Louvain (Belgium): Bibliothèque de l'Université.

MOULIN, LÉO 1953 Les origines religieuses des techniques électorales et délibératives modernes. *Revue internationale d'histoire politique et constitutionnelle* New Series 3:106–148.

PALMER, ROBERT R. 1959 *The Age of the Democratic Revolution: A Political History of Europe and America, 1760–1800.* Volume 1: The Challenge. Princeton Univ. Press.

RYFFEL, HEINRICH 1903 *Die schweizerischen Landsgemeinden.* Zurich: Schulthess.

ULLMANN, WALTER 1961 *Principles of Government and Politics in the Middle Ages.* New York: Barnes & Noble.

MODERN SYSTEMS: GENERAL PROBLEMS

BASTID, PAUL 1948 *L'avènement du suffrage universel.* Paris: Presses Universitaires de France.

BENDIX, REINHARD 1964 *Nation-building and Citizenship: Studies of Our Changing Social Order.* New York: Wiley.

BRAUNIAS, KARL 1932 *Das parlamentarische Wahlrecht: Ein Handbuch über die Bildung der gesetzgebenden Körperschaften in Europa.* 2 vols. Berlin: Gruyter.

DIEDRICH, N. 1965 *Empirische Wahlforschung.* Cologne (Germany): Westdeutscher Verlag.

DUVERGER, MAURICE 1950 *L'influence des systèmes électoraux sur la vie politique.* Paris: Colin.

DUVERGER, MAURICE (1951) 1962 *Political Parties: Their Organization and Activity in the Modern State.* 2d English ed., rev. New York: Wiley; London: Methuen. → First published in French.

EPSTEIN, LEON D. 1964 A Comparative Study of Canadian Parties. *American Political Science Review* 58: 46–59.

GOSNELL, HAROLD F. 1930 *Why Europe Votes.* Univ. of Chicago Press.

GRUMM, JOHN G. 1958 Theories of Electoral Systems. *Midwest Journal of Political Science* 2:357–376.

HOGAN, JAMES 1945 *Election and Representation.* Cork Univ. Press.

INSTITUTE OF ELECTORAL RESEARCH, LONDON 1962 *Parliaments and Electoral Systems: A World Handbook.* Lowestoft (England): Scorpion.

INSTITUTE OF ELECTORAL RESEARCH, LONDON *A Review of Elections.* Published annually. See especially the 1960 and the 1961–1962 volumes.

KEY, V. O. JR. (1942) 1964 *Politics, Parties and Pressure Groups.* 5th ed. New York: Crowell.

KRADITOR, AILEEN S. 1965 *The Ideas of the Woman Suffrage Movement, 1890–1920.* New York: Columbia Univ. Press.

MACKENZIE, W. J. M. 1958 *Free Elections: An Elementary Textbook.* London: Allen & Unwin.

MEYER, GEORG 1901 *Das parlamentarische Wahlrecht.* Berlin: Haering.

PORTER, KIRK H. 1918 *A History of Suffrage in the United States.* Univ. of Chicago Press.

ROKKAN, STEIN 1961 Mass Suffrage, Secret Voting and Political Participation. *Archives européennes de sociologie* 2, no. 1:132–154.

ROKKAN, STEIN 1966a The Comparative Study of Electoral Statistics. International Social Science Council, *Social Sciences Information* 5, no. 2:9–19.

ROKKAN, STEIN 1966b Electoral Mobilization, Party Competition and National Integration. Pages 241–265 in Joseph LaPalombara and Myron Weiner (editors), *Political Parties and Political Development.* Princeton Univ. Press.

ROKKAN, STEIN; and MEYRIAT, JEAN (editors) 1967 *International Guide to Electoral Statistics.* Volume 1: National Elections in Western Europe. Paris: Mouton.

SCHEPIS, GIOVANNI 1955 *I sistemi elettorali: Teoria, tecnica, legislazioni positive.* Empoli (Italy): Caparrini.

SEYMOUR, CHARLES 1915 *Electoral Reform in England and Wales: The Development and Operation of the Parliamentary Franchise, 1832–1885.* New Haven: Yale Univ. Press.

SEYMOUR, CHARLES; and FRARY, DONALD P. 1918 *How the World Votes: The Story of Democratic Development in Elections.* 2 vols. Springfield, Mass.: Nichols.

VALEN, HENRY; and KATZ, DANIEL 1964 *Political Parties in Norway: A Community Study.* Oslo: Universitetsforlaget.

VERNEY, DOUGLAS V. 1957 *Parliamentary Reform in Sweden, 1866–1921.* Oxford: Clarendon.

WESTERATH, HERIBERT 1955 *Die Wahlverfahren und ihre Vereinbarkeit mit den demokratischen Anforderungen an das Wahlrecht.* Berlin: Gruyter.

WIGMORE, JOHN H. 1889 *The Australian Ballot System as Embodied in the Legislation of Various Countries.* Boston: Boston Book Co.

WILLIAMSON, CHILTON 1960 *American Suffrage: From Property to Democracy, 1760–1860.* Princeton Univ. Press.

ZWAGER, HAJO H. 1958 *De motivering van het algemeen kiesrecht en Europa: Een historische studie.* Groningen (Netherlands): Wolters.

MODERN SYSTEMS: TECHNICAL PROBLEMS

ANDRAE, POUL G. (1855) 1926 *Andrae and His Invention: The Proportional Representation Method.* Copenhagen: Privately published. → Chapters 3, 4, and 5 and part of Chapter 9 of the Danish original have been omitted in translation.

COTTERET, JEAN MARIE; ÉMERI, CLAUDE; and LALUMIÈRE, PIERRE 1960 *Lois électorales et inégalités de représentation en France, 1936–1960.* Paris: Colin.

DAVID, PAUL T.; and EISENBERG, RALPH 1961–1962 *Devaluation of the Urban and Suburban Vote: A Statistical Investigation of Long-term Trends in State Legislative Representation.* 2 vols. Charlottesville: Univ. of Virginia, Bureau of Public Administration.

DE GRAZIA, ALFRED 1963 *Essay on Apportionment and Representative Government.* Washington: American Enterprise Institute for Public Policy Research.

DROOP, HENRY R. 1868 *On Methods of Electing Representatives.* London: Macmillan.

HARE, THOMAS 1857 *The Machinery of Representation.* London: Maxwell.

HERMENS, FERDINAND A. 1941 *Democracy or Anarchy? A Study of Proportional Representation.* Univ. of Notre Dame Press.

HERMENS, FERDINAND A. 1951 *Europe Between Democracy and Anarchy.* Univ. of Notre Dame Press.

HOAG, CLARENCE G.; and HALLETT, GEORGE H. 1926 *Proportional Representation.* New York: Macmillan.

HONDT, VICTOR D' 1878 *La représentation proportionelle des partis.* Ghent.

HONDT, VICTOR D' 1882 *Système pratique et raisonné de représentation proportionelle.* Brussels: Muquardt.

JANSON, CARL GUNNAR 1961 *Mandattilldelning och regional röstfördelning.* Stockholm: Idun.

LAKEMAN, ENID; and LAMBERT, JAMES D. 1955 *Voting in Democracies: A Study of Majority and Proportional Electoral Systems.* London: Faber.

MÜLLER, PETER F. 1959 *Das Wahlsystem: Neue Wege der Grundlegung und Gestaltung.* Zurich: Polygraphischer Verlag.

O'LEARY, CORNELIUS 1961 *The Irish Republic, and Its Experiment With Proportional Representation.* Univ. of Notre Dame Press.

ROSS, JAMES F. S. 1959 *The Irish Election System: What It Is and How It Works.* London: Pall Mall.

SAINTE-LAGUË, A. 1910 *La représentation proportionelle et la méthode des moindres carrées.* Académie des Sciences, Paris, *Comptes rendus hebdomadaires* 151: 377–378.

STERNBERGER, ADOLF 1964 *Die grosse Wahlreform: Zeugnisse einer Bemühung.* Cologne (Germany): Westdeutscher Verlag.

UNKELBACH, HELMUT 1965 *Grundlagen der Wahlsystematik: Stabilitätsbedingungen der parlamentarischen Demokratie.* Göttingen (Germany): Vandenhoeck & Ruprecht.

UNKELBACH, HELMUT; and WILDENMANN, RUDOLF 1961 *Grundfragen des Wählens.* Frankfurt am Main (Germany): Athenäum.

MODERN SYSTEMS: REGIONAL AND NATIONAL

BUTLER, DAVID E. (1953) 1963 *The Electoral System in Britain Since 1918.* Enl. ed. Oxford: Clarendon. → First published as *The Electoral System in Britain: 1918–1953.*

CAMPBELL, PETER 1958 *French Electoral Systems and Elections: 1789–1957.* New York: Praeger.

CARSON, GEORGE BARR JR. 1955 *Electoral Practices in the U.S.S.R.* New York: Praeger.

CHARNAY, JEAN PAUL 1965 *Le suffrage politique en France: Élections parlementaires, élection présidentielle, référendums.* Paris: Mouton.

CRUTTI, MARIO; PIZZARI, M.; and SCHEPIS, G. 1951 *Profilo storico degli ordinamenti elettorali.* Empoli (Italy): Caparrini.

GEISMANN, GEORG 1964 *Politische Struktur und Regierungssystem in den Niederlanden.* Kölner Schriften zur politischen Wissenschaft, vol. 4. Frankfurt am Main (Germany): Athenäum.

GERMANY (FEDERAL REPUBLIC), WAHLRECHTSKOMMISSION 1955 *Grundlagen eines deutschen Wahlrechts: Bericht.* Bonn (Germany): Bonner Universitäts-Buchdruckerei.

GILISSEN, JOHN 1958 *Le régime représentatif en Belgique depuis 1790.* Brussels: Renaissance du Livre.

LACHAPELLE, GEORGES 1934 *Les régimes électoraux.* Paris: Colin.

LEWIS, W. ARTHUR 1965 *Politics in West Africa.* London: Allen & Unwin.

MACKENZIE, W. J. M.; and ROBINSON, KENNETH (editors) 1960 *Five Elections in Africa: A Group of Electoral Studies.* Oxford: Clarendon.

MAQUET, JACQUES J.; and HERTEFELT, MARCEL D' 1959 *Élections en société féodale: Une étude sur l'introduction du vote populaire au Ruanda-Urundi.* Académie Royale des Sciences Coloniales, Classe des Sciences Morales et Politiques, Mémoires in 8°, New Series, Vol. 21, part 2. Brussels: Académie Royale.

PEDERSEN, MOGENS N. 1966 Preferential Voting in Denmark. *Scandinavian Political Studies* 1:167–187.

ROKKAN, S.; and HJELLUM, T. 1966 Norway: The Storting Election of September 1965. *Scandinavian Political Studies* 1:237–246.

SCHEPIS, GIOVANNI 1958 *Le consultazioni popolari in Italia dal 1848 al 1957: Profilo storico-statistico.* Empoli (Italy): Caparrini.

SCHEUCH, E.; and WILDENMANN, R. 1965 *Zur Soziologie der Wahl.* Cologne (Germany): Westdeutscher Verlag.

SMITH, T. E. 1960 *Elections in Developing Countries: A Study of Electoral Procedures Used in Tropical Africa, South-east Asia, and the British Caribbean.* New York: St. Martins.

ELECTROCONVULSIVE SHOCK

It has been known for many years that electric current applied to an animal's head can elicit a convulsion. The procedure of eliciting seizures by electrical stimulation is termed "electroconvulsive shock" (ECS). The term "electroshock therapy" (EST) is used in medical references. In the early 1930s drug-induced convulsions (using insulin or Metrazol, for example) were adopted as a treatment for patients with severe mental disorders. In 1938 Cerletti and Bini demonstrated that ECS provided a more highly controlled and reliable means of eliciting convulsions. ECS gradually replaced drugs in convulsive therapy treatments and is still used to some extent as a treatment for mental disorders. It is considered to be particularly effective in the treatment of severely depressed patients (Ulett et al. 1962). Since Cerletti and Bini introduced ECS there have been numerous extensive clinical and experimental studies of the nature and bases of its behavioral effects.

The ECS convulsion. Rats or other rodents have been used as subjects in the majority of experimental studies of ECS. In general, the pattern of the convulsion obtained with rats is similar to that obtained with larger mammals, including humans. Convulsions are usually elicited by stimulating the rats with 25 to 100 milliamperes of current (AC) for approximately 0.2 to 1 second. The current is delivered through electrodes that are either attached to the animal's ear or applied directly to the rat's corneas. The maximal seizure (*grand mal*) consists of a highly stereotyped sequence of movements. The animal's hind legs are first drawn up and then extended. This tonic extension lasts for several seconds and is followed by a brief phase of whole-body clonus. The animal then remains in an immobile state for several minutes. A maximal convulsion can again be elicited in approximately ten minutes. For about 15 minutes following the convulsion the animals are usually hyperirritable. Current below that necessary to elicit a maximal seizure may produce violent running, temporary immobilization, or clonic convulsions. Maximal seizures can be prevented by administering to the animals such depressant drugs as ether, phenobarbital, or diphenylhydantoin prior to the ECS stimulation (Toman et al. 1946). Maximal seizure thresholds increase with the age of the animals and, in different laboratory species, vary directly with the weight of the animals.

Behavioral effects of multiple ECS

In the clinical use of ECS, patients are usually given a series of treatments. Most experimental studies with laboratory animals have adopted this procedure. This procedure is, of course, appropriate for research viewed as an experimental analogue of the clinical treatments. However, recent evidence indicates that ECS has numerous behavioral effects and that the effects of a single ECS treatment are quite different from those produced by a series of treatments.

Activity, sexual and maternal behavior. When rats are given a series of ECS treatments (one or more per day for 7 to 25 days) their behavior is markedly affected. Spontaneous activity is depressed, male sexual arousal is impaired, and maternal behavior (for example, nest building and care of the young) is disrupted (Munn 1950; Beach et al. 1955). The animals' behavior usually returns to normal within a few weeks after the treatments are discontinued.

Learning and retention. Multiple ECS treatments have also been found to impair rats' maze learning and retention. The degree of impairment is directly related to the complexity of the maze task. However, the impairment appears to be temporary. Little impairment is found if a month elapses between the last ECS treatment and the maze learning or retention tests. There is no impairment of performance if convulsions are prevented by the delivering of the ECS stimulation while the animals are anesthetized with ether (Munn 1950; Russell 1948).

Studies of memory in human patients given a series of ECS treatments yield findings similar to those of the rat studies. Patients typically experience impaired memory for several weeks following the termination of the treatments. This deficiency is fairly general and typically involves difficulty remembering well-learned life-history data as well as recently experienced events. Although the deficits generally disappear within a few weeks, deficits have been observed over a period of months in some patients. Some investigators have suggested that temporary memory impairment may contribute in some way to the therapeutic effectiveness of ECS treatments (Janis & Astrachan 1951).

Conditioned emotional response. A number of studies have shown that a series of ECS treatments is particularly effective in attenuating a learned emotional response (Hunt 1965). In these studies rats were first trained to press a lever for a water reward. They then were presented with a series of trials in which a clicking noise was followed by a painful shock delivered to their feet. Within a few trials the clicking noise elicited a conditioned emotional response (CER) consisting of crouching, urination, defecation, and depressed rate of lever pressing. The rats were then given a series of 21 ECS treatments—three per day for seven days. On subsequent tests the clicking noise failed to elicit the CER. Less of an attenuating effect was found if fewer ECS treatments were given or if several weeks elapsed between the CER training and the ECS treatments. The differential effect of ECS on the lever-pressing response and the CER is not due to the fact that the CER was the last response learned. Similar results are obtained when the CER training is given prior to the learning of the lever-pressing response. The effects of multiple ECS on the CER, like those found with

maze learning and retention as well as sexual and maternal behavior, are transient. The CER typically reappears within a month following the treatments. The convulsions appear to play a critical role in attenuating the CER. Multiple ECS treatments do not attenuate the CER if the convulsions are prevented by etherizing the rats prior to each ECS treatment.

It is clear from these studies that a series of ECS treatments markedly affects rats' behavior. The findings indicate, however, that the effects are for the most part temporary. Effects on sexual arousal and learning and retention generally last for only a few weeks following the treatments. Further, it seems clear that the convulsions are essential for the effects observed. There is little evidence of behavioral effects of multiple ECS treatments when convulsions are prevented by anesthetization of the animals prior to the treatments.

Behavioral effects of a single ECS

Shortly after the introduction of ECS clinical observations indicated memory loss as a common consequence of such treatments. In addition to a general loss of ability to remember names, events, and personal life history, patients seemed to have amnesia for events that had occurred shortly before each treatment. This phenomenon has been termed "retrograde amnesia." Systematic studies of memory in patients treated with ECS have confirmed this clinical observation. In an early study, for example, patients were shown a series of pictures prior to receiving an ECS treatment. In tests given the next day they showed poorest retention of the last pictures seen before convulsion (Mayer-Gross 1943).

Evidence that ECS produces retrograde amnesia has been obtained in a large number of experiments with rats. In the first two of such studies (Duncan 1949; Gerard 1955) rats and hamsters, respectively, were given a single ECS treatment after each trial in a learning task. The animals were arranged in different groups and each group was given the ECS treatment at a different time interval after each trial. With the intervals shorter than one hour, the rate of learning increased directly with increases in the length of the interval between the trial and the ECS treatment. Learning was not affected by the treatments given one hour or longer after each trial. Inasmuch as all of the experimental animals were given a series of ECS treatments, it is not possible to discount the possibility that at least some of the effects observed in these studies were due to the cumulative effects of repeated

ECS treatments. It is important to note, however, that treatments did not affect behavior unless they were administered shortly after each training trial. Thus, these findings contrast with findings of a general learning and retention impairment in rats given a series of ECS treatments prior to learning or retention tests.

Evidence of the retrograde amnesic effect of ECS has also been obtained in a large number of studies in which the animals were given only a single ECS treatment. In a series of experiments Thompson and his associates (for example, Thompson & Dean 1955) administered an ECS to different groups of rats at different intervals following massed training trials on a visual discrimination problem. The findings were similar to those obtained by Duncan and Gerard. On retraining trials, 48 hours later, animals given an ECS treatment four hours after the training did not react differently from the controls. In animals treated within one hour after the training, efficiency of relearning varied directly with the interval between the training and the ECS treatments.

In other research Thompson and other investigators have shown that the degree of the retrograde amnesia found with ECS depends upon numerous conditions, including the age and strain of the subjects, degree or strength of original learning, and complexity or difficulty of the learning task. The greatest effects are found when the rats are young or brain damaged and when the learning task is difficult. The duration of the retrograde amnesic effect of ECS is typically limited to a few minutes when a relatively simple learning task is used (Glickman 1961).

Basis of retrograde amnesic effect

During recent years most of the interest in ECS has centered on the problem of the basis of the retrograde amnesic effect. Various hypotheses have been proposed.

Brain damage. A number of investigators have suggested that the amnesic effect of the ECS may be due to brain damage produced by the current. Studies of the brains of experimental animals subjected to ECS treatments indicate that there is some evidence that ECS produces some changes in the brains—particularly small hemorrhages. However, the changes are generally minor and reversible (Madow 1956). It could be that the confusion and general impairment of learning and retention found with a series of ECS treatments is due in part to reversible vascular damage. Such effects could not, however, account for the retrograde amnesic effects of ECS. A single ECS treatment has little or no amnesic effect if the treatment is given several hours after training has been terminated. Further, a single ECS does not impair rats' subsequent ability to learn a new task or perform previously well-learned tasks. Thus, although ECS may produce brain damage, it would be difficult to explain the differential effects of ECS on recent and older memories in terms of brain damage.

Interference with memory consolidation. The most generally accepted interpretation of the retrograde amnesic effect of ECS is that the ECS interferes with the neurophysiological processes involved in storage or consolidation of memory traces (Glickman 1961). Evidence from a variety of clinical and experimental studies has provided strong support for the hypothesis that memory trace consolidation is based upon the perseveration of neurophysiological processes initiated by an experience. In humans retrograde amnesia is a common consequence of head injuries. In experimental studies with laboratory animals retrograde amnesia comparable to that found with ECS treatments has been produced by such treatments as hypoxia, drugs, and audiogenic seizures. The treatments seem to prevent the storage of information acquired during the training trials just prior to the treatment. According to this interpretation the memory loss should be permanent. Available evidence is consistent with this hypothesis. In a study by Chevalier (1965) rats were trained for a task and then given a single ECS. Clear evidence of retrograde amnesia as long as 60 days later was obtained.

Some investigators have assumed that the time required for consolidation to occur after training is indicated by the minimum interval between training and ECS treatment within which no memory impairment is found. However, since different kinds of post-training treatments produce varying degrees of retrograde amnesia, it is more likely that memory storage involves a sequence of processes and that the different treatments are capable of interfering with different processes. For example, with ECS treatments retrograde amnesia is usually obtained only when a few minutes or at most an hour elapses between training trials and treatments. With drugs (for example, Metrazol and puromycin) retrograde amnesia has been found with training-treatment intervals as long as several days (McGaugh & Petrinovich 1965). As indicated above, the deficits in learning and memory observed following a series of ECS treatments tend to disappear within a few weeks.

Most of the experimental studies of ECS effects on memory have used learning tasks employing aversive motivation—usually punishing shock. Consequently, it has been suggested that the ECS treatments may produce only a selective amnesia for the aversive stimulation. This intriguing hypothesis, however, is not supported by the data. Clear evidence of retrograde amnesia has been obtained in studies using food and water rewards. Further, in studies using shock motivation in discrimination learning tasks, the ECS seems to have its primary effects on the memory of the correct cue rather than on the motivation for responding.

Punishing effects of ECS. The findings of several studies suggest that impairment of performance found following repeated ECS treatments may be due in part to aversive effects of the treatments. For example, Friedman (1953) found that rats' performance of a lever-pressing response for food reward was depressed after the animals were given a series of ECS treatments in the apparatus. Behavior of the animals suggested that they had learned to fear the apparatus. The animals urinated, defecated, trembled, approached the lever hesitantly, and then ran away from it. The depression of responses and emotional behavior was considerably less marked in animals given the ECS treatments in a dissimilar apparatus. No effects were observed, however, in subjects treated while under ether anesthesia. The behavioral effects appeared to be due to the convulsions rather than to the ECS current.

Other studies have shown that rats tend to stop performing responses that are repeatedly followed by ECS treatments. These findings have lead some investigators to suggest that the learned fear rather than amnesia may be the cause of the impaired performance of subjects given ECS shortly after training. Recent evidence indicates that, paradoxically, ECS treatments have both amnesic and aversive effects; the amnesic effects, however, cannot be explained in terms of the aversive effects. In one study rats were given a single foot shock as they stepped from a small platform to the floor of a table; half of the rats were given an ECS within a few seconds. The next day the rats were placed on a platform again; those that had received the foot shock but no ECS tended to remain on the platform; those that had been given the ECS treatment displayed little evidence of remembering the previous foot shock and most of them readily stepped off the platform. In a subsequent study using a similar procedure rats were given an ECS in the apparatus each day for eight days immediately after they had stepped from the platform. Latencies of stepping from the platform increased gradually over the eight days. Other rats were given

only a foot shock, and most of these animals learned to stay on the platform within two trials. The performance of rats given foot shocks followed by ECS was similar to that of rats given only ECS treatments. Neither amnesic nor punitive effects were found when the ECS treatments were given one hour after each trial (McGaugh 1965). The results of these studies indicate that the aversive effects of ECS are found with repeated treatments, whereas retrograde amnesia can be obtained with a single ECS treatment. Thus, the amnesic effects of a single ECS cannot be explained in terms of the punishing effects of the treatment.

The paradox remains, however. What is the basis of the punishment if the treatment produces amnesia for events just prior to the ECS stimulation? One possibility is that the subjects learn gradually to associate the apparatus cues with the aftereffects of the convulsion. Patients given a series of ECS treatments tend to develop a fear of the treatments (Gallinek 1956). The patients readily admit that they do not experience any discomfort during the treatment. The fear seems to be based on the severe disorientation experienced while recovering from each treatment. The finding that the aversive effects in rats are eliminated by administering the ECS while the animals are anesthetized lends support to the interpretation that the aversion is based on the aftereffects of the convulsions. A more complete understanding of the basis of the aversive effects of ECS treatments requires additional research [see LEARNING, *articles on* REINFORCEMENT *and* AVOIDANCE LEARNING].

Competing response hypothesis. Lewis and Maher (1965) have proposed still another interpretation of the amnesic effects of ECS. These investigators suggested that through conditioning, the cues in the apparatus elicit behavioral inhibition, that is, a general muscular relaxation and lowered level of activity that competes with and thus interferes with the performance of the previously learned response. Most of the findings of ECS studies, however, are clearly inconsistent with this hypothesis. First, as indicated above, amnesia is found with a single treatment while other behavioral effects, including changes in response latency and freezing and crouching, appear only after a series of ECS treatments. Second, retrograde amnesia is obtained with a single treatment even when the treatment is administered outside of the training apparatus (this, in fact, is the typical procedure). Third, rats given a series of ECS treatments in an apparatus do not appear to be relaxed. They typically urinate, defecate, and tremble. Further, rats will actively avoid a place in an apparatus where they are given repeated ECS treatments (McGaugh 1965). These findings are clearly inconsistent with the conditioned inhibition interpretation of ECS effects.

Contribution of the convulsions. There is clear evidence that the effects of repeated ECS treatments are different from those produced by a single ECS. The effects of repeated ECS treatments seem to be due to the convulsions rather than to the current. Impaired maternal behavior, learning and retention deficits, suppression of a CER, and punishing effects are not found if the convulsions are prevented by the administration of the ECS while the subjects are anesthetized. Recent work indicates, however, that the convulsions are not essential for the production of retrograde amnesia with a single ECS treatment. In unpublished research McGaugh and Alpern obtained clear evidence of retrograde amnesia in animals anesthetized with ether just prior to receiving a single ECS treatment. These findings suggest that the retrograde amnesic effect of ECS is produced by the current rather than the convulsion and are consistent with other recent evidence that retrograde amnesia can be produced by restricted subcortical (and subconvulsive) electrical stimulation of the brain (Williston et al. 1964).

Although many of the effects of ECS remain to be explained, it is clear that ECS has a variety of behavioral effects and that the varied effects are not readily explained in terms of any single hypothesis. In particular, the retrograde amnesic effects of ECS must be considered separately from the diverse and complex effects found when ECS is repeatedly administered. The results of experimental studies of ECS have, as yet, shed little light on the basis of the therapeutic effectiveness of ECS in human patients. The findings have, however, had considerable influence on theories and research concerned with learning and memory. It may be that the therapeutic effectiveness is due to the learning and memory effects; an evaluation of this hypothesis must await further research.

JAMES L. MCGAUGH

[*Other relevant material may be found in* DEPRESSIVE DISORDERS; MENTAL DISORDERS, TREATMENT OF, *article on* SOMATIC TREATMENT; NERVOUS SYSTEM, *article on* BRAIN STIMULATION.]

BIBLIOGRAPHY

BEACH, FRANK A.; GOLDSTEIN, A. C.; and JACOBY, G. A. JR. 1955 Effects of Electroconvulsive Shock on Sexual Behavior in Male Rats. *Journal of Comparative and Physiological Psychology* 48:173–179.

CERLETTI, U.; and BINI, L. 1938 L'elettroshock. *Archivio generale di neurologia, psichiatria, e psicoanalisi* 19:266–268.

CHEVALIER, JACQUES 1965 Permanence of Amnesia After a Single Posttrial Electroconvulsive Seizure. *Journal of Comparative and Physiological Psychology* 59:125–127.

DUNCAN, CARL P. 1949 The Retroactive Effect of Electroshock on Learning. *Journal of Comparative and Physiological Psychology* 42:32–44.

FRIEDMAN, MERTON H. 1953 Electroconvulsive Shock as a Traumatic (Fear Producing) Experience in the Albino Rat. *Journal of Abnormal and Social Psychology* 48:555–562.

GALLINEK, ALFRED 1956 Fear and Anxiety in the Course of Electroshock Therapy. *American Journal of Psychiatry* 113:428–434.

GERARD, R. W. 1955 Biological Roots of Psychiatry. *Science* New Series 122:225–230.

GLICKMAN, STEPHEN E. 1961 Perseverative Neural Processes and the Consolidation of the Memory Trace. *Psychological Bulletin* 58:218–233.

HUNT, HOWARD F. 1965 Electro-convulsive Shock and Learning. New York Academy of Sciences, *Transactions* Series 2 27:923–945.

JANIS, IRVING L.; and ASTRACHAN, MYRTLE 1951 The Effects of Electroconvulsive Treatments on Memory Efficiency. *Journal of Abnormal and Social Psychology* 46:501–511.

LEWIS, DONALD J.; and MAHER, BRENDAN A. 1965 Neural Consolidation and Electroconvulsive Shock. *Psychological Review* 72:225–239.

McGAUGH, JAMES L. 1965 Facilitation and Impairment of Memory Storage Processes. Pages 240–291 in Daniel P. Kimble (editor), *The Anatomy of Memory.* Palo Alto, Calif.: Science and Behavior Press.

McGAUGH, JAMES L.; and PETRINOVICH, LEWIS F. 1965 Effects of Drugs on Learning and Memory. *International Review of Neurobiology* 8:139–196.

MADOW, LEO 1956 Brain Changes in Electroshock Therapy. *American Journal of Psychiatry* 113:337–347.

MAYER-GROSS, W. 1943 Retrograde Amnesia. *Lancet* [1943], no. 2:603–605.

MUNN, NORMAN L. 1950 *Handbook of Psychological Research on the Rat.* Boston: Houghton Mifflin.

RUSSELL, ROGER W. 1948 Contributions of Research on Infrahuman Animals to the Understanding of Electric Convulsive Shock Phenomena. *Journal of Personality* 17:16–28.

THOMPSON, ROBERT; and DEAN, WAID 1955 A Further Study of the Retroactive Effect of ECS. *Journal of Comparative and Physiological Psychology* 48:488–491.

TOMAN, JAMES E. P.; SWINYARD, E. A.; and GOODMAN, L. S. 1946 Properties of Maximal Seizures, and Their Alteration by Anticonvulsant Drugs and Other Agents. *Journal of Neurophysiology* 9:231–239.

ULETT, GEORGE A.; SMITH, K.; and BIDDY, R. 1962 Shock Treatment. *Progress in Neurology and Psychiatry* 17:559–571.

WILLISTON, JOHN S. et al. 1964 Disruption of Short-term Memory by Caudate Stimulation. *American Psychologist* 19:502 only.

ELECTROENCEPHALOGRAPHY
See under NERVOUS SYSTEM.

ELITES

The concept of elites is used to describe certain fundamental features of organized social life. All societies—simple and complex, agricultural and industrial—need authorities within and spokesmen and agents without who are also symbols of the common life and embodiments of the values that maintain it. Inequalities in performance and reward support this arrangement, and the inequality in the distribution of deference acknowledges the differences in authority, achievement, and reward. Elites are those minorities which are set apart from the rest of society by their pre-eminence in one or more of these various distributions. We shall concentrate here on the elites of industrial society.

In modern societies of the West, there is no single comprehensive elite but rather a complex system of specialized elites linked to the social order and to each other in a variety of ways. Indeed, so numerous and varied are they that they seldom possess enough common features and affinities to avoid marked differences and tensions. Leading artists, business magnates, politicians, screen stars, and scientists are all influential, but in separate spheres and with quite different responsibilities, sources of power, and patterns of selections and reward. This plurality of elites reflects and promotes the pluralism characteristic of modern societies in general.

For virtually every activity and every corresponding sphere of social life, there is an elite: there are elites of soldiers and of artists, as well as of bankers and of gamblers. This is the sense in which Pareto (1902–1903) used the term. There is, however, an important factor that differentiates these various elites, apart from their different skills and talents: some of them have more social weight than others because their activities have greater social significance. It is these elites—variously referred to as the ruling elite, the top influentials, or the power elite—which arouse particular interest, because they are the prime movers and models for the entire society. We shall use the term *strategic elites* to refer to those elites which claim or are assigned responsibilities for and influence over their society as a whole, in contrast with segmental elites, which have major responsibilities in subdomains of the society.

Strategic elites are those which have the largest, most comprehensive scope and impact. The boundaries that separate strategic and segmental elites are not sharply defined because of the gradations of authority and the vagueness of the perceptions that assign positions to individuals. The more highly organized elites are, the easier it is to estimate their boundaries and membership. Thus, the more readily identifiable elites in Western societies are those of business, politics, diplomacy, and the higher civil and armed services. Elites in the arts, in religion, and in moral and intellectual life are more vaguely delimited and hence also more controversial.

The differentiation of elites. Even the earliest-known human societies had leading minorities of elders, priests, or warrior kings, who performed elite social functions. A chief in a primitive society, for example, enacted one complex social role in which were fused several major social functions, expressed through the following activities: organization of productive work; propitiation of, and communication with, supernatural powers; judgment and punishment of lawbreakers; coordination of communal activities; defense of the community from enemy attack; discovery of new resources and of new solutions to the problems of collective survival; and encouragement or inspiration of artistic expression. As societies expand in size and in the diversity of their activities, such activities also expand, and more elaborate, specialized leadership roles emerge. Following are some of the major forms of societal leadership.

(1) *Ruling caste.* One stratum performs the most important social tasks, obtains its personnel through biological reproduction, and is set apart by religion, kinship, language, residence, economic standing, occupational activities, and prestige. Religious ritual is the main force that supports the position of this ruling stratum [*see* CASTE].

(2) *Aristocracy.* A single stratum monopolizes the exercise of the key social functions. The stratum consists of families bound by blood, wealth, and a special style of life and supported by income from landed property.

(3) *Ruling class.* A single social stratum is associated with various key social functions, and its members are recruited into its various segments on the basis of wealth and property rather than of blood or religion. Historically, ruling classes have held economic rather than political power, but their influence tends to extend to all important segments and activities of society. Although various differentiated and specialized sectors may be distinguished, they are bound together by a common culture and by interaction across segmental boundaries.

(4) *Strategic elites.* No single social stratum exercises all key social functions; instead, these functions and the elites associated with them are specialized and differentiated. The predominant

justification for holding elite status is not blood or wealth as such but, rather, merit and particular skills. Accordingly, these elites are recruited in various ways adapted to their differentiated tasks and are marked by diversity as well as by impermanence.

In general it appears that where the society as a whole is relatively undifferentiated, elites are few in number and comprehensive in their powers; where social differentiation is extensive, elites are many and specialized. The principal social forces underlying the change from societal leadership based on aristocracy or ruling class to that based on strategic elites are population growth, occupational differentiation, moral heterogeneity, and increased bureaucratization. In a large, industrialized mass society, marked by innumerable ethnic, regional, and occupational differences and stratified as to work, wealth, prestige, style of life, and power, leadership cannot be entrusted to a single ruler, be he chief, warrior, or priest, or to a single stratum marked by hereditary exclusiveness and traditionalism. Instead, the elites of this society will tend to be varied, specialized, and differentiated as to skill, style, background, and rewards. In this way the characteristic attributes of the larger society are mirrored in the strategic elites through whom that society tries to realize its main goals and projects. The division of a society into many groups and strata is therefore paralleled by its reunification around a symbolic center, or core, that signifies the common and enduring characteristics of the differentiated whole. The shape of this center is determined by the complexity and variety of the whole. In this way a society, consisting of a multitude of individuals and groups, can act in concert despite its moral, occupational, and technological diversity and can maintain the sense of unity necessary for collective achievements.

The functions of strategic elites. In every differentiated society, there are patterns of beliefs and values, shared means of communication, major social institutions, and leading individuals or groups concerned with the maintenance and development of the society and its culture. These leading elements, by focusing attention and coordinating action, help keep the society in working order, so that it is able to manage recurrent collective crises.

The best efforts at classifying elites are still those of Saint-Simon (1807) and Mannheim (1935), whose approaches, although separated by a century, have much in common. Saint-Simon divided elites into scientists, economic organizers, and cultural–religious leaders. This classification parallels Mannheim's distinction between the or-

ganizing and directing elites, which deal with concrete goals and programs, and the more diffuse and informally organized elites, which deal with spiritual and moral problems.

Elites may also be classified according to the four functional problems which every society must resolve: goal attainment, adaptation, integration, and pattern maintenance and tension management. Goal attainment refers to the setting and realization of collective goals; adaptation refers to the use and development of effective means of achieving these goals; integration involves the maintenance of appropriate moral consensus and social cohesion within the system; and pattern maintenance and tension management involve the morale of the system's units—individuals, groups, and organizations.

Accordingly, four *types* of strategic elites, which may include a far larger *number* of elites, may be identified: (1) the current political elite (elites of goal attainment); (2) the economic, military, diplomatic, and scientific elites (elites of adaptation); (3) elites exercising moral authority—priests, philosophers, educators, and first families (elites of integration); and (4) elites that keep the society knit together emotionally and psychologically, consisting of such celebrities as outstanding artists, writers, theater and film stars, and top figures in sports and recreation (pattern-maintenance elites).

Thus, the general functions of elites appear to be similar everywhere: to symbolize the moral unity of a collectivity by emphasizing common purposes and interests; to coordinate and harmonize diversified activities, combat factionalism, and resolve group conflicts; and to protect the collectivity from external danger.

Societies differ, however, in the way they incorporate these functions into living institutions. In some societies, usually at simpler stages of development, one agent assumes responsibility for all four system functions; in others, several specialized agents emerge. In advanced industrial societies the tendency is clearly toward several elites whose functional specialization is accompanied by a growing moral and organizational autonomy among them. At the same time, however, the overriding goals of these elites are, as they have always been, the preservation of the ideals and practices of the societies at whose apex they stand.

Recruitment of strategic elites. Elite replacement, which occurs in all societies, involves both the attraction of suitable candidates and their actual selection. What is considered suitable depends on the structure of the elite groups and on whether these elites assume comprehensive or specialized functional responsibilities. Recruitment mechanisms, however varied in practice, reflect only two fundamental principles: recruitment on the basis of biological (and, implicitly, social) inheritance and recruitment on the basis of personal talents and achievements. Although these two systems are not mutually exclusive, one or the other tends to prevail, depending on the system of social stratification, on the values placed on ascription and achievement, and on the magnitude of demand for elite candidates in relation to the supply. Broadly stated, these principles reflect the general tendencies within a social system toward expansion or toward consolidation. Under conditions of expansion, recruitment on the basis of personal achievement is likely to be the rule; under con solidation, recruitment based on inheritance of status. Each principle, moreover, has profound social repercussions on social mobility, on the stimulation of individual ambitions and talents, and on levels of discontent among different social strata. Each, furthermore, affects not only the composition of the elites but also their spiritual and moral outlook.

In modern industrial societies recruitment and selection patterns reflect the changes toward differentiation and autonomy among the elites. According to available evidence from a number of such societies, recruitment based on social inheritance is giving way to recruitment based on individual achievement. This is true for England (Cole 1955; Guttsman 1963; Thomas 1959), Germany (Deutsch & Edinger 1959; Stammer 1951; Dreitzel 1962), France (Aron 1950), the United States (Warner & Abegglen 1955; Mills 1956; Matthews 1960; Keller 1963), and the Soviet Union (Fainsod 1953; Crankshaw 1959), among others. Nonetheless, taking the elite groups as a whole, we note the simultaneous operation of several recruitment and selection principles. Some elites stress ancestry; others, educational attainments; still others, long experience and training. Some elites are elected by the public, others are appointed by their predecessors, and still others are born to their positions. The members of some elites have relatively short tenure, while that of others is lifelong. This is a dramatic contrast to other types of societies with relatively small leadership groups that have diffuse and comprehensive functional responsibilities and comprise individuals trained for their status from birth on.

Of course, looking at modern developments at a single point in time, we note that the hold of the past, with its emphasis on property or birth,

is still very strong among some elites. Conspicuous achievements are still often facilitated, if not determined, by high social and economic position, since wealth and high social standing open many doors to aspiring candidates and instill in them great expectations for worldly success. From a long-range perspective, however, it is clear that the link between high social class and strategic elite status has, in many modern societies, become indirect and informal. Ascribed attributes, such as birth, sex, and race, although they play a greater role in some elites than in others, have decreased in importance in comparison with achieved attributes. This is in line with the general modern trend toward technological and scientific specialization, in which individual skill and knowledge count more than does a gentlemanly upbringing in the traditions and standards of illustrious forebears.

Rewards of strategic elites.   The process of selection or allocation is facilitated by the system of rewards offered to individuals assuming leadership positions in society. Some rewards are tangible material benefits, such as land, money, cattle, or slaves, and others are intangible, such as social honor and influence. The specific rewards used to attract potential recruits to elite positions depend on the social definition of scarce and desirable values and the distribution of these values.

Rewards play a twofold role in the recruitment of elites: they motivate individuals to assume the responsibilities of elite positions, and they maintain the high value placed on these positions. They thus serve as inducements to individuals, as well as indicators of rank.

Rewards, too, have become specialized in modern industrial societies. Some elites enjoy large earnings; others, popularity or fame; and still others, authority and power. Not all elites are equally wealthy, not all have equal prestige; only some have much more power than others, and none have influence in all spheres. The assumption of elite positions thus also involves the acceptance of specific rewards associated with them. Responsibilities and rewards form parts of a whole and may be discussed jointly. And each is linked to recruitment, for rewards are the spur to the expenditure of effort that the duties of strategic positions demand.

The process of recruiting elites and the manner of rewarding them must not be confused with their purposes and status. For although recruitment and rewards affect the composition and performance of elites, they do not alter their functions. As Mosca (1896) clearly demonstrated, democratically and hereditarily recruited elites differ in many important ways, but they nonetheless function as elites.

The tendency toward a pluralization of elites is likely to conflict with the older tendency toward the monolithic exercise of power and leadership. This is a problem in totalitarian as well as in liberal societies. In totalitarian societies, the problem is how to permit the desired flexibility and variety without corroding social stability. Conversely, in liberal pluralist systems, the problem is how to achieve the necessary degree of social cohesion and moral consensus among partly autonomous, highly specialized, yet functionally interdependent elites. The cohesion and consensus are necessary if the society is to pursue common goals and is to be unified in more than name only.

These recent tendencies and trends are neither absolute nor inevitable. They are clearly manifested today in a wide variety of contexts and reflect the tempo of social change in a technologically expanding world. Should this tempo slow down markedly or cease altogether, the impulses toward rigidity and ascription may well come to the fore once again, albeit within a social structure shaped by centuries of industrialism. Some security and stability will be gained, but at the price of adventure and novelty—a familiar exchange in the annals of history and one bound to be reflected in the character and stamp of the strategic elites.

SUZANNE KELLER

[See also BUREAUCRACY; COMMUNITY, article on THE STUDY OF COMMUNITY POWER; POLITICAL SOCIOLOGY; and the biographies of ARISTOTLE; MANNHEIM; MICHELS; MILLS; MOSCA; PARETO; PLATO; SAINT-SIMON.]

BIBLIOGRAPHY

ARON, RAYMOND   1950   Social Structure and the Ruling Class. British Journal of Sociology 1:1–16, 126–143.
BOTTOMORE, THOMAS B.   1964   Elites and Society. London: Watts.
COLE, G. D. H.   1955   Studies in Class Structure. London: Routledge. → See especially pages 101–146 on "Elites in British Society."
CRANKSHAW, EDWARD   1959   Khrushchev's Russia. Harmondsworth (England): Penguin.
DEUTSCH, KARL W.; and EDINGER, LOUIS J.   1959   Germany Rejoins the Powers: Mass Opinion, Interest Groups, and Elites in Contemporary German Foreign Policy. Stanford (Calif.) Univ. Press.
DREITZEL, HANS P.   1962   Elitebegriff und Sozialstruktur: Eine soziologische Begriffsanalyse. Stuttgart (Germany): Enke.
FAINSOD, MERLE   (1953) 1963   How Russia Is Ruled. Rev. ed. Russian Research Center Studies No. 11. Cambridge, Mass.: Harvard Univ. Press.
GUTTSMAN, WILHELM L.   1963   The British Political Élite. London: MacGibbon & Kee.
HUNTER, FLOYD   1959   Top Leadership, U.S.A. Chapel Hill: Univ. of North Carolina Press.
JAEGGI, URS   1960   Die gesellschaftliche Elite: Eine Studie zum Problem der sozialen Macht. Bern (Switzerland) and Stuttgart (Germany): Haupt.
KELLER, SUZANNE   1963   Beyond the Ruling Class: Strategic Elites in Modern Society. New York: Random House.
LASSWELL, HAROLD D.   1936   Politics: Who Gets What, When, How? New York: McGraw-Hill.
MANNHEIM, KARL   (1935) 1940   Man and Society in an Age of Reconstruction: Studies in Modern Social Structure. New York: Harcourt. → First published as Mensch und Gesellschaft im Zeitalter des Umbaus.
MATTHEWS, DONALD R.   1960   U.S. Senators and Their World. Chapel Hill: Univ. of North Carolina Press.
MILLS, C. WRIGHT   1956   The Power Elite. New York: Oxford Univ. Press.
MOSCA, GAETANO   (1896) 1939   The Ruling Class. New York: McGraw-Hill. → First published as Elementi di scienza politica.
PARETO, VILFREDO   1902–1903   Les systèmes socialistes. 2 vols. Paris: Giard.
PARSONS, TALCOTT; BALES, R. F.; and SHILS, E. A.   1953   Working Papers in the Theory of Action. Glencoe, Ill.: Free Press.
SAINT-SIMON, CLAUDE HENRI DE   (1807) 1859   Oeuvres choisis. Volume 1. Brussels: Meenen & Cie.
SERENO, RENZO   1962   The Rulers. New York: Praeger; Leiden (Netherlands): Brill.
STAMMER, OTTO   1951   Das Elitenproblem in der Demokratie. Schmollers Jahrbuch für Gesetzgebung, Verwaltung und Volkswirtschaft 71, no. 5:1–28.
THOMAS, HUGH (editor)   1959   The Establishment: A Symposium. London: Blond.
WARNER, W. LLOYD; and ABEGGLEN, JAMES C.   1955   Occupational Mobility in American Business and Industry: 1928–1952. Minneapolis: Univ. of Minnesota Press.

ELLIS, HAVELOCK

Havelock Ellis was born on February 2, 1859, in Croydon, England, the son of an English sea captain, Edward Peppen Ellis. His mother, Susannah Wheatley Ellis, was a highly energetic and vivacious woman. Ellis felt, however, that he owed much to the mediocrity of his father's family, most of whose males, "whatever their occupation, have all the qualities of trustworthy bank clerks"; and their temperate and cheerful acceptance of the world, according to Ellis, helped to modify his own literary–aesthetic temperament and prevent him from adopting a one-sided, excessive, or eccentric view of life.

Ellis went to a boarding school, the Poplars, at Tooting, where he was well grounded in French, German, and Italian. It was here that one of his masters, Angus Mackay, revealed to him the delights of nineteenth-century English literature and helped arouse his vital interest in philosophic and politico–economic questions of the day. At 16 he began an undistinguished career as a teacher and later headmaster in Australia. At the age of 19, however, he came under the influence of and was in effect converted by the writings of the philosopher–surgeon James Hinton. Hinton's book *Life in Nature* made such a profound impression on young Ellis that he decided to undertake the study of medicine in order to do research and writing in the field of sex. Ellis received his medical training at St. Thomas' Hospital in London, and as a medical assistant he attended a number of patients, many of them women in labor. He obtained his M.D. in 1889 but did not practice medicine; instead, he devoted the rest of his life to editing—for many years his main source of income—and writing.

During the 1880s Ellis wrote on literary and social subjects for first-rate English journals and edited the Mermaid Series of Elizabethan dramatists (a series of scholarly reprints), the Contemporary Science Series, and other works. He made a name for himself in the field of belles-lettres with such books as *The Soul of Spain*, 1908, and *Impressions and Comments*, 1914–1924, and in the field of science and its social implications with such writings as *A Study of British Genius* (1904), *The World of Dreams* (1911), and *The Dance of Life* (1923).

Havelock Ellis is known best as a researcher and philosopher in the field of sex and love. Beginning his studies of human sexuality with a fact-packed book, *Man and Woman* (1894), he went on to write his monumental seven-volume *Studies in the Psychology of Sex* (1897–1928). Although originally banned in his native England, the *Studies* became widely read and cited in all other parts of the world and were without question the most influential and precedent-shattering volumes on human sexuality ever written, up to the time of the publication of the Kinsey reports. They were followed by several other important books on sex–love relations from Ellis' pen, including *The Task of Social Hygiene* (1912), *Little Essays of Love and Virtue* (1922–1931), *Psychology of Sex* (1933), *My Life* (1939), and *Sex and Marriage* (1951).

It is difficult to spotlight the most important and influential of Ellis' contributions to the subject of sex. He produced the first notable scientific book on homosexuality; he pioneered in the presentation of full case histories, diaries, and letters on sexual subjects; he was the first important popularizer of the subject of sex–love relations; he was an outstanding crusader against sex censorship; he convincingly showed the interrelationships between

human sexuality and the love emotions; he did some original research on masturbation, using himself as a subject; and he presented many original and well-formulated ideas on sexual modesty, the biology and psychology of the sexual impulse, sexual periodicity, erotic symbolism, transvestitism, and several other sexual–amative aspects of life. He and Sigmund Freud did more to make sex a respectable word than any other writers of their day. Although Ellis was largely a devotee of the library rather than a clinician or a laboratory scientist, his careful sex research has inspired much clinical and laboratory investigation.

The remarkable thing about Havelock Ellis' sex writings is that while they are factual, objective, and coolly analytical, they are often pervaded with a thoroughly humane, love-centered (rather than sex-centered), and at times aesthetic–mystic quality that makes his views acutely personal as well as dispassionately scientific. He himself was a mild undinist, suffering from sexual shyness and inadequacy during his youth. Ellis was married for 25 years to a basically lesbian woman, Edith Lees Ellis, with whom he nonetheless had a remarkably intense love relationship. He achieved real sexual fulfillment, however, during the last twenty years of his life in his extramarital relationship with Françoise Delisle (he died in 1939 in Suffolk). It seems clear that Ellis' own sex experiences, as well as his personal naturist–humanist philosophy of life (which he carried to almost religious extremes), combined to enable him to view human sexuality in a uniquely realistic yet essentially poetic way and to make him the best and most effective antipuritan of the late nineteenth and early twentieth centuries.

ALBERT ELLIS

[*For discussion of the subsequent development of Ellis' work, see* SEXUAL BEHAVIOR.]

WORKS BY ELLIS

Works of purely literary interest have not been included.

(1894) 1929   *Man and Woman: A Study of Secondary and Tertiary Sexual Characters.* Rev. & enl. ed. Boston: Houghton Mifflin.

(1897–1928) 1936   *Studies in the Psychology of Sex.* 4 vols. Reissued in a new form. New York: Random House. → First published in seven volumes.

(1904) 1926   *A Study of British Genius.* New rev. & enl. ed. Boston: Houghton Mifflin.

(1911) 1926   *The World of Dreams.* New ed. Boston: Houghton Mifflin.

1912   *The Task of Social Hygiene.* Boston: Houghton Mifflin.

(1922–1931) 1937 *On Life and Sex: Essays of Love and Virtue*. 2 vols. in 1. New York: Garden City Pub. → The two volumes were originally published as *Little Essays of Love and Virtue*, 1922, and *More Essays of Love and Virtue*, 1931.

(1923) 1929 *The Dance of Life*. Boston: Houghton Mifflin.

1933 *Psychology of Sex: A Manual for Students*. New York: Emerson; London: Heinemann.

1939 *My Life: Autobiography*. Boston: Houghton Mifflin.

(1951) 1952 *Sex and Marriage: Eros in Contemporary Life*. Edited by John Gawsworth. New York: Random House; London: Williams & Norgate.

WORKS ABOUT ELLIS

COLLIS, JOHN STEWART 1959 *Havelock Ellis; Artist of Life: A Study of His Life and Work*. New York: Sloane. → Published in England as *An Artist of Life: A Study of the Life and Work of Havelock Ellis*.

DELISLE, FRANÇOISE 1946 *Friendship's Odyssey*. London: Heinemann. → An autobiography, with an account of the author's relations with Havelock Ellis from 1916 to 1939.

PETERSON, HOUSTON 1928 *Havelock Ellis: Philosopher of Love*. Boston: Houghton Mifflin.

ELLWOOD, CHARLES A.

Charles Abram Ellwood (1873–1946), known for his efforts to establish a scientific psychological sociology in the United States, was born near Ogdensburg, New York. He entered Cornell University in 1892, initially intending to study law. However, at Cornell he met Edward A. Ross, later a famous sociologist and then, early in his career, teaching economics. Ross induced Ellwood to abandon his plans for a legal career and to turn to the social sciences. Ellwood specialized in sociology and economics. His studies in statistics and demography were mainly directed by Walter F. Willcox; those in political science and economic research by Jeremiah W. Jenks. His instructors were oriented toward social reform, and by the time he was graduated, in 1896, he had become convinced that the main objective of social science should be to improve public well-being. This became the leitmotiv of his sociological writings throughout his life.

Ellwood went to the University of Chicago to pursue graduate work in sociology, being guided by W. I. Thomas and George H. Mead in social psychology, John Dewey in psychology and pragmatic philosophy, and Albion W. Small in systematic sociology and social-reform doctrine. Small advised him to spend a year at the University of Berlin, which he did in 1897/1898, studying historical and reformist economics, mainly under Gustav Schmoller, and philosophy and ethics, under Friedrich Paulsen.

He returned to Chicago in 1898 to complete his doctorate, producing as his dissertation, in 1899, *Some Prolegomena to Social Psychology*. This was the first presentation of social psychology to be firmly based on the principles of academic psychology. The concepts laid down here were amplified and revised in his later systematic works in this field, chiefly under the influence of Charles H. Cooley. Some fifteen years later, in 1914 and 1915, Ellwood studied in England under Leonard T. Hobhouse and Robert R. Marett, leaders in cultural sociology and anthropology, and was led thereby to place psychological sociology within the larger framework of a cultural interpretation of the social process.

Ellwood traveled extensively in Europe in 1927 and 1928 and in Latin America in 1937, thereby developing a deep interest in international relations, which he interpreted from the standpoint of practical pacifism, holding that world peace is essential to any successful program of social amelioration. Ellwood's travels, especially in Europe, led him to form many contacts with foreign sociologists. He developed considerable prestige among them and served as president of the International Institute of Sociology in 1935/1936.

In 1900 Ellwood accepted the newly established chair in sociology at the University of Missouri, and he remained there for three decades, turning out students who became distinguished sociologists, such as E. B. Reuter, Luther L. Bernard, and Herbert Blumer. In 1930 he was called to Duke University to establish a new department of sociology, and he remained there until his death. Among his better-known students at Duke were Paul E. Root, Guy V. Price, Austin L. Porterfield, and Leonard Broom.

Ellwood's most important work in the field of psychological sociology, and the one for which he will also be best remembered as a sociologist, is his *Sociology in Its Psychological Aspects* (1912), which, as a comprehensive psychological interpretation of human behavior, was far ahead of any other work in the field at this time. This synthesis combined contributions from the evolutionary perspective of Darwin; the biological approach of Lloyd Morgan and E. L. Thorndike; the neurology and comparative psychology of Jacques Loeb, as passed on to Ellwood by W. I. Thomas; Thomas' own views of folk psychology; William James's pragmatic and dynamic instrumentalism, especially his emphasis on the importance of habit; the functional psychology of J. R. Angell and John Dewey; the social psychology of G. H. Mead and

C. H. Cooley; and Lester Ward's contention that psychic factors exert dominant control over human and social behavior. Later on, Ellwood's work was far surpassed by that of specialists like L. L. Bernard. Ellwood's *Introduction to Social Psychology* (1917) and *Psychology of Human Society* (1925a), while broader in perspective than his previous works, were less successful as psychological sociology because he tried to weave into them the cultural concepts that had begun to influence him deeply soon after he finished his masterpiece in 1912.

The cultural approach to the social process dominated Ellwood's work in formal sociology during the two decades before his death. He had received some suggestions here from W. I. Thomas during his student days at Chicago, but the main impetus to this shift in emphasis came from his work with Hobhouse and Marett. The cultural interpretation was set forth in his *Cultural Evolution: A Study of Social Origin and Development* (1927a). Primarily because of his contact with Marett, Ellwood was one of the first Americans to cut loose from the unilateral evolutionism of Herbert Spencer, Lewis Henry Morgan, Charles Letourneau, and their associates, which had dominated the historical sociology of the Ward–Giddings–Howard era. Ellwood had a drastically revised and expanded version of his work ready for publication at the time of his death, and it is a serious loss to sociological literature that it was never published.

Ellwood's comprehensive knowledge of the fields and methods of sociology was best and most constructively exhibited in his *Methods in Sociology: A Critical Study* (1933). Ellwood cautioned in a reasonable manner against what he deemed to be danger signs in the sociological trends of the mid-1930s: the attempt to recast sociology in the terms and techniques of natural science; increasing fragmentation; excessive emphasis on quantitative methods; and the repudiation of value judgments and of proper recognition of the ultimate role of social amelioration.

Ellwood's interest in practical sociology was reflected in his 1910 textbook, the first textbook in sociology that appealed to college students. Over 300,000 copies were marketed before it came to be supplanted in the mid-1930s by more substantial and sophisticated textbooks on social problems. Ellwood produced a number of books (see, for example, his 1915 book) that presented his general solutions to social problems, with increasing emphasis on the responsibility of religion. He had planned to expand his introductory treatment of social ethics as a guide to social reconstruction into

a comprehensive and systematic work on social ethics, but the strong impulses from the deep-seated religious experience of his younger days eventually led him to regard a modernized Christianity as the best stimulus and guide to needed social reform. Hence, he revamped his presentation and published *The Reconstruction of Religion* (1922), which became his most widely read book outside college classrooms. This was supplemented by *Christianity and Social Science* (1923). These books gained for Ellwood a large and powerful following among liberally inclined and social-reformist clergymen. Although Ellwood constantly stressed the fact that social change must be guided by scientific and rational principles, he attributed more significance and potency to religious views and values than any other leading American sociologist of his generation. He especially evaded any attempt to apply rational interpretations to sexual problems.

In seeking to summarize Ellwood's place in the development of American sociology, one may safely say that he will be remembered first and foremost for the fact that he executed far and away the most successful of the early attempts to link up scientific psychology with systematic sociology. Other sociologists, such as Tarde, Le Bon, Durkheim, Sighele, Giddings, Ross, and Cooley, had produced more striking interpretations of social behavior from the psychological point of view, but most of them selected some special psychological factor, such as invention, imitation, impression, suggestion, crowd psychological impulses, creativeness, sympathy, and the like, rather than having a comprehensive psychological approach to the subject. Moreover, most of them, save for Durkheim and Cooley, had little technical knowledge of formal psychology and based their analysis and generalization on common-sense and rule-of-thumb psychological concepts.

Influenced by Comte, Ward, and Hobhouse, Ellwood shared with Small the mantle of Ward in presenting social *telesis*, expertly planned social guidance, as the main role and justification of social science in general and of sociology in particular. Ellwood assigned to modern religion a more important role in social telesis than any other leading sociologist of his time.

In our era, which may have settled down to accepting a pattern of "perpetual war for perpetual peace," Ellwood's views on international relations are especially wholesome and pertinent. While primarily concerned with social amelioration, Ellwood, inspired by his reading of Kant, was convinced that there is no likelihood of establishing a social utopia or of perpetuating democratic society unless world peace can be attained, and he believed that this was possible only in connection with a strong world organization.

HARRY ELMER BARNES

[*For the historical context of Ellwood's work, see* SO-CIAL PROBLEMS *and the biographies of* DEWEY; HOBHOUSE; MARETT; MEAD; MORGAN, C. LLOYD; SCHMOLLER; SMALL; THOMAS; WILLCOX; *for discussion of the subsequent development of Ellwood's ideas, see* EVOLUTION; PACIFISM; *and the biography of* BERNARD.]

WORKS BY ELLWOOD

(1899) 1901 *Some Prolegomena to Social Psychology.* Univ. of Chicago Press.
(1910) 1943 *Sociology: Principles and Problems.* New ed., rev. & enl. New York: American Book. → First published as *Sociology and Modern Social Problems.*
(1912) 1921 *Sociology in Its Psychological Aspects.* 2d ed. New York and London: Appleton.
(1915) 1919 *The Social Problem: A Reconstructive Analysis.* Rev. ed. New York: Macmillan.
1917 *An Introduction to Social Psychology.* New York and London: Appleton.
1922 *The Reconstruction of Religion: A Sociological View.* New York: Macmillan.
1923 *Christianity and Social Science.* New York: Macmillan.
1925a *The Psychology of Human Society.* New York: Appleton.
1925b The Group and Society. *Journal of Applied Sociology* 9:401–403.
1925c The Cultural or Psychological Theory of Society. *Journal of Applied Sociology* 10:10–16.
1925d Intolerance [Presidential Address]. American Sociological Society, *Papers and Proceedings* 19:1–14.
1925e *Unsere Kulturkrise: Ihre Ursache und Heilmittel.* Stuttgart (Germany): Kohlhammer.
1927a *Cultural Evolution: A Study of Social Origin and Development.* New York: Century.
1927b Recent Developments in Sociology. Pages 1–49 in *Recent Developments in the Social Sciences.* Philadelphia: Lippincott.
1927c The Social Development of Morality. *Sociology and Social Research* 12:18–25.
1927d The Development of Sociology in the United States Since 1910. *Sociological Review* (London) 19:25–34.
1927e Primitive Concepts and the Origin of Cultural Patterns. *American Journal of Sociology* 33:1–13.
1927f Social Evolution and Cultural Evolution. *Journal of Applied Sociology* 11:303–314.
1929a *Man's Social Destiny in the Light of Science.* Nashville, Tenn.: Cokesbury.
1929b The Background of Good-will. Pages 29–37 in *Pacificism in the Modern World.* Edited by Devere Allen. Garden City, N.Y.: Doubleday.
1929c Sociology in Europe. *Sociology and Social Research* 13:203–210.
1929d Charles Horton Cooley: 1864–1929. *Sociology and Social Research* 14:3–9.
1930a Social Education in the United States. Pages 253–270 in Paul D. Schilpp (editor), *Higher Education Faces the Future: A Symposium.* New York: Liveright.
1930b Recent American Sociology. *Scientia* 47:335–343.

1930c The Uses and Limitations of Behaviorism in the Social Sciences. Pages 187–211 in William P. King (editor), *Behaviorism: A Battle Line.* Nashville, Tenn.: Cokesbury.
1930d Uses and Limitations of Behaviorism in Sociology. American Sociological Society, *Publications* 24:74–82.
1931a The Implications for Religion of Current Trends in the Social Sciences. Pages 74–83 in Milton C. Towner (editor), *Religion in Higher Education.* Univ. of Chicago Press.
1931b Scientific Method in Sociology. *Social Forces* 10: 15–21.
1931c The Philosophy of Protestantism in Its Relation to Industry. *Religious Education* 26:420–426.
1933 *Methods in Sociology: A Critical Study.* Durham, N.C.: Duke Univ. Press.

SUPPLEMENTARY BIBLIOGRAPHY

CRAMBLITT, MARY V. 1944 *A Bibliography of the Writings of Charles Abram Ellwood.* Durham, N.C.: Duke Univ. Press.

ELY, RICHARD T.

Richard Theodore Ely (1854–1943), American economist, probably exerted a greater influence upon American economics during its vital formative period than any other individual. Although Ely's writings were prolific, timely, and vigorous, he made a more lasting impact on his discipline through his achievements as a founder and organizer of scholarly associations, institutes, and research projects.

Ely's career began when the influence of German scholarship upon the United States was at its height. Born in Ripley, New York, of pious Congregationalist stock, he graduated from Columbia College in 1876 and spent the next four years in Germany, primarily at Heidelberg, where he was strongly influenced by Karl Knies, one of the leading historical economists. From 1881 to 1892 Ely taught economics at the then new Johns Hopkins University and produced several books and innumerable articles for scholarly journals, magazines, and newspapers, including pioneer studies of socialism, organized labor, and state taxation. He was an impulsive, outspoken, and contentious man, whose academic friends and foes alike complained of his emotionalism and carelessness. His eager participation in contemporary reform movements brought him both lavish praise and severe condemnation. For example, his sympathetic study *The Labor Movement in America* (1886) provoked his Johns Hopkins colleague Simon Newcomb to declare him unfit to hold a university chair; and in 1894, when he was at the University of Wisconsin, Ely was publicly denounced for preaching socialism and encouraging strikes. In fact, however, he was a moderate reformer, an optimist, and a progressive who favored a mean between individualism and socialism. After a widely publicized "trial," the regents of the university exonerated him and issued a classic declaration in favor of academic freedom.

Ely figured prominently in the controversy between the "old" and "new" schools of American economics during the 1880s. His main contribution to the debate was a polemical monograph entitled *The Past and the Present of Political Economy* (1884), in which he attacked the old school orthodoxy based on Ricardo and Mill and advocated a closer link between economics and ethics and an increased use of a crudely inductive "look and see" method. However, he never rejected Ricardo *in toto* and specifically exempted Ricardian rent doctrine from his general criticism of Ricardian economics. The following year he and several other new school rebels founded the American Economic Association to propagate their ideas and promote the scientific study of economic problems. Ely became the association's first secretary and its most active proponent, but his sentimentalism and reforming zeal at first discouraged more conservative economists from participating. However, even before 1892, when Ely resigned his secretaryship and moved to the Middle West, the organization was turning from social reform to a more neutral scholarly approach. Ely was president of the association from 1900 to 1902. During the 1880s and 1890s, he was prominent in such religious reform organizations as the Christian Social Union and the American Institute for Christian Sociology and was sometimes regarded rather as a preacher than an economist. *An Introduction to Political Economy* (1889a), which Ely prepared for use in connection with his teaching at the Chautauqua Methodist summer school, sold 30,000 copies in a decade, and he subsequently published an even more successful academic textbook, *Outlines of Economics* (1893), which eventually sold more than 350,000 copies.

On his move to Wisconsin in 1892, Ely inaugurated a school of economics, political science, and history. The school, staffed by such scholars as Frederick J. Turner, Edward A. Ross, and John R. Commons, all of whom had been Ely's pupils at Johns Hopkins, became internationally famous because of its collaboration with the Wisconsin government, led by the Progressive politician Robert La Follette. Ely's new school teaching constituted a direct link between German historical economics and twentieth-century institutional economics. His major contribution to this economic tradition was *Property and Contract in Their Relations to the Distribution of Wealth* (1914), and his interest in this field eventually led him to establish in 1920 the Institute for Research in Land Economics and Public Utilities and the associated *Journal of Land and Public Utility Economics* (later called *Land Economics*). Also at Wisconsin Ely helped to launch the American Association for Labor Legislation (of which he became president) and obtained private resources to finance Commons' massive 11-volume *Documentary History of American Industrial Society*, 1910–1911.

Ely was neither an original theorist nor a seminal thinker; he was, however, a stimulating teacher who exerted a profoundly liberating influence on his students, many of whom became distinguished scholars or public figures. Until his death at the age of 89, he remained remarkably active, writing on a variety of topical issues and eventually editing more than a hundred volumes. During his later years he abandoned his earlier defense of the Ricardian rent doctrine and emphasized the parallels between land and capital; one indication of his increasing conservatism is the fact that his Institute for Research was attacked in 1926 as a tool of the public utilities. In a sense, this was a sign of the change in the tone of American economics since Ely's "trial" in 1894.

A. W. Coats

[For the historical context of Ely's work, see ECONOMIC THOUGHT, *articles on* THE HISTORICAL SCHOOL *and* THE INSTITUTIONAL SCHOOL; *and the biographies of* KNIES; MILL; RICARDO.]

WORKS BY ELY

1883   *French and German Socialism in Modern Times.* New York: Harper.

1884   *The Past and the Present of Political Economy.* Baltimore: Johns Hopkins Press.

1885   *Recent American Socialism.* Baltimore: Johns Hopkins Press.

1886   *The Labor Movement in America.* New York: Crowell.

(1888) 1890   *Problems of To-day: A Discussion of Protective Tariffs, Taxation and Monopolies.* New ed., rev. & enl. New York: Crowell.

1888   ELY, RICHARD T.; and FINLEY, JOHN H. *Taxation in American States and Cities.* New York: Crowell.

1889a   *An Introduction to Political Economy.* New York: Chautauqua.

(1889b) 1895   *Social Aspects of Christianity, and Other Essays.* New York: Crowell.

(1893) 1937   ELY, RICHARD T.; and HESS, RALPH H. *Outlines of Economics.* 6th ed. New York: Macmillan.

1894   *Socialism: An Examination of Its Nature, Its Strength, Its Weakness, With Suggestions for Social Reform.* New York: Crowell.

(1900) 1906   *Monopolies and Trusts.* New York: Grosset & Dunlap.

1903   *Studies in the Evolution of Industrial Society.* New York: Macmillan.

(1914) 1922 *Property and Contract in Their Relations to the Distribution of Wealth.* 2 vols. New York: Macmillan.

1924 ELY, RICHARD T.; and MOREHOUSE, EDWARD W. *Elements of Land Economics.* New York: Macmillan.

1938 *Ground Under Our Feet: An Autobiography.* New York: Macmillan.

(1940) 1964 ELY, RICHARD T.; and WEHRWEIN, GEORGE S. *Land Economics.* Madison: Univ. of Wisconsin Press.

SUPPLEMENTARY BIBLIOGRAPHY

COATS, A. W. 1960 The First Two Decades of the American Economic Association. *American Economic Review* 50:555–574.

DORFMAN, JOSEPH 1946–1959 *The Economic Mind in American Civilization.* 5 vols. New York: Viking. → See especially Volumes 3 and 4.

EVERETT, JOHN R. 1946 *Religion in Economics: A Study of John Bates Clark, Richard T. Ely and Simon N. Patten.* New York: King's Crown Press.

FINE, SIDNEY 1951 Richard T. Ely: Forerunner of Progressivism, 1880–1901. *Mississippi Valley Historical Review* 37:599–624.

NOBLE, DAVID W. 1958 *The Paradox of Progressive Thought.* Minneapolis: Univ. of Minnesota Press. → See especially "Richard T. Ely: The Economist as Christian and Prophet," pages 157–173.

EMIGRATION

See MIGRATION *and* REFUGEES.

EMOTION

It is virtually impossible to give a definition of emotion that all psychologists will accept, although there is fair agreement that such phenomena as fear, anger, joy, disgust, and affection should be classified as emotions. Nearly all theorists relate emotion in some way to motivation, and all assign important roles in emotion to the functioning of the autonomic nervous system. All, except the most rigidly behavioristic, classify emotions as *affective* phenomena.

One difficulty in defining emotion is that emotional phenomena are exceedingly complex and must be observed and analyzed from different points of view. An emotional episode can be observed and studied as a conscious experience from the point of view of the experiencing individual. It can be analyzed from the point of view of a behavioral scientist, a physiologist, a social scientist, or a psychiatrist.

Emotion as a conscious experience

Emotions and other affective processes. The term "emotion" is sometimes used to include the whole gamut of affective experiences, but this usage is too broad. Traditionally, the term applies to a single variety of the affective process. The term "affect," in psychiatry, designates a class of experiences including, among others, emotions, moods, and guilt feelings.

The main varieties of affective processes can be classified as follows: (1) A simple feeling of *pleasantness* is associated with such sensory stimulations as the odor of a perfume, a sweet taste, or a musical harmony, and a feeling of *unpleasantness* with a painful burn, a bitter taste, or a bad odor. (2) Pleasant *organic feelings* are associated with good health, buoyancy, or sexual satisfaction, and unpleasant feelings with hunger, thirst, fatigue, cramps, or headaches. (3) *Interests* are mild feelings of pleasantness associated with games, sports, plays, and other activities. *Aversions* are unpleasant affects associated with the rejection of foods, persons, and activities. (4) *Sentiments* are feelings associated with something valued or held sacred; they are based upon past experience and training. There are patriotic, moral, religious, aesthetic, and intellectual sentiments. The term "sentiment" also refers to a stable disposition to react with feeling to a class of objects or situations. (5) *Emotions* are acute affective disturbances arising from the psychological situation and expressing themselves in conscious experience, behavior, and physiological processes. (6) *Moods* are typically less intense and more chronic than emotions but are similar in affective tone and underlying dynamic mechanisms. (7) *Temperament* designates the affective aspect of personality as a whole. Temperaments are said to be apathetic, moody, phlegmatic, cheerful, vivacious, depressed, sanguine, etc. Although temperaments are stable, they are known to change with age, health, and environmental conditions.

In this classification, it will be noted that emotions and moods are distinguished, but they are closely related. An emotion may calm down into a mood or a mood build up into an emotion. Thus a fright may taper off into a mood of anxiety; anger may subside into a mood of hostility or resentment; laughter may become a mood of cheerfulness; weeping, a mood of sorrow or grief. Depression is a mood characterized by the decrease of an individual's vitality, hopes, aspirations, and self-esteem. The mood may be a mild feeling of tiredness or sadness. In psychopathic states a depression may become a profound apathy with psychotic disregard for reality and with suicidal tendencies. Moods and emotions cannot be sharply distinguished; any line of distinction is arbitrary.

"Emotion" is a substantive term; the adjective "emotional" would better characterize the process. Emotional activities are commonly contrasted with rational, intellectual, or even mental processes, as well as with motivational processes.

Emotions and cognition. Emotions are elicited by the awareness of a situation in which an individual finds himself. Magda B. Arnold (1960) argued that emotional behavior follows the intuitive appraisal of a situation. She defined emotion as a felt tendency to move toward anything intuitively appraised as good (beneficial) or away from anything intuitively appraised as bad (harmful). Thus, the feelings of a male enticing a female are emotional; the feelings of a man running a race for his life are emotional.

The cognitive basis of emotion becomes clear when we consider conditions that elicit emotions in different societies. For example, among the Negroes of the Niger delta, it is a rule that if a woman gives birth to twins, she and the twins are put to death. If the mother is allowed to live, her life is little better than a living death, for she becomes an outcast and must live the rest of her days in the forest. But among the Bankundo of the Congo valley, the mother of twins becomes an object of veneration. She is entitled to wear a special badge and her name is changed to "Mother-of-Twins." Obviously, the type of affective arousal by such an event as the birth of twins depends upon the beliefs, attitudes, and practices of a group.

Emotion and motivation. Although it is generally agreed that emotions bear an important relation to motivation, there is disagreement concerning the exact nature of the relationship. In general, there are two main views: First, it is claimed that emotion is a conscious experience associated with purposive, organized activity. Second, it is claimed that emotion is a disorganized experience due to conflict, frustration, thwarted expectation, tension, or the release of tension.

Emotion as organized experience. The first view of emotion is illustrated in the writings of William McDougall (1908), who defined emotion as the consciously felt aspect of instinctive activity. He paired instincts with emotions: the instinct to flee from danger was paired with the emotion of fear; the instinct of pugnacity was paired with the emotion of anger; parental instinct, with tender emotion; sexual instinct, with lust; self-abasement, with the emotion of subjection; self-assertion, with the emotion of elation. McDougall regarded instinctive behavior as always purposive, goal-directed, and integrated, and emotion as the felt equivalent of instinctive behavior.

Other psychologists, e.g., Carl R. Rogers, have emphasized that "emotion" facilitates goal-directed behavior. Feelings of success, self-confidence, and cheerfulness do, in fact, facilitate performance. A question can be raised, however, whether these feelings are properly classified as emotions.

Emotion as disorganized experience. The second view—that emotion is a disorganized experience dependent upon a dynamic disturbance—is widely held by psychiatrists, clinical psychologists, and others who are concerned with health, counseling, and human adjustment. Thus, the psychologist Édouard Claparède argued that emotion occurs precisely when adaptation is hindered for any reason whatever: the man who can run away does not have the emotion of fear; fear occurs only when flight is impossible. Anger is experienced only when one cannot strike his enemy. The uselessness, or even the harmfulness, of emotion is known to everyone, said Claparède.

There has been considerable controversy over these basic concepts. Robert W. Leeper (1948) regards disorganization as a concept inadequate to define emotion and prefers a "motivational" definition. Paul T. Young (1949), in a reply to Leeper, pointed out that the problem is one of definition and emphasis. Some affective reactions are organized and organizing; some facilitate performance. But the term "emotion" has been used traditionally to define a special class of affective processes characterized by disturbance, upset, and disorganization. Affective disturbances, both pleasant and unpleasant, assuredly exist. If there were no disturbances, the term "emotion" could be dropped from the psychological vocabulary, because existing motivational and affective terms and concepts are fully adequate for the descriptive analysis of organized, adaptive activity.

Emotional behavior

The radical behaviorist does not recognize conscious feelings as such but restricts the science of psychology to the phenomena of behavior and associated bodily processes that can be objectively observed. It was John B. Watson, the founder of American behaviorism, who defined emotion as "an hereditary pattern-reaction involving profound changes of the bodily mechanism as a whole, but particularly of the visceral and glandular systems" (1919, p. 165). He described the stimulating situations and the pattern-reactions for three basic emotions in the infant: fear, rage, and love.

The pattern-reaction theory of emotion has been popular with physiologists and physiological psychologists for obvious reasons: The patterns of reaction appear reflectively under specified conditions of stimulation. They resemble simple reflexes but are more complex. They are well integrated. The emotional patterns can be conditioned and extinguished. The neural mechanisms that regulate many of the emotional patterns have been described and localized within subcortical regions of the brain.

Among the patterns of reaction that have been described and analyzed are the following: There is the rage pattern in cats, dogs, and other animals, as well as a similar pattern called "sham rage" in decorticate animals. There are patterns of escape, including impulses to run or fly or dart away when startled and patterns of defense that differ from species to species. There are male and female patterns of sexual response, the startle pattern in man and other animals, and the disgust pattern. There are internal patterns of visceral and glandular response that differ in hostility and fear. There are human patterns of facial expression—smiling, laughing, crying, and weeping. There is no doubt about the objective existence and functional importance of these patterns of reaction.

Critique of the pattern-reaction theory.   Despite the obvious advantages of a pattern-reaction theory of emotion, there are certain difficulties. The theory does not distinguish between emotional and non-emotional patterns. Coughing, sneezing, hiccoughing, sucking, swallowing, and blinking are well-integrated reflexive patterns that are frequently accompanied by changes regulated through the autonomic nervous system. No one regards these reflexes as emotions. Again, the startle pattern, described in detail by Carney Landis and William A. Hunt, was regarded by them as a general skeletal reflex rather than as a true emotional pattern, because startle is completed in the fraction of a second before visceral responses can get under way.

Further, it is difficult to specify the grouping of elements that constitute an emotional pattern. For example, Watson claimed that "fear" is an innate emotional pattern in infants; but his description of "fear" included patterns known to be more elementary: crying, catching the breath, the startle response, possibly the Moro reflex, and an impulse to crawl away. Watson's "fear" is thus a complex of more elementary patterns.

The pattern-reaction concept disregards the acute affective disorganization that is characteristic of emotion. And, further, the observed patterns do not correspond to the "emotions" of everyday life. What patterns, for example, correspond to mother love, pride, embarrassment? It would be wiser, we believe, to describe the patterns of reaction that occur *in* or *during* emotion for their own sake than to define emotion as a pattern of reaction.

The expressions of emotion.   The objective expressions of emotion have been observed and studied since the earliest times. Charles Darwin (1872) made detailed observations on emotional behavior in man and other animals. After studying the data, he formulated three principles of emotional expression.

First, Darwin believed that many expressions of emotion are reduced segments of biologically serviceable acts or acts that once were serviceable in an earlier stage of evolution. Thus an angry man raises the lips involuntarily and shows the canine teeth although he does not intend to bite. The complete expression would be biting and hostile attack.

When a dog is about to attack, it approaches its enemy with a stiff gait and tail erect; the head is slightly raised; the hair, especially along the neck and back, bristles; the ears are pricked up and directed forward; the eyes are wide open and have a fixed stare; the animal shows its teeth and growls. No one is likely to misinterpret the significance of this emotional behavior. Even a small part of the total reaction, e.g., showing the teeth and growling, expresses hostility.

Second, Darwin pointed out that some emotional expressions are directly antithetical to biologically serviceable behavior. To illustrate, suppose the hostile dog suddenly perceives that a man it is approaching is not an enemy but its beloved master. The bearing of the animal instantly changes. Instead of walking upright with a stiff gait, the body sinks downward or even crouches; the animal's movements are flexuous and supple; its tail, instead of being stiff and upright, is lowered and wagging from side to side; the hair is smooth; the ears are depressed and relaxed backwards; its lips hang loosely, and it salivates; the eyelids become elongated, and the eyes no longer appear round and staring. The behavior of the friendly dog is directly antithetical to that of the hostile animal.

Third, Darwin recognized that the above two principles do not explain all expressions of emotion. He formulated a third principle: Some emotional expressions can be explained only in terms of the constitution of the nervous system and associated bodily mechanisms. For example, the writhing of an animal during the birth of young can be explained only in terms of bodily constitution. The excessive activity is neither biologically serviceable nor antithetical to a serviceable act.

Emotional and social expressions.   In an experiment on the facial expressions of emotion, Carney Landis (1924) drew an important distinction between *emotional* and *social* expressions. The emotional expressions, he said, are involuntary and reflexive. They involve changes in the skeletal musculature, glands, and smooth muscles. They are regulated by neural mechanisms that include processes within the autonomic nervous system. The social expressions are voluntary and learned.

Otto Klineberg (1938) studied expressive behavior as recorded in the Chinese novel and drama. He found that many phrases in the Chinese language describe involuntary changes that anyone will recognize as emotional. For example, fear is indicated by such expressions as "every one of his hairs stood on end, and the pimples came out on the skin all over his body" and "they were so frightened that their waters and wastes burst out of them." The meaning of other expressions, however, would not be recognized by persons in Western society. For example, the phrase "they stretched out their tongues" indicates surprise; "he made his two eyes round and stared at him" means anger; "he scratched his ears and cheeks" (in the novel *Dream of the Red Chamber*) means happiness; "he clapped his hands" is likely to mean worry or disappointment.

These conventional expressions are culturebound. They serve to communicate feelings within a group as spoken words convey meanings. We have all learned, of course, to express joy, sorrow, concern, amusement, and other feelings sympathetically, as actors do on the stage. The voluntary and conventional expressions are not true reflexive patterns of emotion. [*See* EXPRESSIVE BEHAVIOR.]

The physiology of emotion

Walter B. Cannon (1915) supplemented and extended the Darwinian doctrine of biological utility by carrying the principle of adaptation to the interior of the body. In a series of experiments, he showed how the bodily changes in pain, fear, and rage are serviceable and adaptive in a struggle for existence. During a biological crisis, widespread organic changes mobilize the energy reserves of the body for a prolonged fight or flight.

During an emergency there is a diffuse discharge across the sympathetic nervous network and increased secretion of the adrenal glands. This neural and glandular discharge produces widespread bodily changes: (1) cessation of processes in the alimentary canal, thus freeing the energy supply for muscles and brain; (2) shifting of blood from abdominal organs to the organs immediately essential to muscular exertion; (3) increased vigor of contraction of the heart; (4) discharge of extra blood corpuscles from the spleen, thus facilitating the process of oxygenation; (5) dilation of the bronchioles, along with deeper respiration; (6)

quick abolition of the effects of muscular fatigue through adrenal discharge; and (7) mobilization of sugar in the circulation. All of these changes, Cannon claimed, are directly serviceable in making the organism more effective in the violent display of energy that fear, rage, or pain may involve.

Critique of the emergency theory. Physiological studies (for example, Arnold 1960) have pointed to weaknesses in Cannon's emergency theory of emotion. Critics agree on the following points: (1) Emotional processes are a function of the entire autonomic nervous system, not of the sympathetic division alone. The sympathetic and parasympathetic divisions of the autonomic system function simultaneously and reciprocally in fear, rage, "sham rage," pain, general excitement, and sexual and other emotions, producing patterns of visceral response that differ from one emotional state to another. (2) Whereas Cannon thought that the secretion of epinephrine was the main hormone in the defensive fight–flight reactions, it is now known that there are two chemical factors —norepinephrine and epinephrine—involved in this reaction. These two hormones are secreted independently and have different physiological effects: norepinephrine appears to be concerned with hostile states, and epinephrine with fear and anxiety. Hormones from the pancreas and pituitary body also are involved in emotional reactions. (3) The autonomic nervous system is on continuous duty 24 hours a day, and the bodily changes produced during a biological crisis correspond to departures from normal conditions. The autonomic system has two main functions: first, it prepares the body to respond defensively to danger; second, it plays its major role in maintaining homeostasis. (4) Cannon emphasized the utility of bodily changes in emotion, but many changes are disruptive, disturbing, and disintegrating rather than an aid in adaptive behavior.

Cannon's work should be brought into relation with that of Hans Selye (1956) upon the general adaptation syndrome and the adjustments of the organism to stress [*see* STRESS].

The neural basis of emotion. The phylogenetically older structures, collectively, and the limbic system and hypothalamus, in particular, are actively involved in pleasurable and painful experiences, in emotional behavior associated with fight, flight, food, and sex. We are just beginning to understand the central dynamics of the emotional reactions.

The hypothalamus is of critical importance in the regulation of emotional behavior. It has long been recognized as a center of endocrine and autonomic-nervous-system control. It forms a critical juncture in the circular feedback system that regulates neural impulses concerned with emotions and neuroendocrine activity. The hypothalamus influences and is influenced by the reticular activating system, the limbic system, secretions of the pituitary, and other endocrine glands, as well as by the neocortex.

The explorations of the reticular activating system by Magoun and associates (Magoun 1958) have altered neurophysiological thinking about motivation and emotion. It is now known that every sensory stimulation has two kinds of effects upon the cerebral cortex: (1) impulses discharged through thalamic nuclei are relayed to the cortex, where they provide sensory information; (2) sensory stimulation also sends impulses through collaterals into the reticular activating system. These impulses are conducted over multisynaptic pathways to the cortex, where they have a nonspecific activating influence. The degree of activation varies with intensity of stimulation. In emotional excitement there is a high level of cortical activation, as Donald B. Lindsley has shown in studies with the electroencephalograph.

The limbic system has been called the "visceral brain" by McLean (1949), who considers that it mediates visceral needs rather than ideational processes; it is concerned with feelings rather than with symbolic activities. The frontotemporal limbic activities may be concerned with self-preservative behavior; the more posterior regions, with sexual behavior and sexual hormones.

The limbic system is involved in positive and negative affective arousals. James Olds (1955) implanted bipolar needle electrodes within the limbic system of rats' brains and demonstrated that electrical stimulation of subcortical points could be either rewarding or punishing. When stimulated within the septal area, the rats acted as if they were pleased; but when stimulated within the *medial lemniscus*, the animals acted as if the stimulation had hurt them and had been unpleasant. Clearly the neural locus of affective arousals, physiological drives, and emotions is being penetrated. [*See* NERVOUS SYSTEM, *article on* BRAIN STIMULATION.]

The dynamics of emotion

A dispositional approach. According to David Rapaport (1942), a good deal of confusion concerning the definition of emotion has been the result of a failure of investigators to distinguish between the phenomena of emotion and the underlying dynamic mechanisms. The phenomena of emotion are complex but can be analyzed from several points of view. The phenomena include (1) the consciously experienced affect, (2) the emotional behavior, and (3) the physiological processes occurring during emotional upheavals. The dynamic mechanisms, in contrast, are always inferred or assumed.

Psychologists assume persistent dispositions that were originally formed by emotional experiences. For example, an intense fright may produce a phobia for high places, enclosures, blood, or some other thing. The grounds of a phobia may seem unreasonable to the subject, but nevertheless the fear persists. Children normally develop fears of thunder, darkness, death, insects, ghosts, and other things on the basis of some fright. The emotion clearly leaves a disposition to fear [*see* PHOBIAS].

Attitudes and motives are formed on the basis of emotional experiences. The story is told that when Abraham Lincoln saw slaves being sold on the New Orleans market, he was so disturbed emotionally that he resolved: "If ever I have the chance, I will hit that thing hard." The emotional disturbance left upon him an indelible imprint that later may have influenced his decisions and actions.

A dispositional approach to the study of emotion implies a *temporal* dimension. Whenever we speak of emotional development, emotional maturity, or emotional stability, we imply a persisting individual with persisting dispositions.

Dispositions include memory traces, attitudes, beliefs, specific motives, expectancies, hopes, and desires, as well as conflicts and unsolved problems. All of these are residues from the past. Among the dynamic conditions that produce emotional upsets, moods of anxiety, depression, and the like are conflicts, frustrations, thwarted expectations, successes, failures, tensions and the release of tensions, painful stimulations, and other factors of stress. A dispositional approach to the complex phenomena of emotion can bring unity out of the diverse data.

Emotion and mental health. In an address to the American Neurological Association in New York City in 1876, George M. Beard maintained that disease might appear and disappear without the influence of any other agent than some form of emotion. Fear, terror, anxiety, grief, anger, wonder, and a definite expectation he regarded as mental conditions likely to produce disease [see Lewis 1959, p. 8]. Beard argued that certain emotional states could neutralize therapeutics and increase the effects of drugs. At the time, his ideas were new and startling; later the ideas were recognized in a movement known as psychosomatic medicine.

Today, it is widely accepted that persistent emotional disturbances constitute an important factor in certain disorders, such as peptic ulcer, essential hypertension, rheumatoid arthritis, ulcerative colitis, bronchial asthma, hyperthyroidism, and neurodermatitis. The health of a patient is strongly influenced by stressful conditions of living that produce emotional traumata, such as financial failure, bereavement, insult, injury, unrequited love, threatened divorce, and loss of self-esteem. These several factors are well recognized by clinical psychologists and psychiatrists.

Emotion plays an important role in psychotherapy. The psychiatric examination is concerned with the whole personality but places special emphasis upon emotions as related to thought processes. During an interview the psychiatrist observes emotional reactions as the patient talks and seeks to elicit thoughts that accompany the emotional reactions. A dominant emotion is associated with something important to the patient, something that affects him deeply. Why it is important can be learned only by getting the patient to tell his thoughts.

Psychoanalysts have long recognized the importance of affects, especially repressed emotional experiences, in the etiology and treatment of neuroses. Some repressed hostility or an unsolved emotional conflict, possibly unknown to the patient, may underlie neurotic symptoms. Free association, aided recall, and the interpretation of dreams, along with free emotional expression, may reveal unconscious motivations and alleviate the mental disorder.

According to Robert W. White (1948), psychotherapy is not an intellectual process. It has wrongly been said that the way to bring about readjustment is to help an individual understand his problems. Awareness of motivations and frustrations on the cognitive level is helpful but not enough to effect a cure. Psychotherapy operates in the sphere of emotion. The main aim of psychotherapy is to provide corrective emotional experience by relaxing the subject's defenses and permitting him to reappraise his anxieties. In the major methods of psychotherapy, the subject is encouraged to *feel*, to express his emotions.

It should be pointed out that emotional upsets are only one manifestation of neurosis. There are other aspects, such as dissociation, delusion, amnesia, tics, and functional paralyses. Emotional upsets appear also in psychoses and disorders that have a definite organic basis as well as in normal everyday living.

In the light of the above discussion, an emotion may be defined as an acute affective disturbance originating within the psychological situation and expressing itself in conscious experience (affect), emotional behavior, and physiological processes. The dynamic determinants of emotion include conflict, frustration, thwarted (or satisfied) expectation, tension or its release, painful stimulation, threat, insult, and similar conditions of stress and relief. Clinically viewed, an emotion is a persisting dynamic disturbance within the individual that may influence his health, happiness, and well-being.

Paul Thomas Young

[*Other relevant material may be found in* Affection; Aggression; Conflict; Drives; Motivation; Sympathy and empathy.]

BIBLIOGRAPHY

Arnold, Magda B. 1960 *Emotion and Personality.* 2 vols. New York: Columbia Univ. Press. → Volume 1: *Psychological Aspects.* Volume 2: *Neurological and Physiological Aspects.*

Cannon, Walter B. (1915) 1953 *Bodily Changes in Pain, Hunger, Fear and Rage: An Account of Recent Researches Into the Function of Emotional Excitement.* 2d ed. Boston: Branford.

Darwin, Charles (1872) 1965 *The Expression of the Emotions in Man and Animals.* Edited by Francis Darwin. Univ. of Chicago Press.

English, Horace B.; and English, Ava C. (1958) 1962 *A Comprehensive Dictionary of Psychological and Psychoanalytical Terms: A Guide to Usage.* New York: McKay.

Klineberg, Otto 1938 Emotional Expression in Chinese Literature. *Journal of Abnormal and Social Psychology* 38:517–520.

Landis, Carney 1924 Studies of Emotional Reactions. 2: General Behavior and Facial Expression. *Journal of Comparative Psychology* 4:447–501.

Leeper, Robert W. 1948 A Motivational Theory of Emotion to Replace "Emotion as Disorganized Response." *Psychological Review* 55:5–21.

Lewis, Nolan D. C. 1959 American Psychiatry From Its Beginnings to World War II. Volume 1, pages 3–17 in *American Handbook of Psychiatry.* Edited by Silvano Arieti. New York: Basic Books.

McDougall, William (1908) 1950 The Principal Instincts and the Primary Emotions of Man. Chapter 3 in William McDougall, *An Introduction to Social Psychology.* London: Methuen. → A paperback edition was published in 1960 by Barnes and Noble.

McLean, Paul D. 1949 Psychosomatic Disease and the "Visceral Brain": Recent Developments Bearing on the Papez Theory of Emotion. *Psychosomatic Medicine* 11:338–353.

Magoun, Horace W. (1958) 1963 *The Waking Brain.* 2d ed. Springfield, Ill.: Thomas.

Olds, James 1955 Physiological Mechanisms of Reward. Volume 3, pages 73–139 in Marshall R. Jones (editor), *Nebraska Symposium on Motivation.* Lincoln: Univ. of Nebraska Press.

Rapaport, David (1942) 1950 *Emotions and Memory.* 2d ed. New York: International Universities Press.

Selye, Hans 1956 *The Stress of Life.* New York: McGraw-Hill.

Watson, John B. 1919 A Schematic Outline of the Emotions. *Psychological Review* 26:165–196.

WHITE, ROBERT W. (1948) 1956 *The Abnormal Personality: A Textbook.* 2d ed. New York: Ronald.

YOUNG, PAUL T. 1949 Emotion as Disorganized Response: A Reply to Professor Leeper. *Psychological Review* 56:184–191.

YOUNG, PAUL T. 1961 *Motivation and Emotions: A Survey of the Determinants of Human and Animal Activity.* New York: Wiley.

EMPATHY

See SYMPATHY AND EMPATHY. *Also relevant is* MODERNIZATION, *article on* SOCIAL ASPECTS.

EMPIRES

The term "empire" has normally been used to designate a political system encompassing wide, relatively highly centralized territories, in which the center, as embodied both in the person of the emperor and in the central political institutions, constituted an autonomous entity. Further, although empires have usually been based on traditional legitimation, they have often embraced some wider, potentially universal political and cultural orientation that went beyond that of any of their component parts. Such "imperial" designation has been attached to a great variety of sociopolitical systems, from relatively ephemeral frameworks like that of the Mongol empires of Genghis Khan and Kublai Khan to the various more modern "colonial" empires, which did not usually evince territorial continuity.

However, the fullest and most succinct development of the major characteristics of empires as distinct political systems can be found in what may be called the "historical bureaucratic empires." In order to explain the meaning of this term, a number of further distinctions need to be made (for a fuller treatment, see Eisenstadt 1963).

Types of imperial systems. The connotation of the term "imperial," as it evolved within political and social consciousness in the history of mankind, evinced throughout its development some common characteristics. At the same time, it also changed greatly between historical, premodern, and modern times. Its basic connotation, as manifest in the Latin *imperium*, is the existence of relatively concentrated authority and rule, focused in a relatively strong center and diffusing its authority over broad territorial contours. In premodern times this designation commonly referred to an authority that extended over territorially contiguous units so that the latter attained some symbols of common political identity. This authority and the concomitant political identity certainly did not connote national sovereignty, but rather the existence of a center of authority that was accepted and hallowed beyond the confines of narrow territorial, kinship, or city limits.

The authority that was enacted in these systems consisted of a special mixture of Weber's three types: the charismatic, the traditional, and the legal–rational. Such authority was usually rooted in a charismatic personality or group whose major orientations were traditional in the sense of upholding a "given" order hallowed by tradition, but not, as we shall see, in the sense of accepting the traditional organizational confines of this order. At the same time, it often contained important elements of a more legal–rational type of authority.

The connotation of imperial has greatly changed in modern times, when it has come to denote rather a type of political system through which one political community or nation has extended its rule over other political units, mostly territorially noncontiguous ones, without fully incorporating them into a framework of common political symbols and identity.

In this article we shall deal only with the first type of imperial system, focusing our analysis on those historical systems within which the basic characteristics of this type of system became most fully developed and institutionalized. Thus we shall not deal with those "conquest" empires, such as those of the Mongols, where the conquering rulers attempted to establish such authority but in which, for a variety of reasons, no such common symbols of identity became accepted and in which the conquerors retained their separate ethnic and political identities. Nor shall we deal with the colonial empires of the nineteenth and twentieth centuries, although this does not preclude examination of their origins.

Formation of bureaucratic empires

Examples of centralized bureaucratic empires are to be found throughout history; the principal ones, which comprise the major historical societies, are as follows:

(*a*) The ancient empires, especially the Egyptian, Babylonian, and, possibly, the Inca and Aztec.

(*b*) The Chinese Empire from the Han period to the Ch'ing.

(*c*) The various Iranian empires, especially the Sassanid and, to a smaller extent, the Parthian and Achaemenid.

(*d*) The Roman Empire and the various Hellenistic empires.

(*e*) The Byzantine Empire.

(*f*) Several ancient Hindu states (especially the Maurya and Gupta) and the Mogul empires.

(*g*) The Arab Caliphate (especially from the reign of the Abbassides and Fatimides), the Arab Muslim states in the Mediterranean and Iran, and the Ottoman Empire.

(*h*) European states during the age of absolutism, and to some extent their initial colonial empires, especially insofar as they were built with the idea of the direct extension of the patrimony and its central authority and not as merchant colonies or purely colonial settlements of small groups. Of these, the Spanish American Empire is probably the nearest to the ideal type of a historical bureaucratic empire.

The majority of these empires developed from one of the following types of political systems: (*a*) from *patrimonial empires* such as the Egyptian and the Sassanid empires; (*b*) from *dualistic nomad–sedentary empires*, necessarily sharing many characteristics in common with the patrimonial type; (*c*) from *feudal systems*, as did the European absolutist states; and (*d*) from *city-states*, as did the Roman and Hellenistic empires.

Despite the great variety of historical and cultural settings, some common features in the first stages of the establishment of such polities may be found. The initiative for the establishment of these polities came, in all cases, from the rulers— emperors, kings, or some members of a patrician ruling elite (like the more active and dynamic element of the patrician ruling elite in republican Rome). In most cases these rulers either came from established patrician, patrimonial, tribal, or feudal families, or they were usurpers, coming from lower-class families, who attempted to establish new dynasties or to conquer new territories. In some cases they were conquerors who attempted to establish their rule over various territories.

In most cases such rulers arose in periods of unrest, turmoil, acute strife, or dismemberment of the existing political system. Usually their aim was the re-establishment of peace and order. They did not, however, attempt to restore the old order in its entirety, although for propagandist and opportunistic reasons they sometimes upheld such restoration as a political ideology or slogan. They always had some vision of the distinctly political goals of a unified polity. They aimed to establish a more centralized, unified polity in which they could monopolize political decision making and the setting of political goals, without being bound by various traditional aristocratic, tribal, or patrician groups. Even when they were conquerors, as in the case of the Roman, Islamic, and Spanish American empires, they also had some such vision and attempted to transmit it to at least part of the conquered population.

Of crucial importance in shaping the activities of these rulers was the geopolitical situation of the polity that they tried to organize—as, for instance, the specific geopolitical situation of Byzantium at the crossroads of Europe and Asia or the vast hydraulic arrangement of China and its special relation with the steppe frontiers. These geopolitical factors indicated, in a sense, the nature of the specific international system to which these empires had to respond, as well as the range of problems to which the rulers were willing and able to address themselves.

The aims of the rulers were very often oriented against, and encountered the opposition of, various social and political groups. However great the turmoil, unrest, and internal strife may have been, there were always some groups that either benefited from this state of affairs—or hoped to do so— or aimed to re-establish the old order, in which they held positions of power and influence. These hostile elements, usually consisting of some aristocratic groups or some of the more traditional urban and cultural elites, usually felt themselves menaced by the new aims and activities of the rulers. They felt that their position was threatened by the trend toward political centralization, and they were therefore unwilling to help in the implementation of this trend. Accordingly, they often attempted to deny resources and support to the rulers, plotting and working against them either in open political warfare or by infiltration and intrigue.

The rulers had to find allies, whether passive or active, in order to be able to implement their aims in the face of these various aristocratic forces. Thus they had to forge various instruments of power and policy with which to mobilize the various resources needed by them—whether economic resources, manpower, or political support. Naturally, the rulers tried to find such allies among the groups and strata whose interests were opposed to those of the more traditional and aristocratic elements and who thus could benefit by the weakening of the latter and by the establishment of a more unified polity. The rulers' allies were therefore of two principal kinds: the more active (mostly urban) economic, cultural, and professional groups who, whether by origin or by their social interests and orientations, were opposed to the aristocratic–traditional groups; and the wider and politically and socially more passive strata, especially the peasants and (to a smaller extent) the urban lower classes.

It was from these various groups and strata that

the rulers hoped to mobilize the various resources they needed. But in order to do this they also had to forge some instruments of political and administrative action on which they could rely and through which they could provide various services to their potential allies. Most rulers were able to form an entourage by recruiting from established administrative and political bodies; however, even when such organs of administration were available, they had to be adapted to the rulers' particular purpose. Insofar as the existing personnel were related to the aristocratic forces, the rulers had in many cases to find replacements. Nor was this enough; loyalty to the ruler had to be secured against bids from opposing forces. Moreover, the rulers had to make sure that these administrative bodies would be effectively organized for their tasks. To this end, the rulers attempted to concentrate the nominations to these positions in their own hands. They tried, as far as possible, to appoint persons who were loyal and who had the necessary administrative qualifications. The rulers also attempted to control the administrative budget, making sure that it was adequate for official salaries as well as other running expenses. This enabled them to lay emphasis on the dependent position of the officials: they were to be "servants," either of the individual ruler or of the polity that he wanted to establish. Accordingly, representation by officials of group or class interests was henceforth to be eliminated.

Thus, in general, the rulers attempted to make these administrative bodies, as far as possible, independent of the more traditional and aristocratic strata and groups and to give them some power and prestige vis-à-vis these strata. Here the rulers had, necessarily, to allow these bodies some measure of autonomy and independence and had to enable them to perform some services to the population. True, the rulers very often wanted to use these administrative bodies only, or mainly, for exploitative purposes. But if the rulers wanted to perpetuate their rule, they had to allow these services to take into account at least some of the needs of some of the social groups, if only to provide them with peace, security, and certain minimal services.

Thus, the development of an imperial system (in the sense of a historical bureaucratic empire) was dependent on two conditions. One condition was the existence, within the preceding social structure, of a relatively high level of societal differentiation, which limited the place of basic ascriptive units—such as family, kinship, or traditional status groups—in the social division of labor and

created many forces cutting across them. On the one hand, this differentiation created problems of integration that called for new solutions, while on the other hand it provided the resources needed for new organizations that could attempt to deal with some of these problems. The second condition was the development of a new type of political leader and elite with wider aims and perceptions of political authority and the ability to serve as a focus of the new imperial authority and symbols and to articulate new, more differentiated, and broader political goals.

The existence of only one of these conditions was not sufficient for the institutionalization of an imperial system. Thus, for instance, in the city-states of Greece, as compared with republican Rome (within which there was a similar level of differentiation), there did not develop such an internally new leadership. Contrariwise, in the Carolingian and Mongol states (or empires), while there did develop rulers with such new styles of leadership, there did not exist an appropriate level of differentiation; thus the imperial system could not become institutionalized, and these polities remained at the level of loosely integrated "conquest" empires, in which the different regions or groups (conquerors and conquered) were not integrated into a polity bound by common symbols of identity.

Although the general existence of a certain level of differentiation was a necessary precondition of the institutionalization of the political systems of such empires, their concrete structures could range from that of the city-state or feudal system to that of the patrimonial empire. Similarly, the social origins, composition, and internal cohesion of the new ruling groups could vary greatly, and the combination of these variations could greatly influence the concrete contours of the developing imperial systems. This tendency was manifest, first, in the tendency toward political centralization; second, in the development by the rulers of autonomous political goals; and third, in the relatively high extent of organizational autonomy of executive and administrative activities.

But the extent of differentiation of political activities, organization, and goals was, in these political systems, still limited by several important factors. First, the legitimation of the rulers was, in these regimes, usually couched in basically traditional–religious terms, even if the rulers tended to stress their own ultimate monopoly of such traditional values and tried to deny that other (traditional) groups could also share in this monopoly. Second, the basic political role of the subject was not fully distinguished from other basic societal roles, such as, for instance, membership in local communities; it was often embedded in such groups, and the citizen or subject did not exercise any direct political rights through a system of voting or franchise. Third, many traditional ascriptive units, such as aristocratic lineages or territorial communities, still performed many crucial political functions and continued to serve as units of political representation. As a consequence, the scope of political activity and participation was far narrower than in most modern and contemporary political systems.

The existence of both traditional and differentiated political orientations, activities, and organizations created within these empires a complex interrelation between the political institutions and other parts of the social structure. The rulers were in need of both traditional and more complex, differentiated political support and were dependent on both. The rulers' traditional dependence on other parts of the social structure was manifest in their need to uphold their traditional legitimation and the traditional, unconditional political attitudes and identifications of many groups. On the other hand, however, the rulers' tendency to political independence and autonomy made them dependent on types of resources that were not available through various traditional ascriptive commitments and relations. In order to implement their various political goals as they pleased, the rulers were in need of more flexible support and resources, which would not be embedded in traditional ascriptive groups or committed for more or less fixed goals (Eisenstadt 1963, chapter 6; Altheim 1955).

Among these flexible resources, the most important were economic and political ones. In the economic field, the rulers needed manpower and goods that could be available not through the fixed commitments of ascriptive kinship and status groups but that could be allocated directly. Among such economic resources, the most important were manpower (military and administrative) for services and for relatively free and flexible occupational choices and various goods and commodities for direct spending or for payment of services.

In principle, such resources could have been the same as those used *within* the various ascriptive groups and in their fixed interrelations. But the very emphasis on their flexibility entailed the possibility of their greater mobility and hence of their necessary translatability into media of exchange such as money, credits, and their equivalents. Once some such media of exchange were established, it was highly necessary to maintain markets and organizational frameworks within which they could flow continuously. Similarly, it was very important to maintain conditions and frameworks in which possibilities of relatively free occupational choices and avenues of mobility could be realized.

A similar situation developed in the field of political support and organization. The rulers were in need of commitments and loyalties that could be made available without the restrictions of such ascriptive groups, and this necessarily entailed the organization of new types of political organizations and leadership that could mobilize such support. Parallel needs could also be found in the cultural, social, and religious fields.

The political demands made on the rulers by the various groups in the society were of both the traditional and the more complex, differentiated types. On the one hand, the rulers were expected to uphold traditional ascriptive rights and benefits; on the other, they were faced with demands for participation in the formulation of the political balance of power—or even in the process of legitimating their own authority. Thus the authority of the rulers, "traditional" though it may have been, was no longer automatic; merely to raise the question of the rulers' accountability was to deny them fixed support.

These different types of political activities and orientations did not coexist in these political systems in separate "compartments," bound together only in some loose and unstable way. They were bound together within the same institutions, and the continuity of each type of political activity was dependent on the existence of both types of political orientation. Because of this, the activities of the rulers were, paradoxically, oriented to maintaining basic *traditional* legitimation through manipulation not only of traditional but also of nontraditional support and to the mobilization also of traditional resources for politically autonomous goals and through nontraditional channels.

Hence, the political system of these empires could subsist only insofar as it was possible to maintain simultaneously and continuously, within the framework of the same political institutions, both the traditional and the more differentiated levels of legitimation, support, and political organization. The continuity of these systems hinged on the continuous existence of a certain balance between political activity and involvement on the part of some segments of the population and of political noninvolvement or apathy toward central political issues by most segments of the population. The limited political involvement could assure some of the more flexible political support, while the apathy, in its turn, was necessary for maintenance of the traditional legitimation of the rulers.

Contradiction and conflict

It was the interplay between these varied orientations of the rulers—their dependence on both traditional and differentiated resources—that greatly influenced their concrete policies and gave rise to some of the basic contradictions that developed within those policies. The rulers of these empires tended to develop three major types of basic political orientations. First, they were interested in the limited promotion of free resources and in freeing them from commitments to traditional aristocratic groups. Second, the rulers were interested in controlling these resources and committing them to their own use. Third, the rulers tended also to engage in various goals—military expansions, for example—which alone could exhaust many of the available free resources. Between these various tendencies of the rulers, serious contradictions easily developed. These contradictions, although not always consciously grasped by the rulers, were nevertheless implicit in their structural position, in the problems and exigencies with which they dealt, and in the concrete policies they employed in order to solve their problems.

These contradictions were exhibited mainly in the sphere of legitimation and stratification. As we have seen, the rulers often attempted to limit the aristocracy's power and to create new status groups. But these attempts faced several obstacles. Regardless of the extent of the monarchs' independent activities in this field, the number of new titles created, and the degree of encouragement of new strata, the symbols of status used by the rulers were usually very similar to those borne by the landed hereditary aristocracy or by some religious elites. The creation of an entirely new secular and rational type of legitimation, in which the social groups or universalistic principles would be the foci of legitimation, was either beyond their horizon or against their basic interest. It would necessarily involve extending the sphere of political participation and consequently increasing the influence of various strata in the political institutions.

Therefore, the rulers were usually unable to transcend the symbols of stratification and legitimation borne by the very strata whose influence they wanted to limit. Consequently, the ability of the rulers to appeal to the lower strata of the population was obviously limited. Even more important, because of this emphasis on the superiority

and worth of aristocratic symbols and values, many middle or new strata and groups tended to identify with them and consequently to "aristocratize" themselves.

The contradiction in the rulers' policies and goals could develop also in a different direction. However tradition-bound the ruling elites may have been, their policies required the creation and propagation of more flexible "free" resources in various institutional fields. Here again, the major types of free resources were, in the economic field, money and easily exchangeable goods, free manpower in general, and free professional manpower in particular; and, in the political and social fields, relatively free commitments and possibilities of support. The propagation of such free resources either gave rise to many religious, intellectual, and legal groups whose value orientations were much more flexible than the traditional ones, or else it promoted such groups. Moreover, the orientations and values of the broader middle strata of the society sometimes were similar to those propagated by these more active elite groups. Although in many cases all these elements were very weak and succumbed to the influence of the more conservative groups and policies of the ruling elite, in other cases—as in Europe—they developed into relatively independent centers of power, whose opposition to the rulers was stimulated only by the rulers' more conservative policies.

The rulers' activities in the economic field were similarly inconsistent. Their main economic aims posed a series of dilemmas that could be extremely acute in relatively undifferentiated economic systems and that could give rise to intensive contradictions between long-term and short-term economic policies. Thus, the continuous necessity to mobilize extensive resources at any given moment could often exhaust the available free resources on which the rulers' economic independence rested. The big landowners and merchants, who constituted important centers of economic power, quite often tried to intensify this contradiction by providing the government with short-term loans or allocations of manpower for very limited periods and purposes; this increased the dependency of the rulers at the same time that it buttressed their own position. Although these allocations were usually insufficient to take care of their long-term needs, the rulers had to pay dearly in terms of the various free resources at their disposal. The rulers had to avail themselves of the various services and other resources of these more tradition-minded groups, giving them in return various concessions that often tended to undermine the long-run availability of free resources. In this way, the position of the rulers gradually became weaker (Eisenstadt 1963, chapter 12).

A similar contradiction existed between the long-range and short-range policies dealing with problems of administrative manpower. In many cases there was not enough manpower available for the execution of various administrative and political tasks, or because of inadequate communication and technical facilities it was very difficult to supervise such personnel effectively. It then became necessary to farm out various functions and positions either to local gentry and landowners or to officials who gradually became "aristocratized."

The best example of how the social groups created by the ruling elite became partially opposed to its aims and basic political premises is the development of the system of sale of offices, which was closely connected, in these empires, with the entire process of recruitment into the bureaucracy (Swart 1949). At first this system was usually introduced by the rulers as a means of solving their financial problems and admitting new (nonaristocratic) elements into their service. But in time, in most of these societies, the bureaucracy came to regard its offices as possessions and either transmitted them in the family or sold them in the market; in this way the rulers, despite many efforts to the contrary, slowly lost control over these offices.

This trend was connected, in general, with the tendency by the bureaucracy itself—the very instrument of power of the rulers—to aristocratize itself, to acquire symbols of aristocratic status, and to ally itself with aristocratic forces. In such cases the bureaucracy very often displaced its goals of service to the rulers for those of self-aggrandizement. Its members used their positions for enriching themselves and their families, thus becoming a growing burden on the economy and losing their efficiency.

This development necessarily affected the nature and extent of political activity and the scope of mobilization of political leadership. Insofar as these processes of aristocratization became intensified, they usually depleted the supply of political leaders to the central political institutions. The more active elements became alienated from the regime, whether their alienation took the form of succumbing to the aristocratic forces, falling into complete political apathy, or becoming centers of social and political upheaval and change.

Politics and social class. Similar contradictions tended also to develop in the political attitudes and activities of the major strata in these societies.

Several basic attitudes of various strata and groups toward the basic premises of the political systems of these empires and toward the basic aims of their rulers can be distinguished. The first attitude, evinced chiefly by the aristocracy, was one of opposition to these premises—an opposition that was often shared by the peasantry and sometimes also by other groups that were interested only in maintaining their own limited local autonomy and their immediate economic interests.

The second attitude consisted of basic identification with the political premises of the imperial system, combined with a willingness to fight for one's own interests within the framework of existing political institutions. This attitude was to be found mostly among the bureaucracy and among various elements of the urbanized professional and cultural elites.

The third attitude, developed mainly by the more differentiated urban groups and professional and intellectual elites, favored changes in the extension of the scope of political systems. This attitude, which was most clearly evinced by the European middle class and intellectual groups at the end of the eighteenth century (Beloff 1954), was manifested in various attempts to change the basic value premises of the political system, to widen the patterns of political participation within it, and to find referents of political orientation that transcended the given political system.

These attitudes often overlapped in concrete instances and varied by group and stratum in different societies and periods. Moreover, the attitudes of any one group were never homogeneous and stable, and they could change greatly according to political conditions. The various political attitudes of the major social groups greatly influenced the extent of their political participation and the scope and the nature of the political leadership that tended to develop from within them. Here again the most significant factor, from the point of view of the continuity of the imperial system, was the bureaucracy's tendency to aristocratize itself and thus to undermine the very conditions of such continuity. No less important was the possibility that the very administrative organs created for the implementation of the rulers' policies could develop autonomous orientations and activities that might become opposed to the basic premises of the imperial system.

Imperial decline

It was the interplay between the policies of the rulers and the political orientations and activities of the major social groups that constituted the crux of the processes of change within the empires and also brought about the development of conditions that could facilitate their downfall. These processes were rooted in the basic characteristics of the social and political structures of all the historical bureaucratic empires. However, the exact ways in which these conditions for change developed, as well as the exact processes that caused them, varied in different empires according to the specific constellation of their structural characteristics, the various external processes that impinged on them, and their unique historical circumstances.

Among the *internal* aspects of the social structure of these empires which influenced the processes of change was, first, the nature of the goals of the rulers. Whether chiefly military and expansionist, or more oriented to the maintenance of a cultural order, or concerned mainly with economic advancement, each kind of goal made different kinds of demands on the various types of resources available in the society. The processes of change and disintegration were also set in motion by (*a*) the policies that the rulers developed for the implementation of their goals and the repercussions of these policies on the relative strength of different social strata; (*b*) changes in the relative strength of such strata as a result of internal economic, religious, or political developments; and (*c*) the development of various internal and external crises and the ways in which the policies developed to deal with them influenced the strength of different groups.

The direction taken by an empire's decline and the rate at which it declined were also greatly influenced by two residual factors: the initial level of social and economic differentiation in the society and the initial strength of its various social groups in relation to one another. Within this context, of special importance was the extent to which there existed common cultural and political bonds encompassing these major social groups and the rulers, as for instance in the case of the Confucian order in China (see Eisenstadt 1963, chapter 11; Balázs 1964, chapters 1–2).

Among the more "accidental" or *external* factors that influenced the processes of change, we should mention different extents of external pressure, major movements of population, conquests of nomads, international economic fluctuations, and the degree to which there existed from the beginning ethnic heterogeneity in a given society. Of equally crucial importance was the specific geopolitical situation of any polity: for instance, the special geopolitical situation of Byzantium at the crossroads of Europe and Asia. In general, it was some combination of external and internal pres-

sures and exigencies that precipitated change in the political systems of these empires. The greater the intensity of these internal contradictions, and the more intractable the external crises by which the empires were faced, the quicker and more intensive was the onslaught of change.

Thus, to give only some very preliminary examples (for a fuller exposition, see Eisenstadt 1963, chapter 12), the fact that in China various invasions, rebellions, and the famous "dynastic cycles" did not undermine for a very long period of time the basic institutional structure of the Chinese Empire (from the Han to the Ch'ing) can be understood if one remembers its geopolitical position, which made it relatively immune to the heavy impact of external forces. Furthermore, in China the relative weakness of the aristocracy and the predominance of the gentry tended to enhance the position of the centralized rulers; and the Confucian literati and bureaucracy, who constituted the backbone of the social and political structure, intervened between the central government and the major social strata and provided an indispensable framework of continuity and unity for the empire. By contrast, the geopolitical exposure of the Byzantine Empire, with its strong sensitivity to invasions and continuous internal struggle between the aristocracy and the free peasantry, led to its complete downfall. Similarly, the Roman and Arabic empires, with their extended boundaries that embraced a great variety of autonomous religions and cultural groups, were unable to contain internal dissension at the same time that they were forced to deal with external pressures.

The foci of change

The policies of the rulers and the political orientations and activities of the major social groups within the empires were greatly influenced by two major sources (both external and internal) of pressure and change. As we have seen above, the external, geopolitical factors, in the broadest sense, provided not only the general setting for these polities but also constituted sources of many concrete pressures, such as external pressures of population and problems of military security or of adjustment to international trade. These geopolitical settings indicated, as we have seen, the nature of the international system within which the rulers of the empires worked and the types of problems to which they were especially sensitive. It has been rightly claimed that in many of these empires there existed, because of their basic structural characteristics, what has been called *Primat der Aussenpolitik* (Altheim 1955), or the priority of foreign policy; this implied a much greater sensitivity to a variety of such external pressures than in many other types of political systems. These external pressures were very often connected with internal problems. For instance, close relations obviously developed between problems of international trade and the situations and activities of merchant groups or between military problems and problems of manpower recruitment. Thus it was the *combination* of external and internal pressures that constituted the major foci of change in the empires.

In more concrete terms, the main factors generating processes of change in these empires were (*a*) the continuous needs of the rulers for different types of resources and especially their great dependence on various flexible resources; (*b*) the rulers' attempts to maintain their own positions of control, in terms of both traditional legitimation and of effective political control over the more flexible forces in the society; (*c*) the great and continuous sensitivity of the internal structure of these societies to various external pressures and to political and economic developments in the international field; (*d*) the consequent needs of the rulers to intensify the mobilization of various resources in order to deal with problems arising out of changes in military, diplomatic, and economic international situations; and (*e*) the development of various autonomous orientations and goals among the major strata and their respective demands on the rulers.

Insofar as there developed strong contradictions between these different factors and especially insofar as the rulers emphasized very expensive goals, which exhausted the available economic and manpower resources, the rulers found themselves in various dilemmas. In such situations, the special sensitivities of these political systems were brought out, and forces were generated that could undermine the delicate balance between political participation and apathy on which the continuity of these systems depended. This meant that the rulers' tendency toward maintenance of active control over different strata could become predominant, thus increasing the power of traditional forces, sharpening the conflicts between them and the more flexible, differentiated strata, and either depleting or alienating the more "free" groups and strata from the rulers. This depletion may have taken varying forms: outright reluctance to have children (or "demographic apathy," as it is sometimes called), weakening of the more independent economic elements and their subordination to more conservative, aristocratic–patrimonial (or feudal) elements, and depletion or flight of mobile capital (Eisenstadt 1963, chapter 12).

These processes were usually closely connected with the aristocratization or ossification of the bureaucracy, with its growing parasitic exploitation of the economy, and with the depletion of active political leadership identified with the regime. Such parasitic exploitation of the economy by the rulers was in a way an intensification of the usual economic activities of the rulers of the empires. The special parasitic nature of their activities in periods of decline—or of the setting in of decline—was evident not so much in the mere extension of the demands for taxes or for manpower as in the fact that the resources mobilized by the rulers were used for the creation of new ascriptive positions and groups. Instead of promoting conditions that could have encouraged the extension of greater resources, through trade or the facilities for training professional manpower, the rulers depleted their resources by adding to their already overdeveloped bureaucracies.

Thus there often developed a continuous flux of foreign elements into the centers of the realms. Initially mere merchants, hirelings, and personal helpers of the rulers, these foreign military groups gradually succeeded in infiltrating some of the most important political posts and finally in totally usurping the supreme political power. This was made possible by the depletion of native strata, together with the mounting internal and external crises. Similar developments could take place with regard to foreign merchants who sometimes, as in Byzantium or the Ottoman Empire, finally managed to monopolize all the trading posts abandoned by the indigenous merchants (Ostrogorski 1940). In those cases, as in Europe, in which these economically and socially more active strata were depleted, they became alienated from the rulers and their policies, as well as from the political institutions of the society, and turned to fomenting change and revolt.

Shmuel N. Eisenstadt

[*See also* Bureaucracy; Civil service; Colonialism.]

BIBLIOGRAPHY

Altheim, Franz 1955 *Gesicht von Abend und Morgen.* Frankfurt (Germany): Fischer.

Balázs, Étienne 1964 *Chinese Civilization and Bureaucracy: Variations on a Theme.* New Haven: Yale Univ. Press.

Baynes, N. H. 1943 The Decline of the Roman Power in Western Europe: Some Modern Explanations. *Journal of Roman Studies* 33:29–35.

Beloff, Max (1954) 1962 *The Age of Absolutism: 1660–1815.* New York: Harper. → See especially pages 170–180, "Absolutism in Transformation."

Boak, Arthur E. R. (1923) 1955 *History of Rome to 565 A.D.* 4th ed. New York: Macmillan.

Cahen, C. 1955 L'histoire économique et sociale de l'Orient musulman médiéval. *Studia islamica* 3:93–116.

Eberhard, Wolfram (1948) 1960 *A History of China.* 2d ed. Berkeley: Univ. of California Press. → First published in German.

Edgerton, William F. 1947 The Government and the Governed in the Egyptian Empire. *Journal of Near Eastern Studies* 6:152–160.

Eisenstadt, Shmuel N. 1963 *The Political Systems of Empires.* New York: Free Press.

Griffin, C. C. 1949 Economic and Social Aspects of the Era of Spanish-American Independence. *Hispanic American Historical Review* 29:170–187.

Hamilton, E. M. 1954 The Decline of Spain. Pages 215–226 in Eleanora Carus-Wilson (editor), *Essays in Economic History.* London: Arnold.

Haring, Clarence H. 1947 *The Spanish Empire in America.* New York: Oxford Univ. Press.

Jones, A. H. M. 1955 The Decline and Fall of the Roman Empire. *History* 40:209–226.

Lewis, Bernard (1950) 1958 *The Arabs in History.* Rev. ed. London: Hutchinson.

Lewis, Bernard 1958 Some Reflections on the Decline of the Ottoman Empire. *Studia islamica* 9:111–127.

Mosca, Gaetano (1896) 1939 *The Ruling Class.* New York: McGraw-Hill. → First published as *Elementi di scienza politica.* See especially paragraphs 6, 7, and 8 in Chapter 2, "The Ruling Class."

Ostrogorski, Georgije (1940) 1957 *History of the Byzantine State.* New Brunswick, N.J.: Rutgers Univ. Press. → First published in German.

Rostovtsev, Mikhail I. (1926) 1963 *The Social and Economic History of the Roman Empire.* New ed., 2 vols. Oxford: Clarendon.

Stange, O. H. 1950 Geschichte Chinas vom Urbeginn bis zur Gegenwart. Pages 363–542 in *Geschichte Asiens,* by Ernst Waldschmidt et al. Munich: Bruckmann.

Swart, Koenraad W. 1949 *Sale of Offices in the Seventeenth Century.* The Hague: Nijhoff.

Weber, Max (1906–1924) 1946 *From Max Weber: Essays in Sociology.* Translated and edited by Hans H. Gerth and C. Wright Mills. New York: Oxford Univ. Press. → See especially pages 162–171, "The Economic Foundations of 'Imperialism.'" First published in German.

Weber, Max (1922) 1957 *The Theory of Social and Economic Organization.* Edited by Talcott Parsons. Glencoe, Ill.: Free Press. → First published as Part 1 of *Wirtschaft und Gesellschaft.*

Wittfogel, Karl A. 1957 *Oriental Despotism: A Comparative Study of Total Power.* New Haven: Yale Univ. Press. → A paperback edition was published in 1963.

EMPLOYMENT AND UNEMPLOYMENT

The commercialization and industrialization of a large part of the world during the past several centuries have involved a radical change in the way in which human labor is directed toward productive ends. Two centuries ago, or more, most of the world's work force tilled the soil, as is still largely true except in North America and Europe. This work was performed in good part under conditions of status, in which a man was tied to a particular place and particular job by institutional arrangements which offered an individual and his family a sense of stability and security.

Today, in the more developed countries and in the commercial–industrial sectors of the less developed economies, command over labor is acquired in the market place. The interaction of demand and supply in the labor market determines, within limits, the level of wages and wage differentials, the volume of employment—and the volume of unemployment. As the relative importance of agriculture and other forms of self-employment has declined, the interplay of demand and supply, in the economy as a whole and in labor markets in particular, has come to be crucial in determining both long-term trends and short-run fluctuations in the volume of employment and unemployment.

The personal insecurity and widespread hardship that frequently resulted from the impersonal market determination of the level of employment began to influence government policies in the most industrialized countries in the latter part of the nineteenth century and became increasingly influential in the twentieth (Beveridge 1909). But intense world-wide concern with the welfare implications of widespread unemployment did not come until the great depression of the 1930s. Out of the shock of that experience and the economic planning that followed came the modern concern with maintaining the level of employment. This development was greatly stimulated by the "Keynesian revolution" in economic thinking, which dates from the mid-1930s.

Today "full employment" is an almost universally espoused goal. Virtually every advanced country that depends to a significant degree on private markets consciously formulates and tries to implement an employment policy. This was not true before the 1930s. The Beveridge Report of 1944, *Full Employment in a Free Society,* represents a landmark in this development. For the United States a comparable landmark is the Employment Act of 1946. The international concern at the end of World War II with the need to maintain a high and stable level of employment is suggested by the pledge, made by the governments subscribing to the United Nations Charter, to take action to promote "higher standards of living, full employment, and conditions of economic and social progress and development" (United Nations . . . 1949, p. 5).

The goal of full employment may conflict with other economic goals. Thus, full employment may not be compatible with the desired degree of stability in the price level, and at times governments have felt compelled to sacrifice some employment in order to correct a disequilibrium in the balance of payments. The question of how to reconcile these goals was being debated vigorously in the Western world in the mid-1960s.

Table 1 offers some historical background on the changing pattern of employment in broad industrial sectors. In the nineteenth century the shift away from agriculture had been most marked in the United Kingdom, and in the first decade of the twentieth century agriculture already accounted for less than 15 per cent of the British labor force. In the other leading industrial countries the agricultural sector of the labor force had already fallen below 50 per cent by the beginning of the twentieth century.

The shift of labor out of farming continued steadily during the first half of the twentieth century and has, indeed, accelerated since the end of World War II (Twentieth Century Fund 1961, pp. 72–74). The movement has been not only toward what is loosely called "industry" (manufacturing, mining, construction, and electric power and gas) but also into the trade and service sectors. This latter movement has been particularly marked in the United States. It is also noteworthy that the relative contribution of industry to total employment actually declined in the United States from 1950 to 1962. Involved here is not only the changing pattern of demand but also a more rapid rise

Table 1 — Percentage distribution of labor force by industrial sector in selected countries, 1910–1962

	1962	About 1950	About 1930	About 1910
France				
Agriculture[a]	21	34	36	43
Industry[b]	40	33	36	32
Service[c]	39	33	27	25
Germany				
Agriculture	14	23	29	34
Industry	49	44	41	40
Service	38	33	30	26
United Kingdom				
Agriculture	4	5	6	12
Industry	48	47	43	43
Service	48	48	51	45
United States				
Agriculture	9	12	22	31
Industry	33	35	31	31
Service	59	53	47	38

a. Agriculture includes forestry and fishing.
b. Industry includes manufacturing, mining, construction, gas, electricity, and water.
c. Service includes trade, banking and finance, transport and communication, and all other services (including government).

Sources: 1910–1950 data from Kuznets 1957, appendix, table 4; 1962 data from Organization for Economic Cooperation and Development 1963.

Table 2 — Percentage distribution of total employment by occupational classification in the United States, 1900–1963

Occupational group	1963	1950	1940	1930	1920	1910	1900
White-collar workers	43.9	36.6	31.1	29.4	24.9	21.4	17.6
Manual workers	36.3	41.1	39.9	39.6	40.2	38.2	35.8
Service workers	13.1	10.5	11.7	9.8	7.8	9.1	9.1
Farm workers*	6.7	11.8	17.4	21.2	27.0	31.1	37.5

* Includes farmers and farm laborers.

Sources: For 1900–1950, U.S. Bureau of the Census 1960; for 1963, U.S. President 1964.

in labor productivity in manufacturing than in the trade and service sectors.

Another change in the pattern of employment involves a gradual shift to white-collar occupations. This change has been particularly notable in the United States, as indicated in Table 2.

Other changes in the composition of employment can be mentioned only in passing; for example, the decline in the importance of self-employment, the rise in the participation of women in the non-agricultural labor force, an upward trend in the age at which children leave school and enter the labor force, and earlier retirement for older workers [see LABOR FORCE]. These trends are expected to continue into the future.

Unemployment

The historical record. During the decade from the mid-1950s to the mid-1960s, unemployment in western Europe was at a lower level than in any earlier peacetime decade in this century. Data on unemployment for selected countries since 1913 are presented in Table 3. By the standards of recent experience, unemployment was high even in the 1920s in a number of countries, notably Germany and the United Kingdom. The catastrophe of the great depression is suggested by the soaring unemployment rates during the 1930s. In the worst year of the depression, a sixth of the German labor force was unemployed, an eighth of the British, virtually a fifth of the Canadian, and as much as a quarter of the American.

The record of the 1950s and 1960s provides a highly encouraging contrast. Since the mid-1950s unemployment rates in western Europe have generally been below 4 per cent, and since 1960 they have typically been below 3 per cent. In contrast, unemployment in the United States, which in the first postwar decade tended to run at a rate of 4 per cent or less except during brief cyclical recessions, failed to fall below 5 per cent in any year after 1957 (through 1964).

This is not to say that European countries have

Table 3 — Unemployment rates in selected countries, 1913–1962[a]
(per cent of the labor force)

Year	France	Germany (later F.R.G.)	Italy	Sweden	United Kingdom	Canada	United States
1913	1.0	1.9	1.7	1.1	1.2	3.0	4.3
1920	b	1.7	b	1.3	1.8	b	5.2
1921	2.5	1.2	b	6.4	9.6	5.8	11.7
1922	b	0.7	b	5.5	8.1	4.4	6.7
1923	b	4.5	b	2.9	6.6	3.2	2.4
1924	b	5.8	b	2.4	5.8	4.5	5.0
1925	b	3.0	b	2.6	6.4	4.4	3.2
1926	1.1	8.0	b	2.9	7.1	3.0	1.8
1927	b	3.9	b	2.9	5.5	1.8	3.3
1928	b	3.8	b	2.4	6.1	1.7	4.2
1929	b	5.9	1.7	2.4	5.9	2.9	3.2
1930	b	9.5	2.5	3.3	9.3	9.1	8.9
1931	2.1	13.9	4.3	4.8	12.6	11.6	16.3
1932	b	17.2	5.8	6.8	13.1	17.6	24.1
1933	b	14.8	5.9	7.3	11.7	19.3	25.2
1934	b	8.3	5.6	6.4	9.9	14.5	22.0
1935	b	6.5	b	6.2	9.2	14.2	20.3
1936	4.2	4.8	b	5.3	7.9	12.8	17.0
1937	b	2.7	5.0	5.1	6.7	9.1	14.3
1938	3.6	1.3	4.6	5.1	8.1	11.4	19.1
1950	1.4	7.2	8.7	1.7	2.5	3.6	5.3
1951	1.3	6.4	9.2	1.6	2.2	2.4	3.3
1952	1.3	6.1	9.8	1.7	2.9	2.9	3.1
1953	1.6	5.5	10.2	1.9	2.6	2.9	2.9
1954	1.6	5.2	8.7	1.8	2.3	4.5	5.6
1955	1.5	3.8	7.5	1.8	2.1	4.3	4.4
1956	1.2	3.1	9.3	1.6	2.2	3.3	4.2
1957	1.0	2.7	8.1	1.7	2.4	4.5	4.3
1958	1.1	2.7	6.4	2.0	3.0	6.9	6.8
1959	1.3	1.9	5.4	1.8	3.1	5.9	5.5
1960	1.3	0.9	4.0	1.6	2.5	6.9	5.6
1961	1.2	0.6	3.4	1.5	2.4	7.1	6.7
1962	1.3	0.5	2.9	1.3	2.9	5.8	5.6

a. The unemployment rates shown for the various countries do not all reflect precisely the same coverage and definitions, although some limited standardization has been applied to the figures. Thus, the figures shown here do not agree completely with those in Table 4, where, for a more limited period, complete comparability with American definitions and coverage has been attempted.

b. Not available.

Sources: For all countries except United States, 1913–1960 from Maddison 1964, table E-1; 1961–1962 adapted from Organization for Economic Cooperation and Development 1963; for United States, 1913–1960 from Lebergott 1964, p. 512; for 1961–1962, from U.S. President 1964, p. 195.

not had pockets of serious unemployment with which to deal. Various countries continue to have their depressed regions—the Italian Mezzogiorno and Northern Ireland, for example—and differentially high unemployment rates may exist in particular countries for teen-agers, the older age groups, or the least skilled.

The relatively high unemployment that persisted in the United States after the mid-1950s gave rise to a vigorous debate as to its causes and appropriate cures (Ross 1964). On the one hand have been those who argued that the high level of unemployment reflected primarily a deficiency of aggregate demand. The argument has run that a higher and more rapidly rising level of total demand, sup-

ported by appropriate monetary–fiscal policies, could increase employment to the point where unemployment would again be brought down to a rate of 4 per cent or less.

Opposing this view has been the structuralist argument that the main problem has been not a lack of jobs in the aggregate but a failure of the labor supply to adjust sufficiently to the rapidly changing pattern of employment opportunities (U.S. Congress, Senate . . . 1963, part 5, pp. 1461–1499). The changing pattern of the demand for labor—resulting from automation and other technological change and from the shift in the composition of output toward services—has greatly increased the demand for highly educated and white-collar workers and reduced the demand for blue-collar, unskilled, and poorly educated workers. And, the argument runs, it has not been possible to make the necessary adjustments in labor supply. As a result, the structuralist position has maintained, merely expanding aggregate demand would lead to labor shortages in occupations in which unemployment rates were already relatively low without materially reducing the rates among the groups that had the highest unemployment.

In the early 1960s the consensus among those who had studied the problem was that the high level of unemployment in the United States was primarily the result of the failure of aggregate demand to expand rapidly enough. There was general agreement also, however, that the heterogeneous character of the American labor force created a persistent structural problem of poor employment opportunities for the underprivileged parts of the labor force (Ross 1964; Gordon 1964). There was increasing recognition on all sides that there was need for a vigorous and comprehensive manpower policy to expedite the absorption into gainful employment of the least qualified groups in the labor force (U.S. Senate . . . 1964).

When is a person unemployed? There is no single unambiguous definition of unemployment. Different purposes call for different definitions. Further, the definitions that are implicit in the official figures published in different countries may vary because of the way in which unemployment statistics are compiled.

The difficulties involved in arriving at a generally accepted definition of unemployment can be illustrated by the household survey utilized in the United States. Information is secured for each person in the household aged 14 and over. For those for whom it is reported that they did not work for pay outside the home at least one hour during the reference week, the question is then asked: "Was . . . looking for work?" An affirmative reply settles the matter; the person is listed as unemployed. A change in this procedure was under consideration in 1966.

This procedure raises the following definitional questions, among others:

(1) Should unemployment be measured in hours or persons? If a person wanting to work full-time can find only a half-time job, should he be counted as half unemployed? Similarly, if an unemployed person seeks only a part-time job, should he be counted as wholly unemployed? In all countries, the official figures refer to persons wholly unemployed, that is, persons who are not working at all

and are seeking full-time or part-time work. But some data on part-time unemployment are available, and the American government now publishes a monthly figure on "percent of labor force time lost" through unemployment.

(2) What should a person have done to look for work, and on what terms should he be willing to accept a job, if he is to be counted as unemployed? What sorts of overt action—such as registering at an employment office or applying personally at a factory or office—should he have taken? And how recently should he have taken such action? Further, if he is willing to work only at his former wage while a job is available to him at a lower wage, should he be counted as unemployed? These are questions that have no single and obvious answer.

(3) A question frequently asked is whether one should include among the unemployed those who are only marginally in the labor force—for example, boys and girls in school seeking part-time jobs or housewives who wish to work to supplement the family income or enjoy a more varied life. Those who would exclude such persons are in effect suggesting that hardship be the primary criterion in defining who is unemployed. Quite clearly, unemployment does not imply the same degree of hardship to all persons seeking jobs at a particular time. The answer here seems fairly clear-cut. An inclusive definition of unemployment should be used by those who compile the data, but the latter should be published in sufficient detail—for example, by age, sex, and marital status—so that the user can combine the subtotals in whatever way best fits the particular definition he wants to use.

(4) The question of marginal attachment to the labor force can cut two ways. The official count of the unemployed may include some persons who are only marginally attached to the labor force. But it also excludes an unknown number who would like to work and would look for work under more favorable conditions. This is not a serious issue if jobs are plentiful, but it does assume importance when unemployment is at a high level. Such a situation of more or less forced withdrawal from the labor force is frequently characterized as one of disguised unemployment.

Disguised unemployment was certainly of some importance in the United States after 1957, when the national unemployment rate remained above 5 per cent. This is an area in which it is difficult to obtain reliable figures. But there has been a growing body of evidence that the lack of jobs created disguised unemployment among women, older persons, the unskilled, those with the least education, and nonwhites (U.S. President 1964, pp. 30–31). Or to put the matter in other terms, labor-force participation rates among these groups were depressed by relatively high unemployment rates.

(5) Some other questions that arise in defining and measuring unemployment can only be mentioned. What should be done about those who are presumably unemployable because of physical or psychological handicaps? Should any attempt be made to measure "underemployment," that is, the extent to which persons are employed at jobs that call for less than their highest current level of skill? While it would certainly be desirable to have even partial measures of such underemployment, the obstacles in the way of developing such data are virtually insuperable.

The problem of underemployment is most frequently discussed in another connection—the very low average productivity and virtually zero marginal productivity of the agricultural populations in some of the least developed parts of the world. Here the pressure of population on natural resources is such that, given the state of production techniques, a moderate decline in the agricultural work force would lead to little if any reduction in total output. This condition is sometimes said to create "disguised unemployment," a term that we have used to mean withdrawal from the labor force because of the scarcity of jobs.

Methods and problems of measurement. It has already been noted that unemployment is measured in different ways in different countries. Systems of compiling unemployment data can be grouped under five headings: (1) sample surveys of the labor force; (2) compulsory unemployment-insurance statistics; (3) unemployment-relief data; (4) trade union records of unemployment; and (5) registrations at government employment offices.

Of these, the first and the last are the most common (U.S. President's Committee . . . 1962, appendix A). In 1964 sample surveys were the source of the official data on unemployment in Canada, Japan, and the United States; and such surveys have been used as a supplementary source of information in a number of other countries—for example, France, Germany, Italy, and Sweden. Employment-office registrations were the primary official source in France, Germany, Great Britain, Italy, Sweden, and elsewhere.

Section A of Table 4 presents the official unemployment rates for a number of countries for the years 1960–1962. Differences in definition and method of measurement, however, mean that a number of adjustments are necessary to make these

Table 4 — Unemployment rates in selected countries, as published and after adjustment to United States definitions, 1960–1962 (per cent of the labor force)

	A. OFFICIAL FIGURES AS PUBLISHED			B. ADJUSTED TO U.S. DEFINITIONS		
	1960	1961	1962[a]	1960	1961[a]	1962[a]
United States	5.6	6.7	5.6	5.6	6.7	5.6
Canada	7.0	7.2	6.0	7.0	7.2	6.0
France	1.0	0.9	0.9	1.9	1.7	1.8
Germany (F.R.G.)	1.2	0.8	0.7	1.0	0.5	b
Great Britain	1.6	1.4	1.9	2.4	2.2	2.8
Italy	8.2	7.6	6.3	4.3	3.7	3.2
Japan	1.0	0.9	0.9	1.1	1.0	1.0
Sweden	1.4	1.2	1.3	b	1.5	1.5

a. Some figures for these years are preliminary.
b. Not available.

Source: Myers 1964, p. 174.

figures fully comparable. Among the points of difference are the following:

(1) Treatment of unpaid family workers. Japan, for example, includes in the labor force unpaid family workers who worked as much as one hour during the survey week. The United States includes them only if they worked 15 hours.

(2) The treatment of persons on temporary layoff and of those waiting to start a new job. Before 1957 these groups were counted as employed in the United States; they are now treated as unemployed. In Japan, they are considered to be employed.

(3) The age at which children are included in the labor force.

(4) The period to which the data apply. In the United States, for example, the period is a week, and anyone working even one hour during the week is counted as employed. In Germany and Great Britain, on the other hand, the reference period is a day. A person not working on that day is counted as unemployed, although he may have worked on one or more other days during that week.

(5) The various unemployed groups that may be excluded from the unemployed. It is fairly common to exclude the self-employed, who are included in the United States. If the data come from unemployment-insurance records, those ineligible for coverage would be excluded. If the figures are based on registrations at employment offices, persons who are seeking jobs but do not register will be excluded.

(6) The computation of the unemployment rate. To compute an unemployment rate it is necessary to divide the number unemployed by some figure that includes the employed. In the United States, the denominator is taken to be the total civilian labor force. The self-employed are included. In a

number of countries, the unemployment rate represents only the percentage of wage-and-salary workers who are unemployed.

In 1962 the U.S. Bureau of Labor Statistics made the first intensive attempt to standardize the unemployment figures in a number of countries, the basis of comparison being the definitions in use in the United States. The results are shown in Section B of Table 4. Of the countries listed, the largest relative adjustments were in the British, French, and Italian figures—the first two upward and the last downward. Even after these adjustments the unemployment rates of all the other countries except Canada were below that of the United States for each of the years 1960–1962.

The kinds of unemployment. For both analytical and policy reasons, it would be extremely useful to be able to distinguish among various kinds of unemployment. In the classifications that have been attempted, the categories that one most frequently encounters bear the titles "frictional," "seasonal," "cyclical" (or "deficiency-of-demand"), and "structural" unemployment (U.S. Congress, Joint Economic Committee 1961).

Virtually all attempts at classification seek to take account of three sets of factors that tend to create a varying gap between the size of the labor force and total employment. These factors may be summarized as follows:

1. *Frictional and seasonal unemployment.* Even with a satisfactory level of aggregate demand and a homogeneous labor force, movement to a new job takes time. Hence, under the best of circumstances, there will be a minimum "float" of workers in the process of moving to new jobs. This can be called "minimum frictional unemployment." Such frictional unemployment is assumed to be balanced by an equal or larger number of job vacancies. If the labor force is not perfectly homogeneous, this frictional minimum may be different for different segments of the working population.

Seasonal unemployment is frequently included in this notion of frictional unemployment. Even if seasonal workers withdraw from the labor force or find other work in the off season, the frictions and time involved in such movements create a seasonal pattern in total unemployment. The seasonal pattern of unemployment does not remain constant over the years, and it is related, in ways which are still not well understood, to changes in the level of aggregate demand.

Seasonal unemployment creates a variety of problems, not the least of which is the problem of measurement. Considerable research has been aimed at improving existing methods of adjusting

unemployment figures for seasonal variation (U.S. President's Committee . . . 1962, chapter 6). And various measures by both government and private employers have had some effect in dampening the amplitude of seasonal movements in unemployment in particular industries. An interesting example was the effect of *Schlechtwettergeld* (bad-weather compensation) in reducing recorded seasonal unemployment in the German construction industry (Germany [Federal Republic] . . . 1962, pp. 56–57).

In Sweden in the early 1960s unemployment in midwinter tended to run three to four times as high as in midsummer. It is not surprising that such countries as Sweden and Norway have devoted considerable effort to reducing these wide seasonal swings. In the United States in 1964 the official seasonal index of the unemployment rate for experienced wage and salaried workers ranged from 84.1 in October to 122.9 in February (see "Rates of Unemployment" 1964). The seasonal amplitude in Canada was still wider.

2. *Cyclical unemployment.* Next is the set of factors implied by what formerly was called "cyclical" and is now frequently termed "deficiency-of-demand" unemployment. What is implied here is that the *total* demand for goods and services, given existent wage rates and labor productivity, is not sufficient to generate jobs for all those who want to work (after appropriate adjustment for minimum frictional unemployment). The number of job vacancies open in the economy as a whole is significantly less than the total number of people seeking work. This is the kind of unemployment that was so predominant during the great depression, and it is to the prevention of this kind of unemployment in particular that so-called full-employment policies are addressed.

3. *Structural unemployment.* The term "structural" unemployment is most frequently associated with the third set of factors. While this term has been used in different ways, structural unemployment almost always implies the following:

(*a*) There are particular sectors of the labor force from which workers cannot easily and quickly move into other sectors in search of jobs.

(*b*) In some or all of these sectors with impaired mobility, unemployment significantly exceeds available vacancies. And because of inadequate mobility, labor supply does not easily adjust to the inadequate level of demand. Hence, unemployment rates are higher in these sectors than in the economy as a whole, and such differentially high unemployment rates tend to persist for relatively long periods.

(c) There may be insufficient demand for particular types of labor for a number of reasons. Three in particular might be cited. First, the demand for particular skills may be reduced because of technological change or a shift in the pattern of demand. Discussions of structural unemployment in the United States in the early 1960s emphasized this factor particularly. Second, there may be a shift of economic activity out of a geographical region not matched by a comparable exodus of workers. This leads to the problem of "depressed areas." And third, there may be an influx of workers—of a particular type or into a particular region —at such a rate that they cannot be quickly absorbed into jobs. The influx of refugees into West Germany after World War II led to considerable debate regarding the size of the structural unemployment problem in that country (Germany [Federal Republic] . . . 1952).

The three kinds of causes of structural unemployment cited in the preceding paragraph all have to do with identifiable shifts in the pattern of demand for or supply of labor, to which the economy finds it difficult to adjust because of some degree of labor immobility. It is also possible that demand and supply for a particular kind of labor may have been out of balance as far back as our records go. Immobility, however it came to exist, may perpetuate such sectoral imbalances and create differentially high unemployment rates that continue indefinitely. Such more or less permanent immobility may be associated with a variety of institutional factors. Thus, we expect to find that unemployment rates are higher among the least skilled and least

educated. We should also expect that unemployment rates would be higher at the extremes of the age distribution than in the prime working ages. In the United States unemployment rates have been higher among Negroes than among whites since unemployment data were first recorded [see DISCRIMINATION, ECONOMIC].

These structural differentials will be the more marked the more heterogeneous is the labor force —and the measure of heterogeneity in this context is intersectoral immobility. These unemployment differentials are particularly marked, and the labor force is particularly heterogeneous, in the United States.

These differentially high unemployment rates may contain a frictional as well as a deficient-demand element. Among construction workers, for example, there may be ample vacancies, but the element of weather plus the need to move from job to job will cause frictional unemployment to be higher than in most other industries. Over and above such differentially high frictional unemployment, there may also be a shortage of jobs in relation to supply of this particular kind of labor.

It might be added that it is not easy in fact to differentiate between unemployment due to an economy-wide deficiency of demand and that due to structural factors in the sense defined above. For one thing, variations in aggregate demand affect different groups differently. For another, even the most persistent structural reasons for differential-employment opportunities tend to weaken in very tight labor markets; the extreme labor tightness during World War II illustrates this. Or, to cite

Table 5 — Unemployment rates for different sectors of the labor force, United States, 1948–1963
(per cent of sectoral labor force)

Sector	1965	1963	1959	1956	1953	1948
All civilian workers[a]	4.6	5.7	5.5	4.2	2.9	3.8
By age and sex[a]						
Men 20 years and over	3.2	4.5	4.7	3.4	2.5	c
Women 20 years and over	4.5	5.4	5.2	4.2	2.9	c
Both sexes, 14–19 years	13.6	15.6	13.2	10.4	7.1	c
Married men[a]	2.4	3.4	3.6	2.3	c	c
By occupation[b]						
White collar	2.3	2.8	2.6	1.7	1.4	2.1
Professional, technical only	1.5	1.8	1.7	1.0	0.9	1.7
Blue collar	5.3	7.2	7.5	5.1	3.5	4.3
Unskilled laborers only	8.4	12.1	12.4	8.2	6.1	7.5
By color[b]						
White	4.1	5.1	4.9	3.3	2.3	3.2
Nonwhite	8.3	10.9	10.7	7.5	4.1	5.2

a. The figures for 1948–1956 in these categories have been adjusted to account for a moderate change in definitions beginning in 1957.
b. The figures for 1948–1956 in these categories have not been so adjusted.
c. Not available.

Sources: "Rates of Unemployment" 1964, pp. 34–35; "Unemployment Rate" 1966; U.S. President 1964, p. 201; 1966, pp. 166–170.

another example, the structural unemployment resulting from the influx of refugees into West Germany largely disappeared in the very tight labor market of the late 1950s and early 1960s.

Table 5 gives some notion of the heterogeneity of the American labor force and of the resulting wide spread in unemployment rates for different parts of the working population. Thus, the unemployment rate for teen-agers has tended to run about 2.5 times the national rate. The rate for white-collar workers has tended to be about half the national rate, while the incidence of unemployment among unskilled laborers is more than twice as heavy as for the labor force as a whole. Similarly, the unemployment rate for nonwhites is about twice the national average. It is hardly necessary to elaborate upon the social and political, as well as economic, consequences of these high unemployment rates. This is particularly so with respect to what is referred to as "the Negro problem" in the United States.

In European countries the labor force is more homogeneous. Also, far fewer data are available on differential unemployment rates by age, occupation, etc., than is the case for the United States. As noted previously, however, every country has some relatively depressed areas, and a regional breakdown of the unemployed is available for a number of countries. Thus, in the United Kingdom in 1962 regional unemployment rates varied from 1.3 per cent in London and southeastern England to 3.7 per cent in Scotland and to no less than 7.5 per cent in Northern Ireland.

The goal of full employment

A high level of employment—or "full employment"—is now an accepted goal of national policy in virtually all of the economically advanced countries of the world. The acceptance of this goal immediately raises two questions. How is the goal of full employment to be defined? And how is this goal related to other economic objectives with which it may sometimes conflict—for example, stability of the price level and equilibrium in a country's balance of payments?

A variety of definitions of full employment has been offered. One made famous by Sir William Beveridge (1944) involves "having always more vacant jobs than unemployed men." The criterion that vacancies should exceed unemployment has frequently been criticized as inflationary, and a common alternative definition runs in terms of approximate equality between vacancies and unemployment.

In recent years, with growing sensitivity to the potential conflict between the goals of full employment and price stability, there has been a tendency

to define the employment objective in an alternative way: as the lowest level to which unemployment can be pushed by an expansion of aggregate demand without bringing about an unacceptable rise in the price level. Here, the definition makes it explicit that the employment target depends on the nature of the trade-off between a fall in unemployment and the associated rise (if any) in the price level.

Most definitions of full employment have sought to describe "a situation in which unemployment does not exceed the minimum allowances that must be made for the effects of frictional and seasonal factors" (United Nations . . . 1949, p. 13). The continued high level of unemployment in the United States between 1957 and 1965, however, raised the question as to how full employment should be defined if a significant amount of structural unemployment exists.

The problem here can be illustrated by Figures 1 and 2. In Figure 1 the job-vacancy rate is measured on the vertical axis and the unemployment rate on the horizontal. The 45° line portrays all possible situations that correspond to an equality of vacancies and unemployed. Curve AA' represents one "structural situation." Vacancies rise as unemployment falls (assuming general expansion with structural rigidities) and vice versa; point C represents a situation of "full" employment, in which vacancies and unemployment are equal—at an over-all unemployment rate of 3 per cent in the diagram.

Assume now that, because of structural changes, the curve shifts to BB'. Vacancies now equal un-

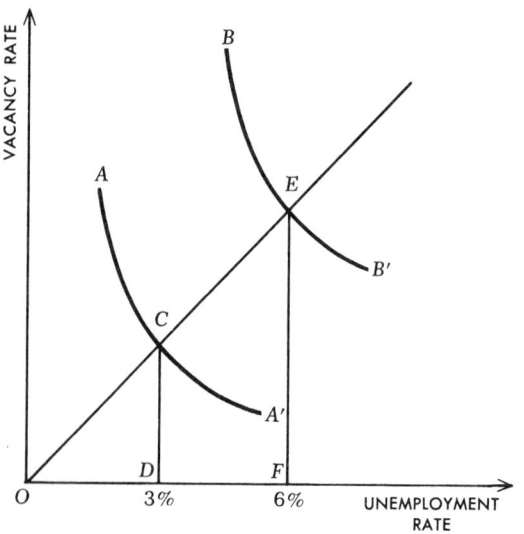

Figure 1

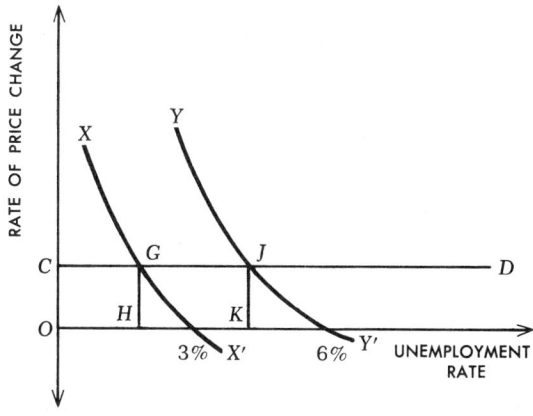

Figure 2

employment at an unemployment rate of 6 per cent. If the attempt were made to force unemployment much below this by expansionary measures, labor shortages would mount while unemployment would decline only slowly and painfully, with substantial upward pressure on wages and prices. Is 6 per cent to be considered the full-employment target, including not only frictional but also structural unemployment?

The second definition cited suggests the relationships illustrated in Figure 2. Here, again, unemployment is measured along the horizontal axis, but now the rate of change in the price level is represented on the vertical axis. This is a variant of what has come to be called the "Phillips curve," which relates wage changes rather than price changes to the level of unemployment (see Phillips 1958). The curves XX' and YY' describe two possible relationships between price-level changes and unemployment. The curve XX' implies that prices can be kept stable at an unemployment rate of 3 per cent. Lower unemployment leads to price increases at an accelerating rate.

Let the situation change to that portrayed by YY'. This upward shift is most commonly associated with labor's increased bargaining strength; but the curve might also shift because of the sort of structural change previously described, with the result that labor shortages in some sectors of the economy are associated with unemployment in excess of vacancies in other sectors. (Not only immobility between sectors but also downward wage rigidity is assumed.) As a result, in the second situation, price stability can be maintained only at an unemployment rate of 6 per cent. Is this full employment?

Since World War II it has been clear that all countries have been willing to settle for something less than absolute price stability. Probably no government would be prepared to pay a significant price in terms of higher unemployment in order to keep the rise in the price level below the rate of, say, 2 per cent per year. This upper limit on the rate of inflation that would be tolerated can be represented by the horizontal line CD in Figure 2. Then OH and OK represent the minimum levels to which unemployment could be reduced in the two cases.

This discussion suggests that the definition of full employment should be approached in two stages. First, we may define "aggregative full employment" as corresponding to that unemployment rate that meets the over-all criterion: total vacancies equal to total unemployment or the smallest amount of unemployment consistent with the desired degree of price stability.

Given the goal of aggregative full employment, which can best be implemented through the use of monetary–fiscal policy, we then need to ask the following question. By means of the various instruments of manpower policy (training and retraining programs, relocation of workers and industry, reduction of discrimination in hiring, and so on), how far is a government prepared to go in reducing the amount of structural unemployment that exists at aggregative full employment? Or, in terms of the diagrams, how far is it prepared to go in seeking to shift the BB' and YY' curves to the left? The answer to this question, when costs and benefits are weighed on the scales of the policy makers' value system, yields what we may call aggregative *and* structural full employment. In the United States, aggregative full employment in the early 1960s was assumed to correspond to an unemployment rate of about 4 per cent, and it was believed by many that unemployment might, by means of an intensive manpower policy, be brought down to 3 per cent—at a cost that was worth incurring in terms of the benefits to be achieved (U.S. Senate ...1964).

It is one thing to conceptualize the goal of full employment; it is another thing to quantify it. Most governments have been reluctant to announce the precise unemployment rate they consider to be equivalent to full employment. One can, however, draw some inferences from recent policy actions and statements. Thus, in 1964–1965 it was reasonable to assume that the full-employment targets in the leading European countries ranged between about 1.5 and 3 per cent unemployment, using American definitions (Gordon 1965). For the United States the corresponding target figure would be about 4 per cent.

The targets cited here correspond to what has been called "aggregative full employment." In addition, governments have various kinds of manpower policies aimed at reducing structural and frictional unemployment.

Other aggregative goals. The potential conflict between full employment and price stability has already been mentioned. There are also at least three other "aggregative" goals that need to be taken into account when a government seeks to pursue a full-employment policy. They are balance-of-payments equilibrium, growth of total output, and what has come to be called "incomes policy" (chiefly keeping the rise in wages in line with the increase in productivity).

There is normally no conflict between the goals of full employment and rapid economic growth. But there is some conflict between full employment and the other goals. Involved here is a set of inter-relationships that can conveniently be discussed in two parts.

First, relative price stability is a goal that is desired to some extent for its own sake. The more rapidly prices rise or fall—apart from balance-of-payments considerations—the greater is the damage to economic welfare as seen by those who frame economic policy. In recent years Germany and the United States have been the two large countries that have shown the greatest sensitivity to inflationary pressures. In most European countries, however, the trade-off between unemployment and price stability seems to be such that the governments concerned would not be willing to sacrifice much, if any, employment in order to reduce the rate of price increase—*provided* that (1) prices in other countries rose also, so that serious balance-of-payments problems did not arise, and (2) the rise in prices did not degenerate into runaway inflation.

This brings us to the second aspect of the potential conflict between full employment and the other aggregative goals. The strongest threat to pursuit of a vigorous full-employment policy comes from the possibility of balance-of-payments disequilibrium. If expansionary policies cause spending and prices to rise faster at home than abroad, a country may incur a deficit in its balance of payments which, if continued long enough, will force it to devalue its currency. This is an especially serious problem for countries for which international trade is particularly important. Such countries will, from time to time, be forced to pursue restrictive monetary and fiscal policies, sacrificing some employment in order to protect international monetary reserves. In the early 1960s the United States was apparently prepared to put up with unemployment considerably in excess of what was widely consid-

ered to be the full-employment target, in part because of the need to reduce the persistent deficit in its balance of payments. In 1966, the British government felt compelled to impose strong deflationary measures to protect the balance of payments.

It is in this connection that price stability plays its most important role. Price stability is a means of achieving balance-of-payments equilibrium. It is primarily a means, rather than an end in itself. It might be noted that what is important here for the balance of payments is not the behavior of the domestic price level by itself but the behavior of domestic prices relative to that of foreign prices.

As the 1960s began, there was increasing recognition on both sides of the Atlantic of the need for an incomes policy that would hold the rise in wages roughly in line with the rise in labor productivity (Organization for Economic Cooperation and Development . . . 1962; U.S. President 1962, pp. 185–190). The Netherlands has had an official, but only partially successful, incomes policy since the end of the war. Here again there is a potential conflict with a vigorous full-employment policy. An incomes policy is extremely difficult to apply unless a government is prepared either to exercise compulsion or to accept a higher level of unemployment than would otherwise be necessary. It is not surprising, therefore, that efforts to implement an incomes policy have not so far been very successful.

The events of the decade from the mid-1950s to the mid-1960s suggest a strong contrast between the ways in which western Europe and the United States reconciled the full-employment and other aggregative goals during this period. The United States was prepared to sacrifice a significant amount of employment in order to keep a relatively stable price level, partly for its own sake but chiefly for the sake of its balance-of-payments position. The relative emphasis put on a fairly strict interpretation of the full-employment goal was considerably stronger in Europe. (For further discussion of the issues in this section see Gordon 1965; Ross 1964, pp. 155–171; Gordon & Gordon 1966.)

Development of manpower programs. The increasing recognition of the need to formulate the goal of full employment in structural as well as aggregative terms calls for not only the appropriate use of monetary–fiscal measures but also the development of a comprehensive manpower program.

Manpower policy is concerned with the structural aspects of employment and unemployment—with facilitating the adjustment of the composition of labor supply to the changing composition of labor demand. A well-developed manpower program would include measures of the following types: (1) an active and comprehensive employment service to assist in placement, to provide vocational guidance, and possibly to collect data on vacancies; (2) an adequate system of unemployment insurance, integrated with a system of subsistence allowances for retraining and aid in the relocation of workers; (3) programs to facilitate the geographical mobility of workers; (4) heavy emphasis on training and retraining to assist workers in acquiring new skills; (5) special programs for the physically and mentally handicapped and for older workers; (6) a well-developed program of projecting the future demand for labor and prospective shortages and surpluses of particular kinds of labor, and wide dissemination of such information; (7) cooperation with the schools in the improvement of vocational education; and (8) special employment projects to assist particular regions or groups of workers in making difficult adjustments to new patterns of demand.

Sweden has a particularly well-developed manpower program that aims to be "so varied, so individualised as—in time—to fit every single person on the employment market" (Olsson 1963, p. 411). Most of the other western European countries have significant manpower programs, which vary in the aspects that have been particularly emphasized. Thus, training and retraining have been stressed in France and Italy; Sweden has emphasized regional labor mobility as well as retraining; regional industrial development has played a key role in manpower policy in the United Kingdom. All of these countries—as well as the other countries of western Europe—have also developed, to different degrees, various of the other dimensions of manpower policy previously listed. It is interesting to note also that elements of an international manpower policy have been developed within the European Common Market.

Spurred by high over-all unemployment and concerned with the especially high unemployment rates in particular segments of the labor force, the United States began to move toward a comprehensive manpower policy at the beginning of the 1960s. A decentralized employment service had existed since the 1930s, as had a system of unemployment insurance. In 1961 the Area Redevelopment Act was passed, followed in 1962 by the much more comprehensive Manpower Development and Training Act. The emphasis in the latter was almost entirely on retraining. Other measures have involved acceleration of public works, federal support of education, special provisions for the training and rehabilitation of underprivileged youth, and special measures to counter discrimination against Negroes (U.S. President 1963; 1964).

By 1965 no country had yet developed a manpower program "so varied, so individualised as to fit every single person on the employment market." But movement toward this goal, more rapid and systematic in some countries than in others, was the trend. Avowed full-employment goals and systematic manpower policies did not exist in the Western world when the great depression struck. Considerable progress toward the formulation of such goals and the implementation of such policies has been made since then.

R. A. GORDON

[See also MONETARY POLICY; FISCAL POLICY; INFLATION AND DEFLATION; and the biography of BEVERIDGE.]

BIBLIOGRAPHY

BEVERIDGE, WILLIAM H. (1909) 1930 Unemployment: A Problem of Industry. London: Longmans.

BEVERIDGE, WILLIAM H. (1944) 1945 Full Employment in a Free Society. New York: Norton.

Employment and Unemployment: Government Policies Since 1950: I. 1956 International Labour Review 74:1–22.

GERMANY (FEDERAL REPUBLIC), BUNDESMINISTERIUM FÜR ARBEIT UND SOZIALORDNUNG 1952 Analyse der westdeutschen Arbeitslosigkeit, Statistik. Bonn: The Ministerium.

GERMANY (FEDERAL REPUBLIC), BUNDESANSTALT FÜR ARBEITSVERMITTLUNG UND ARBEITSLOSENVERSICHERUNG 1962 Ein Jahrzehnt Bundesanstalt für Arbeitsvermittlung und Arbeitslosenversicherung: 1952–1962. Nuremberg: The Institute.

GORDON, R. A. 1964 Has Structural Unemployment Worsened? Industrial Relations 3:53–77.

GORDON, R. A. 1965 Full Employment as a Policy Goal. Pages 25–55 in Arthur M. Ross (editor), Employment Policy and the Labor Market. Berkeley: Univ. of California Press. → From the second Conference on Unemployment and the American Economy, held in 1964 at Boulder, Colorado.

GORDON, R. A.; and GORDON, MARGARET (editors) 1966 Prosperity and Unemployment. New York: Wiley.

KUZNETS, SIMON 1957 Quantitative Aspects of the Economic Growth of Nations: 2. Industrial Distribution of National Product and Labor Force. Economic Development and Cultural Change 5, no. 4, part 2.

LEBERGOTT, STANLEY 1964 Manpower in Economic Growth: The American Record Since 1800. New York: McGraw-Hill.

MADDISON, ANGUS 1964 Economic Growth in the West: Comparative Experience in Europe and North America. New York: Twentieth Century Fund.

MYERS, ROBERT J. 1964 Unemployment in Western Europe and the United States. Pages 172–198 in Arthur M. Ross (editor), Unemployment and the American Economy. New York: Wiley. → From the first Conference on Unemployment and the American Economy, held in 1963 at Berkeley, California.

OLSSON, B. 1963 Employment Policy in Sweden. *International Labour Review* 87:409–434.

ORGANIZATION FOR ECONOMIC COOPERATION AND DEVELOPMENT 1963 *Manpower Statistics: 1950–1962.* Paris: The Organization.

ORGANIZATION FOR ECONOMIC COOPERATION AND DEVELOPMENT, ECONOMIC POLICY COMMITTEE 1962 *Policies for Price Stability: A Report to the Economic Policy Committee by Its Working Party on Costs of Production and Prices.* Paris: The Organization.

PHILLIPS, A. W. 1958 The Relation Between Unemployment and the Rate of Change of Money Wage Rates in the United Kingdom: 1861–1957. *Economica* New Series 25:283–299.

Rates of Unemployment. 1964 U.S. Bureau of Labor Statistics, *Monthly Report on Labor Force, Employment, Unemployment, Hours and Earnings* [1964] January:34–35.

ROSS, ARTHUR M. (editor) 1964 *Unemployment and the American Economy.* New York: Wiley. → From the first Conference on Unemployment and the American Economy, held in 1963 at Berkeley, California.

TWENTIETH CENTURY FUND 1961 *Europe's Needs and Resources: Trends and Prospects in Eighteen Countries.* New York: The Fund.

Unemployment and Structural Change. 1962 International Labour Office, *Studies and Reports* New Series [1962] No. 65.

Unemployment Rate. 1966 U.S. Bureau of Labor Statistics, *Employment and Earnings and Monthly Report of the Labor Force* [1966] February:20–24.

UNITED NATIONS, DEPARTMENT OF ECONOMIC AFFAIRS 1949 *National and International Measures for Full Employment.* Lake Success, N.Y.: United Nations.

U.S. BUREAU OF THE CENSUS 1960 *Historical Statistics of the United States; Colonial Times to 1957: A Statistical Abstract Supplement.* Washington: Government Printing Office.

U.S. CONGRESS, JOINT ECONOMIC COMMITTEE 1961 *Unemployment: Terminology, Measurement and Analysis.* Washington: Government Printing Office.

U.S. CONGRESS, SENATE, COMMITTEE ON LABOR AND PUBLIC WELFARE 1963 *Nation's Manpower Revolution: Hearings Before the Subcommittee on Employment and Manpower of the Committee on Labor and Public Welfare.* Washington: Government Printing Office.

U.S. PRESIDENT 1962 *Economic Report of the President.* Washington: Government Printing Office. → Published annually since 1947.

U.S. PRESIDENT 1963 *Manpower Report of the President.* Washington: Government Printing Office.

U.S. PRESIDENT 1964 *Manpower Report of the President.* Washington: Government Printing Office.

U.S. PRESIDENT 1966 *Manpower Report of the President.* Washington: Government Printing Office.

U.S. PRESIDENT'S COMMITTEE TO APPRAISE EMPLOYMENT AND UNEMPLOYMENT STATISTICS 1962 *Measuring Employment and Unemployment.* Washington: Government Printing Office.

U.S. SENATE, LABOR AND PUBLIC WELFARE COMMITTEE 1964 *Toward Full Employment: Proposals for Comprehensive Employment and Manpower Policy in the United States.* Washington: Government Printing Office.

ENCLAVES AND EXCLAVES

Enclaves and exclaves are discontiguous territories of states which are located within the territory of other states. Seen from the state within which the outlier is located, it is an *enclave;* seen from the state to which the outlier belongs, it is an *exclave.* A typical example is the Spanish town of Llivia in the eastern Pyrenees of France: this is an exclave of Spain, entirely surrounded by French territory and located about four miles from the main Spanish territory; it is also a Spanish enclave within French territory.

Enclaves (exclaves) may be accessible to the main territory of the state to which they belong by land, through the territory of other states, as well as by sea. A typical example is the former German exclave of East Prussia, which from 1919 to 1939, as well as in previous centuries, was separated from the main German territory by Polish territory and the Baltic Sea. However, if discontiguous territories are accessible only by sea, they are usually described as islands; if they are located on other continents, as colonies or associated territories. Thus Hong Kong is regarded as a colony of Great Britain in eastern Asia, although, from the Chinese point of view, it is sometimes described as a British enclave surrounded, on the landward side, by Chinese territory. Gibraltar can similarly be regarded as a British colony on the continent of Europe and as an enclave within Spain. In these cases the nomenclature is necessarily vague; however, this does not detract from the political, economic, and historical significance of enclaves and exclaves.

Territorial waters have the same sovereign attributes as land, and enclaves may therefore exist within territorial waters. A typical example is the islands of Chisamula and Likoma in Lake Nyasa; they are located within the territorial waters of Portuguese Mozambique but are exclaves of Malawi.

States entirely surrounded by territory of one other state, for example, the Vatican, share the characteristics of enclaves and are sometimes referred to as *virtual exclaves.* Contiguous territories of states which for all regular commercial and administrative purposes can be reached only through the territory of other states are called *pene-enclaves* (*pene-exclaves*). These have virtually the same characteristics as complete enclaves (exclaves). A typical example is the Drumully area of the Republic of Ireland, which can be reached by road and rail only through territory of Great Britain (Northern Ireland).

Enclaves (exclaves) should be distinguished

from *neutral territories* that sometimes separate states, for example, those on the northeastern border of Saudi Arabia. Sovereignty in neutral territories is shared between two or more states, and territorial discontiguity is not an essential characteristic. However, for convenience of administration some governmental functions, for example, customs and excise, may be relinquished by the sovereign of the enclave (exclave) to the sovereign of the surrounding territory, and thus an impression of shared sovereignty can result.

Except for the unique cases of East Pakistan and West Berlin, enclaves are today relatively unimportant economically and cover only small areas, usually less than 20 square kilometers. Their political and military value is probably also very limited. Some enclaves (exclaves), for example, West Berlin (including Steinstücken, Papenberger Wiesen, etc.) consist of several parcels of territory, which makes accurate statistical accounting virtually impossible.

Origin of the terms. Use of the terms originated during the late Middle Ages. The first diplomatic document to contain the word "enclave" was the Treaty of Madrid, signed in 1526. Since then the terms have also been used outside political geography; parks, for example, have been described as rural enclaves within cities. Similarly, areas of low prices located within higher price regions, for example, areas along major highways within a high price region where low gasoline prices are posted, are described as low-price enclaves.

Geographical distribution. Most enclaves today are relics of the feudal era, and western Europe contains the largest number, about fifteen. Formerly there were many more; for example, prior to 1866 Prussia alone consisted of more than 270 discontiguous pieces of territory. India also contained large numbers of enclaves prior to independence. During and after the crusades, enclaves were a fairly widespread phenomenon in the eastern Mediterranean region, and presumably they also existed elsewhere during periods of feudal rule. Through accidents of discovery and difficulties of inland penetration, enclaves were also frequently established during the colonial era in or near the coasts of Africa and Asia. Today only a few survive, for example, the Portuguese Cabinda enclave north of the mouth of the Congo. When considered as enclaves, British Hong Kong and Gibraltar fall into this category. Similar Portuguese (Goa, for instance, but also complete exclaves entirely surrounded by non-Portuguese territory, such as Nagar Aveli) and French enclaves (such as Pondicherry, but also complete exclaves, such as Chandernagore) in India have disappeared from the map since India gained independence.

Throughout history, enclaves were sometimes deliberately established to assure control of neighboring areas, for example, by the settlement of Roman veterans in classical times; a modern example is that of the British enclaves on Cyprus created in 1960 to control the eastern Mediterranean and the Middle East. Errors of definition with respect to straight-line boundaries have caused the establishment of two enclaves in North America near the 49th parallel (Point Roberts, Washington, and Lake of the Woods County, Minnesota, both of which are in Canada). Where rivers form boundaries between states, changes of river courses have frequently created enclaves on opposite shores, as on the Mississippi River; where such changes resulted in international boundary problems, these enclaves were usually eliminated by exchange of territory and other compensation, as occurred between the United States and Mexico on the Rio Grande.

The enclaves of West Berlin and of the Hebrew University campus (part of Israel within Jordanian territory) were the result of recent armistice agreements. Similar temporary arrangements have been recorded frequently, particularly in feudal times. The enclaves of East Prussia and of East Pakistan were created in this century to accommodate national or religious aspirations. For the same national reasons the internal spatial organization of the Soviet Union exhibits several enclaves. Parts of former German East Prussia now constitute an enclave of the Russian Soviet Federated Socialist Republic. To what extent the enclaves shown on maps of the Soviet Union are economically or politically significant is not known. Although several enclaves have survived since the early Middle Ages, most have disappeared with the growth of centralized states, and many appear to be only temporary features of modern political geography.

Theories of origin. Most settlements were virtually self-sufficient before the advent of modern transportation, and generally only goods of high value and little bulk were exchanged over distances of more than a few miles. Because of high costs of transportation, most settlements and their environs were surrounded by undeveloped lands separating them from neighboring settlements (Thünen 1826–1863). In the feudal era each of these settlements became dominated by a local ruler who, by war, marriage, or purchase, tried to enlarge his territories. Messengers and the small armies of the era could move through the undeveloped lands between the settlements, and since there was also little trade, there was no need for feudal territories to be contiguous. Thus the pattern of enclaves which is so characteristic of this period gradually evolved. Territorial discontiguity was found not only at the lowest but also at the highest level of the feudal hierarchy. Even self-governing cities contained both enclaves and exclaves. Territorial discontiguity was most marked in Germany but also existed in much more centralized Great Britain, where a few enclaves survive to this day among county areas, for example, in Flintshire.

The modern era. As a result of the growth of the modern state, enclaves were gradually absorbed into the new national territories. Ratzel (1896) and other German geographers, particularly the later German school of "geopolitics," regarded this absorption as an "organic" phenomenon in the evolution of so-called natural boundaries of states. These are frequently related to physical features of geography, such as seacoasts, watersheds, or mountain crests, but usually are poorly definable except in the context of nationalistic ambition. Arguments of this nature were, for example, used by India to defend its action in occupying the Portuguese enclaves and exclaves on the Indian subcontinent. At the time of the French Revolution the process of absorption was already virtually complete in the Iberian Peninsula, Great Britain, and Scandinavia. As a result of the French Revolution the many vestiges of enclaves (particularly with respect to internal tariffs) disappeared from France, and the number of enclaves was considerably reduced in central Europe and Italy. Because of the lesser significance of feudalism in eastern Europe, enclaves were far less important, and they completely disappeared during the nineteenth century.

The final reduction in the number of enclaves to the present low and insignificant figure took place during the period of railway construction. Enclaves came to be regarded as economically and politically absurd, as revealed in the discussion of the problem of German East Prussia during the period between the two world wars. The introduction of motorcars also increased the possibility of smuggling from enclaves (always a serious matter) and assisted public demand for the abolition of enclaves, as in India and Switzerland. Within sovereign states, administrative enclaves, usually relics of the process of state amalgamation following the feudal era, were also greatly reduced in number by the redefinition of local boundaries, as in India and Germany. However, many enclaves have survived in the cantonal system of the Swiss Confederation.

Since World War II the development of air transportation and the building of limited-access highways and railways with systems of overpasses and underpasses have presented new opportunities for connecting enclaves to other territory of the same state. The air lanes, highways, and railways connecting West Berlin to West Germany are an example, although these connections have not worked very satisfactorily. The United Nations partition scheme in 1947 for the former British mandate of Palestine called for a series of discontiguous Arab and Jewish territories, each consisting of a main territory and two exclaves. These exclaves were to touch the main territories at two junction points, where short overpasses and underpasses of limited-access transportation avenues were to connect them with the main territories. While the violent rejection of this partition scheme was the result of other more serious national considerations, there appears to be little doubt that these connecting links between exclaves and main territories were also regarded as highly unsatisfactory. For all these reasons it is unlikely that the new means of transportation will bring about an increase in the number of enclaves.

ALEXANDER MELAMID

BIBLIOGRAPHY

LÖSCH, AUGUST (1940) 1954 *The Economics of Location.* New Haven: Yale Univ. Press. → First published as *Die räumliche Ordnung der Wirtschaft.*

MELAMID, ALEXANDER 1955 The Economic Geography of Neutral Territories. *Geographical Review* 45:359–374.

MELAMID, ALEXANDER 1966 Municipal Quasi-exclaves: Examples From Yonkers, New York. *Professional Geographer* 18, no. 2:94–96.

MINGHI, JULIAN V. 1963 Boundary Studies in Political Geography. Association of American Geographers, *Annals* 53:407–428.

RATZEL, FRIEDRICH 1896 Die Gesetze des räumlichen Wachstums der Staaten. *Petermann's Mitteilungen* 42:97–107.

ROBINSON, G. W. S. 1959 Exclaves. Association of American Geographers, *Annals* 49:283–295. → Contains the best listing of the exclaves existing in 1958.

THÜNEN, JOHANN H. VON (1826–1863) 1930 *Der isolierte Staat in Beziehung auf Landwirtschaft und Nationalökonomie.* 3 vols. Jena (Germany): Fischer.

ENCULTURATION

See SOCIALIZATION.

ENDOGAMY

See INCEST *and* MARRIAGE.

ENGAGEMENT

See MARRIAGE *and* NUPTIALITY.

ENGEL, ERNST

Ernst Engel (1821–1896) was a German statistician. After his early training at a mining academy in Germany, Engel went to the École des Mines in Paris, where he came under the influence of Frédéric Le Play, a pioneer in the study of family budgets, who was a professor there. During a subsequent stay in Belgium he became acquainted with Adolphe Quetelet, well-known for his faith in the possibility of discovering quantitative social laws. Upon his return to Germany Engel took up statistics as a profession and became director of the statistical bureaus of Saxony, 1850–1858, and Prussia, 1861–1882. As a vigorous administrator and inspiring teacher he did much to establish the modern tradition of official statistics; in particular, he insisted on making statistical data accessible and intelligible to the general public. He was also active in the social reform movement, which he supplied not only with figures but also with various practical proposals. In 1881 he published a pseudonymous attack on Bismarck's agricultural protectionism and was promptly relieved of his position on grounds of ill-health. Of the great work on "demology" that he then set out to write only a fragment was completed.

His greatest contribution to the social sciences soon became known as "Engel's law." It states that the proportion of a consumer's budget spent on food tends to decline as the consumer's income goes up, or, in more technical terms, that the income elasticity of demand for food is less than one. Engel derived this generalization from the budgets collected in different countries by his teacher Le Play and from Belgian data compiled by Édouard Ducpétiaux; it has since been invariably confirmed in hundreds of more elaborate surveys in all parts of the world.

Engel published his discovery in the context of a study of the economic development of Saxony (1857), in which he demonstrated that a general rise in productivity requires a shift of population from agriculture to manufacturing because of the effect of an increase in income on the pattern of demand. He also advanced his observations as an argument against Malthus' fears of overpopulation.

From a methodological point of view Engel's law is important as the first significant quantitative law ever established by empirical economic data.

Formulated when economic theory proceeded largely by deduction from a priori assumptions, the law pointed the way to a more reliable approach. It also drew attention to the study of demand, which had been neglected by the classical economists, and suggested that economic development is not merely a matter of capital accumulation. Engel, however, was not much interested in economic theory and considered himself primarily a statistician, as did his numerous followers in the empirical study of family budgets, at least until recently.

Attempts were soon made to find similar generalizations for other categories of expenditure, such as housing and clothing. But here the pattern of demand was not so simple, at least when analyzed in terms of increasing or decreasing budget shares. Thus the "laws" of Schwabe for housing and Schiff for clothing, which state that the share of these categories respectively falls and rises as income increases, are not as universally valid as Engel's law, although they probably hold in a majority of budget surveys. For these two categories the income elasticity is normally so close to one that in a particular survey it may be on either side of unity. From a review of the evidence accumulated during the century following the enunciation of Engel's law, Houthakker (1957) concluded that the typical elasticity with respect to total expenditure is 0.6 for food, 0.8 for housing, 1.2 for clothing, and 1.6 for all other expenditures combined.

The relation between the expenditure on a particular item or group of items on the one hand and income or total expenditure on the other is now generally known as an "Engel curve." Such curves have been extensively studied, especially after the development of regression analysis around the turn of the century. Engel could not avail himself of this technique and had to fit his food–total expenditure relationship by graphical methods. Perhaps the most important instance of an Engel curve is Keynes's consumption function (1936), which relates total expenditure to income and has become the cornerstone of macroeconomic analysis. There is a clear line of descent from Engel's law to Keynes's "fundamental psychological law," according to which the proportion of total consumption to income falls as income goes up.

Engel refined his analysis of family budgets by taking household composition into account. In his little book *Der Kostenwerth des Menschen* ("The Cost of Man"), published in 1883, he proposed what has since become known as an equivalent adult scale to give appropriate weights to persons of different ages and sexes; Engel's unit, however, was not the consumption of an adult male, as in most later scales, but the consumption of an infant under one year. He called this unit "quet" in honor of Quetelet. In this book there are also interesting calculations on some economic aspects of education.

With a little more perseverance Engel could have established another claim to fame, namely, to have initiated not only the cross-section analysis but also the time-series analysis of demand. In a paper of 1861 on the Prussian grain market he derived an empirical demand curve for rye with a price elasticity of about one-half, but he did not consider the results sufficiently trustworthy to pursue the subject, although he did claim to have refuted Gregory King's "law" on the demand for grain. The lack of suitable curve-fitting techniques may have held back his work in this area, and the estimation of empirical demand curves had to wait until the twentieth century.

Engel wrote on many other subjects, including labor and industry, taxation, insurance, banking, and war. His influence extended into many other countries; in the United States, Carroll Wright, founder of the Bureau of Labor Statistics, was his principal follower. Engel was also active in the International Statistical Congresses, the forerunners of the International Statistical Institute of which he was a founder in 1886.

H. S. HOUTHAKKER

[*For the historical context of Engel's work, see the biographies of* KING; LE PLAY; MALTHUS; QUETELET. *For discussion of the subsequent development of his ideas, see* CONSUMERS, *article on* CONSUMPTION LEVELS AND STANDARDS; CONSUMPTION FUNCTION; DEMAND AND SUPPLY, *article on* ECONOMETRIC STUDIES.]

WORKS BY ENGEL

(1857) 1895 Die Productions- und Consumtionsverhältnisse des Königreichs Sachsen. International Statistical Institute, *Bulletin* 9, no. 1, supplement 1. → First published in Volume 3 of Saxony, Statistisches Landesamt, *Zeitschrift des statistischen Bureaus des Königlich Sächsischen Ministeriums des Innern.*

1861 Die Getreidepreise, die Ernteerträge und der Getreidehandel im preussischen Staate. Prussia, Statistisches Landesamt, *Zeitschrift des Königlich Preussischen Statistischen Bureaus* 1:249–289.

(1866) 1872 *Der Preis der Arbeit: Zwei Vorlesungen.* 2d ed. Berlin: Habel.

1872a Beiträge zur Statistik des Krieges von 1870–1871. Prussia, Statistisches Landesamt, *Zeitschrift des Königlich Preussischen Statistischen Bureaus* 12:1–318.

1872b Die Wohnungsnoth: Ein Vortrag auf der Eisenacher Conferenz. Prussia, Statistisches Landesamt, *Zeitschrift des Königlich Preussischen Statistischen Bureaus* 12:379–402.

1875 Die Klassen- und klassificirte Einkommensteuer und die Einkommensvertheilung im preussischen Staat in den Jahren 1852 bis 1875. Prussia, Statistisches Landesamt, *Zeitschrift des Königlich Preussischen Statistischen Bureaus* 15:105–148.

1881 *Deutschlands Getreideproduktion, Brodbedarf und Brodbeschaffung.* By C. Lorenz [pseud.]. Volkswirthschaftliche Zeitfragen, Vol. 3, Part 6. Berlin: Simion. →

1883 *Der Kostenwerth des Menschen.* Berlin: Simion. → Published as Part 1 of Engel's *Der Werth des Menschen,* a projected multivolume edition.

1895 Die Lebenskosten belgischer Arbeiter-familien früher und jetzt. International Statistical Institute, *Bulletin* 9, no. 1:i–vi, 1–124.

SUPPLEMENTARY BIBLIOGRAPHY

ALLEN, ROY G. D.; and BOWLEY, ARTHUR L. 1935 *Family Expenditure: A Study of Its Variation.* London School of Economics and Political Science, Studies in Statistics and Scientific Method, No. 2. London: King.

BLENCK, E. 1896 Zum Gedächtniss an Ernst Engel: Ein Lebensbild. Prussia, Statistisches Landesamt, *Zeitschrift des Königlich Preussischen Statistischen Bureaus* 36:231–238. → Contains a partial bibliography.

FEIG, J. 1907 Ernst Engel. *Allgemeines statistisches Archiv* 7, no. 1:349–359.

FÖLDES, BÉLA 1918/1919 Ernst Engel. *Allgemeines statistisches Archiv* 11:229–245.

HOUTHAKKER, H. S. 1957 An International Comparison of Household Expenditure Patterns, Commemorating the Centenary of Engel's Law. *Econometrica* 25:532–551.

KEYNES, JOHN MAYNARD 1936 *The General Theory of Employment, Interest and Money.* London: Macmillan. → A paperback edition was published in 1965 by Harcourt.

KNAPP, G. F. 1897 *Grundherrschaft und Rittergut.* Leipzig: Duncker & Humblot.

PRAIS, S. J.; and HOUTHAKKER, H. S. 1955 *The Analysis of Family Budgets With an Application to Two British Surveys Conducted in 1937–1939 and Their Detailed Results.* Cambridge Univ. Press.

STIGLER, GEORGE J. 1954 The Early History of Empirical Studies of Consumer Behavior. *Journal of Political Economy* 62:95–113.

ZIMMERMAN, CARLE C. 1936 *Consumption and Standards of Living.* New York: Van Nostrand.

ENGELS, FRIEDRICH

Friedrich Engels was born in Barmen, Germany, in 1820 and died in London in 1895. He was the closest friend of Karl Marx and cofounder of so-called scientific socialism.

Engels was the oldest son in a family of eight children. His father owned a cotton-spinning mill in Barmen and was a partner in another spinning mill, Ermen and Engels, of Manchester and Engelskirchen. Engels attended the *Realschule* in Barmen and the Gymnasium in Elberfeld. To prepare himself for the study of jurisprudence, he studied mercantile problems, first in his father's firm, and then, from 1838 to 1841, in Bremen. Engels then did a year's military service.

He was greatly impressed in his youth with the contrast between the pietistic Calvinism of the middle class in his native city and the misery of the working class, demoralized by drink. Using the pseudonym of Oswald he wrote about this situation in his "Briefe aus dem Wuppertal" (1839), a vivid description of these conditions that shows how early his literary and journalistic ability developed. Little by little he turned away from pietism and religion, strongly influenced by David Friedrich Strauss's critique of the Gospels in *Das Leben Jesu* and, above all, by Ludwig Feuerbach's *Wesen des Christentums*. He affirmed his radical break with religion in his *Schelling und die Offenbarung* (1842a) and in his spirited, witty satire, *Schelling, der Philosoph in Christo* (1842b). These were writings in part aimed at the king of Prussia, who had appointed Schelling to the University of Berlin as Hegel's successor, hoping that he would become the intellectual exponent of his "Christian state." Engels read political criticisms by the members of the "Junge Deutschland," particularly those of Ludwig Börne, and he began to write as a Young Hegelian, one of that group of left-wing intellectuals in Berlin that included the brothers Edgar and Bruno Bauer and the anarchist Max Stirner. Karl Marx also belonged to this group while he was a student in Berlin. Engels' satirical Christian epic, "Die frech bedräute, jedoch wunderbar befreite Bibel: Oder Triumph des Glaubens" (1842c), which was published anonymously, reflected the views of this group. Engels wrote this work when the king of Prussia withdrew Bruno Bauer's *venia legendi* at the University of Bonn because of his criticism of the Gospels. It was Moses Hess who guided Engels to the work of the early French socialists such as Saint-Simon and Charles Fourier and boasted that he had transformed this "revolutionary of the year 1" (i.e., 1793) into a communist.

Engels moved to Manchester in October 1842 to complete his commercial training. He criticized English political and social conditions in the *Rheinische Zeitung*, to which he had contributed since March 1842. At the same time he also wrote for the periodicals of the Chartists and Owenites, describing the development of socialism on the Continent. He supplemented his empirical observations by studying the English economists. In his brilliant "Umrisse zu einer Kritik der Nationalökonomie" (1844), which appeared in the *Deutsch–Französische Jahrbücher*, edited by Marx and the Young Hegelian Arnold Ruge, there is, according to Marx,

an early formulation of the general principles of scientific socialism. Engels here demonstrated the contradictions in liberal economic doctrine and showed that all economic phenomena are, in the end, based on private property. He demanded that private property be abolished. After the publication of this essay, Marx and Engels began to correspond. When they met in Paris in the autumn of 1844, they found, according to Engels, that they were in "complete agreement in all theoretical areas."

There are similarities in the early development of Marx and Engels that seem, on the surface, astonishing: a common literary and poetic bent, a common concern with religious problems, and a similar involvement in juridical–political discussion that led both of them from left-wing Hegelianism to communism. But it was, of course, the situation in Germany during that time that largely determined their common concerns, especially the authoritarianism of Friedrich Wilhelm IV and the political radicalization of the German intellectuals that was a reaction to it. Marx and Engels went beyond bourgeois–liberal criticism, however, thus parting from their former friends, whom they subjected to merciless criticism in *The Holy Family* (1845a), mainly written by Marx, and *The German Ideology* (1845–1846), published posthumously. Their reasons for becoming communists were not identical, to be sure. Engels was brought to the point of revolutionary outrage by his observation of the workers' misery, while Marx, the rationalist, identified the proletariat as the only class that might be fitted by its extreme misery to effect a revolutionary transformation. More subject as Engels was to intense personal and emotional impressions, he always remained second in achievement to Marx. He phrased this aptly himself: "I could never have achieved what Marx did. Marx stood higher, saw farther, and had a broader and quicker grasp of a situation than all the rest of us. Marx was a genius; we others were at best talented" ([1886] 1941, p. 292).

This estimate, however, should not let us overlook the fact that at the beginning of their collaboration it was Engels who was the leading partner, precisely because he assimilated knowledge readily and because his occupation brought him much closer to economics. This is illustrated by *The Condition of the Working Class in England* (1845b), which was planned as a chapter of a comprehensive social history of England. This work by the "doubtless most talented and well-informed of all German writers on sociology," as Hildebrand called him ([1848] 1922, p. 170), is according to Lorenz von Stein, "a picture of the deepest poverty, taken from the dirtiest district of the dirtiest factory town in England, full of incontrovertible facts from this most miserable sphere of the industrial world, beyond any question the best invective ever written in Germany against industrial society and its conditions, a partisan book like no other. That is why the book had so powerful an effect, much more convincing by its exaggerations and errors than by its truths, as is the fate of all such works" (1852, p. 538).

After he and Marx began to work together, Engels seems intentionally to have left to Marx theoretical work, thus acknowledging (and later expressly emphasizing) that the elaboration of the materialist conception of history was essentially Marx's work. He himself took credit for only a "very small part" thereof, asserting that most of the basic ideas, especially in the economic and historical fields, and more particularly their final acute formulations, were due to Marx. While Marx was writing the important theory sections of *The German Ideology* and was criticizing Proudhon in *The Poverty of Philosophy* (1847*a*), Engels was engaged as an agitator. As early as 1843 he had established contact in London with the leaders of a German secret society, the League of the Just. At the end of 1844 he and Moses Hess held communist meetings in the Rhineland, until such meetings were suppressed. In Brussels, where he moved in April 1845 in order to be close to Marx, he was mainly active in the International Communist Committee of Correspondence, founded by Marx and himself. In August 1846 he went to Paris, where after prolonged discussions he succeeded in weaning the local group of the League of the Just from the influence of Wilhelm Weitling, the early German socialist, and P. J. Proudhon, the French anarchist. At the first congress of the League in London in June 1847, he succeeded in transforming it into the Communist League. The second congress, in the fall of 1847, commissioned him and Marx to draw up a party program. Engels prepared a draft of such a program, *Principles of Communism* (1847*b*), written in the form of a catechism. It is significant as a draft of the famous *Communist Manifesto* (1848), but the *Manifesto* itself clearly bears the intellectual and stylistic stamp of Marx.

After the outbreak of the Revolution of 1848, Engels and Marx went to Cologne. There Engels worked as editor of the *Neue Rheinische Zeitung* (published by Marx), since journalism was easier for him than for Marx. At various times there was a warrant out for his arrest because of his journal-

istic activity. He also participated in the Elberfeld civil insurrection, but its leaders repudiated him as a "Red." After the suspension of the *Neue Rheinische Zeitung* in May 1849, he vainly endeavored, together with Marx, to expand the armed uprising in Baden and the Palatinate into a general German revolution. After the uprising collapsed he left for Switzerland and, in October 1849, for London. He portrayed these events in series of articles published in 1849 and 1850.

In London Engels wrote *The Peasant War in Germany* (1850). He hoped that the revolutionary traditions of the peasants might pave the way for a new German revolution, and he was convinced that the success of such a revolution depended on supporting the proletarian revolution by some second edition of the peasants' war of the sixteenth century. Engels' characterization of Thomas Münzer, one of the leaders of that revolt, reveals his insight into his own position. He believed that Münzer had been in a hopeless position: he was the leader of an extremist party, forced to take over a government prematurely, before the dominance of the class he represented could be accepted, and before the measures that the rule of his party implied could successfully be carried out ([1850] 1956, pp. 138–139).

Engels, nevertheless, made a very intensive study of the wars of the French Revolution after 1792 to prepare himself for the military leadership of the future revolution. He expounded principles of revolutionary action in a series of articles, *Germany: Revolution and Counter-revolution* (1851–1852), the authorship of which was wrongly attributed to Marx. Engels' maxims were never to play with insurrection and always to act with the greatest resoluteness and to seize the offensive.

The defensive is the death of every armed rising; surprise your antagonists while their forces are scattering, prepare new successes, however small, but daily; keep up the moral ascendancy which the first successful rising has given you; rally those vacillating elements to your side which always follow the strongest impulse, and which always look out for the safer side; force your enemies to retreat before they can collect their strength against you; in the words of Danton, the greatest master of revolutionary policy yet known: *"de l'audace, de l'audace, encore de l'audace."* (Engels [1851–1852] 1933, p. 100)

From 1854 until 1870, when Engels was an employee and then a partner in his father's firm in Manchester, his writings dealt primarily with military science and earned him the sobriquet "General" among his friends. In the future proletarian revolution he was presumably cast for a role comparable to that of Carnot, the organizer of the *levée en masse* and the army of the French Revolution. He contributed articles to the *New American Encyclopedia* on the army, cavalry, fortifications, infantry, the navy, and so on. As a journalist he repeatedly described the armies of the various countries and evaluated their combat effectiveness. However, his writings went beyond topical journalism. He also concerned himself, in detail, with armaments, with the radical changes in warfare produced by the new industrial technology, and with the political implications of these developments (1859–1861). Thus he advocated expansion of the war of France and Italy against Austria into a German war against Napoleon III, whom he saw as the main adversary of the revolution. His *Die preussische Militärfrage und die deutsche Arbeiterpartei* (1865) was also primarily political: in the Prussian constitutional conflict over expansion of the army, he opposed Ferdinand Lassalle's complete dissociation of the interests of the workers from those of the middle class.

The most important evidence for Engels' activities in this period is his correspondence with Marx, which shows Engels' continuing financial assistance to Marx as well as his encouragement of Marx's writings. Engels' loyal friendship even led him to assume the paternity of Marx's illegitimate son, although this was also an expression of his unconventional conception of relations between the sexes. He himself lived for nearly twenty years with Mary Burns, an Irish working girl, and after her death in 1863 he lived with her sister Lizzy, marrying her only on her deathbed in 1878.

After he moved from Manchester to London in the autumn of 1870, Engels became a member of the General Council of the First International (founded in 1864) and its corresponding secretary for Spain, Portugal, Italy, Ireland, and for a time, Belgium. He played a prominent part in the dispute with Bakunin. He wrote *L'alliance de la démocratie socialiste et l'association internationale des travailleurs* (1873b) together with Marx and "Die Bakunisten an der Arbeit" (see 1873a) by himself. *Anti-Dühring: Herr Eugen Dühring's Revolution in Science* (1878) was aimed at Dühring's strong influence on German social democracy. Notwithstanding its polemics, it was the first popular exposition widely to promote the teachings of Marx. His *Socialism: Utopian and Scientific* (1880), a summary of the first three chapters of the *Anti-Dühring*, was even more popular.

Up to the death of Marx on March 14, 1883, Engels' major effort was devoted to the incomplete *Dialectics of Nature* (1873–1883). Conceived initially as an argument with Ludwig Büchner, it became an attack on the kind of metaphysics in the natural sciences that regarded natural phenomena as immutable, instead of considering them as ever-flowing, changing facts. By including the natural sciences, Engels made dialectics a "science of all interrelationships" and went beyond Marx's materialist conception of history to the *Weltanschauung* of "dialectical materialism." Engels extended the original concept yet further to include prehistory in *The Origin of the Family, Private Property, and the State* (1884a). This work, written after Marx's death, was based on L. H. Morgan's *Ancient Society* of 1877 and on Marx's synopsis of Morgan's book—in fulfillment of a legacy, so to speak.

After Marx's death Engels edited Volume 2 of *Capital* and prepared Volume 3 for the press, using the outlines left by Marx and making some studies of his own. No critical analysis of the extent of Engels' contributions to *Capital* has yet been made.

Engels took care of Marx's works in general, arranging new editions, providing them with his own prefaces, and defending Marx against learned attacks. This greatly overshadowed his own literary activity. Yet he did make important contributions to the history of Marxism: "Marx und die *Neue Rheinische Zeitung*" (1884b); "History of the Communist League" (1885); and *Ludwig Feuerbach and the Outcome of Classical German Philosophy* (1886). In the last years of his life, Engels wrote an important series of letters to Conrad, Schmidt, Bloch, Mehring, and Borgius in which he admitted the possibility that the superstructure could affect the economic infrastructure and thus opposed an overemphasis upon the regularity of historical events. This significant theoretical clarification had a considerable influence upon developments in the Soviet Union.

Engels was Marx's political as well as his literary heir. He played a very important part in the genesis of the Second International in 1889. He continued to act as an adviser to the various socialist parties, through Marx's son-in-law Lafarge in France and through Liebknecht, Bebel, and Bernstein in Germany. His forcing the party to publish Marx's *Critique of the Gotha Programme* (1875–1891), which condemned the theoretical concessions of the Lassalleans, led to violent intraparty disputes. In his "Introduction" to Marx's *The Class Struggles in France* (1895), Engels still defended revolutionary tactics despite the great successes achieved by social democracy after the establishment of universal suffrage. To be sure, he did stress that they must be different from earlier tactics: "The time is past for a revolutionary surprise attack carried out by small conscious minorities at the head of the uncomprehending masses." He attributed special importance to the problem of disarmament (1893) and foresaw the possibility of a future world war. He was stricken with cancer of the esophagus in the midst of his work.

In the influence exerted by Marxism, Engels' work continues to play its part. The extent of the effect of his military–scientific writings on, say, the Russian or the Chinese revolutions cannot yet be assessed, nor has scholarly work distinguishing between his specific views and those of Marx proceeded very far; in view of the decisive influence of Marx and the way in which these thinkers stimulated each other, this distinction is extremely difficult to draw. However, in the intellectual history of Marxism one might say that Engels represented its descent from early socialism, especially early French socialism, while Marx gave it the imprint of classical German philosophy.

THILO RAMM

[For the historical context of Engels' work, see MARXISM; REVOLUTION; SOCIALISM; and the biographies of BAKUNIN; FOURIER; MARX; MORGAN, LEWIS HENRY; PROUDHON; SAINT-SIMON. For discussion of the subsequent development of his ideas, see the biographies of BERNSTEIN; KAUTSKY; LENIN; TROTSKY.]

WORKS BY ENGELS

(1839) 1930   Briefe aus dem Wuppertal. By F. Oswald [pseud.]. Section 1, volume 2, pages 23–118 in Karl Marx and Friedrich Engels, Historisch-kritische Gesamtausgabe: Werke, Schriften, Briefe. Berlin: Marx-Engels Verlag. → First published in Telegraph für Deutschland.

(1839–1895a) 1927–1935   MARX, KARL; and ENGELS, FRIEDRICH Historisch-kritische Gesamtausgabe: Werke, Schriften, Briefe. 12 vols. Edited by David Riazanov; commissioned by the Marx–Engels Institute, Moscow. Frankfurt am Main, Berlin, and Moscow: Marx–Engels Verlag. → Includes manuscripts published posthumously.

(1839–1895b) 1956   MARX, KARL; and ENGELS, FRIEDRICH Karl Marx, Friedrich Engels: Werke. Volume 1. Berlin: Dietz. → The first volumes of a projected 36-volume edition.

1842a   Schelling und die Offenbarung. Leipzig: Bamberg. → Published anonymously.

1842b   Schelling, der Philosoph in Christo: Oder die Verklärung der Weltweisheit zur Gottesweisheit. Berlin: Eyssenhardt. → Published anonymously.

(1842c) 1930   Die frech bedräute, jedoch wunderbar befreite Bibel: Oder Triumph des Glaubens. Section 1, volume 2, pages 173–281 in Karl Marx and Friedrich Engels, Historisch-kritische Gesamtausgabe: Werke, Schriften, Briefe. Berlin: Marx–Engels Verlag. → Published anonymously.

(1843–1895) 1956   MARX, KARL; and ENGELS, FRIEDRICH Karl Marx and Frederick Engels: Selected Correspondence. Moscow: Foreign Languages Publishing House.

(1844) 1930   Umrisse zu einer Kritik der Nationalökonomie. Section 1, volume 2, pages 379–404 in Historisch-kritische Gesamtausgabe: Werke, Schriften, Briefe. Berlin: Marx–Engels Verlag. → First published in the Deutsch–Französische Jahrbücher.

(1845a) 1956   MARX, KARL; and ENGELS, FRIEDRICH The Holy Family. Moscow: Foreign Languages Publishing House. → First published as Die heilige Familie.

(1845b) 1958   The Condition of the Working Class in England. Oxford: Blackwell. → First published as Die Lage der arbeitenden Klasse in England.

(1845–1846) 1939   MARX, KARL; and ENGELS, FRIEDRICH The German Ideology. Parts 1 and 3. With an introduction by R. Pascal. New York: International Publishers. → Written in 1845–1846, the full text was first published in 1932 as Die deutsche Ideologie and republished by Dietz Verlag in 1953.

(1847a) 1963   Introduction. In Karl Marx, The Poverty of Philosophy. New York: International Publishers. → First published in French. A paperback edition was published in 1964.

(1847b) 1952   Principles of Communism. New York: Monthly Review. → Written in 1847; first published posthumously in 1914 as Grundsätze des Kommunismus, edited by Eduard Bernstein.

(1848) 1963   MARX, KARL; and ENGELS, FRIEDRICH The Communist Manifesto. New York: Russell. → A paperback edition was published in 1964 by Washington Square Press.

(1848–1898) 1962   MARX, KARL; and ENGELS, FRIEDRICH Selected Works. 2 vols. Moscow: Foreign Languages Publishing House. → Includes works published posthumously.

(1850) 1956   The Peasant War in Germany. Moscow: Foreign Languages Publishing House. → First published as "Der deutsche Bauernkrieg" in the Neue Rheinische Zeitung: Revue.

(1851–1852) 1933   Germany: Revolution and Counterrevolution. New York: International Publishers. → First published as a series of articles in the New York Daily Tribune.

(1852) 1960   MARX, KARL; and ENGELS, FRIEDRICH Die grossen Männer des Exils. Volume 8, pages 233–335 in Karl Marx, Friedrich Engels: Werke. Berlin: Dietz. → First published in 1930, in Russian. Written in 1852.

(1859–1861) 1915   Po und Rhein; Savoyen, Nizza und der Rhein. Edited by Eduard Bernstein. Stuttgart (Germany): Dietz. → Published anonymously.

(1865) 1963   Die preussische Militärfrage und die deutsche Arbeiterpartei. Berlin: Dietz.

(1870–1871) 1923   Notes on the War. Vienna: Wiener Volksbuchhandlung. → Contains sixty articles reprinted from the Pall Mall Gazette.

(1873a) 1957   Internationales aus dem Volksstaat (1871–1875). Berlin: Dietz. → See especially Chapter 2 on "Die Bakunisten an der Arbeit."

1873b   L'alliance de la démocratie socialiste et l'association internationale des travailleurs. London and Hamburg. → A leaflet.

(1873–1883) 1960   Dialectics of Nature. New York: International Publishers. → First published in German.

(1875–1891) 1959   MARX, KARL; and ENGELS, FRIEDRICH Critique of the Gotha Programme. Moscow: Foreign

Languages Publishing House. → Written by Marx in 1875 as "Randglossen zum Programm der deutschen Arbeiterpartei." First published with notes by Engels in 1891.

(1878) 1959   *Anti-Dühring: Herr Eugen Dühring's Revolution in Science.* Moscow: Foreign Languages Publishing House. → First published as "Herrn Eugen Dührings Umwälzung der Wissenschaft" in *Vorwärts* (Leipzig).

(1880) 1935   *Socialism: Utopian and Scientific.* New York: International Publishers. → First published in French.

(1884a) 1942   *The Origin of the Family, Private Property and the State.* New York: International Publishers. → First published as *Der Ursprung der Familie, des Privateigentums und des Staats.*

(1884b) 1934   Marx und die *Neue Rheinische Zeitung.* Volume 2, pages 27–37 in Karl Marx, *Ausgewählte Schriften.* Edited by V. Adoratskij. Zürich (Switzerland): Ring. → First published in *Der Sozialdemokrat.*

(1885) 1933   History of the Communist League. Pages 120–131 in Friedrich Engels, *Germany: Revolution and Counter-revolution.* New York: International Publishers. → First published as "Zur Geschichte des Bundes der Kommunisten" in *Der Sozialdemokrat* and added to the 1933 edition of Engels 1851–1852.

(1886) 1941   *Ludwig Feuerbach and the Outcome of Classical German Philosophy.* New York: International Publishers. → First published in German.

(1891) 1963   Introduction. In Karl Marx, *The Civil War in France.* Moscow: Foreign Languages Publishing House. → First published in German. A paperback edition was published in 1964 by International Publishers.

1893   *Kann Europa abrüsten?* Nürnberg (Germany): Wörlein.

(1895) 1964   Introduction. In Karl Marx, *The Class Struggles in France: 1848–1850.* New York: International Publishers.

SUPPLEMENTARY BIBLIOGRAPHY

ADLER, MAX   (1920) 1925   *Engels als Denker.* 2d ed. Berlin: Dietz.

BERLIN, ISAIAH   (1939) 1963   *Karl Marx: His Life and Environment.* 3d ed. New York: Oxford Univ. Press.

BOLLNOW, HERMANN   1954   Engels' Auffassung von Revolution und Entwicklung in seinen *Grundsätzen des Kommunismus (1847).* Volume 1, pages 77–144 in *Marxismusstudien.* Schriften der Evangelischen Studiengemeinschaft, No. 3. Tübingen (Germany): Mohr.

BÜNGER, SIEGFRIED   1962   *Friedrich Engels und die britische sozialistische Bewegung, 1881–1895.* Berlin: Rütten & Loening.

COATES, ZELDA (KAHAN)   (1920) 1945   *The Life and Teachings of Friedrich Engels.* London: Lawrence & Wishart. → First published as *The Life and Work of Friedrich Engels.*

CORNU, AUGUSTE   1955–1962   *Karl Marx et Friedrich Engels: Leur vie et leur oeuvre.* Paris: Presses Universitaires de France.

FETSCHER, IRING   1957   Von der Philosophie des Proletariats zur proletarischen Weltanschauung. Volume 2, pages 26–60 in *Marxismusstudien.* Schriften der Evangelischen Studiengemeinschaft, No. 5. Tübingen (Germany): Mohr.

Friedrich Engels: Der Denker. (1935) 1945   Basel: Mundus. → First published in *Bol'shaia sovetskaia entsiklopediia.*

[GOLDENDACH, DAVID B.]   1927   *Karl Marx and Friedrich Engels,* by D. Riazanov [pseud.]. London: Lawrence & Wishart.

HILDEBRAND, BRUNO   (1848) 1922   *Die Nationalökonomie der Gegenwart und Zukunft, und andere gesammelte Schriften.* Jena: Fischer.

KAUTSKY, KARL   (1895) 1899   *Friedrich Engels: His Life, His Work and His Writings.* Chicago: Kerr. → First published in German.

LUCAS, ERHARD   1964   Die Rezeption Lewis H. Morgans durch Marx und Engels. *Saeculum* 15:153–176.

LUCAS, ERHARD   1964   Marx' und Engels' Auseinandersetzung mit Darwin: Zur Differenz zwischen Marx und Engels. *International Review of Social History* (Amsterdam) [1964]:433–469.

MAREK, FRANZ   (1950) 1953   *Friedrich Engels: Denker und Kämpfer.* Leipzig: Fachbuch Verlag.

MAYER, GUSTAV   (1920–1934) 1936   *Friedrich Engels: A Biography.* Introduction by G. D. H. Cole. London: Chapman. → First published in German. The best biography of Engels.

RAMM, THILO   1957   Die künftige Gesellschaftsordnung nach der Theorie von Marx und Engels. Volume 2, pages 26–60 in *Marxismusstudien.* Schriften der Evangelischen Studiengemeinschaft, No. 5. Tübingen (Germany): Mohr.

RUBEL, MAXIMILIEN   1956   *Bibliographie des oeuvres de Karl Marx: Avec en appendice un répertoire des oeuvres de Friedrich Engels.* Paris: Rivière. → A 74-page supplement was published in 1960.

SEEGER, REINHARD   1935   *Friedrich Engels als "junger Deutscher"* . . . . Halle (Germany): Klinz.

STEIN, LORENZ VON   1852   Der Sozialismus in Deutschland. *Gegenwart: Eine encyklopädische Darstellung der neuesten Zeitgeschichte für alle Stände* 7:517–563. → Translation of the extract in the text was provided by Thilo Ramm.

THIER, ERICH   1954   Etappen der Marxinterpretation. Volume 1, pages 1–38 in *Marxismusstudien.* Schriften der Evangelischen Studiengemeinschaft, No. 3. Tübingen (Germany): Mohr.

ENGINEERING

Engineering is a relatively new profession compared with the professions of law, medicine, and the ministry. Like other professions, engineering struggles with such problems as redesigning the curricula of its professional schools and raising standards for entry to the field. In addition, engineering has some distinctive occupational problems. Can it increase the commitment of its members to the profession in the face of mounting pressures not to pursue it as a lifelong career? Can it assume the responsibility for the social effects of technological change? As the progenitors of new technologies that are transforming modern society, engineers are among the most important agents of social change. This article will consider some of the problems and potentialities of the profession, that is, some of the factors favoring or inhibiting the further professionalization of engineering as an occupation.

Professionalism and professionalization. In identifying various attributes of a profession, sociologists have often taken as their model the older professions of law, medicine, and the ministry. Although there is no consensus as to the definition of a profession, there is a growing awareness that professionalism is a multidimensional phenomenon and that occupations differ in their degree of professionalism.

An index of professionalism may be based on ratings of such attributes as (a) the possession of a body of technical and systematic knowledge that guides professional practice; (b) an orientation of service to society rather than self-interest; (c) autonomy in rendering professional service; and (d) societal sanction of professional authority. To develop and transmit the body of technical and systematic knowledge, professional schools and training programs are established. To contribute to the fund of professional knowledge, to promote a service orientation, and to increase autonomy in professional practice, professional associations are formed and codes of ethics are developed. To protect professional authority and enhance occupational prestige, societal sanction is sought in various forms, such as the licensing of graduates and the exercising of control over the curricula of professional schools.

The process of professionalization involves the transformation of an occupation in accordance with the ideal–typical components of professionalism. Although the dynamics of professionalization may differ for different occupations, and possibly for the same occupation in different countries, one study suggests that it entails the following sequence of stages: (1) full-time performance of the occupational function; (2) establishment of a school that is not connected with a university; (3) establishment of a university school; (4) formation of a local professional association; (5) formation of a national professional association; (6) enactment of a licensing law; and (7) development of a formal code of ethics (Wilensky 1964). Even if this sequence of stages is neither invariant nor exhaustive, it may provide a useful description and prediction of the process of professionalization.

Whatever stages of professionalization are postulated or demonstrated, it does not follow that a particular profession has reached the same level of professionalization in all countries. Nor does it follow that professionalization of a given occupation is irreversible. It is frequently assumed, however, that newer professions will follow the pattern of development established by the older professions and that this pattern is irreversible. The question of the conditions under which an occupation may be deprofessionalized has hardly been raised.

Before examining some current problems of the professionalization of engineering, we shall briefly review the factors that led to the emergence of this profession.

Emergence of the engineering profession. Engineering as art long antedates engineering as a profession. The invention of the stone ax in the Paleolithic age was among man's first engineering achievements. In the civilizations of antiquity considerable technological progress was made, as evidenced by such accomplishments as pyramids, aqueducts, canals, bridges, and lighthouses. Directing these engineering feats were highly gifted individuals, some of whom we would today consider engineers. But despite the outstanding work of individual engineers, no professional group came into being for many centuries. Several factors delayed the formation of a profession of engineering. The economies of ancient civilizations did not require the organized development and application of technology, for which an engineering profession was necessary. The prevailing technology was a product of trial and error, intuition, artistry, and the gross synthesis of experience, unsupported by science. In fact, there was pronounced contempt for technology in ancient times. Finally, the tradition of "craft mystery" interfered with the codification and public transmission of technical knowledge. This pattern persisted through the Middle Ages.

During the Renaissance the demand for engineering skills increased. The urgent and recurrent demands of war stimulated the development of many engines of battle, whence came the term "engineer." With the advent of modern science, in the sixteenth and seventeenth centuries, there was a gradual transition from "craft mystery" to science as a basis for technology. The founding of learned societies such as the Royal Society of London, in 1662, the Académie des Sciences, in 1666, and several decades later, the Berlin Academy of Sciences and the Academy of St. Petersburg, reflected and promoted the growing influence of science on technology. During the eighteenth century the services of engineers were enlisted to perform a variety of functions in civilian, as well as in military, life. In France the Corps des Ingénieurs des Ponts et Chaussées, established by the government in 1716, was considered as necessary as the Corps des Ingénieurs de Génie Militaire. In Great Britain engineers were commissioned to drain mines, build roads and canals, and perfect navigational techniques. Thus, the initial stage of the development of engineering as a profession—the need for trained, full-time engineers—comes into view.

Engineering schools were gradually established in place of traditional methods of apprenticeship and pupilage. Among the earliest engineering schools to be founded were the École de Ponts et Chaussées in 1747 and the École Polytechnique in 1795. During the American Revolution, George Washington, deploring the shortage of engineers, asked the Continental Congress to provide facilities for the training of a corps of engineers; in 1802 his proposal was implemented with the establishment of the military academy at West Point, modeled after the École Polytechnique. Efforts were made to provide professional training, not only through special technical schools but also at institutions of higher learning. In England a first chair in civil engineering was established in 1841.

Local professional associations had been established in various parts of England and Scotland during the latter part of the eighteenth century. One was the Society of Civil Engineers, founded in 1771 by John Smeaton, a member of the Royal Society, who is alleged to have been the first Englishman to describe himself as a "civil engineer." In 1818 the first national professional association for engineers was established in England. Similar organizations came into existence in the United States in 1852 and in Canada in 1887.

Thus, the sequence of early developments leading to the emergence of the engineering profession conforms approximately to the first five stages of professionalization mentioned earlier. As engineering became a full-time occupation, in the seventeenth and eighteenth centuries, schools not connected with a university were established, local professional societies were formed, followed by national associations, and engineering was gradually introduced into the curriculum of universities.

Social structure and engineering. The emergence of the engineering profession in western Europe and in North America points up the impact of industrialization on this occupation. Economic development requires and generates technological development, for which engineers and other professionals are essential. Since societies differ markedly in their level of economic development, we would also expect them to differ in their technological capabilities and in the nature and role of their engineering professions. In effect, we are hypothesizing that the relationship between the economic

development and technological development of a society is partly mediated by its engineering profession. Some data bearing on the economic and technological development of various countries and the size of their engineering professions are presented in Table 1.

For present purposes, economic development is indexed by per capita share of gross national product (GNP), and technological development is indexed by the number of patents issued in a year and the percentage of GNP expended for research and development (R & D) in any given year. In Table 1, countries for which data are available are ranked according to the GNP per capita variable. The higher the ranking of a country on GNP per capita, the more likely it is that it ranks higher on the size of its engineering profession and the number of patents issued, and on the percentage of GNP expended for research and development. These data suggest one possible systemic pattern of relationships between these variables. A highly industrialized society has the resources to educate a sizable number of engineers, some of whom, together with scientists, engage in research and development, for which a substantial proportion of such a society's resources is expended; this organized approach to scientific discovery and invention results in increasing numbers of patents; and in turn, the process of invention—in which engineers play a prominent role (Gilfillan 1935, pp. 52, 82–91)—stimulates economic development, which then confronts the engineering profession with new technical problems.

Another feature of the social structure (apart from the economy and technology) that influences the engineering profession is the political system. In highly centralized and relatively unindustrialized societies, such as some under communist regimes, the engineering profession may be disproportionately large because of the government's concern with accelerating the process of industrialization. Under such conditions, the autonomy of the profession may be circumscribed and it may be called upon to perform functions other than those of a technological nature.

The level of industrialization of a society has another effect on the engineering profession, which is not reflected in the statistics in Table 1. As industrialization increases, there is a concomitant increase in the number of specialties in the occupation. From the relatively undifferentiated field of engineering existing in the seventeenth and eighteenth centuries, civil engineering emerged and itself gave rise to mechanical engineering, mining and metallurgical engineering, and electrical and

Table 1 — Gross national product (GNP) per capita, number of engineers, number of patents issued, and percentage of GNP expended for research and development (R & D) in selected countries

	GNP PER CAPITA IN 1957	NUMBER OF ENGINEERS			PATENTS ISSUED IN 1964[a]	PER CENT OF GNP FOR R & D	
	U.S. dollars	Number	Per 10,000 population	Year of information	Number	Percentage	Year of information
United States	2,577	783,000[b]	4.4	1959	47,378	2.8	1960/1961
Canada	1,947	60,400[c]	3.2	1963	24,589	1.2	1960
Switzerland	1,428	14,440[b]	2.9	1955	10,350		
Sweden	1,380	52,400[b]	6.8	1965	6,125	1.8	1959
Belgium	1,196	30,492[b]	3.3	1964			
United Kingdom	1,189	156,000[b]	2.9	1963	34,060	2.5	1958/1959
Norway	1,130	32,020[b]	8.6	1965	1,985	0.7	1960
Denmark	1,057	20,900[b]	4.5	1963	2,833		
France	943	112,000[c]	2.3	1963	33,850	1.3	1961
West Germany	927	226,200[b, d]	4.5	1956	20,150	1.4	1959
Netherlands	836	36,139[b]	2.9	1959; 1965[e]	13,900		
Austria	670	36,559[b]	5.2	1961	6,850		
Soviet Union	600	1,325,000[b]	6.0	1962	6,850	2.3	1960
Ireland	550	2,800[c]	1.0	1962	434		
Italy	516	190,000[b]	3.9	1957			
Argentina	490	15,400[c]	.8	1960			
Greece	340	5,756[c]	.7	1959			
Spain	293	13,035[c]	.4	1960			
Yugoslavia	265	27,429[c]	1.4	1965		0.7	1960
Turkey	220	9,106[c]	.3	1960			
Iran	108	7,510[c]	.4	1960			
Communist China	73	175,000[f]	.3	1957			

a. Calculated by subtracting the number of patents on hand in January 1964 from the number on hand in January 1965 and adjusting the difference to put it on an annual basis.
b. Combined total of engineers with university training and those with formal training just below the university level.
c. University-trained engineers.
d. Includes chemists.
e. Count of university-trained engineers in 1965, other count in 1959; number per 10,000 population is based on 1965 population data and probably is an underestimate.
f. Engineering and technical personnel.

Sources: GNP from Russett et al. 1964, pp. 155–157. Number of engineers from Organization for Economic Cooperation and Development 1963, pp. 225–229, tables 13 and 14; Korol 1965, p. 244, table A-1; Emerson 1965, p. 138, table 7; Horowitz 1965, p. 7, table 1.4; Baldwin 1965, p. 155, table 5.2; Demographic Yearbook 1963. Patents from U.S. Patent Office, *Official Gazette* . . . 1964, p. 777, and 1965, p. 2. Per cent of GNP for R & D from Dedijer 1962.

chemical engineering, which were followed by automotive and aeronautical engineering. In the decades since World War II various economic, scientific, and political developments have stimulated the rise of new specialties, such as nuclear engineering, computer technology, astronautical engineering, and systems engineering.

As the engineering profession becomes increasingly differentiated and heterogeneous, a recurrent question arises regarding the identity of engineers. Periodically, engineering educators, officials of professional societies, and census officials discuss the question, Who is an engineer? In the United States the census definition relies, in effect, on the respondent's decision as to whether he is an engineer. Professional engineering societies emphasize formal training in an engineering school and/or a minimum number of years of engineering experience. This concern with clarifying the definition of an engineer reflects a changing social and technical environment of the occupation, which is due to the accelerating rate of growth of scientific knowledge and increasing levels of industrialization. The

changing environment confronts the occupation with dilemmas as to the meaning of professionalism and the direction of further professionalization. These dilemmas arise in connection with the process of recruitment to the profession, the education of engineers, the career decisions of engineers, the functions of professional societies, the problem of responsibility for the social impact of technological change, and the prestige of the profession.

The recruitment process. In highly industrialized societies engineering is one of the fastest-growing occupations. The average annual rate of growth of the profession in some countries tends to exceed the rates of growth of the economy and of the population. In Communist China the engineering profession had an average annual growth rate of 67.1 per cent during the years 1955 through 1962 (computed on the basis of data in Chêng 1964, pp. 111–113); and in the Soviet Union the comparable rate for these years was 32.2 per cent (based on data in Korol 1965, pp. 242–244, table A-1). In comparison, the annual rate of growth for the engineering profession in Great Britain during the years 1959 through 1963 was 5.5 per cent; in France it was 3.2 per cent for the same period; and in Sweden it was only 2 per cent for the period 1955 through 1960 (Organization for Economic Cooperation and Development 1963, pp. 136–175). Maintaining a balance between the demand for and the supply of engineers has been a problem in the post-World War II period and will probably continue to be a problem in the future (e.g., U.S. Department of Commerce 1963).

The engineering profession, probably more than the older, established professions, tends to recruit its members—at least in highly industrialized societies—from heterogeneous social origins. According to one study, a substantial proportion of graduate engineers in Great Britain have middle-class or working-class backgrounds: 36 per cent of their father's occupations are white-collar and 22 per cent are blue-collar (Gerstl 1963, p. 19; see also Jahoda 1963, p. 54). Several studies of engineering students in the United States also indicate a substantial degree of recruitment from middle-class and working-class backgrounds: 44 per cent of the fathers of engineering students at Northwestern University pursue manual or white-collar occupations (Krulee 1963, p. 20); and 50 per cent of engineering students at the University of California at Berkeley come from working-class or middle-class backgrounds (Trow 1959, p. 68). In the Netherlands, on the other hand, opportunities for entry into the engineering profession appear to be more limited than in the United States and Great Britain: approximately 28 per cent are recruited from working-class and middle-class backgrounds (Kuiper 1956, p. 233, table 2).

The more heterogeneous the social origins of engineers, the more diverse, in all likelihood, are the motivations and values involved in their choice of occupation. In a study of students at 11 American universities who chose engineering as a career, 38 per cent stressed the "chance to earn a great deal of money"; 52 per cent, the opportunity to be creative and original; and 28 per cent, the opportunity to be helpful to others (Goldsen et al. 1960, pp. 43–44). A study of American students from 135 colleges and universities who chose engineering as a career in the freshman year found that 25 per cent mentioned money as a factor, 26 per cent mentioned opportunity to be original, and 7 per cent gave "people" as a reason (Davis 1965, p. 188). In Great Britain a study of sixth-form boys found that, of those interested in engineering, 32 per cent gave "money" or "good prospects" as their reason; 19 per cent mentioned that it affords an opportunity to be creative; and 13 per cent said that they were interested because it combines theory

and practice (Oxford University 1963, pp. 37–38). At two London polytechnics a survey of evening students which inquired into their motivations for attendance found that 36 per cent hoped for a better-paid job, 10 per cent for more job security, 16 per cent for a more interesting job, and 9 per cent for a job with a higher social standing (Cotgrove 1958, pp. 102–103). In short, the values of money, prestige, security, creativity, integration of theory and practice, and helping people are but a few of the values affecting the choice of engineering as a career. The old hypothesis of a relationship between social-class heterogeneity and occupational attrition has recently found some support in a study of the occupational structure of the United States: "The more heterogeneous in social origins the young men entering an occupation are, . . . the greater is their tendency to leave it later for a variety of other occupations. This finding suggests that homogeneity in background fosters social solidarity, which lessens the inclination of its members to leave an occupational group" (Blau 1965, p. 490). Thus, we may infer that social-class heterogeneity among engineers very likely contributes to occupational attrition, because of reduced social solidarity.

The diversity of motives prompting students to enter the field of engineering also creates various difficulties for the profession. First, the very existence of a diversity of values regarding engineering acts to lower the feeling of solidarity among engineers as an occupational group. Second, the prevalent "extrinsic" values, such as money, prestige, and security, contrast with such "intrinsic" work values as the opportunity to be creative or to link theory with practice. Intrinsic values are probably more associated with commitment to a profession than are extrinsic values. Finally, the socially heterogeneous recruits to engineering impose an even greater demand for professional socialization during and after the period of formal education than would socially homogeneous recruits.

Educational patterns. The educational resources of a society, which vary with the level of industrialization, greatly affect not only the number of engineers recruited but also their quality and, in turn, their capability to contribute to technological development. The feedback effects of an adequate supply of well-trained engineers and scientists on economic growth has stimulated widespread interest in developing educational institutions and enlarging enrollments, as an investment in "human capital." That facilities for educating engineers vary in large measure with the level of industrialization of a society can be shown by examining the relationship between the number of enrolled engineering students in various countries and the GNP per capita for these same countries. The higher the degree of industrialization, as measured by GNP per capita, the greater is the number of engineers enrolled (unpublished research by the author, based on data in Russett et al. 1964, pp. 155–157; UNESCO, *Statistical Yearbook 1963*, pp. 226–249, table 16; DeWitt 1961, p. 318). It is noteworthy that, in their effort to accelerate economic growth, communist countries have greatly expanded their facilities for the education of engineers. In China engineering enrollment increased from 30,300 in 1949, when the new regime was established, to 177,600 in 1957 (Orleans 1961, pp. 68–69); in the same year, 40 per cent of all students enrolled in Chinese institutions of higher learning were majoring in engineering (*ibid.*). In the Soviet Union the comparable percentage was 39 per cent in 1958 (DeWitt 1961, p. 318), and in the United States it was 5 per cent in 1962 (computed from statistics in U.S. Office of Education 1965, p. 81, table 58, and in U.S. Bureau of the Census 1963, p. 136, table 177).

Critical as is the *quantity* of engineers educated for the economic and technological development of a society, the principal problems of professionalism and professionalization revolve around the *quality* of their education. Engineering curricula are periodically reviewed by engineering educators and professional societies. This, to be sure, is necessary because the rapid rate of growth of science and technology requires that engineering schools continually revise their curricula to insure that they are transmitting the new state of the art. The task of reducing the time lag between the development of new knowledge and its incorporation into the curriculum is often fraught with difficulty. A case in point is the time lag involved in introducing courses on computers in engineering schools.

Designing and redesigning engineering curricula in response to technological change is beset by many problems other than recruiting a competent and adaptable faculty. One of the problems is that the practice of engineering is generally based on an undergraduate level of education. The fact that relatively high proportions of engineers in some countries have not received even this minimal level of training highlights the unsolved problems of professionalizing this occupation. For example, in China only 35 per cent of engineers had undergraduate engineering degrees in 1955 (Chêng 1964, p. 35), and in the United States only 56 per cent had such degrees in 1960 (Organization for Economic Cooperation and Development 1966). The length of full-time training in engineering

schools ranges from three to five and one-half years, with many European countries and the Soviet Union at the high end of this scale (Conference of Representatives 1960, vol. 2, p. 42).

Associated with the time limitation of an undergraduate level of engineering education is the problem of determining how much of the curriculum should be devoted to fundamental sciences, to engineering sciences, to engineering applications, to specialization in the various fields of engineering, and to nonengineering subjects (American Society for Engineering Education 1955, pp. 11–23; Wood 1961). This problem is closely related to another, which is bound to receive more attention in the future, namely, whether engineers should be trained in a specific branch of engineering or in the fundamentals of engineering. The fact that the main branches of engineering—civil, mechanical, electrical, chemical, and aeronautical—are becoming increasingly interrelated in new technologies makes this problem increasingly significant.

As might be expected, countries differ in the degree to which engineering education is oriented to the acquisition of knowledge in a particular specialty. In the United Kingdom, where about one-half the engineers are trained in part-time, "sandwich," or cooperative programs in technical colleges, and in the United States, where the variation in quality in the more than 250 engineering schools is considerable, there is probably a greater degree of specialization than in some countries in continental Europe. In the Soviet Union and Communist China the degree of specialization appears to be greater still (Korol 1957, pp. 252–253; Chêng 1964, p. 98). In underdeveloped countries, which tend to emulate the educational systems of developed countries, an argument has been advanced for training *general* engineers, rather than specialists, in order to help initiate the process of industrialization (Hunt 1960).

The role of nonengineering subjects in the curriculum—what types and how many courses should be offered in the humanities, in problems of management, or in social sciences—is also an open question. There is notable variation between countries in this respect, as shown by a recent study of some systems of engineering education (Conference of Representatives 1960, vol. 2, p. 44). In part the variation is due to differences in the quality of secondary school education; in part it reflects variation in the assessment of the kinds of knowledge and skills required of a practicing engineer.

Rarely considered in the recurrent reappraisals of engineering education is the question of the inculcation of basic values of professionalism in the training of engineers (see National Society of Professional Engineers 1963). Among the basic professional values to which engineering students might be socialized are: (*a*) the importance of contributing to technological innovation, rather than accepting the technological *status quo*; (*b*) the awareness of and concern for the social impact of technological innovations; and (*c*) the conception of professional education as a lifelong activity that is not confined to the years of formal training in engineering schools. Whether and how to inculcate these and other professional values are still frontier problems in professionalizing engineering. For example, the novel and presumably controversial practice, at a French institution of higher learning at Sacley, of awarding a degree in reactor engineering for a limited period—subject to revalidation after five years by means of attendance at refresher courses and success at future examinations—is based on a conception of engineering education as a lifelong process (King 1965).

Problems of redesigning engineering curricula in a quickly changing technological and social environment defy easy and durable solutions. They are even more resistant to solution without full cognizance of the types of careers pursued by engineers following graduation from an engineering school.

Career patterns. The process of professional socialization obviously does not end upon graduation from an engineering school. The organizational context in which an engineer works and the type of function he performs affect not only the course of his career in engineering but also his career orientation and his degree of commitment to the profession.

Unlike the members of some of the older professions, engineers are predominantly salaried employees, with the exception in some countries of a small subgroup of engineers who are self-employed and engage in consulting work (see, for example, Engineers Joint Council 1965, p. 17). Typically, engineers are employed in manufacturing organizations and in various construction operations of a governmental nature. Within the past several decades, as the number of research-and-development laboratories has rapidly increased, new work contexts have opened up for engineers. In the less industrialized countries most engineers still perform various production functions, whereas in the more industrially developed countries a rising proportion are engaged in research-and-development activities. This variation in function is suggested by the data in Table 2. In the United States and the Soviet Union, two of the more highly industrialized countries, approximately one-third and one-fifth, respectively, of the engineers work in research and development.

As several studies of occupations other than engineering have shown, the first job after graduation usually has more effect on career opportunities than do subsequent jobs. Engineering is no exception to this. Among the factors affecting the engineer's first career decision is the quality of the engineering school he attended. A graduate of an elite school often has the opportunity to begin his career in an organization which is in the main stream of technological development. He also has the opportunity—as is true, for example, of the graduate of the École Polytechnique—to orient his career toward top management (Granick 1962, pp. 26–30).

If the engineer begins his career in a production setting, he is unlikely to subsequently enter a research-and-development organization or engage in teaching and research in an academic environment. The only two probable career lines open to him are management of a technical or a nontechnical function and the pursuit of an occupation other than engineering. The career path of an engineer in a research-and-development organization or in a university is probably quite different from that of an engineer employed in a production organization. In either case, the probability is

Table 2 — Distribution of engineers by type of work, for selected countries: per cent

	Year	Production	Management and administration	Research and development	Teaching	Other
Austria	1961	51	33.5	3	3.5	9
Canada	1959	30	28	23	3	15
Greece[a]	1959	80	7	3	8	1
Soviet Union	1964	33	10	22	7	28
United States	1959	40	8	30		21[b]

a. Includes scientists.
b. Includes engineers engaged in teaching.

Source: Organization for Economic Cooperation and Development 1963, pp. 134 ff. Data for the Soviet Union are estimates computed for the author by Alexander G. Korol.

higher that he will not leave engineering for another occupation; on the other hand, the likelihood is that, after some years in research-and-development work, the engineer may transfer to a production or a management function, especially management of a technical operation. The relatively small percentage of engineers who enter teaching and research in an academic environment, as shown in Table 2, in all likelihood continue in this function; if they leave the academic environment, their career paths are likely to be in research rather than in production (LeBold et al. 1960; Gerstl & Hutton 1966).

As a salaried employee, the engineer experiences organizational constraints that he finds difficult to reconcile with his expectations as a professional (Kornhauser 1962). The type of function he performs as an engineer affects his role conception, as well as the length of his career in engineering. In a production function his role relationships involve interaction with production workers and engineering technicians, on the one hand, and with managers, on the other. As a staff engineer, he lacks the authority of the manager, and he tends to be treated, in some organizational contexts, in the same manner that an engineering technician or a production worker is treated. The norm of obedience is more characteristic of the relationship he has with his superiors and subordinates than the norm of service, which is typical of a professional, or the norm of autonomy, which is typical of a scientist (Evan 1962, p. 352).

In a research-and-development organization the engineer's role tends to subject him to the typical dilemmas of a marginal man (Shepard 1957). The scientist regards him as a "nuts-and-bolts" engineer; the manager, as someone who is insufficiently sensitive to cost factors in engineering. In a research-and-development setting, however, there is less likelihood for his role to be confused with the role of an engineering technician or a production worker. (For an analysis of the occupational marginality of engineering technicians, see Evan 1964.) Probably only the small proportion of engineers engaged in basic or applied research escape some of the problems of marginality: their work is governed, not by a norm of service, but rather by a norm of autonomy.

As a consequence of the rapid rate of technological change, there is a growing tendency for the careers of engineers to be abbreviated. The knowledge and skills of engineers obsolesce so quickly that engineers, especially in highly industrialized countries, find it necessary to shift into management work or nonengineering occupations in the middle of their careers (see, for example, Evan 1963). No longer can the new graduate engineer assume, as some of his predecessors did years ago, that he will spend his entire working career in engineering.

To cope with the growing problem of technical obsolescence, programs of continuing education are being established in the United States, France, Germany, and some other countries. The theory and methodology required for the retraining of engineers in the middle of their careers remain to be developed. As yet there is scant evidence as to the effectiveness of continuing-education programs in helping engineers to cope with their technical-updating problems. Another career problem is the flattening of the salary curve with age, which may be related to the declining market value of older engineers undergoing technical obsolescence (see, for example, Kornhauser 1962, pp. 128–130). These and other career problems of engineers are solved in some countries, not by changing employers, labor markets, or occupations, but by means of emigration. The limited statistics on the migration of engineers makes it difficult to ascertain the countries of origin and destination of engineers who emigrate. However, we do know that this mode of adaptation to career problems has created concern in the countries of emigration. In the face of a shortage of technically trained manpower in most countries of the world, emigration of engineers is looked upon as a "brain drain." This is particularly true in the case of a relatively underdeveloped country, such as Argentina, where engineers have emigrated in substantial numbers to the United States (Oteiza 1965).

In short, the organizational contexts in which engineers are employed, the types of functions they perform, and the types of role relationships in which they are involved have not been conducive to an effective process of professional socialization. After his graduation from engineering school, his work experiences often do not tend to imbue the engineer with a dedication to the occupation (Wilensky 1964, pp. 150–155) or an increasing awareness of the social consequences of technological change. Professional associations have a significant function to perform in making up for the deficiencies of the work context as an agent of professional socialization.

Professional associations.   Only some of the career problems encountered by engineers have thus far received attention by professional associations of engineers. Economic problems have largely been ignored, although licensing regulations may have had an indirect beneficial effect on the earnings of some engineers. Sporadic efforts in some countries to organize trade unions of engineers to promote their economic interests have not been successful (see, for example, Goldstein 1954; Walton 1961). Unlike the medical profession, engineering has not acted in unison to enhance the economic position of its members. One factor that has hindered the professional societies in performing an economic function has been the lack of organizational unity within the profession. Instead of there being a single professional association of all engineers in a country, there has been a tendency toward the "Balkanization" of the occupation. As new specialties in engineering arise, new professional associations come into being, and the proliferation of such societies makes for ever greater difficulties in unifying the profession. This tendency has occurred both in the United States and in the United Kingdom, as well as in western Europe. In the more industrialized societies, where the profession is further developed, there are a greater number of professional associations and correspondingly more difficulty in unifying them.

The principal function that professional societies appear to perform is that of a learned society. In other words, they see themselves principally as an instrument for advancing and disseminating engineering knowledge, thus supplementing the functions performed by universities and research institutes. It follows, therefore, that they can contribute significantly to the engineer's need for continuing education. In the future, even more than in the present, they are likely to help engineers continue their professional development by means of seminars, abstracting services, and special conferences. Thus, participation by engineers in the activities of professional associations may increasingly reflect the degree of their professional commitment. In the more industrialized countries, where the educational services of professional societies are apt to be in greater demand, memberships of engineering societies are likely to be larger than in the less industrialized societies.

Another noteworthy feature about professional associations of engineers is the relatively modest progress they have made to date in organizing international professional associations. Since World War II several regional associations of engineering societies have come into being, notably the Conference of Engineering Societies of Western Europe and the United States of America, the European Federation of National Associations of Engineers, and the Pan-American Federation of Engineering Societies. Another significant development was the founding of the Union of International Engineering Organizations, under the aegis of UNESCO, in 1950. These are in the nature of nongovernmental organizations, whose unit of membership is the national society of engineers, not the individual engineer. The strength of such international bodies depends very much upon the strength of the constituent societies. In their relatively brief history these organizations have not yet contributed noticeably to new modes of international cooperation between engineers, to new media for dissemination of technological knowledge, or to an awareness of membership in a world-wide profession.

In addition to performing economic, educational, and knowledge-advancing functions, professional associations seek to regulate their members' conduct by establishing codes of ethics. To the extent that professional engineering associations have concerned themselves with ethical issues, they have attended mostly to the relations of the engineer with his fellow engineer and his employer. Ethical codes have set forth very general guidelines regulating conduct in these spheres. Only in most general terms do canons of ethics touch upon the relations of the engineer to the public or to society as a whole (National Society of Professional Engineers 1962). Thus far, ethical codes have scarcely concerned themselves with the complex and diffuse ethical question of the responsibility of the engineering profession for the social consequences of technological change.

Dilemmas of social responsibility. One reason for the widespread neglect on the part of engineers of the problem of social responsibility for technological change is the difficulty of accepting responsibility for events over which they exercise virtually no control. As salaried employees, performing in the main a staff function, engineers are rarely in a position to make policy decisions concerning the wisdom of developing or not developing a new engineering product or concerning what, if any, action might be taken to counteract its potential or actual negative social effects. This is particularly true for the overwhelming proportion of engineers engaged in production or in development research, where the norms governing their conduct emphasize obedience to directives from management (Evan 1962). Since management makes the decision to produce or not to produce a particular engineering product or service, the salaried engineer probably feels that he scarcely has an occasion for any ethical decision concerning the possible adverse effects of a technological innovation.

In the past the staff function of the engineer has in fact absolved him from actively concerning himself with the question of responsibility for adverse social consequences of technological innovations (Merton [1949] 1957, p. 568). However, it is unlikely that this absolution of responsibility will be acceptable to engineers in the future, as technological advances generate problems of unemployment, environmental pollution, invasion of privacy, and an increasing threat of accidental or deliberate nuclear war. Pressures from within and without the profession will probably stimulate engineers to come to grips with the social ramifications of the technological changes they help develop.

Some of these ethical dilemmas may be solved by new innovative technology; others may require innovative social changes. Although it is unlikely that the individual engineer will succeed in coping with the many complex ethical dilemmas that arise in the process of technological innovation, collective action by professional associations might prove effective. In other words, if the engineering profession assumes a social responsibility for the problems of negative effects of technological change, it may contribute significantly to their solution.

Prestige of the profession.   The prestige of the engineering profession may be affected by, among other things, the attitudes of the public toward the engineer's role in generating positive or negative social consequences of technological innovations. The increasing prominence of the role of technology in society has probably elevated the prestige of engineering in recent years. On the other hand, the fact that engineering does not require a formal education as prolonged as some other professions and the fact that the members are recruited from heterogeneous social origins may contribute to a lowering of its prestige, relative to other professions, in some countries.

The prestige of engineering has received some attention from sociologists in several countries. As a result of the interest among sociologists in studying systems of social stratification in different societies, several parallel studies of the prestige of various occupations, including engineering, have been undertaken. The methodological differences between these studies make a comparison of the findings hazardous. Nevertheless, on the basis of these studies, it is clear that engineering does not have the same prestige in all countries. For example, in the Soviet Union engineers ranked second in prestige as compared with other occupations (Inkeles & Rossi 1956, pp. 336–337); in the Philippines engineers ranked fourth (Tiryakian 1958, p. 394); in Great Britain they were in eighth place (Hutton & Gerstl 1964, p. 13); in West Germany they were in tenth place (Inkeles & Rossi 1956,

pp. 336–337); and in the United States their prestige rank was 21.5 (Hodge et al. 1964, p. 290). Moreover, the data suggest that the prestige of the engineering profession varies inversely with the degree of industrialization as indicated by GNP per capita. Presumably, as the division of labor becomes more specialized in more industrialized societies and as the proportion of professionals in the labor force increases, engineering faces more competition from other occupations for rewards, monetary and other. In addition, as a society becomes more industrialized, the engineering profession tends to increase in size, which may also become a factor in lowering its prestige. Changes in the internal structure of the engineering profession and in its social role are likely to affect its prestige in the future.

Potential social roles.   What types of roles engineers will play in the future depends in part on the course of professionalization of the occupation and in part on the course of political and economic development. If the occupation becomes increasingly professionalized, we may observe a threefold division.

The appreciable segment of the occupation that has received limited or low-quality training in engineering schools and whose knowledge is based largely on practical experience will tend to coalesce with engineering technicians (Evan 1964, p. 108). This tendency will be encouraged by the progressive application of automation to some of the production and design functions performed by engineers, thus, in effect, de-professionalizing some members of the occupation. At the opposite end of the expertise continuum within the profession, there is a relatively small but probably increasing proportion of engineers working at the frontiers of engineering knowledge, who will tend to merge with applied scientists. The intermediate and by far the largest segment of the occupation will continue to perform a high caliber of technical engineering work. This group may be impelled in one of two directions in the future: toward the acquisition of power at organizational levels or at the national level or toward a new conception of professional service.

In his manifesto to engineers in the 1920s, Veblen ([1919] 1921, pp. 138–169) urged them to replace "absentee owners" and to run industry rationally, in accordance with the "instinct of workmanship" rather than the principles of the "price system." Unlike Marx and Engels in their manifesto to the proletariat, Veblen expressed no hope that his technocratic vision would be real ized. In the decades since Veblen's essay was published, the rise of highly centralized political systems has increased the need for engineers to assist in the planning and decision-making process. In communist countries the political and economic exigencies in domestic and foreign affairs may require, in the decades ahead, an even greater reliance on engineers to perform a technocratic role. In France, as we have seen, the recruitment of engineering graduates from the École Polytechnique and several other *grandes écoles* to commanding positions in industry and in the civil service is another example of a trend for engineers to perform a technocratic role (Granick 1962, pp. 60–72). The engineer imbued with the technocratic vision believes, on the one hand, in the capacity of technology to solve all social problems without recourse to value considerations and, on the other hand, in the importance of integrating engineers into the political power structure of society.

An alternative role for engineers is that of a professionally self-conscious agent of the technological and economic development of a society. Although performing principally a staff function, engineers would explicitly concern themselves with developing technology for human welfare and, more specifically, with the predictable social ramifications of any new engineering design, product, or service (see, for example, Boguslaw 1965, pp. 23–29, 181–204). To distinguish this type of social role from both the technocratic role and the prevailing amoral professional role, we might designate it a "professional-technologist" role. In accordance with this role model, an engineer would be guided by an explicit orientation of professional service in his relations with the technological system of a society.

If the new role of professional technologist is to become institutionalized, at least two developments would have to occur. First, if the tempo of development in science and technology stimulates a large proportion of practicing engineers to acquire a postgraduate degree, say at the master's level, such a trend would increase the exposure of engineers to professional socialization in the context of engineering schools. Second, if a "technological community" transcending national boundaries (and parallel to the prevailing "scientific community") comes into being, it would provide the normative foundations for the professional-technologist role. Such a community would be guided by a set of norms and values concerning technical as well as social facets of engineering, not unlike some of the norms current in the scientific community (Merton [1949] 1957, pp. 550–561). The implementation of past proposals for an international institute of science and technology (Killian 1962) and the emergence of *transnational* professional societies of engineers—whose unit of membership is the individual engineer—in addition to the present international societies, would probably contribute to the emergence of a technological community.

Which of these two new potential social roles—that of the technocrat or that of the professional technologist—will predominate in the years ahead or whether both roles will become institutionalized, albeit in different societies, is obviously difficult to predict. A conditional prediction, however, may be ventured: the professional-technologist role is likely to become institutionalized in societies where a democratic and antielitist ethos predominates; conversely, in societies with a nondemocratic and elitist ethos, the technocratic role of the engineer is likely to become institutionalized. A political–ecological factor that may affect this prediction is the relationship between international conflict and the course of technological development. If international conflict in the next decades comes under effective international regulation—thus reducing the chances of nuclear war—technology, and in turn the engineering profession, will be able to continue its development largely independent of international political and military conflicts. Such an international political environment would be conducive to the institutionalization of the role of the professional technologist, particularly in industrialized societies, and to the growth of a technological community, both of which would usher in a new level of professionalization of engineering.

WILLIAM M. EVAN

[*See also* AUTOMATION; LICENSING, OCCUPATIONAL; OCCUPATIONS AND CAREERS; PROFESSIONS; TECHNOLOGY.]

BIBLIOGRAPHY

AMERICAN SOCIETY FOR ENGINEERING EDUCATION, COMMITTEE ON EVALUATION OF ENGINEERING EDUCATION 1955 *Report on Evaluation of Engineering Education, 1952–1955.* Urbana, Ill.: The Society.

ARMYTAGE, W. H. G. 1961 *A Social History of Engineering.* London: Faber.

BALDWIN, GEORGE B. 1965 Iran's Experience With Manpower Planning: Concepts, Techniques and Lessons. Pages 140–172 in Frederick H. Harbison and Charles A. Myers (editors), *Manpower and Education: Country Studies in Economic Development.* New York: McGraw-Hill.

BLAU, PETER M. 1965 The Flow of Occupational Supply and Recruitment. *American Sociological Review* 30: 475–490.

BOGUSLAW, ROBERT 1965 *The New Utopians: A Study of System Design and Social Change.* Englewood Cliffs, N.J.: Prentice-Hall.

CHÊNG, CHU-YÜAN 1964 *Scientific and Engineering Manpower in Communist China, 1949–1963.* Washington: Government Printing Office.

CONFERENCE OF REPRESENTATIVES FROM THE ENGINEERING SOCIETIES OF WESTERN EUROPE AND THE UNITED STATES OF AMERICA 1960 *Report on Education and Training of Professional Engineers.* 3 vols. Brussells: EUSEC.

COTGROVE, STEPHEN F. 1958 *Technical Education and Social Change.* London: Ruskin House.

DAVIS, JAMES A. 1965 *Undergraduate Career Decisions: Correlates of Occupational Choice.* National Opinion Research Center, Monographs in Social Research, No. 2. Chicago: Aldine.

DEDIJER, STEVAN 1962 Measuring the Growth of Science. *Science* 138:781–788. → Data in Table 1, copyright 1962 by the American Association for the Advancement of Science.

Demographic Yearbook 1965. 1965 New York: United Nations. → Data in Table 1, copyright United Nations 1965. Reproduced by permission.

DEWITT, NICHOLAS 1961 *Education and Professional Employment in the U.S.S.R.* Washington: National Science Foundation.

EMERSON, JOHN P. 1965 *Nonagricultural Employment in Mainland China, 1948–1958.* U.S. Bureau of the Census, International Population Reports, Series P-90, No. 21. Washington: Government Printing Office.

ENGINEERS JOINT COUNCIL 1965 *Engineering Manpower in Profile.* New York: The Council.

EVAN, WILLIAM M. 1962 Role Strain in the Norm of Reciprocity in Research Organizations. *American Journal of Sociology* 68:346–354.

EVAN, WILLIAM M. 1963 The Problem of Obsolescence of Knowledge. Institute of Electrical and Electronics Engineers, Engineering Management Group, *IEEE Transactions on Engineering Management* EM 10: 29–31.

EVAN, WILLIAM M. 1964 On the Margin: The Engineering Technician. Pages 83–112 in Peter L. Berger (editor), *The Human Shape of Work: Studies in the Sociology of Occupations.* New York: Macmillan.

GERSTL, JOEL E. 1963 Social Origins of Engineers. *New Society* 36:19–20.

GERSTL, JOEL E.; and HUTTON, S. P. 1966 *Engineers: The Anatomy of a Profession.* London: Tavistock.

GILFILLAN, S. COLUM 1935 *The Sociology of Invention: An Essay in the Social Causes of Technic Invention and Some of Its Social Results.* Chicago: Follett.

GOLDSEN, ROSE K. et al. 1960 *What College Students Think.* Princeton, N.J.: Van Nostrand.

GOLDSTEIN, BERNARD 1954 Unions and the Professional Employee. *Journal of Business* 27:276–284.

GRANICK, DAVID 1962 *The European Executive.* Garden City, N.Y.: Doubleday.

HODGE, ROBERT W. et al. 1964 Occupational Prestige in the United States, 1925–1963. *American Journal of Sociology* 70:286–302.

HOROWITZ, MORRIS A. 1965 High-level Manpower in the Economic Development of Argentina. Pages 1–36 in Frederick H. Harbison and Charles A. Myers (editors), *Manpower and Education: Country Studies in Economic Development.* New York: McGraw-Hill.

HUNT, J. B. 1960 Engineer Training in the New Nations. *Engineering* 189:287 only.

HUTTON, S. P.; and GERSTL, JOEL E. 1964 Engineering Education and Careers. Part 3F, pages 1–17 in Institution of Mechanical Engineers, Conference on Engineering Education and Career Patterns, London, *Proceedings.* London: The Institution.

INKELES, ALEX; and ROSSI, PETER H. 1956 National Comparisons of Occupational Prestige. *American Journal of Sociology* 61:329–339.

JAHODA, MARIE 1963 *The Education of Technologists.* London: Tavistock.

KILLIAN, J. R. 1962 An International Institute of Science and Technology. *NATO Letter* 10:7–11.

KING, ALEXANDER 1965 *Education and Change.* London: Junior Club Publications.

KORNHAUSER, WILLIAM 1962 *Scientists in Industry: Conflict and Accommodation.* Berkeley: Univ. of California Press.

KOROL, ALEXANDER G. 1957 *Soviet Education for Science and Technology.* Cambridge, Mass.: M.I.T. Press.

KOROL, ALEXANDER G. 1965 *Soviet Research and Development: Its Organization, Personnel and Funds.* Cambridge, Mass.: M.I.T. Press.

KRULEE, GILBERT 1963 Engineers at Northwestern. *Northwestern Engineer* 22:20–36.

KUIPER, G. 1956 The Recruitment of the Learned Professions in the Netherlands. Volume 3, pages 230–238 in World Congress of Sociology, Third, *Transactions.* London: International Sociological Association.

LEBOLD, WILLIAM K. et al. 1960 *A Study of the Purdue University Engineering Graduate.* Purdue University Engineering Extension Series, No. 99. Lafayette, Ind.: Purdue Univ.

MERTON, ROBERT K. (1949) 1957 *Social Theory and Social Structure.* Rev. & enl. ed. Glencoe, Ill.: Free Press. → See Chapter 16 on "Science and Democratic Social Structure" and Chapter 17 on "The Machine, the Worker and the Engineer."

NATIONAL SOCIETY OF PROFESSIONAL ENGINEERS 1962 *Ethics for Engineers: Canons of Ethics, Creed and Rules of Professional Conduct.* Washington: The Society.

NATIONAL SOCIETY OF PROFESSIONAL ENGINEERS 1963 *Engineering College Instruction in Professionalism: A Survey of Faculty Attitudes.* Washington: The Society.

ORGANIZATION FOR ECONOMIC COOPERATION AND DEVELOPMENT 1963 *Resources of Scientific and Technical Personnel in the OECD Area: Statistical Report.* Paris: The Organization.

ORGANIZATION FOR ECONOMIC COOPERATION AND DEVELOPMENT 1966 Deployment and Utilization of Highly Qualified Personnel, Statistical Index. Unpublished manuscript.

ORLEANS, LEO A. 1961 *Professional Manpower and Education in Communist China.* Washington: Government Printing Office.

OTEIZA, ENRIQUE 1965 Emigration of Engineers From Argentina: A Case of Latin American "Brain Drain." *International Labour Review* 92:445–461.

OXFORD UNIVERSITY, DEPARTMENT OF EDUCATION 1963 *Technology and the Sixth Form Boy.* Oxford and Cambridge Schools Examination Board.

RUSSETT, BRUCE M. et al. 1964 *World Handbook of Political and Social Indicators.* New Haven: Yale Univ. Press.

SHEPARD, HERBERT A. 1957 Engineers as Marginal Men. *Journal of Engineering Education* 47:536–542.

TIRYAKIAN, EDWARD A. 1958 The Prestige Evaluation of Occupations in an Underdeveloped Country: The

Philippines. *American Journal of Sociology* 63:390–399.

TROW, MARTIN 1959 Some Implications of the Social Origins of Engineers. *Scientific Manpower* [1958]: 67–74.

UNESCO *Statistical Yearbook, 1963.*

U.S. BUREAU OF THE CENSUS 1963 *Statistical Abstract of the United States.* Washington: Government Printing Office.

U.S. CONGRESS, JOINT COMMISSION ON ATOMIC ENERGY 1956 *Engineering and Scientific Manpower in the United States, Western Europe, and Soviet Russia.* Washington: Government Printing Office.

U.S. DEPARTMENT OF COMMERCE 1963 *Studies in Scientific and Engineering Manpower.* Washington: Government Printing Office.

U.S. OFFICE OF EDUCATION, DIVISION OF EDUCATIONAL STATISTICS 1965 *Digest of Educational Statistics,* by Kenneth V. Simon and W. Vance Grant. Bulletin, 1965, No. 4. Washington: Government Printing Office.

U.S. PATENT OFFICE *Official Gazette of the U.S. Patent Office.* → See especially January 28, 1964, 798:777 only and January 5, 1965, 810:2 only.

VEBLEN, THORSTEIN (1919) 1921 *The Engineers and the Price System.* New York: Huebsch. → A series of papers reprinted from the *Dial.* A paperback edition was published in 1963 by Harcourt.

WALTON, RICHARD E. 1961 *The Impact of the Professional Engineering Union: A Study of Collective Bargaining Among Engineers and Scientists and Its Significance for Management.* Boston: Harvard Univ., Graduate School of Business Administration, Division of Research.

WILENSKY, HAROLD L. 1964 The Professionalization of Everyone? *American Journal of Sociology* 70:137–158.

WOOD, J. F. D. 1961 Development in Engineering Education Overseas. *Journal of the Institution of Engineers* (Australia) 33:75–83.

ENGINEERING PSYCHOLOGY

Engineering psychology is a branch of applied psychology specifically concerned with the discovery and application of information about human behavior and its relation to machines, tools, and jobs so that their design may best match the abilities and limitations of their human users. The field is also referred to, from time to time, as psychotechnology or applied experimental psychology, but these two names appear to be gradually dropping out of use.

Engineering psychology can be properly viewed as part of *industrial psychology.* The latter includes such additional topics as personnel procurement, selection, training, classification, and promotion; labor relations; morale and human relations; organizational management; and consumer behavior. The field of engineering psychology can also be identified as a subarea of *human factors engineering,* or *human engineering,* as it is generally known in the United States, or of *ergonomics,* as it is usually called in the United Kingdom and Europe. The broader field of human factors engineering includes, in addition to engineering psychology, portions of such human sciences as anatomy, anthropometry, applied physiology, environmental medicine, and toxicology.

These distinctions between engineering psychology, industrial psychology, and human factors engineering are more academic than real. In his practical work, the engineering psychologist needs to know enough about all of these disciplines so that he can make use of them in arriving at sensible and informed design decisions. Rather than calling engineering psychology a distinct entity, it would be more correct to say that this name is more a convenient focus around which training is offered in many universities.

Historical development

In a certain sense it is correct to say that people have been concerned with engineering psychology of a sort ever since man began fashioning implements for his own use. Nonetheless, engineering psychology has emerged as a separate discipline only within the past few decades. It was not until the end of the nineteenth century that the first systematic investigations were conducted on man's capacity to work as it is influenced by his job and his tools. Frederick W. Taylor (1898) made empirical studies of the best design of shovels and of the optimum weight of material per shovelful for handling different products, such as sand, slag, rice coal, and iron ore. Taylor's interests, however, were primarily in rates of doing work and in the effects of incentives and worker motivation on rates of working. It remained for Frank B. Gilbreth to set a firm foundation for this field with his classic study of bricklaying (1909). Among other things, Gilbreth invented a scaffolding which could be quickly adjusted so that the bricklayer could work at the most convenient level at all times. A shelf held the bricks and mortar at their most convenient positions. By further changes of a similar nature Gilbreth was able to increase the number of bricks laid from 120 to 350 per man per hour. This pioneering work of Taylor and Gilbreth was the beginning of that branch of industrial engineering now known as time and motion study.

In the years that followed, time and motion engineers developed a number of principles of motion economy, of the arrangement of work, and of work design that have been widely applied throughout modern industry. Insofar as they have focused on human capacities and limitations and have used this information to redesign the machine, the task, or the work environment, it is correct to say that time and motion engineers are predecessors of the modern engineering psychologist.

Still, the primary emphasis in time and motion engineering has been on man as a worker, that is, as a source of mechanical power. During the two world wars there appeared a new class of machines —machines that made demands upon the operator not in terms of his muscular power but rather in terms of his sensory, perceptual, judgmental, and decision-making abilities. The job of a sonar operator, for example, requires virtually no muscular effort, but it makes severe demands on his sensory capacity, his attentiveness, and his decision-making ability. Problems of this type could no longer be dealt with by common sense or by the time and motion engineer's principles of motion economy.

World War I.   When the United States entered World War I in 1917, a group of psychologists under Robert M. Yerkes was organized as the Psychology Committee of the National Research Council. In volunteering their services to the military establishment, they were met at first with considerable skepticism about what they could do of any value in the hard business of war. Gradually these psychologists were able to make some substantial contributions and eventually win the enthusiastic endorsement of the military services.

By and large the psychologists in World War I were concerned with such things as the selection, classification, and training of recruits, and with morale, military discipline, recreation, and problems of emotional stability in soldiers and sailors. A few of them, however, notably Raymond Dodge, Knight Dunlap, and Carl E. Seashore, encountered problems of a different sort—those in which the design of machines and equipment had to be related to the user. These early problems were found in gas masks, in binoculars and monoculars for spotters, in listening devices for locating submarines, and in aircraft. Questions were more numerous than answers, and the war ended before many solid accomplishments had been made.

World War II.   After the armistice in 1918 this pioneering work in engineering psychology was almost entirely abandoned. A few scattered studies appeared between the two world wars under the auspices of the Industrial Health Board and the Industrial Fatigue Research Board of the Medical Research Council (Great Britain), but the field was largely neglected until World War II. At that time the machines and problems foreshadowed by World War I reappeared in profusion. Radar, sonar, high altitude and high speed aircraft, naval combat information centers, and air traffic control centers

placed demands upon their human operators that were often far beyond the capabilities of human senses, brains, and muscles. Operators sometimes had to look for targets which were all but invisible, understand speech against backgrounds of deafening noise, track targets simultaneously in the three dimensions of space with both hands, and absorb large amounts of information to reach life-and-death decisions within seconds. As a result, bombs and bullets often missed their mark, planes crashed, friendly ships were sunk, and whales were depth-charged. The response to the need was so vigorous and dramatic that only a few highlights can be mentioned here.

Having entered the war before the United States, Great Britain faced these problems first and established a pattern that, in broad outlines, was followed later in the United States. The Medical Research Council was responsible for sponsoring much research on man–machine problems in several large universities and in the military services through the Flying Personnel Research Committee, the Royal Naval Personnel Research Committee, and the Military Personnel Research Committee. In the military services, important work was done at such laboratories as the Royal Aircraft Establishment, Farnborough; the Admiralty Naval Motion Study Unit, London; and the Admiralty Research Laboratory, Teddington, Middlesex.

Although entering the conflict later, the United States met problems equally urgent and dealt with them in substantially the same way. The National Defense Research Committee through the Office of Scientific Research and Development set up numerous research contracts in universities and industries to study these problems. All three military services incorporated civilian and military scientist-psychologists into their research and development laboratories in order that research findings would be put to immediate use. Some of the pioneering work in this area was carried out by the Aero Medical Laboratory of the (then) Army Air Forces Air Materiel Command, Wright Field, Dayton, Ohio; the Army Air Forces School of Aviation Medicine, Randolph Field, Texas; the U.S. Navy Electronics Laboratory, San Diego, California; the Naval Research Laboratory, Washington, D.C.; and the Armored Medical Research Laboratory, Fort Knox, Kentucky.

Present status of the field.   Since World War II the growth of engineering psychology has been very rapid. The Society of Engineering Psychologists, Division 21 of the American Psychological Association, had 360 members in 1965. About 770 psychologists are members of the Human Factors Society and, indeed, make up over 60 per cent of the membership of that organization. Psychologists also figure prominently in the Ergonomics Research Society (centered in Great Britain), the Société d'Ergonomie de Langue Française (centered in France), the Nederlandse Vereniging voor Ergonomie, and the Japanese Ergonomics Research Society. Engineering psychologists are employed in every branch of the military service, in many independent research and consulting organizations, and in the aviation, automotive, electronics, communications, and home appliance industries.

At the present time, engineering psychology is most fully developed and exploited as a specialty in the United States. Other countries which give training in this area or make use of it in practical affairs to some degree or other are Australia, Belgium, France, Germany, Great Britain, Israel, Japan, the Netherlands, Sweden, Switzerland, and the U.S.S.R.

Methodology

Engineering psychologists aim to discover principles that can be cast into the form of recommendations for machine design. Unfortunately, they can usually find specific answers for only a small proportion of the questions they face. Part of the difficulty is that man–machine interactions occur in an almost infinite variety. Moreover, the range of these problems is diverging rather than converging. Engineers are busy designing new and complex machines, destined to operate not only in the prosaic world of our everyday lives but in hostile and exotic environments where man has never lived—from the crushing Stygian abysses of our oceans to the infinite voids of deep space. Literally millions of people are actively engaged in the business of designing and constructing machines and machine systems, but there are scarcely a thousand people who make it their primary business to study man in his intimate relations with these machines. For reasons such as these, man–machine problems appear to be multiplying faster than we can do research on them.

The practicing engineering psychologist finds that he spends a considerable portion of his time "trying things out." In some industries and in some laboratories, experimentation of one kind or another may well take up the major part of the engineering psychologist's working time. As one might suppose from the historical development of the field and the nature of the work, methodologies in engineering psychology are diverse and adapted from several disciplines (see Chapanis 1959). The

discovery of new methodologies is also a topic of continuing and active interest in the literature of engineering psychology. For this reason the techniques mentioned below should be regarded as a sample of the ways in which problems have been answered in the past rather than as an exhaustive list of the tools available to the practitioner in this field.

Whenever he can, the engineering psychologist uses full-scale experimentation with the same rigor and sophistication that one expects of the best tradition of experimentation. Because of the complexity of his problems and the many variables that normally influence human behavior in machine situations, the engineering psychologist typically employs experimental designs using several variables, deriving, for example, from methods of analysis of variance. In addition, the psychophysical methods are widely used for obtaining useful data on sensory capacities, as are articulation test methods for measuring the effectiveness of speech communication devices and systems. In preliminary exploratory work on complex systems, the study of critical incidents, accidents, and near accidents has proven widely useful in locating potential sources of man–machine conflict.

From the industrial engineer, the engineering psychologist has borrowed and adapted a number of techniques for directly observing systems in operation. Some of these are activity sampling procedures, process analysis, and micromotion methods. Finally, from more conventional techniques of industrial psychology the engineering psychologist has adapted to his own needs methods of job analysis, task analysis, personnel requirement inventories, questionnaires, tests, and rating scales.

Subject matter

Almost everything that is known about man as a living, feeling, behaving organism is relevant to the engineering psychologist. Current thinking even extends to man as a social organism: a number of recent research findings show clearly that the effectiveness of complex man–machine systems is determined to a considerable extent by the compatibility of the team of men who work in the system. Examples are nuclear submarines and advanced space vehicles, where men are forced to live and work together for extended periods of time in cramped quarters while under unusual stress.

For all that, the amount of information about human behavior that may be required for particular applications varies enormously. In the design of a space vehicle, the engineering psychologist may be faced with problems that cover the full range of human psychology. He needs to consider the sensory capacities of operators as they relate to instrument displays and the sensing of information from inside and outside the vehicle. Knowledge about man's ability to make rapid and correct decisions is vital. Working hours and work–rest cycles are certain to be different from those on earth, and it is important to know how well man can perform under these altered working conditions. The engineering psychologist also needs to consider the human ability to make correct control actions of a great variety. Human reactions to exotic environments, the ability to learn new and complex skills, emotional reactions and personality problems that might arise from the stresses of space flight, social behavior—all of these are relevant for the engineering psychologist. [*See* SPACE, OUTER.]

By contrast with the complexity of a space vehicle, there are many problems in engineering psychology that are much simpler and more circumscribed. The engineering psychologist who works with common consumer items may be faced with questions like: How should the controls be placed on a stove so that housewives correctly turn the correct control to activate a burner? What size and spacing of letters, numbers, and symbols should be used on the labels of household appliances so that they will be easily legible? How should the numbers and letters be arranged on push-button telephones? All of these are examples of relatively restricted but genuine problems encountered in the practical business of engineering psychology.

The man–machine model. In their work engineering psychologists regard man as an element in a man–machine system. Basically, a person who uses or operates a piece of equipment has to do three things. He has first to sense something and to perceive what this something means. The thing the human operator senses is termed a machine *display*. It may be any of a thousand different things—the position of a pointer on a dial, the print-out of a digital computer, a voice coming over a loudspeaker, a red light flashing on a control panel, a highway sign along a speedway, or the resistance felt in a certain kind of control.

Having sensed a machine output, the man next has to interpret what the display means, understand it, perhaps do some mental computation, and reach a decision of some sort. In so doing, the human operator often uses other important human functions—the ability to remember and recall, to compare what he now perceives against past experiences, to recall operating rules he may have learned during training, or to put what he now

experiences into the context of strategies he may have formed for handling events such as this. A man is not necessarily aware that he is doing any or all of these things, of course. His behavior may be so well practiced and routine that the decision to do one thing or another may be made almost by reflex, just as the experienced driver may decide almost unconsciously whether or not he should stop when he sees a green traffic light change to yellow. All of the functions discussed in this paragraph are ordinarily subsumed under the heading of *higher mental processes* in textbooks of psychology. Engineering psychologists often use machine terminology instead of more familiar psychological terms and, in keeping with this trend, refer to all these higher mental processes collectively as *data processing*.

Having reached a decision about the information he has received through his sense organs and dealt with in his nervous system, the human operator then normally takes some action. The action is normally exercised on some sort of a control—a push button, lever, crank, pedal, switch, or handle. Man's action upon one or more of these controls exerts in turn an influence on the behavior of the machine, its output and displays. Many times, of course, a machine operator monitoring a process may decide to do nothing. This is still regarded as an important human output.

A man–machine system does not exist in isolation but in an environment. The character of this environment influences man's efficiency and performance, and the engineering psychologist is often vitally concerned with these factors. Among the more important environmental influences are such commonplace ones as temperature, humidity, ventilation, lighting, noise, and movement. Some less common but still important ones are vibration and a whole host of noxious gases and contaminants. In more exotic systems the engineering psychologist may also have to be concerned with the effects of increased acceleration, weightlessness (zero gravity conditions), anoxia caused by reduced oxygen at high altitudes, radiation, and the effects of reduced barometric pressures on the body.

The display of information. The man–machine model described above provides a convenient framework for summarizing the main content areas of engineering psychology. Machine displays, in a manner of speaking, represent the starting point of the man–machine cycle, for it is through such displays that the machine communicates to its human operator. For this reason, a considerable amount of work has been devoted to studies of displays and the ways in which they should be selected and designed. Although man has available a dozen or so sense channels that could conceivably be used to receive information from machine systems, only three—vision, hearing, and the sense of touch or vibration—have been exploited to any great extent.

In the area of visual displays, research has been done on such problems as the design of mechanical indicators; scales; cathode-ray tubes (radar scopes); charts, tables, and graphs; warning lights and signals; abstract visual dimensions (symbols varying in color, shape, brightness, or size) for coding information; and general and specialized lighting systems (for ready rooms and radar rooms).

Problems of auditory displays can be grouped into two broad classes: those dealing with tonal or noise signals (sirens, diaphones, horns, buzzers, bells, gongs, and so on), and those dealing with speech communication systems. Research on the former class of problems has been generally concerned with signal processing and control: the selection of signals and signal characteristics, the filtering of signals to eliminate unwanted or interfering noise, and the use of signals for coding information. Research on speech communication systems has been aimed at the design of special or efficient languages, the design of the components of speech communication systems (microphones, amplifiers, and so on), and the design of speech communication systems as a whole. [See HEARING; PERCEPTION, *article on* SPEECH PERCEPTION; VISION.]

Machine displays for senses other than vision and hearing have not been used very much, and perhaps for this reason, research on such displays is relatively meager. Within recent years, however, it has been shown that the vibratory sense can be used for an efficient communication system. Using a special kind of vibratory code applied to a man's chest, Geldard (1957) trained one subject to receive up to 38 words per minute. However, because of the awkwardness of the equipment and the possibility of interference from other sources of vibration, it is doubtful whether that particular system will be put into any operational situation. This research shows, however, that there may be unexplored possibilities for communication through these other senses.

Data processing. One important function which man serves in many man–machine systems is that of data processing. He may be required to perceive things, assimilate large masses of data, evaluate or assess a situation, do computations, and make decisions. Despite much research on these higher mental processes our understanding of the mechanisms by which people do these things is still imperfect. As a result, it is in this area of engineering psychology that one finds the fewest principles and concrete recommendations about the ways in which man can be best integrated into man–machine systems. As more and more systems become automated, however, man's role in the system becomes more and more that of a monitor and decision maker. One may expect therefore that some of the greatest research gains are yet to be realized in this area.

Machine controls. Research on the design of machine controls has yielded a substantial number of useful and practical principles. These are concerned with such things as the factors involved in selecting the correct control for a job, control–display ratios, direction-of-movement relationships, control resistance, ways of preventing accidental activation, and control coding. Among the more complex kinds of controls are those involved in what are called closed-loop tracking systems. (Driving a car along a winding road is a simple example of a closed-loop tracking task.) Research on the last kind of problem involves considerations of the mathematical relationships between the movements of the control and the dynamics of the system.

Environmental problems. Although the study of environmental problems might seem to fall exclusively within the province of the applied physiologist, the fact is that psychologists have studied the effects of a wide range of environmental factors on gross behavior. These studies have been concerned with problems of illumination, noise, anoxia (lack of oxygen at high altitudes), certain kinds of noxious gases and contaminants, heat and cold, vibration, and most recently, weightlessness.

The aim of research. In common with research in most other areas of science, research in engineering psychology has as its first aim *understanding*. Beyond this, however, the engineering psychologist hopes that his researches will yield principles which can be put into the form of definite recommendations for machine design. A large number of these are now available, and they can be found in textbooks and guides on this subject (see, for example, Chapanis 1965; McCormick 1957; Morgan et al. 1963). The following example from research on control design will illustrate one of the concepts that originated in engineering psychology and some of the design recommendations that followed from it.

The results of control movements are often shown on a display. The tuning knob on a radio is a familiar example. As you turn the tuning knob, you change a variable condenser inside the radio. At the same time, a pointer moves along a linear or circular scale to show you what frequency or wave length the radio has been tuned to. Examples of linked controls and displays are common in the world of machines. The controls may be knobs, cranks, levers, or translatory controls. Sometimes a control may be in one plane (for example, on the horizontal working surface in front of an operator) and the display in another plane (for example, directly in front of the operator's eyes and at right angles to the surface on which the control is mounted). The number of permutations of controls, displays, and orientations is, of course, very great.

In the case of many control–display combinations it turns out that most people have consistent expectations about the way in which a control should move in order to produce a change in the display. When these expectations are strong and found universally, they are called *population stereotypes*. Controls that conform to these population stereotypes are responded to much more quickly and with far fewer errors than are controls that do not. Human beings are remarkably adaptable and, given sufficient training, can learn to use controls and displays that do not agree with population stereotypes. The interesting thing, however, is that if such an operator is subjected to great stress or to an emergency situation, he frequently regresses or reverts to his natural expectancies. Many accidents in aircraft have been traced to this single factor alone. The design recommendation which follows from this research is clear: Whenever strong population stereotypes exist, control and display movements should agree with them.

Man–machine system design

Although, as was remarked earlier, the scope of engineering psychology covers a range from relatively simple devices to enormously complex machine systems, it is the latter which are the most challenging, most complex, and most difficult to deal with. The design of an air traffic control system, an automated mail handling system, a new guided missile system, or a deep space vehicle system is a problem of gigantic proportions. Thousands of technical and professional experts of a hundred or more different varieties may work for years to bring such a large system into being. Engineering psychologists are generally recognized as important members of such design teams.

In the preceding section the subject matter of engineering psychology has been presented from the standpoint of the way it is organized by the psychologist himself. When we look at the field from the standpoint of what the engineering psychologist contributes to the design of man–machine systems, a somewhat different order of topics results.

Design and planning. The first step in the creation of any large system is generally called a study phase. It is at this time that engineers study in detail the specifications and requirements of the system. Alternative ways of designing the system to meet the requirements are thought up, tested, tried out, and discarded, modified, or accepted. Contrary to what many lay people think, there is much trial and error involved in this stage of the process, and the final conceptualization of the system may be quite different from initial ideas. During this study phase, engineering psychologists are called upon to study and decide about man's role in the system. They usually assist in making decisions about precisely which functions of the system should be allocated to humans and which to machine components. They prepare estimates of the number and types of people that will be required to man the system when it is completed, the so-called QQPRI (Qualitative and Quantitative Personnel Requirements Information). If personnel with specialized training will be needed, engineering psychologists plan and design training programs and curricula to ensure that qualified people are available to operate the system when it is completed. Finally, they may try to anticipate the social consequences of the system on its human operators or society in general.

Project engineering. After preliminary designs and plans have been completed, the system goes into actual construction. The first model of any large system is seldom built as originally planned. Difficulties appear at this point which had not been anticipated in the largely paper-and-pencil study phase, and the changes and modifications that must be made often number in the thousands. During the production phase of system design the engineering psychologist usually makes substantial contributions to the man–machine combination, although ultimate responsibility for design usually rests with an engineer. The engineering psychologist studies, tests, and makes recommendations about specific workplace arrangements, solves specific problems of display and control, and makes design recommendations about the solution of environmental problems.

Another important task of the engineering psychologist is that of studying the system from the standpoint of its reliability and maintenance and of anticipating special problems of maintenance. With the increase in the number of highly automated systems, problems of faultfinding and maintenance are becoming increasingly important. For one thing, the cost of a highly automatic system is so great that the user cannot afford to have it idle for long periods of time. At the same time, such systems are so complex that it is becoming increasingly difficult for repairmen to diagnose what is wrong with them and decide how they can be most quickly repaired. As one illustration of the magnitude of the problem, the U.S. Air Force estimates that to repair and maintain a typical system (for example, an aircraft) during its normal lifetime may cost up to ten times the original purchase price of the system. Further, of the total time spent in actively repairing most large systems, as much as 80 per cent of a maintenance man's time is spent in merely discovering what is wrong with it. The engineering psychologist's contributions here are in planning effective faultfinding strategies and in seeing to it that the equipment is so designed (with sufficient test points, accesses, and so on) that it can be easily maintained, that it is installed where it can be readily reached, that appropriate, well-written maintenance manuals are ready as soon as the equipment is completed, that special tools and test equipment are properly designed and constructed, that maintenance men are trained, that adequate work and storage facilities are provided, and that an adequate supply of spare parts and replacements is provided.

The end result of this part of system development is what is usually termed a *prototype,* a first full-scale working model of the system.

Test and evaluation and operational use. Once a protoype of a system is constructed, it usually goes through a series of tests, often termed operational suitability tests or evaluations, to discover if the system really does what it is supposed to do. It is generally recognized that a man–machine system has to be tested as a complete entity and that the human components in a system may make or break it. The problems of testing systems that contain people are far more difficult than conducting simple engineering or physical tests. Because of their special training in experimental methodology and in the problems of conducting studies on people, engineering psychologists are often given major responsibility for the design and conduct of such tests.

When a large system has been tested, accepted, and put into operational use, it may undergo still further modifications as experience with it accumulates. These are usually far fewer in number and less sweeping than those which occur earlier in the design. Although the engineering psychologist may still play some role in this stage of the lifetime of the system, it is usually a much less important one than in earlier design phases. It is at this time that the training and personnel specialist replaces the engineering psychologist in terms of importance.

ALPHONSE CHAPANIS

[*See also* INDUSTRIAL RELATIONS, *article on* INDUSTRIAL AND BUSINESS PSYCHOLOGY. *Other relevant material may be found in* MILITARY PSYCHOLOGY; PSYCHOPHYSICS.]

BIBLIOGRAPHY

CHAPANIS, ALPHONSE 1959 *Research Techniques in Human Engineering.* Baltimore: Johns Hopkins Press.

CHAPANIS, ALPHONSE 1965 *Man–Machine Engineering.* Belmont, Calif.: Wadsworth.

GELDARD, FRANK A. 1957 Adventures in Tactile Literacy. *American Psychologist* 12:115–124.

GILBRETH, FRANK B. 1909 *Bricklaying System.* New York: Clark.

McCORMICK, ERNEST J. (1957) 1964 *Human Factors Engineering.* 2d ed. New York: McGraw-Hill. → First published as *Human Engineering.*

MORGAN, CLIFFORD T. et al. (editors) 1963 *Human Engineering Guide to Equipment Design.* New York: McGraw-Hill.

TAYLOR, FREDERICK W. (1898) 1911 *Scientific Shoveling.* Wyoming, Pa.: The Wyoming Shovel Works.

ENTERTAINMENT

See COMMUNICATION, MASS; DRAMA; FILM; LEISURE; LITERATURE.

ENTREPRENEURSHIP

There are some unresolved differences in the definitions of entrepreneurship, but there is agreement that the term includes at least a part of the administrative function of making decisions for the conduct of some type of organization. One group of scholars would restrict the term to strategic or innovating decisions, and an overlapping group would apply it only to business organizations. The basis for these differences can be understood from the history of the concept.

The word *entrepreneur* appeared in the French language long before there was any general concept of an entrepreneurial function. By the early sixteenth century, men engaged in leading military expeditions were referred to as entrepreneurs. From this usage, it was easy to move to applying entrepreneur to other types of adventurers. After about 1700, entrepreneur was frequently applied by the French to government road, bridge, harbor, and fortification contractors and, somewhat later, to architects (Hoselitz 1951, p. 195). Seeing such activities as the entrepreneurial function, the mid-eighteenth-century French writer Bernard F. de

Belidor further defined it as buying labor and materials at uncertain prices and selling the resultant product at a contracted price (Hoselitz 1951, pp. 198–199).

Richard Cantillon's *Essai sur la nature du commerce en général* (1755), probably written a generation before its publication date, drew attention to *entrepreneur* as a technical term. The essence of the function of the entrepreneur was to bear uncertainty. Conversely to the Belidor emphasis, Cantillon saw the entrepreneur as anyone who bought and sold at uncertain prices. Obviously, there is no contradiction between Belidor and Cantillon in theory, but merely in the type of examples chosen. Except for princes, landowners, and salaried workers, Cantillon regarded everyone engaged in economic activity as an entrepreneur.

The physiocratic economists of the later eighteenth century, such as François Quesnay and Nicolas Baudeau, called the agricultural cultivator an entrepreneur. Since the physiocrats also thought that only the land was a source of social product, this put the entrepreneur in a key position. In the sphere of agriculture, Baudeau credited the entrepreneur with all the essential characteristics of risk taking and innovation that were to be elaborated in later definitions (in his *Première introduction à la philosophie économique*). At about the same time A. R. J. Turgot, in his *Réflexions sur la formation et la distribution des richesses*, spoke of the entrepreneur in manufacturing as one who risked capital (Hoselitz 1951, pp. 205–212).

Thus, by 1800, many French economists had given special meanings to entrepreneur and entrepreneurship, with differences arising largely from the characteristics of the sector of the economy that chiefly attracted their attention. Those economists interested in government saw the entrepreneur as a contractor, the specialists on agriculture as a farmer, and the proponents of industry as a risk-taking capitalist. The "classic" definition, which was to survive until the twentieth century, was written by an aristocratic industrialist who had had unpleasant practical experience, Jean Baptiste Say.

In the *Catechism of Political Economy*, Say wrote of the entrepreneur as the agent who "unites all means of production and who finds in the value of the products . . . the re-establishment of the entire capital he employs, and the value of the wages, the interest, and the rent which he pays, as well as the profits belonging to himself" ([1815] 1816), pp. 28–29). This idea appeared earlier in *A Treatise on Political Economy* (1803), which was not translated into English until 1827. Say's

entrepreneur commonly, but not necessarily, supplies either his own or borrowed capital. To succeed, he must have "judgment, perseverance, and a knowledge of the world as well as of business. He must possess the art of superintendence and administration" (1803, p. 295 in the 1827 edition). Say does not, however, discuss the entrepreneur in relation to innovation or capital creation. As in the case of the British classicists, he was unable to make entrepreneurship a ponderable factor in his general economic theory.

In contrast to the tolerably consistent and expanding French definitions of entrepreneur, the English appear to have made rather less use of three terms: *adventurer*, *undertaker*, and *projector*. While the Merchant Adventurers of the sixteenth century were the equivalent of French entrepreneurs, *adventurer* did not come into general use. The seventeenth-century French use of entrepreneur for government contractor had its English counterpart in the term *undertaker*. Near the close of the century, the third term, *projector*, came into use. Daniel Defoe, in *An Essay Upon Projects*, equates the term *projector* with *inventor*, but also with *fraud* or *swindler*. In Malachy Postlethwayt's *Universal Dictionary of Trade and Commerce* the words *adventurer* and *undertaker* are referred to but these terms are not given precise definitions (Redlich 1949, p. 9). Bert F. Hoselitz (1951) finds that by the time of Postlethwayt, *undertaker* could be applied to businessmen in general but that the term was, in fact, becoming obsolete. [*See the biographies of* CANTILLON; QUESNAY; SAY; TURGOT.]

Early treatment in economic theory. As economic theory became more carefully formulated in all the western European nations, no operative place was found for the entrepreneur. This was particularly evident in English classic theory from Smith to Marshall, where many writers made no effort either to define or include entrepreneurship.

The difficulty was that English theory was based upon a normal state of equilibrium, established by the multiple reactions of businessmen, consumers, investors, and workers to the prices of goods and services. Individual variations in behavior were seen either as canceled out in the aggregate or suppressed by competition. In this highly aggregative system, any unknown element was to be derived from the relations of theoretically measurable quantities. Such a system could obviously not utilize unmeasurable social or cultural factors such as entrepreneurship. To say that the entrepreneur was rewarded for risk taking, that is, for uncertainty, was the negation of a proper theoretical explanation.

In addition to the inhospitability of classic theory, the mid-nineteenth-century business structure of small-sized to medium-sized family firms, or closely held firms, obscured the distinctive character of the entrepreneurial function. With few exceptions, the men performing this function were also capitalist owners. Their rewards could be seen as a return on capital rather than as special compensations for entrepreneurial ability per se. In his *Principles of Economics*, Alfred Marshall perceived the changed situation inherent in big, managerially run business: "Those general faculties, which are characteristic of the modern businessman," he wrote, "increase in importance as the scale of business increases" (1891, p. 644). Yet Marshall did not elaborate upon the theoretical significance of this increasing factor, and in discussing the growth of English manufacturing he used capitalist and undertaker interchangeably (1891, pp. 40–43).

Perhaps the relatively early development of big corporations in the United States led American economists to think of entrepreneurship as a function separate from either ownership or the supply of capital. In the late 1870s, Francis A. Walker emphasized the distinction between capitalists and entrepreneurs and called the latter the engineers of industrial progress and the chief agents of production (Dorfman 1946–1959, vol. 3, p. 109). Frederick B. Hawley, writing in 1882, saw risk taking as the distinguishing attribute of the entrepreneur, and ranked this as a factor in production on a par with land, labor, and capital (*ibid.*, p. 32). At the end of the century, the unorthodox John R. Commons gave an explanation of risk-taking entrepreneurship and profit that anticipated some of the more fully elaborated ideas of Joseph A. Schumpeter (*ibid.*, p. 283). According to Commons, one type of profits arose from the ability and risk taking of the entrepreneur and was temporary and contingent on changes in the economic situation. But Schumpeter himself, in 1912, gave John Bates Clark credit for being the first to connect "entrepreneurial profits considered as a surplus over interest (and rent), with successful introduction into the economic process of technological, commercial, or organizational improvements" (*ibid.*, vol. 4, p. 166n). The basic problem of finding an operative role for entrepreneurship in economic theory, however, remained unsolved; and economic theorists, in general, well aware of the incongruity of a nonmeasurable human element in a theoretical structure based on quantifiable assumptions,

moved in other directions, such as the study of business cycles, income, saving, and investment. [*See the biographies of* CLARK, JOHN BATES; COMMONS; MARSHALL; WALKER.]

Schumpeter–Cole views. Schumpeter's acceptance of a chair at Harvard, the translation of *The Theory of Economic Development* into English in 1934, and the great depression all called new attention to his position regarding the essential role of the entrepreneur in creating profits. According to Schumpeter, both interest and profit arose from progressive change, and would not exist in a static society, as he defined it. Change, in turn, was the work of innovating businessmen or entrepreneurs. Since one change was likely to stimulate others, there was a tendency for innovations to cluster and produce long upswings in profits and business activity.

Much additional interest in entrepreneurship arose from the work of two of Schumpeter's colleagues at Harvard, economic historians Edwin F. Gay and Arthur H. Cole. In 1944, in his presidential address to the Economic History Association, Cole offered a historical analysis of the changing character of entrepreneurship. Four years later, he and Schumpeter cooperated in establishing at Harvard the Research Center in Entrepreneurial History. From the work of the center, influenced greatly by Cole and Leland H. Jenks, there emerged an approach to entrepreneurship differing from Schumpeter's.

In the Schumpeterian view, innovation was the criterion of entrepreneurship: ". . . the defining characteristic is simply the doing of new things or the doing of things that are already being done in a new way (innovation)" (Schumpeter 1947, p. 151). The "new way" was a "creative response" to a situation that had, at least, three essential characteristics.

First . . . it can practically never be understood *ex ante*. . . . Secondly, creative response shapes the whole course of subsequent events and their "long-run" outcome. . . . Thirdly, creative response . . . has . . . something to do (*a*) with the quality of personnel available in the society, (*b*) . . . with quality available to a particular field of activity, and (*c*) with individual decisions, actions and patterns of behavior. Accordingly a study of creative response in business becomes coterminous with a study of entrepreneurship. (Schumpeter 1947, p. 150)

Thus, to Schumpeter, a manager was an entrepreneur only while he was making a creative or innovative response.

The Cole view of entrepreneurship, however,

equates it with the continuing general activities of managers. It is "the purposeful activity (including an integrated sequence of decisions) of an individual or group of associated individuals, undertaken to initiate, maintain or aggrandize a profit oriented business unit for the production or distribution of economic goods and services" (Cole 1959, p. 7). "Novelty is successful in the business world only if the institution introducing it is being effectively maintained" (p. 15).

Since the difference in the two definitions involves only the scope within which the term may be applied, the followers of Cole and Schumpeter have worked together with a minimum of friction. Both definitions implied broad social approaches, close to the Germanic tradition of Gustav Schmoller, who had seen the need for "a deeper insight into the social context of the enterprise" (Lane & Riemersma 1953, p. 6), or Alfred Weber, who had regarded entrepreneurship as a socioeconomic function separate from profit making. Both definitions also suggest time spans longer than those of dynamic economic theory. [*See the biography of* SCHUMPETER.]

Recent thought. In spite of the difficulties inherent in long-run analysis and in unmeasurable human factors, the increasing interest of economists in economic development has directed their attention to entrepreneurship. While economists in this field include the entrepreneurial function in empirical studies of situations and in recommending appropriate economic policies, the theoretical problem of finding a place for unmeasurable and socially influenced forces in a mathematically oriented theory has not been solved. More specifically, the difficulty is that entrepreneurial earnings would have to be accounted for in a theory of profit, but no theoretical cost of entrepreneurship can be set.

Entrepreneurial study continues, however, in the unoccupied territory bordered by economics, history, and sociology. Two publications—*Explorations in Entrepreneurial History* (started by R. Richard Wohl and Hugh G. J. Aitken at the research center at Harvard and continued in the 1960s under the editorship of Ralph L. Andreano at Earlham College) and *Economic Development and Cultural Change* (initiated by Bert F. Hoselitz at the University of Chicago)—emphasized, during the 1950s and 1960s, the importance of entrepreneurship. In addition to scores of articles in these two publications, the Harvard center inspired a number of larger empirical studies. Of these, Fritz Redlich's volumes on the military entrepreneur in Europe cover the longest historical time span. In all, a new field of specialization, not firmly

attached to any single discipline, appears to have been established.

Students of entrepreneurship generally have come to agree that while it is a definable function, entrepreneur is a term denoting an ideal type rather than a term continuously applicable to a real person. Any businessman or other official may exercise entrepreneurship, but a classification cannot be devised that would empirically separate entrepreneurs and nonentrepreneurs.

One group of scholars has expanded the Cole point of view that entrepreneurship is a continuous function in business organization.

To the extent that behavior in a business firm is organized (formally or informally), to that extent we have entrepreneurship; to the extent that it is disorganized, random, or self-defeating, to that extent entrepreneurship is lacking. . . . The characteristics conventionally associated with entrepreneurship—leadership, innovation, risk-bearing, and so on—are so associated precisely because, in a highly commercialized culture such as ours, they are essential features of effective business organization. By the same logic, in a differently oriented culture, the typical characteristics of entrepreneurship differ. (Aitken 1963, p. 6).

Another school of thought prefers to keep the Schumpeterian distinction between the entrepreneurial function of making strategically important or innovating decisions and the managerial function of maintaining the more routine operations of a business organization. Nonspecialists, also, tend to emphasize strategic decision making in distinguishing entrepreneurship from management.

THOMAS C. COCHRAN

[*See also* HISTORY, *article on* BUSINESS HISTORY.]

BIBLIOGRAPHY

AITKEN, HUGH G. J. 1963 The Future of Entrepreneurial Research. *Explorations in Entrepreneurial History* Second Series 1:3–9.

CANTILLON, RICHARD (1755) 1952 *Essai sur la nature du commerce en général.* Paris: Institut National d'Études Démographiques.

COLE, ARTHUR H. 1946 An Approach to the Study of Entrepreneurship: A Tribute to Edwin F. Gay. *Journal of Economic History* 6 (Supplement):1–15.

COLE, ARTHUR H. 1959 *Business Enterprise in Its Social Setting.* Cambridge, Mass.: Harvard Univ. Press.

DORFMAN, JOSEPH 1946–1959 *The Economic Mind in American Civilization.* 5 vols. New York: Viking. → See especially volumes 3 and 4.

HOSELITZ, BERT F. 1951 The Early History of Entrepreneurial Theory. *Explorations in Entrepreneurial History* 3:193–220.

LANE, FREDERIC C.; and RIEMERSMA, JELLE C. (editors) 1953 *Enterprise and Secular Change: Readings in Economic History.* Homewood, Ill.: Irwin.

MARSHALL, ALFRED 1891 *Principles of Economics.* 2d ed. New York and London: Macmillan. → The first edition was published in 1890. A ninth, variorum edition was published in 1961.

REDLICH, FRITZ 1949 The Origins of the Concepts of "Entrepreneur" and "Creative Entrepreneur." *Explorations in Entrepreneurial History* 1:1–7.

SAY, JEAN BAPTISTE (1803) 1964 *A Treatise on Political Economy: Or, the Production, Distribution and Consumption of Wealth.* New York: Kelley. → First published as *Traité d'économie politique: Ou, simple exposition de la manière dont se forment, se distribuent, et se consomment les richesses.*

SAY, JEAN BAPTISTE (1815) 1816 *Catechism of Political Economy: Or, Familiar Conversations on the Manner in Which Wealth Is Produced, Distributed, and Consumed by Society.* London: Sherwood. → First published as *Catéchisme d'économie politique.*

SCHUMPETER, JOSEPH A. (1912) 1934 *The Theory of Economic Development.* Cambridge, Mass.: Harvard Univ. Press. → First published in German.

SCHUMPETER, JOSEPH A. 1947 The Creative Response in Economic History. *Journal of Economic History* 7:149–159.

ENVIRONMENT

Environment has been defined as "the aggregate of all the external conditions and influences affecting the life and development of an organism" (Webster's *New Collegiate Dictionary*). The aim, then, with either individual organisms or communities, is to distinguish between factors arising from outside the system and factors inherent in the system itself. This sounds simple enough, but in practice the distinction between organism and environment is not always easy to make.

In the first place, there is a problem of *limits.* This is essentially a matter of definition; to illustrate with an absurd example, when does an apple that a person eats cease to be a part of the environment and start to be a part of the man? Perhaps as soon as it enters the mouth; perhaps not until digestion has been completed. Most people, in any case, would consider indigestion caused by eating a green apple to be an environmental effect. Similarly, internal parasites would be considered part of the environment of the individual in which they live, even though they are entirely inside the system: the question is one of origin rather than present position.

The limit problem is not very serious. More confusing is the problem of *interaction* between organism and environment. The earth's atmosphere, for instance, with oxygen and carbon dioxide as component gases, is an essential part of the environment for life as we know it. Yet we now believe that these gases were not part of the early atmosphere of the planet; their existence is a consequence of the action of living organisms, as well as a necessary condition for life. The relation between vegetation and soil provides another type of example. The kind of forest growing in a particular region is at least partly the consequence of the type of soil in that region; yet the nature of the soil is partly determined by the sort of vegetation that has grown on it.

The interaction problem is particularly confusing in the case of man and the human environment. In orienting and judging our surroundings, we depend on our sensory systems; yet, as psychologists can so easily show, what we perceive is in part a consequence of conditioning and learning. We have thus really *created* many aspects of the shapes, colors, sounds, and smells in the world about us, at least as they influence our behavior.

The concept of *culture* is responsible for many difficulties in this connection. Should culture be looked at as a part of the individual or of the community? Is it a part of the environment? The answer surely varies, depending on the nature of the study.

For instance, if we are concerned with the ways in which peoples (or individuals) cope with their natural environment, we almost necessarily look at the physical man with the cultural equipment at his disposal for this purpose. Thus the same physical surroundings, the same environment, may have quite different meanings for, say, a food-gathering pygmy, an agricultural Bantu, or a western European. We are here concerned primarily with cultural adaptations or maladaptations. This is the case with many sorts of geographical and anthropological studies; in extreme cases, human nature may be taken as a constant to be ignored and study concentrated on the interaction between culture and environment in this sense of the term.

In many kinds of psychological studies, on the other hand, cultural traits are dealt with as parts of the environment: we become interested in the ways in which individuals are taught to accept their culture, or the ways in which they are frustrated by it and the forms that rebellion takes. In physiological studies, by contrast, culture may or may not be considered as environmental at all. Work on heat stress, for instance, may involve a naked man on a treadmill under controlled climatic conditions, in an attempt to eliminate cultural effects; alternatively, it may involve clothed men under natural conditions. Investigations of such concepts as "comfort zones" assume that people will be wearing culturally acceptable clothing.

Clothing illustrates nicely many aspects of the man–culture–environment relationship. Clothing is definitely external, stemming from outside the system of the individual organism. Yet in many kinds of practical studies, we must assume that people are wearing clothes and observe environmental effects on clothed individuals. Furthermore, the kind of clothing worn may influence individual personality—witness the effect of uniforms, of formal dress, or of work clothes.

Organism and environment, then, are not contrasting or mutually exclusive terms; rather, they represent interacting systems, and the distinction is useful in analysis only when this is kept in mind. Environment is often contrasted with heredity, as in the long controversy over "nature versus nurture" in shaping human personality. There is no "versus." Every individual is the product of a certain genetic potentiality finding expression in a particular environment or series of environments.

In studies of biological communities, the concept of *ecosystem* has proved useful: this term covers both the living organisms and the abiotic factors of the environment in which they occur. Biologists thus avoid the dangers of looking at the living members of the community as separate from their surroundings. The extension of this idea to man, to human ecosystems, will surely be rewarding.

Ecologists have tried various ways of analyzing environments to study and compare their different components, but no single system is completely satisfactory. One way involves the separation of the biological and physical environments: the living and the nonliving elements in the surroundings of an individual organism or a species. Thus, one can isolate climate as an aspect of the physical environment. In the case of man, some geographers have thought climate to be a controlling factor in cultural development, considering civilization, for instance, to be a response to a particularly stimulating climatic situation. On the other hand, they see climates that are too warm, too humid, or too cold as having a retarding effect on cultural development.

Climate illustrates another aspect of environment, that of *scale*. Climate is ordinarily measured in standard meteorological stations that reflect conditions under which few organisms live. Conditions in a forest or meadow, within the soil, or in a pond may be quite different from those where the standard measurements are made. It is, in fact, useful to distinguish among three levels of climate: the *microclimate* in which an individual lives, perhaps conditions in a cranny in bark or on the underside of a leaf; the *ecological climate* of some particular habitat, like a forest; and the *geographical climate* measured by the standard station. The

same kind of difference, depending on the focus of interest, applies to many other aspects of the environment.

In the case of man, we have to consider the cultural as well as the biological and physical environments, bringing up the whole series of problems mentioned earlier.

Another way of analyzing environmental factors is in terms of whether or not they affect the particular organism under consideration, and whether or not they are perceived. The sum of the forces and materials in any situation can be looked at as the total environment, but this includes many elements that have no influence on behavior. We live, for instance, in the magnetic field of the earth, but this does not affect our physiology in any known way; and we cannot perceive it without the aid of some instrument like a compass. Similarly, we cannot perceive viruses without instruments, but many of them do affect us by causing disease. Viruses would, then, form part of our operational environment, although not a part of our perceptual environment.

We tend to confuse our own perceptual environment with total reality: to think, for instance, that the forest we see is the "real" forest—for squirrels, birds, and insects as well as for ourselves. Yet it is obvious enough, when we stop to think about it, that each kind of animal lives in a particular sort of perceptual world of its own. The forest that a dog sees, hears, and smells is quite different from the forest that we perceive. This is something that must be clearly kept in mind in studying animal behavior as well as animal ecology.

When we turn to man, the concepts of operational and perceptual environments are inadequate by themselves, just as are those of biological and physical environments. For primitive man, the world is full of spirits which form a very real and important part of his surroundings—form what has sometimes been called the supernatural environment.

This sounds a little condescending; we can see that the people themselves created the spirits that so dominate their lives—that the spirits are merely ideas. Yet our own actions are equally governed by ideas. We may not call them spirits or propitiate them with elaborate rituals, but ideas play roles in our lives that often are at least comparable. We might call this world of ideas the *conceptual environment*. This differs somewhat from the cultural environment: the latter would include all human artifacts, such as clothing, housing, and tools; the former is concerned with the ideas that govern the form and use of the constructs.

When we look at the human environment, the continuing interaction between organism and surroundings is very evident. It is often said that man, far more than any other animal, has developed the ability to modify environment and thus to live under a wide range of physical and biological conditions. He has, in fact, created a new "biome" or ecological formation—the man-altered landscape, which is rapidly replacing other terrestrial landscapes as forests are cleared, grasslands plowed, and deserts irrigated. Man, assuming ecological dominance within this biome, has affected directly or indirectly all other organisms living there; he has become a new geological force.

Most members of the human species now live within this man-altered landscape. But this environment is not only a consequence of human activity; it is also a determinant of that activity. For instance, man has created the city; but the nature of the city, of the urban environment, governs his behavior much as the nature of the forest governs the behavior of tree squirrels. We could perhaps most profitably look at this new kind of biome as forming the human ecosystem.

It is, of course, not a single system; it includes a varied collection of differing environments: cities, towns, rice paddies, orchards, pastures, highway rights of way, abandoned fields, rubber plantations, and areas devastated by industrial wastes. Curiously, both social and biological scientists tend to neglect the study of this human ecosystem, perhaps because its study requires a blending of both social and biological knowledge.

MARSTON BATES

[See also CONSERVATION; CULTURE; ECOLOGY; GEOGRAPHY; PLANNING, SOCIAL, *article on* RESOURCE PLANNING; REGION; REGIONAL SCIENCE.]

BIBLIOGRAPHY

The biological concept of environment is developed in ecological textbooks such as Odum & Odum 1953; *the sociological, in books like* Hawley 1950. *The various textbooks of human geography discuss environmental relationships; the point of view of geographical determinism is expressed in* Huntington & Cushing 1921. International Symposium 1956 *contains much environmental material, with good bibliographies. The point of view of an architect is expressed in* Glikson 1963. Bates 1962 *develops the idea of the conceptual environment.* Dubos 1964 *expresses well the need for intensive study of man's environmental relationships.*

BATES, MARSTON 1962 *The Human Environment.* Berkeley: Univ. of California Press.

DUBOS, RENÉ 1964 Environmental Biology. *BioScience* 14:11–14.

GLIKSON, ARTUR 1963 Man's Relationship to His Environment. Pages 132–152 in Gordon Wolstenholme (editor), *Man and His Future.* Papers and discussion of a conference sponsored by the Ciba Foundation. Boston: Little.

HAWLEY, AMOS H. 1950 *Human Ecology: A Theory of Community Structure.* New York: Ronald Press.

HUNTINGTON, ELLSWORTH; and CUSHING, S. W. (1921) 1951 *Principles of Human Geography.* 6th ed. Revised by E. B. Shaw. New York: Wiley.

INTERNATIONAL SYMPOSIUM ON MAN'S ROLE IN CHANGING THE FACE OF THE EARTH, PRINCETON, N.J., 1955 1956 *Man's Role in Changing the Face of the Earth.* Edited by William L. Thomas et al. Univ. of Chicago Press.

ODUM, EUGENE P.; and ODUM, HOWARD T. (1953) 1959 *Fundamentals of Ecology.* 2d ed. Philadelphia: Saunders.

ENVIRONMENTALISM

The question of the relations between man in society and the geographical environment in which he lives is a very old one. Hippocrates (fifth century B.C.) wrote a treatise, "On Airs, Waters, and Places," which is generally regarded as the first formed expression of an environmentalist doctrine, although in view of the limited data available to him it is not appropriate to regard this as a statement sufficiently definitive for a serious critique of environmentalism, as Toynbee does (1934). Environmental considerations, especially climatic ones, play a considerable role in Montesquieu (1748) and perhaps reached their peak in the mid-nineteenth century, with Victor Cousin's "give me the [physical] map of a country . . . and I pledge myself to tell you, a priori, . . . what part that country will play in history, not by accident, but of necessity; not at one epoch, but in all epochs" (quoted in Febvre [1922] 1925, p. 10). Such extreme necessitarianism could hardly go unchallenged, and the first serious attack on geographical determinism is associated with the name of Paul Vidal de la Blache, who about the turn of the century became in effect the founder of an opposed doctrine known as "possibilism."

Possibilist doctrine is perhaps best, or at least most characteristically, summed up in a dictum of Lucien Febvre ([1922] 1925, p. 235): "There are nowhere necessities, but everywhere possibilities; and man, as master of the possibilities, is the judge of their use." A protest against crude predestinarianism was certainly in order; but Vidal's own qualifications are perhaps not always faithfully mirrored by his disciples, and Febvre's epigrammatic statements distracted attention from the real task of assessing the probabilities posed by the indisputable fact that the possibilities are distributed over the face of the earth with great inequality. This has recently been elegantly demonstrated by Lukermann (1965). It is also, perhaps, insufficiently noted that French possibilism was itself to some extent determined by a reaction to what we would now call an expansionist *Geopolitik*, expressed in Friedrich Ratzel's *Politische Geographie* of 1897 (Febvre 1922; cf. Spate 1957).

Be that as it may, the French school of geography, particularly noted for its meticulous and luminous style of regional description, was by that very technique often able, quite plausibly, to evade the issue, while more general works, such as those of Brunhes (1910) and Vallaux (1911), tempered possibilism by some allowance for the "influences," although not the "controls," exercised by the physical environment. In Germany, also, the broad strokes of Ratzelian anthropogeography were gradually succeeded by the more subtle chorographic analyses of *Landschaft*, and already in 1907 Alfred Hettner had arrived at a formulation not dissimilar from Febvre's (cf. Hartshorne 1939, p. 123).

In English-speaking countries the evolution was different. With the popularization, or (in both senses) vulgarization, of Ratzel's basically determinist outlook by Semple's *Influences of Geographic Environment* (1911), a somewhat naïve view of environmental "controls" became paramount among geographers in the United States and Britain, and this is what is generally known as "environmentalism." Another powerful influence was that of Ellsworth Huntington, whose numerous works attached a preponderating role to broad climatic factors. But the antienvironmentalist reaction, if much later than in France and Germany, was all the more complete. To some extent both the acceptance and the reaction stemmed from a rather uncritical empiricism, and this was especially notable in Britain. While in Britain possibilism in its purest form held undisputed sway in the 1930s, in the United States environmentalism was not so much negated as simply sidetracked. There were indeed plenty of overt rejections (Sauer 1925; Platt 1948—an extremist case), but on the whole the emphasis was on geography as simply the study of areal differentiation. This, of course, has clear analogues with the German development, and Hettner in particular was a strong influence, especially through the comprehensive methodologic study of Richard Hartshorne (1939). In Britain there was no comparable searching out of fundamentals, and indeed possibilism fitted well into a rather superficial and characteristically "English" empirical distrust of theory. The qualifications, subtle and unstressed but nonetheless significant, of the French school were ignored, and geography became in effect an entirely idiographic study in which it would be indecent to draw conclusions.

There were, of course, heretics: in the United States, Peattie (1940); in Britain, Markham (1942); but they had no effect.

The old view of geography as primarily a study of man–environment relations is now outmoded, and it is probable that a reasonable consensus would be found in favor of Hartshorne's formulation (1959, p. 21): *"accurate, orderly, and rational description and interpretation of the variable character of the earth surface."* However, relationships vary with the distribution of the phenomena that are in relation, and provided that we do not prejudge the issue by insisting that they are confined to those between man and natural environment or are one-way only, there is still ample scope for the examination of environmental problems. It is not, as Toynbee says (1961, p. 635), modern arrogance, but humility in face of data still inadequate, which refuses to take his refutation of Hippocrates as a final judgment. Moreover, while it may be true that external demands (as from history and sociology) for environmental assessments may represent a hangover from days when geographers were all too ready with crude causal explanations (and they got the habit from historians), it yet remains true that very often historical, sociological, economic, anthropological, political, and even religious and aesthetic phenomena cannot be properly comprehended without careful attention to environmental considerations.

Thus, the question is by no means so decisively closed, in an antienvironmentalist sense, as it seemed two or three decades ago; and as we shall see, it has taken on an entirely new aspect with the application of new techniques to geographical inquiry. While there have always been individual divergences from the general trend and, not infrequently, internal inconsistencies in the work of individuals, whether styling themselves environmentalists or possibilists, the question (as in many controversies) has been bedeviled by the assumption by both sides of a too rigid dichotomy. Whether tenable in strict logic or not, a more balanced probabilistic hypothesis seems warranted. This seems avoidable only if, as Hartshorne hints (1959, p. 55), we altogether abandon any distinction between man and nature; and this repudiation, dubiously metaphysical as it is, in practice seems impossible to maintain (Spate 1963a, pp. 255–259). In practice, except on an absurdly mechanistic plane, it is impossible to hold that all man's activities are absolutely conditioned or determined by his natural environment, even if we resort to intricate rationalizations as to its expression through social institutions. But it is absurd, also, to take

Febvre's dictum at face value and so slide into the position of ignoring the fact that possibilities vary greatly from milieu to milieu and, hence, in any given milieu are in fact limited. One may in a sense overcome this by saying that anything is possible anywhere if only one is willing to pay the price; but then, paying the price is itself a compelled adjustment to the environment. The flight from "controls" into a denial of "influences" takes us nowhere; or, if anywhere, into solipsism.

A reaction against possibilism became apparent around 1950. It avoided the crudity of the earlier concept of environmental control, as well as the dead end of possibilism, by stressing in any given situation the balance of probability, as, of course, both environmentalists and possibilists had often done in practice without admitting it. Some signs of *rapprochement* are found even in contributions avowedly committed to one side or the other (Tatham 1951; Taylor 1951). Perhaps the first really vigorous reassertion of geographic determinism was that of Martin (1952).

This newer and more cautious environmentalism gives more play to social factors than did the old. It recognizes that the geographical environment is only a part of the total environment and allows for the modifications of environment introduced by human activity; geographical influences act through society, and cultural tradition has a certain autonomous and reciprocal effect. Strands of causation may therefore be extremely subtle, and dogmatism is avoided. At the same time, it is firmly held that there is a larger irreducible minimum of influence by the physical environment than possibilism allows for. Although the impact of this will vary with the converse impact of human technological levels, nevertheless there will always be at least the adjustment by price and very often a much more direct adjustment.

The mandates of the geographical milieu are, however, often more negative and permissive than positively imperative. Thus, a total of 200 frost-free nights does not enforce the growing of cotton but does permit it, and fewer frost-free nights inhibit it. Further, while in a given situation the general cast of development may be very strongly influenced or conditioned by geographical factors, the detail may be dependent on quite other factors. This introduces a margin-of-error concept and may be illustrated by the difference between the general location of a frontier zone or a communications node (given the existence of a society with these features), which may be fully conditioned by geography, and the precise siting of a boundary within the frontier zone or of a city near the node, which

may depend on historical accident and which may, perhaps, in turn become a geographical factor in a new chain of relationships (Spate 1957).

This revival of methodological debate in geography owes much to the general increase in sophistication in the social sciences. This is perhaps more particularly true of the newer, quantitative approaches, but is by no means confined to them. It may fairly be said that the net result of the debate has been a material change in the general temper of geographical writing. If there has been no return to the compulsions of the older environmentalist school, as exemplified perhaps not so much in Ratzel himself as in Semple's rendition of him in the *Influences of Geographic Environment* (1911), it is equally true that pure possibilism, in the Febvre version, seems also to be dead. Stimulating as a protest, it was in the long run stultifying. Perhaps its most valuable residuum is that, indirectly at least, it helped to break away from the static concept of environment as a once-and-for-all given thing in itself, and it raised the question, Environment for what? This, however, seems to have no necessary connection with a possibilist view, and it may indeed have gone too far in the direction of a metaphysical identification of man with nature. The newer, probabilistic approach in regional writing is more likely to draw conclusions of general import than possibilism did, or at any rate to draw them more consciously and responsibly.

The debate has not been entirely internal to geography. One factor was the interest aroused by Toynbee's somewhat cavalier direct treatment of environmentalism and by the large if sometimes erratic importance he attached to it in such concepts as "the stimulus of New Ground" and the effects of a *Völkerwanderung* by sea (1934). Toynbee's analyses are of great interest, although vitiated by unfamiliarity with the main current of geographical writing and lack of a sense of scale; but both negatively and positively he contributed to putting environmentalism on the map again. The environmental component in such studies as Wittfogel's *Oriental Despotism* (1957) or, on a different scale, Sahlins' *Moala* (1962) is obvious.

The new trend has not, of course, gone unchallenged. As has been noted, it places some stress on probability, and the almost accidental introduction of the rather clumsy term "probabilism" (for which this writer must regretfully accept responsibility) has naturally attracted some dialectical criticism. Important contributions to the debate are those of Montefiore and Williams (1955) and the Sprouts (1956; 1957; 1965).

The former appear to approach the problem from

the standpoint of logical positivism. Their criticism of a too naïve acceptance of cause and effect as the only way of looking at scientific explanation is acute and vigorous, and they end with calling a plague on both houses: ". . . there can be no further point in their continuing a dispute which has virtually no bearing on their activities as working geographers." However, it may be suggested that this does not dispose of the issue. Belief does normally have some bearing on activity, and the dichotomy has been resurrected in a new (and, to some, alarming) fashion by quantifiers of the type of Warntz and Isard. The fundamentally important papers by the Sprouts include a very careful semantic analysis of hypotheses under the categories "environmental determinism," "mild environmentalism," "environmental possibilism," "environmental probabilism," and "cognitive behaviorism." They point out the logical residuum of environmentalist thinking implied in the possibilist approach and give at least a qualified blessing to probabilism; but it may be said that to a geographer their possibilism looks more like probabilism, and their probabilism seems in turn to hold a more predictive element than those who would not call themselves environmentalists *tout court* would allow.

The rise of applied and quantitative geography has in some respects given a new emphasis to environmental studies. One may instance Soviet geography, in which there is theoretically no problem: the laws of nature govern physical geography but are entirely separate from the social laws which govern man, and therefore there can be no unified geography (which is the essence of environmentalism) but only physical and economic geographies. Practice, and large-scale planning do, however, compel very meticulous attention to environmental factors, and even "influences" are not altogether banned, as they are in pure possibilism (Spate 1963b). In practically all fields involving the physical application of technology, whether under Soviet or Western auspices, very careful attention to problems of the physical environment is essential, if only as part of estimating costs.

It is often stated that the impact of modern technology has minimized, even annihilated, the significance of the environmental factor. However, on analysis it will frequently appear that the role of the physical milieu, if less "brutal" than it may be for a primitive-subsistence society, is pervasive in a more subtle way. It may be theoretically possible to grow anything almost anywhere, at a price; but the effect of price itself, in alliance with modern communications, may well be not to widen the range of a given crop but to narrow it to the area physically best suited for it: witness the formerly wide and presently restricted extent of flax growing in Europe and cotton growing in India. Large-scale technical installations may often depend for their economic efficiency on a nice balance of environmental considerations.

The basic assumptions of the new, quantifying schools have strong determinist, if not mechanistic, overtones, as suggested by the very title "social physics" (Stewart & Warntz 1958). At the least, they are strongly probabilistic, as is well demonstrated by Burton (1963). They aim at being nomothetic rather than idiographic, as were possibilism and much of the work of the chorographic approach standard in the Hartshorne era. They avowedly seek out laws with a capital *L*, as did Semple (Dodd & Pitts 1959). They work largely in models, and a high degree of prediction is regarded as the ideal. A culmination of this attitude is that of Isard (1956) in his desire for a "true" set of regions suitable for all purposes. There is often a tendency, as in the concept of population potential (Stewart & Warntz 1958), to abstract all but one or two factors, considered determinative; but these, also, are considered as some sort of summing up of the essence of the total environment.

It cannot, therefore, be assumed, as it was only a few years ago, that the ancient debate regarding the role of environmental factors is played out. That role changes with every change in technology, but it also must enforce technological changes, if the full and effective deployment of technical potential is to be made possible. Nor would the conquest of space necessarily mean the supersession of environment; there may be other than terrestrial environments for man, and these will compel special adjustments, social and technical. Meanwhile, the study of environment on this earth is far from complete; and while claims that it would provide an all-embracing rationale of society are justly dead, its significance must always be reckoned with in such studies as anthropology, archeology, sociology, and political science, to say nothing of history, and it forms an essential bridge between these social studies and the natural sciences.

O. H. K. SPATE

[*See the entries listed under* GEOGRAPHY. *See also* REGIONAL SCIENCE *and the biographies of* FEBVRE; HETTNER; HUNTINGTON; RATZEL; VIDAL DE LA BLACHE.]

BIBLIOGRAPHY

BRUNHES, JEAN (1910) 1924 *Human Geography.* London: Harrap. → First published in French. A fourth French edition was published in 1934 by Alcan.

BURTON, IAN 1963 The Quantitative Revolution and Theoretical Geography. *Canadian Geographer* 7, no. 4:151–162.

DODD, STUART C.; and PITTS, FORREST R. 1959 Proposals to Develop Statistical Laws of Human Geography. Pages 302–309 in International Geographical Union, Regional Conference in Japan, Tokyo and Nara, 1957, *Proceedings of IGU Regional Conference in Japan, 1957*. Tokyo: Science Council of Japan.

FEBVRE, LUCIEN (1922) 1925 *A Geographical Introduction to History*. New York: Knopf. → First published as *La terre et l'évolution humaine*.

HARTSHORNE, RICHARD (1939) 1964 *The Nature of Geography: A Critical Survey of Current Thought in the Light of the Past*. Lancaster, Pa.: Association of American Geographers.

HARTSHORNE, RICHARD 1959 *Perspective on the Nature of Geography*. Association of American Geographers, Monograph Series, No. 1. Chicago: Rand McNally. → A restatement and, in part, an extensive revision of Hartshorne 1939.

HIPPOCRATES On Airs, Waters, and Places. Pages 54–59 in Eric H. Warmington (editor), *Greek Geography*. London: Dent, 1934.

HUNTINGTON, ELLSWORTH (1915) 1924 *Civilization and Climate*. 3d ed., rev. New Haven: Yale Univ. Press.

HUNTINGTON, ELLSWORTH 1945 *Mainsprings of Civilization*. New York: Wiley; London: Chapman.

ISARD, WALTER 1956 *Location and Space-economy: A General Theory Relating to Industrial Location, Market Areas, Trade and Urban Structure*. Cambridge, Mass.: M.I.T. Press; New York: Wiley.

LUKERMANN, F. 1965 The "Calcul des Probabilités" and the École Française de Géographie. *Canadian Geographer* 9:128–137.

MARKHAM, SYDNEY F. (1942) 1947 *Climate and the Energy of Nations*. 2d American ed., rev. & enl. New York: Oxford Univ. Press.

MARTIN, A. F. 1952 The Necessity for Determinism. Institute of British Geographers, *Publications* 17:1–11.

MONTEFIORE, A. C.; and WILLIAMS, W. M. 1955 Determinism and Possibilism. *Geographical Studies* 2:1–11.

MONTESQUIEU, CHARLES (1748) 1962 *The Spirit of the Laws*. 2 vols. New York: Hafner. → First published in French. See especially Book 14, Chapters 12 and 13.

PEATTIE, RODERICK 1940 *Geography in Human Destiny*. New York: Stewart.

PLATT, ROBERT S. 1948 Environmentalism Versus Geography. *American Journal of Sociology* 53:351–358.

RATZEL, FRIEDRICH (1882–1891) 1921–1922 *Anthropogeographie*. 2 vols. Stuttgart (Germany): Engelhorn. → Volume 1: *Grundzüge der Anwendung der Erdkunde auf die Geschichte*, 4th ed. Volume 2: *Die geographische Verbreitung des Menschen*, 3d ed.

RATZEL, FRIEDRICH (1897) 1923 *Politische Geographie*. 3d ed. Edited by Eugen Oberhummer. Munich and Berlin: Oldenbourg.

SAHLINS, MARSHALL D. 1962 *Moala: Culture and Nature on a Fijian Island*. Ann Arbor: Univ. of Michigan Press.

SAUER, CARL O. (1925) 1963 The Morphology of Landscape. Pages 315–350 in Carl O. Sauer, *Land and Life: A Selection From the Writings of Carl Ortwin Sauer*. Berkeley: Univ. of California Press.

SEMPLE, ELLEN C. 1911 *Influences of Geographic Environment, on the Basis of Ratzel's System of Anthropo-geography*. New York: Holt.

SPATE, O. H. K. 1952 Toynbee and Huntington: A Study in Determinism. *Geographical Journal* 118:406–428. → Contains four pages of discussion.

SPATE, O. H. K. 1957 How Determined Is Possibilism? *Geographical Studies* 4:3–12.

SPATE, O. H. K. 1963a Islands and Men. Pages 253–264 in Francis R. Fosberg (editor), *Man's Place in the Island Ecosystem: A Symposium*. Honolulu: Bishop Museum Press.

SPATE, O. H. K. 1963b Theory and Practice in Soviet Geography. *Australian Geographical Studies* 1:18–30.

SPROUT, HAROLD H.; and SPROUT, MARGARET 1956 *Man–Milieu Relationship Hypotheses in the Context of International Politics*. Princeton Univ., Center of International Studies.

SPROUT, HAROLD H.; and SPROUT, MARGARET (1957) 1964 Environmental Factors in the Study of International Politics. Pages 61–80 in William A. D. Jackson (editor), *Politics and Geographic Relationships: Readings on the Nature of Political Geography*. Englewood Cliffs, N.J.: Prentice-Hall. → First published in Volume 1 of the *Journal of Conflict Resolution*.

SPROUT, HAROLD H.; and SPROUT, MARGARET 1965 *The Ecological Perspective on Human Affairs, With Special Reference to International Politics*. Princeton Univ. Press.

STEWART, JOHN Q.; and WARNTZ, WILLIAM 1958 Macrogeography and Social Science. *Geographical Review* 48:167–184.

TATHAM, GEORGE (1951) 1957 Environmentalism and Possibilism. Pages 128–162 in Thomas G. Taylor (editor), *Geography in the Twentieth Century: A Study of Growth, Fields, Techniques, Aims and Trends*. 3d ed., enl. New York: Philosophical Library.

TAYLOR, THOMAS GRIFFITH (1951) 1957 Introduction: The Scope of the Volume. Pages 3–27 in Thomas G. Taylor (editor), *Geography in the Twentieth Century: A Study of Growth, Fields, Techniques, Aims and Trends*. 3d ed., enl. New York: Philosophical Library.

TOYNBEE, ARNOLD J. 1934 *A Study of History*. Volume 2: The Geneses of Civilization. Oxford Univ. Press.

TOYNBEE, ARNOLD J. 1961 *A Study of History*. Volume 12: Reconsiderations. Oxford Univ. Press.

VALLAUX, CAMILLE 1911 *Géographie sociale: Le sol et l'état*. Paris: Doin.

VIDAL DE LA BLACHE, PAUL 1902 Les conditions géographiques des faits sociaux. *Annales de géographie* 11:13–23.

WITTFOGEL, KARL A. 1957 *Oriental Despotism: A Comparative Study of Total Power*. New Haven: Yale Univ. Press. → A paperback edition was published in 1963.

EPIDEMIOLOGY

Epidemiology is a branch of ecology that includes both the sum of what is known concerning the differential distribution of disease throughout a population and the techniques for collecting and analyzing data dealing with the prevalence and incidence of disease among different social groups. While originally limited to the study of epidemics or the spread of contagious disease, epidemiology today covers all types of disease, degenerative as well as communicable, and all population characteristics—social and psychological as well as biological and physical—that may help to describe or explain the prevalence of disease.

Methods of epidemiology. In the broad sense of the term, epidemiology deals with the occurrence and distribution of disease among different population groups, whether human, animal, or plant. The discovery or description of these differences has been called *descriptive*, or comparative, epidemiology, whereas the analysis of the causal factors and conditions producing these differences is usually referred to as *explanatory*, or analytic, epidemiology. As epidemiology becomes increasingly concerned with the study of the origin and course of disease, rather than solely with its distribution, this distinction is gradually disappearing.

Because of its emphasis upon the relationship between environmental factors and disease, epidemiology is properly regarded as a major branch of human ecology, or "the study of the relations between man and his environment, both as it affects him and as he affects it" (Rogers 1960, p. vii). In general, three main sets of interacting factors form the focus of epidemiological interest: the *host*, or human individual varying in genetic resistance, susceptibility, and degree of immunity to the disease; the *agent*, or carrier of the disease, including any adverse process, whether it be an excess, deficiency, or interference of a microbial, toxic, or metabolic factor, and varying according to infectivity, virulence, and pathogenesis; and the *environment*, or surrounding medium, social as well as physical, which affects both the susceptibility of the host, the virulence of the agent or disease process, and the quantity and quality of contact between host and agent (Paul 1950, pp. 53–54). These three sets of factors do not exist in any simple one-to-one relationship but maintain a complex, ever-changing balance. The occurrence of disease, especially mass disease, is the result of a multiplicity of causal factors, each of which contributes to, rather than accounts for, the appearance of the disease.

Epidemiological knowledge consists of the available facts and theories concerning the relationships between these three factors and the various disease entities and health conditions. *Social* epidemiology, as a subdivision of epidemiology, concentrates on the social, as opposed to the physical or biological, factors in the incidence and prevalence of disease. In the case of the chronic, degenerative diseases and the mental and behavioral disorders, both of which constitute primary targets of modern epidemiology, distinctions between host, agent, and environmental factors and between social and biological or physical factors are becoming increasingly difficult to maintain.

As a research method, epidemiology refers to "the application of scientific principles to investigations of conditions affecting groups in the population [*constructive* epidemiology]" (Clark [1953] 1958, p. 65). Predominantly, this involves the observation of the occurrence of disease under natural conditions in whole populations, as opposed to clinical or laboratory investigations. Epidemiological method, for the most part, uses the research techniques of the population survey to discover the relationship between the occurrence of disease and the presence of various biological, physical, and social factors. The kind of "proof" that it tries, for the most part, to obtain is statistical association between the presumed "causal" factor and the occurrence of the disease. Dawber and Kannel (1963, pp. 433–434) have spoken of "macroscopic" studies, which correlate rates of a disease with other statistical measures for an area or population group (ecological correlations), as contrasted with "microscopic" studies, which correlate personal characteristics with the presence or absence of disease within the individual (individual correlations). *Experimental* epidemiology, involving the controlled introduction of epidemic conditions into populations of experimental animals in the laboratory (Greenwood 1932), field experiments to test the efficacy of various immunizing agents, or various types of preventive measures (MacMahon et al. 1960, pp. 268–279), represents an attempt to apply the experimental method to epidemiological problems.

Historical background. The scope of epidemiology, which was "originally concerned only with epidemics, . . . was extended first to include infectious diseases which do not ordinarily occur in epidemic form, such as leprosy, syphilis, and tuberculosis, and later to noninfectious diseases" (Doull 1952, p. 76). The birth of epidemiology as we know it may be traced back to England in the late seventeenth century, when John Graunt in 1662 developed the first mortality tables. However, it was not until the mid-nineteenth century that men like Johann Süssmilch and Adolphe Quetelet utilized these statistics to help identify etiological factors in disease. The major emphasis of epidemiology under such eminent pioneers as John Snow (cholera), Peter Panum (measles), William Budd (typhoid), and Kenneth Maxcy (endemic typhus) was upon the discovery of host, agent, and environmental factors associated with the spread of these highly contagious diseases, or what has been called "the mass-phenomena of infectious diseases" (see Frost 1910–1939).

The dramatic conquest of the infectious diseases in the present century, together with the growing importance of the chronic, degenerative diseases, soon made it apparent that epidemiology could no longer be restricted to epidemics. As a matter of fact, epidemiological studies of nutritional (James Lind on scurvy) and occupational (Henry B. Baker on lead colic) diseases had already demonstrated the applicability of epidemiological method to noninfectious diseases. The use of statistical associations based upon population surveys became one of the foremost methods for studying the occurrence of cancer, cardiovascular disease, and mental illness and for the difficult task of identifying specific etiological agents. Today, the value of epidemiological research for the study of all diseases is well established (James & Greenberg 1957).

Uses of epidemiology. As a standard tool of medical investigation, epidemiology has been brought to bear upon almost all aspects of the prevention and treatment of disease. Morris (1957) has listed seven fundamental applications: the determination of individual risks on the basis of morbidity tables and cohort analysis—for example, the chances of a forty-year-old male getting cancer; the securing of data on subclinical and undetected cases; the identification of syndromes or clusters of symptoms; the determination of historical trends of disease; the diagnosis of community health needs and resources; program planning, operation, and evaluation; and the search for causes of disease. Similar uses are described by Breslow (1957) for a large-scale epidemiological survey of chronic diseases in California. These include a demographic description of the changing population composition, a broad picture of the state of health and illness in the community, more extensive knowledge about disease prevalence, data on the utilization of health services, case rosters for follow-up investigations, and data on etiological factors. Thus, epidemiology provides a large portion of the scientific base for public health practice.

The diversity of these applications would suggest that epidemiological surveys are often combined, or confused, with general community health surveys. A survey that asks questions about health conditions and medical care of a population sample does not automatically become an epidemiological study. From a more rigorous point of view, the major contribution of epidemiological research should be in the development and testing of hypotheses concerning specific factors that may influence the distribution of some particular disease in a defined population. On the basis of existing knowledge, theory, or observation, the epidemiologist identifies subgroups of the population believed to have varying incidence rates of the disease being investigated. He then hypothesizes certain etiological factors related to the disease and also believed to differ among the subgroups being studied. By means of a field survey or the analysis of existing data, he then tests the direction and degree of association between the occurrence of the disease and the presence or absence of the group characteristic hypothesized as the etiological factor.

Epidemiology and social science. Epidemiology has theoretical and methodological ties to the social sciences. Both the epidemiologist and the social scientist are concerned with demography and ecology—the relationship of man to his environment (Fleck & Ianni 1958). When the environment includes sociocultural factors as possible "causes" of disease, either indirectly (as in the case of poverty leading to malnutrition or unsanitary living conditions) or directly (as in the case of emotional disturbance leading to mental disease or addictive disorders, such as drinking and alcoholism or drug addiction), then all three basic components of epidemiology—host, agent, and environment—take on important social dimensions (King 1963). Epidemiology is becoming increasingly concerned with "the social component of environment . . . that part which results from the association of man with his fellow man . . . the attainments, beliefs, customs, traditions, and like features of a people" (Gordon 1952, pp. 124–125). In the current era of chronic, degenerative diseases, in which an individual's whole way of life may become more important than any single infectious agent in the disease process, social factors become a primary target for epidemiological investigation.

Methodologically, both the epidemiologist and the social scientist rely heavily upon the population survey and field experiment. Similar problems of research design confront both groups, while technical considerations such as sampling, questionnaire construction, interviewing, and multivariate analysis are objects of mutual methodological interest (Wardwell & Bahnson 1964).

Recent research. All major diseases today are the subject of epidemiological research, and almost all of these include, at the minimum, such social groupings as sex, age, marital status and family composition, occupation, socioeconomic status, religion, and race. In addition, many studies are specifically aimed at the investigation of social factors, such as social stress, as possible etiological agents in the occurrence of the disease. Comprehensive reviews have been prepared by Glock and Lennard (1956) on hypertension, Graham (1960) on cancer, Mishler and Scotch (1963) on schizophrenia, Dawber and others (1959) on heart disease, Jaco (1960) and Hoch and Zubin (1961) on mental disease, Suchman and Scherzer (1960) on childhood accidents, King and Cobb (1958) on rheumatoid arthritis, among others. The state of knowledge in this field is advancing rapidly, and the findings of epidemiological surveys appear regularly in such periodicals as the *American Journal of Public Health* and the *Journal of Chronic Diseases*.

In general, these studies reveal a large number of significant differences in the occurrence of disease among different subgroups of the population (Pemberton 1963). For example, coronary artery disease is found to vary according to such sociocultural variables as occupation, economic status, race, and rural–urban residence. Cancer of the uterine cervix occurs much less frequently among Jewish women; men are more likely to incur cardiovascular disease; and mental illness is found more often among the lower socioeconomic groups. On a more psychological level, insecurity and stress tend to be associated with a higher incidence of mental illness, alcoholism, narcotics addiction, heart disease, arthritis, and a host of psychosomatic conditions (Leighton 1959). Perhaps the most famous of these epidemiological correlations deals with the association between smoking behavior and lung cancer (Dorn & Cutler 1958).

Some problems of research design. The major conceptual and methodological problems in epidemiological research stem from its dependence, by and large, upon associational evidence. The basic research design of epidemiological method consists in the comparison of two groups, each with varying rates of a disease, with respect to other characteristics hypothesized as explanatory of these varying disease rates. This is essentially an ex post facto form of survey research and one that may undertake *demographic* studies of existing vital statistics or several other types of study using data specially gathered for the purpose. These can be classified as being either *retrospective* studies, which secure data on different group characteristics hypothesized as etiological factors from at least two groups with varying rates of the disease being investigated, or *prospective* studies, which follow up groups of individuals with and without the hypothesized etiological characteristics in order to determine the differential development of the disease.

In all three study designs, the objective is the determination of a series of statistical associations from which etiological inferences may be drawn. These three types of design offer progressively more rigorous and plausible evidence of causality. The demographic method, relying as it does on ecological correlations, is the weakest, since variations in rates of occurrence between phenomena do not necessarily mean that these phenomena are related (Clausen & Kohn 1954); it is possible to have high ecological associations with little or no individual correlation. Retrospective studies do provide individual correlations, but there is often no way of knowing which of the two factors in an observed correlation came first. Prospective studies using a longitudinal study of cohorts are strongest, since these enable one to define the population at risk *in advance* of the development of disease and then to check one's predictions over time [*see* COHORT ANALYSIS].

Smoking and lung cancer. The association between smoking and lung cancer provides an excellent example of the progression from demographic to retrospective and finally to prospective studies. The initial association was suggested by demographic comparisons showing a much higher incidence of lung cancer among men than women. Retrospective studies revealed a correlation between smoking histories and the occurrence of lung cancer. Finally, intensive prospective studies following up smokers and nonsmokers showed a higher development of lung cancer among the former. The continuing controversy today, however, demonstrates the further need and demand to prove, through experimental rather than epidemiological studies, that smoking can "cause" cancer.

Validity of epidemiological method. The inability of the epidemiologist to "randomize" his experimental and control groups and to alter deliberately the characteristics of his experimental group constitutes an intrinsic conceptual and methodological shortcoming that requires a continuing close working relationship between epidemiological and experimental research. Certain basic prerequisites must be satisfied if epidemiological method is to produce reliable and valid associations. First, the representativeness and generalizability of the sample from whom data are obtained must be ascertainable. This sample should include not only persons who are known to have the disease but also who are free of the disease.

The definition of what is a "normal," or disease-free, control group presents a particularly difficult problem for epidemiological study of the chronic diseases, since these may not become apparent until a fairly late stage. Second, the disease being studied must be defined in such a way that it can be reliably and validly diagnosed using field techniques. Errors due to *false positives* (the proportion of individuals classified as diseased among those truly not diseased) and *false negatives* (the proportion classified as not diseased among those truly diseased) can often lead to spurious associations (Rubin et al. 1956). Third, the hypothesized etiological factors must be similarly capable of objective definition and measurement. These are difficult conditions to meet, especially in relation to the chronic diseases, which often lack both clear-cut diagnostic criteria and well-developed theories of etiology and process (Pollack & Krueger 1960).

Future developments. Epidemiological method is bound to increase in importance as the search for etiological factors in the chronic diseases forces the medical researcher to supplement his laboratory experiments with field studies, both as source and proof of his hypotheses. The multiple nature of etiological factors (many, if not most, of which cannot be reproduced or controlled in the laboratory) will require greater reliance upon population surveys and field trials. Probabilities of disease will replace certainties, and associated conditions rather than specific causes will dominate the picture. Prominent among these conditions will be the cultural, social, and psychological forces that determine how man lives and which in later years influence the degenerative processes. Today we deal with these social factors on the most elementary level, that of descriptive group memberships. Tomorrow we may hope to be able to determine the dynamic factors underlying these group memberships and to develop and test specific hypotheses of how and why social factors relate to the origin and course of disease.

EDWARD A. SUCHMAN

[*See also* DRINKING AND ALCOHOLISM; DRUGS, *article on* DRUG ADDICTION: SOCIAL ASPECTS; ECOLOGY, *article on* HUMAN ECOLOGY; PUBLIC HEALTH; VITAL STATISTICS; *and the biographies of* GRAUNT *and* QUETELET.]

BIBLIOGRAPHY

BRESLOW, LESTER 1957 Uses and Limitations of the California Health Survey for Studying the Epidemiology of Chronic Disease. *American Journal of Public Health* 47:168–172.

CLARK, E. GURNEY (1953) 1958 An Epidemiological Approach to Preventive Medicine. Chapter 3 in Hugh R. Leavell et al., *Preventive Medicine for the Doctor in His Community: An Epidemiologic Approach.* 2d ed. New York: McGraw-Hill.

CLAUSEN, JOHN A.; and KOHN, MELVIN L. 1954 The Ecological Approach in Social Psychiatry. *American Journal of Sociology* 60:140–151.

DAWBER, THOMAS R.; and KANNEL, WILLIAM B. 1963 Coronary Heart Disease as an Epidemiology Entity. *American Journal of Public Health* 53:433–437.

DAWBER, THOMAS R. et al. 1959 Some Factors Associated With the Development of Coronary Heart Disease. *American Journal of Public Health* 49:1349–1356.

DORN, HAROLD F.; and CUTLER, SIDNEY J. 1958 *Morbidity From Cancer in the United States.* U.S. Public Health Service Publication No. 590; Public Health Monograph No. 56. Washington: Public Health Service.

DOULL, JAMES A. 1952 The Bacteriological Era (1876–1920). Pages 74–113 in Franklin H. Top (editor), *The History of American Epidemiology.* St. Louis, Mo.: Mosby.

FLECK, ANDREW C.; and IANNI, FRANCIS A. J. 1958 Epidemiology and Anthropology: Some Suggested Affinities in Theory and Method. *Human Organization* 16, no. 4:38–40.

FROST, WADE HAMPTON (1910–1939) 1941 *Papers of Wade Hampton Frost, M.D.: A Contribution to Epidemiological Method.* Edited by Kenneth F. Maxcy. New York: Commonwealth Fund; Oxford Univ. Press. → These essays provide a brilliant description of the transition to modern epidemiology.

GLOCK, CHARLES Y.; and LENNARD, HENRY L. 1956 Studies in Hypertension. *Journal of Chronic Diseases* 5:178–196.

GORDON, JOHN E. 1952 The Twentieth Century—Yesterday, Today, and Tomorrow (1920–   ). Pages 114–167 in Franklin H. Top (editor), *The History of American Epidemiology.* St. Louis, Mo.: Mosby. → Contains a comprehensive bibliography and discussion of modern developments.

GRAHAM, SAXON 1960 Social Factors in the Epidemiology of Cancer at Various Sites. New York Academy of Sciences, *Annals* 84:807–815.

GREENWOOD, MAJOR 1932 *Epidemiology, Historical and Experimental.* Baltimore: Johns Hopkins Press; Oxford Univ. Press.

HOCH, PAUL H.; and ZUBIN, JOSEPH (editors) 1961 *Comparative Epidemiology of the Mental Disorders.* Proceedings of the 49th annual meeting of the American Psychopathological Association, February 1959. New York: Grune & Stratton.

JACO, E. GARTLY 1960 *The Social Epidemiology of Mental Disorders: A Psychiatric Survey of Texas.* New York: Russell Sage Foundation.

JAMES, GEORGE; and GREENBERG, MORRIS 1957 The Medical Officer's Bookshelf on Epidemiology and Evaluation. Part 1: Epidemiology. *American Journal of Public Health* 47:401–408. → Contains a brief review and bibliography on the epidemiology of various diseases.

KING, STANLEY H. 1963 Social Psychological Factors in Illness. Pages 99–121 in Howard E. Freeman et al. (editors), *Handbook of Medical Sociology.* Englewood Cliffs, N.J.: Prentice-Hall.

KING, STANLEY H.; and COBB, SIDNEY 1958 Psychosocial Factors in the Epidemiology of Rheumatoid Arthritis. *Journal of Chronic Diseases* 7:466–475.

LEIGHTON, ALEXANDER H. 1959 *My Name Is Legion: Foundations for a Theory of Man in Relation to Culture*. The Stirling County Study of Psychiatric Disorder and Sociocultural Environment, Vol. 1. New York: Basic Books. → Contains a theoretical discussion of social stress as a factor in mental illness.

MACMAHON, BRIAN; PUGH, THOMAS F.; and IPSEN, JOHANNES 1960 *Epidemiologic Methods*. Boston: Little. → Contains a critical review of current concepts and methods.

MISHLER, ELLIOT G.; and SCOTCH, NORMAN A. 1963 Sociocultural Factors in the Epidemiology of Schizophrenia. *Psychiatry* 26:315–351.

MORRIS, JEREMY N. 1957 *Uses of Epidemiology*. Baltimore: Williams & Wilkins; Edinburgh: Livingstone.

PAUL, JOHN R. 1950 Epidemiology. Pages 52–62 in David E. Green and W. Eugene Knox (editors), *Research in Medical Science*. New York: Macmillan.

PEMBERTON, JOHN (editor) 1963 *Epidemiology: Reports on Research and Teaching, 1962*. Oxford Univ. Press.

POLLACK, HERBERT; and KRUEGER, DEAN E. (editors) 1960 Epidemiology of Cardiovascular Diseases: Methodology. *American Journal of Public Health* 50 (Supplement): 1–124.

ROGERS, EDWARD S. 1960 *Human Ecology and Health: An Introduction for Administrators*. New York: Macmillan.

RUBIN, THEODORE; ROSENBAUM, JOSEPH; and COBB, SIDNEY 1956 The Use of Interview Data for the Detection of Associations in Field Studies. *Journal of Chronic Diseases* 4:253–266.

SUCHMAN, EDWARD A.; and SCHERZER, ALFRED L. 1960 Current Research in Childhood Accidents. Part 1 in Association for the Aid of Crippled Children, *Two Reviews of Accident Research*. New York: The Association.

U.S. SURGEON GENERAL'S ADVISORY COMMITTEE ON SMOKING AND HEALTH 1964 *Smoking and Health*. U.S. Department of Health, Education and Welfare, Public Health Service Publication No. 1103. Washington: Government Printing Office. → Contains a thorough analysis of the epidemiological evidence on smoking as a cause of cancer and other diseases.

WARDWELL, WALTER I.; and BAHNSON, CLAUS B. 1964 Problems Encountered in Behavioral Science Research in Epidemiological Studies. *American Journal of Public Health* 54:972–981.

EQUALITY

I

THE CONCEPT OF EQUALITY

In the context of the social sciences, the concept of equality refers sometimes to certain *properties* which men are held to have in common but more often to certain *treatments* which men either receive or ought to receive. Traditional characterizations of kinds of treatment as either egalitarian or inegalitarian often turn out to be disguised value judgments or empty statements. It is possible, however, to find descriptive criteria apt to capture the egalitarian and inegalitarian features of principles which have been advocated at different times.

Equality of characteristics. Equality must be construed here in the sense of similarity, that is, of agreement in certain properties. That men are equal means that men share some qualities; these must be specified. Men are evidently unequal in many characteristics. There are natural differences (sex, color, character traits, natural endowments, etc.) and institutional variations (citizenship, religion, social rank, etc.). Other properties are common to all but in varying amounts (age, strength, intelligence, possessions, power, etc.). To claim that all men are equal in such respects can only mean that the resemblances are in some way more significant than the differences, as when Hobbes states that "nature hath made men so equal, in the faculties of the body and mind" that the weakest can kill the strongest and no one can outwit the other.

Men are sometimes held to be equal in the sense of having a common "human nature"—a tautological assertion, unless it is specified that all are naturally good or sinful or that they have the same basic motives (say, self-interest), or common basic needs, or similar capacities to feel pleasure and pain, or the same ability to act deliberately and to choose rationally.

Equality of treatment. Moralists ever since the Stoics have claimed that men, in spite of differences of character or intelligence, are of equal dignity, worth, or desert. Statements of this kind are to be interpreted in a normative sense, to the effect that all men are *entitled* to be *treated* equally. The same applies to the allegation that all men have the same moral or natural rights. To say that I have a moral right implies that others should let me exercise it (whereas to have a legal right means that it is conferred by positive law). Thus, Locke interprets his own statement "that men by nature are equal" as referring, not to "all sorts of equality," since men differ as to "age or virtue," but to "the equal right that every man hath to his natural freedom"; this means that men "should also be equal amongst another," that is, that they *should* be given the corresponding legal rights. Analogously, to claim that those of one nation or race or class are "superior" to all others is to hold that they *ought* to receive preferential treatment.

Whether individuals or groups are, in fact, treated equally or unequally by others depends on the way in which benefits or burdens are allotted to them. These may be legal rights (e.g., to own property, to vote) and legal duties (e.g., to respect the rights of others); material benefits (e.g., wages, unemployment benefits, social services) and liabilities (e.g., punishment, taxation, military service); and opportunities (e.g., to hold certain positions or offices).

Factual statements about equality may be about equality of either characteristics or treatment. Normative statements about equality are always concerned with treatment but may contain references to characteristics as well, as when it is being argued that men *should* be treated equally because they *are* equal in certain characteristics. References to both characteristics and treatment are also contained in general rules of the type: all persons having a certain characteristic are to be allotted a certain benefit or burden (in such and such an amount). This leads to the question of how to determine whether an actual or proposed kind of treatment is egalitarian.

Traditional criteria of egalitarianism

(1) *Impartiality.* Equal treatment means, first of all, the impartial allocation of some benefit or burden by one actor to another, say, by a judge to a claimant. Equality before the law thus means impartial application of the law. Allocations are impartial or partial only by reference to a rule of allocation. With respect to a specified legal or moral rule, a person is treated impartially by another provided his allotment is determined exclusively by the rule itself and not by other factors, such as the latter person's like or dislike of the former. Partiality (allotments made in violation of some given rule) would be the only kind of inegalitarian treatment in this sense. Since any rule—for example, one restricting suffrage to adult citizens or to white citizens—can be applied impartially or partially, we must determine the conditions under which rules themselves are to be considered egalitarian.

(2) *Equal shares to all.* According to the utilitarians, "everybody [is] to count for one, nobody for more than one" in the allocation of benefits and burdens—not of every conceivable kind, of course, but of certain specified types. Similarly, "equality" to the French revolutionaries meant that the same basic legal rights should be granted by every government to all its citizens. Rules which allocate a benefit or burden in equal amounts to everyone are undoubtedly egalitarian.

(3) *Equal shares to equals.* Most rules of allocation grant equal shares of some kind, not to all generally but to all who are equal with respect to some property; for example, all adult citizens have the right to vote; whoever commits a certain

crime shall suffer a certain punishment; persons within the same income bracket are liable to the same income tax. According to the previous criterion, such rules would not be egalitarian. The concept of egalitarianism has therefore been enlarged to cover rules which allot "equal shares to equals"; and a rule is considered inegalitarian by Aristotle "when either equals are awarded unequal shares or unequals equal shares."

Now, every rule may be considered egalitarian in this sense; for a rule stipulates that all, or else that only those who are equal in a specified respect, receive the same specified treatment. Universal suffrage means that the right to vote is given to all adult citizens but not to minors and aliens. A graduated income tax treats any two taxpayers within the same bracket equally and any two within different brackets unequally. To treat all whites alike and all Negroes alike but persons of different color differently is to practice racial discrimination. Every conceivable rule treats equals (in some specified respect) equally and unequals unequally.

(4) *Proportional equality.* To narrow down the criterion again, unequal allotments have been held, ever since Aristotle, to be egalitarian if and only if they satisfy the requirement of "proportional equality." A rule is generally considered to satisfy this requirement if it provides that the amount of benefit or burden is a monotonically increasing function of the specified characteristic; that is, the more of the characteristic, the more benefit or burden. And any two persons are treated "in proportion to their inequality," provided the difference in the amount allotted to each is similarly correlated to the degree in which they differ in the characteristic specified by the rule. But again, any rule which allots "equal shares to equals" implicitly not only allots "unequal shares to unequals" but also allots them "in proportion to their inequality." Both rules—"to each according to his need" and "to each according to his height"—assign different shares to different persons in the proportion in which they differ as to need or as to height. A flat rate and a graduated income tax both fulfill the requirement of proportional equality.

(5) *Unequal shares corresponding to relevant differences.* Inequality in allotment has been held to be egalitarian provided it is based on *relevant* differences in personal characteristics. Thus, age and citizenship are relevant to voting rights but not so sex or race or wealth; it is therefore held egalitarian to limit the franchise to adult citizens but inegalitarian to restrict it to men or whites or poll-tax payers. Wealth *is* relevant to taxation; hence, a graduated income tax is viewed as egali-

tarian but not a sales tax, which disregards this relevant criterion by taxing poor and wealthy buyers at the same rate.

Judgments to the effect that characteristic x is relevant to treatment y are valuational, not factual. That color is not relevant to voting but age is means that it is unjust to base the franchise on color and just to require a minimum age. Equality becomes tantamount to distributive justice: "The unjust is unequal, the just is equal" (Aristotle); that is, it is unjust to make unequal awards to those who share a relevant characteristic. Or, in a recent formulation: to be egalitarian, "a difference of treatment requires *justification* in terms of *relevant* and sufficient differences between the claimants" (Ginsberg 1965, p. 79; italics added). The same purely normative criterion underlies the idea of "equality of consideration," that is, "that none shall be held to have a claim to better treatment than another, in advance of good grounds being produced" (Benn & Peters 1959, p. 110; italics removed). This principle is not only purely valuational but also purely procedural—compatible with whatever substantive discriminatory rule may be established on "good grounds."

(6) *To each according to his desert.* According to Aristotle, a person's desert is the only characteristic relevant to allocations. To be both egalitarian and just, these must therefore be based on proportionate equality on the basis of desert. The problem is here merely pushed a step further back, since judgments of someone's relative desert are again valuational. Unless there are objective criteria for relevant or just or good grounds for differential treatment or for a person's desert or worth, it is impossible to refute the racist's counterclaim that color *is* relevant to franchise or that whites are of superior worth. (His claim that color is relevant to intelligence would be an empirical one and could be refuted on empirical grounds, but it is intelligence rather than color or desert which he proposes in this case as a relevant criterion for granting franchise.) According to criteria 3 and 4, *every* rule of allocation is egalitarian, and *any* rule may be considered just and hence egalitarian according to criteria 5 and 6.

Operational criteria of egalitarianism

(1) *Egalitarian rules of allocation and distribution.* Even advocates of racial discrimination are likely to consider it egalitarian to give preferential treatment to the needy regardless of race but inegalitarian to give it to whites regardless of need. The reason seems to be that the first policy aims at the equal satisfaction of everybody's basic needs, while the second is incompatible with that principle. This points to a distinction which must be made between (1) rules which determine how some benefit or burden is to be *allocated* among persons, that is, how much of it is to be *given* to each or to be *taken* from each, and (2) rules concerning the *distribution* of a benefit or burden which is to result from some allocation, that is, how much each person is to *have* at the end.

Rules of allocation and rules of distribution may be (*a*) egalitarian or (*b*) inegalitarian. Rules of allocation are egalitarian if they allocate the same kind or amount of benefit or burden to all. Similarly, rules of distribution are egalitarian if they stipulate that all are to have equal shares. Here are some examples: (*1a*) universal suffrage, universal head tax; (*1b*) suffrage only for whites, graduated income tax; (*2a*) political equality, equality of possessions; (*2b*) political inequality, inequality of possessions.

(2) *Inegalitarian allocations compatible with egalitarian distributions.* Egalitarian allocations often lead to egalitarian distributions and inegalitarian allocations to inegalitarian distributions. Universal suffrage promotes political equality, not so suffrage for whites only. But an egalitarian distribution does not necessarily require an egalitarian allocation. For example, to bring about an equal *distribution* of the holdings of A, who has 8 units, and of B, who has 2, it is necessary to take, say, 3 from A and to give 3 to B. But taking 1 from A and 1 from B would leave the previous inequality of their distribution unaffected. Egalitarian allocations may thus result in inegalitarian distributions. With respect to an egalitarian rule of distribution, a rule of allocation may be said to be egalitarian if its application is a means to, or a consequence of, the former's implementation and inegalitarian if it is incompatible with the former. A rule of allocation which is intrinsically inegalitarian may thus be egalitarian with respect to some egalitarian rule of distribution, while an intrinsically egalitarian rule of allocation may be inegalitarian in this respect. With respect to equality (or rather, to reducing inequality) of wealth, a graduated income tax is egalitarian and a head tax is inegalitarian.

(3) *Degrees of egalitarianism.* A rule of allocation or of distribution may be considered more egalitarian (or less inegalitarian) than another if it insures "that a larger number of persons (or classes of persons) shall receive similar treatment in specified circumstances" (Berlin [1955–1956] 1961, p. 135)—or rather, similar preferential treat-

ment. Universal suffrage which excludes only minors and aliens is more egalitarian than suffrage which excludes also Negroes and may therefore be considered fully egalitarian for practical purposes. Disenfranchising women is more inegalitarian than disenfranchising Negroes if the latter constitute a small segment of the population but less inegalitarian if Negroes form a large percentage.

On the basis of these purely descriptive criteria, persons with divergent value commitments can agree (or disagree) on an empirical level whether a given rule of allocation or of distribution is egalitarian and to what degree, and whether a rule of allocation is egalitarian with respect to some egalitarian rule of distribution. The resulting classification corresponds in a satisfactory way to our everyday distinctions between egalitarian and inegalitarian treatment.

Instances of egalitarianism

Equality of opportunity. Equal treatment of all in every respect was advocated by some nineteenth-century anarchists: equality of occupation (for example, intellectuals would participate in manual work), of consumption (all would eat and even dress alike), and especially of education would ultimately wipe out existing inequalities of talent and capacity. Most egalitarians, however, consider such an ultimate goal neither desirable nor possible. They realize that in every society individuals are bound to have varying degrees of ability and to hold positions that yield varying degrees of status if not of remuneration. How to match unequal individuals with unequal positions has been their central concern and equality of opportunity their principal answer. This rule deals with the distribution of access to positions in society, not with the allocation of the positions themselves. Opportunities to occupy all positions, including the most attractive ones, are to be distributed in an egalitarian way to all on a competitive basis, regardless of such differences as social status or economic resources and regardless even of differences of ability, since "the least able and the most able are given an equal start in the race for success" (Pennock 1950, p. 81). If everyone has an equal start, then the position he will occupy at the end will, in theory at least, depend exclusively on how far and how fast he runs, that is, on his own resourcefulness (but also on his luck). As the French Declaration of the Rights of Man proclaimed: all citizens "are equally eligible to all honors, places and employments, according to their different

abilities, without any other distinction than that of their virtues and talents."

Legal equality. "Equality of opportunity, in the broad sense of the career open to personality, is and has been the inclusive goal within which the partial goals of the special equalities have their significance" (Hofstadter 1956, p. 137). Equality of legal rights has been, historically, the first of these special equalities. Classical liberalism held that the equal distribution of opportunities required merely the equal allocation of the basic rights of "life, liberty, and property." If legal privileges are abolished and legal rights protected, no obstacle will stand in the way of anyone's pursuit of happiness.

Equal satisfaction of basic needs. Increasing industrialization brought about an increasing awareness that equality of opportunity cannot be achieved by the "majestic equality of the law which forbids rich and poor alike to steal bread and to sleep under bridges" (Anatole France). Equality of opportunity does presuppose the equal allotment of certain rights, but it also requires the application of another egalitarian rule of distribution, namely, equality of the satisfaction of certain basic needs, which in turn calls for an inegalitarian rule of allotment: privileges for the economically underprivileged. Indeed, those who lack the basic physical or educational necessities do not have the same opportunities to reach the higher positions as do the better endowed. To bring the former up to the general starting line, government must compensate them for these initial disadvantages by means of social legislation and social services such as minimum wages, tax exemptions, unemployment benefits, free public schools, and scholarships.

Equality of opportunity is not simply a matter of legal equality. Its existence depends, not merely on the absence of disabilities, but on the presence of abilities. It obtains in so far as, and only in so far as, each member of a community, whatever his birth, or occupation, or social position, possesses in fact, and not merely in form, equal chances of using to the full his natural endowments of physique, of character, and of intelligence. (Tawney [1931] 1965, pp. 103–104)

To condemn such inegalitarian allotment is to oppose equality of opportunity. Herbert Spencer agreed with his neoliberal opponents that "insuring to each the right to pursue within the specified limits the objects of his desires without let or hindrance is quite a separate thing from insuring him satisfaction" but insisted that the state should "confine itself to guaranteeing the rights of its members" and not "assume the role of Relievergeneral to the poor." Such advocacy of mere equality of rights had by that time become an inegalitarian policy which deprived the poor of equality of opportunity and promoted the "survival" of the wealthy at their expense.

Privileges for nobles or property owners and disabilities imposed on a particular sex, religion, or race are inegalitarian, not only in themselves but probably also with respect to any conceivable egalitarian rule of distribution. But privileges for religious, racial, or ethnic minorities may constitute an egalitarian policy when these are considered as constituting economically or socially disadvantaged groups.

Economic equality. Equality of the right of property is compatible with extreme inequality in the distribution of property. Equality of opportunity does not imply equalization of wealth either, certainly not at the end of the "race for success." Nevertheless, to give all an equal start, some must be lifted up and others moved down. The equal satisfaction of basic needs as a precondition for equality of opportunity does require economic equality, that is, a reduction of extreme inequalities in the distribution of commodities. "By equality, we should understand, not that the degree of power and riches be absolutely identical for everybody, but that . . . no citizen be wealthy enough to buy another, and none poor enough to be forced to sell himself" (Rousseau). "The socialist seeks a distribution of rewards, status, and privileges egalitarian enough to . . . equalize opportunities" (Crosland [1956] 1957, p. 113). With respect to this goal, unequal taxation of unequal incomes is egalitarian.

Common ownership of the means of production. Marx, too, realized that "one man is superior to another physically and mentally" and interpreted equality—at least in the first phase of communism —as the opportunity for each to occupy the position which corresponds to his ability. Contrary to the neoliberals and socialists, Marx believed that this goal could not be reached through a redistribution of the means of consumption (the demand for fair distribution as well as for equal rights was to him "obsolete verbal rubbish") but only through the abolition of private control of the means of production. Their "common ownership" would eliminate the possibility of exploitation and class struggle; and "with the abolition of class distinctions, all social and political inequality arising from them would automatically disappear by itself."

To each according to his merit. If there is equality of opportunity and if higher positions bring higher salaries, both will go to those of greater merit or ability. The result would ideally be, "not an aristocracy of birth, not a plutocracy of wealth, but a true meritocracy of talent" (Young [1958] 1959, p. 19). Unequal allocation of rewards, correlated with inequality of ability, is a consequence of equal distribution of opportunities. With respect to equality of opportunity, rewards according to merit in the sense of ability is therefore an egalitarian principle.

This is not so with rewards according to merit in the sense of desert. Plato and Aristotle held not only that people's relative desert or moral worth can be objectively ascertained but also that "there are *innate* differences which fit them for different occupations" (Plato), that "a distinction is already marked, immediately *at birth* between those who are intended for being ruled and those who are intended to rule" (Aristotle), and between those who are "by nature" either slaves or free. Each is to be assigned the function corresponding to his pre-established desert. Aristotle's principle of "proportional equality according to desert" is really inegalitarian, not only intrinsically but also with respect to equality of opportunity and probably every other egalitarian rule of distribution. For the same reason, all rigidly stratified societies are inegalitarian, from feudalism to the Indian caste system.

To each according to his need. Equality of opportunity does not, however, necessarily entail that rewards (as well as positions) go to each according to his ability. Marxists believe that the first stage of communism, in which means of consumption are distributed according to the work performed, will inevitably evolve, in Lenin's words, "from formal equality to real equality, i.e., to realizing the rule: 'From each according to his ability, to each according to his need.'" Positions would still be correlated to ability, but everyone (so Marxists believe) will work spontaneously to the best of his ability even without incentives, and compensations will differ according to need, regardless of the type of work. With respect to equality of opportunity to occupy various positions, this would be another egalitarian rule of allocation.

Political equality. While some political thinkers have advocated the equalization of political power through direct democracy or predicted the abolition of political power through the withering away of the state, it is generally assumed that political power is ubiquitous and always unevenly distributed and that political equality can only mean equality of opportunity to participate in the political process. Political equality has therefore been associated with the democratic institutions of suffrage, representation, and majority rule. Early liberals did not include political rights among the basic rights to be given to all; they demanded merely that wealth should replace birth as a criterion for franchise. Extending suffrage to all property owners was originally an egalitarian demand directed against hereditary privileges of the nobility. Property qualifications for voting rights became an inegalitarian rule when it was invoked in defense of vested property interests against proponents of universal suffrage (which was not instituted in most countries until the decline of laissez-faire liberalism).

Egalitarianism and other social goals

Egalitarian rules may conflict not only with one another (for example, equality of rights and of opportunities, equality of opportunities and of welfare) but also with other social goals. The equal distribution of welfare does not necessarily lead to its maximization. The latter goal might be most effectively realized by slavery or by wage incentives to higher production far greater than would be compatible with equality of welfare and even of opportunity. Equal welfare and equal freedom, too, are competing goals, since the former goal requires government to impose greater restrictions on the freedom of economically dominant groups. Freedom of all citizens with respect to government may result in suppression of freedom of the minority of individualists by the majority of conformists. Equalization of wealth does away with the leisure class, which some consider essential to cultural development. Egalitarianism may thus lead to downward leveling and stifle individuality, diversity, and cultural excellence. Greater equality of opportunity may also generate more frustration and greater unhappiness. Political equality entails majority rule, but the majority may decide on inegalitarian policies. Both Edmund Burke and J. S. Mill were in substantial agreement as to these causal ramifications; yet, the former drew the balance in favor of inegalitarianism, while the latter espoused egalitarianism.

Inegalitarian rules are usually advocated as means to other goals, such as order, efficiency, diversity, and cultural excellence. Egalitarianism, on the other hand, is more often considered intrinsically desirable and morally right. Both egalitarian and inegalitarian principles have been held demonstrably valid on the ground that they are "in agreement with nature." That men should receive equal treatment has been taken as a normative conclusion from the factual premise that "men are equal"—unless this statement itself is interpreted in a normative sense (see above). But it has also been argued that men ought to be treated unequally because they are of unequal rank or ability or race.

Yet, normative principles cannot be derived from factual generalizations; neither equality nor inequality of characteristics entails the desirability of either egalitarian or inegalitarian treatment. There is surely no inconsistency in maintaining that men should be treated equally (e.g., as to rights) in spite of the fact that they are unequal (e.g., as to natural endowments) or that they should be treated unequally (e.g., as to salary) regardless of their common features (e.g., as to basic needs). Once the causal connections between egalitarianism or inegalitarianism and other social goals have been clarified, the adoption of one or the other of these two normative doctrines remains a matter of subjective commitment.

FELIX E. OPPENHEIM

[*See also* DEMOCRACY; JUSTICE; POLITICAL THEORY.]

BIBLIOGRAPHY

BENN, STANLEY I.; and PETERS, RICHARD S. 1959 *Social Principles and the Democratic State.* London: Allen & Unwin. → See especially Chapters 5 and 6.
BERLIN, ISAIAH (1955–1956) 1961 Equality as an Ideal. Pages 128–150 in Frederick A. Olafson (editor), *Justice and Social Policy: A Collection of Essays.* Englewood Cliffs, N.J.: Prentice-Hall. → First published in Volume 56 of Aristotelian Society, *Proceedings.*
CROSLAND, CHARLES A. R. (1956) 1957 *The Future of Socialism.* New York: Macmillan.
GINSBERG, MORRIS 1965 *On Justice in Society.* Ithaca, N.Y.: Cornell Univ. Press. → A paperback edition was published in 1965 by Penguin.
HOFSTADTER, ALBERT 1956 The Career Open to Personality. Pages 111–142 in Conference on Science, Philosophy and Religion in Their Relation to the Democratic Way of Life, *Aspects of Human Equality: Fifteenth Symposium of the Conference on Science, Philosophy, and Religion.* Edited by Lyman Bryson et al. New York: The Conference; Harper.
LAKOFF, SANFORD A. 1964 *Equality in Political Philosophy.* Cambridge, Mass.: Harvard Univ. Press.
PENNOCK, J. ROLAND 1950 *Liberal Democracy: Its Merits and Prospects.* New York: Rinehart.
PENNOCK, J. ROLAND (editor) 1967 *Equality.* Nomos No. 9. New York: Atherton.
SARTORI, GIOVANNI 1962 *Democratic Theory.* Detroit, Mich.: Wayne State Univ. Press. → A paperback edition was published in 1965 by Praeger.
TAWNEY, R. H. (1931) 1965 *Equality.* 4th ed., rev. New York: Barnes & Noble.
WILLIAMS, BERNARD (1962) 1963 The Idea of Equality. Pages 110–131 in Peter Laslett and W. G. Runciman

(editors), *Philosophy, Politics and Society (Second Series): A Collection.* New York: Barnes & Noble.

WOLLHEIM, RICHARD (1955–1956) 1961 Equality and Equal Rights. Pages 111–127 in Frederick A. Olafson (editor), *Justice and Social Policy: A Collection of Essays.* Englewood Cliffs, N.J.: Prentice-Hall. → First published in Volume 56 of Aristotelian Society, *Proceedings.*

YOUNG, MICHAEL D. (1958) 1959 *The Rise of the Meritocracy, 1870–2033: The New Elite of Our Social Revolution.* New York: Random House.

II
EQUALITY AS AN IDEAL

Among the definitions of "equality" provided by the *Oxford English Dictionary* are the following three: (1) "the condition of having equal dignity, rank, or privileges with others"; (2) "the condition of being equal in power, ability, achievement, or excellence"; (3) "fairness, impartiality, equity, due proportion, proportionateness."

A moment's contemplation will reveal that these three definitions of "equality," although all of them are consistent with common usage, are not entirely or necessarily consistent with one another. If, for example, men are unequal in power, ability, achievement, or excellence, then an adherence to definition (3) will lead to a violation of definition (1), while an adherence to definition (1) will lead to a violation of definition (3). It is only if men *are* in fact equal in power, ability, and excellence that equity preserves a condition of equal rank.

But, in fact, men are not equal in power, ability, and excellence. From this it would seem to follow that justice requires a certain measure of inequality. And, indeed, in all social orders, no matter how vehement their passion for equality, we observe that some inequalities are regarded as inevitable and natural. At the same time, no egalitarian society can have an easy conscience about the inequalities within it. There is a sentiment, inchoate yet profound, that no matter how unequal men may be in their abilities, in some deeper sense all men are equal merely by virtue of being men.

The issue of legitimacy. It is certainly true that, in Western civilization at least, men have always believed that equality is in some sense the norm from which inequality represents a deviation. As Wollheim and Berlin have pointed out (1955–1956, pp. 281 ff.), the "naturalness" of the idea of equality seems to derive from the dual assumption that (*a*) men are all members of one species, of a simple class of objects (i.e., human beings) and (*b*) all members of a class should be treated uniformly, unless there is good and sufficient reason not to do so. This assumption, Berlin emphasizes, is so pervasive that it has almost the status of a category (in the Kantian sense) of human rationality:

If I have a cake, and there are ten persons among whom I wish to divide it, then if I give exactly one tenth to each, this will not, at any rate automatically, call for justification; whereas if I depart from this principle of equal division I am expected to produce a special reason. It is some sense of this, however latent, that makes equality an ideal which has never seemed intrinsically eccentric . . . . (*ibid.*, p. 305)

This being the case, it is not surprising that all the golden ages, all the utopias, and all the paradises created by the human imagination are egalitarian (although not necessarily democratic—there may be an infinitely benevolent, if scrupulously egalitarian, despot). However, whereas in classical antiquity, utopia is located in word, not in deed, and in the succeeding Christian centuries it is located in transcendent hope rather than in actuality, in the modern era utopia has become an "ideal" to be realized (if never fully realized) by human effort.

For Plato, as later for Augustine and Aquinas, utopia is conceived as prehistorical, as existing prior to some primordial Fall—a catastrophe that implicates the entire human race and that sets the conditions of its destiny and its progress. The outstanding consequence of this Fall is the abolition of original equality and the establishment of the principle of hierarchy as the "natural" principle of cosmic and social order. The original, harmonious prehistorical unity is shattered, and the universe becomes subject to differentiation—soul and matter, spirit and flesh, idea and reality are now opposite poles, between which the tension of existence tries to maintain an equilibrium. The most perfect equilibrium (indeed, the only enduring one) is, obviously, that which recognizes the superiority of the noble over the base—of soul over matter, spirit over flesh, idea over actuality. The articulation of this order results in a metaphysics of hierarchy, in which both the cosmos and human society are envisaged as part of a "great chain of being," with precedence and consequence clearly defined and with *noblesse oblige* and humble obedience the only two reasonable political perspectives available to the human imagination.

It requires more empathy than most twentieth-century men possess to realize how utterly "natural" the idea of hierarchy came to seem to classical and medieval thinkers—and even to most modern thinkers prior to the American and French revolutions. We are inclined to view this as an anti-egalitarian mode of thought, but the idea of hierarchy saw itself as containing the only feasible idea of political equality, rather than as in any way opposing equality. For equality was defined in terms of justice—of giving each man his due, so that equal men received equal rewards. That all men were not equal—and certainly not equal in all respects—was a platitude confirmed daily by the most casual observation. The hierarchical idea was accepted in good faith and good conscience by almost everyone; if we now deem it an ideology, then it was the ideology not of a class but of an entire historical epoch.

It is Shakespeare, through the sublimity of his language, who makes the older idea of hierarchy available to us better than any political philosopher. Ulysses' speech on "degree," in *Troilus and Cressida*, is the *locus classicus*:

The heavens themselves, the planets, and this centre
Observe degree, priority, and place, . . .
But when the planets
In evil mixture to disorder wander,
What plagues and what portents! what mutiny!
What raging of the sea! shaking of earth!
Commotion in the winds! Frights, changes, horrors,
Divert, and crack, rend and deracinate
The unity and married calm of states
Quite from their fixture! O, when degree is shak'd,
Which is the ladder to all high designs,
Then enterprise is sick! How could communities,
Degrees in schools, and brotherhoods in cities,
Peaceful commerce from dividable shores,
The primogenitive and due of birth,
Prerogative of age, crowns, sceptres, laurels,
But by degree, stand in authentic place?
Take but degree away, untune that string,
And, hark, what discord follows! Each thing meets
In mere oppugnancy. . . .   (Act I, scene 3)

Yet even as Shakespeare wrote these lines, the planets were on their way "in evil mixture to disorder wander." As Sanford A. Lakoff pointed out in his historical survey *Equality in Political Philosophy* (1964), the new astronomy replaced the cosmos with a neutral universe in which "the laws of nature" applied without distinction to heavenly and earthly bodies. Simultaneously, the rise of experimental science and the overthrow of Aristotelian teleology nullified previous distinctions between "base" and "noble" in nature—and, most especially, in human nature. Just as the new physical science declared all the parts of nature to be equal, so the new scientific (i.e., materialistic) psychology declared all the parts of man to be equal—none was intrinsically base or intrinsically noble. The denial of the superiority of spirit over matter, and of mind over body, inevitably suggested that there was no good reason for those who worked with their hands to have an inferior status compared with those whose work was nonmanual and nonmenial. In this way the philosophical foundations of modern bourgeois society were established.

Christianity itself, in the course of its several "reformations," buttressed these new foundations (without, however, necessarily intending this result). Luther's denial of the distinction between "spiritual" and "carnal" authorities and vocations was destructive of churchly hierarchy. The keys of St. Peter were distributed among the congregation of believers, as the monopoly of the Catholic clergy over the apostolic succession was denied and as its exclusive authority to interpret Scripture faithfully was transferred to the entire body of Christendom. Successive generations of reformers carried this antiauthoritarian impulse forward, so that Christendom itself experienced the multiplication of new self-governing and (in the literal sense of the term) self-righteous sects and denominations.

The response to inequality. But while these secular and religious trends were to create the bourgeois world, energies were being released that were to point beyond this world. Even during the Middle Ages, Christian Messianism was only with difficulty kept within the confines of the church; and as the authority of the church crumbled, this messianism became an independent spiritual and political force. The kingdom of God was transferred from a transcendental hereafter to this world, this time, this place.

It was during the English revolution of 1640–1660 that Christian Messianism first revealed its full political ambitions. There had been previous incidents, to be sure (e.g., the Anabaptist revolts in Germany), but these had as their primary aim the creation of local utopias. In contrast, the left-wing Commonwealth's-men sought not only to transform their own national society but also to prescribe principles for all truly Christian and truly just societies. Overton, the Leveller, spoke in the recognizable accents of modernity when he said: "Every man by nature being a king, priest, prophet in his own natural circuit and compass, whereof no second may partake but by deputation, commission, and free consent from him whose right and freedom it is" (Lakoff 1964, p. 65). In declarations such as these, the metaphysical foundations of egalitarian, representative self-government were firmly outlined. It required only the slightest amendment for these metaphysical foundations to be entirely secularized, with "rights" and "freedoms" the prerogatives of men qua men, rather than merely men qua Christians. The political philosophers of the seventeenth and eighteenth centuries moved steadily in this direction, and the political ideologists of the American and French revolutions acted violently upon these new principles of civic organization.

As has been noted, however, even as modern, liberal society was being formed, there was an egalitarian perspective that looked beyond it. This perspective delineated not merely an equality of rights and freedoms but a fraternal equality of condition. Thus, Winstanley, the Digger, prefigured the socialist idea of equality with his declaration that "the earth was made by Almighty God to be a common treasury of livelihood for whole mankind in all his branches . . ." (Lakoff 1964, p. 79). This is socialism, but of a premodern kind. The "common treasury" is a static conception of wealth, and all premodern socialist thinkers envisaged a good society as one of economic modesty rather than of economic abundance—goods were to be distributed equally, and everyone was to be content with what he had. It was not until the nineteenth century that modern socialism, alert to the possibilities of the industrial and technological revolutions it was witnessing, put forward the prospect of equality conjoined to increasing wealth for all. Since premodern socialism demanded a certain measure of asceticism from its adherents, while modern socialism could appeal simultaneously to human idealism and to human appetites, it is not surprising that modern socialism has a far more powerful popular appeal.

It is a distinguishing characteristic of the modern age that "equality" should be not merely an abstract ideal but also a politically aggressive idea. It is generally accepted—it is, indeed, one of the most deeply rooted conventions of contemporary political thought—that the existence of inequality is a legitimate provocation to social criticism. Every inequality is on the defensive, must prove itself against the imputation of injustice and unnaturalness. And where such proof is established, it never asserts itself beyond the point where inequality is to be tolerated because it is, under particular conditions, inescapable. That inequality may be per se desirable is a thought utterly repugnant to the modern sensibility.

The modern egalitarian impulse has had its objective social correlatives. Modern society tends to have a more equal distribution of income and wealth than previous social orders in Western history. Statistics are fragmentary and are open to dispute as to their significance. But, for France, Jean Fourastié ([1951] 1960, p. 30) has made the following estimate: "The salary of a councilor of state increased by a factor of at least 40 from 1800

to 1948; the salary of a professor at the Collège de France by 100; the average salary of an office boy in a government agency by 220; the hourly wages of labourers in provincial cities by more than 400." The general tendency would seem to be unmistakable.

The limits and potential of equality. Nevertheless, there is considerable controversy over the issue of whether equality has been adequately realized in our modern social arrangements. This controversy derives in large part from the ambiguities inherent in the idea of equality. Thus, a comparative percentile increase for lower-income groups represents a step toward equality only from a limited, statistical point of view. In another perspective, it can be regarded as a movement toward further inequality. For when a man's income is increased from a million dollars a year to two million (i.e., doubled), while another's income is increased from one thousand to five thousand (i.e., quintupled), it can fairly be said that the rich man has benefited more notably—in absolute magnitudes—than the poor. Whether one wishes to make such an assertion will depend entirely upon one's conception of equality—whether, that is, one is measuring equality by absolute or relative standards. The progressive income tax represents an effort by the modern state to mediate between these two notions of equality.

A similar ambiguity—between equality of condition and equality of opportunity—plays a most significant role in American social and political thought. Equality of opportunity will inevitably result in inequality of condition, since some men are more able, more energetic, and more fortunate than others. The American creed sanctions such inequality—but only halfheartedly. For there has always been an implicit corollary—derived from the premise that all men are created equal—that equality of opportunity ought to lead to approximate equality of condition, and that failure to realize this goal reflects a deficiency (if not a positive error) in the existing social and economic arrangements. The tides of American politics flow between these two polar conceptions of equality.

In recent years, some of the leading thinkers of American sociology have attempted to transcend this debate over equality by declaring inequality to be a necessary condition of all social organization. To some extent, this effort originates in the experience of just how little effect popular or political ideas about equality have on comparable social structures. The distribution of income in all modern industrialized nations is astonishingly similar, no matter whether the governing ideology of this nation be socialist (e.g., Sweden) or capitalist (e.g., the United States). Instead of wondering about the origins of inequality and of social classes —as did the sociologists of the eighteenth and nineteenth centuries—such thinkers as Talcott Parsons, Kingsley Davis, and Wilbert E. Moore have attempted to demonstrate that social differentiation and social stratification are indispensable to the very existence of a social structure—that each society has functional "norms," both inwardly and outwardly coercive, which prescribe the acceptable degrees and kinds of inequality to be tolerated.

This sociological thesis represents a covert return to the hierarchical principles of distributive justice and proportional equality elaborated by Aristotle in Book v of the *Ethica nicomachea* and Book III of the *Politics*. And since the history of the idea of equality in the Western world is to a considerable extent a record of intermittent, and sometimes violent, dissatisfaction with these principles, it is understandable that the debate over equality should be an unending one, with every new resolution the occasion for a new beginning.

IRVING KRISTOL

[*See also* DEMOCRACY; HUMAN RIGHTS; JUSTICE.]

BIBLIOGRAPHY

ARISTOTLE *Ethica nicomachea*. Translated by W. D. Ross. Oxford: Clarendon Press, 1925.
ARISTOTLE *Politics*. With an English translation. London: Heinemann; Cambridge, Mass.: Harvard Univ. Press, 1959.
DAHRENDORF, RALF 1962 On the Origin of Social Inequality. Pages 88–109 in Peter Laslett and W. G. Runciman (editors), *Philosophy, Politics and Society (Second Series): A Collection*. New York: Barnes & Noble.
EMERSON, RALPH WALDO (1844) 1920 Politics. Pages 310–323 in Ralph Waldo Emerson, *Essays: First and Second Series*. New York: Dutton.
FOURASTIÉ, JEAN (1951) 1960 *The Causes of Wealth*. Glencoe, Ill.: Free Press. → First published in French.
LAKOFF, SANFORD A. 1964 *Equality in Political Philosophy*. Cambridge, Mass.: Harvard Univ. Press.
WOLLHEIM, RICHARD; and BERLIN, ISAIAH 1955–1956 Equality. Parts 1–2. Aristotelian Society for the Systematic Study of Philosophy, London, *Proceedings* 56: 281–326.

EQUILIBRIUM
See ECONOMIC EQUILIBRIUM *and* HOMEOSTASIS.

ERASMUS

Desiderius Erasmus (1466?–1536) (he was baptized Erasmus Rogerii, or Gerards—Desiderius was his own addition), a Dutch humanist, spent his early youth in Gouda and later attended the Latin schools at Deventer and 's Hertogenbosch. There he had contact with the *devotio moderna* and joined the canons regular of the Augustinian monastery of Steyn near Gouda, taking his monastic vows in 1488. Between 1493 and 1516 he lived a wandering life: in service with the bishop of Cambrai, studying at the University of Paris with Robert Gaguin, Jean Vitrier, and Lefèvre d'Étaples, making three visits to England, where he met John Colet and Thomas More and studied theology and Greek, and visiting Italy and Basel. From 1517 to 1521 he taught at Louvain, then lived in Basel until the Reformation was instituted there, and in Freiburg from 1529 to 1535; he died in Basel.

Erasmus was above all a remarkable classical scholar. He fiercely deplored the corrupt state of the Latin of his time and advocated the use of Cicero's language, which he used in all his writings and for which he wrote manuals. Following the example of the Italians, he sought out what, in his opinion, were the most authentic texts of the classics, of which he drew up annotated editions, the Greek with Latin translations. In addition to many classical works he edited the New Testament and the writings of the church fathers.

Erasmus also had great influence on his contemporaries through his hortatory works: humorous and satirical sketches of the life of his contemporaries (*Colloquia* 1518; Eng. trans. *The Colloquies of Erasmus*), paraphrases of the Gospels and Epistles, and his most famous essays: *Enchiridion militis christiani* (1503) and *Moriae encomium* (1511; Eng. trans. *In Praise of Folly*). In them he bitterly mocked stupidity, selfishness, and vanity and pointed out that man can find the true happiness that lies in harmony and peace only through leading a truly Christian life and increasing one's knowledge. Rulers, including the pope, were sharply criticized by Erasmus for their destructive and useless wars. Education to rationality can and must be the key to a better public life; to this end he wrote, among other things, *Institutio principis christiani* (1515–1516; Eng. trans. *The Education of a Christian Prince*), dedicated to Charles v.

Erasmus took up arms early in his career against the idle disputations of the Scholastics, the formalism of the church of his time, the wealth and temporal power of the priesthood, and later, above all, against the monks, whom he regarded as his archenemies and whose monastic life he saw as useless. He hoped for a reconstruction of the church in line with what he saw as primitive Christianity: not a doctrine of redemption from sin and death, but a *philosophia Christi* that teaches man to live in conformity with the commandments of love of neighbor, mercy, self-control, and reason, as the best of the classics also taught. He did not regard the sacraments as means of grace. He condemned the church's doctrine of absolution by penance and good works, the worship of saints and their relics, and the practice of pilgrimages. Edification by word and example, he held, is the only task of the priest. At the same time, he wanted to retain the principal dogmas (including papal power, provided it was confined to matters of faith). However, his interpretation of these dogmas differed so far from that professed by the church that the authorities, even after the Council of Trent, condemned his writings. But his ideas found much support and are still alive, both among Catholics and liberal Protestants.

Erasmus greeted Luther's public stand against the church's doctrine of penance with sympathy. But he soon realized that Luther had in mind an entirely different reformation of the church than he himself desired. At the same time, he continued to advocate a conciliatory attitude toward Luther and opposed his condemnation. It was only after much pressure had been exerted that Erasmus wrote the *Diatribe de libero arbitrio* (1524; Eng. trans. *Discourse on Free Will*) against Luther. In it he set forth his own conception of human dignity and free will, which was related to the ideas of the Italian humanists and the classics, as opposed to the total depravity of man that Luther preached. However, he did this in such a way that his book pleased the Catholics no more than the Protestants. Until his death he pleaded for reconstruction of the church and a *rapprochement* between the Roman and Lutheran factions.

H. A. ENNO VAN GELDER

WORKS BY ERASMUS

(1484–1521) 1962 *The Epistles of Erasmus: From His Earliest Letters to His Fifty-fifth Year.* 3 vols. New York: Russell & Russell.

(1484–1536) 1906–1958 *Opus epistolarum Des. Erasmi Roterodami.* Edited by P. S. Allen. 12 vols. Oxford: Clarendon Press.

(1503) 1963 *The Enchiridion.* Translated and edited by Raymond Himelick. Bloomington: Indiana Univ. Press.

(1511) 1942 *In Praise of Folly.* With a short biography of Erasmus by Hendrik Willem van Loon. New York: Black.

(1515–1516) 1936 *The Education of a Christian Prince.* New York: Columbia Univ. Press.

(1518) 1965 *The Colloquies of Erasmus.* A new translation by Craig R. Thompson. Univ. of Chicago Press.

(1524) 1961 *Discourse on Free Will.* Translated and edited by Ernest F. Winter. New York: Ungar.

Ausgewählte Werke. Edited by Hajo Holborn. Munich: Beck, 1933.

Desiderii Erasmi Roterodami opera omnia. 10 vols. Leiden (The Netherlands): Vander, 1703–1706. → Volume 1: *Qvae ad institvtionem literarvm spectant.* Volume 2: *Adagia.* Volume 3: *Epistolae.* Volume 4: *Qvae ad morvm institvtionem pertinent.* Volume 5: *Qvae ad pretatem institvvnt.* Volume 6: *Novvm Testamentvm.* Volume 7: *Paraphrases in N. Testamentvm.* Volume 8: *Versa e patribvs graecis.* Volume 9: *Apologia I.* Volume 10: *Apologia II.*

Erasmi opuscula. A supplement to the *Opera omnia*, edited with introduction and notes by Wallace K. Ferguson. The Hague: Nijhoff, 1933.

Poems. With introductions and notes by Cornelis Reedijk. Leiden (The Netherlands): Brill, 1956.

SUPPLEMENTARY BIBLIOGRAPHY

BATAILLON, MARCEL 1937 *Érasme et l'Espagne: Recherches sur l'histoire spirituelle du XVIᵉ siècle.* Paris: Droz.

Bibliotheca Erasmiana. (1897–1915) 1964 Pages 271–1048 in *Bibliotheca Belgica.* Volume 2: *Bibliographie générale des Pays-Bas.* Brussels: Culture et Civilisation.

EIJL, E. J. M. VAN 1963 Erasmus en de hervorning van de theologie. *Archief voor de geschiedenis van de katholieke kerk in Nederland* 5: 129–219.

FLITNER, ANDREAS 1952 *Erasmus im Urteil seiner Nachwelt: Das literarische Erasmus-Bild von Beatus Rhenanus bis zu Jean Le Clerc.* Tübingen (Germany): Niemeyer.

GELDER, H. A. ENNO VAN (1961) 1964 *The Two Reformations in the Sixteenth Century: A Study of the Religious Aspects and Consequences of Renaissance and Humanism.* The Hague: Nijhoff.

HUIZINGA, JOHAN (1924) 1952 *Erasmus of Rotterdam.* 3d ed. London: Phaidon. → First published in Dutch.

MESTWERDT, PAUL 1917 *Die Anfänge des Erasmus: Humanismus und "Devotio Moderna."* Leipzig: Haupt.

RENAUDET, AUGUSTIN (1916) 1954 *Préréforme et humanisme à Paris pendant les premières guerres d'Italie 1494–1517.* 2d ed., rev. Paris: Librairie d'Argences.

RENAUDET, AUGUSTIN 1926 *Érasme, sa pensée religieuse et son action d'après sa correspondance (1518–1521).* Paris: Alcan.

RENAUDET, AUGUSTIN 1939 *Études érasmiennes (1521–1529).* Paris: Droz.

RENAUDET, AUGUSTIN 1954 *Érasme et l'Italie.* Travaux d'humanisme et renaissance, No. 15. Geneva: Droz.

RHENANUS, BEATUS 1536 *Desiderii Erasmi Roterodami viri incomparabilis vita, et epitaphia quaedam.* Antwerp (Belgium): Vorstermann. → The first biography of Erasmus.

ROTTERDAM, BIBLIOTHEEK EN LEESZALEN DER GEMEENTE 1937 *Catalogus van geschriften over leven en werken van Desiderius Erasmus aanwezig in de Bibliotheek der gemeente Rotterdam.* Rotterdam (The Netherlands): The Library.

SMITH, PRESERVED 1923 *Erasmus: A Study of His Life, Ideals and Place in History.* New York and London: Harper.

SMITH, PRESERVED 1927 *A Key to the Colloquies of Erasmus.* Oxford Univ. Press.

ERGONOMICS

See ENGINEERING PSYCHOLOGY.

ERRORS

I. Nonsampling Errors   *Frederick Mosteller*
II. Effects of Errors in
    Statistical Assumptions   *Robert M. Elashoff*

I
NONSAMPLING ERRORS

The view has sometimes been expressed that statisticians have laid such great emphasis on the study of sampling errors (the differences between the observed values of a variable and the long-run average of the observed values in repetitions of the measurement) that they have neglected or encouraged the neglect of other, frequently more important, kinds of error, called nonsampling errors.

Errors in conception, logic, statistics, and arithmetic, or failures in execution and reporting, can reduce a study's value below zero. The roster of possible troubles seems only to grow with increasing knowledge. By participating in the work of a specific field, one can, in a few years, work up considerable methodological expertise, much of which has not been and is not likely to be written down. To attempt to discuss every way a study can go wrong would be a hopeless venture. The selection of a kind of error for inclusion in this article was guided by its importance, by the extent of research available, by the ability to make positive recommendations, and by my own preferences.

Although the theory of sampling is generally well developed, both the theory and practice of the control of nonsampling errors are in a less satisfactory state, partly because each subject matter, indeed each study, is likely to face yet uncatalogued difficulties. Empirical results of methodological investigations intended to help research workers control nonsampling errors have accumulated slowly, not only because of myriad variables but also because the variables produce results that lack stability from one study to another.

This article deals mainly with techniques for reducing bias. The portions on variability are not exceptions, for they offer ways to avoid underestimating the amount of variability. The presentation deals, first, with the meaning of bias and with conceptual errors; second, with problems of nonsampling errors especially as they arise in the sample survey field through questionnaires, panel studies, nonresponse, and response errors; and, third, with errors occurring in the analysis of nearly any kind of quantitative investigation, errors arising from variability, from technical problems in analysis, in calculations, and in reporting. Some discussions of nonsampling errors restrict themselves to the field of sample surveys, where problems of bias and blunder have been especially studied, but this article also treats some nonsampling errors in experimental and observational studies.

Bias and conceptual errors

Bias and true values. What is bias? Most definitions of bias, or systematic error, assume that for each characteristic to be measured there exists a true value that the investigation ideally would produce. Imagine repeatedly carrying out the actual proposed, rather than the ideal, investigation, getting a value each time for the characteristic under study, and obtaining an average value from these many repetitions. The difference between that average value and the true value of the characteristic is called the bias. The difference between the outcome of *one* investigation and the true value is the sum of bias and sampling error. The point of averaging over many repetitions is to reduce the sampling error in the average value to a negligible amount. (It is assumed that for the process under study and for the type of average chosen, this reduction is possible.)

Is there a true value? The concept "true value" is most touchy, for it assumes that one can describe an ideal investigation for making the measurement. Ease in doing this depends upon the degree of generality of the question. For example, the measurement of "interventionist attitude" in the United States during World War II is discussed below. For such a broad notion, the concept of a true value seems vague, even admitting the possible use of several numbers in the description. It is easier to believe in a true value for the percentage of adults who would respond "Yes" to "Should we go to war now?" Even here the training of the interviewers, the rapidly changing fraction of the population holding given opinions, and the effect of the social class and opinions of the interviewer upon the responses of those interviewed must raise questions about the existence of a true value. At the very least, we wonder whether a true value could represent a time span and how its conditions of measurement could be specified. In designing an ideal sample survey, what kind of interviewer should be used?

Today some scientists believe that true values do not exist separately from the measuring process to be used, and in much of social science this view can be amply supported. The issue is not limited to social science; in physics, complications arise from the different methods of measuring microscopic and macroscopic quantities such as lengths. On the other hand, because it suggests ways of improving measurement methods, the concept of "true value" is useful; since some methods come much nearer to being ideal than others, the better ones can provide substitutes for true values. (See the discussion on describing response error in the section on "Response error," below.)

To illustrate further the difficulty of the notion of a true value, consider an example from one of the most quantitative social sciences. When the economist assesses the change in value of domestic product, different choices of weights and of base years yield different results. He has no natural or unique choice for these weights and years. He can only try to avoid extremes and unusual situations. While, as noted above, the belief in a true value independent of the measuring instrument must be especially weak in the area of opinion, similar weaknesses beset measures of unemployment, health, housing, or anything else related to the human condition. [See INDEX NUMBERS.]

Conceptual errors. Since the variety of sources of biases is practically unlimited, this article discusses only a few frequently encountered sources.

Target population–sampled population. Often an investigation is carried out on a sample drawn from a population—the sampled population—quite different from that to which the investigator wants to generalize—the target population. This mismatch makes the inference from sample to target population shaky. To match target and sampled population perfectly is usually impossible, but often the expenditure of time and money or the use of special skills or cooperation can patch what cannot be made whole.

Some examples of this process follow: (1) The psychologist wants to establish general laws of learning for all organisms, and especially for man, but he may choose to study only the college sophomore, usually in his own college and rarely outside his own country. His principal alternatives are the rat and the pigeon. Reallocation of time and money may extend the sampled population and bring him closer to the target he has in mind.

(2) The sociologist may want to study the actual organization of trade unions and yet be hard pressed to study in depth more than a single union. This limitation is impossible for an individual to overcome, but cooperative research may help. (For a remarkable cooperative anthropological study of child rearing, see *Six Cultures: Studies of Child Rearing* [Whiting 1963].)

(3) The historian or political scientist may want to exposit the whole climate of opinion within which an important decision is made, yet he must pick some facts and omit others, emphasize some and not others. The sampling of historical records offers a compromise between scanning everything, which may be impossible or unsatisfactorily superficial, and the case study of a single document or of a small collection.

(4) The man who generalizes on educational methods on the basis of his studies in one class, or one school subject, or one grade, or one school, or one school system, or even one country, needs to consider whether the bases of his investigations should be broadened.

(5) The investigator, especially in studies where he does not regard his investigation as based on a sample, but on a population or census, would be wise to consider what population he hopes his investigation applies to, whether the full breadth of it has had an appropriate chance to contribute cases to his study and, if not, how he might get at the rest. He may be satisfied with describing the population under study, but often he is not.

(6) More narrowly, in sampling the membership of a professional society, the investigator may find his published membership list out of date by some years. For a fee the society may be willing to provide its current mailing list, which is probably as close as one can get to the target population. Obviously, the target population changes even while the study is being performed.

Incompatibility of meaning. While arguing for statistical thinking in the attempt to generalize one's results, one must not fall into the pit of statistical nonsense. Both anthropologists and historians call attention to mistakes that can come from regarding seemingly like objects, rituals, or behavior in different cultures as exchangeable commodities for statistical purposes. The notion of "father" without distinction between "pater" and "genitor" offers an example. In the Trobriands, a boy lives with his benign, biological father until he is nine or ten years old, then moves to his mother's brothers' village for training and discipline, and there he inherits property. In the United States the biological father theoretically plays the role of disciplinarian, and the uncles frequently play benign, indulgent roles.

Pilot studies. Toward the completion of a study, investigators usually feel that it would have been better done in some other way. But a study can be petted and patted so long that, before completion, its value is past. The huge, never-completed study usually damages the investigator's reputation, however wise the termination. Much can and must be learned by trying, and therefore nearly any investigation requires pilot work. Pilot work is little written about, perhaps because it is hard to summarize and perhaps because the results usually sound so obvious and often would be were they not hidden among thousands of other possible obvious results that did not occur. The whole spectrum from the tightest laboratory experiment to the loosest observational study requires careful pilot work. Pilot studies pinpoint the special difficulties of an investigation and, by encouraging initial action, overcome doctrines of omniscience that require a complete plan before starting. While it is true that the statistician can often give more valuable aid at the planning stage by preventing errors than by salvaging poor work through analysis, firm plans made in the absence of pilot studies are plans for disaster.

Hawthorne effects. Psychologists sadly say that even under the most carefully controlled conditions, laboratory animals do as they please. Humans do even worse. When Roethlisberger and Dickson (1939) carried out their experiments to find conditions that would maximize productivity of factory teams at the Hawthorne Works of Western Electric, they found that every change—increasing the lighting or reducing it, increasing the wage scale or reducing it—seemed to increase the group productivity. Paying attention to people, which occurs in placing them in an experiment, changes their behavior. This rather unpredictable change is called the Hawthorne effect. Instead of trying to eliminate this effect, it has been suggested that all educational efforts should be carried out as portions of experiments, so as to capitalize on the Hawthorne effect. No doubt boredom, even with experimentation, would eventually set in.

The existence of Hawthorne effects seriously restricts the researcher's ability to isolate variables that change performance in a consistent manner. Although experimenters, by adjusting conditions, may create substantial changes in behavior, what causes the changes may still be a mystery. Reliable repetition of results by different experimenters using different groups can establish results more firmly.

What treatment was applied? In experimental work with humans, it is especially difficult to know whether the treatment administered is the one that the experimenter had in mind. For example, in an unsuccessful learning experiment on the production of words by individuals, subjects in one group were instructed that every word in the class of words that they were seeking contained the same letters of the alphabet. When no differences in learning rates emerged between these subjects and those told nothing about the class of words being sought, further investigations were made. It turned out that few subjects listened to this particular instruction, and among those who did, several forgot it during the early part of the experiment. If a particular instruction is important, special efforts have to be made to ensure that the subject has received and appreciated it.

One approach to the problem of Hawthorne effects uses, in addition to experimental groups, two kinds of control groups: groups who are informed that they are part of an experiment and other groups who are not so informed. As always, the investigator has to be alert about the actual treatment of control and experimental groups. L. L. Thurstone told me about experimenting for the U.S. Army to measure the value of instruction during sleep for training in telegraphy. Thurstone had control squads who were not informed that they were in the study. The sergeants instructing these control squads felt that the "sleep learning" squads were getting favored treatment, and to keep their squads "even," they secretly instituted additional hours of wide-awake training for their own squads, thereby ruining the whole investigation.

Randomization. Generally speaking, randomization is a way to protect the study from bias in selecting subjects or in assigning treatments. It aids in getting a broad representation from the population into the sample. Randomization helps to communicate the objectivity of the study. It provides a basis for mathematical distribution theory that has uses in statistical appraisals and in simulations. [*See* EXPERIMENTAL DESIGN; RANDOM NUMBERS.]

Bad breaks in random sampling. Valuable as randomization is, chance can strike an investigator stunning blows. For example, suppose that a psychological learning experiment is intended to reinforce 5 randomly chosen responses in each burst of 20. If the randomization accidentally gives reinforcement to the first 5 responses in each burst of 20, the psychologist should notice this and realize that he has selected a special kind of periodic reinforcement. The objectivity of the random assignment cannot cure its qualitative failure.

Similarly, suppose that in preparing to study fantasy productions under two carefully controlled conditions the clinical psychologist observes that his randomizing device has put all his scientist subjects into one group and all his humanist subjects into another. In that case, he should reconsider the grouping.

In principle, one should write down, in advance, sets of assignments that one would not accept. Unfortunately, there are usually too many of these, and nobody is yet adept at characterizing them in enough detail to get a computer to list them, even if it could face the size of the task. One solution is to describe a restricted, but acceptable, set of assignments and to choose randomly from these. Omitting some acceptable assignments may help to make the description feasible while keeping the list satisfactorily broad.

If this solution is not possible, then one probably has either to trust oneself (admittedly risky) or else get a more impartial judge to decide whether a particular random assignment should be borne.

If there are many variables, an investigator cannot defend against all the bad assignments. By leaning upon subject matter knowledge and accepting the principle that the variables usually thought to be important are the ones to be especially concerned about, stratification, together with randomization, can still be of some assistance. For example, the stratification might enforce equal numbers of each sex, with individuals still randomly chosen from the potential pools of men and women. In studying bad breaks from randomization, the investigator can afford to consider rejecting only the assignments too closely related to proved first-order or main effects and not second-order effects or boomerang possibilities conceived in, but never observed from, armchairs.

Random permutations. Although arranging objects in a random order can easily be done by using an ordinary random number table, few people know how to do it. In any case, making these permutations is tedious, and it is worth noting the existence of tables of random permutations in some books on the design of experiments and in the book by Moses and Oakford (1963) that offers many permutations of sets numbering 9, 16, 20, 30, 50, 100, 200, 500, 1,000 elements. A set of any other size less than 1,000 can be ordered by using the permutations for the next larger size. With larger sets, some stratification is almost sure to be valuable.

Example. One (nonstratified) permutation for a set of 30 elements is shown in Table 1 (read left

Table 1

11	5	29	26	3
1	19	14	4	20
24	25	27	6	9
30	15	13	18	12
28	22	7	8	17
2	21	16	10	23

to right). To arrange at random the letters of the alphabet, we might assign the integers, starting with 1 for *a* and ending with 26 for *z*, to the positions of the letters in the alphabet. Then, according to the permutation of Table 1, 11 and 5 correspond to *k* and *e*. 29 is omitted, 26 corresponds to *z*. Continuing gives the permutation:

kezcasndtxyfiomrlvghqbupjw.

For a random sample of 5 letters from the alphabet, drawn without replacement, we could just take the first 5 listed.

Simulations for new statistical methods. Large-scale simulation of economic, political, and social processes is growing in popularity; social scientists who invent new statistics would often find it profitable to try these out on idealized populations, constructed with the aid of random number tables, to see how well they perform their intended functions under perfectly understood conditions. This sort of exploration should be encouraged as part of the pilot work. To illustrate the lack, many books and hundreds of papers have been written about factor analytic methods, yet in 1966 it is hard to point to more than a single published simulation (Lawley & Swanson 1954; Tucker 1964) of the methods proposed on artificially constructed populations with random error.

Nonsampling errors in sample surveys

Questionnaires. Questionnaires themselves present many sources of bias, of which the wording of questions and the options offered as answers are especially important. Some topics discussed below ("Panel studies," "Nonresponse," and "Response error") also treat questionnaire matters. [*See especially* SAMPLE SURVEYS; SURVEY ANALYSIS; *see also* INTERVIEWING.]

Wording. The wording and position of questions on questionnaires used in public opinion polls and other investigations illustrate the difficulties surrounding the notion of true value mentioned earlier. Rugg and Cantril's survey article (1944) analyzes and illustrates the effects of the manner of questioning on responses. For example, prior to the U.S. entry into World War II, variations on a question about American aid to Great Britain, asked of American citizens within a period of about six weeks, produced the following percentages in favor of the "interventionist" position: 76, 73, 58, 78, 74, 56. Here the interventionist position meant approval of "giving aid even at the risk of war." At much the same time, unqualified questions about "entering the war immediately" produced the following percentages in favor, 22, 17, 8, numbers substantially different from those in the previous set. Although one would be hard put to choose a number to represent degree of support for intervention, the interval 55 to 80 per cent gives a range; this range was clearly higher than that in support of entering the war immediately.

Pilot studies of the wordings of questions test their meaning and clarity for the intended population. Phillip Rulon recalls interviews with very bright second graders from a geography class to discuss a test item that they had "missed": "Wind-eroded rocks are most commonly found in the (*a*) deserts, (*b*) mountains, (*c*) valleys." They chose "valleys" because few people would *find* wind-eroded rocks in the mountains or the deserts, however many such rocks might be in those places. After a question previously found to be unsatisfactory is reworded, bitter experience advises the testing of the new version.

In single surveys, one needs to employ a variety of questions to get at the stability and meaning of the response. The use of "split ballots" (similar but modified questionnaires administered to equivalent samples of individuals) offers a way to experiment and to control for position and wording.

Changing opinions. To ignore the results of the polls because of the considerable variation in responses would be as big a mistake as to adopt their numbers without healthy skepticism. Since opinion in time of crisis may move rapidly, it is easy to misappraise the tenor of the times without a systematic measuring device. For example, between July 1940 and September 1941, the per cent of U.S. citizens saying that they were willing to risk war with Japan rather than to let it continue its aggression rose from 12 to 65 per cent. Again, although in June 1940 only 35 per cent thought it more important to help England than to keep out of war, by September 1940 the percentage had risen to the 50s (Cantril 1944, p. 222). In September 1940, President Roosevelt made a deal that gave Great Britain 50 destroyers in return for leases of bases (Leuchtenburg 1963, pp. 303–304); in the face of the fluctuations of public opinion a historian considering the destroyer deal might easily believe that Roosevelt acted against, rather than with, the majority. (As I recall from experience at the Office of Public Opinion Research, Roosevelt had his own personal polls taken regularly, with reports submitted directly to him, usually on a single question.)

Seemingly minor variations in questions may change the responses a good deal, and so to study changes over time, one needs to use one well-chosen question (or sequence) again and again.

Naturally, such a question may come under attack as not getting at the "true value." If the question is to be changed, then, to get some parallel figures, it and the new question should be used simultaneously for a while.

Intercultural investigations. Considering the difficulty of getting at opinions and the dependence of responses upon the wording of the questions asked, even within a country, the problem of obtaining comparable cross-cultural or cross-national views looks horrendous. Scholars planning such studies will want to see three novel works. Kluckhohn and Strodtbeck's (1961) sociological and anthropological *Variations in Value Orientations* especially exploits ranking methods in the comparison of value orientations in Spanish-American, Mormon, Texas, Zuñi, and Navajo communities. Subjects describe the many values of their culture by ordering their preferences, for example, for ways of bringing up children: past (the old ways), present (today's ways), or future (how to find new ways to replace the old). Cantril's (1966) social-psychological and internationally oriented *Pattern of Human Concerns* uses rating methods and sample surveys to compare values and satisfactions in the populations of 15 nations. For example, the respondent's rating, on a scale of 0 to 10, expresses his view of how nearly he or his society has achieved the goal inquired about, and another rating evaluates how much either might expect to advance in five years. In international economics, measurements may be more easily compared, although the economist may be forced to settle for measuring the measurable as an index of what he would like to evaluate. Harbison and Myers' study, *Education, Manpower, and Economic Growth* (1964), illustrates this approach.

Panel studies. Although the single sample survey can be of great value, in some problems it is desirable to study the changes in the same people through time. The set of people chosen for repeated investigation is called a panel. One advantage of the panel study over the single survey is the deeper analysis available. For instance, when a net 5 per cent change takes place, does this mean that only 5 per cent of the people changed, or perhaps that 15 per cent changed one way and 10 per cent another? Second, additional measurement precision comes from matching responses from one interview to another. Third, panel studies offer flexibility that allows later inquiries to help explain earlier findings. [*See* PANEL STUDIES.]

Dropouts. Panel studies, even when they start out on an unbiased sample, have the bias that the less informed, the lower-income groups, and those not interested in the subject of the panel tend to drop out. Sobol (1959) suggested sampling these people more heavily to begin with, and she tried to follow movers. According to Seymour Sudman of the National Opinion Research Center, in national consumer panels and television rating panels where a fee is paid to the participant, the lower-income groups do not drop out.

Beginning effects. When new individuals or households first join a panel, their early responses may differ from their later ones. The "first-month" effect has unknown origins. For example, after the first month on the panel, the fraction of unemployed reported in private households decreases about 6 per cent. Over the course of several panel interviews, more houses become vacant and consumer buying decreases (Neter & Waksberg 1964*a*; Waksberg & Pearl 1964). Household repairs decreased by 9 per cent between the second and third interview. In consumer panels, the reports made during the first six or eight weeks of membership are usually not included in the analysis. The start-up differences are not clear-cut and emphatic but unsettling enough that the data are set aside, expensive as that is.

Sample surveys are not alone in these "first-time" effects. Doctors report that patients' blood pressures are higher when taken by a strange doctor. In the Peirce reaction-time data, presented in Table 4, the first day's average reaction time was about twice those of the other 23 days.

Long-run effects. A most encouraging finding in consumer panel studies has been the stability of the behavior of the panelists. By taking advantage of the process of enlarging two panels, Ehrenberg (1960) studied the effects of length of panel membership in Great Britain and in Holland. When he compared reports of newly recruited households (after their first few weeks) with those of "old" panel members, he found close agreement for purchasing rates, brand shares of market, and diary entries per week.

Panels do have to be adjusted to reflect changes in the universe, and panel families dissolve and multiply.

Nonresponse. The general problem of nonresponse arises because the properties of the nonrespondents usually differ to some degree from those of respondents. Unfortunately, nonresponse is not confined to studies of human populations. Physical objects can be inaccessible for various reasons: records may be lost, manholes may be paved over, a chosen area may be in dense jungle, or the object may be too small to be detected. One tries to reduce nonresponse, adjust estimates for it, and allow for it in measures of variability.

Mail questionnaires. The following advice, largely drawn from Levine and Gordon (1958–1959) and Scott (1961), is intended to increase response from mail questionnaires:

(1) Respondent should be convinced that the project is important.

(2) Preparatory letter should be on the letterhead of a well-known organization or, where appropriate, should be signed by a well-known person. In the United States and in Great Britain, governmental agencies are more likely to obtain responses than most organizations. Indeed, Scott (1961) reports 90 per cent response! Special populations respond to appeals from their organizations.

In pilot studies preparatory to using mailed census questionnaires in the initial stage of enumeration for the 1970 census (enumerator to follow up nonrespondents), the U.S. Bureau of the Census got the percentages of responses to the mailing shown in Table 2.

Table 2

	PERCENTAGE OF RESPONSE	
	Long form	Short form
Cleveland, Ohio	78	80
Louisville, Kentucky	85	88

(3) Rewards may be used (gifts, trading stamps, sweepstakes). Do not offer a copy of the final report unless you are prepared to give it.

(4) Make questionnaire attractive (printing on good paper is preferred), easy to read, and easy to fill in, remembering that many people have trouble reading fine print. Longer questionnaires usually lower the response rate.

(5) Keep questions simple, clear, as short as possible, and where multiple-choice answers appear, make sure that they do not force respondent to choose answers that do not represent his position.

(6) Try to keep early questions interesting and easy; do not leave important questions to the end; keep related questions together, unless there are strong reasons to act otherwise.

(7) Use a high class of mail, first-class, airmail, and even special delivery, both for sending the questionnaire and on the return envelope. Do not expect respondent to provide postage. In Great Britain, Scott (1961) found that compared with a postcard a card to be returned in an envelope raised response.

(8) Follow hard-core resistance with repeat questionnaire (the sixth mailing may still be rewarding), telegram, long-distance phone call, or even personal interview, as discussed below. Small response from early mailings may be badly biased;

for example, successful hunters respond more readily than unsuccessful ones to questions about their bag (Kish 1965, p. 547).

(9) Do not promise or imply anonymity and then retain the respondent's identity by subterfuge, however worthy the cause. Views on the effects of anonymity are mixed. If respondent's identity is needed, get it openly.

The principles set out above for mail questionnaires and those below for personal interviews may well be culture-bound for they are largely gathered from Western, English-speaking experience. For example, where paper is expensive, questionnaires on better paper may be less likely to be returned than those on poorer paper.

Sample surveys using personal interviews. In personal interviews, 80 to 90 per cent response has been attained even on intimate topics. In 1966, 85 per cent was regarded as rather good for pre-designated respondents in household surveys. In addition to the relevant maxims given above for mail surveys, to reduce nonresponse in personal interview surveys Sharp and Feldt (1959), among others, suggest some of the following:

(1) Send preview letter; use press to announce survey. In three lengthy surveys on different topics, according to Reuben Cohen of the Opinion Research Corporation, a letter sent in advance led to an average gain of 9 per cent in reaching, after four calls, urban adult respondents randomly drawn from the household list. Cohen also suggests that follow-up letters, after unsuccessful interviewing attempts, can reduce urban nonresponse by about one-third. Some students of polling believe that the actual impact of the preview letter is largely on the interviewer, who thinks that obtaining cooperation will be easier because of it—and so it is.

(2) Use trained interviewers, that is, interviewers trained especially to handle opening remarks, to explain the need for full coverage, and to get information about profitable times to make later calls ("callbacks") to reach respondents who are initially not at home. Experienced interviewers have had 3 per cent to 13 per cent fewer nonrespondents than inexperienced ones.

(3) Be flexible about calling at convenience of respondent, even at his place of work or recreation, on evenings and on week ends.

(4) Allow interviewer to call back many times to locate assigned respondent.

(5) Employ interpreter when appropriate.

(6) In more esoteric situations, know the culture. Do not plan to interview farmers in the peak periods of farm activity. An anthropologist scheduled a survey of current sexual behavior among South Sea islanders during the season when women were taboo to fishermen—the natives, finding it a great joke, were slow to explain.

Extra effort. When a survey carried out in the usual way produces a surprisingly large nonresponse, an all-out effort may be mounted using many of the devices mentioned earlier. A rule of thumb is that the nonresponse can be reduced by about half.

Oversampling nonrespondents. Repeated callbacks are the traditional method for reducing nonresponse in personal interviews, and careful cost analysis has shown that their cost per completed interview is lower than was at first supposed when quota sampling was popular. Kish and Hess (1959) report a procedure for including in the current sample nonrespondents from similar previous surveys, so as to have in advance an oversupply of persons likely not to respond. Then the sample survey, although getting responses from these people at a lower rate than from others, more nearly fills out its quotas.

Subsampling nonrespondents. To reduce nonresponse in mail surveys, subsampling the nonrespondents and pursuing them with personal interviews has been used frequently (formulas for optimum design are given in Hansen & Hurwitz 1946). In methods thus far developed the assumption is made that nonrespondents can surely be interviewed. When this assumption is unjustified, the method is less valid.

Adjusting for respondents not at home. The next method adjusts for those not at home but does not handle refusals, which often come to about half the nonresponse. Bartholomew (1961) has got accurate results by assuming that most of the bias arises from the composition of the population available at the first call. By finding out when to call back, the interviewer reduces later biases from this source. The interviewer gets information either from others in the house or from neighbors. To illustrate, in empirical investigations of populations of known composition, Bartholomew studied the percentage of men in political wards of a city. In four wards, differences between first-call and second-call samples in percentage of men were 17 per cent, 29 per cent, 36 per cent, and 38 per cent, substantial differences. But the differences between the second-call percentage of men and the actual percentage of men not reached by the first call were only 6 per cent, 2 per cent, 2 per cent, and 2 per cent, supporting Bartholomew's point.

Suppose that proportion p of the population has the characteristic of interest. It is convenient to regard p as the weighted average $\rho p_1 + (1 - \rho)p_2$, where ρ is the proportion of first-call responders in the population, p_1 is the proportion of first-call responders having the characteristic, and p_2 is the proportion of others in the population having the characteristic. (It is assumed that p_2 is independent of response status after the first call.) Now if N, the total sample size, is expressed as $N = N_1 + N_2 + N_3$, where N_1 is the number of first-call responders in the sample, N_2 is the number of second-call (but not first-call) responders in the sample, and N_3 is the number of others, then ρ is naturally estimated by N_1/N (the proportion of first-call responders in the sample), and p_1 by n_1/N_1 (the proportion of first-call responders in the sample who have the characteristic) and p_2 by n_2/N_2 (the proportion of second-call responders in the sample having the characteristic). Putting these estimators in the weighted average gives, as estimator of p,

$$\frac{1}{N}\left[n_1 + \frac{n_2(N - N_1)}{N_2} \right].$$

For example, if the number of men in the first call is $n_1 = 40$ out of $N_1 = 200$ interviewed, the second-call data are $n_2 = 200$, $N_2 = 400$, and the original sample size is $N = 1,000$, then the estimate of the proportion of men is 0.44. Even if the theory were exactly true, some increase in variance would arise from using such weights instead of obtaining the whole sample (Kish 1965, secs. 11.7B, 11.7C).

Extrapolation. Hendricks (1956) suggests plotting the variable being measured against the percentage of the sample that has responded on successive waves and extrapolating to 100 per cent. This simple, sensible idea could profit from more research, empirical and theoretical.

Effect on confidence interval. In sample surveys, nonresponse increases the lengths of the confidence intervals for final estimates by unknown amounts. For dichotomous types of questions, the suggestion is often made that all the nonresponses be counted first as having the attribute, then as not having it. The effect on the 95 per cent confidence interval is shown in Table 3. When such extreme allowances are required, the result of, say, 20 per cent nonresponse is frequently disastrous. For large random samples, this treatment of nonresponse, as may be seen from Table 3, adds approximately the per cent of nonresponse to the total length of the confidence interval that would have been appropriate with 100 per cent response. For example, with a sample of 2,500 from a large population, a 95 per cent confidence interval from 58 per cent to 62 per cent would be lengthened by 20 per cent nonresponse to 48.5 per cent to 71.5 per cent. This additional length gives motivation enough for wanting to keep nonresponse low.

Table 3 — Allowance to be added to and subtracted from the observed percentage to give at least 95 per cent confidence of covering the true value*

PER CENT NONRESPONSE	SAMPLE SIZE		
	100	2,500	Infinite
0	9.8	2.0	0.0
5	10.7	4.1	2.5
10	12.9	6.6	5.0
15	15.1	9.0	7.5
20	17.4	11.5	10.0

* These numbers are approximately correct for percentages near 0.50; they are likely to be conservative otherwise.

Source: Cochran, Mosteller, and Tukey 1954, p. 280.

No one believes that these "worst possible" limits represent the true state of affairs, nor should anyone believe the optimist who supposes that the nonrespondents are just like the respondents. In large samples, differences as large as 28 per cent in the fraction possessing a characteristic between the first 60 per cent interviewed and the next 25 per cent have been reported. To develop a more sensible set of limits in the spirit of Bayesian inference would be a useful research job for sample survey workers and theoretical statisticians. [See BAYESIAN INFERENCE.] This urgently needed work would require both empirical information (possibly newly gathered) and theoretical development.

The laboratory worker who studies human behavior rarely has a defined target population and he frequently works with a sample of volunteers. Under such circumstances we cannot even guess the extent of nonresponse. Again the hope is that the property being studied is independent of willingness or opportunity to serve as a subject—the position of the optimist mentioned above.

Since a few experimenters do sample defined populations, the argument that such sampling is impossible has lost some of its strength. The argument that such sampling is too expensive has to be appraised along with the value of inferences drawn from the behavior of undefined sampled populations.

Studying differences between groups offers more grounds for hope that bias from nonresponse works in the same direction and in nearly the same amount in both groups and that the difference may still be nearly right. This idea comes partly from physical measurements where sometimes knowledge can make such arguments about compensating errors rigorous. But, as Joseph Berkson warns, no general theorem states "Given any two wrong numbers, their difference is right."

Response error. When incorrect information about the respondent enters the data, a response error occurs. Among the many causes are misunderstandings, failures of memory, clerical errors, or deliberate falsehoods. The magnitudes of some of these errors and some ways to reduce them are discussed below.

Telescoping events. In reporting such things as amount of broken crockery or expenditures for household repairs, some respondents telescope the events of a considerable period into the shorter one under study. As a possible cure, Neter and Waksberg (1964*b*) have introduced a device called "bounded recall." In a study of household repairs, the respondent was interviewed twice, first under unbounded recall, during which the full story of the last month, including the telescoping from previous months, was recorded by the interviewer. Second, in an interview using bounded recall a month later, the respondent was deliberately aided by the record of repairs from the first interview. The magnitudes of the effects of telescoping are considerable, because the "unbounded" interview for household repairs gave 40 per cent more jobs and 55 per cent higher expenditure than did the "bounded" interview. Data from a "bounded" interview produce less bias.

Forgetting. Although telescoping occurs for some activities, chronic illness (Feldman 1960), which had already been clinically diagnosed, was reported only at a 25 per cent rate in household interviews. Others report rates in the 40 per cent to 50 per cent range. Feldman despairs of the household interview for this purpose; but if improvement in reports is to be attempted, he recommends more frequent interviews by competent, trained interviewers and, in a panel study, the use of a morbidity diary to improve self-reporting. One limitation, not attributable to forgetting, is set because physicians choose not to inform their patients of every illness they diagnose.

Sudman (1964) compared consumer panel reports based upon diary records with reports based upon unaided recall. First, he shows that for 72 grocery products (55 being food), the purchases recorded in the diary underestimate the amount shipped by the manufacturer (after adjustment for nonhousehold use) by a median of about 15 per cent. The underreporting was highly predictable, depending on both the properties of the product (frequency of purchase, where most often purchased) and its treatment in the diary (type size, page number, position on page). Second, when recall was compared with diary, the median ratio of purchases (purchases recalled divided by purchases in diary) was 1.05 for nonfood products, 1.83 for perishable food, 1.54 for staple foods. Leading nationally advertised brands have their market shares overstated under recall by 50 per cent compared to diary records, and chain brands are understated.

Use of experts. After respondents had valued their own homes, Kish and Lansing (1954) obtained expert appraisals for a sample of the homes. The comparison of the experts' appraisal with the homeowners' appraisal can be used to adjust the total valuation or to adjust valuations for groups of houses. For example, the homeowners may average a few per cent too high.

Editing records. Whenever a comparison of related records can be made, the accuracy of records can probably be improved. For example, Census Bureau editors, experienced in the lumber business, check annual sawmill production reports against those of the previous year, and large changes are rechecked with the sawmill.

Describing response errors. One common measure in the analysis of nonsampling errors puts bias and sampling variability into one index, called the mean square error. The larger the mean square error, the worse the estimate. The mean square error is the expected squared deviation of the observed value from the true value. This quantity can be separated into the sum of two parts, the variance of the observation around its own mean and the square of the bias. Although true values are not available, in the United States, the Bureau of the Census, for instance, tries to find standards more accurate than the census to get an estimate of the response bias to particular questions. For example, using the Current Population Survey as a standard, the Bureau of the Census not only finds out that the census underestimates the percentage in the labor force, but the bureau also gets data on the portions of the population not being satisfactorily measured, either because of variability or bias. Using such information, the bureau can profitably redesign its inquiries because it knows where and how to spend its resources.

Response uncertainty. In attitudinal studies (Katz 1946), the investigator must be especially wary of reports obtained by polling the public on a matter where opinion is not crystallized. The No Opinion category offers one symptom of trouble: for example, Katz reports that in 1945 only 4 per cent had No Opinion about universal military training in the United States, 13 per cent had No Opinion about giving the atom bomb secret to the United Nations, and 32 per cent had No Opinion about U.S. Senate approval of the United Nations charter. Even though the vote was 66 per cent to 3 per cent in favor of approving the charter, the 32 per cent No Opinion must suggest that the 69 per cent who offered an opinion contained a large subgroup who also did not hold a well-formed opinion.

Errors in analysis

Troubles with variability. In analyzing data, the presence of variability leads to many unsuspected difficulties and effects. In addition to treating some of the common traps, this section gives two ways to analyze variability in complicated problems where theoretical formulas for variance are either unavailable or should be distrusted.

Inflated sample size. The investigator must frequently decide what unit shall be regarded as independent of what other unit. For example, in analyzing a set of responses made by 10 individuals, each providing 100 responses, it is a common error to use as the sample size $10 \times 100 = 1,000$ responses and to make calculations, based perhaps on the binomial distribution, as if all these responses were independent. Unless investigation has shown that the situation is one in which independence does hold from response to response both within and between individuals, distrust this procedure. The analysis of variance offers some ways to appraise both the variability of an individual through time and the variation between individuals.

Use of matched individuals. Some investigators fail to take advantage of the matching in their data. Billewicz (1965, p. 623) reports that in 9 of 20 investigations that he examined for which the data were gathered from matched members in experimental and control groups, the analysis was done as if the data were from independent groups. Usually the investigator will have sacrificed considerable precision by not taking advantage in his analysis of the correlation in the data. Usually, but not always, the statistical significance of the results will be conservative. When matched data are analyzed as if independent, the investigator owes the reader an explanation for the decision.

Pooling significance tests. In the same vein, investigators with several small effects naturally wish that they could pool these effects to get more extreme levels of significance than those given by the single effects. Most methods of pooling significance tests depend upon independence between the several measures going into the pool. And that assumption implies, for example, that data from several items on the same sample survey cannot ordinarily be combined into a significance test by the usual pooling methods because independence cannot be assured. Correlation is almost certainly present because the same individuals respond to each item. Sometimes a remedy is to form a battery or scale that includes the several items of interest and to make a new test based upon the battery (Mosteller & Bush 1954, pp. 328–331). Naturally, the items would be chosen in advance for the purpose, not based *post hoc* upon their results. In the latter case, the investigator faces problems of multiplicity, discussed below.

Outlying observations. Frequently data contain suspicious observations that may be outliers, observations that cannot be rechecked, and yet that may considerably alter the interpretation of the data when taken at their face value. An outlier is an observation that deviates much more from the average of its mates or has a larger residual from a predicted value than seems reasonable on the basis of the pattern of the rest of the measurements. The classic example is given by the income distribution for members of a small college freshman class, exactly one member of which happens to be a multimillionaire. The arithmetic mean is not typical of the average member's income; but the median almost ignores an amount of income that exceeds the total for all the others in the class. Sometimes the outliers can be set aside for special study.

One current approach tailors the analysis to the type of outlier that is common in the particular kind of investigation by choosing statistics that are both appropriate and not especially sensitive to outliers. For example, as a measure of location, one might systematically use the median rather than the mean, or for more efficiency, the trimmed mean, which is the average of the measurements left after the largest and smallest 5 per cent (or 100α per cent) of the measurements have been removed (Mosteller & Tukey 1966, secs. *A5*, *B5*). In normal populations, the median has an efficiency of about 64 per cent, but the trimmed mean has most of the robustness of the median and an efficiency of about $1 - \frac{2}{3}\alpha$, where α is the proportion trimmed off each end. For $\alpha = 0.10$, the efficiency is 93 per cent. [*See* ERRORS, *article on the* EFFECTS OF ERRORS IN STATISTICAL ASSUMPTIONS; NONPARAMETRIC STATISTICS, *article on* ORDER STATISTICS; STATISTICAL ANALYSIS, SPECIAL PROBLEMS OF, *article on* OUTLIERS.]

Shifting regression coefficients. When one fits a regression equation to data, this regression equation may not forecast well for a new set of data. Among the reasons are the following:

(1) The fitted regression coefficients are not true values but estimates (sampling error).

(2) If one has selected the best from among many predictive variables, the selected ones may not be as good as they appeared to be on the basis of the sample (regression effect).

(3) Worse, perhaps none of the predictive variables were any good to start with (bad luck or poor planning).

(4) The procedure used to choose the form of the regression curve (linear, quadratic, exponential, . . .) has leaned too hard on the previously available data, and represents them too well as compared with the total population (wrong form).

(5) The new sample may be drawn from a population different from the old one (shifting population).

What are the effects of (2) and (5)? Consider the regression of height (Y) on weight (X) for a population of boys. Suppose that the true regression equation for this population is

$$E(Y) = a + b(X - \mu_x),$$

where a and b are unknown constants, $E(Y)$ is the expected value of Y for a given value of X, and μ_x is the mean of X. Suppose that an individual's height has a predictive error e that has mean 0, variance σ^2, and is unrelated to X, Y, and the true values of a and b.

Suppose that the experimenter chooses fixed values of X, x_i, such as 70, 80, 90, 100, 110, 120, 130, 140 pounds, obtaining boys having each of these weights and measuring their heights y_i. Then the data are paired observations (x_i, y_i), $i = 1, 2, \cdots, n$.

Estimating a and b from the sample by the usual least squares formulas one gets $\hat{a}$ and $\hat{b}$. Given a new sample with the same values of X from the same population, one can estimate the Y's for the new sample by

$$\hat{Y}_i = \hat{a} + \hat{b}(x_i - \bar{x}),$$

(where $\bar{x}$ is the average of the X_i) and then the expected mean square error of the estimates for the new sample is

expected value of $\sum(Y'_i - \hat{Y}_i)^2/n = \sigma^2(1 + 2/n)$,

where Y'_i is the height for an individual in the new sample. Note that σ^2 is the expected mean square error that would obtain were a and b known exactly instead of having been estimated.

Suppose that in addition to this population, there is a new population with different values of a and b, say a' and b'. Both populations come from a group of several populations with a and b varying from population to population and having $\bar{a}$ and $\bar{b}$ as the mean values of a and b, respectively, and σ_a^2 and σ_b^2 as the variances of these sets of regression coefficients. For the example of the boys' weights, consider the distribution of values of a and b from one city to another.

The regression line fitted on the basis of the sample from one population and then used on another population yields expected mean square error

$$\left(1 + \frac{2}{n}\right)\sigma^2 + 2(\sigma_a^2 + \sigma_x^2\sigma_b^2),$$

where σ_x^2 is the variance of the chosen set of x's. The first term comes as before from ordinary sampling variation of the Y's around the fitted regression line (the 2 of $2/n$ being the dimension of the parameter space), but the $2(\sigma_a^2 + \sigma_x^2\sigma_b^2)$ comes from drawing two sets of regression coefficients from the population of regression coefficients. This term may be substantial compared to $2\sigma^2/n$ or even σ^2.

We need extensive empirical results for such experiments to get a notion of the size of $2(\sigma_a^2 + \sigma_x^2\sigma_b^2)$ in various settings of interest to social and natural scientists. These investigations have not yet been carried out. The formulas for mean square error in this realistic situation must cause concern until more empirical studies are done. The existence of the added term should be recognized and an attempt made to assess its contribution numerically.

Uncontrolled sources of variation. Although the important formula $\sigma_{\bar{x}} = \sigma/\sqrt{n}$ for the standard deviation of a mean $\bar{X}$, a random variable, is correct when n uncorrelated measurements are drawn from a distribution with standard deviation σ, two difficulties arise. The measurements may not be uncorrelated, and the distribution may change from one set of measurements to another.

Peirce's data illustrate these difficulties. In an empirical study intended to test the appropriateness of the normal distribution, C. S. Peirce (1873) analyzed the time elapsed between a sharp tone stimulus and the response by an observer, who made about 500 responses each day for 24 days. Wilson and Hilferty (1929) reanalyzed Peirce's data. Table 4 shows sample means, $\bar{x}$, estimated standard deviations of the mean $s_{\bar{x}}$, and the ratio of the observed to the estimated interquartile range, $Q_3 - Q_1$. The observed interquartile range is based on percentage points of the observed distribution; the estimated interquartile range is based on the assumption of a normal distribution and has the value $2(0.6745s)$, where s is the sample standard deviation. In passing, note that the ratio is systematically much less than unity, defying the normality assumption. More salient for this discussion is the relation of day-to-day variation to the values of $s_{\bar{x}}$ based on within-day variation. The latter varies from 1.1 to 2.2 (after the first day's data, whose mean and standard deviation are obviously outliers, are set aside). These limits imply naive standard

Table 4 — Daily statistics from Wilson and Hilferty's analysis of C. S. Peirce's data

Day	$\bar{x} \pm s_{\bar{x}}$ (milliseconds)	$\dfrac{Q_3 - Q_1}{2(0.6745s)}$
1	475.6 ± 4.2	0.932
2	241.5 ± 2.1	0.842
3	203.1 ± 2.0	0.905
4	205.6 ± 1.8	0.730
5	148.5 ± 1.6	0.912
6	175.6 ± 1.8	0.744
7	186.9 ± 2.2	0.753
8	194.1 ± 1.4	0.840
9	195.8 ± 1.6	0.756
10	215.5 ± 1.3	0.850
11	216.6 ± 1.7	0.782
12	235.6 ± 1.7	0.759
13	244.5 ± 1.2	0.922
14	236.7 ± 1.8	0.529
15	236.0 ± 1.4	0.662
16	233.2 ± 1.7	0.612
17	265.5 ± 1.7	0.792
18	253.0 ± 1.1	0.959
19	258.7 ± 1.8	0.502
20	255.4 ± 2.0	0.521
21	245.0 ± 1.2	0.790
22	255.6 ± 1.4	0.688
23	251.4 ± 1.6	0.610
24	243.4 ± 1.1	0.730

Source: Wilson & Hilferty 1929.

deviations of the difference between means for pairs of days ranging from 1.6 to 3.1. If these applied, most differences would have to be less than twice these, 3.2 to 6.2, and practically all less than 4.8 to 9.3. Table 4 shows that the actual differences −38, +2, −57, +27, ⋯ , +11, −4, −8 impolitely pay little attention to such limitations.

In the language of analysis of variance, Peirce's data show considerable day-to-day variation. In the language of Walter Shewhart, such data are "out of control"—the within-day variation does not properly predict the between-days variation [see QUALITY CONTROL, *article on* PROCESS CONTROL]. Nor is it just a matter of the observer "settling down" in the beginning. Even after the twentieth day he still wobbles.

Need for a plurality of samples. The wavering in these data exemplifies the history of the "personal equation" problem of astronomy. The hope had been that each observer's systematic errors could be first stabilized and then adjusted for, thus improving accuracy. Unfortunately, attempts in this direction have failed repeatedly, as these data suggest they might. The observer's daily idiosyncrasies need to be recognized, at least by assigning additional day-to-day variation.

Wilson and Hilferty (1929, p. 125) emphasize that Peirce's data illustrate "the principle that we must have a plurality of samples if we wish to

estimate the variability of some statistical quantity, and that reliance on such formula as $\sigma/\sqrt{n}$ is not scientifically satisfactory in practice, even for estimating unreliability of means" (see Table 4).

Direct assessment of variability. One way to get a more honest estimate of variability breaks the data into rational subgroups, usually of equal or nearly equal sizes. For each subgroup, compute the statistic (mean, median, correlation coefficient, spectral density, regression equation, or whatever), base the estimate for the whole group on the average of the statistic for the subgroups, and base the estimate of variability on Student's t with one degree of freedom less than the number of subgroups. That is, treat the k group statistics like a sample of k independent measurements from a normal distribution. [*This method, sometimes called the method of interpenetrating samples, generalizes the method for calculating the sampling error for nonprobability samples described in* SAMPLE SURVEYS, *article on* NONPROBABILITY SAMPLING.]

At least five groups (preferably at least ten) are advisable in order to get past the worst part of the t-table. This suggestion encourages using more, not fewer, groups. For two-sided 5 per cent levels, see Table 5.

Two major difficulties with this direct assessment are (*a*) that it may not be feasible to calculate meaningful results for such small amounts of data as properly chosen groups would provide, or (*b*) even if the calculations yield sensible results, they may be so severely biased as to make their use unwise.

A method with wide application, intended to ameliorate these problems, is the *jackknife*, which offers ways to reduce bias in the estimate and to set realistic approximate confidence limits in complex situations.

Assessment by the jackknife. Again the data are divided into groups, but the statistic to be jackknifed is computed repeatedly on all the data except an omitted group. With ten groups, the statistic is

Table 5 — Two-sided 5 per cent levels for Student's t for selected degrees of freedom

Degrees of freedom	5 per cent critical point
1	12.7
2	4.3
3	3.2
5	2.6
10	2.23
20	2.09
60	2.00
500	1.96
∞	1.96

computed each time for about 90 per cent of the data.

More generally, for the jackknife, the desired calculation is made for all the data, and then, after the data are divided into groups, the calculation is made for each of the slightly reduced bodies of data obtained by leaving out just one of the groups.

Let $y_{(j)}$ be the result of making the complex calculation on the portion of the sample that omits the jth subgroup, that is, on a pool of $k - 1$ subgroups. Let y_{all} be the corresponding result for the entire sample, and define *pseudo values* by

$$(1) \quad y_{*j} = ky_{all} - (k - 1)y_{(j)}, \quad j = 1, 2, \cdots, k.$$

These pseudo values now play the role played by the values of the subgroup statistics in the method of interpenetrating samples. For simple means, the jackknife reduces to that method.

As in the method of interpenetrating samples, in a wide variety of problems, the pseudo values can be used to set approximate confidence limits through Student's t, as if they were the results of applying some complex calculation to each of k independent pieces of data.

The jackknifed value y_*, which is the best single result, and an estimate, s_*^2, of its variance are given by

$$y_* = \frac{1}{k}(y_{*1} + \cdots + y_{*k}),$$

$$s^2 = \left[\sum y_{*i}^2 - ky_*^2\right] \Big/ (k - 1),$$

$$s_*^2 = s^2/k.$$

If the statistic being computed has a bias that can be expressed as a series in the reciprocal of the sample size, N, the jackknife removes the leading term (that in $1/N$) in the bias. Specifically, suppose that $\hat{\mu}$, the biased estimate of μ, has expected value

$$E(\hat{\mu}) = \mu + \frac{a}{N} + \frac{b}{N^2} + \cdots,$$

where a, b, and so on are constants. If $\hat{\mu}_*$ is the jackknifed estimate, its expected value is

$$E(\hat{\mu}_*) = \mu + \frac{\alpha}{N^2} + \frac{\beta}{N^3} + \cdots,$$

where α, β, and so on are constants. To give a trivial example, $\sum(X_i - \bar{X})^2/N$ is a biased estimate of σ^2. Its expected value is $\sigma^2 - (\sigma^2/N)$, and so it has the sort of bias that would be removed by jackknifing.

To understand how the first-order bias terms are removed by jackknifing, one might compute the expected value of y_* for the special case where

$$E(\hat{\mu}) = \mu + a/N.$$

Then with the use of k groups of equal size, n, so that $kn = N$,

$$E(y_{(j)}) = \mu + a/(k-1)n$$
$$E(y_{all}) = \mu + a/kn$$
$$E(y_{*j}) = E[ky_{all} - (k-1)y_{(j)}]$$
$$= k\mu + a/n - [(k-1)\mu + a/n]$$
$$= \mu.$$

Finally,

$$E(y_*) = k\mu/k = \mu.$$

The leading term in the bias was removed in the construction of the y_{*j}'s. Even if the sample sizes are not equal, the leading term in the bias is likely to have its coefficient reduced considerably.

Example of the jackknife: ratio estimate. In expounding the use of ratio estimates, Cochran ([1953] 1963, p. 156) gives 1920 and 1930 sizes (number of inhabitants) for each city in a random sample of 49 drawn from a population of 196 large U.S. cities. He wishes to estimate the total 1930 population for these 196 cities on the basis of the results of the sample of 49, whose 1920 and 1930 populations are both known, and from the total 1920 population. The example randomly groups his 49 cities into 7 sets of 7 each. Table 6 shows their subtotals.

The formula for the ratio estimate of the 1930 population total is

$$\frac{(1930 \text{ sample total})}{(1920 \text{ sample total})} \times (1920 \text{ population total}),$$

so that the logarithm of the estimated 1930 population total is given by $\log(1930 \text{ sample total}) - \log(1920 \text{ sample total}) + \log(1920 \text{ population total})$. Consequently the jackknife is applied to $z = \log(1930 \text{ sample total}) - \log(1920 \text{ sample total})$, since this choice minimizes the number of multiplications and divisions.

Further computation is shown in Table 7 where in the "all" column the numbers 5,054 and 6,262 come directly from the totals of the previous table, and in the "$i = 1$" column the numbers $4,303 = 5,054 - 751$ and $5,347 = 6,262 - 915$ are the re-

Table 6 — Subtotals in thousands for sets of 7 cities

	1920	1930
First 7	751	915
Second 7	977	1,122
Third 7	965	1,243
Fourth 7	385	553
Fifth 7	696	881
Sixth 7	830	937
Seventh 7	450	611
Total	5,054	6,262

Source: Cochran [1953] 1963, p. 156.

Table 7 — Details of jackknifing the ratio estimate

	all	$i=1$	$i=2$	$i=3$	$i=4$	$i=5$	$i=6$	$i=7$
$x_{(i)}$ (1920 sample)	5,054	4,303	4,077	4,089	4,669	4,358	4,224	4,604
log $x_{(i)}$	3.70364	3.63377	3.61034	3.61162	3.66922	3.63929	3.62572	3.66314
$y_{(i)}$ (1930 sample)	6,262	5,347	5,140	5,019	5,709	5,381	5,325	5,651
log $y_{(i)}$	3.79671	3.72811	3.71096	3.70062	3.75656	3.73086	3.72632	3.75213
$z_{(i)} = \log [y_{(i)}/x_{(i)}]$	.09307	.09434	.10062	.08900	.08734	.09157	.10060	.08899
$z_{*i} = 7z_{all} - 6z_{(i)}$	—	.08545	.04777	.11749	.12745	.10207	.04789	.11755
rounded z_{*i}	—	.085	.048	.117	.127	.102	.048	.118

$$\text{Sum} = .645; .645/7 \cong .092 = \text{mean} = z_\circ$$

$$\text{Sum Sq.} = .065979; .065979 - (.645)^2/7 = .006547 = \text{sum sq. deviations}$$

$$\frac{.006547}{6 \times 7} \cong .00015588 = s_*^2$$

$$\sqrt{.00015588} \cong .0125 = s_\circ$$

$$|t_6|_{.95} = 2.447; (.0125)(2.447) = .0306 = \text{allowance}$$

sults of omitting the first 7 cities, and so on for the other columns. Five-place logarithms have obviously given more than sufficient precision, so that the pseudo values of z are conveniently rounded to three decimals. From these are computed the mean $z_\circ$ and the 95 per cent limits = mean ± allowance. Table 8 gives all the remaining details. The resulting point estimate is 28,300, about 100 lower than the unjackknifed estimate. (Since the correct 1930 total is 29,351, the automatic bias adjustment did not help in this instance. This is a reminder that bias is an "on the average" concept.) The limits on this estimate are ordinarily somewhat wider than would apply if each city had been used as a separate group, since the two-sided 95 per cent level for Student's t with 6 degrees of freedom is $|t_6|_{.95} = 2.447$, while with 47 degrees of freedom it is $|t_{47}|_{.95} = 2.012$. The standard error found here was .0125 in logarithmic units, which converts to about 840 in the final total $(4.360 + z_\circ + s_\circ = 4.464;$ antilog $4.464 \cong 29,140; 29,140 - 28,300 = 840)$. The conversion from logarithmic units to original units for the confidence interval represent an approximation that may not always be appropriate [see STATISTICAL ANALYSIS, SPECIAL PROBLEMS OF, *article on* TRANSFORMATIONS OF DATA]. (Further material on the jackknife can be found in Mosteller and Tukey 1966, sec. E).

Table 8 — Final computations for the ratio estimate*

	VALUE OF ESTIMATE	95 PER CENT CONFIDENCE INTERVALS
log ratio	$z_\circ = 0.092$	0.062 to 0.123
log total	$4.360 + z_\circ = 4.452$	4.422 to 4.483
total	antilog $4.452 = 28,300$	26,000 to 30,400

* Base data: 1920 total = 22,919, log (1920 total) = 4.360
 log total = log (1920 total) + log ratio

Analytical difficulties. In analyzing data or planning for its analysis, the choice of a base for rates is not always obvious; comparing many things leads to biases that need adjustment, selection reduces correlation, and selection for excellence leads to disappointments. This section treats these matters.

Bases for rates. The investigator should think about more than one possible base for a percentage or a rate and consider the value of reporting results using different bases. Examples from accident statistics may suffice. Are young women safer drivers than young men? Yes: in the United States in 1966 insurance rates for young women were ordinarily lower because they caused less expensive damage. On the other hand, these rates were based on total disbursements in a fixed period of time. Young women may well drive much less than young men, and if so, their accident rate per mile may be the higher.

Coppin, Ferdun, and Peck (1965) sent a questionnaire on driving in 1963 to a sample of 10,250 California drivers who were aged 16 to $19\frac{1}{2}$ at the beginning of the period. Based on the information from the 65 per cent of questionnaires returned, where respondents estimated mileage driven per week, and on accidents reported in the respondents' Motor Vehicle Department files, the accident rates per 100,000 miles shown in Table 9 were found. On accidents, nonrespondents were very similar to respondents, but nonrespondents had considerably more violations. Since the mileage is estimated, the evidence is weak; but it seems to be the best available. Boys had more accidents per mile at 16, girls at 17, and after that their rates were nearly equal.

How should airplane safety (or danger) be as-

Table 9 — Accidents and violations per 100,000 miles

	ACCIDENTS		VIOLATIONS	
Age	Males	Females	Males	Females
16	2.9	2.1	7.1	4.9
17	1.9	2.3	6.1	4.2
18	1.4	1.4	5.6	3.7
19	1.4	1.5	5.4	3.5

Source: Coppin et al. 1965, pp. 27–28.

sessed? Deaths per million passenger miles, deaths per trip, and casualties per hour flown suggest themselves, and each can be supported.

In general, different answers may be appropriate for different questions, as was the case in the insurance companies' view versus the accident-per-mile view of the safety of young drivers given above. Ease and economy may recommend giving several answers as well as the investigator's judgment about their merits. In some problems, no resolution may be possible, and then the investigator would do well to admit it.

Problems of multiplicity. When methods of appraisal designed for single comparisons are used to compare many things, the multiplicity may mislead. When means of two samples drawn from the same normal population are compared, they differ by more than twice the standard deviation of their difference in less than 5 per cent of the sample pairs. Among ten sample means from the same population, some pair is more likely than not to differ this much (Table 11). Although statistics has come a long way in providing honest methods of making comparisons when there are many to be made, it has largely done this in the framework of a closed system, where the particular items to be compared have already been specified. For example, many workers have offered suitable ways to measure the significance not only of all possible differences but also of all possible linear contrasts (weighted sums, the weights adding to zero) on the same data. [*See* LINEAR HYPOTHESES, *articles on* MULTIPLE COMPARISONS.]

Statistics has not yet provided a way to test the significance of results obtained by peeking at large bodies of data and developing hypotheses as one goes along. The facility of the human brain for rationalizing almost any observed fact immediately after its realization is something that cannot yet be allowed for. This means that it is rarely possible to validate a hypothesis on the same body of data that suggested it and usually new studies are necessary to test hypotheses developed on completely different data (Mosteller & Tukey 1966, sec. B6).

Selection effects. Users of tests for purposes of selection (admission to college, personnel selection) often complain that the scores used to make the selection do not correlate well with the in-service performance of the individuals after selection. Possibly the chosen test does not give scores that correlate well with the performance being measured, but one must remember that when a population is truncated on one of its variables, the correlation of that dimension with the others is likely to be reduced toward zero. To illustrate, suppose that freshman calculus grades Y and pre-course examination grades X are bivariately normally distributed with correlation coefficient ρ. Suppose that only individuals whose pretest scores exceed a certain value $X = x$ are admitted to the calculus course. This means that selection is based on the variable X with the criterion x. The new correlation ρ' between the grades of those taking the course and their pretest scores would be given (see Cochran 1951, p. 453) as

$$\rho' = \rho \sqrt{\frac{1-A}{1-A\rho^2}},$$

where

$$A = \frac{z}{p}\left(\frac{z}{p} - t\right),$$

p = proportion that the selected group is of the whole population,

t = standard normal deviate having proportion p to the right,

z = height of the standard univariate normal at the position t.

If the proportion selected $p = 0.05$, then $t = 1.645$, $z = 0.1031$. Values of ρ' for selected values of ρ and p are shown in Table 10. To return to the example, if pretest scores and calculus grades had originally been correlated $\rho = 0.8$, in the 5 per cent selected the correlation would drop to 0.44.

Table 10 shows that as the percentage truncated increases the correlation in the remaining population slowly decreases from its initial value. For initial correlations between .1 and .8 the reduction is between a half and a third of the original correlation when 75 per cent of the population has been removed. A very rough approximation for ρ' is $(.7p + .3)\rho$ for $p > .25$ and $0 \leqslant \rho \leqslant .7$. The new correlation decreases sharply for the higher initial correlation coefficients when more than 90 per cent of the population is deleted. Unfortunately, these results may be rather sensitive to the detailed shape of the bivariate population studied and so this bivariate normal example can only illustrate the possibilities.

Table 10 — Values of ρ' for various values of 100(1−p), ρ pairs

100(1−p) PER CENT TRUNCATED	VALUES OF ρ							100p PER CENT SELECTED
	.100	.300	.500	.700	.800	.900	.950	
5	.090	.272	.461	.661	.768	.881	.939	95
10	.085	.256	.438	.637	.747	.867	.932	90
25	.073	.224	.389	.583	.698	.834	.912	75
50	.060	.186	.329	.509	.626	.780	.878	50
75	.049	.153	.273	.434	.548	.712	.831	25
90	.041	.128	.231	.374	.481	.647	.781	10
95	.037	.116	.210	.342	.444	.609	.749	5
99	.031	.098	.178	.293	.385	.542	.689	1

Regression effect. Suppose that a fallible measure selects from many individuals a few that appear to be best. On a reassessment based on fresh performance data, the selected ones will ordinarily not do as well as they originally appeared to do on the selection test. The reason is that performance varies and on the occasion of the test some individuals accidentally perform much better than their average and are selected. Happily, individuals selected to be worst do not do as badly on reassessment. This phenomenon is known as regression toward the mean; instances are sometimes called regression effects or shrinkage effects. To illustrate, Mosteller and Wallace (1964, p. 209) selected words and obtained weights for their rates of use with intent to discriminate between the writings of Alexander Hamilton and James Madison. Writers differ in their rate of use of such words as *of, and, the, to,* and *upon.* On the basis of the writings used for the selection and weighting of the word counts, the two statesmen's writings were separated by 6.9 standard deviations. When the same words and weights were applied to fresh writings not used in selecting or weighting, the new writings were separated by 4.5 standard deviations—still good discrimination, but a loss of 2.4 standard deviations is substantial and illustrates well the effect. Losses are usually greatest among the poorer discriminants. Usages of the word *upon* originally separated the writings by 3.3 standard deviations, and did even better, 3.8, in the fresh validating materials; but a less effective set of words giving originally a separation of 1.3 standard deviations dropped to 0.3 on retesting. The lesson is that optimization methods (such as least squares and maximum likelihood) do especially well on just the data used to optimize. Plan for validation, and, where hopes are high for much gain from many small effects, prepare for disappointment.

Weights. If individuals are sampled to find out about their families, as in investigations carried out in schools, unless some account is taken of weights, a peculiar distribution may arise. For example, if a sample of girls is asked to report the numbers of sons and of daughters (including themselves) in their families, it turns out that the average number of daughters observed in the sample is approximately one more than the average number of sons. (More precisely, mathematics not given here shows the difference to be: [*variance of number of daughters* minus *covariance of number of sons and daughters*] divided by [*average number of daughters*]. When the distribution of the number of daughters is approximately Poisson and the numbers of sons and of daughters are independent, the ratio is approximately unity.) Essentially, families of three girls report three times as often as families with one girl, and families with no girls do not report at all. If account is taken of the dependence of frequency of reporting upon the number of daughters, this matter can be adjusted, provided information about families with no daughters is available or is not needed.

Similarly, in studying the composition of special groups, unless the analysis is done separately for each family size, one needs to remember that more children are first-born than second, and so on.

Errors in calculation. A well-planned format for laying out calculations and careful checking aid in getting correct answers. To give a base line, a sample survey by the Internal Revenue Service (Farioletti 1952, pp. 65–78) found arithmetical errors in only 6 per cent of 160,000 personal income tax returns. Considering that the task is sometimes troublesome and often resented, this record appears good.

In scientific work, misreadings of numbers, misplaced decimals, errors in the application of formulas all take their toll. As a first step in the control of error, regard any unchecked calculation as probably wrong.

Overmechanization. Overmechanization of computing puts great pressure on the analyst to make one enormous run of the data and thereby economically get all the analyses he wished. Alas, one great sweep is never the way of good data analysis. Instead, we learn a little from each analysis and return again and again. To illustrate, in deciding whether to transform the data to square roots, logarithms, inverse sines, or reciprocals before launching on the major analysis, tests may be run for each function separately, leading to the choice of one or two transformations for use in the next stage. Otherwise the whole large calculation must be run too many times because there are many branch points in a large calculation with several choices available at each. Furthermore, data analysis requires extensive printout, little of which will be looked at; therefore the data analyst must resist the notion that the good computer user makes the machine do all the work internally and obtains very little printout. He must also resist the idea of having ever speedier programs at the cost of more and more time for programming and less and less for analysis. Fine programs are needed, but the cost of additional machine time from slow programs may be less than the cost of improvements in programming and of the waiting time before analysis can begin.

Possibly with the increase of time-sharing in high-speed computation and the handy packaging of general purpose programs for the analysis of data, the opportunities for making studied choices at each point in the analysis will become easier and less time-consuming.

Preserving data from erasure. After processing, data should usually be preserved in some form other than a single magnetic tape. Contrary to theory and rumor, magnetic tapes containing basic data are occasionally erased or made unusable in the high-speed computing process, and all the explanations in the world about how this could or could not have happened cannot restore a bit of information. One remedy is to have a spare tape with your data or program copied upon it. When disaster strikes, remember that few things seem more likely to recur than a rare event that has just happened, and so copy your spare tape before you submit it to the destroyer.

Hand copying. Since human copying is a major source of error, keep hand copying to a minimum and take advantage where possible of the high-speed computer's ability to produce tables in immediately publishable form and of mechanical reproduction processes. Editing can be done by cutting, pasting, and painting out. When copying is necessary, checks of both column totals and row totals are believed superior to direct visual comparisons of individual entries with the manuscript.

Checks. Checking the programming and calculations of a high-speed computer presents a major unsolved problem. One might suppose that once a machine began producing correct answers, it always would thereafter. Not at all. It may respond to stimuli not dreamed of by the uninitiated. To find, for example, that it throws a small error into the fifth entry in the fourth column of every panel is disconcerting and scary, partly because small errors are hard to find and partly because one wonders whether undetected errors may still be present. Thorough and systematic checking is advised. Some ways are through sample problems; through fuller printout of the details of a problem already worked by hand; by comparing corresponding parts of several problems, including special cases whose answers are known by outside means; and by solving the problem in more than one way.

In addition to the checks on the final calculations, check the input data. For input punched on cards, for example, some process of verifying the punching is required. Methods of checking will vary with the problem. Partly redundant checking may not be wasteful. Look for impossible codes in columns, look for interchanges of columns. Try to set up checks for inconsistency in cards. (In Western cultures, nursery school children are not married, wives don't have wives, and families with 42 children need verification.) Consider ways to handle blanks based on internal consistency.

In working with computers, be wary of the way symbols translate from keyboard to card or tape— dashes and minus signs or zeros, letter O's, and blanks are a few sources of confusion. In dealing with numbers using, say, a two-digit field, a number such as 6, unless written 06, may wind up as 60 or as a meaningless character. The possibilities here are endless, but in a given problem it is usually worth organizing systematic procedures to combat these difficulties.

Order-of-magnitude checking. When calculations are complete, order-of-magnitude checks are always valuable. Are there more people in the state of New York than in the United States? Does leisure plus work plus sleep take much more than 24 hours per day? Exercises in calculations of comparative orders of magnitude can be rewarding in themselves because new connections are sometimes made between the research and the rest of the subject matter.

Significant figures. Both hand and high-speed calculations require numbers to be carried to more places than seem meaningful and to more places than simple rules learned in childhood would suggest. These rules seem dedicated to rounding early so as not to exaggerate the accuracy of one's result. But they may erase the signal with the noise. About the only reassuring rule for complex calculations is that if the important digits are the same when the calculation is carried to twice as many places, enough accuracy has likely been carried.

The old rules for handling significant figures come from a simplified idea that a number can report both its value and its accuracy at the same time. Under such rules the numbers 3.26 and 0.0326 were thought of as correct to within half a unit in the last place. Sometimes in mathematical tables this approach is satisfactory. For data-based numbers, the uncertainty in a number has to be reported separately.

One-of-a-kind calculations. One-of-a-kind calculations, frequent in scientific reports, are especially error prone, both because the investigator may not set up a standard method of calculation, complete with checks, and because he does not have the aid of comparisons with other members of a long sequence. For example, some pollsters believed that their wrong forecast about a vote would have been close had proper weighting for household size been applied, a claim worth checking. Their ultimate error was in thinking that this claim was right. How did they make it? Pages of weightings carefully checked down to, but not including, the final estimate showed no error in their reanalysis. But their one-of-a-kind calculation leading to the final estimate was a ratio composed of an inappropriate numerator and an inappropriate denominator grabbed from the many column totals. By accident this meaningless quotient gave a number nearly identical with that produced by the voters. And who checks further an answer believed to be correct? Actually, the weighting for household size scarcely changed their original forecast. The moral is that the one-of-a-kind calculation offers grave danger.

Consequently, each new calculation can well be preceded by a few applications of the method to simple made-up examples until the user gets the feel of the calculation, of the magnitudes to be expected, and of a convenient way to lay out the procedure. Having someone else check the calculation independently requires that the investigator not teach the verifier the original mistakes. Yates has suggested that, in a large hand calculation, independence could nearly be preserved when different individuals calculate on separate machines in parallel in two different numerical units; for ex-

ample, one computes in dollars, the other in pounds. At the end, the final answers are converted for comparison.

Gross errors in standard deviations. Since the sample range w (largest measurement minus smallest measurement) is easy to compute, it is often used to check the more complicated calculation of a sample standard deviation s. In the same sample, the ratio w/s must lie between the lower and upper bounds given in Table 11 or else the range, sample standard deviation, or quotient is in error. The table shows the 2.5 per cent and 97.5 per cent point of the distribution of w/s for a normal distribution. When calculations lead to ratios falling outside these limits but inside the bounds, they are not necessarily wrong; but further examination may pay.

Table 11 also shows the median of the distribution of the range of a sample of size n drawn from a standard normal distribution. It gives one an idea of the spread measured in standard deviations to be expected of the sample means of n equal-sized groups whose population means are identical. Note that through $n = 20$ a rough rule is that the

Table 11 — Bounds on the ratio: range/standard deviation[a]

n	Lower bound	w/s 2.5%	w/s 97.5%	Upper bound	Median of w/σ
2	1.41	1.41	1.41	1.41	.95[b]
3	1.73	1.74	2.00	2.00	1.59[b]
4	1.73	1.93	2.44	2.45	1.98
5	1.83	2.09	2.78	2.83	2.26
6	1.83	2.22	3.06	3.16	2.47
7	1.87	2.33	3.28	3.46	2.65
8	1.87	2.43	3.47	3.74	2.79
9	1.90	2.51	3.63	4.00	2.92
10	1.90	2.59	3.78	4.24	3.02
15	1.94	2.88	4.29	5.29	3.42
20	1.95	3.09	4.63	6.16	3.69
30	1.97	3.37	5.06	7.62	4.04
50	1.98	3.73	5.54	9.90	4.45
100	1.99	4.21	6.11	14.07	4.97
200	1.99	4.68	6.60	19.95	5.49[c]
500	2.00	5.25	7.15	31.59	6.07[c]
1,000	2.00	5.68	7.54	44.70	6.48[c]

a. Lower bound, 2.5% point, 97.5% point, and upper bound for the ratio: range/sample standard deviation (w/s); median of the distribution of the ratio: range/population standard deviation (w/σ); the sample size is n. The upper and lower bounds apply to any distribution and sampling method; the percentage points and the median are computed for random sampling from a normal distribution, but they should be useful for other distributions.

b. This is not an error. The median is expressed as the multiplier of the *population* standard deviation, whereas the bounds relate range and *sample* standard deviation.

c. The mean of the distribution is given as an approximation to the median because the latter is not available.

Sources: Pearson & Stephens 1964, p. 486, for lower and upper bounds and for 2.5% and 97.5% points; Harter 1963, pp. 162–164, for medians; Pearson & Hartley 1954, p. 174, for means.

median distance between the largest and smallest sample mean is $\sqrt{n}\sigma_{\bar{x}}$.

Reporting. When writing the final report, remember that making clear the frame of reference of a study helps the reader understand the discussion.

Need for full reporting. In reporting on the investigation, be sure to give detailed information about the populations studied, the operational definitions used, and the exceptions to the general rules. Unless the details are carefully reported, they are quickly forgotten and are soon replaced by cloudy fancies. Discussions of accuracy, checks, and controls are needed in the final report.

Full and careful reporting can lead to ample prefaces, numerous appendixes, some jargon, and lengthy discussions. Shrink not from these paraphernalia, so amusing to the layman, for without them the study loses value; it is less interpretable, for it cannot be properly compared with other studies. Jargon may be the price of brevity.

The reader may object that editors will not allow such full reporting. Certainly the amount of detail required does vary with the sort of report to be made. Many studies that are published in short reports turn out to present a long sequence of short articles, and these, in one place or another, can give the relevant details.

Try to go beyond bare-bones reporting by giving readers your views of the sorts of populations, circumstances, or processes to which the findings of the study might apply. Warn the reader about generalizations that you are wary of but that he, on the basis of your findings, might reasonably expect to hold. While such discussions can be criticized as speculation, you owe it to the reader to do your best with them and to be as specific as you can be.

Beyond all this, where appropriate, do write as nontechnical a summary as you can for the interested public.

Suppression of data. In pursuit of a thesis, even the most careful may find it easy to argue themselves into the position that the exceptions to the desired proposition are based upon poorer data, somehow do not apply, would be too few to be worth reporting if one took the trouble to look them up, would mislead the simpleminded if reported, and therefore had best be omitted. Whether or not these views are correct, and some of them may well be, it is preferable to present the whole picture and then to present one's best appraisal of all the data. The more complete record puts readers in a much better position to consider both the judgments and the proposition.

FREDERICK MOSTELLER

[*Directly related are the entries* EXPERIMENTAL DESIGN; FALLACIES, STATISTICAL; SAMPLE SURVEYS.]

BIBLIOGRAPHY

BARTHOLOMEW, D. J. 1961 A Method of Allowing for "Not-at-home" Bias in Sample Surveys. *Applied Statistics* 10:52–59.

BILLEWICZ, W. Z. 1965 The Efficiency of Matched Samples: An Empirical Investigation. *Biometrics* 21:623–644.

CANTRIL, HADLEY (1944) 1947 The Use of Trends. Pages 220–230 in Hadley Cantril, *Gauging Public Opinion.* Princeton Univ. Press.

CANTRIL, HADLEY 1966 *The Pattern of Human Concerns.* New Brunswick, N.J.: Rutgers Univ. Press.

COCHRAN, WILLIAM G. 1951 Improvement by Means of Selection. Pages 449–470 in Berkeley Symposium on Mathematical Statistics and Probability, Second, *Proceedings.* Edited by Jerzy Neyman. Berkeley: Univ. of California Press.

COCHRAN, WILLIAM G. (1953) 1963 *Sampling Techniques.* 2d ed. New York: Wiley.

COCHRAN, WILLIAM G.; MOSTELLER, FREDERICK; and TUKEY, JOHN W. 1954 *Statistical Problems of the Kinsey Report on Sexual Behavior in the Human Male.* Washington: American Statistical Association.

COPPIN, R. S.; FERDUN, G. S.; and PECK, R. C. 1965 The Teen-aged Driver. California, Department of Motor Vehicles, Division of Administration, Research and Statistics Section, *Report 21.*

EHRENBERG, A. S. C. 1960 A Study of Some Potential Biases in the Operation of a Consumer Panel. *Applied Statistics* 9:20–27.

FARIOLETTI, MARIUS 1952 Some Results From the First Year's Audit Control Program of the Bureau of Internal Revenue. *National Tax Journal* 5, no. 1:65–78.

FELDMAN, JACOB J. 1960 The Household Interview Survey as a Technique for the Collection of Morbidity Data. *Journal of Chronic Diseases* 11:535–557.

HANSEN, MORRIS H.; and HURWITZ, WILLIAM N. 1946 The Problem of Non-response in Sample Surveys. *Journal of the American Statistical Association* 41:517–529.

HARBISON, FREDERICK; and MYERS, CHARLES A. 1964 *Education, Manpower, and Economic Growth: Strategies of Human Resource Development.* New York: McGraw-Hill.

HARTER, H. LEON 1963 The Use of Sample Ranges and Quasi-ranges in Setting Exact Confidence Bounds for the Population Standard Deviation. II. Quasi-ranges of Samples From a Normal Population—Probability Integral and Percentage Points; Exact Confidence Bounds for σ. → ARL 21, Part 2. Wright-Patterson Air Force Base, Ohio: U.S. Air Force, Office of Aerospace Research, Aeronautical Research Laboratories.

HENDRICKS, WALTER A. 1956 *The Mathematical Theory of Sampling.* New Brunswick, N.J.: Scarecrow Press.

KATZ, DANIEL 1946 The Interpretation of Survey Findings. *Journal of Social Issues* 2, no. 2:33–44.

KISH, LESLIE 1965 *Survey Sampling.* New York: Wiley.

KISH, LESLIE; and HESS, IRENE 1959 A "Replacement" Procedure for Reducing the Bias of Nonresponse. *American Statistician* 13, no. 4:17–19.

KISH, LESLIE; and LANSING, JOHN B. 1954 Response Errors in Estimating the Value of Homes. *Journal of the American Statistical Association* 49:520–538.

KLUCKHOHN, FLORENCE R.; and STRODTBECK, FRED L. 1961 *Variations in Value Orientations.* Evanston, Ill.: Row, Peterson.

LAWLEY, D. N.; and SWANSON, Z. 1954 Tests of Significance in a Factor Analysis of Artificial Data. *British Journal of Statistical Psychology* 7:75–79.

LEUCHTENBURG, WILLIAM E. 1963 *Franklin D. Roosevelt and the New Deal: 1932–1940.* New York: Harper. → A paperback edition was published in the same year.

LEVINE, SOL; and GORDON, GERALD 1958–1959 Maximizing Returns on Mail Questionnaires. *Public Opinion Quarterly* 22:568–575.

MOSES, LINCOLN E.; and OAKFORD, ROBERT V. 1963 *Tables of Random Permutations.* Stanford Univ. Press.

MOSTELLER, FREDERICK; and BUSH, ROBERT R. (1954) 1959 Selected Quantitative Techniques. Volume 1, pages 289–334 in Gardner Lindzey (editor), *Handbook of Social Psychology.* Cambridge, Mass.: Addison-Wesley.

MOSTELLER, FREDERICK; and TUKEY, JOHN W. 1966 Data Analysis, Including Statistics. Unpublished manuscript. → To be published in the revised edition of the *Handbook of Social Psychology,* edited by Gardner Lindzey and Elliot Anderson.

MOSTELLER, FREDERICK; and WALLACE, DAVID L. 1964 *Inference and Disputed Authorship: The Federalist.* Reading, Mass.: Addison-Wesley.

NETER, JOHN; and WAKSBERG, JOSEPH 1964a Conditioning Effects From Repeated Household Interviews. *Journal of Marketing* 28, no. 2:51–56.

NETER, JOHN; and WAKSBERG, JOSEPH 1964b A Study of Response Errors in Expenditures Data From Household Interviews. *Journal of the American Statistical Association* 59:18–55.

PEARSON, E. S.; and HARTLEY, H. O. (editors) (1954) 1958 *Biometrika Tables for Statisticians.* Volume 1, 2d ed. Cambridge Univ. Press.

PEARSON, E. S.; and STEPHENS, M. A. 1964 The Ratio of Range to Standard Deviation in the Same Normal Sample. *Biometrika* 51:484–487.

PEIRCE, CHARLES S. 1873 On the Theory of Errors of Observations. U.S. Coast and Geodetic Survey, *Report of the Superintendent* [1870]:200–224.

ROETHLISBERGER, FRITZ J.; and DICKSON, WILLIAM J. (1939) 1961 *Management and the Worker: An Account of a Research Program Conducted by the Western Electric Company, Hawthorne Works, Chicago.* Cambridge, Mass.: Harvard Univ. Press. → A paperback edition was published in 1964 by Wiley.

RUGG, DONALD; and CANTRIL, HADLEY (1944) 1947 The Wording of Questions. Pages 23–50 in Hadley Cantril, *Gauging Public Opinion.* Princeton Univ. Press.

SCOTT, CHRISTOPHER 1961 Research on Mail Surveys. *Journal of the Royal Statistical Society* Series A 124:143–205.

SHARP, HARRY; and FELDT, ALLAN 1959 Some Factors in a Probability Sample Survey of a Metropolitan Community. *American Sociological Review* 24:650–661.

SOBOL, MARION G. 1959 Panel Mortality and Panel Bias. *Journal of the American Statistical Association* 54:52–68.

SUDMAN, SEYMOUR 1964 On the Accuracy of Recording Consumer Panels: I and II. *Journal of Marketing Research* 1, no. 2:14–20; 1, no. 3:69–83.

TUCKER, LEDYARD R. 1964 Recovery of Factors From Simulated Data. Unpublished manuscript.

WAKSBERG, JOSEPH; and PEARL, ROBERT B. 1964 The Effects of Repeated Household Interviews in the Current Population Survey. Unpublished manuscript.

WHITING, BEATRICE B. (editor) 1963 *Six Cultures: Studies of Child Rearing.* New York: Wiley.

WILSON, EDWIN B.; and HILFERTY, MARGARET M. 1929 Note on C. S. Peirce's Experimental Discussion of the Law of Errors. National Academy of Sciences, Washington, D.C., *Proceedings* 15:120–125.

II
EFFECTS OF ERRORS IN STATISTICAL ASSUMPTIONS

All physical and social laws or models rest ultimately upon assumptions. These laws do not yield exact numerical statements. Even the much admired exactness of the physicists' laws means only very close approximation—how close depends upon the circumstances. So, too, techniques for statistical analysis require assumptions about the data to justify the use of the techniques in particular situations. When these assumptions are not correct for the data under study, the results of the statistical analysis may be very misleading. This article discusses the effects on statistical analysis of incorrect assumptions and considers some ways of mitigating the problem. The discussion is set in the frameworks of the matched-pairs design, a time-series design, the one-way analysis of variance, and a repeated-measurements design.

The matched-pairs design

In the matched-pairs design two treatments or conditions are studied by assigning one treatment to eacn member of a pair of matched individuals. For example, a department of Slavic languages is interested in finding out whether one of two different teaching methods for a first-year language course is better than the other. A language aptitude and proficiency examination is given on the first day of class, and the scores on these tests are used to pair students who have approximately the same aptitude and proficiency. Then, for each pair of students, one student is randomly assigned to one teaching method and the other student is assigned to the other method. An examination is given at the end of the term to determine whether differences exist between the teaching methods.

Comparisons between the treatments are based on the difference between the responses to the treatments within each pair. Thus the data consist of the n differences $X_1, X_2, \cdots, X_n$, where X_j denotes the difference between the response scores in the jth pair. It is assumed that $X_1, X_2, \cdots, X_n$ constitute a simple random sample from some population; possible further assumptions will be discussed in the next section.

A social scientist may want to make inferences about several features of the probability distribution underlying his matched-pairs experiment. He may ask which estimators or formulas should be used to estimate the unknown mean or median μ. In addition, he may want to know which significance test to use to find out whether the treatments differ. The following sections indicate how answers to these questions may be obtained.

Criteria for point estimation. An investigator is frequently faced with a dilemma in his choice of an estimator. Suppose in the matched-pairs design he wants to estimate μ, the mean difference between treatments. If he is willing to assume that the observations are randomly drawn from a normal distribution, then the sample mean $\bar{X} = (1/n)\sum X_j$ is the unique "best" unbiased estimator for μ.

Evidence may exist, however, that although the underlying distribution is symmetrical, there are too many extreme values for the normality assumption to be correct. For distributions of this long-tailed kind, the sample mean may have a very large variance. The sample median is generally a reasonable estimator to use for such distributions but has a higher variance than the sample mean for more nearly normal distributions. How can one achieve a reasonable compromise—an estimator that is good under reasonable assumptions?

Here, consideration is restricted to long-tailed symmetrical distributions and, in particular, to compound normal distributions that arise in the following way: (1) An observation is randomly drawn from one of two normal populations. (2) With probability $1 - \tau$, this observation is randomly drawn from a normal population that has mean μ and variance σ^2. (3) With probability τ, this observation is randomly drawn from another normal population having mean μ and variance $K^2\sigma^2$. The values of K and τ that are considered are $K \geqslant 2$ and $0 \leqslant \tau \leqslant .10$. In short, the compound normal distributions considered are *mixtures* of two normal distributions with a common mean. [See DISTRIBUTIONS, STATISTICAL, *article on* MIXTURES OF DISTRIBUTIONS.]

A useful way to compare any two unbiased estimators of the same parameter is to compute their efficiency. The *efficiency* of estimator 1 relative to estimator 2 is defined as

$$e(1, 2) = \frac{\text{variance of estimator 2}}{\text{variance of estimator 1}} \times 100.$$

An estimator is chosen that compares favorably in terms of efficiency with its competitors over the range of plausible distributions. An estimator has robustness of efficiency relative to another if the above ratio does not dip far below 100 per cent for plausible alternatives.

Estimators of the mean (or median). One possible compromise between the sample mean and the sample median is

$$\frac{X_{(2)} + X_{(3)} + \cdots + X_{(n-1)}}{n - 2},$$

where $X_{(j)}$ is the jth smallest observation; that is, the largest and smallest observations are discarded and the mean of the remaining observations computed. [See NONPARAMETRIC STATISTICS, *article on* ORDER STATISTICS.]

In general, an arbitrary percentage of the observations may be discarded. Define the α per cent *trimmed mean*, $\bar{X}_\alpha$, as the mean of the observations remaining after the smallest $(\alpha/100)n$ observations and the largest $(\alpha/100)n$ observations are excluded. The 0 per cent and 50 per cent trimmed means are the sample mean and the sample median, respectively; thus, in particular, $\bar{X}_0 = \bar{X}$.

Efficiency comparisons of the 0 and 6 per cent trimmed means for the compound normal distribution in large samples with $K = 3$ and $0 \leqslant \tau \leqslant .10$ are given by Tukey (1960). He shows, for example, that the 0 per cent trimmed mean $\bar{X}$ is the best possible estimator if $\tau = 0$ (that is, if all observations are from one population), but that, even in this extreme case, $\bar{X}_6$ has efficiency 97 per cent relative to $\bar{X}$. On the other hand, if $\tau = .05$, $\bar{X}_6$ has approximately 143 per cent efficiency with respect to $\bar{X}$. These computations (and many more) indicate that there is more to gain than to lose by discarding some extreme observations. It is important to add that in many problems the study of extreme observations may give important clues to the improvement of the experimental or observational technique. [See STATISTICAL ANALYSIS, SPECIAL PROBLEMS OF, *article on* OUTLIERS.]

Test and confidence interval criteria. A test is to be chosen to compare the null and alternative hypotheses

$$H_0: \mu = 0$$
$$H_1: \mu \neq 0 \quad (\text{or } H_1': \mu > 0),$$

respectively. From the test, confidence intervals for μ are to be obtained. The one-sided and two-sided t tests are the "best" tests of H_0 against H_1 or H_1' if the underlying distribution is normal, but the goal is to choose a good test under less stringent assumptions.

Two requirements for a good test are that it must possess robustness of validity and robustness of

Table 1 — Values of γ_1 and γ_2 for some familiar distributions

	CHI-SQUARE (χ^2_{df}) DISTRIBUTION*			COMPOUND NORMAL DISTRIBUTION		
				$\tau = 0$	$\tau = .05$	$\tau = .10$
	$df = 1$	$df = 5$	$df = 10$	$K = 3$	$K = 3$	$K = 3$
γ_1	2.83	1.26	0.89	0.00	0.00	0.00
γ_2	12	2.40	1.20	0.00	4.65	5.33

* Degrees of freedom denoted by *df*.

efficiency over the range of plausible underlying distributions (Box & Tiao 1964; Tukey 1962).

A statistical test or confidence interval has validity if the basic probability statements asserted for the procedure are correct or nearly so. Thus, from *t* tables, the one-sided *t* test with 9 degrees of freedom has probability .05 of exceeding 1.833 under the null hypothesis $\mu = 0$. This statement is valid if the normal assumption holds. But suppose the normality assumption is in error. Can *t* tables still be used to find the probability that *t* will be greater than an arbitrary value t_0 for plausible underlying distributions? If the answer to this question is "yes," then the one-sided *t* test and associated confidence intervals are said to have robustness of validity. Robustness of validity has not been defined rigorously. A quantitatively precise definition of robustness of validity is difficult to give, since it must depend upon the interpretation of the outcome of a significance test in the given experiment.

In addition to possessing robustness of validity, the test should be a good discriminator between the hypotheses. The discriminating ability of a test is measured by its power, which is the probability of rejecting H_0 given that H_1 (or H'_1) is true [see HYPOTHESIS TESTING]. Both the one-sided and two-sided *t* tests have the strong property that their power is higher than the power of any other reasonable test if the normality assumption obtains. This is no longer true for nonnormal distributions, however, and competitors must be sought.

Thus a way to compare two tests is necessary. It is natural to make such comparisons by defining a concept of relative efficiency for two tests, 1 and 2, representable by a numerical index $e(1, 2)$. Efficiency of tests and estimators are related concepts [see NONPARAMETRIC STATISTICS for a discussion of efficiency]. If $e(1, 2)$ is greater than one, test 1 is more powerful than test 2. A test is said to have robustness of efficiency if its efficiency relative to its competitors is not appreciably below one for credible alternative distributions.

Tests and confidence intervals. The information available on the validity and efficiency properties of the *t* test, the Wilcoxon signed-rank test,

and the sign test under nonnormality is now summarized [see NONPARAMETRIC STATISTICS for these tests]. The trimmed *t* promises to be a strong competitor to the preceding tests (Tukey & McLaughlin 1963).

The one-sided and two-sided *t* tests are valid in large samples, although this validity does not extend to very high significance levels, such as .001, and .0001 (see Hotelling 1961).

The validity of the *t* test will be considered for two different nonnormal distributions. First, assume that the nonnormal distribution has the compound normal form considered above. Second, the nonnormal distribution is assumed to be an Edgeworth distribution with skewness parameter γ_1 and kurtosis (or peakedness) parameter γ_2.

Langley and Elashoff (1966) have conducted a Monte Carlo investigation of the performance of the one-sided *t* test. One thousand samples of *n* ($n = 6, 9, 16$) observations each were taken from compound normal distributions with $K = 3$ and $\tau = 0.0, 0.20, 0.40$. In all these situations, the empirical probability of *t* being greater than the normal theory .05 point was between .04 and .06.

The effects on the one-sided *t* test when sampling is from an Edgeworth population with parameters γ_1, γ_2 will be studied next. For symmetrical distributions $\gamma_1 = 0$, while $\gamma_1 > 0$ for distributions with a long right tail; for normal distributions $\gamma_2 = 0$, but $\gamma_2 > 0$ for bell-shaped symmetrical distributions with long tails and $\gamma_2 < 0$ for similar distributions with short tails (see Scheffé 1959, pp. 331–333). In order to provide some feel for the descriptive meaning of the γ_1, γ_2 parameters, Table 1 gives values of γ_1 and γ_2 for several nonnormal distributions. For normal distributions $\gamma_1 = \gamma_2 = 0$.

Table 2 indicates the performance of the one-sided *t* test on a sample of 10. Each entry denotes the probability that $t \geqslant 1.833$ if the null hypothesis that $\mu = 0$ is true (under normal theory this probability is .05). The performance of the one-tailed *t* test as shown in Table 2 may be summarized as follows: (1) The true significance level α is always slightly less than .05 for long-tailed symmetrical distributions and slightly greater than .05 in short-

Table 2 — Probability that $t \geqslant 1.833$

		γ_1			
	−0.6	−0.2	0	0.2	0.6
−1.0	.072	.057	.051	.045	.036
0.0	.071	.056	.050	.044	.035
γ_2 1.0	.070	.055	.049	.043	.034
2.0	.069	.054	.048	.043	.033

Source: Srivastava 1958, p. 427.

tailed symmetrical distributions. (2) Skewness (γ_1) is more important than kurtosis (γ_2). In fact, the true significance level is almost constant in each column. A long right tail means that the true significance level is much less than .05; a long left tail leads to a true significance level much greater than .05. The skewness values covered in Table 2 represent very moderate skewness. The two-sided t test is less affected by skewness and kurtosis (see Srivastava 1958).

The Wilcoxon signed-rank test is the most frequently used competitor to the t test. It was designed to have perfect robustness of validity with respect to significance level for symmetrical distributions; its validity in asymmetrical distributions is unknown. The sign test has perfect robustness of validity with respect to significance level for both symmetrical and asymmetrical distributions.

Some efficiency computations are reported here [*they use the definition of large sample efficiency given in the article* NONPARAMETRIC STATISTICS, *which also discusses the properties of these tests*]. Table 3 presents some efficiency computations of the Wilcoxon and sign tests relative to the t test when the underlying distribution is a compound normal type. If the underlying distribution is normal, the corresponding efficiencies are $e(w, t) = .955$ and $e(s, t) = .636$.

The preceding validity analysis and suggestive efficiency study permits these recommendations: (1) The Wilcoxon signed-rank test should be used for symmetrical distributions with moderately long tails. If confidence intervals are desired, the Walsh

Table 3 — Efficiency of the Wilcoxon and sign tests relative to the t test

	\(K\) 2		3		5	
	τ		τ		τ	
	.05	.10	.05	.10	.05	.10
$e(w,t)$[a]	1.23	1.53	1.45	2.07	2.20	3.52
$e(s,t)$[b]	0.69	0.74	.83	.99	1.29	1.83

a. The efficiency of the Wilcoxon signed-rank test relative to the t test.
b. The efficiency of the sign test relative to the t test.

procedure should be employed. (2) If samples are large and the underlying symmetrical distribution has long tails, the routine use of the Wilcoxon test and Walsh confidence procedure may require a large computing cost. In these instances, if the distribution has only moderately long tails, the t test and its confidence procedure should be a reasonable compromise. If the distribution has very long tails, the sign test and its associated confidence interval procedure provide a reasonable compromise.

A simple time-series design

Nonrandomness among observations can occur in two ways: (1) the observations may not be independent or (2) the observations may not have a common distribution. Each type of nonrandomness will be considered below to show the important effects such nonrandomness may have on statistical methods based upon the assumption of randomness.

Dependence among the observations. A psychologist observes an individual's response at n points in time. Suppose that X_t, $t = 1, 2, \cdots, n$, denotes the individual's response at time t. The psychologist assumes that the response has a linear regression over time; that is,

$$(1) \qquad X_t = \alpha + \beta\left(\frac{t}{n} - \frac{n+1}{2n}\right) + e_t.$$

(The use of $(t/n) - [(n+1)/(2n)]$ instead of just t represents merely a convenient coding of the t values. In particular, $(n+1)/(2n)$ is just the average of the (t/n)'s: $(n+1)/(2n) = (1/n) \cdot \sum_{t=1}^{n} (t/n)$.) The e_t may represent errors of measurement or errors in the assumption of linear regression and are assumed to be random. The psychologist suspects that the e_t, and hence the X_t, may be correlated; that the e_t all have the same distribution is not questioned here. The goal of the experiment is to estimate and test hypotheses about the intercept, α, and the slope, β.

In the estimation problem only two estimators for α and two estimators for β will be studied here. Furthermore, each estimator is a linear combination of the X's ($a_1X_1 + a_2X_2 + \cdots + a_nX_n$). The reasons for this restriction are that such estimators have been studied most thoroughly and that under normality they have optimal properties. Johnston (1963) studies the estimation problem in some detail.

Suppose, at first, that the psychologist believes that there is no dependence among the observations. Then reasonable estimators for α and β are found by the method of unweighted least squares, which gives

$$\hat{\alpha} = \sum_{t=1}^{n} X_t/n,$$

$$\hat{\beta} = \sum_{t=1}^{n} (X_t - \bar{X})\frac{t}{n} \Big/ \sum_{t=1}^{n} \left(\frac{t}{n} - \frac{n+1}{2n}\right)^2.$$

If no dependence exists, then these estimators have minimum variance among all linear estimators that are unbiased. The standard errors of $\hat{\alpha}$ and $\hat{\beta}$ are

$$(2) \qquad \text{s.e. } \hat{\alpha} = \sqrt{\sigma^2/n},$$

$$\text{s.e. } \hat{\beta} = \sqrt{\sigma^2 \Big/ \sum_{t=1}^{n} \left(\frac{t}{n} - \frac{n+1}{2n}\right)^2},$$

where σ^2 is the variance of X_t.

Now, suppose that dependence exists among the observations and assume that the correlation between X_t and X_s, denoted by ρ_{st}, is given by the relation

$$(3) \qquad \rho_{st} = \rho^{|s-t|},$$

where $|s - t|$ denotes the absolute value of the difference $s - t$. What are the effects of nonzero values of ρ on the estimators $\hat{\alpha}$ and $\hat{\beta}$? First, while these estimators are still unbiased, they are in this case no longer the minimum variance linear unbiased estimators (see Johnston 1963 for the way to construct the latter estimators). Efficiency computations comparing $\hat{\beta}$ and the minimum variance linear unbiased estimator, β^*, are given in Table 4, where cell entries are the ratio of the variance of β^* to the variance of $\hat{\beta}$ for a sample of size 5.

Table 4 — Efficiency comparison of $\hat{\beta}$ and β^*

ρ	−.40	−.20	0	.20	.40
var β^*/var $\hat{\beta}$	.921	.982	1	.990	.972

The estimator β^* used in Table 4 is computed under the assumption that ρ is known. When the sample size is large, $\hat{\beta}$ has efficiency one compared with β^* for the particular pattern of correlation considered.

A second effect of nonzero ρ is that the standard errors $\hat{\alpha}$ and $\hat{\beta}$ given in (2) are incorrect. The correct standard errors in large samples for the example are

$$(4) \qquad \text{s.e. } \hat{\alpha} = \sqrt{\frac{\sigma^2}{n}\left(1 + \frac{2\rho}{1-\rho}\right)},$$

$$\text{s.e. } \hat{\beta} = \sqrt{\frac{\sigma^2}{\sum_t \left(\frac{t}{n} - \frac{n+1}{2n}\right)^2}\left(1 + \frac{2\rho}{1-\rho}\right)}.$$

These standard errors may depart quite radically from (2) as Table 5 shows. The ratios obtained in Table 5 are identical to the corresponding ratios of s.e. $\hat{\alpha}$. Since the standard errors in (2) may be in serious error, it is clear that the standard error of prediction, that is, the standard error of $\hat{\alpha} + \hat{\beta}[(t/n) - (n+1)/(2n)]$, may also be very wrong. The third effect of ignoring correlation between the observations concerns s^2, the conventional estimator of σ^2, the underlying variance;

$$s^2 = \sum_{i=1}^{n}\left[X_t - \hat{\alpha} - \hat{\beta}\left(\frac{t}{n} - \frac{n+1}{2n}\right)\right]^2 \Big/ (n-2).$$

If $\rho \neq 0$, then s^2 is a biased estimator of σ^2. Some sampling experiments by Cochrane and Orcutt (1949) suggest that the expected value of s^2 is less than σ^2; when there are a large number of observations, the bias is negligible.

Table 5 — Ratio of incorrect to correct s.e. $\hat{\beta}$

ρ	−.50	−.20	−.10	0	.10	.20	.50
s.e. $\hat{\beta}$ from (2) / s.e. $\hat{\beta}$ from (4)	1.73	1.22	1.10	1	.90	.82	.57

In testing hypotheses about α and β a primary concern is with the behavior of the standard t test,

$$t = \sqrt{\sum\left(\frac{t}{n} - \frac{n+1}{2n}\right)^2} \cdot \hat{\beta}/\sqrt{s^2},$$

to examine $H_0: \beta = 0$ against the alternative $H_1: \beta \neq 0$ in the presence of the correlation model (3). Table 6 gives the probability that $|t_j| \geqslant 1.96$ if $H_0: \beta = 0$ is true when the sample size is large (if $\rho = 0$ this probability is .05). Table 6, and additional tables when H_1 is true, vividly demonstrates the sensitivity of the standard t test to nonzero correlation between the observations when (1) and (3) hold. The nonrobustness of t comes primarily from the use of an incorrect standard error of $\hat{\beta}$ in the denominator of t. The probability computations in Table 6 also hold when $H_0': \alpha = 0$ is tested against $H_1': \alpha \neq 0$ using the statistic $t = \sqrt{n}\,\hat{\alpha}/\sqrt{s^2}$. In many social science problems $\rho > 0$; as seen from Table 5 the null hypothesis would be rejected more often than the nominal 5 per cent level in such situations, assuming that the null hypothesis is true.

Hoel (1964) has reported on a sampling experiment to assess the effects of correlation in small sample sizes on an F test for a polynomial trend. His results support the conclusions reached in the preceding paragraph. Readers interested in robust tests, assuming the correlational structure (3), should consult Hannan (1955).

Table 6 — Large sample probability that $|t| \geqslant 1.96$ when correlation exists

ρ	−.50	−.40	−.30	−.20	−.10	0	.10	.20	.30	.40	.50
Probability	.00068	.0026	.0076	.0164	.0302	.0500	.0762	.1096	.1498	.1994	.2576

It is important to remember that the magnitude of effects on a statistical technique from dependence among the observations is a function of the technique, the model of dependence, and the values of correlational parameters.

Nonidentically distributed observations. Suppose that the psychologist is principally interested in testing the hypothesis $H_0: \alpha = 0$ against $H_1: \alpha \neq 0$. Now, however, assume that strong evidence exists that $\rho = 0$. The psychologist believes $\beta = 0$ in (1), but he is not certain about this belief. Thus he asks the question, "What is the effect on the t test of examining $H_0: \alpha = 0$ against $H_1: \alpha \neq 0$, assuming $\beta = 0$, if in fact $\beta \neq 0$?" The t statistic the psychologist wants to employ (assuming $\beta = 0$) is $t = \sqrt{n}\, \bar{X}/\sqrt{s^2}$, where now s^2 is given by $\sum (X_t - \bar{X})^2/(n-1)$.

Table 7 gives the probability that $|t| \geqslant 1.96$ if $H_0: \alpha = 0$ is correct for various values of $|\beta|$ and σ^2 when n is large (the nominal significance level is .05).

Table 7 — Probability that $|t| \geqslant 1.96$ when a slope, assumed zero, is not zero

		$|\beta|$		
	0	.25	.50	1.0
σ				
.25	.05	.0414	.0238	.0028
.50	.05	.0477	.0414	.0238
1.00	.05	.0488	.0477	.0414
2.00	.05	.0500	.0488	.0477

Two important effects of incorrectly assuming that $\beta = 0$ are apparent from Table 7: (1) the behavior of the t statistic depends upon the unknown σ^2 as well as $|\beta|$, and (2) the stated significance level .05 is always at least as large as the true significance level.

It must be remembered that the effects of nonidentically distributed observations depend on the model underlying the observations and the statistical method being used.

The one-way analysis of variance

The one-way analysis of variance may arise when n individuals are randomly assigned to k treatments. The data consist of the n_i response scores x_{ij} ($i = 1, \cdots, k$; $j = 1, \cdots, n_i$) with $\sum_{i=1}^{k} n_i = n$. The observations are assumed to be independent, and the probability distributions of the response variable are assumed identical for individuals receiving the same treatment.

The one-way layout is frequently employed to estimate the means or medians, μ_i, and the variances, σ_i^2, of the treatments, to establish confidence intervals on the differences, $\mu_i - \mu_j$, and to test hypotheses about the μ_i and σ_i^2. The point estimation problems present no essentially new questions.

Tests and confidence intervals for the median or mean. To discriminate between the null and alternative hypotheses

$$(5) \qquad H_0: \mu_1 = \mu_2 = \cdots = \mu_k$$
$$(6) \qquad H_1: \mu_i \neq \mu_j \text{ for some } i, j,$$

one ordinarily employs the F test, the Kruskal–Wallis H test, or the k sample median test [see NONPARAMETRIC STATISTICS, article on RANKING METHODS; LINEAR HYPOTHESES, article on ANALYSIS OF VARIANCE]. The F test is usually a very good way to make this discrimination if (1) the observations are drawn from a population in which each treatment has the same underlying normal distribution except for possible differences among the μ_i, and (2) the alternative hypothesis is not further specified.

The following sections discuss the validity of these tests. Note that the discussion is germane to the validity of Scheffé's method of multiple comparisons [see Scheffé 1959, chapter 3; see also LINEAR HYPOTHESES, article on MULTIPLE COMPARISONS], since that method is equivalent to the confidence set based on the F test.

Validity assuming $\sigma_i^2 = \sigma^2$ for all i. The F test has perfect validity for all sample sizes if the populations are normal with equal variances and the observations are independent; that is, if the k samples are drawn from the same normal distribution. In large samples the standard F statistic

$$F_{k-1,\, n-k} = \frac{\sum n_i (\bar{X}_i - \bar{X})^2/(k-1)}{\sum\sum (X_{ij} - \bar{X}_i)^2/(n-k)}$$

provides a valid test for the hypothesis (5) except at high significance levels. For small samples it will be assumed that departures from normality can be represented by an Edgeworth distribution with skewness and kurtosis parameters γ_{1i} and γ_{2i} in each population. Table 8 gives the probability that $F \geqslant 2.87$ if (5) is true (under normal theory this probability is .05) for $\gamma_{1i} = \gamma_1$ and $\gamma_{2i} = \gamma_2$ for all i, $k = 5$, all n_i's = 5.

Table 8 — Probability that $F \geqslant 2.87$ for $k = 5$ and all $n_i = 5$

		γ_2			
		−1	−0.5	0	0.5	1
γ_1^2	0	0.053	0.051	0.050	0.049	0.048
	0.5	0.053	0.051	0.050	0.049	0.048
	1	0.053	0.052	0.050	0.050	0.049

Source: Box & Andersen 1955, p. 14.

Table 8 and other work indicate that the F test for (5) possesses robustness of validity relative to significance levels (type 1 error) and power when $\gamma_{1i} = \gamma_1$, all i (Gayen 1949; Pearson 1931). The kurtosis parameter γ_2 has practically no effect on the F test for (5). However, when $\gamma_{11} \neq \gamma_{12}$, it is known that for $k = 2$ the one-sided t test does not have robustness of validity.

The Kruskal–Wallis test and the median test are valid under the null hypothesis that the k samples come from the same population. When $k = 2$, the Kruskal–Wallis test is equivalent to the two-tailed Wilcoxon rank-sum test. In this case of $k = 2$, if $\gamma_{11} \neq \gamma_{12}$ and $\gamma_{21} \neq \gamma_{22}$, the one-sided Wilcoxon test appears to be less robust than the one-sided t test relative to significance levels when the null hypothesis is (5) and μ is a median or mean (Wetherhill 1960).

Inequality of variance. The validity of the preceding tests and some further tests when the assumption of equal variances is dropped will be studied; the normality assumption is retained unless otherwise indicated.

It is necessary at this point to examine the rationale for carrying out a test. Suppose a random sample of n mental patients is drawn and n_1 are assigned to treatment 1 and n_2 ($= n - n_1$) are assigned to treatment 2. After a period of treatment, each patient is tested and given a score that is assumed to be normally distributed in each population. The null hypothesis tested is that $\mu_1 = \mu_2$ (μ_i is the mean for treatment i); suppose the conclusion is that $\mu_1 < \mu_2$. If high scores are indicative of improvement, a decision is made to use the second treatment. Why?

When the variances are equal, the treatment with the higher mean is more likely to give rise to scores greater than or equal to any given score w_0. Thus the significance test gives the psychiatrist usable results, especially if a score at w_0 or above means release from the psychiatric hospital.

Suppose now that each treatment has a different variance and that $\mu_1 < \mu_2$. Then it is by no means uniformly true that the treatment with the higher mean is more likely to give rise to scores greater

than or equal to a release score of w_0. For example, suppose that the scores for treatment 1 and treatment 2 follow normal distributions with $\mu_1 = 0$, $\sigma_1^2 = 9$ and $\mu_2 = 1$, $\sigma_2^2 = 1$, respectively ($\sigma_i^2 = $ variance of treatment i scores). In this case Table 9 gives the probability that a randomly chosen score on treatment i exceeds w_0, $i = 1, 2$.

Nonetheless, it is often appropriate to test equality of means even when the variances may be different, and the remainder of this section deals with that case. This problem is often called the Behrens–Fisher problem. Consider, first, the large sample validity of the two-tailed, two-sample t test (equivalent to F when $k = 2$) based on

$$t = \frac{\bar{X}_1 - \bar{X}_2}{\sqrt{\left(\dfrac{1}{n_1} + \dfrac{1}{n_2}\right) s^2}},$$

where

$$s^2 = \frac{(n_1 - 1)\, s_1^2 + (n_2 - 1)\, s_2^2}{n_1 + n_2 - 2}.$$

The denominator of t is not a consistent estimator of the standard error of $\bar{X}_1 - \bar{X}_2$ unless either $\sigma_1^2 = \sigma_2^2$ or $n_1 = n_2$. This fact partly explains the nonrobustness of t clearly shown in Table 10.

Table 10 gives the probability that $|t| \geqslant 1.96$ for different values of $\theta = \sigma_1^2/\sigma_2^2$ and $R = n_1/n_2$ when the null hypothesis of equal means holds. Table 10 indicates the importance of equal sample sizes in controlling the effects of unequal variances: the significance level remains at .05 irrespective of the value of θ if $R = 1$. Moreover, if $\theta < 1$ and $R > 1$ so that the most variable population has the smallest sample, the true significance level is always larger than .05 and may be seriously so. On the other hand, if $\theta > 1$ and $R > 1$, the true significance level is always less than .05. These results are essentially independent of γ_1 and γ_2 because of the large sample sizes. This lack of robustness of significance-level validity extends to power. The small sample validity of t follows along the lines of the large sample theory (see Scheffé 1959, p. 340).

Since equal sample sizes are sometimes difficult to obtain, even approximately, considerable research has been focused upon alternative ways to

Table 9 — Probability that a randomly chosen score on treatment i exceeds w_0

Release score w_0	Treatment	
	1	2
1.0	.3707	.5000
1.5	.3085	.3085
2.0	.2514	.1587
2.5	.2033	.0668

Table 10 — Large sample probability that $|t| \geqslant 1.96$ when sample sizes and variances differ

| | | θ | | | |
	.20	.50	1.0	2.0	5.0
1	0.050	0.050	0.050	0.050	0.050
R	2	0.120	0.080	0.050	0.029	0.014
5	0.220	0.120	0.050	0.014	0.002

Source: Scheffé 1959, p. 340.

test (5) versus (6). Transformation of the response variable may achieve equality of variance for the transformed variable, so that t may be used. But the user must note that a hypothesis on the means of the *transformed* variates is being tested. [*See* STATISTICAL ANALYSIS, SPECIAL PROBLEMS OF, *article on* TRANSFORMATIONS OF DATA.]

Welch (1938; 1947) investigates the alternative test statistic,

$$v = \frac{\bar{X}_1 - \bar{X}_2}{\sqrt{\dfrac{s_1^2}{n_1} + \dfrac{s_2^2}{n_2}}},$$

and indicates how to obtain significance levels (see also Dixon & Massey [1951] 1957, p. 123). Note that the statistics v and t are the same if $n_1 = n_2$. Furthermore, Welch (1938) shows that the approximate significance level of v may be obtained from tables of the t distribution with f degrees of freedom, where

$$f = \frac{\left(\dfrac{s_1^2}{n_1} + \dfrac{s_2^2}{n_2}\right)^2}{\dfrac{s_1^4}{n_1^2(n_1-1)} + \dfrac{s_2^4}{n_2^2(n_2-1)}}.$$

The v test is valid for both significance level and power in large samples and is much less sensitive to θ than the usual t in small samples. For example, if $\theta = 1$ and $n_1 = 5$, $n_2 = 15$, the exact probability that $|v| \geqslant 5.2$ is .05, where 5.2 is the 5 per cent point of the exact distribution of v. The probability that $|v| \geqslant 5.2$ for any other θ value is always between .035 and .085. In addition, even if $\theta = 1$, so that the t test is valid, the v test is nearly as efficient as t. When both n_1 and n_2 are small, s_1^2 and s_2^2 will have low precision. In these situations, compute f from the following formula:

$$f = \frac{\left(\dfrac{1}{n_1} + \dfrac{1}{n_2}\right)^2}{\dfrac{1}{n_1^2(n_1-1)} + \dfrac{1}{n_2^2(n_2-1)}}.$$

Alternative testing methods for $k = 2$ exist (see Behrens 1963; Cochran 1964).

Inequality of variance also affects the signifi-

cance levels of the Wilcoxon rank-sum test w and the median test. H. R. van der Vaart (1961) gives significance levels of the Wilcoxon test for various θ values, assuming normal distributions and large samples. Pratt (1964) extends van der Vaart's investigation in several ways. Surprisingly, w is sensitive to θ in the case of equal samples, while t remains unaffected. The median test appears to have greater robustness of significance-level validity than t or w near $\theta = 1$ when the three tests are comparable.

The conclusions concerning the effects of inequality of variance on the usual F test for $k = 2$ generally hold for arbitrary k. Robust tests along the lines of Welch's v test have been developed for general k (see James 1951).

Efficiency considerations. When the shapes (including variances) of the k distributions are different, it is important to be precise about which null hypothesis is being tested. The null hypothesis of equality of means is tested by F; the null hypothesis that $p = \frac{1}{2}$ is tested by the Kruskal–Wallis method (when $k = 2$, p is the probability that a random observation under treatment 1 is greater than a random observation under treatment 2). The null hypothesis of equality of medians is tested by the median test. The means may be equal but the medians different, or conversely. Either the means or the medians may be equal, but $p \neq \frac{1}{2}$, or conversely. These facts imply the noncomparability of the three tests if shape differences exist. They also imply that a satisfactory analysis of the data may require an investigator to assemble evidence from all three significance tests—and possibly additional tests.

If the k distributions have the same shape, the following conclusions are justified: the F test does not have robustness of efficiency for bell-shaped symmetrical distributions with moderately long tails. No adequate study has been made of the robustness of efficiency of the Kruskal–Wallis test, but for distributions such as that described above, no competitor is in sight. The median test should have high efficiency for very long tailed symmetrical distributions.

Tests for equality of variances. In many data analyses an investigator is interested in comparing variability among the k treatments; thus he may carry out a test of

$$H_0: \sigma_1^2 = \sigma_2^2 = \cdots = \sigma_k^2$$

against

$$H_1: \sigma_i^2 \neq \sigma_j^2 \text{ for some } i, j.$$

and find confidence intervals for all ratios σ_j^2 / σ_i^2, $i \neq j$ [*see the article on* VARIANCES, STATISTICAL

STUDY OF]. The robustness of validity of Bartlett's test for homogeneity of variance, and hence the validity of confidence intervals derived from Bartlett's test, will next be investigated. Bartlett's test is based upon the statistic M:

$$M = (\sum n_i - k) \ln s_w^2 - \sum (n_i - 1) \ln s_i^2,$$

where

$$s_w^2 = \sum (n_i - 1) s_i^2 / (\sum n_i - k),$$
$$s_i^2 = \sum (X_{ij} - \bar{X})^2 / (n_i - 1).$$

The significance level of M may be approximated from a χ^2 table with $k - 1$ degrees of freedom. The M test requires normality and has almost no robustness of validity, as may be seen from Table 11 where the nonnormality is characterized by the γ_2 parameter ($\gamma_1 = 0$).

The disastrous behavior of M for long-tailed symmetrical distributions may be explained by the following suggestive argument by Box (1953). Let T denote a statistic; for example, $\bar{X}$, s_1^2/s_2^2, M are statistics. Then, in large samples, T divided by its estimated standard error is usually normally distributed by the central limit theorem and associated mathematical facts. Thus, even though sampling may be from a nonnormal distribution, $\bar{X}/(s/\sqrt{n})$ is normally distributed. This result explains the robustness to nonnormality of the t test in the matched-pairs design and the F test in the one-way analysis of variance when the populations have the same shape. But Bartlett's M test does not have this structure of T divided by its standard error; hence, it does not find protection under the central limit theorem.

The nonrobustness of the M test requires the use of an alternative test. Scheffé (1959) has developed a robust test and a robust multiple comparison method for this problem from a suggestion by Box (1953).

The extreme sensitivity of the M test for equality of variances to the value of γ_2 indicates that one may expect trouble with the normal theory analysis of the random effects model, sometimes called model II [see LINEAR HYPOTHESES, article on ANAL-

YSIS OF VARIANCE; see also Dixon & Massey (1951) 1957, p. 174]. Real difficulties do exist with such analyses, even in large samples.

A repeated-measurements design

An investigator records the response of each individual to a stimulus repeated at each of p different points in time. The data consist of response scores, X_{it}, where X_{it} denotes the score of the ith individual at time t, $i = 1, 2, \cdots, n$ and $t = 1, 2, \cdots, p$. Each individual has p response scores. The investigator assumes that

$$(7) \qquad X_{it} = \mu + \alpha_i + \tau_t + e_{it}.$$

The α_i and τ_t denote the individual and time effects, respectively. It is assumed that the random errors e_{it} have a common distribution and that the correlation between e_{it} and e_{is} is given by $\rho^{|t-s|}$. It is assumed then that an individual's response at time t is correlated with his response at another time s, but that the responses of different individuals are independent. The investigator's principal interest lies in testing the hypotheses.

$$(8) \qquad H_0^\alpha: \alpha_1 = \alpha_2 = \cdots = \alpha_n;$$
$$\text{against } H_1^\alpha: \alpha_i \neq \alpha_j \text{ for some } i, j$$

$$(9) \qquad H_0^\tau: \tau_1 = \tau_2 = \cdots = \tau_p;$$
$$\text{against } H_1^\tau: \tau_t \neq \tau_s \text{ for some } t, s.$$

Assume that the e_{it} are normal and study the effects of nonzero ρ on the standard F tests in the two-way analysis of variance.

The hypotheses (8) and (9) may be examined, respectively, by the statistics

$$F_{n-1, (n-1)(p-1)}^\alpha = \frac{\sum\limits_{i=1}^{n} (\bar{X}_{i.} - \bar{X})^2 / (n-1)}{\text{MSE}},$$

$$F_{p-1, (n-1)(p-1)}^\tau = \frac{\sum\limits_{t=1}^{p} (\bar{X}_{.t} - \bar{X})^2 / (p-1)}{\text{MSE}},$$

where MSE represents the mean square error, that is, $\sum (X_{it} - \bar{X}_{i.} - \bar{X}_{.t} + \bar{X})^2 / (n-1)(p-1)$. Table 12 gives the probability that $F^\alpha \geq 3.01$ for different values of ρ (the exact probability is .05 for $\rho = 0$) and the probability that $F^\tau \geq 3.01$ when $n = p = 5$.

Table 12 shows clearly the considerable effect of correlation on the test for individuals and the slight effect such correlation has for the test on times. In the terminology of the two-way analysis of variance, if individuals denote the rows and times denote the columns, then correlation within a row seriously affects the test on rows and only slightly affects the test on columns—with the given model for the correlation. Two explanations for the

Table 11 — True probability of exceeding the .05 normal theory point of M in large samples

		γ_2			
		−1	0	1	2
	2	.0056	.05	.11	.166
k	3	.0025	.05	.136	.224
	5	.0008	.05	.176	.315
	10	.001	.05	.257	.489

Source: Box 1953, p. 320.

Table 12 — Probability that $F^\alpha \geq 3.01$ and probability that $F^\tau \geq 3.01$ in the presence of correlation*

	Correlation, ρ				
	-0.40	-0.20	0.0	$+0.20$	$+0.40$
Exact probability for the F^α test on individuals	.0003	.0101	.05	.1305	.2470
Exact probability for the F^τ test on different times	.0590	.0527	.05	.0537	.0668

* The cell entries were computed assuming $\rho^{|t-s|} = \rho$ if $|t-s| = 1$ and $\rho^{|t-s|} = 0$ if $|t-s| \geq 2$ in order to simplify the computations. This approximation correctly indicates the order of magnitude of the more general model $\rho^{|t-s|}$.

Source: Box 1954, p. 497.

nonrobustness of the F^α test are (1) the numerator and denominator of F^α are correlated, contrary to the ideal condition, and (2) essentially the wrong standard error of the means for individuals is used.

It has been shown that statistical analyses based on assumptions that are incorrect for the data can produce misleading inferences. Furthermore, ways have been indicated to choose good statistical analyses, based on plausible assumptions, so that inferences will not be distorted. The question arises, "How does one decide which assumptions to make?" For example, suppose that there is interest only in making inferences about the mean difference. It then seems preferable to use an inference procedure that is robust against suspected departures from assumptions rather than to make preliminary significance tests of the assumptions of equality on variances, normality and/or symmetry, randomness, and so forth. A procedure that is robust against all failures in assumptions cannot be found, so a procedure must be chosen that is robust against those failures in assumptions that are known to be likely from experience with the problem under study or that would distort the inferences most severely.

ROBERT M. ELASHOFF

[*See also* FALLACIES, STATISTICAL; NONPARAMETRIC STATISTICS.]

BIBLIOGRAPHY

ASPIN, ALICE A. 1949 Tables for Use in Comparisons Whose Accuracy Involves Two Variances, Separately Estimated. *Biometrika* 36:290–293.

BEHRENS, W.-U. (1963) 1964 The Comparison of Means of Independent Normal Distributions With Different Variances. *Biometrics* 20:16–27. → First published in German. Discusses alternative tests to *t* or *v* based upon Fisher's fiducial theory of inference and the use of Bayesian methods.

BOX, GEORGE E. P. 1953 Non-normality and Tests on Variance. *Biometrika* 40:318–335. → Readers will find sections 1, 2, 7, 8, 9 accessible in general. The discussion section is particularly important.

BOX, GEORGE E. P. 1954 Some Theorems on Quadratic Forms Applied in the Study of Analysis of Variance Problems. II: Effects of Inequality of Variance and of Correlation Between Errors in the Two-way Classification. *Annals of Mathematical Statistics* 25:484–498.

BOX, GEORGE E. P.; and ANDERSEN, S. L. 1955 Permutation Theory in the Derivation of Robust Criteria and the Study of Departures From Assumptions. *Journal of the Royal Statistical Society* Series B 17:1–34. → The discussion on pages 26–34 presents some of the best thinking on statistical practice and is accessible in general.

BOX, GEORGE E. P.; and TIAO, G. C. 1964 A Note on Criterion vs. Inference Robustness. *Biometrika* 51:168–173. → The authors discuss robustness of validity and efficiency with a concrete example.

COCHRAN, WILLIAM G. 1964 Approximate Significance Levels of the Behrens–Fisher Test. *Biometrics* 20:191–195.

COCHRANE, DONALD; and ORCUTT, G. H. 1949 Application of Least Squares Regression to Relationships Containing Auto-correlated Error Terms. *Journal of the American Statistical Association* 44:32–61.

DIXON, WILFRID J.; and MASSEY, FRANK J. JR. (1951) 1957 *Introduction to Statistical Analysis.* 2d ed. New York: McGraw-Hill.

GAYEN, A. K. 1949 The Distribution of "Student's" *t* in Random Samples of Any Size Drawn From Non-normal Universes. *Biometrika* 36:353–369. → The method and tables (like Table 2) and discussion are the important features of this and the next reference.

GAYEN, A. K. 1950 The Distribution of the Variance Ratio in Random Samples of Any Size Drawn From Non-normal Universes. *Biometrika* 37:236–255.

GEARY, R. C. 1966 A Note on Residual Heterovariance and Estimation Efficiency in Regression. *American Statistician* 20, no. 4:30–31.

HANNAN, E. J. 1955 An Exact Test for Correlation Between Time Series. *Biometrika* 42:316–326.

HOEL, PAUL G. 1964 Methods for Comparing Growth Type Curves. *Biometrics* 20:859–872.

HOTELLING, HAROLD 1961 The Behavior of Some Standard Statistical Tests Under Nonstandard Conditions. Volume 1, pages 319–359 in Berkeley Symposium on Mathematical Statistics and Probability, Fourth, University of California, 1960, *Proceedings.* Berkeley and Los Angeles: Univ. of California Press.

JAMES, G. S. 1951 The Comparison of Several Groups of Observations When the Ratios of the Population Variances Are Unknown. *Biometrika* 38:324–329. → The author's method for testing the null hypothesis (eq. 5) is accessible.

JOHNSTON, JOHN 1963 *Econometric Methods.* New York: McGraw-Hill. → An exposition of regression methods.

LANGLEY, P. A.; and ELASHOFF, R. M. 1966 A Study of the Hodges–Lehmann Two Sample Test. Unpublished manuscript.

PEARSON, EGON S. 1931 The Analysis of Variance in Cases of Non-normal Variation. *Biometrika* 23:114–133. → The author investigates the validity of the *F* test by Monto Carlo sampling.

PRATT, JOHN W. 1964 Robustness of Some Procedures for the Two-sample Location Problem. *Journal of the American Statistical Association* 59:665–680. → Readers with a modest statistical background will find sections 1 and 2 accessible. The author investigates the validity of several tests under inequality of variance.

SCHEFFÉ, HENRY 1959 *The Analysis of Variance.* New York: Wiley. → Chapter 10 is one of the most comprehensive accounts of the effects of departures from statistical assumptions. Readers with a modest statistical background will find pages 360–368 accessible.

SRIVASTAVA, A. B. L. 1958 Effect of Non-normality on the Power Function of *t*-Test. *Biometrika* 45:421–429.

TUKEY, JOHN W. 1960 A Survey of Sampling From Contaminated Distributions. Pages 448–485 in *Contributions to Probability and Statistics: Essays in Honor of Harold Hotelling*. Edited by Ingram Olkin et al. Stanford Univ. Press. → The author reviews his previous research on robust estimators for μ and σ^2 and gives a good bibliography.

TUKEY, JOHN W. 1962 The Future of Data Analysis. *Annals of Mathematical Statistics* 33:1–67, 812. → The author outlines his views on data analysis and makes several specific suggestions for handling spotty data. The first 21 pages are accessible; thereafter, some parts are accessible, others are not.

TUKEY, JOHN W.; and McLAUGHLIN, DONALD H. 1963 Less Vulnerable Confidence and Significance Procedures for Location Based Upon a Single Sample: Trimming/Winsorization. *Sankhyā: The Indian Journal of Statistics* Series A 25:331–352. → The trimmed *t* is discussed. The beginning sections of the paper are accessible.

VAN DER VAART, H. R. 1961 On the Robustness of Wilcoxon's Two Sample Test. Pages 140–158 in Symposium on Quantitative Methods in Pharmacology, University of Leiden, 1960, *Quantitative Methods in Pharmacology: Proceedings*. Amsterdam: North-Holland Publishing. → The introduction and conclusion, together with the table and graphs, are accessible.

WELCH, B. L. 1938 The Significance of the Difference Between Two Means When the Population Variances Are Unequal. *Biometrika* 29:350–362.

WELCH, B. L. 1947 The Generalization of "Student's" Problem When Several Different Population Variances Are Involved. *Biometrika* 34:28–35.

WETHERHILL, G. B. 1960 The Wilcoxon Test and Nonnull Hypotheses. *Journal of the Royal Statistical Society* Series B 22:402–418.

ESPIONAGE

See INTELLIGENCE, POLITICAL AND MILITARY.

ESTATE TAXES

See TAXATION, *article on* DEATH AND GIFT TAXES.

ESTHETICS

See AESTHETICS.

ESTIMATION

I

POINT ESTIMATION

How many fish are in this lake? What proportion of the voting population favors candidate A? How much paint is needed for this particular room? What fuel capacity should this airplane have if it is to carry passengers safely between New York and Paris? How many items in this shipment have the desired quality? What is the specific gravity of this metal? Questions like these represent problems of point estimation. In present-day statistical methodology, such problems are usually cast in the following form: A mathematical model describing a particular phenomenon is completely specified except for some unknown quantity or quantities. These quantities must be estimated. Galileo's model for freely falling bodies and many models in learning theory, small group theory, and the like provide examples.

Exact answers are often impossible, difficult, expensive, or merely inconvenient to obtain. However, approximate answers that are quite likely to be close to the exact answer may be fairly easily obtainable. The theory of point estimation provides a guide for obtaining such answers; above all, it makes precise, or provides enough framework so that one could make precise, such phrases as "quite likely to be close" and others such as "this estimator is better than that one."

As an introduction to some of the problems involved, consider estimating the number N of fish in a given lake. Suppose that M fish are taken from the lake, marked, and returned to the lake unharmed. A little later, a random sample of size n of fish from the lake is observed to contain x marked fish. A little thought suggests that probably the ratio x/n is near M/N or that the unknown N and the ratio Mn/x (defined only if $x > 0$) are not too far apart. For example, if $M = 1,000$, $n = 1,000$, and $x = 20$, it might be reasonable to believe that N is close to 50,000. [*A similar example, concerning moving populations of workers, is discussed in* SAMPLE SURVEYS.]

Clearly, this procedure *may* lead one badly astray. For example, it is possible, althoughly highly unlikely, that the same value $x = 20$ could be obtained, and hence, using the above procedure, N be estimated as 50,000, even if N is actually as small as 1,980 or as large as 10,000,000. Clearly, considerations of probability are basic here. If $L(N)$ denotes the probability of obtaining 20 marked fish when N fish are in the lake, it can be shown that
$$0 = L(1,979) < L(1,980) < \cdots < L(49,999) = L(50,000) \text{ and } L(50,000) > L(50,001) > \cdots;$$
that is, $N = 50,000$ maximizes the *likelihood* of obtaining 20 marked fish.

Design of experiments. What values of M and n are most satisfactory in the above experiment? Clearly, the bigger n is, the better it is for estimation purposes, but the more expensive the experiment [*see* EXPERIMENTAL DESIGN]. A balance has to be reached between the conflicting goals of minimizing error and minimizing expense. Also, perhaps another experimental design might give better results. In the above problem, let $M = 1,000$, but instead of pulling a fixed number of fish out of the lake, pull out fish until exactly x marked fish have been obtained, where x is fixed in advance. Then n, the sample size, is the observation of interest [see SEQUENTIAL ANALYSIS]. Which design, of all the possible designs, should be used? This kind of question is basic to any estimation problem.

Testing hypotheses. An altogether different problem would arise if one did not really want the value of N for its own sake but only as a means of deciding whether or not the lake should be restocked with small fish. For example, it might be desirable to restock the lake if N is small, say less than 100,000, and undesirable otherwise. In this case, the problem of whether or not the lake should be restocked is equivalent to testing the hypothesis that N is less than 100,000 [see HYPOTHESIS TEST-ING]. In general, a good estimator does not necessarily lead to a good test.

Confidence intervals. The value of an estimator, that is, a point estimate, of N for a particular sample is a number, hopefully one close to N; the value of a confidence interval, that is, an interval estimate, of N for a particular sample is an interval, hopefully one that is not only small but that also contains N [see ESTIMATION, *article on* CONFIDENCE INTERVALS AND REGIONS]. The problem of finding a good interval estimate is more closely related to hypothesis testing than it is to point estimation.

Note that certain problems are clearly point estimation problems rather than problems of interval estimation: when deciding what the fuel capacity of an airplane should be, the designers must settle on one particular number.

Steps in solving an estimation problem

The first step in the solution of an estimation problem, as suggested above, is to design an experiment (or method of taking observations) such that the outcome of the experiment—call it x—is affected by the unknown quantity to be estimated, which in the above discussion was N. Typically, x is related to N probabilistically rather than deterministically. This probability relation must be specified. For example, the probability of obtaining x marked fish in a sample of size n is given by the hypergeometric distribution,

$$\binom{M}{x}\binom{N-M}{n-x} \Big/ \binom{N}{n},$$

provided the sample has been drawn randomly without replacement [see DISTRIBUTIONS, STATIS-TICAL, *article on* SPECIAL DISCRETE DISTRIBUTIONS]. (The denominator is the number of combinations of N things taken n at a time, and so forth.) If the randomness assumption is not quite satisfied, then the specified probability relation will be only approximately true. Such specification problems and their implications will be discussed later. Next, after the experiment has been designed and the probability model specified, one must choose a function f defined for each possible x such that if x is observed, then $f(x)$, the value of the function f at x, is to be used as a numerical estimate of N. Such a function f is called an *estimator* of N. The problem of the choice of f will be discussed later. Finally, after a particular estimator f has been tentatively settled on, one might want to calculate additional performance characteristics of f, giving further indications of how well f will perform on the average. If the results of these calculations show that f will not be satisfactory, then changes in the design of the experiment, for example, an increase in sample size, might be contemplated. Clearly, there is a good deal of interplay among all the steps in the solution of an estimation problem outlined here.

Terminological note. Some authors distinguish terminologically between the *estimator*, the function f, and its numerical value for a particular sample, the *estimate*. Another distinction is that between a random variable and a generic value of the random variable. (Some authors use X for the former and x for the latter.) Such distinctions are sometimes important, but they are not generally made in this article, although special comments appear in a few places. Otherwise it should be clear from context whether reference is made to a function or its value, or whether reference is made to a random variable or its value.

Choice of estimator

As a means of illustrating the various considerations influencing the choice of an estimator, a few typical examples will be discussed.

Example 1. Let x be the number of successes in n independent trials, the probability of a success on an individual trial being p. (For example, x might be the number of respondents out of n questioned in a political poll who say they are Democrats, and p is the probability that a randomly chosen individual in the population will say he is a Democrat.) Here p is unknown and may be any number between 0 and 1 inclusive. An estimator f of p ideally should be such that $f(x)$ is close to p no matter what the unknown p is and no matter what the observation x is. That is, the error $f(x) - p$ committed by using $f(x)$ as an approximation to p should always be small. This is too much to expect since x can, by chance, be quite misleading about p. However, it is not too much to expect that the error be small in some average sense. For example, the mean squared error,

$$E_p(f - p)^2 = \sum_{x=0}^{n} [f(x) - p]^2 \binom{n}{x} p^x (1 - p)^{n-x},$$

should be small no matter what the unknown p is, or the mean absolute error $E_p|f - p|$ should be small no matter what p is, or the like. For the time being, estimators will be compared only on the basis of their mean squared errors. A more general approach, the underlying ideas of which are well illustrated in this special case, will be mentioned later. The first question that arises is, Can one find an estimator f such that, for every p satisfying $0 \leqslant p \leqslant 1$, the mean squared error of f at p is smaller than (or at least not greater than) the mean squared error at p of any other estimator? Obviously, such an estimator would be best in this mean squared error sense. Unfortunately, and this is what makes the problem of choosing an estimator a nontrivial problem, a best estimator does not exist. To see this, consider the estimates f_1 and f_2 defined by $f_1(x) = x/n$ and $f_2(x) = \frac{1}{2}$. It is not hard to show that $E_p(f_1 - p)^2 = p(1 - p)/n$, and clearly, $E_p(f_2 - p)^2 = (\frac{1}{2} - p)^2$. If a best estimator f existed it would have to satisfy $E_p(f - p)^2 \leqslant E_p(f_2 - p)^2$. But the latter quantity is zero for $p = \frac{1}{2}$, implying that $f = f_2$. However, f_2 is not best since $E_p(f_1 - p)^2$ is smaller than $E_p(f_2 - p)^2$ for p near 0 or 1.

Although no best estimator exists, many good estimators exist. For example, there are many estimators f satisfying $E_p(f - p)^2 \leqslant 1/(4n)$ for $0 \leqslant p \leqslant 1$. The estimator f_1, defined above, is such an estimator. The estimator f_3 defined by $f_3(x) = [\sqrt{n}(x/n) + \frac{1}{2}]/(\sqrt{n} + 1)$ with mean squared error $E_p(f_3 - p)^2 = 1/[4(1 + \sqrt{n})^2]$ is another. If n is large, the mean squared error of any such estimator is small for each possible value of p. In this problem, as is typical, any one of many good available estimators would no doubt be reasonable to use in practice. Only by adding further assumptions, for example, assumptions giving some information about the unknown p, can the class of reasonable estimators be narrowed. Note that estimators are still being compared on the basis of their mean squared errors only.

The estimator f_3 is *minimax* in the sense that f_3 minimizes $\max_{0 \leqslant p \leqslant 1} E_p(f - p)^2$ with respect to f. The minimax approach focuses attention on the worst that can happen using f and chooses f accordingly [see DECISION THEORY]. Note that the estimator f_1 ($f_1(x) = x/n$) does have slightly larger mean squared error than does f_3 for values of p near $\frac{1}{2}$; for values of p near 0 or 1 the advantage lies

wholly with f_1. Other properties of these estimators will be discussed later.

Example 2. Suppose that $x_1, x_2, \cdots, x_n$ are observations on n independent random variables, each having the Poisson distribution with parameter λ, where λ is unknown and may be any nonnegative number [see DISTRIBUTIONS, STATISTICAL, *article on* SPECIAL DISCRETE DISTRIBUTIONS]. For example, x_k could be the number of occurrences during the kth time interval of unit length of any phenomenon occurring "randomly" over time, possibly telephone calls coming into an exchange, customers coming into a store, and so forth [see QUEUES]. Knowing that λ is both the mean and variance of the Poisson distribution, it might not be unreasonable to suppose that both the sample mean,

$$m(x) = m(x_1, \cdots, x_n) = \sum_{k=1}^{n} x_k/n = \bar{x},$$

and the sample variance,

$$s^2(x) = \sum_{k=1}^{n} (x_k - \bar{x})^2/(n - 1)$$

(here, one must assume that $n > 1$), provide good estimators of the unknown λ. It is not hard to show that m is *better* than s^2, that is, $E_\lambda(m - \lambda)^2 \leqslant E_\lambda(s^2 - \lambda)^2$ for all $\lambda \geqslant 0$, with strict inequality for some $\lambda \geqslant 0$.

An estimator is *inadmissible* (with respect to a given criterion like mean squared error) if a better one exists; accordingly, the estimator s^2 is here inadmissible. An estimator is admissible if it is not inadmissible. Although it is not obvious, the estimator m is admissible. In fact the class of admissible estimates is very large here, as is typically the case. In example 1, all three estimators discussed, f_1, f_2, and f_3, are admissible.

Example 3. Let $x_1, x_2, \cdots, x_n$ be observations on n independent random variables each having the normal distribution with mean μ and variance σ^2, where both μ and σ^2 are unknown; μ may be any real number and σ^2 may be any positive number. One might be interested in estimating only μ, only σ^2, the pair (μ, σ^2), or perhaps some combination such as μ/σ.

Example 4. Let $x_1, x_2, \cdots, x_n$ be observations on n independent random variables each having the uniform distribution over the set of integers $\{1, 2, \cdots, N\}$, where N may be any positive integer. For example, in a state where automobile license plates are numbered from 1 to N, each x_i would be the number of a randomly chosen license plate. What is a good estimator of N?

Sufficient statistics. A simple and effective way to narrow the class of estimators that one ought to consider when choosing a good estimator is to identify a sufficient statistic for the problem and to consider only those estimators that depend on the sufficient statistic [*see* SUFFICIENCY]. Roughly speaking, if t is a sufficient statistic, knowing $t(x)$ is as useful as knowing x. The following result is important. If t is a sufficient statistic and f is an estimator with finite mean squared error and f does not depend on t (that is, f is not essentially expressible as $f = h(t)$ for some function h), then there is another estimator f_0 that does depend on t and such that f_0 is better than f (in the technical sense defined above). One f_0 that works is the conditional expectation of f relative to t.

In example 2, m is a sufficient statistic, hence only estimators depending on m need be considered. In particular s^2, which does not depend on m in the sense defined above, need not be considered. In example 3, the ordered pair (m, s^2), where m and s^2 are defined as in example 2, is a sufficient statistic. In example 4, the estimator $2m$ might seem at first to be a plausible estimator of N. However, it does not depend on the sufficient statistic u defined by $u(x) =$ the largest of the x_k. Much better estimators than $2m$ exist. For example, the rather complicated

$$f_4 = \frac{u^{n+1} - (u-1)^{n+1}}{u^n - (u-1)^n}$$

is such an estimator. (Note that f_4 is approximately equal to $(n+1)u/n$.)

Further criteria for choice of estimator. So far estimators have been compared on the basis of their mean squared errors only. Since no best estimator exists, a unique solution to the problem of choosing an estimator is generally not obtainable by this approach. This is not really too regrettable since many good estimators usually exist. Even demanding that an estimator be minimax, not necessarily always a reasonable demand, does not always lead to a unique estimator. In example 2, every estimator of λ has unbounded mean squared error; and in example 3 every estimator of μ has unbounded mean squared error. Hence, in these two examples, all estimators of λ and μ, respectively, are minimax, but the concept loses all interest. In example 1, demanding minimaxity does lead to the unique minimax estimator f_3. A unique minimax estimator is clearly admissible.

The strong intellectual and psychological tendency of human beings to be satisfied only with unique answers has often led to further demands being placed on estimators in addition to the one that their mean squared errors be small.

Unbiasedness. An estimator is *unbiased* if the mean value of the estimator is equal to the quantity being estimated. In example 1, f_1 is unbiased since $E_p f_1 = p$, $0 \leqslant p \leqslant 1$. Both m and s^2 are unbiased estimators of λ in example 2. In example 3, m is an unbiased estimator of μ and s^2 is an unbiased estimator of σ^2. In example 4, both $2m$ and f_4 are unbiased estimators of N. The search for a best unbiased estimator often leads to a unique answer. In example 2, an estimator f would be best unbiased (or minimum variance unbiased) if it is unbiased and satisfies

$$E_\lambda(f-\lambda)^2 \leqslant E_\lambda(f^*-\lambda)^2$$

for every $\lambda \geqslant 0$ and every unbiased estimator f^*. The estimator m is such an estimator for this problem and is the only such estimator. The estimator f_1 is the best unbiased estimator of p in example 1; the estimator m is the best unbiased estimator of μ in example 3; and the estimator f_4 is the best unbiased estimator of N in example 4. The *relative efficiency* of two unbiased estimators is the ratio of their reciprocal variances. Relative efficiency may well depend on the parameter value.

Unbiased estimators fail to exist in some important problems. Using the first design mentioned in the problem of estimating the number of fish in a lake, N, no unbiased estimator of N exists. Although in example 3, s^2 is a best unbiased estimator of σ^2, another estimator of σ^2, $(n-1)s^2/(n+1)$, despite being biased, is actually better than s^2 in the sense of mean squared error. This shows that placing extra demands on estimators can actually come into conflict with the small mean squared error demand. Of course, the relative importance of the various properties an estimator may have will no doubt be judged slightly differently by different reasonable individuals.

Invariance. Notions of invariance can sometimes be invoked so that a best invariant estimator exists. For example, if $x = (x_1, \cdots, x_n)$, b is a real number, and $y = (x_1 + b, \cdots, x_n + b)$, the estimator m is invariant in the sense that it satisfies $m(y) = m(x) + b$. It turns out that among all the estimators of μ in example 3 with this property of scale invariance, the estimator m is best in the usual mean squared error sense. The argument for invariance may be stated rather loosely as follows. Irrelevancies in the data (for example, whether time is measured from 12 noon New York time or from 12 noon Greenwich time) should not make a fundamental difference in the results obtained from the analysis of the data.

A different kind of invariance problem can be troublesome in some circumstances. Suppose in example 1 that interest centers not on p but on some function of p, say $1/p$. If f is a satisfactory estimator of p, it need not follow that $1/f$ is a satisfactory estimator of $1/p$, for properties like unbiasedness, mean squared error functions, etc., can change drastically under nonlinear transformations. Fortunately, in many problems the parameter itself, or a single function of it, is of central interest, so that this kind of noninvariance is not serious.

Specification problems. So far, estimators have been chosen relative to given probability models. If an estimator seems satisfactory for a given probability model, it may be relevant to ask if this estimator is also good for probability models closely related to the given one. For example, it is too much to expect that a model postulating normal distributions describes exactly the practical situation of interest. Fortunately, in many common problems slight changes in the probability model will not materially affect the goodness of an estimator reasonable for the original model [see ERRORS, *article on the* EFFECTS OF ERRORS IN STATISTICAL ASSUMPTIONS]. For example, the estimator m of μ in example 3 is actually a fairly reasonable estimator of the population mean μ in a large variety of cases, particularly if the population variance σ^2 is finite and the sample size n is not too small, as can be seen from the formula for its mean squared error, σ^2/n. Circumstances arise, however, in which alternative estimators, for example, the sample median, not so much affected by slight changes in the tails of the distribution, may need to be considered. [*A process for arriving at other such estimators, called Winsorization, is discussed in* NONPARAMETRIC STATISTICS, *article on* ORDER STATISTICS; *the closely related concept of trimming is discussed in* ERRORS, *article on the* EFFECTS OF ERRORS IN STATISTICAL ASSUMPTIONS.]

More than one parameter. Most of the material of this article deals with estimation of a single parameter. The multiparameter case is, of course, also important and multiparameter analogues of all the topics in this article exist. They are treated in the references, for example by Kendall and Stuart (1946), Cramér (1945), and Wilks (1962).

Constructive estimation methods

Maximum likelihood estimators. In example 1, the estimator f_1 is the maximum likelihood estimator of p: For each x, $f_1(x)$ is that value of p maximizing $\binom{n}{x} p^x (1-p)^{n-x}$, the probability of obtaining x. In example 2, m is the maximum likelihood estimator of λ. In example 3, $(m, [n-1]s^2/n)$ is the maximum likelihood estimator of (μ, σ^2). In example 4, u is the maximum likelihood estimator of N. In the problem of estimating the number of fish in a lake, N, using the first design, no maximum likelihood estimator exists since no such

estimate can be defined for $x = 0$, although for $x > 0$ no trouble occurs. In some examples, there is no unique maximum likelihood estimator.

Maximum likelihood estimators are often easy to obtain. A maximum likelihood estimator does not necessarily have small mean squared error nor is it always admissible. So the maximum likelihood principle can sometimes conflict with the small mean squared error principle. Nevertheless, maximum likelihood estimators are often quite good and worth looking at. If the sample size is large, they tend to behave nearly as nicely as the estimator m of μ in example 3.

Maximum likelihood estimation is often constructive, that is, the method provides machinery that often gives a unique estimating function. There are other constructive methods, three of which are described here: the method of moments, least squares, and Bayes estimation. One or another of these constructive methods may provide a simpler or a better behaved estimator in any particular case.

The method of moments. The approach of the method of moments (or of expected values) is to set one or more sample moments equal to the corresponding population moments and to "solve," if possible, for the parameters, thus obtaining estimators of these parameters. The method is particularly appropriate for simple random sampling. In example 1, if the sample is regarded as made up of n observations, the kth being a 1 (success) or 0 (failure), the sample mean is x/n and the population mean is p, so the resulting method of moments estimator is x/n. In example 4, the method of moments, as it would ordinarily be applied, leads to a poor estimator. The method can, nonetheless, be very useful, especially in more complex cases with several parameters.

Least squares. The least squares approach is especially useful when the observations are not obtained by simple random sampling. One considers the formal sum of squares $\sum_k (x_k - EX_k)^2$, where x_k is an observation on the random variable X_k with expectation EX_k (depending on the parameters to be estimated). Then one attempts to minimize the sum of squares over possible values of the parameters. If a unique minimum exists, the minimizing values of the parameters are the values of their *least square estimators*.

The method is particularly appropriate when the X_k are independent and identically distributed except for translational shifts that are given functions of the parameters. If the X_k all have the same expectation, as in examples 1–4, the least squares estimator of that expectation is the sample mean. Least squares estimation, without modification or extension, does not provide estimators of parameters (like σ^2 in example 3) that do not enter into expectations of observations. [*A fuller treatment of this topic appears in* LINEAR HYPOTHESES, *article on* REGRESSION.]

Bayes estimation. Consider example 1 again, this time supposing that the unknown p is itself the outcome of some experiment and that the probability distribution underlying this experiment is known. For example, x could be the number of heads obtained in n tosses of a particular coin, the probability of a head for the particular coin being p where p is unknown, but where the coin has been picked randomly from a population of coins with a known distribution of p values. Then it would be reasonable to choose an estimator f that minimizes the mean value of the squared error $[f(x) - p]^2$ where the averaging is done with respect to the *known* joint distribution of x and p. Such a minimizing estimator is called a *Bayes estimator*; of course it depends on the distribution assigned to p [*see* BAYESIAN INFERENCE]. A distribution may be assigned to p merely as a technical device for obtaining an estimator and completely apart from the question of whether p actually is the outcome of an experiment. This is the spirit in which Bayes estimators are often introduced, as a way of obtaining an estimator that may or may not have good properties. On the other hand, one may assign a distribution to p in such a way that those values of p that seem more likely to obtain are given greater weight. Of course, different individuals might assign different distributions, for this is a matter of judgment. However, this approach does provide one possible method for using any previously obtained information about p that may be available. It would be rather rare that the *only* information available about p before the experiment is that $0 \leqslant p \leqslant 1$.

Examples of Bayes estimators include the estimator f_3 of example 1, obtained by assigning a certain beta distribution to p, and the estimator f_5 of p, defined by $f_5(x) = (x + 1)/(n + 2)$, obtained by assigning to p the uniform distribution on the interval between 0 and 1. [*See* DISTRIBUTIONS, STATISTICAL, *article on* SPECIAL CONTINUOUS DISTRIBUTIONS, *for discussions of these specific distributions.*] Even f_2 is a Bayes estimator. However, f_1 is not a Bayes estimator but is rather the limit of a sequence of Bayes estimators.

Restricting attention to estimators that are Bayes or the limits (in a certain sense) of sequences of Bayes estimators usually assures one of not overlooking any admissible estimator. Bayes methods frequently prove useful as technical devices in solving for minimax estimators and in many other situations.

Asymptotic estimation theory

Because it is often difficult to compare estimators for small sample sizes, much research on point estimation is in terms of large sample sizes, working with limits as the sample size goes to infinity. In this context, an estimator itself is not considered, but rather a *sequence* of estimators, each member of which corresponds to a single sample size. For example, consider the sequence of sample means $m_1, m_2, \cdots$, where $m_n(x_1, \cdots, x_n) = \sum_{k=1}^{n} x_k/n$. If a sequence of estimators has desirable properties in a limiting large sample sense, it is often presumed that particular members of the sequence will to some extent partake of these desirable properties.

Consistency. An asymptotic condition that is often regarded as essential is that of *consistency*, in the sense that the sequence of estimators is close to the true value of the parameter, with high probability, for large sample sizes. More precisely if $\{t_n\}$ is the sequence of estimators, and if θ is the parameter being estimated, the sequence $\{t_n\}$ is said to estimate θ consistently if, for every interval I containing θ in its interior, the probability that the value of t_n belongs to I approaches 1 as n approaches infinity, no matter what the value of θ is. (There is also a nonasymptotic concept of consistency, closely related to the above. Both ideas, and their applications, originated with R. A. Fisher.)

Comparison of estimators. For simplicity, consider now independent identically distributed random variables with common distribution depending on a single parameter, θ. Let ϕ_θ be the density function (or frequency function) corresponding to that common distribution for the parameter value θ. A large number of regularity conditions are traditionally, and often tacitly, imposed on ϕ_θ; for example, distributions like those of example 4 do not come under the standard theory here. In this brief summary, the regularity conditions will not be discussed. With almost no modifications, the discussion applies to qualitative, as well as numerically valued, random quantities.

Two sequences of estimators, competing as estimators of θ, are often compared by considering the ratios of their asymptotic variances, that is, the variances of limit distributions as n approaches infinity. In particular, one or both sequences may have the lowest possible asymptotic variance. In discussing such matters, the following constructs, invented and named by R. A. Fisher, are important.

Score, Fisher information, and efficiency. The *score* of the single observation x_k is a function of both x_k and θ, defined by

$$s_\theta(x_k) = \frac{\partial}{\partial \theta} \ln \phi_\theta(x_k),$$

and it provides the relative change in ϕ (for each possible value of x_k) when θ is slightly changed. Two basic facts about the score are $E_\theta s_\theta = 0$, $\text{var}_\theta s_\theta = -E_\theta(\partial s_\theta/\partial\theta)$. The quantity, $-E(\partial s_\theta/\partial\theta)$, is often called the *Fisher information* contained in a single observation and is denoted by $I(\theta)$.

For the entire sample, $x = \{x_1, x_2, \cdots, x_n\}$, the *sample score* is just the sum of the single observation scores,

$$s_{\theta n}(x) = \sum_{k=1}^{n} s_\theta(x_k).$$

The Fisher information $I_n(\theta)$ contained in the entire sample is defined as above with $s_{\theta n}$ replacing s_θ; it is just the sum of the Fisher information values for the n single observations. Under the assumptions, each observation contributes the same amount to total information—that is, $I(\theta)$ is the same for each observation—so that $I_n(\theta) = n \, I(\theta)$.

Except for sign, $I_n(\theta)$ is the curvature of the likelihood function near the true value of θ. Roughly speaking, sharp curvature of the likelihood function corresponds to sharper estimation, or lower variance of estimation. The *information inequality* says that, for sequences of estimators $\{t_n\}$ such that $\sqrt{n}\,(t_n - \theta)$ converges in distribution to a distribution with mean zero and variance σ^2,

$$\sigma^2 \geqslant \frac{1}{I(\theta)}.$$

Nonasymptotic variants of this inequality have been explored by Darmois, Dugué, Cramér, Rao, and others. The basic variant, for an unbiased estimator t_n, based on a sample of size n, is

$$\text{var}_\theta t_n \geqslant \frac{1}{I_n(\theta)}.$$

(This is usually called the Cramér–Rao inequality.) Under the tacit regularity conditions, this inequality becomes an equality just when

$$t_n = \theta + \frac{s_{\theta n}}{I_n(\theta)}.$$

This can happen only if the right side is not a function of θ, and this in turn occurs (under regularity) when and only when the distributions given by ϕ_θ form an exponential family [see DISTRIBUTIONS, STATISTICAL, *article on* SPECIAL CONTINUOUS DISTRIBUTIONS].

The maximum likelihood estimator of θ based on $x = (x_1, \cdots, x_n)$, say $\hat{\theta}_n$, is (under regularity) the solution of the *likelihood equation* $s_{\theta n}(x) = 0$. Under these circumstances, $s_{\theta n}/\sqrt{I_n(\theta)}$ and $\sqrt{I_n(\theta)}\,[\hat{\theta}_n - \theta]$ are both asymptotically normal with zero mean and variance unity. Further, the difference between these two quantities converges to zero in probability as n increases.

Thus the maximum likelihood estimator is *asymptotically efficient*, in the sense that its asymptotic variance is as low as possible, for it satisfies the asymptotic information inequality. In general there exist other (sequences of) estimators also satisfying the information inequality; these are called *regular best asymptotically normal* (RBAN) estimators. The RBAN estimators are those that are indistinguishable from the maximum likelihood estimator in terms of asymptotic distribution, as it is traditionally construed. Often some RBAN estimator distinct from the maximum likelihood estimator is easier to compute and work with.

The word "regular," used above, refers in part to regularity conditions on the estimators themselves, considered as functions of the sample. Without that restriction, somewhat strange *superefficient* estimators can be constructed.

The concept of asymptotic treatment has been extended recently in other directions than those summarized above, in particular by the work of R. R. Bahadur and C. R. Rao.

A more general approach to estimation

So far the discussion has been based largely on comparing estimators through their mean squared errors. The mean absolute error could, of course, have been used. More generally, suppose that $W(\theta,d)$ is the *loss* incurred when the numerical estimate d is used as if it were the value $g(\theta)$. Here θ is the unknown parameter of the probability distribution underlying the outcome x of an experiment, and $g(\theta)$ is to be estimated. If f is an estimator, x has been observed, and $f(x)$ is used as if it were the value of $g(\theta)$, then the loss incurred is $W[\theta,f(x)]$. The mean loss, $E_\theta W(\theta,f)$, denoted by $r(\theta,f)$, a function of both θ and f, is of interest. The function r is called the *risk function*. Now such terms as *better, admissible, minimax, Bayes,* and so forth could be defined using the risk function, r, rather than mean squared error. For example, f is better than f^* (relative to the loss W) if $r(\theta,f) \leqslant r(\theta,f^*)$ for all θ with strict inequality for some θ [see DECISION THEORY].

In the earlier discussion, W was taken to be $W(\theta,d) = [d - g(\theta)]^2$ and r was therefore mean squared error.

In the more general multiparameter context mentioned earlier, $\boldsymbol{\theta}$ is a vector of more than one ordinary (scalar) parameter, and so may be $\boldsymbol{g}(\boldsymbol{\theta})$, the quantity to be estimated. For example, in example 3, $\boldsymbol{\theta} = (\mu,\sigma^2)$, $\boldsymbol{g}(\boldsymbol{\theta})$ could be $\boldsymbol{\theta}$, and $W(\boldsymbol{\theta},\boldsymbol{d})$ could be $(d_1 - \mu)^2 + (d_2 - \sigma^2)^2$, where $\boldsymbol{d} = (d_1,d_2)$

is an ordered pair of real numbers. Or consider the following example in which an infinite number of quantities are simultaneously estimated.

Example 5. Let $x_1, x_2, \cdots, x_n$ be observations on n independent random variables each having the same distribution function F, where F may be any distribution function on the real line. The problem is to estimate the whole function F, that is, to estimate $F(a)$ for each real number a. Here $\theta = F$, $g(\theta) = F$, d may be any distribution function, and $W(\theta, d)$ may be given, for example, by $\sup |d(a) - F(a)|$, where the supremum (least upper bound) is taken over all real a. A quite satisfactory estimator, the sample distribution function, exists here. For large n, its risk function is near 0. For $x = (x_1, x_2, \cdots, x_n)$, the value of the sample distribution function is that distribution that places probability $1/n$ on each of $x_1, x_2, \cdots, x_n$ if these values are distinct, with the obvious differential weighting otherwise.

One difficulty with the more general approach to estimation outlined here is that the loss function W is often hard to define realistically, that is, in such a way that $W(\theta, d)$ approximates the actual loss incurred when d is used as if it were the value of $g(\theta)$. Fortunately, an estimator that is good relative to one loss function, say squared error, is often good relative to a wide class of loss functions.

Perhaps the key concept in estimation theory is *better*. Once it has been decided what "this estimator is better than that one" should mean, a large part of the theory follows naturally. Many definitions of *better* are possible. Several others besides the one mentioned here appear in the literature, but none has been so deeply investigated.

History

The theory of point estimation has a long history and a huge literature. The Bernoullis, Moivre, Bayes, Laplace, and Gauss contributed many important ideas and techniques to the subject during the eighteenth century and the early part of the nineteenth century. Karl Pearson stressed the method of moments and the importance of computing approximate variances of estimators. During the early twentieth century, no one pursued the subject with more vigor than R. A. Fisher. His contributions include the development of the maximum likelihood principle and the introduction of the important notion of sufficiency. Neyman's systematic study of interval estimation appeared in 1937. Although the possibility of a loss function approach to statistical problems had been mentioned by Neyman and E. S. Pearson in 1933, its extensive development was not initiated until the work of Abraham

Wald in 1939 [*see the biographies of* BAYES; BERNOULLI FAMILY; FISHER, R. A.; GAUSS; LAPLACE; MOIVRE; PEARSON; WALD].

New and nonstandard estimation problems requiring new and nonstandard techniques of solution will no doubt continue to arise. Remarkable solutions to two such problems have recently been proposed under the general name of *stochastic approximation* [*see* SEQUENTIAL ANALYSIS].

Ideally, scientific constructs should possess not only great explanatory power but simplicity as well. The search for both will, no doubt, encourage more and more mathematical model building in the social sciences. Moreover, it is quite likely that these models will have to become more and more probabilistic if they are to achieve these aims. As a consequence, the statistical problems involved, checking the goodness of fit of the model, estimating the unknown parameters, and so forth, will have to be handled with ever-increasing care and knowledge.

D. L. BURKHOLDER

[*See also* STATISTICS, DESCRIPTIVE.]

BIBLIOGRAPHY

Many elementary textbooks on statistical theory discuss the rudiments of point estimation, for example, Hodges & Lehmann 1964. *Fuller treatments will be found in* Cramér 1945, Wilks 1962, *and* Kendall & Stuart 1946. *Large sample theory is treated at length in* LeCam 1953. *Further discussion of estimation from the loss function point of view will be found in Chapter 5 of* Wald 1950. Lehmann 1959 *treats sufficiency and invariance in some detail. Chapter 15 of* Savage 1954 *contains many illuminating comments on the problem of choosing a good estimator.*

CRAMÉR, HARALD (1945) 1951 *Mathematical Methods of Statistics.* Princeton Mathematical Series, No. 9. Princeton Univ. Press.

FISHER, R. A. (1922) 1950 On the Mathematical Foundations of Theoretical Statistics. Pages 10.308a–10.368 in R. A. Fisher, *Contributions to Mathematical Statistics.* New York: Wiley. → First published in Volume 222 of the *Philosophical Transactions,* Series A, of the Royal Society of London.

FISHER, R. A. (1925) 1950 Theory of Statistical Estimation. Pages 11.699a–11.725 in R. A. Fisher, *Contributions to Mathematical Statistics.* New York: Wiley. → First published in Volume 22 of the *Proceedings* of the Cambridge Philosophical Society.

HODGES, JOSEPH L. JR.; and LEHMANN, E. L. 1964 *Basic Concepts of Probability and Statistics.* San Francisco: Holden-Day.

KENDALL, MAURICE G.; and STUART, ALAN (1946) 1961 *The Advanced Theory of Statistics.* Volume 2: Inference and Relationship. New York: Hafner; London: Griffin. → Kendall was the sole author of the 1946 edition.

KIEFER, J.; and WOLFOWITZ, J. 1952 Stochastic Estimation of the Maximum of Regression Function. *Annals of Mathematical Statistics* 23:462–466.

LeCam, Lucien 1953 On Some Asymptotic Properties of Maximum Likelihood Estimates and Related Bayes' Estimates. California, University of, *Publications in Statistics* 1:277–329.

Lehmann, Erich L. 1959 *Testing Statistical Hypotheses.* New York: Wiley.

Neyman, Jerzy 1937 Outline of a Theory of Statistical Estimation Based on the Classical Theory of Probability. Royal Society of London, *Philosophical Transactions* Series A 236:333–380.

Pitman, E. J. G. 1939 The Estimation of the Location and Scale of Parameters of a Continuous Population of Any Given Form. *Biometrika* 30:391–421.

Robbins, Herbert; and Monro, Sutton 1951 A Stochastic Approximation Method. *Annals of Mathematical Statistics* 22:400–407.

Savage, Leonard J. 1954 *The Foundations of Statistics.* New York: Wiley.

Wald, Abraham 1939 Contributions to the Theory of Statistical Estimation and Testing Hypotheses. *Annals of Mathematical Statistics* 10:299–326.

Wald, Abraham (1950) 1964 *Statistical Decision Functions.* New York: Wiley.

Wilks, Samuel S. 1962 *Mathematical Statistics.* New York: Wiley.

II

CONFIDENCE INTERVALS AND REGIONS

Confidence interval procedures—more generally, *confidence region procedures*—form an important class of statistical methods. In these methods, the outcome of the statistical analysis is a subset of the set of possible values of unknown parameters. Confidence procedures are related to other kinds of standard statistical methods, in particular to point estimation and to hypothesis testing. In this article such relationships will be described and contrasts will be drawn between confidence methods and superficially similar methods of other kinds, for example, Bayesian estimation intervals [*see* Bayesian inference; Estimation, *article on* point estimation; Hypothesis testing].

As an example of this sort of procedure, suppose the proportion of voters favoring a candidate is to be estimated on the basis of a sample. The simplest possible answer is to give a single figure, say 47 per cent; this is the type of procedure called *point estimation.* Since this estimate of the proportion is derived from a sample, it will usually be different from the true proportion. How far off the true value is this estimate likely to be? This question can be answered by supplementing the estimate with error bounds, say ±.5 per cent. Thus, one might say that the true proportion lies between 46.5 per cent and 47.5 per cent. This statement might be false. One task of the statistician is to develop a procedure for the computation of such intervals, a procedure that guarantees that the statements are true in, say, 99 per cent of all appli-

cations of this procedure. Such procedures are called confidence procedures.

Estimation by confidence intervals. It is perhaps easiest to begin with a simple example from normal sampling theory.

Example 1. Let $X_1, \cdots, X_n$ be a random sample of size n from a normal distribution with unknown mean μ and known variance σ^2. Then the sample mean $\bar{X} = \sum_i X_i / n$ is a reasonable point estimator of μ. Hence $\pm 2.58\sigma/\sqrt{n}$ are reasonable error bounds in the following sense: the estimator $\bar{X}$ lies between $\mu - 2.58\sigma/\sqrt{n}$ and $\mu + 2.58\sigma/\sqrt{n}$ with probability .99. In other words, the interval $(\mu - 2.58\sigma/\sqrt{n}, \mu + 2.58\sigma/\sqrt{n})$ contains the estimator $\bar{X}$ with probability .99; that is, whatever the value of μ really is,

$$P_\mu \{\mu - 2.58\sigma/\sqrt{n} < \bar{X} < \mu + 2.58\sigma/\sqrt{n}\} = .99.$$

This probability statement follows directly from the facts that $(\bar{X} - \mu)/(\sigma/\sqrt{n})$ has a unit normal distribution and that a unit normal random variable lies in the interval $(-2.58, +2.58)$ with probability .99.

This statement can be given a slightly different but equivalent form: the interval $(\bar{X} - 2.58\sigma/\sqrt{n}, \bar{X} + 2.58\sigma/\sqrt{n})$ covers μ with probability .99, or whatever μ really is,

$$P_\mu \{\bar{X} - 2.58\sigma/\sqrt{n} < \mu < \bar{X} + 2.58\sigma/\sqrt{n}\} = .99.$$

The interval $(\bar{X} - 2.58\sigma/\sqrt{n}, \bar{X} + 2.58\sigma/\sqrt{n})$ is called a confidence interval for μ with confidence coefficient (or confidence level) .99. The confidence interval is a random interval containing the true value with probability .99. Note that it would be incorrect to say, after computing the confidence interval for a particular sample, that μ will fall in this interval with probability .99; for μ is an unknown constant rather than a random variable. It is the confidence interval itself that is subject to random variations.

Generally speaking, there is an unknown parameter, say θ, to be estimated and an estimator $f(X)$ depending on the sample $X = (X_1, \cdots, X_n)$. In example 1, θ is called μ and $f(X)$ is $\bar{X}$. As this estimator f is based on a random sample, it is itself subject to random variations. If f is a good estimator, its probability distribution will be concentrated closely around the true value, θ. From this probability distribution of f, one can often derive an interval, with lower bound $\underline{c}(\theta)$ and upper bound $\bar{c}(\theta)$, containing the estimator $f(X)$ with high probability β (for example, $\beta = .99$). That is, whatever the actual value of θ,

$$(1) \qquad P_\theta \{\underline{c}(\theta) < f(X) < \bar{c}(\theta)\} = \beta.$$

Often these inequalities can be inverted, that is, two functions $\underline{\theta}(X)$ and $\bar{\theta}(X)$ can be specified such that $\underline{\theta}(X) < \theta < \bar{\theta}(X)$ if and only if $\underline{c}(\theta) < f(X) < \bar{c}(\theta)$. Then, whatever θ really is,

$$(2) \qquad P_\theta\{\underline{\theta}(X) < \theta < \bar{\theta}(X)\} = \beta.$$

This means that the interval $(\underline{\theta}(X), \bar{\theta}(X))$ contains the true value θ with probability β. Quantities like $\underline{\theta}(X)$ and $\bar{\theta}(X)$ are often called confidence limits. In example 1, the bounds $\underline{c}(\theta)$, $\bar{c}(\theta)$ and $\underline{\theta}(X)$, $\bar{\theta}(X)$ are given by $\mu \pm 2.58\sigma/\sqrt{n}$ and $\bar{X} \pm 2.58\sigma/\sqrt{n}$, respectively.

It is also possible to develop the concept of a confidence region procedure in general, without reference to point estimation. Denote by P_θ the assumed probability distribution depending on a parameter θ (which may actually be a vector of several univariate, that is, real valued, parameters). Let Θ be the set of all possible parameter values θ. By a confidence procedure is meant a rule for assigning to each sample X a subset of the parameter space, say $\Theta(X)$. If $\Theta(X)$ contains the true value θ with probability β, regardless of the true value of θ (that is, if for all $\theta \in \Theta$, $P_\theta\{\theta \in \Theta(X)\} = \beta$), then $\Theta(X)$ is called a confidence region for θ. The probability β that the true parameter value is covered by $\Theta(X)$ is called the confidence coefficient.

In example 1, the interval $(\bar{X} - 2.58\sigma/\sqrt{n}, \bar{X} + 2.58\sigma/\sqrt{n})$ is the confidence region for the sample $X = (X_1, \cdots, X_n)$ with confidence coefficient .99.

The probability specified by the confidence coefficient has the following frequency interpretation: If a large number of confidence regions are computed on different, independent occasions, each with a confidence coefficient β, then, in the long run, a proportion β of these confidence regions will contain the true parameter value. There is some danger of misinterpretation. This occurs if θ itself is erroneously considered as a random variable and the confidence statement is given the following form: the probability is β that θ falls into the computed confidence set $\Theta(X)$. It should be clear that $\Theta(X)$ is the random quantity and not θ.

In the simplest applications, θ is a real parameter and the confidence region $\Theta(X)$ is either a proper interval $(\underline{\theta}(X), \bar{\theta}(X))$ or a semi-infinite interval: $(-\infty, \bar{\theta}(X))$ or $(\underline{\theta}(X), +\infty)$. If for all θ, $P_\theta(\theta < \bar{\theta}(X)) = \beta$, then $\bar{\theta}(X)$ is called an upper confidence bound for θ with confidence coefficient β. Similarly, $\underline{\theta}(X)$ is a lower confidence bound.

Let $\underline{\theta}(X)$ and $\bar{\theta}(X)$ be lower and upper confidence bounds with confidence coefficients β_1 and β_2,

and suppose that $\underline{\theta}(X) < \bar{\theta}(X)$ for all samples X. Then the interval $(\underline{\theta}(X), \bar{\theta}(X))$ is a confidence interval with confidence coefficient $\beta_1 + \beta_2 - 1$. If $\beta_1 = \beta_2$, that is, if $P_\theta\{\bar{\theta}(X) < \theta\} = P_\theta\{\theta < \underline{\theta}(X)\}$, the confidence interval $(\underline{\theta}(X), \bar{\theta}(X))$ is called central.

Example 2. As in example 1, let $X = (X_1, \cdots, X_n)$ be a sample of n independent normally distributed random variables with unknown mean μ and known variance σ^2. Then $\bar{\theta}(X) = \bar{X} + 2.33\sigma/\sqrt{n}$ is an upper confidence bound for μ at confidence level .99. Thus $(-\infty, \bar{X} + 2.33\sigma/\sqrt{n})$ is a semi-infinite confidence interval for μ with confidence coefficient .99, as is $(\bar{X} - 2.33\sigma/\sqrt{n}, +\infty)$. Hence $(\bar{X} - 2.33\sigma/\sqrt{n}, \bar{X} + 2.33\sigma/\sqrt{n})$ is a central confidence interval for μ with confidence coefficient $.98 = .99 + .99 - 1$. This central confidence interval differs from that in example 1 in that the latter has confidence coefficient .99 and is correspondingly wider.

Example 3. Let $X = (X_1, \cdots, X_n)$ be a random sample from a normal distribution with known mean $\mu = 0$ and unknown variance σ^2. In this case $S_1^2 = \sum_i X_i^2/n$ is a reasonable estimator of σ^2. (A subscript is used in "S_1^2" because "S^2" will later denote a more common, related, but different quantity.) Suppose $n = 10$. Then the central confidence interval for σ^2 with confidence coefficient .98 is given by $(10S_1^2/23.21, 10S_1^2/2.56)$. The constants 23.21 and 2.56 are readily obtained from a table of quantiles for the chi-square distribution, for nS_1^2/σ^2 has a chi-square distribution with 10 degrees of freedom. This example shows that the endpoints of a confidence interval are generally not symmetric around the usual point estimator.

Relation to point estimation. The computation of confidence intervals is often referred to as *interval estimation*, in contrast to *point estimation*. As outlined above, in many practical cases, interval estimation renders information about the accuracy of point estimates. The general definition of confidence intervals is, however, independent of the problem of point estimation.

In many cases, a particular point estimator is related to the set of central confidence intervals. One forms the estimator for a given sample by thinking of the progressively narrowing intervals as the confidence level decreases toward zero. Except in pathological cases, the interval will squeeze down to a point, whose numerical value furnishes the estimator. Such an estimator is, for continuous distributions, median unbiased; that is, it is equally likely to be above and below the parameter under estimation.

Relation to hypothesis testing. The theory of confidence intervals is closely related in a formal way to the theory of hypothesis testing [*see* HYPOTHESIS TESTING].

Example 4. In example 1, the confidence interval for μ with confidence coefficient .99 was given by $\bar{X} - 2.58\sigma/\sqrt{n} < \mu < \bar{X} + 2.58\sigma/\sqrt{n}$. To test the hypothesis $\mu = \mu_0$ against the alternative $\mu \neq \mu_0$ at significance level .01, accept the hypothesis if

$$(3) \quad \mu_0 - 2.58\sigma/\sqrt{n} < \bar{X} < \mu_0 + 2.58\sigma/\sqrt{n};$$

reject it otherwise. This is the customary two-sided test.

Observe that, given $\bar{X}$, the confidence interval consists of all those values μ_0 for which the hypothesis $\mu = \mu_0$ would be accepted. In other words, the confidence interval consists of all μ_0 whose acceptance region contains the given $\bar{X}$.

On the other hand, given the confidence interval with confidence coefficient .99, it is easy to perform a test of a hypothesis $\mu = \mu_0$: Accept the hypothesis if the hypothetical value μ_0 belongs to the confidence interval; otherwise reject the hypothesis. Proceeding in this way, the pattern is precisely that of testing the hypothesis $\mu = \mu_0$, since μ_0 belongs to the confidence interval if and only if (3) is fulfilled, that is, if the hypothesis $\mu = \mu_0$ would be accepted according to the test procedure.

This duality is illustrated generally in Figure 1. The figure is directly meaningful when there is a single (real) parameter θ and when the sample can be reduced to a single (real) random variable. The latter reduction can frequently be accomplished via a sufficient statistic [*see* SUFFICIENCY]. When the problem is more complex, the figure is still of schematic use.

The figure shows that for each value of θ there is an acceptance region, $A(\theta)$, illustrated as an interval. The two curves determine the lower and upper bounds of this interval respectively. The set of all those θ for which $A(\theta)$ contains a given X, $\Theta(X)$, is the interval on the vertical through X between the two curves.

If the graphic representation is considered in a horizontal way (in terms of the X axis), the lower curve represents the lower confidence bound $\underline{\theta}(X)$ as a function of X, and similarly the upper curve represents the upper confidence bound $\bar{\theta}(X)$. If it is considered from the left (in terms of the θ axis), the functions $\underline{\theta}(X)$ and $\bar{\theta}(X)$ depending on X are inverted into the functions $\bar{c}(\theta)$ and $\underline{c}(\theta)$ respectively, depending on θ. (For this reason the letters are turned.)

The general duality between the testing of simple hypotheses and confidence procedures may be described as follows: Let Θ be the set of unknown parameter values and assume that to each sample X a confidence set $\Theta(X)$ is assigned, such that $P_\theta\{\theta \in \Theta(X)\} = \beta$ for all $\theta \in \Theta$. On the basis of such a confidence procedure, a test for any hypothesis $\theta = \theta_0$ can easily be defined as follows: Let $A(\theta)$ be the set of all X, such that $\theta \in \Theta(X)$. Then the events $X \in A(\theta)$ and $\theta \in \Theta(X)$ are equivalent, whence $P_\theta\{X \in A(\theta)\} = P_\theta\{\theta \in \Theta(X)\} = \beta$. Therefore, if $A(\theta_0)$ is taken as the acceptance region for testing the hypothesis $\theta = \theta_0$, a test with acceptance probability β (or significance level $\alpha = 1 - \beta$) is obtained. On the other hand, given a family of acceptance regions (that is, for each hypothesis $\theta \in \Theta$ an acceptance region $A(\theta)$ contains the sample X with probability β when θ is the case), it is possible to define a confidence procedure by assigning to the sample X the set $\Theta(X)$ of all θ for which $A(\theta)$ contains X (that is, the set of all parameter values θ for which the hypothesis θ would be accepted on the evidence X). Then, again $\theta \in \Theta(X)$ if and only if $X \in A(\theta)$, whence $P_\theta\{\theta \in \Theta(X)\} = P_\theta\{X \in A(\theta)\} = \beta$. These remarks refer only to the case of simple hypotheses. In practice the more important case of composite hypotheses arises if several real parameters are present and the hypothesis consists in specifying the value of one of these. (This case is dealt with in "Nuisance parameters," below.)

Under exceptional circumstances the confidence set $\Theta(X)$ may show an unpleasant property: For some X, $\Theta(X)$ might be empty, or it might be identical with the whole parameter space, Θ. Those cases are usually of little practical relevance.

Thus a confidence statement contains much more information than the conclusion of a hypothesis test: The latter tells only whether a specified

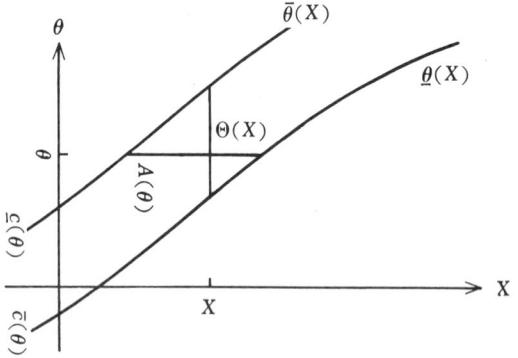

Figure 1 — A confidence region for the parameter θ

hypothesis is compatible with the evidence or not, whereas the confidence statement gives compatibility information about *all* relevant hypotheses.

Optimality. The duality between confidence procedures and families of tests implies a natural correspondence between the optimum properties of confidence procedures and optimum properties of tests.

A confidence procedure with confidence region $\Theta'(X)$ is called *most accurate* if $\Theta'(X)$ covers any value different from the true value with lower probability than any other confidence region $\Theta(X)$ with the same confidence coefficient:

$$P_{\theta_0}\{\theta \,\epsilon\, \Theta'(X)\} \leqslant P_{\theta_0}\{\theta \,\epsilon\, \Theta(X)\} \quad \text{for any } \theta \neq \theta_0.$$

Another expression occasionally used instead of "most accurate" is "most selective." The term "shortest," originally introduced by Neyman, is now unusual because of the danger of confusing shortest confidence intervals and confidence intervals of minimum length.

The family of tests corresponding to most accurate confidence procedures consists of uniformly most powerful tests: Let $A'(\theta)$ and $A(\theta)$ be the acceptance regions corresponding to the confidence regions $\Theta'(X)$ and $\Theta(X)$ respectively; then

$$\begin{aligned} P_{\theta_0}\{X \,\epsilon\, A'(\theta)\} &= P_{\theta_0}\{\theta \,\epsilon\, \Theta'(X)\} \\ &\leqslant P_{\theta_0}\{\theta \,\epsilon\, \Theta(X)\} = P_{\theta_0}\{X \,\epsilon\, A(\theta)\} \\ &\qquad\qquad \text{for any } \theta \neq \theta_0. \end{aligned}$$

Therefore, by using the acceptance region A' the false hypothesis θ is accepted with lower probability than by using A.

Uniformly most powerful tests exist only in exceptional cases. Therefore, the same holds true for most accurate confidence procedures. If, however, the class of tests is restricted (to unbiased tests or invariant tests, for example), the restricted class often contains a uniformly most powerful test within that class. Similarly, tests most powerful against a restricted class of alternatives can often be obtained. In the case of a real parameter a test for the hypothesis θ_0 that is most powerful against all $\theta > \theta_0$ may typically be found. All these restricted optimum properties of tests lead to corresponding restricted optimum properties of confidence procedures.

A confidence procedure is called unbiased if the confidence region covers no parameter value different from the true value with probability higher than its probability of covering the true value. The corresponding property of tests is also called unbiasedness. Therefore, families of uniformly most powerful unbiased tests lead to most accurate un-

biased confidence procedures, that is, confidence procedures that are most accurate among the unbiased confidence procedures: No other unbiased confidence procedures exist leading to confidence regions that contain any value different from the true value with lower probability. The confidence interval given in example 1 is unbiased and most accurate among all unbiased confidence procedures with confidence coefficient .99. On the other hand, the confidence interval given in example 3 is not unbiased.

The optimum properties discussed above are related to concepts of optimality derived from the duality to the testing of hypotheses. A completely different concept is that of minimum length. For instance, the confidence interval given in example 1 is of minimum length. In general the length of the confidence interval is itself a random variable, as in example 3. It is therefore natural to consider a confidence procedure as optimal if the expected length of the confidence intervals is minimal. This concept is appropriate for two-sided confidence intervals. For one-sided confidence intervals the concept is not applicable immediately, as in this case the length is infinite. However, the expected value of the boundary value of the one-sided confidence interval can be substituted for expected length.

In general, confidence intervals with minimum expected length are different from, for example, most accurate unbiased confidence intervals (where such intervals exist). Under special circumstances, however (including the assumption that the distributions of the family have the same shape and differ only in location), invariant confidence procedures are of minimum expected length. The confidence procedure given in example 3 is not of minimum expected length.

Two objections that may be raised against the use of expected length as a criterion are (1) when a confidence interval fails to cover the true parameter value, a short interval is undesirable in that it pretends great accuracy when there is none, and (2) expected length depends strongly on the mode of parameterization, for example, there is no sharp relation between the expected length of a confidence interval for θ and that of the induced interval for θ^3.

Discrete distributions. In the general consideration above it was assumed that there exists a confidence procedure with confidence coefficient β in the sense that, for all θ in Θ, the probability of covering the parameter θ is exactly β when θ is the true parameter. This means that for each θ there exists an acceptance region $A(\theta)$ such that

$P_\theta\{A(\theta)\} = \beta$. This is, however, in general true only for distributions of the continuous type, not for discrete distributions such as the binomial and Poisson distributions [see DISTRIBUTIONS, STATISTICAL]. Thus acceptance regions $A(\theta)$ of probability approximately β must be chosen, with the degree of approximation depending on θ. In practice the acceptance region is selected such that $P_\theta\{A(\theta)\}$ approximates β as closely as possible, either with or without the restriction $P_\theta\{A(\theta)\} \geq \beta$. These acceptance regions $A(\theta)$ define the confidence regions $\Theta(X)$ with (approximate) confidence coefficient β. When the restriction $P_\theta\{A(\theta)\} \geq \beta$ is made, the term "bounded confidence region" is often used, and the region is said to have bounded confidence level β.

Example 5. Let X be the number of successes in n independent dichotomous trials with constant probability p of success. Then X is binomially distributed, that is, $P_p\{X = k\} = \binom{n}{k}p^k(1-p)^{n-k}$. Choose the confidence coefficient $\beta = .99$. Choose for each $p, 0 \leq p \leq 1$, the smallest integer $c(p)$ such that

$$\sum_{k=0}^{c(p)} \binom{n}{k} p^k(1-p)^{n-k} \geq 0.99.$$

Inverting the bound $c(p)$ one obtains one-sided confidence intervals of confidence coefficient .99 for p.

As an illustration, let $n = 20$ and $p = .3$. Since $P\{X \leq 11\} = .995$ and $P\{X \leq 10\} = .983$, the smallest integer such that $P\{X \leq c(p)\} \geq 0.99$ is $c(p) = 11$. Troublesome computations of $c(p)$ can be avoided by use of one of the tables or figures provided for this purpose. For references see Kendall and Stuart ([1943–1946] 1961, p. 118).

Nuisance parameters. In many practical problems, more than one parameter is involved. Often the interest is concentrated on one of these parameters, say θ, while the others are regarded as nuisance parameters. The aim is to make a confidence statement about θ that is true with high probability regardless of the values of the nuisance parameters. The corresponding test problem is that of testing a composite hypothesis that specifies the value of θ without making any assertion about the nuisance parameters. The test is required to have significance level less than or equal to a prescribed α regardless of the nuisance parameters. The corresponding confidence procedure will yield confidence intervals that cover the true value at least with probability $1 - \alpha$ regardless of the nuisance parameters, that is, confidence intervals with bounded confidence level $1 - \alpha$. A special role is played by the so-called similar tests, having exactly

significance level α for all values of the nuisance parameters. They lead to confidence intervals covering the true value with probability exactly $1 - \alpha$ regardless of the nuisance parameters.

Example 6. Let $X_1, \cdots, X_n$ be a random sample from a normal distribution with unknown mean μ and unknown variance σ^2. The variance σ^2 is to be considered a nuisance parameter. Let $\bar{X} = \sum_i X_i/n$ and $S^2 = \sum_i (X_i - \bar{X})^2/(n-1)$. For $n = 10$ a (similar) confidence interval for μ with confidence coefficient .99 is given by $\bar{X} - 3.17\, S/\sqrt{10} < \mu < \bar{X} + 3.17\, S/\sqrt{10}$. For general n, the confidence interval with confidence coefficient .99 is given by $\bar{X} - t_{.005,n-1}\, S/\sqrt{n} < \mu < \bar{X} + t_{.005,n-1}\, S/\sqrt{n}$, where $t_{.005,n-1}$ is the upper .005 point of the tabled t-distribution with $n - 1$ degrees of freedom, for example $t_{.005,9} = 3.17$. Hence the above confidence procedure corresponds to the usual t-test. As for large n, because $t_{.005,n-1}$ is close to 2.58, the confidence interval given here corresponds for large n to the confidence interval given in example 1. The confidence procedure given here is most accurate among unbiased confidence procedures.

Example 7. Consider μ in example 6 as the nuisance parameter. Define S^2 as in example 6 and again take $n = 10$. Then a one-sided confidence interval for σ^2 of confidence coefficient .99 is given by $\sigma^2 \leq 9\, S^2/2.09$. In general, the one-sided confidence interval for σ^2 with confidence coefficient .99 is given by $\sigma^2 \leq (n-1)S^2/\chi^2_{.01,n-1}$, where $\chi^2_{.01,n-1}$ is the lower .01 point of the chi-square distribution with $n - 1$ degrees of freedom. Observe that here the number of degrees of freedom is $n - 1$ while in example 3 it is n.

Confidence coefficient. The expected length of the confidence interval depends, of course, on the confidence coefficient. If a higher confidence coefficient is chosen, that is, if a statement that is true with higher probability is desired, this statement has to be less precise; the confidence interval has to be wider.

It is difficult to give general rules for the selection of confidence coefficients. Traditional values are .90, .95, and .99 (corresponding to significance levels of .10, .05, and .01, respectively). The considerations to be made in this connection are the same as the considerations for choosing the size of a test [see HYPOTHESIS TESTING].

Nested confidence procedures. One would expect the wider confidence interval (belonging to the higher confidence level) to enclose the narrower confidence interval (belonging to the lower confidence level). A confidence procedure with this property is called "nested." All the usual confidence procedures are nested, but this is not a fully general property of confidence procedures.

Sample size. Given the confidence coefficient, the expected length of the confidence interval depends, of course, on the sample size. Larger samples contain more information and therefore lead to more precise statements, that is, to narrower confidence intervals.

Given a specific problem, the accuracy that it is reasonable to require can be determined. In order to estimate the number of housewives knowing of the existence of the superactive detergent X, a confidence interval of ± 5 per cent will probably be sufficiently accurate. If, on the other hand, the aim is to forecast the outcome of elections and the percentage of voters favoring a specific party was 48 per cent in the last elections, an accuracy of ± 5 per cent would be quite insufficient. In this case, a confidence interval of length less than ± 1 per cent would probably be required.

Given the accuracy necessary for the problem at hand, the sample size that is necessary to achieve this accuracy can be determined. In general, however, the confidence interval (and therefore the necessary sample size as well) depends on nuisance parameters. Assume that a confidence interval for the unknown mean μ of a normal distribution with unknown variance σ^2 is needed. Although in example 6 a confidence interval is given for which no information about σ^2 is needed, such information is needed to compute the expected length of the confidence interval: The length of the confidence interval is $2t_{.005,n-1} S/\sqrt{n}$, the expected value for large n is therefore nearly equal to $2t_{.005,n-1} \sigma/\sqrt{n}$. Therefore, in order to determine the necessary sample size n, some information about σ^2 is needed. Often everyday experience or information obtained from related studies will be sufficient for this purpose. If no information whatsoever is at hand, a relatively small pilot study will yield a sufficiently accurate estimate for σ^2. This idea is treated rigorously in papers on sequential procedures for obtaining confidence intervals of given length (Stein 1945). In the case of the binomial distribution, no prior information at all is needed, for $\sigma^2 = p(1-p) \leqslant \frac{1}{4}$, whatever p might be. Using $\frac{1}{4}$ instead of σ^2 can, however, lead to wastefully large samples if p is near 0 or 1.

Robustness—nonparametric procedures. Any statistical procedure starts from a basic model on the underlying family of distributions. In example 1, for instance, the basic model is that of a number of independent normally distributed random variables. Since it is never certain how closely these basic assumptions are fulfilled in practice, desirable statistical procedures are those that are only slightly influenced if the assumptions are violated. Statistical procedures with this property are called *robust* [see HYPOTHESIS TESTING]. Another approach is to abandon, as far as possible, assumptions about the type of distribution leading to nonparametric procedures.

As the duality between families of tests and confidence procedures holds true in general, robust or nonparametric tests lead to robust or nonparametric confidence procedures, respectively. [*Examples showing the construction of confidence intervals for the median of a distribution from the sign test and from Wilcoxon's signed rank test are given in* NONPARAMETRIC STATISTICS.]

Relationship to Bayesian inference. If the parameter is not considered as an unknown constant but as the realization of a random variable with given prior distribution, Bayesian inference can be used to obtain estimating intervals containing the true parameter with prescribed probability [see BAYESIAN INFERENCE].

Confidence statements can be made, however, without assuming the existence of a prior distribution, and hence confidence statements are preferred by *statisticians* who do not like to use "subjective" prior distributions for Bayesian inference. A somewhat different, and perhaps less controversial, application of subjective prior distributions is their use to define so-called subjective accuracy. Subjectively most accurate confidence procedures are defined in analogy to the most accurate ones by averaging the probability of covering the fixed parameter with respect to the subjective prior distribution. It can be shown that a most accurate confidence procedure is subjectively most accurate under any prior distribution with a positive density function (Borges 1962).

Relation to fiducial inference. Fiducial inference was introduced by R. A. Fisher (1930). This paper and succeeding publications of Fisher contain a rule for determining the fiducial distribution of the parameter on the basis of the sample X [see FIDUCIAL INFERENCE].

As in Bayesian inference, this distribution can be used to compute "fiducial intervals," giving information about the parameter θ. The fiducial interval is connected with a probability statement, which admits, however, no frequency interpretation (although some advocates of fiducial methods might disagree).

For many elementary problems, fiducial intervals and confidence intervals are identical. But this is not true in general. One of the attractive properties of fiducial inference is that it leads to solutions even in cases where the classical approach failed until now, as in the case of the Behrens–Fisher problem.

Many scholars, however, find it difficult to see a convincing justification for Fisher's rule of computing fiducial distributions and to find an intuitive interpretation of probability statements connected with fiducial intervals.

A reasonable interpretation of fiducial distributions would be as some sort of posterior distributions for the unknown parameter. It can be shown, however, that fiducial distributions cannot be used as posterior distributions in general; a Bayesian inference, starting from two independent samples and using the fiducial distribution of the first sample as prior distribution to compute a posterior distribution from the second sample, would in general lead to a result different from the fiducial distribution obtained from both samples taken together. For the comparison of fiducial and Bayesian method, see Richter (1954) and Lindley (1958).

Prediction intervals, tolerance intervals. Whereas confidence intervals give information about an unknown parameter, prediction intervals give information about future independent observations. Hence prediction intervals are subsets of the sample space whereas confidence intervals are subsets of the parameter space.

Example 8. If $X_1, \cdots, X_n$ is a random sample from a normal distribution with unknown mean μ and unknown variance σ^2, the interval given by $(\bar{X} - t_{\alpha,n-1}S\sqrt{(n+1)/n}, \bar{X} + t_{\alpha,n-1}S\sqrt{(n+1)/n})$ is a prediction interval containing a future independent observation X_{n+1} with probability $1 - 2\alpha$, if $t_{\alpha,n-1}$ is the upper α point of the t-distribution with $n-1$ degrees of freedom. Note that the probability of the event

$$\bar{X} - t_{\alpha,n-1}S\sqrt{(n+1)/n}$$
$$< X_{n+1} < \bar{X} + t_{\alpha,n-1}S\sqrt{(n+1)/n}$$

is $1 - 2\alpha$ before the random variables $X_1, \cdots, X_n$ are observed. For further discussion of this example see Proschan (1953); for discussion of a similar example, see Mood and Graybill (1950, pp. 220–244, 297–299).

The prediction interval, computed in example 8 above, must not be interpreted in the sense that it covers a proportion α of the population. In a special instance, the interval computed according to this formula might cover more or less than the proportion α. Only on the average will the proportion be α.

In many cases, there is a need for intervals covering a proportion γ with high probability, say β. This is, however, not possible. In general, it is possible only to give rules for computing intervals covering *at least* a proportion γ with high probability β. Intervals with this property are called γ-proportion tolerance regions with confidence coefficient β. In the normal case, one might, for example, seek a constant c, for given γ and β, such that, whatever the values of μ and σ,

$$P\left\{\int_{\bar{x}-cs}^{\bar{x}+cs} f(u;\mu,\sigma)\,du \geq \gamma\right\} = \beta,$$

where $f(u;\mu,\sigma)$ is the normal density with mean μ and variance σ^2.

The constants c, leading to a γ-proportion tolerance interval $(\bar{X} - cS, \bar{X} + cS)$ with confidence coefficient β, cannot be expressed by one of the standard distributions (as was the case in the example of the prediction interval dealt with above). Tables of c can be found in Owen (1962, p. 127 ff.). For further discussion see Proschan (1953), and for nonparametric tolerance intervals see Wilks (1942). [*See also* NONPARAMETRIC STATISTICS.]

Confidence regions. In multivariate problems, confidence procedures yielding intervals are generalized to those yielding confidence regions.

Example 9. Let X and Y be two normally distributed random variables with unknown means μ and ν, known variances 2 and 1, and covariance -1. A confidence region for (μ, ν) with confidence coefficient .99 is given by $(X - \mu)^2 + 2(X - \mu)(Y - \nu) + 2(Y - \nu)^2 \leq 9.21$. The figure 9.21 is obtained from a chi-square table, since the quadratic form on the left is distributed as chi-square with two degrees of freedom. The confidence region is an ellipse with center (X, Y). When such a region is described in terms, say, of pairs of parallel tangent lines, the result may usefully be considered in the framework of multiple comparisons. [*See* LINEAR HYPOTHESES, *article on* MULTIPLE COMPARISONS.]

J. PFANZAGL

BIBLIOGRAPHY

The theory of confidence intervals is systematically developed in Neyman 1937; 1938b. *Prior to Neyman, this concept had been used occasionally in a rather vague manner by a number of authors, for example, by Laplace 1812, section 16, although in a few cases the now current meaning was clearly stated, perhaps first by Cournot 1843, pp. 185–186. A precise formulation without systematic theory is given in Hotelling 1931. A more detailed account of the history is given in Neyman 1938a.*

BORGES, RUDOLPH 1962 Subjektivtrennscharfe Konfidenzbereiche. *Zeitschrift für Wahrscheinlichkeitstheorie* 1:47–69.

COURNOT, ANTOINE AUGUSTIN 1843 *Exposition de la théorie des chances et des probabilités.* Paris: Hachette.

FISHER, R. A. (1930) 1950 Inverse Probability. Pages 22.527a–22.535 in R. A. Fisher, *Contributions to Mathematical Statistics.* New York: Wiley. → First published in Volume 26 of the *Proceedings* of the Cambridge Philosophical Society.

FISHER, R. A. 1933 The Concepts of Inverse Probability and Fiducial Probability Referring to Unknown Parameters. Royal Society of London, *Proceedings* Series A 139:343–348.

HOTELLING, HAROLD 1931 The Generalization of Student's Ratio. *Annals of Mathematical Statistics* 2:360–378.

KENDALL, MAURICE G.; and STUART, ALAN (1943–1946) 1961 *The Advanced Theory of Statistics.* Volume 2: Inference and Relationship. New York: Hafner; London: Griffin. → See especially pages 98–133 on "Interval Estimation: Confidence Levels" and pages 518–521 on "Distribution-free Tolerance Intervals." (Kendall was the sole author of the first edition.)

LAPLACE, PIERRE SIMON DE (1812) 1820 *Théorie analytique des probabilités.* 3d ed., rev. Paris: Courcier. → Laplace's mention of confidence intervals first appeared in the 2d (1814) edition.

LEHMANN, ERICH L. 1959 *Testing Statistical Hypotheses.* New York: Wiley. → See especially pages 78–83, 173–180, and 243–245.

LINDLEY, D. V. 1958 Fiducial Distributions and Bayes' Theorem. *Journal of the Royal Statistical Society* Series B 20:102–107.

MOOD, ALEXANDER M.; and GRAYBILL, FRANKLIN A. (1950) 1963 *Introduction to the Theory of Statistics.* 2d ed. New York: McGraw-Hill. → See especially pages 220–244 on "Interval Estimation." (Mood was the sole author of the 1950 edition.)

NEYMAN, JERZY 1937 Outline of a Theory of Statistical Estimation Based on the Classical Theory of Probability. Royal Society of London, *Philosophical Transactions* Series A 236:333–380.

NEYMAN, JERZY (1938a) 1952 *Lectures and Conferences on Mathematical Statistics and Probability.* 2d ed. Washington: U.S. Dept. of Agriculture. → See especially Chapter 4, "Statistical Estimation."

NEYMAN, JERZY 1938b L'estimation statistique traitée comme un problème classique de probabilité. *Actualités scientifiques et industrielles* 739:26–57.

OWEN, DONALD B. 1962 *Handbook of Statistical Tables.* Reading, Mass.: Addison-Wesley. → A list of addenda and errata is available from the author.

PROSCHAN, FRANK 1953 Confidence and Tolerance Intervals for the Normal Distribution. *Journal of the American Statistical Association* 48:550–564.

RICHTER, HANS 1954 Zur Grundlegung der Wahrscheinlichkeitstheorie. *Mathematische Annalen* 128:305–339. → See especially pages 336–339 on "Konfidenzschluss and Fiduzialschluss."

SCHMETTERER, LEOPOLD 1956 *Einführung in die Mathematische Statistik.* Berlin: Springer. → See especially Chapter 3 on "Konfidenzbereiche."

STEIN, CHARLES 1945 A Two Sample Test for a Linear Hypothesis Whose Power Is Independent of the Variance. *Annals of Mathematical Statistics* 16:243–258.

WILKS, S. S. 1942 Statistical Prediction With Special Reference to the Problem of Tolerance Limits. *Annals of Mathematical Statistics* 13:400–409.

ETHICS

I

ETHICAL SYSTEMS AND SOCIAL STRUCTURES

In a consideration of the relationship of ethical systems to social structure, it is important to show how these terms are being used; different meanings can represent different degrees of abstraction, and the kinds of relationship possible will vary accordingly.

"Social structure" has been taken by Radcliffe-Brown (1952, p. 11; compare pp. 188–204) to mean "an arrangement of persons in institutionally controlled or defined relationships"; in this case, the term stands for a social organization with actual individuals as its constituents. It may be taken, as by Evans-Pritchard ([1940] 1963, p. 262), to exclude relations between persons, but to describe such relations between *groups* as have a high degree of constancy and consistency. Or it may be taken in a still more abstract sense—as a network of relationships between sets of institutionalized social roles (Firth 1954; Nadel 1957; Emmet 1960; 1966).

The view here adopted is that although observation must start from the first of these senses (interactions between persons) and may proceed through the second (regularities in group interactions), the systematic notion of a "social structure" will need to be couched in the abstract terminology of relationships between *roles*.

The notion of an ethical system is even less clearly determined. It may be taken to mean (*a*) the mores of a given society as a sociologist observes them; (*b*) a systematic code of moral principles, such as that of the Roman Catholic church; and (*c*) a philosophical theory about the rationale of moral action, such as utilitarianism.

Ethics and social structure. In considering relationship to a social structure, we would be tempted to say that we need be concerned only with (*a*). This, however, would be unsatisfactory, since to talk of an ethical system is to imply far more than a pattern of observed forms of behavior; rules of conduct, as derived from ethical notions, may be honored in the breach as well as in the observance. In order to discover a people's ethical system even in sense (*a*), it will therefore be necessary to take into account their statements about what is considered right and wrong and why, as well as to describe conformities in their behavior and the working of sanctions against deviation.

For this reason, it might be logically preferable to consider an ethical system simply in sense (*b*), as a body of beliefs about right and wrong, although these are unlikely in many cases to be as systematic as those connected with a formulated theological position, such as that of the Roman Catholic church. Sense (*b*), however, can be related to social structure only by showing how the ethical beliefs in question affect the ways members of the society behave in their social roles.

Social structure in theory and practice. We also need to distinguish here between an *idealized* view of the social structure, seen as a network of roles played according to the rules (or, where rules are broken, corrected by sanctions) and the social structure as a generalized *description* of typical role behavior that may fall short of official ethical prescriptions. In the latter case, however, ethical prescriptions must be taken into account in seeking to understand the behavior, if only to show ways in which the prescriptions are being evaded; the notion of "role expectations," often used in speaking of social structures, can thus be ambiguous. It may stand for predictions of how a person is likely to behave in a given role. It may also stand for "what is expected of him" (normatively) in that role; and notoriously people do not always live up to these "expectations." An ethical system as a set of norms for action needs to be distinguished, therefore, from a descriptive account of the mores as customary ways of behavior (cf. Sumner [1906] 1959, chapter 2).

Distinctiveness of ethical judgments. It is also important to try to distinguish those aspects of the mores that should properly be called ethical from those more properly called religious, legal, political, or matters of etiquette. This is a matter in which the anthropologists of the late nineteenth and early twentieth centuries, such as Westermarck, were interested, but to which less direct attention has been paid more recently, perhaps because moral values pervade these other aspects of social life and are difficult to isolate from them (Edel 1962). Some recent work has been done by moral philosophers on what may be the distinctive criteria of moral as distinct from other kinds of judgment (Ladd 1957; Brandt 1954; cf. Macbeath 1952). But the question of whether these criteria are logically necessary to anything that can be called an ethical system, or whether they are culture bound, is a matter calling for cooperative work between philosophers and anthropologists. Until there is a larger body of material for comparative study directed to such questions as whether primitive peoples have specifically *ethical* notions that are independent of their religious or political notions, the field of study will remain largely speculative.

Two kinds of ethical relativism. The distinction between the logical criteria of what makes a system an ethical system and the substantive principles it contains has not always been drawn by writers on the cultural conditioning of ethical beliefs. While generally holding that ethical beliefs are "relative" to a culture, they do not always distinguish the "reductionist" form of ethical relativism, which presents the ethical beliefs of a people as functionally dependent on their other beliefs and practices, and the kind of "content" relativism which, while allowing that substantive ethical beliefs and practices may be affected by other factors within the society, nevertheless recognizes that there may be distinctive *moral* interests not exhaustively explicable in terms of other interests. The difference between these two approaches can be summarized by saying that the reductionist maintains that the ethical beliefs of a people can be exhaustively rendered in terms of their non-ethical interests, such as the familial or economic, whereas the "content" relativist is prepared to admit that the belief that "X is right" can provide a bona fide reason for acting accordingly, although the content of X may be culturally variable (Emmet 1966, chapter 5).

The latter approach would be concerned with seeing how these different interests may affect each other in producing a particular "way of life"; an instance is Max Weber's well-known thesis on the relation between the Puritan ethic and capitalism in the seventeenth century (Weber 1904–1905). This need not be taken (as by some Marxists) to mean that the ethical ideas of the Puritans were simply a superstructure rationalizing their economic behavior. On the contrary, it can mean that the kinds of behavior, such as hard work and thrifty living, prescribed by their ethical beliefs fitted the kinds of behavior needed for successful entrepreneurial activity in the early stages of a capitalist economy. Thus, a mutual reinforcement of two strong human interests—the ethical and the economic—would be produced and a way of life with survival value established. This type of analysis aims at finding functional interrelations between ethical and other practices within a society without prejudging the question of whether, nevertheless, there may not be *distinctively* ethical motives and interests; for instance, the belief that hard work is morally commendable need not only be a disguised way of saying hard work is economically profitable, nor is it *necessarily* caused by the fact that hard work is profitable.

Ethical systems—form and content.   The question of the distinctive criteria of ethical as distinct from other kinds of judgment has not been overlooked, however, by all writers on the social relativism of morals. Westermarck, in particular, held that there was a universal form of ethical judgments inasmuch as they expressed *disinterested* retributive emotions (1906–1908; 1932). This question of the distinction between the general logical character and the particular substantive content of an ethical system is a point where the third meaning of the term that we distinguished earlier—philosophical theories about the nature of ethical systems—becomes relevant. Edel and Edel (1959) have suggested that an ethical system may be distinguished by certain broad notions that any such system may be supposed to provide for; for example, it will contain some kind of sanction, reasons justifying some kinds of conduct and not others, and, more specifically, some means of controlling aggression and some notion of distributive justice. This may be compared with what Hart (1961, p. 189) has called the minimum content of natural law. This is not a notion of natural law as a universal rational code of ethical principles but a listing of certain basic requirements that any code must somehow meet if people are to live together sufficiently permanently to satisfy the logical and empirical requirements of constituting a "society" (see also Levy 1952, chapter 4 on "The Functional Requisites of Any Society"). Comparative work on these requirements, and on what differences of emphasis may be given them, would be one of the ways in which the study of ethical systems and social structures could be brought together.

Some alternatives to functionalism.   The structural–functionalist approach reflected in the terms "ethical system" and "social structure" has sometimes been interpreted as assuming a more highly integrated and normatively controlled unity within a society than need in fact obtain. The work of Parsons, especially *The Social System*, 1951, has been criticized on these grounds (Lockwood 1956; see also Emmet 1958 for a more extended discussion of the issues). An approach of perhaps more immediate empirical applicability has been outlined by Merton (1957, chapters 8 and 9), who uses the term "reference group" to denote the group or groups from which an individual may take his ethical cues. Modern societies in particular may contain many persons who, although they are conformists from the point of view of their own refer-

ence group, are deviants by the values of the larger society of which their group is a part. Study of deviance and conformity in terms of reference groups may have the effect of reviving interest in the *formal* means, such as political and legal systems, of preserving social cohesion within pluralistic societies. Structural–functional studies, on the other hand, have been mainly concerned with the less formal sanctions of custom and unplanned institutional practices [*see* REFERENCE GROUPS].

Students of organizations have also drawn attention to the importance of informal as well as formal structures. The workings of a large industry cannot be understood simply by looking at the organization chart or by consulting official statements of aims; it is also necessary to discover the unofficial networks of communication, interaction, and leadership. In some cases, elements within these unofficial structures may have their own ethical systems (for example, views on the amount of work that ought to be done), and these can frustrate the official system unless they are taken into account [*see* ORGANIZATIONS, *article on* EFFECTIVENESS AND PLANNING OF CHANGE].

Role, status, and the individual.   If we recognize the looseness of the texture of actual social life, in contrast with any simplified model of the social structure, we see the individual not only as carrying specified role obligations but also as having to meet the demands of a number of different and perhaps conflicting roles. A variety of social structures can be abstracted from the whole field of human relationships: professional, political, family, and friendship roles may all be played by the same individual and are likely to produce competing pressures. Barnard (1938) has called attention to this in the case of high executives, showing how positions of responsibility produce conflicting claims that make heavy demands on an individual's intellectual and moral resources. It is unlikely that any ethical system can be so structured as always to show the priorities among these claims, or any social structure be so simple as not to produce these conflicts.

In relating ethical systems to social structure, therefore, it may be asked whether the former can thereby be *explained* in terms of the latter. A "sociological explanation," following Durkheim (1895), may here be taken to mean an account of behavior not in terms of historical or psychological causation, but in terms of the ways groups are related to one another within the society. Role behavior in social groups is defined partly with reference to ethical norms of expected conduct (cf. Durkheim 1893 on how this is so even in the economic field);

we may therefore say that the ethical system of defining role obligations can be considered as an *aspect* of the social structure, insofar as ethical notions enter into the ways roles are seen and performed. Here a mutual conditioning between ethical beliefs and social arrangements, as we have said, seems more plausible than a one-way causation of the one by the other.

Role performance and social change. It may, of course, be asked whether an *individual* may not be conditioned by the training he receives through the institutions of his society in order to see his role obligations in only one particular way. However, individuals can have their own styles in role performance; they may deviate in various ways; they will have to decide between conflicting role obligations; and in some cases they may create a new role for themselves. There may thus be much individual behavior that will not enter into the description of a social structure except insofar as it may produce innovations that alter the image of an existing role or create a new one. Indeed, it may be said that individual innovation becomes sociologically important only when it modifies role behavior to such an extent that social structure is affected (Emmet 1966, chapters 7 and 8). Individual conduct, therefore, is not being considered as such and is more properly left to psychologists and philosophers.

Nevertheless, the study of social structure can show how certain kinds of behavior will be expected and certain possibilities will be foreclosed because of features in the social situation; and to study the nature of ethical systems in relation to the social structures in which they are embedded may help us to understand why certain actions are thought of as right or wrong in particular societies. These two kinds of understanding can thus fructify one another without being thought of as mutually reducible.

DOROTHY EMMET

[*See also* ROLE; SOCIAL STRUCTURE; STATUS, SOCIAL; UTILITARIANISM; *and the biographies of* BARNARD; DURKHEIM; WESTERMARCK.]

BIBLIOGRAPHY

BARNARD, CHESTER I. (1938) 1962 *The Functions of the Executive.* Cambridge, Mass.: Harvard Univ. Press.

BRANDT, RICHARD B. 1954 *Hopi Ethics: A Theoretical Analysis.* Univ. of Chicago Press.

DURKHEIM, ÉMILE (1893) 1960 *The Division of Labor in Society.* 2d ed. Glencoe, Ill.: Free Press. → First published in French.

DURKHEIM, ÉMILE (1895) 1958 *The Rules of Sociological Method.* 8th ed. Edited by George E. G. Catlin. Glencoe, Ill.: Free Press. → First published in French.

EDEL, ABRAHAM 1962 Anthropology and Ethics in Common Focus. *Journal of the Royal Anthropological Institute of Great Britain and Ireland* 92:55–72.

EDEL, MAY; and EDEL, ABRAHAM 1959 *Anthropology and Ethics.* Springfield, Ill.: Thomas.

EMMET, DOROTHY M. 1958 *Function, Purpose and Powers.* London: Macmillan; New York: St. Martins.

EMMET, DOROTHY M. 1960 How Far Can Structural Studies Take Account of Individuals? *Journal of the Royal Anthropological Institute of Great Britain and Ireland* 90:191–200.

EMMET, DOROTHY M. 1966 *Rules, Roles and Relations.* London: Macmillan; New York: St. Martins.

EVANS-PRITCHARD, E. E. (1940) 1963 *The Nuer: A Description of the Modes of Livelihood and Political Institutions of a Nilotic People.* Oxford: Clarendon.

FIRTH, RAYMOND 1954 Social Organization and Social Change. *Journal of the Royal Anthropological Institute of Great Britain and Ireland* 84:1–20.

HART, HERBERT L. A. 1961 *The Concept of Law.* Oxford: Clarendon.

LADD, JOHN 1957 *The Structure of a Moral Code: A Philosophical Analysis of Ethical Discourse Applied to the Ethics of the Navaho Indians.* Cambridge, Mass.: Harvard Univ. Press.

LEVY, MARION J. 1952 *The Structure of Society.* Princeton Univ. Press. → See especially Chapter 4.

LOCKWOOD, DAVID 1956 Some Remarks on *The Social System. British Journal of Sociology* 7:134–146.

MACBEATH, ALEXANDER 1952 *Experiments in Living: A Study of the Nature and Foundations of Ethics or Morals in the Light of Recent Work in Social Anthropology.* London: Macmillan; New York: St. Martins.

MERTON, ROBERT K. 1957 *Social Theory and Social Structure.* Rev. & enl. ed. Glencoe, Ill.: Free Press. → The first edition was published in 1949.

NADEL, SIEGFRIED F. 1957 *The Theory of Social Structure.* London: Cohen & West; Glencoe, Ill.: Free Press.

RADCLIFFE-BROWN, A. R. 1952 *Structure and Function in Primitive Society.* London: Cohen & West.

SUMNER, WILLIAM GRAHAM (1906) 1959 *Folkways: A Study of the Sociological Importance of Usages, Manners, Customs, Mores, and Morals.* New York: Dover.

WEBER, MAX (1904–1905) 1930 *The Protestant Ethic and the Spirit of Capitalism.* Translated by Talcott Parsons, with a foreword by R. H. Tawney. London: Allen & Unwin; New York: Scribner. → First published in German. The 1930 edition has been reprinted frequently.

WESTERMARCK, EDWARD A. (1906–1908) 1924–1926 *The Origin and Development of the Moral Ideas.* 2 vols., 2d ed. London: Macmillan.

WESTERMARCK, EDWARD A. 1932 *Ethical Relativity.* New York: Harcourt. → A paperback edition was published in 1960 by Littlefield.

II

ETHICAL ISSUES IN THE SOCIAL SCIENCES

Ethics is concerned with standards of conduct among people in social groups; for this reason, research in social science is inextricably bound up in ethical problems. The initial choice of a problem for investigation by the social scientist is often value-laden. The process of inquiry in the social sciences, engaging as it frequently does the lives of people, must meet moral as well as scientific standards. And the product of inquiry constantly adds new data and new theories requiring the revision of established ethical systems. Ethics and social science thus move in contrapuntal relationship, each adding to the character of the other (Shils 1959).

Old issues and new. There are a number of principles of ethics in social science research that are so widely recognized and honored that they do not need detailed discussion. Among these are maintaining highest standards of work, reporting procedures and results faithfully, protecting information given in confidence, giving appropriate credit to co-workers, making appropriate acknowledgment of other writers' materials, representing accurately one's own qualifications, and acknowledging, when appropriate, sources of financial support. The central issue in all of these is integrity, as indeed it is in every step of a true research endeavor. For this reason some social scientists have objected to proposals to define ethical standards for research, arguing that the canons of science are an exacting and sufficient guide to conduct. However, new problems arise as scientists move into new areas under new auspices; old problems appear in new contexts and require new solutions. Ethical standards must be redefined continually to keep them relevant to contemporary situations. Below are several issues that are subjects of concern and of lively debate as this article is written. If these issues are soon dated and no longer lively, it is probably a healthy sign that consensus is being reached on them and that new issues are capturing concern.

Deception in social science research. In many experiments or inquiries in the social sciences, it is necessary, or has been widely considered necessary, to disguise the nature of the task assigned to the subject. The procedure arises usually from the need to control the "set" or "expectancy" with which the subject approaches the task, since set is known to be an important determinant of responses. While in most instances the consequences are trivial, in some instances they may not be trivial at all. In all instances the issue is raised, Is deception ever justified?

Clearly, scientists think that deception is sometimes required to achieve a good that would not otherwise be achievable. For example, it is common practice in medical research to administer a placebo to a control group in order to assess the effects of a drug. No harm is done; the control subjects might still be given the drug if it proves effective. But the outcome of deception is not always benign. In one of the classical experiments on deceit, the investigators tempted children to steal and deceived them into believing that their action could not be detected. Some children did indeed steal. The investigators concluded that honesty is often influenced by the situation, a point demonstrated as much in their own behavior as in that of the children (Hartshorne & May 1928). In a second well-known investigation, social psychologists infiltrated a religious group, posing as converts (Festinger et al. 1956); their conduct has been questioned (Smith 1957). In an experiment on the effects of group pressure on judgment, five co-workers of the experimenter were represented as uninstructed subjects, just like the person whose resistance to social pressure was to be tested (Asch 1948). Both the deception and the stress generated thereby may be questioned, from an ethical viewpoint. Russian psychologists investigating the same problem have avoided the need for deception by using all naive subjects and analyzing the data for trends that occur naturally, accepting the loss in experimental efficiency.

A reasonable ethical standard for such a situation would be that the investigator has an obligation to inform his prospective subject of any aspect of the experiment that might be considered an important factor in the subject's decision to serve. While such an ethical policy obviously has much to commend it, the losses would be great; many experiments concerned with the dynamics of human behavior would be made impossible. Ethics aside, there are pragmatic arguments in favor of a policy of full disclosure of intent. With growing sophistication, the public may come to regard all social science experiments as situations in which deception is to be expected. At this point even truth is suspect. The problem is not simple, nor is it unimportant. Perhaps a minimum obligation of the social scientist is to make the public aware of the problem.

Stress in social science research. While many experimenters have subjected participants in research to stress, one investigator has been taken to task for his seeming insensitivity to the excruciating ordeal his subjects were going through and for his failure to see the larger implications of his methodology. The critic (Baumrind 1964) very reasonably questioned the ethics of subjecting people to extreme stress and pointed out the moral parallels to historical situations in which innocent people have been tortured in the interest of science. The experimenter's rejoinder (Milgram 1964) provides further instruction in the complexity of the problem and demonstrates the value of a continuing debate of ethical issues in research.

The customary routine is to talk with the subject after an experiment involving stress, to explain the procedure, and to try to relieve any residual discomfort. This procedure may suffice in many investigations, but there are others reported in the literature in which the stress is so severe that one could not realistically hope to repair the damage by such a postsession conference. A suitable topic for cross-disciplinary research would be an investigation of possible lingering or delayed effects of experiments involving stress or deception.

It has been proposed that there is already enough stress in life arising from natural causes and that social scientists should not add to it. An alternative is to study stress reactions in natural settings. Many of these are unpredictable and are amenable only to observational study after the event, but some excellent research has been done following disasters, such as tornadoes and earthquakes, by sociologists who were prepared to take advantage of an unpredictable event. There are also predictable and necessary stressful situations that are a normal part of living and could be used in research. A first-grade classroom on the first day of school and the father's waiting room at a maternity hospital are settings where stress can be studied without the investigator's causing it. Webb and his co-workers (1966) have provided an imaginative and useful examination of methodological options in "nonreactive research in the social sciences," including attention to ethical problems.

Protection of research data. The right of the clinician to keep data confidential is widely (though not universally) recognized by custom and in some states and countries by law. But the scientific investigator does not as clearly enjoy such protection. For example, the social scientist engaged in survey research may encounter a serious ethical problem, and lack clear guidelines for conduct, when his evidence is introduced in a court as legal testimony. The court or either contending party may have a legitimate interest in the reliability of the survey and may demand that respondents be identified in order to call them as witnesses. But survey data are generally obtained with assurances of anonymity; a violation of this pledge would not only involve a betrayal of confidence but would also impair the survey method as a research technique by diminishing public confidence in agencies

that use the procedure. In at least one ruling, a court has sustained the right of a survey agency to keep confidential the names of persons interviewed, but other judges may rule differently. Obviously, the social scientist engaged in survey research has a minimum obligation to inform himself on the issues involved so that he can behave responsibly toward people who supply him with information (King & Spector 1963). He might also be expected to anticipate such problems in the planning stages of a study and to take protective measures against a number of contingencies. The issue of proper protection of data, here discussed with reference to surveys, may be equally relevant in other kinds of research. The problem is complicated by the investigator's obligation to keep his work open for scrutiny by competent scientists.

The invasion of privacy. Privacy is a most cherished right of the individual in a free society, and it may well be an important condition for the integration of experience and the achievement of autonomous selfhood. Social scientists are engaged in a number of enterprises that can lead to a reduction of individual privacy. The ethical issue that seems most frequently involved is that information about a person or his family may be collected, and perhaps used officially, without the individual's being aware of what is happening. The use of personality tests for appraising prospective employees, screening school children, and so on has recently attracted public attention. In some instances, restrictive regulations have been imposed to prevent what is seen as an undue invasion of privacy.

Privacy is not always an individual matter but may involve social institutions which depend for their effectiveness on assurances against intrusion; such is true of the jury system in the United States. In 1955, some sociological investigators, with the permission of the trial judge and the contending lawyers, concealed microphones in a jury room and recorded the jury's deliberation. Although the information obtained was treated with scrupulous care by the investigators, the incident created a national furor. The jurors had clearly been deceived and were appropriately indignant. An issue of broader concern involved in this instance was the appropriateness of scientific inquiry into an established social institution; the social scientist who undertakes such studies must be uncommonly concerned with ethical issues, since damage may be done both to social science and to the institutions studied by social scientists.

As computers become increasingly available and efficient in both storage and processing capacities, we face the prospect of an invasion of privacy of quite a different sort. With various agencies collecting diverse data about an individual over a sufficient period of time, and with the data centrally stored and processed, the possibility is imminent that extensive and reliable inferences can be made about an individual that far exceed his intentions of disclosure. The protection of privacy that has come from fragmentation of information or from the sheer tedium and expense of analysis may indeed be lost.

One example may suffice to indicate the further significance of technological developments: it is now possible to obtain, by mail order, a detailed analysis of an individual's responses to the Minnesota Multiphasic Personality Inventory; the evaluation that once required the services of a highly skilled clinician can be provided now, in much shorter time, by a computer. The ethical implications of advances in computer technology are yet to be explored.

The invasion of privacy issue arises at the point of intersection of two highly valued social goods: the need for knowledge about problems, opinions, motivations, and expectancies of people and the need for preservation of personal rights. While the conflict of social values involved is an ancient one (the rack and screw were information-obtaining devices), the problem is of notable contemporary importance because of the steady increase in amount of, and reliance on, social science research, on the one hand, and the advances in the technology of inquiry, including electronic listening devices, recorders, cameras, computers, personal inventories, projective techniques, and planted informers or confederates, on the other hand.

Among the issues that must be considered in achieving a proper balance of conflicting social and individual interest are the importance of the investigation, the informed consent of subjects, the preservation of confidentiality, and the judicious use of records of research. The individual scientist's decisions about these moral issues must be harmonious with the opinion of his peers or with a community consensus. As the social scientist comes to have more of value to offer the community, he can expect more community understanding and support of the unavoidable violation of privacy attendant upon much social science research. (For an informed and sophisticated analysis of the problem of privacy, see Ruebhausen & Brim 1965.)

The issue of informed consent. In medical research it has generally been the practice to obtain the informed consent of a patient as a condition for his participation in an investigation; however, loose definitions of what is meant by *informed* have permitted great latitude in practice. In a decision that will have implications for all research involving human subjects, the Board of Regents of the University of the State of New York in 1966 stringently defined expectations for medical investigators:

No consent is valid unless it is made by a person with legal and mental capacity to make it, and is based on a disclosure of all material facts. Any fact which might influence the giving or withholding of consent is material. A patient has the right to know he is being asked to volunteer and to refuse to participate in an experiment for any reason, intelligent or otherwise, well-informed or prejudiced. A physician has no right to withhold from a prospective volunteer any fact which he knows may influence the decision. It is the volunteer's decision to make, and the physician may not take it away from him by the manner in which he asks the question or explains or fails to explain the circumstances.   (Langer 1966, p. 664)

In this statement the words *social scientist* might be substituted for *physician* and *subject* for *patient* to arrive at an important guideline for research in the social sciences.

But again the issue is not simple. Is a patient in a control group in a medical experiment to be told that the treatment he will receive is known to have no physiological effect but will be administered to control for psychological effects? If such candor were required, much medical research would be impossible. And so it is with social science research, where possible gains in socially valuable knowledge must be weighed against possible losses of individual prerogatives. For a clear joining of the issue, in regard to psychological research, see the correspondence of Miller and Rokeach (1966). Rokeach wrote, to define the complexity of the problem: "What is typically involved in making a decision about moral values, whether in or out of science, is not a choice between good and evil but a choice between two or more positive values, or a choice between greater and lesser evils" (1966, p. 15). All-or-none solutions are seldom satisfactory.

Cross-cultural studies.   The many ethical issues involved in cross-cultural and transnational investigations, long a concern of the professional anthropologist (see, for example, Redfield 1953 and also the "Statement on Ethics of the Society for Applied Anthropology" 1963–1964), were thrust into public prominence, in 1965, by the debacle of Project Camelot, an inquiry sponsored by the U.S. Department of Defense into "the causes of revolutions and insurgency in underdeveloped areas of the world." Exposure of the project in a South American country led to protests from the U.S. ambassador, a Congressional investigation, the cancellation of the project, and a policy requiring that all government-sponsored, foreign-area research be approved by the U.S. Department of State. The fact that Camelot became a national and international *cause célèbre* involving ambassadors, senators, cabinet members, newspapermen, university officials, social scientists, and the president himself, and that it was interpreted as a cloak-and-dagger operation in spite of the sincerity and good will of the participating scientists, has served to obscure the ethical issues involved, issues that demand serious and sophisticated consideration by the social scientist, whether involved in cross-cultural studies or not.

Among the ethical issues are these: Should the intentions of a sponsoring agency be the concern of a social scientist even when he is personally allowed full freedom of inquiry? Should the social scientist be concerned with the uses to which the results of his studies will be put? What is the responsibility of the social scientist for ensuring that the very process of inquiry does not have a deleterious effect on the people being studied? Does the social scientist have an obligation to preserve access to people for subsequent investigators? Is there a point at which inadequacies of design or procedure, or lack of scientific merit in a study, become intrinsically ethical issues by virtue of their imposition on others? These and similar questions may appear to have easy answers, but a sympathetic study of Project Camelot will show their complexity and emphasize the need for social scientists to consider them anew in the context of every proposed investigation (Horowitz 1965).

Social science and social issues. Social science may often have relevance to crucial matters of public policy. With increasing frequency advocates of diverse political and social policies turn to the social scientist for support of their position. Or the social scientist himself, exercising the prerogative of a citizen to make public statements on social and political issues, may find his statements given credence beyond what could be supported by data, by virtue of his being recognized as a scientist, regardless of his competence on the particular topic. Drawn into such an unaccustomed arena, the social scientist must be especially mindful of how he presents his qualifications and of the ethical implications of his statements. Issues related to racial characteristics, for example, have so conjoined science and public policy that they

have been made the subject of study by the Committee on Science in the Promotion of Human Welfare of the American Association for the Advancement of Science ("Science and the Race Problem" 1963).

Care of animals in research. The psychologist has relied heavily on animals—rats, dogs, birds, primates—as subjects in research. To protect laboratory animals from neglect or abuse, formal regulations governing the management of animal laboratories have been developed. These require the provision of adequate food, water, and medical care, the maintenance of sanitary living quarters, the use of anesthetics to prevent pain in operations and other procedures, the provision of postoperative care, and the destruction of animals by humane means. Committees on care of laboratory animals review problems periodically. The U.S. Public Health Service publishes a booklet entitled "Guide for Laboratory Animal Facilities and Care" (Animal Care Panel 1963) and requires recipients of grant support to observe the requirements to assure proper and humane treatment of research animals. The American Psychological Association requires posting in "all rooms where animals are housed and where animal experimentation is conducted" of regulations titled "Guiding Principles for the Humane Care and Use of Animals." In spite of these efforts to assure highest ethical standards in the care of laboratory animals, there is a perennial demand for federal legislation to control practices, especially with respect to dogs and cats. In 1964 there were eight bills introduced in the 88th Congress of the United States, two of which would have been severely restrictive. Although there are occasional cases of negligence or of needless infliction of pain, animals are generally well cared for, and the Congress has shied away from enacting legislation on the matter (Brayfield 1963).

Communication in social science research. Marin Mersenne promoted science in seventeenth-century France by copious letter writing; the problem of communication in science has since become exceedingly complex, with many attendant ethical issues. Ethical problems have involved such issues as plagiarism, misrepresentation of data, the betrayal of confidence, claiming undue credit, and other clearly unacceptable behavior. With the development of what has been called "big science" with extensive government support, problems of a new and more subtle character have emerged. For example, the assignment of credit for research accomplished by a large organization seems to be solved neither by crediting the director alone, as has been done and protested, nor by crediting

30 contributors, as was done in a recent listing of authors. Although promotions may depend on publications, there is a growing need to limit publication to significant findings likely to be of value to others. The sheer volume of reports threatens to overwhelm our most efficient systems for coding, storing, and finding information. Thus, for an investigator to impose the same findings twice on about the same audience constitutes an offense to the development and dissemination of knowledge. The following statement has been proposed to control the volume of publication: ". . . *scientific publication [should] be considered a privilege consequent upon the finding of something which people may need to read, rather than as a duty consequent upon the spending of time and money. . . .* Furthermore . . . no paper [should] be committed more than once to the published literature without very special pleading" (Price 1964).

Research on moral development. Thus far certain theoretical and practical problems relating to ethics and social science research have been considered. It should be noted now that social science research itself is a potential major source of understanding of ethical conduct, of the origins and development of moral standards. Pioneer work was done by Hartshorne and May (1928). Piaget (1932) provided a theoretical matrix for illuminating stages in the moral development of the child. Anthropologists and social psychologists (Whiting 1963) have studied the influence of the family on character formation in different cultures. Russian pedagogical specialists are working explicitly to provide educational experiences to instill communist values in children (Bronfenbrenner 1962). In the United States, the establishment of the National Institute of Child Health and Human Development, to promote research on normal development, can be expected to encourage basic research on the problem.

Social control of scientific inquiry. Various professional, trade, labor, and fraternal groups exert a major influence on the behavior of individuals in contemporary society. Perhaps because of their very diversity they escape attention as instruments of social control, yet it has been contended that they speak with more authority today than do organized religious groups and, further, that they influence day-by-day conduct even more than do local, state, and national governments.

Many of these associations have formal codes of ethics. For the most part these codes have been found to have little effect on the behavior of members of the group (American Academy of Political and Social Science 1955). They are one of the appurtenances of associations and are designed with an eye to building public confidence. However, the traditions, mores, and expectancies that are generated in professional groups do affect behavior, often holding members to extraordinarily high standards of conduct. When codes of ethics are in harmony with long-established tradition (as in *The Principles of Medical Ethics*) or when they are backed up by effective machinery for enforcement, they can be powerful instruments of social control.

The American Psychological Association has applied social science theory and methodology to the task of developing a code of ethics (Hobbs 1948). The critical incidents technique was used to obtain the basic data for the construction of the code. Members of the association were asked to supply descriptions of situations in which a psychologist took some action that either upheld or violated ethical standards. From over a thousand such incidents a committee extracted the principles that appeared to be involved in the behavior reported. The result is two documents: a succinct code (American Psychological Association 1963) and a book-length statement (American Psychological Association 1953) of ethical standards that includes principles, discussions of issues, and illustrations drawn from the collection of critical incidents. Now underway is a new inquiry directed specifically at ethical issues in psychological research; the critical incident technique is again being used to develop basic data from which ethical principles will be derived.

The psychologists' statement of ethical standards is being augmented by a collection of case studies drawn from the files of ethics committees responsible for the enforcement of the code. The assumption is made that the definition of ethical standards is an ongoing, never-finished process and that participation in the process by members of the association may be more important than the written code itself in nurturing high ethical standards in the profession. The Committee on Cooperation Among Scientists of the American Association for the Advancement of Science is collecting similar descriptions, not necessarily to prepare a code of ethics but to illuminate the ethical problems encountered by scientists in all fields.

When scientists fail to regulate their own behavior to the satisfaction of informed members of the community, one can confidently predict that controls will be imposed by legislation or by administrative regulations. In 1965–1966, two major federal agencies adopted procedures governing ethical issues in research supported by their grants.

One agency requires that tests, questionnaires, and other data-gathering devices be approved in Washington by a special review group composed of staff members, with the assistance of consultants. The other agency has established a requirement that grant requests involving possible ethical issues must be reviewed by a recognized local committee of peers of the investigator. The second solution appears to offer protection to research subjects on the basis of competent review without the danger of overcentralized control of scientific inquiry. However, there are responsible investigators who contend that a prescribed review by local peers is an invidious requirement implying incompetence and guilt when competence and rectitude should be assumed, with intervention indicated only when there is some evidence to the contrary. Here again a social process to define appropriate procedures is underway, with the proper resolution still unclear.

It can be expected that society will develop, in time, a productive balance between its need for knowledge and the individual's need for protection against intrusion, inconvenience, or discomfort. A dialectic tension involving values fundamental to a democracy must be resolved, both in terms of general principles and in terms of particular instances. For example, freedom of inquiry must be balanced against rights of privacy, both cherished values in our society. While the issues are complex, resolution is possible. The accommodation, both in substance and in process, will probably be comparable in character to rules governing the right of eminent domain and the right of the individual to own property.

The individual investigator is not without common-sense guidelines. While the answers may not always be clear, some of the questions are: Is the knowledge to be gained worth the imposition involved in obtaining it? Would another design be equally productive but less intrusive? Has fullest advantage been taken of the subject's informed willingness to cooperate? Has the proposed inquiry been designed to minimize effects on the subject population so that subsequent investigators will not be handicapped? To what extent are the proposed procedures consonant with emerging standards, or a calculated departure from them?

Nor is the investigator without criteria to assess and perhaps discover the adequacy of his answers to such questions: first, his own standards as an investigator, concerned quite as much with ethical as with statistical elegance of design; then the approbation of other competent scientists; and,

finally, the appreciation of the larger community, or of significant sections of it, whose support is essential to the continued development of the social sciences.

It is of greatest importance to keep ethical problems under continuing scrutiny and debate, in journals, in training programs, in public forums, with social scientists themselves taking the initiative in the process, in order to provide increasingly instructive principles for clarifying ethical issues in social science research.

NICHOLAS HOBBS

[*See also* MORAL DEVELOPMENT; PRIVACY; SCIENCE.]

BIBLIOGRAPHY

AMERICAN ACADEMY OF POLITICAL AND SOCIAL SCIENCE 1922 *The Ethics of the Professions and of Business.* Edited by Clyde L. King. Annals, Vol. 101, no. 190. Philadelphia: The Academy.

AMERICAN ACADEMY OF POLITICAL AND SOCIAL SCIENCE 1955 *Ethical Standards and Professional Conduct.* Edited by Benson Y. Landis. Annals, Vol. 297. Philadelphia: The Academy.

AMERICAN PSYCHOLOGICAL ASSOCIATION 1953 *Ethical Standards of Psychologists.* Washington: The Association.

AMERICAN PSYCHOLOGICAL ASSOCIATION 1963 Ethical Standards of Psychologists. *American Psychologist* 18:56–60.

AMERICAN STATISTICAL ASSOCIATION, BOSTON, DECEMBER, *1951* 1952 Standards of Statistical Conduct in Business and Government. *American Statistician* 6, no. 1:6–20.

ANIMAL CARE PANEL, ANIMAL FACILITIES STANDARDS COMMITTEE 1963 *Guide for Laboratory Animal Facilities and Care.* U.S. Public Health Service, Publication No. 1024. Washington: Government Printing Office.

ASCH, SOLOMON E. 1948 The Doctrine of Suggestion, Prestige and Imitation in Social Psychology. *Psychological Review* 55:250–276.

BARNES, JAMES A. 1963 Some Ethical Problems in Modern Fieldwork. *British Journal of Sociology* 14:118–134.

BAUMRIND, DIANA 1964 Some Thoughts on Ethics of Research: After Reading Milgram's *Behavioral Study of Obedience. American Psychologist* 19:421–423.

BRAYFIELD, ARTHUR H. 1963 Humane Treatment of Laboratory Animals. *American Psychologist* 18:113–114.

BRONFENBRENNER, URIE 1962 Soviet Methods of Character Education: Some Implications for Research. *American Psychologist* 17:550–564.

BURGESS, ROBERT W. 1947 Do We Need a "Bureau of Standards" for Statistics? *Journal of Marketing* 11:281–282.

COMMISSION DE DÉONTOLOGIE DE LA SOCIÉTÉ FRANÇAISE DE PSYCHOLOGIE 1960 Projet de code déontologie à l'usage des psychologues. *Psychologie française* 5:1–27.

FESTINGER, LEON; RIECKEN, H. W.; and SCHACHTER, STANLEY 1956 *When Prophecy Fails.* Minneapolis: Univ. of Minnesota Press.

FREEMAN, WILLIAM W. K. 1963 Training of Statisticians in Diplomacy to Maintain Their Integrity. *American Statistician* 17, no. 5:16–20.

HARTSHORNE, HUGH; and MAY, MARK A. 1928 *Studies in Deceit*. 2 parts. New York: Macmillan.

HOBBS, NICHOLAS 1948 The Development of a Code of Ethical Standards for Psychology. *American Psychologist* 3:80–84.

HOBBS, NICHOLAS 1959 Science and Ethical Behavior. *American Psychologist* 14:217–225.

HOROWITZ, I. L. 1965 The Life and Death of Project Camelot. *Trans-action*, 3, no. 1:3–7, 44–47.

KELMAN, HERBERT C. 1965 Manipulation of Human Behavior: An Ethical Dilemma for the Social Scientist. *Journal of Social Issues* 21:31–46.

KIMBALL, A. W. 1957 Errors of the Third Kind in Statistical Consulting. *Journal of the American Statistical Association* 52:133–142.

KING, ARNOLD J.; and SPECTOR, AARON J. 1963 Ethical and Legal Aspects of Survey Research. *American Psychologist* 18:204–208.

LANGER, ELINOR 1966 Human Experimentation: New York Verdict Affirms Patient's Rights. *Science* 151:663–666.

MILGRAM, STANLEY 1964 Issues in the Study of Obedience: A Reply to Baumrind. *American Psychologist* 19:848–852.

MILLER, SAMUEL E.; and ROKEACH, MILTON 1966 [Letters] Psychology Experiments Without Subjects' Consent. *Science* 152:15 only.

PIAGET, JEAN (1932) 1948 *The Moral Judgment of the Child*. Glencoe, Ill.: Free Press. → First published in French.

PRICE, DEREK J. DE SOLLA 1964 Ethics of Scientific Publication. *Science* 144:655–657.

REDFIELD, ROBERT 1953 *The Primitive World and Its Transformations*. Ithaca, N.Y.: Cornell Univ. Press.

RUEBHAUSEN, OSCAR M.; and BRIM, ORVILLE G. JR. 1965 Privacy and Behavioral Research. *Columbia Law Review* 65:1184–1211.

SAUVY, ALFRED 1961 La responsibilité du statisticien devant l'opinion et les pouvoirs publics. International Statistical Institute, *Bulletin* 38, no. 2:573–578.

Science and the Race Problem: Report of the AAAS Committee on Science in the Promotion of Human Welfare. 1963 *Science* 142:558–561.

SHAKOW, DAVID 1965 Ethics for a Scientific Age: Some Moral Aspects of Psychoanalysis. *Psychoanalytic Review* 52:335–348.

SHILS, EDWARD 1959 Social Inquiry and the Autonomy of the Individual. Pages 114–157 in Daniel Lerner (editor), *The Human Meaning of the Social Sciences*. New York: Meridian.

SILVERT, K. H. 1965 American Academic Ethics and Social Research Abroad: The Lesson of Project Camelot. American Universities Field Staff [*Reports From Foreign Countries*]: West Coast South America Series 12, no. 3.

SMITH, M. BREWSTER 1957 Of Prophecy and Privacy: [A Book Review of] *When Prophecy Fails*, by L. Festinger, H. W. Riecken, and S. Schachter. *Contemporary Psychology* 2, no. 4:89–92.

SNOW, CHARLES P. 1961 The Moral Un-neutrality of Science. *Science* 133:255–262. → With comments by Warren Weaver, Theodore M. Hesburgh, and William O. Baker.

Statement on Ethics of the Society for Applied Anthropology. 1963–1964 *Human Organization* 22:237 only.

U.S. OFFICE OF SCIENCE AND TECHNOLOGY 1967 *Privacy and Behavioral Research*. Washington: Government Printing Office.

WEBB, EUGENE et al. 1966 *Unobtrusive Measures: Nonreactive Research in the Social Sciences*. Chicago: Rand McNally.

WHITING, BEATRICE B. (editor) 1963 *Six Cultures: Studies of Child Rearing*. New York: Wiley.

ZIRKLE, CONWAY 1954 Citation of Fraudulent Data. *Science* 120:189–190.

ETHNIC GROUPS

An ethnic group is a distinct category of the population in a larger society whose culture is usually different from its own. The members of such a group are, or feel themselves, or are thought to be, bound together by common ties of race or nationality or culture. The nature of an ethnic group's relationships with the society as a whole, and with other groups in it, constitutes one of the main problems in describing and analyzing such societies. As Ruth Benedict said of race conflict, it is not *race* that we need to understand, but *conflict;* so, for an understanding of ethnic groups in a social system, it is not on racial or cultural differences that we need to focus our attention, but on group relations.

Historical outline

The existence of distinct ethnic and cultural groups within societies is widespread and ancient and occurs at most levels of culture, ranging from the Bushmen of the Kalahari, who live within the framework of Tswana society, to modern Europe and America. Ethnic groups in the Near East were recorded by Herodotus almost 2,500 years ago and remained a persistent feature of the Byzantine, the Ottoman, and other Near Eastern empires. Similar situations also occurred in ancient India and in Chinese civilization at all stages of its expansion.

Although scholars in the past have often noted the existence of multiracial and multicultural societies, systematic examination of the sociological consequences of the phenomenon did not begin before the eighteenth century. And then it was principally in connection with the concepts of race and race relations as developed in the next century by writers such as Gobineau (1853–1855) and Chamberlain (1899). Linguistic scholars like Sir William Jones, the Grimm brothers, and Max Müller not only examined the construction and development of Indo-European languages but also inadvertently encouraged the growth and elevation of the idea of race as an ideology and as the most significant index distinguishing culturally different groups from one another.

Earlier historians, including the writers of the

Old Testament, had noted that ethnic groups might be found in a society as a result of the gradual migration of either whole populations or of segments, such as religious refugees, traders, craftsmen, or manual laborers. They also observed that military conquest might bring in its train soldiers and civilians, who either settled permanently in the area or administered their conquests for a period of years before retiring and being replaced from the homeland. Or, again, ethnic groups might be incorporated into a society by altered political boundaries. Sometimes a combination of processes was at work; but however a multiracial or multicultural system came into existence, the types of society in which ethnic groups could be found varied as widely as the processes that brought them into being.

Most investigations of ethnic groups have been made in connection with studies of race relations and stratified societies such as are found in Africa (MacCrone 1937; Patterson 1953), the southern states of the United States (Dollard 1937), parts of the Caribbean (Smith 1955; 1956), Central and South America (Freyre 1933), and in the plural societies of former colonial areas of Asia (Furnivall 1942). Ethnic groups that are not an integral part of a system of over-all social stratification are also found in countries like Switzerland and Nigeria, where they form units in the political system which, although perhaps internally stratified, are not ranked in relation to one another. Other types of multiracial and multicultural situations, as, for example, in northern Laos, Thailand, Burma, and India, have as yet hardly been examined. Frequently in these countries adjacent villages, or even sections of one village, may be linguistically and culturally different and yet be held together in a traditional system of social relations that is not part of the apparatus of a central government (Leach 1954). Similar conditions have been observed, although seldom analyzed, in the Indonesian archipelago, New Guinea, and parts of Africa.

Definitions. At this point it would be wise, for the sake of clarity, to make the distinction between a social group and a social category. By a group, sociologists usually mean an aggregation of people recruited on clear principles, who are bound to one another by formal, institutionalized rules and characteristic, informal behavior. Unless a group is to be no more than a temporary aggregation, it must in addition be organized for cohesion and persistence; that is to say, the rights and duties of membership must regulate internal order and relations with other groups. Members usually identify themselves with a group and give it a name. In practice social groups vary in the degree to which they are corporate; and in certain situations one of the principal difficulties of analysis may be to decide whether a particular social entity is in fact a social group or a mere category of the population, such as red-haired people, selected by a criterion that in the context is socially neutral and that does not prescribe uniform behavior. For any study of group relations this distinction is essential.

In east Africa, the African, the Arab, the European, and the Indian elements of society are closer to being categories of the population than social groups. Although, for example, a fully institutionalized Indian group, recruited from the general category of Indians, is likely to act in the Indian sphere of life, there is no certainty that it will; relations between the ethnic categories may therefore become blurred. The sections of an ethnically and culturally divided population may, according to circumstances, be institutionalized groups related to one another in a system of stratification, or they may be groups living side by side and related in other ways. Ethnic divisions may simply be categories of the population, as are Welshmen and Scotsmen living in England, or Indians, Chinese, and Creoles in Mauritius, who are beginning to lose a sense of ethnic separateness. It is, therefore, always important to be sure what is the exact sociological status of an ethnic or cultural division. Clarity in analysis depends upon it.

Ethnic groups in stratified societies

The division of society into broad *strata*, which form a hierarchy of prestige, wealth, and power, is a feature common to most societies and is one that has been used for classification. A few societies, mostly primitive or small in size, may not be stratified; social positions may not be sufficiently numerous or diverse to be easily grouped into strata or aggregates of individuals sharing an equivalent status that would differentiate them from members of other similar aggregates. This is not to say, of course, that statuses in such small societies may not be ranked but is merely to point out that they do not constitute groups. Sociologists traditionally classify the types of stratification as caste, estate, or class systems. As ethnic and subcultural groups may form the basis of a system of stratification, a closer examination of the matter is needed.

In any system of social stratification the following apply: (1) Individuals belong to strata that are *groups* in the sense that everybody in them shares some obligatory ways of acting that are typically and intentionally different from those in other strata. (2) Strata must be *exclusive*, so that nobody may belong to more than one at the same time. (3) Strata must be *exhaustive*, so that everybody in the society belongs to one. (4) Strata must be *ranked*. In using this criterion, differential access to political and economic resources is taken to be the most significant aspect of the ranking. These criteria do not distinguish different types of stratification, any one of which may be exemplified in a society where ethnic groups are a component element of the system.

Caste groups. One sociological definition of a caste system is that it is a hierarchy of endogamous groups in which status is rigidly ascribed by birth and in which mobility from one group to another is not possible. Correct relations between groups are maintained and validated by religious rules, especially the rule that improper contact between castes produces a state of impurity that entails ritual, legal, and other penalties.

In this definition no careful distinction is usually made between the four-fold division of Indian society into castes (*varna*) and subcastes (*jati*). In early literature the *varna* (priests, soldiers, businessmen, and laborers) are sometimes described in terms of what appear to be ethnic differences; but in historical times they have not constituted more than categories of value against which individuals and members of subcastes could measure their own and other people's prestige. They were not groups, in the sense of imposing duties that were uniform throughout India. In short, the *varna* were ranked categories, not stratified groups. Not dissimilar arrangements are also found in some of the multiracial societies of Africa and the Caribbean.

Empirically, Indian society was made up of many small self-contained caste systems, each of which was a hierarchy of subcaste groups. Subcastes in turn were organized so that social labor was divided among them. Each subcaste traditionally held a monopoly of a particular service, so that all washermen, for example, although not bound to that occupation, could prevent others from practicing it. The essence of this division of labor was that it was cooperative and complementary, not competitive. In these small, closed caste systems relationships between individuals tended to be multiple in that two individuals could fill a number of roles in relation to each other. This "summation" or "involution" of roles is an attribute of small-scale and not large-scale social systems (Nadel 1957, pp. 64–72). The argument may be summarized

thus: (1) Caste groups must be recruited by birth, that is to say, they must be *closed*. (2) Relationships between groups must be *cooperative*, not *competitive*.

In India subcastes are not usually separate ethnic or cultural groups, but an understanding of caste systems is essential in the analysis of society in Iran and parts of the Near East where a multiplicity of ethnic and cultural groups appears to be organized in small-scale caste systems (Barth 1960). It is possible, too, that society in certain parts of the southern states of the United States is similarly arranged (Dollard 1937).

If we are content to say, as are many students, that South Africa and India both exhibit a caste system, then no further distinctions need be sought. But writers on India do not usually agree that "color-bar" societies are *ipso facto* caste systems. Although the population of India was always very large, society there was characteristically composed of separate small-scale involute caste systems. South Africa, although less populous, is typical of large-scale Western society where relationships between roles are usually single-stranded and not the multiple ties of a small-scale society.

In certain ways the system of closed groups in South Africa is nearer the model of an estate system than that of a caste or social-class system, but the sociological status of "color-bar" societies needs to be carefully re-examined. Studies of them have for the most part either used the concepts of stratification without careful consideration or have directed attention to economic functions (Boeke 1953) or to attitudes and other psychological concomitants of the existence of ethnic groups. [*See* Caste.]

Social class groups. In some places, such as parts of the West Indies, ethnic groups are regarded as, and may in fact be, *social classes*. Sociologists generally consider a class to be an aggregate of people occupying roughly the same status, which is different from that of people in other classes and which, unlike status in a caste or estate system, allows movement from one stratum to another. It is never easy to decide to what degree a social class is an institutionalized group or exactly how it is related to economic and political status and prestige. When some of the qualifications for membership are also those for belonging to an ethnic category or group, the difficulties of analysis may become very great indeed. An aggregate of people is not a social class just because they think of themselves as one; it is a social class because some activities are obligatory to all or most members and act as a sign that the people form a group and are eligible for access (appropriately graded according to their class) to resources that are valued by the society. When these activities are also qualifications for membership of ethnic or cultural groups, then ethnic and class groups coincide.

The types of stratification that have been mentioned are, of course, models; and a particular system, whether its constituent elements are ethnic groups or not, may not correspond with the model. Racial differences used as insignia or badges to mark off groups from one another are not different in kind from clothing, speech, manners, property, or other cultural emblems that may serve the same ends. But since physical differences are permanent and may be strikingly visible and may also carry much emotion, the understanding of societies such as are found in Mexico, Nigeria, or Kenya has been made difficult by treating them as if they were altogether different from those more familiar to sociologists. The fact that signs of a special kind are used for distinguishing groups in multiracial societies does not mean that such societies are radically different from others.

In a study of early twentieth-century Burma and Netherlands Indonesia, Furnivall argued that countries in which "there is a plural society, with different sections of the community living side by side, but separately, within the same political unit" ([1948] 1956, p. 304) were "a distinctive form of society with a characteristic political and economic constitution" (1942, p. 195). In such a situation, he believed, members of society are unable to develop the common values and demands generated by sharing common institutions. Another writer, M. G. Smith, regards Furnivall's concepts as essential to comparative sociology, arguing that a plural society is composed of readily identifiable sections held together only by the fact that they are part of one central political system. Such sections, it should be noted, are not necessarily *ethnic* groups. Each is distinguished by having its own "core" of "basic" or "compulsory" institutions. Social systems may therefore be placed on a scale ranging from those that are fully plural with distinct sections fulfilling particular economic, political, religious, or other functions, to homogeneous systems in which one set of basic institutions is shared by all members (Smith 1960). Models of this kind have attracted anthropologists, historians, and economists, especially those working in multiracial or multicultural areas; but most sociologists have found the concept of a basic core of differentiating institutions even harder to define and handle than the concepts with which they were more familiar,

and they have preferred to rely on older and better tested theories of social differentiation. [*See* STRATIFICATION, SOCIAL.]

Ethnic groups in nonstratified societies

Not all societies having ethnic groups within their boundaries incorporate them into a unified system of social stratification, and relations among ethnic groups may (to use a political metaphor) be more of a "federal" nature than one of ranked access to social resources.

Societies with a single administrative system. In Switzerland or Canada, for instance, cultural groupings are clearly differentiated and maintained, and each may be separately stratified; but access to power in the wider society is not limited by either ethnic or cultural origins, nor is it conditioned by a ranked evaluation of ethnic groupings within the society. In Malaya, too, although there are distinct ethnic groups, they are not stratified in relation to one another. The population is divided between Malays and immigrant Chinese and Indians. Constitutionally the machinery of government is in the hands of people selected by voting. The workings of electoral procedures and the staffing of the civil service and the armed forces have, in fact, placed most of the political machinery in the hands of Malays, leaving economic power largely with the Chinese. This distribution of the different kinds of power, with its open possibilities of real loss or gain, has tended to consolidate ethnic categories into political parties (Freedman 1960).

In Mexico, on the other hand, ethnic criteria have, on the whole, been abandoned in the formation of social groups because they no longer mark off differences considered significant. The people who control political, legal, and economic matters attain their positions without reference to race, although not without acquiring the dominant Spanish culture. In Thailand, too, the balance struck between demographic, political, economic, and cultural factors is such that the dominant Buddhist, Thai-speaking group is able to pursue a policy of assimilating ethnic minorities. The policy has had a measure of success with Chinese immigrants, but no attempt has been made to absorb the Muslim, Malay-speaking inhabitants of the southern provinces.

Where ethnic or cultural differences coincide with groups that tenaciously hold different religious opinions, the relationships of one group to another and to the central government may become very complex indeed and lead to serious conflict. But the problem is not one peculiar to ethnically diverse societies. In the sixteenth century, the division of

France into Roman Catholic and Protestant Christians did not make it a plural society, even though some Protestants, especially in the south, were culturally and linguistically separate. Nor did it mean that groups that held these different opinions were different in kind from other groups that had been competing for political power before the religious differences arose.

The point here is an essentially simple one. In any society the immediately effective determinants of most social action lie in the political, legal, and economic spheres; and whether or not the main component groups of the society are stratified in relation to one another, an examination of the social system must be primarily concerned not only with relations between groups but also more specifically with those between rulers and ruled. The latter problem is an aspect of the former, but in a society with groups that differ ethnically, whose interests are in fact opposed to one another, the ensuing conflict may be phrased in racial terms and thus provoke more bitter hostility than in other struggles of the ruled against their rulers.

Societies without a single administrative system. In the examples considered so far, ethnic or cultural groups have formed part of an organized administrative and political system. Understanding the significance and range of such groups and their economic, political, religious, and cultural importance has revolved around the problem of ascertaining the exact position that they occupy in the system. In northern Thailand, Burma, and New Guinea, where small ethnic and cultural groups are dispersed and mingled over a wide area without traditionally being under the direct control of a single administrative system, it is also necessary to determine their exact relationship to one another.

A number of such "tribal" groups have been studied, but because anthropological fieldwork tends toward village studies and because the linguistic difficulties of examining such a heterogeneous system are very great, students have seldom made the study of the wider system the main focus of their attention. Groups of this kind appear to be linked to one another in a network of political, economic, ritual, and marriage alliances about which little information is available. But here, as in more politically unified systems, the balance struck in one place is seldom exactly the same as that in another, where the weighting of economic, political, cultural, and ideological forces may be different. The use of models of the kind that have been discussed in this article is essential in the analysis of any society; and where useful models do not exist, as is probable in the study of such

tribally mixed areas as those just noticed, then they must be constructed. But their usefulness must not be misunderstood. It is highly unlikely that any model will correspond in detail with the complexity and variety of real life, especially that of multiracial and multicultural societies.

Specialization of ethnic groups

This article is concerned mainly with the theoretical problems of describing and analyzing the place of ethnic and cultural groups within social systems of different types. Most studies of societies of this kind have dealt less with theoretical problems than with the consequences of economic, political, or religious specialization of such groups within the wider society. Often these consequences are the result of the structural position of the group, but this in turn may be the result of the specialized tasks that it performs.

When Europeans first began to govern east Africa the difficulties of setting up an administration and of stimulating the trade needed to produce a revenue gave an opening to Indian immigrants, who were ethnically and culturally very different from the African and Arab inhabitants of the region. Even where common beliefs in Islam were held, this fact did not submerge ethnic or cultural differences or the hostility to, and suspicion and fear of, the immigrants, whose interests as middlemen and skilled workers brought them into conflict with all other ethnic categories of the population. Such a conflict tends to make a structural alignment even more rigid and to confirm and perpetuate associated attitudes.

The point can be illustrated in many parts of the world. Studies of Jewish ethnic groups have long been concerned with the political and other social results of economic specialization and the ways in which specialized minority groups, once established, are modified and maintained. Similarly, in all parts of southeast Asia, economic and political developments have produced ethnic specialization with a wide range of conflict.

The political consequences of the specialization of ethnic groups by occupation, and therefore of the kinds of power that they hold in society, is a problem of which all historians of colonial empires, from that of the Romans and the imperial Chinese to the sixteenth-century Spanish and the modern Europeans, are well aware. But it is also a problem that needs even closer attention in postcolonial societies, where, although the structural alignment of groups within them may have altered, the problems of cultural and ethnic diversity remain.

With the growth of good communications and

the spread of travel, ethnically and culturally diverse societies are likely, in the short term, to increase in number rather than diminish. As the sociological study of society ceases to be solely a Western discipline, the need to find appropriate conceptual tools for analyzing ethnic and cultural variation will undoubtedly become a major preoccupation of the discipline.

H. S. MORRIS

[See also MINORITIES; PEASANTRY; RACE RELATIONS; SOCIAL STRUCTURE; TRIBAL SOCIETY. Other relevant material may be found in ASIAN SOCIETY, article on SOUTH ASIA; CARIBBEAN SOCIETY; LINGUISTICS, article on THE SPEECH COMMUNITY.]

BIBLIOGRAPHY

BARTH, FREDRIK 1960 The System of Social Stratification in Swat, North Pakistan. Pages 113–146 in Edmund R. Leach (editor), Aspects of Caste in South India, Ceylon and North-west Pakistan. Cambridge Papers in Social Anthropology, No. 2. Cambridge Univ. Press.

BENEDICT, BURTON 1962 Stratification in Plural Societies. American Anthropologist New Series 64:1235–1246.

BOEKE, JULIUS H. 1953 Economics and Economic Policy of Dual Societies as Exemplified by Indonesia. New York: Institute of Pacific Relations.

CHAMBERLAIN, HOUSTON STEWART (1899) 1910 Foundations of the Nineteenth Century. New York and London: John Lane. → First published in German.

COX, OLIVER C. 1948 Caste, Class and Race: A Study in Social Dynamics. Garden City, N.Y.: Doubleday.

DOLLARD, JOHN (1937) 1957 Caste and Class in a Southern Town. 3d ed. Garden City, N.Y.: Doubleday.

FREEDMAN, MAURICE 1960 Growth of a Plural Society in Malaya. Pacific Affairs 33:158–168.

FREYRE, GILBERTO (1933) 1956 The Masters and the Slaves: A Study in the Development of Brazilian Civilization. 2d ed., rev. New York: Knopf. → First published in Portuguese.

FURNIVALL, JOHN S. 1942 The Political Economy of the Tropical Far East. Journal of the Royal Central Asian Society 29:195–210.

FURNIVALL, JOHN S. (1948) 1956 Colonial Policy and Practice: A Comparative Study of Burma and Netherlands India. Issued in cooperation with the International Secretariat, Institute of Pacific Relations. Cambridge Univ. Press; New York Univ. Press.

GOBINEAU, JOSEPH ARTHUR DE (1853–1855) 1933 Essai sur l'inégalité des races humaines. 6th ed., 2 vols. Paris: Firmin-Didot. → Partially translated into English in 1915 as The Inequality of Human Races.

JAYAWARDENA, CHANDRA 1963 Conflict and Solidarity in a Guianese Plantation. London School of Economics and Political Science, Monograph on Social Anthropology, No. 25. London: Athlone.

LEACH, EDMUND R. 1954 Political Systems of Highland Burma: A Study of Kachin Social Structure. London School of Economics and Political Science; Cambridge, Mass.: Harvard Univ. Press.

MACCRONE, IAN D. 1937 Race Attitudes in South Africa: Historical, Experimental and Psychological Studies. Oxford Univ. Press.

MORRIS, H. S. 1957 The Plural Society. Man 57:124–125.

NADEL, SIEGFRIED F. 1957 The Theory of Social Structure. London: Cohen & West; Glencoe, Ill.: Free Press.

PATTERSON, SHEILA 1953 Colour and Culture in South Africa. London: Routledge; New York: Humanities.

REX, JOHN A. 1959 The Plural Society in Sociological Theory. British Journal of Sociology 10:114–124.

SMITH, M. G. 1955 Framework for Caribbean Studies. Mona (Jamaica): University College of the West Indies.

SMITH, M. G. 1956 Community Organization in Rural Jamaica. Social Economic Studies 5:295–312.

SMITH, M. G. 1960 Social and Cultural Pluralism. New York Academy of Sciences, Annals 83, no. 5:763–785.

ETHNOCENTRISM

See CULTURE, article on CULTURAL RELATIVISM.

ETHNOGRAPHY

The data of cultural anthropology derive ultimately from the direct observation of customary behavior in particular societies. Making, reporting, and evaluating such observations are the tasks of ethnography. Although the successful carrying out of these tasks is intimately related to the validity of cultural and social anthropological interpretations, ethnography itself has received little serious attention. However, as the social sciences have become more critical of their source materials, more concerned with how data are recorded, verified, and analyzed, interest has developed in ethnographic method and theory and in the more technical and personal aspects of conducting ethnographic research.

While the scope and definition of ethnography have varied considerably and opinions differ on many details, contemporary usage does permit a few general terminological distinctions and implications. An ethnographer is an anthropologist who attempts—at least in part of his professional work—to record and describe the culturally significant behaviors of a particular society. Ideally, this description, an ethnography, requires a long period of intimate study and residence in a small, well-defined community, knowledge of the spoken language, and the employment of a wide range of observational techniques including prolonged face-to-face contacts with members of the local group, direct participation in some of that group's activities, and a greater emphasis on intensive work with informants than on the use of documentary or survey data. Used nonspecifically, ethnography refers to the discipline concerned with producing such cultural descriptions. With a regional reference (e.g., "Polynesian ethnography"), the term designates either the way in which ethnography is conceived and practiced in the area or the collective or comparative treatment of the ethnographies written about the peoples living in the region. This last usage is frequently referred to as comparative ethnology, or simply ethnology [see ETHNOLOGY].

History of ethnography

Although the roots of ethnographic description are lost in antiquity and most observations and interpretations (or misinterpretations) of human societies have continued to be transmitted orally, some early written accounts have been preserved. Permanent documentation of such observations increased markedly with European voyages of discovery and exploration. Despite organizational and stylistic differences, it is possible to discern in the literature the transition from the curious recountings of strange, exotic, or bizarre practices to the present attempts at producing valid cultural descriptions. In comparing the successive steps in this transition, one should note changes not only in the content and purpose of ethnography but also in the preparation and background of the investigators and in the circumstances under which field work is conducted. (It is impossible to treat in detail many individual and institutional differences, such as the varying views of ethnographic work among American, British, and European anthropologists; see, for example, Eggan 1961; Firth 1957; Gluckman 1961; Griaule 1957; Kroeber 1957; Lowie 1953; Richards 1939.)

Early ethnography. Beginning in the late fifteenth century and continuing for several hundred years, descriptions of unfamiliar cultural practices were written largely as a result of explorations, missionizing, and the establishment of colonial governments and outposts (see Howell 1642; Rowe 1964). Although there were some exceptional reports such as Pigafetta's observations on Cebu, included in his chronicle of the Magellan voyage (1525), and the extensive Mexican texts recorded in the sixteenth century by Sahagún (see Sahagún, *General History of the Things of New Spain*), the dominant form of early ecclesiastic and governmental records was ethnographically unimpressive. In the nineteenth century, as territorial exploration intensified and the writings of natural historians, travelers, and museum collectors began to augment missionary and official documents, ethnographic inquiry became a somewhat more organized procedure. Many questionnaires, lists, instructions,

and regional guides were written (see Lewis 1814; British Association . . . 1852; Neumayer 1875). In Europe and the United States, professional anthropological societies were supported at first by travelers, government employees, and other amateurs and later encouraged by museums. Institutionalization stimulated the publication of monograph series devoted largely to cultural descriptions (notably, for example, the publications of the Bureau of American Ethnology, the American Ethnological Society, and the larger natural history museums). Landmarks include Morgan's account of Seneca culture (1851), such turn-of-the-century reports of field research as Rivers' study of the Toda (1906), and a few refreshingly innovating works like Barton's study of Ifugao law (1919), in which the value of the case-method approach is demonstrated. Up to the end of World War I vast quantities of published ethnographic material had accumulated from many regions, but although some scholars (such as Boas) had begun to work in depth with informants on particular linguistic and other cultural problems (see Jakobson 1959; Smith 1959), most of this literature had been produced by nonanthropologists (e.g., Morgan was a lawyer, Barton a schoolteacher and dentist), who for a variety of reasons had become attracted to the subject matter, and in the course of short visits, surveys, or by accidental association, had acquired sufficient field experience to write interesting accounts of their observations. Toward the end of this period, museums provided most of the support for field research. In general, ethnographic inquiry was correspondingly dominated by object-centered interests, a standardized topical format for observation and recording, and extensive use of interpreters. [See BOAS; MORGAN, LEWIS HENRY; RIVERS.]

Ethnography before World War II. By 1925 ethnographic field work had become an established professional activity. There was a distinct shift away from mere acceptance of field work toward a more critical and craftsmanlike attention to its execution, a shift from a dominant concern with data accumulation to the deeper analysis of particular cultural patterns. Many of these changes resulted directly from the influence of Malinowski's reports (especially 1922; 1935) based on his lengthy and detailed observations in the Trobriand Islands. His insistence on using the local language, residing for a long time with the group being studied, and delineating functionally related cultural phenomena in specifiable contexts spurred serious rethinking of many aspects of ethnographic research [see MALINOWSKI]. Increased interest in cultural contexts led to a concern with the ethnographer's role in the field situation and a more careful assessment of the way in which field data are recorded (Mauss 1947; Mead 1947; Osgood 1940). Partly as a result of developments in linguistics, sociology, and psychology, ethnographers began to show greater interest in general theory and descriptive methods, as well as to take advantage of an expanded range of research techniques such as the recording of life histories, the administering of projective tests, and the extensive use of film. Field inquiry was increasingly guided by an interest in general problems of cultural variability and of the nature of cultural universals. In the 1930s, attempts to provide needed ethnographic information for trait analysts and hypothesis testers led to various forms of standardization, such as the *Outline of Cultural Materials* (Yale University 1938), to help organize the recording and cross-indexing of field observations. This development aided quantitative and comparative studies and expanded significantly the existing inventories of cultural detail.

The detail, however, often lacked contextual specification, and these efforts thus drew attention to the inherent weakness of relying on prepared formats to guide functionally oriented field research. Similar criticism and experimentation with many field methods and techniques helped to meet the new demands of higher research standards. During this phase the influence of museum sponsorship and amateur ethnography declined. Field workers were mostly trained as anthropologists in graduate university departments and were supported by private foundation and government grants.

Ethnography after 1950. Following World War II, ethnography began to attract more theoretical and methodological attention. Of particular note was the renewed and expanded interest in classification, which is crucially important (Needham 1963, pp. vii–ix). There was also an increased emphasis on communications systems and structural models (e.g., Lévi-Strauss 1958); on the extension of principles developed in structural linguistics to ethnographic descriptions (e.g., Goodenough 1951); on the detailed study of cultural subsystems (e.g., Conklin 1957; Frake 1964b; Pospisil 1958); on contrasts between qualitative and quantitative aspects of field observations (Leach 1961); and on the development of more effective means of accounting for both cultural and personal variables in actual field situations (Condominas 1966). At the beginning of this phase there was a marked increase in the numbers of professional ethnographers, in sources of support, and in opportunities for field work.

Theory and method

The cumulative efforts of ethnographers to go beyond the uncritical narrative and rambling presentation of assumed cultural detail have focused on determining what constitutes a valid cultural description, on developing a theory that permits evaluation of alternative descriptions, and on formulating methods that may be most effective in deriving general statements from recorded observations. For example, it has been suggested that ideally an ethnography constitutes a cultural grammar, an abstract theory which provides the rules for producing, anticipating, and interpreting appropriate cultural behaviors in given settings (Conklin 1964; Frake 1964a; Goodenough 1957). Ethnographic theory, in this view, is concerned with evaluative criteria such as completeness (in both depth and breadth), conciseness, and accuracy. New approaches for providing reliable, valid, and more revealing field analyses have included (1) the formal treatment of cultural subsystems in which the relevant cultural phenomena are discretely organized or relationally describable in terms of a small number of dimensional contrasts or processes—componential definitions and formulaic reduction and rearrangement of terms by specified rules have been applied most frequently to kinship analysis (see Lounsbury 1964); and (2) the intracultural analysis of folk classifications, especially those of natural phenomena. The study of folk science (see Colby 1964) has led to a number of developments such as the more specific analysis of folk taxonomies (Berlin et al. 1966; Conklin 1962). Together with other types of contrast-set, subsegregate, and network linkage analysis, these efforts have sometimes been referred to as *ethnoscience* (Sturtevant 1964). Problems of alternative methodological procedures (Burling 1963) and of multiple contexts and code channels (Hymes 1962) are also being examined. The principles guiding many recent efforts reflect influences from linguistics, logic, mathematics, and systematic biology. Early results of their application in ethnography are, in turn, stimulating developments in such fields as sociology (Cicourel 1964) and archeology (Chang 1967). Furthermore, it is generally agreed, even where opinions on the nature of valid evidence differ widely (e.g., Metzger 1965), that theory and method as well as technique must be constantly tested in the field. [*See* Cognitive theory; Communication; Componential analysis.]

Techniques

Instruments for gathering, storing, retrieving, rearranging, expressing, and using field data while still in the field have multiplied with technical developments (Kano & Segawa 1945; Rowe 1953). Tape recording, cinematography, photogrammetry, aerial mapping, and the use of computers in text and demographic analysis are only a few of the frequently employed technical developments in the treatment of ethnographic data. Selecting from among these many devices and varied interactional techniques those most appropriate for keeping ethnographic records is a complex task. The ethnographer tries not to rely upon published outlines and questionnaires; he shuns interviews with informants carried out in artificial settings; and he avoids premature quantification or overdifferentiated measurement. Initially, at least, flexibility, curiosity, patience, and experimentation with many alternative devices and procedures are desirable. In everyday conversations between field worker and informant, for example, attention to and use of such verbal techniques as the following have been used profitably, although not always with equal success: recording and using natural question and comment frames (i.e., the ways in which information is normally solicited and transmitted in the local language); noting and using question–response sequences and implications; testing by intentional substitution of acceptable and incongruent references; testing by paraphrase; testing by reference to hypothetical situations; testing by experimental extensions of reference; and testing by switching styles, channels, code signals, message content, and roles (by reference or impersonation). Similarly, in the making of visual and nonverbal observations initial experimentation and flexibility help to determine focuses and boundaries of scenes, scheduled events, key roles, etc. Graphic and plastic modeling media have provided additional dimensions for the exploration of actual or hypothetical situations otherwise not easily investigated. Furthermore, ethnomodels, often ignored or treated only anecdotally, may clarify and facilitate field observation. When local systems have been qualitatively established, other procedures such as scaling techniques may be applied to increase the range of observations and provide some basis for quantification by various kinds of discrete, direct, or indirect measures. As available technology makes more elaborate manipulation of field data possible, greater attention can be given to informant–ethnographer interaction, not only in terms of eliciting routines but also with reference to critical and probabilistic changes in the microsociological environment. [*See* INTERVIEWING.]

Personnel. Because ethnographers interact personally and socially with informants, they find themselves carrying on a unique type of natural history, in which the observer becomes a part of (and an active participant in) the observed universe. The extent of this involvement and its importance for ethnographic recording depend on many situational considerations, including the personalities of the ethnographer and his informants. In some types of field inquiry the ethnographer's practical success or failure may depend as much on those impressions he makes locally (Goffman 1956) as on the cultural events being observed. Informal recognition of these variables is frequently reflected in the nontechnical literature and in humorous anecdotes circulated among colleagues. More systematic accounts of these personal background factors and their consequences have appeared with increasing frequency (e.g., Berreman 1962; Casagrande 1960). Especially where long-term investigation of intimate personal relationships is concerned, most anthropologists would agree with Condominas (1965, p. 35) in stressing the "nécessité d'ethnographier les ethnographes." Methods of assessing such contextual information are not yet well developed, but more careful and sensitive reporting of the kinds of transactions involved in ethnographic inquiry (Oliver 1958) and of the total spectrum of social involvements affecting these transactions (Junker 1960; Mintz 1960) may lead to the desired awareness, and thus to appropriate adjustments in continued research. The possibility of combining such sensitivity with technical mastery of ethnographic analysis has been dramatically illustrated in recent contributions by Paul Friedrich (see Tagari 1964) and Laura Bohannan (1966). [*See* OBSERVATION.]

Translation. The problems of ethnography are in the largest sense those of translation. Eventually, all observations must be "translated" into the ethnographer's descriptive code. Thus, linguistic theory, and translation theory in particular, has special relevance for ethnography (Gumperz & Hymes 1964; Nida 1964). And although ethnography and linguistics are not identical, they are to some extent mutually dependent (Hockett 1954). Furthermore, in spite of the fact that much ethnographic research concerns nonverbal behaviors, observations of even the most inarticulate cultural process are often identified, tallied, and even quantified by means of informant-expressed judgments. General linguistic and anthropological interest in semantic theory has been very responsive to discussions of ethnographic problems (e.g., Colby 1966; Conklin 1962; Lamb 1966; Romney & D'Andrade 1964; cf. Malinowski 1935). In particular, attention has been drawn to the diversity of semiotic relations, the multiplicity of contexts and related communication systems, and the importance of contrastive analysis of complete terminological sets [see SEMANTICS AND SEMIOTICS].

Since 1950 the critical re-evaluation of theory and practice has led to greater appreciation of the technical and human problems that are inherent in ethnographic research. Intellectual excitement and controversy have intensified efforts to refine methods for reducing apparent cultural complexity and indeterminacy to clear, systematic, and effective statements.

HAROLD C. CONKLIN

[*Directly related are the entries* ANTHROPOLOGY; COMPONENTIAL ANALYSIS; FIELD WORK; LANGUAGE, *article on* LANGUAGE AND CULTURE; LINGUISTICS; SEMANTICS AND SEMIOTICS.]

BIBLIOGRAPHY

Significant sources other than those listed below may be found in the bibliographies of Colby 1966; Conklin 1962; 1964; Nida 1964; Sturtevant 1964. The articles and appended references in the following collections should also be consulted: Adams & Preiss 1960; Casagrande 1960; Firth 1957; Gumperz & Hymes 1964; Romney & D'Andrade 1964. Most of the early references in this bibliography consist of guides, questionnaires, or sets of instructions to explorers, travelers, and collectors. Other items are listed only if cited in the text.

ADAMS, RICHARD N.; and PREISS, JACK J. (editors) 1960 *Human Organization Research: Field Relations and Techniques.* Homewood, Ill.: Dorsey.

BARTON, ROY F. 1919 *Ifugao Law.* University of California Publications in American Archaeology and Ethnology, Vol. 15, No. 1. Berkeley: Univ. of California Press.

BERLIN, BRENT; BREEDLOVE, DENNIS E.; and RAVEN, PETER H. 1966 Folk Taxonomies and Biological Classifications. *Science* 154, no. 3746:273–275.

BERLIN, K. MUSEEN, MUSEUM FÜR VÖLKERKUNDE 1896 *Instruction für ethnographische Beobachtungen und Sammlungen in Central Ostafrika.* Berlin: The Museum.

BERREMAN, GERALD D. 1962 *Behind Many Masks: Ethnography and Impression Management in a Himalayan Village.* Society for Applied Anthropology, Monograph No. 4. Ithaca, N.Y.: The Society.

BOHANNAN, LAURA 1966 Shakespeare in the Bush. *Natural History* 75, no. 7:28–33.

BRITISH ASSOCIATION FOR THE ADVANCEMENT OF SCIENCE 1852 *A Manual of Ethnological Inquiry: Being a Series of Questions Concerning the Human Race, for the Use of Travellers and Others, in Studying the Varieties of Man.* London: Taylor & Francis.

BRITISH ASSOCIATION FOR THE ADVANCEMENT OF SCIENCE (1874) 1951 *Notes and Queries on Anthropology.* 6th ed., rev. London: Routledge.

BRITISH MUSEUM, DEPARTMENT OF THE BRITISH AND MEDIAEVAL ANTIQUITIES AND ETHNOGRAPHY, BUREAU OF ETHNOGRAPHY 1905 *Anthropological Queries for Central Africa.* Compiled by C. H. Read. London: The Museum.

BURLING, R. 1963 Garo Kinship Terms and the Analysis of Meaning. *Ethnology* 2:70–85.

CASAGRANDE, JOSEPH B. (editor) 1960 *In the Company of Man: Twenty Portraits by Anthropologists.* New York: Harper.

[CASS, LEWIS] 1823 *Inquiries Respecting the History, Traditions, Languages, Manners, Customs, Religion, etc., of the Indians Living in the United States.* Detroit, Mich.: Sheldon & Reed.

CHANG, KWANG-CHIH 1967 *Rethinking Archaeology.* New York: Random House.

CICOUREL, AARON V. 1964 *Method and Measurement in Sociology.* New York: Free Press.

COLBY, B. N. 1964 Folk Science Studies. *Palacio* 70, no. 4:5–14.

COLBY, B. N. 1966 Ethnographic Semantics: A Preliminary Survey. *Current Anthropology* 7:3–32.

CONDOMINAS, GEORGES 1965 *L'exotique est quotidien: Sar Luk, Viet-nam Central.* Paris: Plon.

CONKLIN, HAROLD C. 1957 *Hanunóo Agriculture: A Report on an Integral System of Shifting Cultivation in the Philippines.* FAO Forestry Development Paper No. 12. Rome: Food and Agriculture Organization.

CONKLIN, HAROLD C. 1962 Lexicographical Treatment of Folk Taxonomies. Pages 119–141 in Conference on Lexicography, Indiana University, 1960, *Problems in Lexicography.* Edited by Fred W. Householder and Sol Saporta. Bloomington: Indiana Univ., Research Center in Anthropology, Folklore, and Linguistics. → Also published as Volume 28, no. 2, part 4 of the *International Journal of American Linguistics,* and as Publication No. 21 of Indiana University, Research Center in Anthropology, Folklore, and Linguistics.

CONKLIN, HAROLD C. 1964 Ethnogenealogical Method. Pages 25–55 in Ward H. Goodenough (editor), *Explorations in Cultural Anthropology: Essays in Honor of George Peter Murdock.* New York: McGraw-Hill.

EGGAN, FRED 1961 Ethnographic Data in Social Anthropology in the United States. *Sociological Review* 9: 19–26.

FIRTH, RAYMOND (editor) (1957) 1964 *Man and Culture: An Evaluation of the Work of Bronislaw Malinowski.* New York: Harper.

FOUCART, GEORGE 1919 *Introductory Questions on African Ethnology.* Cairo: Printing Office of the French Institute of Oriental Archaeology.

FRAKE, CHARLES O. 1964a Notes on Queries in Ethnography. *American Anthropologist* New Series 66, no. 3, part 2:132–145.

FRAKE, CHARLES O. 1964b A Structural Account of Subanun "Religious Behavior." Pages 111–129 in Ward H. Goodenough (editor), *Explorations in Cultural Anthropology: Essays in Honor of George Peter Murdock.* New York: McGraw-Hill.

FRAZER, JAMES G. (1907) 1916 *Questions on the Customs, Beliefs and Languages of Savages.* Cambridge Univ. Press.

GLUCKMAN, MAX 1961 Ethnographic Data in British Social Anthropology. *Sociological Review* 9:5–17.

GOFFMAN, ERVING (1956) 1959 *The Presentation of Self in Everyday Life.* Garden City, N.Y.: Doubleday.

GOODENOUGH, WARD H. 1951 *Property, Kin, and Com-*

munity on Truk. Yale University Publications in Anthropology, No. 46. New Haven: Yale Univ. Press.

GOODENOUGH, WARD H. (1957) 1964 Cultural Anthropology and Linguistics. Georgetown University, Washington, D.C., Institute of Languages and Linguistics, *Monograph Series on Languages and Linguistics* No. 9:167–173.

GRIAULE, MARCEL 1957 *Méthode de l'ethnographie.* Paris: Presses Universitaires de France.

GUMPERZ, JOHN J.; and HYMES, DELL H. (editors) 1964 The Ethnography of Communication. *American Anthropologist* New Series, Special Issue 66, no. 6, part 2.

HOCKETT, CHARLES (1954) 1958 Chinese Versus English: An Exploration of the Whorfian Theses. Pages 106–123 in Harry Hoijer (editor), *Language and Culture: Conference on the Interrelations of Language and Other Aspects of Culture.* Univ. of Chicago Press. → See also Hockett's comments in the discussion.

HOCKETT, CHARLES 1964 Scheduling. Pages 125–144 in F. S. C. Northrop and Helen H. Livingston (editors), *Cross-cultural Understanding: Epistemology in Anthropology.* New York: Harper.

HOWELL, JAMES (1642) 1895 *Instructions for Forreine Travell.* London: Moseley.

HYMES, DELL H. 1962 The Ethnography of Speaking. Pages 13–53 in Anthropological Society of Washington, *Anthropology and Human Behavior.* Washington: The Society.

JACKSON, JOHN R. 1834 *Aide-mémoire du voyageur: Ou questions relatives à la géographie physique et politique, etc.* Paris: Bellizard.

JAKOBSON, ROMAN 1959 Boas' View of Grammatical Meaning. Pages 139–145 in Walter Goldschmidt (editor), *The Anthropology of Franz Boas.* American Anthropological Association, Memoir No. 89. Menasha, Wisc.: The Association.

JUNKER, BUFORD H. (1960) 1962 *Field Work: An Introduction to the Social Sciences.* Univ. of Chicago Press.

KANO, TADAO; and SEGAWA, KOKICHI (1945) 1956 *An Illustrated Ethnography of Formosan Aborigines.* Volume 1: The Yami. Rev. ed. Tokyo: Maruzen.

KELLER, ALBERT G. 1903 *Queries in Ethnography.* New York and London: Longmans.

KIRSCHBAUM, FRANZ J.; and FÜRER-HAIMENDORF, CHRISTOPH VON 1934 *Anleitung zu ethnographischen und linguistischen Forschungen mit besonderer Berücksichtigung der Verhältnisse auf Neuguinea und den umliegenden Inseln.* St. Gabriel-Mödling (Austria): Verlag "Anthropos."

KROEBER, ALFRED L. 1957 *Ethnographic Interpretations: 1–6.* University of California Publications in American Archaeology and Ethnology, Vol. 47, No. 2. Berkeley: Univ. of California Press. → See especially Chapter 1, "What Ethnography Is."

LAMB, SYDNEY M. 1966 Epilegomena to a Theory of Language. *Romance Philology* 19:531–573.

LEACH, EDMUND R. 1961 *Pul Eliya, a Village in Ceylon: A Study of Land Tenure and Kinship.* Cambridge Univ. Press.

LÉVI-STRAUSS, CLAUDE (1958) 1963 *Structural Anthropology.* New York: Basic Books. → First published in French.

LÉVI-STRAUSS, CLAUDE 1966 Anthropology: Its Achievements and Future. *Current Anthropology* 7:124–127.

LEWIS, MERIWETHER (1814) 1922 *History of the Expedition Under the Command of Captains Lewis and Clark to the Sources of the Missouri, . . .* 3 vols.

New York: Allerton. → A questionnaire for Lewis and Clark's ethnographic observations is included in Volume 1, pages xxvii–xxviii. A paperback edition was published in 1965 by Dover.

LOUNSBURY, FLOYD G. 1964 A Formal Account of the Crow- and Omaha-type Kinship Terminologies. Pages 351–393 in Ward H. Goodenough (editor), *Explorations in Cultural Anthropology: Essays in Honor of George Peter Murdock.* New York: McGraw-Hill.

LOWIE, ROBERT H. 1953 Ethnography, Cultural and Social Anthropology. *American Anthropologist* New Series 55:527–534.

LUSCHAN, FELIX VON (1904) 1909 *Anleitung für ethnographische Beobachtungen und Sammlungen in Afrika und Oceanien.* 3d ed. Berlin: Unger.

LUSCHAN, FELIX VON 1906 Anthropologie, Ethnographie und Urgeschichte. Volume 2, pages 1–123 in Georg von Neumayer (editor), *Anleitung zu wissenschaftlichen Beobachtungen auf Reisen.* 3d ed. Hanover (Germany): Jänecke.

MALINOWSKI, BRONISLAW (1922) 1960 *Argonauts of the Western Pacific: An Account of Native Enterprise and Adventure in the Archipelagoes of Melanesian New Guinea.* London School of Economics and Political Science, Studies, No. 65. London: Routledge; New York: Dutton. → A paperback edition was published in 1961 by Dutton.

MALINOWSKI, BRONISLAW (1935) 1965 *Coral Gardens and Their Magic.* 2 vols., with a new introduction by E. R. Leach. Bloomington: Indiana Univ. Press. → Volume 1: *Soil-tilling and Agricultural Rites in the Trobriand Islands.* Volume 2: *The Language of Magic and Gardening.*

MARIN, LOUIS (1924) 1925 *Questionnaire d'ethnographie: Tables d'analyse en ethnographie.* Alençon (France): Laverdure. → First published in the *Bulletin* of the Société d'Ethnographie de Paris.

MAUSS, MARCEL 1947 *Manuel d'ethnographie.* Paris: Payot.

MEAD, MARGARET 1947 *The Mountain Arapesh: III. Socio-economic Life. IV. Diary of Events in Alitoa.* American Museum of Natural History, *Anthropological Papers* 40, part 3.

METZGER, DUANE 1965 [A Review of] *The Nature of Cultural Things,* by Marvin Harris. *American Anthropologist* New Series 67:1293–1296.

MINTZ, SIDNEY W. 1960 *Worker in the Cane: A Puerto Rican Life History.* Caribbean Series, II. New Haven: Yale Univ. Press.

MORGAN, LEWIS HENRY (1851) 1962 *The League of the Iroquois.* New York: Citadel. → First published as *The League of the Ho-dé-no-sau-nee, or Iroquois.* A 1901 edition was edited with many notes by Herbert M. Lloyd. A two-volume paperback edition, a reprint of the 1901 edition, was published by the Human Relations Area Files in 1954.

NEEDHAM, RODNEY 1963 Introduction. Pages vii–xlvii in Émile Durkheim and Marcel Mauss, *Primitive Classification.* Translated and edited by Rodney Needham. Univ. of Chicago Press.

NEUMAYER, GEORG VON (editor) 1875 *Anleitung zu wissenschaftlichen Beobachtungen auf Reisen.* 2 vols. Berlin: Oppenheim.

NIDA, EUGENE A. 1964 *Toward a Science of Translating.* Leiden (Netherlands): Brill.

OLIVER, DOUGLAS 1958 An Ethnographer's Method for Formulating Descriptions of "Social Structure." *American Anthropologist* New Series 60:801–826.

Osgood, Cornelius 1940 *Ingalik Material Culture.* Yale University Publications in Anthropology, No. 22. New Haven: Yale Univ. Press.

Pigafetta, Antonio (1525) 1906 *Magellan's Voyage Around the World.* Edited by James A. Robertson. 2 vols. Cleveland: Clark.

Pospisil, Leopold 1958 *Kapauku Papuans and Their Law.* Yale University Publications in Anthropology, No. 54. New Haven: Yale Univ., Dept. of Anthropology.

Richards, Audrey I. 1939 The Development of Field Work Methods in Social Anthropology. Pages 272–316 in Frederic C. Bartlett et al. (editors), *The Study of Society.* New York: Macmillan.

Rivers, William H. R. 1906 *The Todas.* New York and London: Macmillan.

Romney, A. Kimball; and D'Andrade, Roy Goodwin (editors) 1964 Transcultural Studies in Cognition. *American Anthropologist* New Series 66, no. 3, part 2. → A special issue.

Rowe, John H. 1953 Technical Aids in Anthropology: A Historical Survey. Pages 895–940 in International Symposium on Anthropology, New York, 1952, *Anthropology Today.* Edited by Alfred L. Kroeber. Univ. of Chicago Press.

Rowe, John H. 1964 Ethnography and Ethnology in the Sixteenth Century. Kroeber Anthropological Society, *Papers* No. 30:1–19.

Sahagún, Fray Bernadino de *General History of the Things of New Spain, Florentine Codex.* Books 1–13. Translated by A. J. O. Anderson and C. E. Dibble. Santa Fe, N.M.: School of American Research, 1950–1964.

Smith, Marian W. 1959 Boas' "Natural History" Approach to Field Method. Pages 46–60 in Walter Goldschmidt (editor), *The Anthropology of Franz Boas.* American Anthropological Association, Memoir No. 89. Menasha, Wisc.: The Association.

Sturtevant, William C. 1964 Studies in Ethnoscience. *American Anthropologist* New Series, Special Issue 66, no. 3, part 2:99–131.

Tagari Shivashankara Pillai 1964 Under the Mango Tree. *Texas Quarterly* 7, no. 2:54–63. → Translated and edited by Paul Friedrich and K. N. Parameshwaran Nayar.

Yale University, Institute of Human Relations (1938) 1961 *Outline of Cultural Materials.* 4th ed., revised by George P. Murdock et al. New Haven: Human Relations Area Files.

ETHNOHISTORY

See under History.

ETHNOLINGUISTICS

See Language, *article on* Language and Culture; Linguistics.

ETHNOLOGY

Ethnology is generally regarded as one of the major subdivisions of cultural anthropology, the others being anthropological archeology and anthropological linguistics. Anthropology is prefixed to the latter two terms because they refer to the archeology and linguistics largely of preliterate and preindustrial peoples. The archeology of classical Greece and the linguistics of contemporary France would rarely, if ever, be taught in an anthropology department. The claim that anthropology embraces all peoples past and present has been exaggerated by some anthropologists, although the present trend, especially in ethnology, is toward giving attention to a wider range of peoples. In the United States today, but less so in Europe, ethnology is joined to social anthropology. [*See* Anthropology, *articles on* Cultural anthropology *and* Social anthropology.]

Interesting insight into the scope of ethnology can be gained by looking at the names of early anthropological societies. In 1843 the Ethnological Society was founded in England, and in that same year it published the first edition of its guide to field work, an inventory of data to be obtained. This guide included some material on all fields of anthropology but gave the most space to social anthropology. In 1863 the Anthropological Society was founded in England; this was a group of former members of the Ethnological Society who wanted to stress political issues, such as slavery, more heavily. In 1871 the two societies joined to form the Anthropological Institute of Great Britain and Ireland, to which name the word "Royal" was prefixed in 1907. In the United States, the American Ethnological Society was founded in 1842, the Anthropological Society of Washington in 1879, and the American Anthropological Association in 1902. In France, the Société Ethnologique de Paris was established in 1838 and the Société d'Anthropologie de Paris in 1858. In Germany, the Gesellschaft für Anthropologie, Ethnologie, und Urgeschichte was founded in 1869.

It is clear from these examples that "ethnology" was used as a blanket term to cover the entire range of the subject we now label "anthropology" and that the latter term came to be used in the wider sense at a later date. Through much of the nineteenth century the concepts of biological race, language, and culture were confused; one was inferred from the other, and reconstructions of human development combined all three aspects. Ethnology was historically oriented from the start and attempted to account for extant races, languages, and cultures in terms of migration, diffusion, and other historical processes [*see* Diffusion].

In the twentieth century, "ethnology" has come to mean the comparative study of documented and contemporary cultures and has largely excluded their bioanthropology, archeology, and linguistics. "Ethnography," in contrast, is best used to describe the study of the culture of a single tribe or society; but because almost all ethnographies make comparisons at least with neighboring peoples, the distinction between ethnography and ethnology is not sharp and may be compared to that between geography and geology. This article is limited almost completely to comparative ethnology.

Oscar Lewis (1956) gives an excellent idea of the contemporary scope of comparative ethnology. Comparisons may range from two ethnic units (societies) to hundreds, the largest sample so far being Murdock's "Ethnographic Atlas" (Murdock et al. 1962–1966), which is approaching one thousand ethnic units. They may deal with a few adjacent peoples, or a larger number in a culture area, a continent, a hemisphere, or the entire world. The content to be compared may vary from a single culture element to a long list of elements and assemblages of them covering practically every aspect of culture. Verne Ray's list of 7,633 culture elements for the plateau area of North America (1942) is the longest enumerated list so far, and Murdock's world-wide "Ethnographic Atlas" has reached nearly one thousand culture trait categories. Data for comparison may be based on library research, field research, or a combination of the two. The purpose of comparisons may be limited to uncovering the range and kind of variations for the subject at hand and to locating them in space and time; or it may be aimed at establishing culture area groupings, cross-cultural regularities, evolutionary trends, or other hypotheses. The research design may range all the way from a few illustrations of loose-jointed generalizations to a rigid statistical method.

The subject coverage of ethnology includes that of social anthropology and sociology, but it is much broader. For instance, ethnology also includes technology and crafts, plastic and graphic arts, music, dancing, oral literature, dream analysis, religion, world view, ethics, and ethnomedicine. For a much longer list of the subject content of ethnology, see the *Outline of Cultural Materials* (Yale Univ. 1938).

The dominant trend in nineteenth-century ethnology–social anthropology was an evolutionary explanation of how things came to be as they are. In its most extreme form, unilinear evolution, it was assumed that culture change came about largely from causes operating within single societies and that all peoples would, sooner or later, evolve through a half-dozen or more stages of development in the same sequence if their progress were not interrupted by some catastrophe, such as military invasion by an alien power [see EVOLUTION, *article on* CULTURAL EVOLUTION].

Historical ethnology

Toward the end of the nineteenth century two schools of ethnology were founded, one by Boas in the United States and the other by Ratzel and Frobenius in Germany. Both schools emphasized the historical processes of diffusion and migration. Boas' best demonstrations of the process of relay diffusion are to be found in his comparative studies of North American Indian folklore (1895; 1916). By tracing motifs and tale types among groups of contiguous tribes, he showed the overwhelming tendency of these phenomena to cluster into areal types which crosscut language-family boundaries, thus suggesting diffusion. If such material were independently invented over and over again, tribes separated by great distances would exhibit as many resemblances in folklore as neighboring tribes do; but because contiguous tribes shared much more folklore inventory than distant tribes did, diffusion was the obvious explanation.

Boas' diffusion emphasis was most fully developed by A. L. Kroeber and by Clark Wissler, trained as a psychologist but long curator of anthropology in the American Museum of Natural History. Although the earliest American culture area scheme was that of Livingstone Farrand (1904), his work had less impact than that of Kroeber and Wissler. In 1904 Kroeber was the first to classify California Indian cultures, and in 1906 Wissler was the first to mention major North American areas. Wissler (1917) published the first map of culture areas for the hemisphere, and Kroeber (1923) followed Wissler closely in a parallel scheme. In these and later works both authors postulated that the most significant aspects of culture in each area arose at the center and tended to diffuse outward toward the margins. On the assumption that all aspects of culture diffused at about the same rate, the age–area hypothesis, by which the age of a culture trait or complex was determined by the extent of its geographical distribution, was employed by both men.

In addition to the scheme of 15 culture areas for the two American continents endorsed by both men, each also regarded the area from Mexico to Peru as the culture center of a vast Pan-American culture area. Kroeber (1923, fig. 35) presented a large histogram in which the supposedly oldest traits occurred at the bottom, as in archeological stratification, and the youngest at the top. Age was determined largely by the extent of geographical distribution, but typological complexity was also taken into account, as well as a little direct sequential evidence from archeology. Although the horizontal dimension represented dispersal of the culture elements by diffusion and migration, the vertical dimension clearly showed an evolution from the simple to the complex. Thus, in Mexico the sequence included basketry, shamanism, and family groups in the earliest level; then patrilineal clans, simple weaving frame, domesticated plants, pottery, solstitial calendar, stone buildings, town life, cotton growing and loom weaving, matrilineal clans, textile clothing, priesthood, confederacy, sculpture, metallurgy, markets, human sacrifice, temples, empire, mathematics, astronomy, cycle calendar, writing, and books, in that order. Kroeber rejected nineteenth-century unilinear evolution and the theory of many independent origins of cultural resemblances, but he constructed a new kind of evolution with few independent origins and many diffusions and migrations from tribe to tribe and area to area. The age–area hypothesis demands a sequential arrangement of the material, and when this shows a temporal progression in complexity, it becomes evolutionary.

A major weakness of culture area and age–area theory is that culture areas are of varying sizes. Local developments may originate in the "centers" of small areas and tend to spread toward the margins, but at the same time new culture elements and assemblages may arise in the "centers" of larger culture areas and spread by diffusion or migration to the smaller ones, thus mixing elements of internal and external origin; and still more invention may occur in "centers" of each hemisphere and spread widely throughout many culture areas of different sizes in the same hemisphere. The hope of unscrambling this sort of mixture without the help of archeology and historical linguistics is dim. [See ARCHEOLOGY; HISTORY, *article on* CULTURE HISTORY; LINGUISTICS, *article on* HISTORICAL LINGUISTICS.]

Wissler's derivation of historical inferences from geographical distributions was so bold an attempt that he was heavily criticized, especially by Dixon (1928). Kroeber, in contrast, modified his views as new evidence came to light, and in 1939 he published his well-received "Cultural and Natural Areas of Native North America." This was fundamentally an intuitive scheme of culture areas without detailed supporting geographical or historical evidence. Between the time this book was finished —1931—and the time it was published—1939— Kroeber supervised the University of California Culture Element Survey, which, with the help of 13 field workers, collected responses to questionnaires from old informants in 254 localities in western North America, from the continental di-

vide to the Pacific and from the Mexican border to Alaska. This was aimed at collecting enough data to produce a definitive taxonomy of the nineteenth-century cultures, which Kroeber hoped would lead to a fuller set of interpretations. After all this effort, interest in areal classification ebbed to the extent that no one has yet used this vast quantity of data to produce a much superior areal scheme based on a wealth of specific detail. The largest comparative study incorporating this culture element material is still that of Driver (1941), who limited his subject coverage to girls' puberty rites [see CULTURE AREA; KROEBER; WISSLER].

In Germany, Friedrich Ratzel (1887) introduced the "criterion of form," which argued that all specific resemblances in the form of two or more museum objects, other than those determined by the material from which they were made or the use to which they were put, must be explained by a single origin and subsequent diffusion to the localities from which the museum specimens were obtained in the field, no matter how widely separated these localities might be. This was a much more extreme diffusionist position than that of Boas, Boas' pupils, or even Wissler. Frobenius (1898) was the first to use the term *Kulturkreis*, best translated as "culture area" or "culture region"; he also introduced the criterion of quantity, which argued that the larger the number of arbitrary resemblances not due to the nature of the material or the use to which the object was put, the stronger the case for diffusion.

Two early applications of the *Kulturkreis* rules for determining areal clusters, time sequences, and dispersal, those of Graebner (1905) and Ankermann (1905), were fairly well received and not much less tenable than the works of Wissler. They, too, emphasized material culture and arranged their data in a series of temporal strata, or *Schichten*. Neither author gave any explicit technique for packaging culture elements into *Kreise* or *Schichten*, but Czekanowski (1911) showed clearly that the reality of Ankermann's two African *Kreise* could be demonstrated with a correlation technique. Using Yule's Q coefficient, Czekanowski intercorrelated Ankermann's 17 traits of material culture among 47 African tribes and arranged the correlations in a single matrix which clearly showed two distinct intertrait clusters. When mapped, these clusters yielded a twofold areal classification, which conformed to Ankermann's intuitive grouping.

Although no one today subscribes to the idea of single origin and subsequent world-wide dispersal by migration and diffusion of any of the *Kreise* or *Schichten* of, say, Schmidt and Koppers (1924), some of the correlations and functional associations of the *Kreise* and *Schichten* have been confirmed or repostulated by later researchers of different schools. For example, the correlation between moieties and matrilineal descent, challenged by Lowie (1937, p. 182), has been confirmed by Murdock (1949, p. 49). The functional complex of hoe farming by women, matrilocal residence, matrilineal descent, monogamy, and bride service, and the temporal sequence from division of labor to residence to descent has been confirmed or postulated by Murdock (1949), Driver (1956), and Aberle (1961).

The world-wide inferred temporal strata of the *Kulturkreis* school produce an evolution which differs from that of the nineteenth century in calling for single origins or a very small number of independent origins and subsequent dispersal of the phenomena by migration and diffusion; but since such dispersals are multiple, they overlap each other geographically and produce a "layer cake" of temporal stages. Kroeber and Wissler confined their postulated dispersals to a culture area or a hemisphere for the most part, while Schmidt and Koppers more often included the entire world [*see* GRAEBNER; KOPPERS; RATZEL; SCHMIDT].

Kroeber's interest in culture areas and diffusion stimulated Clements (Clements et al. 1926; Clements 1928; 1931) and Driver (see Driver & Kroeber 1932) to determine areal groupings of ethnic units by intercorrelating their inventories of culture traits. These papers were read by three young men in Europe who were familiar with *Kulturkreis* theory and the intertrait correlations of Czekanowski (1911). Almost simultaneously they published four papers which combined the intertrait correlations of Czekanowski with the intertribe correlations of Kroeber, Clements, and Driver (Fürer-Haimendorf 1934; Klimek 1935; Milke 1935; Klimek & Milke 1935). They computed the coefficient Q_6 for three sets of traits: intertribe, intertrait, and tribal cluster with trait cluster. All three assembled their coefficients in rectangular matrices and converted them to shades of gray (as Czekanowski had done in 1911) for quick comprehension. They also mapped their clusters. Interpretation of the resemblances and the groupings was limited to historical factors, but because all of these studies were confined to small regions of culture area size, this wholesale historical explanation was probably not far from the truth although incomplete. A simplified explanation in English of their technique may be found in Driver (1961).

Knowledge of statistical mechanics was so scant

among ethnologists of both schools that few at the time understood that these studies integrated the approaches of the American culture area and the German *Kulturkreis* schools. They offered an objective method for determining both intertribal (culture area) and intertrait (*Kulturschicht-Kulturkreis*) groupings. If every writer in these schools had empirically demonstrated his intertribal and intertrait groupings in this manner, the differences between the schools would have been less marked and much useless polemic would not have been written. Differences in interpretation of the data grouped in these ways still exist, but the reality of the groupings themselves could have been established objectively.

Driver, in his "Girls' Puberty Rites in Western North America" (1941), used a multiple clustering technique parallel to that of the Europeans, but his interpretation of the results went beyond any of that group. His area was larger and posed more problems of interpretation. He distinguished several kinds of resemblances: universals, cultural heritages spread by migrations, relayed diffusions, and convergences. He pointed out (1) that elements of universal or near universal occurrence should not be used to establish historical connection between ethnic units in limited areas; (2) that elements closely associated with a language family might be regarded as a cultural heritage from the protoculture associated with the protolanguage of the group; (3) that continuously distributed resemblances which crossed over language-family boundaries were best regarded as diffusions; and (4) that the group ceremony for pubescent girls among the Apacheans represented an independent origin and a convergence with that held in southern California. He also wrote a chapter on the psychological aspects of menstrual taboos, described the functional position and significance of the girls' puberty rite in each of the subareas into which the entire area had been divided, and assessed the influence of geographical environment on the data.

Functionalism

In addition to the American and German historical schools just described, there arose in the early part of this century the functional schools, which rebelled against not only the nineteenth-century unilinear evolutionists but also the culture historicalists. Malinowski and Radcliffe-Brown are both identified as functionalists, although some significant divergences exist. Malinowski was generally both antihistorical and anticomparative, while Radcliffe-Brown was antihistorical (except in his later years) but never anticomparative. For this reason the latter figures more prominently in comparative ethnology and will be singled out for brief appraisal here.

Radcliffe-Brown discovered a number of generalizations that would now be called correlations. One of the earliest (1913) was his discovery that preferred marriage to a first cross-cousin was associated with kinship terminology of one type, while preferred marriage to a second cross-cousin was found with kinship terminology of another type. This and other perfect or high correlations are given in his important *The Social Organization of Australian Tribes* (1931), where he used the term "correlation" but did not compute any coefficients. In 1935 he wrote: ". . . we can expect to find, in the majority of human societies, a fairly close correlation between the terminological classification of kindred or relatives and the social classification," as revealed "in the attitudes and behavior of relatives to one another" (Radcliffe-Brown 1935, p. 531). His greatest contribution lies in the emphasis on this relationship.

The principal opponent of Radcliffe-Brown was Kroeber, who said:

Kin-term systems, . . . are subject to modification from within and without. There is always a sufficient number of such "accidents" to disguise the basic patterns more or less. . . . the essential features of the pattern are . . . likely to be the ones which have the greatest historic depth. The search for them therefore implies a willingness and ability to view data historically. Without such willingness, it is as good as impossible to separate the significant from the trivial . . . and the work done becomes merely sociological, an affair of schemes. . . . (Kroeber 1934, pp. 21–22)

This position is echoed by E. W. Gifford, a colleague of Kroeber, who wrote: ". . . kinship systems are first of all linguistic phenomena . . . and only secondarily social phenomena. As such they . . . constitute an archaic and highly refractory nucleus, which yields unevenly and only here and there to influences from . . . social structure" (Gifford 1940, pp. 193–194). Kroeber (1936) modified his view in the direction of that of Radcliffe-Brown in a conciliatory paper, and a year later (1937) made the first reconstruction of a protokinship terminology for a language family.

No historian of ethnological thought has yet pointed out that the opposing views of Radcliffe-Brown and Kroeber stem directly from the areas with which each was most familiar. The kinship terminologies and social organization of native Australia are among the most highly integrated of any in the world. High correlations are the rule rather than the exception. California native cultures, in contrast, are among the least integrated in this respect, and correlations are low or nonexistent, as Tax (1937), a pupil of Radcliffe-Brown, showed in an excellent and very thorough study. Australia remained one of the most isolated areas in the world, with little contact with the outside, while California, in contrast, has been exposed to contact on all sides except the Pacific, and the multiplicity of language families and phyla suggests much migration into and out of the area. Australian social organizations and languages had centuries and millennia to simmer down and become integrated, while those of California were constantly being disturbed by intrusions from without. Radcliffe-Brown and Kroeber both failed to understand the limitations of their samples, and it was not until Murdock's *Social Structure* (1949) that an adequate sample and statistical technique were combined to produce more tenable generalizations on this subject [*see* KINSHIP].

Cross-cultural studies

In the United States cross-cultural studies were founded by G. P. Murdock and carried on by his pupils, including J. W. M. Whiting, Whiting's pupils, and others. Murdock has concentrated on kinship and social organization, and his *Social Structure* (1949) is a monumental work in its field. He studied the association between rules of marriage, residence, and descent, as well as kinship terminology, in 250 societies in all the major areas of the world. He used no explicit sampling technique, but his selection was large and widely distributed, and his results have not been seriously challenged to date. Using functional theory, he ran off a list of hypotheses and then confirmed most of them with the Q coefficient of association and chi-square. His general conclusions were that the semantic categories of kinship terms are the result of social organization rather than the cause, and that they are determined principally by forms of marital residence and rules of descent. Marriage prescriptions showed practically no correlation with kinship terminology, while residence and descent yielded many significant correlations.

Murdock further postulated three kinds of developmental cycles, two of which began with the dominance of one sex in the economy, followed by corresponding forms of residence, descent, and kinship terminology. Thus a patri-dominated economy would give rise to patrilocal residence, patrilineal descent, and Iroquoian or Omaha kinship categories. In a similar fashion a matri-dominated economy would produce matrilocal residence, matrilineal descent, and Iroquoian or Crow kinship classification. A sexually balanced economy, in turn, would give rise to bilocal residence, bilateral descent, and Eskimo or Hawaiian kinship terminology. This cyclical theory was confirmed statistically by Driver (1956), who found that the correlations based on about 250 North American peoples could be arranged in a matrix which could be explained in this way. However, Driver failed to measure the potency of genetic factors at this time, although he did so in 1966 in a more methodologically rigorous study (Driver 1966).

Whiting and his followers have centered their interests in the socialization process, the ways and means by which a child acquires the culture in which he is born and reared. The basic work in this field is Whiting and Child (1953). Before their work, good field studies in this subject were so rare that the authors were able to assemble fewer than fifty societies for their comparisons. They used no sampling technique because the total number of tribes was so small, but since every continental area in the world, plus Oceania, was represented, their sample is a rough approximation to a random one. Three "judges" carefully read the same field reports and coded the various societies independently on multistep rating scales. The published ratings are the scores of all three judges combined by summation.

Whiting and Child tested a number of neo-Freudian hypotheses with this method. For instance, they divided severity of socialization into the following five aspects, each of which was rated separately by each of the "judges": anal, oral, sexual, dependence, aggression. The ratings on these five aspects were intercorrelated, and the highest positive correlation turned out to be that between the oral and dependence aspects. These ratings were also correlated with other aspects of culture; for instance, amount of oral socialization anxiety correlated with presence of oral explanations of illness showed a high degree of relationship. On the other hand, they found a zero correlation between anal socialization anxiety and anal explanations of illness. [See SOCIALIZATION.]

A later and more transparent study by Whiting, Kluckhohn, and Anthony (1958) revealed a positive correlation between male initiation ceremonies at puberty, patrilocal residence, exclusive mother–infant sleeping arrangements, and a long *post partum* sex taboo. These variables are also positively correlated with a long lactation period and other kinds of long and close association of the infant with the mother. The authors' explanation was that the resulting strong attachment to the mother had to be broken by an initiation rite which separated the boy from his mother entirely and prepared him for an adult masculine role. Societies

which lacked the long and close association of mother and young son did not need an initiation because there was no strong attachment to sever. Although the results achieved so far in this difficult field of psychological ethnology are less impressive than those in the field of social organization, the difference is due to the inherent complexities of the problems and the scarcity of field material rather than to methodology.

These cross-cultural studies of world-wide scope stem from the evolutionary interests of the nineteenth century. When Tylor (1888) read his now famous paper in which he anticipated correlation methods, Francis Galton challenged the historical independence of Tylor's 350 cases (societies). Tylor's use of probabilities and his conclusion that, for instance, mother-in-law–son-in-law avoidance was caused by matrilocal residence implied that this form of residence occurred first in each society and that it gave rise to this form of avoidance independently over and over again in each society where the avoidance was found. This is a functional–causal–evolutionary explanation. When such explanations include the Oedipus complex or the incest taboo, they may be called psychofunctional–causal–evolutionary. The contrasting explanation has been called geographical–historical, historical, or genetic; it holds that once a custom becomes established, it may be relayed from society to society by means of intermarriage and other kinds of contact. It is not necessary to postulate any necessary antecedent because a behavior may spread like a fashion. Continuity of geographical distribution is generally regarded as evidence of such diffusion. Tylor failed to provide an answer to the question Galton raised, and it plagued cross-cultural research until the 1950s.

Stephens in 1959 paired his 56 societies on the basis of membership in the same genetic language family and geographical proximity, and he concluded that geographical–historical factors determined about as much association as did psychofunctional ones. Landauer and Whiting (1964) compared, in a similar way, associations found within culture areas with those found across culture areas and concluded that the latter were relatively free of historical factors. Raoul Naroll (1961) and Naroll and D'Andrade (1963) have developed other specific techniques to show the effect of genetic versus psychofunctional–evolutionary factors on correlations. Their general conclusion is that both kinds of explanations must be used to account for most correlations and that they are of about equal potency. Cultural behaviors with functional or causal relationships, such as unilateral descent, cross-cousin marriage, and corresponding types of kinship terminology, tend to diffuse as a unit; or if part of such an assemblage is already present, the other members will diffuse more readily because they are compatible with it. Thus both internal and external factors determine the cultural inventory of societies.

Driver (1966) employed still another method and found that genetic factors were a little more powerful than psychofunctional–evolutionary ones but that both were at work. He used a sample of 277 peoples from native North America alone and postulated only four or five historically independent origins of the kin avoidances, which formed the subject of his study. This was determined by a combination of areal clustering, culture-area membership, and language-family affiliation. If other areas show a similar number of origins, this would add up to no more than about twenty for the world. With only twenty cases for a test of the significance of correlations involving kin avoidances, it would require a rather high correlation to achieve significance. Many of the cross-cultural correlations so far computed, for which significance is claimed on the assumption of the historical independence of every positive instance, would by this criterion be judged to be not significant at all.

The principal weakness of most cross-cultural studies so far is that their instances hop, skip, and jump across the map in such a manner that continuity of geographical distribution and other clues to genetic explanations are missing. A world-wide study of a well-reported subject, such as kinship behavior, would require data from at least a thousand societies in order to insure sufficient geographical continuity to permit valid inferences about the number of independent origins of the phenomena. This has not yet been achieved.

Although significant positive correlations in cross-cultural research are relatively easy to find, causal relationships are more difficult to establish, and the direction of causation is still more elusive. Nevertheless, progress has been made in this respect. The direction of causation and sequence of stages in evolution have been determined by constructing a Guttman cumulative scale (Carneiro & Tobias 1963), and the direction of cycling by arranging correlations in a temporal matrix (Driver 1956; Ascher & Ascher 1963; Blalock 1960).

Naroll (1964) has drawn attention to the many problems surrounding the nature of the ethnic unit used in cross-cultural research. Because this is the unit counted in all intertrait cross-cultural correlations, its definition is crucial to such studies. Although there were more differences than agreements in the comments on this article, the major

issues are now aboveboard, and refinements of definitions of ethnic units will surely follow. The nature of culture traits or variables also needs to be re-evaluated.

Coult and Habenstein (1965) give over 500 pages of cross tabulations of raw frequencies, phi-coefficients, and tests of significance for the 210 culture categories and 565 ethnic units of Murdock's 1957 sample.

Textor (1966) offers a still more massive package of similar measures computed largely from the data of Murdock's 1962–1966 sample. These two compilations provide important sources of reference to tens of thousands of relationships which can test many hypotheses, but they are so myopic that they may obscure some of the broader relationships within the data.

Sawyer and Levine (1966) have reduced Murdock's 1957 sample to thirty variables, intercorrelated and factor-analyzed these variables, and produced some compact generalizations about the whole sample which run only to article length. They have also run the same correlations separately for each of the six areas into which Murdock divided the world and have found rather marked areal differences. Some correlations are significantly positive in one area and significantly negative in another, or zero in one area and significantly positive or negative in another. Such areal differences can only be explained by ecological and historical factors. They cast doubt on the importance of universal "laws" or regularities but do not demolish such concepts entirely. What is needed next is a series of correlation studies intermediate between the highly particularized computer print-outs and the grosser generalizations.

It is thus apparent that recent studies have made considerable gains in understanding both genetic and evolutionary relationships and in the statistical rigor with which these relationships have been demonstrated. Although few ethnologists claim that their explanations of relationships among the cultures of nonliterate peoples are of timeless infallibility, validation of hypotheses has reached a respectable level which compares favorably with that of other behavioral sciences.

HAROLD E. DRIVER

[*See also* ANTHROPOLOGY, *article on* THE COMPARATIVE METHOD IN ANTHROPOLOGY.]

BIBLIOGRAPHY

ABERLE, DAVID F. 1961 Matrilineal Descent in Cross-cultural Perspective. Pages 655–727 in David M. Schneider and Kathleen Gough (editors), *Matrilineal Kinship*. Berkeley: Univ. of California Press.

ANKERMANN, B. 1905 Kulturkreise und Kulturschichten in Afrika. *Zeitschrift für Ethnologie* 37:54–84.

ASCHER, MARCIA; and ASCHER, ROBERT 1963 Chronological Ordering by Computer. *American Anthropologist* New Series 65:1045–1052.

BLALOCK, H. M. JR. 1960 Correlation Analysis and Causal Inferences. *American Anthropologist* New Series 62:624–631.

BOAS, FRANZ 1895 *Indianische Sagen von der nordpacifischen Küste Amerikas.* Berlin: Asher.

BOAS, FRANZ 1916 *Tsimshian Mythology.* Smithsonian Institution, Bureau of American Ethnology, Annual Report No. 31. Washington: Government Printing Office.

CARNEIRO, ROBERT L. 1962 Scale Analysis as an Instrument for the Study of Cultural Evolution. *Southwestern Journal of Anthropology* 18, no. 2:149–169.

CARNEIRO, ROBERT L.; and TOBIAS, STEPHEN F. 1963 The Application of Scale Analysis to the Study of Cultural Evolution. New York Academy of Sciences, *Transactions* Second Series 26:196–207.

CLEMENTS, FORREST E. 1928 Quantitative Method in Ethnography. *American Anthropologist* New Series 30:295–310.

CLEMENTS, FORREST E. 1931 Plains Indian Tribal Correlations With Sun Dance Data. *American Anthropologist* New Series 33:216–227.

CLEMENTS, FORREST E.; SCHENCK, SARA M.; and BROWN, T. K. 1926 A New Objective Method for Showing Special Relationships. *American Anthropologist* New Series 28:585–604.

COULT, ALLAN D.; and HABENSTEIN, ROBERT W. 1965 *Cross Tabulations of Murdock's "World Ethnographic Sample."* Columbia: Univ. of Missouri Press. → See Murdock 1957.

CZEKANOWSKI, JAN 1911 Objektive Kriterien in der Ethnologie. Deutsche Gesellschaft für Anthropologie, Ethnologie, und Urgeschichte, *Korrespondenz-Blatt* 42:1–5.

DIXON, ROLAND B. 1928 *The Building of Cultures.* New York: Scribner.

DRIVER, HAROLD E. 1941 Girls' Puberty Rites in Western North America. California, University of, *Anthropological Records* 6:21–90.

DRIVER, HAROLD E. 1956 An Integration of Functional, Evolutionary, and Historical Theory by Means of Correlations. Indiana University, *Publications in Anthropology and Linguistics* Memoir No. 12.

DRIVER, HAROLD E. 1961 Introduction to Statistics for Comparative Research. Pages 303–331 in Frank W. Moore (editor), *Readings in Cross-cultural Methodology.* New Haven: Human Relations Area Files.

DRIVER, HAROLD E. 1962 The Contribution of A. L. Kroeber to Culture Area Theory and Practice. Indiana University, *Publications in Anthropology and Linguistics* Memoir No. 18.

DRIVER, HAROLD E. 1966 Geographical–Historical *Versus* Psycho–Functional Explanations of Kin Avoidances. *Current Anthropology* 7:131–148.

DRIVER, HAROLD E.; and KROEBER, A. L. 1932 Quantitative Expression of Cultural Relationships. California, University of, *Publications in American Archaeology and Ethnology* 31:211–256.

DRIVER, HAROLD E.; and MASSEY, WILLIAM C. 1957 Comparative Studies of North American Indians. American Philosophical Society, *Transactions* 47:165–456.

FARRAND, LIVINGSTONE (1904) 1964 *The Basis of American History.* New York: Harper.

FROBENIUS, LEO 1898 *Der Ursprung der afrikanischen Kulturen.* Berlin: Gebrüder Borntraeger.

FÜRER-HAIMENDORF, C. VON 1934 Völker- und Kulturgruppen im westlich Hinterindien, dargestellt mit Hilfe des statistischen Verfahrens. *Anthropos* 29:421–440.

GIFFORD, E. W. 1940 A Problem in Kinship Terminology. *American Anthropologist* New Series 42:190–194.

GRAEBNER, FRITZ 1905 Kulturkreise und Kulturschichten in Ozeanien. *Zeitschrift für Ethnologie* 37:28–53.

GRAEBNER, FRITZ 1911 *Methode der Ethnologie.* Heidelberg (Germany): Winter.

HYMES, DELL H. (editor) 1965 *The Use of Computers in Anthropology.* The Hague: Mouton.

KLIMEK, STANISLAW 1935 The Structure of California Indian Culture. California, University of, *Publications in American Archaeology and Ethnology* 37:1–70.

KLIMEK, STANISLAW; and MILKE, WILHELM 1935 An Analysis of the Material Culture of the Tupi Peoples. *American Anthropologist* New Series 37:71–91.

KLUCKHOHN, CLYDE (1953) 1961 Universal Categories of Culture. Pages 89–105 in Frank W. Moore (editor), *Readings in Cross-cultural Methodology.* New Haven: Human Relations Area Files Press. → First published in International Symposium on Anthropology, 1952, *Anthropology Today.* Edited by A. L. Kroeber.

KROEBER, ALFRED L. 1904 Types of Indian Culture in California. California, University of, *Publications in American Archaeology and Ethnology* 2:81–103.

KROEBER, ALFRED L. (1923) 1948 *Anthropology: Race, Language, Culture, Psychology, Prehistory.* New ed., rev. New York: Harcourt. → First published as *Anthropology.*

KROEBER, ALFRED L. 1934 Yurok and Neighboring Kin Term Systems. California, University of, *Publications in American Archaeology and Ethnology* 35:15–22.

KROEBER, ALFRED L. 1936 Kinship and History. *American Anthropologist* New Series 38:338–341.

KROEBER, ALFRED L. 1937 Athabascan Kin Term Systems. *American Anthropologist* New Series 39:602–608.

KROEBER, ALFRED L. 1939 Cultural and Natural Areas of Native North America. California, University of, *Publications in American Archaeology and Ethnology* 38:1–242.

KROEBER, ALFRED L. 1940 Stimulus Diffusion. *American Anthropologist* New Series 42:1–20.

KROEBER, ALFRED L. 1962 *A Roster of Civilizations and Culture.* Viking Fund Publications in Anthropology, No. 33. New York: The Fund.

LANDAUER, THOMAS K.; and WHITING, JOHN W. M. 1964 Infantile Stimulation and Adult Stature of Human Males. *American Anthropologist* New Series 66:1007–1028.

LEWIS, OSCAR 1956 Comparisons in Cultural Anthropology. Pages 259–292 in Yearbook of Anthropology, 1955, *Current Anthropology: A Supplement to* Anthropology Today. Edited by William L. Thomas, Jr. Univ. of Chicago Press.

LOWIE, ROBERT H. 1937 *The History of Ethnological Theory.* New York: Farrar & Rinehart.

MILKE, WILHELM 1935 *Südostmelanesien: Eine ethnostatistische Analyse.* Würzburg (Germany): Triltsch.

MURDOCK, GEORGE P. 1945 The Common Denominator of Cultures. Pages 123–142 in Ralph Linton (editor),

The Science of Man in the World Crisis. New York: Columbia Univ. Press.

Murdock, George P. 1949 *Social Structure*. New York: Macmillan. → A paperback edition was published in 1965 by the Free Press.

Murdock, George P. 1957 World Ethnographic Sample. *American Anthropologist* New Series 59:664–687.

Murdock, George P. et al. 1962–1966 Ethnographic Atlas. *Ethnology* 1–4: last article in every issue.

Naroll, Raoul 1961 Two Solutions to Galton's Problem. *Philosophy of Science* 28:15–39.

Naroll, Raoul 1964 On Ethnic Unit Classification. *Current Anthropology* 5:283–312.

Naroll, Raoul; and D'Andrade, Roy G. 1963 Two Further Solutions to Galton's Problem. *American Anthropologist* New Series 65:1053–1067.

Radcliffe-Brown, A. R. 1913 Three Tribes of Western Australia. *Journal of the Royal Anthropological Institute of Great Britain and Ireland* 43:143–194.

Radcliffe-Brown, A. R. (1931) 1948 *The Social Organization of Australian Tribes*. Glencoe, Ill.: Free Press. → First published in Volume 1 of *Oceania*.

Radcliffe-Brown, A. R. 1935 Kinship Terminologies in California. *American Anthropologist* New Series 37:530–535.

Ratzel, Friedrich 1887 Die geographische Verbreitung des Bogens und der Pfeile in Afrika. Akademie der Wissenschaften, Leipzig, *Berichte über die Verhandlungen* Philologisch-historische Klasse 39:233–252.

Ray, Verne F. 1942 Culture Element Distributions: XXII Plateau. California, University of, *Anthropological Records* 8:99–258.

Sawyer, Jack; and Levine, Robert A. 1966 Cultural Dimensions: A Factor Analysis of the World Ethnographic Sample. *American Anthropologist* New Series 68:708–731.

Schmidt, Wilhelm (1937) 1939 *The Culture Historical Method of Ethnology: The Scientific Approach to the Racial Question*. New York: Fortuny. → First published as *Handbuch der Methode der kulturhistorischen Ethnologie*.

Schmidt, Wilhelm; and Koppers, Wilhelm 1924 *Völker und Kulturen*. Regensburg (Germany): Habbel.

Tax, Sol (1937) 1955 Some Problems of Social Organization. Pages 3–34 in Fred Eggan (editor), *Social Anthropology of North American Tribes*. 2d ed. Univ. of Chicago Press.

Textor, Robert B. 1966 A Cross-cultural Summary. Unpublished manuscript, Human Relations Area Files.

Tylor, Edward B. (1888) 1961 On a Method of Investigating the Development of Institutions: Applied to Laws of Marriage and Descent. Pages 1–28 in Frank W. Moore (editor), *Readings in Cross-cultural Methodology*. New Haven: Human Relations Area Files. → First published in Volume 18 of the *Journal of the Royal Anthropological Institute of Great Britain and Ireland*.

Whiting, John W. M.; and Child, Irvin L. 1953 *Child Training and Personality: A Cross-cultural Study*. New Haven: Yale Univ. Press. → A paperback edition was published in 1962.

Whiting, John W. M.; Kluckhohn, Richard; and Anthony, Albert 1958 The Function of Male Initiation Ceremonies at Puberty. Pages 359–371 in Society for the Psychological Study of Social Issues, *Readings in Social Psychology*. 3d ed. New York: Holt.

Wissler, Clark 1906 Ethnic Types and Isolation. *Science* 23:147–149.

Wissler, Clark (1917) 1957 *The American Indian: An Introduction to the Anthropology of the New World*. 3d ed. Gloucester, Mass.: Smith.

Wissler, Clark (1923) 1938 *Man and Culture*. New York: Crowell.

Yale University, Institute of Human Relations (1938) 1961 *Outline of Cultural Materials*. 4th ed., revised by George P. Murdock et al. New Haven: Human Relations Area Files.

ETHNOMEDICINE
See under Medical care.

ETHNOMUSICOLOGY
See under Music.

ETHNOSCIENCE
See Ethnography.

ETHOLOGY

Ethology has existed as a concept since 1762 when it was defined in France as the study of animal behavior. In this sense it carries the same meaning as the Greek word "ethos," from which the modern term ethology is derived. However, a separate meaning of the word ethology, related to the term "ethics," has been used in the Anglo-Saxon literature to define the "science of character."

The founder of modern ethology is Konrad Z. Lorenz, physician, zoologist, and comparative anatomist. By systematic application of biological research methods to the analysis of animal behavior, he provided the initial impetus in the 1930s. The first modern ethology textbook, *The Study of Instinct*, was written by Nikolaas Tinbergen in 1951, and E. H. Hess (1962) and Eibl-Eibesfeldt (1966) recently produced summaries of the modern concepts of behavior. The observations of a number of pioneers, including Spalding (1873), Darwin (1872), Whitman (1898), Altum (1868), Heinroth (1911), and Craig (1918), awakened scientific interest in animal behavior, and ethology came to be considered an independent branch of zoology around 1910. As with every young science, ethology inevitably suffers, on the one hand, from the incorporation of concepts whose meaning has oscillated or has already become too specialized (such as "instinct") and, on the other hand, from the application of provisional concepts, which may alter in meaning with advances in knowledge, to contemporary working hypotheses.

The term "ethology" is now attached to the scientific investigation of the behavior of animals and of some aspects of human behavior. Pronouncements about inaccessible psychic phenomena are avoided; the term "animal psychology" is still occasionally used but on purely historical grounds. Ethology is concerned with the investigation of animals, whether these be single cells—either as individual protozoans or as parts of metazoans—or more complex animal structures, that is, individuals, groups, or so-called animal colonies (e.g., ants, bees, and termites).

The behavior of an animal is equated with changes brought about by effectors (e.g., movements, sounds, scent production, color changes). Such effector responses are temporal events. For this reason only effector responses which repeatedly and identifiably occur are open to scientific analysis; they are then termed "fixed action patterns." It is important to note that these temporal events can be recorded by tape and film, except in the case of chemical or tactile signals. The locomotion of an animal can be subdivided into the movement of the extremities, of antagonistic muscle groups, of single muscles, and ultimately of the muscle fibers. The smallest identifiable effector components, occurring either singly or in combination with other components, are chosen as the units of ethological study.

The aim of ethology is to explain both phylogenetically and physiologically the functional relationships of all factors involved in behavior. This is evident in the modern definition of instinct suggested by Tinbergen: " . . . a hierarchically organized nervous mechanism which is susceptible to certain priming, releasing and directing impulses of internal as well as of external origin, and which responds to these impulses by coordinated movements that contribute to the maintenance of the individual and the species" (1951, p. 112). The touchstone for ethological hypotheses is the reliable prediction of the behavior of a living system in any given situation.

Ethologists are zoologists; they are thus interested in the biology of a species, and their prime interest is behavior as it occurs under natural conditions. The ethologist always begins by compiling an "action catalogue," or *ethogram* of the species in question, that is, as complete a description as possible of the behavior throughout the animal's life cycle. This simply describes what the animal does, not why it does it.

The various behavior patterns are then classified and compared with those of other species, especially with closely related species. It is important that the animals should be observed in their natural habitats or in surroundings which closely resemble them. Additional observations in captivity are often necessary. A very useful expedient, first known to have been practiced by Baron Ferdinand Adam von Pernau in 1702, is to rear the animals to be both tame and unconfined.

Learning, maturation, and genetics. Although learning is considered to be very important in animal behavior, the first concern of the ethologist is with behavior patterns typically performed by all animals of a species, because it is necessary for him to know the basic predetermined responses before proceeding to study changes brought about by learning. This is important, since not every change of form or effectiveness of a given behavior pattern occurring during the life of an individual involves learning in the form of acquisition by experience. As early as 1760 a professor in Hamburg, Hermann Samuel Reimarus, discovered the phenomenon of *maturation* of instincts and pointed out the difference between innate and acquired skills. The innate skills, for example, the collection of food or the performance and "understanding" of the dance language in bees, are present from the time of birth or of hatching from the egg or pupa. Without involving a definition of learning, the problem can be formulated as follows: the majority of behavior patterns in most animals are adapted (adjusted) to special situations in their respective environments. Since this fact cannot be explained as a chance phenomenon and since it is not a self-evident phenomenon, an explanation must be provided. In order to behave adaptively, the animal must have at its disposal information about the environment. This information can be stored either in the chromosomes or in memory; that is, it can be either innate or acquired. In complex behavior patterns, there is often an interaction between innate and acquired elements. However, although we know of perceptual and motor skills in which learning plays no part, it is impossible to postulate a completely learned element of behavior that is not based on genetically determined and, therefore, delimited capabilities. Further, no one has so far been able to demonstrate the infinite modifiability of any arbitrarily chosen, innately determined element of behavior or the possibility that learning could be the function of a nonorganized aggregate of neural elements. In learning, the fact that the organism selects "good" and not "bad" behavioral responses or stimuli logically implies a built-in mechanism which is able to direct learning toward survival value.

A particularly good method for distinguishing between the learned and innate elements of behavior is contained in the *deprivation experiment*: the animal, usually isolated from members of its own species, is deprived of certain experiences and later tested in the situation to which the behavior pattern in question is normally adapted. As a control a normal animal must be tested in the same situation. (This is one of several safety precautions which are necessary in the evaluation of the deprivation experiment.) The majority of behavior patterns do not follow the all-or-none law but can occur at varying intensities. The lowest intensities, where it is just possible to recognize which pattern has been activated, are referred to as *intention movements*. The intensity with which a behavior pattern is performed depends upon both internal and external factors.

The appearance of a particular fixed action pattern in animals isolated from their own species is clear evidence of genetic fixity. It is a constant characteristic of the species concerned and is based upon a specific central nervous mechanism that is inherited just as are morphological and physiological characteristics. (This had already been stated by the English naturalist Spalding in 1873.) A particularly good example is provided by many bird songs which develop into the species-specific pattern even in completely isolated animals. Research into the genetic basis of behavior patterns is developing as an important part of ethology. For example, crossing two duck species which differ in their courtship behavior can give rise to hybrids exhibiting courtship motor sequences not evident in any known species of duck or sometimes to hybrids possessing behavior patterns absent in both parent species but present in some presumed ancestral type (Wall 1963). However, it is still not clear what changes in the complex physiological basis of such behavior patterns are responsible for these differences. Dilger investigated the carrying of nest material in F_1 hybrids of *Agapornis roseicollis parrat* (male) × *A. personata fischeri* (female). Both parent species cut strips of paper or leaves and carry them to the nest. Females of the first species carry the strips in their bills, while females of the second species tuck the strips under special feathers on the lower back. The hybrids attempted to perform this latter pattern but failed for various reasons. For example, some were unable to let go of the strip of paper and tried to carry the strips in the bill *and* under the feathers at the same time. Within two years the behavior of the hybrids improved through learning, but they continued to perform ineffective tucking movements (Dilger 1962).

The genetic fixity of elements of behavior and the fact that they are nearly always to be found in more than one species prove their taxonomic value. In fact they are often characteristic of genera, families, or even higher taxonomic categories. For this reason it is possible to employ behavior patterns in the investigation of the relationships between animals. Indeed, Whitman (1898) and Heinroth (1911) investigated the behavior of doves and ducks respectively in the hope of finding characteristics useful for a more systematic analysis of their interrelatedness. In some grasshopper and toad species, species-specific calls or songs are used for species recognition; thus they represent barriers to interspecific reproduction. On the other hand, it is possible to reconstruct the phylogeny of behavior patterns on the basis of variations in the form of the same basic pattern between closely related species, as was pointed out by Darwin in *The Expression of the Emotions in Man and Animals* (1872). Exactly the same method is used in comparative anatomy and morphology. Although no behavioral fossils exist, more transitional forms exist between different behavioral types than is the case with morphological characteristics; behavioral characteristics occur repeatedly and at different intensities, while a leg is formed only once. The individual elements of various behavior patterns are, however, more open to formation of novel combinations (e.g., in contrast to the bones of the skull in vertebrates). For this reason, the phylogeny of behavior patterns must be based on the simplest possible elements.

We know that no behavioral characteristic is dependent upon only one gene, that each hereditary component affects several characteristics, and that there are not two separate sets of hereditary material governing body construction and behavioral features. The interaction of a behavior pattern with its effector organ is thus just as labile as the coadaptation of several functionally correlated organs.

Evolution and selection. Reimarus pointed out that in many instances behavior patterns adapted to the use of certain organs are performed, at times, even before these organs are developed. Apart from differences in speed of development of behavior patterns and their effector organs, it is also possible that one survives when the other is lost; a cerambycid beetle will continue to preen its antennas after they have been removed by dissection, mutant fruit flies (*Drosophila*) with no wings still perform the wing-preening movements typical of the species, stump-tailed monkeys, when they run along a branch, still show the balancing movements once effective in their long-tailed ancestors. Such historical carry-overs can also be observed in behavior patterns originally adapted to certain environmental conditions which have since changed. Ground-breeding birds regularly use the beak to perform specific behavior patterns for rolling the eggs back into the nest if they are found outside. Tree-breeding birds do not show this, since the eggs that fall disappear. However, Poulsen (1953) was able to show that some birds which have recently evolved from ground-living stock to a tree-living habit still exhibit egg-rolling patterns, while some recently evolved ground-breeding birds lack this pattern. There are other examples which show that fixed action patterns can be extremely conservative in the evolution of a species. On the other hand, closely related species occupying the same area exhibit rapid phylogenetic changes in the sexual behavior patterns serving for sexual recognition. In fact, in some such species greater differences in species recognition signals are seen where two species occur together than where either species occurs in isolation. This phenomenon has been called *character displacement.*

Intraspecific signals usually undergo selection for better recognition (to avoid "misunderstandings") and tend to become more and more conspicuous and outlandish. The behaviors involved are performed more conspicuously and are emphasized by morphological characteristics of color, form, or odor. In addition such behaviors are often rhythmically repeated. This fixed patterning often ceases to show different degrees of intensity. The level of motivation is no longer expressed in the intensity of the behavior but in how often it is repeated at one and the same *fixed intensity* (Morris 1957), much as the urgency of a telephone call is indicated by *how often* the bell rings and not *how loud* it rings. Finally such a recently formed fixed action pattern may become motivationally autonomous of the situation in which it was originally aroused by a process that Tinbergen has called *emancipation.* These and other changes in signal behavior patterns, leading to improved communication between signal sender and signal receiver, are referred to as *ritualization.* We still know very little regarding the physiological and neuroanatomical basis of both nonritualized and ritualized behavior patterns. [*See* COMMUNICATION, ANIMAL.]

It is commonplace to say that no animal performs the behavior patterns in its repertoire in random order. An animal responds to signals according to set principles. It is the task of the behavioral physiologist to analyze this phenomenon. This task involves large-scale studies of sensory physiology, since the animal receives the stimuli with its sense organs; of hormone physiology, since hormones can decide whether the sight of the female elicits courtship by the male, and so on; and of the physiology of the central nervous system, which is responsible for the analysis of the stimuli and for the coordination of the requisite behavior patterns.

Releasing mechanisms.   The carnivorous water beetle *Dysticus marginalis* does not react to the sight of prey (e.g., a tadpole in a glass tube), although it has perfectly developed eyes, but it does react to the chemical stimuli emanating from the prey. If some prey-extract solution is added to the water, the beetle will clasp even inanimate objects immersed in the water. A male robin will attack a bundle of red feathers but not a perfect dummy of a male lacking the characteristic red breast. Such examples show that animals respond with quite specific reactions to quite specific stimuli among the many perceived from the environment. These relevant stimuli are called *sign stimuli,* or *releasers.*

Sign stimuli act upon specific functional units of the central nervous system, the so-called *releasing mechanisms.* The specific properties of these units may likewise be either genetically determined, in which case they are termed *innate releasing mechanisms* (IRM), or partially determined by learning. The releasing mechanism filters out the sign stimuli and thereby triggers off specific behavior patterns. Some behavior patterns čan be elicited by more than one stimulus (e.g., an odor or a vibration). The vigor of the reaction generally depends upon the strength of the stimulus, and heterogeneous stimuli may summate (the same intensity of a reaction may be shown toward a strong odor or a strong vibration or a weak odor together with a weak vibration). Sometimes it is possible to present the animal with an abnormally strong stimulus and obtain a response stronger than that released by the naturally occurring stimulus; Magnus (1958) has shown that the males of the silver-washed fritillary butterfly react with courtship toward the orange and black color pattern of the female's fluttering wings. By placing orange and dark stripes on a cylinder and rotating it, he proved that more rapid color–dark alternation than the rate characteristic of the female was more effective in eliciting the male's reaction. The greater the speed of rotation of the cylinder, the greater were the courtship responses, right up to the physiologically demonstrated flicker-fusion frequency for the species concerned. [*See* SEXUAL BEHAVIOR, *article on* ANIMAL SEXUAL BEHAVIOR.] This susceptibility of animals to *supernormal releasers* provides us with an insight into the reason for the development of bizarre morphological signal structures such as the feathers of the peacock. Some parasitic birds even capitalize on this phenomenon when their young are larger and more babyish than, and therefore preferred to, the host's own young.

Motivation and drives. It has been observed that one individual will sometimes respond to a weak stimulus with a strong response, while at other times respond only at the same intensity or not at all to a much stronger releasing stimulus. It is therefore necessary to measure independently the specific "readiness" of the animal to react, apart from the strength of the stimulus. The strength of a reaction often decreases sharply with repeated equivalent stimulation, as is the case with escape attempts in aquarium fish in response to tapping on the glass pane or with gaping in young birds when the nest is lightly shaken. The readiness of an animal to perform certain patterns exhibits extensive and independent variation; an animal which is not prepared to eat may nevertheless exhibit readiness to flee. The readiness to perform a certain pattern is referred to as the *motivation*. Motivation (e.g., in hunger) often increases with the time interval from the last elicitation of the type of behavior concerned ("damming effect," an effect which is related to the corresponding stimulus threshold). In the extreme case the action pattern can occur without any evident external elicitation—as *vacuum activity*. However, an animal with high motivation to perform specific behavior patterns (where the "drive" is under restraint) usually performs certain behavior patterns suitable for attainment of a stimulus situation appropriate to the motivated patterns. In simple terms, the animal "searches." Craig (1918) observed the occurrence of restlessness, varied movements, and searching behavior as symptoms of a physiological state of appetite for specific stimuli and labeled such behavior *appetitive* behavior, as distinct from *consummatory* behavior, which lowers the degree of motivation when performed and leads to a *state of satisfaction*. It is important to note that the animal does not attempt to achieve the biological effect associated with the consummatory act but merely the performance of the consummatory behavior itself. The state of satisfaction can also be achieved by abreaction in response to models. In the simplest case, appetitive behavior consists of undirected locomotion, but many animals (especially higher-developed forms) learn from experience and modify the appetitive behavior, so that it more rapidly leads to success. They learn when, where, and how they can attain the releasing situation. Briefly, appetitive behavior is typically variable (plastic), whereas the consummatory act is relatively fixed (stereotyped).

Motivational analysis attempts to demonstrate how many behavior patterns are dependent upon the same motivational source and how many partially or completely independent motivational centers are present in a given animal species. It is taken as axiomatic that there are fewer independent sources of motivation than observably distinct behavior patterns and that behavior patterns which regularly occur within short intervals from one another are thus commonly motivated—the motivational state of the animal oscillates more slowly than the alternation of behavior patterns. Further, it is known that behavior patterns exist which are characteristic for specific conflict situations; in the conflict between attack and flight these are represented by threat behavior. Such patterns are certainly motivated from different sources, which may vary independently from one another. It is not known from the outset how many of the behavior patterns observed have mixed motivation, but for the purposes of analysis it is assumed that it is the minimum possible. Wiepkema, a Dutch ethologist, carried out the following model experiment (1961) with the European bitterling: First he recorded the occurrence of the behavior patterns which he had identified for this species (ramming the flank of a conspecific with the head, scouring of the substrate, tail-beating, swimming before the female, etc.) over a long period of time. In this process typical locomotory sequences are found to occur regularly, while some behavior patterns are seen to be mutually exclusive within a given time interval. Wiepkema computed the minimum number of independent variables (i.e., motives) necessary to account for the observed distribution of action patterns. Mixed motivation was taken into account, but it was assumed that one given motive was predominant in each case. For the reproductive period of the bitterling it was found that three independent motivational sources are necessary and that each source governs a group of motor patterns which are totally or predominantly dependent upon the source concerned. These groups are comprised of (1) behavior patterns directed at the rival, objectively termed "fight," (2) behavior patterns directed away from the rival, termed "flight," and (3) the patterns carried out in combination with the female in association with spawning. Accordingly it is possible to refer to the predominant motivation in each case as (1) fight drive, (2) flight drive, and (3) sex drive. Some behavior patterns lie between these groups, however, and are thus more or less equally dependent upon more than one motive. For example, spreading of the fins combined with an undulating movement of the entire body, which wᵉ refer to as "threat," is motivated by both fight and flight drives; a specific courtship pattern is motivated by both fight and sex drives. Using factor analysis it is even possible to rank the action patterns according to a scale of ratios between different drives. [*See* DRIVES; MOTIVATION.]

Various phenomena occur in conflict situations; the animal may combine two behavior patterns (e.g., warding off a rival and eating), it may oscillate between the intention movements of different action patterns (e.g., oscillation between motions toward attack and flight without actually attacking or fleeing), it may exhibit abreaction of an inhibited behavior pattern by transferring the direction to a neutral object (e.g., gulls which do not dare to attack a stronger rival may tear and pluck at tufts of grass), or it may exhibit a behavior pattern which does not belong to either of the motivational sources directly involved in the conflict. This last pattern is referred to as *displacement activity*. For example, domestic cocks will start to eat when they are involved in a conflict between attack and flight, while avocets will assume a sleeping posture. The physiological foundations of displacement activities have been investigated only in a few cases and appear to vary from case to case. Some behavior patterns may be dependent upon the same releasing stimuli as well as upon the same motivational sources. [*See* CONFLICT, *article on* PSYCHOLOGICAL ASPECTS.]

Sequential and hierarchical organization. The fact that some elements of behavior can give rise to conflict at corresponding integrational levels, while others are mutually exclusive, indicates that groups of elements are governed by superior systems which can similarly show mutual interference, promotion, inhibition, or exclusion. In this way, we arrive at the concept of a hierarchical system of dominant and subordinate drives. The same concept emerges from the comparison of releasing situations and appetitive behavior.

A hungry squirrel (1) climbs (2) trees (3) looking for cones; when motivated to build a nest, it (1) climbs (2) trees (3) looking for twigs. Thus different motivations may employ the same "lower" motor and orientation components. The latter are called *taxes*, a taxis being defined as orientation of the whole body or parts of it with respect to the source of stimulation. Further, the distinction between appetitive behavior and consummatory be-

havior is a relative one. Normally, certain appetitive behavior leads to a stimulus situation which initiates another, more specific, appetitive behavior. This fact has been carefully worked out by Baerends (1941) and Tinbergen (1951). The three-spined stickleback is brought into reproductive motivation by the gradual increase in day length in spring and begins migration inland into shallow fresh-water habitats. This factor, together with the rise in water temperature and the visual stimulation of heavily vegetated sites, is a releasing mechanism for the establishment of a suitable territory by the males. A territory is necessary for the male to acquire its characteristic red belly. Only then does it begin to react to particular stimuli which previously had no effect. The male will build a nest with suitable material, fight against rival males (where the releasing stimulus is the red belly of the male intruding into his territory), and court passing females, which present their silvery, swollen, egg-filled bellies to the male in a characteristic manner. Thus, the stimuli emanating from a territory will activate the fighting, building, and mating drives, which must then be elicited by special releasers. Fighting itself consists of a number of behavior patterns (chasing, threatening, tail-beating, biting), each dependent upon still further, highly specific stimuli emanating from the intruder's behavior. The behavioral sequences of male and female form an alternating chain of reactions, each action of one partner releasing the following appropriate reaction of the other partner until the female spawns and the male fertilizes the eggs. The act of fertilization initiates brood care in the male; he now fans fresh water onto the eggs and continues to drive off rivals but does not exhibit further courtship until the young hatch. It is thus clear that there are chains of behavioral tendencies connected at higher and lower levels of integration and that these different levels are organized into a hierarchical system. The advantage of a hierarchy, as opposed to a stereotyped series of single fixed actions, lies in its adaptability to unpredictable sequences of events.

Neurophysiological aspects. It seems evident that some structural organization must exist within the central nervous system, paralleling the observed organization of behavioral responses—in particular the hierarchical organization. Neurophysiological investigation of fixed action patterns has therefore become an important branch of ethological research. Extending the earlier experiments of W. R. Hess (1949), Holst and Saint Paul (1959) demonstrated the existence of structural hierarchical organization of the mechanisms underlying behavior by electrically stimulating specific areas of the brain in chickens. Well-coordinated, complete sequences of movements identical with those observed in normal behavior were elicited. All these sequences of behavior were composed of single actions, each of which could be obtained in isolation by stimulation of specific brain areas. Holst and Saint Paul combined brain stimulation with the normal releasing stimuli, electrically changed the "mood" (motivational state) of the animal and studied artificial conflict between drives by producing interaction of different behavior patterns with simultaneous elicitation.

Neurological research has substantiated the conclusion, derived from ethological field studies, that the coordination of many locomotive patterns arises from impulses generated in the central nervous system. Potent support has also been provided for Lorenz' hypothesis postulating constant production of *action-specific potentials* in the central nervous system.

Habituation and imprinting. Most of the original schemata postulated for the functional structure of behavior have been shown to be simplifications, though correctly describing special cases. In order to arrive at a generalized schema, it is still necessary to modify repeatedly such hypothetical schemata. Even the hierarchical system must be altered to a multidimensional network. The concept of *habituation* likewise increases in complexity with time. A behavior pattern repeatedly elicited by a particular sign-stimulus will cease to occur after a given time. The sense organ can nevertheless be demonstrated to be fully capable of functioning, and it is not even necessary to presume that the motivation of the animal to perform this pattern is entirely extinguished; it is often possible to elicit the same behavior pattern immediately afterward with another sign-stimulus. In such cases, it is necessary to assume that central cut-off systems are involved. Such systems are capable of very complex functions; mechanisms of this type in turkeys extinguish flight behavior in response to all relatively slow-flying objects which occur frequently, and the adult animal flees only in response to uncommon flying objects. In fact, the most infrequently occurring objects which (relative to their own size) are slow-flying are birds of prey. The adult turkey thus shows a well-adapted flight reaction in response to predatory birds—but also to advertising balloons. It is a question of definition whether or not one refers to this effect as learning; it takes place without marked exogenous reward or punishment. The same is true of *imprinting*, which was described by Spalding as early as 1873. In

imprinting, a specific reaction of the animal (which need not be functional at the time of imprinting) becomes attached to an object which later functions as the releasing agent. This occurs within a limited sensitive period, usually at a young age. In contrast to learning by association, there is no reward (as in the previous example), and even punishing stimuli have a reinforcing effect. If ducks or doves are reared by other species they will later show a pairing preference toward a partner belonging to the foster species, even when a conspecific partner is available. [*See* IMPRINTING.]

Phenomena similar to imprinting have been discovered in many fields. Some juvenile birds learn the song entirely from the "father" and will learn the song of a foster-father even in the midst of conspecifics. Since later offspring learn from these birds, the possibility of "speech dialects" arises. In different mammal species there have been cases of *traditions* which largely concern food preferences or forms of food acquisition, although traditions may also arise in the avoidance of enemies.

IRENÄUS EIBL-EIBESFELDT
AND WOLFGANG WICKLER

[*Directly related are the entries* PSYCHOLOGY, *article on* COMPARATIVE PSYCHOLOGY; SOCIAL BEHAVIOR, ANIMAL. *Other relevant material may be found in* COMMUNICATION, ANIMAL; DRIVES; EVOLUTION; GENETICS; IMPRINTING; INSTINCT; LEARNING; MOTIVATION.]

BIBLIOGRAPHY

ALTUM, BERNARD (1868) 1910 *Der Vogel und sein Leben.* 9th ed. Munster (Germany): Schöningh.
BAERENDS, G. P. 1941 Fortpflanzungsverhalten und Orientierung der Grabwespe *Ammophila campestris* Jur. *Tijdschrift voor entomologie* 84:68–275.
CRAIG, WALLACE 1918 Appetites and Aversions as Constituents of Instincts. *Biological Bulletin* 34:91–107.
DARWIN, CHARLES (1872) 1965 *The Expression of the Emotions in Man and Animals.* Edited by Francis Darwin. Univ. of Chicago Press.
DILGER, WILLIAM C. 1962 The Behavior of the Lovebirds. *Scientific American* 206, no. 1:88–98.
EIBL-EIBESFELDT, IRENÄUS 1966 Ethologie: Die Biologie des Verhaltens. Volume 5, pages 341–549 in *Handbuch der Biologie.* Edited by Ludwig von Bertalanffy. Potsdam (Germany): Akademische Verlagsgesellschaft Athenaion.
HEINROTH, OTTO 1911 Beiträge zur Biologie, namentlich Ethologie und Psychologie der Anatiden. Pages 589–702 in International Ornithological Congress, Fifth, Berlin, 1910, *Verhandlungen.* Berlin: Deutsche Ornithologische Gesellschaft.
HESS, ECKHARD H. 1962 Ethology: An Approach Toward the Complete Analysis of Behavior. Pages 157–266 in *New Directions in Psychology,* by Roger Brown et al. New York: Holt.
HESS, WALTER R. (1949) 1954 *Das Zwischenhirn: Syndrome, Lokalisationen, Functionen.* Basel: Schwabe.

HOLST, ERICH VON; and SAINT PAUL, URSULA VON   (1959) 1963   On the Functional Organisation of Drives. *Animal Behaviour* 11:1–20. → First published in German.

LORENZ, KONRAD Z.   1965   *Evolution and Modification of Behavior.* Univ. of Chicago Press.

MAGNUS, DIETRICH   1958   Experimentelle Untersuchungen zur Bionomie und Ethologie des Kaisermantels Argynnis paphia (lep. Nymph). *Zeitschrift für Tierpsychologie* 15:397–426.

MORRIS, DESMOND   1957   "Typical Intensity" and Its Relation to the Problem of Ritualization. *Behaviour* 11: 1–12.

POULSEN, HOLGER   1953   A Study of Incubation Responses and Some Other Behaviour Patterns in Birds. Dansk Naturhistorisk Forening, Copenhagen, *Videnskabelige meddelelser* 115:1–131.

REIMARUS, HERMANN S.   (1760) 1798   *Allgemeine Betrachtungen über die Triebe der Thiere, hauptsächlich über ihre Kunsttriebe.* Hamburg (Germany): Bohn.

SPALDING, DOUGLAS A.   (1873) 1954   Instinct, With Original Observations on Young Animals. *British Journal of Animal Behaviour* 2:2–11.

THORPE, WILLIAM H.   (1956) 1963   *Learning and Instinct in Animals.* 2d ed., rev. & enl. Cambridge, Mass.: Harvard Univ. Press.

TINBERGEN, NIKOLAAS   1951   *The Study of Instinct.* Oxford: Clarendon.

WALL, W. VON DE   1963   Bewegungsstudien an Anatinen. *Journal für Ornithologie* 104:1–15.

WHITMAN, C. O.   1898   Animal Behavior. Woods Hole, Mass., Marine Biological Laboratory *Biological Lectures* [1898]:285–338.

WIEPKEMA, P. R.   1961   An Ethological Analysis of the Reproductive Behaviour of the Bitterling (Rhodeus amarus Bloch). *Archives néerlandaises de zoologie* 14:103–199.

ETHOS

See CULTURE, *article on* CULTURAL RELATIVISM; VALUES, *article on* VALUE SYSTEMS; WORLD VIEW; *and the biography of* REDFIELD.

EUGENICS

Eugenics is an applied science that seeks to maintain or to improve the genetic potentialities of the human species. In practice, eugenics is concerned with any qualities that parents confer on their children, because genetic and cultural traits are often correlated or indistinguishable, and because measures that improve one at the expense of the other are to be avoided. Genetics provides the core of eugenic theory, while any implementation must be broadly based on demography, medicine, psychology, and sociology.

Founded by Sir Francis Galton at the end of the nineteenth century, before the rediscovery of Gregor Mendel's laws of heredity, the early eugenics movement had an insecure scientific foundation and soon became contaminated with class and race prejudice. In the first half of the twentieth century, eugenics was challenged by the growth of equalitarian sentiments and suffered especially from the demonstration of perverted eugenics in Nazi Germany. Since mid-century, the movement has gained respectability by repudiating its early errors and by assimilating scientific advances.

False concepts are still widely propounded in the name of eugenics, and there is disagreement even among geneticists as to the desirability and the urgency of eugenic measures. While some deterioration of hereditary capacities is sure to result from preservation of physically or mentally handicapped persons and from increased irradiation of the population, the rate of this deterioration may be exceedingly slow. Furthermore, medical procedures that ameliorate genetic handicaps do not usually restore complete physical and social normality, so that natural selection still operates against the defects. Although intelligent parents have in the recent past tended to have fewer children than the less intelligent, early predictions of declining general intelligence have not been borne out. Analysis of present trends in reproduction indicates that the increased use and effectiveness of contraception may reverse this fertility difference (Osborn 1963*a*; 1963*b*).

The case for eugenics.   Three lines of reasoning support the case for eugenics. First, individual families can be spared suffering and disruption if severe hereditary defects are identified and the parents given medical advice or assistance in preventing further births.

Second, the high correlation between parents and children in mental characteristics has some of the same implications whether attributed mainly to heredity or mainly to cultural transmission. Mentally handicapped persons, whose children stand the greatest risk of mental handicap, should at least be assisted if they wish to limit their offspring. More intelligent parents who can provide healthy home environments should be encouraged to bear as many children as they can support.

Third, even a very small improvement in the intelligence of a large civilized population may be expected to increase available leadership significantly. The argument for eugenics does not depend on proving that present trends are downward but on evidence that in important respects the population would be better off with eugenic measures than without them (Shapiro 1959). The only assurance against genetic deterioration is demonstrable genetic improvement.

Modern governments and institutions cannot avoid taking action in the sphere of eugenics. Every large-scale social or economic measure alters the distribution of births among segments of the population, and this distribution determines the genetic potentials of the next generation.

Present problems and applications

Radiation effects. In the past two decades public attention has been focused on possible genetic effects of radiation, namely, gene mutations. Children born to survivors of the atomic bombs in Japan have not shown significant genetic effects, and this supports the belief that to date the deleterious effects of atomic bursts on human heredity are small in comparison with natural mutations already accumulated in concealed form. Yet in absolute numbers, the new induced mutations are probably numerous and destined to take a proportionate toll in death and suffering spread over many generations.

In medically advanced countries the population receives radiation from medical X rays that may greatly exceed the present dosage from fall-out of atomic tests. The debt incurred for future generations by use of X rays or atomic testing must be weighed against the supposed immediate gains in health or national security. Some drugs also induce mutations, and these may need to be controlled in the future. Among the consequences of induced mutations, it is likely that physical defects would be less of a threat to man's survival under civilization than innumerable small mental impairments.

Race mixture. There is a broad consensus among geneticists that race mixture in man is no eugenic hazard. In plants and animals, the crossing of races may have unpredictable results. Especially if the parent populations were closely inbred, the new generation may show "hybrid vigor"; some other hybrids may show serious disharmonies. In the case of man there is little evidence for either hybrid vigor or hybrid disharmony, and if they occur they are overshadowed by social and cultural phenomena (Chung & Morton 1961). If some small hybrid populations appear to be genetically and culturally inferior to surrounding peoples, this may be due to isolation, inbreeding, or the quality of people who originate or who join such groups. Gene frequencies are not altered by race crossing but only by mutations and selection.

Population policies. The immediate problem of curbing world population growth overshadows problems of population quality. Nevertheless, population policies adopted now are likely to exert qualitative effects for a long time in the future, and these effects should be weighed.

Birth rate differences between educational classes or between occupations appear in most civilized countries to be unfavorable to social and genetic progress. Eugenically sound population policies would therefore reduce or reverse these differentials at the same time that they accomplish their main purpose. A program to reduce births might, for example, facilitate voluntary family limitation and at the same time extend and advertise the economic benefits of such limitation to the more fertile and less secure economic classes. A program to increase births might best achieve this by assisting with higher education and other goals that deter reproduction by persons of high ability.

Genetic counseling. Genetic factors undoubtedly play some role in nearly all diseases and abnormalities, but avoidance of reproduction is genetically indicated only in conditions for which the risk is known to be high. Even in these instances the advisability of reproduction depends on the nature of the disease, on other genetic variables, on socioeconomic circumstances, and above all on the parents' willingness to sustain the risk. People who avoid childbearing for fear of hereditary defects sometimes have negligible genetic risks and are potentially superior parents. Yet those who seek genetic advice often fail to make use of it. Many universities now have centers for genetic counseling, but hereditary diseases will remain unchecked until family planning becomes general and effective. Whether it will ever be possible to transform harmful genes to the normal form by artificial means is a subject of speculation (Hotchkiss 1965).

Theoretical aspects of eugenics

Heredity and behavior. Galton believed that human behavior could be improved by genetic as well as by cultural progress (1883). Is there today any secure basis for such a belief? On theoretical grounds, the answer to this question is clearly yes. Over the past million years man's forebears made rapid genetic progress with respect to intelligence and social behavior. The only known mechanism of genetic progress is natural or artificial selection of favorable variations, and selection produces permanent gains only if the selected variations are hereditary. Therefore, hereditary variation must have existed as long as mental capacities were evolving, and there is no theoretical reason to suppose that it has now disappeared. Such hereditary variation in behavior provides the necessary basis for further genetic improvement.

Many psychologists and geneticists have adduced what they regard as evidence for hereditary psychological differences. The most important variation seems to be that between individuals, whereas the observed differences between races and social classes are mainly cultural in origin. Even the concept of good and bad "family stock" is erroneous; both good and bad may occur in any family, and psychological traits shared with grandchildren or cousins must be attributed in large part to common environmental factors or to assortative (selective) mating.

Natural selection.   Natural selection is the only known guiding influence in organic evolution and is a necessary correlate of reproduction in a genetically variable organism. Individuals who contribute more progeny than others to the next generation have, by definition, greater *biological fitness*. So far as the differences in fitness may be hereditary and the environment stable, the next generation will have a higher average ability to survive and reproduce. At equilibrium the gain in each generation is offset by new harmful mutations. The first test of fitness is survival; but even among the survivors, natural selection operates through differences in fertility.

Although it acts on whole organisms, natural selection produces evolutionary effects by changing the relative frequencies of single genes. In each generation, sexual reproduction recombines genes so that all are tested in new combinations. The ultimate frequency of a gene depends on its average effect on survival and reproduction; if it is to become frequent, a new gene must be consonant with the major existing adaptations of the species. Natural selection is therefore conservative, tending usually to stabilize established norms.

Natural selection is inefficient for at least three reasons: (1) Many deaths or reproductive failures are due to chance. (2) Individual differences in fitness are often not hereditary. (3) Most hereditary differences in fitness are small. Some of this inefficiency can be overcome under artificial selection, but at a price. When it entails breeding from a few selected individuals, artificial selection may sacrifice both genetic stability and reserve variability. The artificial reproductive success conferred by the breeder on animals with commercially valuable traits may result in feeble or sterile strains. On the other hand, natural selection adapts a species only to its present environment or set of environments, and when the environment changes radically the species may become extinct. Man can foresee some changes in the environment and can, if he will, select for long-term fitness. In the last analysis this is probably a crucial advantage of scientific eugenics over natural selection.

The genetic stability of populations.   Evolution is slow not only because natural selection is inefficient but because natural populations have a great inherent genetic stability. This stability is considerable even in small populations, for example, with a few hundred breeding individuals. Because of large numbers and small individual contributions to the next generation (compared with most species), civilized human populations should be very resistant to change.

Genetic stability resides primarily in the "gene pool" of a population. Each gene has a characteristic frequency, usually determined by a stable equilibrium between opposing forces of selection and mutation. Sudden changes in selective pressures may have more effect on complex traits than on the underlying gene frequencies, but even such traits are not likely to change fast. Thus, if lactation ceases to have survival value, its dependence on several physiological systems may make it vulnerable to mutations in any of a great many genes. Before any single genetic defect reached a frequency of 2.0 per cent, most women might have one or two rarer defects that prevented lactation. But an increase from 0.1 per cent to 2.0 per cent by mutation would take at least a hundred generations. Defects of lactation that were positively selected because of effects on other traits might increase ten times this fast, but they would be few and represent coincidence only.

Probably all human behavioral traits, except some grossly pathological ones, are controlled by multiple genetic factors and by the environment. Most of these traits are graded or continuous. Natural selection tends to eliminate both extremes in such a continuum and produces evolutionary change mainly from slight differences in fitness among the more numerous intermediate individuals. Thus, the gene pool retains a large reserve of variability and accommodates any new variations that do not have extreme effects.

Sources of variation.   It has been suggested that ionizing radiation may speed human evolution by inducing more mutations. While mutations are the raw material of evolution, increased mutation rates now would probably do much more harm than good. First, nearly all mutations are harmful and must be eliminated by impaired fitness of the carriers, often extending over many generations. Second, nearly all of the possibly beneficial mutations have occurred before and are already so frequent that rare additions will not help. Third, the few new useful mutations would increase so slowly under moderate selective pressures that they would remain very rare for centuries.

Variations already present in human populations would suffice to carry human evolution forward a very long distance. New useful mutations that have arisen in the past few millennia are still in the early stages of response to natural selection. The great majority of variable genes, kept at intermediate frequencies by conflicting or inefficient selection, should have an immense potential for improving the species. Some useful genes may be mainly restricted to small populations or to certain races; intermarriage between nationalities and between races will make these generally available. Finally, man's constantly changing environment under civilization changes the survival value of genes, making some useful that were previously neutral or harmful.

The role of an optimum environment. Early Darwinian enthusiasts supposed that natural selection was inevitably cruel and that human evolution could proceed only in a harsh environment. Diverse environments are desirable since they develop diverse potentials and, under natural selection, maintain genetic variability. But present human environments are often restricting and largely beyond control of the individual and even of the family.

Man's future environment will probably be closer to the best than to the worst of present living standards. Eugenic planning for long-term adaptation should seek not only to equalize opportunity but to equalize it at a high economic and educational level. This would have no eugenic effect by itself but would enhance whatever selection was operative, either negative or positive.

Direction and choice in programs. A number of experts have warned that man may become dangerously dependent on medical technology. Such dependence, on a genetic basis, may develop gradually over centuries or millennia, but it is evident that throughout human evolution innate physical capacities have tended to deteriorate as compensatory mental abilities increased. In subhuman evolution, adaptability has repeatedly proved superior to specialized adaptation, and intelligence in its many aspects opens the way to almost unlimited adaptability. In any eugenic program, therefore, intelligence, broadly defined, should take precedence over physical fitness.

The above implied choice is an example of problems that would continually arise in eugenics. It is sometimes contended that the planning of human evolution would require superhuman wisdom. In practice, eugenics need not imply detailed foresight or genetic planning but would select for adaptability and diversity among variations already discernible. If the problems were faced one by one and periodically reviewed, they should be no more grave or insoluble than present political, educational, and social problems.

Dysgenic and eugenic environments. The environment is the instrument of natural selection since it sets the conditions for individual biological fitness, that is, the ability to survive and reproduce. For the continuation of our culture, and perhaps ultimately of the species, some other traits are as important as fertility. A society in which culturally important traits are positively correlated with fertility may be defined as a eugenic environment; the opposite is a dysgenic environment. One society may be eugenic within some social strata and dysgenic in others. Any discussion of a eugenic environment requires specification of the traits considered culturally important. One might assume that the greatest need in our culture is for traits leading to superior achievement in one's chosen occupation. A thorough treatment of the subject would give weight to more specific traits such as intelligence, social maturity, and parental responsibility.

Proposed systems of selection

Promoting optimum expression of each person's genetic capacities would not by itself constitute genetic progress. Eugenic selection, either natural or artificial, is also needed. Any deliberate program to promote eugenic selection would require much research before it could be instituted and careful monitoring of its progress.

Breeding programs. Next to preoccupation with race, the advocacy of artificial breeding programs has probably done most to make eugenics unacceptable. Early proposals were incompatible with concepts of conventional marriage and families as social units. Since the introduction of artificial insemination, the possibility of multiplying the progeny of selected men has become real. If artificial insemination from donors is practiced, all eugenists would agree that the donors should be carefully selected. But proposals for large-scale use of semen from a few great men (Muller 1960) may attach too much importance to fortunate combinations of genes that have little general value in the gene pool or in ordinary environments.

Assistance to selected families. British eugenists, especially, have advocated financial assistance, resembling scholarships, to parents with good eugenic prognosis (Blacker 1952, p. 307). This would enable them to have as many children as they wanted. Economically dependent families, with generally poorer prognosis, would be assisted in limiting their progeny.

With exceptions for grossly pathological heredity, eugenic prognosis in such a program ought to be based upon a couple's social and cultural attainments and on physical and mental health of their earliest progeny. Discrepancies between attainments and genetic potential might be compensated by social transmission of traits, so that this eugenic program would achieve limited cultural improvement if not also genetic improvement. If future environments achieve near equality of opportunities, attainments will more closely reflect genetic capacities.

Automatic selection. Some eugenists have been dissatisfied with the potential for error or misuse in any arbitrary system of selection. Others see eugenic processes as requiring both broad application across all families and stability beyond that of most political systems. From these concerns have come suggestions for automatic selection: economic measures or social conditions under which natural selection will favor qualities of greatest value to society.

If the newest methods of contraception become widely available, they may eliminate nearly all unwanted pregnancies. This in itself would bring family size more in line with parents' capacities for education and achievement (Osborn 1963*a*). The rewarding of fertility with uniform family allowances is not eugenically effective, but some countries offer other benefits. Highly effective automatic selection would require a more carefully planned eugenic environment (Osborn 1940). This might include high degrees of (1) social mobility, (2) individual opportunity, and (3) voluntary assortative marriage, that is, between persons with similar abilities. It might also require special educational, economic, and social measures to make child rearing more acceptable to socially competent persons and less so to the socially inadequate.

GORDON ALLEN

[*Other relevant material may be found in* EVOLUTION; GENETICS; RADIATION; *and in the biographies of* DARWIN *and* GALTON.]

BIBLIOGRAPHY

BLACKER, CHARLES P. 1952 *Eugenics: Galton and After.* London: Duckworth.

CHUNG, C. S.; and MORTON, N. E. 1961 Genetics of Interracial Crosses in Hawaii. Volume 1, pages 134–138 in International Congress of Human Genetics, Second, Rome, *Proceedings.* Rome: Istituto G. Mendel.

DOBZHANSKY, THEODOSIUS 1962 *Mankind Evolving.* New Haven: Yale Univ. Press. → An authoritative exposition for the general scientist of genetic principles relevant to human evolution.

Evolution and Man's Progress. 1961 *Dædalus* 90:409–586. → A symposium. See especially pages 416–476, dealing with genetic evolution.

GALTON, FRANCIS (1883) 1952 *Inquiries Into Human Faculty and Its Development.* London: Cassell.

HALLER, MARK H. 1963 *Eugenics: Hereditarian Attitudes in American Thought.* New Brunswick, N.J.: Rutgers Univ. Press.

HOTCHKISS, ROLLIN D. 1965 Portents for a Genetic Engineering. *Journal of Heredity* 56:197–202.

MEDAWAR, PETER B. 1960 *The Future of Man.* New York: Basic Books; London: Methuen. → A simple discussion of some central questions.

MULLER, HERMAN J. 1960 The Guidance of Human Evolution. Pages 423–462 in Sol Tax (editor), *The Evolution of Man.* Volume 2: Evolution After Darwin. Univ. of Chicago Press.

OSBORN, FREDERICK H. (1940) 1951 *Preface to Eugenics.* Rev. ed. New York: Harper.

OSBORN, FREDERICK H. 1963*a* Excess and Unwanted Fertility. *Eugenics Quarterly* 10:59–72.

OSBORN, FREDERICK H. 1963*b* Eugenics and the Races of Man. *Eugenics Quarterly* 10:103–109.

SHAPIRO, HARRY L. 1959 Eugenics and Future Society. *Eugenics Quarterly* 6:3–7.

WORLD HEALTH ORGANIZATION 1957 *Effect of Radiation on Human Heredity.* Geneva: The Organization.

EUROPEAN SOCIETY

See the entries ANGLO–AMERICAN SOCIETY; SOCIETAL ANALYSIS.

EVALUATION RESEARCH

Ours is an age of social-action programs, where large organization and huge expenditures go into the attempted solution of every conceivable social problem. Such programs include both private and public ventures and small-scale and large-scale projects, ranging in scope from local to national and international efforts at social change. Whenever men spend time, money, and effort to help solve social problems, someone usually questions the effectiveness of their actions. Sponsors, critics, the public, even the actors themselves, seek signs that their program is successful. Much of the assessment of action programs is irregular and, often by necessity, based upon personal judgments of supporters or critics, impressions, anecdotes, testimonials, and miscellaneous information available for the evaluation. In recent years, however, there has been a striking change in attitudes toward evaluation activities and the type and quality of evidence that is acceptable for determining the relative success or failure of social-action programs.

Two trends stand out in the modern attitude toward evaluation. First, evaluation has come to be expected as a regular accompaniment to rational social-action programs. Second, there has been a movement toward demanding more systematic, rigorous, and objective evidence of success. The application of social science techniques to the appraisal of social-action programs has come to be called evaluation research.

Examples of the applications of evaluation research are available from a wide variety of fields. One of the earliest attempts at building evaluation research into an action program was in the field of community action to prevent juvenile delinquency. The 1937 Cambridge–Somerville Youth Study provided for an experimental and a control group of boys, with the former to receive special attention and advice from counselors and other community agencies. The plan called for a ten-year period of work with the experimental group followed by an evaluation that would compare the record of their delinquent conduct during that decade with the record of the control group. The results of the evaluation (see Powers & Witmer 1951) showed no significant differences in conduct favorable to the program. A subsequent long-term evaluation of the same program failed to find new evidence of less criminal activity by persons in the experimental group but added a variety of new theoretical analyses to the evaluation (McCord et al. 1959).

Several evaluations of programs in citizenship training for young persons have built upon one another, thus providing continuity in the field. Riecken (1952) conducted an evaluation of summer work camps sponsored by the American Friends Service Committee to determine their impact on the values, attitudes, and opinions of the participants. His work was useful in specifying those areas in which the program was successful or unsuccessful as well as pointing up the importance of measuring unsought by-products of action programs. Subsequently, Hyman, Wright, and Hopkins carried out a series of evaluations of another youth program, the Encampment for Citizenship (1962). Their research design was complex, including a comparison of campers' values, attitudes, opinions, and behavior before and after a six-week program of training; follow-up surveys six weeks and four years after the group left the program; three independent replications of the original study on new groups of campers in later years; and a sample survey of alumni of the program. These various studies demonstrated the effectiveness of the program in influencing campers' social attitudes and conduct; they also examined the dynamics of attitudinal change.

Evaluations have been made in such varied fields as intergroup relations, induced technological change, mass communications, adult education, international exchange of persons for training or good will, mental health, and public health. Additional examples of applications of evaluation research, along with discussions of evaluation techniques, are presented by Klineberg and others in a special issue of the *International Social Science Bulletin* (1955) and in Hyman and Wright (1966).

Defining characteristics

A scientific approach to the assessment of a program's achievements is the hallmark of modern evaluation research. In this respect evaluation research resembles other kinds of social research in its concern for objectivity, reliability, and validity in the collection, analysis, and interpretation of data. But it can be distinguished as a special form of social research by its purpose and the conditions under which the research must be conducted. Both of these factors affect such components of the research process as study design and its translation into practice, allocation of research time and other resources, and the value or worth to be put upon the empirical findings.

The primary purpose of evaluation research is "to provide objective, systematic, and comprehensive evidence on the degree to which the program achieves its intended objectives plus the degree to which it produces other unanticipated consequences, which when recognized would also be regarded as relevant to the agency" (Hyman et al. 1962, pp. 5–6). Evaluation research thus differs in its emphasis from such other major types of social research as exploratory studies, which seek to formulate new problems and hypotheses, or explanatory research, which places emphasis on the testing of theoretically significant hypotheses, or descriptive social research, which documents the existence of certain social conditions at a given moment or over time (Selltiz et al. 1959). Since the burden is on the evaluator to provide firm evidence on the effects of the program under study, he favors a study design that will tend toward maximizing such evidence and his confidence in conclusions drawn from it. Although good evaluation research often seeks explanations of a program's success or failure, the first concern is to obtain basic evidence on effectiveness, and therefore most research resources are allocated to this goal.

The conditions under which evaluation research is conducted also give it a character distinct from other forms of social research. Evaluation research is applied social research, and it differs from other modes of scholarly research in bringing together an outside investigator to guarantee objectivity and a client in need of his services. From the initial formulation of the problem to the final interpretation of findings, the evaluator is duty-bound to keep in mind the very practical problem of assessing the program under study. As a consequence he often has less freedom to select or reject certain independent, dependent, and intervening variables than he would have in studies designed to answer his own theoretically formulated questions, such as might be posed in basic social research. The concepts employed and their translation into measurable variables must be selected imaginatively but within the general framework set by the nature of the program being evaluated and its objectives (a point which will be discussed later). Another feature of evaluation research is that the investigator seldom has freedom to manipulate the program and its components, i.e., the independent variable, as he might in laboratory or field experiments. Usually he wants to evaluate an ongoing or proposed program of social action in its natural setting and is not at liberty, because of practical and theoretical considerations, to change it for research purposes. The nature of the program being evaluated and the time at which his services are called upon also set conditions that affect, among other things, the feasibility of using an experimental design involving before-and-after measurements, the possibility of obtaining control groups, the kinds of research instruments that can be used, and the need to provide for measures of long-term as well as immediate effects.

The recent tendency to call upon social science for the evaluation of action programs that are local, national, and international in scope (a trend which probably will increase in future years) and the fact that the application of scientific research procedures to problems of evaluation is complicated by the purposes and conditions of evaluation research have stimulated an interest in methodological aspects of evaluation among a variety of social scientists, especially sociologists and psychologists. Methodological and technical problems in evaluation research are discussed, to mention but a few examples, in the writings of Riecken (1952), Klineberg (1955), Hyman et al. (1962), and Hayes (1959).

While it is apparent that the specific translation of social-science techniques into forms suitable for a particular evaluation study involves research decisions based upon the special nature of the program under examination, there are nonetheless certain broad methodological questions common to most evaluation research. Furthermore, certain principles of evaluation research can be extracted from the rapidly growing experience of social scientists in applying their perspectives and methods to the evaluation of social-action programs. Such principles have obvious importance in highlighting and clarifying the methodological features of evaluation research and in providing practical, if limited, guidelines for conducting or appraising such research. The balance of this article will discuss certain, but by no means all, of these compelling methodological problems.

Methodological steps and principles

The process of evaluation has been codified into five major phases, each involving particular methodological problems and guiding principles (see Hyman et al. 1962). They are (1) the conceptualization and measurement of the objectives of the program and other unanticipated relevant outcomes; (2) formulation of a research design and the criteria for proof of effectiveness of the program, including consideration of control groups or alternatives to them; (3) the development and application of research procedures, including provisions for the estimation or reduction of errors in measurement; (4) problems of index construction and the proper evaluation of effectiveness; and (5) procedures for understanding and explaining the findings on effectiveness or ineffectiveness. Such a division of the process of evaluation is artificial, of course, in the sense that in practice the phases overlap and it is necessary for the researcher to give more or less constant consideration to all five steps. Nevertheless it provides a useful framework for examining and understanding the essential components of evaluation research.

Conceptualization. Each social-action program must be evaluated in terms of its particular goals. Therefore, evaluation research must begin with their identification and move toward their specification in terms of concepts that, in turn, can be translated into measurable indicators. All this may sound simple, perhaps routine, compared with the less structured situation facing social researchers engaged in formulating research problems for the oretical, explanatory, descriptive, or other kinds of basic research. But the apparent simplicity is deceptive, and in practice this phase of evaluation research repeatedly has proven to be both critical and difficult for social researchers working in such varied areas as mental health (U.S. Dept. of Health, Education & Welfare 1955), juvenile delinquency (Witmer & Tufts 1954), adult education (Evaluation Techniques 1955), and youth programs for citizenship training (Riecken 1952; Hyman et al. 1962), among others. As an example, Witmer and Tufts raise such questions about the meaning of the concept "delinquency prevention" as: What is to be prevented? Who is to be deterred? Are we talking only about "official" delinquency? Does prevention mean stopping misbehavior before it occurs? Does it mean reducing the frequency of misbehavior? Or does it mean reducing its severity?

Basic concepts and goals are often elusive, vague, unequal in importance to the program, and sometimes difficult to translate into operational terms. What is meant, for example, by such a goal as preparing young persons for "responsible citizenship"? In addition, the evaluator needs to consider possible effects of the program which were unanticipated by the action agency, finding clues from the records of past reactions to the program if it has been in operation prior to the evaluation, studies of similar programs, the social-science literature, and other sources. As an example, Carlson (1952) found that a mass-information campaign against venereal disease failed to increase public knowledge about these diseases; nevertheless, the campaign had the unanticipated effect of improving the morale of public health workers in the area, who in turn did a more effective job of combating the diseases. The anticipation of both planned and unplanned effects requires considerable time, effort, and imagination by the researcher prior to collecting evidence for the evaluation itself.

Research design.   The formulation of a research design for evaluation usually involves an attempt to approximate the ideal conditions of a controlled experiment, which measures the changes produced by a program by making comparisons of the dependent variables before and after the program and evaluating them against similar measurements on a control group that is not involved in the program. If the control group is initially similar to the group exposed to the social-action program, a condition achieved through judicious selection, matching, and randomization, then the researcher can use the changes in the control group as a criterion against which to estimate the degree to which changes in the experimental group were probably caused by the program under study. To illustrate, suppose that two equivalent groups of adults are selected for a study on the effects of a training film intended to impart certain information to the audience. The level of relevant information is measured in each group prior to the showing of the film; then one group sees the film while the other does not; finally, after some interval, information is again measured. Changes in the amount of information held by the experimental group cannot simply be attributed to the film; they may also reflect the influence of such factors in the situation

as exposure to other sources of information in the interim period, unreliability of the measuring instruments, maturation, and other factors extraneous to the program itself. But the control group presumably also experienced such nonprogrammatic factors, and therefore the researcher can subtract the amount of change in information demonstrated by it from the changes shown by the experimental group, thereby determining how much of the gross change in the latter group is due to the exclusive influence of the program.

So it is in the ideal case, such as might be achieved under laboratory conditions. In practice, however, evaluation research seldom permits such ideal conditions. A variety of practical problems requires alterations in the ideal design. As examples, suitable control groups cannot always be found, especially for social-action programs involving efforts at large-scale social change but also for smaller programs designed to influence volunteer participants; also ethical, administrative, or other considerations usually prevent the random assignment of certain persons to a control group that will be denied the treatment offered by the action programs.

In the face of such obstacles, certain methodologists have taken the position that a slavish insistence on the ideal control-group experimental research design is unwise and dysfunctional in evaluation research. Rather, they advocate the ingenious use of practical and reasonable alternatives to the classic design (see Hyman et al. 1962; and Campbell & Stanley 1963). Under certain conditions, for example, it is possible to estimate the amount of change that could have been caused by extraneous events, instability of measurements, and natural growth of participants in a program by examining the amount of change that occurred among participants in programs similar to the one being evaluated. Using such comparative studies as "quasi-control" groups permits an estimate of the relative effectiveness of the program under study, i.e., how much effect it has had over and above that achieved by another program and assorted extraneous factors, even though it is impossible to isolate the specific amount of change caused by the extraneous factors. Another procedure for estimating the influence of nonprogrammatic factors is to study the amount of change which occurs among a sample of the population under study during a period of time prior to the introduction of the action program, using certain of the ultimate participants as a kind of control upon themselves, so to speak. Replications of the evaluation study, when possible, also provide safeguards against attributing too much or too little effect to the program under study. Admittedly, all such practical alternatives to the controlled experimental design have serious limitations and must be used with judgment; the classic experimental design remains preferable whenever possible and serves as an ideal even when impractical. Nevertheless, such expedients have proven useful to evaluators and have permitted relatively rigorous evaluations to be conducted under conditions less perfect than those found in the laboratory.

Error control. Evaluation studies, like all social research, involve difficult problems in the selection of specific research procedures and the provision for estimating and reducing various sources of error, such as sampling bias, bias due to nonresponse, measurement errors arising in the questions asked or in recording of answers, deliberate deception, and interviewer bias. The practices employed to control such errors in evaluation research are similar to those used in other forms of social research, and no major innovations have been introduced.

Estimating effectiveness. To consider the fourth stage in evaluation, a distinction needs to be made between demonstrating the effects of an action program and estimating its effectiveness. Effectiveness refers to the extent to which the program achieves its goals, but the question of just how much effectiveness constitutes success and justifies the efforts of the program is unanswerable by scientific research. It remains a matter for judgment on the part of the program's sponsors, administrators, critics, or others, and the benefits, of course, must somehow be balanced against the costs involved. The problem is complicated further by the fact that most action programs have multiple goals, each of which may be achieved with varying degrees of success over time and among different subgroups of participants in the program. To date there is no general calculus for appraising the over-all net worth of a program.

Even if the evaluation limits itself to determining the success of a program in terms of each specific goal, however, it is necessary to introduce some indexes of effectiveness which add together the discrete effects within each of the program's goal areas. Technical problems of index and scale construction have been given considerable attention by methodologists concerned with various types of social research (see Lazarsfeld & Rosenberg 1955). But as yet there is no theory of index construction specifically appropriate to evaluation research. Steps have been taken in this direction, however, and the utility of several types of indexes has been tentatively explored (see Hyman et al. 1962). One type of difficulty, for example, arises

from the fact that the amount of change that an action program produces may vary from subgroup to subgroup and from topic to topic, depending upon how close to perfection each group was before the program began. Thus, an information program can influence relatively fewer persons among a subgroup in which, say, 60 per cent of the people are already informed about the topic than among another target group in which only 30 per cent are initially informed. An "effectiveness index" has been successfully employed to help solve the problem of weighting effectiveness in the light of such restricted ceilings for change (see Hovland et al. 1949; and Hyman et al. 1962). This index, which expresses actual change as a proportion of the maximum change that is possible given the initial position of a group on the variable under study, has proven to be especially useful in evaluating the *relative* effectiveness of different programs and the relative effectiveness of any particular program for different subgroups or on different variables.

Understanding effectiveness. In its final stage, evaluation research goes beyond the demonstration of a program's effects to seek information that will help to account for its successes and failures. The reasons for such additional inquiry may be either practical or theoretical.

Sponsors of successful programs may want to duplicate their action program at another time or under other circumstances, or the successful program may be considered as a model for action by others. Such emulation can be misguided and even dangerous without information about which aspects of the program were most important in bringing about the results, for which participants in the program, and under what conditions. Often it is neither possible nor necessary, however, to detect and measure the impact of each component of a social-action program. In this respect, as in others noted above, evaluation research differs from explanatory survey research, where specific stimuli are isolated, and from experimental designs, where isolated stimuli are introduced into the situation being studied. In evaluation research the independent variable, i.e., the program under study, is usually a complex set of activities no one of which can be separated from the others without changing the nature of the program itself. Hence, explanations of effectiveness are often given in terms of the contributions made by certain gross features of the program, for example, the total impact of didactic components versus social participation in a successful educational institution.

Gross as such comparisons must be, they nevertheless provide opportunities for testing specific hypotheses about social and individual change, thereby contributing to the refinement and growth of social science theories. It is important to remember, however, that such gains are of secondary concern to evaluation research, which has as its primary goal the objective measurement of the effectiveness of the program.

Certain forms of research design promise to yield valuable results both for the primary task of evaluation and its complementary goal of enlarging social knowledge. Among the most promising designs are those that allow for *comparative* evaluations of different social-action programs, *replication* of evaluations of the same program, and *longitudinal* studies of the long-range impact of programs. Comparative studies not only demonstrate the differential effectiveness of various forms of programs having similar aims but also provide a continuity in research which permits testing theories of change under a variety of circumstances. Replicative evaluations add to the confidence in the findings from the initial study and give further opportunity for exploring possible causes of change. Longitudinal evaluations permit the detection of effects that require a relatively long time to occur and allow an examination of the stability or loss of certain programmatic effects over time and under various natural conditions outside of the program's immediate control.

Viewed in this larger perspective, then, evaluation research deserves full recognition as a social science activity which will continue to expand. It provides excellent and ready-made opportunities to examine individuals, groups, and societies in the grip of major and minor forces for change. Its applications contribute not only to a science of social planning and a more rationally planned society but also to the perfection of social and psychological theories of change.

CHARLES R. WRIGHT

[*See also* EXPERIMENTAL DESIGN; SURVEY ANALYSIS.]

BIBLIOGRAPHY

CAMPBELL, DONALD T.; and STANLEY, J. S. 1963 Experimental and Quasi-experimental Designs for Research on Teaching. Pages 171–246 in Nathaniel L. Gage (editor), *Handbook of Research on Teaching*. Chicago: Rand McNally.

CARLSON, ROBERT O. 1952 The Influence of the Community and the Primary Group on the Reactions of Southern Negroes to Syphilis. Ph.D. dissertation, Columbia Univ.

Evaluation Techniques. 1955 *International Social Science Bulletin* 7:343–458.

HAYES, SAMUEL P. 1959 *Measuring the Results of Development Projects: A Manual for the Use of Field Workers*. Paris: UNESCO.

HOVLAND, CARL I.; LUMSDAINE, ARTHUR A.; and SHEFFIELD, FREDERICK D. 1949 *Experiments on Mass Communication*. Studies in Social Psychology in World War II, Vol. 3. Princeton Univ. Press.

HYMAN, HERBERT H.; and WRIGHT, CHARLES R. 1966 Evaluating Social Action Programs. Unpublished manuscript.

HYMAN, HERBERT H.; WRIGHT, CHARLES R.; and HOPKINS, TERENCE K. 1962 *Applications of Methods of Evaluation: Four Studies of the Encampment for Citizenship*. Berkeley: Univ. of California Press.

KLINEBERG, OTTO 1955 Introduction: The Problem of Evaluation. *International Social Science Bulletin* 7: 346–352.

LAZARSFELD, PAUL F.; and ROSENBERG, MORRIS (editors) 1955 *The Language of Social Research: A Reader in the Methodology of Social Research*. Glencoe, Ill.: Free Press.

McCORD, WILLIAM; McCORD, JOAN; and ZOLA, IRVING K. 1959 *Origins of Crime: A New Evaluation of the Cambridge–Somerville Youth Study*. New York: Columbia Univ. Press.

POWERS, EDWIN; and WITMER, HELEN L. 1951 *An Experiment in the Prevention of Delinquency*. New York: Columbia Univ. Press; Oxford Univ. Press.

RIECKEN, HENRY W. 1952 *The Volunteer Work Camp: A Psychological Evaluation*. Reading, Mass.: Addison-Wesley.

SELLTIZ, CLAIRE et al. (1959) 1962 *Research Methods in Social Relations*. New York: Holt.

U.S. DEPT. OF HEALTH, EDUCATION & WELFARE, NATIONAL INSTITUTES OF HEALTH 1955 *Evaluation in Mental Health: Review of Problem of Evaluating Mental Health Activities*. Washington: Government Printing Office.

WITMER, HELEN L.; and TUFTS, EDITH 1954 *The Effectiveness of Delinquency Prevention Programs*. Washington: Government Printing Office.

EVIDENCE, LEGAL

See LEGAL REASONING; PSYCHIATRY, *article on* FORENSIC PSYCHIATRY; STATISTICS AS LEGAL EVIDENCE.

EVOLUTION

I. THE CONCEPT OF EVOLUTION	*R. C. Lewontin*
II. PRIMATE EVOLUTION	*Elwyn L. Simons*
III. HUMAN EVOLUTION	*S. L. Washburn and Jane B. Lancaster*
IV. CULTURAL EVOLUTION	*Elman R. Service*
V. SOCIAL EVOLUTION	*Shmuel N. Eisenstadt*
VI. EVOLUTION AND BEHAVIOR	*Theodosius Dobzhansky*

I

THE CONCEPT OF EVOLUTION

There are few concepts that appear in the history of ideas that are common to many realms of thought in social and natural science and to philosophy in general. Evolution is such a concept, and its origin as a doctrine was deeply embedded in the social and economic conditions of the industrial West. Like all such world views, it embodies many principles, not all of which are admitted in its various uses, so that even those concerned with organic evolution are unable to agree on the essence of the idea of evolution.

Toward a definition

There is a hierarchy of principles in the evolutionary world view: *change, order, direction, progress,* and *perfectibility.* Evolutionary theories are distinguished by how many of these are successively included as essential. Some evolutionists include only change and order, others add direction, and some few, like Teilhard de Chardin, believe in perfectibility as well.

Change.   The idea of evolution, in its simplest form, is that the current state of a system is the result of a more or less continual change from its original state. The qualification that the change be continual, or at least frequent or regular, is an essential one and distinguishes evolutionary from static world views. For example, many opponents of organic evolution in the nineteenth century accepted the authenticity of fossils but regarded them as antediluvian, as evidence of one or several floods that caused a total replacement of the world's fauna. Diluvianism, like the closely related vulcanism, which postulated a series of inundations of the earth by lava, was a theory of catastrophic and irregular change. There is no fundamental difference between a theory of special creation that populates the world once with unchanging beings and one that populates it several times. They are both theories of special intervention of unique forces in an otherwise normally static system. The distinction between such a world view and an evolutionary one is important for our understanding of the social and economic origins of evolutionism.

Closely related to the idea that change is a characteristic of a system is the principle of *uniformitarianism,* the principle that the forces causing change are themselves unchangeable general laws that govern the system. Thus, geological evolution is seen as the result of processes of mountain-building, sedimentation, and erosion that have gone on throughout the history of the earth, at least since the time when liquid water was present in appreciable quantities. In like manner the processes of natural selection and mutation that can be seen occurring in the organic world today are assumed to have been the operative forces in all the past history of life. Moreover, since such forces are operating at present, it must be concluded that evolution is still going on. A com-

mitment to an evolutionary viewpoint represents a commitment to the instability of the present order as well as the past. In its simplest and irreducible form, evolutionism is the doctrine that change of state is an unvarying characteristic of natural systems and human institutions and that such change follows immutable laws.

Order.   While all evolutionary thought assumes continual change, there is some problem of distinguishing "real" change from a stasis that has only the appearance of change. Let us imagine a deck of cards being shuffled over and over again. In one sense it is obvious that the state of the deck is undergoing continual change, since the cards are being rearranged. But is the deck evolving? For Bergson and Whitehead it is not, because only alternate states of chaos are succeeding each other. *Plus ça change, plus c'est la même chose.* Out of this chaos some organization must appear to be true evolution, and the appearance of new organization, in the view of Whitehead and his followers, is the characteristic of an evolutionary process. In *Science and the Modern World* Whitehead says: "Evolution, on the materialistic theory, is reduced to the rôle of being another word for the description of changes of the external relations between portions of matter. There is nothing to evolve, because one set of external relations is as good as any other set of external relations. There can merely be change, purposeless and unprogressive" ([1925] 1960, p. 157).

But how can we know order as against chaos, except that we have a preconception of order and purpose? To return to the analogy of the deck of cards, if after repeated shuffling, the deck turned out to be grouped by suits, we would certainly say that order had been created. An even higher degree of order would be ascribed to the deck if, in addition, the cards within the suits were arranged in ascending sequence. After all, in poker a royal flush wins and a mixed hand loses. Yet, on any objective criterion a royal flush has exactly the same probability as any given mixed hand, and a completely ordered deck is not less probable than any other given arrangement. The appearance of order is the correspondence between the arrangement of objects and a preconception.

The demand that an evolutionary process create order, or at least that there be a change from one order to a different order, shows clearly that evolution, in this sense, is neither a fact nor a theory, but a way of organizing knowledge.

In contrast to Whitehead, some modern evolutionists are willing to accept any rearrangement of the parts of a structure as evolution. Thus

Dobzhansky (1937) defines organic evolution as "a change in the genetic composition of populations," and he speaks for most students of organic evolution when he says that there are no differences between organisms that cannot be accounted for in this way. But a change in the genetic composition of populations is not different in essence from a reshuffling of cards in that it is for the most part only a change in the relative frequency of elements, all of which are already present. The question of order marks the separation between the completely positivistic evolutionism inherent in Dobzhansky's definition and the creative evolutionism of Bergson and Teilhard. For, once it is proposed that order is the natural outcome of an evolutionary process, ideas of direction, progress, and perfectibility follow swiftly.

Direction. By direction in evolution we mean the concept that there is some natural linear order of states of the system and that an evolutionary process can be described as passing through successive states in this linear order. That is, evolution can be described by a line on a two-dimensional graph with time on one axis and some description of the system on the other. Moreover, this line is supposed to be always ascending or descending. But this description limits evolution to those attributes for which the human mind can make a sensible linear order. It must be possible to describe an evolutionary process as one in which something or other "tends to increase." Thus, it is insufficient to describe the evolution of human culture in terms of a change from hunting and gathering to agriculture, from agriculture to industry. These modes of organization must somehow be placed on a graded scale as, for example, the degree of division of labor (Durkheim) or the degree of complexity (Spencer).

The attempt to find the proper scale on which such a directionality can be measured has been a preoccupation of nonpositivist evolutionists and is the chief point at issue among them. *Complexity* is the scale most appealed to in organic and social evolution. For organic evolution it is supposed that modern organisms have a more complex structure than primitive ones, just as mammals are thought to be more complex than bacteria. Coupled with this idea of increase in structural complexity is the theory that the information content of modern organisms is greater than for past forms. Evolution is, on this theory, a process of accumulation of information about the environment in the complex structure of organisms. Finally, the supposed accumulation of information is thought to be a reversal of the second law of thermodynamics, which

prescribes an increase of entropy with time and thus an increase in the randomness of the universe. Evolutionists sometimes talk of the accumulation of "negentropy" in organic evolution, marking off life from the inorganic cosmos.

This view of organic evolution, which is supposed to apply not only to the structure of organisms but to the interrelations between organisms in the total biosphere, suffers from a number of serious difficulties. First, it would be difficult to show exactly in what sense mammals are more complex than bacteria. There is no doubt that there are many more kinds of tissues in mammals, but bacteria are capable of carrying out many synthetic reactions not possible for mammals. At the level of cell physiology and metabolism, bacteria—bringing a greater synthetic repertory—must be regarded as more complex. Moreover, even if we assume that modern organisms are more complex structurally than those of the Cambrian, no criterion of complexity can distinguish between mammals and bony fish, although there are 270 million years between the first appearance of each. Second, the relation between structural complexity and information about the environment is not perfectly clear. No one knows exactly how to measure the information contained in any organism. It might be done, as in the Shannon–Wiener solution, by regarding the genes as a code made up of three-letter words with a four-letter alphabet, corresponding to what is known about the molecular basis of heredity. If this is done, however, many invertebrates turn out to have more information than many vertebrates, and among bacteria there is a very great variation. The real difficulty is that the equation between complexity and information has been chiefly a metaphorical rather than an exact one.

Finally, the equation of information and complexity with a thermodynamic measure of entropy is based on a misunderstanding of the kinetic theory of gases. The second law of thermodynamics, in the early nineteenth century, represented the beginning of modern evolutionary cosmology. The term "entropy," used for a property of the universe that always increases, has the same meaning, etymologically, as "evolution." Originally, the increase in entropy only signified that different parts of a physical system became more and more alike in their energy content, so that less and less useful work could be obtained from an interaction between them. The kinetic theory of gases provided a picture of molecules moving and colliding, and thus explained the gross observation of heat and work. This, in turn, led to a new interpretation of the second law as guaranteeing that a collection of molecules in any region of space would eventually have the same distribution of kinetic energies as in any other region. Two confusions have arisen about the kinetic theory of gases that have had an important effect on evolutionary thinking. First, it is supposed that individual molecules will all have the same kinetic energy rather than that assemblages of molecules will have the same *statistical distribution* of energies. Second, there is a confusion of kinetic energy of molecules with general kinetic and potential energies, especially gravitational and electromagnetic potential. These two confusions give rise to an erroneously derived generalized second law stating that all the molecules in the universe will eventually be equally spaced out from each other. Given such a formless and orderless end, the evolution of life does indeed seem to go in the opposite direction.

The tendency to turn the second law of thermodynamics into a generalized evolutionary world view (with life as an exceptional countercurrent) has been further encouraged by confusion of thermodynamics with yet another evolutionary cosmology, the "expanding universe." According to this cosmogony, the material universe came into being on the order of 10 thousand million years ago in a small region of space, the matter exploded outward, and the material cosmos will continue to expand forever from this original point in space. A consequence of a fixed amount of matter occupying a larger and larger volume is that matter is becoming more thinly spread globally but not necessarily locally. The theory of the expanding universe does not demand, for example, that the earth break up and its pieces spread apart.

In its own way the theory of the expanding universe is another example of the search for directionality in evolutionary systems. More recently, Bondi, Gold, Hoyle, and others have given currency to nondirectional theories of the cosmos. One is a steady-state theory that allows for expansion but holds density everywhere in dynamic equilibrium by continual creation of new matter. The other is an oscillation theory, which postulates a cyclic expansion and contraction of the material cosmos.

Homeostasis, introduced by Cannon as a principle of physiology and evolution, is related to complexity. Homeostasis is the property of a system to hold constant certain of its elements despite external disturbing forces. What is held constant are those qualities of the system that are necessary for its maintenance, such as body temperature in a mammal or ionic strength of the blood. This property of homeostasis is then extended by evolutionists to include communities of organisms occupying different but coordinated positions in the natural economy. Thus, the relation between numbers and efficiency of carnivores that prey on herbivores and herbivores that crop the grass is thought to be stabilized by the process of evolution, so that fluctuation in the abundance of any of these organisms is compensated by changes in the others. The result is a stable community structure. The notion of *stability* is appealing to modern evolutionists, who see evolution as self-fulfilling, as a stabilization of life in a capricious universe. For the nineteenth century it was quite another matter. Is Nature

> "So careful of the type?" But no.
> From scarped cliff and quarried stone
> She cries, "A thousand types are gone:
> I care for nothing, all shall go."
> Tennyson, *In Memoriam*, Part 56, Stanza 1

Perhaps the only evolutionist doctrine that contains no important element of direction is evolutionary geology, which is entirely a cyclic theory. Mountain-building revolutions are followed by erosion, the formation of featureless peneplains, the deposition of sediments in the seas, followed by new uplift and new mountain-building. Of course, it is supposed that the final cooling of the earth's core will at last put an end to the cycle, but this cooling is the only vestige of directionality that is apparent. Geology remains, among the historical sciences, obdurately materialistic and positivist.

Progress. It is not always easy to differentiate evolutionist doctrines of simple direction from those with an element of progress. I distinguish them by the moral or, better, moralistic tone of progressivism, but moralism is sometimes well hidden. For example, the doctrine that homeostasis gives direction to evolution is sometimes arrived at because man is assumed a priori to be the measure of evolution, and it is fairly easy to make the case that man, the rational mammal, is most homeostatic. "L'Homme, seul paramètre absolu de l'Évolution" is even more anthropocentric than it seems at first sight, for Teilhard de Chardin (1956) is referring not simply to the history of life but *cosmic* evolution! But this is simply Whitehead brought up to date, Whitehead who, in *Modes of Thought*, divides occurrences in nature into six types: "The first type is human existence, body and mind. The second type includes all sorts of animal life, insects, the vertebrates, and other genera. . . . The third type includes all vegetable life. . . . The sixth type is composed of the happenings on an infinitesimal scale, disclosed by the minute analysis of modern physics" (1938, p. 214). Man leads all the rest. The shibboleths of progressivism are the superiority of man in the cosmos, industrial man in the world economy, and liberal democratic man in world society.

Spencer makes extensive use of the term "progress," but in a way that seems not to have a normative or moralistic overtone: "From the earliest traceable cosmical changes down to the latest results of civilization, we shall find that the transformation of the homogeneous into the heterogeneous is that in which progress essentially consists" ([1857] 1915, p. 10). In "Progress: Its Law and Cause," Spencer shows that this transformation has occurred in music, poetry, society, government, manufacturing, commerce, language, and so on. He cautions against normative definition of progress. "Leaving out of sight concomitants and beneficial consequences, let us ask what progress is in itself" (*ibid.*, p. 9). But this is a very curious question to ask, what progress is *in itself*, for does not progress, as opposed to simple change, imply a moral direction? What Spencer has done is to equate progress with change, to say that change, whatever its direction may turn out to be, is progressive by its very nature. We come again to that nineteenth-century belief that change is good, in Spencer's words, "a beneficent necessity."

Most modern students of natural evolution, both organic and social, have taken a step toward materialism in omitting the idea of progress from their systems. An exception is B. Rensch (1947), who distinguishes higher and lower forms of life and devotes a special category of evolutionary change, *anagenesis*, to evolution of higher from lower. While he includes under this rubric increases in stability, homeostasis, and complexity that are discussed here simply as directional rather than progressive, Rensch clearly regards man and especially human freedom as the highest and best product of evolution.

Perfectibility. With the exception of the philosopher Teilhard, modern evolutionism does not contain a utopian element. On the contrary, evolution is generally envisaged as an endless process with no particular perfect end or goal. There is some logical difficulty, however, in maintaining that evolution leads to greater homeostasis, greater cerebralization, greater adaptation, while ignoring the possibility of perfect homeostasis, complete cerebralization, or absolute adaptation. It is not at all obvious how homeostasis of individuals or communities can continue to increase forever. Nevertheless, this issue is generally ignored or, as in the case of Spencer, deliberately set aside. The single

important exception is in evolutionary economics, especially various utopian socialisms. Marxism, especially as interpreted by Lenin and Trotsky, is a straightforward progressivist, perfectionist evolutionary theory. A stage of primitive capitalist accumulation through exploitation of the workers and colonies enriches the society. This is accompanied by the bourgeois revolution that leads to liberal bourgeois democracy. In turn comes the proletarian revolution, proletarian democracy, a breakdown of national interests in the face of class interests, and a final total leveling of the class structure. In this utopian scheme there will still be division of labor, but the "entropy" of the social order will be at a maximum. The parallel is with thermodynamic evolution, which is also a leveling theory and is in contrast with those views of organic evolution that depend upon an increase in differentiation, complexity, storage of information, and a decrease in entropy.

Evolution and history

There are close parallels between the methods and statements of evolutionist doctrines in the natural sciences and the methods and statements of historiography. Geology, cosmology, and organic evolution are historical sciences in that they are descriptions of, and attempts to explain, past events in the light of present occurrences. The problems of making laws or lawlike statements about the past and prediction of the future are the same whether the focus of interest is human history or the history of all organic life. Karl Popper, in *The Poverty of Historicism* (1957), asks the question, "Can there be a *law* of evolution?" and answers, " 'No,' the search for the law of the 'unvarying order' in evolution cannot possibly fall within the scope of scientific method, whether in biology or in sociology. . . . The evolution of life on earth, or of human society, is a unique historical process" (pp. 107, 108).

The chief difficulty of the historical sciences is that they fail to meet what is widely accepted as the norm for a science, Popper's criterion of falsifiability. For Popper, scientific laws are universal statements ("All swans are black, all planets move in ellipses," etc.) and therefore are really prohibitions ("A white swan cannot be found, no planet moves in a circle," etc.). Such prohibitions provide a program for testability, for if one wishes to test the universal law about swans, he does not look for black ones but white ones. If a white swan is found, the law is disproved. A white swan is a *potential* falsifier of the law, and any statement that has no potential falsifier (any existentially quantified statement falls in this category) is *metaphysical* and ought to be excluded from a science.

The trouble with historical sciences like organic evolution is that they are almost entirely made up of existential rather than universal statements. We may take modern Darwinism as an example. It asserts that the organisms now living have evolved from ancestral organisms of a different nature and offers the fossil record as direct evidence. Moreover, it asserts that the mechanism of this change is embodied in three principles: (1) different individuals in a species have different morphologies, physiologies, behaviors, that is, there is variation; (2) there is a correlation between the form of the parents and the offspring, that is, the variation is heritable; and (3) different variants have different rates of survival and reproduction in different environments.

Let us now examine these assertions in the light of Popper's criterion. The evidence that evolution has in fact occurred is contained in the succession of fossils found in different geological strata. From the fossil record we can state with confidence that there are many kinds of animals and plants that, having once existed, no longer exist. But that statement of itself, far from being a universal statement, is an existential one; in fact it is a historical statement, exactly corresponding to the assertion that Napoleon once lived or that Martin Luther died on February 18, 1546, at Eisleben.

Can we push this observation further and say that *all* animals and plants in the fossil record are of a kind no longer represented? No, because that does not happen to be true. But can we at least make the much more interesting and important hypothesis that all kinds of animals and plants eventually will be supplanted by other forms? This also is not falsifiable and is really identical to the assertion that every man has his price. It says, in fact, that every species is mortal, that there exists a time in the future at which any given species will no longer exist. If statements about the universality of evolution are historicist rather than scientific, it still might be that the principles underlying the mechanism of evolution are falsifiable in explaining any particular case of evolution. But that is clearly not the case. The statement of natural selection is that there exists an environment—a combination of temperature, humidity, food, soil, competition of other forms—in which different variants will have different relative reproductive rates. But applied to the past or the future, such a statement has such vast explanatory and predictive power that it is empirically empty. To say that the dinosaurs became extinct because *some* change in environment caused their rate of reproduction to be lowered below the replacement point, or to say that certain amphibia gave rise to reptiles because some environment existed which favored heritable variation in that direction, is, by Popper's criterion, to say nothing.

An example of this difficulty is the argument of the selectionist in explaining the observed differences among populations of present-day organisms. Why are the frequencies of blood types different in different human races? The selectionist says these have arisen by natural selection, and even if no differential survival can presently be discovered (as none can), things used to be different and, at one time, the different races lived in such different environments that they were differentially selected. Such an argument bears more than a little similarity to the claim of Hegel that one cannot act on principles deduced from history, because "each period is involved in such peculiar circumstances, exhibits a condition of things so strictly idiosyncratic, that its conduct must be regulated by considerations connected with itself, and itself alone."

Both historical explanation and evolutionary sciences can be concerned only with offering *sufficient* explanations for past events and with prescribing *possible* future events on the basis of the observation of present processes.

Evolutionism—social and economic matrix

While there is no doubt that the publication of Darwin's *On the Origin of Species* (1859) led to an almost immediate explosion of evolutionary thought, it was only the percussion cap for a charge already set. Because a theory of organic evolution touched upon man's origin and presented a materialistic challenge to his preordained primacy in the universe, it was bound to excite great interest. Nevertheless, the *Origin of Species* appeared in the middle of a period of rampant evolutionism and radical political and social change. It served as the issue over which the battle between stasis and change could be fought, a battle for the final supremacy of a world view that had been making steady gains since the beginning of the eighteenth century.

Darwin was the inheritor, not the creator, of the general preoccupation with evolutionism. This is made clear by Spencer in his *Principles of Biology* (1864–1867), when he argues that one of the chief evidences for organic evolution is that, after all, everything else evolves.

It is now universally admitted by philologists, that languages, instead of being artificially or supernaturally formed, have been developed. And the histories of religion, of philosophy, of science, of the fine arts, of the industrial arts show that these have passed through stages. . . . If, then, the recognition of evolution as the law of many diverse orders of phenomena, has been spreading, may we not say that there thence arises the probability that evolution will be recognized as the law of the phenomena we are considering? ([1857] 1915, pp. 432–433)

The theory of organic evolution will be in its proper historical perspective if it is remembered that evolutionary cosmology had been founded in Kant's *Metaphysical Foundations of Natural Science* of 1786 and in Laplace's nebular hypothesis of 1796. At about the same time, Hutton was forming modern geology by his rejection of the catastrophic theories of the origin of geological formations and his introduction of the principle of uniformitarianism. Although the term "entropy" was not introduced until 1865 by Clausius, the second law of thermodynamics was formulated by Sadi Carnot thirty years earlier. By the time of the publication of the *Origin of Species*, the physical sciences were already thoroughly evolutionist in outlook. Moreover, the fact of the evolution of living forms, although not a mechanism for that evolution, was accepted widely in scientific and literary circles. Darwin's grandfather, Erasmus Darwin, in the *Temple of Nature* (1803, p. 3) invokes the Muse to say "How rose from elemental strife, organic forms, and kindled into life." And his Muse reports that even "imperious man, who rules the bestial crowd, . . . arose from rudiments of form and sense" (p. 28). Less romantic students of natural history like Buffon and especially Lamarck, had, by the beginning of the nineteenth century, fully developed theories of the transformation of species. Even Diderot in 1769 in *Le rêve de d'Alembert* asks: "Qui scait les races d'animaux qui nous ont precedes? Qui scait les races d'animaux qui succederont aux notres? *Tout change, tout passe, il n'y a que le tout qui reste*" ([1830] 1951, p. 56, my italics). Seventy years later we hear the echo in Tennyson: "The old order changeth, yielding place to new" ("Morte d'Arthur," l. 408).

It is often thought obvious that scientific discovery influences the direction of social and economic change, or at least its rate. But what must be even more true is that social and economic world views must permeate science. No appeal to a *Zeitgeist* is implied by such a relationship, for the meaning of *Zeitgeist* is that science and other social activities respond equally to some spirit of the age whose source and power are unknown. To appeal to *Zeitgeist* is to reject any legitimate theory of historical causation. On the other hand, there is nothing mystical about the way in which notions of cause and effect, choice and chance, determinacy and freedom, spread from one science to another. Equally, it is entirely within the normal picture of historical causation that general social attitudes and economic relationships between social classes should have a profound effect upon the acceptability and apparent reasonableness of scientific hypotheses. Science is, after all, a social activity.

Prior to the eighteenth century, European social systems were characterized by a determinist world view. A man was born to his estate and occupied it by divine providence. Fixity and static stability were the mark of society, and radical changes in position could occur only as *exceptional* withdrawals or extensions of divine grace. Although Charles I was king of England *Dei gratia*, he could be deposed because, as Cromwell said, divine grace had been removed from him. The fact of his severed head was sufficient proof of that. Occasionally a man might rise from low estate to be the counselor of kings, but again only an extraordinary grace made this possible. Species were fixed as was the position of the earth in the universe. Galileo's heresy was not that the earth was not at the center of the cosmos but that *it moved*. Men reason by analogy from the condition of their lives to the condition of the universe, and a static society could hardly believe in a dynamic cosmos.

In the eighteenth century a change became felt in the condition of society as the influence of the industrial revolution spread. Social mobility became more common, and classes of parvenus acquired political and social power.

"And it is a remarkable example of the confusion into which the present age has fallen" . . . says Sir Leicester, . . . "that Mrs. Rouncewell's son has been invited to go into Parliament."
Miss Volumnia utters a little sharp scream. . . . "Good gracious, what is the man?"
"He is called, I believe—an—Ironmaster."
Charles Dickens, *Bleak House*, 1853

The phase of bourgeois revolution had begun and from it developed bourgeois revolutionary science. As change became the rule and characteristic of society, catastrophism lost ground in natural science, and a uniformitarian principle of change took its place. It is surely no coincidence that Josiah Wedgwood, who began as a potter's apprentice and ended as one of the great eighteenth-century magnates, was Charles Darwin's maternal grandfather.

Darwin's paternal grandfather, Erasmus, belonged to the circle of new Midland industralists: James Watt, James Keir, Matthew Boulton, and, of course, Wedgwood. Although from the middle class, Erasmus was a self-made man and his son, Robert (Charles's father), emulated him by accepting 40 pounds of his father's money and building it into a respectable fortune with no further aid.

The bourgeois revolution not only established change as the characteristic element of the cosmos but added direction and progress as well. A world in which a man could rise from humble origins must have seemed, to him at least, a good world. Change per se was a moral quality. In this light, Spencer's assertion that change *is* progress is not surprising. Moreover, for those still rising or hopeful of improvement, there is a vested interest in the perpetuity of change, in a uniformitarian principle of replacement of the old by the new.

The bourgeois revolution reached its peak in England in the Reform Bill of 1832 based on Bentham's principle of the "greatest happiness for the greatest number," while on the Continent it took the more violent form of the revolutions of 1848. By the time Darwin published the *Origin of Species*, the ascent of the middle classes was complete and the supremacy of change and progress established in all the natural sciences except biology. The furor against Darwinism was only the last hopeless struggle of an already fatally wounded adversary. It is, of course, true that the principle of natural selection, converted by Spencer to the "survival of the fittest," was used in the last half of the nineteenth century as a justification for laissez-faire practices. But it was only the borrowing of a metaphor to further justify a system already in full operation. It would be quite wrong to propose that Darwinism was an effective agent promoting unlimited economic competition.

Like all revolutions the bourgeois revolution gave way slowly to a period of consolidation, a period in which we still find ourselves. Once the new classes had gained power, it was clearly to their advantage to prevent the revolution from going further. The static hereditary society could hardly be reconstituted, but in its place a system of dynamic stability was erected. Change and social mobility are still accepted as characteristic of society, but it is a running-in-place rather than an overturn of the existing order. Liberal democracy of the twentieth century has a vested interest in maintaining the world social order but allowing individuals, on the basis of relative competitive ability, to find their own place in the social structure.

It is not remarkable, then, that evolutionary theories of the twentieth century are marked by a concern for equilibrium condition and dynamic stability, a playing down of progressivist and perfectionist elements, and a general reliance on the principle that *plus ça change, plus c'est la même chose*. In cosmogony there has been the rise of the steady-state theory of perpetual creation and also of the cyclic expansion–contraction model. Both are characterized by constant movement and change, but neither allows that the universe is going anywhere in particular. In thermodynamics and statistical mechanics there has been emphasis on the local rather than global nature of the law of increase of entropy. It is now admitted that entropy may decrease in other parts of the universe or at other times and that a global statement of the second law of thermodynamics may be too strong. In the realm of organic evolution, progressivism has been entirely abandoned except for a few metaphysical writers. The direction in which evolution is supposed to lead, when a direction is admitted, is that of greater complexity and greater integration leading to greater *stability*. Modern students of evolution are preoccupied with dynamic stability and equilibrium in a global sense. The technical literature of evolutionary genetics is filled with reference to and studies of stable equilibria. This preoccupation would have seemed strange to the evolutionists of the nineteenth century, who saw, reflected in the process of organic evolution, the tendency toward a better world. The evolutionist of the twentieth century presumably sees, in his view of evolution, "the best of all possible worlds."

R. C. LEWONTIN

BIBLIOGRAPHY

BERGSON, HENRI (1907) 1944 *Creative Evolution*. New York: Modern Library. → First published in French.

DARWIN, CHARLES (1859) 1964 *On the Origin of Species*. Cambridge, Mass.: Harvard Univ. Press.

DARWIN, ERASMUS 1803 *Temple of Nature: Or, the Origin of Society; a Poem With Philosophical Notes*. London: Johnson.

DIDEROT, DENIS (1830) 1951 *Le rêve de d'Alembert, Entretien entre d'Alembert et Diderot, et suite de l'entretien*. Edited by Paul Vernière. Paris: Didier. → Written in 1769, but first published in 1830.

DOBZHANSKY, THEODOSIUS G. (1937) 1951 *Genetics and the Origin of Species*. 3d ed., rev. New York: Columbia Univ. Press.

MAYR, ERNST 1963 *Animal Species and Evolution*. Cambridge, Mass.: Belknap Press.

POPPER, KARL R. 1957 *The Poverty of Historicism*. Boston: Beacon. → A paperback edition was published in 1964 by Harper.

RENSCH, BERNHARD (1947) 1960 *Evolution Above the Species Level*. New York: Columbia Univ. Press. → First published as *Neuere Probleme der Abstammungslehre: Die transspezifische Evolution*.

SPENCER, HERBERT (1857) 1915 Progress: Its Law and Cause. Volume 1, pages 8–62 in Herbert Spencer, *Essays: Scientific, Political, and Speculative.* New York: Appleton. → First published in the *Westminster Review.*

SPENCER, HERBERT (1864–1867) 1914 *The Principles of Biology.* 2 vols. New York: Appleton.

TEILHARD DE CHARDIN, PIERRE (1956) 1963 *La place de l'homme dans la nature: Le groupe zoologique humain.* Paris: Éditions du Seuil. → First published as *Le groupe zoologique humain: Structure et directions évolutives.*

WHITEHEAD, ALFRED NORTH (1925) 1960 *Science and the Modern World.* New York: Macmillan.

WHITEHEAD, ALFRED NORTH 1934 *Nature and Life.* Univ. of Chicago Press.

WHITEHEAD, ALFRED NORTH 1938 *Modes of Thought.* New York: Macmillan. → Lectures delivered between 1934 and 1938. A paperback edition was published in 1958 by Capricorn.

II

PRIMATE EVOLUTION

When Darwin published the *Origin of Species* in 1859, only a handful of fossil primates had been found and recognized as such. But during the last three decades of the nineteenth century a considerable series of fossil primates of Tertiary age were recovered in Europe and the Americas. The earliest scholarly attempts to analyze the course of primate evolution from the evidence of these fossils were made by Schlosser in Munich (1887), by Osborn in New York (1902), and by Wortman at Yale (1903–1904). Among the earliest monographic studies of early Tertiary primates were those of William K. Gregory of the American Museum of Natural History, who best summarized his views on primate evolution in a detailed review of the North American lemurlike primate *Notharctus* (1920). Only a little earlier Stehlin (1912–1916) at Basel had published a complementary review of European Eocene prosimians.

Inadequacies of material and methods. There have been several factors holding back full analysis of the course of primate evolution. A major problem results from their presumed early emergence in the tropical forests of the equatorial zones. Because Tertiary vertebrate fossils from these regions are poorly known, the early history of primates remains relatively obscure. Primates of the past, like those of today, were apparently restricted to relatively warm climates, often to tropical forests, and prosimian remains dating after warm, early Tertiary times are not generally found in the northern continents. Exploration for sites in the tropics where Tertiary land vertebrate fossils do occur is being actively carried out today, and it is from these paleontologically little-known regions that most important future additions to knowledge of primate evolution may be expected.

Most of the primate fossils from the early Tertiary (Paleocene and Eocene epochs) consequently are not found in the equatorial regions, where presumably the mainstream of primate evolution has always been located. Therefore, reconstruction of primate history must, at present, be extrapolated in part from fossil evidence from marginal areas. This gap in knowledge of ancient tropical faunas is somewhat lessened because we know that many extinct primates were wide-ranging species and that the higher Old World primates, particularly apes and pre-men, never diversified into a host of separate lineages, as did some groups of mammals, such as bats and rodents.

Thus, differentiation of the main groups and their interrelationships can be reasonably well understood, even from the occasional sampling typical of our imperfect paleontological finds. This is particularly true for the late Tertiary relatives and ancestors of man. However, two theories, originating outside the realm of paleontological evidence, appear to have been responsible for creating a contrary impression. Although the outlook is seldom specifically articulated, some students seem to believe that in order to produce the brain capacities of modern man there must have been many competing early hominid species. With this goes the assumption that the mental capacities of apes and those presumed for pre-men would have made them near masters of their environment and, therefore, so successful that many species would have arisen. These views, together with an overeagerness to create new species and genera, led some early anthropologists and a few modern students to the false conclusion that a great diversity of fossil apes and prehuman species once existed. A confusing welter of ill-founded names exists in the literature on such extinct primates. Those applied to Tertiary apes and hominids have recently been revised by Simons and Pilbeam (1965). Although over a thousand individual specimens of extinct great apes (pongids) and early hominids are now known from European, Asian, and African Miocene–Pleistocene deposits, only a few genera, *Pliopithecus, Oreopithecus, Dryopithecus, Ramapithecus,* and *Gigantopithecus,* can be shown to be distinct and valid. Thus, the main types of close fossil relatives and forerunners of man (Hominoidea) that can convincingly be demonstrated to have existed in the past are about the same in number as the genera of this group that exist today—*Hylobates* (gibbon), *Symphalangus* (siamang), *Pan* (chimpanzee), *Pongo* (orangutan), *Gorilla* (gorilla), *Homo* (man).

As a consequence of the foregoing problems of approach, the study of primate evolution has been hampered. First, the early history of primates is obscured by inadequate knowledge of equatorial vertebrate faunas; and second, understanding of the later history of the particular group that included man's ancestors has been confounded by the tendency to proliferate invalid genera and species.

Origin of primates

Undoubted primates first appear in the fossil record in North American deposits of early Paleocene age, which are more than sixty million years old. By middle Paleocene, the order had already diversified into three or four different main groups, or families. This would suggest that the initial separation of the order from primitive, insectivore-like stock was considerably earlier, perhaps in the late Cretaceous. Indeed, a species possibly primate, but based only on one tooth, has been reported from late Cretaceous beds in Montana.

The best-known primates of Paleocene times appear to represent specialized side branches, which did not long survive the beginning of the Eocene epoch. Although not directly ancestral, these early species do indicate the starting point of the basic primate arboreal adaptation and give evidence of the gradual transition from nonprimate to primate. It may be that some of the less completely known American Paleocene primates, such as *Palaechthon* and *Plesiolestes,* will eventually prove to be near the ancestry of one or more of the primate families of initial early Eocene appearance.

Origin of major surviving groups

Lemurs. At the beginning of the Eocene, prosimians of lemurlike and tarsierlike aspect appear, nearly simultaneously, in the vertebrate assemblages of Europe and North America but are as yet unknown elsewhere. Three major sorts of primates can be characterized.

The most generalized of these early Eocene prosimians are the loosely defined Adapidae, including such well-known forms as *Pelycodus,* and later *Notharctus* and *Smilodectes* in North America, and *Adapis* in Europe. Species of these genera, together with allied forms, apparently did not advance during the Eocene beyond the "lemuroid" condition represented today by the Malagasy lemurs, whom they resemble both in limb-bone structure and in the structure of the ear region of the skull. However, dental patterns in notharctines and adapines do not show trends evolving toward those of modern lemurs; this appears to indicate that known Eocene species of Adapidae were not directly ancestral to the living varieties of lemurs. On the other hand, the family Adapidae—now rather broadly defined—could well represent the family from which modern lemurs and possibly the lorises differentiated (Simons 1962a).

How and when the true lemurs reached their present limited range of distribution in the island of Madagascar is a most intriguing and nearly insoluble problem on the basis of present evidence. If their introduction to this island was by way of the African continent, it might be expected that some evidence of true lemurs would by now have been recovered from the Egyptian Oligocene or east African Miocene deposits, both of which contain warm-climate forest faunas. Although small, evidently arboreal primates have been found in some abundance in these deposits in Egypt and east Africa, none show any significant similarities to the Malagasy lemurs. On the other hand, similarities between lorises and two European late-Eocene primates, *Pronycticebus* and *Anchomomys,* at present classified as Adapinae, suggest that the introduction of this group into Africa could have been by way of Europe.

Tarsiers. Enough is now known of the craniology and dentition of the so-called "tarsioid" primates to demonstrate the falsehood of the extravagant opinion of Wood-Jones that Hominidae are to be derived directly from *Tarsius*-like forms through an ancestral line not shared by the Old World apes and monkeys. What is perhaps more significant is that the Eocene tarsioids so far discovered could not have given rise to the common stem of monkeys, apes, or men either, for they possess noncatarrhine specializations, and all had apparently lost one pair of lower incisors. All surviving members of Anthropoidea have retained these teeth. Nevertheless, these early tarsioids are of great interest because they presumably represent the general level of organization the unknown forerunners of the living higher primates must have reached as far back as the beginning of the Eocene epoch.

The first Anthropoidea. Another major group of primates appeared in the early Eocene, in Europe, Asia, and North America, and is, with one or two exceptions, restricted in temporal range to this epoch. (Gazin 1958 has reviewed the distribution of middle-Eocene members of this family, together with other contemporary North American primates.) Collectively, members of Omomyidae show greater resemblances to Anthropoidea than do other early prosimians. They could well represent the taxon from which all true Anthropoidea differentiated, a probability that is also sound zoogeographically, in view of their Holarctic distribution. Certainty on this point must wait, however, until better knowledge of cranial and postcranial anatomy is available for members of this family. Partial evidence, derived mainly from remains of a species of the North American middle-Eocene omomyid genus *Hemiacodon gracilis*, shows that this species cannot be regarded as "tarsioid" postcranially (Simpson 1940). This observation, in turn, implies that Anthropoidea in its earliest differentiation may not have passed through a definably tarsioid grade of organization. Rather, the anatomy of both Eocene *Necrolemur* and Holocene *Tarsius* clearly indicates that so-called "tarsioids" and the Anthropoidea probably originated in the same segment of early Prosimii. Although serious gaps in the geologic record of primates prevent any very definite attachment of early Tertiary species successions to those of the later Cenozoic, it is likely that some known Paleocene and Eocene types, at least at the generic level, do pertain to the ancestry of living forms. Because climates were much more equable throughout the early Tertiary, with regions as far north as Montana and England supporting a subtropical flora, we can suppose that many of these Paleocene–Eocene genera contained species having a broad north–south range of distribution. Some of the species we now know from northern areas must have had very close allies in the unknown southern faunas. An example of this sort of distribution is provided by one of the large Eocene herbivores. Skulls and jaws of species of the Wasatch pantodont genus *Coryphodon* found in the Big Bend region of Texas, near the Mexican border, cannot be distinguished from remains of this animal found in northern Wyoming. This represents a north–south separation of about one thousand miles; if paleontological information on Wasatch faunas were available from Canada to Guatemala, this distribution could probably be extended even farther. Nevertheless, as with most attempts to trace phyletic lineages in given groups of fossils, the need to discover a great many more connecting links remains, and the search in the more nearly equatorial regions for early Cenozoic faunas containing primates is one of our major objectives.

For the Oligocene two sets of primate data from equatorial regions have become available through recent research projects.

The first of these projects has provided new evidence on the question of differentiation of cercopithecoid monkeys and hominoids. Discoveries made in Oligocene deposits in Egypt between 1961 and 1966 by Yale expeditions under the writer's direction have added new data on the nature of the initial appearance of these two superfamilies. A jaw fragment of a new small primate, *Oligopithecus savagei* (Simons 1962*b*), shows the typical lower dental formula of Miocene–Holocene Old World Anthropoidea, in combination with what are the most primitively constituted lower molars known in this suborder. Premolar heteromorphy and slightly bilophodont molars, plus certain other characters, suggest relationships, on the one hand, to Eocene Omomyidae, and on the other, to Miocene–Holocene cercopithecoids. Further finds of this small mammal could strengthen the possibility, which now rests almost entirely on the evidence of this single fragmentary jaw, that cercopithecoids arose from Old World omomyids. Miocene monkeys are known from deposits in Egypt and east Africa. The early history of Old World monkeys remains very poorly understood, and much of the known earliest material has not been described.

The emergence of Hominoidea

To date no significant information whatever on upper tooth structure of earliest (Eocene–Oligocene) African or Eurasian Anthropoidea has been published. This has been a serious gap in our knowledge because upper premolars and molars, being somewhat more complex than lower-cheek teeth, allow for more accurate appraisal of taxonomic affinity. Restudy of the previously poorly known upper molars of *Pondaungia cotteri* from the late Eocene of Burma, together with discovery by the recent Yale expeditions of several partial upper dentitions of *Apidium* and of isolated upper teeth of *Aegyptopithecus* and *Parapithecus*, has greatly added to the data available for consideration of the prosimian sources of the higher primates of the Eastern Hemisphere. Briefly, the dental evidence of these three early species bears on the crucial point of emergence of Hominoidea from Prosimii: the upper molars of *Apidium* and *Pondaungia* show the three primary cusps of the trigon unconnected by ridges. The hypocone is large, and a pitted lingual cingulum is usually present. In both these genera several small accessory cusps occur in the trigon between the three main cusps. In their over-all upper molar morphology, species of these two genera equally resemble prosimians and higher primates. Cheek teeth of *Apidium*, particularly, also show similarities to those of *Oreopithecus*. This may be due to retention of a comparatively primitive molar cusp pattern in the otherwise advanced latter hominoid. Upper molars of *Propliopithecus*, on the other hand, show the typical pattern characteristic of much later apes, near men, and men. However, the cingulum on the inner side of the upper molars is large, which strengthens the view that this is a primitive character of ape dentitions.

Pondaungia cotteri was described by Pilgrim (1927). This specimen was recovered from the Pondaung sandstone of Burma together with a small mammal fauna, which indicates a late Eocene age for this as well as for another primate, *Amphipithecus*. Comparisons based primarily on the anthracotheres of the Pondaung sandstone and those of the Fayum early Oligocene of Egypt suggest that the Burmese fossils may be earlier, but the question is by no means definitely settled. At present it seems best to regard *Amphipithecus* and *Pondaungia* as of late Eocene age, and since both appear to be hominoids, this indicates the upper limit of differentiation for this major group of primates. As Colbert (1937) has already pointed out for *Amphipithecus*, both appear to show close ties with Pongidae. Tentative assignment of *Amphipithecus* and *Pondaungia* to this family does not seem questionable on grounds of their antiquity, inasmuch as a considerable number of presently existing mammalian families have now been traced back to the late Eocene.

Pilgrim's illustrations and comments on *Pondaungia* left much to be desired, and in fact, on the basis of the information he provided, it was hardly possible to accept the species as belonging to the primates. As he mentioned, part of the source of his weak case lay in the fact that a web-like erosion of the enamel of the lower teeth in the type of *Pondaungia* had obscured their crown patterns. He supposed this to be also the case with the upper molars. Microscopic examination of this material indicates that, while the lower molars do appear to have suffered some erosive damage, the crenulations on the upper teeth represent the natural surface except in one or two broken areas. This sort of crenulation is not unusual among primates, being of frequent occurrence in Eocene Omomyidae and in Miocene–Holocene apes. In conclusion, these features of the upper molars, together with some distinguishable details of the lower teeth and mandibles, suggest an assignment to the Pongidae. Indeed *Pondaungia* may not be far from the direct ancestry of such forms as *Propliopithecus* and its less well-known allies from the Oligocene of Egypt. A less likely possibility is that *Pondaungia* is an advanced omomyid primate with teeth paralleling those of early pongids.

All finds of primates from the Old World Oligocene are distributed throughout some six or seven hundred feet of mainly continental sediments of the Qatrani formation, Fayum province, Egypt—generally regarded as being of early Oligocene age. The classic finds of *Parapithecus, Propliopithecus,* and *Moeripithecus* are from the lower part of this series, in the "Fossil Wood Zone," while the type of *Apidium* came from about five hundred feet higher. The new species of *Apidium* and one of *Propliopithecus* have been found stratigraphically between the two earlier known levels. There are then three primate-yielding levels, of unknown age separation. Enough time had elapsed between their successive depositions, however, to bring about evolutionary changes among the respective primate lineages represented. In December 1963 the Yale expedition recovered from the upper Fayum deposits two new genera and species of primates. One of these, *Aegyptopithecus,* appears to be a good candidate for the ancestry of *Dryopithecus,* of Miocene–Pliocene age, and was possibly a forerunner of all subsequent apes. The second new find, *Aeolopithecus,* resembles gibbons, living and fossil.

Turning to a consideration of primates of the Miocene epoch, which began perhaps about 25 million years ago, there is more abundant information. From South American deposits, located mainly in Argentina and Colombia, a series of monkey species is known. These have most recently been discussed by Stirton (1951). At least partial skulls and jaws are known for species of three genera, *Homunculus, Dolicocebus,* and *Cebupithecia.* These materials show that by Miocene times South American monkeys were structured much as they are today, and therefore they do not provide much evidence as to the origins of this group. Old World monkeys of Miocene age are known only from sites in east Africa and Egypt. The east African Miocene monkey has not yet been named, but that from Egypt was given the rather unfortunate generic name of *Prohylobates* by Fourtau (Egypt 1918).

Broadly contemporary with these monkeys are species of the *Dryopithecus* group of apes (including subgenera *Sivapithecus* and *Proconsul*), which are apparently close to the ancestry of the living African apes. Also represented in Miocene faunas of Europe and Africa are species of *Pliopithecus,* an ancient relative of the present-day gibbons and siamangs of southeast Asia.

Toward the end of the Miocene epoch in Eurasia and Africa, perhaps about fourteen million years ago, species of *Dryopithecus* are contemporary with the oldest undoubtedly manlike primate, *Ramapithecus punjabicus.* Originally discovered in the Siwalik Hills of north India in beds of Miocene–Pliocene age, this species was named by Pilgrim in 1910, but he did not recognize that it belonged to a major new variety of primate and so considered it a species of *Dryopithecus*. Lewis (1934) defined the genus *Ramapithecus*, to which Pilgrim's species has subsequently proved to belong. Lewis initially pointed out that *Ramapithecus* has many manlike features in the upper tooth series. Thus, it can reasonably be placed in Hominidae, the taxonomic family of man (Simons 1963; 1964). To date, however, only parts of upper and lower jaws of this animal have been found. Apparently *Ramapithecus* was a successful and wide-ranging primate. Outside north India, teeth and jaws just like those of the *Ramapithecus punjabicus* have been found at Fort Ternan in Kenya, east Africa; in Yunnan, China; and just possibly in Europe.

Apart from the fact that facial displays and diet in *Ramapithecus* must have been more similar to that of true man than to that of the apes (in view of incisor, canine, and premolar reduction—relative to cheek teeth) little can be inferred about this earliest hominid. It cannot be called man or human, because there is no evidence that *R. punjabicus* manufactured tools. Moreover, nothing is known of its brain size and limb or body skeleton. After this we know little of fossil primates until the earlier Pleistocene.

The Pleistocene and hominid evolution

The Pleistocene was a time of rapid hominid evolution, during which toolmaking first appeared among the ancestors of modern man. In 1925 Dart described an infant skull that he named *Australopithecus africanus*. In spite of the name, which means "African southern ape," Dart recognized *Australopithecus* to be a hominid belonging to the same taxonomic family as modern man, *Homo sapiens*. Nevertheless, his views were not generally accepted until a large number of fossil men or near men of similar age and structural type were recovered by Dart, Broom, and Robinson in south Africa.

More recently, *Australopithecus* has apparently been identified in Java and in north and east African deposits. The proposed name *Homo habilis*, recently coined by Leakey and his associates (1964) on the basis of specimens from Olduvai Gorge in Tanganyika, covers mixed materials, some assignable to the prior south African species *Australopithecus africanus* and some to *Telanthropus capensis* and to *Homo erectus*. In the view of many students (Campbell 1964a), even the first two species are not distinguishable, both belonging to the same small and gracile variety of early man. In addition to the species *A. africanus*, there is a large and more specialized early hominid form in east and south Africa, which should most correctly be called *Australopithecus robustus*. Both of these species appear to have been habitual bipeds; the postcranial skeletons are similar to that of *Homo sapiens* and little like those of apes. Their jaws and teeth, although relatively large, are strongly reminiscent of teeth of later and better-known fossil men. However, in both species, known brain size was apparently little more than a third that of the average present-day *Homo sapiens*. The small brain size initially caused many students to place *Australopithecus* close to or with the apes. This early and erroneous placement of *Australopithecus* has continued to affect balanced understanding of their relationship to living man. Several poorly known or juvenile *Australopithecus* specimens have been made the "types" of new taxa, said to be more advanced and more like *Homo sapiens*. Both *Telanthropus capensis* and *Homo habilis* fall in this category. As Campbell (1964b) demonstrates, they have not been shown to be different enough from each other or from members of *Australopithecus africanus* to warrant species identification.

Clarification of these taxonomic problems is crucial to discussion of the course of the mainstream of the early evolution of man and is one of the prime areas for future advance in this science. Definition and delineation of species populations is requisite to understanding of the ancestral lineage of modern man. Unfortunately, most anthropologists and anatomists who have been the namers of fossil men and near men were not adequately trained to define taxa in harmony with the concepts of modern systematics and population genetics. That these inadequacies are still leading to confusion in understanding of human evolution was confirmed in the technically incorrect diagnosis of *Homo habilis*. Such neglect of the new taxonomy and systematics has seriously affected understanding of primate and human history. In all discussion of earliest men and pre-men, mammalian taxonomy is an area that needs much more sober scientific attention than it has been given so far.

ELWYN L. SIMONS

BIBLIOGRAPHY

CAMPBELL, BERNARD G. 1964a Just Another "Man-ape"? *Discovery* 25, no. 6:37–38.

CAMPBELL, BERNARD G. 1964b Science and Human Evolution. *Nature* 203:448–451.

CLARK, WILFRID E. LEGROS (1955) 1964 *The Fossil Evidence for Human Evolution*. Rev. ed. Univ. of Chicago Press.

CLARK, WILFRID E. LeGROS 1960 *The Antecedents of Man.* Chicago: Quadrangle Books.

COLBERT, EDWIN H. 1937 A New Primate From the Upper Eocene Pondaung Formation of Burma. *American Museum of Natural History Novitates* 951:1–18.

EGYPT, SURVEY DEPARTMENT (1918) 1920 *Contribution à l'étude des vertébrés miocènes de l'Égypte,* by René Fourtau. Cairo: Government Press.

GAZIN, C. LEWIS 1958 *A Review of the Middle and Upper Eocene Primates of North America.* Smithsonian Miscellaneous Collections, Vol. 136. Washington: The Institution.

GREGORY, WILLIAM K. 1920 On the Structure and Relations of *Notharctus,* an American Eocene Primate. American Museum of Natural History, *Memoirs* New Series 3:49–243.

GREGORY, WILLIAM K. 1922 *The Origin and Evolution of the Human Dentition.* Baltimore: Williams & Wilkins.

LEAKEY, L. S. B.; TOBIAS, P. V.; and NAPIER, J. R. 1964 A New Species of the Genus *Homo* From Olduvai Gorge. *Nature* 202:7–9.

LEWIS, G. EDWARD 1934 Preliminary Notice of New Man-like Apes From India. *American Journal of Science* Fifth Series 227:161–179.

OSBORN, HENRY F. 1902 American Eocene Primates and the Supposed Rodent Family Mixodectidae. American Museum of Natural History, *Bulletin* 16:169–214.

PILGRIM, GUY E. 1910 Notices of New Mammalian Genera and Species From the Tertiaries of India. India, Geological Survey, *Records of the Geological Survey of India* 40, no. 1:63–71.

PILGRIM, GUY E. 1927 A *Sivapithecus* Palate and Other Primate Fossils From India. India, Geological Survey, *Palaeontologia indica* New Series 14:1–24.

SCHLOSSER, MAX 1887 Die Affen, Lemuren, Chiropteren usw. des europäischen Tertiärs. *Beiträge zur Paläontologie und Geologie Österreich-Ungarns* 6:1–162.

SCHLOSSER, MAX 1911 Beiträge zur Kenntnis der Oligozänen Land-Säugetiere aus dem Fayum: Ägypten. *Beiträge zur Paläontologie und Geologie Österreich-Ungarns* 24:51–167.

SIMONS, ELWYN L. 1962a A New Eocene Primate Genus, *Cantius,* and a Revision of Some Allied European Lemuroids. British Museum of Natural History, *Bulletin* 7, no. 1:1–36.

SIMONS, ELWYN L. 1962b Two New Primate Species From the African Oligocene. *Postilla* (Yale Peabody Museum) 64:1–12.

SIMONS, ELWYN L. 1963 Some Fallacies in the Study of Hominid Phylogeny. *Science* 141:879–889.

SIMONS, ELWYN L. 1964 On the Mandible of *Ramapithecus.* National Academy of Sciences, *Proceedings* 51, no. 3:528–535.

SIMONS, ELWYN L.; and PILBEAM, DAVID R. 1965 Preliminary Revision of the Dryopithecinae (Pongidae, Anthropoidea). *Folia primatologica* 3:81–152.

SIMPSON, GEORGE G. 1940 Studies on the Earliest Primates. American Museum of Natural History, *Bulletin* 77:185–212.

STEHLIN, H. G. 1912–1916 Die Säugetiere des schweizerischen Eocaens. Schweizerische Paläontologische Gesellschaft, *Abhandlungen* 38:1165–1298; 41:1299–1552.

STIRTON, R. A. 1951 Ceboid Monkeys From the Miocene of Colombia. California, Univ. of, Publications of the Department of Geological Sciences, *Bulletin* 28, no. 11:315–355.

WORTMAN, J. L. 1903–1904 Studies of Eocene Mammalia in the Marsh Collection, Peabody Museum, Part 2: Primates. *American Journal of Science* Fourth Series 15:163–176, 399–414, 419–436; 16:345–368; 17:23–33, 133–140, 203–214.

III

HUMAN EVOLUTION

The modern or synthetic theory of evolution considers evolution to be the result of changes in the gene frequencies in populations. Gene frequencies are altered by means of mutation, selection, migration, and certain chance factors such as drift. When mutations are considered relative to their usefulness to the organism and to the population, mutations occur at random. They are not at random relative to the chemical structure of the organism, and mutations are commoner at some locations on the chromosomes than at others. Mutations are mostly disadvantageous, and their frequency is increased by radiation and by certain chemicals. Selection is the primary agent for bringing order to this process. Over the course of time, those genetic combinations that favor reproductive success become more common; and, conversely, those combinations that are less viable decline. It should be stressed that selection is for reproductively successful populations, and, from the viewpoint of evolution or of the species, the individual is only important insofar as he helps or hinders the success of the population. Variability itself is very important, as it permits the species to adapt to changing conditions; and selection is often for variability rather than for homogeneity which demands a single, limited environment. Migration from one population to another may introduce new genes or change gene frequencies, and this means that genes that are favored by selection may spread throughout the species. Partial reproductive isolation permits adaptation to local conditions and the formation of races, but in the long run it is the species that is the evolutionary unit. Especially when the number of individuals in the breeding population is small—as, in fact, was the case throughout most of human history—chance may cause the gene frequencies of one generation to differ from those of the preceding one. This has been called drift, and it can be a source of variability between small populations of a single species. If populations are founded by very few individuals, on the basis of statistical probabilities their gene frequencies are unlikely to be the same as those of the parent population. In summary, evolution is the result of changing gene frequencies. These changes originate by chance and are ordered by selection. They are modified by migration and certain chance factors. The process of natural selection has both directly and indirectly favored highly variable populations, and there has been no tendency for evolution to produce genetically uniform types.

Biological history

The synthetic theory of evolution has many important implications for social science, but it must be remembered that the concepts most frequently borrowed by the social scientists long antedate modern evolutionary theory. The greatest misunderstanding comes from the notion that evolution is directed toward a particular goal, frequently man himself, and that its course is determined by trends (orthogenesis). The reproductive success of populations is determined by the conditions of the moment, not by ultimate desirability or by the remote future. Reptiles succeeded the amphibians because of structural, physiological, and behavioral advantages that led to numerical and adaptive success, not because reptiles were to give rise to mammals, one of which was to become man. The trends seen in evolution are descriptions of what has actually taken place, and if a trend continues it is because selection in each generation has favored a particular course of events. When there are only a few fossils, the course of evolution may appear simple; but when the record is rich, biological history appears as an incredibly complex web of adapting organisms.

These points are made particularly incisively by Simpson (1964). As he emphasizes, evolution is biological history. The mechanism is revealed in the geneticist's laboratory, and the record is discovered in the rocks. But there are no laws in the usual scientific sense determining the course of evolution. In biological history there are no ultimate goals, inevitable trends, or vitalistic explanations.

The contrast between thinking about evolution in terms of inevitable trends and as the result of selection may be illustrated by consideration of the length of the toes of man and his ancestors. Since human toes have become much shorter compared to those of any possible ancestral primate, it is often asked whether this trend will continue; and men of the future are pictured as having still smaller toes. But the length of human toes has not been determined by a trend which is continuing into the future, regardless of the circumstances. When our ancestors became terrestrial animals to a greater extent, selection favored more efficient bipedal locomotion. Selection for shorter toes was a part of this process, but the fact that selection was for different proportions in the foot does not mean

that selection continues to be for even shorter toes. Probably an equilibrium was reached more than a million years ago, and selection for shorter toes has not continued. There is no trend determining the foot proportions of the future; the notion of an inevitable man of the future with a huge brain, tiny face, small limbs, and so forth finds no support in modern evolutionary theory. Future gene frequencies will be determined by selection (i.e., by reproductive success), and man will become more intelligent only if those individuals with the combinations of genes favoring the development of high intelligence leave more offspring. Evolutionary trends are statements of what has actually taken place in the history of forms of life, but there is no biological momentum that carries past trends into the future.

The study of human evolution is particularly beset with the notions of goal and trend and of evolution as a magic process. It might clarify thinking on the subject to omit the word "evolution" for the moment and to consider the history of the forms of life as revealed by the fossil record, the mechanism of change as shown in the laboratory, and the interpretations of these two kinds of data. The study of man's biological history means precisely the same thing as the study of human evolution, and it does not carry the suggestion of inevitable trend or progress toward some desired goal. The statement that we may study human biological history, human cultural history, and the interrelation of the two should mean precisely the same thing as that we may study human biological and cultural evolution. Understanding comes from the study of the data, and no information is added by using the word "evolution" in preference to the word "history."

The importance of using modern concepts is well illustrated by the change in the meaning of the word "origin." In human evolution "origin" has usually meant a relatively restricted time and place in which a new type arose. Thus one theory held that Neanderthal man arose in Europe, another that he evolved in central Asia. But if the populations of the genus *Homo* were not reproductively isolated during the latter half of the Pleistocene period, mutations and gene combinations favored by selection might have spread throughout the whole species. The origin of the Neanderthal populations that inhabited Europe during the last interglacial period was not limited to Europe but depended on the extent to which European populations were in contact with populations in other parts of the Old World. In the traditional typological, local sense there really is no "origin" of Neanderthal but many origins at different times and places which became incorporated in the European gene pool some 50 to 150 thousand years ago. The origins of Neanderthal were going on steadily over large areas for long periods of time, and the populations named Neanderthal were in part the result of events (mutations, drift, selection, migration) taking place in other races of the species.

Stages in human evolution

The characteristics of the main stages of human evolution are based on the fossils and on the structure and behavior of the primates that exist today. Both kinds of evidence are necessary to reconstruct the course of human evolution, and it is important to keep in mind the nature of the understanding that each kind of evidence can give. The fossils are the only direct clue to what the ancestors were like, the only evidence on many forms that have no close living relatives, and the only evidence as to the actual time of appearance of the various groups of primates. But the fossils are limited to those hard parts that do not easily deteriorate, largely jaws and teeth. Study of the contemporary primate forms supplements this record in two ways. The changes that are seen in the fossils may be interpreted more meaningfully if knowledge of the living animals is used. For example, changes in the form of the ethmoid bone may be directly related to changes in the sense of smell; or a particular form of limb bone may be interpreted as showing a special locomotor pattern. In a quite different way the contemporary forms may indirectly suggest characteristics that probably existed in extinct forms. For example, primitive mammals and contemporary prosimians have tactile hairs, scent glands, and a well-developed sense of smell. It is highly probable that these conditions were general for all the primates of the first half of the Age of the Mammals, but there is direct evidence only on the sense of smell. It is probable that this whole complex was reduced at the end of the Eocene or the beginning of the Oligocene, but this may have happened much earlier or later, and different parts of the complex may have changed at different times. If one is interested in general statements about what happened, the evidence is very good. But the more detailed questions one asks, the more the answers are limited to those that may be derived from teeth and bones.

For the first half of the Age of the Mammals the ancestors of man were small, long-snouted prosimians, not distinguished from the other primates of their time in any remarkable way. The prosimians of the Eocene were successful and highly diversified, and the group underwent a major adaptive radiation resulting in the formation of many distinct families. Many of the most successful groups evolved elongated incisor teeth; and if one examined only the Eocene primates, it might be concluded that these were to be the ultimately successful forms. But the majority of these Eocene primates became extinct after the true rodents appeared, and it may be that competition with the rodents was a major factor in their extinction. Unfortunately, the fossil record is particularly scant at the end of the Eocene and at the beginning of the Oligocene, so it is impossible to determine just which of the families of the early primates are ancestral to the later ones. But the main changes, as outlined below, would be similar regardless of just which lineage is eventually proved to be the correct one. While maintaining hands and feet adapted for climbing by grasping and a primitive quadrupedal posture, some primates in both the New World and the Old World independently evolved a new organization of the special senses and the brain. The primitive sense of smell was reduced, and binocular, stereoscopic color vision evolved. The reduction of the sense of smell is directly reflected in the fossil bone. The changes in vision are inferred from the conditions found in contemporary primates and are mirrored, at least to some extent, in the structure of the bony orbit. The brain increased in size at least four or five times and changed in organization from a primitive dependence on the sense of smell to an organization based on vision as the dominant sense. The change from prosimian to monkey is primarily in the brain and special senses, but in addition the face became shorter and deeper. The special senses and the brain determine what aspects of the external world can be perceived and appreciated and how sensations are organized. In a very real sense the world that we think of as normal (a stereoscopic world of color, in which activity is diurnal) began with the monkeys of the end of the Eocene or the beginning of the Oligocene. Judging from contemporary prosimians, the increase in the size of the brain made a great difference in intelligence. But it must be remembered that this reorganization of the structural basis of experience was an adaptation to a particular kind of arboreal life which took place independently in both the New World and the Old World. Although this organization forms the basis for human experience, it initially evolved because it was useful to monkeys, not to prepare the way for man.

Monkeys (Cercopithecidae) have remained quadrupedal, but the apes (Pongidae) evolved a different locomotor pattern. Apes climb by reaching far up above the head and may hang by one arm, swing below a branch, or reach to the side. This manner of locomotion in the trees probably evolved first as a way of feeding out near the ends of small branches. The structures that make this mode of living possible are complex and include a shallow, wide chest, a long clavicle, a special shoulder joint that involves modification of all bones near the joint, and changes in the elbow, wrist joint, and hand. The fossil record is exceedingly scanty, but this whole complex probably evolved during the Miocene, long after the separation between monkeys and apes. At least many monkeylike features persist in the arm bones of such forms of early Miocene ape as *Proconsul* and *Pliopithecus*. Man is similar to the apes in this structure of the trunk and arms (including the form and numbers of vertebrae, the disposition of the viscera, the form of joints and muscles, and the proportions of the trunk and limbs). Again it must be remembered that this complex evolved for a special life in the trees, and it is shared by all the contemporary apes. Man has these features because his ancestors were arboreally adapted apes, not because there was a trend toward man.

By the beginning of the Pleistocene, possibly two million years ago, the family of which man is the sole living representative (Hominidae) was represented by a genus of bipedal, small-brained creatures (*Australopithecus*). The direct fossil evidence shows that the Hominidae must be at least two million years old; but *Australopithecus* already had small canine teeth of human form and a pelvis closely approximating that seen in man (*Homo*), and the foot differed from that of *Homo* only in details. Prior to the Pleistocene, the Hominidae must have been separated from the Pongidae for some substantial period of time during which these characters evolved. Fragments of jaws dating from the end of the Miocene in India (*Ramapithecus*) and Africa (*Kenyapithecus*) suggest that the line leading to the Hominidae may have been distinct at that time; but since the rate of evolution may be very different for different functional complexes, there is no way to tell if these forms were beginning to be bipedal. It has been repeatedly shown that conclusions drawn from such fragmentary remains are likely to be wrong. [See EVOLUTION, *article on* PRIMATE EVOLUTION.]

Stone tools and animal bones have been found with the remains of *Australopithecus;* and it is probable that these creatures made the tools and hunted small animals, just as from their anatomy it appears that the behavior of *Australopithecus* was far more human than apelike. There were at least two species, *A. africanus* and *A. robustus*, a small one and a large one. Judging from the evidence of the teeth and from the associated archeological remains, both probably made tools. The small species may have been directly ancestral to the genus *Homo* of the Middle Pleistocene. The large form lived at the same time as the small one and continued on to be a contemporary of *Homo* before becoming extinct. As man is approached, there is a tendency to label each specimen as distinct and to emphasize differences instead of similarities. The result is a multiplication of species and genera the more the forms resemble man. Actually, the reverse should be the case. The more a primate is bipedal, tool-using, and hunting, the less likely the form is to speciate and the more likely it is to occupy wide areas with only racial differences.

By the Middle Pleistocene men of the genus *Homo* were fully bipedal, and there is every indication that their locomotor system had evolved to virtually its present form. Brains were approximately twice the size of those of *Australopithecus*. Tools were made according to complex traditions of manufacture, which were widely distributed geographically. Large animals were hunted, and fire was used. This fully human way of life appears to have been established by half a million years ago, but it changed very slowly. Approximately fifty thousand years ago men of modern form appeared. Undoubtedly evolution continued, and the populations adapted to local conditions by biological as well as cultural means. But the main events of human evolution had taken place before that time, and culture became increasingly more important in human adaptation. With agriculture and particularly with modern science the whole pattern shifted, numbers increased from a few millions to billions, and recently it is man who has altered the world. Mutation, selection, and migration are changed by the human way of life and at least in part may be brought under human control.

Since the fossil record is so fragmentary, it is important to note that the latest biochemical and cytological evidence supports the classification of the primates and the general stages of human evolution noted above. Immunochemical studies (especially Williams 1964 and Goodman 1963) show that man's closest living relatives are the great apes, especially the chimpanzee and the gorilla. The small apes, the gibbons, are much less similar both in their immune reactions and in chromosome number and types. The Old World monkeys are still further removed, and the prosimians are both very different and highly diversified. For the first half of the Age of the Mammals man's ancestors were prosimians whose primary adaptation was climbing by grasping. At the end of the Eocene a monkey–ape group evolved, characterized by changes in the brain and special senses. This group diversified in the Oligocene, and the special ape locomotor and feeding patterns evolved in the Miocene. A human bipedal group separated later and was fully evolved in locomotor and dental characters by the beginning of the Pleistocene, some two million years ago.

It should be stressed that the Eocene prosimians evolved into many different forms, most of which became extinct. Subsequently, monkeys and apes evolved into dozens of different genera. No general trend dominates the evolution of the primates, and most of primate evolution has no relation to that of man.

Evolution of behavior

The direct evidence for the course of human evolution outlined above is fragmentary and limited primarily to teeth and jaws. Changes in locomotor patterns are directly reflected in the bones, and in a general way the stages outlined above are probably correct; but so few limb bones are preserved that a very wide variety of interpretations is possible. Turning to the evolution of other behaviors, the evidence is even more indirect and is based primarily on the contemporary forms. The general logic in the use of information from the contemporary primates is that if a structure or behavior is common in a group of living primates it was probably present in closely allied fossil forms. Both parallel evolution and convergence may render such conclusions invalid; and since it is highly adaptable, behavior is particularly liable to these sources of error. An example may make the situation clearer. Primitive mammals probably had a litter of several young. In the primates the number of young is usually reduced to one at a time, and that infant is carried by the mother. The general kind of change is clear, but the details cannot be determined from the record. Marmosets do have twins and galagos more than one young. It is probable that the reduction took place several times, and it is possible that the ancestral apes had more than one young. But the most probable interpretation is that in arboreal primates a single infant carried by the mother was more likely to survive, and that this behavioral adaptation had evolved in the prosimians prior to the evolution of the later primate forms.

The human infant is remarkable in being unable to hold onto its mother, and this not only alters the pattern of human mother–child relations but introduces a division of labor and many social problems that are unique to man. George B. Schaller

(1963) observed that the female gorilla also must help her infant for the first six weeks. Thus man is a little less different than had been thought, and perhaps the particular group of apes from which we are descended were more like gorillas in this regard than like all the other apes and monkeys. The matter cannot be proved one way or the other, but it is most likely that the main difference between man and the other primates came with the evolution of large brains in the Pleistocene, long after the human lineage had separated from the other apes.

A problem exists in the examples that follow which is similar to that encountered in our consideration of the number of young in a litter and the degree of dependency of the newborn: that is, comparison of the living forms highlights a situation of importance in the behavior of man, but the time of origin of the behavior can be suggested in only the most general way. However, many important aspects of human evolution can be appreciated only in this way. For example, length of life has increased greatly in man. In small primitive mammals maturity is a matter of months and old age of two or three years. Comparable figures for monkeys are maturity in three or four years and a life span of well over twenty years. In chimpanzees full maturity is in approximately eight to ten years, and the life span is more than forty years. Comparable figures for man are nearly twice as long. Although there is much variation, the time during which the human young enjoy a protected and privileged position has increased, and a human of eight or ten is still learning and playing at an age when most primates would be fully adult. Clearly, selection has favored the long period of development and learning, even at a great biological cost. It might appear that a process based on reproductive success would favor several young and rapid growth, but in the human way of life selection has been for a single infant, growing slowly. Prolonged dependency and the presence of experienced adults have been major factors in the evolution of human society.

In monkeys and apes there is a menstrual cycle of approximately a month in duration. Sexual activity is concentrated in a period of estrus close to the time of ovulation. Females do not come into estrus for a period of some months during the later part of pregnancy and the first part of lactation. These physiological facts have the effect of concentrating sexual activity when conception is most probable and of spacing the infants. The spacing may be further reinforced by a breeding season, or at least a much greater frequency of births in one part of the year. In the human female the basic cycle continues, but estrus behavior has been lost.

Human females experience a period of lowered fertility during early lactation which is probably comparable to that in many monkeys. However, this period is not long enough for the requirements of human infant spacing; the human infant cannot feed itself when it is six months or even a year old. In man the spacing of infants must be extended by taboos and customs which supplement the physiological mechanisms of birth spacing in the nonhuman primate. The loss of the estrus cycle in the human female may be related to the economic division of labor and the interdependency of the sexes, which is unique to man. This loss may be due to the need of the human female to keep the interest of the food-sharing male; but there may well have also been selective pressure against estrus behavior, which would have been disruptive to the stable, interdependent relationships of a family unit.

The monkeys and apes are almost entirely vegetarian, although most will eat birds' eggs and insects. Hunting of small mammals has been observed rarely in chimpanzees and baboons. The range in which monkeys and apes forage is small, varying from much less than a square mile in gibbons to some fifteen square miles in baboons and gorillas. From a human point of view it is remarkable that animals with keen eyesight, who are capable of climbing into trees and surveying the scene and who are well adapted for locomotion on the ground, so restrict their normal activities. It is probable that hunting is the behavioral adaptation that caused the change in man's relation to his physical environment. Intensive hunting would drive game from a small range, and the location of game and the pursuit of wounded animals would lead to the establishment of large territories. In most nonhuman primates ranges are not defended, and the areas occupied by groups of monkeys or apes usually overlap. Human defense of territory may also be the result of hunting.

Tool use is one of man's most distinctive attributes, and the skillful use of objects is unique to man. Manipulative skills depend on the brain as well as on the hand, and the large area in the human brain devoted to the hand is probably the result of the new selection pressures that came into being with the beginnings of tool using. Both the evidence of the teeth and of the associated tools and animal bones suggest that *Australopithecus* was a tool user and had been so for a long time. If this interpretation is correct, then the increase in size of the human brain came long after the use of tools and probably in response to the new ways of life that tools made possible.

Intelligence and learning are not general but are related to specific abilities. For example, human children play with objects as well as with other children. They enjoy practicing using and throwing, and many games are built around objects. In marked contrast, monkeys and apes are tool-dumb, so to speak. Tasks that the human child easily masters are very difficult or impossible for nonhuman primates. Only the chimpanzee uses some minor tools (Goodall 1964). The same principle can be seen in language. In spite of major efforts, it has proved impossible to teach monkeys or apes to speak. This is because the nonhuman primates lack the neural mechanisms necessary for speech. The sounds of the nonhuman primates convey emotion (such as fear) and the location of the calling animal, and they are important especially when combined with gestures in social interaction. The sound systems of primates are not more complex than those of many other mammals; and, like other mammals, primates can be trained to respond to human sounds. The distinctive character of human speech is the naming of objects, and this requires the linking of visual and auditory parts of the cortex of the brain (Geschwind 1964). The necessary connections are not present in the brains of the nonhuman primates. Once naming of objects had commenced in even the most minor way, the success of this revolution changed selection pressures so that the course of evolution of the brain changed, and structures evolved that ultimately made possible language as we now know it. It is likely that the situation which led to object naming was tool use, and it is the uniqueness of this combination of tools and language to man that accounts for why the other primates did not develop even the simplest languages. If language began at the time the brain was doubling in size between *Australopithecus* and *Homo*, this would give a minimum of two million years of stone toolmaking by small-brained bipeds as a time in which the first naming of objects might have occurred. It is tempting to attribute this great increase in brain size to language and all the ways of life that language made possible. But it must be remembered that it is not just increase in size that separates the brain of modern man from that of the contemporary apes. There have been changes of organization in the brain too, and without these changes skills in tool use, language, and social planning would be impossible. Human intelligence is built on specific abilities which are the products of the evolutionary process.

But the world in which man evolved was a very different one from that in which we are living today. Our bodies had evolved to practically their present form some fifty thousand years ago, and since then human adaptations to the environment have been increasingly by technology and custom. This does not mean that evolution has stopped, but it does mean that the direct interrelation that selection had forged between man and his ways of life is no longer functional. As stone tools improved over vast intervals of time, the biology of the users had time to evolve along with their way of life. In the human head we see the product of the interrelations of biology and a succession of ways of life in which selection was for smaller faces and bigger brains. But since the agricultural and scientific revolutions customs have changed so rapidly that there has been no time for corresponding biological evolution to fit the human actors for the modern world. Human biology evolved to be adaptive in a world of small society, great hazards, and personal skill. The human actor in modern society is too aggressive, too dominance seeking, too acquisitive. The kind of planning necessary in the modern world is difficult for an organism built along the lines of *Homo sapiens*. Many acts which now would be judged undesirable (acts of selfishness, cruelty, and war) are easily learned because they are in accord with basic human biology (Hamburg 1963).

Natural selection can bring about adaptation between biology and a way of life only in very long periods of time, and there is no orthogenesis carrying trends of the past into the future. The fit between organism and society must now be determined by science, and for the first time in all of biological evolution both biology and social life can be planned. But planning can be more efficient if planners remember that the actors in modern technical society are products of the past, of times and ways of life long gone.

S. L. WASHBURN AND JANE B. LANCASTER

BIBLIOGRAPHY

BUETTNER-JANUSCH, JOHN (editor) 1963–1964 *Evolutionary and Genetic Biology of Primates*. 2 vols. New York: Academic Press.

DEVORE, IRVEN (editor) 1965 *Primate Behavior: Field Studies of Monkeys and Apes*. New York: Holt.

DOBZHANSKY, THEODOSIUS 1962 *Mankind Evolving: The Evolution of the Human Species*. New Haven: Yale Univ. Press.

GESCHWIND, NORMAN 1964 The Development of the Brain and the Evolution of Language. Georgetown University, Washington, D.C., Institute of Languages and Linguistics, *Monograph Series on Languages and Linguistics* 17:155–169.

GOODALL, JANE 1964 Tool-using and Aimed Throwing in a Community of Free-living Chimpanzees. *Nature* 201: 1264–1266.

GOODMAN, MORRIS 1963 Man's Place in the Phylogeny of the Primates as Reflected in Serum Proteins. Pages 204–234 in Sherwood L. Washburn (editor), *Classification and Human Evolution*. Chicago: Aldine.

HAMBURG, D. A. 1963 Emotions in the Perspective of Human Evolution. Pages 300–317 in Symposium on Expression of the Emotions in Man, New York, 1960, *Expression of the Emotions in Man*. Edited by Peter H. Knapp. New York: International Universities Press.

Index medicus. → Published since 1960. Articles are listed by subject matter and author.

MAYR, ERNST 1963 *Animal Species and Evolution*. Cambridge, Mass.: Belknap Press.

NAPIER, J. R. 1964 The Evolution of Bipedal Walking in the Hominids. *Archives de biologie* (Liège) 75 (Supplement): 673–708.

OAKLEY, KENNETH P. 1964 *Frameworks for Dating Fossil Man*. Chicago: Aldine. → A comprehensive discussion of methods of dating and the dates of fossil man.

PIVETEAU, JEAN (editor) 1957 *Traité de paléontologie*. Volume 7: Vers la forme humaine. . . . Paris: Masson. → The best general source on fossil primates, including man.

SCHALLER, GEORGE B. 1963 *The Mountain Gorilla: Ecology and Behavior*. Univ. of Chicago Press.

SIMONS, ELWYN L. 1963 Some Fallacies in the Study of Hominid Phylogeny. *Science* 141:879–889.

SIMONS, ELWYN L.; and PILBEAM, D. R. 1965 Preliminary Revision of the Dryopithecinae (Pongidae, Anthropoidea). *Folia primatologica* 3:81–152. → Classification of apes and the origin of man.

SIMPSON, GEORGE G. 1964 *This View of Life: The World of an Evolutionist*. New York: Harcourt.

TOBIAS, PHILIP V. 1965 Early Man in East Africa. *Science* 149:22–33. → Most recent review of *Australopithecus* and the problems of the origin of man.

WASHBURN, SHERWOOD L. (editor) 1963 *Classification and Human Evolution*. Chicago: Aldine.

WILLIAMS, C. A. JR. 1964 Immunochemical Analysis of Serum Proteins of the Primates: A Study in Molecular Evolution. Volume 2, pages 25–74 in John Buettner-Janusch (editor), *Evolutionary and Genetic Biology of Primates*. New York: Academic Press.

Zoological Record. → Published since 1865. Covers classification and fossils, topics not in the *Index medicus*.

ZOOLOGICAL SOCIETY OF LONDON 1963 *The Primates*. Proceedings of the Symposium held on April 12–14, 1962, Symposia 10. London: The Society.

IV

CULTURAL EVOLUTION

The grand movement of origin, transformation, and differentiation of our universe, our earth, and life itself is called evolution. Within this total process we are concerned with the transformations that occurred when the biological, or organic, phase arose out of the inorganic and when the later, cultural phase arose from the organic. Despite their interconnections, however, each of these stages has its own characteristic mode and tempo of evolution.

The cultural phase transcended the organic and inorganic when populations of men created new ways of adapting to each other and to the environment. These adaptations occurred after certain gradual changes in the size and complexity of the hominid forebrain made symbolic thought and communication possible. The capacity for, and use of, symbolic manipulation brought forth unprecedented kinds of social behavior. These new ways of behaving were *supra*biological in the sense that such natural primate characteristics as jealousy, fear, sex and food appetites, and so on, were so often channeled, sublimated, or otherwise altered by means of social rules. In a few striking respects, in fact, the new modes of social behavior were *contra*biological inasmuch as they actually repressed such powerful urges as the sexual, for example, and required sharing rather than competing for scarce food.

The sum total of the social and political rules, technological inventions and economic institutions, the arts, shared beliefs and practices—that is, the culture—tends to persist through time because any particular society maintains these parts integrated with each other and with its environment. Evolutionary changes, therefore, do not correspond to a single world-wide pattern, and each society maintains a certain distinctiveness in the course of change. Thus the culture of mankind generally is an evolutionary stage in the universal process, while particular societies differentiate into cultural genera and species, creating heterogeneity. Sometimes this adaptive process brings forth striking advances that permit greater dominance, all-round adaptability, and growth.

All anthropologists would agree that the earliest human societies must have been small and simple in social organization, poor in technological equipment, without formal legal or governmental institutions, and with an ideology based more on the supernatural than on science. Since these characteristics contrast greatly with modern industrial states, we think of evolution as directional: generally from small to large societies, from simple to complex organizations, from informal to formal political institutions, and so on. The idea of directionality is important because it provides the criteria for classifying separate societies into general stages of the evolution of culture as a totality.

A second characteristic of evolution is the relatedness of the sequence of forms. An important aspect of the interpretation of any particular unit is the investigation of the ancestral forms from which it "unfolded"—its phylogeny.

Not many social scientists are evolutionists, and even the anthropologists who agree that there has been general evolutionary growth disagree about whether there has been enough orderliness in the process for the theory to be useful in classifying cultures or in interpreting a purely historical succession of discrete events. But then, of course, even if the orderliness is agreed upon, it is natural to want to know what causes it, and here further disagreement arises. Most of the different conceptions of the nature and causes of cultural evolution arose in the eighteenth and nineteenth centuries, and a brief historical sketch is useful in describing them.

History of the concept

As primitive societies in various parts of the world became known to Europeans during the age of discovery, two different explanations of their primitiveness were offered. The most widespread belief was theological: they had "degenerated" further from an original state of grace than had civilized peoples. The other, the rationalist explanation that became usual among intellectuals in the seventeenth and eighteenth centuries, was that civilization had evolved from earlier primitive types that must have been similar to the culture of contemporary savages and barbarians. There had been, to be sure, evolutionary notions held by philosophers of the classical traditions—by the Greek Epicurus and the Roman Lucretius, for example—but modern ideas about cultural evolution were propounded most influentially by Turgot, Montesquieu, Rousseau, Condorcet, Helvétius, Diderot, and others in France; Kant and Herder in Germany; Vico in Italy; and Hume, Hobbes, and Ferguson in Britain.

As opposed to degenerationism, all of these writers held to a theory of progress. Although modern anthropologists have commonly thought that this theory was merely a happy giddiness induced by the great economic and political advances of the period, most European scholars were actually pessimistic about progress in the future. While all agreed that progress had taken place in the past, and that discernible, orderly stages of its evolution could be demarcated, only Kant, Turgot, and Condorcet thought that progress was inevitable. There were variations in the names and numbers of stages that were proposed, but most accepted either Turgot's stages of hunting, pastoralism, and farming, or Montesquieu's similar typology of savagery, barbarism, and civilization.

Although the modern holistic concept of culture was lacking, the elements that were seen to be evolving were the human institutions of which culture is composed. There was one emphasis in the evolutionary theory that was peculiar to the times —rationalism. Human institutions were viewed as products of the human mind (as indeed in some sense they must be), a mind that was mistaken or irrational in the past, but increasingly less superstitious and more reasonable as time went on. Since civilized man had literally thought himself out of a "state of nature," the degree of orderliness that lay in human history was due to the progressive improvement of mentality.

In the nineteenth century, evolutionary thought became less philosophical and more influenced by empirical aspirations. Tylor in England and Morgan in the United States were prominent in the creation of ethnological evolutionism; Spencer in England, Saint-Simon, Comte, and Durkheim in France were pioneers in sociology; the reworking of Hegel by Marx and Engels was a creative contribution to political–revolutionary theory. They differed from their predecessors and from one another mainly with respect to the following problems: (1) *What* is it that evolves—culture in general or only the institutions of specific societies? (2) *How* does it evolve—by orthogenetic, inevitable progress, by rational thought and intention, survival of the fittest, or an unconscious dialectical struggle? (3) *Where* is the locus of the evolutionary impulse— in the improvements of technology and the material aspect alone, in the division of labor, the political or ideological aspect, or as a force in the cosmos?

The nature of culture. The ethnologists of the late 1800s, convinced of orderliness in evolution, directed themselves to the delineation of stages of *culture*, which E. B. Tylor defined in the anthropological sense in 1871. L. H. Morgan (1877) did not use that word, but in his usage, "society" and "ethnical periods" (for stages) referred essentially to the subject matter of Tylor's concept. Tylor and Morgan, and most ethnologists of their time as well, were concerned with the world-wide manifestation of cultural stages, not with the culture of a particular society. A specific primitive tribe was of interest only as an illustration of aspects of the culture of an entire stage and of a large geographical area.

This concern with culture in its most general sense rather than with particular societies caused a misunderstanding of the ethnological evolutionists by later commentators. Modern anthropologists frequently criticize the nineteenth-century evolutionists as "unilinear," meaning that the latter believed that all societies inevitably progress through the same stages. This would be a powerful blow at nineteenth-century evolutionary theory, if it were true, but it seems doubtful that any of the evolutionists believed such manifest nonsense. In the statement that seems best to serve modern critics, Morgan said:

Since mankind were one in origin, their career has been essentially one, running in different but uniform channels upon all continents, and very similarly in all the tribes and nations of mankind down to the same status of advancement. It follows that the history and experience of the American Indian tribes represent, more or less nearly, the history and experience of our own remote ancestors when in corresponding conditions.   ([1877] 1964, pp. 6–7)

This sounds "unilinear" to a modern ethnologist, whose concern has been restricted to the structure and functioning of unit systems, but inasmuch as ethnologists were not making such studies in the nineteenth century, it seems apparent that Morgan must have meant nothing more than that wherever barbarism (defined by the traits of horticulture or pastoralism) was found, a general stage of hunting– gathering society (savagery) had preceded it and that stages of both had preceded civilization on continents that had achieved civilization. Such a judgment is attested by archeology now as well as by common sense and should evoke no comment, but in Morgan's day it was worth stating because theories of degeneration and catastrophe were still commonly opposed to evolutionism.

The sociologists tended toward the organismic model for society. A society was thought of as a contained unit made up of interdependent parts, each subserving the others. Evolution was seen as the development of more parts and greater differentiation of them. The "parts" are individuals, groups, and specialized persons and groups. Religions, morals, and political, social, and economic institutions function largely to bolster, integrate, and smooth the relations between the social parts. This early model, refined as nonevolutionary structural functionalism, became characteristic of modern American sociology and British social anthropology but had its roots in the eighteenth-century concern with progress.

The third group, the Marxists, was closer to ethnology than to sociology, at least in its beginning phases under Marx and Engels. In fact, Engels' *Origin of the Family, Private Property and the State* (1884) was inspired by Morgan's *Ancient Society* (1877) and borrowed heavily from it. The theory of general developmental stages was the same, and the conception of the evolving unit did not have the organismic particularism of the sociologists. As in Morgan's case, the concept of culture was absent but would have been appropriate, for institutions (especially technological and economic) were not merely subserviently integrative in function but had more of an initiating "prime mover" status than the sociologists believed.

How does culture evolve?   The eighteenth-century evolutionists thought of the progressive improvement of the human condition as a mentalistic evolution and thus took an idealist view of the evolutionary process. Some of the language of nineteenth-century ethnological evolutionism reflects this, so that we find such expressions as Morgan's "growth of the idea of government" and Tylor's frequent use of "mind" and "mental life" as near synonyms of many aspects of culture. But a very important change occurred in the nineteenth-century view of evolution. As it became more scientifically oriented it posited causal and functional connections between different aspects of culture. Tylor, in his greatest book, *Primitive Culture* (1871), devoted much of the introductory chapter ("The Science of Culture") to describing not only cause–effect relations in culture but also the determining of these cultural relations and the thought and will of the individual. The ethnological school of evolution thus made significant moves toward determinism and against assumptions of free will in human affairs.

The "how," the mechanics of the evolutionary process, was not explicitly described, beyond the suggestion that it was unconscious. We are told that new elements tend to replace older ones if they are better, sometimes, but beyond that one has the impression that evolution was taken as a "given," that orthogenetic forces had moved mankind ever upward, however fitfully.

There is a recurrent note reminiscent of the eighteenth-century rationalist ancestry: "Now that we understand evolution we can more consciously control it." Tylor called anthropology a "reformer's science," and Morgan said, "The time will come . . . when human intelligence will rise to the mastery over property. . . ." This was the deterministic paradox: We can scientifically analyze the evolution of culture because it *is* orderly (because it *is* determined); knowing this we can somehow influence the future as we pass, as Tylor put it, "from the age of unconscious to that of conscious progress."

The sociological wing of nineteenth-century evolutionism pursued the implications of the biological analogy. The rationalist optimism of Condorcet was outdated by the obvious attendant evils of industrialization, especially in England, as illustrated by Malthus' pessimistic *Essay on the Principle of Population*. After the great intellectual success of Dar-

win's theory of selection by survival (itself suggested by Malthus' essay), a theory of "social Darwinism" arose, which, whatever its demerits, at least provided a "how" for the evolutionary process: as a result of conflict between societies superior ones replace the inferior. Some added an "internal conflict" aspect: out of the struggle between classes, groups, and even individuals within the society comes the improvement of the society. Walter Bagehot, Auguste Comte, Herbert Spencer, and Ludwig Gumplowicz were the leaders in this mode of thought.

Marx and Engels were even more consistently deterministic and materialistic than the ethnologists and had a much more definite theory of the mechanics of evolution. This theory was orthogenetic in that the impetus for change came from within the society, from the "dialectic" of the class struggle, the resolution of contradictions in terms of either failure or a higher unity. It should be noted that this internal-conflict theory is not like social Darwinism: the ruling or propertied class is not superior. Marx and Engels, like the ethnologists, were insistent on the lawful, determined nature of evolution, and they also believed that evolution could be oriented by the conscious action of man once he understood its processes. Then, by abolishing the capitalist form of production, "Man, at last the master of his own form of social organization, becomes at the same time the lord over nature, his own master—free" (Engels [1882] 1935, p. 75).

Most of the sociologists became less interested in evolution itself than in the more immediate problems of the organismic nature of a society, particularly that of integration. What holds a society together? Following the social contract theories of the eighteenth century, there were psychological theories, mental interaction theories, and imitation theories, all of which took society to be an organismic entity somehow *mentally* constituted. This was the time when sociology became nonevolutionary, as it mostly remains to this day.

The locus of the evolutionary impulse.   Morgan thought that cultural evolution consisted of two distinct aspects—"inventions and discoveries" (the technical order), which evolve in connected, progressive, cumulative relations to one another, and "institutions" (the forms of the family, of government, religion, architecture, property), which stand in "unfolding relations." By this expression he meant that social institutions originate in a few "primary germs of thought" and thereafter independently change form as well as replace previous forms. Tylor also, although not so explicitly, thought that technology, science, and other aspects of material culture undergo evolution rather independent of religion and "intellectual and moral" progress. Nowhere is it demonstrated, however, that one of these aspects is the "prime mover" and the other a dependent variable or superstructure. But again it should be remembered that Morgan and Tylor were not talking about the process of systemic change in any particular society, hence the matter of functional priority of one part over another simply did not concern them.

The sociologists, preoccupied with social integration, psychology, and mentalism, did not see the initiating locus of evolutionary change in any aspect of culture at all. Spencer and his followers saw evolution as a grand cosmic force that generated complexity out of simplicity and heterogeneity out of homogeneity, aided somewhat by Darwinian "conflict and survival." A few Frenchmen, most notably Émile Durkheim (1893), posited that the division of labor in society, like the functional specialization of organs in biological entities (again, the organismic model), is related to population increases, greater social density, and larger, stronger societies. But it is not clear what the causes of these developments are, and Durkheim explicitly denied that the division of labor is increased for utilitarian reasons like "the greatest happiness for the greatest number" or by any other kind of intention or plan.

The Marxians, on the other hand, were firm in the conviction that the locus of evolutionary change lies in the technoeconomic (or material) sector, which then affects the nature of the social classes and their interrelations, and that ideology is mere superstructure. As such, it is the last part of culture to change. This form of the old materialist versus idealist philosophical argument persists strongly to this day.

Twentieth-century evolutionism

Most American ethnologists in the first half of the twentieth century repudiated an evolutionism that they misunderstood in favor of a raw ethnographic, "natural history" approach to the study of primitive culture. In Britain and France, and in sociology nearly everywhere, evolutionism succumbed intellectually to a structural functionalism that had greater utility for the practical solution of social problems through political administration in the colonies and at home.

A. G. Keller, an American sociologist, Leslie A. White and Julian H. Steward, American ethnologists, and V. Gordon Childe, a British archeologist, were virtually alone in opposing the antievolutionary temper of the times. It was not until after mid-century that there was any larger shift of opinion toward an evolutionary outlook again, but this took place only in America, only in anthropology, and there only in part.

Twentieth-century evolutionism differs from previous theories in two major respects. The first concerns the cultural adaptations through which evolutionary changes are believed to occur. The concept of cultural adaptation has supplanted the orthogenesis of earlier evolutionists, who had found the only generative impulse in the internal classstruggle dialectic proposed by Marx and Engels and in the social Darwinism of some sociologists. Second, a new theoretical synthesis has been made by the reworking and integration of some of the earlier perspectives that had been thought to be contradictory.

The significance of the adaptation of culture to the natural environment as an important aspect of the evolutionary process was presented as "cultural ecology" by Julian H. Steward. Others have proposed further that in the process of adaptation, the environment includes not only the natural environment but adjustments to other social systems as well. According to this view, inventions and discoveries, borrowings, unconscious historical "accidents," changes from whatever source, are the raw materials for evolutionary change in culture. Some of these "fit" as improvements in the internal functional arrangements, while others solve external environmental problems with respect to nature or competition: thus they are selected simply because they are superior instruments. The advance of this perspective over eighteenth-century and nineteenth-century ideas of the "inevitability of progress" and orthogenesis is manifest: the evolutionary perspective is not mystical and can accommodate and make more intelligible the variety of historical data we now possess.

One of the historical facts of life that has plagued all orthogenetic schemes is that different societies manifest great variation in rates of evolution, from drastic revolution to the other extreme of nonevolution—i.e., stabilization. And in so many instances a society makes a very rapid rise only to reach a long-term plateau. The theory that evolution proceeds by adaptation, however, allows for all of these eventualities, taking stabilization as much for granted as progress. Stabilization, after all, merely bespeaks the success of the adaptive process: when the culture is successfully adapted, it tends to reject subsequent possible changes. This can render explicable what might seem paradoxical: that a culture "high" in one stage might fail to advance to further heights in the next simply because of its earlier success. And, of course, the more specialized its form of adaptation, the more deeply entrenched and committed to its present environment it becomes.

The perspective of cultural adaptation and selection is particularly useful in reconciling opposing viewpoints derived from the nineteenth century.

What is it that evolves? Is it culture in general, through grand stages, or only particular social systems? The reconciliation of these two views is easy: both are correct. The evolution of the totality is the product of the evolution of particular societies. To be sure, there is but a single evolutionary process, the selection of traits and their functional adjustment *via* adaptation in particular systems. This is the way societies become differentiated one from the other, but it is also the way some become superior to others in measurable ways. Thus, two different theoretical perspectives are possible with respect to the same data. These are what Sahlins (Sahlins & Service 1960) calls the *specific* evolutionary perspective as compared with the *general* evolutionary perspective. The former refers merely to the creation of diversity by adaptive modification of related particular societies. The latter is the measurement of progress; some specific evolutionary changes are significant breakthroughs that can be measured by such objective directional criteria of progress as greater all-round adaptability, greater dominance, or greater complexity of organization. In short, specific evolution refers to our concern with descent-with-modification or adaptive variation; general evolution refers to the progressive emergence of superior forms, stage by stage, which can be related to the directional evolution of the total culture of the human species.

How does culture evolve? Is it in some measure intentionally planned, or is it an unconscious and nonrational process, determined by events outside human awareness? Surely an improvement in ideas has something to do with it, and sometimes ideas must be conscious and rational; this is most obvious in science and engineering but also holds true in the institutional realm. Many political institutions, for example, result from attempts to solve social or economic problems purposefully. But, of course, there are often latent and unintended consequences of even the most manifest political expediency.

Again, it would seem that a reconciliation of the opposed views can be made by means of the adaptation–selection perspective. New culture traits or modifications can have any number of sources: inventions, purposeful borrowings, accidents, unconscious functional shifts, and so on. The selection or rejection of any of these could also involve conscious intentionality, even if but rarely. The selective process in cultural evolution is only roughly analogous to natural selection in biology; certainly the capacity of a person to analyze his own behavior, predict future events, and rearrange his affairs on that basis is a distinctively human trait. It is more difficult to plan and arrange things on a social or political basis, and the greater the demographic scope the more difficult it is; but it does happen. The adaptation–selection perspective has the great virtue of not prescribing either conscious intention or unconsciousness; it can accommodate either and still lead to greater comprehension of cultural change. And further, determinism in human affairs is not equated with unawareness, indeterminism with awareness. Determinism is a perspective that the analyst takes, not a property of the subject matter under investigation.

Where is the locus of the evolutionary impulse? Does it lie in the mode of production, in technology, in the relations of production, in the class struggle, in the division of labor, in man's view of destiny; or is it a mystical force in the cosmos? It would seem that those who posited mode of production, class struggle, technology, or division of labor were much influenced by the industrial revolution, which has been, of course, a most striking evolutionary prime mover for the past century and a half and promises even more wondrous cultural transformations almost immediately. But has the material, technoeconomic aspect always been the prime mover? The change from primitive chiefdoms to early states and then to empires in Mesoamerica, Peru, and probably elsewhere seems to have been first in the political sector; even the important inventions of writing and mathematics could have originated in the occult mumbo jumbo of priests. The modern evolutionist accordingly wants to know more about particular instances of change and finds no need to insist that the initial loci must be always in the same sector of culture.

Evolutionists of the nineteenth century were more empirical than their predecessors, but their use of ethnographic data was often mere illustration rather than proof of hypotheses. The "comparative method" of some, such as Sir James Frazer, was simply an uncritical, but energetic, "clip and paste." E. B. Tylor (1888) was a notable exception: he originated a method of statistical correlations in his comparative study of marriage and descent rules. Hobhouse, Wheeler, and Ginsberg's work (1915) was another important application of statistics to problems of cultural evolution. Otherwise, both evolutionary theory and the comparative method nearly perished from inattention until mid-twentieth century.

The use of the comparative method began to revive in America during the 1950s, particularly stimulated by George P. Murdock's creation of the Human Relations Area Files and later the "Ethnographic Atlas." Formal graphical means of showing correlations and sequences of culture traits in the course of evolutionary changes have attracted attention recently. (See Naroll 1956; Freeman & Winch 1957; Gouldner & Peterson 1962; and Carneiro & Tobias 1963.) The results of these efforts are meager so far, and several unsolved difficulties attend them. The problems of how to define the significant cultural units to be counted and how to select a random sample of them in the absence of an adequate number of ethnographies of unacculturated societies are serious.

The gravest difficulty of all is caused by the tendency of a culture to become specialized as it adapts to its environment, for to the extent that it is special it is incommensurable. Walter Goldschmidt has aptly called this "the Malinowskian dilemma": Malinowski argued (and successfully demonstrated) that every cultural institution must be understood as a unique product of the cultural whole within which it developed. It would seem to follow, therefore, that the comparative method is wrong, comparing incomparables. Yet, paradoxically, Malinowski often extrapolated from his insights into Trobriand culture to the primitive world in general. Goldschmidt argues that the solution is to compare functions, not institutions: "What is consistent from culture to culture is not the institution; what is consistent are the social problems. What is recurrent from society to society is solutions to these problems" (1966, p. 31).

Julian H. Steward's studies (1955) of "multilinear evolution" show an awareness of these difficulties. He recommends comparative studies of specific holocultures in evolution, rather than comparisons of isolated traits, in order to find the "regularities" of evolution.

There is a different test of theory that is bound to be used more frequently—the test of fruitfulness. Since one of the main purposes of evolutionary theory is to provide intelligibility to historical data, then the better it fulfills this function, the greater must be its empirical as well as logico-didactic virtues. Guy Swanson's study of religion (1960) is a good example: light is cast on the development of religion, and at the same time evolutionary theory proves to be useful.

Such empirical applications of evolutionary theory can result in its refinement only to the extent that evolutionists maintain an empirical orientation, willing to change the theory in the service of its intellectual functions. Some of the older evolutionary philosophies, particularly those of Marx and Spencer, were too grand in scope and too schematic to be useful. They also became stultified dogmas as they were used by political parties and academic "schools of thought." A better fate may be expected of recent evolutionism, judging from the evidence of new empirical attitudes, particularly if its proponents remain guarded against unnecessary and untested preconceptions that can so easily impede a true evolutionary science of culture.

ELMAN R. SERVICE

[See also ANTHROPOLOGY, articles on THE FIELD and THE COMPARATIVE METHOD IN ANTHROPOLOGY; ARCHEOLOGY, article on THE FIELD; CULTURE; ECOLOGY. Also related are the entries INTEGRATION; SOCIAL DARWINISM; SOCIOLOGY, article on THE DEVELOPMENT OF SOCIOLOGICAL THOUGHT; and the biographies of CHILDE; MORGAN, LEWIS HENRY; SPENCER; TYLOR.]

BIBLIOGRAPHY

CARNEIRO, ROBERT L.; and TOBIAS, STEPHEN F. 1963 The Application of Scale Analysis to the Study of Cultural Evolution. New York Academy of Sciences, *Transactions* Second Series 26, no. 2:196–207.

CHILDE, V. GORDON (1936) 1965 *Man Makes Himself.* 4th ed. London: Watts.

CHILDE, V. GORDON 1951 *Social Evolution.* New York: Schumann.

COTTRELL, WILLIAM F. 1955 *Energy and Society: The Relation Between Energy, Social Change, and Economic Development.* New York: McGraw-Hill.

DOBZHANSKY, THEODOSIUS 1962 *Mankind Evolving: The Evolution of the Human Species.* New Haven: Yale Univ. Press.

DURKHEIM, ÉMILE (1893) 1960 *The Division of Labor in Society.* 2d ed. Glencoe, Ill.: Free Press. → First published in French.

ENGELS, FRIEDRICH (1882) 1935 *Socialism: Utopian and Scientific.* New York: International Publishers. → First published as *Die Entwicklung des Sozialismus von der Utopie zur Wissenschaft.*

ENGELS, FRIEDRICH (1884) 1942 *The Origin of the Family, Private Property and the State.* New York: International Publishers. → First published in German.

FERGUSON, ADAM (1767) 1819 *An Essay on the History of Civil Society.* 8th ed. Philadelphia: Finley.

FREEMAN, LINTON C.; and WINCH, R. F. 1957 Societal Complexity: An Empirical Test of a Typology of Societies. *American Journal of Sociology* 62:461–466; 63:78–79.

GOLDSCHMIDT, WALTER R. 1959 *Man's Way: A Preface to the Understanding of Human Society.* Cleveland: World.

GOLDSCHMIDT, WALTER R. 1966 *Comparative Functionalism: An Essay in Anthropological Theory.* Berkeley and Los Angeles: Univ. of California Press.

GOULDNER, ALVIN W. and PETERSON, R. A. 1962 *Notes on Technology and the Moral Order.* Indianapolis, Ind.: Bobbs-Merrill.

HOBHOUSE, LEONARD T.; WHEELER, GERALD C.; and GINSBERG, MORRIS (1915) 1965 *The Material Culture and Social Institutions of the Simpler Peoples: An Essay in Correlation.* London School of Economics and Political Science Monographs on Sociology, No. 3. London: Routledge.

HUXLEY, JULIAN S. 1942 *Evolution: The Modern Synthesis.* London and New York: Harper.

HUXLEY, JULIAN S. 1955 Evolution, Cultural and Biological. Pages 3–25 in *Yearbook of Anthropology.* New York: Wenner-Gren Foundation.

KELLER, ALBERT G. (1915) 1931 *Societal Evolution.* Rev. ed. New York: Macmillan.

MAINE, HENRY J. S. (1861) 1960 *Ancient Law: Its Connection With the Early History of Society, and Its Relations to Modern Ideas.* Rev. ed. New York: Dutton; London and Toronto: Dent.

MONTAGU, ASHLEY 1962 *Culture and the Evolution of Man.* New York: Oxford Univ. Press.

MORGAN, LEWIS H. (1877) 1964 *Ancient Society.* Cambridge, Mass.: Harvard Univ. Press.

MUNRO, THOMAS 1963 *Evolution in the Arts and Other Theories of Culture History.* Cleveland (Ohio) Museum of Art.

NAROLL, RAOUL S. 1956 A Preliminary Index of Social Development. *American Anthropologist* New Series 58:687–715.

SAHLINS, MARSHALL D.; and SERVICE, ELMAN R. (editors) 1960 *Evolution and Culture.* Ann Arbor: Univ. of Michigan Press.

SERVICE, ELMAN R. 1962 *Primitive Social Organization: An Evolutionary Perspective.* New York: Random House.

SPENCER, HERBERT 1915 *Works.* 18 vols. New York and London: Appleton.

STEWARD, JULIAN H. 1955 *Theory of Culture Change: The Methodology of Multilinear Evolution.* Urbana: Univ. of Illinois Press.

SUMNER, WILLIAM GRAHAM; and KELLER, ALBERT G. 1927 *The Science of Society.* 4 vols. New Haven: Yale Univ. Press. → Maurice R. Davis was a co-author of Volume 4.

SWANSON, GUY E. 1960 *The Birth of the Gods: The Origin of Primitive Beliefs.* Ann Arbor: Univ. of Michigan Press.

SYMPOSIUM ON THE EVOLUTION OF MAN'S CAPACITY FOR CULTURE, CHICAGO, 1957 1959 *The Evolution of Man's Capacity for Culture.* Detroit: Wayne State Univ. Press.

TYLOR, EDWARD B. (1871) 1958 *Primitive Culture: Researches Into the Development of Mythology, Philosophy, Religion, Art and Custom.* 2 vols. Gloucester, Mass.: Smith. → Volume 1: *Origins of Culture.* Volume 2: *Religion in Primitive Culture.*

TYLOR, EDWARD B. (1888) 1961 On a Method of Investigating the Development of Institutions: Applied to Laws of Marriage and Descent. Pages 1–28 in Frank W. Moore (editor), *Readings in Cross-cultural Methodology.* New Haven: Human Relations Area Files Press.

WARD, LESTER F. (1883) 1926 *Dynamic Sociology: Or, Applied Social Science, as Based Upon Statical Sociology and the Less Complex Sciences.* New York: Appleton.

WHITE, LESLIE A. 1949 *The Science of Culture: A Study of Man and Civilization.* New York: Farrar, Straus. → A paperback edition was published in 1958 by Grove.

WHITE, LESLIE A. 1959 *The Evolution of Culture: The Development of Civilization to the Fall of Rome.* New York: McGraw-Hill.

V

SOCIAL EVOLUTION

Evolutionary theory dominated sociological thought in the nineteenth and early twentieth centuries, but since about 1920 interest in it has, on the whole, given way to preoccupation with systematic analysis of social systems, analysis of broad social and demographic trends, and investigation of the social determinants of behavior (Ginsberg 1932). The recent tentative revival of interest in an evolutionary perspective is closely related to growing interest in historical and comparative studies. It does not, however, denote a mere return to the assumptions of the classical evolutionists, but rather it implies revision and reappraisal of evolutionary theory in the light of recent advances in sociological theory and research.

From the point of view of sociological analysis, the older evolutionary models broke down mainly over two stumbling blocks. The first was the assumption that the development of human societies is relatively cumulative and unilinear and that the major "stages" of development are universal—even if there are many differences in detail and even if not all societies reach every stage of evolution. The second stumbling block was the failure to specify fully the systemic characteristics of evolving societies or institutions or the mechanisms and processes of change through which the transitions from one "stage" to another were effected. Most of the classical evolutionary schools tended, rather, to point out general causes of change (economic, technological, spiritual) or some general trends (for example, the trend to complexity) inherent in the development of societies. Very often they confused such general tendencies with the causes of change or assumed that these general tendencies explained concrete instances of change (Bock 1963).

Attempts to reappraise evolutionary perspectives, therefore, must address themselves to several basic problems inherent in the new analytical developments in sociological theory, on the one hand, and in the general setting of the evolutionary problem, on the other (Wolf 1964; Parsons 1964; Eisenstadt 1963a). The first crucial problem concerns the extent to which change from one type of society to another is not accidental or random but, rather, evinces over-all evolutionary or developmental trends. Second is the question of the extent to which such changes are cumulative within any given society and within any given institutional sphere in different societies (Wolf 1964). Third is the problem of the extent to which such changes do indeed enhance the adaptive potential of a society in relation to its cultural and natural environment—however such adaptation and environment are defined (White 1959; Sahlins & Service 1960).

Furthermore, even if some such common characteristics or trends can be found within different and disparate societies, the question remains as to the validity of talking about the evolution of human society or culture as a whole. Here three subproblems exist: the first is the extent to which other societies constitute the "environment" of any society—that is, the environment to which any given single society has to adapt and which can enhance the general reservoir of its techniques of adaptation. The second is a question of the extent to which institutions and forms of organization that have adaptive value can be borrowed and transplanted from one society to another, thus enhancing their adaptive potential. And, finally, we must ask to what extent human society is a "system of points" with some common adaptive and integrative mechanisms. As distinct from the general theory of cultural evolution, which in a way assumes the unity of mankind and hence also the internal transferability of institutions or techniques, the focus of sociological analysis is on the relations between the systemic characteristics of societies in interaction with their natural, social, and cultural environments, on the one hand, and some possible broader trends of changes and transformations in their "transbiological" or superorganic abilities and traditions, on the other (Mead 1964).

The starting point of all these discussions, especially from the point of view of the relation between the transformative capacities of any single society and any possible general trends in the development of human societies and human society in general, is the problem of the extent to which such changes may be envisaged as crystallizing into developmental "stages"—a key concept in classical evolutionary thought (Ginsberg 1932). In the older evolutionary school such stages were construed mostly in terms of "specialization" and "complexity," whereas in recent works these concepts have been to a large extent replaced by that of "differentiation."

Differentiation and institutional growth

Differentiation, like complexity or specialization, is first of all a classificatory concept. It describes the ways through which the main social functions or the major institutional spheres of society become dissociated from one another, attached to specialized collectivities and roles, and organized into relatively specific and autonomous symbolic and organizational frameworks within the confines of the same institutional system. In broad evolutionary terms, such continuous differentiation has usually been conceived as a continuous development starting from the "ideal" type of the primitive society or band, in which all the major roles are allocated on an ascriptive basis and the division of labor is based primarily on family and kinship units. Development then proceeds through various stages of specialization and differentiation.

Specialization is first manifest when each of the major institutional spheres, through the activities of people placed in strategic roles within it, develops its own organizational units and complexes and its specific criteria of action. The latter tend to be congruent with the basic orientations of a given sphere, facilitating the development of its potentialities: technological innovation, cultural and religious creativity, expansion of political power or participation, or development of complex personality structure.

Second, different levels or stages of differentiation denote the degree to which major social and cultural activities as well as certain basic resources —such as manpower and economic resources— have been disembedded or freed from kinship, territorial, and other ascriptive units (Parsons 1964; Bellah 1964; Eisenstadt 1963*a*). Although these "free-floating" resources pose new problems of integration, they may also become the basis for a more differentiated social order that is, at least potentially, better adapted to deal with a more variegated environment. Thus, a new set of problems—those of integration—emerges as the very crux of the way in which such resources can be utilized for the crystallization of some general transformative potentials within a society.

Problems of integration. As the more differentiated and specialized institutional spheres become more interdependent and potentially complementary in their functioning within the same over-all institutionalized system, this very complementarity creates more difficult and complex problems of integration. The growing autonomy of each sphere of social activity, and the concomitant growth of interdependence and mutual interpenetration among them, pose for each sphere ever more difficult problems in crystallizing its own tendencies and potentialities and in regulating its normative and organizational relations with other spheres. And at each more "advanced" level or stage of differentiation, the increased autonomy of each sphere creates increasingly more complex problems of integrating these specialized activities into one systemic framework.

The growing autonomy of the different institutional spheres and the extension of their organizational scope not only increase the range and depth of social and human problems but also open up new possibilities for technological development, expansion of political power or rights, and cultural creativity. Growing differentiation also enhances systemic sensitivity to a much wider physical–technical environment and to more comprehensive intersocietal relations. But the growth of systemic sensitivity to new problems and exigencies does not necessarily imply a concomitant development of the ability to deal with these problems, nor does it indicate the ways in which these problems may be solved. At any given level of differentiation an institutional sphere may or may not achieve an adequate degree of integration, and the potentialities unfolded through the process of differentiation may be "wasted"—that is, they may fail to become crystallized into an institutional structure.

Recognition of the integrative problems that are attendant on new levels of differentiation constitutes the main theoretical implication of the concept of differentiation, and it is in the light of the analytical problems raised by this implication that the various questions pertinent to a reappraisal of the evolutionary perspective in social science have to be examined. We are as yet far from any definitive answers to these questions, but at least we can point out some of the most important problems of research in this direction.

Responses to differentiation

The passage of a given society from one stage of differentiation to another is contingent on the development within it of certain processes of change which create a degree of differentiation that cannot be contained within the pre-existing system. Growing differentiation and the consequent structural breakthroughs may take place through a secular trend of differentiation, or through the impact of one or a series of abrupt changes, or both. These tendencies may be activated by the occupants of strategic roles within the major institutional spheres as they attempt to broaden the

scope and develop the potentialities of their spheres. The extent to which these changes are institutionalized and the concrete form they take in any given society necessarily depend on the basic institutional contours and premises of the pre-existing system, on its initial level of differentiation, and on the major conflicts and propensities for change within it (Eisenstadt 1964b).

We need not assume that all changes in all societies necessarily increase differentiation. On the contrary, the available evidence shows that many social changes do not give rise to over-all changes in the scope of differentiation but result, instead, mainly in changes in the relative strength and composition of different collectivities or in the integrative criteria of a particular institutional sphere. Largely because the problem has not yet been fully studied, we do not know exactly what conditions facilitate or precipitate these different types of change in different societies and what makes for variations in innovative or transformative capacities among different societies (Eggan 1963; Sahlins 1964).

Even when social change increases differentiation, the successful, orderly institutionalization of a new, more differentiated social system is not always a necessary outcome. Moreover, at any level of development, response to the problems created by the process of differentiation may take one of several different forms (Weber 1922a; Eisenstadt 1963a). The most extreme outcome is failure to develop any adequate institutional solution to the new problems arising from growing differentiation. Aside from biological extinction, the consequences may be total or partial disintegration of the system, a semiparasitic existence at the margin of another society, or total submersion within another society.

A less extreme type of response tends to lead to "regression," that is, to the institutionalization of less differentiated systems within the more differentiated system that has broken down. Examples include the establishment of small patrimonial or semifeudal chiefdoms on the ruins of the Achaemenid Empire, the development of dispersed tribal–feudal systems at the downfall of the Roman Empire, and similar developments on the ruins of Greek city-states. Many such regressive developments are only partial, in the sense that within some parts of the new institutional structure some nuclei of more differentiated and creative orientations may survive or even develop. Sometimes, but certainly not always, these nuclei "store" entrepreneurial ability for possible—but not inevitable—future developments.

Another possibility, which perhaps overlaps with the last one but is not always identical with it, is the development of a social system in which the processes of differentiation and change go on relatively continuously in one part or sphere of a society without becoming fully integrated into a stable, wider framework. In such situations a continuous process of unbalanced change may develop, resulting either in a breakdown of the existing institutional framework or in stabilization at a relatively low level of integration. Perhaps the best examples of such developments can be found in various "dual conquest" societies (for example, conquest of the sedentary population by nomads in the Mongol Empire) and especially in the pre-independence stages of modern colonial societies.

A fourth, and perhaps the most variegated, type of response to growing differentiation consists of some structural solution that is on the whole congruent with the relevant problems. Within this broad type a wide variety of concrete institutional arrangements is possible. Such different solutions usually have different structural results and repercussions. Each denotes a different structure crystallized according to different integrative criteria and is interpenetrated in a different way by the other major social spheres.

Thus, drawing on examples from the great centralized empires of history, we see that although the initial stages of socioeconomic differentiation were relatively similar in Byzantium, in the later (Abbasside) caliphate, and in post-Han China, each of these societies developed different over-all institutional structures (Eisenstadt 1963a). The Byzantine Empire became a highly militarized and politically oriented system, whereas the caliphate developed a theocratic structure, which was based on continuous attempts to institutionalize a new type of universalistic politicoreligious community. China developed a centralized system based on the power of the emperor and the bureaucracy and, at the local level, on the relative predominance of the gentry; the selective channels of the examination system and the elite formed by the literati were the major mechanisms for integrating the local and central levels.

One very interesting structural solution is the development of a relatively stable system in which the major institutional spheres *vary* in degree of differentiation. One of the most important examples of such variation occurs in feudal systems, which are characterized by a relatively high degree of differentiation in some of the central cultural roles as against a much smaller degree of differentiation in the economic and political roles.

In cases of such uneven differentiation the more differentiated units of such related societies (for example, the church in feudal or patrimonial systems) often tend to develop a sort of international system of their own, apart from that of their "parent" societies.

The variety of integrative criteria and institutional contours at any level of differentiation is, of course, not limitless. The very notion of interdependence among major institutional spheres negates the assumption that any number of levels of differentiation in different institutional spheres can coalesce into a relatively stable institutional system. The level of differentiation in any one sphere necessarily constitutes, within broad limits, a precondition for the effective institutionalization of certain levels of differentiation in other social spheres. But within these broad limits of mutual preconditioning a great deal of structural variety is possible.

The intersocietal environment. The processes of change and of differentiation, on the one hand, and the development of different integrative responses to them, on the other, do not take place within single, closed societies. They are closely related to the international system that constitutes the broader environment of any society. Each society is related to many others geopolitically, ecologically, and socioculturally. These relations constitute the environment to which each society has to adapt and which may also influence its ability to evolve institutional responses to the processes of change.

Such international geopolitical factors, in the broadest sense, not only provide the general setting for any given society but also give rise to many of the concrete pressures upon it, such as external pressures of population, problems of military security, or adjustment to international trade. Such an intersocietal environment need not always consist of societies of the same type or level of differentiation; it may, indeed, contain many different types of societies. In general, it can be assumed that the more differentiated a society is, the greater is its *systemic* sensitivity—although not necessarily its ability to cope with these problems—to a wider and more variegated international setting.

Thus, at any given level of differentiation, the crystallization of different institutional orders is shaped by the interaction between the broader structural features of the major institutional spheres, on the one hand, and, on the other, the development of elites or entrepreneurs in some of the institutional spheres of that society, in some of its enclaves, or even in other societies with which it is in some way connected.

The variability in the concrete components of such interaction helps to explain the great (but not limitless) variety of structural and integrative forms that may be institutionalized at any given level of differentiation. Although different societies may arrive at broadly similar stages of evolution in terms of the differentiation of their major institutional and symbolic spheres, yet the concrete institutional contours developed at each such step, as well as the possible outcomes of such institutionalization in terms of further development, breakdown, regression, or stagnation, may differ greatly among them.

Reappraising evolutionary theory

The preceding analysis of processes of change and differentiation and of concomitant institutionalization of new structures indicates some of the problems that are posed by any attempt to reappraise the evolutionary perspective in sociological theory.

First is the exploration of the different mechanisms of social change and the distinction between those conditions and processes of change that create potentialities for transformation and those that do not. It is obvious, as indicated above, that not all processes of social change necessarily give rise to changes in over-all institutional systems. Although the potentialities for such systemic changes (as distinct from changes in patterns of behavior, in the composition of subgroups, or in the contents of the major integrative criteria of different spheres) exist in all societies, the very actualization of these potentialities, as well as the tempo and direction of such changes, varies greatly among different societies (Eggan 1963; Eisenstadt 1963a).

Second, and closely connected with the first, is the problem of how cumulative the development is of different types of institutional organization. Here it seems that in some institutions there may indeed be a "scale" or "semiscale" order of development, although the application of scale analysis to this type of phenomenon has so far failed to detect any perfect regularities (Carneiro 1962; Goodenough 1963). Such scale order is probably to be found least in the sphere of kinship or family institutions, whereas it is more pronounced in those institutional spheres, such as economics, politics, and law, that are most closely connected with technology or with organizational problems (Wolf 1964; Schwartz & Miller 1964).

However, even the existence of such scale order does not necessarily imply that developments in any institutional sphere are necessarily cumulative in the sense that they can be transferred easily from one society to another at a similar general level of differentiation; neither does it imply that their development within any single society or their transfer from one to another must necessarily proceed in a certain order or that "jumps" are not possible. Studies of the modernization of traditional societies are especially relevant from the point of view of the possibilities of such jumps, although similar cases can probably be found in other types of societies also (Eisenstadt 1963b). At most, studies of such scale order indicate that a certain trait or organizational type may be a necessary, but certainly not a sufficient, condition for the emergence of another; even here, the findings of "quasi scales" indicate the possibility of many functional equivalents of any such trait in a sequential series—especially in cases of rapid social change (Schwartz & Miller 1964).

Third is the question of the extent to which the problems arising from growing differentiation and the institutional solutions to these problems are indeed the same in different societies, thus creating some common trend of development. This problem is very close to that of the relation, to use Sahlins' and Service's nomenclature (1960), between "specific" and "general" evolution or that of the feasibility of the assumption, as put by Eggan (1963, p. 355), "that these particular developments necessarily add up to 'the succession of culture through stages of overall progress,' which is general evolution." But there appears to be no reason why all societies should reach certain stages of differentiation or why they should necessarily develop the same types of institutional contours once they attain such stages. The most that can be claimed at present is that the processes of differentiation in different societies exhibit similar formal and structural characteristics and that these create somewhat similar integrative problems.

It is in these common characteristics and problems that the fact of the common humanity of all human societies, as well as the possibilities of some common understanding and of intersocietal borrowing and transfer of institutions, is rooted; moreover, these characteristics indicate the existence of some "evolutionary universals" in the development of different human societies (Parsons 1964). However, the variety of possible "functional equivalents" of institutionalized solutions to such problems, as well as the possibilities of "regression," stress the fact that the paths of development of different societies are neither necessarily common nor given. In other words, there is no reason to assume that there is a *necessary* relation and congruity between the mechanisms of genetic (here cultural or social) "transmission and change and the route of development of this or that organism or species" (Gellner 1965, p. 17).

This discussion is closely related to the fourth, very crucial problem involved in the reappraisal of evolutionary perspectives: the explanation of the variability of institutionalized solutions to the problems arising from the development of a given level of structural differentiation. Here it should be recognized that the conditions giving rise to structural differentiation and to "structural sensitivity" to a greater range of problems do not necessarily create the capacity to solve these problems.

Creative entrepreneurial elites.   The crucial factor is the presence or absence, in one or several institutional spheres, of an active group of special "entrepreneurs"—that is, an elite that is able to offer solutions to the new range of problems. Among modern sociologists Weber came closest to recognizing this factor when he stressed that the creation of new institutional structures depends heavily on the "push" given by various "charismatic" groups or personalities and that the routinization of charisma is critical for the crystallization and continuation of new institutional structures (Weber [1922b] 1963, chapters 4, 10, and 11). The development of such "charismatic" personalities or groups constitutes perhaps the closest social analogy to genetic mutation. It is the possibility of such mutation that explains why, at any level of differentiation, a given social sphere contains not one but several, often competing, possible orientations and potentialities for development.

As yet, we know little about the specific conditions (as distinct from the more general trend toward structural differentiation) that facilitate the rise of new elites—that is, the conditions which influence the nature of their basic orientations as well as their relations with broader groups, strata, and trends of development, and their ability to forge out and maintain a viable institutional order. There are indications, however, that factors beyond the general trend toward differentiation are important. For example, various special enclaves, such as sects, monasteries, and sectarian intellectual groups or scientific communities, play an important role in the formation of such elites. Furthermore, a number of recent studies (see, for instance, McClelland 1961; Hagen 1962) have indicated the importance of certain familial, ideological, and educational orientations and institutions.

Within this context, it is necessary to re-examine the whole problem of the extent to which institutional patterns are crystallized through diffusion from other societies rather than through independent invention within a society. Cases of diffusion might be partially due to successful importation, by entrepreneurial groups on the margins of a given society, of acceptable solutions to latent problems or needs within that society.

Intersocietal borrowing.   The problems of the interaction between processes of change and "mutative" elites are closely related to a set of problems bearing on the intersocietal nature of evolution. We have seen that the international setting not only constitutes the environment to which any single society has to adapt itself but also provides a reservoir of responses that may be available to it; for instance, the setting may provide enclaves from which new elites or adaptive techniques and organizations can be borrowed.

The existence of such interrelationships—in terms of both common problems and the possibility of "borrowing" solutions—necessarily underlies the basic mutual resemblance of human societies, and it is in turn closely related to the problem of the extent to which it is possible to talk about general "social" evolution or the evolution of human society as a total entity. However, the existence of such mutual resemblance certainly does not ensure that the development of "human society" as a unified system with common adaptive mechanisms necessarily increases its ability to deal with over-all problems of adaptation. Paradoxically, the very interrelatedness of societies may create problems with which they may not be able to deal. What may seem to be a positive accumulation of available mechanisms and a repertoire of adaptations from the point of view of human society as a whole may yet, because of the lack of intersocietal integrative and adaptive mechanisms, constitute a very grave problem.

Limitations of evolutionary theory

The considerations presented above constitute the background for a reappraisal of the evolutionary perspective within the framework of recent sociological theory. An evolutionary perspective, from the point of view of human societies, makes sense only so far as at least some of the processes of change that are inherent in any social system create the potentialities for the institutionalization of more differentiated social and symbolic systems. From the point of view of human society or culture as a whole, such a perspective makes sense only insofar as there exist some mechanisms for the transmission of various institutional and adaptive techniques and for creating some common, intersocietal, adaptive and integrative capabilities and frameworks.

With regard to all these areas, several problems for which there exist as yet no adequate solutions have been pointed out above. They have, in a way, all focused on the interaction between processes of social differentiation, on the one hand, and the formation and activities of different elites, on the other. It is this interaction that makes possible the institutionalization of different integrative principles and concrete structures at a given level of societal differentiation. Any search for solutions to these problems must concentrate on the various aspects of these processes. In this endeavor broad evolutionary considerations indicate ranges of possibilities and types of potential breakthroughs but do not in themselves provide answers.

SHMUEL N. EISENSTADT

[Directly related are the entries on EMPIRES; FEUDALISM; SOCIAL INSTITUTIONS. Other relevant material may be found in ANTHROPOLOGY; DIFFUSION.]

BIBLIOGRAPHY

BELLAH, ROBERT N. 1964 Religious Evolution. American Sociological Review 29:358–374.

BOCK, KENNETH E. 1963 Evolution, Function and Change. American Sociological Review 28:229–237.

CARNEIRO, ROBERT L. 1962 Scale Analysis as an Instrument for the Study of Cultural Evolution. Southwestern Journal of Anthropology 18, no. 2:149–169.

EGGAN, FRED 1963 Cultural Drift and Social Change. Current Anthropology 4:347–355.

EISENSTADT, SHMUEL N. 1963a The Political Systems of Empires. New York: Free Press. → Contains an extended bibliography.

EISENSTADT, SHMUEL N. 1963b Modernization: Growth and Diversity. Bloomington: Indiana Univ., Department of Government.

EISENSTADT, SHMUEL N. 1964a Social Change, Differentiation and Evolution. American Sociological Review 29:375–386.

EISENSTADT, SHMUEL N. 1964b Institutionalization and Change. American Sociological Review 29:235–247.

GELLNER, ERNEST 1965 Thought and Change. London: Weidenfeld & Nicolson.

GINSBERG, MORRIS (1932) 1961 The Concept of Evolution in Sociology. Volume 1, pages 180–199 in Morris Ginsberg, Essays in Sociology and Social Philosophy. London: Heinemann.

GOODENOUGH, WARD H. 1963 Some Applications of Guttman Scale Analysis to Ethnography and Culture Theory. Southwestern Journal of Anthropology 19: 235–250.

HAGEN, EVERETT E. 1962 On the Theory of Social Change. Homewood, Ill.: Dorsey.

MCCLELLAND, DAVID C. 1961 The Achieving Society. Princeton, N.J.: Van Nostrand.

MEAD, MARGARET 1964 Continuities in Cultural Evolution. New Haven: Yale Univ. Press.

PARSONS, TALCOTT 1964 Evolutionary Universals in Society. American Sociological Review 29:339–357.

SAHLINS, MARSHALL D. 1964 Culture and Environment: The Study of Cultural Ecology. Pages 132–147 in Sol Tax (editor), Horizons of Anthropology. Chicago: Aldine.

SAHLINS, MARSHALL D.; and SERVICE, ELMAN R. (editors) 1960 Evolution and Culture. Ann Arbor: Univ. of Michigan Press.

SCHWARTZ, RICHARD D.; and MILLER, JAMES C. 1964 Legal Evolution and Social Complexity. American Journal of Sociology 70:159–169.

WEBER, MAX (1922a) 1957 The Theory of Social and Economic Organization. Edited by Talcott Parsons. Glencoe, Ill.: Free Press. → First published as Part 1 of Wirtschaft und Gesellschaft.

WEBER, MAX (1922b) 1963 The Sociology of Religion. Boston: Beacon. → First published in German.

WHITE, LESLIE A. 1959 The Evolution of Culture: The Development of Civilization to the Fall of Rome. New York: McGraw-Hill.

WOLF, ERIC R. 1964 The Study of Evolution. Pages 108–119 in Sol Tax (editor), Horizons of Anthropology. Chicago: Aldine.

VI
EVOLUTION AND BEHAVIOR

The fundamental postulate of the modern biological theory of evolution is that the guiding agency of evolutionary changes is adaptation to the environments that a species inhabits. This is equally true of changes in structural features, physiology, and behavior of organisms. Evolutionary developments maintain the adaptedness of the species when the environments change, or they improve the adaptedness if the environments are more or less stationary. The environment does not, however, impose changes on the organism, as was believed by some early evolutionists, particularly by the adherents of the now almost completely abandoned Lamarckian hypothesis. It is more accurate to say that the environment presents challenges, to which a living species may respond by adaptive modification of its genetic endowment (genotype). If a response is elicited, the adaptedness is preserved or improved; if the species fails to respond, its fitness declines and it may become extinct. The genetic raw materials from which evolutionary changes may be constructed are mutations, that is, alterations in the gene or chromosome structures. The effects that mutations produce vary in magnitude all the way from alterations so drastic that the mutant is inviable (lethal, as a fatal hereditary disease causing death before sexual maturity) to changes so slight that the change in fitness, if any, that they produce can be detected only by means of refined statistical study. Mutant genes may be favorable only in heterozygous carriers (hybrid vigor, or heterosis) but unfavorable in double dose (in homozygous condition). Or a genetic change may be favorable in some environments and unfavorable in others. Or, finally, a mutant gene may be favorable in combinations with some genes but unfavorable in combination with others.

The great evolutionary importance of sexual reproduction lies in that it constantly combines and recombines the various genes present in the species population, enabling the favorable gene combinations to arise and to be tested by natural selection. In sexually reproducing and outbreeding species, such as man, no two individuals (except identical twins) have the same genotype. We inherit our genes from our parents and pass them to our children, but the gene constellation, the genotype, of every individual is unique. By and large, the greater the change a mutation produces, the greater the chance it will be harmful to the organism.

The adaptive evolutionary changes are compounded almost exclusively of the slight mutational changes (sometimes termed polygenic changes). Changes of greater magnitudes are important rather as the source of the genetic pathology, incapacitation, or weakness. Such diseases as phenylketonuria, with its associated mental defects, and schizophrenia, to name only two, are examples of deleterious mutants affecting behavior. Apart from their negative importance for public health, mutations that produce strikingly visible alterations are also important as materials for genetic studies. Most of the pioneering work in genetics was done with genetic variants that must be classed as more or less pathological deviants and that play only negative roles in evolution, contributing to the "genetic load" the population carries.

Natural selection. Mutational changes, those affecting behavior as well as those responsible for structural and physiological alterations, are mostly harmful to the organism. This is the reason why any increase of the frequency of mutations in human populations (for example, through exposure to X rays, other mutagenic radiations, or chemical mutagens) can result only in a reduction of the average fitness of the populations concerned. How, then, can mutations serve as building blocks for adaptive evolutionary changes? The answer is that mutational changes and their combinations are sorted out by natural selection. The majority of mutations that decrease the fitness of their carriers in all environments and in all combinations are cast out of the populations by natural selection; those that are useful in at least some environments and in some combinations are preserved and multiplied.

The action of natural selection is sometimes compared to that of a sieve, separating the useful genetic variants from the harmful ones. This analogy is misleading if it is taken too literally. Human populations, and those of most sexually reproducing and outbreeding species, always carry great stores of genetic variants which arose by mutation in the immediate or remote past. The genetic reassortments, combined with natural selection in changing environments, become a cybernetic process in which the genetic developments that occur at a given time depend upon the changes that have taken place earlier, and, in turn, they condition the developments that may take place in the future.

Mutation, the process that supplies the raw materials from which evolutionary changes can be constructed, is repeatable and reversible; it is a physiological and, in the last analysis, a mechanical process. But the evolution controlled by natural selection becomes a creative process that is unlikely to be reversed or to be repeated. Evolutionary transformations, such as the transformations that have led to the emergence of the human species, are chains of unique, nonrecurrent events.

Importance of environment. Another consideration, particularly relevant in relation to the evolution of behavior, is that heredity determines not fixed "characters" or "traits" but reactions of the developing organism to the environment. The trait "behavior" obviously cannot be transmitted in inheritance, because it is not present in the sex cells, which are the only material bridge connecting the parents with their progeny. But neither is the skin color inherited in this sense, because no skin pigment is present in the sex cells. What the sex cells do carry are genes, and the genes determine the pattern, or path, that the development of an individual will follow in a given sequence of environments. Another individual with similar genes, an identical twin, may develop differently if his environments are different. A carrier of a different set of genes might also develop differently in similar environments.

We observe that human beings vary with respect to a great many traits—skin color, height, weight, head shape, intelligence, temperament, and special abilities, among countless others. As a broad generalization, it is fair to say that whenever the variation in any trait has been adequately studied genetically, it has been found to be influenced by both genetic and environmental factors. In the past, investigators have often tried to determine which traits are genetic or hereditary and which are environmental; such a dichotomy is now recognized as naive and misleading. All traits, or at any rate a great majority of them, are both genetic and environmental. If everybody had the same genes, as identical twins do, people would look and behave more nearly alike than they actually do. Likewise, if the environments in which people grow and develop were made uniform, this would also result in a reduction of the observed structural and behavioral diversity.

Fixity and conditioned plasticity. No living species inhabits an absolutely uniform and constant environment. Organisms have to face many environments, variable both in space and in time. For example, the inhabitants of the temperate and cold climates must survive in both summer and winter environments. Man achieves more and more effective control over his physical environments, but he must face a great and growing diversity of sociocultural environments. There are two ways to become adapted to a diversity of environments, and both have actually been used in the evolutionary process, including human evolution. One is genetic fixity and genetic specialization; the other is genetically conditioned developmental plasticity. In general, genetic fixity is characteristic of traits whose presence and precise form are indispensable for survival and reproduction. The developmental processes giving rise to such traits are said to be homeostatically buffered, so that they can occur in all environments that the species normally encounters in its habitats. Thus, with very few exceptions, all infants are born with two eyes, a four-chambered heart, physiological systems which digest food and maintain a constant body temperature, ability to learn a symbolic human language, etc. Genetic specialization makes the species polymorphic (consisting of two or more genetically distinct forms living and interbreeding in the same territory) or polytypic (consisting of races that inhabit different territories and are genetically adapted to the environments of their respective territories). For example, the darker and the lighter skin pigmentation of some human races is plausibly supposed to fit them to the climatic conditions of the lands in which they originally lived.

Genetically conditioned developmental plasticity is advantageous when the organism profits by having some traits shaped differently in the different environments that it encounters. The tanning of human skin on exposure to sunlight is an example of such a plasticity. It is important to realize that both fixity and plasticity are genetically determined. Natural selection favored the spread and establishment of mutant genes which in some populations make the skin permanently darkly pigmented and in other races make the pigmentation contingent on sun exposure.

Culture. The most significant product, and the paramount determining factor, of human evolution is culture. The relationships between the biological evolution and culture are frequently misunderstood, and it is important to make them clear. Culture is not transmitted biologically through some special genes; it is acquired anew in every generation by learning and instruction, in large part through the medium of the symbolic language. However, the capacity to learn and to instruct and, most essential of all, the capacity to use the symbolic language, is biologically and genetically vouchsafed to every nonpathological human being. An individual whose genes deprive him of these capacities is an obvious misfit, and his genes are likely to be eliminated by natural selection. Conversely, it is safe to assume that the genetic equipment that made the human species capable of developing and maintaining culture has been compounded by natural selection in the course of the prehuman, subhuman, and human evolution.

Of the many existing forms of human culture, the particular one an individual acquires is determined by the society in which this individual is brought up, rather than by his genes. And yet, not only the ability to acquire any culture at all but also the capacity and inclination to choose this or that occupation, role, or trade within a culture may well be genetically conditioned, facilitated, or hindered. The ability to speak is genetically determined, but what a person will actually say is largely independent of genetics.

Human acquired, extrabiological culture is man's most potent adaptive instrument; it is chiefly by brain, not by brawn, that man controls his environments. Since, however, human environments are preponderantly created by culture, the possession of a genetic endowment that enables members of human populations to adapt themselves to these cultural environments becomes overwhelmingly important. The evolution of the biological basis of human behavior has been controlled by this fact. In all cultures, primitive as well as advanced, the vital ability is, and always was, for every individual to be able to learn whatever is necessary to become a competent member of the culture of which the individual is a part. For this reason, natural selection has favored in human evolution a remarkable plasticity of the behavioral development; man's cardinal adaptive trait is his educability, that is, his capacity to adjust his behavior to circumstances in the light of experience.

Most individuals can be trained, with a greater or lesser facility, for many or most of the occupations and roles that a given culture requires to be filled. Almost everybody could become, if properly brought up, a fairly competent farmer, craftsman, soldier, sailor, teacher, or priest. This is the valid premise of the *tabula rasa* theory, from which this theory draws an erroneous conclusion. First clearly stated by John Locke in 1690, this theory is still popular in many circles. It asserts that a human being at birth is a clean slate on which the environment will inscribe a collection of attributes and qualities. The genetically secured developmental plasticity of human behavior, however, is not at all incompatible with genetic diversity. It is eminently probable that an infant at birth is not a clean slate and that some individuals are, because of their genetic endowments, more easily trainable for some occupations than for others. This is certain for some specialized professions; by no means does everybody have the genetic wherewithal to become a fine singer or a first-class composer or performer of music, or to achieve peak performance in sports or in art.

Biologically, this makes sense; the development of cultures and civilizations has not caused the diversity of vocations to become smaller; on the contrary, this diversity increases by leaps and bounds. The biologically adaptive response to this situation is obviously a combination of an educability or trainability, with an underlying genetic diversity to facilitate the division of labor.

The fallacy of racism.   While the variants of the *tabula rasa* theory would make us believe that all the observed differences, especially all the differences in behavior, between people are the products of upbringing and education, the even more pernicious fallacy of racism would claim that these differences are genetically fixed and largely independent of the environment. One superficially plausible argument often given in favor of racist views is worth discussing here, because it will enable us to bring out clearly an important feature of the evolution of human behavior. It is claimed that the variation in psychic or behavioral traits among human individuals and races must be genetically fixed to about the same extent as it is among breeds of domestic animals. Different breeds of dogs, horses, or cattle are indeed clearly different in behavior, temperament, disposition, intelligence, trainability, etc. These differences are very largely genetically fixed, although by careful training and discipline one can modify them to some

extent. Why then, it is argued, should the differences between humans be supposed to be anything but genetic?

This argument overlooks a profound dissimilarity between the evolutionary histories of the human species and of the animals that man has domesticated. The behavior of a breed of a domestic animal is an essential part of the complex of characteristics that are selected to fit this breed for its intended use. A work horse should not behave like a race horse, because this would make it dangerous and inefficient, and a race horse should not behave like a work horse if it is to win any races. The laboratory mouse and the laboratory rat are sluggish, unaggressive, and apparently dim-witted compared to the wild mouse and the wild rat. They would hardly survive under the conditions in which their wild ancestors thrive; it has been claimed that these species have degenerated when man has furnished their food and shelter. It is, however, obvious that wild mice and wild rats are inconvenient as laboratory animals, and that is why they are seldom used in laboratories.

What would be rated as degenerate in the wild state is a desirable trait in an animal living in a laboratory cage. Man has seen to it that the genes for fixing and stabilizing desirable behavior are established and that the genes for undesirable behavior are bred out of the animals he has domesticated. Although some writers have seen fit to call man a "self-domesticated" animal (a designation accepted by few biologists), his evolutionary pattern is in many ways just the reverse. As previously stated, natural selection may favor mutant genes that confer a developmental fixity on some traits and developmental plasticity on others; the latter is the case with human behavior. A person who is able to learn whatever modes of behavior fit various professions and vocations available in a human society, and to adjust himself to the ways of life that go with these professions and vocations, is likely to have both a social and a biological advantage. An individual set in his ways, always aggressive or always yielding, unable and unwilling to learn or to be trained, is likely to be discriminated against by natural selection. The great developmental plasticity of psychic traits in man is, thus, no biological accident but, on the contrary, a fundamental evolutionary adaptation that distinguishes man from nonhuman animals.

Ethics.   A considerable amount of speculation has been devoted to the problem of whether human ethics could have arisen through the action of natural selection in the evolutionary process. Natural selection is obviously not a benevolent spirit guiding the evolution but a blind and opportunistic process. It is opportunistic in the sense that it promotes the establishment of genes which confer an advantage for survival or reproduction when and where the selection acts, regardless of whether these same genes may be disadvantageous later on. The extinction of countless species of organisms has been due to such a narrow, overspecialized adaptation to the environments that did not endure. Now, it is conceivable that natural selection might encourage genes for altruistic behavior in a species broken up into numerous small colonies or subpopulations. "Altruistic" is in this case to be defined as a behavior benefiting the group (family, clan, tribe) to which the individual so behaving belongs and detrimental to that individual himself. A small population in which genes for such behavior occur may prosper and multiply, despite some of the carriers of these genes sacrificing themselves for the sake of their fellows and thus not transmitting their genes to their own progeny. Conversely, in a large, undivided population, genes for "egotistic" or "criminal" behavior may secure an advantage, if their carriers survive and leave progeny at the expense of other members of the population.

Another possibility is that altruism and egotism are not products of some kind of special genes but, rather, products of cultural developments transmitted not by genes but by learning. C. H. Waddington (1960) has argued that natural selection acts to make man an "ethicizing being" and an "authority acceptor." Particularly in childhood but also during his entire life, a person is able and even eager to acquire, from his parents or from other persons, ideas about what is good and what is evil and to accept instruction or counsel concerning the desirable ways of living in a society with other human beings. According to this view, man is not born virtuous or vicious but with a capacity for both virtue and vice. Biological evolution does not make man ethically better or worse, but it does promote intellectual alacrity and perhaps a sensitivity to ethical issues.

Future developments. Even more speculative and uncertain are the attempts to prognosticate the future evolutionary developments of human behavioral traits and capacities. This is evidently a part of a more general problem of the evolutionary perspectives of the human species. An opinion often expressed is that the biological evolution of man has virtually completed its course, and from now on any further development will be in the cultural realm. This is true to the extent that cultural changes are more rapid than the genetic ones, and this is, in fact, the reason why the development of the capacity for culture has conferred upon the human species an unprecedentedly high biological fitness. It should, however, be kept in mind that the maintenance, not to speak of further expansion, of cultural capacities is possible only on the basis of sound human genetic endowments. Improvement, maintenance, and prevention of deterioration of these genetic endowments is the task of the applied science of eugenics. Many eugenists have been extremely pessimistic about the genetic future of mankind, believing that the genetic processes which go on in human populations trend inexorably toward biological disaster. Others have urged various remedial schemes, such as sterilization of the unfit, or the artificial insemination of women by semen collected from biologically superior donors and preserved in frozen condition for extensive use over the years. During the first third of the twentieth century, eugenics was often used as a support of ultraconservative social philosophies and racist doctrines. All this has made many social scientists, and the public at large, properly skeptical and suspicious of eugenic schemes. Yet eugenics undoubtedly has a sound core; sooner or later man will be forced to take the management of his evolution in his own hands.

THEODOSIUS DOBZHANSKY

[*Other relevant material may be found in* EUGENICS; GENETICS; PSYCHOLOGY, *article on* COMPARATIVE PSYCHOLOGY; *and in the biography of* DARWIN.]

BIBLIOGRAPHY

DOBZHANSKY, THEODOSIUS 1962 *Mankind Evolving: The Evolution of the Human Species.* New Haven: Yale Univ. Press.

DOBZHANSKY, THEODOSIUS 1964 *Heredity and the Nature of Man.* New York: Harcourt.

FULLER, JOHN L.; and THOMPSON, W. ROBERT 1960 *Behavior Genetics.* New York: Wiley.

HALLER, MARK H. 1963 *Eugenics: Hereditarian Attitudes in American Thought.* New Brunswick, N.J.: Rutgers Univ. Press.

HIRSCH, JERRY 1962 Individual Differences in Behavior and Their Genetic Basis. Pages 3–23 in Eugene L. Bliss (editor), *Roots of Behavior: Genetics, Instinct, and Socialization in Animal Behavior.* New York: Harper.

ROE, ANNE; and SIMPSON, GEORGE G. (editors) 1958 *Behavior and Evolution.* New Haven: Yale Univ. Press.

WADDINGTON, CONRAD H. 1960 *The Ethical Animal.* London: Allen & Unwin.

EXCHANGE, ECONOMIC

See EXCHANGE AND DISPLAY; SPECIALIZATION AND EXCHANGE.

EXCHANGE, SOCIAL

See under INTERACTION.

EXCHANGE AND DISPLAY

Exchange refers to the transaction of labor, resources, products, and services within a society. Exchange is not limited to the market economies of industrial societies. Market economies appeared late in world history and until recently were few in number. Even today most of the world's societies do not have fully developed market economies; the range extends from those with no market institutions whatsoever, through those with peripheral markets, to those with important but by no means fully developed market institutions. For such economies as these, it is necessary to consider modes of exchange other than market exchange.

Karl Polanyi (1944; Polanyi et al. 1957) identified and defined three modes of exchange: reciprocal, redistributive, and market. The three modes of exchange are found singly or in combination in the economic organizations of the diverse societies of the world. They seem to be capable of clear and evident definition whatever the complexities required in the analysis of their operation in an economic system. In brief, reciprocity is obligatory gift exchange; redistribution is obligatory payment to an allocative center; and market exchange is purchase and sale with reference to a price system. The three modes subsume all the types of exchange recognized in any society. Transfers or transactions that cannot be included in these categories are considered by a society to be illegitimate or wrong for that very reason.

Most important of all, however, the three modes are the functioning aspects of the integrative structures of various types of economies. A society can be structurally integrated by its social, political, or economic organization, or by some combination of these organizations. When one of these structures predominates or, more rarely, is the sole structure present in the society, a clear model type is discernible. There are three such clear model types. For example, a social economy is one in which the social organization integrates economic life; here reciprocity is the prevailing mode of exchange. In a political economy, the political organization integrates economic life; redistributive exchange prevails. In a market-integrated economy, market exchange prevails. It follows that there will be mixed types of economy ranging through those in which two of the three possible structures of the society seem to be of about equivalent importance, but predominate over the third, to one in which all three have a roughly equivalent importance.

In the comparative study of exchange, the subject of gift giving has a historical and continuing place. It was Marcel Mauss who first investigated the socioeconomic nature of gift giving, and his ideas form part of the present discussion of reciprocal exchange.

The subject of display, which has excited analytical interest since Thorstein Veblen's *The Theory of the Leisure Class* (1899), will be discussed in relation to the three modes of exchange. It will be shown that there are three types of display, each of which is specific to one of the three modes of exchange and its type of economy and social context.

Reciprocity and social economy

Marcel Mauss pointed out the completely obligatory character of gift exchange. He described it as one of the many forms of obligatory reciprocity that expressed and maintained the articulated individual and group relationships of primitive social systems (1925). There existed no "natural," or "pure," market economy in primitive societies. Goods had social or moral value but not some separate economic value. They were exchanged in the same social way as were courtesies and respects or as "entertainments, ritual, military assistance, women, children, dances, and feasts; and fairs in which the market is but one element and the circulation of wealth but one part of a wide and enduring contract." Gift exchange, therefore, was part of a system of "total prestations," as Mauss termed it, in which individuals in a society had both to give and receive in all social exchanges under the "sanction of private or open warfare." If gift giving (or any other sort of social exchange) is often thought of as free and voluntary, it is because the members of a social group far more willingly receive and give than they act in any way that would threaten their membership in the group. The ideas of Mauss continue to be useful but require reworking.

Reciprocity, the receiving and giving of goods and services, is built into the human life cycle and the social order. Without it the nonproducing young could not live and mature to provide the next generation with its livelihood and the social order its continuity. There would be no cushioning of misfortune or infirmity, and the world would be without festivity, hospitality, and benefice. Reciprocity as a mode of exchange is a different matter. It is not universally an important mode of exchange except in those societies that are called primitive by the anthropologist. In nonprimitive folk, peasant, or state-organized societies, reciprocities involve one or both of the other two modes of exchange. For example, for reciprocal gift giving to take place in industrial society, it is necessary for the donors to go into the market for the gifts they will exchange; even the crudest *Kindergarten Handarbeit* will have required for its manufacture some tool or material obtained in the market.

The distinctive character of primitive societies is that they are organized by their social structures. Primitive societies are without independent economic or political structuring. The economic order is "embedded" in the social order as is the political order (Polanyi 1944, p. 57). The rigorous study of such societies is the study of kinship and its extensions and affiliations and of the interrelations of the roles and social groupings formed on a kinship base. Economic aspects can be analyzed out of this social matrix, but such analysis will prove only that in so socialized a situation economic facts are social facts as well, and their ordering follows or is the social organization of the group concerned. It is proposed here that the economic systems of all such groups be called *social economies*. The use of this term sets out the distinguishing features of such systems and prevents the confusions that arise when the economy of such a group is spoken of as if it were a version, albeit a primitive version, of the separable and independent economic systems referred to by the economist.

Reciprocity is the prevailing and characteristic mode of exchange in the world's social economies, which is to say a majority of the world's societies up to the industrial revolution. Nothing other than a social economy existed until the development in the Neolithic of some state organizations or political economies. It is only in the past two centuries that the intrusions of Western market economies or Western political power exerted along economic lines have brought about the extinction of almost all pure social economies save, perhaps, those in Amazonas and the interior of New Guinea. Today, therefore, there are few going social economies in which reciprocity is the sole mode of exchange; but the number in which it is still the dominant mode of exchange is not insignificant, containing as it does a large number of African tribal societies and some Oceanic and American Indian societies.

A full illustration of how reciprocal exchanges follow the lines and groupings of the social structure in a social economy cannot be presented here. The reader is referred to such classic studies as Malinowski's study of the Trobriand Islanders (1922) and Firth's study of the Tikopia (1939). Certain famous institutions of primitive cultures, such as bridewealth, *kula*, and the potlatch have excited interest precisely because each demonstrates the essentially social nature of reciprocal exchange involving valued goods. Anthropologists and other social scientists have examined and re-examined these three institutions as somehow exemplary statements of some key part of the problem of the relation between the economic and the noneconomic in human society.

Bridewealth comprises goods, and sometimes labor services, transferred from the groom's social group to that of the wife. The institution of bridewealth is widespread in Africa, where it is almost always a vitally important institution and quite often highly elaborated. The goods used as bridewealth range from cattle to such items as hoes and pots. Elaborations occur in the amount of the bridewealth; in the number of installments in which it is transferred; in the presence, amount, and number of reciprocal goods (dowry) the wife may bring to the marriage; or in "cattle linking," in which a given marriage and transfer of bridewealth in cattle is determined by past marriages and predetermines future ones. The earlier term used for the institution was "brideprice," but the substitution of the term "bridewealth," suggested by Evans-Pritchard (1931, pp. 36–39), is now widely accepted. "Price" is a term that cannot be lifted out of the context of market economy free of the connotations of purchase and sale. The problem is therefore set: if there is an exchange in which goods of value and a woman are transferred, why is this not a matter of purchase and sale? The anthropologists' answer, although some are not in agreement on this point (Gray 1960), is that this transfer occurs in the context of a rearrangement of the social structure. The marriage creates new reciprocal roles, with new obligations and expectations; the giving of bridewealth is more important symbolically than it is economically. It is thus part of a vast series of social reciprocities and reciprocal exchanges of, as Mauss would say, courtesies, respects, women, dances, and so on, as well as of goods of value. The difference lies precisely in the fact that reciprocal exchange is part of continuing social process and behavior, while market exchange is an isolated, one-time economic act.

Kula is an institution of reciprocal exchange in which permanent partners give and receive recognized treasure items. There are two types of such treasure, which circulate in opposite directions around a *kula* ring made up of a number of island societies of the western Pacific. The institution is best known from the description of the Trobriand Islands by Malinowski (1922). The treasure items are shell armlets and spondylus shell necklaces, which are surrounded by lore and myth and which cannot be exchanged for anything besides one another in the *kula* ring. *Kula* partners engage in reciprocal exchanges of second-grade items (Bohannan 1963, p. 236) as an earnest of the generosity with which they will reciprocate gifts of the treasure items of the greatest possible value in the lore and myth that attaches to them. The whole affair is fraught with the real and magical hazards of long sea voyages by canoe, with elaborate ritual and ceremonial attesting to its importance and assuring its proper conduct and success, and with thrill and wonder about the treasures that have been or might be received. There is no question about the noneconomic nature of the *kula*. It is a reciprocal exchange devoid of economic motive, basis, or gain. This noneconomic interpretation of *kula* itself has been generally accepted, even by those who have claimed that *kula* was a pretext for carrying on a higgling pedestrian trade in very ordinary goods on the side—never with *kula* partners—during *kula* voyages. The problem *kula* sets is the same whatever emphasis is given to the non-*kula* trading on the side. Why is the institution so elaborated, and why are its opportunities so enthusiastically pursued? The only possible answer is that the reciprocal exchange of goods without economic value, no less than economic goods, acknowledges social worth by giving content to the playing of a social role. In *kula*, as is sometimes the case in bridewealth, there is feedback between the recognition of an individual's social prestige within his own society and outside it with his *kula* partners of other societies.

The potlatch of the Indian societies of the northwest coast of North America is an institution of reciprocal exchange in which the frequency, size, and system of exchanges became so great in some cases as to seem not only unique but also bizarre and incredible. It was among the Kwakiutl, in the first quarter of the twentieth century, that the potlatch reached its most extreme development (Codere 1950; 1961). At a potlatch, goods were ceremoniously displayed and then distributed by the potlatcher to a number of individuals of higher and lower social rank. The recipients returned the gift with an increment when they potlatched at some later date. Although the individuals concerned received their potlatch positions through inheritance, it was only by potlatching that the social rank and worth of these positions was maintained or enhanced. Enormous inventories of goods were involved in the over-all system of potlatching and even on the occasion of a single potlatch. The Kwakiutl earned Canadian dollars, particularly in the commercial fishing industry. These earnings were converted into vast quantities of mass-produced Western industrial goods, such as cheap blankets, clothing, housewares, and so on, all of which circulated in the potlatch system in amounts far above consumption needs and possibilities,

along with such traditional non-European goods as wooden canoes. The great season for potlatching was the wintertime, which was largely a time of vacation from economic effort. However, the only vacation from potlatching was just after giving one. The cycle of accumulating property by hard work and by making loans at interest began again as did the accumulation of new indebtedness through receiving goods as new or as returned gifts from other potlatchers. As in the case of *kula*, an immense lore captured the interest of the people. Twenty-five years after the effective end of potlatching, former participants were still recounting the details of past potlatches and the titles, rhetoric, and historical and mythical background associated with them.

The problem set by the potlatch is by now a familiar one with a familiar answer. In a social economy, the ends of all efforts are social; and they are organized along the lines of the social system itself, according to the reciprocal form of all social exchanges.

Redistribution and political economy

Redistribution is the form of exchange that occurs when taxes or other exactions are collected and reallocated by an administrative center. The term is not of the same descriptive accuracy as Polanyi's other two terms, since it does not make clear the nature of the exchange that takes place. Perhaps a better term would be "politically enforced exchange." It is political power that is behind the exaction of goods and services in exchange for membership in good standing in the polity along with whatever reallocations might be received in return. Such reallocations may be in the form of benefit from internal and territorial policing, judicial institutions, and public works or distributions.

Some redistributive exchange exists in many social economies. A rudimentary form of it would be the collection of foodstuffs by a headman for the giving of a feast in which all share. Redistribution also occurs in the relatively few predominantly market economies of the mid-nineteenth-century industrial nations, since some taxation was present in all of them. However, redistribution is the dominant mode of exchange in the political economies that include all those centralized state organizations, archaic and recent, from ancient Egypt, medieval Europe, and pre-Columbian Peru, to precolonial African and Asiatic states. In the political economy, the market is either relatively undeveloped or secondary and subservient to the polity, which, in large part, controls distribution of goods.

The precontact kingdom of Rwanda in east central Africa corresponds to the model of a political economy in which redistribution is the dominant mode of exchange. In Rwanda social life as well as economic life was politicized, although it is the latter that is of concern here (Codere 1962). The masses of the people were peasants who were forced to contribute goods and services to the support of a vast and complex political administration headed by the king, or *mwami* as he was called. Although they are said to have gloried in their poverty and subjugation, which is a matter in doubt, they received little beyond the minimum reallocations in return for almost the entirety of their production over and above what was needed for their own bare subsistence. From their feudal overlords, who were members of the governing caste and often simultaneously their local civil or military administrators, they received the custody and usufruct of a cow. This was probably more important as a symbol of being in good standing with the ruling caste than it was as an economic asset. From their administrators they received military protection, courts, and whatever benefits were inherent in the idea that the entire fertility and welfare of the land and the people depended upon the going order of things with the *mwami* at the head of the centralized state and its administration. The chief redistribution in Rwanda's economy was, in fact, the contribution made by the masses to the support of the few. The ruling caste comprised 15 per cent of the total population and was supported at a level of living that was always higher, and often astronomically higher, than that of the masses. The use or threat of force perpetuated the system.

The use of Rwanda as an example is not to suggest that all political economies have been similarly despotic or similarly one-sided in exacting much and reallocating very little in exchange. Rwanda, however, presents a type case of a political economy in which redistribution is the predominant mode of exchange. Market exchange was virtually nonexistent; and reciprocal exchange was cut back to a minimum, since the masses had neither the kinship organization development nor the economic wherewithal for it. In order to achieve such political ends as improving and maintaining their own power positions within the political hierarchy, the ruling caste engaged in a small number of reciprocal exchanges and in some exchanges of a redistributive character.

Market exchange and market economies

In the comparison of modes of exchange in diverse societies and economies, the salient features of market exchange are purchase and sale at a money price determined by the impersonal forces of supply and demand. It is important to emphasize the abstract and impersonal nature of market exchange as compared to the other two modes. Features that are the essence of reciprocal and redistributive exchange can be, and usually are, eliminated as irrelevancies in market exchange. These include, for example, the social and political roles of the exchangers, the obligatory sociability or ceremoniousness connected with the act of exchange, and social and political restrictions and specifications concerning which goods are exchangeable. To be sure, mutual courtesies and recognition of social worth or political position may accompany any instance of purchase and sale; but they are not necessary. Where they are present, it is either as an irrepressible human element or as part of the amount on the price tag, adjusted to cover such costs as time-consuming courtesy and the elegance of the place of sale.

Although economists have treated most industrial national economies as though they were analogs of the pure market economy model, it is those of the nineteenth century that fit the model best, since they entailed less regulation for any social or political end. Of them, Polanyi wrote (1944, p. 57): "Instead of economy being embedded in social relations, social relations are embedded in the economic system"; and he also stated that "a market economy is an economic system controlled, regulated and directed by markets alone" (p. 68). In a pure market economy, social and political relations are economized. It is not that social and political relations cease to exist; the former are necessary for the continuation of society and the latter for the policing of the market and enforcement of the principle of contract, by means of which it works. Where market exchange prevails, social and political organization give way to economic organization. It was in the dehumanizing and desocializing consequences of market autonomy that such critics of the system as Marx, Engels, Veblen, and Polanyi found their target, just as critics of totalitarian regimes have centered on the human costs of the politicizing of society.

Mixed modes of exchange

Perhaps in no empirical economy in the contemporary world is reciprocity, redistribution, or market exchange the sole mode of exchange, although typically one of the modes may predominate. In primitive societies, the usual situation today is a mixture of the three modes. This has sometimes come about through internal development but more often through the political and economic intrusions of the expanding industrial nations of the West.

In primitive societies where developments, especially of marketlike exchange, have been indigenous and contact influences slight, the three modes of exchange have frequently coexisted as separate spheres that have remained relatively compartmentalized. These have been termed "multicentric" economies by Bohannan and Dalton (1962, p. 3). An example would be Trobriand society (Malinowski 1922; Bohannan 1963, pp. 233–240), in which reciprocity is found in *kula* and kinship relations, redistribution in the exchanges of chiefs and others, and marketlike exchange, or an imperfect and moneyless market exchange, is represented by the ordinary trade accompanying the *kula* and in internal island trade. Another example is provided by Kwakiutl society (Codere 1950; 1961), as it existed from the turn of the century to the depression of the 1930s. Reciprocity characterized many exchanges of subsistence goods between kin and villagers, as well as exchange between individuals in the potlatch system. Market exchange in the Canadian market economy was the source of most of the goods used in potlatching, and some redistribution occurred in the special type of potlatching involved in the purchase of "coppers."

When the three modes of exchange are linked and cross-linked in contemporary economies, they rarely appear as distinct spheres but are relatively integrated by market exchange and the use of money. Thus, many economies today, industrial or nonindustrial, seem to be genuinely mixed economies. Africa furnishes many examples of social or social–political economies that have been permeated by market exchange. Western industrial nations exemplify the process in reverse as their nineteenth-century pure market exchange economies have been transformed into mixed ones. In Africa the European imposition of a money head tax on tribesmen forced the African into market exchange. By the time a man worked for the European to earn money to pay his own tax and that of his kinsmen, and returned with gifts purchased in the market and with money with which to buy a cow or cows for bridewealth, the three modes of exchange were linked and cross-linked. In the Western industrial nations, it was perhaps inevitable that where political power became more widely distributed among the people they would use it to regulate and use the market economy for social ends. For example, the social reciprocity of supporting aged kinfolk is in part taken care of by the payment of taxes and the redistribution to them of money they use in market exchange for purchases to meet their own needs, for gifts to give

reciprocally, and for redistributive payments such as property or sumptuary taxes.

Display

Veblen's *The Theory of the Leisure Class* (1899) is the point of departure for all inquiries into the meaning and uses of display in human society. His terms "conspicuous consumption," "conspicuous waste," and "conspicuous leisure" are still telling, and useful in discussions patterned after his on the universal association of display with social position and prestige. Contemporary social scientists, however, find universals of interest only if they can be fruitfully used in explanations of social behavior. They are not content to conclude, as Veblen did, that display is irrational from an economic point of view, or to leave the discussion of display, irrationality, prestige, and society on a generalized level.

By centering attention on display as it is associated with exchange, it seems possible to discern its essential role in society. This enables us to explain why it takes the forms it does and why it is associated with social prestige, political power, or economic importance.

The most frequent, most important, and most elaborate laying out of goods before the eyes of others will be connected with exchange and specific to the particular mode of exchange. To return to the model systems, in social economies, where reciprocal exchange predominates, the great displays are associated with those exchanges. Similar generalizations can be made for the political and market economies. The great displays are also great events that give visible proof of the productive effort and exchange relations that can be mobilized. They reaffirm and celebrate the system, even while they are part of it.

Displays connected with reciprocal exchange in social economies are frequently modest ones. There is not the production capacity in many cases to achieve anything much more impressive than sufficient food and drink for feasting and sufficient time to prepare for the festivities and participate in them. For example, the Papago Indians of southwestern North America had a saguaro, or cactus-fruit, wine feast, for which everyone produced and set out as many pots of wine as possible and then got publicly, communally, and "beautifully" drunk. In their desert environment and with their specific technology, this was probably the greatest abundance they could have produced; it was witnessed and enjoyed, and it was a great yearly event.

At the other extreme, in the rich natural environment of the northwest coast of North America the displays connected with potlatching were probably the greatest of any ever associated with reciprocal exchange in any primitive society. Wooden statues were often set up a hundred feet or so apart, marking the boundaries of the beachfront display of the goods that had been given away in a potlatch. Of course, these statues then measured the impressiveness of subsequent potlatch displays. The eye of the witness was delighted as well as impressed by various devices of presentation. Gold and silver bracelets, suspended from small stakes planted on the beach, stirred in the breeze and caught the sunlight. Display was part of the actual distribution of goods; every item was publicly and often glowingly mentioned as it was given away, and every lot, of blankets, for example, was publicly counted out. Feasting and entertainment, special carved wooden feast dishes, and special costumes were all part of the show.

Whether modest or pretentious, such displays showed the social worth of the individuals or groups who were responsible for them. Their ability and desire to support social relationships for social as well as private ends were on view.

Display connected with redistributive exchange consists of processions, panoply, public works, and state festivals and entertainments; it is inspiring or intimidating depending upon the nature of the political power concerned and the onlooker's or participant's relation to it.

In the African kingdom of Rwanda, the greatest displays were redistributive. The king's retinue, court, and capital; the review of the royal cattle; the performances of the royal dancers; the magnificence of the royal progress whenever the *mwami* traveled about; and the conspicuous bounty of goods, foodstuffs, milk pots, beer pots, and everything that poured into his household were all part of the pattern. It was repeated on a smaller scale for every lesser political figure in the system.

Other examples of redistributive displays include the Panathenaic festival and the Parthenon; the Roman triumph; and the Coliseum and its circuses. In these societies, which were political economies, however different their polities, the displays connected with redistributive exchange were the most important of any displays that were made in the society. These displays were part of the redistributive exchange itself. The thousands of citizens or subjects whose accumulated tax or tribute payments made such displays possible may have received little in addition to spectacle. The function of such display was the demonstration of political power and its ability to organize all aspects of a society, including the economic aspect.

Display connected with market exchange is so familiar it requires little discussion. Its means are the market place, the fair, the store, the showcase, and so on, not forgetting the ubiquitous extensions of the market place via printing and electronics. While the general purpose of such display is to entice and facilitate purchase, each instance of display has the particular purpose of enabling the particular goods concerned to compete, on as favorable terms as possible, with all the other goods of the market. It is for this reason that its arts and artifices are so highly developed, for they must make up the difference needed for successful sales competition. Display in market economies can be institutional in nature and aim, like some of the great trade fairs. It can also proclaim the ramifications of the system and the general wealth of goods it has made available. However, this is a small part of the total amount of display connected with market exchange; the typical appeal is not "Buy!", but "Buy such-and-such!" It can therefore be said of the display connected with market exchange that its functions and purposes in society are practically the same, that is, to maximize and to integrate the market.

Research on exchange along comparative and behavioral lines will be increasingly developed by anthropologists, if not by economists, since it promises a more profound understanding of the economic aspects of society. There is a need for more detailed and quantified field study of exchange in its full social and cultural context. When such a field as that of kinship and social organization has been developed to the point of rigorous and quasi-mathematical treatment, there seems no good reason why the field of exchange, with its clear factual basis (something being exchanged for something with someone), cannot be reduced to similar clarity, detail, and order.

HELEN CODERE

[*See also* ECONOMIC ANTHROPOLOGY; TRADE AND MARKETS. *Other relevant material may be found in the biographies of* MALINOWSKI; MAUSS; POLANYI; VEBLEN.]

BIBLIOGRAPHY

BOHANNAN, PAUL 1963 *Social Anthropology.* New York: Holt.

BOHANNAN, PAUL; and DALTON, GEORGE (editors) 1962 *Markets in Africa.* Northwestern University Africa Studies, No. 9. Evanston, Ill.: Northwestern Univ. Press.

CODERE, HELEN 1950 *Fighting With Property: A Study of Kwakiutl Potlatching and Warfare, 1792–1930.* American Ethnological Society, Monograph No. 18. New York: Augustin.

CODERE, HELEN 1961 Kwakiutl. Pages 431–516 in Interuniversity Summer Research Seminar, University of New Mexico, 1956, *Perspectives in American Indian Culture Change*. Univ. of Chicago Press.

CODERE, HELEN 1962 Power in Ruanda. *Anthropologica* New Series 4:45–85.

DALTON, GEORGE 1961 Economic Theory and Primitive Society. *American Anthropologist* New Series 63:1–25.

DOUGLAS, MARY 1962 Lele Economy Compared With the Bushong: A Study of Economic Backwardness. Pages 211–233 in Paul Bohannan and George Dalton (editors), *Markets in Africa*. Evanston, Ill.: Northwestern Univ. Press.

EVANS-PRITCHARD, E. E. 1931 An Alternative Term for "Bride-price." *Man* 31:36–39.

FIRTH, RAYMOND W. (1929) 1959 *Economics of the New Zealand Maori*. 2d ed. Wellington: Owen. → First published as *Primitive Economics of the New Zealand Maori*.

FIRTH, RAYMOND W. (1936) 1957 *We, the Tikopia: A Sociological Study of Kinship in Primitive Polynesia*. 2d ed. London: Allen & Unwin. → A paperback edition was published in 1963 by Beacon.

FIRTH, RAYMOND W. (1939) 1965 *Primitive Polynesian Economy*. 2d ed. Hamden, Conn.: Shoe String Press.

FIRTH, RAYMOND W. 1951 *Elements of Social Organization*. London: Watts.

GRAY, ROBERT F. 1960 Sonjo Bride-price and the Question of African "Wife Purchase." *American Anthropologist* New Series 62:34–57.

HERSKOVITS, MELVILLE J. (1940) 1952 *Economic Anthropology: A Study in Comparative Economics*. 2d ed., rev. & enl. New York: Knopf. → First published as *The Economic Life of Primitive Peoples*.

MALINOWSKI, BRONISLAW 1921 The Primitive Economics of the Trobriand Islanders. *Economic Journal* 31:1–16.

MALINOWSKI, BRONISLAW (1922) 1960 *Argonauts of the Western Pacific: An Account of Native Enterprise and Adventure in the Archipelagoes of Melanesian New Guinea*. London School of Economics and Political Science, Studies, No. 65. London: Routledge; New York: Dutton. → A paperback edition was published in 1961 by Dutton.

MANNERS, ROBERT A. 1962 Land Use, Labor, and the Growth of Market Economy in Kipsigis Country. Pages 493–519 in Paul Bohannan and George Dalton (editors), *Markets in Africa*. Evanston, Ill.: Northwestern Univ. Press.

MAUSS, MARCEL (1925) 1954 *The Gift: Forms and Functions of Exchange in Archaic Societies*. Glencoe, Ill.: Free Press. → First published as *Essai sur le don: Forme et raison de l'échange dans les sociétés archaïques*.

MYRDAL, GUNNAR (1956) 1957 *Rich Lands and Poor: The Road to World Prosperity*. Rev. ed. New York: Harper. → First published as *Development and Underdevelopment*.

NASH, MANNING 1964 The Organization of Economic Life. Pages 171–180 in Sol Tax (editor), *Horizons of Anthropology*. Chicago: Aldine.

POLANYI, KARL 1944 *The Great Transformation*. New York: Rinehart. → A paperback edition was published in 1957 by Beacon.

POLANYI, KARL; ARENSBERG, CONRAD; and PEARSON, HARRY W. (editors) 1957 *Trade and Market in the Early Empires*. Glencoe, Ill.: Free Press.

UNDERHILL, RUTH (1937) 1939 *Social Organization of the Papago Indians*. 2d ed. Columbia University Contributions to Anthropology, Vol. 30. New York: Columbia Univ. Press.

VEBLEN, THORSTEIN (1899) 1953 *The Theory of the Leisure Class: An Economic Study of Institutions*. Rev. ed. New York: New American Library. → A paperback edition was published in 1959.

EXCHANGE RATES

See under INTERNATIONAL MONETARY ECONOMICS.

EXCISE TAXES

See under TAXATION.

EXCLAVES

See ENCLAVES AND EXCLAVES.

EXECUTIONS

See CAPITAL PUNISHMENT.

EXECUTIVE, POLITICAL

See POLITICAL EXECUTIVE. *Related material may be found under* ADMINISTRATION *and* LEADERSHIP.

EXISTENTIAL PSYCHOLOGY

See under PSYCHOLOGY.

EXOGAMY

See INCEST *and* MARRIAGE.

EXPECTATIONS, ECONOMIC

See ECONOMIC EXPECTATIONS.

EXPERIMENTAL DESIGN

I. THE DESIGN OF EXPERIMENTS	*William G. Cochran*
II. RESPONSE SURFACES	*G. E. P. Box*
III. QUASI-EXPERIMENTAL DESIGN	*Donald T. Campbell*

I
THE DESIGN OF EXPERIMENTS

In scientific research, the word "experiment" often denotes the type of study in which the investigator deliberately introduces certain changes into a process and makes observations or measurements in order to evaluate and compare the effects of different changes. These changes are called the *treatments*. Common examples of treatments are different kinds of stimuli presented to human subjects or animals or different kinds of situations with which the investigator faces them, in order to see how they respond. In exploratory work, the objective may be simply to discover whether the stimuli produce any measurable responses, while at a later stage in research the purpose may be to verify or disprove certain hypotheses that have been put forward about the directions and sizes of the responses to treatments. In applied work, measurement of the size of the response is often important, since this may determine whether a new treatment is practically useful.

A distinction is often made between a controlled experiment and an uncontrolled observational study. In the latter, the investigator does not interfere in the process, except in deciding which phenomena to observe or measure. Suppose that it is desired to assess the effectiveness of a new teaching machine that has been much discussed. An observational study might consist in comparing the achievement of students in those schools that have adopted the new technique with the achievement of students in schools that have not. If the schools that adopt the new technique show higher achievement, the objection may be raised that this increase is not necessarily caused by the machine, as the schools that have tried a new method are likely to be more enterprising and successful and may have students who are more competent and better prepared. Examination of previous records of the schools may support these criticisms. In a proper experiment on the same question, the investigator decides which students are to be taught by the new machine and which by the standard technique. It is his responsibility to ensure that the two techniques are compared on students of equal ability and degree of preparation, so that these criticisms no longer have validity.

The advantage of the proper experiment over the observational study lies in this increased ability to elucidate cause-and-effect relationships. Both types of study can establish associations between a stimulus and a response; but when the investigator is limited to observations, it is hard to find a situation in which there is only one explanation of the association. If the investigator can show by repeated experiments that the same stimulus is always followed by the same response and if he has designed the experiments so that other factors that might produce this response are absent, he is in a much stronger position to claim that the stimulus causes the response. (However, there are many social science fields where true experimentation is not possible and careful observational investigations are the only source of information.) [See, for example, EXPERIMENTAL DESIGN, article on QUASI-EXPERIMENTAL DESIGN; OBSERVATION; SURVEY ANALYSIS.]

Briefly, the principal steps in the planning of a controlled experiment are as follows. The treatments must be selected and defined and must be relevant to the questions originally posed. The *experimental units* to which the treatments are to be applied must be chosen. In the social sciences, the experimental unit is frequently a single animal or human subject. The unit may, however, be a group of subjects, for instance, a class in comparisons of teaching methods. An important point is that the choice of subjects and of the environmental conditions of the experiment determine the range of validity of the results.

The next step is to determine the size of the sample—the number of subjects or of classes. In general, the precision of the experiment increases as the sample size increases, but usually a balance must be struck between the precision desired and the costs involved. The method for allocating treatments to subjects must be specified, as must the detailed conduct of the experiment. Other factors that might influence the outcome must be controlled (by *blocking* or *randomization*, as discussed later) so that they favor each treatment equally. Finally, the responses or criteria by which the treatments will be rated must be defined. These may be simple classifications or measurements on a continuous scale. Like the treatments, the responses must be relevant to the questions originally posed.

History. The early history of ideas on the planning of experiments appears to have been but little studied (Boring 1954). Modern concepts of experimental design are due primarily to R. A. Fisher, who developed them from 1919 to 1930 in the planning of agricultural field experiments at the Rothamsted Experimental Station in England. The main features of Fisher's approach are as follows (*randomization, blocking,* and *factorial experimentation* will be discussed later):

(1) The requirement that an experiment itself furnish a meaningful estimate of the underlying variability to which the measurements of the responses to treatments are subject.

(2) The use of randomization to provide these estimates of variability.

(3) The use of blocking in order to balance out known extraneous sources of variation.

(4) The principle that the statistical analysis of the results is determined by the way in which the experiment was conducted.

(5) The concept of factorial experimentation, which stresses the advantages of investigating the effects of different factors or variables in a single complex experiment, instead of devoting a separate experiment to each factor.

These ideas were stated very concisely by Fisher in 1925 and 1926 but more completely in 1935.

Experimental error

Some sources of experimental error. A major problem in experimentation is that the responses of the experimental units are influenced by many sources of variation other than the treatments. For example, subjects differ in their ability to perform a task under standard conditions: a treatment that is allotted to an unusually capable group of subjects will appear to do well; the instruments by which the responses are measured may be liable to errors of measurement; both the applied treatment and the environment may lack uniformity from one occasion to another.

In some experiments, the effects of subject-to-subject variation are avoided by giving every treatment to each subject in succession, so that comparisons are made within subjects. Even then, however, learning, fatigue, or delayed consequences of previously applied treatments may influence the response actually measured after a particular treatment.

The primary consequence of extraneous sources of variation, called *experimental errors*, is a masking of the effects of the treatments. The observed difference between the effects of two treatments is the sum of the true difference and a contribution due to these errors. If the errors are large, the experimenter obtains a poor estimate of the true difference; then the experiment is said to be of low precision.

Bias. It is useful to distinguish between random error and error due to bias. A bias, or systematic error, affects alike all subjects who receive a specific treatment. Random error varies from subject to subject. In a child growth study in which children were weighed in their clothes, a bias would arise if the final weights of all children receiving one treatment were taken on a cold day, on which heavy clothing was worn, while the children receiving a second treatment were weighed on a mild day, on which lighter clothing was worn. In general, bias cannot be detected in the analysis of the results, so that the conclusions drawn by statistical methods about the true effects of the treatments are misleading.

It follows that constant vigilance against bias is one of the requisites of good experimentation. The devices of randomization and blocking, if used intelligently, do much to guard against bias. Additional precautions are necessary in certain types of experiments. If the measurements are subjective evaluations or clinical judgments, the expectations and prejudices of the judges and subjects may influence the results if it is known which treatment any of the subjects received. Consequently, it is important to ensure, whenever it is feasible, that neither the subject nor the person taking the measurement knows which treatment the subject is receiving; this is called a "double blind" experiment. For example, in experiments that compare different drugs taken as pills all the pills should look alike and be administered in the same way. If there is a no-drug treatment, it is common practice to administer an inert pill, called a *placebo*, in order to achieve this concealment.

Methods for reducing experimental error. Several devices are used to remove or decrease bias and random errors due to extraneous sources of variation that are thought to be substantial. One group of devices may be called refinements of technique. If the response is the skill of the subject in performing an unfamiliar task, a major source of error may be that subjects learn this task at different rates. An obvious precaution is to give each subject enough practice to reach his plateau of skill before starting the experiment. The explanation of the task to the subjects must be clear; otherwise, some subjects may be uncertain what they are supposed to do. Removal from an environment that is noisy and subject to distractions may produce more uniform performance. The tasks assigned to the subjects may be too easy or too hard so that all perform well or poorly under any treatment, making discrimination between the treatments impossible. The reduction of errors in measurement of the response often requires prolonged research. In psychometrics, much of the work on scaling is directed toward finding superior instruments of measurement [see SCALING].

Blocking. In many experiments involving comparisons between subjects, the investigator knows that the response will vary widely from subject to subject, even under the same treatment. Often it is possible to obtain beforehand a measurement that is a good predictor of the response of the subject. A child's average score on previous tests in arithmetic may predict well how he will perform on an arithmetic test given at the end of a teaching experiment. Such initial data can be used to increase the precision of the experiment by forming blocks consisting of children of approximately equal ability. If there are three teaching methods, the first block contains the three children with the best initial scores. Each child in this block is assigned to a different teaching method. The second block contains the three next best children, and so on. The purpose of the blocking is to guarantee that each teaching method is tried on an equal number of good, moderate, and poor performers in arithmetic. The resulting gain in precision may be striking.

The term "block" comes from agricultural experimentation in which the block is a compact piece of land. With human subjects, an arrangement of this kind is sometimes called a *matched pairs* design (with two treatments) or a *matched groups* design (with more than two treatments).

A single blocking can help to balance out the effects of several different sources of variation. In a two-treatment experiment on rats, a block comprising littermates of the same sex equalizes the two treatments for age and sex and to some extent for genetic inheritance and weight also. If the conditions of the experiment are subject to uncontrolled time trends, the two rats in a block can be tested at approximately the same time.

Adjustments in the statistical analysis. Given an initial predictor, x, of the final response, y, an alternative to blocking is to make adjustments in the statistical analysis in the hope of removing the influence of variations in x. If x and y represent initial and final scores in a test of some type of skill, the simplest adjustment is to replace y by $y - x$, the improvement in score, as the measure of response. This change does not always increase precision. The error variance of $y - x$ for a subject may be written $\sigma_y^2 + \sigma_x^2 - 2\rho\sigma_y\sigma_x$, where ρ is the correlation between y and x. This is less than σ_y^2 only if ρ exceeds $\sigma_x/2\sigma_y$.

A more accurate method of adjustment is given by the analysis of covariance. In this approach, the measure of response is $y - bx$. The quantity b, computed from the results of the experiment, is an estimate of the average change in y per unit increase in x. The adjustment accords with common sense. If the average x value is three units higher for treatment A than for treatment B, and if b is found to be $\frac{2}{3}$, the adjustment reduces the difference between the average y values by two units.

If the relation between y and x is linear, the use of a predictor, x, to form blocks gives about the same increase in precision as its use in a covariance analysis. For a more detailed comparison in small experiments, see Cox (1957). Blocking by means of x may be superior if the relation between y and x is not linear. Thus, a covariance adjustment on x is helpful mainly when blocking has been used to balance out some other variable or when blocking by means of x is, for some reason,

not feasible. One disadvantage of the covariance adjustment is that it requires considerable extra computation. A simpler adjustment such as $y - x$ is sometimes preferred even at some loss of precision.

Randomization. Randomization requires the use of a table of random numbers, or an equivalent device to decide some step in the experiment, most frequently the allotment of treatments to subjects [*see* RANDOM NUMBERS].

Suppose that three treatments—A, B, C—are to be assigned to 90 subjects without blocking. The subjects are numbered from 1 to 90. In a two-digit column of random numbers, the numbers 01 to 09 represent subjects 1 to 9, respectively; the numbers 10 to 19 represent subjects 10 to 19, respectively, and so on. The numbers from 91 to 99 and the number 00 are ignored. The 30 subjects whose numbers are drawn first from the table are assigned to treatment A, the next 30 to B, and the remaining 30 to C.

In the simplest kind of blocking, the subjects or experimental units are arranged in 30 blocks of three subjects each. One in each block is to receive A, one B, and one C. This decision is made by randomization, numbering the subjects in any block from 1 to 3 and using a single column of random digits for the draw.

Unlike blocking, which attempts to eliminate the effects of an extraneous source of variation, randomization merely ensures that each treatment has an equal chance of being favored or handicapped by the extraneous source. In the blocked experiment above, randomization might assign the best subject in every block to treatment A. The probability that this happens is, however, only 1 in 3^{30}. Whenever possible, blocking should be used for all major sources of variation, randomization being confined to the minor sources. The use of randomization is not limited to the allotment of treatments to subjects. For example, if time trends are suspected at some stage in the experiment, the order in which the subjects within a block are processed may be randomized. Of course, if time trends are likely to be large, blocking should be used for them as well as randomization, as illustrated later in this article by the crossover design.

In his *Design of Experiments*, Fisher illustrated how the act of randomization often allows the investigator to carry out valid tests for the treatment means without assuming the form of the frequency distribution of the data (1935). The calculations, although tedious in large experiments, enable the experimenter to free himself from the assumptions required in the standard analysis of variance. Indeed, one method of justifying the standard methods for the statistical analysis of experimental results is to show that these methods usually give serviceable approximations to the results of randomization theory [see NONPARAMETRIC STATISTICS; see also Kempthorne 1952].

Size of experiment. An important practical decision is that affecting the number of subjects or experimental units to be included in an experiment. For comparing a pair of treatments there are two common approaches to this problem. One approach is to specify that the observed difference between the treatment means be correct to within some amount $\pm d$ chosen by the investigator. The other approach is to specify the power of the test of significance of this difference.

Consider first the case in which the response is measured on a continuous scale. If σ is the standard deviation per unit of the experimental errors and if each treatment is allotted to n units, the standard error of the observed difference between two treatment means is $\sqrt{2}\,\sigma/\sqrt{n}$ for the simpler types of experimental design. Assuming that this difference is approximately normally distributed, the probability that the difference is in error by more than $d = 1.96\sqrt{2}\,\sigma/\sqrt{n}$ is about 0.05 (from the normal tables). The probability becomes 0.01 if d is increased to $2.58\sqrt{2}\,\sigma/\sqrt{n}$. Thus, although there is no finite n such that the error is certain to be less than d, nevertheless, from the normal tables, a value of n can be computed to reduce the probability that the error exceeds d to some small quantity α such as 0.05. Taking $\alpha = 0.05$ gives $n = 7.7\sigma^2/d^2 \cong 8\sigma^2/d^2$. The value of σ is usually estimated from previous experiments or preliminary work on this experiment.

If the criterion is the proportion of units that fall into some class (for instance, the proportion of subjects who complete a task successfully), the corresponding formula for n, with $\alpha = 0.05$, is

$$n \cong 4[p_1(1-p_1) + p_2(1-p_2)]/d^2,$$

where p_1, p_2 are the true proportions of success for the two treatments and d is the maximum tolerable error in the observed difference in proportions. Use of this formula requires advance estimates of p_1 and p_2. Fortunately, if these lie between 0.3 and 0.7 the quantity $p(1-p)$ varies only between 0.21 and 0.25.

The choice of the value of d should, of course, depend on the use to be made of the results, but an element of judgment often enters into the decision.

The second approach (specifying the power) is

appropriate, for instance, when a new treatment is being compared with a standard treatment and when the investigator intends to discard the new treatment unless the test of significance shows that it is superior to the standard. He does not mind discarding the new treatment if its true superiority is slight. But if the true difference (new − standard) exceeds some amount, Δ, he wants the probability of finding a significant difference to have some high value, β (perhaps 0.95, 0.9, or 0.8).

With continuous data, the required value of n is approximately

$$n \cong 2\sigma^2(\xi_\alpha + \xi_{1-\beta})^2/\Delta^2,$$

where

ξ_α = normal deviate corresponding to the significance level, α, used in the test of significance,

and

$\xi_{1-\beta}$ = normal deviate for a *one-tailed* probability $1 - \beta$.

For instance, if the test of significance is a one-tailed test at the 5% level and β is 0.9, so that $\xi_\alpha = 1.64$ and $\xi_{1-\beta} = 1.28$, then $n \cong 17\sigma^2/\Delta^2$. The values of Δ, α, and β are chosen by the investigator.

With proportions, an approximate formula is

$$n \cong 2(\xi_\alpha + \xi_{1-\beta})^2\bar{p}\bar{q}/(p_2 - p_1)^2,$$

where $\bar{p} = (p_1 + p_2)/2$ and $\bar{q} = 1 - \bar{p}$ and $p_2 - p_1$ is the size of difference to be detected. One lesson that this formula teaches is that large samples are needed to detect small or moderate differences between two proportions. For instance, with $p_1 = 0.3$, $p_2 = 0.4$, $\alpha = 0.05$ (two-tailed), and $\beta = 0.8$, the formula gives $n = 357$ in each sample, or a total of 714 subjects.

More accurate tables for n, with proportions and continuous data, are given in Cochran and Cox (1950) and a fuller discussion of the sample size problem in Cox (1958).

If the investigator is uncertain about the best values to choose for Δ, it is instructive to compute the value of Δ that will be detected, say with probability 80% or 90%, for an experiment of the size that is feasible. Some experiments, especially with proportions, are almost doomed to failure, in the sense that they have little chance of detecting a true difference of the size that a new treatment is likely to produce. It is well to know this before doing the experiment.

Controls. Some experiments require a *control*, or comparison, treatment. For a discussion of the different meanings of the word "control" and an account of the history of this device, see Boring (1954). In a group of families having a prepaid medical care plan, it is proposed to examine the effects of providing, over a period of time, additional free psychiatric consultation. An intensive initial study is made of the mental health and social adjustment of the families who are to receive this extra service, followed by a similar inventory at the end. In order to appraise whether the differences (final − initial) can be attributed to the psychiatric guidance, it is necessary to include a control group of families, measured at the beginning and at the end, who do not receive this service. An argument might also be made for a second control group that does not receive the service and is measured only at the end. The reason is that the initial psychiatric appraisal may cause some families in the first control group to seek psychiatric guidance on their own, thus diluting the treatment effect that is to be studied. Whether such disturbances are important enough to warrant a second control is usually a matter of judgment.

The families in the control groups, like those in the treated group, must be selected by randomization from the total set of families available for the experiment. This type of evaluatory study presents other problems. It is difficult to conceal the treatment group to which a family belongs from the research workers who make the final measurements, so that any preconceptions of these workers may vitiate the results. Second, the exact nature of the extra psychiatric guidance can only be discovered as the experiment proceeds. It is important to keep detailed records of the services rendered and of the persons to whom they were given.

Factorial experimentation

In many programs of research, the investigator intends to examine the effects of several different types of variables on some response (for example, in an experiment on the accuracy of tracking, the effect of speed of the object, the type of motion of the object, and the type of handle used by the human tracker). In factorial designs, these variables are investigated simultaneously in the same experiment. The advantages of this approach are that it makes economical use of resources and provides convenient data for studying the interrelationships of the effects of different variables.

These points may be illustrated by an experiment with three factors or variables, A, B, and C, each at two levels (that is, two speeds of the object, etc.). Denote the two levels of A by a_1 and

a_2, and similarly for B and C. The treatments consist of all possible combinations of the levels of the factors. There are eight combinations:

(1) $a_1b_1c_1$ (3) $a_1b_2c_1$ (5) $a_1b_1c_2$ (7) $a_1b_2c_2$
(2) $a_2b_1c_1$ (4) $a_2b_2c_1$ (6) $a_2b_1c_2$ (8) $a_2b_2c_2$

Suppose that one observation is taken on each of the eight combinations. What information do these give on factor A? The comparison $(2) - (1)$, that is, the difference between the observations for combinations (2) and (1), is clearly an estimate of the difference in response, $a_2 - a_1$, since the factors B and C are held fixed at their lower levels. Similarly, $(4) - (3)$ gives an estimate of $a_2 - a_1$, with B held at its higher level and C at its lower level. The differences $(6) - (5)$ and $(8) - (7)$ supply two further estimates of $a_2 - a_1$. The average of these four differences provides a comparison of a_2 with a_1 based on two samples of size four and is called the *main effect* of A.

Turning to B, it may be verified that $(3) - (1)$, $(4) - (2)$, $(7) - (5)$, and $(8) - (6)$ are four comparisons of b_2 with b_1. Their average is the main effect of B. Similarly, $(5) - (1)$, $(6) - (2)$, $(7) - (3)$, and $(8) - (4)$ provide four comparisons of c_2 with c_1.

Thus the testing of eight treatment combinations in the factorial experiment gives estimates of the effects of each of the factors A, B, and C based on samples of size four. If a separate experiment were devoted to each factor, as in the "one variable at a time" approach, 24 combinations would have to be tested (eight in each experiment) in order to furnish estimates based on samples of size four. The economy in the factorial approach is achieved because every observation contributes information on all factors.

In many areas of research, it is important to study the relations between the effects of different factors. Consider the following question: Is the difference in response between a_2 and a_1 affected by the level of B? The comparison

$$(a_2b_2 - a_1b_2) - (a_2b_1 - a_1b_1),$$

where each quantity has been averaged over the two levels of C, measures the difference between the response to A when B is at its higher level and the response to A when B is at its lower level. This quantity might be called the effect of B on the response to A. The same expression rearranged as follows,

$$(a_2b_2 - a_2b_1) - (a_1b_2 - a_1b_1),$$

also measures the effect of A on the response to B. It is called the *AB two-factor interaction*. (Some writers introduce a multiplier, $\frac{1}{2}$, for conventional reasons.) The AC and BC interactions are computed similarly.

The analysis can be carried further. The AB interaction can be estimated separately for the two levels of C. The difference between these quantities is the effect of C on the AB interaction. The same expression is found to measure the effect of A on the BC interaction and the effect of B on the AC interaction. It is called the ABC three-factor interaction.

The extent to which different factors exhibit interactions depends mostly on the way in which nature behaves. Absence of interaction implies that the effects of the different factors are mutually additive. In some fields of application, main effects are usually large relative to two-factor interactions, and two-factor interactions are large relative to three-factor interactions, which are often negligible. Sometimes a transformation of the scale in which the data are analyzed removes most of the interactions [see STATISTICAL ANALYSIS, SPECIAL PROBLEMS OF, *article on* TRANSFORMATIONS OF DATA]. There are, however, many experiments in which the nature and the sizes of the interactions are of primary interest.

The factorial experiment is a powerful weapon for investigating responses affected by many stimuli. The number of levels of a factor is not restricted to two and is often three or four. The chief limitation is that the experiment may become too large and unwieldy to be conducted successfully. Fortunately, the supply of rats and university students is large enough so that factorial experiments are widely used in research on learning, motivation, personality, and human engineering [see, for example, TRAITS].

Several developments mitigate this problem of expanding size. If most interactions may safely be assumed to be negligible, good estimates of the main effects and of the interactions considered likely to be important can be obtained from an experiment in which a wisely chosen fraction (say $\frac{1}{2}$ or $\frac{1}{3}$) of the totality of treatment combinations is tested. The device of *confounding* (see Cochran & Cox 1950, chapter 6, esp. pp. 183–186; Cox 1958, sec. 12.3) enables the investigator to use a relatively small sized block in order to increase precision, at the expense of a sacrifice of information on certain interactions that are expected to be negligible. If all the factors represent continuous variables $(x_1, x_2, \cdots)$ and the objective is to map the *response surface* that expresses the response, y, as a function of $x_1, x_2, \cdots$, then one of the designs specially adapted for this purpose may be used. [*For discussion of these topics, see* EXPERIMENTAL DESIGN, *article on* RESPONSE SURFACES; *see also* Cox 1958; Davies 1954.]

In the remainder of this article, some of the commonest types of experimental design are outlined.

Randomized groups. The randomized group arrangement, also called the one-way layout, the simple randomized design, and the completely randomized design, is the simplest type of plan. Treatments are allotted to experimental units at random, as described in the discussion of "Randomization," above. No blocking is used at any stage of the experiment; and, since any number of treatments and any number of units per treatment may be employed, the design has great flexibility. If mishaps cause certain of the responses to be missing, the statistical analysis is only slightly complicated. Since, however, the design takes no advantage of blocking, it is used primarily when no criteria for blocking are available, when criteria previously used for blocking have proved ineffective, or when the response is not highly variable from unit to unit.

Randomized blocks. If there are v treatments and the units can be grouped into blocks of size v, such that units in the same block are expected to give about the same final response under uniform treatment, then a randomized blocks design is appropriate. Each treatment is allotted at random to one of the units in any block. This design is, in general, more precise than randomized groups and is very extensively used.

Sometimes the blocks are formed by assessing or scoring the subjects on an initial variable related to the final response. It may be of interest to examine whether the comparative effects of the treatments are the same for subjects with high scores as for those with low scores. This can be done by an extension of the analysis of variance appropriate to the randomized blocks design. For example, with four treatments, sixty subjects, and fifteen blocks, the blocks might be classified into three levels, *high, medium,* or *low,* there being five blocks in each class. A useful partition of the degrees of freedom (df) in the analysis of variance of this "treatments × levels" design is as follows:

	df
Between levels	2
Between blocks at the same level	12
Treatments	3
Treatments × levels interactions	6
Treatments × blocks within levels	36
Total	59

The mean square for interaction is tested, against the mean square for treatments × blocks within levels, by the usual F-test. Methods for constructing the levels and the problem of testing the over-all effects of treatments in different experimental situations are discussed in Lindquist (1953). [*See* LINEAR HYPOTHESES, *article on* ANALYSIS OF VARIANCE.]

The crossover design. The crossover design is suitable for within-subject comparisons in which each subject receives all the treatments in succession. With three treatments, for example, a plan in which every subject receives the treatments in the order *ABC* is liable to bias if there happen to be systematic differences between the first, second, and third positions, due to time trends, learning, or fatigue. One design that mitigates this difficulty is the following: a third of the subjects, selected at random, get the treatments in the order *ABC*, a third get *BCA*, and the remaining third get *CAB*. The analysis of variance resembles that for randomized blocks except that the sum of squares representing the differences between the over-all means for the three positions is subtracted from the error sum of squares.

The Latin square. A square array of letters (treatments) such that each letter appears once in every row and column is called a Latin square. The following are two 4×4 squares.

	(1)					(2)		
C	A	B	D		A	B	C	D
A	B	D	C		B	C	D	A
B	D	C	A		D	A	B	C
D	C	A	B		C	D	A	B

This layout permits simultaneous blocking in two directions. The rows and columns often represent extraneous sources of variation to be balanced out. In an experiment that compared the effects of five types of music programs on the output of factory workers doing a monotonous job, a 5×5 Latin square was used. The columns denoted days of the week and the rows denoted weeks. When there are numerous subjects, the design used is frequently a group of Latin squares.

For within-subject comparisons, the possibility of a residual or carry-over effect from one period to the next may be suspected. If such effects are present (and if one conventionally lets columns in the above squares correspond to subjects and rows correspond to order of treatment) then square (1) is bad, since each treatment is always preceded by the same treatment (*A* by *C*, etc.). By the use of square (2), in which every treatment is

preceded once by each of the other treatments, the residual effects can be estimated and unbiased estimates obtained of the direct effects (see Cochran & Cox 1950, sec. 4.6*a*; Edwards 1950, pp. 274–275). If there is strong interest in the residual effects, a more suitable design is the *extra-period Latin square.* This is a design like square (2), in which the treatments *C, D, A, B* in the fourth period are given again in a fifth period.

Balanced incomplete blocks. When the number of treatments, v, exceeds the size of block, k, that appears suitable, a balanced incomplete blocks design is often appropriate. In examining the taste preferences of adults for seven flavors of ice cream in a within-subject test, it is likely that a subject can make an accurate comparison among only three flavors before his discrimination becomes insensitive. Thus $v = 7$, $k = 3$. In a comparison of three methods of teaching high school students, the class may be the experimental unit and the school a suitable block. In a school district, it may be possible to find twelve high schools each having two classes at the appropriate level. Thus $v = 3$, $k = 2$.

Balanced incomplete blocks (BIB) are an extension of randomized blocks that enable differences among blocks to be eliminated from the experimental errors by simple adjustments performed in the statistical analysis. Examples for $v = 7$, $k = 3$ and for $v = 3$, $k = 2$ are as follows (columns are blocks):

$v = 7, k = 3$								$v = 3, k = 2$		
A	B	C	D	E	F	G		A	B	C
B	C	D	E	F	G	A		B	C	A
D	E	F	G	A	B	C				

The basic property of the design is that each pair of treatments occurs together (in the same block) equally often.

In both plans shown, it happens that each row contains every treatment. This is not generally true of BIB designs, but this extra property can sometimes be used to advantage. With $v = 7$, for instance, if the row specifies the order in which the types of ice cream are tasted, the experiment is also balanced against any consistent order effect. This extension of the BIB is known as an *incomplete Latin square* or a *Youden square.* In the high schools experiment, the plan for $v = 3$ would be repeated four times, since there are twelve schools.

Comparisons between and within subjects. Certain factorial experiments are conducted so that some comparisons are made within subjects and others are made between subjects. Suppose that the criterion is the performance of the subjects on an easy task, T_1, and a difficult task, T_2, each subject attempting both tasks. This part of the experiment is a standard crossover design. Suppose further that these tasks are explained to half the subjects in a discouraging manner, S_1, and to the other half in a supportive manner, S_2. It is of interest to discover whether these preliminary suggestions, S, have an effect on performance and whether this effect differs for easy and hard tasks. The basic plan, requiring four subjects, is shown in the first three lines of Table 1, where O denotes the order in which the tasks are performed.

The comparison $T_2 - T_1$, which gives the main effect of T, is shown under the treatments line. This is clearly a within-subject comparison since each subject carries a $+$ and a $-$. The main effect of suggestion, $S_2 - S_1$, is a between-subject comparison: subjects 3 and 4 carry $+$ signs while subjects 1 and 2 carry $-$ signs. The TS interaction, measured by $T_2S_2 - T_1S_2 - T_2S_1 + T_1S_1$, is seen to be a within-subject comparison.

Since within-subject comparisons are usually more precise than between-subject comparisons, an important property of this design is that it gives relatively high precision on the T and TS effects at the expense of lower precision on S. The design is particularly effective for studying interactions. Sometimes the between-subject factors involve a classification of the subjects. For instance, the subjects might be classified into three levels of anxiety, A, by a preliminary rating, with equal numbers of males and females of each degree included. In this situation, the factorial effects A, S (for sex), and AS are between-subject comparisons. Their interactions with T are within-subject comparisons.

The example may present another complication. Subjects who tackle the hard task after doing the easy task may perform better than those who tackle the hard task first. This effect is measured by a TO interaction, shown in the last line in Table 1. Note that the TO interaction turns out to be a between-subject comparison. The same is true of the TSO three-factor interaction.

In designs of this type, known in agriculture as

Table 2

Source	df
Between subjects	
S	1
TO	1
TSO	1
Error b	$4(n-1)$
Within subjects	
O	1
T	1
TS	1
SO	1
Error w	$4(n-1)$

split-plot designs, separate estimates of error are calculated for between-subject and within-subject comparisons. With $4n$ subjects, the partition of degrees of freedom in the example is shown in Table 2 (if it is also desired to examine the TO and TSO interactions).

Plans and computing instructions for all the common types of design are given in Cochran and Cox (1950); and Lindquist (1953), Edwards (1950), and Winer (1962) are good texts on experimentation in psychology and education.

WILLIAM G. COCHRAN

[*Directly related are the articles under* LINEAR HYPOTHESES.]

BIBLIOGRAPHY

BORING, EDWIN G. 1954 The Nature and History of Experimental Control. *American Journal of Psychology* 67:573–589.

CAMPBELL, DONALD T.; and STANLEY, J. S. 1963 Experimental and Quasi-experimental Designs for Research on Teaching. Pages 171–246 in Nathaniel L. Gage (editor), *Handbook of Research on Teaching.* Chicago: Rand McNally.

COCHRAN, WILLIAM G.; and Cox, GERTRUDE M. (1950) 1957 *Experimental Designs.* 2d ed. New York: Wiley.

Cox, D. R. 1957 The Use of a Concomitant Variable in Selecting an Experimental Design. *Biometrika* 44: 150–158.

Cox, D. R. 1958 *Planning of Experiments.* New York: Wiley.

DAVIES, OWEN L. (editor) (1954) 1956 *The Design and Analysis of Industrial Experiments.* 2d ed., rev. Edinburgh: Oliver & Boyd; New York: Hafner.

EDWARDS, ALLEN (1950) 1960 *Experimental Design in Psychological Research.* Rev. ed. New York: Holt.

FISHER, R. A. (1925) 1958 *Statistical Methods for Research Workers.* 13th ed., rev. New York: Hafner. → Previous editions were also published by Oliver & Boyd.

FISHER, R. A. (1926) 1950 The Arrangement of Field Experiments. Pages 17.502a–17.513 in R. A. Fisher, *Contributions to Mathematical Statistics.* New York: Wiley. → First published in Volume 33 of the *Journal of the Ministry of Agriculture.*

FISHER, R. A. (1935) 1960 *The Design of Experiments.* 7th ed. New York: Hafner; Edinburgh: Oliver & Boyd.

Table 1

Subject	1		2		3		4	
Order	O_1	O_2	O_1	O_2	O_1	O_2	O_1	O_2
Treatment	T_1S_1	T_2S_1	T_2S_1	T_1S_1	T_1S_2	T_2S_2	T_2S_2	T_1S_2
$(T_2 - T_1)$	$-$	$+$	$+$	$-$	$-$	$+$	$+$	$-$
$(S_2 - S_1)$	$-$	$-$	$-$	$-$	$+$	$+$	$+$	$+$
TS	$+$	$-$	$-$	$+$	$-$	$+$	$+$	$-$
TO	$+$	$+$	$-$	$-$	$+$	$+$	$-$	$-$

KEMPTHORNE, OSCAR 1952 *The Design and Analysis of Experiments.* New York: Wiley.
LINDQUIST, EVERET F. 1953 *Design and Analysis of Experiments in Psychology and Education.* Boston: Houghton Mifflin.
WINER, B. J. 1962 *Statistical Principles in Experimental Design.* New York: McGraw-Hill.

II
RESPONSE SURFACES

Response surface methodology is a statistical technique for the design and analysis of experiments; it seeks to relate an average response to the values of quantitative variables that affect response. For example, response in a chemical investigation might be yield of sulfuric acid, and the quantitative variables affecting yield might be pressure and temperature of the reaction.

In a psychological experiment, an investigator might want to find out how a test *score* achieved by certain subjects depended upon *duration* of the period during which they studied the relevant material and the *delay* between study and test. In mathematical language, the psychologist is interested in the presumed *functional relationship* $\eta = f(\xi_1, \xi_2)$ that expresses the *response score*, η, as a function of the two *variables* duration, ξ_1, and delay, ξ_2. If repeated experiments were made at any fixed set of experimental conditions, the measured response would nevertheless vary because of measurement errors, observational errors, and variability

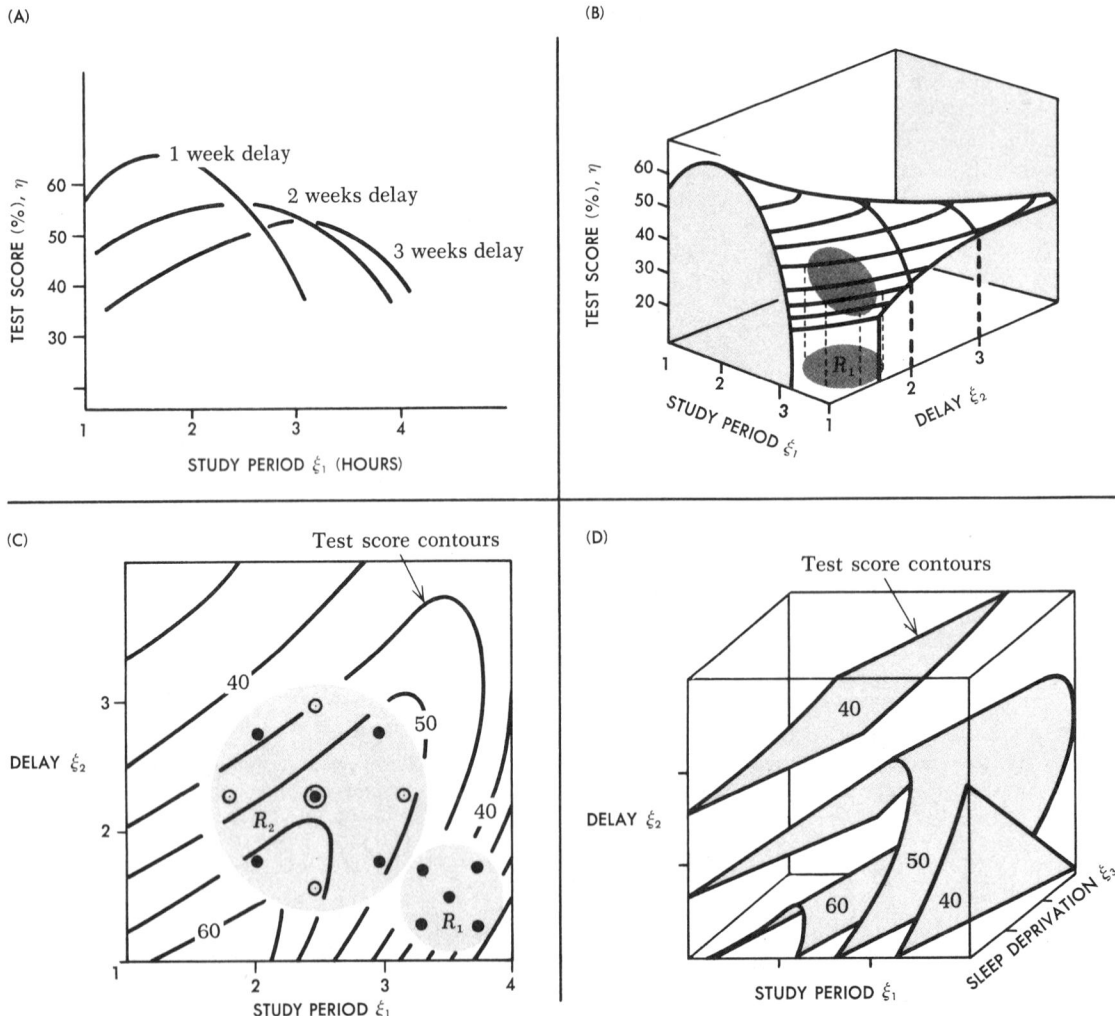

Figure 1 — Geometrical representations of a relationship connecting test scores with study period, delay, and sleep deprivation

in the experimental material. We regard η therefore as the *mean response* at particular conditions; y, the response actually observed in a particular experiment, differs from η because of an (all-inclusive) error e. Thus $y = \eta + e$, and a mathematical model relating the observed response to the levels of k variables can be written in the form

$$(1) \qquad y = f(\xi_1, \cdots, \xi_k) + e.$$

The appropriate investigational strategy depends heavily on the state of ignorance concerning the functional form, f. At one extreme the investigator may not know even which variables, ξ, to include and must make a preliminary screening investigation. At the other extreme the true functional form may actually be known or can be deduced from a mechanistic theory.

Response surface methods are appropriate in the intermediate situation; the important variables are known, but the true functional form is neither known nor easily deducible. The general procedure is to approximate f locally by a suitable function, such as a polynomial, which acts as a "mathematical French curve."

Geometric representation of response relationships. The three curves of Figure 1A, showing a hypothetical relationship associating test score with study period for three different periods of delay, are shown in Figure 1B as sections of a *response surface*. This surface is represented by its response *contours* in Figure 1C. Figure 1D shows how a third variable may be accommodated by the use of three-dimensional *contour surfaces*.

Local graduation. It is usually most convenient to work with coded variables like $x_1 = (\xi_1 - \xi_1^0)/S_1$, $x_2 = (\xi_2 - \xi_2^0)/S_2$ in which ξ_1^0, ξ_2^0 are the coordinates of the center of a region of current interest and S_1 and S_2 are convenient scale factors.

Let $\hat{y}$ represent the calculated value of the response obtained by fitting an approximating function by the method of least squares [*see* LINEAR HYPOTHESES, *article on* REGRESSION]. In a region like R_1 in Figure 1C an adequate approximation can be obtained by fitting the first-degree polynomial

$$(2) \qquad \hat{y} = b_0 + b_1 x_1 + b_2 x_2 .$$

The response contours of such a fitted plane are, of course, equally spaced parallel straight lines. In a region like R_2 a fair approximation might be achieved by fitting a second-degree polynomial

$$(3) \quad \hat{y} = b_0 + b_1 x_1 + b_2 x_2 + b_{11} x_1^2 + b_{22} x_2^2 + b_{12} x_1 x_2.$$

Flexibility of functions like those in (2) and (3) is greatly increased if the possibility is allowed that y, x_1, and x_2 are suitable transformed values

of the response and of the variable. For example, it might be appropriate to analyze log score rather than score itself. [*Ways of choosing suitable transformations are described in* STATISTICAL ANALYSIS, SPECIAL PROBLEMS OF, *article on* TRANSFORMATIONS OF DATA; *and in* Box & Cox 1964 *and* Box & Tidwell 1962.]

Uses of response surface methodology

A special pattern of points at which observations are to be made is called an experimental design. In Figure 1C are shown a first-order design in R_1, suitable for fitting and checking a first-degree polynomial, and a second-order design in R_2, suitable for fitting and checking a second-degree polynomial. Response surface methodology has been applied (*a*) to provide a description of how the response is affected by a number of variables over some already chosen region of interest and (*b*) to study and exploit multiple response relationships and constrained extrema. In drug therapy, for example, the true situation might be as depicted in Figure 2. First-degree approximating functions fitted to *each* of the three responses—η_1, therapeutic effect, η_2, nausea, and η_3, toxicity —could approximately locate the point P where maximum therapeutic effect is obtained with nausea and toxicity maintained at the acceptable limits $\eta_2 = 5$, $\eta_3 = 30$. Response surface methodology has also been applied (*c*) to locate and explore the neighborhood of maximal or minimal response. Because problems in (*c*) often subsume those in (*a*) and (*b*), only this application will be considered in more detail.

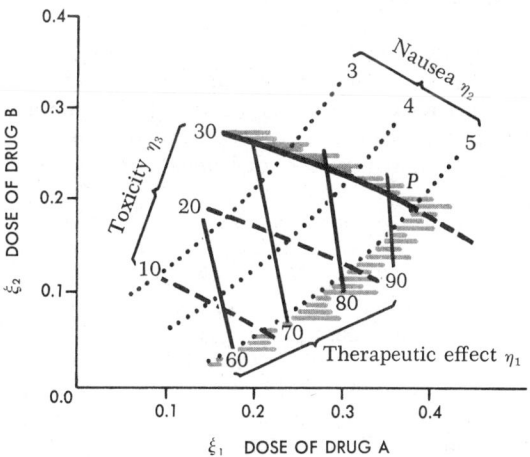

Figure 2 — Dependence of three responses on combined dosages of drugs

Location and exploration of a maximal region. Various tactics have been proposed to deal with the problem of finding where the response surface has its maximum or minimum and of describing its shape nearby. Because the appropriateness of a particular tactic usually depends upon factors that are initially unknown, an adaptive strategy of multiple iteration must be employed, that is, the investigator must put himself in a position to learn more about each of a number of uncertainties as he proceeds and to modify tactics accordingly. It is doubtful whether an adaptive strategy could be found that is appropriate to every conceivable response function. One such procedure, which has worked well in chemical applications and which ought to be applicable in some other areas, is as follows: When the initially known experimental conditions are remote from the maximum (a parallel strategy applies in the location of a minimum) rapid progress is often possible by locally fitting a sloping plane and moving in the indicated direction of greatest slope to a region of higher response. This tactic may be repeated until, when the experimental sequence has moved to conditions near the maximizing ones, additional observations are taken and a quadratic (second-order) fit or analysis is made to indicate the approximate shape of the response surface in the region of the maximum.

An example. In this example iteration occurs in (A) the amount of replication (to achieve sufficient accuracy), (B) the location of the region of interest, (C) the scaling of the variables, (D) the transformation in which the variables are considered, and (E) the necessary degree of complexity of approximating functions and of the corresponding design. The letters A, B, C, etc., are used parenthetically to indicate the particular type of iteration that is being furthered at any stage. Suppose that, unknown to the experimenter, the true dependence of percentage yield on temperature and concentration is as shown in Figure 3A and the experimental error standard deviation is 1.2 per cent.

A first-degree approximation. Suppose that five initial duplicate runs made in random order at points labeled 1, 2, 3, 4, and 5 in Figure 3B yield the results $y_1 = 24$, $y_1' = 27$, $y_2 = 38$, $y_2' = 40$, $y_3 = 42$, $y_3' = 42$, $y_4 = 42$, $y_4' = 41$, $y_5 = 50$, $y_5' = 53$. The average yields at the five points are then $\bar{y}_1 = 25.5$, $\bar{y}_2 = 39$, $\bar{y}_3 = 42$, $\bar{y}_4 = 41.5$, $\bar{y}_5 = 51.5$. At this stage it is convenient to work with the coded variables $x_1 = (\text{temp.} - 70)/10$ and $x_2 = (\text{conc.} - 42.5)/2.5$. Using standard least squares theory the coefficients b_0, b_1, b_2 of equation (2) are then easily estimated

(for example, $b_1 = \frac{1}{4}\{-\bar{y}_1 + \bar{y}_2 - \bar{y}_4 + \bar{y}_5\} = 5.9$) and the locally best-fitting plane is

$$(4) \qquad \hat{y} = 39.9 + 5.9\,x_1 + 7.1\,x_2.$$

The differences in the duplicate runs provide an estimate $s = 1.5$, with five degrees of freedom, of σ, the underlying standard deviation. The standard errors of b_0, b_1, and b_2 are then estimated as 0.5, and no further replication (A) appears necessary to obtain adequate estimation of y.

Checking the fit. To check the appropriateness of the first-degree equation it would be sensible to look at the size of second-order effects. For reason of experimental economy a first-order design usually contains points at too few distinct levels to allow separate estimation of all second-order terms. The design may be chosen, however, so as to allow estimates of "specimen" second-order coefficients or combinations thereof. In the present case estimates can be made of $b_{12} = \frac{1}{4}(\bar{y}_1 - \bar{y}_2 - \bar{y}_4 + \bar{y}_5) = -0.9 \pm 0.5$ and $(b_{11} + b_{22}) = \frac{1}{4}(\bar{y}_1 + \bar{y}_2 + \bar{y}_4 + \bar{y}_5) - \bar{y}_3 = -2.6 \pm 1.2$. Some inadequacy of the first-degree equation is indicated, therefore, but this is tentatively ignored because of the dominant magnitude of b_1 and b_2.

Steepest ascent. It is now logical to explore (B) higher temperatures and concentrations. The points 6, 7, and 8 are along a steepest ascent path obtained by changes proportional to $b_1 \times S_1 = 5.9 \times 10° = 59°$ in temperature and $b_2 \times S_2 = 7.1 \times 2.5\% = 17.75\%$ in concentration. Suppose that $y_6 = 59$, $y_7 = 63$, and $y_8 = 50$. Graphical interpolation indicates that the highest yield on this path is between runs 6 and 7, and this is chosen (B) as the center of the new region to be explored.

The path calculated as above is at right angles to contours of the fitted plane when 10-degree units of temperature and 2.5 per cent units of concentration are represented by the same distances. That the experimenter currently regards these units as appropriate is implied by his choice of levels in the design.

Scaling correction. To correct unsuitable scaling (C) the investigator can adopt the rule that if a variable produces an effect that is small compared with that produced by the other variables, the center level for that variable is moved away from the calculated path and a larger change is made for this variable in the next set of runs. No change of relative scaling is indicated here, but progress up the surface would normally be accompanied by reduction in the sizes of b_1 and b_2. Also, the checks have already indicated that second-order effects can scarcely be estimated with adequate accuracy

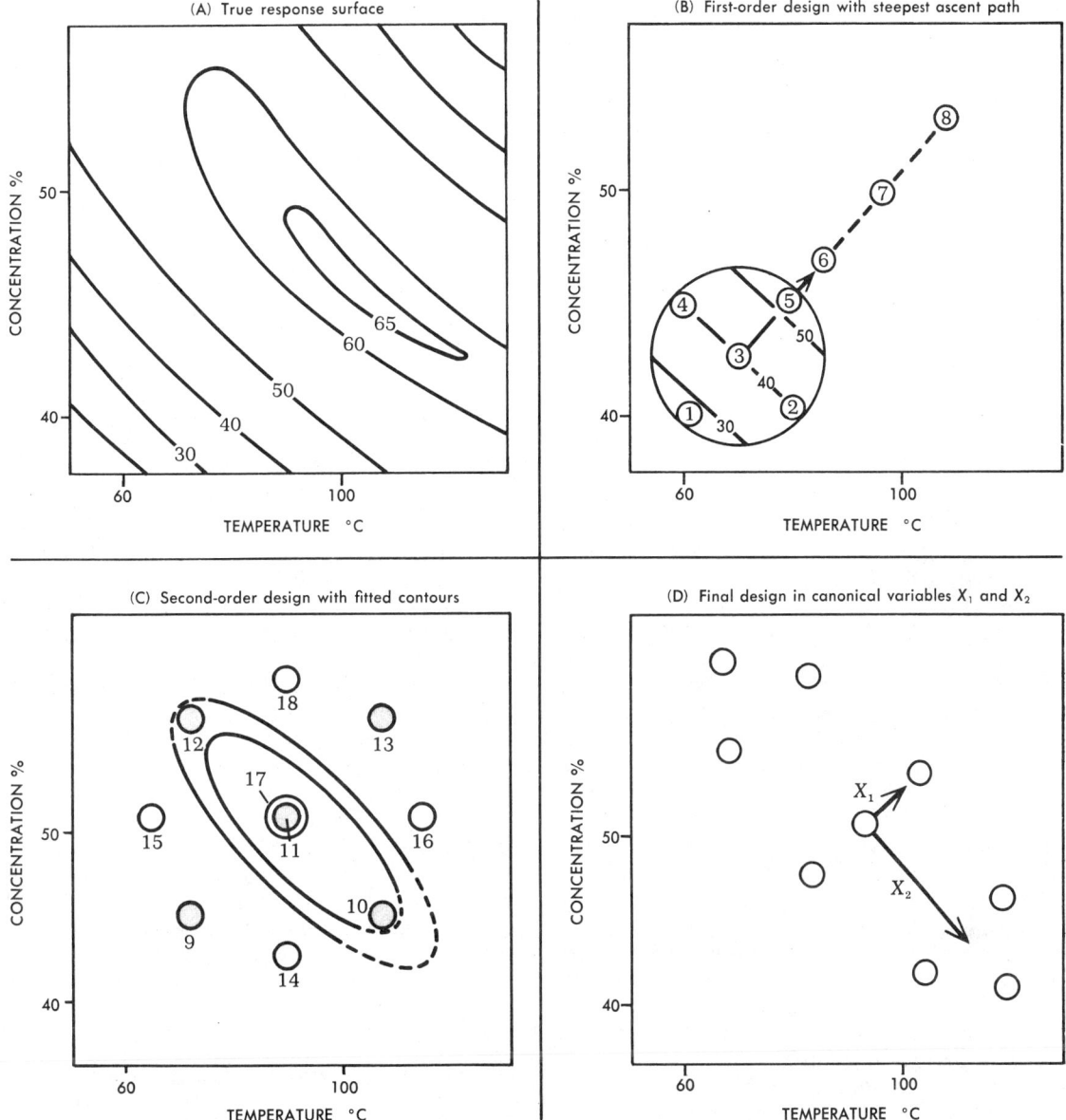

Figure 3 — A true response surface and three successive design patterns

in the present scaling. Thus, wider ranges in both variables should be employed in a second design.

A second-degree approximation. A widened first-order design at the new location might give $y_9 = 50$, $y_{10} = 66$, $y_{11} = 66$, $y_{12} = 63$, and $y_{13} = 52$, as in Figure 3C.

Then $\hat{y} = 59.4 + 1.3\,x_1 - 0.3\,x_2$ is the best-fitting plane, in which x_1 is given by (temp. -90)/15,

x_2 is given by (conc. -18.75)/3.75, and the estimated standard error of the coefficients is about 0.8. In the new scaling the check quantities are now $b_{12} = -6.75 \pm 0.8$ and $b_{11} + b_{22} = 8.25 \pm 1.7$. It is clear, without this time duplicating the design, that first-order terms no longer dominate, and no worthwhile further progress can be made by ascent methods. To make possible the fitting and checking of a second-degree polynomial (E), five additional observations might be taken, say $y_{14} = 54$, $y_{15} = 54$, $y_{16} = 57$, $y_{17} = 65$, $y_{18} = 55$. The last ten observations now form a second-order design. A second-degree equation fitted to these observations gives

$$(5) \qquad \hat{y} = 65.50 + 1.16\, x_1 + 0.05\, x_2$$
$$- 4.31\, x_1^2 - 4.81\, x_2^2 - 6.75\, x_1 x_2.$$

The design allows a check on the adequacy (E) of the second-degree equation by providing estimates of certain "specimen" combinations of third-order terms

$$b_{111} - b_{122} = \tfrac{1}{4}\, \{y_9 - y_{10} + y_{12} - y_{13} - \sqrt{2}y_{15} + \sqrt{2}y_{16}\}$$
$$= -0.19 \pm 1.03$$

and

$$b_{222} - b_{112} = \tfrac{1}{4}\, \{y_9 + y_{10} - y_{12} - y_{13} - \sqrt{2}y_{14} + \sqrt{2}y_{18}\}$$
$$= -0.60 \pm 1.03.$$

The estimated standard errors of the linear coefficients b_1 and b_2, of the quadratic coefficients b_{11} and b_{22}, and of the interaction coefficient b_{12} are, respectively, 0.52, 0.62, and 0.73.

Before an attempt is made to interpret equation (5) there must be some assurance (A) that the change in response it predicts is large compared with the standard error of that prediction. For a design requiring N observations and an approximating equation containing p constants, the average variance of the N calculated responses $\hat{y}$ is $(p/N)s^2 = (6/12) \times 2.1 = 1.1$ for this example. The square root (1.0 for this example) gives an "average" standard error for $\hat{y}$. This may be compared with the range of the predicted $\hat{y}$'s, which is 17.08, the highest predicted value being $\hat{y}_{11} = \hat{y}_{17} = 65.50$ and the lowest $\hat{y}_9 = 48.42$.

A more precise indication of adequacy may be obtained by an application of the analysis of variance, but a discussion of this is outside the scope of the present account [see LINEAR HYPOTHESES, *article on* ANALYSIS OF VARIANCE]. It is to be noted, however, that bare statistical significance of the regression would *not* ensure that the response surface was *estimated* with sufficient accuracy for the interpretation discussed below.

Interpretation.   Once adequate fit and precision have been obtained, a contour plot of the equation over the region of the experimental design is helpful in interpretation. Especially where there are more than two variables, interpretation is further facilitated by writing the second-degree equation in canonical form (D). In most cases, this means that the center of the quadratic system is chosen as a new origin, and a rotation of axes is performed to eliminate cross-product terms.

In a final group of experiments the new canon-
ical axes and scales could be used to position the design. In Figure 3D the design points are chosen so that they roughly follow a contour and make a rather precise final fitting possible.

It might be asked, Why not simply use the twenty or so experimental points to cover the region shown in Figure 3A with some suitable grid in the first place? The answer is that it is not known initially that the region of interest will be in the area covered by that diagram. The "content" of the space to be explored goes up rapidly as the number of dimensions is increased.

Suitable designs.   From the foregoing discussion it will be clear that the arrangements of experimental points suitable for response surface study should satisfy a number of requirements. Ideally, a response surface design should (1) allow $\hat{y}(x)$ to be estimated throughout the region of interest, R; (2) ensure that $\hat{y}(x)$ is as "close" as possible to $\eta(x)$; (3) give good detectability of lack of fit; (4) allow transformations to be fitted; (5) allow experiments to be performed in blocks; (6) allow designs of increasing order to be built up sequentially; (7) provide an internal estimate of error; (8) be insensitive to wild observations; (9) require a minimum number of experimental points; (10) provide patterning of data allowing ready visual appreciation; (11) ensure simplicity of calculation; and (12) behave well when errors occur in settings of the x's.

A variety of designs have been developed, many of which have remarkably good over-all behavior with respect to these requirements. When maximum economy in experimentation is essential, designs that fail to meet certain of these criteria may have to be used at some increased risk of being misled.

G. E. P. Box

BIBLIOGRAPHY

ANDERSEN, S. L. 1959 Statistics in the Strategy of Chemical Experimentation. *Chemical Engineering Progress* 55:61–67.

BOX, GEORGE E. P. 1954 The Exploration and Exploitation of Response Surfaces: Some General Considerations and Examples. *Biometrics* 10:16–60.

BOX, GEORGE E. P. 1957 Integration of Techniques in Process Development. Pages 687–702 in American Society for Quality Control, National Convention, Eleventh, *Transactions*. Detroit, Mich.: The Society.

BOX, GEORGE E. P. 1959 Fitting Empirical Data. New York Academy of Sciences, *Annals* 86:792–816.

BOX, GEORGE E. P.; and COX, D. R. 1964 An Analysis of Transformations. *Journal of the Royal Statistical Society* Series B 26:211–252. → Contains eight pages of discussion.

BOX, GEORGE E. P.; and TIDWELL, PAUL W. 1962 Transformations of the Independent Variables. *Technometrics* 4:531–550.

Box, George E. P.; and Wilson, K. B. 1951 On the Experimental Attainment of Optimum Conditions. *Journal of the Royal Statistical Society* Series B 13:1–45. → Contains seven pages of discussion.

Davies, Owen L. (editor) (1954) 1956 *The Design and Analysis of Industrial Experiments.* 2d ed., rev. New York: Hafner; London: Oliver & Boyd.

Hill, William G.; and Hunter, William G. 1966 A Review of Response Surface Methodology: A Literature Survey. *Technometrics* 8:571–590.

Hotelling, Harold 1941 Experimental Determination of the Maximum of a Function. *Annals of Mathematical Statistics* 12:20–45.

III
QUASI-EXPERIMENTAL DESIGN

The phrase "quasi-experimental design" refers to the application of an experimental mode of analysis and interpretation to bodies of data not meeting the full requirements of experimental control. The circumstances in which it is appropriate are those of experimentation in social settings—including planned interventions such as specific communications, persuasive efforts, changes in conditions and policies, efforts at social remediation, etc.—where complete experimental control may not be possible. Unplanned conditions and events may also be analyzed in this way where an exogenous variable has such discreteness and abruptness as to make appropriate its consideration as an experimental treatment applied at a specific point in time to a specific population. When properly done, when attention is given to the specific implications of the specific weaknesses of the design in question, quasi-experimental analysis can provide a valuable extension of the experimental method.

History of quasi-experimental design. While efforts to interpret field data as if they were actually experiments go back much further, the first prominent methodology of this kind in the social sciences was Chapin's ex post facto experiment (Chapin & Queen 1937; Chapin 1947; Greenwood 1945), although it should be noted that because of the failure to control regression artifacts, this mode of analysis is no longer regarded as acceptable. *The American Soldier* volumes (Stouffer et al. 1949) provide prominent analyses of the effects of specific military experiences, where it is implausible that differences in selection explain the results. Thorndike's efforts to demonstrate the effects of specific coursework upon other intellectual achievements provide an excellent early model (for example, Thorndike & Woodworth 1901; Thorndike & Ruger 1923). Extensive analysis and review of this literature are provided elsewhere (Campbell 1957; 1963; Campbell & Stanley 1963) and serve as the basis for the present abbreviated presentation.

True experimentation. The core requirement of a true experiment lies in the experimenter's ability to apply experimental treatments in complete independence of the prior states of the materials (persons, etc.) under study. This independence makes resulting differences interpretable as effects of the differences in treatment. In the social sciences the independence of experimental treatment from prior status is assured by randomization in assignments to treatments. Experiments meeting these requirements, and thus representing true experiments, are much more possible in the social sciences than is generally realized. Wherever, for example, the treatments can be applied to individuals or small units, such as precincts or classrooms, without the respondents being aware of experimentation or that other units are getting different treatments, very elegant experimental control can be achieved. An increased acceptance by administrators of randomization as the democratic method of allocating scarce resources (be these new housing, therapy, or fellowships) will make possible field experimentation in many settings. Where innovations are to be introduced throughout a social system and where the introduction cannot, in any event, be simultaneous, a use of randomization in the staging can provide an experimental comparison of the new and the old, using the groups receiving the delayed introduction as controls.

Validity of quasi-experimental analyses. Nothing in this article should be interpreted as minimizing the importance of increasing the use of true experimentation. However, where true experimental design with random assignment of persons to treatments is not possible, because of ethical considerations or lack of power, or infeasibility, application of quasi-experimental analysis has much to offer.

The social sciences must do the best they can with the possibilities open to them. Inferences must frequently be made from data obtained under circumstances that do not permit complete control. Too often a scientist trained in experimental method rejects any research in which complete control is lacking. Yet in practice no experiment is perfectly executed, and the practicing scientist overlooks those imperfections that seem to him to offer no plausible rival explanation of the results. In the light of modern philosophies of science, no experiment ever *proves* a theory, it merely *probes* it. Seeming proof results from that condition in which there is no available plausible rival hypothesis to explain the data. The general program of quasi-experimental analysis is to specify and examine those plausible rival explanations of the results that are provided by the uncontrolled variables. A failure to control that does not in fact lend plausibility to a rival interpretation is not regarded as invalidating.

It is well to remember that we do make assured causal inferences in many settings not involving randomization: the earthquake caused the brick building to crumble; the automobile crashing into the telephone pole caused it to break; the language patterns of the older models and mentors caused this child to speak English rather than Kwakiutl; and so forth. While these are all potentially erroneous inferences, they are of the same type as experimental inferences. We are confident that were we to intrude experimentally, we could confirm the causal laws involved. Yet they have been made assuredly by a nonexperimenting observer. This assurance is due to the effective absence of other plausible causes. Consider the inference about the crashing auto and the telephone pole: we rule out combinations of termites and wind because the other implications of these theories do not occur (there are no termite tunnels and debris in the wood, and nearby weather stations have no records of heavy wind). Spontaneous splintering of the pole by happenstance coincident with the auto's onset does not impress us as a rival, nor would it explain the damage to the car, etc. Analogously in quasi-experimental analysis, tentative causal interpretation of data may be made where the interpretation in question is consistent with the data and where other rival interpretations have been rendered implausible.

Dimensions of experimental validity. A set of twelve dimensions, representing frequent threats to validity, have been developed for the evaluation of data as quasi-experiments. These may be regarded as the important classes of frequently plausible rival hypotheses that good research design seeks to rule out. Each will be presented briefly even though not all are employed in the evaluation of the designs used illustratively here.

Fundamental to this listing is a distinction between *internal validity* and *external validity*. Internal validity is the basic minimum without which any experiment is uninterpretable: Did in fact the experimental treatments make a difference in this specific experimental instance? External validity asks the question of *generalizability*: To what populations, settings, treatment variables, and measurement variables can this effect be generalized? Both types of criteria are obviously important, even though they are frequently at odds in that features increasing one may jeopardize the other. While internal validity is the *sine qua non*, and while the question of external validity, like the question of inductive inference, is never completely answerable, the selection of designs strong in both types of validity is obviously our ideal.

Threats to internal validity. Relevant to internal validity are eight different classes of extraneous variables that if not controlled in the experimental design might produce effects mistaken for the effect of the experimental treatment. These are the following. (1) *History:* other specific events in addition to the experimental variable occurring between a first and second measurement. (2) *Maturation:* processes within the respondents that are a function of the passage of time per se (not specific to the particular events), including growing older, growing hungrier, growing tireder, and the like. (3) *Testing:* the effects of taking a test a first time upon subjects' scores in subsequent testing. (4) *Instrumentation:* the effects of changes in the calibration of a measuring instrument or changes in the observers or scorers upon changes in the obtained measurements. (5) *Statistical regression:* operating where groups of subjects have been selected on the basis of their extreme scores. (6) *Selection:* biases resulting in differential recruitment of respondents for the comparison groups. (7) *Experimental mortality:* the differential loss of respondents from the comparison groups. (8) *Selection–maturation interaction:* in certain of the multiple-group quasi-experimental designs, such as the nonequivalent control group design, an interaction of maturation and differential selection is confounded with, that is, might be mistaken for, the effect of the experimental variable [see LINEAR HYPOTHESES, *article on* REGRESSION; SAMPLE SURVEYS].

Threats to external validity. Factors jeopardizing external validity or *representativeness* are: (1) The *reactive or interaction effect of testing,* in which a pretest might increase or decrease the respondent's sensitivity or responsiveness to the experimental variable and thus make the results obtained for a pretested population unrepresentative of the effects of the experimental variable for the unpretested universe from which the experimental respondents were selected. (2) *Interaction* effects between *selection* bias and the *experimental variable.* (3) *Reactive effects of experimental arrangements*, which would preclude generalization about the effect of the experimental variable for persons being exposed to it in nonexperimental settings. (4) *Multiple-treatment interference,* a problem wherever multiple treatments are applied to the same respondents, and a particular problem for one-group designs involving equivalent time samples or equivalent materials samples.

Types of quasi-experimental design.   Some common types of quasi-experimental design will be outlined here.

One-group pretest–posttest design.   Perhaps the simplest quasi-experimental design is the one-group pretest–posttest design, $O_1 \ X \ O_2$ (O represents measurement or observation, X the experimental treatment). This common design patently leaves uncontrolled the threats to internal validity of history, maturation, testing, instrumentation, and, if subjects were selected on the basis of extreme scores on O_1, regression. There may be situations in which the investigator could decide that none of these represented plausible rival hypotheses in his setting: A log of other possible change-agents might provide no plausible ones; the measurement in question might be nonreactive (Campbell 1957), the time span too short for maturation, too spaced for fatigue, etc. However, the sources of invalidity are so numerous that a more powerful quasi-experimental design would be preferred. Several of these can be constructed by adding features to this simple one.

Interrupted time-series design.   The interrupted time-series experiment utilizes a series of measurements providing multiple pretests and posttests, for example:

$$O_1 \ O_2 \ O_3 \ O_4 \ X \ O_5 \ O_6 \ O_7 \ O_8 \ .$$

If in this series, O_4–O_5 shows a rise greater than found elsewhere, then maturation, testing, and regression are no longer plausible, in that they would predict equal or greater rises for O_1–O_2, etc. Instrumentation may well be controlled too, although in institutional settings a change of administration policy is often accompanied by a change in record-keeping standards. Observers and participants may be focused on the occurrence of X and may speciously change rating standards, etc. History remains the major threat, although in many settings it would not offer a plausible rival interpretation.

Multiple time-series design.   If one had available a parallel time series from a group not receiving the experimental treatment, but exposed to the same extraneous sources of influence, and if this control time series failed to show the exceptional jump from O_4 to O_5, then the plausibility of history as a rival interpretation would be greatly reduced. We may call this the multiple time-series design.

Nonequivalent control group.   Another way of improving the one-group pretest–posttest design is to add a "nonequivalent control group." (Were the control group to be randomly assigned from the same population as the experimental group, we would, of course, have a true experimental design not a quasi-experimental design.) Depending on the similarities of setting and attributes, if the nonequivalent control group fails to show the gain manifest in the experimental group, then history, maturation, testing, and instrumentation are controlled. In this popular design, the frequent effort to "correct" for the lack of perfect equivalence by matching on pretest scores is *absolutely wrong* (e.g., Thorndike 1942; Hovland et al. 1949; Campbell & Clayton 1961), because it introduces a regression artifact. Instead, one should accept any initial pretest differences, using analysis of covariance, gain scores, or graphic presentation. (This, of course, is not to reject blocking on pretest scores in true experiments where groups have been assigned to treatments at random.) Remaining uncontrolled is the selection–maturation interaction, that is, the possibility that the experimental group differed from the control group not only in initial level but also in its autonomous maturation rate. In experiments on psychotherapy and on the effects of specific coursework this is a very serious rival. Note that it can be rendered implausible by use of a time series of pretest for both groups thus moving again to the multiple time-series design.

Other quasi-experimental designs.   There is not space here to present adequately even these four quasi-experimental designs, but perhaps the strategy of adding specific observations and analyses to check on specific threats to validity has been illustrated. This is carried to an extreme in the recurrent institutional cycle design (Campbell & McCormack 1957; Campbell & Stanley 1963), in which longitudinal and cross-sectional measurements are combined with still other analyses to assess the impact of indoctrination procedures, etc. through exploiting the fact that essentially similar treatments are being given to new entrants year after year or cycle after cycle. Other quasi-experimental designs are covered in Campbell and Stanley (1963), Campbell and Clayton (1961), Campbell (1963), and Pelz and Andrews (1964).

Correlational analyses.   Related to the program of quasi-experimental analysis are those efforts to achieve causal inference from correlational data. Note that while correlation does not prove causation, most causal hypotheses imply specific correlations, and examination of these thus probes, tests, or edits the causal hypothesis. Furthermore, as Blalock (1964) and Simon (1947–1956) have emphasized, certain causal models specify uneven patterns of correlation. Thus the $A \to B \to C$ model implies that r_{AC} be smaller than r_{AB} or r_{BC}. However, their use of partial correlations or the use of Wright's path analysis (1920) are rejected as tests of the model because of the requirement that the "cause" be totally represented in the "effect." In the social sciences it will never be plausible that the cause has been measured without unique error and that it also totally lacks unique systematic variance not shared with the effect. More appropriate would be Lawley's (1940) test of the hypothesis of *single factoredness*. Only if single factoredness can be rejected would the causal model, as represented by its predicted uneven correlation pattern, be the preferred interpretation [*see* MULTIVARIATE ANALYSIS, *articles on* CORRELATION].

Tests of significance. A word needs to be said about tests of significance for quasi-experimental designs. It has been argued by several competent social scientists that since randomization has not been used tests of significance assuming randomization are not relevant. On the whole, the writer disagrees. However, some aspects of the protest are endorsed: Good experimental design is needed for any comparison inferring change, whether or not tests of significance are used, even if only photographs, graphs, or essays are being compared. In this sense, experimental design is independent of tests of significance. More importantly, tests of significance have mistakenly come to be taken as thoroughgoing *proof*. In vulgar social science usage, finding a "significant difference" is apt to be taken as *proving* the author's basis for predicting the difference, forgetting the many other plausible rival hypotheses explaining a significant difference that quasi-experimental designs leave uncontrolled. Certainly the valuation of tests of significance in some quarters needs demoting. Further, the use of tests of significance designed for the evaluation of a single comparison becomes much too lenient when dozens, hundreds, or thousands of comparisons have been sifted. And in a similar manner, an experimenter's decision as to which of his studies is publishable and the editor's decision as to which of the manuscripts are acceptable further bias the sampling basis. In all of these ways, reform is needed.

However, when a quasi-experimenter has, for example, compared the results from two intact classrooms employed in a sampling of convenience, a chance difference is certainly *one*, even if only one, of the many plausible rival hypotheses that must be considered. If each class had but 5 students, one would interpret the fact that 20 per cent

more in the experimental class showed increases with less interest than if each class had 100 students. In this case there is available an elaborate formal theory for the plausible rival hypothesis of chance fluctuation. This theory involves the assumption of randomness, which is quite appropriate when the null model of random association is rejected in favor of a hypothesis of systematic difference between the two groups. If a "significant difference" is found, the test of significance will not, of course, reveal whether the two classes differed because one saw the experimental movie or for some selection reason associated with class topic, time of day, etc., that might have interacted with rate of autonomous change, pretest instigated changes, reactions to commonly experienced events, etc. But such a test of significance will help rule out what can be considered as a ninth threat to internal validity; that is, that there is no difference here at all that could not be accounted for as a vagary of sampling in terms of a model of purely chance assignment. Note that the statement of probability level is in this light a statement of the plausibility of this one rival hypothesis, which always has some plausibility, however faint.

DONALD T. CAMPBELL

[*Other relevant material may be found in* HYPOTHESIS TESTING; PERSONALITY MEASUREMENT, *article on* SITUATIONAL TESTS; PSYCHOMETRICS; REASONING AND LOGIC; SURVEY ANALYSIS.]

BIBLIOGRAPHY

BLALOCK, HUBERT M. JR. 1964 *Causal Inferences in Nonexperimental Research.* Chapel Hill: Univ. of North Carolina Press.

CAMPBELL, DONALD T. 1957 Factors Relevant to the Validity of Experiments in Social Settings. *Psychological Bulletin* 54:297–312.

CAMPBELL, DONALD T. 1963 From Description to Experimentation: Interpreting Trends as Quasi-experiments. Pages 212–242 in Chester W. Harris (editor), *Problems in Measuring Change.* Madison: Univ. of Wisconsin Press.

CAMPBELL, DONALD T.; and CLAYTON, K. N. 1961 Avoiding Regression Effects in Panel Studies of Communication Impact. *Studies in Public Communication* 3: 99–118.

CAMPBELL, DONALD T.; and McCORMACK, THELMA H. 1957 Military Experience and Attitudes Toward Authority. *American Journal of Sociology* 62:482–490.

CAMPBELL, DONALD T.; and STANLEY, J. S. 1963 Experimental and Quasi-experimental Designs for Research on Teaching. Pages 171–246 in Nathaniel L. Gage (editor), *Handbook of Research on Teaching.* Chicago: Rand McNally.

CHAPIN, FRANCIS S. (1947) 1955 *Experimental Designs in Sociological Research.* Rev. ed. New York: Harper.

CHAPIN, FRANCIS S.; and QUEEN, S. A. 1937 *Research Memorandum on Social Work in the Depression.* New York: Social Science Research Council.

GREENWOOD, ERNEST 1945 *Experimental Sociology: A Study in Method.* New York: Columbia Univ. Press.

HOVLAND, CARL I.; LUMSDAINE, ARTHUR A.; and SHEFFIELD, FREDERICK D. 1949 *Experiments on Mass Communication.* Studies in Social Psychology in World War II, Vol. 3. Princeton Univ. Press.

LAWLEY, D. N. 1940 The Estimation of Factor Loadings by the Method of Maximum Likelihood. Royal Society of Edinburgh, *Proceedings* 60:64–82.

PELZ, DONALD C.; and ANDREWS, F. M. 1964 Detecting Causal Priorities in Panel Study Data. *American Sociological Review* 29:838–848.

SIMON, HERBERT A. (1947–1956) 1957 *Models of Man: Social and Rational; Mathematical Essays on Rational Human Behavior in a Social Setting.* New York: Wiley.

STOUFFER, SAMUEL A. et al. 1949 *The American Soldier.* Studies in Social Psychology in World War II, Vols. 1 and 2. Princeton Univ. Press. → Volume 1: *Adjustment During Army Life.* Volume 2: *Combat and Its Aftermath.*

THORNDIKE, EDWARD L.; and RUGER, G. J. 1923 The Effect of First-year Latin Upon Knowledge of English Words of Latin Derivation. *School and Society* 18: 260–270.

THORNDIKE, EDWARD L.; and WOODWORTH, R. S. 1901 The Influence of Improvement in One Mental Function Upon the Efficiency of Other Functions. *Psychological Review* 8:247–261, 384–395, 553–564.

THORNDIKE, R. L. 1942 Regression Fallacies in the Matched Groups Experiment. *Psychometrika* 7:85–102.

WRIGHT, S. 1920 Correlation and Causation. *Journal of Agricultural Research* 20:557–585.

EXPERIMENTAL PSYCHOLOGY

The subject matter of the field that is traditionally called experimental psychology is included under the entries DRIVES; EXPERIMENTAL DESIGN; FORGETTING; LEARNING; MOTIVATION; PERCEPTION; PSYCHOLOGY, *article on* PHYSIOLOGICAL PSYCHOLOGY.

EXPLANATION

See CAUSATION *and* SCIENTIFIC EXPLANATION.

EXPLORATION OF DATA

See STATISTICS *and* SURVEY ANALYSIS, *article on* METHODS OF SURVEY ANALYSIS.

EXPLORATORY DRIVES

See STIMULATION DRIVES.

EXPORTS

See INTERNATIONAL TRADE.

EXPRESSIVE BEHAVIOR

The term "expressive behavior" refers to those aspects of behavior which manifest motivational states. "Motivational state" is used here to cover emotional attitudes and moods, cognitive attitudes (attention, concentration), activation states (arousal, fatigue), and more-or-less permanent attitudes that are personality attributes.

The study of expressive behavior has a dual origin in psychodiagnostics (falsely attributed to Aristotle) and in rhetoric (Quintilian). Interest in art and, particularly, in the stage (e.g., Engel 1785) stimulated detailed descriptions of expressive movement. More recently, expressive behavior has been discussed in connection with the philosophical problem of knowing other minds (Bain 1859; Lipps 1905; Scheler 1913). At present, the main impetus for the investigation of expressive behavior stems from the study of social perception, emotion, and personality.

"Expressive behavior" is a somewhat misleading term. Many behaviors which are not to be classified as "expressions" still have expressive aspects, e.g., the "deliberate" or "determined" manner of performing actions; the "hesitant" or "emphatic" intonational patterns in speech. The term is misleading, again, since it might suggest an expressive intention or purpose on the part of the subject that in fact is not presupposed. Labeling some behavior as "expressive" does not imply anything about its function or purpose. Expression is not a specific category of behavior, but expressiveness is the result of a perspective on all behavior. Every behavior is expressive when viewed with respect to the motivational state suggested by it. The term "expressive behavior" is misleading, finally, in that it suggests the presence of something, an inner experience, which is expressed but exists distinct from its expression. This, again, is not necessarily the case. Some behavior is expressive without the subject's experiencing the emotions suggested by his behavior, as in a theatrical performance or in an act of deceit. Actually, the investigation of the relationship of expressive behavior to inner states or other dispositions is one of the main tasks in this area.

Phenomena that are functionally quite different are usually classed as expressive behavior; they vary in the manner in which they manifest motivational states:

(*a*) In both expressive movements (movements of limbs, head, facial features, and body) and the manner of performing purposive actions, the movement pattern itself is expressive, that is, it manifests the motivational state. Expressive aspects of vocal behavior and visceral manifestations of emotion can be classed along with expressive movement.

(*b*) In expressive actions, the way in which the environment is treated, rather than the movement pattern itself, is expressive.

(c) Verbal–symbolic behavior is expressive to the extent that it evidences some motivational state of the speaker.

(d) The products of creative behavior, in contrast to the behavior pattern itself, are considered expressive. Professional dancing and singing can, of course, be classified under both (a) and (d).

Expressive movement—descriptive analysis. The study of expressive movement implies (1) carefully describing behavior patterns and (2) ascertaining their meaning, in terms of the subject's introspective report, his earlier or subsequent behavior, or the stimulus situation; or in terms of independently assessed personality traits.

The traditional source for descriptive data on expressive movement is the theater. While posed expressions are still used as stimuli in experiments on recognition of expression, they present obvious and unnecessary difficulties for the analysis of expressive behavior as such. Spontaneous expressions can be collected systematically by exposing the subject to specific stimuli (sudden noises, sweet music, pain); by time sampling during standardized or experimentally varied conditions (stress, task failure); or by electrical brain stimulation (Hess 1962). For recording these movements, refined techniques are sometimes utilized, such as high-speed cinematography (Landis & Hunt 1939) or electromyography (Sainsbury 1955). Sometimes it has been feasible to obtain introspective reports as well (Frijda 1953). Some response patterns have been described in detail, such as the startle pattern (Landis & Hunt 1939) or animal rage patterns (Bard 1950). Correlational studies have been used to identify patterns of individual differences (e.g., Allport & Vernon 1933; for visceral response patterns, see Lacey et al. 1963). Many studies have established the existence of stable individual differences in single expressive traits, such as frequency of nervous movements (Sainsbury 1955) or muscular tension during stress (see Duffy 1962, chapter 11), or size and speed variables, such as size of writing, length, and speed of stride, and rate of speech, as used in the Allport and Vernon study (1933).

A somewhat different approach has been followed in a series of German studies that originated in the work of Piderit (1867). These studies try to describe the variables of expressive movement for various body areas (facial expression, Lersch 1932; general body movement, Strehle 1954; gait, Kietz 1956; gesture, Kiener 1962). They present a large number of hypotheses on personality attributes presumably revealed by the various expressive traits; interpretations are based upon impressions gained during psychodiagnostic sessions. There are no validation studies, however. In general, very little has been established on the relationship between expressive movement and personality, except for some group-comparison studies. For example, patients classified as neurotic or as anxious tend to manifest a higher habitual degree of muscular tension and more frequent nervous movements than normal or nonanxious controls (see Duffy 1962, chapter 11; Sainsbury 1955).

Specificity and meaning. Traditionally it is held that expressive movement expresses emotion; also, that for every linguistically distinguishable emotion there is a corresponding distinct expressive movement pattern. The existence of expressions of other aspects of personality presents difficulties for the first hypothesis. Experimental investigation disproves the second. Landis (1924) elicited spontaneous emotional reactions from a group of subjects. Comparison of these reactions with the subjects' introspective reports revealed that no emotion invariably leads to the same expression in every person and at every moment. Recognition experiments, in which observers are presented with photographs or films showing facial or other expressions, indicate that interpretations of expression are quite often incorrect. Observers attach widely different labels to one and the same expression (see Woodworth & Schlosberg 1955, chapter 5).

The variety of interpretations for a given expression does not mean, however, that expression of emotion is highly ambiguous. Woodworth demonstrated (1938) that there was a high degree of agreement among observers when expressions were judged in terms of emotion groups rather than separate emotions; Schlosberg (1954) showed the same for judgment in terms of three dimensions—pleasantness–unpleasantness, attention–rejection, and level of activation—and demonstrated at the same time the equivalence of these dimension judgments to judgment in terms of emotion groups. These studies suggest that expression does not represent emotions as distinct and discontinuous states; it represents, rather, a set of continuous emotional dimensions. This conclusion is supported by high correlations between dimensional values and measurements of facial features (Frijda & Philipszoon 1963). Every emotion occupies some place in this multidimensional expression space. However, several different motivational states may occupy the same place; hence the confusion in recognition experiments. As yet there is still some uncertainty about the dimensions involved. One of Schlosberg's dimensions, attention–rejection, seems superfluous in view of multidimensional scalings based upon similarity judgments (Abelson & Sermat 1962; Shepard 1962). On the other hand, the importance of additional dimensions is suggested by other studies (Frijda & Philipszoon 1963).

Expressive movement, then, appears to represent the person's state as defined by these dimensions, whose psychological nature can be summarized as the person's attitude, or his readiness to relate to his environment, and his state of activation. Expressive movement, consequently, cannot properly be said to represent emotion. It may manifest some aspect of emotion, emotion being defined by the type of situational determinant in addition to the attitude and the activation state (Frijda 1958; Schachter & Singer 1962). However, the attitude and activation state may instead be part of a cognitive, nonemotional attitude. They may also represent some habitual attitude or activation *modus,* in which case they constitute a personality trait.

Origin.   In order to understand the origin and function of expressive movement, a distinction has to be made. Expressive movements which arise spontaneously out of the actual motivational state are called primary; expressions which are made more or less intentionally are called secondary. Secondary expressive behavior overlays and modifies the primary. People frequently exaggerate their spontaneous reactions for reasons of communication or social participation. Sometimes they produce expressive movements when no corresponding emotional attitude is experienced, as to give a social signal, to be polite, or to deceive. They also produce symbolic expressive movements—gestures of doubt, disbelief, denial, or approval—which serve linguistic functions, underlining or replacing verbal behavior.

Primary expressions seem to be unlearned. The evidence comes from different sources: developmental observations; data on generality over species (which in humans means ethnological evidence); and neuropsychological research [*see* INSTINCT].

Within the first few weeks of life a limited but still differentiated repertory of reactions can be observed: crying, generalized excitement, startle, orienting responses, quiet relaxation, and facial contortions typical of disgust (Malrieu 1960). Somewhat later, smiling appears. These expressions can be observed under conditions that make social learning unlikely: absence of social reinforcement (Dennis 1938); blindness; and even a combination of blindness and deafness (Thompson 1941). The blind manifest these expressions in situations that would call forth the same reactions in normal children.

Systematic cross-cultural research on expressive behavior has been rare since 1867, when Darwin sent a questionnaire to informants around the world. Yet, from scattered reports the generalization seems warranted that the same primary expressive patterns are present in every culture, where they indicate the same motivational states; or, rather, that everywhere they appear at least with this common meaning. Laughter is used everywhere to express joy, even if occasionally it may express other things as well and even if joy occasionally is expressed differently.

Some expressive reactions—those considered indicative of rage, fear, or attention—have been evoked in animals by midbrain stimulation (Hess 1962); laughter, smiling, and weeping occur in human subjects who have cerebral lesions or who are subjected to electrical stimulation in the thalamic region (Hassler & Riechert 1961). Still, these data may be interpreted (e.g., by Hess) as the evocation of emotional impulses as such, and these impulses, of course, might also utilize learned behaviors.

Social determinants.   The inborn forms of expressive behavior are supplemented by and modified by social learning. To what extent this is the case has been demonstrated by Efron's (1941) comparison of gestural behavior of Jews and Italians in New York City. Jews and Italians who have been minimally acculturated to the general American way of life possess quite different gestural habits, although both gesticulate considerably more than the average American. Among more acculturated groups these differences largely disappear. The findings concerning cultural differences, however, in no way conflict with the notion of universal human expressive patterns with fixed meanings.

The influence of culture on expression can be summarized as follows.

(*a*) Culture determines to what extent emotional impulses are shown and, consequently, how frequent and pronounced expressive behavior is. The extent to which expressive behavior is encouraged is culturally determined.

(*b*) Culture may determine under what conditions certain expressions are allowed or prescribed. Weeping by men is, in Western culture, permitted only under special circumstances; in prerevolutionary China the amount of weeping when a relative died was carefully graded by a codex, according to the closeness of the relationship (Granet 1922).

(*c*) There are cultural differences with regard to the events that elicit given emotional reactions.

In these cases there is not so much difference in expressive behavior as in emotional behavior.

(*d*) Certain more-or-less general motor habits— manner of walking or sitting, gestural accompaniment of speech, intonement of speech—may be culturally determined. Such habits can be quite typical for people of a given culture (Efron 1941; LaBarre 1947). They may reflect some culturally determined mental attitude or they may be the expression of nothing but a cultural-movement norm.

(*e*) Secondary expressive movements, particularly those with linguistic meanings, are based upon cultural conventions: the gestures for "yes" and "no" are well-known examples.

Nature of expressive movement. Why should there be expressive movement, and why does it take a particular form? Several explanatory principles have been adduced, which are all supported by some empirical evidence.

(*a*) Expressive behavior is either adaptive behavior or conditioned but originally adaptive behavior. The addition of "originally adaptive" is obviously needed, since people make "disgusted" faces, possibly useful for getting rid of bad-tasting substances, when they hear morally disgusting stories. It seems certain that much in expressive movement is adaptive not only with regard to our forebears, as Darwin would have it, but here and now. Facial expressions of fear often form part, or the beginning, of general protective responses. Expressive movement, if it is adaptive, is so in a rather special way: not by modifying the environment, but by modifying the organism's relationship to his environment, through approach and withdrawal tendencies and through increase or decrease of sensory readiness of different kinds. To be sure, expression may sometimes be adaptive in only a subjective way—for instance, when a child tries to hide from people's glances by holding its hands before its face. To the extent that expressive movement is adaptive, it is connected to the motivational states in a quite intimate and intrinsic manner, since motives are by definition tendencies for establishing or destroying certain kinds of relationships. Primary expressive movement, according to this view, is the execution of behavior tendencies that define or partly define emotions and other motivational states.

(*b*) Expressive behavior is the direct manifestation of emotional (or other) activation. Drowsiness, energy, joy, and alertness refer to hardly more than quantitative variations of activation; the corresponding expressive movements are indeed mainly different degrees of generalized muscular activity, as correlation studies indicate (Frijda & Philipszoon 1963). In addition, expressive behavior embodies the degree of activity control. When emotions disrupt orientation and planning, behavior becomes disorganized and is, consequently, "expressive" of the disrupted state. In this reformulation of Darwin's "irradiation principle," the expressive components again are connected to the emotional impulses in no fortuitous manner. The expressive components are the consequences of the motivational impulses.

(*c*) Expressive movement might be communicative behavior either instinctively, by means of hereditary patterns, or intentionally, by means of conventional symbols. There is ethological evidence for instinctiveness in animal mating ceremonies or warning calls but little evidence to support or suggest instinctiveness in human expression, except, perhaps, the crying of the infant. Voluntary communicative expression is, of course, evident in verbal behavior and in secondary expressive movement. Primary expressions are rapidly utilized for communication, as is notable in the development of infant crying.

(*d*) Expressive movement might be a release phenomenon, serving to discharge emotional tensions. Introspectively, expressing emotions often gives relief. Freeman and Pathman (1942) found that experimentally induced emotional tension dissipated more rapidly in subjects manifesting much restless behavior than in those manifesting little. The fact that there is tension discharge does not, of course, imply that this is the *raison d'être* for the discharging behavior. The explanation may hold, however, for those nervous movements which arise during emotional stress or conflict ("autistic gestures," Krout 1935), such as scratching, rubbing the nose, nail-biting, etc.

The foregoing principles seem to account for most expressive movement; they seem to apply equally well to extralinguistic vocal expression. There are two important exceptions, however. Laughter and weeping do not seem to allow of any interpretation in terms of past or present adaptive movement, although such an interpretation was tried by Darwin; they cannot be smoothly interpreted as activation *modi* or mere consequences of loss of activity control; and their release function does not explain their form either. As yet, laughter and weeping are riddles of human behavior.

Expressive actions. Every human activity indicates some attitude and is thereby expressive, even if only of unemotional matter-of-factness. This holds particularly for choice behavior—choice of interests, of mates, of possessions, of clothing, etc. Activities which demand special mention, however, are those that are clearly objectively useless and clearly motivated by some sort of emotional excitement—a child's hiding under its mother's skirt, banging on the table, tearing its clothes, etc. In part these are what Lewin (1927) called field actions, which try to change the relationship with the environment. In part they have the distinct function of releasing emotional tensions which cannot find their outlet in a more proper, more adequate way. Little systematic study has been made of these phenomena notwithstanding their social importance, which is shown by the behavior of youthful audiences.

Verbal–symbolic behavior. Verbal–symbolic behavior is expressive, of course, primarily in that the subject desires to communicate his feelings, attitudes, or ideas. There is little relationship between a definition of expressive behavior that covers these phenomena and one that is focused upon expressive movement.

Expressive creative behavior. Creative behavior can justifiably be called expressive: its products stem from some drive to structure and shape. It is primarily this drive, which may get its energy from various sources, which art expresses. Artistic production may also, occasionally, serve the purpose of communication of feelings or ideas. Artistic products are frequently expressive, moreover, in the sense in which this term is primarily used here. Paintings, music, and poetry appear invested with emotional meanings for the spectator; they evidence motivational states. Still, there is an important distinction which separates artistic production from the execution of expressive movements. Functionally, both belong to entirely different classes of phenomena. Expressive movement is a direct manifestation of tendencies inherent in the emotional impulse. Expression in art is, as Langer (1942) emphasized, a representation of some motivational state in the language of the particular artistic mode—pictorial, musical, etc. It is a symbol of a motivational state that need not even be actually experienced at the time of creation. In the fact of its being a representation resides an effect, and possibly a function, of artistic production: in the creative process emotional impulses or experiences become structured, and this may facilitate coming to grips with them. Sometimes artistic products may be pervaded by traces of primary expressive movement: this is clearest in dancing and singing, but it is also true of painting and of some aspects of writing style. Yet the intention to create shape or structure in a conventional symbol system—even if the convention is peculiar to the individual artist—makes this class of phenomena irreducible to other kinds of expressive behavior.

NICO H. FRIJDA

[*Directly related is the entry* EMOTION. *Other relevant material may be found in* ATTENTION; CREATIVITY; SYMPATHY AND EMPATHY; TRAITS.]

BIBLIOGRAPHY

ABELSON, ROBERT P.; and SERMAT, VELLO 1962 Multidimensional Scaling of Facial Expressions. *Journal of Experimental Psychology* 63:546–554.

ALLPORT, GORDON W.; and VERNON, PHILIP E. 1933 *Studies in Expressive Movement.* New York: Macmillan.

ASCH, SOLOMON (1952) 1959 *Social Psychology.* Englewood Cliffs, N.J.: Prentice-Hall. → See especially "The Expression of Emotions," pages 183–204.

BAIN, ALEXANDER (1859) 1899 *The Emotions and the Will.* 4th ed. London: Longmans.

BARD, PHILIP 1950 Central Nervous Mechanisms for the Expression of Anger in Animals. Pages 211–237 in International Symposium on Feelings and Emotions, Second, Mooseheart, Ill., 1948, *Feelings and Emotions.* Edited by Martin L. Reymert. New York: McGraw-Hill.

DARWIN, CHARLES (1872) 1965 *The Expression of the Emotions in Man and Animals.* Edited by Francis Darwin. Univ. of Chicago Press.

DENNIS, WAYNE 1938 Infant Development Under Conditions of Restricted Practice and of Minimum Social Stimulation: A Preliminary Report. *Journal of Genetic Psychology* 53:149–157.

DUFFY, ELIZABETH 1962 *Activation and Behavior.* New York: Wiley. → See especially Chapters 5, 10, and 11.

DUMAS, GEORGES 1948 *La vie affective: Physiologie, psychologie, socialisation.* Paris: Presses Universitaires de France.

EFRON, DAVID 1941 *Gesture and Environment.* New York: King's Crown Press.

ENGEL, JOHANN J. 1785 *Ideen zu einer Mimik.* Berlin: Mylin.

FREEMAN, G. L.; and PATHMAN, J. H. 1942 The Relation of Overt Muscular Discharge to Physiological Recovery From Experimentally Induced Displacement. *Journal of Experimental Psychology* 30:161–174.

FRIJDA, NICO H. 1953 The Understanding of Facial Expression of Emotion. *Acta psychologica* 9:294–362.

FRIJDA, NICO H. 1958 Facial Expression and Situational Cues. *Journal of Abnormal and Social Psychology* 57: 149–154.

FRIJDA, NICO H.; and PHILIPSZOON, ELS 1963 Dimensions of Recognition of Expression. *Journal of Abnormal and Social Psychology* 66:45–51.

GRANET, MARCEL 1922 Le langage de la douleur d'après le rituel funéraire de la Chine classique. *Journal de psychologie* 19:97–118.

HASSLER, R.; and RIECHERT, T. 1961 Wirkungen der Reizungen und Koagulationen in den Stammganglien bei stereotaktischen Hirnoperationen. *Nervenarzt* 32: 97–109.

HESS, WALTER R. (1962) 1964 *The Biology of Mind.* Univ. of Chicago Press. → First published in German.

See especially "Psychic Functions and Cerebral Organization," pages 38–149.

KIENER, FRANZ 1962 *Hand, Gebärde und Charakter.* Munich: Reinhardt.

KIETZ, GERTRAUD 1956 *Der Ausdrucksgehalt des menschlichen Ganges.* Leipzig: Barth.

KIRCHHOFF, R. (editor) 1965 *Handbuch der Psychologie.* Volume 5: Ausdruckspsychologie. Göttingen (Germany): Hogrefe.

KLAGES, LUDWIG (1943) 1950 *Grundlegung der Wissenschaft vom Ausdruck.* 7th ed., rev. Bonn: Bouvier.

KROUT, MAURICE 1935 Autistic Gestures: An Experimental Study of Symbolic Movement. *Psychological Monographs* 46, no. 4.

LABARRE, WESTON 1947 The Cultural Basis of Emotions and Gestures. *Journal of Personality* 16:49–68.

LACEY, JOHN I. et al. 1963 The Visceral Level: Situational Determinants and Behavioral Correlates of Autonomic Response Patterns. Pages 161–196 in Symposium on Expression of the Emotions in Man, New York, 1960, *Expression of the Emotions in Man.* Edited by Peter H. Knapp. New York: International Universities Press.

LANDIS, CARNEY 1924 Studies of Emotional Reactions. II: General Behavior and Facial Expression. *Journal of Comparative Psychology* 4:447–501.

LANDIS, CARNEY; and HUNT, WILLIAM A. 1939 *The Startle Pattern.* New York: Farrar.

LANGER, SUSANNE (1942) 1957 *Philosophy in a New Key: A Study in the Symbolism of Reason, Rite and Art.* 3d ed. Cambridge, Mass.: Harvard Univ. Press.

LERSCH, PHILIP 1932 *Gesicht und Seele.* Munich: Reinhardt.

LEWIN, K. 1927 Kindlicher Ausdruck. *Zeitschrift für pädagogische Psychologie* 28:510–526.

LIPPS, T. 1905 Die Erkenntnis von fremden Ichen. *Psychologische Untersuchungen* 1:695–719.

MALRIEU, PHILIPPE 1960 Les conditions de l'évolution des émotions dans la première année. *Schweizerische Zeitschrift für Psychologie* 19:207–222.

PIDERIT, THEODOR (1867) 1925 *Mimik und Physiognomik.* 4th ed. Detmold (Germany): Meyer.

SAINSBURY, P. 1955 Gestural Movement During Psychiatric Interview. *Psychosomatic Medicine* 17:458–469.

SCHACHTER, STANLEY; and SINGER, JEROME 1962 Cognitive, Social and Physiological Determinants of Emotional State. *Psychological Review* 69:379–399.

SCHELER, MAX (1913) 1954 *The Nature of Sympathy.* London: Routledge. → First published as *Zur Phänomenologie und Theorie der Sympathiegefühle.* The second revised and enlarged edition, which was later translated into English, was published in 1923 as *Wesen und Formen der Sympathie.*

SCHLOSBERG, HAROLD 1954 Three Dimensions of Emotion. *Psychological Review* 61:81–88.

SHEPARD, ROGER N. 1962 The Analysis of Proximities: Multidimensional Scaling With an Unknown Distance Function. *Psychometrika* 27:125–140, 219–246.

STREHLE, HERMANN 1954 *Mienen, Gesten und Gebärden.* Munich: Reinhardt.

THOMPSON, JANE 1941 Development of Facial Expression of Emotion in Blind and Seeing Children. *Archives of Psychology* No. 264.

WOODWORTH, ROBERT S. 1938 *Experimental Psychology.* New York: Holt.

WOODWORTH, ROBERT S.; and SCHLOSBERG, HAROLD 1955 *Experimental Psychology.* 3d ed., rev. London:

Methuen. → The first edition was published in 1938 with Woodworth as sole author.

YOUNG, PAUL T. 1961 *Motivation and Emotions: A Survey of the Determinants of Human and Animal Activity.* New York: Wiley. → See especially Chapter 9.

EXPROPRIATION
See NATIONALIZATION.

EXTERNAL ECONOMIES AND DISECONOMIES

The concepts of external economies and diseconomies ("externalities") treat the subject of how the costs and benefits that constrain and motivate a decision maker in a particular activity may deviate from the costs or benefits that activity creates for a larger organization. Most of the economic literature on externalities has focused on the operation of an entire economic system, with particular reference to the effectiveness of prices, markets, competition, and profit motivation as regulators of production and consumption.

Economic theory suggests that a system characterized by private ownership of resources and sufficient competition will maximize total income and economic welfare. The system will establish an equilibrium in which product prices equal their costs on their respective margins of production. Costs include an opportunity rate of return on invested capital, which is an element of business accounting profit, and the rewards, or "rent," that especially endowed resources may command. Production costs also reflect technological constraints, and producers employ the least costly method of producing any given output. A further characteristic of the equilibrium is that similar resources, including capital, obtain equal earnings or returns in all activities. If earnings were unequal, resources would enter more profitable activities and leave less lucrative ones until earnings equality comes about. The resulting allocation of resources is also consistent with consumers' preferences. Finally, consumers' demands, through their influence on market prices and hence profits, determine the allocation of resources.

The system works in such a way that the wide diffusion of decision making which is necessary if complex systems are to operate at all is permitted. Each decision maker only needs to have knowledge about the things he consumes, or produces, or his occupation. That individuals can so narrow their focus permits a division of labor and, in turn, the resulting gains of specialization. The vital mechanism (and social institution) that facilitates such specialization is the price system, or market organization. The price system is an "information system" that provides producers and consumers with the signals that guide their behavior. Hence, the economic system is highly interdependent: the combined behavior of individual decision makers spontaneously determines relative prices and quantities of items produced and consumed, while relative prices are the signals, constraints, and opportunities to which individual decision makers respond and adapt.

Such a general equilibrium system has two specific qualities: (1) Production costs of each item, on its respective margin of production, when viewed in a social cost sense, equal the price of each item. (2) The price of each end product accurately reflects the incremental satisfaction that consumers attach to it. These two qualities constitute a "social optimum" in that national income and economic welfare are maximized [see, however, WELFARE ECONOMICS]. Note that it is only optimal if the marginal *social costs* of each activity equal the *social benefits* they create. If the social cost of an activity exceeds the costs relevant to the decision makers in the activity, there is an external diseconomy. If the benefits of an activity exceed its marginal cost, there is an external economy.

Due to the extreme interdependence within an economy, the behavior of a given industry can increase the cost of other industries in ways which need not be socially undesirable. Some of these phenomena, too, have been associated with the subject of external economies and diseconomies. One of the difficulties in the evaluation of externalities is the problem of determining which are socially desirable or undesirable and should be promoted or counteracted by public policy measures and which do not warrant government interference with the private sector.

The subject of external economies and diseconomies thus treats possible mechanical shortcomings of an economy that cause individual decision makers to operate in a fashion that thwarts the full attainment of broad social objectives. To some students the possible wide extent of externalities is sufficient basis to justify extensive government intervention in the private sector of the economy. To other students this point is debatable. The resolution of these differences has been, and remains, a major unsettled issue in economics.

External diseconomies

Technical external diseconomies. Technical external diseconomies, sometimes called "nuisance effects," were extensively discussed by A. C. Pigou

([1920] 1960, part 2, chapter 9). They arise from undesirable by-products of a production process. An example used by Pigou is the case of steam locomotives emitting sparks that cause fires. A farmer's livestock that eats his neighbor's crops is another example. Extensive lists of unwanted by-products may be drawn up in modern societies— from air and water pollution to traffic congestion associated with the automobile.

Such unwanted by-products are a natural consequence of many production processes. They impose a cost upon society similar to the cost of productive resources necessary to produce the desired product. They create a social problem insofar as their cost may not be properly allocated between different segments of the economy.

Let us consider further Pigou's example of spark-emitting steam locomotives. Assume that the marginal cost of employing resources to produce a ton-mile of railroad freight service may be 3 cents. The railroad system, however, "causes" 0.5 cents worth of damage per ton-mile because of fires inflicted on farmers' crops adjoining the right-of-way. Whether such behavior creates an unwarranted social cost, and what the appropriate social policy should be to deal with it, pose some subtle and complex issues.

The main force of Pigou's treatment of the subject is that the "social cost" of producing a ton-mile of freight is 3.5 cents (3 cents for the railroad's own costs, plus 0.5 cents for the destroyed crops). The policy prescription is that the railroad should be made to pay farmers for their destroyed crops or that railroads should be taxed or restrained in other ways that will prevent damage.

Coase (1960) has demonstrated, however, that this traditional approach to "nuisance effects" is wrong. The relationship is reciprocal. Crop damage is "caused" just as much by the farmer's growing crops along the railroad's right-of-way as by locomotives emitting sparks (indeed, the doctrine of "causation" is spurious). Moreover, to restrain railroads in arbitrary ways may impose a greater social loss (due to higher-cost railroad services) than the loss of some crops. The proper solution is to design a system that maximizes the economy's total product.

Such a solution might be found by recognizing that in producing the crops associated with the 0.5 cents per ton-mile of damage, farmers must purchase resources worth, say, 0.4 cents. Under these conditions, the railroad could pay farmers 0.1 cent *not* to grow crops along its right-of-way. Farmers would be just as well off as if there were no railroad; freight costs would be 3.1 cents per ton-mile, instead of 3.5 cents if farmers were arbitrarily awarded "full" damages; and 0.4 cents worth of resources would be freed to produce other products. Indeed, this kind of solution is often worked out spontaneously by bargaining between the concerned parties or is brought about through legal adjudication.

The social problems associated with external "nuisance effects" arise when certain scarce resources are treated as if they were "free goods"—because of faulty specification of property rights, or because it is difficult to identify in some quantitative way who causes the nuisance or who suffers from it (or both), or because the administrative costs of "solving" the problem may be more costly than the nuisance itself. Many students suggest that activities imposing unregistered social costs upon society be subjected to special excise taxes; however, the precise design of excise taxes that would not themselves distort resource allocation is difficult. Other students urge extensive state regulation. However, a distressing number of nuisance effects are due to activities that are already either regulated or managed by the state, for example, highway systems and government-owned public utilities, suggesting that effective solutions may not be easily attained from that quarter.

Sweeping solutions to the nuisance effect problem do not appear readily available. Thus far in virtually all social systems they have been coped with on an *ad hoc* basis. Perhaps one of the best ways to achieve better social guidelines for treatment of these problems is for economists to give more attention to the precise content of property rights, in terms of their economic effects, and for lawyers to employ economic analysis to evaluate the social utility of legal principles applied to torts.

Pecuniary external diseconomies. Consider industry A (for illustrative simplicity we assume that it only requires labor as a resource) which expands its output (see Table 1).

Table 1

Output	Workers	Wage	Total cost	Average and marginal cost per unit to firm	"Marginal cost" per unit to industry
100,000	100,000	$10.00	$1,000,000	$10.00	—
101,000	101,000	$10.50	$1,060,500	$10.50	$60.50

This example illustrates an "increasing cost" industry. The wage increase is necessary to induce more workers to enter the industry. The operators responsible for hiring the additional workers, by forcing up the wage, may be said to impose an addi-

tional cost upon their colleagues. This kind of cost increase has been termed an "external diseconomy."

It was with reference to cases like this that some students suggested (e.g., Pigou [1920] 1960, pp. 223–225) that the free operation of private business firms resulted in too much output by "increasing cost industries" and that they should be subject to taxation to restrict output. The implication, as illustrated by the arithmetical example, is that the $60.50 is the "social cost" per unit of the additional output; whereas the price that actually emerges in the market is $10.50.

The implication that the increasing cost was a social diseconomy raised some fundamental questions about the nature of costs. The clarification was achieved by D. H. Robertson ([1924] 1952, pp. 143–159) and especially F. H. Knight ([1924] 1952, pp. 160–179) and reiterated by Ellis and Fellner ([1943] 1952, pp. 242–263). The essential points are as follows:

Under competition, with many producers in an industry, each producer will view the cost (or wage) of hiring an additional worker as his marginal cost. In our example, it is $10.50. The $10.50 is also the average cost of production. In a private, competitive equilibrium, the average cost, the marginal cost to each producer, and the market price will be equal. If we take a collective view of the industry (which might be the case if it were operated by a socialist trust or a private monopoly) the "marginal cost" of $60.50 appears, which results from reckoning the possible impact of industry expansion upon the wage level. The question is: Which marginal cost concept is valid from an overall social welfare viewpoint?

The $10.50, rather than the $60.50, is the relevant measure of the marginal social cost. It represents what workers on the margin of production in the given industry could earn producing alternative products in other industries. Increasing the output of industry A requires enticing workers from industry B. If $10.50 is necessary to attract a worker into A, it is because he can earn $10.50 in B. Consumers give up $10.50 worth of B to get an increment of A. The marginal social cost of A is therefore $10.50. It is also the marginal cost upon which private decision makers focus and the signal that the price system generates.

That the shift in consumer demand and the consequential raising of the wage level in industry A operate to create an apparent marginal cost of $60.50 is simply a result of the fact that product prices and wages (and other resource earnings rates) are mutually determined by the operation of the price system. For a central authority to try to prevent the wage increase in industry A would (apart from thwarting consumer preferences) create many problems. First, other means to get additional workers into the industry would have to be found. If, even after getting additional workers into the industry, authorities sought to maintain the $10.00 wage and product price, they would create a rationing problem insofar as consumers would demand more of the commodity at $10.00 than they would at $10.50. Finally, the higher wage of $10.50 for all workers would induce the proper use of the specialized resources: at a $10.00 wage, production managers would not use the workers as efficiently as they would at a $10.50 wage. [*For a further discussion of these points, see* COST.]

External economies

Technical external economies. Consider the situation where a group of farmers dam a stream in order to obtain a supply of irrigation water. The resulting pond may stimulate the fish population and thus enhance fish output and the earnings of fishermen. Increased irrigated acreage devoted to apples will increase the supply of nectar, improve the productivity of bees, and increase the output of honey; conversely, a larger bee population can increase pollenization and raise apple yields.

Such external economies are creatures of multiproduct activities and are similar to the technical external diseconomies cited above. They are probably not as frequent because private producers are adroit at forming arrangements whereby they can capture their by-products and derive a profit from them. For example, in our irrigation pond–fish example, neither the value of irrigation water nor the extra fish may—separately—justify the expense of the dam that makes both possible. But a merger between a fisherman and a farmer would create the necessary arrangement by which the full gain could be captured privately and thus accrue to society.

Technical external economies may nevertheless exist in important areas—where property arrangements are inadequate to capture privately the full benefits of an activity—and are sufficient to justify state intervention. For example, public education and health are areas where, while it may be of some economic worth to an individual to educate himself (or his child) and to keep his family healthy, greater social benefits are obtained if the state pushes the activity beyond the margins that individual incentive would achieve. Multiple-purpose river development projects are further cases in point. Such projects can provide electric power, flood control, navigable waterways, irrigation, and recreational facilities. In principle, a private group with a charter granting it proprietary rights over an entire river basin could construct and operate an appropriate multipurpose river development project. But such a monopoly would have to be carefully controlled by the state to prevent the private group from exploiting such a powerful ownership right in unsocial ways. Hence, it is simpler for the state to design, create, and operate such multipurpose projects.

It should be recognized, however, that this type of argument is used to justify or rationalize many kinds of subtle and not-too-subtle forms of state intervention in support of various industries or forms of consumption. In prewar Germany agriculture enjoyed state subsidies on the ground that peasant boys made good soldiers; in the United States at present the maritime industry enjoys subsidies and the mineral industries enjoy preferential tax treatment in the cause of national defense. Whether the relationship between the costs and the benefits of each of the many government interventions warrants the government action is moot: very few such programs are actually subjected to rigorous cost–benefit analysis based upon modern quantitative and analytical techniques.

Economies of scale. When an industry expands its output, it will normally procure additional goods and services from other firms or industries. Some of the supplying industries may operate under conditions which would permit them to enjoy "economies of scale." Such a condition means that an industry is not fully utilizing its capacity, perhaps because the market demand is not large enough to take all of the output the plant is efficiently capable of producing. Where economies of scale exist, it is possible to produce additional output at lower average unit costs. Because the industry utilizes its capacity more intensively, it spreads its overhead and fixed capital costs over a larger output and enjoys an "internal economy." Industries that can exploit internal economies are also termed "decreasing cost industries."

When a given industry expands its output in a way that necessitates purchases from decreasing cost industries, the industry that expanded initially may also enjoy lower costs. For example, as coal mines in a given district increase output, the railroad serving the mines may experience lower average unit costs. If the lower unit costs are passed on to the coal mine operators, the latter experience a "pecuniary external economy."

The extent to which such pecuniary external economies occur, and the impact they have on market prices, depends on several factors that can only be determined empirically on a case-by-case basis. First, it is a question of fact as to just how important economies of scale are in the economic system and how important their variation between different industries. Although railroads and electric utilities are often cited as examples of decreasing cost industries, what if the railroad or power plant is already fully utilized? Second, when a firm enjoys economies of scale, the activity is imperfectly competitive, or even monopolistic. As illustrated by the coal mining–railroad example, the railroad enjoys a monopoly subject only to the competitive constraint imposed by, say, motor trucks. Unless there is some institutional arrangement such as a public utility commission that forces a rate reduction, the larger coal traffic and consequent lower unit costs will only increase railroad profits. The "internal economy" will not become an external economy to anyone else.

Finally, whether an external pecuniary economy actually permits lower prices for the expanding industry's end product depends upon two opposing forces: the external pecuniary economy will lower cost; however, the industry's expansion can bid up the prices of hired resources and other inputs. The net balance of these opposite forces can only be determined through examination of the composition of the expanding industry's required inputs.

Division of labor and economic growth. Another set of external economies is dynamic and closely associated with economic growth and development. As an industry expands, the growth can create a number of supplying firms and activities which, through increased specialization, afford lower-cost products and labor services. There can arise specialized banking and financial facilities, firms that specialize in machinery design and repair, warehousing and transportation specialists, and numerous other activities oriented to servicing the industry. A labor force will emerge that is more sophisticated. If an industry is concentrated in a given region, knowledge gained in one segment rapidly spreads and speeds the rate at which cost reductions occur and are "competed away" through lower prices. The phenomenon was well treated by Young (1928).

Thus industry expansion stimulates the division of labor. The keener division of labor lowers costs. The lower costs and resulting lower prices increase output even more, which permits a further division of labor. Such a process helps explain the historical development of great regional industrial areas. The phenomenon, when it cuts across an entire economy, can provide a basis for a "take-off" toward the goal of a high degree of economic development.

The external economies associated with industrial development and growth (as well as those associated with economies of scale) pose special problems in the planning and public policy of undeveloped countries. These countries usually produce raw materials or semifinished goods for export and import finished products. Policy makers thus face interesting but perhaps difficult options. To exploit externalities originating in the division of labor at a minimum cost of scarce capital, the best place to start might be the industries that are already the most developed. However, these industries are likely to be the raw material or semifinished product export industries. If they are developed further, the external economies may accrue mainly to foreigners through lower-priced exports. It may thus appear more attractive to concentrate on the development of industries that will produce products which are extensively imported. The foundation for such a development strategy may be meager, however, and the cost-effectiveness per unit of investment may be low.

But it is in manufacturing industries where great gains—apparently resulting from exploiting both the dynamics of the division of labor and economies of scale—have eventually occurred. In recognition of these historical phenomena in Western developed countries, some students (e.g., Rosenstein-Rodan 1943) have advanced the doctrine of "balanced growth." This doctrine suggests that economic development should be promoted on a wide front so that the external economies of each industry will be mutually reinforcing, thus generating a cumulative process of over-all industrial development.

The precise investment strategy that a developing country should adopt is not evident on a purely theoretical basis. Much depends upon the price elasticities and income elasticities of its traditional export industries. Moreover, a country can design a structure of tariffs and export duties that could prevent an inordinate amount of the benefits due to external economies from accruing to foreigners. And by earning more foreign exchange through more efficient operation of its export industries, a country may more effectively gain the resources to finance its internal capital investment programs; or resources may be freed from the export industries to be available for domestically oriented endeavors. Finally, careful attention should be given to the precise qualities of the economy's resources that may provide the basis for the proposed state-supported domestic—as contrasted with export-oriented—industries. At a minimum, it appears that a development program must be integrated with a foreign trade policy. [*For further discussion of the issues in this section, see* ECONOMIC GROWTH, *articles on* THEORY *and* MATHEMATICAL THEORY.]

Growth repercussions. Another variety of external economies may be designated as growth or investment repercussions. They were labeled "pecuniary external economies," however, by Scitovsky (1954). Consider the example where the steel industry enjoys high profits. It expands its capacity and consequently increases its output. The larger output reduces steel prices. The cost to steel-using industries thus falls, and they enjoy higher profits. Their enhanced profits, although external to the steel industry, may be attributed to additional investment in the steel industry.

From this sort of sequence, Scitovsky developed the following line of argument: The profit signal revealed to the steel industry alone is an inadequate measure of the profit that should guide investment in the steel industry. If the steel-using industries were integrated with the steel-producing industry, managers of the integrated industries would have a better guide for their decisions. However, the repercussions and interactions of investment in a major industry can extend throughout the entire economy, which would suggest that the entire economy be "integrated."

Thus it is asserted that the price system provides a poor guide for investment decisions. The policy implication is that central planning and decision making is a better way to allocate investment than is decentralized decision making, since the central authority can explicitly take into account such external economies. A milder policy prescription is that private investors be provided with better information about one another's intentions, which may be done through the French variant of economic planning [*see* PLANNING, ECONOMIC, *article on* WESTERN EUROPE].

The contention that private investors may be unable to exploit this class of pecuniary "external economies" recognizes that, in fact, a market mechanism and its system of price indicators do not provide "perfect" intelligence of what the future holds. But the price system is not the sole source of information in an economic system: businessmen communicate with one another in other ways; they communicate with engineers and scientists on technological possibilities, and they conduct consumer surveys. Conversely, central planners or government officials also operate under imperfect knowledge. The critical substantive issue here is therefore: can the aggregate of private investors— each highly knowledgeable about his own business and responding to prices he confronts in the market place—more efficiently use investable resources than can a central authority, which may have less detailed knowledge about consumer preference and technology but a broader view of the economy in its entirety? Both types of decision making will be "imperfect" because all decision makers have imperfect knowledge. In part, the question will turn upon how highly developed the price system and private communication systems are in a particular society. In a developing economy the information system may be poor. Hence, a case may be made for a high degree of central planning in such a setting.

However, even if an instance can be found of the price system being an inferior information system, the case for central planning and control of investment is not established. The price system combined with private investment decision making provides widely diffused control over investable resources. Centrally controlled investment decision making is subject only to constraints that affect the entire economy. The choice is therefore one between many small decision makers making many small mistakes because of a poor information system, as opposed to the central authority possibly making fewer mistakes but perhaps making monumental ones. Which system is the most efficient is not obvious.

External economies and diseconomies are a manifestation of the fact that, in complex systems, one man's decision or behavior can often have an undesigned impact upon others. The trick in system design is to establish arrangements by which the mutually interacting and dependent behavior of all decision makers harmonizes so that the larger system operates in an optimal or efficient way.

The kinds of problems and phenomena we have discussed are not unique to the operation of a private enterprise social economy, although they have been most extensively treated by economists in such a context. The large multiproduct corporation, the government agency, a military service, or a university—organizations that may be characterized as "closed" systems and may be "centrally managed" to a high degree—have identical problems. Decision making and authority are necessarily diffused (governments consist of departments and bureaus, armies consist of divisions and squads, etc.); the decisions of many must nevertheless result in some coordinated and mutually consistent behavior; decision makers must be constrained as well as motivated; finally, they must be able to obtain knowledge about their constraints and opportunities, which includes the impact of the behavior of others. In varying degrees, discussions of externalities focus on these fundamental aspects of system or organization design and management.

The problems are basically those of specifying over-all system objectives, measuring effectiveness criteria, identifying and measuring the relevant cost concept, determining the relative merits of alternative information systems (with particular reference to the cost and worth of obtaining and communicating information), and specifying the appropriate "decision rules" that should guide individual decision makers.

Much of the economic literature on "externalities" suggests that economists have often failed to meet these problems head-on. On the other hand, the discipline of economics and much of the literature on the general operation of the price system —the product of nearly two hundred years of effort to understand the workings of a complex social economy—provide worthwhile insights into the problems that confront all large organizations.

J. A. STOCKFISCH

[See also WELFARE ECONOMICS.]

BIBLIOGRAPHY

COASE, R. H.   1960   The Problem of Social Cost. *Journal of Law and Economics* 3:1–44.

ELLIS, HOWARD S.; and FELLNER, WILLIAM   (1943) 1952   External Economies and Diseconomies. Pages 242–263 in American Economic Association, *Readings in Price Theory.* Homewood, Ill.: Irwin. → First published in Volume 33 of the *American Economic Review.*

FLEMING, MARCUS   1955   External Economies and the Doctrine of Balanced Growth. *Economic Journal* 65:241–256.

KNIGHT, F. H.   (1924) 1952   Some Fallacies in the Interpretation of Social Cost. Pages 160–179 in American Economic Association, *Readings in Price Theory.* Homewood, Ill.: Irwin. → First published in Volume 38 of the *Quarterly Journal of Economics.*

MEADE, J. E.   1952   External Economies and Diseconomies in a Competitive Situation. *Economic Journal* 62:54–67.

PIGOU, ARTHUR C.   (1920) 1960   *The Economics of Welfare.* 4th ed. London: Macmillan.

ROBERTSON, D. H.   (1924) 1952   Those Empty Boxes. Pages 143–159 in American Economic Association, *Readings in Price Theory.* Homewood, Ill.: Irwin. → First published in Volume 34 of the *Economic Journal.*

ROSENSTEIN-RODAN, PAUL N.   1943   Problems of Industrialization of Eastern and Southeastern Europe. *Economic Journal* 53:202–211.

SCITOVSKY, TIBOR   1954   Two Concepts of External Economies. *Journal of Political Economy* 62:143–151.

STOCKFISCH, J. A.   1955   External Economies, Investment, and Foresight. *Journal of Political Economy* 63:446–449.

VINER, JACOB   (1931) 1952   Cost Curves and Supply Curves. Pages 198–232 in American Economic Association, *Readings in Price Theory.* Homewood, Ill.: Irwin. → First published in Volume 3 of the *Zeitschrift für Nationalökonomie.*

YOUNG, ALLYN A.   1928   Increasing Returns and Economic Progress. *Economic Journal* 38:527–542.

EXTRASENSORY PERCEPTION (ESP)

See PARAPSYCHOLOGY.

EXTREME VALUES

See NONPARAMETRIC STATISTICS, *article on* ORDER STATISTICS.

EYE MOVEMENTS

See under VISION.

F

FACTOR ANALYSIS

I. Statistical Aspects   *A. E. Maxwell*
II. Psychological Applications   *Lloyd G. Humphreys*

I
STATISTICAL ASPECTS

In many fields of research—for example, agriculture (Banks 1954), psychology (Burt 1947), economics (Geary 1948), medicine (Hammond 1944; 1955), and the study of accidents (Herdan 1943), but notably in psychology and the other social sciences—an experimenter frequently has scores for each member of a sample of individuals, animals, or other experimental units on each of a number of variates, such as cognitive tests, personality inventories, sociometric and socioeconomic ratings, and physical or physiological measures. If the number of variates is large, or even moderately so, the experimenter may wish to seek some reduction or simplification of his data. One approach to this problem is to search for some hypothetical variates that are weighted sums of the observed variates and that, although fewer in number than the latter, can be used to replace them. The statistical techniques by which such a reduction of data is achieved are known collectively as *factor analysis*, although it is well to note here that the principal component method of analysis discussed below (see also Kendall & Lawley 1956) has certain special features. The derived variates are generally viewed merely as convenient descriptive summarizations of the observed data. But occasionally their composition is such that they appear to represent some general basic aspects of everyday life, performance or achievement, and in such

cases they are often suitably labeled and are referred to as *factors*. Typical examples from psychology are such factors as "numerical ability," "originality," "neuroticism," and "toughmindedness." This article describes the statistical procedures in general use for arriving at these hypothetical variates or factors.

Preliminary concepts. Suppose that for a random sample of size N from some population, scores exist on each of p jointly normally distributed variates x_i $(i = 1, 2, \cdots, p)$. If the scores on each variate are expressed as deviations from the sample mean of that variate, then an unbiased estimator of the variance of x_i is given by the expression

$$a_{ii} = (N - 1)^{-1} \sum x_i^2,$$

summation being over the sample of size N. Similarly, an unbiased estimator of the covariance between variates x_i and x_j is given by

$$a_{ij} = (N - 1)^{-1} \sum x_i x_j.$$

Note that this is conventional condensed notation. A fuller, but clumsier, notation would use $x_{i\nu}$ for the deviation $(\nu = 1, \cdots, N)$ so that $\sum x_i^2$ really means $\sum_{\nu=1}^{N} x_{i\nu}^2$.

In practice, factor analysis is often used even in cases in which its usual assumptions are known to be appreciably in error. Such uses make the tacit presumption that the effect of the erroneous assumptions will be small or negligible. Unfortunately, nearly nothing is known about the circumstances under which this robustness, or nonsensitivity to errors in assumptions, is justified. Of course, the formal manipulations may always be carried out; the assumptions enter crucially into distribution theory and optimality of the estimators.

275

The estimated variances and covariances between the p variates can conveniently be written in square matrix form as follows:

$$\mathbf{A} = \begin{bmatrix} a_{11} & a_{12} & \cdots & a_{1p} \\ a_{21} & a_{22} & \cdots & a_{2p} \\ \vdots & \vdots & & \vdots \\ a_{p1} & a_{p2} & \cdots & a_{pp} \end{bmatrix}.$$

Since $a_{ij} = a_{ji}$, the matrix $\mathbf{A}$ is symmetric about its main diagonal.

From the terms of $\mathbf{A}$, the sample correlations, r_{ij}, between the pairs of variates may be obtained from

$$r_{ij} = \frac{a_{ij}}{(a_{ii}a_{jj})^{\frac{1}{2}}},$$

with $r_{ii} = 1$. The corresponding matrix is the *correlation matrix*.

The partial correlation concept is helpful here. If, to take the simplest case, estimates of the correlations between three variates are available, then the estimated correlation between any two, say x_i and x_j, for a given constant value of the third, x_k, can be found from the expression

$$\frac{r_{ij} - r_{ik}r_{jk}}{(1 - r_{ik}^2)^{\frac{1}{2}}(1 - r_{jk}^2)^{\frac{1}{2}}}$$

and is denoted by $r_{ij \cdot k}$.

In terms of a correlation matrix, the aim of factor analysis can be simply stated in terms of partial correlations (see Howe 1955). The first question asked is whether a hypothetical random variate f_1 exists such that the partial correlations $r_{ij \cdot f_1}$, for all i and j, are zero, within the limits of sampling error, after the effect of f_1 has been removed. (If this is so, it is customary to say that the correlation matrix, apart from its diagonal cells, is of rank *one*, but details will not be given here.) If the partial correlations are not zero, then the question is asked whether *two* hypothetical random variates, f_1 and f_2, exist such that the partial correlations between the variates are zero after the effects of both f_1 and f_2 have been removed from the original matrix, and so on. (If f_1 and f_2 reduce the partial correlations to zero, then the matrix, apart from its diagonal cells, is said to be of rank *two*, and so on.) The aim of the procedure is to replace the observed variates with a set of derived variates that, although fewer in number than the former, are still adequate to account for the correlations between them. In other words, the derived variates, or factors, account for the variance common to the observed variates.

Historical note. Factor analysis is generally taken to date from 1904, when C. E. Spearman published an article entitled " 'General Intelligence' Objectively Determined and Measured." Spearman postulated that a single hypothetical variate would in general account for the intercorrelations of a set of cognitive tests, and this variate was his famous factor "g." For the sets of tests that Spearman was considering, this hypothesis seemed reasonable. As further matrices of correlations became available, however, it soon became obvious that Spearman's hypothesis was an oversimplification of the facts, and multiple factor concepts were developed. L. L. Thurstone, in America, and C. Burt and G. H. Thomson, in Britain, were the most active pioneers in this movement. Details of their contributions and references to early journal articles can be found in their textbooks (Thurstone 1935; 1947; Burt 1940; Thomson 1939). These writers were psychologists, and the statistical methods they developed for estimating factors were more or less approximate in nature. The first rigorous attempt by a mathematical statistician to treat the problem of factor estimation (as distinct from principal components) came with the publication in 1940 of a paper by D. N. Lawley entitled "The Estimation of Factor Loadings by the Method of Maximum Likelihood." Since 1940, Lawley has published other articles dealing with various factor problems, and further contributions have been made by Howe (1955), by Anderson and Rubin (1956), and by Rao (1955), to mention just a few. Modern textbooks on factor analysis are those of Harman (1960) and Lawley and Maxwell (1963).

While methods of factor analysis, based on the above model, were being developed, Hotelling in 1933 published his *principal components* model, which, although it bears certain formal resemblances to the factor model proper, has rather different aims. It is widely used today and is described below.

The basic factor equations. The factor model described in general correlational terms above can be expressed more explicitly by the equations

$$(1) \qquad x_i = \sum_{s=1}^{k} l_{is}f_s + e_i, \qquad k < p.$$

In these equations k (the number of factors) is specified; f_s stands for the factors (generally referred to as *common* factors, since they usually enter into the composition of more than one variate). The factors are taken to be normally distributed and, without loss of generality, to have zero means and unit variances; to begin with, they will be assumed to be independent. The term e_i refers to a residual random variate affecting only the variate x_i. There are p of these e_i, and they are assumed to be normally distributed with zero means and to be independent of each other and of the f_s. Their variances will be denoted by v_i; the diagonal matrix of the v_i is called $\mathbf{V}$. The l-values are called *loadings* (weights), l_{is} being the loading of the ith variate on the sth factor. The quantities l_{is} and v_i are taken to be unknown parameters that have to be estimated. If a subscript for individual were introduced, it would be added to x_i and f_s, but not to l_{is} or v_i.

If the population variance–covariance matrix corresponding to the sample matrix $\mathbf{A}$ is denoted by $\mathbf{C}$, with elements c_{ij}, then it follows from the model that

$$(2) \qquad c_{ii} = \sum_{s=1}^{k} l_{is}^2 + v_i,$$

and

$$(3) \qquad c_{ij} = \sum_{s=1}^{k} l_{is} l_{js}, \qquad (i \neq j).$$

If the loadings for p variates on k factors are denoted by the $p \times k$ matrix $\mathbf{L}$, with transpose $\mathbf{L}'$, eqs. (2) and (3) can be combined in the single matrix equation

$$(4) \qquad \mathbf{C} = \mathbf{LL}' + \mathbf{V}.$$

Estimating the parameters in the model. Since the introduction of multiple factor analysis, various approximate methods for estimating the parameters l_{is} and v_i have been proposed. Of these, the best known is the *centroid*, or *simple summation*, method. It is well described in the textbooks mentioned above, but since the arithmetic details are unwieldy, they will not be given here. The method works fairly well in practice, but there is an arbitrariness in its procedure that makes statistical treatment of it almost impossible (see Lawley & Maxwell 1963, chapter 3). For a rigorous approach to the estimation of the factor parameters, I turn to the method of maximum likelihood, although this decision requires some justification. The maximum likelihood method of factor estimation has not been widely used in the past for two reasons. First, it involves very onerous calculations which were well-nigh prohibitive before the development of electronic computers. Second, the arithmetic procedures available, which were iterative, frequently did not lead to convergent estimates of the loadings. But recently, largely because of the work of the Swedish statistician K. G. Jöreskog, quick and efficient estimation procedures have been

found. These methods are still being perfected, but a preliminary account of them is contained in a recent paper (Jöreskog 1966). When they become better known, it is likely that the maximum likelihood method of factor analysis will become the accepted method. An earlier monograph by Jöreskog (1963) is also of interest. In it he links up work by Guttman (1953) on *image theory* with classical factor analytic concepts (see also Kaiser, in Harris 1963). (The image of a variate is defined as that part of its variance which can be estimated from the other variates in a matrix.)

The first point to note about eqs. (1) is that since the p observed variates x_i are expressed in terms of $p + k$ other variates, namely, the k common factors and the p residual variates, which are not observable, these equations are not capable of direct verification. But eq. (4) implies a hypothesis, H_0, regarding the covariance matrix $\mathbf{C}$, which can be tested, that it can be expressed as the sum of a diagonal matrix with positive diagonal elements and a symmetric positive semidefinite matrix with at most k latent roots: these matrices are respectively $\mathbf{V}$ and $\mathbf{LL}'$. The value postulated for k must not be too large; otherwise, the hypothesis would be trivially true. If the v_i were known, it would only be necessary to require $k < p$, but in the more usual case, where they are unknown, the condition can be shown to be $(p + k) < (p - k)^2$. Since the x_i are assumed to be distributed in a multivariate normal way, the log-likelihood function, omitting a function of the observations, is given by

$$(5) \qquad L = -\tfrac{1}{2} n \ln |\mathbf{C}| - \tfrac{1}{2} n \sum_{i,j} a_{ij} c^{ij},$$

where $n = N - 1$, $|\mathbf{C}|$ is the determinant of the matrix $\mathbf{C}$, and c^{ij} is the element in the ith row and jth column of its inverse, $\mathbf{C}^{-1}$. To find maximum likelihood estimators of l_{is} and v_i, (5) is differentiated with respect to them and the results are equated to zero. A difficulty arises, however, when $k > 1$, for there are then too many parameters in the model for them to be specified uniquely. This can be seen by an examination of eq. (4), for if $\mathbf{L}$ is postmultiplied by an orthogonal matrix $\mathbf{M}$, the value of $\mathbf{LL}'$, which is now given by $\mathbf{LMM}'\mathbf{L}'$, is unaltered since $\mathbf{MM}' = \mathbf{I}$, the identity matrix. This means that the maximum likelihood method, although it provides a unique set of estimates of the c_{ij}, leads to equations for estimating the l_{is} which are satisfied by an infinity of solutions, all equally good from a statistical point of view.

In this situation all the statistician can do is to

select a particular solution, one that is convenient to find, and leave the experimenter to apply whatever rotation he thinks desirable. Thus the custom is to choose L in such a way that the $k \times k$ matrix $J = L'V^{-1}L$ is diagonal. It can be shown that the successive elements of J are the latent roots, in order of magnitude, of the matrix $V^{-\frac{1}{2}}(A - V)V^{-\frac{1}{2}}$, so that for a given value of V, the determination of the factors in the factor model resembles the determination of the principal components in the component model.

The maximization of eq. (5) with the above diagonalization side condition leads to the equations

$$\hat{c}_{ii} = a_{ii}$$

or

(6)
$$\hat{v}_i = a_{ii} - \sum_{s=1}^{k} l_{is}^2,$$

and

(7)
$$\hat{L}' = \hat{J}^{-1}\hat{L}'\hat{V}^{-1}(A - \hat{V}),$$

where circumflex accents denote estimates of the parameters in question. Eq. (7) can usually be solved by iterative methods and details of those in current use can be found in Lawley and Maxwell (1963), Howe (1955), and Jöreskog (1963; 1966). The calculations involved are onerous, and when p is fairly large, say 12 or more, an electronic computer is essential.

A satisfactory property of the above method of estimation, which does not hold for the centroid and principal component methods, is that it can be shown to be independent of the metric used. A change of scale of any variate x_i merely introduces proportional changes in its loadings.

Testing hypotheses on number of factors. In the factor analysis of a set of data the value of k is seldom known in advance and has to be estimated. To begin with, some value of it is assumed and a matrix of loadings L for this value is estimated. The effects of the factors concerned are now eliminated from the observed covariance (or correlation) matrix, and the residual matrix, $A - LL'$, is tested for significance. If it is found to be statistically significant, the value of k is increased by one and the estimation process is repeated. The test employed is of the large sample chi-square type, based on the likelihood ratio method of Neyman and Pearson, and is given by

(8)
$$X^2 = n \ln(|\hat{C}|/|A|),$$

with $\frac{1}{2}\{(p-k)^2 - (p+k)\}$ degrees of freedom. A good approximation to expression (8), and one easier to calculate, is

(9)
$$X^2 = n \sum_{i<j} (a_{ij} - \hat{c}_{ij})^2/(\hat{v}_i\hat{v}_j).$$

There is also some evidence to suggest that the test can be improved by replacing n by $n' = n - \frac{1}{6}(2p + 5) - \frac{2}{3}k$.

Factor interpretation. As already mentioned, the matrix of loadings, L, given by a factor analysis is not unique and can be replaced by an equivalent set LM where M is an orthogonal matrix. This fact is frequently used by experimenters when interpreting their results, a matrix M being chosen that will in some way simplify the pattern of loadings or make it more intuitively meaningful. For example, M may be chosen so as to reduce to zero, or nearly zero, as many loadings as possible in order to reduce the number of parameters necessary for describing the data. Again, M may be chosen so as to concentrate the loadings of variates of similar content, say verbal tests, on a single factor so that this factor may be labeled appropriately. Occasionally, too, the factors are allowed to become correlated if this seems to lead to more meaningful results.

It is now clear that given a matrix of loadings from some analysis, different experimenters might choose different rotation matrices in their interpretation of the data. This subjective element in factor analysis has led to a great deal of controversy. To avoid subjectivity, various empirical methods of rotation have been proposed which, while tending to simplify the pattern of loadings, also lead to unique solutions. The best known of these are the *varimax* and the *promax* methods (for details see Kaiser 1958; Hendrickson & White 1964). But another approach to the problem, proposed independently by Howe (1955), Anderson and Rubin (1956), and Lawley (1958), seems promising. From prior knowledge the experimenter is asked to postulate in advance (*a*) how many factors he expects from his data and (*b*) which variates will have zero loadings on the several factors. In other words, he is asked to formulate a specific hypothesis about the factor composition of his variates. The statistician then estimates the nonzero loadings and makes a test of the "goodness of fit" of the factors structure. In this approach the factors may be correlated or uncorrelated, and in the former case estimates of the correlations between them are obtained. The equations of estimation and illustrative examples of their application can be found in Howe (1955) and in Lawley and Maxwell (1963; 1964); the latter gives a quick method of finding approximate estimates of the nonzero loadings.

Estimating factor scores. As the statistical theory of factor analysis now stands, estimation is a twofold process. First, the factor structure, as described above, of a set of data is determined. In practice, however, it is often desirable to find, in addition, equations for estimating the scores of individuals on the factors themselves. One method of doing this, developed by Thomson, is known as the "regression method." In it the l_{is} are taken to be the covariances between the f_s and the x_i, and then for uncorrelated factors the estimation equation is

$$(10) \qquad \hat{f} = L'C^{-1}x,$$

or, more simply from the computational viewpoint,

$$(11) \qquad \hat{f} = (I + J)^{-1}L'V^{-1}x,$$

where $\hat{f} = \{\hat{f}_1, \hat{f}_2, \cdots, \hat{f}_k\}'$, $x = \{x_1, x_2, \cdots, x_p\}'$, and, as before, $J = L'V^{-1}L$, and I is the identity matrix. If sampling errors in L and V are neglected, the covariance matrix for the errors of estimates of the factor scores is given by $(I + J)^{-1}$.

If the factors are correlated and their estimated correlation matrix is denoted by P, then eqs. (10) and (11) become, respectively,

$$(12) \qquad \hat{f} = PL'C^{-1}x,$$

and

$$(13) \qquad \hat{f} = (P^{-1} + J)^{-1}L'V^{-1}x,$$

while the errors of estimates are given by $(P^{-1} + J)^{-1}$.

An alternative method of estimating factor scores is that of Bartlett (1938). Here, the principle adopted is the minimization, for a given set of observations, of $\sum_i e_i^2/v_i$, which is the sum of squares of standardized residuals. The estimation equation now is

$$(14) \qquad \hat{f}^* = J^{-1}L'V^{-1}x.$$

It is of interest to note that although the sets of estimates gotten by the two methods have been reached by entirely different approaches, a comparison shows that they are simply related. For uncorrelated factors the relationship is

$$\hat{f}^* = (I + J^{-1})\hat{f};$$

for correlated factors it is

$$\hat{f}^* = (I + J^{-1}P^{-1})\hat{f}.$$

Comparing factors across populations. If factors can be viewed as representing "permanent" aspects of behavior or performance, ways of identifying them from one population to another are required. In the past, identification has generally been based on the comparison of matrices of loadings. In the case of two matrices, a common approach, developed by Ahmavaara (1954) and Cattell and Hurley (1962), is to rotate one into maximum conformity in the least square sense

with the other. For example, the matrix required for rotating L_1 into maximum conformity with L_2, when they both involve the same variates, is obtained by calculating the expression $(L_1'L_1)^{-1}L_1'L_2$ and normalizing it by columns. The factors represented by L_1 in its transformed state are likely to be more or less correlated, but estimates of the correlations between them are given by $(M_0'M_0)^{-1}$, standardized so that its diagonal cells are unity, where $M_0 = (L_1'L_1)^{-1}L_1'L_2$ and M_0' is its transpose. This procedure is fairly satisfactory when the sample *covariance* matrices involved do not differ significantly. When they do, the problem of identifying factors is more complicated.

A possible approach to it has been suggested by Lawley and Maxwell (1963, chapter 8), who make the assumption that although two covariance matrices, C_1 and C_2, involving the same variates may be different, they may still have the same L-matrix. This could occur if the two $k \times k$ covariance matrices Γ_1 and Γ_2 between the factors themselves were different. To keep the model fairly simple, they assume that the residual variances in the populations are in each case V and then set up the equations

$$(15) \qquad \begin{aligned} C_1 &= L\Gamma_1L' + V, \\ C_2 &= L\Gamma_2L' + V. \end{aligned}$$

For this model Lawley and Maxwell show how estimates of L, V, Γ_1, and Γ_2 may be obtained from two sample covariance matrices A_1 and A_2. They also supply a test for assessing the significance of the difference between the estimates of Γ_1 and Γ_2, and also for testing the "goodness of fit" of the model.

The method of principal components

The principal component method of analyzing a matrix of covariances or correlations is also widely used in the social sciences. The components correspond to the latent roots of the matrix, and the weights defining them are proportional to the corresponding latent vectors.

The model can also be stated in terms of the observed variates and the derived components. An orthogonal transformation is applied to the x_i $(i = 1, 2, \cdots, p)$ to produce a new set of uncorrelated variates $y_1, y_2, \cdots, y_p$. These are chosen such that y_1 has maximum variance, y_2 has maximum variance subject to being uncorrelated with y_1, and so on. This is equivalent to a rotation of the coordinate system so that the new coordinate axes lie along the principal axes of an ellipsoid closely related to the covariance structure of the x_i. The transformed variates are then standardized to give a new set, which will be denoted z_s. When this method is used, no hypothesis need be made about the nature or distribution of the x_i. The model is by definition linear and additive, and the basic equations are

$$(16) \qquad x_i = \sum_{s=1}^{p} w_{is} z_s, \qquad i, s = 1, 2, \cdots, p,$$

where z_s stands for the sth component, and w_{is} is the weight of the sth component in the ith variate. In matrix notation eqs. (16) become

$$x = Wz,$$

where $x = \{x_1, x_2, \cdots, x_p\}'$, $z = \{z_1, z_2, \cdots, z_p\}'$, and W is a square matrix of order p with elements w_{is}.

Comparison of eqs. (16) with eqs. (1) shows that in the principal component model residual variates do not appear, and that if all p components are obtained, the sample covariances can be reproduced exactly, that is, $A = W'W$. Indeed, there is a simple reciprocal relationship between the observed variates and the derived components.

A straightforward iterative method for obtaining the weights w_{is} is given by Hotelling in his original papers; the details are also given in most textbooks on factor analysis. In practice, all p components are seldom found, for a small number generally accounts for a large percentage of the variance of the variates and can be used to summarize the data. There is also a criterion, developed by Bartlett (1950; 1954), for testing the equality of the remaining latent roots of a matrix after the first k have been extracted; this is sometimes used to help in deciding when to stop the analysis.

The principal component method is most useful when the variates x_i are all measured in the same units. Otherwise, it is more difficult to justify. A change in the scales of measurement of some or all of the variates results in the covariance matrix being multiplied on both sides by a diagonal matrix. The effect of this on the latent roots and vectors is very complicated, and unfortunately the components are not invariant under such changes of scale. Because of this, the principal component approach is at a disadvantage in comparison with the proper factor analysis approach.

A. E. Maxwell

[See also Clustering; Distributions, statistical, *article on* mixtures of distributions; Latent structure; Statistical identifiability.]

BIBLIOGRAPHY

Ahmavaara, Y. 1954 Transformational Analysis of Factorial Data. Suomalainen Tiedeakatemia, Helsinki, *Toimituksia: Annales* Series B 88, no. 2.

Anderson, T. W.; and Rubin, Herman 1956 Statistical Inference in Factor Analysis. Volume 5, pages 111–150 in Berkeley Symposium on Mathematical Statistics and Probability, Third, *Proceedings*. Edited by Jerzy Neyman. Berkeley: Univ. of California Press.

Banks, Charlotte 1954 The Factorial Analysis of Crop Productivity: A Re-examination of Professor Kendall's Data. *Journal of the Royal Statistical Society* Series B 16:100–111.

Bartlett, M. S. 1938 Methods of Estimating Mental Factors. *Nature* 141:609–610.

Bartlett, M. S. 1950 Tests of Significance in Factor Analysis. *British Journal of Psychology* (Statistical Section) 3:77–85.

Bartlett, M. S. 1954 A Note on the Multiplying Factor for Various χ^2 Approximations. *Journal of the Royal Statistical Society* Series B 16:296–298.

Burt, Cyril 1940 *The Factors of the Mind: An Introduction to Factor-analysis in Psychology.* Univ. of London Press.

Burt, Cyril 1947 Factor Analysis and Physical Types. *Psychometrika* 12:171–188.

Cattell, Raymond B.; and Hurley, John R. 1962 The Procrustes Program: Producing Direct Rotation to Test a Hypothesized Factor Structure. *Behavioral Science* 7:258–262.

Geary, R. C. 1948 Studies in Relationships Between Economic Time Series. *Journal of the Royal Statistical Society* Series B 10:140–158.

Gibson, W. A. 1960 Nonlinear Factors in Two Dimensions. *Psychometrika* 25:381–392.

Hammond, W. H. 1944 Factor Analysis as an Aid to Nutritional Assessment. *Journal of Hygiene* 43:395–399.

Hammond, W. H. 1955 Measurement and Interpretation of Subcutaneous Fats, With Norms for Children and Young Adult Males. *British Journal of Preventive and Social Medicine* 9:201–211.

Harman, Harry H. 1960 *Modern Factor Analysis.* Univ. of Chicago Press. → A new edition was scheduled for publication in 1967.

Harris, Chester W. (editor) 1963 *Problems in Measuring Change: Proceedings of a Conference.* Madison: Univ. of Wisconsin Press. → See especially "Image Analysis" by Henry F. Kaiser.

Hendrickson, Alan E.; and White, Paul O. 1964 Promax: A Quick Method for Rotation to Oblique Simple Structure. *British Journal of Statistical Psychology* 17:65–70.

Herdan, G. 1943 The Logical and Analytical Relationship Between the Theory of Accidents and Factor Analysis. *Journal of the Royal Statistical Society* Series A 106:125–142.

Horst, Paul 1965 *Factor Analysis of Data Matrices.* New York: Holt.

Hotelling, Harold 1933 Analysis of a Complex of Statistical Variables Into Principal Components. *Journal of Educational Psychology* 24:417–441, 498–520.

Howe, W. G. 1955 Some Contributions to Factor Analysis. Report No. ORNL-1919, U.S. National Laboratory, Oak Ridge, Tenn. Unpublished manuscript.

Jöreskog, K. G. 1963 *Statistical Estimation in Factor Analysis: A New Technique and Its Foundation.* Stockholm: Almqvist & Wiksell.

Jöreskog, K. G. 1966 Testing a Simple Hypothesis in Factor Analysis. *Psychometrika* 31:165–178.

Kaiser, Henry F. 1958 The Varimax Criterion for Analytic Rotation in Factor Analysis. *Psychometrika* 23:187–200.

KENDALL, M. G.; and LAWLEY, D. N. 1956 The Principles of Factor Analysis. *Journal of the Royal Statistical Society* Series A 119:83–84.

LAWLEY, D. N. 1940 The Estimation of Factor Loadings by the Method of Maximum Likelihood. Royal Society of Edinburgh, *Proceedings* 60:64–82.

LAWLEY, D. N. 1953 A Modified Method of Estimation in Factor Analysis and Some Large Sample Results. Pages 35–42 in *Uppsala Symposium on Psychological Factor Analysis, March 17–19, 1953.* Nordisk Psykologi, Monograph Series, No. 3. Uppsala (Sweden): Almqvist & Wiksell.

LAWLEY, D. N. 1958 Estimation in Factor Analysis Under Various Initial Assumptions. *British Journal of Statistical Psychology* 11:1–12.

LAWLEY, D. N.; and MAXWELL, ALBERT E. 1963 *Factor Analysis as a Statistical Method.* London: Butterworth.

LAWLEY, D. N.; and MAXWELL, A. E. 1964 Factor Transformation Methods. *British Journal of Statistical Psychology* 17:97–103.

MAXWELL, A. E. 1964 Calculating Maximum-likelihood Factor Loadings. *Journal of the Royal Statistical Society* Series A 127:238–241.

RAO, C. R. 1955 Estimation and Tests of Significance in Factor Analysis. *Psychometrika* 20:93–111.

SPEARMAN, C. E. 1904 "General Intelligence" Objectively Determined and Measured. *American Journal of Psychology* 15:201–293.

THOMSON, GODFREY H. (1939) 1951 *The Factorial Analysis of Human Ability.* 5th ed. Boston: Houghton Mifflin.

THURSTONE, LOUIS L. 1935 *The Vectors of Mind: Multiple-factor Analysis for the Isolation of Primary Traits.* Univ. of Chicago Press.

THURSTONE, LOUIS L. 1947 *Multiple-factor Analysis.* Univ. of Chicago Press. → A development and expansion of Thurstone's *The Vectors of Mind,* 1935.

II
PSYCHOLOGICAL APPLICATIONS

The essential statistical problem of factor analysis involves reduction or simplification of a large number of variates so that some hypothetical variates, fewer in number, which are weighted sums of the observed variates, can be used to replace them. If psychological experimenters were satisfied with this sole, statistical objective, there would be no problem of psychological interpretation and of meaning of factors. They would simply be convenient abstractions. However, psychologists and psychometricians, starting with Charles Spearman (1904), the pioneer factor analyst, have wanted to go beyond this objective and have thereby created the very large psychological literature in this field. The goal of factor analysts following in the Spearman tradition has been to find not only convenient statistical abstractions but the elements or the basic building blocks, the primary mental abilities and personality traits in human behavior. Such theorists have explicitly accepted chemical elements— sometimes even the periodic table—as their model

and factor analysis as the method of choice in reaching their goal.

Factor interpretation and methodology

Factor extraction methods. There are several variations of factor methods, certain of which are more amenable to psychological interpretation than others. For example, the experimenter can start his analysis from a variance–covariance matrix or from a correlational matrix with estimated communalities (discussed below) in the principal diagonal. If he is interested in psychological interpretations of factors, he almost uniformly selects the latter, since use of the variance–covariance procedure results in obtaining factors that contain unknown amounts of common-factor, nonerror-specific, and error components. For purposes of psychological interpretation, including generalizing to new samples of psychological measures, the inclusion of nonerror-specific and error variance in the factors is undesirable. The intercorrelations and communalities, on the other hand, are determined only by the common factors.

The experimenter also has a choice among several methods of factor extraction, including the centroid, principal components (sometimes called principal axes), and maximum likelihood methods. Choice among these is based largely on feasibility criteria. The first was used almost exclusively before the advent of high-speed digital computers. The third is generally acknowledged to be superior statistically to the second, but it is too expensive in time and computer to use. The second is at present the method most frequently used by psychologists, since it extracts a maximum amount of variance with each successive factor. The centroid method only approximates this criterion, although frequently it is a close approximation. There is thus no pressing need to redo all previous work involving the centroid method now that computational facilities are available. The maximum likelihood method can and should be used, as a check on conclusions reached with the more economical principal components, when size of matrix and computer availability make it feasible.

The communality problem. When the experimenter elects to analyze correlations and communalities, he must estimate the latter. These communalities represent the proportion of common factor variance in the total variance of a variable: the amount that a variable has in common with other variables in a particular study. Unfortunately, from the methodological viewpoint, there is no way to obtain an unbiased estimate of the communality. Several rule-of-thumb methods are available, and there are theoretically sound upper and lower bounds for the communality estimate.

An unbiased reliability estimate can be used as an upper bound for the estimated communality. Reliability and communality differ to the extent that reliability includes specific nonerror variance. A lower-bound estimate in the population of persons is the squared multiple correlation between each variable and all of the others (Guttman 1954). The reader should note, however, that while this procedure provides a lower-bound estimate for the population, a sample value can be seriously inflated. The multiple correlation coefficient capitalizes on chance very effectively. For example, when the number of variables equals the number of observations, the multiple correlation in the sample is necessarily unity, although the population value may in fact be zero. The investigator who wants a lower-bound estimate may still utilize the Guttman theorem if he estimates the population values from sample values that are corrected for their capitalization on chance.

Number of factors. If he is interested in the psychological meaning of his factors, the experimenter has a further choice among criteria for determining the number of factors to retain and interpret. When estimated communalities are employed, no one of the possible criteria is more than a rule of thumb. The various criteria lead to radically different decisions concerning the number of factors to be retained; and different investigators, in applying one, several, or all of these criteria, will reach different conclusions about the number of factors.

One class of criteria for determining the number of factors has been characterized as emphasizing psychological importance without regard to sampling stability. Some investigators use some absolute value of the factor loadings, e.g., .30, either rotated or unrotated or both, without regard to the number of observations on which the correlations are based. A more recent suggestion has been to retain factors whose principal roots were greater than unity (Kaiser & Caffrey 1965). Such criteria appear to make an assumption that the number of observations is very large, so that the factors and loadings that are large enough psychologically are at the same time not the result of sampling error.

A second class of criteria has been characterized as emphasizing the number of observations, even though there are no known sampling distributions for factors or factor loadings. In several related criteria, factor loadings and/or residuals are compared in one way or another with the standard error of correlation coefficients of zero magnitude for the sample size involved. Factoring of the intercorrelations of random normal deviates as a method of obtaining empirical sampling errors has also been used.

A third criterion involves the "psychological meaning" of the rotated factors: the investigator merely states in effect that he is satisfied with the results of his analysis. Since any behavioral scientist of any modest degree of ingenuity can rationalize the random grouping of any set of variables, this does not appear to be a useful criterion scientifically. Without agreement on an objective criterion, however, psychological meaning of the factors tends to be the principal criterion used in deciding upon the number of factors to interpret.

Even in situations where probabilities of alpha and beta errors can be estimated, different investigators, depending on their temperaments or on social consequences, may set quite different standards for such errors. In determining the number of factors, however, there are no objective methods of error estimation, and the range of probabilities of alpha and beta errors resulting from differences among investigators or differences in social consequences is increased several-fold. For example, for one matrix of personality variables two investigators differ by a ratio of four to one in their assessment of the proper number of factors to retain and interpret. The difference between 12 and 3 factors is far from trivial. Such discrepancies reduce factor analysis to a hypothesis formation technique. As a method of discovery of psychological principles, or of hypothesis testing generally, ambiguities of this magnitude cannot be tolerated. The lack of a suitable test for number of factors has opened the door for a great deal of poor research.

Factor rotations. After the factors are extracted, the experimenter has to decide whether to rotate or not. Rotation of axes to psychologically meaningful positions follows inevitably from an interest in finding the psychological elements.

The rotation problem is seen most clearly in the two-factor case. First, the two factors are conceptualized as orthogonal (perpendicular) dimensions extending from values of -1.00 to $+1.00$. Then the points representing the loadings of the tests on these factors are fixed in the space defined by these dimensions. Imagine now that a pin is inserted at the origin of the two dimensions and that these are now rotated about the pin. Wherever they stop, new coordinates can be determined for the test points. It must be noted that the test points are located as accurately by the new dimensions as by the original ones, and that the intercorrelations of the tests are described with equal accuracy. There are, in point of fact, an infinite number of positions of the coordinates and thus an infinite number of mathematical solutions to the factor problem. The investigator interested in psychological meaning rotates the dimensions into some psychologically unique position. It is important, where possible, that factor descriptions of measures remain stable from sample to sample of either persons or measures, or both. This can be achieved, apparently in the great majority of cases, with an adequate rotational solution.

Rotation is almost uniformly performed when factors obtained are from a correlation matrix having communality estimates in the diagonal. Factors obtained from the variance–covariance matrix, on the other hand, are generally not rotated and are preferred by the experimenter interested in description alone rather than in explanation. The experimenter also has a choice among several different rotational methods, based upon different criteria and leading to either orthogonal or oblique factors.

Orthogonal versus oblique rotation.   Orthogonal rotations offer the simplicity of uncorrelated dimensions in exchange for a poorer fit of the test points. Oblique rotations offer a better fit for the test points in exchange for a complexity of correlated dimensions. If oblique rotations are used, the investigator can also elect to factor in the second and perhaps higher orders; i.e., he can factor the intercorrelations among his first-order factors, among his second-order factors, and so on. After factoring in several orders, the investigator also has the option of presenting and interpreting his results in the several orders, or, by means of a simple transformation, he can convert the oblique factors in several orders to orthogonal, hierarchical factors in a single order.

Until the advent of high-speed digital computers, basically the only method for achieving a given rotational result was hand rotation. There are now several computer programs for rotation to either orthogonal or oblique structure.

If the investigator elects an orthogonal solution to his problem, he has a number of programs among which to choose. One of the earlier programs is the quartimax of Neuhaus and Wrigley (1954). This was followed by Kaiser's varimax program (1958). An important difference between the two is that quartimax typically produces a general factor in ability data which is a function of the sampling of test variables, i.e., the general factor may reflect verbal, perceptual, or other specific emphasis, depending upon the nature of the tests

sampled. Varimax provides results that are more stable from one test battery to another. This is achieved by a more even distribution of variance among the rotated factors. In the opinion of many investigators, varimax rotations have achieved a near-ultimate status for the orthogonal case, but Schonemann (1964) has now developed a program that he calls varisim, which spreads existing variance more evenly among the several factors than varimax does. Results from the two programs are not completely parallel even for well-defined factors. There is as much rationale for varisim as for varimax. In consequence, the ultimate status of varimax has been dislodged, and we are again faced with a somewhat arbitrary choice among orthogonal rotational methods.

Oblique rotational programs are now fairly numerous and exhibit variability in results comparable to that among orthogonal ones. There is one important difference: no oblique program has as yet achieved the status that varimax once had. Because of the various sources of dissatisfaction with existing programs, there is much more research activity in the area of oblique rotation than in orthogonal rotation. There is still frequent resort to visually guided rotations if the investigator is striving for an oblique structure.

Methodological summary.   The investigator who wishes to find psychological meaning in his data, the one who is trying to discover the basic building blocks or causal entities in human behavior, has a difficult task. Important decisions for which there are no sound foundations must be made at several steps in the procedure. Communalities must be estimated; the estimate of the number of factors to be extracted and retained for rotations must be based upon inadequate criteria; and although subjective bias possibly resulting from hand rotations has been eliminated by rotations obtained on high-speed computers, the choice of rotational program among either oblique or orthogonal solutions may lead to quite different results.

In the absence of sound estimation methods, the criterion of replicability is typically offered as a substitute. Replicability is a very important criterion in science generally. When applied to factor analysis, however, one must be aware that seemingly parallel results may have been forced on the data, typically without intention on the part of the experimentalist to do so. For example, considerable congruence of factor patterns can be obtained from the intercorrelations of two independent sets of random normal deviates by extracting as many factors as variables and by rotating to oblique simple structure. The result will be one-to-one correspondence of the factors. The intercorrelations of the factors will differ, but even these differences will not be large, since they are randomly distributed about zero.

Methods of assessing the congruence of factor patterns also leave something to be desired. The most common method by far is that of visual inspection and unaided judgment. The most precise, the correlation between two estimated factor scores in the same sample, is rarely seen. Claimed replication of a factor is frequently without adequate foundation.

Early general factor interpretations

Mental energy. Spearman did not have available any of the above-described techniques for the factor analysis of relationships among variables. Neither did he have access to the multitude of tests now available. He hypothesized that one general factor was sufficient to account for the intercorrelations among his variables, and he developed relatively simple methods to test this hypothesis. (Present methods of multiple factor analysis include Spearman's single factor as a special case.) In psychological interpretation Spearman is of interest, however, because he interpreted his single factor as "mental energy." This was considered the sole basis or building block of mental ability or intelligence. [See SPEARMAN.]

Multiple bonds. Spearman's interpretation was challenged by Godfrey Thomson (1919) and by Edward Thorndike (Thorndike et al. 1926). Thomson proved that correlational matrices having the form required to satisfy Spearman's one-factor interpretation could also be "explained" by the presence of many overlapping elements. Thorndike discussed connections (bonds) between stimuli and responses as an alternative to Spearman's mental energy concept. Considering that there are many thousands of stimuli to which a person will respond differentially, and that tests sample these, the extent to which there is overlap in the elements sampled by two measures determines the degree to which they are correlated. If the intercorrelations of several measures have the formal properties necessary for Spearman's unitary mental energy explanation (one factor), they also can be explained by multiple bonds or overlapping elements (multiplicity of factors). [See THORNDIKE.]

Unitary mental energy is a basic building block, a general influence or "cause"; multiple bonds are a complex of stimulus–response connections that are acquired in a dynamic, complex physical and social environment. Multiple bonds that underlie the behavior under observation cannot be said to

cause that behavior in the same sense that mental energy is said to cause intellectual performance.

Recourse to parsimony in this instance is not an acceptable solution, since the two explanations are so different. It should come as no surprise, for example, to learn that Spearman and his followers have stressed genetic bases for intelligence, while the multiple bonds notion lends itself most readily to a stress on environmental forces and learning.

Multiple factors

Thurstone's primary mental abilities. Although Thurstone (1938) is considered to have broken with Spearman, the break was related only to the number of factors required to account for intelligence. Thurstone considered that some seven to nine factors were sufficient to account for the intercorrelations of the more than fifty tests he used. However, Spearman himself had come to doubt the single-factor explanation; the break was more apparent than real. On the issue of what lies behind factors there was no break. Careful reading of Thurstone's writings makes it quite clear that to him factors were much more than descriptive devices. Factors were functional unities; their ubiquity strongly suggested genetic determiners; after all, they were called primary mental abilities. [See THURSTONE.]

Ferguson's learning emphasis. However, just as a single factor can be replaced by multiple overlapping bonds, so also can multiple group factors be replaced by sets of overlapping bonds. One need only assume that environmental pressures and learning come in somewhat separate "chunks." Demographic differences, e.g., parental occupation, region of the country, rural–urban differences, etc., could account for some of the "chunking" required. Ferguson (1956) has produced a very satisfactory explanation along these lines in which learning and transfer are important variables. Various kinds of learning are facilitated or inhibited by the variety of environments in which children develop. Learning transfers, both positively and negatively, to novel situations. The amount and direction of the transfer are determined by stimulus and environmental similarities. Learning and transfer, along with environmental differences, produce the clustering of measures on which the factors depend. [See LEARNING, article on TRANSFER.]

Physical analogies. Thurstone (1947), in order to convince himself and others that factors were "real," constructed a factor problem that has attracted a good deal of attention. He showed that if dimensions of boxes were factored, the result was a three-factor solution which could be rotated into a position such that the factors represented the dimensions of length, breadth, and depth, the three basic dimensions of Euclidean space. He also showed that these factors were correlated, i.e., an oblique solution gave a better fit to the data than did an orthogonal one. The obliquity reflects, of course, the fact that the dimensions of man-made boxes tend to be correlated, i.e., long boxes tend to be big boxes.

In a situation more relevant to behavior Cattell and Dickman (1962) have demonstrated that the intercorrelations of the performance of balls in several "tests" yield four factors that can be identified as size, weight, elasticity, and string length. It is clear from this and the preceding example that factor analysis can sometimes identify known physical factors in data.

One question about these examples is the certitude with which the factors can be identified after rotation, granting that the correct number of factors can be obtained by present methods. Thurstone suggested the criteria of simple structure for the adequacy of rotations. Generally speaking, simple structure is achieved when the number of zero loadings in a factor table has been maximized while increasing the magnitude of loadings on a small number of variables. The application of these criteria to the examples described resulted in clearcut identification of the three and four factors. It has been shown by Overall (1964), however, that if Thurstone had started with a different set of measurements, the criteria of simple structure for rotations would have led to differently defined factors, i.e., they would not have been the "pure" physical dimensions but would have represented complex combinations of those dimensions.

A more basic question is whether psychological data are similar to physical data, i.e., whether psychological dimensions obtained by factoring are similar to physical dimensions. The demonstration that three or four physical factors, as the case may be, can be recovered from correlational data does not prove that factors in psychological data have a similar functional unity. Not only is Thomson's alternative explanation theoretically acceptable for multiple factors, but it makes good psychological sense as well. Psychological tests measure performance on each of a series of items. These performances make up the total score. Although Thomson would not have suggested a one-to-one correspondence between item and element or stimulus–response bond, one can conclude that there are at least as many elements represented in a test as there are items. Thus the multiple bonds approach fits the actual measurement situation so well that

the adherents of the other point of view must bear the burden of proof—and for psychological, not physical, data.

Guilford's structure of intellect. The work of J. P. Guilford has been most influential in the factor analysis of human abilities (e.g., 1956). It has increased by ten times the small number of primary mental abilities proposed by Thurstone, but the approach to their interpretation remains much the same. Guilford's thinking about the nature of factors is modeled very closely after the periodic table of the chemical elements; he has in fact proposed a structure which points out missing factors and has proceeded in his own empirical work to "discover" many of these.

In spite of similarities in thinking about the nature of factors, the discrepancy in numbers between Guilford and Thurstone is highly significant, and it illustrates a basic difficulty with psychological tests and the attempts to find causal entities from the analysis of their intercorrelations. Not only do psychological tests measure performance on a relatively large number of pass–fail items, but there is at present no necessary or sufficient methodological or theoretical basis for deciding which items should be added together to make up a single test score (Humphreys 1962). The number of factors has proliferated in Guilford's work because he has produced large numbers of homogeneous experimental tests. By additional test construction, making each test more and more homogeneous, the number of factors could be increased still further. As a matter of fact, there is no agreed-upon stopping place short of the individual test item, i.e., a single item represents the maximum amount of homogeneity. This logic results in the same number of primary mental abilities as there are ability test items.

The progression from Thurstone to Guilford can be interpreted as further evidence for the multiple bonds theoretical approach. On the other hand, positing a functional unity inside the organism for each item represents a scientific dead end.

Cattell's structure of personality. The work of R. B. Cattell has been most influential in the factor analysis of the domain of personality (e.g. 1957). Cattell's thinking about the character of factors does not differ materially from that of Spearman, Thurstone, and Guilford in that for Cattell, factors are real influences.

The number of identified personality factors has increased considerably under Cattell's direction. Although measurement problems differ, Cattell's work parallels that of Guilford with human abilities. Self-report questionnaires present the multiple items problem with yes–no scoring of items. Personality investigators also have the problem of deciding which items should be added together in any given score. A great deal of additional work, however, has been done with rating scales and with so-called objective tests of personality. "Density" of sampling of the test or rating domain, a concept introduced by Cattell, is still involved in the proliferation of factors, even though the mechanism is not that of item selection. Thus, in obtaining ratings, one must decide on the number and overlap in meaning of traits to be rated. One must decide whether to include both extroversion and sociability or, even closer, both ascendance and dominance. While there is no rigorous method to depend on in the sampling of measures, decisions about what will be tested still affect the number of factors and their importance.

Furthermore, it is also typical of many experimental designs that large numbers of variables relative to the number of observations are analyzed; that many of these variables have low reliability and thus low communality; that many factors are retained for rotational purposes; and that rotations are made to an oblique structure. All of these elements contribute to possible capitalization on chance.

It is of interest that Cattell uses as a primary rotational criterion a count of the number of variables in the hyperplane, i.e., the multidimensional plane defined by all factors other than the one in question. (More simply, a measure having a zero loading on a factor is located geometrically someplace in the factor's hyperplane.) This criterion places a premium on the extraction of a large number of factors relative to the number of measures, on the use of variables of low reliability, and on the use of variables unrelated to the major purpose of the analysis. In the opinion of many critics Cattell has increased the probability of making Type i errors beyond tolerable bounds, although neither he nor his critics can assign a value to alpha in this situation.

A dramatic example of the difficulties that may be involved in typical factor analytic research is given by some data described by Horn (1967). He obtained a good fit to an oblique factor pattern derived from an analysis of ability and personality variables by factoring the intercorrelations of the same number of random normal deviates, based upon the same number of observations, as the psychological variables. This finding highlights the principle that replication of findings may be of little import in factor analytic investigations.

It is also apparent that the essential reason for factor analyzing intercorrelations, to seek some reduction or simplification of data, has not been realized. The number of variables and the number of factors have grown astronomically, and the end is not yet in sight. It is highly possible that the search for psychological meaning, the search for the basic building blocks or elements, has been responsible. If psychological data are different from physical data in important respects, and if the multiple bonds are a more accurate representation of the data than the chemical elements point of view, researchers would profit from taking another look at the reasons why they factor analyze. An economical description of complex data is itself an important scientific goal.

Lloyd G. Humphreys

[*Directly related are the entries* Clustering; Multivariate analysis; Traits. *Other relevant material may be found in* Intelligence and intelligence testing; Psychology, *article on* constitutional psychology; *and in the biographies of* Spearman *and* Thorndike.]

BIBLIOGRAPHY

Cattell, Raymond B. 1957 *Personality and Motivation Structure and Measurement.* New York: World.

Cattell, Raymond B.; and Dickman, Kern 1962 A Dynamic Model of Physical Influences Demonstrating the Necessity of Oblique Simple Structure. *Psychological Bulletin* 59:389–400.

Ferguson, George A. 1956 On Transfer and the Abilities of Man. *Canadian Journal of Psychology* 10:121–131.

Guilford, J. P. 1956 The Structure of Intellect. *Psychological Bulletin* 53:267–293.

Guttman, Louis 1954 Some Necessary Conditions for Common Factor Analysis. *Psychometrika* 19:149–161.

Horn, John 1967 On Subjectivity in Factor Analysis. Unpublished manuscript.

Humphreys, Lloyd G. 1962 The Organization of Human Abilities. *American Psychologist* 17:475–483.

Kaiser, Henry F. 1958 The Varimax Criterion for Analytic Rotation in Factor Analysis. *Psychometrika* 23:187–200.

Kaiser, Henry F.; and Caffrey, John 1965 Alpha Factor Analysis. *Psychometrika* 30:1–14.

Neuhaus, Jack O.; and Wrigley, Charles 1954 The Quartimax Method: An Analytical Approach to Orthogonal Simple Structure. *British Journal of Statistical Psychology* 7:81–91.

Overall, John E. 1964 Note on the Scientific Status of Factors. *Psychological Bulletin* 61:270–276.

Schonemann, P. H. 1964 A Solution of the Orthogonal Procrustes Problem With Applications to Orthogonal and Oblique Rotation. Ph.D. dissertation, Univ. of Illinois.

Spearman, Charles 1904 "General Intelligence" Objectively Determined and Measured. *American Journal of Psychology* 15:201–293.

Thomson, Godfrey H. 1919 The Proof or Disproof of the Existence of General Ability. *British Journal of Psychology* 9:321–336.

THORNDIKE, EDWARD L. et al. 1926 *The Measurement of Intelligence*. New York: Columbia Univ., Teachers College.

THURSTONE, LOUIS L. 1938 *Primary Mental Abilities*. Univ. of Chicago Press.

THURSTONE, LOUIS L. 1947 *Multiple-factor Analysis*. Univ. of Chicago Press. → A development and expansion of Thurstone's *The Vectors of Mind*, 1935.

FACTORIAL DESIGNS
See EXPERIMENTAL DESIGN.

FADS
See COLLECTIVE BEHAVIOR; FASHION; MASS PHENOMENA.

FAHLBECK, PONTUS ERLAND

Pontus Fahlbeck (1850–1923) was one of the cultural leaders of Sweden around the turn of the century. Successful in a career which combined scientific, political, and business interests, he was, at first, professor of history and political science at the University of Lund and, later, professor of political science and statistics at that university. It was largely thanks to his efforts that a chair in statistics, the first in Sweden, was established at Uppsala in 1910. In addition, he endowed a widely known foundation at the University of Lund that supports research in political science.

His scientific and political books and articles reflect, on the one hand, his broad socioeconomic perspectives and, on the other, his keen interest in the political problems of the day. Some influence from German *Kathedersozialismus* and social-law theory can be traced in his treatment of social problems. He described himself as moderately right wing in political matters and radical in social matters.

Fahlbeck began his academic career in history, concentrating on problems of European medieval history, and then took up political science, dealing with the Swedish constitution and its development in relation to social organization. His involvement deepened as he gradually moved toward general social science, or sociology in a broad sense. His interest focused on human society as a system of classes, the socioeconomic functions of class differentiation, and the transition from feudal society, with its class privileges, to the free groupings of modern society. In modern society, as he saw it, the legal differences between the social strata have been erased.

Fahlbeck's magnum opus is *Sveriges adel* ("The Swedish Nobility"; 1897–1902). Volume 1 is a historical study tracing each family from its en-noblement through subsequent generations. Out of a total of 2,735 families, some 25 per cent were extinct by 1898. The statistical analysis focuses on the process of extinction and includes death rates and survival tables, calculated by family. The second part is a demographic–statistical study of the then contemporary nobility. This many-faceted analysis has been referred to as a pioneering work. Throughout, Fahlbeck developed his argument on two planes—careful statistical analysis and speculative discussion. Notable are his strong emphasis on the importance of social circulation and of the leadership of the upper classes, his resigned attitude toward the deadly dangers resulting from the excessive refinement of the upper classes, and his dissatisfaction with Malthus and, in particular, neo-Malthusianism.

In general, Fahlbeck will be remembered not so much for the concrete results he produced but for the way in which he understood and dealt with some of the key issues which then confronted scientists. Like other brilliant men of his epoch, Fahlbeck was in a frustrating situation. He was aware of rapid socioeconomic developments and their great challenge to the rising social sciences, and he was also vaguely aware that the available scientific methods were inadequate to meet the challenge. At times he seemed to be far ahead of his contemporaries, groping for something that he could not articulate and that has perhaps still not been reached.

Fahlbeck's attitude toward statistical methods was ambivalent. He set forth his views on statistics, as an independent branch of social science, in two programmatic articles (1897; 1918). In the first he enthusiastically supported the actual and potential use of statistics and the numerical method in the social sciences. By the time he wrote the second article, Fahlbeck's attitude had changed. During the interval between the appearance of the two articles, the flourishing period of German demographic and social statistics had been cut off by the emergence of a strong, antitheoretical position in official statistics (von Mayr, Zahn). In England, in the meantime, the use of statistics in the biological sciences had begun, leading to a rapid and epoch-making development of advanced statistical methods, especially in the experimental area. In the period between the writing of the two articles, Fahlbeck had himself successfully used statistical methods in his study of the nobility. Yet, in his 1918 article he dismissed the advanced methods of statistics as "higher mathematics" and argued that in the social application of statistics there is room only for simple methods.

Despite the loose arguments and clichés of the

1918 article, Fahlbeck's position is not without its merits. Although his argument that the study of human behavior and social phenomena is the crucial area for statistical work is extreme, he was right to stress the key importance of studying them statistically. And his untenable view that simple methods suffice for the social sciences may have been an outgrowth of his frustration with the methods then available. His primary goal was the development of appropriate methods, comparable with those of the natural sciences, for dealing with the highest order of phenomena in the scientific hierarchy, that is, with human phenomena.

HERMAN WOLD

[See also ELITES; STRATIFICATION, SOCIAL; and the biography of GALTON.]

WORKS BY FAHLBECK

1897   Den statistika typen eller regelbundenheten uti de menskliga företeelserna: Ett bidrag till statistikens teori (The Statistical Type, or the Regularity of Human Phenomena: A Contribution to the Theory of Statistics). Lund (Sweden): Malströms Boktryckeri.

1897–1902   Sveriges adel (The Swedish Nobility). 2 vols. Lund (Sweden): Gleerup.

1900   La régularité dans les choses humaines ou les types statistiques et leurs variations. Journal de la Société de Statistique de Paris 41:188–201.

1918   Statistiken och den numeriska kunskapsmetoden: Ett bidrag till frågan om statistikens ställning som vetenskap (Statistics and the Numerical Method of Knowledge: A Contribution to the Question of the Status of Statistics as a Science). Lunds universitets årsskrift, No. 14. Lund (Sweden): Gleerup.

SUPPLEMENTARY BIBLIOGRAPHY

Festskrift till Pontus Fahlbeck den 15 oktober 1915.   1915   Lund (Sweden): Gleerup.

LAGERROTH, FREDRIK   1924   Minnesord över Pontus Erland Fahlbeck. Humanistika Vetenskapssamfundet i Lund, Årsberättelse [1923/1924]:20–28. → An obituary.

WALLENGREN, SIGFRID   1923   Pontus Fahlbeck. Statsvetenskaplig tidskrift för politik–statistik–ekonomi 26: 211–228. → An obituary.

FAIR TRADE LAWS
See RESALE PRICE MAINTENANCE.

FALANGISM

Falangism is the Spanish variant of the fascist doctrines that gained vogue in Europe during the 1930s. Its origins are purely theoretical, for falangism existed as an ideology on paper for several years before it became a significant political movement. The originators of Falangist doctrine were Ramiro Ledesma Ramos (1905–1936), sometime postal clerk and unemployed intellectual, and José Antonio Primo de Rivera (1903–1936), a young aristocrat and son of the former dictator General Miguel Primo de Rivera. The ideological basis of Falangist doctrine was first expounded by Ledesma in 1931 under the label "national syndicalism." Intoxicated by the spectacle of German national socialism, Ledesma endeavored singlehandedly to fabricate a Spanish fascistic program that would combine the two main radical forces in early twentieth-century Europe—nationalism and socialism. Ledesma's notion of "national syndicalism" was that of a revolutionary movement that would carry out the socioeconomic program of Spanish anarchosyndicalism under the aegis of a dictatorial nationalist state.

Falangism took formal shape in 1933–1934, after the founding of a new political movement called Falange Española (Spanish Phalanx). This organization was largely the creation of José Antonio Primo de Rivera, a restless, romantic, and energetic young man who wanted to complete the work begun by his father. Amid the frustrating experiences of the first two years of the Second Spanish Republic, he groped for a formula that could unify all the Spanish people and promote national rejuvenation. Like Ledesma, he thought it could be supplied by some kind of "Spanish fascism," which would combine nationalistic dictatorship and sweeping socioeconomic reform. Certain conservatives helped him found the Falange on October 29, 1933, and it soon absorbed the tiny group of radicals who followed Ledesma.

The classic doctrine of falangism was defined at the end of 1934 in a program written principally by Ledesma and referred to as the "Twenty-seven Points" (see Primo de Rivera 1942). The major principles announced were:

(1) Political unity of Spain and elimination of regional separatism.

(2) Abolition of political parties.

(3) Establishment of a nationalist dictatorship led by the party.

(4) Use of violence in regenerating Spain.

(5) Development of Spanish imperial power.

(6) Expansion and strengthening of the armed forces.

(7) Recognition and support of Catholicism as the official religion of Spain but rejection of any clerical influence in government.

(8) A sweeping economic reform, referred to as "revolution," which emphasized the following:

(a) Establishment of a complete system of national syndicates, embracing employers and employees, to organize, coordinate, and represent all of Spain's economic activity.

(*b*) Sweeping agrarian reform, reclaiming waste-land, improving techniques, concentrating scattered holdings, and reorganizing the great latifundia.

(*c*) Stimulation of industrial expansion.

(*d*) Basic respect for private property, but nationalization of all credit facilities to eliminate capitalist usury.

Together with these specific goals, a general mystique of Spanish nationalism and an interpretation of Spanish history exalting certain peculiarities of Spanish life were expounded, and almost all of Spanish liberalism and the nation's experience with constitutional parliamentary government were denounced. The fanaticism in the Spanish past was interpreted as a triumph of the nation's spirit. The Inquisition and some of the nation's more absolutist rulers were exalted and used as evidence that Spaniards needed forceful, authoritarian rule.

At the time this program was drafted the Falange probably had the support of only one per cent of the Spanish people. Its economic program remained vague because almost none of the party's few intellectuals had concrete experience with economic matters. One of the more confusing of the Twenty-seven Points was the declaration "We have a will to empire," for the Falangist notion of "empire" was never made clear. One Falangist leader soon went out of his way to indicate that "empire" meant only cultural influence and diplomatic leadership and not political or territorial domination. Other Falangists spoke in more aggressive terms, proposing the annexation of Portugal.

In October 1934 José Antonio Primo de Rivera was made *jefe nacional* (national chief) of the movement. In his person the *jefe* summarized the contradictions of Falangist doctrine, for he was an intellectual liberal and manifestly uncomfortable with the fascist aggressiveness of Falangist ideology. Most Falangists had originally referred to their movement as "fascist," but Primo de Rivera and other party leaders soon became worried about close identification with Italian fascism and German Nazism. By 1935 they were emphasizing that falangism was not intended to be "fascist" at all, but merely a native development of Spanish nationalism.

Since falangism began as an intellectual abstraction and changed greatly when finally placed in practice, it can be adequately understood only through a study of its historical evolution. The Falange was a rabid foe of the Spanish Republic, but it lacked popular support and had already been driven underground by the police and rendered physically impotent when the rebellion against the republic broke out, on July 17, 1936. The revolt was organized entirely by the Spanish Army, and the Falange, which had no official standing, was forced to collaborate with the rebels on the army's terms. During the first months of the civil war the movement lost most of its original leaders, for José Antonio Primo de Rivera, Ramiro Ledesma, and others were shot by the Republicans.

Nonetheless, in this climate of civil war, the membership of the party swelled enormously, for falangism was the only radical new ideology with which the Spanish right could combat the militant left. The military dictatorship had few clear political ideas, and after Generalissimo Francisco Franco emerged as head of the new Nationalist government, he and his advisers searched for some kind of official political ideology and structure. Falangism seemed the answer, for it stressed the defense of traditional Spanish institutions, proposed a solution to class warfare, and was the ideology most congenial to Nazi Germany and fascist Italy, the two states on which the military dictatorship had to rely to win the war. On April 19, 1937, the Falange was therefore elevated to the role of the state party of Spain, and the Twenty-seven Points were adopted as a government program.

Falangism was thus taken over as a tool of the military dictatorship; the Falangists did not in any way take over the Franco state. Franco became head of the Falange, which was reorganized, watered down, and mixed with a variety of more conservative groups. Officially, the party was fused with the reactionary, monarchist Carlist militia and renamed "Falange Española Tradicionalista de las Juntas de Ofensiva Nacional Sindicalista." The 27th point of the Falangist program, which had prohibited any such fusion, was then dropped. Power rested securely in the hands of Franco and the military hierarchy, almost none of whom was truly "Falangist." Indeed, most Spanish officers tended to sneer at the orthodox Falangists, calling them "our Reds."

Falangism had two main tasks after the end of the civil war, in 1939. The first was the creation of a nationwide system of workers' and employers' syndicates. This soon blanketed all urban and industrial regions, although it was slow to include the rural areas. The syndicates were organized by state functionaries from the top downward. They did not represent the workers but controlled them in the interests of the state and of the employers. Such a situation contrasted sharply with the original Falangist theory, in which the syndicates were supposed to be dynamic revolutionary organisms, helping to carry out a national economic reformation.

The second major task of falangism was ideological: to provide an authoritarian nationalist political theory that would supply intellectual and emotional support for the dictatorship. Falangism furnished the substance of the state propaganda machine, its antiliberal, antiparliamentary ideology being used to discredit all elements not within the Franco government and to indoctrinate the new generation of Spanish youth with loyalty to the regime. Falangist demagogy was widely employed in an attempt to convince the workers and the rest of the population that the present conservative dictatorship, protecting propertied interests and the *status quo*, was somehow a dynamic national revolution.

At no time was the Falange party organization allowed a position of independent authority inside the state, but Falangists were given a near monopoly on bureaucratic positions and many jobs in the lower echelon of the government apparatus. At the same time, the Falange National Council was packed with conservatives and army men so that there would be no danger of the movement's original ideological radicalism becoming more than rhetoric. As a result of the great influx of wartime members, the majority of Falangists had little sense of revolutionary national-syndicalist doctrine. They were largely an amorphous collection of opportunists and timeservers, who supported the regime as a means of gaining employment.

Since the nationalistic authoritarianism of Falangist propaganda was extended, on the international plane, to intense enmity against Britain, the United States, and the other Western democracies, falangism was especially useful to the Franco regime during the years 1937–1942, when the Nazi–fascist star was rising and the Spanish regime hoped to find a place inside the fascist new order. During this period it was often found convenient to revert to the original definition of falangism and to call it "Spanish fascism."

After 1943, however, with fascism on the wane in Europe, this definition came to be as much a liability as an asset to the Franco regime. From that time on, great efforts were made to erase the overtly fascistic, imperialistic aspects of Falangist ideology. The official government spokesmen and even Falangist leaders began to place especially heavy emphasis on the "Catholic" nature of falangism, to play up the "religious" aspect of the regime's political orientation. Falangist ideologues now began to say that not everything done by liberal regimes was bad, that in fact the Falange

itself was rather "liberal," or at least broad-minded and forgiving. The amount of money provided the Falangist organization fell off rapidly by 1945, as the Spanish regime tried anxiously to provide itself with a new façade. No more was heard about the Spanish "empire" or the virtues of violence. There was even some speculation that the Falange would be dismantled altogether. However, there was never any danger of the Franco regime's going that far, for the vague Falangist ideology was the only political ideology the military dictatorship possessed. Rather, the Falangist "new line" was expanded. "National revolution" now meant merely the continuation of the existing syndical system to keep the workers in their place. "Nationalism" and "antiliberalism" were used mostly to provide propaganda support for the regime and not to defame the progressive nations of the Western world.

Franco had always stressed the fact that falangism had not achieved final form as a doctrine, that the program of the state would continue to change. Presumably, it would never cease to do so. After 1945 emphasis was placed on the wide variety of political and ideological forces in the original "movement" behind the Franco government. Conservatives, moderate liberals, constitutional monarchists, clericals, and reactionary Carlists, who had always resented the relative ideological monopoly of falangism, were now permitted more voice.

In 1947 Franco arranged a plebiscite to turn his regime into a sort of regency, with some member of the Spanish Bourbon dynasty slated to succeed him when he wearied of his role as dictator or died. Falangist doctrine had always been more or less antimonarchist. In fact, much of the rank and file of the Falangist organization was rabidly so, deeming monarchism incompatible with any kind of vigorous modern political movement. Therefore, Franco's official establishment of the monarchy as his successor seemed to reduce the function of falangism even further.

The true result of the transformation of the regime into a pseudo regency was nonetheless that it increased the significance of falangism for the dictatorship. Franco's own monarchism was largely fraudulent; he had primarily sought a way to pacify restlessness about the future. Publicly favoring monarchist interests, Franco actually sustained Falangist propaganda and the Falangist bureaucracy so that monarchist influence would not become too strong. The Spanish dictator could thus threaten the monarchists with a revival of extreme falangism whenever they tried to place any pressure on his regime.

Although he cared even less about ideology than

before, Franco probably felt more comfortable with falangism and the party bureaucracy than with most other elements of his regime. The Falangists were so completely dependent on his personal benevolence that they dared not seriously oppose him, and their ideology of nationalism and authoritarian rule was still the most comfortable political rationale for his heterogeneous, but increasingly light-handed, tyranny.

The immediate future of the regime was assured in 1951, when the United States began its policy of *rapprochement* with Franco. It became clear that the regime would no longer suffer international pressure because of its quasi-fascist texture, and Franco responded by placing a regular Falangist at the head of the bureaucracy and appointing four new Falangist ministers in the 1951 cabinet shake-up. Falangist propagandists felt freer to return to some of their old prejudices. Nonetheless, and despite the fact that the United States was still, in the classic Falangist definition, a decadent liberal parliamentary democracy, the new doctrine had to be one of friendship with America, for the latter had indirectly become a principal supporter of the Franco dictatorship.

The growing prosperity of Spain in the 1950s finally made it possible for the regime to attempt to realize a few peripheral aspects of the original Falangist program of economic reform. A program of state-operated industrialization, directed by the National Institute of Industry (INI), lavished vast amounts of money on a great variety of industrial projects between 1951 and 1958. At a much slower pace, a new beginning was made in state irrigation projects and agrarian reform. This, however, had little to do with falangism per se, being directed by separate bureaucracies and paying little heed to the incomplete plans of the creators of falangism.

The last effort to define falangism politically and to turn it into a living, controlling force was made in 1956–1957. The growth of political opposition had made a mild shake-up of the government necessary. A commission of old-guard Falangists was called together, and three separate *anteproyectos* (draft proposals) were drawn up to define the Falangist position. (The *anteproyectos* were not officially published, but copies of them were made available to this author by one of the Falangist leaders involved.) These made it clear that the Twenty-seven Points were quite dead. There was no mention of "empire" or "violence." Instead, the new catechism stressed the pre-eminence of Catholicism, national unity, and social justice and the viability of a moderated capitalism.

With regard to the structure of the state, the Falangists approved Franco's Cortes (parliament), a rubber-stamp assembly elected indirectly from a state-controlled list of nominees. However, they requested the elevation of the Falangist National Council to a sort of upper chamber or senate. Their project acknowledged a king as successor to Franco in the role of chief of state but requested the appointment of a prime minister, or chief of government, who would carry on ordinary executive functions. He was to be responsible primarily to the chief of state, although it was stipulated that three adverse votes by the Falangist National Council should bring his resignation. Continuation of the one-party system was projected, and the Franco system of establishing a series of "fundamental laws" in lieu of a constitution was approved.

Such a project contained a wholly original statement of Falangist notions of political structure, for at no time previously had the party's organic goals been made so clear. Nonetheless, the *anteproyectos* were irrelevant, for there was no chance that they would ever be realized. The most influential pressure groups in Franco Spain—the hierarchy of the army and the Roman Catholic church—reacted with extreme anger. The *anteproyectos* were quietly buried without ever having been made public, and in the 1957 cabinet change falangism was further downgraded.

By that time the major interest in Spain was economic development, not politics. The Franco regime preferred to give the appearance of liberalization and a more purely technical kind of government. The tendency was thus toward the transcendence of falangism by a more "prismatic" political doctrine, permitting expression of pluralistic tendencies, within a limited range, under one-man rule. Such an orientation was much more effective in an era of increasing integration with liberal western Europe.

It was perhaps impossible to expect that Falangism, as an ideology or as a movement, could survive and flourish in the postfascist epoch of western Europe. Having attained a position of pseudo responsibility without effective power, it had served as an effective scapegoat, to be blamed or downgraded whenever the regime felt a show of "liberalization" to be necessary. Nonetheless, it did leave a significant legacy, since it provided the principal rationale for authoritarian unity and government in Spain. At the same time, by its rhetorical emphasis on economic reform and social justice, it probably constituted the most liberal force within the regime.

STANLEY G. PAYNE

[*See also* DICTATORSHIP; FASCISM; SOCIAL MOVE-MENTS.]

BIBLIOGRAPHY

The changing emphases of Falangist doctrine are best seen in the publications of its creators and leaders. For the pre-World War II *period these are* Aparicio 1939; Ledesma Ramos 1935; Primo de Rivera 1942 *and* 1956; Redondo 1939. *For the later period see* Fernández Cuesta 1951; Arrese 1943, 1947, *and* 1957; *and the official journal of the movement,* Revista de estudios políticos. *General historical accounts and critiques are* Payne 1961 *and* Nellessen 1963.

APARICIO, JUAN (editor) 1939 *Antología: La conquista del estado.* Barcelona (Spain): Ediciones FE. → A compilation of articles that originally appeared in the periodical *La conquista del estado* in 1931.

ARRESE, JOSÉ LUIS DE 1943 *Escritos y discursos.* Madrid: Vicesecretaría de Educación Popular.

ARRESE, JOSÉ LUIS DE 1947 *Capitalismo, comunismo, cristianismo.* Madrid: Ediciones Radar.

ARRESE, JOSÉ LUIS DE 1957 *Hacia una meta institucional.* Madrid: Ediciones del Movimiento.

FERNÁNDEZ CUESTA, RAIMUNDO 1951 *Intemperie, victoria y servicio: Discursos y escritos.* Madrid: Ediciones del Movimiento.

[LEDESMA RAMOS, RAMIRO] 1935 *¿Fascismo en España? (Sus origines, su desarrollo, sus hombres),* by Roberto Lanzas [pseud.]. Madrid: Ediciones "La Conquista del Estado."

NELLESSEN, BERND 1963 *Die verbotene Revolution: Aufstieg und Niedergang der Falange.* Hamburg (Germany): Leibniz.

PAYNE, STANLEY G. 1961 *Falange: A History of Spanish Fascism.* Stanford Studies in History, Economics and Political Science, No. 22. Stanford (Calif.) Univ. Press.

PRIMO DE RIVERA, JOSÉ ANTONIO 1942 *Norma programática de la Falange.* Pages 589–597 in José Antonio Primo de Rivera, *Obras completas.* Compiled and edited by Augustín del Río Cisneros and Enrique Conde Gargollo. Madrid: "Diana."

PRIMO DE RIVERA, JOSÉ ANTONIO 1956 *Textos inéditos y epistolario.* Madrid: Ediciones del Movimiento.

REDONDO, ONÉSIMO (1939) 1954–1955 *Obras completas.* 2 vols. Madrid: Publicaciones Españolas.

Revista de estudios políticos (Madrid). → Published bimonthly since 1941.

FALLACIES, STATISTICAL

This article will be mainly concerned with statistical fallacies, but it should be noted that most other fallacious types of reasoning can be carried over into statistics.

Most fallacies seem foolish when pinpointed, but they are not the prerogative of fools and statisticians. Great men make mistakes, and when they admit them remorsefully, they reveal a facet of their greatness. The reason for mentioning the mistakes of eminent people in this article is to make it more fun to read.

Many fallacies, statistical or otherwise, have their origin in wishful thinking, laziness, and busyness. These conditions lead to oversimplification, the de-

sire to win an argument at all costs (even at the cost of over*complication*), failure to listen to the opposition, too-ready acceptance of authority, too-ready rejection of it, too-ready acceptance of the printed word (even in newspapers), too-great reliance on a machine or formal system or formula (*deus ex machina*), and too-ready rejection of them (*diabolus ex machina*). These emotionally determined weaknesses are not themselves fallacies, but they provoke them. For example, they provoke special pleading, the use of language in more than one sense without notice of the ambiguity (if the argument leads to a desirable conclusion), the insistence that a method used successfully in one field of research is the only appropriate one in another, the distortion of judgment, and the forgetting of the need for judgment.

A logical or syntactical fallacy. We begin with an example of a fallacious argument in which the conclusion is correct:

"No cat has no tail. One cat has one more tail than no cat. Therefore one cat has one tail."

A good technique for exposing fallacious reasoning is to use the same form of argument in order to deduce an obviously false result:

"No cat has eight tails. One cat has one more tail than no cat. Therefore one cat has nine tails."

The fallacy can be explained by careful attention to syntax, specifically by noting that the following two propositions have been confused: (1) It is false that any cat has eight tails, and (2) the object named "no cat" has eight tails. P. M. S. Blackett once said, exaggerating somewhat, that a physicist is satisfied with an argument if it leads to a result that he believes to be true.

Arguments from authority. The book *Popular Fallacies* by Alfred S. E. Ackermann is more concerned with fallacies of fact than of reasoning, and here many fallacies depend on the acceptance of authority. It is interesting to see that the author was himself misled by authority on at least two occasions.

First, he argues that it is a fallacy "that cigarette smoking is especially pernicious," appealing to the opinions of several authorities: for example, "Of the various forms of smoking, cigarette smoking is the most wholesome, preferably without a holder," according to Sir Robert Armstrong-Jones, F.R.C.P., in the *Daily Mail*, January 1, 1927 (Ackermann [1907] 1950, pp. 174–175). (The current medical opinion is that, of cigarettes, cigars, and pipes, cigarettes are the least wholesome, at any rate in regard to lung cancer. Of course, Armstrong-Jones *might* be right after all.)

Then Ackermann refers to the thesis "that there is a prospect of atomic energy being of practical use." Lord Rutherford is quoted, from the *Evening News*, September 11, 1933, as saying that "anyone who expects a source of power from the transformation of these atoms is talking moonshine" (*ibid.*, pp. 708–709).

It would be unfair to blame Ackermann for relying on these authorities, but it is useful to hold in mind that the highest authorities can be wrong, even when they are emphatic in their opinions. Their desire not to seem too academic should sometimes be allowed for, especially when they hold an administrative appointment.

What should the question really be? When Gertrude Stein was on her deathbed, one of her friends asked her, "What is the answer?" After a few seconds she whispered back, "What is the question?"

It is important for the statistician to satisfy himself that a *right* question is being asked, by inquiring into the purposes behind the question. Chambers (1965) states that when a member of Parliament asked for some inland revenue figures that were not available from the published statistics, his invariable rule was to find out the purpose for which the information was needed. More often than not he found that the figures sought were irrelevant, that other figures already published were more helpful, or that the M.P. was misguided over the whole business.

It is often reasonable to make exploratory investigations without a clear purpose in mind. The fallacy we have just pointed out is the assumption that the questioner necessarily asks for information that is very relevant to his purposes, whether those purposes are clear or vague. The fallacy of giving the "right answer to the wrong question" is further discussed by A. W. Kimball (1957).

Ignoring the "exposure base." Consider, for example, the reports on traffic deaths that are issued after public holidays. Many readers conclude from the increased number of deaths that it is more dangerous to drive on public holidays than on ordinary days. The conclusion may or may not be correct, but the reasoning is fallacious, since it ignores the fact that many more people drive automobiles on public holidays and thus more people are exposed to the possibility of an accident. If holidays and ordinary days are compared on the basis of deaths per passenger mile, it might turn out that the holiday death rate is lower, since the reduction of the average speed caused by the vol-

ume of traffic also may reduce the seriousness, if not the number, of accidents.

"Deus ex machina"—the precision fallacy. When we know a machine or formal system that can produce an exact answer to a question, we are tempted to provide an answer and inquire no further. But exact methods often produce exact answers to wrong questions.

One of the main aims of statistical technique is to fight the danger of wishful thinking and achieve a measure of objectivity in probability statements. But absolute objectivity and precision are seldom if ever attainable: there is always, or nearly always, a need for judgment in any application of statistical methods. (This point is especially emphasized in Good 1950.) Inexperienced statisticians often overestimate the degree of precision and objectivity that can be attained. An elementary form of the precision fallacy, which is less often committed by statisticians than by others, is the use of an average without reference to "spread." A related trap is to gauge closeness by some measure of spread but to ignore systematic errors (bias) [*see* ERRORS, *article on* NONSAMPLING ERRORS].

The use of an average without a measure of spread can be especially misleading, or even comic, when the sample is small and the spread is therefore large. But even if the mean and standard deviation of the *population* are given, they can be misleading if the population is very skew. For skew populations it is better to give some of the quantiles [*see* STATISTICS, DESCRIPTIVE, *article on* LOCATION AND DISPERSION].

Randomization. An example of the precision fallacy occurs in connection with the important technique of randomization. Let us consider the famous tea-tasting experiment (see Fisher 1935, chapter 1; Good 1956). A lady claims to be able to tell by tasting, with better than random chance, whether the milk is put into her tea first or last. We decide to test her by giving her twenty cups of tea to taste, in ten of which the milk is poured first, and in ten last. If the lady gets many more than ten of her assertions right and if we have not randomized the order of the twenty trials, we might suspect that whatever sequence we selected for some psychological reason, the lady might have tended to guess for similar psychological reasons. So we randomize the order and can then apparently make use of the hypergeometric tail-area probability as a precise, objective, and effectively complete summary of the statistical significance of the experiment [*see* EXPERIMENTAL DESIGN *and* RANDOM NUMBERS].

But suppose we now examine the random sequence and spot some pattern in it—for example, that cups 3, 6, 9, 12, 15, and 18 had the milk in first. This would at once undermine the precise validity of our result in relation to its relevance to the hypothesis under investigation. We can partly remove this difficulty by means of "restricted randomization," but we cannot completely remove it, because every finite sequence exhibits some special features, however recondite. Only by judgment, necessarily subjective, can we decide that any given feature is unimportant. The only way we can preserve the precision is to make use of a "statistician's stooge" to perform the experiment for us, including the randomization (Good 1960–1961). He must report the number of successes to us but must on no account tell us the randomized order. Precision in a randomized experiment can be obtained only at the price of suppressing some of the information. The point made here is not universally accepted by statisticians.

If the number of cups of tea is very large, then the importance of the above criticism of randomization will usually be negligible. But long experiments are expensive, and in the statistical design of experiments the expense can never be ignored.

Randomization in itself is by no means a fallacious technique; what is fallacious is the notion that without the suppression of information, it can lead to a precise tail-area probability relevant only to a null hypothesis.

The suppression of information. In its crudest forms the suppression of information is often at least as wicked as an outright lie. We shall later refer to some of the cruder forms. But we have just seen that randomization loses its precision unless some information is suppressed, and we shall now argue more forcibly that it is a fallacy to suppose that the suppression of information is always culpable.

One way of seeing this is in terms of digital communication. When an electrical "pulse" of a given shape is liable to have been attenuated and distorted by noise, some circuitry is often incorporated for the purpose of re-forming ("regenerating") the pulse. This circuitry, as it were, accepts the hypothesis that the pulse is supposed to be present rather than absent. Since noise in the electronic system makes the probability less than one that the supposed pulse is present, the regeneration loses some information. But allowing for the nature of the *subsequent* communication channel, it can be proved that the loss is often more than compensated. (This will not be proved here, but it is not surprising to common sense.) In pedagogy the corresponding principle is that simplification is necessary when teaching beginners. In statistics the corresponding device is known as the *reduction of the data*, that is, the reduction of a mass of data to a more easily assimilable form. If the statistics are "sufficient," then there is no loss of information, but we often have to be satisfied with "insufficient" statistics in order to make an effective reduction of the data. Thus it is fallacious to say that the suppression of information is always a statistical crime. (Note that apparently sufficient statistics might not really be so if the model is wrong. People sometimes publish, say, only a mean and variance of a sample, and this prevents readers from checking the validity of the model for which these statistics would be sufficient.) [*See* SUFFICIENCY.]

Terminological ambiguities. Important examples of terminological ambiguities occur both in the philosophy of statistics and in its practical applications. Often they are as obvious as the "no cat" ambiguity, once they are pointed out. But before they are pointed out, they lead to a great deal of argument at cross purposes. Thus, many of the problems in the philosophy of probability clear themselves up as soon as we distinguish between various kinds of probability (see Good 1959a). (We shall not discuss here whether they can all be reduced to a single kind or whether they all "exist." But they are all talked about.) [*See* PROBABILITY, *article on* INTERPRETATIONS.]

There is tautological, or mathematical, probability, which occurs in mathematical theories and requires no operational definition. It occurs also in the definition of a "simple statistical hypothesis," which is a hypothesis for which some probabilities of the form $P(E|H)$ are assigned *by definition*. (Here E represents an event or a proposition asserting that an event obtains, and the vertical stroke stands for "given" or "assuming.") There are *physical*, or material, probabilities, or *chances*. These relate to tautological probabilities by means of the *linguistic axiom* that to say that H is true is to say that the physical probability of E is $P(E|H)$, for some class of events, E. There are *logical* probabilities, or credibilities. There are *subjective*, or personal, probabilities, which are the intensities of conviction that a man will use for betting purposes, after mature consideration. There are *multisubjective* probabilities, belonging to groups of people. And there are *psychological* probabilities, which are the probabilities that people behave as if they accept, even before applying any criterion to test their consistency. By confusing pairs of these six kinds of probability, *fifteen different kinds of fallacy can be generated*. For example, it is often said that there is no sense in talking about the probability that a population parameter has a certain value, for "it either has the value or it does not, and therefore the probability is either 0 or 1." It need hardly be mentioned, to those who are not choked with emotion, that the probability need not be 0 or 1 when it is interpreted not as a physical probability but as a logical or as a subjective probability.

Even physical probabilities can be confused with each other, since they can be mistakenly referred to the same event. For example, apparent variations in the incidence of some crime or disease from one place or time to another are very often found to be due to variations in the methods of classification. Adultery would appear to increase enormously if Christ's definition were suddenly to be accepted in the law—"Whosoever looketh on a woman to lust after her hath committed adultery with her already in his heart" (Matthew 5.28). Since partners to adultery do not often turn in official reports, perhaps a better example is that of crime records. An example with documentation, quoted by Wallis and Roberts (1956), is that of felonies in New York. It was alleged that there had been an increase of 34.8 per cent from 1949 to 1950, but later it appeared that this was at least largely due to a revised method of classification.

This class of practical statistical fallacies is extremely common in the social sciences, and one should be very much on guard against it. As a further example, two standard definitions of the number of unemployed in the United States differ by a factor of over 3, namely, the "average monthly rate" and the "total annual rate." Putting it roughly, one measure for any given year is the average monthly number of people unemployed; the other, larger measure is the number of people who were unemployed at any time during the year. [*See* EMPLOYMENT AND UNEMPLOYMENT.]

An example of a terminological fallacy is the confusion of "some" and "all." It is perpetrated by John Hughlings Jackson in the following excerpt: "To coin the word, verbalising, to include all ways in which words serve, I would assert that both halves of the brain are alike in that each serves in *verbalising*. That the left half does is evident, because damage of it makes a man speechless. That the right does is inferable, because the speechless man understands all I say to him in ordinary matters" (quoted in Penfield & Roberts 1959, p. 62). Some damage to the left hemisphere seems here to have been confused with destruction of all of it.

Another example of the "some and all" fallacy is to assume that since some poems are better than others in the opinion of any reasonable judge, then, given any set of poems, one of them must be the best. More generally, the possibility of *partial* ordering is easily overlooked. But sometimes the assumption of partial ordering, although truer than complete ordering, is too complicated for a given application. In a beauty competition, for example, each girl might be the best of her kind, but it might be essential to award the prize to only one of them.

In some social surveys respondents are asked to rank several objects in order of merit. An alternate design, which will often be less watered down by the need to reach decisions in doubtful cases, is to ask for comparisons of pairs of objects but to permit "no comparison" as a response for any given pair.

Ignoring a relevant concomitant variable. "The death rate in the American Army in peacetime is lower than that in New York City. Therefore leave New York and join the army." The fallacy is that the methods of selection for the army are biased toward longevity, both by age and by health, and these clearly relevant variables have been ignored. The fallacy can also be categorized as failure to control for exposure, since many inhabitants of New York City are subject to the possibility of death from infant diseases, chronic diseases, and old age, whereas very few men in the army are so exposed. The example can also be regarded as one of "biased sampling," a category of fallacy to be considered later.

Ignoring half of a contingency table. It is commonly believed that government scientists in the United Kingdom earn more on the average than university teachers. But, as Rowe pointed out (1962), the average age of university teachers is less than that of government scientists, because a large proportion of lecturers leave the universities before their mid-thirties. Rowe showed that the median earning of university teachers above the age of 35 is greater than that of government scientists. But he did not estimate what these men *would* have earned in government service. Thus, although he refuted the original argument, he did not ask the really relevant question. This question is very difficult to answer. A possible approach, which would shed some light, would be to find out the distribution of salaries as a function of job, age, and intelligence quotient.

The perennial problem here is which covariates to choose and where to stop choosing them, since the list of possibilities is typically impracticably large. A related issue is that the greater the number of conditioning classificatory variables (dimensionality of the contingency table), the fewer the cases in the relevant cross-classification cell. This is one of the unsolved problems of actuarial science, where the problem of estimating probabilities in multidimensional contingency tables is philosophically basic (for some discussion of this problem, with references, see Good 1965).

It sometimes happens that a fact is almost universally ignored, although in retrospect it is clearly highly relevant. In the late 1950s people in the United States were arguing that the standard of college teaching staffs was deteriorating, since the proportion of newly employed teachers who held a doctorate was decreasing. What was overlooked was that the proportion of teachers who took their doctorates after becoming teachers was increasing. Cartter (1965) states that Bernard Berelson was almost alone in his correct interpretation of the situation.

Biased sample. At one time, most known quasistellar radio sources lay approximately in a plane, and this seemed to one writer to have deep cosmological significance. But these radio sources could not be definitely identified with optical sources unless they were located with great accuracy, and for this purpose they had to be occluded by the moon. Also, as it happened, most of the observations had been made from the same observatory. Hence there was a very strong bias in the sampling of the sources (this was mentioned by D. W. Dewhurst in a lecture in Oxford on January 28, 1965). As Sir Arthur Eddington once pointed out, if you catch fish with a net having a 6-inch mesh, you are liable to formulate the hypothesis that all fish are more than 6 inches in length. [*See* ERRORS, *article on* NONSAMPLING ERRORS.]

It is sometimes overlooked that atrocity stories usually form a biased sample. Newspapers tend to report the atrocities of political opponents more than those of friends. An exception was the Nazi atrocities, which were so great that the evidence for them had to be overwhelming before they could be believed. (For example, there appears to be no reference to them in the 1951 edition of the *Encyclopaedia Britannica*.)

Sometimes inferences from a sample are biased because of seasonal variations. According to Starnes (1962), Democratic Secretary of Labor Willard Wirtz stated just before an election that over "four and a half million more Americans have jobs than when this Administration took office in January of 1961." Wirtz later admitted that the figure should have been 1.224 million, and he said, "It isn't proper to compare January figures with October figures without a seasonal adjustment." Similarly, the Republican governor of New York, Nelson D. Rockefeller, once referred to a "net increase of

450,000 jobs" since he had taken office. The figure is worthless because it again ignores the adjustment for seasonal variations.

Bias is difficult to avoid in social surveys, for example, in the use of questionnaires, where poor wording is frequent and where one sometimes (especially in political and commercial surveys) finds tendentious wording.

Even with an unbiased sample, it is possible to get a biased conclusion by computing the significance level of various tests of the null hypothesis and selecting the one most favorable to one's wishes. Although these tests are based on the same sample and are therefore statistically interdependent, there will be a reasonable probability that one out of twenty such tests will reach a 5 per cent significance level. A suggestion of how to combine such "parallel" tests is given by Good (1958a).

The suppression of the uninteresting. Suppose we have done an experiment, and it reaches a significance level of 5 per cent. Should we reject the null hypothesis? Perhaps the experiment has been performed by others without significant results. If these other experiments were taken into account, the total significance of all the experiments combined might be negligible. Moreover, the other results might have been unpublished because they were nonsignificant and therefore uninteresting. This explains why some apparent medical advances do not fulfill their early promise. The published statistics are biased in favor of what is interesting. As one physician said, "Hasten to use the remedy before it is too late" (Good 1958b, p. 283; Sterling 1959).

Sample too small. One of the most frequent and elementary statistical fallacies is the reliance on too small a sample. In 1933 Meduna, believing that schizophrenia and epilepsy were incompatible because of the rarity of their joint occurrence, started to induce convulsions in mental patients by chemical means. Consequently, the beneficial effect of convulsions on depressives was eventually accidentally discovered. Meduna's sample was too small, and in fact it has now been found that schizophrenia and epilepsy are *positively* correlated (Slater & Beard 1963). One moral of this story is that experiments can be worth trying without theoretical reason to believe that they might be successful.

Misleading use of graphs and pictures. Graphs and pictures are often used in newspapers in the hope of misleading readers who are not experienced in interpreting them. Sometimes graphs are inadequately labeled; sometimes the scale is chosen so as to make a small slope appear large; sometimes the graph is drawn on a board and the board is pictured in perspective so as to accentuate the most recent slope; sometimes too little of a time series is shown, and the graph is started at a trough (a device that is useful for salesmen of stocks, when they wish the public to invest in a particular equity).

A useful method for misleading with pictures is to depict, say, salaries by means of objects such as cash boxes whose *linear* dimensions are proportional to the salaries. In this way an increase is made to appear much larger than it really is. Another useful method for misleading the public is attributed by Huff (1954) to the First National Bank of Boston. The bank represented governmental expenditure by means of a map of the United States in which states of low population densities were shaded to indicate that total government spending was equal to the combined income of the people of those states. The hope was that the reader would get the impression that federal spending, as a fraction of the total income of the United States, was equal to the total area of the shaded states divided by the whole area of the country. [*See* GRAPHIC PRESENTATION.]

"Smaller" versus "smaller than necessary." The confusion of "smaller" with "smaller than necessary" will be illustrated in a hereditary context, and an oversimplification of the theory of natural selection will be pointed out. Let us suppose that it is true that intelligent people tend to have fewer children than less intelligent people and that the level of intelligence is hereditary. (We are not here concerned with whether and where this supposition is true, nor with the precise interpretation of "intelligent.") It then appears to follow that the average level of intelligence will necessarily decline. This fallacy will be perpetrated on most readers of Chapter 5 of the book by the eminent zoologist Peter B. Medawar (1960, p. 86), in spite of the words italicized by us in the following quotation: "If innately unintelligent people tend to have larger families, then, *with some qualifications*, we can infer that the average level of intelligence will decline." In order to show that the argument without the qualification is invalid it is sufficient to use a mathematical model that, for other purposes, would be much oversimplified (see Behrens 1963). Imagine a population in which 10 per cent of men are intelligent and 90 per cent are unintelligent and that, on the average, 100 intelligent fathers have 46 sons, of whom 28 are intelligent and 18 unintelligent, whereas 100 unintelligent fathers have 106

Table 1 — Hypothetical proportions of intelligent and unintelligent sons

		SONS	
		Intelligent	Unintelligent
FATHERS	100 *intelligent*	28	18
	900 *unintelligent*	72	882
	Total	100	900

sons, of whom 98 are unintelligent and 8 are intelligent. It will be seen from Table 1 that the proportion of intelligent males would remain steady in expectation.

But now it must be determined whether the right question is being asked. Suppose we were convinced that the general level of intelligence was decreasing, and we made suggestions accordingly for encouraging the more intelligent to have more children. Should we not put these suggestions forward even if the general level of intelligence were *increasing*? Would we not like to see the rate of increase also increase? Yes, of course. Looking from this point of view, we might not fully agree with Medawar's arguments, but we might well agree with some of his recommendations.

"Regression fallacy." If we select a short or tall person at random, the chances are that his relatives will be closer in average height than he is to the mean height of the population. Francis Galton described this phenomenon as "regression." If now we consider the heights of the sons of tall men and of short men, we might infer that the variability of heights is decreasing with time. This would be an example of the regression fallacy. One way of seeing that the argument must be fallacious is by considering the heights of the parents of short and tall people: we would then infer that the variability of heights is *increasing* with time!

Wallis and Roberts (1956) mention several other examples of the regression fallacy. One is the widespread belief that the second year in the major leagues is an unlucky one for new baseball players who have successfully finished their first year.

Invalid use of formulas or theorems. The use of formulas or theorems in situations where they are not valid is a special case of the *deus ex machina* class of fallacies and is very frequent. The following are a few examples.

Implicit assumption of independence. In an experiment consisting of n trials, each successful with probability p, is the variance (the square of the standard deviation) of the number of successes equal to $np(1 - p)$, as it would be if independence held? (An example would be the quality inspection of items on an assembly line.) The formula is so familiar that it is tempting to assume that it is always a good approximation. But familiarity breeds mistakes. For a Markov chain the variance can be quite different (see, for example, Good 1963), as it can also be when sampling features of children in families or fruit on trees.

Another example of a fallacious assumption of independence relates to the variability of physiological traits. Why, even if there were only eight traits, each trichotomized into equal thirds, only one person out of $3^8 = 6561$ would be in the middle (normal) group for all eight traits!

Assuming form determines distribution. Let n_{ij} be the frequency of the "dinome," that is, pair of adjacent digits (i,j), in a sequence of N random sampling digits $(i,j = 0,1,2, \cdots, 9)$. Clearly $\sum n_{ij} = N - 1$. Let

$$\psi^2 = \frac{10}{N-1} \sum_{i,j} \left(n_{ij} - \frac{N-1}{100} \right)^2.$$

It has been erroneously assumed at least four times in the statistical literature that ψ^2 has asymptotically (for large N) a tabular chi-squared distribution. In one case this led to the unfair rejection of a method of producing pseudo random numbers. Presumably the erroneous distribution arose from the typographical identity of the expression for ψ^2 with the familiar statistic of the chi-square test. (For references to three of these papers and to a paper that gives a correct method of using ψ^2, see Good 1963.) The misapplication of the above so-called serial test is particularly disastrous when working with binary digits (0 and 1), that is, with base 2.

Assuming the winner leads half the time. There is a fallacy in assuming that in a long sequence of statistically independent fair games of chance between two players the ultimate winner will be in the lead about half the time. This is a misapplication of the law of large numbers. That it *is* a fallacy depends on one of the most surprising theorems in the theory of probability, the so-called arc sine law. In fact, the probability that a specified player will be in the lead for less than a fraction x of the time is approximately $(2/\pi)$ arc sin $x^{\frac{1}{2}}$ (see, for example, Feller 1950–1966, vol. 1, p. 251). This implies that however long the game, it is much more likely that a specified player will be ahead most of the time or behind most of the time than that he will be about even; for example, the probability that a specific player will be ahead 90 per cent or more of the time, or behind 90 per cent or more of the time, is about .40, while the probability that the player will be ahead between 40 and 60 per cent

of the time is only about .13. As Feller says, the arc sine law "should serve as a warning to those who easily discover 'obvious' secular trends" in economic and social phenomena.

The "maturity of the chances." An elementary misapplication of the law of large numbers, or "law of averages," is known as the maturity of the chances. In World War I many soldiers took shelter in bomb craters on the grounds that two bombs seldom hit the same spot. For the same reason P. S. Milner-Barry, the British chess master, decided to retain his London flat after it was bombed in World War II. As a matter of fact it *was* bombed again. At roulette tables, it is said, the chips pile up on the color that has not occurred much in recent spins. Of course, in practice, if a coin came down heads fifty times running, it would be *more* likely than not, in logical probability, to come down heads on the next spin, not *less* likely. In fact, it would probably be double-headed. There are circumstances, of course, when an event is less likely to occur soon after it has just occurred: this would be true for some kinds of accidents and in many situations where one is sampling without replacement. Usually the question is basically empirical, but the expression "maturity of the chances," or "Monte Carlo fallacy," usually refers to sequences of events that are statistically independent, at least to a good approximation.

Law of large numbers misapplied to pairs. A mnemonic for the fallacy of misapplying the law of large numbers when considering pairs of objects selected from a set is the well-known "birthday problem." If 24 people are selected at random, then it is more likely than not that at least one pair of them will have the same birthday (that is, month and day). This is simple to prove, but a good intuitive "reason" for it is that the number of pairs of people in a group of 24 people is 276, and $\exp(-276/365) < \frac{1}{2}$. (The crude argument here is based on a Poisson approximation to the probability of no "successes" in 276 roughly independent trials with common success probability 1/365.) The result is true a fortiori if births are not distributed uniformly over days of the year.

C. R. Hewitt, in a "Science Survey" program of the British Broadcasting Corporation in February, 1951, stated that the probability is less than 1/64,000,000,000 that two fingerprints of different people will be indistinguishable. From this he inferred that no two people have indistinguishable fingerprints and thus committed the birthday fallacy. The argument is fallacious even if we ignore resemblances of fingerprints among relatives, since the number of *pairs* of people in the world exceeds

4,000,000,000,000,000,000. The conclusion might be correct.

A similar fallacy arises in connection with precognition. Suppose, entirely unrealistically, that there is just one remarkable and well-documented case of somebody in the world having an apparently precognitive dream. How small must the apparent probability be in order that the report, if true, should by itself convince us of precognition? Presumably its reciprocal should be at least of the order of the population of the world times the number of dream experiences of a man times the number of his waking experiences. This triple product might be as large as 1,000,000,000,000,000,000,-000,000,000 (or 10^{27}). This informal application of statistics should discourage a too ready assumption that the evidence from apparently precognitive dreams is overwhelming. A formal application of statistical methods to this problem is very difficult. This discussion is not intended to undermine a belief in the possibility of precognition, but it is a plea for a better evaluation of the evidence.

Failure to use precise notation. An example of the fallacy of failure to use sufficiently explicit notation is given by the "fiducial argument." The purpose of R. A. Fisher's fiducial argument (1956, pp. 52–54) was to produce a final (posterior) distribution for a parameter without assuming an initial (prior) distribution for it. This was ambitious, to say the least, since *de nihilo nihilum.*

The argument starts off from a parametric distribution for a random variable, X. Fisher selected an example of which the following is a special case. For each positive number x_0, suppose that

$$P(X > x_0 \mid \theta) = \exp(-x_0\theta),$$

where θ is a positive parameter in whose value and final distribution we are interested. Writing $x_0 = u/\theta$, we get $P(X\theta > u \mid \theta) = \exp(-u)$. From this it can be proved, using the usual axioms of probability theory (although Fisher omitted the proof), that $P(X\theta > u) = \exp(-u)$ for any positive number, u, provided that an initial distribution for θ is assumed to exist. (It is not necessary to assume that this distribution is in any sense known.) Hence $P(\theta > \theta_0) = \exp(-x\theta_0)$, where $\theta_0 = u/x$. Fisher infers from this that

$$P(\theta > \theta_0 \mid x) = \exp(-x\theta_0),$$

where θ_0 is any real positive number. But this last equation does not follow from the axioms of probability unless the initial probability density of θ is proportional to $1/\theta$. The fallacy in the fiducial argument was due to Fisher's failure to indicate what is "given" in his probability notation. So great

was Fisher's authority that there are still many statisticians who make use of the fiducial argument; thus the analysis given here is currently considered controversial [*see* FIDUCIAL INFERENCE].

Assuming order of operations reversible. An example of the fallacy of assuming that the order of two mathematical operations can be interchanged is the assumption that the expectation of a square is equal to the square of the expectation. This occurs in M. J. Moroney (1951, p. 250), where he says that evidently the expected value of chisquare for a multinomial distribution is zero.

Correlation and causation. *Positive correlation does not imply causation, either way round.* There is a positive correlation between the number of maiden aunts one has and the proportion of calcium in one's bones. But you cannot acquire more maiden aunts by eating calcium tablets. (Younger people tend to have more maiden aunts and more bone calcium.) In New Hebrides people in good health are lousier than people with fever. The advice to acquire lice cannot be rationally given, since lice avoid hot bodies [*see* Huff 1954, p. 99; *see also* CAUSATION].

Zero correlation does not imply statistical independence, although it does so for a bivariate normal distribution and for some other special families of distributions.

If there is a positive correlation between A and B and also between B and C, this does not imply that the correlation between A and C is positive, even for a trivariate normal distribution. But the implication *does* follow if the sum of the squares of the first two correlation coefficients exceeds unity.

If the time order is wrong, then causation is unlikely, to say the least. In one survey vaccination was found to be positively correlated with various infectious diseases, when one looked at different districts in India. This was used by antivaccinationists for propaganda. If they had not been emotionally involved, they would probably have noticed that in several districts increased vaccination had *followed* an increase in the incidence of disease (Chambers 1965).

Post hoc, ergo propter hoc ("after this, therefore because of this"). D. O. Moberg, in a lecture in Oxford on February 2, 1965, stated that premarital intercourse seemed to be positively correlated with divorce and inferred that the propensity to divorce was increased by premarital intercourse. The inference *might* be correct, but an equally good explanation is that premarital intercourse and divorce are both largely consequences of the same attitude toward the institution of matrimony. It is also possible that untruthful responses are associated with a propensity to divorce or with a propensity to avoid divorce.

Ecological correlation. Suppose we find that in American *cities* the illiteracy rate and the percentage of foreign-born are associated. This does not imply the same association for *individuals* (see Goodman 1959). It would even be possible that every foreign-born person was highly literate. Cities might attract foreign-born people and also attract or produce illiteracy.

Wrong criteria for suboptimization. Granted that in most decision problems it is not so much a matter of optimization as of "suboptimization," that is, of approximate optimization, there is still an acute problem in choosing *what* to suboptimize. Various fallacies arise through choosing a wrong criterion or through not using a criterion at all (see Koopman 1956; Good 1962). Often a criterion is selected from too narrow a point of view, ignoring questions of consistency with higher-level criteria. For example, when coeducation at New College, Oxford, was being discussed at another Oxford college, the question of the relative requirements for education of men and women was ignored, but the effect on the atmosphere of the senior common room was mentioned. Another fallacy is to ignore the "spillover," or side effects, of some project. Sometimes, when an urgent decision is required, the cost in delay of detailed theory is unjustifiably ignored. At other times the cost of the theory is said to be too heavy, and the fact is overlooked that the results of this theory might be valuable in similar circumstances in the future and that the training of the theoretician is important. Sometimes the criterion of profitability is given too little weight, sometimes too much (see also McKean 1958; Hitch & McKean 1954).

Statistics of statistical fallacies. There is some unpublished work by Christopher Scott on the statistics of statistical fallacies and errors for the specialized field of sample surveys conducted by mail. Scott read the 117 articles and research reports that had been written in English on this topic up to the end of 1960. He excluded 22 of the reports either because they were duplicates of others or because they gave almost no details of method. Of the remaining 95 articles, he found one or more definite errors in 54 and definite shortcomings in another 13. Among the definite errors there were 14 cases in which the experimental variable was not successfully isolated, that is, a change in technique was reported as causing a change in the result, whereas the latter change could reasonably be ascribed to variation in some concomitant variable.

There were 9 cases in which obviously relevant data, such as sample size or response rate, were not reported, and 7 cases in which a necessary significance test was not given. There is not space here for further details, and hopefully they will be published elsewhere.

For misuses of the chi-square test, see Lewis and Burke (1949).

Good fallacies. It is a fallacy to suppose that all fallacies are bad. A clearly self-contradictory epigram can be a neat way of conveying truth or advice, to everybody except quibblers. For example:

"Only a half-truth can be expressed in a nutshell."

"Everything in moderation."

"It would be a *non sequitur* if it were not a tautology."

"Races in which people were immortal became extinct by natural selection."

"There's nothing wrong with chess players that not being people wouldn't put right."

In this article it has been necessary to omit reference to many kinds of fallacies. A more complete listing is given in the categorization of logical and statistical fallacies by Good (1959*b*).

IRVING JOHN GOOD

[*See also* ERRORS, *article on* NONSAMPLING ERRORS.]

BIBLIOGRAPHY

Further literature on fallacies is mentioned in Good 1959b. *In particular,* Thouless 1932 *for fallacies in ordinary reasoning and chapter 3 of* Wallis & Roberts 1956 *for fallacies in statistics are both very useful.* Wagemann 1935 *also gives an interesting general treatment.*

ACKERMANN, ALFRED S. E. (1907) 1950 *Popular Fallacies: A Book of Common Errors, Explained and Corrected With Copious References to Authorities.* 4th ed. London: Old Westminster Press.

BEHRENS, D. J. 1963 High IQ, Low Fertility? Statistical "Non Sequitur." *Mensa Correspondence* (London) no. 50:6 only.

CARTTER, ALLAN M. 1965 A New Look at the Supply of College Teachers. *Educational Record* 46:267–277.

CHAMBERS, S. PAUL 1965 Statistics and Intellectual Integrity. *Journal of the Royal Statistical Society* Series A 128:1–15.

FELLER, WILLIAM 1950–1966 *An Introduction to Probability Theory and Its Applications.* 2 vols. New York: Wiley. → The second edition of Volume 1 was published in 1957.

FISHER, R. A. (1935) 1960 *The Design of Experiments.* 7th ed. New York: Hafner; London: Oliver & Boyd.

FISHER, R. A. (1956) 1959 *Statistical Methods and Scientific Inference.* 2d ed., rev. New York: Hafner; London: Oliver & Boyd.

GOOD, I. J. 1950 *Probability and the Weighing of Evidence.* London: Griffin.

GOOD, I. J. 1956 Which Comes First, Probability or Statistics? *Journal of the Institute of Actuaries* 82:249–255.

GOOD, I. J. 1958a Significance Tests in Parallel and in Series. *Journal of the American Statistical Association* 53:799–813.

GOOD, I. J. 1958b How Much Science Can You Have at Your Fingertips? *IBM Journal of Research and Development* 2:282–288.

GOOD, I. J. 1959a Kinds of Probability. *Science* New Series 129:443–447.

GOOD, I. J. (1959b) 1962 A Classification of Fallacious Arguments and Interpretations. *Technometrics* 4:125–132. → First published in Volume 11 of *Methodos*.

GOOD, I. J. 1960–1961 The Paradox of Confirmation. *British Journal for the Philosophy of Science* 11:145–149; 12:63–64.

GOOD, I. J. (1962) 1965 How Rational Should a Manager Be? Pages 88–98 in *Executive Readings in Management Science*. Edited by Martin K. Starr. New York: Macmillan. → First published in Volume 8 of *Management Science*.

GOOD, I. J. 1963 Quadratics in Markov-chain Frequencies, and the Binary Chain of Order 2. *Journal of the Royal Statistical Society* Series B 25:383–391.

GOOD, I. J. 1965 *The Estimation of Probabilities: An Essay in Modern Bayesian Methods*. Cambridge, Mass.: M.I.T. Press.

GOODMAN, LEO A. 1959 Some Alternatives to Ecological Correlation. *American Journal of Sociology* 64:610–625.

HITCH, CHARLES; and MCKEAN, RONALD 1954 Suboptimization in Operations Problems. Volume 1, pages 168–186 in *Operations Research for Management*. Edited by Joseph F. McCloskey and Florence N. Trefethen. Baltimore: Johns Hopkins Press.

HUFF, DARREL 1954 *How to Lie With Statistics*. New York: Norton. → Also published in paperback edition.

JACKSON, JOHN H. (1931) 1958 *Selected Writings of John Hughlings Jackson*. Vol. 2. Edited by James Taylor. New York: Basic Books.

KIMBALL, A. W. 1957 Errors of the Third Kind in Statistical Consulting. *Journal of the American Statistical Association* 52:133–142.

KOOPMAN, B. O. 1956 Fallacies in Operations Research. *Journal of the Operations Research Society of America* 4:422–426.

LEWIS, D.; and BURKE, C. J. 1949 The Use and Misuse of the Chi-square Test. *Psychological Bulletin* 46:433–489. → Discussions of the article may be found in subsequent issues of this bulletin: 47:331–337, 338–340, 341–346, 347–355; 48:81–82.

MCKEAN, RONALD N. 1958 The Criterion Problem. Pages 25–49 in Ronald N. McKean, *Efficiency in Government Through Systems Analysis*. New York: Wiley.

MEDAWAR, PETER B. 1960 *The Future of Man*. New York: Basic Books; London: Methuen.

MORONEY, M. J. (1951) 1958 *Facts From Figures*. 3d ed., rev. Harmondsworth (England): Penguin.

PENFIELD, WILDER; and ROBERTS, LAMAR 1959 *Speech and Brain-mechanisms*. Princeton Univ. Press.

ROWE, P. 1962 What the Dons Earn. *The Sunday Times* (London) October 21.

SLATER, ELIOT; and BEARD, A. W. 1963 The Schizophrenia-like Psychoses of Epilepsy: Psychiatric Aspects. *British Journal of Psychiatry* 109:95–112.

STARNES, RICHARD 1962 Age of Falsehood. *Trenton Evening Times* December 19.

STERLING, THEODORE D. 1959 Publication Decisions and Their Possible Effects on Inferences Drawn From Tests of Significance—Or Vice Versa. *Journal of the American Statistical Association* 54:30–34.

THOULESS, ROBERT H. (1932) 1947 *How to Think Straight*. New York: Simon & Schuster. → First published as *Straight and Crooked Thinking*.

WAGEMANN, ERNST F. (1935) 1950 *Narrenspiegel der Statistik; Die Umrisse eines statistischen Weltbildes*. 3d ed. Salzburg (Austria): Verlag "Das Bergland-Buch."

WALLIS, W. ALLEN; and ROBERTS, HARRY V. 1956 *Statistics: A New Approach*. Glencoe, Ill.: Free Press. → An abridged paperback edition was published in 1965 by the Free Press.

FAMILY

The articles under this heading discuss the central aspects of the family as a universal institution in society. Closely related are the entries KINSHIP; MARRIAGE. *The reproduction function of the family is discussed in* FERTILITY; FERTILITY CONTROL; *the socializing function of the family is reviewed in* SOCIALIZATION *as well as in* CULTURE AND PERSONALITY; DEVELOPMENTAL PSYCHOLOGY; INFANCY; PERSONALITY, *article on* PERSONALITY DEVELOPMENT; MORAL DEVELOPMENT. *Stages in family life are reviewed in* ADOLESCENCE; AGING; DEATH; LIFE CYCLE; *as well as in* FAMILY, *article on* DISORGANIZATION AND DISSOLUTION. *Specialized aspects of the family are reviewed in* ADOPTION; AFFECTION; INCEST; NUPTIALITY; PATERNALISM; SEXUAL BEHAVIOR. *Many anthropologists, psychologists, and sociologists have contributed to an understanding of the family; the following biographies are of particular relevance:* BACHOFEN; BURGESS; ENGELS; FRAZER; FREUD; GESELL; HALL; LE PLAY; MCLENNAN; MAINE; MALINOWSKI; MORGAN, LEWIS HENRY; RADCLIFFE-BROWN; TYLOR; WALLER; WESTERMARCK.

I

COMPARATIVE STRUCTURE

One of the few widely accepted generalizations of social science asserts that "the family" is an institution found in all human societies. There is controversy over just what constitutes the family and what its functions might be, but the generalization itself is widely accepted. In modern Euro–American societies it is accepted that the normal family is a coresidential group which consists of a married couple and their own children and which lives apart from other kin. This has become the reference type for comparative study, and it is argued that in modern, highly differentiated societies such as those of North America and Europe the family has become a highly specialized agency exhibiting the *essential* and irreducible characteristics which are significant for cross-cultural comparison (Parsons & Bales 1955, p. 10).

In all human societies provision must be made for biological and social reproduction if the society is to continue, and it is generally assumed that the family performs at least these functions. Mating is never simply random, and children require a long period of care by a limited number of individuals with whom they develop relations of intimacy if they are to grow up as normal human beings capable of playing adult roles. This conclusion is based partly upon experimental evidence (Bowlby 1951) and partly upon inference from the fact that in all known societies children are raised in small kinship-based groups and there are customary modes of regulation between children and their socially recognized parents and between the parents themselves. Looked at in this way there is a very close relationship between the family and the domestic group, and both constitute systems of relationship which vary over time. The form of these systems is tied to the physical processes of individual birth, maturation, and death, so that families, like individuals, pass through developmental stages (Fortes 1958). The processes of individual maturation and death are social as well as physical, since individuals are participants in social systems as well as in biological processes. Societies live longer than either individuals or families, but societies exist only through the patterned interaction of individuals who share common understandings. Mating and procreation provide for the continuity of the biological species, while socialization relates it to the equally important continuity of social structure and cultural pattern. It has been argued on both theoretical and empirical grounds that the primary function of the family is socialization, so that an intimate relation is established between biological and social processes, a relation which is reflected in the dependence of demographic trends upon social custom.

The generalizations set out above seem to hold true in a large number of different societies, but it is not certain to what extent the observations and descriptions used have been influenced by the definitions adopted by field investigators. Some writers have expressed doubt that the family is a universal human institution, but both the assertion and its refutation depend upon some agreed identification of what is being discussed.

Definitions

Domestic groups.   A domestic group may be defined as a group of people who habitually share a common dwelling and a common food supply. These minimal activities of domestic groups may be greatly extended, and domestic groups may vary in size and stability. The word "family" has its origin in a Latin word which could be roughly equated with "domestic group," but for sociological purposes the two must be sharply distinguished. Domestic groups may be made up of individuals between whom no kinship ties exist, and, conversely, members of one family may be distributed over two or more domestic groups. The term "household" may be used interchangeably with "domestic group."

Biological family.   In Euro–American societies the basic model of kinship and family ties is that of biological relatedness and sexual intercourse, so that kin and familial relations are thought of in terms of physical descent or sexual relations. This is not so in all societies, even though it appears that family relations are almost invariably intimately associated with sexual regulation and reproduction. Social relations of family and kinship can develop independently of genetic links or sexual relations, so that adoption or other forms of fictive kinship are just as real as blood ties. Even where actual genetic links exist they do not constitute *social* relations; these must be learned and developed separately. Similarly, marriage is always more than sexual mating. Schneider (see *Aspects of the Analysis . . .* 1965) has expressed in a particularly pointed and convincing way the objections to confusing an analytical definition of kinship with definitions stressing biological relatedness.

The relation between mother and child appears to be in a rather special category, since the human infant is part of its mother's physical being before birth and continues to be dependent upon her or a substitute for a considerable period afterward. The development of artificial feeding has modified this close dependence, but experience in rearing motherless infants has shown that adverse effects result from deprivation of close continuous contact with a mother figure in early infancy. The "mother figure" can be any suitable person, and experiments with monkeys have shown that, for them, even contraptions of wire and cloth can serve as "mothers" in some sense. This raises the question of just what we mean when we use words such as "mother" and should lead to a careful distinction between the activities involved in mothering on the one hand and the biological relationship of the mother to the child on the other. In the case of the father–child relationship, the more frequent disjunction between biological and social paternity has led to a distinction between *pater* and *genitor*. The former term is used to refer to a child's legally recognized father and the latter to his supposed biological father. In some societies a child's father (*pater*) may be a woman or a dead man. Among the Nuer of east Africa, the kin of a man killed in war before he had married would sometimes marry a woman to "his name." After payment of the bride price the woman cohabited with a lover, but any children born to her were the legal offspring of the dead "husband," inheriting from him and sacrificing to him as their ancestor. Cases such as this make clear the differences between biological and social links, and although the family is frequently, or even usually, coincident with a particular constellation of biological links, it cannot be defined in terms of them.

Nuclear family.   The term "nuclear family" (or "elementary," "simple," or "basic") is most frequently used to refer to a group consisting of a man, a woman, and their socially recognized children. This is a straightforward use of the term; it refers to concrete groups, and the qualification "nuclear" suggests that this is the unit out of which more extensive family groups are built or grow. The group need not be coresidential provided regular relationships are maintained among its members. It need not exist as a separate and isolated entity but may be contained within more extensive groups provided it is given some recognition. It has been suggested that the nuclear family is *the* universal form of family relations, always fulfilling "distinctive and vital functions—sexual, economic, reproductive, and educational . . ." (Murdock 1949, p. 3). "The nuclear family is a universal human social grouping. Either as the sole prevailing form of the family or as the basic unit from which more complex familial forms are compounded, it exists as a distinct and strongly functional group in every known society" (p. 2). The evidence for this statement is far from conclusive, and much of it that does seem to support the generalization may be biased simply because of the way in which the data have been collected and presented. Cases such as the Nayar and the Ashanti (see below) tend to disprove the assertion, and this has now been recognized by Murdock.

Parsons has argued that the nuclear family exhibits characteristics which seem to be necessary (on theoretical grounds) for the socialization of children and the stabilization of adult personalities (Parsons & Bales 1955). He has argued elsewhere that the incest taboo is also universal in human societies for similar reasons and that taboo results in the perpetual creation of new nuclear-family groups through marriage (Parsons 1954). Even if one accepts the ideas that sexual intercourse must be regulated and that children must be cared for and socialized within small groups with the characteristics exhibited by the nuclear family, this does not necessarily mean that the nuclear family, as defined by Murdock, is universal. Levy and Fallers (1959) have suggested that a distinction should be made between the nuclear family as a concrete group and the "nuclear-family relationship complex." The latter would consist of the relationships of husband–wife, mother–son, mother–daughter, father–son, father–daughter, brother–sister, brother–brother, and sister–sister considered as a system of interaction between roles. By looking at the nuclear family as a system of roles rather than as a concrete grouping of individuals, it is possible to see that role behavior appropriate to this complex might be distributed among a number of individuals, groups, or agencies that do not themselves constitute a single group. Malinowski showed that certain aspects of what he considered to be the normal "father" role are played by the mother's brother in some societies with matrilineal inheritance and descent. Similarly, in some societies the "mother" role is played in whole or in part by mother surrogates, such as mother's sisters, mother's mothers, paid nurses, or teachers. In order to make statements such as these it is necessary to assume that we know what the "real" or "normal" nuclear-family role complex is, and here it is evident that there is a tendency to take the Euro–American family pattern as the type case. Despite this drawback, the concentration of attention upon a role complex rather than concrete groups is a step toward freeing the concept of nuclear family from the rigidity imposed upon it by Murdock. If one asserts that the nuclear-family relationship complex is institutionalized in all human societies—instead of speaking of the universal occurrence of nuclear-family *groups*—then it is possible to account for the normal development of children brought up in groups that are not nuclear families in the restricted sense. Where one parent is missing or no siblings are present, children may still be affected by the institutionalized nuclear-family role complex, different elements of which are activated by other kinsmen, neighbors, teachers, or even more remote individuals. We may also relate the necessary biological and social functions to this role complex rather than to concrete nuclear families and leave it to empirical investigation to show just how the roles are embodied in a particular society. While this goes some way toward freeing investigation from the analytical restrictions imposed by the concept of the universality of the nuclear family, there are good grounds for going even further and asking just what is meant by the roles involved in the supposedly universal nuclear-family role complex.

Compound family.   The term "compound family" is used to refer to a concrete group formed through the amalgamation of nuclear-family units or parts of them. A polygynous household consisting of one man, his three wives, and their respective children would constitute a compound family, as would a family group constituted by remarried widows or divorcees with children from a previous marriage. A compound family need not constitute a coresidential group.

Joint family.   According to the handbook *Notes and Queries on Anthropology* (see British Association . . . 1874), a joint family exists when "two or more lineally related kinsfolk of the same sex, their spouses and offspring, occupy a single homestead and are jointly subject to the same authority or single head." An example would be a group consisting of a man and his wife with their married sons and their wives and children. It would be wrong to think of such a group as being a mere mechanical aggregate of nuclear families. Joint families generally arise, exist, and persist because they carry out activities more extensive than would be possible for a nuclear-family group. Joint families grow as younger members bring in spouses rather than setting up independent households. As the younger married couples beget children, it may be possible to detect the existence of a number of nuclear-family cells within the structure of the joint family. The younger married couples will often have their own living quarters and may establish their own cooking facilities. If they have their own budgetary arrangements, then the joint family has really split—even if the young couples do not actually move out of the house. On the other hand, the joint family may be such a cohesive unit that it is difficult to see nuclear families within it as separate groups in any meaningful sense. The men may form one solidary group and the women another; the children may regard all the women of the house as their "mothers." Eventually, as the original family grows too big,

the joint family will either split or some persons will leave to form separate groups.

Extended family.   An extended family is a dispersed version of the joint family. That is, the members of the constituent groups of an extended family do not all live together in one dwelling. They usually live close together and engage in common activities.

The concept of extended family really exhausts the usefulness of the word "family" for this kind of empirical classification, since an extended family is already a short lineage and can be discussed in terms of lineage theory, or it is a kindred and may be analyzed as such. Since birth is the criterion of membership in lineages and kindreds, they tend to develop considerable interest in the birth, training, and ultimate loyalties of their recruits, so that there is a close fit between these formations and the "families" which provide and train the recruits.

Comparative family studies

Because they are a part of all human experience and such a powerful agency in the formation of adult attitudes, familial relations have always been a subject of interest and discussion. Their changing and varied forms have been studied by such diverse and ancient disciplines as theology, classics, law, and philosophy. This interest quickened during the period known in Europe as the Enlightenment, but it was the late nineteenth-century interest in evolution that stimulated extensive comparative studies of family forms. Fantastic theories were proposed in an attempt to reconstruct the history of mankind and to account for the existence of seemingly pointless customs and strange kinship terminologies among non-European peoples. Bachofen's postulated development of society from promiscuity through a great period of mother right and female dominance to father right and patriarchy was an attempt to account for the recognized importance of matrilineal descent systems and the universal importance of motherhood. Other writers of the period argued in much the same way, although disagreeing on developmental priorities. Such writers as Sir Henry Maine, Edward Tylor, J. F. McLennan, Lewis H. Morgan, Friedrich Engels, Sir James Frazer, E. Westermarck, and Robert Briffault carried forward the debate on origins, and, although their theories were highly speculative, they encompassed a wide range of cases and paid particular attention to historical sources. Despite the shortcomings of both theories and sources, these writers laid the foundations for modern studies by systematizing existing information on the family, and they are still worth reading for their insight into problems that have been neglected.

It is surprising that students of the family have not paid more attention to a series of basic sociological works which concern themselves with the classification of social relationships. Maine, Tönnies, and Durkheim, in particular, set up dichotomous categories which they believed to represent fundamentally different types of social relationship: relations of status as opposed to contract; relations of *Gemeinschaft* as opposed to *Gesellschaft;* mechanical versus organic solidarity. In all these systems one pole was most clearly represented by relations of a familial or kinship type. Since it was generally assumed that we know what familial relations are, this reference was intended to be illustrative, although Tönnies, in his *Gemeinschaft und Gesellschaft*, attempted to show how natural will develops within the complex of relations that go to make up the family. The crux of the matter is that what we term familial relations are relations exhibiting a particular kind of solidarity that involves persons in total and permanent social relations. This type of relationship is contrasted with the partial and specialized character of *Gesellschaft* or contractual relations. Just where the boundaries of familial relations are drawn varies from one society or subgroup to another and is, of course, affected by a large number of empirical factors.

Intensive field-work methods developed during the early twentieth century by Boas, Kroeber, Lowie, and others in the United States and by Malinowski and Radcliffe-Brown in Britain produced a new body of detailed information on kinship, marriage, and the family. Malinowski's work on the family in Australia and Melanesia was a study of primitive matriliny and was intended to show (in part at least) that the nuclear family emerges naturally even where there is ignorance of the male role in the physiological process of reproduction. The Trobriand Islanders studied by Malinowski asserted that children are conceived when a spirit enters the body of a woman and that sexual intercourse is simply a matter of mutual satisfaction to the persons involved. Malinowski was impressed by the fact that men developed important social relationships with their wives' children even though they did not consider that there was any biological connection involved. Furthermore, men did not exercise the kind of authority over their children that is often associated with "paternity"; the mother's brother was more important in that respect. He concluded from these observations that the nuclear family is a universal institution but does not al-

ways assume the emotional configuration suggested by Freud's theory of the Oedipus complex; it is rather a "functional formation dependent upon the structure and upon the culture of a society" (Malinowski [1927] 1953, pp. 142–143). The implication of this idea was that the nuclear-family complex could be activated by various persons and agencies—in the case of societies with matrilineal descent groups it may be that repressed hatred between uncle and nephew replaces that found between father and son in patriarchal societies.

Radcliffe-Brown's brilliant and lucid treatment of the jural significance of kinship ties enabled him to look at the family in terms of the formal duties, rights, and obligations between the members and between them and external groups. Whereas Malinowski regarded wider kinship ties as "mere extensions" of the nuclear-family complex and the sentiments generated within it, Radcliffe-Brown spoke of the varying modes of incorporation, for jural purposes, of the unit of mother and children. He saw the relationship between a mother and her children as being somehow "basic" because of the close emotional and nurturant ties involved, while other kinship ties could be stressed or neglected to varying degrees depending upon the structure of the whole social and kinship system. In other words, Radcliffe-Brown's concern was not with the family as a locus of emotional solidarity, or socialization functions, or sexual satisfactions; he was more concerned to explore the ways in which the empirical reference points of birth, sexual relations, and child rearing could be variously stressed for legal purposes. Apart from the apparent invariability of the mother–child relationship, he was prepared to accept the fact that all the other activities and functions could be distributed in widely varying ways.

In the generation since these pioneers of field investigation, detailed work has been carried out in many parts of the world, yielding new information and continuous refinement of theory. The development of the Yale cross-cultural survey is an attempt to organize material from a wide range of sources in order to make inductive generalizations about human societies or to test particular hypotheses. Other writers make similar generalizations based upon a more selective use of sources. In either case it is evident that the generalizations are no better than the observations on which they are based. This is well demonstrated by Murdock's generalizations based on the cross-cultural survey files. Observations reported in monographic studies depend to a considerable extent upon the investigator's preconceived ideas and categories or upon his interests. In the field of family studies all these may be severely limited.

Parallel to the development of a wide-ranging comparative study of kinship and family structure, there has been a continuing tradition of interest in the family life of Europe and America. In the nineteenth century, Le Play constructed a typology of European family structures ranging from the patriarchal systems of the semifeudal eastern European areas, which resulted in the development of extended families, through the *famille-souche*, or stem-family, of the semi-industrial areas to what he considered to be the unstable and disorganized systems of the urban industrial areas. Le Play's typology, or something very like it, seems to have regained favor as a universal system of classification (see Levy in *Aspects of the Analysis . . . 1965*). The stem-family type is of particular interest because it seems to combine an emphasis upon the ideal of family continuity with an actual situation where most of the domestic units are small and self-liquidating.

As a result of their work on the development of capitalism and its institutional structure, Marx and Engels became interested in the development of the family, an interest which was quickened by the publication of Lewis H. Morgan's *Ancient Society* (1877). Marx read this work and made extensive notes on it, but it was Engels who published an extensive commentary on it after Marx's death, under the title *The Origin of the Family, Private Property and the State*. In this work Marx's general theories of social and economic history are combined with Morgan's speculative history of kinship institutions. The most general conclusion of the book is that a stable monogamous family system, dominated by male authority and prescribed and supported by law, has really developed as a device for the perpetuation of the private ownership of property. This conclusion has been widely misinterpreted to mean that Engels was opposed to any sort of family relationships and that the family should be abolished in socialist societies. On the contrary, Engels went out of his way to point out that the emotional and sexual elements involved in family relations can only be paramount when considerations of property do not enter into the picture. Thus, he argued that the proletariat make and break marital unions only upon the basis of mutual attraction, whereas in bourgeois marriage the conjugal pair are indissolubly united even when they have no love for each other and perhaps engage in adultery with other available partners.

The influence of Freud's work upon comparative family studies can only be mentioned in passing. It has produced some of the most penetrating hypotheses concerning the content of family relationships, particularly in European and American societies where psychoanalysis' has been most widely practiced as a therapeutic technique. Studies of the relation between culture and personality focus upon the familial milieu as the context of personality development, and students of this field have produced some of the most detailed and intimate documentation of family life in non-Western cultures. It is also evident that Freud's thought has influenced the formation of hypotheses about the nature and functions of family structure, at least since the work of Malinowski.

Theoretical and research problems

Despite the considerable time and effort devoted to family studies and despite the refinement of definitions and the improvement of concepts, our knowledge of the family remains rudimentary. We use the term "family" in the loosest possible way, perhaps because of the very nature of the data themselves. For comparative study it is necessary to exercise great care in the construction of theoretical models in order to avoid distortions in observation and description. The bulk of family theory is derived from the Euro–American cultural tradition and from the study of European and American societies. The development and extension of psychoanalysis has produced both a large collection of empirical data and a growing sophistication in its interpretation. But this has been accompanied by a tendency to attribute functional necessity to observed patterns, so that there is a danger of assuming that the functions performed by small family groups in Euro–American societies *must* be performed by similar groups, similarly defined and constituted, in all societies. Parsons (see Parsons & Bales 1955) has tried to show the systematic relation between nuclear-family structure on the one hand and socialization for participation in wider social systems on the other. This analysis is very convincing in its establishment of the general conditions which seem to be necessary for adequate human socialization, but those conditions can be expressed in very general terms and could be met by a wide variety of actual persons and groups. If the nuclear family is to be thought of as that group that carries out primary socialization, then it is necessary to investigate the empirical composition of such groups in a wide range of societies.

Should we continue to use the model of nuclear family or even of nuclear-family relationship complex as a measure for cross-cultural comparison?

Is this anything more than a device for making all observations fit our conception of what should exist? Or is it mainly a problem of language? Will more flexible terms that are not derived directly from a particular cultural tradition enable us to overcome these difficulties? Similar problems have arisen in debates over the question of whether all societies have "law" or "a political system." In spite of some recent defense of the idea of the universality of the nuclear family from linguistic analysts (Lounsbury 1965), it would seem to be desirable to keep an open mind on the question.

Much of the work already done in the study of comparative family structure has been based upon the collection of information about norms, that is, the ideal modes of behavior in different societies; and, as we have suggested above, these have usually been translated into terms of the norms of Euro–American society. Many anthropologists have supplemented interview data and informant's statements with case material, genealogical investigation, sample surveys, and statistical analyses. The aim has been either to try to determine what the system "really is" or to discover the manner in which norms work out in practice. Pioneering work in this regard was done by Audrey Richards, John Barnes, and Meyer Fortes. Fortes has always stressed the importance of regarding the family as a process in time and of looking at the cyclical development of family structure. As the individuals who compose family groups grow older and as new members are born and others die, the structure of the group changes as well as the relationships between the individuals concerned. New possibilities for this type of analysis are presented by the development of computers. With the aid of these machines it is possible to simulate the experience of a whole community of families over a long time period by constructing models of family structure or household composition and then applying to them such variable elements as birth and death rates, age at marriage, duration of unions, and fertility patterns. In this way it is possible to determine what varieties of family and household types would be produced under varying circumstances over varying time periods.

A major controversy that has developed within anthropology has considerable bearing on the whole subject of comparative family studies. This controversy starts with Lévi-Strauss' idea that the building block of kinship systems is not the biological or nuclear family but a constellation of roles which includes the siblings of a marrying couple as well as their children. In disagreeing with Radcliffe-Brown's contention that it is the relations between

members of the "elementary family" that constitute the unit of structure from which all kinship systems are built, he says:

Of course, the biological family is ubiquitous in human society. But what confers upon kinship its socio-cultural character is not what it retains from nature, but, rather, the essential way in which it diverges from nature. A kinship system does not consist in the objective ties of descent or consanguinity between individuals. . . . The essence of human kinship is to require the establishment of relations among what Radcliffe-Brown calls "elementary families." Thus, it is not the families (isolated terms) which are truly "elementary," but, rather, the relations between those terms.   (Lévi-Strauss [1958] 1963, pp. 50–51)

From this starting point Lévi-Strauss proceeds to a complex analysis of preferential and prescriptive marriage systems, but the perspective which he introduced leads to a new assessment of intrafamilial relations.

Briefly, the question is whether the relations of nuclear family and of filiation always constitute a basic "natural" system which tends to counterbalance particular kinship ties stressed for jural purposes, or whether we should regard nuclear-family relations as being nothing more than a fortuitous complex of highly variable relations some of which may be dispensed with altogether. For example, if filiation is always bilateral (because every child must have a "father" and a "mother"), then where patrilineal descent is stressed for jural purposes the strong jural tie between father and child will be balanced by the tie between mother and child and, by extension, between the child and its mother's kin—a tie of complementary filiation. Conversely, it could be argued that where matrilineal descent is stressed, a compensating bond will exist between father and children and between the child and the father's kin. The point to be noted in this argument is that the ties between parents and children may be accorded great legal significance or may be simply affective, but they derive ultimately from the bonds of filiation and descent which arise within the nuclear-family relationship complex. These relations are socially rather than biologically defined, but they focus upon activities which are familial.

The contrary view is that relationships between a child and its parents may derive from the fact that the parents are married to each other rather than from any bond of filiation. Thus, the Trobriand Islanders assert that there is no genetic link between fathers and their children. A man is a "father" because he is the husband of the child's mother. Of course this ideological view of the matter seems to be related to the political and legal sphere rather than to the field of domestic relations, where fatherhood may be rooted in a set of activities rather than a set of abstract principles.

It is not necessary to document the details of this controversy here; adequate references will be found in Leach (1961) and Schneider (see Association of Social Anthropologists . . . 1966). The point of interest here is Leach's contention that relations between children and parents may be as variable as any other social relations and that we should be prepared to find societies in which even the mother–child relationship is conceived of as one wholly derivative from the fact of the mother's marriage to the father, who is thought of as the person with whom the child has a real consanguineal relationship. In such a situation the mother is an affine; she is not "mother" necessarily at all, but "father's wife."

The controversy outlined here does not focus upon the internal relations or the structure of the family as such; it is concerned with an understanding of the structure of total social systems. But it does bring into quite sharp focus the need to abandon a dogmatic view of the universality of nuclear-family relations and the need to differentiate clearly between the activities involved in domestic relations, the facts of biological interconnectedness, and the interlocking of familial and wider kinship relations. It seems likely that future research will operate with a bigger collection of more differentiated concepts derived from a splitting up of such notions as descent, filiation, sibling bonds, alliance, and, of course, the general notion of nuclear family.

Throughout the discussion so far it has been assumed that comparative family studies refer to comparisons between different *societies* and that "structure" means societal norms. Some of the most interesting modern research is concerned with the study of differences in family structure *within* societies; studies which throw light upon the nature of society itself. It has long been recognized that the structure of family relations appears to vary with class, ethnic group, and other factors. This raises the question of whether the variation lies at the level of culture (that is, in the norms themselves) or whether the actual distribution of empirically ordered "types" of family is the result of constraints operating to prevent the full realization of cultural ideals. For example, it is generally accepted that Hindus value a joint family system in which marriages are contracted at an early age and are indissoluble and in which brides are brought to live in their husband's father's house, where they

come under the authority of the senior woman and the men form a corporate group. In fact, it would seem that such ideal patterns are met only by the wealthier families, where a common interest in property serves as a binding factor, while the poorer families tend to be small and to consist of only a couple with their own minor children. It has also been suggested that the size of households would be limited under preindustrial conditions everywhere by the early death of parents and high infant mortality rates. Such arguments ignore the fact that purely demographic constraints can be circumvented, since family and kinship relations are not biological relations and since adoption or other forms of culturally defined kinship ties can be used as the basis of household formation.

Important though adoption and the collapsing of relationships may be as a means of keeping functioning groups intact, it must be realized that the exigencies of birth-and-death rates and other demographic variables do have an effect upon household composition, just as the biological processes of maturation have an effect. Sociologically, a more important consideration is the extent to which norms vary from group to group and result in the precipitation of different configurations of family organization. In the United States there has been discussion of "the culture of poverty" in relation to the incidence of fatherless families among lower-status and lower-income groups. In such cases it is difficult to determine whether the pattern of family living among these lower-income groups is determined by a simple inability to command the means of achieving valued patterns of behavior or whether different values are operative. In such cases the study of family life becomes a very sensitive index to the whole mode of integration of the over-all social system. This question is discussed further below.

Although knowledge of the genesis of emotional disturbance and social deviance is much more extensive than it was 25 years ago, it is still inadequate. The complexity of the relationship system of family groups is understood in only the most general terms despite the considerable body of detailed information pertaining to Euro–American families. The profound hatreds and bitter rivalries which are the counterpart of the relations of familial solidarity are well known to anthropologists, both as the source of conflicts with political and economic significance and as the basis of witchcraft beliefs and magical and religious practices. These conflicts are the product of the interaction systems themselves within small "multibonded" groups and may have considerable significance for wider system organization. It has often been remarked that the family is the unit within which primary socialization takes place and within which the growing child is taught the ultimate value orientations of the whole society. This is not necessarily done formally, but the values may be implicit in the general structure of the familial relationship system itself. If this is so, then it is important to know how these relationships are structured in different societies and just how the values are internalized by the growing child.

The range of variability

In the large Ashanti villages of central Ghana one can often see children carrying pots of food from their mother's house to the house of their father. The children may eat with their father and then go home to sleep at the house where their mother lives, while the mother may visit the father for the night. This pattern of divided residence and visiting back and forth seems to exist because the Ashanti traditional social system stresses matrilineal descent for important social purposes, such as inheritance of land, succession to office, and political status. Women often value the tie to their brother as highly as, or higher than, the relationship to their husband, since it is from the brother that their children will inherit. Because the child's place in society is mainly determined through its relationship to its mother and her matrilineal kin, the breaking of a marital tie is of little legal consequence either for the spouses or for the children. It is true that fathers have always had responsibility for the upbringing of their own children, including the provision of food and the teaching of crafts and skills, but these duties could be carried out even when the child did not reside with the father and even after the parents had broken their conjugal tie. According to Fortes (1949) another factor inducing women to remain in their own homes even after marriage is the very close relationship between mother and children, and particularly between mothers and daughters. This case demonstrates the way in which interests and relationships can cut right across the solidarity of the nuclear family, and it would be very difficult to demonstrate that the nuclear family is either a normal or a necessary coresidential unit among the Ashanti. The Ashanti concept of family is quite different from the European concept; Fortes mentions that persons who speak English often say, "Your mother is your family, your father is not."

The most extreme and best known example of the effect of matrilineal descent upon familial relationships was to be found among the Nayar caste of southern India in the period before the full effects of British rule were felt. Among the Nayar, it appears that the marital relationship was reduced to a merely symbolic level, being contracted at around the time that the girl reached puberty and shortly thereafter being ritually broken. Afterward, the women were allowed to have informal love affairs with men who visited them at night. The households consisted of a group of brothers and their sisters and the sisters' children, and any children born to the woman of the household became members of the matrilineal joint family. The children were discouraged from developing any strong attachments to either their *pater* or *genitor*, and while it would be impossible to argue that the role of father was completely absent from this social system, it was obviously diminished in favor of the solidarity of the property-owning matrilineal group. It seems likely that many of the functions that are normally fulfilled by fathers in relation to socialization and personality development were carried out by male members of the matrilineage (Gough 1952).

Cases such as these have led some writers, including Radcliffe-Brown, to suggest that the basic structural unit of kinship systems is the unit of mother and children, in other words, to separate the nuclear family into a number of paired relationships, or dyads, and to see how, in differing societies, they fit in relation to each other and to other groups. This is certainly a step in the right direction toward loosening the categories involved in the nuclear-family complex and exploring more fully their independent connections. Even in societies with pronounced patriarchal authority we find that the mother–children unit often forms an important subgroup, given special recognition and marked by close emotional ties among its members.

Among the Swazi as described by Hilda Kuper (see Radcliffe-Brown & Forde 1950), descent, inheritance of economically valuable possessions, and succession to office is patrilineal, but women are given a position of great prominence in the organization of domestic life. Homesteads are built in the form of a semicircular group of huts surrounding a cattle pen, each hut being occupied by a mother and her children. In the center of the arc is the "great hut" occupied by the mother of the male head of the compound (or one of his senior wives if his mother is dead). When a young man or a group of full brothers sets up a new homestead, their mother is installed in the place of honor, for it was she who reared them, watched over their rights, guarded their inheritance, fed and nurtured them. The father is respected as the head of the group, revered, and eventually worshiped as an ancestor, but the mother is loved and cherished. This pattern is common in patriarchal societies where the father is an authoritarian figure and the holder of property that the heir requires in order to attain full maturity—thus introducing an underlying tension into the formally respectful relationship. Parsons has suggested that the father role is always an "instrumental" one as opposed to the more emotional or "expressive" quality of the mother role (Parsons & Bales 1955, pp. 157–158). In a penetrating study comparing two adjacent groups in west Africa which share a basically similar culture, Goody has shown that in one of them the matrilineal inheritance of certain types of property alters the interpersonal relationships between close kin and even alters the mode of ancestor worship (1962). Since intrafamilial relationship patterns seem to be so responsive to the effect of outside influences, it is premature to assert too many conclusions about the structure of the nuclear family as such. The specialization of males and females in instrumental and expressive roles may be an aspect of sex-role differentiation in this case rather than of role specialization within a small group structure. Certainly women take on instrumental roles in the absence of men, but they retain the predominantly expressive quality appropriate to females.

In tribal societies where kinship is the basis of recruitment to all or most important social roles, the family must articulate directly with descent groups and becomes a mechanism for the continuous generation of new kinship ties. As Fortes says, "the workshop, so to speak, of social reproduction, is the domestic group" (Goody 1958, p. 2). In more differentiated social systems with an increased division of labor, a literary tradition, and a well-developed class or caste system, it is still true that families may be large, multifunctional units. In China and India, for example, the whole weight of tradition, values, and religious sentiment favored the growth of large patrilineal joint families and patriarchal authority. The uneven distribution of wealth and status seems to affect the realization of these ideals, so that the majority of households are small and contain only parents and children. This is not simply a matter of demographic determinism; the absence of a sufficient property base leads to the early secession of mature sons, who try to make out for themselves. Large joint families are found mainly among landowning and merchant groups, where sons have a continuing material interest in the patrimony to reinforce and sustain filial piety. Such large "families" are really lineages or descent groups which constitute perpetual corporations managing a common enterprise.

Le Play thought of the *famille-souche*, or stem-family, as preserving familial continuity while adapting to the demands of industrialism. While many of the younger members of the family migrated or went off to work in industrial centers, the main family, or stem, continued and was usually located on its own land or in its own house. A regular mode of inheritance designed to prevent fragmentation was imposed to ensure both the continuity and the integrity of the familial estate. The existence of such a system in twentieth-century rural Ireland has been described by Arensberg and Kimball (1940), and its presence in parts of the United States has been depicted (Zimmerman & Frampton 1935). On the small farms of rural Ireland it is customary for one son to inherit the family farm, while the other children marry out or migrate to the towns. The heir usually postpones his marriage until his father is nearly ready to hand over control, thus ensuring that the farm will not have to support more persons than it can carry and ensuring the continuity of one male line on an undivided farm. The stem-family is not a product of industrial society. Recent work by Laslett indicates that the preindustrial family system in England did not encourage the growth of large extended families occupying single dwellings; on the contrary, the nuclear-family household seems to have been the normal type of dwelling group, and when large household groups are found, they appear to have been made up by servants or craft laborers rather than by kin. There was also a continuous process of downward mobility in which the children of wealthy or high-status families were sloughed off into lower positions, while the main heir took over an intact patrimony (Laslett 1965).

The urban family system of modern Europe and America developed out of the system found in agrarian society (or "the world we have lost," as Laslett terms it). It has been a constant preoccupation of writers on the modern family to think of it as being somehow stripped of functions and reduced to a pale shadow of its former ample self. The ideal is that of a nuclear-family group living in its own house independently of other kin and subsisting upon the wages or salary of the husband–father. Falling birth rates, an increase in the incidence of divorce, a decline in home food processing, clothes making, and so on—all these have been held to signify a decline in family living and a shift toward increasing individualism and material values. Parsons and others have argued that the family system of the urban United States is not a denuded form of a more "normal" or "natural" family system but is itself a highly specialized form that articulates most satisfactorily with a highly differentiated economic and political system and with institutionalized values that stress achievement rather than inheritance. It is argued that the smallness and relative isolation of the family from other kinship ties is an adaptation that makes possible the spatial and status mobility of its members. The unit of mother and children remains the basic affective group within which there is close emotional identification, and the husband–father is closely integrated with it both emotionally and in terms of his status-conferring and economic-support functions. It is upon his position in the occupational system that the status and the style of life of the whole family group depends. This functional interpretation of the importance of the nuclear family in industrial society may be considerably weakened by the work of Laslett, referred to above. If the nuclear family has been the major form of European family structure for many centuries, predating the industrial revolution, and if this family form was the product of social values rather than of demographic or other constraints, then the modern family forms may be simply the continuation of a culturally preferred form.

Studies of the structure of kinship and family relations in modern industrial societies are rare in spite of the considerable literature on special problems of family living. Recent work in Britain has shown that lower-class families often live in close proximity to near kin and maintain intimate contact with them despite the "isolation" of the nuclear family (Young & Willmott 1957). The cooperation between mother and married daughters is particularly noticeable, and most writers have remarked upon the great importance of women in their role as mothers of grown-up children. Fathers are important, of course, as wage earners and supporters of their families, but in the lower class the status of the family tends to be fixed less by the occupation of the husband–father than by birth into a particular neighborhood and class. The network of relations between female kin is reinforced by daily contact, mutual help, and support in times of economic hardship, and is balanced by a tendency for men to spend their leisure time together rather than with the members of their own nuclear family.

A more extreme form of matrifocal family structure occurs in low-status ethnic groups where there appears to be some correlation with insecurity in male employment. In the plantation areas of the southern United States, the West Indies, and Latin America and in the urban areas of developing societies in Africa and Asia, one often finds high illegitimacy rates and unstable mating patterns. An array of types of domestic group is produced, the most distinctive being those in which a mother is surrounded by adult children and some of her daughter's children. Money income flows into such a household from a variety of sources, such as children's earnings, payment to daughters for the support of illegitimate children, the older woman's own labor, and perhaps government relief funds. This income is reallocated around the essential tasks of child rearing and nurturance, and it appears that a household group of this kind is a useful adaptation to conditions of economic insecurity. This form of domestic group appears to be always regarded as a deviant form, partly because of the instability of male roles in relation to it. Unlike the matrilineal situation, men do not have important legal ties to their sisters; it is the mother who is the focus of the familial solidarity, and her position derives from affective rather than jural relations. It would be wrong to suggest that this is the *typical* household or familial form in the societies in which it occurs. Even at the class levels where it is most frequently found it constitutes only a small proportion of actual household groups, but its significance is as an expression of the strength of mother–child relations and the relative weakness of marital ties.

This brief sketch has outlined only some of the major features of family structure. Variations within single societies have hardly been touched upon, and nothing has been said about pathological forms. Nor has attention been directed toward the attempts which have been made from time to time to do away with family solidarity in favor of allegiance to other groups, although such attempts provide valuable experimental data. The Israeli cooperative communities are probably the best recent examples of this, although no definite conclusions about the necessity or otherwise of nuclear-family relationships can be drawn (Spiro 1958). What these cases do perhaps indicate, along with some of the matrilineal and matrifocal cases, is that marriage is not the only means of securing social "legitimacy" for children. Spiro shows that children brought up in central nurseries and schools are in a sense children of the whole community, in spite of the specific relationships they may develop with their "own" parents. This is possible because of the relatively small size of the communities.

However the family may be defined or structured, it always constitutes an area of diffuse and permanent solidarity between a limited number of individuals, and this is probably its most important distinguishing characteristic. This is a view at least suggested by W. H. Rivers in his *Social Organization* when he deliberately identifies the family of parents and children as the basic unit in European society but points out that in other societies the family may be much bigger, that biological connection is no guide to kinship, and that genealogies express kinship ties but may be fabricated to fit social reality. Rivers is very wary about drawing any precise line between family relationships and other kinship ties. Such lines can be drawn in particular cases but are very difficult to define a priori.

RAYMOND T. SMITH

[*Directly related are the entries* KINSHIP *and* MARRIAGE; *see also* CONFLICT, *article on* ANTHROPOLOGICAL ASPECTS.]

BIBLIOGRAPHY

ARENSBERG, CONRAD M.; and KIMBALL, SOLON T. (1940) 1961 *Family and Community in Ireland.* Gloucester, Mass.: Smith.

Aspects of the Analysis of Family Structure, by Ansley J. Coale et al. 1965 Princeton Univ. Press.

ASSOCIATION OF SOCIAL ANTHROPOLOGISTS OF THE COMMONWEALTH, CONFERENCE ON NEW APPROACHES IN SOCIAL ANTHROPOLOGY, CAMBRIDGE, *1963* 1966 *The Relevance of Models for Social Anthropology.* Edited by Michael Banton. London: Tavistock. → See especially "Some Muddles in the Models" by David M. Schneider.

BACHOFEN, JOHANN J. (1861) 1948 *Das Mutterrecht.* 2 vols. 3d ed. Edited by Karl Meuli. Basel: Schwabe.

BELL, NORMAN W.; and VOGEL, EZRA F. (editors) 1960 *A Modern Introduction to the Family.* London: Routledge; Glencoe, Ill.: Free Press.

BOTT, ELIZABETH 1957 *Family and Social Network: Roles, Norms, and External Relationships in Ordinary Urban Families.* London: Tavistock.

BOWLBY, JOHN 1951 *Maternal Care and Mental Health.* Geneva: World Health Organization.

BRITISH ASSOCIATION FOR THE ADVANCEMENT OF SCIENCE (1874) 1954 *Notes and Queries on Anthropology.* 6th ed., rev. London: Routledge.

EVANS-PRITCHARD, E. E. 1951 *Kinship and Marriage Among the Nuer.* Oxford Univ. Press.

FORTES, MEYER (1949) 1963 Time and Social Structure: An Ashanti Case Study; Radcliffe-Brown's Thesis. Pages 54–84 in Meyer Fortes (editor), *Social Structure: Studies Presented to A. R. Radcliffe-Brown.* New York: Russell.

FORTES, MEYER 1958 Introduction. Pages 1–14 in Jack R. Goody (editor), *The Developmental Cycle in Domestic Groups.* Cambridge Papers in Social Anthropology, No. 1. Cambridge Univ. Press.

FRAZIER, E. FRANKLIN (1939) 1957 *The Negro in the United States.* Rev. ed. New York: Macmillan. → First published as *The Negro Family in the United States.*

GOODY, JACK R. (editor) 1958 *The Developmental Cycle in Domestic Groups.* Cambridge Papers in Social Anthropology, No. 1. Cambridge Univ. Press.

GOODY, JACK R. 1962 *Death, Property and the Ancestors: A Study of the Mortuary Customs of the Lodagaa of West Africa.* Stanford Univ. Press.

GOUGH, KATHLEEN 1952 Changing Kinship Usages in the Setting of Political and Economic Change Among the Nayars of Malabar. *Journal of the Royal Anthropological Institute of Great Britain and Ireland* 82: 71–87.

HALPERN, JOEL MARTIN 1958 *A Serbian Village.* New York: Columbia Univ. Press.

LASLETT, PETER 1965 *The World We Have Lost.* London: Methuen.

LEACH, EDMUND R. 1961 *Rethinking Anthropology.* London School of Economics and Political Science Monographs on Social Anthropology, No. 22. London: Athlone.

LÉVI-STRAUSS, CLAUDE (1958) 1963 *Structural Anthropology.* New York: Basic Books. → First published in French.

LEVY, MARION J. 1949 *The Family Revolution in Modern China.* Cambridge, Mass.: Harvard Univ. Press.

LEVY, MARION J.; and FALLERS, L. A. 1959 The Family: Some Comparative Considerations. *American Anthropologist* New Series 61: 647–651.

LOUNSBURY, FLOYD G. 1965 Another View of the Trobriand Kinship Categories. *American Anthropologist* New Series 67, part 2: 142–185.

MALINOWSKI, BRONISLAW (1927) 1953 *Sex and Repression in Savage Society.* London: Routledge; New York: Harcourt. → A paperback edition was published in 1955 by Meridian.

MEAD, MARGARET 1949 *Male and Female: A Study of the Sexes in a Changing World.* London: Gollancz; New York: Morrow.

MORGAN, LEWIS HENRY 1871 *Systems of Consanguinity and Affinity of the Human Family.* Smithsonian Contributions to Knowledge, Vol. 17, Publication No. 218. Washington: Smithsonian Institution.

MORGAN, LEWIS HENRY (1877) 1964 *Ancient Society.* Edited by Leslie A. White. Cambridge, Mass.: Belknap.

MURDOCK, GEORGE P. 1949 *Social Structure.* New York: Macmillan.

PARSONS, TALCOTT (1949) 1959 The Social Structure of the Family. Pages 241–274 in Ruth N. Anshen (editor), *The Family: Its Function and Destiny.* Rev. ed. New York: Harper.

PARSONS, TALCOTT 1954 The Incest Taboo in Relation to Social Structure and the Socialization of the Child. *British Journal of Sociology* 5: 101–117.

PARSONS, TALCOTT; and BALES, ROBERT F. 1955 *Family, Socialization and Interaction Process.* Glencoe, Ill.: Free Press.

RADCLIFFE-BROWN, A. R.; and FORDE, C. DARYLL (editors) 1950 *African Systems of Kinship and Marriage.* Published for the International African Institute. Oxford Univ. Press.

SCHNEIDER, DAVID M.; and GOUGH, KATHLEEN (editors)
1961 *Matrilineal Kinship*. Berkeley: Univ. of California Press.

SPIRO, MELFORD E. 1958 *Children of the Kibbutz*. Cambridge, Mass.: Harvard Univ. Press.

THOMAS, WILLIAM I.; and ZNANIECKI, FLORIAN (1918–1920) 1958 *The Polish Peasant in Europe and America*. 2 vols., 2d ed. New York: Dover.

YOUNG, MICHAEL; and WILLMOTT, PETER 1957 *Family and Kinship in East London*. Institute of Community Studies, Report No. 1. London: Routledge; Glencoe, Ill.: Free Press. → A paperback edition was published in 1963 by Penguin.

ZIMMERMAN, CARLE C. 1947 *Family and Civilization*. New York: Harper.

ZIMMERMAN, CARLE C.; and FRAMPTON, MERLE E. 1935 *Family and Society: A Study of the Sociology of Reconstruction*. London: Williams & Norgate; Princeton, N.J.: Van Nostrand.

II
DISORGANIZATION AND DISSOLUTION

Aside from some slight semantic disagreements, most social scientists agree that some form of a familial group is universal among human beings. Likewise in every society some of the familial groups are imperfect in their functioning and deserving of the label "disorganized." Generally there is some relationship between disorganization and a more climactic, terminal situation called "dissolution." Family groups are eventually dissolved by death or some form of separation, insofar as these groups are organized around the matings of men and women. Of course, a family process, in the sense of overlapping and interacting generations, is immortal, providing there is reproductive replacement before the familial group of a particular generation disintegrates (Kirkpatrick [1955] 1963, pp. 192–195).

Nature and significance

The significance of familial disorganization and dissolution depends upon the institutional arrangements for family life in a particular culture. If stress is laid on the nuclear family, then kinfolk are less available to aid members of the smaller familial group. Some families are vulnerable in the sense that their members expect permanence, have made deep emotional commitments, and do not readily redirect affection and loyalty. On the other hand, people may be less hurt by familial instability in cultures where instability is an established norm and where kinfolk are helpful and meaningful.

In most cultures, the familial group helps prepare children both for membership in a society and for effective functioning as parents. Disorganization and dissolution are significant in that they tend to interfere with this socialization process. Furthermore, disorganization and dissolution are often cumulative and recurrent in the family process. There is a convergence of evidence in the United States that people with happy marriages tend to come from happy homes. Divorce also runs in families; divorced persons are divorce-prone, and children suffering from bereavement or parental divorce may be involved with delinquency, illegitimacy, and unwise marriage. The consequences of disorganization and dissolution experienced by the parents are commonly visited upon the offspring, perhaps for several generations. Some children, however, are warned by the fate of their parents and in marriage make an effort to reverse a trend toward disorganization.

Terminology.   It is impossible to make a useful analysis of the nature and significance of family disorganization and dissolution without precise terminology. In current usage "disorganization" seems to imply maladjustment, malfunctioning, psychological decay, and the existence of family problems. Goode defines family disorganization as "the breakup of a family unit, the dissolution or fracture of a structure of social roles when one or more members fail to perform adequately their role obligation." He lists five types of family disorganization, namely, illegitimacy, dissolution, whether as a result of divorce, annulment, separation, or desertion; "empty shell family"; unwilled absence of one spouse; and "unwilled" major role failures (Goode 1964, pp. 91–92).

Clearly, such taxonomy makes no distinction between disorganization and dissolution. It seems from the inclusion of illegitimacy that a family can be "disorganized" by role failure even before it is organized. Caplow defines an organization as "a social system that has an unequivocal collective identity, an exact roster of members, a program of activity, and procedures for replacing members" (1964, p. 1). Following this line of thought, it would seem more proper to regard the "illegitimate family" as unorganized rather than as a type of family disorganization.

Distinction between disorganization and dissolution.   In the present discussion a distinction will be made between family disorganization and family dissolution, and marital disorganization will be regarded as a special case of family disorganization. Family *dissolution* means disintegration, disruption, or chronic instability; it is characterized by "dependence, agency intrusion, member extraction, premature atypical departure and family violence" (Kirkpatrick [1955] 1963, p. 565).

Marital dissolution, as a special form of family

dissolution, may take the form of suicide, murder of spouse, annulment, separation (ranging from psychological withdrawal to legal separation), and, finally, divorce. The withdrawal from spouse may be accompanied by substitution for wife of a co-wife, concubine, mistress, or prostitute. Sometimes dissolution is by stages, for example, in a sequence of avoidance, suit for separate maintenance, legal separation, an interlocutory divorce decree, and finally an absolute divorce with the right of re-marriage.

Family dissolution is an imperfect index of family *disorganization*. Divorce is an imperfect index of marital disorganization because there may be disorganization without divorce. For example, divorce was very difficult to obtain in England prior to liberalization of the laws in 1857 and again in 1937. When the divorce door is closed, marital disorganization may be inconspicuously endured. On the other hand, a couple with high expectations of marital bliss but relatively little marital disorganization may seek divorce as an exit from marriage. That marital disorganization is often not extreme is shown by the frequency of reconciliation, dropping of divorce suits, and remarriage to the former spouse. Thus, Harvey J. Locke (1951, pp. 54–55) found that about a fourth of the divorced couples he studied were in the same marital adjustment category as the less happy fourth of the married couples.

Religious and moralistic viewpoints. Family disorganization and dissolution are viewed by many people in moralistic and religious terms. The family at one time performed functions so important that disharmony and disruption were viewed with alarm. One assumption of the patri-archal system in western European culture was that paternal authority could insure efficiency and stability in family life. It is probably still the as-sumption of middle-class people in the United States that "nice" people get on together and as spouses stay together.

The Roman Catholic viewpoint concerning family disorganization and dissolution has re-mained rather clear and constant since the Council of Trent, 1545–1563. The ideal is patriarchal har-mony established by a marriage sacrament directed toward the goals of parenthood and marital love. The Catholic doctrine assumes various impedi-ments, such as disparity of religion, lack of con-sent, or intention to seek a divorce. Given the impediment of disparity of religion, the marriage of a Catholic to a non-Catholic, especially one un-baptized, can be nullified, thus permitting the Catholic party to obtain a civil divorce and marry

a Catholic partner "in favor of the Faith." Even a marriage between Catholics may be dissolved by papal dispensation if the marriage is unconsum-mated and grounds exist for the marital disruption. In addition to nullification and dissolution by dis-pensation, the church grants separation from bed and board, which does not include the right of re-marriage. The consummated and valid marriage between two Catholics is indissoluble and permits no remarriage unless terminated by death. Certain Protestant denominations hold equally religious and moralistic views (Kirkpatrick [1955] 1963, pp. 573–575).

The legalistic viewpoint. The legalistic view, which is prevalent in the United States, had its origins in canon law and was influenced by the common law of England. It is complicated by the lack of uniformity among the various statutes and decisions of the 50 states; the practice of seeking divorce in states other than the state of residence has brought controversial cases to the U.S. Su-preme Court (Harper & Skolnick [1952] 1962, pp. 451–458).

Basic to the legalistic doctrine of divorce in the United States is *adversary procedure*. It is assumed that a relatively innocent party may be granted a divorce because of the relative guilt of the other party with reference to "grounds" specified in the statutes of the various states. There are four legal doctrines associated with the basic adversary pro-cedure. If spouses cooperate in providing evidence calculated to obtain a divorce on certain grounds, that is *collusion*, and the divorce should be denied. If one party forgives an offense such as adultery and continues to live with the spouse, *condonation* is assumed, and the derivative inference is made that the damage to the innocent party was not great enough to justify a divorce. If one party shows that the other party is equally guilty, *suc-cessful recrimination* is established and the divorce is not to be granted. If one party plots the guilty behavior of the other party, that is *connivance*, and the divorce would be denied to the allegedly innocent party. Thus the legal operation of divorce is withheld from marriages so sick as to menace the well-being of both adults and children in the familial group (Kirkpatrick [1955] 1963, p. 595).

Social pathology. Disorganization and dissolu-tion are subject to a third viewpoint, that of social pathology. This viewpoint assumes that well-func-tioning, organized families are "normal"; malad-justment and disruptions are regarded as deviant behavior. The families with problems should be brought back into line by monetary aid, psycholog-ical manipulation, and a therapy designed to help people achieve conformity to the social norms. With little reflection upon alternative frames of reference, there is concern for the cure of pathological situations.

Sociological viewpoint. A fourth viewpoint is that of scientific sociology. In the choice of this label there is no intended implication that sociology is a distinct, mature, and sophisticated science. Perhaps at the present time it is merely an attempt at clear, honest, abstract thinking about social phenomena, increasingly aided by systematic observation and analysis. From such an intellectual orientation, which is relatively free from concealed value assumptions and distorting preconceptions, family dissolution is sometimes seen as a relief of family disorganization. For certain infections, amputation is the choice of a lesser evil as compared with further spread of infection. So it may be with divorce.

The sociological viewpoint is generally deterministic and assumes that social changes make inevitable certain reactions in terms of disorganization and reorganization. According to this view, familial institutions, groups, and relationships are part of a larger social structure in which every aspect of the total configuration is related to every other aspect. Family disorganization may be one facet of a larger social disorganization.

Methods and trends in research

Family crisis. Research concerning crises of the family has been extensive. The great depression in the United States brought forth books on unemployment as a crisis for the family, and World War II brought an interest in bereavement and other trials visited upon the family by wartime conditions. More recently scholars have speculated as to the devastating influence that an atomic war would have on the family.

The confusion of terminology in regard to disorganization and dissolution is compounded by the concept of *family crisis*. Death, like divorce, can cause the dissolution of family units, and often bereavement is placed in the category of family crisis. Hill writes of the event (A) which interacts with the ability of the family to meet a crisis (B); both (A) and (B) interact with the definition which the family makes of the event (C), and thus the situation is an (X)—the crisis for a particular family. One family may take in its stride an impact which would crush another family that is lacking in resources and prone to regard a trifle as a crisis (Waller [1938] 1951, p. 460).

Endogenous and exogenous disorganization. Kirkpatrick drew a distinction between endoge-

nous and exogenous disorganization, the former having an internal origin and the latter a relatively external origin. Distinctions were also made between the normal and atypical, the timely and the premature, and the objectively severe as compared with the objectively trivial. It was suggested that the term "crisis" be restricted to exogenous disorganization due to an objectively severe atypical or premature event (Kirkpatrick 1955, p. 503). Insofar as family dissolution results from exogenous disorganization, as defined above, it would seem proper to speak of exogenous family dissolution; an example would be the wiping out of a family by flood or fire.

Bereavement. The assassination of President Kennedy in 1963 was a conspicuous atypical, extreme experience which brought premature bereavement. The disorganization in the Kennedy family, in the sense of shock and sorrow, was exogenous disorganization; and the dissolution, in the sense of the loss of the head of the family, could be regarded as exogenous dissolution. Perhaps all bereavement, save that due to violence within the family group, could be regarded as exogenous, and if premature or atypical, it would be a family crisis. An expected death from natural causes of old age would be less clearly a crisis by the criteria which have been set forth, although some degree of disorganization and dissolution might result. There is no claim of exclusive categories in the suggested terminology, and the distinctions are relative.

It is important to make a distinction between father-deceased bereavement and mother-deceased bereavement in view of their differential implications for the family in terms of economic consequences and implications for the offspring in terms of sex typing, identification, and preparatory affectional relationships with parents of the opposite sex. Many aspects of bereavement experience have been probed by Howard Becker, Willard Waller, Thomas D. Eliot, David M. Fulcomer, and others. Perhaps more attention should be paid to the loss of common memories. If a beloved person is no longer available to confirm a happening, there may be doubt about the reality of prior experience and uncertainty about personal identity. If the identity of A is essentially the identity of A *in relation to* B, the loss of B drastically alters the subjective identity of A. Improved knowledge of familial disorganization and dissolution calls not only for greater precision of terminology but also for further exploration of bereavement as a family crisis that may lead to subtle forms of exogenous disorganization.

Demographic investigation. Investigators have explored the distribution of familial disorganization and dissolution over *space*, by *social categories*, and in *time*. For example, relief cases of a certain type may be more prevalent in certain urban areas and within social categories such as "nonwhites." Furthermore, there may be fluctuations in the case load of social welfare agencies by time periods. Unemployment associated with the business cycle has generally meant an increase in the number of families dependent upon external financial assistance.

The most extensive investigation has been that of divorce regarded as a measure of familial dissolution and, more specifically, of marital dissolution. Numerous studies have noted variations in divorce rates by geographical region, sometimes considered in combination with various social categories. Paul Glick has studied "marriage instability" as measured by separation ratios, divorce ratios, and proportion of children not living with both parents. His hypothesis that marital disruption in the United States tends to be more closely related to urbanization than to regions of residence was only partially supported (1963, pp. 47–54).

Various writers such as William J. Goode, Robert Winch, and Christine H. Hillman have stressed the higher divorce ratios among persons of lower socioeconomic status (Goode 1964, pp. 88–90; Winch [1952] 1963, pp. 706–708). However, this evidence contains some inconsistencies when men and women are considered separately. One finds a rather high incidence of divorce among college women as compared both with less educated women and with men at the same college level (Kirkpatrick [1955] 1963, p. 589). It should be stressed that the proportion divorced in a particular group or category of people is affected by remarriage and the rapidity of remarriage. If every person receiving a divorce decree remarried on the same day, there would be no residue of unmarried "divorced persons" in the population.

Desertion, another mode of marital dissolution, may not be accurately reflected in the census categories "separated," "spouse absent," and "divorced," because of remarriage. During 1955 a Philadelphia court recorded 4,224 desertions handled, in contrast to only 2,812 divorces (Kephart 1961, p. 548). Desertion may be a substitute for divorce or preliminary to the legal action of divorce.

The demographic approach stresses the changing prevalence of divorce in various countries. The trend of the divorce rate after World War II was upward in many European countries, such as France, England, and Sweden, as well as in the United States and Canada (Jacobson 1959, table 42, p. 90; table 47, p. 98; Kirkpatrick [1955] 1963, p. 586). For the United States, rates are available from 1920 through 1960, expressed as divorces per year per one thousand married females 15 years of age and over. A curve based on such rates shows a drop during the depression in the 1930s, a huge peak in 1946 following the war, a decline to a plateau, and a figure of 9.2 on that plateau in 1960 as compared with 8.0 in 1920 (Carter & Plateris 1963). From a sociological point of view, this increase is far from spectacular.

The clinical approach. For many decades investigators have utilized methods less objective but perhaps more penetrating than those of the demographers. The various theories of Freud concerning emotion-laden interaction in the family group were integrated by J. C. Flügel. Waller, in his brilliant pioneer study of divorced couples (1930), drew upon psychoanalytic concepts in his analysis of alienation and postdivorce adjustment. He expressed original intuitions concerning motivation, as, for example, the suspicion that some ex-wives seek alimony not out of greed but because of jealous disinclination to see an ex-husband financially capable of marrying another woman. Some psychiatrists probably go to an extreme in regarding the seeking of divorce as an expression of neuroticism.

Historical and comparative studies. The older and well-known accounts of the family, such as those by Edward Westermarck, George Elliott Howard, and Arthur W. Calhoun, contain much historical and comparative information concerning disorganization and dissolution. A book by Lichtenberger, published in 1931, gives a thoughtful and comprehensive analysis of divorce.

More recently, Murdock (1950) made a systematic survey of divorce practices in 40 nonindustrial societies. In many of these societies he found divorce to be more frequent than in the United States, but he also found more preventives and functional adaptations. From this anthropological perspective, the American family does not seem to be in a state of hopeless decay. Following Murdock's lead, various anthropologists have investigated determinants of divorce rates in various cultures. Ackerman (1963), from a study of 62 societies, found certain forms of homogamy to be associated with low divorce rates. Christensen (1963) has given an elegant demonstration of the fact that the association between premarital pregnancy and divorce varies with a culture's sexual permissiveness.

Measurement and prediction. Beginning in the 1930s, researchers attempted to measure and predict marital disorganization. The investigators often collected information concerning background factors at the same time that information was requested concerning marital adjustment. Some of the correlations between the so-called prediction scales (based upon various items, for the most part premarital) and the adjustment scales probably involved a "halo effect" (see Kirkpatrick [1955] 1963, chapters 15, 18, and appendix). Well-adjusted respondents tended to report favorably on both their marriages and their childhood backgrounds. The reverse was probably true for maladjusted couples.

In the longitudinal or forecasting studies of such authors as Ernest W. Burgess and Paul Wallin, Truman L. Kelley and Louis M. Terman, information was first obtained on a sample of individuals, and then after a period of years further information was gathered concerning their marital adjustment. [*See the biography of* BURGESS.] In general, correlations between scores on a prediction instrument and some categories of outcome tended to be lower when the halo effect was controlled by the passage of time.

In connection with this body of research, a great deal of information was collected concerning factors associated with "marital adjustment" or other criteria of success. The findings of many of these studies were brought together, with the revelation that there was rather a striking lack of convergence in evidence (Kirkpatrick 1947). Cautious verbal generalizations about the convergence of findings concerning factors related to marital adjustment and a guide to the sources from which these findings were derived are available (see Kirkpatrick [1955] 1963, chapter 15 and appendix A).

Improvement of scientific knowledge

More precise terminology, pertinent distinctions, and rigorous theory would all be helpful in furthering scientific knowledge in the area under discussion. Since disorganization and dissolution are aspects of family behavior, any advance in knowledge of family systems in general would indirectly contribute to knowledge in this specific area.

Theories of mating. Winch has systematically carried over his functional theory of the family to the area of family disorganization and dissolution. If he is correct in his theory of complementary mating, a foundation would be laid for generalizations concerning the kind of matings which would avoid family disorganization and dissolution ([1952] 1963, pp. 567–655).

Kirkpatrick derived a theory of mating from a basic postulate concerning the influence of prior satisfactions and dissatisfactions in the course of family experience; this theory was called a theory of "selective needs" based on prior satisfactions and dissatisfactions. In some respects it is different from the Winch theory, and in other respects it is convergent and supplementary (Kirkpatrick [1955] 1963, pp. 300–307). According to the Kirkpatrick theory, an extreme of marital disorganization and perhaps consequent familial disorganization would exist when the spouse violates "minus–plus needs" by providing more of the particular kind of dissatisfaction which was distressing during a prior phase of family experience. For example, the wife who fails to compensate for the dissatisfactions experienced by her husband with his mother and aggravates these same dissatisfactions by behavior similar to that of the mother, risks marital disorganization and possibly divorce.

Criteria of scientific worth. Improvement of scientific knowledge in this as in other areas depends upon meeting five different criteria of scientific worth (Kirkpatrick 1939; 1959). One criterion is that of *verifiability*. In one sense verifiability implies repeatability of procedure, as in the case of experiments in the natural science field. There is some assurance that research is verifiable by others when it is presented as already verified by the investigators in the sense of proper sampling, validity and reliability of instruments, and correctness of logical inference. It is striking that so many findings concerning factors favorable to success in marriage have been nonverifiable or unverified.

A second criterion is *transmissibility*. A marriage counselor may achieve striking success and yet be unable to transmit his art or technique to a pupil. Often a description of divorce rates in a certain country cannot be transmitted to another scholar because symbols lack identical meanings for each person.

A third criterion of scientific worth is *consistency*. The contribution having this quality is logically sound, and the terms are carefully defined and consistently used with reference to their assigned meanings. Theory, hypotheses, research design, findings, and conclusion are interrelated. Any convergence or discrepancy in evidence is systematically presented.

The fourth criterion is *scope*. Family disorganization and disruption may be analyzed in a single brief case study, or a massive three-volume work may describe this aspect of family systems with global coverage. For example, Goode made an admirable study of divorce as affecting a sample of women in Detroit (1956) and in another book analyzed the family patterns as affected by industrialism in varied countries of the world (1963).

A fifth and somewhat multiple criterion is that of *implication*. Research having the quality of implication has one or more of four characteristics —namely, prediction, practical application, methodological innovation, and creative integration. It would be useful to construct a questionnaire that would predict divorce with 100 per cent accuracy. A study would have implications when, if applied to family counseling, it prevented 90 per cent of the needless divorces. It would be a methodological contribution to integrate the various measures of marital dissolution into an improved index of marital disorganization. Finally, the subcriterion of creative integration would be illustrated by a new integration of existing theories concerning family disorganization into a generalized theory that generated hypotheses subject to definitive verification by empirical research.

Statistics and indices. The improvement of scientific knowledge concerning disorganization and dissolution depends upon improved statistics. In recent years some improvements have been made in marriage and divorce statistics in the United States, which are often inferior to those of less wealthy countries. In 1958 a reporting system known as the "divorce registration area" was established. For inclusion in the divorce registration area a state must have central files of divorce records; include on its record forms certain standard items; receive regularly reports from local areas such as counties; and cooperate with the National Vital Statistics Division in regard to testing data for completeness and accuracy (Carter 1960). Further support to the movement for improved statistics was given by a committee on marriage and divorce statistics of the American Sociological Association, which published a report in June 1958. As part of an action program initiated by the federal agencies concerned with marriage and divorce statistics, a national sample of marriage and divorce transcripts was collected for the year 1960, and the official improved statistics for 1960 are based on this new source, which extends coverage beyond the 18 states in the divorce registration area.

There are various ways in which scientific knowledge would be advanced by improvement of marriage and divorce statistics. Certain needs and research possibilities will be mentioned.

The duration of marriage prior to divorce is a very important item of information. While it is claimed that the duration of marriage to the time of the decree is known for 96.2 per cent of all divorces granted in the United States during 1960, this information has not been fully used to compute the probability of divorce for couples marrying at a particular time. Such true probabilities for earlier years have been computed by Monahan (1959) and Jacobson (1959), but there is a tendency to regard mistakenly the ratio of divorces to marriages of the same year as expressing the risk of divorce.

Improved divorce statistics would reveal on a national basis the details of prior experience with marriage and divorce prior to a particular divorce that is being recorded and tabulated.

It would also be helpful to have national statistics on the total number of persons of various types who have been affected by divorce. People pass out of categories which imply a record of divorce, but they may carry the subjective experience of divorce with them into a remarriage or a relationship with a stepparent.

Statistics concerning divorce should be more closely related to improved statistics concerning separation and desertion. It may be that concern about the divorce of a particular date is inappropriate in view of the fact that the granting of a decree is merely a legal event far removed in time from significant experiences of the individual concerned (Monahan 1962).

It is highly important to have national statistics which are cross tabulated, showing the characteristics of one divorced spouse as matched with those of the other spouse. For research purposes it would be useful to have such cross tabulations by previous marital experience, religion, age at divorce, education, occupation and social status, and children resulting from prior marriages of the divorced spouses.

An interrelation of divorce, marriage, and birth statistics on a national basis would be helpful. Christensen (1963) has already demonstrated that such comparisons are useful in showing the association of premarital pregnancy with divorce. It may be that computer storage and retrieval of data will make the method of "record linkage" increasingly applicable.

Statistics concerning family dissolution which permit valid international comparisons would be desirable. Obviously, a country which regards divorce as a private family matter and lacks a governmental agency concerned with divorce may seem to have a low divorce rate because of underreporting. A logical extension of trends in the United States would be an international divorce registration area, having as members countries with acceptable statistics. Other countries might seek then to improve their indices of family dissolution.

Given the process of changing marital status, which is conspicuous in the United States and in other industrialized countries, there is need for statistics that contribute to an index of what might be called the *velocity* of family dissolution. The speed of separation, divorce, remarriage and redivorce, could be known only with the aid of information concerning prior family experience, which would be reported at each transition. It is known from unusually good statistics in Iowa for 1953 that the duration of marriage prior to a divorce ranges from an average of 6.3 years for primary marriages, to 3.2 when both parties have been married before, to 1.8 for couples breaking up their third marriage (Monahan 1959). Kirkpatrick attempted a crude measure of velocity of family dissolution by dividing the number of divorces per year by the number of persons who in the year following were in the status of divorced (1955, p. 534). A good index of velocity of family dissolution would require improved statistics and would take into account the speed with which children lose natural parents to acquire a stepparent and perhaps a series of such stepparents.

Knowledge of causes and consequences. The distinction between disorganization and dissolution must again be stressed. As compared with couples equally disorganized but undivorced (either contemporary or living in a previous century), certain modern couples seek divorce for special reasons. Often the woman is able to get a job and hence can insist on a high standard of marital happiness. Thus, dissolution may be a *preventive* of disorganization. Some people are less tied to marriage than others; family functions, religious taboos, or life-long commitment to parental roles may simply have less meaning for them (Landis 1963). The door of divorce is more open to certain couples than to others because of lenient laws in their locality, relative freedom to migrate elsewhere for an easy divorce, encouragement of relatives, opportunities for remarriage, and in general, the prospect of freedom without the economic, religious, and psychological penalties which have threatened other couples in various times and places. It can even be argued that divorce itself is a cause of divorce, in that frequent divorce weakens the norm of marital stability. Divorce frees bad matrimonial risks for remarriage and subsequent divorce; offspring imitate divorced parents; and the divorce of numerous friends makes the choice of divorce more normal and respectable (Kirkpatrick [1955] 1963, pp. 577–582).

Persons facing divorce during the latter half of the twentieth century in the United States have varied problems. Variations in the divorce laws of the 50 states contribute to the possibility of legal tangles. The divorce procedure is neither consistently routinized nor consistently established as an individualized therapeutic procedure; certainly, as compared with the bereaved person, the divorced person lacks a clearly defined role to play. The more meaningful any marriage is, the more painful will be its dissolution. But the confusion involved in divorce as compared with bereavement is often almost as disturbing as the previous frustration and deprivation. Seriously maladjusted couples are confused and torn between the choices of continued sickness in their marriage and the amputation brought about by the choice of divorce. The grim challenge is to find the choice which brings the lesser evil.

Effect on children. It can be argued that research concerning the effect of disorganization and disintegration on children is important, even if it is imperfect by the criteria previously mentioned. Children are the helpless victims of the mistakes of their elders; they have little control over their destinies and usually cannot select the stepparent who comes to them in the course of the divorce–remarriage process.

Much of the research has failed to compare the children of disorganized but undissolved homes with those from disorganized and broken homes of specific types. Landis and Nye found that children from broken homes fared as well or better, according to certain criteria, than children from intact but unhappy homes (Nye 1957). Burchinal (1964) considered homes reintegrated by remarriage, as well as broken and unbroken homes, and found no differential effect on adolescents.

In regard to the convergence of valid findings, much depends on the methods used, the type of effect on children, and the age of offspring at which possible effects are investigated. Landis (1963) found rather impressive evidence that happy parental marriages were favorably related to the dating experience of offspring. Robert R. Bell and James DeBurger, both using the sibling-cooperator method (Kirkpatrick & Cotton 1951, p. 82), found that parental divorce showed greater influence than bereavement on the marital adjustment of grown offspring (see Kirkpatrick [1955] 1963, pp. 665–674).

Applications of knowledge

Effective application of improved knowledge of family disorganization and dissolution depends on the emerging pattern of interprofessional cooperation. Lawyers, doctors, psychologists, social workers, educators, home economists, clergymen, and demographers, as well as social scientists, draw upon the growing body of knowledge in this area. That thriving interdisciplinary organization in the United States—the National Council on Family Relations—draws members from all of the above-mentioned professions. Furthermore, the emerging international organizations concerned with the family tend to be interprofessional in character.

Legal changes.   Legal changes, both actual and proposed, tend to reflect a sharper international perspective. Varied explanations of the divorce trends in England include the influence of changes in the divorce laws. However, Max Rheinstein (1960) found little influence of legal changes on divorce rates in Germany. In the United States, a tabulation of the divorce laws in the various states as of 1952 was cross tabulated by the crude divorce rates of 1950 and the percentages of respondents in the various states answering "No" to a question on a poll of 1936 which read, "Should divorces be easier to obtain in your state?" There was a striking lack of correspondence between severity of the laws, behavior as to obtaining divorces, and public opinion concerning legal restrictions (Kirkpatrick 1955, p. 538). Of course, extreme differences in divorce law among various countries or extreme changes within an area, for instance, in South Carolina, do correspond in some degree with divorce rates.

David and Vera Mace note a more "folksy" and less legalistic type of divorce procedure in Russia than in the United States (Mace & Mace 1963, pp. 203–226). Olson (1961) makes similar observations with regard to Japan. In view of the long and, thus far, futile campaign in the United States to achieve either a uniform divorce law in the various states or federal control by a change in the constitution, it is interesting to observe that Australia established such a uniform federal law in 1959. This may well have some effect on the pattern of Australian divorce rates.

Family counseling.   Counseling and therapy offer one means of applying improved knowledge concerning family disorganization and dissolution. At times, legal reforms converge with provisions for family counseling. In Australia the Matrimonial Causes Act (mentioned above) restricts dissolution before three years of marriage and provides for marriage counseling and conciliation; it authorizes federal payment for such services to approved marriage guidance organizations (Harvey 1964). The provision for counseling in connection with the divorce procedure in Australia and Japan may give encouragement to persons in the United States who, like Judge Paul W. Alexander, plead for a therapeutic approach, abolition of adversary procedure, and family courts that provide for counseling prior to the granting of a divorce (Kirkpatrick [1955] 1963, pp. 631–632).

There is some agreement, furthered by experience with counseling and therapy, that prevention of family trouble should be sought by a focus on education and counseling at an early period in the life span. Since family dissolution results in no small measure from the coming together of the wrong combinations of people, there is an argument for premarital counseling and guidance in the process of selecting mates. Many issues, however, remain controversial. For example, the small number of trained counselors in relation to potential demand provides an incentive to sacrifice quality to quantity by approving the activity of many relatively untrained persons as counselors.

Perhaps the dilemma of quality versus quantity may be solved to some extent by group counseling and therapy instead of individual treatment. The mutual support found in such groups is impressive. Certain instruments constructed for measuring attitudinal agreement, marital adjustment, and empathy in dyadic relationships might be adapted for self-analysis on the part of individuals and couples with minimal outside aid from experts (Kirkpatrick & Hobart 1954, pp. 10–19).

International trends.   The international outlook with regard to family disorganization and dissolution offers an intellectual challenge that goes beyond the parochial applications of existing knowledge. However, some promising beginnings have been made; Goode, for instance, has noted the influence of industrialization upon differential family instability among the different social classes of various countries. These classes may vary, of course, as to degree of urbanization, type of kinship system, and feministic orientation (de Visscher 1956). The most valid generalization seems to be that with the spread of Western technology there tends to be increasing similarity in the family systems of the world, including their provision for marital dissolution. The diffusion of feminism may temporarily increase family dissolution, as women demand equality in the privilege of divorce and become economically independent of both husbands and kinfolk (Sysiharju 1960).

Family systems tend to have a certain resiliency under the impact of drastic social change. The free divorce of the 1920s in communist Russia has been replaced by a conservative and restrictive procedure. Hitler attempted reactionary change of the

German family (Kirkpatrick 1938), but after the political and military crisis had passed, the general feministic and egalitarian trends characteristic of Western civilization reappeared (Schelsky 1953). As the dominance of the independent nuclear family is proclaimed, evidence appears of the survival of functional kinship systems. Carle C. Zimmerman, who expressed concern about the return of the unstable "atomistic family," found substantial evidence that "friend-families" tend to be supportive and homogeneous in regard to low incidence of divorce (Zimmerman & Cervantes 1956, pp. 91–117; see also Shanas & Streib 1965).

Improved facilities for communication are characteristic of the modern world, on the international, the national, and the familial level. Cultural interaction may increase both the similarity of familial institutions and agreement concerning human goals such as peace, freedom, and happiness— ends to which social institutions are means. If improved communication reduces repression, hollow ritual, and pretense at every level, the pursuit of happiness and freedom may lead to an increase in divorce rates or other indices of familial dissolution in conservative areas of society. Nevertheless, if dissolution be distinguished from disorganization, certain increases in dissolution may mean merely a spread of higher aspirations and a reluctance to endure familial disorganization with its associated misery.

CLIFFORD KIRKPATRICK

[*See also* MARRIAGE, *article on* FAMILY FORMATION; *and the biographies of* WALLER; WESTERMARCK.]

BIBLIOGRAPHY

ACKERMAN, CHARLES 1963 Affiliations: Structural Determinants of Differential Divorce Rates. *American Journal of Sociology* 69:13–20.

BURCHINAL, LEE G. 1964 Characteristics of Adolescents From Unbroken, Broken and Reconstituted Families. *Journal of Marriage and the Family* 26:44–51.

CAPLOW, THEODORE 1964 *Principles of Organization.* New York: Harcourt.

CARTER, HUGH 1960 Plans for Improved Statistics on Family Formation and Dissolution in the United States. *Social Forces* 39:163–169.

CARTER, HUGH; and PLATERIS, ALEXANDER 1963 Trends in Divorce and Family Disruption. U.S. Dept. of Health, Education, and Welfare, *Health, Education, and Welfare Indicators* [1963], September:5–14.

CHRISTENSEN, HAROLD T. 1963 Timing of First Pregnancy as a Factor in Divorce: A Cross-cultural Analysis. *Eugenics Quarterly* 10:119–130.

GLICK, PAUL C. 1963 Marriage Instability: Variations by Size of Place and Region. *Milbank Memorial Fund Quarterly* 41:43–55.

GOODE, WILLIAM J. 1956 *After Divorce.* Glencoe, Ill.: Free Press.

GOODE, WILLIAM J. 1963 *World Revolution and Family Patterns.* New York: Free Press.

GOODE, WILLIAM J. 1964 *The Family.* Englewood Cliffs, N.J.: Prentice-Hall.

HARPER, FOWLER V.; and SKOLNICK, JEROME H. (1952) 1962 *Problems of the Family.* Rev. ed. Indianapolis, Ind.: Bobbs-Merrill.

HARVEY, LESLIE V. 1964 Marriage Counseling and the Federal Divorce Law in Australia. *Journal of Marriage and the Family* 26:83–86.

JACOBSON, PAUL H. 1959 *American Marriage and Divorce.* New York: Holt.

KEPHART, WILLIAM M. 1961 *The Family, Society, and the Individual.* Boston: Houghton Mifflin.

KIRKPATRICK, CLIFFORD 1938 *Nazi Germany: Its Women and Family Life.* Indianapolis, Ind.: Bobbs-Merrill.

KIRKPATRICK, CLIFFORD 1939 A Methodological Analysis of Feminism in Relation to Marital Adjustment. *American Sociological Review* 4:325–334.

KIRKPATRICK, CLIFFORD 1947 *What Science Says About Happiness in Marriage.* Minneapolis, Minn.: Burgess.

KIRKPATRICK, CLIFFORD (1955) 1963 *The Family as Process and Institution.* 2d ed. New York: Ronald Press.

KIRKPATRICK, CLIFFORD 1959 Sociological Significance of This Research. Pages 289–295 in Winston Ehrmann, *Premarital Dating Behavior.* New York: Holt.

KIRKPATRICK, CLIFFORD 1965 The Family. Pages 298–305 in *Encyclopedia of Social Work.* Edited by Harry L. Lurie. New York: National Association of Social Workers.

KIRKPATRICK, CLIFFORD; and COTTON, JOHN 1951 Physical Attractiveness, Age and Marital Adjustment. *American Sociological Review* 16:81–86.

KIRKPATRICK, CLIFFORD; and HOBART, CHARLES 1954 Disagreement, Disagreement Estimate, and Nonempathetic Imputations for Intimacy Groups Varying From Favorite Date to Married. *American Sociological Review* 19:10–19.

LANDIS, JUDSON T. 1963 Social Correlates of Divorce or Non-divorce Among the Unhappily Married. *Marriage and Family Living* 25:178–180.

LICHTENBERGER, JAMES P. 1931 *Divorce: A Social Interpretation.* New York: McGraw-Hill.

LOCKE, HARVEY J. 1951 *Predicting Adjustment in Marriage: A Comparison of a Divorced and a Happily Married Group.* New York: Holt.

MACE, DAVID; and MACE, VERA 1963 *The Soviet Family.* Garden City, N.Y.: Doubleday.

MONAHAN, THOMAS P. 1959 The Duration of Marriage to Divorce: Second Marriages and Migratory Types. *Marriage and Family Living* 21:134–138.

MONAHAN, THOMAS P. 1962 When Married Couples Part: Statistical Trends and Relationships in Divorce. *American Sociological Review* 27:625–633.

MURDOCK, GEORGE P. 1950 Family Stability in Non-European Cultures. American Academy of Political and Social Science, *Annals* 272:195–201.

NYE, F. IVAN 1957 Child Adjustment in Broken and in Unhappy Unbroken Homes. *Marriage and Family Living* 19:356–361.

OLSON, LAWRENCE 1961 How the Japanese Divorce. American Universities Field Staff, *East Asia Series* 9, no. 8.

RHEINSTEIN, MAX 1960 Divorce and the Law in Germany: A Review. *American Journal of Sociology* 65:489–498.

Schelsky, Helmut (1953) 1955 *Wandlungen der deutschen Familie in der Gegenwart.* 3d ed., enl. Stuttgart (Germany): Enke.

Shanas, Ethel; and Streib, Gordon F. (editors) 1965 *Social Structure and the Family: Generational Relations.* Englewood Cliffs, N.J.: Prentice-Hall.

Sysiharju, Anna-Liisa 1960 *Equality, Home, and Work: A Socio-psychological Study on Finnish Student Women's Attitudes Towards the Woman's Role in Society.* Helsinki: Tekijä.

U.S. National Center for Health Statistics 1964 *Marriage and Divorce: A Selected Bibliography of Statistically Oriented Studies.* Washington: Government Printing Office.

Visscher, Pierre de 1956 *Attitudes antiféministes et milieux intellectuels.* Louvain (Belgium): Institut de Recherches Économiques et Sociales.

Waller, Willard W. 1930 *The Old Love and the New: Divorce and Readjustment.* New York: Liveright.

Waller, Willard W. (1938) 1951 *The Family: A Dynamic Interpretation.* Revised by Reuben Hill. New York: Dryden.

Winch, Robert F. (1952) 1963 *The Modern Family.* Rev. ed. New York: Holt.

Zimmerman, Carle C.; and Cervantes, Lucius F. 1956 *Marriage and the Family: A Text for Moderns.* Chicago: Regnery.

FAMINE

"Famine is like insanity, hard to define but glaring enough when recognized. . . . one country will define as food shortage what another country would call famine" (Taylor 1947, pp. 98, 102). In recent years, and particularly in the United States, where food surpluses have been embarrassing politically (perhaps also morally), journals have been prone to report from abroad as "famines" what subsequently appear as shortages or merely threats of shortage. Shortages are not infrequently relieved before they become famines.

True famine is shortage of total food so extreme and protracted as to result in widespread persisting hunger, notable emaciation in many of the affected population, and a considerable elevation of community death rate attributable at least in part to deaths from starvation. Criteria do not exist to measure the degree of hunger, emaciation, or elevation of death rate serving to differentiate famine from shortage. The archetypical famine extends over a wide area and affects a large population. Starvation deaths on a small scale, as among members of an isolated family, a small hamlet, a group of travelers in wild country, an icebound ship, would not commonly be characterized as famine. Acute shortage of food for a few weeks, such as preharvest hunger in some parts of the underdeveloped world, is not famine. Lack of a particular customary food, such as sugar or beef, is not fam-

ine if there is abundance of other items. Shortage of a particular vitamin or mineral in a population, evidenced perhaps by uncommonly heavy incidence of scurvy, beriberi, pellagra, rickets, or impaired vision, is not famine, although in recent decades the word has been applied to such shortages.

The members of a community beset by famine gradually become greatly emaciated and increasingly weak and listless—eventually to the point of lying in homes or along the streets and roads, utterly inactive, skeletonized, often with swollen bellies, waiting for death. In famine-stricken regions beggars are encountered in abnormal numbers. There are riots, aimless wanderings, purposeful migrations; men, women, and children comb fields, alleys, and dumps, hoping to find a scrap of edible material. Livestock owned by the poor are sold or eaten.

A house-to-house survey in north China during the famine of 1920–1921 revealed that people were eating, among other items not in their normal diets, "flour made of ground leaves, fuller's earth, flower seed, poplar buds, corncobs, . . . sawdust, . . . cotton seed, elm bark, . . . peanut hulls, sweet potato vines ground . . ." (Mallory 1926, p. 2). Kravchenko (1946, p. 113), who as an official of the government witnessed the famine of 1932–1933 in the Soviet Union, quotes a young peasant woman: "I will not tell you about the dead. . . . The half-dead, the nearly-dead are even worse. There are hundreds of people in Petrovo bloated with hunger. I don't know how many die every day. Many are so weak that they no longer come out of their houses. A wagon goes around now and then to pick up the corpses. We've eaten everything we could lay our hands on—cats, dogs, field mice, birds. When it's light tomorrow you will see the trees stripped of their bark. . . . And the horse manure has been eaten. . . . Sometimes there are whole grains in it." Upon such horrors in a famine-ridden area are superimposed an upsurge of burglary, robbery with violence, murder for gain. Cannibalism occurs but is a rare as well as secret event of which little can be known. Sorokin (1942, p. 81) holds the opinion that less than one-third of one per cent of a population in noncannibalistic societies would practice cannibalism under pressure of starvation. Disease flourishes abnormally as resistance is reduced by low food intake.

The calamity of famine falls most heavily upon the poor, unless the state is dispossessing and punishing a former aristocracy or bourgeoisie. Food prices begin to rise even before damages to crops or military or political interferences with food inflow become generally apparent. People with ample purchasing power begin to accumulate stocks of food, either for their own future use or for sale at higher prices in weeks to come. Markets are swept clear of foodstuffs. Employment shrinks, and wages, where there is employment, seem not to rise in proportion to food prices. Families with low incomes (if not dependents of the wealthy) feel the pinch of hunger first. They sell their possessions—their clothing, household furnishings, house timbers; even the means customarily used to provision themselves with food are sold. According to Woodham Smith, during the great Irish potato famine of the 1840s fishermen all over Ireland pawned or sold their gear to buy meals (1962, p. 291). During that and other famines many poor peasants have eaten the seed necessary to produce a new crop. Children have been sold in Chinese famines; and men have sold themselves into slavery. Prostitution burgeons. Buyers seem always to appear, for although famine may decimate a large population, it does not annihilate. Some members of a stricken community profit from the circumstances of famine. Some are protected by their position in, or by power of, the government.

Causes. Famine has many causes. Nearly a century ago Walford (1878–1879, p. 450) listed 12, classifying them into natural causes beyond human control and artificial causes within human control. This distinction remains valid in a general way, although it is certainly true that man has learned to modify some of the natural causes as well as to minimize their impact. Natural causes include drought, excessive rains and flood, unseasonably cold weather, typhoons and other high winds, tidal waves, depredations by vermin and such insects as locusts, and plant diseases. They tend chiefly to reduce production of food and to destroy stocks. Occasionally, though mostly for short periods, floods or frosts restrict the flow of foodstuffs from surplus to deficit areas. The artificial causes—commonly political—include warfare that involves siege or blockade, or destruction of food stocks or growing grain; and wartime strains on economies that diminish manpower, machines, or fertilizers, thus reducing cultivated acreage, yields, and production. Revolutions, particularly when they involve a struggle between peasantry and officialdom, may reduce food acreages and yields and thus contribute to famine; so may excessive taxation or collection from peasants of grain surpluses, which happened in Soviet Russia in 1932–1933. It is difficult to perceive in the vague history of famines a major one in which political causes alone were operative, although this may be said of a good many minor famines—typified in

sieges of cities. An age-old device of war is to impose famine on the enemy.

The great famines of the world have been due to natural forces, frequently intensified, however, by political factors. Sometimes economic or demographic situations—prevalence of poverty, including unemployment, peasant agriculture of the bare subsistence type, or many landless agricultural laborers in a population of high density—are regarded as causes of famines. They certainly make for vulnerability to famine, but unlike natural or political catastrophes are chronic rather than episodic in character.

The principal natural causes of major famines have been deficiency of rainfall (drought) or excess of rainfall (flood). Probably no major famines, but only localized and minor ones, have been due to excessively cold weather, high winds, or infestations of insects or vermin. Even a great swarm of locusts consuming every growing plant would rarely spread over an area more than a fraction as large as that covered by major drought or flood. Plant disease in the form of potato blight, however, did emerge on one occasion—in Ireland in 1845–1849—as the outstanding natural cause of a famine of great severity. Drought outranks flood as a major cause, except perhaps in north China, where in some summers the Yellow River may rise so high that it overflows its diked banks and renders unproductive the vast agricultural plains of its valley. Few flood famines of major proportions are recorded elsewhere, but one did occur, in the years 1315, 1316, and 1317, in the British Isles and on the Continent east and north of the Pyrenees and Alps at least through present-day Poland; mortality was high (Lucas 1930). Continuous rain greatly reduced the harvests of grain crops, and pestilence (murrain) killed many farm animals.

Famine follows upon extreme shortage, insufficiently relieved by inshipment, of the staple starchy food crop of the afflicted area. That crop is usually grain—usually wheat or rye in temperate zones; rice, a millet, or sorghum in warmer climates. Famine or general food shortage in northeastern Brazil, however, will chiefly represent deficiency of the manioc crop; in Ireland it was the potato crop. The grains and starchy roots provide the bulk of the energy-yielding food for most of the world's population. In the absence of shortage of grain crops or (rarely) of starchy roots, a major natural famine is unlikely to occur. Grain is relatively cheap per thousand calories of nutriment, readily storable, and easily transported and processed into meal or flour. It is the most serviceable foodstuff to be brought in to ward off or relieve famine.

Geographical incidence. Whether natural or artificial, famine is always regional or local, never world-wide or continent-wide—or even nationwide in such vast countries as India, China, Russia, and Brazil. Conceivably, some large areas of the world have escaped, if judgment can be based upon the two major chronicles of famine (see Walford 1878–1879; Minnesota . . . 1950). Therein no mention is made of famine in Australia, in the great islands of the East Indies, or in Africa south of the Sahara. In North America and Central America, the only listing is of a famine in Mexico in 1051 ("Famine which caused the Toltecs to migrate"), and this is perhaps not clearly authenticated. South America seems to have experienced major famine only in northeastern Brazil (the *sertão*), an area subject to recurrent severe droughts. Although the chroniclers of world famine make no mention of Japan, historians record three famines there in different regions, in 1732–1733, 1783–1787, and 1832–1836, severe enough to provoke violent riots (Sansom 1963, p. 222).

Europe west of Russia has witnessed no natural famine since the great Irish calamity of the 1840s, although artificial famines on a much smaller scale accompanied World War II, at least in Greece and in the western part of Holland. There were food shortages elsewhere both then and during and after World War I. Ancel Keys (see Minnesota . . . 1950, p. 1251) lists since 1850 one famine in Persia (1871), one in Asia Minor (1874–1875), one in Egypt (1897), one in Brazil (1877), and one or two in Morocco (1877–1878), indicating infrequent occurrence in those countries. In Russia over the same period no fewer than ten famines are noted, and in India 13, not counting the most recent one, the great Bengal famine of 1943. The number of famines in China since 1850 is uncertain, but a severe one occurred in 1877–1878; others in 1919–1920 and 1929–1930; and lesser ones in 1906, 1911, 1916, and 1924. Russia, India, and China over the past century have encompassed the outstanding famine areas of the world. Each contains regions adjacent to deserts, where rainfall is regularly low, highly variable, and of summer incidence; crops tend to fail in the exceptionally low-rainfall years. These regions also have a rather dense and impoverished agricultural population. In Russia the region most frequently drought-ridden centers in the Volga basin; in China, the valley of the Yellow River; in India, the northwest and the Deccan plateau. Each country also contains regions of abundant and dependable rainfall, where famine rarely occurs. But in all the great famines of the twentieth century natural and artificial causes worked simultaneously—drought and flood, war and revolution.

Relation to disease. Since famine stimulates human diseases, statistical differentiation between deaths from starvation and deaths from disease is practically impossible, as is close measurement of the degree to which famine elevates death (and morbidity) rates above normal levels. A dependable ranking of the famines of even the past century from most to least lethal is out of the question. Nevertheless, it can probably be said that there was mortality of a million persons or more above average at least in the Irish famine of 1845–1849; the Indian of 1877–1878, 1896–1897, 1899–1900, and 1943; the Russian of 1921–1922 and 1932–1933; and the Chinese of 1877–1878 and 1929–1930.

Famine reduces resistance to many diseases, including malaria, influenza, and tuberculosis; smallpox, cholera, typhus, or relapsing fever may plague the afflicted regions, especially if the population is crowded into unsanitary refugee camps, as on the fringes of cities. Acute deficiency diseases take a much larger toll than usual, for reduced food consumption is certain to bring intake of some of the essential vitamins and minerals below requirements. Acute and protracted diarrhea ("bloody flux"), induced by polluted water and the eating of improper materials, appears to be a lethal scourge, particularly among children. Famine not only increases death rates but also reduces birth rates, thus slowing growth of population. Advancing scientific knowledge of diseases and growth of both national and international health services in the twentieth century have greatly lessened the risk of high mortality as a result of famine.

Relation to migration. The circumstances of famine induce people to flee from it, not only to escape but also to seek work that will permit them to restore purchasing power in some form to family and friends left behind. Refugees from the countryside often flock to cities, especially centers of government. Of those who flee, many return upon the abatement of famine conditions, but others find new homes. The drought-ridden *sertão* of northeastern Brazil has witnessed both the flight and return and the permanent export of population—not abroad, but to other parts of the nation (James 1942, p. 425; Smith 1879, pp. 398–435). Scarcity-induced migration that crosses national frontiers has not been common. The conspicuous example in history is the great migration of more than a million people from Ireland during and after the famine of the 1840s, the bulk of whom came to the United States, remaining to participate in and influence that country's development. Internal migrations that may have occurred in Russia, China, and India have not been carefully recorded or studied. In general, demographers appear not to lay much stress on famine as a cause of the surging migrations of history or prehistory. The unrecorded breakup of families attributable to famine migration must have caused millions of individual catastrophes. The famine in Ireland led to the conviction in Great Britain that at all times basic food must be available as cheaply as possible to the poor, and the Corn Laws that had long held grain-prices high were repealed in 1846. Famines or shortages there and elsewhere have tended to force a lightening of the burden of taxes and rents upon peasant farmers and a wider acceptance by governments of responsibility for prevention and relief.

Remedial measures. Five centuries ago famine was regarded almost throughout the world as inevitable and was so accepted, often as a manifestation of divine wrath. Occasionally, however, there were rulers who sought to prevent or relieve it. The Biblical story of Joseph in Egypt, storing grain in "fat" years against the "lean" that might follow, exemplifies probably the most common method of famine prevention in antiquity and medieval times. The rulers of the Inca Empire guarded against famine by storage and by construction of irrigation canals. Irrigation, a safeguard against famine because it both elevates and stabilizes the acre-yields of crops, was practiced some 5,000 years ago in Sumer and is very ancient elsewhere in Asia and north Africa, but famine can hardly have been the sole stimulus for irrigation. Flood control by dikes and dams is also an ancient device which militates against famine but has other values. Destruction of stores of grain and of irrigation and flood-control works is obviously a method of creating artificial famine.

Natural famines having their origin mainly in drought or flood, sometimes in plant disease or insect pest, are not now regarded as inevitable. Within nations, a naturally induced or threatened food shortage is certain to be met by domestic efforts to ward off or relieve it. This was not true in the Soviet Union as late as 1932–1933 but occurred there in 1963–1964, following a very severe drought, when a huge quantity of grain was imported and paid for. So it was in China a year or two earlier. India and Pakistan have been able since war ended in 1945 to arrange, partly on the basis of international credits, for sporadic grain imports sufficient to preclude famine; so also have Brazil and Yugoslavia. The disposition of all governments by the 1960s was to prevent or relieve famine or shortages within their own borders; and of some governments to donate or loan funds or food surpluses to prevent or relieve famine beyond their own borders. The capacity of nations to pay or to loan or donate has increased. International cooperation in famine relief or prevention has increased in the past century, as evidenced by such organizations as the Red Cross, the China Relief commissions, the American Relief Administration of World War I, the United Nations Relief and Rehabilitation Administration following World War II, and the Food and Agriculture Organization of the United Nations. Supplies have been available despite the huge growth of world population; and with the advancement in agriculture everywhere, few localities stand in such risk of drought or pests or plant disease as prevailed even half a century ago. If, nevertheless, natural calamity strikes, the network of transport, by ship overseas, by barge on canal and river, by rail, by truck on roads, even by air, has so grown and is now so far-flung and efficient that stricken regions can be reached. Governments have learned how to ration food in short supply in a manner more equitable than was possible earlier.

Progress in coping with natural famine is thus apparent politically, economically, and socially. Until the end of the twentieth century there seems no reason why true famine of natural origin should be endured in any country, for over so short a time world population seems unlikely to outrun food supplies. What the more distant future holds is purely conjectural. But even in the shorter term, it cannot be said that artificial famine, induced by war or revolution, may not again appear.

M. K. Bennett

[*See also* Food.]

BIBLIOGRAPHY

Bhatia, B. M. 1963 *Famines in India: A Study in Some Aspects of the Economic History of India, 1860–1945.* New York: Asia Publishing House.

Fisher, Harold H. 1927 *The Famine in Soviet Russia, 1919–1923: The Operations of the American Relief Administration.* New York: Macmillan.

Golder, Frank A.; and Hutchinson, Lincoln 1927 *On the Trail of the Russian Famine.* Stanford Univ. Press.

James, Preston E. (1942) 1959 *Latin America.* 3d ed. New York: Odyssey.

Jasny, Naum 1949 *The Socialized Agriculture of the USSR: Plans and Performance.* Stanford Univ. Press.

Knight, Henry 1954 *Food Administration in India: 1939–47.* Stanford Univ. Press.

Kravchenko, Victor 1946 *I Chose Freedom: The Personal and Political Life of a Soviet Official.* New York: Scribner.

LOVEDAY, ALEXANDER 1914 *The History and Economics of Indian Famines.* London: Bell.

LUCAS, HENRY S. 1930 The Great European Famine of 1315, 1316, and 1317. *Speculum* 5:343–377.

MALLORY, WALTER H. 1926 *China: Land of Famine.* New York: American Geographical Society.

MINNESOTA, UNIVERSITY OF, LABORATORY OF PHYSIOLOGICAL HYGIENE 1950 *The Biology of Human Starvation.* 2 vols. Minneapolis: Univ. of Minnesota Press.

SALAMAN, REDCLIFFE 1949 *The History and Social Influence of the Potato.* Cambridge Univ. Press.

SANSOM, GEORGE B. 1963 *A History of Japan.* Volume 3: 1615–1867. Stanford Univ. Press.

SMITH, HERBERT H. 1879 *Brazil: The Amazons and the Coast.* New York: Scribner.

SOROKIN, PITIRIM A. 1942 *Man and Society in Calamity: The Effects of War, Revolution, Famine, Pestilence Upon Human Mind, Behavior, Social Organization and Cultural Life.* New York: Dutton.

TAYLOR, A. E. 1947 Famine. Unpublished manuscript, Stanford Univ., Food Research Institute.

WALFORD, CORNELIUS 1878–1879 The Famines of the World: Past and Present. *Journal of the Royal Statistical Society* 41:433–526; 42:79–265.

WOODHAM-SMITH, CECIL B. 1962 *The Great Hunger: Ireland 1845–1849.* New York: Harper. → A paperback edition was published in 1964 by New American Library.

FANON, FRANTZ

Frantz Fanon (1925–1961), political theorist, was born in Martinique. He studied medicine in France after World War II, became a psychiatrist, and served in a government hospital in Algeria. In 1956 he resigned from French government service and joined the Algerian National Liberation Front (FLN), becoming first an editor of the party's journal and then, under the Provisional Government of the Algerian Republic, an ambassador to Ghana and a special envoy to the Congo. When he died in Bethesda, Maryland, of leukemia, he had established a reputation as the leading ideologist of the Algerian revolution. Subsequently, he came to be regarded as a major theorist of anticolonialism. His last work, *The Wretched of the Earth* (1961), is the clearest extant statement of this ideology.

Fanon began as a psychiatrist. He argued that neuroses can be understood and treated only if they are related to the cultural situation that gives rise to them, what he called their "sociogenesis." For Fanon, the crucial aspect of a social structure is the extent to which it creates institutions that fulfill men's needs. He maintained that "a society which forces its members to desperate solutions is a nonviable society, which must be replaced" (*Pour la révolution africaine*, p. 61).

Fanon argued that in the eyes of most men the fundamental conflict of the contemporary world is the race conflict: Black men and white men constitute two hostile camps. He was very clear that the source of this conflict, as of all conflicts, is oppression—in this case, a racial oppression which masks the oppression of capitalism and colonialism. "It is the white man who creates the Negro. But it is the Negro who creates negritude" ([1959] 1965, p. 47). Rooted in a tradition of universalistic rationalism, Fanon nevertheless rejected the French idea and policy of assimilation which, he felt, could never transcend paternalism and which tended to justify continued oppression. He defended the wearing of the veil by Algerian women as a symbol of nationalist opposition but thought that the veil would disappear after the success of the fundamental revolution against the colonizers.

Fanon sought ways for the colonized to purge themselves of the degrading effects of colonialism. For an individual or a group, the primary symptom of the fact that it has not attained human status is that it asks—indeed, appeals—for magnanimity. Rights can only be had if they are taken by purgative acts of violence. In a situation of collective denial of rights, there must be "collective catharsis." Violence is the means to this catharsis.

Fanon believed that renewal is not easy. It requires violence, which frees the individual from the mental deformities imposed by colonialism and creates the possibility of renewal. Politicization can then follow; for to politicize is to awaken the mind to the world. Thus, self-consciousness will be the guarantee of cultural openness. The liberation of the oppressed individual from the apathy that has been encouraged in him—Fanon spoke of the "cultural mummification of colonialism"—is the only possible basis of true liberation.

Neither this individual liberation nor real decolonization can be achieved without violence. Violence is "in the atmosphere" and is constantly giving rise to spontaneous outbursts of violent protest. This spontaneity is a great source of strength, placing pressure on the inherently reluctant leadership of protest movements. But it is also dangerous, because it is neither disciplined nor farsighted. Successful revolution requires the proper balance of spontaneity and self-control.

Nationalist movements in the contemporary world have been the principal vehicle of decolonization. However, for Fanon they are an uncertain instrument because they tend to be led by the urban middle classes and because they ignore, insofar as they can, the peasantry. But only the peasantry in the underdeveloped world is really revolutionary, for only it has nothing to lose. The urban proletariat, by contrast, is a privileged group which tends to look down upon the peasants. The chief characteristic of the urban nationalist elite is that its anticolonialism goes hand in hand with its spirit of accommodation. Its propensity to compromise, combined with the peasants' often premature acceptance of concessions, constitutes the chief danger to the anticolonialist revolution.

Fanon saw the colonial powers and their agents as following a policy of making minimal concessions which are intended to undermine the unity of the oppressed classes. He analyzed the guided steps to independence in much of Asia and Africa in these terms. Under pressure, the colonial powers cede authority to each national bourgeoisie, thus effectively in most cases creating new allies. The single-party systems of the "third world"—the underdeveloped world—have been "dictatorships of the bourgeoisie."

The struggle for national liberation of colonial countries can, according to Fanon, be understood only in the context of the struggle of the "third world" for full equality and self-realization. Fanon drew on Hegel and Marx for his analysis of the underlying contradictions of the capitalist world. He followed Sorel and Lenin in their emphasis on the necessity of organized violence to polarize society. And he drew on a modified version of Freud's theories for his analysis of how changes in the social structure lead to shifts in the personality structure, which in turn determine the possibilities of political action.

Fanon sought to go beyond nationalism to the world revolution of the colonized against the colonizers. He considered the attainment of national sovereignty to be insufficient. Fundamental emancipation of the once-colonial peoples can come about, according to Fanon, through their participation in this world-wide revolution. He thought that a "new man" must be created and that only through the reawakened self-consciousness of the oppressed peoples can a true international consciousness be created and man's humanity be established.

IMMANUEL WALLERSTEIN

[See also COLONIALISM; IMPERIALISM. Other relevant material may be found in MODERNIZATION.]

BIBLIOGRAPHY

1952 Peau noire, masques blancs. Paris: Seuil.
(1959) 1965 Studies in a Dying Colonialism. New York: Monthly Review Press. → First published as L'an V de la révolution africaine.
(1961) 1965 The Wretched of the Earth. Preface by Jean-Paul Sartre. New York: Grove. → First published as Les damnés de la terre.
Pour la révolution africaine: Écrits politiques. Paris: Maspero, 1964.

SUPPLEMENTARY BIBLIOGRAPHY

ISAACS, HAROLD R. 1965 Portrait of a Revolutionary. Commentary 40, no. 1:67–71. → An insightful discussion of Fanon.

FANTASY

Fantasy, man's capacity to "give to airy nothing a local habitation and a name," has long intrigued poets, playwrights, and painters but has only during the twentieth century become a formal area of scientific inquiry in psychology. In current usage the term is almost synonymous with "daydream." Within the area of experimental or clinical study, however, the term "fantasy" has a broader significance since it deals not only with imaginary activity spontaneously produced as part of the ongoing stream of thought (daydreams) but also with products of thought elicited upon demand from a clinician or in response to inkblots or ambiguous pictures. In effect, whether as a privately occurring daydream or as a publicly elicited story or imaginative response, fantasy generally seems to involve a complex associative activity in which events from the past are integrated into some more or less elaborate ongoing image. This image, usually visual but often auditory or verbal, is generally an inner "event" in which a new situation, possibility, personal role, or sequence of behavior is formulated either on a "mental screen" or as a story told to an examiner. Deriving from the Greek phantasia and still often spelled in Greek style as "phantasy," fantasy refers to man's remarkable ability to create an "as if" world either spontaneously or upon demand. It is possible that at one time such a capacity was not so widely developed, and people were more prone to regard their own fleeting imagery or brief daydreams as actual visions, omens, or appearances of deities, much as they responded to nocturnal dreams. Prophetic visions, like Ezekiel's "wheel" or John's Apocalypse, probably represent literary expressions of elaborate daydreams or fantasies used for expository or hortatory purposes.

History

Within psychology the formal study of fantasy as a behavioral phenomenon is probably traceable to Francis Galton's classic studies of individual differences in imagery. Although imagery itself as a field of inquiry has a somewhat separate history, the fact that much fantasy behavior involves some form of imagery led Galton to touch on issues involving the differences between persons in their internal private constructions. By 1890 William James in his great work, *The Principles of Psychology*, devoted portions of several chapters, including the famous one on the "stream of thought," to issues closely related to fantasy processes. James was among the first great psychologists to sense a continuity between normal phenomena characteristic of the ongoing self-stimulating properties of the living brain and the bizarre delusions or hallucinations of the insane or the inspirational visions of religious mystics. James also called attention to what he termed the reproductive and memorial facets of imagery, or the degree to which the image is of an object recently perceived or one called forth from the distant past. The fantasy presumably may represent a response to a stimulus perceived momentarily which triggers off a complex associative process in the ongoing stream of thought. The taste of the *madeleine* crumb produced in Proust a vivid memory of his childhood in Combray, a strong memorial association, whereas the sound of the song of the nightingale touched off a more "fanciful" association in Keats, the song that

> oft-times hath
> Charm'd magic casements, opening on the foam
> Of perilous seas, in faery lands forlorn.

> "Ode to a Nightingale," stanza 7, ll. 8–10

Psychoanalytic contributions. Although the nineteenth and early twentieth centuries were times of considerable research and controversy within psychology with respect to imagery and the possible existence of "imageless" thought, little attention was paid to the daydream itself as a spontaneously produced image complex. Interest in fantasy processes and dreams was limited at that period (and particularly following the emergence of Watsonian behaviorism in America) to the clinical psychiatrist and especially to the psychoanalyst. Freud's elucidation of the structure and interpretative possibilities of the phenomena of nocturnal dreaming, based largely on remarkable self-observation and intensive clinical work, also led quite naturally to explorations of other dreamlike phenomena, such as daydreams. When Freud realized that patients' accounts of infantile seductions (which he believed to be the foundation of neurotic developments) could not possibly have occurred, he was compelled to pay more attention to the nature of childhood fantasy as the source of such material. The free-association process of psychoanalysis itself also led to frequent reports of fantasies or daydreams, the most important, from a technical

psychotherapeutic sense, being those involving the relationship between analyst and patient. Many psychoanalysts, therefore, paid careful attention to daydreams of patients and began in some instances to experiment with eliciting fantasies when patients were resistant to or incapable of recalling night dreams. Freud himself during the early part of the twentieth century speculated on the psychological significance of the daydream in his papers "The Relation of the Poet to Day-dreaming" (1908) and "Formulations on the Two Principles of Mental Functioning" (1911).

Throughout the early decades of the twentieth century psychoanalysts made regular use of reports of spontaneous fantasies and published many papers in which myths or popular stories and literature were interpreted as forms of fantasy.

Projective methods. Some attempts were made to study children's fantasies through stories elicited from them or through their drawings, but the most influential advances in the psychological study of fantasy came from the development of so-called projective techniques.

Rorschach technique. The first and most famous of the projective methods was the Rorschach Inkblot Technique, developed by Hermann Rorschach, a Swiss psychiatrist. Of particular interest to him was his finding that persons who reported numerous "human movement" responses to the inkblots, such as "two footmen bowing, two ladies dancing," were characterized on the one hand by considerable motor inhibition or awkward motility and on the other by a heightened capacity for "inner living," imagination, or fantasy production. In contrast, persons who produced numerous color-dominated responses were more likely to be outgoing, motorically affective, and emotionally labile. The juxtaposition of the human-movement and color responses provided an indication of what Rorschach called the "experience type," the relative degree to which capacity for fantasy behavior and inner living were balanced with tendencies toward emotionality and direct action.

Rorschach's method, somewhat modified, spread slowly through Europe and was introduced into the United States in the late 1920s and early 1930s by David Levy and Samuel Beck. In the United States by the time of World War II it had been adopted by clinical psychologists, who saw the method as a means of exploring the private fantasy world of patients without direct questioning and of eliciting behavioral data that could be quantified, thus meeting to some extent the objections of academic psychology to the purely qualitative approach of clinical psychoanalysis and psychiatry. With the introduction of more formal academic courses within the universities and private seminars on Rorschach technique, a great deal of systematic research was generated to check specific features of the technique or to compare cultures, psychopathological groups, or dimensions of individual difference through the use of the elicited fantasy response to the inkblots. A summary of much of the work in this field and of the methodological and theoretical issues involved in the use of the Rorschach method is available in *Rorschach Psychology,* edited by Rickers-Ovsiankina (1960) [*see* PROJECTIVE METHODS, *article on* THE RORSCHACH TEST].

Thematic Apperception Test. Beginning in the early 1930s at Harvard University's Psychological Clinic, a group of psychologists under the leadership of Henry A. Murray undertook extensive studies of various techniques using elicited fantasies to study the nature of the normal personality. A specific technique that emerged was Murray's Thematic Apperception Test, a method for eliciting imaginative stories in response to somewhat ambiguous pictures, for example, of a boy staring at a violin set before him on a table. The stories elicited by each of a series of 20 pictures were then analyzed in terms of the motivational pattern presumably involved in the story content, in effect an application of psychoanalytic interpretative methods, perhaps more systematic, quantifiable, and suitable for rigorous research requirements. With various modifications in scoring categories and picture content, the basic method is in widespread use today for clinical, industrial, and research purposes. Such scoring of motivational patterns from elicited fantasy products has been especially instrumental in the careful study by David McClelland, John Atkinson, and their numerous students of achievement motivation through fantasy. Because of the relatively objective scoring techniques available and high reliability of trained judges scoring for such motives as *achievement* and *affiliation,* the Thematic Apperception Test or related methods for scoring story material as a fantasy expression of a need or motive are perhaps more widely used in systematic research than the more diffuse Rorschach method. [*For relevant summaries of literature, see* Atkinson 1958; *see also* ACHIEVEMENT MOTIVATION; PROJECTIVE METHODS, *article on* THE THEMATIC APPERCEPTION TEST.]

Other projective methods. Within clinical practice and, to a lesser extent, in formal research, a large variety of fantasy-eliciting techniques are used. These include various drawing procedures or such studies of artistic activity as finger painting,

eliciting responses to incomplete sentences or to requests like "Name your three wishes," choices of various symbolic objects, organization of mosaic patterns, and puppet play. All make some general assumptions that a long-standing personality predisposition or style, as well as a motive pattern or aspects of bizarre thought and pathology, will be manifested by such elicited quasi-fantasy expressions. The proliferation in the use of these projective techniques has not, however, been the fruit of sufficient systematic prior experimentation with any one technique as a rule, nor have any really significant contributions to systematic psychological theory resulted from their widespread application. Individual clinical psychologists may be especially gifted at eliciting material using a particular technique with which they have much experience, but such personalized effectiveness does not usually add to the general body of psychological knowledge.

Experimental approaches. More recently, as a result of particular theoretical developments within psychoanalytic theory and progress in research in psychology and neurophysiology, greater attention has been paid to experimental efforts to study the nature of ongoing imagery or fantasy and daydream experience. New techniques—some involving electrophysiological measurement or systematic inquiry of subjects during sensory isolation, under the influence of special drugs, or during monitoring or vigilance tasks—have led to some increased sophistication and rigor in the study of the "stream of thought" in the normal adult. Recent developments in this area are summarized in Holt (1964) and Singer (1966).

Current theories and relevant research

Surprisingly little as yet is known of the range and variation of fantasy in normal adults and children or of differences in the content, frequency, or structure of daydreams among various cultural groups (Singer 1966). There has emerged, however, chiefly from psychoanalysis, a preliminary theoretical formulation of the function of daydreaming in the economy of the personality. Research reflects efforts to examine and test the implications of the theory of fantasy, which derives chiefly from the specific formulations of Freud.

Defensive or cathartic models. One of Freud's more fascinating insights was his observation that the capacity to delay gratification, a vitally significant step in man's adaptive development, was somehow linked to his imaginative capacity. Two general conceptions of the relation between thought or fantasy and control mechanisms can be discerned in Freud's work and in that of most psychoanalytically oriented investigators or learning theorists who have developed the implications of the notion of the relations of thought and delay. One conception stems from Freud's early paper on the poet and daydreaming (1908), in which he stated that "unsatisfied wishes are the driving power behind fantasies" and pointed out the degree of similarity between daydreams and night dreams in their wish-fulfilling function. The daydreams that the poet transforms into artistic productions are disguised representations of unfulfilled infantile desires, defenses against direct recognition of these desires. As Freud put it: "Happy people never daydream."

This view that the daydream is an outgrowth of an unsatisfied wish and is a defense against its direct manifestation pervades much psychoanalytic thinking. Closely related to the defensive function of fantasy but perhaps more precise in formulation is Freud's second conception that all processes of thought, including fantasy, by allowing partial satisfactions (expenditure of small quantities of energy), partially reduce the drive and thereby permits delay in gross motor discharge. This theory of the catharsis or drive reduction obtained through play and fantasy in children or daydreams in adults has many important implications (see Rapaport 1956).

In effect, it proposes that where there is a delay in the opportunity to discharge a certain amount of energy through satisfaction of a need or through movements associated with attaining such satisfaction, the fantasied reproduction "in the mind's eye" of the gratifying activity or associated movements will partially reduce the amount of energy at least enough, say, so that rash or fruitless action will not occur. From a psychoanalytic standpoint (where the emphasis is on the inner origin of stimulation) such partial discharges may effectively control maladaptive overt discharge of many antisocial or asocial tendencies. Thus, regular watching of wrestling or boxing on television may curb man's tendency to assault his neighbor upon minimal provocation, and the conscious acceptance of daydreams of sexual conquest may effectively prevent rape, whereas inability to experience such thoughts may lead to overt impulse-gratifying behavior that has unfortunate consequences.

Within academic psychology the learning-theory formulation of the catharsis model does not specify the amount of instinctual energy but does emphasize that fantasied behavior has, in effect, secondary-reinforcing qualities that may lead to a lowering of drive strength consequent to engaging in a daydream about the goal object. It is assumed that if a child is hungry he begins to make motor reactions associated with searching for food. To the extent that he can, at an ideational level, reproduce an image of the movements that would gratify his hunger or of his mother coming in with the food, and if just about that time his mother does indeed come in, then the ideational representation acquires secondary-reinforcing properties. Provided his mother comes regularly but perhaps not invariably (intermittent reinforcement being superior in preventing extinction), the fantasy activity will be learned as one means of response in a state of need.

A number of interesting lines of research have been developed in attempts to test the cathartic theory of fantasy and some of the implications of this drive-reduction model. The theory also has some important implications for the logic of projective testing where, for example, one faces the interpretative task of deciding whether the person who provides a certain frequent response pattern to inkblots or photographs is likely to show the same or opposite pattern in overt behavior. In the case of the Rorschach, for example, there is evidence for an inverse relationship between perception of movement on the blots and overt movement, impulsivity, and other ego functions (Rickers-Ovsiankina 1960). Most of the evidence supports Rorschach's notion that human-movement responses are linked with controlled motility, on the one hand, and imaginative development on the other. An experiment by Page (1957) has provided an important link in this chain by demonstrating that only this human-movement response of all Rorschach factors is significantly associated with reported frequency of daydreaming.

Criticism of the cathartic model. When the focus in the projective method is not on the *structural* aspect of fantasy and motor behavior but on the relation of specific content to projective fantasy, a different finding emerges. The controversy between the alternative channel and direct expression theories of Thematic Apperception Test interpretation seems to be resolved by the large majority of studies in favor of direct expression. The literature on fantasied aggression as summarized by Buss (1961) and the extensive work by McClelland (1961) and Atkinson (1958) has certainly supported the idea that persons who produce aggressive or achievement-oriented themes behave accordingly in daily life.

An important step in the effort to test the drive-reduction model of fantasy came in Feshbach's study (1955) in which it was demonstrated that when insulted Ss were given an opportunity to express aggression through storytelling they showed less aggression in subsequent ratings than did a group given no opportunity for fantasied aggressive expression. Feshbach also found that viewing a filmed prize fight after induction of anger would partially reduce later aggressive ratings. It should be noted, however, that the very writing of the stories is perhaps a more motorically involved expression than pure daydreaming, the daily life phenomenon associated with drive reduction.

Where experimental efforts have focused attention not upon experimentally aroused anger but upon the arousal of stress, anxiety, or fear, the cathartic significance of daydream or fantasy activity is less in evidence or unsupported (Singer 1966). These results suggest that when we turn to stress rather than anger as the drive or affect involved, the effects of daydreaming are more complex; engaging in fantasy may enhance anxiety when the future situation is unstructured but may reduce it when a short-term stress is imminent by distracting the person from continued thought.

Particularly telling evidence against a catharsis theory has come in the works of Berkowitz (1964) and Bandura, Ross, and Ross (1963). These studies, concentrating on aggressive expression, seem to offer a body blow to the cathartic theory and to point up the importance of considering the pattern of environmental stimulation more thoroughly in understanding the meaning of fantasy play in relation to direct motor expression. Berkowitz, for example, found that Ss who viewed a movie scene in which a prize fighter was taking a "justifiable" beating showed a heightened tendency to aggressive behavior toward a fellow student soon after the show, compared with Ss who had been told the beating was undeserved [see AGGRESSION, article on PSYCHOLOGICAL ASPECTS]. The studies by Bandura, Ross, and Ross of modeling behavior indicate, too, that young children aroused to anger by frustration are likely to imitate directly the aggressive behavior of a previously witnessed live or filmed model [see IMITATION].

The evidence for a catharsis theory of fantasy seems weak, at best, in view of recent research and a restudying of the problem. The data, of course, are chiefly from the study of aggressive behavior, and in general there has been little concern either with naturalistic daydreaming behavior and its consequences (as against filmed or thematically stimulated responses) or with affects other than anger and aggressive behavior.

Fantasy as a cognitive skill. An alternative approach may be proposed that at least conceptually reconciles the Rorschach data on movement perception and motor inhibition and the results of the direct expression or modeling theories of fantasy aggression. Heinz Hartmann, while developing his concept of the autonomous ego, noted that fantasy may serve to prepare the person for a greater mastery of the outside world through increased insight into his own psychic processes. It seems preferable to go further than Hartmann and begin again with a fresh look at the origin of fantasy and imagery without the burden of concepts of cathectic dynamics or neutralized versus libidinized energy. One may start, instead, by regarding the development of fantasy behavior or daydreaming as a cognitive skill, a capacity for gradual internalization of response and for attending to the ongoing "reverberatory" behavior of one's brain—responses available to most children. Conceivably, children may differ constitutionally in their capacity to form visual or auditory images, but these differences for the most part account for only a small amount of the variance in subsequent development of daydreaming skills or styles. Special handicaps do exist, and it has been found that congenitally blind children are less imaginative in their spontaneous play and storytelling than otherwise matched sighted children (Singer 1966).

Fantasy play is thus an important feature in the development of children, a part of the continuous assimilation–accommodation pattern, as Piaget put it (1945). There are, however, certain particular factors that increase the likelihood that fantasy play will become an integrated skill, rather than a sporadic response pattern, and, thus, a capacity to manipulate or to attend to an inner dimension, which may be one of man's greatest assets. Similarly, if we recognize more clearly the potential of man's inner skills, we may make possible a further advance in man's fullest use of his capacities.

Factors in development of fantasy. What, then, are some circumstances conducive to fantasy development?

Identification and imitation. The modeling theory suggests that imitation of parents is probably an important element in fantasy development. The child who perceives his parents as benign persons will strive for identification more readily and learn more of their behaviors, and there is some evidence that persons showing more imagination on the Rorschach (human-movement responses) also report that their parents were benign and loving (Singer 1960). Identification with a specific adult figure, usually the mother, who represents inhibition of impulse, socialization, and storytelling, may be an important feature in fostering internalization. Several studies on daydreaming have yielded evidence of more frequent daydreaming by male and female adults who were more closely identified with their mother than with their father or who perceived their father as further from their ideal (Singer 1966). A similar finding was reported by Sharef (1959) in a doctoral dissertation at Harvard: he noted that young men who had a history of being chosen as a mother's confidant showed greater imaginative or introceptive tendencies. Some degree of modeling and imitation caused in part by eagerness to please, by the availability of copying of certain types of responses, and by the parent's rewarding these responses may foster fantasy skill. A well-known quotation from Goethe serves to make this point:

> From father I have looks and build
> And the serious conduct of living.
> My mother gave me gaiety
> And zest for fantasizing.
>
> *Xenions*

Opportunity for play. Given the closeness to at least one adult who encourages verbal interchange or fantasy play, a child still requires some opportunity to practice such activities. There are indications that extensive contact with other children is likely to provide less opportunity for such fantasy play unless the children are older and play a quasi-parental role, for example, a much older sister who plays "house" or "school" with a younger child. By and large, the extensive kaleidoscopic ebb and flow of physical motion and varied external stimulation provided by a group of children is most likely to involve a child in external behaviors and afford him little chance to practice fantasy play. A study carried out with children aged six to nine (Singer 1966) produced evidence that indicated that children reporting more fantasy play had significantly fewer older siblings, that is, they tended to be either first-born or only children and not members of large families.

One might argue that daydreaming thus becomes a defense against loneliness. At the same time many children who take great pleasure in elaborate fantasy games and who are eager to share these with others are frustrated by the disorganization of the other children and return to solitary play or, if they have some influence on the group, develop a more organized fantasy game, for example, pirates or detectives. Chance factors of being alone, of being encouraged to read, of storytelling or fantasy making as part of the family tradition as well as cultural aspects that strongly emphasize imaginative exchange or intellectual exploration, achievement motivation, upward mobility in society—all increase the likelihood of extensive involvement in fantasy play by a given child (Singer 1966). In effect, the child who plays extensively by creating fantasy people, situations, imaginary worlds, or scientific make-believe is practicing a complex series of skills related to what Kurt Goldstein has called the "attitude toward the possible." These children have a more complex vocabulary, develop structural and organizational skills, see relationships that others may have to be taught in school, and, perhaps most important, carve out for themselves a dimension of experience —attentiveness to their own associational flow— which may be a realm they can enter or leave at will. This dimension can, of course, become the basis of an extensive defensive maneuver should the outside world become too stressful or should the child fail to develop positive social skills with his peers. The development of an extensive inner life by no means excludes the possibility of enjoyment and skill in social experience, group games, or sports. It merely provides an additional medium for play and satisfaction. There is as yet no evidence that psychotic patients show any excessive predisposition toward daydreaming. Indeed, chronic patients are often characterized more by an impoverishment of inner living and daydreaming than by the excessive involvement in "private worlds" so often attributed to them [*see* DEFENSE MECHANISMS].

Adaptive aspects of fantasy. It is obvious that enhanced vocabulary and abstract skills represent great evolutionary advances in man. But let us also consider the adaptive manifestations of the more "fantastic" aspects of thought, daydreams, and reverie. The Rorschach findings about the inverse relationship between imagination and motor impulsivity are better explained not by a relatively mechanical catharsis theory but by viewing the person who has imagination as having a whole set of alternative responses in addition to motor activity. In a waiting room he need not be so restless (as was found in several studies) if he can provide himself with an inner source of stimulation to engage his interest and provide positive affective experience. He may voluntarily set up an inner sequence (imagining a movie, replaying a baseball game) or he may permit the ongoing stream of consciousness, the reverberatory activity of his brain, to hold his attention. In situations of reduced sensory cues, this capacity may be an asset, as was found in studies of sensory deprivation (Holt 1964). Similarly, it was found (Singer 1966, p. 108) that persons required to monitor a blinking light in a dark room with all external cues reduced were more likely to remain awake and comfortable if at the same time they could engage in free associative talk. When these same persons were limited to monotonous counting, they tended to fall asleep and became quite irritable. There is also evidence that persons who have a history of daydreaming, that is, for whom attention to inner experience is a well-established pattern, are less susceptible to hallucination.

The person who has developed a considerable ability to picture events or scenes concerning people through reading and imaginative play has available a tool for greatly increasing his own response repertory. The ability to imagine a variety of social responses or scenes concerning people may enhance a person's ability to deal with novel or difficult social demands. Obviously, practice in actual situations is also necessary, but it is possible that such learning will come more quickly to a person who has engaged in some preparatory fantasy. The fact that fantasy originates in play brings it closer to humor and wit and makes it possible for the person who employs fantasy when anxious or in conflict to see a humorous, bizarre, or unusual facet to his dilemma and to obtain at least some temporary positive affective experience or to alleviate the stress through a comical fantasy. The development of an inner cognitive style of differentiated attentiveness to ongoing thoughts, memories, or marginal associations, or of an ability to manipulate such material at will, thus can be seen as an important feature of the over-all ego strength of the personality, a skill, much as is motor ability, empathic capacity, or precision in communication [see HUMOR].

Recent research developments

In addition to the research centering on theoretical issues, other areas of significant ongoing experimental work in the field of fantasy may be cited briefly. The extensive work of McClelland interpreting the fantasy content of stories in third-grade readers as evidence of achievement motivation has been particularly fruitful. McClelland's work has shown, for example, that indications of the degee of achievement motivation expressed in the fantasy products of various countries around the world are highly related to the *actual* economic development of the country over a period of years (McClelland 1961). These striking results suggest either that the inclusion of such achievement-oriented materials in the stories used in teaching young children stimulates them to become more achievement oriented or, what is more likely,

that an already ongoing national achievement-oriented pattern is then consciously or unconsciously reflected in the thematic materials provided children. Most of the work of Atkinson and McClelland has emphasized the nature of motivation rather than the study of the fantasy process for its own sake. McClelland, however, has attempted a formulation of the relationship between degree of deprivation and the occurrence of a fantasy expression of the deprived need.

The greater awareness that during periods of reduced sensory stimulation man becomes increasingly responsive to internally produced stimulation, as well as the methodological advances in the study of night dreaming by electroencephalographic patterns and oculoretinograms, have encouraged studies of man's waking pattern of ongoing thought. A series of investigations has suggested, for example, that adult Ss who are engaging in daydreaming show relatively little eye movement but that ocular motility increases when attempts at suppression of ongoing thought occur (Singer 1966). Similarly, experimental studies of the relative degree of external stimulation necessary to prevent subjects from actually engaging in passing fantasies also suggest that a remarkable degree of ongoing thought activity occurs, at least for college adults, despite great demands on attention from the outside (Singer 1966). It seems likely that man's relative willingness or ability to attend to what appears to be an almost continuous ongoing stream of internal reverberatory associative activity may be a significant dimension for personality study [see DREAMS].

As yet, however, relatively little is known of the physiological basis of this stream of thought or of the factors that lead to relative priorities in attention to such internal processes. We also know little in a systematic way of individual differences in daydreaming and the personality correlates of such differences, although some studies have opened the way for further work in these areas. Formal data on whether there are differences between cultural or national groups in frequency, content, and structure of daydreaming or resort to inner living are scant indeed. Singer and McCraven (Singer 1966, pp. 57–63) did find some evidence that American-born subcultural groups (Negro, Jewish, Italian, Irish, German, and Anglo-Saxon) did differ in reported daydream frequency, with the more upwardly mobile groups (or less socially secure ones) showing more fantasy activity. An earlier comparison of American-born Irish and Italian schizophrenic adults by Singer and Opler also yielded evidence of differences in degree of fantasy activity between persons of differing cultural background (Singer 1966, pp. 64–65).

JEROME L. SINGER

[*Directly related are the entries* CREATIVITY; STIMULATION DRIVES. *Other relevant material may be found in* AESTHETICS; FINE ARTS; LITERATURE; PSYCHOANALYSIS.]

BIBLIOGRAPHY

ATKINSON, JOHN W. (editor) 1958 *Motives in Fantasy, Action, and Society.* Princeton, N.J.: Van Nostrand.

BANDURA, ALBERT; ROSS, DOROTHEA; and ROSS, SHEILA A. 1963 Vicarious Reinforcement and Imitative Learning. *Journal of Abnormal and Social Psychology* 67: 601–607.

BERKOWITZ, LEONARD 1964 The Effects of Observing Violence. *Scientific American* 210:35–41.

BUSS, ARNOLD H. 1961 *The Psychology of Aggression.* New York: Wiley.

FESHBACH, SEYMOUR (1955) 1958 The Drive-reducing Function of Fantasy Behavior. Pages 160–175 in John W. Atkinson (editor), *Motives in Fantasy, Action, and Society.* Princeton, N.J.: Van Nostrand.

FREUD, SIGMUND (1908) 1925 The Relation of the Poet to Day-dreaming. Volume 4, pages 173–183 in Sigmund Freud, *Collected Papers.* London: Hogarth. → First published as "Der Dichter und das Phantasieren."

FREUD, SIGMUND (1911) 1959 Formulations on the Two Principles of Mental Functioning. Volume 12, pages 215–226 in Sigmund Freud, *The Standard Edition of the Complete Psychological Works.* London: Hogarth. → First published as *Formulierungen über die zwei Prinzipien des psychischen Geschehens.*

HOLT, ROBERT R. 1964 Imagery: The Return of the Ostracized. *American Psychologist* 19:254–264.

McCLELLAND, DAVID C. 1961 *The Achieving Society.* Princeton, N.J.: Van Nostrand.

McKELLAR, PETER 1957 *Imagination and Thinking: A Psychological Analysis.* London: Cohen & West.

PAGE, HORACE A. 1957 Studies in Fantasy: Daydreaming Frequency and Rorschach Scoring Categories. *Journal of Consulting Psychology* 21:111–114.

PIAGET, JEAN (1945) 1951 *Play, Dreams, and Imitation in Childhood.* New York: Norton; London: Heinemann. → First published in French as *La formation du symbole chez l'enfant.* A paperback edition was published in 1962 by Norton.

RAPAPORT, DAVID (editor and translator) 1956 *Organization and Pathology of Thought: Selected Sources.* Austen Riggs Foundation, Monograph No. 1. New York: Columbia Univ. Press.

RICKERS-OVSIANKINA, MARIA C. (editor) 1960 *Rorschach Psychology.* New York: Wiley.

SHAREF, M. R. 1959 An Approach to the Theory and Measurement of Introception. Ph.D. dissertation, Harvard Univ.

SINGER, JEROME L. 1960 The Experience Type: Some Behavioral Correlates and Theoretical Implications. Pages 223–259 in Maria C. Rickers-Ovsiankina (editor), *Rorschach Psychology.* New York: Wiley.

SINGER, JEROME L. 1966 *Daydreaming: An Introduction to the Experimental Study of Inner Experience.* New York: Random House.

FARMING

See AGRICULTURE; LAND; LAND TENURE; PLANTATIONS; RURAL SOCIETY.

FASCISM

"Fascism" is used primarily to identify the political system by which Italy was ruled from 1922 to 1945. It is also used to identify a prototype of totalitarianism and is applied to variations of political systems thought to parallel the Italian one.

Historical development

Historically, fascism has its origins in the crisis of Italian parliamentary institutions. This crisis was caused in large part by a failure in the process of adjustment of the traditional parliamentary parties to new mass parties. It occurred at a moment of intensified difficulties caused by World War I, as deep economic and social upheavals were complicated by an upsurge of nationalism and the aftermath of the Bolshevik Revolution of 1917. Thus, the combination of the weakness of the liberal ruling class, the revolutionary aspirations of the working classes, the extremism of patriotism, the dissatisfaction with the 1919 peace settlements, the psychological dislocation of war veterans, the fears of property-owning classes, and the political role played by the army and the crown produced, four years after the armistice of 1918, the episode known as the March on Rome and the beginnings of a 23-year dictatorship of the Fascist party under the leadership of Mussolini.

As fascism sought, not without difficulty but with final success, to organize itself for the seizure of power, the clash of different ideological trends and the contradictions that were to mark its entire life stood out clearly. In the beginning, fascism showed a strong socialist inspiration. Many of the leaders had come to fascism from socialist and syndicalist movements, but they had differentiated themselves from orthodox socialists by maintaining an aggressive nationalistic attitude that had caused them to favor Italy's intervention in World War I, to be against what they described as the "unjust" peace settlements, and to support the political adventure of D'Annunzio's seizure of Fiume. Mussolini backed the occupation of the factories by the workers as part of a revolutionary program intended to give to the industrial working classes the political role they did not have. But, by playing on the themes of national grandeur and power, he was also enlisting the support of nationalistic activists, who thought in terms of territorial expansion and colonialism.

By the end of 1920, however, nationalism rather than socialism was providing the main driving force of fascism. The government of the time, headed by the liberal leader Giovanni Giolitti, rightly thought that a specific revolutionary danger did not exist and that prudent handling of the situation would lead, as it did, to a peaceful resolution of that particular conflict. But Italy's middle classes, the landowners, the business world, the army, and the crown saw in fascism the militant movement that, properly led, could make Italy safe from the Marxist peril. In 1921/1922 the original, and small, fascist movement was swamped by hundreds of thousands of new members, most of them of middle-class provenance, while it received subsidies from industrial quarters and weapons from the military establishment.

Fascism reoriented itself along fresh lines, with policies that stressed, above all, the need to restore the authority of the state at home and abroad. The state was conceived as the defender of law and order and as the unyielding supporter of the national interest in foreign affairs. The younger party members were organized into blackshirted squads that proceeded to destroy the physical structure and to liquidate the leadership of socialism and communism, which by then had become the chief targets.

When, after the 1919 elections, Giolitti failed to reach agreement with either the Socialists or the Christian Democrats, he imagined that fascism would see Italy through the political impasse by taming these two mass parties and that in the end liberalism would return to power. Liberal Italy greeted October 28, 1922, the day of the fascist seizure of power, as the beginning of an interlude that would stabilize political life, restore the authority of the state, and prepare the return to tradition shortly afterward.

The second period in the history of fascism goes from 1922 to 1925. In the course of these three years the fascist regime sought to answer a number of questions about its own direction and purpose. After the bloody violence of the preceding two years, these years appeared mild enough on the surface, and some of the liberal leaders even thought that their forecasts would be realized. Laissez-faire was the prevailing economic policy. Parties and the press seemed to function almost normally. The word "totalitarian" had not yet been invented.

But the inherent logic of the system was already at work. First, the blackshirted army had not been dissolved, and the dualism typical of a totalitarian state was born, with two sets of institutions—one answerable to the government, the other to the Fascist party. Second, the use of violence accepted as normal since 1922 could not be given up. Force was still the foundation of the regime. One after the other, the voices of the opposition were stilled. The climax was the murder of Matteotti, the Socialist party leader. For the old ruling class, this proved to be the final test of its sense of responsibility and its understanding of the nature of the modern political process. In the summer of 1924 the crown might still have succeeded in obtaining Mussolini's resignation. The advice it received was that no change should be attempted. The Vatican joined in this appraisal when it drove Luigi Sturzo, the leader of the Christian democratic movement, into exile.

In 1925, exploiting this extraordinary vote of confidence, fascism built the totalitarian structure. The press was silenced or taken over. All parties were abolished except the Fascist party. Constitutional changes were begun that created the unique figure of the leader embodying in his person the sum total of power.

The next ten years, from 1925 to 1935, represented a period of both practical consolidation and theoretical doctrinal development. With power safely in his hands, Mussolini began to consider the problem of the place of fascism in history. Fascism had been criticized as being a naked, pragmatic movement. It was necessary to acquire ideas and to develop an overview on the nature of man and of nations that could promise the recognition of fascism as one of the important revolutionary movements of the twentieth century.

The enemies were identified with great precision. Marxism still was the foremost opponent. But liberalism became another enemy to be fought. Showing little regard for those who had put him in office, Mussolini began to cultivate the ideas that led by 1927 to the labor charter, by 1930/1931 to the beginnings of the corporate state, and by 1934 to the establishment of the corporations themselves.

Some of these economic ideas did provide a certain amount of lively discussion at the time among those whose aim was primarily to find some third way between Marxism and liberalism. The key notions were that (a) the community alone was to have the right to determine what the national interest required; (b) therefore, the conflicting interests of owners, workers, technicians, and the state were to be brought together in a single unit, the corporation, operating under public control; (*c*) strikes and lockouts were to be forbidden; and (*d*) the doctrine of the primacy of the politician over the expert was to be abandoned. The divisiveness of politics was to be eliminated by the unity of expertise.

The world-wide depression that had hit the Western world after 1929 facilitated Mussolini's task. By 1931 the industrial and banking systems of Italy were in serious trouble. The totalitarian regime made possible a quick salvage operation, which placed the key industrial and financial sectors of the country under direct government ownership or control. By 1935 fascism had realized, at least on paper, the goals of a state-controlled society. In its repression of the individual and of social groups, fascism was steadily strengthening and centralizing its power, which was exercised in the name of an ideology that had become a key operational tool in the hands of the new elite.

In its third period, 1935 to 1943, violence and war became the substance of fascism. The first important manifestation of this totalitarian characteristic took place in 1935 with the aggression against Ethiopia, which provided the regime with a testing ground for its military policies, challenged the League of Nations, and furnished German Nazism with evidence of the might of fascist Italy. The second act was played on the battlefields of Spain, where both Nazism and fascism joined hands against republican Spain. Historically, this armed clash was of great significance, for it gave the enemies of Mussolini some idea of their strength and of guerrilla-warfare techniques. The third act was played in 1940, when Mussolini entered World War II on the side of Hitler after the defeat of France. Italy's defeat came soon, and by 1943 the fascist regime collapsed, as it had begun, through an intervention of the crown.

From 1943 to 1945 the Fascist Social Republic came feebly and fleetingly to life under the control of the Germans. The only point worthy of note is that Mussolini, on the eve of the final collapse and of his own death, tried in a clumsy way to go back to his syndicalist origins and appear as a defender of the proletariat. Industrial plants were now to be turned over to the workers themselves. But it was 1945 and too late.

The fascist regime—ideal and reality

As a movement based on a pragmatic appraisal of the conditions necessary to retain power, fascism was never too preoccupied with the task of a theoretical definition of its own origins and goals. The

philosopher Giovanni Gentile sought to link it to Hegelian idealism, the jurist Alfredo Rocco attempted to develop a heavy-handed theory of the state, while Mussolini himself sought to provide the ideology of totalitarianism.

Instruments of power. But the real drive of fascism was in the building of instruments of power and not in the building of theory. Between 1925 and 1939, four main tools of power were developed and refined: charismatic leadership, single-party rule, terror, and economic controls.

Leadership. Around the leader, Benito Mussolini, a series of institutional privileges were built, intended to make his position unchallenged. Constitutionally, he was chief of state and, as such, was placed in a position that was not subordinate to that of the king. Although the monarchy was kept, the Great Council of Fascism had been given certain rights on questions affecting the succession to the throne which placed the monarchy in a dependent position. Politically, the constant rotation in office of Mussolini's subordinates kept competitors out of the way. Psychologically, the unique position of the leader was carefully maintained by all the devices of communication and propaganda typical of totalitarian states. The identification of fascism with Mussolini was made compulsory in meetings of parliamentary assemblies, of the Fascist party, of economic bodies, of schoolchildren, of every form of group life.

Party rule. The party became a capillary instrument of power going from its highest body, the Great Council of Fascism, which met from time to time to decide major questions of policy, through the secretary of the party and the provincial federations to the thousands of party units, which at the communal level were the daily instruments of propaganda and contact with the country. The party reached out in all directions with its subsidiary organizations, affecting the activities of schoolchildren and the cultural and sport activities of the people. The party became the carrier of the ideology and slogans of the leader, and, more important, the channel through which most of the life of the country had to flow. Jobs, advancement, and preferment had to be cleared in most instances through the party. Membership in the party was, at first, a right belonging to the small elite group that in the pre-1922 days had supported the party's fight for power; in a second phase which lasted into the early 1930s, membership was made available to all who applied; in a third and final phase, one could become a member only by moving up through the youth organizations that by then had been created. Thus, membership in the Fascist party was reserved at first to the fighters, later to the opportunists, and finally to the perfect citizens of a fascist state nurtured on the ideals of fascism from their most tender age.

Terror. Although between 1925 and 1943 the party was the chief vehicle for the consolidation of the regime, it was no longer the chief instrument of terror, as it had been between 1920 and 1925. "Legalized" repressive functions were carried out by the Special Tribunal for the Safety of the State and by the secret police under the Ministry of the Interior. But from 1943 to 1945, the years of renewed bloody civil war between fascist militias and the resistance groups, the party again undertook the task of meting out summary justice to the increasingly rebellious population and was guilty of massacres that exceeded in scope anything that had been witnessed between 1920 and 1925.

Economic controls. As the pseudo liberalism of the initial years gave way to controls on economic life equaling those on political life, fascism developed two principal instruments of policy. The first was the Institute for Industrial Reconstruction (IRI), which, started in 1931 as an antidepression device, was soon changed into an agency to pursue the military goals that after 1935 became the heart of the dictatorship. Controlling all major financial institutions and nearly all heavy industry through the IRI, the regime transformed it into an ever-expanding industrial complex on which fascist war production plans were based. The second was the corporation, which imposed central controls over all forms of economic activity, including all remaining so-called private activities. Before becoming a "political" tool in 1939, with the establishment of the Chamber of Corporations, the corporation had helped the government control both labor unions and employers' associations by bringing them all under the rule of a central bureaucracy. The corporations were the best example of a basic tenet of fascist doctrine: the supremacy of the expert over the politician. They were the evidence of the triumph of economics over politics, as parliamentary institutions, made up of representatives of the general interests of the community, were superseded by experts talking the language of economics and technology, given to the hard-headed discussion of facts and not to the empty rhetoric of parliamentarism.

Fascism in operation. All told, this structure represented something new. As Mussolini said, "A party holding 'totalitarian' rule over a nation, is a new departure in history. There are no points of reference nor of comparison" ([1932] 1935, p. 36). Later analysts were to agree in large part with this statement and to say that totalitarianism did, indeed, represent a twentieth-century departure in the political evolution of mankind. In addition, the essence of totalitarianism was to be found in a combination of leadership, an ideologically inspired mass party, and violence, and in so total a claim by the ruling group over the lives of the individuals that no separateness, no autonomous legal system, and no group life could survive.

The totalitarian pattern of fascism, however, falls short of this model, in part because Mussolini gave too much weight to the state: "For Fascism the State is absolute, individuals and groups relative. Individuals and groups are admissible insofar as they [cannot attack the state]. . . . The Fascist state . . . has a will of its own. For this reason it can be described as 'ethical' " ([1932] 1935, pp. 37–38). And in article 1 of the labor charter of 1927 the Italian nation was described as an "organism having ends, a life and means superior in power and duration to the single individuals or groups of individuals composing it" (National Fascist Party [1927] 1935, p. 53). These were Hegelian influences that reflected the early role of the idealism of Gentile, whose presence could not be fully reconciled with the nihilism of authentic totalitarianism.

The party itself was one additional field in which fascist totalitarianism did not ring true. The party efforts to maintain ideological coherence, discipline, and a sense of mission were thwarted by the Italian belief in relativism, the spirit of compromise, and the refusal to take ideology seriously. The history of other totalitarian parties has shown that the party purge is of the essence in a totalitarian system. A domesticated totalitarian party, not wracked by fear, not cowed by the brooding image of the leader, but rather reduced to a mere vehicle for the securing of jobs, is no longer a revolutionary movement. The events from 1943 to 1945 showed that the behavior of blackshirted killer squads, the trial and execution of a few high-placed fascist leaders, including Mussolini's own son-in-law, were evidence only of the extremes of panic to which the surviving fascists were driven under the twin pressures of partisans' attacks and of German controls. The ease with which the country shed its fascist trimmings showed that in 25 years an effective hard core of fascist militants had not developed.

Hence, terror on a large scale and for preventive or repressive purposes never quite materialized. Fascism suffers by comparison with the apocalyptic liquidations for which Hitler and Stalin will be known to history. Instead of millions, Mussolini had on his conscience only a few tens of thousands of dead, excluding casualties due to direct military action during World War II. The will was lacking. Mussolini's cynical boasting was nearly always accompanied by a most lively sense of his inadequacy. The assured appearance of the leader on the public square was not matched by equal confidence in his private political activities. He had been a member of a democratic socialist party for too long to forget entirely the habit of doubt and skepticism. Hidden admiration for certain traditional forms of Italian culture stopped him from exercising his powers to the fullest extent. His ignorance made him avoid direct confrontation with established forms of conducting public business, which could therefore continue as before.

Mussolini's most persistent feeling probably was that of the crisis of the modern capitalistic order. He kept asking certain questions over and over again, without necessarily providing the answers. In 1932 he had asked, "Is this crisis, which has held us in its grip for the past four years . . . a crisis 'within' the system or 'of' the system?" (1935, p. 10). He felt he could not give an answer then, but in November 1933 he was to say, "Today my answer is: the crisis has sunk so deep into the system that it has become a crisis 'of' the system. . . . We can now assert that the capitalistic mode of production has been superseded" (pp. 10–11). Why is this so? Because by its very size capitalism has turned "into a social phenomenon, and it is precisely at this moment that capitalistic enterprise . . . falls like a dead weight into the arms of the State" (p. 16).

This is a purely Marxian analysis of the problem (the dominant socialized characteristics of a highly developed capitalistic system, the sudden crisis) up to the point at which the heir of capitalism is not the armed proletariat sitting on the ruins of the institutions of the bourgeois state, but is the "ethical state itself."

Mussolini tried hard, with the labor charter and the laws on the corporations, to give some unity to the new system. He made large theoretical claims for the corporations, which were to unite workers, owners, experts, the state, and the party and to which powers had been given extending from wage fixing to the regulation of production, the settlement of disputes, the drafting of collective labor contracts, and the prevention of strikes and lockouts.

But in his vaguely socialist dream, he was limited, on the one hand, by his recognition of private property as necessary to the fulfillment of the human personality and, on the other, by the overwhelming bureaucratic complexities of the all-or-nothing paper structure of the corporate state, and this made it necessary for him to appoint to the governing boards of the corporations representatives not only of wine but also of vinegar producers, not only of umbrella but also of button manufacturers. The resistance of the property owners who had put Mussolini in power was subtle and stubborn. They saw, in the immense Roman bureaucracy and in a party where the stout of heart and the believers were few, the chance to use the state capitalism of fascism in the same way in which public systems in other countries have been used by anxious capitalists in trouble, that is, as a prop to keep them going until better times.

The easy way out for everybody was military adventure. Again, the final flare-up of the Social Republic in the spring of 1945 is evidence of the decay of a system on the eve of its liquidation. Until then, the vast structure of the production system had been used only to prepare for war and to enable the regime to find overseas the outlets not found at home.

Interpretations

As a phenomenon that, having spread from Italy to other countries, affected the course of history between the two world wars, fascism has been subjected to a 40-year effort at interpretation. The variety of analyses has been correspondingly great, with sharp contrasts among the points of view depending on the time, the interests, and the approaches of those dealing with it.

The fascists themselves, those with a more speculative frame of mind and able to write with some detachment after the event, have tended to see in fascism one phase of the world-wide shifting of the political discourse from multiparty to one-party systems and of the transfer of power from the legislative to the executive, in which violence was discipline and military aggression was reaction to foreign hostility. They still believe that some of the trends and programs foreshadowed by the fascist era should be developed in the future as part of the needs of modern government. Fascism without ideology, war, and concentration camps could find expression in a depoliticized society that would turn its back on the rhetoric of the nineteenth century, but not on deeply felt national sentiments, and seek its way under the guidance of stable and efficient leadership.

The parties in power at the end of World War I, when the crisis began, saw the fascist movement in a different light. To them it was the unavoidable reaction of the "healthier" political forces in the country to the process of disintegration of the community and the constitutional system, caused by forces largely identified with Marxism. Marxism, in its twin embodiment of socialism and communism, loomed as a many-sided assault on the traditional institutions. The infrastructure agencies (cooperatives, peasants' leagues, trade unions) moved against the state with excessive economic claims and with a systematic onslaught on the processes of production. The authority of the state itself was being weakened by a series of strikes that affected vital public services. Fascism was a reaction of certain social groups, primarily the middle classes and the well-educated urban youth, intended to restore law and order.

But the undermining of the liberal constitutional order was not carried out at this level alone, for at the national political level Marxist parties were acting in alliance with another large and new political formation, the Christian Democratic party. Marxism and Christian democracy as mass parties joined hands here in their attempt to deprive the parliament and cabinet of their traditional roles by imposing rigid programs, which, the liberals thought, were not in keeping with the discussion and compromise typical of a constitutional democracy. Party bosses, who were constitutional "outsiders," sought to dominate political life. Fascism was to restore the constitutional system through the destruction of mass parties, those intruders which, since 1919, had upset the apple cart. Hence, a dual purpose was attached to fascism: the immediate restoration of normalcy against communist subversion and the long-range return to parliamentary government freed from the obnoxious influence of mass party rule. In brief, fascism was an interlude at the end of which the forward march of liberalism could be resumed.

This view did not survive the events of 1924/1925, when the institutions of totalitarianism were set up and a fuller view of fascism stood revealed. The realization by the liberals of the illiberal realities of single-party dictatorship took place by stages between 1923 and 1925. By then, from Giolitti to Croce, Italian liberalism presented a united antifascist front. But what stood out most clearly was the liberals' singular attachment to certain constitutional values that ruled out modern variations, chiefly the constitutional transfer of power to mass democratic parties. Liberal elitism was in the end confronted and defeated by brutal and stronger varieties of fascist elitism. The critics of the liberals' position have pointed out that this was a historical mistake of which they were the first victims.

Many of the spokesmen for the new mass parties, from Sturzo to Tasca, have pointed out that it was the refusal of the old ruling class to come to terms with the new elite emerging from the mass upheavals of postwar Italy that was at the root of the triumph of fascism. Socialists and Christian Democrats, far from seeing in themselves the agents for the destruction of the state, saw in their programs the only hope for a democratic renovation of Italian life and institutions. Their view was that the liberals were the accomplices of fascism in an attempt to stop the normal democratic evolution of a society in rapid transformation.

The Marxists follow orthodox lines. Fascism was the defender of capitalistic society, threatened by the steady widening of the power of the Russian Revolution and of the influence of Marxism in Italy. Fascism was a repressive movement developing along the lines Marx had anticipated for the final phase of bourgeois society.

This understanding of fascism as a class phenomenon, deprived of mystery and uncertainty, simplified the task of the Marxist opposition, which, after 1925, was to be essentially communist opposition. The socialists were no longer an effectively organized force, whereas other Marxist groups, aware of the evolution of Stalinism, had moved toward the center with reformulation of a modern liberal–socialist faith. Through their firm rejection of fascism, the communists were to derive great political benefits after 1945, for they could then identify themselves with one clear alternative in which they claimed to have believed all along. However, the communist interpretation of fascism did run into some difficulties. At the beginning the difficulty lay in the fact that the clear-cut class lines which would have had to be present as capitalism engaged in a supreme attempt at survival were not there at all. Fascism drew mass support from lower middle classes, intellectuals, peasants, and workers. Ten years later the noncapitalistic inclinations of fascism had become apparent, at least in theory, even though the fledgling corporate state was submerged by the requirements of fascist military policy. At this stage, however, the communists could point to war as the logical outcome of a capitalistically inspired tyranny. But at the end the lines were confused once more as fascism tried to revert to one of its ideological roots, socialism. These difficulties, however, did not substantially weaken the appeal of the communist interpretation, because its key element was the condemnation of the bourgeoisie, which it made responsible for fascism. And to this analysis many non-Marxists found it possible to accede. Moreover, the Marxist interpretation had the advantage of appearing to deal seriously with the phenomenon of fascism. Whatever it was, it was not to be taken lightly. It was a phase in the development of certain contemporary societies.

Such views stand a better chance of withstanding the test of history than predominantly literary interpretations, widely accepted at times, of fascism as a bad dream, as an inexplicable and certainly short-lived aberration that would fade away with a return to rational behavior. This caustically ironic attitude was justified perhaps by the frequency with which fascism appeared clothed in grotesque garments or supported policies that, because they were unacceptable on the basis of tradition, could not be sustained. But it suffered from an incomplete analysis of the crisis of Italian society and from a belief that Italian history since 1870 had shown nothing but favorable progress along the lines of modern democracy and that the anarchy prevailing deep in the hearts of so many Italians had been conquered by a growing sense of community.

Related to the bad-dream school was the historical one of fascism as a periodic phenomenon of Italian history. Mussolini was linked to the long series of tyrants, large and small, adventurers, and Machiavellian princes, who for many centuries had dotted the Italian landscape. Italy was the victim of one more manifestation of an endemic disease. A lack of discrimination, a tendency to vague generalizations, and a belief in cyclical recurrence afflicted an account that later could not explain the unprecedented catastrophic events marking the end of fascism and the difficulties that have continued to beset Italy since 1945.

Evaluation

No adequate review of the fascist era, from the point of view of the social scientist, has been undertaken since 1945. The literature has tended to be reminiscent, episodic, and introspective. At best we have detailed narratives of short critical periods in the history of fascism. Slowly, however, general reflections and lines of agreement appear to emerge and suggest some preliminary conclusions.

The first concerns the weakness of Italy's prefascist ruling class, a class whose credit ledger in the years from 1848 to 1922 was certainly not a mean one. But between 1912 and 1922 that class had been guilty of a series of decisions taken outside the liberal constitutional system and against the interests of the country. The Libyan war was a surrender to nationalistic and colonial interests. The parliamentary manipulations of the spring of 1915 had brought the country into World War I under unfavorable conditions and against the inclinations of the country at large. The acceptance of the dismal rhetoric of D'Annunzio as the official ideology of a country at war released the worst aspect of the sentimental patriotism and aggressive nationalism that formed such a large part of the post-1919 crisis. The failure of the machinery of the state and of the administration to maintain order and, worse still, the arming by the government of the Black Shirts were the final evidence of the liquidation of a ruling class that no longer ruled, had no views of what it should do, and was ready to step aside in the hope of recovering the past sometime in the future.

The second is the recognition of the depth of a phenomenon that today is playing a decisive role in the transformation and behavior of social groups, that of anomie. World War I had imposed an altogether excessive and cruel effort upon Italy. The idiocy of generals who sent hundreds of thousands of young men to a useless death, the social upheavals caused by war industries and profiteering, the opening up, under the strains of conflict, of regions that for centuries had been cut off from communication not only with the rest of the world but almost with their neighbors, and the lack of any recognition after 1918 of the seriousness of the problems which peacetime Italy would confront caused an unendurable strain on the weak texture of Italian society. This created large and vague expectations on the part of millions of unemployed and uprooted peasants, war veterans, frontline heroes, and dissatisfied students. Liberal Italy was not prepared to meet them or even to recognize them.

Under such anomic conditions, the appeal of mass movements—Marxism, Christian democracy, fascism—was bound to be great. That of Marxism was notable, even though the Socialist party dated back to the late nineteenth century. Although the theoretical weaknesses of the old warrior had been exposed, its half-hearted revolutionary enthusiasm could not be concealed. The mass appeal of Christian democracy was based on yet untested slogans and on new men, and it quickly gathered strength. But Italian liberalism had lumped Christian democracy together with Marxism. Both were forms of the revolt of upstart political elites against the majesty of the liberal state. The last of the three, fascism made its appearance as something new, promising shelter, food, stability, jobs, and a vigorous political system to those who were looking for such assurances. It had the advantage over Marxism and Christian democracy of being helped by the ruling class and by the weapons placed at its disposal.

Fascism can thus be seen as a mass movement to which an anomic society turned in a period of crisis for reassurance and the promise of satisfaction of essential community needs. But the promise was not kept. Behind the seemingly innovative façade, economic and social stagnation prevailed. Perhaps the most typical fascist law was the one that attempted to stop internal migrations. By freezing population movements, by keeping the peasant on the land, fascism strengthened the anarchism of individuals and acted directly contrary to the needs of the country, preventing the modernization of its ancient, quasi-feudal structures.

Thus, fascism did not resolve the anomic state of Italian society that had made its rise possible in the first place. The process of integration and modernization could start in earnest only after 1945. Among all the industrialized countries of western Europe, Italy is still the one most substantially removed from the conditions of a modern state. This, in part, is the result of the long frost of fascism.

At the same time, however, fascism functioned as if it had understood the new conditions of economic life. Bits of the largely unused machinery and ideas of the corporate state have been retained in post-1945 Italy in such fields as collective bargaining, where national and compulsory uniformities are now imposed. Labor agreements binding even on those who have not participated in their negotiation and massive state intervention in the settlement of labor disputes are part of the practice of republican Italy. Equally significant has been the resurfacing of fascist corporativism, the acceptance of its features in Gaullist France. The controlling factor everywhere is found in the deep malaise of European capitalism, which in its support of monopoly practices, sharp dealings with public authority, secrecy of managerial decisions, and drive for sheltered markets has deepened many of the accepted defects and realized few of the expected promises of the industrial revolution.

MARIO EINAUDI

[*See also* CAUDILLISMO; DICTATORSHIP; FALANGISM; NATIONAL SOCIALISM; SOCIALISM.]

BIBLIOGRAPHY

ALATRI, PAOLO 1956 *Le origini del fascismo*. Rome: Editori Riuniti.

DEAKIN, FREDERICK W. 1962 *The Brutal Friendship: Mussolini, Hitler and the Fall of Italian Fascism*. New York: Harper; London: Weidenfeld & Nicolson.

DELZELL, CHARLES F. 1961 *Mussolini's Enemies: The Italian Anti-Fascist Resistance*. Princeton Univ. Press.

DORSO, GUIDO 1949 *Mussolini alla conquista del potere*. Edited by C. Muscetta. Turin: Einaudi.

FELICE, RENZO DE 1965— *Mussolini*. Volume 1: Il rivoluzionario, 1883–1920. Turin: Einaudi.

FINER, HERMAN (1935) 1964 *Mussolini's Italy*. Hamden, Conn.: Shoe String Press.

GAROSCI, ALDO 1943 *La vita di Carlo Rosselli*. 2 vols. Rome: Edizioni "U."

GOBETTI, PIERO 1960 *Scritti politici*. Edited by Paolo Spriano. Turin: Einaudi.

GRAMSCI, ANTONIO 1947 *Opere*. Vol. 1— Turin: Einaudi. → Eleven volumes published up to 1966.

MEGARO, GAUDENS 1938 *Mussolini in the Making*. Boston: Houghton Mifflin.

MUSSOLINI, BENITO (1932) 1935 *The Doctrine of Fascism*. Florence: Vallecchi. → First published in the *Enciclopedia italiana*. Reprinted in 1942 in Michael Oakeshott (editor), *The Social and Economic Doctrines of Contemporary Europe*, published by Macmillan.

MUSSOLINI, BENITO 1935 *Four Speeches on the Corporate State*. Rome: "Laboremus."

NATIONAL FASCIST PARTY, GRAND COUNCIL OF FASCISM (1927) 1935 The Labour Charter. Pages 51–62 in Benito Mussolini, *Four Speeches on the Corporate State*. Rome: "Laboremus."

ROCCO, ALFREDO 1926 *The Political Doctrine of Fascism*. New York and Worcester, Mass.: Carnegie Endowment for International Peace.

ROSSELLI, CARLO (1930) 1945 *Socialismo liberale*. Rome: Edizioni "U."

SALVATORELLI, LUIGI; and MIRA, GIOVANNI (1956) 1962 *Storia d'Italia nel periodo fascista*. 4th ed. Turin: Einaudi.

SALVEMINI, GAETANO 1936 *Under the Axe of Fascism*. New York: Viking; London: Gollancz.

SALVEMINI, GAETANO 1961 *Scritti sul fascismo*. Edited by Roberto Vivarelli. Milan: Feltrinelli.

STURZO, LUIGI (1919–1926) 1956–1957 *Il Partito Popolare Italiano*. 3 vols. Bologna: Zanichelli.

STURZO, LUIGI (1926) 1927 *Italy and Fascismo*. New York: Harcourt; London: Faber & Gwyer. → First published in Italian.

[TASCA, ANGELO] 1938 *The Rise of Italian Fascism, 1918–1922*, by Angelo Rossi [pseud.]. London: Methuen. → First published in French in 1938. Translated into Italian in 1950 as *Nascita e avvento del fascismo*.

VALERI, NINO (1956) 1958 *Da Giolitti a Mussolini: Momenti della crisi del liberalismo*. 4th ed. Florence: Parenti.

FASHION

Fads and fashion are related yet fundamentally different social phenomena. Fashion is the more important of the two. Its general nature is suggested by the contrasting terms "in fashion" and "outmoded." These terms signify a continuing pattern of change in which certain social forms enjoy temporary acceptance and respectability only to be replaced by others more abreast of the times. This parade of social forms sets fashion apart from custom, which is to be seen as established and fixed. The social approbation with which fashion is invested does not come from any demonstration of utility or superior merit; instead, it is a response to the direction of sensitivities and taste.

Although conspicuous in the area of dress, fashion operates in a wide assortment of fields. Among them are painting, music, drama, architecture, household decoration, entertainment, literature, medical practice, business management, political doctrines, philosophy, psychological and social science, and even such redoubtable areas as the physical sciences and mathematics. Any area of social life that is caught in continuing change is open to the intrusion of fashion. In contrast, fashion is scarcely to be found in settled societies, such as primitive tribes, peasant societies, or caste societies, which cling to what is established and has been sanctioned through long usage.

The picture of fashion as a distinctive social process in which collective judgment of what is proper and correct shifts in response to the direction of sensitivity and taste sets three major questions: What is the nature of the situation in which the fashion process operates? What is responsible for its operation? What societal role or function does the fashion process perform?

Areas of fashion. Areas amenable to fashion are those that have been pulled into an orbit of continuing social change. The structuring of social life in such areas tilts away from reliance on established social forms and toward a receptiveness to novel ones that reflect new concerns and interests; thus, these areas are open to the recurrent presentation of prospective models of new social forms that differ from each other and from prevailing social forms. These models compete for adoption, and opportunity must exist for effective choice among them. Most significant in this selective process are prestigeful personages who through their advocacy of a model give social endorsement or legitimacy to it. Means and resources must be available for the adoption of the favored models.

Explanations of fashion

Most theoretical analysis of fashion centers on the major question of what is responsible for the operation of fashion. We may dismiss trivial answers such as that fashion is a crazelike outburst of collective disturbance or that it is a hoax perpetrated by venal-minded sets of persons seeking financial or personal gain. The more serious analyses fall into two categories. One type seeks to account for fashion in terms of psychological motives, the other in terms of societal or structured processes.

Psychological theories. Psychological explanations generally treat fashion as an expression of feelings of revolt against the confinement of prevailing social forms. Scholars identify different feelings. Some regard as most important the effort to escape from ennui, or boredom, especially in the leisure class. Some ascribe fashion to playful and whimsical impulses to embroider the routines of life. Some attribute major weight to the excitement that comes from venturing into novel forms of conduct. Others regard fashion as a symbolic expression of hidden sexual interests. Particularly important is the view, most clearly expressed by Edward Sapir (1931), that fashion is an effort to add to the attractiveness of the self, especially under conditions which impair the integrity of the ego; fashion is seen as a means of rediscovering the self through novel yet socially sanctioned departures from prevailing social forms. Finally, some scholars trace fashion to desires for personal prestige or notoriety.

These various psychological explanations are deficient in that they do not explain how or why the various feelings give rise to a fashion process. Such feelings are present and operate in societies and areas of life in which fashion does not occur. We are given no account of why the feelings should lead to the formation of fashion rather than taking other channels of expression available to them. Instead of accounting for fashion, the feelings presuppose its existence as a medium for their play.

Simmel's view of fashion. Most sociological explanations center on the idea that fashion is basically an emulation of prestige groups. Georg Simmel (1904) has given the most sophisticated presentation of this view. He contends that in an open-class society the elite class seeks to set itself apart visibly by distinctive insignia, such as dress and modes of living. Members of subjacent classes seeking higher status adopt these insignia. It is then necessary for the elite class to introduce new differentiating insignia, which in turn leads to a new wave of emulation. Simmel's scheme characterizes fashion as a recurring process. It provides an explanation of how new fashions are introduced and acquire sanction, an account of their spread, and an explanation of their disappearance. It also supplies an explanation for the absence of fashion from folk and caste societies and from certain areas in modern society, such as the area of utility and that of the sacred, in which status considerations are irrelevant.

However, this scheme fails to see fashion as a process that transcends and embraces the elite. The elite, although in the vanguard of fashion, is itself required to follow fashion's direction. Its prestige does not assure that anything it introduces will become the fashion; instead, its introductions must coincide with the direction of what is acceptable. People adopt a new model to be "in fashion" rather than to emulate prestige groups. Any concern of the elite to set itself apart as a distinctive status group takes place within the ongoing process of fashion; such concern does not account for the process or set it in motion.

Processes of social change

Fashion should be seen as a process of reaching out for new congenial social forms in an area that is a part of a continually changing world. The movement of that world introduces new horizons, germinates new inclinations and interests, and shifts orientation away from the past to the proximate future. The fashion process meets this kind of developing world through two major stages—innovation and selection. In the *innovative stage* new models or proposals—such as new dress designs, styles of furniture, themes in entertainment, approaches in philosophy, or theoretical schemes in science—are presented. Such models are geared to the current state of their respective fields; each seeks to sketch out a prospective line of movement. The models appear as rival claimants for adoption and thus initiate a *selective process*, which results in a new fashion. Prestigeful individuals and groups occupy a key role in the selection; they make the initial choices, and they give a stamp of endorsement to the model they embrace. To influence others, however, they must be qualified to give an endorsement. Further, the model they endorse must be found congenial to current trends in order to gain general dissemination. The history of fashion shows dramatic instances of the failure of a model to become fashionable despite an effective marshaling of prestige groups on its behalf, for example, the failure of the highly organized effort to check the trend toward shorter skirts in 1922–1923. Fashion leaders are the unwitting surrogates of the larger body of people sharing in the movement of fashion. The vague tastes and proclivities aroused in such people by their moving world are the ultimate source and shaper of fashion.

Historical continuity. The underlying connection between fashion and emerging taste helps to explain two important features of fashion: its historical continuity and its modernity. The history of fashion shows that new fashions are related to and grow out of their immediate predecessors. The typical picture is that of fashion trends—a feature that enables us to identify fashion periods and to speak of fashion cycles. Changing tastes and proclivities, while moving toward something new, must also take into account what is currently defined as proper and correct. Correspondingly, in devising their new models, fashion innovators always have to consider the prevailing fashion. Although the intrinsic nature of the object of fashion may set a limit to a trend (as in the case of the lengthening or shortening of the skirt), and although a trend may reach a point of exhausting its possibilities, a reversal or abrupt redirection of fashion necessarily has temporal linkage with the preceding fashion form.

Modernity. The feature of modernity in fashion is particularly significant. Fashion is always modern; it always seeks to keep abreast of the times. Fashion is sensitive to the movement of current developments not only in its given field but also in adjacent fields and, indeed, to general movements in the larger social world. Thus, fashion in women's dress is responsive to its own trend, to developments in fabrics, ornamentation, and in the fine arts, to exciting events such as the discovery of the tomb of Tutankhamen, to political happenings, and to major social shifts such as the emancipation of women or the rise of the "cult of youth." In an indirect and attenuated way, fashion in every field responds to the general or over-all direction of modernity itself. This responsiveness seems to be the chief factor in the formation of a "spirit of the times" or *Zeitgeist.*

Social functions of fashion

The remaining major question—what is the social role or function of fashion—has not received satisfactory consideration. The conventional answers are that fashion allows for the harmless play of fancy and caprice, for a mild and legitimate escape from the tyranny of custom, for socially sanctioned adventure into an area of novelty, for the display and parading of the ego, for a cloaked expression of sexual interests, for the invidious demarcation of elite classes, and for an external and spurious identification by lower status people with a higher status group.

Control functions. Fashions at different points in their careers may serve varied purposes; yet, the function of the fashion process cannot be reduced to such purposes. The functions of fashion derive, instead, from the fact that it introduces controlling social forms into a moving area of divergent possibilities. As such, it performs three significant functions. First, it introduces uniformity by selecting from many models one which is to carry the stamp of propriety and thus compel adherence. If all proposed models were to be followed, social life in a given fashion area would become chaotic. In this respect, fashion performs in a moving society the control function that custom performs in a settled society.

Second, fashion provides for an orderly march from the immediate past to the proximate future. By presenting new models and subjecting them to the process of competition and collective selection, the fashion process offers a continuous means of adjusting to a changing and shifting world. The fashion mechanism detaches social forms from the grip of the past, as suggested by the derogatory connotation of such expressions as "old-fashioned" and "out of date"; yet, in growing out of the preceding mode fashion maintains continuity of development.

Third, the fashion process nurtures and shapes a common sensitivity and taste, as is suggested by the congeniality and naturalness of current fashion in contrast to the oddness and incongruity of past fashions. This common sensitivity and taste is analogous on the subjective side to a "universe of discourse." Like the latter, it provides a basis for a common approach to the world and for handling and digesting the experiences the world yields. The value of a pliable and re-forming body of common taste to meet a shifting and developing world is apparent.

Collective taste

The term "taste," which is central in the above discussion, deserves clarification. It represents an organic sensitivity to objects of social experience, as when we say, for example, that "vulgar comedy does not suit our taste" or that "they have a taste for orderly procedure." Taste has a trifold character: it is like an appetite in seeking positive satisfaction; it operates as a sensitive selector, giving a basis for acceptance or rejection; and it is a formative agent, guiding the development of lines of action and shaping objects to meet its demands. Thus, it appears as a subjective mechanism, giving orientation to individuals, structuring activity, and molding the world of experience.

Tastes are themselves a product of experience; they usually develop from an initial state of vagueness to a state of refinement and stability, but once formed they may decay and disintegrate. They are formed in the context of social interaction, responding to the definitions and affirmations given by others. People thrown into areas of common interaction and having similar runs of experience develop common tastes.

The fashion process involves both a formation and an expression of collective taste in the given area of fashion. The taste is initially a loose fusion of vague inclinations and dissatisfactions that are aroused by new experiences in the field of fashion and in the larger surrounding world. In this initial state, collective taste is amorphous, inarticulate, and awaiting specific direction. Through models and proposals, fashion innovators sketch possible lines along which the incipient taste may gain objective expression and take definite form. Collective taste is an active force in the ensuing process of selection, setting limits and providing guidance; yet, at the same time it undergoes refinement and organization through its attachment to, and embodiment in, specific social forms. The origin, formation, and career of collective taste constitute the huge problematic area in the study of fashion. Major advancement in our knowledge of the fashion mechanism depends on the charting of this area.

Fads

Fads, like fashion, may occur in widely different areas of group life, such as games, recreation, entertainment, dietary practice, health and medical practice, dress, ornamentation, language, and popular beliefs. Although superficially fads seem to be similar to fashion, they actually constitute a separate genre of collective behavior. The most noticeable difference is that fads have no line of historical continuity; each springs up independent of a predecessor and gives rise to no successor. This separate, detached, and free-floating character signifies that fads, unlike fashion, are not part of a regulating social process that gives shape and structure to group life. The derogatory connotation of the term "faddish" points to the alien and questionable status of fads. We may note other significant differences. Fads do not require endorsement by a qualified prestige group in order to gain acceptance; they may spread from any section of hierarchized society. Fads are ephemeral, leaving no residue except in the occasional remnants of a detached cult. Fads follow the pattern of a craze or boom, thriving on spectacular and excitatory appearance, suddenly riveting attention and inducing a quasi-impulsive adoption, only to exhaust their attractiveness and undergo a rapid demise.

Fads, unlike fashion, may occur in any type of society, traditional or modern. Their universality suggests that they have a natural root in human existence. But we know little about the generic conditions that bring them into being. Most of the psychological explanations advanced to explain fashion seem far more appropriate as explanations of fads.

HERBERT G. BLUMER

[*See also* COLLECTIVE BEHAVIOR; STYLE.]

BIBLIOGRAPHY

BARBER, BERNARD; and LOBEL, LYLE S.   1952   Fashion in Women's Clothes and the American Social System. *Social Forces* 31:124–131.

BELL, QUENTIN   1947   *On Human Finery.* London: Hogarth.

BERGLER, EDMUND   1953   *Fashion and the Unconscious.* New York: Brunner.

CLERGET, PIERRE   1914   The Economic and Social Role of Fashion. Pages 755–765 in Smithsonian Institution, *Annual Report: 1913.* Washington: The Institution.

FISHBEIN, MORRIS   1932   *Fads and Quackery in Healing.* New York: Covici.

FLÜGEL, JOHN C.   (1930) 1950   *The Psychology of Clothes.* London: Hogarth.

GREGORY, PAUL M.   1947   An Economic Interpretation of Women's Fashions. *Southern Economic Journal* 14: 148–162.

HURLOCK, ELIZABETH B.   1929a   Motivation in Fashion. *Archives of Psychology* 17, no. 111.

HURLOCK, ELIZABETH B.   1929b   *The Psychology of Dress: An Analysis of Fashion and Its Motive.* New York: Ronald Press.

JACK, NANCY K.; and SCHIFFER, BETTY   1948   The Limits of Fashion Control. *American Sociological Review* 13: 730–738.

KELLETT, ERNEST E.   1931   *Fashion in Literature: A Study of Changing Taste.* London: Routledge.

KROEBER, ALFRED L.   1919   On the Principle of Order in Civilization as Exemplified by Changes of Fashion. *American Anthropologist* New Series 21:235–263.

LANG, KURT; and LANG, GLADYS   1961   *Collective Dynamics.* New York: Crowell. → See especially Chapter 15 on "Fashion: Identification and Differentiation in the Mass Society."

MEYERSOHN, ROLF; and KATZ, ELIHU   1957   Notes on a Natural History of Fads. *American Journal of Sociology* 62:594–601.

MOROWITZ, HAROLD J.   1953   Fashions in Science. *Science* 118:331–332.

NYSTROM, PAUL H.   1928   *Economics of Fashion.* New York: Ronald Press.

RICHARDSON, JANE; and KROEBER, ALFRED L.   1940   Three Centuries of Women's Dress Fashions: A Quantitative Analysis. California, University of, *Anthropological Records* 5, no. 2:111–153.

SAPIR, EDWARD   1931   Fashion. Volume 6, pages 139–144 in *Encyclopaedia of the Social Sciences.* New York: Macmillan.

SIMMEL, GEORG   (1904) 1957   Fashion. *American Journal of Sociology* 62:541–558.

SMELSER, NEIL J.   (1962) 1963   *Theory of Collective Behavior.* London: Routledge; New York: Free Press. → See especially Chapter 7.

SOMBART, WERNER   1902   *Wirtschaft und Mode.* Wiesbaden (Germany): Bergmann.

SUMNER, WILLIAM GRAHAM   (1906) 1959   *Folkways: A Study of the Sociological Importance of Usages, Manners, Customs, Mores, and Morals.* New York: Dover.

VEBLEN, THORSTEIN   (1899) 1953   *The Theory of the Leisure Class: An Economic Study of Institutions.* Rev. ed. New York: New American Library. → A paperback edition was published in 1959. See especially Chapter 7.

YOUNG, AGNES B.   1937   *Recurring Cycles of Fashion: 1760–1937.* New York: Harper.

FATIGUE

Fatigue is an experienced state of discomfort, aversion, and inability to perform, otherwise known as tiredness or weariness (Bartley 1943; Bartley & Chute 1947). The term applies to the total individual (the organism-as-a-person) and not properly to an organ or tissue. Fatigue is to be distinguished from impairment, which refers to the inability of cells or tissues to perform. Fatigue is sometimes confused with work decrement, for quite often the inquirer is actually interested in work output rather than in the state of the performer.

Fatigue is brought about in various ways, one common cause being discomfort in muscles induced by exertion, another being impairment. Very often, however, fatigue arises from some sort of disorganization within the individual. This is induced, in part, through confrontation with circumstances that are disliked or considered futile and useless. The disorganization referred to here can be described at various body-process levels. Disorganization can involve a disruption in the proper timing of various processes or a conflict between these processes with subsequent tension, awkwardness, and forgetfulness that result in discomfort and the realization of inadequacy.

Chronic fatigue often represents an unwholesome outlook on daily routine or life in general or arises from personality disorganization rather than some debilitating body processes at a lower level (Muncie 1941).

Critique of common conceptions. The common outlook that confuses fatigue with impairment is characterized by several points, some of which are acceptable and some not (Bartley 1951). First is the view that activity modifies the acting system, and that the modification is a chemical one. Fatigue is taken to be such a modification. However, this is really *impairment* and is a phenomenon that takes place at the tissue level, whereas fatigue is a phenomenon at the personality level— the experience, the self-awareness of condition. It is also assumed that fatigue can be either a general body condition or specifically localized. The slowing down of a process is taken to be the evidence of fatigue or, by some writers, to be fatigue itself. Here again, it seems to be impairment that is at issue.

Conventional assumptions shift from considering fatigue as tissue effects to considering it as the way the organism-as-a-person behaves. Even at this level compensation is generally overlooked in human performance. This is evidenced in the tacit assumption made by many that the subject has only one way of performing a given task. For example, it is not presumed that one muscle fiber group may be recovering while some other group is taking its place in carrying on over-all performance. But this type of compensation does occur, and it makes many of the simple, customarily performed "fatigue" experiments inappropriate and inadequate.

It is also false to assume that fatigue developed in one kind of performance may be measured by using an altogether different performance as a test.

The concern with fatigue as distinct from work output arises most directly and forcefully in medical practice and is even encountered in athletics. Physicians are being constantly confronted with patients who complain of tiredness, sometimes in connection with convalescence from debilitating disease or simply as a syndrome of its own (Alvarez 1941; Harms & Soniat 1952; Muncie 1941). On the other hand, work output is generally the main concern in industry (Dill et al. 1936; Edwards et al. 1935). Fatigue is often a term incorrectly *inferred* when an individual notices certain symptoms. In this case, what is called fatigue is self-diagnosis rather than something that arises as a directly felt inability to perform. Thus, a patient may tell an ophthalmologist that he has visual fatigue, inferring this (a self-diagnosis) from the fact that after reading awhile what he sees becomes blurred. This is different than his reporting how he feels. Such a usage of fatigue is to be avoided if the language on fatigue is to be consistent.

Finally, according to the conventional view, there are several kinds of fatigue. The more basic categorization distinguishes *objective* fatigue (work decrement); *subjective* fatigue (the experience of tiredness); and *physiological* fatigue (change or reduction in a specific body process).

Although there are various additionally specified kinds of fatigue, when fatigue exists it is essentially the same in all cases. The core of fatigue is the self-realization of relative inability to carry on. It is a negative orientation toward a task demand. Although the stance toward demand is always es-

sentially the same, various fringe details (various sensory and other components) may vary from case to case, but they are mere details in the unique over-all syndrome that is distinguishable as fatigue.

For example, fatigue arising in intellectual tasks should not be called mental fatigue, if by that one means a special kind of fatigue. Mental fatigue is only the fatigue that arises in intellectual (mental) tasks. Despite the fact that many kinds of tasks may lead to fatigue, no implication that there are many *kinds* of fatigue should be made.

So many loosely related phenomena have been called fatigue that it has been suggested that the word be done away with entirely (Muscio 1921). Bartley and colleagues (Bartley 1943; 1951; 1957; Bartley & Chute 1945; 1947) have chosen rather to retain the word in its original meaning (i.e., for the phenomena first labeled "tiredness") and rename other phenomena associated with it.

Problems in studying fatigue. Many studies that are meant to be studies of fatigue begin with questions about the experience of tiredness and inability to continue performance and end up by bypassing these questions and by providing information about other problems. For example, an investigator may note that workers in a plant feel sluggish and ineffective during mid-morning and mid-afternoon. He may suppose that this has something to do with blood sugar level. In his study he finds that at these times blood sugar level is lowest. He may then try a plan whereby the workers take in the same total amount of food per day but eat varying numbers of meals. Some eat two, some three, some four, and some even five meals per day. Blood sugar level is then tested periodically throughout the day. It is found that where many meals are eaten the blood sugar level never falls as low at any part of the work day as it does when few meals are eaten. At this point, the investigator assumes his study is completed. He should continue and determine whether the feeling of sluggishness is eliminated or greatly reduced by redistributing food intake into a greater number of meals, with the total intake held constant. It is only when he has performed this additional step that the original questions of sluggishness and inefficiency receive an answer. It is only then that the investigation becomes a fatigue investigation.

One of the persistent problems in dealing with fatigue is its measurement. It is always expected that if an entity exists it can be measured. The definition of fatigue as a relation to demand in which the individual *feels* his own inability to go on makes easy measurement unattainable. When work output is all that is to be measured, such measurement is easily made. However, the problem of measuring fatigue as defined here is no different from the problem of measuring anxiety, depression, boredom, hope, anger, or a virtually uncountable number of other states of the organism-as-a-person. Thus, the concept of fatigue should not be singled out for criticism because it refers to a phenomenon difficult to quantify. Nevertheless, such criticism has been leveled, at times, against what is conventionally called "subjective fatigue," for that reason.

The first point to be recognized is that the phenomenon in question must exist in order to be measured or dealt with in any way. The first step in studying it is to produce it. The second is to manipulate conditions under which it occurs. The next point to realize is that the person fatigued is the only one able to state when it exists. The observations made by all others have to do with overt performance, body process, or both, which are not fatigue although they may be closely related to it in some way. It is also to be recognized that the problem of quantitatively dealing with fatigue involves either developing a fatigue scale or choosing a fatigue point, such as the point at which the performer is no longer able to continue.

It will become quickly evident that in most cases the crucial conditions that lead to fatigue lie within the subject himself rather than the external conditions that produce the demand. Whatever is done to study fatigue, the organism-centered approach is necessary. In fact, it is necessary in trying to understand work output as well.

In certain ways, the phenomena that are personalistic rather than environmental can be studied more concretely than might be supposed. For example, it certainly is possible to manipulate goals (which are personalistic phenomena). In setting a task for a subject one can tell him something that will indicate the amount of time required to perform the task. One can then vary the amount of time so indicated to see what remoteness of goals has to do with the self-assessments of the subjects at various moments during performance and whether this variable has anything to do with the point at which "exhaustion" is reached. Other such dimensions and their body-process concomitants can also be chosen.

Another problem in studying fatigue has to do with how far various subjects will push themselves either in their use of energy resources or in experiencing bodily discomfort. This problem is related to motivation, and its solution may actually be a way of dealing with or measuring motivation. This problem is encountered not only in psycho-

logical experimentation but also in the physiological treadmill experiments. Some subjects "reach their limits" in muscular exertion before oxygen debt occurs, while others do not. No physiologist would expect that a subject would be exhausted before oxygen debt appears. These results illustrate the difference in the amount that individuals will push themselves. Thus the problem of subjectivity is as inherent in many phases of physiology as in psychology. Hence it cannot be disposed of by assuming that it occurs only in nonbehavioristic types of research.

Relieving fatigue. Various drugs and other substances have been tried by investigators to relieve fatigue and improve performance in athletic activities (Karpovich 1959; Smith & Beecher 1959).

Fatigue may often be relieved by inducing a change of attitude or attention or by shifting from one task to another rather than by rest (inactivity). Supposedly the needed change involves reorganization within the individual rather than a replenishment of energy.

Fatigue and the syndrome called *stress* by Selye (1956) have a lot in common, particularly certain factors of origin. Selye's discoveries and concepts go a long way toward providing a bodily basis for human incapacity, and when this is coupled with a monistic psychology, which attempts to understand human behavior, considerable progress seems to be possible.

S. HOWARD BARTLEY

[*Other relevant material may be found in* ACHIEVEMENT MOTIVATION; INFANCY, *article on* THE EFFECTS OF EARLY EXPERIENCE; SLEEP; STRESS.]

BIBLIOGRAPHY

ALVAREZ, W. C. 1941 What Is the Matter With the Patient Who Is Chronically Tired? *Journal of the Missouri State Medical Association* 38:365–368.

BARTLEY, S. HOWARD 1943 Conflict, Frustration and Fatigue. *Psychosomatic Medicine* 5:160–163.

BARTLEY, S. HOWARD 1951 Fatigue and Efficiency. Pages 318–347 in Harry Helson (editor), *Theoretical Foundations of Psychology.* New York: Van Nostrand.

BARTLEY, S. HOWARD 1957 Fatigue and Inadequacy. *Physiological Reviews* 37:301–324.

BARTLEY, S. HOWARD; and CHUTE, ELOISE 1945 A Preliminary Clarification of the Concept of Fatigue. *Psychological Review* 52:169–174.

BARTLEY, S. HOWARD; and CHUTE, ELOISE 1947 *Fatigue and Impairment in Man.* New York: McGraw-Hill.

DILL, D. B. et al. 1936 Industrial Fatigue. *Journal of Industrial Hygiene and Toxicology* 18:417–431.

EDWARDS, H. T.; THORNDIKE, A.; and DILL, D. B. 1935 The Energy Requirement in Strenuous Muscular Exercise. *New England Journal of Medicine* 213:532–535.

HARMS, H. E.; and SONIAT, T. L. L. 1952 The Meaning of Fatigue. *Medical Clinics of North America* 36:311–317.

KARPOVICH, P. V. 1959 Effect of Amphetamine Sulfate on Athletic Performance. *Journal of the American Medical Association* 170:558–561.

MUNCIE, WENDELL 1941 Chronic Fatigue. *Psychosomatic Medicine* 3:277–285.

MUSCIO, B. 1921 Is a Fatigue Test Possible? *British Journal of Psychology* 12:31–46.

SELYE, HANS 1956 *The Stress of Life.* New York: McGraw-Hill.

SMITH, G. M.; and BEECHER, H. K. 1959 Amphetamine Sulfate and Athletic Performance. *Journal of the American Medical Association* 170:542–557.

WHITING, HELEN F.; and ENGLISH, HORACE B. 1925 Fatigue Tests and Incentives. *Journal of Experimental Psychology* 8:33–49.

FEARS

See PHOBIAS.

FEBVRE, LUCIEN

Lucien Febvre (1878–1956) was born in Nancy, the capital of Lorraine, where his father was, at that time, teaching at the university. Both his father and his mother, however, came from Franche-Comté, and it was to this province that Febvre was deeply attached. He spent all his vacations there; he taught at the lycée at Besançon from 1897 to 1911; he was always interested in the life, the scenery, and the people of Franche-Comté; and he died there and was buried at Saint-Amour, on the border of Bresse and the Jura. Just as Michelet, to whom Febvre liked to compare himself, was a child of Paris, so Febvre might well be called a "peasant" of Franche-Comté—this, indeed, is what his friend, the novelist Léon Werth, called him.

Febvre's studies took him from the lycée at Nancy to the faculty of letters there, then to the Lycée Louis-le-Grand in Paris, and finally, from 1899 to 1902, to the École Normale Supérieure, from which he was graduated as agrégé in history and geography. His closest and most influential friend during these formative years was Henri Wallon, philosopher, psychologist, and physician, who later became his colleague at the Collège de France.

Febvre attained full intellectual maturity very early, well before 1911 when he defended his thesis at the Sorbonne. This brilliant thesis, *Philippe II et la Franche-Comté* (1911*a*), is a broad historical and geographical, as well as economic and social, study of this province in the second half of the sixteenth century. The work may be compared to the volumes of the *Histoire de Belgique*

that Henri Pirenne was then writing: while the Franche-Comté "route" was certainly not as important as the "crossroads" of the Low Countries, Febvre's study is more profound and more erudite than Pirenne's and, since it is in the mainstream of historiography, has not dated as much.

At the École Normale Febvre came into contact with Paul Vidal de la Blache, who had established geography as an autonomous discipline in France, and with Lucien Gallois, another geographer. From the beginning of his scholarly life Febvre, in effect, had two professions, history and geography. His enthusiasm for geography was great, as is shown by the geographical preface to his thesis, by his numerous reviews of geographical books, and by his masterly work, *A Geographical Introduction to History* (1922). This volume is a long, vigorous, and brilliant argument against narrow determinism and in favor of a subtle possibilism that encompasses human evolution and history.

Geography was his first love, but he soon gained familiarity with all the sciences of man by spending time in the office of the new *Revue de synthèse historique,* founded in 1900 by Henri Berr and edited by him. Berr's editing communicated his own outgoing spirit: he tried to bring together in a kind of continuous conversation all the different kinds of history—intellectual, cultural, social, economic, institutional, political, and so forth—and the new human sciences, especially sociology. During his stay in Paris at the Fondation Thiers, from 1903 to 1906, Febvre established close ties with Berr and his group, soon becoming a key contributor to the *Revue de synthèse* and later to the other undertakings that arose out of it: the *Semaines de synthèses* and the vast series, *L'évolution de l'humanité.* Thus, when Febvre wrote in 1911 on the Franche-Comté, he was already something of a historian, a geographer, a sociologist, an economist, a psychologist, and a linguist.

Given this background, there is nothing surprising either in the appearance in 1922 of his *Geographical Introduction to History,* a book which had a tremendous impact on the small world of French historians and geographers, or in the founding in 1929 of the *Annales d'histoire économique et sociale,* which marked a decisive turning point in French historiography. It may seem that these achievements came relatively late in Febvre's career, but for five solid years he had been involved in World War I, always in the front line, ending up as captain of a machine gun company. In 1912 he had been appointed professor in the faculty of letters at Dijon and in 1919 he moved to the University of Strasbourg. There he and Marc Bloch became close friends, and it was with Bloch that he was to found, edit, and, indeed, to a large extent write the *Annales*.

The effect of the *Annales* was to establish a kind of hegemony of history over the other human sciences: while in general barriers were eliminated between disciplines, these disciplines were not considered equal in importance, history being accorded a preferred position, especially vis-à-vis social psychology and sociology and even more so vis-à-vis economics. This intellectual position might be labeled "historicism" if this term did not have such pejorative connotations and particularly if it were not so easily confused with the *Historismus* of German thinkers. The essential point is to make clear the differences between the *Revue de synthèse*, whose theme was the colloquy of the human sciences, and the *Annales*, which constituted a sort of Common Market, with history as the preponderant power.

Yet great as is Febvre's contribution in the *Annales*, it does not represent the true scope of his intellectual role. The key to this scope is his generosity, his deep-felt need to share his knowledge. Just as Paul Langevin, 1872–1946, was the "banker" for the physicists of his generation—that is, the lender, the disseminator of ideas, what Diderot had been for many of the writers of his time, so also was Febvre a banker: he never became tired of having people come in to see him, of listening, of guiding. When conversation did not suffice he wrote what he called his "letters of guidance." It was in this way that he trained Marc Bloch, his junior by eight years, and the present author as well. Often his "guidance" consisted of simply surrendering his own projects to others, especially after 1929, when work on the *Annales* became his principal activity. Himself a "peasant" and a marvelous historian of the land, he turned over this subject to Bloch, who produced *Les caractères originaux de l'histoire rurale française* (1931); later, after 1946, he turned over to the present author the task of establishing relationships between historical and economic studies. His own relatively brief writings on the work of François Simiand, Earl J. Hamilton, Giuseppe Parenti, Frederic C. Lane, and others, show how receptive he was to new ideas in economics.

Although Febvre thus abandoned some of his favorite topics to others, he does seem to have found, outside his primary field of intellectual activity, even outside the *Annales*, a kind of subject that delighted him: the history of art, of religion, or even, in the broad sense, of culture. History was *one* for him and whatever his particular concern, he surveyed the entire landscape. In 1928 he published *Martin Luther: A Destiny*, a book that he clearly enjoyed writing and that is written beautifully. Luther was not for Febvre simply a problem in biographical research, nor even a difficult subject made attractive by its very difficulty; Luther represented the problem of the unique individual in history and of the unpredictable power of such an individual.

All his life, indeed, Febvre liked to consort with the great minds of "his" century, the sixteenth. He was wonderfully well acquainted with them; to hear him read Rabelais was a pleasure. His excellent humanist education (which he received from his father and from an uncle rather than in school) explains his delight in writing his charming little book, *Autour de l'*Heptaméron (1944), or that masterpiece of classical erudition, *Origène et Des Périers* (1942a).

Increasingly, he fought for one kind of history while writing rather a different kind himself. In 1942, with the publication of *Le problème de l'incroyance au XVIᵉ siècle: La religion de Rabelais* (1942b), he seems to have emerged victoriously from this conflict: this time he had all the reins in his hand, and the book is his best one. In the first two parts of the work he treated Rabelais in the traditional way, using evidence from his life and his works, but he devoted the third part to the "mental apparatus" of the period—the words, the feelings, the concepts that are the infrastructure of the thought of the century, the basis on which everything was constructed or could be constructed, and which may have prevented certain things from being constructed.

Although the book was much praised, its originality limited its appreciation by historians. Febvre's work was ahead of its time, and it is only recently that the structuralists of the new literary criticism (for example, Michel Foucault, in his *Les mots et les choses: Une archéologie des sciences humaines*, 1966) have done similar research into the culture of a society.

Yet Febvre did not pursue his ideas, and his work remained incomplete. As he worked in the area of psychological, social, and cultural history, he seems to have had difficulty in stating problems, fixing bench marks, and drafting a methodology. Thus he was always uncertain about the nature of civilization, to use that convenient term. Often he insisted that civilization must be located in a particular time, that its changeful nature must be pinned down, and he protested against the frequent assertion that "man is always the same." But at the same time his *Rabelais* presupposes the long continuation of what he aptly called the mental apparatus of men, something beyond the individual or the unique. He might have stressed this transcendence more had he not been excessively impressed, as laymen tend to be, by the implications of the concept of relativity as formulated by Einstein. He was tormented by the perennial problem of the objective status of the "observer"—the historian—and of the events being observed—history.

He did not doubt, however, that history provides an understanding of one's own time and that such an understanding is indispensable to the historian. This is why to the very end of his life Febvre never left the intellectual battleground. It is no accident that he entitled the first volume of his collected articles *Combats pour l'histoire* (1953).

In 1947 he created the section of economic and social sciences of the École Pratique des Hautes Études, serving as chairman of this section until his death. He also revived the *Annales*, whose publication had been hampered by the war; he even tried, without any real success, to revive the project of publishing the *Encyclopédie française*, begun in 1933 by Anatole de Monzie and himself. And once again he did whatever he could to help other scholars. Really to appreciate the intellectual force of Febvre one must read not only his books but also his many articles and reviews and his marvelous letters. Those who were privileged to enjoy his informal conversation are certain that he is among the greatest of modern French historians.

FERNAND BRAUDEL

[*See also* HISTORY; *and the biographies of* BLOCH; PIRENNE; VIDAL DE LA BLACHE.]

WORKS BY FEBVRE

1911a *Philippe II et la Franche-Comté: Étude d'histoire politique, religieuse et sociale*. Paris: Champion.
1911b *Notes et documents sur la Réforme et l'Inquisition en Franche-Comté: Extraits des archives du Parlement de Dole*. Paris: Champion.
(1912) 1922 *Histoire de Franche-Comté*. 7th ed. Paris: Boivin.
(1922) 1925 *A Geographical Introduction to History*. New York: Knopf. → First published as *La terre et l'évolution humaine*.
(1928) 1929 *Martin Luther: A Destiny*. New York: Dutton. → First published as *Un destin: Martin Luther*.
1930 FEBVRE, LUCIEN et al. *Civilisation*. Paris: Renaissance du Livre.
(1931) 1935 DEMANGEON, ALBERT; and FEBVRE, LUCIEN *Le Rhin: Problèmes d'histoire et d'économie*. Paris: Colin.
1932 *L'individualité en histoire: Le personnage en histoire*. Paris: Renaissance du Livre.
1942a *Origène et Des Périers: Ou, l'énigme du Cymbalum mundi*. Paris: Droz.
(1942b) 1962 *Le problème de l'incroyance au XVIe siècle: La religion de Rabelais*. 2d ed. Paris: Michel.
1944 *Autour de l'Heptaméron: Amour sacré, amour profane*. Paris: Gallimard.
1946 Introduction. In Jules Michelet, *Michelet*. Paris: Éditions des Trois Collines.
1953 *Combats pours l'histoire*. Paris: Colin. → A collection of previously published articles.
1957 *Au coeur religieux du XVIe siècle*. Paris: S.E.V.P.E.N. → A collection of previously published articles.
1962 *Pour une histoire à part entière*. Paris: S.E.V.P.E.N. → A collection of previously unpublished articles.

SUPPLEMENTARY BIBLIOGRAPHY

BLOCH, MARC (1931) 1952–1956 *Les caractères originaux de l'histoire rurale française*. New ed., 2 vols. Paris: Colin. → Volume 2, *Supplément établi d'après les travaux de l'auteur: (1931–1944)*, was written by Robert Dauvergne.
FOUCAULT, MICHEL 1966 *Les mots et les choses: Une archéologie des sciences humaines*. Paris: Gallimard.

FECHNER, GUSTAV THEODOR

Gustav Theodor Fechner (1801–1878) is considered to be the founder of psychophysics and thus of experimental psychology as a whole. He was also the founder of experimental aesthetics. Fechner was born in Lower Lusatia, then part of German northern Silesia. His father and both of his grandfathers were clergymen. Fechner studied medicine first at the University of Dresden and then at the University of Leipzig, obtaining his degree in 1822. His interests turned more and more to physics, however, and he was appointed instructor of natural philosophy at Leipzig the following year. During his years as a student, the lectures of Lorenz Oken on natural philosophy and of E. H. Weber on physiology made the most lasting impressions on Fechner. Oken is now forgotten, but he was then a renowned romantic natural philosopher and cured Fechner of his "man, the machine" approach. Fechner hailed Weber, the discoverer of "Weber's law," as the real father of psychophysics. [*See* WEBER, ERNST HEINRICH.]

After his appointment to the university faculty, Fechner began experimental studies of physical and chemical problems and supported himself by translating, revising, and publishing reference works and textbooks on physics and chemistry. The sheer volume of the work he did during these years is extraordinary. In addition to 28 investigations of his own, published between 1827 and 1840, he annually turned out 1,500 to 2,000 printed pages of textbooks and reference works between 1822 and 1838. He even found time to write several literary pieces, which he published under the pseudonym of "Dr. Mises."

Fechner was married in 1833, and in 1834 he was appointed professor of physics at Leipzig. But he occupied the chair only until 1839; after repeated attacks of severe exhaustion he was, for three years, completely incapacitated by a mysterious illness. The major symptoms were disturbances of vision, with hypersensitivity to bright light, sporadic total failure of digestion, obsessions, and, finally, more and more terrifying hallucinations. He recovered quite suddenly. It seems most likely that the illness was an atypical form of schizophrenia.

The initial impetus for the work on which Fechner's fame is based doubtless came from Oken, who fascinated him so much that at first he was resolved to emulate Oken's unrestrained philosophizing. However, Fechner's empirical research in physics and physiology saved him, and in the guise of "Dr. Mises," he himself participated in mocking this kind of romantic inventing of concepts, which appears to prove everything, while actually it proves nothing. Oken continued to exert some influence on Fechner, however, and later he returned to this kind of thinking without surrendering to it completely.

Psychophysics

The problem that concerned Fechner most was the connection between body and mind. His *Elemente der Psychophysik* (1860) aims at utilizing experimental procedures, such as those employed by Weber previously, to explore this connection more precisely, arriving, if possible, at mathematically formulated laws. Earlier, Johann Friedrich Herbart had demanded that psychological laws be formulated in mathematical terms, but he despaired of the likelihood that psychology would ever obtain the necessary experimental data. Fechner saw in Weber's threshold experiments the possibility of securing such data. He assumed that the difference between two sensations may be defined by the number of "just noticeable differences" (jnd) between them, and that these jnd's can be represented mathematically. He used the number of jnd's above the lower absolute threshold as a measure of the intensity of sensation evoked by a stimulus. In order to be able to describe the relationship between psychic and physical quantities mathematically, Fechner sought to establish a general functional relationship between sensations and stimuli of whatever magnitude. In the range within which Weber's law is valid—Weber's law states that jnd's are proportional to the magnitude of the stimuli—integration yields a function that describes the intensity of a sensation in terms of the logarithm of the stimuli, measured from the absolute threshold.

Since the acuity of the sensory apparatus fluctuates from instant to instant and from person to person, thresholds can be defined only statistically. Fechner perfected the experimental strategies that had earlier been used by Weber and by Vierordt, as well as by such astronomers and physicists as Lambert, Steinheil, and Laugier, to determine the degree of uncertainty or the accuracy of measurement in comparisons of stimuli. According to the nature of variation of the stimulus in comparisons of successive sensations, he distinguished three kinds of psychophysical methods of data collection: (1) the method of jnd's, in which the difference between the stimuli compared is gradually increased until it is perceptible or diminished until it is no longer perceptible; this is also called the method of limits; (2) the method of right and wrong cases, in which a standard stimulus is compared with randomly varied comparison stimuli; this method is also called the constancy method; and (3) the method of average error, in which a comparison stimulus is adjusted by the subject to correspond to a standard; this is also referred to as the reproduction method.

In calculating threshold values, Fechner employed the law of errors formulated by Gauss and Laplace, and in his posthumous *Kollektivmasslehre* (1897) he set forth the applicability of the law of errors to many other problems in psychology. The *Kollektivmasslehre* also contains his contributions to correlation statistics. It is the first textbook of statistics to be designed especially for behavioral scientists. Using carefully planned experiments, whose layouts resemble those today used in the analysis of variance, he endeavored to exclude from the calculation of reaction variability, which defines the threshold difference, those constant errors that arise from the particular features of the experimental procedure.

Fechner realized that "psychophysics" (his coinage) was an innovation of great importance: he called it a science "in the initial state of becoming," and his own work for all its scope, merely "a modest beginning of a beginning." His work was soon taken up by some of the greatest scientists of his time. As far back as 1858, Ernst Mach and Hermann von Helmholtz had begun to experiment on their own, stimulated by Fechner's preliminary report. Wilhelm Wundt followed in 1862, A. W. Volkmann in 1864, H. Aubert and J. R. L. Delboeuf in 1865, and J. Bernstein and Vierordt in 1868. Of the outstanding specialists in the field of psychology only one remained a skeptic: William James, who as late as 1890 declared that despite all its acumen and all its care, the psychological yield of the *Elemente* was "just nothing," not important enough to merit mention in even a footnote.

The methods of measurement developed by Fechner are now generally adopted in quantitative experimental psychology, although some of the mathematical implications of his derivations are open to serious criticism (Luce & Galanter 1963). They are employed with equal success in all sorts of fields and for the most diverse problems. In recent years, the problem of psychological scaling, which Fechner was the first to appreciate and deal with, has again come to the forefront; it has been remarkably clarified and given new depth, especially in the work of S. S. Stevens and G. Ekman (for example, Stevens 1934).

Fechner is remembered almost exclusively as a methodologist. The fundamental theoretical postulates he presented in his psychophysics have gone unnoticed and are generally attributed to later authors. Most noteworthy is his working hypothesis of "concrete parallelism," which assumes an isomorphism between phenomena of consciousness and "psychophysical phenomena," that is, those processes occurring in the cerebrum that are directly associated with the phenomena of consciousness. This assumption and its elaboration is usually attributed to Ewald Hering, Georg Elias Müller, Max Wertheimer, and, above all, Wolfgang Köhler, although it was clearly formulated in Volume 2 of Fechner's *Elemente*.

Aesthetics

Following his work in psychophysics, Fechner ventured also to transform the field of aesthetics from speculation to exact factual research. He summarized the results of his efforts in his *Vorschule der Aesthetik* (1876). He tried to derive the conditions that determine what is pleasing and what is displeasing, not from a higher ideal of beauty but from below, by systematic empirical comparison of the beautiful with the less beautiful. This endeavor was not as successful as his work in psychophysics. Fechner was the victim of a then prevalent confusion: to him, as to his contemporaries, "from below" meant not only "from perception to concept," but also "from the simple to the more complex," and the properties of the complex, it was then believed, are those of its simple constituents. The study by Christian von Ehrenfels, who proved that this postulate is false—and thereby not only opened up a new era in psychology but also made possible a more relevant theory of beauty—did not appear until three years after Fechner's death.

Fechner did, however, conduct a study—in line with his attempt to establish an experimental science of aesthetics—which makes him one of the earliest forerunners of modern opinion research. Two nearly identical versions of a Madonna reputed to have been painted by Hans Holbein were then being exhibited in Dresden, and Fechner asked the visitors to the exhibition to note on a sheet of paper which of the two they thought was more beautiful. At that time the public was unfortunately not accustomed to such questionnaires, and only 116 of the 11,000 visitors took the trouble to write their comments. Of these 116, some were art critics who had previously formed judgments, while others failed to follow instructions, thus rendering the results useless. Nonetheless, the experiment made a contribution to methodology that might have become as influential as psychophysics, had its significance been understood.

Analysis of systems

Around 1850, Fechner tackled another fundamental problem, that of the apparent finality of particular processes in animate and inanimate nature. In contrast to the neovitalists, he insisted that this finality be explained within the framework of the principle of causality. He laid down the axiom that every system in nature that is delimited with respect to its environment and hence is more or less closed, as well as every relatively autonomous part of such a system, tends, after a longer or shorter period of dislocation, to return to its previous state, and he specifically speaks of a "tendency toward stability." From this there is a direct road, via Ernst Mach's observation that the stable states of comparatively closed structures are formally distinct, to the concepts of equilibrium of Wolfgang Köhler and Ludwig von Bertalanffy. As Fechner used the concept of "stability," it was broader than it is today; it included not only what he called "simple stability" but also "complex stability," examples of which he found primarily in organisms. These examples are identical with Köhler's "stationary states" and Bertalanffy's "steady states." Thus, Fechner's works contain a surprising number of stimulating ideas which are still influential, though they may sometimes appear under different names [*see* PERSONALITY: CONTEMPORARY VIEWPOINTS; SYSTEMS ANALYSIS, *article on* PSYCHOLOGICAL SYSTEMS].

WOLFGANG METZGER

[*For the historical context of Fechner's work, see the biographies of* GAUSS; LAPLACE; WEBER, E. H. *For discussion of the subsequent development of his ideas, see* AESTHETICS; PSYCHOPHYSICS; QUANTAL

RESPONSE; SCALING; *and the biographies of* HELM-
HOLTZ; THURSTONE; WUNDT.]

WORKS BY FECHNER

(1836) 1943 *Life After Death.* Pages 21–90 in Gustav
Theodor Fechner, *Life After Death.* New York: Pantheon. → First published as *Das Büchlein vom Leben
nach dem Tode.*

1848 Ueber das Lustprinzip des Handelns. *Zeitschrift für
Philosophie und philosophische Kritik* New Series 19:
1–30, 163–194.

(1860) 1907   *Elemente der Psychophysik.* 2 vols. 3d ed.
Leipzig: Breitkopf & Härtel.

1871 *Ueber die Aechtheitsfrage der holbein'schen Madonna: Discussion und Acten.* Leipzig: Breitkopf &
Härtel.

1873 *Einige Ideen zur Schöpfungs- und Entwickelungsge-
schichte der Organismen.* Leipzig: Breitkopf & Härtel.

1874 *Ueber den Ausgangswerth der kleinsten Abweich-
ungssumme, dessen Bestimmung, Verwendung und
Verallgemeinerung.* K. Sächsische Gesellschaft der
Wissenschaften, Mathematisch-physische Klasse, Abhandlungen, 11, no. 1. Leipzig: Hirzel.

(1876) 1897–1898 *Vorschule der Aesthetik.* 2d ed. 2 vols.
in 1. Leipzig: Breitkopf & Härtel.

1877 *In Sachen der Psychophysik.* Leipzig: Breitkopf &
Härtel.

1882 *Revision der Hauptpuncte der Psychophysik.* Leipzig: Breitkopf & Härtel.

1888 Ueber die psychischen Massprincipien und das
weber'sche Gesetz: Discussion mit Elsas und Köhler.
Philosophische Studien 4:161–230.

Kollektivmasslehre. Edited by G. F. Lipps. Leipzig: Engelmann, 1897.

SUPPLEMENTARY BIBLIOGRAPHY

BORING, EDWIN G. (1929) 1950 *A History of Experimental Psychology.* 2d ed. New York: Appleton. → See
especially pages 275–296.

BORING, EDWIN G. 1942 *Sensation and Perception in
the History of Experimental Psychology.* New York:
Appleton.

BRETT, GEORGE S. 1921 *A History of Psychology.* Volume 3: Modern Psychology. London: Allen & Unwin.
→ See especially pages 127–239.

BURT, C. 1960 Gustav Theodor Fechner: *Elemente der
Psychophysik,* 1860–1960. *British Journal of Statistical Psychology* 13:1–10.

HALL, G. STANLEY 1912 *Founders of Modern Psychology.* New York: Appleton. → See especially pages
123–177, "Gustav Theodor Fechner."

KÜLPE, O. 1901 Zu Gustav Theodor Fechners Gedächtnis. *Vierteljahresschrift für wissenschaftliche Philosophie und Soziologie* 25:191–217.

LASSWITZ, KURD (1896) 1910 *Gustav Theodor Fechner.*
3d ed. Stuttgart (Germany): Frommann.

LUCE, R. DUNCAN; and GALANTER, EUGENE 1963 Psychophysical Scaling. Volume 1, pages 245–308 in
R. Duncan Luce, Robert R. Bush, and Eugene Galanter (editors), *Handbook of Mathematical Psychology.*
New York: Wiley.

MICHELS, WALTER C.; and HELSON, HARRY 1954 A
Reconciliation of the Veg Scale With Fechner's Law.
American Journal of Psychology 67:677–683.

STEVENS, S. S. 1934 The Volume and Intensity of Tones.
American Journal of Psychology 46:397–408.

THURSTONE, L. L. 1929 Fechner's Law and the Method
of Equal-appearing Intervals. *Journal of Experimental
Psychology* 12:214–224.

WIRTH, WILHELM 1912 *Psychophysik: Darstellung der
Methoden der experimentellen Psychologie.* Leipzig:
Hirzel.

WUNDT, WILHELM 1901 *Gustav Theodor Fechner: Rede
zur Feier seines hundertjährigen Geburtstages.* Leipzig: Engelmann.

FECUNDITY

See FERTILITY.

FEDERALISM

Federalism and its kindred terms—e.g., "federal"
—are used, most broadly, to describe the mode of
political organization which unites separate polities
within an overarching political system so as to
allow each to maintain its fundamental political
integrity. Federal systems do this by distributing
power among general and constituent governments
in a manner designed to protect the existence and
authority of all the governments. By requiring that
basic policies be made and implemented through
negotiation in some form, it enables all to share
in the system's decision-making and decision-
executing processes.

Different conceptions

No single definition of federalism has proved
satisfactory to all students, primarily because of
the difficulties in relating theoretical formulations
to the evidence gathered from observing the actual
operation of federal systems. Attempts at definition
have also foundered on the problems of distinguishing between (1) the federal principle as a broad
social concept and federalism as a narrower political device; (2) two classic but different conceptions
of federalism; (3) authentically federal *systems*
and political systems which utilize elements of the
federal *principle*; (4) mature and emergent federal
systems; and (5) federalism and "intergovernmental relations" as distinct political phenomena.

Social and political principle. Federalism, conceived in the broadest social sense, looks to the
linkage of people and institutions by mutual consent, without the sacrifice of their individual identities as the ideal form of social organization. First
formulated in the covenant theories of the Bible
(Kaufman 1937–1948), this conception of federalism was revived by the Bible-centered "federal"
theologians of seventeenth-century Britain and New
England (Miller 1939), who coined the term
"federal"—derived from the Latin *foedus* (covenant)—in 1645 to describe the system of holy and

enduring covenants between God and man which lay at the foundation of their world view. This conception of federalism was given new theoretical form by nineteenth-century French and German social theorists. Closely related to the various theories of social contract, it is characterized by the desire to build society on the basis of coordinative rather than subordinative relationships and by the emphasis on partnership among parties with equal claims to legitimacy who seek to cultivate their diverse integrities within a common social order (Boehm 1931). [See SOCIAL CONTRACT.]

As a political device, federalism can be viewed more narrowly as a kind of political order animated by political principles that emphasize the primacy of bargaining and negotiated coordination among several power centers as a prelude to the exercise of power within a single political system, and stress the value of dispersed power centers as a means for safeguarding individual and local liberties. This means, in effect, that political institutions common to different political systems, when combined within a federal system and animated by federal principles, are effectively endowed with a distinctive character. For example, while political parties are common in modern political systems, parties animated by the federal principle show unique characteristics of fragmentation and lack of central discipline that increase the power of local groups within the system as a whole (Grodzins 1960a).

Federation and confederation. Federal ideas have been systematically conceptualized in two different ways. On the one hand, federalism has been conceived as a means to unite a people already linked by bonds of nationality through distribution of political power among the nation's constituent units. In such cases, the polities that constitute the federal system are unalterably parts of the national whole, and federalism invariably leads to the development of a strong national government operating in direct contact with the people it serves, just as the constituent governments do. On the other hand, federalism has also been conceived as a means to unify diverse peoples for important but limited purposes, without disrupting their primary ties to the individual polities that constitute the federal system. In such cases the federal government is generally limited in its scope and powers, functioning through constituent governments which retain their plenary autonomy, and, to a substantial degree, is dependent upon them.

Both conceptions of federalism have evolved from early federal experiments. The principles of strong national federalism were first applied by the ancient Israelites, beginning in the thirteenth cen-

tury B.C., to maintain their national unity through linking their several tribes under a single national constitution and at least quasi-federal political institutions (Bright 1959). Several centuries later, the Greek city-states experimented with federal-style institutions as means for the promotion of intranational harmony and cooperation, primarily for defensive purposes, through associations (e.g., the Achaean League) that came close to what were later defined as confederations (Freeman 1863). A modified form of the Greek view was developed by the sixteenth-century theorists (Gierke 1913). They held that federalism meant a permanent league of states united through a perpetual covenant, binding under international law, in which the constituent states delegated enumerated powers to a general government while retaining full rights of internal sovereignty.

However, when the American system—the prototype of modern federal systems—emerged in the late eighteenth century, its architects developed a conception of federalism much like that of ancient Israel. From the first, American federalism functioned to serve a people with a single national identity and was constituted with a strong national government to serve that people on a national basis, though, as late as 1789, *The Federalist* could. describe the new American constitution as "partly national and partly federal" in deference to the then-accepted views. The successful efforts of the supporters of that constitution to appropriate the term "federalist" for their own use (Main 1961, pp. ix–xi) restored to common usage the older conception of federalism as a noncentralized national union bound by municipal law, with a general government superior to the governments of the constituent states (Diamond 1963).

Just as the American system became the prototype for other modern federal systems, so the American conception of federalism became the generally accepted one. The other conception was ultimately subsumed under the word "confederation" and its kindred terms. The two systems described by these different conceptions reflect, in part, the distinctions implied in the German *Staatenbund* (confederation) and *Bundesstaat* (federation), terms developed in the mid-nineteenth century (Mogi 1931). A certain degree of confusion remains because the terms invented to describe both systems were used indiscriminately for many years.

Though the American conception of federalism is today almost universally accepted as the most accurate usage, the confederal conception remains a living and legitimate aspect of the federal idea in its largest political sense. Today, the latter is most prominent among certain advocates of limited European union (the Common Market exemplifies a confederal form) and among many so-called world federalists. [See INTERNATIONAL INTEGRATION.]

Federalism and related systems. Federal systems are often confused with four other forms of political order which make use of specific federal principles. The use of some federal principles in multiple monarchies, legislative unions, empires, and decentralized unitary systems can have important consequences similar to those in authentically federal systems. But the fact that such principles do not permeate the four systems makes the distinctions between them and true federations extremely important.

Federal systems differ from *multiple* (or *dual*) *monarchies* in two essential ways. The central constitutional characteristic of the multiple monarchy is that union exists only in the person of the sovereign and is maintained only through the exercise of executive power in his name. No significant common institutions exist to unite the constituent polities—no common legislatures, no common legal system, and little in the way of a common political substructure. On the contrary, each constituent polity maintains its own political system, which the monarch guarantees to support under the terms of his compact with the realm. Multiple monarchies have historically been less than democratic regimes. Even where there have been tendencies toward democratization, the very fact that union exists only by virtue of the common sovereign has tended to elevate the position of the monarch to one of real power. Attempts to transfer sovereignty or the attributes of sovereignty elsewhere by their very nature stimulate the division of this kind of association of civil societies into separate polities. Thus, the Austro–Hungarian Empire was held together by the Hapsburg emperors and disintegrated when that family ceased to rule (Sharma 1953, chapter 7). The dual monarchy of Sweden and Norway ceased to function when democratic government was introduced, transferring the attributes of sovereignty from the monarch to the nation(s). In Spain, on the other hand, the inability of the Spaniards to transform a multiple monarchy into a federal system, in a locale which by nature demanded peninsular union of some sort, led to the consolidation of the constituent polities into something approximating a unitary state which remained highly unstable because of the local barriers to consolidation that could neither be accommodated nor eradicated (Elliott 1964). [See MONARCHY.]

Multiple monarchies have been transformed into stable and unified polities through *legislative union*. The United Kingdom is a case in point. The centrifugal tendencies of the seventeenth-century dual monarchy linking England and Scotland were finally eliminated through a legislative union of the two nations in 1707. Legislative union bears very close resemblance to federal union at several crucial points. Though designed to direct public allegiance to a single national authority, the terms of the union encourage the political system to retain certain noncentralizing elements. The government of the nation remains national rather than central in character, since it is created by a perpetual covenant which guarantees the constituent parties their boundaries, representation in the national legislature, and certain local autonomies, such as their own systems of municipal law. Legislative unions usually unite unequal polities. The centralizing tendencies induced by this are somewhat counterbalanced by the residual desire for local self-government in the constituent states. Thus, in the United Kingdom the cabinet has acquired a supremacy not foreseen in 1707, but within the framework of cabinet government Scotland has acquired a national ministry of its own with a separate administrative structure, based in Scotland, for most of its governmental programs (Milne 1957).

Federal systems also differ from *empires* allowing cultural home rule. Such empires have often been termed federal—in some cases because they claim to be. The Roman Empire was the classic example of this kind of political system in the ancient world, and the Soviet Union may well be its classic modern counterpart. In both cases, highly centralized political authorities possessing a virtual monopoly of power decide, for reasons of policy, to allow local populations with different ethnic or cultural backgrounds to maintain a degree of cultural home rule, provided that they remain politically subservient to the imperial regime. While this often appears to offer a substantial degree of local autonomy, its political effects are purposely kept minimal. Any local efforts to transform cultural home rule into political power are invariably met with suppressive force from the central government, even to the point of revoking cultural rights, as examples from the history of both empires reveal.

Federal systems are clearly different from *decentralized unitary states*, even though such states may allow local governments considerable autonomy in some ways. In such states local powers are invariably restricted to local matters, as determined by the central authorities, and are subject to national supervision, restriction, and even withdrawal, though tradition may mitigate against precipitous action by the central government in areas where local privileges have been established. Still, as the English experience has shown, even powerful traditions supporting local autonomy have not stood in the way of great reconcentration of power by democratically elected parliaments when such action has been deemed necessary by a national majority.

Mature and emergent federal systems. Several recent studies (Macmahon 1955; Wheare 1946) have attempted to draw distinctions between mature and emergent federal systems. The thrust of their argument is that federalism, when used to unify separate political systems to form a new nation, and federalism, as a form of decentralized government in an established nation, encourage markedly different kinds of political behavior. In the former case, federalism serves as a means to bring tenuous unity to nations composed of highly autonomous polities, with the locus of power remaining among the constituent units. As federal systems mature, so the argument goes, power is increasingly concentrated at the center, and federalism remains only to promote a certain amount of decentralization within an otherwise highly unified political system. Wheare goes so far as to argue that federalism is a transitional phenomenon useful in promoting progressively larger polities which are then gradually discarded (in fact, if not in form) as an unnecessary encumbrance. This argument may have some validity in describing the history of nonfederal political systems which have utilized federal principles to promote national unity. For example, it can be used to describe the evolution of the United Kingdom into its present constitutional state. It cannot be applied, however, to any of the three exemplary federal systems—Canada, Switzerland, and the United States. Their national ties existed from the first, and their national governments were granted broad powers at the outset. Nor has federalism declined in importance as those nations have matured.

There are undoubtedly differences between mature and emergent federal systems, but those differences are more likely to relate to the character of conflict and negotiation between the general and constituent governments than to their relative strengths.

Federalism and intergovernmental relations. Because the study of federalism at its most immediately empirical level heavily stresses the study of intergovernmental relations, the two are often considered to be synonymous. Federalism, however, is something much more than the relationships between governmental units, involving as it does principles which are designed to establish the proper character of those relationships and which must also affect the character of other political institutions within federal systems. As already indicated, federalism concerns the way in which federal principles influence party and electoral systems in federal polities just as much as it concerns the way in which local governments relate to their regional or national ones, or to each other. Moreover, the study of intergovernmental relations exists apart from the study of federalism, since such relationships are to be found in all political systems, federal or otherwise, where there is more than one government extant within a given polity.

Characteristics and operational principles

The most useful way to attempt to understand federalism as a political phenomenon is to undertake a survey of the basic characteristics of federal systems, principles, and processes in order to understand both the manner and the direction of their development.

As a first step it seems necessary to identify the various federal systems that exist today or have existed in the past; only then can we analyze them as operating political systems. However, identifying federal systems is no simple matter, as we have just seen. The difficulties are heightened by the wide functional differences easily observed in the various political systems which call themselves federal and by the often greater operational similarities between self-styled "federal" and "unitary" systems. Contrast, for example, the political systems of Australia and the Soviet Union, Canada and Mexico, Switzerland and Yugoslavia, or compare the United States and Great Britain.

Moreover, federal systems have historically been marked by great internal distinctions between theory and practice, perhaps more so than other political systems. In the United States, the measure of the maintenance of federalism was long considered to be the degree of separation of government activities by level, because it was generally believed that such separation actually existed. In fact, American federalism from the first had been characterized by extensive intergovernmental functional collaboration within the framework of separate governmental structures (Elazar 1962). Similarly, the Canadian federal system has always been described as one in which the federal government is clearly dominant—the repository of all powers not explicitly granted to the provinces. Yet since the brief period of federal supremacy in the years immediately following confederation, the provinces have consistently gained power at federal expense (Smiley 1965). The Russian federal constitution goes so far as to grant each Soviet republic the right of secession—a patent impossibility under the realities of the Russian political system.

Nevertheless, some basic characteristics and operational principles common to all truly federal systems can be identified, and help us to define such systems. These may be divided into three essential elements and a number of supplementary ones.

Written constitution. First, the federal relationship must be established or confirmed through a perpetual covenant of union, inevitably embodied in a written constitution that outlines, among other things, the terms by which power is divided or shared in the political system and which can be altered only by extraordinary procedures [*see* CONSTITUTIONS AND CONSTITUTIONALISM]. Every existing federal nation possesses a written constitution, as do most of the other nations incorporating elements of the federal principle. Juridically, federal constitutions are distinctive in that they are not simply compacts between the rulers and the ruled but involve the people, the general government, and the polities constituting the federal union. Moreover, the constituent polities retain local constitution-making rights of their own.

Noncentralization. The political system must reinforce the terms of the constitution through an actual diffusion of power among a number of substantially self-sustaining centers that are generally coincident with the constituent polities established by the federal compact. Such a diffusion of power may be termed *noncentralization*. It differs from decentralization—the conditional diffusion of specific powers to subordinate local governments by a central government, subject to recall by unilateral decision. It is also more than devolution—the special grant of powers to a subnational unit by a central government, not normally rescindable. Noncentralization ensures that no matter how certain powers may be shared by the general and constituent government at any point in time, the authority to participate in exercising them cannot be taken away from either without mutual consent. Constituent polities in federal systems are able to participate as partners in national governmental activities and to act unilaterally with a high degree of autonomy in areas constitutionally open to them —even on crucial questions and, to a degree, in opposition to national policies, because they possess effectively irrevocable powers.

Areal division of power. A third element that appears to be essential in any federal system is the internal division of authority and power on an areal basis (Maass 1959), what in the United States has been called territorial democracy. It is theoretically possible to create a federal system whose constituent units are fixed but not territorially based. There were premodern protofederations of nomadic tribes, and some observers have seen federal elements in nations constitutionally structured to accommodate social and political divisions along ethnic, religious, or even ideological lines. Nevertheless, no authentic federal system has existed without an areal basis for the federal division. Historically, when areal divisions of power have given way to divisions on the basis of functional interest, federalism has been replaced by pluralism. In modern democratic theory the argument between federalists and antifederalists has frequently revolved around the respective values of areal and functional diffusions of power. Theorists who have argued the obsolescence of federalism while endorsing the values used to justify its existence have generally based their case on the superior utility of pluralism (Mogi 1931, pp. 1059–1115). Proponents of the federal-areal division argue that the deficiencies of territorial democracy are greatly overshadowed by the neutrality of areal representation of functional interests, and they argue further that any other system devised for giving power to these interests has proved unable to cope with the complexities and changes of interest endemic in a dynamic age while certainly limiting the advantages for local differentiation inherent in the areal system.

Studies of federal systems indicate the existence of other elements that supplement the three basic ones. While all of them are not always present in every federal system, their near universality leads to the conclusion that they serve important functions in the maintenance of federalism in each. Similarly, while many of them are found individually in various kinds of political systems, it is their combination within a single system structured around the basic elements that is characteristic of federalism.

Maintaining union. Generally characteristic of modern federal systems are direct lines of communication between the public and both the general and the constituent governments, which allow the public to exert direct influence on both governments and permit them to exercise direct authority over a common citizenry. The people may (and usually do) elect representatives to all governments which serve them. All of the governments may (and usually do) administer programs so as to serve the individual citizen directly. The courts may serve both levels of government, applying the relevant laws directly.

The existence of those direct lines of communication—one of the major features distinguishing federations from leagues—is usually predicated on the existence of a sense of common nationality binding the constituent polities and peoples of federal nations together, another element requisite for the maintenance of a successful federal system. In some countries this sense has been inherited, but in most it has had to be invented. Federalism in Germany has been based on a common sense of an inherited German nationhood. In the United States, Argentina, and Australia a sense of nationhood had to be at least partly invented. National consciousness soon became second nature in those countries, since none of their constituent states ever had much more than a partially developed national consciousness of its own. Canada, Switzerland, and Yugoslavia have had to invent a sense of common nationality strong enough to embrace "nationality groups" whose intense national feelings are rooted in the constituent polities. In such newly formed federal systems as India, Malaysia, and Nigeria, the future of federalism is endangered by the absence of a common sense of nationality. Contrary to some theories, federalism has not proved to be a particularly good device for integrating diverse nationalities into a single political system unless it has been accompanied by other factors compelling integration.

Geographic necessity has been a major factor promoting the maintenance of union within federal systems, even in the face of strong pressures toward disunion. The Mississippi Valley in the United States, the Alps in Switzerland, the island character of the Australian continent, and the mountains and jungles surrounding Brazil have served as direct geographic influences promoting unity. More political than "natural," but no less compelling geographically, have been the pressures for Canadian union generated by that country's neighbor to the south or for the federation of the German states generated by their neighbors to the east and west.

Maintaining noncentralization. It has been well demonstrated that the constituent polities in a federal system must be fairly equal in population and wealth or at least balanced geographically or numerically in their inequalities, if noncentralization is to be maintained. The United States has been able to overcome its internal inequities because each geographic section has included both great and small states. In Canada, the ethnic differences between the two largest provinces have served to inject balance into the system. The existence of groups of cantons in different size categories has helped maintain Swiss federalism. Similar distributions exist in every other system whose federal character is not in question.

The existence of a large polity dominating smaller states with which it is nominally federated on equal terms has often been one of the major reasons for the failure of federalism. In the German federal empire of the late nineteenth century, Prussia was so obviously dominant that the other states had little opportunity to provide national leadership or even a reasonably strong hedge against the desires of its king and government. Similarly, even without the problem of the Communist party, the existence of the Russian Soviet Federal Socialist Republic, which occupies three-fourths of the area and contains three-fifths of the population of the Soviet Union, would have severely crippled the possibilities of maintaining authentic federal relationships in that country.

Successful federal systems have also been characterized by the permanence of the boundaries of their constituent units. This does not mean that boundary changes cannot occur, but it does mean that as a matter of constitutional law such changes can be made only with the consent of the polities involved and that, as a matter of political policy, they are avoided except in the most extreme situations. Boundary changes have occurred in the "classic" federal systems—the United States divided Virginia during the Civil War, Canada has enlarged the boundaries of its provinces, and Switzerland has divided cantons—but they have been the exception rather than the rule, and in every case at least the formal consent of the constituent polities was given. Even in weaker federal systems, such as those of Latin America, state boundaries have tended to remain relatively secure. When boundary changes have been made, as in the postwar redrawing of *Länder* boundaries in West Germany to account for the diminished territory of the Federal Republic and the alteration of state lines to recognize linguistic unities in India, the essential heartlands of the polities involved have been preserved.

In a few very important cases, noncentralization is both reflected and supported through the constitutionally guaranteed existence of different systems of law in the constituent polities. Though the differences in those systems are likely to be somewhat eroded over time—the extent of their preservation varying from system to system—their continued existence as separate systems and the national mixture of laws which their existence promotes act as great bulwarks against centralization [see LEGAL SYSTEMS]. In the United States, each state's legal system stems directly and to a certain extent uniquely from English law, while federal law occupies only an interstitial position binding the systems of the fifty states together insofar as necessary. The resulting mixture of laws keeps the administration of justice, even in federal courts, substantially noncentralized (Macmahon 1955, chapter 11). In Canada, the existence of common law and civil law systems side by side is one constitutional guarantee of French-Canadian cultural survival. Noncentralized legal systems, a particularly Anglo-American device, are often used in legislative as well as federal unions. They are rare in other political cultures and have become less common in all federal systems established since 1900. More common is the provision for modification of national legal codes by the subnational governments to meet special local needs, as in Switzerland.

The point is generally well taken that unless the constituent polities have substantial influence over the formal or informal amending process the federal character of the system is open to question. Since many constitutional changes are made without recourse to formal constitutional amendment, the position of the constituent polities must be additionally protected by a constitution designed so that any serious changes in the political order can be made only by the decision of dispersed majorities which reflect the areal division of powers. This protection, which federal theorists have argued is important for popular government as well as for federalism (Diamond 1963), is a feature of the most truly federal systems.

Noncentralization is strengthened in all federal systems by giving the constituent polities guaranteed representation in the national legislature and, often, by giving them a guaranteed role in the national political process. In some federal systems, notably those of the United States and Switzerland, the latter is guaranteed in the written constitution. In others, such as Canada and those in Latin America, certain powers of participation have been acquired and have become part of the traditional constitution.

Recent studies have shown that the existence of a noncentralized party system is perhaps the most important single element in the maintenance of federal noncentralization (Macmahon 1955). Noncentralized parties initially develop because of the constitutional arrangements of the federal compact, but once they have come into existence, they tend to be self-perpetuating and to function as decentralizing forces in their own right.

The United States and Canada provide two examples of the different forms which can be assumed by a noncentralized party system. In the United States, where party responsibility is minimal and virtually nonexistent on the national level, a two-party system has developed, with the parties actually coalitions of the several state or, in some cases, local party organizations functioning as national units only for the quadrennial presidential elections or for purposes of organizing the national Congress. Party financing and decision making are functions which are dispersed either among the state organizations or among widely divergent factions operating nationwide. In Canada, on the other hand, the parliamentary form of government, with its concomitant requirement of party responsibility, means that at the national level considerably more party cohesiveness must be maintained simply in order to gain and hold power.

The noncentralized party system in Canada has developed through a fragmentation of the parties along regional or provincial lines. The parties with nationwide bases are still divided internally along provincial lines, with each provincial organization autonomous. Individual provinces are frequently dominated by regional parties that send only a few representatives to the national legislature, adding to the fragmentation of the system. Very often, the party victorious in national elections is the one which is briefly able to expand its base to most nearly national proportions.

European-style federal systems where parliamentary government is the norm follow the Canadian model. Australia and Switzerland come closest to paralleling it, and traces of it can be found in the German Federal Republic. A more centralized variation of the same pattern exists in countries like India, in which the national government is dominated by one very large and diffuse national party which is held together nationally by personal leadership but is quite factionalized in the states where it must share the governing power with other parties.

Federal nations with less developed party systems frequently gain some of the same decentralizing effects through what the Latins call *caudillismo*—noncentralized personal leadership systems which diffuse power through strong local leaders operating in the constituent polities. Caudillistic noncentralization is most characteristic of Latin American federal systems but apparently exists in such new federations as Nigeria and Malaysia as well [see CAUDILLISMO].

The importance to federalism of a noncentralized party system is well illustrated by contrast with those formally federal nations dominated by one highly centralized party, such as the Soviet Union, Yugoslavia, and Mexico. In all three cases, the dominant party has operated to limit the power of the constituent polities in direct proportion to the extent of its dominance.

Ultimately, however, noncentralization is maintained to the extent that there is respect for the federal principle within each federal system. Such respect is necessarily reflected in the immediate recognition by the decision-making publics that the preservation of the constituent polities is as important as the preservation of the nation as a whole. In the words of the American Chief Justice Salmon P. Chase, federalism looks to "an indestructible Union, composed of indestructible States" (*Texas* v. *White*, 7 Wallace [1869]). This recognition may be based on loyalty to particular constituent polities or on an understanding of the role played by federalism in animating the political system along certain unique lines. Thus, those who value government by conciliation and partnership, with emphasis on local control, are likely to have respect for the federal principle.

Citizens of a federal nation must show that respect in two ways, by showing self-restraint and by cultivating the political art of negotiation. Federalism can exist only where there is considerable tolerance of diversity and willingness to take political action through conciliation even when the power to act unilaterally is available. The usual prerequisite to action in federal systems is the ability to build consensus rather than the power to threaten coercion. Western federal nations can furnish many examples of the exercise of national self-restraint in dealing with difficult federal problems. Even in a federal system as centralized as that of India, the constitutional right of the national government to assume control of the state governments is exercised as little as possible— notably when the communists win local elections— and is then clearly a temporary action.

The historical record indicates that the dual purpose implied in Chase's dictum has been at least as responsible for the creation of federal systems as has the single interest in political unification. The Canadian confederation came into being not only to create a new nation out of the British North American colonies but also to give Ontario and Quebec autonomous political systems of their own. Similarly, every move toward greater union in the Swiss confederation has been made in order to preserve the independence of the cantons from both outside encroachment and revolutionary centralism (Sharma 1953, pp. 269–275). A good case

can be made that similar motivations were important in the creation of Australia, Malaysia, Nigeria, and the United States.

Maintaining the federal principle. Several of the devices commonly found in federal systems serve to maintain the federal principle per se and are consequently supportive of both the national government and the constituent polities. Two of these are particularly common and important.

The maintenance of federalism requires that the nation and its constituent polities each have a substantially complete set of governing institutions of their own with the right—within limits set by the compact—to modify those institutions unilaterally. Separate legislative and administrative institutions are both necessary. This does not necessarily mean that all governmental activities must be carried out by separate institutions at each level. It is possible for the agencies of one government to serve as agents of the other by mutual agreement. But each government must have the needed institutions to function independently in the areas of its authority and the structural resources to cooperate freely with the other government's counterpart agencies.

In this regard, the contractual sharing of public responsibilities by all governments in the system appears to be a central characteristic of federalism. Sharing, broadly conceived, includes common involvement in policy making, financing, and administration of government activities. In contemporary federal systems, it is characterized by extensive intergovernmental collaboration. Sharing can be based on highly formal arrangements or informal agreements. In federal systems, it is usually contractual in nature. The contract—politically a limited expression of the compact principle—is used in formal arrangements as a legal device to enable governments responsible to separate polities to engage in joint action while remaining independent entities. Even where government agencies cooperate without formally contracting to do so, the spirit of federalism that pervades ongoing federal systems tends to infuse the participating parties with a sense of contractual obligation.

In any federal system, it is likely that there will be continued tension between the federal government and the constituent polities over the years and that different "balances" between them will develop at different times. The existence of this tension is an integral part of the federal relationship, and its character does much to determine the future of federalism in each system. The question of federal–state relations which it produces is perennially a matter of public concern because virtually all other political issues arising in a federal system are phrased in terms of their implications for federalism. In this way federalism imposes a way of looking at problems that stands apart from the substantive issues raised by the problems themselves. This is particularly true of those issues which affect the very fabric of society. In the United States, for example, the race question is a problem of federal–state as well as Negro–white relations, and the same is true of the cultural question in Canada and the linguistic question in India.

The end product. The very terminology of federalism is characterized by a revealing ambiguity that is indicative of the end product of federal systems. The word "federalize" is used to describe the unification of "sovereign" states into a federal polity and also the permanent devolution of authority and power within a nation to subnational governments. In this ambiguity lies the essence of the federal principle—the perpetuation of both union and noncentralization.

Viewed from the top, the combination of the elements discussed above results in a federal rather than a central government—i.e., a government composed of a nationwide coalition of political institutions, some with predominantly local power bases (such as the national legislature), others with predominantly national power bases (such as the national bureaucracy). This government, whose power is thus diffused vertically and laterally, functions in cooperation with the constituent polities which it must conciliate in order to act. Decision making is characterized by heavy reliance upon negotiation and bargaining and by minimal reliance upon the exercise of force. Operations are characterized by a measure of disorder, since noncentralization breeds multiple power centers located at or cutting across all levels of government. Each of these centers seeks to keep open routes of access to the others, usually succeeding because it is in the best interests of all to maintain this kind of disorder as part of the "rules of the game."

Viewed locally, a federal system consists of governmental inputs from different sources whose local connections normally serve to fragment local authority. However, because such a system rewards those who actively seek to reconcile the diffuse elements and bind them together for a larger purpose, local political leaders can control these inputs to a great extent. While this may not prevent the national government from exercising great power at any given time or from increasing its total power over time, it does mean that as long as the federal principle remains operative, the public can and almost invariably does limit certain kinds of national government actions or guides such actions

into particular channels (often directed toward strengthening the constituent governments) by invoking the terms of the compact.

Viewed theoretically, these patterns of behavior and the arguments advanced to justify them serve to reaffirm the fundamental principles that (1) the strength of a federal polity does not stem from the power of the national government but from the authority vested in the nation as a whole; (2) both the national government and the governments of the constituent polities are possessed of delegated powers only; and (3) all governments are limited by the common national constitution.

All this should make it apparent that federalism is a form of popular government embodying elements of both republicanism and democracy. The federal structures occasionally adopted by nondemocratic systems must generally be considered "window dressing" except insofar as the injection of the federal principle may serve as a democratizing force in itself. In Yugoslavia, for example, the existence of a federal superstructure has proved useful in fostering such decentralization as the Communist party leadership wished to allow and may even have played a role in stimulating decentralizing tendencies.

Empirical and theoretical development

Ancient protofederal systems. Long before the term "federal" was invented, there were political systems that embodied elements of the federal principle. The Israelite political system was probably the first example in recorded history of a union of constituent polities based on a sense of common nationality, with national and tribal political institutions and some division of functions between the two partly formalized by a written constitution. As a republic it was never able to overcome the problems of national executive leadership and succession and, after some two hundred years, revised its constitution to superimpose a limited monarchy on its federal institutions. Still, as many of the seventeenth-century federalists noted, it came closer to resembling a modern federal system than any comparable premodern nation. Its classic intellectual product, the Bible, was the first book to discuss the problems of a federal polity.

Permanent leagues of independent states united by a sense of common need but without any sense of common nationhood were found in various parts of the Greek world. They were entrusted with certain matters in the realm of foreign affairs and defense but were in every respect accountable to their member states. The classic example of this system was the Achaean League (251–146 B.C.), a protofederal system often erroneously considered to be the first federal polity (Freeman 1863). The Greeks left some descriptions of their leagues but no theoretical discussions of the league as a political system. Except for Aristotle's criticisms, the great Greek political theorists ignored federalism as a political principle because the very idea contradicted their conception of the small, unified polis as the only basis upon which to build the good regime.

Several of the great ancient empires, notably the Persian, Hellenic, and Roman, structured their political systems around the principle of cultural home rule. Since political life was virtually inseparable from the religious and cultural aspects of society in the ancient world, imperial recognition of local constitutions offered a measure of contractual devolution of political power; however, as in more recent examples of this form of imperialism, such home rule was not a matter of local right but represented a conditional grant subject to unilateral revocation by the imperial rulers.

Medieval experiments. Elements of the federal principle are foreshadowed in medieval feudalism through its emphasis on essentially immutable contractual relationships that permanently link the contracting parties while guaranteeing their rights. However, the hierarchical character of these relationships, coupled with the lack of practical mechanisms to maintain the terms of the contracts, led to the degeneration of those elements in most feudal societies. Another movement in the direction of federalism grew out of the development of medieval commercial towns in central Europe which formed leagues for mutual defense and assistance following the Greek model. The most important development in this period was the first confederation of Swiss cantons in 1291 for mutual aid in defense of their independence. The success of this effort was in no small measure due to its connection, from the beginning, with quasi-popular government. These embryonic federal experiments all proceeded pragmatically while federal theory was confined to juridical discussions of the corporate relationships between polities in the Holy Roman Empire.

Ultimately a fusion of contractual elements from feudalism with political mechanisms from the commercial confederacies gave rise to the immediate antecedents of modern federalism. The Christian states on the Iberian Peninsula created a political system which in its most advanced stages came very close to authentic federalism. During the years of the reconquest, most of the peninsula was reorganized under the *fuero* system, which established local governments with relatively liberal political institutions in order to encourage resettlement. New states were formed through feudal-style contractual relationships designed to protect local rights. Three of these states joined in a quasi-federal arrangement under the crown of Aragon, each of them (plus several in Italy added later) retaining its own constitution and governing institutions as well as acquiring representation in the over-all Aragonese government. Unification of Spain under a multiple monarchy in 1469 left most of these federal elements intact for the next two and a half centuries, but the demands of the monarchy ultimately subverted them, transforming Spain into a precariously centralized state.

In the sixteenth century, certain emergent civil societies, influenced by the Reformation to return to Scripture as a political source and by the Spanish system of political organization, as well as by local necessity, began to apply federal principles for state-building purposes. The Hapsburg heirs to the Spanish crown had applied Iberian principles to the organization of their other European possessions. Their governmental reforms in the Netherlands provided an organizational basis for the federation of the United Provinces in the late sixteenth century. When that country gained its independence, it established a political system which, while unable to solve the most crucial technical problems of federalism, maintained itself in federal style for two hundred years, until Napoleon put an end to its existence, leaving a residue of noncentralization that marks the Netherlands today.

The Swiss, in the meantime, were developing their own techniques for combining feudal and commercial elements to create a loose confederation of cantons, which was also influenced by Biblical ideas and, perhaps negatively, by contacts with Hapsburg Spain. Achieving full independence in 1648, the Swiss confederation remained loosely leagued for two centuries (except for the Napoleonic interlude), until it adopted a federal constitution in 1848.

First modern formulations. The protofederalism of the United Provinces and the Swiss cantons, coming at the outset of the age of nationalism, also stimulated the first serious efforts to formulate federal theories based on modern political ideas. Jean Bodin analyzed the possibilities of federation in light of the problem of sovereignty. Hugo Grotius and Samuel Pufendorf examined federal arrangements as aspects of international law. These theorists all treated federalism as an aspect of international law. Johannes Althusius (1603), analyzing the Dutch and Swiss constitutions, was the first to perceive that federalism was really concerned with problems of national unity. The real father of modern federal theory, he was also the first to connect federalism with popular sovereignty and to distinguish between leagues, multiple monarchies, and confederations. His retention of hierarchical principles and his emphasis on the corporate organization of society both flawed the federal character of his work and reflected the empirical roots of his analysis.

Thus the rise of the nation-state in the sixteenth and seventeenth centuries stimulated federal solutions to the problems of national unification. In all but a few countries on the periphery of western Europe, the application of federal principles foundered on three problems: (1) the conciliation of feudally rooted hierarchies with a system demanding fundamental social equality in order to facilitate the sharing of power; (2) the reconciliation of local autonomy with national energy in an era of political upheaval that required most nations to maintain a state of constant mobilization basically incompatible with the toleration of local differences; and (3) the problem of executive leadership and succession, which is particularly complex in federal systems and was not solved until the United States invented the elected presidency.

Modern federalism. The rise of modern imperialism also contributed to the emergence of federalism, as indicated by the works of the important prerevolutionary political theorists of the eighteenth century, e.g., Montesquieu and Adam Smith. Here, too, the Spanish experience was influential, but it remained for the British to create the requisite popular institutions in their colonization of North America and for the Biblically influenced colonists to create the theoretical justification for these institutions. The theoretical ambiguity of those quasi-federal institutions led Americans to assume that their relationship to the British government was federal, while London entertained no such notion (Becker 1922). The Americans' response to their view of the imperial system helped them develop the federal ideas they were later to use so creatively.

The founders of the United States of America can be said to have transformed and organized the principles of federalism into a practical system of government. They were able to do so partly because their nation developed without the disadvantages that plagued earlier federal systems. As a postfeudal society, the United States had no serious problem of coping with hierarchies. As a relatively isolated nation, external pressures for centralization were not present for nearly 150 years. American political inventiveness took care of the internal

problems of applying the federal principle, though not without having to fight a major civil war to resolve some of them. Though the specific forms of American federalism were not widely imitated with success, its basic principles of organization were emulated by almost every other nation attempting the federal solution to the problems of popular government in a pluralistic civil society. The creation of the theoretical framework for those principles was part and parcel of the invention of federalism. Set forth in its basics in the debate over ratification of the constitution, that framework had at its core *The Federalist* (1787–1788), the classic formulation of the principles of modern federalism. Equally important to the evolution of federal systems, however, were the arguments of those who wished to preserve even greater state autonomy; many of these arguments were transformed into tools to promote extraconstitutional decentralization during the nineteenth century.

From the first, American contributions to federal theory—even those of the few theorists not actively involved in politics—have been rooted in the practical concerns of maintaining a federal system. Most of these contributions have, accordingly, been formulated as discussions of constitutional law. The courts, particularly the federal Supreme Court, have conducted continuing debate on the meaning and character of federalism through the medium of case law. Leading political figures, such as Gallatin, Calhoun, Lincoln, Wilson, and the Roosevelts, have made real contributions through their state papers. The pragmatic orientation of those contributions, however, has tended to obscure their more lasting theoretical importance (Anderson 1955).

The French Revolution, while stimulating the development of popular government, was essentially hostile to the spirit and institutions of federalism. Its immediate heirs tried to destroy federal institutions in western Europe in the name of democracy, and the subsequent bearers of its tradition have proved equally hostile to federal ideas—except insofar as some of them have equated federalism with decentralized government.

In the nineteenth century, several of the new Latin American nations, following the United States example and also influenced by the federal elements in the Hispanic imperial tradition, experimented with federalism, with distinctly mixed results. Even where federalism survived in theory, the instability of Latin American governments and the frequent recourse to dictatorial regimes hampered its effective operation. Even so, the three largest Latin American nations—Argentina, Brazil, and Mexico—retain federal systems of varying political significance; federal principles are also included in the political systems of Colombia and Venezuela.

In the mid-nineteenth century European politicians and political theorists, stimulated by necessity, the American example, and the very influential studies of Tocqueville (1835), turned to consider federalism as a form of democratic political organization. Though practical applications remained few, numerous works were produced, primarily in the German-speaking countries, where doctrinaire and metaphysical analyses of federalism in relation to the problems of nationalism, sovereignty, and popular consent were in vogue. The most important of these works were the theoretical formulations of Bluntschli (1849–1852), based on his observations of federal reorganization in Switzerland, and the historical studies of Gierke. In the end, federal principles were used in the unification of Germany, and Switzerland adopted a modern federal constitution. Fully federal solutions were rejected in other nations, but several adopted quasi-federal institutions to meet particular problems of unification and decentralization.

During the late nineteenth century, British interest in imperial federalism was manifested in several ways. Canada and Australia were given federal constitutions and dominion status in 1867 and 1901, respectively, and the foundations were laid for the federal unification of India. British political theorists interested in imperial unity and internal devolution explored contemporary (Bryce 1888) and historical (Freeman 1863) federal experiments and presented arguments of their own as to the utility and proper organization of federal systems (Labillière 1894).

Whereas in the nineteenth century federalism was used to abet ethnic nationalism, in the twentieth it has been used as a means to unify multiethnic nations. Several of the ethnically heterogeneous nations created or reconstructed after World War I, including the Soviet Union and Yugoslavia, formally embraced federalism as a nominal solution to their nationality problems. The United Kingdom added a federal dimension at the same time to accommodate the Irish. Extension of nation-building activities to Asia and Africa, where ethnic diversity is even greater than in Europe, has led to new efforts in the same vein. In nations outside of the totalitarian orbit, such as India and Malaysia, federalism has been used to secure political and cultural rights for the larger ethnolinguistic groups. In Africa, where the survival of separate ethnic groups has been called into question by the native nationalists, federalism has been applied in several

nations, including Nigeria and Cameroon, as a device for sharing political power rather than a way to maintain cultural autonomy.

The contemporary study of federalism. The emergence of political science as a discipline in the late nineteenth century stimulated a shift from an explicitly normative to a predominantly empirical interest in federalism. Such noted British scholars as Bryce (1901) and Dicey (1885) were the first to study federalism as part of their general interest in political systems. American scholars began their work in the 1870s, as the Civil War generation was passing into history, but their first works still reflected the issues of the war. Thus Burgess (1886) concluded that the utility of the states was dissipated by modern technology, just as their power was destroyed by the war, while Wilson (1885) accepted the view that the war had wrought great changes but still saw federalism as alive and vital.

Though these men and their colleagues laid the foundations for the empirical study of federal systems with the tools of contemporary political science, federalism as a field of study was neglected for many years. The rise of other problems to attract the attention of scholars, the negation of earlier legalistic and metaphysical approaches, and the decline of normative interest in the federal principle combined to dissuade younger political scientists from examining questions of federal government, except incidentally, until the twentieth century was well advanced.

Renewed interest in the field first developed when American students of public administration found themselves confronted with problems of intergovernmental relations at nearly every turn. The study of intergovernmental relations in the administrative realm brought about significant gains in the understanding of the process of federal government, not the least of which was a growing recognition that the assumptions about federalism underlying their work, borrowed whole from nineteenth-century theorists, needed serious re-examination. Beginning in the 1930s and 1940s, American and British political scientists began to raise fundamental questions about the nature of federal systems and the interrelationships of their governmental components (Anderson 1946). In the 1950s these questions were expanded to include, among others, problems of political influence, the role of political parties, the historical development of federal systems, and the meaning of earlier federal theories (Bachelder & Shaw 1964). By the early 1960s, students of existing federal governments were rediscovering the need to clarify the principles of federalism in order to understand the operation of those governments. Students of comparative government were also becoming increasingly interested in problems of political integration, centralization, and decentralization—all of which stimulated new interest in the systematic study of federalism.

Evaluation

While many attempts to establish federal systems have ended in failure, such systems, once established, have proved to be most durable. No authentic federal system that has lasted for even 15 years has ever been abandoned except through revolutionary disruption (as in the case of Germany), and in every such case federalism—showing remarkable resilience—has ultimately been restored. Certain theories to the contrary, there is no evidence that federalism represents a transitional stage on the road to unitary government. No federal system in history has ever "evolved" into a unitary one, nor has any established system been structurally consolidated by internal decision. On the contrary, federal devices to conciliate minority populations have been used in place of force to maintain unity even in consolidated systems. Moreover, federal systems or systems strongly influenced by the federal principle have been among the most stable and long-lasting of polities.

At the same time, relatively few cultures have been able to utilize federal principles in government. Anglo–American civil societies have done so most successfully. Even those not fully committed to federalism have, without exception, included elements of the federal principle in whatever systems they have chosen, no doubt because both constitutionalism and noncentralization rate high on the scale of Anglo–American political values.

Of the 16 formally federal nations that exist in the world today, Australia, Cameroon, Canada, India, Malaysia, Nigeria, and the United States were created under British colonial tutelage. These seven include all the nations established since World War II that have been able to maintain federal systems, and they provide most of the successful examples of federalism in operation. Of the nine remaining federal nations, Argentina, Brazil, and Mexico fall directly within the Hispanic political tradition and Austria, Germany, and Switzerland, though they follow the Germanic political tradition, were also influenced by Hispanic ideas at some point in their development. Both political traditions have been influential in stimulating federal inclinations in many of the nonfederal nations, but they have been notably less successful in fostering lasting federal institutions; the Hispanic tradition has failed to combine federalism and stability, while the Germanic has tended toward authoritarian centralization. (The three remaining nations, Libya, the Soviet Union, and Yugoslavia, are federal in name and formal structure but hardly in any meaningful sense of the term.)

The successful operation of federal systems requires a particular kind of political environment, one which is conducive to popular government and has the strong traditions of political cooperation and self-restraint that are needed to maintain a system which minimizes the use of coercion. Beyond the level of tradition, federal systems operate best in societies with sufficient homogeneity of fundamental interests—or consensus—to allow a great deal of latitude in political operations and to place primary reliance upon voluntary collaboration. The existence of severe strains on the body politic which lead to the use of force to maintain domestic order is even more inimical to the successful maintenance of federal patterns of government than of other forms of popular government. Moreover, federal systems are most successful in civil societies with the human resources to fill many public offices competently and with material resources plentiful enough to allow a measure of economic waste in payment for the luxury of liberty.

DANIEL J. ELAZAR

[*See also* CENTRALIZATION AND DECENTRALIZATION; CONSTITUTIONAL LAW, *article on* DISTRIBUTION OF POWERS; PRESIDENTIAL GOVERNMENT. *Other relevant material may be found in* GOVERNMENT; INTERNATIONAL INTEGRATION; NATION; STATE.]

BIBLIOGRAPHY

ALTHUSIUS, JOHANNES (1603) 1932 *Politica methodice digesta*. Edited by Carl J. Friedrich. Cambridge, Mass.: Harvard Univ. Press. → The first European book directed entirely to the discussion of federalism. Text in Latin with a comprehensive English introduction.

AMERICAN ACADEMY OF POLITICAL AND SOCIAL SCIENCE 1965 *Intergovernmental Relations in the United States*. Edited by Harry W. Reynolds, Jr. Annals, Vol. 359. Philadelphia: The Academy.

ANDERSON, WILLIAM 1946 *Federalism and Intergovernmental Relations: A Budget of Suggestions for Research*. Chicago: Public Administration Service.

ANDERSON, WILLIAM 1955 *The Nation and the States: Rivals or Partners?* Minneapolis: Univ. of Minnesota Press. → One of the best descriptions of the American federal system.

ASPATURIAN, VERNON V. 1950 The Theory and Practice of Soviet Federalism. *Journal of Politics* 12:20–51.

BACHELDER, GLEN L.; and SHAW, PAUL C. 1964 Federalism: A Selected Bibliography. Unpublished manuscript, Michigan State Univ., Institute for Community Development and Services.

BECKER, CARL L. (1922) 1958 *The Declaration of Independence: A Study in the History of Political Ideas.* New York: Vintage. → An important study of the origins of American federal ideas.

BIRCH, ANTHONY H. 1955 *Federalism, Finance and Social Legislation in Canada, Australia, and the United States.* Oxford: Clarendon.

BLUNTSCHLI, JOHANN K. 1849–1852 *Geschichte des schweizerischen Bundesrechtes.* 2 vols. Zurich: Meyer & Zeller. → A theory of federal organization based on the reconstruction of the Swiss Confederation in 1848.

BOEHM, MAX H. 1931 Federalism. Volume 6, pages 169–172 in *Encyclopaedia of the Social Sciences.* New York: Macmillan. → Devoted primarily to a discussion of federalism as a social theory.

BONDURANT, JOAN 1958 *Regionalism vs. Provincialism: A Study in Problems of Indian National Unity.* India Press Digests, Monograph Series, No. 4. Berkeley: Univ. of California Press.

BRETT, LIONEL (editor) 1961 *Constitutional Problems of Federalism in Nigeria.* Lagos (Nigeria): Times Press.

BRIGHT, JOHN 1959 *A History of Israel.* Philadelphia: Westminster Press. → The best description of federal institutions in ancient Israel.

BRYCE, JAMES (1888) 1909 *The American Commonwealth.* 3d ed., 2 vols. New York and London: Macmillan. → An abridged edition was published in 1959 by Putnam. A classic work whose descriptions of federal–state relations follow conventional American opinions of the period.

BRYCE, JAMES 1901 *Studies in History and Jurisprudence.* New York: Oxford Univ. Press. → Includes Bryce's theoretical considerations of federalism.

BURGESS, JOHN W. 1886 The American Commonwealth. *Political Science Quarterly* 1:9–35. → One of the earliest pronouncements on the "demise of the states" in the United States.

CANADA, ROYAL COMMISSION ON DOMINION–PROVINCIAL RELATIONS 1940 *Report.* 3 vols. Ottawa: Patenaud. → Volume 1: *Canada: 1867–1939.* Volume 2: *Recommendations.* Volume 3: *Documentation.* The most comprehensive survey of the Canadian federal system.

CLAREMONT MEN'S COLLEGE, CLAREMONT, CALIF., INSTITUTE FOR STUDIES IN FEDERALISM 1961 *Essays in Federalism,* by George C. S. Benson et al. Claremont, Calif.: The College.

CODDING, GEORGE A. 1961 *The Federal Government of Switzerland.* Boston: Houghton Mifflin.

COWEN, ZEHMAN 1959 *Federal Jurisdiction in Australia.* New York: Oxford Univ. Press.

DIAMOND, MARTIN 1963 The Federalist. Pages 573–593 in Leo Strauss and Joseph Cropsey (editors), *History of Political Philosophy.* Chicago: Rand McNally. → An important discussion of *The Federalist* as a major contribution to democratic political theory.

DICEY, ALBERT V. (1885) 1961 *Introduction to the Study of the Law of the Constitution.* 10th ed. With an introduction by E. C. S. Wade. London: Macmillan; New York: St. Martins. → First published as *Lectures Introductory to the Study of the Law of the Constitution.* The classic liberal work on the British constitution that considers the questions of federalism in comparison with legislative union.

ELAZAR, DANIEL J. 1962 *The American Partnership: Intergovernmental Co-operation in the Nineteenth-century United States.* Univ. of Chicago Press. → A study of the evolution of intergovernmental relations in the United States.

ELAZAR, DANIEL J. 1966 *American Federalism: A View From the States.* New York: Crowell.

ELLIOTT, JOHN H. 1964 *Imperial Spain: 1469–1716.* New York: St. Martins. → Historical description of Spanish protofederal systems and their decline.

Federalism and Economic Growth in Underdeveloped Countries: A Symposium, by Ursula K. Hicks et al. 1961 New York: Oxford Univ. Press.

FREEMAN, EDWARD A. (1863) 1893 *The History of Federal Government in Greece and Italy.* 2d ed. London and New York: Macmillan. → A classic attempt to trace the origins of federalism.

GIERKE, OTTO VON (1913) 1934 *Natural Law and the Theory of Society: 1500 to 1800.* Translated with an introduction by Ernst Barker. Cambridge Univ. Press. → A study of the early modern origins of federal ideas. A translation of five subsections of Volume 4 of *Das deutsche Genossenschaftsrecht.* A paperback edition was published in 1957 by Beacon.

GOLDWIN, ROBERT A. (editor) 1963 *A Nation of States: Essays on the American Federal System.* Chicago: Rand McNally.

GRAVES, W. BROOKE 1964 *American Intergovernmental Relations: Their Origins, Historical Development, and Current Status.* New York: Scribner.

GRODZINS, MORTON 1960a American Political Parties and the American System. *Western Political Quarterly* 13:974–998. → A very important descriptive analysis of the role of a noncentralized party system in the maintenance of federalism.

GRODZINS, MORTON 1960b The Federal System. Pages 265–282 in U.S. President's Commission on National Goals, *Goals for Americans.* Englewood Cliffs, N.J.: Prentice-Hall. → A comprehensive description of the American federal system.

GRODZINS, MORTON 1966 *The American System: A New View of Government in the United States.* Chicago: Rand McNally.

HAMILTON, ALEXANDER; MADISON, JAMES; and JAY, JOHN (1787–1788) 1961 *The Federalist.* Edited with introduction and notes by Jacob E. Cooke. Middletown, Conn.: Wesleyan Univ. Press. → The classic foundation of federal theory.

KAUFMANN, YEHEZKEL (1937–1948) 1960 *The Religion of Israel: From Its Beginnings to the Babylonian Exile.* Univ. of Chicago Press. → An abridgment and translation of *Toldot Hā-emūnāh Hā-yisrāelit.* An important discussion of the origins of covenant theory in the Bible.

LABILLIÈRE, FRANCIS P. DE 1894 *Federal Britain: Or, Unity and Federation of the Empire.* London: Low, Marston. → A compendium of studies relating to the idea of British imperial federalism.

LIVINGSTON, WILLIAM S. (editor) 1963 *Federalism in the Commonwealth: A Bibliographical Commentary.* London: Cassell.

MAASS, ARTHUR (editor) 1959 *Area and Power: A Theory of Local Government.* Glencoe, Ill.: Free Press. → Pioneering effort to formulate theories about the areal distribution of power and its consequences.

MACMAHON, ARTHUR W. (editor) (1955) 1962 *Federalism: Mature and Emergent.* New York: Russell. → An excellent collection of articles on federalism in theory and practice, with emphasis on the United States and Europe.

MAIN, JACKSON T. 1961 *The Anti-Federalists: Critics of the Constitution, 1781–1788.* Chapel Hill: Univ. of North Carolina Press. → A study of the movement opposed to the ratification of the American constitution.

MILLER, PERRY (1939) 1961 *The New England Mind: The Seventeenth Century.* Boston: Beacon. → An important discussion of seventeenth-century "federal theology" and its application in the New World.

MILNE, DAVID 1957 *The Scottish Office and Other Scottish Government Departments.* New York: Oxford Univ. Press. → A survey of the history and functions of the separate ministries for Scotland.

MOGI, SOBEI 1931 *The Problem of Federalism: A Study in the History of Political Theory.* 2 vols. London: Allen & Unwin. → Compendious historical survey of the various theories of federalism.

RIKER, WILLIAM A. 1964 *Federalism: Origin, Operation, Significance.* Boston: Little.

SCHMIDHAUSER, JOHN R. 1958 *The Supreme Court as Final Arbiter in Federal–State Relations: 1789–1957.* Chapel Hill: Univ. of North Carolina Press.

SHARMA, BRIJ M. 1953 *Federalism in Theory and Practice.* 2 vols. Chandausi (India): Bhargava. → One of the few comprehensive studies of federal systems throughout the world; gives special emphasis to the Indian situation.

SMILEY, DONALD V. 1962 The Rowell–Sirois Report, Provincial Autonomy, and Post-war Canadian Federalism. *Canadian Journal of Economics and Political Science* 28:54–69.

SMILEY, DONALD V. 1965 The Two Themes of Canadian Federalism. *Canadian Journal of Economics and Political Science* 31:80–97.

TOCQUEVILLE, ALEXIS DE (1835) 1945 *Democracy in America.* 2 vols. New York: Knopf. → First published in French. Paperback editions were published in 1961 by Vintage and by Schocken.

U.S. COMMISSION ON INTERGOVERNMENTAL RELATIONS 1955 *A Report to the President for Transmittal to the Congress.* Washington: Government Printing Office.

U.S. CONGRESS, HOUSE, COMMITTEE ON GOVERNMENT OPERATIONS (1955) 1956 *Intergovernmental Relations in the United States: A Selected Bibliography.* Washington: Government Printing Office.

WELLS, ROGER H. 1961 *The States in West German Federalism: A Study of Federal–State Relations, 1949–1960.* New York: Bookman.

WHEARE, KENNETH C. (1946) 1964 *Federal Government.* 4th ed. New York: Oxford Univ. Press.

WILSON, WOODROW (1885) 1961 *Congressional Government: A Study in American Politics.* New York: Meridian. → The classic study of a legislature-centered federal government.

FEEBLEMINDEDNESS

See MENTAL RETARDATION.

FEEDBACK

See CYBERNETICS; HOMEOSTASIS; MODELS, MATHEMATICAL; SIMULATION.

FERENCZI, SÁNDOR

Sándor Ferenczi, one of the earliest psychoanalysts, was born in Miskolc, Hungary, in 1873 and died in Budapest, in his house in the Buda hills, in 1933. He was for a time Sigmund Freud's closest friend and collaborator.

Early life. Ferenczi was one of 11 children. His parents, whose surname had originally been Fraenkel, were well-to-do, owning the largest bookstore in Miskolc. A biographer, Izette De Forest (1954), tells us that Ferenczi's parents were unusually enlightened in the freedom and companionship they gave to their children and that the life of the family was gay and spontaneous, devoted to the enjoyment of scholarship, music, drama, poetry, and languages. The famous psychoanalyst Ernest Jones (1953–1957)—who knew Ferenczi well—tells us, however, that Ferenczi was haunted throughout life by a quite inordinate and insatiable longing for his father's love. Ferenczi himself said in a letter to Freud that his feelings about Freud and other colleagues were bound up with his childhood difficulties with his father and brothers.

After graduating from the local Gymnasium, Ferenczi studied medicine in Vienna, receiving his degree in 1894. He had a year of compulsory service as a physician in the Austro-Hungarian army and then interned in various hospitals in Budapest, notably St. Rókus Korház. There he specialized in neurology and neuropathology, also developing his skill in hypnotism. In 1900 he opened an office in Budapest for the practice of neurology.

Development of interest in psychoanalysis. When Ferenczi first read Freud's *The Interpretation of Dreams* he was not able to assimilate its teachings. It was his rereading of Breuer and Freud's *Studies on Hysteria* that impressed him with the claims of psychoanalysis. He wrote to Freud in 1907 and, accompanied by Dr. F. Stein of Budapest, who introduced him, called on Freud in February 1908. The impression that he made brought an invitation to spend a fortnight in August with the Freud family at their summer place. He became a member of the Vienna Psychoanalytic Society, the small group that met on Wednesday evenings with Freud.

Later career. Ferenczi and Freud traveled together extensively, and between 1908 and 1933 they exchanged more than a thousand letters. In 1909 Ferenczi accompanied Freud on a trip to the United States, where Freud lectured at Clark University. In 1910, at Freud's suggestion, Ferenczi proposed the founding of the International Psychoanalytic Association; and in 1913 he founded the Hungarian Psychoanalytic Society. In 1916 he underwent a brief personal analysis with Freud; it lasted only three weeks, for two hours a day, since Ferenczi had to return to his military duties as a medical officer in Hungary. According to Freud, the analysis was continued later. In 1918 Ferenczi was elected president of the International Psychoanalytic Society; he relinquished the presidency in 1919. His failure to be invited again to be president of the society was a keen disappointment to him and may have been a consequence of his advocacy of lay analysis.

In 1919, after 18 years of indecision, Ferenczi married. The marriage was a very happy one, and although there were no children, Ferenczi delighted in his relationship with his wife's daughters by a former marriage.

Ferenczi came to New York City for eight months in 1926–1927 to give a course of lectures at the New School for Social Research. During his visit he gave analytic training to eight or nine people, mostly laymen.

As Ferenczi's views on psychoanalytic technique diverged more and more from Freud's in later years, he gradually withdrew from Freud. Although there was never a sharp break, a sense of estrangement developed between them.

Personality. Ernest Jones described Ferenczi as follows:

He [Ferenczi] had an altogether delightful personality which retained a good deal of the simplicity and a still greater amount of the imagination of the child; I have never known anyone better able to conjure up, in speech and gesture, the point of view of a young child. . . . He had a very keen and direct intuitive perception, one that went well with the highest possible measure of native honesty. . . . He had an exceptionally original and creative mind. . . . As is often the way, however, with people who throw out masses of ideas like sparks, their quality was very uneven, since judgment—objective and critical judgment—was the one gift denied to Ferenczi. . . . (1959, pp. 199–200)

At times, Jones says, Ferenczi could be somewhat masterful, and even dictatorial; and toward the end of his life, especially during his final illness, he "lost most of his old cheerfulness and vitality, became heavy, depressed, and ungracious, withdrew from his friends, and—most serious of all—allowed his scientific judgment to be gravely deflected" (Jones 1959, p. 200).

Early contributions to psychoanalysis. Freud always gave Ferenczi generous credit for ideas the two had worked out in common, and at times it is not possible to distinguish their respective shares. Among Ferenczi's important early papers are "Stages in the Development of the Sense of Reality" (1913); a paper on the relationship of homosexuality and paranoia (1912*a*); and a paper describing transitory symptom formation during psychoanalytic treatment (1912*b*). He worked out in detail the implications of Freud's explanation of

hypnosis as depending on the masochistic attitude of the person hypnotized; and he discriminated between the different forms of homosexuality.

In the paper on the development of the sense of reality—praised by Jones as "the best he [Ferenczi] ever wrote" (Jones 1933)—Ferenczi listed four stages through which the child passes in moving from domination by the pleasure principle to acceptance of the reality principle. These four periods are the period of unconditional omnipotence (intrauterine), the period of magical–hallucinatory omnipotence (earliest infancy), the period of omnipotence by the help of magic gestures, and the period of magic thoughts and magic words. He showed that the child at first has all his wishes gratified and believes himself omnipotent. Later, when the child finds that wishes are no longer immediately gratified and has to accept some limitations upon his power, he attempts to circumvent these frustrations by imagining the gratification of his wishes, or by making magical gestures, or by using magical thoughts and words. When at last the individual realizes that the environment does not conform to his wishes, that gratification is entirely conditional upon work, and that even work does not always lead to success, then the sense of reality may be said to be fully developed.

Theory of genital sexuality. Influenced by Darwin and Lamarck as well as by psychoanalytic thought, Ferenczi sought in *Thalassa: A Theory of Genitality* (1924) to explicate the relationship of sexuality to the evolution of the race. Ferenczi pointed out that pregenital sexual impulses can be expressed and gratified by genital activity. For instance, a man can express urethral or anal tendencies in the way he performs and experiences sexual intercourse. Such a mixture of partial sexual drives, and indirect expression of them, Ferenczi chose to call "amphimixis." Sexual intercourse can also express various fantasies, including the fantasy of reunion with the mother through return to the womb, a fantasy revealed in the course of psychoanalysis of patients. Since the penis goes into the birth canal during intercourse and the seminal fluid does go into the uterus, sexual intercourse is well suited to the acting out of this fantasy.

Assuming a phylogenetic origin for this fantasy, Ferenczi speculated that it derives from the marine background of the race; mankind's ancestors were fishes. Thus, in wishing to return to the womb, man is also expressing the wish to return to the sea, the origin of all life.

In general, psychoanalysts have ignored these

speculations. They believe that Ferenczi did not have a satisfactory way of testing his speculations by an appeal to evidence.

Contributions to technique. Ferenczi is acknowledged to have been a gifted therapist. He proposed a number of innovations in technique: at first these centered on the so-called "active" technique; later they had to do with a greater participation by the therapist in the psychoanalytic interaction, a participation that included the granting of more— and more direct—gratifications to patients than most analysts believed advisable. These later experiments led Freud to write, "He was persuaded that we could accomplish far more with our patients if we gave them enough of the love they had longed for in childhood" (1933, pp. 297–299). Most analysts reject Ferenczi's belief that granting more gratification to patients is therapeutic. Ferenczi's strong interest in the reactions of disappointment and mistrust that the child suffers in his relationship with his parents has led a few of his pupils, notably Alice Balint (1949), to investigate early parent–child relationships.

Ferenczi's early contributions to psychoanalysis have been so fully assimilated that their origin is often forgotten, although his later writings, which were more speculative and deviated from Freudian orthodoxy, have been less widely accepted.

FRANK AULD, JR.

[*For the historical context of Ferenczi's work, see* PSYCHOANALYSIS *and the biography of* FREUD. *For discussion of the subsequent development of his ideas, see* SEXUAL BEHAVIOR, *articles on* SEXUAL DEVIATION: PSYCHOLOGICAL ASPECTS *and* SEXUAL DEVIATION: SOCIAL ASPECTS.]

WORKS BY FERENCZI

(1908–1914) 1952 *First Contributions to Psycho-analysis.* London: Hogarth. → Contains a selection of Ferenczi's essays that were originally published in German. First published in English as *Contributions to Psychoanalysis.* Later editions have the title *Sex in Psychoanalysis.*

(1908–1925) 1927 *Further Contributions to the Theory and Technique of Psycho-analysis.* New York: Liveright. → Contains a collection of some of Ferenczi's most important contributions to psychoanalysis. Translated from the German.

(1908–1933) 1955 *Final Contributions to the Problems and Methods of Psycho-analysis.* London: Hogarth. → A collection of papers written in or first published in German.

(1912a) 1950 On the Part Played by Homosexuality in the Pathogenesis of Paranoia. Pages 154–184 in Sándor Ferenczi, *Selected Papers.* Volume 1: Sex in Psychoanalysis. New York: Basic Books. → First published in German.

(1912b) 1950 Transitory Symptom Constructions During the Analysis. Pages 193–212 in Sándor Ferenczi, *Selected Papers.* Volume 1: Sex in Psychoanalysis. New York: Basic Books. → First published in German.

(1913) 1950 Stages in the Development of the Sense of Reality. Pages 213–239 in Sándor Ferenczi, *Selected Papers.* Volume 1: Sex in Psychoanalysis. New York: Basic Books. → First published in German.

(1924) 1949 *Thalassa: A Theory of Genitality.* New York: Psychoanalytic Quarterly. → First published as *Versuch einer Genital-theorie.*

(1924) 1925 FERENCZI, SÁNDOR; and RANK, OTTO *The Development of Psychoanalysis.* New York: Nervous and Mental Disease Pub. → First published as *Entwicklungsziele der Psychoanalyse.*

Selected Papers. 3 vols. New York: Basic Books, 1950–1955. → Volume 1: *Sex in Psychoanalysis,* 1950. Volume 2: *Theory and Technique of Psychoanalysis,* 1952. Volume 3: *Problems and Methods of Psychoanalysis,* 1955.

SUPPLEMENTARY BIBLIOGRAPHY

BALINT, ALICE 1949 Love for the Mother and Mother-love. *International Journal of Psycho-Analysis* 30: 251–259.

BALINT, MICHAEL 1949 Sándor Ferenczi: Obiit 1933. *International Journal of Psycho-Analysis* 30:215–219.

DE FOREST, IZETTE 1954 *The Leaven of Love.* New York: Harper.

FREUD, SIGMUND 1933 Obituary: Sándor Ferenczi. *International Journal of Psycho-Analysis* 14:297–299.

JONES, ERNEST 1933 Obituary: Sándor Ferenczi, 1873–1933. *International Journal of Psycho-Analysis* 14: 463–466.

JONES, ERNEST 1953–1957 *The Life and Work of Sigmund Freud.* 3 vols. New York: Basic Books. → Volume 1: *Formative Years and the Great Discoveries,* 1953. Volume 2: *Years of Maturity,* 1955. Volume 3: *Last Phase,* 1957. See especially Volumes 2–3.

JONES, ERNEST 1959 *Free Associations: Memoirs of a Psycho-analyst.* New York: Basic Books.

FERGUSON, ADAM

"I hear he [Ferguson] is about to publish . . . a natural history of man: exhibiting a view of him in the savage state, and in the several successive states of pasturage, agriculture and commerce" (Reid [1764–1788] 1895, p. 42). Thus wrote Thomas Reid on December 20, 1765, to his friend Dr. David Skeene. Reid had just succeeded Adam Smith in the chair of moral philosophy at Glasgow. Nearly a century later, Karl Marx singled out Ferguson, although not with complete accuracy, as the first in modern times to develop the theory of the division of labor in economy and society. Still later, Gumplowicz, distinguished exponent of the conflict theory of society, saw in Ferguson's *History of Civil Society* "the first natural history of society" and in Ferguson himself "the first sociologist" (Gumplowicz 1892, p. 67). William Dunning found in him one who combined "the critical spirit of Hume and the historical spirit of Montesquieu" most attractively and "studied society and its institutions . . . to determine by the light of history whither society was moving, not by superhuman wisdom to fix its course" (Dunning [1920] 1936, p. 63).

These brief characterizations may serve to epitomize the thought, and the place in the history of social thought, of one of the outstanding "moral philosophers" of Scotland of the later eighteenth century.

Adam Ferguson was born in the manse of Logierait, Perthshire, in 1723, and was educated for the Christian ministry (like so many leaders of thought in the Scotland of his day) at St. Andrews and Edinburgh. At the age of 21, he was appointed deputy-chaplain—and later chaplain—of the famous Highland "Black Watch" regiment. In 1757, Ferguson succeeded Hume as keeper of the Advocates' Library in Edinburgh, and in 1759 he was appointed to the chair of natural philosophy in the university there; he was transferred five years later to the chair of pneumatics and moral philosophy. He filled this post with distinction until 1785, when for reasons of health he resigned it. He continued literary activities at a more leisurely pace in retirement.

In 1767, he published his *Essay on the History of Civil Society*, using "history" in the then current static–descriptive sense as well as in a "temporalizing" sense. This work strongly reflects, by Ferguson's own admission, the influence of Montesquieu. Two years later, Ferguson published the *Institutes of Moral Philosophy*, an outline of the course of lectures that he followed, with variations, throughout his teaching career. In 1783, he published *The History of the Progress and Termination of the Roman Republic*, a work that reached many editions. His two-volume *Principles of Moral and Political Science*, "being chiefly a Retrospect of Lectures delivered in the College of Edinburgh," was published in 1792. This was in reality only a greatly expanded and more finished version of the *Institutes*, with some variations. Most of these works appeared almost immediately in translation in Germany and France, and some also in Italy and Russia. He was also widely known and read in America.

Ferguson was a principal founder and charter member of the Royal Society of Edinburgh; on a visit to the Continent in 1793, he was made an honorary member of the Berlin Academy of Science. He was closely associated, through personal friendship, various literary clubs, and correspondence, with others from Edinburgh, such as Hume, Lord Kames, William Robertson, John Home, Adam Smith (with whom he had a temporary falling-out), and Edward Gibbon, all of whom had high regard for Ferguson. Abroad he received the acclaim of men like Baron d'Holbach in France and Schiller, Jacobi, Herder, and others in Germany. He spent his last years, with failing eyesight, at St. Andrews, where he died in 1816, at the age of 92. He was buried in the old cathedral churchyard, and the beautiful epitaph that Sir Walter Scott, boyhood playmate of the Ferguson children, wrote for him is still to be seen there.

Whereas Ferguson's fame at home and abroad rested chiefly on his *Civil Society*, this work is best understood in the broader setting of his entire social and moral philosophy, which is more adequately stated in his *Principles*. "Moral philosophy" covers comparative anthropology, individual and social psychology, and "natural religion" and is applied to jurisprudence, economics and politics, and ethics. The basic concern of moral philosophy is human nature itself. "Human nature," Ferguson once observed, "is my trade"—meaning, no doubt, the business of his chair. Man is viewed as a rationally intelligent, morally evaluating, active, and therefore progressive animal, always and everywhere living in society. He is to be studied, therefore, not only as an individual but also as a member of the community. The community is at once the source of his being, the field of his operations, the end of most of his actions, and the indispensable means—through the invention and use of language as his principal instrument of communication—to the realization of his essential humanity.

Key elements in Ferguson's social theory are a clear-cut distinction between "physical law," which he saw as a generalization of behavioral fact on every level, and "moral law," which he saw as a generalization of values and norms of conduct; a sharp differentiation of the cultural and traditional from the biological; a juxtaposition of the principles of "union" and of "rivalship" or conflict; the division of labor in economy and society; and a consistently evolutionistic viewpoint skeptical of planned progress—evolution, however, usually in an ontogenetic and cultural, rather than a biological, application.

Ferguson's moral philosophy in particular was essentially that of the ancient Stoics: Man is by his very nature an active being and a social being; all action involves choices, both of ends and of means to ends; choices are made between moral values and result in either happiness or misery, both for the actor and for his fellow men. If norms of conduct and systems of such norms are to be effective, they must be rationally based on empirical knowledge both of human nature and "of the situation in which [man] is placed." "Men of real fortitude, integrity and ability are well placed in every scene" ([1767] 1819, p. 506). "Everyone indeed is answerable only for himself; and, in preserving the integrity of one citizen, does what is required of him for the happiness of the whole" (1792, vol. 2, p. 512).

Like most of his Scottish contemporaries, Ferguson was averse to "metaphysics," or abstract philosophizing; yet he was not without philosophical acumen, a regard for system, a sense of "wholism," and a clear understanding of basic methodology. In this sense, he was an exponent of the "common-sense" philosophy and one of its founders.

WILLIAM C. LEHMANN

[*For the historical context of Ferguson's work, see the biography of* HUME.]

WORKS BY FERGUSON

(1767) 1819 *An Essay on the History of Civil Society.* 8th ed. Philadelphia: Finley.
(1769) 1800 *Institutes of Moral Philosophy.* New ed., enl. Basel: Decker.
(1783) 1841 *The History of the Progress and Termination of the Roman Republic.* 3 vols. Philadelphia: Wardle.
1792 *Principles of Moral and Political Science.* 2 vols. Edinburgh: Trahan.

SUPPLEMENTARY BIBLIOGRAPHY

DUNNING, WILLIAM A. (1920) 1936 *A History of Political Theories From Rousseau to Spencer.* New York: Macmillan.
GUMPLOWICZ, LUDWIG 1892 *Die soziologische Staatsidee.* Graz (Austria): Leuschner & Lubensky.
JOGLAND, HERTA H. 1959 *Ursprünge und Grundlagen der Soziologie bei Adam Ferguson.* Berlin: Duncker & Humblot.
KETTLER, DAVID 1965 *The Social and Political Thought of Adam Ferguson.* Columbus: Ohio State Univ. Press.
LEHMANN, WILLIAM C. 1930 *Adam Ferguson and the Beginnings of Modern Sociology.* New York: Columbia Univ. Press.
REID, THOMAS (1764–1788) 1895 *Works.* 2 vols. London: Longmans.
SMALL, JOHN 1864 Biographical Sketch of Adam Ferguson, LL.D.: Professor of Moral Philosophy in the University of Edinburgh. Royal Society of Edinburgh, *Transactions* 23:599–665.

FERTILITY

Demographers distinguish fertility (actual reproduction) from fecundity (the capacity for reproduction). The distinction is important, because in all societies actual reproduction is less, often much less, than the potential maximum. The rather wide variations in actual fertility among societies have no known general relation to differences in fecundity. In specific instances, low fertility may be explained by such biological factors as venereal disease. However, it is likely that group fertility levels vary generally in relation to social factors that affect either the social norms about the proper number of children or a limited number of means of fertility control. These means are *intermediate* between the social organization or social norms, on the one hand, and actual fertility, on the other hand.

Davis and Blake (1956) have provided the following useful classification of these "intermediate variables":

Factors affecting exposure to intercourse:
(*A*) Those governing the formation and dissolution of unions in the reproductive period:
(1) Age of entry into sexual unions.
(2) Permanent celibacy: proportion of women never entering sexual unions.
(3) Amount of reproductive period spent after or between unions.
(*a*) When unions are broken by divorce, separation, or desertion.
(*b*) When unions are broken by death of husband.
(*B*) Those governing the exposure to intercourse within unions:
(4) Voluntary abstinence.
(5) Involuntary abstinence (from impotence, illness, unavoidable but temporary separations).
(6) Coital frequency (excluding periods of abstinence).
Factors affecting exposure to conception:
(7) Fecundity or infecundity, as affected by involuntary causes.
(8) Use or non-use of contraception:
(*a*) By mechanical and chemical means.
(*b*) By other means.
(9) Fecundity or infecundity, as affected by voluntary causes (sterilization, subincision, medical treatment, etc.).
Factors affecting gestation and successful parturition:
(10) Foetal mortality from involuntary causes.
(11) Foetal mortality from voluntary causes.

Most of the intermediate variables are regulated by a complex structure of normative prescriptions (Nag 1962; Freedman 1963). For example, how many children a couple should have is a problem so recurrent and with so many social ramifications in each society that it would be a sociological anomaly if appropriate social norms did not develop as a social solution to guide behavior. Moreover, different combinations of values for these variables may produce identical fertility levels, whereas societies or groups with very different fertility levels may have similar values on some of the intermediate variables. Of course, the connection between some of these intermediate cultural variables and a society's fertility level need not be apparent to members of the society.

Measurement of fertility

Fertility can be defined as the number of births occurring in a population unit during a specified time period. The unit may be the individual male or female, the male–female couple, the social stratum or other groupings of individuals or couples, or the whole society. For any of these levels, birth rates or frequency distributions may be computed separately or adjusted for a large variety of social, economic, or demographic characteristics. In most official statistics, the time period is short, giving a cross-section picture of what happens in a particular year or period. An important departure from cross-section rates is the measurement of fertility over the childbearing span of historical cohorts of women [*see* COHORT ANALYSIS].

"Period" measures. The most common fertility measure is the *crude birth rate*, or number of births per thousand population per annum. It is usually computed for whole nations or for major demographic strata within nations, such as the urban population. More refined measures are important for some purposes, but the crude birth rate is still often used in evaluating the contribution of fertility to population growth in relation to mortality and migration. Table 1 shows the considerable variation in crude birth rates among major world regions.

Birth rates are called *age-specific* when they are computed for fairly narrow age groups (usually one or five years), usually with reference to the female population only. Since the crude birth rate is a function of both the age–sex distribution of the population and of the age-specific fertility rates, various methods are used to eliminate the effect of varying age–sex distributions in a comparison of different populations. This may be done either by standardization (in this case, the use of a common age–sex distribution to weight the different age-specific rates) or by the computation of one of the four remaining measures in common use by demographers:

(1) Births per annum per thousand women in the childbearing years (the *general fertility rate*).

(2) Births per annum per thousand women in specified age groups (*age-specific birth rates*).

Table 1 — Crude birth rates and gross reproduction rates for less and more economically developed regions of the world, 1963

	Crude birth[a] rate	Gross reproduction[a] rate
Less developed regions	41–42[b]	2.6–2.7[b]
Africa	48	3.0
North	46	2.9
West	54	3.4
South and east	45	2.7
Asia (excluding Soviet Union)	40–41[b]	2.5–2.6[b]
Southwest	45	3.0
South central	44	2.9
Southeast	49	2.9
East	35–37[b]	2.1–2.3[b]
America (excluding North America)	41	2.8
Middle	45	3.0
South	40	2.7
More developed regions	22	1.4
North America	24	1.8
Europe	19	1.3
Northern and western	18	1.3
Central	18	1.2
Southern	21	1.3
Oceania	24	1.8
Soviet Union	25	1.4
World total	35–36[b]	2.25–2.31[b]

a. Provisional weighted averages of most recent rates available in 1963 for countries within each region.

b. No absolute figure obtainable because of varying estimates for mainland China; figures given here correspond to range of best alternative estimates.

Source: Adapted from "Conditions and Trends . . ." 1965.

(3) The *gross reproduction rate* or "total fertility rate" (a simple summation of the age-specific birth rates for female babies or all babies).

(4) The *net reproduction rate* (an adjustment of the gross reproduction rate to take into account the effect of mortality on reproduction rates).

These are all "period" measures—that is, measures based on the births and deaths of a *particular* year or other time period considerably shorter than the reproductive span of the couples in the population. The rates do not take into account the earlier reproductive history of the units measured; they may therefore be misleading about long-run reproductive trends, especially for populations in which efficient family-planning methods are widely used. Short-run variations in conventional period rates may result from variations in the number of women marrying at each age and in child-spacing patterns, rather than from the number of children born over the childbearing span. For example, marriage rates and the birth of a first child are rather closely correlated with the business cycle in highly industrialized countries (Kirk & Nortman 1959).

Fertility measures of historical cohorts. A major methodological advance in recent years is the measurement of the cumulative fertility of historical *cohorts* of women, taking into account the family-building sequence of marriage and the spacing of successive children (France . . . 1953). Ideally the data needed for each historical birth cohort include the percentage of each cohort dying, the percentage of the single marrying, the percentage with one previous birth having another, and so on. From annual empirical probabilities of this type, it is possible to reconstruct, to date, the cumulative fertility of a particular cohort or of the whole population. But only a few countries are beginning to collect these data.

In cohort analysis, the stages of family building are related to specific historical dates, not just to abstract age categories. It is therefore possible to link variations in family-building patterns for particular cohorts to time series for economic or other social phenomena.

Data for fertility studies. The newer, more sophisticated measures cannot be used in most countries at present, because they lack even the elementary data required for the simpler conventional measures. However, special efforts are being made to improve fertility statistics in some of the developing countries in order to measure the success of programs to reduce the birth rate [*see* POPULATION, *article on* POPULATION POLICIES].

Sample surveys are used increasingly to estimate fertility and other related phenomena, especially where other statistical resources are lacking. For example, a series of sample surveys is the principal basis for our knowledge of African populations. The sample survey is also often used to collect information about social factors that may affect fertility, since some of the most important intermediate variables, such as age at marriage or use of contraception, do not appear at all in the official series.

Fertility in preindustrial societies

Despite the lack of statistical data, it can be asserted with some confidence that fertility rates have been moderately high to very high in almost all preindustrial societies throughout history. With the high mortality levels that have prevailed in such societies, fertility had to be moderately high for the society to survive.

An increasing volume of data for contemporary preindustrial societies indicates, without exception, that fertility is at least moderately high (see Table 2). With the exception of the Tikopia, the

Table 2 — Distribution of less and more economically developed countries by level of crude birth rate, 1963

Crude birth rate (per thousand population)[a]	Less developed regions[b]	More developed regions[b]
Under 15.0	—	3
15.0–19.9	1	17
20.0–24.9	4	10
25.0–29.9	1	3
30.0–34.9	3	—
35.0–39.9	11	—
40.0–44.9	21	1
45.0–49.9	28	1
50.0–54.9	12	—
55.0–59.9	5	—
60.0 and over	2	—
Total countries[c]	88	35

a. Wherever a crude birth rate had not yet been published for 1963, the most recent available rate was used.

b. See Table 1 for geographical composition of these regions.

c. Excluding countries having fewer than 250,000 inhabitants in 1960, countries having no satisfactory data, and a few countries for which examination of available data had not been completed in 1963.

Source: Adapted from "Conditions and Trends . . ." 1965.

only substantiated instances of relatively low fertility in preindustrial societies are those subject to extreme social disorganization (Lorimer 1954, chapter 3). From the point of view of a preindustrial society, of course, high fertility is a functional adjustment to high mortality; but from the point of view of the reproducing couple, high fertility is motivated by the central importance of familial and kinship ties in their lives. Motivations for larger numbers of children are increased when children enhance the ability of the familial unit to attain socially valued goals, and when such goals are attained through kinship and familial ties rather than through other social relationships.

Fertility and social values. Although a reasonably large number of children may be vitally important to parents in a preindustrial society, this does not necessarily mean that the normative value is for the highest possible fertility. But evidence on the existing norm in preindustrial societies is less than satisfactory. Ford (1945) has indicated that the normative pressures against childlessness and against very small families are great and probably universal in preindustrial societies. However, he has also concluded that mothers are ambivalent about childbirth in many circumstances and that considerable social pressure may be required to ensure adequate reproduction. Davis and Blake (1956) have pointed out that since to have some children is very important, a society with high and variable mortality is likely to have built into its structure very strong pressures for bearing children early in marriage, before the death of one or both parents, and also to have additional children as a safeguard against the catastrophic loss of the essential minimum number. On the other hand, if unfavorable conditions develop, this may result in "too many" children. Therefore, there may be a delicate balance between pressures that tend toward higher fertility, to ensure at least a certain minimum number of children, and contrary pressures that encourage abortion or infanticide in order to minimize or eliminate what, under difficult subsistence conditions, becomes an intolerable surplus. In any case, although there is general agreement that fertility is likely to be high in almost all preindustrial societies, there is also a body of evidence about the existence of control practices that keep fertility below a potential biological maximum, and about cultural and social factors that produce variations in fertility through these practices.

Cultural effects on intermediate variables. On the question of control, there is evidence that the "natural fertility" of man is probably higher than that reported for most preindustrial societies (Lorimer 1954, chapter 1; Henry 1961), but genetic differentials in fecundity cannot be ruled out. Health conditions reducing fecundity and increasing fetal mortality may constitute a functional, if unintended, adjustment to keep fertility below maximum levels.

Evidence has been assembled on the use of a wide variety of control measures—including contraception, abstinence, abortion, and infanticide—in many preindustrial societies (Himes 1936; Devereux 1955; Nag 1962). Unfortunately, the evidence usually demonstrates the existence of certain practices in a culture without specifying either the extent of use or the effect on fertility. Nevertheless, there is a basis for the tentative generalization that more or less effective methods of control potentially were available in many preindustrial societies, probably affected fertility levels in some, and, presumably, might have had a much wider use and effect were it not for the rewards derived from having children in such societies and the risk that these rewards would be lost because of unpredictably high mortality [see FERTILITY CONTROL].

There are no empirically validated general explanations for the variations in fertility from high to very high among preindustrial societies. It is often possible to point to particular intermediate variables as the immediate causes of less than maximum fertility, but even in these instances the *level* of the intermediate variables is a topic that so far has given rise to explanations that are at best speculative.

Among the most important attempts at general explanation are those linking variations in kinship structure to variations in fertility (Lorimer 1954, chapter 2). A specific example of importance is the hypothesis that neolocal nuclear family systems and related economic arrangements led to late marriage or nonmarriage in preindustrial Europe, producing relatively low birth rates (Eversley 1963). If this is true, it runs counter to the most commonly held theories, which associate such birth rates with industrialization. It has also been suggested that some institutions may function to limit fertility, although this is not their deliberate purpose. For example, many religious systems prescribe periods of sexual abstinence, which usually (although not always) have the indirect effect of limiting fertility (Nag 1962).

Another unintended restraint on fertility is the possible reduction in fecundity resulting from poor nutrition and health conditions, whether these affect the whole society or only the lowest strata. This is one possible explanation for the fact that in some Indian studies the poorest rural workers have the lowest fertility. Another finding is that the period of amenorrhea and temporary sterility following a pregnancy apparently is lengthened if an infant lives and is breast-fed. This suggests that variations in infant mortality and in weaning practices may also affect fertility (Potter et al. 1966).

Lack of an adequate contraceptive technology has been suggested as an explanation for high fertility in preindustrial societies (Davis & Blake 1956, p. 223). An opposing point of view is that contraceptive practices are not developed or widely disseminated when available, because the structure of such a traditional society provides little motivation for small rather than large families. *Coitus interruptus*, probably the principal means for modern fertility decline in England and France, has been practiced for centuries by some couples within many preindustrial societies. If sufficient motivation for small families had been present, such a method might have been adopted more widely, in at least a few preindustrial societies.

These are only illustrations of theories and studies indicating that a variety of cultural factors in preindustrial societies affect the intermediate variables in such a way as to keep fertility below its maximum biological potential. Since many of the limits on fertility are based on cultural patterns without consciously recognized links to family size, changes in such practices initially may lead to higher fertility before modern family-planning practices take their place. For example, this might be the result of a further relaxation of traditional sanctions against the remarriage of widows in India.

Fertility in industrial countries

Transitional decline of fertility.   The large decline in fertility in economically developed countries in the nineteenth and twentieth centuries is unprecedented. Most sociologists and demographers would probably agree that there have been two basic causes for the general decline. In the first place, there has been a major transfer of functions from the family to other specialized institutions, so that fewer children are required to achieve socially valued goals. Second, a sharp reduction in mortality has reduced the number of births necessary to have any desired number of living children.

The historical timing of fertility decline in most countries, rather long after the beginning of the modern process of economic development and social change, has been explained in terms of a descriptive model of the "demographic transition." This model assumes that fertility and mortality are both high in the preindustrial period. The rapid population growth associated with modern economic development is then attributed to a decline in mortality that occurred while fertility remained relatively stable at rather high levels. It is further assumed that after a considerable time lag, fertility begins to fall, reducing the rate of population growth as it approaches the level of mortality. The usual explanation of this time lag is that whereas low mortality is always positively valued, there are no low fertility norms to carry over from the preindustrial period; they must be developed gradually in a trial-and-error process, under the influence of lower mortality and the changing consequences of varying numbers of children.

This simple model of the demographic transition is under revision as the result of a number of important studies. Some have shown a considerable variability in the actual course of the demographic transition (Hatt et al. 1955; Ryder 1957). Especially significant has been the work of a number of economic historians (for instance, Eversley 1963) probing, in detail, European data for the medieval period and for the seventeenth and eighteenth centuries. These studies have tried to relate changes in economic organization and in family structure to changes in age at marriage, rate of marriage, and illegitimacy. An important, if controversial, hypothesis emerging from this work is that a rise in fertility rather than a fall in mortality may be responsible for the population growth during the early stages of industrialization.

Explanations for the decline in fertility that eventually occurred throughout the Western world sometimes concentrate on the intermediate variables and sometimes on the changes in social structure, which first produced the small family norms and then affected the intermediate variables.

The role of contraception.   Most scholars probably would agree that the mass adoption of contraception is the most important change immediately responsible for the decline in fertility in modern industrial countries. Notable exceptions are Ireland, where men have tended to marry late or not at all, and Japan and the countries of eastern and central Europe, where abortion has been widely practiced since World War II.

It has generally been assumed that contraception was the most important factor in the development of the small family that gradually became the norm for western Europe. But this assumption must remain, at best, a plausible hypothesis, since there is an almost complete lack of systematic comparative data for many of the other intermediate variables affecting fertility. The only study providing a series of historical statistics on the use of contraception is that by Lewis-Faning for England (Great Britain . . . 1949). He demonstrated that as the use of contraception increased, fertility declined, and that contraception was adopted first in those social classes whose fertility fell first. The practice was found to have spread to other social classes in reasonably close correspondence to observed patterns of differential fertility. There is also illustrative evidence about the adoption of contraception—especially *coitus interruptus*—by significant elements in the French population in the late eighteenth and early nineteenth centuries; and it so happens that this was the period in which fertility in France began to fall (France . . . 1960).

Since the war several studies have provided statistical evidence of the mass use of contraception in a number of Western countries and have related the practice to fertility levels (e.g., Freedman 1961, pp. 116–118). These studies do indeed demonstrate that many populations with a history of marked secular decline in fertility now practice family planning on a massive scale; but another finding that they also have in common is that contraceptive practice is not necessarily highly rational and effective, even when the *average* number of children per family is limited to two or three. Even in the United States, where contraception is virtually universal for the fecund at some time in married life, many couples use ineffective means, many do not begin contraception early in marriage (although they do not want all their children immediately), some begin only after having more children than they want, and many conceive despite contraceptive efforts to postpone pregnancies (Freedman et al. 1959, chapters 3–6). In Japan and a number of east European countries, the failure of contraception as practiced to produce the small families desired has been followed by massive supplementary use of legal abortion.

Biological theories.   Before World War II, it was not uncommon to attribute the decline in fertility to a decrease in biological fecundity. The main argument was that development of industrial–urban society brought about a decrease in fecundity. This was held to be a consequence either of genetic selection or of the stresses supposedly associated with urban life—especially for the higher status groups, whose fertility fell fastest. Although such explanations may be valid for special situations, the prevailing scholarly opinion does not assign it great importance in the over-all fertility decline in Western countries. Kiser and Whelpton, in the Indianapolis study, demonstrated both that a modern urban population can have a high fertility rate during periods when contraception is not used and that fecundity differences are not associated with socioeconomic status in the way that they should be if the biological argument about fecundity decline is true (see Whelpton 1943–1958, vol. 2, pp. 303–416). This argument has also been weakened by the difficulty of reconciling it with the temporal changes in fertility that have been observed to follow changes in economic conditions.

Whatever combination of intermediate variables was responsible, there is no question that fertility fell rapidly in all the developed Western countries, so that just before World War II small families averaging closer to two than three children were characteristic. In many countries, fertility was below the level required for replacement even with the very low prevalent mortality, and concern about a declining and aging population led to national investigations and official pronatalist policies.

Sociological theories.   Many explanations were advanced for these unprecedented fertility declines. The dominant ideas before World War II, however, were all related to the changing functions of family and children in an urban–industrial society. To summarize the theories: Industrial urbanization was associated with a complex division of labor in all spheres of life; with the associated high rate of social and physical mobility, this inevitably led to a growth of secularism and rationalism, the declining influence of such traditional forces as religious faith, and the shattering of traditional family and other primary group associations. An essential element in this view of urban life was the idea that the family would lose its functions to other specialized institutions. On the one hand, children would cease to be productive assets in a familially based economy, and, on the other hand, they would be impediments to active participation in the larger organizations from which the rewards of an urban society would come. The dominant view was that as whole populations became involved in the urban market and society, family planning would become universal and the size of family planned would continue to decline.

It is plausible that a shift in functions from the family to other institutions is one basic explanation for the secular decline in fertility in the developed countries. But in retrospect there is little systematic evidence in prewar studies linking *specific* changes in the functions of the family to the decline of fertility at *specific* times and places. There are still no satisfactory answers to some important comparative historical questions, for example: Why did fertility begin to decline much earlier in France than in England, where urban–industrial development was earlier and more intense? Why has fertility remained higher in the Netherlands than elsewhere, despite that country's early involvement in the nexus of international trade?

One line of theory and research has stressed the joint role of social mobility and rising standards of living in motivating couples to restrict family size. This is one explanation offered for the early decline of fertility in France (Blacker 1957). Banks (1954) has linked the onset of the fertility decline in England with a change in economic conditions that made restriction of family size necessary for the maintenance and advance of living standards in the rising middle class. More recent statistical studies produce conflicting results, with some indicating no correlation between mobility and fertility in the United States (Westoff et al. 1961) and others finding a relationship in France (Bresard 1950), England (Berent 1952), and Brazil (Hutchinson 1961). Even in those cases in which a relationship is found, it is possible that the distinctive fertility of the mobile population is simply an averaging of the fertility levels of their positions of origin and destination, and not a distinctive consequence of social mobility itself.

Postwar fertility increase in the West. A decrease in childlessness is only one of the important postwar demographic trends that direct attention to the need for a re-evaluation of the role of family and children in society. In most of the developed countries in which fertility reached very low levels before the war, there has been an increase in the proportion of people marrying, a decrease in the age at marriage, and an increase or stabilization in the average family size of those who marry. There is, however, little evidence of a return to large families since the war; the shift is from having no children or one child to having from two to four. In a number of countries, an increase in the number of marriages, rather than in the number of children per marriage, accounts for a significant part of the postwar rise in fertility.

Since the war, urban sociologists have given increasing recognition to the persistence and even the resurgence of primary groups, including the family, as the means by which stable individual personality organization is maintained in impersonal specialized societies. Part of this revaluation of urban society involves more attention to the persistent influence of traditional ideologies in religious and other associations with ends that are not primarily economic or political. Such associations had been doomed to extinction by prewar sociologists, who were fond of stressing the growth of secular rationalism. By contrast, a community study by Lenski (1961) shows the persistence of Catholic ideology in many areas of life, including fertility, even after the consideration of the influence of rising education, socioeconomic status, and urbanization. These results are confirmed, with more demographic detail for fertility, in the Princeton study (Westoff et al. 1961).

Some sociologists and demographers have suggested that the leveling off in the long-run secular decline in fertility may mean that family size has reached a level appropriate to its functions under urban–industrial conditions. From this viewpoint, considerable experimentation may be required before a stable social norm is developed governing the size of such an important unit as the family. The very low fertility of the 1930s is seen as an experimental "overshooting" of an "equilibrium solution," with a readjustment following when the dysfunctional consequences were widely felt. The increasing convergence of family size in many countries to a small range of one to four children may be additional evidence that a family-size pattern appropriate to urban–industrial societies is developing (Universities–National Bureau Committee for Economic Research 1960, pp. 36–76).

Differential fertility

Differential fertility refers to variation in fertility among significant subgroups in a population. In principle, almost any classification of the population may be a basis for measuring fertility differences. Scholarly attention, however, has centered on groups of people whose differing positions in the society give them different resources, styles of life, and power. Such groups frequently are distinctive in social norms and culture traits affecting fertility.

General principles. Classifications used in studies of differential fertility include those based on education, occupation, income, wealth, landholding, caste, social class, labor-force status of the wife, religion, ethnic–racial groupings, regional divisions, bureaucratic positions, intelligence, and size of place of residence. Occupation and education have been the most frequently used bases for classification, both because they are readily available in censuses and in official vital statistics and because they are significant indicators of status and style of life in most modern societies.

Social groups or strata that differ in their fertility differ also on one or more of the intermediate variables affecting fertility. Differentials may result from *deliberate* controls, such as contraception, or from the *unintended consequences* of other variations. For example, in some places, the rate of spontaneous abortions is higher in lower-status than in higher-status groups, and this has an unintended effect on the status differentials.

For a number of contemporary societies, there is evidence that the low-fertility subgroups have used deliberate family-limitation practices—mainly contraception and abortion—more extensively and effectively than other groups. Substantiating data are available, for example, for the United States, England, Japan, Hungary, Czechoslovakia, Puerto Rico, Turkey, India, and Taiwan.

It is more difficult to establish unequivocally whether the higher fertility subgroups have larger families because they want them or because they do not have the knowledge or means to restrict family size. Low motivation toward a small-family goal may reduce interest in learning and practicing effective family-planning methods. In the United States, there is evidence that the practice of contraception for spacing births becomes more effective as the number of children born to a couple approaches the desired total. This suggests that ineffective family planning may reflect a desire for more children rather than inability to use the proper means. On the other hand, the important Indianapolis study by Kiser and Whelpton in 1940 found that low-status and high-status groups expressed similar attitudes about desired family size but that the low-status groups had more children because they practiced contraception less effectively (Whelpton 1943–1958).

At least in societies in which socially significant groups of people deliberately practice family limitation, differential fertility levels will be affected by distinctive subgroup attitudes about how many children a family should have. Presumably, fertility will be higher and family limitation practices less prevalent or effective in subgroups in which larger numbers of children are rewarding in various ways. The relatively high fertility of the agricultural sector of many populations, for example, can be linked to the utility of children, whether as laborers in the family enterprise, as an alternative to urban social-security programs to meet the risks of illness, disability, and old-age, or as the members of essential primary social groups. Similar functions have been ascribed to larger numbers of children among low-status urban groups during the period of transition to a modern economy.

Fertility differentials often do not correspond to the differentials in the *rate of reproduction*—a measure that also takes mortality into account. For example, in countries as different as India and England, the mortality rate is considerably higher in lower-status than in higher-status groups. Therefore, by the time a given cohort of women has reached the end of the childbearing period, differences between social strata in the number of living children per mother often vary considerably from differences in the average number of children ever born to each mother.

Fertility differentials by status measures. Such stratification measures as education, occupation, or income have been studied most extensively in relation to fertility, partly because data are available in standard demographic sources, but also because stratification is important in social and economic theory (United Nations . . . 1953, chapter 5). Socially patterned differences in life style and economic activity presumably may influence either the social norms about family size or the variables immediately determining fertility, such as fetal mortality and effective access to contraception. But there is no single, universally valid relation between status measures and fertility, because such particular indications of status as education or land-ownership vary in their significance in different societies and because the value attached to large families is greater in some societies than in others. Indeed, the resources that go with high status are

likely to be used to achieve large families in some societies and small families in others.

For preindustrial societies, there is evidence in some studies of a positive correlation between fertility and status, especially among agricultural populations (Stys 1957). The nature of the evidence varies. Fertility has been found to increase with size of landholding; agricultural tenants or workers have been found to have lower fertility than landholders; persons with low-status occupations have been reported to have lower-than-average fertility. The evidence for a positive correlation is reported in regional studies for England, Germany, Poland, China, the United States, India, and the Philippines for various periods between the seventeenth and twentieth centuries.

A plausible explanation of positive correlations between fertility and status in *pre*industrial societies is that dependence on relatives and children for a variety of social needs increases the social valuation of large families, so that those with higher status use their power to increase family size (for example, by early marriage). It is also plausible that in some instances poor health, poor nutrition, the absence of males seeking work, or high maternal mortality among fertile lower-status mothers may explain the lower fertility for lower-status groups. The thesis that higher fertility invariably goes with higher status in all preindustrial societies is certainly not supported by the evidence. For example, in some contemporary regional studies of peasant populations in India, there is no correlation between status measures and fertility (Chandrasekaran 1963).

A negative correlation between occupational status and fertility in Western urban populations appears with the earliest pertinent census data in the nineteenth century (United Nations 1953). In the period of transition to a mature industrial–urban society, negative correlations between broad status measures and fertility are found wherever systematic data are available. Although the evidence is mainly for Western countries, similar negative relationships have been reported for the advanced changing urban sectors in such diverse places as India, Taiwan, Chile, Puerto Rico, and Lebanon. Plausible explanations for these negative correlations center on the idea that high-status groups live first in the developing urban–industrial sectors in which they enjoy a number of advantages. These would include superior access to information about the means for fertility control, later marriage because of higher educational standards, and lower mortality rates (making fewer births necessary for any desired number of children). Such families, it is argued, would find the economic value of children relatively small in the course of acquiring higher living standards for themselves and their children. They would also be likely to participate in extrafamilial activities, which could occupy time that might otherwise have been given to additional children. Whatever the explanation, the existence of the negative relation between status and fertility is well documented for many places.

The lower fertility of high-status groups in the period of transition to advanced industrialization may be the result of both the smaller proportion marrying at important child-bearing ages and the use of contraception to limit family size within marriage. Historical data for status differentials in the use of contraception corresponding to differentials in fertility are available only for England, as already mentioned (Great Britain . . . 1949). However, similar differentials in use of contraception have appeared later in other countries, as data become available. More recently, there is evidence that the differential use of legal abortion is producing fertility status differentials in Japan and in some countries of eastern Europe.

At least in the United States, the higher fertility of low-status groups is partly a consequence of their rural origin rather than of their status in the urban community (Goldberg 1959). There is a high proportion of farm-reared persons in low-status groups, whether these are defined in terms of occupation, income, or education. When only couples living in cities for at least two generations are considered, either the status differentials become slightly positive or the negative correlation is reduced. This is consistent with the thesis that the negative correlation is part of the *transition* to a mature urban society rather than an intrinsic characteristic of such a society.

The negative relation of status to fertility is most pronounced in data for the period before World War II. However, even at that time there were many exceptions within broad occupational groups. For example, low fertility is reported among service workers, such as barbers and waiters, having frequent contact with higher-status groups. For the period between the world wars, the highest income groups sometimes had higher fertility rates than the next income group, especially when comparisons are made for persons of high educational or occupational status.

There was a sharp contraction in fertility differentials in many countries in the "baby boom" following World War II. Fertility generally increased most in those social strata which had the lowest fertility before the war. However, even in the United States, where this phenomenon was very pronounced, there continued to be significant negative correlations between various status measures and fertility (Grabill et al. 1958).

Postwar studies, mainly in the United States, indicate that there is now very little relationship between measures of social status and the number of children desired and expected. It is not yet known whether the expectations and desires of each stratum will be realized in action. Apart from possible changes in what is desired, the present evidence is that lower-status groups still are less effective in planning their fertility to attain desired family size.

Some scholars believe that in a mature urban–industrial society fertility eventually will be positively correlated with status—and especially with income (Universities–National Bureau . . . 1960, pp. 209–240). A basic assumption is that effective use of contraception, together with very low mortality rates, will diffuse throughout the society, so that the fertility of each stratum will directly reflect the value of varying numbers of children in that stratum. Children, it is argued, having lost their differential utility as laborers or as social security resources, will be valued by all social classes for direct satisfactions, such as those yielded by durable consumer goods. The higher-income groups will then be able to afford and will choose to have more children than low-income groups. There is some support for this argument in data showing that there is a small positive correlation of income and fertility among couples who plan family size effectively and that this correlation is highest for couples with an urban background (Whelpton 1943–1958, vol. 3, pp. 360–415).

This projection of a positive correlation in the mature urban society makes assumptions, still unverified, about the elasticity of demand for children. One could just as well argue that the higher educational status generally found with higher income may lead to a broadening of interests, which will compete for attention with the demands of larger families. The theory also assumes that in the modern welfare state even the lowest status groups can receive from nonfamilial institutions assistance formerly received from children in meeting the risks of illness, disability, unemployment, old age, and loneliness.

Differentials by city size and farm residence. In industrialized countries, fertility is almost always highest in the farm sector and tends to decrease as the size of the community increases. The explanation generally offered is twofold: it is said that contraception diffused from larger to smaller cities, and from there to the farms, and that the functional advantages of larger families are greatest, and their costs least, in smaller communities and on farms.

With the postwar rise in birth rates, fertility differentials by city size probably decreased in many countries, since fertility increased most in the status groups concentrated in large cities. Nevertheless, the traditional differentials persist in most Western countries for which there are adequate data. It is not yet clear whether the remaining inverse relation of fertility to city size in developed countries is a permanent feature of their structure, or a transitional phenomenon.

In the United States, at any rate, urban–rural fertility differentials have existed from a very early time. Declines in fertility in the rural and urban sectors followed parallel courses until about 1940, but since then urban fertility rates have risen more than the rural rates, thus reducing the differential. In a number of preindustrial countries (India, for example) urban–rural fertility differentials either do not exist or are minimal (Robinson 1961). In such societies, cities are often administrative and political centers in which familial organization does not differ greatly from that in rural areas; the city lacks the specialized institutions that take over many family functions in industrial societies.

Religious differentials. Most research on religious fertility differentials deals with the specific influence of the Roman Catholic church in limiting the practice of family planning (except by periodic abstinence) and in supporting norms for larger families. The doctrines of the church do not require large families, but they do restrict the means that may be used to achieve smaller families. The fact that empirical findings differ with the country studied suggests that the influence of the church depends on other variables in the society. In the United States, close attachment to the church is associated with higher fertility and with lesser use of the most effective fertility-control practices, even among higher-status groups. Lenski (1961) explains this result by an emphasis in Catholicism on familial rather than economic mobility values. But studies in Puerto Rico and other Latin American areas find no relation between attachment to the church and fertility. Indeed, international comparisons of fertility do not show any significant correlation between fertility and the percentage of Catholics in the population, when the level of general social development is taken into account.

Most of the other major world religions do not have specific doctrines about family limitation. However, religious practices frequently have an indirect effect on fertility. For example, in both India and China major religious traditions support a strong preference for at least one and preferably two sons, thus increasing the pressures for additional children. A pervasive fatalism in a religious ideology may have a greater effect than a specific injunction against contraception in impeding rational planning of fertility.

Other differentials. In industrial societies, wives who work away from home are found to have fewer children than those who stay at home. Some women work because they cannot have children, but the lower fertility of working women persists even when only fecund women are considered. Where the wife's work is closely tied to the home, lower fertility may not result. In Japan and Puerto Rico, women who worked at home or in small family enterprises were found to have higher fertility than other working wives.

Fertility differentials between ethnic, racial, or regional populations are extensively studied, because of their practical economic or political significance. But the *meaning* of the differentials depends on their specific historical and cultural context. Sometimes it is possible to explain such differentials in terms of status or rural–urban differences; otherwise, no successful analytic generalization of these studies has been made.

Consequences of differential fertility. Much of the early interest in differential fertility was eugenic. It was feared that the genetic quality of the population would deteriorate if low-status groups had higher-than-average fertility. This assumes that lower-status groups are more poorly endowed genetically—for example, with respect to intelligence—but this has not been scientifically established. Certain types of mental abnormality have a known genetic basis, but they are not sufficiently numerous to affect broad status differentials. It is likely that high or low fecundity itself may have a genetic basis, but this also is not known to have any specific connection to broad socially significant strata. Whether there are important genetic differences between social strata is still an open question. Probably, there is greater consensus that differential fertility may produce a social problem, regardless of the genetic origin of the problem, if fertility is high in groups with limited personal or social resources for child-rearing. There is some evidence that intellectual development is greater for children reared in small families; but the apparent contraction of fertility differentials in the postwar period in industrial countries has reduced the earlier concern about the social and biological consequences of differential fertility.

Differential fertility may affect the rate and character of social mobility. Varying rates of reproduction of different social strata affect the relative number of opportunities available in each stratum, depending on the extent of social inheritance of position. More generally, the rate of recruitment of new members is one important determinant of the continuity, structure, and power of any subgroup in the population. Recruitment from other groups by adoption or invasion is an alternative to reproduction, but differential fertility is often the principal determinant of the relative growth of population subgroups from generation to generation. Where success of groups contesting for political power depends on their size, a lively concern about comparative reproduction rates often is evident.

RONALD FREEDMAN

[*Directly related are the entries* GENETICS, *article on* DEMOGRAPHY AND POPULATION GENETICS; POPULATION. *Other relevant material may be found in* MIGRATION; MORTALITY; NUPTIALITY.]

BIBLIOGRAPHY

BANKS, JOSEPH A.   1954   *Prosperity and Parenthood: A Study of Family Planning Among the Victorian Middle Classes.* London: Routledge.

BERENT, JERZY   1952   Fertility and Social Mobility. *Population Studies* 5:244–260.

BLACKER, J. G. C.   1957   Social Ambitions of the Bourgeoisie in 18th Century France, and Their Relation to Family Limitation. *Population Studies* 11:46–63.

BRESARD, MARCEL   1950   Mobilité sociale et dimension de la famille. *Population* 5:533–566.

CHANDRASEKARAN, C.   1963   Physiological Factors Affecting Fertility in India. Volume 2, pages 89–96 in International Population Conference, New York, 1961, *Proceedings.* London: International Union for the Scientific Study of Population.

Conditions and Trends of Fertility in the World.   1965   *Population Bulletin of the United Nations* No. 7.

DAVIS, KINGSLEY; and BLAKE, JUDITH   1956   Social Structure and Fertility: An Analytic Framework. *Economic Development and Cultural Change* 4:211–235.

DEVEREUX, GEORGE   1955   *A Study of Abortion in Primitive Societies: A Typological, Distributional, and Dynamic Analysis of the Prevention of Birth in 400 Preindustrial Societies.* New York: Julian.

DUNCAN, OTIS DUDLEY   1965   Farm Background and Differential Fertility. *Demography* 2:240–249.

EVERSLEY, D. E. C.   1963   Population in England in the Eighteenth Century: An Appraisal of Current Research. Volume 1, pages 573–582 in International Population Conference, New York, 1961, *Proceedings.* London: International Union for the Scientific Study of Population.

FORD, CLELLAN S.   1945   *A Comparative Study of Human Reproduction.* Yale University Publications in Anthropology, No. 32. New Haven: Yale Univ. Press.

FRANCE, INSTITUT NATIONAL D'ÉTUDES DÉMOGRAPHIQUES   1953   *Fécondité des mariages: Nouvelle méthode de mesure,* by L. Henry. Travaux et Documents, Cahier No. 16. Paris: Presses Universitaires de France.

FRANCE, INSTITUT NATIONAL D'ÉTUDES DÉMOGRAPHIQUES   1960   *La prévention des naissances dans la famille: Ses origines dans les temps modernes,* by H. Bergues et al. Travaux et Documents, Cahier No. 35. Paris: Presses Universitaires de France.

FREEDMAN, RONALD   1961   The Sociology of Human Fertility: A Trend Report and Bibliography. *Current Sociology* 10, no. 2:35–121. → A report on research since 1945 with an annotated bibliography of 636 items.

FREEDMAN, RONALD   1963   Norms for Family Size in Underdeveloped Areas. Royal Society of London, *Proceedings* Series B 159:220–245.

FREEDMAN, RONALD; WHELPTON, P. K.; and CAMPBELL, A. A.   1959   *Family Planning, Sterility, and Population Growth.* New York: McGraw-Hill.

GLASS, DAVID V.; and EVERSLEY, D. E. C.   1965   *Population in History.* London: Arnold.

GOLDBERG, DAVID   1959   The Fertility of Two-generation Urbanites. *Population Studies* 12:214–222.

GRABILL, WILSON H.; KISER, C. V.; and WHELPTON, P. K.   1958   *The Fertility of American Women.* Prepared for the Social Science Research Council in cooperation with the U.S. Department of Commerce, Bureau of the Census. New York: Wiley.

GREAT BRITAIN, ROYAL COMMISSION ON POPULATION   1949   *Papers.* Volume 1: Family Limitation and Its Influence on Human Fertility During the Past Fifty Years, by E. Lewis-Faning. London: H.M. Stationery Office.

HATT, PAUL K.; FARR, N. L.; and WEINSTEIN, E.   1955   Types of Population Balance. *American Sociological Review* 20:14–21.

HENRY, LOUIS   1961   La fécondité naturelle: Observation, théorie, résultats. *Population* 16:625–636.

HIMES, NORMAN E.   (1936) 1963   *Medical History of Contraception.* New York: Gamut; London: Allen & Unwin.

HUTCHINSON, BERTRAM   1961   Fertility, Social Mobility and Urban Migration in Brazil. *Population Studies* 14: 182–189.

KIRK, DUDLEY; and NORTMAN, DOROTHY L.   1959   Business and Babies: The Influence of the Business Cycle on Birth Rates. Pages 151–160 in American Statistical Association, Social Statistics Section, *Proceedings.* Washington: The Association.

LENSKI, GERHARD E.   (1961) 1963   *The Religious Factor: A Sociological Study of Religion's Impact on Politics, Economics, and Family Life.* Rev. ed. Garden City, N.Y.: Doubleday.

LORIMER, FRANK   1954   *Culture and Human Fertility: A Study of the Relation of Cultural Conditions to Fertility in Non-industrial and Transitional Societies.* Paris: UNESCO.

NAG, MONI   1962   *Factors Affecting Human Fertility in Non Industrial Societies: A Cross-cultural Study.* Yale University Publications in Anthropology, No. 66. New Haven: Yale Univ. Press.

POTTER, R. G. et al.   1966   Application of Field Studies to Research on the Physiology of Human Reproduction. A chapter in M. Sheps (editor), *Public Health and Population Change.* Univ. of Pittsburgh Press.

ROBINSON, WARREN C.   1961   Urban–Rural Differences in Indian Fertility. *Population Studies* 14:218–234.

RYDER, NORMAN B.   1957   The Conceptualization of the Transition in Fertility. *Cold Spring Harbor Symposia on Quantitative Biology* 22:91–96.

RYDER, NORMAN B.   1960   The Structure and Tempo of Current Fertility. Pages 117–136 in Universities–National Bureau Committee for Economic Research, *Demographic and Economic Change in Developed Countries*. Princeton Univ. Press.

STYS, W.   1957   The Influence of Economic Conditions on the Fertility of Peasant Women. *Population Studies* 11:136–148.

UNITED NATIONS, DEPARTMENT OF SOCIAL AFFAIRS, POPULATION DIVISION   1953   *The Determinants and Consequences of Population Trends: A Summary of the Findings of Studies on the Relationship Between Population Changes and Economic and Social Conditions.* Population Studies, No. 17. New York: United Nations. → See especially Chapter 5.

UNIVERSITIES–NATIONAL BUREAU COMMITTEE FOR ECONOMIC RESEARCH   1960   *Demographic and Economic Change in Developed Countries*. National Bureau of Economic Research, Special Conference Series, No. 11. Princeton Univ. Press.

WESTOFF, CHARLES F. et al.   1961   *Family Growth in Metropolitan America*. Princeton Univ. Press.

WHELPTON, P. K.   1943–1958   *Social and Psychological Factors Affecting Fertility.* 5 vols. New York: Milbank Memorial Fund. → Volume 1: *The Household Survey in Indianapolis.* Volume 2: *The Intensive Study: Purpose, Scope, Methods and Partial Results.* Volume 3: *Further Reports on Hypothesis in the Indianapolis Study.* Volume 4: *Further Reports on Hypotheses and Other Data From the Indianapolis Study.* Volume 5: *Concluding Reports and Summary of Chief Findings From the Indianapolis Study.*

FERTILITY CONTROL

"Fertility control," as the term is used in this article, refers to patterns of human behavior that have as their primary objective the prevention of unwanted pregnancies and births. Individuals and couples adopt these patterns in accordance with their cultural values, reinforced by formal or informal social pressures.

The methods of fertility control are traditionally grouped into four categories: abstinence, contraception, sterilization, and induced abortion. The boundaries between these categories, however, are not clearly delineated and will become even less so in the future. The rhythm method, for example, is a method of contraception, but it also requires abstinence during a portion of the menstrual cycle. Oral contraception interferes with reproduction for periods of time and is sometimes referred to as temporary sterilization, while surgical sterilization has been called permanent contraception.

The term "birth control," coined by Margaret Sanger in 1914 (Lader 1955), is generally used as a synonym for contraception. From the beginning, the term was intended to exclude abortion, and, in general, sterilization and abstinence have also been excluded. A number of terms substituted for birth control, such as family limitation, child spacing, family planning, and planned parenthood, appear, for the most part, to be intended to promote social acceptance rather than to improve communication.

History.   Under some circumstances pregnancy and/or childbearing have been considered undesirable or have actually been proscribed in human societies since the dawn of history. Anthropologists have noted the practice of abortion among many preliterate peoples throughout the world. It is also probable that abstinence and *coitus interruptus* became known as methods of fertility control at the same time as the connection of coitus with pregnancy. It would appear, however, that fertility control was practiced only sporadically throughout most of man's long history. Since levels of mortality were generally high in premodern societies, only those societies survived where the level of natality was also high.

The practice of fertility control on a scale sufficient to influence the trend of the birth rate began in France toward the end of the eighteenth century (France . . . 1960) and in other countries during the nineteenth century (Himes 1936). Generally, it spread from the well-to-do and educated classes to the underprivileged, and from the cities to the countryside. In some countries, however, farm owners were among the first to restrict the size of their families in order to avoid property division.

At present, fertility control is practiced in one form or another and with varying degrees of success by most couples in the industrialized countries of the world and by social minorities, mainly urban, in nonindustrialized countries. However, even in societies where fertility control is not widely practiced, many recent surveys have shown that the majority of couples approve the idea of family limitation (see, for example, Berelson 1966). The preferred size of family, as indicated by the respondents, tends to be substantially smaller than the average number of children per family in the community.

Methods of contraception

Contraception, according to the usage of most writers on the subject, includes all nonpermanent measures to prevent coitus from resulting in conception. In older demographic literature, it has been customary to distinguish between "appliance methods," that is, mechanical devices and spermicides, and "nonappliance methods," such as withdrawal or the rhythm method. More recently, the major distinction is between the "traditional methods" and the "modern methods," the latter referring to oral and intrauterine contraceptives. Still another classification is made by the Roman Catholic church, which distinguishes between "natural birth control," that is, the rhythm method (see below), and "artificial birth control," comprising all other methods.

Folk methods. The principal folk methods of contraception are *coitus interruptus* and the douche. *Coitus interruptus* or withdrawal of the male prior to ejaculation is the oldest contraceptive procedure known to man. It appears in the Old Testament (Genesis 38) and has been noted by anthropologists in many parts of the world. In western and northern Europe, where relatively late marriage has long coexisted with close and frequent social contacts between unmarried adults and with a strong condemnation of pregnancy out of wedlock, withdrawal appears to have been the method by which premarital pregnancies were averted. At a later time, the practice was transferred into married life. There can be no doubt that *coitus interruptus* was the principal method by which the historical decline of the birth rate in the West was achieved. Statistical studies suggest a level of effectiveness similar to that of vaginal methods (see Table 3).

Postcoital douches with plain water, vinegar, and various products advertised under the name of "feminine hygiene," long used for purposes of family limitation, have lost popularity in recent decades. Since sperm has been found in the mucus of the cervical canal within 90 seconds after ejaculation, medical opinion considers the contraceptive effectiveness of douching as quite unsatisfactory.

Vaginal methods. Vaginal contraceptive methods are designed to prevent the entry of sperm into the uterus by a mechanical barrier and/or to kill the sperm by chemical action. The condom or sheath, a cover for the penis during intercourse, made its first appearance in England in the eighteenth century. Since the latter part of the nineteenth century, the early "skin" condoms, made from the intestines of sheep and other animals, have gradually been replaced by the cheaper and more convenient rubber sheaths. A large proportion of the condoms sold in the United States prior to 1938 were inferior in quality. Since supervision over condoms has been assumed by the Food and Drug Administration, their quality has improved greatly.

The condom offers protection not only against unwanted pregnancy but also against venereal disease. It can be used without special instruction and elaborate preparation in any situation where coitus is possible.

The diaphragm, known in the United Kingdom as the Dutch Cap, was invented by a German physician, Wilhelm P. J. Mensinga, prior to 1882. Before the advent of oral contraceptives, it was the contraceptive device most often recommended by physicians in private practice and in birth control clinics throughout the United States and Europe. The diaphragm, inserted into the vagina and covering the cervical *os*, prevents the entry of sperm into the uterus. To fit a diaphragm, a pelvic examination by a physician or other trained health worker is necessary. Because of this requirement, the method is not suitable for general use in countries where medical personnel and medical facilities are scarce.

The contraceptive effectiveness of the condom and diaphragm is high and appears to be approximately equal for the two methods. Occasional failures occur, for example, if a condom tears or a diaphragm is displaced during coitus. A rate of 2 to 3 pregnancies per 100 women per year would seem to be a high estimate for consistent users. If motivation is weak, much higher pregnancy rates must be expected.

Chemical contraceptives consist of a spermicidal compound and a vehicle for its introduction and distribution within the vagina. Various creams and jellies and, more recently, foams with a highly spermicidal action, have been developed by the pharmaceutical industry. Insertion into the vagina is accomplished, prior to intercourse, by means of an applicator. The effectiveness of these methods seems to be lower than that of the diaphragm or the condom. Because vaginal tablets can be manufactured easily and cheaply and because no pelvic examination, fitting, or apparatus is needed, they have been considered eminently suitable for programs of population control in the economically underdeveloped regions of the world. However, the results of clinical and field trials have not been encouraging, and it does not appear likely that this method will prove sufficiently acceptable and effective to be of value in reducing the rate of population growth.

Rhythm method. The rhythm or safe period method of contraception, also known as periodic continence, is based on the fact, recognized independently in the early 1920s by Ogino in Japan and Knaus in Austria, that conception is possible during only a small fraction of each menstrual cycle. The fertile days can be determined either by the application of a simple formula to the menstrual history of the woman or by the observation of changes in basal body temperature during the menstrual cycle, or by a combination of both.

Rhythm is at present (that is, in 1966) the only method of fertility control, other than complete abstinence, sanctioned by the Roman Catholic church. Its contraceptive effectiveness has been the subject of much controversy. The theoretical effectiveness of the method, correctly taught and understood, and consistently practiced according to the Ogino formula, is roughly comparable to that of vaginal methods. The use-effectiveness, on the other hand, which may be modified by errors of instruction or comprehension and by the couple's willingness to take chances, has been consistently less than that of vaginal methods in comparable situations.

Oral methods. The contraceptive "pill," long thought of as an attractive solution to the problem of fertility control, became a reality in the late 1950s. Since 1956 several oral contraceptives have been extensively tested in many countries. No permanent or serious side effects were noted in any of the clinical trials, but laboratory studies of various organ systems have in some instances revealed deviations from normal values. The significance of these changes cannot yet be evaluated. Women who discontinue the medication conceive promptly. Oral contraceptives have established themselves not only as virtually 100 per cent effective, if taken according to prescription, but also as highly acceptable to most users, including many women in the lower socioeconomic strata who had been unsuccessful with other contraceptive methods.

Intrauterine methods. Intrauterine contraceptive devices (IUDs) are small, variously shaped objects (rings, spirals, loops, etc.) which are inserted into the uterus by a physician. The procedure takes only a few minutes and requires no anesthesia. The devices are made of chemically inert materials, such as polyethylene or stainless steel, and may remain in the uterus for an indefinite period. The mechanism of action of the IUDs is not fully understood. The best available evidence suggests that the presence of a foreign body in the uterus reduces the time required for the movement of the ovum through the Fallopian tube from three to four days to one day or less and that the fertilized ovum, therefore, reaches the uterus at a time when neither it nor the endometrium is ready for implantation. There is some evidence, however, that the ovum may not be fertilized at all.

Since 1960 several types of IUDs have been carefully studied in the United States and elsewhere

(Tietze 1966; International Conference . . . 1964). In some cases the uterus expels the device, usually during a menstrual period and occasionally without the woman being aware of it, or the device must be removed because of side effects such as bleeding and/or pain. No evidence has been produced that the IUDs are carcinogenic, nor does their use interfere with fertility after they have been removed. During use, 2 to 3 accidental pregnancies per 100 women per year must be expected even with the more successful types of IUDs. These failures may occur after an unnoticed expulsion or, more frequently, with the device *in situ*. No case of fetal malformation attributable to an IUD has been reported.

The sociological importance of the IUDs lies in the fact that they offer the only fully reversible method of birth control now available which requires a single decision rather than sustained motivation on the part of the users. The insidious dissipation of user interest, which has played so frustrating a role in all other methods of contraception, is of little importance with the IUD. Regardless of apathy, fatigue, or sexual excitement, the contraceptive device is in place and no further action is required of either the man or the woman.

Extent of contraceptive practice

The first nationwide investigation of the extent of contraceptive practice in the United States was the Growth of American Families (GAF) Study, conducted in 1955 (Freedman et al. 1959). A second survey along similar lines was carried out in 1960 (Whelpton et al. 1965). According to these surveys, the proportions of white couples with wives 18–39 years of age who had taken up the practice of birth control prior to the interview were

Table 1 — Per cent of white couples ever using contraception: United States, 1955 and 1960

	1955	1960
Religion of wife:		
Catholic	57	70
Protestant	75	84
Jewish	86	95
Education of wife:		
Grade school	48	66
High school, 1–3	65	78
High school, 4	74	83
College	84	88
Income of husband:		
Under $3,000	58	70
$3,000–$3,999	69	77
$4,000–$5,999	74	80
$6,000 or more	79	85
Entire sample	70	81

Source: Adapted from Whelpton et al. 1965.

70 per cent in 1955 and 81 per cent in 1960. Among couples who had never tried to prevent conception, many were found to be sterile or subfecund. The extent and type of contraception varied with religious affiliation and with such indications of socioeconomic status as wife's education and husband's income (see Table 1).

Among nonwhite couples, included for the first time in the 1960 GAF Study, only 59 per cent reported use of contraception, a substantially lower proportion than among the lowest educational and income groups of white couples.

The great majority of couples using birth control relied on one or more of five methods (see Table 2). It should be noted that the 1960 survey was completed before oral contraceptives came into general use.

Close correlations were found in the GAF surveys between choice of contraceptive method and level of education, as well as other indicators of socioeconomic status. Use of the rhythm method by Catholics was strongly associated with advanced education. A similar association was found for the diaphragm among Protestants and among those Catholics who had experience with "artificial birth control." Conversely, use of the douche and especially of withdrawal were inversely associated with educational level, while the condom was a popular method at all socioeconomic levels. The findings of the GAF Study have been confirmed, to a large extent, by the Family Growth in Metropolitan America (FGMA) Study (Westoff et al. 1961). According to a nationwide survey taken in late 1965 (Ryder & Westoff 1966), about

Table 2 — Per cent distribution of users by last method used: United States, 1955 and 1960

Last method used	Entire sample	RELIGION OF WIFE		
		Protestant	Catholic	Jewish
1955				
Condom	29	31	16	56
Diaphragm	25	29	12	37
Rhythm	24	14	56	2
Douche	9	11	6	—
Withdrawal	8	8	8	3
All other	5	7	2	2
	100	100	100	100
1960				
Condom	28	30	17	49
Diaphragm	22	26	7	35
Rhythm	23	14	55	5
Douche	9	11	5	2
Withdrawal	8	8	10	2
All other	10	11	6	7
	100	100	100	100

Source: Adapted from GAF Study, 1955 and 1960 (special unpublished tabulations, privately communicated).

Table 3 — Per cent of married women, under 45 years of age, ever using and currently using oral contraception: United States, 1965

	Ever using	Currently using
Age:		
Under 20	42	28
20–24	46	30
25–29	37	22
30–34	24	13
35–39	15	8
40–44	9	5
Education:		
Grade school	12	7
High school, 1–3	26	15
High school, 4	26	16
College, 1–3	32	19
College, 4	37	22
Race and religion:		
White	27	16
Catholic	21	11
Non-Catholic	29	18
Negro	19	12
Entire sample	26	15

Source: Adapted from Ryder & Westoff 1966.

6.4 million married women under 45 years of age (26 per cent) had used oral contraception, while 3.8 million were relying on the "pill" at the time of the interview. Use was found inversely associated with age and directly with education (see Table 3).

In the United Kingdom the first major investigation of the contraceptive habits of the population was conducted in 1946–1947 on behalf of the Royal Commission on Population. In 1959–1960 new data were obtained from the Population Investigation Committee's marriage survey (Rowntree & Pierce 1961). In terms of religious affiliation and socioeconomic status, the patterns of contraceptive practice were found to be similar to those reported in the United States. In regard to methods, there are important differences. While the condom is the most widely used method in both countries, British couples tend to rely far more often on *coitus interruptus* and far less often on the diaphragm than American couples. Catholic couples in the United Kingdom showed less preference for the rhythm method than Catholic couples in the United States.

In Japan ten surveys on birth control were conducted between 1950 and 1965 (Muramatsu 1966). During this period the proportion of couples who reported current use of contraception increased from 19 per cent to 52 per cent. The proportion of couples practicing contraception was higher in the six major cities of Japan than in the other urban areas and was lowest in the rural districts. The familiar socioeconomic gradient was also present. The condom, the most widely used method of contraception in Japan, was reported by a majority of users in each survey since 1952. Next in popularity was the rhythm method, an example of a prophet (Ogino) honored in his own country.

The extent of contraceptive practice and the methods used have also been studied in a number of other countries throughout the world. Generally speaking, the practice of contraception is inversely correlated with the level of the birth rate and rarely reaches 10 per cent of all couples in the rural areas of the developing countries. The proportion tends to be higher in towns and among the better educated. It has been suggested that the more widespread practice of contraception in industrialized societies is connected with the decline, in these societies, of the extended family and the correspondingly greater opportunities afforded to young, unmarried adults for training in contraceptive practices (Ryder 1959).

Effectiveness

Study of the effectiveness of contraception requires a distinction between "theoretical effectiveness" and "use-effectiveness." Theoretical effectiveness is the effectiveness of a method under ideal conditions, that is, used consistently and according to instructions, without any omissions or errors of technique. Use-effectiveness refers to the contraceptive practice of a particular population and reflects such variables as the socioeconomic and cultural characteristics and the degree of motivation of the couples concerned.

Theoretical effectiveness is not accessible to measurement and can only be inferred from the performance of the most successful group of users. Use-effectiveness is measured in terms of failure rates per 100 woman-years of use, according to the formula first proposed by Raymond Pearl (1932), or preferably by means of cumulative failure rates, according to the life table procedure described by R. G. Potter (1963).

Comprehensive information on the effectiveness of contraception, as practiced by young urban couples in the United States during the 1950s, was obtained during the course of the FGMA Study (Westoff et al. 1961, pp. 83–101). During the 28,607 months of exposure to the use of contraception reported by the couples included in the survey, 534 accidental pregnancies occurred, corresponding to a failure rate of 22.4 per 100 years of exposure. Failure rates for individual methods ranged from about 14 per 100 years of exposure for the condom and the diaphragm to about 40 for the rhythm method and the postcoital douche (*ibid.*, Table B-2). These rates reflect use-effectiveness—not theoretical effectiveness. Some of the couples admitted that they were "taking chances" in their contraceptive practice. Without such omissions, both admitted and unadmitted, it must be presumed that the failure rate for each method would have been much lower.

This conclusion is strongly supported by the results of reinterviews with the same couples about three years later. It was found that the couples who had used contraceptive measures since marriage and already had the number of children they desired experienced a failure rate of only 3.7 per 100 years of exposure for all contraceptive methods combined and a rate of 2.6 if they used the condom, the diaphragm, or withdrawal (Westoff et al. 1963, pp. 38–44). Couples who intended to have additional children and who, therefore, wanted to postpone pregnancy rather than prevent it altogether had much higher failure rates, similar to those experienced prior to the first interview.

Sterilization

Surgical sterilization was originally used to protect women whose life or health was threatened by pregnancy. Dr. James Blundell of London is credited with having first proposed the procedure in 1823. Effective techniques were developed in the latter part of the nineteenth century when aseptic surgery and anesthesia became available. At about the same time, sterilizing operations began to be widely used on males, mainly in connection with operations on the prostate. Growing confidence in the efficacy and safety of surgical sterilization led to its use for eugenic purposes, that is, to prevent persons suffering from hereditary disabilities, especially mental deficiency, various psychoses, and idiopathic epilepsy, from having offspring.

In the United States, 32 states adopted legislation between 1907 and 1937 regulating the practice of eugenic sterilization. Some of these laws have been declared unconstitutional, but the majority are still in force. However, few states have used their authority extensively, and the total number of persons sterilized under these eugenic laws from their inception up to the end of 1965 was 65,000. During the early 1960s the number of eugenic sterilizations averaged about 500 per year.

Outside the United States sterilization for eugenic reasons is legally regulated in a few countries, notably in Scandinavia and in Japan. In Germany eugenic sterilization, involving a minimum of 200,000 persons, was practiced under the Eugenic Law of July 14, 1933, until 1945. This estimate does not include inmates of concentration camps who were sterilized without legal authorization.

In recent years discussion has centered on the legality and/or propriety of voluntary sterilization as a method of family limitation and on the use of sterilization in countries where high birth rates and rapid population growth threaten to produce serious economic and social difficulties (Blacker 1962).

Permanent sterilization in women is ordinarily accomplished by salpingectomy, that is, by the cutting, ligation (tying), and partial removal of the Fallopian tubes. In the male, the sterilizing operation (vasectomy) consists of the cutting, ligation, and removal of a portion of the spermatic duct. Since sterilization does not involve removal of the sex glands, it does not produce loss or impairment of sexual desire or of capacity for sexual response. Restoration of fertility by a second operation is possible but not certain. This fact restricts sterilization to persons permanently ineligible for parenthood and to mature couples who have all the children they want or are likely to want in the future. According to a number of studies, the great majority of sterilized patients are satisfied with the result, feel relieved from the nagging fear of pregnancy, and have no complaints. Regrets and more serious psychological side effects have, however, been occasionally noted in sterilized persons of both sexes, who were poorly chosen and/or not suitably prepared for the operation. Such undesirable side effects are most likely to occur if the marriage is unhappy or on the brink of breaking up, or when the operation is accepted reluctantly, under pressure from a spouse or other persons.

The number of voluntary sterilizations in the United States during the late 1950s is estimated at 110,000 annually, including 65,000 operations on women and 45,000 vasectomies. Later estimates are not available. Sterilization of women has been popular in Puerto Rico since the 1940s and has also gained wide acceptance in Japan (Koya 1961). In India the government encourages voluntary sterilization as a method of population control. By mid-1965 about 900,000 operations had been reported, two-thirds on men and one-third on women. South Korea, too, has included vasectomy in its national family planning program, and 49,000 vasectomies were performed from 1962 to 1964.

Abortion

Induced abortion, that is, termination of unwanted pregnancy by destruction of the fetus, has been performed throughout man's history. Some cultures prescribe abortion under specific circumstances, others tolerate it, still others condemn it. In the United States most state laws stipulate prevention of the death of the pregnant woman as the sole ground on which pregnancy may be interrupted. In practice, many (but by no means all) reputable hospitals permit therapeutic abortion in cases where a serious threat to health is to be averted and for certain eugenic reasons, as when a pregnant woman catches a disease that is likely to cause malformations in the fetus. In New York City the number of therapeutic abortions equaled about one-fifth of one per cent of the number of live births in 1960–1962 (Gold et al. 1965). In a few countries, such as Denmark and Sweden, the interpretation of medical necessity for abortion is far more liberal, since it takes into account less serious threats to the woman's physical or mental health, as well as her economic situation. In 1963 legal abortions amounted to about 5 per cent of the number of live births in Denmark, and to about 3 per cent in Sweden (Tietze 1966).

In still other countries, abortion is legally available either at the request of the pregnant woman or on broadly interpreted social indications. In the Soviet Union abortion was legalized after World War I. In 1936 this policy was reversed, and for the next two decades abortion was permitted on medical grounds only. In 1955 another reversal took place, and abortion on request was once more legalized. The adoption of similar legislation in most countries of eastern Europe has been followed by very rapid increase in legal abortions. In Hungary legal abortions have outnumbered live births since 1959 (Mehlan 1966). In Japan the Eugenic Protection Law of 1948 authorized interruption of pregnancy for economic as well as medical reasons. The subsequent interpretation of this law has been tantamount to making abortion available unconditionally.

In several countries where the practice of abortion is restricted by law, estimates of its incidence have been obtained by the survey method (see, for example, Armijo & Monreal 1965; Hong 1966). This approach has not yet been used successfully in the United States. In 1959 a committee appointed by the Conference on Abortion at Arden House, New York, concluded that a "plausible estimate of the frequency of induced abortion . . . could be as low as 200,000 and as high as 1,200,000 per year . . ." (Planned Parenthood . . . 1958, p. 180). No new data which would permit a more precise evaluation are available.

Methods of the future

Continuing research in the field of human and animal reproduction promises new methods of fertility control, which may become available over the coming decade. Among the following procedures, some are now undergoing clinical evaluation, others are being studied in selected human volunteers, and still others are in various stages of development with laboratory animals: long-acting ovulation suppressants administered by injection; compounds suppressing spermatogenesis, for use as oral or injectable contraceptives in males; immunization of females against sperm; immunization of males against sperm, resulting in suppression of spermatogenesis; blocking of the spermatic duct by injections of plastic material which can be easily removed; compounds acting on the fertilized ovum prior to implantation; and compounds with destructive action on the young embryo.

CHRISTOPHER TIETZE

[See also FERTILITY; POPULATION, articles on POPULATION GROWTH and POPULATION POLICIES.]

BIBLIOGRAPHY

Publications in the field of fertility control, both medical and sociological, are extremely numerous, and the rate of publication will undoubtedly increase; accordingly, the works cited in this article constitute only a minute fraction of the available literature and may be rapidly superseded by new developments. A classified bibliography covering all aspects of the field (but with emphasis on the medical side) is Tietze 1965. Studies in Family Planning, an occasional publication of the Population Council, regularly summarizes much current research, especially that which deals with the social and demographic aspects of fertility control. The proceedings of the many international conferences on fertility control are published by the Excerpta Medica Foundation of Amsterdam.

ARMIJO, ROLANDO; and MONREAL, TEGUALDA 1965 Epidemiology of Provoked Abortion in Santiago, Chile. *Journal of Sex Research* 1:143–159.

BERELSON, BERNARD 1966 KAP Studies on Fertility. Pages 655–668 in International Conference on Family Planning Programs, Geneva, 1965, *Family Planning and Population Programs: A Review of World Developments.* Univ. of Chicago Press.

BLACKER, C. P. 1962 Voluntary Sterilization: The Last Sixty Years. *Eugenics Review* 54:9–23; 143–162.

CALDERONE, MARY S. (editor) 1964 *Manual of Contraceptive Practice.* Baltimore: Williams & Wilkins.

CONFERENCE ON RESEARCH IN FAMILY PLANNING, NEW YORK, *1960* 1962 *Research in Family Planning: Papers Presented at a Conference Sponsored Jointly by the Milbank Memorial Fund and the Population Council, Inc.* Princeton Univ. Press.

FRANCE, INSTITUT NATIONAL D'ÉTUDES DÉMOGRAPHIQUES 1960 *La prévention des naissances dans la famille: Ses origines dans les temps modernes,* by H. Berques et al. Travaux et Documents, Cahier No. 35. Paris: Presses Universitaires de France.

FREEDMAN, RONALD; WHELPTON, P. K.; and CAMPBELL, A. A. 1959 *Family Planning, Sterility, and Population Growth.* New York: McGraw-Hill.

GOLD, EDWIN M. et al. 1965 Therapeutic Abortions in New York City: A Twenty-year Review. *American Journal of Public Health* 55:964–972.

GREAT BRITAIN, ROYAL COMMISSION ON POPULATION 1949 *Papers.* Volume 1: Family Limitation and Its Influence on Human Fertility During the Past Fifty Years, by E. Lewis-Faning. London: H.M. Stationery Office.

HIMES, NORMAN E. (1936) 1963 *Medical History of Contraception.* New York: Gamut.

HONG, SUNG BONG 1966 *Induced Abortion in South Korea.* Seoul: Dong-A.

INTERNATIONAL CONFERENCE ON FAMILY PLANNING PROGRAMS, GENEVA, *1965* 1966 *Family Planning and Population Programs: A Review of World Developments.* Univ. of Chicago Press. → Edited by Bernard Berelson and others.

INTERNATIONAL CONFERENCE ON INTRA-UTERINE CONCEPTION, SECOND, NEW YORK, *1964* 1964 *Proceedings.* Excerpta Medica Foundation, International Congress Series, No. 86. Amsterdam: The Foundation.

JAFFE, FREDERICK S. 1964 Family Planning and Poverty. *Journal of Marriage and the Family* 26:467–470.

KOYA, YOSHIO 1961 Sterilization in Japan. *Eugenics Quarterly* 8, no. 3:135–141.

LADER, LAWRENCE 1955 *The Margaret Sanger Story and the Fight for Birth Control.* New York: Doubleday.

MEHLAN, K.-H. 1966 The Socialist Countries of Europe. Pages 207–226 in International Conference on Family Planning Programs, Geneva, 1965, *Family Planning and Population Programs: A Review of World Developments.* Univ. of Chicago Press.

MURAMATSU, MINORU 1966 Japan. Pages 7–19 in International Conference on Family Planning Programs, Geneva, 1965, *Family Planning and Population Programs: A Review of World Developments.* Univ. of Chicago Press.

PEARL, RAYMOND 1932 Contraception and Fertility in 2,000 Women. *Human Biology* 4:363–407.

PLANNED PARENTHOOD FEDERATION OF AMERICA 1958 *Abortion in the United States.* New York: Hoeber.

POTTER, R. G. JR. 1963 Additional Measures of Use-effectiveness of Contraception. *Milbank Memorial Fund Quarterly* 41:400–418.

ROWNTREE, GRISELDA; and PIERCE, RACHEL M. 1961 Birth Control in Britain. Part 1: Attitudes and Practices Among Persons Married Since the First World War. Part 2: Contraceptive Methods Used by Couples Married in the Last Thirty Years. *Population Studies* 15:3–31, 121–160.

RYDER, NORMAN B. 1959 Fertility. Pages 400–436 in P. M. Hauser and O. D. Duncan (editors), *The Study of Population.* Univ. of Chicago Press.

RYDER, NORMAN B.; and WESTOFF, CHARLES F. 1966 Use of Oral Contraception in the United States, 1965. *Science* 153:1199–1205.

TIETZE, CHRISTOPHER (editor) 1965 *Bibliography of Fertility Control: 1950–1965.* New York: National Committee on Maternal Health.

TIETZE, CHRISTOPHER 1966 Contraception With Intra-uterine Devices: 1959–1966. *American Journal of Obstetrics and Gynecology* 96:1043–1054.

TIETZE, CHRISTOPHER; and NEUMANN, LUSSIA (editors) 1962 *Surgical Sterilization of Men and Women: A Selected Bibliography.* New York: National Committee on Maternal Health.

WESTOFF, CHARLES F.; POTTER, ROBERT G.; and SAGI, PHILIP S. 1961 *Family Growth in Metropolitan America.* Princeton Univ. Press.

WESTOFF, CHARLES F.; POTTER, ROBERT G.; SAGI, PHILIP C.; and MISHLER, ELIOT G. 1963 *The Third Child: A Study in the Prediction of Fertility.* Princeton Univ. Press.

WHELPTON, PASCAL K.; CAMPBELL, ARTHUR A.; and PATTERSON, JOHN E. 1965 *Fertility and Family Planning in the United States.* Princeton Univ. Press.

FEUD

Feud has been defined by Lasswell as ". . . relations of mutual animosity among intimate groups in which a resort to violence is anticipated on both sides" (1931, p. 220). This definition includes two important concepts—"violence" and "intimate [or related] groups"—that require amplification.

Nature of violence. Concerning the concept of violence, the question arises, Is any type of violence between intimate groups a feud, or are there specific characteristics that denote the violence of a feud? The concept is commonly refined in terms of intensity and duration. Thus, there appears to be general agreement that the violence typical of a feud may range from beating, which leaves only slight injuries, to killing several members of the opposite group. A feud involves prolonged and intermittent hostilities. As a logical consequence, a single fight or a single killing cannot be defined as a feud. Long intervals of relative peace sometimes elapse between the fights and slayings (Lowie [1920] 1947, p. 414). Bohannan says that "feud occurs when the principle of self-help gets out of hand" (1963, p. 290), implying that if an injury is redressed through violence and the self-redress is final and more or less accepted by the other party, such violence does not merit the term "feud." Lasswell states that feuds often continue so long after they begin that the precipitating episodes are even forgotten (1931, p. 221). Evans-Pritchard (1940, p. 293) agrees with the criterion of prolonged violence. However, he points out that a feud cannot go on indefinitely; otherwise the relationship of the fighting groups (among the Nuer, their membership in the same tribe) would be severed, and further hostilities, not occurring between related groups, could no longer by implication be called feud (1940, pp. 279, 283).

We may conclude, then, that feud involves prolonged, often intermittent violence which must end at some point short of the obliteration of the second criterion of feud—the intimate relationship of the feuding groups. Of course, concluding a feud does not necessarily mean that mutual hostility is transformed into indifference or friendship. A new feuding cycle most likely erupts between the old combatants any time that a new crime or injury is committed by an individual against a member of the other side.

The chain of violent acts that marks the feud is initiated in order "to secure revenge, reprisal, or glory for a particular individual or family within the group" (Wright 1942). Another common characteristic of the violence that may be classified as feud is the claim that the actual acts of hostility are regulated by customs shared by the two fighting groups (Radcliffe-Brown 1952, p. 215). In other words, the hostilities of the two groups are patterned upon, and subject to, rules which both sides observe. Furthermore, the initial act of violence is regarded as injury to the whole group to which the victim belongs (family, clan, or village), and the members consequently stand under an obligation to avenge the injustice (Radcliffe-Brown 1952, p. 215; 1940, p. xx; Nadel 1947, p. 151). Paraphrasing Durkheim, Radcliffe-Brown calls their duty an expression of "collective solidarity." However, this principle works also with regard to the opposite party, where it produces a group liability, with the effect that any member of the offender's group may be slain for the crime of his relative, his friend, or a coresident (Radcliffe-Brown 1952, p. 215; Nadel 1947, p. 151).

According to Radcliffe-Brown (1952, p. 215; 1940, p. xx), another aspect of the violence of feuds is that it is justified by "public sentiment." Unfortunately, he fails to specify whether this public sentiment pertains to the group of avengers, to both of the groups in conflict, or to the society at large. If we recall his statement that the acts of violence are regulated by custom, we may conclude that this public sentiment pertains to the larger society of which the two fighting groups are constituent segments. Not all acts of violence justify development of such a sentiment: in order that a violent revenge be considered a justifiable act, its magnitude should be valued as an equivalent to the injury suffered (Radcliffe-Brown 1952, p. 215, 1940, p. xx; Nadel 1947, p. 151). Who, however, determines the equivalent? Implied in the writings of Radcliffe-Brown and Nadel is the notion that the criteria for equivalence are sufficiently objective, i.e., part of a general custom known to all, so that it is often unnecessary for a specified authority to deliver an opinion on the balance between the injury and revenge. Among the Nuba, for example, "equivalence" is so specific that not only must a man be killed for a man and a woman for a woman, but the age of the person killed in revenge should approximate that of the original victim. For death in excess of requirement a compensation must be offered in the form of a person who is adopted into the offended clan (Nadel 1947, pp. 151–152). In most other primitive societies such compensation is usually tendered in terms of a payment known in the literature as "blood money." Bearing in mind Bohannan's important point that feud occurs when "self-help gets out of hand," Radcliffe-Brown's and Nadel's principle of equivalence of revenge applies to feud only when such equivalence is not achieved by the first retaliation of the injured party. There have to be more than two acts of violence to justify the application of the term "feud."

The characteristics of violence that form one of the two major criteria of feud may be summed up as follows: (1) the violence of a feud ranges in intensity from injury to killing; (2) it is initiated on behalf of a particular individual or family that is a member of the more inclusive "injured group"; and (3) it is of long duration, involving at least three instances of violence—injury, revenge, and counterrevenge. Hostile acts consisting of an injury and of an equivalent revenge that is accepted as final by both parties do not merit the term feud and should more properly be called self-redress. The nature of self-redress is, in most cases, basically different from the prolonged violence called feud.

Nature of feuding groups. The second major criterion of feud, which requires the committed violence to occur between two "intimate [or related] groups," is far more important and complex (Lasswell 1931). It is almost generally agreed that the two groups fighting each other must be related in order to qualify such hostilities as a feud. However, various authors differ in their explanation of the nature of this relationship. An imprecise position is assumed, for example, by Wright, who states that "most primitive groups observe different war practices toward a related group with which friendship normally exists and toward a wholly alien group. Hostilities of the first type, although group sanctioned, are usually of the nature of a feud to secure revenge, reprisal, or glory for a particular individual or family within the group" (1942). Others who have studied feuds—for example, Malinowski ([1941] 1964, p. 261)—go further, claiming that relationship between the two groups obtains from the fact that they both belong to "the same larger cultural unit." Similarly, those who use the phrase "members of the same society" do not necessarily identify the political unit involved. For example, Max Gluckman (1940, p. 41) speaks of a type of intertribal feud within a larger nation, while Hobhouse and his associates restrict the relationship of feuding groups to membership in the same tribe: "Feuds would thus also be the appropriate name for reprisals exercised by one branch of a community upon another, e.g., as between two clans or two local groups within a tribe" (Hobhouse et al. [1915] 1930, p. 228). Besides this type of an "internal self-redress" called feud, these authors recognize another type of redress which exists between two segments of otherwise unrelated communities and is labeled "external self-

redress." A similar limitation of the application of the concept of feud to the fighting done by groupings that belong to the same tribe is upheld quite explicitly by Evans-Pritchard. He contrasts these hostilities with the intertribally organized violence which he calls war: "Thus, if a man of one tribe kills a man of another tribe, retribution can only take the form of intertribal warfare" (1940, p. 278). "Between segments of the same tribe, opposition is expressed by the institution of the feud" (1940, p. 283).

Some authors theorize that marriage ties constitute the link between the two feuding groups. Accordingly, hostilities in a society with exogamous subgroups such as clans, lineages, or local communities are all regarded as feuds and not as wars (Schneider 1964, p. 282; also implied by Colson 1962, p. 120).

The relationship between the hostile groups is far less nebulous and more related to the feuding itself than the marriage-tie hypothesis would imply. Evans-Pritchard has the following to say about those Nuer who engage in intratribal fighting: "Then either the contradiction of feuds is felt and they are settled, the unity of the tribe being maintained thereby, or they remain so long unsettled that people give up all hope and intention of ever concluding them and finally cease to feel that they ought to be concluded, so that the tribe tends to split and two new tribes come into being" (1940, p. 279). This statement suggests that the nature of the relationship of two feuding groups lies in the fact that the more inclusive group of which the two are members is, at least to some degree, politically organized. The political organization may mean that there exists a formally designated authority with jurisdiction over both feuding groups; in other cases it may consist of only the most informal arbiters or go-betweens, who customarily settle internal political problems. Gluckman ([1956] 1959, p. 20) went so far as to claim that feuding, by creating a necessity for the existence of such go-betweens, tends to unite the members of the larger grouping. There are good examples of formal political authority terminating feuds between subgroups by the use of force, in the event that the customary exchange has failed. The present author would hesitate to designate as a feud fighting which occurs between politically unrelated groupings and would criticize Wagner (1940, p. 223) and Schneider (1964, p. 279) for holding that an overall political organization is not necessary to qualify a condition of strife as a feud. Wherever feuds do occur, there exists a politically influential authority (a formal chief, an informal headman, a council of important men, or an individual of very limited power, such as a go-between), who is usually too weak or disinterested in controlling his constituents, with the result that prolonged fighting is not prevented. The weaker the political control, the longer the feuds last and the harder it is to conclude them (see especially Evans-Pritchard 1940, pp. 278–279; and Gluckman [1956] 1959, p. 19).

Feud and war. The criterion of an over-all political organization that relates the two feuding groups may also be used to mark the boundary between feud and war. Whereas feuds can occur only within a politically organized whole, war occurs beyond such an organization and always involves two groups that are politically unrelated (Nadel 1947, p. 301). One should not, however, go to the extreme and claim that it would be "advisable to include all external, group-sanctioned violence against other human beings in the conception of primitive war" (Schneider 1964, p. 276). There seem to be two kinds of hostility external to politically organized groupings: hostility which is "exercised by a part of a community only upon members of another community" and which should properly be called "external self-redress," or retaliation; and hostility which means "an operation conducted in the name of the community as a whole," and which thus deserves to be regarded as war (Hobhouse et al. [1915] 1930, p. 228).

These structural criteria that distinguish feud, external redress, and war appear to be more politically relevant and suitable than the following, which are of only circumstantial nature. For example, the claim that only publicly initiated hostilities should be called war, while the privately initiated ones should be labeled feuds, constitutes a most impractical criterion. However, Schneider's criticism of anthropologists for misusing the term "war" is erroneous; it is based on his contention that hostilities within a society that is segmented into exogamous groups (such as clans, lineages, or communities) cannot be called war (Schneider 1964, pp. 279, 282). He disregards the fact that exogamy is a social-structural feature and war is a political phenomenon and that, therefore, presence or absence of exogamy is irrelevant to this problem. To make the term "war" cross-culturally applicable and meaningful, one should define it in terms of political-structural features. Data on the Kapauku Papuans of New Guinea bear out the fallacy of such an analysis (Pospisil 1958). These Papuans live in localized exogamous lineages. Several lineages, belonging to different sibs, unite for defense purposes into a political confederacy. Beyond this unit no political organization exists. Interconfeder-

ational strife, which is true war, is marked by organization, by participation of whole confederacies as units in the fighting, and by ferocity involving slaughter, arson, rape, etc. On the contrary, fighting within a confederacy is done, as a rule, with sticks, not with bows and arrows, and does not result in death. No raping of women, burning of houses, killing of pigs, or destruction of gardens accompany these internal hostilities. To consider both types of fighting as feud would be to obscure rather than clarify the ethnological reality. Bearing the political-structural criteria of feud and war in mind, one can readily see how erroneous are the claims that war is uncommon or nonexistent in "the lowest stages" of social development (Hobhouse et al. [1915] 1930, p. 228) and that it requires for its existence a "certain development of social organization." Indeed, it is the feud that requires a complex social development—a large social entity with an over-all political organization that is segmented into subgroups.

Feud and law. The fact that feuds are fought between subgroups of a more inclusive grouping possessing an over-all network of political relations has led to the conclusion that feud is a primitive juridical mechanism and that it is an expression, or manifestation, of primitive law. Accordingly, Malinowski writes, "Fighting, collective and organized, is a juridical mechanism for the adjustment of differences between constituent groups of the same larger cultural unit" ([1941] 1961, p. 261). Spencer contends that after a north Alaskan Eskimo was killed, ". . . his own kin became embroiled and the legal mechanism of the feud was put into motion" (1959, p. 161). The notion that feuding is a manifestation of primitive law led Lasswell to the conclusion that there must be two types of feuds: "While the blood vengeance feud was itself the expression of primitive law, the modern feud is at least formally illegal and characteristically fills the interstices left in the functioning of the prevailing system of legal organization" (1931, p. 220). Many anthropologists have disagreed with the idea that feud is the expression of primitive law and have proposed or implied a unitary definition of feud. Hoebel (1949, p. 3) considers that feud lies outside the sphere of law. He bases this distinction on the fact that the counter-killings do not stop and that there is nothing one may regard as a mutually recognized coercive sanction against the killer and his group. Similarly, Bohannan (1963, p. 290) calls feud "a faulty jural mechanism" because it does not lead to a final settlement—to peace and rectitude. Radcliffe-Brown, on the other hand, refuses to regard feud as law, not because of its functional aspect, but because it lacks "the exercise of recognized authority in settling disputes" (1940, p. xx).

Pospisil (1956) defines law by means of four criteria, none of which is inherent in the phenomena of feuds: (1) law is manifested in a decision made by a political authority; (2) it contains a definition of the relation between the two parties to the dispute (*obligatio*); (3) it has a regularity of application (intention of universal application); (4) it is provided with a sanction. Law, which is characterized by these four criteria, is present in all societies—indeed, in every functioning group or subgroup of people—that he has investigated. In the primitive societies in which feud is endemic, law exists in those subgroups which have developed leadership, thus coexisting with feuds without incorporating them into the jural mechanism. Whereas law presupposes decisions passed by an authority holding jurisdiction over both litigants and a regular respect for, and compliance with, these decisions by the parties to the dispute, a feud represents an intergroup fight in which all the participants ignore and even defy the jurisdiction of the over-all political authority, which is usually weak or uninterested. Consequently, whereas law is a means of intragroup settlement of disputes, a feud—because of the feuding parties' defiance of the superordinated political structure—is basically an intergroup phenomenon, although it occurs within a more inclusive, politically organized unit. The difference between law and feud is again of political-structural nature, as are the differences between feud, war, and external redress. That law stands in opposition to feud and that the latter is actually the antithesis of the former rather than its manifestation, is well documented in those societies in which feuds are stopped by legal decisions of the over-all authority, who either has enough power to enforce his will or possesses the skill to persuade the quarreling parties to accept his solutions (see especially Nadel 1947, p. 154; Evans-Pritchard 1940, pp. 278–279).

Finally, it should be pointed out that not every case of "internal self-redress" constitutes a feud. When a counterkilling is accepted by the over-all political authority as a just punishment of the culprit or of his subgroup and the subgroup of the defender is induced or forced to accept such a verdict and to refrain from further counterkillings, the sanctioned reprisal constitutes a case of legal self-redress that is true law (Hoebel 1949, p. 3; Pospisil 1958, p. 256; Bohannan 1963, p. 290). Hoebel, for example, writes, "If the kin group of the original killer customarily accepts the action of the avengers as just, and stays its hands from further counterkilling, then we have legal law" (1949, p. 3).

In conclusion, we may summarize the salient features of feud and set it off from the related concepts of law, war, external self-redress, and legal self-redress. The essence of feud has been found to be a series (at least three instances) of acts of violence, usually involving killings, committed by members of two groups related to each other by superimposed political-structural features (often involving the existence of an over-all political authority) and acting on the basis of group solidarity (a common duty to avenge and a common liability). This definition sets feud apart from war and external self-redress because the last two terms refer to acts of violence committed by members of politically unrelated groups: in war both combat groups act as units in the organized fighting; in external self-redress members of two subgroups only, each belonging to a different, politically unrelated group, participate in the hostilities. This definition also distinguishes feud from law. Feud is an internal affair, conducted by members of the subgroups of an over-all political organization who ignore or even defy its political authority. In its conduct, then, feud refers to intergroup phenomena. Law, on the contrary, is an intragroup affair in the full sense of the term: a decision of the authority who holds jurisdiction over both parties to the dispute is passed, and both disputing parties are induced or forced to comply with its provisions.

LEOPOLD POSPISIL

[*See also* War. *Other relevant material may be found in* Judicial process, *article on* comparative aspects; Law, *article on* law and legal institutions; Political anthropology, *article on* political organization.]

BIBLIOGRAPHY

Bohannan, Paul 1963 *Social Anthropology.* New York: Holt.

Colson, Elizabeth 1962 *The Plateau Tonga of Northern Rhodesia.* Manchester (England) Univ. Press.

Evans-Pritchard, E. E. 1940 The Nuer of the Southern Sudan. Pages 272–296 in Meyer Fortes and E. E. Evans-Pritchard (editors), *African Political Systems.* Oxford Univ. Press.

Gluckman, Max 1940 *The Kingdom of the Zulu of South Africa.* Pages 25–55 in Meyer Fortes and E. E. Evans-Pritchard (editors), *African Political Systems.* Oxford Univ. Press.

Gluckman, Max (1956) 1959 *Custom and Conflict in Africa.* Glencoe, Ill.: Free Press.

Hobhouse, Leonard T.; Wheeler, Gerald C.; and Ginsberg, Morris (1915) 1930 *The Material Culture and Social Institutions of the Simpler Peoples: An*

Essay in Correlation. London School of Economics and Political Science Monographs on Sociology, No. 3. London: Chapman.

HOEBEL, E. ADAMSON 1949 Introduction. Pages 1–5 in Roy F. Barton, *The Kalingas.* Publications in Anthropology, Social Anthropological Series. Univ. of Chicago Press.

HOEBEL, E. ADAMSON 1954 *The Law of Primitive Man: A Study in Comparative Legal Dynamics.* Cambridge, Mass.: Harvard Univ. Press.

HONIGMAN, JOHN J. 1960 [Review of] *The North Alaskan Eskimo,* by Robert F. Spencer. *American Anthropologist* New Series 62:340–341.

LASSWELL, HAROLD D. 1931 Feuds. Volume 6, pages 220–221 in *Encyclopaedia of the Social Sciences.* New York: Macmillan.

LOWIE, ROBERT H. (1920) 1947 *Primitive Society.* New York: Liveright. → A paperback edition was published in 1961 by Harper.

MALINOWSKI, BRONISLAW (1941) 1964 An Anthropological Analysis of War. Pages 245–268 in Leon Bramson and George W. Goethals (editors), *War: Studies From Psychology, Sociology, Anthropology.* New York: Basic Books.

NADEL, SIEGFRIED F. 1947 *The Nuba: An Anthropological Study of the Hill Tribes in Kordofan.* London and New York: Oxford Univ. Press.

POSPISIL, LEOPOLD 1956 The Nature of Law. New York Academy of Sciences, *Transactions* 18:746–755.

POSPISIL, LEOPOLD 1958 *Kapauku Papuans and Their Law.* Yale University Publications in Anthropology, No. 54. New Haven: Yale Univ. Press.

POSPISIL, LEOPOLD 1964 Law and Societal Structure Among the Nunamiut Eskimo. Pages 395–431 in Ward H. Goodenough (editor), *Explorations in Cultural Anthropology: Essays in Honor of George Peter Murdock.* New York: McGraw-Hill.

RADCLIFFE-BROWN, A. R. 1940 Preface. In Meyer Fortes and E. E. Evans-Pritchard (editors), *African Political Systems.* Oxford Univ. Press.

RADCLIFFE-BROWN, A. R. 1952 *Structure and Function in Primitive Society: Essays and Addresses.* London: Cohen & West; Glencoe, Ill.: Free Press.

SCHNEIDER, JOSEPH 1964 Primitive Warfare: A Methodological Note. Pages 275–283 in Leon Bramson and George W. Goethals (editors), *War: Studies From Psychology, Sociology, Anthropology.* New York: Basic Books.

SPENCER, ROBERT F. 1959 *The North Alaskan Eskimo.* U.S. Bureau of American Ethnology, Bulletin No. 171. Washington: Government Printing Office.

WAGNER, GUNTHER 1940 The Political Organization of the Bantu of Kavirondo. Pages 197–238 in Meyer Fortes and E. E. Evans-Pritchard (editors), *African Political Systems.* Oxford Univ. Press.

WEDGWOOD, CAMILLA H. 1930 Some Aspects of Warfare in Melanesia. *Oceania* 1:5–33.

WRIGHT, QUINCY (1942) 1965 *A Study of War.* 2d ed. Univ. of Chicago Press.

FEUDALISM

Feudalism conventionally denotes the type of society and the political system originating in western and central Europe and dominant there during the greater part of the Middle Ages. However, the term is also applied to other societies and systems of government with similar characteristics, in antiquity and in modern times; in the Marxist usage it refers to a type of society and economy characterized by serfdom, generally succeeding the economic systems based on slavery and preceding capitalism.

The word from the Germanic *fehu-od* (from which is derived the English and French *fief*)—that is, "property in cattle" and, later, "tenure" or "property in land"—stresses the importance, in the system, of land tenure and the rights and privileges attached to it. Since the seventeenth century, the complex of tenurial and personal relationships and economic, social, and political dependencies that centered on the fief have increasingly been regarded as a scaffold of social stratification and political organization. This view, often reflecting actual political and social problems in eighteenth-century England and France, created the notion of a period dominated by "feudal laws" (Montesquieu) that were comprehensive enough to denote a regime and to dominate and rule a society. The later meaning of the word, although basically rooted in eighteenth-century usage, came to denote, through abuse of language, such social realities as the political predominance of a landholding aristocracy and the exploitation of the small and weak by the powerful. It also came to denote any political system in which the power of the state was weakened or paralyzed by the privileges of the few and made inefficient by the fractioning of political power, or by the opposition of powerful political or economic aristocratic factions.

Historical scholarship since the nineteenth century has brought to light more and more of the variety of economic, social, and political forms to be found in feudal societies at any one time, as well as the changes inevitable in any social and political framework lasting over five hundred years. Nevertheless, some major features do recur, and a certain rhythm of evolution seems to have been common to rather large areas as they reacted to similar economic, social, and political changes. Hence, it is possible to speak about feudal institutions without implying that all aspects of economic, social, and political life predominant in the greater part of the European Middle Ages were always present. Such institutions can also be found in other societies; sometimes they evolve from similar conditions, but often they are isolated phenomena in different frameworks or without the interrelations deemed essential in the European system. (In these cases the term "feudal tendencies" might be a better description.)

Despite the great variety of definitions of feudalism, some minimal common characteristics of a fully developed feudal system would be accepted by most scholars. These include: (1) lord–vassal relationships; (2) a personalized government that is most effective on the local level and has relatively little separation of political functions; (3) a system of landholding consisting of the granting of fiefs in return for service and assurance of future services; (4) the existence of private armies and a code of honor in which military obligations are stressed; and (5) seignorial and manorial rights of the lord over the peasant (see Coulborn 1956; Hall 1962).

Perhaps the fullest definition of feudalism in the political sphere was given by Weber ([1922] 1957, pp. 375–376), who considered feudalism one type of "patriarchal authority." According to Weber: (1) The authority of the chief is reduced to the likelihood that the vassals will voluntarily remain faithful to their oaths of fealty. (2) The political corporate group is completely replaced by a system of relations of purely personal loyalty between the lord and his vassals and between these, in turn, and their own subvassals (subinfeudation). (3) Only in the case of a "felony" does the lord have a right to deprive his vassal of his fief. (4) There is a hierarchy of social rank, corresponding to the hierarchy of fiefs, but it is not a hierarchy of authority in the bureaucratic sense. (5) The elements in the population who do not hold fiefs with some political authority are "subjects"—that is, patrimonial dependents. (6) Powers over the individual budgetary unit (domains, slaves, and serfs), the fiscal rights of the political group to the receipt of taxes and contributions, and powers of jurisdiction and compulsion to military service are all objects of feudal grants.

In the social sector an important element of feudalism is the bearing of arms as a class-defining profession. Here feudalism is distinguished by a relative closing of the social status system in which (for the groups dependent primarily on the land) the distribution of goods and services is closely integrated with the hierarchy of social statuses. Within the economic sector feudal government and society appear uniformly to rest upon a landed, or locally self-sufficient, economic base as distinguished from a pastoral, commercial, or industrial one. The merchant community, although it may play a significant role in the economy, is essentially outside the feudal nexus. The appearance of certain technological features of government and economy, notably centralized communications and means of large-scale political organization, serve to undermine the feudal institutions (Hall 1962).

Whatever the variations within the economic, social, or political sphere, perhaps the most important problem in the analysis of feudal societies or systems is the extent to which in any given place we can find these feudal characteristics developing or coexisting in all the major institutional spheres. The classical age of feudalism is usually dated from the eleventh to the thirteenth centuries and located in northern France. Other societies in different historical periods, whether European or non-European, are compared to this northern French society to determine the extent to which feudal institutions and tendencies developed within them.

Feudalism in western Europe

The specific features of feudalism were the outcome of the encounter of two types of society, the Romanized and the Germanic. Their fusion into a new society, the Romano–Germanic, was accompanied by a merging and reshaping of their respective institutions. Neither the German nor the Roman traditions were homogeneous, and throughout central and western Europe they differed according to the strength of the local (often pre-Roman, Celtic) institutions and the effectiveness of Romanization, on the one hand, and the distance of the new Germanic societies from their earlier, preinvasion habitats, on the other.

At the time of their encounter, both societies were in a state of transition. The late Roman or Romanized West was passing through the profound crisis of a disintegrating empire, a weakening of central power, and a dislocation of the bureaucratic state machinery; the economic breakdown was seen in the diminishing importance of cities as centers of administration and of specialized economic activities, in the process of devaluation, and in the slowing down of the money economy. State and society were groping for new norms of existence. Public authority was delegated to the great landowners, who already exercised some authority over their immediate dependents; economic life was shifting from city to countryside and was concentrated on the larger estates, which tried to achieve autarchy in supplying their needs; insecurity was creating private warrior bands; freed slaves were being absorbed into the peasantry, who lost their status as free men to become the dependent semiservile "colonate." The Germanic tribes (*Sippen*), through migration and settlement, had loosened or lost their tribal ties. There remained the cohesion of families and of the newer and weaker village communities, which in time came to represent territorial units rather than strong kinship relations. The transition from tribal to state organization continued in the fifth and sixth centuries, but the lack of a competent administration combined with an extremely low level of literacy and restricted money circulation helped to weaken the traditional units; nowhere was a state structure able to take over and to fulfill its public duties.

The early medieval state, like that of the Frankish Merovingians (end of the fifth to beginning of the eighth century), presents, consequently, a juxtaposition of divergent elements of state and society (hardly ever integrated into a coherent whole). From this point of view, the features associated with feudalism are the direct outcome of a society striving for patterns of organization and cohesion in a period of declining state power and the disruption of traditional kinship security groups.

The most striking feature of the developing system is the new stratification of society. Roman social hierarchy was far more polarized than that of the Germanic tribes. The latter, although not egalitarian, as some nineteenth-century historians claimed, was basically a society of free men with a charismatic and hereditary chieftainship. The new administrative and military needs had already singled out the royal Merovingian entourage of warriors and officials and had sanctioned their standing by a higher *Wergeld*. At the beginning of the eighth century, however, the permanent need for professional, highly trained military men (mounted warriors) brought about a radical change in society. The former peasant–warrior lost his military value. Private bands of warriors, a phenomenon that had its antecedents as much in the imperial bodyguard and in the private armies of the Roman senatorial class as in the ancient Germanic followers (*Gefolgschaft*) of the chieftain, sprang up around the king and local magnates.

Vassalage. The nexus between the chieftain and his free followers was taken over by the institution of *vassalage* (although the word itself points to a more humble origin, as "vassal" derives from the Celtic *gwas*, meaning "youngster" or "servant"). Beginning in the early Carolingian period (eighth century), the new institution was integrated into the framework of state and society until it became official, recognized and sanctioned in public law and put to the service of the state. With the tremendous expansion of the empire of Charles the Great and for two centuries thereafter, vassalage as a type of social cohesion became the normal way of assuring not only military service but also public authority. Although the ancient oath of fealty of subjects to the ruler remained, it was felt that it did not sufficiently assure either loyalty or political allegiance. Consequently, an oath of vassalage, more binding and directly linked with the ruler, was demanded from appointed officials. The

heads of military and administrative circumscriptions—dukes, marquis, and counts—became vassals of the king. This new type of relation, which abandoned the charismatic character of the earlier period, was based mainly on the notions of fealty and absolute loyalty, strengthened by the religious element inherent in the oath itself, and it bound the contracting parties in a contractual relation.

The principles of vassalic relations, first applied at the highest state level, spread rapidly to the lower rungs of the social ladder. Magnates and royal officials assured their own standing and the performance of the services of their office by contracting vassals, and the same process continued downward to the simple warrior and local administrative officer. Thus, a pyramidal structure of bonds and dependencies arose, a scaffold of state structure and state machinery, the apex of which, ideally, was the king.

Economic and social relations. The economic premises of the new social order were rooted in early medieval economy and grew out of the same social changes that made vassalic relations possible. The weakening of the *Sippe* not only created insecurity but also changed the economic bases of existence. The village community, far weaker than the *Sippe* organization, could not offer adequate security, and social cohesion took the new form of individuals seeking the protection of the powerful man in their vicinity, drawing both on the patron–client pattern of the Roman tradition and on the Germanic notion of *Grundherr*, the rich and strong proprietor, whose influence transcended the boundaries of his property and his direct dependents. Such proprietors included ecclesiastical institutions as well as secular lords. The peasants—and often whole villages—commended themselves into the protection of the powerful, relinquishing their property and receiving it back as a "precarium" (from *preco*, "to beg for"), a possession (later, hereditary tenure) burdened by certain economic obligations. Conversely, they received the protection of the establishment or the lay lord. This protection against outside (fiscal, administrative, military, or juridical) pressures not only made the peasant economically dependent but also initiated the process through which he lost his standing as free man and citizen. His dealings with state authority were henceforth channeled through his overlord. In this sense, the king, who combined competences of state sovereignty (often theoretical in the ninth and tenth centuries) and vassalic suzerainty, lost his subjects, whom he could reach only through the mediation of their overlords.

The material basis of the vassalic contract was

the fief. This was usually an agricultural territory (but there existed also money fiefs) granted by the lord to the vassal at the "homage" (from *homo*, "man") ceremony when the vassal swore to serve the lord as his "man." At the highest level of the feudal echelon the fief was usually a seigniory— that is, an economic and political entity invested with public powers of administration, taxation, and jurisdiction. A seigniory might comprise anything from a single village to a large complex of villages. It was the degree of public authority and the degree of immunity from the interference of an overlord which differentiated it from a simple fief and fixed its place in the hierarchy of fiefs in the kingdom. The seigniory comprised, as a rule, a large territory where the exercise of public rights was shared, in different degrees, by the lord and the men who became his vassals ("subvassals" of the overlord) through enfeoffment and homage. Public power became an object of inheritance, since it accompanied the inheritance of the fiefs and seigniories.

At the bottom of the feudal ladder was the simple knight who owed to the overlord his own service and was supported by a fief just large enough to assure him a living in keeping with the standards of his class. Such a fief could coincide with a village or part of it, and its economic organization was usually described as a manorial economy. The lord of the manor also had noneconomic rights over the tenants on his manor, the most characteristic being the rights of jurisdiction deriving from land tenure.

The movement of commendation, common to all strata of society, brought about a complete transformation of its social stratification and cohesion and, finally, of the concepts of the state and its authority. Thousands of links of dependence ran from the apex to the lowest echelons of society. Their scope, meaning, and aim changed from step to step. Whereas in higher echelons commendation created a professional caste of warriors soon to become the nobility, in the lower echelons it created a class of people serving the lords in different capacities. As long as the service was basically military, the link of commendation created vassalage, which had come to be regarded as the only condition fitting a free man. Lower down, commendation created serfdom of varying degrees, but always connoting economic dependence, social degradation, and exclusion from the community of free men and subjects.

The hierarchic principle of cohesion and dependence was sustained economically by the legal hierarchy of land and by the fixed relation of men to land. Only where feudalization did not penetrate the depth of society were there free communities, direct subjects of royalty, and allodial (entirely independent) property. Ireland and Scotland preserved clannish cohesion; Frisia preserved independent communities; in Saxony and parts of Spain there were free men; and German nobility kept allodial property late into the twelfth century. In all other territories all land except the royal domain had the legal status of tenure or dependent possession.

The main economic feature of the fief was the holder's privilege not to work the land himself but to receive income in specie, money, and work from the peasant population. The peasants themselves held their land as servile tenures astricted as to payments and services, which varied widely according to the type of servile tenure. But it is a striking feature of the system that the obligations of the peasant were those deriving from his own legal status and that of the land he held. The theoretical symmetry between the status of a man and that of his holding was soon destroyed by marriage and inheritance. A serf might, for example, be the tenant of a "free mansus" (*mansus*, "a unit of family holding"), his duties deriving from his status as serf and the obligations inherent in the free mansus.

Stabilization of the system. Around 1100 the major features of feudalism began to stabilize and integrate into a coherent politico–economic system. Yet, complete integration was never achieved. Rights of possession, economic privileges, and public authority often remained undefined, consequently competing and overlapping. Starting in the second half of the twelfth century, political theoreticians with legal training tried to describe the institutions of government and society as forming a logical whole. One of the stabilizing factors was the general rule linking vassalage with fiefs and their regular, hereditary transmission. Occurring on all levels of the feudal hierarchy, it assured a solid scaffold of social structure. Not only were the simple knight, his immediate overlord, and every lord up to the apex of the feudal hierarchy henceforth concerned with fiefs and seigniories, as pure vassalage links would have postulated, but the family as a whole became a major factor in the feudal mechanism. On the upper level of the hierarchy, that of the great tenants-in-chief of the crown with quasi-state authority, it was the dynasty that counted. Below them, the traditional vassals of the dynasty were often regarded not only as members of the household (*maisnie*) but as a part of the noble lineage (*lignage*). The relations between lords and vassals were often conceived in terms of family relations, and the competences of the lord were not unlike the Germanic *mundeburdum* or the Roman *patria potestas*. The custom of sending the vassals' children to be raised at the court of the overlord strengthened this type of relation, as did the meetings of the vassals at the lord's court in times of festivity, which were held as much for business reasons as for socializing.

Rise of the nobility. In the twelfth century a two-hundred-year-old process of class formation came to an end, producing a class of nobility. The old warrior class of the eighth century was by then a class pursuing the profession of arms, which assured it a privileged place in society and a major share in political power; moreover, it was a class which could transmit its economic, social, and political standing to its descendants, becoming, consequently, a hereditary nobility. Despite the marked differences within the class itself, differences based primarily on the extent of political power and the control of economic resources, all fief holders regarded themselves, and were regarded by others, as the highest class in society.

The most characteristic feature of the military nobility was its new warrior ideal—the knight. "Knighthood" was a designation of rank and dignity; it was, by implication, the expression of the new ethos—chivalrousness. Fusing ancient Germanic ideals of the "heroic age" with newer concepts of ecclesiastical origin, chivalry (from *chevalier*, "a mounted warrior") expressed the worldly ideals of the fighting class and the new ethical teachings of the church. Fighting should not be an end in itself but should serve social and religious ideals in a basically other-world-oriented society. Biblical virtues—the protection of women, the weak, and the poor and the defense of religion—were the aims that enabled the church to sanction war and bloodshed. The ideal of the "Christian knight" (*miles Christianus*) which represented the ethos of the warrior caste, imprinted its character on the period. Its early, extreme theoretical formulation was by Bernard of Clairvaux, who regarded the knight as a permanent candidate for martyrdom, and its early institutionalization was in the military orders created at the time of the Crusades in the Holy Land and the Christian reconquest of Spain.

The ideals of monasticism and warriorship merged into the ideal of the Christian knight par excellence. Chivalry became institutionalized, adopting a military–ecclesiastical initiation rite ("dubbing") and elaborating a code of behavior and a set of virtues fitting a member of the class. Henceforth, membership in the nobility depended not only on origin but on the formal act of "knighting." The chivalrous virtues and rules of behavior and the image the class had of itself were perpetu-ated by upbringing and education. The noble child passed a period of graded apprenticeship, living with a noble family (very often the vassal's overlord) before dubbing, which could be given only by someone who was himself a knight. The introduction of chivalric rites and what became in the later part of the thirteenth century a formal code of chivalrous behavior made the noble class more exclusive, thus affecting social mobility. The code became, especially after the fourteenth century, extremely formalized and served to exclude nonmembers who acquired economic position in nonnoble pursuits (commerce and banking) and who, by buying fiefs, tried to penetrate the ranks of nobility. It also excluded knights who engaged in commercial pursuits.

While the nobility was guarding its ranks against outsiders, its own internal differentiation proceeded swiftly. The baronial class, in many cases, split into magnates, "greater barons," or *grandes*; beneath them "smaller barons," or *hidalgos*; and below them simple knights. Although social mobility existed, it tended to be rather limited. Marriages and dowries were usually contracted in a closed class market, and marriage with a lower-born noble was regarded with disdain. Local variations always existed—for example, social mobility was greater in England than on the Continent, and German *ministeriales* (sometimes serfs but in any case not nobles) in royal military service were ennobled and could exercise the highest state functions, even at the end of the twelfth century (although Germany at this time was not yet entirely feudalized). The features and ideals of the nobility that are described above survived long after the class lost its political standing and parts of its economic position or even economic privileges.

Growth of political units. As the links of cohesion strengthened, the administrative framework, grouping fiefs and seigniories into larger political units, became clearer. Generally speaking, there were two main lines of development. One was the creation of strong local principalities (Anjou, Normandy, Flanders), which at the turn of the eleventh century succeeded in dominating the different seigniories in their territories, recapturing some of the public authority (control of castles and mints —in some places a monopoly of the princely dynasty), and often developing princely bureaucratic administrations. This process built up the strong centralized provinces, which during the next hundred years were taken over by the Capetians and became the foundations of the kingdom of France.

The second line was followed by Germany. In twelfth-century Germany, less feudalized than France, public authority was often still in the hands of local princely dynasties with allodial possessions, who exercised their competences not as the king's vassals but, theoretically, as his officials. Their power was strengthened at the beginning of the century when the "quarrel of investiture" weakened the standing of royalty. To create stronger cohesion and forge links of dependence, the crown tried to bring the highest nobility into direct vassalic dependence, in the process resigning to it public authority in the principalities. The principalities, by forging vassalic links with the local nobility, were supposed to become well-ordered administrative units directed by the crown. The principalities achieved, indeed, strong governments, but the crown never succeeded in bringing them into a rigid state framework. Germany, especially after the interregnum at the end of the Hohenstaufen dynasty (middle of thirteenth century), was made up of principalities and their rulers (*Länder* and *Landesherren*) within a loose framework of the empire. Legislation forced the emperor to enfeoff noble escheats, which could otherwise have enlarged the royal domain and thus strengthened his position at the expense of the princely class. Finally, the principle of election of the emperor by the imperial electors (*Kurfürsten*) assured their dominance. Consequently, Germany never reached any degree of state unity. On the contrary, the principalities became independent, strongly organized states, with princely power based on authority delegated by the emperor and on vassalic links obligatory within their territories. In England, after the Norman conquest, sovereignty and suzerainty assured a preponderant power to the crown. Feudal particularistic tendencies, brought to light in the middle of the twelfth century by rival claims to the throne, were quickly checked, leaving royalty in full possession of its powers. In Italy the development followed the lines of Germany, but the place of the principalities was taken by the emerging cities, the "communes," which created territorial units virtually independent of the central power.

The decline of feudalism. The decline of feudalism was a general phenomenon of European history that owed as much to the economic transformations of the twelfth and thirteenth centuries as it did to features inherent in the feudal system itself. The economic transformations were the result of the twelfth-century "urban revolution." The revival of money economy, the renewal of city life with its more complex division of labor, the rise of the new social stratum of burgesses—all proclaimed new needs and new possibilities. They enabled the state to perform and enlarge its functions without constant recourse to feudal services. The new mar-

ket situation enabled the peasants to accumulate money from the sale of surplus production and initiated the commutation of manorial services into money payments. The final result was the disruption of the manorial economy and a profound change in the standing of the nobility.

Insecurity decreased in the far better policed states of the central Middle Ages, and the rural population did not depend for its survival or defense on the local magnate. The political power he wielded could be, and was, more efficiently used by state officials. Inherited political power consequently lost its practical and moral justification.

The change in the position of the feudal lord is even more marked when compared with the all-important lord–vassal relations of the earlier period. As already mentioned, the inheritance of fiefs greatly contributed to the solidity of the system. At the same time, it brought with it a notable change in the feudo–vassalic establishment. As heredity was the rule and the renewal of the vassalic oath usually only a formality, the economic element in the relationship overshadowed the personal and intimate elements. Previously undefined and unlimited duties of service were replaced by fixed and measured obligations. Thus, the military service was fixed for 40 days yearly; other aids and services were measured in stereotyped proportions according to the size of the fief. The fact that from the end of the tenth century a vassal could hold fiefs from different lords created a problem of multiple, often opposed, loyalties.

The weakening of the ties of dependence in the upper strata of society and the process of dissolution on the manorial level brought about a complete transformation in patterns of social cohesion and state organization. Different strata of society became crystallized in the pattern of "estates." The estate grouped people of the same social class, who had a similar economic standing and enjoyed the same privileged position in the state in relation to the crown and to other estates. Unlike the former feudal links of cohesion, which were vertical, the new links binding man to man were horizontal. Men joining others of their own class sought assurance and confirmation of their privileged position more than security and protection. A man's standing was no longer described in terms of dependence on a feudal overlord, but in terms of his belonging to a given "estate." The hierarchic pattern continued to exist but as a hierarchy of strata of society rather than a hierarchy of individuals. Moreover there were no formal links of dependence between the different estates. In a sense, all were in direct relation to the crown, and all claimed a share in political power, whether on the national or the local level.

Feudalism in other areas

Japan. Outside western Europe, the greatest convergence of feudal characteristics in the various institutional spheres probably occurred in Japan, where it developed at the end of the twelfth century and persisted in its "pure" form until the Tokugawa regime. Here we may follow Hall's analysis (1962).

The origin of feudalism in Japan seems to have coincided with the establishment of the Kamakura shogunate by Minamoto Yoritomo in 1192. Although vassalage and enfeoffment may have existed even before the twelfth century, only a small portion of Japanese society was organized around these practices by 1192. In Japan during the Kamakura period (1185–1333) the legal government was still centered on the emperor. It operated through the traditional civil administration (greatly weakened) and an expanding system of semipublic domains (*shōen*). Independent of these administrative and fiscal relationships, there were numerous more informal hierarchies based upon clan ties and military allegiances. Military hierarchies tended to form around the local magnates. It was primarily through the development of hierarchies of such allegiances as they came to center upon the office of shogun, or military dictator (or on certain other high military posts), that feudal institutions crystallized.

Yoritomo's importance to the development of feudalism in Japan lay in regularizing and extending the practice of pledges of military allegiance combined with protection of landholdings. Yoritomo's authority to appoint *shugo*, or "constables," and *jitō*, or "stewards," and to interfere in the *shōen* system was based on his assertion of supreme military command in a time of national crisis. Through such appointments and through the increase of legal powers, the feudal nexus in government and society steadily encroached upon the imperial–*shōen* complex, giving rise to a new type of institutional nexus.

At the apex of the state structure military authority gradually overshadowed civil authority, and during the thirteenth century the balance between civil and military power shifted steadily in the direction of the latter. Similarly, at the provincial level, military interests gained over civilian as the *shugo* increasingly took on the stature of military governors. Locally, the *shugo* were able to build up their economic support largely through the plural holding of *jitō* rights to numerous *shōen*. They used their superior status in the shogunal hierarchy to assert their influence among local *bushi*, or members of the military class. Before long the *shugo* had absorbed many civil administrative powers at the same time that they achieved personal leadership of province-wide military bands, which they organized increasingly on a lord–vassal basis. Below the *shugo* the step-by-step expansion of the *jitō*'s land rights among the *bushi* also served to extend the feudal element in Japanese society.

As local *bushi* became *ryōshu*, or landed proprietors, they began to divide these lands among family members or retainers, extending the practice of combining grants of land with ties of military loyalty. The new military bonds forged between *shugo* and proprietary *jitō* or between *jitō* and vassal families became the basis of this ever-widening feudal system of social and political organization.

The warfare that embroiled most of Japan during the middle of the fourteenth century hastened feudal trends in all parts of the country. Under the Ashikaga shogunate (1338–1573) the imperial center lost all of its effective power. The shogunate, now located at the very seat of the imperial court in Kyoto, absorbed most of the powers and functions of the civil government, although even now the emperor continued to play a crucial role as the ritual symbol of sovereignty and the source of the shogun's delegated authority.

In the provinces the key figures were the *shugo*, who by the end of the fourteenth century had developed into true regional overlords, having acquired the combined powers of the former civil and military governors. They held title, under the shogun, to territories the size of entire provinces, serving as the ultimate authority in both civil and military affairs.

By 1500, however, most of the jurisdictional territories of the *shugo* had been broken into fragments and a wave of new magnates of local origin had inherited the pieces. The *shugo* had disappeared and with them not only a generation of *bushi* leaders but also the last remnants of imperial law and civil land management based on the *shōen*.

The end of this relatively "pure" type of feudalism came in Japan with the more centralized Tokugawa regime (1603–1867). Although based on the feudal structures and to some extent perpetuating them, this regime, through its policy of centralization, in fact froze the feudal institutions, depriving them of vitality and autonomy.

Japanese feudalism differed from the European pattern in several important respects: (1) the continuous importance of the imperial center in spite of its loss of political function; (2) the weakness, perhaps even total absence, of contractual elements in the relations between lords and vassals; (3) the full, personal, familistic expression of these relations; and (4) the lack of any representative institutions. Nevertheless, like the European pattern, it is a major example of feudalism, since it clearly demonstrated a relatively high degree of convergence of feudal characteristics in the different institutional spheres.

Russia. In other societies the extent of such convergence was smaller. The regime of the feudal (patrimonial) principality in medieval Russia was accompanied by a certain immunity from political authority, conferred by private possession of land. The connection became firmly established because of the importance of military functions in local politics in pre-Muscovite central Russia and, later, its national importance in Muscovy. Whenever possession of land was hereditary, the authority connected with it was also hereditary. This was the normal pattern in pre-Muscovite times, and it again became general in the seventeenth century, the nonhereditary *pomest'e* ("benefice" or "military holding") being merely a historical interlude, even if a rather long one. In pre-Muscovite Russia the essential sociopolitical relation was not between lord and vassal but between the *votchinnik* ("patrimonial lord") and the population of his *votchina* ("landed possession" or "patrimony"), which came close to that of ruler and subject. There was no link between the prince's service and possession of land, and although there was hereditary landholding, the prince's service was not hereditary, and subjects were free to leave their principalities. Yet, even though the *pomest'e* was not hereditary, there was a connection between military function and possession of land. It was based not on a feudal contract involving mutual fealty between a suzerain and a vassal, but rather on the absolute sovereignty of the tsar, who, requiring service from any of his subjects, granted a *pomest'e* in return for such service (Szeftel 1956).

Three distinct types of sociopolitical structure are relevant to Russian feudalism: the *votchina* regime, the *pomest'e* regime, and Western feudalism.

The *votchina* regime was characterized by the growth of the manorial power of the lord of the estate over the population laboring on it or merely settled in its vicinity. Such power could be enforced by immunity privileges. The *votchina* estates were owned by political rulers (princes), by private persons, or by the church. Although it represented, to a certain extent, the social aspects of feudal tendencies the *votchina* system did not contain a counterpart to the political aspects. There was no formal political connection between the vassal's service and the control of the land.

The *pomest'e* regime tended to make the control of the land depend on service rendered to the state by the landholder. There was no dispersion of political power in this regime as it grew up in the Muscovite state of the sixteenth and seventeenth centuries. The power was concentrated in the person of the supreme ruler, the tsar.

In the *standard type* of feudalism (Western feudalism) some characteristics of both the *votchina* and the *pomest'e* regimes are combined. However, for this type to develop, certain traits which were lacking in either or both of these regimes are essential. Like the *votchina* regime, the standard type of feudalism presupposes the expansion of the manor and the growth of the manorial rights of the lord. On the other hand, like the *pomest'e* regime, feudalism of the standard type is characterized by the conditionality of rights on the land. The control of the land by the lower-class landlord depends on the service he renders to the seignior.

The important point of difference between the *pomest'e* regime and feudalism of the standard type is that while in the former political power is concentrated in the hands of the supreme ruler, in the latter the political authority is usually dispersed. Thus, no lord–vassal relationship of the western European type could develop in pre-Muscovite Russia, no code of chivalry was based on it, and there could be no consistent heredity of functions.

The key to understanding the differences between the Russian and Western developments is the great migratory and resettlement movement in medieval central Russia. This mobility of the rural population was fundamentally caused by the rapid exhaustion of soil that was not too fertile to begin with and by extensive primitive agriculture. Although the movement produced some feudal traits in Russian life, it was also the source of instability in social relationships. In Russia the shifting local population did not provide the "free servant" with many bases to rely on, and there was no other protection for his liberty than the temporary character of his service and the right of free departure.

Byzantium. The constellation of feudal characteristics in the Byzantine Empire was rather different from that found in Russia, centering primarily on the system of the *pronoia* ("providence," "foresight," "care"). To give lands to a person in *pronoia* is to give lands into his care. In practice it meant that estates were given for administration to high officers of the state or army, to monasteries, and to private persons, as a reward for services.

The grants differed from simple donations in that the *pronoia* land was bound to the recipient, the *pronoiarios*; that he received it for a definite period only, usually for life; that he could not sell the *pronoia* estate; and that it was not hereditary.

The system developed under the eleventh-century Byzantine rulers who tried to reduce the power of the military class and to increase that of the civil bureaucracy by demilitarizing the administration. This policy clearly reflected the decay of the former organization of the military–peasant colonies (*themes*). The military commander (*strategos*), who usually served as governor of a province, was replaced by the *practor*, who had been the supreme justice on the staff of the *strategos*. The *practor*, of course, was a civilian, and thus, the primacy of the military command in the *themes* gave way to the primacy of a civilian administration based upon the new aristocracy of scholars and civilians in the capital.

But the preponderance of the civilian aristocracy in the capital did not lead to a strengthening of the central power in the rural districts. Generals and great landowners outweighed the civilians. The emperors of the Ducas dynasty had already been compelled to give great privileges both to their civilian adherents and to their military or landowning adversaries; with the accession of Alexius Comnenus, 1081–1118, the military aristocracy took over the state. It was under the Ducas that the *pronoia* system was first developed and that Byzantium approached quasi feudalization. The new class of the *pronoia* owners became liable for military service, replacing the former class of peasant soldiers of the decaying system. The owner of a *pronoia* estate, when summoned, had to appear with a certain number of horsemen, according to the size of the *pronoia*.

Since within the *pronoia* the formerly free peasants became more or less serfs, they came under the jurisdiction of the *pronoiarios*, although this jurisdiction was restricted. The central government, thus, gave up many of its prerogatives including that of direct taxation, and the *pronoiarios* became small rulers, whose estates appeared as little kingdoms within the empire. The crown became more and more dependent on them, which contributed to the weakening of the central government and to the decline and disintegration of the empire (Ostrogorski 1940; Kantorowicz 1956).

In sum, Byzantine feudalism was characterized by the relative predominance of economically independent small estates combined with a growing political decentralization—without, however, the concomitant development of an over-all system of vassalage, a feudal–chivalrous military class, or special feudal political institutions.

Parallel cases. The Byzantine type of feudalism is found in many other societies, especially in periods of the decline of great empires—to some extent at the end of the Roman Empire, in the later Sassanid period in Iran, and in the aftermath of Aśoka's kingdom in India. In many cases institutions of this type of feudalism developed when officials abused their rights to collect taxes and turned their offices into hereditary fiefs. In other cases the political traits of feudalism (usually many politically self-sufficient patrimonial units having some interrelations and an orientation toward one budding center) were more highly developed than feudal economic characteristics. Such cases can be found in China under the Shang and, even more clearly, under the Chou; in ancient Mesopotamia under the Kassites, in Mittani, in the Iran of the Parthian regime, in the *iqtâ'* institution of medieval Islam, and possibly in ancient Egypt.

In none of these cases, however, was there a fully developed system of vassal–lord relations or a full-fledged social organization of a military–political class. At most, only rudiments of each existed.

Emergence and demise of feudal systems

In spite of all the differences in their origins and features, the feudal systems of the various societies analyzed above—and many more could be included —manifest some common characteristics. Perhaps most important is that they played a major role in the development of "high" cultures or civilizations. Feudal systems can be found, even if in varying degrees, in almost all of the great civilizations of the past, where they were central in keeping and developing great traditions under circumstances often inimical to their maintenance.

The importance of this characteristic can best be seen by examining the varying conditions under which feudal institutions develop. One such set of conditions is the *partial* dismemberment of relatively comprehensive, widespread sociopolitical systems (Hintze 1929; Coulborn 1956). The reasons for such dismemberment may vary greatly: the clash of cultures, the invasions of nomads, or the development of internal contradictions that cause the imperial system to lose its effectiveness and its essential resources. However, the dismemberment is not by itself crucial to the development of feudalism; rather, it is the combination of the dismemberment and the persistence or development of the ideals of a "great empire" and of orientations toward broader societal frameworks among some of the elite groups (such as the church or the new military class) who gain control over the governmental and economic functions and the contradictions between the idea of an empire and the lack of material and administrative positions to administer one. In some cases, such as that of Chinese feudalism, these orientations were developed by active groups that were unable to establish any viable broader system but, nevertheless, developed some vision of such a system. [See EMPIRES.]

Within most feudal systems, ideological orientations to such broader frameworks were of great importance, even if they were only partially institutionalized. Any feudal system is, thus, always characterized by some inherent imbalances in its structure, as it contains more and less differentiated centripetal and centrifugal structures and orientations. However, the exact location of such institutional imbalances in any feudal system—whether in the economic, political, or cultural sphere—varies greatly.

The demise of the feudal system is predicated on changes in those conditions—technological, political, and economic—that increase the effectiveness of the wider frameworks and that may enable the restoration or the establishment of unitary frameworks and of central powers within them. In less differentiated societies this can give rise to a restoration of patrimonial or imperial systems. In more differentiated societies—as in western Europe and in Japan—the feudal background made the later transition to modernity easier and more stable, and in some cases, it might have facilitated—after a period of the "estate" system or of absolutism—the development of a relatively pluralistic system.

JOSHUA PRAWER AND
SHMUEL N. EISENSTADT

[See also BUREACRACY; EMPIRES; MANORIAL ECONOMY; VILLAGE. Other relevant material may be found in EVOLUTION, article on SOCIAL EVOLUTION; KINSHIP; STATUS, SOCIAL; and in the biographies of BLOCH; BÜCHER; FUSTEL DE COULANGES; GIERKE.]

BIBLIOGRAPHY

BARRACLOUGH, GEOFFREY (editor) (1938) 1948 Mediaeval Germany, 911–1250: Essays by German Historians. 2 vols. Oxford: Blackwell.

BLOCH, MARC 1931 (1952–1956) Les caractères originaux de l'histoire rurale française. New ed. 2 vols. Paris: Colin.

BLOCH, MARC 1932 Feudalism, European. Volume 6, pages 203–210 in Encyclopaedia of the Social Sciences. New York: Macmillan.

BLOCH, MARC (1939–1940) 1961 Feudal Society. Univ. of Chicago Press. → First published in French.

BLOCH, MARC (1941) 1942 The Rise of Dependent Cultivation and Seigniorial Institutions. Volume 1, pages 224–277 in The Cambridge Economic History of Europe From the Decline of the Roman Empire. Cambridge Univ. Press.

BODDE, DERK 1956 Feudalism in China. Pages 49–92 in Rushton Coulborn (editor), Feudalism in History. Princeton Univ. Press.

BOUTRUCHE, ROBERT 1959 Seigneurie et féodalité. Volume 1: Le premier âge des liens d'homme à homme. Paris: Aubier.

BRUNDAGE, BURR C. 1956 Feudalism in Ancient Mesopotamia and Iran. Pages 93–119 in Rushton Coulborn (editor), Feudalism in History. Princeton Univ. Press.

CAHEN, CLAUDE 1940 Le régime féodal de l'Italie normande. Paris: Geuthner.

CAHEN, CLAUDE 1953 L'évolution de l'iqtâ' du IXᵉ au XIIIᵉ siècle: Contribution à une histoire comparée des sociétés médiévales. Annales: Économies, sociétés, civilisations 8:25–52.

CAHEN, CLAUDE 1960 Réflexion sur l'usage du mot "féodalité." Journal of the Economic and Social History of the Orient 3:2–20.

CALMETTE, JOSEPH (1923) 1947 La société féodale. 6th ed. Paris: Colin.

CAM, HELEN M. (1950) 1963 England Before Elizabeth. 2d ed., rev. London: Hutchinson's University Library.

CHARANIS, PETER 1944/1945 On the Social Structure of the Later Roman Empire. Byzantion 17:39–57.

CHARANIS, PETER 1948 The Monastic Properties of the State in the Byzantine Empire. Dumbarton Oaks Papers No. 4:51–118.

CHARANIS, PETER 1951 On the Social Structure and Economic Organization of the Byzantine Empire in the Thirteenth Century and Later. Byzantinoslavica 12:94–153.

COULBORN, RUSHTON (editor) 1956 Feudalism in History. Princeton Univ. Press.

CRONNE, H. A. 1939 The Origins of Feudalism. History New Series 24:251–259.

DUBY, GEORGES 1961 Une enquête à poursuivre: La noblesse dans la France médiévale. Revue historique 226:1–22.

EDGERTON, WILLIAM F. 1956 The Question of Feudal Institutions in Ancient Egypt. Pages 120–132 in Rushton Coulborn (editor), Feudalism in History. Princeton Univ. Press.

EHTÉCHAM, MORTÉZA 1946 L'Iran sous les Achéménides. Contribution à l'étude de l'organisation sociale et politique au premier empire des Perses. Fribourg (Switzerland): Imprimerie Saint Paul.

GANSHOF, FRANÇOIS L. (1944) 1961 Feudalism. With a foreword by F. M. Stenton. New York: Harper. → First published as Qu'est-ce que la féodalité?

GENICOT, L. 1962 La noblesse au moyen âge dans l'ancienne "Francie." Annales: Économies, sociétés, civilisations 17:1–22.

GRANET, MARCEL 1952 La féodalité chinoise. Instituttet for Sammenlignende Kulturforskning, Oslo, Serie A: Forelesninger, 22. Oslo: Aschehoug.

GUILHIERMOZ, PAUL 1902 Essai sur l'origine de la noblesse en France au moyen âge. Paris: Picard.

HALL, JOHN W. 1962 Feudalism in Japan: A Reassessment. Comparative Studies in Society and History 5:15–51.

HALPHEN, L. 1933 La place de la royauté dans le système féodal. *Anuario de historia del derecho español* 9:313–321.

HINTZE, OTTO 1929 Wesen und Verbreitung des Feudalismus. Akademie der Wissenchaften, Berlin, Philosophisch-historische Klasse, *Sitzungsberichte* [1929]: 321–347.

KANTOROWICZ, ERNST H. 1956 "Feudalism" in the Byzantine Empire. Pages 151–166 in Rushton Coulborn (editor), *Feudalism in History.* Princeton Univ. Press.

KEES, HERMAN 1932–1933 Beiträge zur altägyptischen Provinzialverwaltung, und der Geschichte des Feudalismus. Gesellschaft der Wissenschaften zu Göttingen, Philologisch-historische Klasse, *Nachrichten* [1932]: 85–119; [1933]: 579–598.

KOSMINSKII, E. A. 1955 *Osnovnye problemy zapadno-evropeiskogo feodalizma v sovetskoi istoricheskoi nauke* (Basic Problems of West European Feudalism as Reflected in Soviet Historical Science). Moscow: Akademiia Nauk SSSR. → Text in Russian and English.

MITTEIS, HEINRICH 1933 *Lehnrecht und Staatsgewalt: Untersuchungen zur mittelalterlichen Verfassungsgeschichte.* Weimar (Germany): Böhlaus.

MITTEIS, HEINRICH (1940) 1959 *Der Staat des hohen Mittelalters: Grundlinien einer vergleichenden Verfassungsgeschichte des Lehnszeitalters.* Weimar (Germany): Böhlaus.

MOR, CARLO G. 1952 *L'età feudale.* 2 vols. Milan: Vallardi.

OSTROGORSKI, GEORGIJE 1929 Die wirtschaftlichen und sozialen Entwicklungsgrundlagen des byzantinischen Reiches. *Vierteljahrschrift für Sozial- und Wirtschaftsgeschichte* 22:129–143.

OSTROGORSKI, GEORGIJE (1940) 1957 *History of the Byzantine State.* New Brunswick, N.J.: Rutgers Univ. Press. → First published in German.

OSTROGORSKI, GEORGIJE 1941 Agrarian Conditions in the Byzantine Empire in the Middle Ages. Pages 194–223 in *The Cambridge Economic History of Europe From the Decline of the Roman Empire.* Volume 1: The Agrarian Life of the Middle Ages. Cambridge Univ. Press.

OSTROGORSKI, GEORGIJE (1948–1951) 1954 *Pour l'histoire de la féodalité byzantine.* Brussels: Institut de Philologie et d'Histoire Orientales et Slaves. → A translation of two separate works, first published in Russian and Serbian respectively.

Les peuples de l'orient méditerranéen. 4th ed. Volume 2: L'Égypte, by Étienne Drioton and Jacques Vandier. (1938) 1962 Paris: Presses Universitaires de France.

POLIAK, ABRAHAM N. 1939 *Feudalism in Egypt, Syria, Palestine and the Lebanon, 1250–1900.* London: Royal Asiatic Society.

PRAWER, JOSHUA 1959 La noblesse et le régime féodal du royaume latin de Jérusalem. *Moyen âge* 65:41–74.

PRAWER, JOSHUA 1966 Estates, Communities and the Constitution of the Latin Kingdom. Israel Academy of Sciences and Humanities, *Proceedings* 2:1–42.

PRESTAGE, EDGAR (editor) 1928 *Chivalry: A Series of Studies to Illustrate Its Historical Significance and Civilizing Influence.* New York: Knopf.

REISCHAUER, EDWIN O. 1956 Japanese Feudalism. Pages 26–48 in Rushton Coulborn (editor), *Feudalism in History.* Princeton Univ. Press.

SANCHEZ-ALBORNOZ Y MENDUIÑA, CLAUDIO 1942 *En torno a los orígenes del feudalismo.* 3 vols. Mendoza (Argentina): Univ. Nacional de Cuyo.

SEVČENKO, IHOR 1952 An Important Contribution to the Social History of Late Byzantium. Ukrainian Academy of Arts and Sciences in the United States, *Annals* 2: 448–459.

SOCIÉTÉ JEAN BODIN POUR L'HISTOIRE COMPARATIVE DES INSTITUTIONS 1936 Les liens de vassalité et les immunités. Brussels, Université Libre, Institut de Sociologie Solvay, *Revue* 16:7–118.

SOCIÉTÉ JEAN BODIN POUR L'HISTOIRE COMPARATIVE DES INSTITUTIONS 1938 *La tenure.* Recueil, Vol. 3. Brussels: Librairie Encyclopédique.

SOCIÉTÉ JEAN BODIN POUR L'HISTOIRE COMPARATIVE DES INSTITUTIONS 1949 *Le domaine.* Brussels: Librairie Encyclopédique. → See especially Georgije Ostrogorski's "Le grand domaine dans l'empire byzantin."

STEINDORFF, GEORG; and SEELE, KEITH C. (1942) 1957 *When Egypt Ruled the East.* Univ. of Chicago Press. → A paperback edition was published in 1963.

STENTON, F. M. (1932) 1961 *The First Century of English Feudalism, 1066–1160.* 2d ed. Oxford: Clarendon.

SZEFTEL, MARC 1956 Aspects of Feudalism in Russian History. Pages 167–182 in Rushton Coulborn (editor), *Feudalism in History.* Princeton Univ. Press.

THORNER, DANIEL 1956 Feudalism in India. Pages 133–150 in Rushton Coulborn (editor), *Feudalism in History.* Princeton Univ. Press.

VASILIEV, A. A. 1933 On the Question of Byzantine Feudalism. *Byzantion* 8:584–604.

VERNADSKY, GEORGE 1939 Feudalism in Russia. *Speculum* 14:300–323.

WEBER, MAX (1922) 1957 *The Theory of Social and Economic Organization.* Edited by Talcott Parsons. Glencoe, Ill.: Free Press. → First published as Part 1 of *Wirtschaft und Gesellschaft.*

FIDUCIAL INFERENCE

R. A. Fisher (1930) proposed a statistical method for obtaining from observed data a probability distribution concerning a parameter value; he called the distribution a *fiducial probability distribution.* The theory of confidence intervals, as developed by J. Neyman, was initially presented in the literature as a clarification and development of fiducial probability [*see* ESTIMATION, *article on* CONFIDENCE INTERVALS AND REGIONS]. Fisher denied the equivalence and in his subsequent theoretical papers developed and extended fiducial probability.

As an example, consider a sample of independent measurements, $X_1, \cdots, X_n$, on a physical characteristic μ, and suppose that the measurement error is normally distributed with mean 0 and known variance σ_0^2. Fisher requires that fiducial inference be based on the simplest statistic containing all the information about the parameter, in this case, on the sample mean $\bar{X}$. [*The sample mean here is a minimal sufficient statistic; see* SUFFICIENCY.] The expression $W = \bar{X} - \mu$, involving the variable $\bar{X}$ and the characteristic μ, has a known distribution: normal with mean 0 and variance σ_0^2/n. In an application of the method, the value of $\bar{X}$ is obtained and substituted in the expression $W = \bar{X} - \mu$; the expression is solved for μ in terms of W, giving $\mu = \bar{X} - W$; the fiducial distribution of μ then derives from the known distribution of W: μ is normal with mean $\bar{X}$ and variance σ_0^2/n. A 95 per cent fiducial interval is $\bar{X} \pm 1.96\sigma_0/\sqrt{n}$.

Fisher claimed that a fiducial probability statement has the same meaning as an ordinary probability statement. In the example, suppose that the 95 per cent fiducial interval as calculated in a specific application is 163.9 ± 0.8. The fiducial statement is that there is 95 per cent probability that the unknown value of μ lies in this interval. The interval 163.9 ± 0.8 is also a 95 per cent confidence interval, but as a confidence interval its interpretation is different [see ESTIMATION, article on CONFIDENCE INTERVALS AND REGIONS]. Confidence methods and fiducial methods do not, however, always lead to the same numerical results.

The proponents of the confidence method claim that in this context probability statements concerning μ cannot be made; the value of μ is something that exists: either it *is* in the interval or it *is not*, and we don't know which.

The proponents of the fiducial method reply that probabilities concerning realized values are commonplace: in the play of card games, for example, a player may observe his own hand and perhaps other cards (say, those already played) and make a probability statement concerning the distribution of cards in the concealed hands.

The rejoinder is that μ did not arise from a random process such as the card shuffling and dealing. The relevance of this rejoinder is perhaps the key element to criticisms of the fiducial method.

In more complex problems the fiducial method may give a result different than the confidence method. In one prominent problem mentioned below, the Behrens–Fisher problem, the fiducial method gives an answer where confidence methods have not yet produced an entirely satisfactory result.

In his original paper on the fiducial method, Fisher (1930) considered a statistic, T, obtained by the maximum likelihood method for estimating a parameter, θ. Let $F(T, \theta)$ be the cumulative distribution function for the statistic T. The probability density function for T is obtained by differentiating with respect to T: $f(T, \theta) = \partial F(T, \theta)/\partial T$. Correspondingly, the fiducial density function for θ, given an observed value for T, is obtained by differentiating with respect to θ: $g(\theta, T) = \partial F(T, \theta)/\partial \theta$.

Fisher illustrated the method with the correlation coefficient r of a sample from a bivariate normal distribution with population correlation coefficient ρ.

For more complex problems, Fisher proposed the use of a *pivotal quantity*, $W = h(T, \theta)$, a function of the statistic T and the parameter θ that has a fixed known distribution regardless of the value of θ. For the first example, $W = \bar{X} - \mu$ is a pivotal quantity. In an application, the observed value of the statistic T is substituted in the expression $W = h(T, \theta)$; the parameter θ is expressed in terms of W; and the fiducial distribution of θ is obtained from the known distribution of W.

Fisher's original method for obtaining a fiducial distribution is a special case of the pivotal method. As a function of a continuous statistic, T, the cumulative distribution function $W = F(T, \theta)$ has a uniform distribution on the interval $(0, 1)$; this relationship is called that of the *probability integral transformation*. The fiducial density of θ for fixed T is obtained from the uniform distribution of W, in the same way as the density of T for fixed θ is obtained by differentiation.

As a second example, consider a random sample, $X_1, \cdots, X_n$, from a normal distribution with mean μ and variance σ^2, both unknown, and suppose that interest centers on the parameter μ. The quantity $t = \sqrt{n}(\bar{X} - \mu)/s_x$, using the sample mean $\bar{X}$ and sample standard deviation s_x, has a known distribution, the t-distribution on $n - 1$ degrees of freedom. In an application, the values of $\bar{X}$ and s_x are substituted and the parameter is solved for: $\mu = \bar{X} - ts_x/\sqrt{n}$. This equation gives a fiducial distribution for μ that is of t-distribution form ($n - 1$ degrees of freedom), located at $\bar{X}$ and scaled by the factor $s_x/\sqrt{n}$.

The Behrens–Fisher problem is an extension of this example. Consider a first random sample, $X_1, \cdots, X_n$, from a normal distribution with mean μ_x and variance σ_x^2, and a second independent random sample, $Y_1, \cdots, Y_m$, from a normal distribution with mean μ_y and variance σ_y^2. The Behrens–Fisher problem concerns inference about the parameter difference, $\mu_x - \mu_y$. The fiducial method gives a distribution described by $\bar{X} - t_1 s_x/\sqrt{n}$ for μ_x and a distribution described by $\bar{Y} - t_2 s_y/\sqrt{m}$ for μ_y. (Here t_1 and t_2 are independent t variables with $n - 1$, $m - 1$ degrees of freedom.) The fiducial distribution for $\mu_x - \mu_y$ is that of the difference, $\bar{X} - \bar{Y} - (t_1 s_x/\sqrt{n} - t_2 s_y/\sqrt{m})$; some percentage points are given in Fisher and Yates ([1938] 1949, p. 44).

For many problems involving normal and chi-square distributions, the fiducial distribution has the form of a Bayesian posterior distribution as based on a prior distribution with uniformity characteristics [see BAYESIAN INFERENCE].

Fisher (1956) considers a wide range of statistical problems and derives the corresponding fiducial distributions.

A central criticism of the fiducial method has been concerned with whether fiducial probabilities are in fact probabilities in an acceptable sense. Some recent analysis, mentioned later, has clarified this question.

Other criticism seems to fall under three headings. First, fiducial probabilities in some examples may not add or integrate to a total of 1. James (1954) and Stein (1959) produce examples that can yield fiducial distributions that do not integrate to 1. Second, in some examples more than one reasonable pivotal quantity may be present; these can lead to several inconsistent fiducial distributions (see Creasy 1954; Fieller 1954; Mauldon 1955). In other examples no reasonable pivotal quantity may be present. Third, if a fiducial distribution from a collection of data is used as a prior distribution for a Bayesian analysis on a second collection of data, the resulting distribution may be different from the fiducial distribution based on the combined collection of data [see Lindley 1958; see also BAYESIAN INFERENCE].

Fraser (1961) uses transformations to investigate fiducial probability. The transformation approach applies to a large proportion of Fisher's examples, and it introduces an additional range of problems for which fiducial distributions can be obtained.

In a later paper (Fraser 1966) the emphasis in the transformation approach is focused on error variables. Consider the example involving a sample of measurements, $X_1, \cdots, X_n$, on a physical quantity, μ. Let e be a variable describing the error introduced by the measuring instrument: in the example, e is normally distributed with mean 0 and variance σ_0^2. A measurement, X_i, can then be expressed in the form $X_i = \mu + e_i$. Correspondingly, the sample mean takes the form $\bar{X} = \mu + \bar{e}$, where $\bar{e}$ is normally distributed with mean 0 and variance σ_0^2/n. Now consider an application and suppose there is no information concerning μ. With no information concerning μ, there is no information concerning $\bar{e}$ other than that describing its distribution. Probability statements can then be made concerning the unknown $\bar{e}$ just as the card player makes statements concerning the realized but unrevealed cards in his opponents' hands.

Suppose the normal distribution of $\bar{e}$ with vari-ance σ_0^2/n gives a 95 per cent probability for $\bar{e}$ lying in the interval 0.0 ± 0.8. Then, with an observed $\bar{x} = 163.9$, the probability statement concerning $\bar{e}$ is equivalent to the statement that μ is in the interval 163.9 ± 0.8 with probability 95 per cent.

This analysis involving error variables applies to many of Fisher's examples, and it extends to other problems. The name structural probability has been introduced (Fraser 1966) to distinguish it in cases where the method conflicts with the fiducial method. None of the criticisms mentioned concerning fiducial probability apply to structural probability.

D. A. Sprott (1964) uses a more general class of transformations to analyze a wider range of fiducial distributions.

Some alternative methods have been proposed for obtaining probability distributions concerning parameter values: Dempster (1963; 1966) proposes direct probabilities, and Verhagen (1966) proposes induced probabilities.

D. A. S. FRASER

[See also ESTIMATION, article on CONFIDENCE INTERVALS AND REGIONS.]

BIBLIOGRAPHY

A survey of fiducial methods and criticisms may be found in Fraser 1964.

CREASY, MONICA A. 1954 Limits for the Ratio of Means. Journal of the Royal Statistical Society Series B 16:186–194.

DEMPSTER, A. P. 1963 On Direct Probabilities. Journal of the Royal Statistical Society Series B 25:100–110.

DEMPSTER, A. P. 1966 New Methods for Reasoning Towards Posterior Distributions Based on Sample Data. Annals of Mathematical Statistics 37:355–374.

FIELLER, E. C. 1954 Some Problems in Interval Estimation. Journal of the Royal Statistical Society Series B 16:175–185.

FISHER, R. A. (1930) 1950 Inverse Probability. Pages 22.527a–22.535 in R. A. Fisher, Contributions to Mathematical Statistics. New York: Wiley. → First published in Volume 26 of the Proceedings of the Cambridge Philosophical Society.

FISHER, R. A. (1956) 1959 Statistical Methods and Scientific Inference. 2d ed., rev. New York: Hafner; London: Oliver & Boyd.

FISHER, R. A.; and YATES, F. (1938) 1949 Statistical Tables for Biological, Agricultural, and Medical Research. 3d ed., rev. & enl. New York: Hafner; London: Oliver & Boyd.

FRASER, D. A. S. 1961 The Fiducial Method and Invariance. Biometrika 48:261–280.

FRASER, D. A. S. 1964 On the Definition of Fiducial Probability. International Statistical Institute, Bulletin 40, part 2:842–856.

FRASER, D. A. S. 1966 Structural Probability and a Generalization. Biometrika 53:1–9.

James, G. S. 1954 Discussion on the Symposium on Interval Estimation. *Journal of the Royal Statistical Society* Series B 16:214–218.

Lindley, D. V. 1958 Fiducial Distributions and Bayes' Theorem. *Journal of the Royal Statistical Society* Series B 20:102–107.

Mauldon, J. G. 1955 Pivotal Quantities for Wishart's and Related Distributions, and a Paradox in Fiducial Theory. *Journal of the Royal Statistical Society* Series B 17:79–85.

Sprott, D. A. 1961 Similarities Between Likelihoods and Associated Distributions a Posteriori. *Journal of the Royal Statistical Society* Series B 23:460–468.

Sprott, D. A. 1964 A Transformation Model for the Investigation of Fiducial Distributions. International Statistical Institute, *Bulletin* 40, part 2:856–869.

Stein, Charles 1959 An Example of Wide Discrepancy Between Fiducial and Confidence Intervals. *Annals of Mathematical Statistics* 30:877–880.

Verhagen, A. M. W. 1966 The Notion of Induced Probability in Statistical Inference. Division of Mathematical Statistics, Technical Paper No. 21. Unpublished manuscript, Commonwealth Scientific and Industrial Research Organisation, Melbourne, Australia.

FIELD THEORY

In psychology, the term "field theory" is used primarily to designate the point of view of Kurt Lewin and his co-workers. Although the term has its origin in physics, where it is employed to refer to the conceptualization of electromagnetic phenomena in terms of fields of electromagnetic forces, field theory in psychology is not an attempt to explain psychological events in terms of physical processes. Rather, it refers to a "method of analyzing causal relations and of building scientific constructs" (Lewin 1943*a*), which Lewin felt could be applied as fruitfully in psychology as it had been in physics. [*See* Lewin.]

Lewin's early interests and writings—much influenced by the German philosopher Ernst Cassirer—were concerned with the nature of theory in science. Much of his own research orientation and of his great impact on psychology arose from his way of thinking about theorizing. His approach to theorizing in psychology was characterized by several major themes:

(1) *An emphasis on the psychological explanation of behavior* focuses on the purposes which underlie behavior and the goals toward or away from which behavior is directed; it stresses that one has to deal with what exists psychologically, what is real for the person being studied.

(2) *An emphasis on the total situation* stresses that the most fundamental construct is that of the psychological "field," or life space. All psychological events are conceived to be a function of the life space, which consists of the person and the environment viewed as *one* constellation of interdependent factors. Lewin made it evident that it is meaningless to explain behavior without reference to both the person and his environment and that psychological events are not determined by the characteristics of the individual—"instincts," "heredity," "needs," "habits"—acting independently of the situation.

(3) *An emphasis on systematic rather than historical causation* indicates that psychological events have to be explained in terms of the properties of the field which exist *at the time* when the events occur. Lewin rejected the notion of "action at a distance" and stressed that past events can have a position only in the historical causal chains whose interweaving creates the present situation.

(4) *The dynamic approach*, like that of the gestalt school, accepts the view that living systems tend to maintain a dynamic equilibrium in relation to their environments. Related to this view was Lewin's interest in the processes by which equilibrium is restored when it is disturbed and his interest in such motivational processes as the arousal of need tensions, the setting of goals, goal-directed action, and the release of tension.

Lewin was not only a metatheoretician but also a bold and original experimentalist. However, the themes underlying Lewin's approach to theorizing have played a central role in his empirical work on psychology. These themes are reflected in his research preoccupation with the psychological environment (the person's perception of the situation confronting him), his emphasis on social and group influences upon behavior, his stress on the contemporaneous rather than the historical determinants of behavior, and his focus on dynamics (motivation, conflict, and change). The range and impact of the work of Lewin and his associates is indicated by a list of some of the research areas in psychology which they opened up for experimental investigation: dynamic studies of memory, resumption of interrupted activities, substitute activity, satiation, level of aspiration, studies of different types of group leadership, group decision. Many of the terms associated with Lewin are now part of the common vocabulary of psychologists—e.g., "life space," "valence," "locomotion," "overlapping situation," "cognitive structure," "action research." In the space available here, it will be impossible to do more than sketch some of Lewin's central theoretical notions. This is done in five sections which deal with (1) dynamic concepts, (2) structural concepts, (3) socially induced change, (4) level of aspiration, and (5) group dynamics.

Dynamic concepts

After several years of work at the University of Berlin on the more traditional problems of perception and learning, Lewin turned to the study of motivation. In 1926 he published the first of a series of over twenty brilliant articles by himself and his students, "Untersuchungen zur Handlungs- und Affektspsychologie" ("Investigations Into the Psychology of Behavior and Emotion"), which appeared in *Psychologische Forschung*. Here most of the concepts which later became so famous first appeared. Among them are the concepts "tension," "valence," "force," and "locomotion," which play a key role in Lewin's theorizing about motivation.

A system in a state of *tension* is said to exist within the individual whenever a psychological need or an intention (sometimes referred to as a quasi need) exists. Tension is released when the need or intention is fulfilled. Tension has the following conceptual properties: (*a*) it is a state of a region in a given system which tries to change itself in such a way that it becomes equal to the state of surrounding regions, and (*b*) it involves forces at the boundary of the region in tension. A *positive valence* is conceived as a force field in which the forces are all pointing toward a given region of the field (the valent region which is the center of the force field); all the forces point away from a region of *negative valence*. The construct *force* characterizes the direction and strength of the tendency to change at a given point of the life space. Change may occur either by actual locomotion (i.e., change in position) of the person in his psychological environment or by a change in the structure of his perceived environment.

There exists a definite relation between tension systems of the person and certain properties of the psychological environment. In particular, a tension may be related to a positive valence for activity regions in the psychological environment which are perceived as tension reducing, and a negative valence for the region in which the behaving self is at present. However, the existence of a region of positive valence (a goal region) depends not only upon the existence of tension but also upon whether there are perceived possibilities for reducing the tension.

When a goal region which is relevant to a system in tension exists in the psychological environment, one can assert that there is a force acting upon the behaving self to locomote toward the goal. A tension for which there is a cognized goal leads not only to a tendency to actual locomotion toward the goal region but also to thinking about

this type of activity. This may be expressed by saying that the force on the person toward the goal exists not only on the level of doing (reality) but also on the level of thinking (irreality).

The Zeigarnik quotient. From the foregoing assumptions about systems in tension it is possible to make a number of derivations. Thus, it follows that the tendency to recall or resume interrupted activities should be greater than the tendency to recall or resume finished ones. Zeigarnik (1927) and many others have conducted experiments in which subjects are given a series of tasks to perform and are then prevented from completing half of them. Later, the subjects are asked to recall the tasks they had performed. The results are presented in the form of a quotient, commonly called the Zeigarnik quotient (ZQ):

$$\frac{\text{uncompleted tasks recalled } (RU)}{\text{completed tasks recalled } (RC)}.$$

Zeigarnik predicted a quotient of greater than 1. The obtained quotient was approximately 1.9, clearly supporting Lewin's assumptions. However, since many completed tasks were also recalled, it was obvious that additional factors were involved. Analyzing the situation of the subject at the moment of recall, Zeigarnik concluded that in addition to the force on the person to think about, and hence to recall, the uncompleted tasks, there was also present a force to recall both uncompleted and completed tasks exerted upon the person by the experimenter's instructions to "try to recall the tasks you worked on earlier." The Zeigarnik quotient could be viewed as a function of the relative strengths of the induced force to recall all tasks and of the force to recall the uncompleted tasks. As the strength of the force induced by the experimenter increases in relation to the force toward the task goals, the quotient should decrease toward 1; as it decreases in relative strength, the quotient should increase beyond 1. These additional predictions, which follow from an analysis of the situation at recall, were borne out in experiments by Zeigarnik and others. Thus, if the strength of motivation associated with the interrupted task is relatively high, or the strength of the experimenter's pressure to recall is low, or if the task is interrupted near its end, the Zeigarnik quotient will be high.

A number of more recent experiments have indicated that the situation of recall is frequently even more complex than indicated above. When not finishing a task is interpretable as a personal failure (e.g., in an experiment where the tasks are presented as measures of a socially esteemed ability) and when recall of failure threatens one's self-esteem, or when the recall of success raises a lowered self-esteem, the Zeigarnik quotient tends to be less than 1.

Substitute value. Käte Lissner initiated the study of the value which one activity has for reducing a tension originally connected with another activity by a technique involving resumption of the interrupted task; some of the other experimenters have employed the technique of recall. The substitute value is measured by the amount of decrease in resumption or recall of the interrupted original activity after a substitute activity has been completed. The results of the experiments on substitute value can be summarized as follows: (1) Substitute value increases with the perceived degree of similarity between the original and the substitute activity and with the degree of difficulty of the substitute activity (Lissner 1933). (2) Substitute value increases with increasing temporal contiguity between the original and the substitute activity and with the attractiveness of the substitute activity (Henle 1942). (3) The substitute value of an activity (e.g., thinking, talking, or doing) depends upon the nature of the goal of the original task. Tasks that are connected with the goal of demonstrating something to another person (e.g., the experimenter) require an observable substitute activity (not merely "thinking" without social communication); "realization tasks," in which the building of a material object is the goal, require "doing," not only telling how it can be done; for intellectual problems, talking (or telling how it can be done) can have a very high substitute value (Mahler 1933). (4) "Magic solutions," "make-believe solutions," or solutions which observably violate the requirements of the task have little substitute value for tasks at the reality level. However, if the situation is a make-believe or play situation, make-believe substitutions will have substitute value (Sliosberg 1934; Dembo 1931). (5) A substitute activity which is identical with the original activity will have little substitute value if it does not serve the same goal. Thus, building a clay house for Tony will have little substitute value for building a clay house for Nicky. If the emphasis is on building a clay house and not upon the "for somebody," then, of course, substitution will occur (Adler & Kounin 1939). (6) Having someone complete the subject's interrupted task tends to have little substitute value, particularly when completion of the task is related to self-esteem. However, when pairs of individuals work cooperatively on a task, the completion of the task by one's partner has considerable substitute value (e.g., Lewis & Franklin 1944).

The research findings with respect to substitute value have implications for a wide range of problems in psychology—from the relative gratification value of individual versus socially shared projective or fantasy systems to the development of specialized roles within a group. Let us briefly illustrate with the very important finding that the actions of another person can be a substitute for one's own actions if there is a cooperative relationship. The fact of substitutability enables individuals who are working cooperatively on a common task to subdivide the task and to perform specialized activities, since none of the individuals in a cooperative situation has to perform all the activities by himself. In contrast, the individual in a competitive situation is less likely to view the actions of others as substitutable for similarly intended actions of his own. Thus, when a competitive situation exists in a group, specialization of activities is less likely to develop (Deutsch 1949a; 1949b).

Satiation. The concept of tension systems has also been fruitfully employed in experimental studies of satiation. With regard to most needs, one can distinguish a state of deprivation, of satiation, and of oversatiation. These states correspond to a positive, a neutral, and a negative valence of the activity regions which are related to a particular need or tension system. Karsten (1928) has studied the effect of repeating over and over again such activities as reading a poem, writing letters, drawing, and turning a wheel. The main symptoms of oversatiation appear to be (1) the appearance of subunits in the activity that lead to the disintegration of the total activity and a loss of meaning of the activity; (2) increasingly poorer quality of work and greater frequency of errors in performing the task; (3) an increasing tendency to vary the nature of the task, accompanied by a tendency for each variation to be quickly satiated; (4) a tendency to make the satiated activity a peripheral activity by attempting to concentrate on something else while doing the task—this is usually not completely successful, and the mind wanders; (5) increasing dislike of the activity and of similar activities, accompanied by an increased valence for different tasks; (6) emotional outbursts; (7) development of "fatigue" and similar bodily symptoms which are quickly overcome when the individual is shifted to another activity.

Satiation occurs only if the activity has, psychologically, the character of marking time or of getting nowhere. If the activity can be viewed as making progress toward a goal, the usual symptoms of satiation will not appear. Embedding an activity in a different psychological whole, so that its meaning is changed, has practically the same effect on satiation as shifting to a different activity. The rapidity with which satiation occurs depends upon factors such as the nature of the activity— with increasing size of its units of action and with increasing complexity satiation occurs more slowly —and the state of the person—the more fluid the state of the person, the more quickly he is satiated. The rate of satiation and cosatiation of similar activities (i.e., the spread of satiation effects from one activity to similar activities) decreases with age and with lack of intelligence (Kounin 1941).

Structural concepts

Lewin attempted to develop a geometry, which he termed "hodological space," to represent a person's conception of the means–end structure of the environment, of what leads to what. Although Lewin's "hodological space" was never developed adequately from a mathematical viewpoint, it served to highlight the necessity of considering a person's conception of his environment in analyzing his behavior possibilities and in characterizing the direction of his behavior. For example, an individual who walks around a fence to get to a ball behind it is, psychologically, walking toward the ball as he physically walks away from it.

Cognitive structure.   The view that direction in the life space is dependent upon cognitive structure has been applied to provide insights into some of the psychological properties of situations which are cognitively unstructured.

Most new situations are cognitively unstructured, since the individual is unlikely to know "what leads to what." As he strikes out in any direction, he does not know whether he is going toward or away from his goal. His behavior will be exploratory, trial-and-error, vacillating, and contradictory rather than efficient and economical. If reaching the goal has positive significance and not reaching it has negative significance for the individual concerned, then being in a region that has no clear cognitive structure results in psychological conflict, since the direction of the forces acting upon him is likely to be both toward and away from any given region. There will be evidences of emotionality as well as cautiousness in such situations. In addition, the very nature of an unstructured situation is that it is unstable; perception of the situation shifts rapidly and is readily influenced by minor cues and by suggestions from others.

Lewin has employed his characterization of cognitively unstructured situations to give insight into the psychological circumstances of the adolescent (1939–1947) as well as those of minority group members (1935), of people suffering from physical handicaps (Barker 1946), of the *nouveaux riches*, and of other persons crossing the margins of social classes. It may be applied to any situation in which the consequences of behavior are seemingly unpredictable or uncontrollable; in which benefits and harms occur in an apparently inconsistent, fortuitous, or arbitrary manner; or in which one is uncertain about the potential reactions of others.

Conflict.   Lewin has brilliantly employed his structural concepts, in conjunction with his dynamic concepts, to give insight into the nature of *conflict situations*. He distinguishes three fundamental types of conflict:

(1) The individual stands midway between two positive valences of approximately equal strength. This type of conflict is unstable. As the individual, due to the play of chance factors, moves from the point of equilibrium toward one goal region rather than the other, the resultant force toward that region increases, and, hence, he will continue to move toward that region. This follows from the assumption that the strength of force toward a goal region decreases with increasing distance from the goal.

(2) The second fundamental type of conflict occurs when the individual finds himself between two approximately equal negative valences. The punishment situation is an example. This type of conflict is very much influenced by the structure of the situation. Let us illustrate three varieties of this type of conflict: (*a*) the individual is between two negative valences, but there are no restraints keeping him in the situation—e.g., a girl who will have to marry an unpleasant suitor or become an impoverished spinster if she remains in her village (there is nothing to prevent her from leaving her village); (*b*) the individual is between two negative valences, but he cannot leave the field—e.g., a group member who is faced with the prospect of losing social status or of performing an unpleasant task (he cannot leave the group); (*c*) the individual is in a region of negative valence and can leave it only by going through another region of negative valence—e.g., a man is cited for contempt of Congress for not testifying whether or not some of his acquaintances were members of the Communist party (to purge himself of contempt he must become an informer).

It is evident that the situation depicted in (*a*) will lead the person to go out of the field. Only if restraints prevent the individual from leaving the field will such a situation result in more than momentary conflict. Restraints as in (*b*) introduce a conflict between the driving forces related to the negative valence and the restraining forces related to the barrier. There is a tendency for a barrier to acquire a negative valence which increases with the number of unsucccessful attempts to cross it and which, finally, is sufficiently strong to prevent the individual from approaching it (Fajans 1933). Thus, the conflict between driving and restraining force is replaced by a conflict between driving forces, as in (c) above. This fact is particularly important for social psychology since, in many situations of life, the barriers are social. When a person turns against the barrier, he is in effect directing himself against the will and power of the person or social group to whom the erection of the barrier is due.

(3) The third fundamental type of conflict situation occurs when the individual is exposed to opposing forces deriving from a positive and a negative valence. One can distinguish at least three different forms of this conflict: (a) a single region has both positive and negative valence. (The Freudian concept of ambivalence is subsumable under this variety of conflict.) For example, a person wishes to join a social group but fears that being a member will be too expensive. (b) A person is encircled by (but not actually in) a negative or a barrier region and is attracted to a goal which is beyond it—e.g., a person who has to go through the unpleasant ordeal of leaving his home or his group in order to pursue some desired activity. In this situation, the region of the person's present activity tends to acquire negative valence as long as the region which encircles the person hinders locomotion toward desired outer goals. Thus, being a member of a minority group or being in a ghetto or in a prison often takes on negative valence, apart from the inherent characteristics of the situation, because one can get to desired goals from the region only by passing through an encircling region of negative valence. (c) A region of positive valence is encircled by or is accessible only through a region of negative valence. This type of situation differs from (b) in that the region of positive valence rather than the region in which the person is to be found is encircled by the negative valence. The "reward situation," in which the individual is granted a reward only if he performs an unpleasant task, is an example of this type of conflict.

Lewin ([1939–1947] 1963, p. 259), as well as Miller (1944), has pointed out that the forces corresponding to a negative valence tend to decrease more rapidly as a function of psychological distance than do the forces corresponding to a positive valence. The amount of decrease depends also upon the nature of the region which has a positive

or negative valence. It is different in the case of a dangerous animal which can move about than it is in the case of an immovable unpleasant object. The difference in the gradients of decrease for forces deriving from positive and negative valences accounts for the apparent paradox that a strong fear or a strong tendency to withdraw may be taken as evidence of a strong desire for the goal. Only with a very attractive goal will the equilibrium point between approach and avoidance tendencies be close enough to the negatively valent region to produce a strong force away from the goal. On the other hand, strengthening the negative valence of a region may very well have the effect of weakening the forces in conflict, since the equilibrium point may be pushed a considerable distance away from the valent regions. [See CONFLICT, *article on* PSYCHOLOGICAL ASPECTS.]

Socially induced change

It should be noted that Lewin's motivational concepts do not presuppose that motivation is primarily induced by physiological deficits; his conceptualization suggests that tension and valences may be aroused socially (e.g., by an experimenter's instructions to perform a task); he also indicated that the forces acting upon an individual may be "imposed" or may directly reflect the individual's own needs.

The concept of *powerfield* is relevant in this connection. It is an inducing field; it can induce changes in the life space within its area of influence. The distinction between *own* and *induced* forces has been found to be useful in explaining some of the differences in behavior under autocratic and democratic leadership (Lippitt & White 1943). Thus, children in a club led by authoritarian leaders (who determined policy, dictated activities, and were arbitrary and personal in evaluation of activities) tended to develop little of their own motivation with respect to club activities. Although the children worked productively when the leader was present (i.e., when his powerfield was psychologically effective), the lack of personal motivation toward group goals clearly evidenced itself in (1) change of behavior when the leader left the club, (2) absence of motivation when the leader arrived late, (3) lack of carefulness in the work, (4) lack of initiative in offering spontaneous suggestions in regard to club projects, (5) lack of pride in the products of club effort. [See LEADERSHIP.]

The distinction between own and induced forces has also been employed to explain why workers are usually happier and more productive when they can participate in the decisions which affect their work. Participation in goal setting is more likely to create own forces toward the goal and thus reduce the necessity to exert continuous social influences toward the same end (Coch & French 1948).

Level of aspiration

Perhaps no other area of research that Lewin and his students have opened to experimental investigation has been the object of so many studies as that of level of aspiration. The level of aspiration may be defined as the degree of difficulty of the goal toward which the person is striving. The concept of level of aspiration is relevant only when there is a perceived range of difficulty in the attainment of possible goals and a variation in valence among the goals along the range of difficulty.

In discussing the level of aspiration, it may be helpful to consider a sequence of events which is typical for many of the experimental studies in this area: (1) A subject plays a game (or performs a task) in which he can obtain a score (e.g., throwing darts at a target); (2) after playing the game and obtaining a given score, he is asked to tell what score he will undertake to make the next time he plays; (3) he then plays the game again and achieves a different score; (4) he reacts to his second performance with feelings of success or failure, with a continuing or new level of aspiration, etc. In the foregoing sequence, point (4) (reaction to achievement) is particularly significant for the dynamics of the level of aspiration.

In outline form, the theory of the level of aspiration is rather simple (Lewin et al. 1944). It states that the resultant valence of any level of difficulty will be equal to the valence of achieving success times the subjective probability of success, minus the valence of failure times the subjective probability of failure. The level of aspiration (i.e., the goal an individual will undertake to achieve) will be the level of difficulty that has the highest resultant positive valence. The subjective experience of success or failure is determined by the relation of the individual's performance to his level of aspiration (providing, of course, that the performance is seen to be self-accomplished) and not simply by his absolute accomplishments.

Experimental work on the level of aspiration has brought out the variety of influences which affect the positive and negative valences of different levels of difficulty. It has indicated that cultural and group factors establish scales of reference which help to determine the relative attractiveness of different points along a difficulty continuum. Some of these influences are rather stable and permanent in their effects. It has been found, for example, that most people in Western cultures, under the pervasive

cultural pressures toward "self-improvement," when first exposed to a level of aspiration situation initially give a level of aspiration which is above the previous performance score, and under most conditions they tend to keep their level of aspiration higher than their previous performance. In addition to broad cultural factors, the individual's level of aspiration in a task is likely to be very much influenced by the standards of the group to which he belongs. The nature of the scales of reference set up by different group standards may vary. Reference scales do not derive solely from membership in a definitely structured social group; they also may reflect the influence of one's self-image, of other individuals, or of groups that either establish certain standards for performance or that serve as models for evaluating self-performance. Thus, the level of aspiration of a college student with respect to an intellectual task will vary, depending upon whether he is told that a given score was obtained by the average high school student, the average college student, or the average graduate student.

Research has given some insight into the factors determining the values on the scale of subjective probability. A main factor which determines the subjective probability of future success and failure is the past experience of the individual in regard to his ability to reach certain objectives. If the individual has had considerable experience with a given activity, he will know pretty well what level he can expect to reach, and the gradient of values on the subjective probability scale will be steep. However, it is not only the average of past performances which determines an individual's subjective probability scale but also the trend—whether he is improving, getting worse, or remaining the same. Furthermore, there is experimental evidence to indicate that the last or most recent success or failure has a particularly great influence on the individual's expectation of his future achievement level. In addition, there is evidence that the subjective probability scales, as well as the performance of others, can influence the subject's own probability scale. Personality factors—for example, self-confidence—may also influence subjective probability.

The level of aspiration theory has widespread implications for many social phenomena. It gives insight into the reasons for social apathy in the face of pressing political and international problems. People are not likely to attempt to achieve even highly valued objectives when they see no way of attaining them. Similarly, it sheds some light upon why social revolution tends to occur only after there has been a slight improvement in the situation of the oppressed groups—the improvement raises their level of aspiration, making goals which were once viewed as unattainable now perceived as realistic possibilities.

Concepts of group dynamics

Apart from papers dealing with group decision and social change (Lewin 1935–1946; 1947*a*; 1947*b*) Lewin actually wrote very little on the theory of group dynamics. However, from the research investigations of his colleagues and students at the Research Center for Group Dynamics a formidable array of concepts has emerged. [*See* Groups.]

Let us begin our discussion of the concepts of group dynamics by briefly considering the concept of group. Lewin ([1935–1946] 1948, p. 48) wrote:

The essence of a group is not the similarity or dissimilarity of its members, but their interdependence. A group can be characterized as a "dynamic whole"; this means that a change in the state of any subpart changes the state of any other subpart. The degree of interdependence of the subparts of members of the group varies all the way from a loose "mass" to a compact unit.

French (1944) pointed out that in addition to interdependence, membership in a group presupposes identification with the group. Deutsch (1949*a*) indicated that the interdependence is promotive or cooperative rather than, for example, competitive. Thus, a group may be tentatively defined as being composed of a set of members who mutually perceive themselves to be cooperatively or promotively interdependent in some respect(s) and to some degree.

Cohesiveness. One of the key concepts, which has been the subject of much experimental investigation, is that of cohesiveness. Intuitively, cohesiveness refers to the forces which bind the parts of a group together and which, thus, resist disruptive influences. Hence, the study of conditions affecting group cohesiveness and of the effects upon group functioning of variations in group cohesiveness is at the heart of the study of group life. Festinger, Schachter, and Back (1950) have defined cohesiveness, in terms of the group member, as "the total field of forces which act on members to remain in the group." The nature and strength of the forces acting upon a member to remain in the group may vary from member to member.

Various measures of individuals' "cohesiveness" to their groups have been employed in experimental investigations: desire to remain in the group, the ratio of "we" remarks to "I" remarks during group discussion, ratings of friendliness, evaluations of the group and its sociometric choice versus outgroup sociometric choice, and others. Deutsch

(1949*a*), in a theoretical paper, provides a rationale for the use of a wide variety of measures by developing the hypotheses that members of more cohesive (cooperative) groups, as compared with members of less cohesive (competitive) groups, would, under conditions of success: (*a*) be more ready to accept the actions of other group members as substitutable for similarly intended actions of their own (and therefore would not have to perform them also); (*b*) be more ready to accept inductions (i.e., be influenced) by other members; and (*c*) be more likely to cathect positively the actions of other group members. From these core hypotheses, with the addition of more specific assumptions, it is possible to derive the influence of more or less cohesiveness upon many aspects of group functioning. Thus, from the substitutability hypothesis, it is possible to predict that more specialization of function, more subdivision of activity, and more diversity of membership behavior would occur in the more cohesive groups. The inductibility hypothesis leads to the prediction that members of more cohesive groups would be more attentive to one another, be more understood by one another, be more influenced by one another, and be more likely to change and have more internalization of group norms than members of less cohesive groups. The cathexis hypothesis leads to predictions of greater friendliness, greater ratio of in-group sociometric choices, etc., in the more cohesive groups. Data in a variety of experiments (e.g., Deutsch 1949*b*; Schachter 1951; Back 1951) support the foregoing predictions. [*See* Cohesion, social.]

Communication. In a well-integrated program of research, Festinger and his co-workers have developed a series of fertile hypotheses (Festinger 1950) and have conducted some ingenious experiments on the communication process within groups. In brief, these investigators have been concerned with three sources of pressures to communicate within groups: (*a*) communications arising from pressures toward uniformity in a group (Back 1951; Festinger & Thibaut 1951; Schachter 1951); (*b*) communications arising from forces to locomote in a social structure (Kelley 1951; Thibaut 1950); and (*c*) communications arising from the existence of emotional states (Thibaut 1950; Thibaut & Coules 1952). [*See* Interaction.]

Pressures toward uniformity. Festinger (1950; 1954) has indicated two major sources of pressures toward uniformity in a group: social reality and group locomotion. He indicates that when there is no single objective basis for determining the validity of one's beliefs, one is dependent upon social reality to establish confidence in one's beliefs. Thus, to evaluate the validity of his opinions or to evaluate his abilities or even the appropriateness of his emotions (Schachter 1959), he will compare them with those of others. Festinger (1954) posits that to facilitate accuracy of evaluation of their opinions or abilities, people will seek out others with similar opinions or abilities for comparison and will avoid dissimilarity or attempt to reduce it when it exists. Also, lack of agreement among members of a group provides an unstable basis for beliefs which depend upon social consensus for their support, and hence —in line with Heider's discussion of the tendency toward cognitive balance (1958) or Festinger's theory of cognitive dissonance (1957)—forces will arise to produce uniformity. [See CONFORMITY.]

Pressures toward uniformity among members of a group may also arise because such uniformity is desirable or necessary in order for the group to locomote toward some goal. Greater uniformity in opinion within a group can be achieved in either of the following ways: (a) by actions (i.e., communications) that are directed at changing the views of others or one's own views or (b) by actions to make others incomparable in the sense that they are no longer effective as a comparison for one's opinions —e.g., by rejecting or excluding people with deviating opinions from the group.

Experiments have shown that increasing the attraction to the group, and thus increasing the importance of the group as a comparison object, increases the amount of influence which is attempted and the amount of opinion change which occurs when there is opinion discrepancy within a group (Back 1951). It has also been demonstrated that the more relevant or important the opinion is for the functioning of the group, the more pressure there will be for uniformity in a group (Schachter 1951; Festinger & Thibaut 1951). Also, as may be expected from theoretical considerations, there is evidence that when pressures toward uniformity exist, the concern is mainly with those members of the group who have opinions most divergent from one's own. Thus, members exert influence mainly on those whose opinions are most divergent from their own.

Pressures toward change.   The experiments revealing the tendency to direct communication toward deviants in the group, and through communication to exert social pressure upon them, provide support for Lewin's theory of group decision and social change. Lewin (1947b) began his analysis of change by pointing out that the *status quo* in social life is not a static affair but a dynamic process that flows on while still keeping a recognizable form. He borrowed the term "quasi-stationary equilibria" from physics to apply to such ongoing processes, which are kept at their present level by fields of forces preventing a rise or fall. The field of forces in the neighborhood of the level of equilibrium presupposes that the forces against exceeding the equilibrium level increase with the amount of raising and that the forces against lowering increase (or remain constant) with the lowering. Thus, if we assume that a group standard is operating to determine the level of worker productivity in a factory, any attempt upon the part of the worker to deviate from the standard by higher productivity will only result in stronger forces being induced upon him by his co-workers in order to push him back into line. That is, as the Festinger experiments have demonstrated, the deviant will be exposed to stronger pressures toward uniformity the more he deviates. However, as Lewin points out, the gradient of forces may change at a distance from the equilibrium level, so that after an individual has gone a certain distance from the equilibrium level, the forces may push him away from rather than pull him toward the group standard.

Lewin's analysis of the *status quo* as a quasi-stationary equilibrium has two major implications. First, it points out that change from the *status quo* can be produced either by adding forces in the desired direction or by diminishing opposing forces. However, the two methods of producing change have different consequences: if forces are added, the process on the new level will be accompanied by a state of relatively high tension, since the strength of forces in opposition will be greater; if the opposing forces are decreased, the new level will be accompanied by lower tension. Second, it highlights the difficulties of attempting to change group-rooted individual conduct and attitudes through efforts directed at the individual and not his group. If one endeavors to change the prejudices of an individual without changing the prejudice of the group to which he belongs, an individual will either be estranged from his group or be under pressure from his group to revert to his initial attitudes. Isolated individuals may perhaps change their attitudes because of their individual experiences, but the person who is deeply enmeshed in the social life of his community is unlikely to be able to resist the pressures to conform on matters of community importance if he wishes to continue in good standing. [See ATTITUDES, *article on* ATTITUDE CHANGE.]

Considerations such as the foregoing have led to a series of experiments in various settings— in the school, with neighborhood groups, in industry, in an interracial workshop—on the relative efficacy of changing behavior by efforts directed at individuals or at a group (Lewin 1935–1946). A typical procedure has been to compare the results of a lecture or individual instruction in changing behavior regarding the use of certain foods with the results of a group decision favoring the use. Results have clearly indicated that the group decision method produces more change.

The present status of field theory

In previous sections of this article, work that was directly initiated or stimulated by Lewin or his immediate associates has been described. The large sweep of this work, the brilliant innovations, the experimental ingenuity cannot help but be impressive. Even though Lewin died in 1947, his impact on psychology continues to be felt in the extension and application of his ideas by others. We turn, briefly, to a discussion of some current work in psychology—a theory of achievement motivation, balance and dissonance theory, and T-group training (laboratory training groups) which extends Lewin's ideas.

A theory of achievement motivation. Atkinson (1957; 1964) has developed a theory of achievement motivation that is an extension and elaboration of ideas advanced in the theory of level of aspiration developed by Lewin, Festinger, and Sibylle Escalona. Atkinson's theory attempts to account for the determinants of the direction, magnitudes, and persistence of achievement-motivated performance. Achievement motivation is the resultant of two opposed tendencies: $T_s - T_f$ (the tendency to achieve success minus the tendency to avoid failure. In Atkinson's notation this is represented as T_{-f}.).

The tendency to achieve success is assumed to be a multiplicative function of the motive to achieve success (M_s) which the individual carries about with him from situation to situation, the subjective probability of success (P_s), and the incentive values of success at a particular activity (I_s): $T_s = M_s \times P_s \times I_s$. Similarly, the tendency to avoid failure is assumed to be a multiplicative function of the motive to avoid failure (M_{af}), the subjective probability of failure (P_f), and the negative incentive value of failure (I_f): $T_f = M_{af} \times P_f \times I_f$.

So far, Atkinson's analysis parallels the level of aspiration theory, if one assumes, quite properly, that the Lewinian concept of valence is equivalent to Atkinson's motive times incentive: namely, that the valence of success $= M_s \times I_s$ and that the valence of failure $= M_{af} \times I_f$. He, however, introduces the additional assumptions that $I_s = 1 - P_s = P_f$

and that $I_f = -P_s$. In other words, his theory details more unequivocally the relationship between the perceived level of difficulty and the incentive values of success and failure. It states, in effect, that the value of success increases with the perceived difficulty of the task, while the displeasure at failure increases with the perceived ease of the task. (Notice that in Atkinson's theory $P_s \times I_s$ must equal $-P_f \times I_f$ and, hence, that whatever differences in strength there are between T_s and T_f will be due solely to the differences between M_s and M_{af}.) In addition, he has specified methods of measuring M_s and M_{af}; M_s is measured by the methods developed by McClelland and his associates (1953) to measure need achievement and M_{af} is measured by the Mandler–Sarason Test of Anxiety (1952).

Atkinson (1964) summarizes a considerable amount of research that is consistent with his theory. The wide applicability of the theory is indicated by the range of content to which the theory has been applied: motivational effect of ability grouping in schools, strength of achievement motive and occupational mobility, fear of failure and unrealistic vocational aspiration, preferences for degrees of risk, and the effects of success and failure. [See ACHIEVEMENT MOTIVATION.]

Cognitive balance. One of the notions implicit in Lewin's view of the life space as cognitively structured, and generally in the gestalt view that organization tends to be as "good" as possible, is that when a structure of beliefs and attitudes is imbalanced or disharmonious, a tendency will arise to change one's beliefs and attitudes until they are balanced. Lewin's view is brought out most clearly in his discussion of cognitively unstructured situations and in his discussion of the cognitive structure of different types of conflict situations. Heider (1946; 1958), one of Lewin's most brilliant associates, has extended this notion in his theory of cognitive balance. [See THINKING, *article on* COGNITIVE ORGANIZATION AND PROCESSES.]

Heider points out that cognitive stability requires a congruence among causal expectations with respect to related objects. That is, for a state of complete cognitive harmony to exist, the various implications of a person's expectations or judgments of any aspect of the cognized environment cannot contradict the implications of his expectations or judgments of any other aspect of the cognized environment. Thus, if a person judges X to be of potential benefit to his welfare, he cannot at the same time judge that Y (which is also judged to be of benefit to his welfare) and X are antagonistic and still have a stable or balanced cognitive structure. (Let X and Y be things, people, the products of people, or the characteristics of people.) When the cognitive structure is in a state of imbalance or is threatened by imbalance, forces will arise to produce a tendency toward locomotion that will change the psychological environment or produce a tendency toward change in the cognition of the environment. Under conditions which do not permit locomotion, the tendency for cognitive change is enhanced.

Heider specifies further that (*a*) in regard to attitudes directed toward the same entity, a balanced state exists if positive (or negative) attitudes go together; a tendency exists to see a person as being positive or negative in all respects; (*b*) in regard to attitudes toward an entity combined with belongingness, a balanced state exists if a person is united with the entities he likes and if he likes the entities he is united with; the converse is true for negative attitudes; (*c*) if two entities are seen as parts of a unit, a balanced state will exist if the parts are seen to have the same dynamic character (positive or negative). If the two entities have different dynamic characters, a balanced state can exist if they are seen to be segregated (i.e., by breaking up the unit).

Heider's theory has had wide ramifications in social psychology. Cartwright and Harary (1956) extended balance theory to cover a greater range of phenomena and also removed some of its ambiguities by using the mathematical theory of linear groups. Newcomb (1953; 1961) has applied Heider's theory to the "balancing" of interpersonal relations, particularly in his analysis of communicative acts and the development of friendships. Rosenberg and Abelson (1960) have applied a modification of Heider's theory to the problems of attitude change.

Dissonance theory. Leon Festinger, one of Lewin's most renowned students, has developed a theory (1957) which is similar to balance theory in its stress on the need to avoid cognitive inconsistency (dissonance) but differs from it in emphasizing postdecisional processes. Lewin (1939–1947), in a discussion of the behavior of a housewife who buys food, had suggested that behavior before and after decisions about purchasing food differed: prior to the decision, the more expensive the food, the less likely it was to get to the family table; after the decision, the higher its cost, the more likely it was to be used. Festinger's theory generalizes the idea that the postdecision situation may differ from the predecision situation. It makes the original assumption that making a decision per se arouses dissonance and pressure to reduce the dissonance. [*See* THINKING, *article on* COGNITIVE ORGANIZATION AND PROCESSES.]

Postdecision dissonance results, according to Festinger, from the fact that the decision in favor of the chosen alternative is counter to the beliefs which favor the unchosen alternative(s). To stabilize or freeze the decision after it has been made, the individual will attempt to reduce dissonance by changing his cognitions so that the relative attractiveness of the chosen, as compared with the unchosen, alternative is increased, or by developing cognitions which permit the alternatives to be substitutable for one another, or by revoking the decision psychologically. In Festinger's view (1964), the crucial difference from the predecision state of dissonance is that the predecisional conflict is "impartial" and "objective"; it does not lead to any spreading apart of the attractiveness in favor of the to-be-chosen alternative. Festinger writes: "Once the decision is made, however, and dissonance–reduction processes begin, one should be able to observe that the differences in attractiveness between the alternatives change, increasing in favor of the chosen alternative" (1964, pp. 8–9).

A variety of interesting and ingenious experiments have been stimulated by Festinger's view of the postdecision process. (See Brehm & Cohen 1962, for a detailed review.) These experiments have often involved "nonobvious" predictions which appear to defy common sense. Many of these predictions derive from the notion that if a decision produces insufficient rewards, the person will change his beliefs so as to make the decision seem more rewarding. Festinger (1961, p. 11) writes: "Rats and people come to love the things for which they have suffered." Presumably they do this to reduce the dissonance induced by the suffering, and their method of dissonance-reduction is to enhance the attractiveness of the choice which led to their suffering in order to justify it.

The theory of dissonance has stimulated extensive research into many aspects of social psychology: attitude and behavioral change, perceptual distortion, selective exposure to information, work productivity, and so forth. Recently, dissonance theory has been the subject of methodological criticism (Chapanis & Chapanis 1964) and theoretical criticism (Deutsch et al. 1962; Rosenberg 1965) which pose some difficult but perhaps not unresolvable problems for the theory.

T-group training. T-group training (laboratory training in groups) utilizes the experiences and interpersonal relations which occur in a temporary, laboratory-created group to help the participants develop insights into group processes, insights into the way that they themselves function in groups, and skills of participation in groups. The National Training Laboratories, which has become one of the key institutions concerned with the application of behavioral science to social practice, was established in 1947 with the cosponsorship of Lewin's Research Center for Group Dynamics and has been very much influenced by Lewin's ideas. His articles "Conduct, Knowledge, and Acceptance of New Values" (Lewin & Grabbe 1945) and "Frontiers in Group Dynamics" (1947) present the intellectual base for the development of the conception of laboratory training groups. These articles highlight the importance of the group in the process of individual re-education and change. In recent years, a considerable literature has been developed in connection with the laboratory method of training individuals in groups (see Bradford et al. 1964). While some of this literature is evangelistic in tone, this, too, is consonant with Lewin's active and continuing concern that social science be used to make the world a better place in which to live.

Although it cannot be said that Lewin's specific theoretical construct—his structural and dynamic concepts—are central in current research in psychology, his impact on psychology has been a major one. His impact is reflected in the general orientations which, today, are more and more taken for granted. These are that psychological events have to be explained in psychological terms; that central processes in the life space (e.g., distal perception, cognition, motivation, goal-directed behavior) rather than the peripheral processes of sensory input or of muscular action should be the focus of investigation; that psychological events have to be studied in their interrelations with one another; that the individual has to be studied in his interrelations with the group to which he belongs; that the attempt to bring about change in a process is the most fruitful way to investigate it; that important social psychological phenomena can be studied experimentally; that the scientist should have a social conscience; and that a good theory is valuable for social action as well as for science.

Morton Deutsch

[*Directly related are the entries* Gestalt theory; Personality; Phenomenology; Social psychology; Thinking, *article on* cognitive organization and processes; *and the biography of* Lewin. *For comparison, other relevant approaches to psychological phenomena may be found in* Personality: contemporary viewpoints; Psychoanalysis. *Relevant also are* Achievement motivation; Attitudes; Cohesion, social; Conflict; Groups; Leadership; Systems analysis, *article on* psychological systems; *and the biographies of* Brunswik; Cassirer; Hull; Tolman.]

BIBLIOGRAPHY

Adler, Dan L.; and Kounin, Jacob S. 1939 Some Factors Operating at the Moment of Resumption of Interrupted Tasks. *Journal of Psychology* 7:255–267.

Atkinson, John W. (1957) 1958 Motivational Determinants of Risk-taking Behavior. Pages 322–339 in John W. Atkinson (editor), *Motives in Fantasy, Action, and Society: A Method of Assessment and Study.* Princeton, N.J.: Van Nostrand. → First published in Volume 64 of *Psychological Review.*

Atkinson, John W. 1964 *An Introduction to Motivation.* Princeton, N.J.: Van Nostrand.

Back, Kurt W. 1951 Influence Through Social Communication. *Journal of Abnormal and Social Psychology* 46:9–23.

Barker, Roger G. (1946) 1953 *Adjustment to Physical Handicap and Illness.* 2d ed. New York: Social Science Research Council.

Bradford, Leland P.; Gibb, Jack R.; and Benne, Kenneth D. (editors) 1964 *T-group Theory and Laboratory Method: Innovation in Re-education.* New York: Wiley.

Brehm, Jack W.; and Cohen, Arthur R. 1962 *Explorations in Cognitive Dissonance.* New York: Wiley.

Cartwright, Dorwin; and Harary, Frank 1956 Structural Balance: A Generalization of Heider's Theory. *Psychological Review* 63:277–293.

Chapanis, Natalia P.; and Chapanis, Alphonse 1964 Cognitive Dissonance: Five Years Later. *Psychological Bulletin* 61:1–22.

Coch, Lester; and French, John R. P. 1948 Overcoming Resistance to Change. *Human Relations* 1:512–532.

Dembo, Tamara 1931 Der Ärger als dynamisches Problem. *Psychologische Forschung* 15:1–144.

Deutsch, Morton 1949a A Theory of Cooperation and Competition. *Human Relations* 2:129:152.

Deutsch, Morton 1949b An Experimental Study of the Effects of Co-operation and Competition Upon Group Process. *Human Relations* 2:199–231.

Deutsch, Morton; Krauss, Robert M.; and Rosenau, Norah 1962 Dissonance or Defensiveness? *Journal of Personality* 30:16–28.

Fajans, Sara 1933 Die Bedeutung der Entfernung für die Stärke eines Aufforderungscharakters beim Säugling und Kleinkind. Untersuchungen zur Handlungs- und Affektpsychologie, No. 12. *Psychologische Forschung* 17:215–267.

Festinger, Leon 1950 Informal Social Communication. *Psychological Review* 57:271–282.

Festinger, Leon 1954 A Theory of Social Comparison Processes. *Human Relations* 7:117–140.

Festinger, Leon 1957 *A Theory of Cognitive Dissonance.* Evanston, Ill.: Row, Peterson.

Festinger, Leon 1961 The Psychological Effects of Insufficient Reward. *American Psychologist* 16:1–11.

Festinger, Leon 1964 *Conflict, Decision, and Dissonance.* Stanford Studies in Psychology, No. 3. Stanford Univ. Press.

Festinger, Leon; Schachter, Stanley; and Back, Kurt (1950) 1963 *Social Pressures in Informal Groups: A Study of Human Factors in Housing.* Stanford Univ. Press.

FESTINGER, LEON; and THIBAUT, JOHN 1951 Interpersonal Communication in Small Groups. *Journal of Abnormal and Social Psychology* 46:92–99.

FRENCH, JOHN R. P. 1944 Organized and Unorganized Groups Under Fear and Frustration. Pages 229–308 in *Authority and Frustration*, by Kurt Lewin et al. Univ. of Iowa Press.

HEIDER, FRITZ 1946 Attitudes and Cognitive Organization. *Journal of Psychology* 21:107–112.

HEIDER, FRITZ 1958 *The Psychology of Interpersonal Relations*. New York: Wiley.

HENLE, MARY 1942 *An Experimental Investigation of Dynamic and Structural Determinants of Substitution*. Contributions to Psychological Theory, Vol. 2, No. 3, Serial No. 7. Durham, N.C.: Duke Univ. Press.

KARSTEN, ANITRA 1928 Psychische Sättigung. *Psychologische Forschung* 10:142–254.

KELLEY, HAROLD H. 1951 Communication in Experimentally Created Hierarchies. *Human Relations* 4:39–56.

KOUNIN, JACOB S. 1941 Experimental Studies of Rigidity. Parts 1–2. *Character and Personality* 9:251–282. → Part 1: The Measurement of Rigidity in Normal and Feeble-minded Persons. Part 2: The Explanatory Power of the Concept of Rigidity as Applied to Feeble-mindedness.

LEVY, S. 1953 Experimental Study of Group Norms: The Effects of Group Cohesiveness Upon Social Conformity. Ph.D. dissertation, New York Univ.

LEWIN, KURT (1935) 1948 Psycho–Sociological Problems of a Minority Group. Pages 145–158 in Kurt Lewin, *Resolving Social Conflicts: Selected Papers on Group Dynamics*. New York: Harper. → First published in Volume 3 of *Character and Personality*.

LEWIN, KURT (1935–1946) 1948 *Resolving Social Conflicts: Selected Papers on Group Dynamics*. New York: Harper.

LEWIN, KURT (1939–1947) 1963 *Field Theory in Social Science: Selected Theoretical Papers*. Edited by Dorwin Cartwright. London: Tavistock.

LEWIN, KURT (1943a) 1963 Defining the "Field at a Given Time." Pages 43–59 in Kurt Lewin, *Field Theory in Social Science: Selected Theoretical Papers*. London: Tavistock.

LEWIN, KURT (1943b) 1948 The Special Case of Germany. Pages 43–55 in Kurt Lewin, *Resolving Social Conflicts: Selected Papers on Group Dynamics*. New York: Harper. → First published in Volume 7 of *Public Opinion Quarterly*.

LEWIN, KURT (1946) 1948 Action Research and Minority Problems. Pages 201–218 in Kurt Lewin, *Resolving Social Conflicts: Selected Papers on Group Dynamics*. New York: Harper. → First published in Volume 2 of the *Journal of Social Issues*.

LEWIN, KURT (1947a) 1963 Frontiers in Group Dynamics. Pages 188–237 in Kurt Lewin, *Field Theory in Social Science: Selected Theoretical Papers*. Edited by Dorwin Cartwright. London: Tavistock. → First published in Volume 1 of *Human Relations*.

LEWIN, KURT (1947b) 1958 Group Decision and Social Change. Pages 197–211 in Society for the Psychological Study of Social Issues, *Readings in Social Psychology*. 3d ed. New York: Holt.

LEWIN, KURT; and GRABBE, PAUL (1945) 1948 Conduct, Knowledge, and Acceptance of New Values. Pages 56–68 in Kurt Lewin, *Resolving Social Conflicts: Selected Papers on Group Dynamics*. New York: Harper.

→ First published in Volume 1 of the *Journal of Social Issues*.

LEWIN, KURT et al. 1944 Level of Aspiration. Volume 1, pages 333–378 in J. McV. Hunt (editor), *Personality and the Behavior Disorders*. New York: Ronald Press.

LEWIS, HELEN B.; and FRANKLIN, MURIEL 1944 An Experimental Study of the Role of the Ego in Work. Part 2: The Significance of Task-orientation in Work. *Journal of Experimental Psychology* 34:195–215.

LIPPITT, RONALD; and WHITE, RALPH K. 1943 The "Social Climate" of Children's Groups. Pages 485–508 in Roger G. Barker, Jacob S. Kounin, and Herbert F. Wright (editors), *Child Behavior and Development*. New York: McGraw-Hill.

LISSNER, KÄTE 1933 Die Entspannung von Bedürfnissen durch Ersatzhandlungen. Untersuchungen zur Handlungs- und Affektspsychologie, No. 18. *Psychologische Forschung* 18:218–250.

McCLELLAND, DAVID C. et al. 1953 *The Achievement Motive*. New York: Appleton.

MAHLER, WERA 1933 Ersatzhandlungen verschiedenen Realitätsgrades. Untersuchungen zur Handlungs- und Affektspsychologie, No. 15. *Psychologische Forschung* 18:27–89.

MANDLER, GEORGE; and SARASON, SEYMOUR B. 1952 A Study of Anxiety and Learning. *Journal of Abnormal and Social Psychology* 47:166–173.

MILLER, NEAL E. 1944 Experimental Studies of Conflict. Volume 1, pages 431–465 in J. McV. Hunt (editor), *Personality and the Behavior Disorders*. New York: Ronald Press.

NEWCOMB, THEODORE M. 1953 An Approach to the Study of Communicative Acts. *Psychological Review* 60:393–404.

NEWCOMB, THEODORE M. 1961 *The Acquaintance Process*. New York: Holt.

ROSENBERG, MILTON J. 1965 When Dissonance Fails: On Eliminating Evaluation Apprehension From Attitude Measurement. *Journal of Personality and Social Psychology* 1:28–42.

ROSENBERG, MILTON J.; and ABELSON, R. P. 1960 An Analysis of Cognitive Balancing. Volume 3, pages 112–163 in *Attitude Organization and Change*, by Milton J. Rosenberg et al. New Haven: Yale Univ. Press.

SCHACHTER, STANLEY 1951 Deviation, Rejection and Communication. *Journal of Abnormal and Social Psychology* 46:190–207.

SCHACHTER, STANLEY 1959 *The Psychology of Affiliation: Experimental Studies of the Sources of Gregariousness*. Stanford Studies in Psychology, No. 1. Stanford Univ. Press.

SLIOSBERG, SARAH 1934 Zur Dynamik des Ersatzes in Spiel- und Ernstsituationen. *Psychologische Forschung* 19:122–181.

THIBAUT, JOHN 1950 An Experimental Study of the Cohesiveness of Underprivileged Groups. *Human Relations* 3:251–278.

THIBAUT, JOHN; and COULES, JOHN 1952 The Role of Communication in the Reduction of Interpersonal Hostility. *Journal of Abnormal and Social Psychology* 47:770–777.

ZEIGARNIK, BLUMA 1927 Das Behalten erledigter und unerledigter Handlungen. Untersuchungen zur Handlungs- und Affektspsychologie, No. 3. *Psychologische Forschung* 9:1–85.

FIELD WORK

Field work is the study of people and of their culture in their natural habitat. Anthropological field work has been characterized by the prolonged residence of the investigator, his participation in and observation of the society, and his attempt to understand the inside view of the native peoples and to achieve the holistic view of a social scientist. A society can be said to provide a ready-made laboratory for the social scientist in somewhat the same way that the human organism serves the biologist.

Field studies have long been the mark of cultural anthropologists and to a somewhat lesser degree of sociologists; they are increasingly being done by political scientists, social psychologists, and other social scientists. A difference exists between anthropology and sociology in the history, problems, and methods of field work. Today, however, the trend is toward similarity.

Anthropologists began to do field studies toward the end of the nineteenth century, although Morgan's study of the Iroquois appeared somewhat earlier. The major emphasis on anthropological field work has been primarily British and American, with such notable exceptions as the work of Thurnwald in Germany and of Lévi-Strauss in France. Among the first expeditions were those of Boas in British Columbia and of Haddon with his associates in the Torres Strait region of the Pacific. Their goal was to extend the boundaries of the knowledge of man by studying wide variations in his cultures.

The publication of Malinowski's *Argonauts of the Western Pacific* in 1922 revealed the great potentialities of field work. This study of Trobriand Islanders, among whom Malinowski had lived for almost three years, set new standards for field workers which continue to operate. Field work came to mean immersion in a tribal society—learning, as far as possible, to speak, think, see, feel, and act as a member of its culture and, at the same time, as a trained anthropologist from a different culture. It is significant that this method was forged in the study of small, homogeneous tribal societies in which it would have been difficult for the investigator to have avoided face-to-face relations. In recent years the range in type and size of societies studied by anthropologists has been much extended. With this extension, new problems and new methods have developed, but certain others have remained constant.

Beginning field work

The anthropologist chooses the geographical and cultural area for his field project, studies the litera-ture, and, if the language has been recorded, learns as much of it as possible before going into the field. Today, he will most likely also be interested in a specific problem and in social or culture theory, and he will endeavor to be *au courant* with the literature.

He then has to consider whether he goes to the field alone, with his family, or as part of a team. In the past the norm was the lone field worker; today it is common for the investigator's spouse and children to travel into the field. The research team—a number of anthropologists or scientists representing different disciplines—is a new trend. Each method has its advantages and disadvantages. Being alone gives a greater intensity to the field experience and may provide more intimate data, since the field worker is thrown upon the native people for company. On the other hand, it has the disadvantages of loneliness and of being limited to what one person can accomplish. The family has an advantage in reducing loneliness, and a mate and children may be useful entering wedges into the community and in securing data from their own sex and age groups. A team obviously extends the range of data which can be collected. A disadvantage of a family or team is that relationships with native peoples may be more difficult if one is quickly accepted and the other (or others) disliked.

Whether the field worker goes alone or with his family or as a member of a team, approval for the project and, if possible, cooperation must be secured from those who have authority in the society. Authority may reside in a group of clan elders, a chief, a tribal king, officials of a colonial government or an independent nation, the general manager of an industrial company, or the leaders of any other dominant economic, social, or political group. The questions of those in power, whoever they be, are usually concerned with whether the investigator threatens the *status quo* and whether he can be trusted not to reveal any information which they would consider harmful to the individual or the community. The traditional position of the anthropological field worker is that he is there as scholar to learn rather than as an instrument of change and that he never betrays an informant. (In applied social science, anthropologists, sociologists, economists, and others sometimes both study and help to implement social change, but this is a quite different type of field work [*see, for example*, ANTHROPOLOGY, *article on* APPLIED ANTHROPOLOGY].)

The nod of approval from those in power is only the first step. The field worker must then gain the good will of the people he wishes to study. He has to explain his presence to them, as he did to those in authority, as simply and as honestly as possible. In general there is no substitute for honesty. In some societies, both tribal and modern, people may be flattered by someone being interested enough to travel a long way to find out about their customs and to learn their language. The anthropologist must from the beginning differentiate himself from other aliens of his race or culture, such as missionary, government official, trader, planter, or work supervisor, whom the indigenous people may have known. It is extremely important that they have opportunities to observe and to know the field worker. The nearer his house is to the hub of activities, the easier it is for reciprocal observations and for easy social relations. The location of the house may also symbolically establish an important difference between the field worker and other aliens.

Gradually the field worker's role evolves. It usually has many facets and will not be the same in all situations or for all field workers. He may begin by rendering certain services. In a tribal society he often brings material goods ranging from ornaments to useful spades and knives. He may dispense simple remedies, such as aspirin and antimalarial medicine, to those needing them. In modern societies he often accepts invitations to speak to meetings of teachers, to church congregations, a chamber of commerce, and any other significant group that invites him. He is not only being helpful; he is making it easy for people to see and to know him.

The first steps

During the first month or so the field worker proceeds very slowly, making use of all his sensory impressions and intuitions. He walks warily and attempts to learn as quickly as possible the most important forms of native etiquette and taboos. When in doubt he falls back on his own sense of politeness and sensitivity to the feelings of others. He likewise has to cope with his own emotional problems, for he often experiences anxieties in a strange situation. He may be overwhelmed by the difficulties of really getting "inside" an alien culture and of learning an unrecorded or other strange language. He may wonder whether he should intrude into the privacy of people's lives by asking them questions. Field workers vary in their degree of shyness, but most people of any sensitivity experience some feelings of this type when they first enter a new field situation.

Sooner or later, when the field worker has established rapport with the people and has learned how to handle his own anxieties, he establishes a routine of work. It is usually wise to begin with relatively impersonal tasks. If he has not already done so, learning the language is among the first essentials. Field workers naturally vary in their linguistic abilities, and languages differ in degrees of complexity. But learning any unrecorded language presents manifest difficulties for anyone. Margaret Mead (1939) has made the useful distinction between *using* and *learning* the native language. The field worker frequently learns to speak and understand a language without learning it as a linguist would. In parts of Oceania where pidgin English is common, a combination of it and the native language may be the method of communication. In Africa, the field worker may have to know the language of the former or present colonial power, a lingua franca such as Swahili, and as much as possible of a native language. Often he works through an interpreter, either all the time or on certain problems where his fluency in the appropriate language is not sufficient for understanding. The status, sex, and personality of the interpreter may present difficulties in certain situations, and it may be useful, therefore, to have several interpreters. No easy solution to the language problem exists. Ideally, the field worker should be an expert in the native language. Usually he simply does the best he can within the limitations of time and the inherent difficulties of the situation.

Making a census is another early task which has the value of being impersonal and essential. It is necessary to locate people in space and to know the composition of households. As the field worker goes from one household to another, he also gets acquainted with the occupants. (In modern large societies, a government census is usually available.)

Participation in the culture

Participating and observing become an ever more important part of the routine. The field worker somewhat resembles a natural historian: he observes and notes, as far as possible, whatever comes within his range, even though he may not always know the relevance of all his observations. He follows long and devious sequences, such as those involved in initiation, marriage, and death rituals, which may be six or more months in preparation, and, at the same time, he observes the minutiae of daily life in which they occur. He accompanies the people on their economic tasks—hunting, fishing, planting, cooking, and others. He listens to them converse and gossip when they are at ease and picks up new clues which he later follows up. A woman anthropologist alone in the field can usually participate more fully than a man alone, because a man is generally restricted to being with other males. But even where social segregation between the sexes is strict, a woman can work with men as well as with women. No one fears her.

The intensity of the field worker's participation varies from one situation to another and between investigators. Among the Nuer, Evans-Pritchard was given little choice. The Nuer were "persistent and tireless" visitors, in and around his camp all the time, and he suffered from a lack of privacy (Evans-Pritchard 1940). Some anthropologists participate in ritual dances, feasts, and similar social events; others limit themselves to taking notes. The field worker's sense of the social situation and his personal desires and limitations dictate how much and when he will participate.

Whatever the degree of the field worker's participation in the whole society, friendships with a few people develop, and they help him to find a niche in the community. It is these friends who often become his best informants. They may include servants or other employees, a chief, medicine man, and many others. Often, too, an informal adoption as a "son," "daughter," "sister," or "brother" helps the anthropologist find his place and extends or deepens his range of knowledge. *In the Company of Man* (Casagrande 1960) provides profile sketches of key informants who were close associates and important teachers for each of the contributing anthropologists.

When the field worker has become familiar with the social contours and feels more or less accepted, he begins to work systematically on such anthropological problems as kinship systems, forms of marriage and residence, economic and political organization, witchcraft and magical beliefs and practices, or any other aspect of life which is significant in the society and interesting to him. He asks questions in structured and unstructured interviews and notes the measure of agreement or disagreement between the patterns which emerge from the answers and the actual behavior he observes. Usually, a discrepancy exists between the ideal and the real. Another method, used effectively by Oscar Lewis (1961), is the tape recording of long interviews with different members of one family, resulting in a significant humanistic account. Hortense Powdermaker (1962) had inter-African conversations recorded by an African assistant, which revealed spontaneous tones of feeling and subtleties of African life.

Unexpected and chance events, such as a quarrel, often reveal facets of a culture which the field worker had not known existed or, perhaps, only dimly suspected. Then, too, lies may be as informative on certain levels as the truth. For instance, in a study in Mississippi, one of the major values of middle-class white people—the straining for an aristocratic family background—was revealed in their consistent lying about their backgrounds (Powdermaker 1939). Failures and newcomers, who reveal the pressures which they resist or try to conform to, may be another excellent source of data.

Whomever the anthropologist is interviewing or however he is participating, there must be a high degree of reciprocal communication between him and the people he studies. This need represents an important difference between the methods of the social and the natural sciences. The chemist and physicist do not communicate personally with molecules or atoms, but communication for the social scientist depends to a large degree on his psychological involvement. The field worker faces a special problem, however, for he must be both detached and involved. If this dual role is an inherent part of the anthropologist's personality or self image (strengthened by his training), he plays it spontaneously and easily. As Goffman (1961) puts the problem, the degree of tension felt by a field worker corresponds to the level of congruence between spontanous and unspontaneous (playing the rules of the game) roles.

The notion that involvement connotes a lack of scientific objectivity is mistaken. It is only when an anthropologist is aware of his involvements that he can then detach himself and observe. Hidden or unconscious involvements (positive or negative) are dangerous, for the obvious reason that the investigator cannot step outside of them. An obsessive identification with either the underdog or the top social levels limits the field worker's communication and his objectivity. In a highly stratified society it is important for him to move easily within its different segments.

In addition to a capacity for open involvements and for becoming detached from them, personal qualities such as kindness, patience, tact, endurance, and the ability to "take" both loneliness and ambiguity are helpful. Other idiosyncratic characteristics may be useful in one field situation and not in another.

Despite its reputation, the so-called culture shock is not often one of the problems of a trained anthropologist. First, he arrives with a general knowledge of the people and their culture through having immersed himself in the literature. Second, his penetration into the culture is so gradual that by the time he achieves any understanding of it, he is apt to take it for granted. In fact, he has to be on his guard against this tendency. Culture shock is more likely to be experienced when he returns to his own modern urban society after an extended period in a tribal one.

The theoretical orientation of the field worker is significant from the beginning. Historical reconstruction, functionalism, a structural or cultural approach, and psychological anthropology are among the major frames of reference. Each influences the field worker's choice of problems, the type of data he collects, the kind of clues he picks up, some of his techniques, his hypotheses, and his interpretations. The collecting of data and theorizing are not necessarily separate processes. As the field worker participates, observes, and interviews, much of the time he is also thinking of hypotheses, of comparative data, and of relevant theories; it is also true, of course, that problems and hypotheses frequently arise out of empirical data in the field. Because of the personal nature of field work, it is imperative that while in the field the anthropologist accurately record empirical data separately from hypotheses and interpretations and distinguish the impressions from the definitive data. Thus, he should tell us the number of informants he used; give details of their age, sex, and social status; and provide precise descriptions of the methods used in securing data. Scientific standards demand as complete honesty as possible and data that may be negative as well as positive in terms of hypotheses. It should be possible for a reader to make different interpretations from the data. One of the most rigorously honest presentations is Cora DuBois's study of the Alorese (1944).

New trends in field work

The above points are relatively constant in all anthropological field work. Among the new trends are an emphasis on specific problems rather than on holistic studies; working in larger and more complex societies; a greater concern with sampling; the use of sociological surveys along with the traditional participation, observation, and interviewing; and a frank recognition of the fact that the field worker is a human instrument and part of the situation studied.

A team has obvious advantages in working on complex problems and in large societies. One of the early cross-disciplinary teams in the field was that of the anthropologist Clyde Kluckhohn and the physician Dorothea Leighton, who studied the Navajo (1946). An experiment in regional research was made by a team of 12 social scientists, all anthropologists except one historian and one political scientist, who worked on political development in Uganda and Tanganyika under the direction of

Audrey Richards (1960), then the director of the East African Institute of Social Research. The members of this team worked independently. A comparative study of child rearing in six cultures by six research teams, each consisting of a man and a woman worker, under the direction of John and Beatrice Whiting (1963), represents still another kind of team. A more extensive cross-disciplinary approach was used in a study (Rogler & Hollingshead 1965) of schizophrenia in Puerto Rico conducted by a sociologist, psychiatrists, an anthropologist, and social workers. As yet there have been relatively few field teams initiated by anthropologists which cover a large number of disciplines.

Anthropologists in the past were not unaware of the problem of sampling. An adequate sample might be almost impossible in historical reconstruction. But in small functioning communities, the whole population of the village usually appeared in the field worker's genealogical charts, and it was relatively easy for him to establish the frequency of forms of behavior without any elaborate statistical methods. Today, working in larger societies, the anthropologist often employs assistants to make a random survey at the beginning of the field study to establish patterns, or toward the end to substantiate or negate qualitative aspects of the research. But getting a truly random sample may present difficulties if the investigator and his assistants have no access (or much less) to one group.

Another new problem arises in working in those complex contemporary societies which have dual power structures representing different ideologies. To work with both is decidedly not easy. There is also the problem of centricity: most anthropologists find it more difficult to overcome ideological centricity than ethnocentricity. Training enables an anthropologist to study cannibalism, witchcraft, and other tribal customs with relative objectivity. It is less easy to be objective on issues which threaten strong political or other social commitments. On the other hand, a person who has no commitments would not be able to understand those of others.

Field work in sociology

As they work on problems in complex modern societies, anthropologists come closer to sociology. Field work has long been the practice of sociology, although its history and methodology have differed from those of anthropology. In contrast with the early anthropologists, who traveled far for comparative materials, the first field workers in sociology were primarily interested in the reform of their own society, in which the industrial revolution and the rise of an urban proletariat had brought many urgent social problems. In England, Beatrice Potter (later Mrs. Sidney Webb) and Charles Booth and, in France, Le Play did field studies among the poor through involvement with them, direct observation, and interviewing.

American sociologists followed in the European tradition of being critics of modern society. Initial empirical research included the *Hull-House Maps and Papers* (1895) and W. E. B. DuBois's *The Philadelphia Negro* (1899). Field work among the urban poor was developed at the University of Chicago by such men as Louis Wirth, Robert E. Park, and their many able students. They studied conditions among ethnic and racial minorities and such groups as criminals, hoboes, and prostitutes. These people were foreign, perhaps with an exotic quality, to many of the middle-class American sociologists. They explored at home, while the anthropologists of the same period were studying exotic peoples in distant lands.

The traditional distinction in subject matter is weakening. Members of both disciplines and of other social sciences increasingly study "primitive" preliterate and modern literate societies. Problems, too, become interchangeable; studies such as those of social structure, communities, social change, and interpersonal relations (e.g., those involved in social mobility, social conditioning, role playing) are common to both disciplines.

A few sociologists, such as Robert and Helen Lynd and William Foote Whyte, in their respective eminent studies, *Middletown* (1929) and *Street Corner Society* (1943), have used anthropological methods and techniques as models. But in general, the trend in sociology has been to emulate the natural sciences as far as possible and to limit field problems to those on which quantifiable data can be secured, primarily through the use of surveys. In 1959 Nathan Glazer wrote, "The sociologist today—whether his field of interest is the community, criminology, marriage and the family, world politics, social classes, housing—is a man who asks people questions and then statistically analyzes the answers to them. If he does not ask the questions himself, he hires some one else to ask them; or, if not that, he analyzes the statistics gathered by those who *have* asked questions—census-takers, social workers, and others" ([1959] 1964, pp. 43–44). The beginning of sociology in England coincided with the development of statistics there, and the relationship between the two is, thus, no accident.

Many sociological field studies lack personal participation and detailed observation; formal questionnaires can be a barrier to establishing relations between the field worker and the people he studies. According to John Bennett and Kurt Wolff (1955), the typical sociologist attempts to have the detachment and objectivity of the natural scientist and to view the people he studies as objects or, at best, "subjects" rather than as fellow human beings with whom he enters into some kind of personal relations.

There seems to be a new trend in which anthropology and sociology change places methodologically, at least to some degree. Increasingly anthropologists try to eliminate or deny the humanism of their approach and to select those field problems which they think lend themselves to a rigorous scientific method. Some anthropologists try to emulate the methods of the natural scientists, but the imitation, unfortunately, is often of the mechanistic notions of causality common to nineteenth-century science. These have now been replaced by principles of indeterminacy and by probability curves. It was a sociologist, Melville Dalton, who pointed out this time lag. He wrote, "Influenced by the dogmatism of nineteenth century science, research methodology in the social and psychological sciences is now more cocksure than in the increasingly humbler physical sciences" (Dalton 1959, p. 273).

The field worker as an individual

A quite new development, not yet strong enough to be called a trend, is the recognition that the field worker is himself an inherent part of the situation studied and that his personal as well as his scientific reactions are an important part of the research process. Field workers, of course, have long known that they are *human* instruments of research, although some have tried to be, or to present an image of, faceless robots. But there has been a reluctance to recognize the scientific significance of the field worker's personality and his all-too-human characteristics. Relatively little space has been given in publications to his mistakes, to the trial-and-error nature of some of his procedures, to the role of chance, to the influence of his reactions on a strange people and on their culture, and other such important personal factors. With a few exceptions, anthropologists have included only a few paragraphs or pages on these points in the introductions to their monographs or have relegated them to private conversations. After a long period of emulating natural scientists, some sociologists now recognize the peculiarly human characteristics of their discipline. In *Sociologists at Work* (Hammond 1964) 13 eminent sociologists give candid personal accounts of how their field research projects evolved, of their frustrations as well as their achievements in the field, of what actually happened rather than of what should have happened. *Stranger and Friend: The Way of an Anthropologist* (Powdermaker 1966) gives probably the frankest and most detailed account of one anthropologist's field studies, of mistakes as well as successes, of relationships between the field worker and the peoples studied, and of how her personality and training related to the type of work done.

The field is a laboratory in which the role of the investigator is significant and relevant to the study of the people and their culture, and obviously the more candid and revealing the field worker is about his role, the more scientific is the report and the more helpful it is to other investigators. The recognition of the significance of the personal characteristics of the field worker to his research confirms the point that field work is an art as well as a science.

HORTENSE POWDERMAKER

[*See also* ETHNOGRAPHY; INTERVIEWING; OBSERVATION.]

BIBLIOGRAPHY

ADAMS, RICHARD N.; and PREISS, JACK J. (editors) 1960 *Human Organization Research: Field Relations and Techniques.* Homewood, Ill.: Dorsey.

ARENSBERG, CONRAD M.; and KIMBALL, SOLON T. 1965 *Culture and Community.* New York: Harcourt. → See especially pages 28–47, "The Community-study Method."

BENNETT, JOHN W.; and WOLFF, KURT H. 1955 Toward Communication Between Sociology and Anthropology. *Yearbook of Anthropology* 1:329–351.

BERREMAN, GERALD D. 1962 *Behind Many Masks: Ethnography and Impression Management in a Himalayan Village.* Society for Applied Anthropology, Monograph No. 4. Ithaca, N.Y.: The Society.

[BOHANNAN, LAURA] (1954) 1964 *Return to Laughter,* by Elenore Bowen [pseud.]. Garden City, N.Y.: Doubleday.

CASAGRANDE, JOSEPH B. (editor) 1960 *In the Company of Man: Twenty Portraits by Anthropologists.* New York: Harper.

DALTON, MELVILLE 1959 *Men Who Manage: Fusions of Feeling and Theory in Administration.* New York: Wiley.

DUBOIS, CORA A. (1944) 1960 *The People of Alor: A Social-psychological Study of an East Indian Island.* Cambridge, Mass.: Harvard Univ. Press.

DUBOIS, W. E. B. 1899 *The Philadelphia Negro: A Social Study, Together With a Special Report on Domestic Service by Isabel Eaton.* Series in Political Economy and Public Law, No. 14. Philadelphia: Univ. of Pennsylvania.

EVANS-PRITCHARD, E. E. (1940) 1963 *The Nuer: A Description of the Modes of Livelihood and Political Institutions of a Nilotic People.* Oxford: Clarendon.

FIRTH, RAYMOND W. (1936) 1957 *We, the Tikopia: A Sociological Study of Kinship in Primitive Polynesia.* 2d ed. London: Allen & Unwin. → A paperback edition was published in 1963 by Beacon.

GILLIN, JOHN 1949 Methodological Problems in the Anthropological Study of Modern Cultures. *American Anthropologist* New Series 51:392–399.

GLAZER, NATHAN (1959) 1964 The Rise of Social Research in Europe. Pages 43–72 in Daniel Lerner (editor), *The Human Meaning of the Social Sciences.* New York: Meridian.

GOFFMAN, ERVING (1956) 1959 *The Presentation of Self in Everyday Life.* Garden City, N.Y.: Doubleday.

GOFFMAN, ERVING 1961 *Encounters: Two Studies in the Sociology of Interaction.* Indianapolis, Ind.: Bobbs-Merrill.

HAMMOND, PHILLIP E. (editor) 1964 *Sociologists at Work: Essays on the Craft of Social Research.* New York: Basic Books.

HENRY, JULES; and SPIRO, MELFORD E. 1953 Psychological Techniques: Projective Tests in Field Work. Pages 417–429 in International Symposium on Anthropology, *Anthropology Today.* Edited by A. L. Kroeber. Univ. of Chicago Press.

Hull-House Maps and Papers: A Presentation of Nationalities and Wages in a Congested District of Chicago, Together With Comments and Essays on Problems Growing Out of the Social Conditions. 1895 New York: Crowell.

JUNKER, BUFORD H. (1960) 1962 *Field Work: An Introduction to the Social Sciences.* Univ. of Chicago Press.

KLUCKHOHN, CLYDE 1945 The Personal Document in Anthropological Science. Pages 79–173 in Louis R. Gottschalk, Clyde Kluckhohn, and Robert Angell, *The Use of Personal Documents in History, Anthropology and Sociology.* New York: Social Science Research Council.

KLUCKHOHN, CLYDE; and LEIGHTON, DOROTHEA (CROSS) (1946) 1951 *The Navaho.* Oxford Univ. Press.

KLUCKHOHN, FLORENCE R. 1940 The Participant–Observer Technique in Small Communities. *American Journal of Sociology* 46, no. 3:331–343.

LEWIS, OSCAR 1953 Controls and Experiments in Field Work. Pages 452–475 in International Symposium on Anthropology, *Anthropology Today.* Edited by A. L. Kroeber. Univ. of Chicago Press.

LEWIS, OSCAR 1961 *The Children of Sánchez: Autobiography of a Mexican Family.* New York: Random House. → A paperback edition was published in 1963 by Vintage.

LYND, ROBERT S.; and LYND, HELEN M. (1929) 1930 *Middletown: A Study in Contemporary American Culture.* New York: Harcourt. → A paperback edition was published in 1959.

MALINOWSKI, BRONISLAW (1922) 1960 *Argonauts of the Western Pacific: An Account of Native Enterprise and Adventure in the Archipelagoes of Melanesian New Guinea.* London School of Economics and Political Science, Studies, No. 65. London: Routledge; New York: Dutton. → A paperback edition was published in 1961 by Dutton.

MEAD, MARGARET 1939 Native Languages as Field-work Tools. *American Anthropologist* New Series 41:189–205.

NADEL, S. F. 1939 The Interview Technique in Social Anthropology. Pages 317–327 in F. C. Bartlett et al. (editors), *The Study of Society: Methods and Problems.* London: Routledge; New York: Macmillan.

NASH, DENNISON 1963 The Ethnologist as a Stranger: An Essay in the Sociology of Knowledge. *Southwest Journal of Anthropology* 19, no. 2:149–167.

OSGOOD, CORNELIUS 1953 *Winter.* New York: Norton.

PAUL, BENJAMIN D. 1953 Interviewing Techniques and Field Relationships. Pages 430–451 in International Symposium on Anthropology, *Anthropology Today.* Edited by A. L. Kroeber. Univ. of Chicago Press.

POWDERMAKER, HORTENSE 1939 *After Freedom: A Cultural Study in the Deep South.* New York: Viking.

POWDERMAKER, HORTENSE 1962 *Copper Town; Changing Africa: The Human Situation on the Rhodesian Copperbelt.* New York: Harper.

POWDERMAKER, HORTENSE 1966 *Stranger and Friend: The Way of an Anthropologist.* New York: Norton.

RICHARDS, AUDREY I. (editor) 1960 *East African Chiefs: A Study of Political Development in Some Uganda and Tanganyika Tribes.* London: Faber; New York: Praeger.

RIESMAN, DAVID; and BENNEY, MARK 1956a The Sociology of the Interview. *Midwest Sociologist* 18:3–15.

RIESMAN, DAVID; and BENNEY, MARK (editors) 1956b The Interview in Social Research. *American Journal of Sociology* 62, no. 2. → See especially pages 137–252.

ROGLER, LLOYD H.; and HOLLINGSHEAD, AUGUST B. 1965 *Trapped: Families and Schizophrenia.* New York: Wiley.

WAGLEY, CHARLES; and GALVÃO EDUARDO 1949 *The Tenetehara Indians of Brazil: A Culture in Transition.* Columbia University Contributions to Anthropology, No. 35. New York: Columbia Univ. Press. → See especially the preface.

WAX, ROSALIE H. 1952 Reciprocity as a Field Technique. *Human Organization* 11, no. 3:34–37.

[WITHERS, CARL] (1945) 1961 *Plainville, U.S.A.,* by James West [pseud.]. New York: Columbia Univ. Press.

WHITING, BEATRICE B. (editor) 1963 *Six Cultures: Studies of Child Rearing.* New York: Wiley.

WHYTE, WILLIAM F. (1943) 1961 *Street Corner Society: The Social Structure of an Italian Slum.* 2d ed., enl. Univ. of Chicago Press.

WHYTE, WILLIAM F. 1957 On Asking Indirect Questions. *Human Organization* 15, no. 4:21–23.

FIGGIS, JOHN NEVILLE

The work of John Neville Figgis (1866–1919) in political philosophy constitutes the fusing of two interests and two careers. Born in Brighton, England, and educated at Cambridge University, he developed and matured as a student of history and political thought under the influence of Maitland. Influenced also by another distinguished Cambridge teacher, Mandell Creighton, he recognized a call to the religious life, which led him to the Church of England and eventually to a monastic order of that church, the Community of the Resurrection. He continued writing and occasional lecturing on both religious and political–historical topics until his death.

In his historical works on political theory, Figgis laid greatest emphasis, in the tradition of Gierke and Maitland, on the importance of man's corporate life as the foundation of the state. His *Churches in the Modern State* (1913) is a popular exposition of the nature of corporate life and an application of his theory to the question of the nature of a church and its relation to the state. It exhibits a passionate concern for freedom in the face of the growing power and authority of the state.

From his scholarly studies of the history of political thought, especially that of the Middle Ages and the early modern period, Figgis concluded that there are two ways of understanding the corporation. He assumed that a corporation is "a society of men bound together for a permanent interest," and he recognized as corporations such bodies as the family, the club, the union, the college, and the church. Bodies other than the state must be understood *either* as creatures of the state *or* as real persons with lives of their own and an origin independent of the state. From Figgis' point of view, the former approach is wrong, and the latter is true to the facts of history and social life.

The monistic theory

Figgis traced the theory that the corporation is a creature of the state to the concept of absolute sovereignty, which in turn he traced to the abstract idea of unity. Modern monism (the theory of the unitary or all-embracing state) derives, he suggested, from the ancient conception of the city-state as an organic unity and from the view developed in Roman law of the position and authority of the emperor as sovereign. These notions were imported into the Roman Catholic church in the medieval period and developed (with only a slight setback—the conciliar movement in the fifteenth century) into the nineteenth-century doctrine of the absolute power and infallibility of the pope. In the course of this "*crescendo* of Papal claims," attempts were made by some popes—for example, Boniface VIII, 1294–1303, and John XXII, 1316–1334—to claim secular power as well as spiritual power and authority. With the rise of national states after the Renaissance, these attempts failed, but a political theory was developed by Machiavelli, Bodin, and Hobbes that claimed for the ruler in the secular realm the same authority that the popes had been able to establish for themselves in the church. According to this theory, as Figgis described it, the sovereign of the state, whether one man, a few men, or all men, is the sole source of social authority and social life; no other society (corporation) has a life of its own. Each society in the state exists, carries on its affairs, and exercises its authority over its members with the permission, tacit or express, of the sovereign. All such societies are merely creatures of the state; they have no innate life of their own and no original right or authority.

This theory of corporations is rejected by Figgis on two main grounds: first, that it does not square with the facts of history; and second, that the implications of this doctrine are inimical to the self-development and freedom of the individual. The evidence to support the first argument was developed by Gierke in his monumental *Das deutsche Genossenschaftsrecht*. Gierke had shown that there is another way to conceive of corporations and even a spirit of corporate life. Figgis accepted Gierke's approach and developed evidence of his own from his analysis of the situation in his own day of social groups vis-à-vis the state. He was especially concerned with the problem of the relation of churches to the state in a period of religious heterogeneity. Put simply, the question is, What authority does a modern state (for example, England in the late nineteenth or early twentieth century) have over the churches that have been organized within its borders? (The problem of England is especially complicated because it has both an established church and unestablished churches, which are both national and international.) The state clearly has the right to prevent or punish violations of law. But does not a church have the right to determine its membership conditions, its ritual, and even its purpose without state interference? The issue had been met in the courts where some members of a church sued to prevent church leadership supported by a majority of the membership from amalgamating with another church (1913, pp. 18–20). The results of these cases pointed sometimes to the monistic theory (when churches were prevented from changing) and sometimes to the other theory (when churches were left to themselves). Similar cases arose and continue to arise in connection with trade unions, and the issue has not really been settled.

The second argument against the monistic theory, namely, that its implications for individual freedom are repugnant, hinges on the demonstration that there is a growing trend, independent both of the development of one-man rule and of democratic rule, toward the destruction of smaller organizations either by their consolidation into larger ones or by their absorption into the state. Believers in freedom for the individual must condemn this development because it cuts off from more and more individuals their sources of social power and their support against the might of the state. It does not matter that the state is one which exhibits popular sovereignty. The life of man is a social life, and if ultimately there is no society other than the state, man becomes a creature of the state. Figgis did not live to see the rise of modern totalitarianism in the third and fourth decades of the twentieth century, but he did foresee it. Much evidence could be found in the later period to confirm his fears.

The corporation as a real person

A more adequate theory of corporate life, Figgis held, sees any corporation (especially such a voluntary association as a church) as possessing an inherent life of its own, generated out of the spirit and will of its members. He recognized the affinities of his approach to that of Rousseau. A corporation is a living force with powers of self-development. It has a life greater than the mere sum of the individuals composing it and is not merely a matter of contract. Each such body has its own individuality, its own ethos. The existence of such bodies is a "social fact" that may or may not be recognized by the state. Failure to recognize it leads to a condition akin to that of individuals in slavery. Recognition of the real personality of corporations by the state leads to a conception of the state as a *communitas communitatum*.

Groups that arise in society out of the efforts of individuals to realize themselves do not develop without genuine authority over their members, and this authority manifests itself in a government that has legislative, executive, and judicial powers. The authority of the group comes from the consent of its members. The group carries on activities that are public for its members, but private in relation to the state. But Figgis realized that this distinction between public and private does not satisfactorily describe life in modern societies. Instead of seeing society as a collection of individuals confronting an entity called the "state" and being unified by it, he saw society as a complex of individuals, groups, and corporations presided over by a rather special sort of group called the "state." Figgis was part of that pluralistic movement that saw the state as one group in society having distinctive functions, but one which was not in all ways superior to every other group, either in its claims on the individual or in its benefits to him. The state is a strong power that is needed to prevent injustice between groups and to secure to each group its rights. It does not create the groups, but in pursuing its own goals it has to regulate them, limit their activities, and settle conflicts among them. However, the resolution of conflicts has tended to produce, Figgis believed, unwarranted interference in the internal life of groups. His doctrine, reminiscent of that of Mill, is that the state has the right to limit the activities of groups only insofar as they impinge on other groups or individuals and that the internal life of the group is inviolable. For Figgis, this is the meaning of the doctrine of the real personality of corporations, and it seems to stand or fall on the adequacy of the distinction between the internal (private) and the external (public) activities of groups.

Although Figgis never developed a systematic political theory in any detail, he offered hints as to the proper point of view of an adequate political theory, and from these hints his readers may gain some idea of the sort of theory he would defend. The recognition of the real personality of groups, the importance of "self-realization" for groups, and the characterization of the state as the *communitas communitatum* suggest that his theory would derive from Gierke and Maitland on the one hand and from the British Hegelians on the other. His concern for freedom speaks of the influence of Mill and Acton. Yet he never does come to grips with the question, What is a state? If corporations are real persons, it is self-contradictory to say that it is a *communitas communitatum*, for if the state is taken to be a real person, what happens to other groups which are internal to it? If, however, the other groups are seriously thought to be independent of the state, in what sense does it continue to be a *communitas*? The doctrine of the real personality of corporations seems to introduce rigidities of its own that inhibit the clear observation of the facts of social life. The subsequent development of pluralism (political, social, and economic) carried further the "discrediting" of the state and provoked, in turn, a reaction in the direction of statism that Figgis would have deplored.

HENRY M. MAGID

[*For the historical context of Figgis' work, see* PLURALISM *and the biographies of* ACTON; GIERKE; GREEN; MAITLAND; MILL. *For other relevant material see* SOVEREIGNTY; STATE; VOLUNTARY ASSOCIATIONS.]

WORKS BY FIGGIS

(1896) 1922   *The Divine Right of Kings.* 2d ed. Cambridge Univ. Press. → First published as *The Theory of the Divine Right of Kings.* A paperback edition was published in 1965 by Harper.
1907   *Studies of Political Thought: From Gerson to Grotius, 1414–1625.* Cambridge Univ. Press.
(1913) 1914   *Churches in the Modern State.* 2d ed. London and New York: Longmans.
1917   *The Will to Freedom, or the Gospel of Nietzsche and the Gospel of Christ.* New York: Scribner.
1921   *The Political Aspects of St. Augustine's* City of God. London: Longmans.

SUPPLEMENTARY BIBLIOGRAPHY

MAGID, HENRY M.   1941   *English Political Pluralism: The Problem of Freedom and Organization.* Columbia University Studies in Philosophy, No. 2. New York: Columbia Univ. Press. → See especially pages 10–30 on "Figgis: The Significance of the Real Personality of Groups."
TUCKER, MAURICE G.   1950   *John Neville Figgis: A Study.* London: Society for Promoting Christian Knowledge.

FILM

Cinema, which by now should mean both motion pictures for theaters and films for television, is simultaneously an art and an industry because its means of creation and its systems of distribution involve expensive technology. This has been true since the early nickelodeon days of the public viewing parlor, when five cents illuminated a 50-foot-long scene. Today's distribution of color television into living rooms at the rate of $105,000 for a 50-second commercial only inflates the problem in terms of the costs involved and the relative quality of the product.

What effect this artistic, social, and economic phenomenon has on the cultural values of both creators and viewers is an international problem of the first magnitude, since cinema is a world-wide language that can be grasped by the illiterate as well as by the educated. Nothing less than the control of men's minds and emotions is at stake. Since aesthetics, in this case, has become linked both with economics and with political action responsive to the uses of visual communication, cinema is the major cultural force in the second half of the twentieth century.

The relation between those who create the picture and those who pay its costs is a conflict between the front office and the sound stage as old as Michelangelo's quarrels with the papacy, or as complex as Shakespeare's efforts to gain the good graces of his patrons. What is unique to cinema is the degree of interdependence between artistry and finance.

The question cannot be dismissed as a matter of preference. What is art to one may indeed be an industry to another, and vice versa. The inseparability of the equation makes it difficult to evaluate. The union of film art and the picture industry is a marriage contracted in hell, lived on earth, and rewarded in heaven.

Problems of film production.   A poet needs only paper and pen to be in business; a novelist has the option of adding typewriter and ribbons to these tools; a painter can start work once he has brushes, paints, and canvas; and a sculptor can fashion almost any durable material. A musician is not obliged to own or rent an orchestra to compose a symphony. But a motion picture director requires a fully equipped studio to compose a motion picture. An impoverished painter could steal hair from a cat to make a brush, but a film director will find that cameras, lenses, lights, developing tanks, and editing apparatus are relatively inexpensive compared with actors' salaries, set construction, or shooting on location.

Cinema is the only art form solely dependent on machinery. The electronic extension of motion pictures via television is more expensive and involves more machinery. Never before in man's artistic history has the artist been so subordinate to the means which shape his ends; and, conversely, never before has the patron or sponsor or producer been so dependent on talent for the utilization of his machinery for production, distribution, and exhibition. A camera collecting dust is not a money-making gadget, nor is a script collecting dust a motion picture that can be projected.

A writer–director in cinema is like an orchestral conductor; his script, or score, cannot be experienced without the collaboration of myriad different craftsmen employing different instruments. Ideally, they should be hired for their specific competence in dealing with a special challenge. This is a problem of correct casting of craftsmen, but under strict union regulations of seniority the writer–director is obliged to accept the run-of-the-mill worker, who is not generally inclined to support artistic adventures. Also, the number of employees allotted to an assignment has been prescribed by union rules. There are qualitative considerations aside from the quantity of workers, assistants, and collaborators. A studio may employ specialists as diverse as architects (to design sets) and experts in Zen Buddhism (to do "research").

Since the basic concepts of a motion picture must be filtered through so many individuals before the picture reaches its final version, and since these concepts are primarily visual, the relation of the number of individuals involved to the degree of aesthetic coherence in the picture's imagery is obviously crucial. A cinematic law might be postulated: The greater the number of collaborators in the creation of a picture, the less coherent its imagery will be.

Production problems begin with the "source," which is either a story or a body of factual material. The source may be a novel, a play, a short story, or an "original treatment"; it may even be a social essay, a political theme, or a report on actualities. The author of the source will usually have his ideas and emotions translated into script form by other writers; the final shooting script may be prepared by yet another batch of writers, including dialogue specialists. Such has been the prevailing pattern in Hollywood's film and television studios; the same is true of Italy, France, Yugoslavia, Hungary, Czechoslovakia, Poland, the Soviet Union, Japan, Nationalist China, and the Chinese People's Republic. In England and Sweden the tendency has been to use an individual writer, as is the preference in independent production in the United States. In fact, the writer–director personality as a single force explains the rising quality throughout the world of the feature film. Such figures as Ingmar Bergman, Federico Fellini, Michelangelo Antonioni, Jean-Luc Godard, François Truffaut, David Lean, Tony Richardson, Stanley Kubrick, and Sidney Lumet are directors who also serve as their own writers, in close cooperation with a scenarist.

Final decisions over script in terms of plot and story values, over casting of stars and other actors, and over the editing of the shots were made by producers or executive producers during the years of the mass production system. Thus a studio like Twentieth Century-Fox, Metro-Goldwyn-Mayer, or Warner Brothers used to program its merchandise, during the heyday of studio monopoly, by planning ten westerns, five musical comedies, a dozen social dramas (with love interest), half a dozen situation comedies, five war dramas, and a flock of Grade B thrillers. Depending on how these products sold in the market place, the program for the following year was adjusted. The producer system reigned. In the 1930s and 1940s the producer was like a lord commanding his manor, but he was also in competition with a neighboring producer under company management whose power also rose or fell according to the success of his product. Executive producers were like dukes ruling over a collection of lordly producers. Such duchy strongholds were set up at M-G-M, for example, under the supreme authority of the king, Louis B. Mayer. Industry ruled over art (Crowther 1957; Ross 1952).

For the creative talent there was no choice; Faust was compelled to sell his soul to the devil. Throughout the 1930s novelists and playwrights from the East (whose fate is perhaps epitomized by that of F. Scott Fitzgerald) accepted front office control; there was no other, since Samuel Goldwyn ran a one-man M-G-M.

Rise and fall of the independents. The celebrated case of *United States* v. *Paramount* ended the reign of the studio chiefs when the Supreme Court held that a producer cannot be an exhibitor. This bill of divorcement, known as the Anti-Block Booking Decision, separated the ownership of studios from ownership of movie theaters (Conant

1960). The principle behind the Supreme Court's decision was the Sherman Anti-Trust Act of some seven decades earlier, a principle never before applied to the distribution of an American art form. The 1907 Patents Trust case had already broken the production monopoly held by the Edison interests, so that dozens of new producing companies were founded at that time. These were consolidated or eliminated throughout the first two decades of the century, climaxing in the monolithic studios of the 1930s and 1940s. Following the Anti-Block Booking Decision, independent production boomed, mainly through stars and directors forming their own companies. It would naturally be assumed that the liberation of talented creators from the assembly line production system would permit more audacious pictures with fresh plots and deeply delineated characterizations. Such hopes have proven hallucinatory. Although the economic base shifted in the 1950s, the cultural superstructure remained solidly attached to box office values. Men of talent had been conditioned by formula, and upon risking their own money and reputations, they played the new game in the safe style of the old one.

In the 1960s no longer does the producer represent the banker; he may be the same person. Or the actor may be his own director, and the writer his own producer. But the Muse Unchained can inspire only those who are capable of appreciating freedom and adventure. On the whole, the product of a company dominated by an actor or director cannot be distinguished from the run-of-the-mill product of a major manufacturer. The suspicion grew that Faust couldn't deliver any more than the devil. To give the devil his due, it must be said that the banker began to suspect that the artist (actor, director, or writer–producer) was not interested so much in creating a new art as in accumulating new money.

Films and audiences in the 1960s. The artistic bankruptcy of Hollywood existed before the coming of television. There were, of course, a few good pictures made during the early 1950s, among which *High Noon, Shane, On the Waterfront,* and *Marty* were outstanding. But bad money makes more bad money—all, unfortunately, of an identical green. Major manufacturing companies took on serials for TV; the Saturday serial of silent days became nightly, national, and network. Artistic values have continued to suffer, while the major portion of many studios' income has come from the sale or rental of previous features to television, the production of serials and features for television, and the rental of studio space and facilities to television.

Hollywood in the mid-1960s continues at an artistic low level, with an accompanying hostility toward serious pictures. Artistic initiative has shifted from Hollywood to abroad. The American motion picture audience has been fragmented, thanks to television. The fragmentation is quite similar to the division in other entertainments, such as the theater, books, and magazines. The potential market for quality pictures is at an all-time high; for instance, there are over four thousand film societies at American universities, with an attendance of over 2.5 million. Nevertheless, the old answers to the problem of quality continue in force. The "blockbuster" produced by the major studio—one thinks of *Ben Hur, Spartacus, Guns of Navarone, Cleopatra*—has been an old answer. Independent production, which has given us such pictures as *The Bridge on the River Kwai, Anatomy of a Murder,* and *Lawrence of Arabia,* is still an old answer.

What is new is that the fragmented audience may be as small as that of art houses or film societies, or as large as that of national circuits. Moreover, producers realize that there is less financial risk in a good low-budget film than in a good high-budget film. *Lawrence of Arabia,* for example, did not make the profit, in proportion to its costs, that was made by *Tom Jones.* In Europe, where governments frequently underwrite a portion of production costs, financing is both less complex and more easily arranged; dual producerships involving partners from different European countries assure lower costs. Among the major film-producing countries, only the United States does not in some measure subsidize film production. Also, there is greater artistic freedom in Europe, where the film is recognized as a director's medium.

Ingmar Bergman, more than any foreign director, has demonstrated that artistic independence can collect, however modestly in his case, at box offices. Of American producer–directors, Stanley Kramer has been the most successful in proving that political subjects can also collect; his *The Defiant Ones, On the Beach, Judgment at Nuremberg,* and *Ship of Fools* all dealt with unmistakably political themes, and all made money. It is possible that successes like these may slowly be encouraging the major producers to abandon their reliance on time-worn formulas. For instance, a "sleeper" like *David and Lisa*—a small-budget picture with virtually unknown actors that dealt with the theme of mental illness with unusual realism—may have influenced one of the more progressive major studios to distribute *Love With a Proper Stranger,* in which a young girl's love affair was treated with an absence of conventional moralizing that was quite new to the American screen. In this way even a few examples of artistic boldness may have an impact on the entire industry. At any rate, by the late 1960s the foreign director, the native producer, and the major releaser were all influencing and in turn being influenced by a more enterprising production outlook.

What was hopefully different about this outlook was a greater reliance on the individual. Stanley Kubrick was able to make *Dr. Strangelove*, the most independently audacious American film since *Citizen Kane*, because the distributor who paid for the production (Columbia) did not have script-approval rights. The result was a uniquely stylized and satirical film that could not otherwise have been made and that in certain categories achieved box office records. Carl Foreman, who enjoyed script freedom for *The Victors*, did a controversial picture that was more successful financially than D. W. Griffith's masterpiece *Intolerance*, which had to wait several decades for its proper recognition. It is clear that the fragmented movie audience of the 1960s can be reached if the proper means are employed.

Of gods and bankers. If a signature, as John Houseman terms it, is now more possible on a film than before, then the artistic prospects appear good. In Europe, films are advertised through the name of the director as well as the stars. This emphasis on basic creative talent is beginning to receive recognition in America, but only a few directors, such as George Stevens, John Huston, and Stanley Kramer, are widely known to the public. Stanley Kubrick, Sidney Lumet, and John Frankenheimer are relatively unfamiliar except to younger, serious audiences. The clearer the director's own contribution becomes, the more likely he is to be recognized as a factor in box office receipts and the greater the support he is likely to gain from the bankers who finance motion pictures. It is not so crucially important that the mass of people can't tell one Ford from another, except on wheels; the gentlemen who own and control the apparatus of manufacture and distribution know who is most likely to return profits on their loans. Ingmar Bergman has rejected offers from every major American owner of the apparatus. That he was wanted makes it easier for younger directors to enter doors. Fellini's financial success in Europe with *La Dolce Vita* gave him the opportunity to be his own boss in *8½* after years of hocking his soul to Roman financiers. The artistic and financial success of *8½* permitted Fellini to exercise his freedom with wider scope in *Giulietta degli Spiriti*, but not, unfortunately, with similar success. It is doubtful whether a single creative person is capable of having the

judgment to control objectively the writer as well as the director in him. Both Wall Street and the studios should take note that the single gifted individual is sufficient unto himself in any art except the film. Indeed, the varied talents of the writer–director–producer are inherently at odds with each other. Even so catholic a genius as Leonardo da Vinci would have found himself hard put to be the following (all in his own image): writer, director, producer, editor, promoter, manager of a seven-ring circus, handholder, advertiser, salesman, and psychoanalyst for actors. It is excessive to expect so much, even from a cinematic god.

The writer in him will tell the director how to shoot, but the director will prevent the editor in him from trimming shots before the saturation point. Conversely, the promoter in him will cast actors or actresses who have box office appeal but are not necessarily suitable for the characters they are to portray. When all these talents work well together in one body and one mind, we have the rarest of exceptions: a work of art that is a financial success. Who can deny how different the second half of *Lawrence of Arabia* might have been had David Lean, a truly gifted director, been able to maintain an artistic coherence? Or—conversely—how much more gratifying *Cleopatra* could have been for the mass audience had an administrative intelligence controlled excesses of writing and direction.

Casting of artistry by financial authority is as important for total achievement as the casting of financial acumen by the creator. Louis B. Mayer is as dead as Erich von Stroheim, the director he defeated in the cutting room when *Greed* was mutilated. History is always on the side of the creator, but this is of little consolation during periods of creative struggle. Stroheim, who never had the opportunity to cast bankers, would soon be a cinematic god if he were alive in today's market place.

Nevertheless, living gods are rare in cinema. Orson Welles was once such a demon, Federico Fellini is today in Italy, Ingmar Bergman in Sweden, and Akira Kurosawa in Japan. Perhaps the greatest of them all is Luis Buñuel, an enigmatic genius who has been making and breaking rules for forty years. No American director can be said to enjoy this stature. Those who are their own producers—John Ford, Elia Kazan, Stanley Kubrick, George Stevens, Billy Wilder, William Wyler, Fred Zinnemann—obviously produce the better American pictures. Should this trend expand through one fragmented audience into others, it could parallel the first golden age, the years of D. W. Griffith, Thomas H. Ince, Mack Sennett,

Charles Chaplin, Douglas Fairbanks—when directors did their own casting of bankers. The question of for whom a picture is intended is more important now than previously, primarily because art and industry are wedded as never before. It is a different kind of liaison, a marriage made in heaven, lived in hell, and rewarded on earth.

The television monopoly. In the nonfragmented audience of television viewers, the film writer–director lives in a serfdom unparalleled in the history of creativity in America. Since television has become the center of every home and the heart of the advertising world, the financial prizes are tempting beyond imagination. Not even in the decades when Hollywood's monetary rewards were reckoned as phenomenal has there been so much money paid out to so many people for so little talent.

Following the exposure of the rigged quiz shows, the TV networks assumed programming control in 1960. Between that year and 1966 network profits rose from about $21 million to more than $80 million. The prime time between 7:30 P.M. and 10:30 P.M. is controlled by the three networks, who produce the programs on film or tape, either directly or through affiliates or associates, and sell the time and costs to the sponsor. Thus the networks act as both producers and distributors, in violation of the Sherman Anti-Trust Act and in direct contravention of the *United States* v. *Paramount* Supreme Court ruling. Although the attorney general of the United States could go to court and win a decree that would separate television program production (90 per cent of which is on film or tape and comes out of Hollywood) from television program exhibition, no action is taken. The advertisers remain in show business and get more powerful every year, though they are, in turn, dependent on the networks for time slots and programs. The competition between advertisers for prime time strengthens the monopoly power of the networks.

Hollywood film producers of programs for sale to the networks claim, and rightly so, that they cannot get their shows on television unless they invite a network to participate in (1) a portion of the copyright ownership, meaning a share of present and future profits; (2) domestic syndication rights, which are the major profit source in booking films into local television stations; (3) foreign syndication rights, which are increasingly profitable and are cushions for future income during a producer's dry period or his old age. "Residuals"— the profit from replays—are highly lucrative in the rebooking of such popular serials as *Gunsmoke*, *Bonanza*, *I Love Lucy*, and dozens more.

The box office standard of judgment for motion pictures has been replaced by the television rating systems, which estimate, with varying degrees of inaccuracy, the alleged millions viewing a given program at a given time. Although quality drama and public affairs documentaries may have audiences in the millions—larger than audiences in the past who viewed such programs in theaters or classrooms—these films are unceremoniously scuttled in favor of more shows with mass appeal. The lowest common denominator ensures the advertiser of the widest market for his sales pitch. Thus *Playhouse 90* and *Matinée*, which provided quality entertainment and a proving ground for fresh acting, writing, and directing talent, were replaced by soap operas and quiz shows. Protest letters went unheeded; economics wrote the ticket.

The four major sources of sponsorship—the automobile, cigarette, drug, and soap industries—are in competition among themselves for prime time, and so are the companies that make up each of these industries. The packager of filmed shows for television syndication knows in advance what kind of story his writers need write, what sort of flashy, attention-arresting direction his directors should deliver, and what name stars will attract ratings. What this attitude does to the quality of programs can be seen nightly. Newton Minow's "vast wasteland"—the term he used as chairman of the Federal Communications Commission (FCC) in describing their world to the National Association of Broadcasters—has become in a few years an expanding Sahara with an occasional oasis on a Sunday afternoon.

Proposals for federal regulation. The cultural future of film in America for the mass audience lies in the hands of the FCC, which, however, is disinclined to use the powers given it by Congress to police the abuses of both stations and networks in their violations of frequency and length of commercials and in their failure to provide the statutory proportion of public service programming. Since a third of the Congress is personally interested in commercial returns of local broadcasting stations and/or in stock ownership in broadcasting companies, there has been no effort to strengthen the spine of the FCC. The Johnson administration is known as the broadcaster's ally in Washington.

Nonetheless, the proposals of the FCC to control and foster competition in television program production and procurement of programs should be noted for the sake of their historical interest. The proposed rules would prohibit network corporations from (1) engaging in syndication in the United States or distributing independent programs for exhibition outside the United States; (2) acquiring syndication and foreign sales rights in programs produced by other persons and licensed directly to the network corporations for exhibition; (3) acquiring rights to share in the profits from syndication and foreign sales of such programs. They would also require network corporations to divest themselves of distribution and profit-sharing rights in domestic syndication and overseas sales of which they are presently possessed.

To achieve these ends the proposed FCC rules would set a limit on undue concentration and would stimulate competition. A network could not offer a weekly evening program schedule in which more than 50 per cent of the time, or a total of 14 hours per week, whichever is greater, is occupied by programs produced by the network or in which it has acquired the first-run license from an independent producer. This stricture is exclusive of newscasts and special news programs and sustaining programs. The net result of the rule—if ever passed and rigorously administered—would be to make prime time available every evening for the exhibition of some programs in which the network corporations have no financial or proprietary interests. The market would then be broadened for the independent program producer and competition among such producers would be encouraged. The films would then reflect the program judgments not only of the network corporations but also of a large number of competitive elements who wish to reach the American people through television.

What this ruling would do for the television audience is what the Anti-Block Booking Decision did for the motion picture audience, namely, encourage the tastes of the multiple public. This would make for a more democratic atmosphere in a pluralistic society.

The aesthetics of film.   The closed market place for stories and ideas has limited experiments with program content while indulging technical maneuvers to hook and hold the attention of the majority. Cinema aesthetics, catering to Nielsen ratings tastes, have emphasized excessive movements of frame and camera, excessive pacing to shots, and unrelated camera angles or compositions—all superimposed on a superficial story line and on thin characterizations. On the other hand, in the open market place of international film production for theaters, the aesthetic advances are remarkable, as seen in the color utilizations, for example, of An-

tonioni in *Deserto Rosso* and Fellini's *Giulietta degli Spiriti*. Alain Resnais, Jean-Luc Godard, and François Truffaut fragment time and space in ways which enhance theme, plot, and characters.

Cinema aesthetics is being furthered through the works of such gifted artists rather than through the theories of critics, many of which are unrelated to contemporary cinema. For example, Kracauer (1960) has revealed the realistic nature of photography as a phenomenon affecting credibility; Lawson (1964) has emphasized the audio–visual nature of cinema that makes it a new art form. In contemporary cinema it is clear, as never before, to what degree movements and light affect meaning. This approach comes closer to the *sui generis* possibilities of cinema, which set it apart as a language, a craft, and an art. Knowledge of these possibilities is helpful in assisting the viewer to analyze the factors affecting his reactions and his judgment. With such a "grammar of cinema" at his fingertips, he is armed to withstand the hourly assault of TV programs and the clever techniques of popular film productions. This grammar, rooted in movements and light, finds that the frame, with its composition and inner action and frame movement; the shot, with its variety of frame movements in conjunction with edited movements between shots; and the edit, with its various jugglings of time through the juxtaposition of shots, comprise what might be called the "seven faces of time" (Gessner 1965).

Unless in the second half of the 1960s the federal government of the United States moves to protect its citizens in their free access to the best in cinema, the American people will continue to be denied full participation in the most dominant art of the twentieth century. In practical terms, such protection can be achieved through breaking the TV monopolies and by offering government subsidies for production, as is already the practice in Sweden, France, Italy, and the United Kingdom. The British Broadcasting Corporation (BBC), subsidized by government funds and a tax on receiving sets, is a particularly good example for study, since it is wholly free in making creative judgments. Some of the more interesting films produced anywhere emerge under BBC sponsorship. In the United States, only the National Educational Television approximates, on a smaller scale, the BBC approach, but not with the BBC's imaginative audacity. Sweden taxes every seat in its movie theaters to support a cinema training program for talented youth and to subsidize experimental productions not designed for box office success. These examples, it is to be hoped, might influence the eventual creation in America of a national film academy which would train and produce youthful talent, and of an audacious cinema in the tradition of the country where the art and industry were born.

ROBERT GESSNER

[*See also* COMMUNICATION, MASS; DRAMA.]

BIBLIOGRAPHY

AGEE, JAMES (1958) 1963 *Agee on Film: Reviews and Comments.* London: Owen.

ANDERSON, JOSEPH L.; and RICHIE, DONALD 1960 *The Japanese Film: Art and Industry.* New York: Grove.

ARNHEIM, RUDOLF (1957) 1960 *Film as Art.* Berkeley: Univ. of California Press.

BABITSKY, PAUL; and RIMBERG, JOHN 1955 *The Soviet Film Industry.* New York: Praeger.

BATZ, JEAN-CLAUDE 1963 *À propos de la crise de l'industrie du cinéma.* Brussels: Université Libre de Bruxelles, Institut de Sociologie.

COMMISSION ON FREEDOM OF THE PRESS 1947 *Freedom of the Movies: A Report on Self-regulation,* by Ruth A. Inglis. Univ. of Chicago Press.

CONANT, MICHAEL 1960 *Antitrust in the Motion Picture Industry: Economic and Legal Analysis.* Berkeley: Univ. of California Press.

CROWTHER, BOSLEY 1957 *Lion's Share: The Story of an Entertainment Empire.* New York: Dutton.

EMERY, F. E. 1959 Psychological Effects of the Western Film: A Study in Television Viewing. II. The Experimental Study. *Human Relations* 12:215–232.

FABREGAT CUNEO, ROBERTO 1957 El proceso del cine en el mundo y en la cultura y la deformación de los temas culturales al través del cine. *Revista mexicana de sociología* 19:387–404.

FARBER, MANNY 1963 The Fading Movie Star. *Commentary* 36:55–60.

GANS, HERBERT J. 1962 Hollywood Films on British Screens: An Analysis of American Popular Culture Abroad. *Social Problems* 9:324–328.

GESSNER, ROBERT 1963–1964 On Teaching Cinema in College: A Modest Proposal for an Ideal Academic Program. *Film Culture* No. 31:47–50.

GESSNER, ROBERT 1965 Seven Faces of Time: An Aesthetic for Cinema. Pages 158–167 in György Kepes (editor), *The Nature and Art of Motion.* New York: Braziller.

GOODMAN, EZRA 1961 *The Fifty Year Decline and Fall of Hollywood.* New York: Simon & Schuster.

HANDEL, LEO A. 1950 *Hollywood Looks at Its Audience: A Report of Film Audience Research.* Urbana: Univ. of Illinois Press.

HARRIS, THOMAS 1957 The Building of Popular Images: Grace Kelly and Marilyn Monroe. *Studies in Public Communication* 1:45–48.

HUACO, GEORGE A. 1965 *The Sociology of Film Art.* New York: Basic Books.

JACOBS, LEWIS 1960 *Introduction to the Art of the Movies: An Anthology of Ideas on the Nature of Movie Art.* New York: Noonday.

KAUFFMANN, STANLEY 1966 *A World on Film.* New York: Harper.

KRACAUER, SIEGFRIED 1960 *Theory of Film: The Redemption of Physical Reality.* New York: Oxford Univ. Press.

LAWSON, JOHN H. 1964 *Film, the Creative Process: The Search for an Audio–Visual Language and Structure.* New York: Hill & Wang.

LINDGREN, ERNEST (1948) 1963 *The Art of the Film.* 2d ed. New York: Macmillan.

MACCANN, RICHARD D. 1964 *Film and Society.* New York: Scribner.

POWDERMAKER, HORTENSE 1950 *Hollywood, the Dream Factory: An Anthropologist Looks at the Movie-makers.* Boston: Little.

ROSS, LILLIAN (1952) 1953 *Picture.* London: Gollancz. → A paperback edition was published in 1962 by Doubleday.

ROSTEN, LEO C. 1941 *Hollywood: The Movie Colony, the Movie Makers.* New York: Harcourt.

SCOTCH, NORMAN A. 1960 The Vanishing Villains of Television. *Phylon* 21:58–62.

STORK, LEOPOLD 1962 *Industrial and Business Films.* London: Phoenix House.

TALBOT, DANIEL (editor) 1959 *Film: An Anthology.* New York: Simon & Schuster.

TYLOR, PARKER 1960 *The Three Faces of the Film.* New York: Yoseloff.

WOLFENSTEIN, MARTHA; and LEITES, NATHAN 1950 *Movies: A Psychological Study.* Glencoe, Ill.: Free Press.

FINANCE, LOCAL

See LOCAL FINANCE.

FINANCIAL INTERMEDIARIES

Financial intermediaries issue (indirect) debt of their own to buy the (primary) debt of others. Their issues attract funds from alternative expenditures by nonfinancial spending units on consumption, tangible investment, or primary debt. Their lending directs the flow of funds to expenditure by borrowers on consumption, tangible investment, or primary debt. They intermediate between the sources of funds that flow to them and the ultimate users of these funds.

The intermediaries may be identified by their balance sheets, which show a high proportion of financial to tangible assets and of indirect debt to equity. Their income statements report high ratios of income from interest and dividends to total income and of expense for interest and dividends to total expense.

There are bank (monetary) intermediaries and nonbank (nonmonetary) intermediaries. The former are commercial banks and the central bank, together constituting the monetary system, which issues indirect debt, subject to unique regulations, in the form of money. The indirect debt which is issued by nonbank intermediaries is not used as a means of payment.

Both types of intermediary are to be distinguished from other institutions that transmit funds from ultimate lenders to ultimate borrowers. These other institutions do not issue their own indirect debt in soliciting funds. They include security dealers, brokers, and exchanges.

Types of intermediary. The principal nonbank financial intermediaries in the United States are the following:

Depositary intermediaries
    Credit unions
    Mutual savings banks
    Savings and loan associations
Insurance and pension intermediaries
    Casualty and miscellaneous insurance companies
    Fire and marine insurance companies
    Fraternal insurance organizations
    Government retirement, pension, insurance, and social security funds
    Group health insurance
    Private life insurance companies
    Private noninsured pension funds
    Savings bank life insurance departments
Finance companies
    Factors
    Mortgage companies
    Personal finance companies
    Sales finance companies
Investment companies
    Closed-end companies
    Face-amount certificate companies
    Industrial loan companies
    Open-end companies
Agricultural credit organizations
    Federal land banks
    Livestock loan companies
    National farm loan associations
    Production credit associations
Government lending institutions
    Banks for cooperatives
    Federal Home Loan Banks
    Federal intermediate credit banks
    Federal National Mortgage Association
    Federal Savings and Loan Insurance Corporation

This list is not complete; it omits such domestic intermediaries as the American Express Company, the Export–Import Bank, small business investment corporations, and pawnbrokers, as well as international intermediaries in which the United States participates, including the International Monetary Fund and the International Bank for Reconstruction and Development. (Detailed classifications of intermediaries in the United States may be found in the following sources: "A Quarterly Presentation of Flow of Funds . . ." 1959; Goldsmith 1958, pp. 50–55; Goldsmith & Lipsey 1963, vol. 1, pp. 27–36.)

Nonbank intermediaries may be classified in many ways. In terms of proprietorship, they may be governmental or private, and the private organizations may be stock, unincorporated, mutual, or cooperative. They may be primary, dealing with the general public, or secondary, dealing with other financial institutions. Grouped according to assets, they may be lenders principally on real estate, for example, or agricultural products or consumer durables. Grouped according to liabilities, they may borrow mainly at short term or at long term, and their obligations may or may not carry insurance benefits. They pay their creditors interest, dividends, capital gains, or indemnities. They vary in regional distribution, rate of growth, cyclical stability, degree of concentration, and tax status. Each of them reflects an opportunity for private enterprise to profit from transmission of funds between lenders and borrowers or a governmental desire to supplement private financial arrangements.

Growth in the financial system of the United States has consisted partly in proliferating types of intermediary. At the beginning of the nineteenth century, commercial banks and private insurance companies were available for the deposit and borrowing of funds. Savings banks and savings and loan associations were operating before mid-century, and by 1880 there were mortgage companies. The pace and quality of economic growth in the first two decades of the twentieth century were especially congenial to financial innovation: to this period one may credit the postal savings system, credit unions, finance companies, investment companies, and federal agencies for agricultural credit. Pension funds and various additional federal lending agencies, especially in the area of mortgage finance, were generated by the circumstances of the 1920s and 1930s. International intermediaries have been the notable innovations of the 1940s and 1950s (Goldsmith 1958, chapter 4; Kuznets 1961, pp. 304–305). It is one aspect of relative economic maturity that the pace of innovation in financial intermediaries has diminished. Existing intermediaries introduce adaptations in service which seem to provide a sufficient flow of funds at full employment and at an acceptable rate of growth in national income.

Dimensions of intermediation in the U.S. At the end of 1963, financial assets held by nonbank intermediaries amounted to one-fifth of all financial assets in the national balance sheet—to about $510,000 million in an aggregate of $2.42 billion. In terms of their portfolios, they were three-fifths larger than the monetary system. The bulk of their assets, approximately $360,000 million, was financed by indirect debt to consumer households and nonprofit organizations. This debt amounted to one-third of the financial assets in those sectors.

The distribution of financial assets among the types of nonbank intermediary is unequal. Intermediaries in the insurance and pension categories accounted for one-half of all intermediary assets at the end of 1963, savings and depositary institutions for one-third, and the remainder was widely dispersed among other categories.

Nonbank intermediaries do not grow at a uniform rate. The reason is that they sell indirect debt in specialized forms to different classes of savers, buy primary debt at different terms from different classes of investors, encounter dissimilar regulatory restraints and stimuli, and experience diverse changes in technical conditions of producing the service of intermediation. Each responds uniquely to the phases of short and long cycles in real economic development; to changes in life expectation and age distribution of the population; to variations in the price level, in the distribution of income between sectors, and in relative growth rates for various kinds of real capital. During a recent decade, 1948–1958, growth among intermediaries varied from 521 per cent for credit unions to 35 per cent for mutual savings banks (Goldsmith et al. 1963, vol. 2, pp. 114–115; see also Friend 1963, pp. 666–667; 1964, pp. 16–45).

Theory of financial intermediation. Nonbank financial intermediaries participate in four markets. They are net buyers on markets for primary securities; on markets for money balances—to be held as reserves of liquidity either voluntarily or by regulatory rule; and on markets for productive factors—labor in particular, but also capital goods and land. They are sellers on markets for their own issues of indirect debt—in such forms as savings and loan shares, savings bank deposits, and pension claims. (See Patinkin 1956.) This last market will be discussed first. (We neglect here operations by intermediaries on foreign exchange markets and the bearing of intermediation on international balances of payments.)

Markets for nonbank indirect financial assets (NIFA). Demand for NIFA, issued by nonbank intermediaries as their own indirect debt, comes mainly from consumer households. Consumers demand NIFA as a component of their personal wealth along with such other components as money balances, primary securities, business equity, housing, and durable goods. NIFA are relatively more important in the personal wealth of consumers at medium income levels than of consumers at extremes of the income distribution.

Consumers add to their portfolios of NIFA by saving, borrowing, and displacing funds from alternative assets. NIFA qualify as a superior, or luxury, good in the consumer budget.

Economists have experimented with many forms of demand function for NIFA (Brown & Friend 1964, pp. 125–128; Tobin & Brainard 1963). Demand rises with the real rate of interest paid by intermediaries relative to rates of return on other assets. It rises with permanent disposable income, and apparently it responds to intermediaries' advertising. It is depressed by risks involved in holding NIFA and increased by insurance against these risks. These are typical arguments in demand functions for NIFA, but others are relevant for particular assets. A stock market boom intensifies demand for shares in investment funds. Age distribution of consumers is significant to demand for insurance. Growth in union membership enhances demand for uninsured pension fund claims.

Demand for NIFA is confronted by conditions of supply—a supply function for individual intermediaries and for the industry. (Studies of the supply function include Hensley 1958; *Trade Association Monographs for the Commission on Money and Credit* 1962.) The supply of NIFA offered by intermediaries varies inversely with the rate of interest on NIFA. At each such rate of interest, supply tends to rise as rates of interest on the primary securities that intermediaries hold rise. It is the spread between primary (lending) rates and NIFA (borrowing) rates that creates opportunity for profit in intermediation. Since, in the long run, the primary rate tends to vary with the marginal productivity of tangible wealth, the supply of intermediation is responsive to opportunities for real investment.

Because intermediation incurs costs for wages and depreciation, its supply is depressed by increases in wage rates and in prices of capital goods and is increased by technological advance that economizes labor and capital. Increases in risk and uncertainty of investment in primary securities, which typically are at long term, and of the much more liquid NIFA debt, which is typically at short term, inhibit the supply of NIFA. Conditions of supply in intermediation are affected, perhaps more profoundly than in any other industry, by governmental intervention in the form of subsidy, special tax terms, and sundry regulatory devices. The net effect of governmental intervention in the United States has probably been to stimulate both supply and demand. The justification may be that there are external benefits of intermediation that wholly free markets would not realize.

There is a separate industry of firms supplying each variety of NIFA. These industries are imperfectly competitive, and some of them satisfy the specifications of oligopoly. Governmental restrictions on freedom of entry of new firms are accountable for some loss of competitive impulse. In addition, there is reason to suspect the existence of internal economies of scale for the intermediary firm that are not compatible with free competition. The evident imperfections of competition have led to numerous governmental restraints on the structure of the intermediary industry and its market behavior.

Taken in conjunction, the demand and supply functions for nonmonetary intermediation determine the volume of NIFA and their market rates of interest. These functions determine the spread between primary rates and NIFA rates and the gross profit to intermediation. The gross profit, adjusted principally for labor and capital costs, determines net profit, which, in relation to profit opportunities elsewhere, regulates the desired flow of equity funds into the industry. It is equity funds, in turn, which help to provide the factor of safety for NIFA that induces consumer households to invest in these assets at yields below primary rates of interest.

Markets for primary securities. Nonmonetary intermediaries are net buyers of primary securities: they acquire securities with funds that flow to them on the market for NIFA and, in much smaller volume, sell primary securities of their own, mainly equities, to finance increases in their net worth. The latter may be dropped from consideration here with the generalization that they increase in response to governmental capital requirements, to gains in intermediaries' net earnings, and to general advances in prices of common stocks.

Historically the development of intermediaries has been a necessary condition for broad and active markets in primary securities. Intermediation supports an infrastructure of security exchanges, dealers, and brokers. Reciprocally, efficient market facilities for primary securities reduce the operating costs, risks, and uncertainties of intermediaries' portfolios. (For illustrations see Basch 1964, chapter 6; Nevin 1961, chapter 4.)

By supplying attractive media for savings and by support of markets for investors' issues of primary securities, nonbank intermediation facilitates division of labor between saving and investment. One result is that primary securities accumulate in amounts that are relatively large in comparison with national income.

Aside from stimulating the organization of security markets and growth in primary securities, intermediaries influence the allocation of savings among investment opportunities and, hence, the quality of primary securities. Successful intermediation depends heavily on arbitrage between opportunities to finance investment and to acquire primary securities. From the standpoint of society, such arbitrage promotes allocative efficiency in the saving–investment process. On markets for primary securities, one manifestation of allocative efficiency is uniformity in interest rates and other terms of lending for similar securities. Intermediation works against fragmentation of security markets.

By encouraging saving, and so accelerating growth of capital, intermediation tends to reduce interest rates on primary securities. To the extent that intermediation allocates savings efficiently, it results in a capital stock of high productivity and so tends to raise interest rates on primary securities. The net effect of intermediation on interest rates, in the long run, is probably to raise them.

Efficient nonbank intermediation increases the short-run stability of rates of interest on primary securities. Each increase in primary rates first widens profit margins in intermediation and then induces increases in rates paid on NIFA. Insofar as more attractive yields on NIFA stimulate saving and divert the public's demand from money balances, the effect is to intensify the flow of funds through nonbank intermediaries toward purchase of primary securities. Conversely, short-period declines in primary rates may shrink the flow of funds toward purchase of primary securities. If intermediation does temper short-run fluctuations in primary rates, the result is a reduction in market-risk premia on primary securities. (For an alternative view see Minsky 1964.)

Markets for goods. Nonbank intermediation influences aggregate propensities to consume, the quality of consumption, and the stability of consumption. There is a dual effect on total consumption, since NIFA attract savings, while consumer credit, financed through intermediaries, facilitates consumption. Intermediation is important for the quality of consumption, partly because it changes relative costs to consumers of different classes of goods, partly also because it permits flexible adjustments in life-cycle patterns of consumption. Finally, intermediation is pertinent to temporal stability in consumption to the extent that changes in consumer stocks of NIFA and in consumer debt, as well as in yields and costs of NIFA and debt, lead to acceleration or deferral of consumer spending (Enthoven 1957–1964; [U.S.] Board of Governors . . . 1957).

Influences of intermediation can be traced through markets for goods other than consumption goods. As the savings outlet that provides the alternative to financing investment from internal sources, through direct issues of primary securities to savers, through the monetary system, and through government, nonbank intermediation participates in selecting investment opportunities and in shaping the structure of the capital stock. It is involved in allocating savings between private and governmental investment, between domestic and foreign uses. Furthermore, it is a factor in the short-run stability both of total investment and of components including housing and business inventory (Grebler & Maisel 1963).

Measurements of national income originating in nonbank intermediation are ambiguous. It may be estimated that saving by these institutions on their own account is less than 1.5 per cent of national saving in the United States, that their tangible investment is about 0.25 per cent of national investment, and that they employ about 1.5 per cent of the civilian labor force. Their impact on markets for goods and factors is mainly indirect, through the saving–investment decisions of other sectors.

Market for money. There has been intensive debate regarding the effect of growth and innovation in NIFA, and of changes in their yields, on the demand for and the supply of money. The central issue has been the degree of substitutability between NIFA and money balances in the asset portfolios of consumer households especially, but also of business firms.

If demand for money is negatively elastic to yields on NIFA, changes in these yields resulting from a monetary policy that raises (lowers) the rate of growth in the supply of money may raise (lower) growth in demand for money and so offset the intended effects of monetary policy on markets for goods, factors, and primary securities. Since substitutability of NIFA for money is not perfect, interference from NIFA with monetary policy may presumably be overcome by sufficiently large and timely adjustments in the money supply. Alternatively, interference of NIFA with monetary policy might be overcome by bringing within the orbit of monetary control those nonbank intermediaries which issue NIFA most closely resembling money.

If NIFA are near substitutes for money, tradi-

tional monetary controls can also be obstructed by responses of nonbank intermediaries. There are other implications. For example, if commercial banks must be restrained more tightly over long periods or subjected to more vigorous and volatile control for short periods because nonbank intermediaries weaken monetary discipline, there is discrimination against banks. The discrimination may be criticized on grounds of equity or because it undermines the capitalization and solvency of banks. If banks dispose of savings differently than do nonbank intermediaries, the discrimination may also be criticized for its allocative effects on the stock of capital. (The literature concerning effects of nonbank intermediation on monetary controls is very large. It includes Commission on Money and Credit 1961, pp. 78–81; Gurley & Shaw 1960, chapter 6; Johnson 1962; Great Britain, Committee on the Working of the Monetary System 1959, pp. 129–135.)

Equilibrium of the market for money, at a relatively stable price level, appears to be an important prerequisite for development of nonbank intermediation and of NIFA, even with price-escalator provisions. Inflation is a tax not only on money balances but also on the real value of NIFA as well, and correspondingly diminishes real demand for NIFA. Furthermore, inflation often concentrates savings in sectors of the community that prefer other dispositions of savings than NIFA. International data suggest that nonmonetary intermediation lags where inflation is habitual and erratic.

Integration between nations, in monetary and trade institutions and policies, has important implications for nonbank intermediation, with regard both to markets for NIFA and to intermediary portfolios of primary securities. For example, one can expect innovations in NIFA, such as Euro-currencies, and international arbitrage by intermediaries, such as investment funds, that will tend to unify markets for savings.

Regulation. Nonbank intermediation is typically subject to intensive governmental regulation and intervention. At the extreme, there is government ownership and management. Short of this limit, regulation and intervention include subsidy and other stimulants as well as various restraints on private enterprise in intermediation.

There are seven common objectives of regulation: to increase propensities to save, to guide the allocation of savings to investment, to limit short-period instability of growth, to strengthen the solvency of intermediaries, to improve intermediaries' operating efficiency, to correct the distribution of income and wealth, and to stabilize the balance of payments. (The last will not be discussed here.)

The basic technique of accelerating savings through nonbank intermediaries is to intensify demand for NIFA, relative to consumption, at given levels of national income. Rates of interest may be raised on NIFA, innovations introduced, savers' safety guaranteed. For these objectives, competition may be intensified among intermediaries, tax concessions granted to them, deposits insured, and portfolio limits relaxed.

Regulation of intermediaries is traditionally concerned with savings allocation. For the benefit of housing or, say, investment in agriculture and small business firms, regulation has provided incentives for intermediaries that guide savings to desired ends. Programs to overcome regional lags in development have included subsidized allocations of loanable funds through intermediaries. Measures against restraint of competition among intermediaries are partly concerned with allocative efficiency.

Nonbank intermediaries have contributed at times to short-period turbulence in the saving–investment process. Measures to correct their influence toward overinvestment include minimal requirements for liquidity and net worth. Measures to correct their influence toward underinvestment include guarantee of their portfolios and provision of rediscount facilities.

The solvency of intermediaries has been an objective of high priority in regulation. The costs of insolvency that have seemed to justify intensive regulation include inequity to savers, misallocation of savings, and contagious economic instability. Measures to protect solvency include net-worth requirements, supervision of operations, limits on portfolio selection, and loan insurance. There is basis for argument that regulatory preoccupation with solvency has imperiled some other objectives, such as allocative efficiency.

Operating efficiency is not often a primary objective of regulation. Its purpose is to liberate real resources for other uses, to reduce spreads between rates of interest on primary securities and rates on NIFA, and to strengthen solvency. Economic operation can be essential for the comparatively primitive forms of intermediation that are appropriate in early stages of national economic development. It has counted heavily in the growth of such intermediaries in the United States as credit unions.

Distributive considerations enter into some regulatory techniques. The purpose may be merely to prevent inequitable incidence on some social classes of gains and losses from intermediation, or it may be to change the distribution of income and wealth. The first purpose is illustrated by regulation of insurance companies' portfolios in the interest of beneficiaries, or of investment funds to limit conspiratorial gains of insiders. The second purpose is illustrated by various special credit arrangements for agriculture or war veterans or regions suffering a slow tempo of development.

These objectives of regulation have given rise, especially in the United States, to a complex apparatus of federal and state regulatory techniques administered by governmental departments, commissions, and institutions. Dissatisfaction with this apparatus has inspired intensive re-evaluation by both private and governmental bodies. The principal occasions in the United States were during the decade before World War I, during the 1930s, and in the early 1960s by the Commission on Money and Credit. There were other national investigations in the course of the 1960s: in Japan the Committee on Financial System Research; in the United Kingdom, Committee on the Working of the Monetary System; in Canada, Royal Commission on Banking and Finance.

These recent studies of regulations concerning both monetary and nonbank intermediaries had to do, in part, with irrationalities in regulatory agencies and techniques. They were also directed to goals of regulation and, for the first time, to possible benefits of applying a general theory and compatible techniques to regulation of various classes of intermediaries. There is no precedent for their attempts to define optimality in the financial superstructure of capitalism. They did not reach common conclusions on either principles or techniques of regulation.

International differences. There is notable diversity of nonbank intermediation between countries. First, NIFA per capita vary widely (Kuznets 1955; Goldsmith 1955). This is explained partly by differences in real income and wealth per capita, since income and wealth elasticities of demand for NIFA are high. It is explained, too, by differences in centralization of decisions to save and invest: economic centralism is not a fertile environment for nonbank intermediation. Again, NIFA appear to be high, relative to income, where price inflation has been modest and low where inflation has been rapid, chronic, and erratic. Nonbank intermediaries are relatively strong where the monetary system does not practice broad diversification of portfolios and indirect debt, where public debt is not finely differentiated, and where social security is not financed mainly from current government revenues. The evidence is that non-bank intermediation has been retarded by social instability and defects of legal structure. There are also imponderables of social framework, social mobility, and personal motivation that affect the pace of intermediation. Governmental assistance and foreign aid figure prominently in growth of NIFA. Finally, development in intermediation varies between countries according to the accessibility and quality of complementary institutions. All of these and other factors relating to international differences can be classified according to their effects on conditions of demand and supply for NIFA.

The quality as well as the scale of nonbank intermediation varies internationally. There is variation in primary securities acquired by intermediaries, in NIFA, and in institutional structure. One observes rough correspondence of qualitative with quantitative development: such intermediaries as investment funds appear where real income per capita is high; small cooperatives for agricultural credit, where income is lower. Still, the quality of intermediation is not uniform between countries at comparable stages of economic development. Differences in composition of wealth and output are partly responsible, and the form of political organization is pertinent. The distribution of income by level of income is another factor, as is the distribution of population by age and degree of urbanization. Within the orbit of capitalism, the social choice between alternative methods of mobilizing and allocating savings deeply affects the environment of nonbank intermediation. One can trace in the quality of intermediation the unique historical experience of each society that has given momentum to some intermediaries rather than others; the mores and traditions that condition savers for or against lotteries, perhaps, and for or against concentrations of financial power; the mobility of ownership in enterprise; and the geographic extent of the economic system. From differences in savers' tastes to differences in technological conditions of intermediation and patterns of governmental intervention, there are numerous factors to explain the international diversity in intermediation. One may infer that optimal development of intermediation will have strikingly indigenous characteristics.

E. S. Shaw

[*See also* Banking; Banking, central; Money.]

BIBLIOGRAPHY

Alhadeff, David A. 1960 Credit Controls and Financial Intermediaries. *American Economic Review* 50:655–671.

Basch, Antonin 1964 *Financing Economic Development*. New York: Macmillan.

Birnbaum, Eugene A. 1958 The Growth of Financial Intermediaries as a Factor in the Effectiveness of Monetary Policy. International Monetary Fund, *Staff Papers* 6:384–426.

Brown, Murray; and Friend, Irwin 1964 An Econometric Model of the United States With Special Reference to the Financial Sector. Pages 117–172 in Irwin Friend, Hyman P. Minsky, and Victor L. Andrews (editors), *Private Capital Markets*. Published for the Commission on Money and Credit. Englewood Cliffs, N.J.: Prentice-Hall.

Brunner, Karl; and Meltzer, Allan H. 1963 The Place of Financial Intermediaries in the Transmission of Monetary Policy. *American Economic Review* 53, no. 2:372–382.

Canada, Royal Commission on Banking and Finance 1964 *Report*. Ottawa: Queen's Printer and Controller of Stationery.

Commission on Money and Credit 1961 *Money and Credit: Their Influence on Jobs, Prices, and Growth*. Englewood Cliffs, N.J.: Prentice-Hall.

Enthoven, Alain C. 1957–1964 The Growth of Instalment Credit and the Future of Prosperity. *American Economic Review* 47:913–929.

Ettin, Edward C. 1963 The Development of American Financial Intermediaries. *Quarterly Review of Economics and Business* 3:51–69.

Feige, Edgar L. 1964 *The Demand for Liquid Assets: A Temporal Cross-section Analysis*. Englewood Cliffs, N.J.: Prentice-Hall.

Friend, Irwin (1963) 1964 Determinants of the Volume and Composition of Saving With Special Reference to the Influence of Monetary Policy. Pages 649–688 in Commission on Money and Credit, *Impacts of Monetary Policy*. Englewood Cliffs, N.J.: Prentice-Hall.

Friend, Irwin 1964 The Effects of Monetary Policies on Nonmonetary Financial Institutions and Capital Markets. Pages 1–116 in Irwin Friend, Hyman P. Minsky, and Victor L. Andrews (editors), *Private Capital Markets*. Published for the Commission on Money and Credit. Englewood Cliffs, N.J.: Prentice-Hall.

Gies, Thomas C.; Mayer, Thomas; and Ettin, Edward C. 1963 Portfolio Regulations and Policies of Financial Intermediaries. Pages 157–264 in *Private Financial Institutions*. Englewood Cliffs, N.J.: Prentice-Hall.

Goldsmith, Raymond W. 1955 Financial Structure and Economic Growth in Advanced Countries: An Experiment in Comparative Financial Morphology. Pages 113–167 in Universities–National Bureau Committee for Economic Research, *Capital Formation and Economic Growth*. Part 1: Sources and Channels of Finance in Capitalist Countries. Princeton Univ. Press. → Includes eight pages of comment by Edward S. Shaw and a reply by Raymond W. Goldsmith.

Goldsmith, Raymond W. 1955–1956 *A Study of Saving in the United States*. 3 vols. Princeton Univ. Press.

Goldsmith, Raymond W. 1958 *Financial Intermediaries in the American Economy Since 1900*. National Bureau of Economic Research, Studies in Capital Formation and Financing, No. 3. Princeton Univ. Press.

Goldsmith, Raymond W.; and Lipsey, Robert E. 1963 *Studies in the National Balance Sheet of the United States*. 2 vols. National Bureau of Economic Research, Studies in Capital Formation and Financing, Vol. 11. Princeton Univ. Press. → The second volume was pub-

FINE ARTS: Art and Society 439

FINE ARTS: Art and Society   *439*

lished under the joint authorship of Raymond W. Goldsmith, Robert E. Lipsey, and Morris Mendelson.

GREAT BRITAIN, COMMITTEE ON THE WORKING OF THE MONETARY SYSTEM 1959 *Report.* Papers by Command, Cmnd. 827. London: H.M. Stationery Office. → Commonly known as the Radcliffe Report.

GREAT BRITAIN, COMMITTEE ON THE WORKING OF THE MONETARY SYSTEM 1960 *Principal Memoranda of Evidence.* 3 vols. London: H.M. Stationery Office.

GREBLER, LEO; and MAISEL, SHERMAN J. (1963) 1964 Determinants of Residential Construction: A Review of Present Knowledge. Pages 475–620 in Commission on Money and Credit, *Impacts of Monetary Policy.* Englewood Cliffs, N.J.: Prentice-Hall.

GURLEY, JOHN G.; and SHAW, E. S. 1955 Financial Aspects of Economic Development. *American Economic Review* 45:515–538.

GURLEY, JOHN G.; and SHAW, E. S. 1956 Financial Intermediaries and the Saving–Investment Process. *Journal of Finance* 11:257–276.

GURLEY, JOHN G.; and SHAW, E. S. 1960 *Money in a Theory of Finance.* With a mathematical appendix by Alain C. Enthoven. Washington: Brookings Institution.

HARBRECHT, PAUL P. 1959 *Pension Funds and Economic Power.* New York: Twentieth Century Fund.

HENSLEY, R. J. 1958 Economies of Scale in Financial Enterprise. *Journal of Political Economy* 66:389–398.

JOHNSON, H. G. 1962 Monetary Theory and Policy. *American Economic Review* 52:335–384.

KHUSRO, A. M. 1957 Liquidity Preference in India. *Indian Economic Review* 3, no. 3:24–40.

KUZNETS, SIMON 1955 International Differences in Capital Formation and Financing. Pages 19–111 in Universities–National Bureau Committee for Economic Research, *Capital Formation and Economic Growth.* Part 1: Sources and Channels of Finance in Capitalist Countries. Princeton Univ. Press.

KUZNETS, SIMON 1961 *Capital in the American Economy: Its Formation and Financing.* National Bureau of Economic Research, Studies in Capital Formation and Financing, No. 9. Princeton Univ. Press.

MINSKY, HYMAN P. 1964 Financial Crisis, Financial Systems, and the Performance of the Economy. Pages 173–380 in Irwin Friend, Hyman P. Minsky, and Victor L. Andrews (editors), *Private Capital Markets.* Published for the Commission on Money and Credit. Englewood Cliffs, N.J.: Prentice-Hall.

NEVIN, EDWARD 1961 *Capital Funds in Underdeveloped Countries: The Role of Financial Institutions.* London: Macmillan; New York: St. Martins.

NIHON GINKŌ (BANK OF JAPAN) 1959 *Outline of the Financial System in Japan.* 3d rev. ed. Tokyo: The Bank.

OTT, DAVID J. 1961 The Financial Development of Japan. *Journal of Political Economy* 69:122–141.

PAAUW, DOUGLAS S. 1960 *Financing Economic Development: The Indonesian Case.* Glencoe, Ill.: Free Press.

PATINKIN, DON (1956) 1965 *Money, Interest, and Prices: An Integration of Monetary and Value Theory.* 2d ed. New York: Harper.

PATINKIN, DON 1961 Financial Intermediaries and the Logical Structure of Monetary Theory. *American Economic Review* 51:95–116.

A Quarterly Presentation of Flow of Funds, Savings, and Investment. 1959 *Federal Reserve Bulletin* 45:828–859.

SMITH, WARREN L. 1959 Financial Intermediaries and Monetary Controls. *Quarterly Journal of Economics* 73:533–553.

THORN, RICHARD S. 1958 Nonbank Financial Intermediaries, Credit Expansions, and Monetary Policy. International Monetary Fund, *Staff Papers* 6:369–383.

TOBIN, JAMES; and BRAINARD, WILLIAM C. 1963 Financial Intermediaries and the Effectiveness of Monetary Controls. *American Economic Review* 53, no. 2:383–400.

Trade Association Monographs for the Commission on Money and Credit. 1962 Englewood Cliffs, N.J.: Prentice-Hall. → Monographs include American Mutual Insurance Alliance, *Property and Casualty Insurance Companies: Their Role as Financial Intermediaries;* Miles L. Colean, *Mortgage Companies: Their Place in the Financial Structure;* Investment Company Institute, *Management Investment Companies;* Leon T. Kendall, *The Savings and Loan Business: Its Purposes, Functions, and Economic Justification;* Life Insurance Association of America, *Life Insurance Companies as Financial Institutions;* National Association of Mutual Savings Banks, *Mutual Savings Banking: Basic Characteristics and Role in the National Economy;* and National Consumer Finance Association, *The Consumer Finance Industry.*

[U.S.] BOARD OF GOVERNORS OF THE FEDERAL RESERVE SYSTEM 1957 *Consumer Installment Credit.* 4 parts in 3 vols. Washington: Government Printing Office. → See especially Part 2.

U.S. COMMITTEE ON FINANCIAL INSTITUTIONS 1963 *Report to the President of the United States.* Washington: Government Printing Office.

U.S. CONGRESS, HOUSE, COMMITTEE ON BANKING AND CURRENCY, SUBCOMMITTEE ON DOMESTIC FINANCE 1963 *Comparative Regulations of Financial Institutions.* Washington: Government Printing Office.

FINANCING, POLITICAL
See POLITICAL FINANCING.

FINE ARTS

I. ART AND SOCIETY — *Francis Haskell*
II. THE RECRUITMENT AND SOCIALIZATION OF ARTISTS — *Mason Griff*

I
ART AND SOCIETY

Societies of all kinds and of all periods have given birth to what can today be classified as art, but there exist no significant propositions as to the nature of the relationship between particular social systems and the kinds of art that develop under them. The problem was first seriously posed during the Enlightenment, when philosophers arguing in favor of differing political organizations suggested that desirable art would necessarily follow desirable government. But the view of Shaftesbury and others that freedom was a prerequisite of great art was hardly borne out either by the previous or subsequent history of England, where architecture, sculpture, and painting, although reaching a higher peak than they had for some centuries, were hardly superior to those engendered under despotic regimes in Italy, France, and central Europe.

In more recent years the problem has been raised in more sophisticated terms: quality, it is admitted, may be capricious in its incidence, but style will necessarily be governed by fundamental social laws. E. H. Gombrich has demonstrated the fallacies that usually underlie such reasoning [see STYLE], but it will in any case be impossible to make any authoritative large-scale statements about the relationship of art to society until the very few studies of particular societies and their arts have been greatly increased in number, scope, and depth. History remains our only source of guidance.

The artist in history

Research into the status of artists at different periods, while of interest in itself, does not seem to throw much light on the nature or quality of the art produced, nor does it even give an indication of the esteem in which art has been held. Moreover, for many societies and epochs the data are extremely scanty.

Greece. In Greece between the sixth and third centuries B.C. a flowering of the arts so spectacular that it influenced all subsequent history appears to have been almost totally neglected by the innumerable writers of genius who lived through it. However, outlines of the artists' lives and a few anecdotes of their personalities must have been recorded, because later historians such as Pliny evidently drew on lost sources of this kind. But nowhere in classical Greek literature is there anything to suggest that individual artists were held in serious consideration, and by inference we can assume that they were considered as being little superior to craftsmen. This, however, certainly does not imply that the Greeks were indifferent to the masterpieces that were produced: indeed, Plutarch points out in a much-quoted phrase (in *Pericles*) that "no generous youth, from seeing the Zeus at Olympia or the Hera at Argos, longs to be Phidias or Polyclitus, for it does not of necessity follow that if the work delights you with grace, the one who wrought it is worthy of your esteem."

It is noteworthy that in all the discussions that took place during the golden age on the nature of inspiration, examples were never chosen from among sculptors or painters, and it is clear that although artists in classical times could be either slave or free, the mere association of their work with manual labor was enough to prevent their being highly esteemed. For this reason, which was to recur later in the Middle Ages, an architect stood a greater chance of earning renown than a painter or sculptor, for, when successful, he would be considered more as an entrepreneur than a manual laborer. However, as frequently occurs in the social history of the arts, sufficient skill could on occasion enable its possessor to overcome this indifference to the individual artist and defy even the most rigid conventions. There are, for instance, records indicating that as early as the last quarter of the sixth century B.C., "several potters . . . were able to erect impressive dedications on the Acropolis" (Cook 1960, p. 272), and it is also well known that at much the same time we begin to find frequent examples of signed work.

During the Hellenistic period the social status of the artist certainly improved, and legends about the relations between Alexander the Great and Apelles, which are recorded by Pliny, indicate at the very least an ideal that was no longer held to be absurd—and incidentally set a highly important precedent for subsequent royal patronage. We are, however, still very largely ignorant not only about the status of the artist in antiquity but also about the nature of his training and mode of life generally, although we do find hints of exhibitions, dealers, and other features of the artistic scene that later became commonplace. If we are entitled to assume, as seems probable, that the artist in classical antiquity was considered to be little more than a craftsman, it remains the more surprising that the development of sculpture and painting was so extraordinarily striking. For it is often held that artistic change is encouraged by the notion of the artist's individuality, whereas, almost by definition, the craftsman is employed exclusively to satisfy public demand.

Rome. For Roman times, too, the evidence is scattered, fragmentary, and conflicting. It seems clear that to Cato and those who thought like him art was something essentially foreign—even degrading—and this view must clearly have been reflected in their opinion of the artists themselves. On the other hand, archeological research and literary references illustrate obviously enough the admiration felt for Greek sculpture, and Pliny's stories of the Greek artists must surely have suggested to many that the superior ones among them could achieve recognition far higher than that likely to have been granted to mere craftsmen. If, however, we risk the premise that some acknowledgment of the artist as an individual with a will of his own, who does not merely respond to the pressures of the market, is at least a likely prerequisite of adventurous art, then the highly derivative nature of Roman sculpture (and also the extremely conservative tendencies of the ancient Egyptians) might imply that the position of the artist was a very lowly one. But the dangers of such a circular argument are too great to make it worth pursuing. Certainly the Romans never included the visual arts among the *artes liberales,* and this, together with the physical destruction and chaos that followed the collapse of the Western Empire, proved to be of decisive importance for the Middle Ages.

Middle Ages. The state of our researches into the artist's position in medieval times must reinforce our skepticism about any broad-based conclusions to be drawn from antiquity. For here too the arts were almost completely ignored by serious writers. However, a considerable number of scattered documents—of the very kind which have not survived from ancient Greece or Rome—can still be traced, and these show us how complex the situation was. Their investigation has recently been undertaken by Andrew Martindale (1966). Since his researches constitute by far the most valuable contribution that has yet been made to the subject, they have been heavily drawn upon in the following discussion.

Enough documentation certainly survives to prove what was only conjecture in any discussion of earlier periods: until the fifteenth century most artists were generally considered superior craftsmen. In 1323, for instance, a Paris scholar listed among "those craftsmen working with their hands" not only "the most ingenious makers of all sorts of image, whether contrived in sculpture or in painting or in relief" but also "the most cunning constructors of instruments of war" and the "makers of bread." Moreover, from tax returns and other sources we can see that artists, like other craftsmen, tended to live together in communities in particular parishes and that they made no distinction between work that would now be considered mechanical, such as decorating saddles (in London the painters' guild was a branch of the saddlers'), and painting devotional images. The artist was incorporated into a guild, and his training followed the usual practice by which, as a youth of about 12, he would enter a master's shop as an apprentice. There he would help out and familiarize himself with technical processes, to emerge after some years as a journeyman, before finally becoming an independent master able to engage apprentices of his own. Thus Lorenzo

Ghiberti, after winning in 1403 the competition for the second set of bronze doors for the baptistery of San Giovanni in Florence (this was a means of attracting artists which was always to remain popular with committees), was in a position to employ as many as 21 apprentices a few years later. The guilds also served other purposes, some of which, such as the maintenance of a certain status and ritual dignity, have been carried on by the academies into our own day. In general, however, their concern was essentially with more practical matters, above all, to protect both the artist and his client from fraud.

But a too-uniform pattern must not be read into the Middle Ages, and many of the striking developments that occurred in Renaissance Italy were already present in embryo. Then, as later, the law of supply and demand operated powerfully in favor of change. It is true, as Martindale stresses, that a king might bring painters into his household for reasons that had little to do with their professional ability and treat them, once there, with scant respect or reward—he instances a "Jack of St. Albans," who was required to dance on a table, and Giotto, whose gift of repartee seems to have been at least as highly prized as his art; yet it is hard to believe as he does that such appointments did nothing to raise the status of painting as an occupation (all our experience of psychology surely suggests the contrary). Martindale himself implies that the occasional institution of the post of "town painter" (a practice adopted, above all, in Venice) may well have been inspired by imitation of such royal gestures. Competition between towns was also of the greatest importance. The terms of Giotto's nomination in 1334 as city architect of Florence ("architect"— though he had made his name as a painter) will serve as an example:

As in the whole world there is to be found none better qualified . . . than Master Giotto di Bondone, the painter of Florence, he shall therefore be named in his native city as Magnus Magister and publicly regarded as such, so that he may have occasion to abide here; for by his presence many can have the advantage of his wisdom and learning, and the city shall gain no small honour because of him.

These terms show what lip service burghers were prepared to pay to the arts—and artists—for enhancing their own reputations (and doing down a rival city).

It is true that Italy in general and Florence in particular were exceptional in paying such honors, but the wording of the appointment reminds us that the rivalry between secular and religious communities, towns and courts, and one city and another could play as significant a part in elevating the position of the artist as could the rivalries between individual patrons in later years. Certainly the artists often thought of themselves as much more than mere craftsmen, as can be seen from the very many self-laudatory inscriptions that they put on their own works: we find examples of these as early as 1100.

Renaissance. The Renaissance did, of course, bring great changes in the status of the artist—one could instance a fragment of a letter from Prince Frederico Gonzaga, who was trying to get hold of any example of Michelangelo's

never-sufficiently-to-be-praised work . . . sculpture or painting, as he chooses, we do not mind which it is as long as it is by him . . . at least a drawing, if it is well done in charcoal. . . . And you must tell him that his work will be placed in a most honourable position, and that we shall feel eternal gratitude towards him, and that we shall never forget such a special favour, and will always be ready to do anything we possibly can to give him pleasure. (quoted in Luzio 1913, pp. 246–247)

But it must always be remembered that Michelangelo's position was a wholly exceptional one and that many of the customs of the Middle Ages were carried on well after his death. However, the letter does point up the new role that had been assumed ever since the fifteenth century by secular patrons in Burgundy, Italy, and elsewhere.

The early humanists who did so much to raise the value of art seem themselves to have been more interested in the remains of antiquity than in contemporary painting or sculpture, but by the middle of the fifteenth century a number of rulers were aware of the possibilities of private patronage as distinguished from the traditional construction and decoration of public buildings. And toward the end of the century Lorenzo de' Medici, whose role as an art lover has been much exaggerated, did anticipate the modern practice of advertising abroad the supremacy of his country's artists in order to enhance its prestige. Other collectors all over Italy, and soon all over Europe, acquired contemporary works of art, which were then evidently kept accessible to other artists and connoisseurs. From these princely collections sprang most of the great national museums, following the example of Anna Maria Ludovica, the last of the Medici, who in 1743 left the accumulated family treasures to the city of Florence. Elsewhere, beheading or exile usually proved a more effective means of acquiring art treasures.

Nonetheless, appreciation of art, and even admiration for the artist, could go hand in hand with habits formed in earlier ages. Well into the seventeenth century, for example, we come across patrons insisting on the use of specified colors in the canvases painted for them, and the nature of commissions generally shows how little individuality was allowed to the artist and how much he was still treated as a craftsman. It was usual for a patron when ordering a picture to pay for the stretcher and the priming, and frequently also the canvas and some of the more expensive colors. He would then indicate the dimensions, insist on a specific time limit for its completion, and make arrangements about the subject matter. As these specifications must have usually taken the form of spoken agreements, it is difficult for us to gauge how strictly they were enforced; yet the survival of preliminary drawings and, later, of painted oil sketches can occasionally give us an idea of any changes required. Most significant of all in this context is the method of payment. The price of the picture was decided in advance—according to a seventeenth-century Italian author, this could be done by finding out how long the work would take and estimating what the painter's daily earnings should be "by comparison with the pay of a craftsman engaged in similar work." A proportion of this was paid at once, and further sums were paid at different stages in its progress, ending, on completion, with the final settlement, to which would be added a bonus. This bonus was the only allowance made for the vagaries of independence. Further indications of the artist's status (and perhaps of the very nature of artistic creativity) can be deduced from the fact that in certain cities, notably Venice, it was a custom until the end of the eighteenth century for artists to work together in families. All this should be borne in mind when the "individualism" of Renaissance artists is being assessed.

In Italy especially, artists were keenly preoccupied with their place in society throughout the fifteenth century, and innumerable arguments were produced to establish their claim to be considered wholly superior to craftsmen. Particular attention was concentrated on the "intellectual" as opposed to the "manual" aspects of their work. Leonardo, whose respect for antiquity led him to the erroneous conclusion that painting had then been one of the liberal arts, only to be "driven out" at a later date, stressed above all the painter's need to have a thorough knowledge of mathematics. It is through instances such as this that we can probably see most clearly how a study of social pressures on the artist can sometimes help us to understand the nature of his art. The Renaissance stressed imagination and science at the expense of the faithful portrayal of reality, and categories of subject matter were tentatively drawn up and later codified to put these ideas into effect, with "history painting" at the top of the list and "genre" at the bottom.

The social status of artists was largely determined by their choice of subject matter until well into the nineteenth century. At the same time, the guilds, which had once been of such service to the artist, were now considered degrading to him through their association with other crafts, and their dissolution was gradually achieved not so much by theoretical arguments as by the practice, adopted first by sovereigns and then by private citizens, of employing artists in defiance of all established traditions. But the process was a slow one, and into the seventeenth and even the eighteenth century the guilds continued to play a significant, if increasingly marginal, part in the life of artistic communities in Italy, France, and elsewhere; nor was the distinction between "arts" and "crafts" made final before the French Revolution.

The rise of the modern artist

The decay of the guilds has sometimes been held responsible not only for the "individualism" and enormous increase in the speed of artistic change that characterize the Renaissance but also for the emergence of the "neurotic" artist so much associated with the early and mid-sixteenth century—and indeed with later times. The force of this argument would be much increased were it possible to conduct any serious research into the state of mind of artists in earlier times. What is certain, however, is that as the guilds decayed, new associations arose that took their place and assumed some of the same functions (Pevsner 1940).

Academies. The Accademia dei Virtuosi al Pantheon, founded in Rome in 1543, was concerned with the same sort of charitable works that had been carried out by medieval guilds. The Accademia del Disegno, established in Florence in 1563, had the grand duke of Tuscany and Michelangelo as its first copresidents (the juxtaposition itself is revealing). While it was intended primarily to promote the newly won status of artists, one of its aims was teaching young men to maintain a high standard of art—but significantly, the instruction was more in the realm of general education than in the technical field, which had been the aim of the earlier guilds.

Dealers. Other features of the present situation first began to emerge during the sixteenth and seventeenth centuries. The enormous reputation of Italian art attracted the attention of collectors else-

where in Europe who, as they were unable to travel themselves, either had to summon particular artists to their courts or mansions or, when this was impossible, to rely on dealers and international agents. Hitherto, such men, who had been operating ever since the Middle Ages, had included works of art among innumerable other commodities. But now they began to assume much greater importance, as can be seen by studying the career of Jacopo Strada (immortalized in a magnificent portrait by Titian), who supplied pictures and antiques to the German courts.

Venice was the most commercialized of Italian cities, and it is there that we find in the person of Aretino the prototype for so many dubious figures familiar since his day—the man who is at once artistic adviser to the great (he received a gold chain from François I), dealer, and collector (in the pursuit of which activity he tried to blackmail Michelangelo). In general, however, dealers in contemporary art played a relatively small role in Italy and confined their often extortionary attentions to young painters who had as yet had no chance of finding patrons directly or to those who suffered during the many financial crises that upset what was always a precarious economic situation. It was in the north, where both courtly patronage and contempt for trade were of much less importance than in Italy, that art dealing first assumed really significant proportions. In sixteenth-century Antwerp and, much more so, in seventeenth-century Amsterdam artists often dealt with middlemen who sometimes—as is the modern practice—paid them a regular allowance in return for their entire output. This breakup in the direct relationship between patron and artist and the consequent "rationalization" of the market obviously played its part in encouraging that specialization of subject matter—flowers, genre, portraiture, etc.—for which Dutch artists were particularly renowned.

Exhibitions. It is in the north too that we can find the origins of the modern picture exhibition. During the later Middle Ages these had been frequently associated with religious festivals at which artists and other craftsmen had shown their wares, but such occasions (which continued until a much later period) belong more to the history of commerce than to the history of art. By the mid-sixteenth century, however, exhibitions were organized by the artists' guilds in Antwerp, and some kinds of formal arrangements had come into being. Meanwhile, another tradition of almost equal importance was slowly beginning to develop in Italy, whereby churches and their cloisters were decorated with pictures on particular saints' days. At first these occasions had no commercial purpose whatsoever and were designed, for instance, by the Virtuosi al Pantheon, purely as an act of homage to a patron saint. By the early seventeenth century, however, artists had seen the possibilities for self-advancement that were inherent in the custom and were anxious to display their pictures on the various opportunities available each year—even though there was as yet still no question of selling them. Nor were there any catalogues or other regular promotional procedures.

The Paris salon.   By far the most important step in the development of the modern exhibition was taken in Paris in 1667, when for the first time, what was intended to be an annual *salon* was organized for its members in the Louvre by the Académie Royale, the most authoritative of the early academies. Exhibitions took place thereafter at irregular intervals, although they were well established by the second quarter of the eighteenth century, and printed catalogues were sold. For the first time, the general public, as opposed to a highly restricted circle of the rich and powerful, had the opportunity to see current production without having to crane their necks in dark churches or wheedle their way into the palaces of the aristocracy. As an inevitable result the artist could appeal to a wider circle than ever before, the much-debated phenomenon of "bourgeois taste" began to make itself seriously felt, and criticism sprang into being.

Art criticism.   Criticism had hitherto been confined to historians and theorists, usually arguing from basic principles, and to amateur poets, who were likely to write laudatory sonnets about works they particularly admired. It had been bedeviled by the problem of whether a person who was not a practicing artist was in a position to make any useful comments, and in any case, it had only rarely dealt with new works. Yet critics could prove to be very influential. Often the critic, who was never in any sense a professional, served as adviser to the more important patrons. Thus G. P. Bellori, the most prominent critic of the seventeenth century, whose idealizing theories profoundly affected his own and all future generations, worked for Queen Christina of Sweden and for the popes; and Winckelmann, his even more important successor in the eighteenth century, was employed by Cardinal Albani.

In any case, such great theorists, historians, and scholars belong to a wholly different class from the pamphleteers who in 1738 began—much to the justified indignation of the artists—to review the salons. Their tone was often low and scurrilous, but the popularity of their work can be gauged from the fact that there were 2 written criticisms in 1738, 10 in 1773, and 28 ten years later. While most of their articles are now forgotten, they are of importance for the historian of art because they anticipate later writers who reached the far larger and more ignorant publics of the nineteenth and twentieth centuries and because they include one genius, Diderot.

Connoisseurs.   One other extremely important phenomenon occurred during the period under consideration: the arrival on the scene of the *connoisseur*, the "man of taste," often holding little political power and of relatively small means but deeply concerned with the arts. He was able to exert considerable influence, particularly on artists whose talents were not easily adaptable to official commissions likely to be offered by great princes or clerics. Such a man in seventeenth-century Rome was Cassiano dal Pozzo, who employed Poussin for many years, or Pierre Crozat (admittedly of infinitely greater wealth), who nourished the very unusual genius of Watteau. Indeed, many of the most beautiful houses, pictures, and statues of the eighteenth century were produced for such individuals, who, being far removed from the court or church, proved to be extremely rewarding patrons—and friends.

By the end of the eighteenth century many of the institutions associated with today's artistic scene were already in being: the private collector, the dealer, the exhibition, the critic, and even the museum of modern art (in the form of state purchases, in France especially, of promising new works). Huge fortunes could be earned—Sir Joshua Reynolds left £100,000 on his death in 1792—and huge reputations gained (Reitlinger 1961).

The ideology of genius.   It cannot be denied that the artist's situation has changed radically since the late eighteenth century. Once again the main cause must be attributed to a new conception of the artist's status. The idea of wayward "genius" and "inspiration," which had been confined by the ancients to poets and thinkers, was extended during the Renaissance to artists—at first rather tentatively and then with growing assurance. The towering achievements of Michelangelo and his strange, austere character, notable for its *terribiltà*, were, more than any theoretical writing, responsible for the acceptance of this concept. In the sixteenth century Benvenuto Cellini implied that artists were entitled to live above the law, and in the seventeenth Salvator Rosa claimed to be unable to paint unless "carried away by the transports of enthusiasm." He refused to accept the traditional advance payment for commissioned pictures, claiming he could not know when a painting would be finished.

By the seventeenth century it was a commonplace that artists were likely to have difficult characters, at the very least, and that this might even be a prerequisite of their talent—this despite the strenuous efforts of nearly all the leading artists of the day to conform to established patterns of social behavior so as to raise their status.

In the eighteenth century William Blake was only one among many who denied that art could be taught—an assumption underlying the many new academies that had been founded all over Europe to improve standards of design—and soon afterward Goya claimed for the artist the right to look to his own fantasies rather than to the outer world for the subject matter of his art. It is, however, exceedingly important to stress that scarcely one, if any, of the serious artists of the nineteenth century ever put into practice the vast claims that had been made for the rights of genius by their predecessors and encouraged by the German *Sturm und Drang*.

Nonetheless, nearly all of them did maintain that where artist and public conflicted, it was the artist's moral duty to be true to himself rather than to his patrons. This was a stand that had hitherto been possible only for the very great, whose reputations were already assured and whose "difficult" works could therefore be taken on trust even when they were not fully understood. But this change of attitude occurred when, because of the increased birth rate and the urbanization that had been stimulated by the industrial revolution, a much bigger and presumably rather different public began to have the opportunities to see, and then to buy, modern art. Unfortunately, not even the minimum basic research into this change of patronage from a "cultivated aristocracy" to a "*nouveau-riche*, ignorant bourgeoisie" has yet been undertaken. The general validity of this traditional view will merely have to be assumed.

Art and politics. Two other important new developments took place at this time, about which we can be much more certain. First, there was the great politicization of life that occurred as a result of the French Revolution. Artists had occasionally played a part in the important issues of their day —Tilman Riemenschneider had suffered torture for his support of the Peasants' Revolt of 1525, Lucas Cranach had strongly backed the Reformation, Michelangelo had helped to defend Florence against the Medici in 1527, and so on—but never before had their styles, as opposed to their occasional subject matter, been associated with political views. In the eighteenth century, it is true, some writers—notably Diderot—had tried to identify certain artists with certain social and political causes (again, as in the case of John Baptiste Greuze,

usually on the basis of subject matter), but their lack of success had been total. And those who see in the classicism of David some sort of bourgeois opposition to court circles are merely projecting into the past what would never have been suspected—by him or his patrons—before 1789. Nonetheless, David's career does mark a watershed. Actively engaged in politics himself (and always, until his last years in exile, on the winning side, whichever it was), he initiated a great stylistic revolution that was inevitably confused with political revolution. Thereafter, art and politics became inextricably confused, so that in 1825 we can find the writer Louis Vitet exclaiming, "Le goût en France attend son 14 Juillet" (quoted in Grate 1959, p. 17), although in fact he was calling for an end to Davidian classicism in the name of that painterly romanticism whose leading exponent was Delacroix, soon to become a convinced reactionary!

Public galleries. The other important innovation was the widespread inauguration of public art galleries, above all, the Louvre in 1793 and in 1824 the National Gallery in London. They kept on permanent view collections of old masters, often dimmed by yellowing varnish, as a sort of standing reproach to any artistic change—this danger had been anticipated by Constable, one of the first to suffer in this way, and countless innovators could have echoed his fear that "the manufacturers are made the criterions of perfection, instead of nature." This was particularly ironic because most public art galleries had been founded not only because of the general belief of the Enlightenment that art could improve the quality of civilization and help to "soften manners," but above all, because it was hoped that galleries, like the academies, would benefit living artists: the Louvre was at first opened only to artists on seven out of every ten days.

The artist and the bourgeoisie

A new conception of the artist, of "ignorant" public opinion, and of the politicization of all culture (so that every new step, previously welcomed, was now looked upon as potentially subversive by a public that dreaded above all else a new social upheaval)—all these factors played a vital and often tragic role in the history of nineteenth-century art, especially as the century drew to a close. In almost every country in Europe, but particularly in France, an "official art," sponsored by the principal dealers, the academies, and the richer collectors, confronted those painters, sculptors, and, later, architects whom today we look upon as the finest artists of their times. Controversy centered particularly (but not only) on the "lack of finish" characteristic of nearly all that vital art which was trying to break away from the formulas imposed by David and his school—formulas which were clung to with savage and paradoxical obstinacy by those very academies that he had wanted to abolish. There is ample evidence to show that lack of finish was equated with excessive ease and superficiality, and the now familiar charge, usually made in the presence of great and unfamiliar pictures, that "my little daughter aged ten can paint better than that" is first to be found early in the nineteenth century. More damaging to adventurous artists than public scorn was the hostility of their conservative colleagues, for no mechanism for showing their work had yet replaced the salon or academy exhibitions. In France the organization of such exhibitions was until 1880 under the direct control of the government.

In the earlier part of the century royal or other patrons were sometimes sufficiently powerful to ignore the pressures of the academy, and Delacroix received important public commissions long before he was grudgingly admitted to the Institut de France in 1857, after his eighth application. Later this dichotomy tended to disappear, and more and more artists found themselves excluded from the *salons* (and hence public attention) by restrictive juries. Unsuccessful efforts were made to organize independent exhibitions, and some artists, such as Courbet and Manet, followed an eighteenth-century precedent set by Greuze and others and showed their work privately. The Revolution of 1848 brought a "free" exhibition, Napoleon III organized the Salon des Refusés in 1863, and a group of artists (later to be called the impressionists) showed their works together in 1874 and thereafter at irregular intervals until 1886. Above all, the year 1884 saw the first Salon des Indépendants—a direct rival at last to the official exhibition—which did away with the jury system altogether.

Meanwhile the *salon* itself was beginning to break down, at first under the sheer weight of numbers (White & White 1965) and then, in 1890, because of a split due more to personal quarrels than to any conflict of principle. Gradually, independent dealers began to take over the function of sponsoring modern art, although how important official backing remained can be seen from the fact that in 1900, when he was already the most famous artist in France and possibly in the world, Auguste Rodin said that unless he was successful at the Great Exhibition of that year, he would have to enter the Institut, "parce que c'est à *eux* seuls que vont les grandes commandes."

Dealers as patrons. The dealers who now came to the fore were very different from any that had been seen hitherto. According to Durand-Ruel, the most conspicuous of them, a mature picture dealer should be at the same time an enlightened patron ready, if necessary, to sacrifice his immediate interests to his artistic convictions and a man who would rather fight against the speculators than associate with their interests (Venturi 1939, vol. 1, p. 17). He himself is of additional interest because, while supporting the impressionists at a time when they were looked upon as dangerous revolutionaries —the potential instigators of a new Commune—he remained a staunch reactionary, bitterly hostile to the republican regime; and there is some reason to believe that he relished this double assault on the values of the triumphant *tiers état*. The eventual rewards that came to Durand-Ruel when the impressionists achieved popularity may have played their part in encouraging other dealers, such as Vollard and Kahnweiler, who, like their Dutch predecessors in the seventeenth century, tended to monopolize the output of their favorite artists but whose role in the development of modern painting is analogous to that of Renaissance patrons— as can be seen from their portraits, like those of Pope Leo x or Philip ii of Spain, painted by the greatest artists of their times.

Along with a new type of dealer went a new type of critic, concerned not only with reviewing the annual salons but also with interpreting the "misunderstood artist" and explaining him to the public: witness the writings of Baudelaire on Delacroix, Duranty and Duret on the impressionists, Fénéon on the neo-impressionists, and so on.

The avant-garde. The concept of the avantgarde, that is, of an art that will by its very nature be in conflict with received opinion, had been aired in passing early in the nineteenth century, but only toward its end became the doctrine that has affected all subsequent thinking on the arts. Manifestoes and apologists began to accompany every new movement, culminating in those of the Italian futurists in 1910, in which for the first time, artists and writers went out of their way to court public hostility: there could be no better indication of how far the situation had changed since 1874, when Degas had asked his friend Giuseppe de Nittis to exhibit with the impressionists, explaining that "puisque vous exposez au Salon, les gens mal documentés ne pourront pas dire que nous sommes l'exposition des refusés" (Nittis 1895, p. 237).

Yet despite all this, the critics (and the public) of the end of the nineteenth century were already chastened by the ridicule that now covered those who had rejected first the romantics and then the realists. Opposition to new developments reached a final paroxysm of fury and then, in Western countries at least, tended to disappear following World War II, so that it is now not unusual for an art that appears to defy the traditional rules to be backed by conservative governments; for ever since the intensification of artistic rivalries induced by the international exhibitions of the nineteenth century, all governments have felt the need to encourage artistic output. Similarly, museum directors, warned by the sad experiences of their predecessors who lost so many vital opportunities of enriching their collections with modern works at accessible prices, now pay increasing attention to contemporary developments. Especially in the United States, such directors have often been indirectly assisted by a national policy of taxation that assists patrons intending to bequeath their collections to public museums—a policy often deplored not only on grounds of social morality but also because it has curtailed the role of the museum as an arbiter of taste.

All these developments, combined with the more cautious attitude of critics, have necessarily robbed the avant-garde of its original significance to the extent that works which are considered the most modern of their day are often rapidly acquired by the very people whom they were originally designed to challenge. Dissatisfaction with "academic art" and a recognition of past misunderstandings, as well as the actual nature of much twentieth-century painting and sculpture, have also led to an obsession with the act of creation itself (sometimes at the expense of the created work), so that universities and other educational bodies have been anxious not only to acquire contemporary art but also to observe the artist at work by incorporating him within their communities—often with no specific duties. The nature of artistic development is as yet too-little understood for it to be clear whether or not this new relationship with society is a beneficial one.

FRANCIS HASKELL

[See also CREATIVITY, article on SOCIAL ASPECTS; STYLE. A guide to other relevant material will be found under ART.]

BIBLIOGRAPHY

ANTAL, FREDERICK 1948 Florentine Painting and Its Social Background. London: Routledge.

COOK, R. M. 1960 Greek Painted Pottery. Chicago: Quadrangle Books.

CROZET, RENÉ 1954 La vie artistique au 17ème siècle. Paris: Presses Universitaires de France.

DIDEROT, DENIS (1759–1767) 1957–1963 Salons. Edited by Jean Seznec and Jean Adhémar. 3 vols. Oxford: Clarendon.

EASTON, MALCOLM 1964 Artists and Writers in Paris: The Bohemian Idea, 1803–1867. London: Arnold.

FRANCASTEL, PIERRE 1965 La réalité figurative: Éléments structurels de sociologie de l'art. Paris: Gonthier.

GOMBRICH, E. H. 1960 The Early Medici as Patrons of Art. Pages 279–311 in Italian Renaissance Studies. Edited by E. F. Jacob. London: Faber.

GOMBRICH, E. H. 1963 Meditations on a Hobby Horse, and Other Essays on the Theory of Art. London: Phaidon. → See especially pages 86–94, "The Social History of Art," for criticism of Arnold Hauser's Social History of Art. A number of research projects are implied by the criticism.

GRATE, PONTUS 1959 Deux critiques d'art de l'époque romantique: Gustave Planche et Théophile Thoré. Stockholm: Almqvist & Wiksell.

HASKELL, FRANCIS 1963 Patrons and Painters: A Study in the Relations Between Italian Art and Society in the Age of Baroque. New York: Knopf.

HAUSER, ARNOLD 1951 Social History of Art. 2 vols. London: Routledge.

LUZIO, ALESSANDRO (editor) 1913 La galleria dei Gonzaga; venduta all'Inghilterra nel 1627–1628: Documenti degli archivi di Mantova a Londra. Milano (Italy): Cogliati. → The translation of the extract in the text was provided by Francis Haskell.

MARTIN, ALFRED VON (1932) 1944 Sociology of the Renaissance. London: Routledge. → First published in German. A paperback edition was published in 1963 by Harper.

MARTIN, W. 1907 The Life of a Dutch Artist. Part 6: How the Painter Sold His Works. Burlington Magazine 9:357–369.

MARTINDALE, ANDREW 1966 The Rise of the Artist. Pages 281–314 in Joan Evans (editor), The Flowering of the Middle Ages. New York: McGraw-Hill.

NITTIS, GIUSEPPE DE 1895 Notes et souvenirs du peintre Joseph de Nittis. Paris: Librairies-imprimeries Réunies.

PELLES, GERALDINE 1963 Art, Artists and Society. Englewood Cliffs, N.J.: Prentice-Hall.

PEVSNER, NIKOLAUS 1940 Academies of Art: Past and Present. New York: Macmillan.

REITLINGER, GERALD 1961 The Economics of Taste: The Rise and Fall of Picture Prices, 1760–1960. London: Barrie & Rockliff.

SALMON, PIERRE 1958 De la collection au musée. Brussels: Office de Publicité.

SCHLOSSER, JULIUS VON 1965 L'arte di corte nel sècolo XIV. Milan (Italy): Edizioni di Comunità.

VENTURI, LIONELLO 1939 Les archives de l'impressionnisme. 2 vols. Paris and New York: Durand-Ruel. → The translation of the extract in the text was provided by Francis Haskell.

WACKERNAGEL, MARTIN 1938 Der Lebensraum des Künstlers in der florentinischen Renaissance. Leipzig: Seemann.

WHITE, HARRISON; and WHITE, CYNTHIA 1965 Canvases and Careers: Institutional Change in the French Painting World. New York: Wiley.

WITTKOWER, RUDOLF; and WITTKOWER, MARGOT 1963 Born Under Saturn; the Character and Conduct of Artists: A Documented History From Antiquity to the French Revolution. London: Weidenfeld & Nicolson.

II

THE RECRUITMENT AND SOCIALIZATION OF ARTISTS

"Recruitment" is a term used to refer to the underlying processes for bringing new members into a group. Sociologists are especially interested in understanding those social forces that encourage individuals to join, or repel them from joining, an occupational or professional group and to embark on a particular career within that group.

In many occupations the process of recruitment can be readily understood. For example, consider the military, from whom the word "recruitment" was originally borrowed. We know in clear terms the subjective and objective meaning of the professional soldier. We are aware of the symbols, such as money, glory, social advancement, travel, and adventure, which attract persons to become soldiers. We are equally aware of the symbols that distract, discourage, and repel the individual from this profession—fear, lack of sympathy with the cause, discipline, death, separation from loved ones and from one's community.

By contrast, there is a great vagueness concerning the recruitment of the artist. It is very difficult, first of all, to define the term "artist"; any attempt at an essential, or even an operational, definition of the artist—an attempt in which many generations of aesthetes have failed—is bound to founder (see Gabor 1963, p. 148, who makes the same point for the definition of "art"). The reasons for this become apparent as soon as several crucial questions are asked. For example, who is an artist, and why is he one? Does it depend on the amount of time spent working as an artist? Then how does one include individuals like Charles Ives, an American composer whose entire working career was spent in an insurance company?

Does working as an artist qualify one to be included in this category? Then we must exclude individuals of high artistic potential whose creative urge is latent or shows itself in activities other than art. Can we rely on contemporary recognition by institutions within the art world, such as galleries, museums, or private collectors? But to do this would exclude practically all the impressionist painters, not to mention Rembrandt at the time that he created some of his most important masterpieces. In view of these difficulties, we must rely on connotative and denotative examples in order to define our term "professional artist," while keeping in mind the shortcomings of this method.

When speaking of a professional artist, I think of Pablo Picasso, Marc Chagall, Alberto Giacometti, Ernest Hemingway, William Faulkner, Anton Webern, and Arnold Schönberg, to name a few outstanding figures from the first half of the twentieth century. Such men devote their time and psychic energy to creative endeavors or would do so if circumstances permitted. In other words, their primary work is or would be directed toward ex-

ploring the "fundamental categories" of human existence, the attempt to exalt or denigrate authority, "to explore or explain the universe, to understand the meaning of events, to enter into contact with the sacred or to commit sacrilege, to affirm the principles of morality and justice and to deny them, to encounter the unknown, . . . to stir the senses by the control of and response to words, sounds, shapes, and colors" (Shils 1960a, p. 290).

Control of the arts. In some countries and during some eras there has been fairly tight control of the arts, both in the number of recruits and in the course of their careers. For example, during the guild era in Europe no disciple could change masters unless his first teacher agreed to break his contract, and all disciples had to remain with the master for three years (Tomasini 1953, pp. 135, 140). Furthermore, there was an attempt to establish mastership as a hereditary privilege (Dobb 1947, pp. 116–117). Willetts writes that during the existence of the Sung Academy in China (12th century) "its appointments seem to have been sinecures with promotions through four ranks." The French Académie Royale de Peinture et de Sculpture had a similar elaborate hierarchy. In both academies "admission and promotion were by competitive examination. In both, the candidate was required to submit his personal version of a set theme, after gaining official approval of his proposed treatment by means of a preliminary sketch" (Willetts 1958, p. 518).

In twentieth-century Europe and the United States the arts are characterized by a relative absence of centralized occupational control, as compared, for example, with the academies mentioned above or with the medical profession in the United States, with its institutional self-awareness, its standards of competence and discipline, and its relatively stabilized recruitment. Moreover, in these countries the demand for the visual arts—and for other arts as well—is rapidly and vastly expanding. This combination of an expanding market and an absence of tight controls suggests that the world of art—fine and commercial—must recruit in a rather generous, if not excessive, fashion. Unlike certain occupations, the world of art need not underrecruit for the purpose of controlling a valuable skill, with its accompanying monetary rewards, prestige, and honor.

Much of the rather "open" recruitment in art is reflected in various gentle practices and policies of many art schools in the United States. Probably few applicants are refused admittance. Students occasionally drop out of school of their own volition but are rarely expelled as from medical or engineering schools. There are few or no crucial tests or other hurdles that a student must pass to remain in school. Grades seem mainly to yield encouragement or prestige and seem not to be utilized to restrict enrollment or to force the repeating of courses. Anyone who has the time and money can go to any number of commercial and fine arts schools. (These data on art schools, as well as the following section on the students' family background and public school experience, are based on Strauss 1955a; see also Griff 1960; 1964a; 1964b.)

Early socialization of the artist

Because recruitment into the art world is neither tightly limited nor carefully controlled, we should not be led to assume that artists somehow drift into art. There exists a whole social paraphernalia for getting persons committed to their artistic identities; and the fact that the machinery is not usually visible to the person himself does not, of course, make it any less real.

The chief mechanism for pumping a flow of talent into art today is the public-school system—aided by the art schools and often abetted unknowingly and unwillingly by the student's family. This is true, among other reasons, because nowadays artists do not appear to come from very high or very low social classes. An artistic career is not generally initiated by an education at prep school or an elite college, nor do persons of low economic standing usually become artists by emulating models found in their communities (they are far more likely to emulate athletes). Parents in various strata introduce their offspring to art, stressing humanist, hobbyist, and other values; but not many parents consider the visual arts a propitious locale on which to fight the battle for class and occupational success. As a consequence, few parents directly influence their children to enter the field of art. Moreover, attendance at galleries and museums, with or without parents, plays no discernible part in recruitment; it is, in fact, a rare art student who reports having any art "in his background." Nor do students entering art school usually know artists of any kind except their public-school teachers; nor are they especially acquainted with art history or with the biographies of famous artists.

Public-school experiences. The public-school art teachers begin to exert their influence quite early in the career of the artist, generally in grammar school. Impoverished or misguided though their teaching may be, they may introduce the youngster to the satisfactions and delights of drawing and painting. These teachers serve to keep interest in art alive throughout the school years by bestowing approval upon the child, singling him out for special honors, placing his work in public view, or assigning him honorific tasks, such as decorating the blackboards. Some students mention that as early as kindergarten, teachers singled them out for praise and isolated them from their classmates so that they could concentrate on their art.

In high school the child who has been recognized for his artistic virtuosity continues to take art courses and often has the opportunity to major in art. Art teachers may begin to suggest that he go on to art school—a step that otherwise might not occur to some—and may procure information and even scholarships for their protégés. The high-school milieu affords additional prestige, for the child may win a school prize, or even a national one, or receive acclaim for decorating a stage set, drawing for the school paper, and other such activities.

Saturday morning art classes. Complementing the role of the high school in the recruitment process are the typical Saturday morning classes sponsored by the community art museum. These special classes, which are to be found in Europe as well as in the United States, play a crucial role in encouraging an art career. For school children whose art instruction is limited (especially in the private or parochial schools, where art instruction may be absent), they provide the first exposure to advanced courses and qualified teachers. The Saturday classes provide students not only with material facilities, such as oils, brushes, and models, but also with professional instruction and the encouragement offered by the milieu of a museum. Also, for both children and adolescents, this may be their first (and perhaps only) opportunity to come into contact with peers having similar dispositions toward art.

Another important effect of the Saturday morning classes is that they single out the artistic person: that is, they signify to those in his social milieu, as well as to himself, that he has been socially recognized as having an unusual ability, absent in others, which has certain rewards. In addition, these classes stimulate the nascent attributes of independence and freedom from external restraint that are associated with artists, because they separate the individual from his social milieu perhaps for the first time in his life. This *may* accelerate for these children the normal personality development from unilateral to autonomous thinking, studied by Piaget (1923). Finally, the experience of the Saturday classes may reinforce a sense of security for some children; in the childhood and adolescent world of comparisons, they can brag about their painting ability, which may, indeed, be the only outstanding skill they have.

Parental attitudes

The portrait that emerges from a study of the childhood and adolescent social experiences of the individual who possesses artistic skills reveals the congruence of encouragement and reward, of aspiration and fulfillment. He learns that his contribution is socially meaningful and constructive, and at the same time he is encouraged to exercise freely that which he most basically feels is himself. Except for the normal tensions of childhood and adolescence all the factors favoring the retention and nourishment of an artist's career are present.

Discontinuities in this pattern become apparent when the person declares publicly that he wishes to prepare for a career in art. The parents of the would-be artist make two very strenuous objections to his desire. The first is that the painter cannot hope to support himself solely from the sale of his paintings and that this will make it impossible for him to attain many of the symbols of success that families cherish. The second objection is directed at the bohemian stereotype of the artist, which the family wishes to avoid because it violates the professed mores of our culture. (The fact that artists often seem to become bohemians is, of course, closely related to their financial problems.)

When the student's intention to become an artist is discovered, there is a reversal in the attitude of his parents toward him. Thus, a crisis is engendered, which becomes aggravated during the period beginning with the announcement of his intentions and ending with the termination of his formal education. The entire family makes a determined effort to dissuade him. They remove his paintings from the walls where they were prominently displayed. Artistic achievements and the large remunerations for paintings received by artists become topics to be avoided.

It is at this point that the germ of self-estrangement (commonly referred to as alienation) is first implanted. Going contrary to the wishes of one's parents causes one's conscience to suffer. It suffers because of the strong affective relationship between parents and child, because of intensive cultural imperatives emanating from the mores and reinforced by religious institutions—particularly the dogma concerning filial duties—and because of the acute sensitivity and imagination characteristic of the artist qua artist. While the exertion of the individual toward independence is normal during this period, this breaking away may have added significance for the career of the artist. Rank, for

example, in discussing the creation of individuality said:

The gradual freeing of the individual from dependence by a self-creative development of personality replaces the one-sided . . . dependence on the mother. . . . The person in the third and highest level of development, the creative type, such as the artist or the philosopher, creates a world for himself which he can accept without wanting to force it on others; and he accepts himself. Such a person creates his own inner ideals, which he affirms as his own commandments. At the same time he can live in the world without falling into continual conflict with it. (1932; quoted in Mullahy 1948, pp. 177, 183–184)

There appears to be an inconsistency in parental attitudes toward the child who chooses the artistic career. It has been stated that the young artist is encouraged and rewarded and that his early success in art is a source of gratification for his parents as well as for him. However, the parents' later disapproval of his career choice becomes understandable if the difference between school success and occupational success is considered. School success is confined largely to the yardstick of the report card ("My daughter gets all A's in art"), and there is also recognition in the form of prizes, articles in the local newspaper, or acknowledgment on graduation programs. However, when a child graduates from high school new standards and criteria of judgment are applied, which are associated with symbols of financial success and social prestige. Art is not an avenue leading to the attainment of these symbols, and parents know this. Moreover, these reactions reflect some significant attitudes toward the fine artist and toward art in contemporary culture.

Cultural variations. Contemporary industrial culture stresses conformity, respectability, rationality, practicality, and security. These are a few of the essential values incorporated in the cultural complex that Max Weber called "rational bourgeois capitalism." Art and the life of the artist are antinomies of this. Fine art is nonutilitarian. Moreover, the artist tends to be nonconformist and to violate many of the behavioral patterns prescribed by society. His choice of career opposes the success theme so strongly emphasized and so pervasive in contemporary culture. The parents of artists may themselves have failed to achieve success, and they, with all good intentions of loving parents, want their children to avoid the disappointments that they have experienced. Also, to parents who value success for their children as an affirmation and confirmation of their worthiness as parents, there is little comfort in the notion that the young artist may achieve recognition posthumously. Yet, this is frequently all the young artist can offer as justification for the sacrifices he proposes.

Parental opposition to a career in art is neither recent nor geographically confined; nor, for that matter, is parental encouragement. The way in which a son is forced to struggle against his parents because he suffers from an internal ebullition of artistic desire, which they try to suppress, has become a classic ritual (Fry 1929, p. 6 in the 1958 edition). Yet, instances of the encouragement of artistic careers have also been notable (Haskell 1963, pp. 20–21; Tomasini 1953). The experience of the contemporary composer Gian-Carlo Menotti provides an example:

How well I remember as a child watching the profound sorrow of all Milan as the funeral of Puccini passed through the streets. It was a loss for each of us as well as for our country. No wonder that a young Italian boy's wanting to be a composer could only be a source of satisfaction and pride to his family and friends. But the family's regard for music was only a reflection of the general public's esteem in which the composer was held in Italy. (1953, pp. 42–43)

The explanation for this variation in attitudes is open to debate and awaits further research. Two hypotheses, however, immediately come to mind. One is suggested by Menotti:

It is my contention that the average American has little or no respect for the creative artist and is apt to consider him as an almost useless member of the community. The average American father still views with dismay the fact that one of his sons may choose to become a composer, writer, or painter. He will consider any such pursuit a sign of "softness," an unmanly and, I venture to say, un-American choice.

I must add in all frankness that this hostility toward the arts is not uncommon in Europe within a certain class of society. But it exists only in a very small percentage of the population, mostly among the *nouveaux riches* and the very orthodox members of the aristocracy who still feel that it is more noble to patronize than to create. Moreover, even in this latter small moribund class, artistic activity is at least looked upon as an essential element of gracious living rather than the adornment of uneventful Sunday afternoons. (1953, pp. 39–40)

An alternative hypothesis is suggested by an artist turned popular writer: "Art needs a proper climate. The average Frenchman is no more artistic than the average American. . . . But the French climate is good for art, because in France an artist isn't expected to earn as much as a stockbroker. He is justified in his existence even if he is just a *little* artist. He doesn't have to be a Picasso. He counts as a necessary human factor although he hasn't reached the very top" (King 1958, p. 8).

Preparation for a career in art

After graduating from high school the neophyte artist enrolls in an art school or art institute, where he takes a basic course in the fundamentals of drawing, painting, and illustration. There he is thrown together with a large group of individuals having a variety of talents and backgrounds. For many, the first year is a joy. They work and learn (perhaps for the first time) in a milieu that is permeated with art. The school may be in a museum, or at least very near one, and the students are socially united by their common interest in art.

Specialization ensues during the subsequent years. In the second year, the students are divided into fine arts, commercial or applied arts, and art education sections. Further specialization takes place during the third and fourth years, but the most important specialty, in terms of the recruitment process, is fine arts.

The fine arts student searches for a teacher compatible to his temperament both as an artist and as an individual. Some seek and readily accept technical instruction; others expect to get instruction only upon request; still others are hostile to any instruction, asseverating that it is a violation of artistic mores for an instructor even to touch their canvases.

Competition for grades is discouraged because of the inherent difficulty in judging art; both talented and untalented students, as well as instructors, mention this. Usually, the only institutionally fostered competition that is meaningful is the rivalry for the traveling fellowships, which takes place during the senior year. Both students and instructors have suggested that some students deliberately alter their natural style during the fellowship competition in order to cater to the known tastes of the judges. However, in general, we can say that the art school does not constitute a disruptive force, in terms of the unity of the self, as other types of schools frequently do. In other words, the intensive competition that tempts or forces students to engage in subterfuge or parroting their mentors in order to receive passing or superior grades is not present in the art school. What emerges in the art school is a consistency between self and fulfillment. Thus, the self-estrangement that for the average person begins with formal schooling and continues indefinitely does not, for the most part, affect the art student.

Vocational choices. As the student nears the end of his academic training he becomes anxious over what he will do when he graduates. Some may succumb to the prodding of their parents (or fiancées or wives) and take a few commercial art courses before they graduate. For the same reasons, others may take courses in art education or may return for a year after they graduate to take courses in art education. Still others pass through four years of training and delay their decisions until they graduate. A very few will win traveling fellowships lasting for a year or two and thereby postpone their decisions temporarily. A few, both those who have completed their fellowships and those who did not win one, will find galleries that will give them small subsidies. Eventually, however, each must find a source of steady income. Some will find work in the post office or in stores and will paint in the evenings or on weekends. A prolonged siege of this work is disheartening, especially when the individual realizes that he may have to do this for many years—that is, until he is recognized—or that he may have to work at whatever he is doing for the rest of his life. In the end, most return to art in secondary ways—some as art educators and many as commercial artists.

Whichever alternative is chosen, it will be a secondary choice and one that implies taking a job which the person feels is not his basic calling. It is at this point in the recruitment process of the artist that the state commonly referred to as alienation begins to be seriously experienced. As mentioned above, the first signs of alienation appear in connection with the students' conflict with their parents, as they finish high school, but in art school this parental opposition is usually overcome or disregarded. However, there is this important difference between finishing formal art school and finishing high school. While parents will strenuously object to their child's going to art school, they will, in most cases, continue to support their child because the mores demand it. After graduation, however, there are no moral imperatives necessitating continued support and certainly none that would obligate the parents to support the child indefinitely. It must also be pointed out that it is at this point in the student's life that the philosophies to which he has been exposed in his intellectual quest as artist—no matter how ingenuous they may appear—begin to fructify.

These circumstances raise a number of important questions concerning the artist. One of the most important of these is, What happens to one's artistic identity when one enters various types of employment? Griff (1960; 1964b) has sought the answer to this question in a study of commercial (i.e., advertising) artists. Commercial artists were selected for study because it was believed that these people had chosen the extreme alternative among the possibilities available to the artist. It was felt that the role of the commercial artist differs in so many fundamental ways from that of the fine artist that a study of it could serve as a paradigm for what happens in the case of less extreme vocational choices.

Art and advertising

There are few institutions whose basic values are more opposed to one another in all fundamental respects than are those of art and advertising—their vocabularies, their traditions, their standards and rules, beliefs and symbols, criteria for the selection of subject matter and problems, modes of presentation, canons for the assessment of excellence—are all antithetical.

The traditions of art seem by their very nature to entail a measure of tension with the traditions of advertising and its close allies, commerce and industry. The very intensity and concentration of commitment to these value orientations reflect the distance that separates the two. Art, like genuine religion, continues to be vitally concerned with the sacred or the ultimate ground of thought and experience and the aspiration to enter into intimate contact with it. Thus, art involves the search for truth, for the principles embedded in events and actions, or for the establishment of a relationship between the self and the essential, whether the relationship be cognitive, appreciative, or expressive (Shils 1960b).

In contrast, the traditions of advertising emphasize the selection of the mundane as subject matter; its presentation in terms of immediate perception as well as by the use of standardization, classification, and clichés; the necessity for certainty of cognition and direction; the deliberate attempts to manipulate through the use of visual stimuli based upon emulation, fear, and sex; and the assessment of excellence in terms of attention value, consumption, and fidelity (called brand loyalty) to the product of one's client.

In addition, there are innumerable technical differences between advertising and the fine arts, based upon the problems of graphic reproduction. The commercial artist must consider the different qualities of papers and printing inks and the effect these will have on the final version of his work. He must consider that the painting as seen in the original and then on the printed page will be different, because the flat surface of the paper eliminates the third dimension together with the brush strokes and canvas pores. Since it is necessary to make the product and accompanying message stand out (known technically as highlighting), a sharp linear style is used; a firm principle of advertising art is recognition through a silhouette.

The differences in compositional techniques are also readily apparent. For example, in many automobile ads there appears to be an illusion of deep space, but upon careful analysis it can be seen that the eye does not move from the front plane to deep space; compare this to a painting by a Dutch master, where the eye moves into the interior from the front of the room and then into the distance through an open door or window. In the advertisement the automobile covers the horizon, extends along most of the composition, and blocks the eye from easy recession into the background. Even the space in the background is indeterminate and has the function of forcing the nearer objects toward the eye, thus forcing the viewer to concentrate on the advertised product (Parker 1937, pp. 119–122).

Role identification and artistic values. Commercial artists range in type from those who remain symbolically attached to the role of the fine artist to those who reject this role completely. Between these two extremes lies a third group that identifies with both roles (see Griff 1960, pp. 219–241, for an extended account of the three roles mentioned here).

The traditional role. Some artists work as commercial artists, but subjectively identify themselves as fine artists "temporarily" engaged in the commercial field. In other words, they identify with what they regard as the artist's *traditional role*; their rationalization for working in the commercial field is that the normative standards of contemporary society preclude any economically feasible alternative. Underlying this assumption is the belief that society will give lip service to, but in reality will not support, the artist's primary identity—that of the fine artist as he emerged at the end of the nineteenth century. In supporting their premise they cite numerous examples, both past and present, of other individuals who have tried, without success, to live exclusively from their paintings. In addition, there is the actual attempt by many of them to live from the sale of their paintings. Finding this to be an impossibility, they may have turned to commercial art. Also, there is the further realization that other aspects of the reward system of society are absent (i.e., prestige, praise, or admiration of others for their dedication to their ideals). Instead, in many cases, negative sanctions have been applied against them in the form of derision and questions concerning the practicality of their labors, as well as their "sanity."

The commercial role. Artists who assume the "commercial role" see art (both fine and commercial) as a utilitarian product, and they conceive of themselves as instruments for the transformation of verbal symbols (dictated by a client) into visual ones. Consequently, their ideological orientation is directed toward pleasing and satisfying their clients. Conceiving their roles in this manner the commercial-role artists refrain from interjecting or altering in any way the intent of their clients unless specifically directed to do so. Thus, they accept a norm that is not only upheld by their occupational group but also sanctioned by the larger society: The customer is always right. In carrying out this belief, they define their roles as having been successfully fulfilled when the requirements of their clients have been met as parsimoniously as possible. This means the creation of illustrations in the quickest and cheapest fashion.

In contrast to the attitudes held by the traditional-role artists, the commercial-role artists reject the notion that they are artists working in the commercial field because of extenuating circumstances. On the contrary, they believe that the traditional role is a nineteenth-century anachronism and therefore should be discarded by the contemporary artist.

The compromise role. The "compromise role" is a mixture of both the traditional and the commercial roles. Like the commercial-role artists, those who assume the compromise role believe that they are instruments of the clients; however, they conceive of themselves as active, rather than as passive, agents. In carrying out this conception of themselves, they translate the demands of the client but at the same time attempt to persuade him to accept innovations, specifically the interjection of fine arts symbols into their illustrations. Thus, many feel that they are involved in a crusade for better art. They believe that by raising the standards of their clients' art, they are at the same time raising the level of taste of the public.

The resemblance between the compromise role and the traditional role lies in the fact that both are concerned with fine arts. However, the artists who choose the compromise role do not consider the commercial field onerous or harmful to fine arts or believe that their status should be independent of the secular realm. They believe, as do the commercial-role artists, that their legitimate position in society lies in the commercial field. They reflect to a great extent the Bauhaus definition of the artist. This definition stresses the importance of the artist's working in a society rather than being isolated from it. The definition also stresses that the artist, while working in a society, should exert all his technical, moral, and aesthetic skills to influence the products of mass production (Moholy-Nagy 1929).

The study of the recruitment of the artist is part of a broader field called the sociology of art. This field is still in its infancy, and much fundamental work must be done before its outlines, contributions, and limitations will be known and understood. Griff's study (1964a) of art students in Chicago is a step in that direction; further research will confirm, invalidate, or suggest revisions of it. Meanwhile, what is needed now are similar data from the other fine arts and from those areas that are emerging as new fine arts, such as photography and the film. In this connection, important research could be accomplished by studying how an area emerges as a fine art. Other important questions and areas of needed research are: What are the career patterns of successful and unsuccessful artists? What are the social conditions responsible for the fame of an artist, the capriciousness of fame, and immortality; the social conditions hindering or encouraging creative endeavors; the relationship between contemporary patrons and styles of art; the social and psychological conditions impeding artists or aiding them to break with traditional and acceptable styles of art, thus innovating new styles; and the social roles of critics and patrons? Once research on these questions has been undertaken, it will be possible to clarify the more significant and elusive questions, such as whether the artist is a reflection of his society, or whether art is a reflection of the age.

MASON GRIFF

[*Directly related are the entries* CREATIVITY *and* PROFESSIONS. *Other relevant material may be found in* ARCHITECTURE; CRAFTS; FASHION; LITERATURE; STYLE; *and in the biographies of* LUKÁCS *and* RANK.]

BIBLIOGRAPHY

CLARK, KENNETH 1956 *The Nude: A Study in Ideal Form.* New York: Pantheon. → A paperback edition was published in 1959 by Doubleday.

COOMARASWAMY, ANANDA K. 1946 *The Religious Basis of the Forms of Indian Society.* New York: Orientalia. → A social-psychological analysis of Indian art.

COWAN, LOUISE 1959 *The Fugitive Group: A Literary History.* Baton Rouge: Louisiana State Univ. Press. → An excellent study of the effect that face-to-face interaction has upon the emergence of an original poetical style.

DOBB, MAURICE (1947) 1964 *Studies in the Development of Capitalism.* Rev. ed. New York: International Publishers.

DUDEK, LOUIS 1960 *Literature and the Press.* Toronto (Canada): Ryerson. → This study parallels in many important ways Griff's studies of painters; however it concentrates on the literary artist. Contains a wealth of material and a source of innumerable research possibilities, as well as insights into the problem of contemporary literature being overwhelmed by mass society. It also explores the effects of mass society on the creative product of literary authors.

FRY, ROGER (1929) 1952 *Cézanne: A Study of His Development.* 2d ed. New York: Macmillan; London: Hogarth. → A paperback edition was published in 1958 by Noonday.

GABOR, DENNIS (1963) 1964 *Inventing the Future.* New York: Knopf. → A paperback edition was published in 1964 by Penguin.

GIMPEL, JEAN (1958) 1961 *The Cathedral Builders.* New York: Grove. → First published in French. A technical, historical, and sociological account of the building of cathedrals in Europe from 1050–1350.

GRIFF, MASON 1959 Alienation and the Artist. *Arts in Society* [1959], Fall: 43–54. → A social and historical study of the alienation of the artist during the nineteenth century.

GRIFF, MASON 1960 The Commercial Artist: A Study in Changing and Consistent Identities. Pages 219–241 in Maurice Stein, A. Vidich, and D. White (editors), *Identity and Anxiety.* Glencoe, Ill.: Free Press.

GRIFF, MASON 1961 Creativity and Syrenes. Unpublished manuscript. → Suggests the relationships between creativity and social factors; also contains a number of specific research suggestions.

GRIFF, MASON 1964a The Recruitment of the Artist. Pages 61–94 in Robert N. Wilson (editor), *The Arts in Society.* Englewood Cliffs, N.J.: Prentice-Hall. → A discussion of the problems of the neophyte artist; based on a study of students attending a large art school in Chicago.

GRIFF, MASON 1964b Conflicts of the Artist in Mass Society. *Diogenes* 46:54–68. → A report based on a social-psychological study of the artist who, unable to earn a living from his paintings, becomes a commercial (advertising) artist.

HARRISON, JANE E. (1913) 1927 *Ancient Art and Ritual.* London: Butterworth. → An important sociological study of dramatic art. See especially pages 119–169 on "The Transition From Ritual to Art."

HASKELL, FRANCIS 1963 *Patrons and Painters: A Study in the Relations Between Italian Art and Society in the Age of the Baroque.* New York: Knopf; London: Chatto & Windus. → Contains innumerable suggestions for further research in the sociology of art; also serves as an example of scholarship in this area.

KING, ALEXANDER 1958 *Mine Enemy Grows Older.* New York: Simon & Schuster.

MACK, GERSTLE 1935 *Paul Cézanne.* New York: Knopf. → A less technical and more sociological account of Cézanne than Fry 1929.

MENOTTI, GIAN-CARLO 1953 A Plea for the Creative Artist. Pages 37–45 in Fernando Puma (editor), *The 7 Arts.* Garden City, N.Y.: Doubleday.

MOHOLY-NAGY, LÁSZLÓ (1929) 1946 *The New Vision.* New York: Wittenborn. → First published in German.

MULLAHY, PATRICK 1948 *Oedipus: Myth and Complex.* New York: Hermitage. → See especially pages 162–207 for the section entitled "The Theories of Otto Rank."

MUMFORD, LEWIS (1952) 1960 *Art and Technics.* New York: Columbia Univ. Press.

PARKER, PAUL 1937 The Analysis of the Style of Advertising Art. Master's thesis, Univ. of Chicago, Department of Art. → A technical and social analysis of advertising art compared with fine art; written by a commercial artist.

PARKER, PAUL 1938 The Iconography of Advertising Art. *Harper's* 177:80–84.

PEVSNER, NIKOLAUS 1940 *Academies of Art: Past and Present.* Cambridge Univ. Press; New York: Macmillan.

PIAGET, JEAN (1923) 1959 *The Language and Thought of the Child.* 3d ed., rev. New York: Humanities Press. → First published as *Le langage et la pensée chez l'enfant.*

RANK, OTTO 1932 *Art and Artist: Creative Urge and Personality Development.* New York: Knopf.

SHILS, EDWARD 1958 Ideology and Civility: On the Politics of the Intellectual. *Sewanee Review* 66:450–480.

SHILS, EDWARD 1960a Mass Society and Its Culture. *Dædalus* 89:288–314.

SHILS, EDWARD 1960b The Traditions of Intellectuals. Pages 55–61 in George B. de Huszar (editor), *The Intellectuals.* Glencoe, Ill.: Free Press. → Discusses the tension between intellectuals and the business class.

STERN, L. 1958 George Lukács: An Intellectual Portrait. *Dissent* 5:162–173. → Includes discussion of Lukács' theories concerning art and mass society.

STRAUSS, ANSELM 1955a The Art School and Its Students: A Study and Interpretation. Unpublished manuscript. → A report based on the same research as that discussed in Griff 1964a.

STRAUSS, ANSELM 1955b Some Aspects of Recruitment Into the Visual Arts. Unpublished manuscript. → Derived from the same study as that described in Griff 1964a.

TOMASINI, WALLACE J. 1953 The Social and Economic Position of the Florentine Artist in the 15th Century. Ph.D. dissertation, Univ. of Michigan.

WILLETTS, WILLIAM 1958 *Chinese Art.* 2 vols in 1. New York: Braziller. → See especially pages 501–652 on "Painting and Calligraphy," and within that chapter, the section "Status of the Artist." A paperback edition was published in 1958 by Penguin.

FIRM, THEORY OF THE

The theory of the firm is that branch of economic theory which deals with the determination of the most important economic variables associated with the individual business unit, such as price, output, and growth. There are no readily defined boundaries for the theory, although it is usually distinguished from the theory of production, which deals with the selection of inputs and techniques of production by the firm; from programming, which explains how optimal techniques of production may be discovered; and from the study of business enterprise and the corporation, which have a more institutional focus [see CORPORATION; PRODUCTION; PROGRAMMING]. The theory of the firm is closely associated with the concept of the industry; the industry is composed, roughly, of those firms producing similar products. The relationship between the firm and the industry will be described in some detail later in this article.

The theory of the firm has a considerable his-

tory in economic thought, going back at least as far as Cournot (1838) and appearing implicitly a good deal earlier. The development of consumer theory and the basing of economics upon a theory of individual choice obviously called for an analogous development in the treatment of units of production, and after 1900 more and more attention was directed to the theory of the firm.

There are many possible approaches to the theory of the firm. These approaches may be categorized in various ways, the most fruitful of which seem to result from the division between: (a) static and dynamic approaches; (b) those theories that derive their results from the assumption of profit maximization and those that do not; and (c) deterministic and probabilistic theories.

Static and dynamic approaches. By a static theory of the firm we mean a theory that describes the characteristics of a firm in a position of equilibrium. We will deal first with the case in which this equilibrium arises when the firm is maximizing its profits.

The first part of the static theory to be well developed was the theory of the price and output policy of a profit-maximizing monopolist. A monopolist is defined as the only supplier of a particular "commodity." He is therefore confronted by a market demand curve giving a total revenue (R) that varies with output:

$$(1) \qquad R = f(x), \qquad f'(x) < 0,$$

where x is the quantity produced and sold. (Inventories are seldom allowed for in the simple theory.) Total costs (C), which include normal profits, are also affected by output. Normal profits are defined as those only just sufficient to keep the entrepreneur and his firm in the given industry:

$$(2) \qquad C = g(x).$$

Profit is maximized when $R - C$ is maximized, when

$$(3) \quad \frac{dR}{dx} - \frac{dC}{dx} = 0 \quad \text{and} \quad \frac{d^2R}{dx^2} - \frac{d^2C}{dx^2} < 0,$$

i.e., output is set at a profit maximizing level when marginal cost equals marginal revenue and marginal cost is rising faster (or falling less quickly) than marginal revenue.

Perhaps one of the most striking things about this solution is that it makes no assertion about the level of profits. In fact, it is often assumed that the monopolist must make in the normal way profits that are in some sense "supernormal."

It was the achievement of Pigou (1928) and others to see that some of the results obtained above are in fact of wider applicability and hold for the static theory of the firm in perfect competition as well as in monopoly. The chief differences between the two cases arise from the fact that in perfect competition price is treated as fixed, so that marginal revenue equals price. Thus

$$(4) \qquad \frac{dR}{dx} = P, \qquad \frac{d^2R}{dx^2} = P,$$

where P is the price of the product as seen by the firm. It follows that

$$(5) \qquad \frac{dC}{dx} = P, \qquad \text{and} \qquad \frac{d^2C}{dx^2} > 0.$$

This is to say that in perfect competition marginal cost equals price and that marginal cost is rising at the point of equilibrium output. Since in perfect competition entry is free and all factors of production are freely available at given prices, it is also deduced that average cost is equal to price in equilibrium and that average cost is at its lowest at the point of equilibrium output.

The above results are very important in welfare economics and form a part of the basis for asserting the optimality of perfectly competitive systems. [*See* WELFARE ECONOMICS.] But this fact has led to much confusion in the theory of the firm. It has led some writers to the paradoxical view that the theory of the firm is merely a part of welfare economics and that no evidence of the actual behavior of firms is relevant to the theory. Others have been unwilling to accept any evidence that tends to cast doubt on the universality of perfect competition in the real world. Both of these pitfalls should be carefully avoided.

It was pre-eminently Chamberlin's contribution (1933) to the static theory of the firm to notice that some degree of monopoly power is consistent with free entry and that the equality of average costs and prices is consistent with monopolistic equilibrium. (This point was noted also by Robinson [1933], but she was, on the whole, more concerned with considering certain special aspects of monopoly theory.) Chamberlin centered the bulk of his attention on achieving the marriage of monopoly and competition, and he proceeded in an elaborate diagrammatic exposition to show how it could be accomplished in certain hitherto unexplored situations.

The Chamberlinian relationship which is best known is summarized in Figure 1. Here all firms are assumed to have identical cost curves and identical demand curves. CC' is the average cost curve of any one of the firms. DD' is the demand curve confronting any one of the firms, after allowance is made for exit and entry of firms and for the assumption that all firms charge identical prices: dd'

is the demand curve that would face the firm if it could alter its prices without action or reaction by its competitors. In equilibrium the number of firms must adjust until all firms make only normal profits, and each firm still remaining in the industry believes that it is making maximum profits. This will occur at point T in Figure 1 if each firm believes its rivals will ignore its price policy.

Chamberlin's argument for the universal applicability of his models seems, in retrospect, somewhat unconvincing. Even if the economic world is in the main some blend of monopolistic and competitive elements, there is no reason to think that it is the very simplified blend that Chamberlin has assumed. If the world is more complex than Chamberlin has surmised, it is at least possible that other models, and perhaps simpler models, may be more useful predictors of economic behavior. The merits of any consistent model are not to be determined so much by argument as by performance.

An alternative to Chamberlin's approach has emerged from the development of the theory of oligopoly. Indeed, some writers seem to claim that oligopoly is in fact the norm in nonperfectly competitive markets. Unfortunately there are many competing oligopoly theories; they are not always presented in testable form; those that are testable in principle would often be difficult to distinguish empirically; and little testing has so far been attempted.

The dynamic theory of the firm has, on the other hand, received only limited treatment. The out-

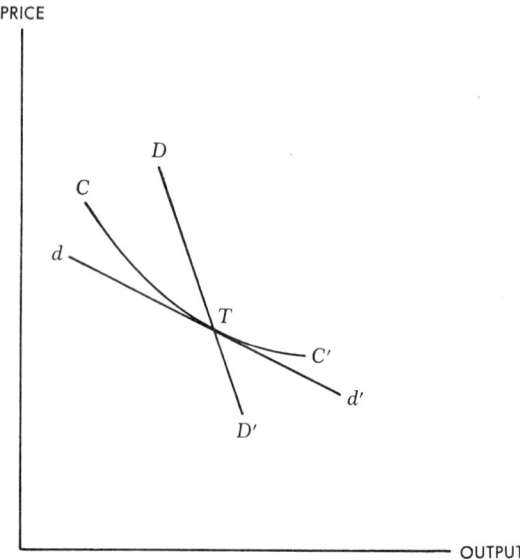

Figure 1 — Equilibrium under monopolistic competition

standing contribution to the subject is probably contained in Hicks (1939). Hicks's treatment is, however, confined to a discussion of intertemporal equilibrium. The question of the path of adjustment to a new equilibrium position, or the extent to which the costs of the firm depend upon the production experience of the firm, has been largely ignored until recent years (Clower 1959; Arrow 1962).

Profit maximization. Next we turn to the controversy over the role of profit maximization in the theory of the firm. The assumption of profit maximization has proved a very useful starting point for investigations in many areas closely connected with the theory of the firm, particularly in the theory of investment and replacement. But some economists have been suspicious of the profit maximization assumption and have preferred to substitute something else. This substitute has usually taken one of two forms: utility maximization or behavioral relations. The former is generally used in static equilibrium systems, the latter are usually not. An example of utility maximization is provided by the work of Scitovsky (1943). He shows in effect that if entrepreneurs maximize utility rather than profit, if utility is influenced by effort, and if effort is related to the size of output, then the traditional deductions of minimum average costs, in equilibrium, of perfect competition will be falsified.

An alternative utility maximization hypothesis asserts that utility is affected by the level of expected profits and by the variance of these profits. If variance decreases with output, the entrepreneur might, for example, decide to operate at outputs above minimum cost output, even under conditions of perfect competition.

One group of writers, of whom the best known is Papandreou (1952), has tended to argue that a large number of considerations will enter the utility function of the entrepreneur, so that propositions derived from profit maximizing assumptions are bound to be misleading. This approach is no doubt highly plausible, but the advantage of plausibility is purchased at the expense of any meaningful hypothesis. Putting it another way, while we increase the immediate acceptability of the theory of the firm by increasing the number of variables that the firm is said to consider in maximizing utility, we achieve this by reducing the number of testable results of the theory.

Some writers have felt that the deduction of the behavior of the firm from static equilibrium models is beyond the present powers of the economist and have instead directed their attention to the formu-

lation of behavioral hypotheses about the firm. Such hypotheses may or may not be consistent with the profit maximization hypothesis. One of the leading species of this genus is the so-called "full-cost pricing principle." Roughly, this asserts that prices of manufactured products will be set at a level that will yield a "normal" profit to a firm operating with modern equipment at a high level of capacity utilization. A great deal of effort has been expended in trying to show that such behavior is consistent with profit maximization. However, the behavioral hypothesis itself, which was first suggested by interviews with businessmen, cannot be said to have been subjected to rigorous statistical testing.

Somewhat similar remarks can be made about many of the alternative behavior hypotheses that have been offered for consideration. It has, for example, been suggested that firms aim at maximizing their share of the market rather than their profits. It has also been suggested that firms "satisfice"—that is, that they only seek to increase profits if profits fall below a certain "acceptable" level. In both these cases it can be said that discussion has been aimed more at finding justifications for these hypotheses than at testing their validity by observation. A similar difficulty has plagued efforts to develop a behavioral theory of the growth of the firm.

The theories discussed above have been concerned with explaining only the main features of the behavior of firms. Recently, however, effort has been devoted to the development of models that could predict the detailed conduct of business units in particular aspects of their work. Thus the detailed pricing policy of a particular department of a department store may be studied and a formula found that will enable us to predict this behavior. Much of this work has been stimulated by the suggestions of H. A. Simon (1959), and it remains until now largely descriptive in character. Little effort has been directed toward rationalizing the observed behavior in terms of profit maximization or utility maximization. It may indeed be surmised that simple explanations of detailed behavior patterns would be difficult in models excluding uncertainty and decision costs.

Probabilistic theories. Another line of development in the theory of the firm involves a twofold departure from the neoclassical formulation. First, the notion of static equilibrium of the individual firm is abandoned. Second, the focus changes from deterministic theories of the behavior of a single firm to probabilistic rules about the behavior of large groups of firms. This approach is also behavioral in orientation. While there may be a recognition of the desire for profit maximization, its effect is in many individual cases swamped by a myriad of other forces. As a result, the impact of any change in parameters at best changes the probabilities that govern the conduct of the firm.

The originator of this approach to the theory of the firm appears to have been Alfred Marshall. In the second edition of his *Principles of Economics* (1890) Marshall introduced the notion of the "representative firm" to explain the determination of long run supply price. The representative firm is not any particular firm; rather it is a descriptive fiction by means of which Marshall attempted to amalgamate a dynamic probabilistic theory of the firm with an essentially static and deterministic theory of price determination for the industry.

Marshall's attempt to harness the static with the dynamic approaches was vigorously rejected by most of his successors. Foremost among the critics was Robbins (1928), who objected correctly but irrelevantly that Marshall's implied theory of the firm was inconsistent with static equilibrium assumptions.

Marshall's approach fell into disuse for nearly 25 years but was re-established by P. K. Newman and J. N. Wolfe (1961). They showed that the Marshallian doctrine could be interpreted in terms of the stationary state of a probabilistic (Markov) process. [See MARKOV CHAINS.] It was shown that if the probabilistic laws governing the rise and decline of firms were affected by the price of the product, then a particular size distribution of firms and consequently a particular output would emerge from each price. It will be seen that this formulation allows by means of a single process the simultaneous determination of price, output, and the size distribution of firms.

More concretely, we may imagine the probability that a firm will change its size in any period as being governed by a "transition matrix," or matrix of transition probabilities, $\mathbf{A}$. This takes the following form:

$$\mathbf{A} = \begin{matrix} & \begin{matrix} 1 & 2 & \cdots & n \end{matrix} \\ \begin{matrix} 1 \\ 2 \\ \vdots \\ n \end{matrix} & \begin{bmatrix} a_{11} & a_{12} & \cdots & a_{1n} \\ a_{21} & a_{22} & \cdots & a_{2n} \\ \vdots & \vdots & & \vdots \\ a_{n1} & a_{n2} & \cdots & a_{nn} \end{bmatrix} \end{matrix}$$

where a_{12}, for example, is the probability that a firm in the first size-class at a particular period will be in the second size-class one period later. (The figures on the left-hand margin and across the top of the matrix are of course the various size-classes.)

If the matrix $\mathbf{A}$ obeys certain so-called Markovian assumptions, its continued application to a large group of firms will ultimately produce a definite size distribution that is independent of their initial distribution. And if the entries in the transition matrix are not fixed but are different for each price prevailing, there will be a different size distribution of firms for each particular equilibrium price. [See MARKOV CHAINS.]

This sketch of the probabilistic theory of the firm is necessarily incomplete. It will, however, be seen that this theory has the merit of dealing with the firm more nearly in the context in which it appears in real life than does a static theory. Nevertheless, the theory remains highly abstract, and its practical usefulness has yet to be demonstrated.

It will be apparent that the theory of the firm is moving increasingly in the direction of empirical science—that is, toward the formulation and testing of hypotheses about how firms actually behave. This is true whether the hypothesis being put forward is cast in deterministic or probabilistic form. It is at the same time less tied to the assumption of profit maximization. But profit maximization has not lost its usefulness, however frequently it may seem to be contradicted as a descriptive hypothesis. Profit maximization will always be the aim of at least some firms during at least some portion of their history. And so we would expect that profit maximization would continue to play an important role in the *normative* aspect of the theory of the firm.

The firm and the industry. The notion of the industry goes far back in economic thought; it probably derived intact from the market place. By the time of Marshall's *Principles of Economics* (1890) it had come to occupy an important place in economic theory. The industry was there defined as a group of firms producing an identical product. This definition is highly ambiguous, but to some it seemed to imply a homogeneity of output that was most easily related to a state of perfect competition. Chamberlin's assumption of identical cost and demand curves for all firms enabled him to work with "groups" that behaved rather like Marshallian industries. But the abandonment of perfect competition created difficulties for the concept of the industry, once differences in cost and demand conditions between firms were admitted. In the first place, firms might be selling apparently identical products at different prices. Moreover, as Robinson (1933) pointed out, a shift of demand in a perfectly competitive industry would (in the absence of external economies at any rate) have an unambiguous effect upon price and output, while in an imperfectly competitive "industry" it might not. The latter seemed a particularly damaging point, since one of the main motives for the development of the theory of the firm seems to have been to obtain greater certainty about the shape of the industry supply curve. Finally, Triffin (1940) argued that general equilibrium under conditions of nonperfect competition admitted no clear conceptual division between industries. Perhaps partly as a result of these arguments there has been a tendency for theoretically oriented economists to avoid using the concept of the industry and to some extent to neglect the study of the determinants of supply.

From a pragmatic point of view these developments seem ill judged. Ever since Plato and Aristotle, philosophers have been vexed by the problems of finding useful categories under which the large numbers of slightly differing objects we see about us can be grouped. Any such grouping is almost always an abstraction, and the important question is not whether it is a truly homogeneous grouping but whether it is a useful grouping. On the basis of the experience of students of economic institutions, the concept of the industry appears a highly useful abstraction for many purposes, although not for all. The spread of quantitative techniques seems likely to reinforce that conclusion, since statistics are usually available only on an industry basis. Indeed, from the statistical point of view the problem of defining the industry appears to arise from asking the wrong questions. The question should be whether some characteristics of a group of firms (e.g., the mean output of the firms or the mean price charged by them for their products) change in a statistically significant way as the result of changes in some specified variable. It would be difficult in an uncontrolled situation to test for the effects of a very large number of variables. The preponderating influence of a small number of strategic variables is an assumption that must be satisfied if testing is to give useful results. These strategic variables may be those predicted by standard theory or they may not, but this question is one of fact and not of theory.

The conclusion seems to be that the concept of the industry may well remain of great practical use whatever theory of the firm is adopted. This was one of the essential messages of Marshall's "representative firm." In that construct the "industry" is preserved, although firms are neither in equilibrium nor perhaps even operating under conditions of perfect competition. In this respect at least, Marshallian notions appear to have had a more "modern" empirical flavor than most of the later work on the theory of firm and industry. [*See* MARKETS AND INDUSTRIES.]

External economies. A good deal of attention has been given to the effect of changes in the total output of the industry upon the costs of the individual firms in the industry. These effects are termed "external economies" when the costs of production of the firms in the industry are lowered by an increase in the output of the industry. Since it is commonly argued that all firms have identical minimum costs in the long run equilibrium of perfect competition, all firms will in this case be affected equally.

It is usual to distinguish between pecuniary external economies, which arise through reduced factor prices, and technological external economies, which arise through improved organization of industry. The latter are most significant from the welfare point of view, but much doubt has been expressed about the frequency of their occurrence in a perfectly competitive milieu. However, for political or other reasons it may be impossible to enforce perfect competition, and the external economies associated with monopoly may be of great practical importance in some lines.

Scitovsky (1954) has suggested that a further source of external economies would arise if different stages of production were expanded (or contracted) in an uncoordinated way. Such external economies are essentially temporary in character. However, where monopolistic conditions are present, this type of external economy may lead to the permanent neglect of otherwise profitable investment opportunities.

It would appear that the estimation of the actual size of external economies in particular industries would be extremely useful. The task is made difficult, however, by the absence of data, by the uneven pace of technical advance, and by the great variation among the production processes performed by firms that are perforce lumped together in the same "industries." [*See* EXTERNAL ECONOMIES AND DISECONOMIES.]

J. N. WOLFE

[*See also* COMPETITION; MONOPOLY; OLIGOPOLY. *Other relevant material may be found in* DECISION MAKING, *article on* ECONOMIC ASPECTS.]

BIBLIOGRAPHY

AMERICAN ECONOMIC ASSOCIATION 1952 *Readings in Price Theory.* Edited by Kenneth E. Boulding and George J. Stigler. Homewood, Ill.: Irwin.

ARROW, KENNETH J. 1962 The Economic Implications of Learning by Doing. *Review of Economic Studies* 29:155–173.

CHAMBERLIN, EDWARD H. (1933) 1956 *The Theory of Monopolistic Competition: A Re-orientation of the Theory of Value.* 7th ed. Harvard Economic Studies, Vol. 38. Cambridge, Mass.: Harvard Univ. Press.

CLOWER, ROBERT W. 1959 Some Theory of an Ignorant Monopolist. *Economic Journal* 69:705–716.

COURNOT, ANTOINE A. (1838) 1960 *Researches Into the Mathematical Principles of the Theory of Wealth.* New York: Kelley. → First published in French.

CYERT, RICHARD M.; and MARCH, JAMES G. 1963 *A Behavioral Theory of the Firm.* Englewood Cliffs, N.J.: Prentice-Hall.

DORFMAN, ROBERT 1951 *Application of Linear Programming to the Theory of the Firm, Including an Analysis of Monopolistic Firms by Non-linear Programming.* Berkeley: Univ. of California Press.

HICKS, JOHN R. (1939) 1946 *Value and Capital: An Inquiry Into Some Fundamental Principles of Economic Theory.* 2d ed. Oxford: Clarendon.

MARSHALL, ALFRED (1890) 1961 *Principles of Economics.* 9th ed., 2 vols. New York and London: Macmillan. → The second edition was published in 1891.

NEWMAN, PETER K.; and WOLFE, J. N. 1961 A Model for the Long-run Theory of Value. *Review of Economic Studies* 29:51–61.

PAPANDREOU, ANDREAS G. 1952 Some Basic Problems in the Theory of the Firm. Pages 183–219 in Bernard F. Haley (editor), *A Survey of Contemporary Economics.* Volume 2. Homewood, Ill.: Irwin.

PENROSE, EDITH T. 1959 *The Theory of the Growth of the Firm.* New York: Wiley.

PIGOU, ARTHUR C. 1928 An Analysis of Supply. *Economic Journal* 38:238–257.

ROBBINS, LIONEL 1928 The Representative Firm. *Economic Journal* 38:387–404.

ROBINSON, JOAN (1933) 1961 *The Economics of Imperfect Competition.* London: Macmillan; New York: St. Martins.

SCITOVSKY, TIBOR 1943 A Note on Profit Maximisation and Its Implications. *Review of Economic Studies* 11:57–60.

SCITOVSKY, TIBOR 1954 Two Concepts of External Economies. *Journal of Political Economy* 62:143–151.

SIMON, HERBERT A. 1959 Theories of Decision-making in Economics and Behavioral Science. *American Economic Review* 49:253–283.

STIGLER, GEORGE J. 1951 The Division of Labor is Limited by the Extent of the Market. *Journal of Political Economy* 59:185–193.

TRIFFIN, ROBERT 1940 *Monopolistic Competition and General Equilibrium Theory.* Harvard Economic Studies, Vol. 67. Cambridge, Mass.: Harvard Univ. Press.

WOLFE, J. N. 1961 Co-ordination Assumptions and Multiple Equilibria. *Quarterly Journal of Economics* 75:262–277.

FISCAL POLICY

I. OVERVIEW   *Herbert Stein*
II. WARTIME FISCAL POLICY   *Roy Blough*

I

OVERVIEW

Fiscal policy is an aspect of public finance, of making and financing government expenditures. It is distinguished from other aspects of public finance in being concerned with decisions about certain "over-all" variables—such as total expenditures, total revenues, and total surplus or deficit—in terms of their "over-all" effects—such as their effects on national income, total employment, and the general level of prices.

The management of their total revenues and expenditures and of the relation between them has become one of the principal instruments by which governments seek to achieve a high level of economic activity and general price stability. This effort encounters many problems—including the compatibility of these two objectives with each other and with other goals, the uncertainty of the size and timing of the necessary actions, and the difficulty of making and carrying out decisions in a large and political organization. Nevertheless, there is widespread confidence that the fiscal instrument is sufficiently powerful, and its use sufficiently understood, to make a substantial contribution to successful economic performance.

The distinction between fiscal policy and the other aspects of public finance that deal with particular expenditures and taxes and their particular consequences is an abstraction from the complexity of the real world. In fact, decisions about the "over-all" variables are made up of decisions about particulars. Also, any decision that has "over-all" effects will also have particular effects on particular individuals, industries, or sectors of the economy.

While the boundary between fiscal policy and other aspects of public finance is necessarily arbitrary, the concept of fiscal policy is useful for analysis and for policy making. Every particular expenditure, tax, and debt issue may have a different over-all effect from every other. Yet for certain purposes it may be both convenient and safe to regard some large categories of expenditures, taxes, and debt issues, or even their totals, as single variables. In fact, it may be impossible to do otherwise, since existing knowledge is too crude to permit distinction among all possible variables.

It is necessary to distinguish fiscal policy not only from other aspects of public finance but also from monetary policy, which also consists of over-all measures usually evaluated in terms of over-all effects—on national income, total employment, or the price level, for example. This distinction can be drawn in various ways, depending upon the definition given to monetary policy. The distinction and connection are clearest if monetary policy is defined as policy with respect to the quantity of money. Fiscal policy can then be defined as policy with respect to total government sources and uses of funds and their composition. Certain sets of actions are a mixture of both monetary and fiscal policy—such as an increase of government expenditures financed by an increase in government borrowing, which in turn causes or is permitted to cause an increase in the money supply. Even in the mixed cases it is possible to distinguish between the monetary and fiscal aspects and to consider what effects flow from each. Its relation to monetary policy is one of the central problems of fiscal policy; this will be discussed below.

Pre-Keynesian theory. Fiscal policy began to assume a leading role in economic thinking, economic controversy, and economic policy only in the 1930s. But as long as there have been governments there has been fiscal policy, and a substantial body of doctrine about it existed long before the 1930s. Although we shall be concerned here mainly with "modern," i.e., post-1930, fiscal policy, a few words should be said about earlier ideas and practice. Modern thinking about fiscal policy, after first abandoning much of prior doctrine, has since reincorporated a great deal of it.

Neither fiscal theory nor fiscal practice before the 1930s was primarily concerned with maintaining high employment and stabilizing the rate of growth of total national output. Economic thinking and policy in general were much less dominated by the high employment problem than they later came to be and were more focused on problems of long-run growth, efficiency in the use of employed resources, and equity in the distribution of income. It was believed that in the long run the economy would tend to produce at a rate determined by "real" factors—the supply of labor and capital and the state of technology. Prices and wage rates would tend to adjust to changes in total money expenditures for goods and services so as to leave real output unchanged.

This view still left the possibility that variations in the general level of prices would have unwanted distributional effects in the long run and would cause unemployment in the short run. This was commonly regarded as a monetary problem, which could be handled by appropriate management of the quantity of money. At the same time, certainly by the 1920s, the possible contribution of budget policy, particularly variation of public works expenditures, to short-run economic stabilization, was widely but not universally recognized. However, a well-developed theory of how budget policy worked was lacking. There was uncertainty and disagreement about whether budget policy was an independent instrument of economic stabilization or only a particular way of carrying out monetary policy which might nevertheless be helpful in special circumstances. Moreover, the small size of government budgets relative to national incomes

severely limited the possibility of a major contribution of budget policy to economic stabilization.

Before the depression, attention in economic thinking about fiscal policy focused on its consequences for the distribution of the total output among uses, rather than on its consequences for the level of output in the short run. The main consequences of fiscal policy were considered to be its effects on (a) the division of output between consumption and investment and (b) the division of output between public and private use. Standards of good fiscal policy were largely derived from the desired objectives for these two divisions of the national output. (There was, of course, a vast literature on aspects of public finance other than "fiscal policy" which was concerned with other consequences.)

A major theme was the connection among budget balancing, saving, investment, and economic growth. If government expenditures were larger than tax receipts, the deficit would have to be financed by borrowing. The government's borrowing would absorb part of the nation's current private saving, which would therefore not be available to finance private investment. Investment would be lower than if the budget had been balanced, and consequently the rate of economic growth would also be lower.

This argument that total savings will be larger if there is a budget surplus than if there is a deficit is true only if the taxes used to achieve the surplus depress private savings by an amount less than the tax collections. Kinds of taxes are conceivable of which this would not be true. However, it is not necessary to adopt such taxes. Indeed, the same argument that calls for balancing the budget and running a surplus in order to promote economic growth also calls for avoiding kinds of taxation that depress private saving.

The conclusion that government budgets should be balanced was also reached by consideration of the proper division of the national product between private and public uses. The requirement that government expenditures should be financed by taxation was considered necessary to prevent a politically dangerous and economically wasteful excess of government spending. Ultimately the citizen might be thought of as buying services from the government and as obtaining the right amount when he acquires the amount whose cost he is willing to pay in taxes.

It is not demonstrable a priori that the total amount of government expenditures that would be made if they had to be paid for in taxes is the "best" amount, or even better than the amount that would be made if they could be financed by borrowing.

Government expenditures have a real cost in private expenditures that must be forgone, however they are financed. The "discipline" argument for budget balancing is that citizens will not accurately appraise this real cost if they can borrow to pay it. Once this possibility of error is admitted, it becomes a question of fact in what direction the errors run. If the citizens may underestimate costs which are financed by borrowing, so may they overestimate costs financed by taxation and either overestimate or underestimate the benefits of expenditures.

As has been noted, consideration of the desirable division of the national product between consumption and investment and between public and private uses led economists before the 1930s to budget balancing as a basic principle of fiscal policy. But the common popular support for the budget-balancing idea was probably not chiefly based on the economists' argument. The idea that government budgets should be balanced has a direct and intuitive appeal as a particular application of principles of conduct accepted as having moral and utilitarian validity in a much broader field. The "folk wisdom" basis of popular thinking about budgets probably explains the strong resistance of that thinking to the revolutionary change in economists' views of the matter that began in the 1930s.

Post-Keynesian theory. Earlier thinking about fiscal policy was challenged in the 1930s at its root—namely, the proposition that fiscal policy does not affect total national output. Successful challenge to this proposition brought the level of total output and total employment to the forefront of the objectives of fiscal policy. It also radically altered thinking about policy to achieve the traditional objectives.

The revolution in thinking about fiscal policy can be dated from the publication of John Maynard Keynes's *General Theory of Employment, Interest and Money* in 1936. This work had its precursors and was subsequently explained, extended, refined, and in part controverted by others. But the *General Theory* was the turning point. All serious argument about fiscal policy since it was published, even the argument that completely denied the Keynesian conclusions, has been influenced by it.

The first step in the new approach to fiscal policy was to loosen the link between the quantity of money and total money expenditures or total money income. If the ratio of total money income to the supply of money was fixed (or if not fixed, at least determined by factors that fiscal policy could not influence), fiscal policy that did not affect the supply of money would not affect total money income.

The new theory provided a way for fiscal policy to affect total money income, without a change in the supply of money. This, of course, implied a change in the ratio of money income to money supply. For example, suppose the government increases its expenditures without equally increasing taxes and without increasing the supply of money. The increase in government expenditures will initially increase the incomes of individuals and businesses. Since there has been no increase in the money supply, the ratio of their money holdings to their incomes has declined. Older theory would have emphasized reactions to a decline in this ratio which took the form of attempts of individuals and businesses to build up their money holdings by cutting their expenditures, which would in turn reduce total income. The newer theory emphasized two other possibilities. One was that money holdings were already "redundant," so that there would be no felt need to increase money holdings as incomes increased. The other possibility was that individuals and businesses would try to build up their money holdings by selling interest-bearing securities (rather than by cutting their expenditures). This would reduce the prices of such securities, and raise the interest rates they yielded, until a point was reached at which people would no longer consider it worthwhile to sell securities at low prices, or give up interest, in order to get more money.

In the early years of the "new fiscal theory" there was some disposition to carry the argument even further. That is, not only was the effectiveness of fiscal policy asserted, but the effectiveness of monetary policy was denied. If people were willing to absorb a change in their money holdings without any reaction, or if they reacted in a way that affected only interest rates, which did not in turn affect either private investment or saving, there would be no route by which a change in the money supply could affect total money income.

Controversy between the pre-Keynesian view and the extreme post-Keynesian view raged for some years in the late 1930s. But in time a consensus emerged on an intermediate position. The ratio of total money income to the money supply is not fixed, but can be affected by changes in interest rates, which can be changed by fiscal policy; but the ratio is not infinitely variable, and a change in the money supply will affect money income, either through an effect on interest rates and investment, or directly. Under this formulation the national money income may be affected by fiscal policy, or by monetary policy, or by various combinations of the two. Wide disagreement remains, however, about the probable magnitudes of the effects of each kind of action.

The foregoing discussion has run entirely in

terms of the effect of fiscal action upon total money income and money expenditures. It will be recalled that earlier thinking held that variations in money income and expenditures would not in any case affect real output and employment, except temporarily, but would affect only prices and wage rates. The Keynesian analysis assumed that as long as employment was below some level, considered the full employment level, wage rates would be stable and variations in money income would be directly reflected in employment and real output. Some of Keynes's early followers tended to argue as if this assumption, made for purposes of analysis, were also descriptive of the real world. However, there has since been a general recognition that the actual situation is more complicated. There is no single point of "full employment" below which variations in money income affect only employment and output without affecting prices and wage rates and above which only prices and wage rates, but not employment and output, would be affected. At least over a considerable range of employment levels, variations in money income will affect both prices and output, although the price effect will presumably be larger and the output effect smaller, the higher the initial level of employment. This makes the choice of the "desired" behavior of money income difficult, but it still leaves the behavior of money income an important objective of fiscal policy.

Sources and uses of funds. Discussion of the new fiscal policy initially concentrated on the effects of variations in government expenditures, taxes being given. Emphasis was placed on the stimulative effects of "deficit spending," that is, of government spending not offset by tax revenues. It was shown that on certain assumptions the increase in the national income resulting from an increase in deficit spending would be a multiple of the increase in deficit spending. The increase in government spending initially causes private incomes to rise by an equal amount. Recipients of the additional private income will be induced to spend more, which will generate more income for others, who in turn will spend more, and so on in a "multiplier" process whose limit depends on the proportion of their additional income that people spend.

It soon became clear that similar effects could be expected from variations in taxes, expenditures being given. A reduction in taxes would increase, and an increase in taxes would reduce, private spending, which would affect private incomes, and thereby affect private spending, and so on in the multiplier process.

If an increase of government expenditure would increase the national income by some multiple of the increase, and an increase of taxes would reduce the national income by some multiple of the tax increase, an equal increase of expenditures and taxes would affect the national income in one direction or the other if the expenditure and tax multipliers were unequal. There is no a priori reason to think that the multipliers are equal. In the 1940s and 1950s there was a great deal of discussion of the implications of equal changes of expenditures and revenues. Most of it revolved about the "balanced-budget multiplier theorem," which showed that on certain assumptions the multiplier of an equal increase in expenditures and revenues will be 1; that is, the total increase in spending from an equal increase in government spending and taxes will equal the increase in government spending.

The balanced-budget multiplier theorem demonstrated that the budget deficit or surplus could not logically be regarded as the sole source and measure of the effects of the budget on total spending, and opened the way to a more general view of the possibilities of fiscal policy.

The government may be conceived of as obtaining funds from a variety of sources and using funds in a variety of ways. The total sources and total uses are equal, if borrowing and the use of existing balances are considered sources of funds. Each of the sources and uses of funds has some effect on total national spending, but the effects of different sources and uses need not be equal per dollar. If every dollar used has an equal positive effect on total spending, and if every dollar obtained, including dollars borrowed, has an equal negative effect, then fiscal policy can have no net effect.

The new fiscal policy first said that the effect of borrowing funds to finance a deficit was less per dollar than the effect of obtaining funds from taxes and also less, and of opposite sign, than the effect of spending funds. Therefore, an equal increase of government spending and borrowing, or an equal decrease of taxes and increase of borrowing, would have an effect on total spending.

The balanced-budget multiplier discussion said that the effect of obtaining funds by taxing was different, per dollar, and of opposite sign from the effect of spending funds. Therefore an equal increase of taxes and government expenditures would have a net effect on total expenditures—an expansive effect if the expenditure multiplier was larger than the tax multiplier.

Once we have gone this far, it is a logical next step to say that different government expenditures and different taxes have different effects per dollar. In this case a shift from one kind of government expenditure to another, or from one kind of tax to another, would have a net effect on total expenditure. This net effect could be achieved without a change in the size of the deficit or surplus or in the total size of the budget.

Formally the possibility exists of obtaining any desired effect on total spending through any one of a large number of combinations of sources and uses of government funds. Any differences in the effect per dollar of any two sources or uses of funds would constitute a lever that could be used to affect total spending. Whether in fact the number of such levers is large depends on whether the differences in the effects of various sources and uses of funds are significant, whether the differences are known with some certainty, and whether the various sources and uses of funds can in practice be manipulated to serve some objective with respect to total spending.

Little is reliably known about the differences in the effects of various fiscal actions upon total spending. There is fairly general agreement that an increase in spending or a decrease in taxes has a larger expansive effect, per dollar, than the contractive effect of an increase in government borrowing, although even this would be disputed with respect to some kinds of government borrowing. If this is true, then any combination of fiscal actions that includes expenditure increases and tax decreases, but no expenditure decreases or tax increases, will have an expansive effect. But if the combination includes tax and expenditure actions that separately have effects of different directions, the direction of the net effect would be uncertain.

Modern theory opens up the possibility of a large number of combinations of fiscal actions that could affect total spending, some but not all of which would affect the surplus or deficit. We do not know even the direction of the effect of many of these combinations, including some that affect the surplus or deficit. Where there is considerable confidence about the direction of the effect, the magnitude of the effect is still uncertain, to a degree that varies with the particular action.

Theories concerning implementation. The new theory held out the possibility of achieving any desired level or rate of change of money national income. It said that given any objective for the behavior of money national income, and given all the factors other than fiscal policy that affect its behavior, there is some combination of government expenditure programs and tax rates that will achieve the objective. However, this proposition stops far short of specifying what the proper fiscal policy is at any time.

The implementation of fiscal policy must contend with several difficulties:

(1) It is not certain what behavior of money national income should be the objective of fiscal policy. The money national income is an intermediate objective, important because of its influence on employment, production, prices, economic growth, and the balance of payments. What the effect of a particular level and rate of change of money national income will be on these aspects of the economy is always impossible to tell precisely. Even if it were known what the effects would be, what would be the "best" effects would still have to be determined.

(2) The fiscal policy necessary to achieve any given course of money national income will depend upon the other autonomous factors that affect the national income in the future period in which the fiscal decisions will operate. If these other factors —which may be summed up as private tendencies to invest and consume—are strong, a less expansive fiscal policy will be required than if they are weak. These other factors are variable, and prediction of them is subject to a wide margin of error.

(3) The effects of various fiscal actions upon the money national income are known only very roughly. Presumably, for example, a one-point reduction in the basic rate of the individual income tax will make the money national income higher than it would otherwise have been. But informed estimates of the magnitude and timing of the effects will vary widely, and this will also be true of other fiscal actions.

(4) Even if the target for behavior of money national income, the autonomous factors affecting the national income, and the effects of all fiscal actions are precisely known, the proper fiscal policy is not uniquely determined. There will almost certainly be more than one combination of tax and expenditure actions that would yield the target national income. A choice will have to be made among these combinations, and it will have to be made on criteria other than the effect on national income, since the combinations are alike in that respect.

(5) Since the behavior of money national income is affected to some, much-disputed, degree by monetary policy, the policy packages among which a choice must be made consist not only of various combinations of fiscal actions but also of various combinations of fiscal and monetary policy.

(6) For all the foregoing reasons, the range and variety of fiscal policies that might reasonably be thought at any time to give a good combination of effects on employment, production, prices, etc., will be large, and it will not be possible objectively and certainly to select one policy as best. The selection of a policy to follow will be made in the political process, by people who are sensitive to

the political consequences of the selection. This may introduce a bias into the selection, causing it to depart systematically from what is probably the best choice.

This list of difficulties does not constitute an argument against fiscal policy or even against using fiscal policy to achieve desired effects on employment, production, growth, prices, and the balance of payments. There will be a fiscal policy as long as there is government. This fiscal policy will have effects, and it is obviously desirable that it should have good rather than bad effects. But the difficulties listed here do suggest the problems that must be overcome to assure the choice of the fiscal policy that will have the best effects, or is most likely to have the best effects.

General strategies of implementation. Two main lines of thinking about the strategy of implementing fiscal policy have emerged in the postwar period, although each has variants and the two lines tend to meet when each is elaborated with regard to the conditions of the real world. One approach is direct and activist, the other indirect and passive.

The direct, activist approach might be called the "do your best" approach. It recognizes that the appropriate target for money national income, the future state of the economy upon which fiscal policy will operate, and the future effects of various fiscal actions cannot be known with certainty. Nevertheless, in this view, the responsible authorities in government must make, and act upon, their best estimates of these factors. While there will be departures from the ideal result, these departures, it is believed, will be smaller than would be yielded by any alternative system.

The indirect, passive approach would call for fiscal policy to adhere to some predetermined objective rule or standard which would not require forecasting short-run economic fluctuations. An effort was made to find such a rule which would, first, keep fiscal policy from being an independent destabilizing force and, second, insofar as consistent with the first objective, make fiscal policy a stabilizing force. This effort was more evident in the United States than elsewhere, perhaps because the American political process did not leave budget policy to "experts," and this generated more public interest in specifying guides to budget policy.

The rule commonly suggested set as a standard a fixed relation between expenditure programs and tax rates such that revenues would exceed expenditures by some constant amount X (which might be positive, zero, or negative) when the national income was at some standard level Y. Examples of proposed budget rules may be found in the articles by the Committee for Economic Development and by Milton Friedman included in American Economic Association, *Readings in Fiscal Policy* (1955). Thus the actual surplus would be constant when the actual national income was at the standard. To this degree the budget would be neutral. If this rule were followed, the actual surplus would be below X when the actual national income was below the standard Y, and the surplus would be above X when the actual national income was above the standard Y. The farther the national income was below the standard, the less the government would subtract from the private income stream in taxes, and the more it would add in expenditures, so that the larger the government's support for total spending and income would be. To this degree the budget would be stabilizing; it would resist variations in the actual national income relative to the standard. The standard level of national income would rise through time with the growth of potential national output. If actual national income did not rise as fast as potential, adherence to the rule would generate a rising deficit (or falling surplus), which would tend to accelerate the growth of actual national income.

The logic of the rule did not require that the standard national income should be equal to the potential or "full employment" national income, although it did require that the standard bear a certain constant relation to potential national income. However, in fact, the standard was usually prescribed as the full-employment national income, and the rule called for balancing the budget (or running some specified constant surplus or deficit) at full employment. Thus discussion of the rule focused attention on what the surplus or deficit would be at full employment, as distinguished from the actual surplus or deficit. The "full employment surplus" became a widely-used shorthand measure of the impact of fiscal policy. Whereas changes in the actual surplus or deficit result from changes in other economic conditions as well as from changes in budget policy, changes in the full employment surplus result almost entirely from changes in budget policy. Use of the full employment surplus for analysis or prescription did not necessarily imply that the full employment surplus should be constant, and the concept came to be used in the 1960s by many who did not accept the rule of constant full employment surplus.

Supporters of the indirect, passive approach recognized that in principle an active policy based on perfect foresight would yield superior stabilization results. However, perfect foresight was not possible, and actual decisions, if freed of all conventional rules, would not even be governed by the best possible economic forecasts. The political decisions might be random and destabilizing, or might be biased in an inflationary, expenditure-increasing direction. Therefore, a less ambitious and more restrained policy would lead to better results. In fact, a high degree of stability (meaning steadiness of growth) could be expected from a passive fiscal policy, especially if combined with a stabilizing monetary policy. In some variants this stabilizing monetary policy is also considered to be governed by a rule, such as a constant rate of growth of the money supply; in other variants the monetary policy is flexible and discretionary.

Probably the basic criticism of the indirect approach is that the establishment of a budget rule requires a forecast of what economic conditions will be on the average during the period when the rule is in force. A rule that might be highly inflationary in one set of conditions might be highly deflationary in another. Therefore the rule does not eliminate the need for forecasting but requires a more difficult, because longer-run, kind of forecast than a more active and flexible policy requires.

The choice between these two approaches reflects differences of opinion about the operation of the economic and political systems as well as some differences in evaluating the consequences of inflation and rising government expenditures. While these differences have not been resolved, experience and discussion have tended to narrow the difference between the two approaches. Advocates of what is called here the direct approach do not want or expect a continuous adjustment of fiscal policy to actual or forecast economic conditions, but only an adjustment at intervals. They would also recognize that it may not be desirable to change fiscal policy to deal with economic changes that are small or quite uncertainly forecast. And they have had, at least when in responsible positions, to accept as some restraint the popular sentiment favoring balanced budgets.

At the same time, at least many supporters of a "rule" of fiscal policy would recognize that it may be necessary or desirable to change the rule from time to time. They would also accept the possible necessity at some time to depart temporarily from the rule.

Once these points are reached, the differences between the two approaches come down to questions about the frequency of changes in fiscal policy and the strength of the evidence required to justify a change. These are matters of gradation, on which a continuous graduation of positions may be taken.

The fiscal–monetary "mix." If fiscal policy is not the only instrument by which the government can influence the money national income, it is not a sufficient guide to fiscal policy to say that it must be so managed as to bring about the desired national income. It can only be said that the available instruments should be used in combination to effect the desired result, but this leaves open the question of the combination in which the various instruments should be used. The main question of combining instruments concerns the combination of fiscal and monetary policy.

Even though fiscal and monetary policy may both be capable, in general, of affecting the national income, there may be special circumstances in which they are not alternative instruments. For example, it has been thought that at the bottom of a deep depression, profit prospects may appear so bleak that no expansion of the money supply would stimulate an increase in investment or other private spending. In this case monetary policy would not be an alternative to fiscal policy for promoting recovery. However, whether this is a realistic possibility has been disputed, and there is no suggestion that such circumstances have emerged in the postwar world.

Fiscal actions and monetary actions may differ in the speed with which they can be taken, have effect, and be modified or reversed if necessary. This may provide the basis for a division of labor between fiscal and monetary policy, the more flexible instrument being used in those circumstances in which a quick and possibly reversible effect is needed. In much of the earlier postwar writing it was assumed that monetary policy was the more flexible instrument and therefore should be relied upon for short-run adjustments of the impact of the combined fiscal–monetary package. However, later study suggested that the lag between monetary action and its effects might be long and variable. This raised the question whether monetary policy was in fact the more flexible and manageable element in the monetary–fiscal combination. Thus, the principle remains that in the division of labor between fiscal and monetary policy, the more flexible instrument should be used for the more rapid and frequent adjustments, but which is the more flexible instrument is uncertain.

If the desired money national income for any period can be achieved by one of several combinations of fiscal and monetary policy, the choice among these combinations requires the invocation of some additional objective. Two such objectives have seemed particularly relevant: economic growth and balance-of-payments equilibrium.

On certain assumptions, the economy will grow more rapidly with a large budget surplus than with a small budget surplus or deficit, if in each case there is the appropriate monetary policy to attain the desired current rate of money national income. Unless there are fully offsetting effects, the larger surplus will mean larger total savings and larger total investment. Some offsets may be expected. Getting the larger surplus will require some combination of higher taxes, which may reduce private saving or have other growth-restraining effects, and lower public expenditures, some of which might have had growth-promoting effects. Also, the more expansive monetary policy required to accompany the larger surplus may depress private saving. Therefore, a larger-surplus policy cannot be said to be a faster-growth policy without further specification, but it is probably possible to design a larger-surplus policy that will be a faster-growth policy. Even this would not, of course, by itself make the larger surplus preferable. A larger surplus leads to faster growth only at some cost, in the form of reduced current consumption and possibly also in other forms; whether it is legitimate or wise for government to decide to pay that cost is a question that would still have to be answered.

In the late 1950s and early 1960s attention was focused on the balance-of-payments implications of the combination of fiscal and monetary policy. This new interest was largely derived from concern with the position of the United States, which was running a persistent balance-of-payments deficit along with more unemployment and less inflation than most of the rest of the world. A country in such circumstances seeks both domestic expansion and contraction of its external deficit. It was suggested that these two objectives might be simultaneously approached by a more expansive fiscal policy combined with a less expansive monetary policy. More generally, it could be shown that if domestic income and the balance of payments depend upon monetary and fiscal policy and on no other, and if these two policies affect no other objectives, the two objectives determine the best combination of the two policies. While these conditions may never be fully met, they may be approximated for short periods.

Definition of the budget. Any fiscal policy which uses the budget position—the size of the deficit or surplus—as a guide to action requires a decision on what is to be included in the budget—how it is to be defined. As was indicated earlier, government fiscal operations can be described by a statement of the sources and uses of government funds, the sources and uses being necessarily equal. The creation of a budget that can have a surplus or a deficit requires the selection of some but not all of these sources and uses of funds for inclusion in the budget. Which items should be included depends on the policy purpose to be served by the over-all budget figures. Aside from this purpose, there is no "true" budget.

The appropriate definition of the budget depends on whether the main purpose of budget policy is (a) to affect the money national income, (b) to exercise "discipline" over government spending, by requiring that expenditure be matched by taxation, or (c) to affect national saving by controlling the relation between government revenues and the government expenditures that are not for investment. Different emphases on these three objectives lead to different answers to the questions that arise about the definition of the budget. These questions relate chiefly to four kinds of transactions:

(1) Trust account transactions in which the government accumulates a fund from a particular class of individuals, out of which payments are made, simultaneously or subsequently, for specified purposes. Social insurance funds are a leading example.

(2) Loan transactions in which the government at some times lends money to private borrowers or to other governments or purchases their debt, and at other times receives repayment or sells the debt.

(3) Capital expenditures for the acquisition by government of assets (including loans) that yield a subsequent return, whether in money or in non-monetary benefits.

(4) Transactions in which there is a considerable lapse of time between the accrual of a liability to or from the government and the corresponding cash payment.

Different treatments of these kinds of transactions are illustrated by the three "budgets," or statements of government receipts and payments, commonly used in the United States:

The *administrative* budget, which excludes trust account transactions, is almost entirely on a cash basis, and makes no distinction between loan or capital transactions and current transactions;

The *cash-consolidated* budget, which includes trust account transactions and is entirely on a cash basis;

The government sector of the *national income accounts*, which also includes trust account transactions, but excludes loan transactions and reflects corporate-profits-tax liability accruals rather than cash payments.

None of these three financial accounts used in the United States distinguishes between capital and current transactions. However, many other governments use capital budgets which do make this distinction.

Since the main object sought in postwar thinking about fiscal policy has been a certain effect, presumably stabilizing, upon money national income, the search for definitions of the budget has focused on that which would be most revealing of the effects of fiscal policy on money national income. What is desired is the most comprehensive definition of the budget consistent with the requirement that all fiscal policies yielding an equal surplus in the budget so defined have, under similar general economic conditions, equal effects on money national income. This test can be literally met only if every expenditure has the same effect, per dollar, as every other expenditure and the same effect, with sign reversed, as every receipt. This is to say that the test cannot be literally met by any real budget. The test does suggest the desirability of excluding from the budget transactions that are markedly different in their effect per dollar from the transactions included and that vary substantially in magnitude relative to the transactions included. However, if important items are excluded in order to make the budget more homogeneous and thus to give the size of the surplus or deficit a more stable meaning, problems arise in establishing criteria and mechanisms for controlling the excluded items. In practice, some compromise beween homogeneity and comprehensiveness in defining the budget must be found.

It seems clear that if the budget is intended to reveal the effects of fiscal transactions on money national income, there is no good reason for excluding trust account transactions from the budget. Many, and probably most, of the receipts and expenditures made by trust accounts are quite similar in their aggregate economic effects to many of the receipts and expenditures included in the regular budget. A more difficult problem is the treatment of loan transactions. If the government makes a loan to a private business, a local government, or a foreign government, is this more like a government grant or purchase, in which case it should be treated as an expenditure, or more like government purchase (repayment) of its own securities, in which case it should not be treated as an expenditure? Probably the answer depends upon the terms and circumstances of particular kinds of loans.

If the main objective of budget policy is to stabilize, or otherwise influence, total money expenditures, there is no good reason to distinguish between the current and capital expenditures of government. Capital spending, at least when it is for purchase of real goods and services, is likely to

have as great a direct and indirect effect on total spending in the economy as does current spending. The amount of taxation needed for economic stabilization does not depend on whether the government's expenditures are for current or capital purposes.

Emphasis on the "disciplinary" function of a budget rule may provide a rationale for excluding the trust accounts from the budget. The purpose of requiring that the budget be balanced may be to assure that government expenditures are not made unless taxpayers have demonstrated their willingness to pay taxes for them. However, this purpose does not require the inclusion in the budget of transactions that have their own disciplinary safeguards. If the government undertakes a particular expenditure program to which specific revenues are assigned, with a definite plan and commitment over some period, the disciplinary function of budget balancing does not require inclusion of these transactions in the budget. The cogency of this argument for excluding a trust fund from the budget depends upon whether the trust fund actually conforms to this description, which is sometimes, but not always, the case.

A similar case on "disciplinary" grounds can be made for excluding from the budget capital transactions where the productivity of government capital investments can be objectively measured and compared with the cost of capital. This would provide a test of the desirability of public investments that would be superior to the test of the willingness of the community to pay taxes for them. Where the investment yields a product that is sold in the market—as is the case with a government-owned railroad—this objective test of productivity may be available. But there are many kinds of government investment—education being one example—where the product is difficult to measure or even to define. To remove the requirement that such expenditures be financed by taxation may leave no adequate limits to their expansion.

One case for use of a capital budget may be found in the desire to separate the government decision about the total amount of saving in the economy from the decision about the total amount of government investment. The total saving of the economy is equal to private saving plus the excess of taxes over current, noninvestment expenditure of government. The government, or the community through the government, may decide to make this total larger or smaller by deciding on a larger or smaller excess of taxes over current expenditures. (This assumes that private savings do not increase or decrease by an amount equal to the change in the excess of taxes over current expenditures.) The government may decide to run a large current surplus in order to generate large total savings and thus permit large total investment and a high rate of growth. This decision by itself logically implies nothing about the proportions in which the investments would be private and government. On the other hand, the government may decide on a larger or smaller amount of public investment. This by itself implies nothing about what total saving should be. The decision to have a large amount of public investment may reflect a judgment that many public investments are more productive (or otherwise desirable) than private investments and should be made instead of them—not in addition to them. The existence of large opportunities for productive investment may be a reason for wanting high savings and a large excess of taxes over current expenditure. But this would be equally true whether the opportunities were for public or private investment.

If a capital budget is used, the government would decide, by deciding on the size of its current surplus, how much it should contribute to total saving. It would decide this in terms of the value the community places on economic growth and the supply of productive investment opportunities, public and private. The government would also decide on the desirability of particular public investments in terms of their productivity, taking into account the cost of capital. Proponents of the capital budget maintain that this would result in better decisions about both the government's contribution to saving and the government's investment than does a budget which lumps together current and capital expenditure.

A different kind of concern with the effect of budget policy on total saving may justify the exclusion of trust accounts from the budget. It may be desired to balance the budget so that all private savings will be available to finance private investment, either on the grounds that growth will be promoted thereby or that "consumers' sovereignty" requires that the amount of private investment should be determined by private saving. If individual citizens voluntarily make payments into a government-managed fund from which they will subsequently receive benefits, these savings should, on this principle, not be available to finance government expenditures, as would happen if they were lumped into the budget. The force of this argument depends upon the degree to which the trust account in fact has the character of a private voluntary savings institution.

The idea of the capital budget does not neces-

sarily imply that the current budget should be balanced by taxation; the rule may be a surplus or deficit in the current budget. However, much discussion of the idea has assumed that the issue was between balancing the current budget and balancing the total budget. Since net government capital expenditures are likely to be positive, balancing the current budget will be more expansionary than balancing the total budget. This has won some support for the capital budget idea from those who believe there is need for an expansionary fiscal policy but who do not want to violate community sentiment in favor of balancing "some" budget.

Budget flexibility.   Fiscal action taken at any time has its effects on some future time. The appropriateness of the action is its appropriateness to the future time at which its effects occur. Fiscal action therefore requires or implies a forecast. The reliability of the forecast will be greater the nearer the future period to which it relates. For this reason attention has been directed to increasing the flexibility of fiscal policy, so that it will have its effects more quickly and the time for which forecasts have to be made will be shortened. Increased flexibility has been sought along three main lines, sometimes called built-in flexibility, formula flexibility, ·and discretionary flexibility.

Built-in flexibility.   The stabilizing effect of the variation in government tax receipts or liabilities and unemployment compensation payments that automatically accompanies variation in the national income has already been noted. Recognition of the value of this automatic response of the budget has naturally led to the question whether this response could be strengthened. However, a basic difficulty arises in considering possible ways to strengthen the built-in stabilizing response. The extent to which tax receipts vary with a change in the national income depends upon the tax rates applied to individual and corporate incomes at the margin —the proportion of an increase in an individual's or corporation's income that is taken in taxes. If these marginal rates are high, the proportion of a change in national income that is absorbed in a change in tax receipts will be large, and this will have a stabilizing effect on the economy. However, if these rates are high, taxes will take a large proportion of the additional income that an individual or corporation may earn by productive activity. At least beyond some point this will weaken the incentive to productive activity and will adversely affect economic efficiency and growth. Thus the stabilizing value of high marginal tax rates can be obtained only at the cost of other important economic objectives.

In general, the marginal rates of tax, and also the rates of unemployment compensation payments, have been so closely determined by a combination of other factors economically and politically more important as to leave no room for adjusting them to increase "built-in" stabilization.

To get around this difficulty there have been proposals intended to increase the automatic responsiveness of tax collections or unemployment compensation to changes in the over-all state of the economy without increasing their responsiveness to the condition or activity of any individual. The general principle may be illustrated by the following hypothetical scheme: Weekly withholding of income tax from each taxpayer will be reduced by $2.00 for every percentage point by which the latest published seasonally adjusted figure for the rate of unemployment exceeds 4 per cent (and annual liability will be correspondingly reduced). Such a scheme would greatly increase the variability of tax collections in response to variations in the rate of unemployment without increasing the amount of tax taken out of an additional dollar of income earned by any individual.

Formula flexibility. Consideration of proposals for formula flexibility has not proceeded beyond an elementary and formal stage. One difficulty is that while, once the formula is adopted, reliance on long-term forecasting is eliminated, the formula itself implies a long-run forecast of the way in which fiscal policy should respond to changes in the economy. Formula flexibility buys speed of response in exchange for discretion in deciding what the response should be. This may be a worthwhile exchange, but that has not been satisfactorily demonstrated. Possibly a more serious difficulty is political. Governments may be willing to take active fiscal measures when the need is clear and present but unwilling to commit themselves in advance to the automatic occurrence of such measures.

Discretionary flexibility. Efforts to increase the flexibility of the budget have been largely concentrated on discretionary measures. Preparations are sought which, while leaving the government in all cases free to act or not, will enable the government to decide more quickly and will speed up the effects of the decisions taken. The classic case of such preparations is the "shelf of public works." Ideally this is a reserve of government construction projects for which legislative authorizations and appropriations have been made, plans drawn, and sites obtained, so that work can be started quickly when the Executive decides to do so. Interest in the shelf of public works has diminished, at least in the United States, since the end of World War II. Federal nonmilitary public works activities have not been large, and the volume of projects that seem desirable enough to authorize but not urgent enough to begin immediately has been small relative to the size of the economy and its potential fluctuations. The volume of these that could quickly reach a high rate of operation and, if necessary, be stopped without great loss is even smaller. Also, it has appeared that the need for expansive action might arise when construction is running at a high rate, so that increasing public works would not be appropriate.

The revenue side of the budget seems to hold out greater possibility for quick and powerful fiscal action. Federal revenues in the United States are about 20 per cent of the gross national product. Changes in tax rates that are administratively feasible could increase or decrease the available after-tax incomes of individuals or businesses by large amounts in a short time. The period required for legislative enactment of a tax change may be long, however, and there have been a number of proposals for shortening this period. These involve advance legislative authorization to the president to make a specified tax cut, possibly subject to Congressional veto within a limited period, or an agreement by Congress to act upon a presidential recommendation within a limited period. In fact, even without such arrangements the legislative process would allow quick Congressional action on a tax change if a strong majority of Congress were agreed on the need for it.

Deliberate and systematic effort to use fiscal policy to keep the economy operating close to its potential while avoiding inflation and serving other objectives became standard practice in most Western industrial countries after World War II. The results of that experience were varied and interpretation of the results even more varied. But the experience did not contradict the idea that fiscal policy, at least when accompanied by appropriate monetary policy, is a powerful instrument for affecting economic performance in basically free economies. This instrument by itself may be unable to reconcile inconsistencies where they arise between some objectives, such as full employment and price stability or domestic stabilization and international equilibrium. Even aside from this, knowledge and institutions are inadequate for management of the fiscal instrument to achieve its ideal effectiveness. Yet there is little doubt that the results of freeing fiscal policy from older inhibitions have on the whole been beneficial and that further opportunities for improved use of the fiscal instrument, based on experience and study, remain.

HERBERT STEIN

[See also DEBT, PUBLIC; MONETARY POLICY; MONEY; PUBLIC EXPENDITURES; TAXATION.]

BIBLIOGRAPHY

AMERICAN ECONOMIC ASSOCIATION 1955 *Readings in Fiscal Policy.* Homewood, Ill.: Irwin. → Contains an extensive classified bibliography.

ANDO, ALBERT; and MODIGLIANI, FRANCO 1965 The Relative Stability of Monetary Velocity and the Investment Multiplier. *American Economic Review* 55:693–728.

COLM, GERHARD 1955 *Essays in Public Finance and Fiscal Policy.* Oxford Univ. Press.

DEPRANO, MICHAEL; and MAYER, THOMAS 1965 Tests of the Relative Importance of Autonomous Expenditures and Money. *American Economic Review* 55:729–752.

DOW, J. C. R. 1964 *The Management of the British Economy: 1945–1960.* Cambridge Univ. Press.

Economic Policy in Our Time, by Étienne S. Kirschen et al. 3 vols. 1964 Amsterdam: North-Holland Publishing. → Describes the experience of eight industrial countries.

FRIEDMAN, MILTON (1951) 1959 The Effects of a Full-employment Policy on Economic Stability: A Formal Analysis. Pages 117–132 in Milton Friedman, *Essays in Positive Economics.* Univ. of Chicago Press. → First published in French in Volume 4 of *Économie appliquée.*

FRIEDMAN, MILTON; and MEISELMAN, DAVID 1964 The Relative Stability of Monetary Velocity and the Investment Multiplier in the United States: 1897–1958. Pages 165–268 in *Stabilization Policies: A Series of Research Studies Prepared for the Commission on Money and Credit.* Englewood Cliffs, N.J.: Prentice-Hall.

FRIEDMAN, MILTON; and MEISELMAN, DAVID 1965 Reply to Ando and Modigliani and to DePrano and Mayer. *American Economic Review* 55:753–785. → Contains a rejoinder by Ando and Modigliani on pages 786–790 and by DePrano and Mayer on pages 791–792.

KEYNES, JOHN MAYNARD 1936 *The General Theory of Employment, Interest and Money.* London: Macmillan. → A paperback edition was published in 1965 by Harcourt.

KIMMEL, LEWIS H. 1959 *Federal Budget and Fiscal Policy: 1789–1958.* Washington: Brookings Institution. → Contains a description of and references to early writings of economists and others.

LEWIS, WILFRED 1962 *Federal Fiscal Policy in the Postwar Recessions.* National Committee on Government Finance, Studies in Government Finance. Washington: Brookings Institution.

MUNDELL, ROBERT A. 1962 The Appropriate Use of Monetary and Fiscal Policy for Internal and External Stability. International Monetary Fund, *Staff Papers* 9:70–77.

SAMUELSON, PAUL A. 1942 Fiscal Policy and Income Determination. *Quarterly Journal of Economics* 56: 575–605.

SIMONS, HENRY C. (1942) 1948 Hansen on Fiscal Policy. Pages 184–219 in Henry C. Simons, *Economic Policy for a Free Society.* Univ. of Chicago Press. → First published in the *Journal of Political Economy.*

U.S. CONGRESS, JOINT COMMITTEE ON THE ECONOMIC REPORT 1947 *Economic Report of the President: Hearings Before the Joint Committee on the Economic Report.* Washington: Government Printing Office.

U.S. COUNCIL OF ECONOMIC ADVISERS 1947 *Annual Report to the President, Second.* Washington: Government Printing Office.

U.S. PRESIDENT 1947 *Economic Report of the President.* Washington: Government Printing Office. → Published annually since 1947.

II
WARTIME FISCAL POLICY

The objectives and methods of peacetime fiscal policy are not invalidated by the onset of a major war. However, the overriding goal of winning the war modifies both the relative emphasis placed on the various objectives and the mixture of procedures adopted to achieve them.

The experience of the United States in World War II will serve to illustrate the points involved. The magnitude of that war and its grave threat to the nation demanded the greatest feasible effort. The public, with minor exceptions, strongly supported the war. On balance there could be no recourse to the resources of other countries; instead, the United States supplied large amounts of matériel to its allies. However, the war was considered a temporary interlude in the national life, as is evidenced by the speed and completeness of demobilization at its conclusion.

The magnitude of the war required policies designed to achieve maximum engagement and utilization of human and material resources: a substantial proportion of the resources previously employed in producing civilian goods had to be shifted quickly to the military effort. Patriotic fervor was such that people were willing to sustain exactions, toil, inconvenience, and hardship not acceptable at other times, but only if they believed these burdens were being fairly shared by everyone. In the absence of both the opportunity and the reason to borrow abroad, all borrowing had to come from the same public that paid the taxes and bore the other burdens of the war, although not necessarily in the same proportions. Because of the expectation that the war would be a temporary condition, people were willing to postpone the purchase of many durable and semidurable goods, thus freeing resources for the war effort. The same expectation also strengthened public resistance to efforts by particular groups to use the wartime emergency as an occasion for permanently altering the social and economic structure of the economy.

These wartime conditions had several implications for fiscal policy. The use of a draft to select persons for military service was an obvious necessity, but its superior equity over "buying" recruits also gave it a superficial attractiveness as a method of recruiting industrial and other supporting efforts. It was not, however, a practical method for eliciting the intensive, tedious, continued efforts required in war production. Moreover, such use of the draft and concomitant military command system would have threatened the postwar economy with the perpetuation of a totalitarian economic system.

Accordingly, it was deemed imperative to rely as much as possible on governmental expenditures and fiscal incentives to stimulate maximum utilization of human and material resources, and on taxation and borrowing to support the resulting financial costs of the war. However, certain direct controls were required to reinforce and complement the fiscal measures. To have diverted resources from civilian to military use through fiscal measures alone would have been a slow, incomplete, and very costly process; priorities and direct allocations were an effective addition, which, although sometimes drastic, were justified in the public mind by the war emergency. Furthermore, it was clear that, despite heavy taxation, persons with large incomes and accumulated wealth could virtually monopolize the purchase of scarce, necessary consumer goods, while persons with small incomes suffered intense hardship. Rationing, although administratively difficult and sometimes arbitrary, could assure broad distribution of the supply. For reasons of economy and morale price and wage controls were needed to prevent spiraling inflation, gross inequities, and permanent shifts in the economic positions of different persons and groups.

While fiscal measures alone cannot be expected to achieve the objectives, or cope with the economic problems, of a major war, they should be made to do as much as possible, thereby reducing the need to employ measures disruptive of the market economy. The major objectives of an effective wartime fiscal program are fairness of burden distribution, stimulation of military and supporting production, avoidance of inflation, and salutary consequences for the postwar economy. In practice these goals must be pursued through political and administrative processes in which policy and action are determined by what people believe, whether or not it is in accord with reality.

Taxation versus borrowing. The major alternatives for financing governmental expenditures are taxation, borrowing of private savings, and expansion of the money supply. The last usually takes the form of loans from commercial and central banks rather than direct money issue. Because of its inflationary effects, it is the least desirable alternative. No case has yet been noted of a major war financed by taxation alone. During World War II the U.S. federal government collected in taxes 45 per cent of its expenditures, a somewhat higher percentage than during World War I or the Civil War and a somewhat lower percentage than was collected by Great Britain and Canada in World War II.

The relative shares of war costs to be paid from taxation and from borrowing have been determined by various factors. A traditional belief that still seems to be influential is that through borrowing, a country can shift much of the cost of the war to "future generations" in the postwar years. This belief has no validity for a country relying on internal resources. While a relatively small part of the real economic burden of the war can in some sense be shifted to postwar years, the amount thus postponable cannot be increased by financing the war through borrowing instead of taxing. What can be changed by this means is the distribution of the cost among persons. Wartime borrowing places financial burdens during the war on lenders, who after the end of the war are repaid out of taxes, which in turn are paid by the lenders and nonlenders alike. [See DEBT, PUBLIC.]

The desirability of the redistribution resulting from wartime borrowing can be measured by applying the criteria listed above. With respect to fairness of burden distribution, there are conflicting considerations. Financing through taxation avoids the injustice of levying a double burden on members of the armed forces; once on the battlefield and again through taxation to reimburse wartime lenders. However, to pay the total cost of a major war through currently collected taxes would require imposing a heavier burden on low-income groups than would be necessary if part of the cost were met by accumulating debts to be serviced after the war out of collections from progressive taxes.

With respect to production incentives, lending to the government has a less adverse effect than paying taxes does, since the patriotic efforts of workers, farmers, and businessmen are strengthened by the assurance of a tangible reward in the form of current assets and postwar spending power.

Taxation is distinctly superior to wartime borrowing as a means of minimizing inflation both during and after the war. To the citizen's mind his tax payments are gone forever, while what he loans to the government creates for him an asset that psychologically encourages his continued expenditure. To minimize this effect, the government seeks through shortages, rationing, and patriotic appeals to maximize private savings and to tap them through the sale of war bonds and other securities. The inadequacy of voluntary savings commonly necessitates borrowing from banks as well, with consequent expansion of the money supply. If the economy moves into war from a low level of output, as was the case in the United States in 1940–1941, some growth in the money supply is needed to finance expanded production and any price increases that may be required to stimulate and transfer resource utilization. Also, the chances for a prosperous postwar economy are improved by sufficient wartime borrowing from the public and from banks to provide the reserves of liquid assets needed to support demand during the postwar transition period. However, such borrowing throughout the war greatly exceeded these needs and created an excessive volume of liquid assets. Although the resulting inflationary pressures were largely suppressed during the war, the liquid assets contributed importantly to the inflationary spending of the postwar period.

All these considerations may be variously evaluated and balanced in choosing between more taxes or more borrowing. The conclusion almost certainly will be that more should be paid through taxation than will be politically feasible, because the psychological limits to taxation are undoubtedly much below the economic limits set by adverse effects on production incentives. The psychological limits appear to be determined more by the rapidity and extent of rate increases than by the previous level of the rates. In the United States the political and psychological limits undoubtedly were closely approached by 1943, when Treasury Department efforts to secure substantial tax increases met with great political resistance and a minimum of public support.

Use of income taxes.   The major sources of expanded revenue to finance World War II were taxes on net income, particularly the personal income tax but also the corporation income tax and excess profits tax. The characteristics of progressive income taxation are especially needed in time of war. The progressive income tax is highly flexible in that rates and exemptions can be readily changed, yields at given rates increase more than proportionately to the rise in national income, and with current collection, rate increases can be quickly reflected in government revenues. The income tax is the best adapted of all taxes for adjusting the tax load in accordance with the social consensus on what is equitable. Taxes on net income do not drive businesses into bankruptcy and are less likely than most other taxes to be shifted forward in higher prices with consequent wage and price escalation. However, despite its merits, the income tax can be overused; very high income tax rates may impair incentives to produce and unquestionably stimulate the search for ways to avoid or evade the tax. [*See* TAXATION.]

Use of sales taxes.   An exception to the heavy use of the income tax by nations fighting World War II was in the Soviet Union, where sales taxation is part of the apparatus of socialist income distribution. In other countries the use made of sales taxes and other gross transactions taxes differed greatly, but the rates generally were not greatly increased during the war, perhaps because of the regressive incidence of the taxes and their tendency to upset wage stabilization programs. In the United States the pre-emption of the sales tax field by the states was a factor, as was a political reluctance to introduce a general sales tax that might well remain as a permanent element of the postwar system. In Great Britain a heavy "purchases tax" on sales at the wholesale level was imposed, at rates ranging up to 100 per cent. The objective was not only to raise revenue but also to discourage the purchase of scarce, less necessary goods. A very modest use of this principle was made in the United States in the form of moderate excise taxes on scarce durable goods, with the unintended sequel that they were treated as purely revenue taxes and their repeal was delayed long after the shortages had turned to surpluses.

Special taxation.   A major question regarding the concept of fairness in war taxation is to what extent higher rates or special taxes should be imposed on increases of income realized because of the war. The corporate excess profits tax, which has become an expected element in wartime tax structures, is the principal illustration of taxation used for this purpose. It has the twofold objective of raising revenue where psychologically and economically it will presumably hurt the least and of preventing businesses from reaping unconscionable profits from the common emergency. In practice, the excess profits tax has proved to be extremely difficult to administer in harmony with its objectives; in a complex business society truly excessive profits are hard to define with precision and even harder to measure. Yet having in the tax system an "excess profits tax," even a weak or arbitrary one, seems to be essential to promote morale and make more acceptable the wartime controls that limit the incomes of workers and farmers.

The principle of special taxation on increases of income was not extended to individuals, despite considerable support for such action, no doubt because both the formulation and administration would have been even more difficult than for corporate business. The tax would also have damaged the war effort by impairing the incentives of war workers, whose new-found prosperity was indeed the target of the proposals.

Substantial resistance appeared to any tax changes that would permanently modify the relative economic positions of taxpaying groups and might therefore be considered reforms. Perhaps the clearest illustration is the estate tax, which was increased only moderately. The reasoning of the Congress seemed to be that if higher wartime rates continued into the postwar years, the result would be a major shift in the distribution of wealth and income; while strictly as wartime levies the rate increases would arbitrarily fall only on the estates of persons who died during the war.

New methods of raising revenue did not prove popular with the wartime congresses. An effort by the Treasury Department late in the 1942 session to secure a progressive tax on personal expenditures was summarily rejected. The idea of distinguishing part of the income tax as a refundable, compulsory loan, proposed by J. M. Keynes in 1940, was strongly supported by some economists in the United States administration, and it was incorporated to a small degree in the "victory tax" on income—a tax designed to hit lower incomes, with war workers again the main target. The compulsory loan feature was in effect repealed before collection. The compulsory loan was, however, used in Great Britain and, for a short time, in Canada. The experience can scarcely be considered a success (Heller 1951). Keynes's objective in proposing compulsory lending was to raise the psychological limits of wartime taxation, but apparently the taxpayers rarely distinguished between the loan part and the tax part of the payment.

External resources. Countries in a position to supplement their domestic resources with resources from other countries have used various methods to accomplish the transfer. For the most part, intergovernmental loans were used during World War I, but the repayment mechanism broke down after the war; the United States, which was the principal creditor, imposed such heavy protective tariffs as to make repayment in goods virtually impossible. In World War II the use of intergovernmental loans was minimized, and large use was made of the Lend-Lease program, which in effect was a method of common burden sharing with no postwar indebtedness liability. At the opening of World War II the British nationalized foreign securities held by citizens and, as the situation required, either sold them for foreign exchange or used them as collateral for loans. The British also incurred large foreign exchange debts in Commonwealth countries, some of which were not liquidated until long after the war. The Germans made substantial drafts on the resources of countries that they occupied during the war (Lindholm 1947).

"In-between" periods.   Turning from major wars to periods marked by minor war or heavy cold war defense budgets, we find that some of the characteristics discussed above are absent. The economic and financial requirements during such periods impose burdens that large and growing economies may absorb with little difficulty—except for potentially greater inflationary pressures than would be present in time of real peace. There is little sense of national emergency or outpouring of patriotic fervor and willingness to sacrifice. There is gradual although reluctant recognition that the problem may continue indefinitely rather than be quickly ended. It may prove to be significant that thus far the experience of the United States with modern fiscal policy has not been during periods of substantially unimpaired peace but during periods of major war, reconversion from war, minor war, and the "gray area" between war and peace.

In a situation falling between peace and war the appropriate fiscal policies tend to be similar to those of a peacetime period, although of course much depends on the size and rate of growth of defense and military expenditures. At times, even the need for further fiscal stimulus may emerge. In an "in-between" period the use of control measures to supplement fiscal policy is usually resisted, and if they are imposed, their administration is less successful in achieving compliance than in a time of major war.

Fiscal measures must be carefully oriented. The policy toward borrowing should depend on current conditions, not on projections into a doubtful "postwar" period. The tax system should be developed for the long run, not for a short-run emergency. An excess profits tax, for example, would be less appropriate in an "in-between" period than in time of major war, as well as more difficult to design and administer, since there is no valid base period against which to measure the excessiveness of profits.

In short, a period between peace and major war is an unusually difficult one in which to operate fiscal policy. The economy may develop too much inflationary pressure for successful containment through fiscal and monetary policy alone, while the absence of patriotic fervor and sense of urgency prevents wartime controls from being either acceptable or readily administrable. It is a period in which quasi controls, "voluntary" restraints, and other halfway measures, unsatisfactory as they are for all concerned, may represent the only feasible supplement to fiscal and monetary policies.

ROY BLOUGH

BIBLIOGRAPHY

British White Paper on War Finance.   1946   [U.S.] Board of Governors of the Federal Reserve System, *Federal Reserve Bulletin* 32:723–748. → First published as *National Income and Expenditures in the United Kingdom: 1938–1945*. Great Britain, Parliament, Papers by Command, Cmd. 6784.

CHICAGO, UNIVERSITY OF, LAW SCHOOL   1952   *Defense, Controls, and Inflation: A Conference*. Edited by Aaron Director. Univ. of Chicago Press.

COLM, GERHARD   1935   War Finance. Volume 15, pages 347–352 in *Encyclopaedia of the Social Sciences*. New York: Macmillan.

CRUM, WILLIAM L.; FENNELLY, JOHN F.; and SELTZER, LAWRENCE H.   1942   *Fiscal Planning for Total War*. New York: National Bureau of Economic Research.

HARRIS, SEYMOUR E.   1951   *The Economics of Mobilization and Inflation*. New York: Norton.

HELLER, WALTER W.   1951   Compulsory Lending: The World War II Experience. *National Tax Journal* 4: 116–128.

KEYNES, JOHN MAYNARD   1940   *How to Pay for the War: A Radical Plan for the Chancellor of the Exchequer*. New York: Harcourt; London: Macmillan.

LINDHOLM, RICHARD W.   1947   German Finance in World War II. *American Economic Review* 37:121–134.

MURPHY, HENRY C.   1950   *The National Debt in War and Transition*. New York: McGraw-Hill.

PAUL, RANDOLPH E.   1954   *Taxation in the United States*. Boston: Little.

STUDENSKI, PAUL; and KROOS, HERMAN E.   (1952) 1963   *Financial History of the United States: Fiscal, Monetary, Banking, and Tariff, Including Financial Administration and State and Local Finance*. 2d ed. New York: McGraw-Hill.

SUMBERG, THEODORE A.   1946   The Soviet Union's War Budgets. *American Economic Review* 36:113–126.

TAX INSTITUTE   1944   *Curbing Inflation Through Taxation*, by Marriner S. Eccles et al. New York: The Institute.

FISHER, IRVING

Irving Fisher (1867–1947), American economist, had originally intended to become a mathematician. He studied at Yale with the eminent mathematician J. Willard Gibbs but was drawn toward economics under the influence of William Graham Sumner. As Fisher himself reported, he was fascinated by Sumner. He was also deeply influenced by the astronomer Simon Newcomb, who had published a number of economic texts, including the remarkable *Principles of Political Economy*.

From 1892 to 1895 Fisher taught mathematics at Yale, with an interval in 1893 and 1894, when he visited Europe, spending time in Berlin and Paris. After 1895 he transferred from the mathematics to the economics department, remaining at Yale until his retirement in 1935.

A prolific writer, gifted in the most varied subjects, active as a mathematician, statistician, demographer, economist, businessman, reformer, and teacher, Fisher left behind him some thirty books and hundreds of papers and theoretical studies, as well as many popular articles dealing with a wide spectrum of subjects, ranging from economic theory to public health.

Fisher made a fortune from his invention of a visible card index file system, which he marketed in 1910. The corporation he founded merged with others in 1926 to form Remington Rand, Inc., of which he was a director until his death. He was also a founder and director of several agencies for economic analysis and forecasting, and a director of a considerable number of other companies. Part of Fisher's fortune was lost in the 1929 stock-market crash.

He was connected with a large number of associations and interested in many public causes. He was concerned with the problems of world peace and campaigned for six months throughout the United States in favor of U.S. participation in the League of Nations. He published two books (1923; 1924) and many articles on the subject. He was an ardent proponent of prohibition (see 1926; 1928a). His objectivity in selecting statistical data for these books has been questioned by some of his opponents.

Fisher also devoted a good deal of his time to campaigning for improved hygienic, sanitary, and eugenic practices. These crusades were an outcome of his own severe attack of tuberculosis in 1898, which interrupted his work for four years and gave him an interest in problems of health. In 1913, together with H. A. Ley and ex-President Taft, he founded the Life Extension Institute, with a view to generating public awareness of the contribution that sound living and periodic medical examinations can make to good health. He published *How to Live* (see Fisher et al. 1915), which has run into 90 editions and sold more than 400,000 copies in the

United States; it has also been translated into ten languages. None of Fisher's economic writings was as successful.

His deep concern with problems of eugenics arose from his belief that civilization could be saved only if the trends of physiological decadence of the superior elements and excessive reproduction of the inferior were reversed. Fisher served as president of the Eugenics Research Association, the American Eugenics Society, the Life Extension Institute, and the Vitality Records Office.

Like Walras, and like Pareto in the earlier part of his life, Fisher was always actively concerned with public policy, trying to modify the existing situation and to protect the organization of the economic system. He saw clearly that economic difficulties are very often monetary difficulties, and he constantly recommended active intervention by the public authorities in monetary affairs. He was an apostle of managed currency and of stabilization of the purchasing power of money. In his book on stable money he related that between 1912 and 1934 he prepared no less than 99 speeches, 37 letters to newspapers, 161 special articles, 9 submissions to appropriate governmental bodies, 12 circulars, and 13 books, a total of 331 documents intended to disseminate his ideas on monetary stabilization. Fisher was founder and president of the Stable Money League, a body whose aim was to make propaganda in favor of the "compensated" dollar.

Contributions to economics

The very lucidity of Fisher's thought may have led superficial minds to undervalue its true worth. Since no effort is necessary to comprehend his meaning, there is a tendency to underestimate the complexity and, in many instances, the originality of his thinking. In contrast to Marx and Keynes, he could develop his ideas fully, specify them, and so strip them of their obscurities and contradictions that the formulas which emerged were extraordinarily plain and clear. Whatever the difficulty of the subject, Fisher excelled at distinguishing the theoretical from the practical, at using only perfectly defined concepts, at identifying problems, treating each in a concise, clear paragraph, and at relegating to appendixes elements that were accessory to the main theme. His essential contribution lay, first, in his reduction of the copious accumulation of inconsistent notions in earlier writings to a contradiction-free synthesis that made full use of their valid elements and, second, in his lucid presentation of this synthesis.

The remarkable characteristic of Fisher's work is that it contains no *basic* error. Taken as a whole, and aside from a few minor errors of detail, it offers only valid ideas. His work is characterized by the ability to clarify, whether analytically or synthetically, rather than by the power of creative imagination. This is where Fisher's true originality is to be found.

Use of mathematics. Fisher must be considered one of those who laid the foundations of modern economics, particularly of econometrics. He contributed more than any other scholar to the introduction into economics of scientific methodology and mathematical thinking, and he played an essential role in the development of specific concepts and theories which lie at the base of today's economics.

Even as a student, Fisher perceived the immense potential that a scientific approach offered in the field of economics, and he became one of the most brilliant pioneers in the cause of mathematical economics. He believed that sooner or later every science tends to become mathematical and that the social sciences are therefore only more backward than astronomy, physics, and mathematics. He was convinced that all those who, like Gibbs, systematically relied on mathematics as a working tool would find their reward in the form of important discoveries. But he was also aware of the need to limit the use of mathematics. He was an economist; while mathematics was one of his tools, he never fell into the trap of mere formalism, characteristic of so much of the work done today. His work, like that of Pareto, teems with judicious comments on the scope and nature of theories, on the power and limits of the application of mathematical techniques, and on scientific method in general.

In 1929 two young mathematical economists, Charles Roos and Ragnar Frisch, proposed to Fisher that he join them in founding a society aimed at disseminating mathematical thinking in economics. He welcomed the suggestion with enthusiasm. The international Econometric Society was founded the next year, with Fisher as its first president. By now this society has several thousand members, including many of the most distinguished economists. [*See* ECONOMETRICS.] This may serve to indicate how much the atmosphere has changed since the young Fisher noted, in 1891, that mathematical economics was still almost as much on the defensive as it was during the 1870s and 1880s, when Jevons and Walras were pleading for it so ardently, and so vainly.

Theory of value and prices. In the *Mathematical Investigations in the Theory of Value and Prices* (1892), a work of his youth, Fisher's aim was to present a general mathematical model of the determination of value and prices. He claimed to have specified the equations of general economic equilibrium for the case of independent goods (chapter 4, sec. 10), although the only mathematical economist whose work he had consulted was Jevons. With commendable honesty he recognized the priority of Walras's *Éléments d'économie politique pure* (1874) as far as the equations of the general equilibrium are concerned and likewise the priority of Edgeworth's *Mathematical Psychics* (1881) as regards the concept of utility surfaces. It appears that, although only a student, Fisher had independently developed a theory of general economic equilibrium that was identical to part of Walras's and included the concept of the indifference surface, one of the fundamental bases of modern economic theory [*see the biography of* WALRAS].

Given the existence of these earlier formulations, the truly new elements in the *Investigations* were its clarity of presentation, its illustration of the general theory of equilibrium by a mechanical model in the case of independent goods, and its generalization of equilibrium theory to the case in which the utility of each good depends on the quantities of other goods consumed. A comparison of Fisher's text with Walras's will show how much more clear and concise Fisher's exposition is. Fisher, however, apparently did not perceive the distinction between ordinal and cardinal utility; it was Pareto who emphasized the concept of ordinal utility and used it systematically. Although the *Investigations* does have a valuable appendix on utility and the history of the mathematical method in economics, on balance, the assessment made by Ragnar Frisch (see Schumpeter 1948), that the *Investigations* is a work of monumental importance, seems exaggerated and unjustified.

Capital and income. Fisher's study of capital and income (1906) was intended to place the fundamental concepts in this field on a rational and rigorous basis and to develop the theorems flowing from these concepts. According to Fisher, his aim was to supply the long-missing link between the ideas and habits that govern business management and the theories of abstract economics.

This aim was satisfactorily realized. *The Nature of Capital and Income* contains the theoretical foundations of accounting science, both at the enterprise level and for the economy as a whole, as well as of actuarial science. Moreover, it presents these fundamentals in the framework of a general economic theory. Thus, Fisher prepared a

rigorous foundation for the subsequent work on national income and wealth.

With this book Fisher apparently became the first economist to develop a theory of capital (including human capital) on an actuarial and accounting basis; both disciplines are essential parts of any economic calculus. His theoretical constructions issued from a concrete examination of accountancy and actuarial operations; this is the only valid approach, and many economists (even including Keynes, in the *Treatise on Money* as well as in the *General Theory*) have erred by postulating a priori relationships between economic aggregates.

Also in *The Nature of Capital and Income* Fisher presented a systematization of the two concepts of capital and income, both rigorously defined. He showed very clearly how these two concepts are linked through the rate of interest. Capital consists of a stock of goods; income is a flow of services. The value of capital is given by the present value of the future flow of income from it. The direction of the causal relation is not from capital to income but from income to capital; it is not from the present to the future but from the future to the present. In other words, the value of capital is the discounted value of expected income. [*See* CAPITAL.]

He saw with unprecedented clarity that the economic present is no more than the capitalization of the future and that therefore the economic present is only a synthetic projection of the anticipated future. Fisher demonstrated convincingly that in economics only the future counts, and that past costs have no direct relevance to value. In point of fact, his research resulted in a rigorous definition of the bases on which it is possible to ground a valid theory of interest.

The only notable omission in this work is Fisher's failure to give the mathematical relations between capital and income in continuous notation. Such a formulation, which could well have found a place in an appendix, would have shown even more clearly the link between capital and income (see Allais 1965a).

The analysis of capital and income in this book is so satisfactory that it is hardly possible to go beyond it, and it retains all its relevance today. Curiously enough, *The Nature of Capital and Income*—which is Fisher's masterpiece, in my opinion—was not duly appreciated, and Pareto and Schumpeter are among the few economists who have recognized its value.

Monetary theory. In *The Purchasing Power of Money* (1911) Fisher completely recast the theory of money, giving a full demonstration of the principles that determine the purchasing power of money in the formal framework of the equation of exchange

$$(1) \qquad MV + M'V' = PQ$$

and applying these principles to the study of historical changes in purchasing power.

It is impossible, without doing grave injustice to the author, to analyze or even summarize this book, which is powerfully original in its close association of theory and econometric analysis with factual data. For Fisher, the purchasing power of money (or its reciprocal, the general price level) depends wholly on five well-defined factors: (1) the stock of money in circulation, M; (2) its velocity of circulation, V; (3) the volume of deposits, M'; (4) their velocity of circulation, V'; and (5) the over-all volume of transactions.

In his preface Fisher stated that, fundamentally, his ambition was only to renovate and amplify the old "quantity theory" of money. He claimed that if the previously presented version is modified appropriately, it must be accepted as a basically correct theory.

Although Fisher is all too widely believed to have been an intransigent quantity theorist, he specified in many places the limiting conditions on the quantity theory's validity. A few quotations should dissipate any doubt as to his real position:

. . . the theory is correct in the sense that the level of prices varies directly with the quantity of money in circulation, provided the velocity of circulation of that money and the volume of trade which it is obliged to perform are not changed. . . . ([1911] 1920, p. 14)

The strictly proportional effect on prices of an increase in M is only the *normal* or *ultimate* effect after transition periods are over. The proposition that prices vary with money holds true only in comparing two imaginary periods for each of which prices are stationary or are moving alike upward or downward and at the same rate. . . . (*ibid.*, p. 159)

Therefore the "quantity theory" will not hold true strictly and absolutely during transition periods. . . . (*ibid.*, p. 161)

There is no doubt that the weak point in Fisher's theory is his inability to free himself from the trammels of the *ceteris paribus* assumption, which Bishop Berkeley had introduced in the eighteenth century. In his attempt to show the correctness of the quantity theory, Fisher shed fresh light on a significant number of questions, but in a sense he wanted to prove too much and was led into giving insufficient weight to short-term transitional phenomena.

Long before *The Purchasing Power of Money* first appeared in 1911, Walras had attempted to escape from this blind alley by defining the concept of "real wanted cash balances." The Cambridge school, including Pigou and Keynes, did no more than take up Walras's idea, but nobody was able to develop an operational formulation of the theory of money, and the coefficients that were defined could not be rendered determinate. An operational formulation has only been developed in the recent past, for example, by the present author (Allais 1965*b*). The equation of exchange $MV = PQ$ had already been used by Newcomb in his *Principles of Political Economy*, and indeed it was to Newcomb that Fisher dedicated his book on money.

From a monetary viewpoint, the main contributions of Fisher's work seem to be a notable clarification of the significance of the formal framework of the equation of exchange; the definition of statistical methods for estimating the different parameters of this equation, in particular the velocities of circulation of notes and coin and of deposit money, and for estimating the over-all volume of transactions; the estimates themselves; and finally, a definitive clarification of the influence of demand deposits on prices and of the need to include them in the definition of the supply of money.

Although Fisher was responsible for remarkable progress in monetary theory, he was not exempt from errors of judgment. Thus, chapters 11 and 12 are devoted to the verification of the equations of exchange. But an equation of this kind, which is the definition of the velocity of circulation, cannot be verified; all that the statistics can demonstrate is the compatibility of the different estimates of the velocity of circulation.

Whatever its limitations, *The Purchasing Power of Money* clarified much that had been confused. Fisher did not use the fertile Walrasian concept of desired cash balance explicitly, nor did he attain the fruitful Keynesian concept of liquidity preference. And it is true that he did not reach a satisfactory synthesis of the theory of money with price theory (although taking his work as a whole, he came nearer to such a synthesis than did Keynes). Nevertheless, he produced analyses of monetary questions—in particular of the velocity of circulation and of the equation of exchange—that in many respects are definitive. [*See* MONEY, *articles on* QUANTITY THEORY *and* VELOCITY OF CIRCULATION.]

Theory of interest. For Fisher, the rate of interest is governed by the balance between the supply of capital, as determined by the psychology of savers, and the demand for capital, as determined by the possibilities of, and the outlook for, investment.

As with some of his other works, the major contribution of *The Theory of Interest* (1930*a*) is not so much the presentation of major new ideas as the clarity and rigor of exposition of an extremely complex subject. The fundamental theses of the book had already been developed before Fisher by John Rae (1834) and, above all, by Böhm-Bawerk (1884–1912). Fisher, indeed, underlined his debt in the dedication of his book: "To the memory of John Rae and of Eugen Böhm-Bawerk, who laid the foundations upon which I have endeavored to build."

At the outset, Fisher made the distinction between nominal interest and real interest. The major part of the book (chapters 4–18) is devoted to the theory of the determination of the real rate of interest. Then follows a special chapter, 19, on the relation of interest to money and prices. Fisher's theory of the real rate of interest is a synthesis of psychological theories, such as the theory of abstinence, and physical theories, such as the theory of productivity. The objectivity with which he accomplished this synthesis enabled him to give due weight to the significance of each of the different aspects. While the central themes of the book are all to be found in greater or lesser measure in Böhm-Bawerk's work, the clarity of Fisher's presentation and the rigor of his analysis are incomparably greater.

Throughout his analysis, Fisher quite correctly distinguished two problems, namely, how the interest rate is determined and why it is always positive. He contended correctly, and in contrast to the approach taken by many earlier writers, that the determination problem should be the one studied first. He stressed, again quite correctly (chapter 8, secs. 4, 5), that from a psychological or technical viewpoint there is nothing in the nature of men or things that should lead one to expect that the rate of interest, expressed in terms of whatever good is chosen as unit, will be positive rather than negative. Long before Keynes, Fisher showed clearly that the rate of interest in terms of a given good cannot become negative if the good can be stocked without significant expense, a condition that is met by money (chapter 2, sec. 3, chapter 11, sec. 9). In his discussion of the case of the interest on unredeemable bonds (chapter 13, sec. 10), he also pointed out the impossibility of a zero or negative interest rate. But since he does not appear to have seen that land rents, like unredeemable bonds, are in practice a kind of perpetual income, he failed to realize that in a social organization based on private land ownership the rate of interest cannot be zero or negative (see Allais 1947, vol. 2, pp. 479–499).

Fisher's theory of interest, like that of Böhm-Bawerk, is a capitalistic theory springing from an examination of the nature of capital. In a sense, it is the opposite pole to a theory such as that of Keynes, which is essentially a monetary theory of the rate of interest. (The present author has discussed this point: Allais 1947, vol. 1, p. 27.) Neither Fisher nor Keynes succeeded in approaching the indispensable synthesis of the two points of view. In discussing the repercussions of the theory of interest on monetary problems, Fisher showed conclusively that when prices are at peak levels, interest rates are high, not because the price level is high but because it has risen; and that when prices are low, interest levels are low, not because the price level is low but because it has declined (chapter 19, sec. 10).

Fisher's *Theory of Interest* is not entirely free of error. For example, in the discussion of the optimum date for tree felling (chapter 7, sec. 6), Fisher stated that the date is given by the equality of the marginal growth rate of the forest and the rate of interest. This result is wrong and leads to an overestimation of the optimum length of the interval between two fellings—for no account is taken of the fact that the earlier the trees are felled, the earlier will it be possible to repeat the cycle. The quantity to be maximized is not the present value of a single felling, but the present value of all the income from successive fellings. Elsewhere, Fisher appears to have considered that the reason for the difference between long-term and short-term interest rates reflects the nearness or distance of the redemption date (chapter 13, sec. 11). He failed to observe what Keynes saw clearly, namely, that short-term loans have the advantage of being relatively more liquid and are therefore remunerated at a lower rate. Finally, Fisher stated that the productivity of nature is a factor tending to support the interest rate (chapter 8, sec. 6). Counterexamples showing that this point of view is untenable can be found (see, among others, Allais 1947, vol. 2, p. 721).

Nevertheless, in an over-all view allowing for these minor criticisms, Fisher's analysis of interest represents a successful attack on one of the most difficult problems of economic theory, one that such men as Walras, Pareto, and Marshall had not fully grasped and for whose first deep analysis the credit goes to Böhm-Bawerk.

While it is true that Fisher did not completely resolve the issues of the basis of interest and the relation between the physical productivity and the value productivity of capital, he was responsible for a remarkable growth of understanding in this field. His analyses, particularly of the propensities to save and invest and of the interdependence of the rate of interest with other components of the economic system, prepared the way for his followers. [*See* INTEREST.]

Monetary policy.   Three of Fisher's works are devoted to projects for monetary reform: *Stabilizing the Dollar* (1920), *Stamp Scrip* (1933*b*), and *100% Money* (1935). It is not unfair to say that throughout his life he was absorbed, even obsessed, by concern for the maintenance of a stable purchasing power of money—in other words, the avoidance of both inflation and deflation.

Stabilization of purchasing power.   Fisher's first book on monetary policy (1920) contains a plan for a reform of the gold standard, intended to stabilize purchasing power. Its principle, which was stated as early as 1911 in *The Purchasing Power of Money* (chapter 13, sec. 5), is very simple. If prices in terms of gold rise by one per cent, the official price of gold should be lowered by one per cent in order to maintain the purchasing power of the dollar; conversely, if prices in terms of gold decline by one per cent, the official price of gold should be raised by one per cent. In this system, the increase (or decrease) of the official price of gold must apply to all currencies if the principle of fixed exchange parities is to be respected. But a single country can also apply the system, as long as it is prepared to accept variations in its currency exchange rate in line with the price fixed for gold in terms of national currency. *Stabilizing the Dollar* also contains a systematic bibliography on the stabilization of the purchasing power of money, in which Fisher cited many authors (e.g., Rooke 1824; Newcomb 1879; Marshall 1887) whose ideas corresponded closely to his own.

Despite Fisher's assertions to the contrary (appendix 2, 1D) the cogency of his propositions is based on the quantity principle, which is valid only over the long term. Although his plan therefore applies only to long-term price movements, it would have been entirely viable and effective during the nineteenth century. Certainly, if the system had been in operation in that period, the long-run increases and declines in the price level, which actually occurred and whose drawbacks are evident, could have been avoided. It is also certain that it would have enabled full internal and external currency convertibility to be maintained after World War I. One might even claim that the introduction of this system would have been a necessary condition for the maintenance of convertibility. Indeed, as Fisher himself stressed, the link with gold is not strictly indispensable, and under a system of paper money, price stability can be underpinned by appropriate limitation of the volume of newly issued means of payment. He himself stated that the operation of his plan would be facilitated rather than hindered by the internal demonetization of gold, the sole essential feature of his scheme being the full convertibility of paper money into gold ingots (chapter 4, sec. 6). These ideas still have some potential value. In point of fact, they had been applied during the Middle Ages to prevent nominal prices from declining, and the fixed price of gold, introduced in the nineteenth century, was in a way a regression of practice.

Stamped money plan.   The objective of Fisher's stamped money plan of 1932 and 1933 was to furnish an efficient method of combating the hoarding of money, which has extremely injurious effects in a period of depression, the more so as the rate of hoarding tends to accelerate. Here again, the original idea was not Fisher's own but was first suggested by Silvio Gesell in his book *The Natural Economic Order* (1906–1911, part 2) as a means of lowering the rate of interest.

In the system advocated by Gesell, notes in circulation would retain their value only if validated each month by a stamp sold through the post office network. The price of the stamp could be fixed in the light of circumstances; Gesell proposed a figure equivalent to a depreciation of the order of 5 per cent per annum. Gesell's aim was not so much to combat depression as to lower the rate of interest toward zero in order to suppress all unearned income in a market economy.

In *Booms and Depressions* Fisher took up the idea with his customary clarity, pointing out that it constitutes a method of discouraging hoarding. He wrote:

Let one hundred of these dollars be given to each citizen. . . . This "gift" would be to all of us from all of us (and so no gift at all). . . . After all the 12 stamp spaces have been filled, the dollar could be redeemed either by another of the same kind or by an ordinary dollar, at the option of the government. If the stamped dollar, renewed, runs for nine years (108 months), the funds for this redemption will have already been provided to the government by the public. . . . This strange-appearing plan will not seem so strange if we think of it as a loan to the public from the government, to be repaid in monthly installments of one per cent.   (1932, pp. 227–229)

Gesell's suggestion was taken up by Keynes also, who pointed out that it would permit the level of interest rates to be lowered (1936, chapter 23, sec. 6).

There is no doubt that a scheme of this kind is a valid antidepression weapon, provided it is extended also to cover bank deposits—which is feasible. Fisher believed that in normal times there would be no need to have recourse to this system but that if the need for it became evident, it could be introduced with beneficial effect. It has been objected that anyone wishing to hoard would not be prevented from hoarding land, precious stones, or precious metals, but from a monetary viewpoint this is not a valid objection: what is at issue is how to avoid generalized overproduction by rendering it undesirable to hoard *money*.

The proposals for monetary reform by Gesell, Keynes, and Fisher have not been understood. The idea of stamped money has been derided as an economic absurdity. Yet the only objection that may validly be raised is that in normal circumstances, i.e., when monetary policy is implemented reasonably, hoarding is moderate and the stamping of money is unnecessary. So far as the monetary aspect is concerned, the policy of validation of money through stamps is recommended by Fisher only in case of need. As for Keynes's notion that lower interest rates would increase the real national income, it can be shown that losses are wholly negligible by comparison with the capitalistic optimum situation with an interest rate of a few per cent (see Allais 1962).

Today the danger is not deflation but inflation, and the current interest in the stamped money plan is quite limited, if it exists at all. But from a theoretical point of view, this system—as well as that of the stable dollar—has many features that merit reflection.

The aim of *Stamp Scrip*, which was published in 1933, a few months after *Booms and Depressions*, was to describe the stamped-money experiments made in the Austrian towns of Schwanenkirchen and Wörgl and in a score of American cities in 1932, to assess the merits of these experiments, and to reply to certain objections that had been put forward. In Fisher's own words, the book was prepared "in a few days of fast and furious work"; the speed with which it was written had, to say the least, unfortunate consequences for its quality.

Hundred per cent reserve. Fisher's aim in *100% Money* was to show that economic fluctuations can be largely eliminated if demand deposits are totally backed by a corresponding amount of cash, thus depriving the banking system of its right— more or less erratically exercised—to create money; and to show that a system of this kind "would actually stop the irresponsible creation and destruction of circulating medium by our thousands of commercial banks which now act like so many private mints" (1935, p. xi).

The fact is that the degree of potential instability of a banking system becomes greater as the coverage ratio departs farther from unity. Credit is generally the process in which a banker makes a loan of money he does not possess to a client who nevertheless considers the money as available. The system can continue to operate as long as depositors as a whole have sufficient confidence in its stability. But once confidence is shaken, the banks are unable to honor demands for withdrawals. In its basic conception this system is irrational, and its only justifications are its historical acceptance and the savings of gold that it permitted in the nineteenth century, when the price of gold was fixed—the possible consequence of this fixity under a gold standard being long-term decreases of the price level. Fisher's *100% Money* sets forth a valid plan to rationalize the monetary system. Some of the aims of the plan have been implemented since 1934, when the Federal Deposit Insurance Corporation was founded: since then a bank failure caused by depositors withdrawing funds from the banking system has become a practical impossibility. However, the present system has the drawback that the management of the over-all money supply is less easy than it would have been under a "100 per cent money" system.

Again, the original idea was not Fisher's, as he acknowledged in his preface. He himself gave the credit for the suggestion to a group of economists from the University of Chicago, including, among others, Henry C. Simons, Aaron Director, Frank H. Knight, Henry Schultz, Paul H. Douglas, and A. G. Hart. In November 1933 this group circulated an unsigned 26-page mimeographed paper entitled 'Banking and Currency Reform" (see Walker 1935; Hart 1935). However, the credit for the original idea should not go to the Chicago school. Much earlier, in 1898, Walras was stressing the unstable nature of the system of issue of banknotes and was proposing a 100 per cent coverage ratio (1898, pp. 348, 365, 374, 375 of the 1936 French edition). Ludwig von Mises adopted much the same position in 1928 in his book *Geldwertstabilisierung und Konjunkturpolitik*.

A system of 100 per cent money is perfectly feasible providing that banking activity is split into two clearly separated branches, deposits and lending. Depositors would pay charges to cover the cost of managing their accounts, and banks would make loans with funds they had borrowed for that purpose. Introducing the system would involve certain transitional problems, but they could easily be overcome, and their resolution would give governments a much greater mastery of monetary policy than could be acquired in any other way. The idea of this reform has generally been abandoned today; its only proponents are a few economists such as Milton Friedman in the United States (1959) and Maurice Allais in France (1947).

Other works on monetary policy. Three other books written for the lay public should be mentioned among Fisher's published works on monetary reform. These are *The Money Illusion* (1928*b*), *Booms and Depressions* (1932), and *Inflation?* (1933*a*). The first and last of these are, by comparison with his other works on the subject, of limited interest.

Booms and Depressions is of more importance. It has three parts, dealing with theories, facts, and remedies, respectively. Nine main factors are considered: overindebtedness, volume of currency, price level, net worth, profit, production, psychological factors, currency turnover, and rates of interest. Most stress is placed on the factor of overindebtedness.

When the 1929 slump occurred, Fisher was over 60 years old; yet he tackled the very difficult theory of economic fluctuations. He finally reached the conclusion—which contains a large element of truth—that business cycles are due on the one hand to the existence in the banking system of uncovered demand deposits and on the other to the opportunities for hoarding offered by the circulating monetary media. These views led him to recommend regulation of the demand for and supply of money through steadily depreciating circulating money and 100 per cent coverage of demand deposits as a cure for business cycle ills (see 1933*b*; 1935).

Appraisal of monetary policy. Nowhere in his writings did Fisher really take up the central problem of variations in the demand for money with the level of economic activity, and despite the reservations he himself made, his approach was too narrowly oriented toward quantity theory. As Schumpeter aptly put it, "the scholar was misled by the crusader." His propaganda in favor of the compensated dollar resulted in his misinterpretation of the price stability that ruled up to 1929 and, correspondingly, his total unawareness of the gravity of the situation. He was one of the most optimistic supporters of the doctrine of the "new economic era." Although he had done quite well from his investments in the 1920s, he had to absorb large losses in the 1929 crisis. But as soon as he assessed its scope properly, he became an indefatigable proponent of the various plans for the restoration of prosperity that have been summarized above. To-

gether with George Frederick Warren, he persuaded President Roosevelt to devalue the dollar in order to stimulate a rise in the price level in the United States.

Contributions to statistics

Fisher's work on money and prices, in particular his propositions for stabilization of the dollar, led him to considerable advances in two branches of statistical science: price indices and distributed lags.

Index numbers. The aim of Fisher's book *The Making of Index Numbers* (1922) is to identify the characteristics of the best feasible index of prices for use in measuring changes in the purchasing power of money. This book, in which he tried to systematize and rationalize index number theory by defining a certain number of criteria, is in fact an extension of chapter 10 of his *Purchasing Power of Money* and of the appendix to that book. His research into the qualities of a satisfactory price index was a by-product of his general analysis of the equation of exchange.

Whereas Fisher's approach in *The Purchasing Power of Money* was deductive, in *The Making of Index Numbers* it was inductive and empirical: he compared the results of using different formulas on the same historical data. He used two principal criteria of evaluation, the "time reversal test" and the "factor reversal test," and recommended use of the "ideal" index, the geometric mean of the Paasche and Laspeyre indices.

There can be no doubt that Fisher's study, which was the most extensive at that time in the field of index numbers, was a fruitful springboard for much of the progress made subsequently [see INDEX NUMBERS].

Distributed lags. Fisher was the first to envisage a systematic dependence of the present on the past in economics, and thus he opened up a whole new area. The existence of systematic effects explains why it has been possible successfully to analyze economic and geophysical time series using autoregressive equations

$$(1) \qquad b_0 y_t + b_1 y_{t-1} + \cdots + b_h y_{t-h} + \cdots = \epsilon_t,$$

which when inverted can be written formally as

$$(2) \quad y_t = a_0 \epsilon_t + a_1 \epsilon_{t-1} + a_2 \epsilon_{t-2} + \cdots + a_p \epsilon_{t-p} + \cdots,$$

in which y_t is the cumulative effect of earlier actions, ϵ_{t-p}, weighted by coefficients a_p, which decline with distance in time. The accepted English term for this formulation, "distributed lags," was coined by Fisher. This term is intended to convey that each ϵ_{t-p} acts with a certain delay, so that lags of different length must be taken into account when studying the influence of the past.

In his study "Our Unstable Dollar and the So-called Business Cycle" (1925) Fisher proposed a formulation of the type

$$y(t) = y_0 + \int_0^\infty \alpha(\theta) p(t - \theta) \, d\theta,$$

in which the weights $\alpha(\theta)$ are distributed lognormally, for study of the interdependence of the level of economic activity $y(t)$ and past values $p(t - \theta)$ of the general level of prices.

Later, in his *Theory of Interest* (chapter 19, sec. 6), he used weights α, which declined linearly with time, to study the relationship between the rate of interest and earlier rates of increase of the price level.

The line of approach initiated by Fisher was later to prove particularly fertile in econometric thought. [See DISTRIBUTED LAGS.]

Influence

Unlike Adam Smith, John Stuart Mill, and Alfred Marshall, Fisher wrote no systematic treatise. The reason for this is doubtless that Fisher was preoccupied above all with research and that his manifold practical activities took much time. In Schumpeter's well-chosen words, Fisher's works "are the pillars and arches of a temple that was never built. They belong to an imposing structure that the architect never presented as a tectonic unit" ([1948] 1960, p. 237). But these foundations are solid.

Fisher was not an eminent philosopher, like Cournot, and he did not have a universal mind, like Pareto; he did not share Walras's preoccupation with social problems or try to study the philosophy of the social and economic organization of the time, as did Keynes and Schumpeter. But the fact remains that he made major contributions to the fundamental problems of capital, interest, and money.

As Schumpeter observed in his remarkable biographical article, Fisher, unlike Marx, Marshall, and Keynes, did not found a school. He had many pupils, but few disciples. In his crusades he joined forces with many other groups and individuals, but he remained almost alone in his scientific work. Perhaps it was the derision aroused by his crusading activity that led to his isolation; one of his critics has written: "His career was marked by neglect at its inception and ridicule at its close" (Lekachman 1959, p. 293).

For many years, Fisher's influence was nonetheless considerable. He was president of the American Statistical Association, of the international Econometric Society, of the National Institute of the Social Sciences, and of the American Association for Labor Legislation. The appearance of a book by Fisher was invariably an event, and it would be reviewed widely, though the reception might be favorable or hostile. In the case of both *Stamp Scrip* and *100% Money*, the reaction among Fisher's fellow economists and in official circles was unfavorable. In fact, Fisher was often considered prone to draw too rapid conclusions from abstract conceptions and therefore inclined to suggest measures whose chances of success were correspondingly uncertain.

Although there has never been a Fisher school in the sense that there has been a Keynesian school, Fisher's influence on a great number of young economists was nevertheless profound (see Sasuly 1947). As a disciple of Fisher, the author of the present article is among those who have recently produced systematizations, generalizations, or extensions of Fisher's theoretical and econometric work on capital, income, interest, and money (see Allais 1943; 1947; 1954; 1965a; 1965b).

Assessment

The opinion of Fisher's work has not generally been as high as its merit warrants, especially in the United States, where its value has been grossly underestimated.

To a remarkable extent Fisher combined within himself the eminently Anglo-Saxon preoccupation with facts and practical action and the essentially Latin quality of clarity of conception and exposition. He was at one and the same time theorist and practitioner, having the characteristics, therefore, of a great engineer.

Fisher had, above all, an extraordinary feeling for things concrete, and the whole body of his work is permeated by an unceasing search for numerical applications. For him no theory was of use unless it led to applied work and the quantitative analysis of factual data. Fisher always maintained close contact with businessmen and tried to familiarize himself with their reactions and preoccupations, so as to analyze them and compare them with the theoretical models of economic science. He was deeply interested in practical action. Economic science, as he saw it, was not merely pure philosophical speculation; it should be used, as engineering is, to achieve practical ends.

Fisher's normative approach tended to lower the esteem in which he might otherwise have been held. This unfortunate fate he shares with Marx, whose remarkable sociological accomplishments have been partially discredited by his political attitude, and with Walras, whose normative propositions have been considered by many as unsophisticated or even downright infantile.

Men who are accepted as geniuses have been known to spout nonsense on certain issues. As Pareto wrote: "It is somewhat hard to believe, although it is no more than the truth, that the great Newton wrote a book which proved that the prophecies of the Apocalypse had come to pass." No one would conclude from this that Newton's *Mechanics* is not a first-level achievement of the human spirit.

Fisher marks a decisive stage in the history of economic science. He was the first economist to combine profound theory and authoritative observation. He contributed powerfully to the construction of theoretical mathematical models aimed at the explanation of reality, and at the same time, whether in working out his assumptions or interpreting his results, he never lost his extraordinary preoccupation with reality, which he observed and analyzed with a refined sense of the concrete.

Simultaneously a theorist and a practitioner, Fisher combined to the highest degree two supposedly incompatible characteristics: an *esprit de géometrie* and an *esprit de raffinement*; these are, despite Pascal's opinion, but two sides of one and the same medal—intelligence. Because of these qualities, Fisher ranks with the greatest contributors to economic science. Like physics, economics calls for the study of abstract constructions at the same time that it requires the observation and analysis of facts. When Fisher died in 1947, the present author wrote (Allais 1947) that it was because of the combination of these two qualities that Fisher had to be given a place in the hall of fame of modern economics. A year later Schumpeter described him as America's greatest scientific economist. The future will certainly confirm this judgment. Fisher opened up a new horizon. Others will go beyond the point he reached; they have done so already, for it is easier to progress when the way is posted with signs.

MAURICE ALLAIS

[*For the historical context of Fisher's work, see the biographies of* BÖHM-BAWERK; NEWCOMB; PARETO; RAE; SUMNER; *and* WALRAS.]

WORKS BY FISHER

(1892) 1961 *Mathematical Investigations in the Theory of Value and Prices.* New Haven: Yale Univ. Press.

(1896) 1925 *Elements of Geometry.* New York: American Book Co. → In collaboration with Andrew W. Phillips.

(1897a) 1960 A Bibliography of Mathematical Economics. Pages 173–209 in Antoine A. Cournot, *Researches Into the Mathematical Principles of the Theory of Wealth.* New York: Kelley.

(1897b) 1943 *A Brief Introduction to the Infinitesimal Calculus.* New York: Macmillan.

(1906) 1927 *The Nature of Capital and Income.* New York and London: Macmillan.

1907 *The Rate of Interest: Its Nature, Determination and Relation to Economic Phenomena.* New York: Macmillan.

(1910a) 1912 *Elementary Principles of Economics.* New York: Macmillan. → First published as *Introduction to Economic Science.*

1910b *National Vitality: Its Wastes and Conservation.* U.S. 61st Congress, 2d Session, Senate Document No. 419. Washington: Government Printing Office.

(1911) 1920 *The Purchasing Power of Money: Its Determination and Relation to Credit, Interest and Crises.* New ed., rev. New York: Macmillan.

1914 *Why the Dollar Is Shrinking? A Study in the High Cost of Living.* New York: Macmillan.

(1915) 1946 FISHER, IRVING et al. *How to Live: Rules for Healthful Living Based on Modern Science.* 21st ed., rev. New York: Funk & Wagnalls.

1920 *Stabilizing the Dollar: A Plan to Stabilize the General Price Level Without Fixing Individual Prices.* New York: Macmillan.

(1922) 1927 *The Making of Index Numbers: A Study of Their Varieties, Tests, and Reliability.* 3d ed., rev. Boston: Houghton Mifflin.

1923 *League or War?* New York: Harper.

(1924) 1926 *America's Interest in World Peace.* Rev. ed. New York: Funk & Wagnalls. → A revised edition and condensation of *League or War?*

1925 *Our Unstable Dollar and the So-called Business Cycle. Journal of the American Statistical Association* 20:179–202.

(1926) 1927 *Prohibition at Its Worst.* 5th ed. New York: Alcohol Information Committee.

1928a *Prohibition Still at Its Worst.* New York: Alcohol Information Committee.

1928b *The Money Illusion.* New York: Adelphi. → Contains a systematic bibliography.

(1930a) 1961 *The Theory of Interest.* New York: Kelley. → Revision of *The Rate of Interest* 1907.

1930b *The Stock Market Crash—and After.* New York: Macmillan.

1932 *Booms and Depressions: Some First Principles.* New York: Adelphi. → Contains a systematic bibliography.

1933a *Inflation?* New York: Adelphi.

1933b *Stamp Scrip.* New York: Adelphi.

1933c *After Reflation, What?* New York: Adelphi.

1934 FISHER, IRVING; and COHRSSEN, HANS R. L. *Stable Money: A History of the Movement.* New York: Adelphi.

(1935) 1945 *100% Money: Designed to Keep Checking Banks 100% Liquid; to Prevent Inflation and Deflation; Largely to Cure or Prevent Depressions; and to Wipe Out Much of the National Debt.* 3d ed. New Haven: City Printing.

1937 Note on a Short-cut Method for Calculating Distributed Lags. International Statistical Institute, *Bulletin* 29, no. 3:323–328.

1942 *Constructive Income Taxation: A Proposal for Reform.* New York: Harper.

SUPPLEMENTARY BIBLIOGRAPHY

ALLAIS, MAURICE (1943) 1952 *Traité d'économie pure.* 2d ed. Paris: Imprimerie Nationale. → First published in 1943 as *Économie pure.*

ALLAIS, MAURICE 1947 *Économie & intérêt: Présentation nouvelle des problèmes fondamentaux relatifs au rôle économique du taux de l'intérêt et de leurs solutions.* 2 vols. Paris: Librairie des Publications Officielles.

ALLAIS, MAURICE 1954 *Les fondements comptables de la macro-économique: Les équations comptables entre quantités globales et leurs applications.* Paris: Presses Universitaires de France.

ALLAIS, MAURICE 1962 The Influence of the Capital-output Ratio on Real National Income. *Econometrica* 30:700–728.

ALLAIS, MAURICE 1965a The Role of Capital in Economic Development. Pages 697–978 in Study Week on the Econometric Approach to Development Planning, Vatican City, 1963 [*Travaux scientifiques et discussions*]. Pontificia Accademia delle Scienze, Rome, Scripta Varia, Vol. 28. Chicago: Rand McNally; Amsterdam: North-Holland Publishing.

ALLAIS, MAURICE 1965b *Reformulation de la théorie quantitative de la monnaie: La formulation héréditaire, relativiste et logistique de la demande de monnaie.* Paris: SEDEIS. → An abridged version was published in the December 1966 issue of the *American Economic Review.*

BÖHM-BAWERK, EUGEN VON (1884–1912) 1959 *Capital and Interest.* 3 vols. South Holland, Ill.: Libertarian Press. → First published as *Kapital und Kapitalzins.* See especially Volume 1: *History and Critique of Interest Theories,* 1884; and Volume 2: *Positive Theory of Capital,* 1889.

CAGAN, PHILLIP 1956 The Monetary Dynamics of Hyperinflation. Pages 25–117 in Milton Friedman (editor), *Studies in the Quantity Theory of Money.* Univ. of Chicago Press.

DAVIS, HAROLD T. 1941 *The Analysis of Economic Time Series.* Bloomington, Ind.: Principia Press.

DOUGLAS, PAUL H. 1947 Irving Fisher. *American Economic Review* 37:661–663.

EDGEWORTH, FRANCIS Y. (1881) 1953 *Mathematical Psychics: An Essay on the Application of Mathematics to the Moral Sciences.* New York: Kelley.

FISHER, IRVING NORTON 1956 *My Father, Irving Fisher.* New York: Comet.

FISHER, IRVING NORTON 1961 *A Bibliography of the Writings of Irving Fisher.* New Haven: Yale Univ. Library.

FRIEDMAN, MILTON (1959) 1961 *A Program for Monetary Stability.* New York: Fordham Univ. Press.

GESELL, SILVIO (1906–1911) 1958 *The Natural Economic Order.* London: Owen. → First published in German as *Die Verwirklichung des Rechtes auf den vollen Arbeitsertrag* and *Die neue Lehre vom Geld und Zins.*

HART, ALBERT G. 1935 The "Chicago Plan" of Banking Reform. *Review of Economic Studies* 2:104–116.

KEYNES, JOHN MAYNARD 1936 *The General Theory of Employment, Interest and Money.* London: Macmillan. → A paperback edition was published in 1965 by Harcourt.

KOYCK, LEENDERT M. 1954 *Distributed Lags and Investment Analysis.* Amsterdam: North-Holland Publishing.

LEKACHMAN, ROBERT 1959 *A History of Economic Ideas.* New York: Harper. → Published in French in 1960.

MARGET, ARTHUR W. 1938 *The Theory of Prices: A Reexamination of the Central Problems of Monetary Theory.* Vol. 1. Englewood Cliffs, N.J.: Prentice-Hall.

MARSHALL, ALFRED 1887 Remedies for Fluctuations of General Prices. *Contemporary Review* 51:355–375.

MORET, JACQUES 1915 *L'emploi des mathématiques en économie politique.* Paris: Giard & Brière.

NERLOVE, MARC 1958 *Distributed Lags and Demand Analysis for Agricultural and Other Commodities.* U.S. Dept. of Agriculture, Handbook No. 141. Washington: Government Printing Office.

NEWCOMB, SIMON 1879 The Standard of Value. *North American Review* 129:223–237.

RAE, JOHN (1834) 1905 *The Sociological Theory of Capital.* New ed. annotated by C. W. Mixter. New York: Macmillan. → First published as *Statement of Some New Principles on the Subject of Political Economy Exposing the Fallacies of the System of Free Trade and of Some Other Doctrines Maintained in the Wealth of Nations.*

ROOKE, JOHN 1824 *An Inquiry Into the Principles of National Wealth, Illustrated by the Political Economy of the British Empire.* Edinburgh: Balfour.

SASULY, MAX 1947 Irving Fisher and Social Science. *Econometrica* 15:255–278.

SCHUMPETER, JOSEPH A. (1948) 1960 Irving Fisher: 1867–1947. Pages 222–238 in Joseph A. Schumpeter, *Ten Great Economists: From Marx to Keynes.* New York: Oxford Univ. Press. → First published in Volume 16 of *Econometrica* as "Irving Fisher's Econometrics."

SCHUMPETER, JOSEPH A. (1954) 1960 *History of Economic Analysis.* Edited by E. B. Schumpeter. New York: Oxford Univ. Press.

SELIGMAN, BEN B. 1962 *Main Currents in Modern Economics: Economic Thought Since 1870.* New York: Free Press.

SUDELA, AMELIA G. 1937 Biographical Sketch of Irving Fisher; Selected Bibliography of the Economic Writings of Irving Fisher. Pages 441–450 in *Lessons of Monetary Experience: Essays in Honor of Irving Fisher.* New York: Farrar & Rinehart.

VILLARD, HENRY H. (1948) 1957 Monetary Theory. Volume 1, pages 314–351 in Howard S. Ellis (editor), *A Survey of Contemporary Economics.* Homewood, Ill.: Irwin.

VON MISES, LUDWIG 1928 *Geldwertstabilisierung und Konjunkturpolitik.* Jena (Germany): Fischer.

WALKER, CHARLES H. 1935 The "Chicago Plan" of Banking Reform. II: The Application of the Proposals in England. *Review of Economic Studies* 2:117–121.

WALRAS, LÉON (1874–1877) 1954 *Elements of Pure Economics: Or, the Theory of Social Wealth.* Translated by William Jaffé. Homewood, Ill.: Irwin; London: Allen & Unwin. → First published as *Éléments d'économie politique pure.*

WALRAS, LÉON 1898 *Études d'économie politique appliquée: Théorie de la production de la richesse sociale.* Lausanne (Switzerland): Rouge.

WESTERFIELD, RAY B. 1947 Irving Fisher. *American Economic Review* 37:656–661.

FISHER, R. A.

Ronald Aylmer Fisher (1890–1962) achieved world-wide recognition during his lifetime as a statistician and geneticist. He continued the work begun in England by Karl Pearson at the beginning of the twentieth century, but he developed it in new directions. Others also contributed to the tremendous surge in the development of statistical techniques and their application in biology; but these two men, by their energetic research and example, in turn held the distinction of dominating the statistical scene for a generation.

Fisher was born in East Finchley, near London. Apart from a twin brother who did not live long, he was the youngest of seven children. His father, George Fisher, was an auctioneer; no particular scientific ability is evident in the achievements of his relatives, except perhaps those of an uncle who, like Ronald Fisher, was a wrangler in the mathematical tripos at Cambridge. Fisher attended school at Stanmore Park and then went to Harrow, where he was encouraged in his mathematical interests and won a scholarship to Gonville and Caius College, Cambridge. His leanings in mathematics followed the English tradition in natural philosophy, and his university student years, from 1909 to 1913, culminated in his receiving first a distinction in optics for his degree papers in 1912 and then a studentship in physics during his postgraduate year. He had, however, already noticed from studying Karl Pearson's *Mathematical Contributions to the Theory of Evolution* that natural philosophy need not stop with the physical sciences.

After leaving Cambridge, Fisher spent a short time with the Mercantile and General Investment Company. When World War I broke out in 1914, his very bad myopia prevented him from joining the army, and he taught mathematics and physics for four years at various English public schools. In 1917 he married Ruth Eileen Guinness, who was to bear him eight children.

Fisher did not really begin his full-time statistical and biological career until 1919, when he became statistician at Rothamsted Experimental Station, an agricultural research institute in Harpenden, Hertfordshire. His earlier years had, however, been a valuable gestation period. In a short paper published in 1912 while he was still at Cambridge, he had already proposed the method of maximum likelihood for fitting frequency curves. Two more solid papers established his permanent reputation for research. The first was his remarkable paper on the sampling distribution of the correlation coefficient, published in Karl Pearson's journal *Biometrika* in 1915, in which his geometrical powers of reasoning were first fully displayed. The second, published in 1918, examined the correlation between relatives on the basis of Mendelian inheritance and exhibited his ability to resolve crucial problems of statistical genetics. Fisher received from Karl Pearson an offer of a post at University College at the same time that he received the Rothamsted offer, but he wisely chose Rothamsted, largely because of the much greater scope and independence of this new statistical post but also, perhaps, because his contacts with Pearson had not been particularly promising. Pearson was apt to bulldoze his way into research problems without worrying unduly about territorial rights. Having been previously stymied by the correlation distribution problem, he took over Fisher's solution with enthusiasm but without the further close consultation that professional etiquette would seem to require. Fisher was aggrieved by this treatment, and it may well have been the start of the long and bitter feud that developed over the years. Fisher had reason to criticize much of Karl Pearson's work, but the personal animosity that developed between them was something more than a substantive disagreement. As late as 1950, when a selection of Fisher's best statistical papers was published, the omission of the 1915 *Biometrika* paper was a silent reminder of Fisher's feelings.

The period at Rothamsted, from 1919 to 1933, was the most brilliant and productive of Fisher's career. The institute, with its teams of biologists and congenial research atmosphere, was precisely the environment Fisher needed. His own wide range of biological interests enabled him to understand his colleagues' problems and to discuss their statistical aspects constructively with them. His statistical activities were represented by the publication of his best-known book, *Statistical Methods for Research Workers* (1925a), which has been published in 13 English editions and also translated into several foreign languages. Fisher's varied accomplishments included doing much of his own computing and initiating many of his own genetical experiments on poultry, snails, and mice, although it is for his creative theoretical ability that he will be remembered. By 1929 he had been elected a fellow of the Royal Society of London. He published his classic on population genetics, *The Genetical Theory of Natural Selection* (1930a), in which he did much to reconcile Darwin's theory of evolution by natural selection with Mendel's genetical principles, which were unknown to Darwin. In the later chapters of this work he discussed the theory, first suggested by Francis Galton, of the evolution of a genetic association between infertility and ability. This could result from marriages between those successful because of high innate ability and those successful because of social advantages due to relatively infertile parents' having concentrated their material resources on one or two children. His energetic views included proposals for family allowances proportional both to size of family and to size of income, which would offset the penalty imposed on children by parental fertility.

Fisher's genetic and eugenic interests were soon

to be reflected in his move to London in 1933, when he was appointed Galton professor at University College as successor to Karl Pearson. This move, however, no doubt fanned the flames of their feud. When Pearson retired, the college isolated the teaching of statistics in a new department of statistics, under his son Egon; the Galton professor was left with eugenics and biometry. In spite of Egon Pearson's greater tolerance and appreciation of Fisher's new statistical techniques, which emphasized precise methods of analysis in small samples, Fisher felt frustrated, as he indicated at the time in a letter to W. S. Gosset. Moreover, Jerzy Neyman, who held a post in the statistics department from 1935 to 1938, incurred Fisher's wrath by publishing work that Fisher regarded as unnecessary or misguided; their proximity in the same building at University College exacerbated Fisher's sense of injury. The recurrence of feuds of this kind was by now beginning to be as much a manifestation of Fisher's own temperament as of his antagonists'. His wide interests and strong personality made him a charming and lively companion when he chose to be and a generous colleague to those who were in sympathy with his work, as many have testified. But his emotions as well as his intellect were too bound up in his work for him to tolerate criticism, to which he replied in vigorous and sometimes quite unfair terms. Apart from such lapses from objectivity, Fisher proceeded to consolidate his scientific reputation both by the development of the study of genetics (especially human genetics) in his department and by the continued publication of statistical works, such as *The Design of Experiments* (1935*a*), *Statistical Tables for Biological, Agricultural, and Medical Research* (with F. Yates, in 1938), and further original papers in his departmental journal (the *Annals of Eugenics*) and elsewhere.

The third main phase of Fisher's scientific career was his appointment to the Arthur Balfour chair of genetics at Cambridge, from 1943 until his retirement in 1957. During this time he wrote two more books—*The Theory of Inbreeding*, in 1949, and *Statistical Methods and Scientific Inference*, in 1956—and also edited the collection of his papers published in 1950 (see 1920–1945); but most of his important work was already under way. Honors continued to accumulate, including three medals from the Royal Society (a royal medal in 1938, a Darwin medal in 1948, and a Copley medal in 1955), a knighthood in 1952. Shortly before he retired, he became master of his Cambridge college. He was an honorary member of the American Academy of Arts and Sciences, a foreign associate of the National Academy of Sciences, a member of the Pon-

tifical Academy of Sciences, and a foreign member of the Royal Danish Academy of Sciences and Letters and of the Royal Swedish Academy of Sciences.

After retirement he visited the division of mathematical statistics of the Commonwealth Scientific and Industrial Research Organisation in Adelaide, Australia, where he was a research fellow at the time of his death.

Contributions to statistics and genetics

Statistics.   To turn in somewhat more detail to Fisher's original work, a formal listing of his contributions to statistics item by item might result in an underemphasis of the strength of their impact, which was due to their simultaneous variety and depth. Moreover, a formal listing is unsatisfactory since the intimate relation of Fisher's contributions to the practical problems arising from his professional environment sometimes meant that their academic presentation was incomplete or late, or both. Work of great value, such as the technique of analysis of variance, received inadequate discussion in *Statistical Methods for Research Workers* because it had hardly reached any degree of finality when this book was published in 1925, and it was still rather cluttered with ideas of intraclass correlation; apparently, Fisher never bothered to redraft the discussion for the later editions.

Excluding Fisher's mathematical work in genetics, it is nevertheless convenient to try to list his chief contributions to statistical theory under two main headings: (1) fundamental work in statistical inference, and (2) statistical methodology and technique. The first group would include his important work on statistical estimation, mainly represented by two papers, one published in the *Philosophical Transactions* of the Royal Society (1922), and the other published in the *Proceedings* of the Cambridge Philosophical Society (1925*b*). Before writing these papers, Fisher had already been much concerned with precise inference in small samples for familiar quantities, such as the correlation coefficient, chi-square, etc., and had produced a steady flow of papers on their sampling distributions, of which his 1915 paper on the correlation coefficient is the best known. He was very careful to distinguish between an unknown population parameter and its sample estimate. When the sampling distribution of the estimate was available in numerical form, a test of the significance of any hypothetical value of the parameter became possible. These precise tests of significance—for example, of an apparent correlation r in the sample on the "null hypothesis" of no real correlation ($\rho = 0$)—were particularly valuable at the time because of the tendency among biologists and other research workers not to bother with them. Fisher's own emphasis on them was, however, rather inconsistent with his subsequent attack on the Neyman–Pearson theory of testing hypotheses, especially since an unthinking use of these significance tests by some workers, as in the failure to recognize that a nonsignificant result does not imply the truth of the hypothesis tested (e.g., $\rho = 0$), caused some reaction against their use later on.

It is evident that Fisher had begun to think about his general theory of estimation before 1922; apart from his advocacy of maximum likelihood in 1912, the notion of sufficiency had also arisen in the special case of the root mean square deviation as an estimate of the true standard deviation σ in the case of a normal, or Gaussian, sample. Nevertheless, the general theory was first systematically developed in the two papers cited, and it included a discussion of the concept of consistency and a heuristic derivation of the asymptotic properties of maximum likelihood estimates in large samples [see ESTIMATION, article on POINT ESTIMATION]. It also included a crystallization of the concept of information on a parameter θ in the formula

$$I = E\left\{ \left(\frac{\partial L}{\partial \theta} \right)^2 \right\},$$

where $L = \log p(S|\theta)$ is the logarithm of the probability of the sample S when the parameter has true value θ. The importance of this work lay in (1) examining the actual sampling properties of maximum-likelihood estimates, particularly in large samples (the *method* of maximum likelihood goes back quite a long way, at least as it is analogous to maximum a posteriori probability by Bayes' inverse-probability theorem on the assumption of a uniform a priori distribution); and (2) emphasizing that a sample provides, in some appropriate statistical sense, a definite amount of information on a parameter. Fisher's concept of information, preceding Shannon's, which was introduced in quite a different context (see Shannon 1948), was especially appropriate for large samples because of the possible ordering of normally distributed estimates in terms of their variances (squared standard deviations). [See INFORMATION THEORY.] Fisher justified his concept more generally in the use of small samples by thinking in terms of many such samples; it is curious that he missed the exact inequality relating the information function and the variance of an unbiased estimate known as the Cramér–Rao inequality. In any case, however, the arbitrariness of the variance and unbiasedness remains; and in small samples Fisher introduced the general notion of a sufficient statistic, which, by

rendering conditional distributions of any other sample quantities independent of the unknown parameter, exhausted the "information" in the sample [see SUFFICIENCY].

The next remarkable contribution in this general area came with Fisher's brief paper entitled "Inverse Probability" (1930b). Fisher had always been derisory of the estimates and inferences resulting from the Bayes inverse-probability approach. He felt that a unique and more objective system of inferences should be possible in fields where statistical probabilities operate and noted that an exact sampling distribution involving a sample quantity or statistic T and an unknown parameter θ leads (under appropriate regularity and monotonicity properties) to the feasibility of assigning what he termed a "fiducial interval," with a known fiducial probability that the parameter θ is contained in the interval. The interpretation accepted at the time, and implied by Fisher's own wording in this paper, was that this interval, which is necessarily a function of the statistic T, is in consequence a random interval and that fiducial probability is a statistical probability with the usual frequency connotation. Referring to the case of a true correlation coefficient ρ, he said, "We know that if we take a number of samples of 4, from the same or different populations, and for each calculate the fiducial 5 per cent value for ρ, then in 5 per cent of cases, the true value of ρ will be less than the value we found" ([1930b] 1950, pp. 22, 535). With some restrictions (for example, to sufficient statistics) it was thus apparently identical with the theory of confidence intervals developed about the same time by Neyman (1937). [See ESTIMATION, article on CONFIDENCE INTERVALS AND REGIONS; FIDUCIAL INFERENCE.]

On inductive inference questions, Fisher often did not make it clear· what he was claiming; but it should be stressed that regardless of what his interpretation was or of its relevance to the problem at hand, it still was formulated in terms of an assumed statistical framework. Nevertheless, its formal bypassing of Bayes' theorem was a masterly stroke which received attention outside statistical circles (cf. Eddington's remark, "We can never be sure of particular inferences; therefore we should aim at a system of inference that will give conclusions of which in the long run not more than a stated proportion, say $1/q$, will be wrong" [1935a] 1960, p. 126).

Later, Fisher attempted to extend fiducial theory to more than one parameter. His first paper (1935b) discussing this extension took as one example the problem of inferring the difference in population means of two samples coming from normal populations with different variances. The difficulty here (which Fisher may not have realized at the time, since he himself never examined in detail the logical relations of sufficient statistics in the case of more than one parameter) is that the effect of the unknown variance ratio cannot be segregated in the absence of a "sufficient" quantity for it that does not involve unwanted parameters, such as the individual population means. In rejecting a criticism along these lines by the present author (Bartlett 1936; for further details see, for example, Bartlett 1965), Fisher explicitly gave up the orthodox frequency interpretation for fiducial probability which he appeared to have assumed earlier. He and others attempted to formulate a theory for several parameters that would be both unique and self-consistent, but this has yet to be achieved in any generality, and to many this search is misguided in that it does not eliminate from fiducial theory the arbitrariness that Fisher had so strongly criticized in the Bayes approach.

A rather different and somewhat more technical estimation problem that Fisher solved in 1928 is the derivation of sample statistics that are unbiased estimates of the corresponding population quantities and of the sampling moments of these statistics. The population quantities are the cumulants or semi-invariants first introduced by Thiele (1903), and Fisher's combinatorial rules for obtaining the appropriate sample statistics and their own cumulants constituted a striking example of Fisher's intuitive mathematical powers. Another paper published in 1934 is worth noting as an original and independent contribution to the theory of games developed about the same time by von Neumann and Morgenstern. [*See* GAME THEORY, *article on* THEORETICAL ASPECTS.]

Fisher's work on the design of experiments is so important logically as well as practically that it may be regarded as one of his most fundamental contributions to the science of statistical inference. It is, however, convenient to consider it in the second general area of statistical methodology and technique, in conjunction with analysis of variance. Fisher perceived the simultaneous simplicity and efficiency of balanced and orthogonal experimental designs in agriculture. Replication of the same treatment in different plots is essential if any statistical assessment of error is to be made, and formally equal numbers of plots per treatment are desirable. However, simplification in the statistical analysis is illusory if the analysis is not valid. When observations are collected haphazardly, the most sensible assumptions about statistical varia-

bility have to be made. In controlled experiments there is the opportunity for deliberately introducing randomness into the design so that systematic variation can be separated from purely random error. This is the first vital point Fisher made; the second naturally accompanied it. With the analysis geared to the design, all variation not attributable to the treatments does not have to inflate the error. With equal numbers of plots per treatment, each complete replication can be contained in a separate block, and only variability among plots in the same block is a source of error; variability between different blocks can be automatically removed in the analysis as irrelevant. The third point arose from treatment combinations, such as different fertilizer ingredients. For example, if nitrogenous fertilizer (N) and phosphate (P) are to be tested, the recommended set of treatment combinations is

Control (no fertilizer), N, P, NP,

where NP denotes the treatment consisting of both the ingredients N and P (each in the same amount as when given alone). This design maintains simplicity and may improve efficiency, for if phosphate has no effect, or even if its effect is purely additive, the plots are balanced for nitrogen and doubled in number, and similarly for phosphate. Moreover, if both ingredients do not act additively, an interaction term can be defined that measures the difference in effect of N (or P) in the presence and absence of the other ingredient. Such a definition, although to some extent arbitrary, completes the specification of the treatment effects; and the whole technique of *factorial experimentation* typified by the above example is of the utmost importance both in principle and in practice. As Fisher put it:

The modifications possible to any complicated apparatus, machine, or industrial process must always be considered as potentially interacting with one another, and must be judged by the probable effects of such interactions. If they have to be treated one at a time this is not because to do so is an ideal scientific procedure, but because to test them simultaneously would sometimes be too troublesome, or too costly. In many instances . . . this impression is greatly exaggerated. (1935a, p. 97)

A further device that naturally arose in factorial designs was that of *confounding*, by which some of the higher-order interaction effects in designs with three or more factors are assumed to be unimportant and are deliberately arranged to coincide in the analysis with particular block contrasts. This enables the number of plots per block to be smaller and the accuracy of the remaining treatment effects thereby to be increased.

To a large extent the practical value of these experimental methods was not dependent on the statistical analysis, but the simplicity and clarity of the analysis greatly contributed to the world-wide popularity of these designs. This analysis was in principle classical least-squares theory, but the orthogonality of the design rendered the estimation problem trivial, and the concomitant assessment of error was systematized by the technique of "analysis of variance." Basically, this technique is a break-down of the total sum of squares of the observations into relevant additive parts containing any systematic terms ascribable to treatments, blocks, and so on. Once the technique was established and the appropriate tests of significance were available (on the assumption of normality and of homo-geneity of error variance) from Fisher's derivation and tabulation of the "variance-ratio" distribution, it could handle more complicated least-squares problems, such as more complex and even non-orthogonal experimental designs or linear and curvilinear regression problems. One useful ex-tension was the adjustment of observed experi-mental quantities, such as final agricultural yield, by some observed quantity measured prior to the application of treatments. This technique was re-ferred to as analysis of covariance, although this last term seems more appropriate for the simul-taneous analysis of two or more variables—that is, the technique of multivariate analysis.

Fisher was active in the development of multi-variate analysis. Earlier workers had of course encountered multivariate problems in various con-texts, and Fisher had followed up his geometrical distribution of the correlation coefficient with a derivation of the distribution of the multiple corre-lation coefficient (1928b), again brilliantly using his geometrical approach. The problem exercising Harold Hotelling in the United States and P. C. Mahalanobis in India, as well as Fisher, was the efficient use of several correlated variables for dis-criminatory and regression problems. Fisher's name is particularly associated with the concept of the discriminant function, some function of the varia-bles that will efficiently distinguish from the meas-urements of these variables for a single individual whether he came from one or another of two different populations.

Contributions to genetics.   Fisher's work in ge-netics was comparable in importance to his purely statistical contributions and equally reflected his originality and independence of outlook. In the first decade of the twentieth century, Mendelian genet-ics was still a new subject, and its quantitative con-sequences were not yet properly appreciated. It was in dispute whether they were consistent with Dar-win's theory of evolution by natural selection or even with the observed inheritance of metrical characters. Fisher took the second and lesser prob-lem first, and in his 1918 paper he gave a pene-trating theoretical analysis of correlation, breaking it down into nongenetic effects, additive gene ac-tion, and further complications, such as genic inter-action and dominance. He was thus able to demon-strate the consistency of Mendelian principles with the observed correlations between sibs or between parents and offspring. Then, in his book on the genetic theory of natural selection, he tackled the larger problem. He pointed out that the atomistic character of gene segregation (in contrast to Dar-win's hypothetical "blending" theory of heredity) is essential for maintaining variability, which in turn is the basis of the process of natural selection. He clarified the theoretical role of mutations, show-ing that mutations provide a reservoir from which eventually only favorable ones can survive. He emphasized the possibility of the selection of modi-fier genes, for example, in rendering the action of many mutant genes recessive by modifying the heterozygote phenotypically toward the natural wild type. The relative importance of this theory of the evolution of dominance was queried, for example, by Sewall Wright, among others, but this did not prevent it from being a relevant thesis that stimu-lated further research. The effect of modifier genes was also shown to be important in the phenomenon of mimicry.

At the Galton laboratory, Fisher's work in human genetics included linkage studies and the initiation of serology research on the human blood groups. An exciting moment in the work on serology came when G. L. Taylor and R. R. Race studied the Rhesus blood groups. Fisher was able to predict, from the experimental results to date, the effective triple structure of the gene, and hence two more anti-sera and one more allele, which were soon suc-cessfully traced. Such predictions may be compared with Fisher's earlier theoretical predictions in the theory of evolution, for example, on the evolution of dominance. They made possible the maintenance of a healthy link with experimental and observa-tional work, which was often initiated or encour-aged by Fisher himself. It was in this spirit that he collaborated for several years with E. B. Ford in sampling studies of natural populations.

In retrospect, Fisher's wholehearted immersion in his own research problems, fundamental and broad as these were, did cause him to ignore some important theoretical trends. His neglect of purely mathematical probability, which had been rigor-ously formulated by A. N. Kolmogorov (1933), seemed to extend to developments in the theory of random or stochastic processes, although these were very relevant to some of his own problems in evolutionary genetics. In England, A. G. McKendrick had published some brilliant papers on stochastic processes in medicine, and G. U. Yule on the analysis of time series, but Fisher never appeared to appreciate this work; in particular, his own papers on the statistical analysis of data recorded in time sometimes showed a rather overrigid adherence to classical and unduly narrow assumptions. In appraising Fisher's work, one must consider, in addition to these general boundaries that demarcate it, his occasional specific errors and, more importantly, his temperamental bias in controversy. Fisher's scientific achievements are, however, so varied and so penetrating that such lapses cannot dim their luster or reduce his ranking as one of the great scientists of this century.

M. S. BARTLETT

[*For the historical context of Fisher's work, see* STATISTICS, *article on* THE HISTORY OF STATISTICAL METHOD; *and the biographies of* GALTON; GOSSET; PEARSON; YULE. *For discussion of the subsequent development of Fisher's ideas, see* ESTIMATION; EXPERIMENTAL DESIGN; FIDUCIAL INFERENCE; HYPOTHESIS TESTING; LINEAR HYPOTHESES, *article on* ANALYSIS OF VARIANCE; MULTIVARIATE ANALYSIS.]

WORKS BY FISHER

1912 On an Absolute Criterion for Fitting Frequency Curves. *Messenger of Mathematics* New Series 41: 155–160.

1915 Frequency Distribution of the Values of the Correlation Coefficient in Samples From an Indefinitely Large Population. *Biometrika* 10:507–521.

1918 The Correlation Between Relatives on the Supposition of Mendelian Inheritance. Royal Society of Edinburgh, *Transactions* 52:399–433.

(1920–1945) 1950 *Contributions to Mathematical Statistics.* New York: Wiley.

(1922) 1950 On the Mathematical Foundations of Theoretical Statistics. Pages 10.308a–10.368 in R. A. Fisher, *Contributions to Mathematical Statistics.* New York: Wiley. → First published in Volume 222 of the *Philosophical Transactions*, Series A, of the Royal Society of London.

(1925a) 1958 *Statistical Methods for Research Workers.* 13th ed., rev. New York: Hafner. → Previous editions were also published by Oliver & Boyd.

(1925b) 1950 Theory of Statistical Estimation. Pages 11.699a–11.725 in R. A. Fisher, *Contributions to Mathematical Statistics.* New York: Wiley. → First published in Volume 22 of the *Proceedings* of the Cambridge Philosophical Society.

(1928a) 1950 Moments and Product Moments of Sampling Distributions. Pages 20.198a–20.237 in R. A. Fisher, *Contributions to Mathematical Statistics.* New York: Wiley. → First published in Volume 30 of the *Proceedings* of the London Mathematical Society.

(1928b) 1950 The General Sampling Distribution of the Multiple Correlation Coefficient. Pages 14.653a–14.763 in R. A. Fisher, *Contributions to Mathematical Statistics.* New York: Wiley. → First published in Volume 121 of the *Proceedings* of the Royal Society of London.

(1930a) 1958 *The Genetical Theory of Natural Selection.* 2d ed., rev. New York: Dover.

(1930b) 1950 *Inverse Probability.* Pages 22.527a–22.535 in R. A. Fisher, *Contributions to Mathematical Statistics.* New York: Wiley. → First published in Volume 26 of the *Proceedings* of the Cambridge Philosophical Society.

1934 Randomization and an Old Enigma of Card Play. *Mathematical Gazette* 18:294–297.

(1935a) 1960 *The Design of Experiments.* 7th ed. New York: Hafner. → Previous editions were also published by Oliver & Boyd.

(1935b) 1950 The Fiducial Argument in Statistical Inference. Pages 25.390a–25.398 in R. A. Fisher, *Contributions to Mathematical Statistics.* New York: Wiley. → First published in Volume 6, part 4 of the *Annals of Eugenics.*

(1938) 1963 FISHER, R. A.; and YATES, FRANK *Statistical Tables for Biological, Agricultural, and Medical Research.* 6th ed., rev. & enl. New York: Hafner.

1949 *The Theory of Inbreeding.* Edinburgh: Oliver & Boyd; New York: Hafner.

(1956) 1959 *Statistical Methods and Scientific Inference.* 2d ed., rev. New York: Hafner. → Previous editions were also published by Oliver & Boyd.

SUPPLEMENTARY BIBLIOGRAPHY

BARTLETT, M. S. 1936 The Information Available in Small Samples. Cambridge Philosophical Society, *Proceedings* 32:560–566.

BARTLETT, M. S. 1965 R. A. Fisher and the Last Fifty Years of Statistical Methodology. *Journal of the American Statistical Association* 60:395–409.

EDDINGTON, ARTHUR STANLEY 1935 *New Pathways in Science.* New York: Macmillan.

KOLMOGOROV, ANDREI N. (1933) 1956 *Foundations of the Theory of Probability.* New York: Chelsea. → First published in German.

NEYMAN, JERZY 1937 Outline of a Theory of Statistical Estimation Based on the Classical Theory of Probability. Royal Society of London, *Philosophical Transactions* Series A 236:333–380.

NEYMAN, JERZY 1967 R. A. Fisher (1890–1962): An Appreciation. *Science* 156:1456–1462. → Includes a two-page "Footnote" by William G. Cochran.

SHANNON, C. E. 1948 Mathematical Theory of Communication. *Bell System Technical Journal* 27:379–423, 623–656.

THIELE, THORWALD N. 1903 *Theory of Observations.* London: Layton.

YATES, F.; and MATHER, K. 1963 Ronald Aylmer Fisher. Volume 9, pages 91–129 in Royal Society of London, *Biographical Memoirs of the Fellows of the Royal Society.* London: The Society. → Contains a bibliography on pages 120–129.

FLETCHER, ALICE CUNNINGHAM

Alice Cunningham Fletcher (1838–1923), American ethnologist, was born in Cuba during a temporary residence of her American parents on the island. She traveled widely in her early years and eventually settled in the Boston area, where she studied American archeology and ethnology at the Peabody Museum at Harvard University. It was out of intense concern for the welfare and rights of the American Indian that she began her scientific studies of them. Although she was eventually to gain great and well-merited recognition as a scholar, the recommendations in behalf of American Indians that she made in the name of anthropological authority suffered from an uncritical commitment to benevolent philosophies of the nineteenth century. The policy she advocated was based on the assumption that it was both inevitable and desirable for the Indians to be assimilated into white society and for their tribal culture to be rapidly destroyed.

In 1870 she held a post with the Women's National Indian Association as administrator of funds from which small loans were made to Indians so that they might buy their own lands and build homes. Then, in 1879, she met Thomas Henry Tibbles—frontiersman, minister, journalist, and ardent worker in the cause of Indian rights—and asked that she be allowed to take part in his work on the frontier. Tibbles found it difficult to take seriously the plans of the small, seemingly delicate woman, already 40 years old and a product of city life, but Alice Fletcher prevailed. On September 1, 1881, she arrived in Omaha, Nebraska, to begin work on field studies that were to become standard references in North American ethnology. But many anthropologists familiar with Fletcher's work are not aware of the fact that this field work permitted her to initiate the large-scale implementation of her well-intentioned but misguided notions and thus to affect the course of Indian affairs throughout the country up to the present day.

In Omaha, she was met by Tibbles and Bright Eyes La Flesche, an educated Omaha Indian woman associated with Tibbles' work and soon to become his wife. Tibbles' autobiography, *Buckskin and Blanket Days* (1957), reflects both his admiration for Alice Fletcher's determination and exasperation at her cheerful obliviousness to what wiser minds had heretofore recognized as realities in dealing with Indians and Indian agents. He never identified her by name but referred to her only as "High Flyer," the name bestowed on her by his Omaha helper, Wajapa. After introductions to members of the Omaha tribe, the two women, Tibbles, and Wajapa set off on a journey to the Winnebago reservation—the Ponca settlement north of the Niobrara River which was made up of removed and demoralized remnants of the tribe whose members had returned to their old haunts—and finally to the Rosebud Sioux reservation in South Dakota. Tibbles had not underestimated the hardships, bad weather, and inconveniences that

could be expected on the trip, but Alice Fletcher withstood them all equably.

She was impressed by Tibbles, Wajapa, and Bright Eyes and was grateful to them. Although they could converse in the several languages encountered on this first journey and could communicate with equal ease with her, a lady newly arrived from Boston, it apparently never occurred to her that the two Indians were highly atypical and that for all of Tibbles' vast knowledge of Indian life, his Indian policy derived entirely from the white Christian values he shared with her.

Alice Fletcher had long since decided that what was best for the Indians was a Congressional act whereby every adult Omaha would be allotted 80 acres, to remain tax-free and to be held in trust by the government for a period of 25 years. After that time those who were judged competent would be granted fee patents and control over their holdings. Reservation lands left over after the distribution of allotments were to be sold for the benefit of the tribe to finance development of their farms. It is doubtful that the Omaha understood the nature of Fletcher's solution for their problems; they only feared dispossession, as their neighbors the Ponca had experienced, and were in no position to question her narrow interpretation of their plea, "Make my home secure" (La Flesche 1923).

Alice Fletcher had influential friends in Washington, and the act was quickly pushed through legislative procedures and passed August 7, 1882. She was appointed special agent to oversee the surveying and allotment. In subsequent years she performed similar work among the Winnebago and Nez Percé, who, along with many other tribes, were allotted land under the Dawes Severalty Act of 1887, patterned after the Omaha Act.

In 1910, after an absence of many years, she returned to the Omaha for a brief visit. She observed, ". . . the act has not been altogether evil nor has it been wholly good for the people" (Fletcher & La Flesche 1911, p. 640). The Omaha were certainly far better off materially and were more cheerful than they had been when she first knew them, and it is small wonder that she viewed their future with optimism. She saw the tendency to lease rather than work the land as nothing more than an unfortunate phase of adjustment to land ownership, although it was really an indication of a major trend. The few well-run farms that she thought would be models proved to be short-lived exceptions. Finally, those items which she noted as "quaint survivals of old customs under a new guise" were really instances of adaptations, of cultural persistence, and of a desperate clinging to tribal identity that characterize Omaha life to the present day.

Margaret Mead spent the summer of 1930 with the Omaha (Mead 1932, *passim*). In keeping with her desire to conceal the identity of the group, which she called the "Antlers," Mead did not mention Fletcher by name but paid respectful tribute in her statement that the traditional life and history had been so completely recorded for the Antlers that she chose to work with this group because she would be able to devote her attention entirely to modern conditions. Mead did not disclose that the same scholar who had provided such excellent ethnographic data was also the "well-intentioned lady of missionary leanings" whose benevolent efforts resulted in the social and economic chaos Mead observed. But Mead thought that philanthropic Americans of that time could not have been expected to understand that individual landownership by Indians would not solve the economic problems that the loss of the buffaloes had created. In any case, the inadequacy of the Omaha plan was demonstrated wherever allotment took place. Between the time that fee patents were issued and the beginning of the administration of John Collier as commissioner of Indian affairs in 1938, two-thirds of allotted Indian lands had passed into white ownership (Fey & McNickle 1959, p. 78). Fletcher's "strong paper" on individual allotments was far weaker than the tribal treaty relating to undivided lands.

In matters unrelated to economics her outlook was scientifically objective. Tibbles always disapproved strongly of her interest in Indian dancing and singing and of her desire to observe and record ceremonies: to him such matters were part of Indian "savagery" to be rigorously discouraged and repressed. Alice Fletcher, however, was impressed by the artistry, poetic sophistication, and scientific significance of these customs in contrast to the Indians' material life, and she made important pioneering studies of Indian music and ceremony. Her obviously sincere concern for Indian welfare and her untiring efforts to record ceremonial life accurately won the esteem of her informants. She collected highly secret data with relative ease and maintained generally excellent relations with both colleagues and informants by a combination of humor, patience, total unselfishness, and lack of vindictiveness when crossed. Her small stature and seeming frailness apparently disarmed people who did not appreciate her strength and determination. During one field trip she suffered a siege of "inflammatory rheumatism," which was to leave her crippled for the rest of her life.

As she lay in pain, her Indian friends gathered daily to cheer and console her with songs. As soon as she was able, and with an amazing display of musical aptitude and memory, she carefully transcribed a large number of the songs (Hough 1923, p. 255).

Fletcher's theoretical interests were influenced by nineteenth-century evolutionary concepts but went beyond mere collection of facts or broad ascription of traits to given stages of development. Her investigations of Omaha religion carried her into comparative work among other Siouan speakers of the Plains, and as she suspected the existence of yet older layers of cosmology and ritual from other sources, she turned to the Caddo as the likely carriers of more ancient forms. She had observed the Pawnee hako ceremony in the 1880s, and as her awareness of problems of diffusion increased, she returned as an experienced field worker to the Pawnee in the 1890s and recorded the ceremony (Fletcher 1904).

Her scientific endeavors won rapid recognition in the anthropological profession. From 1883 onward, her name appears often in the *Proceedings* of the American Association for the Advancement of Science (AAAS) in connection with papers dealing with aspects of Plains culture. In 1896 she was vice president of the AAAS. In 1884/1885 she was in charge of Indian exhibits at the New Orleans industrial exposition. It pained her that Indians were represented by crude artifacts, and she wrote a letter, which was published and circulated among Indian groups, stressing the importance of education if Indian people were to take their rightful place in creating technological wonders like those of the white man (Fletcher 1885, pp. 1–4).

The Chicago world's fair of 1893 included a special congress of anthropology, and she took an active part in the proceedings along with the major anthropologists of her day, such as Frederic Ward Putnam, Franz Boas, and Zelia Nuttall.

After 1890, when she made her home in Washington, D.C., Alice Fletcher was a member of the Women's Anthropological Society (WAS) and served as its president in 1895. The WAS was founded in 1885 by Matilda Stevenson, famous for her studies of Pueblo groups, and was disbanded in 1899, when the group was received as a whole into the heretofore all-male Anthropological Society of Washington. Alice Fletcher was elected president of that society in 1903 and of the American Folklore Society in 1906. She worked closely with Frederic Ward Putnam in his research on the Serpent Mound in Ohio, and in 1900 they engaged in a fund-raising campaign to buy the site as a historic landmark, turning the deed over to the Ohio Archeological and Historical Society.

By the time of her death, at the age of 85, Alice Fletcher had become sort of a living legend in anthropology, active to the end in promoting scholarly enterprises and good works.

NANCY OESTREICH LURIE

[*Other relevant material may be found in* INDIANS, NORTH AMERICAN.]

WORKS BY FLETCHER

1885 *A Letter From the World's Industrial Exposition at New Orleans to the Various Indian Tribes Who Are Interested in Education.* Carlisle, Pa.

1904 *The Hako: A Pawnee Ceremony.* U.S. Bureau of American Ethnology, *Twenty-second Annual Report, 1900–1901.* → The entire issue is devoted to Alice C. Fletcher's work.

1911 FLETCHER, ALICE C.; and LA FLESCHE, FRANCIS *The Omaha Tribe.* U.S. Bureau of American Ethnology, *Twenty-seventh Annual Report, 1905–1906.* → Much of the research on the volume as a whole antedated that done on the hako ceremony published earlier. The entire issue is devoted to Alice Fletcher's and Francis La Flesche's work.

SUPPLEMENTARY BIBLIOGRAPHY

Alice C. Fletcher Memorial Meeting. 1923 *El palacio* 15, no. 5:83–88. → Contains sentimental tributes by Alice C. Fletcher's friends.

FEY, HAROLD E.; and MCNICKLE, D'ARCY 1959 *Indians and Other Americans: Two Ways of Life Meet.* New York: Harper. → Although Alice Fletcher's role is not noted, this account reviews the devastating effects of the Dawes Act of 1887 and the amount of land loss up to 1933.

HOUGH, WALTER 1923 Alice Cunningham Fletcher. *American Anthropologist* New Series 25:254–258. → An obituary containing the most extensive biographical data in the form of a chronology of events and achievements and a bibliography of Alice C. Fletcher's writings.

LA FLESCHE, FRANCIS 1923 Alice C. Fletcher. *Science* New Series 58:115 only. → An obituary stressing the nature of Alice C. Fletcher's personality.

LAMB, DANIEL S. 1906 The Story of the Anthropological Society of Washington. *American Anthropologist* New Series 8:564–579.

LUMMIS, CHARLES F. 1923 In Memoriam: Alice C. Fletcher. *Art and Archeology* 16:75–76.

MEAD, MARGARET 1932 *The Changing Culture of an Indian Tribe.* Columbia University Contributions to Anthropology, Vol. 15. New York: Columbia Univ. Press.

TIBBLES, THOMAS H. 1957 *Buckskin and Blanket Days: Memoirs of a Friend of the Indians Written in 1905.* Edited by Theodora B. Cogswell. New York: Doubleday. → Thomas H. Tibbles' memoirs were written in 1905 but checked and expanded, with a biographical introduction by T. Cogswell, in 1957. Tibbles takes full credit for inspiring the Dawes Act of 1887, and although he often refers to Alice Fletcher as "High Flyer" and pays her grudging respect as a remarkable woman, it is clear that he resented her overshadowing him in the role of friend and benefactor to the Indians.

FLEURE, H. J.

Herbert John Fleure, British geographer and anthropologist, has done much to further the view that the study of man and his societies should not be divorced from the study of their environments and that an evolutionary approach to the condition of man and his cultures in the various regions of the world is essential to the discipline of human geography. He vigorously championed this subject at a time when it was not generally recognized as a university discipline in Britain.

Fleure grew up in Guernsey. In 1897, when he was 20, a scholarship to the University College of Wales, Aberystwyth, enabled him to take courses in the natural sciences; he specialized in marine zoology. He spent the year 1903–1904 studying at the University of Zurich, where Rudolf Martin stimulated his interest in anthropology. The following year he returned to Wales and received the degree of D.SC. He then began to teach courses in zoology, geology, and botany at Aberystwyth and in 1907 was elected to a newly established lectureship in geography. His intellectual development was influenced by Darwinism and by the works of such German earth scientists as Eduard Suess and Ferdinand von Richthofen.

Fleure became professor of zoology in 1910 but continued to teach geography, and in 1917 his persistent advocacy of this subject was rewarded by his appointment to the endowed (Gregynog) chair of geography and anthropology. In the same year he became honorary secretary of the Geographical Association and editor of its journal (now *Geography*), and through these agencies he worked strenuously to advance the cause of human geography in education. From 1930 until his retirement in 1944, Fleure was professor of geography in the University of Manchester. He has been president of three sections of the British Association for the Advancement of Science, and of many learned societies. In 1936 he was elected fellow of the Royal Society.

Fleure quickly established his reputation as an anthropologist with an anthropometric survey of Wales conducted in 1916 (Fleure & James 1916). He first outlined a scheme of world regions, defined by the quality of life within them, in an article published in 1917. Suspicious of the concept of "natural regions," he saw, long before prehistoric archeology and paleoecology had established the antiquity and extent of man's alteration of his surroundings, that human societies can fashion their own environments and that "environment" is a term of cultural appraisal. In his *Human Geography in Western Europe* (1918) he first presented his conception of that discipline. The first of the ten volumes of *The Corridors of Time,* written in collaboration with Harold Peake, appeared in 1927, and the last volume appeared in 1956. From the first volume (*Apes and Men*) to the last (*Times and Places*), this series presents Fleure's mature views on the development of human societies in the major regions of the world since prehistoric times. A balanced judgment on such issues as diffusion and independent development springs from a broad training in the sciences of man.

Fleure has stressed the significance of culture contacts in all periods of human history as leading to the questioning of routine, the cross-fertilization of ideas, objective thought, and the release of innovative effort. Always guarded in his conclusions, Fleure has been chary of general laws in human geography, where the likelihood prevails that different responses will arise in different regions at different times.

In addition to the works mentioned, Fleure has contributed extensively to encyclopedias and also to journals of geography, anthropology, sociology, folklore, and archeology.

E. ESTYN EVANS

[*See also* GEOGRAPHY; REGION.]

WORKS BY FLEURE

1916   FLEURE, H. J.; and JAMES, T. C. Geographical Distribution of Anthropological Types in Wales. *Journal of the Royal Anthropological Institute of Great Britain and Ireland* 46:35–153.

(1917) 1919   Human Regions. *Scottish Geographical Magazine* 35:94–105. → A revision of the paper "Régions humaines" published in May 1917 in *Annales de géographie.*

1918   *Human Geography in Western Europe: A Study in Appreciation.* London: Williams & Norgate.

1922   *The Peoples of Europe.* Oxford Univ. Press.

1923   *The Races of England and Wales: A Survey of Recent Research.* London: Benn.

(1927) 1929   *The Races of Mankind.* Garden City, N.Y.: Doubleday.

1927–1956   PEAKE, HAROLD; and FLEURE, H. J. *The Corridors of Time.* 10 vols. New Haven: Yale Univ. Press. → Volume 1: *Apes and Men,* 1927. Volume 2: *Hunters and Artists,* 1927. Volume 3: *Peasants and Potters,* 1927. Volume 4: *Priests and Kings,* 1927. Volume 5: *The Steppe and the Sown,* 1928. Volume 6: *The Way of the Sea,* 1929. Volume 7: *Merchant Venturers in Bronze,* 1931. Volume 8: *The Horse and the Sword,* 1933. Volume 9: *The Law and the Prophets,* 1936. Volume 10: *Times and Places,* 1956.

1951   *A Natural History of Man in Britain: Conceived as a Study of Changing Relations Between Men and Environments.* London: Collins.

FLOURENS, PIERRE

Pierre Flourens (1794–1867) was a French neurophysiologist who came from Languedoc. His intellectual aptitude became apparent to his family when he was still very young, and his education was accelerated. By the time he was 15 he was a student at the celebrated faculty of medicine at Montpellier; he received his medical degree before he was 20.

Flourens was drawn to Paris, where he became a protégé of Georges Cuvier, who introduced him to the intellectual elite of the city. In 1828 he became deputy professor to Cuvier at the Collège de France; in 1830, professor at the Musée d'Histoire Naturelle; and in 1855, professor at the Collège de France. He also became a member of the Académie des Sciences in 1828 and was made perpetual secretary of that institution in 1833. In 1840 Flourens was elected to the Académie Française.

While still a young experimenter, Pierre Flourens devised a rigorous technique for investigating the brain. Before him, researchers had plunged a trocar into the brain through a trephined aperture that permitted no precise localization and that concealed pressures and hemorrhages from the investigator. Flourens carefully uncovered the brain and its meninges, avoiding damage to the blood vessels, and precisely excised the area to be studied.

In 1822 Flourens began to study the effects of extirpation of successive layers of the cerebellum. He found that at an intermediate point of extirpation a loss of stability and motor skill appears, as if the animal, although still able to walk, run, fly, or swim, has lost its "balance wheel." This was the original discovery of the function of coordination.

Flourens also studied the effects of eliminating one of the semicircular canals of the ear. The result was "an impetuous movement of the head," which shifted violently in the spatial plane of the canal in question. This again was an original discovery, opening up the further study of the semicircular canals as distinct from the cochlear apparatus.

Flourens also experimented on the brain stem. In the lower portion, in the medulla oblongata, he precisely delimitated the small point that is the seat of the "vital node," which if punctured causes instantaneous death by suddenly terminating respiration. In the upper portion a selective extirpation, anterior to the corpora quadrigemina, gave the first experimental indication of a relay in the central nervous apparatus of sight.

Finally, he made experiments on the cerebral hemispheres. This work was particularly difficult and time consuming. The terrain had been little explored by anatomists, and little was known of the connections and relays. Flourens' work was divided into two series: in one he performed complete ablations of the cerebral hemispheres; in the other, limited ablations by regions, sometimes by progressive removal.

The series of total ablations produced the following results: loss of intelligence and judgment; loss of all voluntary initiative; and relative diminution of instinctive activities, with retention of automatic motility and locomotion.

The series of limited ablations produced losses of the same kind, greater or lesser according to the region and the individual case; but these losses were only partial and proved to be capable of attenuation or compensation.

Above all, Flourens reached the fundamental conclusion that the degree of disorder in any particular faculty seemed to depend *only* on the quantity of cerebral tissue removed, regardless of its location. Generalizing from this fact, Flourens became opposed in principle to all attempts to establish "cerebral localizations"; and his own doctrine of the "homogeneity" of the brain became the focus of a historic dispute.

There is, to be sure, a case against Flourens, but it should be reviewed with detachment. In the first place, Flourens, like others at that time, failed to recognize the significance of certain paralytic effects because he did not experiment on primates. Next, it should be noted that the first indisputable demonstration of cerebral localization did not occur until 1870, after Flourens had died. Last, Flourens' conclusions with regard to the "homogeneity" of the brain and the theory that effects are related to the magnitude of the ablation were again based on experiments limited to lower mammals. Indeed, even so great an investigator as Lashley was similarly misled to conclude from his famous experiments on rats that there are "mass-action" effects.

Lately, with the refinement of physiological conceptions, the problem of homogeneity has again been raised, and some researchers have concluded that in the neocortex the highest functions of nervous integration go beyond "analytical" regional localization. These researchers explicitly evoke the memory of Flourens.

AUGUSTE TOURNAY

[*See also* NERVOUS SYSTEM; *and the biographies of* BROCA *and* LASHLEY.]

WORKS BY FLOURENS

(1824) 1842   *Recherches expérimentales sur les propriétés et les fonctions du système nerveux dans les animaux vertébrés.* Paris: Baillière.

(1841) 1858   *Histoire des travaux de Georges Cuvier.* 3d ed. Paris: Garnier. → First published as *Analyse raisonnée des travaux de G. Cuvier.*

(1844) 1850   *Histoire des travaux et des idées de Buffon.* 2d ed. Paris: Hachette. → First published as *Buffon.*

1856–1862   *Recueil des éloges historiques lus dans les séances publiques de l'Académie des Sciences.* 3 vols. Paris: Garnier.

SUPPLEMENTARY BIBLIOGRAPHY

[A Bibliography of] Marie Jean Pierre Flourens. 1868 Volume 2, pages 642–646 in Royal Society of London, *Catalogue of Scientific Papers (1800–1863).* London: Clay.

VULPIAN, M. 1888 Éloge historique de M. Flourens. Académie des Sciences, Paris, *Mémoires* 2d series 44:cxlix–clxxxiv.

FLOW-OF-FUNDS ACCOUNTS
See NATIONAL INCOME AND PRODUCT ACCOUNTS.

FOLK MEDICINE
See MEDICAL CARE, *article on* ETHNOMEDICINE.

FOLK MUSIC
See MUSIC, *article on* ETHNOMUSICOLOGY.

FOLK SOCIETY
See COMMUNITY–SOCIETY CONTINUA; PEASANTRY; REGION; TRIBAL SOCIETY; VILLAGE; *and the biographies of* ODUM *and* REDFIELD.

FOLKLORE

Folklore means folk learning; it comprehends all knowledge that is transmitted by word of mouth and all crafts and techniques that are learned by imitation or example, as well as the products of these crafts. Objects which are mass produced and knowledge which is acquired through books or formal education are a part of culture, which includes the total body of learning, but they are not folklore. In nonliterate societies folklore is virtually identical with culture, but in literate industrialized societies it is only a fragment of culture. Anthropologists and humanists have defined folklore differently, but their definitions are in fundamental agreement in excluding all learning that is transmitted by writing.

Folklore includes folk art, folk crafts, folk tools, folk costume, folk custom, folk belief, folk medicine, folk recipes, folk music, folk dance, folk games, folk gestures, and folk speech, as well as those verbal forms of expression which have been called folk literature but which are better described as verbal art. Verbal art, which includes such forms as folktales, legends, myths, proverbs, riddles, and poetry, has been the primary concern of folklorists from both the humanities and the social sciences since the beginnings of folklore as a field of study, and it is with this principal segment of folklore that this article is concerned.

European interest in folklore goes back at least to the sixteenth century and the age of exploration, but the modern study of folklore is generally considered to date from the early years of the nineteenth century, when the Grimm brothers began collecting German folktales in the field. The term folklore was first introduced into English in 1846 by William John Toms, who urged that accounts of "the manners, customs, observances, superstitions, ballads, proverbs, &c., of the olden time" be recorded in Britain for future study and for comparison with the materials which were being recorded in Germany by the Grimm brothers and other scholars.

Forms of verbal art

A variety of forms or genres of verbal art have been distinguished by folklorists, but neither the categories nor the terminology has been standardized. The following categories have proved useful.

Prose narrative. Myths, legends, and folktales are three important kinds of prose narrative or "tale," which is one of the most widespread forms of verbal art. The differences between myths, legends, and folktales are hotly disputed, but distinctions similar to those made here are recognized in some nonliterate societies and have long been employed by students of European folklore.

Myths. In the society in which they are told, myths are considered to be truthful accounts of what happened in the past. They are taught to be believed, and they can be cited as authority in answer to ignorance, doubt, or disbelief. Myths are the embodiment of dogma; they are usually sacred, and they are often associated with theology and ritual. Their characters are usually not human beings, but they often have human attributes. Myths account for the origin of the world, of mankind, of death; for characteristics of birds and animals; or for features of the landscape. They may recount the activities of the deities, their victories and defeats, their friendships and enmities, their love affairs, and their family relationships. They may "explain" details of ceremonial paraphernalia or ritual, or why taboos must be observed.

Legends. Like myths, legends are regarded as true by the narrator and his audience, but they are usually secular rather than sacred. Their principal characters are human, and they concern a period less remote than that of myths. They tell of migrations, wars and victories, deeds of past chiefs and kings, and succession in ruling dynasties. They include local tales of buried treasure, ghosts, fairies, and saints. Legends correspond to *Sagen* in German and *traditions populaires* in French.

Folktales. Prose narratives that are regarded as fiction are called folktales. They usually recount the adventures of animals or humans, but ogres and even deities may appear in them. A variety of subtypes can be distinguished, including drolls or noodles, trickster tales, tall tales, dilemma tales, formulistic tales, and moral tales or fables. Folktales are known as *Märchen* in German and as *contes populaires* in French. They have been known as fairy tales in English, but this is inappropriate both because fairies seldom appear in folktales and because narratives about fairies are usually regarded as true. Some folklorists use the term *Märchen* in English while employing "folktale" to include all three categories, but this is unnecessary when "prose narrative" better serves this purpose.

The distinction here between truth and fiction refers only to the beliefs of those who tell and hear these tales, and not to our beliefs, to historical or scientific fact, or to any ultimate judgment of truth and falsehood. In diffusing from one society to another, a myth or legend may be accepted without being believed, thus becoming a folktale in the borrowing society. Occasionally the reverse may also happen. In a period of rapid cultural change an entire belief system and its mythology may be discredited. Even in cultural isolation there may be some skeptics who do not accept the traditional system of belief. Nevertheless, it is important to know what the majority in a society believes to be true at any given point of time, for people act upon what they believe to be true.

Aphorisms. Proverbs, maxims, and similar terse, sententious sayings can be grouped together. Again usage varies, but in this article proverbs are distinguished from "proverbial phrases" or metaphorical comparisons and from maxims or mottoes like "Honesty is the best policy," which can be applied only in the literal sense. Proverbs have a deeper meaning, one which can be understood only through the analysis of the social situations to which they are appropriate. While prose narratives are world-wide in their distribution, proverbs are primarily an Old World genre, important throughout Europe, Asia, and Africa. Proverbs have been reported from the Americas and from Oceania, but not in large numbers and not with sufficient documentation to determine whether they are in fact proverbs or some other form of aphorism.

Riddles. Riddles differ from proverbs in that they require an answer, but they may also be concisely stated. African riddles are usually phrased as short declarative sentences, rather than as questions, so that they resemble proverbs in form and so that initially it may be difficult for an outsider to recognize the implicit question to which he is expected to provide the correct answer. Riddles vary considerably in their form of statement; and many European riddles take the form of rhyming poems, as in the case of Humpty Dumpty. Riddles again are primarily an Old World genre, although some have been recorded in other parts of the world.

Poetry, tongue-twisters, and verbal formulas. Poetry is widespread, at least in the form of song texts, but has received far less attention than the forms of verbal art mentioned thus far. Tongue-twisters have been recorded in various parts of the world but have been little studied. Incantations, invocations, passwords, greetings, and other verbal formulas have also been neglected by folklorists, although they appear in linguistic studies and in ethnographic descriptions of ritual and etiquette. Like tongue-twisters and some song texts, verbal formulas are often obscure in meaning and both difficult and almost pointless to translate. Comprehension is often less important than correct recitation, and verbatim accuracy may be essential to their religious, magical, or social effectiveness. In view of this it is not surprising that these forms have received less attention than prose narratives, proverbs, and riddles, in all of which both comprehension and communication are involved.

These forms of verbal art are not watertight compartments, as the case of rhyming riddles suggests. Dilemma tales, which are widespread in Africa, leave the solution up to the audience. Often classified with riddles, they are clearly a borderline form; they seem usually to call for argumentation rather than a correct answer. Trickster tales may be either myths or folktales; and ballads are narratives in songs. Some tales incorporate songs in the development of the plot, and others end by quoting a proverb to summarize a moral. The social significance of verbal art is stressed in the following section, but its aesthetic attributes are also important. Their study provides a common meeting ground for the humanities and the social sciences that is rarely if ever equaled in other data on human behavior. Language imposes limitations on the artist in folklore as the medium of expression does in the graphic and plastic arts, music, or the dance. In the case of verbal art the medium of expression is the spoken word, and verbal art is subject to the limitations of the phonetics, grammar, and vocabulary of the language. For this reason linguists are best qualified to consider the question of style, which can be defined as what the artist is able to achieve within the limitations of his techniques and media. Linguists have, in fact, contributed several important discussions of this subject. More often they have recorded prose narratives as a convenient means of collecting texts for linguistic analysis, with the result that many of the most accurately recorded and carefully transcribed collections of verbal art are to be found in linguistic studies.

Some functions of verbal art

Amusement is an obvious function of folktales, riddles, and tongue-twisters, but verbal art has other, more important functions.

Education. In nonliterate societies verbal art plays a major and often explicitly recognized role in education. It is important to learn myths and legends because they contain information that is believed to be true. Proverbs are often characterized as the distilled wisdom of past generations. Learning the values of a culture as they are expressed in proverbs is similarly considered important in its own right; without some command of proverbs, individuals in many African societies cannot effectively fulfill their roles as adults. Whereas African proverbs are considered to be the province of adults, riddles are for children. Riddles teach the characteristics of plants, animals, and other things in nature, as well as some features of technology, material culture, and social structure. Even folktales that are regarded as fictitious are recognized by Africans as important in the education of children, because so many of them are moral tales. The importance of verbal art in education has been noted in nonliterate societies throughout the world. Verbal art provides a medium for the transmission of knowledge, values, and attitudes from one generation to another and thus contributes to the continuity of culture.

Social control. Verbal art helps to maintain conformity to cultural values and accepted patterns of behavior. It is widely used to express social approval and disapproval, to apply social pressure, and to exercise social control. Proverbs, songs of ridicule, and even riddles and folktales may be used to criticize those who deviate from the accepted norms and social conventions. On the other hand, proverbs, praise names, and praise songs give recognition and reward to those who conform. African proverbs are especially important in this respect. When action is contemplated that may lead to social friction, open hostilities, or direct punishment by society, proverbs can be used to express warning, defiance, or derision of a rival or enemy. They may also express advice, counsel, or warning to a friend.

Because of the high regard in which they are held, and because they are considered especially appropriate to adult life, African proverbs are highly effective instruments of social control. Because they express the morals and ethics of a society, they are convenient standards for appraising behavior in terms of the approved norms. And because they are pungently, sententiously, and wittily stated, they are ideally suited for commenting on the behavior of others.

Social authority. Verbal art serves to validate social institutions and religious rituals. Malinowski showed how, in the Trobriand Islands of the Pacific, myth provides a warrant and a charter for magic, ceremony, ritual, and social structure. Myths can be cited as authority on questions of religious belief and ritual procedure, and to justify rights to land, fishing grounds, social position, tribute, or political authority. This important function can be seen in many societies, but it is not confined to myth. When dissatisfaction with or skepticism of an accepted pattern is expressed, or when doubts about it arise, there is usually a myth or legend to validate it; however, a moral folktale or a proverb may serve the same purpose.

Sociopsychological function. Verbal art provides a psychological release from the restrictions imposed on the individual by society. Ever since Greek myths were recorded in writing, it has been recognized that characters in myths do things that are regarded as shocking, sinful, and even criminal in daily life. Myths and folktales provide an opportunity for people to talk about kinds of behavior that society prohibits them from indulging in, and about kinds of success that they can scarcely hope to achieve themselves.

This can be illustrated in our own society by "dirty jokes" and, formerly, mother-in-law jokes. In the case of the latter, their popularity has declined as fewer young couples live with their in-laws and the family is increasingly fragmented. In American Indian societies that practice mother-in-law avoidance, the trickster violates his own mother-in-law. Tales of polygynous marriages feature far more prominently among the monogamous Pueblo groups than in societies where polygyny is accepted. In West Africa the Ashanti and Dahomeans recognize the value of being able to criticize and laugh at authority and other matters, both secular and sacred, in a way they cannot do normally, through folktales and songs. Even riddles and tongue-twisters, although considered the province of children, sometimes involve sexual references that are considered off-color by adults.

The familiar theme of rags to riches, the widespread tale of the magic flight or of the seven-league boots, and tales of resurrection after death are also meaningful in terms of psychological release. Viewed in this light, verbal art reveals man's attempt to escape in fantasy from the restrictions of his geographic environment, from his own biological limitations as a member of the human species, and from the repressions imposed upon him by society, whether these result from social and economic inequalities, from sexual taboos, or from the Ashanti taboo against laughing at a person afflicted with yaws.

Cultural continuity. When the functions of education, control, authority, and release are viewed together, it can be seen that verbal art has the broader function of maintaining the continuity and stability of culture. It is used to inculcate customs and ethical standards in the young, to reward the adult with praise when he conforms or to punish him with criticism or ridicule when he deviates, to provide him with rationalizations when he questions the institutions and conventions of his society, and at the same time to provide him with a compensatory escape from the hardships and injustices of everyday life. It operates to ensure cultural continuity from generation to generation through its role in education, by emphasizing conformity to the accepted cultural norms, and through the validation of social and religious institutions. By providing a psychological escape from the institutions and norms which it sanctions and enforces and by providing discontented individuals an opportunity to talk about forbidden forms of behavior, rather than practicing them, verbal art preserves the established customs and institutions from direct attack and change.

Political uses of verbal arts. Despite the fact that verbal art serves to continue and stabilize culture, it has also been used for the purposes of political propaganda and social change. During the emergence of the independent nations of Africa, myths, legends, and song texts have been used to promote ethnic unity, regionalism, nationalism, anticolonialism, and pan-Africanism.

The Yoruba creation myth provided the basis for the Society of the Children of Oduduwa (Egbe Omo Oduduwa), established for the purpose of uniting the people of the Western Region of Nigeria, and Bakongo mythology has been used for political purposes by Joseph Kasavubu's Abako party in the Congo. In Katanga a common myth has been cited by politicians to show why the

Lunda, Luena, and Chokwe should unite in support of Tshombe and his Conakat party, or, conversely, why the Luena and Chokwe should join in opposition to the Lunda. African praise songs have been adapted to honor new political leaders; songs of allusion have been used to criticize colonial officials and rival politicians; and the hymn "God Bless Africa," first sung publicly in 1899, has been adopted as a closing anthem by the African National Congress and as the unofficial national anthem of several African countries, and it was sung at the 1958 Conference of Independent African States in Accra, Ghana.

In the Soviet Union in 1936, the Communist party "discovered" the effectiveness of folklore as a political weapon. Scholars reversed earlier theories that regarded folklore as a product of the upper classes filtering down to the lower classes, and claimed that the working people were the creators of folklore.

Folktales and songs have been used to advance the theme of the class struggle in the Soviet Union, in China, in Cuba, and elsewhere. The Nazis used Teutonic mythology to promote their idea of a master race. In earlier times Krylov used fables to needle the Russian aristocracy, and the first Chinese edition of *Aesop's Fables* was suppressed by officials who recognized their satire and suspected that they had been invented locally. Further study of the political uses of verbal art, which have only recently been recognized by folklorists, will undoubtedly reveal other instances of this kind.

The recording of verbal art is a well-recognized field technique in linguistic and anthropological research, and it can be helpful in studying political attitudes. Verbal art provides useful materials for school curricula and important data for the study of law, values, psychology, and history in nonliterate societies. Writing and industrialization have undermined its social significance far more in urban United States than in most literate societies, but they have never destroyed verbal art or the other segments of folklore.

WILLIAM BASCOM

[*Directly related are the entries* COMMUNICATION; DRAMA; HISTORY, *article on* ETHNOHISTORY; MUSIC, *article on* ETHNOMUSICOLOGY. *Other relevant material may be found in* CRAFTS; HISTORIOGRAPHY; MYTH AND SYMBOL; PRIMITIVE ART.]

BIBLIOGRAPHY

BASCOM, WILLIAM (1954) 1965 Four Functions of Folklore. Pages 279–298 in Alan Dundes (editor), *The Study of Folklore*. Englewood Cliffs, N.J.: Prentice-Hall. → First published in Volume 67 of the *Journal of American Folklore*.

BASCOM, WILLIAM 1955 Verbal Art. *Journal of American Folklore* 68:245–252.

BASCOM, WILLIAM 1965a Folklore and Literature. Pages 469–490 in Robert A. Lystad (editor), *The African World: A Survey of Social Research*. New York: Praeger. → A bibliography appears on pages 558–560.

BASCOM, WILLIAM 1965b The Forms of Folklore: Prose Narratives. *Journal of American Folklore* 78:3–20.

BENEDICT, RUTH 1935 *Zuni Mythology*. 2 vols. Columbia University Contributions to Anthropology, Vol. 21. New York: Columbia Univ. Press.

DORSON, RICHARD M. 1959 *American Folklore*. Univ. of Chicago Press.

FISCHER, JOHN L. 1963 The Socio-psychological Analysis of Folktales. *Current Anthropology* 4:235–295.

Funk & Wagnalls Standard Dictionary of Folklore, Mythology and Legend. Edited by Maria Leach. 2 vols. 1949 New York: Funk & Wagnalls.

GRIMM, JAKOB; and GRIMM, WILHELM (1812–1815) 1948 *Grimm's Fairy Tales*. Complete ed., rev. Translated by Margaret Hunt; revised by James Stern. London: Routledge. → First published in German.

HERSKOVITS, MELVILLE J.; and HERSKOVITS, FRANCES S. 1958 *Dahomean Narrative: A Cross-cultural Analysis*. Northwestern University African Studies, No. 1. Evanston, Ill.: Northwestern Univ. Press.

JACOBS, MELVILLE 1959 *The Content and Style of Oral Literature: Clackamas Chinook Myths and Tales*. Wenner-Gren Foundation for Anthropological Research Publications in Anthropology, No. 26. Univ. of Chicago Press.

MALINOWSKI, BRONISLAW (1926) 1948 Myth in Primitive Psychology. Pages 72–124 in Bronislaw Malinowski, *Magic, Science and Religion and Other Essays*. Glencoe, Ill.: Free Press; Boston: Beacon. → A paperback edition was published in 1954 by Doubleday.

OPLER, MORRIS E. 1940 *Myths and Legends of the Lipan Apache Indians*. Memoirs of the American Folk-Lore Society, Vol. 36. Philadelphia: The Society.

RATTRAY, R. S. 1930 *Akan-Ashanti Folk-tales*. Oxford: Clarendon.

RAUM, O. F. 1940 *Chaga Childhood: A Description of Indigenous Education in an East African Tribe*. Oxford Univ. Press.

THOMPSON, STITH 1946 *The Folktale*. New York: Dryden.

THOMPSON, STITH 1953 Advances in Folklore Studies. Pages 587–596 in International Symposium on Anthropology, New York, 1952, *Anthropology Today: An Encyclopedic Inventory*. Univ. of Chicago Press.

FOLKWAYS

See the biography of SUMNER.

FOLLETT, MARY PARKER

Mary Parker Follett (1868–1933) was a social philosopher who attempted to apply the principles she deduced to practical problems in business, politics, and social work. She was born a member of an old Quincy, Massachusetts, family and was educated at Thayer Academy, Radcliffe College, and the Sorbonne. While still a student at Radcliffe she spent the year 1890–1891 at Newnham College, Cambridge, England, where she formed many lifelong friendships. Her intellectual contribution to the social sciences is contained in two books, *The New State* (1918) and *Creative Experience* (1924), and a posthumous collection of papers, *Dynamic Administration,* published in 1942 (see 1926–1930). She died in London.

Among the earliest to see the importance of the group in understanding an individual and his thoughts, she rejected schemes which postulate a dualism between the individual and society, as well as most other forms of causal interaction between these two entities, in favor of the notion of integration.

The New State is a plea for a political order based on an interlocking hierarchy of membership groups, beginning at the neighborhood level. The unit of the community is the socialized individual, that is to say, the individual who, through associational membership, has become a fully participating member of society. This is the new individualism of the new state. In the ideal democracy, therefore, integration of the individual personality and the society is so complete that no conflict, either psychological or social, is conceivable. "Democracy does not register various opinions; it is an attempt to create unity" (1918, p. 209).

In *Creative Experience* Follett discussed the prevention and elimination of the failure of integration, that is, of social conflict. She was particularly interested in problems of social change and conflict in small-scale social systems, such as factories, wage boards, regulating commissions, community centers, and neighborhoods.

The concept of circular response, developed in *Creative Experience* and in later essays and lectures, is her principal contribution to the analysis of failures of integration. Circular response rests upon the theory that the unit of social analysis is the pattern of relations between actors, conceived as a single situation produced by a union of their interests (1924, p. 188). No response by an actor is wholly predictable for he must continually modify his behavior to adjust to the expected responses of others, who constitute his environment. This modulation of both the activity and the sentiments of the actors in an environment constitutes circular response. As Follett put it: "The most fundamental thought about all this is that reaction is always reaction to a relating. . . . I never react to you but to you-plus-me; or to be more accurate, it is I-plus-you reacting to You-plus-me" (1924, p. 62). Somewhat similar theories have been used by Foote and

Cottrell (1955), but their chosen unit of analysis is the episode or event rather than the single social act.

Thus, the only good solution to social conflict is not compromise, not conquest, but integration. Integration in this context means the creation of a novel solution that penalizes no one and that becomes the only sure base for progress toward an ideal democracy. If integration is to be achieved, various forms of coordination must be introduced as fundamental principles of organization: (1) *direct contact* between the responsible people who have to carry out policies, rather than hierarchical control; (2) *early contact* between these responsible people, so that policy may be created by them, rather than later meetings that can only try to resolve differences between policies already evolved by isolated groups; (3) the reciprocal relating of all factors in a situation, that is, equal attention to all the variables in the social system.

Coordination in these various forms is a continuing process, since in any complex social environment there exist many points of creativity, and established policies can never be executed as designed but must constantly be reformed in consonance with basic goals.

The sources of Follett's ideas are to be found in the thinking of her own time: she borrowed much from Cooley's concept of the primary group, which became her ideal social setting, and from G. H. Mead's analysis of the "I" and the "me." Her work also reflects the psychological approach to politics of such English political philosophers as Graham Wallas as well as the emphasis on purpose or will or thought in contemporary idealist political thinking. Follett did not appreciate the role of institutional structures, bureaucracy, or force. She firmly rejected Durkheim's proposition that social facts may be conceived of as "things," and her approach to the concept of the state was unsophisticated. She never mentioned the existence of legitimate power or the prevalence of legitimized and idealized peace that has its source in bloody conquest.

Her early papers were in political analysis, but she later found that she could more conveniently study the operation of political influences in industrial systems. Her positions in the Department of Vocational Guidance of the Boston school system and on the Massachusetts Minimum Wage Board gave her access to basic data with which to test her generalizations. She never presented her data in the form of tables, preferring to communicate by generalization and illustrative story.

Professional sociologists have tended to ignore Follett's writings, although they contain many interesting and sensible statements on the subjects of primary group analysis and the creative process in society. Nor are there many references to her work in writings on industrial relations or political science. Curiously, the pluralistic concept of the state is occasionally attributed to her by political scientists (for example, de Grazia 1952), although she had been highly critical of that concept in *The New State:* her emphasis on integrative behavior is not compatible with the concept of the state as an amalgam of discrete political groups.

JOHN MOGEY

[*See also* CONFLICT, *article on* POLITICAL ASPECTS; GENERAL WILL; POLITICAL PROCESS; REPRESENTATION, *article on* THEORY; *and the biographies of* COOLEY; MEAD; WALLAS.]

WORKS BY FOLLETT

1892   Henry Clay as Speaker of the United States House of Representatives. American Historical Association, *Annual Report* [1891]:255–265.
(1896) 1909   *The Speaker of the House of Representatives.* New York: Longmans.
1918   *The New State: Group Organization, the Solution of Popular Government.* New York: Longmans.
(1924) 1951   *Creative Experience.* Gloucester, Mass.: Smith.
(1926–1930) 1942   *Dynamic Administration: The Collected Papers of Mary Parker Follett.* New York: Harper. → Contains a bibliography.

SUPPLEMENTARY BIBLIOGRAPHY

DE GRAZIA, ALFRED (1952) 1962   *Politics and Government: The Elements of Political Science.* 2 vols. New ed., rev. New York: Collier. → First published as *The Elements of Political Science.*
FOOTE, NELSON N.; and COTTRELL, LEONARD S.   1955   *Identity and Interpersonal Competence: A New Direction in Family Research.* Univ. of Chicago Press.
WOOD, ARTHUR E.   1926   The Social Philosophy of Mary P. Follett. *Social Forces* 4:759–769.

FOOD

I. WORLD PROBLEMS   *Nevin S. Scrimshaw*
II. CONSUMPTION PATTERNS   *Yehudi A. Cohen*

I
WORLD PROBLEMS

Low per capita food production and high rates of population growth in underdeveloped areas cause food shortages in many less developed countries, particularly in tropical and semitropical regions. Even though 60 to 80 per cent of the people in these countries are engaged in farming, their productivity is so low that it does not meet the needs of the population. By contrast, in some industrialized countries less than 8 per cent of the population is engaged in an agricultural industry that produces vast surpluses. Although these surpluses help to meet the needs of many other parts of the world, malnutrition is widespread and persistent in the underdeveloped areas and is responsible for much of the high mortality in these areas, whether by itself or in combination with infections of various types.

Factors limiting adequate food production are primarily social and economic rather than physical. The lack of knowledge and the illiteracy of the rural population complicate attempts to increase food production as well as to control population in underdeveloped countries. Long-standing customs, limited agricultural training activities, and inadequate storage and distribution facilities help to perpetuate low agricultural production in these areas. Lack of the tools of scientific agriculture and scarcity of money or credit for their purchase are major additional factors. Moreover, this inadequacy of the food supply is part of a vicious circle that keeps productivity low: malnourished populations are more vulnerable to disease and less capable of sustained work than are well-nourished populations.

Continued increases in food production can be anticipated in most of the less developed countries although in many areas they will not be large enough to maintain adequate per capita food supplies. The additional food necessary to give at least a subsistence ration to most persons is likely to continue to come from the food surpluses of the industrialized countries and to be augmented by the exploitation of new protein sources.

The over-all world food supply is failing to keep pace with population growth but is not yet limiting the world's explosive population increase (Food and Agriculture Organization . . . 1966).

Food and history.   The replacement of exclusive dependence upon hunting, fishing, and gathering by the beginnings of agriculture was the first great step in human development. The rate and scope of social evolution have depended to a major extent on the development of more effective means of obtaining food. In primitive cultures, man's struggle for food consumes most of his time, thought, and energy. The creation of a surplus of food over and above what is needed to live leads to successive refinements in the subdivision of labor, which in turn make possible social and technical advances and thus the production of even greater quantities of food.

For millennia the food supply was a major factor limiting the growth of human populations and determining their density in any particular area. It is only in the last century that improvements in agricultural production have become sufficiently widespread to remove food as the limiting factor in most population growth. In combination with improved control and prevention of infectious and other diseases, an exponential increase in numbers of people has been the result.

Pressure for good agricultural land for the production of food has been a major factor in the turbulent warfare of the historical record. Crop failures have resulted in population losses through death and emigration, which have impoverished and impeded the social and economic development of populations and even whole countries. For example, Ireland has never recovered from the high losses from starvation and emigration as a direct consequence of the potato famine of the 1840s; the political history of the United States and Canada has perhaps been equally changed by hundreds of thousands of Irish immigrants. Another example of the importance of food problems is found in the major political and economic consequences of the failure of agricultural production in the communist countries.

Contemporary problems

Paradoxically, the principal nutrition problem of the industrialized countries today is one of overeating, with a consequent increase in obesity, cardiovascular disease, diabetes, and hypertension. [See OBESITY.]

In contrast, nutritional difficulties in underdeveloped countries are similar to those experienced in the industrialized countries 50 to 100 years ago. Children under five years of age and, to a lesser extent, pregnant and nursing mothers are most affected.

Common deficiencies.   The most common severe nutritional deficiencies are those of protein and vitamin A. The best indicator of the prevalence of protein deficiency ("kwashiorkor") is the mortality rate for children one to five years of age, which is commonly 20 to 50 times higher in underdeveloped countries than in areas like western Europe, the United States, Australia, New Zealand, and Japan. Infant mortality rates (deaths of children under one year of age) are two to four times higher in most less developed countries than in those that are industrialized. Early weaning with improper substitutes and inadequate supplementation of breast milk are important factors in high mortality rates for infants who survive the dangerous first months of life.

Vitamin A deficiency is also most common among preschool children; it causes severe eye lesions which often result in blindness. In Indonesia and other countries of southeast Asia, deaths from secondary infection are particularly common in children with vitamin A deficiency. This deficiency could be readily prevented by the green and yellow vegetables that are, or could be, widely available in most countries.

Another common problem—marasmus, or partial starvation—is seen most often among infants who have been prematurely weaned and fed watery gruels that are deficient in both calories and protein. A form of acute thiamine deficiency (infantile beriberi) is a cause of death among nursing infants in some southeast Asian countries, where a polished rice diet results in thiamine (vitamin B_1) deficiency in mothers. Beriberi also still occurs among many adults in these areas. Pellagra, caused by inadequate niacin and tryptophan intake, is seen in those populations of Africa that subsist on maize as the principal staple, but it is seldom seen in the maize-eating populations of Latin America, where additional niacin is provided by both beans and coffee.

Women experiencing repeated cycles of pregnancy and lactation are likely to develop iron deficiency anemia, loss of bone calcium, and reduced lean body mass. Malnutrition in other adults is less common, except in times of famine, although individuals unable to obtain work, or too old or sick to work, may be seriously undernourished because they cannot afford to buy adequate food. Alcoholism is a common cause of malnutrition in both underdeveloped and industrialized countries because money is spent on alcohol rather than on proper food.

The cost of malnutrition.   The cost of malnutrition to less developed areas is exceedingly high; it includes the waste of resources in rearing infants who die before they can become useful citizens and the reduced working capacity of malnourished adults. From a quarter to a third or more of the children die before they reach school age, largely from infections that would not be fatal to a well-nourished child or from clinical malnutrition precipitated by a prior episode of acute infectious disease (Scrimshaw 1966). Nearly all children among the less privileged populations of underdeveloped countries show retarded growth and development at the time they reach school age; and although they are rarely seriously malnourished during school years, they do not make up for the deficit acquired during preschool years. Recent evidence suggests that the retardation in physical development in infancy is paralleled by impaired mental development, which is probably permanent. This means that the future development of a country is compromised by serious malnutrition in young children. Moreover, attempts to provide adequate medical care are complicated and made more costly by both the greater amount and the longer duration of illness of both malnourished children and adults.

An unfortunate aspect of malnutrition in adults is that the workers so adapt themselves to malnutrition by reduced vitality and activity that they scarcely realize they are underfed. The final result is lethargy, lack of drive, and loss of initiative. For both industrial and farm workers it leads to absenteeism because of sickness and to higher accident rates because of early fatigue. In general, the countries of the world with the lowest per capita consumption of food are also those where the efficiency of the workers is lowest.

Reasons for malnutrition

Although for the world as a whole the long-term trend of per capita food production has been upward, there has been a decline in per capita food production in communist Asia and in India, as well as in many parts of Latin America and southeast Asia (Food and Agriculture Organization of the United Nations 1963). If the high population growth rates in the less developed countries increase as projected, still more of these countries will soon be unable to maintain present levels of per capita food production. It is important to recognize that increased food needs will continue to arise not only from a growing population but also from greater per capita income. As people in the less developed countries improve their financial status, much of the increase is spent for food. In some countries where food production has not kept pace, this situation has led to a substantial rise in imports of food, and in others the effect of growth in income has been balanced by rising food prices. Either result has serious economic and political consequences.

Using food shipments from regions of high per capita productivity to meet part of the food needs of the increased numbers of people in the less developed countries is not a satisfactory solution, because it involves considerable problems of transporting and financing, which are further complicated by political issues. Ideally, adequate food production should be achieved in each area, unless foreign exchange is available for food purchases from cash crop or industrial exports.

Physical waste. Unfortunately, the largest loss of food to insects and rodents occurs in those countries with the greatest food shortages. For example, in some of the grain storage bins of India, the loss to rodents alone is over 30 per cent. Conservative official estimates of total such *preventable* food losses in India indicate that they are greater than the present large annual food deficit and constitute at least 25 per cent of the total grain production; if such losses were prevented, India would have food for export.

In tropical regions of the food-short countries, mold causes additional spoilage. In the case of peanuts, an important source of protein in Africa and India, one type of mold (*Aspergillus flavus*) produces a substance called "aflatoxin," which even in trace amounts is highly carcinogenic for experimental animals. This mold also grows freely on cereal grains, sweet potatoes, and legumes, and even slightly moldy food is likely to be unfit for human consumption. Lack of refrigeration also results in spoilage of fruits and vegetables, which are a glut on the market when in season and unavailable or prohibitively expensive the rest of the time.

The great majority of the malnourished populations of the world depends on either a cereal staple such as rice, wheat, or corn, or starchy roots such as manioc or potatoes. The former are more nutritious, but the latter produce more calories per acre, require less labor, and are somewhat easier to store without serious loss.

Cultural waste. It is a mistake to conclude that the malnutrition of less developed areas is solely due to inadequate food production, lack of storage facilities, or even lack of purchasing power. Ignorance of the nutritional needs of young children and lack of understanding of the relationship between food and health are of equal or greater importance. The failure to give any food supplement to breast-fed infants before 9 to 12 months of age in many countries; the use of rice-water, barley-water, cornstarch or even sugar-water as a weaning food; and the variety of taboos surrounding the giving of eggs to young children are examples of common practices which lead to malnutrition and death of children under five years of age, even among families whose older children and adults do not suffer from malnutrition. In underdeveloped countries, one often sees a critically malnourished child with a woman who is wearing new clothes and jewelry and who is totally unaware of the true reason her child is dying.

The various erroneous beliefs surrounding the proper feeding of children with infections are often the most important factors in the chain of multiple causation leading to acute nutritional disease. For example, in both south India and Central America children with measles are given water in which a small amount of cereal and various local herbs has been cooked—a diet grossly deficient in protein and calories. Such beliefs also cause the family to spend money for charms, ceremonies, and useless proprietary medicines.

In underdeveloped areas the seemingly irrational beliefs regarding food may be quite elaborate. Particularly common is the practice of classifying foods and prohibiting certain combinations. In Peru, for instance, foods are "hot, cold, heavy, or light." A complex of beliefs indicates when and to whom a given class of foods can be fed. Certain classes of food are considered appropriate or inappropriate, without relation to their nutritive value, at times such as pregnancy or during one or another illness. Few societies recognize the true relationship of foods to health.

Improving production and conservation

The yield increases of the industrialized countries are due to chemicals, mechanization, good seeds and animal breeds, and their effective use. Chemicals and machinery could achieve miracles in the less developed areas, but they require greater capital investment and know-how than are presently available. Selective breeding of plants and animals could also be extremely effective: types of both have been developed which are much more productive and sometimes also more resistant to disease. For example, virus-resisting potatoes, rust-resistant wheat, hybrid corn and, most recently, high lysine corn and gossypol-free cottonseed are part of the "miracle" of food production in the industrialized countries, along with greatly improved breeds of poultry, cattle, sheep, and swine.

Some of these superior varieties can be introduced directly into less developed countries, but most require additional research for their adaptation to different environmental conditions. Agricultural research and its application through agricultural extension have been a major factor in high yields in the developed countries. Production of most improved varieties requires considerable knowledge of scientific agriculture as well as much initial capital investment, and the education of government officials is also an important factor. Poorly informed administrative and policy officials often block the efforts of extension workers and farmers by ill-considered taxes or import controls, unwise emphasis on cash crops, neglect of agricultural research, indifference or hostility to producer cooperatives, and failure to provide for rural credit.

Limiting physical waste. Solution of the food problems of less developed areas will require extensive improvements in the conservation and handling of food as well as in its production. Of first importance is reducing preventable food losses through the use of insecticides and rodenticides, construction of rat-proof and dry storage facilities, fumigation of grain, and improved distribution by using protective packaging materials and more rapid transportation. Controlled atmosphere and cold storage facilities are useful for some seasonal and highly perishable crops, and refrigeration is essential for the proper conservation of meat, poultry, and fish.

Smoking and salting are simple and effective means of preserving meat and fish for adult consumption, but in general they do not provide food that is suitable as major protein sources for infants and young children. Sun-drying is widely used for many foods, but this has serious limitations in a hot, moist climate, especially when proper storage conditions are unavailable. Using artificial heat is more costly and involves the same problems of storage and packaging. Thermal processing or canning represents a big economic step because it requires sealable containers as well as higher temperatures. In industrialized countries spray-drying has been extensively employed for milk and a variety of other products that are fluid before processing. Obviously, the handling of frozen foods in tropical underdeveloped countries in the early stages of industrial development poses problems that preclude the widespread application of freezing as a method of food storage. Freeze-drying seems too expensive to apply to food staples, but the shelf life of certain types of food may be extended by low doses of ionizing radiation. Chemical preservatives and other additives that have been important in the efficient utilization of the food supply in modern nations are also needed in underdeveloped countries. Examples are antioxidants to slow down the process by which fats become rancid and propionates to inhibit molds.

New food sources. Nutritional requirements can be satisfied by an adequate source of calories and sufficient quantities of each of the essential amino acids, fatty acids, vitamins, and minerals in any utilizable form, whether natural or synthetic. There are many compelling reasons why most nutrients will continue to be supplied largely from plants and animals for a long time to come, but new and exotic sources of food are being explored.

Oilseed meals, such as cottonseed flour, can serve as valuable new sources of proteins provided that they are carefully processed. Furthermore, much nutritional benefit can be derived from the enrichment of certain foods. For example, the quality of most protein-containing foods of vegetable origin can be improved by combining them with foods of complementary essential amino acid content or by adding the missing amino acids in synthetic form. Other examples include the enrichment of salt with potassium iodide for the prevention of goiter, a measure which has proved as practical and effective in Guatemala and Colombia as in the United States and Switzerland; the prevention of beriberi and pellagra by the addition of B-complex vitamins to cereal products; the enrichment of margarine and skim milk with vitamins A and D so that they are nutritionally acceptable substitutes for butter and whole milk, respectively, and the addition of the amino acid lysine to wheat and wheat flour.

In a number of underdeveloped areas where milk cannot be depended upon to furnish needed protein, vegetable mixtures that were developed to serve this purpose are proving to be commercially successful and are bringing about important nutritional improvements. Furthermore, the world catch of marine fish has increased enormously in recent years, and processes have been developed for the production of a low-cost fish protein concentrate. In the meantime, fresh, canned, and smoked fish are compensating for the protein inadequacy of the diet in Japan and a number of other countries. Attempts to use algae, green leaves, and even grass as sources of protein have met with little success because of poor palatability and excessive costs, but this could be changed by technological developments. Other possible protein sources are food yeast, which can be grown with several inexpensive carbohydrates, such as molasses and sulfite liquor of the paper industry. Other microorganisms can be produced by using petroleum by-products or natural gas as their source of energy.

Synthetic foods. Palatable synthetic foods simulating bacon, hamburger, ham, chicken, fish, and scallops have already been developed from soy protein isolate. Protein fibers are spun like nylon and reconstituted into textured foods that can be flavored in any desired manner. At present these are as expensive as the foods they simulate, but as the number of mouths to feed increases and costs of the process are brought down they are likely to prove useful. The nutritional needs of the body can already be reduced to chemically known substances that can be synthesized or extracted from natural products. To meet the demands of an enormously increased world population, the eventual use of wholly synthetic foods seems likely. Ironically, most of the efforts to achieve this are being stimulated by the nutritional requirements of man in space rather than by terrestrial food problems.

Social science research. Much of the malnutrition in the world today, particularly among young children, can be prevented by changes in feeding practices. Increased production and purchasing power will not alone automatically eliminate malnutrition; too often the additional money is spent on soft drinks, alcohol, or other consumer items that will not improve inadequate diets. Nutritional education must be a major part of efforts to eliminate malnutrition.

There is much that the social scientist can contribute to solving world food problems. Persons responsible for nutrition and health education need to understand the reasons for food practices and beliefs, yet these have too often been neglected by social scientists even when studying a culture in detail. Even less research has been done on the most appropriate and effective means of inculcating food habits in various cultures (See Mead 1943; 1964).

An exception was the introduction in Guatemala of the low-cost protein-rich vegetable mixture, Incaparina, which benefited from preliminary field studies by anthropologists. The success of this product is attributable in large part to its introduction as a variant on the traditional *atole* rather than as a new food product. It will not always be possible to use this technique, for new foods often will have no local counterpart. The guidance of social scientists who have made advance studies will be particularly needed for the introduction of products that have never before been used for human feeding, such as fish protein concentrate or bacterial protein.

There is also need to study changes in food habits or attempts to impose new foods, for their impact on other aspects of culture. Gifts of unfamiliar surplus foods may simply be unused or they can upset patterns of life that are oriented about indigenous staples. Authoritarian methods of forcing nutritional standards on a child or a community may endanger cooperation in other important matters.

A major obstacle to introducing agricultural techniques is the lack of local technological knowledge and competence. Agricultural extension agents and teachers often attempt to induce change blindly without understanding the existing beliefs and traditions that they are trying to alter. Similarly, although technology is making rapid progress in devising practical techniques for family planning, motivating people to make use of them remains a problem. In order to make such programs more effective, there is an urgent need for studies of the ways in which the desired changes can be achieved.

The agricultural revolution

The world is now in the midst of a revolution in food production, conservation, and distribution that is as far-reaching in its effects on societies as the original development of agriculture; it is comparable in significance to the industrial revolution, with which it is closely allied. Farm production in the industrialized countries has risen spectacularly within a few decades, simultaneously with a sharp reduction in the numbers of persons engaged in farming and the actual amount of land under cultivation. This has meant food for greatly increased numbers of people. Equally important, the workers no longer needed in agriculture are freed for the production of consumer goods and services to an extent beyond any previously seen in history. It is this freedom which has made possible modern economic and social development.

With the need for farm labor decreasing, the cities of the industrialized countries have received the increase in population. Nevertheless, food production in these countries is rising despite the diminishing farm population, thus providing enough food for the growing urban markets. In many of the less developed countries, population is outgrowing available land, and people from the rural areas are migrating to the cities in ever larger numbers. However, in most such countries farming remains largely at subsistence levels, and transportation and storage facilities are inadequate to meet the demands of the cities for food distribution.

An efficient agriculture thus becomes a prime requisite of economic and social development. Subsistence agriculture adds nothing to the national economy; and until enough farm families contribute to meeting the food needs of urban families, the manpower and capital required for industrialization will not be available. Once food production rises sufficiently to provide a firm basis for economic and social development, the process tends to accelerate. Research results accumulate and are applied; capital is amassed and invested; machines are constructed and put to work. As the process continues, more and more people are available, educated, and trained for the complex tasks of a technically advanced society. Unless the health and intelligence of the people are such that they can make good use of modern knowledge and tech-

nology, no amount of investment in material things can ensure satisfactory social and economic development. A good food supply is needed to prevent excessive morbidity and mortality from disease as well as the poor learning and working capacity that result from malnutrition. At present, the growing per capita shortage of food in many countries will continue to thwart the ambitions and make a mockery of the goals of economic planners.

NEVIN S. SCRIMSHAW

[*Other relevant material may be found in* AGRICULTURE; MORTALITY; POPULATION, *article on* POPULATION GROWTH; TECHNICAL ASSISTANCE; *and in the biography of* SAUER.]

BIBLIOGRAPHY

ALTSCHUL, AARON M. 1965 *Proteins: Their Chemistry and Politics.* New York: Basic Books.

BROWN, LESTER R. 1963 *Man, Land and Food: Looking Ahead at World Needs.* U.S. Department of Agriculture, Foreign Agricultural Economic Report No. 11. Washington: Government Printing Office.

BROWN, LESTER R. 1965 *Increasing World Food Output.* U.S. Department of Agriculture, Foreign Agricultural Economic Report No. 25. Washington: Government Printing Office.

BURGESS, ANNE; and DEAN, REGINALD F. A. (editors) 1962 *Malnutrition and Food Habits: Report of an International and Interprofessional Conference.* New York: Macmillan.

CONFERENCE ON MEETING PROTEIN NEEDS OF INFANTS AND PRESCHOOL CHILDREN, WASHINGTON, D.C., *1960* 1961 *Progress in Meeting Protein Needs of Infants and Preschool Children: Proceedings.* . . . National Research Council Publication No. 843. Washington: National Academy of Sciences–National Research Council.

FOOD AND AGRICULTURE ORGANIZATION OF THE UNITED NATIONS *The State of Food and Agriculture.* → Published since 1947. The authoritative annual review of developments in the world food and agricultural situation. See especially the 1966 volume.

FOOD AND AGRICULTURE ORGANIZATION OF THE UNITED NATIONS 1963 *Third World Food Survey.* Freedom From Hunger Campaign Basic Study No. 11. Rome: FAO.

JELLIFFE, D. B. 1955 *Infant Nutrition in the Subtropics and Tropics.* Monograph Series, No. 29. Geneva: World Health Organization.

MEAD, MARGARET 1943 The Problem of Changing Food Habits. Pages 20–31 in National Research Council, Committee on Food Habits, *The Problem of Changing Food Habits: Report of the Committee on Food Habits; 1941–1943.* National Research Council Bulletin No. 108. Washington: National Academy of Sciences–National Research Council.

MEAD, MARGARET 1964 *Food Habits Research: Problems of the 1960's.* National Research Council Publication No. 1225. Washington: National Academy of Sciences–National Research Council.

RITCHIE, JEAN A. S. 1950 *Teaching Better Nutrition: A Study of Approaches and Techniques.* Food and Agriculture Organization of the United Nations, Nutritional Studies, No. 6. Washington: Government Printing Office.

SCRIMSHAW, NEVIN S. 1966 The Effect of the Interaction of Nutrition and Infection on the Pre-school Child. In International Conference on Prevention of Malnutrition in the Pre-school Child, Washington, D.C., 1964, *Pre-school Child Malnutrition: Primary Deterrent to Human Progress.* National Research Council Publication No. 1282. Washington: National Academy of Sciences–National Research Council.

II
CONSUMPTION PATTERNS

The consumption of food, like other biologically supportive activities, is an aspect of cultural behavior. In no society are people permitted to eat everything, everywhere, with everyone, and in all situations. Instead, the consumption of food is governed by rules and usages which cut across each other at different levels of symbolization. These symbolizations define the social contexts and groupings within which food—or a particular kind of food—is consumed, and prohibit or taboo the consumption of particular foods. An important dimension of the social contexts regulating the consumption of food is the principle that patterns of consumption and distribution must be examined as one. For example, there are some societies in which it is believed that a person will die if he eats food which he has grown himself, while in others it is felt that a person may eat only food which he himself has grown or acquired by purchase or other exchange. Between these two extremes are several other patterns.

In all societies the distribution and consumption of food is an expression of a variety of social relationships: those of social proximity and distance, religious-ritual fraternity and status, political superordination and subordination, bonds within and between families, and the like. The definition of food, its distribution, and its consumption always take place with reference to individuals as occupants of statuses and categories within institutionalized groupings.

In other words, food is used symbolically to represent only some social forms and personal feelings in a society, and these are usually among the important forms and personal feelings in the group's life. Thus, by noting the specific and bounded social contexts—clan, village, in-law relationships, friendship, and the like—within which food is employed symbolically, it is often possible to infer which are the important groupings and relationships within the society. For example, a taboo on eating the totemic animals associated with one's clan is indicative of the significance of clans in the organiza-

tion of the society's institutions; it is not the taboo per se which suggests the importance of clan relationships but the fact that some rule governing the consumption of food—in this case, forbidding it—is associated with the clan. Why clans usually prohibit their members from eating the animals associated with these groups is a separate question, and one about which there is still considerable uncertainty.

Among some Melanesian people the rule that a man must give part of the harvest of a crop to his sister, while his wife receives a similar prestation from her brother, provides a clue to the importance of certain matrilineal ties; in societies that have a caste system the rule that the members of different castes may not eat together indicates the importance of formal distance between castes as well as the caste organization itself. Correlatively, when food ceases to be employed as a vehicle for the expression of social sentiments within a grouping, e.g., in a clan, or when proscriptions concerning the consumption of food are attacked, it can be assumed that significant changes are taking place in the socioeconomic structure of that society.

The rules governing the distribution of food within a society reflect and reinforce prevailing ethical and moral orientations in that society. For example, when the government of the United States willingly distributes food supplies to poor people in other societies but not within American society itself, it appears that its dominant values implicitly tend to define poverty as an indication of moral failure, if not as sinful. Hence, the assumption often appears to be that if there were gratuitous distributions of food to poor Americans, such action would be construed as reward or even approval of such moral failure. But since it is characteristic that the criteria pertaining to the distribution of food within a social system differ entirely from those relating to other groupings or societies, American society can make prestations of food to people in other societies while refusing (or being unable) to do so within its own social boundaries.

Almost every society defines a few foods as acceptable for consumption under some circumstances but wholly unacceptable in others. For example, foods which are associated with amusement and relaxation are usually considered inappropriate to ritual or ceremonial occasions. In pluralistic and stratified societies, most foods which are grown indigenously are eaten by people in all groups; however, in almost all such societies, there are a few foods and drinks which are not universal or which will be consumed by members of different groups in different contexts or situations. Thus, for example, the same alcoholic beverages in a pluralistic society will be drunk under different conditions and in entirely different places by members of different groups. Such definitions both symbolize and reinforce the consciousness of separateness and distance existing between bounded groups in pluralistic and stratified societies.

For reasons which are not yet completely clear, the major transitional crises of the life cycle—the *rites de passage*—are marked in almost all societies by ritual or ceremonial distribution and consumption of food. One possible hypothesis to explain these nearly universal customs is that each of the three transitional crises (birth, marriage, death) initiates a significant alteration in socioeconomic relationships and reciprocities and that these are symbolically noted in displays, distributions, prestations, token exchanges, and consumption of food. An individual's birth automatically establishes reciprocal rights and duties between him and others to whom he is related in a series of interlocking social networks; marriage in all societies is a transitional ceremony which establishes bonds and reciprocities between the kin groups of the marrying couple; an individual's death terminates, and requires readjustments in, reciprocal economic relationships.

In addition to these ritual celebrations through distribution and consumption of food, as well as other forms of wealth (e.g., bride wealth), a great many societies celebrate historical or ceremonial events according to calendrical systems. These recurrent and fixed celebrations are usually governed by ritual consumptions of food, as in the American Thanksgiving feast or in the custom of many Americans to celebrate their Independence Day with family picnics. Calendrically regulated religious events are similarly celebrated.

One of the fundamental principles governing the organization of social relationships in all societies is the division of labor by sex; most societies also stipulate divisions of labor according to the additional criteria of age, status or ranking, group membership, and the like. Although the division of labor is most apparent in the production of food, it also plays a major role in the consumption of food. There is probably considerable, even systematic, overlap between rules governing the division of productive labor and those governing food consumption, of which kinship is undoubtedly of prime importance; thus far, little work has been done on this problem. A possible model for such an analysis would be a horticultural society in which the wife does most of the productive work, raising food which her husband then gives to his sister.

The distribution and consumption of food within the nuclear family also symbolize institutionalized relationships. For example, among the Tallensi of west Africa there are many expressions of the separateness of father and son and of the father's absolute authority. One of these symbolizations is the rule that a son may not look into his father's granary during the father's lifetime. After the father's death, his eldest surviving son is conducted ritually by his father's brothers to peer into the deceased's granary. This son thus acquires control over the distribution of the food stored in the granary, and this prerogative, among others, symbolizes and supports his control over the patrilocal extended family.

To cite another illustration, where it is the assigned task of the woman of a household to distribute the food within the nuclear family, e.g., by serving meals to members of the household, the manner in which she distributes the food may symbolize relationships to her husband and children at different stages of the family cycle (and to other members of the household, if present). Thus, status relationships within the family are sharply delineated by such rules as whether a woman eats with her husband or separately, when and whether a man eats with his children, etc. Among the Manus of the Admiralty Islands, near New Guinea, the estrangement between husband and wife during the first few years of marriage, and the competitive relationship in which each stands in relation to the kin of the other, is symbolized in part by the shame they feel in eating together. The most competitive relationships among the Manus are between brothers-in-law and between sisters-in-law: these people may not eat together.

The special significance of food in the symbolization of kinship relationships generally can be seen in the fact that behavior with respect to food in the nuclear family often varies with the degree of segregation or division of role relationships; the latter is in turn dependent on the degree to which the nuclear family is connected to a wider nexus of kinship networks. Thus, one of the symbolizations of the greatly reduced segregation of role relationships between husband and wife in modern complex societies—attendant on the weakening of wider kinship matrices—has been the tendency to minimize and blur the division of labor with respect to the distribution of food within the family. In the lower social strata of Western societies, for example, men do not cook or otherwise participate in the distribution of food within the family; in these strata there is usually a strong connection between the nuclear family and wider kinship groupings and a marked degree of segregation in role relationships between husband and wife. In higher social strata in some Western societies, on the other hand, there are situations in which men do cook and participate in the distribution of food within the nuclear family; these situations tend to arise as segregation in role relationships between spouses becomes weakened as part of the attenuation of wider kinship relationships.

Most societies provide for separateness between nuclear families. One of the symbolizations of this separateness is in the confinement of the preparation and consumption of food to the social boundaries of the nuclear family. In most polygynous organizations, each wife has her own hearth or kitchen; she and her children eat separately, the husband either eating with each nuclear family serially or eating with his senior wife. While such arrangements are usually interpreted by anthropologists as being designed to maintain peace among co-wives, these patterns of consumption must also be understood as representations of the social-structural differentiations which most societies make between nuclear families. Among some Mexican Tarascan groups who possess a stem-family organization, in which a son continues to live with his father after marrying, the son's wife and her mother-in-law share a common kitchen, and the two nuclear families eat jointly. When dissension occurs, or in anticipation of the son's plans to found an independent household, his wife will sometimes establish her own kitchen, and the two families will eat separately. Among the Cheyenne Indians of North America, where men were forbidden to speak directly to their mothers-in-law, the men were required to provide all the meat by hunting; this was cooked in the mother-in-law's lodge, but then her daughters carried the food to their respective tepees for eating. The hunting and gathering Tiwi of Northern Australia are one people who do not separate the component nuclear families of polygynous households into consumption units. Instead, each polygynous household cooks and eats as a unit. This is probably because each household head has many more wives, especially elderly ones, than he has children; hence, there are few component nuclear families in each household.

There are four patterns which govern the distribution of food, and hence the consumption of food; three of these are patterns of sharing. Although they have a tendency to shade off into one another, they are easily identifiable and clearly illustrate the basic principle that it is a characteristic of social systems to symbolize social relationships by means of different patterns of distributing and consuming food. These four patterns are (1) recurrent exchange and sharing of food; (2) mutual assistance and sharing in times of need; (3) narrowed and reluctant sharing; and (4) nonsharing.

(1) *Recurrent exchange and sharing.* There are several variations on this pattern of sharing; all, however, are associated with and symbolize a combination of factors which tend to give rise to maximal solidarity within the community: social affiliation based on consanguineal kinship; physical proximity between households; the prescription or careful control of residence by, among other factors, rules of residence; the conduct of interpersonal communication in stable and consistently functioning primary or face-to-face groupings. In brief, the combination of highly integrated kin groups, physical proximity, and sedentary life appear to yield strong feelings of social proximity. Recurrent exchange and sharing of food is one of the symbolic representations of this solidary state.

Among most peoples characterized by this kind of social organization, there is a constant flow of gifts of food from household to household within the solidary grouping. Among other societies, whose cultures are suffused with religious ceremonial (e.g., the Hopi and Tallensi), the recurrent distribution of food, too, takes place in a religious ceremonial context. Among still others (e.g., the Kurtatchi and the Papago), there are unelaborated but repeated donations, prestations, and exchanges of small token amounts of food among kinsmen.

Regardless of the variations on the theme, these recurrent and repetitive exchanges of food almost always take place within the sociological boundaries of the solidary community. Also, such recurrent exchanges of food are in addition to ceremonialized or ritualized feasts.

(2) *Mutual assistance and sharing in times of need.* The primary difference between type (1) and the social organization with which mutual assistance in times of need is associated is that in the latter the ties and alignments of kinship are not solidified into corporate kin groups. The bonds of kinship, qualitatively speaking, are equally strong in both social organizations, but in the present instance these ties are not elevated to the level of exclusive and solidary groupings.

A degree of social and emotional solidarity arises in such a community from the strong and marked tendency to affiliate primarily with kinsmen, real or fictive. Usually the members of such a community are mostly kinsmen, and sometimes entirely kinsmen. An element of fissility, and a corresponding degree of social distance, is introduced into such a social organization by a variety of factors. First, physical mobility and change in community membership are usually permitted, thus resulting in the simultaneous presence of kinsmen and non-kinsmen within the group. Where nonkinsmen join the community, they are sometimes addressed and treated as kinsmen; preference for consanguineal ties is the mainspring of such relationships. But of equal, if not greater, significance is the fact that kinsmen have the right to sever relationships with their group and either establish or join an entirely independent one. While extreme personalization of relationships is the rule in this social organization, social cohesiveness and proximity are proportionately weakened by movement away from kinsmen and by the intrusion of nonkinsmen into the community. Among many peoples (e.g., the Andamanese, Arunta, South African Bushmen, Plains Indian tribes) the exigencies of the food-producing environment, rather than tensions and quarrels, appear to have necessitated such adjustments on the social-structural level. In either event, the consequences, in terms of fission and social distance, are similar.

It is possible to observe a process of compromise in this social organization between forces which give rise to social proximity and those resulting in social distance. Any of these, when taken alone, is productive of either solidarity or fissility. For example, clanship among the Navajo or the peasants of Shantung province in pre-Republican China would, when taken separately, produce a high degree of social solidarity. Obversely, the isolation of the family—geographically, and hence emotionally, among the Navajo and almost entirely emotionally among Shantung peasants—gave rise to the emotional inbreeding of the family vis-à-vis the community. The simultaneity of factors making both for solidarity and for fissility produces a compromise between the two and places such peoples at this point along the continuum of social cohesiveness and solidarity rather than at the point of maximal or minimal solidarity. Mutual assistance in times of need is characteristic of such societies.

In nomadic hunting and gathering societies having this type of social organization, mutual assistance and sharing in times of need often take the form of the immediate dispensation of meat to almost all the households of the community as soon as an animal is captured or slain, especially to those who do not have meat. In sedentary societies, mutual assistance in times of need takes the form of aid rendered to kinsmen, real or fictive, when

economic help is objectively required. There is, of course, mutual assistance in time of need in societies which practice recurrent exchange and sharing; however, as the present instance indicates, there are many societies in which there is mutual assistance without the elaboration of recurrent exchange.

This is not meant to imply that there are no feasts and exchanges whatever in this social organization; these are present, but they occur only on specific occasions, e.g., religious events and the life crises marked by *rites de passage*. Nor is the idea or concept of recurrent prestation unknown in such societies, but such exchange is almost always confined to gifts of goods, not food.

(3) *Narrowed and reluctant sharing.* By this is meant that whatever assistance is rendered to people is given very reluctantly and grudgingly. This pattern of food distribution is ordinarily associated with fragmented social systems in which the isolated nuclear family unit is the significant unit of association; socially, geographically, and emotionally isolated from all other family units, it constitutes neither a society nor a community. Nor do the several family units constitute a society, structurally or functionally, when they come together.

The primary characteristic of this social system is the presence of relatively great geographic distances between households and families and, concomitantly, clearly demarcated social boundaries. Physical space or distance in this social organization serves as a boundary-maintaining force only indirectly and incidentally; this is an important consideration, because even when the family units in such a social system unite for temporary amalgamations, they continue to maintain their great social distance from each other. Although the ties of kinship in this social organization may be highly formalized, there are rarely any functioning kin groups outside the family, and kinship ties become increasingly diffuse as the physical distance between kinsmen increases.

One of the material symbolizations of this social atomism or fission is the pattern of narrowed and reluctant sharing, as among the Kaska and Ojibwa Indians. Even when individuals in these societies are willing to extend aid, they are willing to do so only to a very limited number of people. The cultures of such peoples generally contain the ideal prescription of generosity and mutual assistance in times of need, but this ideal is rarely, if ever, achieved; in actual behavior, generosity and assistance are extremely restricted—qualitatively and in the number of persons toward whom such behavior is manifest. Another way of stating this is that behavior with respect to food in such societies approaches parsimoniousness but never quite achieves it, reflecting the atomization of social relationships beyond the nuclear family.

(4) *Nonsharing.* This is a general category; it has thus far not been possible to determine different types of nonsharing behavior with respect to food, as has been done in connection with patterns of sharing, because there are too few societies in the category of nonsharing from among which discrete types of nonsharing could be elicited.

Here "nonsharing" means the absence in a culture of enforceable prescriptions to share food with others, no matter how great their need; where nonsharing is found as the dominant pattern, the individuated accumulation of wealth is an end in itself, rather than a means to cooperative or competitive generosity. That is, people in many societies, as in the first two categories described above, amass food or other forms of wealth in order to be able to distribute it in socially prescribed forms of generosity, and there is often competition to be the most generous.

In societies characterized by nonsharing, there are rarely, if ever, any closed groups within the community in which membership, feeling of belonging, and reciprocity are fixed and inalienable. Few, if any, institutionally significant statuses are ascribed; authority, group cohesiveness, interfamilial support, and mutual assistance are almost always absent. Similarly, allegiances are expedient and frequently contractual. While considerations of kinship appear to play occasional roles in interpersonal associations, such considerations are decidedly secondary; instead, kinsmen and nonkinsmen alike enter into the economically competitive struggle, and personal profit and success emerge as predominant values. Power resides among those who are monetarily powerful rather than among those persons whose social dominance derives from ascribed high status or who have succeeded in other spheres of competitive activity.

Societies characterized by this system superficially resemble societies in which narrowed and reluctant sharing is found, in that the effective socioeconomic unit appears to be the independent nuclear family. The resemblance, however, is superficial. In societies in which nonsharing is the dominant pattern, the social isolation of the family does not derive from physical distance between family units. Instead, the principal isolating factor appears to be the search for individually accumulated wealth. Examples of societies characterized by nonsharing of food are the Alorese, the Marquesans,

highland peasants in Jamaica, the Yakut of Siberia, and the Yurok Indians.

The comparative ethnographic data reveal with marked clarity that no matter how highly elaborated a pattern of recurrent exchange and sharing might be, to say nothing of other patterns, in no society is an individual expected to give up everything he possesses. In no society is true "selflessness" an expected or imposed value to which the individual must adhere. For example, among the Arapesh of New Guinea, who have elaborated recurrent exchange to an extreme and among whom a man does not eat food which he himself has grown, personal ownership and rights in property are clearly delineated with definite notions of "mine" and "yours." The Kwoma, too, who believe that a man would die if he ate his own harvest, also specify individual ownership of the yield of the land, each person's crop being put in a separate bin in a storehouse. The Copper Eskimo prescribe that even if only one seal is caught, it must be distributed equally throughout the community. However, it has been observed among them that during the winter, when each woman cooks indoors, she can hide the choicer portions of meat for her husband and herself until after visitors have left; in the summer, on the other hand, when most of the cooking is done out-of-doors and everyone can see what is in the pot, no concealment is possible. It can be suggested that the provision in all cultures for personal ownership and retention—no matter how great the pressures to share—is due, at least in part, to the need for material representations of individuation and personal separateness, i.e., self-awareness. As Hallowell noted in his paper "The Self and Its Behavioral Environment," "It seems necessary to assume self-awareness as one of the prerequisite psychological conditions for the functioning of any human social order, no matter what linguistic and culture patterns prevail" ([1937–1954] 1955, p. 75).

At the same time that the social forces which make for extreme degrees of social proximity maximize predispositions to share food, factors making for social distance within a maximally solidary community will mitigate the predisposition to share. That is, it can be assumed that every society contains some forces, however few and small, which help to make for social distance. In a society in which extreme social proximity helps to produce a pattern of recurrent food sharing, those factors making for social distance in the same society will help to produce a proportionate reluctance to share.

For example, high social status, such as chieftainship, is determined in a variety of ways. It can be postulated that social distance is greater between persons of high and low ascribed statuses than between persons of high and low achieved statuses. Assuming some degree of reluctance in most people to share food with others, even in societies in which people appear strongly predisposed to share, it follows logically that reluctance to share would covary with ascribed high status even in societies in which there is strong social cohesiveness and solidarity. In other words, it can be assumed that persons with ascribed high status in solidary communities will employ their social distance from the "masses" or "commoners" as a mechanism which enables them to amass and retain more for themselves; this is not necessarily conscious on their part. For example, among the Manuans of Samoa, who have an elaborate hierarchy of chieftainship, a high income is one of the few feudal privileges. Although chiefly wealth is kept in circulation by the requirement that chiefs be generous to commoners, the chiefs nevertheless generally have more food than anyone else. Among the Dahomeans, the economic organization was usually characterized by a surplus which eventually brought about the concentration of wealth in the hands of the hereditary leisure classes.

The evidence is conclusive that patterns in the consumption of food are almost always governed by cultural symbols and that the ways in which food is distributed and consumed reflect a society's dominant modes of social relationships and groupings, especially those pertaining to kinship ties.

YEHUDI A. COHEN

[*See also* DRINKING AND ALCOHOLISM; EXCHANGE AND DISPLAY; *and the biography of* MAUSS.]

BIBLIOGRAPHY

COHEN, YEHUDI A. 1961 Food and Its Vicissitudes: A Cross-cultural Study of Sharing and Nonsharing. Pages 312–350 in Yehudi A. Cohen, *Social Structure and Personality: A Casebook.* New York: Holt.

COHEN, YEHUDI A. 1964a The Establishment of Identity in a Social Nexus: The Special Case of Initiation Ceremonies and Their Relation to Value and Legal Systems. *American Anthropologist* New Series 66:529–552.

COHEN, YEHUDI A. 1964b *The Transition From Childhood to Adolescence: Cross-cultural Studies of Initiation Ceremonies, Legal Systems, and Incest Taboos.* Chicago: Aldine.

DURKHEIM, ÉMILE (1893) 1960 *The Division of Labor in Society.* Glencoe, Ill.: Free Press. → First published as *De la division du travail social.*

FIRTH, RAYMOND W. (1939) 1965 *Primitive Polynesian Economy.* 2d ed. Hamden, Conn.: Shoe String Press.

HALLOWELL, A. IRVING (1937–1954) 1955 *Culture and Experience.* Philadelphia Anthropological Society, Publications, Vol. 4. Philadelphia: Univ. of Pennsylvania Press. → A collection of essays by one of the most influential thinkers in American anthropology; in the classical anthropological tradition but with a strong orientation toward psychological conceptualizations of cultural processes. Included are many papers on the Ojibwa Indians.

MAUSS, MARCEL (1925) 1954 *The Gift: Forms and Functions of Exchange in Archaic Societies.* Glencoe, Ill.: Free Press. → First published as *Essai sur le don: Forme et raison de l'échange dans les sociétés archaïques.*

MEAD, MARGARET (editor) 1937 *Cooperation and Competition Among Primitive Peoples.* New York: McGraw-Hill. → A paperback edition was published in 1961 by Beacon. Descriptions of social and economic life in thirteen primitive societies, and interpretive chapters by the editor. One of the milestones in comparative studies in anthropology.

RICHARDS, AUDREY I. (1932) 1948 *Hunger and Work in a Savage Tribe: A Functional Study of Nutrition Among the Southern Bantu.* Glencoe, Ill.: Free Press. → A paperback edition was published in 1964 by World Publishing. A classic study of patterns of food consumption in one culture area, but with generalizations of wide applicability.

SAHLINS, MARSHALL D. 1965 On the Sociology of Primitive Exchange. Pages 139–236 in Conference on New Approaches in Social Anthropology, Jesus College, Cambridge, 1963, *The Relevance of Models for Social Anthropology.* New York: Praeger.

FORCED LABOR

See INTERNMENT AND CUSTODY; SLAVERY.

FORECASTING

See POPULATION, *especially the article on* POPULATION GROWTH; PREDICTION; PREDICTION AND FORECASTING, ECONOMIC. *Related material may be found under* TIME SERIES.

FOREIGN AID

I. POLITICAL ASPECTS   *George Liska*
II. ECONOMIC ASPECTS   *Gerald M. Meier*

I
POLITICAL ASPECTS

Pecuniary grants and other material donations by one government to another are among the recurrent features of interstate relations. The two basic types of grants are *tribute* and *subsidy.* Tribute is typically a donation from a state that is somehow more vulnerable to a less vulnerable state in exchange for protection or immunity; subsidy originates typically with a state that is at least financially stronger, and the donor expects in return a performance that serves his security strategy.

Contemporary foreign aid may comprise elements of tribute, when it secures immunity from verbal hostility and feelings of guilt, for instance. But its direct line of descent is from subsidies. The elementary political economy of subsidies is unchanging: the subsidy is an inducement for the recipient to behave in a way that would supplement the donor's exertions or substitute for them, and do it at a cost that is less than the cost of alternative courses of action, including war and greater national exertions in war. The basic assumption is clearest in aid for military effort. It holds that there is a definable unit of fighting power or defense power that can be had more cheaply from outside the donor's military establishment. The assumption is vindicated whenever domestic armaments have reached one or more of the limits set by internal supply of material resources, conditions of social stability within a political order, and countervailing responses by third states. The same basic principle of diminishing returns of strictly internal efforts can be applied to economic welfare and other non-military components of national security and international stability, and serves as the rationale of foreign aid.

Objectives

The ultimate objective of the donor is to convert superior economic power into a pattern of political alignments that would improve his regional or global position. The recipient expects foreign aid to generate new resources of power, welfare, and prestige. His principal aim may be to consolidate the regime's authority with respect to opposition forces, to keep abreast of growing popular needs or of growth in other states, or to equip himself for effective or even offensive action with regard to other countries. Calculation of political advantage to be derived from aid is at its most pragmatic when diplomacy of maneuver and alignment predominates in a relatively flexible and relaxed multipolar situation; it may be temporarily subordinated to ideological determinants, or to the compulsions of force or the general interest when the global or regional balance of power is exposed to a hegemonial drive and polarized in consequence. Subsidies then become an emergency expedient to confirm lesser states in their readiness to resist the onslaught or to convert to resistance those states reluctant to subordinate their immediate concerns to the maintenance of the existing international system.

The expanded foreign aid activities following World War II conformed, on the whole, to the fundamental principles of the statecraft of subsidies. Foreign aid was part of a policy of coalition building by the United States, the preponderant yet defensive power in the system; it became part of a coalition-frustrating policy in the hands of the Soviet Union in a later phase of the cold war. The peculiar character of the contest enlarged the meaning of the coalition to be built or frustrated and drew into the compass of foreign aid not only active, military allies; economic and military aid were used to attract the uncommitted, floating allegiance of "independents" as well as to consolidate established commitments. The need to win the apparently decisive uncommitted states made both contestants edge away from damaging antecedents and associations. The more conservative United States repudiated the paternalistic and colonial elements in its past and among its allies; the revolutionary Soviet Union disclaimed its militant tradition as an export commodity and disowned its overly expansionist Chinese ally whenever expedient for reassuring alarmed neutrals. Yet the need to retain the allegiance of the inner core of committed partisans has imposed a limit on profitable opportunism also in the international contest; it is a dubious electoral and diplomatic strategy to woo untested new friends in such a way as to alienate old comrades-in-arms.

Difficulties in implementing the objectives. Three special circumstances have warped the implementation of the political economy of subsidies beyond the unavoidable measure of distortion introduced by hegemonial conflict.

One was an *overemphasis on the role of economic changes and processes in assuring political stability and on the role of domestic politics in unstabilizing foreign policy activities.* In this respect, the effect of liberal predispositions was comparable with the affirmations of Marxist ideology and was reinforced by the need of meeting the Soviet practice of internal political subversion and manipulation of economic malcontents. Growing demands for external assistance consequently acquired great authority, but the recipients all too often lacked the will and ability to use this assistance responsibly and effectively.

Another deforming influence has been the *association of foreign aid with decolonization;* it added psychological and propagandistic biases to those imparted by a deterministic ideology and an opportunistic political strategy. Foreign aid came to be widely regarded as a duty for the advanced states and as a reparation for the uncritically asserted grievances of recipients.

The consequent moral advantage of recipient countries was enhanced by a political advantage owing to the third distorting circumstance, the *sharp increase in military–technological inhibitions on warlike settlements of conflicts between major powers.* A demonstrable capacity to wage a major nuclear war has remained a fundamental condition of the efficacy of all political action by the principal powers, including dispensation of foreign aid; at the same time, however, the economic power and activities of the donor states have been largely deprived of their essential support in usable conventional military force. Thermonuclear stalemate and severance of economic power from the ultimate military sanction behind political control have combined to increase the ability of the more ambitious among the lesser states to act with impunity. Competitive economic growth has become the prime functional substitute for war as a test of superiority for the two competing superpowers and politico-economic systems. Consequently, foreign aid activities, the principal device for extending the economic competition to third and lesser states, were temporarily overstrained.

The distorting ideological, psychological, and military circumstances produced a disparity between power and control or influence that was unfavorable to the donors. This disparity at first intensified the donors' competition over the Afro–Asian nations; only progressively and uncertainly has the disparity begun to foster a tacit understanding between the superpowers, regarding the rules and limits of foreign aid competition, that may eventually match comparable understandings in the domain of the arms race.

American and Soviet approaches. Undeniable differences of style and spirit have separated the so-called capitalist and the so-called socialist major donors. But both have been confounded by comparable uncertainties regarding the objectives of foreign aid and the means or strategies for attaining the objectives. The immediate, short-term objective of both the United States and the Soviet Union has been negative: to prevent forces favorable to the competitor from becoming established or consolidated to the detriment of one's allies and sympathizers in embattled lesser countries. The long-term, positive objective has been to promote a structure of world order that would reflect the internal organization, or the domestic ideal, of the superpowers: the supremacy of one class or elite in one case, pluralism of competing forces within the limits of consensus on essentials in the other. The uneasy coexistence of short-term preventive objectives and long-term constructive objectives compelled both major donors repeatedly to decide between often uncongenial, immediate beneficiaries of foreign aid and ultimate, actually favored beneficiaries. In practice, this often meant that the

Soviet Union aided or appeared to aid bourgeois-nationalists against local communists and that the United States helped dictatorial oligarchs, at least temporarily, against local liberals or democrats.

The ambiguity of objectives has been reflected in uncertainties over strategies. The unresolved issue has been whether to choose a strategy keyed to individual countries or a strategy keyed to the international system as a whole. A one-country strategy of foreign aid as implemented by the United States would promote the capacity for political independence of individual recipients, on the assumption that the exercise of such independence would be consistent with American interests. As implemented by the Soviet Union, this strategy would aim at subverting the identity of a noncommunist regime, on the assumption that formal political independence no less than formal political democracy is only a disguise for rule by elements hostile to the Soviet Union. In both cases, the stress is on the peculiar needs, conditions, and opportunities in the target country, while the repercussions of aid to that country in comparable or related countries are downgraded.

The one-system strategy would reverse the priorities, assigning high priority to the foreign policy behavior of recipients and its international repercussions. An American one-system strategy of longer range would promote behavior conducive to an elementary world order and, secondarily, to the progressive breakup of the Sino–Soviet bloc. The corresponding strategy of the Soviet Union would promote the progressive erosion of Western positions in the less developed countries as a group, producing an irretrievable breakdown of the Western system rather than piecemeal subversion in one country after another.

No clear choice between the two principal kinds of strategy has been made by either superpower, in part because of the untoward relationships between domestic and external political behavior of many recipient regimes. The United States has had to cope with the problem of regimes that are internationally pro-Western but internally antireform; the Soviet Union has had the problem of countries that are internationally neutralist and outwardly anti-West but domestically anticommunist. On the whole, doctrinaire supporters of foreign aid as a panacea in the West and of communism and local Communist parties as paramount concerns in the Sino–Soviet bloc have tended to favor the one-country approach, concentrating on immediate and locally promising conditions. Those primarily concerned with foreign policy have stressed the immediate needs of a coherent foreign aid policy and the long-range requirements of a propitiously evolving international system, in view of the unlimited stakes of the global conflict and the limited efficacy of foreign aid in any one country, if administered in separation from over-all political and military strategies.

Types of aid

However used, foreign aid has differed from its antecedents in the modern European state system. Chief among them are the more or less overt dynastic subsidies for military manpower, chiefly in the seventeenth and eighteenth centuries, and the more or less officially sponsored but privately subscribed loans in the nineteenth and early twentieth centuries. Throughout, the principles and practices of "foreign aid" were adjusted to the type of control over individuals, whether authoritarian or constitutional, and to the prevailing scope of governmental functions, whether they were mercantilist, laissez-faire, or welfare-statist. They were also adapted to the predominant ways of managing international political alignments and military conflicts—as relatively temporary or hopefully indefinite commitments, implemented by levies of manpower or by advance building of infrastructures such as railroads and air bases.

However, political and technological changes have, on the whole, fostered a growing temporal and qualitative gap between grant and anticipated performance. The difference between economic grant and expected political performance was always there; but even in the field of military aid and security the typical performance of the recipient came to differ radically from the donor's whenever concession of facilities replaced supplementary manpower as the principal return for the aid given. The balance between specific and immediate acts and slowly evolving general conditions, as the purposes of foreign aid, has tended to shift in favor of the conditions expected to generate policies congenial to the donor even after the termination of the aid relationship.

The growing gap between grant and performance has become increasingly hard to span for two interacting sets of reasons. One has had to do with the instability of governing elites and their frequent replacement by competing elites. Revolutionary break and repudiation of indebtedness, anticipated in the lot of French loans to the tsarist regime in Russia, has become the rule, albeit with exceptions. The other set of reasons has had to do with the diffusion of aid relationships as an apparently stable and permanent feature of international relations. Aid from a richer or well-established state

has come to constitute a well-nigh automatic counterpart to diplomatic recognition and practically its most valuable by-product. However, this recognition in kind has not been governed by norms comparable with those of recognition in law, regarding effective internal political control, responsible international conduct, and nonidentification of material aid with moral approval.

Acquisitive and creative aid. The distance between grant and anticipated performance, whatever may be its long-range effect on foreign aid, helps distinguish between two types of aid in the post-World War II era through the maze of administrative and propagandistic nomenclature. One kind of aid may be described as acquisitive; it is closest to traditional subsidies in that it is extended in the anticipation of a relatively specific, tangible, or immediate advantage for the donor. The acquisition may range from a facility such as a military base or a base for political operations, through an alliance commitment (or repudiation of alliance commitment to the donor's adversary), to the control over large segments of a country that would otherwise be economically and politically nonviable. Alternatively, the donor can give aid in anticipation of a long-range economic and political development in a favored direction. Such aid may be called creative or developmental. Acquisitive aid generally has large military components for internal or external security; creative aid typically is economic, even though it may release indigenous resources for military outlays. Although a few aid relationships may be wholly acquisitive or creative in motive and purpose, most are primarily one or the other. The volume of aid determines whether aid is merely token aid, designed to manifest the donor's interest in the country as an encouragement to friendly groups, or whether more important aid constitutes a down-payment, committing the donor to long-term contributions as long as the recipient goes on displaying willingness and capacity to administer a politically and economically promising development process.

The two main types of aid, acquisitive and creative, have a different bearing upon two classes of problems that are raised by foreign aid: the distribution of aid and the control over aid and related policies. The problem of distribution has so far concerned chiefly the choice between military and economic aid and choice among alternative recipients.

Distribution of aid

Military versus economic. In the United States, allocation of resources between economic and military forms of assistance has been a major, if sometimes distracting, issue. The faith in economic means, in the guise of liberalized trade and private investments, was marked in American foreign policy before, during, and after the period of planning for peace during World War II. It received a confirmation from the successful economic reconstruction of western Europe under the European Recovery Program, which became the doubtfully valid model for subsequent programs of economic assistance elsewhere, following the disappointment of exaggerated expectations from technical-assistance programs short of large-scale aid for development. The military–political crises of the cold war produced countervailing stresses in favor of military assistance to countries and regimes threatened from within or without. The resulting debate over the proper ratio between economic and military aid was confused by ambiguous official categories of aid, such as "defense support." The outcome of this debate was marked by the contrast between nominal victories for advocates of economic aid and the less spectacular shifts in the actual ratio, due in large part to the continuing demand by many recipients for substantial military aid.

The issue between economic and military aid has been largely a false one. As long as economic aid promotes development, it also fosters social mobilization and, thereby, some political instability. Not all governmental elites that administer outside assistance are anxious to be self-liquidating. To neutralize their increased vulnerability, they found that military aid for internal security was both necessary and legitimate. Moreover, military assistance can be a means to the goal of economic assistance by providing a developing country with forces not only for local defense but also for internal development that a nationwide, properly controlled and used military establishment can generate. The United States has, therefore, been justified in granting military assistance not only for the immediate purposes of its containment and alliance policy. On its part, the Soviet Union has been led to disseminate military assistance to willing takers by the desire to break open the containment ring and secure immediate political gains in crucially important or vulnerable noncommitted countries.

Alternative recipients—allies or neutrals? With regard to the distribution of aid among alternative recipients, both major donors have faced a related problem: whether to give preferential or exclusive assistance to their allies or to distribute aid widely among noncommitted countries as well. Only a minority power willing to remain so or prepared to rely on military conquest could probably afford the purism of aid only to allies. There is no other ready criterion. Different flaws vitiate such criteria as that of the need of potential recipients, their capacity to effect and absorb changes with outside assistance, or their ability and willingness to make their internal conduct or external policies conform to the interests and policies of the donor.

A distribution following any one criterion or coherent set of criteria becomes well-nigh impossible once there is an aid race between major donors. Such competition occurred between the United States and the Soviet Union and reached its peak in the late 1950s. The competition was aggravated by failures of perception. For one thing, the competing powers long ignored the similarity or identity of many of their problems and frustrations in the domain of foreign aid. For another, both insiders and outsiders tended to judge and compare the performance of the superpowers in not really comparable situations. The temporary beneficiary of the political and intellectual misapprehension was the Soviet Union, which gained easy, and apparently lasting, initial successes in the conflict-ridden Western orbit, displaying largesse toward noncommunist countries and reserving strict aid policies for communist countries.

Multilateral versus bilateral aid. Multilateral administration and distribution of foreign aid through international agencies has been widely advocated as a way out of the frustrations of bilateral methods. A change-over on a major scale has been inhibited, however, by the growing structural disequilibrium in the United Nations. The disequilibrium has favored numbers over the intrinsic weight of states and their contributions, and has been inimical to progressive expansion of the organization's functional scope in regard to the dispensing of aid and similar long-range activities. Moreover, most recipient countries have actually been reluctant to rely primarily on multilateral modes of allocation and control of economic assistance.

A more practical way of dispersing donor–recipient relations, and distributing aid in a quasi-multilateral manner, may occur by means of the multiplication of both Western and communist donors. A deliberately planned division of labor among ex-colonial powers has been preached in the West and practiced by the Soviet-bloc countries (excepting Communist China) in the late 1950s and early 1960s. The alternative way of dividing labor is a less concerted and even superficially competitive one, whenever one power acts in the place of and over the protests of another in an alienated country or part of the world. In the postwar period, the United States acted in countries bent upon repudiating both the presence and the presents of former colonial masters. As psychological decolonization in the former European empires advanced, as experience with powers other than the former metropoles grew, and as the colonial revolt spread to Latin America, the process has tended to be reversed. West Germany has been developing her economic activities abroad; France and Britain have been recovering their positions of the preferred donors in parts of Asia and Africa and have even moved to act by means of trade or aid on behalf or in lieu of the United States in disaffected countries of Latin America. It is unclear at the time of writing whether the competitive trade-and-aid activities of Communist China and the Soviet Union in Africa and Asia will ultimately prove to have been instruments of a break or of a more or less reluctant division of labor. In any event, the over-all result has been a larger total bulk of aid and its wider diffusion, if not a more rational distribution.

Control of aid

The other major problem is that of control. It concerns such issues as those of "strings" and "intervention," and it has remained unresolved in either theory or practice, although regularization of foreign aid depends on a general acceptance of a few principles or propositions. Some form of control over each other's behavior is the precondition of any cooperation between self-willed sovereign actors, not least in the sphere of foreign aid. Control becomes reciprocal whenever lesser states extract a greater leeway from stalemate among greater powers. Some strings are inevitably attached to grants by one state to another but are likely to be effective as well as legitimate only if they are adapted to suit particular types of aid and the corresponding kinds of anticipated performance. And no effort can do away with at least indirect or unintended intervention by the donor once a government accepts aid and thus admits its inability to cope with its tasks in a strictly internal manner. The donor's right to intervention generally stops short of forcible or dictatorial interference, but there are two exceptions. First, the assistance may be so massive that it creates responsibility for the recipient's existence, and circumstances could be so critical that they endanger the vital interests of both recipient and donor. Alternately, an invitation to intervene may be extended by the recipient, induced by past or anticipated assistance from the interventionist power and directed against a force other than clear majority will of the people concerned.

The occasions for intervention would be reduced by a policy that may be described as one of remote control. Under such a policy, the donor seeks to act on policies of sensitive governing elites by way of precedent-creating action in comparable situations accessible to a more direct exercise of influence. Alternatives to remote control are direct control, over the internal or external activities of a pliant or trustful government, and indirect control, obtained by promoting congenial political groups likely to sway politics in the direction favored by the donor without his constant interference. The previously noted one-country strategy overtaxes the capacity for relatively direct forms of controls, notably if the donor is unable to act upon reliable theoretical knowledge of relationships between economic aid and economic development and between economic development and political stability. The one-system strategy by contrast heightens the bearing of remote control by consistent policies in comparable situations, creating a body of rules by way of discernible authoritative precedents; flexibility is subordinated to the rule-making function of policy and reserved for diplomatic instruments with an immediate, predictable, and easily manipulable impact on men and events.

Critique and prospects

The problems besetting foreign aid indicate its shortcomings. The political future of foreign aid depends on its qualities as an instrument of current policies and as a foundation of a new system of international politics and of a new world order. There is a possible conflict between the two tests insofar as the traits that constitute the standing of foreign aid as an instrument of national policy tend to endear assistance to proponents of new forms of relations among nations. Foreign aid as an economic weapon too frequently tends to be separated from a complementary exercise of political influence and military power. Furthermore, aid is often rendered in the anticipation of counter-performance, the maturity of which is commonly all the more delayed and uncertain the more voluminous is the assistance. Consequently, results are not forthcoming, cannot be convincingly related to the grant, or are reversible by contrary developments before they are consolidated. The paucity of demonstrable positive returns encourages negative appraisals of foreign aid: as a waste or an expedient without which things would be still worse. The difficulty in consolidating provisional results is frustrating to the donor, even though it may be stabilizing internationally if it besets all the rival donors.

The shortcomings of foreign aid as an instrument of foreign policy become critical when changes in the international system reduce the donors' needs that commonly motivate aid. Among such changes are technological developments that lessen the dependence of the major powers on alliances and military facilities on foreign soil, and political events that dampen the intensity of competition over intermediate unaligned states. The task of controlling aid relationships from a position of exploitable political weakness becomes less impossible for major donors, but also less pressing. Military–political competition that has polarized the state system is apt to give way either to an outright military clash or to international politics of increasing diplomatic flexibility, marked by a shift of the focus of sought gains and feared losses from small, uncommitted states to relations and combinations among middle and great powers. Insofar as trends of this kind prevail, international agencies might get a chance to supersede bilateral foreign aid activities and routinize the allocation and administration of aid for economic development through application of objective criteria of need and capacity; the agencies themselves might, however, first have to undergo a change in their structure or spirit, and conform more realistically to the balance of material needs and contributions of the aid-giving and the aid-receiving countries. Conversely, if foreign aid were made multilateral, it might be hampered in a multipolar world by the diffusion of the tendency for each major economic power center to claim and obtain a preferential right to foreign aid activities in its regional orbit.

As long as the rendering of foreign aid and its results remain in large part the function of more pressing and compelling political, military, and diplomatic strategies, foreign aid activities in themselves are unlikely to constitute a basis of a new system of international politics. Such a system would implement a scientific theory of economic and political development, so far largely lacking, and would rest on the willingness of both donors and recipients to implement common interests in the expansion of individual and group welfare, of political choices, and of exchanges of all kinds. A sustained program of foreign aid free from subservience to political contests would provisionally take the place of free trade as the chief integrating element in a system of international relations governed by the distribution of developmental functions among unevenly endowed states. So conceived, the new system of international politics would supplement the older ideal of dividing the production and consumption of security among more or less favored states in a system of collective security; and it would supplant the diametrically opposed view of foreign aid as a perpetuation of subsidies by partly altered means in a still essentially mercantilist statecraft marked by contest over insufficiently expanding and expandable assets.

Barring unpredictable upheavals, the ultimate test of foreign aid as a positive and enduring factor in but slowly evolving international politics is a long-range one. It concerns the fitness of foreign aid to contribute to a stable world order. To a limited but real extent, international order and stability rest on domestic orders. Foreign aid makes a contribution in this area when it promotes coalitions of political and functional elites, meaning especially the modernizers and the guardians of the modernization process in developing countries. To be both stable and stabilizing, the coalitions must be able to agree on the scope and rate of manageable change, to be implemented by the elites and absorbed by the masses, in a process of growth that is largely independent of intercessions, restraints on modernizers, and compensations to dispossessed groups from the outside. Only very few underdeveloped countries, not necessarily representative of the fundamental problem, have managed to initiate and perpetuate such a process that would be largely self-sustaining politically as well as economically. The liberal explanation that failure to overcome underdevelopment in backward countries is a source of instability and war has been gaining ground over its Leninist counterpart, that the source is found in maladjustments due to economic overdevelopment in industrialized, capitalist–imperialist countries. To the extent that these hypotheses are valid and foreign aid helps relieve critical economic maladjustments, not least by reducing the gap between unequally developed countries, foreign aid can promote international stability.

In the international arena, foreign aid activities tend to promote stability when they provide rival powers with outlets for moderately competitive behavior, reducing the incentive to violent forms of rivalry. Foreign aid activities can relieve international tensions when they are informed by a realistic appraisal of possible gains for either side, and they may stabilize the international system both in the short and the long run insofar as contemporary major powers accept the fact that they are building up new economic and military powers that may eventually recast alignments to their disadvantage. The generation of reserve power may reduce the pressures on governments to avert by force unfavorable developments that may be foreshadowed by trends in the arms race or by rates of competitive economic growth. Such an anticipation may have been partly responsible for some major wars in the past, including both world wars of the twentieth century.

Two decades after the end of World War II, there has been a widespread desire to evaluate the intervening experience with different forms of large-scale governmental aid. A continuing retreat of foreign aid from the forefront of direct great-power competition would favor a new balance between acquisitive and creative aid. This might entail depoliticization of foreign aid in one respect, that of allowing considerable autonomy to objective needs of development, and its politicization in another respect, that of a progressive definition and acceptance of reciprocal rights and obligations on the part of recipients as well as donors. The new balance would reflect the growing need for the so-called revolution or rising expectations to come to terms with the less spectacular but no less significant decline of expectations attached to foreign aid. Any new compromise between the demands of the revolution in the less developed countries and the consequences of the evolution in the industrial donor countries could not but alter the manifestation of a technique that can be shown to be a recurrent, but not continuous, and a useful, but not indispensable, feature of international statecraft.

GEORGE LISKA

[See also ALLIANCES; COLONIALISM; IMPERIALISM; MODERNIZATION; TECHNICAL ASSISTANCE. *A guide to other relevant material will be found under* INTERNATIONAL RELATIONS.]

BIBLIOGRAPHY

The writings on foreign aid in the West, and in the United States in particular, can be grouped into categories of official and scholarly publications.

Among the official sources, the most important are records of the annual hearings before the foreign relations committees of the two houses of Congress and the special reports occasionally ordered by both branches of the government. Major examples are U.S. Congress 1957, *prepared for a special committee of the 85th Congress;* U.S. President's Committee 1959; U.S. Committee . . . 1963.

Among the scholarly sources, the executive–legislative process in relation to foreign aid is analyzed in Haviland 1958. *The school of thought stressing the long-range economic development of foreign aid is represented by* Millikan & Rostow 1957 *and* 1958. *The school of thought stressing short-range political control and objectives is represented by* Liska 1960 *and* Morgenthau 1962. *The background writings for the two contrasting approaches are* Rostow 1960 *and* Staley 1954, *respectively. A successful attempt to present a balanced approach is* Millikan & Blackmer 1961.

A larger body of scholarly literature is concerned with the description, analysis, and evaluation of particular forms and programs of economic and military aid, with reference to particular countries or regions. Outstanding among these are Brown & Opie 1953; Price 1955; Mont-gomery 1962; Jordan 1962. *While also regionally focused,* Wolf 1960 *is valuable mainly as an attempt to evolve theoretical criteria for the allocation of aid.*

The foreign aid activities of the communist-bloc countries have been described in U.S. Department of State 1958; Berliner 1958; Allen 1960. *Important information regarding assistance through the United Nations can be found in* Asher et al. 1957 *and* Sharp 1952 *and in such periodicals as* Foreign Affairs, International Organization, *and* International Conciliation.

Sources on the antecedents of foreign aid are uneven. A classic source on the liberal period is Feis 1930, *which can be supplemented with* Michon 1927. *No single source deals exhaustively with dynastic subsidies. However, see* Braubach 1923 *and less systematic references in* Horn 1930 *and* Pinkham 1954. *Relevant for the understanding of the broader contemporary context of foreign aid activities are* Calvocoressi 1962; Emerson 1960; Ehrhard 1957; Martin 1962.

ALLEN, ROBERT L. 1960 *Soviet Economic Warfare.* Washington: Public Affairs Press.

ASHER, ROBERT E. et al. 1957 *The United Nations and Promotion of General Welfare.* Washington: Brookings Institution.

BERLINER, JOSEPH S. 1958 *Soviet Economic Aid: The New Aid and Trade Policy in Underdeveloped Countries.* Published for the Council on Foreign Relations. New York: Praeger.

BRAUBACH, MAX 1923 *Die Bedeutung der Subsidien für die Politik im spanischen Erbfolgekriege.* Bonn and Leipzig: Schroeder.

BROWN, WILLIAM ADAMS; and OPIE, REDVERS 1953 *American Foreign Assistance.* Washington: Brookings Institution.

CALVOCORESSI, PETER 1962 *World Order and New States.* London: Chatto & Windus.

EHRHARD, JEAN (1957) 1958 *Le destin du colonialisme.* 3d ed. Paris: Éditions Eyrolles.

EMERSON, RUPERT 1960 *From Empire to Nation: The Rise to Self-assertion of Asian and African Peoples.* Cambridge, Mass.: Harvard Univ. Press. → A paperback edition was published in 1962 by Beacon.

FEIS, HERBERT (1930) 1961 *Europe, The World's Banker, 1870–1914: An Account of European Foreign Investment and the Connection of World Finance With Diplomacy Before the War.* New York: Kelley.

HAVILAND, H. FIELD 1958 Foreign Aid and the Policy Process: 1957. *American Political Science Review* 52:689–724.

HORN, DAVID B. 1930 *Sir Charles Hanbury Williams and European Diplomacy (1747–1758).* London: Harrap.

JORDAN, AMOS A. 1962 *Foreign Aid and the Defense of Southeast Asia.* New York: Praeger.

LISKA, GEORGE 1960 *The New Statecraft: Foreign Aid in American Foreign Policy.* Univ. of Chicago Press.

MARTIN, LAURENCE W. (editor) 1962 *Neutralism and Nonalignment: The New States in World Affairs.* New York: Praeger.

MICHON, GEORGES (1927) 1929 *The Franco–Russian Alliance, 1891–1917.* London: Allen & Unwin. → First published in French.

MILLIKAN, MAX F.; and BLACKMER, DONALD L. M. (editors) 1961 *The Emerging Nations: Their Growth and United States Policy.* A study from the Center for International Studies, Massachusetts Institute of Technology. Boston: Little.

MILLIKAN, MAX F.; and ROSTOW, W. W. 1957 *A Proposal: Key to an Effective Foreign Policy.* A study from the Center for International Studies, Massachusetts Institute of Technology. New York: Harper.

MILLIKAN, MAX F.; and ROSTOW, W. W. 1958 Foreign Aid: Next Phase. *Foreign Affairs* 36:418–436.

MONTGOMERY, JOHN D. 1962 *The Politics of Foreign Aid: American Experience in Southeast Asia.* Published for the Council on Foreign Relations. New York: Praeger.

MORGENTHAU, HANS J. 1962 A Political Theory of Foreign Aid. *American Political Science Review* 56:301–309.

PINKHAM, LUCILE 1954 *William III and the Respectable Revolution: The Part Played by William of Orange in the Revolution of 1688.* Cambridge, Mass.: Harvard Univ. Press.

PRICE, HARRY B. 1955 *The Marshall Plan and Its Meaning.* Ithaca, N.Y.: Cornell Univ. Press.

ROSTOW, W. W. (1960) 1963 *The Stages of Economic Growth: A Non-Communist Manifesto.* Cambridge Univ. Press.

SHARP, WALTER R. 1952 *International Technical Assistance: Programs and Organization.* Chicago: Public Administration Service.

STALEY, EUGENE (1954) 1961 *The Future of Underdeveloped Countries: Political Implications of Economic Development.* Rev. ed. Published for the Council on Foreign Relations. New York: Harper.

U.S. COMMITTEE TO STRENGTHEN THE SECURITY OF THE FREE WORLD 1963 *The Scope and Distribution of United States Military and Economic Assistance Programs: Report to the President of the United States.* Washington: Government Printing Office. → Known as the Clay Committee report.

U.S. CONGRESS, SENATE, SPECIAL COMMITTEE TO STUDY THE FOREIGN AID PROGRAM 1957 *Foreign Aid Program: Compilation of Studies and Surveys.* 85th Congress, 1st Session, Senate Document No. 52. Washington: Government Printing Office.

U.S. DEPARTMENT OF STATE 1958 *The Sino–Soviet Economic Offensive in the Less Developed Countries.* Department of State Publication No. 6632; European and British Commonwealth Series, No. 51. Washington: Government Printing Office.

U.S. PRESIDENT'S COMMITTEE TO STUDY THE UNITED STATES MILITARY ASSISTANCE PROGRAM 1959 *Composite Report.* 2 vols. Washington: Government Printing Office. → Known as the Draper Committee report.

WOLF, CHARLES JR. 1960 *Foreign Aid: Theory and Practice in Southern Asia.* Princeton Univ. Press.

II

ECONOMIC ASPECTS

The international transfer of economic resources is the essence of foreign economic aid. The flow of public assistance consists of grants and loans in cash and kind, including technical assistance, from a donor government or international organization to other governments or enterprises in recipient countries. The sources, forms, and purposes of financial and technical assistance are extremely varied [see TECHNICAL ASSISTANCE]. Of primary importance, however, is the flow of resources to poor countries in order to accelerate their development. The purely economic function of this aid should be distinguished from that of direct military assistance, which may also be received by a developing country; moreover, aid should properly be considered as only that part of the foreign capital inflow that normal market incentives do not provide. [See INTERNATIONAL MONETARY ECONOMICS, *article on* PRIVATE INTERNATIONAL CAPITAL MOVEMENTS.]

Several aspects of foreign economic aid require particular emphasis: the historical evolution of aid programs; the determination of the objectives and magnitude of aid; the appraisal of the relative merits and demerits of different types of aid; the criteria of effective use of aid; and the burden of aid.

Evolution of aid programs. Foreign assistance programs have evolved through a series of legislative measures and administrative procedures required at different times for various purposes. Before World War II economic aid came mainly from metropolitan countries in support of overseas colonies and dependencies, was on a purely bilateral basis, and involved relatively small amounts of financial grants. [See COLONIALISM, *article on* ECONOMIC ASPECTS.]

The United States, however, early supported a large-scale assistance program through loans from the Export–Import Bank of Washington; since 1954 this bank has concentrated increasingly on capital assistance to less-developed countries. Aside from the lend–lease arrangements, which provided economic support to wartime allies, the first general foreign aid program supported by the United States came with the Economic Cooperation Act of 1948. This initiated the European Recovery Program (Marshall Aid Program), which during 1948–1952 furnished loans and grants to 17 western European countries that confronted problems of reconstruction and balance of payments pressures. Although aid under this program was not directly related to the problems of newly developing countries, it demonstrated the potential of international aid and was a prototype for subsequent aid programs.

In 1950 the U.S. Congress passed the Act for International Development, which incorporated a technical assistance program ("Point Four"). This was the first of a series of Foreign Assistance Acts. A variety of agencies have administered U.S. aid in the course of these successive programs. The United States has also provided, under Public Law 480 and "Food for Peace" programs, for the sale of surplus agricultural commodities for local currencies. In 1957 the Development Loan Fund was

Table 1 — United States government foreign aid by program: fiscal years 1941–1960ᵃ
(converted to millions of U.S. dollars)

	1941–1948	1949–1952	1953–1956	1957	1958	1959	1960	Total
Gross total—all programsᵇ	70,318	21,529	23,893	5,472	5,429	6,690	5,077	138,408
Investment in international financial institutions	3,385	—	—	35	—	1,375	80	4,875
Gross grants	57,167	18,959	20,924	4,142	3,963	3,860	3,654	112,669
Lend–lease	48,672	—	—	—	—	—	—	48,672
UNRRA and related aidᶜ	3,473	53	—	—	—	—	—	3,526
Aid to occupied areas	3,591	2,791	270	1	1	2	2	6,658
ERP, MSA, and other economic aidᵈ	514	11,778	6,622	1,502	1,244	1,369	1,314	24,343
Farm surplus disposalᵉ	—	49	653	281	365	312	314	1,974
MDAP and MSA military aidᶠ	—	3,073	13,377	2,358	2,353	2,177	2,023	25,361
Other grantsᵍ	914	1,214	2	—	—	—	—	2,130
Gross creditsᵇ	9,766	2,570	2,969	1,295	1,466	1,455	1,343	20,864
Lend–lease settlement	2,957	56	—	6	—	—	—	3,019
Export–Import Bank	2,570	880	1,547	237	760	708	399	7,101
British loan	3,750	—	—	—	—	—	—	3,750
ERP and MSA economic aid	—	1,532	512	106	232	240	315	2,937
Farm surplusʰ	—	—	860	937	474	506	629	3,406
Other credits	487	102	49	9	i	i	i	647

a. Fiscal years ending June 30; details may not add to totals because of rounding.
b. Includes net accumulation of foreign currency claims deriving from farm surplus disposal.
c. Includes post-UNRRA and Interim Aid.
d. ERP—European Recovery Program; MSA—Mutual Security Act; other aid includes contributions to UN agencies, technical assistance to Latin America, Inter-American and related highways, Trust Territory development, Libyan Special Purpose Fund, etc.
e. Donations of agricultural products plus dollar equivalent of foreign currency grants derived from farm surplus disposal.
f. MDAP—Mutual Defense Assistance Program.
g. Greek–Turkish, Chinese stabilization, and military aid; Philippine, Korean, and other Far East aid grants.
h. Dollar equivalent of loans made in foreign currencies derived from the farm surplus disposal programs, plus the net accumulation of such currencies.
i. Less than $500,000.

Sources: Foreign Grants and Credits by the United States Government, 1952, p. 81, appendix B; U.S. National Advisory Council on International Monetary and Financial Problems; Higgins 1962, table 3-1.

created to administer long-term, low-interest loans from the United States. The magnitude of American foreign aid from 1941 to 1960 is summarized by program in Table 1.

Although the United States has been the largest donor, many other countries have also participated in international economic assistance. Since 1954 the Soviet Union has entered into assistance agreements with developing countries and has also extended technical assistance on an increasing scale. While a considerable part of aid from non-communist Western countries has consisted of grants, the Soviet system has concentrated on long-term "bulk" credits, under which agreements for deliveries of goods on credit are negotiated. Although there has not been much difference in the length of loans and terms of repayment between Soviet and Western agreements, a larger proportion of Soviet aid has allowed for repayment in local currency or local products, and Soviet loans have had lower interest rates.

Soviet technical assistance has usually been supplied as part of a larger, integrated program

Table 2 — Commitments by the centrally planned economies of bilateral economic aid to underdeveloped countries, 1954–1960 (millions of U.S. dollars)

	Before 1958	1958	1959	1960	Total
Donor:					
China (mainland)	82	26	—	21	129
Czechoslovakia	21	68	76	50	215
East Germany	7	—	22	—	29
Poland	—	—	6	30	36
Rumania	—	11	—	—	11
U.S.S.R.	712	345	782	804	2,643
Yugoslavia	—	10	67	58	135
Total, donor countries	822	460	953	963	3,198
of which:					
Credits	769	460	945	939	3,113
Grants	53	—	8	24	85
Recipient:					
Africa	—	—	181	60	241
Latin America	4	102	6	120	232
Middle East	203	282	272	270	1,027
Southeast Asia	615	76	494	513	1,698
Total, recipient countries	822	460	953	963	3,198

Source: UN, Department of Economic and Social Affairs 1961, table 16, p. 34.

consisting of loans, development goods, and bilateral trade; in contrast, technical aid from Western countries has usually been connected to individual projects or to specific training objectives. Communist-bloc technical experts have also concentrated on relatively few conspicuous projects that entail complex technology, while American technical assistance has emphasized the broader and more basic needs of agriculture, health, and education.

As may be noted in Table 2, commitments (which were not in all instances implemented) made by the centrally planned economies to the underdeveloped countries amounted, by the end of 1960, to approximately $3,200 million. Table 3 compares the magnitude of aid from the Sino–Soviet bloc with that of the United States.

Other countries have also sponsored bilateral aid programs—notably the United Kingdom, France, West Germany, Canada, and Japan. Table 4 summarizes the magnitude of bilateral aid during 1958–1960.

Regional organizations have also been significant contributors to aid: the Colombo Plan for Cooperative Economic Development in South and Southeast Asia, inaugurated in 1950; the Organization for American States, formed in 1951 and strengthened by the Inter-American Development Bank in 1959, the Act of Bogotá of 1960, and the Charter of Punta del Este, which launched the "Alliance for Progress"; and the Organization for Economic Cooperation and Development (OECD), which in 1961 succeeded the Organization for European Economic Cooperation (OEEC).

Finally, the United Nations and a number of its specialized agencies play a prominent role in foreign aid: the International Bank for Reconstruction and Development (IBRD), International Finance Corporation (IFC), United Nations Special Fund (UNSF), International Development Association (IDA), Technical Assistance Board (TAB), World Health Organization (WHO), Food and Agriculture Organization (FAO), and regional economic commissions.

Utilizing the capital subscribed by member nations, the loans raised in the markets of member countries, and the return on its own operations, the IBRD has been the principal development-financing institution of the United Nations. The IDA has provided loans at very long term and with no or low interest, and it has had great latitude in its selection of projects for financing. This has enabled the IDA to meet the special needs of developing countries that, for balance of payments reasons, were nearing the limit of their capacity

Table 3 — Comparison of economic credits and grants extended to less-developed countries by the Sino–Soviet bloc and the United States (millions of U.S. dollars)

	SINO–SOVIET BLOC	UNITED STATES*	
	Mid-1955–December 1961	Mid-1955–December 1961	Mid-1948–December 1961
Total	4,371	9,449	12,727
Latin America	465	1,341	2,080
Argentina	104	360	524
Brazil	4	961	1,515
Cuba	357	20	41
Middle East	1,077	1,896	2,723
Cyprus	1	10	10
Egypt	615	394	479
Iran	6	411	672
Iraq	216	13	21
Syria	178	69	70
Turkey	17	980	1,452
Yemen	44	19	19
Africa	601	502	512
Ethiopia	114	115	125
Ghana	182	35	35
Guinea	110	4	4
Mali	65	2	2
Somalia	62	15	15
Sudan	22	64	64
Tunisia	46	267	267
Asia	2,112	4,881	5,973
Afghanistan	204	138	184
Burma	93	68	90
Cambodia	65	195	232
Ceylon	58	77	77
India	963	2,726	3,221
Indonesia	641	308	541
Nepal	55	40	44
Pakistan	33	1,329	1,584
Europe	116	829	1,439
Iceland	5	35	70
Yugoslavia	111	794	1,369

* U.S. figures include credits and grants from ICA obligations; DLF loans approved; Export–Import Bank long-term loans authorized; and Public Law 480 funds earmarked for country use under Title I, authorizations under Title II, and shipments under Title III.

Source: U.S. Congress, Committee on Appropriations, p. 207.

to borrow abroad for development projects on conventional terms. The IFC has been instrumental in assisting private industrial development by investing without government guarantee in productive private enterprises. During the year 1961/1962, the IBRD and its two affiliates, the IFC and IDA, made new commitments of more than $1,000 million. Although not itself a lending agency, the UNSF has made greater investment feasible and more effective by granting assistance for preinvestment work in the form of surveys, training, and applied research. Contributions to the United Na-

Table 4 — Bilateral aid to underdeveloped countries, 1958–1960
(millions of U.S. dollars)a

Contributing country	CALENDAR YEAR 1958			CALENDAR YEAR 1959			CALENDAR YEAR 1960		
	Grants	Loans	Repayments	Grants	Loans	Repayments	Grants	Loans	Repayments
Australiab	37.0	1.2	—	34.4	0.6	—	39.2	1.7	—
Belgiumc	4.0	—	—	30.0	—	—	86.0	—	—
Canada	47.3	9.5	—	60.3	1.3	—	48.1	—	—
Denmark	—	—	—	—	—	—	0.7	—	—
France	524.5	227.6	41.2	665.2	176.2	42.4	687.0	87.0	19.0
Germany (FRG)	5.2	74.4	16.0	6.6	46.1	17.5	6.2	77.5	16.9
Italy	10.2	—	1.7	9.0	30.5	8.9	8.9	16.8	10.0
Japan	177.4	—	—	4.0	—	—	2.5	78.6	—
Netherlands	20.8	1.7	—	21.7	2.3	—	28.2	3.6	—
New Zealandd	4.2	0.2	—	5.0	0.3	—	6.3	—	—
Norway	1.2	—	—	1.0	—	—	0.9	—	—
Sweden	0.8	—	—	0.9	—	—	1.0	—	—
Switzerland	0.1	—	—	0.1	—	—	—	—	—
United Kingdom	143.0	67.0	20.0	151.0	137.0	25.0	165.0	176.0	22.0
United States	1,132.0	796.0	167.0	1,157.0	733.0	205.0	1,320.0	723.0	220.0
Yugoslavia	—	—	—	—	—	—	0.3	26.0	—

a. Omits aid from Sino–Soviet bloc.
b. Fiscal years ending 30 June of years stated.
c. Advances to Ruanda–Urundi with no specific schedule of repayment are treated as grants.
d. Fiscal years ending 31 March of years stated.

Source: UN, Statistical Office 1961, table 157, p. 467.

tions Expanded Program of Technical Assistance amounted to over $41.5 million in 1961, compared with less than $20 million a decade earlier.

The amount of capital assistance from the United Nations has been small in comparison with bilateral programs, but it has particular importance because of its multilateral character. The same is true for the technical assistance programs provided by the United Nations itself and by several of its specialized agencies. Table 5 indicates the magnitude of multilateral aid, 1958–1960, while Table 6 shows the magnitude of public aid by source and type, 1953/1954–1958/1959. In recent years the relative share of the flow of capital to underdeveloped countries has been approximately 90 per cent on a bilateral basis and only 10 per cent on a multilateral basis, with the IBRD, IFC, and IDA accounting for slightly over one-half of the multilateral aid.

Objectives and magnitude of aid. Foreign aid is usually a component of a nation's foreign policy; for this reason its objectives are diverse. The underlying objectives may be mixed even for a particular act of assistance by a single government

Table 5 — Multilateral aid to underdeveloped countries, 1958–1960
(millions of U.S. dollars)

Source*	CALENDAR YEAR 1958			CALENDAR YEAR 1959			CALENDAR YEAR 1960		
	Grants	Loans	Repayments	Grants	Loans	Repayments	Grants	Loans	Repayments
EDF	—	—	—	0.1	—	—	3.4	—	—
IBRD	—	345.7	47.0	—	310.3	68.5	—	340.1	91.5
IFC	—	4.9	—	—	7.8	—	—	13.6	—
UNICEF	18.3	—	—	20.4	—	—	18.3	—	—
UNRWA	31.8	—	—	34.1	—	—	34.7	—	—
UNSF	—	—	—	0.3	—	—	2.0	—	—
UNEPTA	25.9	—	—	24.7	—	—	24.1	—	—
Other UNTA	10.8	—	—	11.3	—	—	13.5	—	—

* The following abbreviations have been introduced in the table: EDF, Development Fund of the European Economic Community; IBRD, International Bank for Reconstruction and Development; IFC, International Finance Corporation; UNICEF, United Nations Children's Fund; UNRWA, United Nations Relief and Works Agency for Palestine Refugees in the Near East; UNSF, United Nations Special Fund; UNEPTA, United Nations Expanded Programme of Technical Assistance; and other UNTA, all programs of technical assistance administered by the United Nations, the specialized agencies, and the International Atomic Energy Agency, other than EPTA.

Source: UN, Statistical Office 1961, table 157, p. 467.

Table 6 — Total governmental aid, multilateral and bilateral, by type, 1953/1954–1958/1959

	1953/1954–1955/1956 ANNUAL AVERAGE			1957/1958–1958/1959 ANNUAL AVERAGE		
	Grants	Loans (net)	Total	Grants	Loans (net)	Total
Total aid in billions of U.S. dollars	1.5	0.5	2.0	2.2	1.1	3.3
Bilateral aid	1.4	0.4	1.8	2.1	0.8	2.9
Multilateral aid	0.1	0.1	0.2	0.1	0.3	0.4
Total aid as percentage distribution by type	74.4	25.6	100	66.0	34.0	100
Bilateral aid	77.0	23.0	100	70.9	29.1	100
Multilateral aid	48.3	51.7	100	27.2	72.8	100

Source: UN, Secretary-General 1961, p. 48.

to another—since humanitarian motives, military interests, and political purposes tend to fuse with the purely economic objective.

Solely in terms of the direct economic goal, foreign aid is intended to augment the resources of the recipient country so that its rate of development may be raised. The largest proportion of the flow of public funds has been devoted to investment projects in industry, agriculture, mining, and basic "overhead" facilities, such as power and transportation [see CAPITAL, SOCIAL OVERHEAD]. To achieve a higher rate of economic development, however, a country must also experience social development through investment in human resources, introduction of new techniques of production, and institution building. Technical assistance programs fulfill some of these requirements by improving health and education and supporting rural community development. Even though social projects are difficult to evaluate in terms of economic criteria alone and hence are a questionable objective of economic aid, financial and technical assistance may nonetheless be necessary to initiate social programs that will contribute to higher productivity. An even more controversial objective of foreign aid is stabilization assistance in the form of balance of payments, or general purpose, loans to a country that has current external liabilities in excess of its international reserves or to a country that cannot meet its current liabilities out of current foreign exchange earnings without restricting essential imports.

Clarity on the objectives of foreign aid is the necessary first step in determining how much aid is needed by a recipient country. But even when the objectives are clearly defined, it is still extremely difficult to calculate the magnitude and duration of external assistance required to attain these objectives. Nonetheless, such calculations are commonly attempted, especially in relation to the recipient country's development plan. Although the statistical exactitude of this type of calculation

is illusory, its logic is of interest, and improvement of the concepts and methodology underlying these quantitative estimates may result from more intensive consideration of the problems involved.

The usual type of calculation proceeds as follows: A target is set for the desired increase in per capita real income over a given time period. On the basis of estimated annual population growth and the economy's marginal capital–output ratio (the ratio between the value of additional capital and the value of additional annual output produced), it is concluded that a certain percentage of national income must be saved and invested to attain the per capita income target. If domestic saving is less than this amount and cannot be immediately raised by domestic policy measures, the balance must be sought from external sources. To the extent that private foreign investment does not fill the gap, public funds from abroad are required.

This exercise is, however, a highly oversimplified way to calculate aid requirements. Capital–output ratios have not yet been measured accurately enough to justify their use in deriving quantitative conclusions. Moreover, exclusive concentration merely on the relationships between a capital–output ratio, a savings ratio, and population growth is a much too mechanical and narrow interpretation, for it misses the inner complexity and subtleties of the development process. Other factors besides investment are strategic in accelerating development, and the full implications of external aid cannot be appreciated without a more comprehensive analysis of the role of foreign capital. In the broadest context the analysis should consider how the foreign aid relates to a greater national effort to increase the rate of development, and it should examine the differential impact of various forms of capital assistance in terms of their costs and benefits.

Although the calculation of foreign aid requirements is difficult, the underlying rationale for such aid is clear. It is not possible to relate any one source of funds to a specific type of use, but the net capital imports can offset, or "finance," the difference between the value of products used and the value of products produced domestically; or the difference between net investment and net domestic savings; or the value of imports and factor payments abroad *minus* the value of exports and factor receipts. All these differences constitute a shortfall in real resources that results when the claims of the development plan exceed the available domestic resources. This gap in real resources is in turn reflected in a foreign exchange gap. To the extent that the use of foreign exchange reserves or an inflow of private capital does not fill the gap, public capital assistance from abroad will be necessary to give command over the additional resources. The size of a development plan is therefore constrained by the amount of foreign economic aid that is forthcoming.

While the dependence on external aid may have to be large at the outset of the development program, most plans aim for a progressive reduction in aid and the eventual realization of a self-financing plan. To achieve this the plan relies on a high marginal rate of domestic saving. It is expected that the proportion that can be saved out of an increase in output will be much higher than the average savings ratio at the plan's beginning. The proportion of national income invested and financed by domestic savings would then increase, and the ratio of net foreign capital imports to additional investment would decline. The reliance on foreign aid will also diminish if, as development proceeds, the composition of investment alters toward projects with a lower import content, the production of import-substitutes increases, export revenue expands, and total domestic output grows without inflationary financing.

Forms of aid. The significance of foreign aid depends not only on its magnitude but also on the terms on which it is made available. The various forms of financial assistance can be differentiated by their terms—whether "hard" loans, "soft" loans, or grants; by the parties they involve—whether government-to-government or government-to-enterprise and whether furnished by national or multilateral agencies; and by their conditions—whether for specific projects or for a general development program.

Hard loans carry a commercial rate of interest, have a relatively short amortization period, and require repayment in foreign currency. Various types of soft loans are possible: very long-term loans repayable in foreign currency at a low rate of interest or without interest; loans repayable in local cur-

rency; long-term loans at low interest with a long grace period for payment of principal and interest.

Since they require neither servicing nor repayment, grants rather than loans are sometimes proposed for projects involving "social" development. It is thought that loans are appropriate for self-liquidating "economic" projects, where the criterion can be ability to service the loan, but that grants should be made for such nonself-liquidating projects as education, health, and community development, where the criterion is simply "need." International grants do have the merit of adding no burden of interest and amortization charges upon the recipient country, and they are a clear manifestation of the donor's willingness to offer a unilateral income transfer.

There is, however, little justification in differentiating between "social" and "economic" capital, insofar as both can contribute to an expansion of total output, which is the basic consideration in determining the recipient country's capacity to service foreign obligations. If in the interest of assuring effective use of grants, the granters attempt to exercise more control over the recipient country than would be the case for loans, then grants may, of course, be resented. And while it may be politically inexpedient for a donor nation to offer grants, there may be less political opposition to loans—even with generous low-interest and long-term provisions.

Although the greater part of all economic aid has been on a bilateral basis, several arguments are advanced in favor of providing more aid through multilateral channels: better coordination of assistance activities can be achieved; the aid is more acceptable to recipient nations; the practice of discrimination among recipients is more difficult, and the aid program is less susceptible to political influences; tied loans (requiring expenditure in the lending country) are avoided; and more appropriate technical assistance may be obtained by drawing upon the experience of all nations.

In some areas and for some activities international auspices may not be feasible. And few would insist that all types of aid be administered by international agencies. Short of complete multilateralism, however, there is still considerable scope and need for the multilateral coordination of bilateral programs—multilateral supervision of the technical, financial, and commodity aid supplied by individual countries.

Another major issue is whether aid should be given only for a specific project or extended for general purposes too. Advocates of the project approach claim that only by financing soundly conceived projects will foreign aid contribute to an increase in productive capital. The IBRD, for instance, has tended to give prime consideration to the foreign exchange requirements of specific projects, emphasizing the economic soundness of the projects and their direct contribution to the productivity of the borrowing country. Moreover, it is claimed that the review of specific projects has some educational value and allows the donor to act more readily as a critic of the details of the recipient's development plan.

It has become increasingly clear that the effectiveness of aid depends not merely on the productivity of specific projects but more generally on the complementarity of different projects and the appropriateness of the developing country's allocation of total investment expenditures from both domestic and foreign sources. Similarly, the narrow view that aid should be confined to the foreign exchange component of specific projects misses the fundamental principle that the receipt of aid allows the country to acquire command over resources in general, not simply to increase command of foreign resources in particular. Insofar as changes occur in the general program of development, it is impossible to identify exactly the inflow of capital with a specific project; the inflow contributes to the whole program. The effectiveness of aid depends upon the country's allocation of its general resources. The same consideration is relevant for determining the country's capacity to service foreign debt, as noted below.

Use of aid. Even if aid is provided in substantial amounts and on favorable terms, there remains the ultimate problem of achieving its most effective use. External assistance should add to—not substitute for—the country's own developmental efforts. If capital assistance is to result in a higher rate of investment, it must be prevented from simply substituting for domestic sources of financing investment, and it should not be dissipated in supporting higher personal consumption or an increase in nondevelopment current expenditure by the government.

If external assistance were to be used for bolstering current consumption, the scope for the use of foreign capital would obviously be practically boundless. When this use is excluded, the economically warranted demand for capital is limited by the country's ability to use capital productively— that is, by the country's "capital absorptive capacity." In the short run, even if not in the long run, there may be a limit to how much capital assistance can be effectively used when the investment must not only cover its costs but also yield a reasonable increase in income. It should also be recognized that the effective use of capital assistance may depend in large part upon the effectiveness of technical assistance. For the purpose of contributing technical aid is essentially to raise absorptive capacity. Once the pace of development gains momentum, the absorptive capacity will be higher, and foreign capital can then be utilized more effectively.

When capital assistance is not confined to specific investment projects but is available on a general-purpose basis, the allocation of the foreign capital is decisive in determining whether it contributes as much as possible to raising the growth potential of the recipient economy. An efficient allocation of investment resources then depends upon the application of investment criteria based on the country's entire development program and the adoption of appropriate domestic policy measures to supplement the use of foreign aid. Since the formation of capital depends, in the last resort, on domestic action, there can be no simple equivalence between the amount of aid received and the subsequent rate of development. The effectiveness of the use made of foreign aid in the country's entire development program will be more decisive in determining whether development is to be sustained than is the initial amount of aid received.

It is therefore proper to emphasize the necessity of self-help measures, as American aid programs have increasingly done. Unless recipient governments adopt measures to mobilize fully their own resources and to implement their plans, the maximum potential from aid will not be realized. It has become increasingly evident that to realize this objective in many poor countries it is necessary to undertake basic reforms in land tenure systems, the tax structure, education, and governmental administration. Additional attention must therefore be given to the sociocultural and political aspects of aid.

Burden of aid. Significant as the benefits from aid may be, they are not without their costs. For the donor there is a burden in mobilizing aid; for the recipient, a burden of debt servicing and repayment.

Although the mobilization of aid is not limited by a physical incapacity on the part of donor countries to provide the needed resources, there is a problem of paying for the transference of the resources. Unless inflation is to be endured, it is necessary to withdraw—by taxation or government borrowing—the money equivalent of the resources to be transferred.

Moreover, the donor nation may be intensifying the difficulty of maintaining equilibrium in its balance of payments, unless it requires that its loans and grants be expended in the country of origin. If such "tied" aid is necessary out of balance of payments considerations, and the alternative to tied funds would be no aid at all, then the larger amount of tied aid is to be preferred, even though the condition that the aid be expended in the donor country may diminish the value of the aid to the recipient country as compared with freedom to import from a third country.

The willingness of an individual country to bear the burden of providing resources out of public funds may depend on the willingness of other countries to share in the burden. An increase in the total flow of aid becomes politically more feasible if there is a belief that the burden is being shared equitably. But there is no unambiguous formula for determining what constitutes an equitable distribution among the contributors of aid. A refined proposal would have the developed countries contribute according to a progressive tax schedule applied to the country's per capita real gross national product. Perhaps the most practicable solution is to accept the commonly advocated proposal of a flat-rate levy on national income—say, one per cent of the national income of the donor nations.

For the recipient country the burden of foreign aid depends upon the country's capacity to service its external obligations. When the return flow of interest and of amortization payments exceeds the inflow of new capital assistance, the country confronts a transfer problem in servicing the debt. It will have to generate an export surplus to cover the net outward transfer of amortization on capital account and of interest payments on current account. This entails a transformation of the economy such that resources can be reallocated to the sector producing exports or import-substitutes. To accomplish this the country may have to endure internal and external controls or experience exchange depreciation. The adverse effects of these measures of balance of payments adjustment might be interpreted as the indirect costs of foreign aid, to be added to the direct costs.

The direct cost of servicing capital assistance, however, is not a burden in itself. Even though part of the increased production from the use of foreign capital has to be paid abroad in interest—and this is a deduction that would not be necessary if the savings were provided at home—nonetheless the country has benefited from additional investment. What does matter in mitigating the burden of the debt is the country's ability to avoid the necessity of adopting restrictive measures in order to find sufficient foreign exchange for the remittance of the external service payments. To minimize these indirect costs the country's development program must give due consideration to the debt-servicing capacity of the country.

This becomes part of the problem of selecting appropriate investment criteria. To provide for adequate servicing of the foreign debt the capital should increase productivity sufficiently to yield an increase in real income greater than the interest and amortization charges. If this is done, the economy will have the capacity to raise the necessary funds—either through a direct commercial return or greater taxable capacity. Moreover, to provide a sufficient surplus of foreign exchange to avoid a transfer problem, the capital should be utilized in such a way as to generate a surplus in the other items of the balance of payments equal to the transfer payments abroad. If it is realized that the ability to create a sufficiently large export surplus depends on the operation of all industries together, not simply on the use made of foreign investment, it is then apparent that a project financed by foreign aid need not itself make a direct contribution to the balance of payments. Instead of such a narrow balance of payments criterion, the basic test for the allocation of capital aid is simply that it should be invested in the form that yields the highest social marginal product. As long as capital is distributed according to its most productive use and the excess spending associated with inflation is avoided, the necessary export surplus can be created indirectly. The essential point is that the allocation of foreign aid according to the criterion of productivity will also be the most favorable for debt servicing, since it maximizes the increase in income from a given amount of capital and thereby contributes to the growth of foreign exchange availabilities.

The problem of debt servicing will also be eased for the aid-receiving country when capital assistance is offered at lower interest, for longer terms, and with more stability and when the creditor country follows a more expansionary domestic policy and a more liberal trade policy.

Need for further research. Foreign aid has been extended mainly in an *ad hoc* fashion in response to immediate policy situations and without the opportunity for a substantial amount of prior research. Its practice, however, has suggested several areas of basic research that merit considerably more investigation. Of fundamental importance is the need for clear criteria in determining aid requirements, its optimal allocation among recipients, and its most effective use.

Since foreign economic aid is only a single component of the total flow of resources from rich to poor countries, it is important to investigate more thoroughly the relationships between capital assistance, private foreign investment, and international trade. Under what conditions can loans and grants stimulate private foreign investment? And under what conditions are they competitive? To what extent are the benefits of foreign aid being offset by adverse foreign trade policies? Might not more be gained from policies that stabilize the poor countries' foreign exchange earnings than from additional capital assistance?

Insofar as the effective use of foreign aid may depend on social and political reforms, it would be instructive to examine more systematically the sociocultural and political aspects of foreign aid. This should serve to correct the tendency to overemphasize capital productivity and technical productivity at the expense of noneconomic variables that are strategic in the development process. [See ECONOMIC GROWTH, *article on* NONECONOMIC ASPECTS.]

The impact of technical assistance might also be greater if additional research were undertaken on the special problems of adapting techniques of production to the special circumstances of the poor countries. Not only should research be directed toward new scientific advances of particular utility to underdeveloped economies, but the problems of diffusing the new technology and gaining its acceptance in the recipient society must also be solved.

Further, attention should be given to the possible means of coordinating the many different actual and potential sources of foreign assistance and to feasible arrangements for giving greater continuity to the flow of aid.

Finally, on the basis of accumulated experience in a variety of countries it would be useful to have a number of case studies of foreign aid as a basis for a comparative study of the conditions under which different types of aid have proved effective.

GERALD M. MEIER

[*See also* COMMUNITY, *article on* COMMUNITY DEVELOPMENT; ECONOMIC GROWTH; PLANNING, ECONOMIC, *article on* DEVELOPMENT PLANNING; TECHNICAL ASSISTANCE.]

BIBLIOGRAPHY

ALTER, G. M. 1961 The Servicing of Foreign Capital Inflows by Underdeveloped Countries. Pages 139–162 in International Economic Association, *Economic Development for Latin America*. Edited by Howard S. Ellis. New York: St. Martins.

ASHER, ROBERT E. 1961 *Grants, Loans, and Local Currencies: Their Role in Foreign Aid*. Washington: Brookings Institution.

BENHAM, FREDERIC C. 1961 *Economic Aid to Underdeveloped Countries*. Oxford Univ. Press.

BERLINER, JOSEPH S. 1958 *Soviet Economic Aid: The New Aid and Trade Policy in Underdeveloped Countries*. New York: Praeger.

BROWN, WILLIAM A.; and OPIE, REDVERS 1953 *American Foreign Assistance*. Washington: Brookings Institution.

CHENERY, HOLLIS B.; and STROUT, ALAN M. 1966 Foreign Assistance and Economic Development. *American Economic Review* 56:679–733.

FEI, J. C. H.; and PAAUW, D. S. 1965 Foreign Assistance and Self-help: A Reappraisal of Development Finance. *Review of Economics and Statistics* 47:251–267.

Foreign Grants and Credits by the United States Government. → Issued since 1948, under various titles, by the U.S. Department of Commerce, Office of Business Economics. Reports prior to No. 15 (1948) are classified restricted and are available only to authorized officials of the U.S. Government. See especially the issue for 1952, page 81, Appendix B.

HIGGINS, BENJAMIN 1962 *United Nations and U.S. Foreign Economic Policy*. Homewood, Ill.: Irwin.

LITTLE, I. M. D.; and CLIFFORD, J. M. (1965) 1966 *International Aid: A Discussion of the Flow of Public Resources From Rich to Poor Countries, With Particular Reference to British Policy*. London: Allen & Unwin; Chicago: Aldine.

NEALE, ALAN D. 1961 *The Flow of Resources From Rich to Poor*. Cambridge, Mass.: Harvard Univ., Center for International Affairs.

OHLIN, GORAN 1966 *Foreign Aid Policies Reconsidered*. Paris: Organization for Economic Cooperation and Development, Development Center.

PINCUS, JOHN A. 1965 *Economic Aid and International Cost Sharing*. Baltimore: Johns Hopkins Press.

ROSENSTEIN-RODAN, P. N. 1961 International Aid for Underdeveloped Countries. *Review of Economics and Statistics* 43:107–138.

SINGER, H. W. 1965 External Aid: For Plans or Projects? *Economic Journal* 75:539–545.

UN, DEPARTMENT OF ECONOMIC AND SOCIAL AFFAIRS 1961 *International Flow of Long-term Capital and Official Donations: 1951–1959*. New York: United Nations. → See especially page 34, Table 16.

UN, SECRETARY-GENERAL 1961 *International Economic Assistance to the Less-developed Countries: Report to the Economic and Social Council*. New York: United Nations. → See especially page 48.

UN, SECRETARY-GENERAL 1962 *The United Nations Development Decade; Proposals for Action: Report*. New York: United Nations.

UN, STATISTICAL OFFICE 1961 *Statistical Yearbook, 1960*. New York: United Nations. → See especially Table 157, page 467. Copyright United Nations 1961. Data reproduced by permission.

U.S. CONGRESS, HOUSE, COMMITTEE ON APPROPRIATION *Foreign Operations Appropriations: Hearings*. → See especially the hearings for 1963.

U.S. CONGRESS, JOINT ECONOMIC COMMITTEE 1961 *Economic Policies Toward Less Developed Countries*. 87th Congress, 1st Session. Washington: Government Printing Office.

U.S. NATIONAL ADVISORY COUNCIL ON INTERNATIONAL MONETARY AND FINANCIAL PROBLEMS *Report of Activities*. → Published since 1945.

WOLF, CHARLES JR. 1960 *Foreign Aid: Theory and Practice in Southern Asia*. Princeton Univ. Press.

FOREIGN POLICY

For half a century the making of foreign policy has been studied in Western democratic countries as a field of specialization separate from the making of public policy in general. This intellectual differentiation rests upon implicit and explicit assumptions about the way the foreign policy field differs from other areas of public policy. The leading assumption is that foreign policy is "more important" than other policy areas because it concerns national interests, rather than special interests, and more fundamental values. A second assumption builds upon the first: since foreign policy questions evoke a different political response, it is assumed that political institutions function differently when they confront foreign policy issues. In addition, of course, different institutions are also involved, in that some governmental agencies are concerned exclusively or substantially with foreign policy. There is growing uncertainty among political scientists, in the United States at least, as to the validity of these assumptions. There is also considerable skepticism concerning the theoretical value of treating foreign policy processes as analytically distinct—a skepticism that will undoubtedly draw all the different public policy research fields closer together in the future. Nevertheless, the present state of our knowledge reflects, for better or worse, a set of beliefs about the uniqueness of foreign policy processes within the political order.

This orientation toward foreign policy making can be traced to World War I and the events leading up to it—although it might have developed in the United States in any case, since these were America's first years of great-power status and a period in which increasing attention was given to foreign relations. In the United States the war experience convinced some people that isolationism was no longer an appropriate response to international problems and that the United States must remain actively involved in the affairs of the world. Foreign policy became, for these people, the most important area of public policy, and responsible international participation the only viable political stance. And in both England and the United States the war gave rise to movements to end the traditional secretive practices of the world's statesmen and diplomats, movements that found concrete expression in Wilson's plea for "open covenants of peace, openly arrived at" and in the conference diplomacy of the League of Nations. Points One and Fourteen, and Wilsonian philosophy generally, were major building blocks in the progressive "democratization" of foreign policy.

Logically, this struggle for greater public participation in, and control over, foreign relations could have resulted in the assimilation of foreign policy to the working principles and practices of everyday politics in democratic countries. That it has not may be attributed to the prior claim for the "primacy of foreign policy," to the ineluctable requirements of secrecy imposed by the demands of national political and military strategies, and to the small amount of interest in foreign policy on the part of the general public.

Nevertheless, the study of foreign policy making was permanently affected by the liberal, rationalist, democratic ideology, with its twin convictions that the people, once they were educated, would make liberal and wise decisions in foreign policy and that man could improve his political institutions and their policy outputs if he would only think about them intelligently. These convictions explain the focus of attention, down to the present day, on the search for "better" ways to handle foreign policy, both organizationally and politically, so that public values and common sense might be more freely admitted into policy-making circles, and "better" policies (that is, responsible international participation) might eventuate.

The bulk of scholarly enterprise in the field of foreign policy making lies along one or the other of these two lines of concern, which I shall summarize here as "rationality" and "ideology." By "rationality" I mean a concern for the organization and structure of policy making which generally (but by no means exclusively) reflects a belief that certain policy-making relationships or arrangements can be found that are for one reason or another more "rational" than any others—that is to say, better designed to implement the values and decisions of intelligent and responsible foreign policy makers. By "ideology" I mean a concern for democratic control of foreign policy making which generally (although, again, not exclusively) reflects a belief that foreign policy decisions should be made by politically responsive or responsible individuals or groups and that the foreign policy of a democratic society can be wise and strong only to the extent that it commands the understanding and support of the public. Cutting across these two major approaches to the subject of foreign policy making are three different levels of analysis: the individual, the institutional, and the systemic. There are thus six major classifications, or clusters, into which the political scientist's study of foreign policy making may be conveniently divided for explanatory purposes. We shall look at each of these in turn, largely in the American context, since by its intellectual antecedents and history this subject has been of interest predominantly to American scholars. Having done this, we will be in a better position to identify and discuss research on foreign policy making in other countries and research through cross-national comparisons.

The rational approaches

Rational–institutional approach. The central focus of the study of foreign policy making has long been on the institutions of government that are chiefly responsible for the formulation and administration of foreign policy. And in the present period, as in the past, the motivating force seems to be the uncovering of more efficient, effective ways of organizing the policy-making machinery so that it rationally serves the interests or purposes of the analyst, whether these purposes are economy, speed of decision, singularity of authority, or coherence in execution. The executive departments and agencies—the Executive Office of the President, the Department of State, the Foreign Service, the Department of Defense, the Central Intelligence Agency, the U.S. Information Agency, the Peace Corps—have been studied and, in many cases, restudied from different perspectives in the various historical periods that mark America's development as a major power in world affairs. And certain of the functions of these institutions have come in for some scrutiny—diplomacy, for one, because the work of the diplomat is involved in so many of the processes of foreign policy making and execution, and intelligence, for another, because of the steady enlargement in the scope of covert political operations. Some examples of studies in this area are the works by Ransom (1958), Ilchman (1961), and McCamy (1964) on the executive side and Carroll (1958) on the congressional side.

In recent years, also, growing attention has been paid to the planning function in foreign affairs; this has been in response to the fear that without the assignment of adequate institutional responsibilities for thinking about the future, no one will have the time to give advance thought to emerging problems and to their avoidance or solution. (Current concern with foreign policy planning represents, perhaps better than anything else, the faith that political problems, like scientific or engineering problems, can be solved by the timely application of rational thought and organization.)

Because of the complexity of the institutional framework for making foreign policy and the frequency with which the institutions are altered either formally or through usage, the rational–institutional outlook has also focused on interagency coordination as a technique for rationalizing the continuously unwieldy processes of foreign policy formulation and agreement within the government. Actually, the phrase "administration of foreign affairs" refers as much to the coordination of powerful and nearly autonomous foreign policy agencies both at home and "in the field" as it does to the processes of policy making and execution within these agencies (Brookings Institution 1960). The development of high-level coordinating mechanisms like the National Security Council has drawn the interest of scholars, government officials, and members of Congress (see Hammond 1961) who have feared that the coordinating institutions may take over important policy-making functions.

Rational–individual approach. The development of the social sciences, especially of psychology, under the impetus of the political and social crises of World War II resulted in a new orientation toward the individual as the organizing point for political research. In opposition to what was felt to be the empty formalism of traditional institutional and administrative analyses, some students of foreign policy making shifted their focus to individuals and the ways in which they perceived the internal and external factors that came to bear on their institutional settings. The major products of this new line of inquiry have been decision-making studies (e.g., Snyder et al. 1962) that attempt to understand both the factors in human choice and the logic of administrative structure in the foreign policy field by examining the processes of individual and group decision making in institutional settings.

Recent developments in organization theory, although based on research in other types of institutions (e.g., Cyert & March 1963), have considerable relevance to the study of behavior in foreign policy agencies and should be an important influence on future research. The behavior of individuals when they occupy policy-making roles is central to the analysis of decision making, in game models as in the real world, and it explains the continuing interest in biographies and memoirs of policy officials. Students of foreign policy look to political biography, both conventional and psychoanalytic (see George & George 1956), for life experiences that help to illuminate the relations between individuals possessing particular personality types, backgrounds, and the like and the operating norms of particular policy-making offices.

Rational–systemic approach. At still another level, the search for more rational arrangements of organization and structure in the foreign policy field has led scholars to study the patterned interactions of individuals and institutions that constitute the universe of foreign policy making. These studies of interactions or systems cover dyadic relationships between political actors as well as more inclusive studies of how men and institutions handle problems or produce policies. And if the focus, on the individual level, is on reality as perceived by persons in policy-making roles, here the focus may be said to be on the objective reality created by the interactions of two or more political institutions.

The interactions of individuals and institutions involve accommodations of power and interest that we customarily associate with politics rather than administration. This is the case whether the individuals or institutions stand in some hierarchical relationship to one another or are relatively autonomous, deriving their power independently from other sources. Yet much of the scholarly work at the systemic level overlooks these sources of conflicts of power and interest, approaching the subject instead as if there were some arrangements of the foreign-policy-making institutions of government that were rationally or optimally designed to achieve a superior kind of foreign policy. Some commonly studied partial systems of foreign policy making, described in the phrases "executive–legislative relations" and "bipartisanship," are often treated in this way. The three-cornered relationship of the president, his party in Congress, and the opposition party in Congress has often been examined (e.g., Woodrow Wilson Foundation 1952) to see if a way could be discovered to remove the friction in the system that is presumed to interfere with the smooth functioning of a unified, national-interest-oriented policy machinery. [See BIPARTISANSHIP.]

Recent scholarship, however, has begun to change this emphasis on the structural aspects of foreign policy interactions. Instead of attempting to eliminate or bypass the political features of foreign-policy-making systems by emphasizing administrative arrangements, contemporary scholars have been concentrating precisely on these features (Huntington 1961; Robinson 1962; Schilling et al. 1962). They have begun to study the interactions of individuals within and between foreign policy agencies as sets of bargaining relationships, which are similar to the bargaining processes that take place in other areas of public and political life where competitions of power and of interest are more overt and accepted. This bargaining orientation is thus less committed to the "rational" aspect of foreign policy making; its normative implications tend rather to be those of science in general —that is, one needs to understand how a system operates before one can calculate the consequences of attempting to make any given change in it.

Another body of literature that might appropriately be described in this category consists of "case studies" that reconstruct the way specific issues, policies, or events were handled by the governmental participants in the foreign-policy-making process. These are more likely to be historical–descriptive (e.g., Jones 1955) than analytical in nature, and they find their rationale in the assumption that the mysteries of the governmental process will yield to the accumulated weight of information on how the system has actually worked in specific instances in the past.

The ideological approaches

The second major approach to the study of foreign policy making I have called "ideological," because in one form or another it is concerned with the democratization of foreign policy—with the possibilities and procedures for introducing a substantial measure of public values into every stage in the formulation of foreign policy. This approach starts from the general premise that the foreign policy area has different roots and different requirements of interest and support in the political system than do other policy areas. It then branches out in two directions. One line of inquiry, based explicitly on the primacy of the foreign policy area over other policy areas, seeks to alter the bases of interest and support in order to optimize public knowledge of, participation in, and control over, foreign policy decision making. A second line of inquiry seeks to discover what the different roots and requirements of interest and support are, in order to understand the operative political processes, sometimes for the purpose of facilitating democratic control and sometimes for more general social science purposes. In both of these lines of inquiry, the central objects of study are most often either nongovernmental groups or the interactions between the nongovernmental and the official elements.

Ideological–institutional approach. Just as the foreign policy institutions of government have been the central focus of study for those seeking better modes of organizing the foreign policy machinery, so the institutions of nongovernmental foreign policy activity have come in for a large share of the attention of those interested in a greater democratic perspective for foreign policy. In this context, foreign policy has benefited from an inclination in political science generally to explore the group basis of politics; thus, the role of organized interest groups in foreign policy making has become an important area of study (Cohen 1959). Much of this research has been limited to the positions, interests, and demands of particular organizations, and thus it has shared in the empty formalism of some of the rational–institutional studies. But increasingly, interest-group activities are being examined at the points where they intersect the domains of other participants in the process of foreign policy making: that is, they are more and more being treated as parts of a political system. And attention is also being turned to skill groups of a comparatively unorganized nature, such as scientists and "academic strategists," which are playing a larger role in the technical complexities of foreign policy making in a nuclear environment (Gilpin & Wright 1964).

The widespread conviction that a sound and stable foreign policy requires an interested, informed, intelligent public opinion has led to extensive, although far from satisfactory, investigations of the major channels through which foreign policy attitudes and information are transmitted to public audiences. The role of the universities as factors in the development of interest in, and knowledge about, foreign affairs has been a subject of study for some years, although precise measures of the impact of educational institutions at all levels on the foreign policy thinking of students are still lacking. The media of mass communication have been intensively scrutinized for many years (see Hero 1959), although their impact on foreign policy attitudes and information is still largely a matter of intelligent speculation (guided by deep concern) rather than of demonstrable fact.

It was noted above that most of the ideologically oriented studies of foreign policy making were nongovernmental in nature. An important exception concerns the treatment of the U.S. Congress. Part of the study of Congress as a foreign-policy-making institution is approached from the point of view of clarifying its internal organization and procedures and of understanding its interactions as part of the governmental process; hence, it was discussed under the rational–institutional heading. But important parts of this study of Congress are approached from the point of view of understanding and improving its representative role in the foreign policy field, and so they merit inclusion here also. This ideological perspective on the Congress is concerned with that body as a major object of public representation on foreign policy matters and as a channel through which public preferences and aspirations are made a constituent ingredient of foreign policy (Dahl 1950).

Ideological–individual approach. One of the most important and durable approaches to the subject of popular participation in foreign policy making has been through public opinion studies— through sampling and aggregating the attitudes of ordinary citizens. These studies find their rationale in the belief that if foreign policy were to be formulated both democratically and wisely, the average man would have to be interested, well-informed, and enlightened. And in order to discover the conditions of public interest, information, and attitudes at any point in time, as well as possible changes in these conditions over time, it has been necessary to explore the many dimensions of public opinion on foreign policy. In fact, the phrase "public opinion and foreign policy" generally refers to the foreign policy outlook of ordinary citizens rather than of those groups or publics that might be politically more effective in presenting their views.

After thirty years of public opinion research, the data on public attitudes toward foreign policy questions have reached mountainous proportions and have formed the bases for many studies of the public opinion process, both in its political and its psychological dimensions (see especially Almond 1950; Scott & Withey 1958; Deutsch & Edinger 1959). Normatively, these data, which continually show the large majority of the population to be uninterested and uninformed on foreign policy, have been used to justify and guide governmental and private efforts to capture public attention and to enlighten the public on foreign policy matters.

A growing feeling that data drawn from samples of the general population have already yielded whatever significance they contain is leading to new directions in research on public opinion. Scholars are beginning to use opinion data more imaginatively, seeking to relate the foreign policy opinions of attentive and interested individuals to more formal steps in governmental foreign policy making. Similarly, students of public opinion are focusing their attention more narrowly on the leadership elements among nongovernmental groups—on those persons who, by virtue of their special positions or qualifications, have an especially powerful role in shaping the views and the policies of public groups. [See PUBLIC OPINION; see also Rosenau 1963.]

Ideological–systemic approach. Careful study of the processes of public participation and control in foreign policy making has led rather directly to the systemic level, since it has been readily observed that any effort to explore the influence of public factors on governmental decision makers almost automatically compels the investigator to study the patterns of interaction between public and governmental actors. The broadest studies of a systemic variety are, once again, case studies of the interactions of the governmental and the non-governmental spheres as they have actually taken shape in a particular policy-making circumstance (e.g., Cohen 1957; Bauer et al. 1963) or as they may be traced out through a detailed analysis of how a single nongovernmental group or institution confronts the governmental process (Cohen 1963). Still lacking in this effort to understand how the public influences foreign policy making, however, are studies at the decision-making points to establish with some accuracy the constraints and opportunities that foreign policy officials read into the public mood: too often the subject is approached as if "the public" were always a source—if not *the* source—of constraints on wise governmental initiative and decision making in foreign policy.

A more circumscribed but still striking pattern of interactions that has been studied from the perspective of "who is to control" is the civil–military relationship. For many years the main concerns of these studies were the devices and techniques for maintaining civilian—hence, ultimately, public—control over military personnel and institutions, which were generally presumed to pose a threat to democratic government by their very existence, if not by their hidden aspirations to power. This simplistic viewpoint has given way in recent years to more complex approaches to the question of civil versus military contributions to public policy, since the military have perforce been accorded a larger role even while civilian authority has been substantially strengthened (Stein 1963).

Research needs

The persistent and increasingly imaginative exploitation of the approaches to the study of foreign policy making discussed above has taught us a great deal about the subject, but in a rather segmented way. This review points up how little there is in the way of explicit general models of the foreign-policy-making process—or, more precisely, processes, since there is no single combination of forces that is always operative and no single path that is followed in every instance. While much necessary work remains to be done in each of the above classifications before we can lay claim to confident understanding of how the parts of the foreign-policy-making system operate, such work would be helped immeasurably by more elaborate theories governing the whole system of foreign policy making.

In addition to a dearth of general theories, and perhaps as a contributing factor to that dearth, there has been very little comparative analysis in the study of foreign policy making. Rather, our analyses of institutions, individuals, and even systems have been singular and for that reason not always cumulative. At the present time we cannot have very great confidence in the generality of our hypotheses and insights. Comparisons are possible between similar institutions or similar policy-making functions in different countries or different political settings, or with respect to the same institutions or functions operating in different historical periods. It is also possible to compare the behavior and interactions of participants across a representative range of policy issues arising in any one political system. Such comparative analyses seem to be a very promising means of formulating a generally applicable model of foreign policy making.

We noted at the beginning of this article that the subject of foreign policy making has been most extensively pursued in the United States. Much less work—and much less sophisticated work—has been done on foreign policy making elsewhere in the world. How does one account for this situation?

In the first place, the historical circumstances and the political setting that have inspired this research in the United States have not been present to any important extent in other countries. Even in Great Britain, where the movement for open diplomacy had some force during World War I, the stronger political traditions of executive discretion in foreign affairs have discouraged an open exploration of foreign policy making, especially where one could detect in that exploration some aspirations for greater public participation. In countries that did not undergo political experiences comparable to those of the United States, the political culture has directed the attention of scholars to other kinds of problems.

Second, interest in modern methods of social science research has developed more slowly elsewhere in the world than in the United States. Apart from public opinion research, which has had an extensive development, research on foreign policy making that has been done in other countries has usually been historical–descriptive in nature and can be characterized as rational–institutional. With few exceptions (e.g., Frankel 1963), the major works on foreign policy making in countries other than the United States have dealt with the formal administrative apparatus for the conduct of foreign relations.

Third, the lack of a tradition of comparative analysis in this field has meant that even American scholars have been slow to turn their attention to aspects of foreign policy making in other countries. Quality studies dealing with individual countries have only recently started to appear (e.g., Speier & Davison 1957; Bishop 1961; Mendel 1961); genuinely comparative studies have still to be made.

There is no reason to believe that our growing knowledge of foreign-policy-making processes in the United States will help us to understand what these processes are like in other countries: we have long since learned that propositions drawn from the American political system are of limited relevance to other political contexts. The comparative study of political systems is now expanding rapidly; the comparative study of foreign-policy-making processes could be made an important part of that endeavor.

BERNARD C. COHEN

[See also CIVIL–MILITARY RELATIONS; INTERNATIONAL RELATIONS; MILITARY POLICY; NATIONAL INTEREST; NATIONAL SECURITY; PUBLIC POLICY; SCIENCE, article on SCIENCE–GOVERNMENT RELATIONS.]

BIBLIOGRAPHY

ALMOND, GABRIEL A. (1950) 1960 The American People and Foreign Policy. New York: Praeger.

BAUER, RAYMOND A.; POOL, ITHIEL DE SOLA; and DEXTER, L. A. 1963 American Business and Public Policy: The Politics of Foreign Trade. New York: Atherton.

BISHOP, DONALD G. 1961 The Administration of British Foreign Relations. Syracuse Univ. Press.

BROOKINGS INSTITUTION, WASHINGTON, D.C. 1960 United States Foreign Policy: The Formulation and Administration of United States Foreign Policy. Washington: Government Printing Office.

CARROLL, HOLBERT N. 1958 The House of Representatives and Foreign Affairs. Univ. of Pittsburgh Press. → A paperback edition was published in 1966 by Little.

COHEN, BERNARD C. 1957 The Political Process and Foreign Policy: The Making of the Japanese Peace Settlement. Princeton Univ. Press.

COHEN, BERNARD C. 1959 The Influence of Non-governmental Groups on Foreign Policy-making. Boston: World Peace Foundation.

COHEN, BERNARD C. 1963 The Press and Foreign Policy. Princeton Univ. Press.

CYERT, RICHARD M.; and MARCH, JAMES G. 1963 A Behavioral Theory of the Firm. Englewood Cliffs, N.J.: Prentice-Hall.

DAHL, ROBERT A. 1950 Congress and Foreign Policy. New York: Harcourt.

DEUTSCH, KARL W.; and EDINGER, LOUIS J. 1959 Germany Rejoins the Powers: Mass Opinion, Interest Groups, and Elites in Contemporary German Foreign Policy. Stanford Univ. Press.

FRANKEL, JOSEPH 1963 The Making of Foreign Policy: An Analysis of Decision-making. Oxford Univ. Press.

GEORGE, ALEXANDER L.; and GEORGE, JULIETTE 1956 Woodrow Wilson and Colonel House. New York: Day.

GILPIN, ROBERT; and WRIGHT, CHRISTOPHER (editors) 1964 Scientists and National Policy-making. New York: Columbia Univ. Press.

HAMMOND, PAUL Y. 1961 Organizing for Defense: The American Military Establishment in the Twentieth Century. Princeton Univ. Press.

HERO, ALFRED O. 1959 Mass Media and World Affairs. Boston: World Peace Foundation.

HILSMAN, ROGER 1956 Strategic Intelligence and National Decisions. Glencoe, Ill.: Free Press.

HUNTINGTON, SAMUEL P. 1961 The Common Defense: Strategic Programs in National Politics. New York: Columbia Univ. Press.

ILCHMAN, WARREN F. 1961 Professional Diplomacy in the United States, 1779–1939: A Study in Administrative History. Univ. of Chicago Press.

JONES, JOSEPH M. 1955 The Fifteen Weeks: February 21–June 5, 1947. New York: Viking.

KOGAN, NORMAN 1963 The Politics of Italian Foreign Policy. New York: Praeger.

MCCAMY, JAMES L. 1964 Conduct of the New Diplomacy. New York: Harper.

MENDEL, DOUGLAS H. 1961 The Japanese People and Foreign Policy: A Study of Public Opinion in Posttreaty Japan. Berkeley: Univ. of California Press.

PHILLIPS, CLAUDE S. JR. 1964 The Development of Nigerian Foreign Policy. Evanston, Ill.: Northwestern Univ. Press.

RANSOM, HARRY H. 1958 Central Intelligence and National Security. Cambridge, Mass.: Harvard Univ. Press.

ROBINSON, JAMES A. 1962 Congress and Foreign Policy-making: A Study in Legislative Influence and Initiative. Homewood, Ill.: Dorsey.

ROSENAU, JAMES N. 1963 National Leadership and Foreign Policy: A Case Study in the Mobilization of Public Support. Princeton Univ. Press.

SCHILLING, WARNER R.; HAMMOND, P. Y.; and SNYDER, G. H. 1962 Strategy, Politics and Defense Budgets. New York: Columbia Univ. Press.

SCOTT, WILLIAM A.; and WITHEY, STEPHEN B. 1958 The United States and the United Nations: The Public View, 1945–1955. New York: Manhattan.

SNYDER, RICHARD C.; BRUCK, H. W.; and SAPIN, B. (editors) 1962 Foreign Policy Decision Making: An Approach to the Study of International Politics. New York: Free Press.

SPEIER, HANS; and DAVISON, W. PHILLIPS (editors) 1957 West German Leadership and Foreign Policy. Evanston, Ill.: Row, Peterson.

STEIN, HAROLD (editor) 1963 American Civil–Military Decisions: A Book of Case Studies. Birmingham: Univ. of Alabama Press.

U.S. CONGRESS, SENATE, COMMITTEE ON GOVERNMENT OPERATIONS 1961 Organizing for National Security. Inquiry of the Subcommittee on National Policy Machinery. Washington: Government Printing Office.

WOODROW WILSON FOUNDATION 1952 United States Foreign Policy: Its Organization and Control. A report by William Y. Elliott. New York: Columbia Univ. Press.

FOREIGN TRADE
See INTERNATIONAL TRADE.

FORENSIC PSYCHIATRY
See under PSYCHIATRY.

FORGETTING

It seems quite unnecessary to be concerned with a definition of "forgetting." Each of us has had innumerable experiences, often painful, with this phenomenon, and we know that, in general, the longer the period between the point at which we learn something and the point at which we try to remember it, the less likely we are to remember correctly. The growth of living organisms is always accompanied by deterioration processes. Forgetting is the behavioral deterioration process that may be likened to organic deterioration and is in opposition to the growth process called "learning." We do not, in fact, know much about the organic or physiological correlates of forgetting, and it is not easy to understand why, in the evolutionary process, forgetting should remain so powerful a process in man when, from almost any point of view, it is unadaptive. It is almost as if we have "room" for only so much learning, and when more learning is to be added than the room will hold, some of the old learning must go. Indeed, in a manner of speaking, the theories of forgetting are based on this notion.

Learning must occur before forgetting can occur. This fact, seemingly trivial, is the key to an understanding of the processes causing forgetting and must also be the foundation of any applied program aimed at retarding forgetting.

Sources of evidence

A review of the experimental studies of forgetting can but lead to the impression that the evidence on which we base our knowledge of forgetting comes from quite a restricted set of materials and procedures, and thus our generalizations about forgetting may be severely restricted. It is a fact that most of our data come from what is classically known as rote-learning tasks, and the subjects for experimentation have been preponderantly college students. The study of the forgetting of motor skills has lagged; the memory for ideas, concepts, and principles has never been systematically investigated. Yet, when probes into these areas have been made, the results have given us no reason to believe that the basic laws are different from those derived from rote-learning tasks. The extensive use of college students—whose use has not been dictated by theoretical concern but has been largely a matter of convenience—may make us wary of generalizing these conclusions to all ages and ability levels. But again, the evidence available does not indicate that any serious distortions in the laws of forgetting are attendant upon the particular subjects that have been used in experimental work.

Nonsense syllables and nonwords. We must look to the tasks and materials from which most of our contemporary knowledge of forgetting is derived. The materials are simple verbal units. These may be words, or they may be a sequence of letters not found in English dictionaries. Calling these latter units "nonsense syllables," or "nonsense material," has produced considerable misunderstanding. It has often been assumed that a nonsense syllable (for example, RUH) is an artificial unit which removes the study employing such units from contact with real-life situations. It might be argued that experimentation is always, in fact, artificial (a vacuum does not exist in nature) and that it is only by such procedures that fundamental laws are obtained, because these procedures allow for the control of variables. In fact, the original use of nonsense syllables by Ebbinghaus in his pioneering studies on memory was, to a large extent, based on this premise. But there are three other facts that must be set forth and that may be more critical than an argument based on a philosophy of science.

To say that a nonsense syllable is not related to real life is simply erroneous. A word common to an adult must be, in essence, a nonsense syllable to a child before its meaning is acquired. The use of verbal units not in dictionaries may be tapping the same or similar processes that are involved when the child changes from a nonverbal organism to an organism with a verbal repertoire that can be correctly applied. Or a nonsense syllable may be likened to a word in a foreign language, and thus to the college student it is anything but removed from real life.

The second point is that a derogation of the use of nonsense syllables assumes a dichotomy between what is meaningful and what is nonsense. But measurements of meaning, by any of many techniques, do not support such a schism. There is a continuum between words and nonwords. Many so-called nonsense syllables have greater meaning than some words. Nonsense words, like "real" words, have varying affective connotations. Indeed, it could probably be demonstrated that affective reactions to such nonsense syllables as WOR are much more intense than those to such common words as THE. A nonsense unit, therefore, should mean only a word that does not appear as an entry in a dictionary, but this distinction per se between words and nonwords appears to have little psychological relevance.

The third reason for not viewing nonwords as

something significantly apart from words is probably the most critical when reference is made to the use of these materials only in the study of forgetting. This reason is simply that the evidence indicates that words and nonwords "behave" the same as far as forgetting is concerned. This point will be given elaboration at a later point in the discussion.

Manner of presenting verbal units. In the bulk of the studies on forgetting, verbal units are formed into lists, so that in a single task the subject learns several items. The items might be formed into a *serial* list in which the subject must learn to reproduce not only the items but also a particular order of the items. A second widely used type of list is the paired-associate list. The subject is presented a series of pairs and is required to learn to reproduce the second member of each pair when the first member is shown alone. Acquiring the order of the pairs is not a part of the task; indeed, the investigator usually prevents his subject from learning the order by presenting the pairs in a different order from time to time. The paired-associate task is a counterpart of the task of learning a vocabulary of a foreign language, in which the first member of the pair is a word in the learner's native language and the second member is its foreign equivalent.

Other tasks that have also been used include prose passages, sentences, and lists of words to be recalled in any order. But for reasons that need not be detailed here, at the present stage in the development of psychological research, the paired-associate task possesses properties that make it a superior vehicle for studying forgetting, and much of the discussion will be cast around this task. This does not imply that there is evidence that forgetting varies as a function of the task. Such comparisons are difficult to make, although insofar as they have been made there is no convincing evidence that the type of task is a critical variable in the study of forgetting.

Rapid single-unit technique. Most of the research on forgetting has been with multiple-unit tasks (for example, several pairs of items in a paired-associate task). What must be considered a most amazing technical breakthrough was made in 1959 by Lloyd R. Peterson and Margaret J. Peterson. These investigators were able to devise a situation in which a *single* verbal unit was presented for learning and the subsequent course of forgetting could be measured over a period of time. A syllable, such as RZL, was presented for study for two seconds. Then, in order to prevent the subject from rehearsing the syllable, he was given a neutral task (for example, counting) for a few seconds. Finally, he was asked to recall the syllable originally shown to him. The startling fact is that lawful and reliable forgetting curves were obtained in which forgetting was essentially complete (the subject could not reproduce the unit) after 20 *seconds*. The exploitation of this technique has been, and is being, pursued by many investigators. The classical studies have used forgetting intervals of hours or days, and thus the sheer labor and mechanical problems in the performance of these studies were great. Although it is perhaps too early to say with assurance that the laws of forgetting observed under the Peterson–Peterson technique are the same as those for classical studies, the evidence thus far points strongly to this conclusion. If this is true, the study of forgetting may proceed at a pace hitherto impossible with classical procedures. In the Peterson–Peterson technique, seconds are comparable to hours or even days with the classical list method.

Single-task studies of forgetting

We may turn next to an examination of the reliable experimental facts in single-task studies of forgetting. A distinction must be drawn between single-task and multiple-task studies if we are to focus on the processes believed critical for an understanding of forgetting.

The laboratory situation can be described as follows. A subject who has not previously served in a laboratory experiment involving verbal learning is given a single list of verbal units to learn. These are normally presented over and over, each unit being exposed for a short interval of time (for example, two seconds), until the subject is just able to reproduce the list perfectly. Assume, further, that the subject returns 24 hours later and is asked to recall all of the units he can. We ask now about the general quantitative aspects of forgetting in such a situation and, in particular, what variables cause the amount of forgetting to vary.

Amount forgotten. Over the 24-hour period, the subject will forget from 15 to 20 per cent of the units. Thus, if the list contained ten paired associates, we will expect about eight of these to be recalled correctly. Under the conditions specified above, this amount of forgetting remains fairly constant across a wide range of materials and tasks. Some gross measures may indicate a degree of forgetting as great as 30 per cent, but when refined techniques of measurement are used, the 15 to 20 per cent loss will usually be found. With intervals longer than 24 hours, more forgetting will, of course, occur, but we do not know with any precision the rate of fall for many longer intervals with various materials. Because of the relatively large amount of data available on forgetting after 24 hours, we will use this interval as a basic reference interval.

Significance of the degree of learning. We may now ask about variables that influence the amount of forgetting during the 24-hour period. The facts, as viewed at the present time, provide a conclusion that seems not only to be opposite to that expected as research in an area proceeds but also opposite to that often expected according to "common sense." For we can name only one variable that substantially influences the rate of forgetting in the single-task situation. Obviously, considerable clarification and elaboration are needed.

Characteristics of the verbal units will produce enormous differences in the rate at which the list is learned. As might be expected, a list of common words is learned much more rapidly than a list of difficult nonwords. The differences are so large that even the casual reader will be convinced that this is true. Thus, it is clear that a list of five 3-letter words, such as CAT, PEN, BUS, FAR, and ELK, would be learned more rapidly than a list of five nonwords, such as RZL, DBQ, HFG, BJX, and PCR. Technically, we say the words have a higher level of meaningfulness than do the nonwords. But if both sets are learned to an equal degree, they will be equally remembered 24 hours later. The critical point is the "equal degree of learning," because degree of learning is the one variable that does influence the amount of forgetting. This can be demonstrated in two ways. First, when the number of practice trials is varied within a given task, it will be found that the greater the number of practice trials, the less the forgetting. Second, when units within the task are examined, one may note that those units which have been given correctly many times during learning will prove to be remembered better after 24 hours than those given correctly only a few times. So we say that if the degree of learning is equal for materials of widely different meaningfulness, they will be forgotten at the same rate.

Meaning related to degree of learning. The foregoing conclusion might seem contradictory to the experience of many, because most of us have long believed that retention of more meaningful material is better than that of less meaningful material. But this belief may have arisen as follows. If we spend an equal amount of time in learning the two kinds of material, retention of the list of words would assuredly be better after 24 hours than the retention of the list of nonwords. Even if a subject spent twice as much time study-ing the nonword list, retention of the words might still be better. This is because differences in rate of learning such lists vary so markedly that even after a longer study period on the nonwords the degree of learning will still be less than the degree of learning for words. But under such circumstances, the differences in amount remembered after 24 hours must be ascribed to the degree of learning achieved and not to the differences in the material. Differences in the material produce differences in learning, but if the level of learning achieved for materials of different difficulty prior to the introduction of the retention interval is equivalent, we may expect essentially equal amounts of forgetting, which, as noted earlier, will be about 15 to 20 per cent over 24 hours.

Similarity related to degree of learning. Let us consider another variable that produces wide differences in learning. If the number of duplicated letters among nonwords is varied within a list of paired associates, the greater the number of duplicated letters, the more difficult it is to learn the task. Technically, this is called "variation in intralist formal similarity." But again, if the level of learning achieved for a list with high similarity is equivalent to that for a list with low similarity, the amount of forgetting will not differ measurably over a 24-hour period. The same situation will prevail if we use a list of synonyms and a list of words with very little similarity of meaning. The former will be more difficult to learn, but differences in forgetting cannot be demonstrated if the levels of learning attained are equivalent.

Individual differences in rate of learning. The general principle that degree of learning is the only critical variable in the single-task situation can be pursued one step further. There is evidence leading to the conclusion that there are no individual differences in forgetting. One proposition that has been ubiquitous in psychological research is that any set of measurements will produce a distribution of reliable individual differences. Some individuals are slow learners; others are fast learners. Some have excellent depth perception; others have poor depth perception. Measurements on living organisms of all levels have supported the proposition that there is a consistent range of individual differences. To suggest that this proposition does not hold true for forgetting requires a careful exposition of the extent of the data available for its support.

For one characteristic of individuals, the data are quite clear. The rate at which a person learns a given task is not related to rate of forgetting. A subject who learns a list very slowly will show no more forgetting than a subject learning the same task very rapidly, if the level of learning attained is equivalent. Such a fact is not without some support in incidental observations. It is not unusual for students in the author's classes to observe (when discussing their performance in the course) that they do not learn rapidly, but once they have learned something well, they remember it well. A slow-learning student, therefore, may take much longer to achieve a level of learning attained by a rapid-learning student, but given the equivalent degree of learning, forgetting does not differ.

Rate of learning is, of course, only one of hundreds of characteristics on which people differ reliably. Some people are more emotional than others; some are more conservative than others. Do none of these many possible characteristics produce differences in rate of forgetting? Here the evidence is less convincing, but it is pointing toward the conclusion that if these characteristics are related to rate of forgetting, the magnitude of their effect is small.

Consider, for example, the following situation. Subjects of widely different learning abilities are given the same period of time to study a given task, and immediately following this study period they are tested. The test scores will show a wide range, indicating that rate of learning differed markedly among the subjects. After 24 hours, a recall test is given. The recall scores are then correlated with the scores taken immediately after learning. Such a procedure will produce very high correlations across a wide variety of materials. The high correlations can be taken to indicate again the strong relationship between degree of learning and retention. If there were wide individual differences in rate of forgetting that vitiate the relationship between learning and retention, such high correlations would not be found. This is to say that a given person's retention score can be predicted with a high degree of accuracy if only his learning score is known. Under such circumstances, it does not seem possible to attribute to individual differences a role of consequence in forgetting. That such a conclusion runs contrary to the conclusions concerning the role of individual differences in many other situations is indeed a puzzle, and perhaps future research will change the conclusion. But the available data allow at least a tentative conclusion that individual differences in forgetting are, at best, of very small magnitude.

Multiple tasks and forgetting theory

The reason for making the distinction between single-task forgetting and multiple-task situations may now be examined. Very early in the period in which the study of learning and memory was brought into the laboratory, it was discovered that if two tasks were learned in immediate succession and the subject's retention of the first task was then tested, severe forgetting was observed. That the second task was in some way responsible for this forgetting was shown by control conditions in which only the single task was learned and tested for retention.

Retroactive and proactive inhibition. The amount of forgetting produced by the learning of a second task, interpolated between the learning and recall of a first task, is called "retroactive inhibition." The amount of retroactive inhibition that can be produced in the laboratory is very great; under appropriate conditions recall of the first task can be reduced to zero.

The discovery of retroactive inhibition had two important consequences. First, it became an object of study per se, and hundreds of experiments have been performed in which such variables as the similarity between tasks, the degree of learning of the interpolated task, and various time relationships have been studied.

The second consequence of the work on retroactive inhibition is that it has largely set the theoretical thinking of investigators. This thinking has preponderantly tended toward the use of *interference* as a fundamental cause not only of forgetting observed in the retroactive situation but of all forgetting. Certainly the role of interference in retroactive inhibition cannot be disputed: the higher the similarity between the two tasks, the greater the amount of retroactive inhibition. Furthermore, subjects are regularly observed to give items from the interpolated task when they are asked to recall the first task. A theory built around an interference notion seemed quite appropriate.

In more recent years, a second source of interference was discovered that has only served to refine and reinforce the notion that interference must be a major cause of forgetting. This second source of interference is identified as "proactive inhibition." Again, a subject learns two tasks, but this time he is asked to recall the task subsequently learned. Of course, some time must elapse between the learning of the second task and the request for its recall to expect forgetting to occur, but given this situation, there will be greater forgetting than would occur for a single list. It is as if the originally learned task interferes with the recall or retention of the subsequently learned task. The magnitude of proactive inhibition increases with time between the learning of the second task and its recall. After 24 hours, we may expect the amount of forgetting produced by proaction to be as great as that produced by retro-action. The combined effects of both retroaction and proaction may be studied by having the subject learn three lists and then subsequently requesting the recall of the second.

Interference theory. The refinements in the interference theory have consisted of increased specification of the mechanisms involved. In order to study these mechanisms, certain fairly standard interference paradigms have been devised. The most widely used is known as the "A–B, A–C paradigm." This may be visualized as representing a paired-associate arrangement in two successive lists in which the left-hand unit (stimulus term) is identical in both lists and the right-hand unit (response term) differs. With the first list the subject learns to give a response to a specific stimulus, but with the second list he must learn a new response to the same stimulus. When the several items in the two lists have this relationship, interference or negative effects are observed in learning the second list.

Extinction and spontaneous recovery. It is an easy step to assume that the negative effect in learning the second list must somehow be related to the forgetting observed in the retention tests for either list at some later point in time. The evidence points to the fact that something akin to an extinction process occurs in learning the second list. More particularly, the associations developed in learning the first list are extinguished or unlearned in the process of learning the second list. Therefore, if immediately after learning the second list, recall of the first list is requested, serious retroactive inhibition should occur. It does; it is as if the response terms of the first list are not available to the subject. But now, assume that 24 hours elapse before recall of the first list is requested. Retroactive inhibition will occur, but it will be less in magnitude than the amount measured immediately after second-list learning. Independent evidence suggests that following extinction a form of spontaneous recovery occurs, just as in the case of an extinguished conditioned response. Such spontaneous recovery would account for the decreased retroactive inhibition observed after the 24-hour retention interval.

Next, let us examine the role of extinction and spontaneous recovery in proactive inhibition. If following learning of the second list there is a recovery over time of the associations in the first list, these recovered associations should interfere with the recall of the second list. The greater the recovery, the greater the interference; hence, such a mechanism would account for the fact that proactive inhibition increases with time.

The use of extinction and recovery mechanisms in an interference theory of forgetting has further implications. Suppose the second list is learned by distributed practice; that is, we carry out a trial or two, let an interval elapse, give another trial or two, another interval, and so on. These intervals, inserted in learning, should allow some spontaneous recovery of the first-list associations. But the next learning trials should produce some extinction of the first-list associations. Thus, over a series of such learning and rest cycles, we would have successive recovery and extinction cycles. Again, generalizing from work in other areas of learning, we find that such extinction–recovery cycles may lead to more permanent extinction of the first-list associations. Distributed practice on the second list, therefore, should decrease the amount of proactive inhibition. Tests of this proposition are positive. Indeed, when the distribution intervals are long (such as 24 hours), enormous reduction in proactive inhibition will occur. In general, it is fair to say that the use of extinction–recovery notions, as subprocesses under a general interference theory of forgetting, have proved very useful.

Rapid single-unit technique. Earlier we discussed the technique of studying retention of single items over very short intervals and, in addition, noted that near-complete forgetting had been observed in as short a period as 20 seconds. Experimental evaluations of this phenomenon have now made it fairly reasonable to assume that this rapid forgetting is produced by proactive interference. It is common to use a single subject many times in the single-item studies. The subject is given different units at different times, and retention is tested at various intervals following presentation. Thus, in effect, the subject builds up a repertoire of units as the experiment proceeds. If it is assumed that the previously presented units interfered proactively, the rapid forgetting of the item of the moment may be accounted for. The interpretation seems to hold. Given the appropriate arrangement of conditions, it can be shown that the greater the number of previous items presented, the greater the rate of forgetting the item at hand. The first item presented to the subject shows little, if any, forgetting over time. It seems reasonable to conclude, therefore, that we are not confronted with new principles of forgetting when studying retention of singly presented items over short intervals of time.

Pre-experimental associations. We now come to the final step in the analysis of the interference theory of forgetting. As previously discussed, when the subject learns a single list, forgetting will be approximately 15 to 20 per cent over 24 hours. The facts of retroactive and proactive inhibition produced in the laboratory made it reasonable to suspect that interference also accounted for this 15 per cent to 20 per cent loss. More particularly, it would appear that the interference must arise proactively from sources outside the laboratory. The reasoning is as follows. Assume that the subject is 20 years old at the time he learns this single list. If forgetting the list is to be attributed to interference, it is much more probable that he would have learned "something" that would interfere during these previous 20 years than during the 24-hour retention interval. The latter, of course, would be a source of retroactive interference. The longer the retention interval, the more important would interference from retroactive sources become.

What could be the source of interference from outside the laboratory? The subject has a large verbal repertoire that he has built up during the years. This includes not only a great many verbal units but also associations among those units. It is known, furthermore, that there are varying strengths of associations among letters, and a major reason for the difficulty of learning nonwords is that the required associations are contrary to the existing stronger habits or associations. In effect, then, when a subject is required to learn a nonword, he must extinguish, or at least suppress, the associations he brings to the laboratory session. If one were to apply the extinction–recovery theory, it would be expected that during the retention interval the older associations would recover and interfere with those built up in the laboratory, thus producing the forgetting observed at recall. Or, if the materials involved words, pre-experimental associations among those words and with other words would have to be extinguished if the task of the laboratory required new associations. But again, the old habits should recover with time and interfere with recall. Thus the interference theory, as refined and shaped by the facts derived from the studies of retroactive and proactive inhibition in the formal laboratory setting, was given a direct counterpart in the single-list situation, with the interference stemming from habits the subject had learned outside the laboratory. This translation seemed quite appropriate, and the magnitude of the interference to be expected from outside sources could surely account for the 15 per cent to 20 per cent forgetting observed.

To test the application of the theory to the single-list situation requires the construction of learning tasks that will be differentially interfered with by associative habits that the subject brings to the laboratory. This, in turn, requires a knowledge of the associative habits that the subject has, in fact, developed over the years. From various word-association tables and letter-association tables, something *is* known of the associative network of the average college student. For example, it is known that words occurring with great frequency in our language have more and stronger associations than do words occurring with low frequency. It might be expected, therefore, that if a verbal task were constructed of frequently used words in such a way that the already established habits were inappropriate or contrary to the habits that must be acquired to master the task, an effective proactive situation would be devised. Furthermore, proactive inhibition should be greater than for a task constructed of infrequently used words, since the pre-experimental associations among the infrequently used words are minimal. Clearly, it would be predicted that more of the task constructed of frequently used words would be forgotten; forgetting should be greater because proactive interference after a day, a week, or a month should be greater.

Tests of such expectations have been disappointing. Little, if any, difference in the forgetting of the various tasks has been observed. The same has been true when associations among letters have been used to construct nonwords that should be differentially susceptible to previous habits.

We can see that although the interference theory has been quite successful in accounting for observed facts in the formal retroactive-inhibition and proactive-inhibition paradigms, the translation of this theory to account for the forgetting observed for a single list has not. In study after study we find that 15 to 20 per cent of the task is forgotten over a 24-hour period; we cannot get differential forgetting of any appreciable amount for different materials. The success of the interference theory in other contexts will not allow it to be given up easily. Rather, it would appear that the more fruitful approach would be to continue to devise tasks in which the amount of interference from already established habits would be different. This, in turn, may require further extensive assessment of the habit repertoires of the subjects.

Implications of interference theory. There are further untested implications of the interference theory as outlined above. If proactive inhibition from outside sources is responsible for the forgetting of a single list, we would expect more forgetting for a given task for older people than for younger people. For example, a college student should show more forgetting of a verbal task than should a first-grader. This should follow because the number of potential interfering associations should be greater for the college student. We might also predict that a genius would show more forgetting than an imbecile. The genius has, in his lifetime, learned infinitely more than the imbecile; hence, the sources of potential interference should be greater. Other similar propositions can be deduced from the interference theory. It will probably not be abandoned despite its inadequacy in the single-list situation until a variety of tests of the theory have been negative.

BENTON J. UNDERWOOD

[See also LEARNING. Other relevant material may be found in the biography of EBBINGHAUS.]

BIBLIOGRAPHY

McGEOCH, JOHN A. 1932 Forgetting and the Law of Disuse. Psychological Review 39:352–370.

MELTON, ARTHUR W. 1963 Implications of Short-term Memory for a General Theory of Memory. Journal of Verbal Learning and Verbal Behavior 2:1–21.

PETERSON, LLOYD R.; and PETERSON, MARGARET J. 1959 Short-term Retention of Individual Verbal Items. Journal of Experimental Psychology 58:193–198.

POSTMAN, LEO 1961 The Present Status of Interference Theory. Pages 152–179 in Conference on Verbal Learning and Verbal Behavior, New York University, 1959, Verbal Learning and Verbal Behavior: Proceedings. New York: McGraw-Hill.

UNDERWOOD, BENTON J. 1957 Interference and Forgetting. Psychological Review 64:49–60.

UNDERWOOD, BENTON J.; and POSTMAN, LEO 1960 Extraexperimental Sources of Interference in Forgetting. Psychological Review 67:73–95.

FOUNDATIONS

The foundation may be defined as an instrument for the contribution of private wealth to public purpose. In this broad sense, foundations existed in antiquity and include perpetuities set up by the pharaohs for religious purposes, Greek and Roman endowments, and the ecclesiastical and charitable trusts made in Tudor England and later.

Early charitable trusts. For example, Plato established his famous Academy on land that Cimon the Athenian had given for public use. Before his death in 347 B.C., Plato directed that the income of his own adjacent fields should be used for the perpetual support of the school. This foundation survived nearly nine hundred years, until it was finally suppressed by the Christian Emperor Justinian in A.D. 529 for teaching pagan doctrines.

The corporate personality, able to receive and hold property in perpetuity, was primarily a Roman legal concept. In the Roman Empire during the first two centuries of the Christian era, foundations to aid the needy—usually associated with municipalities but sometimes private associations—became common. Under Constantine special laws were passed extending this principle to the churches.

The foundation in perpetuity (vaqf, vakif) has been common in Islamic countries. Examples of deeds of trust appeared in the early Hittite civilization (c. 1200 B.C.), but after the foundation principle was given specific approval by Muhammad it spread widely. A vaqf has been defined as the appropriation of a particular article in such manner that it becomes subject to the rules of divine property: the appropriator's right in such objects is extinguished and they become the property of God, who returns the derivative benefits to his people. Three broad categories of obligation are recognized: first and foremost, a man's duty to his own family; second, the maintenance of God's worship according to the tenets of Islam; and, finally, charity in the everyday sense, including works of public utility. No world estimates of either the number or accumulated wealth of vakiflar are available, but they are reported to exist in considerable numbers in Turkey, Saudi Arabia, India, Iran, and other countries with substantial Muslim populations. In 1964 the Turkish administrator of vakiflar reported more than seventeen thousand properties under his supervision.

In England, after Henry VIII dissolved the monasteries, the secular charities grew to such numbers that in 1601, under Elizabeth I, a special act was passed. Commonly called the Statute of Charitable Uses, it became the legislative cornerstone for the creation, control, and protection of such funds. The registry of charitable trusts compiled in the 1960s in England may record as many as 200,000, many of them surviving from Tudor and Stuart times.

As early examples of foundations in the United States, consider the two funds established in Boston and Philadelphia in 1791, under the will of Benjamin Franklin, to assist "young married artificers of good character." Portions of these funds were to accumulate for two hundred years and are still accumulating. But the first substantial fund that corresponds to the more modern concept of a foundation was the Peabody Education Fund, set up in 1867 by George Peabody, with a principal sum of over $2 million to "aid the stricken South."

Development of the foundation concept. About the beginning of the twentieth century the foundation idea began to take deeper root in American soil, and with a significant difference from the old concept of the fixed charitable trust. Large endowments were set up, often in perpetuity, but with wide latitude in their use. The new doctrine asserted that the funds of foundations are largely the venture capital of philanthropy, best invested in activities requiring risk and foresight that are not likely to be supported either by government or private individuals. The usual purpose is not relief or even cure; it is prevention, research, and discovery "to promote the well-being of mankind." Characteristically, the larger foundations have great freedom of action, with their trustees devoting less time to conserving money than to exploring new and enterprising ways of spending it.

Andrew Carnegie was a chief architect of these ideas, first through his essay *The Gospel of Wealth* (first published as *Wealth* in 1889; see Carnegie 1886–1899) and then through the foundations he himself established. In 1902 he set up his first important foundation, the Carnegie Institution of Washington, ". . . to encourage, in the broadest and most liberal manner, investigation, research, and discovery, and the application of knowledge to the improvement of mankind" ("Articles of Incorporation" [1902] 1965, p. 577). In the same year John D. Rockefeller's General Education Board was established with Mr. Carnegie as an active trustee.

Others that are now well known—like the Milbank Memorial Fund and the Russell Sage Foundation—followed rapidly. In 1911 various Carnegie benefactions culminated in the Carnegie Corporation of New York, the largest and most general of the Carnegie group. The Rockefeller Foundation, giant of the early foundations and still the world's second largest, was initiated in 1913; in 1914 appeared the Cleveland Foundation, the first of the community foundations inviting multiple trust funds.

The first three decades of the twentieth century constituted a period of increasing but gradual growth. Of the 5,050 foundations with known dates of origin included in the latest *Foundation Directory*, some 285, or less than 6 per cent of the group, had been established by the end of the lush 1920s. The fourth decade, the depression 1930s, seemed scarcely conducive to accumulations of surplus wealth; and some foundations did disappear or find their assets severely impaired. However, the *Foundation Directory* tabulates 288 new foundations originating in that decade, including the incorporation in 1936—with an initial endowment of $25,000—of the now gigantic Ford Foundation.

Postwar growth. By the middle 1940s a new group of foundations had sprung up in various sections of the United States, induced in part by high postwar levels of taxation resulting from World War II. Many of these were family foundations, set up by a living individual, with contributions and direction closely held within the family group. Another large segment was composed of company-sponsored foundations set up by business corporations to receive substantial contributions in years of good profits—or especially high taxes—and to disburse these funds, through good years and bad, in customary patterns of corporation giving. Both of these types of foundations differ in one significant respect from the older, traditional type: they usually have no large initial corpus but carry on their often substantial programs with moneys received currently. They may eventually accumulate substantial assets, but presently they are conduit foundations rather than the fixed-endowment type.

By 1964, date of publication of the second edition of the *Foundation Directory*, it was estimated that there were somewhat more than fifteen thousand foundations in the United States; but nine thousand were too small to meet the *Directory*'s size qualifications. Assets totaled $14,500 million, and grants were in the neighborhood of $800 million annually. These, however, are not large sums in the total American economy or even in its philanthropic segment. All foundations together are able to spend only about 8 cents of the annual dollar of private philanthropy. The significance of the foundation contribution lies in its special qualities and directions rather than in its gross total.

Moreover, although foundations are numerous and have been increasing at a rate of about 1,200 a year, most assets are in the hands of a relatively small number of large foundations. The 176 large foundations, each possessing $10 million or more, accounted for $11,000 million in assets, or 76 per cent of the total for the whole group. Among this group were 10 foundations with assets exceeding $150 million, headed by the gigantic Ford Foundation which, at market values of its stock holdings in late 1964, had assets of over $4,000 million.

The foundation as it exists in America has not spread extensively in other countries. England has less than a dozen foundations of substantial size which have freedom in programming. Canada has a growing number of foundations. A few examples exist in continental Europe, South America, Australia, India, and the Far East. In 1964 New Zealand issued its first directory (*A Directory of Philanthropic Trusts* 1964), including 63 trusts. Evidence increases of lively interest in other countries, and as surplus wealth becomes available and changes are made in tax structures, this typically American development may be extensively copied.

Types of foundations. Foundations differ so widely that description is difficult without some effort at classification. One such division is into grant-making and operating foundations. The former carry out their objectives by making gifts to independent agencies or persons and usually have small staffs merely to evaluate (or, in some cases, stimulate) requests for support. The latter themselves conduct operations in the fields of their choice and may have professional staffs of considerable size.

General foundations. Nearly all the larger, well-known foundations such as Ford, Rockefeller, Carnegie, Kellogg, and Sloan are general foundations. Operating under broad charters, they support the research projects in education, health, and welfare that characterize foundation work in the public mind. Usually they have large endowments, but some smaller foundations also support programs of national significance and properly fall within this category. Foundations of this type have a board of trustees (directors, managers) with broad interests, and a trained professional staff to serve as the "eyes" of the foundation, seeking out promising new ventures, evaluating projects offered, handling details of grants—or actual operations, if the foundation is of the operating type—and following through on results, so that future programs may be guided by past experience.

Special purpose foundations. Special purpose foundations are created—many of them by will or trust instrument rather than by incorporation—to serve a charitable purpose closely detailed, usually in the charter or perhaps in a letter of gift. The purpose may be as narrow as that of the Prairie Chicken Foundation of Illinois, devoted to preserving remnants of prairie chicken flocks, or as broad as advancement of education. Criticism of such foundations is not directed against program concentration on particular needs or projects, as some of these foundations efficiently serve useful ends, but against rigid restrictions freezing concentration for a long period or perpetually.

Community foundations. Community foundations are composite foundations, usually set up as trusts rather than as corporations, and functioning under community control in a way seldom found in other philanthropic endowments. Capital gifts are received, and the principal is administered by the trust departments of local banks. Income is distributed, together with such portions of the principal as may be authorized in any trust, under the supervision and control of a distribution committee. The foundation reserves the power to transfer to other similar purposes any funds which can no longer be effectively used for the ends originally designated. The donors may be numerous; each donor may specify how his gift is to be used or leave it to the discretion of the distribution committee, but usually the use of the donation is limited to the city or county within which the community foundation is situated.

Company-sponsored foundations. Typically, the company-sponsored foundation is a tax-exempt, nonprofit legal entity separate from the parent company but with a trustee board consisting wholly or principally of corporation officers and directors. Except in the case of foundations associated with large national companies, their programs are likely to be confined to the communities within which the parent company has offices and to center on philanthropies that benefit the corporation, its employees, its stockholders, or its business relationships. They are conduit foundations in that they not only disburse their investment income, as do nearly all foundations, but typically receive substantial new funds every year, or at least every year of good corporate profits.

Family foundations. Family (or personal) foundations are usually established by a living person or persons rather than by bequest. Generally they are initially small and may have no administrative organization or headquarters other than the office of the donor or a law firm. The trustees are apt to be the donor or donors, his immediate family, and perhaps his lawyer, banker, or business associate. At the outset, programs may differ little from the personal giving of wealthy men and women who have not incorporated their charity and probably include gifts to the local community fund, hospital, the donor's college or church, etc. Assets are no adequate measure of potential; such foundations may make substantial grants out of new annual gifts. Many of these initially small foundations may become recipients of large bequests upon the deaths of donors; and as experience accumulates, programs may change. Nearly all the large general foundations of today began as family foundations with limited funds oriented toward personal charities.

The relative numbers, assets, and grant activities of these five types of foundations are indicated by Table 1, taken from the *Foundation Directory* and including all American foundations of substantial size at the time of its publication.

Table 1 — Assets and grants of 6,007 foundations by type of foundation, 1964

CLASS	NUMBER	ASSETS		GRANTS	
		Amount (in millions)	Per cent	Amount (in millions)	Per cent
General	190	$ 9,289	64	$384	49
Special purpose	479	1,277	9	62	8
Community	102	425	3	18	2
Company-sponsored	1,716	1,177	8	143	19
Family and miscellaneous	3,520	2,343	16	173	22
Total	6,007	$14,511	100	$779*	100

* Entries do not add to this total because of rounding.

Source: *Foundation Directory 1964, p. 22.*

Fields of foundation activity. Table 2 shows education to be the most favored field of foundation activity, although before large governmental expenditures were channeled into medical research, grants made in the field of health were equally important. Similarly, expansion of social security, private insurance and retirement plans, and increased governmental involvement in relief and similar fields formerly supported largely by voluntary contributions have resulted in declining foundation support in social welfare areas. The great recent expansion of research within educational institutions makes them logical channels for an ever-broadening stream of foundation activities in the sciences and international affairs.

The rise of international activities into second place is the most notable recent change, and later data indicate continuing growth in this area. Not all of these sums go abroad; many of these grants are made to American universities for area studies and like projects. It needs to be added that the Ford Foundation is the major factor in this increase in internationally oriented dollars, although other foundations have been entering the field or expanding their programs within it.

Welfare and health receive only modest founda-

Table 2 — Grants of 6,007 foundations, by major fields, 1964

Field	Amount (in millions)	Per cent
Education	$315	40
International activities	106	14
Welfare	96	12
Health	90	12
Sciences	86	11
Religion	46	6
Humanities	40	5
Total	$779	100

Source: *Foundation Directory 1964, p. 44.*

tion support. Closer analysis of the data reveals that this pattern is characteristic of the larger rather than the small foundations. Some five thousand small foundations, for example, gave 34 per cent of their grants in the field of welfare, as compared with a mere 6 per cent for foundations with assets above $10 million.

The sciences have been an expanding research interest. In the *Directory* tabulation, support for the physical sciences mounted to 40 per cent of the total science expenditure, with the life sciences—formerly the unchallenged leader—at 32 per cent. The social sciences received 28 per cent of the total.

Religion receives only 6 per cent of foundation grants, although as a category it receives an estimated half of all private philanthropic gifts in the United States. But most of this giving is done personally, rather than through a foundation, even where an individual could choose either channel.

The humanities come last in the *Directory* tabulation, at 5 per cent of the total. However, still more recent figures indicate a substantial rise in this area, stimulated through such special projects as Lincoln Center in New York.

Foundations in American society. Because foundations are numerous and some of them bear the names of wealthy families, a popular misconception exists that they have tremendous assets and are able to make almost unlimited expenditures. Relatively, the resources of foundations are not large in the American economy and may be shrinking. In 1913 the federal government's total expenditures for education came to $5 million. The Carnegie Corporation of New York in that year spent a total of $5.6 million, so that if it had devoted all its funds to education, it could have more than equaled the federal government total. The Rockefeller Foundation is known around the world for its extensive fellowship program, on which it has spent $61 million in the past fifty years; but this total is less than the amount the American government spends in a single year today for its fellowship program alone.

Although in relative terms foundations constitute a minor segment of the American economy, their still considerable growth in numbers and in wealth has at times occasioned concern. As early as 1915 the Walsh Committee of the U.S. Senate charged that foundations were dominated by big business and were exerting strong conservative and reactionary influences. In the late 1940s it became evident that business enterprises in some numbers were seeking tax shelter under the foundation umbrella. To correct this and other abuses, the Revenue Act of 1950 set up "prohibited transactions" involving dealings between foundations and their donors or related persons. It taxes at ordinary corporation rates foundation profits from business enterprises not substantially related to the foundation's tax-exempt purposes, and it makes unreasonable accumulations of income a basis for loss of exempt status.

In the House of Representatives in 1952 the Cox Committee, and again in 1954 the Reece Committee, held special hearings on foundations, concentrating on program; but the charge then was the opposite of the Walsh charges. The Reece Committee attempted to demonstrate that foundations and certain educational institutions were engaged in a "diabolical conspiracy" to weaken and discredit the capitalistic system in the United States and to promote Marxist socialism. Neither the Walsh nor the Reece thesis was supported by substantial evidence, and no legislation followed.

In the 1960s the spotlight turned back to financial aspects, with allegations that certain foundations were serving primarily as tax shelters and business conveniences for their donors.

Some present tendencies. A few foundations now have more than a half century behind them, and a substantial record of experience is available for all foundations. The administration of foundations is becoming professionalized. While there are no institutions of special training for this field, national and regional conferences, informal luncheon groups, and other similar devices increasingly offer opportunities for exchange of experience. Foundations have resisted the formation of any closely knit national association, perhaps because of the high degree of individualism that characterizes the field and perhaps partially to avoid charges of collusion and wealth concentration.

Literature in the field, once sparse, is rapidly increasing. About two hundred foundations issue printed reports, usually annually; and histories of a number of the older foundations have recently been published. A few critical studies have appeared, and more are in progress.

Foundations are in some respects unique among American social institutions. They are the only important agencies in America free from the political controls of legislative appropriations and pressure groups, and free from the lay controls of having to temper programs with the judgments and prejudices of current contributors. Because of this position of unusual freedom, the foundations have an opportunity—and perhaps a special responsibility —to attack the longer range, more difficult, and often controversial questions which face the nation and the world; and many of them do spend a substantial part of their funds in pioneering ventures that would have difficulty in obtaining support from other private sources or from government.

F. EMERSON ANDREWS

[*See also* PHILANTHROPY.]

BIBLIOGRAPHY

ANDREWS, F. EMERSON 1956 *Philanthropic Foundations.* New York: Russell Sage Foundation.

ANDREWS, F. EMERSON 1958 *Legal Instruments of Foundations.* New York: Russell Sage Foundation.

ANDREWS, FRANK M. 1960 *A Study of Company-sponsored Foundations.* New York: Russell Sage Foundation.

Articles of Incorporation. (1902) 1965 Carnegie Institution of Washington, *Yearbook* 64:577–579.

CARNEGIE, ANDREW (1886–1899) 1962 *The Gospel of Wealth, and Other Timely Essays.* Cambridge, Mass.: Belknap Press. → Contains articles first published in various periodicals.

Community Foundations in the United States and Canada: 1964 Status. 1965 New York: Council on Foundations.

A Directory of Philanthropic Trusts. 1964 Wellington (New Zealand): Whitcombe & Tombs.

EMBREE, EDWIN R.; and WAXMAN, JULIA 1949 *Investment in People: The Story of the Julius Rosenwald Fund.* New York: Harper.

FORD FOUNDATION 1949 *Report of the Study for the Ford Foundation on Policy and Program.* Detroit: The Foundation.

FOSDICK, RAYMOND B. 1952 *The Story of the Rockefeller Foundation.* New York: Harper.

FOSDICK, RAYMOND B. 1962 *Adventure in Giving: The Story of the General Education Board, a Foundation Established by John D. Rockefeller.* New York: Harper.

Foundation Directory. 2d ed. Edited by Ann D. Walton and Marianna O. Lewis. 1964 New York: Russell Sage Foundation.

Foundation News. → Bulletin of the Foundation Library Center. Published since 1960.

GLENN, JOHN M.; BRANDT, LILIAN; and ANDREWS, F. EMERSON 1947 *Russell Sage Foundation: 1907–1946.* 2 vols. New York: Russell Sage Foundation.

GREAT BRITAIN, COMMITTEE ON THE LAW AND PRACTICE RELATING TO CHARITABLE TRUSTS 1952 *Report.* Papers by Command, Cmd. 8710. London: H.M. Stationery Office.

HOWARD, NATHANIEL R. 1963 *Trust for All Time: The Story of the Cleveland Foundation and the Community Trust Movement.* The Cleveland Foundation.

KEELING, GUY W. (editor) 1953 *Trusts and Foundations: A Select Guide.* Cambridge: Bowes & Bowes.

KELLOGG (W. K.) FOUNDATION 1956 *The First Twenty-five Years: The Story of a Foundation.* Battle Creek: The Foundation.

KEPPEL, FREDERICK P. 1930 *The Foundation: Its Place in American Life.* New York: Macmillan.

KIGER, JOSEPH C. 1954 *Operating Principles of the Larger Foundations.* New York: Russell Sage Foundation.

LINDEMAN, EDUARD C. 1936 *Wealth and Culture: A Study of One Hundred Foundations and Community*

Trusts and Their Operations During the Decade 1921–1930. New York: Harcourt.

LOMASK, MILTON 1964 *Seed Money: The Guggenheim Story.* New York: Farrar.

MACDONALD, DWIGHT 1956 *The Ford Foundation: The Men and the Millions.* New York: Reynal.

NATIONAL INDUSTRIAL CONFERENCE BOARD 1955 *Company-sponsored Foundations.* Studies in Business Policy, No. 73. New York: The Board.

NEW YORK UNIVERSITY 1963 *Proceedings of the Sixth Biennial Conference on Charitable Foundations.* Edited by Henry Sellin. New York: Bender.

RUSK, DEAN 1961 *The Role of the Foundation in American Life.* Claremont (Calif.) Colleges.

SHAPLEN, ROBERT 1964 *Toward the Well-being of Mankind: Fifty Years of the Rockefeller Foundation.* Garden City, N.Y.: Doubleday.

U.S. CONGRESS, HOUSE, SELECT COMMITTEE ON SMALL BUSINESS 1962 *Tax-exempt Foundations and Charitable Trusts: Their Impact on Our Economy.* Chairman's Report, 87th Congress. Washington: Government Printing Office.

FOURIER, CHARLES

Charles Fourier, French socialist thinker, was born at Besançon in 1772 and died in Paris in 1837. The sources of his thought remain obscure. To a great extent he was an autodidact, who owed much to his reading and still more to his reflections on what he read. Fourier's inclination was to become a military engineer, but his family—wealthy merchants—made him a tradesman in Marseilles. A setback in business in 1799, combined with his lack of business ability, reduced Fourier to the role of civil servant at Lyons. After 1816, when he inherited an income from his mother, he was finally able to devote himself entirely to his writing. In 1823 he settled permanently in Paris. Although he left a large body of published writings as well as many unpublished manuscripts, he never did write the "Grand Traité" that was to lay out his whole system in detail.

To use the language of the time, Fourier was a capitalist whose personal experience made him sensitive to the social plagues and the vices of a civilization based on commercial lies. The sole thought of his life was to find a "way out" that he might propose to his contemporaries. His first major book (1808) painted a cosmic fresco, showing blind humanity the path toward happiness and abundance. All his life he waited for the benefactor (king, minister, or financier) who would enable him to make even a partial test of his social "invention," or scheme.

This scheme assumes a correspondence between the cosmic order and the social order. It applies to the latter order the law of gravity established for the former by Newton and then applies to both orders a law of evolution, with eight ascending periods followed by the same number of descending periods. The peak is the reign of "harmony," in which "association" will be fully triumphant; however, humanity is still immersed in the fifth period, called "civilization" to distinguish it from the barbarism from which humanity has only recently emerged. The goal is the free governance of things by individuals who are at once completely free, fully mature, and highly organized. This goal explains the importance that Fourier attached to education, his criticism of the family and of the relations between the sexes, and finally his theory that the "passions" should be put to use instead of being repressed. The means of achieving this goal is the "phalanstery," a basic social unit whose organization rests on the mathematical rationality of social phenomena (the dimensions of groups, the balance of age groups, the alternation of activities) and which encompasses all aspects of the life of its members.

Fourier, an antirevolutionary and a strong opponent of Saint-Simon and Owen, believed his social system to be consistent with any form of government, including the monarchical one. Had not the French monarchy already shown great adaptability, having been feudal in the Middle Ages, absolute under Louis XIV, and bourgeois under Louis Philippe? There seemed to Fourier no reason why it could not also adapt to the new industrialism. This strange man thus combined traits that in others are generally mutually exclusive—political conservatism, social reformism, moral anarchism (at least in his conception of free love), and anti-Christian religiousness. Fourier believed in the goodness of human nature and rejected the dogma of original sin. He saw harmony as the law of the cosmos and held that what is true for nature must be true for society. This is why he gave to Newton's work the same importance that Marx was to see in that of Darwin; however, Marx abstracted from Darwinism a process of struggle, while Fourier found in Newton's theory a mechanism of attraction.

Fourier had only a limited influence on the development of society: his realm was that of thought, not of action. Yet the only thinkers who acknowledged a direct debt to Fourier were the Russian revolutionaries Herzen, Petrachevsky, and Tchernichevsky. While he was in some ways far ahead of his time, in many other respects he was a man of the past: his views apply much more to an agricultural and trading society than to one that is industrial and technological. Marx, of course, scorned him as a "utopian socialist." Nevertheless, Fourierism did not remain an abstract utopia. For thirty to forty years Fourierist ideas were realized in a series of community experiments, both in France and in a number of other countries, especially in the United States. For the most part, these experiments were attempts at the collective operation of a large rural estate, and they foreshadowed more modern forms of social organization. One of these enterprises took on an urban and industrial aspect—the *familistère* at Guise (in northern France). Today there remains not only a factory (like any other factory) but also a set of dwellings that is a unique example of Fourierist architecture. Some of Fourier's disciples put little trust in the success of these partial realizations of his scheme and held that a total transformation of society was called for. Rallying around Victor Considérant, 1808–1893, they entered into political life and became a real force for some years, but with the advent of Napoleon III they could do no better than merge into the bourgeois opposition to the Second Empire. As Charles Gide pointed out some time ago (1924), there is a direct relationship between Fourierism and the cooperative movement which played an important role before 1914 and of which there are now new developments, for example, in Yugoslavia, Israel, and the countries of the Third World.

ÉMILE POULAT

[*For the historical context of Fourier's work, see* SOCIALISM; UTOPIANISM; *and the biographies of* MARX; OWEN; SAINT-SIMON.]

WORKS BY FOURIER

(1808) 1857   *The Social Destiny of Man: Or, Theory of the Four Movements.* New York: Dewitt. → First published as *Théorie des quatre mouvements et des destinées générales: Prospectus et annonce de la découverte.*

1822   *Traité de l'association domestique agricole.* 2 vols. Paris: Bossange.

1829–1830   *Le nouveau monde industriel et sociétaire: Ou invention du procédé d'industrie attrayante et naturelle distribuée en séries passionnées.* Paris: Bossange.

1835–1836   *La fausse industrie morcelée, répugnante, mensongère, et l'antidote: L'industrie naturelle, combinée, attrayante, véridique donnant quadruple produit.* 2 vols. Paris: Bossange.

1841–1845   *Oeuvres complètes de Ch. Fourier.* 6 vols. Paris: Librairie Sociétaire.

1851–1858   *Publication des manuscrits de Charles Fourier.* 4 vols. Paris: Librairie Phalanstérienne.

SUPPLEMENTARY BIBLIOGRAPHY

BESTOR, ARTHUR E. 1950   *Backwoods Utopias: The Sectarian and Owenist Phases of Communitarian Socialism in America, 1663–1829.* Philadelphia: Univ. of Pennsylvania Press.

Bibliothèque internationale de sociologie de la coopération. → A monographic series published since 1955; each volume has a separate author and publisher.

BO, GIUSEPPE DEL 1957   *Charles Fourier e la scuola societaria: 1801–1922.* Milan (Italy): Feltrinelli. → A very valuable catalogue of the Fourierist collection assembled by the Giangiacomo Feltrinelli Institute.

BOURGIN, HUBERT 1905   *Fourier: Contribution à l'étude du socialisme français.* Paris: Société Nouvelle de Librairie et d'Édition. → Still the basic work on Fourier, in part outdated but not replaced.

DESROCHE, HENRI CH. 1962   Fouriérisme ambigu: Socialisme ou religion? *Revue internationale de philosophie* 16:200–220.

DESROCHE, HENRI CH. 1964   *Coopération et développement: Mouvements coopératifs et stratégie du développement.* Paris: Presses Universitaires de France.

GAUMONT, JEAN 1924   *Histoire générale de la coopération en France: Les idées et les faits, les hommes et les oeuvres.* 2 vols. Paris: Fédération Nationale des Coopérateurs de Consommation.

GIDE, CHARLES 1924   *Fourier: Précurseur de la coopération.* Paris: Association pour l'Enseignement de la Coopération.

HÉMARDLINQUER, J. J. 1964   La "découverte du mouvement social": Notes critiques sur le jeune Fourier. *Mouvement social* 3, no. 48:49–70.

Phalange: Revue de la science sociale. → Published from 1832–1849 under varying titles by the Bureau de Phalange. Fourier was a frequent contributor from 1832–1840.

POULAT, ÉMILE 1957   *Les cahiers manuscrits de Fourier: Étude historique et inventaire raisonné.* Paris: Entente Communautaire. → Contains an important chapter by Henri Desroche.

POULAT, ÉMILE 1962   Écritures et tradition fouriéristes. *Revue internationale de philosophie* 16:221–233.

ZIL'BERFARB, JOGANSON J. 1964   *Sotsial'naia filosofiia Sharlia Fur'e i ee mesto v istorii sotsialisticheskoi mysli pervoi poloviny XIX veka* (The Social Philosophy of Charles Fourier and Its Place in the History of Socialist Thought in the First Half of the Nineteenth Century). Moscow: Nauka.

FRANK, JEROME

Jerome N. Frank (1889–1957) was an American lawyer, public official, judge, law teacher, and writer on law and social philosophy. As an active participant in public affairs, first as a middle-ranking figure in the New Deal and later as a United States circuit court judge, Frank was respected as an effective, if sometimes turbulent, influence for change. He had opponents but few enemies. He was a generous person, kind, unpretentious, enthusiastic in behalf of his friends, and a witty companion as well. His passion was writing, and even in the most demanding periods of his service in Washington, he produced books and articles on a wide variety of subjects. They remain the chief source of his influence.

Frank was born in New York but grew up in Chicago; he attended the University of Chicago, taking his law degree in 1912. The university left in Frank's mind strong traces of attitudes that were typical of the institution's early outlook: a sense of identification with the liberal and progressive theme in the spirit of the nation; a wide-ranging enthusiasm for ideas, particularly new ideas; and a preference for innovations, especially if they could be called "reforms." After leaving the university, Frank practiced law for 17 years in Chicago, where he was a conspicuous and successful counselor and attorney, mainly in the field of commercial and financial transactions. He and his wife, a well-known poet, also belonged to the literary world of Chicago.

Intellectual interest and a sense of immediate need led Frank to undergo psychoanalysis, an event in his personal history that had a far-reaching impact on his thinking. In 1930 Frank published his most famous book, *Law and the Modern Mind*, which views the law in a Freudian perspective and interprets the methods and processes of law as social magic. Thus, judges are shown as father figures of mystical authority, dressed in robes and required to sit on high benches so that they evoke irrational deference. This kind of magic, according to Frank, helps maintain social order. The book came at a moment when Freudian insights were just beginning to touch the literature of political science, anthropology, literary criticism, sociology, and law; and it created a storm. Its sparkle and force made it a conspicuous factor in the acceptance of psychoanalysis as an important element in American views of man as a social being.

Frank had moved to New York in 1929; there he continued to practice law and joined a number of intellectual circles. He lectured at the New School for Social Research and in 1930 began an intermittent association with the Yale Law School, which lasted until his death.

The Yale Law School of the early 1930s was a lively place, well suited to Frank's personality and interests. The staff included William O. Douglas, Walton H. Hamilton, Thurman Arnold, Abe Fortas, Underhill Moore, and a number of psychologists, economists, and statisticians, as well as more orthodox law professors. The school imbued Frank with the sense that the world was about to be remade, if not reborn. It was one of the centers of American "legal realism," a controversial philosophical movement, which was concerned with directing attention from the "law in the books," the doctrinal law of the appellate courts, to "the law in action," the patterns of usage and practice that actually prevail in daily life, in the lower courts, and in business. Frank fought zestfully for the latter view of the law, a view which was strongly resisted.

After this stimulating experience he joined several members of the Yale faculty in the adventurous first wave of President Roosevelt's New Deal and was appointed general counsel of the Agricultural Adjustment Administration. This radical experiment in direct controls was headed by George Peek, a rural conservative and, like most of his agrarian staff, suspicious of urban, volatile, intellectual types like Frank himself and the extraordinary group he assembled, a group which included Arnold and Fortas from Yale, Adlai Stevenson, and Alger Hiss, among many others. The conflict between this group, led by Frank, and the older breed of agricultural experts lasted nearly two years; it ended in one of the spectacular explosions of the New Deal, with Frank and a considerable number of his allies in the Department of Agriculture being dismissed. Frank was soon reappointed, first to the staff of the Reconstruction Finance Commission and then as a member—from 1937 to 1939—and as the chairman—from 1939 to 1941—of the Securities and Exchange Commission, where he played an active part in the development of policy, particularly under the Public Utility Holding Company Act of 1935.

During this period he published *Save America First* (1938), a far-ranging comment on the economic element in social experience, which included an argument against American participation in the European war. It was written in the spirit of senators Borah and Norris and the older tradition of agrarian Populism; before June 1940 Frank took part as an isolationist in the national debate over America's interest in the war.

In 1941 he was appointed judge of the United States Court of Appeals for the Second Circuit, sitting in New York; he later moved to New Haven when he began to teach regularly at the Yale Law School. Frank found stimulus in the company of his judicial colleagues, especially judges Learned Hand, Augustus Hand, and Charles E. Clark, as well as at the law school, where he maintained an active office and saw students and faculty members regularly. His opinions were colorful and often unorthodox in form, reflecting the range of his reading and the mannerisms of a style that had become unusually free and personal in tone. He did important judicial work in several fields of law, including procedure, finance, criminal law, and civil liberties. He was widely quoted on obscenity, immigration, the rights of the accused in criminal trials, and other subjects; and his views were much discussed in the law reviews.

The books and articles of the final period in Frank's life embody the unresolved contradictions of his view of law and of the social process. Quick, agile, and known for his brilliant *aperçus*, Frank did not have the discipline of a systematic scholar and permitted himself the luxury of inconsistent positions. In his teaching at Yale and in his writing, especially in *Courts on Trial* (1949), he stressed the importance, as well as the uncontrollable irrationality, of fact-finding in the processes of law, arguing that fact-finding constitutes a step in the trial of cases that dominates the apparently superior legal rules laid down by appellate judges. He deplored and ridiculed man's yearning for strict and predictable legal rules, but in the end his proposals for law reform aimed to bring trials under the more effective control of those rules and to make the rules clearer, more uniform, and more predictable. He argued that legal education should be brought closer to trial practice and also that legal practice should correspond more closely to the law taught in law schools. For many years he saw "natural law" as a dangerously vague and misleading slogan, but he never ceased to contend that the administration of law should give a larger place to ideas of ethics and individual justice.

In his work Frank revealed the strengths and shortcomings of the legal and social philosophy of which he was a militant partisan. He spoke persuasively for sensible reform, for simplicity, and for humane values in the law and in the social order generally. By preaching the need to relate theories to facts he helped men to build the law anew on the foundation of social need. If he never realized the equal need of relating facts to theories, he shared his faith in the autonomy of fact with many pragmatists.

EUGENE V. ROSTOW

[*See also* JUDICIARY; JURISPRUDENCE; *the detailed guide to related articles under* LAW; *and the biographies of* HAMILTON, WALTON H.; LLEWELLYN; POUND.]

WORKS BY FRANK

(1930) 1949   *Law and the Modern Mind.* New York: Coward.
1938   *Save America First: How to Make Our Democracy Work.* New York: Harper.
1942   *If Men Were Angels: Some Aspects of Government in a Democracy.* New York: Harper.
(1945) 1953   *Fate and Freedom: A Philosophy for Free Americans.* Rev. ed. Boston: Beacon.

1949   *Courts on Trial: Myth and Reality in American Justice.* Princeton Univ. Press. → A paperback edition was published in 1963 by Atheneum.
1957   FRANK, JEROME; and FRANK, BARBARA *Not Guilty.* Garden City, N.Y.: Doubleday.
1965   *A Man's Reach: The Philosophy of Judge Jerome Frank.* Edited by Barbara Frank Kristein. New York: Macmillan. → A selection of Frank's writings.

SUPPLEMENTARY BIBLIOGRAPHY

In Memoriam; Judge Jerome N. Frank: 1889–1957.   1957   *University of Chicago Law Review* 24:625–708. → See especially pages 706–708 for a bibliography of the nonjudicial writings of Frank.
PAUL, JULIUS   1957   *The Legal Realism of Jerome N. Frank: A Study of Fact-skepticism and the Judicial Process.* The Hague: Nijhoff. → See especially pages 157–162 for a bibliography of the writings of Frank.
SCHLESINGER, ARTHUR M. JR.   1959   *The Age of Roosevelt.* Volume 2: The Coming of the New Deal. Boston: Houghton Mifflin.

FRAZER, JAMES GEORGE

Sir James George Frazer (1854–1941), British social anthropologist, folklorist, and classical scholar, was born in Glasgow. He attended the University of Glasgow from 1869 to 1874 and then went to Trinity College, Cambridge. He became a fellow of the college in 1879 and remained at Cambridge for the rest of his life. For one year, 1907/1908, he visited Liverpool University as professor of social anthropology, being the first to hold a chair with that name. Throughout his career he made little or no direct contact with the remote peoples who figure so extensively in his writings, and much of his simplification of their ideas (which explains some of his popular success) may be attributed to this absence of personal experience.

It is difficult now to appreciate Frazer's theories of magic and religion, since they have either been thoroughly assimilated or else outdated by extensive field research, yet in the intellectual life of his time, and particularly in the field of social anthropology, his work was of great importance. He himself appears to have anticipated the obsolescence of his work when he stressed that firsthand observation of foreign societies would furnish the science of man with a solid foundation which could never be shaken, and which would endure when many of the theories of his time, his own included, were forgotten or remembered only as curiosities. And with a characteristic skepticism that may now appear sententious he wrote that

magic, science, and religion are nothing but theories of thought. . . . And as science has supplanted its predecessors, so it may hereafter be itself superseded by some more perfect hypothesis, perhaps by some totally different way of looking at the phenomena—of registering the shadows on the screen—of which we in this generation can form no idea. The advance of knowledge is an infinite progression towards a goal that for ever recedes. (1890, pp. 712–713 in the abridged edition)

Although Frazer was directly in that current of opposition to established clerical orthodoxy that swept so many thinkers of his time (notoriously his friend William Robertson Smith) into socially painful controversy, he himself was consistently held in respect amounting to veneration. He treated Christianity as comparable with pagan religions and thus, at least by implication, deprived Christianity of its uniqueness, but he did so too tactfully to give real offense. He undermined rather than attacked the doctrinal convictions of his contemporaries. He was rewarded in his lifetime with public and academic honors, among them a civil list pension granted in 1905 for services to literature and anthropology. (It is interesting to note that he received his honorary D.C.L. at Oxford in the company of Lord Kitchener and Cecil Rhodes.) His wife was single-mindedly devoted to his reputation; indeed, R. R. Marett likened her to the guardian–wife of a priest of ancient Rome.

To his admirers Frazer appeared as a modern seer, a role that he accepted. He was revered by colonial administrators and missionaries as few anthropologists have been, and his extensive correspondence with them, together with his published questionnaire (1907), produced firsthand information about many peoples of the world. Men of letters (Kipling, Tennyson, T. S. Eliot, Ezra Pound, and D. H. Lawrence, to mention only a few) also took account of Frazer's writings, which have probably influenced the poetry of this century as much as they have the anthropology. A. E. Housman identified some of the characteristics that account for the popular appeal of Frazer's work when he described it as ". . . a museum of dark and uncouth superstitions invested with the charm of a truly sympathetic magic" and said it illuminated "the forgotten milestones of the road which man has travelled" (Dawson 1932, p. xi). Frazer's success in popularizing his subject and consolidating its practical relevance must be seen as one of his great claims to fame in the social sciences.

The development of the psyche. *The Golden Bough*, a reconstruction of the whole history of modes of human thought, orders a vast range of exotic beliefs and customs in terms of man's search for true knowledge and effective control of his environment and his condition. Frazer posited

three elements in the development of the human psyche, and in the spirit of the evolutionary thinking of his time, he saw these as characterizing three stages in human mental advance: magical, religious, and scientific thought.

Magical thought assumed that the universe is regulated by impersonal and unchanging laws (in this respect, Frazer believed, magic is like science). These laws were known to the magician through his art and applied by him in a quasi-technical way to control events. But magical beliefs and procedures (unlike scientific ones) were derived from faulty reasoning by analogy and from superficial associations: the qualities of one object were supposed to induce similar qualities in another. (One of the many examples given by Frazer is the ancient Greek custom of eating ravens' eggs to produce black hair.) This homeopathic magic assumed a "law of sympathy," which operates in such a way that like produces like. In addition, there was "contagious magic," which assumed that things once in intimate contact would subsequently act upon one another: a man's hair or nail clippings, for example, were used to work evil upon him. Although Frazer oversimplified the problems of symbolic thought that such beliefs now present to anthropologists, his distinctions continue to have some elementary taxonomic value.

Magical thought, which was gradually discredited, in Frazer's opinion, because its failures became apparent, gave way to religious thought. In this phase superhuman beings were thought to control the world. The uniformity of nature ceased to be taken for granted, since the occurrence of natural events was assumed to depend upon the will of conscious personal agents. Man sought to gain the help of these agents by acts of supplication and propitiation.

Finally, recognizing more clearly the limits of his own powers of control and applying logico-experimental methods, man achieved the scientific stage.

Assessment of "The Golden Bough." The main value of *The Golden Bough* for many of Frazer's contemporaries lay in its wide range of reference, its bold ordering of complex and varied information, and its perception of similarities in beliefs and customs that to them might have appeared quite distinct from one another. Frazer greatly overstressed the part played by deliberate reasoning in religious and magic belief and created a primitive man whose intellectual ambitions and processes of thought were those of a scholar like himself. (Even his evolutionary sequence reflects, psychologically, the process of growing up as many people with a pious upbringing like Frazer's experienced it: magical fantasies of power in early childhood, followed by adolescent religious belief, yielding in maturity to "scientific" agnosticism.)

Often Frazer preached the dangers of misinterpretation that he himself had failed to avoid. What he said of Robertson Smith's *Religion of the Semites* may be said of his own explanations of primitive thought: namely, that what now seems to be their inherent plausibility is in fact a presumption against them. Similarly Rousseau's views on the origin of society commended themselves to the most reasonable people of the previous century just because, if *they* had to reconstruct society from its foundations, they would have proceeded much as Rousseau supposed primitive men did. Thus Frazer and many of his contemporaries explained magical and religious thought by imputing a "natural" form of their own reasoning to very different peoples. Moreover, lacking knowledge of local languages and cultures, they were satisfied to take reports of isolated customs and beliefs quite out of their social context, and in this process they sometimes distorted even such evidence as they had.

An early critique of Frazer's work is that of W. Ridgeway (1924), who discussed divine kingship, one of Frazer's central themes in *The Golden Bough*. The divine king, according to Frazer, has a vitality that is believed to be the source of vitality in society and nature, and therefore, when his powers fail, he must be put to death so that a vigorous successor may continue to ensure prosperity. Ridgeway admitted that Frazer's exposition of the sacredness of kingship and the symbolism surrounding it did draw attention to these subjects and stimulate further investigation, but he charged that for many years Frazer's mode of analysis also distracted attention from the practical politics of ancient tribal monarchies. A more recent examination of Frazer's interpretation is Evans-Pritchard's *Divine Kingship of the Shilluk of the Nilotic Sudan* (1948). This shows in a particularly interesting way the hold Frazer's imagination had even on professional field observation: thus C. G. Seligman's investigations among the Shilluk, which used Frazer's concept of divine kingship, revealed just the set of beliefs and practices that fitted the Frazer argument. As Evans-Pritchard points out, there is very slight evidence for the actual ritual killing of the kings of Shilluk, while there is considerable evidence for the important role played by political conflicts within the ruling house. Many anthropologists thus became "enslaved," as Seligman was and as Malinowski once claimed to have been, by Frazerian anthropology (see also Leach 1965).

Influence of Frazer's ideas. Frazer's detailed contributions to anthropological thinking—his studies of the soul, of death, and of totemism and taboo, for example—belong to a framework of discussion that has now largely been abandoned, although it should be granted to him that in his time his was a more modern view than many others. He recognized, for example, that the notion of taboo has something to do with the Roman concept of *sacer*, with its dual connotation of "sacred" and "accursed," and though his general theory of totemism was crudely mechanistic, he did go some way toward identifying the bond of a common life that frequently links men and their totemic species.

But the significance of Frazer does not depend finally upon his anthropological theories. What he did was to introduce a comparative approach to the study of human social institutions. Here the very ambivalences and contradictions in his attitudes toward "the savage" may have served a purpose. While he had a certain ethnocentric contempt for the "dark and uncouth superstitions" he recorded, he also constantly implied that primitive thought is part of a single body of human tradition, linking his contemporaries (and himself) with much they despised. His self-deceived magicians and priests were also agents of human progress, the ablest and most intelligent of their time. In keeping with his own political philosophy, he also commended them for establishing intellectual despotism—and any statesman of his time who agreed with Frazer in principle was thereby accepting comparison with savages.

Frazer denied that all savages have an equal propensity to accept mystical explanations, asserting that in "savage as in civilized society there are sceptics as well as mystics" ([1923] 1931, p. 416); indeed, he believed that the "primitive mentality" that Lévy-Bruhl attributed exclusively to savages also characterizes such modern thinkers with mystical proclivities as Pascal, Newton, and Hegel. And on various occasions he stressed not only the common qualities of the thought of savage and civilized men but the positive contributions the former have made to the latter. Thus, in *Psyche's Task* (1909) he made a plea for the value of "superstitions": he saw their function in the maintaining of such institutions as civil order, private property, marriage, and the sanctity of human life. In a sense he anticipated the interest in "function" of Malinowski and Radcliffe-Brown. And in *The Golden Bough* he wrote that

of [all] the benefactors whom we are bound thankfully to commemorate, many, perhaps most, were savages. For when all is said and done, our resemblances to the savage are still far more numerous than our differences from him; and what we have in common with him, and deliberately retain as true and useful, we owe to our savage forefathers who slowly acquired by experience and transmitted to us by inheritance those seemingly fundamental ideas which we are apt to regard as original and intuitive. (1890, p. 264 in the abridged edition)

It is, then, as a powerful solvent of contemporary prejudices that Frazer's work stands out. Without him, the struggle to introduce anthropological knowledge and anthropological viewpoints to authorities in academic and public life would have been longer and harder. In an essential way, he made modern anthropology possible.

R. G. LIENHARDT

[For discussion of the subsequent development of Frazer's ideas, see ANTHROPOLOGY, article on THE COMPARATIVE METHOD IN ANTHROPOLOGY; CULTURE; MYTH AND SYMBOL; RELIGION; RITUAL; and the biographies of LÉVY-BRUHL; MALINOWSKI; SELIGMAN, C. G.; SMITH, WILLIAM ROBERTSON.]

WORKS BY FRAZER

(1887) 1910 Totemism and Exogamy. 4 vols. London: Macmillan.

(1890) 1955 The Golden Bough: A Study in Magic and Religion, 3d ed., rev. & enl. 13 vols. New York: St. Martins; London: Macmillan. → A one-volume abridged edition was published in 1922, and reprinted in 1955.

(1907) 1910 Questions on the Customs, Beliefs and Languages of Savages. Cambridge Univ. Press.

(1909) 1920 Psyche's Task: A Discourse Concerning the Influence of Superstition on the Growth of Institutions. 2d ed., rev. & enl. London: Macmillan.

(1923) 1931 Garnered Sheaves: Essays, Addresses, and Reviews. London: Macmillan.

SUPPLEMENTARY BIBLIOGRAPHY

BESTERMAN, THEODORE 1934 A Bibliography of Sir James George Frazer, O.M. London: Macmillan.

DAWSON, WARREN R. (editor) 1932 The Frazer Lectures: 1922–1932. London: Macmillan.

EVANS-PRITCHARD, E. E. 1948 The Divine Kingship of the Shilluk of the Nilotic Sudan. Cambridge Univ. Press.

LEACH, EDMUND R. 1965 Frazer and Malinowski. Encounter 25, no. 5:24–36.

RIDGEWAY, W. 1924 The Methods of Manhardt and Frazer, as Illustrated by the Writings of the Mistress of Girton (Miss Phillpotts, O.B.E.), Miss Jessie Weston, and Dr. B. Malinowski. Cambridge Philological Society, Proceedings Nos. 124–126:6–19.

FRAZIER, E. FRANKLIN

The most significant contributions of E. Franklin Frazier (1894–1962) to the literature of sociology are embodied in his writings in the fields of family behavior and race and culture contacts.

Although these fields are commonly demarcated as separate areas of study, they were not always so conceived by Frazier.

Frazier's major contribution to the literature of the family is The Negro Family in the United States (1939). Building on earlier research (1932a; 1932b), the book analyzes the impact first of slavery and then of emancipation and urbanization upon the Negro family. These experiences produced in the Negro family variations from the dominant American family pattern—to wit, a more important role for the female; attachment of great significance to variations in skin color; and a higher incidence of illegitimacy, of common law relationships, and of other forms of family disorganization. Frazier's viewpoint that the structure and values of the Negro family in the United States are to be understood, except in the most isolated instances, as products of the Negro's American experiences involved him in a lively controversy with the anthropological scholar and Africanist, Melville Herskovits, whose studies led him to the conclusion that the major institutions of Negro life, including the family, incorporate African survivals to a significant extent.

Frazier's sociological conceptions were shaped mainly by his graduate training at the University of Chicago, from which he received the doctoral degree in 1931. There he studied with Ellsworth Faris, Robert E. Park, William F. Ogburn, and Ernest Burgess. He became associated with the program of research on the urban community and on race relations, directed by Park and conducted by a group of brilliant graduate students and young instructors that included Louis Wirth, Everett C. Hughes, and Herbert Blumer. Although critics labeled this group the "Chicago ecological school," its basic conception of sociology was in fact much broader than the study of ecological phenomena. The group believed that any social phenomenon may be understood within the context of the larger social system and that the larger social system may be coterminous with society itself.

The influence of this approach is reflected in Frazier's work on culture contacts (1949a; 1957). In his Race and Culture Contacts in the Modern World (1957), he analyzed the ecological and demographic relationships that result from contacts between people of diverse racial and cultural backgrounds and the effects of these relationships on economic, political, and social organization.

Perhaps the most interesting result of Frazier's work on culture contacts is his Black Bourgeoisie (1955), an analysis of the evolution, composition, and style of life of the Negro middle class in the United States. The Negro middle class, according to Frazier, differs from middle classes in general not only in composition but also in values. Frazier pointed out that the Negro middle class lacks the strong entrepreneurial tradition that has been the backbone of the middle classes in general. Negro business is small business, mainly of the service variety—restaurants, beauty parlors, food stores, undertaking establishments. Negro insurance companies and the Negro press may be exceptions, but even these are small compared to white organizations of the same type. Similarly, Negro banks are few and possess limited capital.

The black bourgeoisie, therefore, "is constituted of those Negroes who derive their principal income from services they render as white-collar workers." This class of white-collar workers, mainly professionals and clerical and sales personnel, has acquired a dominant position among Negroes. Although their incomes are limited, they have lost much of the old virtues identified with the middle class—industry, thrift, belief in the substantive values of education—and have, instead, emphasized conspicuous consumption and attractive social life, values more commonly associated with a leisure class. This emphasis upon society and social life represents "status without substance." This theme, that Negro values are distorted, recurs in many of Frazier's articles on Negro life in the United States: he saw the racial system as forcing the Negro to live in isolation and as endowing him with a sense of dependency and inferiority.

Frazier was born in Baltimore, Maryland. An apt and intellectually curious student, he received a B.A. degree with honors from Howard University in 1916. His first serious, formal encounter with sociology was as a graduate student at Clark University, from which he received an M.A. degree in 1920. There he studied with Frank Hankins, whom he credited with opening up to him the possibilities of sociology as a systematic study. In addition to graduate study at Chicago, his formal education included a year of study at the New York School of Social Work, 1920–1921, and a year in Denmark as a fellow of the Scandinavian–American Foundation, 1921–1922. His major academic affiliation was with Howard University, where he was professor of sociology from 1934 until he died.

Frazier was president of the American Sociological Society in 1948 and was awarded honorary degrees by Morgan College, Baltimore, in 1955 and by the University of Edinburgh in 1960.

G. Franklin Edwards

[For the historical context of Frazier's work, see the biographies of Burgess; Hankins; Herskovits; Ogburn; Park; for discussion of the subsequent development of his ideas, see Race relations.]

WORKS BY FRAZIER

1932a   The Negro Family in Chicago. Univ. of Chicago Press.
1932b   The Free Negro Family: A Study of Family Origins Before the Civil War. Nashville, Tenn.: Fisk Univ. Press.
1939   The Negro Family in the United States. Univ. of Chicago Press. → A revised and abridged edition was published in 1948 by Dryden Press.
1949a   Race Contacts and the Social Structure. American Sociological Review 14:1–11.
(1949b) 1963   The Negro in the United States. Rev. ed. New York: Macmillan.
(1955) 1957   Black Bourgeoisie. Glencoe, Ill.: Free Press. → First published in French. A paperback edition was published in 1962 by Collier.
(1957) 1965   Race and Culture Contacts in the Modern World. Boston: Beacon.
1964   The Negro Church in America. Liverpool University Studies in Sociology, No. 1. New York: Schocken; Liverpool (England) Univ. Press. → Published posthumously.

SUPPLEMENTARY BIBLIOGRAPHY

Davis, A. P.   1962   E. Franklin Frazier 1894–1962: A Profile. Journal of Negro Education 31:429–435.
Edwards, G. Franklin   1962   Edward Franklin Frazier: 1894–1962. American Sociological Review 27:890–892.
Odum, Howard W.   1951   American Sociology: The Story of Sociology in the United States Through 1950. New York: Longmans. → See especially pages 233–239 on "Franklin Frazier: 1894—."

FREE TRADE

See International trade and International trade controls.

FREEDOM

The word "freedom," with its synonym "liberty," has a strong laudatory connotation. It has therefore been applied to whatever actions, policies, or institutions may be deemed valuable, from obeying the law to attaining economic affluence. Political writings seldom provide explicit definitions of "freedom" in descriptive terms, but it is often possible to infer descriptive definitions from the context. If this is done, it will be seen that the concept of freedom refers most frequently to social freedom, which must be distinguished from other descriptive and valuational usages. Descriptive definitions of "freedom" designate empirically specifiable states of affairs and can therefore be accepted by anyone, regardless of his normative views on liberty. "Freedom" in a valuational sense is used to commend rather than to describe; it therefore means different things to writers committed to different ethical standards.

Social freedom

The concept of interpersonal or social freedom refers to relationships of interaction between persons or groups, namely, that one actor leaves another actor free to act in certain ways. This concept is best defined by reference to another interaction relation, that of interpersonal or social unfreedom.

Social unfreedom defined. With respect to actor B, actor A is unfree to perform action x if and only if B makes it either impossible or punishable for A to do x. "B makes it impossible for A to do x" means that B performs some action y such that were A to attempt x, his attempt would fail. By denying a citizen a passport, the government makes him practically unable to travel abroad and, hence, unfree to do so. With respect to the United States, Communist China is unfree to conquer Formosa, and vice versa, since U.S. forces would presumably prevent either power from invading the other. If the Ku Klux Klan forcibly prevents Negroes from entering a public school, the Negroes are unfree to do so with respect to the Klan, but not with respect to the government. "B makes it punishable for A to do x" means that were A to carry out x, B would perform some action y that would deprive A. Governmental sanctions against illegal acts are only one example of punishability as an instance of social unfreedom. With respect to a union, a company would be unfree to withhold certain benefits if the union were to picket the company. Residents in a typical block of modern suburbia are unfree to deviate from certain tacit norms with respect to the "neighborhood," which tends to penalize nonconformists.

Social freedom defined. Social freedom is not the contradictory of social unfreedom. I am not officially unfree to pay incomes taxes, yet, I am not free to pay them either; rather, I am unfree to withhold payment. A relationship of freedom refers to a set of at least two alternative actions or types of actions. I am unfree to do this; I am free to do this *or* that. An actor is free to act in any one of several ways, provided there is no other actor who makes him unfree to perform any of these actions. Thus, with respect to B, A is free to do either x or z if and only if B makes it neither impossible nor punishable for A to do either x or z. "Freedom to vote" means freedom either to vote or to abstain; but "freedom to propagate the truth" really means unfreedom to spread "erroneous" views. Furthermore, I may be free to act in one way or another with respect to one person or group, whereas another actor makes me unfree to engage in one of these activities. Officially, Americans are free to adopt any religion or to adhere to none, but many Americans are unfree to be agnostics with respect to certain nonofficial groups who subject "atheists" to all kinds of informal sanctions.

Testing statements about social freedom. Whether an actor *was* *un*free to do what he actually did can be determined with certainty, but only ex post facto. If A's attempt to do x was frustrated by B, or if A succeeded in doing x but was penalized by B for having done so, it follows by definition that A was, with respect to B, unfree to do x. That A is *un*free to do x, or that A was or is or will be *free* to do x or z, are empirical hypotheses that can be asserted only with a certain degree of probability, depending on the answers to such questions as: were A to carry out x, would B penalize him? If 60 per cent of all speeders in France are convicted, every French driver is to that extent unfree to speed, regardless of how many comply. A person's social freedom does not depend on his actual behavior. We often perform actions that we are unfree to do (for example, speeding) and refrain from actions that we are free to perform (for example, driving at any speed lower than the speed limit).

Social freedom and political freedom. Relationships of interpersonal or social freedom and unfreedom may hold between any two persons or groups, for example, members of a family, buyers and sellers, legislature and executive, pope and emperor, members of the Common Market. A government's freedom may or may not be limited by an international organization, another government, a church, its own citizens, some interest group within or outside of its jurisdiction, etc. Political freedoms are a subclass of social freedoms and usually refer to the freedom of citizens or associations with respect to the government. Interest in political liberty has in various periods of history centered on freedom of religion, of speech and writing, of association (religious, political, economic), and of participation in the political process (suffrage). The idea of political freedom has been extended to cover demands for economic liberty, "freedom from want," national self-determination, etc.

Social freedom and control. Social *un*freedom and control are overlapping categories. By *preventing* A from doing x, B makes A unfree to do x and controls his behavior. If B *punishes* A for having done x, one may infer that A was, with respect to B, unfree to do x; but B did not control A's behavior, since his threat of punishment failed to deter A from doing x. *Influence* is another form of control; however, if B succeeds, for example, in persuading A to vote Democratic, B does not thereby restrict A's freedom to vote Republican (or Democratic). Here, both control and freedom relationships hold between B and A.

Social freedom and power. Although there may be unfreedom without control and control without unfreedom, the concept of power had best be taken as comprising both control and unfreedom relationships. If B either has influence over A's not doing *x*, or prevents A from doing *x*, or makes it punishable for him to do so, B may be said to have power over A in this respect. The example of B persuading A to vote Democratic illustrates that power and freedom relationships may hold between the same pair of actors. The same is true in the following situations: B has power over A with respect to a limited range of alternatives; A is free within that range. Government, for example, has the power to compel citizens to serve in the armed forces but may leave them free either to submit to the draft or to volunteer. A may be, with respect to B, free to do *x*, either because B has no power to limit A's freedom or because he permits A to do *x*. The United States Congress is free to legislate as it pleases as far as the president is concerned, to the extent that he chooses not to exercise his veto power. To affirm that freedom of speech prevails in a given society is to refer to the following relationships of both freedom and unfreedom (and power) between any two of its members, A and B: A and B each leave the other free to say what he wants; with respect to B, A is unfree to prevent him from expressing his views, and vice versa; A and B are unfree to do so, not only with respect to each other but also with respect to the government, which protects everybody's *right* to free speech.

Social freedom and legal rights. It is true both that liberty depends "on the silence of the law" (Hobbes) and that "where there is no law there is no freedom" (Locke). I am socially free to act in a certain way only if (1) there is no effectively enforced law prohibiting or ordering me to do so and if (2) I have an effectively protected legal right to that effect, that is, if all others are unfree to hinder me from doing so. We must distinguish between freedom in the behavioral sense and in the legal sense. All drivers have the legal duty not to speed, but they are socially unfree to speed only to the extent that speeders are actually fined. Thus, driver A, who sped on a particular occasion without being detected, was socially free to do so on that occasion, even though he had no legal right to that effect. If 40 per cent of all speeders in France escape conviction, French drivers are to that extent socially free to speed.

Other descriptive meanings

Freedom of choice. Whereas social freedom refers to two actors and their respective actions, freedom of choice signifies a relationship between one actor and a series of alternative potential actions. "A has freedom of choice as to *x* or *z*" means that it is possible for A to do either *x* or *z*, or that both *x* and *z* are open as well as avoidable to A, or that A will bring about *x* provided he chooses to do *x*. Conversely, if it is either impossible or necessary for A to do *x*, A has no freedom of choice as to *x*. It is in this sense that Hume defines liberty as "the power of acting or not acting, according to the determinations of the will." Freedom of choice is neither a necessary nor a sufficient condition for social freedom. If A cannot do *x*, he is unfree to do so only if his inability has been caused by some other actor B. Otherwise, A remains free to do *x*, even though he has no freedom of choice as to *x*. Most men are incapable, yet at liberty, to become millionaires or to run for high political office. Unemployment during a recession diminishes freedom of choice, not social freedom, unless the recession itself can be causally linked, for example, to specific governmental policies. The high cost of television time renders this medium inaccessible to most; this restricts freedom of choice for prospective broadcasters, not their freedom of speech. Everybody is socially "free to sleep under bridges" or at home, including the homeless, who have no choice in the matter. (In all such cases, the illusion of paradox arises because the actor is likely to value the opportunity he lacks, not the freedom he has.) Conversely, we do have freedom of choice with respect to most punishable actions; we can be made unfree to do them precisely because they are open to us.

Free will. Indeterminists often hold that human beings have "free will," that is, that their actual choices and resulting behavior are not causally determined but constitute chance events. Determinists can with perfect consistency deny this doctrine and yet affirm that men often have freedom of choice. They argue that the fact that A *has* the choice of doing either *x* or *z* does not preclude the possibility of explaining and predicting A's *actual* choice by virtue of causal (for example, psychological or sociological) laws.

Free actions. Of an action itself, it can be said that it was either a free or an unfree one, as when we say: "this murder was a free action," or "he paid his taxes, but not freely." Involuntary behavior is unfree, and so are nondeliberate actions, for example, those that the actor has been conditioned to perform. Voluntary actions are free, unless they are motivated by fear of punishment. A's handing over his money to B, who points a gun at him, is an unfree action (yet it is a voluntary action, determined partly by B's threat and partly by A's desire to save his life). But if A refuses to comply with B, then A acts freely. One may do freely what one is unfree to do. Again, if B persuades A to do x without threats of punishment, A's action x is a free one. Sometimes, however, "free" is used more broadly to refer to actions that are autonomous, that is, determined exclusively by the actor's own decisions and not by the influence of others, as when John Stuart Mill said: "The only freedom which deserves the name is that of pursuing our own good *in our own way.*"

Free persons.   "Free" often refers to a characteristic, not of actions but of persons. A person may be said to be free to the extent that he has the disposition to act freely, or to act autonomously, or to develop his capacities to the fullest. Marx, for example, prophesied a society "in which the free development of each is the condition for the free development of all." "Freedom" becomes a synonym for "self-realization." Laski uses the term almost exclusively in this sense in his article on liberty (1933).

Feeling free.   Liberty is often said to consist in doing what one desires. It would be more accurate to say that an actor *feels* free to the extent that he does what he wants. Freedom as a state of mind must be distinguished from freedom as a state of affairs. Among the things I want to avoid doing, there may be some I am free to do and others I am unfree to do. Some persons derive a feeling of freedom from the fact that they are left free to act out any one of several alternatives. Others feel free when they "escape from freedom" into submission to some authority that conditions them to want to do its will. Dostoevski's grand inquisitor plays on these two meanings of the word: "Today, people are more persuaded than ever that they have perfect freedom; yet they have brought their freedom to us and laid it humbly at our feet."

A free society.   Is it legitimate to use "free" as a characteristic of a group, such as when democracy is held to be a free society? There is no such thing as freedom in general; every organized society consists of an intricate network of specific relations of both freedom and unfreedom. Citizens in a democracy have the political freedom to partici-

pate in the governmental process through "free" elections. Voters, parties, and pressure groups are thereby empowered to *limit* the freedom of their elected officials. Democracy also requires that "civil liberties" be protected by legal rights and duties, and these duties again imply limitations of freedom. In a perfect dictatorship, the ruler has unlimited freedom with respect to his subjects, whereas they are totally unfree with respect to him. In a democracy, both liberties and restrictions of freedom are distributed more evenly, for example, among the various branches of government, between government and governed, majority and minority. *Equal* freedom, not *more* freedom, is the essence of democracy. (Strictly speaking, it is not meaningful to say that there is "more" freedom in one *society* than in another; but it is possible to define degrees of social freedom in the sense that one *actor* has greater freedom in a certain respect than another.) A society in which liberties are evenly distributed may be called a free society. However, here we come close to using "freedom" in a valuational sense: a society is free in which those and only those freedom relations hold that are *desirable.*

Valuational meanings

Because of the laudatory connotation of the word "freedom," writers have been inclined to define it to cover those and only those relationships of *both* social freedom and unfreedom that they happen to value and wish to commend to others. Such persuasive definitions of freedom are useful not as tools of the empirical social sciences but as rhetorical devices; they enable the writer to express his normative views in assertive form. For example, by stating that "to obey the laws laid down by society is to be free," Rousseau in effect exhorts citizens to obey such laws; he is not trying to explicate the meaning of freedom. Persuasive definitions of freedom have been used to propound almost every political ideology, as is illustrated by the following examples.

Freedom as protection of basic rights.   Classical liberalism from Locke to Spencer and his followers advocated that government ought to restrict a person's freedom when and only when necessary to protect another person's basic rights (often held to correspond to natural rights). Accordingly, "*no society* in which these liberties are not, on the whole, respected, *is free*" (Mill). Conversely, a society *is free*, provided it is based on these laissez-faire principles. And a person who enjoys these legal rights and is subject to the corresponding legal duties is free, however unfree he may be in other regards and with respect to actors other than the government, for example, because of economic exploitation or social pressure. Thus, the United States Supreme Court once held that minimum-wage and maximum-hour laws violate the constitutional principle of liberty, because such regulations are not necessary to the protection of basic rights but constitute "arbitrary" limitations of "freedom of contract" of both employer and employee.

Freedom as satisfaction of basic needs. Neo-liberals point out that the right to acquire the necessities of life is of little value to those who lack the opportunity to acquire them, that government ought to make them available to all, and that this may require governmental restriction of individual freedom through regulations concerning public health, education, and welfare. Social welfare, not social freedom, is their ultimate goal; but they still use the word "freedom" to designate this end. "Personal freedom means, in fact, the power of the individual to buy sufficient food, shelter, and clothing" (Sidney and Beatrice Webb). And so, "the distinction between welfare and liberty breaks down altogether" (Ralph Barton Perry). Conversely, those who are unable to bring about what society ought to enable them to achieve, but who are free with respect to the government to make the attempt, are said to lack "true freedom." "Freedom from want," unlike freedom of speech, does not refer directly to social freedom, but to absence of want and presence of a satisfactory living standard for all. It is only in an indirect sense that "necessitous men are not free men" (Franklin D. Roosevelt). They have little freedom of choice and are socially unfree with respect to the economically powerful. "Freedom" is applied not only to the welfare goal itself but also to whatever restrictions of social freedom are deemed necessary to achieve it. The Supreme Court now interprets liberty to be compatible with minimum-wage laws and other "reasonable regulations and prohibitions imposed in the interest of the community." "Freedom" includes desirable social unfreedom and excludes undesirable social freedom.

Freedom as government by consent. This persuasive definition of freedom is used to express the norm that government ought to be based on consent of the governed, and this usually means representative government and majority rule. For example, "the liberty of man in society is to be under no other legislative power but that established by consent in the commonwealth" (Locke). Under such a system, men are free because their freedom is limited only by measures in the enactment of which they were free to participate. With a slight shift in emphasis, "freedom" stands no longer for the government's duty to be responsive to the will of the citizens but for the citizen's duty to obey governmental enactments reflecting the will of the majority or the "general will." According to Rousseau, the citizen is free whether he fulfills this obligation freely or whether he has been "compelled to be free." And so "freedom" comes to refer no longer to having the choice of acting in one way or another, but to acting in no other way than that prescribed by authority.

Freedom as moral constraint. The definitions of freedom taken up so far, including even the persuasive ones, are made up entirely of descriptive terms. However, definitions of freedom often include ethical words, such as "right," "ought," or "virtue." In such cases, not only the term to be defined (freedom) but also the defining expression has valuational meaning. For example, "Liberty can consist only in the power of doing what we ought to will" (Montesquieu). Similarly, a person is often said to be free, not if he acts freely or develops his capacities, but if he realizes his "best" or "essential" self. For example, "Liberty may be defined as the affirmation by an individual or group of his or its own essence" (Laski 1933, p. 444). Some have held that a person is most likely to realize his essence if he is left free to choose for himself.

According to another tradition, which extends from Plato via the Stoics and Christian thought to Neo-Hegelianism, man reaches the highest form of self-realization by submitting to some moral norm imposed by his own "higher self," which is usually identified with faith, reason, or moral conscience. "I call him free who is led solely by reason" (Spinoza). "Obedience to a law which we prescribe to ourselves is liberty" (Rousseau). Freedom no longer signifies the absence of unwelcome, but the presence of welcome restraints. "For freedom is not acquired by satisfying yourself with what you desire, but by destroying your desire" (Epictetus). In short, freedom is unfreedom to do wrong, whereas freedom to deviate from the prescribed path is license. "If unbridled license of speech and of writing be granted to all, nothing will remain sacred and inviolate. . . . Thus, license will gain what liberty loses" (*Encyclical libertas* 1888).

If "freedom" becomes a label for anybody's moral or political ends, then everybody's value commitment to freedom will be vacuous. All will agree that liberty is the supreme good, but they will agree on nothing else. Meaningful disagreement about the *value* of freedom presupposes agreement about the *meaning* of freedom in nonvaluational terms. The concept of social freedom provides an adequate basis for a fruitful discussion of the normative, as well as the empirical, aspects of liberty. In this discourse, the divergent views about which social freedoms ought to be extended or limited will depend on the value one assigns to such other social goals as equality, justice, or welfare, which may compete with the goal of freedom.

FELIX E. OPPENHEIM

[*See also* DEMOCRACY; EQUALITY; JUSTICE; NORMS; POLITICAL THEORY; VALUES.]

BIBLIOGRAPHY

ADLER, MORTIMER J. 1958–1961 *The Idea of Freedom.* 2 vols. Garden City, N.Y.: Doubleday. → Contains significant quotations about freedom selected from all major writings from the Greeks to the present. Bibliography covers anthologies and periodical literature.

AMERICAN SOCIETY FOR POLITICAL AND LEGAL PHILOSOPHY 1962 *Liberty.* Edited by Carl J. Friedrich. Nomos 4. New York: Atherton. → A collection of essays.

ARON, RAYMOND 1965 *Essai sur les libertés.* Paris: Calmann-Lévy.

BAY, CHRISTIAN 1958 *The Structure of Freedom.* Stanford (Calif.) Univ. Press.

BERLIN, ISAIAH 1958 *Two Concepts of Liberty.* Oxford Univ. Press.

CRANSTON, MAURICE (1953) 1955 *Freedom: A New Analysis.* 2d ed. London: Longmans.

HAYEK, FRIEDRICH A. VON 1960 *The Constitution of Liberty.* Univ. of Chicago Press; London: Routledge.

LASKI, HAROLD 1933 Liberty. Volume 9, pages 442–446 in *Encyclopaedia of the Social Sciences.* New York: Macmillan.

MULLER, HERBERT J. 1960 *Issues of Freedom: Paradoxes and Promises.* New York: Harper.

OPPENHEIM, FELIX E. 1961 *Dimensions of Freedom: An Analysis.* New York: St. Martins; London: Macmillan.

FRENKEL-BRUNSWIK, ELSE

Else Frenkel-Brunswik (1908–1958) was born of Polish-Jewish parents in the town of Lemberg, then part of the Austro–Hungarian Empire, and received her doctorate in psychology in 1930 at the University of Vienna. She continued at the university, as lecturer and research associate, until shortly after the Nazi *Anschluss* in 1938. With her husband, Egon Brunswik, she then moved to the University of California at Berkeley, where she remained until her death.

The professional life of Else Frenkel-Brunswik covers a period that was not one of great new theories or startling discoveries in psychology. It was, rather, a time of expansion and ferment. The boundaries of academic psychology were being extended from the study of segmental psychological processes in the experimental laboratory to a more profound conception of human personality in its development over time and its engagement with a complex sociocultural environment. Psychologists sought to grasp the implications of the revolutionary changes stemming from psychoanalysis, from the physical sciences, and from cataclysmic societal developments. To an unusual degree, Frenkel-Brunswik's career reflected these major intellectual and social developments and at the same time influenced the course of psychology.

Her doctoral thesis (1931) under Karl Bühler attempted a *rapprochement* between traditional associationism and the newer concepts of gestalt psychology. Subsequently, on the staff of the Psychological Institute, headed by Charlotte Bühler, she collaborated in a series of developmental studies (see, for example, Frenkel & Weisskopf 1937) derived from the biographies of 400 persons selected from various historical periods and walks of life. This research, although theoretically limited, exemplifies enduring features of her approach: the developmental view of personality; the combined use of phenomenological and behavioral data and of multiple assessment methods; and the functional view of behavioral striving in terms of adaptation and goal achievement.

The situation in Vienna provided three additional formative influences. First, there was the philosophical influence of the logical positivism of the "Vienna circle," which included such men as Neurath, Schlick, and Carnap. This produced an enduring concern with problems of theory development, conceptual and operational definition of terms, and the role of inference in personality measurement.

Second, there was the influence of psychoanalysis, which was of fundamental importance in shaping her future work. She had a personal analysis in Vienna. Although she did not become a practicing psychoanalyst, a clinical mode of thought continually informed her research, her teaching, and her experience of life. One of her initial studies drawing upon psychoanalytic theory was "Mechanisms of Self-deception" (1939).

A third influence derived from the sociopolitical situation during the 1930s. Frenkel-Brunswik was deeply affected by the tragic events of that period. However, it was only after she came to the United States that these concerns were explicitly reflected in her intellectual work.

Although the emigration from Austria in 1938 was in many respects painful, her situation in the United States offered tremendous opportunity and stimulation. She flourished there. Her first position in California was at the Institute of Child Welfare, and she maintained this association for the rest of her career.

Personality theory

One of her first publications in the United States was the paper "Psychoanalysis and Personality Research" (1940), which was read at the now-historic Symposium on Psychoanalysis by Analyzed Experimental Psychologists. In this paper, she wrote, not as an "analyzed experimental psychologist," but as a personality theorist in the broadest sense. She recognized that there was complementarity as well as conflict between the psychoanalytic, phenomenological, and behaviorist schools. Rather than starting with one of these theoretical positions, she sought to identify, in terms meaningful to all of them, the basic theoretical domains in the study of personality. She posited four such domains: the *central* and the *peripheral* levels of personality (following and enlarging upon Henry A. Murray's formulation); and the *proximal* and *distal* effects of behavior upon the environment (a perspective on behavior utilizing the distinction made by gestalt theorists and by Egon Brunswik). A truly comprehensive personality theory, she maintained, must encompass relationships between all four domains rather than being encapsulated within one or two. She argued also for the combined use of clinical and experimental modes of investigation. Although many of her then-radical proposals are now widely accepted, this paper stands as a fresh statement of the theoretical and methodological tasks of dynamic personality research.

In her monograph "Motivation and Behavior" (1942) Frenkel-Brunswik applied and developed further the theoretical position outlined in her 1940 article. This empirical study of adolescents made use of concepts and measures in several theoretical domains. There were self-reports obtained through questionnaires, observers' ratings of behavior in specific social situations, projective test material, and clinical ratings of underlying (central) motives based upon inferences from a wide variety of observational and test data. The concept of *alternative manifestation* was developed and operationalized, to help account for the relationships of underlying motives to overt behavior and conscious self-report, and theoretically sophisticated use was made of partial and multiple correlation techniques. In this study Frenkel-Brunswik provided one of the earliest models of systematic personality research. She dealt with various levels of personality, seen as dynamically interdependent, and she contributed to the methodology of inferential clinical ratings, relating

them to more-directly behavioral measures and giving them a legitimate place within the academic psychological investigation of personality. Her work on the clinical ratings was innovative in at least two respects. On the one hand, she developed techniques to increase the explicitness and reliability of clinical inferences. On the other, she anticipated the later research on social perception in her study of the influence of the rater's personality on his judgments of subjects' motivation and behavior.

Her sociopsychological interests took form in the early 1940s. In 1942 she had a Social Science Research Council fellowship for work in sociology and anthropology at the University of Chicago, Harvard, the Langley Porter Institute, and with Kroeber and others at the University of California. In 1943 she joined Sanford and Levinson in a study of personality and prejudice, and Adorno became their collaborator soon after. The study expanded over the next few years and was published under the title *The Authoritarian Personality* (1950). During this period she was also engaged in a related study of prejudice in children and families (see Frenkel-Brunswik & Havel 1953).

"The Authoritarian Personality"

Frenkel-Brunswik made certain distinctive and specifiable contributions to *The Authoritarian Personality;* these will be noted below. She also contributed in significant but less identifiable ways to the character of that work as a whole. The basic theoretical conception and methodology of the research were an emergent product of intimately collaborative effort by the four coauthors and reflected their common intellectual concerns. Without attempting to allocate specific credit to individual authors, I shall simply indicate the major features of this comprehensive project. It will be evident that they express Frenkel-Brunswik's earlier interests and are of importance in her subsequent work.

Theoretically, *The Authoritarian Personality* represented a convergence of previously disparate viewpoints: attitude theory in academic psychology; the sociological analysis of ideology; and psychoanalysis and related personality theories, notably that of Murray. Consciously held attitudes, values, and ideologies were regarded as aspects of personality. They were related to contemporaneous character traits, cognitive–emotional styles, ego defenses, and less conscious wishes and fantasies. The formation of ideology was seen in developmental perspective and was related to more general processes of ego and superego development. In retrospect, the approach may be seen as a form of psychoanalytic ego theory; that is to say, it drew upon traditional psychoanalytic concepts and at the same time emphasized and conceptualized ego processes that link the person more directly with his social environment. This approach, now widely held in various forms, was at the time a major innovation in social psychology.

Methodologically, the research on authoritarianism involved the conjoint use of previously disparate techniques: scales and other questionnaire devices, projective techniques, and semistructured clinical interviews. Intensive case studies were used to develop hypotheses and to guide the explicit formulation of variables that were then measured by means of questionnaires administered to groups. The continuing interplay of clinical and statistical analysis was an essential feature of the methodology. The Authoritarianism (F) Scale, perhaps the most widely used and most poorly understood product of the study, was one result of this interplay.

The most clearly identifiable contributions by Frenkel-Brunswik are in the chapters bearing her name. These deal with the construction and analysis of the intensive, semistructured interviews. The interviews were standardized in the sense that they covered a predefined set of topical areas and theoretical issues, and they required considerable advance training of the interviewers. At the same time they had a clinically "open" quality in that the interviewer tried to follow the threads of the subject's thought and feeling; within the loose structure of the topical areas and issues, the content and sequence of the interview were largely determined by the interviewee. This was, in short, a qualitatively distinct hybrid—a cross between the survey and the therapy interview—and an important contribution to personality–social research.

In the analysis of the interviews Frenkel-Brunswik developed an extensive series of categories that distinguish "high-authoritarian" from "low-authoritarian" subjects. The rating of each category required clinical inference on the part of the rater. To help control for the subjectivity in this process, the categories were defined in some detail and were scored by two independent raters, so that reliability could be determined. Categories were developed in three broad domains: parents and childhood; sex, people, and self; and dynamic and cognitive personality organization. The interpretive integration of findings in these domains led to the formulation of a smaller number of major themes and patterns.

One of the concepts developed here (and given greater prominence in her subsequent research) is *intolerance of ambiguity* (1949). This concept has a complex, many-faceted character. Its referents include a tendency toward oversimplification in perceptions and conceptions of the external world; a deep uneasiness about ambiguity and lack of order in personal relationships and social structures; a proclivity to engage in moralistic, all-good or all-bad value judgments, without recognition of moral ambiguities; an inability to acknowledge ambivalence (emotional ambiguity) in one's experience of parents and significant others. This concept thus has motivational, emotional, cognitive, and moral aspects, and it refers to the person's experience of both self and external world. Although subsequent evidence has not fully supported Frenkel-Brunswik's initial formulation of intolerance of ambiguity as a relatively unified, pervasive *trait*, it does indicate the usefulness of this kind of multiple-component concept as a *genotype* underlying diverse overt behaviors.

Later career

The period from 1950 to 1955 was a lively and productive one for Frenkel-Brunswik. She visited Europe for the Rockefeller Foundation and reported on the condition of European psychology. She wrote a number of papers that reflected the growing breadth of her theoretical interests: on the interaction of sociological and psychological variables (1952; 1954*b*); on perceptual–cognitive functioning as an aspect of personality (1951); on psychoanalysis and the unity of science (1954*a*; 1957). In 1953 she began a study of aging; this work was completed and published by colleagues (Reichard et al. 1962) after her death. In 1954/1955, she was a fellow at the Center for Advanced Study in the Behavioral Sciences.

This period of great vitality was cut short by the tragic death of her husband, Egon, in 1955—a blow from which she never fully recovered. Her final dream had been a major treatise on values, a book that would bring together her lifelong interests in psychoanalysis, sociology, and philosophy. This hope was ended by her own premature death in 1958.

Frenkel-Brunswik's intellectual commitment, warmth, and intensity were reflected in her relationships with students. Although she did not do much formal teaching, she developed unusually close relationships through seminars, research collaboration, and informal contacts. She had a charismatic femininity. The number of present-day psychologists who feel a special gratitude to her and who regard her as a major formative influence in their personal and professional development is large indeed.

The contributions of Frenkel-Brunswik can perhaps best be grasped within the context of the radical new developments in American psychology during the period of roughly 1935 to 1950. She was a founding figure in the establishment of the new fields of personality psychology and social and clinical psychology. She forged important links between psychoanalysis and academic personality research. She contributed to the development of a conception of man that takes account of both reason and passion, of the most primitive and the most mature, of the autistic and the socially embedded aspects of his nature. Finally, she was multidisciplinary in the best sense of the word. She was ready to engage in disciplined search for the relevant, no matter how far it led from her disciplinary origins.

DANIEL J. LEVINSON

[*For the historical context of Frenkel-Brunswik's work,* see GESTALT THEORY; PERSONALITY: CONTEMPORARY VIEWPOINTS, *article on* COMPONENTS OF AN EVOLVING PERSONOLOGICAL SYSTEM; *and the biographies of* BRUNSWIK; BÜHLER; SCHLICK. *For discussion of the subsequent development of Frenkel-Brunswik's ideas, see* ATTITUDES; PERSONALITY, POLITICAL, *article on* CONSERVATISM AND RADICALISM.]

BIBLIOGRAPHY

The author was given access to an unpublished manuscript dealing with the life and work of Else Frenkel-Brunswik by Joan Havel Grant and Nanette Heiman. The manuscript is scheduled for publication in Psychological Issues *in 1968. It should be noted that Frenkel-Brunswik's works are sometimes listed in bibliographies and in library catalogues under Brunswik.*

WORKS BY FRENKEL-BRUNSWIK

1931   Atomismus und Mechanismus in der Assoziationspsychologie. *Zeitschrift für Psychologie* 123:193–258.
1937   FRENKEL, ELSE; and WEISSKOPF, EDITH Wunsch und Pflicht im Aufbau des menschlichen Lebens. Volume 1 in *Psychologische Forschungen über den Lebenslauf.* Edited by Charlotte Bühler and Else Frenkel. Vienna: Gerold.

1939   Mechanisms of Self-deception. *Journal of Social Psychology* 10:409–420.
1940   Psychoanalysis and Personality Research. *Journal of Abnormal and Social Psychology* 35:176–197.
1942   Motivation and Behavior. *Genetic Psychology Monographs* 26:121–265.
1949   Intolerance of Ambiguity as an Emotional and Perceptual Personality Variable. *Journal of Personality* 18:108–143.
1950   *The Authoritarian Personality,* by T. W. Adorno et al. New York: Harper. → Else Frenkel-Brunswik was a coauthor.
1951   Personality Theory and Perception. Pages 356–419 in Robert R. Blake and Glenn V. Ramsey (editors), *Perception: An Approach to Personality.* New York: Ronald.
1952   Interaction of Psychological and Sociological Factors in Political Behavior. *American Political Science Review* 46:44–65.
1953   FRENKEL-BRUNSWIK, ELSE; and HAVEL, JOAN Prejudice in the Interviews of Children. Part 1: Attitudes Toward Minority Groups. *Journal of Genetic Psychology* 82:91–136.
1954a   Psychoanalysis and the Unity of Science. *Dædalus* 80:271–350.
1954b   Environmental Controls and the Impoverishment of Thought. Pages 171–202 in American Academy of Arts and Sciences, *Totalitarianism: Proceedings of a Conference.* Cambridge, Mass.: Harvard Univ. Press.
1957   Perspectives in Psychoanalytic Theory. Pages 150–182 in Henry P. David and Helmut von Bracken (editors), *Perspectives in Personality.* New York: Basic Books.

SUPPLEMENTARY BIBLIOGRAPHY

REICHARD, SUZANNE K.; PETERSON, PAUL C.; and LIVSON, FLORINE 1962 *Aging and Personality: A Study of Eighty-seven Older Men.* New York: Wiley. → A report on a study directed by Else Frenkel-Brunswik.

FREQUENCY CURVES

See DISTRIBUTIONS, STATISTICAL; STATISTICS, DESCRIPTIVE.

International Encyclopedia of the SOCIAL SCIENCES

DAVID L. SILLS EDITOR

VOLUME 6

The Macmillan Company & The Free Press, New York
COLLIER-MACMILLAN PUBLISHERS, LONDON

[C O N T I N U E D]

FREUD, SIGMUND

Sigmund Freud was born May 6, 1856, in Freiberg, Moravia (now Czechoslovakia), and died September 23, 1939, in exile in London. When the boy was three, his father, a small wool merchant, was forced by economic reverses to move for a year to Leipzig and thence to Vienna, where Freud spent the rest of his life—1860 to 1938—except for his last year. His biographers agree that the unusual structure of the family into which he was born was partly responsible for his interest in intimate human relationships: Freud's father had two sons by his first wife; when he remarried after her death, it was to a woman of their age. Sigmund, her first child, often played with his year-older nephew. A brother who was born when Sigmund was not yet a year old died after eight months; then came four sisters and another brother.

A dedicated student, Freud graduated *summa cum laude* from the Gymnasium at age 17 and entered the University of Vienna medical school. After three years Freud became deeply involved in research, which delayed his M.D. until 1881; research was to remain his main interest. In 1882 he met and became engaged to Martha Bernays, and he began clinical training in order to be able to earn a living from the practice of medicine. He continued research and publishing, was made *Dozent*, and received a grant in 1885 to study for several months with Charcot in Paris. The next year he married and began practicing neurology; three sons and three daughters were born between 1887 and 1895.

Since existing therapies were not effective for his patients, most of whom were neurotic, he turned to hypnotic suggestion and in 1889 briefly visited Bernheim and Liébeault to perfect his technique. He learned a more helpful method, however, from a close friend, Josef Breuer, whose patient "Anna O." (Bertha Pappenheim) had managed to overcome some hysterical symptoms by talking freely about the circumstances of their first occurrence. Freud's successful experiences with and modifications of this "cathartic" treatment were reported in the book he wrote jointly with Breuer, *Studies on Hysteria* (1893–1895). For the next five years, he continued to develop this psychotherapeutic method into psychoanalysis, gradually withdrawing from neurology, although by then he had an international reputation in that field. [*See* HYSTERIA; PSYCHOSOMATIC ILLNESS.]

The way his own self-analysis contributed to the growth of his ideas during this period may be seen in the letters and drafts of papers sent to a Berlin colleague, Wilhelm Fliess, who became a close friend and confidant (see 1887–1902; 1895). The first major statement of his theories was *The Interpretation of Dreams* (1900). In 1902 he was made professor extraordinarius at the University of Vienna, and about that time his publications and lectures began to attract a group of followers, which became in 1908 the Vienna Psychoanalytical Society.

The principal focus of Freud's life thereafter was the growth of psychoanalysis—as a theory, a form of treatment, and a movement. The movement did not remain monolithic: dissident followers who withdrew and formed their own schools included Adler (in 1911), Stekel (in 1912), Jung (in 1913), and Rank (in 1926). As Freud's ideas began to become more widely known, they attracted respect and scientific interest, but also met with a great deal of hostility as well as extreme rejection. A truly objective weighing of these two kinds of reactions at various periods of Freud's career has yet to be done, but in any event Freud seems to have been more keenly aware of the negative than of the positive reception. An especially welcome early sign of recognition was the award of an honorary degree by Clark University in 1909, on which occasion he visited America with Jung, Ferenczi, and Jones and delivered a series of lectures.

In 1923 he had the first of many operations for cancer of the upper jaw, which finally proved fatal. During his last 16 years, Freud suffered almost constant pain and difficulty in speaking because of an awkward prosthesis, but he continued psychoanalyzing and writing into his final year. Only after the Nazi *Anschluss* could he be persuaded to leave Vienna, though he often had declared his detestation for the city. Long before the end, he had achieved world-wide acclaim and recognition as one of the decisive shapers of the twentieth century.

The development of Freud's ideas

Freud's first scientific contribution was published in 1877; his last was written only a few months before his death. Only the most superficial sketch of the development of his thought in the six hundred-odd papers and books he produced over these 63 years can be given here. There were four major and overlapping phases of that development.

(1) His prepsychoanalytic work, which lasted about twenty years, may be subdivided into an initial ten years of primarily histological–anatomical research and a partly overlapping 14 years of clinical neurology, with increasing attention to psychopathology, beginning in 1886 when he returned from Paris.

(2) The first theory of neurosis dates from the decade of the 1890s, when Freud used hypnosis and Breuer's cathartic method of psychotherapy, gradually developing the psychoanalytic methods of free association, dream interpretation, and the analysis of transference. The first dozen truly psychoanalytic papers appeared during this time, expounding the view that neurosis is a defense against intolerable memories of a traumatic experience— infantile seduction at the hands of a close relative. With the discovery of his own Oedipus complex, however, Freud came to see that such reports by his patients were fantasies, which led him to turn his interest away from traumatic events in external reality and toward subjective psychic reality. A notable but only recently discovered event in the development of Freud's thought occurred in 1895 after the publication of the book he wrote with Breuer: he wrote but did not publish a "Psychology for Neurologists" (or "Project for a Scientific Psychology"; see Freud 1895), presenting a comprehensive anatomical–physiological model of the nervous system and its functioning in normal behavior, thought, and dreams, as well as in hysteria. He sent it to Fliess in high excitement, then quickly became discouraged by the difficulties of creating a thoroughgoing mechanistic and reductionistic psychology, tinkered with the model for a couple of years in letters to Fliess, and finally gave it up.

The turn of the century marked many basic changes in Freud's life and work: he severed his close and dependent friendships with colleagues (first Breuer, then Fliess) and his contacts with the Viennese medical society; his father died; his last child was born; he psychoanalyzed himself; he gave up neurological practice, research, and conceptual models; and he created his own new profession, research method, and theory, in terms of which he worked thereafter.

(3) Freud's topographic model was the foundation of two decades of work, during which he published his major clinical discoveries, notably, *The Interpretation of Dreams* (1900) and *Three Essays on the Theory of Sexuality* (1905); his papers on the technique used in psychoanalytic treatment; his five major case histories, the central works of metapsychology; and a series of important surveys and popularizations of his ideas, in addition to his principal applications of his theories to jokes, literature and art, biography, and anthropology. A complete or metapsychological explanation, Freud wrote in 1915, requires "describing a psychical process in its dynamic, topographical and economic aspects"—that is, in terms of a theoretical model in which the central concepts are psychological forces, structures, and quantities of energy (Rapaport & Gill 1959). Hence, we speak of three metapsychological points of view. The topographic model, which was first set forth in Chapter 7 of *The Interpretation of Dreams* and was further elaborated in the metapsychological papers (1915), conceptualizes thought and behavior in terms of processes in three psychological systems: the conscious, preconscious, and unconscious (none of which has an explicit locus in the brain).

(4) In the final period, extending between the two world wars, Freud made four main types of contributions: the final form of his theory of instinctual drives (*Beyond the Pleasure Principle*, 1920); a group of major modifications of both general and clinical theory—most notably, the struc-

tural model of the psychic apparatus (*The Ego and the Id*, 1923) and the theory of anxiety and defense (*Inhibitions, Symptoms and Anxiety*, 1926); applications of psychoanalysis to larger social problems; and a group of books reviewing and reformulating his theories.

To grasp the structure of Freud's work, it is useful not only to adopt such a developmental approach but also to view his theories from the perspective of the following threefold classification:

First and best known is the clinical theory of psychoanalysis, with its psychopathology, its accounts of psychosexual development and character formation, and the like. The subject matter of this type of theorizing consists of major events (both real and fantasied) in the life histories of persons, events occurring over spans of time ranging from days to decades. This theory is the stock in trade of the clinician—not just the psychoanalyst, but the vast majority of psychiatrists, clinical psychologists, and psychiatric social workers. Loosely referred to as "psychodynamics," it has even penetrated into general academic psychology via textbooks on personality.

Second, there is what Rapaport (1959) has called the general theory of psychoanalysis, also called metapsychology. Its subject matter—processes in a hypothetical psychic apparatus or, at times, in the brain—is more abstract and impersonal; and the periods of time involved are much shorter—from fractions of a second up to a few hours. The processes dealt with are mostly those occurring in dreams, thinking, affect, and defense; Freud's reasoning in working out this theory is much closer, and he made more use of theoretical models of the psychic apparatus. The main works are the "Project for a Scientific Psychology," Chapter 7 of *The Interpretation of Dreams*, and the metapsychological papers.

Third is what might be called Freud's phylogenetic theory. The subject matter is man as a species or in groups, and the periods of time involved range from generations to eons. Here are Freud's grand speculations, largely evolutionary and teleological in character; they contain no explicit models of a psychic apparatus, employing instead many literary, metaphorical concepts. The principal works of this type are *Totem and Taboo* (1913), *Beyond the Pleasure Principle* (1920), *Group Psychology and the Analysis of the Ego* (1921), *The Future of an Illusion* (1927), *Civilization and Its Discontents* (1930), and *Moses and Monotheism* (1934–1938).

His clinical contributions are among the earliest of Freud's papers that are still being read, and he continued to write in this vein all of his life. As far as the other two types of theory are concerned, however, they overlap fewer developmental periods: the major metapsychological works came early, the main phylogenetic ones late. As Freud's concepts became more metaphorical and dealt with such remote issues as man's ultimate origins and the meaning of life and death, he became less concerned with describing or systematically accounting for the course and fate of an impulse or thought.

The rest of this article will concentrate on hypotheses and observations about two groups of Freud's ideas: what now appear to have been his major, lasting contributions, those that have been most influential on and most assimilated into the behavioral sciences (not to mention literature, art, and other aspects of contemporary Western culture); and his major errors, those concepts that have been most cogently criticized by psychoanalysts and other scientists. Finally, it will discuss historical antecedents of his ideas and influences upon them. The literature on these topics is already large and growing rapidly, so this survey must be highly selective.

Major contributions and weaknesses

Contributions. Freud may be said to have made five major contributions.

(1) He based his work on the assumption of *psychic determinism*: the lawfulness of all psychological phenomena, even the most trivial, including dreams, fantasies, and slips of the tongue.

(2) The lastingly valued aspects of Freud's complex doctrine of the unconscious include the general proposition that cognitive and other psychological events can go on outside of awareness; the influence of unconscious motivation on behavior; and the special qualitative characteristics of unconscious processes—the primary process and symbolism. The primary process is the kind of primitive functioning of the "psychic apparatus" that characterizes the unconscious id; indeed, it is the principal property by means of which the latter is defined. Processes characterized by magical rather than rational logic and by wishfulness—a seeking for immediate gratification of crude sexual or aggressive impulses—are called primary. Freud emphasized the concepts of displacement and condensation of psychic energy in his conceptualization of the primary process and noted that it often makes use of symbols, which differ from other types of displacement substitutes in having been shared by many persons for generations. These were the main theoretical resources Freud called upon to explain dreams, neurotic symptoms, psy-

chotic thought and language, normal character traits, myths, creative thought, art, and humor.

(3) Of the many contributions Freud made to our understanding of *sexuality*, the following seem to enjoy the most acceptance: his stress on its great importance in human life generally; his broad definition, which includes oral, anal, and other bodily pleasures and links them to the phallic–genital; his conception of its plasticity—it can be delayed, transformed, or fixated, and interest can be shifted from one "component drive" or "partial instinct" to another; his discovery that it appears early in human life (infants and young children masturbate, have sexual curiosity, etc.) and follows a typical developmental sequence; his insistence that bisexuality and "polymorphous perversity" are universal endowments or potentialities; his explanation of sexual perversions as pathological developments, not (or not wholly) as constitutional givens and not as sins; and his elaborations of many aspects of the Oedipus complex—the fact of inevitable but tabooed incestuous attraction in families, the associated phenomena of anxiety about castration (or, more generally, mutilation), and of intrafamilial jealousy, hatred, and envy, much of it unconscious.

(4) Three of Freud's concepts—*conflict, anxiety*, and *defense*—are so interrelated that we may look on them as constituting one major contribution. He saw the pervasive importance of conflict (not merely the traditional opposition of reason and passion, or ego versus id, but also ego versus superego and superego versus id) in both normal and abnormal behavior. One of his earliest insights was that defenses—structuralized means of controlling impulse and preventing the outbreak of anxiety, thus being in effect resolutions of conflict —are major factors in the formation of symptoms and character traits and are shaping influences on the organization of thought. He also described the specific mechanisms of defense, such as repression, projection, reaction formation, isolation, and mastery via the turning of passivity into activity. [*See* ANXIETY; CONFLICT, *article on* PSYCHOLOGICAL ASPECTS; DEFENSE MECHANISMS.]

(5) A number of Freud's lasting discoveries and insights make up the *genetic point of view*. He showed the necessity of knowing facts of development in order to understand personality; the importance of the events of early life for the main features of character, including the specific syndromes of the oral and anal character types as outgrowths of events at the corresponding psychosexual stages; the role of identification as a principle of learning and development; the importance

of drive delay and control in development; and the nature of psychopathology as regression along a developmental path.

As Shakow and Rapaport (1964) have pointed out, in each instance it is the general conception and the observations that have been accepted, not the specific concepts and the explanatory theory in which they are embedded. But this is to be expected: theories necessarily age, and any theory in the behavioral sciences formed as long ago as Freud's is bound to contain many anachronisms, obsolete assumptions, and unfortunate turns of thought.

Flaws.   Three weaknesses in Freud's work seem to have had the most extensive negative effects upon theory, research, and practice (see Holt 1965a; 1966). However necessary they may have been to his positive contributions, they are logically separable from them.

(1) His basic operating model (at first, of the central nervous system; later, of the psychic apparatus) was a passive reflex apparatus with no energies of its own, operating only to rid itself of inputs from the body (instinctual drive) and from the environment (reality), these inputs being conceptualized as quantities of energy (subjectively experienced as tension), and the regulative rule formulated as the principle of constancy. Consequently, the fundamental principle of motivation and affect is tension reduction.

Even in Freud's fourth period, when he said little directly about it, the passive reflex model seems to have operated as a silent pressure in the following directions:

(*a*) Freud tended to overemphasize quantitative as against qualitative aspects of behavior and thought, though only the latter were observable. The quantitative emphasis would have been more defensible if it had actually led to measurement, which is needed, but it did not. The result was a relative neglect of the phenomenology of affects in favor of a primary emphasis on pleasure and unpleasure, including anxiety (Kardiner et al. 1959), and a relative neglect of the phenomenology of the primary process, such as the various specific forms taken by condensation and displacement, in favor of an elaborate theory about unmeasurable energies of various qualitatively and directionally specific types.

(*b*) Similarly, Freud tended to reduce motivation to the somatically based; for example, he assumed that love and affection are derivative forms of a seeking after sensuous pleasure.

(*c*) There was a relative neglect of motives that do not easily fit the tension-reduction conception, such as curiosity and positive interest in stimuli and the seeking of challenges to master (White 1963).

(*d*) The passive reflex model suggests a simple theory of pleasure and unpleasure as perceived concomitants of rises and falls in energic tension. Yet from the beginning, Freud was aware of conflicting data, and he was never able either to abandon the original theory entirely or to account for the anomalous observations in a way that was consonant with the model.

(*e*) There were other shortcomings in the metapsychological economic point of view—the notion of a fixed and limited amount of energy which has to be withdrawn from one locus if used at another: for example, a scarcity economics of love, according to which the more one loves others the less self-esteem is possible—and in the quasi-vitalistic, unmeasurable, and overelaborated concept of psychic energy (Holt 1966).

(*f*) The model was hospitable to the death instinct and nirvana principle as ultimate extensions of tension reduction. But outwardly directed aggression was difficult to fit into the model and was relatively neglected for years.

(2) The second fundamental flaw was Freud's originally physicalistic conception of reality: basically, as "masses in motion and nothing else" ([1895] 1954, p. 369); more generally, as a welter of dangerous energies in which may be found some tension-reducing objects. In this conception, reality lacks significant organization on a large scale, as in the social structures or value systems (especially the latent ones) postulated by modern sociology and anthropology. To be sure, Freud did not consistently hold to such reductionism; he always dealt with meanings as such. Nevertheless, a physicalistic notion of reality lingered in his mind as an implicit conceptual ideal, with several consequences:

(*a*) Without a way to conceptualize an enduring structure of society and culture, Freud needed to assume individual genetic transmission of stable but latent cultural themes by way of a Lamarckian inheritance of acquired characteristics and to assume also that much of what he observed was inherited and universal, not culturally specific (for example, the Oedipus complex, or the inferior status of women as determined by anatomical differences).

(*b*) Freud tended to neglect the problems of adaptation and the relations to reality studied more recently in ego psychology.

(*c*) There were problems in the theory of object relations: for example, the "primary hate of objects," which the model requires, conflicts with the facts of infant observation; the theory also had difficulty in accounting for sustained interest and affection in a sexually consummated relationship, and psychoanalysts were led to a relative neglect of the natural history of subtleties in human relations.

(3) Freud's third basic error was his unclear and ambivalent handling of the mind–body problem, alternating between psychophysical parallelism and interactionism. The consequences began to show up as soon as he gave up the neurological model of 1895: he carried over its basic assumptions (the passive reflex model and the implicitly physicalistic concept of reality) in his later, ostensibly psychological, theories. There were several consequences of Freud's failure to take a consistent position on the mind–body problem.

(*a*) The status of the basic model remained undeveloped, unclear with regard to the existential status both of psychic energies and forces and of psychic structure.

(*b*) Since the basic model was not made fully explicit, there followed a relative neglect of structural considerations in favor of a "motivational reductionism" (Gill 1959), the explanation of the control and restraint of impulses (especially aggressive ones) in terms of instinctual *fusion and defusion* instead of in structural terms, and the neglect of adaptive and health-maintaining capacities in favor of an emphasis on pathology.

(*c*) A further consequence was Freud's tendency to reify functions as structures and to personify theoretical entities of uncertain existential status.

(*d*) Psychoanalysis became isolated from progress in medical and physiological sciences because of the difficulty in assimilating their findings.

It should be emphasized that none of these shortcomings was as crippling as it might have been if the underlying assumptions had been applied rigidly and consistently. As a group, they did steer Freud's thinking to a demonstrable extent, but thanks to the creative looseness of his cognitive style (Holt 1965*b*) he was able to observe much and to develop many specific theories that were logically incompatible with them.

Historical background

Before examining the antecedents of those ideas of Freud's that have been outlined above, it will be helpful to sketch in some of the grand trends of intellectual history in the nineteenth century.

"Naturphilosophie" and its rejection. The way for the romantic revolt that broadly characterized all aspects of intellectual life in the early 1800s had been prepared by *Naturphilosophie*, a mystical and often rhapsodic view of Nature as perfused with spirit and with conflicting unconscious forces and as evolving according to an inner, purposive design. Not a tightly knit school, its constituent thinkers included (in chronological order) Kant, Lamarck, Goethe, Hegel, Schelling (perhaps the central figure), Oken, and Fechner. With the exception of Fechner, who lived from 1801 to 1887, they all lived athwart the eighteenth and nineteenth centuries. *Naturphilosophie* encouraged the recrudescence of vitalism in biology, championed by the great physiologist Johannes Müller, and stimulated a humanistic school of romantic medicine (Galdston 1956). In psychiatry, the early part of the century was dominated by the reforms of Pinel, Esquirol, and their followers, who introduced an era of "moral treatment": firm kindness in place of restraints, therapeutic optimism based on etiological theories of a more psychological than organic cast, and an attempt to involve inmates of asylums in constructive activities.

The tough-minded reaction to this tender-minded era was greatly aided by the strides being made in physics and chemistry. Three of Müller's students, Brücke, du Bois-Reymond, and Helmholtz, met Carl Ludwig in 1847 and formed a club (which became the Berlin Physical Society) to "constitute physiology on a chemico–physical foundation, and give it equal scientific rank with Physics" (Ludwig, quoted by Cranefield 1957, p. 407). They did not succeed in their frankly reductionist aim but did attain their other objectives: to promote the use of scientific observation and experiment in physiology and to combat vitalism. Among themselves, they held to the following program:

No other forces than the common physical–chemical ones are active within the organism. In those cases which cannot at the time be explained by these forces one has either to find the specific way or form of their action by means of the physical–mathematical method, or to assume new forces equal in dignity to the chemical–physical forces inherent in matter, reducible to the force of attraction and repulsion. (du Bois-Reymond, quoted by Bernfeld 1944, p. 348)

In Germany especially, this materialistic ferment of physicalistic physiology, mechanism, and reductionism became the mode, gradually putting romantic medicine and other aspects of *Naturphilosophie* to rout. Where earlier there had been Psychic, Psycho-somatic, and Somatic schools in German psychiatry (Earle 1854, see in Hunter & Macalpine 1963, pp. 1015–1018), the Somatic gradually won out; Meynert, for example, conceived mental disorders to be diseases of the forebrain. Despite its therapeutic successes, moral treatment was banished along with its psychogenic (often sexual) theories as "old wives' psychiatry," in favor of strictly organic–hereditarian views and very little by way of therapy (Bry & Rifkin 1962).

The University of Vienna medical school was an outpost of the new hyperscientific biology, with one of its promulgators, Brücke, holding a major chair and directing the physiological institute (Bernfeld 1944). Ironically, Freud tells us that his decision to enter medical school was determined by hearing the "Fragment on Nature" attributed to Goethe read aloud at a public lecture. This short prose poem is an epitome of *Naturphilosophie*, and it must have swayed Freud because of his long-standing admiration for Goethe and perhaps because of a "longing for philosophical knowledge," which had dominated his early years, as he said later in a letter to Fliess. Evolution had been a major tenet of *Naturphilosophie*; so it is not surprising that this 1780 dithyramb could be part of a lecture on comparative anatomy, the discipline that furnished much of the crucial evidence for Darwin's *Origin of Species* (1859).

Energy and evolution. Perhaps the two most exciting concepts of the nineteenth century were energy and evolution; both of these strongly influenced Freud's teachers at the medical school. Helmholtz had read to the 1847 group his fundamental paper on the conservation of energy—presented as a contribution to physiology. Thirty years later, Brücke's lectures were full of the closely related (and still poorly differentiated) concepts of energy and force. To use these dynamic concepts was the very hallmark of the scientific approach; Brücke taught that the "real causes are symbolized in science by the word 'force'" (Bernfeld 1944, p. 349). It seems obvious that the first of Freud's three metapsychological points of view, the dynamic (explanation in terms of psychological forces), had its origins in this exciting attempt to raise the scientific level of physiology by the diligent application of mechanics and especially of dynamics, that branch of mechanics dealing with forces and the laws of motion. The heavily quantitative emphasis of the school of Helmholtz and its stress on energy are clearly the main determinants of metapsychology seen from the economic point of view (explanations in terms of quantities of energy). The fact that, among authors Freud respected most, such disparate figures as Fechner and Hughlings Jackson held to dynamic and economic viewpoints no doubt strengthened Freud's unquestioning conviction that these viewpoints are absolutely necessary elements of an explanatory theory.

Despite its physicalistic program, the actual

work of Brücke's institute was largely classical physiology and histology. Freud had had his Darwinian scientific baptism under Claus in a microscopic search for the missing testes of the eel, and his several attempts at physiological and chemical experiments under other auspices were fruitless. He was happy, therefore, to stay at the microscope where Brücke assigned him neurohistological studies, inspired by and contributing to evolutionary theory. When he worked with Meynert, it was again in a structural discipline with a genetic method— the study of brain anatomy using a series of fetal brains to trace the medullar pathways by following their development. His subsequent clinical practice was in neurology, a discipline which, as Bernfeld (1951) has noted, was "merely a diagnostic application of anatomy." Moreover, Freud's first full-scale theoretical model, the "Project" of 1895, is foremost a theory about the structural organization of the brain, both gross and fine. His early training thus demonstrably convinced him that a scientific theory has to have a structural (or topographic) base.

Of Freud's enduring contributions listed above, the two that are most plausibly traced to the intellectual climate of physicalistic physiology and to specific teachings of Brücke and Meynert are psychic determinism and the genetic point of view. The evolutionary surge of *Naturphilosophie*, given a modern, scientific, and nonteleological form in Darwinism, inspired all the biological sciences of the late nineteenth century with a conviction that phenomena of life cannot be understood without the elucidation of how the organism develops—out of its own parental germ plasm and out of a phylogenetic series. This point of view pervaded all of Freud's work in this first period; it would have been surprising if he had not carried it over and extended it when he turned to psychopathology, as Spencer was doing in academic sociology and psychology.

The assumption of exceptionless determinism was so fundamental a principle of mechanistic science as hardly to need discussion. Freud was exposed to it on all sides in the university and in much of his reading, then and later. Doubtless, this conviction that all phenomena are lawful and are thus legitimate subjects of scientific interest helped Freud to pay attention to the trivia of mental life and underlay his conviction that even if a patient relaxed the controls of conscious purpose in favor of free association, the material he produced would not be random but would betray an inner organization, a deeper and more meaningful set of psychological laws.

The unconscious. But the existence of psychological forces determining a meaningful inner organization required the assumption of a dynamic unconscious realm of the mind, besides consciousness. Many writers have shown how much a part of the thought of the time one part of this assumption was: "the general conception of unconscious mental processes was *conceivable* . . . around 1700, *topical* around 1800, and *fashionable* around 1870–1880" (Whyte 1960, pp. 168–169). Among the scientists known to have been familiar to Freud during his formative years (before 1900)—Charcot, Bernheim, Breuer, Lipps, H. Jackson, Galton, Fechner, and Helmholtz—all had one or another concept of the unconscious; other such concepts are to be found in writings known to have influenced Freud: those of the philosophers Plato, Kant, and Spinoza (Aron 1963–1964), the Bible, and the works of his favorite writers of fiction, Goethe, Shakespeare, Cervantes, and Dostoevski. Moreover, the Herbartian psychology taught in all Austrian secondary schools when Freud was in the Gymnasium was presented "not as one of several schools of psychology but as a well-established semi-official psychology" (Andersson 1962); together with associationism, it was adopted by Meynert and translated into neurological terms. It was a theory of the dynamic interaction of ideas, some of which may *repress* others below the threshold of consciousness, whence they may be hindered from rising by the *resistance* of the more or less integrated *masses of ideas*. This is, not surprisingly, precisely the terminology used by Breuer and Freud in 1893 ([1893–1895] 1955, chapter 1) in their first attempt at a psychological explanation of hysteria.

It is possible to find some predecessor who expressed one or another of most components of Freud's conception of the unconscious (though it is not established that any of them were known to Freud before he formed his own hypotheses)—for example, symbolism in dreams (von Schubert, Scherner), the role of dream symbols in myths (Carus, von Schubert), dreams as wish fulfillments (Plato, Maass), and the unconscious as the source of powerful motives (Herder, Richter) and of artistic creativity (Goethe, Schiller). Nevertheless, these were mostly isolated *aperçus*; even von Hartmann, whose *Philosophy of the Unconscious* touches on all of them, was not able to integrate these fragmentary insights into a coherent theory, like the psychoanalytic theory of the primary process. Furthermore, Freud differed from all his "anticipators" in that they remained outside the cave and made remarks—often profound ones—on what they glimpsed inside, but Freud went boldly in and devoted himself for decades to its painstaking (and painful) empirical exploration. Although the idea of unconscious processes had been around for centuries, Freud forced us to see the true power and pervasiveness of these processes in man's thought, feeling, and behavior.

Sexuality. The enormous importance of sexuality as a basic human motive had long been explored by poets and dramatists, and there had been many times when it was freely discussed in science and medicine as well as in everyday conversation. The prevailing belief today is that the second half of the nineteenth century, when Freud grew to maturity, was an era of unusually strong shame about sexuality and of moralistic attempts to suppress even its scientific study in the name of Christian morality; this climate of opinion influenced Freud's own personality and behavior, so characterized by propriety, self-control, and conventional monogamy. Yet our stereotype of Victorian prudery is probably oversimple; in any case, by the end of the nineteenth century the tide had begun to turn; Bry and Rifkin (1962) and Rieff (1959, chapter 10) have documented many social, literary, artistic, and scientific countermovements. In addition, it might be mentioned that sexology was already an established (if minor) science when Freud's contributions first appeared. Though Freud and Fliess felt like lonely pioneers, Magnus Hirschfeld and Krafft-Ebing had preceded both of them, and Havelock Ellis and G. Stanley Hall were their contemporaries. We know little about how a *Zeitgeist* of slowly liberalizing attitudes about sex may have been transmitted to Freud. We do know that there were contemporary moves to broaden the concept of sexuality and extend it backward in the life span, such as the observations of diffuse sexuality in children by Bell (1902), the relation of sucking and masturbation in the first year by Roehmer (1891), and the plasticity of the sexual drive in children (Barnes 1892).

Again, diligent historical scholarship can uncover predecessors for many, perhaps most, of Freud's lastingly valid formulations about sex. For example, Shakow and Rapaport (1964) have pointed to James's (1890) recognition of the potentiality for perversion in all of us; and many authors have discussed the similarities between Freud's and Plato's broad concept of eros. Freud himself acknowledged that the idea of universal bisexuality had first been suggested to him by Fliess. In the era of moral treatment, various sexual etiologies had been suggested for a number of neurotic conditions, which made Freud's first psychoanalytic papers

seem more reactionary than radical to many of his organically minded psychiatric colleagues.

As with the difference between Freud and earlier writers on the unconscious, so here again it was he alone who really devoted himself to prolonged, focused empirical as well as theoretical work on sexuality. In addition, however, Freud differs from most of the others who have helped to liberalize sexual mores in his mode of presenting his conclusions: he always refused to pull his punches, to make any concessions to prudishness in hopes of gaining a more sympathetic hearing; but at the same time, he had not the slightest tendency to glorify or romanticize sexuality. He presented his facts and theories dryly and as directly as his own distaste allowed him. In the short run, he antagonized the bluestockings and undermined the feminists, while disappointing the libertines and disillusioning the sexual utopians. By overstating the centrality of sexuality and stretching the concept of libido, he laid himself open to misunderstanding as a pansexualist and attained the unwelcome notoriety of a *succès de scandale*. In the long run, however, the net effect was to force the world's attention to the problems of sex, greatly advancing the contemporaneous anti-Victorian movements and, despite vicious opposition and vilification, probably getting his ideas a hearing and ultimate acceptance faster than he could have done in any other way.

Role of conflict. Views of man's behavior as the outcome of interior conflicts have been propounded since ancient times. The pervasive human tendency to think in terms of dichotomies is speculatively traceable to anatomical bilateral symmetry and to the diurnal cycle of light and dark. In any case, a probable shaping influence on Freud's conceptual orientations is the centrality of conflict between unconscious purposive forces in the world view of *Naturphilosophie*. More immediately, the Herbartian psychology of Lindner that Freud studied in the Gymnasium treats the life of the mind in terms of conflicting ideas, which could be smoothly absorbed into the paradigm of parallelograms of forces in physicalistic physiology. Hughlings Jackson, whom Freud greatly admired, held to even more proto-Freudian views on the role of conflicting forces (Stengel 1954a; 1954b).

The substance of the conflicting forces in Freud's final model is clearly related to traditions in Western thought going at least as far back as Empedocles, for whom love alternated with its antithesis, strife, and to religious sources: God versus Satan and the doctrine of conscience as the opponent of the base passions. In the era of moral treatment, there had been no dearth of psychiatrists who saw these inner battles as a cause of neurosis. Carter, writing in 1853, observed the conflict between sexual desire and moral scruple in chaste hysterics of both sexes and even blamed "the modern necessity of [a single woman's] entire concealment" of her sexuality as the social cause of most hysteria (see Hunter & Macalpine 1963, pp. 1002–1003).

Defense and repression. Freud's conception of defense, more particularly his ideas about defense against anxiety, seems to be a more original clinical innovation than most other parts of psychoanalytic theory. Perhaps its model was the medical conception of the body's defenses against pathogenic invasion; and the proposition that ideas can be repressed was familiar in Herbartian psychology. Nietzsche described the general outlines of several specific defenses—according to Brandt (1955), repression, isolation, reaction formation, sublimation, and projection—but there is no evidence that Freud knew about it. These conceptions and the closely related signal theory of anxiety are as directly derived from clinical observation as any in psychoanalysis and are among Freud's most original contributions.

Regression. The Darwinian origins of the genetic viewpoint in psychoanalysis have been briefly mentioned. An important specific mediator of Darwinism was Hughlings Jackson, from whose view of the evolutionary organization of the brain Freud took the conception of a hierarchic organization of psychic structures (Rapaport 1959), and from whose correlated theory of neurological diseases as "reversals of evolution," Freud derived the concept of regression as an explanation of psychopathogenesis (Stengel 1954a; 1954b). The genetic discipline of embryology had been given an enormous impetus by Darwin; Freud's use of fetal materials in his medullar researches must have caused him to study this discipline with particular care and to become familiar with the epigenetic principle that is implicit in his doctrine of psychosexual development. The phenomenon of identification and its role in interpersonal and social relations of all kinds, as well as its outstanding importance in development, appears to be largely the outgrowth of clinical observation; Rieff's (1959) hint that it may owe something to the "sympathy" of earlier social theorists (for example, Adam Smith) remains unexplored. By contrast, it is easy to find plenty of antecedent recognition of the importance of impulse control in the growth of character.

Passive reflex model. Freud put his personal stamp upon all the conceptions he drew—directly or indirectly—from his broad intellectual heritage. His reworking of the ideas of others often brought to the forefront their latent potentialities for advancing the understanding of the central problems—the innermost longings and agonies—of real persons. At times, however, the usefulness of Freud's ideas was marred by his need to fit them into his set of basic working assumptions, the passive reflex model of the nervous system.

This model was synthesized by Freud from the physicalistic physiology of his teachers and was more clearly enunciated in the "Project" than in any of the works of Brücke, Meynert, Breuer, or Exner, in which its elements may be clearly discerned (Amacher 1965). Anticipations of the dynamic, economic, and topographic points of view are plainly to be seen in books that Freud cited, for example, those by Fechner (Ellenberger 1956) and Jackson (Stengel 1954a; Spehlmann 1953); the economic point of view is also traceable to Darwin (Andersson 1962). It seems safe to conclude, therefore, that this set of principles was concurrently developed by many leading scientists in Germany and Austria in their attempts to apply the physics of Helmholtz and his school to biology and to generalize the reflex arc as a model of all mental processes in order to close the doors to such romantic notions as spontaneity, free will, and vitalism. Although virtually all of the assumptions underlying the passive reflex model are demonstrably untrue, much of the same doctrine underlies the behavioristic schools of psychology and is only now being painfully modified.

When Freud put aside explicit neurological theorizing, he was unable to give up the passive reflex model and the closely related physicalistic concept of reality (Spehlmann 1953; Holt 1965a). Although he explicitly postponed any attempt to relate the terms of metapsychology to processes and loci in the body, he substituted psychological theories that carry the same burden of anachronistic assumptions.

Nevertheless, Freud did not make a clean break from neurology, which fact contributed to his unclear and inconsistent stand on the mind–body problem (Rubinstein 1965; Holt 1965a). Jones (1953–1957, vol. 1) and a number of other authors portray him as a consistent follower of Jackson in a psychophysical parallelism that makes mind an "independent concomitant" of brain. But neither Jackson himself, who at times postulated that physical energy is directly transformed into psychic energy (Spehlmann 1953), nor Freud's teachers held to a consistent position (Amacher 1965); it was common to slip into interactionism, and Freud followed suit (Andersson 1962, p. 107). The concept of hysterical conversion is the most obvious instance of interactionism.

Speculative elements. The concept of Freud's most frequently rejected, at least among psychoanalysts, is the death instinct; not surprisingly, many of them have attributed this concept to Freud's own needs and conflicts. While the evidence is impressive that for many years Freud had an unusual and probably pathological preoccupation with death, there are plenty of less tendentious hypotheses about sources for this notion. Freud himself traced it to the ancient Greeks; it has been likened to the Christian concept of original sin; pessimistic, late romantic philosophers like Nietzsche contributed a strain of thought of which Freud could not have been unaware, however little he read them directly. More generally, the works in which he developed the theory of the repetition compulsion (clearly related as it is to the ancient conception of "the eternal return") and the virtually mythic concepts of life- and death-instincts are part of his phylogenetic theory. It is tempting to interpret this last development in Freud's thought as a kind of return of the repressed: that youthful speculative bent and yearning for broad philosophical knowledge which he repeatedly admitted fearing in himself and suppressed for many years (Holt 1963). His exposure to and enthusiasm for *Naturphilosophie* antedated his conversion to physicalistic physiology, which helped him put such unscientific ways of thought out of mind. Even the philosopher with whom he studied, Brentano, strongly opposed *Naturphilosophie* and advocated the scientific method as the only valid source of knowledge.

Yet the old mode of thought remained an undercurrent in his thinking, as it did in that of his friend Fliess (Galdston 1956). Finally, after Freud's change of identity at the turn of the century, after his great discoveries, the establishment of the psychoanalytic movement, and his first international recognition, the old mode of thought may have seemed less threatening. In *Totem and Taboo* (1913), one of his favorites among his own books, he created what he himself called a "scientific myth" (the slaying of the Darwinian primal horde's father). Shortly thereafter, he first read Lamarck, who was strongly identified with *Naturphilosophie*. It is Fechner the *Naturphilosoph*, not the psychophysicist, whom he cited in *Beyond the Pleasure Principle* (1920), and the loose, analogical, teleological, and personifying mode of thought he employed there is in marked contrast to the cognitive style of his metapsychological works (Holt 1965*b*).

Many properties of his concept of psychic energy can be traced to the vitalism that was a prominent feature of *Naturphilosophie* (Holt 1966). Some of the specific fallacies in his phylogenetic works can be traced to sources on the more mechanistic-materialistic side: Haeckel's "biogenetic law" that ontogeny recapitulates phylogeny seemed to provide respectable scientific auspices for the extension of genetic speculations based on individuals to the development of all mankind; Spencer and various post-Darwinians were the source of his linear-evolutionary conception of anthropology; and the inheritance of acquired characters had been a general assumption of the organic-hereditarian psychiatrists of Freud's formative period (Andersson 1962), as well as having been given some currency by Darwin himself (Ritvo 1965). Nevertheless, the major flaws of both manner and matter in Freud's speculative works show the unmistakable earmarks of *Naturphilosophie*.

Freud's stature is too great for his errors to require any whitewashing; it is not an apology for him but a fact that the least tenable aspects of his theories are traceable to influences that shaped his basic outlook when he was still a student, while his enduring achievements seem to owe less to antecedent influences. It appears to be one of the marks of a genius that he finds more sources of ideas in his reading and observation and subjects them to a truer integration and transmutation than does the less gifted man. The great contributor to knowledge (who may or may not be a genius) does not only toss off brilliant sparks of ideas; he lights and tends an enduring fire. Freud had both of these innovative capacities and more: his ideas have the remarkable property of being self-transcending. He taught us how to know more than he could, how to find and use the best in what he left by testing it against reality.

ROBERT R. HOLT

[*For a listing of articles describing Freud's influence upon psychology, psychiatry, and the other social sciences, see the detailed guide under the entry* PSYCHOANALYSIS. *Directly related to Freud's work and influence are the biographies of* ABRAHAM; ADLER; ALEXANDER; CHARCOT; ELLIS; FECHNER; FERENCZI; HELMHOLTZ; HORNEY; JONES; JUNG; KLEIN; MÜLLER, JOHANNES; RANK; RAPAPORT; REICH; RÓHEIM; SULLIVAN.]

WORKS BY FREUD

(1887–1902) 1954 *The Origins of Psychoanalysis: Letters to Wilhelm Fliess, Drafts and Notes: 1887–1902.* New York: Basic Books.

(1893–1895) 1955 BREUER, JOSEF; and FREUD, SIGMUND Studies on Hysteria. Volume 2 of *The Standard Edition of the Complete Psychological Works of Sigmund Freud*. London: Hogarth; New York: Macmillan.

(1895) 1954 Project for a Scientific Psychology. Pages 347–445 in Sigmund Freud, *The Origins of Psychoanalysis*. New York: Basic Books.

(1900) 1953 The Interpretation of Dreams. Volumes 4–5 of *The Standard Edition of the Complete Psychological Works of Sigmund Freud*. London: Hogarth; New York: Macmillan.

(1905) 1953 Three Essays on the Theory of Sexuality. Volume 7, pages 123–245 in *The Standard Edition of the Complete Psychological Works of Sigmund Freud*. London: Hogarth; New York: Macmillan.

(1913) 1959 Totem and Taboo. Volume 13, pages ix–162 in *The Standard Edition of the Complete Psychological Works of Sigmund Freud*. London: Hogarth; New York: Macmillan.

(1915) 1957 Papers on Metapsychology. Volume 14, pages 109–243 in *The Standard Edition of the Complete Psychological Works of Sigmund Freud*. London: Hogarth; New York: Macmillan.

(1920) 1955 Beyond the Pleasure Principle. Volume 18, pages 7–66 in *The Standard Edition of the Complete Psychological Works of Sigmund Freud*. London: Hogarth; New York: Macmillan.

(1921) 1955 Group Psychology and the Analysis of the Ego. Volume 18, pages 69–134 in *The Standard Edition of the Complete Psychological Works of Sigmund Freud*. London: Hogarth; New York: Macmillan.

(1923) 1961 The Ego and the Id. Volume 19, pages 12–63 in *The Standard Edition of the Complete Psychological Works of Sigmund Freud*. London: Hogarth; New York: Macmillan.

(1926) 1959 Inhibitions, Symptoms and Anxiety. Volume 20, pages 77–178 in *The Standard Edition of the Complete Psychological Works of Sigmund Freud*. London: Hogarth; New York: Macmillan.

(1927) 1961 The Future of an Illusion. Volume 21, pages 5–58 in *The Standard Edition of the Complete Psychological Works of Sigmund Freud*. London: Hogarth; New York: Macmillan.

(1930) 1961 Civilization and Its Discontents. Volume 22, pages 64–148 in *The Standard Edition of the Complete Psychological Works of Sigmund Freud*. London: Hogarth; New York: Macmillan.

(1934–1938) 1964 Moses and Monotheism: Three Essays. Volume 23 in *The Standard Edition of the Complete Psychological Works of Sigmund Freud*. London: Hogarth; New York: Macmillan.

Gesammelte Schriften. 12 vols. Leipzig, Vienna and Zurich: Internationaler Psychoanalytischer Verlag, 1924–1934.

Gesammelte Werke. 18 vols. London: Imago, 1940–1952.

The Standard Edition of the Complete Psychological Works of Sigmund Freud. 24 vols. London: Hogarth; New York: Macmillan, 1953–1964.

SUPPLEMENTARY BIBLIOGRAPHY

AMACHER, PETER 1965 *Freud's Neurological Education and Its Influence on Psychoanalytic Theory.* Psychological Issues, Vol. 4, No. 4; Monograph No. 16. New York: International Universities Press.

ANDERSSON, OLA 1962 *Studies in the Prehistory of Psychoanalysis: The Etiology of Psychoneuroses and Some Related Themes in Sigmund Freud's Scientific Writings and Letters, 1886–1896.* Stockholm: Svenska Bokförlaget Norstedts.

ARON, WILLIAM 1963–1964 Freud and Spinoza. *Harofé haivri* [1963] no. 2:260–242; [1964] no. 1:284–265; [1964] no. 2:260–242.

BARNES, E. 1892 Feelings and Ideas of Sex in Children. *Pedagogical Seminary* 2:199–203. → Now called the *Journal of Genetic Psychology*.

BELL, SANFORD 1902 A Preliminary Study of the Emotion of Love Between the Sexes. *American Journal of Psychology* 13:325–354.

BERNFELD, SIEGFRIED 1944 Freud's Earliest Theories and the School of Helmholtz. *Psychoanalytic Quarterly* 13:341–362.

BERNFELD, SIEGFRIED 1951 Sigmund Freud, M.D.: 1882–1885. *International Journal of Psycho-analysis* 32:204–217.

BRANDT, RUDOLF 1955 Freud and Nietzsche: A Comparison. Ottawa, University of, *Revue* 25:225–234.

BRY, ILSE; and RIFKIN, ALFRED H. 1962 Freud and the History of Ideas: Primary Sources, 1886–1910. Pages 6–36 in Academy of Psychoanalysis, *Science and Psychoanalysis.* Volume 5: Psychoanalytic Education. New York: Grune.

CRANEFIELD, PAUL F. 1957 The Organic Physics of 1847 and the Biophysics of Today. *Journal of the History of Medicine* 12:407–423.

DARWIN, CHARLES (1859) 1964 *On the Origin of Species.* Cambridge, Mass.: Harvard Univ. Press.

ELLENBERGER, HENRI F. 1956 Fechner and Freud. Menninger Clinic, *Bulletin* 20:201–214.

GALDSTON, IAGO 1956 Freud and Romantic Medicine. *Bulletin of the History of Medicine* 30:489–507.

GILL, MERTON M. 1959 The Present State of Psychoanalytic Theory. *Journal of Abnormal and Social Psychology* 58:1–8.

HOLT, ROBERT R. 1963 Two Influences on Freud's Scientific Thought: A Fragment of Intellectual Biography. Pages 364–387 in Robert N. White (editor), *The Study of Lives.* New York: Atherton.

HOLT, ROBERT R. 1965a A Review of Some of Freud's Biological Assumptions and Their Influence on His Theories. Pages 93–124 in Norman S. Greenfield and William C. Lewis (editors), *Psychoanalysis and Current Biological Thought.* Madison: Univ. of Wisconsin Press.

HOLT, ROBERT R. 1965b Freud's Cognitive Style. *American Imago* 22:163–179.

HOLT, ROBERT R. 1966 Beyond Vitalism and Mechanism: Freud's Concept of Psychic Energy. Unpublished manuscript.

HUNTER, RICHARD A.; and MACALPINE, IDA (editors) 1963 *Three Hundred Years of Psychiatry, 1535–1860: A History Presented in Selected English Texts.* Oxford Univ. Press. → See especially pages 1002–1003 and 1015–1018.

JAMES, WILLIAM (1890) 1962 *The Principles of Psychology.* 2 vols. New York: Smith.

JONES, ERNEST 1953–1957 *The Life and Work of Sigmund Freud.* 3 vols. New York: Basic Books. → Volume 1: *Formative Years and the Great Discoveries,* 1953. Volume 2: *Years of Maturity,* 1955. Volume 3: *Last Phase,* 1957.

KARDINER, ABRAM; KARUSH, AARON; and OVESEY, LIONEL 1959 A Methodological Study of Freudian Theory. *Journal of Nervous and Mental Disease* 129:11–19, 133–143, 207–221, 341–356.

PARSONS, TALCOTT (1952) 1953 The Superego and the Theory of Social Systems. Pages 13–29 in Talcott Parsons, Robert F. Bales, and Edward A. Shils, *Work-*

ing Papers in the Theory of Action. Glencoe, Ill.: Free Press.

PARSONS, TALCOTT (1958) 1964 Social Structure and the Development of Personality: Freud's Contribution to the Integration of Psychology and Sociology. Pages 78–111 in Talcott Parsons, *Social Structure and Personality.* New York: Free Press.

RAPAPORT, DAVID 1959 The Structure of Psychoanalytic Theory: A Systematizing Attempt. Pages 55–183 in S. Koch (editor), *Psychology: A Study of a Science.* Volume 3: Formulations of the Person and the Social Context. New York: McGraw-Hill.

RAPAPORT, DAVID; and GILL, MERTON 1959 The Points of View and Assumptions of Metapsychology. *International Journal of Psycho-analysis* 40:153–162.

RIEFF, PHILIP 1959 *Freud: The Mind of the Moralist.* New York: Viking.

RITVO, LUCILLE B. 1965 Darwin as the Source of Freud's Neo-Lamarckianism. *Journal of the American Psychoanalytic Association* 13:499–517.

ROEHMER, A. 1891 Ueber psychopatische Minderwertigkeiten des Säuglingsalter. *Medizinisches Korrespondenzblatt für Würtemberg* 61:265–269, 273–279, 281–285, 289–292.

RUBINSTEIN, B. B. 1965 Psychoanalytic Theory and the Mind–Body Problem. Pages 35–56 in Norman S. Greenfield and William C. Lewis (editors), *Psychoanalysis and Current Biological Thought.* Madison: Univ. of Wisconsin Press.

SHAKOW, DAVID; and RAPAPORT, DAVID 1964 *The Influence of Freud on American Psychology.* Psychological Issues, Vol. 4, No. 1. New York: International Universities Press.

SPEHLMANN, RAINER 1953 *Sigmund Freuds neurologische Schriften: Eine Untersuchung zur Vorgeschichte der Psychoanalyse.* Berlin: Springer.

STENGEL, E. 1954a A Re-evaluation of Freud's Book *On Aphasia:* Its Significance for Psychoanalysis. *International Journal of Psycho-analysis* 35:85–89.

STENGEL, E. 1954b The Origins and Status of Dynamic Psychiatry. *British Journal of Medical Psychology* 27:193–200.

WHITE, ROBERT W. 1963 *Ego and Reality in Psychoanalytic Theory: A Proposal Regarding Independent Ego Energies.* Psychological Issues, Vol. 3, No. 3. New York: International Universities Press.

WHYTE, LANCELOT L. 1960 *The Unconscious Before Freud.* New York: Basic Books.

FRIENDSHIP

Friendship is a voluntary, close, and enduring social relationship. The behavior of friends varies greatly among societies and situations and according to personality variables. Values about friendship vary less and can be summarized as involving closeness, solidarity, absence of ulterior ends, reciprocity, impulsiveness in mutual choice, and, perhaps, independence of social distinctions such as age, sex, and class. Friendship is intimate but less so than love and some family ties. Supplementing sexual and familial ties, friendship is a residual cultural category subsuming close and expectedly enduring ties. Since friendship involves voluntary

commitment, intimacy, and spontaneity, its consequences for the individual and for society, through individual growth and security, are presumably crucial. Possibly for this reason, to be without friends often involves shame.

Most other important social relationships exclude friendship. Even highly compatible and close brothers are brothers rather than friends, and friendship tends to be incompatible with such relationships as those of mother and child, lovers, and employer and employee. This incompatibility is probably due to the fact that the obligations and rights of friends typically are subject to overruling by other ties. The impulsiveness of choice and the reciprocity or symmetry of the friendship relation also rule out various choices. If friends are impulsively chosen, few brothers will be friends. Reciprocity and symmetry imply rough equality in mutual rights and obligations and in qualities and performances, requiring fairly equal status in significant respects between friends. In general, friendship can be logically and culturally expected to occur only when there is a low probability of higher or strongly sanctioned obligations intervening directly between friends.

Like distant kinship terms, "friend" is a relational designation: "friend" and "friendship" refer to a relationship between two or more persons rather than to the characteristics of one or more persons. This is in contrast to close kinship terms, which are simultaneously relational and categorical, and to occupational designations, which are on the whole categorical. Accordingly, while friendship is significant in personal terms, it is no less an interpersonal structure. It follows that variants of friendship structure may well be a characteristic of collective units.

In theoretical terms, friendship is definitely a relational phenomenon: it is impossible to assign meaning to statements such as "He is a friend" without implying to whom "he" is related in this way. However, empirically the matter is less clear, partly because the friendship role is vague. Also, the friendship relationship as a social type is made ambiguous by personal descriptions such as "He is friendly," "He is a great friend," or "He is everybody's friend." The suggestion has been made that a highly differentiated society with a high degree of mobility and an emphasis on specific performance cannot also support enduring and important intimate relationships beyond those of the nuclear family. This may be the structural source of "pseudo *Gemeinschaft*"—that is, appeals, usually commercial, that use a presumption of closeness to transfer modes of behavior from a friendship setting to strangers, with the consequent growth of values of superficial friendship, friendliness, and popularity.

Friendship is a distinct institution. In Western societies (loosely the basis for the above considerations) it is a vague institution, whereas in other societies friendship is often more salient and differentiated. In either case, friendship is a low-order (as well as a crosscutting) institution: it is found everywhere but is not a distinct, comprehensive segment of society. It is comparable to money, language, and love rather than to religion, the family, or the economy. Partly for this reason, friendship is not at present a specialized field of inquiry in sociology. While few studies focus on friendship, many find it, since closeness to others is a pervasive potentiality in man.

Friendship as an institution

To say that friendship is an institution is to ask the cross-cultural question: What links are there between variations in the structure of friendship and in the structure of society? Two studies have initiated the general cross-cultural study of friendship (Eisenstadt 1956; Cohen 1961). At the least, these studies provide a spectrum of variation in friendship institutions; at their best, they provide hypotheses or findings about the place of friendship in encompassing social structures.

Variations between societies. S. N. Eisenstadt's subject is "ritualized personal relations," including blood brotherhood, blood friendship, "best" friends, *compadre* and godparent relations, and cases of contractual servitude. All these relationships are particularistic, personal, voluntary, and fully institutionalized (usually in ritual terms). They are both diffusely affective and instrumental, always in the economic sphere, often more broadly (politics, etc.). Eisenstadt hypothesizes that these kinshiplike but voluntary relations are to be found in predominantly particularistic (that is, kinship-dominated or caste-dominated) societies because they alleviate strains in and between the groups that constitute such societies. In effect, Eisenstadt proposes that ritualized personal relations, similar to friendship in Western terms in that they are voluntary and personal or intimate, are mechanisms of social integration. They are parallel to such institutions as kinship extension, extralineage kinship obligations, various types of associations, hospitality toward strangers, and joking relationships in providing ties cutting across groups and categories. Ritualized personal relations are also mechanisms of social control. [*See* KINSHIP, *article on* PSEUDO-KINSHIP.]

Yehudi A. Cohen presents a typology of friendship institutions that loosely expresses a dimension of degree of commitment between friends. *Inalienable* friendship is a variant characterized by ritual or ceremonial entry and, ideally, permanence—in the main corresponding to Eisenstadt's ritualized personal relations. Three other somewhat separate categories are *close*, *casual*, and *expedient* friendships. In a sample of about sixty societies, twenty have the inalienable type of friendship as the dominant form, thirty have close friendship, three have casual friendship, and four have expedient friendship (there are no data for ten societies, and some are counted twice because of structural changes). Activities in the friendship relation commonly include material exchange (and/or economic assistance) and sociopolitical and emotional support; in some cases they include the more specialized activities of go-between in love affairs and marriage arrangements, homosexuality, sponsorship in rites of passage, mourning obligations, and exchange of children. Formalized friendship is far more frequent among men than women and is rare across sex lines. Inalienable friendship carries with it incest taboos in half the cases. It is almost invariably joined with just one partner, who in some cases has to be chosen inside the local solidary group and in other cases outside of it; in a few societies either choice is open.

Cohen predicts covariation between type of friendship and the nature of the significant solidary grouping to which the individual is attached. He expects inalienable friendship to coincide with the *maximally solidary* community (generally, localized descent groups where nuclear families and households are socially, physically, and emotionally close as a societal nucleus sharply distinguished from other groupings). Close friendship is expected to be associated with the *solidary-fissile* community (where solidarity is split between kinship group and community). The *nonnucleated* society (where isolated, solidary nuclear families are tied loosely together) is expected to be associated with casual friendship. Finally, an expedient type of friendship institution is expected to occur in *individuated* social structures (where there is emphasis on individual amassing of wealth and relatively little solidarity even in the nuclear family).

Roughly speaking, Cohen's hypotheses are supported by his data. There is an association between the degree of solidarity in the local community and the degree of commitment in the friendship institution (although the number of cases in extreme types of friendship and solidarity is small). Of 13 societies with maximally solidary communities, 11 have predominantly the inalienable type of friendship; of 35 societies with solidary-fissile communities, 27 have close friendship.

Cohen's interpretation of this finding is in terms of holistic compatibility in culture and personality. A dimension of personal generosity versus withholding seems to be the basic variable that unites community structure with friendship structure. There is a correlation between childhood gratification versus deprivation, on the one hand, and adult food sharing versus individual amassment of food or money on the other. For the present, it remains an open question as to how this holistic pressure can be translated into detailed questions about the operation of social arrangements.

Cohen's study raises formal questions about his variables: To what extent are his four-point variables adequate and reliable in use? Is inalienable friendship a more significant category than formalized friendship? Further, under what conditions, and with what effects, are intragroup and intergroup friendships mandatory or preferred? The most crucial and stimulating question would seem to be this: Is institutionalized friendship (i.e., ideal and/or dominant forms) a more relevant variable than distribution of actual forms of friendship? This question leads to interesting problems in Western societies. What, in various settings, is the distribution of close, casual, and expedient friendships? Is degree of differentiation of societies correlated with dominance of expedient friendships? Is a possible dominance of expedient friendships to be contrasted with some of our values concerning friendship rather than with our past—or has there been a real change in the friendship institution over, say, the last fifty years, concomitant with industrialization and increasing differentiation?

Variation within one society. Additional demonstrations of the dependence of norms regulating friendship on an encompassing social structure emerge if we compare separate settings within one society rather than comparing different societies. In a study of the merchant marine in a society where it is a significant element economically and culturally, Aubert and Arner (1959) found that the culture and the social structure of the Norwegian merchant marine include a near taboo on personal friendships. This trait is probably a consequence of (as well as a contribution to) other structural elements: the ship is a "total institution" (Goffman 1958); top positions can only be reached from the bottom; there is an extraordinarily high rate of turnover; work roles dominate (to the extent that terms of address and reference are largely job titles, the alternative being home region); there is a cultural and realistic emphasis on crises requiring discipline; and, finally, there is a peculiar combination of equality and inequality (in a number of respects the crew are sailors "in the same boat," yet each man and his position is unique through pay and shift arrangements). In outline, the occurrence and forms of friendship among the crew are reinforcing consequences of the nature of the ship as a place of work, in particular through its arrangements for interaction, physical closeness, and recruitment. In a significant contrast, friendship is a standard occurrence among the crew in the Hull distant-water fishing fleet (Tunstall 1962); the distant-water trawler lacks the character of the total institution that is inherent in the Norwegian merchant vessel.

Friendship as interaction

Perhaps the most penetrating study of friendship yet to appear is W. F. Whyte's *Street Corner Society* (1943), a description and analysis of life in an immigrant slum in the late 1930s. Whyte's topic is the interaction between young men, the significance of this interaction for individuals, and its relationship to career, welfare work, and politics. In the first place, Whyte gives a vivid picture of voluntary association among "Cornerville" young adults. This association is marked by a strong informal structure. Loosely integrated gangs, consisting of small cliques, have a clearly hierarchic structure in terms of influence and prestige. Participation and acceptance in these groups are crucial for the balance of individual personalities. Changing and stable group structure is symbolically expressed in interaction. The typical group ties the individual to his community in many ways; it takes membership in atypical groups to foster career ambitions beyond Cornerville. In the first place, then, Whyte describes the social realities, of which friendship is the predominant one, for young men in Cornerville. Second, he analyzes the interrelations of friendship and the Cornerville culture with racketeering and politics, which are intimate, as well as with traditional welfare work, which cuts itself off from the mainstream of Cornerville life.

The kind of friendship structure that Whyte describes is, in all likelihood, unusual. Friendship groups are rarely as highly structured in a hierarchy as in Whyte's community; friends are rarely as dependent on leadership; they are rarely as significant for each other and so often and so regularly in each other's presence; friends are rarely so sharply segregated from nonfriends; and friends of one person are rarely to such an extent also friends of each other. Whyte described a situation that was unusual, arising as it did from the historical accident of a major depression in a lower-class environment of second-generation immigrants.

Several themes above have been investigated in later, more specific studies of friendship. Elizabeth Bott (1957) has investigated friendship networks, stressing the difference between connected networks, where one's friends are also friends of each other, and open ones, where friends do not make up an interconnected group. Her exploratory study of families and their friends indicates that if a married couple is involved in a close-knit set of friends, the couple tends to have a rigid separation of roles in the household. On the other hand, if the network of friends is loosely connected, separation of roles among husband and wife is at a minimum.

Adolescent friendship. In his study of friendship among young men, Whyte related variants of friendship to career ambitions in distinguishing between "corner boys" and "college boys." Friendship among adolescents may be more significant than at earlier and later ages, both in general and specifically for career choice. What is the nature and significance of friendship among adolescents? In a discussion of David Riesman's hypothesized "other-directed" personality type, with its assumed peer dependence among adolescents, Parsons and White (1961) see adolescent friendship as a mechanism for loosening children's dependence on parents and as a channel for the testing of career choice. Relying on findings from studies of friendship choices in high schools, they conclude that the adolescent's dependence on peers is far from a seeking of free-floating approval; relations among peers partially consist of commitments to normative standards. Parsons and White emphasize that there are two kinds of normative culture among high school students: one is rather hedonistic, characterized by much value on popularity and reluctance to accept the achievement orientation in the adult world, and the other, which is somewhat less frequent, includes a strong commitment to mastery of this achievement orientation. The availability of friendship cliques (of either type of culture) is both a sorting mechanism and a testing ground for long-term educational and career commitments.

The finding of two distinct normative cultures among adolescents, one centering on hedonism and the other, nearly as important, on scholastic achievement, is unusual. Coleman (1961) found widely varying social climates in the ten high schools that he studied. In all of them, athletic achievement was the major basis for recruitment to the informal elite of the school; scholastic achievement was always a decidedly minor basis; the strongest position of all was held by the all-rounder. Gordon (1957), in a case study of a Midwestern high school, found a salient structure of dominant cliques, within which close friendship might occur. Cliques centering on scholastic achievement were quite unimportant, although students showed increasing fulfillment of school expectations for scholastic achievement with each additional year in school. The students' school and social life seemed to be dominated by a fierce competition for prestige that was achieved on the basis of conformity to highly developed normative patterns. Adolescent life in school was dominated by efforts to achieve a differentiated social status —that is, essentially a search for identity. Membership in a group gives the protection of being visibly and actively "somebody," but friendship appears to be largely an instrumental and regulative structure rather than a supportive and permissive one. However, the detailed regulation of behavior implied in the adolescent culture is partly (as in dress) a symbol of autonomy relative to adult society and partly (as in puritan morals) an acceptance of explicit adult values.

In spite of variation in content of adolescent culture and friendship groupings, Parsons and White's main points are valid: adolescent culture, with cliques forming around variant values, affords standards of right and wrong, affects career choice, and enforces a degree of independence from parents. Nevertheless, the central place of popularity in this adolescent culture leaves Riesman's claim of a growing "other-directedness" an open issue.

Friendship in work groups. Adolescent friendship approaches being a way of life, although a transitional one, related to love and a future family as well as to work and a future career. Friendship is also important in careers. The influence of friendship on recruitment to and work in a career has been shown in community studies (Warner & Lunt 1941, pp. 188–199; Seeley et al. 1956, p. 135). The importance of friendship in one line of work was shown dramatically by Coleman, Katz, and Menzel (1957): doctors' adoption of new therapeutic drugs depends to a considerable extent on membership in informal friendship cliques.

The theme of friendship in work has been a significant one in social science at least since the Hawthorne studies in the 1930s. In one setting it was found that a differentiated set of friendship relations among male workers supported a broad normative orientation, including a norm limiting productivity (Roethlisberger & Dickson 1939, part 4). In another setting, friendly relations among female workers were suggested as an explanatory variable behind a continuously climbing curve of productivity under varying and controlled external work conditions (*ibid.*, part 1). The concept of an informal social structure in organizations has been with us since these studies. With respect to friendship or friendly human relations, these two findings have been duplicated over and over again, in industrial and bureaucratic settings as well as in research on problem solving in laboratory groups: friendly relations may lead to either increased or decreased productivity. The normative basis of friendship, particularly the definitions of relations to higher authorities, is presumably one decisive differentiating variable.

Selection of friends

The initial view of friendship given in this article is a romantic one; it is empirical in that it formulates surface values concerning friendship in our culture. However, while it may be true that friends are culturally expected to be chosen impulsively, it is certain that choice follows socially structured paths. Friends tend to share social position. The tendency of friends to be alike is well illustrated by a finding in a study of a political election that compared voters' choices with those of their best friends. A sample of voters was divided into four subgroups according to whether three, two, one, or none of their best friends intended to vote for the Republican party; among those whose friends were all intending to vote Republican, 61 per cent expressed strong intentions of voting Republican, and the percentage dropped to 37, to 23, and to 2 for the other three subgroups, respectively (Berelson et al. 1954, p. 99). Two explanatory principles are needed: friends select each other on the basis of similarity, and they influence each other to become similar. The systematic study of similarity and dissimilarity between friends was opened up by Lazarsfeld and Merton (1954) when they asked how selectivity comes about and how it varies for different kinds of attributes and within different kinds of social structures. While they clarify many issues in their article (for example, by distinguishing between status-homophily and value-homophily), their contribution has remained programmatic.

Similarity in attitude is one basis on which friendships are formed. Longitudinal studies (e.g., Newcomb 1961) indicate that the explanatory principle of selectivity in terms of similarity outweighs the principle of similarity resulting from friendship. The balance of the evidence for the view that friends select each other on the basis of complementarity of needs rather than on the basis of similarities is negative (Secord & Backman 1964). Findings based on sociometric studies of friendship concerning other bases of choice have been summed up as follows:

> . . . a person is likely to choose the following individuals: (1) those with whom he has a greater opportunity to interact, (2) those who have characteristics most describable in terms of the norms and values of the group, (3) those who are most similar to him in attitudes, values, and social-background characteristics, and (4) those whom he perceives as choosing him or assigning favorable characteristics to him, (5) those who see him as he sees himself, and (6) those whose company leads to gratification of his needs. (Secord & Backman 1964, p. 247)

Two theoretical formulations with implications for the study of friendship have appeared in recent years (Thibaut & Kelley 1959; Homans 1961). Both are exchange theories of interaction, where basic terms are costs, rewards, outcomes, and comparison levels. This framework allows the analysis of steps in attraction processes (Secord & Backman 1964, chapter 7): friendship is the outcome of sampling and estimation, bargaining, commitment, and, finally, institutionalization.

Problems for research

Both sociometric findings on friendship and Secord and Backman's exchange analysis of friendship focus on the *initiation* of friendship structures; that is, their central theoretical topic is attraction rather than established friendship relations. Research on friendship needs more concentration on the substantive contents of friendship itself. How, in fact, are rights and obligations in friendship experienced in various social environments? What are the institutional and actual encouragements and limits to friendship in various contexts—politics, business, everyday life? What are the major rewards and strains in friendships? Is the ambiguity of friendship a circumstance that serves to initiate as well as to terminate other kinds of relationships? Under what conditions will friendships end? Is friendship, more often than other types of relationships, a subjectively sustained reality in the face of decreased overt interaction? For partial answers to such questions, and for the generation of other specific and significant questions about friendship, analysis of detailed reports on the behavior and orientations of friends, acquaintances, strangers, and enemies in everyday life is required. It would seem that such studies, which demand more descriptive patience than we now see in social science, can give a rich yield, since friendship, as a kind of cement in personality and social fabrics, is probably more strategically related to other social relationships than research has indicated so far.

ODD RAMSØY

[*Other relevant material may be found in* LEADERSHIP *and* SOCIOMETRY.]

BIBLIOGRAPHY

AUBERT, VILHELM; and ARNER, ODDVAR 1959 On the Social Structure of the Ship. *Acta sociologica* 3:200–219.

BERELSON, BERNARD; LAZARSFELD, PAUL F.; and McPHEE, WILLIAM N. 1954 *Voting: A Study of Opinion Formation in a Presidential Campaign.* Univ. of Chicago Press.

BOTT, ELIZABETH 1957 *Family and Social Network: Roles, Norms, and External Relationships in Ordinary Urban Families.* London: Tavistock.

COHEN, YEHUDI A. 1961 *Social Structure and Personality.* New York: Holt.

COLEMAN, JAMES S. 1961 *The Adolescent Society: The Social Life of the Teenager and Its Impact on Education.* New York: Free Press.

COLEMAN, JAMES S.; KATZ, ELIHU; and MENZEL, HERBERT 1957 The Diffusion of an Innovation Among Physicians. *Sociometry* 20:253–270.

EISENSTADT, SHMUEL N. 1956 Ritualized Personal Relations. *Man* 56:90–95.

GOFFMAN, ERVING 1958 The Characteristics of Total Institutions. Pages 43–84 in *Symposium on Preventive and Social Psychiatry.* A symposium held at the Walter Reed Army Institute of Research in 1957. Washington: Government Printing Office.

GORDON, C. WAYNE 1957 *The Social System of the High School: A Study in the Sociology of Adolescence.* Glencoe, Ill.: Free Press.

HOMANS, GEORGE C. 1961 *Social Behavior: Its Elementary Forms.* New York: Harcourt.

LAZARSFELD, PAUL F.; and MERTON, ROBERT K. 1954 Friendship as a Social Process: A Substantive and Methodological Analysis. Pages 18–66 in Morroe Berger, Theodore Abel, and Charles H. Page (editors), *Freedom and Control in Modern Society.* Princeton, N.J.: Van Nostrand.

NAEGELE, KASPAR D. 1958 Friendship and Acquaintances: An Exploration of Some Social Distinctions. *Harvard Educational Review* 28:232–252.

NEWCOMB, THEODORE M. 1961 *The Acquaintance Process.* New York: Holt.

PARSONS, TALCOTT; and WHITE, WINSTON 1961 The Link Between Character and Society. Pages 89–135 in Seymour Lipset and Leo Lowenthal (editors), *Culture and Social Character: The Work of David Riesman Reviewed.* New York: Free Press.

ROETHLISBERGER, FRITZ J.; and DICKSON, WILLIAM J. (1939) 1961 *Management and the Worker: An Account of a Research Program Conducted by the Western Electric Company, Hawthorne Works, Chicago.* Cambridge, Mass.: Harvard Univ. Press. → A paperback edition was published in 1964 by Wiley.

SECORD, PAUL F.; and BACKMAN, CARL W. 1964 *Social Psychology.* New York: McGraw-Hill.

SEELEY, JOHN R. et al. 1956 *Crestwood Heights: A Study of the Culture of Suburban Life.* New York: Basic Books.

THIBAUT, JOHN W.; and KELLEY, HAROLD H. 1959 *The Social Psychology of Groups.* New York: Wiley.

TUNSTALL, JEREMY 1962 *The Fishermen.* London: MacGibbon & Kee.

WARNER, W. LLOYD; and LUNT, PAUL S. 1941 *The Social Life of a Modern Community.* New Haven: Yale Univ. Press.

WHYTE, WILLIAM F. (1943) 1961 *Street Corner Society: The Social Structure of an Italian Slum.* 2d ed., enl. Univ. of Chicago Press.

FRINGE BENEFITS
See under WAGES.

FROBENIUS, LEO

Leo Frobenius (1873–1938) was one of the last of the great explorers that the nineteenth century turned out in such profusion; he was also one of the first ethnologists who did not confine himself to an ethnographic description of the facts but elaborated a method for organizing in space and time the confused welter of discrete observations about the world's nonliterate peoples.

Frobenius was born in Berlin. In his early youth, he devoted his time to the ethnology of Africa, at the age of 21 publishing a bulky volume on African secret societies (1894). As a scientist, he was self-taught. And although he combined an intuitive mind with tremendous industry, emotional involvement with his material often led him to lapse into pathos.

His works on cultural morphology grew out of a profound knowledge of primitive cultures. In 1893 he began a collection of photographs and other ethnographic materials that later formed the basis of the Africa Archives. Frobenius made 12 expeditions to Africa from 1904 to 1935, devoting himself to ethnological field work and the photographing of rock pictures. He also made a trip to India. The holdings of the Africa Archives were greatly expanded by his expeditions, and in 1922 the archives became the Forschungsinstitut für Kulturmorphologie. In 1932 he was invited to teach cultural anthropology at the University of Frankfurt am Main as an *Honorarprofessor.* In 1934 he was appointed director of the Municipal Museum of Ethnology in Frankfurt am Main. He died in Biganzolo on Lago Maggiore.

As a historian, Frobenius endeavored through his research to provide historical background for the civilizations that had formerly been regarded as having no history because their past was not illuminated by any written records, and thereby to incorporate them into world history. This work stimulated an expansion of the historical perspective, which at the turn of the twentieth century had been almost exclusively confined to the advanced and literate civilizations of Europe and the Near East. The historical field of vision was expanded not only in spatial–geographical terms, by the inclusion of previously neglected parts of the world, but in ethnological terms as well; many primitive cultures have preserved forms of thought, of behavior, and in general, of cultural patterns that are obviously much older than those of the earliest advanced and literate civilizations of the Near East. In his works on the philosophy of history and civilization, Frobenius sought to comprehend not only a particular culture, but culture as such, and therewith the entire history of the world. He tried to grasp and to explain the forces and motives that lead to the origin of a culture, the laws governing its course, the relationship between man and culture, and the meaning and goal of historical development. The broad scope of his research contributed insights and findings of fundamental importance to historically oriented ethnology.

"Kulturkreise."   At the close of the nineteenth century, there were two conflicting doctrines in ethnology, represented in the German-speaking world by Adolf Bastian on the one hand, and by Richard Andree and Friedrich Ratzel on the other. Both doctrines proceeded from the same set of facts, i.e., the observation that elements of mental and material culture identical in form and function may be found in regions of the world that are far apart, frequently separated by oceans, and among peoples speaking different languages and often belonging to different races. The doctrine advocated by Bastian in *Der Mensch in der Geschichte: Zur Begründung einer psychologischen Weltanschauung* (1860) explained such occurrences by assuming that the evolution of mankind has always, and in all parts of the world, been subject to the same laws; that this evolution has been a linear one; and that, consequently, upon reaching a certain stage of development, all societies are independently compelled by the rigid law of evolution to create and shape the cultural objects that correspond to the given stage of development.

This evolutionary view was opposed by the doctrine advocated by Andree in *Ethnographische Parallelen und Vergleiche* (1878) and by Ratzel in "Geschichte, Völkerkunde und historische Perspective" (1904), who attributed the occurrence of identical elements of culture in different regions of the world to the migrations either of entire cultures or of individual cultural elements and to direct or indirect cultural contact. Frobenius was always a convinced champion of this latter doctrine, which is known as the diffusion or migration theory.

Building on the ideas of Andree, Ratzel, and his own teacher, H. Schurtz, Frobenius made a giant step through his two pioneering works "Der westafrikanische Kulturkreis" (1897) and "The Origin of African Civilizations" (1898*a*), which cleared the way for a new scientific approach in ethnology. He demonstrated that many elements of material and mental culture are by no means scattered at random over the world but are always densely concentrated in certain areas and always occur in a characteristic combination with other cultural manifestations. Frobenius inferred from the identical geographical distribution of certain elements of culture that these could not be fortuitous combinations, but that there had to be a close relationship among several of the elements. He therefore grouped areas of identical distribution into what he called *Kulturkreise;* these, in turn, he arranged in relative chronological order so as to provide a historical background for nonliterate cultures. The core of this method was cultural comparison, and its technical tool was cartography. As the creator of the theory, Frobenius became the trail-blazer of the historical approach in ethnology, for even today, cultural comparison constitutes an important means to the construction of historical accounts of cultures without written traditions. Later on, the theory of *Kulturkreise* was extended by Fritz Graebner and Bernhard Ankermann, and it finally became part of the theory of the "Vienna school" of Wilhelm Schmidt. However, this school did not develop the concept of *Kulturkreise* as Frobenius understood it but instead allowed it to become static, thus impairing its effectiveness.

Although the concept of *Kulturkreise* continued to play a major role in Frobenius' work, he soon came to realize clearly the methodological shortcomings of his own early works that dealt with it. He sharply attacked the use of statistical methods to establish *Kulturkreise*—methods which amounted only to a summation of isolated and often quite heterogenous elements, often totally unrelated and of different historical significance. What he had described as *Kulturkreise* in his initial works were in fact bloodless, empty constructions, mere accumulations of data. Frobenius demanded a morphological mode of considering cultures—a meaningful combination of individual elements into an organic whole and the comprehension of a culture in its complexity and its historical context. As Frobenius saw it, *Kulturkreise* obtained from a cartographic picture of distribution were not cultures in the real sense of the term, but merely starting points for further research, skeletons that must be fleshed out, or auxiliary constructions that might enable him to penetrate to the core of the problem: the question of the nature of culture. The provisional nature of his *Kulturkreise* becomes especially manifest when they are compared to the *Kulturkreise* of Graebner and the Vienna school, which were by no means intended to have a provisional, skeletal character. The latter were of a definitive nature and of fixed, rigid magnitudes; arranged chronologically and combined, they were even supposed to furnish an outline of the history of mankind.

Development of culture.   Frobenius' intellectual objective was to understand the essential nature of culture. His first book devoted to this problem was *Die naturwissenschaftliche Kulturlehre* (1899, *Probleme der Kultur*, vol. 1). It foreshadowed the concepts of his subsequent theory of *paideuma* (1921), in which he endeavored to provide an answer to the question of the nature, the morphology, and the development of a culture. Frobenius regarded the several cultures as living organisms in the biological sense that every culture is subject to the laws of the organic world, springing up like seed, growing, and attaining its apogee at maturity, after which it begins to age and finally dies. He used the terms *Ergriffenheit* (emotional involvement), *Ausdruck* (expression), and *Anwendung* (application) to characterize the stages of youth, maturity, and age traversed by a culture, comparing them to a life curve.

Frobenius regarded the *Ergriffenheit* of man as the crucial event in the emergence of a culture. Once man is gripped by the world about him, the particular nature of the things in his world and the existential order within which he lives are revealed to him. In this process, man plays a rather passive role, being object rather than subject, affected by the phenomena that overcome him, move him, and shake him to his innermost being. It would be wrong, however, to exaggerate his passivity: in the last analysis, only alert, active, and creative spirits are open to the phenomena of the world around them; only they are capable of reproducing these phenomena and putting together a comprehensive and valid picture of the reality that surrounds them.

Frobenius attributed decisive importance to the creative qualities of man. In his eyes, *Ergriffenheit* and creative will are the motive forces that give rise to the emergence of a culture. The emergence of culture occurs almost exclusively in the realm of ideas, for the process begins not simply with objects but with the inner nature of the objects and phenomena in man's environment. Therefore the *Ergriffenheit*, the youth stage, of a culture is always characterized by fundamental and magnificent spiritual–religious creations. More simply stated: Religion stands at the beginning of a culture. Because the rise and formation of the spiritual–religious foundations generally take place quietly and without any visible indications, it is very difficult to establish precisely the emergent phase of a culture; in the case of nonliterate peoples, precision is almost impossible. As a rule, the historian can identify and describe only those fully developed cultures that already possess a stamp of their own and have reached the stage of maturity, while the decisive mental processes that form a culture are not accessible to observation; at best they can be reconstructed from its mature state.

If the *Ergriffenheit* of man is the crucial event in the origin of a culture, man's environment must be of decisive importance, for it alone is able to move him. That is why Frobenius regarded environment as a factor of overriding significance and recognized the primary bond between every culture and its location, while the factor of race seemed to him unimportant. He attributed differences between various cultures largely to the differences in environmental conditions. The cartographic method he employed in mapping *Kulturkreise* and the patterns of distribution he obtained greatly aided him in reaching this conclusion. Thus, he believed that the extensive rain forests of the equatorial regions, with their uniformity of scenery and climate, give rise to a different form of *Ergriffenheit* than that of the savanna and steppes, with their pronounced alternations of drought and rainy periods.

The second stage that a culture must pass through is that of *Ausdruck*, maturity, the apex of the life curve. At this point of development, men continue to be affected by things, but they have now assimilated the experience of their environment and mastered it in the philosophical sense. They are able to express the essential nature of things and of the existential order, as well as of their own existence, in religious, artistic, and social constructs. Only when man has risen above the level of things can he make them completely his own and shape them creatively. In the period of the maturity of a culture, ideas take on visible shape; they are manifested in religious rites, in the forms of social order, in artistic creations, as well as in the complexity of daily life and the economy. A culture in the stage of maturity is in a state of harmony and draws on abundant resources.

Frobenius' researches were always aimed at comprehending the spiritual center of a culture, from which its impulses proceed and all actions of the culture are controlled. He called this spiritual center the *paideuma*, the soul of the culture, which permeates man and gives his action a direction and goal. Every movement and every expression of a culture, even the simple implements of daily use, are related to the spiritual center and bear the stamp of the particular *paideuma*. All elements are conceived as intimately interrelated in function, which is not true of the elements of the early conception of *Kulturkreise*; this is why Frobenius refused to regard the early *Kulturkreise* as true cultures in the *paideuma* sense.

The last stage is called by Frobenius *Anwendung* (application) because in this phase he saw the rational aspect of reality and the question of the usefulness and possible applications of a cultural asset coming increasingly to the fore. An implement or a social institution is no longer evaluated solely as the expression of a central spiritual idea but is regarded only from the standpoint of its utility. The rational utilitarian aspect of many cultural assets, especially of the material objects, is no doubt inherent from the very outset, but in the *Anwendung* phase it predominates over ideal values. The bonds linking the individual elements of culture to the spiritual center become ever looser, and their progressive isolation finally results in the disintegration of the entire culture. The *Anwendung* stage of a culture is characterized by overemphasis on technical–civilizing forces. The nonpurposeful striving for knowledge of the *Ergriffenheit* phase recedes, and creative spiritual ideas are "applied" and "turned to account" according to their usefulness. An increasing semantic depletion makes itself felt in the religious field, and symbols and religious rites are dominated by routine. When the creative forces are paralyzed, meaningful content dwindles away, cultural forms become petrified, and the culture gradually dies away.

As Frobenius saw it, the various cultures are closed organisms, subject to the same law that governs all living things in this world. Every culture has a soul of its own, a unique character, and an individuality otherwise found only in animate nature. Frobenius therefore attributed to every culture an autonomous set of laws that determines its development, largely independent of its particular human members. This is an inevitable although often misunderstood conclusion if cultures are regarded as living organisms that are governed by the laws of life. Man cannot stem the natural development of a culture. For example, he cannot prevent the aging of a culture; all he can do is prolong or shorten the process. When Frobenius ventured the opinion that culture might exist even without human beings, he meant that culture is not a fiction but a reality that "takes hold of" men just as do the phenomena of their environment. This notion is supported by the historical fact that cultures tend to expand beyond the boundaries of their original centers, especially in the stage of maturity, and "seize," as it were, people of alien cultures, putting them under their sway.

Although Frobenius was the target of violent attacks, his thoughts and ideas fell upon fertile soil in the German-speaking world. His scientific work in the field of culture founded cultural morphology in ethnology, which is the special concern of the Frobenius Institute. The work of his disciple Adolf E. Jensen on comparative religion refined and advanced Frobenius' description of the history of culture and increased its depth. All work in the cultural-historical aspects of ethnology has been profoundly influenced by Frobenius' doctrines. For a time, he was closely associated with Oswald Spengler, who advocated similar ideas about the essential nature of culture. Outside of Germany, and especially in the English-speaking world, Frobenius was accepted only with reservations.

HELMUT STRAUBE

[For the historical context of Frobenius' work, see the biographies of BASTIAN and RATZEL. For discussion of the subsequent development of Frobenius' ideas, see CULTURE; CULTURE AREA; HISTORY, article on CULTURE HISTORY; and the biographies of GRAEBNER; KOPPERS; NORDENSKIÖLD; SCHMIDT.]

WORKS BY FROBENIUS

1894   *Die Geheimbünde Afrikas: Ethnologische Studie.* Hamburg: Actien-Gesellschaft.

1897   Der westafrikanische Kulturkreis. *Petermanns Geographische Mitteilungen* 43:225–236, 262–267.

(1898a) 1899   The Origin of African Civilizations. Smithsonian Institution, *Annual Report* [1899]:637–650. → First published in German.

1898b   *Die Masken und Geheimbünde Afrikas.* Halle: Karras.

1898c   *Der Ursprung der Kultur.* Berlin: Bornträger.

1899–1901   *Probleme der Kultur.* 4 vols. Berlin: Dümmler. → Volume 1: *Die naturwissenschaftliche Kulturlehre,* 1899. Volume 2: *Die Mathematik der Oceanier,* 1900. Volume 3: *Die Schilde der Oceanier,* 1900. Volume 4: *Die Bogen der Oceanier,* 1901.

1907   *Im Schatten des Kongostaates: Bericht über den Verlauf der ersten Reisen der D.I.A.F.E. von 1904–1906.* Deutsche inner-afrikanische Forschungs-Expedition, No. 1. Berlin: Reimer.

1910   *Der schwarze Dekameron: Belege und Aktenstücke über Liebe, Witz und Heldentum in Innerafrika.* Berlin: Vita.

(1912–1913) 1918 *The Voice of Africa: Being an Account of the Travels of the German Inner African Exploration Expedition in the Years 1910–1912.* 2 vols. London: Hutchinson. → First published as *Und Afrika sprach.*

1916 *Der kleinafrikanische Grabbau. Praehistorische Zeitschrift* 8:1–84.

(1921) 1928 *Paideuma: Umrisse einer Kultur- und Seelenlehre.* 3d ed., rev. & enl. Frankfurt am Main: Societäts-Druckerei.

1921–1928 FROBENIUS, LEO (editor) *Atlantis: Volksmärchen und Volksdichtungen Afrikas.* 12 vols. Munich: Veröffentlichungen des Forschungsinstituts für Kulturmorphologie. → Volumes 1–3: *Volksmärchen der Kabylen.* Volume 4: *Märchen aus Kordofan.* Volume 5: *Dichten und Denken im Sudan.* Volume 6: *Spielmannsgeschichten der Sahel.* Volume 7: *Dämonen des Sudan: Allerlei religiöse Verdichtungen.* Volume 8: *Erzählungen aus dem West-Sudan.* Volume 9: *Volkserzählungen und Volksdichtungen aus dem Zentral-Sudan.* Volume 10: *Die atlantische Götterlehre.* Volume 11: *Volksdichtungen aus Oberguinea.* Volume 12: *Dichtkunst der Kassaiden.*

(1921–1931) 1937 FROBENIUS, LEO; and FOX, DOUGLAS C. *African Genesis.* New York: Stackpole. → First published in German.

1922–1933 FROBENIUS, LEO; and WILM, LUDWIG VON (editors) *Atlas Africanus: Belege zur Morphologie der afrikanischen Kulturen.* 8 parts. Munich: Beck.

1923 *Das unbekannte Afrika: Aufhellung der Schicksale eines Erdteils.* Munich: Beck.

1925 FROBENIUS, LEO; and OBERMAIER, HUGO *Hádschra Máktuba: Urzeitliche Felsbilder Kleinafrikas.* Munich: Wolff.

1925–1929 *Erlebte Erdteile.* 7 vols. Frankfurt am Main: Societäts-Druckerei. → Volume 1: *Ausfahrt: Von der Völkerkunde zum Kulturproblem,* 1925. Volume 2: *Erschlossen Räume: Das Problem Ozeanien,* 1925. Volume 3: *Vom Schreibtisch zum Äquator,* 1925. Volume 4: *Paideuma,* 1928. Volume 5: *Das sterbende Afrika,* 1928. Volume 6: *Monumenta africana,* 1929. Volume 7: *Monumenta terrarum,* 1929.

(1929) 1938 *Die Waremba: Träger einer fossilen Kultur. Zeitschrift für Ethnologie* 70:159–175.

1931a *Erythräa: Länder und Zeiten des heiligen Königsmordes.* Berlin and Zurich: Atlantis.

1931b *Madsimu Dsangara: Südafrikanische Felsbilderchronik.* 2 vols. Berlin: Atlantis.

1932 *Schicksalskunde im Sinne des Kulturwerdens.* Leipzig: Voigtländer.

1933 *Kulturgeschichte Afrikas: Prolegomena zu einer historischen Gestaltlehre.* Zurich: Phaidon.

1937 *Ekade Ektab: Die Felsbilder Fezzans.* Leipzig: Harrassowitz.

1937 *The Story of Rock Picture Research.* Pages 13–28 in New York, Museum of Modern Art, *Prehistoric Rock Pictures in Europe and Africa.* New York: The Museum.

SUPPLEMENTARY BIBLIOGRAPHY

ANDREE, RICHARD 1878 *Ethnographische Parallelen und Vergleiche.* Stuttgart: Maier.

BASTIAN, ADOLF 1860 *Der Mensch in der Geschichte: Zur Begründung einer psychologischen Weltanschauung.* 3 vols. Leipzig: Wigand. → Volume 1: *Die Psychologie als Naturwissenschaft.* Volume 2: *Psychologie und Mythologie.* Volume 3: *Politische Psychologie.*

Leo Frobenius: Ein Lebenswerk aus der Zeit der Kulturwende, dargestellt von seinen Freunden und Schülern. 1933 Leipzig: Köhler & Amelang.

HAHN, EDUARD 1926 Leo Frobenius. *Preussische Jahrbücher* 205:205–222.

JENSEN, ADOLF E. 1938 Leo Frobenius: Leben und Werk. *Paideuma* 1:45–58.

LOWIE, ROBERT H. 1913 *Und Afrika sprach* . . . A Book Review. *Current Anthropological Literature* 2:87–91.

MÜHLMANN, WILHELM 1939 Zum Gedächtnis von Leo Frobenius. *Archiv für Anthropologie* New Series 25:47–51.

NIGGEMEYER, HERMANN 1939 Leo Frobenius. *Ethnologischer Anzeiger* 4:268–272.

RATZEL, FRIEDRICH 1904 Geschichte, Völkerkunde und historische Perspective. *Historische Zeitschrift* 93, no. 1:1–46.

FRUSTRATION

See AGGRESSION, *article on* PSYCHOLOGICAL ASPECTS; STRESS.

FUNCTIONAL ANALYSIS

I. STRUCTURAL–FUNCTIONAL ANALYSIS   *Marion J. Levy, Jr.*

II. VARIETIES OF FUNCTIONAL ANALYSIS   *Francesca M. Cancian*

I
STRUCTURAL–FUNCTIONAL ANALYSIS

Few concepts in modern social science history have generated as much discussion as those of structure and function and the type of analysis associated with them. The main difficulty in speaking of structural–functional analysis in general arises from five sources. One, there is the feeling in many quarters that there is something new and special about structural–functional analysis. Two, in general usage elementary procedures in definition have not been observed. The same term has frequently been used for more than one distinct referent. Three, teleology in the sense of scientific fallacy—in this case structural teleology, functional teleology, or both—has frequently been committed in connection with such analysis. Four, the use of stability assumptions in models generally has been both misunderstood and misconstrued. Five, unintentionally, evaluations have been written into the analysis, thereby raising questions about its objectivity.

Structural–functional analysis is not new in either the social or the natural sciences; it has a pedigree that stretches indefinitely back in both fields. The only new aspect of it is its formidable new name, structural–functional analysis. Discussion of it as something new under the sun is the social scientist's counterpart of M. Jourdain's discovery that he had been speaking prose. The only possible novelty associated with this form of analysis is the attempt in recent years to be carefully explicit in the use of these concepts and to differentiate special subsidiary forms of the analysis, although none of the latter are substantively new either. Shorn of careless uses of definitions and of teleology, structural–functional analysis is simply a synonym for explicit scientific analysis in general. In scientific fields marked by greater theoretical development and associated applications of mathematical forms of expression, the increased verbal explicitness that has recommended the various concepts of structure and function to many in the biological and social sciences is more cumbersome than available alternatives. Corresponding increases in theoretical development in the biological and social sciences will lead to similar alternatives there.

Simply speaking, structural–functional analysis consists of nothing more complicated than phrasing empirical questions in one of the following several forms or some combination of them: (1) What observable uniformities (or patterns) can be discovered or alleged to exist in the phenomena studied? (2) What conditions (empirical states of affairs) resultant from previous operations can be discovered or alleged to exist in the phenomena studied? (3) When process (or action, i.e., changes in the patterns, conditions, or both, depending on one's point of view, are discernible between any two or more points in time) can be discovered (or alleged) to take place in terms of observable uniformities, what resultant conditions can be discovered? The first question asks, "What structures are involved?" The second asks, "What functions have resulted (or have been performed)?" And the third asks, "What functions take place in terms of a given structure(s)?" Many special forms of these three questions are useful and necessary for the analysis of different types of problems; for example, one might ask about the possibility of adjustment in terms of a system, the normative content of a system, the "necessary" features of a system, the degree of planning or consciousness involved, etc. All of these are variants of the three basic questions or some combination of them. In addition to the most general form of the concepts of structure and function, six subsidiary sets of concepts most generally associated with this form of analysis, either explicitly or implicitly, are defined and discussed below in terms of the special purposes generally associated with them.

Function and structure. These explicit concepts, ostensibly in their most general form, are fre-quently encountered in the biological and social sciences. In both fields somewhat similar difficulties have been associated with the use of the concepts. Joseph H. Woodger in biology and Robert K. Merton in the social sciences (Woodger 1924, pp. 326–330; Merton 1949, pp. 21–28) have pointed to the profusion of different referents given to the term "function" even in the scientific sense. These different referents have for the most part been left implicit by both authors although the confusion is noted. Perhaps the major difficulty associated with the general concept of function has been the use of a single term to cover several distinctly different referents. This difficulty is much greater with the concept of function than with the associated concept of structure. Most of the general discussions in the literature have been largely preoccupied with the concept of function. The concept of structure has, more often than not, been left undiscussed. To prevent confusion, the most general form of the concepts "structure" and "function" used for purposes of scientific analysis must be defined in such a way that the other uses of the terms represent specific subcategories. The term "function" may be defined as any condition, any state of affairs, resultant from the operation (including in the term "operation" mere persistence) of a unit of the type under consideration in terms of a structure(s). In the case of the biological sciences that unit is usually an organism or a subsystem of an organism. In the case of the social sciences the unit is usually a system of action involving a set of one or more persons (actors). The term "structure" may be defined as a pattern, i.e., an observable uniformity, in terms of which action (or operation) takes place.

In ordinary usage the term "function" is most generally identified with the term "eufunction" defined below. Similar confusion of the term "structure" with "eustructure" is not common. The concept of structure in this general form explicitly covers a wide range of possibilities from highly stable uniformities to highly fleeting ones. Any event may contain an element indicative of a structure if it is considered with regard to nonunique aspects or parts.

Much of the interest of scientific social analysis is centered on the structure of societies and other social systems (or the structures of social action in general), that is, on the interrelationships among different kinds, aspects, and parts of structures. The relationship between the concepts of function and structure is close. Structure refers to an aspect of empirical phenomena that can be divorced from time. The patterns of action, qua patterns, do not exist as concrete objects in the same sense that sticks and stones do. The patterns of action in this sense are abstractions from concrete empirical phenomena, and they "exist" and are empirically verifiable in the same sense that the squareness of a box exists and is empirically verifiable. What has been said here of patterns qua patterns does not apply to the patterns when they are considered in operation. Structures in operation (i.e., the exemplifications of particular patterns) are empirical in the same sense as sticks and stones. In this sense the term "structure" in social science is no departure from the usage of the natural sciences.

The concepts of structure and function fall into a peculiar set of concepts. Classification of a referent as a function or a structure depends in part on the point of view from which the phenomena concerned are discussed. What is a function from one point of view is a structure from another. The concepts of consumption and production are more familiar examples of this peculiar set. The manufacture of automobiles is production from the point of view of an automobile user and consumption from the point of view of a steelmaker. Thus functions in this sense are themselves structures (i.e., patterns) or have important structured (i.e., patterned) aspects, and all structures are the results of operations in terms of other structures (i.e., they are functions). The politeness of small children may be considered as a structure of their behavior or as a function of operation in terms of the structures (i.e., patterns) of discipline indulged in by their parents.

Functional and structural requisites. The concepts functional and structural requisites are primarily oriented to the development of systems of analysis for any cases of a particular type of unit. A functional requisite may be defined as a generalized condition necessary for the maintenance of the type of unit under consideration, given the level of generalization of the definition and the most general setting of such a unit. In seeking to discover the functional requisites of a unit one asks the question, "What must be done to maintain the system concerned in its setting on the level under consideration?" A given condition is a functional requisite if its removal (or absence) would result in (*a*) the total dissolution of the unit, or (*b*) the change of one of the structural elements of the unit on the level under consideration (i.e., one of the structural requisites).

A structural requisite may be defined as a pattern (or observable uniformity) of action (or operation) necessary for the continued existence of the type of unit under consideration, given the level of generalization of the definition and the most general

setting of such a unit. In trying to discover the structural requisites of a unit one seeks an answer to the question, "For a given unit, what structures (i.e., patterns) must be present such that operations in terms of these structures will result in the functional requisites of the unit?" Briefly, functional requisites are answers to the question, "What must be done?"; structural requisites are answers to the question "How must what must be done, be done?" Both questions involve the qualifying phrase "if the unit is to persist in its setting on the level of generalization given." Most of the misunderstanding about stability mentioned above has been associated with this question of persistence. One utilizes an assumption of stability to get at a list of requisites, but this does not imply that any unit analyzed must in fact be stable. To make such units stable by definition is to reduce most discussions of this sort to trivia. To use a stability assumption as an element in a model (i.e., paradigm) does not. Structural–functional requisite analysis includes the following steps in any specific case: (1) *define* the unit of phenomena to be studied; (2) *discover* (or hypothesize about) the setting (i.e., those factors determining the limits within which the ranges of variations of the unit concerned take place); (3) *discover* what general conditions must be met (i.e., functional requisites) if the unit is to persist in its setting without change (i.e., alteration of structures) on the level under consideration; (4) *discover* what structures must be present in the system, as a minimum, if action in terms of the system is to result in the persistence of the unit in its setting without any change on the level under consideration (i.e., the structural requisites).

Several things should be kept in mind. One, although the definition of the unit is arbitrary, whether empirical referents of such a unit exist is not. Two, the setting of such a unit is not a matter of definition but of discovery. Three, neither structural requisites nor functional requisites can be alleged to exist "because they are requisites." Such allegations constitute the commission of structural or functional teleology. To assert that requisites exist *because they are requisites* is to imply that the unit must continue to exist for some preordained reason. Scientifically speaking, *nothing* can be alleged to exist "because it is a requisite." The fact that this form of teleology is fallacious is in no way contradicted by the fact that it is frequently a useful element of models of action to assume or allege that the action concerned is oriented to future states of affairs. Four, the determination of the functional requisites of a unit is the determination of the minimum implications of interrelationships between the factors setting the limits of variation of the unit and the unit itself, and in this type of analysis it is never necessary to deal with more than these minimal implications. However, when material is collected in these terms, more than the minimum will always be collected, since such minimal materials never exist neatly separated from all others. Five, there is a systematic test for error in requisite analysis. If a structure is alleged to be a requisite of the unit concerned, and if examination of a particular case of such a unit uncovers no material on this score, one of three or some combination of three things is an explanation of the lack of data. First, the hypothesis that the structure is a requisite of the unit concerned may be an incorrect one. Second, the observer may have misobserved; there may be data he has overlooked. Third, the unit concerned, although it may closely resemble the unit as defined, may in fact not be a case of such a unit.

There is nothing new about requisite analysis. There has never been a time in which people failed completely to ask questions as to whether given conditions or patterns were not in some sense necessary for the continued existence of certain types of units.

Functional and structural prerequisites. The requisite concepts are not in and of themselves oriented to questions of change; the concepts of functional and structural prerequisites are. All questions of change implicitly or explicitly involve comparisons between at least two of at least three possible distinctions with regard to the units under consideration. These distinctions are those of an initial, a transitional, and a resultant stage. Systematic knowledge about any two of these stages makes possible systematic derivation (prediction or postdiction) of knowledge about the third. Requisite analysis can be used for examining any two of these three or more stages in terms of a constant frame of reference. Constants and variables are therefore more easily detected.

A functional prerequisite may be defined as a function that must pre-exist if a given unit is to come into being in a particular setting. Correspondingly, a structural prerequisite may be defined as a structure that must pre-exist if a given unit is to come into being in a particular setting. The closer two stages of a given unit under consideration are in point of time the greater is the probability that the requisites and the prerequisites of a given unit will be identical. To illustrate this, one of the commonest mistakes in trying to understand the problems of development in "underdeveloped areas"

is the implicit assumption that requisites and prerequisites must or do coincide. It is neither obvious nor tenable to take the position that all of the structures that must be maintained if the United States is to continue as a highly modernized society are identical with the structures that have to pre-exist if Nigeria is to become a highly modernized society, or even that they are identical with all the structures that had to pre-exist, say, in the beginning of the nineteenth century, if the United States was to become a highly modernized society.

Implicitly or explicitly, some form of requisite analysis always underlies any form of prerequisite analysis. Teleology must be avoided in uses of the concepts of structural and functional prerequisites as well as in uses of the concepts of structural and functional requisites. To assert that some structure must pre-exist because it is a structural prerequisite of a given unit is to fall into teleological dynamics as distinguished from the teleological statics described in the case of requisites.

Eufunction, dysfunction; eustructure, dysstructure. These concepts focus attention on questions of adjustment and maladjustment of the units under consideration. Although the term "function" is ordinarily used in several different senses in the social sciences, most often it refers to the concept of eufunction as defined here. With respect to a given unit, "eufunction" may be defined as any function that increases or maintains adaptation or adjustment of the unit to the unit's setting, thus making for the persistence of the unit as defined in its setting. With respect to a given unit, "dysfunction" may be defined as any function that lessens the adaptation or adjustment of the unit to its setting, thus making for lack of persistence (i.e., change or dissolution) of the unit as defined in its setting. The terms "eustructure" and "dysstructure" are similarly defined, *mutatis mutandis*. Alternatively, eustructures may be defined as structures in terms of which operations result in eufunctions, and dysstructures may be defined as structures in terms of which operations result in dysfunctions. Eufunctions or dysfunctions and the corresponding variants of structure may exist, as far as a given unit is concerned, as elements of that unit (i.e., internal to it) or as elements of the setting of the unit concerned. Not all eufunctions *for* a unit are eufunctions *of* the unit, although ordinarily, when one uses the concept of eufunction, attention is focused on functions associated with the unit itself rather than on functions of operation in terms of other units in that setting.

The concept of "nonfunction," in the sense of being neither a eufunction nor a dysfunction, is inutile. Where questions of adjustment are not involved, the general concept of function as used here or another of its special forms will serve. Where questions of adjustment are involved, nothing is less probable than a precisely poised function with no implications for adjustment or maladjustment. Indeed, such considerations define precisely what might be called the category of irrelevant functions, i.e., those lacking any implications for the focus of interest at the time. Such functions would also have to lack any interdependencies with the eufunctions or dysfunctions *for* or *of* the systems concerned.

It is in connection with the terms "eufunction" and "dysfunction" (and the corresponding forms of the concept of structure) that most allegations of building evaluations into structural functional analysis are made. In rough terms, a eufunction is a function that tends to preserve the unit as defined and a dysfunction is one that tends to dissolve it. However, loose usage of these concepts results in the use of eufunctional to refer to conditions making for "good adaptations" and dysfunctional to refer to conditions making for "bad adaptations." Such judgments are a function of one's evaluation of the unit concerned—if one cares to make such an evaluation. No condition or aspect of a condition is inherently eufunctional or dysfunctional. Without identification of the unit concerned and its setting, no judgment of the eufunctional or dysfunctional character of the condition can be made. The same condition that is eufunctional from one point of view may be dysfunctional from another. For example, conditions that were eufunctional for Meiji Japan were dysfunctional for the continuation of Tokugawa Japan and vice versa.

While these concepts are susceptible to the uncritical inclusion of value judgments, they are also a useful vehicle for the explicit consideration of policy-oriented analyses. Either implicitly or explicitly, in seeking to maximize a given policy goal, one asks the questions, "What conditions make for maximal adjustment of the system concerned to that state of affairs (i.e., the eufunctions for that system in that setting)?" and "What conditions should be avoided as interfering with the maintenance of that system in that setting (i.e., are dysfunctional for it)?" Two other points should be carefully kept in mind. First, teleology is to be avoided in this connection too. No function or structure exists *because* it is a eufunction or a eustructure, nor is it tenable to hold that any function or structure that persists must be eufunctional or eustructural. Second, a given element with important eufunctional or eustructural implications for a given unit in its setting may also contain aspects with dysfunctional or dysstructural implications. A functional requisite of a given unit is certainly at least in part eufunctional for that unit, but a given function, even though it is a requisite, may also contain dysfunctional implications as well, although presumably in this case they would not be sufficiently pronounced to overcome the requisite nature of the function.

The concepts of eufunction, dysfunction, eustructure, and dysstructure focus on the question of the maintenance or lack of maintenance of a system in its setting. The requisite concepts focus on the question of what a system is like if it is maintained. The prerequisite concepts focus attention on what conditions must pre-exist before a given type of unit can come into being. The requisite concepts are useful primarily for static theories, although dynamic analysis is involved in discovery of the requisites of a given system in its setting. Like the prerequisite concepts, those of eufunction, dysfunction, eustructure, and dysstructure focus attention on dynamic interrelationships—on the implications of the operation of a particular structure or the presence of a particular function for the state of the system concerned at some future point in time.

Latent, manifest, UIR, and IUR functions and structures. This set of terms is adapted from Merton's suggestion many years ago about latent and manifest functions. Usage here is somewhat changed, since Merton did not envisage their use apart from the concepts of eufunction and dysfunction as defined here, nor did he develop the implications of the fact that his defining conditions could vary independently. Following Merton's usage an element will be termed "manifest" if it is intended and recognized by the participants in the system of action concerned. It will be termed "latent" if it is neither intended nor recognized. It will be termed "UIR" if it is unintended but recognized and "IUR" if it is intended but unrecognized. These concepts focus attention on the level of explicitness and sensitivity of the members of a given system to the structures in terms of which they operate. Such distinctions are vital to any discussions involving rationality, planning, and so forth. The concept of manifest dysfunction is explicitly included as a possibility here. Failure to consider it explicitly has built implicit evaluations into a great deal of analysis. Social reformers usually concentrate all their efforts on being manifestly dysfunctional for the system they are trying to reform and manifestly eufunctional for what they consider to be a better world.

The concepts of function and structure in general, the requisites, the prerequisites, and eufunction–dysfunction, eustructure–dysstructure, are concepts generally applicable to social and nonsocial phenomena and to human as well as to nonhuman phenomena. Concepts of latent, manifest, IUR, and UIR specifically focus attention on the point of view of the actor and involve the assumptions that such actors can and do orient their behavior to future states of affairs about which they are capable of explicit thinking and observation, and that the presence or absence of such explicit thinking, observation, or both has, in turn, implications for their subsequent behavior. Although it is conceivable that such concepts be utilized with regard to nonsocial phenomena, it is not likely that they will prove useful in such a field nor have they generally been so employed. It is quite conceivable that they could be employed with regard to some animate but nonhuman phenomena, but by far their greatest applications are to human social phenomena.

Concrete and analytic structures. The distinction between concrete and analytic structures is oriented to the type of abstraction involved in certain concepts useful for empirical analysis. Concrete structures may be defined as those structures (i.e., patterns) that define the units that are at least in theory capable of physical separation (in time, space, or both) from other units of the same sort. As the term will be applied for social analysis, it refers more specifically to the structures that define the membership units involved in social action, i.e., units in regard to which any given individual may be classified as included or excluded, or some combination of the two. Society, as that term is generally used, is a concrete structure considered in operation. So are organizational contexts generally, such as families, business firms, and governments. Concrete structures other than societies are the structures of action that define the membership units within a given society or those relating to two or more societies, i.e., they are all other social systems. All concrete structures are social systems; all societies are social systems; and all social systems other than societies are either subsystems of a given society or the results of interdependencies among two or more societies. The family, as that term is often used, is a concrete structure; its structures define a membership unit. So are business firms. A given individual may at one and the same time be a member of both a given business firm and a given family; nevertheless, the social structures characterizing the business firm are not part of the social structures characterizing the family concern, however complex the interrelationships may be, unless the firm is specifically and completely a family affair. It is at least conceivable that all the members of a given family could be put in one room, that the members of a given business firm could be put into another, and if necessary, those individuals who are members of both could be removed from the two rooms and put into a third.

Analytic structures are defined as structures (i.e., patterns) that define the aspects of units that are not even theoretically capable of concrete separation from other structured aspects. If one defines the economic aspect of action as having to do with the allocation of goods and services and political aspects as having to do with the allocation of power and responsibility, then economic and political structures are analytic structures, since there are no social systems that are totally devoid of either economic or political aspects.

Failure to keep this sort of distinction straight constitutes the fallacy of reification (or misplaced concreteness). Thus the terms "economy" and "polity" as generally used cannot occupy the same position in a system of analysis as the term "family." As these concepts are generally defined, they represent analytic structures, and the concept "family" refers to a concrete one. This distinction, though difficult in the context of social phenomena, is a generally familiar one in the natural sciences. Concepts such as atoms, molecules, cells, organs, and elementary particles are concrete structures. Aspects such as mass, shape, color, temperature, and mitosis are analytic structures.

In actual analysis one always uses some combination of both sorts of concepts. One cannot identify analytic structures without some specification sooner or later of the concrete structures of which they are aspects. Correspondingly, one cannot discuss the nature of concrete structures without sooner or later making reference to aspects that cut across such units. Careful observance of the distinction and the avoidance of the fallacy of reification is the key par excellence to the avoidance of much disciplinary parochialism in the social sciences.

Apart from considerations of methodological elegance there is another reason for being careful about this distinction. One of the most general distinctions between concrete structures or organizations is that between those which are specialized in the predominant orientation of their members to one or another of these analytic structures and those which are not specialized in this way. (Organizations may, of course, be specialized in other ways, e.g., in terms of the product orientations of the members.) Thus, a business firm may be spoken of as a predominantly economically oriented structure (or perhaps more accurately, though more cumbersomely, as a specially economic–analytic-structure-oriented concrete structure). A family unit is not specialized in any one of these aspects in any clear-cut predominance over the others.

Institutions, tradition, and utopian structures. The three terms "institution," "tradition," and "utopian structure" refer to different types of structure. The concept "institution" may be defined as any normative pattern, conformity to which is generally expected and failure to conform with which is generally met with moral indignation or some other form of sanction by the individuals who are involved in the same general social system and are aware of the failure. This is the sense of the term employed by Talcott Parsons in his early work. A given structure may be more or less well-institutionalized to the degree to which conformity with the structure is generally to be expected and the degree to which failure to conform to the structure is met by the moral indignation or sanctions of the individuals who are involved in the system and who are aware of the failure. Thus, the two sources of variability with regard to the level of institutionalization may be referred to as conformity aspects and sanction aspects. An institution may be regarded as crucial or more or less strategic. A given institution will be called a crucial institution if it is a structural requisite of the system in which it appears. It may be regarded as a more or less strategic institution to the extent that: (1) it is the institutionalized form of all or a portion of a structural requisite; and (2) the structure concerned may not or may be altered without destroying the structural requisite involved. A completely strategic institution *is* a crucial institution. The first of the two aspects of the strategic quality of an institution will be called its substantive aspect, and the second will be called its critical aspect. The critical aspect is a special form of consideration of the general problem of functional substitutes, equivalents, or alternatives (i.e., the question of the possibility of a given condition being the result of behavior in terms of one or more alternative structures).

A great deal of nonsense is talked and written as a result of misunderstanding the problem of functional substitutability. Many use this nonsense to argue the severe limitation of what can be done in these terms. Much of the confusion results from initially posing a question implicitly on one level of generality and in the course of the discussion proceeding, still implicitly, on a different and less general level. If the argument is correct that role differentiation on the basis of absolute age is a requisite of all societies, there can be no functional substitutability for that. The fact that the members of one society handle role differentiation in terms of five absolute age distinctions whereas those of another handle it in terms of ten simply indicates the fact that a particular solution to absolute age distinctions is not determinant for all societies. For a particular society, however, either five or ten distinctions may be just as much a requisite as some sort of role differentiation on the basis of absolute age is for all societies. Some discussions of functional substitutability imply that the structures involved can be changed without other changes on the level of generality on which the treatment has been focused. There are, of course, instances in which a given function may result from operation in terms of various alternative structures on specific lower levels of generality without changes on the most general level under scrutiny, but that question is by no means settled by the analyst's simply being able to conceive of another structure from action in terms of which the function in question could result—and so asserting his conclusions.

The term "tradition" may be defined as an institution whose perpetuation is institutionalized—that is to say, as a special form of institution. An institution may be considered more or less traditional, or more or less traditionalized, to the extent that its perpetuation is institutionalized without regard to changes of the functional implications of operations in terms of it—whether these be eufunctional or dysfunctional implications. In this sense, monogamous marriage in the United States would seem to be much more highly traditional and traditionalized than the structure of driving on the right-hand side of the road. A tradition in this sense is a double institutionalization: (1) the structure concerned is an institution; and (2) the perpetuation of the structure is also an institution. Traditions may vary in at least two radically different ways. One, they may, of course, vary with regard to the institution that is traditionalized, although implicit in the concept of any institution in its conformity aspects is some degree of traditionalization. More important, traditions—like other institutions—may vary with regard to their combinations of conformity and sanction aspects. For example, the tradition of driving on the right-hand side of the road in the United States has very high conformity aspects and relatively minor sanction aspects, whereas the tradition of the incest taboo has very high conformity aspects and very high sanction aspects.

Utopian structures may be defined as those particular sets of normative patterns which, though not institutionalized, do require allegiance to them as institutionalized ideals. Allegiance to them as ideals is highly traditionalized in both conformity and sanction aspects. Thus, one does not in fact expect conformity to the principle of "Love they neighbor as thyself," but expression of it as an ideal is certainly institutionalized in some social contexts, and its perpetuation is institutionalized. In the social systems in which they are found, utopian structures often have the function of making it easier to teach the actual institutional structures of the system and of setting the framework in terms of which actual conformity to less extreme expectations is, in fact, expected.

Ideal and actual structures. Ideal structures may be defined as those structures that the members of any given system (or systems) feel should be the structures of their behavior or those of others. Actual structures may be defined as the structures (i.e., patterns) in terms of which the members of the system in fact behave as they would be described by an observer with theoretically perfect scientific knowledge. The terms "ideal" and "actual" in these respects may be applied in other connections, but they are most generally applied to the concepts of structure. The following generalizations in terms of them are relevant in almost any analysis. One, there are no peoples who do not make some distinction between ideal and actual structures. Two, ideal and actual patterns of a given system never coincide perfectly. Three, the members of the systems concerned are always to some extent aware of the fact that the ideal and actual structures do not coincide perfectly. Four, some sources of stress and strain in any social system inhere in the fact that the ideal and actual structures do not coincide perfectly. Five, not paradoxical relative to the fourth generalization, some of the possibilities of integration in terms of any social system inhere in the fact that the ideal and actual structures do not coincide perfectly. Six, failure of the ideal and actual structures to coincide perfectly is never explicable solely in terms of hypocrisy. Seven, perfect coincidence of the ideal and actual structures would require both perfect knowledge and perfect motivation on the part of all of the members of the system concerned in all possible situations. This would (a) overload any known set of cognitive capacities of individuals; and (b) were it possible to have perfect coincidence of the ideal and actual structures, the resultant system would be totally brittle, since any change of setting factors necessitating or causing any change internal to the system would require complete resetting of all of the cognitive capacities of the members of the system.

These concepts can be further elaborated; e.g., there may be ideal ideal structures (i.e., utopian structures) as well as many pseudo or pretended ideal structures (i.e., hypocrisies which are ideal structures which are not actual ideal structures).

Structural–functional analysis in the most general sense, shorn of confusion of terminology, misuses of stability assumptions, teleology, and implicit evaluations, is synonymous with scientific analysis in general. The special forms of structural–functional analysis are not new, although the attempt to be explicit about them in general is recent. Of the various special forms of structural–functional analysis, there is one sense in which requisite analysis underlies the rest. It is oriented to the derivation of a system of analysis for any unit of the sort under discussion, and all of the other forms of structural–functional analysis, whether in terms of prerequisites, manifest, latent, UIR, and IUR elements, eufunction–dysfunction, eustructure–dysstructure, etc., presuppose two or more states of some sort of unit(s) which presumably can be analyzed systematically. Of the various special forms of structural–functional analysis, those having to do with the latent, manifest, UIR, and IUR elements, the concepts of institutions, traditions, and utopian structures, and the ideal and actual structures are the most specifically oriented to the analysis of human social phenomena. The other special forms are much more generally oriented.

MARION J. LEVY, JR.

BIBLIOGRAPHY

DAVIS, KINGSLEY 1959 The Myth of Functional Analysis as a Special Method in Sociology and Anthropology. *American Sociological Review* 24:757–772.

FIRTH, RAYMOND 1955 Function. *Yearbook of Anthropology* [1955]: 237–258.

HEMPEL, CARL G. 1959 The Logic of Functional Analysis. Pages 271–307 in Llewellyn Gross (editor), *Symposium on Sociological Theory*. New York: Harper.

LEVY, MARION J. JR. 1952 *The Structure of Society.* Princeton Univ. Press.

LEVY, MARION J. JR. 1954 Comparative Analysis of Societies in Terms of Structural–Functional Requisites. *Civilisations* 4, no. 2:191–197.

MALINOWSKI, BRONISLAW 1944 *A Scientific Theory of Culture and Other Essays.* Chapel Hill: Univ. of North Carolina Press. → A paperback edition was published in 1960 by Oxford Univ. Press.

MALINOWSKI, BRONISLAW 1945 *The Dynamics of Culture Change: An Inquiry Into Race Relations in Africa.* New Haven: Yale Univ. Press. → A paperback edition was published in 1961.

MERTON, ROBERT K. (1949) 1957 *Social Theory and Social Structure: Toward the Codification of Theory and Research.* Rev. ed. Glencoe, Ill.: Free Press.

NADEL, SIEGFRIED F. 1951 *The Foundations of Social Anthropology.* London: Cohen & West: Glencoe, Ill.: Free Press.

NADEL, SIEGFRIED F. 1957 *The Theory of Social Structure.* London: Cohen & West; Glencoe, Ill.: Free Press. → Published posthumously.

NAGEL, ERNEST 1957 *Logic Without Metaphysics, and Other Essays in the Philosophy of Science.* Glencoe, Ill.: Free Press.

NAGEL, ERNEST 1961 *The Structure of Science: Problems in the Logic of Scientific Explanation.* New York: Harcourt.

PARSONS, TALCOTT 1937 *The Structure of Social Action: A Study in Social Theory With Special Reference to a Group of Recent European Writers.* New York: McGraw-Hill.

RADCLIFFE-BROWN, A. R. 1952 *Structure and Function in Primitive Society: Essays and Addresses.* London: Cohen & West; Glencoe, Ill.: Free Press.

WOODGER, JOSEPH H. (1924) 1948 *Biological Principles: A Critical Study.* London: Routledge.

II
VARIETIES OF FUNCTIONAL ANALYSIS

For the past few decades functional analysis has been a major approach to understanding the organization of society. But at the same time it has become the target of very serious criticism and has been attacked as illogical, value-laden, and incapable of explaining anything. As one would expect, there is a serious problem of definition.

The term "functional analysis" or "structural-functionalism" has been applied to a great variety of approaches (Merton 1949; Firth 1955) that share only one common element: an interest in relating one part of a society or social system to another part or to some aspect of the whole. Within this variety, three aspects or types of functionalism can be distinguished: the first is based on the concepts and assumptions of sociology; the second, on the theoretical orientation that all major social patterns operate to maintain the integration or adaptation of the larger social system; the third, on a model of self-regulating or equilibrating systems. Most functional analyses contain all three aspects, but a clear description and evaluation of functionalism requires their separate consideration.

A nondistinctive type. The first type of functionalism consists in stressing sociological analyses as opposed to psychological or historical analyses. It is based on the assumption that the social traits existing in a society at a given time are interrelated in a systematic way and that ordered relationships can be discovered among "social facts" or social institutions without necessarily bringing in psychological or historical factors. This guiding assumption is accompanied by an implicit consensus on the important elements of social structure and by a developing set of hypotheses on their interrela-

tions. The crucial elements of social structure include: the composition and formation of groups, the organization of economics and religion, and the distribution of authority and prestige. These are the now-traditional concerns of sociology and social anthropology, the elements stressed by the major theorists from Émile Durkheim and Max Weber to A. R. Radcliffe-Brown, Talcott Parsons, and George C. Homans.

This type of functional analysis is most characteristic of the monographs of British social anthropologists and their adherents in the United States, and of the essays of sociologists, especially Kingsley Davis and Talcott Parsons, on some aspect of modern societies. The anthropologists typically present a careful description of a primitive society. The sociologists begin with a more impressionistic account of some institution in their own society. Then both go on to show how the various parts of the society or institution are interrelated, how the whole system "hangs together" despite some strains and inconsistencies. This type of work has led to many valuable hypotheses, such as those relating the isolated nuclear family and the modern economic system, or matrilocal residence and divorce rates.

Careful description and a search for general patterns are obviously necessary to social science, and, as Davis (1959) points out, functionalism has been an effective banner under which to fight for these qualities. In anthropology, functionalism successfully opposed the diffusionists and the empiricists, who tended to ignore general patterns, and the evolutionists and the rigid monocausalists, who tended to ignore the necessity of careful description.

However, as Davis also argues, this type of functionalism is essentially equivalent to sociological analysis, and it is misleading to distinguish it by a special name. The functionalist position that societies should be viewed as systems having definite structure or organization means primarily that the parts of a society are interrelated in some nonrandom way; i.e., that there are regular patterns and relationships, and, therefore, it is reasonable to try to construct a science of society. This position underlies all sociological analysis, although there is considerable disagreement on whether all parts of a society are interrelated or whether there are relatively autonomous subsystems. The elements of society that these functionalists consider are also not distinctive, nor are the kinds of relationships among elements. Functionalists do stress reciprocal relationships, but the typical monograph or essay also includes relationships based on similarity, one-way causation, fulfillment of a psychological or social need, etc. The problems and accomplishments of this kind of functional analysis are the same as the problems and accomplishments of sociology and social anthropology in general. Therefore, the discussion below will concern only the other two types of functionalism, both of which are distinct forms of analysis.

Two distinctive types. The first of the two remaining types of functional analysis will be called traditional functional analysis because it is the most widely used type. It is based on the theoretical orientation that all major social patterns operate to maintain the integration or adaptation of the larger system, and it is further distinguished by two crucial attributes, both of which make it very difficult to construct adequate explanations. First, a social pattern is explained by the effects or consequences of the pattern, and, second, these consequences must be beneficial and necessary to the proper functioning of society. The traditional approach includes those functionalists who focus on a few aspects of a society at a time and attempt to link one social pattern with one need and thereby "explain" the pattern. It also includes those who deal with a complex system of many elements and try to show how these elements are interrelated so as to form an adaptive and consistent system.

Traditional functional analysis can be contrasted with the second type: formal functionalism. This approach is concerned with homeostatic, or equilibrating, systems, and so with feedback and self-regulation. It abandons the two distinctive attributes of the traditional approach. The effects of a trait for some part of the system are used to explain that part and not to explain the trait; and there is no restriction on the kinds of consequences to be considered. They may or may not be beneficial or necessary to society. This approach is called "formal" because it does not include a theoretical orientation or a substantive hypothesis about empirical events. It is a model of kinds of relationships between elements, like a mathematical model.

The distinctiveness of traditional functionalism from other forms of analysis can be readily illustrated. For example, a traditional functionalist explanation of adolescent rebellion in the United States might point to the positive effects or functions of rebellion in securing independence from parents, which is crucial in our society. A nonfunctionalist explanation might focus on causes of rebellion, such as parental ambivalence about the desirability of being stable and mature. Formal functionalism would produce an interpretation different from both of the above, since it is concerned

with equilibrating or feedback systems and not with relationships of one-way effect or cause. It should be noted again that these different types of analysis are usually combined in practice. Thus Parsons' discussion of adolescence (1942) includes both of the arguments in the above example, as well as many more.

Functional analysis clearly is not distinct in some ways. It does not have any necessary monopoly on the empirical problems of analyzing total societies or comparing institutions cross-culturally, even though historically these fields have been dominated by functionalists. It is also not the case that complex, formal models of functional systems include some logically special types of propositions. Any model that can be communicated to social scientists can be reduced to a combination of simple statements such as: "if a then b," and "$a = (f)b$." Nor does traditional functional analysis involve a distinctive form of explanation; rather, it must be evaluated according to the general standards of adequate scientific explanations.

Traditional functional analysis

Scientific explanation. The criteria of an adequate scientific explanation are extremely difficult to state precisely, and the philosophers of science continue to struggle with the problem. However, Nagel (1961), Hempel (1965), and other philosophers have stated the criteria in a way that seems close to the actual practice of scientists and that is based on the idea that explaining a statement necesarily involves deducing it from some more general statement or statements. This is the view of explanation that will be used here.

A scientific explanation consists of deducing the proposition to be explained (the explicandum) from some true or plausible general assumptions in conjunction with a statement of initial or antecedent conditions. The statement of initial conditions connects the explicandum to the assumptions. For example, if one wanted to explain the existence of witchcraft among the Navajo, using the two assumptions: (1) "if a society is subjected to externally imposed change then there will be a high level of aggression within the society," and (2) "if high aggression then witchcraft"; then the appropriate statement of initial conditions would be "imposed change has occurred among the Navajo."

The minimal requirements for an adequate explanation are (1) all the propositions must be clearly stated, that is, stated clearly enough to enable recognition of a negative case; (2) the assumptions must not be empirically false; (3) the statement of initial conditions must be true; and

(4) the explicandum must be derivable from the assumptions and initial conditions according to the rules of logic. Formulating an explanation is equivalent to constructing a theory, for if the assumptions are general it will be possible to deduce from them many verifiable propositions and not only the explicandum. In other words, the logical structure of explanation is identical with prediction if the prediction is based on a theory. In both cases one demonstrates that the phenomenon in question had to occur, given the assumptions. The only difference is that in prediction one starts with the assumption and proceeds to deduce testable propositions; in explanation one begins with a tested proposition and searches for some appropriate assumptions from which it can be deduced. Explanation, no less than prediction, requires precise propositions with clear empirical implications.

Traditional functional "explanations" usually fail to meet most of the minimal requirements of an adequate explanation. It is, of course, difficult to construct adequate explanations or theories in social science, regardless of the type of analysis that is used. However, the concepts and strategy of traditional functionalism create formidable problems, and the problems are especially tenacious. Many contemporary functional analyses contain the same errors that have been pointed out for decades in numerous papers (for an excellent presentation of the problems of functional analysis, see Durkheim 1895, chapter 5).

Vacuous functional explanations. The problems of functional explanation are illustrated in Kluckhohn's sophisticated and complex interpretation of Navajo witchcraft (1944). He uses the three major types of functional arguments: (1) a vacuous explanation in terms of various unrelated, adaptive effects of witchcraft; (2) a more adequate explanation in terms of a functional prerequisite theory; and (3) an interpretation of witchcraft as part of an equilibrating system, using the model of a functional system.

Kluckhohn first explains Navajo witchcraft patterns simply by demonstrating that they have a variety of beneficial effects. He states that the major question (explicandum) is why witchcraft patterns have survived through a given period of time and that his basic postulate is "that no cultural forms survive unless they constitute responses which are adjustive or adaptive, in some sense, for the members of the society or for the society considered as a perduring unit" (1944, p. 46). This postulate is very similar to Merton's statement of the three basic postulates of functional analysis: "Substantially, these postulates hold first, that

standardized social activities or cultural items are functional for the *entire* social or cultural system; second, that *all* such social and cultural items fulfill sociological functions; and third, that these items are consequently *indispensable*" ([1949] 1957, p. 25). These postulates have been criticized for leading to a static, conservative orientation (Dahrendorf 1958); for if every pattern helps to maintain every other pattern, then the system will not generate conflict or change; and if every social pattern is indispensable, then it is clearly unwarranted and probably dangerous to change any pattern.

The postulates also lead to vacuous explanations like Kluckhohn's. After stating the major question and basic postulate, Kluckhohn proceeds to describe many adjustive and adaptive consequences of witchcraft. They include (1) expressing aggression outside the group, since accused witches are generally outsiders; (2) retarding the accumulation of wealth, since rich people are frequently accused; and (3) preventing adultery, since fear of witches keeps people from leaving their homes at night.

The form of this type of explanation is:

(1) Social patterns persist if and only if they are adaptive (or functional or fulfill needs);

(2) Pattern X is adaptive;

Therefore, pattern X has persisted.

Such explanations are vacuous because the term "adaptive" or "needs" or "functional" is so loosely defined that all social patterns can be viewed as adaptive (or maladaptive). "Adaptive" is used to include anything that is beneficial to some groups or system. With a little imagination, one can show that any social pattern has adaptive consequences for some states of some systems and maladaptive consequences for some states of the same or other systems. Therefore, the presence or absence of any social pattern can be "explained" by this assumption, and any social pattern can be used to confirm or falsify the assumption. For example, one could focus on the maladaptive consequences of witchcraft and argue that since witchcraft has persisted and is maladaptive, the assumption is falsified.

This problem has been pointed out clearly in many critiques of functional analysis (Merton 1949; Nagel 1957); it is usually stated as the necessity for clear system reference or for defining "functional" or "adaptive" relative to specific states of specific systems. Kluckhohn is aware of the problem, and Merton discusses it explicitly and at length in his famous paper "Manifest and Latent Functions" (1949). Nonetheless, Kluckhohn, Merton in his explanation of city bosses (1949), and many less competent functionalists often point to the functions or beneficial effects of the phenomenon being considered and write as if this constituted an explanation of the phenomenon. These interpretations often contain valuable hypotheses about how the phenomenon is related to other parts of the society, but they typically ignore the maladaptive consequences of the phenomenon and hinder the development of theory by implying that the task of explanation has already been partially accomplished.

The form of functional explanations. Kluckhohn's second line of argument in explaining Navajo witchcraft is based on the beginnings of a theory of functional prerequisites which limits the relevant consequences of witchcraft to the effective management of anxiety and hostility. The outline of his argument, leaving out many complications, is (1) if a society is to survive as an integrated system, it must provide a relatively nondisruptive way of expressing or dealing with hostility and anxiety; (2) hostility and anxiety can be managed through witchcraft and related scapegoating behavior or through withdrawal, passivity, sublimation, or other functionally equivalent patterns; (3) because of various conditions of Navajo society, the functional equivalents of witchcraft cannot be the main ways of dealing with anxiety and hostility; and finally (4) Navajo society has survived. From these assumptions (1 and 2) and initial conditions (3 and 4), Kluckhohn derives his explicandum: Navajo witchcraft patterns have survived.

The form of the argument is represented in the following scheme:

(1) If a society survives (A), then hostility is managed (B);

(2) If hostility is managed (B), then witchcraft (C) or a functional equivalent (D) is present;

(3) The functional equivalents of witchcraft (D) are not present in Navajo society;

(4) Navajo society has survived (A);

   Therefore, witchcraft is present in Navajo society (C).

Kluckhohn's argument here is one of the most sophisticated and precise attempts to construct a general functional explanation. It also illustrates one form of an adequate functional explanation,

which henceforth will be referred to as the paradigm of functional explanations: (1) if a system survives or is integrated, then a functional prerequisite is fulfilled; (2) if this prerequisite is fulfilled, then pattern X or its equivalent is present in the system; (3) the functional equivalents are not present in system S; (4) S has survived or is integrated, and therefore X is present in S. There are other forms of explanation that use the basic concepts of functionalism, but this form seems to be implicit in most traditional functional analyses.

Let us first consider the simplest question: the logic of the explanation. Substituting symbols for the phrases in Kluckhohn's argument, it is apparent that the logic is sound: (1) if A then B; (2) if B then C or D; (3) D is false; (4) A is true, and therefore C is true. Hempel (1959) has argued that in the typical functional explanation the second assumption is usually stated in reverse. Ignoring the functional equivalent term D for purposes of clarity, this means changing assumption (2) to "if C then B." The argument is then logically incorrect and contains the fallacy of affirming the consequent: if A then B; if C then B and A is true; therefore C is true. However, Hempel has misinterpreted the functionalists, which is easy to do given the discursive-essay style of most functional explanations.

In logic, the statement "if A then B" or "$A \supset B$" is identical with the statement "if not–B then not–A" (Kemeny, Snell & Thompson 1956). But when a functionalist says, "witchcraft results in the effective management of hostility," he does not mean "if witchcraft, then management of hostility." This would be identical to saying, "if hostility is not managed, then there will not be witchcraft," and most functionalists would not want to say that, since they would hypothesize that managing hostility depends on several factors in addition to witchcraft (and its functional equivalents). What they mean to say is "if witchcraft (or its equivalent) is not present, then hostility is not managed," which is logically identical with assumption (2) in the above paradigm. In other words, a given social pattern and its equivalents are typically interpreted as necessary but not sufficient conditions for fulfilling a functional prerequisite.

The major problems in Kluckhohn's explanation concern the basic concepts of functional theory: adaptation or survival, integration, functional prerequisites, and functional equivalents. An adequate theory or explanation requires clear definition of these concepts and direct or indirect verification of the assumptions in which they are interrelated.

However, this requirement is so difficult that almost all functionalists, including Kluckhohn, fail to meet it. It is so difficult that at this stage of the development of social science it might be advisable to abandon the attempt to construct functional theories or explanations at the total society level.

System reference.   In Kluckhohn's first assumption, the crucial terms are survival and management of hostility. Neither term is defined precisely enough to allow discrimination between societies that have survived or have managed hostility and those that have not. Some of the problems involved in conceptualizing survival, integration, and functional prerequisites will be discussed in later sections.

The remaining term in the first assumption is "society," and here again we run into difficulties. Any theory must specify its scope—the units to which it applies and under what conditions, and "society" is a unit that is notoriously difficult to define. Kluckhohn himself states that it is questionable whether the Navajo as a whole constitute an integrated society, and a crucial part of his interpretation refers not to Navajo society, but to the consumption unit of several families. Witchcraft accusations are generally made outside the consumption unit but within Navajo society; therefore the statement that witchcraft manages hostility by directing aggression outside the group is true only of the consumption groups. Yet Kluckhohn's first assumption refers to a different unit—society. This shift invalidates his argument. His assumptions here are essentially: if a society survives (A), then hostility is directed outside the society (B); if hostility is directed outside consumption groups (C), then witchcraft is present (D). It is impossible to deduce anything from these assumptions since B and C are not the same.

Functional equivalents.   In Kluckhohn's second assumption we come to the most admirable part of his argument, for, unlike most functionalists, Kluckhohn explicitly faces the issue of functional equivalents. His inability to handle it adequately indicates the difficulty of the task.

The concept of functional equivalents is based on the idea that several social patterns can fill the same function or have the same consequence; to put it colloquially, "there's more than one way to skin a cat." The concept has been useful in suggesting the classification of social patterns on the basis of common function. Such classification often reveals important similarities among apparently different social patterns, for example, the similarities between witchcraft and racial prejudice

when both are viewed as ways of focusing aggression outside the group. However, the concept leads to great difficulties in functional explanations of a particular social pattern.

Kluckhohn's second assumption states that witchcraft or its functional equivalent is a necessary condition of managing hostility. The assumption is meaningful (directly or indirectly testable) only if it is possible to distinguish between patterns that are and are not equivalents of witchcraft. This requires listing all functional equivalents, or categorizing them, or stating their distinctive attributes. This must be done in such a way that the assumption is falsifiable—in this instance, so that it is logically possible for a society to manage hostility and not contain witchcraft or any equivalent pattern.

Kluckhohn's approach is to list the functional equivalents of witchcraft, and he states: "Withdrawal, passivity, sublimation, conciliation, flight and other responses" are alternative adjustive responses to hostile feelings (1944, p. 51). One problem with this and all lists is that there is no reason not to add more items, thereby making assumption (2) virtually unfalsifiable. Kluckhohn also attempts to identify the distinctive attributes of all the patterns on this list: they are all adjustive responses to hostility. But this only makes assumption (2) a tautology: if hostility is managed, then there will be witchcraft or some other way of managing hostility.

The need for theory.   After defining the functional equivalents of a pattern, another task remains. In order to explain why a particular social pattern is present instead of another, functionally equivalent pattern, it is necessary to develop a set of assumptions or a theory that specifies which pattern will occur under which conditions. Kluckhohn implicitly states such theories as he eliminates the functional equivalents on his list on the basis of specific conditions of Navajo society or its environment. For example, he says that withdrawal is of limited effectiveness because Navajo "types of shelter and the needs for co-operation for economic ends sharply limit the privacy of individuals" (1944, p. 52). Kluckhohn is moving in the right direction here, but he is clearly a long way from formulating a clear and explicit theory about the conditions determining the occurrence of a particular social pattern.

It should be noted that if such theories are developed, functional explanations would be expanded to include the cause of origin of social patterns and the cause of their persistence (Bredemeier 1955). Most traditional functional explanations of a social pattern X refer to the causes of X only if there is a reciprocal relationship in which X causes itself, that is, if X has certain effects on Y that in turn cause X. In the paradigm of functional explanations, social pattern X is explained by its effects and not by its causes, "cause" here meaning the necessary or sufficient antecedent conditions for pattern X. But the paradigm can be expanded to include assumptions about the conditions determining the presence of a particular pattern, following Kluckhohn's procedure, and these assumptions would probably take the form of stating the causes of the origin and persistence of pattern X.

Such an expansion has the additional advantage of making it easier to include social change in traditional functional analyses. If one excepts the concept of functional differentiation (Parsons 1964), which has limited applicability, it must be admitted that traditional functional analysis is not very useful in dealing with change. However, with the specification of antecedent conditions determining particular social patterns, it would be possible to predict the change from one social pattern to another, functionally equivalent pattern.

Kluckhohn's explanation of Navajo witchcraft illustrates two major problems in traditional functional explanations: consistent system reference and functional equivalents. Other traditional explanations will be considered in the following discussion of the concepts of functional prerequisites, adaptation, and integration. We will return to Kluckhohn in the discussion of models of functional systems.

Functional prerequisites. The remaining problems in traditional functional explanations concern the definition of the concepts in the first assumption of such explanations: if a system survives or is integrated, then a certain functional prerequisite is fulfilled.

The best-known attempt to formulate a list of needs or prerequisites is that of Aberle and his co-workers (1950). They start with a definition of the survival of a society, which includes biological survival of its members and the absence of general apathy, and then state nine functional prerequisites, such as regulating affect and controlling disruptive behavior. The list is presented as a tentative set of cross-cultural categories, an improvement on the standard chapter titles in monographs.

This type of list is not very helpful in constructing functional explanations, because it does not limit the domain of functional prerequisites. The needs are so broad that almost any social process can be seen as contributing to at least one of them, and, being a list, there are few constraints on adding more needs. But a limited set of prerequisites is essential to functional explanation; without it, an imaginative investigator can "explain" any social pattern merely by describing some consequence or effect of the pattern and arguing that this consequence is a functional prerequisite.

There are two main approaches to arriving at a limited set of prerequisites. One is to construct a set of prerequisites and empirically test whether they have been fulfilled in surviving societies, while other conceivable prerequisites have not. The second approach is to devise a theory that includes an assumption specifying social prerequisites. The assumption would not be directly testable. It would have to be combined with other propositions stating the empirical implications of (1) asserting that all societies must meet these prerequisites or (2) classifying social patterns according to the prerequisites they meet.

Parsons (1961) is using the second approach when he asserts that all systems must meet the prerequisites of latent pattern maintenance, integration, goal attainment, and adaptation. He is not making an empirical statement but is proposing that it would be fruitful to categorize and interpret social structures in terms of their contributions to these functions. His system is not directly useful in explaining social patterns because, as yet, he has not developed a clear set of propositions that specify the empirical relevance of placing a structure in one of the four categories as opposed to another. This crucial step was made in Bales's general theory of functional prerequisites (1950). He specifies two basic functions—adaptation and integration—and supplements this nonempirical assertion with a complex set of propositions about the empirical processes that accompany each function. For example, adaptation is associated with increasing division of labor, stratification, and formality, while the opposite characterizes integration. This suggests specific predictions about the attributes of organizations oriented to adaptation, or of task leaders as opposed to expressive leaders, or of small groups in the adaptive phase. Although Bales's theory still awaits precise formulation, it is a rare example of a theory that is both general and functional and that leads to adequate explanations or precise predictions [see INTERACTION, *article on* INTERACTION PROCESS ANALYSIS].

Adaptation and integration. The difficulty in defining the prerequisites for the adaptation or integration of social systems is based in part on the ambiguity of the concepts "adaptation" (or "survival") and "integration." These concepts are crucial to the first assumption in the paradigm of functional explanations: if a system survives or is integrated, then certain functional prerequisites are fulfilled. The assumption requires a definition that will discriminate between systems that are adapted or integrated and those that are not; and this has proved to be difficult. The concept of adaptation is further complicated by its association with evolutionary theory.

The difficulty in defining adaptation has long been recognized (Radcliffe-Brown 1952). Adaptation may be equated with physical survival, but this runs into the problem that societies, unlike organisms, rarely fail to survive in the sense of keeping enough of their members alive and together. Most recorded cases of the physical death of societies are the direct result of hostile action by overwhelmingly powerful outsiders who are new to the environment, and this is not the kind of situation with which functionalists are usually concerned. Since almost all societies survive, barring sudden catastrophe, it is impossible to test a statement of the form "X is necessary for survival" if X is universal. It is also impossible to test a statement of the form "X_1 is necessary for the survival of social system S_1" if X_1 has always been present in S_1.

Adaptation or survival may also be defined as maintenance of the social organization or structural continuity. Survival in this sense is by no means universal; in fact it might be difficult to find a society that has survived over the last century, i.e., one that has not undergone basic change. This leads to new problems, because functional explanations of the persistence of social patterns require the assumption that the system has survived (statement 3 in the paradigm). Precise definitions of "stability" or "structural continuity" would have to be worked out, and such explanations would be limited to societies that fit the definition of "stable." Alternatively, adaptation can be defined as ensuring high reproduction rates following the biologists' revision of Darwin (Simpson 1949). This definition has the advantage of discriminating among societies, being easy to measure, and making it possible to distinguish different degrees of adaptation, as opposed to the all-or-nothing criteria of physical survival. These two later definitions or others probably could be formulated precisely and could be used in specifying the prerequisites of adaptation. If the problem of functional equivalents could be solved, it would then be possible to explain social patterns according to the paradigm of functional explanations.

However, many interpretations in terms of adaptation do not follow the paradigm. They often use the form of argument discussed in the section on vacuous explanations (patterns persist only if they are adaptive; pattern X is adaptive; therefore X persists). This type of argument is not vacuous if "adaptive" is precisely defined, and some investigators seem to be moving toward a fairly precise definition which equates "adaptation" with "maintaining adequate levels of nutrition and health for most members of the society." Harris' interpretation of the sacred cows of India (1965) and other recent papers on economics and ecology in primitive societies (Leeds & Vayda 1965; Suttles 1960) are examples of this kind of argument, in which a social pattern is interpreted by showing how it helps to ensure an adequate food supply. These interpretations are unobjectionable if they are viewed as illustrations of a specific hypothesis, such as Harris' hypothesis that here is a "cross-cultural tendency to maximize production of food" (1959, p. 194). However, the interpretations are often presented as if they were explaining a social pattern in terms of the assumption that "social patterns persist only if they are adaptive." Adequate explanations require plausible assumptions, and the plausibility of this assumption rests on shaky grounds.

First, the assumption is plausible if one accepts the idea that there is a process of selection of the fittest social patterns or societies. But I doubt that many social scientists imagine, for example, that some early societies developed the family and therefore survived, while others did not and therefore died out, or that some Northwest Coast Indians developed the potlatch and survived, while the others became extinct. One alternative and somewhat more plausible notion is that some groups developed distinct methods of socialization, or the potlatch, and these groups reproduced faster than the others and eventually dominated the society. However, I know of no data that clearly demonstrate that either of these assumed processes ever occurred except in the few situations where extinction through disease or military aggression was imminent. Another alternative idea is that adaptive social traits are more widespread than less adaptive traits because the weak tend to imitate the strong (Dore 1961). Social patterns may diffuse to weaker groups from groups with more resources and power, that is, with patterns that are more adaptive.

The assumption that only adaptive traits persist is also plausible if restricted to the manifest functions of social patterns, that is, to the effects of the pattern that are recognized and intended by members of the society (Merton 1949). If the decision makers of a society are aware of the adaptive value of a social pattern, this will probably influence whether they want to maintain the pattern. However, the crucial variables here are the decision makers' beliefs about the adaptive or integrative consequences of the pattern. These events are a subset of the class of goal-oriented behavior; people behave so as to maximize certain goals and values, and one of these goals is usually successful adaptation to the environment. In these cases, it would be better to abandon functional terminology for a more cognitive, actor-oriented approach.

The concept of integration is just as problematic as that of survival. Integration is defined in a wide variety of ways and often masks value judgments or unnecessarily complicates a clear nonfunctional statement. This section will focus on the difficulties in defining integration so that it can be used in traditional functional explanations. Many analyses involving integration or adaptation supplement or replace the traditional approach with the use of models of self-regulating systems, and this aspect of functionalism will be considered later in the discussion of formal functionalism.

There are two major approaches to defining integration. One draws on system theory and defines integration in terms of interdependence and frequent interaction among the members of a bounded unit. Although the approach leads to a relatively precise and manageable definition, it excludes many aspects of the intuitive notion of integration. The second approach draws on the ideas of congruency and fit or the absence of conflict, strain, or anxiety. The notion of fit is extremely vague. The statement that pattern X fits with pattern Y means only that there is *some* relationship between X and Y. The type of relationship is often left unspecified.

The typical functionalist approach to the concept of integration is to equate fit with lack of conflict. Four kinds of definitions in terms of absence of conflict can be distinguished. The first defines integration as logical–meaningful consistency among social patterns (Sorokin [1937–1941] 1962, vol. 1, pp. 15, 23). Integration means that similar themes, values, or principles are used in all spheres of social life. One ambiguity in this definition is the meaning of absence of integration. It could mean conflict within the cultural system; however, many functionalists seem to mean conflict within individuals, and they make the dubious assumption

that logical inconsistency among the beliefs will produce psychological conflict. The second definition of integration focuses on the absence of aggression and exploitation of the powerless among members of a social system. An integrated system is marked by cooperation, consensus on mutual rights and duties, and loyalties that crosscut the subgroups within the system. The third definition focuses on the absence of conflicting demands on individuals as to the appropriate behavior or feelings in a specific situation; and the fourth definition concerns the fit between an individual's motivation and the behavior required by the social system.

The obvious general problem in using any of these definitions is that a functional explanation must assume that the society being considered is integrated. This is proposition (3) in the argument: (1) if the system is integrated, then need N is filled; (2) if N, then pattern X; and (3) the system is integrated; therefore X. This limitation is implicitly recognized by functionalists, for they tend to shift to nonfunctional explanations when interpreting social patterns that result in increased conflict. One example of such a shift is Parsons' discussion of the female role in the United States (1942).

It seems very unlikely that any society or large social system is perfectly integrated, regardless of which definition is used. Therefore, integration needs to be defined in a relative way: if a system has Y amount of integration, then N will be fulfilled. This is not an impossible task but a difficult one. It requires extensive theoretical and empirical work on the distribution and implications of different levels of integration, the prerequisites for a given level of integration, and the functionally equivalent social patterns that fulfill each prerequisite. Until some such specification of integration is made, the term cannot be used in explanations [*see* INTEGRATION, *article on* SOCIAL INTEGRATION].

Alternative approaches. Traditional functionalism has been defined as those analyses that use certain concepts (adaptation, integration, functional prerequisites, and equivalents) and that explicitly or implicitly use the paradigm of functional explanation in which social patterns are explained by their effects. Because of the many problems discussed above, few functionalists succeed in formulating adequate explanations or theories. If some of the concepts are abandoned and the paradigm is changed, then alternative types of analysis are revealed that have a better prospect of leading to adequate explanations. Although some of these alternatives are frequently used, they are not labeled as "functional analysis" as often as the traditional approach.

One frequently used alternative is to turn functional explanations around, that is, to reverse the explicans and the explicandum in the paradigm of explanation so that phenomena are explained by their causes, not by their effects or functions. Instead of explaining a social pattern by deducing it from the assumption that the society has survived, one explains the survival of the society by the patterns whose effect is to ensure survival. For example, the statement that "witchcraft lessens in-group aggression" is used to explain rates of aggression, not witchcraft. This approach, combined with a focus on systems other than total societies, includes studies of the prerequisites for the survival of marriages, utopias, associations, or other social systems. It also includes studies of the prerequisites for the structural continuity of social systems, that is, of the conditions for maintaining a certain type of social organization in a specified environment. This is the approach described by Levy in his outline of "structural–functional requisite analysis" (1952, pp. 34 ff.).

A second possible change of traditional functionalism, as mentioned above, is to consider smaller systems under specified conditions rather than total societies in general. One great advantage in this procedure is that systems such as therapy groups, unions, or lineages often fail to survive or seem to have low levels of integration; therefore, statements about the prerequisites for survival or integration can be tested. In addition, the possible functional prerequisites and equivalents are probably more limited, and, finally, there would be less difficulty in maintaining consistent system reference because there are fewer subsystems than in a society.

A more radical change is to abandon the focus on adaptation and integration and to consider the prerequisites of any state of a system—such states as high suicide rates, for instance, or high or low levels of in-group aggression. With this revision, we have eliminated the distinguishing attributes of functional analysis: explaining patterns by their beneficial (adaptive or integrative) effects. Functionalism so defined includes all analyses of the prerequisites, conditions, or determinants of any attribute or state of human behavior. Very little information is transmitted by labeling all these analyses as "functional," and very few social scientists use the term in this way.

However, there is a type of functionalism that does not involve explaining patterns by their bene-ficial effects and is a distinct form of analysis. This is formal functionalism, which is distinguished by the use of models of self-regulating or functional systems. Traditional functional analyses contain many examples of such systems: of reciprocal relationships, of one pattern varying so as to maintain another within a given range, and of complex feedbacks and causal chains that involve many parts of a system. But some traditional functional explanations do not utilize this type of model. For example, the explanation of the incest taboo in terms of its function of creating alliances among families, or the explanation of rites of passage by their function of reducing conflict between old and new roles, does not involve reciprocal or self-regulating relationships. Therefore, the theoretical orientation of traditional functionalism and the model of self-regulating or functional systems should be kept distinct.

The assumption that models of functional systems fit society is the basis of some of the concepts and procedures of traditional functional analysis. The stress on latent functions—effects that are unintended and unrecognized—is based in part on the assumption that models of complex, self-regulating systems apply to many social systems. Therefore, a change in one social pattern may affect seemingly unrelated patterns or, because of compensating changes in other social patterns, may have effects that are opposite from those intended —or no effects at all. Another instance is the functionalist postulate that all social patterns "are functional for the *entire* social or cultural system" (Merton [1949] 1957, p. 25). This is another way of saying that the whole social system forms some sort of self-regulating system. These are premature judgments about the extent to which models of functional or self-regulating systems accurately represent the relationships found in social systems. The applicability of the models is an empirical question for which the relevant data have not been collected.

Formal functionalism

Formal functionalism consists in the attempt to construct models that describe how the units of a system are interrelated so as to maintain each other or some other state of the system. In contrast to traditional functionalism, it contains no theoretical orientation and has no empirical content. The models must be supplemented by theory and research that specify the empirical units or variables that correspond to the abstract elements in the models.

As an illustration of the use of such models,

Kluckhohn's analysis of Navajo witchcraft is useful again. Kluckhohn supplements his structural analysis with an examination of changes over time. He describes the deprivation and anxiety of the Navajo during their confinement at Fort Sumner and several decades later, during a period of lesser stress that was caused by the livestock reduction program. He notes that warfare was impossible for the Navajo after Fort Sumner, that witchcraft accusations and executions were most frequent shortly after Fort Sumner, and that accusations also increased after the inception of the livestock program. In his interpretation, Kluckhohn assumes, first, that deprivation and frustration cause increased hostile feelings, and, second, that these impulses will cause in-group aggression unless the hostility is directed outside the group; warfare and witchcraft are viewed as social patterns that direct aggression to outsiders. Given these assumptions, the changes in frustration, hostility, aggression, and witchcraft can be accurately represented as a self-regulating system directed to maintaining a low level of in-group aggression. When the environment (the United States government) imposes increased frustration, hostile impulses increase, but this is followed by increased witchcraft accusations, given the impossibility of warfare, and this aggression to outsiders reduces hostile impulses back to a level where they no longer threaten the maintenance of low in-group aggression.

Nagel's model. The model used in Kluckhohn's analysis has been precisely described by Nagel (1957). Starting with Merton's article "Manifest and Latent Functions" (1949), Nagel rigorously describes the model that seems to be implicit in functional analysis in the social sciences.

A functional system, according to Nagel's definition, is made up of two types of variables: G's and state coordinates. G is the property of the system that is maintained or is stable. State coordinates determine the presence or absence of G and may include parts of the system's environment. The values of the state coordinates vary to such an extent that the maintenance of G is threatened, but when one exceeds the "safe" limits for G, the other(s) compensates and G is maintained. Such a system of G and state coordinates may be called functional with respect to G, and the state coordinates may be described as having the function of maintaining G.

For example, a small task-oriented group could be treated as a functional system (Bales 1950). Let G be the solution of the group's task or problem. Let the state coordinates be task-oriented activity and emotionally supportive activity. If these three variables can be usefully treated as a functional system, then: (1) problem solution is dependent on task-oriented activity and emotionally supportive activity; (2) at certain times, there will be such a preponderance of task-oriented activity that problem solution will be threatened because of decreased motivation or resentment over following others' suggestions—at these times emotionally supportive activity will increase, and problem solution will no longer be threatened; (3) at certain times, there will be such a preponderance of emotionally supportive activity that problem solution will be threatened. At these times task-oriented activity will increase to maintain problem solution or G.

By definition, more than one state of the system leads to maintenance of G. Thus, in the preceding example, eventual problem solution might result both from initially high task-oriented activity and low supportive activity, followed by increased supportive activity, and from initially low task-oriented activity and high supportive activity, followed by increased task activity. In a functional system there is more than one combination of the values of certain parts of the system which will result in the same trait or will have the same consequences (maintenance of G). This is one way of stating the notion of functional equivalents.

The other crucial elements in Nagel's model concern the limitations of the variation of state coordinates. Three kinds of limits are relevant. First, there are the limits dictated by physical reality. For example, the amount of interaction in a given period cannot exceed the maximum number of acts possible in that time period. Second, within the limits of physical reality there are limits determined by the definition of the system under consideration. If a property is used to define a system, one cannot analyze conditions under which this property disappears. The third and most important set of limits are those beyond which compensation is impossible and G ceases to exist. The potential stability of a given G in a specific functional system can be expressed in terms of the discrepancy between two of these sets of limits: the possible variation for each state coordinate and the limits of variation within which compensation by other state coordinates will occur. G becomes less stable as the discrepancy between these two ranges increases.

It should be noted that, contrary to the strategy of traditional functionalism, stability of G is not *assumed*. The traditional approach is to assume the stability of G (integration or survival) and explain state coordinates in terms of their efficiency in maintaining G; states of the system are explained by their effects. In Nagel's model, the stability or disappearance of G is explained by the extent to which state coordinates compensate for each other's variation; states of the system are explained by their causes. A rough definition of "cause" is being used here: A causes B if the occurrence of B depends on the previous occurrence of A.

Some functionalists have suggested that the notion of cause is not applicable to complex social systems, but this seems to mean only that social patterns are often caused by a complex set of interrelated factors and not by one simple factor. For instance, in the small group example, task solution depends on: (1) a certain amount of task-oriented activity; (2) emotionally supportive activity; (3) mechanisms which cause a switch from one type of activity to the other when one type is dangerously low; and perhaps additionally on (4) some reciprocal relationship whereby group perception of progress in solving the task is necessary to maintain the two types of activity. This is a complex system, but these four factors can be isolated as the determinants or causes of task solution. The unwillingness to use the term "cause" often indicates only that the analysis is incomplete and that it is not yet possible to clearly define the relevant parts of the system and to specify the direction and magnitude of the relationships among these parts.

To summarize Nagel's model, a functional system is one that satisfies the following conditions: (1) the system can be analyzed into a set of interdependent variables or parts; (2) the values of these variables determine whether or not a certain property G will occur in the system; (3) there are limits on the variation of state coordinates such that variation within the limits is followed by compensating variation of other state coordinates, and G is maintained; (4) variation beyond these limits is not compensated for by other state coordinates, and G disappears.

The type of analysis suggested by Nagel's formalization would probably avoid many problems of traditional functional analysis. As in any formal model, this one specifies the entities that must be clearly and consistently defined: the system, goal state, state coordinates, and the limits on their variation. Any state of any system might be viewed as a G state in a functional system; therefore the problematic concepts of survival and integration are not necessary, although they could be used as the G state (see, for example, the series of analyses

in Leeds & Vayda 1965, in which the G state is the survival of the population in the face of variation in the environment). The model also encompasses various kinds of change: (1) goal states that are moving equilibria; (2) compensating changes in state coordinates; (3) compensating changes in subsystems that are treated as state coordinates of a higher level system; and (4) disappearance of G resulting from state coordinates exceeding the limits of compensation (Cancian 1960–1961).

The contribution of formal functionalism to the explanation of social patterns is quite different from that of traditional functionalism, because a formal model lacks substantive propositions and therefore, by itself, cannot explain anything. If the correspondence between the model and the parts of a specific system are demonstrated, this would constitute, at the least, a precise description of the system. The description might also be called a "little theory" (Cancian 1965, chapter 13)—a "theory" because it would explain and predict how variance in one part of the system would affect other parts of the system, and a "little theory" because the propositions would be limited to one specific system. In order to construct a general theory or explanation, it would be necessary to add an assumption stating that the model fit a certain class of systems, of which the specific system was a member.

Specification of functional equivalents. The major problem left unresolved in this model is that of functional equivalents. An example illustrates the difficulty. Assume that one is investigating the system of relationships between North American college students and their parents and that one attempts to explain independence from parents (G) by the state coordinates of peer-organized rebellion against authority, communication with parents, and other variables. How would one deal with the different types of organized rebellion, such as panty raids, burning draft cards, or picketing for civil rights? The approach suggested by the model would be to consider only the primary function of these activities for the goal state of independence. Panty raids, burning draft cards, etc., would be ranked according to the degree of rebellion involved, and all other differences among the activities would be ignored. The advantage of this method is that it results in a general explanation that includes college students participating in various types of peer-organized rebellion. Note, however, that the idea of functional equivalents then has no special meaning; it merely indicates that a general variable takes various empirical forms. For example, reinforcement can take the form of food or water.

As it is usually used, "functional equivalents" does have a special meaning. There is often an implicit assumption that if one social pattern disappeared, a functionally equivalent pattern would appear or would be more likely to appear. This aspect of functional equivalents can be dealt with by treating the equivalent patterns as a subsystem, with the G of fulfilling the function of the patterns. In this subsystem, as one rebellious activity decreases, some other activity increases so as to maintain peer-organized rebellion, *if* the subsystem is a functional system with respect to rebellion. An examination of this subsystem would indicate the conditions (limits of variance) under which a functional equivalent would take the place of a disappearing activity. The problem of predicting whether a specific rebellious activity would be maintained within certain limits could be handled by considering the subsystem in which the G state is that activity and the state coordinates are the variables that maintain the activity.

Alternative models. Every functional system must contain certain minimal attributes: (1) variable A that is regulated or maintained within a range; (2) variable B that does the regulating; (3) a mechanism that communicates the variation of A to B. These minimal requirements are exemplified by the famous system: room temperature–furnace–thermostat, and by various systems in the social science area (Lennard & Bernstein 1960). Note that the existence of feedback, or reciprocal or mutual causation between A and B, is not enough. The feedback must be of a special kind; it must operate so as to maintain at least one of the variables within a given range. For example, according to many observers, the system of "juvenile crime–reform school" is not a functional system with respect to maintaining low crime rates. There is a reciprocal relationship; reform school does feed back to crime rates, but its effect appears to increase crime.

This minimal functional system can be elaborated in many ways, resulting in alternative functional models. The primary alternative to Nagel's model is based on changing his notion of a G state. Nagel's system is hierarchical, that is, it contains several variables that interact so as to maintain some state of the system within a given range (G), and the effect of G on these variables is not considered. In the alternative, horizontal model, the effects of the variation in G on the state coordinates are included in the analysis. Both G and the state coordinates vary so as to maintain each other within a certain range; therefore there is no reason to discriminate between the two types of variables. There are many illustrations of such systems in the area of complementary roles or interpersonal relations. Thus, an authoritarian professor and a dependent student or a sadistic–masochistic couple often maintain each other in their respective roles.

Within the general framework of a hierarchical or horizontal model, many specific varieties of functional systems can be constructed. The system may be simple and include only the minimal attributes of a functional system, or it may be very complex and contain many parts and subsystems, like McCleery's description of a prison system (Barton & Anderson 1961) or Parsons' model of the social system (1961).

The system may operate so as to maintain one, or several, or all of its components within a given range. Systems also differ in the amount of variation necessary to set off compensating processes, in the limits beyond which compensation is impossible, and in the time required for compensation. When it does occur, the compensation may be too much or too little or out of phase (Scientific American 1955). Compensation for the variance of one component may take the form of pushing back that component within a range that is less threatening to the system, or it may consist of a proportional change in other components. There are many possible complexities and variations in functional systems, some of which are described in the literature, especially in the fields of economics, cybernetics, and systems engineering.

Using models. There are two major procedures for utilizing functional models in constructing theories or general explanations. One approach is to begin with a careful investigation of a single system. After describing the major components of the system and how they are interrelated, the model implicit in the description can be examined. Some previously developed model may fit the description and produce new statements about the system, or it may be necessary to construct a model. The next step is to verify the "fit" by examining the particular system over time, observing variations in the components, and seeing if there is, in fact, compensation that maintains some components within a given range. The final step is to try to generalize this "little theory" to other systems by examining the boundary conditions or parameters of the systems and by restating the components in more general terms. An example of this approach is Sweet's analysis of how bedouin camping units maintain a certain size camel herd by raiding, migration, splitting up the social unit, and other means (1965). Her description could probably be restated as a theory of the bedouin camel complex, that is, as a limited set of propositions about herd size, raiding frequency, etc., and the relations between them. This theory could be tested against the historical record of bedouin behavior. If verified, it might be possible to restate the "little theory" in more general terms, so that, given certain conditions, it applies to camel herders in general, or pastoral peoples, or people dependent on material goods whose availability fluctuates widely.

Another approach is to start with an abstract theory about a general class of phenomena that are interrelated so as to form a functional system. This procedure is exemplified in the research on balance theory in social psychology (Heider 1958). The basic idea in the theory is that individuals will vary their sentiments and evaluations so as to maintain a balanced state. Thus, if two individuals like each other and one of them likes a third person but the other does not, then the individuals will move into a balanced state, that is, they will both come to like or dislike the third person, or they will change their feelings about each other. The relationships among components in this theory correspond to the relationships in mathematical graph theory, and the application of this mathematical model has made the theory more precise and has yielded new propositions (Berger et al. 1962).

These two approaches start with a specific or general empirical system and then examine the model or set of relationships in the system. An alternative would be to start with a model and then search for some empirical systems that fit it. This approach would be much less likely to succeed than the first two because the investigator might not encounter any phenomenon of interest that fits the model, and then the effort of constructing the model would be completely wasted. However, there are some guidelines for locating empirical systems that operate like functional systems.

A primary indicator of the applicability of a functional model is the persistence of a social pattern despite forces that tend to destroy the pattern. For example, the apparent persistence of European gypsies suggests the presence of compensating processes, as does the persistence, despite reform movements, of deviant patterns such as city bosses or prostitution. Of course, it may be that such patterns persist because of some constant, powerful factor or factors, but it would probably be fruitful to try to analyze the persistence in terms of a functional model. Another relevant attribute is the presence of inherently runaway processes that are kept within limits. Some of the social processes that might increase indefinitely, but often do not, are the exploi-

tation of followers by powerful leaders or the rejection of competing loyalties by a sexually attracted couple (Slater 1963). Still another attribute is the presence of reciprocal relationships—that is, of regular sequences of social patterns that return to the point of origin. The most obvious class of phenomena in this category is self–other patterns, or complementary roles, but reciprocal relationships also occur in large social systems, as shown by Leach's analysis of cyclic change between two political systems in Burma (1954). These various attributes provide clues as to the applicability of a functional model, but in every case the appropriateness of a functional model and the fit of different types of models are questions that must be empirically investigated.

The usefulness of models in general cannot be disputed, and the importance of constructing models will surely increase as social scientists attempt to deal with complex systems of variables in a precise manner and as they shift from monocausal theories to the notion of interdependent systems. The usefulness of models of functional systems in particular depends on the extent to which the phenomena investigated by social scientists exhibit equilibrating or self-maintaining processes. Formal functionalism is based on the most valuable part of the research strategy of functional analysis: an attempt to view behavior patterns as mutually reinforcing parts of an equilibrating system. Whether or not this strategy will succeed in yielding general and verified theories is an empirical question that will not be settled until this strategy is given a thorough trial.

FRANCESCA M. CANCIAN

[*Directly related are the entries* INTEGRATION; INTERACTION, *article on* INTERACTION PROCESS ANALYSIS; SYSTEMS ANALYSIS. *Other relevant material may be found in* MODELS, MATHEMATICAL; SIMULATION; SOCIAL STRUCTURE; SOCIOLOGY, *article on* THE DEVELOPMENT OF SOCIOLOGICAL THOUGHT; *and in the biographies of* DURKHEIM; HENDERSON; MALINOWSKI; RADCLIFFE-BROWN; WEBER, MAX.]

BIBLIOGRAPHY

ABERLE, DAVID F. et al. 1950 The Functional Prerequisites of a Society. *Ethics* 60:100–111.

BALES, ROBERT F. 1950 *Interaction Process Analysis: A Method for the Study of Small Groups.* Reading, Mass.: Addison-Wesley.

BARTON, ALLEN H.; and ANDERSON, BO 1961 Change in an Organizational System: Formalization of a Qualitative Study. Pages 400–418 in Amitai Etzioni (editor), *Complex Organizations: A Sociological Reader.* New York: Holt.

BERGER, JOSEPH et al. 1962 *Types of Formalization in Small-group Research.* Boston: Houghton Mifflin.

BLACK, MAX (editor) 1962 *The Social Theories of Talcott Parsons: A Critical Examination.* Englewood Cliffs, N.J.: Prentice-Hall.

BREDEMEIER, HARRY C. 1955 The Methodology of Functionalism. *American Sociological Review* 20:173–180.

BUCKLEY, WALTER 1957 Structural–Functional Analysis in Modern Sociology. Pages 236–259 in Howard Becker and Alvin Boskoff (editors), *Modern Sociological Theory in Continuity and Change.* New York: Dryden.

CANCIAN, FRANCESCA M. 1960–1961 Functional Analysis of Change. *American Sociological Review* 25:818–827; 26:930–931.

CANCIAN, FRANK 1965 *Economics and Prestige in a Maya Community: The Religious Cargo System in Zinacantán.* Stanford Univ. Press.

COLLINS, PAUL W. 1965 Functional Analyses in the Symposium *Man, Culture, and Animals.* Pages 271–282 in Anthony Leeds and Andrew P. Vayda (editors), *Man, Culture, and Animals: The Role of Animals in Human Ecological Adjustments.* Washington: American Association for the Advancement of Science.

DAHRENDORF, RALF 1958 Out of Utopia: Toward a Reorientation of Sociological Analysis. *American Journal of Sociology* 64:115–127.

DAVIS, KINGSLEY 1959 The Myth of Functional Analysis as a Special Method in Sociology and Anthropology. *American Sociological Review* 24:757–772.

DAVIS, KINGSLEY; and MOORE, WILBERT E. 1945 Some Principles of Stratification. *American Sociological Review* 10:242–249.

DORE, RONALD P. 1961 Function and Cause. *American Sociological Review* 26:843–853.

DURKHEIM, ÉMILE (1895) 1958 *The Rules of Sociological Method.* 8th ed. Edited by George E. G. Catlin. Glencoe, Ill.: Free Press. → First published as *Les règles de la méthode sociologique.*

FALLDING, HAROLD 1963 Functional Analysis in Sociology. *American Sociological Review* 28:5–13.

FIRTH, RAYMOND 1955 Function. *Yearbook of Anthropology* [1955]:237–258.

GOLDSCHMIDT, WALTER 1966 *Comparative Functionalism.* Berkeley and Los Angeles: Univ. of California Press.

GOULDNER, ALVIN W. 1960 The Norm of Reciprocity: A Preliminary Statement. *American Sociological Review* 25:161–178.

HARRIS, MARVIN 1959 The Economy Has No Surplus? *American Anthropologist* New Series 61:185–199.

HARRIS, MARVIN 1965 The Myth of the Sacred Cow. Pages 217–228 in Anthony Leeds and Andrew P. Vayda (editors), *Man, Culture, and Animals: The Role of Animals in Human Ecological Adjustments.* Washington: American Association for the Advancement of Science.

HEIDER, FRITZ 1958 *The Psychology of Interpersonal Relations.* New York: Wiley.

HEMPEL, CARL G. 1959 The Logic of Functional Analysis. Pages 271–307 in Llewellyn Gross (editor), *Symposium on Sociological Theory.* Evanston, Ill.: Row, Peterson.

HEMPEL, CARL G. 1965 *Aspects of Scientific Explanation, and Other Essays in the Philosophy of Science.* New York: Free Press.

HOMANS, GEORGE C. 1964 Bringing Men Back In. *American Sociological Review* 29:809–818.

JOHNSON, HARRY M. 1960 *Sociology: A Systematic Introduction.* New York: Harcourt.

KEMENY, JOHN G.; SNELL, J. LAURIE; and THOMPSON, GERALD L. (1957) 1962 *Introduction to Finite Mathematics.* Englewood Cliffs, N.J.: Prentice-Hall.

KLUCKHOHN, CLYDE 1944 *Navaho Witchcraft.* Harvard University, Peabody Museum of American Archaeology and Ethnology, Papers, Vol. 22, No. 2. Cambridge, Mass.: The Museum.

LEACH, EDMUND R. 1954 *Political Systems of Highland Burma: A Study of Kachin Social Structure.* London School of Economics and Political Science; Cambridge, Mass.: Harvard Univ. Press.

LEEDS, ANTHONY; and VAYDA, ANDREW P. (editors) 1965 *Man, Culture, and Animals: The Role of Animals in Human Ecological Adjustments.* Publication No. 78. Washington: American Association for the Advancement of Science.

LENNARD, HENRY L.; and BERNSTEIN, ARNOLD 1960 *The Anatomy of Psychotherapy: Systems of Communication and Expectation.* New York: Columbia Univ. Press.

LEVY, MARION J. 1952 *The Structure of Society.* Princeton Univ. Press.

MALINOWSKI, BRONISLAW 1931 Culture. Volume 4, pages 621–645 in *Encyclopaedia of the Social Sciences.* New York: Macmillan.

MARTINDALE, DON (editor) 1965 *Functionalism in the Social Sciences: The Strength and Limits of Functionalism in Anthropology, Economics, Political Science, and Sociology.* Philadelphia: American Academy of Political and Social Science.

MERTON, ROBERT K. (1949) 1957 Manifest and Latent Functions. Pages 21–84 in Robert K. Merton, *Social Theory and Social Structure.* Rev. & enl. ed. Glencoe, Ill.: Free Press.

MILLS, THEODORE M. 1959 Equilibrium and the Processes of Deviance and Control. *American Sociological Review* 24:671–679.

NAGEL, ERNEST 1957 A Formalization of Functionalism. Pages 247–283 in Ernest Nagel, *Logic Without Metaphysics, and Other Essays in the Philosophy of Science.* Glencoe, Ill.: Free Press.

NAGEL, ERNEST 1961 *The Structure of Science: Problems in the Logic of Scientific Explanation.* New York: Harcourt.

PARSONS, TALCOTT 1942 Age and Sex in the Social Structure of the United States. *American Sociological Review* 7:604–616.

PARSONS, TALCOTT (1961) 1965 An Outline of the Social System. Volume 1, pages 30–79 in Talcott Parsons et al. (editors), *Theories of Society: Foundations of Modern Sociological Theory.* New York: Free Press.

PARSONS, TALCOTT 1964 Evolutionary Universals in Society. *American Sociological Review* 29:339–357.

RADCLIFFE-BROWN, A. R. (1952) 1961 *Structure and Function in Primitive Society: Essays and Addresses.* London: Cohen & West; Glencoe, Ill.: Free Press.

RADCLIFFE-BROWN, A. R. 1957 *A Natural Science of Society.* Glencoe, Ill.: Free Press.

SCIENTIFIC AMERICAN 1955 *Automatic Control.* New York: Simon & Schuster.

SIMPSON, GEORGE G. (1949) 1961 *The Meaning of Evolution: A Study of the History of Life and Its Significance for Man.* New Haven: Yale Univ. Press.

SLATER, PHILIP E. 1963 On Social Regression. *American Sociological Review* 28:339–364.

SOROKIN, PITIRIM A. (1937–1941) 1962 *Social and Cultural Dynamics.* 4 vols. Englewood Cliffs, N.J.: Bedminster Press. → Volume 1: *Fluctuation of Forms of Art*. Volume 2: *Fluctuation of Systems of Truth, Ethics, and Law*. Volume 3: *Fluctuation of Social Relationships, War, and Revolution*. Volume 4: *Basic Problems, Principles, and Methods*.

SUTTLES, WAYNE 1960 Affinal Ties, Subsistence, and Prestige Among the Coast Salish. *American Anthropologist* New Series 62:296–305.

SWEET, LOUISE E. 1965 Camel Pastoralism in North Arabia and the Minimal Camping Unit. Pages 129–152 in Anthony Leeds and Andrew P. Vayda (editors), *Man, Culture, and Animals: The Role of Animals in Human Ecological Adjustments*. Washington: American Association for the Advancement of Science.

TUMIN, MELVIN M. 1953 Some Principles of Stratification: A Critical Analysis. *American Sociological Review* 18:387–394. → See the debate in this issue and in Volume 28, 1963.

VAN DEN BERGHE, PIERRE L. 1963 Dialectic and Functionalism: Toward a Theoretical Synthesis. *American Sociological Review* 28:695–705.

FUNCTIONAL INTERNATIONAL INTEGRATION

See INTERNATIONAL INTEGRATION, *article on* FUNCTIONALISM AND FUNCTIONAL INTEGRATION.

FUNCTIONAL REPRESENTATION

See INTEREST GROUPS.

FUSTEL DE COULANGES, NUMA DENIS

Numa Denis Fustel de Coulanges (1830–1889) devoted his life entirely to the study of the origin, evolution, and transformation of societies. Fustel was born in Paris. He never knew his father, a retired naval lieutenant, who died a few months after his birth. After secondary studies at the Lycée Charlemagne in Paris, he entered the École Normale Supérieure. The reactionary atmosphere then predominant in France pervaded the school and modified Fustel's previous liberalism. Graduating from that school in 1853, he spent two years at the Ecole Française d'Athènes, where he began the study of ancient Greece. Upon his return, he was appointed professor at the *lycée* at Amiens; he defended his theses for the *doctorat-ès-lettres*, the second of which, in Latin, concerned the cult of Vesta and contained in embryo the substance of *The Ancient City*, his first great historical work, published in 1864.

His tastes and his ability destined him for a university career, and in 1860 he was appointed to the chair of history in the Faculté des Lettres at Strasbourg. His brilliant teaching attracted many students, but despite this success he felt alone.

When a vacancy occurred at the Ecole Normale Supérieure, he applied for the post and for five years taught history there. His reputation as a teacher led Victor Duruy, the minister of public instruction, to entrust him with teaching history to the Empress Eugénie, the wife of Napoléon III, but the lessons were interrupted after only a few months by the outbreak of the war with Prussia.

The war had a profound effect on the patriotism of Fustel de Coulanges; it aroused his resentment against the German nation and helped to change the orientation of his investigations. He now plunged into the study of the political institutions of early medieval France and devoted the major part of his scholarly efforts to them from that time on. In December 1875 he was called to the Sorbonne to take the chair of ancient history, and in December 1878 he was appointed to the chair in medieval history, a position he kept until his death in 1889—except for three years, 1880–1883, during which he served, somewhat against his will because his health was poor, as director of the École Normale.

The first of the two principal works of Fustel de Coulanges was *The Ancient City: A Study on the Religion, Laws, and Institutions of Greece and Rome*. In the introduction the author stated that he hoped to reveal the principles and rules by which the societies of Greece and Rome were governed. Fustel's selection of a subject was not determined exclusively by the search for knowledge: what he wanted as well was to prove that the conception of Greece and Rome that people had had ever since the beginning of the French Revolution was false and that the consequences of this erroneous conception had been unfortunate. "They have deceived themselves," he said, "about the liberty of the ancients, and on this very account liberty among the moderns has been put in peril" ([1864] 1956, p. 11). And he added that such errors could be corrected only by an objective study of the history of the Greco–Roman world that would show that modern political conditions were not comparable to those of ancient societies.

According to Fustel, the formation of these societies was, in fact, based on a belief common to all the Aryan races, namely, that after death the soul continues to live, associated with the body, in the tomb. The earliest religion was ancestor worship, and the family unit that tended the sacred fire in the home became the basic unit of the ancient societies. This primitive social organization expanded by gradual stages: the *gens*, the Greek phratry, and the Roman tribe. The end point of the development was the city, which Fustel defined as "a religious association" open only to its citizens, that is, only to the members of patrician families. Over the centuries these primitive institutions lost their simplicity. The priest-kings who had governed the cities lost their political authority. The *gens* lost its cohesion; the plebs, which had been outside the city, entered into it. Then the Roman conquest transformed the character of the old cities bit by bit, by destroying their traditional municipal regimes. The triumph of Christianity was the final blow to traditional city government.

What Fustel de Coulanges argued with great logic, but perhaps at the expense of considering other relevant factors in social development, was that ancient society was founded on a particular belief and that it persisted insofar as that belief prevailed: it changed gradually as the belief weakened, and it did not survive its disappearance.

The *Histoire des institutions politiques de l'ancienne France* (1875–1889) was Fustel's second great historical work. After 1870 he devoted almost all his scholarly activity to it. The many articles that he published after 1872 in the *Revue des deux mondes*, the proceedings of the Académie des Sciences Morales et Politiques (he was elected to membership in 1865), and a number of other journals dealt chiefly with specific problems related to his major work.

The work focuses on the impact of the Germanic invasions. Fustel demonstrated the way in which the political institutions and social organization of Roman Gaul changed gradually, becoming first those of Frankish Gaul and then those of feudal France. According to the prevailing "Germanistic" conception of the great invasions, they were an avalanche that buried the Roman world. Fustel de Coulange's conception was more sophisticated. He saw the invasions as a phenomenon occurring over a long period, a slow infiltration of the empire by barbarian nations. These peoples, whether Visigoths, Burgundians, Franks, or others, were not hostile to Rome; but their invasion, combined with the effects of internal causes, produced a gradual, imperceptible, and nonrevolutionary transformation in the political and social institutions of Romanized Gaul.

This conception of Fustel's has been accepted by most subsequent historians, although they have tried to make the theory somewhat more flexible; Fustel's logician's temperament had left it too rigid.

Fustel de Coulanges has been reproached for having attached exclusive importance to written documents, in particular to charters, at the expense of other historical sources, such as archeological material. Nonetheless his faculty for interpreting texts enabled him to extract the maximum of their historical significance. As the great medievalist Charles Victor Langlois justly observed, Fustel needed only to apply his critical approach to a hundred words such as *villa, marca, allodis*, to revise radically the interpretation of Merovingian times.

Fustel's analysis of texts and vocabulary produced results of considerable value to sociologists. To take one famous example, his method permitted him to show that agrarian collectivism had never really existed, contrary to the theory of *Markgenossenschaft* that was developed by German economists and legal historians and diffused also in Romance countries. Fustel de Coulanges never doubted that the institutions of the family and of individual property were universal and went back to earliest times.

ROBERT LATOUCHE

[*Other relevant material may be found in* FEUDALISM *and in the biography of* GIERKE.]

WORKS BY FUSTEL DE COULANGES

(1864) 1956 *The Ancient City: A Study on the Religion, Laws, and Institutions of Greece and Rome.* Garden City, N.Y.: Doubleday. → First published in French.

(1875–1889) 1888–1892 *Histoire des institutions politiques de l'ancienne France.* 6 vols. Paris: Hachette.

SUPPLEMENTARY BIBLIOGRAPHY

GUIRAUD, PAUL 1896 *Fustel de Coulanges.* Paris: Hachette.

LATOUCHE, ROBERT (1956) 1961 *The Birth of Western Economy.* London: Methuen; New York: Barnes & Noble. → First published in French.

TOURNEUR-AUMONT, JEAN M. 1931 *Fustel de Coulanges.* Paris: Boivin.

G

GALIANI, FERDINANDO

Ferdinando Galiani (1728–1787), Italian economist, was born in Chieti. He received a classical education and took religious orders. Entering government service, he became secretary of the Neapolitan embassy in Paris in 1759 and served there for a decade. During this period he also visited England. The remainder of his life was spent in the service of the kingdom of Naples, where he directed a variety of government offices, for the most part engaging in the formulation and administration of national economic policy.

His published works embrace the humanities as well as the social sciences (a bibliography may be found in Nicolini 1909). He also left a large number of letters that are not only of biographical interest but are also important for the light they cast on the social, economic, and political characteristics of eighteenth-century Europe. Galiani's wide circle of personal contacts—his intellectual correspondents and associates included Voltaire, Diderot, Genovesi, Turgot, Vico, Friedrich M. von Grimm, and others, as well as many highly placed diplomatic colleagues—make his letters invaluable documents.

His ideas as an economist had considerable originality. His economic thinking was influenced by Aristotle as well as by more modern theorists such as Bernardo Davanzati (1529–1606), John Locke (1632–1704), and Geminiano Montanari (1633–1687). He read Vico at an early age, and it was because of Vico's influence that Galiani always placed his economic ideas in a social context. Despite his basic rejection of most of physiocracy, his ideas were close to those current in France, and for a time he had a close intellectual relationship with Turgot and André Morellet. Like the works of other eighteenth-century economists (for example, Cantillon) Galiani's reveal a body of thought that is thoroughly eclectic. It is systematically related to no particular body of ideas, showing traces of scholasticism, of qualified mercantilism (especially where money and wealth are concerned), as well as of the natural-law ideas of the time. A free-thinking rationalist, Galiani appears nevertheless to have retained from mercantilism a protectionist international trade policy, if only with respect to grain.

The theoretical core of Galiani's work is found in *Della moneta* (1750); his policy prescriptions (clothed, incidentally, in a polished polemical literary style) are in *Dialogues sûr le commerce des blés* (1770). His originality lies primarily in the fields of value theory, interest theory, and economic policy.

Value theory. Galiani's value theory was based on the dichotomy between utility and scarcity that had been at the core of value theory from the time of Aristotle. This dichotomy was fundamental to the theories of his predecessors, Davanzati and Montanari (Gordon 1964, pp. 115–116), and of his contemporaries, Quesnay and Adam Smith. But Galiani's value theory departed from that of his contemporaries: it foreshadowed the subjective demand theory that was so highly developed in the 1870s by Menger, Jevons, and Walras (Einaudi 1953, pp. 272–273; Kauder 1953, p. 638; Schumpeter 1954, p. 300 and *passim*). Moreover, his concept of relative scarcity foreshadowed the theory of diminishing marginal utility, another advance of

45

economics in the last quarter of the nineteenth century. (The theory had, in fact, been clearly stated by Herman Gossen in 1854 but did not become widely known until its rediscovery by Jevons.)

Galiani understood the quantity of a commodity demanded as varying inversely with price, probably in a schedule sense rather than in the stock sense common in his day. The idea of price elasticity of demand is present in *Della moneta* (Einaudi 1953), although not in the mathematical terms developed by Alfred Marshall in 1890.

He did not discuss cost in general, but only the factor of labor in cost. For although he believed value to be subjectively determined and to vary from individual to individual, he did not believe that its source or its measurement is subjective. Rather, he believed that labor is not only the source of value but part of its objective measurement.

Interest theory. In economic writing before the seventeenth century, interest theory is rarely discussed, and when it is, the discussion is largely confined to theories of loan interest. This is also true of Galiani's interest theory. Nevertheless, his is one of the first discussions that considers why interest is paid instead of whether interest payments are legal or moral. Using a probability model, Galiani explained that interest is in principle paid to compensate the lender for the risk entailed in parting with his money (here and now)—money that is to be recovered from the borrower sometime in the future (or from a distant shore). Like his subjective value theory, Galiani's interest theory is based on a psychological assumption: men in general prefer present money over money at a future time or at some distant place. This theory has come to be known as the "time preference theory of interest," and Galiani's formulation of it anticipates that of Böhm-Bawerk by more than a century.

Economic policy. In matters of policy, Galiani adopted a position of historicogeographical relativism. Even the best-constructed economic models must be adjusted for circumstances of time and place before being applied to specific problems. This became a basic principle of the German historical school of Friedrich List and Wilhelm Roscher, but unlike that school, Galiani did not reject abstract theory.

It is surely remarkable that Galiani's early ideas in the areas of value and monetary theory anticipated corresponding notions of the neoclassical and Austrian schools, respectively. His later writings clearly foreshadow the views of the German historical school on economic policy.

PETER R. TOSCANO

[*For the historical context of Galiani's work, see* ECONOMIC THOUGHT; *and the biographies of* LOCKE; QUESNAY; SMITH, ADAM. *For discussion of the subsequent development of his ideas, see* UTILITY *and the biographies of* BÖHM-BAWERK; LIST; ROSCHER.]

WORKS BY GALIANI

(1750) 1915 *Della moneta.* Edited by Fausto Nicolini. Bari: Laterza.

(1770) 1803 *Dialogues sur le commerce des blés.* Scrittori classici italiani di economia politica, Vols. 12–13. Milan: Destefanis.

(1818) 1889–1890 *Correspondance avec Madame d'Épinay* . . . 3d ed. 2 vols. Paris: Lévy. → Especially useful as a source of information on Galiani's social activities in Paris.

1880 *Lettere di Ferdinando Galiani al marchese Bernardo T. Tanucci.* Edited by Augusto Bazzoni. Florence: Vieusseux. → An excellent source for students of eighteenth-century diplomatic history.

SUPPLEMENTARY BIBLIOGRAPHY

ARIAS, GINO 1922 Ferdinando Galiani et les physiocrates. *Revue des sciences politiques* 45:346–366.

ARIAS, GINO 1925 Il pensiero economico di Ferdinando Galiani. *Politica* 21:193–210.

BÖHM-BAWERK, EUGEN (1884) 1959 *Capital and Interest.* Volume 1: History and Critique of Interest Theories. South Holland, Ill.: Libertarian Press. → First published in German.

EINAUDI, LUIGI (1936) 1953 The Theory of Imaginary Money From Charlemagne to the French Revolution. Pages 229–261 in Frederic C. Lane and Jelle C. Riemersma (editors), *Enterprise and Secular Change: Readings in Economic History.* Homewood, Ill.: Irwin. → First published in Italian in Volume 1 of *Rivista di storia economica.*

EINAUDI, LUIGI 1953 *Saggi bibliografici e storici intorno alle dottrine economiche.* Rome: Edizioni di Storia e Letteratura. → See especially pages 267–305 on "Galiani economista."

GORDON, BARRY J. 1964 Aristotle and the Development of Value Theory. *Quarterly Journal of Economics* 78:115–128. → A skillful critique of Kauder 1953.

KAUDER, EMIL 1953 Genesis of the Marginal Utility Theory From Aristotle to the End of the Eighteenth Century. *Economic Journal* 63:638–650. → Reprinted in Joseph J. Spengler and William R. Allen (editors), *Essays in Economic Thought: Aristotle to Marshall.*

NICOLINI, FAUSTO 1909 Saggio bibliografico. Pages 405–431 in Ferdinando Galiani, *Il pensiero dell'abate Galiani: Antologia dei suoi scritti editi e inediti.* Bari: Laterza.

NICOLINI, FAUSTO 1918 Giambattista Vico e Ferdinando Galiani: Ricerca storica. *Giornale storico della letteratura italiana* 71:137–207.

NICOLINI, FAUSTO 1931 Ferdinando Galiani. Volume 6, pages 546–547 in *Encyclopaedia of the Social Sciences.* New York: Macmillan.

ROSSI, JOSEPH 1930 *The Abbé Galiani in France.* New York: Institute of French Studies.

SCHUMPETER, JOSEPH A. (1954) 1960 *History of Economic Analysis.* Edited by E. B. Schumpeter. New York: Oxford Univ. Press.

TAGLIACOZZO, GIORGIO (editor) 1937 *Economisti napoletani dei sec. XVII e XVIII.* Bologna: Cappelli. → Contains portions of Galiani 1750 and Galiani 1770, prefaced by the editor's comments.

VICO, GIOVANNI BATTISTA (1725) 1948 *The New Science*. Translated by Thomas G. Bergin and Max Harold Fisch. Ithaca, N.Y.: Cornell Univ. Press. → First published in Italian. A paperback edition was published in 1961 by Doubleday.

GALL, FRANZ JOSEPH

Franz Joseph Gall (1758–1828), German anatomist, founder of cranioscopy (later known as phrenology), and physician, was born in the grand duchy of Baden and died at Montrouge near Paris. He was the sixth child of a merchant. After the usual schooling, he studied medicine first at Strassburg and later at Vienna, where he was graduated in 1785.

He began his medical practice in Vienna and at the same time studied the healing powers of nature, the subject of his first book, *Philosophisch-medicinische Untersuchungen über Natur und Kunst im kranken und gesunden Zustande des Menschen* (1791). In it, Gall discussed the relationship between body and soul; the latter was located in the brain and was the seat of ideas. This concept led him to the notion of the cerebral localization of mental faculties, and he devoted the remainder of his life to exploring this idea.

There was at the time great interest in methods of determining character and temperament from external bodily configurations, especially the facial (physiognomy), and Gall gradually evolved a new method called "cranioscopy," combining the concepts of cerebral localization with the analysis of bodily configurations.

He argued that faculties or talents are inborn and dependent upon cerebral structures; therefore the brain is made up of as many "organs," or areas, as there are moral and intellectual qualities. These "organs" are on the cerebral surface, and as their size is reflected accurately by the overlying skull, they are palpable. He selected and located the "organs" by his empirical observations: having observed that a good memory is associated with protruding eyes, he therefore postulated that the memory organ is on the cerebral orbital surface and its hypertrophy pushes out the eyes. Character and intellect are represented by 27 organs, or psychic qualities, sharply delineated on the cranial surface.

About 1796 Gall began lecturing on cranioscopy in Vienna. Although the theory won great popularity, its materialism, manifested by an attempt to relate mind to matter, also incited opposition, so that in 1802 Gall's teaching was banned for religious reasons. Gall was joined in 1804 by Johann Gaspar Spurzheim, who had recently received his medical degree and who helped with the dissections of the nervous system that Gall undertook. Unlike other physiognomists, Gall attempted to create a scientific basis for his theory.

Seeking a more congenial atmosphere, Gall and Spurzheim left Vienna in 1805, and after an extended tour of Germany and neighboring countries, where their lectures excited widespread controversy, they settled in Paris in 1807. As in Vienna, Gall established an extensive medical practice with many famous patients, and he also resumed his lecturing and writing. In 1808 he published his *Discours d'ouverture au cours de physiologie du cerveau* (1808) and in the same year prepared with the help of Spurzheim a neuroanatomical memoir which was assessed by a group of distinguished French scientists. On the whole the judges were favorably impressed, and in the following year the report, with replies to the criticisms made by the assessors, was published (Gall & Spurzheim 1809). In 1810 Gall's most important and comprehensive work on neuroanatomy and cranioscopy began to appear, entitled *Anatomie et physiologie du système nerveux en général . . .* (1810–1819). Spurzheim helped with the first and second volumes only, for in 1813 he left France to popularize "phrenology," as he, but not Gall, came to call cranioscopy. Gall's last publication was a revised edition of *Anatomie et physiologie. . . .* He died of a cerebrovascular accident and was buried in Père-la-Chaise cemetery in Paris: his skull is preserved in the Musée de l'Homme.

Gall had an insatiable desire to learn and claimed that he was not guided by a desire for power, honors, or riches, although some of each came his way. He was perfectly sincere, if somewhat uncritical, in his ideas of brain function and was by no means a quack as is often thought; the stigma earned by phrenology was largely due to its popularizers, who claimed that phrenological examination could be used in career selection, for all kinds of prophecies, in choosing members of parliament and other professional men, etc. Gall's own intellectual abilities, his powers of observation, and his honesty, integrity, and independence in matters of principle were outstanding. As a product of the eighteenth-century Enlightenment, he was a social reformer, and he emphasized the need for medical ethics. He deduced moral rules from his phrenology and called for state educational systems and reform of current methods of handling criminals and lunatics.

Gall's influence was widespread. His anatomical investigations and cranioscopy turned attention to the brain, and he had an important influence on brain dissection and neuroanatomy in general in the nineteenth century. Moreover, phrenology first popularized the modern concept of cerebral localization of function, although it made no specific contribution to the concept. Gall's basic idea was right, but for the wrong reasons. Phrenology was also important in the development of scientific psychology, of anthropological investigations of the skull, and of criminology.

Phrenology retained popularity throughout the nineteenth century, and societies furthering its practice still exist today. Apart from its general effects upon the study of anatomy and physiology at the beginning of the nineteenth century, it has played no further role in science. However, its influence on social reform, political groups, religion, philosophy, and literature has been extensive, especially in the United States and Britain.

EDWIN CLARKE

[See also NERVOUS SYSTEM, *article on* STRUCTURE AND FUNCTION OF THE BRAIN; *and the biographies of* BROCA; FLOURENS; LASHLEY.]

WORKS BY GALL

(1791) 1800 *Philosophisch-medicinische Untersuchungen über Natur und Kunst im kranken und gesunden Zustande des Menschen.* 2d ed. Leipzig: Baumgärtner.

1808 *Discours d'ouverture . . . au [cours] sur la physiologie du cerveau.* Paris: Didot.

1809 GALL, FRANZ JOSEPH; and SPURZHEIM, J. GASPAR *Recherches sur le système nerveux en général, et sur celui du cerveau en particulier.* Paris: Schoell.

1810–1819 GALL, FRANZ JOSEPH; and SPURZHEIM, J. GASPAR *Anatomie et physiologie du système nerveux en général et du cerveau en particulier, avec des observations sur la possibilité de reconnoître plusieurs dispositions intellectuelles et morales de l'homme et des animaux par la configuration de leurs têtes.* 4 vols. and Atlas. Paris: Schoell. → A revised edition was published in 1825 in six volumes as *Sur les fonctions du cerveau et sur celles de chacune de ses parties.*

(1825) 1835 *On the Functions of the Brain and of Each of Its Parts: With Observations on the Possibility of Determining the Instincts, Propensities, and Talents, or the Moral and Intellectual Dispositions of Men and Animals, by the Configuration of the Brain and Head.* 6 vols. Boston: Marsh, Capen & Lyon. → A partial translation of *Anatomie et physiologie du système nerveux en général, et du cerveau en particulier. . . .* (Rev. ed.)

SUPPLEMENTARY BIBLIOGRAPHY

ACKERKNECHT, ERWIN H.; and VALLOIS, HENRY V. (1955) 1956 *Franz Joseph Gall: Inventor of Phrenology and His Collection.* Madison: Univ. of Wisconsin Medical School, Department of History of Medicine. → First published in French.

DAVIES, JOHN D. 1955 *Phrenology; Fad and Science: A 19th-century American Crusade.* New Haven: Yale Univ. Press.

FOSSATI, JEAN ANTOINE L. 1858 Gall (François Joseph). Volume 19, columns 271–284 in *Nouvelle biographie générale.* Edited by Jean Hoefer. Paris: Didot.

HOLLANDER, B. 1909 *The Unknown Life and Works of Dr. Francis Joseph Gall, the Discoverer of the Anatomy and Physiology of the Brain.* London: Gall Society. → Written by an ardent latter-day phrenologist and therefore very biased.

TEMKIN, OWSEI 1947 Gall and the Phrenological Movement. *Bulletin of the History of Medicine* 21:275–321.

GALTON, FRANCIS

Francis Galton was born in 1822 and died in 1911. He was educated successively at home, at a dame school, at Boulogne, and at Kenilworth. In 1835, at the age of 13, he entered King Edward's School at Birmingham, where he stayed for two years. He spent two years as a medical student, the first at the General Hospital, Birmingham and the second at King's College, London. In 1840 he entered Trinity College, Cambridge, as a mathematics student, but was content to take a poll degree in 1843, when his health broke down.

Galton's father, Samuel Tertius Galton, was a banker. His mother, Violetta Darwin, was the daughter of Erasmus Darwin by his second wife. One of Erasmus Darwin's grandsons through his first wife was Charles Robert Darwin; there was a certain physical resemblance between the two cousins. His mental development is interesting: he is credibly reported to have read a simple book before he reached the age of three, and his restless ingenuity with regard to machinery dates from his early youth. He did not enjoy school, however, nor did he find the profession of medicine, which was chosen for him, congenial. In spite of his interest in mechanics and mathematics, he was not successful in his Cambridge studies.

When his father died in 1844, Galton immediately forsook any idea of continuing his medical career. He found himself the possessor of a more than adequate income and proceeded to spend his time and energy "hunting with a set chiefly noteworthy for their extravagance and recklessness . . . the strange thing [being] that it [shooting] seemed to absorb his whole nature, and to be done not for the sake of the experience, but in the pure pursuit of occupation" (Pearson 1914–1930, vol. 1, pp. 208–209).

It was after these fallow years, as Pearson called

them, that Galton carried out the explorations for which he was later awarded the gold medal of the Royal Geographical Society in 1853. Even before going to Cambridge, Galton had taken an extended trip down the Danube and on to Smyrna, which had perhaps awakened the young man to the delights of foreign scenes and strange peoples. After his father's death he set off again for Egypt, Khartoum, and Syria, but he "was still touring for the boyish fun of movement and of new scenes. He had not yet thoughts of the language, habits, or archaeology of the people he mingled with" (*ibid.*, p. 205). It was not until after four years of idleness in England that he set out on a trip to tropical Africa, the results of which showed that he had come to terms with life and with himself.

In 1850 Galton set off for the Cape and spent two years upcountry exploring from Walvis Bay to Lake Ngami, territory of which little was known. He composed 15 brief laws for the Hottentot chiefs who governed the Damaras of the plain and compiled a rudimentary dictionary for the English who wished to use the local tongue. He returned to England early in 1852 and read a paper to the Royal Geographical Society, which awarded him its gold medal the following year. This award was followed in 1854 by a silver medal from the French Geographical Society. Early in 1853 he met Louisa Butler and married her in August. After an extended honeymoon tour of Europe, punctuated by visits to England, the Galtons finally settled in London, and in 1855 Galton really began to work.

Early publications. As might be anticipated, Galton's first publication was on exploration, and in 1855 *The Art of Travel* was published. There were signs that his scientific curiosity was developing in new directions, since in *Vacation Tourists and Notes of Travel* (1861–1864), which he meant to be an annual magazine, there is a description of the eclipse of the sun in 1860, with a drawing of the curved rays of the corona that he had observed. Galton's first piece of fruitful research was on the weather. He started to plot wind and pressure maps and noted, from very scanty data, that centers of high pressure are associated with clockwise directions of winds around the calm center. He coined the name "anticyclone" for such systems in 1863. Several other papers followed, in which he was clearly feeling his way toward the concepts of correlation and regression.

He tried to determine a linear prediction formula for the velocity of the wind, given the pressure, temperature, and humidity. He did not succeed, possibly because of his failure to realize that the prediction formula for pressure from velocity was not the same as the prediction formula for velocity from pressure. The realization that there are two regression lines was still in the future, as was the concept of correlation. In 1870 he read a paper at the British Association entitled "Barometric Predictions of Weather," in which he was fumbling toward a multiple regression, trying to predict the wind from pressure, temperature, and humidity. He failed in his objective at the time, but he posed the problem for others who were to succeed.

Intellectual influences. In assessing the intellectual influences on Galton, continuing uncertainty exists as to the extent of Quetelet's influence. Pearson tended to minimize the significance of Quetelet for Galton; he wrote, "I am very doubtful how far [Galton] owed much to a close reading of the great Belgian statistician" (Pearson 1914–1930, vol. 2, p. 12), and he placed perhaps undue weight on the fact that Galton possessed no copy of Quetelet's *Letters . . . on the Theory of Probabilities* (1846). Pearson further remarked that Galton "was never a great student of other men's writings: he was never an accumulator like his cousin Charles Darwin" (Pearson 1914–1930, vol. 1, p. 209). Now Pearson was closer to Galton's time and actually knew him, so that some weight must be given to his opinions. Nevertheless, Pearson would appear to have underestimated the influence of Quetelet; he himself pointed out that Galton's work seemed to flow naturally out of that of Quetelet. Further, Galton's obsession with the normal curve of error which, to a certain extent, has unduly influenced the development of statistical method, can only have stemmed from Quetelet. One of Quetelet's great achievements was to consider all human experience as ultimately capable of being described numerically, which was fundamentally Galton's attitude also.

The other great influence on Galton during the period in which he was establishing himself as a research worker affected the whole of the scientific world in the second half of the nineteenth century —the publication in 1859 of Charles Darwin's *The Origin of Species*. The effect of this work on Galton was not immediately apparent in his writings, but there can be no doubt that the book was responsible for transforming him from a geographer into an anthropologist and eugenist. He began with the article "Hereditary Talent and Character" in 1865 and proceeded through *Hereditary Genius* (1869); *English Men of Science: Their Nature and Nurture* (1874); *Inquiries Into Human Faculty* (1883); and *Natural Inheritance* (1889), by which time he was 67 years of age. As Pearson said, "We see that his researches in heredity, in anthropometry, in psychometry and statistics, were not independent studies; they were all auxiliary to his main object, the improvement in the race of man."

Application of statistics. In *Hereditary Genius*, Galton claimed that his discussion of heredity was the "first to treat the subject in a statistical manner" ([1869] 1952, p. vi). He clearly owed much to Quetelet and paralleled Quetelet's use of the normal curve for anthropometric measurements by using it to grade intellectual ability. He was quite explicit about this: "The law is an exceedingly general one. M. Quetelet, the Astronomer-Royal of Belgium, and the greatest authority on vital and social statistics, has largely used it in his inquiries. He has also constructed numerical tables, by which the necessary calculations can be easily made, whenever it is desired to have recourse to the law" (*ibid.*, p. 23).

Galton supplemented Quetelet's tables by a short table of the abscissas of the unit normal curve corresponding to percentiles of area (1889). He examined the abilities of the kin of persons who had achieved eminence of some kind—judges, generals, scientists, statesmen, painters, poets, and clerics. He was concerned with distinguishing between general ability and special ability and regarded each individual personality as a combination of natural ability and the advantages accruing from early environment, i.e., nature and nurture.

This idea of nature and nurture recurs in his writings. Thus we find in *English Men of Science* (1874), "It is, I believe, owing to the favourable conditions of their early training that an unusually large proportion of the sons of the most gifted men of science become distinguished in the same career. They have been nurtured in an atmosphere of free enquiry. . . ." The thesis is that heredity tends to produce eminence in *some* area and that environment tends to be the deciding factor in specifying *what* this area shall be. Galton tried to go beyond this in *Inquiries Into Human Faculty and Its Development* (1883), the book that possibly holds most interest for students of the history of psychology, in which he discussed preliminary results that he had obtained in the psychometric field.

In 1876, at the exhibition of scientific instruments at South Kensington, Galton exhibited his "Whistles for Determining the Upper Limits of Audible Sounds in Different Persons." Both before and after this time he was active in proposing tests for the measurement of muscular sensitivity by weight discrimination, for the perception of differences of tint, for reaction time, for acuteness of hearing, for keenness of vision and judgment of length by the eye, and for the senses of smell and touch. In an attempt to describe the skewed distributions that often resulted from the application of his tests, Galton hypothesized that in some frequency distributions, such as, for example, judgment of length, the geometric mean, rather than the arithmetic mean, is the best "medium" for the distribution, and he wrote a paper on "The Geometric Mean in Vital and Social Statistics" (1879). As usual the mathematical conceptualization was beyond him, and he took the problem to Sir Donald Macalister, who derived what is now known as the log-normal distribution.

At this stage of his work, he was associated with the American psychologist James McKeen Cattell, who on his return to the University of Pennsylvania (and later at Columbia University), began to teach statistical psychology, giving his first course in 1887. Through Cattell, Galton's ideas and experiments exerted possibly the greatest single influence upon American psychology during the last years of the nineteenth century.

From the statistical point of view, *Natural Inheritance* is probably the most important of Galton's writings. As can be seen from his earlier works, the ideas in it had been fermenting in his mind for some time, but it was their expression in *Natural Inheritance* that excited the interest of those whom today we might call the practitioners of applied mathematics. Again he was influenced by the fact that Quetelet was using the normal curve to describe anthropometric data and by the interest in the problems of inheritance aroused in him by *The Origin of Species*.

He began the book with a summary of those properties of the normal curve that appealed to him. He had previously suggested representing a frequency distribution by using grades or percentiles, and he elaborated on this suggestion here, pointing out that the normal distribution is completely determined from a knowledge of the median and one other quantile. Galton had observed that many measured characteristics can be closely described by a normal curve. He used the "quincunx," first shown in print with the publication of his lecture "Typical Laws of Heredity," delivered at the Royal Institution (1877), to illustrate the build-up of the normal curve: He had noticed that a normal curve is reproduced by lead shot falling vertically through a harrow of pins and he tried to explain the stability of measured characteristics by this mechanical device. In this paper he had almost reached the concepts of both regression and correlation but must have felt the need for further thought, since it was at this time that he began to collect data bearing on inheritance in man. Galton published nothing further on heredity for eight years. The foundation of his ideas on regression and correlation did not perhaps become clear to him until a short time before the publication of *Natural Inheritance*.

The regression line arose naturally out of measurements of the sizes of the seeds of mother and daughter sweet pea plants. The sizes of the seeds of daughter plants appeared to "revert" to the mean (the word "revert" was soon replaced by "regress"). This inspired him to look at a bivariate frequency table of the heights of fathers and sons, in which he found a regression to "mediocrity." The arguments he used became familiar ones with the analysis of variance put forward by R. A. Fisher some forty to fifty years later. Suppose, Galton said, that we want to predict the height of brother A, given the height of brother B. We take, therefore, all the individuals who have heights the same as B and form a collection of the heights of all of their brothers. These brothers as a group Galton called a cofraternity, and he proceeded to discuss the variation in height of all individuals about the grand mean, the variation of the cofraternity means about the grand mean, and the variation of the individuals of the cofraternities about their respective cofraternity means. This splitting up of variation had been done previously by Lexis in Germany and Dormoy in France, but Galton was possibly the first to carry out this type of analysis with the idea of assigning the variation.

While studying the bivariate frequency table of heights of fathers and sons, Galton was struck by the observation that the contours of equal frequency in the table were similar and similarly situated ellipses. He also found the lines that fitted the medians of the arrays (possibly drawing them by eye) and the slopes of these lines eventually became his regression coefficients. This early work, as is inevitable with a pioneering effort, is confused and difficult to evaluate, not least because Galton himself was not explicit. When, however, he had determined that he had what would now be termed linearity of regression and homoscedasticity in the arrays of the table, his mathematical powers were not sufficient to enable him to form a mathematical model for his surface, and he took the problem to Hamilton Dickson, a Cambridge mathematician. Dickson's mathematical formulation was published in an appendix to Galton's paper "Family Likeness in Stature," presented to the Royal Society in 1886. Galton was troubled by the fact that the slope of the regression line depends on the variability of the margins, and this concern led to his search for a unit-free measure of association.

Some time earlier, in 1882, Alphonse Bertillon had put forward a scheme for classifying criminals according to 12 physical measurements that was adopted by the prefecture of police in Paris. Galton became interested in this scheme and pondered for some time over which measurements would be the most descriptive—that is, which would discriminate one man most effectively from his fellows. It was from these considerations that he was led to the realization that some measurements might be so highly correlated with other measurements as to be useless for the prescribed purposes and finally to the necessity for describing how any two measurements are related. The slope of the regression line is not adequate for this, since it depends on both the scales of measurement and the choice of dependent variables. However, the regression line fitted between the variables that Galton used (1888) after dividing the heights (reduced by their median) by a measure of their variability (their semi-interquartile range) and similarly dealing with forearm length provides a unit-free measure of association. Given the problem and 65 years of subsequent statistical development, the correlation coefficient may now appear to have been inevitable. There can be no question, however, that at the time at which Galton wrote, 1888–1889, the production of a measure of association that was independent of location and scale was an immense contribution to statistical methodology.

The Bertillon system of measurement also started Galton wondering about the whole procedure of personal identification. In the paper for the Royal Institution in which he discussed bertillonage, he also drew incidental attention to fingerprints. In his book *Finger Prints* (1892), he referred to the work of Jan Purkinje, Kollman, William Herschel, and Henry Faulds, who had preceded him in this study, but it is clear that at the time he wrote little was known. As he himself said:

It became gradually clear that three facts had to be established before it would be possible to advocate the use of finger prints for criminal or other investigations. First it must be proved, not assumed, that the pattern of a finger print is constant throughout life. Secondly that the variety of patterns is really very great. Thirdly, that they admit of being so classified, or lexiconised, that when a set of them is submitted to an expert, it would be possible for him to tell, by reference to a suitable dictionary or its equivalent, whether a similar set had already been registered. These things I did, but they required much labor.

As a result of Galton's book and his evidence to a committee set up by the Home Office in 1893, a fingerprint department was established, the forerunner of many such throughout the world. Galton himself, as might be expected from his previous work and interest, turned to studying the inheritance of fingerprints, a study which was carried on for many years in the laboratory that he founded and that was named after him.

Eugenics. The term "eugenics" was introduced by Galton in his book *Inquiries Into Human Faculty* (1883) and soon won general acceptance. The study of human inheritance and the possibility of improving human stock were undoubtedly linked in his mind, as his public lectures and papers witness. He did more than lecture, however. In 1904 he founded a research fellowship in national eugenics at the University of London which was to develop in a few years into the Galton Laboratory of National Eugenics, with Karl Pearson as its first director. Pearson was succeeded by R. A. Fisher, and the now vast complex of statistical theory and method developed there thus owes its origin to Galton.

It was inevitable that Galton's work should attract the interest of young men able in the mathematical and in the biological fields, and the late 1880s saw Karl Pearson, and W. F. R. Weldon— the one a professor of applied mathematics and the other a professor of zoology and both at University College, London—working in the field of "biometry," i.e., the application of mathematics to problems of biological inheritance. Galton himself said, "The primary object of Biometry is to afford material that shall be exact enough for the discovery of incipient changes in evolution which are too small to be otherwise apparent." Pearson and Weldon met difficulties in their attempts to publish papers relating to biometry in existing journals and determined to start their own. A guarantee was required. Galton, on being asked to help, not only guaranteed the whole amount but followed it up with an additional gift that enabled his admirers to go their way in freedom; the journal *Biometrika*, the first to be devoted to both the theory and practice of statistics, was established on a firm footing. In the last decade of his life, Galton played the part of counselor and adviser to the younger men, but he still worked away at his own problems, as his continued output of letters and papers indicates.

During his last years many honors came his way. He had been elected a fellow of the Royal Society in 1856, receiving a gold medal in 1886, the Darwin medal in 1902, and the much-prized Copley medal in 1910, the year before his death. He was awarded the Huxley medal by the Anthropological Institute in 1901 and the Darwin–Wallace medal by the Linnean Society in 1908. He received honor-

ary degrees from both Oxford and Cambridge universities and became an honorary fellow of Trinity College, Cambridge, his old college, in 1902. The citation for the Darwin medal said, in part, "It may safely be declared that no one living has contributed more definitely to the progress of evolutionary study, whether by actual discovery or by the fruitful direction of thought, than Mr. Galton." Mr. Galton's private comment was, typically, "Well, I am very pleased except that I stand in the way of younger men" (quoted in Pearson 1914–1930, vol. 3A, p. 237).

F. N. DAVID

[*For the historical context of Galton's work, see the biographies of* DARWIN *and* QUETELET. *For discussion of the subsequent development of Galton's ideas, see* EUGENICS; LINEAR HYPOTHESIS, *article on* REGRESSION; MULTIVARIATE ANALYSIS, *articles on* CORRELATION; *and the biographies of* CATTELL; FISHER, R. A.; PEARSON.]

WORKS BY GALTON

(1855) 1856 *The Art of Travel: Or, Shifts and Contrivances Available in Wild Countries.* 2d ed., rev. & enl. London: Murray.

1861–1864 GALTON, FRANCIS (editor) *Vacation Tourists and Notes of Travel in 1860* [1861, 1862–1863]. London: Macmillan.

1863 *Meteorographica: Or, Methods of Mapping the Weather.* London: Macmillan.

1865 Hereditary Talent and Character. *Macmillan's Magazine* 12:157–166, 318–327.

(1869) 1952 *Hereditary Genius: An Inquiry Into Its Laws and Consequences.* New York: Horizon Press. → A paperback edition was published in 1962 by World.

1870 Barometric Predictions of Weather. British Association for the Advancement of Science, *Report* 40 [2]:31–33.

1874 *English Men of Science: Their Nature and Nurture.* London: Macmillan.

1876 Whistles for Determining the Upper Limits of Audible Sounds in Different Persons. Page 61 in South Kensington Museum, London, *Conferences Held in Connection With the Special Loan Collection of Scientific Apparatus, 1876.* Volume 2: Physics and Mechanics. London: Chapman.

(1877) 1879 Typical Laws of Heredity. Royal Institution of Great Britain, *Proceedings* 8:282–301. → First published in Volume 15 of *Nature.*

1879 The Geometric Mean in Vital and Social Statistics. Royal Society of London, *Proceedings* 29:365–367.

(1883) 1952 *Inquiries Into Human Faculty and Its Development.* London: Cassell.

1886 Family Likeness in Stature. Royal Society of London, *Proceedings* 40:42–63. → Supplemented with an appendix by J. D. Hamilton Dickson on pages 63–72.

1888 Co-relations and Their Measurement, Chiefly From Anthropomorphic Data. Royal Society of London, *Proceedings* 45:135–145.

1889 *Natural Inheritance.* London and New York: Macmillan.

1892 *Finger Prints.* London and New York: Macmillan.

1908 *Memories of My Life.* London: Methuen.

SUPPLEMENTARY BIBLIOGRAPHY

BURT, CYRIL 1962 Francis Galton and His Contributions to Psychology. *British Journal of Statistical Psychology* 15:1–49.

DARWIN, GEORGE H. (1912) 1939 Sir Francis Galton. Volume 2, pages 70–73 in *Dictionary of National Biography: Second Supplement.* Oxford Univ. Press.

NEWMAN, JAMES R. 1956 Commentary on Sir Francis Galton. Volume 2, pages 1167–1172 in James R. Newman (editor), *The World of Mathematics: A Small Library of the Literature of Mathematics From A'hmosé the Scribe to Albert Einstein.* New York: Simon & Schuster.

PEARSON, KARL 1914–1930 *The Life, Letters and Labours of Francis Galton.* 3 vols. Cambridge Univ. Press. → Includes a comprehensive bibliography of Galton's works.

QUETELET, ADOLPHE (1846) 1849 *Letters Addressed to H. R. H. the Grand Duke of Saxe-Coburg and Gotha, on the Theory of Probabilities, as Applied to the Moral and Political Sciences.* London: Layton. → First published in French.

GAMBLING

Gambling may be defined as a form of activity in which the parties involved, who are known as bettors or players, voluntarily engage to make the transfer of money or something else of value among themselves contingent upon the outcome of some future and uncertain event.

While the origins of gambling are lost to recorded history, it appears probable that games of chance developed out of various magical and religious practices employed by man to cope with problems of uncertainty and fate. In contemporary societies gambling appears most frequently in recreational contexts and in association with various sports and games. Among the major classes of games, gambling is especially common in those in which chance plays a prominent role, but it also appears in connection with games of skill or strategy and with games of physical prowess. In nonrecreational contexts gambling occurs in the form of wagers on the outcome of future events about which the bettors have strong convictions, as in the case of election outcomes. Elements closely parallel to gambling appear in conjunction with economic activities, especially those in which risk and uncertainty are prominent. In effect, speculators on the commodity markets bet against each other about the rise or fall of commodity prices.

In its various aspects gambling is at once a major recreational institution, a minor vice, a large-scale industry, a powerful source of crime and political corruption, a perennial social problem, a fascinating psychological puzzle, and an intriguing pastime. Like prostitution, it is ancient, widespread, and widely disapproved. It flourishes, in spite of ethical taboo and legal sanction, as an institutionalized deviant pattern and as a form of crime in which the victims are willing accomplices.

Social science perspectives on gambling. Because of gambling's complex and paradoxical nature, it is not surprising that the responses to it by social scientists and others have been extraordinarily diverse. Philosophers and theologians have struggled with the ethical and teleological implications of gambling, viewing it at times as a profane and frivolous stepchild of religion, to which it bears certain disquieting similarities. Mathematicians have exploited gambling to the hilt in the development of probability theory, some of them becoming gamesters in the process. Economists have turned to gambling to clarify the distinction between the functional and dysfunctional aspects of speculation and, more recently, for some sophisticated reformulations of utility theory. In the "theory of games" they have found in gambling a model for analyzing strategies in competitive situations involving risk and uncertainty.

Experimental psychologists have employed gambling situations in studies of probability learning and probability preferences, of levels of aspiration, and of intermittent reinforcement and conflict–drive motivation. Social psychologists have utilized gambling games to study social competition, aggression, and coalition formation. Psychoanalysts and clinical psychologists have concerned themselves with the unconscious motivations and personality structures of gamblers and with the problems of addiction. Sociologists have been interested in the incidence of gambling, its organization in relation to the underworld and the police, its functions for individuals and society, and its control. Finally, ethnographers and social historians have provided some fascinating descriptions of the cultural patterning of gambling in various times and places.

In these many different approaches that have touched on the subject, the interest in gambling has often been peripheral to some other, central interest, with the result that the coverage is piecemeal and fragmentary. While there are scattered bits of useful knowledge and theory, systematic treatises on gambling are sadly lacking. Moreover, many of the treatments that do exist are speculative, impressionistic, and moralistic, and many are also without adequate data.

The psychology of gambling

From a psychological viewpoint, gambling is at once an instrumental activity, directed toward a consciously recognized economic end, and an expressive activity, enjoyed as an end in itself. Interpretations of gambling motivations have varied widely, depending upon which of these facets has commanded the central focus of attention.

Gambling as instrumental behavior. In making their betting decisions, economically oriented gamblers must take two principal factors into account: the odds and the probabilities. In gambling terminology "odds" designates the ratio between the amount staked and the amount the player stands to win if successful. "Probabilities" refers to expectations regarding the outcome of the event bet upon, expressed as a ratio of favorable to unfavorable outcomes or as the percentage of favorable outcomes out of all possible outcomes. The actuarial value of a gambling risk depends upon the relationship between the odds and the probabilities. In gambling situations generally, there is a tendency for these two ratios to approach an inverted balance: as the probabilities of a favorable outcome become smaller, the odds become longer. For example, in horse racing, long shots fetch better prices than favorites. That this tendency exists at all may be taken as evidence for the operation of an element of economic rationality among gamblers.

It is clear, however, that no general theory of gambling behavior can be constructed from the conventional notions of economic rationality alone. In every gambling situation either the odds and probabilities are exactly balanced or they are not. Assume, first, that they are balanced, as in the case of tossing coins for even money. In the gambling world such risks are known as fair risks because neither side has any clear advantage. While it might appear that the rational gambler would have no particular reason to avoid such risks, there is also no apparent reason for him to accept them. Indeed, according to orthodox economic theory, the prudent gambler would presumably assign some element of disutility or cost to risk assumption and to the activity of gambling itself, regarding it as a form of "work." Moreover, if he assigns some function of diminishing utility to successive increments of money income, as economic theory assumes, the utility of each unit of money he might win in a fair-risk situation would be less than that of the money he might lose. Hence, the economically rational gambler would presumably avoid such risks as in this sense "not fair."

In all other gambling situations the odds and probabilities are not in balance. In situations of this sort, since all gambling transactions are between persons, it follows that whereas one player has backed a good risk, his opponent has by definition accepted a poor one. It is evident, therefore, that at least half of all gamblers have lost their rational economic bearings. In fact, in the gambling world the majority of good risks are monopolized by the professional gamblers who operate the various games and devices, always with a comfortable margin of safety. From the lay player's point of view there are no "good risks" at all in any professionally operated gambling house. Yet the market behavior of such gamblers makes it clear that there is always an easy market for poor gambling risks, especially those in which the odds are intriguingly long but offset by disastrously short probabilities.

The "utility of money." Economists and psychologists alike have advanced many arguments and theories designed to show how such apparently nonrational behavior may yet be motivationally intelligible. One line of argument has called for a reappraisal of traditional assumptions about the diminishing utility of money. Thus, Vickrey (1945) reasoned that the behavior of lottery players clearly implies that in this situation the utility of money is an increasing rather than a decreasing function of income. Following this same theme, Friedman and Savage (1948) demonstrated that for the gambler even a small probability of a large reward may have more utility than either a much larger probability of small loss or the certainty, if the risk be rejected, of staying at the same income level. Along similar lines, Mosteller and Nogee (1951) recorded the actual market behavior of experimental subjects in a situation that permitted varying amounts to be won, with varying probabilities of success or failure. Observing that the subjects do not automatically accept the bets with the highest actuarial values, they attempted to construct a series of curves showing the actual utility for their subjects of varying amounts of money (see also Coombs & Komorita 1958).

The "utility of gambling." A second line of analysis has challenged the assumption that the activity of gambling should be reckoned on the cost, or disutility, side of the calculus. In effect, the gambler may justify his losses as a fair payment for the pleasure he has obtained from the activity itself. Royden, Suppes, and Walsh (1959) have proposed a carefully reasoned model for the experimental measurement of the "utility of gambling" itself, which they argue must be kept independent of notions about the "utility of money." This line of analysis, however, is not much help in explaining why gamblers find pleasure in this activity, while nongamblers presumably do not.

Subjective probabilities. A third line of analysis, focusing on the cognitive aspects of gambling orientations, raises the question whether gambling behavior is a function of simple ignorance or error or whether the "subjective probabilities" upon which the gambler premises his behavior are systematically distorted or biased by various motivational factors.

Ignorance or error. Studies of probability learning provide evidence that there is ample scope for error in appraising the probabilities in complex gambling situations. Komorita (1959) has shown that experimental subjects are least accurate in estimating probabilities when the number of events or possible outcomes is large and when the probabilities for unit events depart from .50. Brim and Koenig (1959) found, in a sample of 143 college students, that none knew the correct way to combine the probabilities of independent events. And Cohen and Hansel (1958) found that even highly intelligent subjects tended to interpret multiplicative probabilities as if they were additive. Professional gamblers are less prone to such errors and employ their extra knowledge to design gambling situations in which the true probabilities are subtly concealed.

Faulty reasoning may also serve to distort subjective probability estimates, as, for example, in the widespread belief among gamblers in the "maturity-of-chances" doctrine (Jarvik 1951). Since Dame Fortune must keep her books in balance, reason such gamblers, at roulette, for example, after any unduly long run of black the probabilities of red appearing on the next few plays are greatly increased. In fact, of course, the probabilities on unit events are not affected by preceding sequences. Ironically, perhaps, while the ability to estimate true probabilities generally increases with maturity (Cohen 1957), more sophisticated reasoning errors, such as the maturity-of-chances theory, do not occur among young children and become increasingly common with advancing age (Ross & Levy 1958).

Distorted estimates of the true probabilities also result from erroneous information—a principle much utilized by shrewd professionals. Thus, race tracks abound with false tips and spurious "inside information," much of which is deliberately circulated by touts to mislead the fans and thus to skew the betting odds in some desired direction.

Motivated bias. While there is ample scope for simple ignorance or error in gambling situations, there is also abundant evidence that such errors are not random or merely cognitive but reflect consistent patterns of motivated bias. Very simply, the "errors" are almost invariably such as to distort the subjective probabilities in the gambler's favor. It has been observed again and again that gamblers consistently overestimate their own skill or luck, and it has been demonstrated experimentally that subjects consistently overestimate low probabilities (cf. Preston & Baratta 1948; Nogee & Lieberman 1960).

A variety of possible explanations of this phenomenon have been advanced. Atkinson (1957) demonstrated experimentally that the tendency to overestimate chances to win is especially likely to be associated with a high need for achievement. Another recent study of probability learning has shown that positive events are learned more rapidly and extinguished more slowly than negative events (Crandall et al. 1958). This might help to explain the tendency among gamblers to think they are ahead—to remember the exciting winning play and forget the losses that preceded it. But, of course, most gamblers do know in a cognitive sense that they might lose and that they have lost in the past. Leon Festinger and his associates would regard this as an example of dissonant information that must somehow be suppressed if the gambler wishes to continue, which of course he does; indeed, this circumstance may cause the actor to develop some extra attraction to the activity, harnessing various secondary drives to it to justify his behavior and compensate for the dissonant information (Lawrence & Festinger 1962).

In terms of learning theory more generally, gambling represents an ideal–typical situation of "intermittent reinforcement," or partial reward, and the evidence is overwhelming that activities reinforced in this way are peculiarly resistant to extinction. One plausible explanation of this is advanced in the conflict–drive theory developed by J. M. Whiting and his associates. Basically, this theory argues that when the same activity is sometimes rewarded and at other times nonrewarded or punished, conflict between the contradictory expectations of reward and punishment has the effect of adding drive strength to the originally reinforced action (Sears et al. 1953). Very simply, if the gambler always won or always lost, he would presumably lose interest; however, the conflict between fear and hope helps keep him going.

Gambling as expressive behavior. In considering the purely psychological rewards of gambling, we are clearly getting away from a concern with cognitive orientations and the interpretation of gambling as an instrumental activity directed toward an economic goal and are moving toward interpretations of gambling as an end in itself. It has been shown that even mathematically sophisticated subjects, possessing full information regarding the odds and the probabilities, opt for poor risks most of the time (Scodel et al. 1959). Curiously, it is also clear that there are some kinds of people who would not even bet on a sure thing. Moreover, there are evidently important differences among gamblers themselves: between those who prefer games of pure chance and those who prefer games involving skill or strategy; between system players and long-shot players; or between petty gamblers and addicts, for example. Such differentials as these yield to analysis only in terms of the differential noneconomic needs and motives of different classes of people.

Games as expressive models. Games typically occur in times, places, and contexts that are removed from the workaday utilitarian sectors of social structure and hence from the constraints and disciplines that the reality principle imposes on task-oriented activities. Thus, they tend to become intimately involved with the expressive and social–emotional sectors and to be concerned with problems of tension release and integration. Indeed, because they operate in what Kurt Lewin called a "plane of unreality," games are well suited to function as expressive models, onto which a variety of psychological conflicts and problems can be harmlessly projected. As Menninger noted with respect to games of strategy, they may enable us "to express aggression without reality consequences; one can hurt people without really hurting them; we can even kill them without really killing them" (1942, p. 172). In a similar vein, Phillips (1960) has interpreted certain children's games as exercises in the mastery of anxiety, in which psychological problems can be worked through in a miniature and relatively safe context.

Observing that games are not free and spontaneous expressive activities of individuals but are embedded in culture, Roberts and Sutton-Smith (1962) hypothesize that games will have special relevance for psychological problems that are endemic and widespread in the cultures or subgroups in which they are played. While games provide a buffered learning experience for children, game involvement typically diminishes with maturity as individuals become integrated into the mainstream of their culture. Games among adults are thus presumed to represent unresolved areas of conflict, and addicted players are presumed to be persons in a high state of unresolved inner conflict.

We may go on to inquire, for what kinds of needs or conflicts, for what kinds of persons, in what kinds of groups or societies, are gambling games appropriate expressive models? A number of theories have been proposed, each with at least some evidence in its support.

Teleological motivations in gambling. Since games of chance apparently originated out of religious and magical practices of divination, it has frequently been proposed that gambling may still perform an important teleological function in helping people orient themselves to the problems and conflicts invoked by the intrusions of chance, risk, and uncertainty in a world presumed to be causally and morally ordered. In principle, chance is meaningless and unintelligible, both causally and ethically. Yet, because of its capacity to violate legitimate expectations in important ways, many people feel that it must mean something: why do these things happen? why do they happen to me? For people who find these problems salient, gambling may assume a cosmic significance as a device for probing after the ground of things and of one's personal relationships to fate (am I lucky today?). In one of the earliest psychological studies of gambling, France (1902) argued that in an environment of uncertainty a belief in luck is functional in encouraging a necessary element of risk assumption but that too much reliance on luck would obviate action and lead to a lack of effort. Relevant empirical evidence is provided in a recent cross-cultural study (Roberts et al. 1959) which demonstrates that games of chance are especially likely to be found in preliterate societies in which the deities are regarded as benevolent and nonaggressive and readily subject to compulsion by humans. In contemporary, rationally oriented societies, gambling appeals particularly to superstitous persons, and it is one of the few areas in which permissive attitudes toward superstition are tolerated.

Economic conflicts and gambling. Because of gambling's quasi-instrumental, economic character, it is also peculiarly suitable for the working out of conflicts engendered by the discipline, frustrations, and constraints of the capitalist economic system. Since its rewards are distributed on the basis of chance, gambling would appear to make a mockery of the legitimate economy, with its stress on rationality, discipline, and hard work and its assumed correlations of effort, merit, and reward. Evidence that conflicts in this area are relevant to gambling motivation is provided in another cross-cultural study, which demonstrated that games of chance are most frequently found in preliterate societies in which child-training practices place special stress on responsibility training and arouse high anxiety about achievement performance (Roberts & Sutton-Smith 1962). The authors of this latter study have also demonstrated that in the United States games of chance tend to be preferred by women and low-status economic groups—categories especially involved with positions of frustrating drudgery and with routine responsibilities (Sutton-Smith et al. 1963). A similar hypothesis is tested by Tec (1964) in her study of gambling in Sweden, in which she demonstrated that habitual gambling is especially common in groups that find conventional channels of social advancement blocked (see also Devereux 1949; Caillois 1958).

Competition and aggression. Where gambling occurs in conjunction with games of strategy, as in poker (see Riddle 1925), motivations of personal competition and aggression may also play a prominent role. In a classic analysis of this theme, W. I. Thomas (1901) viewed gambling as a form of sublimated combat and suggested that such games may help to keep this vital "instinct" alive in our civilized, bureaucratic world. Among preliterate societies it has been shown that games of strategy tend to occur most frequently in the relatively complex societies with developed systems of stratification, in which social competition becomes problematic and a source of conflict (Roberts et al. 1959). In the contemporary United States a preference for games of strategy and also games of physical prowess is more common among higher-status persons (Sutton-Smith et al. 1963).

Anxiety and guilt in gambling. Finally, there are theories that have focused upon thrill-seeking motivations in gambling behavior and their relationship to anxiety. There is broad consensus among students of habitual gamblers that, for all their apparent external calm, gamblers are in fact highly anxious persons. The psychological literature on levels of aspiration provides abundant evidence that persons known to be high in anxiety are particularly prone to set goals for themselves that are grossly unrealistic on the basis of past performance, being either much too high or much too low (cf. Lewin et al. 1944). It has also been demonstrated that unrealistic aspirations are more likely to be set in gaming situations, perhaps because of their miniature and fictitious character, than in real life situations (Frank 1935). Addressing himself to such findings, Atkinson (1957) argues that unrealistic aspirations in fact serve the function of minimizing anxiety about failure, for if one did not really expect to succeed, failure has very little sting. In his studies of probability preferences, he was able to demonstrate that persons high in "need achievement" and presumably high in success drives typically prefer risks at intermediate probability levels, in which success or failure are equally probable and, hence, which generate a maximum of tension and anxiety. Subjects low in "need achievement" and presumably more con-

cerned with fear of failure typically preferred risks at extreme probability levels (either sure things or long shots), in which the success–failure tension is greatly reduced. Persons with high success need would presumably prefer games of skill or strategy, while persons with high fear of failure would prefer games of pure chance, in which failure is peculiarly noninvidious [see ACHIEVEMENT MOTIVATION].

Why do people who are high in anxiety and in fear of failure elect to gamble at all? Edmund Bergler, the only psychoanalyst who has dealt extensively with the problem of addicted gamblers, has argued that such gamblers are genuine neurotics, driven by unconscious aggression and latent rebellion "against logic, cleverness, moderation, morals and renunciation. That latent rebellion, based on the inwardly never-relinquished 'pleasure principle,' scoffs ironically at all the rules of education. Heavy inner retaliation is the result . . . rebellion activates a deep unconscious feeling of guilt" (1943, pp. 385–386). This guilt, Bergler argues, becomes in turn a source of anxiety and creates a need for self-punishment. These unconscious feelings are then neatly displaced into the segregated, miniature, and toylike setting of gambling, where they may be more or less harmlessly worked out. The gambler persuades himself that the real source of his guilt and anxiety is the tension of the game itself, and he achieves the needed self-punishment by keeping going until he loses. Thus, unconsciously, the neurotic gambler wants to lose, and he needs to lose in order to keep his psychological books in balance (see also Bergler 1957; Olmsted 1962).

Because gambling provides such a neat, ready-made, institutionalized, and culturally sanctioned mechanism for the handling of neurotic problems of this sort, the neurotic gambler does not feel neurotic and rarely appears voluntarily for treatment. Hence, to date there has been very little empirical research on gambling addiction, and academic psychologists have largely ignored the problem. There is, however, at least some empirical evidence that gambling may also serve somewhat parallel conflict-resolving functions for nonaddicted petty gamblers, along the lines indicated earlier in this article.

The sociology of gambling

From a sociological point of view gambling is of interest primarily as an institutionalized deviant pattern. Although it is widely disapproved of, gambling is nevertheless also widely practiced, and it has given rise to an extensive *sub rosa* organization that is elaborately articulated with the underworld, on the one hand, and with the legitimate world of its clientele, on the other.

Attitudes toward gambling.   The disapproval of gambling is ancient and extremely widespread, although varying greatly in intensity, content, and rationale. At different times and places gambling has been treated as a capital offense or merely as a misdemeanor. Legal restrictions have ranged from total prohibition to selective permissiveness, in which certain types of gambling activities have been permitted or even encouraged while others were forbidden or in which the rules against gaming were lifted during stated holidays or holy days. The laws have often made a distinction between games of pure chance and games of skill or between professional gamblers and their clients. Similarly, the grounds for the disapproval of gambling have varied widely, ranging from views that hold that gambling is fundamentally wrong in principle to views that hold that gambling is wrong only if it produces manifestly evil consequences. Essentially the same conclusions, moreover, have been derived at times from theological and ethical arguments and at other times from rationalistic, scientific, and pragmatic grounds.

In Western society attitudes toward gambling have varied significantly among different religious groups. While the Bible is silent on the subject of gambling, there are numerous references to the use of lots for serious purposes, as when Moses was instructed to allocate the lands of Canaan among the Israelites by lot (Numbers 26.55). Since chance events were considered "acts of God," the use of the lot, with appropriate ritual and respect, was regarded as justified for discerning the divine will in serious matters. However, the use of the lot for frivolous purposes, as in gaming, was regarded as a sacrilege and profanation. While formal opposition to gambling has persisted among Jewish moralists, prevailing attitudes have softened considerably, and they now view gaming as essentially a useless waste of time. Moreover, since the Middle Ages gambling has been widespread within the Jewish community. Roman Catholics have also come to take a liberal attitude toward gambling, holding that there is nothing wrong in principle with gambling, providing only that certain conditions be met: that the game be honest, that the stakes be moderate and within the means of the players, and that the money staked be one's own, for example.

Gambling and the Protestant ethic.   In Western society fundamental opposition to gambling, as a matter of basic ethical principle, is centered squarely in Protestantism and in the cultures where these denominations prevail. These are also, as Weber (1904–1905) observed, the same cultures in which modern bourgeois capitalism has achieved its greatest development. This fact suggests the hypothesis that gambling is somehow peculiarly antithetical, in principle at least, to the core of values embraced in this dominant economic system and in its supporting Protestant ethic.

On the surface, at any rate, the antithesis would seem to be clear enough. Among the core values of bourgeois capitalism are its special emphasis on rationality, disciplined work habits, prudence, thrift, methodical adherence to routine, and the assumed correlation of effort, ethical merit, and reward. The values symbolically embodied in gambling are diametrically opposed to these core virtues. Since its rewards are based on chance, gambling is explicitly and spitefully nonethical and makes a mockery of the required correlation of merit and reward. Thus, it tends to undermine disciplined work habits, prudence, and thrift; and in place of the needed rational–empirical orientations, it tends to foster superstitious beliefs and magical practices. If the values fostered by gambling were to become general in the population, the whole system of ethical sentiments that functions to sustain this dominant economic system would simply wither away. So argue the Protestant moralists.

In fact, of course, even in the dominant economic system the alternative values of initiative, daring, boldness, shrewdness, aggressive competitiveness, and willingness to assume risks also play a prominent role, and sheer luck is not always irrelevant. Because these values do not fit so neatly with those of the ethically sanctioned core, they have been the focus of considerable cultural ambivalence and guilt. The American public is uncomfortably aware, for example, of certain disquieting similarities between gambling and transactions on the stock markets; but open discussion of these similarities is strongly tabooed, and standard economic texts make a frantic effort to focus on the differences. In effect, gambling becomes a whipping boy to serve the precarious distinction between forms of speculation that are functionally useful and hence "legitimate" and those that are functionless or dysfunctional. Thus, when speculation gets out of hand, the obviously dysfunctional consequences for the economy are blamed, not on legitimate businessmen and still less on the stock market system, but on "gamblers," who have somehow invaded the market and should be driven from it. More generally, it is quite possible that the disapproval of gambling, in addition to reinforcing certain functionally appropriate values and attitudes, functions as a mechanism through which society seeks to allay its fears and misgivings about the ethical integrity of the dominant system—a fact that may account for the persistence and intensity of this disapproval in Protestant societies (Devereux 1949, chapter 18).

Functions of gambling for society. The fact that gambling persists in spite of the powerful legal and ethical taboos against it may be taken as evidence that it serves important psychological functions for the gamblers; the preceding discussion of the psychology of gambling has called attention to at least some of these. But what about functions or dysfunctions of gambling for society? This, of course, is an empirical question that cannot be answered on the basis of a priori principle. The fact that the *disapproval* of gambling is functional for society does not in itself establish that the *practice* of gambling is therefore dysfunctional, for the questions of scale, contexts, and side effects must also be considered. Most observers would probably agree that the addicted gambler, like the alcoholic, is a waste for society. Moreover, it is probably true, as the moralists have argued, that if gambling became a major preoccupation for the whole population and if the attitudes and practices of gambling were to permeate the sphere of the dominant economic system, the consequences for society would be seriously dysfunctional.

However, there is no evidence that petty gambling is in any way damaging to character or that petty gamblers differ in significant ways from nongamblers (Tec 1964). On the contrary, petty gambling may function as a kind of institutionalized "solution" for many of the specific psychological problems generated by the conflicts, strains, and ambivalences embedded in the economic system. It may serve to revitalize certain relevant patterns of motivation that are given little scope in routine economic pursuits, such as motives relating to themes of daring, combat, faith, and willingness to take chances. It has also been argued that the existence of institutionalized petty gambling is functional for society in providing a channel into which potentially disruptive speculative tendencies may be safely deflected from the legitimate market place. To these should be added the positive (and perhaps somewhat perverse) value-reinforcing and scapegoating societal function of the disapproval of gambling, for which institutionalized gambling provides a convenient target.

The legalization issue

If recreational petty gambling is harmless enough and may even perform useful functions for personality and society, the question naturally arises, should gambling be legalized? In fact, several forms of gambling have already been legalized during the present century. Gambling casinos flourish in many European countries and in Latin America; many nations, including even the Soviet Union and China, have adopted state lotteries; and legalized football betting pools have captured enormous followings in England and Sweden.

Gambling and law in the United States. In the United States pari-mutuel betting at racetracks has been legalized in approximately half the states. Several states allow the playing of bingo for charitable purposes; two states (New Hampshire and New York) operate a lottery, and only one state (Nevada) permits all forms of gambling. Although there is unmistakable evidence that moral resistance to legalized gambling is weakening rapidly in the United States, until November 1966, with the above exceptions, proposals to legalize any other form of gambling in the United States had been soundly defeated.

Although legal sanctions may have some dampening effect on the amount of gambling that occurs, they have never been able to stop gambling altogether. Sample polls in the United States have indicated over and over again that a majority of American adults do in fact gamble at least occasionally, in spite of moral taboos and legal restrictions. In 1951 the Kefauver committee estimated the volume of illegal betting in the United States at $20,000 million per year (Kefauver 1951), but that estimate is almost certainly too low. In 1963 an officially recorded $2,700 million was wagered legally on horse races alone, through the pari-mutuel machines, and experts are generally agreed that at least ten times as much was wagered illegally with bookmakers. Scarne (1961, p. 1) places the probable total volume of betting, for all types of gambling in the United States, at closer to $500,000 million a year. While this estimate is probably too large, there is ample evidence that the volume of illegal betting in the United States is sufficient to support a major industry. Indeed, since the legalization of the liquor industry in 1933, gambling has become the major source of support of the organized underworld in the United States.

The antigambling laws are unenforced and unenforceable in the United States for two principal reasons. First, the enormous financial resources controlled by the professional gamblers have enabled them to buy protection from excessive police or political harassment. Indeed, gambling has become one of the principal sources of political corruption and graft in America, especially at municipal levels (Devereux 1949; Kefauver 1951). Second, the general public, although sufficiently ambivalent to insist that antigambling statutes remain on the books, does not really want the gambling laws enforced and hence provides grossly insufficient support to reform-administration and routine enforcement efforts. As noted above, gambling is a peculiar form of crime, which is carried on with the willing consent of its victims; even when the victims have been clearly duped or cheated, they are usually loath to complain to the police, because of feelings of embarrassment and shame.

Arguments for legalization. The proponents of legalization argue that gambling—at least regulated petty gambling—is probably harmless, possibly beneficial, and in any case ineradicable. Antigambling statutes can never be effectively enforced. By keeping them on the books, we throw the entire operation into the hands of the underworld, create thereby an enormous source of revenue and power for organized crime, and keep alive a major source of political graft and corruption in America. Moreover, we place an unnecessary burden of guilt and hypocrisy upon the lay public, which must patronize these illegal and frequently dishonest establishments to indulge their gambling propensities. Partial legalization, as it currently exists in the United States, is doubly unsatisfactory, the argument continues, for it is discriminatory, hypocritical, and sabotages the moral convictions needed for effective law enforcement. Legalization will effectively end this sort of hypocrisy, get gambling into the open where it can be suitably regulated and controlled, dry up a major source of underworld income and power, eliminate the occasion and resource for police graft and political corruption, and make available to the state a highly lucrative source of additional revenue, achieved through the most painless known form of taxation. These arguments were ably stated some thirty years ago by a leading American sociologist, E. W. Burgess (1935), and have been repeated ever since. Until now they have not prevailed, even though recent public opinion polls show unmistakable trends in this direction.

Arguments against legalization. The opposition to legalization stems from several sources and draws on a variety of arguments. The core of resistance in the United States is still firmly rooted in the residual Puritan culture, which regards gambling as inherently sinful and placates its restive conscience by keeping the official façade of culture officially against it. Whatever the merits of the moralists' theological or ethical grounds, their arguments tend to be sociologically naive; in the empirical world one drink does not necessarily make an alcoholic or one lottery ticket an addicted gambler. While conceding that a generalized gambling mania might have disastrous consequences for society, it is an empirical question whether legalization would have this consequence. However, the moralists undoubtedly score a strong empirical point in their argument that selective legalization weakens the public will to enforce the statutes which remain.

Arguments from other sources have attempted to grapple more directly with empirical consequences. Would legalization in fact rid gambling of gangster influence? No, answers Virgil Peterson (1945), who was for many years chairman of the Chicago Crime Commission, citing the continued influence of the underworld in the liquor business even after the repeal of prohibition laws, and the unsavory history of graft and corruption which accompanied the later days of legalized lotteries in nineteenth-century America. In rebuttal proponents point out that most European state lotteries have operated successfully for years without major scandal. But perhaps the United States is different.

Would legalization set off a wholesale gambling mania, create a population of gambling addicts, and sabotage work disciplines and the ethical attitudes which maintain them? Undoubtedly the incidence of gambling would increase, perhaps quite substantially, if the taboos were lifted and the facilities made more visible, guilt-free, and accessible, but nobody knows for sure how much it would increase. So far, the legalization of football pools and off-track betting shops in England has not produced any runaway mania. But again, perhaps the United States is different. There is at least some evidence that by the 1820s American lotteries had reached such craze proportions that they had seriously disruptive consequences for some communities (Spofford 1892) and some evidence that during the racing season at local tracks many local businesses suffer, absenteeism increases, installment payments fall off, and petty crimes increase (New Jersey State Chamber of Commerce 1939). Regarding the possible long-run effects of wholesale legalization upon the ethical attitudes and beliefs which underpin the system of bourgeois capitalism, there is no relevant empirical evidence. Opponents of legalization point to Latin America, where permissive attitudes to gambling and generally more fatalistic value systems prevail and where bourgeois capitalism has been slow to develop. Who can say whether gambling is cause or consequence in this relationship? Recalling the functions attributed above to the disapproval of gambling, could the United States afford an attitude of moral indifference?

The solution, of course, does not have to be of an either–or nature. Although few are willing to admit it and still fewer to recommend it, since it violates all the principles of logic and common sense, the United States has again and again shown by its behavior that it still covertly prefers the present type of compromise solution, in which a formal façade of disapprobation and legal taboo is combined with halfhearted enforcement and widespread practice. Through this arrangement it does achieve at least some measure of regulation and constraint, keeps the public conscience appeased, and yet provides generous opportunities for those who would gamble to do so (for a carefully reasoned defense of this arrangement, see Dos Passos 1904). But these gains, if they be that, are not achieved without serious cost; and in any event, in this age of increasing secularization it is highly probable that the proponents of further legalization will have won their battle in the United States before another edition of this encyclopedia appears.

EDWARD C. DEVEREUX, JR.

[*See also* GAME THEORY; LEISURE; SOCIAL CONTROL; SPECULATION, HEDGING, AND ARBITRAGE; UTILITY.]

BIBLIOGRAPHY

ATKINSON, JOHN W. (1957) 1958 Motivational Determinants of Risk-taking Behavior. Pages 322–339 in John W. Atkinson (editor), *Motives in Fantasy, Action, and Society: A Method of Assessment and Study.* Princeton, N.J.: Van Nostrand. → First published in Volume 64 of the *Psychological Review.*

BERGLER, EDMUND 1943 The Gambler: The Misunderstood Neurotic. *Journal of Criminal Psychopathology* 4:379–393.

BERGLER, EDMUND 1957 *The Psychology of Gambling.* New York: Hill & Wang.

BLOCK, HERBERT A. 1962 The Gambling Business: An American Paradox. *Crime & Delinquency* 8:355–364.

BRIM, O. G. JR.; and KOENIG, F. W. 1959 Two Aspects of Subjective Probability Among College Students. *Journal of Communication* 9:19–26.

BURGESS, ERNEST W. 1935 *The Next Step in the War on Crime—Legalize Gambling: A Report to Governor Harry M. Horner.* Chicago: Adair.

CAILLOIS, ROGER (1958) 1961 *Man, Play and Games.* New York: Free Press. → First published as *Les jeux et les hommes.*

COHEN, JOHN 1957 Subjective Probability. *Scientific American* 197:128–138.

COHEN, JOHN; and HANSEL, C. E. M. 1956 *Risk and Gambling: The Study of Subjective Probability.* New York: Philosophical Library.

COHEN, JOHN; and HANSEL, C. E. M. 1958 The Nature of Decisions in Gambling. *Acta psychologica* 13:357–370.

COOMBS, C. H.; and KOMORITA, S. S. 1958 Measuring Utility of Money Through Decisions. *American Journal of Psychology* 71:383–389.

CRANDALL, V. J.; SOLOMON, D.; and KELLAWAY, R. 1958 The Value of Anticipated Events as a Determinant of Probability Learning and Motivation. *Journal of Genetic Psychology* 58:3–10.

DEVEREUX, EDWARD C. 1949 Gambling and the Social Structure: A Sociological Study of Lotteries and Horse Racing in Contemporary America. Ph.D. dissertation, Harvard Univ.

DOS PASSOS, JOHN R. 1904 Gambling and Cognate Vices. *Yale Law Journal* 14:9–17.

FRANCE, CLEMENS J. 1902 The Gaming Impulse. *American Journal of Psychology* 13:364–407.

FRANK, J. D. 1935 Some Psychological Determinants of Level of Aspiration. *American Journal of Psychology* 47:285–293.

FRIEDMAN, MILTON; and SAVAGE, L. J. 1948 The Utility Analysis of Choices Involving Risk. *Journal of Political Economy* 56:279–304.

GALDSTON, IAGO 1951 Psychodynamics of the Triad, Alcoholism, Gambling and Superstition. *Mental Hygiene* 35:589–598.

GREENSON, RALPH R. 1947 On Gambling. *American Imago* 4:61–77.

JARVIK, MURRAY E. 1951 Probability Learning and a Negative Recency Effect in the Serial Anticipation of Alternative Symbols. *Journal of Experimental Psychology* 41:291–297.

KEFAUVER, ESTES 1951 *Crime in America.* Garden City, N.Y.: Doubleday.

KOMORITA, S. S. 1959 Factors Which Influence Subjective Probability. *Journal of Experimental Psychology* 58:386–389.

LAWRENCE, DOUGLAS H.; and FESTINGER, LEON 1962 *Deterrents and Reinforcement: The Psychology of Insufficient Reward.* Stanford Univ. Press.

LEWIN, KURT et al. 1944 Level of Aspiration. Volume 1, pages 333–378 in Joseph McV. Hunt (editor), *Personality and the Behavior Disorders.* New York: Ronald Press.

MENNINGER, KARL 1942 *Love Against Hate.* New York: Harcourt. → A paperback edition was published in 1959.

MOSTELLER, FREDERICK; and NOGEE, PHILIP 1951 An Experimental Measurement of Utility. *Journal of Political Economy* 59:371–404.

NEW JERSEY STATE CHAMBER OF COMMERCE, RESEARCH DEPARTMENT 1939 *The Economic Effects of Parimutuel Horse Racing, as Measured by the Experiences of Other States.* Orange, N.J.: The Department.

NOGEE, PHILIP; and LIEBERMAN, BERNHARDT 1960 The Auction Value of Certain Risky Situations. *Journal of Psychology* 49:167–179.

OLMSTED, CHARLOTTE 1962 *Heads I Win—Tails You Lose.* New York: Macmillan.

PETERSON, VIRGIL W. (1945) 1949 Gambling—Should It Be Legalized? *Journal of Criminal Law and Criminology* 40:259–329. → First published by the Chicago Crime Commission.

PHILLIPS, R. H. 1960 The Nature and Function of Children's Formal Games. *Psychoanalytical Quarterly* 29:200–207.

PRESTON, MALCOLM G.; and BARATTA, PHILIP 1948 An Experimental Study of the Auction Value of an Uncertain Outcome. *American Journal of Psychology* 61:183–193.

RIDDLE, E. M. 1925 Aggressive Behavior in a Small Group. *Archives of Psychology* No. 78.

ROBERTS, JOHN M.; ARTH, MALCOLM S.; and BUSH, ROBERT R. 1959 Games in Culture. *American Anthropologist* New Series 61:597–605.

ROBERTS, JOHN M.; and SUTTON-SMITH, BRIAN 1962 Child Training and Game Involvement. *Ethnology* 1:166–185.

ROSS, B. M.; and LEVY, N. 1958 Patterned Predictions of Chance Events by Children and Adults. *Psychological Reports* 4:87–124.

ROYDEN, HALSEY L.; SUPPES, PATRICK; and WALSH, KAROL
1959 A Model for the Experimental Measurement of
the Utility of Gambling. *Behavioral Science* 4:11–18.

SCARNE, JOHN 1961 *Scarne's Complete Guide to Gambling.* New York: Simon & Schuster.

SCODEL, A.; RATOOSH, P.; and MINAS, J. S. 1959 Some
Personality Correlates of Decision Making Under Conditions of Risk. *Behavioral Science* 4:19–28.

SEARS, R. R. et al. 1953 Some Child Rearing Antecedents of Aggression and Dependency in Young Children. *Genetic Psychology Monographs* 47:135–236.

SPOFFORD, A. R. 1892 Lotteries in American History.
American Historical Association, *Annual Report*
[1892]:173–195.

SUTTON-SMITH, B.; ROBERTS, J. M.; and KOZELKA, R. M.
1963 Game Involvement in Adults. *Journal of Social
Psychology* 60:15–30.

TEC, NECHAMA 1964 *Gambling in Sweden.* Totowa, N.J.:
Bedminster.

THOMAS, W. I. 1901 The Gaming Instinct. *American
Journal of Sociology* 6:750–763.

THORNER, ISIDOR 1956 Ascetic Protestantism, Gambling,
and the One-price System. *American Journal of Economics and Sociology* 15:161–172.

VICKREY, WILLIAM 1945 Measuring Marginal Utility by
Reactions to Risk. *Econometrica* 13:319–333.

WEBER, MAX (1904–1905) 1930 *The Protestant Ethic
and the Spirit of Capitalism.* Translated by Talcott
Parsons, with a foreword by R. H. Tawney. London:
Allen & Unwin; New York: Scribner. → First published in German. The 1930 edition has been reprinted
frequently. See especially pages 35–92.

GAME THEORY

I. THEORETICAL ASPECTS   *Oskar Morgenstern*
II. ECONOMIC APPLICATIONS   *Martin Shubik*

I

THEORETICAL ASPECTS

The theory of games is a mathematical discipline
designed to treat rigorously the question of optimal
behavior of participants in games of strategy and
to determine the resulting equilibria. In such games
each participant is striving for his greatest advantage in situations where the outcome depends not
only on his actions alone, nor solely on those of
nature, but also on those of other participants
whose interests are sometimes opposed, sometimes
parallel, to his own. Thus, in games of strategy
there is conflict of interest as well as possible cooperation among the participants. There may be
uncertainty for each participant because the actions of others may not be known with certainty.
Such situations, often of extreme complexity, are
found not only in games but also in business, politics, war, and other social activities. Therefore, the
theory serves to interpret both games themselves
and social phenomena with which certain games
are strictly identical. The theory is normative in

that it aims at giving advice to each player about
his optimal behavior; it is descriptive when viewed
as a model for analyzing empirically given occurrences. In analyzing games the theory does not
assume rational behavior; rather, it attempts to
determine what "rational" can mean when an individual is confronted with the problem of optimal
behavior in games and equivalent situations.

The results of the interlocking individual actions
are expressed by numbers, such as money or a
numerically defined utility for each player transferable among all. Games of strategy include games
of chance as a subcase; in games of chance the
problem for the player is merely to determine and
evaluate the probability of each possible outcome.
In games of strategy the outcome for a player cannot be determined by mere probability calculations.
Specifically, no player can make mere statistical
assumptions about the behavior of the other players
in order to decide on his own optimal strategy.

But nature, when interfering in a game through
chance events, is assumed to be indifferent with
regard to the player or players affected by chance
events. Since the study of games of chance has
given rise to the theory of probability, without which
modern natural science could not exist, the expectation is that the understanding of the far more
complicated games of strategy may gradually produce similar consequences for the social sciences.

History. In 1710 the German mathematician–
philosopher Leibniz foresaw the need and possibility of a theory of games of strategy, and the
notion of a minimax strategy (see section on "Two-
person, zero-sum games," below) was first formulated two years later by James Waldegrave. (See
the letter from Waldegrave in the 1713 edition of
Montmort 1708; see also Baumol & Goldfeld 1967.)
The similarity between games of strategy and economic processes was occasionally mentioned, for example, by Edgeworth in his *Mathematical Psychics*
(1881). Specialized theorems, such as Ernst Zermelo's on chess, were stated for some games; and
Émile Borel developed a limited minimax strategy,
but he denied the possibility of a general theorem.
It was not until John von Neumann (1928) proved
the fundamental theorem that a true theory of
games emerged (see section on "Two-person, zero-
sum games," below). In their *Theory of Games and
Economic Behavior*, von Neumann and Morgenstern (1944) extended the theory, especially to
games involving more than two players, and gave
applications of the theory in economics. Since then,
throughout the world a vast literature has arisen
in which the main tenets of the theory have been
widened and deepened and many new concepts

and ideas introduced. The four-volume *Contributions to the Theory of Games* (Kuhn & Tucker 1950–1959) and *Advances in Game Theory* (Dresher, Shapley, & Tucker 1964) give evidence of this continuing movement. These works contain extensive bibliographies, but see especially Volume 4 of *Contributions to the Theory of Games*.

Game theory concepts

Games are described by specifying possible behavior within the rules of the game. The rules are in each case unambiguous; for example, certain moves are allowed for specific pieces in chess but are forbidden for others. The rules are also inviolate. When a social situation is viewed as a game, the rules are given by the physical and legal environment within which an individual's actions may take place. (For example, in a market individuals are permitted to bargain, to threaten with boycotts, etc., but they are not permitted to use physical force to acquire an article or to attempt to change its price.) The concrete occasion of a game is called a play, which is described by specifying, out of all possible, allowable moves, the sequence of choices actually made by the players or participants. After the final move, the umpire determines the payments to each player. The players may act singly, or, if the rules of the game permit it and if it is advantageous, they may form coalitions. When a coalition forms, the distribution of the payments to the coalition among its members has to be established. All payments are stated in terms of money or a numerically defined utility that is transferable from one player to another. The payment function is generally assumed to be known to the players, although modifications of this assumption have been introduced, as have other modifications—for example, about the character of the utilities and even about the transferability of payments.

The "extensive" form of a game, given in terms of successive moves and countermoves, can be represented mathematically by a game tree, which describes the unfolding of the moves, the state of information of the players at the moment of each choice, and the alternatives for choices available to each player at each occasion. This description can, in a strict mathematical sense, be given equivalently in a "normalized" form: each player, uninformed about the choices made by any other player, chooses a single number that identifies a "strategy" from his given finite or infinite set of strategies. When all personal choices and a possible random choice are made (simultaneously), the umpire determines the payments. Each strategy is a complete plan of playing, allowing for all contingencies as represented by the choices and moves of all other players and of nature. The payoff for each player is then represented by his mathematical expectation of the outcome for himself. The final description of the game therefore involves only the players' strategies and no further chance elements.

The theory explicitly assumes that each player, besides being completely informed about the alternative payoffs due to all moves made or strategies chosen, can perform all necessary computations needed to determine his optimal behavior. (This assumption of complete information is also commonplace in current economic theory, although seldom stated explicitly.)

The payments made by all players may add up to zero, as in games played for entertainment. In this case the gains of some are exactly balanced by the losses of others. Such games are called zero-sum games. In other instances the sum of all payments may be a constant (different from zero) or may be a variable; in these cases all players may gain or lose. Applications of game theory to economic or political problems require the study of these games, since in a purchase, for example, both sides gain. An economy is normally productive so that the gains outweigh any losses, whereas in a war both sides may lose.

If a player chooses a particular strategy as identified by its number, he selects a *pure* strategy; if he allows a chance mechanism, specified by himself, to make this selection for him, he chooses a *mixed* or *statistical* strategy. The number of pure strategies for a player normally is finite, partly because the rules of games bring the play to an end after a finite number of moves, partly because the player is confronted with only a finite number of alternatives. However, it is possible to treat cases with infinitely many strategies as well as to consider even the borderline case of games with infinitely many players. These serve essentially to study pathological examples or to explore certain mathematical characteristics.

Game theory uses essentially combinatorial and set-theoretical concepts and tools, since no specific calculus has as yet evolved—as happened when differential and integral calculus were invented simultaneously with the establishment of classical mechanics. Differential calculus is designed to determine maxima and minima, but in games, as well as in politics, these are not defined, because the outcome of a player's actions does not depend on his actions alone (plus nature). This applies to all players simultaneously. A maximum (or minimum) of a function can be achieved only when all variables on which the maximum (minimum) depends are under the complete control of the would-be maximizer. *This is never the case in games of strategy.* Therefore, in the equivalent business, political, or military operations there obtains no maximum (minimum) problem, whether with or without side conditions, as assumed in the classical literature of these fields; rather one is confronted there with an entirely different conceptual structure, which the theory of games analyzes.

Two-person, zero-sum games

The simplest game of strategy is a two-person, zero-sum game, in which players A and B each have a finite number of strategies and make their choices unknown to each other. Let P be the payoff to the first player, and let $-P$ be the payoff to the second player. Then P is greater than, equal to, or less than 0, depending on whether A wins, draws, or loses. Let $A_1, A_2, \cdots, A_n$ be the strategies available to player A and $B_1, B_2, \cdots, B_m$ be the strategies available to player B. In the resulting $n \times m$ array of numbers, each row represents a pure strategy of A, each column a pure strategy of B. The intersections of the rows and columns show the payoffs to player A from player B. The first player wishes to maximize this payoff, while the second wishes to minimize it. This array of numbers is called the payoff matrix, an example of which is presented in Table 1, where payments go from B to A. Player A's most desirable payoff is 8; B's is -10. Should player A pick strategy A_1, either of these two events may happen depending on B's action. But if A picks A_1, B in his own interest would want to pick B_3, which would mean that A would have to pay 10 units to B instead of receiving 8. The row minima represent the worst that could happen to A for each of his strategies, and it is natural that he would want to make as great as possible the least gain he can expect from each; that is, he seeks the maximum of the row minima, or the *maximin*, which in Table 1 is -1 (strategy A_3). Conversely, B will wish to minimize the column maxima—that is, seek the

minimax—which is also -1 (strategy B_2). We would say that each player is using a minimax strategy—that is, each player selects the strategy that minimizes his maximum loss. Any deviation from the optimal strategies A_3 and B_2 is fraught with danger for the deviating player, so that each will choose the strategy that contains the so-called *saddle point of the payoff function.* The saddle point is defined as the point at which the maximin equals the minimax. At this point the least that A can secure for himself is equal to the most that B may have to part with. (In the above example A has to pay one unit to B.) If there is more than one saddle point in the payoff matrix, then they are all equal to each other. Games possessing saddle points in pure strategies are called *specially strictly determined.* In these games it is immaterial whether the choice of the pure strategy by either player is made openly before the other makes his choice. Games of *perfect* information—that is, games in which each player at each move is always informed about the entire previous history of the play, so that what is preliminary to his choice is also anterior to it—are always specially strictly determined. Chess belongs in this class; bridge does not, since each of the two players (one "player" being the north–south team, the other the east–west team) is not even completely informed about himself—for example, north does not know precisely what cards south holds.

Most games will have no saddle points in pure strategies; they are then said to be not strictly determined. The simplest case is matching pennies. The payoff matrix for this game is presented in Table 2. Here, if one player has to choose openly before the other does, he is sure to lose. Each player will therefore strive to prevent information about his choice from flowing to the other. This is accomplished by the player's choice of a chance mechanism, which selects from among the available pure strategies with probabilities determined by the player. In matching pennies, the chance mechanism should select "heads" with probability $\frac{1}{2}$ and "tails" with probability $\frac{1}{2}$. This randomization may be achieved by tossing the coin before showing it. If there is a premium, say on matching heads over matching tails, the payoff matrix would reflect this, and the probabilities with which the two sides of the coin have to be played in order to prevent disclosure of a pattern of playing to the benefit of the opponent would no longer be $\frac{1}{2}$ for heads and $\frac{1}{2}$ for tails. Thus, when there is no saddle point in pure strategies a randomization by a chance mechanism is called for. The players are then said to be using mixed, or statistical, strategies. This does *not* trans-

Table 1 — Payoff matrix for a two-person, zero-sum game

A's strategy \ B's strategy	B_1	B_2	B_3	Row minima
A_1	8	-3	-10	-10
A_2	0	-2	6	-2
A_3	4	-1	5	-1
Column maxima	8	-1	6	

Table 2 — Payoff matrix for matching pennies

A's penny \ B's penny	Heads	Tails	Row minima
Heads	1	−1	−1
Tails	−1	1	−1
Column maxima	1	1	

form a game of strategy into a game of chance: the strategic decision is the specification of the randomization device and the assignment of the proper probabilities to each available pure strategy. Whether pure or mixed strategies are needed to assure a saddle point, the theory at no point requires that the players make assumptions about each other's intelligence, guesses, and the like. The choice of the optimal strategy is independent of all such considerations. Strategies selected in this way are perfect from the defensive point of view. A theory of true offensive strategies requires new ideas and has not yet been developed.

Von Neumann proved that each matrix game can be made strictly determined by introducing mixed strategies. This is the *fundamental theorem* of game theory. It shows that each zero-sum, two-person game has a saddle point in mixed strategies and that optimal mixed strategies exist for each of the two players. The original proof of this theorem made use of rather complex properties of set theory, functional calculus, and combinatorics. Since the original proof was given, a number of alternative, simplified versions have been given by various authors. The numerical solution of a matrix game with m columns and n rows demands the solution of a system of linear inequalities of $m + n + 1$ unknowns, the $m + n$ probabilities for the strategies of players A and B and the minimax value. There exist many techniques for solving such systems; notably, an equivalence with solving dual linear programs has proved to be of great importance [*see* PROGRAMMING]. High-speed computers are needed to cope with the rapid rise of the required arithmetical operations. A more modest view of mixed strategies is the notion of behavioral strategies, which are the probability distributions over each player's information sets in the extensive form of the game. For games such as chess, even the optimal pure strategy cannot be computed, although the existence of a saddle point in pure strategies can be proved and either white or black has a winning pure strategy no matter what the other does (or both have pure strategies that enforce a

draw). The problems of finding further computational techniques are actively being investigated.

n-Person, zero-sum games

When the number of players increases to $n \geq 3$, new phenomena arise even when the zero-sum restriction remains. It is now possible that cooperation will benefit the players. If this is not the case, the game is called inessential. In an essential game the players will try to form *coalitions* and act through these in order to secure their advantage. Different coalitions may have different strength. A winning coalition will have to divide its proceeds among its members, and each member must be satisfied with the division in order that a stable solution obtains [*see* COALITIONS].

Any possible division of payments among all players is called an *imputation*, but only some of all possible imputations will be contained in a *solution*. An inessential game has precisely one imputation that is better than any other, that is, one that *dominates* all others. This unique imputation forms the solution, but this uniqueness is trivial and applies only to inessential games. There is no cooperation in inessential games.

A solution of an essential game is characteristically a nonempty set of several imputations with the following properties: (1) No imputation in the set is dominated by another imputation in the set. (2) All imputations not in the set are dominated by an imputation contained in the set. There may be an infinite number of imputations in a solution set, and there may be several solution sets, each of which has the above properties. Furthermore, it should be noted that every imputation in a solution set is dominated by some imputation not in that set, but property (2) assures that such a dominating imputation is, in turn, dominated by an imputation in the solution set.

To be considered as a member of a coalition, a player may have to offer *compensations* or side payments to other prospective members. A compensation or side payment may even take the form of giving up privileges that the rules of the game may attribute to a player. A player may be admitted to a coalition under terms less favorable than those obtained by the players who form the initial core of a coalition (this happens first when $n = 4$). Also, coalitions of different strength can be distinguished. *Discrimination* may occur; for example, some players may consider others "taboo"—that is, unworthy as coalition partners. This leads to the types of discriminatory solutions that already occur when $n = 3$. Yet discrimination is not necessarily as bad for the affected player as defeat is for a nondiscriminated player, because cooperation against the discriminated player may not be perfect. A player who by joining a coalition does not contribute more to it than what he can get by playing for himself merely has the role of a dummy.

The fundamental fact of cooperation is that the players in a coalition can each obtain more than they could obtain by playing alone. This expresses the nonadditivity—specifically, the superadditivity—of value, the explanation of which has long been recognized as a basic problem in economics and sociology. In spite of many efforts, no solution was found, but it is now adequately described by the characteristic function $v(S)$, a numerical set function that states for any cooperative n-person game the proceeds of the coalition S, and an imputation that describes the distribution of all payments among all players (von Neumann & Morgenstern 1944, chapter 6).

Since there may be many solutions to a cooperative (essential) n-person game, the question arises as to which of them will in fact prevail. Each solution may correspond to a specific mode of behavior of the players or a specific form of social organization. This expresses the fact that in the same physical setting different types of social organization can be established, each one consistent in itself but in contradiction with other organizations. For example, we observe that the same technology allows the maintenance of varying economic systems, income distributions, and so on. If a *stable standard of behavior* exists (a mode of behavior accepted by society), then it can be argued that the only relevant solution is the one corresponding to this standard.

The choice of an imputation *not* in the solution set, while advantageous to each of those in the particular coalition that is able to enforce this imputation, cannot be maintained because another coalition can enforce another imputation, belonging to the solution set, that dominates the first one. Hence, a standard is set and proposals for imputations that are not in the solution will be rejected. The theory cannot state which imputation of all those belonging to the standard of behavior actually will be chosen—that is, which coalition will form. Work has been done to introduce new assumptions under which this may become feasible. No imputation contained in the solution set guarantees stability by itself, since each is necessarily dominated from the outside. But in turn each imputation is always protected against threats by another one *within* the solution set that dominates the imputation *not* in the solution set.

Since an imputation is a division of proceeds among the players, these conditions define a certain fairness, such that the classical problems of fair division (for example, cutting a cake) become amenable to game-theoretic analysis.

This conceptual structure is more complicated than the conventional view that society could be organized according to some simple principle of maximization. The conventional view would be valid only if there were inessentiality—that is, if there were no advantage in cooperation, or if cooperation were forbidden, or, finally, if a supreme authority were to do away with the entire imputation problem by simply assigning shares of income to the members of the society. Inessentiality would be the case for a strictly communistic society, which is formally equivalent to a Robinson Crusoe economy. This, in turn, is the only formal setup under which the classical notion of marginal utility is logically valid. Whether cooperation through formation of coalitions is advantageous to participants in a society, whether such cooperation, although advantageous, is forbidden, or whether compensations or side payments are ruled out by some authority although coalitions may be entered—these are clearly empirical questions. The theory should take care of all eventualities, and current investigations explore the different avenues. In economic life, mergers, labor unions, trade associations, cartels, etc., express the powerful tendencies toward cooperation. The cooperative case with side payments is the most comprehensive, and the theory was originally designed to deal with this case. Important results have been obtained for cooperative games without side payments (Aumann & Peleg 1961), and the fruitful idea of "bargaining sets" has been introduced (Aumann & Maschler 1964).

All indications point overwhelmingly to the benefits of cooperation of various forms and hence to the empirical irrelevance of those noncooperative, inessential games with uniquely determined solutions consisting only of one single imputation dominating all others (as described in the Lausanne school's general economic equilibrium).

Cooperation may depend on a particular flow of information among the players. Since the required level may not in fact be attainable, noncooperative solutions become important. Economic markets in which players act independently and have no incentive to deviate from a given state have been studied (Nash 1950). *Equilibrium points* can be determined as those points for which unilateral changes in strategy are unprofitable to everyone. As Nash has shown, every finite game, or the domain of mixed strategies, has at least one equilibrium point. If there is more than one equilibrium point, an intermixture of strategy choices need not give another equilibrium point, nor is the payoff to players the same if the points differ from each other.

There is no proof, as yet, that every cooperative n-person, zero-sum game for any $n > 4$ has a solution of the specified kind. However, every individual game investigated, even with arbitrarily large n, has been found to possess a solution. The indications are that the proof for the general case will eventually be given. Other definitions of solutions—still differing from that of the Lausanne–Robinson Crusoe convention—are possible and somewhat narrow the field of choices. They are inevitably based on further assumptions about the behavior of the participants in the game, which have to be justified from case to case.

Simple games

In certain n-person games the sole purpose is to form a *majority* coalition. These games are the "simple" games in which voting takes place. Ties in voting may occur, and weights may differ from one player to another; for example, the chairman of a committee may have more than one vote. A player's presence may therefore mean the difference between victory or defeat. Games of this nature can be identified with classical cases of production, where the players represent factors of production. It has been proven that even in relatively simple cases, although complete substitutability among players may exist, substitution rates may be undetermined and values are attributed to the players (factors) only by virtue of their *relation* to each other and not by virtue of their individual contribution. Thus, contrary to current economic doctrine, substitutability does not necessarily guarantee equality as far as value is concerned.

Simple games are suited for interpretation of many political situations in that they allow the determination of the weights, or power, of participants in decision processes. A particular power index has been proposed by Shapley. It is based on the notion of the average contribution a player can make to the coalitions to which he may belong, even considering, where necessary, the order in which he joins them. The weight of a senator, a congressman, and the president in the legislative process has been calculated for the United States. The procedure is applicable to other political systems—for example, the Security Council of the United Nations (Shapley 1953).

Composition of games

Every increase in the number of players brings new phenomena: with the increase from two to three players, coalitions become possible, from three to four, ties may occur among coalitions, etc.

There is no guarantee that for very large n an asymptotic convergence of solutions will occur, since coalition formation always reduces large numbers of individual players to small numbers of coalitions acting upon each other. Thus, the increase in the number of players does not necessarily lead to a simplification, as in the case of an enlargement of the numbers of bodies in a physical system, which then allows the introduction of classical methods of statistical averages as a simplification. (When the game is inessential, the number of participants is irrelevant in any case.)

An effective extension of the theory by the enlargement of numbers can be achieved by viewing games played separately as one composite game and by introducing contributions to, or withdrawals from, the proceeds of a given game by a group of players outside the game under consideration. These more complicated notions involve constant-sum games and demonstrate, among other things, how the coalition formation, the degree of cooperation among players, and consequently the distribution of the proceeds among them are affected by the availability of amounts in excess of those due to their own strategies alone. Strategy is clearly greatly influenced by the availability of greater payments than those that can be made by only the other players. Thus, coalitions—namely, social structures—cannot be maintained if outside contributions become larger than specified amounts, such that as a consequence no coalition can exhaust the amounts offered. It can also be shown that the outside source, making contributions or withdrawals, can never be less than a group of three players.

These concepts and results are obviously of a rather complicated nature; they are not always directly accessible to intuition, as corresponds to a truly mathematical theory. When that level is reached, confidence in the mathematical results must override intuition, as the experience in the natural sciences shows. The fact that solutions of n-person games are not single numbers or single sets of numbers—but that the above-mentioned, more complicated structures emerge—is not an imperfection of the theory: it is a fundamental property of social organization that can be described only by game-theoretic methods.

Nonzero-sum games

Nonzero-sum games can be reduced to zero-sum games—which makes that entire theory applicable—by the introduction of a fictitious player, so that an n-person, nonzero-sum game becomes equivalent to an $(n + 1)$-person, zero-sum game. The fictitious player is either winning or losing, but since he is fictitious he can never become a member of a coalition. Yet he can be construed as proposing alternative imputations, thereby influencing the players' strategies and thus the course of the play. He will lose according to the degree of cooperation among the players. If the players cooperate perfectly, the maximum social benefit will be attained. In these games there is an increased role of threats, and their costs to the threatening player, although threats already occur in the zero-sum case.

The discriminatory solutions, first encountered for the three-person, zero-sum game, serve as instruments to approach these problems. Most applications to economics involve gains by the community—an economy being productive and there being no voluntary exchange unless both sides profit—while many other social phenomena fall under the domain of zero-sum games. The non-zero-sum theory is so far the part of game theory least developed in detail, although its foundations seem to be firmly established by the above procedure.

Applications

Game theory is applicable to the study of those social phenomena in which there are agents striving for their own advantage but not in control of all the variables on which the outcome depends. The wide range of situations of which this is true is obvious: they are economic, political, military, and strictly social in nature. Applications have been made in varying degree to all areas; some have led to experiments that have yielded important new insights into the theory itself and into special processes such as bargaining. Finally, the possibility of viewing the basic problem of statistics as a game against nature has given rise to modern statistical decision theory (Wald 1950). The influence of game theory is also evident in philosophy, information theory, cybernetics, and even biology.

OSKAR MORGENSTERN

[*See also the biography of* VON NEUMANN.]

BIBLIOGRAPHY

AUMANN, R. J.; and PELEG, B. 1961 Von Neumann–Morgenstern Solutions to Cooperative Games Without Side Payments. American Mathematical Society, *Bulletin* 66:173–179.

AUMANN, R. J.; and MASCHLER, M. 1964 The Bargaining Set for Cooperative Games. Pages 443–476 in M. Dresher, L. S. Shapley, and A. W. Tucker (editors), *Advances in Game Theory.* Princeton Univ. Press.

BAUMOL, WILLIAM J.; and GOLDFELD, STEPHEN M. (editors) 1967 Precursors in Mathematical Economics. Unpublished manuscript. → To be published in 1967 or 1968 by the London School of Economics and Political Science. Contains the letter from Waldegrave to Rémond de Montmort, first published in the second (1713) edition of Montmort (1708), describing his formulation, and a discussion by Harold W. Kuhn of the identity of Waldegrave.

BERGE, CLAUDE 1957 *Théorie générale des jeux à n personnes.* Paris: Gauthier-Villars.

BLACKWELL, DAVID; and GIRSHICK, M. A. 1954 *Theory of Games and Statistical Decisions.* New York: Wiley.

BRAITHWAITE, RICHARD B. 1955 *Theory of Games as a Tool for the Moral Philosopher.* Cambridge Univ. Press.

BURGER, EWALD (1959) 1963 *Introduction to the Theory of Games.* Englewood Cliffs, N.J.: Prentice-Hall. → First published in German.

DRESHER, MELVIN 1961 *Games of Strategy: Theory and Applications.* Englewood Cliffs, N.J.: Prentice-Hall.

DRESHER, MELVIN; SHAPLEY, L. S.; and TUCKER, A. W. (editors) 1964 *Advances in Game Theory.* Annals of Mathematic Studies, Vol. 32. Princeton Univ. Press.

EDGEWORTH, FRANCIS Y. (1881) 1953 *Mathematical Psychics: An Essay on the Application of Mathematics to the Moral Sciences.* New York: Kelley.

FRÉCHET, MAURICE; and VON NEUMANN, JOHN 1953 Commentary on the Three Notes of Émile Borel. *Econometrica* 21, no. 1:118–127.

KARLIN, SAMUEL 1959 *Mathematical Methods and Theory in Games, Programming and Economics.* 2 vols. Reading, Mass.: Addison-Wesley.

KUHN, HAROLD W.; and TUCKER, A. W. (editors) 1950–1959 *Contributions to the Theory of Games.* 4 vols. Princeton Univ. Press.

LUCE, R. DUNCAN; and RAIFFA, HOWARD 1957 *Games and Decisions: Introduction and Critical Survey.* A Study of the Behavioral Models Project, Bureau of Applied Social Research, Columbia University. New York. → First published in 1954 as *A Survey of the Theory of Games,* Columbia University, Bureau of Applied Social Research, Technical Report No. 5.

McKINSEY, JOHN C. C. 1952 *Introduction to the Theory of Games.* New York: McGraw-Hill.

[MONTMORT, PIERRE RÉMOND DE] (1708) 1713 *Essay d'analyse sur les jeux de hazard.* 2d ed. Paris: Quillau. → Published anonymously.

MORGENSTERN, OSKAR 1963 *Spieltheorie und Wirtschaftswissenschaft.* Vienna: Oldenbourg.

NASH, JOHN F. JR. 1950 Equilibrium in *n*-Person Games. National Academy of Sciences, *Proceedings* 36:48–49.

PRINCETON UNIVERSITY CONFERENCE 1962 *Recent Advances in Game Theory.* Princeton, N.J.: The Conference.

SHAPLEY, L. S. 1953 A Value for *n*-Person Games. Volume 2, pages 307–317 in Harold W. Kuhn and A. W. Tucker (editors), *Contributions to the Theory of Games.* Princeton Univ. Press.

SHAPLEY, L. S.; and SHUBIK, MARTIN 1954 A Method for Evaluating the Distribution of Power in a Committee System. *American Political Science Review* 48:787–792.

SHUBIK, MARTIN (editor) 1964 *Game Theory and Related Approaches to Social Behavior: Selections.* New York: Wiley.

SUZUKI, MITSUO 1959 *Gemu no riron.* Tokyo: Keisho Shobo.

VILLE, JEAN 1938 Sur la théorie générale des jeux ou intervient l'habilité des joueurs. Pages 105–113 in Émile Borel (editor), *Traité du calcul des probabilités et de ses applications.* Volume 4: Applications diverses et conclusion. Paris: Gauthier-Villars.

Vogelsang, Rudolf 1963 *Die mathematische Theorie der Spiele.* Bonn: Dümmler.

von Neumann, John (1928) 1959 On the Theory of Games of Strategy. Volume 4, pages 13–42 in Harold W. Kuhn and A. W. Tucker (editors), *Contributions to the Theory of Games.* Princeton Univ. Press. → First published in German in Volume 100 of the *Mathematische Annalen.*

von Neumann, John; and Morgenstern, Oskar (1944) 1964 *Theory of Games and Economic Behavior.* 3d ed. New York: Wiley.

Vorob'ev, N. N. (editor) 1961 *Matrichnye igry.* Moscow: Gosudarstvennoe Izdatel'stvo Fiziko–Matematicheskoi Literatury. → A collection of translations into Russian from foreign-language publications.

Wald, Abraham (1950) 1964 *Statistical Decision Functions.* New York: Wiley.

Williams, John D. 1954 *The Compleat Strategyst: Being a Primer in the Theory of Games and Strategy.* New York: McGraw-Hill.

II
ECONOMIC APPLICATIONS

The major economic applications of game theory have been in oligopoly theory, bargaining theory, and general equilibrium theory. Several distinct branches of game theory exist and need to be identified before our attention is limited to economic behavior. John von Neumann and Oskar Morgenstern, who first explored in depth the role of game theory in economic analysis (1944), presented three aspects of game theory which are so fundamentally independent of one another that with a small amount of editing their opus could have been published as three independent books.

The first topic was the description of a game, or interdependent decision process, in extensive form. This provided a phraseology ("choice," "decision tree," "move," "information," "strategy," and "payoff") for the precise definition of terms, which has served as a basis for studying artificial intelligence, for developing the behavioral theory of the firm (Cyert & March 1963), and for considering statistical decision making [see DECISION THEORY]. The definition of "payoff" has been closely associated with developments in utility theory [see UTILITY].

The second topic was the description of the two-person, zero-sum game and the development of the mathematical theory based upon the concept of the minimax solution. This theory has formal mathematical connections with linear programming and has been applied successfully to the analysis of problems of pure conflict; however, its application to the social sciences has been limited because pure conflict of interests is the exception rather than the rule in social situations [see PROGRAMMING].

The third subject to which von Neumann and Morgenstern directed their attention was the development of a static theory for the n-person ($n \geqslant 3$), constant-sum game. They suggested a set of stability and domination conditions which should hold for a cooperative solution to an n-person game. It must be noted that the implications of this solution concept were developed on the assumption of the existence of a transferable, interpersonally comparable linear utility which provides a mechanism for side payments. Since the original work of von Neumann and Morgenstern, twenty to thirty alternative solution concepts for the n-person, non-constant-sum game have been suggested. Some have been of purely mathematical interest, but most have been based on considerations of bargaining, fair division, social stability, and other aspects of human affairs. Many of the solution concepts do not use the assumption of transferable utility.

Oligopoly and bargaining

Markets in which there are only a few sellers (oligopoly), two sellers (duopoly, a special case of oligopoly), one seller and one buyer (bilateral monopoly), and so on, lend themselves to game-theoretic analyses because the fate of each participant depends on the actions taken by the other participant or participants. The theory of games has provided a unifying basis for the mathematical and semimathematical works dealing with such situations and has also provided some new results. The methodology of game theory requires explicit and detailed definition of the strategies available to the players and of the payoffs associated with the strategies. This methodology has helped to clarify the different aspects of intent, behavior, and market structure in oligopolistic markets (Shubik 1957). So-called conjectural variations and lengthy statements regarding an oligopolist's (or duopolist's or bargainer's) moves and countermoves can be investigated in a unified way when expressed in terms of strategies.

Oligopoly. Perhaps the most pervasive concept underlying the writings on oligopoly is that of a noncooperative equilibrium. A group of individuals is in a state of noncooperative equilibrium if, in the individual pursuit of his own self-interest, no one in the group is motivated to change his strategy. This concept is basic in the works of Cournot, Bertrand, Edgeworth, Chamberlin, von Stackelberg, and many others. Nash (1951) has presented a general theory of noncooperative games, based on the equilibrium-point solution. This theory is directly related to Chamberlin's theory of monopolistic competition, among others.

The outcome given by a solution is called Pareto optimal if no participant can be made better off without some other participant's being made worse off. Noncooperative solutions, whose outcomes need not be Pareto optimal, have been distinguished from cooperative solutions, whose outcomes must be Pareto optimal. Also, equilibrium points are distinguished on the basis of whether the oligopoly model studied is static or dynamic. In much of the literature on oligopoly, quasi-cooperative solutions have been advanced and quasi-dynamic models have been suggested. Thus, while the Chamberlin large-group equilibrium can be interpreted as the outcome of a static noncooperative game, the small-group equilibrium and the market resolution suggested by Fellner (1949) are cast in a quasi-dynamic, quasi-cooperative framework. A limited amount of development of games of survival (Milnor & Shapley 1957) and games of economic survival (Shubik & Thompson 1959) has provided a basis for the study of multiperiod situations and for an extension of the noncooperative equilibrium concept to include quasi-cooperative outcomes.

New results. The recasting of oligopoly situations into a game-theory context has produced some new results in oligopoly theory (see, for example, Mayberry, Nash, & Shubik 1953; Shubik 1959*a*). Nash (1953) and Shubik (1959*a*) have developed the definition of "optimum threat" in economic warfare. The kinky oligopoly demand curve and the more general problem of oligopolistic demand have been re-examined and interpreted. Other results concern stability and the Edgeworth cycle in price-variation oligopoly; duopoly with both price and quantity as independent variables; and the development of diverse concepts applicable to cartel behavior, such as blocking coalitions (Scarf 1965), discriminatory solutions, and decomposable games.

Selten (1965) has been concerned with the problem of calculating the noncooperative equilibria for various classes of oligopolistic markets. His work has focused on both the explicit calculation and the uniqueness of equilibrium points. Vickrey (1961), Griesmer and Shubik (1963), and others have studied a class of game models applicable to bidding and auction markets. Working from the viewpoint of marketing and operations research, Mills (1961) and others have constructed several noncooperative game-theoretic models of competition through advertising. Jacot (1963) has considered problems involving location and spatial competition.

Behavioristic findings. Game theory can be given both a normative and a behavioristic interpretation. The meaning of "rational behavior" in situations involving elements of conflict and cooperation is not well defined. No single set of normative criteria

has been generally accepted, and no universal behavior has been validated. Closely related to and partially inspired by the developments in game theory, there has been a growth in experimental gaming, some of which has been in the context of economic bargaining (Siegel & Fouraker 1960) or in the simulated environment of an oligopolistic market (Hoggatt 1959). Where there is no verbal or face-to-face communication, there appears, under the appropriate circumstances, to be some evidence in favor of the noncooperative equilibrium.

Bargaining. The theory of bargaining has been of special interest to economists in the context of bilateral monopoly, which can involve two firms, a labor union and a firm, or two individuals engaged in barter in the market place or trying to settle a joint estate. Any two-person, nonconstant-sum situation, be it haggling in the market or international negotiations, can be formally described in the same game-theoretic framework. However, there are several substantive problems which limit application of this framework and which have resulted in the development of different approaches. In nonconstant-sum games communication between the players is of considerable importance, yet its role is exceedingly hard to define. In games such as chess and even in many oligopolistic markets, a move is a well-defined physical act—moving a pawn in a definite manner or changing a price or deciding upon a production rate; in bargaining it may be necessary to interpret a statement as a move. The problem of interpreting words as moves in negotiation is critical to the description and understanding of bargaining and negotiation processes. This "coding" problem has to be considered from the viewpoint of many other disciplines, as well as that of game theory.

A desirable property of a theoretical solution to a bargaining problem is that it predicts a unique outcome. In the context of economics this would be a unique distribution of resources (and unique prices, if prices exist at all). Unfortunately, there are few concepts of solution pertaining to economic affairs which have this property. The price system and distribution resulting from a competitive market may in general not be unique; Edgeworth's solution to the bargaining problem was the contract curve, which merely predicts that the outcome will be some point among an infinite set of possibilities.

The contract curve has the property that any point on it is jointly optimal (both bargainers cannot improve their position simultaneously from a point on this curve) and individually rational (no point gives an individual less than he could obtain without trading). The Pareto-optimal surface is larger than the contract curve, for it is restricted only by the joint optimality condition. If it is assumed that a transferable comparable utility exists, then the Pareto-optimal surface (described in the space of the traders' utilities) is flat; if not, it will generally be curved. Any point on the Pareto-optimal surface that is individually rational is called an imputation. In the two-person bargain the Edgeworth contract curve coincides with two game-theoretic solutions, the *core* and the *stable set*. The core consists of all undominated imputations (it may be empty). A stable set is a set of imputations which do not dominate each other but which together dominate all other imputations. An imputation, α, is said to *dominate* another imputation, β, if (1) there exists a coalition of players who, acting jointly but independently of the others, could guarantee for themselves at least the amounts they would receive if they accepted α, and (2) each player obtains more in α than in β. The core and stable-set solutions can be defined with or without the assumption of transferable utilities. Neither of these solution concepts predicts a unique outcome.

One approach to bilateral monopoly has been to regard it as a "fair-division" problem, and several solution concepts, each one embodying a formalization of concepts of symmetry, justice, and equity, have been suggested (Nash 1953; Shapley 1953; Harsanyi 1956). These are generally known as *value* solutions, since they specify the amount that each participant should obtain. For the two-person case, some of the fair-division or arbitration schemes do predict unique outcomes. The Nash fair-division scheme assumes that utilities of the players are measurable, but it does not need assumptions of either comparability or transferability of utilities (Shubik 1966). Shapley's scheme does utilize the last two assumptions. Other schemes have been suggested by Raiffa (1953), Braithwaite (1955), Kuhn (in Shubik 1967), and others.

Another approach to bargaining is to treat it in the extensive form, describing each move explicitly and showing the time path taken to the settlement point. This involves attempting to parametrize qualities such as "toughness," "flexibility," etc. Most of the attempts to apply game theory in this manner belong to studies in social psychology, political science, and experimental gaming. However, it has been shown (Harsanyi 1956) that the dynamic process suggested by Zeuthen (1930) is equivalent to the Nash fair-division scheme.

General equilibrium

Game theory methods have provided several new insights in general equilibrium economics. Under the appropriate conditions on preferences and production, it has been proved that a price system that clears the market will exist, provided that each individual acts as an independent maximizer. This result holds true independently of the number of participants in the market; hence, it cannot be interpreted as a limiting phenomenon as the number of participants increases. Yet, in verbal discussions contrasting the competitive market with bilateral monopoly, the difference generally stressed is that between the market with many participants, each with little if any control over price, and the market with few participants, where the interactions of each with all the others are of maximum importance.

The competitive equilibrium best reflects the spirit of "the invisible hand" and of decentralization. The use of the word "competitive" is counter to both game-theoretic and common-language implications. It refers to the case in which, if each individual considers himself an isolated maximizer operating in an environment over which he has no control, the results will be jointly optimal.

Game-theoretic solutions. The power and appeal of the concept of competitive equilibrium appears to be far greater than that of mere decentralization. This is reflected in the finding that under the appropriate conditions the competitive equilibrium may be regarded as the limit solution for several conceptually extremely different game-theoretic solutions.

Convergence of the core. It has been noted that for bilateral monopoly the Edgeworth contract curve is the core. Edgeworth had suggested and presented an argument to show that if the number of traders is increased on both sides of the market, the contract curve would shrink (interpreted appropriately, given the change in dimensions). Shubik (1959b) observed the connection between the work of Edgeworth and the core; he proved the convergence of the core to the competitive equilibrium in the special case of the two-sided market with transferable utility and conjectured that the result would be generally true for any number of markets without transferable utility. This result was proved by Scarf (the proof, although achieved earlier, is described in Scarf 1965); Debreu and Scarf improved upon it (1963). Using the concept of a continuum of players (rather than considering a limit by replicating the finite number of players in each category, as was done by Shubik, Scarf, and Debreu), Aumann (1966) proved the convergence of the core under somewhat different conditions. When transferable utility is assumed, the core converges to a single point and the competitive equilibrium is unique. Otherwise it may split and converge to the set of competitive equilibria.

The convergence of the core establishes the existence of a price system as a result of a theory which makes no mention of prices. The theory's prime concern is with the power of coalitions. It may be looked upon as a formalization of countervailing power, inasmuch as it rules out imputations which can be dominated by any group in the society.

Shapley and Shubik (1966) have shown the convergence of the value in the two-sided market with transferable utility. In unpublished work Shapley has proved a more general result for any number of markets, and Shapley and Aumann have worked on the convergence of a nontransferable utility value recently defined by Shapley. Harsanyi (1959) was able to define a value that generalized the Nash two-person fair-division scheme to situations involving many individuals whose utilities are not transferable. This preceded and is related to the new value of Shapley, and its convergence has not been proved.

There are several other value concepts (Selten 1964), all of which make use of symmetry axioms and are based upon some type of averaging of the contributions of an individual to all coalitions.

If one is willing to accept the value as reflecting certain concepts of symmetry and fairness, then in an economy with many individuals in all walks of life, and with the conditions which are required for the existence of a competitive equilibrium satisfied, the competitive equilibria will also satisfy these symmetry and fairness criteria.

Noncooperative equilibrium. One of the important open problems has been the reconciliation of the various noncooperative theories of oligopolistic competition with general equilibrium theory. The major difficulty is that the oligopoly models are open in the sense that the customers are usually not considered as players with strategic freedom, while the general equilibrium model considers every individual in the same manner, regardless of his position in the economy. Since the firms are players in the oligopoly models, it is necessary to specify the domain of the strategies they control and their payoffs under all circumstances. In a general equilibrium model no individual is considered a player; all are regarded as individual maximizers. Walras' law is assumed to hold, and supply is assumed to equal demand.

When an attempt is made to consider a closed economic model as a noncooperative game, considerable difficulties are encountered in describing the strategies of the players. This can be seen im-

mediately by considering the bilateral monopoly problem; each individual does not really know what he is in a position to buy until he finds out what he can sell. In order to model this type of situation as a game, it may be necessary to consider strategies which do not clear the market and which may cause a player to become bankrupt—i.e., unable to meet his commitments. Shapley and Shubik (in Shubik 1967) have successfully modeled the closed two-sided two-commodity market without side payments and have shown that the noncooperative equilibrium point converges from below the Pareto-optimal surface to the competitive equilibrium point. They also have considered more goods and markets on the assumption of the existence of a transferable (but not necessarily comparable) utility.

When there are more than two commodities and one market, the existence of a unique competitive equilibrium point appears to be indispensable in defining the strategies and payoffs of players in a noncooperative game. No one has succeeded in constructing a satisfactory general market model as a noncooperative game without using a side-payment mechanism. The important role played by the side-payment commodity is that of a strategy decoupler. It means that a player with a supply of this type of "money" can decide what to buy even though he does not know what he will sell.

In summary, it appears that, in the limit, at least three considerably different game-theoretic solutions are coincidental with the competitive equilibrium solution. This means that by considering different solutions we may interpret the competitive market in terms of decentralization, fair division, the power of groups, and the attenuation of power of the individual.

The stable-set solution of von Neumann and Morgenstern, the bargaining set of Aumann and Maschler (1964), the "self-policing" properties of certain imputation sets of Vickrey (1959), and several other related cooperative solutions appear to be more applicable to sociology, and possibly anthropology, than to economics. There has been no indication of a limiting behavior for these solutions as numbers grow; on the contrary, it is conjectured that in general the solutions proliferate. When, however, numbers are few, as in cartel arrangements and in international trade, these other solutions provide insights, as Nyblén has shown in his work dealing with stable sets (1951).

Nonexistence of competitive equilibrium. When conditions other than those needed for the existence of a competitive equilibrium hold, such as external economies or diseconomies, joint ownership, increasing returns to scale, and interlinked tastes, then the different solutions in general do not converge. There may be no competitive equilibrium; the core may be empty; and the definition of a non-cooperative game when joint property is at stake will call for a statement of the laws concerning damages and threats. (Similarly, even though the conditions for the existence of a competitive equilibrium are satisfied, the various solutions will be different if there are few participants.) When the competitive equilibrium does not exist, we must seek another criterion to solve the problem of distribution or, if possible, change the laws to reintroduce the competitive equilibrium. The other solutions provide different criteria. However, if a society desires, for example, to have its distribution system satisfy conditions of decentralization and fair division, or of fair division and limits on power of groups, it may be logically impossible to do so.

Davis and Whinston (1962), Scarf (1964), and Shapley and Shubik (1964) have investigated applications of game theory to external economies, to increasing returns to scale, and to joint ownership. In the case of joint ownership the relation between economics and politics as mechanisms for the distribution of the proceeds from jointly owned resources is evident.

It must be noted that the "many solutions" approach to distribution is in contrast to the type of welfare economics that considers a community welfare function or social preferences, which are not necessarily constructed from individual preferences.

Other applications

Leaving aside questions of transferable utility, there is a considerable difference between an economy in which there is only barter or a passive shadow price system and one in which the government, and possibly others, have important monetary strategies. Faxen (1957) has considered financial policy from a game-theoretic viewpoint.

There have been some diverse applications of game theory to budgeting and to management science, as can be seen in the articles by Bennion (1956) and Shubik (1955).

Nyblén (1951) has attempted to apply the von Neumann and Morgenstern concept of stable set to problems of macroeconomics. He notes that the Walrasian system bypasses the problem of individual power by assuming it away. He observes that in game theory certain simple aggregation procedures do not hold; thus, the solutions to a four-person game obtained by aggregating two players in a five-person game may have little in common with the solutions to the original five-person game. He outlines an institutional theory of the rate of interest based upon a standard of behavior and (primarily at a descriptive level) links the concepts of discriminatory solution and excess to inflation and international trade.

MARTIN SHUBIK

[The reader who is not familiar with oligopoly theory and general equilibrium theory should consult ECO-NOMIC EQUILIBRIUM; OLIGOPOLY; WELFARE ECO-NOMICS.]

BIBLIOGRAPHY

AUMANN, ROBERT J. 1966 Existence of Competitive Equilibria in Markets With a Continuum of Traders. Econometrica 34: 1–17.

AUMANN, R. J.; and MASCHLER, M. 1964 The Bargaining Set for Cooperative Games. Pages 443–476 in M. Dresher, Lloyd S. Shapley, and A. W. Tucker (editors), Advances in Game Theory. Princeton Univ. Press.

BENNION, E. G. 1956 Capital Budgeting and Game Theory. Harvard Business Review 34: 115–123.

BRAITHWAITE, RICHARD B. 1955 Theory of Games as a Tool for the Moral Philosopher. Cambridge Univ. Press.

CYERT, RICHARD M.; and MARCH, JAMES G. 1963 A Behavioral Theory of the Firm. Englewood Cliffs, N.J.: Prentice-Hall.

DAVIS, OTTO A.; and WHINSTON, A. 1962 Externalities, Welfare, and the Theory of Games. Journal of Political Economy 70: 241–262.

DEBREU, GERARD; and SCARF, HERBERT 1963 A Limit Theorem on the Core of an Economy. International Economic Review 4: 235–246.

FAXEN, KARL O. 1957 Monetary and Fiscal Policy Under Uncertainty. Stockholm: Almqvist & Wiksell.

FELLNER, WILLIAM J. 1949 Competition Among the Few: Oligopoly and Similar Market Structures. New York: Knopf.

GRIESMER, JAMES H.; and SHUBIK, MARTIN 1963 Towards a Study of Bidding Processes. Naval Research Logistics Quarterly 10: 11–21, 151–173, 199–217.

HARSANYI, JOHN C. 1956 Approaches to the Bargaining Problem Before and After the Theory of Games. Econometrica 24: 144–157.

HARSANYI, JOHN C. 1959 A Bargaining Model for the Cooperative n-Person Game. Volume 4, pages 325–356 in Harold W. Kuhn and A. W. Tucker (editors), Contributions to the Theory of Games. Princeton Univ. Press. → Volume 4 was edited by A. W. Tucker and R. Duncan Luce.

HOGGATT, A. C. 1959 An Experimental Business Game. Behavioral Science 4: 192–203.

JACOT, SIMON-PIERRE 1963 Stratégie et concurrence de l'application de la théorie des jeux à l'analyse de la concurrence spatiale. Paris: SEDES.

MAYBERRY, J. P.; NASH, J. F.; and SHUBIK, MARTIN 1953 A Comparison of Treatments of a Duopoly Situation. Econometrica 21: 141–154.

MILLS, H. D. 1961 A Study in Promotional Competition. Pages 245–301 in Frank M. Bass et al. (editors), Mathematical Models and Methods in Marketing. Homewood, Ill.: Irwin.

MILNOR, JOHN W.; and SHAPLEY, LLOYD S. 1957 On Games of Survival. Volume 3, pages 15–45 in Harold W. Kuhn and A. W. Tucker (editors), *Contributions to the Theory of Games*. Princeton Univ. Press. → Volume 3 was edited by M. Dresher, A. W. Tucker, and P. Wolfe.

NASH, JOHN F. JR. 1951 Non-cooperative Games. *Annals of Mathematics* 54:286–295.

NASH, JOHN F. JR. 1953 Two-person Cooperative Games. *Econometrica* 21:128–140.

NYBLÉN, GÖREN 1951 *The Problem of Summation in Economic Sciences*. Lund (Sweden): Gleerup.

RAIFFA, HOWARD 1953 Arbitration Schemes for Generalized Two-person Games. Volume 2, pages 361–387 in Harold W. Kuhn and A. W. Tucker (editors), *Contributions to the Theory of Games*. Princeton Univ. Press.

SCARF, H. 1964 Notes on the Core of a Productive Economy. Unpublished manuscript, Yale Univ., Cowles Foundation for Research in Economics.

SCARF, H. 1965 The Core of an *n*-Person Game. Unpublished manuscript, Yale Univ., Cowles Foundation for Research in Economics.

SELTEN, REINHARD 1964 Valuation of *n*-Person Games. Pages 577–626 in M. Dresher, Lloyd S. Shapley, and A. W. Tucker (editors), *Advances in Game Theory*. Princeton Univ. Press.

SELTEN, REINHARD 1965 Value of the *n*-Person Game. → Paper presented at the First International Game Theory Workshop, Hebrew University of Jerusalem.

SHAPLEY, LLOYD S. 1953 A Value for *n*-Person Games. Volume 2, pages 307–317 in Harold W. Kuhn and A. W. Tucker (editors), *Contributions to the Theory of Games*. Princeton Univ. Press.

SHAPLEY, LLOYD S.; and SHUBIK, MARTIN 1964 *Ownership and the Production Function*. RAND Corporation Research Memorandum, RM-4053-PR. Santa Monica, Calif.: The Corporation.

SHAPLEY, LLOYD S.; and SHUBIK, MARTIN 1966 *Pure Competition, Coalition Power and Fair Division*. RAND Corporation Research Memorandum, RM-4917. Santa Monica, Calif.: The Corporation.

SHUBIK, MARTIN 1955 The Uses of Game Theory in Management Science. *Management Science* 2:40–54.

SHUBIK, MARTIN 1957 Market Form, Intent of the Firm and Market Behavior. *Zeitschrift für Nationalökonomie* 17:186–196.

SHUBIK, MARTIN 1959a *Strategy and Market Structure: Competition, Oligopoly, and the Theory of Games*. New York: Wiley.

SHUBIK, MARTIN 1959b Edgeworth Market Games. Volume 4, pages 267–278 in Harold W. Kuhn and A. W. Tucker (editors), *Contributions to the Theory of Games*. Princeton Univ. Press. → Volume 4 was edited by A. W. Tucker and R. Duncan Luce.

SHUBIK, MARTIN 1966 Measureable, Transferable, Comparable Utility and Money. Unpublished manuscript, Yale Univ., Cowles Foundation for Research in Economics.

SHUBIK, MARTIN (editor) 1967 *Essays in Mathematical Economics in Honor of Oskar Morgenstern*. Princeton Univ. Press. → See especially Harold W. Kuhn, "On Games of Fair Division"; and Lloyd S. Shapley and Martin Shubik, "Concept and Theories of Pure Competition."

SHUBIK, MARTIN; and THOMPSON, GERALD L. 1959 Games of Economic Survival. *Naval Research Logistics Quarterly* 6:111–123.

SIEGEL, S.; and FOURAKER, L. E. 1960 *Bargaining and Group Decision Making: Experiments in Bilateral Monopoly*. New York: McGraw-Hill.

VICKREY, WILLIAM 1959 Self-policing Properties of Certain Imputation Sets. Volume 4, pages 213–246 in Harold W. Kuhn and A. W. Tucker (editors), *Contributions to the Theory of Games*. Princeton Univ. Press. → Volume 4 was edited by A. W. Tucker and R. Duncan Luce.

VICKREY, WILLIAM 1961 Counterspeculation, Auctions and Competitive Sealed Tenders. *Journal of Finance* 16:8–37.

VON NEUMANN, JOHN; and MORGENSTERN, OSKAR (1944) 1964 *Theory of Games and Economic Behavior*. 3d ed. New York: Wiley.

ZEUTHEN, F. 1930 *Problems of Monopoly and Economic Warfare*. London: Routledge.

GAMING

See SIMULATION.

GANGS

See under DELINQUENCY.

GAUSS, CARL FRIEDRICH

Carl Friedrich Gauss (1777–1855), greatest of German mathematicians, was born in Brunswick on April 30, 1777. (He was baptized Johann Friedrich Carl, but he later dropped his first name and reversed the second and third.) Ranked with Archimedes and Newton as one of the three greatest mathematicians of all time, he combined in a most unusual way a pure mathematician's interest in abstract ideas and logical rigor, a theoretical physicist's interest in the creation of mathematical models of the physical world, an astronomer's talent for keen observation, and an experimentalist's skill in the application and invention of methods of measurement. He was blessed with a stupendous faculty for mental calculation, which enabled him to explore numerical relationships experimentally and to carry out extensive or involved routine computations quickly and accurately; he also had a gift for learning ancient and modern languages, which became his hobby. He contributed mightily to every branch of pure and applied mathematics that existed in his day, some of which he had founded, and he made major contributions in astronomy, geodesy, physics, and metrology. Each of his many interests had its principal, but not exclusive, season: before 1800, philology and number theory; 1800–1820, astronomy; 1820–1830, geodesy, differential geometry, and conformal mapping; 1830–1840, geomagnetism, electromagnetism, and general theory of inverse-square forces; 1840–1855, topology and the geometry of functions of a complex variable. He died in Göttingen on February 23, 1855. Of his many contributions, those used most widely in the physical, biological, and social sciences today relate to the method of least squares, his first formulation of which dates from 1795 to 1798 and his second from 1821 to 1823.

Gauss was the only child of Gebhard Dietrich Gauss, a bricklayer and gardener, by his second wife, née Dorothea Benze, daughter of a stonemason. Gebhard Gauss, being skilled in writing and calculating, kept accounts for a local insurance company; he was esteemed by the townspeople, but at home he was harsh and uncouth, which repelled his brilliant son. Gauss's mother had no special schooling, could not write, and could barely read, but she was cheerful, intelligent, and of strong character. She had a genial and extraordinarily intelligent younger brother, Johann Friedrich, a skilled weaver of artistic damasks, who quickly spotted his nephew's unusual talents and capacities and enjoyed sharpening his wits on those of his sister's young genius. Gauss, as a small boy, thought highly of his uncle and later, lamenting his untimely death in 1809, often declared that a born genius had been lost in him.

Gauss's precocity is unequaled in the history of mathematics. Before he was three, while watching his father's payroll calculations he detected an error and announced the correct result. He was admitted at age ten to the beginners' class in arithmetic at St. Katherine's Volksschule in Brunswick, where the speed and accuracy of his mental calculations so astonished the schoolmaster that he purchased for the boy the best obtainable textbook on arithmetic, which Gauss quickly mastered, convincing the schoolmaster that Gauss had gone beyond him. Luckily the schoolmaster had an assistant who was interested in mathematics. He and Gauss studied algebra and the rudiments of calculus together in the evenings, helping each other over difficulties and amplifying the textbook proofs. Thus in his eleventh year Gauss became acquainted with the binomial theorem and, finding the textbook "proof" unsatisfactory when the exponent n is not a positive integer, devised his own proof of the convergence of the infinite series involved, which established him as one of the first of the "rigorists" and served as an inspiration for some of his greatest later work.

Early in 1791 Gauss's amazing powers came to the attention of Carl Wilhelm Ferdinand, duke of Brunswick, who became Gauss's patron, paid the expenses of his education at Caroline College from 1792 to 1795 and at the University of Göttingen

from 1795 to 1798, and until his death in 1806 gave Gauss considerable additional financial support. At Caroline College, Gauss devoted himself with equal success to classical literature, philosophy, and advanced mathematics. He studied carefully the original works of Newton, Euler, and Lagrange. In March 1795 (Dunnington 1955, p. 391) he rediscovered that invaluable principle of number theory, the law of quadratic reciprocity, which Legendre had published in 1785, and of which Gauss was to publish the first rigorous proof in 1801. Yet, on entering the University of Göttingen in October 1795, he was still undecided whether to make mathematics or philology his career.

Mathematics won on March 30, 1796, the day Gauss discovered that a regular polygon of 17 sides is amenable to straightedge-and-compass construction; such a construction had eluded mathematicians for two thousand years. By June 1, 1796, he had discovered much more: a regular polygon with an odd number of sides is amenable to such construction if and only if the number of its sides is a prime Fermat number, $F_n = 2^{2^n} + 1$, or a product of different prime Fermat numbers (five of which are known today). In 1796 he also developed the first rigorous proof of the fundamental theorem of algebra (i.e., that every nonconstant polynomial has a root), which became the subject of the doctoral dissertation for which he was awarded a PH.D. *in absentia* by the University of Helmstedt in 1799. In the autumn of 1798 Gauss polished the final draft of his greatest masterpiece, *Disquisitiones arithmeticae*, the printing of which began in 1799 but was not completed until September 1801, owing to the sale of the original print shop. Gauss brought together in this work his own original contributions to the theory of integral numbers and rational fractions and all of the principal related, but somewhat disconnected, results of his predecessors, so enriching the latter by rigorous reformulation and blending into a unified whole that this great book is regarded as marking the beginning of the theory of numbers as a separate, systematic branch of mathematics.

Among Gauss's early achievements was his reduction of the ecclesiastical calendar's extremely complicated computational procedure for finding the date of Easter (see *Encyclopaedia Britannica*, 11th ed., vol. 4, pp. 991–999) to a set of simple formulas from which the answer for any given year can be found in a few minutes. His motivation stemmed from his mother's inability to recall the exact date of his birth—only that it was a Wednesday, eight days before Ascension Day. As first published (1800), his procedure gave an incorrect date for Easter in 1734 and would have been incorrect again in 1886. Gauss supplied the necessary correction in 1807 and later provided an additional correction needed from 4200 on. (A semipopular exposition of Gauss's procedure, with a worked example, has been provided by H. Herbert Howe [1954].)

Gauss's first formulation of the method of least squares dates from his student days. In the autumn of 1794 he read (Galle 1924, p. 5) Lambert's discussion (1765, pp. 428–488) of the determination of the coefficients of a linear relationship $y = \alpha + \beta x$ from a set of n (> 2) observational points (Y_i, x_i) by the method of averages. In 1795 Gauss conceived the simpler and more objective procedure of taking for α and β the values a and b that minimize the sum of squared residuals, $\sum_i(Y_i - a - bx_i)^2$, and worked out the computational details, except for the weighting of observations of unequal precision (Galle 1924, p. 7). In 1797 he attempted to justify his minimum-sum-of-squared-residuals (mssr) technique by means of the theory of probability but "found out soon that determination of the most probable value of an unknown quantity is impossible unless the probability distribution of errors of observation is known explicitly" ([1821a] 1880, p. 98). Therefore, "it seemed to him most natural to proceed the other way around" and to seek the probability distribution of errors that "in the simplest case would result in the rule, generally accepted as good, that the arithmetic mean of several values for the same unknown quantity obtained from equally reliable observations shall be considered the most probable value" ([1821a] 1880, p. 98).

The concept of a probability distribution, or "law," of errors originated with Thomas Simpson (1755): he studied the sampling distribution of the arithmetic mean of n independent and identically distributed errors subject to a discrete rectangular or a discrete triangular law of error, and concluded that "the more observations or experiments are made, the less will the conclusion be subject to err, provided they admit of being made under the same circumstances" (p. 93). In 1757 he extended his analysis to samples of n from a continuous triangular distribution. Studies of other continuous laws of error followed: rectangular, by Lagrange, published in 1774; double-exponential $(Ce^{-m|x|}, -\infty < x < +\infty)$, by Laplace in 1774; semicircular $(C\sqrt{r^2 - x^2}, -r \leqslant x \leqslant +r)$, by Daniel Bernoulli in 1778; and double-logarithmic $(C \log a/|x|, -a \leqslant x \leqslant +a)$, by Laplace in 1781 (for further details, see Eisenhart 1964; Todhunter 1865; Merriman 1877).

Using inverse probability, Gauss found $f(v) = (h/\sqrt{\pi}) \exp(-h^2v^2)$ to be the required probability distribution of errors (1809, art. 175–177). He noted that h ($= 1/(\sigma\sqrt{2})$ in modern notation, where σ is the *root-mean-square error*, or *standard deviation*, of the distribution) "can be considered as the measure of precision of the observations" (art. 178). Although De Moivre in 1733 had adduced the *function e^{-t^2}* to approximate sums of successive terms of the binomial expansion of $(a + b)^n$ when n is large (for what he actually wrote, see Smith [1929] 1959, pp. 566–575), and Laplace, in a series of papers published during the period 1774–1786, had explored in great detail the use of this function and its derivatives to approximate various probability distributions arising in games of chance, notably the binomial and hypergeometric distributions and the corresponding incomplete beta-function forms obtained through application of Bayes' theorem, and had suggested tabulation of its integral for use in such problems (see Todhunter [1865] 1949, art. 890–911) neither De Moivre nor Laplace seems to have considered $C \exp(-h^2x^2)$, or an equivalent expression, as a *law of error* or as a *probability distribution* in its own right.

Gauss then went on to deduce his mssr technique from $f(v)$, by what we would today call the method of maximum likelihood, finding that when the respective observations, $Y_i, i = 1, 2, \cdots, n$, are of unequal precision, each residual should be multiplied by the corresponding measure of precision, $h_i, i = 1, 2, \cdots, n$, before squaring (art. 179); derived the formula for the precision, $h(\overline{\overline{Y}})$, of any weighted arithmetic mean, $\overline{\overline{Y}}$, of n independent observations (art. 181), finding that the precision, $h(\overline{Y})$, of the unweighted arithmetic mean, $\overline{Y}$, of n equally precise independent observations is proportional to $\sqrt{n}$ (art. 173); derived for the case of observations on linear functions of several unknown quantities $\alpha, \beta, \cdots$ the rule of formation of (what we call) the *normal equations* that jointly determine optimal estimators $A, B, \cdots$ (art. 180); outlined (art. 182) his famous method of elimination for solving the normal equations—most widely known today through a modification published by M. H. Doolittle (1878)—that provides as a byproduct an easily evaluated expression (art. 182, sec. 5) for the corresponding minimum sum of squared residuals in terms of quantities found in the course of their solution; and gave similar expressions (art. 183) for evaluating the precisions $h_A, h_B, \cdots$ of $A, B, \cdots$ as determinations of $\alpha, \beta, \cdots$.

An entry in Gauss's diary (see *Werke*, vol. 10, p. 533) indicates that he completed the foregoing development of the method of least squares on June 17, 1798. A fragment of his first application of these procedures in the spring of 1799 has been found (see *Werke*, vol. 12, pp. 64–68), and a short note ([1799] 1900, p. 136) dated August 24, 1799, on another application was published in October 1799.

In 1801 Gauss became deeply involved in the development and application of new astronomical methods which, in conjunction with his least squares techniques, resulted in amazingly accurate predictions, despite the scanty data available, of the orbits of some newly discovered planets; the success of his new methods brought about Gauss's immediate recognition as a first-rank astronomer (Bell 1937; Dunnington 1955, pp. 49–57). In 1805 Gauss began preparation (in German) of his second masterpiece, *Theoria motus corporum coelestium . . .* (1809), in which he was to give a complete system of formulas and procedures for computing the motion of a body whose orbit is a conic section, and a general method for determining the orbit of a comet or a planet from only three observed positions. The third section (art. 172–189) he devoted to a detailed exposition of the theory and application of his least squares methods. The German text was completed in 1806 (Galle 1924, p. 10). When the work was offered for publication in 1807, the publisher accepted it only on condition that Gauss translate it into Latin, because of the very unsettled political situation in Germany following the disastrous defeat of the Prussian army (under the leadership of Gauss's patron, the duke of Brunswick) by the Napoleonic forces at the battle of Auerstedt in October 1806. Consequently, full details of Gauss's first formulation of the method of least squares were not published until the Latin translation appeared in 1809. In the meantime, Legendre's independent formulation of his methods of least squares had appeared in print (1805); this went little beyond what Gauss had developed in 1795—no probability considerations are involved, and there is no discussion of precision or weighting of observations. A controversy followed, bitter on Legendre's part, in which many persons became involved, and which, as Bell explains, "was most unfortunate for the future development of mathematics" ([1937] 1956, p. 331).

In his 1809 presentation, Gauss regarded the measures of precision $h_1, h_2, \cdots$ of the respective observations involved as known quantities and said nothing about how to determine their values in practice. F. W. Bessel took the first step in this direction: in 1815 he introduced the *probable error*

as a measure of imprecision (1815, p. 234), which he later defined (1816, p. 142) as the magnitude, r, that an error has an equal chance of exceeding (or being less than) in absolute value; and from 48 determinations of the right ascension of the polestar he obtained a value for the probable error of such determinations (1815, p. 234) by means of the formula $R = 0.8453\sum_i |Y_i - \bar{Y}|/n$, where $\bar{Y} = \sum_i Y_i/n$. (The numerical result given conforms to this formula [cf. Gauss 1816, art. 8], which is not stated.) The following year, Bessel (1816, pp. 141–142) showed that the probable error for Gauss's error distribution, $f(v)$, is given by $r = 0.476936h^{-1} = 0.8453\epsilon = 0.6745\sigma$. In this formulation $\epsilon = 1/(h\sqrt{\pi})$ represents the mean absolute error of the distribution and $\sigma = 1/(h\sqrt{2})$ is the root-mean-square error of the distribution, respectively. Gauss immediately pointed out (1816, art. 3) that given m independent errors $V_1, V_2, \cdots, V_m$ distributed according to his error function, $f(v)$, then for "m large or small" the "most probable values" (or, in modern terminology, the *maximum likelihood estimators*) of h and r are $\hat{H} = \sqrt{m/2\sum_i V_i^2}$ and $\hat{R} = 0.6744897\sqrt{\sum_i V_i^2/m}$, respectively. He showed (art. 4) that for large m, $\hat{H} - h$ and $\hat{R} - r$ are distributed approximately as $f(v)$, with $h_H = \sqrt{m}/h$ and $h_R = \sqrt{m}/r$, and gave (*loc. cit.*) explicit expressions, in terms of $\hat{H}$ and $\hat{R}$, for the "probable limits" of (in modern terminology, 50 *per cent confidence limits* for) "the true values of h and r." Next he considered (art. 5) the estimation of r by $R_p = C_p \sqrt[p]{\sum_i |V_i|^p/m}$, with $C_p = C_p(m,h)$ chosen so that r is the mean of the large-sample distribution of R_p, and found R_2 to be the most precise, noting (art. 6) that R_2 for $m = 100$ is as precise a measure of r as is R_1 for $m = 114$, R_3 for $m = 109$, R_4 for $m = 133$, R_5 for $m = 178$, and R_6 for $m = 251$. Finally, he considered (art. 7) the estimation of r by the "middlemost" (i.e., the *median*) of the absolute errors $|V_i|$ when m is odd and found that this procedure requires $m = 249$ in order to achieve precision comparable to R_2 for $m = 100$. Gauss then evaluated (art. 8) R_1, R_2, R_3, and R_4 for the 48 determinations considered by Bessel (1815), taking the residuals, $Y_i - \bar{Y}$, as measures of the corresponding errors, V_i, and concluded that Bessel had used the formula R_1.

On February 15, 1821, Gauss presented to the Royal Academy of Sciences in Göttingen a completely new formulation of the method of least squares that was entirely free from dependence on any particular probability distribution of errors. Entitled "Theoria combinationis observationum erroribus minimis obnoxiae. Pars prior" (1821*a*), it stemmed from the earlier work of Laplace: Three years before Gauss's birth, Laplace ([1774] 1891, pp. 41–48) had said that to estimate a parameter θ one ought to use that function $T = T(Y_1, Y_2, \cdots)$ of the observations, $Y_1, Y_2, \cdots$, for which the mean (or expected) absolute error of estimation, $E\{|T - \theta|\}$, is a *minimum* for the given probability distribution of errors, and, for the case of independent identically distributed observations, Laplace gave an explicit procedure for finding such a function for estimating the location parameter of their common distribution, $f(y - \tau)$, when this is completely specified except for the value of τ. Finally, Laplace showed that in the case of independent observations of equal (or unequal) precision, Gauss's technique of minimizing the sum of squared residuals leads to the same estimators as Laplace's own procedure for minimizing the mean absolute error of estimation when and only when (Laplace [1812] 1820, book 2, chapter 4, sec. 23) the errors $X_i = Y_i - \tau$ of the respective observations are distributed in accordance with Gauss's law of error,

$$\frac{h_i}{\sqrt{\pi}} \exp \left(-h_i^2 x_i^2\right), \qquad i = 1, 2, \cdots.$$

Gauss ([1821a] 1880, art. 6–7) proposed using instead the mean *square* error of an observation, $E\{(Y - \eta)^2\}$, or of an estimator $E\{(T - \theta)^2\}$, as a better measure of "uncertainty" ("incertitudo") and derived (art. 9) his remarkable inequalities (see Savage 1961, eq. 9) for the probability that a random variable Z with a continuous unimodal probability distribution will differ (positively or negatively) from its modal value z_0 by more than λ times its root-mean-square error measured from z_0. Then he showed (art. 18–23) that when the mean values $E\{Y_i\} = \eta_i$ of a set of n independent observations $Y_1, Y_2, \cdots, Y_n$ are linear functions of k ($< n$) unknown parameters θ_j ($j = 1, 2, \cdots, k$) and (in modern terminology) the *variances* $E\{(Y_i - \eta_i)^2\} = \sigma_i^2$ of the Y_i are all finite, then the mssr technique yields estimators T_j of the θ_j having minimum mean-square error ($j = 1, 2, \cdots, k$), whatever the distribution(s) of errors of the observations. In a second memoir (1823), he extended the preceding result to estimators L_r of linear functions $\Lambda_r(\theta_1, \theta_2, \cdots, \theta_k)$ of the θ's ($r = 1, 2, \cdots, m; m \leqslant k$) and showed (art. 37–40) that the resultant minimum sum of squared residuals is strictly equivalent to the sum of $n - m$ independent errors (i.e., has $n - m$ degrees of freedom). These results, at one time attributed erroneously to A. A. Markov (for explanation, see Neyman ([1938] 1952, p. 228), are derived and discussed by various recent authors (e.g., Graybill 1961; Scheffé 1959;

Zelen 1962) as the "Gauss–Markov theorem," and the method of least squares is thereby endorsed as a procedure for obtaining *minimum variance linear unbiased estimators*.

Gauss definitely preferred his 1821 formulation of the method of least squares above all others (for his statement to this effect on February 26, 1821, see [1821b] 1880, p. 99). In a letter to F. W. Bessel (Gauss & Bessel 1880) dated February 28, 1839 (an excerpt from which is given in his *Werke*, vol. 8, pp. 146–147), he remarked that he had never made a public statement of his reasons for abandoning the metaphysical approach of his first formulation but that a decisive reason was his belief that maximizing the probability of a zero error is less important than minimizing the probability of committing large errors.

In his later years, Gauss took special pride in his contributions to the development of the method of least squares and, despite a lifelong aversion to teaching, gave a course on this subject at the University of Göttingen each year from 1835 until his death. During his lifetime, the method of least squares became a basic tool in astronomy and geodesy throughout the world and has remained one to this day. And when Karl Pearson and G. Udny Yule began to develop the mathematical theory of correlation in the 1890s, they found that much of the mathematical machinery that Gauss devised for finding "best values" for the parameters of empirical formulas by the method of least squares was immediately applicable in correlation analysis, in spite of the fact that the aims of correlation analysis are the very antithesis of those of the theory of errors. As Galton remarked in his *Memories of My Life* (1908, p. 305), "The primary objects of the Gaussian Law of Error were exactly opposed, in one sense, to those to which I applied them. They were to get rid of, or to provide a just allowance for errors. But these errors or deviations were the very things I wanted to preserve and to know about." In consequence, Gauss's contributions to the method of least squares embody mathematics essential to statistical theory and its applications in almost every field of science today.

Gauss was visited in 1829 by the Belgian astronomer–physicist–statistician Adolphe Quetelet, who was engaged in making geomagnetic measurements in Holland, Germany, Italy, and Switzerland. Gauss had been interested in geomagnetism from around the turn of the century and had remarked, in a letter to Heinrich Olbers dated March 1, 1803, "I believe that this offers a greater field for the application of mathematics than has yet been supposed" (Olbers & Gauss, *Briefwechsel . . .*); his intense activity in other fields had thus far prevented his undertaking research in geomagnetism, despite the strenuous efforts of Alexander von Humboldt, in 1804 and again in 1828, to persuade him to do so. When Quetelet arrived, he found Gauss studying Russian for relaxation: "I have been very fatigued," he said, "from occupying myself with astronomy, geodesy, and other subjects that I know fairly well; I wanted to turn my attention to a language that I did not know at all, and now I am reading Russian" (Quetelet 1866, p. 646). Measurement of the intensity of the earth's magnetism was new to Gauss, and he was eager to know how such measurements were made and the precision that could be achieved (p. 645). Quetelet set up his apparatus in Gauss's yard,, and together they conducted a series of experiments, taking observations simultaneously but in slightly different manners. The agreement of the results obtained astonished Gauss, who exclaimed: "But these observations conform to the precision of astronomical observations" (p. 646).

From January 1831 on, geomagnetic measurements were made regularly at Göttingen. By February 1832, Gauss was deeply involved in research on geomagnetism and had found that he could express the intensity of geomagnetism in what he called "absolute units," that is, in terms of units of the three fundamental physical quantities: length, mass, and time. On December 15, 1832, he presented his findings to the Royal Academy of Sciences in Göttingen in a paper entitled "Intensitas vis magneticae terrestris ad mensuram absolutam revocata" (1832), which was promptly recognized as one of the most important papers of the century.

Gauss made electromagnetic measurements for the first time in October 1832. By Easter 1833, he and his young physicist colleague Wilhelm Weber had put into operation an electromagnetic telegraph between Gauss's observatory and Weber's physics laboratory (Dunnington 1955, pp. 147–148, 395). They sent only individual words at first, and later complete sentences. Plans were drawn up in 1835–1836 for its use on the Leipzig–Dresden railroad but were dropped when the railroad authorities declared that the wires would have to be put underground. A monument showing Gauss and Weber discussing their telegraph was erected on the campus of the University of Göttingen.

In 1832 Gauss had begun preparation of his "Allgemeine Theorie des Erdmagnetismus" ("General Theory of Terrestrial Magnetism"); completion was delayed by lack of experimental material. At Gauss's suggestion a magnetic observatory (of nonmagnetic construction) was erected at the University of Göttingen in 1833. By 1836 Göttingen had become the principal European center for research on geomagnetism; and an association of magnetic observatories, known as the Göttingen Magnetic Union, was formed to coordinate simultaneous measurement of geomagnetic phenomena throughout Europe. In 1837 Gauss and Weber collaborated in the invention of a galvanometerlike device, the bifilar magnetometer, for measuring magnetic field intensities; and with it, Gauss verified the inverse-square law of magnetic attraction to which he had already been led by theory. His "Allgemeine Theorie . . ." appeared in 1839 and was followed in 1840 by his (with Weber) "Atlas des Erdmagnetismus" (1840) and his great treatise "Allgemeine Lehrsätze in Beziehung auf die im verkehrten Verhältnisse . . ." (1840)—i.e., what today we call "potential theory"—which marked the peak of his work in physics and the close of his work on magnetism. Near the end of his life, Gauss, like Laplace, Fourier, and Poisson, turned his attention to the social sciences and to the help that they might derive from the physical sciences. In particular, he took an active interest in application of the theory of probability to social laws. Thus, in 1847, he corresponded with the Danish astronomer Heinrich Christian Schumacher on the laws of mortality and on the construction of mortality tables (Quetelet 1866, pp. 653–655).

Called "the prince of mathematicians" even in his lifetime, Gauss received a steady stream of honors (listed chronologically in Dunnington 1955, appendix B), beginning with his election in 1802 as a corresponding member of the Imperial Academy of Arts and Sciences in St. Petersburg. He was elected a fellow of the Royal Society of London in 1804 and received the Copley Medal in 1838; he became a full member of the Royal Academy of Sciences in Berlin in 1810, a fellow of the American Academy of Arts and Sciences in Boston, Massachusetts, in 1822, and a member of the American Philosophical Society in Philadelphia in 1853. In 1842 the highest order conferred by the kingdom of Prussia, *Pour le mérite*, was awarded to him. On July 16, 1849, exactly 50 years after receipt of his doctorate, a Gauss jubilee was held in Göttingen at which honors were showered upon him, including honorary citizenship of Brunswick and Göttingen, which he prized above all the rest.

CHURCHILL EISENHART

[*For the historical context of Gauss's work, see the biographies of* LAPLACE; MOIVRE; *for discussion of the subsequent development of his ideas, see* ESTIMATION; LINEAR HYPOTHESES, *article on* REGRESSION;

MULTIVARIATE ANALYSIS, *articles on* CORRELATION; *and the biographies of* PEARSON; QUETELET; YULE.]

A BIBLIOGRAPHY OF GAUSS

WORKS BY GAUSS

(1799) 1900   Zur Geschichte der Entdeckung der Methode der kleinsten Quadrate. Volume 8, pages 136–141 in *Carl Friedrich Gauss Werke.* Göttingen: Dieterichsche Universitäts-Druckerei.

(1800) 1874   Berechnung des Osterfestes. Volume 6, pages 73–79 in *Carl Friedrich Gauss Werke.* Göttingen: Dieterichsche Universitäts-Druckerei.

(1801) 1966   *Disquisitiones arithmeticae.* English translation by Arthur A. Clarke. New Haven: Yale Univ. Press.

(1807) 1874   Noch etwas über die Bestimmung des Osterfestes. Volume 6, pages 82–86 in *Carl Friedrich Gauss Werke.* Göttingen: Dieterichsche Universitäts-Druckerei.

(1809) 1963   *Theory of Motion of the Heavenly Bodies Moving About the Sun in Conic Sections.* New York: Dover. → First published as *Theoria motus corporum coelestium.* . . .

(1816) 1880   Bestimmung der Genauigkeit der Beobachtungen. Volume 4, pages 109–117 in *Carl Friedrich Gauss Werke.* Göttingen: Dieterichsche Universitäts-Druckerei. → An English translation appears in *Gauss's Work (1803–1826).* See also section 3 of Whittaker and Robinson 1924.

(1821*a*) 1880   Theoria combinationis observationum erroribus minimis obnoxiae. Pars prior. Volume 4, pages 1–26 in *Carl Friedrich Gauss Werke.* Göttingen: Dieterichsche Universitäts-Druckerei. → An English translation appears in *Gauss's Work (1803–1826).*

(1821*b*) 1880   Anzeigen: Theoria combinationis observationum erroribus minimis obnoxiae. Pars prior. Volume 4, pages 95–100 in *Carl Friedrich Gauss Werke.* Göttingen: Dieterichsche Universitäts-Druckerei.

(1823) 1880   Theoria combinationis observationum erroribus minimis obnoxiae. Pars posterior. Volume 4, pages 27–53 in *Carl Friedrich Gauss Werke.* Göttingen: Dieterichsche Universitäts-Druckerei. → An English translation is in *Gauss's Work (1803–1826).*

(1825–1827) 1965   *General Investigations of Curved Surfaces.* Hewlett, N.Y.: Raven Press. → Translations of Gauss's 1827 paper "Disquisitiones generales circa superficies curvas," his abstract of it, and his 1825 fragment "Neue allgemeine Untersuchungen über die krummen Flächen."

(1832) 1877   Intensitas vis magneticae terrestris ad mensuram absolutam revocata. Volume 5, pages 79–118 in *Carl Friedrich Gauss Werke.* Göttingen: Dieterichsche Universitäts-Druckerei. → Magie 1935 contains English excerpts.

(1839) 1966   General Theory of Terrestrial Magnetism. Volume 2, pages 184–251 in Richard Taylor (editor), *Scientific Memoirs, Selected From the Transactions of Foreign Academies of Science, and Learned Societies, and From Foreign Journals.* New York: Johnson. → First published in German.

(1840) 1966   General Propositions Relating to Attractive and Repulsive Forces Acting in the Inverse Ratio of the Square of the Distance. Volume 3, pages 153–196 in Richard Taylor (editor), *Scientific Memoirs, Selected From the Transactions of Foreign Academies of Science, and Learned Societies, and From Foreign Journals.* New York: Johnson. → First published in German.

(1840) 1929   GAUSS, CARL FRIEDRICH; and WEBER, WILHELM Atlas des Erdmagnetismus nach den Elementen der Theorie entworfen: Supplement zu den Resultaten aus den Beobachtungen des magnetischen Vereins unter Mitwirkung von C. W. B. Goldschmidt. Volume 12, pages 335–408 in *Carl Friedrich Gauss Werke.* Göttingen: Dieterichsche Universitäts-Druckerei. → Charts following page 408.

COLLECTIONS OF GAUSS'S WORKS

1855   *Méthode des moindres carrés: Mémoires sur la combinaison des observations.* Translated by J. Bertrand, and published with the authorization of the author. Paris: Mallet-Bachelier.

Abhandlungen zur Methode der kleinsten Quadrate. Thesaurus mathematicae, Vol. 5. Würzburg: Physica-Verlag, 1964.

Carl Friedrich Gauss Werke. 12 vols. Göttingen: Dieterichsche Universitäts-Druckerei, 1870–1933.

Gauss's Work (1803–1826) on the Theory of Least Squares. Translated by Hale F. Trotter. Statistical Techniques Research Group, Technical Report, No. 5. Princeton, N.J.: Princeton Univ., 1957. → Prepared from Gauss 1855.

WORKS CONTAINING EXTRACTS BY GAUSS

MAGIE, WILLIAM F.   (1935) 1963   *A Source Book in Physics.* Cambridge, Mass.: Harvard Univ. Press. → See especially extracts from Gauss 1832.

MIDONICK, HENRIETTA O. (editor)   1965   *The Treasury of Mathematics: A Collection of Source Material in Mathematics.* New York: Philosophical Library.

SMITH, DAVID EUGENE   (1929) 1959   *A Source Book in Mathematics.* 2 vols. New York: Dover.

TAYLOR, RICHARD (editor)   1966   *Scientific Memoirs, Selected From the Transactions of Foreign Academies of Science, and Learned Societies, and From Foreign Journals.* 7 vols. New York: Johnson.

CORRESPONDENCE

Briefe von C. F. Gauss an B. Nicolai. Karlsruhe: Braun, 1877.

GAUSS, CARL FRIEDRICH; and BESSEL, FRIEDRICH W. *Briefwechsel zwischen Gauss und Bessel.* Leipzig: Engelmann, 1880.

GAUSS, CARL FRIEDRICH; and BOLYAI, WOLFGANG *Briefwechsel zwischen Carl Friedrich Gauss und Wolfgang Bolyai.* Leipzig: Teubner, 1899.

GAUSS, CARL FRIEDRICH; and GERLING, CHRISTIAN L. *Briefwechsel zwischen Carl Friedrich Gauss und Christian Ludwig Gerling.* Berlin: Elsner, 1927.

GAUSS, CARL FRIEDRICH; and SCHUMACHER, HEINRICH C. *Briefwechsel zwischen C. F. Gauss und H. C. Schumacher.* 6 vols. Altona: Esch, 1860–1865.

HUMBOLDT, ALEXANDER VON; and GAUSS, CARL F. *Briefe zwischen A. v. Humboldt und Gauss.* Leipzig: Engelmann, 1877.

OLBERS, WILHELM; and GAUSS, CARL F. *Briefwechsel zwischen Olbers und Gauss.* 2 parts. Berlin: Springer, 1900–1909. → Published as Volume 2 of Wilhelm Olbers, *Sein Leben und seine Werke.*

SUPPLEMENTARY BIBLIOGRAPHY

BELL, ERIC T.   (1937) 1956   Gauss: The Prince of Mathematicians. Volume 1, pages 295–299 in James R. Newman (editor), *The World of Mathematics: A Small Library of the Literature of Mathematics From A'h-mosé the Scribe to Albert Einstein.* New York: Simon & Schuster. → A paperback edition was published in 1960.

BESSEL, FRIEDRICH W.   1815   Ueber den Ort des Polarsterns. *Astronomisches Jahrbuch* [1818]:233–241.

BESSEL, FRIEDRICH W.   1816   Untersuchungen über die Bahn des Olbersschen Kometen. Akademie der Wissenschaften, Berlin, Mathematische Klasse, *Abhandlungen* [1812–1813]:119–160.

DOOLITTLE, M. H.   1878   [Method Employed in This Office in the Solution of Normal Equations and in the Adjustment of a Triangulation.] U.S. Coast and Geodetic Survey, *Report of the Superintendent* [1878], Appendix 8, Paper 3:115–120.

DUNNINGTON, G. WALDO   1955   *Carl Friedrich Gauss, Titan of Science: A Study of His Life and Work.* New York: Hafner. → Contains a comprehensive bibliography of works by and about Gauss.

EISENHART, CHURCHILL   1964   The Meaning of "Least" in Least Squares. *Journal of the Washington Academy of Sciences* 54:24–33.

Festschrift zur Feier der Enthüllung des Gauss–Weber-Denkmals in Göttingen. 2 vols.   1899   Leipzig: Teubner.

GALLE, A.   1924   Über die geodätischen Arbeiten von Gauss. Volume 11, part 2, pages 1–165 in *Carl Friedrich Gauss Werke.* Göttingen: Dieterichsche Universitäts-Druckerei.

GALTON, FRANCIS   1908   *Memories of My Life.* London: Methuen.

GRAYBILL, FRANKLIN A.   1961   *An Introduction to Linear Statistical Models.* Vol. 1. New York: McGraw-Hill.

HÄNSELMANN, LUDWIG   1878   *Karl Friedrich Gauss: Zwölf Kapitel aus seinem Leben.* Leipzig: Duncker & Humblot.

HOWE, H. HERBERT   1954   How to Find the Date of Easter. *Sky and Telescope* 13:196.

KLEIN, FELIX et al.   1911–1920   *Materialien für eine wissenschaftliche Biographie von Gauss.* 8 vols. Leipzig: Teubner.

LAMBERT, JOHANN HEINRICH   1765   *Beyträge zum Gebrauche der Mathematik und deren Anwendung.* Vol. 1. Berlin: Buchladen der Realschule.

LAPLACE, PIERRE SIMON DE   (1774) 1891   Mémoire sur la probabilité des causes par les événements. Volume 8, pages 27–65 in *Oeuvres complètes de Laplace.* Paris: Gauthier-Villars. → See especially "Problème III: Déterminer le milieu que l'on doit prendre entre trois observations données d'un même phénomène" on pages 41–48.

LAPLACE, PIERRE SIMON DE   (1812) 1820   *Théorie analytique des probabilités.* 3d ed., rev. Paris: Courcier. → Smith 1929 contains English extracts from Book 2.

LAPLACE, PIERRE SIMON DE   *Oeuvres complètes de Laplace.* 14 vols. Paris: Gauthier-Villars, 1878–1912.

LEGENDRE, ADRIEN M.   (1805) 1959   On the Method of Least Squares. Volume 2, pages 576–579 in David Eugene Smith, *A Source Book in Mathematics.* New York: Dover. → First published as "Sur la méthode des moindres quarrés" in Legendre's *Nouvelles méthodes pour la détermination des orbites des comètes.*

MACK, HEINRICH (editor)   1927   *Carl Friedrich Gauss und die Seinen: Festschrift zu seinem 150. Geburtstage.* Brunswick: Appelhans.

MERRIMAN, MANSFIELD   1877   A List of Writings Relating to the Method of Least Squares, With Historical and Critical Notes. Connecticut Academy of Arts and Sciences, *Transactions* 4:151–232.

MOIVRE, ABRAHAM DE   (1733) 1959   A Method of Approximating the Sum of the Terms of the Binomial $\overline{a+b}\backslash^n$ Expanded Into a Series, From Whence Are Deduced Some Practical Rules to Estimate the Degree of Assent Which Is to Be Given to Experiments. Volume 2, pages 566–575 in David Eugene Smith, *A Source Book in Mathematics.* New York: Dover. → First published as "Approximatio ad summam terminorum binomii $\overline{a+b}\backslash^n$ in seriem expansi."

NEYMAN, JERZY   (1938) 1952   *Lectures and Conferences on Mathematical Statistics and Probability.* 2d ed. Washington: U.S. Department of Agriculture. → See especially Chapter 4, "Statistical Estimation," in the second edition.

QUETELET, ADOLPHE   1866   Charles-Frédéric Gauss. Pages 643–655 in Adolphe Quetelet, *Sciences mathématiques et physiques chez les Belges au commencement du XIXe siècle.* Brussels: Van Buggenhoudt.

SARTORIUS VON WALTERSHAUSEN, WOLFGANG   1856   *Gauss zum Gedächtniss.* Leipzig: Hirzel.

SAVAGE, I. RICHARD   1961   Probability Inequalities of the Tchebycheff Type. U.S. National Bureau of Standards, *Journal of Research, B. Mathematics and Mathematical Physics* 65 B:211–222.

SCHEFFÉ, HENRY   1959   *The Analysis of Variance.* New York: Wiley.

SCHERING, ERNST   (1877) 1909   Carl Friedrich Gauss' Geburtstag nach hundertjähriger Wiederkehr. Pages 176–213 in Ernst Schering, *Gesammelte mathematische Werke.* Berlin: Mayer & Müller.

SIMPSON, THOMAS   1755   A Letter to the Right Honourable George Earl of Macclesfield, President of the Royal Society, on the Advantage of Taking the Mean of a Number of Observations, in Practical Astronomy. Royal Society of London, *Philosophical Transactions* 49, part 1:82–93.

SIMPSON, THOMAS   1757   An Attempt to Show the Advantage Arising by Taking the Mean of a Number of Observations in Practical Astronomy. Pages 64–75 in Thomas Simpson, *Miscellaneous Tracts on Some Curious and Very Interesting Subjects in Mechanics, Physical-astronomy, and Speculative Mathematics.* London: Nourse.

TODHUNTER, ISAAC   (1865) 1949   *A History of the Mathematical Theory of Probability From the Time of Pascal to That of Laplace.* New York: Chelsea.

WHITTAKER, E. T.; and ROBINSON, G.   (1924) 1944   *The Calculus of Observations: A Treatise on Numerical Mathematics.* 4th ed. Princeton, N.J.: Van Nostrand. → Section 103 provides a digest of Gauss 1816.

WINNECKE, F. A. T.   1877   *Gauss: Ein Umriss seines Lebens und Wirkens.* Brunswick: Vieweg.

WITTSTEIN, THEODOR   1877   *Gedächtnissrede auf Carl Friedrich Gauss zur Feier des 30. April 1877.* Hanover: Hahn.

ZELEN, MARVIN   1962   Linear Estimation and Related Topics. Pages 558–584 in John Todd (editor), *Survey of Numerical Analysis.* New York: McGraw-Hill.

GEDDES, PATRICK

Patrick Geddes (1854–1932), British biologist, sociologist, and town planner, was born in Ballater, Scotland, and died in Montpellier, France. His childhood was spent in Perth. Because he was small and frail, Geddes did not go to school until he was eight; but through working in the cottage garden with his father, a retired professional soldier, he acquired his lifelong interest in plants and gardens. When he was 15, his father took him on a walking trip of more than two hundred miles through a series of river valleys. This tour suggested to young Geddes the practice he was to introduce later into both British education and town planning—the city and regional survey. After his graduation when he was barely 16 from the Perth Academy, where he had been a prize-winning student, his father gave him a free year to spend both reading and working with a local craftsman. During that year, Geddes' interests turned toward the biological sciences; and the reading of Thomas Huxley's *Lay Sermons* led to his beginning his career in the study of biology, at first under Huxley himself.

While pursuing zoological studies in Paris, Geddes came under the influence of Edmond Demolins of the *science sociale* group, who introduced him to Frédéric Le Play's detailed occupational and regional studies of *famille, travail, lieu*. These categories, like organism, function, and environment in biology, constituted the basic triad that Geddes used in his later analyses of society; *famille* was replaced by "folk" or "people."

In 1879, on a British Association for the Advancement of Science grant, Geddes went to Mexico. There his health broke down and he suffered a two-month period of blindness. This misfortune had a decisive effect on his intellectual life. To overcome his handicap, he invented a system of graphic notations by means of paper folded into nine squares. It was the first of his "thinking machines" and one of the earliest applications of graphic methods to nonmathematical problems. By the elaboration of these graphs, using as many as 36 squares, Geddes sought to demonstrate the constant interplay of ideas, forces, functions, groups, and institutions, all of which are usually treated by the specialized sciences as if they were independent and isolated. His basic graph, in which the central figure of the triad represents an activity or a function, and the surrounding squares modes of interaction, was an early systematization of field theory; and the holistic view it presented was much later developed independently by J. L. Moreno.

No longer able to use the microscope, Geddes nevertheless produced a steady stream of scientific papers and encyclopedia articles during the 1880s; he even opened up a new area in biology with his lifelong collaborator, J. Arthur Thomson, in their pioneer volume on the evolution of sex (1889) [*see* ECOLOGY, *article on* HUMAN ECOLOGY]. In that year a special chair in botany was established for him at University College, Dundee, a post he occupied for three months annually until 1919. Meanwhile, his widening social, aesthetic, and

historical explorations turned him toward social problems. As early as 1882, Geddes introduced the new concept of energetics, later developed by Wilhelm Ostwald, into the analysis of census statistics; in 1884 he applied functional biological criteria to the more conventional economic analyses of the division of labor.

After his marriage in 1886, Geddes settled in Edinburgh and engaged in a series of activities that laid the basis for his later career as a town planner and as the leading British exponent of regionalism. Among these were the founding of four badly needed university residence halls, run by students; the rehabilitation of sundry sordid tenements of the Old Town; and the transformation by voluntary labor of neglected patches of land into gardens and play spaces. In the 1890s he converted the Outlook Tower atop Castle Hill into what Charles Zueblin described as "the world's first sociological laboratory"—actually a sociological museum, library, and meeting place. In 1891 he instituted a series of 14 collegiate summer meetings at the tower, with scholars like P'etr Kropotkin and Élisée Reclus as lecturers. In the 1890s Geddes gathered round him a group of artists and writers who formed the center of the short-lived Celtic renascence. Among them was the writer of Celtic romances, William Sharp, who called himself Fiona Macleod.

In 1903 Geddes embarked more formally on his career as sociologist and planner by assisting his colleague Victor Branford in the founding of the Sociological Society in London and by entering a planning competition held by the Carnegie Trust for the civic improvement of Dunfermline. Although his ambitious designs for Dunfermline were rejected, Geddes' comprehensive report, *City Development* (1904), remains a landmark in city planning, for it demonstrates his method of "conservative surgery," that is, preserving the complex historic tissue of a city while boldly introducing desirable innovations (see Geddes 1947).

Geddes' own survey of Edinburgh, modest in scale, established the civic survey as an essential first step in town planning, while in a series of city exhibitions and sociological lectures, including numerous extension courses at the University of London, he opened up the neglected study of the city itself. This rediscovery of the city was his outstanding contribution to sociology. Geddes' leadership helped pave the way for the British Housing and Town Planning Act of 1909 and brought him an invitation to put his ideas to work in India. There, between 1914 and 1924, he surveyed and planned some fifty cities; and from 1919 to 1924 he served as professor of civics and sociology at the University of Bombay. His unpublished plans for the Hebrew University of Jerusalem and for Tel Aviv and his remarkable two-volume report on Indore (1918) were also completed between 1914 and 1925. The report on Indore contains his exhaustive critical appraisal of the failings and potentialities of the modern university.

Although Geddes considered his thought a union of the traditions of Comte and Le Play, in his effort at synthesis he was a continuator of Herbert Spencer and more remotely of Aristotle. He treated sociology as a unifying discipline whose main components are geography, economics, and anthropology, all taken in their widest human context. His aim as a systematic thinker was to break down the sterile isolation and impoverished abstraction of specialized knowledge, so as to be able to move and act freely over the entire range of human experience, even that which lay beyond rigorously scientific description. He was as fertile as Bentham in coining neologisms, and many of his new terms, such as "geotechnics," "biotechnics," and "conurbation," have already entered the dictionary, while his characterization of specialism—"knowing more and more about less and less"—has become classic.

The best presentation of Geddes' method, along with his general sociological conspectus, appears in Volume 2 of *Life* (1931, chapters 11–13). These pages reveal the detailed wealth of his scholarship and first-hand experience, which offsets the sometimes arbitrary explications of his graphs. Since he was essentially an oral teacher, like G. H. Mead, his direct influence is best shown in the work of his students and colleagues, such as P. Abercrombie (town planning), V. Branford (sociology), H. J. Fleure (geography), and J. Arthur Thomson (biology). But more important, the influence of his ideas is being felt throughout the world, even in cases where their origin has been forgotten.

LEWIS MUMFORD

[For the historical context of Geddes' work, see CITY, article on FORMS AND FUNCTIONS; and the biographies of COMTE; LE PLAY; SPENCER. For discussion of the subsequent development of his ideas, see HOUSING, article on SOCIAL ASPECTS; REGION; and the biography of FLEURE.]

WORKS BY GEDDES

1882 On the Classification of Statistics and Its Results. Royal Society of Edinburgh, *Proceedings* 11:295–322.
1884 An Analysis of the Principles of Economics. Royal Society of Edinburgh, *Proceedings* 12:943–980.
(1889) 1914 GEDDES, PATRICK; and THOMSON, JOHN A. *The Evolution of Sex.* 2d ed., rev. London: Walter Scott.
1904 *City Development; A Study of Parks, Gardens, and Culture-institutes: A Report to the Carnegie Dunfermline Trust.* Edinburgh: Geddes.
1905–1906 Civics, as Applied Sociology. Sociological Society, London, *Sociological Papers* 1:103–118; 2:57–119.
1907 A Suggested Plan for a Civic Museum (or Civic Exhibition) and Its Associated Studies. Sociological Society, London, *Sociological Papers* 3:197–240.
(1912) 1923 *Dramatisation of History: A Pageant of Education From Primitive to Celtic Times.* 5th ed. Bombay: Modern Publishing Co. → First published as *The Masque of Ancient Learning and Its Many Meanings.*
(1915) 1950 *Cities in Evolution.* New ed., rev. Oxford Univ. Press.
(1917) 1919 BRANFORD, VICTOR V.; and GEDDES, PATRICK *The Coming Polity.* New & enl. ed. London: Williams.
1917 GEDDES, PATRICK; and SLATER, GILBERT. *Ideas at War.* London: Williams & Norgate.
1918 *Town Planning Towards City Development: A Report to the Durbar of Indore.* 2 vols. Indore (India): Holkar State Press.
1931 THOMSON, J. ARTHUR; and GEDDES, PATRICK *Life: Outlines of General Biology.* 2 vols. London: Williams & Norgate.
1947 *Patrick Geddes in India.* Edited by Jacqueline Tyrwhitt, with an introduction by Lewis Mumford. London: Humphries. → Published posthumously.

SUPPLEMENTARY BIBLIOGRAPHY

BOARDMAN, PHILIP L. 1936 *Esquisse de l'oeuvre éducatrice de Patrick Geddes, suivie de trois listes bibliographiques.* Montpellier (France): Imprimerie de la Charité. → Contains a bibliography of Geddes' works.
BOARDMAN, PHILIP L. 1944 *Patrick Geddes: Maker of the Future.* With an introduction by Lewis Mumford. Chapel Hill: Univ. of North Carolina Press.
DEFRIES, AMELIA 1927 *The Interpreter Geddes: The Man and His Gospel.* London: Routledge.
MAIRET, PHILIP 1957 *Pioneer of Sociology: The Life and Letters of Patrick Geddes.* London: Lund Humphries.
Sociological Review. → Published since 1908. Most of Patrick Geddes' papers were published in this journal between 1908 and 1931.

GEIGER, THEODOR

Theodor Geiger (1891–1952) was a German-born sociologist whose chief interests were the fields of general social theory, methodology, social stratification and mobility, the sociology of law, and ideology. Even in Germany, Geiger's work is not widely known, although his writings on social stratification and mobility and on the sociology of law possess current significance. There is practically no secondary literature on Geiger. It was not until some years after his death that his influence was felt at all beyond the confines of Germany and Scandinavia.

Geiger's life mirrors German history in the twentieth century. His numerous publications—a bibliography of his works contains some 160 titles—constitute a courageous and nonideological discussion of the social and methodological problems of his time. He is noteworthy as an early critic of Nazism.

Geiger was the son of a teacher in a Munich Gymnasium; he studied law at the University of Munich and at Würzburg—where he received his doctorate in law—and volunteered for military service in World War I. After the war, until 1932, he was a member of the German Social Democratic party. During this time he began work on some problems relevant to the sociology of law. For some years he was active as a tutor, translator, and writer. He was fluent in the Scandinavian languages and also in Finnish. From 1920 on, he lived in Berlin, collaborating in the publication of the periodical *Die Fremde Presse* and working intensively in the field of adult education. He taught at the Volkshochschule Gross-Berlin and had become the principal of that school by the time he left, in 1928, to occupy the chair of sociology at the Brunswick Institute of Technology. While he was in Berlin he also worked at the National Statistical Bureau.

In 1933 Geiger emigrated to Denmark. For some time his studies in Copenhagen were supported by the Rockefeller Foundation. In 1938 he became professor of sociology at Aarhus. With the German occupation of Denmark, it became desirable for Geiger to leave, and in 1943 he escaped to Sweden. There he was stimulated by contact with the jurists and social scientists of the "Uppsala school." In 1945 he returned to Aarhus and founded the first institute of sociological research in Scandinavia. In collaboration with T. T. Segerstedt (of Uppsala), V. Verkko (of Helsinki), and J. Vogt (of Oslo), Geiger founded a series of publications, *Nordiske studier i sociologi*, Volume 1 of which was published in Copenhagen in 1948. He was also busy with several large-scale empirical studies on stratification and mobility and with developing his ideas on the sociology of law and the critique of ideology —ideas dating back to the stimulation he had received in Sweden. He was one of the founders of the International Sociological Association (ISA) and, together with D. Glass, was a leading spirit in the First International Working Conference on Social Stratification and Social Mobility. In 1951 he went to the University of Toronto as visiting professor; on the return voyage he died suddenly on shipboard.

General social theory. Geiger made important theoretical contributions to the study of social groups and to the refinement of Tönnies' categories of *Gemeinschaft* and *Gesellschaft*. He was also concerned with the role of secondary groups in modern society, notably in two articles, one, "Die Gruppe und die Kategorien Gemeinschaft und Gesellschaft," published in 1927 and the other, "Die Legende von der Massengesellschaft," pub-

lished in 1951. After briefly outlining a sociological theory (which he later partly retracted) in *Die Gestalten der Gesellung* (1928), in the 1930s he wrote his powerful introductory text *Sociologi* (1939), at the time a unique work in Scandinavia and for several decades an important textbook. Subsequently, he shifted entirely from the construction of general theory to the study of specific problems.

Methodology. In the 1920s Geiger was one of the few European sociologists doing empirical research. One of his first studies was an evaluation of illegitimacy statistics (1920). His book *Die soziale Schichtung des deutschen Volkes* (1932) and several articles—on employees (1933*a*), on the self-employed (1933*b*), and on problems of adult education—also have an empirical foundation. After these early works Geiger, influenced by Scandinavian thought and by American sociology, sought to refine the methods of empirical social research. He developed his own methods of inquiry and presentation, notably in his studies of Danish intellectuals and of changes in social stratification in Aarhus. His theoretical considerations of methodology (e.g., several articles written in 1948 and 1949: see *Arbeiten zur Soziologie*) also raised problems of the philosophy of science and of knowledge.

Stratification and mobility. In his studies of social stratification, Geiger initially accepted the Marxist view that German society had a clear-cut class structure, but he departed increasingly from this conception. Under the influence of American sociology and of his own empirical data, he wrote, while he was in Sweden, *Klassesamfundet i støbegryden* ("Class Society in the Melting Pot," 1948). By means of large-scale research he developed a dynamic analysis of social mobility and a typology of social fluctuation, together with a multidimensional model of stratification. A brief article by Geiger on his theory of social stratification was published in the *Wörterbuch der Soziologie*, edited by W. Bernsdorf and F. Bülow (1955).

Sociology of law and ideology. Geiger was early concerned with the sociology of law, and his association with the Uppsala school intensified this interest (1946*a*; 1946*b*; 1947). In several publications he took issue with the views of S. Ranulf, A. Ross, and K. Illum. Geiger linked the sociology of law with the analysis of ideology, discussing juristic concepts—norms, sources of law, consciousness of law, etc.—as phenomena of social reality. He examined the general nature of civil order and broke it down into such partial orders as habit, custom, usage, and law. Although this analysis is based on Continental legal conceptions, it constitutes a theory of social control that has bearing, also, on non-European social structures. Indeed, the *Vorstudien* (1947) are, with the fundamental works of G. Gurvitch and N. S. Timasheff, among the most important contributions to the sociology of law.

Geiger's conception of ideology has frequently been misinterpreted. Ideology, to him, is a concept in the theory of knowledge: *Ideologie ist theoretisch gemeintes A-Theoretisches* ("Ideology is the atheoretical taken theoretically"). He was led to this approach by the Uppsala school, especially by the work of A. Hägerström, although he criticized Hägerström and by the same token departed from the view of Karl Mannheim. Geiger's "value nihilism" must be understood in terms of a theory of knowledge: his value nihilism permits primary value judgments, but not their conversion into theories. In his last work, *Demokratie ohne Dogma* (1960), he made a plea for "intellectual humanism," the "enlightenment of the masses," the "democratization of reason," the "asceticism of emotion," and "abstinence from value judgment." Yet he was a pragmatist: he considered his last work to be his political testament and hoped that his ideas would be put into practice.

PAUL TRAPPE

[*See also* COMMUNITY–SOCIETY CONTINUA; IDEOLOGY; ILLEGITIMACY; LAW; SOCIAL CONTROL; SOCIAL MOBILITY; STRATIFICATION, SOCIAL; *and the biographies of* MANNHEIM *and* TÖNNIES.]

WORKS BY GEIGER

1919 *Die Schutzaufsicht.* Breslau (then Germany): Schletter.

1920 *Das uneheliche Kind und seine Mutter im Recht des neuen Staates: Ein Versuch auf der Basis kritischer Rechtsvergleichung.* Munich: Schweitzer.

1926 *Die Masse und ihre Aktion: Ein Beitrag zur Soziologie der Revolutionen.* Stuttgart (Germany): Enke.

1927 Die Gruppe und die Kategorien Gemeinschaft und Gesellschaft. *Archiv für Sozialwissenschaft und Sozialpolitik* 58:338–374.

1928 *Die Gestalten der Gesellung.* Karlsruhe (Germany): Braun.

(1931*a*) 1959 Führung. Pages 136–141 in *Handwörterbuch der Soziologie.* New ed. Stuttgart (Germany): Enke.

(1931*b*) 1959 Gemeinschaft. Pages 173–180 in *Handwörterbuch der Soziologie.* New ed. Stuttgart (Germany): Enke.

(1931*c*) 1959 Gesellschaft. Pages 201–211 in *Handwörterbuch der Soziologie.* New ed. Stuttgart (Germany): Enke.

(1931*d*) 1959 Revolution. Pages 511–518 in *Handwörterbuch der Soziologie.* New ed. Stuttgart (Germany): Enke.

(1931*e*) 1959 Soziologie. Pages 568–578 in *Handwörterbuch der Soziologie.* New ed. Stuttgart (Germany): Enke.

1932 *Die soziale Schichtung des deutschen Volkes: Soziographischer Versuch auf statistischer Grundlage.* Stuttgart (Germany): Enke.

1933*a* Soziale Gliederung der deutschen Arbeitnehmer. *Archiv für Sozialwissenschaft und Sozialpolitik* 68: 151–188.

1933*b* Statistische Analyse der wirtschaftlich Selbständigen. *Archiv für Sozialwissenschaft und Sozialpolitik* 69:407–439.

1934 *Erbpflege: Grundlagen, Planung, Grenzen.* Stuttgart (Germany): Enke.

1935 *Samfund og arvelighed: En sociologisk undersøgelse.* Copenhagen: Martin.

1939 *Sociologi: Grundrids og hovedproblemer.* Copenhagen: Nyt Nordisk Forlag.

1941 *Konkurrence: En sociologisk analyse.* Aarhus, Universitet, Acta jutlandica, Aarsskrift, Vol. 13, no. 2. Aarhus (Denmark): Universitets Forlaget.

1943 *Kritik af reklamen.* Copenhagen: Nyt Nordisk Forlag.

(1944) 1949 *Aufgaben und Stellung der Intelligenz in der Gesellschaft.* Stuttgart (Germany): Enke. → First published as *Intelligensen.*

1946*a* *Debat med Uppsala om moral og ret.* Copenhagen: Munksgaard.

1946*b* *Ranulf contra Geiger: Et angreb og et offensivt forsvar.* Copenhagen: Nyt Nordisk Forlag.

(1947) 1964 *Vorstudien zu einer Soziologie des Rechts.* Aarhus, Universitet, Acta jutlandica, Aarsskrift, Vol. 19, no. 1. Neuwied (Germany): Luchterhand.

(1948) 1949 *Die Klassengesellschaft in Schmelztiegel.* Cologne (Germany): Kiepenheuer. → First published in Danish.

1949 *Den Danske intelligens fra reformationen til nutiden: En studie i empirisk kultursociologi.* Aarhus, Universitet, Acta jutlandica, Aarsskrift, Vol. 21, no. 1. Aarhus (Denmark): Universitets Forlaget.

1951*a* Die Legende von der Massengesellschaft. *Archiv für Rechts- und Sozialphilosophie* 39:305–323.

1951*b* *Soziale Umschichtungen in einer dänischen Mittelstadt.* Aarhus, Universitet, Acta jutlandica, Aarsskrift, Vol. 23, no. 1. Aarhus (Denmark): Universitets Forlaget.

1952 *Fortidens moral og fremtidens.* Copenhagen: Reitzel.

1953 *Ideologie und Wahrheit: Eine soziologische Kritik des Denkens.* Stuttgart (Germany) and Vienna: Humboldt. → Published posthumously.

1954*a* Intelligenz. Volume 5, pages 302–304 in *Handwörterbuch der Sozialwissenschaften.* Stuttgart (Germany): Fischer. → Published posthumously.

1954*b* Ideologie. Volume 5, pages 179–184 in *Handwörterbuch der Sozialwissenschaften.* Stuttgart (Germany): Fischer. → Published posthumously.

(1955) 1962 Theorie der sozialen Schichtung. Pages 186–205 in Theodor Geiger, *Arbeiten zur Soziologie: Methode, moderne Grossgesellschaft, Rechtssoziologie, Ideologiekritik.* Neuwied (Germany): Luchterhand. → Published posthumously. Originally appeared in the *Wörterbuch der Soziologie,* edited by W. Bernsdorf and F. Bülow.

(1960) 1963 *Demokratie ohne Dogma: Die Gesellschaft zwischen Pathos und Nüchternheit.* Munich: Szczesny. → First published posthumously as *Die Gesellschaft zwischen Pathos und Nüchternheit.*

Arbeiten zur Soziologie: Methode, moderne Grossgesellschaft, Rechtssoziologie, Ideologiekritik. Neuwied (Germany): Luchterhand, 1962.

GEMEINSCHAFT–GESELLSCHAFT

See COMMUNITY–SOCIETY CONTINUA *and the biography of* TÖNNIES.

GENERAL SYSTEMS THEORY
See under SYSTEMS ANALYSIS.

GENERAL WILL

The concept of the general will involves the moral values and the political aspirations that are shared by the members of a community and to which the policies of its government must broadly conform if that government is to be considered legitimate. The term was used in this minimal sense by Jean Jacques Rousseau, its originator, who also used it, more importantly, to describe the will to justice that would characterize his ideal democracy and achieve its authoritative expression in legislative decisions [*see* ROUSSEAU].

Since Rousseau, different and precise meanings, depending upon the political theory in which they are embedded, have been attached to the term; these have had as their primary and common aim its adaptation to the analysis of politics and national character. Typically, some theory of the general will has been used to explain, to justify, and to prescribe for the institutions of constitutional and liberal democracy, especially by thinkers within or influenced by the British idealist school of political thought. Often, existence of a general will is made the cardinal criterion of community and is seen as the essential prerequisite to political stability and self-government.

For Rousseau, the "general will" was the concept by means of which he summarized his theory of political obligation and displayed its logical dependence upon the psychological, ethical, and institutional components of his political philosophy. In Rousseau's ideal society, as presented in *The Social Contract*, the natural right to moral freedom, to live in accordance with the dictates of one's own conscience and sense of morality, is psychologically and institutionally reconciled with the social necessity for political authority, because there law is the reflection of the individual's desire for justice. Laws that express the general will are acceptable both to reason and to conscience and thus are held not so much to restrict freedom as to enlarge and to sustain it.

Rousseau's general will implies that neither a society that lacks a general will nor a government that disregards it can have rightful authority over the individual. Failure to establish the institutions essential to the creation of the general will inevitably means moral distortion of human personality and frustration of man's capacity for natural goodness. According to Rousseau's view of human dynamics and moral development, only in a small and equalitarian society can man become an ethical being for whom the realization of justice and its integration with the claim to moral freedom are paramount and compelling objectives—and then only if men participate directly and steadily in the making of the laws to which they will owe obedience.

The social and institutional requisites of the general will as conceived of by Rousseau would appear to preclude its use for the purpose of legitimating constitutional democracy on the scale of the national state. The fundamentally moral and synthetic nature of the concept, however, opens the way for its modification, inspired by the hope of adapting it to the justification of representative government. This process of reinterpretation began with Kant, who derived from Rousseau's general will his conception of the categorical imperative, which served for him as the supreme criterion of both morality and legality. In contrast to Kant's primarily ethical elucidation of the concept, Hegel's political interpretation of it takes the form of his metaphysical and historical conception of reason. The Hegelian conception of rationality as cumulative may be regarded as a historicizing of the general will. The result is that the reconciliation of the right to moral freedom with the demands of social justice is obtained not in acts of legislation but, rather, in reflective acceptance of and willing adherence to the social and political arrangements that have emerged historically in the shape of the national and constitutional state.

The British idealist T. H. Green spoke of a general will with reference to the hopes and aspirations of a people, on which government depends and to which it should be both responsive and facilitative (1882). The most elaborate effort to employ the idea of a general will in the rationale of liberal constitutionalism was made by Bernard Bosanquet (1899). He conceived of the state as a concrete universal, a dynamic and rationally articulated totality, the fulfillment of whose requirements may be understood in terms of "will," which is the moving system of interlocking attitudes and functions that constitutes a politically organized and sovereign society. Here the general will becomes more an attribute of the polity than a moral characteristic of individuality and, as such, gives both direction and significance to the activities of individuals, who are self-governing insofar as they sense and respond appropriately to the intimations of their society [*see* BOSANQUET *and* GREEN].

Less like Hegel and more like Rousseau in tone is the theory of the "neighborhood group" advocated by Mary Parker Follett (1918). She saw the neighborhood as the necessary source of what Rousseau would have recognized as the general will, and she urged the recasting of democratic institutions so as to make this social unit an integrating force of moral and political importance. Her ideas have found effective application in administration and urban planning [see FOLLETT].

Still other interpretations of the general will seek to locate it in the nature of man in society, in the psychological and social foundations of political authority, rather than directly in political agreement and legislative performance. These include W. Ernest Hocking's "will to power" (1926), which requires the state as its vehicle, and Robert MacIver's redesignation of the general will as the "will for the state" (1926), which derives social unity and political authority from a common root in individual and group freedoms. In the field of jurisprudence, Hugo Krabbe's assertion of the "sense of right" of a community as the criterion of the validity of law (1915) is an attempt to convert the general will into a dynamic type of natural law.

More complex reformulations of the general will, which are more directly in the spirit if not the letter of Rousseau's political theory, are presented in the works of Lindsay (1943) and Barker (1951). Both regard discussion as the process distinctive to democratic society and government by which, fittingly differentiated and articulated, the general will may be generated and expressed. In this perspective, the general will is the formative conception in the theory of the deliberative state as set forth in Frederick Watkins' analysis of liberalism (1948) and in J. Roland Pennock's exposition of the principles of liberal democracy (1950). In a deliberative state, political participation not only is essential to social unity but should also be active and substantive, without excessive dependence upon either leadership or disciplined and programmatic parties. Deliberative democracy is the type of democracy most closely in accord with Rousseau's ideal.

Viewed in the light of its origin and development, the general will does not have any single meaning or accepted role in political theory. There is, however, an agreed *core* of meaning and implication. (1) As a legitimating idea the concept directs attention to the criterion of popular consent, expressed through the methods of representative and responsible government; to the desirability of a diversity of forms of participation and access; and to justice and freedom as the proper ends of the state. (2) As an analytic concept the general will suggests consideration of those conditions of social unity and common purpose sufficiently strong to permit the establishment, acceptance, and control of political authority. (3) From a diagnostic standpoint the concept indicates that a society lacking in moral and political unity is unlikely to be capable of self-government and is liable, therefore, to an imposition of coherence and direction by authoritarian techniques and ideologies. (4) Prescriptively, the general will continues to influence the construction of democratic theory in a liberal, as opposed to a majoritarian, mode and to guide the design of political, urban, and administrative democratic institutions in ways consistent with the meaning Rousseau gave it.

Owing to its fundamentally moral nature, the concept continues to inspire investigation and explication of the ethical purposes of political society and political activity. But in keeping with its composite nature, future research may be conducted in a number of directions: historical investigation of the development of political culture; psychological investigation of the formation of moral and political attitudes, especially those basic to personal independence and resilience; specification and interpretation of the principles of justice; and explanation of the social and political processes integral to liberal constitutionalism in both more mature and less mature industrializing societies. Above all, the concept of the general will invites attention to the interdependence of psychological processes, moral character, and political institutions.

JOHN W. CHAPMAN

[See also AUTHORITY; DEMOCRACY; LEGITIMACY; LIBERALISM; PUBLIC INTEREST; REPRESENTATION; SOCIAL CONTRACT; STATE.]

BIBLIOGRAPHY

BARKER, ERNEST 1951 *Principles of Social and Political Theory.* New York: Oxford Univ. Press.
BOSANQUET, BERNARD (1899) 1951 *The Philosophical Theory of the State.* 4th ed. London: Macmillan. → The 1951 publication is a reprint of the fourth edition, which was first published in 1923.
CHAPMAN, JOHN W. 1956 *Rousseau: Totalitarian or Liberal?* New York: Columbia Univ. Press.
CHAPMAN, JOHN W. 1960 Metropolitan Citizenship: Promises and Limitations. In Carl J. Friedrich (editor), *Responsibility.* Nomos 3. New York: Liberal Arts.
CHAPMAN, JOHN W. 1963 Justice and Fairness. In Carl J. Friedrich and John W. Chapman (editors), *Justice.* Nomos 6. New York: Atherton.
DERATHÉ, ROBERT 1948 *Le rationalisme de J.-J. Rousseau.* Paris: Presses Universitaires de France.
FOLLETT, MARY P. 1918 *The New State: Group Organization, the Solution of Popular Government.* New York: Longmans.

GREEN, THOMAS HILL (1882) 1960 *Lectures on the Principles of Political Obligation.* London: Longmans. → Reprinted from Volume 2 of the three-volume collected *Works of Thomas Hill Green,* edited by R. L. Nettleship and published posthumously in 1885–1888. First published as a separate book in 1895.

HEGEL, GEORG W. F. (1821) 1942 *Philosophy of Right.* Oxford: Clarendon. → First published in German.

HOCKING, WILLIAM ERNEST 1926 *Man and the State.* New Haven: Yale Univ. Press.

JOURNÉES D'ÉTUDE SUR LE "CONTRAT SOCIAL," DIJON, 1962 1964 *Études sur le* Contrat social *de Jean-Jacques Rousseau: Actes des journées d'étude organisées à Dijon pour la commémoration du 200e anniversaire du* Contrat social. Dijon, Université, Publications, New Series, No. 30. Paris: Belles Lettres. → See especially pages 143–164, "Le sens de l'égalité et de l'inégalité chez J.-J. Rousseau," by Raymond Polin.

KRABBE, HUGO (1915) 1927 *The Modern Idea of the State.* New York and London: Appleton. → Translated from the Dutch.

LINDSAY, A. D. (1943) 1947 *The Modern Democratic State.* Published under the auspices of the Royal Institute of International Affairs. Oxford Univ. Press.

MacIVER, ROBERT M. 1926 *The Modern State.* Oxford Univ. Press.

PENNOCK, J. ROLAND 1950 *Liberal Democracy: Its Merits and Prospects.* New York: Rinehart.

PENNOCK, J. ROLAND 1952 Responsiveness, Responsibility, and Majority Rule. *American Political Science Review* 46:790–807.

PLAMENATZ, JOHN P. 1963 *Man and Society: Political and Social Theory.* 2 vols. New York: McGraw-Hill.

Rousseau et la philosophie politique. Annales de philosophie politique, No. 5. 1965 Paris: Presses Universitaires de France.

Jean-Jacques Rousseau et son oeuvre: Problèmes et recherches. 1964 Paris: Klincksieck. → See especially pages 231–247, "La fonction du législateur chez J.-J. Rousseau," by Raymond Polin.

SABINE, GEORGE H. 1952 The Two Democratic Traditions. *Philosophical Review* 61:451–474.

WATKINS, FREDERICK 1948 *The Political Tradition of the West: A Study in the Development of Modern Liberalism.* Cambridge, Mass.: Harvard Univ. Press.

GENERATIONS

I. THE CONCEPT   *Julián Marías*
II. POLITICAL GENERATIONS   *Marvin Rintala*

I
THE CONCEPT

Ever since antiquity, the concept of *generation* has been held in a biological, and consequently in a genealogical, sense of regular descent of a group of organisms from a progenitor. But since the early nineteenth century there has been developed a social and historical concept of generations as comprising the structure not only of societies but also of history itself. Nevertheless, attempts to formulate a sociological theory of generations in the biological sense of kinship descent have been unproductive because the temporal continuity of births makes impossible any determination of *social* generations so long as "generation" is understood in a purely biological sense. It is therefore necessary to arrive at a strictly social and historical interpretation of the generation concept in order for it to acquire relevance in the field of the social sciences.

History of the generation concept. Auguste Comte, the founder of modern sociology, considered the duration of human life a decisive element in determining the velocity of human evolution and therefore the passing of one generation to another, the term of full activity for man being thirty years (1830–1842, pp. 635–639 in part 4 of the 1839 edition). Comte did not deal with the phenomena of individual or simply familial life but with social life based on "the unanimous adhesion to certain fundamental notions" (1851–1854, part 4, p. 679).

John Stuart Mill obtained the concept of social generations from Comte and added further refinements of considerable interest. He argued that in each successive age the "principal phenomena" of society are different, and that the interval which marks these changes most clearly is the generation —that is, the period of time in which a "new set" of individuals reaches maturity and takes possession of society. He believed that each social state is generated not only by the preceding one but also by the whole previous history of humanity; one of the key concepts in understanding this process is that of the generation. "History accordingly does, when judiciously examined, afford Empirical Laws of Society" (Mill [1843] 1961, p. 598).

After this philosophical beginning of the theory of generations, the theory received further development at the hands of statisticians and historians. Antoine Augustin Cournot, the French economist and mathematician, first explicated the fact that epochs succeed themselves in continuity and only historical events give evidence of the articulation of generations: "Through education, each generation transmits to the one immediately following, a certain groundwork of ideas; and while this act of education or transmission is in operation, the *educating generation* is still present; unexpected, moreover, is the influence of the survivors of a preceding generation who have not ceased taking a notable part in the government of the society, on the movement of ideas and affairs" (1872, vol. 1, chapter 8).

Giuseppe Ferrari, Italian historian, politician, and editor of Vico, limited himself to the examination of political history, in which he believed he had discovered that the scene changes every thirty years and that the generation is the decisive element. Starting from this basic premise, he formulated laws of political succession: "Generations behave according to these principles, and are in turn preparatory, revolutionary, reactionary, and conciliatory" (1874, p. 182).

The German historian Wilhelm Dilthey also found the idea of generation useful for studying the culture of an epoch, and he applied it in many of his writings. In 1875 Dilthey arrived at the notion that the generation is at once a space of time, an internal metrical concept of human life of about thirty years' duration, and a contemporary relation of individuals to each other.

The relationship between individuals denoted by the term *generation* is therefore one of simultaneity. We say that certain people belong to "the same generation" when they have, in a certain sense, grown up together, passed through childhood and youth at about the same time, and enjoyed their period of maturity during more or less the same years. It follows, then, that such people are bound together in another, deeper relationship: they also constitute "the same generation" because, in their impressionable years, they have been subject to the same leading influences.   ([1875], 1924, vol. 5, p. 37)

The historian Leopold von Ranke and, to a much greater extent, his disciple Ottokar Lorenz put the theme of generations into a historical context from the point of view of periodization. Ranke took the concept of generation in the usual sense of the word. Lorenz took his point of departure from Ranke and from the French psychologist T. A. Ribot, whose studies of heredity were just beginning to appear; he put forward the conception of a scientific history founded on the study of heredity and genealogy. Lorenz was especially interested in the century as a method of dividing history into periods; thus, he defined a generation as the sum of all those who were employed within a given cultural area during one-third of a century.

In the twentieth century an attempt was begun to study history in terms of generations; thus, new refinements were gradually added to the theory. The principal studies are those of François Mentré (1920), Karl Mannheim (1928), Engelbert Drerup (1933), Pedro Laín Entralgo (1945), and Julián Marías (1949a; 1955). Attempts were also made to apply the doctrine of generations to particular themes: for example, art (Pinder 1926) and literature (Petersen 1930; Peyre 1948). But the most extensive general contribution, based on a philosophical theory of social life, was made by José Ortega y Gasset. His student Julián Marías has continued to write in this tradition.

The reality of generations

In varying degrees, the studies of generations have left in obscurity the questions of what generations are, why they exist, how long they last, what their scope is, and how they are determined. Some attempts have clarified *some* of these aspects, but in general without sufficient justification. Ortega y Gasset's theory of human life and, more concretely, of historical and social life has the merit of dealing with all of these questions. According to Ortega, all purely biological (and therefore genealogical) consideration of human life is insufficient, since human life does not consist in its psychophysical structures alone, but in what man does with them. Human life is a drama with character, plot, and scenery—the world; and this world is primarily a mass of social interpretations of reality: beliefs, ideas, customs, estimations, etc. These have a life independent of our individual wills; like laws, they stand *in force*, and we cannot avoid meeting them and having to deal with them. Ortega called them *vigencias* (states of being in force), giving social value to a juridical term. The world thus is a system of *vigencias*, or reigning norms, that both permits and compels man to orient himself and live his life (Ferrater Mora [1957] 1963, pp. 46–65; Marías 1949b).

The world system at all times presents the aspect of a *determined historical* level in which historical–social generations appear:

The changes in vital sensibility which are decisive in history, appear under the form of the generation. A generation is not a handful of outstanding men, nor simply a mass of men; it resembles a new integration of the social body, with its select minority and its gross multitude, launched upon the orbit of existence with a pre-established vital trajectory. The generation is a dynamic compromise between mass and individual, and is the most important conception in history. It is, so to speak, the pivot responsible for the movements of historical evolution.   (Ortega [1923] 1961, pp. 14–15)

Thus, a generation is a human variation; every generation manifests a certain vital attitude. Generations are born one after the other, each encountering the forms of the previous one. There are *cumulative* epochs and others that are *eliminatory* and polemic.

A distinction must also be made between the *contemporary* (those who live in the same time) and the *coeval* (those who are the same age and are, by turns, young, mature, and old together) who constitute a generation (Ortega [1933] 1962, pp. 42–43). Ortega was, of course, well aware of the criticism that, since men are born every day, and since only those born on the same day are of the same age, the concept of generation is an illusion. But he rejected this kind of mathematical exactitude in dealing with the stuff of human life: "Within the human trajectory of life, age is a certain way of living. . . . Age, then, is not a date, but a 'zone of dates'; and it is not only those born in the same year who are the same age in life and in history, but those who are born within a zone of dates" (*ibid.*, p. 47).

Having defined the concept of generation, Ortega went on to consider the problem of applying it to history. Here he made use of the traditional division of human life into five "ages"—childhood, youth, "initiation" (or early manhood), "dominance" (or maturity), and old age. If the complete life-span is set at 75 years, the "ages" or generations of the life-span can be regarded as equal periods of 15 years each. Ortega pointed out that, since history is made largely by men between the ages of 30 and 60, it is the third and fourth generations that are of crucial interest to historians at any one time. But, from the point of view of individual development, these two generations are very different in character: "from thirty to forty-five is the period of gestation, or creation and conflict; from forty-five to sixty, the stage of dominance and command" (*ibid.*, p. 59). Because of their very great difference in outlook, there is always potential or actual conflict between these two generations, and herein Ortega detected the locus of historical change.

There remains the problem of finding a starting point for the generational series: why should any one division of history into 15-year periods be more valid than another? Ortega thought he had solved this problem by introducing the notion of the "decisive generation"; he argued that since it was already clear, from independent historical considerations, which were the crucial years in which a new era came into being, one had only to seek out the individuals who were the most decisive innovators of that period and note when they entered early manhood. Thus, if we take the Middle Ages as lasting until about 1350, and the modern age as beginning at some time between 1600 and 1650, the late fourteenth and all of the fifteenth and sixteenth centuries being a period of transition, the problem, as Ortega saw it, was to find the individual who most decisively represented the emergence of the modern age. In the present case, Ortega decided that that individual was Descartes, who ended his thirtieth year in 1626; thus the key date of the previous generation was 1611, and that of the generation following Descartes was 1641. Not that these dates were hard-and-fast divisions; Ortega intended them only as major reference points: "the center of the zone of dates which corresponds to the decisive generation" (Ortega [1933] 1962, p. 63). Nor did all generations have their great men, although there was a strong presumption that what Ortega called the "tone" of history changed more or less decisively every 15 years.

Ortega did not pretend to have solved the problem of generations in any final sense; what he offered the historian was a series of challenges, of demands to rethink his conception of the past in the light of the generational approach. Indeed, Ortega was not engaged in the writing of history as such; his main interest, so far as history was concerned, was in isolating and defining those periods of crisis and decisive social change which redefine the entire meaning of human existence. Like Wilhelm Dilthey, he continually stressed the importance of studying the meaning of historical events for those who took part in them. His generational schema was thus an indispensable means of detecting regularities in the seemingly endless variation of human experience.

Dynamics of generations

Most of Ortega's writings were issued as public lectures or newspaper articles, in which forms he excelled. This gives his work great cogency of style but sometimes deters the specialist. A certain amount of systematic elaboration and clarification of his ideas is therefore necessary in order to demonstrate their usefulness to social science and to provide further developments of his method.

The macrostructure of history—epochs—cannot be determined a priori or cyclically, because it is dependent not on any constant structural factor of human life, but on its empirical contents. The microstructure—generations—is based on the mechanism of ages that is constant within certain extensive historical limits. Generations are, by turns, the "actors" and the "acts" of the historical drama, the "who" and the "what" of history whose movement is not continual but gradual. The generation is the elemental historical present, the term of relative stability of a world figure, and the rhythm of historical variation. The empirical determination of generations within a society is difficult and requires investigations that are rigorous and extremely cautious. Only the reigning norms of a society and their variation can be analyzed in detail. If a certain number of representative figures are taken whose origins fall within the same 15-year period (though the boundaries of the generations in question are not known, nor are the generations to which these figures belong), we can at least take each individual as representative of his own generation and study its characteristics in him. If other persons born in subsequent 15-year periods are added to the series, we can continue to assume that each group belongs to the same generation. But if, at a certain moment, a change in the whole series is observed, a "boundary" between two generations is indicated, and an entire generational series can then be established, at least in a provisional manner. This hypothetical series can be applied like a framework to historical reality, which will then confirm or correct it. Thus the proposed scale of generations serves as a provisional "working hypothesis"; its value is methodological.

Generations are not small groups of illustrious men; the latter are only the *representative* men of a generation that comprises innumerable anonymous men born within a certain "zone of dates." If a society is studied from the point of view of generations, it appears to be joined in groups or strata of coevals, each of whom occupies a definite position by virtue of his experiences, his pretensions, and, finally, his social level, since stratification is universal. The generational perspective introduces discontinuity and articulation in place of an amorphous and confused whole. From a historical point of view—inseparable from sociology because society is intrinsically historical—a date "unfolds" itself in several dates that correspond to the different generations. In each date there are four major human strata or generations, coexistents in interaction, with precise and unsubstitutable functions: (*a*) the "survivors" of a previous epoch who indicate the origins of the present situation, that is, the men "of another time" who nevertheless remain in this one; (*b*) those in power in all areas, whose pretensions generally coincide with the actual state of the world; (*c*) the "opposition" or active generation that has not yet triumphed and fights with the previous generation for the transfer of power and the realization of its own innovations; and (*d*) the young, who have new pretensions and look forward to a "putsch" or downfall of the *status quo*. A historical epoch is therefore defined by a principle or form of life that differentiates it from the previous one and affects the totality of a society. It is a process by which an innovation that begins by being individual goes on to permeate a minority and finally becomes dominant throughout the entire society, so that it is the form that individuals encounter as the prevailing way of life. Such a process requires the intervention of at least four successive generations, or about sixty years.

Empirical determination of generational series requires considerable work that has not as yet been accomplished anywhere. It is advisable to take a clearly defined society (a nation, for example) and a not too large space of time, since the normal concatenation of generations can be disturbed by serious historical upheavals. Between two different societies there normally is a time lag in the dates of generations. But the fact that different societies often have certain key dates in common is an indication that the same customs, manners, ideas, beliefs, etc. dominate over a certain historical area; in other words, that this constitutes *one* society, at least on a certain level. For example, it is very probable that the generations of western Europe coincide since the eighteenth century—in our time, perhaps throughout the West. It is certain, on the other hand, that the key dates in the United States are different from those in India or China.

The method of generations would permit a "social cartography" to be arrived at, the difficulties of which would be great but no greater than the requirements for any other empirical investigation of social phenomena. It should be noticed that historical–social generations affect *all* the men of a society in all the dimensions of their life; properly speaking, there is no such thing as (for example) a purely "literary" or "political" generation.

Particular fields can, of course, be investigated to obtain a greater facility of comparison or to pursue a particular interest; it must be borne in mind, however, that the results obtained cannot be extended to the whole society but must be related to a general theory of generations.

JULIÁN MARÍAS

[*Directly related is the entry* COHORT ANALYSIS. *Other relevant material may be found in* HISTORY, *article on* THE PHILOSOPHY OF HISTORY; PERIODIZATION; *and in the biographies of* COMTE; COURNOT; DILTHEY; MANNHEIM; MILL; ORTEGA Y GASSET; RANKE; VICO.]

BIBLIOGRAPHY

BENLOEW, LOUIS 1881 *Les lois de l'histoire.* Paris: Germer-Baillière.

COMTE, AUGUSTE (1830–1842) 1896 *The Positive Philosophy of Auguste Comte.* Freely translated and condensed by Harriet Martineau, with an introduction by Frederic Harrison. 3 vols. London: Bell. → First published as *Cours de philosophie positive.*

COMTE, AUGUSTE (1851–1854) 1875–1877 *System of Positive Polity.* 4 vols. London: Longmans. → First published in French. The translation of the extract in the text was made by the encyclopedia's editorial staff from the 1851–1854 French edition.

COURNOT, ANTOINE A. (1872) 1934 *Considérations sur la marche des idées et des évènements dans les temps modernes.* 2 vols. Paris: Boivin.

CROCE, BENEDETTO (1917) 1960 *History: Its Theory and Practice.* New York: Russell. → First published as *Teoria e storia della storiografia.*

DILTHEY, WILHELM (1875) 1924 Über das Studium der Geschichte der Wissenschaften vom Menschen, der Gesellschaft und dem Staat. Pages 31–73 in Wilhelm Dilthey, *Gesammelte Schriften.* Volume 5: Die geistige Welt. Leipzig and Berlin: Teubner.

DRERUP, ENGELBERT 1933 *Das Generationsproblem in der griechischen und griechisch-römischen Kultur.* Paderborn (Germany): Schöningh.

DROMEL, JUSTIN 1862 *La loi des révolutions: Les générations, les nationalités, les dynasties, les religions.* Paris: Didier.

EISENSTADT, SHMUEL N.   1956   *From Generation to Generation: Age Groups and Social Structure.* Glencoe, Ill.: Free Press; London: Routledge.

FERRARI, GIUSEPPE   1874   *Teoria dei periodi politici.* Milan (Italy): Hoepli.

FERRATER MORA, JOSÉ   (1957) 1963   *Ortega y Gasset: An Outline of His Philosophy.* New rev. ed. New Haven: Yale Univ. Press.

JESCHKE, HANS   1934   *Die Generation von 1898 in Spanien.* Halle (Germany): Niemeyer.

LAFUENTE FERRARI, ENRIQUE   1951   *La fundamentación y los problemas de la historia del arte.* Madrid: Tecnos.

LAÍN ENTRALGO, PEDRO   1945   *Las generaciones en la historia.* Madrid: Instituto de Estudios Políticos.

LORENZ, OTTOKAR   1886   *Die Geschichtswissenschaft in Hauptrichtungen und Aufgaben kritisch erörtert.* Berlin: Hertz.

LORENZ, OTTOKAR   1891   *Leopold von Ranke, die Generationslehre und der Geschichtsunterricht.* Berlin: Hertz.

MANNHEIM, KARL   (1928) 1952   The Problem of Generations. Pages 276–320 in Karl Mannheim, *Essays on the Sociology of Knowledge.* New York: Oxford Univ. Press. → First published in German.

MARÍAS, JULIÁN   (1949a) 1961   *El método histórico de las generaciones.* 3d ed. Madrid: Revista de Occidente.

MARÍAS, JULIÁN   1949b   Ortega and the Idea of Vital Reason. *Dublin Review* 222, no. 445: 56–79; no. 446: 36–54.

MARÍAS, JULIÁN   (1955) 1964   *La estructura social: Teoría y método.* 4th ed. Madrid: Sociedad de Estudios y Publicaciones.

[MARTÍNEZ RUIZ, JOSÉ]   1913   *Clásicos y modernos,* by Azorin [pseud.]. Madrid: Renacimiento.

MENTRÉ, FRANÇOIS   1920   *Les générations sociales.* Paris: Bossard.

MILL, JOHN STUART   (1843) 1961   *A System of Logic, Ratiocinative and Inductive.* London: Longmans.

ORTEGA Y GASSET, JOSÉ   (1923) 1933   *The Modern Theme.* New York: Norton. → First published as *El tema de nuestro tiempo.* A paperback edition was published in 1961 by Harper.

ORTEGA Y GASSET, JOSÉ   (1933) 1962   *Man and Crisis.* New York: Norton. → First published as *En torno á Galileo.*

PETERSEN, JULIUS   1930   Die literarischen Generationen. Pages 130–187 in Emil Ermatinger (editor), *Philosophie der Literaturwissenschaft.* Berlin: Junker & Dünnhaupt.

PEYRE, HENRI   1948   *Les générations littéraires.* Paris: Boivin.

PINDER, WILHELM   (1926) 1928   *Das Problem der Generation in der Kunstgeschichte Europas.* 2d ed. Berlin: Frankfurter Verlags-Anstalt.

RANKE, LEOPOLD VON   (1888) 1954   Über die Epochen der neueren Geschichte. Part 9, section 2 in Leopold von Ranke, *Weltgeschichte.* Leipzig: Duncker & Humblot.

RÜMELIN, GUSTAV   1875   Über den Begriff und die Dauer einer Generation. Volume 1, pages 285–304 in Gustav Rümelin, *Reden und Aufsätze.* Freiburg im Breisgau (Germany): Mohr.

SALINAS, PEDRO   1935   El concepto de generación literaria aplicado á la del 98. *Revista de occidente* 50: 249–259.

SCHLEGEL, FRIEDRICH   (1812) 1889   *Lectures on the History of Literature, Ancient and Modern.* London: Bell. → First published as *Geschichte der alten und neuen Literatur.*

SOULAVIE, JEAN-L. G.   1809   *Pièces inédites sur les règnes de Louis XIV, Louis XV et Louis XVI.* Paris: Colin.

WECHSSLER, E.   1929   Davoser Hochschulvorträge und das Problem der Generationen in der Geistesgeschichte. *Zeitschrift für französischen und englischen Unterricht* 28: 435–438.

II

POLITICAL GENERATIONS

Group consciousness is universally recognized as one of the fundamental elements of political motivation. Individual human beings in every political system seek the security provided by membership in groups. Group consciousness is created by certain basic similarities, and this consciousness in turn creates more homogeneity within the group, a conformity which often leads to common action. Individuals think of themselves as members of a group and therefore act as members of that group. Since the interests of different groups are not always mutually compatible, there is social conflict. Since all individuals have allegiances to more than one group, there is conflict within the individual, who must decide which group is most important to him in given circumstances. In European politics, for instance, there has often been a conflict between national consciousness and class consciousness, which has generally been resolved in favor of the former.

Although political scientists have studied intensively both national consciousness and class consciousness, they have not explored to any considerable extent another kind of group consciousness, that of belonging to a distinct generation. This omission is surprising, for novelists, cultural and political historians, and sociologists have all used the concept of generation with considerable success. Although Turgenev's *Fathers and Sons* is the outstanding example of a literary work in which different generations cannot communicate effectively with each other, generational conflict is one of the major themes running through most of world literature. This fact is perhaps responsible for the emphasis which cultural historians have given to the study of different literary, artistic, and musical generations. Sometimes, indeed, cultural historians have seen only the successive alternation of "romantic" and "classical" generations. Historians, among them Ranke, have speculated about the significance of a generations approach to political history. Sociologists, especially Karl Mannheim (1928) and Rudolf Heberle (1951), have emphasized the importance of generational differences in social movements and social change. Political scientists, however, have used political generation as a conceptual tool only in the study of modern totalitarianism. Sigmund Neumann (1939; 1942) convincingly stressed the generational consciousness of National Socialist leaders and followers. Students of Soviet politics have found basic differences, not attributable merely to life cycle differences, between the responses of younger and older generations to the enforcement of conformity within the Soviet Union.

It could be argued that the concept of political generation can be of major assistance in understanding the motivation of leaders and followers in all political systems, not merely those which are totalitarian. Much of the hesitance of political scientists in applying this concept undoubtedly has arisen from uncertainty as to the precise meaning of a generation in politics. A political generation is not to be equated with a biological generation. Political generations do not suddenly "change" every 30 or 35 years. The process of social change is continuous, and it cannot wait until political power is handed on from father to son. There is undoubtedly much personal conflict between fathers and sons, but most of this conflict has no direct political significance. The history of politics is not primarily that of conflict, or even of consensus, between fathers and sons—although such conflict may take place, as it did between James and John Stuart Mill, with important political consequences. There are always—assuming a minimal rate of social change—more than two generations in politics at any one time. The idea of a "young" generation and an "old" generation as the sole participants in the political process is as oversimplified as Karl Marx's assumption that there are only two classes in modern industrial society. The idea of two generations in politics is frequently linked with the erroneous assumption that the "young" generation is always liberal and the "old" generation is always conservative.

Implicit in a generations approach to politics is the assumption that an individual's political attitudes do not undergo substantial change during the course of his adult lifetime. Once a set of political beliefs has been embraced, it is regarded as unlikely that the individual will abandon his beliefs. Rather than altering his previous outlook on the basis of new facts, the individual either rejects or accepts these new facts depending on whether or not they are consistent with his previous outlook. In this sense, a "liberal" generation will remain "liberal" in terms of the formative years throughout the physical lifetime of its members. Whether this same political attitude will appear liberal under radically changed circumstances is another matter. Much of the confusion in the political vocabulary of any nation may be due to the different meanings given to the same term by members of different generations. In thus explaining the tenacity of "outmoded" policies, generations theory removes these policies from the realm of free choice, from the realm of moral judgments. In this respect, a generations approach has the same fundamental weaknesses and strengths as any other determinist approach.

Especially in times of rapid social change, it is important to know precisely at what period of life political attitudes are formed. It is interesting that no serious advocate of a generations approach has argued that political attitudes are formed during childhood. Rather, it is argued that late adolescence and early adulthood are the formative years during which a distinctive personal outlook on politics emerges, which remains essentially unchanged through old age. The crucial years are regarded as approximately 17 to 25. If these years are in fact formative, neither the years preceding nor the years following them are decisive in the formation of political attitudes. It is during the formative years that the youth discovers his own identity. When he defines who he is in terms of society, he defines his political outlook as well. A political generation is seen as a group of individuals who have undergone the same basic historical experiences during their formative years. Such a generation would find political communication with earlier and later generations difficult, if not impossible.

The size of a political generation. Not all historical events are experienced to the same degree by the same number of individuals in their formative years, and political generations therefore vary widely in size. The 1825 Decembrist conspiracy, for instance, decisively influenced a much smaller number of young Russians than did the Russian Revolution of 1917. Assuming that the total degree of political participation is stable, it is the temporal and spatial "limits" of a given historic event that define the size of the resulting political generation, just as the degree of uniqueness of that event determines the degree of difficulty that generation will have in communicating with earlier and later generations. In this sense, for instance, the political generation created by World War I was a general European phenomenon. It was neither world-wide nor confined to one or a few European nations. The enormous transformation of European society which the war involved meant that a new political generation was created throughout Europe. But the limited nature of the war experience outside Europe meant that the war had far less impact on, say, American or Japanese youth. Those Europeans whose formative years, in whole or in part, occurred during 1914–1918, especially those who actually fought in the war, were not all influenced in the same way; but they were nevertheless all decisively influenced by it. Their reactions to the war were often very different, depending upon their national, class, and, especially, personality differences. In a real sense, the fact that they were all involved in the war in their formative years determined their attitude toward politics for the rest of their lives. Some never recovered from the war and retreated from politics, which had, they felt, led directly to such suffering. Others entered politics after 1918 determined above all to prevent a recurrence of war. Still others never spiritually left the battlefield and as a result engaged in politics as the continuation of war by other means. These three alternatives formed what Karl Mannheim termed "generation units," which together constituted a generation precisely because they were oriented toward one another, if only to fight one another. Politics involves more than knowledge of friend and foe, but many of the personal friendships and enmities which in fact later influence political behavior originate during the formative years. Each generation speaks out with more than one voice—there is conflict within each generation as well as among generations.

The time span of a political generation.   If a political generation is not the same as a biological generation, it becomes all the more important to define the specific time span within which all who experience their formative years can be said to be molded into one distinct political generation. Without such a definition, it is impossible to classify individuals as members of one or another political generation with any precision, especially since few significant historic events "begin" and "end" with as much definiteness as World War I. Such classification cannot be done on an *ad hoc* basis. If the *ad hoc* method is attempted, it may properly be suspected that generational differences are being used as a *deus ex machina* in much the same way that differences in national character are sometimes invoked when there seems to be no other explanation of some political phenomenon. On the other hand, since the concept of political generation is closely related to the process of social change, any arbitrary choice of time span is likely to violate the complexity of reality. The actual time span involved in a generation will differ substantially in periods in which the process of social change is more rapid or less rapid. Karl Mannheim (1928) suggested that whether a new generation

appears every year, every thirty years, or every hundred years, or whether it emerges rhythmically at all, depends entirely on the specific social context. This variability, of course, is merely one aspect of the general problem of applying ideal types to concrete situations. All concepts of comparative analysis must be defined in time and space if they are to be of any use in clarifying reality. This is especially true of the concept of political generation, since membership in the same generation involves common location in time and space. In twentieth-century Western society, in which social change is not only rapid but cataclysmic, the time span of a political generation is considerably shorter than in more stable societies. The most reasonable estimate for the time span of a political generation in twentieth-century Western society is probably ten to fifteen years. In twentieth-century non-Western societies experiencing revolutionary social, economic, and political changes, this time span may be even shorter.

The spatial span of a political generation.   Although the spatial span of a political generation is difficult to define with precision, it is clear that many coevals in the human race are not members of the same generation. Those whose formative experiences are fundamentally different cannot be members of the same generation, even though they may coexist in time. There was, for instance, as Mannheim pointed out, no community of experience between youths in China and Germany about 1800. It could be argued that there is considerable community of experience between youths in East Germany and Communist China today, since their formative years are spent in similar totalitarian political environments. Indeed, such phenomena as the spread of nationalism and of industrialization indicate that the spatial barriers between generations may be breaking down, at the same time that more rapid social change is increasing the importance of the temporal barriers between generations. The effect of the latter development is to make communication between different political generations more difficult, while the effect of the former development is to increase the world-wide significance of this decline in ability to communicate. The implications of these long-range developments for meaningful communication within and among political systems are not entirely encouraging.

Significance of the concept.   Generational consciousness is undoubtedly less significant as a source of political motivation than either national or class consciousness. National consciousness finds its organizational expression in national states, and class consciousness finds its organizational expression in class-based private associations and parties. There is no analogous organizational structure created by generational consciousness, except for occasional loosely knit groups such as "Young Turks," "Young England," or "Young Conservatives." There are many powerful men recognized as primarily national or class leaders, but there are relatively few such men recognized as primarily generational leaders. Political personages nevertheless write, as did one Canadian leader, autobiographies with such titles as *My Generation of Politics and Politicians* (Preston 1927). Indeed, perhaps the most impressive evidence for the existence of generational consciousness in politics is the frequency with which it is articulated in the autobiographical writings of political leaders. These writings often demonstrate that, as Léon Blum put it, "a man remains essentially what his youth has made him" and that there is a special kind of communication, in politics as in other aspects of life, between members of the same generation. This should not be surprising, for the latter are simultaneously experiencing the problems and the promise of the life cycle itself.

Problems for further research. Clearly generational consciousness is not the single key to understanding political motivation, but equally clearly there is enough evidence of its importance to justify further research efforts. An exact evaluation of this importance waits upon full answers to several questions, some of which have their implications for the social sciences in general:

(1) When do an individual's politically formative years begin and end? To what extent is this period different in different societies?

(2) How substantial is the continuity between political attitudes accepted during the formative years and political attitudes in later years? (Care should be taken not to concentrate exclusively in this research on any one single element of political action, such as voting behavior, for the same fundamental attitudes might cause a voter to shift party allegiance in a changing party constellation. In the United States, for instance, an individual who became a Wilsonian liberal in his formative years might consider himself consistent in voting for Republican candidates in elections after the Democratic party was transformed under Franklin Roosevelt. A supporter of the Congress party at the achievement of Indian independence might in later decades feel that his continuing personal beliefs were best articulated by some other—or by no—party.)

(3) How long is the time span necessary to form a distinct political generation? What is the relationship between the rate of social change—and changes in the rate of social change—and the length of this time span?

(4) What is a generation unit? To what extent do generation units see the totality of politics in terms of each other?

MARVIN RINTALA

[*See also* IDENTIFICATION, POLITICAL. *Other relevant material may be found in* COHORT ANALYSIS; SOCIALIZATION; *and in the biography of* MANNHEIM.]

BIBLIOGRAPHY

ALEXANDER, EDGAR (1956) 1957 The Dilemma: The Generations' Problem. Pages 33–42 in Edgar Alexander, *Adenauer and the New Germany: The Chancellor of the Vanquished.* Preface by Alvin Johnson. New York: Farrar, Straus. → First published in German.

BAUER, RAYMOND A.; INKELES, ALEX; and KLUCKHOHN, CLYDE 1956 Generational Differences. Pages 190–198 in Raymond A. Bauer et al., *How the Soviet System Works: Cultural, Psychological and Social Themes.* Cambridge, Mass.: Harvard Univ. Press. → A paperback edition was published in 1961 by Vintage.

EISENSTADT, SHMUEL N. 1956 *From Generation to Generation: Age Groups and Social Structure.* Glencoe, Ill.: Free Press; London: Routledge.

EVAN, WILLIAM M. 1959 Cohort Analysis of Survey Data: A Procedure for Studying Long-term Opinion Change. *Public Opinion Quarterly* 23:63–72.

GUSFIELD, JOSEPH R. 1957 The Problem of Generations in an Organizational Structure. *Social Forces* 35:323–330.

HALPERN, BEN 1961 *The Idea of the Jewish State.* Cambridge, Mass.: Harvard Univ. Press.

HEBERLE, RUDOLF 1951 *Social Movements: An Introduction to Political Sociology.* New York: Appleton. → See especially pages 118–127 on "The Problem of Political Generations."

MANNHEIM, KARL (1928) 1952 The Problem of Generations. Pages 276–320 in Karl Mannheim, *Essays on the Sociology of Knowledge.* New York: Oxford Univ. Press. → First published in German.

NEUMANN, SIGMUND 1939 The Conflict of Generations in Contemporary Europe: From Versailles to Munich. *Vital Speeches of the Day* 5:623–628.

NEUMANN, SIGMUND (1942) 1965 *Permanent Revolution: Totalitarianism in the Age of International Civil War.* 2d ed. New York: Praeger. → First published as *Permanent Revolution: The Total State in a World at War.*

ORTEGA Y GASSET, JOSÉ (1923) 1933 *The Modern Theme.* New York: Norton. → First published as *El tema de nuestro tiempo.* A paperback edition was published in 1961 by Harper.

PINDER, WILHELM 1926 *Kunstgeschichte nach Generationen.* Leipzig: Pfeiffer.

PRESTON, WILLIAM T. R. 1927 *My Generation of Politics and Politicians.* Toronto: Rose.

RINTALA, MARVIN 1958 The Problem of Generations in Finnish Communism. *American Slavic and East European Review* 17:190–202.

RINTALA, MARVIN 1962 *Three Generations: The Extreme Right Wing in Finnish Politics.* Bloomington: Indiana Univ. Press.

Rintala, Marvin 1963 A Generation in Politics: A Definition. *Review of Politics* 25:509–522.

Zeitlin, Maurice 1966 Political Generations in the Cuban Working Class. *American Journal of Sociology* 71:493–508.

GENETICS

I
GENETICS AND BEHAVIOR

Behavior genetics is a relatively new cross-disciplinary specialization between genetics and psychology. It is so new that it hardly knows what to call itself. The term "behavior genetics" is gaining currency in the United States; but in some quarters there, and certainly elsewhere, the term "psychogenetics" is favored. Logically, the best name would be genetical psychology, since the emphasis is on the use of the techniques of genetics in the analysis of behavior rather than vice versa; but the inevitable ambiguity of that term is apparent. Psychologists generally use the terms "genetic" or "genetical" in two senses: in the first and older sense of developmental, or ontogenetic; and in the second, more recent usage relating to the analysis of inheritance. The psychologist G. Stanley Hall coined the term "genetic" before the turn of the century to denote developmental studies (witness the *Journal of Genetic Psychology*), and Alfred Binet even used the term "psychogenetic" in this sense. But with the rapid rise of the discipline now known as genetics after the rediscovery of the Mendelian laws in 1900, William Bateson, one of the founders of this new science, pre-empted the term "genetic" in naming it, thereby investing "genetic" with the double meaning that causes the current confusion. Psychological genetics, with its obvious abbreviation, psychogenetics, is probably the best escape from the dilemma.

Importance of genetics in behavior. The importance of psychogenetics lies in the fundamental nature of the biological processes in our understanding of human social behavior. The social sciences, and psychology in particular, have long concentrated on environmental determinants of behavior and neglected hereditary ones. But it is clear that in many psychological functions a substantial portion of the observed variation, roughly of the order of 50 per cent for many traits, can be ascribed to hereditary causation. To ignore this hereditary contribution is to impede both action and thought in this area.

This manifold contribution to behavioral variation is not a static affair. Heredity and environment interact, and behavior is the product, rather than the sum, of their respective contributions. The number of sources of variability in both heredity and environment is large, and the consequent number of such possible products even larger. Nevertheless, these outcomes are not incalculable, and experimental and other analyses of their limits are of immense potential interest to the behavioral scientist. The chief theoretical interest lies in the analysis of the evolution of behavior; and the chief practical significance, so far as can be envisaged at present, lies in the possibilities psychogenetics has for the optimization of genetic potential by manipulation of the environmental expression of it.

Major current approaches. The major approaches to the study of psychogenetics can be characterized as the direct, or experimental, and the indirect, or observational. The former derive principally from the genetical parent of this hybrid discipline and involve the manipulation of the heredity of experimental subjects, usually by restricting the choice of mates in some specially defined way. Since such techniques are not possible with human subjects a second major approach exists, the indirect or observational, with its techniques derived largely from psychology and sociology. The two approaches are largely complementary in the case of "natural" genetic experiments in human populations, such as twinning or cousin marriages. Thus, the distinction between the two is based on the practicability of controlling in some way the essentially immutable genetic endowment—in a word, the genotype—of the individuals subject to investigation. With typical experimental animals (rats, mice, etc.) and other organisms used by the geneticist, such as the fruit fly and many microorganisms, the genotype can often be specified in advance and populations constructed by the hybridization of suitable strains to meet this specification with a high degree of accuracy. Not so with humans, where the genotype must remain as given, and indeed where its details can rarely be specified with any degree of accuracy except for certain physical characteristics, such as blood groups. Observational, demographic, and similar techniques are therefore all that are available here. The human field has another disadvantage in rigorous psychogenetic work: the impossibility of radically manipulating the environment—for example, by rearing humans in experimental environments from birth in the way that can easily be done with animals in the laboratory. Since in psychogenetics, as in all branches of genetics, one deals with a phenotype—in this case, behavior—and since the phenotype is the end product of the action, or better still, *interaction* of genotype and environment, human psychogenetics is fraught with double difficulty. Analytical techniques to be mentioned later can assist in resolving some of these difficulties.

Definition. To define psychogenetics as the study of the inheritance of behavior is to adopt a misleadingly narrow definition of the area of study, and one which is unduly restrictive in its emphasis on the hereditarian point of view. Just as the parent discipline of genetics is the analysis not only of the similarities between individuals but also of the differences between them, so psychogenetics seeks to understand the basis of individual differences in behavior. Any psychogenetic analysis must therefore be concerned with the environmental determinants of behavior (conventionally implicated in the genesis of differences) in addition to the hereditary ones (the classic source of resemblances). But manifestly this dichotomy does not always operate, so that for this reason alone the analysis of environmental effects must go hand in hand with the search for genetic causation. This is true even if the intention is merely to exclude the influence of the one the better to study the other; but the approach advocated here is to study the two in tandem, as it were, and to determine the extent to which the one interacts with the other. *Psychogenetics is best viewed as that specialization which concerns itself with the interaction of heredity and environment, insofar as they affect behavior.* To attempt greater precision is to become involved in subtle semantic problems about the meanings of terms.

At first sight many would tend to restrict environmental effects to those operating after the birth of the organism, but to do so would be to exclude prenatal environmental effects that have been shown to be influential in later behavior. On the other hand, to broaden the concept of environment to include all influences after fertilization—the point in time at which the genotype is fixed—permits consideration of the reciprocal influence of parts of the genotype upon each other. Can environment include the rest of the genotype, other than that part which is more or less directly concerned with the phenotype under consideration? This point assumes some importance since there are characteristics, not behavioral—at least, none that are behavioral have so far been reported—whose expression depends on the nature of the

other genes present in the organism. In the absence of some of them, or rather certain alleles of the gene pairs, the value phenotypically observed would be different from what it would be if they were present. That is, different components of the genotype, in interplay with one another, modify phenotypic expression of the characteristic they influence. Can such indirect action, which recalls that of a chemical catalyst, best be considered as environmental or innate? It would be preferable to many to regard this mechanism as a genetic effect rather than an environmental one in the usually accepted sense. Hence, the definition of the area of study as one involving the interaction of heredity and environment, while apparently adding complexity, in fact serves to reduce confusion.

It must be conceded that this view has not as yet gained general acceptance. In some of the work reviewed in the necessarily brief survey of the major findings in this area, attempts have been made to retain a rather rigid dichotomy between heredity and environment—nature versus nurture—in fact, an "either/or" proposition that the facts do not warrant. The excesses of both sides in the controversies of the 1920s—for example, the famous debate between Watson and McDougall over the relative importance of learned (environmental) and instinctive (genetic) determinants of behavior—show the fallacies that extreme protagonists on either side can entertain if the importance of the interaction effect is ignored.

Gene action. The nature of gene action as such is essentially conducive to interaction with the environment, since the behavioral phenotype we observe is the end product of a long chain of action, principally biochemical, originating in the chromosome within the individual cell. A chromosome has a complex structure, involving DNA (deoxyribonucleic acid) and the connections of DNA with various proteins, and may be influenced in turn by another nucleic acid, RNA (ribonucleic acid), also within the cell but external to the nucleus. There are complex structures and sequences of processes, anatomical, physiological, and hormonal, which underlie normal development and differentiation of structure and function in the growth, development, and maturation of the organism. Much of this influence is determined genetically in the sense that the genotype of the organism, fixed at conception, determines how it proceeds under normal environmental circumstances. But it would be a mistake to regard any such sequence as rigid or immutable, as we shall see.

The state of affairs that arises when a number of genetically determined biochemical abnormalities affect behavior is illustrative of the argument. Many of these biochemical deficiencies or inborn errors of metabolism in humans are the outcome of a chain of causation starting with genic structures, some of them having known chromosomal locations. Their effects on the total personality—that is, the sum total of behavorial variation that makes the individual unique—can range from the trivial to the intense. The facility with which people can taste a solution of phenylthiocarbamide (PTC), a synthetic substance not found in nature, varies in a relatively simple genetical way: people are either "tasters" or "nontasters" in certain rather well-defined proportions, with a pattern of inheritance determined probably by one gene of major effect. But being "taste blind" or not is a relatively unimportant piece of behavior, since one is never likely to encounter it outside a genetical experiment. (It should perhaps be added that there is some evidence that the ability to taste PTC may be linked with other characteristics of some importance, such as susceptibility to thyroid disease.) Nevertheless, this example is insignificant compared with the psychological effect of the absence of a biochemical link in patients suffering from phenylketonuria. They are unable to metabolize phenylalanine to tyrosine in the liver, with the result that the phenylalanine accumulates and the patient suffers multiple defects, among which is usually gross intellectual defect, with an IQ typically on the order of 30. This gross biochemical failure is mediated by a single recessive gene that may be passed on in a family unnoticed in heterozygous—single dose—form but becomes painfully apparent in the unfortunate individual who happens to receive a double dose and consequently is homozygous for the defect.

Alternatively, a normal dominant gene may mutate to the recessive form and so give rise to the trouble. While mutation is a relatively rare event individually, the number of genes in each individual—probably on the order of ten thousand —and the number of individuals in a population make it statistically a factor to be reckoned with. One of the best documented cases of a deleterious mutation of this kind giving rise to a major defect relates to the hemophilia transmitted, with certain important political consequences, to some of the descendants of Queen Victoria of England. The dependence of the last tsarina of Russia on the monk Rasputin was said to be based in part on the beneficial therapeutic effect of his hypnotic techniques on the uncontrollable bleeding of the Tsarevitch Alexis. Victoria was almost certainly heterozygous for hemophilia and, in view of the absence of any

previous record of the defect in the Hanoverian dynasty, it seems likely that the origin of the trouble was a mutation in one of the germ cells in a testicle of Victoria's father, the duke of Kent, before Victoria was conceived in August 1818.

But however it comes about, a defect such as phenylketonuria can be crippling. Fortunately, its presence can be diagnosed in very early life by a simple urine test for phenyl derivatives. The dependence of the expression of the genetic defect on the environmental circumstances is such that its effect can be mitigated by feeding the afflicted infant with a specially composed diet low in the phenylalanine with which the patient's biochemical make-up cannot cope. Here again, therefore, one sees the interaction of genotype and environment —in this case the type of food eaten. Many of the human biochemical defects that have been brought to light in recent years are rather simply determined genetically, in contrast with the prevailing beliefs about the bases of many behavioral characteristics including intelligence, personality, and most psychotic and neurotic disorders. This is also true of several chromosomal aberrations that have been much studied recently and that are now known to be implicated in various conditions of profound behavioral importance. Prominent among these is Down's syndrome (mongolism) with, again, effects including impairment of cognitive power. [See INTELLIGENCE AND INTELLIGENCE TESTING; MENTAL DISORDERS, *articles on* BIOLOGICAL ASPECTS *and* GENETIC ASPECTS.]

Sex as a genetic characteristic. The sex difference is perhaps the most striking genetically determined difference in behavior and the one that is most often ignored in this connection. Primary sex is completely determined genetically at the moment of fertilization of the ovum; in mammals sex depends on whether the spermatozoon effecting fertilization bears an X or a Y chromosome to combine with the X chromosome inevitably contributed by the ovum. The resulting gamete then has the form of an XX (female) or an XY (male) individual. This difference penetrates every cell of every tissue of the resulting individual and in turn is responsible for the observable gross differences in morphology. These, in turn, subserve differences of physiological function, metabolism, and endocrine function which profoundly influence not only those aspects of behavior relating to sexual behavior and reproductive function in the two sexes but many other aspects as well. But behavior is also influenced by social and cultural pressures, so that the resulting sex differences in behavior as observed by the psychologist are especially good examples of a phenotype that must be the ...d product of both genetic and environmental forces. There is a large literature on sex differences in human behavior and a sizable one on such differences in animal behavior, but there has been little attempt to assess this pervasive variation in terms of the relative contribution of genetic and environmental determinants. This is partly because of the technical difficulties of the problem, in the sense that all subjects must be of either one sex or the other—crossing males with females will always result in the same groups as those one started with, either males or females—there being, in general, no genetically intermediate sex against which to evaluate either and identical twins being inevitably of like sex. It is also partly because the potential of genetic analyses that do not involve direct experimentation has not been realized. This is especially so since the causal routes whereby genetic determinants of sex influence many of the behavioral phenotypes observed are often better understood than in other cases where the genetic determinants underlying individual differences manifest in a population are not so clear-cut. [See INDIVIDUAL DIFFERENCES, *article on* SEX DIFFERENCES.]

Sex linkage. There is one exception to the general lack of interest in the biometrical analysis of sex differences having behavioral connotations: sex-linked conditions. That is to say, it is demonstrated or postulated that the gene or genes responsible for the behavior—often a defect, as in the case of color blindness, which has a significantly greater incidence in males than in females—are linked with the sex difference by virtue of their location on the sex chromosome determining genetic sex. Thus it is that sex can be thought of as a chromosomal difference of regular occurrence, as opposed to aberrations of the sort which give rise to pathological conditions, such as Down's syndrome. Indeed there are also various anomalies of genetic sex that give rise to problems of sexual identity, in which the psychological and overt behavioral consequences can be of major importance for the individual. While the evidence in such cases of environmental modification of the causative genetic conditions is less dramatic than in phenylketonuria, interaction undoubtedly exists, since these chromosomal defects of sex differentiation can in some cases be alleviated by appropriate surgical and hormonal treatment. [See SEXUAL BEHAVIOR, *article on* SEXUAL DEVIATION: PSYCHOLOGICAL ASPECTS; *and* VISION, *article on* COLOR VISION AND COLOR BLINDNESS.]

Human psychogenetics. It is abundantly clear that most of the phenotypes the behavioral scientist is interested in are multidetermined, both environmentally and genetically. The previous examples, however, are the exception rather than the rule, and their prominence bears witness that our understanding of genetics and behavior is as yet so little advanced that the simpler modes of genetic expression have been the first to be explored. In genetics itself, the striking differences in seed configuration used by Mendel in his classic crosses of sweet peas are determined by major genes with full dominance acting simply. But such clear-cut expression, especially of dominance, is unusual in human psychogenetics, and more complex statistical techniques are necessary to evaluate multiple genetic and environmental effects acting to produce the observed phenotype.

Whatever the analysis applied to the data gathered in other fields, in human psychogenetics the method employed cannot be the straightforward Mendelian one of crossbreeding which, in various elaborations, remains the basic tool of the geneticist today. Neither can it be the method of selection —artificial, as opposed to natural—that is otherwise known as selective breeding. Indeed, none of the experimental techniques that can be applied to any other organism, whatever the phenotype being measured, is applicable to man, since experimental mating is effectively ruled out as a permissible technique in current cultures. It may be remarked in passing that such has not always been the case. The experiment of the Mogul emperor, Akbar, who reared children in isolation to determine their "natural religion" (and merely produced mutes) and the eugenics program of J. H. Noyes at the Oneida Community in New York State in the nineteenth century are cases in point. The apparent inbreeding of brother with sister among the rulers of ancient Egypt in the eighteenth dynasty (sixteenth to fourteenth century B.C.), which is often quoted as an example of the absence in humans of the deleterious effects of inbreeding ("inbreeding depression"), may not be all it seems. It is likely that the definition of "sister" and "brother" in this context did not necessarily have the same biological relevance that it has today but was rather a cultural role that could be defined, at least in this case, at will.

Twin study. In the absence of the possibility of an experimental approach, contemporary research in human psychogenetics must rely on natural genetic experiments. Of these, the one most widely used and most industriously studied is the phenomenon of human twinning. Credit for the recognition of the value of observations on twins can be given to the nineteenth-century English scientist Francis Galton, who pioneered many fields of inquiry. He may be justly regarded as the father of psychogenetics for the practical methods he introduced into this field, such as the method of twin study, as well as for his influence which extended, although indirectly, even to the American experimenters in psychogenetics during the early decades of the present century.

Twin births are relatively rare in humans and vary in frequency with the ethnic group. However, the extent to which such ethnic groups differ among themselves behaviorally as a result of the undoubted genetic differences, of which incidence of multiple births is but one example, is controversial. As is well known, there are two types of twins: the monozygotic or so-called identical twins, derived from a single fertilized ovum that has split into two at an early stage in development, and the dizygotic or so-called fraternal twins, developed from two separate ova fertilized by different spermatozoa. These two physical types are not always easy to differentiate, although this difficulty is relatively minor in twin study. Nonetheless, they have led to two kinds of investigation. The first relates to differences in monozygotic twins who have identical hereditary make-up but who have been reared apart and thus subjected to different environmental influences during childhood; and the second relates to the comparison of the two types of twins— usually restricted to like-sex pairs, since fraternal twins can differ in sex. The latter method supposes all differences between monozygotic pairs to be due to environmental origin, whereas the (greater) difference between dizygotic pairs is of environmental plus genetic origin. Thus, the relative contribution of the two sources of variation can be evaluated.

Findings obtained from either method have not been especially clear-cut, both because of intractable problems regarding the relative weight to be placed upon differences in the environment in which the twins have been reared and because of the sampling difficulties, which are likely to be formidable in any twin study. Nevertheless, interesting inferences can be drawn from twin study. The investigation of separated monozygotic twins has shown that while even with their identical heredity they can differ quite widely, there exists a significant resemblance in basic aspects of personality including intelligence, introversion, and neurotic tendencies, and that these resemblances can persist despite widely different environments in which the members of a pair are reared. Such findings emphasize the need to consider the contribution of genotype and environment in an interactive sense—clearly some genotypes represented

in the personality of monozygotic twin pairs are sensitive to environmentally induced variation, whereas others are resistant to it.

Comparisons between monozygotic and dizygotic twins reared together suggest that monozygotic twins more closely resemble each other in many aspects of personality, especially those defining psychological factors such as neuroticism and introversion–extroversion. The increase in the differences between the two types of twins when factor measures are used—as opposed to simple test scores—suggests that a more basic biological stratum is tapped by factor techniques, since the genetic determination seems greater than where individual tests are employed. Here again, the degree to which any phenotype is shown to be hereditary in origin is valid only for the environment in which it developed and is measured; different environments may well yield different results. The problems of environmental control in human samples are so intractable that some students of the subject have questioned whether the effort and undoubted skill devoted to twin study have been well invested, in view of the inherent and persisting equivocality of the outcome.

Multivariate methods.   Methods of twin study, introduced largely to improve upon the earlier methods of familial correlation (parents with offspring, sib with sib, etc.), have been combined with them. Familial correlation methods themselves have not been dealt with here, since within-family environments are bound to be even greater contaminants in determining the observed behavior than environments in twin study methods. Nevertheless, used on a large scale and in conjunction with twin study and with control subjects selected at random from a population, multivariate methods show promise for defining the limits of environmental and genotypic interaction. So far, the solutions to the problems of biometrical analysis posed by this type of investigation have been only partial, and the sheer weight of effort involved in locating and testing the requisite numbers of subjects standing in the required relationships has deterred all but a few pioneers. Despite the undoubtedly useful part such investigations have played in defining the problems involved, the absence of the possibility of experimental breeding has proved a drawback in the provision of socially useful data.

Animal psychogenetics.   Recourse has often been had to nonhuman subjects. The additional problem thereby incurred of the relevance of comparative data to human behavior is probably balanced by the double refinements of the control of both the heredity and the environment of the experimental subjects. Two major methods of genetics have been employed, both intended to produce subjects of predetermined genotype: the crossbreeding of strains of animals of known genotype; and phenotypic selection, the mating of like with like to increase a given characteristic in a population.

Selection. Behavioral phenotypes of interest have been studied by the above methods, often using laboratory rodents. For example, attributes such as intelligence, activity, speed of conditioning, and emotionality have been selectively bred in rats.

Selection for emotional behavior in the rat will serve as an example of the techniques used and the results achieved. Rats, in common with many other mammalian species, defecate when afraid. A technique of measuring individual differences in emotional arousal is based on this propensity. The animal under test is exposed to mildly stressful noise and light stimulation in an open field or arena. The number of fecal pellets deposited serves as an index of disturbance, and in this way the extremes among a large group of rats can be characterized as high or low in emotional responsiveness. Continued selection from within the "high" and "low" groups will in time produce two distinct strains. Control of environmental variables is achieved by a rigid standardization of the conditions under which the animals are reared before being subjected to the test as adults. Careful checks on maternal effects, both prenatal and postnatal, reveal these effects to be minimal.

Such an experiment does little beyond establishing the importance of the genetic effect on the given strains in the given environment. While there are techniques for assessing the relative importance of the genetic and environmental contributions to the variation observed under selection, they are better suited to the analysis of the outcome of experiments using the alternative major genetical method, that of crossbreeding of inbred strains.

Crossbreeding. Strains used in crossbreeding experiments have usually been inbred for a phenotypic character of interest, although not usually a behavioral one. However, this does not preclude the use of these inbred strains for behavioral studies, since linkage relationships among genes ensure that selection for factors multidetermined genetically often involves multiple changes in characteristics other than those selected for, and behavior is no exception to this rule. Moreover, the existence of such inbred strains constitutes perhaps the most important single advantage of animals as subjects, since it enables simplifying assumptions regarding the homozygosity or genetic uniformity of such strains to be made in analysis of the outcome of crosses. Members of inbred strains are theoretically as alike as monozygotic twin pairs, so that genetic relationships—which in human populations can be investigated only after widespread efforts to find them—can be multiplied at will in laboratory animals.

This approach allows a more sensitive analysis of the determinants, both environmental and genetic, of the behavioral phenotype under observation. In addition, the nature of the genetic forces can be further differentiated into considerations of the average dominance effects of the genes involved, the extent to which they tend to increase or decrease the metrical expression of the behavioral phenotype, and the extent to which the different strains involved possess such increasers or decreasers. Finally, rough estimates of the number of these genes can be given. But the analysis depends upon meeting requirements regarding the scaling of the metric upon which the behavior is measured and is essentially a statistical one. That is, only average effects of cumulative action of the relatively large number of genes postulated as involved can be detected. Gone are the elegantly simple statistics derived from the classical Mendelian analyses of genes of major effect, often displaying dominance, like those encountered in certain human inborn errors of metabolism. There is little evidence of the existence of comparable genes of major effect mediating behavior in laboratory animals, although some have been studied in insects, especially the fruit fly.

A typical investigation of a behavioral phenotype might take the form of identifying two inbred strains known to differ in a behavioral trait, measuring individuals from these strains, and then systematically crossing them and measuring all offspring. When this was done for the runway performance of mice, an attribute related to their temperamental wildness, the results, analyzed by the techniques of biometrical genetics, showed that the behavior was controlled by at least three groups of genes (a probable underestimate). The contributions of these groups were additive to each other and independent of the environment when measured on a logarithmic scale but interacted with each other and with the environment on a linear scale. These genes showed a significant average dominance effect, and there was a preponderance of dominant genes in the direction of greater wildness. The heritability ratio of the contributions of "nature" and "nurture" was around seven to three.

The use of inbred lines may be restricted to first

filial crosses if a number of such crosses are made from several different lines. This increases precision of analysis in addition to allowing a proportionate decrease in the amount of laboratory work. One investigation examined the exploratory behavior of six different strains of rats in an open field of the kind used for the selection mentioned above. On a linear scale there were no untoward environmental effects, including specifically prenatal maternal ones. The heritability ratio was high, around nine to one; and while there was a significant average dominance component among the genes determining exploration, there was no preponderance of dominants or recessively acting genes among increasers or decreasers. The relative standing in this respect of the parental strains could be established with some precision.

Limitations. While the methods described above have allowed the emergence of results that ultimately may assist our understanding of the mechanisms of behavioral inheritance, it cannot be said that much substantial progress has yet been made. Until experiments explore the effect of a range of different genotypes interacting with a range of environments of psychological interest and consequence, little more can be expected. Manipulating heredity in a single standard environment or manipulating the environment of a single standard genotype can only provide conclusions so limited to both the genotypes and conditions employed that they have little usefulness in a wider context. When better experiments are performed, as seems likely in the next few decades, then problems of some sociological importance and interest will arise in the application of these experiments to the tasks of maximizing genetic potential and perfecting environmental control for the purpose of so doing. A new eugenics may well develop, but grappling with the problems of its impact on contemporary society had best be left to future generations.

P. L. BROADHURST

[*Directly related are the entries* EUGENICS; EVOLUTION; MENTAL DISORDERS, *article on* GENETIC ASPECTS. *Other relevant material may be found in* INDIVIDUAL DIFFERENCES, *article on* SEX DIFFERENCES; INSTINCT; INTELLIGENCE AND INTELLIGENCE TESTING; MENTAL RETARDATION; PSYCHOLOGY, *article on* CONSTITUTIONAL PSYCHOLOGY.]

BIBLIOGRAPHY

BROADHURST, P. L. 1960 Experiments in Psychogenetics: Applications of Biometrical Genetics to the Inheritance of Behavior. Pages 1–102 in Hans J. Eysenck (editor), *Experiments in Personality*. Volume 1: Psychogenetics and Psychopharmacology. London: Routledge. → Selection and crossbreeding methods applied to laboratory rats.

CATTELL, RAYMOND B.; STICE, GLEN F.; and KRISTY, NORTON F. 1957 A First Approximation to Nature–Nurture Ratios for Eleven Primary Personality Factors in Objective Tests. *Journal of Abnormal and Social Psychology* 54:143–159. → Pioneer multivariate analysis combining twin study and familial correlations.

FULLER, JOHN L.; and THOMPSON, W. ROBERT 1960 *Behavior Genetics*. New York: Wiley. → A comprehensive review of the field.

MATHER, KENNETH 1949 *Biometrical Genetics: The Study of Continuous Variation*. New York: Dover. → The classic work on the analysis of quantitative characteristics.

SHIELDS, JAMES 1962 *Monozygotic Twins Brought Up Apart and Brought Up Together: An Investigation Into the Genetic and Environmental Causes of Variation in Personality*. Oxford Univ. Press.

II

DEMOGRAPHY AND POPULATION GENETICS

The best available definition of population genetics is doubtless that of Malécot: "It is the totality of mathematical models that can be constructed to represent the evolution of the structure of a population classified according to the distribution of its Mendelian genes" (1955, p. 240). This definition, by a probabilist mathematician, gives a correct idea of the "constructed" and abstract side of this branch of genetics; it also makes intelligible the rapid development of population genetics since the advent of Mendelism.

In its formal aspect this branch of genetics might even seem to be a science that is almost played out. Indeed, it is not unthinkable that mathematicians have exhausted all the structural possibilities for building models, both within the context of general genetics and within that of the hypotheses—more or less complex and abstract—that enable us to characterize the state of a population.

Two major categories of models can be distinguished: *determinist* models are those "in which variations in population composition over time are rigorously determined by (*a*) a known initial state of the population; (*b*) a known number of forces or 'pressures' operating, in the course of generations, in an unambiguously defined fashion" (Malécot 1955, p. 240). These pressures involve mutation, selection, and preferential marriages (by consanguinity, for instance). Determinist models, based on ratios that have been exactly ascertained from preceding phenomena, can be expressed only in terms of populations that are infinite in the mathematical sense. In fact, it is only in this type of population that statistical regularities can emerge (Malécot 1955). In these models the composition of each generation is perfectly defined by the composition of the preceding generation.

Stochastic models, in contrast to determinist ones, involve only finite populations, in which the gametes that, beginning with the first generation, are actually going to give birth to the new generation represent only a finite number among all possible gametes. The result is that among these active, or "useful," gametes (Malécot 1959), male or female, the actual frequency of a gene will differ from the probability that each gamete had of carrying it at the outset.

The effect of chance will play a prime role, and the frequencies of the genes will be able to drift from one generation to the other. The effects of random drift and of genetic drift become, under these conditions, the focal points for research.

The body of research completed on these assumptions does indeed form a coherent whole, but these results, in spite of their brilliance, are marked by a very noticeable formalism. In reality, the models, although of great importance at the conceptual level, are often too far removed from the facts. In the study of man, particularly, the problems posed are often too complex for the solutions taken directly from the models to describe concrete reality.

Not all these models, however, are the result of purely abstract speculation; construction of some of them has been facilitated by experimental data. To illustrate this definition of population genetics and the problems that it raises, this article will limit itself to explaining one determinist model, both because it is one of the oldest and simplest to understand and because it is one of those most often verified by observation.

A determinist model. Let us take the case of a particular human population: the inhabitants of an island cut off from outside contacts. It is obvious that great variability exists among the genes carried by the different inhabitants of this island. The genotypes differ materially from one another; in other words, there is a certain polymorphism in the population—polymorphism that we can define in genetic terms with the help of a simple example.

Let us take the case of autosome ("not connected with sex") gene a, transmitting itself in a monohybrid diallely. In relation to it individuals can be classified in three categories: *homozygotes* whose two alleles are a (a/a); heterozygotes, carriers of a and its allele a' (a/a'); and the homozygotes who are *noncarriers* of a (a'/a'). At any given moment or during any given generation, these three categories of individuals exist within the population in certain proportions relative to each other.

Now, according to Mendel's second law (the law of segregation), the population born out of a cross between an individual who is homozygote for a (a/a) and an individual who is homozygote for a' (a'/a') will include individuals a/a, a/a', and a'/a' in the following proportions: one-fourth a/a,

one-half a/a', and one-fourth a'/a'. In this population the alleles a and a' have the same frequency, one-half, and each sex produces half a and half a'. If these individuals are mated randomly, a simple algebraic calculation quickly demonstrates that individuals of the generation following will be quantitatively distributed in the same fashion: one-fourth a/a, one-half a/a', and one-fourth a'/a'. It will be the same for succeeding generations.

It can therefore be stated that *the genetic structure of such a population does not vary from one generation to the other*. If we designate by p the initial proportion of a/a individuals and by q that of a'/a' individuals, we get $p + q = 1$, or the totality of the population. Applying this system of symbols to the preceding facts, it can be easily shown that the proportion of individuals of all three categories in the first generation born from a/a and a'/a' equals p^2, $2pq$, q^2. In the second and third generation the frequency of individuals will always be similar: p^2, $2pq$, q^2.

Until this point, we have remained at the individual level. If we proceed to that of the gametes carrying a or a' and to that of genes a and a', we observe that their frequencies intermingle. In the type of population discussed above, the formula p^2, $2pq$, q^2 still applies perfectly, therefore, to the gametes and genes. This model, which can be regarded as a formalization of the Hardy–Weinberg law, has other properties, but our study of it will stop here. (For a discussion of the study of isolated populations, see Sutter & Tabah 1951.)

Model construction and demographic reality. The Hardy–Weinberg law has been verified by numerous studies, involving both vegetable and animal species. The findings in the field of human blood groups have also been studied for a long time from a viewpoint derived implicitly from this law, especially in connection with their geographic distribution. Under the system of reproduction by sexes, a generation renews itself as a result of the encounter of the sexual cells (gametes) produced by individuals of both sexes belonging to the living generation. In the human species it can be said that this encounter takes place at random. One can imagine the advantage that formal population genetics can take of this circumstance, which can be compared to drawing marked balls by lot from two different urns. Model construction, already favored by these circumstances, is favored even further if the characteristics of the population utilized are artificially defined with the help of a certain number of hypotheses, of which the following is a summary description:

(1) Fertility is identical for all couples; there is no differential fertility.

(2) The population is closed; it cannot, therefore, be the locus of migrations (whether immigration or emigration).

(3) Marriages take place at random; there is no assortative mating.

(4) There are no systematic preferential marriages (for instance, because of consanguinity).

(5) Possible mutations are not taken into consideration.

(6) The size of the population is clearly defined.

On the basis of these working hypotheses, the whole of which constitutes panmixia, it was possible, not long after the rediscovery of Mendel's laws, to construct the first mathematical models. Thus, population genetics took its first steps forward, one of which was undoubtedly the Hardy–Weinberg law.

Mere inspection of the preceding hypotheses will enable the reader to judge how, taken one by one, they conflict with reality. In fact, no human population can be panmictic in the way the models are.

The following evidence can be cited in favor of this conclusion:

(1) Fertility is never the same with all couples. In fact, differential fertility is the rule in human populations. There is always a far from negligible sterility rate of about 18 per cent among the large populations of Western civilization. On the other hand, the part played by large families in keeping up the numbers of these populations is extremely important; we can therefore generalize by emphasizing that for one or another reason individuals carrying a certain assortment of genes reproduce themselves more or less than the average number of couples. That is what makes for the fact that in each population there is always a certain degree of *selection*. Hypothesis (1) above, essential to the construction of models, is therefore very far removed from reality.

(2) Closed populations are extremely rare. Even among the most primitive peoples there is always a minimum of emigration or immigration. The only cases where one could hope to see this condition fulfilled at the present time would be those of island populations that have remained extremely primitive.

(3) With assortative mating we touch on a point that is still obscure; but even if these phenomena remain poorly understood, it can nevertheless be said that they appear to be crucial in determining the genetic composition of populations. This choice can be *positive*: the carriers of a given characteristic marry among each other more often than chance would warrant. The fact was demonstrated in England by Pearson and Lee (1903): very tall individuals have a tendency to marry each other, and so do very short ones. Willoughby (1933) has reported on this question with respect to a great number of somatic characteristics other than height—for example, coloring of hair, eyes and skin, intelligence quotient, and so forth. Inversely, *negative* choice makes individuals with the same characteristics avoid marrying one another. This mechanism is much less well known than the above. The example of persons of violent nature (Dahlberg 1943) and of red-headed individuals has been cited many times, although it has not been possible to establish valid statistics to support it.

(4) The case of preferential marriages is not at all negligible. There are still numerous areas where marriages between relatives (consanguineous marriages) occur much more frequently than they would as the result of simple random encounters. In addition, recent studies on the structures of kinship have shown that numerous populations that do not do so today used to practice preferential marriage—most often in a matrilinear sense. These social phenomena have a wide repercussion on the genetic structure of populations and are capable of modifying them considerably from one generation to the other.

(5) Although we do not know exactly what the real rates of mutation are, it can be admitted that their frequency is not negligible. If one or several genes mutate at a given moment in one or several individuals, the nature of the gene or genes is in this way modified; its stability in the population undergoes a disturbance that can considerably transform the composition of that population.

(6) The size of the population and its limits have to be taken into account. We have seen that this is one of the essential characteristics important in differentiating two large categories of models.

Demography and population genetics

The above examination brings us into contact with the realities of population: fertility, fecundity, nuptiality, mortality, migration, and size are the elements that are the concern of demography and are studied not only by this science but also very often as part of administrative routine. Leaving aside the influence of size, which by definition is of prime importance in the technique of the models, there remain five factors to be examined from the demographic point of view. Mutation can be ruled out of consideration, because, although its importance is great, it is felt only after the passage of a certain number of generations. It can therefore be admitted that it is not of immediate interest.

We can also set aside choice of a mate, because the importance of this factor in practice is still unknown. Accordingly, there remain three factors of prime importance: fertility, migration, and preferential marriage. Over the last decade the progressive disappearance of consanguineous marriage has been noted everywhere but in Asia. In many civilized countries marriage between cousins has practically disappeared. It can be stated, therefore, that this factor has in recent years become considerably less important.

Migrations remain very important on the genetic level, but, unfortunately, precise demographic data about them are rare, and most of the data are of doubtful validity. For instance, it is hard to judge how their influence on a population of Western culture could be estimated.

The only remaining factor, fertility (which to geneticists seems essential), has fortunately been studied in satisfactory fashion by demographers. To show the importance of differential fertility in human populations, let us recall a well-known calculation made by Karl Pearson in connection with Denmark. In 1830, 50 per cent of the children in that country were born of 25 per cent of the parents. If that fertility had been maintained at the same rate, 73 per cent of the second-generation Danes and 97 per cent of the third generation would have been descended from the first 25 per cent. Similarly, before World War I, Charles B. Davenport calculated, on the basis of differential fertility, that 1,000 Harvard graduates would have only 50 descendants after two centuries, while 1,000 Rumanian emigrants living in Boston would have become 100,000.

Measurement of fertility.   Human reproduction involves both *fecundity* (capacity for reproduction) and *fertility* (actual reproductive performance). These can be estimated for males, females, and married couples treated as a reproductive unit. Let us rapidly review the measurements that demography provides for geneticists in this domain.

Crude birth rate.   The number of living births in a calendar year per thousand of the average population in the same year is known as the *crude birth rate*. The rate does not seem a very useful one for geneticists: there are too many different groups of childbearing age; marriage rates are too variable from one population to another; birth control is not uniformly diffused, and so forth.

General fertility rate.   The ratio of the number of live births in one year to the average number of women capable of bearing children (usually defined as those women aged 15 to 49) is known as the *general fertility rate*. Its genetic usefulness is no greater than that of the preceding figure. Moreover, experience shows that this figure is not very different from the crude birth rate.

Age-specific fertility rates. Fertility rates according to the age reached by the mother during the year under consideration are known as *age-specific fertility rates*. Demographic experience shows that great differences are observed here, depending on whether or not the populations are Malthusian—in other words, whether they practice birth control or not. In the case of a population where the fertility is natural, knowledge of the mother's age is sufficient. In cases where the population is Malthusian, the figure becomes interesting when it is calculated both by age and by age group of the mothers at time of marriage, thus combining the mother's age at the birth of her child and her age at marriage. This is generally known as the *age-specific marital fertility rate*. If we are dealing with a Malthusian population, it is preferable, in choosing the sample to be studied, to take into consideration the age at marriage rather than the age at the child's birth. Thus, while the age at birth is sufficient for natural populations, these techniques cannot be applied indiscriminately to all populations.

Family histories.   Fertility rates can also be calculated on the basis of family histories, which can be reconstructed from such sources as parish registries (Fleury & Henry 1965) or, in some countries, from systematic family registrations (for instance, the Japanese *koseki* or *honseki*). The method for computing the fertility rate for, say, the 25–29-year-old age group from this kind of data is first to determine the number of legitimate births in the group. It is then necessary to make a rigorous count of the number of years lived in wedlock between their 25th and 30th birthdays by all the women in the group; this quantity is known as the group's total "woman-years." The number of births is then divided by the number of "woman-years" to obtain the group's fertility rate. This method is very useful in the study of historical problems in genetics, since it is often the only one that can be applied to the available data.

Measurement of reproduction.   Let us leave fertility rates in order to examine rates of *reproduction*. Here we return to more purely genetic considerations, since we are looking for the mechanism whereby one generation is replaced by the one that follows it. Starting with a series of fertility rates by age groups, a *gross reproduction rate* can be calculated that gives the average number of female progeny that would be born to an age cohort of women, all of whom live through their entire reproductive period and continue to give birth at the rates prevalent when they themselves were born. The gross reproduction rate obtaining for a population at any one time can be derived by combining the rates for the different age cohorts.

A gross reproduction rate for a real generation can also be determined by calculating the average number of live female children ever born to women of fifty or over. As explained above, this rate is higher for non-Malthusian than for Malthusian populations and can be refined by taking into consideration the length of marriage.

We have seen that in order to be correct, it is necessary for the description of fertility in Malthusian populations to be closely related to the date of marriage. Actually, when a family reaches the size that the parents prefer, fertility tends to approach zero. The preferred size is evidently related to length of marriage in such a manner that fertility is more closely linked with length of marriage than with age at marriage. In recent years great progress has been made in the demographic analysis of fertility, based on this kind of data. This should enable geneticists to be more circumspect in their choice of sections of the population to be studied.

Cohort analysis.   Americans talk of *cohort analysis*, the French of analysis by *promotion* (a term meaning "year" or "class," as we might speak of the "class of 1955"). A cohort, or *promotion*, includes all women born within a 12-month period; to estimate fertility or mortality, it is supposed that these women are all born at the same moment on the first of January of that year. Thus, women born between January 1, 1900, and January 1, 1901, are considered to be exactly 15 years old on January 1, 1915; exactly 47 years old on January 1, 1947; and so forth.

The research done along these lines has issued in the construction of tables that are extremely useful in estimating fertility in a human population. As we have seen, it is more useful to draw up cohorts based on age at marriage than on age at birth. A fertility table set up in this way gives for each cohort the *cumulative* birth rate, by order of birth and single age of mother, for every woman surviving at each age, from 15 to 49. The progress that population genetics could make in knowing *real* genic frequencies can be imagined, if it could concentrate its research on any particular cohort and its descendants.

Demography of genic frequencies

This rapid examination of the facts that demography can now provide in connection with fertility clearly reveals the variables that population genetics can use to make its models coincide with reality. The models retain their validity for genetics because they are still derived from basic genetic concepts; their application to actual problems, however, should be based on the kind of data mentioned above. We have voluntarily limited ourselves to the problem of fertility, since it is the most important factor in genetics research.

The close relationship between demography and population genetics that now appears can be illustrated by the field of research into blood groups. Although researchers concede that blood groups are independent of both age and sex, they do not explore the full consequences of this, since their measures are applied to samples of the population that are "representative" only in a demographic sense. We must deplore the fact that this method has spread to the other branches of genetics, since it is open to criticism not only from the demographic but from the genetic point of view. By proceeding in this way, a most important factor is overlooked—that of *genic frequencies*.

Sample structure.   Let us admit that the choice of a blood group to be studied is of little importance when the characteristic is widely distributed throughout the population—for instance, if each individual is the carrier of a gene taken into account in the system being studied (e.g., a system made up of groups A, B, and O). But this is no longer the case if the gene is carried only by a few individuals—in other words, if its frequency attains 0.1 per cent or less. In this case (and cases like this are common in human genetics) the structure of the sample examined begins to take on prime importance.

A brief example must serve to illustrate this cardinal point. We have seen that in the case of rare recessive genes the importance of consanguineous marriages is considerable. The scarcer that carriers of recessive genes become in the population as a whole, the greater the proportion of such carriers produced by consanguineous marriages. Thus if as many as 25 per cent of all individuals in a population are carriers of recessive genes, and if one per cent of all marriages in that population are marriages between first cousins, then this one per cent of consanguineous unions will produce 1.12 times as many carriers of recessive genes as will be produced by all the unions of persons not so related. But if recessive genes are carried by only one per cent of the total population, then the same proportion of marriages between first cousins will produce 2.13 times as many carriers as will be produced by all other marriages. This production ratio increases to 4.9 if the total frequency of carriers is .01 per cent, to 20.2 if it is .005 per cent, and to 226 if it is .0001 per cent. Under these conditions, one can see the importance of the sampling method used to estimate the frequency within a population, not only of the individuals who are carriers but of the gametes and genes themselves.

Genealogical method. It should be emphasized that genetic studies based on genealogies remain the least controversial. Studying a population where the degrees of relationship connecting individuals are known presents an obvious interest. Knowing one or several characteristics of certain parents, we can follow what becomes of these in the descendants. Their evolution can also be considered from the point of view of such properties of genes as dominance, recessiveness, expressivity, and penetrance. But above all, we can follow the evolution of these characteristics in the population over time and thus observe the effects of differential fertility. Until now the genealogical method was applicable only to a numerically sparse population, but progress in electronic methods of data processing permits us to anticipate its application to much larger populations (Sutter & Tabah 1956).

Dynamic studies. In very large modern populations it would appear that internal analysis of cohorts and their descendants will bring in the future a large measure of certainty to research in population genetics. In any case, it is a sure way to a dynamic genetics based on demographic reality. For instance, it has been recommended that blood groups should be studied according to age groups; but if we proceed to do so without regard for demographic factors, we cannot make our observations dynamic. Thus, a study that limits itself to, let us say, the fifty- to sixty-year-old age group will have to deal with a universe that includes certain genetically "dead" elements, such as unmarried and sterile persons, which have no meaning from the dynamic point of view. But if a study is made of this same fifty- to sixty-year-old age group and then of the twenty- to thirty-year-old age group, and if in the older group only those individuals are considered who have descendants in the younger group, the dynamic potential of the data is maximized. It is quite possible to subject demographic cohorts to this sort of interpretation, because in many countries demographic statistics supply series of individuals classified according to the mothers' age at their birth.

Other demographic factors. This discussion would not be complete if we did not stress another aspect of the genetic importance of certain demographic factors, revealed by modern techniques, which have truly created a demographic biology. Particularly worthy of note are the mother's age, order of birth, spacing between births, and size of family.

The mother's age is a great influence on fecundity. A certain number of couples become incapable of having a second child after the birth of the first child; a third child after the second; a fourth after the third; and so forth. This sterility increases with the length of a marriage and especially after the age of 35. It is very important to realize this when, for instance, natural selection and its effects are being studied.

The mother's age also strongly influences the frequency of twin births (monozygotic or dizygotic), spontaneous abortions, stillborn or abnormal births, and so on. Many examples can also be given of the influence of the order of birth, the interval between births, and the size of the family to illustrate their effect on such things as fertility, mortality, morbidity, and malformations. .

It has been demonstrated above how seriously demographic factors must be taken into consideration when we wish to study the influence of the genetic structure of populations. We will leave aside the possible environmental influences, such as social class and marital status, since they have previously been codified by Osborn (1956/1957) and Larsson (1956–1957), among others. At the practical level, however, the continuing efforts to utilize vital statistics for genetic purposes should be pointed out. In this connection, the research of H. B. Newcombe and his colleagues (1965), who are attempting to organize Canadian national statistics for use in genetics, cannot be too highly praised. The United Nations itself posed the problem on the world level at a seminar organized in Geneva in 1960. The question of the relation between demography and genetics is therefore being posed in an acute form.

These problems also impinge in an important way on more general philosophical issues, as has been demonstrated by Haldane (1932), Fisher (1930), and Wright (1951). It must be recognized, however, that their form of Neo-Darwinism, although it is based on Mendelian genetics, too often neglects demographic considerations. In the future these seminal developments should be renewed in full confrontation with demographic reality.

JEAN SUTTER

[*Directly related are the entries* COHORT ANALYSIS; FERTILITY; FERTILITY CONTROL. *Other relevant material may be found in* NUPTIALITY; RACE; SOCIAL BEHAVIOR, ANIMAL, *article on* THE REGULATION OF ANIMAL POPULATIONS.]

BIBLIOGRAPHY

BARCLAY, GEORGE W. 1958 *Techniques of Population Analysis.* New York: Wiley.

DAHLBERG, GUNNAR (1943) 1948 *Mathematical Methods for Population Genetics.* New York and London: Interscience. → First published in German.

DUNN, LESLIE C. (editor) 1951 *Genetics in the Twen-*

tieth Century: Essays on the Progress of Genetics During Its First Fifty Years. New York: Macmillan.

Fisher, R. A. (1930) 1958 *The Genetical Theory of Natural Selection.* 2d ed., rev. New York: Dover.

Fleury, M.; and Henry, L. 1965 *Nouveau manuel de dépouillement et d'exploitation de l'état civil ancien.* Paris: Institut National d'Études Démographiques.

Geppert, Harald; and Koller, Siegfried 1938 *Erbmathematik.* Leipzig: Quelle & Meyer.

Haldane, J. B. S. 1932 *The Causes of Evolution.* London and New York: Harper.

Henry, Louis 1953 *Fécondité des mariages: Nouvelle méthode de mesure.* Institut National d'Études Démographiques, Travaux et Documents, Cahier No. 16. Paris: The Institute.

Larsson, Tage 1956–1957 The Interaction of Population Changes and Heredity. *Acta genetica et statistica medica* 6:333–348.

L'Héritier, Philippe 1954 *Traité de génétique.* Volume 2: La génétique des populations. Paris: Presses Universitaires de France.

Li, Ching Chün (1948) 1955 *Population Genetics.* 2d ed. Univ. of Chicago Press.

Malécot, Gustave 1948 *Les mathématiques et l'hérédité.* Paris: Masson.

Malécot, Gustave 1955 La génétique de population: Principes et applications. *Population* 10:239–262.

Malécot, Gustave 1959 Les modèles stochastiques en génétique de population. Paris, Université, Institut de Statistique, *Publications* 8:173–210.

Newcombe, H. B.; Smith, M. E.; and Schwartz, R. R. 1965 *Computer Methods for Extracting Kinship Data From Family Groupings of Records.* Chalk River (Ontario): Atomic Energy of Canada Limited.

Osborn, F. 1956/1957 Changing Demographic Trends of Interest to Population Genetics. *Acta genetica et statistica medica* 6:354–362.

Pearson, Karl; and Lee, Alice 1903 On the Laws of Inheritance in Man. *Biometrika* 2:257–462.

Pressat, Roland 1961 *L'analyse démographique: Méthodes, résultats, applications.* Paris: Presses Universitaires de France.

Sutter, Jean; and Tabah, Léon 1951 Les notions d'isolat et de population minimum. *Population* 6:481–498.

Sutter, Jean; and Tabah, Léon 1956 Méthode mécanographique pour établir la généalogie d'une population: Application à l'étude des esquimaux polaires. *Population* 11:507–530.

United Nations 1961 *The Use of Vital and Health Statistics for Genetic and Radiation Studies.* New York: United Nations.

Whelpton, Pascal K. 1954 *Cohort Fertility: Native White Women in the United States.* Princeton Univ. Press.

Willoughby, Raymond R. 1933 Somatic Homogamy in Man. *Human Biology* 5:690–705.

World Population Conference 1965 *Proceedings.* New York: United Nations. → See especially "Recent Advances in the Theory of Population Genetics" by M. Kimura.

Wright, Sewall 1951 The Genetical Structure of Populations. *Annals of Human Genetics* 15:323–354.

III

RACE AND GENETICS

Since 1900, the study of genetics has made two major contributions to the theoretical understanding of the biology of race. First is the replacement of earlier theories of racial heredity based on the blending of characteristics by the newer, genetical notion of a breeding population incorporating gene frequencies based on the particulate, or Mendelian, theory of heredity. Because of the use of a misleading theory of heredity, nearly all of the writing on subspecific taxonomy of the human species before 1900, and unfortunately much written since then, is incorrect.

The second contribution of genetics has been to place race in the perspective of a general theory of organic evolution. This interpretation of racial biology derives from those parts of population genetics initially developed by Wright (1931; 1951) and Haldane (1932) and interpreted variously by Dobzhansky (1962), Mayr (1963), Simpson (1961), and Morton and Yasuda (1963). We cannot adequately understand the evolutionary history of mankind either in terms of individuals or in terms of the species as a whole because individuals do not evolve and the details of the evolutionary process are not necessarily uniform for all subdivisions of the species. This is why it is of theoretical importance to recognize subspecies in evolutionary biology, whether or not they are given taxonomic recognition.

Race and subspecies. A "race" is a category logically more inclusive than the notion of "individual" and less inclusive than the notion of "species." Most contemporary authorities equate the anthropological concept of race with the zoological concept of subspecies.

Subspecies and races are two or more genetically distinguishable populations of a species that have separate distributions but which can, and do, interbreed freely in overlap zones or when brought into contact. The frequency of gene exchange between races is highest in the contact zone and decreases away from it.

Since the geographical change in gene frequency is gradual, any attempt to separate sharply local populations into races having different gene frequencies is arbitrary. Often groups defined by one set of genetically determined characteristics show a clear geographical distribution. The distribution of a group defined by another set of alleles may be mapped with equal certainty; usually the geographical boundaries of two such classifications will not coincide very closely.

Knowledge of race. Statements about race involve two distinct kinds of knowledge, one about *attributes*, the other about *relationships*. Usually our knowledge of the phenotypes used to define races is direct and observational; in principle there may be full agreement among experts regarding the attributes which characterize a given group of people. Our knowledge about the biological relationships among individuals often is indirect, being based on interviews or inferred from geographical, societal, or cultural circumstances. Two individuals are biological relatives when one developed from a zygote formed by a gamete from the other or both developed from zygotes formed by gametes from a common ancestor. Each individual is connected by gametes to his parents, to the members of one or more races, and, ultimately, to the species. In practice it is rare to know directly all relevant parent–child links connecting the members of a race. Genetics makes rules for predicting the distribution of phenotypes–genotypes among individuals of known relationship. In the study of race such rules are used to infer relationships of populations of individuals whose phenotypes–genotypes are known.

Particulate versus blending heredity.   The molecular, particulate nature of the genetic material and the facts of gene segregation and recombination have great theoretical significance for the biology of race.

If the hereditary materials were blended (as nineteenth-century biologists assumed) like solutes in solvents, every member of a breeding population would soon reach hereditary uniformity and, barring mutation and hybridization, a "pure" race would be established in each locality. The genetic material would become unique to each local breeding population, and genotypes of offspring would necessarily be a midway blend of those of their parents. But, in fact, segregation and recombination do produce novel genic variation within the local breeding population. Genes in body cells occur in pairs (*AA*, *Aa*, *aa*). When gametes are formed, the members of each pair segregate so that each gamete has only one gene from each pair (*A* or *a*) and each child receives only one member of a pair from each parent (i.e., two parents of genotype *Aa* may produce a child who is *AA*, *Aa*, or *aa*). Also, each pair of genes at other loci (nonalleles) is capable of undergoing segregation separately, so that two pairs of genes which are together in one parent (say *AAbb* or *aaBB*) may be recombined in the child (*AaBb*), the recombination rate being slower for linked than for independent nonalleles.

Before the effective start of genetics in 1900, it was believed that hereditary material was a homogeneous substance which could be mixed or diluted but was identical in all members of a "pure" race. If two individuals were alike in one hereditary aspect, they would be alike in all others. Within a "pure" race all variation was due to environmental effects. Genetics now shows that hereditary mate-

rial is a heterogeneous collection of separate particles which need not be the same even in close relatives. Two closely related individuals may have many genes in common but may differ in others. Likewise, because of parallel mutation, unrelated people may have some genes of the same function even though these genes are not derived from a common ancestor.

Before genetics, it was believed that the hereditary material differed in kind between races of the same species, just as two elements differ. The pregenetic view of race involved what Aristotle called the "essence" of material bodies. Just as atoms of copper and tin are of different construction, so two races were thought to have hereditary material different in essence; the difference was, accordingly, not in degree but in kind. As atoms of copper can join those of tin to make bronze, so it was thought "pure" races come together to form a mixed race. It was possible to think of individuals of mixed races as being "mostly Alpine" or "mostly Nordic," in the same way that it was possible to think of alloys with varying fractions of different metals. Using an analogy from ceramics, certain anthropologists even as late as the 1940s spoke of race X having a "wash" of race Y. As is shown below, such beliefs are refuted by the identification of homologous genes in different races.

Kinds of gene differences between races.   It is clear we should not speak of racial characteristics, only of racial differences. Differences between any two races express differently occurring frequencies of autosomal genes. These may be written as follows:

Population 1:
$$(pA + qa)^2(p'B + q'b)^2 \cdots (p''N + q''n)^2 = 1,$$

Population 2:
$$(rA' + sa')^2(r'B' + s'b')^2 \cdots (r''N' + s''n')^2 = 1.$$

Here $A, a, \cdots, N', n'$ represent sets of alleles with frequencies $p + q = 1$, $r + s = 1$, where $0 \leqslant p$, $r \leqslant 1$. (The arrays of possible genotypes can be derived as the products of the squares of the above binomials. If there are k alleles at a locus, the binomial is replaced by a k-nomial. For sex-chromosomal loci, the array of genotypes in the heterogametic sex is given by the first power of the k-nomial.) By identifying and comparing the frequencies of genes between populations, we may distinguish four kinds of differences:

(1) If the same kinds and frequencies are present in both, the two populations are identical.

(2) If gene frequencies equal zero or unity in one population but are not fixed ($0 < p$, $r < 1$) in the other, or if some but not all frequencies are unity in one and zero in the other, the two popula-

tions are qualitatively different in gene frequency at one or more but not at all loci; they show a *specific* difference in kind.

(3) If the allele at all loci is zero in one population and unity in the other, there is a *general* difference in kind.

(4) If none of the frequencies equal zero or unity, the populations differ in degree not in kind.

Prior to the twentieth century, most anthropologists and biologists assumed the differences between local populations within the same race were of sort (1) and those between races were of sort (3). The early students assumed the genetic material of (pure) races was homogeneous within, and qualitatively different between, races.

Today we have frequency information on nearly fifty genes in which some of the alleles at each locus are common enough in one or more human populations to be of anthropological interest. Several hundred rare major genes are known to medical genetics. The knowledge gained from both human and general genetics demonstrates that "pure" races in the sense of homogeneous breeding populations differing in the kind of genes present at all loci do not exist in the human species or in any known sexual species of animals or plants.

For at least eight known human chromosomal loci, specific differences in kind of sort (2) are known to hold between some pairs of human races. For instance, the gene associated with blood group A of the ABO series is present in all known European populations, as is the gene for B, but gene *A* is absent in some, and gene *B* is absent in many American Indian populations. The genes for the Diego, Henshaw, Hunter, Kell, Lutheran, Rhesus, and hemoglobin ACS loci show detectable differences in kind between two or more human races.

Differences of sort (4), i.e., cases where the same kinds of genes are present in different frequency, constitute the most common kind of genetic divergence observed between local and geographical races of man for both normal and nearly all of the identified deleterious major genes. (See Dobzhansky 1962 or recent textbooks of human genetics for further data on the major genes mentioned above.)

Typology and race. The pregenetic typological approach to racial anthropology used at least three different concepts of "types." All are unacceptable to modern genetics, each for a different reason.

(*a*) The *average type* of a population is defined by a set of traits used to identify members of the ("pure") race. Thus Nordics in Sweden and elsewhere are characterized by tall stature, long heads, blond hair, and blue eyes. From the genetic point of view there are two basic difficulties in this approach: Only a small fraction of the members of any local breeding population exhibit the full set of traits used to define the type, and the vast amount of genetic variability known to be present in all sexually reproduced populations is not recognized. Retzius and Fürst found only 10.07 per cent of a large sample of Swedish conscripts had all four of the above diagnostic traits for Nordics (Dahlberg 1942). Since a breeding population has no average genotype, it cannot have an average phenotype; thus, it is misleading to pick out a typical (average) member of any race.

(*b*) *Morphological types*, which occur in groups of two to about ten in a given population, are also defined by a cluster of traits. The racial history of a population is explained by the supposed coming together and intermixture of individuals belonging to the several types, all wrongly assumed to be stable over time and to represent ancestral stocks (see, e.g., Hooton 1926; 1931).

An example of misinterpreted history comes from western Europe, where most people in the north are tall, blond, and blue-eyed; most in the south are short, brunet, and brown-eyed; and those in the midland are assorted in stature and pigmentation, with short blonds, tall brunets, brown-eyed blonds, etc. Those who use morphological types to explain racial history assume the people of the midland are a mixture of migrants from the north and south. But this is not necessarily what happened in history; the "mixed" group may be the actual common ancestor of the two "pure" groups concentrated by natural selection in the two extremes of the geographical range. The rather scanty information with historical depth suggests this latter explanation is the correct one for the origin of the "morphological races" of western Europe.

The processes of gene segregation and recombination, together with those of parallel and recurrent mutation, negate the possibility of sorting the members of an interbreeding population into morphological types representing ancestral stocks. A simple hypothetical example will illustrate this. The initial generation includes two "races" (Table 1). Genes *A* and *a* are autosomal and lack dominance. Since the *A* allele is fixed in one and the *a* allele in the other, each "race" is genotypically invariant for the traits. Now if north and south send migrants to

Table 1

	RACE	
	North	South
Phenotype	X	Y
Genotype	AA	aa

midland and there hybridize, the F_1 hybrids will all have genotype Aa and phenotype XY. Intercrossing of the F_1's will produce all three genotypes in subsequent generations of the new midland "race." But in this mixed "race," individuals of type XY are more closely related (a distance of one parent–child step) to their homozygous parents of type X or Y than are individuals of type X or Y who turn up in subsequent generations (distant by two or more parent–child steps). It may also happen that, through mutation rather than descent, members of the population may come to possess genes identical to those of the founding generation.

Sameness of phenotype represents neither degree of closeness nor the fact of relationship in a mixed population. Further, sameness of some specific phenotype does not guarantee that a given individual in a mixed population will inherit other desirable or undesirable traits from an ancestor of the same specific phenotype. (See Dahlberg 1943 for extension of this argument to other kinds of major genes and to polygenes.)

(c) The *individual types* of the Czekanowski group of Polish anthropologists are "racial elements" defined by a cluster of traits assumed to be controlled by one, or several closely linked, pleiotropic gene(s). These genes simultaneously affect the set of type-defining traits in whatever population they are found. This typology is compatible with population genetics if the frequencies of the "racial elements" have the empirical properties of the frequencies of pleiotropic genes, a possibility, however, not supported by family studies or by the fit of observed population frequencies of "racial elements" to those expected for genotypes in equilibrium Mendelian populations (Bielicki, 1965).

Modes of change in gene frequency. The theory of population genetics builds upon a population model in which gene frequencies are in equilibrium. The relative frequencies of genes and of genotypes remain steady in a randomly mated breeding population if mutation does not preferentially add or subtract genes, if genes flowing into the population from the outside differ neither in kind nor in frequency from those native to the local population, if there is no differential fertility or mortality between genes and genotypes, and if the breeding population is large enough in numbers that genetic drift does not occur. If these equilibrium conditions do not hold, gene and/or genotype frequencies will change until a new steady state is attained.

Inbreeding and assortative mating, the two most important departures from random mating, do not by themselves change gene frequencies but only the relative frequencies of genotypes; such changes are usually in the direction of increased homozygosity.

Mutation. Mutation is the primary source of all gene variation. The molecular basis of mutation is change in the sequence of nucleotides in DNA. Estimated spontaneous mutation rates in man vary from about one to one hundred mutations per million gametes. The rates are specific for loci and alleles but may vary somewhat according to the mutagenic nature of the environment. Probably the mutation rates for the more common human genes are sufficiently small compared with the rates for other modes of change that mutation is not a major determinant of observable local and regional differences in gene frequencies. However, it should be emphasized that mutation is repetitive; within a species, a mutation is not likely to occur only once, nor to occur in one major race and not in another.

Gene flow. Gene flow refers to introduction of genes from outside the local breeding population. The process is general for loci, haploid sets of genes being introduced on each occasion. In terms of the change in frequency, the most important type of gene flow involves recurrent, more or less regular introduction of gametes from neighboring groups which are partially isolated reproductively. When the parental populations are sufficiently dissimilar in gene frequencies, gene flow is called race mixture. Mixture may result in very rapid changes in gene frequencies. When clines are reflections of gene flow, the gene frequencies of several loci should show similar cline distribution when the incoming and native populations differ in those frequencies.

Recurrent gene flow has been an important factor preventing the splitting of mankind into allopatric species. Before the development of extrasomatic modes of transportation, the vast majority of gene flow involved neighboring populations. With the development of more rapid transportation, the rate and distance of gene flow increased. Since A.D. 1600 mixture has been the most significant factor in population differentiation.

Selection. Selection is the main guiding force in race formation. Genes or genotypes which, on the average, increase genetic fitness will become more frequent in later generations. Genetic fitness is defined solely in terms of differential fertility and/or mortality. For a given environment, genes may be harmful, neutral, or beneficial. The population frequencies of harmful genes are determined by the balance between their rate of entry by mutation and their rate of removal by selection. Neutral genes must be very rare, their spread very slow, and their replacement by more successfully adaptive genes very rapid. An important class of genes are those with increased fitness in heterozygotes; such genes spread rapidly through local populations and, given gene flow, through those sections of the species population with similar environmental conditions. These genes with a selective advantage of the heterozygote may have stable equilibrium frequencies largely determined by selection coefficients and nearly independent of initial gene frequencies and mutation rates. If polygenes are additive, selection acts on each locus independently of the others. Linkage between polygenes, unless very strong, is unimportant for selection rates.

Genetic drift. The two genes at each autosomal locus in an individual are a sample, one from each parent, of the four genes at that locus in the parents. With small population numbers, random fluctuation in this sampling process may change gene frequencies, leading to concentration or fixation of some alleles and loss of others in local populations. The resulting irregular and patchy gene-frequency distributions may be nonadaptive.

The origin of races. The formation of races is not characteristic of all sexual species. Race formation requires partial reproductive isolation. Change in gene frequency is the fundamental event in the formation of races. Race formation, i.e., adaptation to local conditions, must occur in all successful, widespread species with partially isolated local populations. Given the raw materials of gene diversity, the genetic subdivision of a species depends largely on local selection pressures, on the one hand, and gene flow, on the other. If there is much gene flow, local races cannot form; if there is less gene flow, clines may develop; if there is little gene flow, local races will differentiate. If any of the local populations are small in number, say under one hundred, there may be considerable loss and fixation of genes by random genetic drift.

Race differences in behavior. Human races differ in languages and culture as well as in genes. One of the most significant contributions of the social sciences to the general knowledge of the twentieth century is the demonstration that a large fraction of functionally important differences between human groups in learned behavior is largely independent of race, or as we put it, independent of genic differences distinguishing races.

Differences in the frequency of major genes between local populations as well as major geographical races are well established for some behavioral traits, e.g., the ability to taste phenylthiocarbamide and the four kinds of X-linked partial color blindness, although these behavioral variations are of limited functional significance in human societies.

One sort of theoretical model in population genetics suggests we should observe statistical differences in the frequencies of polygenes making up the genetical components of intellectual abilities and temperament (e.g., Hogben 1932, p. 169; Sturtevant 1954). Equally valid theoretical models support the opposite conclusion by suggesting that the genotypes making up the capacity underlying cultural learning are a species characteristic maintained in equilibrium in all human populations (e.g., Dobzhansky 1962, p. 320). Since the genetic basis of intelligence is polygenic and since we cannot identify polygenes in man, precise information about racial, i.e., inherited, differences in general intelligence is simply not available. But it seems clear that if differences between major races exist in general intellectual abilities, these differences are small in magnitude compared with the range of genetic variation within all major races (Spuhler & Lindzey 1967).

J. N. SPUHLER

[*See also* EVOLUTION, *article on* HUMAN EVOLUTION; RACE.]

BIBLIOGRAPHY

BIELICKI, TADEUSZ 1965 Population Genetics and the Race Process; Typologists Versus Populationists and Genetic Theory; Intensity of Feedbacks Between Physical and Cultural Evolution. *International Social Science Journal* 17, no. 1:91–99.

DAHLBERG, GUNNAR 1942 An Analysis of the Conception of Race and a New Method of Distinguishing Races. *Human Biology* 14:372–385.

DAHLBERG, GUNNAR (1943) 1948 *Mathematical Methods for Population Genetics.* New York and London: Interscience. → First published in German.

DOBZHANSKY, THEODOSIUS 1962 *Mankind Evolving: The Evolution of the Human Species.* New Haven: Yale Univ. Press.

HALDANE, J. B. S. 1932 *The Causes of Evolution.* London and New York: Harper.

HOGBEN, LANCELOT 1932 *Genetic Principles in Medicine and Social Science.* New York: Knopf.

HOOTON, EARNEST A. 1926 Methods of Racial Analysis. *Science* 63:75–81.

HOOTON, EARNEST A. (1931) 1947 *Up From the Ape.* Rev. ed. New York: Macmillan.

MAYR, ERNST 1963 *Animal Species and Evolution.* Cambridge, Mass: Belknap Press.

MORTON, N. E.; and YASUDA, N. 1963 The Genetical Structure of Human Populations. Pages 185–203 in Centre International d'Étude des Problèmes Humains, *Les déplacements humains: Aspects méthodologiques de leur mesure.* Edited by Jean Sutter. Entretiens de Monaco en sciences humaines, Première session, 1962 (24–29 mai). Paris: Hachette.

SIMPSON, GEORGE G. 1961 *Principles of Animal Taxonomy.* Columbia Biological Series, No. 20. New York: Columbia Univ. Press.

SPUHLER, J. N.; and LINDZEY, GARDNER 1967 Racial Differences in Behavior. Chapter 19 in Jerry Hirsch (editor), *Behavior–Genetic Analysis*. New York: McGraw-Hill.

STURTEVANT, A. H. 1954 Social Implications of the Genetics of Man. *Science* 120:405–407.

WRIGHT, SEWALL 1931 Evolution in Mendelian Populations. *Genetics* 16:97–159.

WRIGHT, SEWALL 1951 The Genetical Structure of Populations. *Annals of Eugenics* 15:323–354.

GENIUS

See CREATIVITY, *especially the article on* GENIUS AND ABILITY; INTELLIGENCE AND INTELLIGENCE TESTING; *and the biography of* TERMAN.

GENNEP, ARNOLD VAN

Charles-Arnold Kurr van Gennep (1873–1957), ethnographer and folklorist, who is best known for his work on rites of passage, was born in Württemberg, Germany, of a Dutch father and a French mother. At his father's death van Gennep was adopted by a French doctor, and thus his already strong ties with France were further strengthened. He received most of his education in France.

His career was not primarily an academic one. He served the French government for two periods, from 1903 to 1910 and again from 1919 to 1921, and worked for such cultural organizations as the Alliance Française and the International Congress of Popular Art. For relatively brief periods he held university appointments at Neuchâtel, Oxford, and Cambridge.

In *The Rites of Passage* (1909), van Gennep systematically compared those ceremonies which celebrate an individual's transition from one status to another within a given society; he concluded that most such ritual observances have a tripartite sequence. The major phases of this sequence are separation (*séparation*), transition (*marge*), and incorporation (*agrégation*). Van Gennep went beyond this analysis of rites of passage to an interpretation of their significance for the explanation of the continuing nature of life. He believed that rites of passage, with their symbolic representation of death and rebirth, illustrate the principles of the regenerative renewal required by any society.

Although van Gennep followed the prevailing system of classification of beliefs and rites associated with magic, when he analyzed rites of passage he introduced a new approach. Instead of utilizing a priori categories as the units of his taxonomy, he abstracted these units from the structure of the ceremonies themselves. This procedure led him to differentiate the rites-of-passage phases: separation, transition, and incorporation. His inductive procedure included consideration of the variables of time and space. Over a quarter of a century later Julian Huxley was to label this method of classification, in biology, as the "new systematics."

Van Gennep was obviously impressed with the importance of the transitional, or liminal, phase that he had noted within a ceremony. One aspect of its importance is related to his concept of social regeneration. When individuals or groups are in a state of suspension (limen), separated from their previous condition and not yet incorporated into a new one, they constitute a threat to themselves and to the entire group. In this state they are outside the sphere of normal control and must be reintegrated in order to avoid becoming disruptive. The liminal period also has its own internal structure, and it is possible to observe stages of entry into the period, the period itself, and departure from the period of transition.

Some other contributions by van Gennep deserve brief mention. He established, for example, that the time of so-called puberty, or initiation, rites does not coincide with physiological puberty; rather, they are scheduled according to societal definitions. He also emphasized the importance of ritual exchange and thus anticipated Malinowski's analysis of reciprocity. Finally, he noted the similarity between the structure of individual and group rites when either kind is in a state of change. The subsequent designation of group ceremonies as "rites of intensification" by Chapple and Coon (1942) is a welcome conceptual extension.

Van Gennep was highly regarded for his work in the field of European folklore. He did much to change its orientation from its historical and antiquarian origins by introducing the methods and perspective of ethnography. European scholars of his time tended to view the customs of rural peoples as quaint reminders of the past and to treat them as elements of history. Van Gennep saw folk literature and practices as aspects of living culture, to be examined within the context of changes among individuals in their relations with each other. His concern with changes in traditional culture led him to study the disappearance of some of its elements in the urban centers of France and the spread of cosmopolitan culture.

Van Gennep was enormously energetic in the accumulation of folklore materials and in their publication. His writings include several score articles, numerous monographs, and the monumental *Manuel de folklore français contemporain* (1937–1958). Van Gennep's editorial activity in this field also was prodigious: for over thirty years, from

1906 to 1939, he edited the section "Ethnographie-Folklore-Religions-Préhistoire" in the *Mercure de France*, and he founded and directed several French journals of ethnography and folklore.

Van Gennep's adherence to the comparative method in ethnography helps us to understand his theoretical formulations. He based his interpretations on the assumption that man is a part of nature and is therefore subject to the great natural laws of stability, variability, and change. He considered his goal to be the formulation of general syntheses. On this basis he challenged the adequacy of the principles of individual psychology and apriorism. He thought regeneration a necessity of social and individual existence, noting similarities between the cyclical shift of seasons and the passage of the individual through the stages of life. In the ceremonies which celebrate both transitions, he noted the recurring theme of death and rebirth. For him, neither the individual nor the rites can be divorced from the social context, nor from time and space. He insisted that ceremonial patterns should be examined as wholes and that comparison should be based upon similarities in structure rather than upon content.

There are resemblances between van Gennep's concerns and those of his contemporaries, but his approach was so radically different from theirs that the resemblances are largely of a superficial kind. For example, the interest in religion, magic, and myth, which he shared with Lang, Frazer, Marett, and others, proceeded from entirely different conceptual assumptions. Their rational, a priori approach was rooted in a historical perspective which sought to isolate stages of development such as fetishism, animism, animatism, or totemism and to provide definitions for each. Frazer in particular sought to ground his conclusions in universal psychological characteristics—the principle of association and the law of sympathy. In contrast, van Gennep was more interested in the dynamics of change than in the statics of classification and definition. For him, impersonal and personal power (dynamism and animism) unite to constitute religion, while magic consists of the techniques of control. In this he differed from Frazer, in whose view magic preceded religion and was in conflict with it. Van Gennep also differed from Hubert and Mauss, who defined religion as official doctrine and magic as socially prohibited (a view incorporated by Durkheim in his polarization of the sacred and the profane).

Thus, van Gennep saw the tradition, methods, and goals of ethnography as different from those of both the French sociologists and the British school of anthropology. The full exposition of these differences awaits future scholarship. A recently renewed interest in the study of rites of passage is evidenced by the writings of Whiting and Child (1953), Young (1965), and Turner (1964). This resurgence may extend to further study of van Gennep's ethnographic method and of his theoretical formulations.

Solon T. Kimball

[*For the historical context of van Gennep's work, see the biographies of* Frazer; Marett; Mauss; *for discussion of the subsequent development of his ideas, see* Life cycle; Myth and symbol; Ritual; Theology, primitive.]

WORKS BY VAN GENNEP

1908–1914 *Religions, moeurs, et légendes: Essais d'ethnographie et de linguistique.* 5th series. Paris: Mercure de France.
(1909) 1960 *The Rites of Passage.* London: Routledge; Univ. of Chicago Press. → First published in French.
1937–1958 *Manuel de folklore français contemporain.* Volumes 1, 3–4 in 9 parts. Paris: Picard. → Volume 2 will not be published.

SUPPLEMENTARY BIBLIOGRAPHY

Chapple, Eliot D.; and Coon, Carleton S. 1942 *Principles of Anthropology.* New York: Holt.
Lecotté, Roger 1958 Arnold van Gennep: 1873–1957. *Fabula* 2:178–180.
Turner, Victor W. 1964 Betwixt and Between: The Liminal Period in *Rites de passage.* American Ethnological Society, *Proceedings* [1964]:4–20.
Whiting, John W.; and Child, Irvin L. 1953 *Child Training and Personality: A Cross-cultural Study.* New Haven: Yale Univ. Press. → A paperback edition was published in 1962.
Young, Frank W. 1965 *Initiation Ceremonies: A Cross-cultural Study of Status Dramatization.* Indianapolis, Ind.: Bobbs-Merrill.

GENOCIDE

See International crimes.

GEOGRAPHY

The articles under this heading describe the main fields of contemporary geography and the field of statistical geography, which is an approach to geography rather than a discrete field. Other material of direct or related interest to geography may be found under Area; Cartography; Central place; City; Conservation; Culture area; Diffusion, *article on* the diffusion of innovations; Ecology; Enclaves and exclaves; Environment; Environmentalism; Industrial concentration; Land; Landscape; Location theory; Planning, social; Population; Rank–size relations; Region; Regional science; Water re-

SOURCES. *Biographical articles of relevance to geography include* BOWMAN; BROWN; FLEURE; HETTNER; HUMBOLDT; HUNTINGTON; KJELLÉN; MACKINDER; MARSH; RATZEL; RITTER; SAUER; TELEKI; VIDAL DE LA BLACHE.

I
THE FIELD

Geography is neither a purely natural nor a purely social science. From its early development as an organized field of knowledge in classical Greece, geography has included animate as well as inanimate things, man and his works as well as nature. This was of little concern as long as man was regarded as an integral part of nature. But geography, although a very old subject, did not become established as a university discipline with an organized academic profession until after the natural and social sciences had become divided into separate faculties. Regular university departments of geography were first established in German-speaking countries in the 1870s and 1880s; in France a little later; and in Great Britain and the United States generally in the present century. In each country the first generation of professors of geography had been trained in other fields, in most cases the natural sciences. Self-taught in geography, few of them outside Germany were familiar with its past development.

One consequence was that geography tended to separate into two parts: one natural, more commonly called physical geography, and one human or social, sometimes called economic geography. (In different countries and in different institutions in the same country practice varies as to whether the subject is part of the natural science faculty, part of the social science faculty, or split between the two.) For many students, on the other hand, it was the connections between the two parts, the man–land relationships, that constituted the distinctive subject matter of geography. During the period of its initial establishment as a university subject in the English-speaking countries, geography was commonly defined as the study of the relationships, in whichever direction, between the natural environment and man. This "environmentalist" concept of the field seems to have been first formulated in Germany, and then in France, late in the nineteenth century, but it was very soon dis-carded, both in theory and practice by German geographers and, to a large degree, in practice by those of France; in both countries geography returned to its historic focus of interest in the study of the distinctive character of the areas of the earth. This concept and its historical background were made familiar to American and British geographers only in the 1920s and 1930s. And although today few geographers would assert the environmentalist concept, many of its aspects, notably the emphasis on a man–nature dichotomy, still color much of their writing. [See ENVIRONMENTALISM.]

Modern geography, like the geography of past centuries, studies the earth as the space in which man lives—his habitat, milieu, or environment. This includes not just part of the environment, the physical or natural part, but the total environment; in any inhabited area the environment of today has been in part produced by man, and the existing population constitutes a living factor in the present environment. Geography, of course, is not alone in studying man's environment. Many fields in the natural and social sciences study a particular category of phenomena, not excluding its distribution and variations over the earth. What geography, and geography alone, studies is the areal character of the earth in which man lives—the form, the content, and the function of each areal part, region, or place and the pattern of and interconnections between the areal parts.

If the total diversity of places and their interrelations were simply the sum of areal variations and connections of physical, biological, and social phenomena, the subject could readily be divided into distinct fields: physical geography, biogeography, and human, or social, geography; or possibly two parts, the geography of nature and the geography of man. In reality, however, the phenomena of these several abstract categories are in many cases very closely interrelated in their areal variations and connections from place to place. Indeed, what the geographer observes as individual features—i.e., a soil, river water, a farm, a transport route—are element complexes in which factors of physical, animate, and social origin are so intricately interwoven as to require study within a single field.

Places or areas, large or small, may be studied either specifically or generically. Human interest in individual places is indicated by the practice from earliest times of giving each area a proper name—"Hudson River," "Pennsylvania," or "the South." Geography, like history, is ultimately concerned with attaining maximum comprehension of individual cases. An essential step in the description as well as the understanding of the individual area is the determination of its generic characteristics. When we speak of places as "deserts," "canyons," "cities," "farms," or "culture areas," we limit the criteria in each case to a few closely interrelated features, overlooking aspects in which places of the same type may be radically different. Comparative study of the characteristics of places by kind may reveal indications of significant correspondence, leading to hypotheses of generic relationships. [*The use of modern statistical methods to discover and determine such correlations is discussed below in* GEOGRAPHY, *article on* STATISTICAL GEOGRAPHY.]

Among the social sciences geography, like history, overlaps the fields which study a particular category—economic, political, or sociological. In geography, as in history, it is the integrated combinations of diverse elements, in their complex interrelationships, that form the direct subjects of study. While the ultimate objective in geography is comprehension of the full integration of areas, analysis requires focusing successively on partial integrations. Comparative study of areas, to establish generic concepts and relationships, must be limited to partial integrations over many areas or over the whole world. Such studies may be confined to a very narrow topic, such as the relation of crop yield to rainfall, or may cover the whole group of features which form the economy of areas. [*Divisions of human geography based on common groupings of social features are treated in the articles that follow.*]

RICHARD HARTSHORNE

BIBLIOGRAPHY

An excellent introduction by a professional geographer is Broek 1965. A much more exhaustive treatment, with lengthy bibliographies, may be found in Hartshorne 1939; 1959; two collections of essays, James & Jones 1954 and Taylor 1951, should also be consulted. The classic work in German geography is Hettner 1927. The French literature is reviewed in Claval 1964. The bibliographies of the articles that follow should also be consulted.

BROEK, JAN O. M. 1965 *Geography: Its Scope and Spirit.* Columbus, Ohio: Merrill.

CLAVAL, PAUL 1964 *Essai sur l'évolution de la géographie humaine.* Cahiers de géographie de Besançon, No. 12. Paris: Les Belles-Lettres.

CRONE, GERALD R. 1951 *Modern Geographers: An Outline of Progress in Geography Since 1800 A.D.* London: Royal Geographical Society.

FREEMAN, THOMAS W. (1961) 1963 *A Hundred Years of Geography.* Chicago: Aldine.

HARTSHORNE, RICHARD (1939) 1964 *The Nature of Geography: A Critical Survey of Current Thought in the Light of the Past.* Lancaster, Pa.: Association of American Geographers.

HARTSHORNE, RICHARD 1959 *Perspective on the Nature of Geography.* Association of American Geographers, Monograph Series, No. 1. Chicago: Rand McNally.

→ A restatement and, in part, an extensive revision of Hartshorne (1939).

HETTNER, ALFRED 1927 *Die Geographie: Ihre Geschichte, ihr Wesen und ihre Methoden.* Breslau (then Germany): Hirt.

JAMES, PRESTON E.; and JONES, CLARENCE F. (editors) (1954) 1964 *American Geography: Inventory and Prospect.* Syracuse Univ. Press.

NATIONAL COUNCIL FOR THE SOCIAL STUDIES 1959 *Yearbook, 29th: New Viewpoints in Geography.* Edited by James E. Preston. Washington: The Council.

TAYLOR, THOMAS GRIFFITH (editor) (1951) 1958 *Geography in the Twentieth Century: A Study of Growth, Fields, Techniques, Aims and Trends.* 3d ed., enl. New York: Philosophical Library.

II
POLITICAL GEOGRAPHY

Political geography may be defined from the disciplinary perspective of either geography or political science. From the former perspective, political geography appears as "the study of political phenomena in their areal context" (Jackson 1964, p. 1). This is amplified in the statement political geography is "the study of areal differences and similarities in political character as an interrelated part of the total complex of areal differences and similarities" (Hartshorne et al. 1954, p. 178). Attention to areal dimensions and patterns—suggested by such terms as location, distance, space, distribution, configuration—is also evident in research under the rubric of political science; the same holds for research in political history and politically oriented research in sociology and other disciplines.

Concepts and techniques

Classical writings on political subjects contain many speculations regarding man's relations to the earth (Thomas 1925). Several contemporary political scientists have given special attention to areal aspects of political institutions, processes, relationships, and policies (e.g., Spykman 1938; 1942; 1944; Spykman & Rollins 1939; Deutsch 1953; Smuckler 1953; Herz 1957; Sprout 1931; 1963; Sprout & Sprout 1946; 1960; 1962; 1965). But with very few exceptions (e.g., Van Dyke 1960, p. 128), commentaries on the political science discipline deal with the areal focus trivially or not at all.

Geographers have given more attention to areal aspects of political phenomena. Although its antecedents go back to the nineteenth century and earlier (Hartshorne 1935), the modern field of political geography dates in America from World War I (e.g., Bowman 1921) and in Europe from somewhat earlier (Ratzel 1897; George 1901; Mackinder 1902; 1904; 1911–1923; Fairgrieve

1915; and others). The American college catalogues of 1930 announced few courses in political geography. Thirty years later the number exceeded 300, a growth accompanied by proliferation of teaching materials and buttressed by theoretical and substantive research. Contributors to theory include Whittlesey (1939), Hartshorne (1935; 1950), Gottmann (1952), and Jones (1954*a*; 1954*b*).

In the idiom of modern geography, geographic quality attaches to any phenomena, human as well as nonhuman, intangible as well as tangible, exhibiting areal dimensions and associations that "give character to particular places" (James & Jones 1954, p. 4). To anticipate a point that will be stressed later, areal patterns of behavior and other intangible human phenomena are becoming increasingly central to research in political geography.

Similarly, the "political" in political science refers to more than the formal apparatus of government; political quality attaches to any aspect of power and influence in society. A community organized on the basis of power is by definition a political community. Every political community (though not every political organization) has a territorial base. Country, often used as a synonym for state, denotes the territorial aspect of a state. Province, city, village, school district, port authority, and other subdivisions of a state all carry territorial connotations. The same holds for empire, political bloc, coalition, and other terms that identify units and combinations of units in imperial and international relationships.

Political areas.   In the idiom of geography, any section of the earth's surface delineated by reference to political criteria is a political area. These criteria include *de jure* jurisdiction and authoritative decision making. Political areas so delineated include nation-states, their formally constituted subdivisions, and empires. These are unquestionably significant political areas, and a great deal of political geography has been written in terms of them. As geographers have emphasized (e.g., Whittlesey 1935), the "impress" of political authority changes both the physical and social aspects of landscapes: it affects, for example, inspection stations and other boundary structures; transportation grids that conform to political requirements (e.g., Wolfe 1963); movements of goods and people within a frame of migration and commercial laws; and linguistic and other cultural homogeneities imposed by political authority.

But delineating political areas by reference only to political authority and legal jurisdiction leaves many phenomena uncovered: for example, it does not account for frontier zones that exhibit political homogeneities of personal behavior at variance with *de jure* jurisdiction (Hartshorne 1950), and areal patterns of behavior that are within a recognized territorial jurisdiction but not coterminous with its boundaries, such as the region of "isolation" in the United States (Smuckler 1953) or the Washington–Boston "megalopolis" (Gottmann 1961).

The criteria of jurisdiction and authority completely fail to delineate areas that exhibit patterns of political interaction but no overarching organization of authority. These are the characteristic patterns of international politics, whether of the society of nations as a global whole or of less-than-global areas such as the communist "realm," the so-called free world, the Atlantic "community," and many others.

Geographers have traditionally emphasized the more tangible aspects of political areas. This emphasis is evident in Sauer's morphological conception of political geography as "the study of political landscapes"—i.e., "the administrative centers, the boundaries, and the defensive lines and positions" (1927, p. 208). With reference to political boundaries, Fischer (1949) noted that geographers have usually stressed the stabilizing influence of physiographic factors, often to the neglect of historical and other cultural processes. Stephen B. Jones (1959) reviewed the geographical literature on boundaries, analyzing the ways in which these have been conceived in different places and periods.

Geographers have given increasing attention to intangible factors and to processes of social change. This trend is evident in the writings noted above. In a plea for more "functional" political geography, Hartshorne (1950) emphasized the importance of "centripetal" and "centrifugal" ideas and social movements in the evolution of state areas. Gottmann (1951) introduced the concepts of *circulation* (a French term for which the nearest English equivalent is probably "movement") and *iconographie* (symbols that foster loyalty, solidarity, and conformity) as organizing ideas for the analysis of change and resistance to change in political areas. Jones (1954*a*) brought these and other ideas together in a "unified field theory."

Political potential.   In a period of history, the results of political interaction, whether within a single national community or upon the broader stage of international politics, exhibit areal patterns of coercion–submission and influence–deference. Within nation-states and empires, these patterns evolve under processes of authoritative decision making, no matter how primitive or obscure these processes may be. The patterns of international politics, however, have evolved in the absence of legitimized overriding authority. In consequence, these patterns are derived in the main from less sharply delineated images of the distribution of power and influence among the interacting national communities.

There is no standard term to denote the aggregate pressure, pull, attraction, or simply effect that one nation or coalition exerts on the behavior of others. The term "power," with its strong military connotations, is too restrictive, since relations of influence–deference are derived from a much broader spectrum of behavior than coercion–submission—i.e., brute force and the threat of it. The term "political potential" has been suggested to denote this broader spectrum (Sprout & Sprout 1962, p. 158).

The concept of political potential has definite areal connotations. It expresses areal variations in the intensity and efficacy of a government's demands on other nations, i.e., when and how it gets what where. In addition, political potential expresses the total, or aggregative, effect of a nation's statecraft plus effects deriving from that nation's sheer presence on the international landscape, which are evident in the behavior of other nations. Common sense, confirmed by observation, indicates that location, distance, space, the configuration of lands and seas, and the distributions of population, raw materials, technology, institutions, ideologies, and other phenomena may all have some bearing on the political potential of every nation and on the resulting patterns of political interaction and relationship [see MILITARY POWER POTENTIAL].

Maps of the international potentials of both particular states and the major regions and the society of nations as a whole might somewhat resemble a topographic contour map. Such maps, however, do not exist; perhaps the available data are too amorphous and ambiguous to render trustworthy mapping possible in the present state of knowledge. But studies of political potential from a geographic perspective, utilizing geographic methods, should help to clarify the areal concepts implicit in the vocabulary of international politics—e.g., bipolarity, polycentricity, balance of power, sphere of influence, political orbit, and many others in common use [see INTERNATIONAL POLITICS].

Geographic areas and political systems. Although geographers and political scientists share an interest in political phenomena, their disciplinary frameworks are recognizably different. Political scientists exhibit interest in areal dimensions and patterns *only* to the extent that these seem to contribute to an understanding of institutions, processes, relationships, and issues of public concern. In consequence, political analysts tend to view geographic dimensions and patterns from a predominantly ecological perspective, i.e., relations between "political actors" and their milieux. The ways in which students of politics generally frame problems tend to focus attention especially on the psychological linkages between actor and milieu (Sprout & Sprout 1965).

For most geographers (but there are many exceptions) interest in ecological relationships, although generally active, tends to be subsidiary to areal patterns per se. However, this contrast in perspective should not be exaggerated. When one considers the increasing attention that geographers are giving to intangible social patterns and their evolution through time and to the values and motivations that underlie such patterns, it may be more nearly correct to say that "area" is simply the frame of reference within which geographers study political behavior and its results.

In political theory the concept of system has come to occupy a position somewhat analogous to the concept of area in geography [see SYSTEMS ANALYSIS]. These organizing ideas are interestingly relatable. What appears from the geographic perspective to be a political area—city, province, state, empire, major political region, etc.—may appear from the viewpoint of political science to be a system, i.e., a constellation of political units (individuals, groups, or organized communities) that interact and relate in describable patterns. Hartshorne and others have emphasized the complementarity of these perspectives (James & Jones 1954, p. 174).

This complementarity comes through strongly in Jones's "unified field theory of political geography" (1954a). Jones's model consists of five interconnecting categories—"political idea–decision–movement–field–political area." These are likened to a "chain of lakes or basins . . . at one level, so that whatever enters one will spread to all the others." There are close counterparts to Jones's "basins" in other vocabularies. His term "political idea" approximates the concepts of image and goal-orientation in behavioral theory. "Decision" is just what it is elsewhere. "Movement" and "field" seem to be more or less analogous to a course of action that changes, even as it is changed by, the encompassing milieu. Finally, "political area" includes "any political organized area" that has "recognized limits, though not necessarily linear or permanent." Thus, the communist international system, the

Atlantic alliance, the British Commonwealth, or any other international system constitutes (with suitable change in perspective and terminology) a political area, just as does a state, a subdivision thereof, or any other areally expressible system of political interaction.

Flow from idea to area, in Jones's model, is the process by which people control and alter their milieu. The idea of man as a geographic agent, refashioning the landscape along with the physical processes of nature, is an important concept of modern geography. It was given arresting expression in the mid-nineteenth century (see Glacken 1956, pp. 70 ff.) and, more recently, by Sauer (1925) and others. The increasing capacity in technically advanced societies to alter the milieu has immense political implications.

The concept of flow from idea to area, in Jones's model—i.e., from image and purpose to operational result in the behavioral idiom—rests (more often implicitly than explicitly) on the general man–milieu hypothesis of "possibilism." This is the proposition that the capacities of the actor and the properties of his milieu set limits to his accomplishment with reference to any *given* course of action and that these limitations may be operative irrespective of whether or how he perceives and takes them into account. One corollary is the hypothesis that the higher the level of technology, the greater becomes human capacity to control and modify nonhuman components of the milieu. Another corollary is that an operator's ability to affect the behavior of human components of his milieu depends on his capabilities in relation to theirs *at the place* where their relative capabilities are tested.

The reverse flow, from area to idea, in Jones's model, is the process by which the milieu is said to condition human behavior. This conditioning process has been a focus of controversy, largely because of the teleological imagery to which many writers (though not Jones) are addicted. The influences ascribed to nature or to other aspects of the milieu can be expressed, free from teleological overtones, by such psychological concepts as perception, cognition, recognition, stimulus, response, feedback, etc. (Sprout & Sprout 1965). Expressing the conditioning process in such terms emphasizes the complementarity of geography and behavioral science. With certain exceptions, usually unimportant in political contexts, the phenomena of psychological stimulus and response provide the only demonstrated path of influence from milieu to actor, from environment to environed organism, from "area" to "ideas." The psychological nature of environmental conditioning of behavior (from which many areal patterns are derived) has long been understood, although not always clearly delineated (e.g., Mackinder 1919, p. 28; Febvre 1922, p. 171; James & Jones 1954, p. 13). At least one contemporary geographer has explicitly restated this process in the idiom of psychological theory (Kirk 1952).

Geographic techniques. A major contribution which geographers have made to the study of political phenomena is the development of graphic techniques. Most political areas are too large to be directly perceived *in toto*. The eye may not differentiate and relate various categories of phenomena distributed over the area, even when they are directly perceivable; hence the value of graphic modes of research, analysis, and presentation, by means of model globes, maps, cartograms, photographs, etc. (Bowman 1934, chapter 4; Boggs 1948). Maps delineating selected features of an area can be compared and superposed (e.g., Bowman [1921] 1928, pp. 146, 460). Large segments of the earth's surface can be examined from different perspectives (Harrison 1944; Boggs 1945). High-altitude and low-altitude photographs and oblique-angle pictures add new dimensions and textures to the perception of smaller areas (e.g., Gutkind 1956, pp. 1 ff.). Maps and cartograms can deceive as well as inform and hence are powerful instruments of political propaganda (Boggs 1946). Maps and other graphic tools not only carry preconceived messages but, when studied, may also evoke new insights and hypotheses [*see* CARTOGRAPHY].

Research in political geography

The substantive literature divides roughly into two categories: (1) works that focus on political areas as such; and (2) works that utilize areal concepts and patterns to explain or to predict political events. This cleavage more or less follows disciplinary lines, but by no means consistently. Some of the more important theoretical works have been cited, and a few teaching books are included in the bibliography, along with works cited in this text. A more comprehensive bibliography is appended to the long essay on political geography in James and Jones (see Hartshorne et al. 1954).

With respect to research on particular political areas, one should distinguish between works that deal primarily with political phenomena in an areal context and those that merely utilize political boundaries as a frame of reference for a wider range of phenomena—e.g., works on areal distributions of agriculture, industry, communication grids, etc.

Works that are politically oriented in the stricter

sense cluster around various focuses. One of these is the formation, expansion, and disintegration of political areas (e.g., Bowman 1921; Whittlesey 1939; Hartshorne 1950; Deutsch 1953). The following are of particular interest: Herz's analysis of the formation of modern "large-area" states and of the advances in technology that are making these states progressively vulnerable to economic, psychological, and military penetration (1957); Vevier's essay on geographical ideas in the territorial expansion of the United States (1960); and Hart's hypotheses regarding the logistical requisites of political areas (1949). There are many studies of functioning political areas which reflect the varied research perspectives and methods of several disciplines. The Searchlight Series, edited by G. W. Hoffman and G. E. Pearcy, offers a continually growing list of short books of this type.

A second focus is on the analysis of political areas in the light of population growth, spreading communication grids, industrialization, and urban sprawl (e.g., Gottmann 1961; Wolfe 1963). Worthy of special mention is Mumford's historical study of cities (1961).

A third focus is on areal patterns delineated not by political authority but by civic attitudes and preferences. This involves studies of integrative and disintegrative ideas and movements within state areas (e.g., Hartshorne 1950); attitudes toward the "national space" (e.g., Herman's study of communist China, 1959); regional variations in civic postures toward public problems such as military defense and foreign policy (e.g., Beard 1934; Sprout & Sprout 1939; Smuckler 1953).

A fourth focus is on the role of political authority in the development, use, depletion, conservation, and renewal of resources. These questions are approached from different angles in International Symposium on Man's Role . . . (1956) and also in Udall (1963) and Herber (1962). The effects of resource use and of regulations governing use constitute important exhibits of the "impress" of political authority upon the earth.

A fifth research focus is on political regions larger than nation-state areas. These include ancient and modern empires (e.g., Fawcett 1951; Fisher 1950) and international regions delineated in various ways (Jones 1955a). Boggs's essay on the Western Hemisphere (1945) focused attention on the need for precise criteria for delineating major political regions. This need is exemplified in some textbooks, in which political regions are variously delineated by physiographic, historical, broadly cultural, or other criteria, sometimes without clear demonstration of political relevance.

The geographic dimensions and patterns of international politics have been analyzed from various perspectives. Virtually every textbook on international politics gives attention to the uneven distribution of people and things among nations. Areal variations are recognized to be strategic in the estimation of state capabilities (e.g., Sprout & Sprout 1962; Jones 1954b). Such variations form the basis of hypotheses invented to explain or to predict patterns of interaction in the society of nations (Jones 1955a; 1955b; Sprout 1963). Such hypotheses represent attempts to identify factors whose uneven distribution in space provides a plausible explanation of international patterns.

Geopolitics

Most attention has been given to hypotheses derived from the global and regional configuration of lands and seas. These include Mahan's sea-power interpretation of history (1900; Sprout & Sprout 1962); Mackinder's hypothesis of trend toward a world empire based in the "heartland" of Eurasia (1904; 1919), later modified considerably (see especially 1911–1923, vol. 2; 1943); and variants and critiques of Mahan's and Mackinder's theories too numerous to list here [see MACKINDER; MAHAN; see also, e.g., Fairgrieve 1915; Dorpalen 1942; Spykman 1944; East & Moodie 1956, chapter 18].

Climatic variations have inspired another set of geopolitical hypotheses and critiques (e.g., Huntington 1915; Wheeler 1946; Mills 1949; Missenard 1954). International political patterns have also been linked with the uneven distribution of the various raw-material requisites of modern industry. There is some disposition to regard areal differentials in technology as the critical variable (e.g., Brown 1956), a hypothesis that has been linked with demographic distribution to produce a prediction that international political patterns will ultimately be determined by the latter. The prediction is based on the premise that technological primacy will vary with relative numbers of superior scientists and other gifted individuals, the incidence of such individuals varying, in the long run, with the size of population (Blount 1957; critique by Sprout 1963).

The adjective "geopolitical" requires some explanation. Political geography in general, and international political geography in particular, is often confused with geopolitics. This word entered the English language as a loose translation of *Geopolitik*, which came, in the interwar period, 1919–1939, to denote mobilization of areal knowledge for purposes of state—in short, geo-*policy*. Geopolitics was associated in particular with the

Institut für Geopolitik in Munich, directed by Karl Haushofer, a general turned geographer and propagandist, who is widely believed (perhaps mistakenly) to have contributed significantly to Hitler's strategy of conquest (e.g., Dorpalen 1942; Fifield 1945).

Because certain Germans exploited the concept of *Lebensraum* and other geopolitical ideas for aggressive purposes, many in America and elsewhere illogically concluded that any mixing of geography and politics must be tainted with war and conquest. Geographers insisted that geopolitics was a part of political science. Political scientists tossed the pariah subject back to the geographers. Time has blurred the odious policy connotations of geopolitics, perhaps more so in America than in Europe. The term has even acquired some respectability, especially in the context of military-defense analysis.

The adjective "geopolitical," never as value-laden as the noun "geopolitics," was employed sparingly in the 1930s (e.g., Whittlesey 1939), and increasingly in more recent years, to denote the *areal aspect of any political pattern* and, in particular, hypotheses that purport to explain or to predict areal distributions and patterns of political potential in the society of nations. All such hypotheses represent assessments of opportunities and limitations implicit in the properties of the interacting political communities and of the milieu in which they operate. Such assessments (in the idiom of ecological theory) are essentially possibilistic, even though they may be expressed in deterministic or near-deterministic rhetoric (Sprout & Sprout 1965).

HAROLD SPROUT

[See also ECOLOGY; INTERNATIONAL POLITICS. *Other relevant material may be found under* ENCLAVES AND EXCLAVES; INTERNATIONAL RELATIONS.]

BIBLIOGRAPHY

ALEXANDER, LEWIS M.   (1957) 1963   *World Political Patterns.* 2d ed. Chicago: Rand McNally. → A college text organized regionally.

BEARD, CHARLES A.   1934   *The Idea of National Interest: An Analytical Study in American Foreign Policy.* New York: Macmillan.

BLOUNT, B. K.   1957   Science Will Change the Balance of Power. *New Scientist* 2, no. 32:8–9.

BOGGS, S. W.   1945   This Hemisphere. U.S. Department of State, *Bulletin* 12:845–850.

BOGGS, S. W.   1946   Cartohypnosis. U.S. Department of State, *Bulletin* 15:1119–1125.

BOGGS, S. W.   1948   Geographic and Other Scientific Techniques for Political Science. *American Political Science Review* 42:223–248.

BOWMAN, ISAIAH   (1921) 1928   *The New World: Problems in Political Geography.* 4th ed. New York: World. → The first edition is important as an early comprehensive American work on political geography; the later editions, considerably revised, have more enduring value.

BOWMAN, ISAIAH   1934   *Geography in Relation to the Social Sciences.* New York: Scribner.

BROWN, HARRISON   1956   Technological Denudation. Pages 1023–1032 in International Symposium on Man's Role in Changing the Face of the Earth, Princeton, N.J., 1955, *Man's Role in Changing the Face of the Earth.* Edited by William L. Thomas et al. Univ. of Chicago Press.

DASMANN, RAYMOND F.   1963   *The Last Horizon.* New York: Macmillan.

DEUTSCH, KARL W.   1953   The Growth of Nations: Some Recurrent Patterns of Political and Social Integration. *World Politics* 5:168–195.

DORPALEN, ANDREAS   1942   *The World of General Haushofer.* New York: Farrar.

EAST, WILLIAM G.; and MOODIE, A. E. (editors)   1956   *The Changing World: Studies in Political Geography.* New York: World. → A symposium textbook in the tradition of Isaiah Bowman's *The New World.*

FAIRGRIEVE, JAMES   (1915) 1941   *Geography and World Power.* 8th ed., rev. New York: Dutton. → After 1915 a new Chapter 18 was included that considerably altered the main thesis of the book.

FAWCETT, CHARLES B.   (1951) 1957   Geography and Empire. Pages 418–432 in Thomas Griffith Taylor (editor), *Geography in the Twentieth Century.* 2d ed., rev. New York: Philosophical Library.

FEBVRE, LUCIEN   (1922) 1925   *A Geographical Introduction to History.* New York: Knopf. → First published as *La terre et l'évolution humaine.*

FIFIELD, RUSSELL H.   1945   Geopolitics at Munich. U.S. Department of State, *Bulletin* 12:1152–1162.

FISCHER, ERIC   1949   On Boundaries. *World Politics* 1:196–222.

FISHER, CHARLES A.   1950   The Expansion of Japan: A Study in Oriental Geopolitics. *Geographical Journal* 115:1–19, 179–193.

FISHER, CHARLES A.   1964   *Southeast Asia: A Social, Economic, and Political Geography.* New York: Dutton.

GEORGE, HEREFORD B.   (1901) 1924   *The Relations of Geography and History.* 5th ed., rev. & enl. Oxford: Clarendon.

GLACKEN, CLARENCE J.   1956   Changing Ideas of the Habitable World. Pages 70–92 in International Symposium on Man's Role in Changing the Face of the Earth, Princeton, N.J., 1955, *Man's Role in Changing the Face of the Earth.* Edited by William L. Thomas et al. Univ. of Chicago Press.

GOBLET, YANN M.   1955   *Political Geography and the World Map.* New York: Praeger.

GOTTMANN, JEAN   1951   Geography and International Relations. *World Politics* 3:153–173.

GOTTMANN, JEAN   1952   *La politique des états et leur géographie.* Paris: Colin.

GOTTMANN, JEAN   (1961) 1964   *Megalopolis: The Urbanized Northeastern Seaboard of the United States.* Cambridge, Mass.: M.I.T. Press. → An urban-economic evaluation of the nature of a continuously urbanized section of the eastern United States.

GUTKIND, E. A.   1956   Our World From the Air: Conflict and Adaptation. Pages 1–44 in International Symposium on Man's Role in Changing the Face of the Earth, Princeton, N.J., 1955, *Man's Role in Changing the Face of the Earth.* Edited by William L. Thomas et al. Univ. of Chicago Press.

HARRISON, RICHARD E. 1944 *Look at the World: The Fortune Atlas for World Strategy.* New York: Knopf.

HART, HORNELL 1949 Technology and the Growth of Political Areas. Pages 28–57 in William F. Ogburn (editor), *Technology and International Relations.* Univ. of Chicago Press.

HARTSHORNE, RICHARD 1935 Recent Developments in Political Geography. *American Political Science Review* 29:785–804, 943–966.

HARTSHORNE, RICHARD 1950 The Functional Approach in Political Geography. Association of American Geographers, *Annals* 40:95–130.

HARTSHORNE, RICHARD 1959 *Perspective on the Nature of Geography.* Association of American Geographers, Monograph Series, No. 1. Chicago: Rand McNally. → A restatement and, in part, an extensive revision of "The Nature of Geography: A Critical Survey of Current Thought in the Light of the Past," published in 1939.

HARTSHORNE, RICHARD et al. 1954 Political Geography. Pages 167–225 in Preston E. James and Clarence F. Jones (editors), *American Geography: Inventory and Prospect.* Syracuse Univ. Press. → An excellent bibliography appears on pages 222–225.

HERBER, LEWIS 1962 *Our Synthetic Environment.* New York: Knopf.

HERMAN, THEODORE 1959 Group Values Toward the National Space: The Case of China. *Geographical Review* 49:164–182.

HERZ, JOHN H. 1957 Rise and Demise of the Territorial State. *World Politics* 9:473–493.

HUNTINGTON, ELLSWORTH (1915) 1924 *Civilization and Climate.* 3d ed., rev. New Haven: Yale Univ. Press.

INTERNATIONAL SYMPOSIUM ON MAN'S ROLE IN CHANGING THE FACE OF THE EARTH, PRINCETON, N.J., *1955* 1956 *Man's Role in Changing the Face of the Earth.* Edited by William L. Thomas et al. Univ. of Chicago Press.

JACKSON, W. A. DOUGLAS 1958 Whither Political Geography? Association of American Geographers, *Annals* 48:178–183.

JACKSON, W. A. DOUGLAS (editor) 1964 *Politics and Geographic Relationships.* Englewood Cliffs, N.J.: Prentice-Hall. → A well-chosen collection of teaching materials drawn from several disciplines.

JAMES, PRESTON E.; and JONES, CLARENCE F. (editors) 1954 *American Geography: Inventory and Prospect.* Univ. of Syracuse Press.

JONES, STEPHEN B. (1954a) 1964 A Unified Field Theory of Political Geography. Pages 101–109 in W. A. Douglas Jackson (editor), *Politics and Geographic Relationships.* Englewood Cliffs, N.J.: Prentice-Hall.

JONES, STEPHEN B. (1954b) 1964 The Power Inventory and National Strategy. Pages 318–338 in W. A. Douglas Jackson (editor), *Politics and Geographic Relationships.* Englewood Cliffs, N.J.: Prentice-Hall.

JONES, STEPHEN B. 1955a Views of the Political World. *Geographical Review* 45:309–326.

JONES, STEPHEN B. 1955b Global Strategic Views. *Geographical Review* 45:492–508.

JONES, STEPHEN B. 1959 Boundary Concepts in the Setting of Place and Time. Association of American Geographers, *Annals* 49:241–255.

KIRK, WILLIAM 1952 Historical Geography and the Concept of the Behavioural Environment. *Indian Geographical Journal* [1952]:152–160.

MACKINDER, HALFORD (1902) 1930 *Britain and the British Seas.* 2d ed. Oxford: Clarendon.

MACKINDER, HALFORD 1904 The Geographical Pivot of History. *Geographical Journal* 23:421–444.

MACKINDER, HALFORD 1911–1923 *Nations of the Modern World.* 2 vols. London: Philip.

MACKINDER, HALFORD (1919) 1942 *Democratic Ideals and Reality: A Study in the Politics of Reconstruction.* London: Constable; New York: Holt.

MACKINDER, HALFORD 1943 The Round World and the Winning of the Peace. *Foreign Affairs* 21:595–605.

MAHAN, ALFRED THAYER (1900) 1905 *The Problem of Asia and Its Effect Upon International Policies.* Boston: Little.

MAULL, OTTO (1925) 1956 *Politische Geographie.* Berlin: Safari Verlag.

MILLS, CLARENCE A. 1949 Temperature Dominance Over Human Life. *Science* 110:267–271.

MISSENARD, ANDRÉ 1954 *À la recherche de l'homme.* Paris: Librairie Istra. → See especially Part 3, "Climat et milieu physique."

MUMFORD, LEWIS 1961 *The City in History: Its Origins, Its Transformations, and Its Prospects.* New York: Harcourt.

PEARCY, GEORGE E. et al. (1948) 1957 *World Political Geography.* New York: Crowell. → A regionally organized symposium textbook.

POUNDS, NORMAN J. G. 1963 *Political Geography.* New York: McGraw-Hill. → A book designed for college teaching.

RATZEL, FRIEDRICH (1897) 1923 *Politische Geographie* 3d ed. Edited by Eugen Oberhummer. Munich and Berlin: Oldenbourg.

SAUER, CARL O. (1925) 1963 The Morphology of Landscape. Pages 315–350 in Carl O. Sauer, *Land and Life: A Selection From the Writings of Carl Ortwin Sauer.* Berkeley: Univ. of California Press.

SAUER, CARL O. 1927 Recent Developments in Cultural Geography. Pages 154–212 in E. C. Hayes (editor), *Recent Developments in the Social Sciences.* Philadelphia: Lippincott.

SCHÖLLER, PETER 1958 Das Ende einer politischen Geographie ohne sozialgeographische Bindung. *Erdkunde: Archiv für wissenschaftliche Geographie* 12:313–316.

SMUCKLER, RALPH H. 1953 The Region of Isolationism. *American Political Science Review* 47:386–401.

SPROUT, HAROLD 1931 Political Geography as a Political Science Field. *American Political Science Review* 25:439–442.

SPROUT, HAROLD 1963 Geopolitical Hypotheses in Technological Perspective. *World Politics* 15:187–212.

SPROUT, HAROLD; and SPROUT, MARGARET 1939 *The Rise of American Naval Power.* Princeton Univ. Press.

SPROUT, HAROLD; and SPROUT, MARGARET (1946) 1960 Atlantic, Command of. Volume 2, pages 628–632 in *Encyclopaedia Britannica.* 14th ed. Chicago: Benton.

SPROUT, HAROLD; and SPROUT, MARGARET (1960) 1964 Geography and International Politics in an Era of Revolutionary Change. Pages 34–51 in W. A. Douglas Jackson (editor), *Politics and Geographic Relationships.* Englewood Cliffs, N.J.: Prentice-Hall.

SPROUT, HAROLD; and SPROUT, MARGARET 1962 *Foundations of International Politics.* Princeton, N.J.: Van Nostrand.

SPROUT, HAROLD; and SPROUT, MARGARET 1965 *The Ecological Perspective on Human Affairs, With Special Reference to International Politics.* Princeton Univ. Press.

SPYKMAN, NICHOLAS J. 1938 Geography and Foreign Policy. *American Political Science Review* 32:28–50, 213–236.

SPYKMAN, NICHOLAS J. 1942 *America's Strategy in World Politics.* New York: Harcourt.

SPYKMAN, NICHOLAS J. 1944 *The Geography of the Peace*. New York: Harcourt.

SPYKMAN, NICHOLAS J.; and ROLLINS, ABBIE A. 1939 Geographical Objectives in Foreign Policy. *American Political Science Review* 33:391–412, 591–614.

TAYLOR, THOMAS G. (editor) (1951) 1957 *Geography in the Twentieth Century*. 3d ed. New York: Philosophical Library.

THOMAS, FRANKLIN 1925 *The Environmental Basis of Society*. New York: Century.

UDALL, STEWART L. 1963 *The Quiet Crisis*. New York: Holt.

VAN DYKE, VERNON 1960 *Political Science: A Philosophical Analysis*. Stanford Univ. Press.

VAN VALKENBURG, SAMUEL; and STOTZ, CARL L. (1954) 1955 *Elements of Political Geography*. Englewood Cliffs, N.J.: Prentice-Hall. → Topically organized text.

VEVIER, CHARLES 1960 American Continentalism: An Idea of Expansion, 1845–1910. *American Historical Review* 65:323–335.

WAGNER, PHILIP 1960 *The Human Use of the Earth*. Glencoe, Ill.: Free Press.

WEIGERT, HANS W.; and STEFANSSON, VILHJALMUR (editors) 1944 *Compass of the World*. New York: Macmillan.

WEIGERT, HANS W.; and STEFANSSON, VILHJALMUR (editors) 1949 *New Compass of the World*. New York: Macmillan.

WEIGERT, HANS W. et al. 1957 *Principles of Political Geography*. New York: Appleton. → Wide-ranging text by several authors, with strong emphasis on economic, demographic, and broadly cultural factors.

WHEELER, RAYMOND H. 1946 Climate and Human Behavior. Pages 78–87 in Philip Harriman (editor), *Encyclopedia of Psychology*. New York: Philosophical Library.

WHITTLESEY, DERWENT 1935 The Impress of Effective Central Authority Upon the Landscape. Association of American Geographers, *Annals* 25:85–97.

WHITTLESEY, DERWENT (1939) 1944 *The Earth and the State*. New York: Holt.

WOLFE, ROY I. 1963 *Transportation and Politics*. Princeton, N.J.: Van Nostrand.

WOLFE, ROY I. 1964 Perspective on Outdoor Recreation: A Bibliographical Survey. *Geographical Review* 54:203–238.

III
ECONOMIC GEOGRAPHY

The subject matter of economic geography is related substantively and historically to both disciplines from which the field receives its name. It obtains from geography an emphasis upon similarities and differences from area to area, large and small, on the earth's surface, and upon linkages or circulations between areas. It acquires from economics an interest in the production, distribution, exchange, and consumption of goods and services. Economic geography therefore may be defined as an inquiry into similarities, differences, and linkages within and between areas in the production, exchange, transfer, and consumption of goods and services. Particular attention is given to the location of economic activity, considered both in theoretical and practical terms [see SPATIAL ECONOMICS].

Relationship to geography and economics. Economic geography is so intimately a part of the whole of geography that separating it from the general field is difficult. Because gaining a livelihood not only is essential to human existence but also involves a wide range of cultural and natural (physical and biological) features and interrelationships between those features, most matters of concern within economic geography are of concern within the over-all discipline, and vice versa. This is especially true if natural and noneconomic cultural features are considered in terms of their positive and negative implications for human use of earth space in gaining a livelihood. However, the emphasis upon livelihood in economic geography does mean a corresponding reduction of attention to those cultural or natural conditions which may be only loosely related to spatial aspects of livelihood. Thus, for example, neither the cultural origin of a religious belief nor the process of landform development is of direct interest to the economic geographer unless applicable in some way— as an advantage or constraint—to the location and interrelationships of economic activities.

As in the whole of geography, the spectrum of the totality of interrelationships in economic geography may be horizontal (involving different areas or different points within a given area), vertical (involving a morphological column of cultural and natural features at a specific point on the earth's surface), or both horizontal and vertical. Horizontal relationships are stressed in most work now being carried on.

We may consider economic geography, therefore, as emphasizing the livelihood aspects of the whole of geography, rather than as a compartment of the parent discipline. The field has a direct tie to economics and, by way of the whole of geography, indirect ties to other disciplines in the social and natural sciences. So considered, the field by definition is sufficiently broad in scope to anticipate any methodological changes from time to time and place to place, although specific approaches, concepts, points of view and emphasis, immediate objectives, and methods have ranged rather widely with change of either time or place.

Trends. However, among economic geographers there is lack of agreement as to specific direction, particularly in the United States and Canada. For a time after its emergence as a separate field in the United States, during the early years of the twentieth century, economic geography relied primarily upon the inductive approach, with individual scholars aggregating ideas and data from field and library work into descriptions, classifications, and qualitative interpretations, utilizing numerical evidence when possible. Partially because of limitations on the amount of information obtainable in these ways, emphasis was placed on the unique or at least the distinctive features and interrelationships in both systematic and regional work; generalizations were made when possible. Although this approach continues to be utilized profitably by many economic geographers, the past decade has marked the emergence of a new school of thought, with immediate roots going as far back as the 1930s and indirect roots into the early portion of the nineteenth century. This school has chosen an explicitly theoretical approach, emphasizing nomothetic research and depending appreciably upon mathematical abstraction. In the early 1960s the suggestion was made that geography basically is concerned with systems analysis (Ackerman 1963) and that the overriding problem of geography is understanding the man–land system of the earth. This giant system in turn is considered by Ackerman to comprise a large number of hierarchically arranged subsystems and processes. Such a concept places economic geography in the position of searching for laws involving livelihood within a context of systems analysis applied to earth space. The degree to which the concept has been generally accepted is not yet certain.

Two basic rationales. Like the over-all discipline, economic geography in the United States and Canada can be visualized in terms of two fundamental rationales—the topical, or systematic (not to be confused with system in systems analysis), and the regional. In economic geography both rationales focus on primary activities (here, as generally in economics, considered to be agriculture, grazing, forest-products industries, mining, fishing, and hunting), secondary activities (manufacturing and construction), and tertiary activities (all other occupations). The two rationales differ especially as to initial starting position. The topical, or systematic, rationale begins with structural aspects and works toward their earth-space expression and relationships, whereas the regional begins with space and works toward structure. The respective starting positions are usually reflected in various emphases in the completed works. Both rationales can be divided into subjects which themselves have become research interests for certain economic geographers. In practice these subjects are usually called systematic or topical specialties. Agricultural geography, manufacturing geography, and marketing geography have been of long-standing interest. Transportation geography and theoretical approaches to certain tertiary activities and domes-

tic trading patterns have been developed actively within the past decade [*see* CENTRAL PLACE]. In addition, increasing attention is being given to recreation geography and to aspects of tertiary activities not yet accorded full consideration, to geographical aspects of international trade, and to the economic geography of primary activities other than agriculture. Work has begun on the geography of consumption and the geography of price.

Because economic activities are earth based and may be clustered, as to location and/or function, into patterns of differing kinds and intensity, regions are important to economic geography. As in the whole of geography, regions in economic geography may be either homogeneous or nodal. The homogeneous region, sometimes called the formal region, is more or less an inventory of static features and relationships within an area that has been delimited on the basis of prevailing homogeneity of at least one feature. Both cultural and natural features and relationships may be so classified: the spring wheat belt, the manufacturing belt between Chicago and New York, and the Appalachian Mountains are three examples in North America of this classification. Each example has been delimited on the basis of a single criterion, but multiple-criterion regions are possible at higher levels of generalization.

The nodal, or functional, region classifies human organization of earth space. This region has a point of focus (such as a city or town), an organized area of mutual interdependence with respect to that point and associated territory (such as the trading area of a city or town), and connecting lines to the territory (such as transportation and communication routes) providing the linkage (such as commuter and freight traffic and communications flows) between the point and the area.

Both the homogeneous and the nodal regions are here envisaged as means of classification and not as objective entities to be discovered in a scientific sense. Either type of region can be considered at various levels of observation and detail. When several levels are superimposed, a pyramidlike framework with hierarchical tendencies may be recognizable.

Realms of interdisciplinary contact. Besides its subfields, economic geography extends into realms of interest shared with other disciplines. The utilization and conservation of natural and human resources is of long-standing interest to some economic geographers. More recently, the development of regional science is of definite interest to some economic geographers, many of whom participated in that development. Especially in the 1960s some economic geographers have become very interested in regional inequalities of economic development, whether within a country or at a continental or global level of observation.

Theoretical and practical implications. The theoretical importance and practical significance of economic geography are inextricably intertwined. Theories seek optimum circumstances and efficiency in human utilization of earth space: what are the most desirable size, spacing, and intermix of specific economic units of production, exchange, transfer, and consumption within selected typologies of cultural and natural conditions? On the other hand, evaluations of historical and current practices indicate the degree to which theoretical models are actually applicable, especially in view of the cultural institutions, personalities and wills of key individuals, and specific natural conditions of a given area. Such evaluations also provide a degree and type of qualitative insight not obtainable through hypothesis alone.

Once a satisfactory relationship between theory and practice has been established, a logical step is application to planning procedures. In economic geography the value of both theoretical and pragmatic study to planning is clear, whether the viewpoint of the planner is the broad outlook of the regional analyst, concerned with an intermix of varied economic activities and resources, or the more restricted and highly specialized view of the expert in finding locations for individual units of economic activity.

Methods of study. Inasmuch as developments and trends in the United States from 1904 to 1954, the first 50 years of geography's existence as a university discipline, have been evaluated elsewhere (James & Jones 1954), the events of succeeding years will be emphasized here. A survey of the literature indicates that research since 1954 can be divided into three categories, on the basis of approach and method: qualitative interpretation, usually with substantial numerical evidence and sometimes making use of the case-study technique; quantitative classification, in a more or less descriptive sense, with qualitative elaboration and explanation and involving a specific procedure applicable to different areas and time periods; and formulation and testing of specific hypotheses and models. These approaches have been applied, with varying degrees of intensity, to most facets of economic geography, but they will be discussed here with respect to agriculture, manufacturing, trade, and transportation.

Agricultural geography. All three approaches are utilized in agricultural geography, which is still a subject of keen interest. Books and articles involving qualitative interpretation are diverse as to

specific subject matter, but most can be classified under certain broad headings. Approximately one-third of the articles on agriculture appearing in four professional journals of the United States and Canada—*Annals* (Association of American Geographers), *Canadian Geographer, Economic Geography, Geographical Review*—treated a specific agricultural activity in a definite area, evaluating such aspects as type and size of enterprises, natural environmental advantages or constraints, combinations of selected crops and livestock with other crops and livestock, allocation of land, general farming practices, and trends. One-fourth emphasized over-all use of agricultural land in a specified area, considering other aspects of agricultural geography in a subsidiary way. Nearly one-fifth were concerned primarily with reclamation of agricultural land—irrigation, drainage, erosion control, etc. A final one-fourth involved miscellaneous interests, such as land redistribution in a given area, agricultural colonies of a minority group in a given area, land tenure in a specified place, the economic development of a country that is heavily dependent on agriculture, and the historical geography of agricultural change in a selected location, etc. These four categories of qualitative interpretation, which cover the most numerous writings on agricultural geography in literature published in the United States and Canada, provide valuable insight into conditions evaluated by each author but have almost no common denominator.

Descriptive and analytic interpretation of a quantitative nature involves a classification based on numerical information, preferably official data continually available. The classification reveals pattern when plotted on a map and hence may be used to construct generic regions (typologies of regions) based on quantitative criteria. Once the criteria become standardized on a world-wide basis, the classifications will become standardized and applicable to all parts of the world. In principle both the homogeneous and the functional region may be so constructed, but in practice the homogeneous region has received the most attention to date in agricultural work. Prior to 1954 most studies were based on inadequate quantitative evidence, rather highly generalized, and presented at continental or even global levels of observation. Weaver (1954, especially pp. 175–184) applied a greater measure of objectivity to an area of intermediate size, aggregating data from county units to compute, for the Middle West of the United States, areal differences in crop combinations on the basis of degree of variance from a theoretical curve of optimal combinations. Subsequent work by other geographers includes a quantitative sampling approach to agricultural regionalization, the application of multiple correlation and regression analysis to rural farm population densities in the Great Plains, and the statistical association of cash grain farming in the Middle West with landforms.

The application of hypotheses to agricultural geography has been based on a rediscovery of implications of Thünen's pioneer work treating the effect of transport cost and market price on crop and livestock combinations (1826–1863). Current research suggests that, while the influence of distance to market on agricultural land use does not result today in patterns so simple as those set down by Thünen, the influence of market price and transport cost does exist and can be analyzed mathematically [*see* RENT].

Manufacturing geography. Qualitative interpretation of manufacturing geography, as indicated in publications of the United States and Canada, has been applied especially to areas other than Anglo–America, usually where numerical information is not fully available. Such an article or monograph may be an appraisal of a specific industry or group of industries or may involve a general examination of all manufacturing. The method of the historical geographer, providing the time dimension, may or may not be utilized. The case study is seldom used. Work involving only qualitative interpretation constitutes a relatively small percentage of all studies in manufacturing geography, largely because numerical data are available to a greater degree than, for example, in agriculture.

Quantitative classifications are numerous in manufacturing geography. Labor force and value added are usually the criteria of measurement, although the list of possibilities is long and includes value of product, wages paid, amount of energy consumed, area of ground space, area of floor space, and land value. One such classification, with labor force used as the measuring criterion, has revealed structural and spatial changes in the manufacturing of the United States. Another has been based on magnitude (number of employees, wages paid, and value added) and intensity (ratios of labor force and value added to selected national totals), the classification being applied, with allowance for kind and amount of data available, to the United States, Japan, and the Soviet Union. In still another classification based on labor force and value added, the author developed a technique for showing change over time on a single map and applied his technique not only to conditions within specific regions but also to differential rates of regional growth, as measured by national totals. Another study classified cities by labor force on

the basis of prevailing industries, after first removing from consideration the city-serving functions of the industries. Several indices of industrial diversification also have been developed, with labor force the prime criterion of measurement. A typology of manufacturing flows relies, on the one hand, upon the orientation of manufacturing to raw materials or agglomerations of input factors and, on the other, upon access to both national and regional markets.

Increased attention is also being accorded theoretical approaches to manufacturing geography. Here, especially, work is being shared—by economic geography and regional science [*see* REGIONAL SCIENCE]. Among initial geographical models was a construction by Harris (1954) showing the importance of market potential to industrial localization. Other geographers have used models to measure association tendencies in manufacturing, concluding that agglomeration is a very important force. Models have been used to examine tendencies of high-value-added manufacturing to concentrate in certain areas, and they have also been used to associate circular and cumulative causation with the growth of manufacturing and associated urbanization. [*See* ECONOMIES OF SCALE *and* EXTERNAL ECONOMIES AND DISECONOMIES.]

Geography of trade. Attention to trade in economic geography has focused especially on domestic trade. Theoretical work is being pursued vigorously under the stimulus of central-place theory. Pragmatic work, whether qualitative interpretation or quantitative classification, also has been of keen interest. This pragmatic work is usually called marketing geography, although some studies in domestic commodity flow would not necessarily be included under such a heading. Early research of this kind was associated especially with urban geography, which developed as a field in the first half of the twentieth century and is becoming increasingly important. This early research has been a valuable antecedent to both central-place theory and marketing geography. From numerous studies of individual urban units and, subsequently, from use of census information three significant contributions were made: the idea of the city-region, a functional region of interdependent units, including an urban unit; the classification of all cities in a country by relatively dominant functions, as measured by nationwide norms; and the concept of an economic base comprised, on the one hand, of trading and related activities or portions of activities which provide financial support for a specified area and, on the other, of activities or portions of activities which merely provide local interaction and have no influence outside that area (James & Jones

[1954] 1964, pp. 142–166, 245–251). Subsequently, Murphy and Vance (1954) developed a technique for delimiting the central business district (CBD), based on land use involving the retailing of goods and services and the provision of office space. Ullman (1957) developed a series of maps interpreting commodity flow within the United States, emphasizing principles of complementarity, transferability, and intervening opportunity. Other writers have been interested in the most appropriate location for shopping centers, especially with respect to market areas shared by competing firms. Questions have been raised as to the necessity of formal theories in marketing geography, but as yet no definite answers have emerged. Meanwhile, in a related area efforts are being made to map and evaluate the spatial distribution of finance as an economic activity and to associate this distribution with trading areas of cities.

Most geographical work in international trade has been pragmatic. One study has associated broad regional patterns (countries or groups of countries) and degree of dependence upon categories of exports and imports, and another has classified countries by degree of dependence upon exports. Still another has examined the free port, concluding that it may have outlived its usefulness in technically advanced, highly industrialized countries. Thoman and Conkling (1967) appraised national and bloc trends in international trade between 1938 and 1963, dependence of individual economies upon exports and export specialties, and logistics and mechanics of such trade.

Transportation geography. Although transportation long has been treated in the literature of economic geography, its full significance is only coming to be realized as the functional region, which depends for interpretation largely upon the flow of commodities and people to and from central places, comes to the forefront of attention. This is especially true of linkage studies involving transportation *and* trade—the carrier and route, plus shipping costs, plus direction and composition of commodity and passenger movement, plus alternative opportunities for such movement. Such linkage studies reveal the dynamic aspects of an area, whether for a specified time or with change over time. Again, all three categories of approach are to be seen, with qualitative interpretation utilized particularly to present an unusual idea or to appraise general conditions over a wide area where adequate numerical information is lacking. Some geographers, however, have produced excellent qualitative interpretations concerning areas, small or large, that are covered rather fully by census and comparable data. In addition, historical geogra-

phers have provided insight into the development of somewhat analogous transportation routes that have evolved at different times and for different purposes.

Classifications by density of route and by general direction and function of route, again usually at continental or global levels of observation, are not new in transportation geography; but these have been augmented, usually at national or regional levels, by more-detailed and more-meaningful studies. Models have also been used to indicate the impact of highways on geographic change, to anticipate the development of transportation networks, and to explain differential rates of growth in passenger traffic between leading airports.

Regional economic geography. Several recent books and monographs have applied regional approaches to economic geography. Gottmann (1961) evaluated the urban-economic aspects of Megalopolis, an urbanized section of the Atlantic seaboard of the United States stretching from Boston southward beyond Washington, D.C. Hance (1964) presented a regional examination of Africa, based on many years of study there. Camu and his associates (1964) produced a regional–systematic survey of the economic geography of Canada, introducing a multiple-criterion regional construct and several new ideas in regionalization, including the areal distribution of the total amount and types of capital investment. These and similar works have carried forward the continuing aspects of traditional economic geography as expressed regionally. In addition, as has been shown, many economic geographers have contributed to regional science and to regional economic development.

Other viewpoints. Economic geography is widely accepted outside the United States and Canada and generally is defined in terms already stated. The field is especially comprehensive in the Soviet Union, by definition virtually replacing human geography (Geograficheskoe Obshchestvo SSSR [1961] 1962, especially pp. 31–44). Under the stimuli of dialectical materialism and national development, economic and physical geographers of the Soviet Union have devoted close attention to pragmatic aspects of their respective subdivisions of the over-all discipline. A keen interest also exists in the Soviet Union in planning, particularly in the roles of theory and measurement. An emerging school of thought there holds that geography should not be compartmentalized but be considered as a unit—a view somewhat similar to Ackerman's concept of the discipline as a man–land system.

Europe and the United Kingdom have continued a long-standing interest in economic geography. German geographers have built on the work of

Thünen and Alfred Weber, fusing these studies with evaluations of management practices, enterprises, and land use to produce a well-founded inductive–deductive concept of the field (Otremba 1953). The term "applied geography" has come into use, particularly in France but also in other parts of Europe and, recently, in the International Geographical Union (Phlipponneau 1960). Although not limited to economic geography, applied geography stresses maximum efficiency in man's use of earth space. In the United Kingdom economic geographers have bridged the gap rather smoothly between the deductive and inductive approaches, providing valuable and well-written reviews that take cognizance of historical development (Estall & Buchanan 1961; Chisholm 1962). Planning is of long-standing interest to British economic geographers, and recent work evinces growth of theoretical work (Haggett 1965). In Scandinavia, notably Sweden, theoretical approaches have been utilized actively for a long time, although pragmatic work continues.

There are many examples in other countries of application of the approaches already mentioned. Qualitative interpretation frequently is a detailed inventory of available resources under specified conditions and cutoff limits. Classifications are becoming more numerous, and there is some experimentation with hypotheses.

No one of the three approaches in economic geography necessarily is superior to the others, and more work is urgently needed in all. As additional data become available and increasingly standardized internationally, classifications and theories probably will become more numerous and will be produced mainly by committee or team efforts. Qualitative interpretations by individuals, however, always will be necessary—not only to provide unusual stimuli and insights but also to bring together cogently the threads of complex ideas, a result that cannot be expected from anthologies.

RICHARD S. THOMAN

[*See also* CENTRAL PLACE; CONSERVATION; REGIONAL SCIENCE; TRANSPORTATION.]

BIBLIOGRAPHY

ACKERMAN, EDWARD A. 1963 Where Is a Research Frontier? Association of American Geographers, *Annals* 53:429–440. → A logical argument for the process–system concept of geography as a nomothetic science.

ALEXANDERSSON, GUNNAR; and NÖRSTRÖM, GÖRAN 1963 *World Shipping: An Economic Geography of Ports and Seaborne Trade.* New York: Wiley. → A thorough assessment of ocean commerce and ports on a worldwide and regional basis.

CAMU, PIERRE; WEEKS, E. P.; and SAMETZ, Z. W. 1964 *Economic Geography of Canada.* Toronto: Macmillan. → An intriguing systematic and regional survey, using a 68-region classification developed over a ten-year period.

CHATTERJEE, SHIBA PRASAD 1964 *Fifty Years of Science in India: Progress of Geography.* Calcutta: Indian Science Congress Association. → Contains a detailed bibliography.

CHISHOLM, MICHAEL 1962 *Rural Settlement and Land Use: An Essay in Location.* London: Hutchinson's University Library. → An able presentation of theoretical approaches to agricultural geography, viewed at different levels of observation and in cognizance of technical change.

ESTALL, R. C.; and BUCHANAN, R. O. 1961 *Industrial Activity and Economic Geography.* London: Hutchinson's University Library. → An excellent survey of selected theoretical and pragmatic considerations, including government policy, in the location of industry.

GARRISON, WILLIAM L. 1959–1960 Spatial Structure of the Economy. Association of American Geographers, *Annals* 49:232–239, 471–482; 50:357–373. → An excellent review of trends and methods in theoretical economic geography.

GEOGRAFICHESKOE OBSHCHESTVO SSSR (1961) 1962 *Soviet Geography: Accomplishments and Tasks.* New York: American Geographical Society. → First published in Russian. A methodological statement by 56 leading Soviet geographers.

GINSBURG, NORTON S. (editor) 1961 *Atlas of Economic Development.* Univ. of Chicago Press. A careful interdisciplinary effort to map economies by specified criteria and, through factor analysis, by combinations of those indices.

GOTTMANN, JEAN (1961) 1964 *Megalopolis: The Urbanized Northeastern Seaboard of the United States.* Cambridge, Mass.: M.I.T. Press → An urban-economic evaluation of the nature of a continuous urbanized section of the eastern United States.

GRÖTEWALD, A. 1959 Von Thünen in Retrospect. *English Geography* 35:346–355.

HAGGETT, PETER (1965) 1966 *Locational Analysis in Human Geography.* New York: St. Martins.

HANCE, WILLIAM 1964 *The Geography of Modern Africa.* New York: Columbia Univ. Press.

HARRIS, CHAUNCY D. 1954 The Market as a Factor in the Localization of Industry in the United States. Association of American Geographers, *Annals* 44:315–348. → An evaluation of the role of market potential in industrial location, especially as expressed in numbers of people and associated sales less shipping charges from specified central places.

JAMES, PRESTON E.; and JONES, CLARENCE F. (editors) (1954)1964 *American Geography: Inventory and Prospect.* Syracuse Univ. Press. → A survey of trends in geography during its first 50 years in the United States and of the status of geography at mid-century. See especially pages 3–68, 142–166, 240–332 and references in bibliographies to monographs by Richard Hartshorne.

JOHNSON, HILDEGARD B. 1962 A Note on Thünen's Circles. Association of American Geographers, *Annals* 52:213–220.

MURPHY, RAYMOND E.; and VANCE, J. E. JR. 1954 Delimiting the CBD. *Economic Geography* 30:189–222.

OTREMBA, ERICH 1953 *Allgemeine Agrar- und Indu-striegeographie.* Stuttgart (Germany): Franckh'sche Verlagshandlung. → Provides a thorough review of the development and mid-1950 status of economic geography in Germany, especially the German Federal Republic.

OTREMBA, ERICH 1957 *Allgemeine Geographie des Welt-handels und des Weltverkehrs.* Stuttgart (Germany): Franckh'sche Verlagshandlung.

PHLIPPONNEAU, MICHEL 1960 *Géographie et action: In-troduction à la géographie appliquée.* Paris: Colin. → Emphasis on the need for study of the functional region, with attention to planning.

TAAFFE, EDWARD J. 1962 The Urban Hierarchy: An Air Passenger Definition. *Economic Geography* 38:1–14. → An experiment in the use of a model to predict trends in air passenger traffic between major cities of the United States.

THOMAN, RICHARD S.; and CONKLING, EDGAR C. 1967 *Geography of International Trade.* Englewood Cliffs, N.J.: Prentice-Hall. → A survey of characteristics and trends in world trade by global, regional, and national patterns, and of the logistics and mechanics involved in such trade.

THÜNEN, JOHANN H. VON (1826–1863) 1930 *Der iso-lierte Staat in Beziehung auf Landwirtschaft und Nationalökonomie.* 3 vols. Jena (Germany): Fischer.

ULLMAN, EDWARD L. 1957 *American Commodity Flow: A Geographical Interpretation of Rail and Water Traffic Based on Principles of Spatial Interchange.* Seattle: Univ. of Washington Press.

WEAVER, JOHN C. 1954 Crop-combination Regions in the Middle West. *Geographical Review* 44:175–200. → A pioneer experiment in close measurement of crop combinations in terms of relative percentages of harvested land.

IV

CULTURAL GEOGRAPHY

Cultural geography as treated here is peculiar to American geography and can be understood as a complement to certain of the trends in American geography in the early part of this century. Cultural geography in a broader sense deals with any part of man's culture in the same way that plant geography deals with the distribution of plant species and vegetation or that economic geography is concerned with the production and distribution of goods and services. Cultural geography in the narrower sense used here is also characterized by certain cultural topics with which it deals, although its unifying thread is its manner of using the anthropological idea of culture to give meaning to its material. The tracing of continuity in space and time can help account for cultures and culture traits whose presence may not seem satisfactorily explained by their function in meeting overt ends. The subject matter of cultural geography has been winnowed by its need of such probing into origins. Cultural geography is not a self-sufficient field of study that produces all its own data and examines them as part of a closed system; it is rather an exchange in which data and interpretations from many sources are examined from one general point of view.

Development. Physiography was emphasized in the formative period of American geography, which occurred around the turn of the century. The first human geography then admitted inquiry into selected relationships between man and his physical environment. Later, concern with the productive capacities of the land came to be coupled with the growth of an economic geography that concentrated on production and trade. Economic geographers either assumed or looked for a functionalism or an adherence to economic laws that assured efficiency.

Carl Sauer (1925; 1931) outlined a new cultural geography dealing with those elements of material culture that give character to area through being "inscribed into the earth's surface." The focus was to be on those works of man rather than on man himself. The study was to be empirical and historical, without preference for environmental or any other selected class of explanation. The elements studied were to be broadly economic as well as material, although Sauer (1941) was later to expand their scope.

Sauer's proposals produced, first, a general change in the direction of American geography and, later, the more special cultural geography, whose early growth was chiefly through his own students. This cultural geography has increasingly occupied the territory its name and rationale have staked out; its content has been limited chiefly by what other fields have previously claimed.

European geography contributes a great portion of the material of cultural geography, especially in dealing with Europe's own rich heritage, but mostly under the heading of a general human geography or a less inclusive social geography. The models for Sauer's program were heavily German, especially Friedrich Ratzel's work on culture spread, Eduard Hahn's work on agricultural development, and regional studies focused on settlement history. *Kulturgeographie* continues as a broad division of geography in Germany, where the modern idea of culture developed, but it does not parallel the American cultural geography as a specific hub for the swapping of ideas (National Research Council . . . 1965). The absence of a recognized cultural geography in Britain and France is hardly surprising, for the culture concept is less used in those countries (the *genre de vie* of Vidal de la Blache is similar in use but much less inclusive).

Content. Most studies in cultural geography develop one or more of the following subjects:

The growth of man's exploitation of his habitat. The study of man's use of his environment includes such topics as the early use of tools and implements, domestication of plants and animals, and the various economies of food production. Human development and human invention both have geographic dimensions in that they are composed of specific events occurring in specific places. The geographer's concern with both the spatial arrangement and the qualities of habitats qualifies him for taking part in the reconstruction of man's past as well as in the understanding of the present. The cultural geographer's interest in the past begins with the beginning of man and follows his wanderings with ever more cultural equipment into new surroundings (Sauer 1952).

Archeology, history, physical geography, and field observation provide much of the raw material for work in this field. Archeology and history, each limited by its sources of data, must remain incomplete records. Cultural geography often asks questions they are least likely to have answered. Thus, many early chapters in man's growth can at best be speculative theories that may remain unverified.

Physical change induced on the surface of the earth by man. Man's material advance leaves its mark on the earth he works. Physical change may be an inadvertent product of man's use of the land: soil erosion induced by cultivation, soil enrichment around human habitations, and vegetation change induced by grazing or burning. It may be a deliberate change, such as the clearing of woods or terracing of hillsides for farming (Spencer & Hale 1961). The actions of man and nature have been of such duration and of such intermixture as to be often no longer separable.

American concern with man's part in the processes of physical geography dates from George P. Marsh's writing, in 1864, of *Man and Nature*. A more recent study, *Man's Role in Changing the Face of the Earth* (International Symposium . . . 1956), explores the earth as the imprint of man's way of life, as a record of his past, and as a material resource for the present and future. The processes that explain the past may serve as guides for the future.

Settlement forms—rural and urban. Settlement forms make up a large part of the features of the man-made landscape. Study of rural settlement has dealt mostly with house types, the arrangement of houses and other structures in relation to each other and to road networks, and the arrangement of fields. Although the settlement of the United States is recent, the history of its house forms is already partly lost, and tracing them is difficult

(Kniffen 1965). The settlement patterns, more easily reconstructed, have converged on variations of the isolated farmstead. For most of Anglo–America the field pattern had to fit the rectangular survey; older areas show the confusion of metes and bounds, but traditional patterns survive, particularly in the old French riverine settlements. Reconstruction of the history of American settlement forms has not proceeded nearly so far as the inventorylike studies of rural patterns in Germany or of rural houses in Italy. Even where inventories are thorough, the forms have resisted satisfactory explanatory generalization.

American geographers have done relatively little with urban settlement forms. Enticing opportunities for study may be found in regionally dominant town and city plans, the pattern of street and lot layout, and cross-city comparison of house types, building materials, and architectural styles.

Nonmaterial culture, such as language and religion. Languages are considered the most reliable ethnic tracers, since the arbitrary choosing of words from a very large pool makes accidental repetition most improbable. Further, language, as a means and a mark of intercommunication, is a maker and a product of group cohesion and, hence, of cultures. Analysis of languages and their distributions has usually been the work of the specialist, but the results are widely used in geography. Toponyms are components of language that are very close to geography because of their fixture on the land and their frequent reference to its qualities.

Religion, also a conservative marker of peoples, is a social institution with significant spatial structure and a molder of the cultural landscape. Geography deals with religion in ways that range from the distribution of specific religions to the expression of a primal sense of order in the landscape—for example, orientation of streets or property lines with the compass (Isaac 1965).

Origin and spread of cultures and civilizations. The spread of culture is most simply studied through particular culture traits, but often an entire complex of culture traits may be welded together by a powerful or influential people and spread over a wide area in relatively uniform fashion. A way of living or a civilization may be traced from its inception to its expansion into a greater territorial base, until finally it reaches its limits and is absorbed or replaced by another expanding culture. The growth of potamic civilizations from their home in Mesopotamia, the growth of the Chinese nation from its culture hearth in the Wei Valley, or the grafting of the Marxist politico–economic complex onto a variety of cultural trunks in the past fifty years would be suitable subjects for such analysis.

Geographers have treated cultures in a variety of ways, such as dividing the world into major culture regions (Russell & Kniffen 1951), examining the development of cultures and subcultures, mapping the core and fringe areas of cultures (Meinig 1965), and studying culture islands.

Cultural evaluation of the environment. The favorite theories of geography are often themselves generalized evaluations of environment. Their change with the passage of time is evidence that they too, however reasoned, are part and parcel of changing culture. What man does with his natural resources depends on his technology, on his perception of his natural resources and of his place among them, and on a complex of values concerning the present and future. Clarence Glacken (1956) has studied man's place in nature from the viewpoint of changes in Western ideas about the habitable world. Non-Western conceptions, as shaped by cosmologies, modified by experience, and revealed in language, are also essential to interpretation of living patterns (Lowenthal 1961).

The environment may be graded in aesthetic terms. Modification of the landscape, including the productive portion of the landscape, may then be guided by aesthetic senses and axioms. Yet the perception of the environment and the responses to environmental stimuli are probably not purely cultural. Sonnenfeld (1965) has asserted the need for isolating the noncultural parts of the behavior that relate to the environment and effect the shaping of the landscape. To do so would better sort the variables with which the cultural geographer deals and would clarify his ideas of causality.

Purposes.   Many studies are undertaken to provide factual answers to specific questions. Some studies are primarily in the geographical tradition of exploration; these include many of the regional inquiries in cultural geography (e.g., Wagner 1958) as well as more specific data-collecting trips (e.g., Zelinsky 1958). Other studies seek links in the solution of specified larger problems, be they geographic in nature or otherwise. A major theme of Kniffen's work has been the use of a particular culture trait as an index to migration and diffusion and the culture regions they shape.

H. C. Brookfield (1964), in a thoughtful critique of American cultural geography, noted its frequent reluctance to compare, generalize, or explain, especially if doing so meant going into social organization or social attitudes. American cultural geographers have often preferred to focus their immediate interest on filling selected gaps in knowledge rather than on using the material gained primarily as a means to further the abstract concepts of the field. There are advantages in developing a reliable body of elaborated description relatively free of the data selection that would be suitable for testing prechosen abstractions. However, cultural geography should also work ahead with generalization as fast as the data and advance of theory permit. Some division of labor may optimize the exchange between description and abstraction.

Purposes of scholarly study are often indeterminate. Idle curiosity may impel the investigator, even while specific hope of practical application accounts for his financial support. Many of the world's problems are not abstract generalizations but are stresses that arise from unique local conditions. A geography that views every place as *sui generis* is a likely source of help. The theme of man's use of his environment, enmeshed in most of cultural geography, gives geography its widest views and most likely application on a world scale. Certainly the cultural geographer is not much drawn to his study by the hope of immediate application, even though it is with past and present application that he constantly deals. Rather he is lured on by the prospect of a better articulated view of man's work and works in their terrestrial frame.

Methods.   Studies of small areas are most likely to depend for their data on field observation. Those on a world-wide scale necessarily depend on secondary sources. Spatial and chronological analysis of the data often form the logical core of the study. The former seeks simplification through the demonstration of spatial order or pattern; the latter emphasizes change in historical depth or the more detailed sequence of change known as process.

Spatial arrangement of data is an essential characteristic of geography. The map is the visual means of arranging the data in its spatial order. (*To spread out* or *to unfold* in this manner approximates the literal meanings of *explanare* and *explicare*, bases for the verb *explain* in English and the modern Latin languages). Mapping the distribution of a culture trait or complex does not constitute an explanation, but it leads to hypotheses as to how the culture trait developed. One common method of map interpretation is to seek correlative distributions that may also be causal associations. A second method is to treat the distribution as a changing product of diffusion and extinction and to seek the conditions that have governed the changes (Zelinsky 1958; Spencer & Hale 1961). An isochronic map is useful in combining both temporal and spatial analysis.

Chronological arrangement of data is essential

to the study of culture. The conservative nature of culture, which follows earlier models even in the process of change, encourages one to study it by tracing its continuity. If a device is not demonstrably functional in every aspect of its design, it may be explained genetically by tracing its origins and movements. John Leighly emphasized this type of cultural explanation in his proposal for a study of the tangible works of man in the landscape in the terms of art history, stressing "the essential time-bond of culture rather than its looser place-bond" (1937, p. 135). The culture concept provides a means of giving intelligibility to what, at least to people removed from the particular cultural context, seems irrational.

Plumbing the basic reasons for cultural choices may provide a functional explanation of what was once considered irrational. Cultural geography would become less dependent on genetic explanation as its mainstay to the extent that culture change—or lack of it—could be explained in terms of human satisfactions. Predictions of the direction of culture change will lead to more application of the findings of cultural geography. Any theory of culture change could have a corresponding theory of cultural geography as the spatial expression of the change. Uses of the culture concept in regional study by geographers and anthropologists have been considered by Thomas (1957).

A battery of general methods is summed up by Wagner and Mikesell (1962, p. 24): "Who? Where? What? When? and How? The themes of culture, culture area, cultural landscape, culture history, and cultural ecology respond to these queries." The themes imply cross sections of investigation, most of them with conceptual dimensions rather than geometrical ones as in the case of the map. Since cultural geography deals with such a great range of phenomena, its methods must also be varied.

Persistent questions. The objects of study in cultural geography may be seen as forms—abstract or concrete, single or complex. Many of the general questions of cultural geography hinge on the derivation of these forms, which is variously sought in environment, function, ideology, technology, ornamentation, previous forms, and the chances of invention and accident. The derivation of one form does not necessarily serve as a model for the derivation of others.

The role of the physical environment. Cultural geography can deal with man's relations with his physical environment at any depth of understanding of this environment. Sauer's work with early man leaned heavily on assessments of environmental change and of environmental opportunity to supply gaps in the a posteriori record. On the other hand, the continuity of culture can be traced over the earth without attention to the physical environments through which the culture spread, although to do so is to ignore a part of the possible explanation.

The reaction against environmental determinism (the doctrine that the physical environment determines the way in which man lives in an area) has united with a culturally oriented geography to produce a new geographic etiology that stresses cultural determinism (a doctrine that emphasizes the role of culture as opposed to that of the environment). One statement of cultural determinism is that culture determines what the environment means to man. An even stronger position holds that man's perception of the environment is all that matters about the physical environment; since perception is culturally controlled, explanation of human behavior is then deemed to be cultural. Cultural determinism presents useful views of the continuity of culture growth, but is less successful as an analysis of cause (a precursor without which the result would have been different). One must remember, first, that perception, by its definition, is not merely hallucination (i.e., independent of external stimulus) and, second, that the environment may not respond to man's management in just the way his perception of it orders.

The difficulties of the man–nature and culture–environment dichotomies are sometimes dissolved in union. Man is often conveniently viewed as a part of nature. Man, culture, and environment in a land have been treated as one in sketches of regional "personality."

Form versus function. What part does function play in cultural design and what part do previous forms play? How fast do forms change to conform to changing needs? Are forms also molded by aesthetic considerations? A barn is built for certain purposes, and a given design is likely to be retained only so long as it fulfills its function reasonably well. But the differences between two barns performing the same functions must be explained on some other basis. Even if the differing features mirror cultural traditions, they may still have originated in functions of other times and other places. Purely decorative features, too, sometimes originate in function. Relic forms may continue to be built or may survive in structures that have outlived their original functions. Whether function or form is stressed in any particular comparison may depend on whether the similarities or the differences are sought.

Form and ideals. A simple feature in the landscape, say a post, serves its function and reflects some particular post-making tradition. It probably has no particular relation to the ethos or set of ideals of the people who use it. A more complicated form with a more complicated function, say the physical form of the village or community built to facilitate a way of living, is more likely to reflect the distinctiveness of that way of living or of the ideals that lie behind it. An ascetic people, not given to social intercourse, probably would not provide their town with plazas and esplanades or decorate it in bright colors. The few geographic studies that deal specifically with form in relation to ideology suggest that rather different peoples may adopt the same readily available forms for the same overt purposes. An account of a Dutch Reformed settlement in Michigan (Bjorklund 1964) tells how immigrants largely gave up their old forms in favor of the common American forms, but it also shows how the American forms still conformed to the old ideology. If identical forms conform to different ideologies, we must assume that the differing peoples see the forms as fulfilling different inner functions and gain different satisfactions from them. In another study Philip Wagner concludes: "Nicoya suggests that thoroughgoing transformations in the social sphere may sometimes produce only moderate variations in technology and landscape, and thus that two or more very dissimilar societies may differ little in the way they conceive and utilize a given habitat" (1958, p. 248). Conversely, peoples with similar ideologies are likely to evolve different community forms for their living. Inquiry into the regulation of form by ideals should be carried further.

Forms of distributions. The forms of distributions are also subject to systematization. The significance of continuous and discontinuous distributions, the relation of area of origin to area of greatest intensity, or the persistence of the core area of a culture region are all aspects of the structure or form of culture areas.

Relation to other fields. Historical geography is the division of geography most closely related to cultural geography. The two complement each other in a cultural–historical geography, in which history provides the explanation of culture and culture provides the organizing concept for the subjects of most geographic interest in history. Historical geography can stand alone, however, for it is often not organized around the culture concept. On the other hand, culture is always dependent on the past for its explanation.

Economic geography and cultural geography could go separate ways as long as one depended primarily on economic laws for its explanation while the other depended on the patterns of the past. But an entire system of economic laws may

be found to be a culture complex that has evolved somewhat accidentally and not in an inescapable mesh of cosmic law. Even in our market economy the prices bid for goods may be but expressions of cultural preference (for example, the American preference for corn-fed ham versus the European for barley-fed). And within a changing economy new institutions, products, and types of enterprise originate and diffuse in a fashion suggestive of the culture traits that they are. On the other hand, the relevant economic laws are also necessary parts of the cultural explanation. Thus, economic and cultural geography join in any broad view of the two fields.

Political geography, like economic geography, is supported by an independent discipline that has its own laws (although less precise), and its systems fulfill stated functions. A nation represents an idea that had an origin and has been spread with some show of power to the borders of the land. The generic idea of nation is again a cultural concept that had an origin and a diffusion that just now seems about to complete the circuit of the earth. Each nation depends on a community of interests, often including such culture traits as a national language and religion. The behavior of its voters, too, reflects persistent patterns in its regional culture.

Cities have both economic and political dimensions, although the economic has loomed larger in urban geographical studies. City planning and urban sociology are cognate disciplines that help provide the rationale for an independent urban geography. At the same time, cities are concentrations of culture that are very sensitive to cultural differences. Internally, the distribution of subcultures within a complex city and the city landscape are equally concerns of cultural geography. Externally, urban functions and rural–urban attitudes vary from culture to culture.

The mathematical formulations now popular in economic and urban studies will be most successful if they can describe the regularities and implications of cultural behavior. Swedish studies have originated quantitative analysis of culture transmission and have attempted to simulate both its rational and random qualities.

The idea of culture provides a frame into which man-made functional systems fit. The narrower cultural geography and the fields that deal with the functional systems that are also a part of culture can fuse into a broader cultural geography in which the culture concept constantly insists on a proper relativity in time and space. Grasp of the concepts of culture and cultures is perhaps the quickest route to a viewpoint not entirely bound by one's own culture and from which one can even see one's own culture in some perspective. Culture is a fit mediator in a study whose point of departure is the comparison of different peoples and lands.

EDWARD T. PRICE

[*Other relevant material may be found in* CARTOGRAPHY; CULTURE; ENVIRONMENTALISM; LANDSCAPE; *and in the biographies of* MARSH; RATZEL; SAUER; VIDAL DE LA BLACHE.]

BIBLIOGRAPHY

BJORKLUND, ELAINE M. 1964 Ideology and Culture Exemplified in Southwestern Michigan. Association of American Geographers, *Annals* 54:227–241.

BROOKFIELD, H. C. 1964 Questions on the Human Frontiers of Geography. *Economic Geography* 40:283–303.

GLACKEN, CLARENCE J. 1956 Changing Ideas of the Habitable World. Pages 70–92 in International Symposium on Man's Role in Changing the Face of the Earth, Princeton, N.J., 1955, *Man's Role in Changing the Face of the Earth.* Edited by William L. Thomas et al. Univ. of Chicago Press.

INTERNATIONAL SYMPOSIUM ON MAN'S ROLE IN CHANGING THE FACE OF THE EARTH, PRINCETON, N.J., *1955* 1956 *Man's Role in Changing the Face of the Earth.* Edited by William L. Thomas et al. Univ. of Chicago Press.

ISAAC, ERICH 1965 Religious Geography and the Geography of Religion. Pages 1–14 in *Man and Earth.* Series in Earth Sciences, No. 3. Boulder: Univ. of Colorado.

KNIFFEN, FRED 1965 Folk Housing: Key to Diffusion. Association of American Geographers, *Annals* 55: 549–577.

LEIGHLY, JOHN B. 1937 Some Comments on Contemporary Geographic Method. Association of American Geographers, *Annals* 27:125–141.

LOWENTHAL, DAVID 1961 Geography, Experience, and Imagination: Towards a Geographical Epistemology. Association of American Geographers, *Annals* 51:241–260.

MARSH, GEORGE P. (1864) 1965 *Man and Nature: Or, Physical Geography as Modified by Human Action.* Edited by David Lowenthal. Cambridge, Mass.: Harvard Univ. Press.

MEINIG, D. W. 1965 The Mormon Culture Region: Strategies and Patterns in the Geography of the American West, 1847–1964. Association of American Geographers, *Annals* 55:191–220.

NATIONAL RESEARCH COUNCIL, AD HOC COMMITTEE ON GEOGRAPHY 1965 *The Science of Geography: Report.* National Research Council Publication No. 1277. Washington: National Academy of Sciences–National Research Council.

RUSSELL, RICHARD; and KNIFFEN, FRED B. 1951 *Culture Worlds.* New York: Macmillan.

SAUER, CARL O. (1915–1962) 1963 *Land and Life: A Selection From the Writings of Carl Ortwin Sauer.* Edited by John Leighly. Berkeley: Univ. of California Press.

SAUER, CARL O. (1925) 1963 The Morphology of Landscape. Pages 315–350 in Carl O. Sauer, *Land and Life: A Selection From the Writings of Carl Ortwin Sauer.* Berkeley: Univ. of California Press.

SAUER, CARL O. (1931) 1962 Cultural Geography. Pages 30–34 in Philip L. Wagner and Marvin W. Mikesell (editors), *Readings in Cultural Geography.* Univ. of Chicago Press. → First published in Volume 6 of the *Encyclopaedia of the Social Sciences.*

SAUER, CARL O. (1941) 1963 Foreword to Historical Geography. Pages 351–379 in Carl O. Sauer, *Land and Life: A Selection From the Writings of Carl Ortwin Sauer.* Berkeley: Univ. of California Press. → First published in Volume 31 of the Association of American Geographers, *Annals.*

SAUER, CARL O. 1952 *Agricultural Origins and Dispersals.* New York: American Geographical Society.

SONNENFELD, JOSEPH 1965 A Behavioral Approach to Cultural Geography. Pages 10–18 in Discussion Papers in Cultural Geography. Unpublished manuscript. → Prepared for the 61st annual meeting of the Association of American Geographers, Columbus, Ohio.

SPENCER, J. E.; and HALE, G. A. 1961 The Origin, Nature, and Distribution of Agricultural Terracing. *Pacific Viewpoint* 2:1–40.

THOMAS, WILLIAM L. JR. 1957 *Land, Man and Culture in Mainland Southeast Asia.* Glen Rock, N.J.: Privately published.

WAGNER, PHILIP L. 1958 *Nicoya: A Cultural Geography.* University of California Publications in Geography, Vol. 12. Berkeley: Univ. of California Press.

WAGNER, PHILIP L.; and MIKESELL, MARVIN W. (editors) 1962 *Readings in Cultural Geography.* Univ. of Chicago Press.

ZELINSKY, WILBUR 1958 The New England Connecting Barn. *Geographical Review* 48:540–553.

V

SOCIAL GEOGRAPHY

No generally accepted definition of social geography exists. The variety of literature which has appeared under the title of social geography is astounding; even within particular schools there are wide disparities of approach and definition. With some notable exceptions, for example, in Sweden and Holland, social geography can be considered a field created and cultivated by a number of individual scholars rather than an academic tradition built up within particular schools. Furthermore, for many people the term "social geography" itself is in disfavor because of its past association with various forms of determinism that postulated a causal connection between society and the geographical environment.

Perhaps, therefore, the best way to examine social geography is to establish a general theoretical outline of the field and, on this basis, to review the existing literature. Naturally, many of the works relevant to what is here called social geography will have been written as contributions to some other discipline.

The argument that social geography is a necessary discipline can be made in at least two ways. One is by analogy with other, better established branches of geography. A widely accepted definition of "human geography" is that it deals with mankind in the context of his total geographical milieu. For the purposes of analysis this milieu has been subdivided into separate categories corresponding to various orders of human activity, for example, the economic, the political, and the cultural. Therefore, one could postulate that social geography is the subdivision of geography that deals specifically with the social order, or that it is the systematic study of the social dimension in areal differentiation.

An alternative way is to begin with the definition of geography as the study of similarities and contrasts between places on the face of the earth. Society, that is, social organization and values, patterns of social movement and interaction, and social dynamics and change, plays such an important role in producing similarities and contrasts between places on the earth that it justifies systematic consideration within the discipline.

The question immediately arises as to how to isolate this social dimension for independent study. In fact, since human activities characteristically are group activities, how can human geography be anything else but social? The virtually interchangeable use of the terms "human" and "social" by several geographers in the British and Dutch schools serves to emphasize the logical (and etymological) basis for this question. Yet, although in the evolution of human geography emphasis has been placed in varying degrees on purely social elements—and although languages, races, and religions have rarely been excluded from consideration—the function of these social elements in the total conceptual framework has not been very clear. In fact, the idea that such social elements could be systematized into a general framework for geographical analysis has been only recently proposed (Bobek 1959; van Paassen 1965).

There are two primary questions social geography must answer: How do mankind's social characteristics vary through space? How do these characteristics affect (or reflect) man's adaptation to and adaptation of his total geographical milieu? Since such questions touch every aspect of human geography, it is difficult to conceive of social geography as a separate field. Its distinctive feature would thus appear to lie more in its focus and objectives than in any clearly delineated subject matter. In practical terms, the traditional twofold method of geography can be applied to these central questions in the following way: by the examination of spatial variations in the distribution and interaction of social groups within their total geographical milieus and by the examination of differential patterns of society's use of the earth, as indicated in settlement forms, livelihoods, circulation networks, and land use patterns. While the first method implies a morphological or formal study of world social patterns, the second method implies a functional interpretation of such patterns in terms of their underlying social processes.

Having thus outlined, in broad terms, the place and function of social geography, let us now see how these fundamental questions have been studied in the past. From such a general and necessarily eclectic survey we may discern some of the major conceptual and technical ingredients from which a definition of social geography can be formulated.

The development of social geography

Studies explicitly or implicitly directed toward the exploration of social geography can be considered under two broad headings: first, the historical precedents, which fall roughly into three major stages, each one characterized by a different approach; and second, the works of twentieth-century geographers.

Historical precedents. Descriptive reports written by explorers and men of letters during classical times, for example, the writings of Herodotus, Thucydides, Strabo, and others, provide the first written recognition of world social differences. Such encyclopedic descriptions continued to appear intermittently in the Occident up to the seventeenth century, for example, the accounts of Marco Polo and the *lettres édifiantes* of Jesuit missionaries. The twofold implication of these works was that social life takes various forms in different parts of the world and that these differences are caused by, or at least are associated with, differences in the physical—particularly climatic—environment.

A second phase consisted of the various philosophical reflections on these and later geographical discoveries. On the one hand, speculative thinkers sought normative principles for an ideal social order from natural law, and, on the other hand, the positivists insisted that such principles should be sought in the existing and empirically observable conditions of society. The essential message of this second phase was that there is a rational order in world society and that this order can be discovered deductively (speculative approach) or inductively (positivistic approach).

A third and far more significant phase began in the nineteenth century, accompanied in France by the emergence of the idea of democracy, in Germany by the rise of national consciousness, and elsewhere by the slow yet effective permeation of a "scientific" approach to knowledge. Ethnographers and historians were among the first to study world social variations in a systematic way. As early as 1725 Giambattista Vico suggested that human development followed an identical series of stages and that the actual variations in world society at any particular time were due to their differential positions within that series. Later in the eighteenth century, Johann Gottfried Herder in Germany and Condorcet in France expressed similar ideas. The geographer Johann Georg Kohl examined the social function and significance of various settlement types; later, his colleague E. Hahn (1896) studied the evolution of livelihoods and demonstrated the religious and social origins of some economic practices. Yet this "scientific" approach to the study of mankind's social differences was also associated with exaggerated single-factor explanations, for example, the biological interpretation first expounded by A. Schäffle (1875–1878) and the psychological interpretation, which found its fullest expression in the Durkheimian school in France. Friedrich Ratzel's *Anthropogeographie* (1882–1891) incorporated both these elements: the ecological view of society within its natural environment and the role of human intelligence (the "idea") in enabling man to overcome physical barriers (1901). Unfortunately, the latter perspective did not emerge too clearly in his monumental work—on which the whole tradition of anthropogeography has been patterned—and so his name has been linked with the idea of society being determined by the physical environment. His *Politische Geographie* (1897) and some articles (1876; 1901) in fact contained hypotheses that were far more relevant to social geography than the *Anthropogeographie*.

One of the most significant precedents to social geography in the nineteenth century was the work of Frédéric Le Play. Disdainful of the various a priori explanations of society prevalent in his day, he set out to study the actual social conditions of worker families in France. His famous monograph technique produced an encyclopedic inventory of social facts, and from a great number of studies he deduced certain basic types, which then served as bases for comparison. Traces of Le Play's analytical formula *lieu–travail–famille*, later adapted by Geddes (1915) into the formula "place–work–folk," can be found in the writings of such early British geographers as H. J. Fleure (1918). French geographers inherited important elements from Le Play, for example, the monograph technique in empirical field studies, but the most important legacy of *lieu–travail–famille* was the social survey movement, which flourished in Britain and America during the early part of the century.

Many geographers, such as Ritter, von Humboldt, Hassinger, Ruhl, and Hettner in Germany, Reclus in France, George Perkins Marsh in America, and H. J. Mackinder in Britain, deserve recognition as pioneers of social geography. However, the three major channels of thought that contained the most useful concepts were those initiated by Le Play (the social survey movement), Ratzel (anthropogeography), and Durkheim (social morphology).

Twentieth-century social geographers. The mutual relations of society and environment was a subject that aroused great speculation and interest at the turn of the century. Yet there was no discipline equipped to embrace the entire question. Ratzel had made an abortive attempt to do so, and his environmentalist disciples exaggerated rather than corrected the deterministic premise of anthropogeography. Many scholars, particularly the Durkheimian sociologists, remained unconvinced that geography had any right to entertain such a monumental task.

At this juncture came one of geography's greatest entrepreneurs, Paul Vidal de la Blache. Society for Vidal (1896; 1902) and his school could not be explained entirely in terms of biological, psychological, or environmental interpretations. It was rather an intricate network of ideas and bonds that provided stability and orientation to human life within particular geographical milieus. In his classical studies of the Mediterranean world and of monsoon Asia (1917–1918), Vidal demonstrated the complex, yet harmoniously balanced, interplay between human institutions and particular natural settings. *Genres de vie* (literally, patterns of living) were the concrete expressions of a society's ongoing contact with nature: sets of techniques, cemented through tradition, whereby human groups secured the material necessities of life within a functional social order (Vidal 1911; Sorre 1948). Repeated experiences in meeting life's common problems within a particular geographical milieu occasioned the development of community consciousness, which made a *genre de vie* truly an ecological system. Variations of this basic concept appear in the literature of other disciplines, for example, social anthropology (Kroeber & Kluckhohn 1952; Redfield 1955), American human ecology (McKenzie 1934) and urban sociology (Park & Burgess 1921). By means of *genre de vie* and other concepts, the French school of human geography replaced the exaggerated Ratzelian notions of environmental determinism by the more elastic concepts of possibilism and dismissed the charges made in the *Année sociologique* between 1890 and 1910 more by substantive works than by theoretical arguments. "La géographie humaine," thus formulated, was a social geography in the broad, integral sense: all other dimensions of the human milieu were studied from the vantage point of society. Many British and American human geographers followed almost identical lines, while the Dutch "sociale geografie" was the direct equivalent of the French "géographie humaine." The kernel of this orientation, namely, society as the source and framework for all human activity, reappears in the work of Hans Bobek (1959) in Vienna. Lucien Febvre's famous apologia (1922) articulated the philosophical and historical *raison d'être* of such a discipline.

To Vidal's essentially ecological approach, his disciple Jean Brunhes added the important dimension of group psychology, asking, for example, why similar environments were used in entirely different ways at different periods in history. He defined social geography as the third level of complexity in human geography's fourfold structure. The fourfold structure included the primary groups of family, kin, and culture; the secondary groupings of livelihood and special interest; the various forms of spatial interaction within and among these groups; and, finally, the legal systems which institutionalize a society's subdivision and access to land and property ([1910] 1924, pp. 36–46). This definition, admirably suited to the study of European—particularly French—rural society of the early twentieth century, remained the basic framework for social geography among British, French, and Dutch scholars up to World War II. Most of the early studies in social geography were regional in character, and their excellence consisted more in their artistic cohesion and integrative descriptions than in their analytical or theoretical expertise. The empirical conditions which favored the use of the regional framework by French scholars did not exist to the same extent elsewhere; this partly explains the divergence of orientation and method which developed among the various schools of human geography.

During the 1930s, British social geographers were involved in methodological controversy. Does social geography consist in merely mapping mankind's social characteristics, or must it also analyze the processes involved in relating a society to its geographical environment? What is the relation between social geography and human ecology? Why not replace the term "human" by "social" as the generic term to signify all the nonphysical aspects of geography?

The fundamental dichotomy between a formal and functional approach expressed in this British debate reiterated the duality that had developed in Holland since the 1920s. While at Utrecht the study of social groups within their territorial framework (de Vooys 1950) was being pursued along the lines of the French school, at Amsterdam Steinmetz' "sociography" was used to study the entire social content of space as a system in itself —aside from any considerations of a group's relation to its natural environment. The birth of sociology in Holland—particularly rural sociology as a separate discipline—has no doubt modified the original disciplinary orientations of these two schools (van Paassen 1965).

Prior to World War II little attempt was made to systematize the elements of social geography. In general, the important associations evident in the spatial organization of society—particularly in the United States—appeared in the literature of human ecology (Theodorson 1961) and urban sociology (Park & Burgess 1921). One major exception, of course, was the work of the environmentalists in examining connections between human behavior and the geographical environment (Thomas 1925).

Pierre George and Maximilien Sorre (1943–1953) were the first great systematizers of social geography. In George's works a close link is maintained between social and economic aspects of human behavior, the social being one facet of the economic (1946, p. 1). For Sorre (1948, pp. 13–16, 66–122) society represented a system of techniques—family and kinship systems, livelihoods (*genres de vie*), languages, and religions, each one having a specific influence on the spatial organization of mankind and his work. Sorre's schema does not make clear, however, whether social geography consists of a series of systematic subfields based on these various kinds of techniques, or whether a distinction is to be made between the "social" and "political" techniques. In his work all forms of organization from family and kin groups to giant political blocs form a continuum (1961, pp. 211–264). Gourou's more comprehensive concept of *civilisation* (1964) comprises both material techniques (modes of production) and spiritual techniques (ideas, values). These three approaches at generalization are important because they try to maintain the integral and holistic character of social geography at the same time that they establish some order and a basis for comparative work. Bobek has made a similar attempt to construct a spatiotemporal framework for world society (1959). His work is a fertile synthesis of French and German traditions: his systematic framework is based on a holistic approach involving types of societies defined in terms of their actual use of their geographical environment (1961).

Several other attempts to formulate the problem of society in geography in terms of a particular systematic framework have appeared: for example, those of Wagner (1960), Ackerman (1963), and van Paassen (1965). Yet more characteristic of postwar work is the development of individual systematic lines of enquiry, for example, geography of rural and urban life, population studies, and geography of religions and political behavior. Associated with this is a more lively *va-et-vient* between geographers and scholars in other disciplines, particularly concerning questions of rural and urban life (Friedmann 1953) and regional planning (Phlipponneau 1960). Studies are still being made within a regional framework, but the focus has changed. Juillard in Alsace (1953) studied particular social problems from a regional perspective, while Rochefort in Sicily (1961) studied regional life from the perspective of the social processes at work. Such reorientations have, of course, raised new methodological problems and prospects. Chatelain (1947; 1953), for example, postulates a duality between the geography of social classes (a kind of social morphology) and the geography of social life (a sociological geography). Claval (1964) envisions the latter as the most feasible future direction for the discipline, citing the work of W. Hartke at Munich as an example. It is difficult, however, to see how these two aspects of the field can be separated.

To label the research being done at Munich as sociological geography may be misleading. Certainly the perspective is social: social-geographic differentiation (*sozialgeographische Differenzierung*) implies that social values—as expressed in the occupational structure—are the primary agents of landscape differentiation. Thus, maps of socioprofessional structure (*Sozialkartierung*) for a series of periods are collated with a corresponding series of land-use patterns (*Nutzflächenkartierung*), and significant associations are sought. This basic formula has been applied successfully both in rural and urban contexts. Geipel's study (1952) of one German region, for example, demonstrated that the sources of regional unity—which varied at different periods—are found essentially in the collective decision-making mechanism of the regional community. This is quite a contrast to the sources of regional unity commonly sought in the natural (physiographic) or economic (agricultural) landscape. Hartke (1956) demonstrated that regions where this phenomenon existed had similar geographic (regional) characteristics. Associations found in urban studies are even more interesting. Hartke's intraurban corridors (*Passagen*) suggest some qualifications to the traditional concentric zone and sector theories of urban structure, while his study of urban expansion

patterns provides new bases for the classification of cities (1961).

In marked contrast to the inductive, empirical, and microscopic approach of the Munich social geographers is the more highly developed theoretical and deductive approach found in Sweden. Torsten Hägerstrand (1952) and Sven Godlund (1956) have applied refined mathematical techniques to the study of migration, rural–urban interaction, circulation, and other dynamic aspects of the field. One of the most interesting developments has been the use of simulation models for the analysis and prediction of spatial movement.

This approach has been adopted and modified in the postwar period by a number of American geographers. At Iowa spatial models have been used to study the distribution patterns of schools, churches, and settlements, often with a view to spatial planning. Morrill's study of Swedish towns (1963) exemplifies this approach. Yet, in general, social geography in the United States is not a unified field: on the one hand there are holistic regional studies, for example, Platt's Saarland study (1961) and Broek's southeast Asian study (1944), and, on the other hand, there are a growing number of systematic studies in racial, linguistic, religious, and other spheres. Some interesting associations have been elaborated, for example, between religion, land use, and livelihood (Isaac 1959), between cultural pluralism and political integration (Lowenthal 1961), and between migration and political behavior within ethnic groups (Lewis 1965). However, the exciting developments in the actual social geography of America have been treated mainly by foreigners (Gottmann 1961) or by scholars in other disciplines.

Résumé of contemporary social geography. In general, the empirical record would seem to characterize social geography as a multifaceted perspective on the spatial organization of mankind. The implication is that some important sources of areal differentiation emanate from society, thus reversing the premises of anthropogeography and other deterministic explanations of social differentiation. Analysis of this social dimension in human geography has involved two basic approaches: the examination of the formal distributions of social phenomena as indices of areal differentiation and the interpretation of these distributions in the light of their underlying social processes. A recent development, particularly in northwestern Europe, is the involvement of social geographers in interdisciplinary research and regional planning.

Nevertheless, the social dimension is one of the least studied aspects of human geography. Social geography lacks definite boundaries and has neither a central unifying concept nor even an agreed content. Instead, there are scattered individual efforts to analyze the changing social patterns of the modern world. Generalizations regarding the nature and potential function of the field, therefore, can only be proffered as suggestions, based on the substantive research directions and ideas of contemporary experts in the field and on the current trends and technical possibilities in other social science disciplines.

The future of social geography

The challenge. Social geography faces a set of challenges that are unprecedented. Revolutionary changes in world social patterns have rendered past analytical techniques obsolete, while philosophical and cultural currents within modern social life tend to increase the propensity to change of both reality itself and its social-psychological significance. Thus, while technological, economic, and commercial evolution tends to produce a certain degree of standardization in society's spatial order, there is a universal tendency to emphasize social, that is, ethnic, religious, or linguistic, differentiation. The philosophical problems of intersubjectivity and coexistence are ubiquitously discussed. "The home of contemporary man," wrote Plattel ([1960] 1965, pp. 1–2) "does not lie primarily in a localized environment, but in his fellow-man." The traditional methods and objectives of social science are being fundamentally challenged. Analysis must somehow be broadened so as to arrive at a more holistic vision of social reality: the classical Cartesian premises underlying accepted research methodology led to the discovery of systems, but mechanics and structures of systems constitute only a partial view of reality. Today both subjective (internal) aspects of reality and objective (external) aspects of reality must be analyzed. Modern psychology and sociology have endeavored to meet this challenge by forging new analytical techniques, and many other social science disciplines have adopted a decidedly behavioristic approach in recent years.

In the light of these developments, the spatial patterns of world society assume a new significance; the immediate challenge for social geographers would seem to be the collaboration with other scholars in the monumental task of describing world society within its geographical setting. For such an endeavor, social geography needs a unifying theme, a conceptual framework that will enable it to contribute toward and benefit from the research efforts of scholars in related social science disciplines. Such a unified framework seems to be

emerging from the work of some contemporary social geographers. Some of its characteristics are described below.

Social space as central theme.   Claval's critique of contemporary social geography concludes that "to understand the geography of a place means to understand the social organization of those who inhabit it, their mentality, their beliefs, their 'representations'" (1964, p. 123). Watson's study of Hamilton demonstrates how "The spatial pattern is, in the last analysis, a reflection of the moral order" ([1951] 1965, p. 476). In this article I have postulated that the *raison d'être* of social geography rests on the fact that the social order is distinct from (even if closely interrelated with) the other orders of human activity in space. In order to describe adequately this social dimension or order, contemporary thought would seem to demand the use of both internal and external perspectives. Is this possible?

Sociologists, for example, Chombart de Lauwe (1956) and Gaston Bardet (1951), and human ecologists, for example, Firey (1960), have demonstrated the technical possibility of exploring a society's perception of its geographical milieu. Geographers, for example, Rochefort (1961), Burton and Kates (1964), and Pataki (1965), have also shown that space has different meanings for different societies, and thus distance and spatial movement can no longer be considered in traditional geodesic terms but must be considered in terms of those dimensions perceived by their human occupants. For example, groups of Italians, Poles, Pakistanis, and Negroes may live side by side in one section of a city. Yet each group, because of economic, historical, cultural, or other reasons, may possess an entirely different conception of space. Some groups may have a social horizon that scarcely transcends the block in which they live or the set of stores in which they work or shop, while others may have social contacts with relatives thousands of miles away. Whether contact with distant relatives is frequent or rare does not influence the fact that a bond is perceived which ignores the barriers of space and time. The social geography of urban neighborhoods cannot ignore these differential attitudes toward space.

This illustration, which challenges traditional notions of space, may lead to the impression that only the social-psychological conception of space matters. Rochefort (1963), in discussing this problem, strongly emphasized that the real dimensions of geographic space must always be kept in mind. Therefore, the central conceptual problem in social geography is to define space in such a way that both subjective and objective dimensions are included.

Sorre's response (1957) to this challenge was the concept of social space: the synthesis of real and perceived dimensions of space. The subjective component of social space in his view is embodied in the distribution of fundamental social groups, while the objective component consists of their concrete geographic setting.

Bobek's concept of social landscape already expressed the main idea that a unit of social space is a region or place in which one or several groups live and have a common set of ideas of their environment (1943; 1948). The fundamental merit of this concept, as a central theme for social geography, is that it incorporates the traditional elements of groups and environment, while redefining them in terms which are relevant to the examination of modern society. Let us see how the methodology of contemporary social geography could be organized around such a central theme.

Subjective component—social groups. Sociology has shown how the dimensions and meaning of space are colored by the beliefs and group affiliations of its human occupants. Sociologists speak of ethnic space, religious space, and other spaces, and social morphology maps the distribution of groups on the premise that their formal spatial configurations imply the values held by the group (Halbwachs 1938). Social geography must go further: these groups, the subjective component of social space, must be studied not only as morphological patterns on the earth but also as formative influences in molding a society's perception of its environment. The relevant groups include those which determine or condition the spatial distribution and interaction of people, for example, language and ethnic groups; those which influence a society's use of space, for example, religious and kin groups; and, most significantly, those which develop as a result of society's mode of material subsistence, namely, the *genres de vie* or livelihood groups. The bonds and values engendered by participation in these groups are not directly observable on the earth's surface, but they are essential to the understanding of the spatial movements and distribution of people on the earth. Classical French geography used such formal categories of relevant groups, but profound transformations in social structure have occurred since the analytical framework of Brunhes, or even Sorre, was first formulated. Even though the choice of relevant grouping will demand close cooperation with sociologists and others, the social geographer does not have to abandon entirely the analytical techniques

of his predecessors. Rather, such traditional concepts should be re-examined in the light of the new analytical possibilities which appear in many social science disciplines. One example which might merit re-examination, for example, is the Vidalian notion of *genre de vie*. Settlements forms, land use, social interaction, and even political integration have been explained by geographers in terms of *genres de vie*. Many feel that the concept has lost its applicability to modern social life (George 1951; Le Lannou 1949), but others argue that it can be reformulated (Sorre 1948; Varagnac 1948). By discounting the various modifications which have accrued through the years and by re-examining the original notion in the light of contemporary developments both in world society and in social science, guidelines for a reformulation may become apparent. A *genre de vie*, in Vidal's opinion (1911), implies more than a means of material subsistence; its geographical significance stems in large part from its spiritual component, the *structures mentales* which persist even after the external modalities of livelihood change. The important point is that both material and spiritual elements are harmoniously integrated in the *genre de vie* community within a particular milieu. Such a conception closely resembles the notion of "community" in rural sociology (Hillery 1950).

Without changing the concept at all, there are some applications in the modern world. Witness the adaptation problems of immigrants from rural to urban areas, the psychological problems involved in the retraining of unemployed miners, the social consequences of colonialism and economic restructuring within the "third world." In the urban industrial world, however, livelihood is a less compelling basis for community consciousness than other similarities, for example, a common racial, professional, or linguistic background or similar consumption habits (Fourastié 1963). But whatever the source, if a recognizable consistency in a group's perception and consequent use of its environment are associated with a common *structure mentale*, why not consider this pattern as a *genre de vie*, for example, that of travel agents, of salesmen, of truck drivers, of commuting students, of social scientists? Chombart de Lauwe (Chombart de Lauwe et al. 1952, p. 243) showed how a deep social rift could prevail in a small dormitory village because the inhabitants belonged to two different *genres de vie*. The same could be said of immigrant ethnic groups in some urban centers (Taeuber & Taeuber 1965). Ideally, within either an urban or a rural region, one could thus identify the component *genres de vie* and see if there is a hierarchy of importance among them, the dominant one giving a character to the place, as in pilgrimage, market, or university towns. Many other possibilities exist, but much more substantive work, preferably in conjunction with other disciplines, is needed before any formal categories of modern *genres de vie* can be made. Until this is done, the existing formal groupings of language, religion, race, etc., may serve to constitute the subjective component of social space; however, if these sociological categories can somehow be integrated into the more geographical concept of *genre de vie*, the result would be an ideal subjective ingredient for social geography.

Objective component—the social environment. The term "social environment" is used here to connote all the socially significant aspects of the total geographic milieu. Traditionally, geographers have tended to exaggerate the distinction between the natural (physical–biotic) environment and the artificial network of human establishments created by society. This dualistic conception tends to ignore the fact that mankind's environment-creating apparatus has by no means entirely destroyed the natural framework and that the interplay of natural and artificial assumes very different forms throughout the world. The social environment, as objective component of social space, includes more than these two levels. It includes, for example, the relation of social attitudes and traditions to nature, resource use, and the ethics of group relations.

Social geographers are far from a satisfactory definition of the social environment; they lack substantive studies which would provide the raw material for such a definition. What is the social significance, for example, of purely physical elements, such as humidity, temperature, or altitude? Geographers have added very little to the "findings" of the Huntingtonian environmentalists. Yet the behavioral sciences are interested in knowing the connections, real or perceived, between society and its natural environment. The research challenges proposed in Sorre's *Géographie psychologique* (1954) remain virtually untouched. In addition, little is known about the "synthetic environment" (Herber 1962): the various consequences of atmospheric and oceanic pollution, or the consumption of medicated foods, stimulants, and sedatives. What are the physiological and pathological consequences of changes in the environment, for example, housing, communication, and diet?

Recently some geographers have viewed the environment as an amalgam of systems (Wagner & Mikesell 1962; Ackerman 1963; van Paassen 1965). This approach is satisfactory from the theoretical and technical points of view, but does it admit of nonsystematic (dysfunctional) elements which often play such an important part in social life? The social geographer must be sensitive to the local exceptions which give special character to individual places, such as Rochefort (1961) demonstrated in her study of Sicilian social environment.

Approaches to the study of social space. We have seen that the study of social groups within their territorial (environmental) framework has constituted the basic traditional methodology of the Dutch, British, and some French social geographers. In theory, this has involved a combination of a morphological approach (mapping of social groups) and an ecological approach (relations of groups to environment). Today, however, the latter (vertical) dimension is perhaps less significant than the horizontal one, namely, the spatial patterns of interaction between social groups, such as Lowenthal's Caribbean study illustrated (Lowenthal 1961). A psychological approach to group attitudes, such as one finds in the *Revue de psychologie des peuples*, may provide clues to the origins of some spatial discontinuities in social interaction.

In terms of the notions of group and environment, as redefined above, let us see what analytical methods can be used in the study of social space. Two of the many possible approaches are (1) to consider social space as a mosaic of social areas defined in terms of the occupant groups, for example, *genres de vie* or ethnic groups; and (2) to view social space as nodally organized, that is, as a network of spatial relations radiating around certain centers (Sorre's *points privilégiés*) and permeated by the arteries of circulation.

Formal approach—social areas. Initially, the formal approach examines the spatial patterns and characteristics of social groups in virtually the same fashion as that used by the disciples of Steinmetz in Amsterdam. On the basis of these distributions a series of regions, homogeneous in terms of individual characteristics, can be compared and associations can be sought. Such associations, however, must then be examined in terms of the social environment in which these social characteristics occur, that is, an ecological approach must supplement the more formal "sociographical" stage of analysis. In addition to these two steps, the geographer must endeavor to see how all these elements combine to form the social whole within a particular region and must seek explanations for the variations through space in the incidence and functional character of these social wholes. Jones sees "social regions" within the city of Belfast (1960), for example, as a product of historical and religious forces, while the "social area analysis" tradition in American human ecology (Theodorson 1961) has demonstrated the use of various other indices in the establishment of intraurban social regions.

Functional approach. A more dynamic and increasingly popular approach is to consider social space in terms of its nodal organization. The orbit of group activities and the related horizons of social consciousness can be examined (cartographically) in terms of their use of these nodes, for example, markets, cinemas, and schools (Chombart de Lauwe et al. 1952). The hinterland of each of these nodes varies in scale and significance, and these variations provide crucial insights into the social character of particular places. The study of nodal regions and of circulation are two examples of a functional approach to the study of social space.

Sorre (1961) suggests that settlement units— towns, cities, metropolises—provide a primary set of nodes on a world scale. Within each of these nodes is an internal system of centers (schools, churches, cinemas) whose social significance can also be examined cartographically. Here again the social geographer can collaborate with and utilize some of the existing principles of central place theorists and perhaps somewhat qualify definitions of centrality currently based on commercial and industrial criteria. Edgar Kant's *Umland* studies (Kant et al. 1951), J. Labasse's circulation studies (1955), and Pierre George's studies of the urban fringe (1962) provide orientation for this kind of study. As world society becomes more urbanized, social geographers will concern themselves more with the urban field, and, here, collaboration with other scholars will be imperative.

The essential clue to the internal dynamism of social space can be found in its circulation system. Circulation here includes all kinds of movement of goods, services, people, and ideas—any kind of spatial movement which occasions social communication. As the Paris study (Chombart de Lauwe et al. 1952) demonstrated, the actual and potential use of a circulation system indicates the concrete social horizons of the group it serves; changes within it may indicate or produce changes in the relation between groups and between a group and its social environment.

A vast number of research questions emanate from this dimension of social space, particularly now that the processes of social differentiation and cultural standardization are so closely tied with large-scale, mass-produced goods and services. Interregional traffic, the currents of the tourist world, pilgrimages, daily and seasonal commuting —these are only a few samples of the many activities the student of circulation could investigate.

To summarize, social geography can be defined as the study of the areal (spatial) patterns and functional relations of social groups in the context of their social environment; the internal structure and external relations of the nodes of social activity; and the articulation of various channels of social communication.

Although the discussion has distinguished between various elements and approaches to social geography, it must be emphasized that one of the fundamental characteristics of the field has been, and must remain, its integral, holistic character. Like social history, it must endeavor to maintain the holistic view, that is, to show how the individual parts and their functional connections integrate to give a specific character to the social whole. French geographers have supplied ample precedent for this kind of holism; so, indeed, have the social anthropologists of the Anglo–American world. The more the field becomes theoretically systematized, the greater will the challenge of integration become.

For social geography to fulfill its potential, the various approaches to the field need to be coordinated into a systematic conceptual framework. Sorre's concept of social space could provide a central theme for such a framework. Its ingredient elements could be considered as bases for systematic subdivisions, for example, geography of language, of religions, and of diet, each of which contributes a valuable perspective on society's spatial order. The definition given here seems to incorporate the various elements which have belonged to the field of social geography and which, given the trends in contemporary social science, could constitute fruitful future directions for the discipline.

ANNE BUTTIMER

BIBLIOGRAPHY

ACKERMAN, EDWARD A. 1963 Where Is a Research Frontier? Association of American Geographers, *Annals* 53:429–440.

BARDET, GASTON 1951 Social Topography: An Analytico–Synthetic Understanding of the Urban Texture. *Town Planning Review* 22:237–260.

BOBEK, HANS 1943 Der Orient als Soziallandschaft. Unpublished manuscript.

BOBEK, HANS 1948 Stellung und Bedeutung der Sozialgeographie. *Erdkunde* 2, no. 1/3:118–125.

BOBEK, HANS 1959 Die Hauptstufen der Gesellschafts- und Wirtschaftsentfaltung in geographischer Sicht.

Die Erde: Zeitschrift der Gesellschaft für Erdkunde zu Berlin 90:259–298.

BOBEK, HANS 1961 Sozialgeographie: Neue Wege der Kultur- und Bevölkerungsgeographie. Deutsche Gesellschaft für Bevölkerungswissenschaft, *Mitteilungen* 3:62–67.

BROEK, JAN O. M. 1932 *The Santa Clara Valley, California: A Study in Landscape Changes.* Utrecht (Netherlands): Oosthoek.

BROEK, JAN O. M. 1944 Diversity and Unity in Southeast Asia. *Geographical Review* 34:175–195.

BROOKFIELD, H. C. 1961 The Highland Peoples of New Guinea: A Study of Distribution and Localization. *Geographical Journal* 127:436–448.

BRUNHES, JEAN (1910) 1924 *Human Geography.* London: Harrap. → First published in French. A fourth French edition was published in 1934 by Alcan.

BURTON, IAN; and KATES, ROBERT W. 1964 The Perception of Natural Hazards in Resource Management. *Natural Resources Journal* 3:412–441.

CHATELAIN, M. ABEL 1947 Les fondements d'une géographie sociale de la bourgeoisie française. *Annales de géographie* 56:455–462.

CHATELAIN, M. ABEL 1953 Horizons de la géographie sociologique. *Revue de géographie de Lyon* 28:225–228.

CHOMBART DE LAUWE, PAUL H. 1956 *La vie quotidienne des familles ouvrières.* Paris: Centre National de la Recherche Scientifique.

CHOMBART DE LAUWE, PAUL H. et al. 1952 *Paris et l'agglomération parisienne.* Volume 1: L'espace social dans une grande cité. Paris: Presses Universitaires de France.

CLAVAL, PAUL 1964 *Essai sur l'évolution de la géographie humaine.* Cahiers de géographie de Besançon No. 12. Paris: Les Belles-Lettres. → Translation of extract in text provided by Anne Buttimer.

DICKINSON, ROBERT E. (1947) 1956 *City Region and Regionalism: A Geographical Contribution to Human Ecology.* London: Routledge.

DURKHEIM, ÉMILE (1893) 1960 *The Division of Labor in Society.* Glencoe, Ill.: Free Press. → First published as *De la division du travail social.*

DURKHEIM, ÉMILE (1895) 1958 *The Rules of Sociological Method.* 8th ed. Edited by George E. G. Catlin. Glencoe, Ill.: Free Press. → First published as *Les règles de la méthode sociologique.*

EVANS, EMYR E. 1942 *Irish Heritage: The Landscape, the People and Their Work.* Dundalk (Ireland): Tempest.

EVANS, EMYR E. 1957 *Irish Folk Ways.* New York: Devin-Adair.

FEBVRE, LUCIEN (1922) 1925 *A Geographical Introduction to History.* New York: Knopf. → First published as *La terre et l'évolution humaine.*

FIREY, WALTER I. 1960 *Man, Mind and Land: A Theory of Resource Use.* Glencoe, Ill.: Free Press.

FLEURE, HERBERT J. 1918 *Human Geography in Western Europe: A Study in Appreciation.* London: Williams & Norgate.

FLEURE, HERBERT J. 1947 *Some Problems of Society and Environment.* London: Institute of British Geographers.

FORDE, DARYLL (1934) 1963 *Habitat, Economy and Society: A Geographical Introduction to Ethnology.* 5th ed. London: Methuen.

FOURASTIÉ, JEAN 1963 *Le grand espoir du XXe siècle.* Paris: Gallimard.

FRIEDMANN, GEORGES (editor) 1953 *Villes et campagnes: Civilisation urbaine et civilisation rurale en France.* Paris: Colin.

GEDDES, PATRICK (1915) 1950 *Cities in Evolution.* New ed., rev. Oxford Univ. Press.

GEIPEL, ROBERT 1952 *Soziale Struktur und Einheitsbewusstein als Grundlagen geographischer Gliederung.* Rhein-Mainische Forschungen, No. 38. Frankfurt am Main (Germany): Kramer.

GEORGE, PIERRE (1946) 1956 *Géographie sociale du monde.* 4th ed. Paris: Presses Universitaires de France.

GEORGE, PIERRE 1951 *Introduction à l'étude géographique de la population du monde.* France, Institut National d'Études Démographiques, Travaux et Documents, Cahier No. 14. Paris: Presses Universitaires de France.

GEORGE, PIERRE 1956 *La campagne: Le fait rural à travers le monde.* Paris: Presses Universitaires de France.

GEORGE, PIERRE 1962 *Précis de géographie urbaine.* Paris: Presses Universitaires de France.

GODLUND, SVEN 1956 The Function and Growth of Bus Traffic Within the Sphere of Urban Influence. *Lund Studies in Geography* Series B, No. 18.

GOTTMANN, JEAN (1961) 1964 *Megalopolis: The Urbanized Northeastern Seaboard of the United States.* Cambridge, Mass.: M.I.T. Press.

GOUROU, PIERRE 1964 Changes in Civilisation and Their Influence on Landscapes. *Impact of Science on Society* 14:57–71.

GROENMAN, S. JOERD (1950) 1953 *Methoden der sociografie: Een inleiding tot de practijk van het sociale onderzoek in Nederland.* Assen (Netherlands): Van Gorcum.

HÄGERSTRAND, TORSTEN 1952 The Propagation of Innovation Waves. *Lund Studies in Geography* Series B, No. 4.

HAHN, EDUARD 1896 *Die Haustiere und ihre Beziehungen zur Wirtschaft des Mensches.* Leipzig: Duncker & Humblot.

HALBWACHS, MAURICE (1938) 1960 *Population and Society: Introduction to Social Morphology.* Glencoe, Ill.: Free Press. → First published as *Morphologie sociale.*

HARTKE, WOLFGANG 1956 *Die Hütekinder im Hohen Vogelsberg: Der geographische Charakter eines Sozialproblems.* Münchner Geographische Hefte, No. 11. Regensburg (Germany): Lassleben.

HARTKE, WOLFGANG 1959 Gedanken über die Bestimmung von Räumen gleichen sozialgeographischen Verhaltens. *Erdkunde* 13:426–436.

HARTKE, WOLFGANG 1961 Die sozialgeographische Differenzierung der Gemarkungen ländlicher Kleinstädte. *Geografiska annaler* 43:105–113.

HARTKE, WOLFGANG 1963 Der Weg zur Sozialgeographie: Der wissenschaftliche Lebensweg von Professor Dr. Hans Bobek. Österreichische Geographische Gesellschaft, *Mitteilungen* 105:5–22.

HARTMANN, F. 1958 Volkach am Main: Kulturgeographische Studien über eine unterfränkische Kleinstadt. Unpublished manuscript.

HARTSHORNE, RICHARD (1939) 1964 *The Nature of Geography: A Critical Survey of Current Thought in the Light of the Past.* Lancaster, Pa.: Association of American Geographers.

HARTSHORNE, RICHARD 1950 The Functional Approach in Political Geography. Association of American Geographers, *Annals* 40:95–130.

HERBER, LEWIS 1962 *Our Synthetic Environment.* New York: Knopf.

HILLERY, GEORGE A. JR. 1950 Definitions of Community: Areas of Agreement. *Rural Sociology* 20:111–123.

INTERNATIONAL SYMPOSIUM ON MAN'S ROLE IN CHANGING THE FACE OF THE EARTH, PRINCETON, N.J., 1955 1956 *Man's Role in Changing the Face of the Earth.* Edited by William L. Thomas et al. Univ. of Chicago Press.

ISAAC, ERICH 1959 Influence of Religion on the Spread of Citrus. *Science* 129:179–186.

JONES, EMRYS A. 1960 *A Social Geography of Belfast.* Oxford Univ. Press.

JUILLARD, ÉTIENNE 1953 *La vie rurale dans la plaine de Basse-Alsace: Essai de géographie sociale.* Strasbourg, Université, Institut des Hautes Études Alsaciennes, Vol. 9. Strasbourg: Le Roux.

KANT, EDGAR et al. 1951 Studies in Rural–Urban Interaction. *Lund Studies in Geography* Series B, No. 4.

KROEBER, A. L.; and KLUCKHOHN, CLYDE 1952 *Culture: A Critical Review of Concepts and Definitions.* Harvard University, Peabody Museum of American Archaeology and Ethnology Papers, Vol. 47, No. 1. Cambridge, Mass.: The Museum. → A paperback edition was published in 1963 by Vintage Books.

LABASSE, JEAN 1955 *Les capitaux et la région, étude géographique: Essai sur le commerce et la circulation des capitaux dans la région lyonnaise.* Paris: Colin.

LE LANNOU, MAURICE 1949 *La géographie humaine.* Paris: Flammarion.

LE PLAY, FRÉDÉRIC (1855) 1877–1879 *Les ouvriers européens,* 2d ed. 6 vols. Tours (France): Mame.

LE PLAY, FRÉDÉRIC (1871) 1907 *L'organisation de la famille: Selon le vrai modèle signalé par l'histoire de toutes les races et de tous les temps.* 5th ed. Tours (France): Mame.

LEWIS, PEIRCE F. 1965 Impact of Negro Migration on the Electoral Geography of Flint, Michigan, 1932–1962: A Cartographic Analysis. Association of American Geographers, *Annals* 55:1–25.

LOWENTHAL, DAVID 1961 *The West Indies Federation: Perspectives on a New Nation.* American Geographical Society, Research Series, No. 23. New York: Columbia Univ. Press.

MCKENZIE, R. D. 1931 Ecology, Human. Volume 5, pages 314–315 in *Encyclopaedia of the Social Sciences.* New York: Macmillan.

MCKENZIE, R. D. 1934 The Field and Problems of Demography, Human Geography and Human Ecology. Pages 52–66 in Luther L. Bernard (editor), *The Fields and Methods of Sociology.* New York: Farrar.

MACKINDER, HALFORD (1919) 1942 *Democratic Ideals and Reality: A Study in the Politics of Reconstruction.* London: Constable; New York: Holt.

MORRILL, RICHARD L. 1963 The Development of Spatial Distributions of Towns in Sweden: A Historical–Predictive Approach. Association of American Geographers, *Annals* 53:1–14.

PAASSEN, C. VAN 1965 *Over vormverandering in de sociale geografie.* Gröningen (Netherlands): Wolters.

PARK, ROBERT E.; and BURGESS, ERNEST W. (1921) 1929 *Introduction to the Science of Sociology.* 2d ed. Univ. of Chicago Press.

PATAKI, K. J. 1965 Shifting Population and Environment Among the Auyuna: Some Considerations on Phenomena and Schema. M.A. thesis, Univ. of Washington.

PELLETIER, JEAN 1959 *Alger; 1955: Essai d'une géographie sociale.* Cahiers de géographie de Besançon, No. 6. Paris: Belles Lettres.

PHLIPPONNEAU, MICHEL 1960 *Géographie et action: Introduction à la géographie appliquée.* Paris: Colin.

PLANHOL, XAVIER DE 1957 *Le monde islamique: Essai de géographie religieuse.* Paris: Presses Universitaires de France.

PLATT, ROBERT S. 1961 The Saarland; an International Borderland: Social Geography From Field Study of Nine Border Villages. *Erdkunde* 15:54–68.

PLATTEL, MARTIN G. (1960) 1965 *Social Philosophy.* Duquesne Studies, Philosophical Series, No. 18. Pittsburgh, Pa.: Duquesne Univ. Press. → First published in Dutch.

RATZEL, FRIEDRICH 1876 *Städte und Culturbilder aus Nordamerika.* Leipzig: Brockhaus.

RATZEL, FRIEDRICH (1882–1891) 1921–1922 *Anthropogeographie.* 2 vols. Stuttgart (Germany): Engelhorn. → Volume 1: *Grundzüge der Anwendung der Erdkunde auf die Geschichte,* 4th ed. Volume 2: *Die geographische Verbreitung des Menschen,* 3d ed.

RATZEL, FRIEDRICH (1897) 1923 *Politische Geographie.* 3d ed. Edited by Eugen Oberhummer. Munich and Berlin: Oldenbourg.

RATZEL, FRIEDRICH (1901) 1902 Man as a Life Phenomenon on the Earth. Volume 1, pages 61–106 in Hans F. Helmolt (editor), *The History of the World: A Survey of Man's Record.* New York: Dodd. → First published in German.

REDFIELD, ROBERT 1953 *The Primitive World and Its Transformations.* Ithaca, N.Y.: Cornell Univ. Press. → A paperback edition was published in 1957.

REDFIELD, ROBERT 1955 *The Little Community: Viewpoints for the Study of a Human Whole.* Univ. of Chicago Press. → A paperback edition, bound together with *Peasant Society and Culture,* was published in 1961 by Cambridge Univ. Press.

REDFIELD, ROBERT; and VILLA ROJAS, ALFONSO (1934) 1962 *Chan Kom: A Maya Village.* Carnegie Institution of Washington, Publication No. 448. Univ. of Chicago Press.

Recherches sociographiques. → Published since 1960 by Laval University, Faculty of Social Sciences, Quebec.

Revue de psychologie des peuples. → Published since 1946 by the Institute Havrais de Sociologie Économique et de Psychologie des Peuples, Le Havre, France.

ROCHEFORT, RENÉE 1961 *Le travail en Sicile: Étude de géographie sociale.* Paris: Presses Universitaires de France.

ROCHEFORT, RENÉE 1963 Géographie sociale et sciences humaines. Association de Géographes Français, *Bulletin* No. 314–315:18–32.

RUPPERT, KARL 1958 *Spalt: Ein methodischer Beitrag zum Studium der Agrarlandschaft mit Hilfe der kleinräumlichen Nutzflächen und Sozialkartierung und zur Geographie des Hopfenbaus.* Münchner Geographische Hefte, No. 14. Regensburg (Germany): Lassleben.

SAUER, C. O. 1931 Geography, Cultural. Volume 6, pages 621–624 in *Encyclopaedia of the Social Sciences.* New York: Macmillan.

SCHÄFFLE, ALLEN (1875–1878) 1896 *Bau und Leben des sozialen Körpers.* 2d ed. 4 vols. Tübingen (Germany): Laupp.

SCHNORE, LEO F. 1961 Geography and Human Ecology. *Economic Geography* 37:207–217.

SORRE, MAXIMILIEN 1943–1953 *Les fondements de la géographie humaine.* 3 vols. Paris: Colin.

SORRE, MAXIMILIEN 1948 La notion de genre de vie et sa valeur actuelle. *Annales de géographie* 57:97–108, 193–204.

SORRE, MAXIMILIEN 1954 *La géographie psychologique: L'adaptation au milieu climatique et biosocial.* Traité de psychologie appliquée, Vol. 3, part 3. Paris: Presses Universitaires de France.

SORRE, MAXIMILIEN 1957 *Rencontres de la géographie et de la sociologie.* Paris: Rivière.

SORRE, MAXIMILIEN 1961 *L'homme sur la terre.* Paris: Hachette.

STEWARD, JULIAN H. 1950 *Area Research: Theory and Practice.* Bulletin No. 63. New York: Social Science Research Council.

TAEUBER, K. E.; and TAEUBER, A. F. 1965 *Negroes in Cities: Residential Segregation and Neighborhood Change.* Chicago: Aldine.

THEODORSON, G. A. (editor) 1961 *Studies in Human Ecology.* Evanston, Ill.: Row, Peterson.

THOMAS, FRANKLIN 1925 *The Environmental Basis of Society: A Study in the History of Sociological Theory.* New York: Century.

Tijdschrift voor economische en sociale geografie. → Published since 1910 by the Nederlandse Vereniging voor Economische en Sociale Geografie.

VARAGNAC, ANDRÉ 1948 *Civilisation traditionnelle et genres de vie.* Paris: Michel.

VIDAL DE LA BLACHE, PAUL 1896 Le principe de la géographie générale. *Annales de géographie* 5:129–142.

VIDAL DE LA BLACHE, PAUL 1902 Les conditions géographiques des faits sociaux. *Annales de géographie* 11:13–23.

VIDAL DE LA BLACHE, PAUL 1911 Les genres de vie dans la géographie humaine. *Annales de géographie* 20:193–212, 289–304.

VIDAL DE LA BLACHE, PAUL 1917–1918 Les grandes agglomérations humaines. *Annales de géographie* 26:401–422; 27:92–101, 174–187.

VOOYS, ADRIAAN C. DE 1950 *De ontwikkelung van de sociale geografie in Nederland.* Inaugural lecture at the University of Utrecht. Groningen (Netherlands): No publisher given.

WAGNER, PHILIP 1960 *The Human Use of the Earth.* Glencoe, Ill.: Free Press.

WAGNER, PHILIP L.; and MIKESELL, MARVIN W. (editors) 1962 *Readings in Cultural Geography.* Univ. of Chicago Press.

WATSON, JAMES W. (1951) 1965 The Sociological Aspects of Geography. Pages 463–499 in Thomas Griffith Taylor (editor), *Geography in the Twentieth Century: A Study of Growth, Fields, Techniques, Aims and Trends.* New York: Philosophical Library.

VI
STATISTICAL GEOGRAPHY

Statistical geography is to geography what econometrics is to economics, sociometrics to sociology, psychometrics to psychology, or even jurimetrics to jurisprudence—an approach to the field rather than a subdivision of that field. Like these other approaches, it is of recent development—the manifestation within geography of the trend to a more quantitative approach that has characterized all the social sciences since the end of World War II. As is also the case with these other approaches, many of the pioneering contributions to statistical geography have come from workers in other fields. The parallel term "geometrics" is not used to describe the work of the statistical geographer, however, not so much because it provides an inappropriate picture of the statistical geographer's attempts to identify and measure regularities observable in spatial distributions as because the branch of mathematics that originated in Greek attempts to measure the earth has a two-thousand-year priority in its right to the name. In addition, mathematical geography, concerned as it is with map projections, is the branch of geography that today relies most heavily and directly upon geometry.

The syndrome that characterizes statistical geography today includes a more formal theoretical orientation than was true of geography in the past, a reliance upon statistical inference and numerical analysis in empirical research, the use of mathematical programming and simulation procedures in applied research, a basic concern with model construction, and an involvement with high-speed computers, mass-data banks, and automated mapping devices.

Yet this assemblage of interests is not monolithic. There are differences in emphasis, corresponding to each of the four main traditions of geographic research: spatial, area studies, man–land, and earth science (Pattison 1964; National Research Council 1965). Statistical geography originated within the spatial tradition, with its emphasis upon analysis of spatial distributions and associations, and initially relied heavily upon exercises in distribution fitting and upon regression and correlation analysis. It spread to area studies when the spatial tradition began using multivariate analysis, then to the man–land tradition via behavioral studies of environmental perception and individual decision making, and to the earth-science tradition as spatial studies and related systematic sciences began using systems analysis. To understand these several facets of statistical geography, with their differences in use of theory, choices, and timing of applications of statistical methods, and their contacts with the rest of science, therefore requires some understanding of the four research traditions. These, in turn, can best be viewed within a formal overview of approaches to regional analysis (Berry 1964*a*).

Approaches to regional analysis

Virtually any sort of regional analysis may be considered as starting from information about one or more *places*. For each place, one or more *properties*, or characteristics, may be measured, and the measurements may be made at one or more points in *time*. It is often convenient to think in terms of a three-dimensional array $\mathbf{X}$ of order $v \times p \times t$. Cell x_{ijk} of this array (or matrix) records the value of variable i at place j in time k. Rows of the array—vectors of array values for fixed i, k—record the distribution of variables over places at some point in time. Column vectors inventory the properties of places at time t. Time vectors report on the t states of variable i at place j.

Operational specification of variables, places, and times varies with the interests of the particular analyst, but a matrix such as $\mathbf{X}$ is (albeit usually implicitly) the object of all forms of geographic study. A row vector of $\mathbf{X}$ is a spatial distribution that can be mapped. A column vector is a locational inventory. Such row and column vectors are the bases of systematic (topical) and regional geography, respectively. Time vectors report changes in spatial distributions and at locations and are basic to historical geography.

The data. Cell x_{ijk} may contain a variety of different records, depending upon specification of i, j, and k. Columns, for example, may be defined as places with area, such as countries, states, counties, census tracts, or quarter-mile-square cells of a half-mile grid. Alternatively, they may be dimensionless points; three such examples are triangulation points used for measuring altitude, weather stations, and soil-sample-core locations (Kao 1963). Rows may be defined as properties of the places (scalar quantities, such as population residing in each of a set of census tracts or altitude at each of a set of triangulation points), or they may refer to connections between places (vector quantities, such as flow of coal from southern Illinois to each of the Midwestern counties). Rows also might be airline traffic flow between cities; in this case columns would represent *pairs* of cities. In addition, any level of measurement may appear, whether nominal, ordinal, interval, or ratio [*see* STATISTICS, DESCRIPTIVE, *article on* LOCATION AND DISPERSION, *for a discussion of levels of measurement*].

Spatial tradition. Geography's spatial tradition is founded upon cartographic portrayal and subsequent study of spatial distributions, thus having as its base row-wise analysis. A few examples of the kinds of spatial distributions studied follow:

(1) A land-use map—scalar, nominal, of areas, an areal distribution.

(2) A map showing the location of major cities by dots—scalar, nominal, at points, a point distribution.

(3) An airline-route map—vector, nominal, joining points.

(4) A map of soil quality—scalar, ordinal, of areas.

(5) A map showing average annual temperature—scalar, interval. If the map shows averages by states or districts, it is also discontinuous and areal (a choropleth map, if different shadings are applied to the units), but if it shows the temperature varying over the country as a surface, it is a continuous generalization. The generalization is of point observations (usually isopleth, since the surface will be depicted by contours) if, for example, weather-station data are used, or of areal data if interpolations were made, for example, with respect to the district averages treated as points central to each of the districts.

(6) A highway map, with routes classified by quality—vector, ordinal, joining points.

(7) A map of city-to-city air-passenger movements—vector, ratio, joining points.

Two dominant themes emerge in spatial analysis of such maps: evaluation of the *pattern* of scalar distributions and of similarities in pattern over a number of such distributions and evaluation of the *connectivity* evidenced by vector distributions and of similarities in the connectivity of several such distributions. Apparently, the fundamental properties of pattern include absolute location (position), relative location (geometry), and scale, with a family of interesting derived properties, including density and density gradients, spacing, directional orientation, and the like. Similarly, accessibility is central to the study of connectivity, and from it are derived such properties as centrality itself, relative dominance, degree of interdependence, etc. The two themes merge in *spatial-systems* analysis, where pattern and connectivity are examined in their association. For example, urban land values decline with increasing distance from the city center, and type of farming varies with distance from market. Such examples are readily generalized to the dynamic, that is, time-dependent, case.

Area-studies (chorographic) tradition. Just as row-wise analysis is the basis of the spatial tradition, so columnwise analysis provides the base for geography's area-studies tradition. The essential problems of this tradition are those of regional intelligence: the characterization of place in terms of the associations between characteristics localized in that place. This approach is often restricted to those features of place that are directly observable as landscape but, especially among the French school of human geographers, is also extended to an evaluation of both tangible and intangible aspects of "regional character" and of the differentiation of places (the study of "areal differentiation") [*see* LANDSCAPE].

An appetite for information, a penchant for the peculiar, emphasis upon field work, attachment to the people and language of a particular part of the world, a strong literary bent, a companionship with history and great reliance upon historical modes of explanation (in contrast to the functional, deterministic, and probabilistic modes of the other geographic traditions)—all these serve to identify the work of the student in the area-studies tradition, whatever the areas examined: countries or continents, regions or culture areas.

Man–land tradition. In the tradition of medieval philosophy, classical geographers distinguished between two major sets of variables: the physical (inorganic plus biotic) and the cultural. The associated methodological argument was that these provided the bases of the two major segments of the field: physical geography and cultural geography. Finer groupings of variables within these categories led to the variety of systematic branches of the subject, such as the geographies of landforms, of plants, of industry, of cities, or of language (the many topical fields and subfields might thus be identified as nested subsets of rows of the matrix $\mathbf{X}$).

The classical modes of thought, however, also led to a particular tradition in geography, the man–land tradition, in which the relationships between physical variables and human characteristics and activities were examined. In combination with the social Darwinism of the late nineteenth century, simple one-way studies were made of the effects of environment on man. These were later complemented by studies of the effects of man on environment, from which emerged much of the original thinking in the field of conservation. More recently the ancient dichotomy has been relaxed with, for example, studies of the effects of environmental perception on resource evaluation and decision making in resources management (Kates 1962) and with the adoption of a systems-analysis frame (Ackerman 1963).

Earth-science tradition. During the eighteenth century, geography was an integral and substantial part of natural philosophy. At that time geographical study embraced all aspects of the earth, air, and waters. Since then, however, most aspects of these studies have branched off as separate systematic sciences, and geography's earth-science tradition has been left with such concerns as the study of landforms and their evolution (geomorphology), descriptive climatology, and certain aspects of the geographies of soils, plants, and animals, together with the attempt to achieve some spatial synthesis of these in order to identify "natural environmental complexes." It is to this latter end that systems-analysis procedures have recently been employed in this research tradition (Chorley 1962).

Antecedents and stimuli

Prior to World War II few papers of a statistical nature had been published by geographers. Perhaps the only contributions worthy of note were Matui's (1932) fitting of the Poisson distribution to quadrat counts of settlements in a portion of Japan and Wright's (1937) discussion of Lorenz measures of concentration in the spatial case. However, two general antecedents can be distinguished, in addition to the pioneering contributions of workers in other fields: centrography and social physics. From the former came the idea of developing a special family of descriptive statistics for spatial distributions, and from the latter the recognition of certain classes of regularities in such distributions.

Centrography. During the early part of the twentieth century there was a lively debate among statisticians concerning such measures as the center of population. Part of the debate stemmed from publication by the U.S. Bureau of the Census of a piece entitled *Center of Population and Median Lines . . .* (U.S. Bureau of the Census 1923). Many articles were published, notably in the *Journal of the American Statistical Association* and in *Metron*, concerning the relative advantages of alternative centers, the center of gravity, the spatial median, and the center of minimum aggregate travel. (The U.S. Census Bureau's geography branch still reports on the center of gravity of the United States' population after each census.) This debate gradually subsided in the United States, but in the Soviet Union centrography flourished during the 1920s and 1930s. A centrographic laboratory was founded at Leningrad, under the auspices of the Russian Geographic Society, in 1925, and its director, E. E. Sviatlovsky, pursued studies of the "actual" and "proper" centers and the distributions of all manner of phenomena. However, the set of "proper" centers of economic activities prepared for the Gosplan of 1929 was at odds with the second Five-Year Plan, and as a result, the laboratory was finally disbanded. Porter (1963) provides a fairly complete bibliography of the relevant literature on centrography. Recently, the Israeli statistician Bachi (1963) has attempted to revive centrography, with the development of a variety of measures of dispersion and association of spatial distributions. Current interest within geography is slight, however, except as embraced by the social physicists (Stewart & Warntz 1958).

Social physics. The attempt to describe human phenomena in terms of physical laws has a long history in every social science [*see* RANK–SIZE RELATIONS].

In geographical studies this has been expressed in two major ways: (1) by use of "gravity models" to describe spatial interaction; and (2) by use of "potential models" as general summaries of interdependency between all places in large areas. Such models are said by their advocates to summarize a wide variety of social and economic distributions in economically advanced societies. Gravity models were first used in a relatively formal way by E. G. Ravenstein, in his seminal study "The Laws of Migration" (1885; 1889). Thereafter, these models found wide application, for example, in marketing geography—Reilly's "law of retail gravitation" (1931)—and in urban transportation studies describing interzonal travel. Carrothers (1956) reviews this work and the basic postulate that interactions or movements between places are proportional to the product of the masses and inversely proportional to some exponent of distance: that is, $I_{ij} \propto M_i \cdot M_j / d_{ij}^x$. Such gravity analogs were generalized by the astronomer J. Q. Stewart (1947) to the case of the potential surface, which simultaneously describes the interactions of each place and every other. Thus, the potential at any point i is given by

$$P_i = \sum_{j=1}^{j=n} (P_j / d_{ij}^x).$$

The surface is interpolated from such measures for a sample set of points. There is still considerable interest within geography in social physics (Stewart & Warntz 1958), and new applications are continually being developed. Mackay (1959), for example, used gravity models to translate the depressing effects upon telephone communications of the French–English language boundary in Canada and of the United States–Canadian political boundary into their physical-distance equivalents, thus showing how social space can be transformed into the metric of physical space. Similar applications are to be found in all branches of cultural geography today.

Pioneering contributions from elsewhere. Workers in other fields provided several significant examples of the application of statistical methods to geographic problems, identified the major statistical problems of regional analysis, and prepared the first text on statistical geography, thereby doing much to set the pace and tone of statistical geography today. A statistician, M. G. Kendall (1939), for example, showed how principal-components analysis could be used to develop a multivariate index that would portray the geographical distribution of crop productivity in England. M. D. Hagood (1943), an agricultural statistician, used multiple-factor analysis to define multivariable uniform regions. An economist, C. Clark (1951), showed that the negative exponential distribution fitted population density patterns within cities. G. K. Zipf (1949), a philologist, developed the rank–size distribution of cities. A mathematical social scientist, H. A. Simon (1955), showed the bases of this distribution in simple stochastic processes, and sociologists found that a repetitive three-factor structure characterized the social geography of cities (Berry 1964*b*; 1965). G. U. Yule and M. G. Kendall ([1911] 1939) identified the problem of *modifiable units*: if data are of areas rather than at points, results of any analysis will be in part dependent upon the nature of the areal units of observation utilized. W. S. Robinson (1950) provided the relevant relationship between individual and ecological (areal, set-type) correlations, subsequently extended by Goodman (1959) in the context of ecological regression. A second problem, that of *contiguity*, or spatial autocorrelation, has been examined by Moran (1948) in the nominal case and by Geary (1954) more generally. Geary also applied his measures of contiguity to evaluating lack of independence of residuals from regression in studies of spatial association. These studies are reviewed in *Statistical Geography* (Duncan et al. 1961), the first general book in the field, written by sociologists. Further examination of autocorrelation in spatial series is to be found in "Spatial Variation" (Matérn 1960), a major contribution to areal sampling by a mathematician. Spatial analysis remains basic to quantitative plant ecology and to epidemiology, and from these fields have come many of the ideas used today in the study of pattern in point distributions and of spatial diffusion processes.

Statistical geography—1950 to 1965

Centrography, social physics, and external stimuli, facilitated by developments in computer technology that for the first time enabled the mass data of geographic problems to be handled conveniently, combined to stimulate workers in geography's spatial tradition to work quantitatively. The older forms of cartographic analysis provided firm bases for this development, and many of the early studies were simply quantitative extensions of analyses cartographically conceived and executed. Arthur H. Robinson (1962), a cartographer, for example, utilized correlation and regression analysis to improve the ways by which he could map spatial associations. McCarty and his associates (1956) used similar procedures to replace older cartographic means of comparison. Thomas (1960) showed the various ways in which residuals from regression could be treated cartographically so as to draw upon traditional geographical means of map analysis in model reformulation and refinement. King (1962) applied the "nearest-neighbor" methods of the quantitative plant ecologist to the study of pattern in point distributions, with, like the 1932 Matui study, expectations derived from the Poisson distribution. These represent but a few examples of the spatial studies concerned with distribution fitting as a means of studying spatial pattern or with uses of correlation and regression in studies of spatial association. Many other examples are to be found in uses of regression to fit gravity models and obtain the distance exponents for different phenomena (Carrothers 1956) or to fit negative exponential distributions to urban population densities and the like (Berry 1965).

These kinds of studies represent the beginnings, from which statistical geography has grown rapidly. Dacey and Tung (1962) have made major advances in point-pattern analysis, for example, by transforming the distribution-fitting exercise into an explicit hypothesis-testing frame, with relevant expectations derived from settlement theory. Curry (1964) views many urban phenomena as the outcome of known-probability mechanisms. The Swedish geographer Hägerstrand (1953) was the first to show that many spatial patterns might be considered as the outcome of diffusion processes that could be simulated, using Monte Carlo methods, and his work led to a burst of similar simulation studies in the United States (Morrill 1963).

New approaches to spatial analysis have also been developed. Most of the examples outlined above use scalar data. Garrison (1960) showed that the mathematical theory of graphs provided an excellent base from which to examine vector distributions, and Nystuen and Dacey (1961) extended his argument to the case of organizational regions, using graph-theoretic measures of accessibility of places to communications networks to define relatively independent subsets of relatively interdependent places. Tobler (1963) showed how

a generalization of map projections, traditionally studied by the mathematical geographer, could be used as the basis for mapping social, economic, cultural, or political space into physical space, as a further means for merging geographical applications of various statistical and mathematical methods with the more traditional means of geographical analysis. Finally, in addition to developments of the descriptive kind, statistical geography has extended its work to embrace investigations of a prescriptive nature. Garrison and Morrill (1960), for example, applied the techniques of spatial price-equilibrium analysis to determining what should be the patterns of interregional trade in wheat and flour in the United States. Other research workers are now much concerned with the procedures of spatial programming. Haggett (1965) has provided an excellent review of the substance of the first decade of quantitative work in the spatial tradition.

With the use of multivariate analysis, statistical geography has spread from the spatial tradition to that of area studies. A traditional geographic problem in this latter tradition is that of regionalization —the attempt to derive areas relatively uniform in terms of a complex of associated characteristics and also relatively different from other areas in terms of that complex. Such problems, involving mass-data analysis, were traditionally handled by overlaying maps. This earlier procedure has been replaced, however, by the use of the modern computer, applying such multivariate procedures as factor analysis to reduce many variables to a few factors representing "complexes" of associated characteristics, and the application of numerical taxonomy to get optimal classification (minimizing within-group variance) of observations into regions on the basis of the distances between observations in the factor space (Berry & Ray 1966). Output from the entire procedure of data analysis and reduction includes the complexes of characteristics that define "regional character," measures of the similarity of the observations, and the regions [*see* CLUSTERING].

Statistical work also characterizes the man–land tradition, largely by virtue of either simple correlation and regression studies that include physical variables, on one side, and cultural variables, on the other (for example, correlations of annual precipitation and population densities in the high plains), or through uses of probability theory. It is the latter, indeterministic type of study that represents new departures. Curry (1962*a*), for example, shows how livestock management in the intensive grassland-farming areas of New Zealand is related to probabilities of fodder availability, which in turn are derived from probabilities of requisite climatic conditions. Much of the basic research goes into establishment of the relevant probabilities, in this case, of the probabilities of repetitive events that play a central role in farm management. Kates (1962), on the other hand, examined relations of management of flood-plain property to flood hazards, rare events. He found management practices to be conditioned, not by reasonably precise evaluations of the situation, as in the case of the New Zealand farmers, but by a widely varying set of preconceptions, at variance with the actual probability mechanisms.

Work in the earth-science tradition of geography has, also, become statistical and ranges from the attempt to reformulate the geography of landforms generated by fluvial mechanisms in the framework of general-systems theory (Chorley 1962) through studies of climatic change as a random series (Curry 1962*b*) to the analysis of precipitation climatology using harmonic methods (Sabbagh & Bryson 1962) or to the development of linear models predictive of some characteristic through prior multivariate analysis, so as to satisfy the assumptions of the model ultimately to be produced (Wong 1963). There is today perhaps more work of a statistical kind in the earth-science tradition than in either the area-studies or man–land tradition.

Statistical geography—analysis of both the statistical and the mathematical kind—is to be found in all branches of geography today. However, in the methods utilized, certain differences between geography's four main research traditions are to be noted. In the spatial tradition, distribution fitting, correlation and regression analysis, uses of such methods as the mathematical theory of graphs, and prescriptive uses of spatial programming dominate, along with uses of probability mechanisms to study diffusion processes. The area-studies tradition relies upon multivariate analysis, particularly factor analysis, and upon numerical taxonomy, to facilitate mass-data analysis. In the man–land tradition, a neat contrast is to be noted between those of traditional deterministic outlook, who use regression methods, and those concerned with decision making in resources management, who focus upon probabilities of the a priori and a posteriori kinds. Finally, in the earth-science tradition those procedures that facilitate systems analysis have been those most rapidly adopted and used. At the end of World War II geography was nonquantitative. Statistical geography has played an integral, even critical, part in the transformation of geography into a modern social science in the postwar years.

BRIAN J. L. BERRY

[*See also* CARTOGRAPHY; CENTRAL PLACE; REGIONAL SCIENCE. *Other relevant material may be found in* CLUSTERING; FACTOR ANALYSIS; MULTIVARIATE ANALYSIS.]

BIBLIOGRAPHY

ACKERMAN, EDWARD A. 1963 Where Is a Research Frontier? Association of American Geographers, *Annals* 53:429–440.

BACHI, ROBERTO 1963 Standard Distance Measures and Related Methods for Spatial Analysis. Regional Science Association, *Papers* 10:83–132.

BERRY, BRIAN J. L. 1964*a* Approaches to Regional Analysis: A Synthesis. Association of American Geographers, *Annals* 54:2–11.

BERRY, BRIAN J. L. 1964*b* Cities as Systems Within Systems of Cities. Pages 116–137 in John Friedmann and William Alonso (editors), *Regional Development and Planning: A Reader*. Cambridge, Mass.: M.I.T. Press.

BERRY, BRIAN J. L. 1965 Research Frontiers in Urban Geography. Pages 403–430 in Philip M. Hauser and L. F. Schnore (editors), *The Study of Urbanization*. New York: Wiley.

BERRY, BRIAN J. L.; and RAY, MICHAEL 1966 Multivariate Socio-economic Regionalization: A Pilot Study in Central Canada. Unpublished manuscript.

CARROTHERS, GERALD A. P. 1956 An Historical Review of the Gravity and Potential Concepts of Human Interaction. *Journal of the American Institute of Planners* 22:94–102.

CHORLEY, RICHARD J. 1962 Geomorphology and General Systems Theory. U.S. Geological Survey, *Professional Paper* 500B.

CHORLEY, RICHARD J. 1963 Geography and Analogue Theory. Association of American Geographers, *Annals* 54:127–137.

CLARK, COLIN 1951 Urban Population Densities. *Journal of the Royal Statistical Society* Series A 114:490–496.

CURRY, LESLIE 1962*a* The Climatic Resources of Intensive Grassland Farming: The Waikato, New Zealand. *Geographical Review* 52:174–194.

CURRY, LESLIE 1962*b* Climatic Change as a Random Series. Association of American Geographers, *Annals* 52:21–31.

CURRY, LESLIE 1964 The Random Spatial Economy: An Exploration in Settlement Theory. Association of American Geographers, *Annals* 54:138–146.

DACEY, MICHAEL F.; and TUNG, TSE-HSIUNG 1962 The Identification of Randomness in Point Patterns. *Journal of Regional Science* 4:83–96.

DUNCAN, OTIS DUDLEY; CUZZORT, RAY P.; and DUNCAN, BEVERLY 1961 *Statistical Geography: Problems in Analyzing Areal Data*. New York: Free Press.

GARRISON, WILLIAM L. 1960 Connectivity of the Interstate Highway System. Regional Science Association, *Papers* 6:121–137.

GARRISON, WILLIAM L.; and MORRILL, RICHARD L. 1960 Projections of Interregional Patterns of Trade in Wheat and Flour. *Economic Geography* 36:116–126.

GEARY, R. C. 1954 The Contiguity Ratio and Statistical Mapping. *Incorporated Statistician* 5:115–145. → Includes four pages of discussion.

GOODMAN, LEO A. 1959 Some Alternatives to Ecological Correlation. *American Journal of Sociology* 64:610–625.

HÄGERSTRAND, TORSTEN 1953 *Innovationsförloppet ur korologisk synpunkt*. Lund (Sweden): Gleerupska Universitetsbokhandeln.

HAGGETT, PETER (1965) 1966 *Locational Analysis in Human Geography.* New York: St. Martins.

HAGOOD, MARGARET D. 1943 Statistical Methods for Delineation of Regions Applied to Data on Agriculture and Population. *Social Forces* 21:287–297.

KAO, RICHARD C. 1963 The Use of Computers in the Processing and Analysis of Geographic Information. *Geographical Review* 53:530–547.

KATES, ROBERT W. 1962 *Hazard and Choice Perception in Flood Plain Management.* Department of Geography Research Paper No. 78. Univ. of Chicago Press.

KENDALL, M. G. 1939 The Geographical Distribution of Crop Productivity in England. *Journal of the Royal Statistical Society* Series A 102:21–62.

KING, LESLIE J. 1962 A Quantitative Expression of Patterns of Urban Settlements in Selected Areas of the United States. *Tijdschrift voor economische en sociale geografie* 53:1–7.

McCARTY, HAROLD H.; HOOK, J. C.; and KNOS, D. S. 1956 *The Measurement of Association in Industrial Geography.* Iowa City: State Univ. of Iowa, Department of Geography.

MACKAY, J. ROSS 1959 The Interactance Hypothesis and Political Boundaries in Canada: A Preliminary Study. *Canadian Geographer* 11:1–8.

MATÉRN, BERTIL 1960 Spatial Variation: Stochastic Models and Their Applications to Some Problems in Forest Surveys and Other Sampling Investigations. Sweden, Statens Skogsforskningsinstitut, *Meddelanden* 49, no. 5.

MATUI, ISAMU 1932 Statistical Study of the Distribution of Scattered Villages in Two Regions of the Tonami Plain, Toyama Prefecture. *Japanese Journal of Geology and Geography* 9:251–256.

MORAN, P. A. P. 1948 The Interpretation of Statistical Maps. *Journal of the Royal Statistical Society* Series B 10:245–251.

MORRILL, RICHARD L. 1963 The Development of Spatial Distributions of Towns in Sweden: A Historical–Predictive Approach. Association of American Geographers, *Annals* 53:1–14.

MOSER, CLAUS A.; and SCOTT, WOLF 1961 *British Towns: A Statistical Study of Their Economic and Social Differences.* Edinburgh: Oliver.

NATIONAL RESEARCH COUNCIL, AD HOC COMMITTEE ON GEOGRAPHY 1965 *The Science of Geography: Report.* National Research Council Publication No. 1277. Washington: National Academy of Sciences–National Research Council.

NYSTUEN, JOHN D.; and DACEY, MICHAEL F. 1961 A Graph Theory Interpretation of Nodal Regions. Regional Science Association, *Papers* 7:29–42.

PATTISON, WILLIAM D. 1964 The Four Traditions of Geography. *Journal of Geography* 63:211–216.

PORTER, P. W. 1963 What Is the Point of Minimum Aggregate Travel? Association of American Geographers, *Annals* 53:224–232.

RAVENSTEIN, E. G. 1885 The Laws of Migration. *Journal of the Royal Statistical Society* Series A 48:167–235. → Includes seven pages of discussion.

RAVENSTEIN, E. G. 1889 The Laws of Migration: Second Paper. *Journal of the Royal Statistical Society* Series A 52:241–305. → Includes three pages of discussion.

REILLY, WILLIAM J. 1931 *The Law of Retail Gravitation.* New York: Putnam.

ROBINSON, ARTHUR H. 1962 Mapping the Correspondence of Isarithmic Maps. Association of American Geographers, *Annals* 52:414–429.

ROBINSON, W. S. 1950 Ecological Correlations and the Behavior of Individuals. *American Sociological Review* 15:351–357.

SABBAGH, MICHAEL A.; and BRYSON, REID A. 1962 Aspects of the Precipitation Climatology of Canada Investigated by the Method of Harmonic Analysis. Association of American Geographers, *Annals* 52:426–440.

SIMON, HERBERT A. 1955 On a Class of Skew Distribution Functions. *Biometrika* 42:425–440.

STEWART, JOHN Q. 1947 Empirical Mathematical Rules Concerning the Distribution and Equilibrium of Population. *Geographical Review* 37:461–485.

STEWART, JOHN Q.; and WARNTZ, WILLIAM 1958 Physics of Population Distribution. *Journal of Regional Science* 1:99–123.

THOMAS, EDWIN N. 1960 *Maps of Residuals From Regression: Their Characteristics and Uses in Geographic Research.* Iowa City: State Univ. of Iowa, Department of Geography.

TOBLER, WALDO R. 1963 Geographical Area and Map Projections. *Geographical Review* 53:59–78.

U.S. BUREAU OF THE CENSUS 1923 *Fourteenth Census of the United States; 1920: Center of Population and Median Lines and Centers of Area, Agriculture, Manufactures, and Cotton.* Washington: Government Printing Office.

WONG, SHUE TUCK 1963 A Multivariate Statistical Model for Predicting Mean Annual Flood in New England. Association of American Geographers, *Annals* 53:298–311.

WRIGHT, JOHN K. 1937 Some Measures of Distributions. Association of American Geographers, *Annals* 27:177–211.

YULE, G. UDNY; and KENDALL, M. G. (1911) 1958 *An Introduction to the Theory of Statistics.* 14th ed., rev. & enl. London: Griffin. → M. G. Kendall has been joint author since the eleventh edition (1937) and revised the 1958 edition. See especially pages 310–325 on "Correlation and Regression: Some Practical Problems."

ZIPF, GEORGE K. 1949 *Human Behavior and the Principle of Least Effort: An Introduction to Human Ecology.* Reading, Mass.: Addison-Wesley.

GEOPOLITICS

See GEOGRAPHY, *article on* POLITICAL GEOGRAPHY, *and the biographies of* KJELLÉN; MACKINDER.

GEORGE, HENRY

Henry George (1839–1897) grew up in Philadelphia. As the author of *Progress and Poverty* he became one of the most telling speakers for social protest anywhere in the world. His father was the son of an English immigrant who had succeeded as a shipper; his mother's family had settled in the city before the Revolution. His father, a Democrat, was a customhouse clerk and for some years a publisher of Episcopalian sunday-school books; he sought to cultivate in his family both Democratic and low-church loyalties. Politically, young Henry George differed from his parents in that he was strongly opposed to slavery and voted Republican during the Civil War and the early Reconstruction period. However, he never abandoned his Episcopalian sympathies: his lifelong belief in the triumph of justice secularized the millennial hope that he had learned as a youngster.

George's family had little money to spare, and he left school when he was only 13. However, the deprivations he suffered were no worse than those of any child in a large family on a white-collar income. He learned how hard life could be for workingmen when, at age 15, shipping to India as a cabin boy, he witnessed a sailors' mutiny. For George himself the trip was pure adventure. His next long voyage, in 1857, which took him to California, was also inspired by restlessness rather than financial need. It was not until he had been in California for about seven years and was responsible for supporting a wife and two children that his inability to find steady work as a printer made him directly aware of the desperation of poverty.

George's journalistic career began with a job on the San Francisco *Alta California* in 1865; subsequently he worked on several other San Francisco papers, the *Times*, the *Chronicle*, and the *Herald*. In the late 1860s he returned to the Democratic party and became an adviser to Henry H. Haight, the state's governor who was crusading against monopoly. Haight put George in charge of the Sacramento *Reporter*, a party organ, but in 1871 George returned to San Francisco as founder, proprietor, and editor of the independent Democratic *Daily Evening Post*. As a business venture (George's only one), the paper failed, but it was a journalistic success. It provided George with the first platform from which he was able to develop fully his critical and reformist ideas.

George's experience with journalists and journalism made him familiar with some of the problems of California's spectacular and troubled economy, but it was several years before he found the "solution" to these problems. When he was still a printer in Sacramento, James McClatchy, the famous editor of the Sacramento *Bee*, acquainted him with the nation's homestead policy and the frustrations of that policy. On the San Francisco *Times*, George fought against private domination of land ownership, arguing that as a legal entity the city of San Francisco had the true ownership of the land it occupied, by devolution of title from the king of Spain through the *pueblo* of San Francisco. This claim was put forward with some success to reduce the claims of land-grabbers and speculators.

While working for the *Herald*, George came face to face with a more general problem, that of technological monopoly. The paper sent him to New York to obtain contracts for telegraphing the news from the Associated Press by way of Western Union. The failure of the negotiations appeared to George to jeopardize the freedom of the press. Deeply disturbed, he experienced "a thought, a vision, a call," and dedicated himself to combat the evil and want he had observed in New York. A few months later he had a second "vision." Riding in the foothills above Oakland, he looked down on the flatland near San Francisco Bay, which the transcontinental railroad had fantastically increased in value. "Like a flash it came upon me that there was the reason of advancing poverty with advancing wealth. With the growth of population, land grows in value, and the men who work it must pay for the privilege" (quoted in *The Life of Henry George*, by Henry George, Jr. [1871–1900] 1906–1911, vols. 9–10, p. 210).

As early as 1870, when he attributed to every man a "natural right" to a parcel of the earth's surface, George had begun to convert his reformist convictions into economic formulas. In 1871 his pamphlet *Our Land and Land Policy* (1871–1900, vol. 8) appeared, which was sizable enough to be considered his first book. It is a classic of economic criticism. George denounced both the prodigality of the national government in giving away the arable domain and that of the California state government, which permitted speculators to acquire much of the best land. He reasoned that in spite of past errors the homestead policy could yet be made to succeed if oversize holdings already granted were reduced by land taxes or inheritance taxes. Although he still accepted private property in land as a useful institution, George began to insist that "in nature" there is "no such thing as fee simple in land." The following year, in the *Daily Evening Post*, he carried this crucial limitation on land ownership a step further: "The land of a country rightfully belongs to all the people of that country; . . . there is no justification for private property in land except the general convenience and benefit; . . . private rights in land should always be held subordinate to the general good" (Barker 1955, pp. 176–177).

Gradually George systematized his economic ideas. Some time in the 1860s in Sacramento he had attended a meeting on the protective tariff, a policy in which he had long believed, and he had made an impromptu speech *against* the tariff. Free trade thus became his first publicly announced economic doctrine, and one from which he never departed; in the *Post* he was to advocate it repeatedly and dogmatically.

He opposed land monopoly because it denied free and just access to the bounties of earth; concerning the new natural monopolies which had been created by technology he felt differently. He demanded in the *Post* that the latter be transferred from private to public ownership—railroads and telegraphs to be owned by the national government and gas and water systems by the cities. His goal was to turn from private to public advantage the benefits of all monopolies that were not artificial and deserving of destruction. His editorials favored trade unions, a policy of high wage levels (other California papers were deflationist), and a policy of reserving the arable domain to actual homesteaders. Although in many of these ideas he was stimulated by socialists, he rejected the general doctrine of socialism.

When *Progress and Poverty* (1871–1900, vol. 1) first appeared in 1879, in San Francisco, the academic profession of economics was inchoate in the eastern United States and had no existence whatever in California. Economic thought in the east followed mainly the British classical school; the American nationalist school, of which H. C. Carey had been the principal figure, was a minority movement among economists, but its influence on Republican and national policy gave it disproportionate importance. The new analytical and institutional economics, then rising in Germany, Austria, and England, was little known at the time in America, and known not at all to George. Therefore, when George used and adapted the terms and logic of Smith, Ricardo, and John Stuart Mill, he was moving in an accepted tradition, and when he rejected the wages fund doctrine and the iron law of wages, he was merely revising the tradition, much as Francis A. Walker in the United States, and Mill himself had done.

The central four-fifths of *Progress and Poverty* is essentially a syllogism. The first premise appears in Book III, "The Laws of Distribution." There George stated his proposition that economic rent, being a product of monopoly—usable land is by nature monopolistic, not something replaceable—always reduces wages and interest. The second premise occurs in Book IV; on the basis of observation, George asserted that modern industrialism increases rent and that, as resource sites and urban sites rise in value, rent flowing into private hands creates social inequity, depression, and poverty. From these two premises—the first, that the landowner inevitably takes from the laborer and the capitalist and the second, that with private land ownership rent increases exacerbate social injustice—George reasoned to his synthesis, "The Rem-

edy," presented in Book VI. It is the historic proposal to do away with private property in land, or at least with the private privileges of tenure. In the following three books, George spelled out the procedures involved in his "Remedy": either land might be nationalized, or there might be taxation that would transfer economic rent from the landholder to the community (the latter alternative eventually became the "single tax"). The rent so placed at the disposal of the state could be distributed or invested, according to public interest.

The remaining one-fifth of the book contains the 15 pages of introduction and the 90 pages of conclusion, which may be called George's moral and religious sequence. There the author restated his paradox—that modern material "progress" actually widens the gap between the economically privileged and the unprivileged—and he stated his belief that a socially just civilization can be based only on a Christian and democratic conscience: "Association in equality is the law of progress."

It was in Europe that *Progress and Poverty* was first received with understanding, if not always with praise. Émile de Laveleye, the Belgian "socialist of the chair," discussed it with critical appreciation in the *Revue scientifique de la France et de l'étranger* (1880); Adolf Wagner of the University of Berlin was unfavorable; but Gustav Schmoller found freshness in the work, although he also found much to criticize. George wanted attention in the United States so much that even a highly critical review by William Graham Sumner in *Scribner's* pleased him.

George's early international reputation increased, however, not so much by reason of his writings as because of his involvement in public affairs abroad. By 1881 he had moved from California to New York, and the *Irish World* of that city sent him as correspondent to Ireland. Conditions in Ireland had not yet been improved by Gladstone's land reform, and George hoped to affect the situation as well as to report it. He distributed *Progress and Poverty* in Ireland, as well as a pamphlet on *The Land Question* ([1881] 1906–1911, vol. 3). He also went to London, where he established an uneasy relationship with H. M. Hyndman, the wealthy Marxist; made friends with Helen Taylor, the literary executor of John Stuart Mill, who said that Mill would have accepted George's ideas as an extension of his own; and became acquainted with Alfred Russel Wallace, the theorist of evolution who was also interested in land nationalization, and with other prominent men like John Morley and Joseph Chamberlain. George made the speech which George Bernard Shaw says converted him to social reform. George proudly assessed the long, semifavorable review of *Progress and Poverty* in the London *Times* as evidence that he was being taken seriously in high places.

The first visit to Europe led to four subsequent ones. The last one, in 1890, rounded out a trip that included a triumphant speaking tour in Australia. As far as the influence of George's ideas in the United Kingdom is concerned, the visits of 1883–1884 and 1884–1885 were the heyday. All the major British journals reviewed *Progress and Poverty*, and distinguished academic economists reacted to the book, albeit often negatively. Sir Henry Fawcett of Cambridge objected to George's opposition to compensating the landlords whose property rights he would destroy; Alfred Marshall, while admitting "freshness and earnestness" in George, concentrated a barrage of statistics on weaknesses in his findings about wages; Philip H. Wicksteed, a Unitarian minister and distinguished economist, acknowledged a major debt to George; and Arnold Toynbee, the young pro-labor Oxford economist, tried just before his untimely death to refute George in public lectures in London. In Scotland, George discovered many admirers: the Land Restoration League there shared his preference for land taxation as the best means of reform. Keir Hardie became the political link between George's impact on Britain in the 1880s and the modern British Labour party. During an Oxford visit, the students treated George outrageously; at Cambridge, things went better. As J. A. Hobson observed in 1897: ". . . Henry George may be considered to have exercised a more directly powerful formative and educative influence over English radicalism of the last fifteen years than any other man" (p. 844).

After his return from Ireland, George's activities in America took several directions. He wrote a series of articles for *Frank Leslie's Illustrated Newspaper* which was polemically directed against a previous series of articles on current problems written by Sumner for *Harper's Weekly*. In book form Sumner's articles became *What Social Classes Owe to Each Other*, the recognized classic of social Darwinist thought. George's articles, gathered and published as *Social Problems* (1871–1900, vol. 2), initially were better received than *Progress and Poverty*.

George also became active on the political scene. In 1886 a major New York City labor union persuaded him to be the Labor party candidate for mayor. He drew considerable support from early social gospelers, the labor unions, and recent immigrant voters. At the polls he came in second, close enough to the winning candidate to give credence to the charge that he would have won if votes had not been stolen. He did succeed in drawing maximum attention to his ideas and in consolidating his followers.

George's next venture was the single-tax reform. Although the phrase "single tax" does not appear in *Progress and Poverty*, the reform idea does. It was George's lasting conviction that land-value taxation could and should be used to transfer the whole product of economic rent from private owners to the community. A transfer of this kind would be politically easier to achieve in America than land nationalization and would have the same economic effect. George began using the term "single tax" during the mid-1880s, but it was a convert to his ideas, Thomas G. Shearman, a New York lawyer, who transformed the term into a slogan and the name of a reform movement. By 1888 single-tax meetings were being held in the principal cities on the eastern seaboard, in the Middle West, and in California. The long-term leaders of the movement —Louis F. Post, Tom Loftin Johnson, Warren Worth Bailey, William Lloyd Garrison II, Jackson S. Ralston, and Lawson Purdy—were already active, and before 1890, 130 single-tax organizations had appeared. The early movement was strained by an inner struggle between "single-tax, limited" men, like Shearman, who wanted only as much rent appropriated as was necessary for ordinary public services, and "single-tax, unlimited" men, like George, who wanted all the rent taken. After George's death, the proponents of "single-tax, limited" predominated. The movement narrowed, but it endured. During the early 1900s its program was incorporated into municipal reform programs and enactments, conspicuously in Ohio; and during the 1910s it influenced Wilsonian, Democratic progressivism. From 1887 to the present, through organizations which have varied from clubs to schools to endowments, the movement has continuously promoted land-value taxation and free trade.

During the 1890s, Henry George left the advocacy of the single tax largely in the hands of others, as he had earlier abandoned labor politics. With the exception of his round-the-world trip and the final campaign for the New York mayoralty in 1897, he gave his time to writing three books, which were essentially testaments. In *The Condition of Labor* ([1891] 1906–1911, vol. 3) he challenged Pope Leo XIII to permit Catholics to enter his movement; in *A Perplexed Philosopher* ([1892] 1906–1911, vol. 5) he fully dissociated himself from the materialism of Spencerian and likeminded belief in progress and repeated his program for land-value taxation; in *The Science of Political Economy* ([1897] 1906–1911, vols. 6–7), which he never completed, he tried, with new elaboration but without mastery of current modes of economic thought, to persuade readers that his economic theories were scientifically sound. These codicils never had the impact of his earlier books, although they too revealed George's passion for justice and freedom and his intellectual boldness and gift for persuasion. The final statements rounded out a dedicated and prophetic life.

CHARLES A. BARKER

[*See also* RENT; TAXATION, *article on* PROPERTY TAXES; *and the biographies of* MILL; SUMNER; TOYNBEE; WALKER; WICKSTEED.]

BIBLIOGRAPHY

BARKER, CHARLES A. 1955 *Henry George.* New York: Oxford Univ. Press.
CORD, STEVEN B. 1965 *Henry George: Dreamer or Realist?* Philadelphia: Univ. of Pennsylvania Press.
DE MILLE, ANNA A. [GEORGE] 1950 *Henry George: Citizen of the World.* Chapel Hill: Univ. of North Carolina Press.
GEIGER, GEORGE R. 1933 *The Philosophy of Henry George.* New York: Macmillan.
GEORGE, HENRY (1871–1900) 1906–1911 *The Writings of Henry George.* 10 vols. Garden City, N.Y.: Doubleday. → Volume 1: *Progress and Poverty.* Volume 2: *Social Problems.* Volume 3: *The Land Question; Property in Land; The Condition of Labor.* Volume 4: *Protection or Free Trade.* Volume 5: *A Perplexed Philosopher.* Volumes 6–7: *The Science of Political Economy; Moses: A Lecture.* Volume 8: *Our Land and Land Policy; Speeches, Lectures, and Miscellaneous Writings.* Volumes 9–10: *The Life of Henry George,* by Henry George, Jr.
HOBSON, J. A. 1897 Influence of Henry George in England. *Fortnightly Review* 68:835–844.
LAVELEYE, ÉMILE DE 1880 La propriété terrienne et le paupérisme. *Revue scientifique de la France et de l'étranger* 2nd Series 18:708–710. → A review of *Progress and Poverty.*
LAWRENCE, ELWOOD P. 1957 *Henry George in the British Isles.* East Lansing: Michigan State Univ. Press.
NEW YORK, PUBLIC LIBRARY 1926 *Henry George and the Single Tax: A Catalogue of the Collection in the New York Public Library,* by Rollin A. Sawyer. The Library.
NOCK, ALBERT J. 1939 *Henry George: An Essay.* New York: Morrow.
YOUNG, ARTHUR N. 1916 *The Single Tax Movement in the United States.* Princeton Univ. Press.

GERSON, JEAN DE

Jean Charlier de Gerson (1363–1429) was born at Gerson-les-Barbey in Champagne. He began his studies at the University of Paris in 1377, becoming a bachelor of arts in 1381 and a doctor of theology in 1392. For much of his life Gerson was a leading academic theologian of his university; he was made chancellor in 1395, succeeding his friend Pierre d'Ailly, with whom he was later to share the intellectual leadership of the conciliar movement.

Gerson was prominent in support of the attempt of the Council of Pisa, 1409, to end the great schism in the papacy by appealing to the allegedly superior authority of the General Council in church government. Later he was a member of the French delegation to the Council of Constance, 1414–1418, where he formulated his mature conciliarist theories. He had strongly alienated the Burgundian faction in French court politics by his strong condemnation of their use of the doctrine of tyrannicide to justify the murder of the anti-Burgundian Duke Charles of Orleans in 1408, and their hostility prevented him from returning to Paris; his surviving years were spent in Vienna and Lyons.

Although he wrote a number of academic theological treatises, in the scholastic manner, Gerson was primarily concerned with the active implementation of the demands of the Christian life. His considerable pastoral experience was gained in Paris and in Bruges, where he was for a time dean of the Church of St. Donatien. A large number of his sermons and pastoral and spiritual treatises, including influential writings on mysticism, survive. His preoccupation with the problem of how best to end the scandal of the papal schism grew out of his pastoral responsibilities.

Theories of church government. Gerson's ideas on church authority in general, and on the position of the General Council within the government of the church in particular, are among the most original and permanently influential parts of his works. He arrived at a full-blown conciliar position only after a slow process of disillusionment with the executive power of the papacy. It was as late as 1409, on the eve of the Council of Pisa, that Gerson first put forward the idea that in case of grave necessity the ordinary canon law of the church could be set aside. Gerson was here dealing with the problem of how a council to end the schism could be summoned without papal approval, hitherto considered essential by the canonists. He solved the difficulty by appealing to the principle of epikeia, or equity, which set aside the letter of the law in order to preserve its spirit (a concept going back via Aquinas and other Scholastics to Aristotle).

Gerson's mature conciliar theory is set forth in *De potestate ecclesiastica,* written in 1416–1417, during the Council of Constance. Gerson argued that the General Council, representing the totality of the faithful, was superior to any other institution in the church, including the papacy, even though, as the executive head of the church, the papacy had the prerogative to oversee its day-to-day governance. The theory of conciliar supremacy was not new; it had been discussed freely in the fourteenth century, but Gerson gave it its most comprehensive expression. His application of the theory of representation to the church, the most articulated social organism of the Middle Ages, is his enduring contribution to political science.

There has been some controversy about Gerson's position in the medieval philosophical and theological spectrum. He certainly had close affinities with the Ockhamist school, sharing with them a dislike of the excessive intrusion of man-made intellectual concepts into the data of revelation, a practice characteristic of the Scotists. But he referred freely also to the authority of pre-Ockhamist writers of the realist tradition, such as St. Bonaventure, St. Thomas Aquinas, and St. Albert the Great, as well as to the authority of patristic sources. The truth may be that Gerson's system was an eclectic one, evolved with a constant eye on the needs of practical Christian teaching.

JOHN B. MORRALL

[*Other relevant material may be found in the biographies of* AQUINAS; MARSILIUS OF PADUA; OCKHAM.]

WORKS BY GERSON

(1417) 1965 *De potestate ecclesiastica*. Volume 6, pages 210–250 in Jean de Gerson, *Oeuvres complètes*. Paris: Desclée.

Oeuvres complètes. 12 vols. Paris: Desclée, 1960—. → To be published in 12 volumes. Volumes 1–6 have been completed.

Opera omnia. 5 vols. in 4. Antwerp (Belgium): Sumptibus Societatis, 1706.

SUPPLEMENTARY BIBLIOGRAPHY

ARIÈS, PHILIPPE (1960) 1962 *Centuries of Childhood: A Social History of Family Life*. New York: Knopf. → First published as *L'enfant et la vie familiale sous l'ancien régime*. Contains a discussion of Gerson's pedagogical ideas.

COMBES, ANDRÉ 1940 *Jean Gerson: Commentateur dionysien*. Études de philosophie médiévale, Vol. 30. Paris: Vrin.

COMBES, ANDRÉ 1942 *Jean de Montreuil et le chancelier Gerson: Contribution à l'histoire des rapports de l'humanisme et de la théologie en France au début du XVe siècle*. Études de philosophie médiévale, Vol. 32. Paris: Vrin.

COMBES, ANDRÉ 1945–1959 *Essai sur la critique de Ruysbroeck par Gerson*. 3 vols. Paris: Vrin.

COMBES, ANDRÉ; MOURIN, LOUIS; and SIMONE, FRANCO 1951 Jean Gerson. Volume 6, pages 185–191 in *Enciclopedia cattolica*. Vatican City: The Encyclopedia.

CONNOLLY, JAMES L. 1928 *John Gerson: Reformer and Mystic*. Louvain, Université Catholique, Recueil de travaux d'histoire et de philologie, 2d Series, fasc. 12. Louvain (Belgium): Librairie Universitaire.

MORRALL, JOHN B. 1960 *Gerson and the Great Schism*. Manchester Univ. Press.

MOURIN, LOUIS 1952 *Jean Gerson: Prédicateur français*. Bruges (Belgium): De Tempel.

SCHWAB, JOHANN B. 1858 *Johannes Gerson; Professor der Theologie und Kanzler der Universität Paris: Eine Monographie*. Würzburg (Germany): Stahel.

GERVAISE, ISAAC

Isaac Gervaise, merchant and writer on economics, was a French Huguenot born in Paris after the mid-seventeenth century. He became a naturalized British citizen. In 1691 his father helped to finance the Royal Lustring Company of England (manufacturers of a fine black silk), and shortly thereafter both father and son became officers of the company.

Gervaise is known for only one work, *The System or Theory of the Trade of the World*, which was published in 1720 but in effect rediscovered by Jacob Viner only in 1935 (see Foreword to Gervaise [1720] 1954). It is a remarkable essay, formulating the first general equilibrium treatment of the international mechanism of adjustment. Gervaise's presentation marks a pioneer application of the "income" or "macroeconomic" approach to problems of international equilibrium and disequilibrium. It analyzes the process that produces disequilibrium and shows under what conditions adjustment is restored or maladjustment persists. Gervaise drew a distinction between disturbances which may arise from fluctuations in trade per se and those which may arise from comparative stability in prices. His formulation embraces domestic and international equilibrium; credit, inflation, and their effects on trade; the role of exchange rates; monopoly, tariffs, and the determinants of free trade.

Although Gervaise's work deserves more attention for its masterly theorizing than for its policy recommendations, it is nevertheless notable as one of the very few unambiguous expressions of a free-trade position in the English economic literature before Adam Smith. Gervaise argued in uncompromising terms that monetary instability and monopoly must be held in strict control. In an age when most writings on economics consisted of special pleading, Gervaise's scientifically objective work was a most unusual achievement. It is the more remarkable since Gervaise was an officer in a company that operated with special monopolistic privileges, and the public policy he advocated was in sharp conflict with his private interests. To be sure, it may have been easier and less noble for him to take an antimercantilist position in 1720, for in that year the Royal Lustring Company had lost its charter. Gervaise wrote in his preface: ". . . this System . . . hath the ill Fate to appear at a time, when I myself could wish it false" ([1720] 1954, p. 3). The statement seems to imply that while repeal was in the public interest it was injurious to his private interests.

Gervaise had not only the advantage of practical experience but also the capacity for general inquiry. A man of his experience and training was in a singularly fortunate position to examine the then existing international mechanism of adjustment, and he examined it with realistic detail and penetrating insight. Every sentence reveals incisive first-hand knowledge of the phenomena he described. The economy of words, the deep insight into the motivations of men and nations, and the vigor of his analysis all contribute to making Gervaise's book a profound study, the wisdom of which appears to grow with each reading.

JOHN M. LETICHE

[See also INTERNATIONAL MONETARY ECONOMICS; INTERNATIONAL TRADE.]

BIBLIOGRAPHY

GERVAISE, ISAAC (1720) 1954 *The System or Theory of the Trade of the World.* With a Foreword by Jacob Viner and an Introduction by John M. Letiche. Baltimore: Johns Hopkins Press.
LETICHE, JOHN M. 1952 Isaac Gervaise on the International Mechanism of Adjustment. *Journal of Political Economy* 60:34–43.
LETICHE, JOHN M. 1959 *Balance of Payments and Economic Growth.* New York: Harper.
MAINTRIEU, JEHAN 1909 *Le traité d'Utrecht et les polémiques du commerce anglais.* Paris: Pichon & Durand-Auzias.
VINER, JACOB 1937 *Studies in the Theory of International Trade.* New York: Harper.

GESELL, ARNOLD L.

Whatever else Arnold Gesell (1880–1961) may have accomplished, he made his name a household word in the United States: his books and articles on child development are legion, and some of the books were best sellers. For example, by 1943 *Infant and Child in the Culture of Today* had gone through 15 printings. At least one generation of American infants and preschoolers was reared according to the manuals provided by Gesell and his colleagues.

Gesell was born in Alma, Wisconsin; by the time he graduated from the local high school he was already deeply committed to science and the profession of teaching. At Clark University, where he earned his PH.D. degree in 1906, he came under the influence of G. Stanley Hall, one of the earliest psychologists to study child development. Gesell's early dedication to teaching, combined with his contact with Hall, probably pointed him in the direction that led to his fame as the "father of scientific child study."

After graduate study at Clark, Gesell spent several years as a teacher and principal in a public school, as a settlement worker, and as a normal-school and university professor. Finally, he found his niche at Yale, where he founded the Clinic of Child Development in 1911 and remained its director until his formal retirement in 1948. Gesell had already gained substantial professional status when he decided that medicine would give him greater depth as a research worker; accordingly, he studied medicine at Yale at the same time that he was an assistant professor, and he received his M.D. degree in 1915. Retirement 33 years later was only a formality for Gesell—he continued his clinical work and research for the Harvard Pediatric Study and at the Gesell Institute of Child Development.

Gesell's power to attract able, almost fanatically devoted disciples is well known to both scientists and laymen. Most of these followers bear his stamp indelibly, have reflected credit on his name and on their apprenticeship to him, and are themselves well known in the field of child development. Not until the 1940s did a group of Young Turks in the fields of child and clinical psychology come to consider Gesell only as a recorder of norms, neatly labeled and classified but without the explanatory power that is psychology's central interest.

Gesell did a basically respectable, and even a notable, job of combining clinical work with scientific observation of children. His photographic and one-way mirror studies of infants brought a new exactitude to the study of the young child. But his data about older children seem to have been less rigorously gathered. His coauthored books, e.g., *The First Five Years of Life* (1940) and *The Child From Five to Ten* (1946), tend to lose the individual child and to specify rather dogmatically an invariance and a genetic or constitutional universality of child development. These works simply assert the cyclical character of child development and underestimate the influence of the complex culture in which the child develops and learns. Development emerges as something mechanical: invariant, unchangeable, almost fatelike. The question may well be asked whether Gesell, with his rigid norms, his lack of individual variation, his strong emphasis on the constitutional, and his neglect of the cultural, has not hindered parents in their rearing of children more than he has helped them.

The Gesell Development Schedules were perhaps not intended as measures of infant intelligence, but they were widely so used and were long considered nearly infallible. In fact, however, they have failed, for the most part, to predict later intellectual development of children, individually or in groups. The harm that has been done by the trusting employment of the schedules is incalculable: many children have been denied adoption and condemned to prolonged and blighting custody in infant-care institutions because their Developmental Quotients were low (and, predictably, became lower the longer the children stayed in the institutions).

Gesell wrote with a bland, almost Olympian certainty about how children develop, and unless his writings are examined carefully they carry the implication that his conclusions are based on the careful study, over an extended period, of untold hundreds of infants and children. Even the fine print does not reveal precisely the actual number of subjects who were studied at different ages. A sympathetic biographer has referred to "follow-up examinations on about 175 cases, with referrals from different agencies and persons of 600 to 700, mostly of preschool age, and 1,000 or more guidance and observational contacts centering on nursery children" (Miles 1964, p. 55). The considerably less sympathetic Milton J. E. Senn, Gesell's successor at Yale, has pointed out that the sample for Gesell's basic 1925 survey was all white and numbered only 107 middle-class children from a single city in New England, while studies of older children were based on even smaller samples—for example, for six-year-olds, only eleven girls and seven boys (1955).

This is slight evidence, indeed, for statements describing the six-year-old as follows: "He tends to go to extremes . . ." (Gesell & Ilg 1946, p. 90), or "An outstanding characteristic of the 6-year-old is his meager capacity to modulate" (p. 92), or "He does not only smile,—he fairly dances with joy. He cries copiously when unhappy, kicks and shakes with his grief. Even during sleep he pitches his whole organism into his dreams. Hence the gross arousals of his nightmares, which come to a peak at the age of six" (p. 94). And so on and on, for 42 pages.

In sum, Gesell no longer appears the superman of child development that he was considered in his heyday, in the 1930s and 1940s. Serious questions must be raised about the quality of his social influence and the advice to parents by his disciples— for example, the flat statement by Louise Ames that the time of first tooth eruption is perhaps the best predictor of later reading success. Yet none can deny him a measure of greatness: he *was* the most scientific of the early students of infant behavior. He did give great impetus to moving "child study" toward "a *science* of child behavior." He fathered and fostered one of the great centers for child study. He trained some of the best workers in the field of child behavior and development and influenced (and still influences) them all. These are no mean achievements.

BOYD R. McCANDLESS

[*For the historical context of Gesell's work, see the biography of* HALL; *for discussion of the subsequent development of Gesell's ideas, see* ADOLESCENCE; DEVELOPMENTAL PSYCHOLOGY; INFANCY; MORAL DEVELOPMENT; SENSORY AND MOTOR DEVELOPMENT; SOCIALIZATION.]

WORKS BY GESELL

1940 YALE UNIVERSITY, CLINIC OF CHILD DEVELOPMENT *The First Five Years of Life: A Guide to the Study of the Preschool Child.* New York: Harper. → Contains "Early Mental Growth" by Arnold Gesell and "The Study of the Individual Child" by Arnold Gesell and Catherine S. Amatruda.

(1943) 1949 GESELL, ARNOLD; and ILG, FRANCES L. *Child Development: An Introduction to the Study of Human Growth.* Part 1: Infant and Child in the Culture of Today. New York: Harper.

(1946) 1949 GESELL, ARNOLD; and ILG, FRANCES L. *Child Development: An Introduction to the Study of Human Growth.* Part 2: The Child From Five to Ten. New York: Harper.

1952 Autobiography. Volume 4, pages 123–142 in *A History of Psychology in Autobiography.* Worcester, Mass.: Clark Univ. Press.

SUPPLEMENTARY BIBLIOGRAPHY

MILES, WALTER R. 1964 Arnold Lucius Gesell, 1880–1961: A Biographical Memoir. National Academy of Sciences, *Biographical Memoirs* 37:55–96.

SENN, MILTON J. E. 1955 The Epoch Approach to Child Development. *Woman's Home Companion* 82, Nov.: 40–42, 60–62.

GESTALT THEORY

The problem that gestalt theory confronts is that of an extended event, whether an experience or an action, that cannot be adequately described as a sum of smaller, independent events. Such an event is called a gestalt; this term can be translated as "form," "configuration," or "structure." Facts of this character were largely ignored in the atomistic psychology of the nineteenth and early twentieth centuries, although a few thinkers had begun to question this neglect.

The gestalt movement introduced a new approach to the treatment of psychological facts. It arose in Germany in the second decade of the twentieth century as a reaction against atomistic psychology. Its founders and pioneers were Max Wertheimer, Wolfgang Köhler, and Kurt Koffka. The first 25 years of its existence were a period of rapid development of ideas and of intensive investigation. Beginning with the 1920s it commanded wide attention in the psychological world. With the rise of Nazism the leading gestalt psychologists left Germany for the United States, and the subsequent course of the movement became, in a measure, part of the history of American psychology. [*See the biographies of* KOFFKA; KÖHLER; WERTHEIMER.]

The gestalt movement advanced a searching examination of the presuppositions of atomism; more important, it introduced an alternative conception that became the basis of many investigations and theoretical proposals. The earliest contributions of gestalt psychology were concerned mainly with problems of perception. Subsequently, its investigations extended to the areas of thinking, memory, and learning, and, more recently, to social psychology and the psychology of art; it also made contact with certain aspects of logic and ethics. As its investigations came to include new areas, gestalt theory stood revealed as a systematic orientation within psychology.

The source of the gestalt movement can be traced to one paramount concern. As a rule the events of mental life possess form, sense, and value; these are its striking characteristics. Yet, the prevailing scientific psychology contained virtually no reference to these attributes, and its accounts appeared correspondingly limited and barren. The customary reply to this stricture was that scientific procedure requires analysis into elements and therefore permits no other outcome. Accepting this reasoning, some thinkers concluded that important human phenomena and problems necessarily fall outside the reach of science. Others, among them the vitalists, appealed to higher and undefined agencies as sources of form and sense. Gestalt psychologists rejected such a solution on the ground that it adopted a questionable postulate about the demands of scientific investigation. An approach that fails to do justice to the most obvious facts of experience cannot, they held, be scientifically correct. They saw in this situation a challenge to re-examine the starting point of psychology.

Perceptual organization

The formulations of gestalt theory were first tested in perception. This was the most advanced part of systematic psychology and the area in which atomism was most strongly entrenched. In the psychology of the early twentieth century the elements of perception were simple and irreducible sensations, each having its unique quality and a constant relationship to a particular excitation of the sense organs. To explain the combinations of these isolated sensations (and their images), this psychology invoked the mechanism of association by contiguity, which, it held, brought order into the initial chaos of sensations. The goals of this psychology were to identify the elements of experience and the corresponding stimulus energies and to describe the manner in which the elements become associated, all based on the method of analytic introspection.

The issue was brought to a head when Wertheimer took the radical step of denying the reality of sensory elements as parts of perceptual experience. His study of apparent movement ([1912–1920] 1925, pp. 1–105), which marks the formal beginning of gestalt theory, provides a specific illustration of this thesis. The experience of motion was traditionally described as a sum of successive sensations of position, each corresponding to successive local excitations. Apparent movement results when two stationary objects in distinct positions—for example, two lines—are exposed in succession with a suitably small time interval between them; the observer sees one line moving from one to the other position in a manner indistinguishable from real motion. This phenomenon, which is at the basis of cinematography, was well known. Wertheimer pointed out that apparent movement is not a series of sensations but an effect of two stimulus events cooperating to produce a new, unitary outcome; perceived movement cannot be split up into successive stationary sensations. The static character of the external situation is not represented in experience, while the movement perceived has no counterpart in the objective situation. From the assumption that experience consists of having one sensation followed by another, one cannot account for the experience of change inherent in motion, a conclusion that applies equally to the perception of real motion.

A further and more important step in this development was the gestalt account of grouping, or unit formation, in perception. Visual experience consists of things that may, in turn, form groups; certain parts of the visual field appear to cohere and to form units that separate themselves from the surrounding space and from other units. The units of perception are trees, houses, persons—not innumerable sensory elements. It was the contribution of gestalt theory to show that the formation and segregation of units cannot be taken as self-evident, as it seems to common sense, but constitutes a central problem for the psychology of perception. The physical energies that are reflected from the points of an external object are entirely discrete; each hits the eye independently of the others, with no indication of whether each comes from the same object. They form a mere mosaic of stimuli that may be grouped in numerous ways and that provide no basis for the veridical organization of the percept. Unity of the physical object does not account for unity of the percept. How then do units emerge from discrete stimulation? Wertheimer described certain fundamental principles of grouping, or unit formation, in perception, among them those of proximity, similarity, closure, common fate, and good continuation (Wertheimer 1925). Working with discontinuous points or lines, he demonstrated that they tend to fall into groups, in accordance with relative spatial proximity and qualitative similarity; grouping also occurs in accordance with closure and good continuation. Wertheimer considered one principle, that of *Prägnanz*, fundamental and inclusive of the others. The principle of *Prägnanz* maintains that grouping tends toward maximal simplicity and balance, or toward the formation of "good form."

The facts of grouping establish, first, that sets of stimuli produce effects not derivable from the effects of the single stimuli. These effects, observable only in extended wholes, are dependent upon strictly objective conditions—namely, specific geometrical relations between stimuli. Second, the stimulus relations logically permit other groupings that do not in fact occur. Thus, the facts of grouping give evidence of selective principles according to which sensory data are organized, and the units of perception must therefore be considered products of organization or specific effects of processes resulting from certain relationships. Third, the same sensory conditions of grouping that usually give rise to veridical perception sometimes produce nonveridical perception. As the facts of camouflage show, physically real units are not necessarily perceived, and perceptual units sometimes arise in the absence of corresponding physical units. Fourth, Wertheimer concluded that he had identified primary principles of grouping in perception. He explicitly included past experience as one determinant of grouping but maintained that it cannot account for the other grouping tendencies that are themselves necessary conditions of learning. Last, the principles of grouping have a broad range of application; foremost is their capacity to explain object and form perception in general.

The treatment of part–whole relations, which is central to the gestalt position, may best be illustrated with the contribution of von Ehrenfels, who in 1890 described perceptual facts that are not a sum of independent local components. A property of a visual entity, such as roundness or symmetry, does not reside in its separate parts or in their sum; the same is true of the character of a temporal unit, such as a melody. Such properties are also transposable; a melody is recognized in a new key, although it shares no tones with that heard originally, and a square is recognizable as such when it is enlarged or reduced or when it appears in a new part of the field. There are innumerable facts of this order that refer to qualities in wholes only, among them those we call straight, closed, hard, smooth, translucent.

These form qualities, or *Gestaltqualitäten*, posed a problem for a psychology that took sensations as the sole contents of experience. Reversing the traditional formulation, Wertheimer proposed not only that a coherent whole has properties and tendencies not discoverable in its isolated parts but also that a part has properties which it does not possess when it stands alone or when it belongs to another unit. The character of a whole often determines whether one of its parts will be perceptible or not and what its properties will be. Given three dots in a linear array, one is perceived as middle, the others as ends; these properties are relationally determined and do not exist for the isolated components. This thesis of part–whole determination asserts that a part is a dependent property of its whole and thus draws a basic distinction between "part" and "element."

Furthermore, a host of discoveries demonstrated that the identical stimulation, at different points in time, of a given region can produce markedly different effects, depending upon the stimulation occurring in neighboring regions. The perceptual constancies and the so-called illusions revealed striking discrepancies between what is in fact observed and what should be observed if local sensations alone were the content of experience. The shapes and sizes of objects remain within limits approximately constant as their orientation and distance are varied, and the colors of objects tend to look the same when the conditions of illumination change widely. The same proximal stimulation may cause perception of bright or dark, of upright or tilted, of large or small, of motion or rest, of motion at a high or at a low velocity, depending upon other stimulus conditions. In an effort to bolster the classical position the interpretation advanced was that the sensations in question were in fact unchanged but were corrected by judgments or "unconscious inferences" formed in the course of past experience. A clearer and more consistent explanation of these and other facts could be given using the assumption that they were effects of perceptual organization initiated by specific stimulus relations. [See PERCEPTION, *articles on* PERCEPTUAL CONSTANCY *and* ILLUSIONS AND AFTEREFFECTS.]

Important support for the gestalt treatment of perception came from the demonstration by Rubin (1915) of the distinction between "figure" and "ground," between the thing-character of the former and the formlessness of the latter. A step in the same direction was the subsequent discovery by Michotte (1946) that particular conditions of successive stimulation produce the experience of causality. When figural units are perceived to move in relation to each other at certain rates, they are experienced as functionally connected; the observer refers to the motion of one object as the cause, while the motion of another object is perceived as the effect. Still other patterns of movements, which can also be clearly specified, produce the impression of animated movement. In the light of these and related findings atomism in perception ceased to be a viable position.

Physical and physiological gestalten. The concept of gestalt received a fundamental elaboration in the work of Köhler (1920; 1940). As a first step Köhler called attention to a striking similarity between certain aspects of field physics and facts of perceptual organization. He pointed to certain instances of functional wholes in physics that cannot be compounded from the action of their separate parts. There are macroscopic physical states that tend to develop toward an equilibrium and in the direction of maximum regularity. One can describe the local conditions in such functional wholes with any desired degree of precision, but they do not function as independent parts. Systems of this character, of which there are numerous instances, are physical gestalten. They meet the criteria of von Ehrenfels (1890) for a gestalt quality.

Following the lead of the phenomenal data, Köhler proposed that there are macroscopic field processes in the brain, involving interactions which account for the effects of grouping and segregation and for the operation of the *Prägnanz* principle. Traditionally, cortical action was described in terms of separate excitations conducted along insulated fibers to circumscribed areas. The relational determination of experiences implies that the neural processes corresponding to separate stimulations must influence each other across distances in a manner that depends on their relative properties.

Köhler proposed a fundamental change in the conception of cortical functioning. A region such as the optic sector may be considered an electrolyte; the processes within it occur according to physical laws of self-distribution rather than according to the microanatomy of neural networks. Local states of excitation are surrounded by fields that represent these states in their environment and interact with other local states similarly represented. On this basis Köhler put forward the hypothesis that there are physiological processes which are special instances of physicochemical gestalten and that these are the correlates of phenomenal gestalten.

Implicit in the preceding examination is the assumption of psychophysical isomorphism, or the proposition that brain processes include some structural features that are identical with those of organized experience. Isomorphism refers not to metrical but to topological correspondences; brain processes are assumed to preserve the functional relations of symmetry, closedness, and adjacency, not the exact sizes and angles of patterns projected on the retina. This formulation diverges from the widely accepted view that phenomenal and physiological events are lawfully correlated but have no further likeness between them. The postulate of isomorphism is intended as a heuristic guide to investigation. In this manner Köhler sought a unified explanation for facts in neurophysiology and psychology among certain facts of physics. [See NERVOUS SYSTEM, *article on* STRUCTURE AND FUNCTION OF THE BRAIN.]

Memory and association

There is a natural transition from the gestalt study of perception to memory. When a form has been perceived it may be subsequently recognized and recalled; thus, the products of perceptual organization are among the contents of memory. The persistence of past experiences requires a concept of memory traces; further, the resemblance between memories and original experiences implies that memory traces preserve the organized character of earlier processes. Gestalt studies of memory start from this assumption; a first effort to elaborate a theory of memory-trace action will be found in Koffka (1935).

The preceding formulations lead directly to one of the problems of memory—recognition. The facts of transposition to which von Ehrenfels first called attention imply the recognition of wholes or gestalten and, further, that recognition occurs on the basis of gestalt similarity and in the absence of identical elements in past and present situations. Since recognition depends upon the activation of specific memory traces and is highly selective, the gestalt proposal is that such memory-trace contact occurs on the basis of distinctive similarity, analogous to grouping by similarity in immediate experience. This formulation further implies that if the process corresponding to a present experience is to contact a corresponding memory trace, it must have its effect beyond its immediate locus and that neural conduction along insulated nerve fibers alone does not suffice to explain recognition. Thus, according to this account recognition depends upon an interaction that is relationally determined.

With respect to the concept of association two points are of main consequence. First, the gestalt account of perceptual organization was intended as a direct alternative to the interpretation that perceptual units are made up of associations between elements. Second, association theories have in practice all but abandoned the phenomena of perception; they tend to take the presence of perceptual units for granted and concentrate instead on connections formed between one unit and another. In treating these facts, one principle, that of association by contiguity, was increasingly singled out as basic. According to this principle, temporal contiguity is the crucial condition of association. In this account an association has the character of a bond that does not alter the terms it connects.

From the standpoint of gestalt theory the concept of an association as a mere bond is not a satisfactory basis of explanation. Processes in nature are as a rule relationally determined. In this connection Köhler (1929; 1941) proposed that an association is not a new process, but an aftereffect of organization and that it is dependent upon the relative properties of the respective terms. When two items are connected they form a unit and leave a corresponding unitary trace; subsequent excitation of a part of this trace will spread to the entire trace. Given this starting point there is no reason to single out the relation of contiguity, to the exclusion of others; all relations, such as those of similarity and good continuation, should bind events to each other. More generally, conditions favorable to organization should be conditions of association. Accordingly, the formation of associations and perceptual organization receive a unified interpretation. There remain unresolved issues in this area, but the available evidence supports the conclusion that relations other than contiguity exert pronounced effects on the formation of associations (Asch 1960). [*See* FORGETTING.]

Thinking

Two themes have been most prominent in the gestalt treatment of thinking: one concerns the occurrence of understanding or insight; the other, the occurrence of processes of discovery. Of these, understanding is the more general phenomenon; it occurs often in the absence of the discovery of solutions and provides a basis for them. To understand is to have an awareness of a required relation between immediately given facts. When such understanding is present the relation is experienced as "following from" the given facts—that is, the nexus between them is itself understandable. Given two premises and a conclusion the latter either develops out of the former or contradicts it. Such relations, which have the character of "if *A*, then *B* and only *B*," contrast most strongly with the association between heterogeneous facts; the terms and their relation form a unit all parts of which are dependent upon one another. An understandable relation between two terms is not a third term added to them; given any two of the parts the third is demanded. The relation in question is thus a dependent part-property of a whole. The first point of the gestalt account of thinking is that understanding or insight in the sense here described pervades human experience and that no thinking is possible in its absence. Understandable relations have the character of requiredness, or "oughtness." This is the outstanding trait of facts of aesthetics and ethics as well as of logic; in each of these realms requiredness is relationally determined, being a property of an interdependent situation. Thus, the concept of value becomes related to that of organization. One observes an important aspect of requiredness when a situation is incomplete; in such cases the gap has particular properties that produce tendencies toward completion in accordance with the character of what is given. Gestalt theorists have sought to explore the conditions of requiredness out of a concern for establishing whether there are ethical invariants; these invariants would provide an alternative to a relativistic foundation for ethics.

Connections between concrete empirical events are not, however, understandable in the same way as logical connections. That heavy bodies fall when dropped cannot be automatically deduced; the underlying functional connections are hidden, and conclusions concerning them must be based on induction. Accordingly, the prevailing tendency of psychology since David Hume has been to stress the role of purely factual regularities in our knowledge of causal action. Gestalt psychology proposes that empirical events too are often related in ways that are structurally simple and that these relations facilitate the learning of the causal interplay. Duncker (1935) has pointed out that there are far-reaching correspondences between the phenomenal properties of causes and of their effects. They are often coincident in space and time and thus stand out against a background of more indifferent events. A sound is heard where an object is seen to strike; a sheet of paper acquires a crease where it is folded; fire burns shortly after a match is applied to an object. There are also pronounced similarities of content and form between cause and effect. The shape of a footprint corresponds to that of a shoe; a hot object transmits heat to its surroundings; a wet object moistens things in contact with it. Further, variations of cause often produce parallel variations of effect. The accelerated rhythm of the motions of knocking parallels the changing rhythm of the sounds produced; the stronger the push one applies to an object, the faster and farther it moves. These relations make possible a systematic ordering of empirical facts, although the relations are not fully intelligible.

Gestalt psychology treats productive thinking as the development of new structures or organizations. The discovery of a solution begins with a situation and a goal that cannot be directly reached; what requires explanation is how the gap is bridged. The principal point of the gestalt account is that the operations of thinking do not occur piecemeal but are effects of organization and reorganization. First, thinking is a directed process based on an initial view of a coherent but incomplete situation. The direction arises from the problem itself—more accurately, from the gap between the view of the given conditions and the goal. The urge to overcome the difficulty creates the tensions and vectors that lead to a re-examination of the materials and of the problem. This formulation asserts a distinction between an aggregate of independent facts and a structure; there can scarcely be productive thinking when the possibility of grasping a principle is excluded. Further, under the stress of the initially incomplete view the material is reorganized; parts and relations previously unnoted or in the background emerge, often abruptly, analogously to the reversal of perceptual forms, and parts previously separated become united. These changes in the meaning of parts, including changes of relation and direction, produce the transition to a new view that has greater coherence. From the outset the steps are guided by the main lines of the problem and

are taken with reference to each other. The operations of centering and recentering, of separating fundamental from peripheral features, spring from the whole character of the situation or from a structural view of the gap and its stresses. These formulations account for the fact that the organization of the problem situation often changes before the more detailed steps can be elaborated.

The preceding account represents only some first steps toward a theory discovery. There is at this time no satisfactory explanation of the occurrence of sudden reorganization that favors the emergence of a solution. Reference to understanding or insight does not constitute an explanation, since these are descriptive terms that do not clarify the underlying operations.

The treatment of thinking in gestalt psychology was formulated in explicit opposition to the associationism of the early decades of the twentieth century, which excluded reference to understandable relations and, indeed, to relations generally. Associationism postulated that connections between psychological events are neutral and devoid of meaning—that is, given events A and B, nothing in the character of A points to B rather than to any other event. Associationism also excluded reference to operations of organization and reorganization. Accordingly, it described the emergence of changed views and of new solutions in terms of the reshuffling of associative chains, the components of which remain constant. This approach defined knowledge as a repertoire or inventory of specific data and of connections between them. From the standpoint of gestalt theory the striking powers of thinking seem to disappear under the associationistic treatment. Thinking involves functions different from association, although it draws some of its materials from associations. No purely contingent associations, however strong, can provide understanding.

Another point at issue is the role of past experience in the process of solution. Associative accounts treat thinking mainly as a product of past experience. Gestalt theory does not question the contribution of past experience but asserts that thinking involves more than recall. Since innumerable associations lead out from a given problem situation, a solution cannot arise on the basis of associative reproduction alone. Some selection must take place. Further, it is questionable whether the products of past experience enter into thinking in unaltered form; they may have to be reorganized in order to meet the demands of the problem. Nor may one neglect the fact that recalled material is itself often the product of understanding that has occurred in the past; reference to past experience does not exclude understanding. Finally, the solution of a problem may not even require recall of added facts; this is the case when the appropriate facts are given as part of the problem. Conversely, one may fail to solve a problem under these conditions.

In recent decades a revised associationism has attempted to encompass the organized character of thinking operations within the framework of a stimulus–response analysis. Realizing the inadequacy of the earlier one-stage associative paradigm, it has postulated the presence of intervening mediational processes, which would bridge the gap between apparently noncontiguous events (e.g., Osgood 1953). The inferred mediating events in question are assigned the same properties as overt stimulus–response connections. Their function is to introduce further associative links between overtly observable connections and, thus, to provide a replacement for cognitive operations. This elaboration admits no organizing principle other than that of association; it continues to adhere to a linear model of thinking operations, treating them as chains of stimulus–response connections. It is too early to evaluate this effort; at this time it is not clear how it can accommodate the presence of rules or principles, the seeing of given materials in a new way, or the achieving of a view in terms of which one can understand a mass of detail.

The psychology of thinking touches upon questions of education, of teaching and learning, since there is no sharp separation between discovering a solution and understanding it when it is explained. This aspect has been treated most extensively by Wertheimer in *Productive Thinking* (1945). In this connection he has contrasted learning by drill and by understanding. A pupil may memorize the steps of a solution and reproduce them without error, but if he has failed to understand, he will become helpless or make senseless errors when the details of the problem are changed. If he has understood the relation of the steps to the goal, he will be able to adapt the solution to a new set of conditions that retains the essential structural relations. Indeed the ability to produce the necessary transpositions constitutes an operational test of understanding (see, e.g., Katona 1940). In teaching and learning, as in the discovery of a solution, to leave out the relation of a given fact to the whole is to take away the essentials of thinking. Educational practices that stress piecemeal preoccupation with details, exactness of repetition, and instantaneous response tend to be inimical to thinking. [*See* LEARNING; PROBLEM SOLVING; THINKING.]

Social psychology

Gestalt theory has in recent decades provided the starting point for a number of systematic efforts in social psychology, among them those of Lewin and Heider. The following are some selected examples of problems studied from this point of view.

(1) Social action in man depends upon the capacity of the participants to perceive and understand one another. These operations involve reference to the mental processes of others; in everyday life one makes sense of the actions of persons by referring to their feelings, perceptions, intentions, and ideas. Yet, it is widely accepted that there is no access to these internal events in others, that one can only observe their actions, and that these actions need not be expressive of internal events. How, then, is one to explain the conviction that another is in pain or is angry or that his voice is charged with sorrow? According to one account such conclusions can only be reached indirectly, on the basis of association and inference by analogy with one's own experiences. A more behavioristic account disregards reference either to the experience of the observer or of the observed; the actions in question are said to acquire significance on the basis of association with other actions and environmental conditions. Each of these formulations treats the perceived actions of others as initially neutral. Gestalt theory proposes a fundamentally different conception of the relation between action observed in others and their experience, holding that these are structurally closely similar. Fearfulness, joy, hesitation, boldness are expressed in action as much as in the dynamics of experience. The outward form of an action is an expression of underlying forces. If so, understanding the mental life of another person is not primarily a question of generalizing from the physical to something unrelated to it.

Perception and understanding of other persons depend to a marked degree on the observation of their expressive, or physiognomic, characteristics. For gestalt theory physiognomic facts are a crucial part of perception (Arnheim 1954; Koffka 1940). Percepts, including those that are inanimate and static, are rarely neutral. One perceives in visual and auditory patterns the dynamic characteristics of tension, balance, rhythm; these are indeed the primary contents of everyday perception. Expressive qualities depend upon the pattern of an entire situation; they tend to be lost when one concentrates on separate parts. They are often more immediately and more vividly observable than shape and color; the clouds that hang in the sky are ominous as well as dark, a face is alert as well as elongated. Expressive qualities are functionally important, since they determine approach and withdrawal. Gestalt theory assumes that certain patterns and movements are initially perceived as inviting or repelling, cheerful or somber; further, the perception of identity of expressions across different media and modalities depends upon similarity of form qualities. Gestalt theory therefore opposes theories that try to derive the expressive character of a whole from those of its separate components. Illustrative of this is the effort to arrive at the expressive characteristics of a face from an analysis of its individual parts or to read character from handwriting based on a list of isolated characteristics. [See EXPRESSIVE BEHAVIOR.]

(2) The proposition that each individual acts in accordance with his wishes and needs has received a particular interpretation in contemporary psychology—namely, that human relations are without exception based on self-interest. So incontrovertible has this assumption appeared that it has dictated that membership in groups and even concern for others and action in behalf of others be treated as derivatives of self-interest. Gestalt psychology calls attention to the far-reaching ambiguity and vagueness in this position. It begins with the observation that the phenomenal self is only one part of the phenomenal field. The world that is represented in the experience of each person and that spurs him to action includes far more than the self; in fact, the self constitutes a small portion of it. The question then arises of specifying the kinds of relations that obtain under different conditions between the phenomenal field and that part of it we call the self; this is a special case of part–whole relations. Seen in this light it becomes evident that the customary formulation confuses the phenomenal self with the entire psychological field. In consequence the correct—and tautological—proposition that motivational vectors have their source in the individual is equated with the quite different proposition that the vectors arise from the self. The latter proposition too is often correct, but its universal validity is no longer self-evident. In perception one finds that under certain circumstances the coordinates of the surroundings become the coordinates for the self—that is, that the self is perceived and localized with respect to the surroundings, and not conversely. Thus, there are conditions that induce a person to perceive himself in motion when he is stationary or tilted when he is upright.

By analogy it becomes necessary to ask whether there are not also motivational conditions in which the individual feels and is moved to act as part of the social field, subject to its demands. In the light of this analysis it is dogmatic to presuppose that acting in accordance with the needs of others or with the demands of a situation must be interpreted as a version of self-centeredness. There may rather be circumstances when self-centered action is unnatural. Actions called right and wrong are particularly instructive in this connection. They cannot be simply equated with preferences since they often go against personal inclination, nor are they always in accord with convention or social approval. The issue as restated becomes a factual one: under what conditions does action become self-centered, and under what conditions is it in accordance with needs and requirements that are located outside the self and to which the self is responsive? No propositions of gestalt psychology prescribe an answer to this question; rather, the example illustrates the role of phenomenological analysis and of a concern with part–whole relations in the formulations of a psychological problem. [See SYMPATHY AND EMPATHY.]

(3) Forming an impression of a person has a place of obvious importance in social psychology. Is it adequate to say, in accordance with an atomistic interpretation, that to have an impression is to possess a number of facts about a person, to know that he has these and these characteristics? Certain initial observations stand in the way of such a conclusion. An impression of a person appears in some sense unitary; also, certain aspects are felt to be more fundamental than others. To this one must add that a change in one characteristic may alter the character of the entire impression. Thus, the discovery of one new fact about a person may have drastic repercussions upon one's entire view of him; one may be compelled to reorganize one's view and to conclude that one had not really known him. Furthermore, even when one "knows" a man, at some point one may realize, without the benefit of new information, that his characteristics are really organized quite differently than one had originally supposed and that one had missed the main point about him.

These observations form the basis of a gestalt theory of impression formation that emphasizes the interrelations among observed characteristics and the manner in which these characteristics modify each other (Asch 1952). An impression has the characteristics of a structure the parts of which cooperate to produce a particular organization. From these initial assumptions the following, more specific propositions emerge from investigation: (*a*) The items of knowledge about a person do not remain isolated but interact and mutually alter each other. (*b*) The interactions depend upon the properties of the items in their relation to one another. (*c*) In the course of interaction the characteristics group themselves into a structure in which some become central and others dependent. (*d*) The resulting interdependence creates a unitary impression which tends to be subjectively completed in the direction of becoming more consistent and coherent. (*e*) It follows that a given item of information or a characteristic functions as a dependent part, not as an element. (*f*) If so, the "same" trait in two persons is not necessarily the same. The issue under discussion is not limited to persons; the same questions arise when one considers the knowledge of any extended and interrelated situation, whether it concerns the perceived character of a group or the structure of an attitude. [*See* PERCEPTION, *article on* PERSON PERCEPTION.]

(4) Acts and utterances of persons and groups are constantly judged and evaluated; how these judgments are made is a problem that has attracted attention. One general observation has been the starting point of considerable investigation: a given act or assertion is often differently evaluated depending upon its source. Thus, one may accept an opinion from one person or group but reject it when it comes from another. The customary explanation of this effect has been in terms of prestige suggestion; a judgment or opinion is said to be changed by the attachment to it of positive or negative prestige. Of theoretical consequence is the assumption that an object of judgment is one thing, its evaluation another, and that these separate factors can be connected at will to produce an arbitrarily desired outcome. An alternative interpretation assumes that actions and evaluations are relationally determined (Asch 1952). Specifically, an act or assertion does not retain a fixed character when it is related to two different sources but functions as a dependent part of its context, altering in content and significance as it is referred to different sources. If so, the datum that is accepted is not psychologically the same as that which is rejected, and the effect in question does not concern primarily a change in the evaluation of an object but of the object being evaluated, not a change of response to a fixed condition but a change in the condition to which one is responding. This interpretation diverges importantly from the usual one for both critical and uncritical judgments. [*See* PERCEPTION, *article on* SOCIAL PERCEPTION.]

(5) A formally similar problem arises at a more comprehensive level in the psychological interpretation of culturally determined values. Thinking must guard against two opposed dangers: taking profound cultural differences too lightly and accepting their incommensurability too readily. Behavioristic learning psychology derives cultural values from the operations of conditioning and reward. The most striking application is to ethical judgments, which are said to be learned by the application of reward and punishment. From this standpoint it follows that the same act evaluated as morally right by one society may well be regarded with indifference or as wrong by another. Gestalt theory introduces several considerations that this approach ignores. First, ethical tendencies may be considered vectors or requirements that follow directly from observation of specific conditions. Second, the relation between conditions having a specific character and the ethical judgment they generate is invariant. This postulate would suffer disproof if it were shown that a situation possesses the same cognitive character for those who judge it differently. However, much evidence in support of ethical relativism fails to consider the definition of the situation, which often varies considerably as a function of differences in knowledge and factual assumptions. Indeed, on the assumption that there are invariant principles of right and wrong, differences of situational meaning must produce differences of evaluation. There is no reason to expect that two people would value identically what they see and hear if they do not see and hear identically, even though they are facing the same objective conditions. A limited conclusion from the available evidence is that the range of cultural relativism is substantially narrowed when one takes the situational context into account. From this examination emerges the following reformulation of the problem of ethical relativism: can one attach different or opposed evaluations to a situation that has a constant cognitive content? Without prejudging a full answer to this difficult question, it appears that such an outcome is far from certain. [*See* CULTURE, *article on* CULTURAL RELATIVISM; ETHICS.]

Major issues

An examination of the main themes of gestalt theory may clarify their mutual relevance and their relations to other directions within psychology and may point to issues that remain unsolved.

Parts and wholes. The most general goal of scientific inquiry is to describe and explain the interdependence of observed events. This has been the aim of both atomistic and gestalt theories in psychology; they are essentially formulations about operations or modes of dependence. Given the atomistic assumption of discrete elements, the connections formed between them are neutral or independent of the terms they join. It follows from this starting point that ordered events, whether simultaneous or successive, are summations of components. This beginning has the appeal of simplicity; it reduces the operations underlying the coherence of phenomena to a bare minimum—namely, to traditional associations. The gestalt treatment of dependence takes as its starting point the evidence of experienced wholes. The observation that a change at one point of a coherent whole creates systematic changes at other points suggests that there is mutual determination of parts within a whole and that there are processes of interaction which depend upon relations between the parts. The recognizability of transposed wholes provides strong support for this formulation. Further, since parts of wholes often have a hierarchical character, their structure is not adequately described in terms of a sum of relations.

The following examples illustrate the point at issue. A child who places a solid geometrical form in a form board appears to be guided by similarity of shape between the object and the area to which he fits it. A gestalt account of this performance would begin with the primary role of perceived similarity in steering the action. An associationistic account finds no place for the direct effect of such an intrinsic relationship; instead it begins with operations based on contiguity and derives the effects of similarity from them. The following quite different illustration bears upon the same point. How can one characterize the relation between an emotional experience and the apprehension of the conditions that produce it? It is customary to suppose that the provoking conditions function as a spark or trigger that releases the emotional effect. In this formulation the connection between the antecedent and consequent conditions is again neutral; nothing in the properties of the former accounts for the properties of the latter. The alternative gestalt account proposes that an intrinsic relation connects the respective events: we flee from the horrible and laugh at what is amusing. More generally, a clarification of interdependence among events may involve more than the statement that A is followed by B; it requires an explanation of how one event grows out of another, how the character of one determines the character of the other.

Despite its pivotal position, the notion of part–whole determination has not been fully clarified. Some students have objected to the gestalt claim that parts do not enter into wholes with a fixed character, on the ground that a whole can alter a part only if the latter has definite properties of its own. This formulation raises no logical difficulties but it does point toward problems that await investigation. Gestalt psychologists have concentrated on two extreme types of conditions: those that give rise to highly coherent units and, in contrast to these, conditions that approximate to a mere aggregate of data. There is doubtless a multiplicity of intermediate instances deserving of study that would clarify the kinds of part–whole relations that occur. Thus, under certain conditions the parts of a unit are clearly perceived and are available in a relatively independent way; the omission of a part may have quite distinct effects depending upon the kind of unit in question.

A difficulty has also arisen over the formulation that an additive analysis is not adequate to account for facts of organization. One generally attempts in investigation to relate a given effect to a number of conditions. The customary procedure in psychology is to trace the total effect to effects produced by pairs of variables—A and B, A and C, B and C, etc.—and to derive the final outcome from an accumulation of these separate effects. This mode of analysis slights the fact that once interaction has occurred between A and B, neither of these is any longer present in its original form when one considers their interactions with C, etc. Given an organized context, the effect cannot be decomposed into independent strands; explanation requires a law of the mutually interacting forces taken as a whole.

Certain misconceptions concerning wholes and parts are probably less widespread at present than in the past. First, it had not been sufficiently understood earlier that experienced gestalten are not related to any possible gestalt characteristics of the objective conditions. These last, when considered as conditions of stimulation, are never gestalten; the consequences of organization on perceptual experience always transcend the conditions of stimulation. Second, emphasis upon wholes does not imply an indiscriminate dependence of facts upon each other or the assumption that there are no facts independent of each other. Wholes are self-limiting, since segregation is the counterpart of unit formation. Third, gestalt psychology is not opposed to analysis. The position it has taken is that analysis is fruitful provided it deals with the units and natural parts actually found in experience. Fourth, the most general implication of whole–part determination is that crucial characteristics of local facts are ignored unless one takes into account their place within a wider scheme. In the early days of gestalt psychology there was a tendency to neglect the converse point, later investigated by Köhler (1958), that a larger organization may suppress the individuality of its parts by obscuring its suborganizations. Last, whether a given experience or action is a sum of components or a product of organization is a wholly empirical question. Thus, the issue of "relational," as against "absolute," choosing in discrimination learning is to be resolved by evidence, as is the question whether an impression one forms of a person consists of a sum of data or of their transformation into organized form. The contribution of gestalt psychology to these problems has been to formulate the alternatives more sharply and, where possible, to devise procedures for testing them.

The principle of "Prägnanz."   No proposition is more characteristic of gestalt thinking than the principle of *Prägnanz*: experienced perceptual wholes tend toward the greatest regularity, simplicity, and clarity possible under the given conditions. This principle also applies to certain physical systems, and Köhler in particular has applied it to the cortical correlates of perception. Two opposed outcomes derive from the tendency of experienced gestalten to turn into particularly simple and clear structures: depending upon given conditions a gestalt will have either a maximum articulation of its parts, or it will be highly simplified. It is also implicit in these formulations that ambiguous conditions, which do not fully prescribe the perceptual outcome, produce a special direction toward the completion of gaps and the resolving of contradictions, so that all parts are determined by the structure of the whole.

Although intended to have a general application, the principle of *Prägnanz* was oriented mainly toward facts of perception. Thus, Wertheimer subsumed the laws of grouping under it. Some thinkers, while accepting good continuation and closure as clear illustrations of *Prägnanz*, have wondered in what sense the latter describes grouping by proximity or similarity. However, in gestalt theory the tendency toward *Prägnanz* is not one process among others, but is inherent in all processes and products. Accordingly, one would say that grouping per se introduces regularity and simplicity and that to group in accordance with proximity and similarity is to have a radically simpler phenomenal field than absence of grouping would yield. This formulation admittedly renders concrete investigation difficult; accordingly, investigators have sought empirical tests to compare actually obtained "good form" with other alternatives that are logically possible under the same stimulus conditions. While it has not been

possible to establish unambiguous criteria for good form, a great deal of selectivity has been demonstrated: where stimulation is compatible with a nearly infinite number of different experienced events, only a limited number—often only one or two—will actually be realized.

There is, however, a set of phenomena that argues convincingly for a principle of maximum simplicity in perceptual experience: where a given stimulus array can be organized in alternate ways, that organization is realized which yields a constant, rather than an ever-changing, perceptual object. A black circle moving across a homogeneous white ground is perceived as such, while the alternative organization, namely, a succession of black areas, each emerging from and returning to the white ground, is not realized. Phenomenal identity as studied by Ternus (1926) and Wertheimer also demonstrates a powerful preference to maintain a constant organization when one views a moving form. Another important instance of this tendency is the kinetic depth effect that Wallach and his associates have described (Wallach & O'Connell 1953). When an observer follows the deforming shadow of a slowly rotating object on a screen, he organizes the successive views so as to see a rigid shape moving in the third dimension; he does not see changing two-dimensional shapes. Wallach (1940) has also shown that in sound localization with head movement, one tends to perceive the sound as coming from a stationary source rather than from a moving source. The perceptual constancies may also be considered instances of the same tendency. [*See* PERCEPTION, *article on* PERCEPTUAL CONSTANCY.]

In areas other than perception the principle of *Prägnanz* has in general resisted conclusive investigation or clear definition. An early hypothesis of Wulf (1922) that memory traces undergo changes in the direction of greater regularity and simplicity has not been supported. In thinking, the discovery of a solution often marks a transition to a simpler structure, but this formulation lacks explanatory power. Equally rudimentary is our present understanding of tendencies in action toward the completion of situations that contain a gap, in accordance with the demands of the given structure. In social psychology the prevalence of extremely simplified views of groups and of public issues is a striking fact, but investigation has not advanced sufficiently to be theoretically relevant. A somewhat nearer approach is the study initiated by Heider (1958) of preferences for balanced configurations of interpersonal relations, and of the tendency to convert unbalanced configurations into a preferred form. Despite the difficulties, interest in the principle of *Prägnanz* persists and continues to be a concern of investigation.

Nativism. Gestalt theory holds that organization in accordance with general principles of physical dynamics is present from the start in psychological functioning. This position leaves wide scope for unlearned processes. At the same time, the widespread view that gestalt theory underestimates the effects of past experience is oversimplified. It is more important to note that the concept of organization determines the treatment of both unlearned and learned functions. Gestalt theory refers unlearned operations mainly to relationally determined physicochemical processes rather than to the action of specific anatomical structures. Similarly, it holds that the effects of past experience are also products of organization, or determined by structural requirements.

The treatment of form perception brings this position into sharp relief. From the standpoint of gestalt theory, unlearned organizing principles determine the perception of form, and past experience cannot exert an influence until the sensory processes are organized. It thus takes issue with the assumption of the empiricists that visual perception consists originally of a mosaic of sensations and that learning transforms them into shaped visual objects. There is in fact substantial evidence that some form perception is unlearned. Figure–ground articulation is governed by an unlearned function, as is articulation in accordance with good form. The selective principles according to which sensory data are organized in perceptual grouping, in perception of visual motion, or in the perception of identity are similarly independent of specific learning. Other perceptual functions also appear to be unlearned, among them stroboscopic motion, brightness contrast, and distance perception in lower organisms. Particularly instructive are observations of perceptually ambiguous situations; the fact that observers markedly agree in favoring one outcome over another indicates that the processes which order perception into coherent entities are not products of specific learning. There is also evidence that spontaneous organization of form often takes effect before an influence of past experience can occur.

The assumption of unlearned organizing principles does not, however, imply neglect of the history of past stimulation. To a degree this becomes evident in the treatment of temporal organization in perception. Gestalt psychology has from the start considered perceptual organization of temporally extended events equal in importance with that of simultaneously given data. The role of successive stimulation in apparent motion was the first phenomenon that Wertheimer formally investigated, and he illustrated the principles of grouping with melodies as well as with static visual forms. Further, he identified one principle of grouping, that of objective set (*objektive Einstellung*), which directly concerns the effect of membership in a temporal sequence upon the phenomenal characteristics of a given structure. In these cases, as in the work of Michotte on phenomenal causality, perceptual organization depends directly on prior stimulation. [*See* TIME, *article on* PSYCHOLOGICAL ASPECTS.]

In addition, recent advances in investigation have brought about a further development in gestalt thinking, as in psychology generally, pointing to the conclusion that a history of prior stimulation is a necessary condition of adequate perceptual functioning. Thus the investigation of figural aftereffects by Köhler and Wallach (1944) demonstrates that all perceptual experiences at a given moment are in some important respects a function of what a person has experienced in the past. The import of this conclusion is that the perceptual system requires not only an adequate amount of previous stimulation but particular kinds and distributions of stimulation. [*See* PERCEPTION, *article on* ILLUSIONS AND AFTEREFFECTS.]

The work of Helson (1964) on the organization of data across time illustrates the continuity of current investigation with gestalt contributions. The "adaptation level" demonstrates that temporally separated stimulations interact, so that the phenomenal intensity of a given stimulation is lawfully determined by preceding stimulation. In addition to establishing that perception depends upon the articulation of a stimulus array in the temporal dimension, it also demonstrates that the same datum may be obtained from different structures, each of which determines its subjective values. This line of inquiry brings to the fore the importance of sensitivity to successive arrays of stimulation.

Furthermore, gestalt psychology does not question the more customary effects of past experience upon perception. Indeed, it finds a definite place for them and has formulated the rudiments of a memory-trace theory to account for them (Koffka 1935). Gestalt psychologists have opposed unexamined and *ad hoc* assumptions about the effects of past experience that were introduced to bolster the atomistic position. Such claims, they maintained, require proof and an account of the operations by which past experience exerts its effects. More specifically, they have combated an elementaristic concept of past experience and insisted that unorganized experience cannot organize perception. Accordingly, they have proposed that the organization of form in past experience can reorganize a percept by means of memory-trace contact. The demonstration of a memory effect of three-dimensional form perception by Wallach (Wallach et al. 1953) provides a clear illustration. A pattern which has previously been experienced as three-dimensional on the basis of appropriate depth cues will subsequently be seen as three-dimensional in the absence of these cues; in this case the outcome is dependent upon past organization. [*See* PERCEPTION, *article on* DEPTH PERCEPTION.]

Gestalt psychology leaves vast room for past experience and education in its treatment of thinking and learning. At the same time, it places emphasis in these areas on processes that have not previously occurred. These draw upon materials of the past, but the organizations that occur are not exclusively products of past experience. A chimpanzee needs relevant past experience with the functional properties of sticks, bars, and food in order to solve problems, but the organization of these experiences is a new step. Similarly, a child's understanding of a relation such as that of transitivity requires knowledge of the terms in question. The latter example raises a new question—namely, whether simple logical operations are learned. The implication of the gestalt position is that once the facts are given, the mental operations of creating a structure from them and of reading them off ensue directly. Such relations are mental products; they are not given as facts about the environment. These formulations are consistent with observations, such as those of Piaget, that a given level of maturation is necessary before a child can grasp a relation such as transitivity, that he must pass through earlier intellectual stages before he is capable of handling it. Other developmental studies of the recent period raise a different problem. Harlow has shown that infrahuman primates require prolonged experience before they can handle relations such as those of oddity and reversal. Do these findings demonstrate that the relations in question are "learned"? An alternative that must be considered is that past experience is necessary in order to find out what relation is important, but that the relation per se is not learned. [*See* DEVELOPMENTAL PSYCHOLOGY, *article on* A THEORY OF DEVELOPMENT; INTELLECTUAL DEVELOPMENT.]

Phenomenological method. Gestalt theory is phenomenologically oriented. It assigns a place of crucial importance in psychological inquiry to the data of immediate experience. They are part of its subject matter and therefore require explanation; in addition, they are indispensable as a basis for the construction of theory. This position has a general affinity with the phenomenological tradition represented in the modern period by Husserl and is in sharp contrast to the direction of behaviorism. [*See* PHENOMENOLOGY *and the biography of* HUSSERL.]

There is an obvious relation between the character of phenomenal events and the initial formulations of gestalt psychology. In the area of perception the primary concern has been to explain why things look, sound, and feel as they do; the phenomenal facts are in this case the facts requiring explanation. More specifically, the observation that wholes and whole qualities are given in immediate perceptual experience was the basis for the rejection of elementarism and for the adoption of the concept of part–whole determination. Similarly, in thinking, the presence of understandable relations and of reorganization serve as primary observations and as first steps toward an eventual theory. This is equally the case in social psychology, where a clarification of the ways in which persons comprehend a given situation often provides crucial information about the phenomena to be studied and a basis for further exploration. The work of Heider (1958) is an example of the possibilities of a phenomenological procedure in the study of interpersonal relations. Finally, it is hard to conceive of a psychology of aesthetics that ignores direct experience [*see* AESTHETICS].

Although the explanatory concepts that gestalt psychology seeks are not themselves phenomenal facts, it assumes an intimate relation between them. It holds, first, that behavior cannot be adequately explained without reference to central processes and that these may be represented in immediate experience. Second, the postulate of psychophysical isomorphism suggests that an examination of what is phenomenally given can be both a source of hypotheses about neural events and a testing ground for them. From this perspective psychology possesses, in contrast to the natural sciences, a unique access to central processes. As Albert Einstein is reported to have once remarked in connection with this issue: "If atoms could talk about their internal processes I would not believe everything they say, but I would certainly listen."

The main requirement of phenomenological observation is to render an unprejudiced report of immediate experience under specified conditions. This general rule at once differentiates phenomenology from analytic introspection, which was dominated by a prior theory about the character of the events to be described. The phenomenological observer must be open to his experiences as they appear to him, independently of prior beliefs or assumptions about them and should not exclude what is strange or contrary to preconceptions. When viewing a visual contour, he will not allow his knowledge to deter him from noting that it appears in front of the ground, while the ground itself appears unbroken in the area that the figure occupies, or that the contour delineates the figure and not the ground. In turn the investigator will consider the explanation of these facts necessary to a theory of figure–ground organization. Although this mode of observation is not quite naive and requires cultivation, its aim is natural observation. The import of phenomenology as a psychological procedure is that it restores everyday experience, with its qualitative diversities, to psychology.

Phenomenal facts would be of reduced import if they were unconnected with action. In fact, the connection is close; persons act in a situation in accordance with the ways they perceive, feel, and think about it. If a person misperceives a situation, he acts in accordance with his misperception, not on the basis of conditions as they are. It is, consequently, of the utmost importance to relate action to the cognitive apprehension of given conditions. However, in the absence of a coherent rationale the relation between direct experience and action reduces essentially to a correlation between incommensurable data. From the standpoint of gestalt psychology the phenomenal facts are, as stated earlier, the most direct, although partial, expressions of those mediating processes that steer action. These processes are organized representations of external and internal conditions. Interposed between stimulation and action, they have the status of cognitive representations, comprising relations and systems of relations between facts, between means and ends, and between grounds and consequents. Since they steer action, they have the status of causes and are necessary to the prediction of action. Phenomenal facts—percepts, ideas, hypotheses, inferences—are more closely related to these central processes than to any other events, and therefore, they throw light on the events that issue in action. The cognitive analysis that gestalt psychology has pursued in different areas of human psychology and that has opened new paths for investigation derives from these assumptions.

At the same time gestalt theory does not favor a purely phenomenological psychology. Central processes are more inclusive and continuous than phenomenal events; therefore, the latter alone cannot provide the basis for a coherent science. In all areas of psychology, including those of perception and

thinking, there are functional relations that are inaccessible to phenomenology. Other areas are at best poorly represented at the phenomenal level; habits and attitudes are formed unawares; the formation of associations and the operations of retention are not open to inspection; and there are always factors outside the phenomenal field that determine action. These considerations point to the need for inductive procedures in psychology; they do not, however, justify the neglect of direct experience when it is accessible.

The importance that gestalt theory attaches to immediate experience rests on a far-reaching examination that cuts across generally accepted categories. It distinguishes sharply between phenomenal and functional facts, the latter referring to events that are outside immediate experience and that are the object of scientific inquiry. Direct experience includes both objective facts, such as rocks and animals, and subjective facts, such as wishes and pains; indeed, the distinction between objective and subjective is one that occurs within the phenomenal domain. Thus, secondary and tertiary qualities are often phenomenally highly objective, since they appear located in specific objects in outside space.

Consequently, direct experience is a condition of all scientific inquiry. Observation consists in the first instance of phenomenal facts; it begins with what is seen, heard, touched. At no point do the procedures of science eliminate these phenomenal components. The most refined observations, such as those represented by pointer readings, are perceptual situations that depend upon the identification of units, the perception of motion, and the discrimination of positions. Moreover, the theoretical constructions erected to explain observations, including the rules of logic and mathematics—in general, the structures of inference and proof necessary to scientific activity—are also strictly phenomenal events. There is thus a necessary continuity of direct experience with the concepts and procedures that science fashions; ultimately all concepts have a phenomenal base. The scientist's picture of the world is based on the achievements of perception and thinking; his choice of units of observation is based on his perception of form, and his inferences must obey logical demands and the cognition of causal relations. Although the investigator who concentrates on a particular problem must take this background for granted, it cannot be ignored in a systematic account of the character of scientific investigation.

These considerations throw a new light on the distrust of phenomenal data in behavioristic psychology. Early behaviorism rejected direct experience in favor of objective data on the ground that the former is private and inaccessible to public check and, therefore, cannot form part of the body of scientific knowledge. Since one cannot place experiences side by side and compare them, behaviorists concluded that one can observe only the behavior of another, not his experiences. However, the assumption that objective data are free of phenomenal components was based on a naive realism that failed to consider the role of the observer. The behaviorist as investigator reports his observations and inferences—that is, the contents of his phenomenal field. It is therefore hardly consistent on his part to rule out the reports of other observers simply because these observers happen to be his subjects. More recently, behaviorists have accepted that the data of science are based on phenomenal reports but have proposed to include only those observations which command agreement among independent observers. It is generally accepted that observations on which qualified observers can agree have a special standing in science. However, the implication that phenomenally subjective events are generally untrustworthy and *ipso facto* fail to command agreement cannot be sustained. [*See* OBSERVATION.]

There are, to be sure, sources of error to be guarded against and difficulties to be resolved when one includes the reports of observers in a system of functional concepts. No doubt it may be more difficult to find the appropriate referents to the report "I am feeling dizzy and confused" than to the report "The rat depressed the bar five times." Nevertheless, the methodological purism of the behavioristic position has in important respects had negative effects. The proposals to reduce perception to overt discriminative responses and to treat the reports of persons as "verbal behavior" have not been fruitful. In fact, they marked an abandonment of interest in phenomena and problems that are most specifically and significantly human. They also discouraged, because they failed to realize, the constructive contribution of free observation and description in the discovery of new phenomena. Consequently, they underestimated the creative phases of scientific activity that precede proof and that set the goals for proof. These attitudes have had a profoundly restrictive effect on human psychology.

The more serious reason for the behavioristic distrust of phenomenal data has been the belief that they are epiphenomena, with no place in a causal–explanatory scheme. Gestalt theory reserves judgment on the mind–body problem, while seeking a bridge between direct experience and the concepts of natural science; it sees in the clarification of this relation a challenge to psychology and to science generally. The distrust, bordering on aversion, of direct experience that behaviorism has demonstrated is also motivated by the attempt to imitate the natural sciences in their progressive elimination of phenomenal data. From the standpoint of gestalt theory human experience is an important part of nature and too significant to be discarded. An account of human functioning that omits reference to direct experiences is as incomplete as would be the description of a musical instrument that included all details of its materials, construction, and functioning but made no mention of the music it produces.

Relation to behaviorism. Certain other divergences between behaviorism and gestalt psychology have to do with the respective problems they have considered. Gestalt psychology grows out of studies in human perception and thinking, while behaviorism takes its start from the study of infrahuman organisms. There are also diverse tendencies within behaviorism itself, some of which are closely connected with gestalt positions. Thus, a concern with the organization of central processes unites gestalt theory with investigators such as Lashley, and the work of Tolman exemplifies an approximation to a gestalt behaviorism in animal psychology [*see the biographies of* LASHLEY *and* TOLMAN].

However, the "stimulus–response" psychologies constitute one variety of behaviorism, highly influential on the American scene, that is strongly opposed to gestalt psychology. Stimulus–response accounts of behavior are atomistic; although their units are molar, they treat behavior as composed of chains of stimulus–response units and changes of behavior as the addition and elimination of such units.

From the perspective of gestalt psychology, action is characterized by organization, and coordination of complex movements poses problems analogous to organization in perception. Accordingly it questions the adequacy of accounts of action that employ isolated stimulus–response units. Further, it holds that organized cognitive representations steer intelligent action in animals and man; sequences of chained units do not do justice to the operations of organizing and reorganizing that external conditions initiate. Also, the "stimulus" of stimulus–response psychologies implicitly refers to perceptual configurations, which are not, however, treated as such.

These problems are magnified when one turns to human psychology. It is a significant feature of the stimulus–response programs that they aspire to base a psychology of man on concepts and methods derived exclusively from the study of infrahuman organisms. This aim presupposes that no problems or processes will be discovered that are unique to human functioning. Instead of freely examining human achievements and asking how one can account for them, they attempt to fit observations to concepts derived from another area. The question arises whether concepts pertaining to one range of facts retain their meaning or relevance when extrapolated to a new area or whether they become mere labels for phenomena that have not been examined in their own right.

Conclusion

Gestalt theory was the first attempt within psychology to give a fundamental treatment to problems of wholes and part–whole relations. It was productive of new discoveries and concepts; it generated new questions and proved relevant to basic issues of psychology. Its contributions laid the foundations for the modern study of perception; it broke new ground in the investigation of thinking, memory, and learning; it initiated new steps in social psychology. These achievements deeply affected the outlook of psychology, not least so when they provoked opposition. They spurred a sharpening of issues and the revision of alternative positions; there is little work of consequence in psychology that has been wholly untouched by gestalt ideas.

It is nevertheless questionable to conclude, as some students have, that the contributions of this movement have been fully absorbed and that it has died of success. It is more likely that its natural development was blocked when it was uprooted from its milieu in Europe following the Nazi catastrophe. To this one must add that there were barriers to a full comprehension of its perspective and of its conception of science in the profoundly different intellectual environment that prevailed in the United States. It is therefore more appropriate to stress that gestalt theory is not a completed system, that many of the issues it raised await resolution, and that it might be best described as a program of investigation or a region of problems. Thus, there is as yet little understanding of the physiological foundations that gestalt theory sought for psychology, and the postulate of isomorphism remains a heuristic principle. Further, gestalt psychologists were selective with respect to the problems they studied; in general they preferred those that lent themselves to exact investigation and clear theoretical decisions. Consequently, there are

large areas to which it has not notably contributed, among them developmental and abnormal psychology and the psychologies of personality, of language, and of action. Neither has it contributed directly to the psychology of motivation, with the exception of Lewin and his group, whose concepts are related to those of gestalt theory. At the same time, the formulations of gestalt theory contain important implications for these areas. [*See* Achievement motivation; Field theory; *and the biography of* Lewin.]

Although there are no procedures peculiar to gestalt investigators, a distinctive style is evident in their formulations of problems and in their manner of studying them that reflects an implicit attitude toward the tasks of science. Perhaps first in order of importance is a sensitivity to the danger of distorting the subject matter by obeying prior prescriptions about the demands of scientific procedure. It is a natural consequence of the phenomenological orientation of gestalt psychology to think it presumptuous to expect phenomena to conform to rules that precede observation. Connected with this starting point is the belief that faithful observation is an essential step to explanation. Consequently, gestalt psychology accords a place of importance to qualitative observation and, while welcoming exact experimentation, rejects the view that measurement is the sole source of valid evidence. Indeed, some of its own most significant discoveries were essentially systematic demonstrations. One consequence of the more customary assumption is that a phenomenon is not considered important if it cannot be studied experimentally; it is, however, more correct to say that experimentation is only one kind of observation. Indeed, there is danger in stressing experimentation before essential questions have been clarified—the danger of aimless experimentation.

An equally prominent theme of gestalt theory is that clarification of fundamentals requires attention to fairly large areas of phenomena. This becomes evident in gestalt investigations of particular questions, as well as in its broad conception of psychology. It specifically included facts of logic, ethics, and aesthetics as part of the subject matter of psychology at the same time that it sought to establish contact with the concepts of natural science. This approach questions whether the study of ever more detailed problems in special fields will yield knowledge of psychology as a whole. Psychology still has to discover its fundamentals; exclusive attention to those questions that can be studied in exact ways may ignore important phases of the subject and may even lose sight of the realization that the discovery of fundamentals is urgently needed. Indeed, facts in a limited area may be seriously misinterpreted, however carefully they are studied, if their reference to a wider scheme remains obscure.

A sense of the human and philosophical import of psychology pervades gestalt writings. Their critique of arbitrary dissection, of focusing on narrow facts, was based on technical considerations; they also expressed a concern about the destructive implications of such procedures for a conception of man. Science is a way to clarify major issues of mankind. If psychology eliminates or distorts essential facts and if these are represented as the main evidence about his nature, man himself will appear of little account. Gestalt theory questioned the assumption that certain convictions prevalent in psychology were scientifically derived. The denial of understanding, the view that actions and judgments are in principle subjectively determined, the treatment of value in terms of neutral facts, and the consequent rejection of valid value did not, it claimed, necessarily follow from scientific thinking. There is also a quality of moral optimism in gestalt psychology, which some may consider extrascientific if not antiscientific. This charge cannot be easily leveled against a movement that strictly opposed the approach of vitalism to facts of life and that sought to find a basis for psychology in natural science. The charge itself may be an expression of moral pessimism.

Solomon E. Asch

[*Directly related are the entries* Field theory *and* Thinking, *article on* cognitive organization and processes. *Contrasting approaches to behavioral phenomena are discussed in* Forgetting; Learning, *especially the articles on* classical conditioning, instrumental learning, reinforcement, *and* discrimination learning; Psychoanalysis. *Other relevant material may be found in* Aesthetics; Attitudes; Groups; Perception; Phenomenology; Problem solving; Social psychology; Systems analysis, *article on* psychological systems; Thinking; *and in the biographies of* Husserl; Katz; Koffka; Köhler; Külpe; Wertheimer.]

BIBLIOGRAPHY

PRIMARY SOURCES

Arnheim, Rudolf 1954 *Art and Visual Perception.* Berkeley: Univ. of California Press.

Asch, Solomon E. (1952) 1959 *Social Psychology.* Englewood Cliffs, N.J.: Prentice-Hall.

Asch, Solomon E. 1960 Perceptual Conditions of Association. *Psychological Monographs* 74, no. 3.

Duncker, Karl (1935) 1945 On Problem-solving. *Psychological Monographs* 58, no. 5. → First published as *Zur psychologie des produktiven Denkens.*

Ehrenfels, Christian von 1890 Über "Gestaltquali-
täten." *Vierteljahrsschrift für wissenschaftliche Philosophie und Soziologie* 14:249–292.

Ellis, Willis D. (1938) 1950 *A Source Book of Gestalt Psychology.* London: Routledge. → Contains excerpts from the technical contributions of gestalt psychology which were first published in *Psychologische Forschung* between 1921 and 1938.

Heider, Fritz 1958 *The Psychology of Interpersonal Relations.* New York: Wiley.

Helson, Harry 1964 *Adaptation-level Theory: An Experimental and Systematic Approach to Behavior.* New York: Harper.

Henle, Mary (editor) 1961 *Documents of Gestalt Psychology.* Berkeley: Univ. of California Press.

Henle, Mary 1965 On Gestalt Psychology. Pages 276–292 in Benjamin B. Wolman and Ernest Nagel (editors), *Scientific Psychology.* New York: Basic Books.

Katona, George (1940) 1949 *Organizing and Memorizing: Studies in the Psychology of Learning and Teaching.* New York: Columbia Univ. Press.

Katz, David (1911) 1935 *The World of Colour.* London: Routledge. → First published in German as *Die Erscheinungsweisen der Farben und ihre Beeinflüssung durch die individuelle Erfahrung.* A revised and enlarged edition was published in 1930 as *Der Aufbau der Farbwelt.*

Koffka, Kurt (1921) 1928 *The Growth of the Mind: An Introduction to Child-psychology.* 2d ed., rev. New York: Harcourt. → First published as *Die Grundlagen der psychischen Entwicklung: Eine Einführung in die Kinderpsychologie.* The first treatment of questions of learning and education from the perspective of gestalt psychology.

Koffka, Kurt 1922 Perception: An Introduction to the *Gestalt-theorie. Psychological Bulletin* 19:531–585.

Koffka, Kurt 1935 *Principles of Gestalt Psychology.* New York: Harcourt. → The only comprehensive treatment of gestalt psychology; by one of its leading figures.

Koffka, Kurt 1940 Problems in the Psychology of Art. Pages 180–273 in *Art: A Bryn Mawr Symposium,* by Richard Bernheimer et al. Bryn Mawr Notes and Monographs, Vol. 9. Bryn Mawr (Pa.) College.

Köhler, Wolfgang (1917) 1956 *The Mentality of Apes.* 2d ed., rev. London: Routledge. → First published in German. A paperback edition was published in 1959 by Random House. A renowned study of intelligence in apes and of the concept of insight.

Köhler, Wolfgang (1920) 1924 *Die physischen Gestalten in Ruhe und im stationären Zustand.* Erlangen (Germany): Philosophische Akademie.

Köhler, Wolfgang (1929) 1947 *Gestalt Psychology.* Rev. ed. New York: Liveright. → A paperback edition was published in 1947 by New American Library. The first general exposition of the movement; a classic in the literature of psychology.

Köhler, Wolfgang 1938 *The Place of Value in a World of Facts.* New York: Liveright.

Köhler, Wolfgang 1940 *Dynamics in Psychology.* New York: Liveright. → A field theory in perception and memory. A work that develops earlier ideas and foreshadows subsequent directions of investigation.

Köhler, Wolfgang 1941 On the Nature of Associations. American Philosophical Society, *Proceedings* 84:489–502.

Köhler, Wolfgang 1951 Relational Determination in Perception. Pages 200–230 in Lloyd A. Jeffress (editor), *Cerebral Mechanisms in Behavior.* New York: Wiley.

KÖHLER, WOLFGANG 1958 Perceptual Organization and Learning. *American Journal of Psychology* 71:311–315.

KÖHLER, WOLFGANG; and WALLACH, HANS 1944 Figural After-effects: An Investigation of Visual Processes. American Philosophical Society, *Proceedings* 88:269–357.

LEWIN, KURT (1926–1933) 1935 *A Dynamic Theory of Personality: Selected Papers.* New York: McGraw-Hill. → Papers first published in German.

LEWIN, KURT (1939–1947) 1963 *Field Theory in Social Science: Selected Theoretical Papers.* Edited by Dorwin Cartwright. London: Tavistock.

MICHOTTE, A. (1946) 1963 *The Perception of Causality.* London: Methuen. → First published in French.

OSGOOD, CHARLES E. (1953) 1959 *Method and Theory in Experimental Psychology.* New York: Oxford Univ. Press.

RUBIN, EDGAR (1915) 1921 *Visuell wahrgenommene Figuren: Studien in psychologischer Analyse.* Copenhagen: Gylendal. → First published in Danish.

TERNUS, JOSEF 1926 Experimentelle Untersuchungen über phänomenale Identität. *Psychologische Forschung* 7:81–136.

WALLACH, H. 1940 The Role of Head Movements and Vestibular and Visual Cues in Sound Localization. *Journal of Experimental Psychology* 27:339–368.

WALLACH, H.; and O'CONNELL, D. N. 1953 Kinetic Depth Effect. *Journal of Experimental Psychology* 45:205–217.

WALLACH, H.; O'CONNELL, D. N.; and NEISSER, U. 1953 The Memory Effect of Visual Perception of Three-dimensional Form. *Journal of Experimental Psychology* 45:360–368.

WERTHEIMER, MAX (1912–1920) 1925 *Drei Abhandlungen zur Gestalttheorie.* Erlangen (Germany): Philosophische Akademie. → Contains three early contributions: "Über das Denken der Naturfölker" first published in Volume 70 in the *Zeitschrift für Psychologie;* "Experimentelle Studien über das Sehen von Bewegung" published in Volume 61; and *Über Schlafsprozesse im produktiven Denken.*

WERTHEIMER, MAX (1925) 1944 Gestalt Theory. *Social Research* 11:78–99. → First published in German.

WERTHEIMER, MAX 1934 On Truth. *Social Research* 1:135–146.

WERTHEIMER, MAX 1935 Some Problems in the Theory of Ethics. *Social Research* 2:353–367.

WERTHEIMER, MAX 1937 On the Concept of Democracy. Pages 271–285 in Max Ascoli and Fritz Lehmann (editors), *Political and Economic Democracy.* New York: Norton.

WERTHEIMER, MAX (1945) 1961 *Productive Thinking.* Enl. ed., edited by Michael Wertheimer. London: Tavistock. → Published posthumously; the product of a lifelong concern with problems of thinking, logic, and education.

WULF, FRIEDRICH 1922 Über die Veränderung von Vorstellungen. *Psychologische Forschung* 1:333–373.

SECONDARY SOURCES

ALLPORT, FLOYD H. 1955 *Theories of Perception and the Concept of Structure.* New York: Wiley.

BORING, EDWIN G. (1929) 1950 *A History of Experimental Psychology.* 2d ed. New York: Appleton.

GUILLAUME, P. 1937 *La psychologie de la forme.* Paris: Flammarion.

HEIDBREDER, EDNA 1933 *Seven Psychologies.* New York: Appleton.

HENLE, MARY 1965 *On Gestalt Psychology.* Pages 276–292 in Benjamin B. Wolman and Ernest Nagel (editors), *Scientific Psychology.* New York: Basic Books.

METZGER, WOLFGANG (1940) 1954 *Psychologie.* 2d ed. Darmstadt (Germany): Steinkopff.

PETERMANN, BRUNO (1929) 1932 *The Gestalt Theory and the Problem of Configuration.* New York: Harcourt. → First published as *Gestalttheorie und das Gestaltproblem.*

PRENTICE, W. C. H. 1959 The Systematic Psychology of Wolfgang Köhler. Volume 1, pages 427–455 in Sigmund Koch (editor), *Psychology: The Study of Science.* New York: McGraw-Hill.

SCHEERER, MARTIN 1931 *Die Lehre von der Gestalt.* Berlin: Gruyter.

WOODWORTH, ROBERT S. (1931) 1964 *Contemporary Schools of Psychology.* 3d ed. New York: Ronald. → See especially pages 214–250 on "Gestalt Psychology."

GIDDINGS, FRANKLIN H.

Franklin Henry Giddings (1855–1931), a founder of American sociological theory and research, was born in Sherman, Connecticut, of strict Puritan ancestry on both sides. His father was a Congregational minister. Giddings' intellectual precocity is shown by the fact that before entering college he had read extensively in the then highly controversial writings of Darwin, T. H. Huxley, John Tyndall, and Spencer. These authors, together with Adam Smith, Comte, and J. S. Mill, provided the foundation of his devotion to individualism—his basic philosophical position—and his primary sociological concepts. Graduating from Union College in 1877, Giddings spent the next decade in newspaper work, mainly on the then famous *Springfield Republican* and *Springfield Union*. He lectured on political science and sociology at Bryn Mawr College from 1888 to 1894 and at Columbia University from 1891 to 1894. In 1894 he was appointed professor of sociology at Columbia; he was the first full-time professor of sociology in the United States.

Among the founders of American sociology he occupies a strategic position as the most influential link in the transition of sociology from moral philosophy and the philosophy of history to inductive research. In this he was influenced by his close association with Richmond Mayo-Smith and by the concurrent rapid spread of statistical studies into related fields. Although he made no historically significant contributions to statistical research, he gave a powerful stimulus to quantitative studies of all aspects of community life through his lectures and books and his influence on hundreds of students, including over fifty PH.D. candidates.

Giddings' basic philosophy was a combination of Comtean positivism and Spencerian evolutionism. He saw social evolution as part of cosmic evolution, as basically an equilibration of energy among individuals and groups that results in differentiation, integration, segregation, and assimilation. He thus viewed every social order as always in a state of moving equilibrium, such equilibrium in power and status being essential for internal justice and order and, on a wider scale, for international peace. He considered sociology both a natural science and the basic elemental social science, giving an account of the origin, growth, structure, and activities of human association through the operation of physical, biological, and psychological forces. At times he thought sociology might become a quantitatively exact science.

In his view, "social process," or social life, results from the interaction of "primary causes," the natural resources and accessibility of a given habitat, and the "secondary causes," the human motives arising within society itself. Since all social energy is physical energy transmuted by means of economic activities, the "social composition," or the number, density, and genetic heterogeneity of a given population, is determined by these primary causes. At the same time, harnessing these resources of food and power increases social dynamics and, hence, the processes of differentiation and integration, thus adding complexity to the "social constitution," that is, the functional and purposive groupings, ranging from social clubs to sovereign states. Giddings thus found the task of sociology to be the integration of subjective with objective processes and concepts in terms of mental activity, organic adjustment, natural selection, and conservation of energy.

This basic position is generally sound if rich and accessible natural resources are considered primary only in the sense of being antecedent in time, or as essential, but culturally viewed, static preconditions for the development of a dense population and a highly dynamic social order, or if it is acknowledged that both the manner and extent of their utilization is dependent on the state of cultural advancement. Giddings would probably agree, since he saw all forms of association as "essentially phenomena of thought and feeling," so that his analyses of the stages of society's evolution from zoogenic to demotic forms, as well as his analyses of the social constitution and the social mind, were all couched in psychosocial terms.

In *The Principles of Sociology* (1896) he declared that the original and elementary subjective fact of society is the "consciousness of kind," or Adam Smith's "sympathy," plus a conscious recognition of likeness. In answer to critics who viewed consciousness of kind as merely another name for herd instinct or gregariousness, he sought repeatedly, but not convincingly, to show that gregariousness is a purely hereditary "biophysical habit" to which man alone adds the purely psychic activity of conscious recognition of likeness and difference of kind. This raises the question of just where in the evolution of neural structures such recognition emerged, but in the light of studies in animal psychology there can be little doubt that it preceded primitive man. Giddings himself declared consciousness of kind to be dependent on in-group communication and to result in mutual aid, both of which traits were well developed among the higher apes.

Although Giddings continued to argue this issue, in the outline of his "system" in *Studies in the Theory of Human Society* (1922, p. 292), he made "pluralistic behavior," or like response of two or more persons to a given stimulus, antecedent to, and the basis of, consciousness of kind. He declared "interstimulation and response" among individuals to be the causal basis of all collective behavior. Social phenomena thus result from two variables: the psychosocial situation and the pluralistic response to it. Hence he offered a new definition: "Pluralistic behavior is the subject-matter of the psychology of society, otherwise called sociology" (1922, p. 252).

Thereafter, he held that "like" response to an idea, symbol, or group value ensures group solidarity, social control, and concerted volition. Moreover, since "unlike" response to an ideal or purpose leads to segregation, competition, rivalry, and conflict among social groups, the internal solidarity and concerted volition of every group rests upon an awareness of likeness in mental attitude. Differences in the speed, intensity, and duration of response give rise to processes of differentiation and integration, to leadership and followers, the emergence of a guiding "protocracy" of more able members, the division of labor, and to social status. Differences in the intensity of consciousness of kind result in wide variation in the permanence of association and the scope of cooperative activities: the range extends from family to political party. Like and unlike responses result in an endless variety of social groupings, serving varied human purposes, from bridge clubs to nations and international alliances, each of which by the same process develops its own folkways, mores, and institutions. It seems safe to say that no elementary subjective sociological facts have been found that supersede in aptness and universality Giddings' pluralistic response and consciousness of kind.

Giddings adopted Lester Ward's distinction between social genesis and social telesis. Like Spencer and Ward he saw a teleological beneficence in the evolutionary processes, aided by increasing scientific knowledge. However, his utopianism was restrained. In the matured views of *The Scientific Study of Human Society* (1924) he argued that the only *means* available for "societal engineering" are the same as those now used by religious, educational, economic, and political agencies in current social adjustments, so that the *processes* of societal engineering are the same as those of social genesis. Indeed, the envisaged ends of telic action are the results of the efficient causes operating in social genesis, so that telesis is "a conditioned and projected genesis." Consequently, the fruits of telic efforts are more or less the same as the inevitable consequences of the genetic processes. Nevertheless, he envisaged the ends of these processes to be the development of more able, more tolerant, and more cooperative members of society, as well as an enhancement of social welfare.

These are obviously logical conclusions from his basic philosophy. Moreover, while the language is different, the meaning harmonizes, in general, with that of such cultural determinists as A. L. Kroeber and L. A. White. Giddings saw society caught up in cosmic evolutionary processes; Kroeber and White see it caught up in a self-determining cultural stream. Giddings, however, manifested a latent utopianism in assuming that the realization of his own ideals was the assured end of cosmic forces.

His lectures, articles, and books abound in shrewd insights into human nature and social problems and processes. As a whole, they represent a pivotal point in the development of American sociology. While his own terms did not win wide usage, they contained the essence of the "social distance," the "social interaction," and the "social situation" of later works.

At the same time, his somewhat questionable distinction between "social" psychology as defining individual reactions and "societal" psychology as defining group reactions led to his ignoring almost entirely the then current advances in dynamic and social psychology. Far more enigmatic is his neglect of the concurrent development of cultural concepts and theories in anthropology. Spencer, his master, had added the "superorganic" as the third distinctive realm of phenomena; Giddings had declared in his *Descriptive and Historical Sociology* (1906, pp. 176, 183) that the past products of interstimulation and response become "the most immediate and most important stimuli in modern social life," but he did not develop the implication of this principle in cultural terms.

FRANK H. HANKINS

[*For the historical context of Giddings' work, see the biographies of* COMTE; DARWIN; MILL; SPENCER; WARD, LESTER F.]

WORKS BY GIDDINGS

1888 CLARK, JOHN B.; and GIDDINGS, FRANKLIN H. *The Modern Distributive Process.* Boston: Ginn.
(1896) 1911 *The Principles of Sociology: An Analysis of the Phenomena of Association and of Social Organization.* New York: Macmillan. → Translated into seven languages. Giddings' most important work.
(1898) 1916 *The Elements of Sociology: A Textbook for Colleges and Schools.* New York: Macmillan. → The most advanced of the early American textbooks.
(1900) 1901 *Democracy and Empire, With Studies of Their Psychologic, Economic and Moral Foundations.* New York: Macmillan. → Views on various public issues; a work of enduring value.
1901 *Inductive Sociology: A Syllabus of Analyses and Classifications and Provisionally Formulated Laws.* New York: Macmillan. → Designed as a basis for statistical studies.
(1906) 1923 *Readings in Descriptive and Historical Sociology.* New York: Macmillan. → Restatement and illustration from literature and history of the concepts outlined in Giddings' *Inductive Sociology.*
1918 *The Responsible State.* Boston: Houghton Mifflin. → Problems of political morality; strong reaction against German militarism.
(1922) 1926 *Studies in the Theory of Human Society.* New York: Macmillan. → Revision and amplification of concepts and analyses; Giddings' second most important work.
1924 *The Scientific Study of Human Society.* Chapel Hill: Univ. of North Carolina Press. → Replaced *Inductive Sociology,* with increased emphasis on statistical researches.
1929 *The Mighty Medicine: Superstition and Its Antidote.* New York: Macmillan. → An exposure of occultism and a plea for enlightened education.
1932 *Civilization and Society: An Account of the Development and Behavior of Human Society.* New York: Holt. → An informal text composed of Giddings' lectures as edited by Howard W. Odum.

SUPPLEMENTARY BIBLIOGRAPHY

ABEL, THEODORE 1930 The Significance of the Concept of Consciousness of Kind. *Social Forces* 9:1–10.
COLUMBIA UNIVERSITY, FACULTY OF POLITICAL SCIENCE 1931 *The Bibliography of the Faculty of Political Science: 1880–1930.* New York. Columbia Univ. Press. → See especially pages 63–76, which list 14 books and at least 200 articles by Giddings.
NORTHCOTT, CHARLES H. 1948 The Sociological Theories of Franklin Henry Giddings: Consciousness of Kind, Pluralistic Behavior, and Statistical Method. Pages 744–765 in Harry E. Barnes (editor), *An Introduction to the History of Sociology.* Univ. of Chicago Press.
ODUM, HOWARD W. 1951 *American Sociology.* New York: Longmans.

GIERKE, OTTO VON

The German jurist Otto von Gierke (1841–1921) was born in Stettin, the son of a Prussian official. He was reared in a highly respectable, patriotic, and Prussian atmosphere. As a student at the University of Berlin, he was influenced by Georg Beseler, a jurist of the Germanist school, who had already sketched and was teaching the idea of a purely German theory of associations (*Genossenschaftstheorie*). After professorships at Breslau (1872–1884) and Heidelberg (1884–1887) Gierke succeeded to Beseler's chair at Berlin, which he occupied until his death.

At the beginning of Gierke's career, German legal scholarship was dominated by the Romanist school of Savigny; but Gierke began and remained a staunch Germanist. The Germanists, like the Romanists, were historically minded; their research, however, did not take them back to the Roman Empire, Justinian's Code, and the Reception, but followed the path marked out by Jacob Grimm to the law of the ancient German *Mark* and the *Gemeinde* (local community), to feudal records, town charters, and the rules of guilds, in search of "truly German" legal principles. The first volume of Gierke's *Das deutsche Genossenschaftsrecht* (1868–1913), dedicated to Beseler, was the first product of his self-imposed task of broadening the foundation for a German theory of associations by a detailed study of successive types of organizations in German history. This task, diligently pursued through much of his life, was not quite completed when, in 1913, he published the fourth and last volume of his most famous work.

He temporarily abandoned historical research for more immediate problems in 1888, when the first draft of the new civil law code disappointed and challenged the Germanists. Gierke wrote a series of critical articles and, when he and his fellow Germanists failed to obtain substantial modifications of the code, settled down to his second major task. Convinced that the materials of a common German law existed and that legal progress could come only through developing deep-rooted German traditions and weeding out Romanist imports, he felt a solemn obligation "to penetrate the new code with a Germanistic spirit; to develop its Germanic content upon an historical basis; to foster the growth of its Germanism in the future" (1868–1913, vol. 4, p. xii). The first volume of his *Deutsches Privatrecht* ("German Private Law," 1895–1917), on *Personenrecht* ("Law of Persons," 1895), was followed by a second on *Sachenrecht* ("Law of Things," 1905) and a third on *Schuldrecht* ("Law of Obligatory Relations," 1917). Their important impact on German civil law is generally acknowledged.

Gierke's influence on legal and political theory derived from his historical and systematic analyses of associations. The four volumes of *Das deutsche Genossenschaftsrecht* trace the changing forms of groups through four periods of history. In the earliest period of German law the free association (*freie Genossenschaft*) was predominant; it was based on natural coherence; all rights remained with the members collectively and no corporate existence of the *Genossenschaft* was postulated. In the second period (800–1200) the lordly union (*herrschaftlicher Verband*) was predominant; in this, rights attached to a single individual (e.g., a king or feudal lord) who represented the legal unity of the group. In the third period (1200–1525), which interested Gierke most, a new type of association, the free union (*freie Vereinigung* or *Einung*), became predominant. Growing out of the free will of its associates, the free union nevertheless resembled the old Germanic association in that the law, rights, and duties of the association were attributed to the collective membership. The guild was the purest example of this type, but it also appeared in towns, leagues of towns, and many other associations of varying importance, permanence, and respectability. The principle of free union, plus that of the federal organization of associations into larger unions, as illustrated by the Hanse, at one time gave promise, Gierke thought, that the feudalized Empire would be reconstituted as a federation. But rural areas continued to be dominated by feudal relationships; once-free associations became privileged corporations; finally, a new authoritarian principle triumphed, exemplified in the sovereign state, conceived as separate from and above the people and as the exclusive embodiment of the common interest. By the end of the fourth period (1525–1806), the absorption or dissolution of privileged corporations by the state and the establishment of individual liberty and equality before the law had opened the way for a rich development of free associations with all the varied and complex characteristics that modern associations have.

The old German association, Gierke explained, had had no clearly defined theory; Germanic conceptions implicit in the legal characteristics of the manifold associations of the thirteenth, fourteenth, and fifteenth centuries failed to reach explicit formulation. The competition, in legal theory, of German and Romanist ideas was paralleled by the competition, in publicistic thought, of "truly medieval" and "antique–modern" tendencies. In the development of medieval association law, Gierke discerned manifestations of a German tendency to construe each group as a purposive entity that acted as a whole and, as a whole, was the subject of rights and obligations. This tendency, however, never reached its logical conclusion, a concept of the group as a real person. As association law was finally formulated by canonists and postglossators, German views were submerged by Romanist influences: the association was construed as an institution (*Anstalt*), whose legal existence derived from a grant of powers by superior authority and whose *Rechtssubjektivität* was located in an artificial personality (*persona ficta*) constructed by positive law. Similarly, "truly medieval" political thought, which conceived society as a complex structure of mutually articulated group-entities, each with its own purpose, group-law, and organic unity, was defeated by "antique–modern" tendencies which, progressively eroding the autonomous claims of intermediate groups, issued in an irreconcilable dichotomy between theories of the all-embracing sovereignty of an organic state and unsatisfactory attempts to explain the state itself as contractually constructed by the human atoms who alone had natural existence and natural rights.

Gierke's historical and systematic theses meet in his assertion of the Germanic doctrine that should be applied to modern associations. Attacking the prevailing doctrine of Savigny, which construed them as creations of positive law on the ground that "originally and from a naturalistic point of view" (1868–1913, vol. 2, p. 25) true legal personality belongs only to individual men, he propounded a doctrine which seemed to him not only more German, but also superior in scientific realism and philosophical validity. When law treats groups as persons, he insisted, it does not distort reality. Joint-stock companies, churches, trade unions are—like the state itself—real collective persons. They exist whether the state recognizes them or not; the role of the state is declaratory, not creative. The *Genossenschaft* is an organic unity, composed of individuals or other associations, with its own original purpose; it organizes itself through its own system of "social law"; it is autonomously capable of willing and acting; it has thus a real personality, which is the proper subject of rights and obligations. Appreciation of the actual nature of associations opens the way to the only sort of legal theory that corresponds with fact and the only sort of social organization that can be ethically satisfactory, one that resolves the conflicts inherent in human strivings toward unity and liberty.

Gierke repeatedly emphasized that his position lay between that of the extreme individualists, who would reduce human relationships to contracts among sovereign individuals, and that of the organicists, who would absorb the individual and all society into the state. A man is born "as a member of a family, a race, a community, in short, as a member of a whole" (1868–1913, vol. 2, p. 47) and "what man is, he owes to the association of man with man" (1868–1913, vol. 1, p. 1). The system of human associations, natural and voluntary, presents a complex pattern of rich and fluid variety. To primitive natural associations based upon "purely physical" ties are added a complex and fluid variety of associations more deliberately created—some highly specialized in purpose and membership, others more generalized and comprehensive. The process of differentiation and specialization is balanced by a process of generalization. But, as an expression of man's social nature, the lowliest and narrowest association has some of the same dignity and value as the highest and most comprehensive one.

The state is the product of the same sort of process as that which produces all other associations. But it is distinguished from other associations in that it is the highest and most comprehensive; thus its purposes include the forceful carrying out of "the general will" and the coercive conciliation of the wills of all individual and collective persons. Accordingly, although it is "not generically different," the state differs qualitatively as well as quantitatively from other associations. Moreover, its function requires both *Genossenschaft* and *Herrschaft*. The history of the German state, Gierke believed, had culminated in an integration of *Genossenschaft* and *Herrschaft*, organically uniting the state's associational basis with the inherent authority of the monarchy at its apex.

Gierke's theory of law corresponded to his theory of associations. In "Die Grundbegriffe des Staatsrechts" (1874) he attacked the formalist conception of law as a creation of the state. "The final source of all law" is "the social consciousness of any social institution whatever" (Gierke in Lewis 1935, p. 176); the declaration that transforms social convictions of right into law is made by other associations besides the state. In the terminology he used in *Das Wesen der menschlichen Verbände* ("The Nature of Human Associations," 1902), the two basic categories of law are not private and public law, but "individual law," through which the state regulates the external relations of individual and collective persons, and the various bodies of "social law," which treat individuals only as members of groups. Social law is the law produced by the collective persons themselves to regulate their internal life, the relations of the whole with its parts, and the integration of narrower into more inclusive entities. The public law that organizes the structure of the state, and those of narrower associations (e.g., local communities, provinces) insofar as they are a part of the state structure, is simply one among many systems of autonomously developed "social law," differing from other systems only in the specific characteristics appropriate to the specific nature and purpose of the state. Gierke's concept of "social law" enables him to construe the internal rules of churches, trade unions, business corporations, etc., as independent of state determination and to put such bodies on an equal basis with human persons in claiming areas of freedom into which the state cannot intrude.

Gierke's conception of the nature of associations could suggest a highly decentralized federal political structure, which might include as constituent members both functional and territorial units. Morris R. Cohen once referred to Gierke as "a sort of patron saint of political pluralists." But Gierke himself was not a political pluralist, nor did he develop the ideal of a functional federalism. The pluralistic elements of his theory were always carefully balanced by the organic and authoritarian, and by the dominant role he assigned to the state and to its law. His devotion to Prussia and the monarchy and his concern for the assured unity of the German people tipped the balance steadily toward authority. He became increasingly convinced that the constitution of the Bismarckian *Reich* achieved an almost perfect harmony of associational and authoritarian principles. Earlier in his career he had demanded decentralizing reforms, but in 1919 his fear of the disruption that would follow the abolition of the monarchy made him a vigorous critic of the Weimar constitution.

Gierke's theory of social law influenced such writers as Léon Duguit and Hugo Krabbe; his insistence on the autonomous origins of associations influenced, directly or indirectly, the thought of S. G. Hobson, G. D. H. Cole, Harold J. Laski, and others. His influence on English pluralism owed much to Frederic William Maitland, who introduced Gierke to English-speaking academic circles in 1900. With a lawyer's interest in the legal interpretation of corporations and other groups, Maitland emphasized Gierke's legal doctrine of the real personality of associations but paid less attention to his view of their organic nature and to the very special role he attributed to the state. J. N. Figgis contributed to Gierke's reputation as a pluralist when in *Churches in the Modern State* he drew heavily from Gierke in vindicating the "real life and personality" of churches and other associations against the "Leviathan state" and the Aus-

tinian concept of sovereignty. In Germany, Gierke's student and follower Hugo Preuss argued in his early writings for a transformation of the authoritarian, Prussia-dominated *Reich* into a decentralized democratic state whose articulation would be unhampered by the outworn dogma of sovereignty; but Preuss did not minimize his divergence from Gierke. In the Weimar period he moved to an uncompromising assertion of the sovereignty of the united German state.

Gierke's historical interpretations have been criticized as generalizing beyond the evidence, as tending to transform social movements into ideological or spiritual movements, as reading his own categories into past thought. But *Das deutsche Genossenschaftsrecht*, with its massive erudition and often perceptive statement, remains a classic which no historian of its topics can ignore. Gierke's systematic theses have also been criticized, even by generally sympathetic writers, for example, in the penetrating analysis by Ernest Barker (1934). Interest in Gierke's theory has declined with the decline of the pluralist school. The normative and juristic conclusions that he drew from recognition of the spontaneous self-assertion of groups have little in common with more recent descriptive analyses of group action in politics.

JOHN D. LEWIS

[*For the historical context and subsequent development of Gierke's ideas, see* NATURAL LAW; PLURALISM; POLITICAL GROUP ANALYSIS; VOLUNTARY ASSOCIATIONS; *and the biographies of* DUGUIT; FIGGIS; LASKI; MAITLAND.]

WORKS BY GIERKE

1868–1913 *Das deutsche Genossenschaftsrecht.* 4 vols. Berlin: Weidmann. → Volume 1: *Rechtsgeschichte der deutschen Genossenschaft*, 1868. Volume 2: *Geschichte des deutschen Körperschaftsbegriffs*, 1873. Volume 3: *Die Staats- und Korporationslehre des Altertums und des Mittelalters und ihre Aufnahme in Deutschland*, 1881. Volume 4: *Die Staats- und Korporationslehre der Neuzeit*, 1913. Reprinted in 1954 by Akademische Druck- und Verlagsanstalt, Graz (Austria). Translations of extracts provided by J. D. Lewis.

(1874) 1915 *Die Grundbegriffe des Staatsrechts und die neuesten Staatsrechtstheorien.* Tübingen (Germany): Mohr. → First published in Volume 30 of *Zeitschrift für die gesamte Staatswissenschaft*.

(1880) 1939 *The Development of Political Theory.* Translated by Bernard Freyd. New York: Norton. → First published in 1880 as *Johannes Althusius und die Entwicklung der naturrechtlichen Staatstheorien* by Koebner, Breslau.

(1881) 1958 *Political Theories of the Middle Age.* Cambridge Univ. Press. → A translation of "Die publicistischen Lehren des Mittelalters," a section of Volume 3 of Gierke's *Das deutsche Genossenschaftsrecht*. Translated with a famous introduction by Frederic William Maitland.

1883   *Labands Staatsrecht und die deutsche Rechtswissenschaft.* Schmollers Jahrbuch für Gesetzgebung, Verwaltung und Volkswirtschaft im Deutschen Reich 7: 1097–1195.

1887   *Die Genossenschaftstheorie und die deutsche Rechtsprechung.* Berlin: Weidmann.

1895–1917   *Deutsches Privatrecht.* 3 vols. Munich and Leipzig: Duncker & Humblot. → Volume 1: *Allgemeiner Teil und Personenrecht,* 1895. Volume 2: *Sachenrecht,* 1905. Volume 3: *Schuldrecht,* 1917.

1902 (1954)   *Das Wesen der menschlichen Verbände.* Darmstadt (Germany): Wissenschaftliche Buchgemeinschaft. → Extracts from this work have been translated as "The Nature of Human Associations" and published on pages 139–157 of Lewis 1935.

(1913) 1934   *Natural Law and the Theory of Society, 1500 to 1800.* 2 vols. Translated with an introduction by Ernest Barker. Cambridge Univ. Press. → A 1934 translation of five subsections of Volume 4 of Gierke's *Das deutsche Genossenschaftsrecht.* A paperback edition was published in 1957 by Beacon Press.

SUPPLEMENTARY BIBLIOGRAPHY

BARKER, ERNEST   (1934) 1950   Translator's Introduction. Pages ix–xci in Otto von Gierke, *Natural Law and the Theory of Society, 1500 to 1800.* Cambridge Univ. Press. → An important work about Gierke.

EMERSON, RUPERT   1928   *State and Sovereignty in Modern Germany.* New Haven: Yale Univ. Press. → See Chapter 4, pages 126–154 on "The School of the *Genossenschaft.*"

GURVITCH, GEORGES   1922   Otto von Gierke als Rechtsphilosoph. *Logos: Internationale Zeitschrift für Philosophie der Kultur* 11:86–132.

LEWIS, JOHN D.   1935   *The Genossenschaft-theory of Otto von Gierke: A Study in Political Thought.* Madison: Univ. of Wisconsin. → An appendix contains translated extracts from Gierke's *Das deutsche Genossenschaftsrecht; Johannes Althusius . . . ; Das Wesen der menschlichen Verbände;* and *Die Grundbegriffe des Staatsrechts.*

MAITLAND, FREDERIC WILLIAM   (1900) 1958   Introduction. In Otto von Gierke, *Political Theories of the Middle Age.* Cambridge Univ. Press.

PREUSS, HUGO   1910   Die Lehre Gierkes und das Problem der preussischen Verwaltungsreform. Volume 1, pages 245–304 in Berlin Universität, Juristische Fakultät, *Festgabe der Berliner juristischen Fakultät für Otto Gierke zum Doktor-Jubiläum 21 august 1910.* Breslau (then Germany): Marcus.

SCHULTZE, ALFRED   1923   Otto von Gierke als Dogmatiker des bürgerlichen Rechts. *Jherings Jahrbücher für die Dogmatik des bürgerlichen Rechts* 73:i–xlvi.

STUTZ, ULRICH   1922   Zur Erinnerung an Otto von Gierke. *Zeitschrift der Savigny-Stiftung für Rechtsgeschichte* (Germanistische Abteilung) 43:vii–lxiii. → Contains a bibliography.

TIERNEY, BRIAN   1955   *Foundations of the Conciliar Theory: The Contribution of the Medieval Canonists From Gratian to the Great Schism.* Cambridge Univ. Press. → Pages 98–105 discuss, with references, some criticism of Gierke's interpretations of medieval political theory and canon law.

GIFFEN, ROBERT

Sir Robert Giffen (1837–1910) was a British statistician, economist, and writer on finance. He was born in the Scottish town of Strathaven and was educated at the local village school. He showed an early aptitude for journalism, he and his brother contributing anonymous poems and articles to the local newspaper. At the age of 13 he entered the office of a Glasgow solicitor in a very minor position but made use of his seven years' stay in that city by attending lectures at the university. Journalism, however, attracted Giffen more than the law, and in 1860 he became reporter and subeditor of the *Stirling Journal.* Like many another Scot before him, he was lured south of the border, and he became connected with the *Globe,* then more or less the official organ of Lord Palmerston's administration. After a short time on the *Fortnightly Review,* in 1868 he became subeditor of the *Economist,* then under the editorship of Walter Bagehot.

The time that Giffen spent in the city of London was to serve him well in his future career. His contact with Bagehot was especially profitable, for he acquired from Bagehot both his style and his methodology. His later connection with the city office of the *Daily News* provided an invaluable acquaintance with the London stock exchange and the ways of the London financial community.

In 1871, when the Report on Local Taxation was published, George Goschen, president of the Poor Law Board and main author of the report, acknowledged Giffen's assistance. The reputation so earned led to Giffen's appointment as chief of the statistical section and controller of corn returns at the Board of Trade. An attempt in 1876 to reorganize this body and transfer some of its functions to the Foreign Office proved unsatisfactory; the old Statistical Department was revived and reorganized with Giffen at its head as assistant secretary. In 1892 he became controller-general of the Commercial, Labour, and Statistical departments, a position he retained until his retirement in 1897, having received the K.C.B. in 1895 in recognition of his service.

When Giffen accepted his position in the civil service he obtained permission to publish his views on matters of economic interest. Indeed, he was very active in the affairs of the Royal Statistical Society and the Royal Economic Society; he was influential in the founding of the latter body in 1890 and president of the former from 1882 to 1884. A frequent, almost prolific, contributor to the journals of both bodies, he was also editor of the

Journal of the Royal Statistical Society from 1876 to 1891 and provided the "city notes" in the *Economic Journal* until he died.

Giffen's reputation rests mainly on his work in "official statistics," a field which had been pioneered by G. R. Porter, who was the first to organize the crude, incomplete mass of statistics relating to revenue and commerce. Richard Valpy made further improvements, instituting the system of statistical abstracts. Giffen was largely responsible for the first attempts to collect figures relating to the wages of manual laborers and for setting up the Bureau of Labour Statistics. Although Giffen appeared to have little knowledge of the mathematical theory of statistics, he had a remarkable intuitive grasp of the significance of facts and figures, a gift that allowed him to clear the way through the most complicated problems by the use of bold estimates. He was always inclined to caution, but his imaginative approach caused him to tackle such problems as the measurement of national income, which had formerly been considered too difficult a task by many an able statistician. In addition, his journalistic flair did much to popularize the use of statistics, and his wide acquaintance and knowledge of the world of finance and business led government departments and official bodies to seek his advice. In fact, some of his most important work is to be found in official reports.

While at the height of his career, Giffen's opinion was respected in the fields both of applied and theoretical economics; today he is chiefly remembered for his "Paradox," mentioned in Book 3 of Marshall's *Principles* ([1890] 1961, p. 132). This exception to the general law of demand was held to operate in a community heavily dependent upon one commodity for its staple diet. If the price of this commodity falls, the real income of the community is increased so that it can afford to buy superior foodstuffs and thereby cut down its consumption of the "Giffen good." The opposite will occur in the case of a price rise, producing the unusual effect of quantity demanded increasing as prices rise and falling as prices fall.

Giffen was among the earliest to analyze the workings of the quantity theory of money, and the role played by the rate of interest, within an economy possessing a banking system. His ideas seem to have had a great deal of influence on Alfred Marshall, over and beyond the "Paradox." Giffen was very much concerned with the way in which the volume of "bank money" affects the level of currency. In *Stock Exchange Securities* (1877) and two essays, "The Effects on Trade of the Supply of Coinage" (in [1879–1885] 1886, pp. 89–104) and "Gold Supply: The Rate of Discount and Prices" (*ibid.*, pp. 37–88), he very clearly indicated the relationship that exists between a banker's cash reserves and the level of deposits, and the part played by the discount rate in bringing about an equilibrium between the supply of gold and the level of prices.

His "dispensation" from refraining to participate in current controversy allowed him to become a leading protagonist in many of the debates of the latter part of the nineteenth century. A staunch laissez-faire economist, he was an avid opponent of the protectionist and socialist schools, both at home and abroad; but he was willing to concede that protection could have political advantages, especially when it concerned colonial produce, and was willing to tolerate it in a mild degree if it was the only alternative to socialism. As might be expected, he was also opposed to much of Gladstone's financial policy and was a foremost antagonist of the bimetallist school.

K. J. PENNEY

[*For the historical context of Giffen's work, see the biography of* BAGEHOT; *for discussion of the subsequent development of his ideas, see the biography of* MARSHALL.]

WORKS BY GIFFEN

(1869–1879) 1890 *Essays in Finance.* First series. 5th ed. London: Bell.

(1869–1902) 1904 *Economic Inquiries and Studies.* 2 vols. London: Bell.

1877 *Stock Exchange Securities: An Essay on the General Causes of Fluctuations in Their Price.* London: Bell.

(1879–1885) 1886 *Essays in Finance.* Second series. New York: Putnam.

1889 *The Growth of Capital.* London: Bell.

1913 *Statistics . . . Written About the Years 1898–1900.* Edited with an introduction by Henry Higgs, and with the assistance of G. Udny Yule. London: Macmillan. → Published posthumously.

SUPPLEMENTARY BIBLIOGRAPHY

ANONYMOUS 1910 Sir Robert Giffen. *Economic Journal* 20:318–321.

BATEMAN, A. E. 1910 Sir Robert Giffen. *Journal of the Royal Statistical Society* Series A 73:529–533.

BROWN, ERNEST H. P.; and BROWNE, M. H. 1963 Carroll D. Wright and the Development of British Labour Statistics. *Economica* New Series 30:277–286.

ESHAG, EPRIME 1963 *From Marshall to Keynes: An Essay on the Monetary Theory of the Cambridge School.* Oxford: Blackwell.

MARSHALL, ALFRED (1890) 1961 *Principles of Economics.* 9th ed. New York and London: Macmillan. → See especially Book 3, page 132.

STIGLER, GEORGE 1947 Notes on the History of the Giffen Paradox. *Journal of Political Economy* 55:152–156.

GIFFORD, EDWARD W.

Edward Winslow Gifford (1887–1959), American anthropologist, was born in Oakland, California. His formal schooling ended with a high school diploma. From 1904 to 1912 he was assistant curator of ornithology in the California Academy of Sciences and a member of academy expeditions to the Revillagigedo Islands in 1903 and to the Galapagos Islands in 1905–1906. He was appointed assistant curator of the Museum of Anthropology at the University of California in 1912 and became, successively, associate curator, curator, and director of the museum. In 1920 he was appointed lecturer in the department of anthropology, in 1938 associate professor, and in 1945 full professor.

In addition to his early interests in natural history (particularly ornithology and conchology), Gifford's range of anthropological interests and competence was very broad, including archeology, folklore, kinship, social organization, material culture, religion, and physical anthropology. In each of these fields he made both substantive and theoretical contributions.

Gifford's major effort was directed toward the ethnology of California Indians. He wrote a number of monographs on tribal groups in California and a number of articles on special aspects of the culture of Californian aboriginal societies. With the exception of those of A. L. Kroeber, Gifford's contributions to California ethnography are quantitatively larger than those of any other worker.

Archeology was a secondary interest, but in 1948, toward the end of his career, he began an investigation of Oceanian archeology that resulted in major excavations in Fiji, New Caledonia, and Yap. The archeology of northwestern Mexico attracted his interest in 1945 and 1946, and he made several important contributions to that field.

Gifford's ethnographies are filled with detail. Informants who contributed information beyond that pertaining to the direct question were apparently allowed to continue, and these bits of volunteered data were usually noted and included. The result of this leniency with informants is that Gifford's ethnographic accounts contain a multitude of data that does not occur in the published ethnographies of any other worker, and these data often provide some fact or allow some insight that cannot be obtained when only those data are reported that relate to generalizations.

Gifford was unusual in sensing the importance of recording individual experiences of aboriginal informants at a time long before this kind of information was considered important. Thus, his study of Clear Lake Pomo society stands as a pioneer attempt to determine the actual composition of local groups by the genealogical method (1922). His monograph on the Northfork Mono includes an extraordinarily detailed history of one informant, recorded in 1918, who could list no fewer than 23 settlements where she had lived in the course of her life, all of which were located within an area of approximately 150 square miles (1922). Such vignettes provide us with a means of viewing life in aboriginal California in terms of individual experience as well as impersonal customs and institutions.

Gifford did not hesitate to take on projects of synthesizing immense bodies of fact. Two of his largest works remain the main sources of primary data on two aspects of the California Indians: their physical characteristics (1926*a*) and their kinship terminologies (1922).

Beyond being a patient collector of facts, Gifford was competent at seeing and solving theoretical or terminological problems. In a paper on Euro-American culture contact in Tonga published in 1929, he became the first American anthropologist to use the term "acculturation" in the modern sense. The same is true of his use of the term "lineage," which he proposed, in a broad survey of political organization (1926*b*), as the basic unit of aboriginal California societies.

In archeology he was the first to devise a method, which has since become important, for segregating the components of refuse deposits, identifying them, and deriving from the proportions of each component economic interpretations, indications of dietary change over time, and reflections of the relations of the occupants to local environment. Gifford was among the first to employ the weight, rather than the count, of potsherds from archeological excavations to assess chronological changes in the ceramic complex.

In addition to his field investigations, Gifford guided the Museum of Anthropology at Berkeley for 44 years and directed its development of one of the major anthropological collections in the United States. The importance of the Berkeley collections rests not so much upon their size as upon the fact that an unusually large proportion of the materials was collected in the field by scholars, including Gifford himself, and is accompanied by information on cultural context. Gifford organized the collections to make the context of the objects as explicit as possible and constructed a card index for cross reference. Consequently, it is possible that no other major research collection in anthropology is more accessible to scholars.

ROBERT F. HEIZER

[*For the historical context of Gifford's work, see the biographies of* KROEBER *and* LOWIE.]

WORKS BY GIFFORD

1916 *Composition of California Shellmounds.* University of California Publications in American Archaeology and Ethnology, Vol. 12, No. 1. Berkeley: Univ. of California Press.

1922 *California Kinship Terminologies.* University of California Publications in American Archaeology and Ethnology, Vol. 18. Berkeley: Univ. of California Press.

1926a *Californian Anthropometry.* University of California Publications in American Archaeology and Ethnology, Vol. 22, No. 2. Berkeley: Univ. of California Press.

1926b *Miwok Lineages and the Political Unit in Aboriginal California. American Anthropologist* New Series 28:389–401.

1929 *Tongan Society.* Bernice P. Bishop Museum, Bulletin No. 61. Honolulu, Hawaii: The Museum.

1939 *The Coast Yuki. Anthropos* 34:292–375.

1949 KROEBER, ALFRED L.; and GIFFORD, EDWARD W. *World Renewal: A Cult System of Native Northwest California.* University of California Anthropological Records, No. 13. Berkeley: Univ. of California Press.

1951 *Archaeological Excavations in Fiji.* University of California Anthropological Records, Vol. 13, No. 3. Berkeley: Univ. of California Press.

SUPPLEMENTARY BIBLIOGRAPHY

FOSTER, GEORGE M. 1960 Edward Winslow Gifford, 1887–1959. *American Anthropologist* New Series 62:327–329.

HARVARD UNIVERSITY, PEABODY MUSEUM OF ARCHAEOLOGY AND ETHNOLOGY, LIBRARY 1963 Edward Winslow Gifford. Volume 9, pages 243–247 in *Catalogue, Part 1, Authors.* Boston: Hall.

GIFT TAXES

See under TAXATION.

GIFTS

See EXCHANGE AND DISPLAY *and the biography of* MAUSS.

GILDS

Gild studies form one of the more obvious links between history and the social sciences. Originating in nineteenth-century romantic interest in early Germanic institutions and the theme of liberty, they have played into three lines of speculation about the role of voluntary associations in societal development. The first began with controversy over the respective influence of "Germanist" theory based on the right to associate freely and of the Romanist theory that the right to associate is a concession from the prince. [*See the biographies of* GIERKE *and* SAVIGNY *for discussion of these theories and the controversy.*] This general dialectic is still being reformulated as a fundamental theoretical element in studies of ecclesiastical influence on the philosophy of law and in studies of the development of representative institutions. Research on this last subject is now, under the direction of an international commission, strongly comparative. But it focuses on the wider political communities of medieval and early modern Europe rather than on the smaller associations, which, to social anthropology, would be of at least equal significance. From the start, however, a second line of thought linked these with the elementary bonds of kinship, seeing them at first as an effort to transcend kinship loyalties and later as partially reverting to them. Research on this problem has lagged, although there are signs of its revival in France and Italy. A third line of thought, prominent in much of the better social history written in the third quarter of the nineteenth century and now revived by the influence of twentieth-century sociology, is concerned with nonpolitical aspects of the social controls that small associations may have exercised.

The tendency now is to interpret the term "gild" —the variant spelling "guild" is from the seventeenth century—as applying only to occupational associations. This was not the original sense of the word. It was specific only in signifying that members were under the obligation to "geld," that is, to make payments for purposes agreed upon. Throughout the Middle Ages, it was also synonymous with *fraternitas*—definable as a pseudo-kinship group of a character in principle congenial to Christianity. Since contemporary terminology varied from one period and one area to another, historians writing in English have found it convenient to adopt "gild" as a generic term for all of the smaller associations with a fraternal aspect; French and Italian usage distinguishes the occupational types (*corporations, corporazioni*) from the purely fraternal (*confréries, confraternitate*). Within Europe, historians can compare their findings on the basis of a common awareness of the political and social context in which any type of association ran its course. But now that ethnologists and historians of other civilizations are singling out occupational gilds for description and comment, comparative study will call for analyses going beyond the tradition of European political theory.

West European studies can, however, be a source of hypotheses, typologies, and, especially, of developmental models useful in all comparative work. The evidence on which they rest has undergone a great deal of critical examination; in the North it covers a thousand years and in Italy almost two thousand, running back into republican Rome. West European experience was, of course, affected by peculiarities of political and religious organization and by historical contingencies that varied from one country to another. It will be compressed here into a scheme of five phases, in each of which the relationship between small voluntary associations and public authority changed. The functions and the organization of the main types of gild characteristic of each phase will then be discussed, but space will not permit even a catalogue of the accompanying types of local power structures or any discussion of the highly influential examples of differentiated corporate bodies within the church (for which see *Histoire de l'église . . .* 1964).

The course of development.   The five phases of development may be described briefly as follows:

(1) In the northern "barbarian" kingdoms of the early Middle Ages, associations contributing to order pass unchallenged by weak monarchies.

(2) Monarchy asserts itself as the source of legitimacy of association. The papacy does the same in regard to religious orders but permits free fraternal association among the laity. This phase culminates in chartered concessions to town governments, which become more or less autonomous organs of public authority.

(3) Town governments, after some lag, permit the differentiation of citizen communities into occupational gilds, which serve both public and private ends.

(4) Gilds are enmeshed in a system of state-regulated privilege. Noneconomic associations in Protestant states survive only through sectarian organization.

(5) Either voluntarily or in consequence of revolution, the state abandons the system of special privilege; economic gilds either atrophy or are abolished.

Phase 1.   In the societies to which phase 1 is applicable, customary law prevailed, and feud rather than royal authority was the chief sanction in the enforcement of law against crimes of violence. In other words, kinship was the traditional source of power in local communities. It is uncertain at what point gilds arose to offer supplementary protection (which was available also from lordship). The earliest known example is from the rules of the gild of thanes at Cambridge, written at some time in the late Anglo-Saxon period. This gild combined five functions: protection of members' property, discouragement of violence, mutual aid in sickness, common worship, and responsibility

for decent burial. An oath bound members, and banquets brought them together. They were men of upper middle rank. Their protective plan, if one of them were robbed, was to track down the thief and compel him to raise the large sum of 8 pounds as compensation. Their way of discouraging violence was simply to add to the normal pecuniary penalties: the rules allow for the possibility of the murder of one "brother" by another and demand only that the murderer pay 8 pounds to the gild in addition to the wergild due to the kindred of his victim. A group strong enough to intimidate thieves and to fine its own members heavily was obviously a formidable power in any local community. Even fraternities professing no purpose but group worship, conviviality, and the support of a loan and burial fund could mobilize power to maintain order.

Phase 2.   The second phase was inaugurated in Frankish territory by Charlemagne's fear that sworn gilds might disrupt the feeble unity of his realm. Gild power, he realized, depended on the oath; the words "to live or die together" could be added to it secretly to create a group as solidary as a kindred, but also expansible and potentially defiant of all law but its own. Charlemagne banned sworn gilds but was unable to suppress them. His edicts, however, bestowed a kind of legitimacy on unsworn gilds for mutual aid. There were probably already merchant gilds among them; they grew as trade grew and by the eleventh century had a more elaborate organization than the earlier protective gilds. The cloth merchants of Valenciennes, for example, had a salaried secretary elected for life, a treasurer, an almoner, a dean, their own priests, an elected judicial board of 12, and, as chief officer, a mayor.

The specific legitimation of gilds by charter came about slowly as part of that piecemeal granting of judicial or fiscal privileges to successive groups of town residents which preceded the full development of town governments. In early twelfth-century London, two artisan gilds received charters authorizing them to hold private courts, and other unchartered gilds of unspecified nature were made to pay for the privilege of existing. The older freedom of association survived only under the shelter of the church, in the form of parish gilds supporting the cult of chosen saints.

Phase 3.   The differentiation of the citizen body into occupational gilds, which characterized the third phase, was a political process. It helped to redefine the line, which rapid immigration had tended to blur, between citizens and noncitizens resident in a town. It domesticated the primitive gild oath, making it a sanction of civic obedience. It turned gild officers into quasi-public officials and used gilds in the assignment of military and night-policing duties. Finally, it fostered political consciousness. Artisan gilds gave the towns whatever drive toward "democratic" reform they had; the new mercantile gilds mobilized resistance to this drive.

In the matter of social controls over economic conduct, the role of the gilds was mainly to introduce collective decisions about how to meet new and difficult situations. The move toward formal organization among artisans did not spread until the late thirteenth century, when, after two centuries of expanding trade, the towns were beginning to face more competitive conditions. The basic values of an ambitious but hard-pressed working population had long been rooted in the master artisan families. The need for hard work, frugality, and calculation had been beaten into many generations of sons and apprentices. Market officials had set checks on dishonesty in selling, and in the export industries merchants and their agents had done the same for manufacturing practices. Neighborhood opinion condemned open quarreling. Above all, Christian doctrine had set a moral and religious value on work and approved of honest gain. In their character as fraternities, both occupational and parish gilds had sharpened sanctions by grudging any grant from their loan or relief funds to members who failed in business through laziness, intemperance, or "folly." The last notion covered bad judgment in not following the regular mercantile practice of dividing capital among separate ventures to reduce risk. Enterprising artisans had undertaken local trade in the materials of their craft as an avenue of upward mobility; in twelfth-century Genoa they had even made small investments in the port's booming overseas trade. The Genoese of that age had already adopted Ben Franklin's maxim that "Time is money," their trade and loan contracts being dated by the hour of the day.

The new formal organizations tried to keep up the reputation of their members' wares for high quality, to lower costs by reducing wages, and to cover up disputes over technical innovations that would lower costs. In all such matters both mercantile and artisan gilds acted to some extent as secret societies. Although gilds had to submit a code of rules to the city authorities in order to be recognized as legitimate, there was no regular check on the interpretation of the rules or their amendment. Disagreement over competitive practices was sometimes so bitter as to lead to the realignment of dissident groups into new gilds.

As is well known, the fund-raising power of the gilds was drawn on to support not only the cult of patron saints but also the major festivals through which the spiritual values of the entire community were reaffirmed. The persistence with which gilds cultivated pleasant manners within their own circles is less well appreciated; at a gild meeting, all overt aggression, whether by word or deed, was relentlessly penalized. This is worth remark in an age when, despite centuries of Christian teaching, overt aggression was still common among the aristocracy, the peasantry, and the floating lower level of the urban population. The gilds may further be credited with inventing the bourgeois pattern of periodic, respectable festivity among married couples.

The Italian gild movement of this period was the first to draw the secular professions into its pattern of organization, and in Tuscany lay "Round Table" clubs imitated the gild practice of employing notaries to draft their "statutes." Neither universities nor military organizations can be dealt with here, but it should be noted that the fraternity form was permitted to alien groups of artisans and that in the Low Countries it was used, at the instigation of lords, to keep archers in training. In illicit, sworn forms it persisted among Frisian pirates, in French resistance to English occupation, and among unfree peasants raising funds to sue for or buy freedom. Heretic groups, on the other hand, preferred hierarchic forms of organization under charismatic leadership.

Phase 4. The fourth phase, especially in provincial towns in the sixteenth and seventeenth centuries, saw the social and economic activity of industrial gilds at its height, but political and economic circumstances were changing. State power standing above town administrations was readier than ever to grant enlarged powers to harass local competitors, gild offices fell more than ever into the hands of mercantile entrepreneurs, and subordinate fraternities of wage workers were suppressed.

Phase 5. The fifth phase, during which gild organization of trade and industry died out, dragged on from the seventeenth into the nineteenth century, according as new industrial development and reaction against the old system of privilege were precocious or late. There had always been skepticism as to whether gilds stood, as they claimed, for the public interest. North of the Alps the spectacle of rural industry, based either on handicrafts or on new mechanization, progressing without benefit of gilds, fanned this skepticism long before it found theoretical exposition in new economic thought and propaganda. Then, too, as "fraternity" flamed up as a national, and international, slogan, the old local fraternal forms of association became obsolete. True, the question of continuity between the old forms and the new craft unions, burial clubs, etc., intrigues historians, but the story remains incomplete.

Comparisons with developmental models that might be constructed for other civilizations, including the rapidly moving kaleidoscope of present-day Africa, would rest, in the first instance, on the place of universalist principles in the legitimation of association. In all their phases European gilds were in part particularistic in spirit, but it was their contributions to order and religion that, from the first, were the basis of their legitimation. In Europe it was through the medieval gilds that universalist principles of policy protecting the consumer against fraud and dangers to health (e.g., from soiled second-hand mattress stuffing, diseased meat, and impure drugs) were first explicitly formulated. After the demise of the gilds, such functions had ultimately to be taken over by the state, and they have been the essential justification for the revival of professional and trade associations. [*See* LICENSING, OCCUPATIONAL.] In Islam, artisan gilds, whose appearance must now be dated no earlier than the thirteenth century (Goitein 1964), were the bearers of a universalist fraternal philosophy. Particularist aspects of Western gilds have been exaggerated by an uncritical acceptance of the notion that a son necessarily followed his father's trade. Comparative study on this point has to be quantitative and has to take account of general demographic trends and the channeling of migration to towns. Far from being a worked-out field, the study of voluntary associations can still illuminate many aspects of society. [*See* VOLUNTARY ASSOCIATIONS.]

SYLVIA L. THRUPP

BIBLIOGRAPHY

ARNAKIS, GEORGE G. 1953 Futuwwa Traditions in the Ottoman Empire: Akhis, Bektashi Dervishes, and Craftsmen. *Journal of Near Eastern Studies* 12:232–247.

BAZANT, JAN 1964 Evolution of the Textile Industry of Puebla: 1544–1845. *Comparative Studies in Society and History* 7:56–69.

DAVIS, NATALIE Z. 1965 Strikes and Salvation at Lyons. *Archiv für Reformationsgeschichte* 56:48–64.

DE ROOVER, RAYMOND 1962 La doctrine scolastique en matière de monopole et son application à la politique économique des communes italiennes. Pages 149–179 in *Studi in onore di Amintore Fanfani.* Volume 1: Antichità e alto medievo. Milan (Italy): Giuffrè.

ESPINAS, GEORGES 1943 Le droit d'association dans les villes de l'Artois et de la Flandre française depuis les origines jusqu'au début du XVIe siècle. Volume 3, pages 179–230 in *L'organisation corporative du moyen âge à la fin de l'ancien régime.* Louvain, Université Catholique, Recueil de travaux d'histoire et de philologie, 3d Series, fasc. 18. Louvain (Belgium): Bibliothèque de l'Université, Bureau du Recueil.

GOITEIN, S. D. 1964 Artisans en Méditerranée orientale au haut moyen âge. *Annales: Économies, sociétés, civilisations* 19:847–868.

Histoire de l'église depuis les origines jusqu'à nos jours. Volume 12, Part 1, Books ii–vi: Institutions ecclésiastiques de la Chrétienté médiévale, by Gabriel Le Bras. 1964 Paris: Bloud & Gay. → Contains a bibliography on Christian fraternities in the footnotes on pages 414–417.

KAHL, WILLIAM F. 1962 A Checklist of Books, Pamphlets, and Broadsides on the London Livery Companies. *Guildhall Miscellany* 2:99–126.

KELLENBENZ, HERMANN 1963 Les industries rurales en occident de la fin du moyen âge au XVIIIe siècle. *Annales: Économies, sociétés, civilisations* 18:833–882.

KELLETT, J. R. 1958 The Breakdown of Gild and Corporation Control Over the Handicraft and Retail Trade in London. *Economic History Review* 2d Series 10:381–394.

LEDOUX, R. 1912 *La suppression du régime corporatif dans les Pays-Bas autrichiens en 1784. Un projet d'édit.* Académie Royale de Belgique, Classe des Lettres et des Sciences Morales . . . , Mémoires, Collection in-8°, 2d Series, Vol. 10, fasc. 1. Brussels: Hayez.

LE TOURNEAU, ROGER 1957 *Les villes musulmanes de l'Afrique du Nord.* Algiers: La Maison des Livres.

LEWIS, BERNARD 1937 The Islamic Guilds. *Economic History Review* 8:20–37.

LITTLE, KENNETH 1957 The Role of Voluntary Associations in West African Urbanization. *American Anthropologist* New Series 59:579–596.

MORSE, HOSEA B. (1909) 1932 *The Gilds of China, With an Account of the Gild Merchant or Co-hong of Canton.* 2d ed. London: Longmans.

SOCIÉTÉ JEAN BODIN POUR L'HISTOIRE COMPARATIVE DES INSTITUTIONS 1954–1955 *La ville.* 2 parts. Recueils, Vols. 6–7. Brussels: Librairie Encyclopédique. → Part 1: *Institutions administratives et judiciaires.* Part 2: *Institutions économiques et sociales.*

THRUPP, SYLVIA L. 1963 The Gilds. Pages 230–280 in *The Cambridge Economic History of Europe From the Decline of the Roman Empire.* Volume 3: Economic Organization and Policies in the Middle Ages. Cambridge Univ. Press. → A bibliography appears on pages 624–634.

WAGNER, DONALD O. 1937 The Common Law and Free Enterprise: An Early Case of Monopoly. *Economic History Review* 7:217–220.

WALTZING, JEAN PIERRE 1895–1900 *Étude historique sur les corporations professionelles chez les Romains depuis les origines jusqu'à la chute de l'empire d'occident.* 4 vol. Louvain (Belgium): Peeters.

GINI, CORRADO

The work of Corrado Gini (1884–1965) has had a profound impact on many fields within the social sciences. The son of a manufacturer, Gini was born in Motta di Livenza, Treviso Province. He studied law at the University of Bologna, where he also took courses in mathematics. The broad scope of his scholarly contributions is reflected in the variety of subjects he taught, successively, at the universities of Cagliari, Padua, and Rome: statistics, political economy, demography, biometrics, constitutional law, and sociology.

Gini also furthered the development of social science in other than academic capacities. From 1926 to 1932 he was chairman of the Central Institute of Statistics. He directed several scientific expeditions to study the demographic, anthropometric, and medical characteristics of particular ethnic groups in Fezzan, Palestine, Mexico, Poland and Lithuania, Calabria, and Sardinia, as well as the processes of assimilation of immigrant groups generally. He was the founder and editor of the international journal of statistics *Metron*, in 1920, and of the journal *Genus*, the organ of the Italian Committee for the Study of Population Problems.

In recognition of his achievements he was awarded honorary doctorates, one in economic science—from the Catholic University in Milan, in 1932—and another in sociology—from the University of Geneva, in 1934; and he was awarded an honorary doctor of science degree by Harvard at the 1936 tercentenary celebration of that university.

The main currents of thought in Italian culture at the time that Gini began his scientific activity were positivism and idealism. Gini's commitment to positivism was limited. His works manifest a remarkable eclecticism, arising from his systematic study of a variety of disciplines: law, economics, statistics, mathematics, and biology. He always placed the phenomena he was studying in a more general context, bringing essential social, economic, and demographic elements to bear on the topic of his immediate concern.

Gini thoroughly understood the importance of descriptive statistics, as is shown by his particular admiration for Luigi Bodio among Italian statisticians, but at the same time he deeply felt the need to study the procedures of inferential statistics and to find suitable criteria for evaluating those procedures. To this end he studied the works of Bernoulli, Lexis, and Czuber, as well as those of the Italians Angelo Messedaglia and Rodolfo Benini.

Contributions to statistical method. Gini's first scientific works deal with the statistical regularity of rare events. To the same period—1908 to 1911—belongs his initial work on the concept and measurement of probability, with special attention and application to the human sex ratio at birth. His findings were contained in a book (1908) in which he presented analyses of extensive empirical materials on sex ratios from different countries. In the same work, he developed a theory of dispersion,

that is, of the quantitative structure of the scatter or variability among measured quantities of the same kind. He later returned to the topic of dispersion (1940; 1941).

Gini made a lengthy critique of the principles of statistics in order to reinforce the logical basis of statistics and to rid it of naïve empiricism. He wished to raise statistics to the level of an independent science, one of whose tasks would be the systematic investigation of the advantages and limitations of various indexes, or descriptive statistics, under differing structures of error.

In an address entitled "I pericoli della statistica" (1939; "The Dangers of Statistics"), inaugurating the first meeting of the Società Italiana di Statistica, Gini warned statisticians about the faulty logical foundations of some statistical methods and stressed the importance of estimating meaningful parameters. He published further papers on this general subject (1943; 1947). In the latter paper, "Statistical Relations and Their Inversions," he pointed out that poor statistical notation may lead to misunderstanding and error. For example, if one writes $y = 3 + 7x$, as a mathematical relationship between the real variables x and y, one may just as well write $x = -\frac{3}{7} + \frac{1}{7}y$; this is called invertibility. On the other hand, in a statistical context of regression, one may loosely write $y = 3 + 7x$, meaning that the expectation (or average) of a random variable Y is thus linearly related to possible values of another random variable X. For clarity, one should use a more complete notation like the now conventional

$$E(Y|X = x) = 3 + 7x,$$

and, in general, $E(X|Y = y) \neq -\frac{3}{7} + \frac{1}{7}y$. On the other hand, taking complete averages, $EY = 3 + 7EX$; this situation is called one of subinvertibility.

In a paper written in collaboration with Luigi Galvani, "Di talune estensioni dei concetti di media ai caratteri qualitativi" (1929; "Extension of Mean Value Theory to Qualitative Characteristics"), Gini made an original contribution in another area. The problem here was to find a meaningful analogue of the usual arithmetic mean for a purely qualitative or nominal distribution. By defining a measure of deviation between any two classes of the qualitative classification and by a minimization argument, Gini showed how to choose one of the classes of the classification as a kind of mean.

The theory of generalized means was of continuing interest to Gini, and he was particularly concerned with its very general expression and with a wide variety of mean values (1938). In another article, again with Galvani, he discussed extensively the topic of location parameters for bivariate distributions, noting especially geographical problems (see Gini et al. 1933).

Next to generalized means, measures of variability are of great importance, and Gini discussed these at length, giving special attention to descriptive statistics not intrinsically tied to the normal distribution (1912). He introduced a new measure of variability, the *mean difference*, which is essentially the expected absolute value of $X_1 - X_2$, where X_1 and X_2 are independent random variables with the same distribution of interest. (Gini thought primarily in terms of the sample version of the mean difference.)

Gini also worked on measures of variability for qualitative or nominal distributions and on measures of variability that are tied to the concentration curve and are considered important in the economic analysis of income and wealth (1921).

Nontypicality of typical census areas. Gini set himself the task of selecting a sample of typical census areas in Italy. To this end, he showed that it is not adequate simply to select the sample in such a way that the averages of various characteristics calculated for the sample are equal to those calculated for the entire territory of Italy. Even when the examination is confined to only the characteristics used in selecting the sample, the sample proves to be unrepresentative with respect to the variability and concentration of those characteristics and to the relations existing between them. Accordingly, Gini included in the criteria of representativeness these last two aspects of the distributions of characteristics, and he examined the conditions to which each of the proposed criteria subjects the other criteria.

Theory of price indexes. To the theory of price indexes, which is of great importance in economic statistics, Gini contributed a classic paper, "Quelques considérations au sujet des nombres indices des prix et des questions analogues" (1924), in which he solved some logical and technical problems connected with elimination methods.

Distinguishing between simple and complex indices, Gini showed how, in general, the methods for obtaining complex indexes can be considered as particular cases of the method of elimination (which consists in separating the different circumstances affecting a phenomenon in order to make comparisons *ceteris paribus* with similar phenomena at different times or places). The problem was to keep the phenomenon of "price variation" distinct from the phenomenon of "quantity variation."

Operating with the general method of the "typical population" organized into four special methods, Gini obtained various formulas for index numbers, at the same time providing criteria for choosing that one of the formulas best suited to the aims of particular problems. (Another of his papers on the same topic is "Methods of Eliminating the Influence of Several Groups of Factors," 1937).

Theory of distributions. Gini made substantial contributions to the study of relationships between two probability distributions and between two random variables with a joint distribution. Particularly important are the following:

(*a*) *Transvariation.* Suppose that one considers two probability distributions, represented for convenience by (independent) random variables X, Y. Suppose further that $EX < EY$; it may still be quite probable that $X > Y$, that is, the difference between the observations X and Y may show a different sign than the corresponding difference between expected values. Gini proposed a specific measure for this phenomenon, which he called transvariation (1953; 1959*a*; see also Kruskal 1957).

(*b*) *Distance between two distributions.* Gini was one of the first to consider the problem of measuring meaningfully how much two probability distributions differ in gross (1914*a*). He proposed a measure of distance, based on the two cumulative distribution functions, that was in fact a metric in the technical mathematical sense (see Fréchet 1947).

(*c*) *Association between two random variables with a joint distribution.* Gini made the basic distinction between *connection* (any kind of statistical dependence) and *concordance* (dependence in which it makes sense to speak of one variable tending to increase—or decrease—along with the other). The correlation ratio, for example, is a measure of connection, while the coefficient of correlation is a measure of concordance. Gini analyzed previously suggested measures of association and proposed new ones both for the case of numerical variates and for that of qualitative variates (see Goodman & Kruskal 1959, which contains relevant references to Gini, Weida, and Pietra).

Demography and biometrics. Gini pioneered in studies that relate demographic phenomena to social and biological phenomena. Thus, he studied the sources of differential fertility (1949), and he related the phenomenon of migration to broader social and demographic considerations (1946*b*).

Gini also proposed a unified research program for analyzing the eugenic and dysgenic effects of war, with special emphasis on the measurement of the effects of war on mortality (1915–1920). Also related to demographic phenomena are Gini's studies of various populations in phases of expansion, regression, and extinction (1934).

Economic and sociological research. From the earliest years of his career, Gini tackled the difficult problem of estimating national wealth. He made a constructive criticism of the method of the interval of devolution and the first calculation by a direct method of the private wealth of Italy (1914b). He followed a methodological organization of the data with a comparative study of the qualitative composition of wealth, clarifying the conditions that make nations wealthy (1959b).

Gini originated the idea of including the value of human capital in the calculation of wealth [see CAPITAL, HUMAN]. This makes it possible to indicate the preponderant cause for the incommensurability in time and territory of the wealth and economic well-being of various collectivities (1956a). The value-as-property of the man who labors becomes a factor in estimating wealth, just as the share derived from human labor is included in income (1914a). This conception clearly links economic considerations with sociological and demographic ones.

Related to Gini's conception of human capital is his cyclical theory of population. Observing the differential rates of reproduction of social classes, Gini formulated a theory of social metabolism that is based on an analogy to organic metabolism: the upper classes, having low rates of reproduction, will tend to extinction unless they get new members from the lower classes, which have higher rates of reproduction (1927). Gini intended this theory to replace Pareto's concept of the circulation of elites.

Gini also developed a theory of phases of population growth, these being related to social and economic phenomena (1923). According to his theory, a particular population grows rapidly in the first phase of its development, then has a diminishing rate of growth until it is approximately stationary, and finally begins a decline that may even lead to total extinction. In the first phase, capital is very scarce and there is little differentiation between social classes; later, as capital is accumulated, classes become increasingly differentiated, and there is a concomitant differentiation of reproductive behavior. As birth control spreads, a deterioration in the quality of the population can be avoided only by the influence of external factors, such as the immigration of young people from populations in the phase of demographic expansion.

Gini's neo-organicist approach makes it possible to distinguish normal economic processes from pathological ones—those in which the state of a society is unbalanced—and to initiate economic processes of restoration. In general, he believed that states of imbalance could be remedied by the regulatory activities of political agencies and of economic organizations.

In Gini's view, an important aspect of the development of society is the transition from forced to free labor and then to spontaneous labor (1956b). This last represents the final stage in a psychological process that raises labor from a primordial means of obtaining a living to a free and autonomous activity that enriches the human personality.

Gini's pre-eminent place in the development of Italian statistics is based on a dual contribution: his work in scientific statistics, which included important teaching and editorial activities; and his efforts toward the development of official statistics, notably, the consolidation in a single institute of all the various agencies for the collection of data and the extension of the number of items about which data are collected.

TOMMASO SALVEMINI

[*Directly related are the entries* SAMPLE SURVEYS; STATISTICS, DESCRIPTIVE; VARIANCES, STATISTICAL STUDY OF. *Other relevant material may be found in* CENSUS; GENETICS; INCOME DISTRIBUTION, *article on* SIZE; INDEX NUMBERS; MIGRATION; POPULATION; *and in the biographies of* BENINI; BERNOULLI FAMILY; LEXIS; PARETO.]

WORKS BY GINI

1908 *Il sesso dal punto di vista statistico: Le leggi della produzione dei sessi.* Milan: Sandron.

(1912) 1955 *Memorie di metodologia statistica.* Volume 1: Variabilità e concentrazione. 2d ed. Rome: Veschi.

1914a *Di una misura della dissomiglianza fra due gruppi di quantità e delle sue applicazioni allo studio delle relazioni statistiche.* Venice: Ferrari.

(1914b) 1962 *L'ammontare e la composizione della ricchezza della nazioni.* 2d ed. Turin: Bocca.

(1915–1920) 1921 *Problemi sociologici della guerra.* Bologna: Zanichelli. → A collection of previously published articles.

1921 Measurement of Inequality of Incomes. *Economic Journal* 31:124–126.

(1923) 1952 *Patologia economica.* 5th ed., rev. & enl. Turin: Unione Tipografico–Editrice Torinese.

1924 Quelques considérations au sujet de la construction des nombres indices des prix et des questions analogues. *Metron* 4:3–162.

1927 *Il neo-organicismo: Prolusione al corso di sociologia.* Catania: Studio Editoriale Moderno.

1929 GINI, CORRADO; and GALVANI, LUIGI Di talune estensioni dei concetti di media ai caratteri qualitativi. *Metron* 8, no. 1/2:3–209.

1933 GINI, CORRADO; BERARDINIS, L. DE; and GALVANI, L. Sulla selettività delle cause di morte durante l'infanzia. *Metron* 11, no. 1:163–183.

1934 Ricerche sulla popolazione. *Scientia* 55:357–373.

1937 Methods of Eliminating the Influence of Several Groups of Factors. *Econometrica* 5:56–73.

1938 Di una formula comprensiva delle medie. *Metron* 13:3–22.

1939 I pericoli della statistica. *Rivista di politica economica* 29:901–924.

1940 Sur la théorie de la dispersion et sur la vérification et l'utilisation des schémas théoriques. *Metron* 14:3–29.

1941 Alle basi del metodo statistico: Il principio della compensazione degli errori accidentali e la legge dei grandi numeri. *Metron* 14:173–240.

1943 I testi di significatività. Società Italiana di Statistica, *Atti* [1943]:241–279.

1946a Actualidades demográficas. *Revista internacional de sociología* 4:147–169.

1946b Los efectos demográficos de las migraciones internacionales. *Revista internacional de sociología* 4:351–388.

1947 Statistical Relations and Their Inversions. International Statistical Institute, *Revue de l'Institut International de Statistique* 15:24–42.

1948 Evoluzione della psicologia del lavoro e della accumulazione. Banca Nazionale del Lavoro, *Moneta e credito* Whole No. 2.

1949 Vecchie e nuove osservazioni sulle cause della natalità differenziale e sulla misura della fecondità naturale delle coniugate. *Metron* 15:207–358.

1950 Metodologia statistica: La misura dei fenomeni collettivi. Volume 3, part 2, pages 245–321 in *Enciclopedia delle matematiche elementari*. Milan: Hoepli.

1951 Caractère des plus récents développements de la méthodologie statistique. *Statistica* 11:3–11.

1952 On Some Symbols That May Be Usefully Employed in Statistics. International Statistical Institute, *Bulletin* 33, no. 2:249–282.

1953 The Measurement of the Differences Between Two Quantity Groups and in Particular Between the Characteristics of Two Populations. *Acta genetica et statistica medica* 4:175–191.

1955 Sur quelques questions fondamentales de statistique. Paris, Université, Institut Henri Poincaré, *Annales* 14:245–364.

1956a Valutazione del lavoro e del capitale nell' *Economia lavorista*. *Rivista bancaria* New Series 12:522–530.

1956b *Economia lavorista: Problemi del lavoro.* Turin: Tipografia Sociale Torinese.

(1956c) 1966 *Statistical Methods.* Rome: Biblioteca del Metron. → Lectures delivered at the International Center for Training in Agricultural Economics and Statistics, Rome.

1958 Logic in Statistics. *Metron* 19, no. 1/2:1–77.

1959a *Transvariazione.* Rome: Libreria Goliardica.

1959b *Ricchezza e reddito.* Turin: Unione Tipografico–Editrice Torinese.

1959c Mathematics in Statistics. *Metron* 19, no. 3/4:1–9.

SUPPLEMENTARY BIBLIOGRAPHY

CASTELLANO, VITTORIO 1965 Corrado Gini: A Memoir With the Complete Bibliography of His Works. *Metron* 24; no. 1–4.

FRÉCHET, MAURICE 1947 Anciens et nouveaux indices de corrélation: Leur application au calcul des retards économiques. *Econometrica* 15:1–30, 374–375.

FRÉCHET, MAURICE 1947–1948 Le coefficient de connexion statistique de Gini–Salvemini. *Mathematica* 23:46–51.

FRÉCHET, MAURICE 1957 Sur la distance de deux lois de probabilité. Paris, Université, Institut de Statistique, *Publications* 6:183–198.

GALVANI, LUIGI 1947 À propos de la communication de M. Thionet: "L'école moderne de statisticiens italiens." Société de Statistique de Paris, *Journal* 88:196–203. → A bitter attack on the 1945–1946 article by Pierre Thionet. See pages 203–208 for Thionet's reply to Galvani.

GOODMAN, LEO A.; and KRUSKAL, WILLIAM H. 1959 Measures of Association for Cross-classifications: II. Further Discussion and References. *Journal of the American Statistical Association* 54:123–163.

KRUSKAL, WILLIAM H. 1957 Historical Notes on the Wilcoxon Unpaired Two-sample Test. *Journal of the American Statistical Association* 52:356–360.

NEYMAN, JERZY (1938) 1952 *Lectures and Conferences on Mathematical Statistics and Probability.* 2d ed., rev. & enl. Washington: U.S. Department of Agriculture, Graduate School.

SALVEMINI, TOMMASO 1943 La revisione critica di Gini ai fondamenti della metodologia statistica. *Statistica* 3:46–59.

THIONET, PIERRE 1945–1946 L'école moderne de statisticiens italiens. Société de Statistique de Paris, *Journal* 86:245–255; 87:16–34.

GIRSHICK, MEYER A.

Meyer Abraham Girshick (1908–1955), American statistician, was born in Russia and immigrated to the United States in 1922. After graduating from Columbia College in 1932, he did graduate work in statistics under Harold Hotelling at Columbia University from 1934 until 1937. (Several years later he received a doctorate from Columbia.) In 1937–1939 he was a statistician with the Bureau of Home Economics, U.S. Department of Agriculture, where he participated in a pioneer study of body measurements of 147,000 American children that helped manufacturers to develop improved sizing of garments. At the same time, he gave evening courses in statistics at the U.S. Department of Agriculture Graduate School, courses that had a profound influence on the dissemination of sound statistical methods in government work and encouraged many new research workers. In 1939–1944 and again in 1945–1946 he was principal statistician for the Bureau of Agricultural Economics. For one year during World War II he participated in the work of the Statistical Research Group at Columbia University, a panel composed of statisticians and designed to develop statistical methods appropriate to wartime problems. Working with others on the panel, particularly Abraham Wald, had a decisive influence on Girshick's subsequent career. After a brief stay at the Bureau of the Census, he became a research statistician and mathematician at the RAND Corporation in Santa Monica, California (a research organization primarily devoted to work for the U.S. Air Force). From 1948 until his untimely death in 1955 he was professor of statistics at Stanford University. He was elected president of the Institute of Mathematical Statistics (one of the principal learned societies for theoretical statistics) in 1951.

His early papers, written between 1936 and 1944, were primarily concerned with problems of multivariate statistical analysis. His major achievement was to find the distribution of the roots and characteristic vectors associated with certain determinantal equations that are used in testing the null hypothesis that two sets of variates are independent (1939). [See MULTIVARIATE ANALYSIS.]

Subsequently he also found the distribution of these roots when the null hypothesis is not true. From this the power function of certain tests can in principle be obtained (1941).

His interest in multivariate analysis and his substantive work at the Bureau of Agricultural Economics combined to turn his attention to newly developing methods of estimation of simultaneous equations in economics. These methods were originated by Trygve Haavelmo and continued by Tjalling Koopmans, T. W. Anderson, and Herman Rubin. In collaboration with Haavelmo, Girshick conducted one of the first major empirical studies on an econometric model for the agricultural sector of the United States economy (1947), and through unpublished work he contributed importantly to the development of the limited-information approach to simultaneous equation estimation. [See SIMULTANEOUS EQUATION ESTIMATION.]

During the period that Girshick was associated with the Statistical Research Group, Wald was originating two major concepts of statistics: sequential analysis and statistical decision theory [see DECISION THEORY; SEQUENTIAL ANALYSIS; and the biography of WALD]. Girshick's subsequent work was almost exclusively confined to these two areas (see Blackwell & Girshick 1954).

His earliest work in sequential analysis concerned the testing of composite hypotheses in which the mean of one process is less than, or equal to, the mean of another, the alternative being that it is greater. He showed that the power functions of such tests were constant on certain curves in the parameter space, and he was able to use this information to derive approximate sequential tests for the parameters of the exponential family of distributions (1946a). He also found exact relations for tests when the variables take on only a finite set of values. As a by-product of his interest in sequential analysis he found, in collaboration with Frederick Mosteller and L. J. Savage, a method of getting unbiased estimates of a parameter from data that have been generated by a sequential, or similar, sampling scheme (Girshick et al. 1946b). He and David Blackwell found a lower bound for the variance of such estimates (Blackwell & Girshick 1947).

His work in decision theory was developed in a series of papers, most of them coauthored with Blackwell, Rubin, Savage, or Arrow. The major results of these studies were systematically presented in *Theory of Games and Statistical Decisions* (1954), written jointly with Blackwell. This book today represents a major study of statistical method using the concepts of the theory of games from the decision-theory point of view. The theory of games, which is closely allied to decision theory, is also given prominence in the book. [See GAME THEORY.] Among its most noteworthy accomplishments are a study of the interrelations of various criteria for complete classes of solutions and related concepts and a systematic treatment of Bayesian and related procedures in statistical contexts. Other special features include rigorous analysis of the concepts of sufficiency and of invariance, a clear exposition and characterization of sequential probability-ratio tests and their optimal properties, a study of Bayesian estimation procedures with special loss functions, particularly the quadratic and the absolute value, and the theory of comparison of experiments.

Girshick's influence on the development of statistical theory occurred as much through his direct personal relations, his enthusiasm and intelligent guidance, as through his published work, important as the latter is.

KENNETH J. ARROW

WORKS BY GIRSHICK

1939 On the Sampling Theory of Determinantal Equations. *Annals of Mathematical Statistics* 10:203–224.

1941 The Distribution of the Ellipticity Statistic L_e When the Hypothesis Is False. *Terrestrial Magnetism and Atmospheric Electricity* 46:455–457.

1946a Contributions to the Theory of Sequential Analysis. *Annals of Mathematical Statistics* 17:123–143, 282–298.

1946b GIRSHICK, MEYER A.; MOSTELLER, FREDERICK; and SAVAGE, L. J. Unbiased Estimates for Certain Binomial Sampling Problems With Applications. *Annals of Mathematical Statistics* 17:13–23.

1947 GIRSHICK, MEYER A.; and HAAVELMO, TRYGVE Statistical Analysis of the Demand for Food: Examples of Simultaneous Estimation of Structural Equations. *Econometrica* 15:79–110.

1947 BLACKWELL, DAVID; and GIRSHICK, MEYER A. A Lower Bound for the Variance of Some Unbiased Sequential Estimates. *Annals of Mathematical Statistics* 18:277–280.

1954 BLACKWELL, DAVID; and GIRSHICK, MEYER A. *Theory of Games and Statistical Decisions.* New York: Wiley.

SUPPLEMENTARY BIBLIOGRAPHY

BLACKWELL, DAVID; and BOWKER, ALBERT H. 1955 Meyer Abraham Girshick: 1908–1955. *Annals of Mathematical Statistics* 26:365–367.

GLOTTOCHRONOLOGY

See LINGUISTICS.

GOALS

See ACHIEVEMENT MOTIVATION; DRIVES; MOTIVATION; ORGANIZATIONS, *article on* ORGANIZATIONAL GOALS; VOLUNTARY ASSOCIATIONS.

GOBINEAU, JOSEPH ARTHUR DE

Joseph Arthur de Gobineau (1816–1882) is best known as the author of the *Essai sur l'inégalité des races humaines* (1853–1855), which made race the principal explanatory factor in history and had an important influence on the development of the concept of race in the nineteenth century. Although during his lifetime Gobineau received little recognition in his native France, after his death his racial theories aroused considerable interest, especially in Germany.

The mystique of elitism and race in Gobineau's thought had its roots in certain circumstances of his life. His family was noble, but the origins of its nobility were obscure. His father, Louis de Gobineau, was a captain in the royal guard, and his mother, Anne-Louise Magdeleine de Gercy, was the daughter (if we believe Gobineau) of an illegitimate son of Louis xv. Gobineau's adolescence was tormented by the marital conflict between his parents, and he began very early to question whether "all kinds of blood and all origins are alike."

Gobineau went to Paris in 1835 and became a member of its literary, artistic, and scientific circles. He attended the salons of Madame de Serre, of Rémusat, and of Tocqueville. Initially he seemed to lean toward a sort of liberalism in politics, but the revolution of 1848 instilled in him a permanent abhorrence of democracy. When Tocqueville served as minister of foreign affairs of the republic in 1849, Gobineau became his private secretary, and upon Tocqueville's fall, Gobineau entered the diplomatic service. The books he wrote about the countries in which he lived—Germany, Persia, Greece, Brazil, and Sweden—were all pervaded by his theories of race.

Aristocratic by temperament himself, Gobineau sought passionately all his life to justify elitism both scientifically and philosophically. From the outset, he defined the elite in ethnic terms, identifying it with a superior race, a "race of masters." He asserted that the white race is superior to the yellow and black races by virtue of its intelligence, its capacity for reflection, its love of order and liberty, its sense of honor, and its pre-emption of all civilized values, and he claimed superiority among the whites for the pure Aryan. Unhappily, however, as he saw it, this ethnic hierarchy has no permanence, for races are constantly mixing; indeed, there are no more pure races. This mixing is disastrous, for it lowers the superior elements to the level of the less gifted and leads eventually to degeneration and to the extinction of civilization. On the political level, the mixing of races finds its expression in democracy, which Gobineau considered the worst form of state. In a draft foreword written in 1877 for a second edition of the *Essai*, he admitted that his race theory was "a natural consequence of [his] horror and disgust at democracy." The *Essai* reveals Gobineau's profound pessimism, ending as it does with an apocalyptic vision of the world in the final stage of decay—an era of uniformity, mediocrity, and passivity on the part of individuals.

Gobineau's pessimism about the fate of civilization came to be reinforced by the justified conviction that he was not being appreciated. His travels to Greece, Persia, and Brazil only served to confirm his idea that the mixture of races causes degeneration. Full of hatred and contempt for the "mixed breeds," he returned from Brazil to France in 1870 to experience the Franco–Prussian War, defeat, the Commune, and the installation of the republic. These events convinced him that the downfall of his country was inevitable, led as it was by the "Gallo–Roman rabble," the "bourgeoisie."

His last ministry was in Stockholm, from 1872 to 1876, and he did much writing there. He finished his novel *Les pléiades* (1874), in which he presented the idea that, as a consequence of racial degeneration, an elite must be sought among individuals—individuals who stand out by virtue of their love of liberty, their sense of honor, and their energy—and he went back to work on his poem *Amadis* (1887), into which he poured his feudal ideas, his hatreds, and his apocalyptic vision of a degenerate world. There too he worked on *Ottar Jarl* (1879), the story of a Norwegian pirate, the imaginary founder of his own family of which he claimed to be the last offshoot; the work is a rather pathetic attempt to prove that he was an elite being. In Stockholm, too, he embraced the pagan spirit, leaving behind not only the Catholicism of his family but also many other forms of religious and philosophical thought that he had accepted successively since childhood.

His growing hostility toward a society that failed to appreciate him led to his being retired prematurely in 1876. He lived out his last years in Italy, full of bitterness and pessimism, separated from his wife, and in financial stringency.

R. THENEN

[*For the historical context of Gobineau's work, see* RACE.]

WORKS BY GOBINEAU

(1847) 1961 *Mademoiselle Irnois, suivi de Adélaïde.* Paris: Gallimard.

(1853–1855) 1933 *Essai sur l'inégalité des races humaines.* 6th ed. 2 vols. Paris: Firmin-Didot. → Partially translated into English in 1915 as *The Inequality of Human Races.*

(1854–1876) 1933 *Correspondance entre le comte de Gobineau et le comte de Prokesh Osten (1854–1876).* Paris: Plon.

(1856–1863) 1959 *Les dépêches diplomatiques du comte de Gobineau en Perse.* Études d'histoire économique, politique et sociale, No. 30. Geneva: Droz.

(1859) 1923 *Trois ans en Asie (de 1855 à 1858).* Paris: Grasset.

1861 *Voyage à Terre-Neuve.* Paris: Hachette.

(1865) 1933 *Les religions et les philosophies dans l'Asie centrale.* Paris: Gallimard.

(1868–1881) 1936 *Lettres à deux athéniennes (1868–1881).* Athens: Castalie.

1869a *Histoire des perses d'après les auteurs orientaux, grecs et latins.* 2 vols. Paris: Nourrit.

1869b *L'Aphroessa.* Paris: Maillet.

(1870–1882) 1938 GOBINEAU, JOSEPH ARTHUR DE; and PEDRO II, EMPEROR OF BRAZIL D. *Pedro IIᵉ o conde de Gobineau (correspondencias ineditas).* São Paulo: Companhia Editora Nacional. → Letters written between 1870 and 1882. See pages 373–619 for the French originals.

1872 *Souvenirs de voyage (Céphalonie, Naxie et Terre-Neuve).* Paris: Plon-Nourrit.

(1872–1882) 1958 *Correspondance, 1872–1882: Comte de Gobineau et Mère Benedicte de Gobineau.* 2 vols. Paris: Mercure de France.

(1874) 1928 *The Pleiads.* New York: Knopf. → First published in French.

(1876) 1965 *Nouvelles asiatiques.* Paris: Garnier.

(1877) 1927 *The Renaissance: Savonarola, Cesare Borgia, Julius II, Leo X, Michaelangelo.* New York: Putnam. → First published in French.

1879 *Histoire d'Ottar Jarl, pirate norvégien, conquérant du pays de Bray en Normandie, et de sa descendance.* Paris: Didier.

1887 *Amadis, poème.* Paris: Plon. → Published posthumously.

1907 *La Troisième République française et ce qu'elle vaut.* Strasbourg: Trübner. → Published posthumously.

(1923) 1924 *The Golden Flower.* New York: Putnam. → Five historical essays published posthumously in French. Written originally as prefaces to the five parts of Gobineau's play *La renaissance,* 1877.

SUPPLEMENTARY BIBLIOGRAPHY

DREYFUS, ROBERT 1905 *La vie et les prophéties du comte de Gobineau.* Paris: Lévy.

Études gobiniennes. 1966 Paris: Klincksieck.

GAULMIER, JEAN 1965 *Spectre de Gobineau.* Paris: Pauvert.

Gobineau et le gobinisme. 1934 *Nouvelle revue française* 49. → The entire issue is devoted to Gobineau.

LANGE, MAURICE 1924 *Le comte Arthur de Gobineau: Étude biographique et critique.* Strasbourg: Librairie Istra.

[Numéro spécial consacré à Gobineau.] 1923 *Europe* No. 9.

[Numéro spécial consacré à Gobineau.] 1923 *Nouveau mercure,* 10.

ROWBOTHAM, ARNOLD 1929 *The Literary Works of Count de Gobineau.* Paris: Champion.

SCHEMANN, LUDWIG 1913–1916 *Gobineau: Eine Biographie.* 2 vols. Strasbourg: Trübner.

SCHEMANN, LUDWIG 1914–1923 *Quellen und Untersuchungen zum Leben Gobineau.* 2 vols. Strasbourg: Trübner.

SEILLÈRE, ERNEST 1903 *La philosophie de l'impérialisme.* Volume 1: Le comte de Gobineau et l'aryanisme historique. Paris: Plon-Nourrit.

SPRING, GERALD M. 1932 *The Vitalism of Count de Gobineau.* New York: Institute of French Studies.

TOCQUEVILLE, ALEXIS DE (1843–1859) 1959 *Oeuvres, papiers et correspondances.* Volume 9: Correspondance d'Alexis de Tocqueville et d'Arthur de Gobineau. Paris: Gallimard.

GÖKALP, ZIYA

Ziya Gökalp (1876–1924) was primarily responsible for introducing the study of sociology into Turkey, and he drew from sociology the intellectual basis for his ardent Turkish nationalism.

Born in Diyarbakir, the son of a civil servant who edited the official local newspaper, Mehmed Ziya (later Gökalp) attended secular schools there and also learned traditional Islamic lore from his uncle, a Muslim lawyer. At 18 he attempted suicide. By the following year, however, he was able to go to Istanbul and enroll at the Veterinary College.

He had already been influenced by the ideas of the Young Turks, and in 1895 he became a member of the secret society of Union and Progress in Istanbul. In 1898 he was arrested; after a year's imprisonment he was banished to his native town, where he devoted all his time to study. In those years the Young Turks who were in exile in Paris were strongly influenced by French sociology. One of them, Prince Sabaheddin, a follower of Le Play, went so far as to declare that only through sociological studies could the Ottomans introduce social change and thus find a way to achieve harmony among the various elements in the empire, a view later supported by Gökalp (in the first issue of his newspaper, *Peyman*, August 28, 1909).

In 1908, after the Young Turk revolution, Gökalp became the representative of the Union and Progress party in Diyarbakir. The next year he was elected a member of the central council of the party at Salonica and given the task of expounding its doctrine and attracting young people to its ranks. In 1910 he received an appointment to teach sociology in Salonica, the first such appointment in Turkey, and five years later he became the first professor of sociology at the University of Istanbul. He taught in the faculty of letters until 1919, making it a center for studies of Turkey as a nation. Exiled to Malta after World War I, he returned to Diyarbakir in 1921 as a wholehearted supporter of Atatürk and edited the *Küçük mecmua* ("Little Review"), in which he wrote a series of sociological essays designed to instruct the national leaders. In 1922 he was appointed director of Cultural Publications in Ankara, a department of the Ministry of Public Education, and there published his famous *Türkçülüğün essasları* (1923; "Foundations of Turkism").

Gökalp believed that the political revolution of the Young Turks needed to be completed by a social revolution that would create a "new life" in such areas as economics, the family, fine arts, morality, and law. A new Turkish civilization could be created only by gaining knowledge of Turkey's genuine national values. As late as 1911 he had believed that values are nothing but *idées-forces* based on philosophical considerations, but after 1912 he accepted the Durkheimian interpretation of values as collective representations. (He considered Durkheim to be the most penetrating sociologist and the founder of scientific sociology.) According to Gökalp, collective representations are realizations in the "collective consciousness," which, when they become fully articulated, are called ideals. "The only source of values is society itself and the experience of collective sentiments by individuals constitutes collective conscience" ([1911–1923] 1959, pp. 62–64).

After her defeat in the Balkan War, a critical period began for Turkey. Discussions of reforms were accompanied by conflicts between the Islamists, Westernists, and Turkists. Gökalp, who had come to Istanbul in 1912, felt that these conflicts had to be reconciled in a broader outlook. He argued that humanity was composed of culture groups, each with its own value system, and of civilization groups, with rules and techniques capable of inter-cultural diffusion and universal acceptance ([1911–1923] 1959, pp. 97–101). It was sociologically valid that Turks belonged at the same time to the Turkish nation, to the Muslim religious community, and to European civilization (Gökalp [1911–1923] 1959, pp. 71–76; Heyd 1950, pp. 149–151). Increasingly Gökalp stressed nationalism as the most powerful ideal of the modern age and nations as the most highly developed species on the scale of culture groups. In the nation he thought it was possible to integrate Turkish culture, Islam, and Western techniques. He later came to identify collective representations with national mores and asserted that "the . . . [discipline] which studies how the culture of a nation is distinguished from the civilization to which it belongs is called *cultural sociology*" ([1911–1923] 1959, pp. 172–173).

Following his belief that the task of the sociologist is to discover the elements of national culture, he embarked on a series of studies on the evolution of the Turkish family and on the pre-Islamic Turkish religion and state. His idea of a modernized Islam was predicated on the theory that the part of the religious law of Islam that is based on consensus is of social rather than divine origin and may therefore change in accordance with secular change ([1911–1923] 1959, pp. 193–196). He was convinced that a national state must be a secular one, and he strongly advocated a national system of education and economy. His programs for secularizing both education and the judiciary and for introducing equal rights for women were partly put into effect in 1917–1918.

Opinion on Gökalp is divided. He himself thought that what was original about his work was his testing of Durkheim's sociological method by applying it to Turkish civilization. His supporters agree that his conceptualizations of the nature of culture and nation are original and that his work represents scientific sociology in the Durkheim tradition; his critics stress that he had a dogmatic and deductive mind with strong collectivist ideas. Above all, he was an impassioned nationalist, and there is no doubt that his teachings provided an intellectual foundation for the modernization of Turkey.

HALIL İNALCIK

[*For the historical context of Gökalp's work, see* ISLAM; NATIONALISM; PAN MOVEMENTS; *and the biographies of* DURKHEIM; LE PLAY.]

WORKS BY GÖKALP

(1911–1923) 1959 *Turkish Nationalism and Western Civilization: Selected Essays.* Translated and edited with an introduction by Niyazi Berkes. New York: Columbia Univ. Press.

(1923) 1940 *Türkçülüğün essaslarĭ* ("Foundations of Turkism"). Istanbul: Arkadas Matbaasĭ.

Külliyat. 2 vols. Ankara: Türk Tarih Kurumu Basĭmevi, 1952–1965. → Volume 1: *Siirler ve halk masallari*. Volume 2: *Ziya Gökalp'ın mektupları*.

Ziya Gökalp'in ilk yazı hayatı, 1894–1909: Doğumu'nun 80. yıldönümü münasebetiyle. Istanbul: Diyarbakırı Tanıtma Dernegi, 1956.

SUPPLEMENTARY BIBLIOGRAPHY

HEYD, URIEL 1950 *Foundations of Turkish Nationalism: The Life and Teachings of Ziya Gökalp.* London: Luzac.

TÜTENGIL, CAVIT O. 1949 *Ziya Gökalp Rakkĭnda bir bibliyografya denemesi.* Istanbul: Berksoy Matbaasĭ.

ÜLKEN, HILMI ZIYA *Ziya Gökalp.* Istanbul: Kanaat Kitavebi. → Date of publication not ascertained.

ZĪYĀ AL-DĪN, FAKHRĪ 1935 *Ziya Gökalp, sa vie et sa sociologie: Essai sur l'influence de la sociologie française en Turquie.* Nancy (France): Berger–Levrault.

GOLD STANDARD

See INTERNATIONAL MONETARY ECONOMICS *and* MONEY.

GOLDENWEISER, ALEXANDER A.

Alexander Alexandrovich Goldenweiser (1880–1940), American anthropologist, was born in Kiev, Russia, the son of a lawyer with broad intellectual interests. He was educated in Kiev and at Harvard and Columbia, where he earned his PH.D. in 1910. A cosmopolitan figure, he achieved few of the rewards his ability might have earned him. He never held a full-time, permanent academic position, but he taught at many schools, including Columbia, the New School for Social Research, Portland Extension Center, Reed College, and the University of Wisconsin. His appointments were in anthropology, psychology, and sociology, and once he was even professor of thought and culture. He was an exciting teacher; although few of his students went on to become anthropologists, few forgot his lectures. He was also one of the first supporters of, and a contributor to, the *Encyclopaedia of the Social Sciences*.

An early student of Franz Boas, Goldenweiser was one of the most gifted American anthropologists of his generation. Yet his works are now often neglected. One reason for this may be that Boas and his students devoted so much of their time to critical attacks on the then prevalent theoretical positions: early in the twentieth century a simplistic, unilinear evolutionism was dominant; geographic determinism and, to a lesser extent, even racialism and other naïvely biological interpretations of behavior were also respectable posi-

tions. Armchair theorists were writing speculative works, many dealing with the "origins" of institutions. All of this was attacked by Boas and his group. Furthermore, although the group was primarily historical in outlook, it also opposed the extreme position of some historical anthropologists who were active particularly in Germany, Austria, and England and who argued against evolutionism on the grounds that cultural change results from migration or diffusion from one or a few original centers.

Theoretical polemics aside, Goldenweiser's writings might be more widely read had he published the kinds of field reports produced in such quantity by Alfred L. Kroeber, Robert H. Lowie, and others. Although he was popular with his Iroquois informants, he evidently did not enjoy field research and engaged in this activity for only a relatively few months. He preferred to concern himself with anthropological theory and with the broader problems of "social theory." He once told a friend that he would rather read bad theory than none at all. Moreover, he knew a number of languages well and did not limit his reading to anthropology.

Goldenweiser made theoretical contributions in more than one area. His article "The Principle of Limited Possibilities in the Development of Culture" (1913) is concerned with the issue of diffusion versus independent invention; it suggests that objects and acts can take only a limited number of forms and that this can lead to convergences among the traits of disparate cultures. Other early writings centered on totemism—for example, his 1910 article "Totemism: An Analytical Study." Ironically, his discussion of totemism contributed to a decreased interest in it among his colleagues, since it led them to conclude that there is no single, definable category of totemic practices but only diverse, if partially similar, phenomena that may be grouped under this term.

In his writings Goldenweiser made extensive use of the concept of culture. On some occasions he took culture for granted, but on others he advanced cultural, as against alternative, interpretations of behavior, as well as exploring particular cultural concepts, such as "patterning" (1936). This concept served him in his consistent attempts to see mankind in the round.

He may have overestimated the extent to which his own analyses and those of his colleagues could properly be characterized as psychological. Despite the fact that he had read a great deal of Wundt, some Freud, and the works of certain social psychologists, it is doubtful whether he made any attempt to keep abreast of developments in the main stream of psychology. He was particularly interested in the relationship between individuals and their culture, but he was not really one of the architects of the "culture and personality" movement. He was curious about the conceptual worlds of nonliterate peoples—what was then frequently called the primitive mind—and he did not think these conceptual worlds differed fundamentally from that of modern men. He was also curious about philosophy, the arts, and culture history, including various aspects of the history of European civilization.

Goldenweiser was not at home in the world as he knew it. Sometimes he was irresponsible in his relations with publishers or with academic systems. He appears to have lacked a substantial theoretical basis for studying the regularities of human life; the writings of his contemporaries did not readily offer such a basis, and even had it been there, his personal anarchistic predilections might have militated against his finding it. While he made few lasting contributions to theory, he did think well and write well on the questions of concern to him.

DAVID H. FRENCH

[*For the historical context of Goldenweiser's work, see the biographies of* BOAS *and* KROEBER.]

WORKS BY GOLDENWEISER

1910   Totemism: An Analytical Study. *Journal of American Folk-lore* 23:179–293.
1913   The Principle of Limited Possibilities in the Development of Culture. *Journal of American Folk-lore* 26:259–290.
1922   *Early Civilization: An Introduction to Anthropology.* New York: Knopf.
1931   *Robots or Gods: An Essay on Craft and Mind.* New York: Knopf.
1933   *History, Psychology, and Culture.* New York: Knopf.
1936   Loose Ends of Theory on the Individual, Pattern, and Involution in Primitive Society. Pages 99–104 in *Essays in Anthropology Presented to A. L. Kroeber in Celebration of His Sixtieth Birthday, June 11, 1936.* Berkeley: Univ. of California Press.
1937   *Anthropology: An Introduction to Primitive Culture.* New York: Crofts.

SUPPLEMENTARY BIBLIOGRAPHY

BUNZEL, RUTH L.   1960   Alexander Goldenweiser (1880–1940). Page 508 in Margaret Mead and Ruth L. Bunzel (editors), *The Golden Age of Anthropology.* New York: Braziller.
WALLIS, WILSON D.   1941   Alexander A. Goldenweiser. *American Anthropologist* New Series 43:250–255.
WHITE, LESLIE A.   1958   Alexander Alexandrovich Goldenweiser. Volume 22, pages 244–245 in *Dictionary of American Biography: Supplement Two.* New York: Scribner.

GOLDSTEIN, KURT

Kurt Goldstein, American neurologist, psychiatrist, and psychologist, was born in 1878 in Kattowitz, Germany, and died in 1965 in New York City.

Goldstein entered medicine with the intention of devoting his life to the treatment of patients with mental diseases. In 1903 he received his medical degree at Breslau, Germany. He studied psychiatry with Karl Wernicke and neuroanatomy with Ludwig Edinger. His first ten papers, all published between 1903 and 1904, are studies of the anatomy of spinal pathways, of the embryology of the brain, and of comparative neuroanatomy. Clinical papers soon followed: one, in 1906, on memory problems and deficits created by neurological and psychiatric disturbances, foreshadowed important distinctions that underlie present-day differential diagnostic testing. In 1906 he joined the staff of the psychiatric clinic at the University of Königsberg, where he found his high expectations thwarted: mental patients were relegated to custodial care without any attempt at treatment. Nor did the prevailing Kraepelinian nosology indicate any conceivable direction for therapy. Goldstein used the opportunity for careful examination and observation of patients and published papers on neurological and psychiatric topics—motor disturbances, sensory disturbances, the nature of hallucinations, alcoholism, manic–depressive states, schizophrenia—and comparisons of clinical symptoms with post-mortem findings.

In 1919 he was appointed professor of neurology and director of the Neurological Institute at the University of Frankfurt. There he established the Institut zur Erforschung der Folgeerscheinungen von Hirnverletzungen, where, under his aegis and in collaboration with the psychologist Adhémar Gelb and many students, a large number of brain-injured soldiers were studied intensively and for long periods of time. These studies led to entirely novel conceptions of such problems as aphasia, agnosia, and tonus disturbances and generally to systematic descriptions of behavioral changes wrought by brain injury. In 1930 Goldstein became professor of neurology at the University of Berlin and director of the Neurological Hospital Moabit, a post he held until Hitler's advent in 1933. After a year's writing in Amsterdam he came to New York City in 1935; until 1940 he was clinical professor of neurology at Columbia University and head physician at Montefiore Hospital. In 1939 Harvard invited him to deliver the William James lectures, which were published under the title

Human Nature in the Light of Psychopathology (1940). From 1940 to 1945 he continued research and teaching as professor of neurology at Tufts Medical School, Boston. He then returned to New York, where he practiced privately and taught at the College of the City of New York, Columbia University, and the New School for Social Research. For many years he was also a guest professor at Brandeis University.

Goldstein's experimental papers and monographs provoked lively discussions among neurologists and psychologists; yet his greatest impact came with the publication of *The Organism: A Holistic Approach to Biology Derived From Pathological Data in Man* (1934), written during his year's exile in Amsterdam. Goldstein viewed behavior as the unified activity of the whole organism, whose basic "motive" is optimum self-actualization in a given environment. Reflexes, clinical symptoms, or functions subjected to laboratory investigation are part processes, and failure to consider that their isolation is artificial results in erroneous interpretation. Study of brain-injured patients reveals the general change underlying specific symptoms and manifestations, namely, an impairment of the patients' "abstract attitude" and a preponderance of "concrete" modes of behavior, affecting all performance fields. The "abstract attitude" is defined, basically, as man's capacity to reason deliberately, to plan and account for his actions, to view particular objects or events as instances of a class. Upon loss of these capacities the individual is at the mercy of the immediate, concrete sensory or mnemonic stimulus situation and is unable to transcend it. The aphasic patient cannot name an object, that is, supply the class symbol, yet he may spontaneously produce the word within a sentence or an action. Thus, aphasia is not a loss of words or word images. Rather, it is a dedifferentiation of language, a loss of concepts and their symbols; in other words, it is the manifestation in language of impaired abstraction. This view has important implications for the problem of cerebral localization. Functions cannot be localized, although defects can be, if we keep in mind the problem of isolated part processes and integrated organismic activity.

Impairment of abstraction is not limited to brain-injured patients. It manifests itself also in psychotic processes. Whatever its cause, impaired abstraction restricts the patient's opportunities for self-realization. Consequently, his conduct becomes rigid; he is vulnerable to anxiety, to the "catastrophic reaction," that is, to the threat of being unable to actualize himself, and to the danger of "losing existence."

Goldstein was only peripherally associated with the gestalt psychologists Wertheimer, Köhler, and Koffka; however, he was an editor of *Psychologische Forschung*, the house organ of gestalt psychology. While he never established a school, his views on aphasia profoundly influenced the English neurologist Sir Henry Head, as well as philosophers concerned with problems of normal language, particularly Goldstein's cousin Ernst Cassirer and the followers of Edmund Husserl. Generally critical of psychoanalytic theory, Goldstein acknowledged the importance of some of Freud's views, especially his broad emphasis on motivation and his discussion of the nature of symptoms. Existential psychology has claimed Goldstein somewhat unsuccessfully. Although phenomenological observation and analysis were fundamental to his work, he did not share the metaphysics of existential psychology and psychiatry.

MARIANNE L. SIMMEL

[*For the historical context of Goldstein's work, see* GESTALT THEORY *and the biographies of* KOFFKA; KÖHLER; WERTHEIMER. *For discussion of subsequent development of his ideas, see* LANGUAGE, *article on* SPEECH PATHOLOGY; MENTAL DISORDERS, *article on* ORGANIC ASPECTS; NERVOUS SYSTEM; SYSTEMS ANALYSIS, *article on* PSYCHOLOGICAL SYSTEMS; *and the biographies of* CASSIRER *and* HUSSERL.]

WORKS BY GOLDSTEIN

1927   Die Lokalisation in der Grosshirnrinde. Pages 600–842 in *Handbuch der normalen und pathologischen Physiologie, mit Berücksichtigung der experimentellen Pharmakologie.* Volume 10: Spezielle Physiologie des Zentralnervensystems der Wirbeltiere. Berlin: Springer.

(1934) 1939   *The Organism: A Holistic Approach to Biology Derived From Pathological Data in Man.* New York: American Book. → First published as *Der Aufbau des Organismus.*

1940   *Human Nature in the Light of Psychopathology.* Cambridge, Mass.: Harvard Univ. Press.

1941   GOLDSTEIN, KURT; and SCHEERER, MARTIN. Abstract and Concrete Behavior: An Experimental Study With Special Tests. *Psychological Monographs* 53, no. 2, serial no. 239.

1942   *Aftereffects of Brain Injuries in War, Their Evaluation and Treatment: The Application of Psychologic Methods in the Clinic.* New York: Grune.

1948   *Language and Language Disturbances: Aphasic Symptom Complexes and Their Significance for Medicine and Theory of Language.* New York: Grune.

1959   Notes on the Development of My Concepts. *Journal of Individual Psychology* 15:5–14.

SUPPLEMENTARY BIBLIOGRAPHY

Goldstein Anniversary Number. 1949 *Confinia neurologica* 9:1–272.

HEAD, HENRY 1926 *Aphasia and Kindred Disorders of Speech.* 2 vols. Cambridge Univ. Press.

MEIERS, JOSEPH I. 1958 *Kurt Goldstein Bibliography, 1903–1958.* Document No. 5816. Washington: American Documentation Institute, Photoduplication Service.

MOURGUE, RAOUL 1937 La conception de la neurologie dans l'oeuvre de Kurt Goldstein. *Encéphale* 32, part 1:32–56.

Papers in Honor of Kurt Goldstein. 1959 *Journal of Individual Psychology* 15:1–99.

RIESE, WALTHER 1948 Kurt Goldsteins Stellung in der Geschichte der Neurologie: Versuch einer Würdigung aus Anlass seines 70. Geburtstages, 6 November 1948. *Schweizer Archiv für Neurologie und Psychiatrie* 62: 2–10.

GOODNESS OF FIT

A goodness of fit procedure is a statistical test of a hypothesis that the sampled population is distributed in a specific way, for example, normally with mean 100 and standard deviation 15. Corresponding confidence procedures for a population distribution also fall under this topic. Related tests are for broader hypotheses, for example, that the sampled population is normal (without further specification). Others test hypotheses that two or more population distributions are the same.

Populations arise because of variability, of which various sources (sometimes acting together) can be distinguished. First, there is inherent variability among experimental units, for example, the heights, IQ's, or ages of the students in a class each vary among themselves. Then there is measurement error, a more abstract or conceptual notion. The age of a student may have negligible measurement error, but his IQ does not; it depends on a host of accidental factors: how the student slept, the particular questions chosen for the test, and so on. There are also other conceptual populations, not properly thought of in terms of measurement error—the population of subject responses, for example, in the learning experiment below.

The distribution of a numerical population trait is often portrayed by a histogram, a density function, or some other device that shows the proportion of cases for which a particular value of the numerical trait is achieved (or the proportion within a small interval around a particular value). The shape of the histogram or density function is important; it may or may not be symmetrical. If it is not, it is said to be *skew*. If it is symmetrical, it may have a special kind of shape called *normal*. For example, populations of scores on intelligence tests are often assumed normally distributed by psychologists. Indeed, the construction of the test may aim at normality, at least for some group of individuals. Again, lifetimes of machines may be assumed to have negative exponential distributions,

meaning that expected remaining life does not vary with age. [*See* DISTRIBUTIONS, STATISTICAL, *article on* SPECIAL CONTINUOUS DISTRIBUTIONS; PROBABILITY; STATISTICS, DESCRIPTIVE.]

It is technically often convenient, especially in connection with goodness of fit tests, to deal with the *cumulative distribution function* (c.d.f.) rather than with the density function. The c.d.f. evaluated at x is the proportion of cases with numerical values less than or equal to x; thus, if $f(x)$ is a density function, the corresponding c.d.f. is

$$F(x) = \int_{-\infty}^{x} f(t)\, dt.$$

For explicitness, a subscript will be added to F, indicating the population, distribution, or random variable to which it applies. It is a matter of convention that cumulation is from the left and that it is based on "less than or equal to" rather than just "less than."

The *sample c.d.f.* is the steplike function whose value at x is the proportion of observations less than or equal to x. Many goodness of fit procedures are based on geometrically suggested measures of discrepancy between sample and hypothetical population c.d.f.'s. Some informal procedures use "probability" graph paper, especially normal paper (on which a normal c.d.f. becomes a straight line).

For nominal populations (for example, proportions of people expressing allegiance to different religions or to none) there is no concept corresponding to the c.d.f. The main emphasis of this article is on numerical populations.

Although goodness of fit procedures address themselves principally to the shape of population c.d.f.'s, the term "goodness of fit" is sometimes applied more generally than in this article. In particular, some authors write of goodness of fit of observed regressions to hypothetical forms, for example, to a straight line. [*This topic is dealt with in* LINEAR HYPOTHESES, *article on* REGRESSION.]

Hypotheses—simple, composite, approximate. A test of goodness of fit, based on a sample from a population, assesses the plausibility that the population distribution has specified form; in brief, *tests* the hypothesis that F_X has shape F_0. The specification may be complete, that is, the population distribution may be specified completely, in which case the hypothesis is called *simple*. Alternatively, the form may be specified only up to certain unknown parameters, which often are the parameters of location and scale. In this case the hypothesis is called *composite*. Still another type of hypothesis is an *approximate* one, which is composite in a certain sense. Here one specifies first what one would consider a material departure from a hypothesized shape (Hodges & Lehmann 1954). For example, in the case of a *simple approximate hypothesis*, one might agree that F_x departs materially from F_0 if the maximum vertical deviation between the actual and hypothesized cumulative distribution functions exceeds .07. The approximate hypothesis then states that the actual and hypothesized distributions do not differ materially in this sense.

Approximate hypotheses specialize to the others, so that a complete theory of testing for the former would be desirable. This is especially true since, as has been pointed out by Karl Pearson (1900) and Joseph Berkson (1938), tests of "exact" hypotheses, being as a rule *consistent*, have problematical logical status: unless the exact hypothesis is exactly correct and all of the sampling assumptions are exactly met, rejection of the hypothesis is assured (for fixed significance level) when sample size is large. Unfortunately, such a complete theory does not now exist, but the strong early interest in "exact" hypotheses was not misspent: The testing and "acceptance" of "exact" hypotheses concerning F_x seems to have much the same status as the provisional adoption of physical or other "laws." If the latter has helped the advancement of science, so has no doubt the former; this is true notwithstanding that old hypotheses or theories will almost surely be discarded as additional data become available. This point has been made by Cochran (1952) and Chapman (1958). Cochran also suggests that the tests of "exact" hypotheses are "invertible" into confidence sets, in the usual manner, thus providing statistical procedures somewhat similar in intent to tests of approximate hypotheses [*see* ESTIMATION, *article on* CONFIDENCE INTERVALS AND REGIONS].

Conducting a test of goodness of fit. Many tests of goodness of fit have been developed; as with statistical tests generally, a test of goodness of fit is conveniently conducted by computing from the sample a *statistic* and its *sample significance level* [*see* HYPOTHESIS TESTING]. In the case of a test of goodness of fit, the statistic will measure the discrepancy between what the sample in fact *is* and what a sample from a population of hypothesized form *ought to be*. The sample significance level of an observed measure of discrepancy, d_0, is, at least for all the standard goodness of fit procedures, the probability, $Pr\{d \geqslant d_0\}$, that d exceeds d_0 under random sampling from a population of hypothesized form. In other words, it is the proportion of like discrepancy measures, d, exceeding d_0, computed on the basis of many successive hypothetical

random samples of the same size from a population of hypothesized form. For many tests of goodness of fit, there exist tables (for extensive bibliography see Greenwood & Hartley 1962) that give those values of d_0 corresponding to given significance level and sample size (n). Many of these standard tests are *nonparametric*, which means that $Pr\{d \geqslant d_0\}$ is the same for a very large class of hypotheses F_0, so that only one such tabulation is required [*see* NONPARAMETRIC STATISTICS].

If, as is usual, the relevant alternative population distributions (more generally, alternative probabilistic models for the generation of the sample at hand) tend to encourage large values of d_0, the hypothesized population distribution will be judged implausible if the sample significance level is small (conventionally .05 or less). If the sample significance level is not small, it means that the statistic has a value unsurprising under the null hypothesis, so that the test gives no reason to reject the null hypothesis. If, however, the sample significance level is very large, say .95 or more, one may construe this as a warning of possible trouble, say, that an overzealous proponent of the hypothesis has slanted the data or that the sampling was not random. Note here an awkward usage prevalent in statistics generally: an observed measure of discrepancy d_0 with *low probability* $Pr\{d \geqslant d_0\}$ usually is described as *highly significant*.

Choosing a test of goodness of fit. Choosing a test of goodness of fit amounts to deciding in what sense the discrepancy between the hypothesized population distribution and the sample is to be measured: The sample c.d.f. may be compared directly with the hypothesized population c.d.f., as is done in the case of tests of the Kolmogorov–Smirnov type. For example, the original Kolmogorov–Smirnov test itself, as described below, summarizes the discrepancy by the maximum absolute deviation between the hypothesized population c.d.f., F_0, and the sample c.d.f. Alternatively, one may compare uncumulated frequencies, as for the χ^2 test. Again, a standard shape parameter, such as skewness, may be computed for the sample and for the hypothesized population and the two compared.

Any reasonable measure of discrepancy will of course tend to be small if the population yielding the sample conforms to the null hypothesis. A good measure of discrepancy will, in addition, tend to be large under the likely alternative forms of the population distribution, a property designated technically by the term *power*. For example, the sample skewness coefficient might have good power if the hypothesized population distribution were normal (zero population skewness coefficient) and the relevant alternative distributional forms were appreciably skew.

Two general considerations. Two general considerations should be kept in mind. First it is important that the particular goodness of fit test used be selected without consideration of the sample at hand, at least if the calculated significance level is to be meaningful. This is because a measure of discrepancy chosen in the light of an observed sample anomaly will tend to be inordinately large. Receiving license plate 437918 hardly warrants the inference that, this year, the first and second digits add to the third, and the fifth and sixth to the fourth. It may of course be true, in special instances, that some adjustment of the test procedure in the light of the data does not affect the significance computations appreciably—as, for example, when choosing category intervals, based on the sample mean and variance, for the χ^2 test (Watson 1957).

Second, a goodness of fit test, like any other statistical test, leads to an inference from a *sample* to the *population sampled*. Indeed, the usual hypothesis under test is that the sample is in fact a *random sample* from an *infinite population* of hypothesized form, and the tabulated probabilities, $Pr\{d \geqslant d_0\}$, almost always presuppose this. (In principle, one could obtain goodness of fit tests for more complex kinds of probability samples than random ones, but little seems to be known about such possibilities.) It is therefore essential that the sample to which a standard test is applied can be thought of as a random sample. If it cannot, then one must be prepared either to do one's own nonstandard significance probability computations or to defend the adequacy of the approximation involved in using the standard tabulations. Consider, for example, starting with a random sample involving considerable repetition, say the sample of response words obtained from a panel of subjects taking a psychological word association test or the sample of nationalities obtained from a survey of the United Nations. Suppose now that one tallies the number of items in the sample (response words, nationalities) appearing exactly once, exactly twice, etc. There results a new set of data, consisting of a certain number of one's, a certain number of two's, etc. This collection of integers has the outward appearance of a random sample, and the literature contains instances of the application of the standard tests of goodness of fit to such observed frequencies. Yet the probability mechanism that generates these integers has no resemblance whatever to random sampling, and the

standard probability tabulations cannot be assumed to apply. Other examples arise when the data are generated by time series; for some of these the requisite nonstandard probability computations have been done (Patankar 1954), while, in other cases, special devices have made the standard computations apply. For example, in the case of the learning experiment by Suppes and his associates (1964), the sample consists of the time series of a subject's responses to successive stimuli. Certain theories of learning predict a particular bimodal long-run response population distribution; but the goodness of fit test of this hypothesized shape, on the basis of a series of subject responses, is hampered by the statistical dependence of neighboring responses. However, theory suggests, and a test of randomness confirms, that the subsample consisting of every fifth response is effectively random, enabling a standard χ^2 test of goodness of fit to be carried out on the basis of this subsample. Whether four-fifths of the sample is a reasonable price to pay for validly carrying out a standard procedure is of course a matter of debate.

Tests of simple hypotheses

The χ^2 test. The χ^2 test was first proposed in 1900 by Karl Pearson. To apply the test, one first divides the possible range of numbers (number pairs in the bivariate case) into k regions. For example, if only nonnegative numbers are possible, one might use the categories 0 to .2, .2 to .5, .5 to .7, and .7 and beyond. Next, one computes the probabilities, p_i, associated with each of these regions (intervals in the example just given) under the hypothesized F_0. This is often done by subtracting values of F_0 from each other: for example, when F_0 is the exponential cumulative distribution function $1 - e^{-x}$,

$$
\begin{aligned}
p_1 &= F_0(.2) - F_0(0) = F_0(.2) = 1 - e^{-.2} &= .18 \\
p_2 &= F_0(.5) - F_0(.2) &= e^{-.2} - e^{-.5} &= .21 \\
p_3 &= F_0(.7) - F_0(.5) &= e^{-.5} - e^{-.7} &= .11 \\
p_4 &= F_0(\infty) - F_0(.7) &= e^{-.7} &= .50
\end{aligned}
$$

The expected numbers E_i of observations in each category are (under the null hypothesis) $E_i = np_i$, where n is the size of the random sample.

After the sample has been collected, there also will be observed numbers, O_i, of sample members in each category. The chi-square measure of discrepancy d_{χ^2} is then computed by summing squared differences of class frequencies, weighted in such a way as to bring to bear standard distribution theory,

$$
d_{\chi^2,0} = \sum_{i=1}^{k} (O_i - E_i)^2 / E_i ,
$$

where the subscript 0 indicates the specific sample value of d_{χ^2}. (Often "X^2" or "χ^2" is used to denote this statistic.)

As is shown, for example, by Cochran (1952), the probability distribution of d_{χ^2}, when $F_X = F_0$, can be approximated by the chi-square distribution with $k - 1$ degrees of freedom, χ^2_{k-1}. This fact, to which the test owes its name, was first demonstrated by Karl Pearson. The larger the expectations E_i, the better is the approximation; this has been pointed out, for example, by Mann and Wald (1942). Hence, the significance, $Pr\{d_{\chi^2} \geqslant d_{\chi^2, 0}\}$, is evaluated to a good approximation by consulting a tabulation of the χ^2_{k-1} distribution. For example, if k, as above, equals 4, and $d_{\chi^2, 0}$ had happened to be 4.6, then $Pr\{d_{\chi^2} \geqslant d_{\chi^2, 0}\} \cong .20$. With a sample significance level of .20, most statisticians would not question the plausibility of F_0. However, were $d_{\chi^2, 0}$ larger, and the corresponding significance equal to .05 or less, the consensus would be reversed.

At what point is the distributional approximation endangered by small E_i? An early study of this problem, performed by Cochran in 1942 (referred to in Cochran 1952), shows that a few E_i near 1 among several large ones do not materially affect the approximation. Recent studies, by Kempthorne (1966) and by Slakter (1965), show that this is true as well when *all* E_i are near 1.

These and other studies indicate that, although some care must be taken to avoid very small E_i, much latitude remains for choosing categories. How is this to be done? To begin with, in keeping with the spirit of remarks by Birnbaum (1953), if the relevant alternatives F^* to F_0 are such that

$$d_{\chi^2}(F^*, F_0) = \sum_{i=1}^{k} (E_i^* - E_i)^2 / E_i$$

is large for a certain choice of k categories, it is these categories that should be selected. Among various sets of k categories, those yielding large $d_{\chi^2}(F^*, F_0)$ are preferred.

In the absence of detailed knowledge of the alternatives, the usual recommendation, at least in the one-dimensional case, is to use intervals of equal E_i. There remains the question of how many such intervals there should be. The typical statistical criterion for this is power, that is, the likelihood that the value of d_{χ^2} will be large enough to warrant rejection of the hypothesis F_0 when the population is in fact a relevant alternative one. If large power is desired for *all* alternative population c.d.f.'s departing from F_0 at some x by at least a given fixed amount, Mann and Wald (1942) recommend a number of categories of the order of $4n^{2/5}$. Williams (1950) has shown that this figure can easily be halved.

The χ^2 test is versatile; it is readily adapted to problems involving nominal rather than numerical populations [*see* COUNTED DATA]. It can also be adapted to bivariate and multivariate problems, as, for example, by Keats and Lord (1962), where the joint distribution of two types of mental test scores is considered. As opposed to many of its competitors, the χ^2 test is not biased, in the sense that there are no alternatives F^* to F_0 under which acceptance of F_0 is more likely than it is under F_0 itself. It is readily adapted to composite and approximate testing problems. Also, it seems to be true that the χ^2 test is in the best position among its competitors with regard to the practical computation of power. As is pointed out by Cochran (1952), such computations are performed by means of the *noncentral* chi-square distribution with $k - 1$ degrees of freedom.

Modifications of the χ^2 test. Important modifications of the χ^2 test, intended to increase its power against specific families $\mathcal{G}$ of distributions alternative to F_0, are given by Neyman (1949) and by Fix, Hodges, and Lehmann (1954). Here $\mathcal{G}$ is assumed to include F_0 and to allow differentiable parametric representation of the category expectations E_i. Note that the inclusion of F_0 in $\mathcal{G}$ differs from the point of view adopted, for example, by Mann and Wald (1942). These modifications are essentially *likelihood ratio* tests of F_0 versus $\mathcal{G}$ and are similar to procedures used to test composite and approximate hypotheses.

Another modification, capable of orientation against specific "smooth" alternatives, Neyman's ψ^2 test, was introduced in 1937. Other important modifications are described in detail in Cochran (1954).

Other procedures. When $(X_1, \cdots, X_n)$ is a random sample from a population distributed according to a *continuous* c.d.f. F_0, then $(U_1, \cdots, U_n) = (F_0(X_1), \cdots, F_0(X_n))$ has all the probabilistic properties of a random sample from a population distributed uniformly over the numbers between zero and one. (If the population has a density function, the c.d.f. is continuous.) No matter what the hypothesized F_0, the initial application of this *probability integral* transformation thus reduces all probability computations to the case of this *uniform* population distribution and gives a *nonparametric* character to any procedure based on the transformed sample $(U_1, \cdots, U_n)$. Most goodness of fit tests of simple hypotheses are nonparametric in this sense, including the χ^2 test itself, when categories are chosen so as to assign specified values, for example, the constant value $1/k$, to the category probabilities p_i.

Another common test making use of the transformation $U = F_0(X)$ is the Kolmogorov–Smirnov test, first suggested by Kolmogorov (1933) and explained in detail by Goodman (1954) and Massey (1951). The test bears Smirnov's name, as well as Kolmogorov's, presumably because Smirnov (as Doob and Donsker did later) gave an alternate derivation of its asymptotic null distribution, tabulated this distribution, and also extended the test to the two-sample case discussed below (1939a). Denote by $F_n(x)$ the *sample c.d.f.*, that is, $F_n(x)$ is the proportion of sample values less than or equal to x. The test is based on the maximum absolute vertical deviation between $F_n(x)$ and $F_0(x)$,

$$d_K = d_K(F_n, F_0) = \sqrt{n}\, (\max_{-\infty < x < +\infty} |F_n(x) - F_0(x)|),$$

the dependence of d_K on the quantities $U_i = F_0(X_i)$ being best brought out by the alternate formula

$$d_K = \sqrt{n} \max\left[\max_i \left(\frac{i}{n} - u_i \right), \max_i \left(u_i - \frac{i-1}{n} \right) \right],$$

where u_1 is the smallest U_i, u_2 is the next to smallest, etc.; the equivalence of the two formulas is made clear by a sketch. As Kolmogorov noted in his original paper, the probabilities tabulated for d_K are *conservative* when F_0 is not continuous, in the sense that, for discontinuous F_0, actual probabilities of $d_K \geqslant d_{K,0}$ will tend to be less than those obtained from the tabulations, leading to occasional unwarranted acceptance of F_0.

Computations (Shapiro & Wilk 1965) suggest that this test has low power against alternatives with mean and variance equal to those of the hypothesized distribution. It has, however, been argued, for example, by Birnbaum (1953) and Kac, Kiefer, and Wolfowitz (1955), that the test yields good minimum power over classes of alternatives F^* satisfying $d_K(F^*, F_0) \geqslant \delta$; these, as the reader will note, are precisely the classes of alternatives envisaged by Mann and Wald (1942) in optimizing the number of categories used in the χ^2 test. A detrimental feature of the Kolmogorov–Smirnov test is its bias, pointed out in Massey (1951).

An important feature of the test is that it can be "inverted" in keeping with the usual method to provide a confidence band for $F_0(x)$ centered on $F_n(x)$, which, except for the narrowing caused by the restriction $0 \leqslant F_0(x) \leqslant 1$, has constant width [see ESTIMATION, *article on* CONFIDENCE INTER-

VALS AND REGIONS]. The construction of such a band has been suggested by Wald and Wolfowitz and is described by Goodman (1954). Attaching a significance probability to an observed $d_{K,0}$ amounts to ascertaining the band width required in order just to include wholly the hypothesized F_0 in the confidence band.

The Kolmogorov–Smirnov test has been modified in several ways; the first of these converts the test into a "one-sided" procedure based on the discrepancy

$$d_{K^+} = \sqrt{n}\,[\max_{-\infty < x < +\infty} (F_n(x) - F_0(x))]$$
$$= \sqrt{n}\left[\max_i \left(\frac{i}{n} - u_i \right) \right].$$

A useful feature of this modification is the simplicity of the large sample computation of significance probabilities associated with observed discrepancies $d_{K^+,0}$; abbreviating the latter to d, one has $Pr\{d_{K^+} \geqslant d\} \cong e^{-2d^2}$. It is verified by Chapman (1958) that d_{K^+} yields good minimum power over those classes of alternatives F^* that satisfy $d_{K^+}(F^*, F_0) = \sqrt{n} \max_x (F^*(x) - F_0(x)) \geqslant \delta$.

Other, more complex modifications provide greater power against special alternatives, as in the weight function modifications (Darling 1957), which provide greater power against discrepancies from F_0 in the tails. Another sort of modification, introduced and tabulated by Kuiper in 1960, calls for a measure of discrepancy d_V that is especially suited to testing goodness of fit to hypothesized *circular* distributions, being invariant under arbitrary choices of the angular origin. This property could be important, for example, in psychological studies involving responses to the color wheel, or in the learning experiment mentioned above. The measure d_V also has been singled out by E. S. Pearson (1963) as the generally most attractive in competition with d_K and the discrepancy measures d_{ω^2} and d_U mentioned below.

A second general class of procedures also making use of the transformation $U = F_0(x)$ springs from the discrepancy measure

$$d_{\omega^2} = n \int_{-\infty}^{+\infty} [F_n(x) - F_0(x)]^2 \, dF_0(x)$$
$$= \frac{1}{12n} + \sum_{i=1}^{n} \left(\frac{2i-1}{2n} - u_i \right)^2,$$

first proposed by Cramér in 1928 and also by Von Mises in 1931 (see Darling 1957). Marshall (1958) has verified a startling agreement between the asymptotic and small sample distributions of d_{ω^2} for sample sizes n as low as 3. Power considerations for d_{ω^2} are similar to those expressed for d_K, and are discussed also in the sources cited by Marshall; the test based on d_{ω^2} can be expected to have good minimum power over classes of alternatives F^* satisfying the conditions $d_{\omega^2}(F^*, F_0) = n \int_{-\infty}^{+\infty} [F^*(x) - F_0(x)]^2 \, dF_0(x) \geq \delta$. However, the test is biased (as is that based on d_K).

As in the case of d_K, d_{ω^2} has weight function modifications for greater power selectivity, and also a modification d_U, analogous to the modification d_V of d_K and introduced by Watson (1961), which does not depend on the choice of angular origin and is thus also suited for testing the goodness of fit to hypothesized circular distributions.

Other procedures include those based on the Fisher–Pearson measures $d_{FP}^{(1)} = -2\sum_{i=1}^{n} \ln u_i$ and $d_{FP}^{(2)} = -2\sum_{i=1}^{n} \ln (1 - u_i)$, apparently first suggested in connection with goodness of fit in 1938 by E. S. Pearson. As pointed out by Chapman (1958), the tests based on $d^{(1)}$ and $d^{(2)}$ are uniformly most powerful against polynomial alternatives to $F_U(x) = x$ of form x^k and $(1 - x)^k$, $k > 1$, and hence are "smooth" in the sense of Neyman's ψ^2 test. Computations by Chapman suggest that, dually to d_K, $d^{(2)}$ has good maximum power over classes of alternatives F° satisfying $d_K(F^*, F_0) \leq \delta$.

Another set of procedures, discussed and defended by Pyke (1965) and extensively studied by Weiss (1958), are based on functions of the spacings, $u_{i+1} - u_i$ or $u_i - (i + 1)^{-1}$, of the u's, from each other or from their expected locations under F_0. Still another criterion (Smirnov 1939b) examines the number of crossings of $F_n(x)$ and $F_0(x)$.

An important modification, applicable to all of the procedures in this section, is suggested in Durbin (1961). This modification is intended to increase the power of any procedure based on the transforms U_i, against a certain class of alternatives described in that paper.

Since there are multivariate probability integral transformations, applying an initial "uniformizing" transformation is possible in the multivariate case as well. However, one of several possible transformations must now be chosen, and, related to this nonuniqueness, the direct analogues of the univariate discrepancy measures are no longer functions of uniformly distributed transforms and do not lead to nonparametric tests (Rosenblatt 1952).

Tests of composite hypotheses

The χ^2 test. In the composite case, the null hypothesis specifies only that $F_X(x)$ is a member of a certain parametric class $\{F_\theta(x)\}$. Typically, but not necessarily, θ is the pair (μ, σ), μ a param-

eter of location, and σ a parameter of scale, in which case $F_\theta(x)$ may be written $F_0[(x - \mu)/\sigma]$. In any event, there arises the question of modifying the measure d_{χ^2} of discrepancy between the sample and a particular cumulative distribution function into a measure D_{χ^2} of discrepancy between the sample and the *class* $\{F_\theta(x)\}$. A natural approach is to set

$$D_{\chi^2} = \min_\theta d_{\chi^2}.$$

If θ is composed of m parameters, it can be shown that, under quite general conditions, D_{χ^2} is approximately distributed according to the χ^2_{k-1-m} distribution when $F_X(x)$ equals any one of the $F_\theta(x)$. Hence significance probability computations can once again be referred to tabulations of the χ^2_ν distribution. The requisite minimization with respect to θ can be cumbersome, and several modifications have been proposed, for example, the following by Neyman (1949):

Suppose that one defines $d_{\chi^2}(\theta)$ as the discrepancy d_{χ^2} between the observed sample and the particular distribution $F_\theta(x)$. Then D is defined also by

$$D_{\chi^2} = d_{\chi^2}(\tilde{\theta}),$$

with the estimator $\tilde{\theta}$ computed from

$$d_{\chi^2}(\tilde{\theta}) = \min_\theta d_{\chi^2}(\theta),$$

that is, with $\tilde{\theta}$ the *minimum chi-square estimator* of θ. The suggested modifications involve using estimators of θ alternate to $\tilde{\theta}$ in this last definition of D_{χ^2}, that is, estimators that "essentially" minimize $d_{\chi^2}(\theta)$; among these are the so-called grouped-data or partial-information maximum likelihood estimators.

Frequently used but *not equivalent* estimators are the ordinary "full-information" maximum likelihood estimators $\hat{\theta}$ of θ, for example, $(\bar{x}, s)$ for (μ, σ) in the normal case. These do *not* "essentially" minimize d_{χ^2} and consequently tend to inflate D_{χ^2} beyond values predicted by the χ^2_{k-1-m} distribution, leading to some unwarranted rejections of the composite hypothesis. However, it is indicated by Chernoff and Lehmann (1954), and also by Watson (1957), that no serious distortion will result if the number of categories is ten or more.

Composite analogues of other tests. Adaptation of the tests based on the probability integral transformation to the composite case proceeds much as in the case of χ^2. With definitions of $d_{\omega^2}(\theta)$ and $d_K(\theta)$ analogous to that of $d_{\chi^2}(\theta)$, Darling (1955) has investigated the large sample probability distribution of $D_{\omega^2} = d_{\omega^2}(\hat{\theta})$ and of $D_K = d_K(\hat{\theta})$ for efficient estimators $\hat{\theta}$ of θ analogous to the estimators $\tilde{\theta}$ for χ^2. Note that in the absence of any χ^2-like categories, the ordinary full-information maximum likelihood estimators now *do* qualify as estimators $\hat{\theta}$.

A major problem now is, however, that the modified procedures are no longer nonparametric. Thus a special investigation is required for every composite hypothesis. This is done by Kac, Kiefer, and Wolfowitz (1955) for the normal scale-location family, and the resulting large sample distribution is partly tabulated.

Tests based on special characteristics. The alternatives of concern sometimes differ from a composite null hypothesis in a manner easily described by a standard shape parameter. Special tests have been proposed for such cases. For example, the sample skewness coefficient has been suggested (Geary 1947) for testing normality against skew alternatives. Again, for testing Poissonness against alternatives with variance unequal to mean, R. A. Fisher has recommended the variance-to-mean ratio $\sum_{i=1}^{n}(X_i - \bar{X})^2/\bar{X}$ (see Cochran 1954). This measure is approximately distributed as χ^2_{n-1} when Poissonness in fact obtains, for $\lambda > 1$ and $n > 15$ (Sukhatme 1938), which follows from the fact that the denominator is then a high-precision estimate of λ, and the numerator is approximately distributed as $\lambda \chi^2_{n-1}$. Analogous recommendations apply to testing binomiality. Essentially the same point of view underlies tests of normality based on the ratio of mean deviation, or of the range, to the standard deviation.

Transforming into simple hypotheses. Another interesting approach to the composite problem, advocated by Hogg and also by Sarkadi (1960), is to transform certain composite hypotheses into equivalent simple ones.

Specifically, there are location-scale parametric families $\{F_0[(x - \mu)/\sigma]\}$ with the following property: A random sample from any particular $F_0[(x - \mu)/\sigma]$ is reducible by a transformation T to a new set of random variables, $Y = T(X)$, constituting in effect a random sample from a distribution $G(y)$ involving no unknown parameters at all. Moreover, *only* random samples from distributions $F_0[(x - \mu)/\sigma]$ lead to $G(y)$ when operated on by T.

It then follows that testing the composite hypothesis H that $(X_1, \cdots, X_n)$ is a random sample from a distribution $F_0[(x - \mu)/\sigma]$ with some μ and some σ is equivalent to testing the hypothesis H' that $(Y_1, \cdots, Y_m)$ is a random sample from the distribution $G(y)$. Any of the tests for simple hypotheses is then available for testing H'. An example is provided by a negative exponential F_0 and uniform G, in which case the ordered exponential random sample $(X_{(1)}, \cdots, X_{(n)})$ is transformed

into an ordered uniform random sample $(Y_{(1)}, \cdots, Y_{(n-2)})$ by the transformation

$$Y_{(i)} = \frac{(X_{(n)} - X_{(n-1)}) + \cdots + i\,(X_{(n-i+1)} - X_{(n-i)})}{(X_{(n)} - X_{(n-1)}) + \cdots + (n-1)\,(X_{(2)} - X_{(1)})}.$$

Conditioning. Another way of neatly doing away with the unknown parameter is to consider the conditional distribution of the sample, given a sufficient estimate of it. This method is advocated, at least for testing Poissonness, in Fisher (1950).

Tests related to probability plots. S. S. Shapiro and M. B. Wilk have quantified in various ways the departure from linearity of the sorts of probability plots mentioned above, in particular of the plot of the ordered sample values against the expected values of the standardized order statistics [*see* NONPARAMETRIC STATISTICS, *article on* ORDER STATISTICS]. This new approach bears some similarity to one given in Darling (1955), which is based on the measure d_{02} modified for the composite case. Both approaches, in a sense, compare adjusted observed order statistics with standardized order statistic expectations. But the approach of Shapiro and Wilk is tailored more explicitly to particular scale-location families, by using their particular order statistic variances and covariances. It is no wonder that preliminary evaluations of this sort of approach (for example, by Shapiro & Wilk 1965) have shown exceptional promise. As an added bonus, the procedure is *similar* over the entire scale-location family; that is, its probability distribution is independent of location and scale.

Approximate hypotheses

The first, and seemingly most practically developed, attempt to provide the requisite tests of approximate hypotheses is found in Hodges and Lehmann (1954). Hodges and Lehmann assume the k typical categories of the χ^2 test and formulate the approximate *simple* hypothesis in terms of the discrepancy $d(p, p_0)$ between the category probabilities p_i under F_X and the category probabilities $p_{0,i}$ under a *simple* hypothesis F_0. A very tractable discrepancy measure of this type is ordinary distance, for which the approximate hypothesis takes the form

$$d(p, p_0) = \sum_{i=1}^{k} (p_i - p_{0,i})^2 \leqslant \delta.$$

Denoting O_i/n by o_i, the suggested test reduces, essentially, to the *one-sided* test of the hypothesis $d(p, p_0) = \delta$ based on the approximately normal statistic $[d(o, p_0) - \delta]/\hat{\sigma}$, where $\hat{\sigma}$ is the standard deviation, estimated from the sample o_i, of $d(o, p_0)$. For example, when F_0 specifies k categories with

$p_{0,i} = 1/k$, one treats as unit normal (under the null hypothesis) the statistic

$$S = \frac{\sqrt{n}\,[d(o, p_0) - \delta]}{2\sqrt{\sum o_i^3 - (\sum o_i^2)^2}}$$

and uses an upper-tail test. Thus a value of S of 1.645 leads to a sample significance level of .05. This approach lends itself easily to the computation of power and is extended as well by Hodges and Lehmann to the testing of approximate *composite* hypotheses.

Extension of other tests for simple hypotheses to the testing of approximate hypotheses has been considered by J. Rosenblatt (1962) and by Kac, Kiefer, and Wolfowitz (1955).

Further topics

That the sample is random may itself be in doubt, and tests have been designed to have power against specific sorts of departure from randomness. For example, tests of the hypothesis of randomness against the alternative hypothesis that the data are subject to a Markov structure are given by Billingsley (1961) and Goodman (1959); the latter work also covers testing that the data have Markov structure of a given order against the alternative that the data have Markov structure of higher order, and the testing of hypothesized values of transition probabilities when a Markov structure of given order is assumed [see MARKOV CHAINS].

Many of the tests described in this article can be extended to *several-sample* procedures for testing the hypothesis that several populations are in fact distributed identically; thus, as first suggested in Smirnov (1939a), if $G_m(x)$ denotes the proportion of values less than or equal to x, in an independent random sample $(Y_1, \cdots, Y_m)$ from a second population, $d_K(F_n, G_m)$ provides a natural test of the hypothesis that the two continuous population distribution functions F_X and G_Y coincide. Many of these extensions are functions only of the *relative ranks* of the two samples and, as such, are nonparametric, that is, their null probability distributions do not depend on the common functional form of F_X and G_Y. [*Several-sample nonparametric procedures are discussed in* NONPARAMETRIC STATISTICS.]

Another topic is that of tests of goodness of fit as preliminary tests of significance, in a sense discussed, for example, by Bancroft (1964). That tests of goodness of fit are typically applied in this sense is recognized by Chapman (1958), and the probabilistic properties of certain "nested" sequences of tests beginning with a test of goodness of fit have been considered by Hogg (1965). The Bayes

and information theory approaches to χ^2 tests of goodness of fit are also important (see Lindley 1965; Kullback 1959).

H. T. DAVID

[*Directly related are the entries* HYPOTHESIS TESTING; SIGNIFICANCE, TESTS OF. *Other relevant material may be found in* COUNTED DATA; ESTIMATION; NONPARAMETRIC STATISTICS.]

BIBLIOGRAPHY

BANCROFT, T. A. 1964 Analysis and Inference for Incompletely Specified Models Involving the Use of Preliminary Test(s) of Significance. *Biometrics* 20:427–442.

BERKSON, JOSEPH 1938 Some Difficulties of Interpretation Encountered in the Chi-square Test. *Journal of the American Statistical Association* 33:526–536.

BILLINGSLEY, PATRICK 1961 Statistical Methods in Markov Chains. *Annals of Mathematical Statistics* 32:12–40.

BIRNBAUM, Z. W. 1953 Distribution-free Tests of Fit for Continuous Distribution Functions. *Annals of Mathematical Statistics* 24:1–8.

CHAPMAN, DOUGLAS G. 1958 A Comparative Study of Several One-sided Goodness-of-fit Tests. *Annals of Mathematical Statistics* 29:655–674.

CHERNOFF, HERMAN; and LEHMANN, E. L. 1954 The Use of Maximum Likelihood Estimates in χ^2 Tests for Goodness of Fit. *Annals of Mathematical Statistics* 25:579–586.

COCHRAN, WILLIAM G. 1952 The χ^2 Test of Goodness of Fit. *Annals of Mathematical Statistics* 23:315–345.

COCHRAN, WILLIAM G. 1954 Some Methods for Strengthening the Common χ^2 Tests. *Biometrics* 10:417–451.

DARLING, D. A. 1955 The Cramér–Smirnov Test in the Parametric Case. *Annals of Mathematical Statistics* 26:1–20.

DARLING, D. A. 1957 The Kolmogorov–Smirnov, Cramér–Von Mises Tests. *Annals of Mathematical Statistics* 28:823–838.

DURBIN, J. 1961 Some Methods of Constructing Exact Tests. *Biometrika* 48:41–55.

FISHER, R. A. 1924 The Conditions Under Which χ^2 Measures the Discrepancy Between Observation and Hypothesis. *Journal of the Royal Statistical Society* 87:442–450.

FISHER, R. A. 1950 The Significance of Deviations From Expectation in a Poisson Series. *Biometrics* 6:17–24.

FIX, EVELYN; HODGES, J. L. JR.; and LEHMANN, E. L. 1954 The Restricted Chi-square Test. Pages 92–107 in Ulf Grenander (editor), *Probability and Statistics*. New York: Wiley.

GEARY, R. C. 1947 Testing for Normality. *Biometrika* 34:209–242.

GOODMAN, LEO A. 1954 Kolmogorov–Smirnov Tests for Psychological Research. *Psychological Bulletin* 51:160–168.

GOODMAN, LEO A. 1959 On Some Statistical Tests for *m*th Order Markov Chains. *Annals of Mathematical Statistics* 30:154–164.

GREENWOOD, JOSEPH A.; and HARTLEY, H. O. 1962 *Guide to Tables in Mathematical Statistics*. Princeton Univ. Press. → A sequel to the guides to mathematical tables produced by and for the Committee on Mathematical Tables and Aids to Computation of the

National Academy of Sciences–National Research Council of the United States.

HODGES, J. L. JR.; and LEHMANN, E. L. 1954 Testing the Approximate Validity of Statistical Hypotheses. *Journal of the Royal Statistical Society* Series B 16: 261–268.

HOGG, ROBERT V. 1965 On Models and Hypotheses With Restricted Alternatives. *Journal of the American Statistical Association* 60: 1153–1162.

KAC, M.; KIEFER, J.; and WOLFOWITZ, J. 1955 On Tests of Normality and Other Tests of Goodness of Fit Based on Distance Methods. *Annals of Mathematical Statistics* 26: 189–211.

KEATS, J. A.; and LORD, FREDERIC M. 1962 A Theoretical Distribution for Mental Test Scores. *Psychometrika* 27: 59–72.

KEMPTHORNE, O. 1966 The Classical Problem of Inference: Goodness of Fit. Unpublished manuscript. → Paper presented at the Berkeley Symposium on Mathematical Statistics and Probability, Fifth, *Proceedings* to be published.

KOLMOGOROV, A. N. 1933 Sulla determinazione empirica di une legge di distribuzione. Istituto Italiano degli Attuari, *Giornale* 4: 83–99.

KUIPER, NICOLAAS H. 1960 Tests Concerning Random Points on a Circle. Akademie van Wetenschappen, Amsterdam, *Proceedings* Series A 63: 38–47.

KULLBACK, S. 1959 *Information Theory and Statistics.* New York: Wiley.

LINDLEY, D. V. 1965 *Introduction to Probability and Statistics From a Bayesian Viewpoint.* Volume 2: Inference. Cambridge Univ. Press.

MANN, H. B.; and WALD, A. 1942 On the Choice of the Number of Class Intervals in the Application of the Chi Square Test. *Annals of Mathematical Statistics* 13: 306–317.

MARSHALL, A. W. 1958 The Small Sample Distribution of $n\omega_n^2$. *Annals of Mathematical Statistics* 29: 307–309.

MASSEY, FRANK J. JR. 1951 The Kolmogorov–Smirnov Test for Goodness of Fit. *Journal of the American Statistical Association* 46: 68–78.

NEYMAN, JERZY 1937 "Smooth Test" for Goodness of Fit. *Skandinavisk aktuarietidskrift* 20: 149–199.

NEYMAN, JERZY 1949 Contribution to the Theory of the χ^2 Test. Pages 239–273 in Berkeley Symposium on Mathematical Statistics and Probability, First, *Proceedings.* Berkeley: Univ. of California Press.

PATANKAR, V. N. 1954 The Goodness of Fit of Frequency Distributions Obtained From Stochastic Processes. *Biometrika* 41: 450–462.

PEARSON, E. S. 1938 The Probability Integral Transformation for Testing Goodness of Fit and Combining Independent Tests of Significance. *Biometrika* 30: 134–148.

PEARSON, E. S. 1963 Comparison of Tests for Randomness of Points on a Line. *Biometrika* 50: 315–325.

PEARSON, KARL 1900 On the Criterion That a Given System of Deviations From the Probable in the Case of a Correlated System of Variables Is Such That It Can Be Reasonably Supposed to Have Arisen From Random Sampling. *Philosophical Magazine* 5th Series 50: 157–175.

PYKE, RONALD 1965 Spacings. *Journal of the Royal Statistical Society* Series B 27: 395–449.

ROSENBLATT, JUDAH 1962 Testing Approximate Hypotheses in the Composite Case. *Annals of Mathematical Statistics* 33: 1356–1364.

ROSENBLATT, MURRAY 1952 Remarks on a Multivariate Transformation. *Annals of Mathematical Statistics* 23: 470–472.

SARKADI, KÁROLY 1960 On Testing for Normality. Magyar Tudományos Akadémia, Matematikai Kutató Intézet, *Közlemények* Series A 5: 269–274.

SHAPIRO, S. S.; and WILK, M. B. 1965 An Analysis of Variance Test for Normality (Complete Samples). *Biometrika* 52: 591–611.

SLAKTER, MALCOLM J. 1965 A Comparison of the Pearson Chi-square and Kolmogorov Goodness-of-fit Tests With Respect to Validity. *Journal of the American Statistical Association* 60: 854–858.

SMIRNOV, N. V. 1939a On the Estimation of the Discrepancy Between Empirical Curves of Distribution for Two Independent Samples. Moscow, Universitet, *Bulletin mathématique* Série Internationale 2, no. 2: 3–26.

SMIRNOV, N. V. 1939b Ob ukloneniiakh empiricheskoi krivoi raspredeleniia (On the Deviations of the Empirical Distribution Curve). *Matematicheskii sbornik* New Series 6, no. 1: 1–26. → Includes a French résumé.

SUKHATME, P. V. 1938 On the Distribution of χ^2 in Samples of the Poisson Series. *Journal of the Royal Statistical Society* 5 (Supplement): 75–79.

SUPPES, PATRICK et al. 1964 Empirical Comparison of Models for a Continuum of Responses With Non-contingent Bimodal Reinforcement. Pages 358–379 in R. C. Atkinson (editor), *Studies in Mathematical Psychology.* Stanford Univ. Press.

WATSON, G. S. 1957 The χ^2 Goodness-of-fit Test for Normal Distributions. *Biometrika* 336–348.

WATSON, G. S. 1961 Goodness-of-fit Tests on a Circle. *Biometrika* 48: 109–114.

WEISS, LIONEL 1958 Limiting Distributions of Homogeneous Functions of Sample Spacings. *Annals of Mathematical Statistics* 29: 310–312.

WILLIAMS, C. ARTHUR JR. 1950 On the Choice of the Number and Width of Classes for the Chi-square Test of Goodness of Fit. *Journal of the American Statistical Association* 45: 77–86.

GOODNOW, FRANK J.

The impact of Frank J. Goodnow (1859–1939) upon the study of public administration in the United States has been quite durable. Goodnow's classic treatise *Politics and Administration* (1900) was the intellectual point of departure, along with Woodrow Wilson's "Study of Public Administration" (1887), for much of the work in the field up to World War II. It is a book still frequently cited today, although not always praised.

Goodnow began teaching administrative law at Columbia in 1883 and remained there throughout his professorial career. In 1914 he resigned from the Columbia faculty to become president of Johns Hopkins University, a position he held until his retirement in 1929. Goodnow was one of the principal founders of the American Political Science Association and became its first president in 1903. He helped to redraft the New York City charter in 1900, served on President Taft's commission on economy and efficiency in 1911–1912, and in 1913 went to China as legal adviser to its president.

Much of Goodnow's scholarly work was in the field of municipal government. Although his approach to the study of municipal institutions was primarily legal in character, his works also reveal a keen awareness of the realities of city politics around the beginning of the twentieth century. They remain quite useful to students of urban political development in the United States, since current trends and problems in urban government and politics are still structured by the cleavage between bossism and reformism, which was so prominent an issue in Goodnow's day.

A focal point of controversy in political science has been the distinction Goodnow delineated in *Politics and Administration* between politics, as the sphere in which the will of the state is articulated, and administration, as the range of methods and techniques through which the state's purposes are carried out. This functional separation of powers had a great deal of practical utility in the early movement to reform the organization and operation of public administration in the United States, since it justified the introduction into the public service of practices and values—e.g., efficiency, hierarchy, and discipline—altogether alien to the egalitarian ethos of American politics itself. The distinction also helped carve out a sphere of autonomy for public agencies at a time when these administrative units were hard pressed to maintain professional standards in the face of pressures from spoils-oriented and sometimes corrupt party organizations. When it was first formulated, the separation between politics and administration was to a large extent an effort to free administrators from political harassment.

Intellectually, however, the separating of these two segments of governmental activity has not fared very well at the hands of recent critics. Since World War II the study of public administration has been largely "politicized"—in the sense at least that the role of bureaucracy in modern government has increasingly been studied from the point of view of the tactics that agencies follow in securing resources upon which their survival depends, including appropriations, constituency support, and statutory authority, or with a focus on the involvement of administrators in the framing of public policy. The modern tendency has been to point up and to some extent justify the role of administrators in the political process.

However, although Goodnow's distinction be-tween politics and administration was to serve more often as a target for criticism than as a model, the issues he first raised in a systematic way are still very much at the center of scholarly concern. Dwight Waldo, for example, has noted that the dichotomy between facts and values in the work of Herbert Simon, since World War II one of the central figures in the study of public administration, is closely analogous to Goodnow's own distinction between administration and politics (Waldo 1963, pp. 187–188). The entire effort to create a "science" of administration in modern times does in fact ultimately turn upon the possibility of singling out a sphere of managerial expertise which is distinct from and independent of political preferences and policy goals. Thus, Goodnow's work retains its intellectual relevance today, even though it no longer has the authority it once commanded.

From the point of view of governmental structure, there can be no disputing the fact that the distinction has been an important force in the development of American institutions. Merit systems and a variety of other devices have been established at all levels of government to provide administrative agencies with some degree of legal protection against the grosser forms of political interference. At the same time, there has been a continued effort to limit the political role of executive agencies, for example, by statutes designed to prevent them from engaging in "propaganda" or lobbying activity. Public policy in the United States has thus sought to separate politics and administration, however much the two spheres may overlap in the actual day-to-day work of government.

FRANCIS E. ROURKE

[See also ADMINISTRATIVE LAW; CIVIL SERVICE; COMMISSIONS, GOVERNMENT; POLITICAL PROCESS; PUBLIC ADMINISTRATION; PUBLIC LAW.]

WORKS BY GOODNOW

(1893) 1903 *Comparative Administrative Law: An Analysis of the Administrative Systems, National and Local, of the United States, England, France and Germany.* 2 vols. New York: Putnam.
(1895) 1897 *Municipal Home Rule: A Study in Administration.* New York and London: Macmillan.
1897 *Municipal Problems.* New York and London: Macmillan.
(1900) 1914 *Politics and Administration: A Study in Government.* New York: Macmillan.
(1904) 1910 *City Government in the United States.* New York: Century.
1905 *The Principles of the Administrative Law of the United States.* New York and London: Putnam.
(1909) 1919 *Municipal Government.* 2d ed. New York: Century.
1911 *Social Reform and the Constitution.* New York: Macmillan.

1916a *The American Conception of Liberty and Government.* Providence, R.I.: Standard Printing.

1916b *Principles of Constitutional Government.* New York and London: Harper.

1926 *China: An Analysis.* Baltimore: Johns Hopkins Press.

SUPPLEMENTARY BIBLIOGRAPHY

HAINES, CHARLES G.; and DIMOCK, MARSHALL E. (editors) 1935 *Essays on the Law and Practice of Governmental Administration: A Volume in Honor of Frank J. Goodnow.* Baltimore: Johns Hopkins Press. → See especially pages v–xv for a biographical sketch.

MACMAHON, ARTHUR W. 1958 Frank Johnson Goodnow. Volume 22, pages 250–251 in *Dictionary of American Biography.* New York: Scribner.

WALDO, DWIGHT 1948 *The Administrative State: A Study of the Political Theory of American Public Administration.* New York: Ronald Press. → See especially pages 106–109.

WALDO, DWIGHT 1963 Comparative Public Administration: Prologue, Performance, Problems and Promise. *Indian Journal of Political Science* 24:177–216.

WILSON, WOODROW (1887) 1953 The Study of Public Administration. Pages 65–75 in Dwight Waldo (editor), *Ideas and Issues in Public Administration: A Book of Readings.* New York: McGraw-Hill.

GOSSEN, HERMANN HEINRICH

Hermann Heinrich Gossen, German writer on economics, was born at Düren in the Rhineland in 1810 and died at Cologne in 1858. His claim to fame is based on a single publication: in 1854 he published a book that develops, with the help of mathematics, a comprehensive theory of the hedonistic calculus. In this work Gossen postulated the principle of diminishing marginal utility and from this derived the following theorem: to maximize utility, a given quantity of a good must be divided among different uses in such a manner that the marginal utilities are equal in all uses. In the Continental literature the postulate is usually referred to as Gossen's First Law and the theorem as his Second Law.

Gossen pioneered in the development of the subjective theory of value on the basis of the marginal principle, but his work was neglected during his life, and he died a disappointed man, having withdrawn the unsold copies of his book from the publisher. His work was briefly mentioned in a history of economic thought published the year of his death and, more appreciatively, in 1870 in the second edition of a book on the labor problem by F. A. Lange, the famed historian of materialism. Gossen's importance in the development of economic thought was first recognized in the late 1870s, when Jevons, Menger, and Walras had already published their own versions of the new theory of value. Gossen's book was brought to the attention of Jevons by a colleague in August 1878, causing him to complain: "I am, therefore, in the unfortunate position that the greater number of people think the theory nonsense, and do not understand it, and the rest discover that it is not new" (Jevons 1886, pp. 387–388). Jevons found comfort, however, in the thought that "the theory in question has in fact been independently discovered three or four times over, and must be true" (*ibid.*, p. 389).

The next month Jevons advised Walras of Gossen's anticipation. Both men publicly recognized Gossen's priority and did much to save his work from oblivion, Jevons in the preface to the second edition of his *Theory of Political Economy* in 1879 and Walras in an article in the *Journal des économistes* (1885). Walras even prepared a French translation of Gossen's book, but this was never published. Much later, in 1950, an Italian translation was brought out.

An estranged Catholic, Gossen offered his work with the messianic fervor of the founder of a new religion: the laws of science were the dogma, the hedonistic calculus was the moral principle, instruction in the laws of science was the cult, experiments the sacraments, and scientists the priests. Some of Gossen's thoughts echo ideas of Bentham, Saint-Simon, and Comte, but since Gossen did not cite authorities, it is uncertain whether, or to what extent, he was indebted to these writers. German translations of two of Bentham's juridical works had appeared in the 1830s, and one of these had been published in Cologne, where Gossen spent many years of his life. He may have come under the influence of Bentham's hedonistic philosophy, but the mathematical treatment was his own work, as probably was his statement of the principle of diminishing marginal utility. There had been other economists who developed the subjective theory of value and the marginal principle, but none of them carried either idea as far as Gossen did.

In matters of economic policy, Gossen's pronounced individualism led him to a modified laissez-faire point of view. All that exists, he held, must by itself create the means to further existence; otherwise it does not deserve to continue to exist. On this basis he rejected government support of religion, art, and science. Public relief of the poor was to be given in the form of loans. A general system of government loans would be established to enable everyone to make the most of his opportunities. Private property was to be protected and freed from restrictions that hamper individual initiative, but land was to be nationalized (purchased by the government) and then auctioned off to the highest bidder in the form of a lifetime lease to facilitate its most productive use.

The reasons for the almost complete neglect of Gossen's work for a quarter of a century are not difficult to trace. His book was the work of a lone outsider, unknown in academic circles. Obedient to his father's wishes, but with great reluctance, Gossen had studied law to prepare himself for a career in the Prussian civil service. After a few years he had relinquished government service and started an unsuccessful venture in the insurance business. When he published his book, with high hopes of recognition, he gave it a forbiddingly pretentious title, which in English translation reads "Development of the Laws of Human Relations, and of the Rules of Human Action Derived Therefrom" (1854). The presentation and style of the work are bizarre and cumbersome. The book is not divided into parts or chapters, and simple dash lines, rather than headings, separate the various topics. Gossen was presumptuous enough to make a favorable comparison, on the first page, of his own study of society with Copernicus' study of the cosmos, and on the penultimate page to claim in enlarged print that the adoption of his system of thought would turn the earth into a paradise. Such claims were bound to appear preposterous to the followers of the historical school, who were beginning to fill the chairs of economics in Germany in Gossen's time, and as late as 1929 Sombart referred to Gossen as a "brilliant idiot." Moreover, Gossen's book abounds with diagrams, formulas, and lengthy arithmetical illustrations. Half a century after its publication, Marshall, under much more favorable circumstances, still deemed it wise to take infinite care to make the mathematical treatment of economics palatable to his readers. Gossen's book might have found some favor because of its polemics against communists and socialists and because the subjective theory of value could be used as a critique of the foundations of socialist economics. The German historical economists, however, had their own ways of coping with the threat of socialism, and several decades after the publication of Gossen's book they were still inclined to deprecate rather than to make use of the ideological weapons available in the armory of the Austrian branch of the new theory of value. The Austrians themselves began to pay attention to Gossen only in 1889.

It is significant also that when Gossen was born, the Rhineland was part of the France of the Emperor Napoleon, in whose revenue service Gossen's father was employed. Gossen's thought was fundamentally un-German, and his fellow countrymen responded as little to his hedonism and utilitarianism as to the idea of natural law. It is thus no accident that recognition eventually came from foreigners.

HENRY W. SPIEGEL

[*For discussion of the subsequent development of Gossen's ideas, see* UTILITY *and biographies of* JEVONS; MENGER; WALRAS.]

WORK BY GOSSEN

(1854) 1927 *Entwicklung der Gesetze des menschlichen Verkehrs und der daraus fliessenden Regeln für menschliches Handeln.* 3d ed. Introduction by Friedrich A. Hayek. Berlin: Prager.

SUPPLEMENTARY BIBLIOGRAPHY

BAGIOTTI, TULLIO 1955 Nel centenale del libro di Gossen. *Giornale degli economisti e annali di economia* 14:236–253.

BAGIOTTI, TULLIO 1957 Reminiszenzen anlässlich des hundertsten Jahrestages des Erscheinens des Buches von Gossen. *Zeitschrift für Nationalökonomie* 17:39–54.

BEHRENS, FRITZ 1949 *Hermann Heinrich Gossen.* Leipzig: Bibliographisches Institut. → A Marxist interpretation of Gossen as the first scientific apologist of capitalism.

BOUSQUET, G. H. 1958 Un centenaire: L'oeuvre de H. H. Gossen et sa véritable structure. *Revue d'économie politique* 68:499–523.

BRAEUER, WALTER 1952 *Handbuch zur Geschichte der Volkswirtschaftslehre.* Frankfurt am Main (Germany): Klostermann.

EDGEWORTH, F. Y. 1896 H. H. Gossen. Volume 2, pages 231–233 in Robert H. Palgrave, *Dictionary of Political Economy.* London: Macmillan. → A good source on Gossen's technical economics.

HAYEK, FRIEDRICH A. 1932 Herman Heinrich Gossen. Volume 7, page 3 in *Encyclopaedia of the Social Sciences.* New York: Macmillan.

JEVONS, WILLIAM S. (1871) 1879 *The Theory of Political Economy.* 2d ed. London: Macmillan.

JEVONS, WILLIAM S. 1886 *Letters and Journal.* London: Macmillan.

LANGE, FRIEDRICH ALBERT (1865) 1870 *Die Arbeiterfrage.* 2d ed. Winterthur (Switzerland): Bleuler.

PANTALEONI, MAFFEO (1889) 1957 *Pure Economics.* New York: Kelley & Millman. → See pages 28 ff. for the best source in English of Gossen's technical economics.

RIEDLE, HERMANN 1953 *Hermann Heinrich Gossen 1810–1858: Ein Wegbereiter der modernen ökonomischen Theorie.* Winterthur (Switzerland): Keller.

STARK, WERNER 1943 *The Ideal Foundations of Economic Thought.* London: Routledge. → See pages 149 ff. for the best source in English of Gossen's economic philosophy and policy proposals.

WALRAS, LÉON (1885) 1952 Walras on Gossen. Pages 470–488 in Henry W. Spiegel (editor), *The Development of Economic Thought.* New York: Wiley. → Originally published in *Journal des économistes.*

GOSSET, WILLIAM SEALY

The impact of W. S. Gosset (1876–1937) on the social sciences was entirely indirect. He was, however, one of the pioneers in the development of modern statistical method and its application to the design and analysis of experiments. He is far better known to the scientific world under the pseudonym of "Student" than under his own name. Indeed all his papers except one appeared under the pseudonym.

He was the son of Colonel Frederic Gosset of the Royal Engineers, the descendant of an old Huguenot family that left France after the revocation of the Edict of Nantes. Gosset was a scholar of Winchester—that is, a boy who was awarded a prize on the basis of a competitive examination to pay for part or all of his education—which shows that his exceptional mental powers had developed early. From Winchester he went, again as a scholar, to New College, Oxford, where he obtained first class degrees in mathematics and natural science.

On leaving Oxford in the autumn of 1899 he joined the famous brewing firm of Guinness in Dublin. He remained with Guinness all his life, ultimately becoming, in 1935, chief brewer at Park Royal, the firm's newly established brewery in London.

At that time scientific methods and laboratory determinations were beginning to be seriously applied to brewing, and this naturally led Gosset to study error functions and to see the need for adequate methods to deal with small samples in examining the relations between the quality of the raw materials of beer, such as barley and hops, the conditions of production, and the finished article. The importance of controlling the quality of barley ultimately led him to study the design of agricultural field trials.

In 1904 he drew up for the directors the first report on "The Application of the Law of Error." This emphasized the importance of the theory of probability in setting "an exact value on the results of our experiments; many of which lead to results which are probable but not certain." He used only the classical theory of errors, such as is found in G. B. Airy's *On the Algebraical, and Numerical Theory of Errors of Observation* (1861) and M. Merriman's *A Text-book on the Method of Least Squares* (1884). But he observed that if X and Y are both measured from their mean, there are often considerable differences between $\sum(X + Y)^2$ and $\sum(X - Y)^2$; in other words, he was feeling his way

toward the notion of correlation, although he had not yet heard of the correlation coefficient.

His first meeting with Karl Pearson took place in 1905, and in 1906/1907 he was sent for a year's specialized study in London, where he worked at, or in close contact with, the biometric laboratory at University College.

Mathematical statistics. Gosset was once described by Sir Ronald Fisher as the "Faraday of statistics." The comparison is apt, for he was not a profound mathematician but had a superb intuitive faculty that enabled him to grasp general principles and see their relevance to practical ends.

His first mathematical paper was "On the Error of Counting With a Haemacytometer" ([1907] 1943, pp. 1–10); here he derived afresh the Poisson distribution as a limiting form of the binomial and fitted it to four series of counts of yeast cells. The derivation presented no particular difficulty (it had in fact been obtained before by several investigators), but it was characteristic of him to see immediately the correct method of dealing with a practical problem. One of these series has become world famous owing to its inclusion as an example in Fisher's *Statistical Methods for Research Workers* (1925).

His next paper, "The Probable Error of a Mean" ([1908] 1943, pp. 11–34), brought him more fame, in the course of time, than any other work that he did, for it provided the basis of Student's t-test.

In his work at the brewery he had been struck by the importance of knowing the accuracy of the mean of a small sample. The usual procedure at the time was to compute the sample average and standard deviation, $\bar{x}$ and s, and to proceed as if $\bar{x}$ were normally distributed with the same mean as that of the population and with standard deviation $s/\sqrt{n}$, where n is sample size. The difficulty here is that s is a fallible estimate of the true population standard deviation. Gosset's intuition told him that the usual procedure, based on large sample considerations, would, for small samples, give a spuriously high impression of how accurately the population mean is estimated.

By a combination of exceptional clearheadedness and simple algebra, he obtained the first four moments of the distribution of s^2. He then proceeded to fit the Pearson curve that has these moments. His results showed that the curve has to be of Type III (essentially the gamma or χ^2 distribution), and he found the distribution of s^2 to be $C(s^2/\sigma^2)^{(n-3)/2} \exp[(-ns^2/2\sigma^2)]d(s^2/\sigma^2)$. He then showed that the correlation coefficient between $\bar{x}^2$ and s^2 was zero, and assuming absolute independence (which does not necessarily follow but was true in this case), he deduced the probability distribution of $z = (\bar{x} - \mu)/s$, where μ is the true mean. With a mere change of notation this is the t-distribution. Here s is defined to be $(1/n)\sum(x - \bar{x})^2$ so that

$$t = (\bar{x} - \mu)\Big/\sqrt{\frac{\sum(x - \bar{x})^2}{n(n - 1)}} = \frac{\bar{x} - \mu}{s}\sqrt{(n - 1)}.$$

He then checked the adequacy of this distribution by drawing 750 samples of 4 from W. R. Macdonell's data on the height and middle-finger length of 3,000 criminals and by working out the standard deviations of both variates in each sample (see Macdonell 1902). This he did by shuffling 3,000 pieces of cardboard on which the results had been written, possibly the earliest work in statistical research that led to the development of the Monte Carlo method.

Later in his paper on "Probable Error of a Correlation Coefficient" ([1908] 1943, pp. 35–42), Gosset used the 750 correlation coefficients of the two variables. Here his remarkable intuition again led him to a correct answer. By correlating the height measurements of one sample with the middle-finger lengths of the next, he was able to obtain 750 values of r, the sample correlation coefficient, for which ρ, the true population correlation coefficient, was presumably zero. He noticed that the observed distribution of r was approximately rectangular. If it were a Pearson curve it would have to be Type II, that is, $C(1 - r^2)^\lambda$, and his result from the 750 samples suggested $\lambda = k(n - 4)$. He guessed that $k = \frac{1}{2}$ and confirmed the result by taking 750 samples of 8 to which $C(1 - r^2)^2$ gave an excellent fit. Six years later Fisher proved that all these brilliant conjectures for the distribution of s^2, t, and r when $\rho = 0$ were indeed correct.

The correlation coefficient between the two measurements in the 3,000 criminals was 0.66. Gosset also examined two sets of 750 samples of sizes 4 and 8 and one set of 100 samples of 30, for which the true value must have been close to 0.66. He could see from his results that the standard deviation given by $(1 - \rho^2)/\sqrt{n}$ was too small and that the distribution could not be of Pearson type except when $\rho = 0$. He succeeded in obtaining the exact repartition of r for any ρ in samples of 2, but the general solution for $\rho \neq 0$ had to await the publication of Fisher's famous paper in 1915.

Gosset's fourth paper ([1909] 1943, pp. 43–48) dealt with the distribution of the means of samples not drawn at random. His brewing experience had repeatedly drawn his attention to the fact that successive observations were not uncorrelated. Here

he supposed a sample of n values to be drawn in such a way that the correlation between every pair of observations is the same (say ρ), so that ρ is effectively an intraclass correlation. He used the algebraical methods of his second paper to determine the first four moments of the mean, in this case employing as an illustration some data published by Greenwood and White (1909) in which 2,000 phagocytic counts had been grouped in samples of 25. Both the original counts and the distribution of means could be fitted by Pearson Type I (Beta) curves. However, the observed values of β_1 and $(\beta_2 - 3)$ for the distribution of means were bigger than would have been anticipated if the usual theory for independent observations had been valid. The modified theory produced much better agreement.

Gosset published five more mathematical papers between 1909 and 1921 ([1913; 1914; 1917; 1919; 1921] 1943, pp. 53–89). With the possible exception of the first of these, they are still of interest. The 1921 paper gave for the first time the correction for ties in calculating Spearman's rank correlation coefficient.

Agricultural and other biometric studies.   It was natural, owing to the high importance of barley quality in brewing, that Gosset should have become interested in agricultural problems. His active interest seems to have started in 1905 when he was first asked for advice by E. S. Beaven, a maltster who had started experimental work in the 1890s. From then onward there was a constant interchange of correspondence and ideas between them, in which the mathematical insight of the younger man supplemented the experimental experience of the older.

Gosset's first meeting with Fisher was at Rothamsted in August 1922; each had the greatest admiration for the other's work and doubtless each had considerable influence on the development of the other's ideas on experimental design. Toward the end of Gosset's life they had a difference of opinion about the relative methods of random and systematic arrangements, but this did not affect the high regard that they always had for one another.

In 1911 Gosset examined the results of some uniformity trials carried out by Mercer and Hall at Rothamsted ([1911] 1943, pp. 49–52). In the most important of these, an acre of wheat had been harvested in 1/500-acre plots. Gosset showed from the results how advantage could be taken of the correlation between the yields of adjacent plots to increase the accuracy of varietal comparisons, and he showed that for a given acreage greater accuracy could be obtained with smaller plots rather than with larger plots.

As early as 1912 and 1913 Beaven had invented the "chessboard" design, and experiments had been laid down, each with eight varieties of barley on yard-square plots, in three centers. These were essentially "block designs," with each variety occurring once in each block; but within the block, the arrangement was balanced rather than random. At this time Gosset discovered the correct estimate of error per plot for the varietal comparisons, precisely the same result as would be obtained from an analysis of variance. He compared every possible pair of varieties and calculated for each pair $\sum(d - \bar{d})^2$, d being the difference in one block. He added these results together for all n varieties and divided by $\frac{1}{2}n(n-1)(m-1)$, where m is the number of blocks. These experiments were discontinued during World War I, but in 1923 Gosset and Fisher discovered, independently, the analysis of variance method of obtaining the result. In a letter to Gosset, Fisher proved the algebraical equivalence of Gosset's original method and the new one.

These chessboard designs were small-scale work. For field trials, Gosset and Beaven favored the "half-drill strip method," in which two varieties were compared on an area of about an acre. In this method, the two varieties are sown in long strips—CAACCAAC, etc.—there being an integral number of "sandwiches" (such as CAAC).

The error of the varietal comparison was obtained from the variances of the differences $(C - A)$ either in individual strips or in sandwiches. In one such experiment, described by Gosset, on something more than an acre, the standard error of a varietal mean was found to be about 0.6 per cent. Gosset was later criticized by Fisher for preferring this method to randomized strips or randomized sandwiches. Gosset welcomed the advances in the science of agricultural experimentation that came from Fisher and his school. His own attitude was a very practical one, based on his extensive experience in Ireland experimenting with barley.

A good account of much of this kind of work is given in Gosset's most important paper on agricultural experimentation, "On Testing Varieties of Cereals" ([1923] 1943, pp. 90–114). The paper also describes some large-scale work carried out by the department of agriculture in Ireland during 1901–1906 to find the best variety of barley to grow in that country. Here two varieties, Archer and Goldthorpe, were carried right through the whole period and each tested on two-acre plots in a large number of centers. With 50 pairs of plots of this size, the standard error of the comparison was still about 10 per cent to 15 per cent. However, the result was based on wide experience. In the half-drill strip experiment the corresponding standard error was only 1 per cent, but the result applied only to an acre, in one place, under very particular conditions of soil and season.

While it was important to plan yield trials in such a way as to reduce experimental error and to obtain an accurate estimate of it, it was only by comparison and analysis of the results from a number of soils, seasons, and climates that one could judge the relative value of different varieties or different treatments. Further, products must also be subjected to tests of quality. *Conclusions drawn in one center could in any case be applicable only to the particular conditions under which the trials were carried out.* While he insisted that "experiments must be capable of being considered to be a *random* sample of the population to which the conclusions are to be applied," in an individual center he often preferred balanced (that is, systematic) arrangements to randomized ones. He liked the Latin square, because of its combination of balance (to eliminate soil heterogeneity) with a random element, thus conforming to all the principles of allowed witchcraft ([1926] 1943, pp. 199–215). He was less happy about randomized blocks because he felt that a balanced arrangement within the blocks often gave a greater accuracy than did a random one. Further, he was unwilling to accept the result of the toss of a coin, or its equivalent, if the arrangement so obtained was biased in relation to already available knowledge of the fertility gradients of the experimental area. In his last paper, "Comparison Between Balanced and Random Arrangements of Field Plots" ([1938] 1943, pp. 193–215), he wrote:

It is of course perfectly true that *in the long run*, taking all possible arrangements, exactly as many misleading conclusions will be drawn as are allowed for in the tables, and anyone prepared to spend a blameless life in repeating an experiment would doubtless confirm this; nevertheless it would be pedantic to continue with an arrangement of plots known beforehand to be likely to lead to a misleading conclusion. (p. 202)

He thought that an experimenter with a knowledge of his job could arrange the treatments within a block so that *real error*, that is, the variance of the different treatment means that would be obtained with dummy treatments in a uniformity trial, would be less than if the treatments had been randomized. This statement was no doubt often true in the domain in which he worked, but its general validity has often been questioned. He distinguished between the *real error* as here defined and the *calculated error*, that is, the error variance of the treatment mean, that would be obtained from usual analysis of variance procedures. He maintained, perfectly correctly, that if the real error were reduced by balancing, the calculated error would be too high. In his last paper, he showed, in addition, that in this situation experiments that have a real error less than the calculated one fail to give as many "significant" results as those that have a greater error, if the real treatment differences are small. When, however, the real treatment differences are large, the reverse is the case. Therefore, if balanced arrangements have a small real error, they will less often miss large real differences and more often miss small ones. He regarded this as a positive advantage; where real differences in a particular center were small, he was satisfied to have an upper limit to his error because he thought that only by collating results from different centers could he arrive at the truth. Where real differences were small, even if statistically significant, the results at different centers were likely to be conflicting.

This last paper was written in reply to one by Barbacki and Fisher (1936), which purported to show that the half-drill strip method is less accurate than the corresponding randomized arrangement. Gosset was right in maintaining that these authors were in error, for they had not compared like with like in the actual data they had examined —a uniformity trial carried out by Wiebe (1935). However the data were not very good for deciding the question, for as subsequently shown by Yates (1939), owing to defective drilling they contained a periodic fluctuation, two drill-widths wide. Gosset would almost certainly have welcomed the combination of balance and randomization achieved by some of the designs invented since his day, which are likely to give a gain in accuracy similar to that obtained by his systematic designs over randomized blocks and at the same time are free from difficulties in error estimation.

In an article on Gosset, Sir Ronald Fisher praised "Student's" work on genetical evolutionary theory (see Gosset [1907–1938] 1943, pp. 181–191). He concluded: "In spite of his many activities it is the 'Student' of *Student's* *test of significance* who has won, and deserved to win, a unique place in the history of scientific method" (Fisher 1939, p. 8).

J. O. Irwin

[For the historical context of Gosset's work, see Distributions, statistical; Statistics, *article on* the history of statistical method; *and the*

biographies of Fisher, R. A.; *and* Pearson. *For discussion of the subsequent development of his ideas,* see Estimation; Experimental design; Hypothesis testing.]

WORKS BY GOSSET

(1907–1938) 1943 "Student's" Collected Papers. Edited by E. S. Pearson and John Wishart. London: University College, Biometrika Office. → William S. Gosset wrote under the pseudonym "Student." The 1943 edition contains all the articles cited in the text.

SUPPLEMENTARY BIBLIOGRAPHY

Airy, George B. (1861) 1879 On the Algebraical and Numerical Theory of Errors of Observations and the Combination of Observations. 3d ed. London: Macmillan.

Barbacki, S.; and Fisher, R. A. 1936 A Test of the Supposed Precision of Systematic Arrangements. Annals of Eugenics 7:189–193.

Fisher, R. A. 1915 Frequency Distribution of the Values of the Correlation Coefficient in Samples From an Indefinitely Large Population. Biometrika 10:507–521.

Fisher, R. A. (1925) 1958 Statistical Methods for Research Workers. 13th ed. New York: Hafner. → Previous editions were published by Oliver & Boyd.

Fisher, R. A. 1939 "Student." Annals of Eugenics 9: 1–9.

Greenwood, M. Jr.; and White, J. D. C. 1909 On the Frequency Distribution of Phagocytic Counts. Biometrika 6:376–401.

Macdonell, W. R. 1902 On Criminal Anthropometry and the Identification of Criminals. Biometrika 1: 177–227.

Merriman, Mansfield (1884) 1911 A Text-book on the Method of Least Squares. 8th ed. New York: Wiley.

Wiebe, G. A. 1935 Variation and Correlation in Grain Yield Among 1,500 Wheat Nursery Plots. Journal of Agricultural Research 50:331–357.

Yates, F. 1939 The Comparative Advantages of Systematic and Randomized Arrangements in the Design of Agricultural and Biological Experiments. Biometrika 30:440–466.

GOVERNMENT

The study of government has followed several main lines of inquiry. These include both an examination of the source and distribution of authority and the classification of types of government (such as presidential systems and monarchies), as well as analysis of levels of government (including such units as national societies, clubs, churches, and trade unions). Although a thorough review is impossible here, we can examine the main themes which unite these various approaches and evaluate their theoretical status.

At the most general level, government consists of a group of individuals sharing a defined responsibility for exercising power. At this level the definition applies to cases where government is sovereign, as well as to cases where it is not. Sovereign government, the most important type, consists of a group of individuals sharing a defined responsibility for the maintenance and adaptation of a national autonomous community, on behalf of which it exercises a practical monopoly of coercive powers. If by "a defined responsibility" we mean its legitimacy (the sanctified right to exercise power on behalf of others by means of decision making), then the characteristics of sovereign government are as follows: a government is a group of individuals exercising legitimate authority, and protecting and adapting the community by making and carrying out decisions. [*See* SOVEREIGNTY *and* STATE.]

These characteristics impose certain limits of variation upon government. One limit is efficacy, i.e., the capacity of a government to cater to community needs. A second refers to the internal structure of a given type of government, i.e., its form. Changes in form which occur when one type of government is transformed into another are ordinarily related to the efficacy, or performance, of a particular government. Hence, the limit upon government is observable when for any reason (inability to make decisions, failures to comply with widely distributed but central values) it can no longer function. If this is not merely a matter which can be remedied by changing the incumbents of political office, i.e., if the political roles and supporting offices are no longer acceptable, then the withdrawal of legitimacy denotes that the system of government is no longer regarded as appropriate by the public; its limits have been breached. At that point, change from one type of government to another is likely.

The most common distinctions that have been made between types of governments include the following: is the government competitive or monopolistic? democratic or totalitarian? pluralistic or monistic? presidential or monarchical? Of course, these well-known categories overlap considerably. For example, it is possible to have a totalitarian presidential system. As is the case with all dichotomous variables, these distinctions force the observer to put a particular government in one category or the other, even when it demonstrates characteristics of both. Such distinctions are based on two criteria: the organization of government and the degree of control it exercises over the community. These criteria combine the moral, or normative, dimension of politics with the dimensions relating to governmental structure and political behavior. These three analytically distinct elements, i.e., the normative, structural, and behavioral aspects of government, will now be separately examined.

Normative aspects of government deal with such abstract questions as justice, equity, equality. Through these, men define their lasting values, their ideas of right and wrong. Normative theory represents, therefore, certain speculations about those aims and activities of government which embody the central values and ultimate ends of a political community; it defines political legitimacy.

In contrast, structural principles are those which deal with the arrangements and instruments involved in governmental decision making. Of course, they are related to normative issues insofar as the form of a government is seen as a means of attaining the ends of society. Preoccupation with the structural dimension leads directly to the analysis of alternative forms of government, with normative considerations employed in order to evaluate those most suitable for realizing the goals of the community by means of governmental decision making. In the past, structural analysis has been mainly concerned with the distribution of political power, describing various types of government in terms of how widely power is shared by the members of a political community.

Classical writers were particularly interested in normative issues and structuralists have been preoccupied with governmental forms. Both groups, to the extent that they considered it at all, assumed behavior to be a condition of conflict. For both, a propensity to conflict is regarded as the normal political expression of human nature, much as economists assumed that man has a natural propensity "to truck, barter, and exchange." Hobbes, for example, put this assumption very sharply as "the war of all against all." Such assumptions led both Plato and Hobbes to seek authoritarian governments as the best means of regulating the condition of conflict. Other theorists have seen a division of powers as the best method to control conflict.

Certain combinations of normative and structural approaches have been called institutionalist theories. Institutionalists, such as Carl Friedrich (1937), Harold Laski (1925; 1935), and Herman Finer (1932), concerned themselves with the normative and structural relations between law, constitutional forms, and governmental procedures in wide historical, religious, and economic contexts. Their considerations included an interest in practical reform as well as theory, and they consciously built on the formulations of Ostrogorskii (1902), Bryce (1921), Graham Wallas (1908), and others.

Emphasis on the behavioral dimension originated largely in the 1930s, with the "Chicago school" and, in particular, with Harold Lasswell, who sought to introduce behavioral explanations into political affairs. This is most explicit in his pioneering work *Psychopathology and Politics* (1930). However, until recently, few theorists followed this lead. It is, therefore, not surprising that the study of socialization processes, motivation, and political culture has been handled mainly by political sociologists. [*See* POLITICAL SOCIOLOGY.]

Analysis today is characterized by the refinement of structural theories of government into a system, i.e., a set of interrelated elements which can be integrated with behavioral theories. The resulting analysis has taken many different forms and has made some advances, but it is particularly weak in its treatment of normative theory. [*See* POLITICAL SCIENCE *and* POLITICAL THEORY.]

Theories of government

Historically, most theories of government have fallen into one or the other of two main analytical sets: mechanistic and organic.

Mechanistic theories. The first set reflects the view that society is composed of competing and interacting interests (both individual and group), that these generate conflict, and that it is the job of government to ameliorate or resolve such conflict. Government is thus a device for finding ways to relax tension in the political system. These theories, relying heavily on the free exchange of information, see government as a point in a flow of activity which is initiated by the political community. Since government has a decision-making apparatus, which responds to tension points in the system, the appropriate actions will be forthcoming. Behavioral tensions represent "inputs," or stimuli affecting political leaders, who by responding to them generate decisions, or "outputs" (see Figure 1).

INPUTS   OUTPUTS

Figure 1 — Government as a dependent variable

In Figure 1, assume that the social system is a national society. Government responds to a variety of societally generated inputs, including customs and beliefs (normative characteristics), classes and interests (structural characteristics), and preferences and perceptions (behavioral characteristics). Democratic theories of government are based on this model. This is why they have been particularly concerned with the establishment of a useful set of intervening structural variables between the

social system and government itself. Hence the preoccupation with the analysis of political parties, electoral systems, and the like, which are seen as devices for improving the relationship between the social system and government in order to raise the quality and appropriateness of policy decisions and increase the efficacy of government.

It is the liberal democratic approach which accepts this view, with government cast in the role of mediator and judge in conflicts between contending parties. The principles of structural organization are embodied in law, which serves as a framework for all other forms of organization. Normative consensus centers around the maintenance of the legal framework itself. Government strengthens consensus by ensuring the widest realization of norms already held. Such liberal theories are contained in the ideas of Diderot and d'Alembert, Holbach and Helvétius, Condillac and Locke, Rousseau and Hume. It is a tradition which includes Voltaire's innocent rationalism and Bentham's equitable utilitarianism. What these thinkers had in common was an emphasis on individual knowledge and shared reason, a position which elevates the individual to the center of the political stage. Rationality is a norm, and it requires a framework in which free ideas and competitive views can be put forward.

The Western democratic governments reflect variants of this model, but it was also accepted, at least in principle, in other areas. For example, the constitutions of many of the new Afro–Asian nations were drawn with this general approach in mind, even where the actual practice of government is wholly different from its normative and structural theory.

To sum up, the normative assumption underlying the model is that a social system is composed of individuals or groups with an equal right to be represented. Structurally, it is assumed that a government must reflect proper representation; the behavioral assumption is that competitive conflict between the members of the social system renders representative forms necessary. The model therefore displays the following characteristics: the unit of which the social system is composed is the individual; the ends of the individual are maximized; the structure of government is organized in such a way that a plurality of ends is maximized; the decisions of government, by maximizing a plurality of ends, maintain balance or harmony in the social system; and the principle of legitimacy is equity. The concern of political theorists following this tradition is with the improvement of devices that government can use to maximize a plurality of ends. Certain structural procedures have, therefore, become endowed with the quality of norms. Moreover, underlying this view is an assumption, rather mechanistic, that government is a contrivance. It does not grow organically. It must be established, with each structural principle becoming endowed with a predictable consequence. Government is, first, a kind of social physics, with particular devices having predictable results.

Organic theories. The classical view is different (as are many contemporary ones). For example, both Plato and Aristotle related government to the evolution of human society from lower to higher forms. Therefore, government was essentially an educational body, embodying a set of ideals and perfecting rationality, thereby directing the state toward a new golden age. Moreover, this conception of government has had as durable a tradition as the liberal democratic one. Although such views were widely accepted in medieval Europe (Gierke 1881), it was Hegel who gave the conception its most powerful rationale and Marx who brought it into popular currency. Marx accepted nineteenth-century notions of progress but saw in the evolution of man's higher purposes a relationship between change in the material world and the unfolding human consciousness. Government is an instrument of this relationship. As such, it has its own cycle. It becomes an instrument of revolutionary action, of insurrection, which, if successful, represents the most dynamic class. It comes to power as the instrument which must transform revolutionary impetus into practical accomplishment. Having accomplished this, it will in turn be rendered anachronistic and vulnerable until the final stage, when government is itself no longer necessary.

Nor was Marx alone in accepting an organismic conception of government. More liberal-minded proponents include Thomas Hill Green, who saw government as an instrument of morality. Herder, a philosophical romantic, also shared the view that government was a transitional phenomenon by means of which an "aristo–democracy" would educate the public and develop a sufficient level of political consciousness to render government superfluous. "The ultimate aim of aristo–democracy, Herder saw in the disappearance of the State as an administrative 'machine' of government, and its replacement by an 'organic' way of ordering social life, in which active cooperation would render all forms of subordination obsolete and superfluous" (Barnard 1965, p. 77). Similar views were expressed by Fichte, Schelling, and Bosanquet. Today this approach is particularly attractive in develop-

ing areas, where government is seen as the instrument of an evolutionary ideal.

The organic evolutionary concept remains an alternative to the liberal democratic one. It implies a role for government, which directs society toward higher ends. Evolutionary in conception, this tradition is often enriched by ecclesiastic and theocratic ideals. It stresses the role of the community over and against the role of the individual. Although modern organic conceptions elevate man to a central position, they emphasize that the community is the instrument of his perfection; such views are endemic in revolutionary governments, which see themselves as the instruments of social transformation. Where the role of government is so central, we can say that it becomes the independent variable (Figure 2).

INPUTS   OUTPUTS

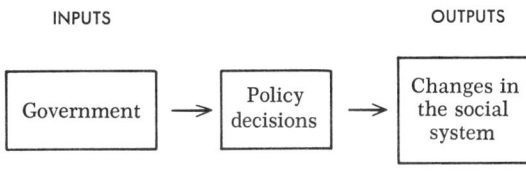

Figure 2 — Government as an independent variable

Government is the instrument by means of which change is produced in the social system. The purposes and objects of such change (normative characteristics) are defined by government. The organization of government (structural characteristics) will depend on the best means to accomplish these purposes. The activities of government will include whatever symbolic manipulation through education, communications media, etc., is necessary to affect both the content and manner of policy decision making pursuant to changes in the social system.

In the first model (Figure 1) government is the dependent variable and social system or community is the independent variable. Power is seen to inhere in the public, which creates the inputs of stimuli to which government must cater (Easton 1957; 1965). In the second model (Figure 2) government is the independent variable and social system the dependent one. Such systems tend to be centralized in the form of their authority. They tend to elevate the goals of the government into norms and make them sacred and ethical precepts, through which legitimacy is defined. Governments resembling the first model tend to be competitive, pluralistic, and democratic; those resembling the second tend to be monopolistic, monistic, and totalitarian. Normatively, the first are more secular than the second. Structurally, they are less hierarchically organized. Behaviorally, they rely heavily on internalized norms and self-control, rather than on external authority. As opposing paradigms, these two generalized types, in their various concrete formulations, are perpetually vulnerable to each other. Indeed, one can see over time that they form a permanent dialogue of conflict. They represent two fundamentally different approaches to government.

Political norms and forms of authority

We can now begin to explore some of the implications of that dialogue of conflict. One way of describing it is in terms of the difference between sacred and secular norms. This difference is important because it draws our attention to the normative basis of a government and, therefore, to its legitimacy. Normative conflict generally takes place between sacred and secular beliefs. [*See* LEGITIMACY.]

Sacred political norms. Governments based on sacred norms cover a wide range of cases, ancient and modern, including ancient China and many of the early Semitic kingdoms. Consider the following description: "The Egyptian of historic times did not have our doubts and difficulties. To him the kingship was not merely part, but the kernel of the static order of the world, an order that was divine just as much as the kingship was divine. . . . From the earliest historic times, therefore, the dominant element in the Egyptian conception of kingship was that the king was a god—not merely godlike, but very god" (Fairman 1958, p. 75). Or take the case of ancient Greece. There the principles of patrilineal authority and ascribed status were linked to an ancestral and religious source, not only for kings but for every citizen (Hignett 1952, p. 63). Ascribed status applied particularly to priests and to the distinction between nobles and commoners. Hence, political norms represented an explicit validation of the structure authority.

Sacredness does not apply only to theocratic or primitive societies. It applies as well to many modern states. The sacred qualities of Marxism–Leninism in the Soviet Union are today enshrined in an elaborate philosophical system. Many of its sacred attributes were cruelly visible in the various purges and trials of the 1930s. It appears, even today, in the controversies over the political role of literature and the arts. Clearer still is the case of modern China. Mao's prescriptive sayings assume such a sacred characteristic as to define the basis of political legitimacy. Many new nations share this characteristic (although to a lesser degree), particularly in cases where an attempt is made to ritualize the authority of a charismatic or highly personalistic leader by endowing his words and teachings with special insight.

No government is entirely free from sacred qualities, whether these be elaborate and ideological or be token symbols, such as a flag, or a constitutional document. These aspects of government may be merely ceremonial, or what Bagehot called the "dignified part," or they may represent high drama in which the solidarity and unity of a community may be expressed.

It is possible to distinguish three main varieties of sacred attachments, which, even if they overlap, are analytically separable. Ranking them in ascending order of sacredness, they are (1) primordial attachments to or beliefs about race, language, and nationality (a typical expression of primordial attachment is nationalism); (2) philosophical attachments (the most generalized moral and philosophical ideal in which a total synthesis is expressed relating man to his environment and specifying the way of the future is to be found today in socialism); and (3) religious attachments (this refers to religious beliefs in which the origin of the society, moral purpose, and a particular pattern of transcendental beliefs are associated in a universal religious doctrine, such as Christianity).

In practice all three of these may be blended. Modern populist and totalitarian regimes, as in Nazi Germany, mixed primordial attachments of race and theological attachments of religion. In the Soviet Union during World War II, the symbols of government were more and more primordial, i.e., nationalist, and less and less philosophical, i.e., Marxist.

Secular political norms. Secular norms rely on a framework of rules rather than on some higher purposes of state. The most common cases of secular systems are those in which the sacred elements have declined through institutionalization. They do not disappear, but they become so completely a part of the accepted pattern of right and wrong that it is not necessary to do more than refer to them on ritual occasions. Thus, ceremony rather than the substance of belief is characteristic of these systems.

By tacit agreement secular systems reserve the "higher" goals to the individual, and these goals inhere in his body of private beliefs. If governments should violate these norms, they run the risk of overstepping their limits of variation and of being eliminated.

We can now cut across the sacred–secular normative distinction with a structural variable, the pattern of centralized or decentralized authority [*see* AUTHORITY]. Once again we must employ a caveat and remind ourselves that it is always difficult to use dichotomous variables to divide concrete cases. What is in theory decentralized may be quite the opposite in practice. Or highly centralized systems may show informal patterns of consultation and accountability to various groups in the community. Indeed, at any given time even the most highly centralized system may act on certain issues in a highly decentralized manner. Moreover, centralized government includes monarchical and bureaucratic systems, represented by ancient empires, that can combine monarchy with decentralized administration [*see* EMPIRES]. This configuration includes different types of government: systems where the hierarchy is based on a king who is a father of his people, with authority deriving from a totemic ancestor, as in many tribal governments, or systems where authority lodges in a patrimonial figure and the relationship between ruler and ruled is that of patron and client [*see* KINGSHIP; *see also* Fallers 1956].

Centralized authority. Let us ignore all these variations in form and say boldly that centralized power begins from the top and is applied downward through a specific delegation of authority. A military organization or a bureaucracy represents a clear-cut "command" case, with autocratic and totalitarian governments defined as those which employ this system of hierarchy. Government may then be represented by a single figure, a king or dictator, or by an oligarchy or junta (Friedrich & Brzezinski 1956). Such highly centralized systems show the following characteristics: concentrated power is subject to few checks; power inheres at the top; subordinate authority is derivative; and there is strong reliance on the personality of a particular leader. [*See* AUTOCRACY; OLIGARCHY.]

Decentralized authority. Decentralized authority represents an opposite conception of power: power is generated by the public through the aggregation of their political wants, is expressed through various groups, and is regulated by an abstract system of rules. (Its usual normative expressions include the acceptance of the principle of majority rule, protection of rights, and representation.) This is what we mean by a democratic government. It is characterized by checks and balances, parliamentary control over the executive, and some form of election as the method of political recruitment to sensitive positions. Of course, such practices do not exhaust the forms of decentralization. Decentralization may be functional, based on the allocation of the economic power in society among various groupings, such as guilds, protective as-

Table 1 — The derivation of political typologies

		CONCENTRATION OF POWER	
		Centralized	Decentralized
PREDOMINANT POLITICAL NORMS	Sacred	A	C
	Secular	B	D

sociations, professional associations, and other interest groups. [*See* CONSTITUTIONS AND CONSTITUTIONALISM.]

The distinctions between sacred and secular and between centralized and decentralized types of government can form the basis of a more general model by means of which to analyze government. Table 1 pinpoints the four combinations that will be examined in detail. To summarize the possibilities, the highly centralized and sacred system, *A*, represents modern populist totalitarian governments. The centralized and secular system, *B*, represents many autocratic forms of government. The sacred and decentralized system, *C*, includes many early forms of theocratic society, from the feudalism of the High Middle Ages in Europe to religious or theocratic governments in America, such as the Puritan colonies of New England. And modern democratic governments fall into the secular and decentralized category, *D*.

Sacred and centralized governments

The modern sacred–centralized type of system is likely to be associated with the establishment of a new political system. Government is the independent variable and is associated with a new moral framework. Such conditions commonly apply after a major revolution or in territories that have recently gained independence. [*See* DICTATORSHIP; TOTALITARIANISM.]

Communist governments. The distinguishing feature of the sacred–centralized communist government is the high degree of centralization encompassing the total community. The sacred object of government is to transform the material conditions of life and the consciousness of the people at the same time. The evolution of the community becomes a moral goal, to be sought under the leadership of a militant vanguard—the Communist party—serving as the spearhead of government. In the classic, Leninist form of the communist regime, no competitive sources of power can be tolerated. In recent times, however, a slight trend toward secularization and decentralization can be seen in the Soviet Union (Brzezinski 1962).

Historically, the Soviet Union is an interesting

case of external beliefs influencing internal social groups to revolt against a highly autocratic monarchy, a weak parliament (the Duma was only founded in 1905), and a centralized bureaucracy liberally sprinkled with foreign, particularly German, immigrants (Pipes 1954). Not only was the revolutionary instrument based on a small but dynamic working-class movement; Marxism itself was largely restricted to Russian middle-class intellectuals. It was essentially an alien doctrine (transformed by Lenin to meet Russian conditions) leading to a revolutionary organization which later became the centralizing mechanism of state power. When the religious beliefs of the Greek Orthodox church were replaced by the secular ideology of Marxism–Leninism, the goals of political development became sacred and formed the new basis of the legitimacy of government. Of course, a wide discrepancy existed between the theory and practice of government. Power was in fact centralized in the hands of the first secretary of the Politburo of the Central Committee of the Communist party, while constitutionally the Soviet Union was a federal system with an elected "supreme organ of state power," the Supreme Soviet, which had, in theory, the exclusive right of legislation. [See COMMUNISM, *article on* SOVIET COMMUNISM.]

This system formed the model of state organization for all other communist systems until relatively recently. Since the death of Stalin, however, two interesting features may be noted. The sacred quality of Marxist–Leninist ideology has declined, particularly as younger generations find it less significant as a doctrine than as a ritual; and a trend toward decentralization has begun. A struggle is on between the communist political leaders and the technical specialists, economists, scientists, and the like. Moreover, as "polycentricism" on an international level becomes more accepted, the necessity for a more "liberal" approach to Marxism–Leninism reduces its orthodoxy. Alternative structural experiments are increasingly common, such as those in Hungary, Yugoslovia, and Poland, in which "cultural" decentralization (in the case of Hungary and Poland) and economic decentralization (in the case of Yugoslavia) represent experiments in greater freedom. [See COMMUNISM, *article on* NATIONAL COMMUNISM; *see also* Laqueur & Labedz 1962.]

The communist examples are of particular relevance because they have become attractive models to governments of developing areas bent on following the Soviet pattern of rapid industrialization (Ulam 1960).

Fascist governments. Fascist governments were more secular in their orientations. The develop-

mental or evolutionary sacred ideology around which communist governments try to organize their societies embodies certain universalized moral aims. In contrast, the sacred attachments of fascist governments showed greater attraction to primordial sentiments, including race and nationality. Although there are structural similarities between communist and fascist governments, particularly with respect to the roles of a powerful totalitarian political leader and a weak set of parliamentary institutions, one important difference should be pointed out. In the communist case, government is monolithic, emphasizing the evolution of the entire community. Fascist governments, in contrast, tolerated certain corporate groupings.

Three fascist governments are of interest here: Germany, Italy, and Spain. All were highly centralized, but they varied considerably with respect to the sacredness and secularity of political norms.

The strongest attachment to sacred primordial political norms was exhibited in Nazi Germany. The supremacy of one race and the liberating effects of war and conflict were embodied in the revived Nordic myths ("Odinism") and blended into a set of nationalist political norms. Structurally, although the government was highly centralized under a personal dictatorship, four main groupings were given exceptional attention: army and secret police, large-scale industrial enterprise, labor organized into fronts and battalions, and military scientists and technicians. The Nazi case also shows that even under a highly centralized form of government, economic control can be kept separate from ownership, with private industry continuing to operate under government regulations. Unlike the situation in communist systems, in Nazi Germany a market system of economic allocation coexisted with government-organized fiscal and credit manipulations. Each corporate group obtained special conditions of privilege. [See NATIONAL SOCIALISM.]

Italian fascism showed less commitment to primordial political norms than Nazism, as well as a somewhat less centralized governmental structure. The norms themselves were composed of ambiguous combinations of primordial sentiments, appeals to historical precedent, and claims to philosophical universality. Primordial claims were mixed with the corporate organization of the state, under the inspiration of the collegia of the late Roman Empire. The "corporation" was thus associated with the great period of Italian imperial and cultural achievement and became the legitimizing basis of the regime.

A second claim to universality, which was of

minor importance during the period of Italian fascism, may yet prove to be highly significant. This is the view that the proper way to organize the state is in corporate groupings functional to development and industrialization. In arguing the case of corporate government, it was pointed out that fascism as a form of government, although totalitarian, emphasized the role of the corporation as both the point of reconciliation between state and individual and the instrument of individual expression (see Barker 1942, pp. 328–366). This possibility remains as an important structural device, midway between highly centralized and decentralized systems. [*See* FASCISM.]

Both the German and Italian systems contained important normative ambiguities, which they attempted to resolve in the apotheosis of violence. This was most apparent in their total repudiation of democratic, decentralized forms of government (which were regarded as catering to human weakness). Italian and German fascism both represented an authentic totalitarian populism (a modern form of tribalism), in which medieval ideas of corporation, organic concepts of the community, and primordial sentiments were intertwined within a highly centralized system of administrative government.

The Spanish case has been less ideological and less centralized. Despite the exceptional power of Generalissimo Franco and the concentration of authority in the national cabinet, the Falange, as a political party, plays a lesser role in government than the National Socialist party did in Germany, or the Fascist party in Italy (Payne 1961). One reason is that within six years of Franco's accession to power, Italy and Germany were defeated. Their systems no longer served as models of successful dictatorship. Even more important is the Catholic tradition, to which the right wing of the Falange and significant proportions of the population generally subscribe. [*See* FALANGISM.]

More decentralized than the others, and therefore more autocratic than totalitarian, the Spanish system remains an extension of an old and established bureaucratic system which traces its roots to the imperial Spanish tradition, the Inquisition, and a centralized monarchy. Even today the Spanish government tries to preserve a vague commitment to monarchy as a traditional form of legitimacy. This allows the government to revive memories of Spanish grandeur, treating communism, secularism, and socialism much as Philip II and Archbishop Carranza of Toledo treated Protestantism, Islam, and Judaism (Davies 1937). This fervor would indicate the presence of sacred political norms, derived from Catholicism and more or less indifferent to the structure of authority. Many of the same norms served equally well in Perón's Argentina, and the more socialist forms of Catholic corporatism are sometimes embodied in modern and decentralized socialist or democratic governments, for example, in Chile. [*See* CAUDILLISMO.]

Secular and centralized governments

The most pronounced characteristics of a secular–centralized system of government are autonomous power in the hands of a president or monarch (or perhaps a presidential monarch); a single political party, whether in the form of an elite (a communist party) or a populist mass party with an elite center (most nationalist parties); a truncated or largely ritualistic parliament, which does not have a real veto power over the executive; and an elections system which does not allow effective competition between candidates for political office.

Such centralized systems show several characteristic problems common to all forms of centralized government with the exception of institutionalized monarchies. The most important of these are, first, succession to high public office (which is usually accompanied by severe struggles for power) and, second, the institutionalization of disagreement.

The normative content of both the communist and fascist forms of government gives direction and shape to the entire society. Historically, however, there have been many cases where the normative content is relatively low (or largely ceremonial and ritualized), while power remains centralized. These include most nineteenth-century monarchical forms of government. Indeed, precisely because their sacred characteristics were emptied of content (while retained in form) they were unable to survive as types and were either transformed or removed. In France the monarchical form, attempted periodically during the nineteenth century, had been effectively destroyed by the French Revolution. Only Bonapartism had any genuine normative success. In Britain the secularization process began with the transformation of the monarchy or, symbolically, with the beheading of Charles I. The Act of Settlement of 1701, whereby the sovereign occupies the throne under a parliamentary title, established parliamentary supremacy, although it took many generations before the full implications were worked out (Dicey 1885). Real structural changes in the form of decentralization were embodied in the widening of parliamentary control over the executive and in popular representation from 1832 onward (Gash 1953). If the record of historical cases of secular–centralized government is any guide, then one useful proposition can be stated as follows: as sacred political norms become secularized through ritualization, government must decentralize, since its legitimacy disappears. [*See* MONARCHY.]

Examples of secular–centralized governments include czarist Russia (although there were important theocratic elements incorporated in the role of the czar), and Bismarck's Germany. More recent cases are colonial administrative governments in British and French Africa, south Asia, the Netherlands, the East Indies, and the Belgian Congo.

Many of the new nations have gone from one form of highly centralized system, under colonialism, to another, in the form of one-party government, but with a change in the quality of political norms. The norms often become endowed with intense attachment to primordial loyalties associated with race and nation and, to a lesser degree, with some aspects of socialism and public ownership, all wrapped up in a particular ideological message, such as Nasserism in Egypt, Nkrumahism in Ghana, or "Communocracy" in Guinea.

Sacred and decentralized governments

Where new constitutional governments have been most successful, they have evolved a shared set of political norms deriving from a previous period when such norms were explicitly sacred, either in an ecclesiastical form, as in the case of the Puritan commonwealths, or in a more directly political form. This suggests the following proposition: decentralized–secular governments are most stable and effective when they have developed out of an earlier centralized–sacred or decentralized–sacred form, with norms of self-control becoming behaviorally widespread. Modern democratic government emerged when the decentralization of authority and secularization of political norms proceeded more or less simultaneously with a corresponding increase in the standard of individual civic obligation (Almond & Verba 1963).

The origins of Western democratic governments derive from a synthesis of generally agreed religious values, which is associated with a generalized Christian ethic. The theocratic origins of democratic government are not to be taken lightly. Even the American experience assumed a unified set of Christian (mainly variants of deistic and Protestant) theological precepts. Law was based on the prior conception of agreed principles of political propriety. The formation of these principles can be found in many different theologically articulated forms, including the religious wars between Catholics and Protestants and between various Protestant groups as well. Nor was the body of precept within the Catholic church much more unified. Certainly the conflicts over conciliarism and the role of the church councils, not to speak of the nationalization of the church itself within each country, all testify to the explicitly political consequences of religion. These issues were so important to politics that much of the process of secularization can itself be traced to the search for some mutually agreeable and satisfactory common denominator of precept in order to render politics more secular. [*See* CHRISTIANITY.]

In the United States this was most clearly recognized in the works of Brooks and Henry Adams, both of whom saw the modern economic state, with its emphasis on instrumental values, economic exchange, and corporate finance, as destroying the implicit basis of the original Christian values. Nowhere is this more explicit than in Henry Adams' essay on Mont-Saint-Michel (1904; see also Brooks Adams 1898). Such views, which tended to idealize the classical and medieval civilizations, were romantic expressions of this religious ideal. But in addition to energy, there was doctrine and creed. The church militant was not always composed of simple stuff. Even in Catholic Spain during the "golden century," the conquistadors, who combined the adoration of the Virgin with great greed in plundering the New World and founding an empire, were vastly different in their political aims from the various religious orders, Jesuit, Benedictine, and Dominican, and these in turn had their constitutionalists, such as Juan de Mariana, Francisco Suárez, and Bellarmine (Lewis 1954).

The secularization of political norms can be seen as occurring in three historic steps. The first was nationalization of the church. By this means the political universalism of the church, symbolized in the term "Holy Roman Empire," was restricted, and various national churches arose.

The second step was the extension of that process to government. It was symbolized in the expression "divine right of kings," whereby authority was traced to the Deity through the principle of royal inheritance and kinship. This established the idea of a sovereign government as a legitimate unit with rights to protect itself against external sacerdotal power.

The third step was the growth of Protestantism, associated first with the unfolding of Christian principles through equity and with the radicalization of instrumental values. The transition was particularly significant because Protestantism emerged as a particular religious ideology with a mutually reinforcing synthesis between sacred values and instrumental objects germane to industrialization. In this sense, Protestantism was the mode of transition from the more explicitly religious form of government to a more secular one, which merely reflected religious values. This is why the roots of modern Western constitutional ideas are so deeply embedded in the Protestant ideal of the community. [See PROTESTANT POLITICAL THOUGHT.]

In a sense, the secularization of religion emerged as a result of the utter loneliness of Protestantism, which in Calvin's doctrine excluded even the church from participation in individual salvation. Weber makes the point that this is the singular difference between Catholic and Protestant doctrine, and the result was an emphasis on an individualism held in check by the concept of a calling embodying good works and sobriety. Rationality was reflected in a political community of individuals. Thus, self-control became the founding ethic of representative government, in conjunction with the economic doctrine of capitalism. Catholic doctrine, in sharp contrast, "punishing the heretic but indulgent to the sinner," retained a conception of the organic community that, although not necessarily antagonistic to decentralized government, did not support its basis in individualism and the doctrine of individual representation (Weber 1904–1905; McNeil 1954).

The consequences of Protestantism and Dutch, British, and American capitalism helped to create the conditions of secularization, with a greater degree of emphasis on legal and constitutional political devices. Weber quotes John Wesley: "I fear wherever riches have increased, the essence of religion has decreased in the same proportion" (Weber 1904–1905, p. 175 in the 1958 edition). This view is central to modern secular democratic government, where law has replaced religion as the foundation of the community. Thus, secularization in political terms is important in the West because, as a process containing a constitutional element the object of which is to establish a framework of government responsive to change, it leads to an explicit acceptance of the idea of the sovereignty of the people. Secularization paid particular attention to the accumulation of wealth as a duty, which favored rapid economic growth. The process is its own problem, however. Secular and decentralized government has wrestled with the question of how to retain the idea of obligation and responsibility in the face of continuous radical secularization.

It should not be assumed that there is a linear progression from centralized to decentralized or from sacred to secular systems. The opposite occurred (and in a peaceful manner) in Weimar Germany. Legitimacy was withdrawn from the constitutional government when the voters freely chose the Nazi party. This implies that the norms of a secular and decentralized system were relatively weak and insufficiently institutionalized. It also means that such a system can operate only when self-control and nonpolitical restraints on behavior predominate.

Secular and decentralized governments

As secularization occurred in Western societies, theological obligations were changed into codes of civic responsibility. Law replaced religion as the basis of political norms. With the rising prosperity of Europe, there developed a general belief that free, democratic governments with maximum political participation for all would provide a beneficial political condition. Indeed, struggles during the nineteenth century were over the speed and thoroughness with which constitutional democracy would incorporate the entire membership of a system rather than over structural principles of government. [See DEMOCRACY.]

A view of government analogous to the approach of classical economics was widely accepted. The community is composed of voters, who are like consumers, and their choice is tantamount to consumer sovereignty. The election system represents the market, in which voters choose their representatives on the basis of stated preferences. Government, consisting of parliament and cabinet as well as administrative cadres, is similar to the productive unit and manufactures decisions, which the public evaluates through the electoral mechanism. The courts are present to ensure that the rules of the system are not violated.

The principles on which the system works include a high level of information, rationality as an attribute of voting and decision making, and equal representation (Downs 1957; Easton 1966). Such principles underlie the American form of presidential government and the utilitarian systems advocated by John Stuart Mill and the Benthamites in England. Advocates of this form emphasize the improvement of information, the uses of education in order to reach rationality (only the informed voter can be rational), and, in particular, the improvement of electoral systems in order to achieve the maximum reproduction of public wants in a representative chamber. Hence, for example, one of the problems considered most important is whether proportional representation is preferable to simple plurality voting or some combination of weighted balloting or lists. [See ELECTIONS, *article* on ELECTORAL SYSTEMS.] Important questions also arise about the role of political parties in government. How do parties, acting as agents by which public desires are transformed into government cognizance, facilitate the political process? In this respect political parties are designed to emphasize certain publicly held priorities and make them explicit, so that as the problems confronting government become more complex and individuals cannot make their views known on all of them, politicians stand for some symposium of priorities and on this basis are accepted or rejected by the voters.

The principle of majority rule implies in effect that the rightness of a doctrine is measured by the degree of support it obtains and that support creates power. Hence, majority rule is a principle of power which credits the rationality of the majority and elevates reason, plus numbers, over abstract morality. It is because of this that instrumentalities begin to take on their own moral proprieties. [See MAJORITY RULE.]

Not all democratic polities accepted this highly individualistic form of government. Two alternative forms, one older and one very modern, have stressed the idea of the organic community rather than the more mechanistic doctrine of individualism. The first of these forms, an extension of medieval doctrine, incorporates Catholic beliefs in the context of a decentralized state. This includes various specific approaches to democratic government, such as Christian socialism and Christian democracy. The second form is democratic socialism, which emphasizes the democratic state as a means of fulfilling conditions of equality and freedom in conjunction with the development of the moral and material basis of the community.

Both of these forms see an inadequacy in democracy, resulting from a contradiction between private ownership of the means of production and the maintenance of civic obligation. How can government be secular and decentralized yet retain authority? If the achievement of democratic government is that it is secular in practice and therefore free of formalized commitments to a higher set of priorities than those desired by a majority, the problem is how to retain that self-control implicit in Calvin's formula. One answer is to study the new roles in government, particularly those which provide a "calling," such as the roles of civil servants, of members of professions, and of scientists, whose sense of responsibility and commitment to the exchange of free ideas is perhaps one of the most important characteristics of democratic government in highly industrial societies. [See BUREAUCRACY and SCIENCE, article on SCIENCE–GOVERNMENT RE-

LATIONS; see also Friedrich 1937; Jouvenel 1963; Sartori 1962.]

Types of democratic governments. Democratic governments require further differentiation. First, they can be divided into unitary and federal forms. Unitary governments are based on the position that all powers not otherwise reserved belong to a central government. Federal governments take the position that residual powers lie with the component geographical units which make up the federation. [See FEDERALISM.]

Second, they can be classified as presidential and parliamentary forms. In a true presidential system, a president elected by the population is responsible to them, rather than to the legislature. The legislature, in turn, is responsible to the population which elects it, and not to the president. This provides checks and balances, with the public acting as arbiters during periodic elections, held at fixed intervals. [See PRESIDENTIAL GOVERNMENT.] The parliamentary system shows parliament supreme, with a prime minister responsible to it and holding office at its pleasure. Through votes of confidence and changes in parliamentary party membership, a government can fall, in which case a new general election to parliament is necessary; the majority or plurality of seats won by a political party provides a mandate to form a government. Under such a system the president (or monarch) is largely a figurehead. Where the parliamentary government is a constitutional monarchy, the transition from earlier forms of monarchy has generally been smooth, rather than abrupt, and has been achieved by virtue of internal structural changes. Notable cases are Holland, Denmark, Sweden, Norway, and Great Britain.

Much of the present concern of democratic government lies with the problems associated with the growing complexity of modern life and the increasingly broad responsibilities which individuals expect a secular government to take upon itself. Whereas the problem in the first half of the twentieth century was the improvement of electoral and representation methods and of local government and administration, the present emphasis is on the work load of parliaments and congresses. Both federal and unitary systems today accept the principle of one man, one vote, and "popular sovereignty" tends to mean a form of parliamentary representation embodying territorial and demographic bases. How to maintain debate on important issues and get through a heavy legislative work load is therefore a critical matter. In Great Britain, for example, the widening of the franchise was accompanied by the decline of the role of the private-member bill as the work load of the committees increased. Parliament divides according to the lines laid down by the party whips, and a free vote, each member voting according to his conscience, becomes rare (see Wheare 1955; McKenzie 1955). Discipline in parliament has given rise to the term "cabinet dictatorship." [See PARLIAMENTARY GOVERNMENT.]

How well parliamentary or cabinet forms of decentralized representative government work depends a great deal on how political parties carry on the work of government. Different structural rules obviously affect this. Since all decentralized and democratic forms of government have some means to control the executive, this may lead, in multiparty systems, to cabinet instability, as it did in France and does in Italy. The stability of such parliamentary governments, therefore, depends on the stability of coalitions. Where two parliamentary parties are characteristic, instability is rare, partly because of rigorous party discipline. [See PARTIES, POLITICAL, article on PARTY SYSTEMS; INTEREST GROUPS; see also Laski 1951.]

How to improve decentralized and democratic government has posed serious problems of political theory. It is not surprising, therefore, that highly individualistic conceptions of democracy have been replaced by notions of group representation, block voting, and the responsiveness of government to various groups, such as professional bodies, business lobbies, trade unions, cooperative movements, civic and veterans' organizations, churches, and educational and cultural groups. [See PLURALISM and POLITICAL GROUP ANALYSIS; see also S. E. Finer 1958.] Indeed, so important have group theories become that interest groups have been called in Britain an "anonymous empire."

All of these questions relate directly to the relations between community and government. More precisely, they are devoted to an examination of intervening variables between community and government, such as political parties and interest groups, and even of subgroups within government itself. (See Figure 3.)

Government in new nations

Governments formed in new nations—those achieving independence after 1945—present some of the most interesting and challenging material confronting constitutional experts, political theorists, and politicians alike. New governments tend to include characteristics of all the forms we have discussed (Apter 1965). For example, in Africa and parts of Asia there are attachments to primitive governments, which remain in competition with central government for the loyalties of the population. Regional clusters associated with a religious or linguistic affiliation may represent powerful primordial loyalties, denying legitimacy to a central government or countering it with a preference for local primordial attachments. Thus, unity and legitimacy within the context of a nation are urgent problems facing political leaders. Inasmuch as certain aspects of primitive government represent a rightful heritage, it may be that traditional qualities of legitimacy should be applied to modern governmental forms, as has been attempted under such ideological forms as "African socialism" or "communocracy." [See NATION.]

Furthermore, new nations commonly emphasize the positive role of government as the great "engine" of social change, actively intervening in all aspects of life, from family relationships to educational opportunities, from road building to the development of local airways. Government in this respect is seen as an independent variable, much as it is, for example, in the Soviet Union.

At the same time, most constitutional patterns follow the line of Western parliamentary government. With sufficient control over parliament, through the instrumentality of party discipline, it is possible to retain popular government, based on

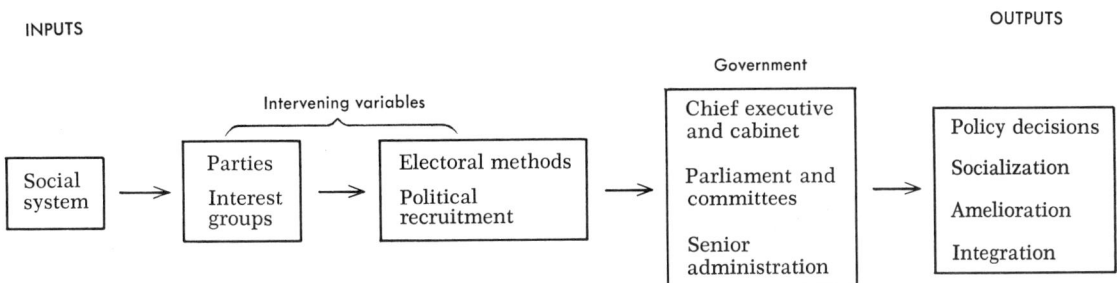

Figure 3 — Intervening variables relating to democratic government

parliamentary practice and a cabinet system, with few formal checks on executive authority.

In a very real sense, then, the governments of new nations tend to become amalgams of the other types we have discussed—theocratic, communist, fascist, and democratic. Their roots in primitive government become identified in normative terms, with a mythical past providing a national identity. The communist emphasis on puritanism, public ownership, and discipline is represented in the recruitment of a developmental elite and in its method of exercising power. The representation of corporate functional groups has much in common with fascist governments. And, the populist democratic emphasis and the pattern of parliamentary government represent Western democratic ideals and some of its procedures.

All this is confusing because the various systems of government described appear to be so antithetical that it would seem impossible to blend them into a viable and effective system. This is to a certain extent true; hence, virtually all new governments are in the process of changing into some more stable type. It is not surprising that quite often what holds such a government together is allegiance to a particular political leader, associated with revolution or the development of a mass movement. Indeed, the outstanding common feature of these new governments is their dependence on a personalized leader supported by a dominant political party. This tends to be the case whether or not the system is *formally* a single-party state, as long as there is a dominant party which is capable of controlling large regional areas. In the special case of new governments, therefore, the crucial factors are the relationship between the leader of the government and the leader of the party, and the role of the party. Ordinarily the first two are the same person, and the party operates government.

In terms of the various models employed here, new governments incline in theory to the position that government is an independent variable. In practice, however, government is likely to be an expression of an elite which manipulates a mass party that is itself a reflection of a wide diversity of interests. In other words, government and social system tend to become incorporated into the broad concept of a single party. Party becomes the independent variable, with government the intervening one, and social system the dependent one. (Even where there is more than one party, the situation is not very different. There may be several dominant regional—tribal or linguistic—parties, rather than one party; however, none are deeply committed to a single ideology, and in this they differ sharply from communist or fascist parties.)

The situation illustrated in Figure 4 is found in its clearest form under conditions of radical transformation from dependent to independent status or directly after a revolution. Since the framework within which the parliamentary and cabinet systems operate is not entirely eliminated, it intervenes between government and changes in the social system. In other words, the role of government, derived through the formal decision-making process, is the making of technical decisions, while the main lines of policy are generally laid down by governmental leaders, who are also senior party leaders. Classic examples are Nyerere's Tanzania, Ghana under Nkrumah, Nasser's Egypt, and Algeria under Ben Bella. [See MODERNIZATION.]

INPUTS   OUTPUTS

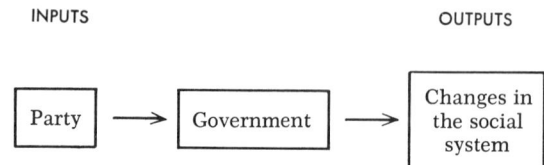

Figure 4 — Government in the pluralistic single-party state

How can new governments be evaluated? Normative criteria involve those associated with democratic systems and would include the adequacy of the protection of individual rights, and the degree of pluralism tolerated in government and parliament. On this score governments in new nations show a mixed record. Some, such as Ghana under Nkrumah, have a declaration of fundamental principles to which the president has sworn adherence, but these declarations cannot be enforced in the courts. Nigeria has a bill of rights. Burma emphasizes the social ownership of the means of production. Ghana and India have preventive-detention ordinances. It is safe to say that the protection of civil rights and liberties varies less with governmental form than with the general spirit in which government functions.

Since the legitimacy of new governments tends to be rather weak and is often associated with highly personalistic leaders (a very vulnerable structural condition), another normative criterion is how successfully a government develops primordial loyalties. The quality of such attachments provides a basis for evaluation of new governments and describes the depth of its emerging political culture. [See POLITICAL CULTURE.]

Primordial attachments tend to become linked to problems of economic growth. Planning, technical skills, manpower surveys, and the like, are important areas of governmental decision making.

[*See* ECONOMIC GROWTH.] In addition, they are moral or normative concepts associated with the objectives which commonly take the form of socialism, since socialism explicitly validates a development ideal and is represented, through party and government, in evolutionary ideal terms. Socialism also justifies political demands for personal sacrifice and loyalty. How well socialism (or its variants) can embody new economic rationality and enforce commitment to savings, work, education, and development becomes a third evaluative criterion. [*See* SOCIALISM.]

Behavioral consequences of normative beliefs thus emerge. A combination of political norms, nationalist primordial sentiments, and philosophical ideological expressions of socialism combine to form the motivational system of the society. Structurally these elements are organized less frequently in parliamentary or representative institutions than in functional or corporate bodies within and around a political party. Party wings and various related interest groups are the devices that link individuals to the government.

Despite all the integrative efforts, the most striking feature of new governments is the behavioral weakness in their population vis-à-vis government. Changing allegiances and ritualization of authority, not to speak of the stresses and strains of rapid economic change and industrialization, all require much study of motivation, of the sources of personal identity, and of learning. Indeed, what is now called the identity problem, involving examination of the conditions under which individuals are able to establish a set of personality boundaries compatible with changing normative and structural conditions, is a growing concern. Only a few studies of the relationship between government and identity have been attempted, though many problems of governing derive from the search for identity (Pye 1962; Erikson 1958; Edelman 1964).

Contemporary research and theory

The author has tried to demonstrate a few of the emphases associated with the study of government and has employed both normative and structural variables to differentiate types of systems. Historically, the most elaborately studied aspect of government has been its normative side, which is still important in trying to determine how governments will evolve because it helps us to relate political means and ends. The structural dimension, almost as well studied in the literature as the normative, has been heavily weighted in favor of the study of the constitution as the foundation of government. Different constitutional systems have been distinguished through enumeration of their characteristics. More recently, work on the structural dimension, developed along the lines of institutionalist analysis and heavily influenced by the work of Max Weber, Karl Mannheim, and others, has related government to art, religion, philosophy, education, and other social institutions. The main concern of these scholars has been to study democracy as a universal system originating in Western civilization and to contrast it with less evolved forms of government, such as monarchy or oligarchy.

This work led to the development of functional analysis in the study of government, with its emphasis on the derivation of more-universalized comparative categories. Such studies have by and large employed one of two forms of systems theory. [*See* SYSTEMS ANALYSIS.] The first tends to follow the organismic analogy. Government is seen in its intimate relationships to society. A good set of functional categories for government will do the following: allow comparison of widely diverse forms and actions in terms of their implications for government as a whole; segregate critical activities from less critical ones; allow one to observe explicit levels of explanatory theory (Almond & Coleman 1960; Apter 1965).

The second emphasis in contemporary systems theory follows a mechanistic tradition. Some of the recent work, based on theories of coalitions, is originally derived from economic theories and attempts to use principles of rational calculation and maximization in order to predict political group behavior [*see* COALITIONS]. Several of the efforts to deal with coalitions begin with the group basis of politics and draw their original inspiration from the writings of A. F. Bentley [*see* POLITICAL GROUP ANALYSIS *and the biography of* BENTLEY]. The most powerful form of systems analysis following this tradition is to be found in cybernetics models and game theory. These represent more-generalized structural models than the ones used for functional analysis. The rules derived for one unit apply to all group behavior. In the game-theory approach these deal primarily with the consequences for action of communications and information. Systems analysis of this type involves analysis of attempts, according to explicit rules, to maximize gains and minimize losses. Formulation of such highly rationalistic models can help us to understand political competition and government actions in priority and other settings. [*See* GAME THEORY; *see also* Downs 1957; Snyder 1961.]

Emphasis on groups has also given rise to an important literature with behavioral, as well as structural, implications. Behavioral and structural aspects of government depend on the analysis of government as a group, with reference to its size, its patterns of communications, and the ways in which motivation and memory are structured within it. Work in this area draws on the theories of psychologists, e.g., Kurt Lewin, R. Lippitt, and Theodore Newcomb, concerning leadership, inter-action processes, cohesiveness, control over devi-ance, internalization of norms, etc., and tends to treat decision making as the main object of analy-sis. [See DECISION MAKING; see also Cartwright & Zander 1953.] Today such an emphasis can be in-tegrated with informational analysis, group theory, and game theory in certain cybernetics models applied to government. This form of systems theory uses the concept of an information grid, in which a political system represents the flow of messages or of "cues" and government the critical "trans-former," i.e., a coding and decision-making instru-ment. It is concerned with adaptability, and em-phasizes the capacity of different systems to learn and adjust, with government performing an essen-tially creative role. One modern political theory which attempts to bring together these functional and other emphases very systematically is Karl Deutsch's application (1963) of the general cyber-netics model, which is an attempt to solve prob-lems of learning, creativity, and adaptation in politics.

To account for these new developments, a more general way of analyzing governments is required. The formulation illustrated in Figure 5 helps to move the analysis of government to a highly gen-eralized level, incorporating the various approaches, new and old, in a single model. In this model politi-cal behavior is the independent variable. Political norms and structures can therefore be treated as intervening variables. Their effectiveness is subject to change because political structure is bound and limited by the legitimacy pattern established by the relationships between political behavior and politi-cal norms. Political structure can be seen in terms of its consequences for decision making, which in turn is designed to maintain a sustained pattern of political behavior consonant with the maintenance of norms.

It is possible, of course, to enlarge the complexity of this model. More important, it is necessary to rotate these variables for different purposes and to hold each of them independent in turn, in order to estimate their effects. Many of the variations in approach to the study of government derive from holding different of these variables independent without realizing the specific methodological impli-cations of doing so. The selection of variables to be held independent is entirely arbitrary. To estimate the effectiveness of different forms of government, however, it might be useful to treat political struc-ture as the independent variable and see how vari-ous types—democratic, totalitarian, centralized, decentralized, monistic, pluralistic, monopolistic, competitive—affect both political norms and politi-cal behavior. How does each of these alternative types allow political learning to take place? How does government preserve continuity? How does it affect the course of change? In addition to rotating the variables, it is possible to add new intervening variables. These may be normative ones, such as ideologies, or structural ones, such as political parties, administrative organizations, and the like.

Any general theory of government will require a model which is sufficiently explicit to account for the limits of variation, sufficiently flexible to handle diverse methodological emphasis, and empirical enough to be fully operationalized. We are still far from able to construct such a model, but the fore-going discussion shows that at least the foundations of the model and the theory have been laid. Still needed are improved techniques of gathering data, as well as analytical paradigms by means of which such data can be related to the appropriate theory. These concerns connect the analysis and study of government to the philosophy of science by empha-sizing logical and epistemological problems, and also cause us to speculate about the application of highly advanced mathematical and statistical techniques and computer programming to the care-ful mapping and testing of propositions about gov-ernment. The concept of government thus remains

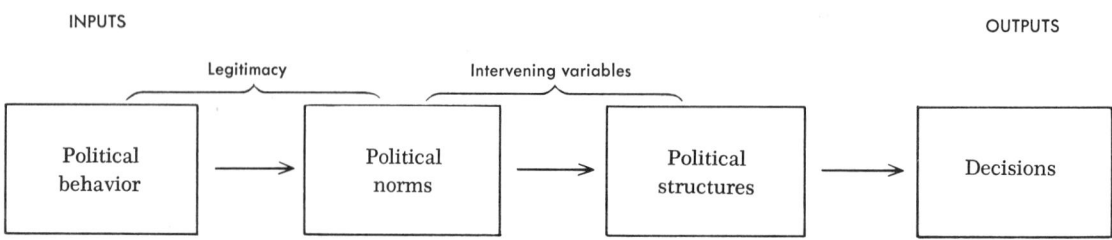

Figure 5 — A generalized model of government

a critical point of departure for both the evaluation of the normative issues of political life and the structural and behavioral analysis of politics.

DAVID E. APTER

[Related to the concept of government are the entries ADJUDICATION; ADMINISTRATION; ELECTIONS; LEGISLATION; POLITICAL EXECUTIVE; REPRESENTATION. Guides to other relevant material may be found under LAW; POLITICAL ANTHROPOLOGY; POLITICAL SCIENCE.]

BIBLIOGRAPHY

ADAMS, BROOKS 1898 *The Law of Civilization and Decay.* New York: Macmillan.

ADAMS, HENRY (1904) 1963 *Mont-Saint-Michel and Chartres.* New York: Collier.

ALMOND, GABRIEL A.; and COLEMAN, JAMES S. (editors) 1960 *The Politics of the Developing Areas.* Princeton Univ. Press.

ALMOND, GABRIEL A.; and VERBA, SIDNEY 1963 *The Civic Culture: Political Attitudes and Democracy in Five Nations.* Princeton Univ. Press.

APTER, DAVID E. 1965 *The Politics of Modernization.* Univ. of Chicago Press.

BARKER, ERNEST (1942) 1958 *Reflections on Government.* New York: Oxford Univ. Press.

BARNARD, FREDERICK M. 1965 *Herder's Social and Political Thought.* Oxford: Clarendon.

BRYCE, JAMES 1921 *Modern Democracies.* 2 vols. New York: Macmillan.

BRZEZINSKI, ZBIGNIEW K. 1962 *Ideology and Power in Soviet Politics.* New York: Praeger.

CARTWRIGHT, DORWIN; and ZANDER, ALVIN (editors) (1953) 1960 *Group Dynamics: Research and Theory.* 2d ed. Evanston, Ill.: Row, Peterson. → A good review of the psychological materials on group behavior.

DAVIES, REGINALD TREVOR 1937 *The Golden Century of Spain.* London: Macmillan.

DEUTSCH, KARL W. 1963 *The Nerves of Government: Models of Political Communication and Control.* New York: Free Press.

DICEY, ALBERT V. (1885) 1961 *Introduction to the Study of the Law of the Constitution.* 10th ed. With an introduction by E. C. S. Wade. London: Macmillan; New York: St. Martins. → First published as *Lectures Introductory to the Study of the Law of the Constitution.*

DOWNS, ANTHONY 1957 *An Economic Theory of Democracy.* New York: Harper.

EASTON, DAVID 1957 Political Structures and Processes. *World Politics* 9:383–400.

EASTON, DAVID 1965 *A Systems Analysis of Political Life.* New York: Wiley.

EASTON, DAVID (editor) 1966 *Varieties of Political Theory.* Englewood Cliffs, N.J.: Prentice-Hall. → See especially "An Individualistic Theory of Political Process," by James M. Buchanan.

EDELMAN, JACOB M. 1964 *The Symbolic Uses of Politics.* Urbana: Univ. of Illinois Press.

ERIKSON, ERIK H. (1958) 1962 *Young Man Luther: A Study in Psychoanalysis and History.* Austin Riggs Monograph No. 4. New York: Norton.

FAIRMAN, H. W. 1958 The Kingship Rituals of Egypt. Pages 74–104 in Samuel H. Hooke (editor), *Myth, Ritual and Kingship: Essays on the Theory and Practice of Kingship in the Ancient Near East and in Israel.* Oxford: Clarendon.

FALLERS, LLOYD A. (1956) 1965 *Bantu Bureaucracy: A Century of Political Evolution.* Univ. of Chicago Press.

FINER, HERMAN (1932) 1949 *The Theory and Practice of Modern Government.* Rev. ed. New York: Holt.

FINER, SAMUEL E. (1958) 1962 *Anonymous Empire: A Study of the Lobby in Great Britain.* London: Pall Mall.

FRIEDRICH, CARL J. (1937) 1950 *Constitutional Government and Democracy: Theory and Practice in Europe and America.* Rev. ed. Boston: Ginn. → First published as *Constitutional Government and Politics: Nature and Development.*

FRIEDRICH, CARL J.; and BRZEZINSKI, ZBIGNIEW K. (1956) 1965 *Totalitarian Dictatorship and Autocracy.* 2d ed., rev. Cambridge, Mass.: Harvard Univ. Press.

GASH, NORMAN 1953 *Politics in the Age of Peel: A Study in the Technique of Parliamentary Representation, 1830–1850.* London and New York: Longmans.

GIERKE, OTTO VON (1881) 1958 *Political Theories of the Middle Age.* Cambridge Univ. Press. → First published as "Die publicistischen Lehren des Mittelalters," a section of Volume 3 of Gierke's *Das deutsche Genossenschaftsrecht.* Translated, with a famous introduction, by Frederic William Maitland.

HIGNETT, CHARLES (1952) 1962 *A History of the Athenian Constitution to the End of the Fifth Century B.C.* Oxford: Clarendon.

JOUVENEL, BERTRAND DE 1963 *The Pure Theory of Politics.* New Haven: Yale Univ. Press.

LAQUEUR, WALTER; and LABEDZ, LEOPOLD (editors) 1962 *Polycentrism: The New Factor in International Communism.* New York: Praeger.

LASKI, HAROLD J. (1925) 1957 *A Grammar of Politics.* 4th ed. London: Allen & Unwin.

LASKI, HAROLD J. (1935) 1956 *The State in Theory and Practice.* London: Allen & Unwin.

LASKI, HAROLD J. (1951) 1962 *Reflections on the Constitution: The House of Commons, the Cabinet [and] the Civil Service.* Manchester Univ. Press. → Published posthumously.

LASSWELL, HAROLD D. (1930) 1960 *Psychopathology and Politics.* New ed., with afterthoughts by the author. New York: Viking.

LEWIS, EWART (editor) 1954 *Medieval Political Ideas.* 2 vols. New York: Knopf.

McKENZIE, ROBERT T. (1955) 1963 *British Political Parties: The Distribution of Power Within the Conservative and Labour Parties.* 2d ed. London: Heinemann; New York: St. Martins. → A paperback edition was published in 1964 by Praeger.

McNEIL, JOHN T. 1954 *The History and Character of Calvinism.* New York: Oxford Univ. Press.

OSTROGORSKII, MOISEI I. (1902) 1964 *Democracy and the Organization of Political Parties.* 2 vols. Edited and abridged by Seymour M. Lipset. Chicago: Quadrangle. → An abridged edition of a 1902 English translation from the French.

PAYNE, STANLEY G. 1961 *Falange: A History of Spanish Fascism.* Stanford Studies in History, Economics and Political Science, No. 22. Stanford Univ. Press.

PIPES, RICHARD (1954) 1964 *The Formation of the Soviet Union.* Rev. ed. Cambridge, Mass.: Harvard Univ. Press.

PYE, LUCIAN W. 1962 *Politics, Personality, and Nation Building: Burma's Search for Identity.* New Haven: Yale Univ. Press.

RIKER, WILLIAM H. 1962 *The Theory of Political Coalitions.* New Haven: Yale Univ. Press.

SARTORI, GIOVANNI 1962 *Democratic Theory.* Detroit, Mich.: Wayne State Univ. Press. → A paperback edition was published in 1965 by Praeger.

SNYDER, RICHARD C. 1961 *Game Theory and the Analysis of Political Behavior.* New York: Free Press.

TALMON, JACOB L. (1952) 1965 *The Origins of Totalitarian Democracy.* 2d ed. New York: Praeger.

ULAM, ADAM B. 1960 *The Unfinished Revolution: An Essay on the Sources of Influence of Marxism and Communism.* New York: Random House.

WALLAS, GRAHAM (1908) 1962 *Human Nature in Politics.* 4th ed. Gloucester, Mass.: Smith.

WEBER, MAX (1904–1905) 1930 *The Protestant Ethic and the Spirit of Capitalism.* Translated by Talcott Parsons, with a foreword by R. H. Tawney. London: Allen & Unwin; New York: Scribner. → First published in German. The 1930 edition has been reprinted frequently. A paperback edition was published in 1958 by Scribner.

WHEARE, KENNETH C. 1955 *Government by Committee: An Essay on the British Constitution.* Oxford: Clarendon.

GOVERNMENT COMMISSIONS

See COMMISSIONS, GOVERNMENT; REGULATION OF INDUSTRY.

GOVERNMENT STATISTICS

Statistical data generated by government sources are referred to and cited in many articles in this encyclopedia, including CENSUS; ECONOMIC DATA; FALLACIES, STATISTICAL; INTERNATIONAL TRADE; SAMPLE SURVEYS; VITAL STATISTICS; *and the biographies of* QUETELET *and* WILLCOX. *This article is confined to over-all aspects: the relation of statistics to the establishment of national states; the range of substantive matters on which statistics are collected; the ways in which that collection is organized in different parts of the world; the business and professional environment within which government statisticians work; the problems and difficulties they face in both developed and underdeveloped countries.*

Government statistics in the modern state are an essential part of a wider information system. The first compilers of statistics did not make a sharp distinction between numerical and other facts, and it is still true that numerical data complement other kinds of information in the process by which decisions are made in private and public undertakings. These data are as indispensable in a centralized as in a pluralistic society; as important in the deliberations of government itself as they are in the firms, commissariats, or other groupings concerned with getting out a product. The effectiveness of the market mechanism of a free society depends on the quality of the information on which its entities base their decisions. Western European economic planning consists in large measure in the provision of supplementary information to private enterprise. A tightly controlled, centralized system needs, more than anything else, a feedback—of which the statistics it collects are a pivotal element —if it is not to be the unwitting victim of its own concentration of power.

Statistics and the state

The history, the present condition, and the problems yet to be solved in government statistics reflect the circumstances of modern national states. A governmental administrative apparatus is a principal user of official statistics, and its existence and efficiency are a main condition for securing them. While sporadic attempts at counting people or goods were known in classical times and in the ancient empires of the Middle East, there is virtually no continuity between these and modern official compilations.

Modern history. Like so much else that pertains to the modern state, its statistical system emerged about the time of the French Revolution. One of the early acts of the Constituent Assembly was to see to the publication of a statistical account of the resources of France, prepared by Lavoisier. In 1800 the Bureau de Statistique was created in Paris. The assembly required a census (Articles I and II of the Law of July 22, 1791, according to Faure 1918, p. 277), which was duly taken in 1791. François de Neufchâteau, in a circular dated the 15th of Fructidor of the year VI (presumably September 1, 1799), saw the census—with characteristic revolutionary exaggeration—as "the measure of the strength, the source of the wealth, the political thermometer of the power of states" (Faure 1918, p. 284).

Just as British nationality erupted less violently than did that of France, so its statistical system had a more gradual inception. Early landmarks were the *Domesday Book* of William the Conqueror in 1086; the record of customs dues collected in the Port of London in the time of Edward III; the Tudor counts of men and resources in the face of the danger of war; and the registration of deaths, initiated by Henry VIII in 1532, when there was widespread fear of the plague.

The dependence of statehood on a statistical system has become more and more clear with the passing of time. The mercantilist writers of the epoch of the absolute monarchs were concerned with the power of the state in peace and war; the monarch and his advisers had to have measures of the stock of men and other resources [*see* ECONOM-IC THOUGHT, *article on* MERCANTILIST THOUGHT]. The British and French colonial administrations in North America, and later the British in India, took censuses, that of the Canadian province of Quebec in 1666 being the first of modern censuses (Linder 1959, p. 330). With democracy there came to be other reasons for statistical compilations. In the first of the major federal constitutions, that of the United States, a means of determining the political weight of the contracting entities was required; their relative populations seemed to provide this, and the first of the regular series of decennial censuses of the United States was taken in 1790, although a printed schedule was not employed until 1830. Confederation in Canada in 1867 was based on a similar provision for representation by population and was followed by a census in 1871; the Australian colonies were united in 1900, and the formation of a statistical office followed in 1905.

Since World War II dynastic, colonial, tribal, and other political forms have been displaced by national organizations throughout the world. Along with attempts to provide themselves with constitutions, elections, and the beginnings of modern industry, new countries have set up statistical systems, both as a precondition for development and as a symbol of nationhood. The new statistical style is far more ambitious than the colonial model that preceded, in proportion as over-all national aims are more extended than colonial aims. An important role in promoting the extension and quality of statistical work was played by the League of Nations, through its Committee of Statistical Experts, and subsequently by the United Nations, through its statistical and population commissions. Under UN auspices a world population census was attempted about 1950 and again in 1960, with a high degree of national cooperation. In the decade of the 1860s censuses were taken in which 17 per cent of the estimated population of the planet was counted; over ten times as many people were counted in censuses around 1960, and these constituted 67 per cent of the population of the globe (*Demographic Yearbook 1962*, p. 1). Results are not uniformly satisfactory; a study of the quality of statistical organization and statistical output of the various countries would undoubtedly show a close relation to the quality of governmental administration in general. Chile is better organized statistically than Burma; Burma than Cambodia.

Government statistics classified. A wide range of statistical data has come to be regarded as appropriate for government compilation and publication.

Classification by source. One way to classify government statistics is according to source: households for population censuses, family-budget surveys, employment and unemployment counts; business establishments for production and employment data; incorporated and unincorporated firms for profit figures; national-government revenue departments for foreign trade and income tax accounts. The categories are not exclusive; households and commercial establishments often provide complementary data bearing on the same matter.

Where economic statistics are essentially a summary record of transactions, they are in principle available through questions addressed to either of the parties to the transaction; retail prices may be ascertained through surveys of retail stores with respect to goods sold or through household surveys with respect to goods bought. If the business establishment is more often used, this is a matter of the greater availability of records and the larger number of transactions implicitly covered by one report; in underdeveloped countries, where business is less organized, questions addressed to the consumer are relatively more favored. For data on employment and unemployment, the household seems on the whole as satisfactory a source as the business establishment. In North America the contest between rival figures of unemployment has been an important stimulus to improvement not only of the sampling and questioning techniques used in household surveys but also of the administration of unemployment insurance itself, in respects that go far beyond statistics.

Classification by time of publication. A grosser form of classification is by the indication of temporal trends that series give. Some are issued promptly and tell the latest news: weekly railway carloadings, department-store sales, stocks of wheat in central elevators, stocks of the several metals. At the other extreme are full censuses of industry and population, taken only at long intervals; their results are released over a period of time, beginning within a few months after enumeration and continuing for some years after the data are collected, and they are valuable for the cross-sectional relations that they reveal. Because of this configuration of prompt summary data and delayed details, the national economic picture of a country with respect to any moment of time is only gradually filled in, over the five or ten years subsequent to that time.

Government statistical activities include analysis and interpretation as well as data collection. Although knowledge of analysis helps in gathering data, and vice versa, the two specializations are different. An example of the division of labor on this basis is that existing between the United States Bureau of the Census and the Department of Labor on statistics of employment and unemployment; the former agency has the responsibility for gathering the material, the latter for the official analysis.

Expansion in modernization. A statistical system seems to start with population censuses and foreign trade as the main items; other kinds of data—for example, counts of starts and completions of residential construction—are added as time goes on. As a country develops, the need for statistics mounts with the variety and difficulty of decisions required by an increased division of labor in the economy. A demand for factual justification, in terms of which people can explain their decisions to themselves and to others, seems to have characterized the North American continent from an early date. General Francis A. Walker, speaking before the International Statistical Institute, pointed this out in 1893: "A strong passion for statistics early developed itself in the life of our people, and such statesmen and publicists as Hamilton . . . became working statisticians. . . . No government in the world has ever lavished money and labor . . . more cheerfully and patiently in this respect" (quoted in Cummings 1918, p. 573). But this culture of facts is no longer confined to the United States, to those of English speech, or to Europeans; it is becoming world-wide.

The proposition that the statistics collected by any government are a function of its interests and responsibilities can be exemplified in the process of decolonization. When much of the world was under the hegemony of the states of western Europe, the statistical system centered on foreign trade. What was important for British administrators was the amount of rice exported from Burma, of jute exported from Bengal; the Netherlands wanted to know the amounts of coffee, sugar, and rubber exported from Java in the periods when each of these commodities was at its height. Another phase of colonial development was the land tax; the land tax made it both necessary and possible to have figures on acreages and production of the main crops. A further stage was some rudimentary concern with people, expressed by population censuses. The building of railways in India and Java, for instance, was followed by the collection of transport statistics—data that no one would have collected when oxcarts, proas, and the backs of men were the principal means of shipping commodities. And the evolution that occurred in the colonies in Asia was paralleled in Latin America, where the several governments, although independent, had interests nearly as restricted as those of the colonial powers.

The advent of independence in Asia and of the welfare state everywhere has increased the range of government statistics. Every country concerned with development is trying to expand its educational system, and statistics of schools, teachers, and pupils are nearly universal. In England and Wales educational statistics of a kind date back to the 1820s and 1830s, when public money was first given to the schools (Baines 1918, p. 377). Vital statistics are being gradually improved, a process that requires the inculcation of the habit of recording births and deaths not only on the part of the hierarchy of the civil registration system but also on the part of the medical profession and the public at large; such institutionalization will take at least a generation or two in the new countries. Meanwhile, sample surveys are being introduced, to observe the birth rate and its changes, as well as many other population and economic phenomena. Family-budget surveys, which had been foreshadowed by colonial governments in their moments of welfare-mindedness (a coolie-budget survey was made in the Netherlands Indies in the 1930s), are becoming more frequent; the government of India, through the Indian Statistical Institute in Calcutta, has been particularly active in this and other types of household survey.

Organization of statistical services

Every government has sooner or later to consider the organizational framework within which its statistics will be collected. When left to themselves, individual departments of the central government tend to collect whatever data their administration generates, and they hardly separate the collection of such information from administrative control of their operations. When the act regulating the collection of duties in the United States was passed in 1789 (Cummings 1918, p. 579), it required the collector of customs to record ships' manifests and other information connected with trade; the series of foreign trade statistics for the United States accordingly dates from 1789. The British Post Office collects and publishes the returns of the postal service; the British Department of Inland Revenues, established in 1849, collects the estate and stamp duties, land taxes, and income taxes. But with increase of scale, such departments come to separate their statistical from their administrative work; the British Board of Trade formed within itself a statistical branch as early as 1833 (Baines 1918, p. 374). Subsequently, labor, local departments of agriculture, and many other departments or boards came to have their own statistical units, not only in the United Kingdom but in the United States, the British dominions, and the countries of western Europe. The Interstate Commerce Commission (ICC) of the United States was from the start insistent on securing data from the railways it regulated, and ICC publications constitute an important series.

Sometimes one of these agencies would be assigned the taking of a decennial census, a periodic task required of the registrar-general in England and Wales, whose continuing work was the civil register and vital statistics. In Canada the decennial census provided for in the British North America Act was the charge of an office established in the Department of Agriculture in 1905. But in all countries, increasing attention to statistics led to proposals for centralization in a specialized agency.

Degree of centralization. With the establishment of even small statistical offices within government departments, the work of statistics began to benefit from some degree of separation from the day-to-day exigencies of administration.

Centralization in national government. The collection into a single office of all the statistical activities of the national government was considered, in order to secure even more of the gains of specialization. To the argument of efficiency (concentration of specialized personnel and equipment to deal with the large scale of centralized statistical work) was added that of avoidance of duplication, a perennial hazard of government work and one which appeared in statistical work from the earliest days. Separating statistical work from the other work of government lessens the pressure on the statistician to distort his results to protect political or administrative interests—reference is made below to the judicial aspect of the statistician's function. The better coordination of a central system, moreover, ought to permit the recognition of gaps in data. It should also make easier the adoption of uniform classifications; it is highly desirable that production and exports, for instance, be recorded on the same commodity classification, so that comparisons may be possible. But anyone who knows the tendency to autonomy of the divisions of a governmental organization will realize that having the several compilations under a single roof is no automatic guarantee of uniformity; the several sections can pursue different courses. One special danger of a centralized organization is that it will become so self-contained as to be immune to the needs of the users of its data. Centralization offers high returns when the central organization is well coordinated internally and alert to the changing requirements of outside users.

The administrative argument for centralization

was early carried into effect, in one degree or another, in the Netherlands, Canada, Australia, Germany, and Italy. About the middle of the 19th century the Netherlands took important steps in this direction; in 1848 a statistical bureau was established in the Department of Home Affairs whose responsibilities were far wider than the tabulation of data generated in the department. Canada and Australia committed themselves to a statistical system that was centralized in the double sense that statistics were at least as much the affair of the central government as of the states or provinces or of any lower level of government and that among the agencies of the central government there was one with pre-eminence in the collection and tabulation of statistics in a number of different fields. The Canadian system has been in principle entirely centralized since the founding of the Dominion Bureau of Statistics in 1918. A degree of centralization was arranged in Germany with the establishment of the Imperial Statistical Office in 1872, the year after the establishment of the German Empire; in Italy centralization was begun in 1861, the year of the constitution of the monarchy, with a directorate of statistics that was the ancestor of the present Istituto Centrale di Statistica.

In the United States and the United Kingdom practice has evolved closer to the decentralized pole of the centralized–decentralized continuum. The means of coordination in the United Kingdom is an office in the Cabinet Secretariat that operates through a series of understandings with the heads of statistical divisions in the Board of Trade, the Ministry of Food, the Ministry of Agriculture, etc. All the statistical divisions in departments are directed by statistician members of the Professional, Scientific, and Technical Class, one of the five classes of the British civil service; appointments anywhere are open to members of the statistician class irrespective of where they are serving. The Treasury approves the expenditures of statistical departments, and on new expenditures they are advised by the Central Statistical Office.

The American arrangement is more formal; the Office of Statistical Standards of the Bureau of the Budget not only reviews all requests for funds to carry out statistical work within the federal government; its approval is required before any federal government questionnaire can be sent to ten or more respondents. This requirement dates back to the Federal Reports Act of 1942 and was intended to reduce the burden on respondents and to eliminate duplication. Where duplication exists, it not only is wasteful of government funds but also arouses the fiercest resentment of respondents who are required to answer the same questions more than once.

The best coordination does not consist exclusively of the negative injunctions of an enforcement agency. An example of a more positive kind is the collaboration of the U.S. Social Security Administration, essentially an operating agency, and the Bureau of the Census in the creation of a publication showing county business patterns based on Social Security Administration records. The U.S. Bureau of the Census has used tax records to eliminate business-census questionnaires for a million retail establishments without employees. By using Social Security records as a source of lists, the Bureau of the Census is able to take the economic censuses at reduced cost.

Coordination requires fine judgment at a thousand points. Should both the U.S. Bureau of Mines and the Bureau of the Census continue to secure mineral statistics? The Bureau of the Census collects benchmark data on an establishment basis every five years from all establishments within the scope of the census, assigning to the mining industry the output of all those that are classifiable as mining. The Bureau of Mines collects information more frequently, on the output of minerals as well as on engineering and technical matters. These data are thought to be independently valuable and different enough not to seem to constitute duplication.

Division of responsibility. Along quite a different dimension is the division of responsibility between the national government and the local governments of states or provinces and cities. In this dimension the United Kingdom is highly centralized, while Germany has problems because of the division of statistical activities among the *Länder*, and even in the Netherlands there is some devolution of statistical activities to organizations in the cities.

Every national statistical system must depend on local sources for its information. At the one extreme is complete central control, as found in the national census of countries such as the United States and Canada, in which the local officers are appointed and instructed by the center through a training ladder that inculcates definitions and procedures that are, at least in principle, fully determined centrally, and which is backed by a central budget from which all participants are paid. More decentralized is the census in countries such as Argentina, where the plans are made by a national statistical office but where the budget does not include the funds for paying enumerators, who are government employees on the payroll of other departments of the center or the provinces (for

example, schoolteachers), co-opted for one or several days' work on the enumeration. Coordination of such an operation requires feats of diplomacy. Further down on the scale of decentralization is the system of vital registration, used in the United States and other countries, in which local registry officials report to a state authority and whatever national uniformity exists is the result of negotiations in which the national office can take leadership more by virtue of its persuasiveness than because of any legal or budgetary power.

Comparability and change. The government statistical agency must have both continuity and adaptation of its output to changing needs, a combination of virtues easier to prescribe than to follow. In some instances an agency is very rigid; the disposition to continue collecting the same data in the same fashion year after year is both the strength and the weakness of government agencies. But at other times it changes arbitrarily; A. L. Bowley charged that the United Kingdom census of 1921 was deliberately made noncomparable with anything that went before, a statement challenged by Greenwood et al. (1932, p. 279). Again, judgment is required; the elimination of old series and the initiation of new ones and the modification of definitions that make a given series more useful for the future but lessen its comparability with the past must be discussed on a more specific level than this article can attain.

Practices that are good in one place and time may not be so in a different economy and society. Attempts to transfer categories of statistical compilation from a country in which money economy dominates to one in which households produce for their own use rather than for exchange may not be satisfactory. Some of the greatest difficulties in collecting statistics within the developed countries are in the sector of subsistence agriculture. The relation of statistics to industrial practice is brought home especially strikingly by the present situation in the United States, where the National Bureau of Economic Research and the Bureau of the Census, among other agencies, are trying to find how individual series can be improved or replaced. With the shift of traffic to trucks and airlines, carloadings have become much less useful. Department-store sales mean less when many of the lines of merchandise are also sold by discount houses and drugstores. The inventive spirit that discovered department-store sales and carloadings as key figures in the economy is needed now to go beyond these.

Interactions with environment. The government statistical agency is by no means a free agent but depends on the administrative practices of other governmental agencies and of business concerns. Statistics of imports depend on valuations made for customs purposes; comparing the exports of newsprint or metals from Canada to the United States, for instance, with the imports of nominally the same commodities into the United States from Canada will show how substantial is the effect of varying definitions of commodities as well as of sources and destinations. Since definitions are often part of procedures for customs valuation, and these are embedded in laws around which substantial material interests have developed, discrepancies between countries are likely to persist despite many conventions and attempts at accommodation, from that of Brussels in 1910 to those of the United Nations Statistical Commission.

Effects of accounting practices. One important network in which the statistical agency is enmeshed is the accounting practices of industry, themselves in part the consequence of the regulations of the government income tax department. The art of statistical collection includes finding modes of definition of the entities about which inquiry is made that are most in conformity with the accounting practices of business and provide the most useful information to the public. The industrial establishment, as against the firm, is generally taken as the primary element for collection of industrial statistics and is defined in practice as the smallest production unit that maintains more or less complete records. The statistical agency does not always play a purely passive role; it is often in a position to exercise influence and initiative. In Canada the federal agency concerned with financial statistics of the 5,000 municipalities of the country was able to persuade them to adopt a standard accounting procedure, which benefited them as well as national statistics.

National professional associations. The environment within which a statistics-producing office of government has to work includes, besides the operating agencies of the same government and the productive units of the country at large, a host of professional associations, as well as individuals interested in statistics. The American Statistical Association in 1844 petitioned the Congress of the United States to recompile the census of 1840; its policy of protesting poor work and supporting good in the federal statistical field has operated to the present day, although the need for its intervention is not as great as when the government service was staffed almost exclusively by amateurs (Bowman 1964).

International professional associations. To the national associations have now been added important international ones. First among these was the International Statistical Institute, from the nineteenth century on a persistent and wholesome influence in favor of high standards and comparable classifications. The Economic and Social Council of the United Nations, through its statistical and population commissions, has had an effect in stimulating countries to take censuses; to adopt a minimum set of questions in these, for which a serious attempt would be made to attain international comparability; to use modern techniques, in the interest of accuracy and promptness of release of data. Sensitive to the desire of nations to be independent of outside interference in statistics as in other fields, the council has made its chief weapon the argument of international comparability in statistics of production, as well as of population. Also of influence have been the regional agencies of the United Nations for Asia, Europe, Latin America, and now Africa; the Inter-American Statistical Association; the specialized agencies of the United Nations, including the United Nations Educational, Scientific, and Cultural Organization (UNESCO), the Food and Agriculture Organization (FAO), the International Labour Organisation (ILO), etc., in their respective fields. The resolutions and the conventions that these have drawn up often suffer from being stated in highly abstract terms, but they are supplemented by technical assistance services to less developed members, including the sending out of advisers and the providing of training facilities. The publications of international bodies have not only been directly useful to scholars and others but also have been an incentive to members to secure data. FAO conferences of groups of neighboring countries have constituted an effective form of pressure for improvement of agricultural statistics.

Other influences. Series of government statistics have often been initiated from the outside. The Metropolitan Life Insurance Company began collecting statistics of labor turnover in the United States in 1926, and these compilations were later taken over by the United States Department of Labor (Hauser & Leonard 1946, p. 363). In Canada statistics of wage rates collected by the Bell Telephone Company for its own purposes have influenced federal government collections. Statistics of stocks on hand have often been started by associations of manufacturers and then continued by a public statistical agency. In the Netherlands one of the influences that led to the centralized system was the private Union for Statistics, founded in 1856 (Stuart 1918, p. 435), which published many volumes of data, although it did no primary collecting. Later this private union was subsidized by the government, and ultimately all of its activities were taken over. Especially well known is the pressure that Quetelet, the Belgian statistician, exerted through his researches as a private citizen between about 1825 and 1841 (when he became a public official). His avid interest in the regularity of certain social phenomena, e.g., the "budget of the scaffold," finds its monument in the extensive series of criminal statistics produced in Belgium and many other countries (Julin 1918, p. 128). In England the first edition of the essay by Malthus that attracted so much attention to population was followed within three years by the census of 1801 [*see the biographies of* QUETELET *and* MALTHUS].

There are many other examples of the influence of men and ideas—as well as outside organizations—on government statistics. The collection of economic data during the present generation has been altered by the recognition of national accounts as a general framework. The concept was developed by scholars in universities in the United States and Great Britain, following suggestions of J. M. Keynes. The notion of national income makes it possible to arrange a great variety of existing series in the pigeonholes of a national-accounts framework; the output of the statistical systems ceases to appear arbitrary, for each portion measures a contribution to the gross national product; certain gaps become visible—for instance, personal services—and there is pressure to fill them. Furthermore, the examination in this fashion of economic statistics as a whole permits the grand total of the country's economic activities to be calculated in at least three ways—by value added, by income received, and by expenditure—which have important elements of independence as to source of data. The confrontation of calculations of a total derived from more or less independent statistical sources has been an incentive to improve the accuracy of all components.

The current prestige of economic planning has had important effects on government statistical work. Planning may be good or bad, effective or ineffective, but in all instances it requires data. One cannot even go through the motions of planning without statistics. Government planning agencies requiring data are in an especially strong position to see that the necessary resources are allocated to their collection.

The statistical profession and government. Underlying recent developments is a rapid professionalization of statistics. Times have changed greatly since Francis A. Walker lamented, in an address before the American Statistical Association in 1896, "I do not know of a single man now holding, or who has ever held, a position in this country as the head of a statistical bureau, or as chief of a statis-tical service, or as a statistician, who had any elementary training for his work" (quoted in Cummings 1918, p. 574). A recent Bureau of the Census survey of its staff showed 576 employees in professional statistical positions, of whom all but 22 had an academic degree, including 36 PH.D.s and 102 M.A.s (Bowman 1964, p. 14). The change has come about through the extension of the field. Statistical method is applied to acceptance sampling and quality control in industry, to experimental design in agricultural trials, to bio-assay, operations research, and sample surveys of national populations. The interchange among these applications and between each application and a rapidly expanding mathematical statistical theory has had a decisive effect. Backed by a theory based on probability and relatively well-established methods of application of the theory; with a rapidly growing body of literature in books and professional journals; with departments of statistics in a number of universities, and courses in nearly all; there is less and less need for the government statistical agency to depend on the gifted amateur like Quetelet in Belgium, Knibbs in Australia, or Coats in Canada. And yet, present-day expansion and progress can be matched in quality by some of the early work. Florence Nightingale had much effect on the British War Office through her statistics showing deaths from battle and from disease separately. Her data on the army hospitals in India led to important reforms. It is not that the modern professional is better than the old-fashioned gifted amateur, but the former is more certain to be on hand when needed and commands the tools that have now been created.

Sampling in the new professionalization. Among the large-scale sample surveys now conducted are those on a monthly basis in the United States and Canada, quarterly in the Federal Republic of Germany and other European countries, and virtually continuously in India. The topics of survey are almost as wide as the topics of statistics itself [*see* SAMPLE SURVEYS].

Like any important change in technique, sampling does not merely attain the earlier objectives at lower cost; it brings a radically new viewpoint on the whole process of data collection. Instead of thinking of himself as charged with passively compiling given data, the statistician orients himself to the purpose of the compilation and the degree of accuracy required if the purpose is to be served; thus, he is led to take account of the nonsampling as well as the sampling error to which his work is subject. He sees himself at his professional best in measuring error, controlling quality, and evaluating results. He comes to measure information, not by the mass of data he can turn out, but rather by the accuracy attained in a single figure. The percentage of the labor force unemployed, for example, may be the occasion for a major decision in regard to the economy. If there is an allotment to improve the figure, he must decide what amount should be spent to improve the accuracy of response and what to increase the sample. In other words, he must decide if there will be more return from applying a given effort to the sampling or to the nonsampling error. The changed attitude toward error—the view that it is both inevitable and to be constantly combated—is seen in the United States Bureau of the Census, where the 1950 and subsequent population censuses have been accompanied by an official estimate of the degree of underenumeration, an estimate in part made by having superior enumerators survey a sample of areas. This practice has been applied in Canada since 1951. It is the mark of the professional statistician that he does not assert that his results are exact; even when he has done the survey by the best means that are available, he is satisfied to consider his one survey as an arbitrary selection from all the surveys that might have been carried out at about the same time and with equally acceptable definitions [see ERRORS, *article on* NONSAMPLING ERRORS].

Enduring problems of official statistics.   A survey of the statistical agencies of any government, even those of a very advanced country, would show the continuance of some out-of-date practices, the publication of some figures that are not usable because they are based on purely administrative definitions of the entities counted or because the error is not stated by the agency but may be presumed to be large. Besides the valuable statistics they contain, library shelves are weighted with irrelevant, useless, and inaccurate statistics, a situation to be deplored in proportion as good techniques are available.

Government statistics' judicial function.   Especially pernicious are those inaccuracies intended to serve some political purpose. The strongest argument for statistical centralization relates to what may be called the judicial function of the official statistician. The statistics of foreign trade may show that the government's trade policy is going badly; the statistics of prices may show that its monetary policy is leading to inflation. Protection of the public requires that the agency responsible for the policy not be the one with exclusive control over the statistics; to give it such control is to ask of it superhuman strength to withstand temptation. In a hundred minor decisions of statistical compilation, an operating agency may be swayed by noting how the result will come out. Presentation also requires impartiality. On issues such as whether a price index ought to be released now, when it has been scheduled to appear, or next week, after a national election has taken place, hangs the virtue of the statistician. Without this virtue and the resulting public confidence in statistics, much of the cost of collecting data is wasted; statistics that are not believed are of no use. In a statistician, as in a judge, ignorance is less dangerous than corruption. The statistician will be most useful to the community when his statistical honor is not in conflict with some nonstatistical responsibility. At a higher administrative level, the political head of the department that includes the statistical office must accept the self-discipline of permitting decisions regarding statistics to be made on statistical considerations, not because such decisions are always correct but because, when they are wrong, they are wrong in a disinterested way. One method that lessens the need for self-discipline is to have a commission entirely outside of politics control the statistical office, as is done in the Netherlands.

Much less subtle than the issues of the preceding paragraph are the distortions as a matter of policy that have been seen in some totalitarian countries. During the Stalin period in the Soviet Union, statistics were not considered to pertain to science but to revolution and to mobilization of the people for national construction. If the statistics do not show progress, the masses will become discouraged and their effort will flag. The same attitude was found in China in the 1950s (Li 1962). The competition between districts to be in the van of socialist production was extended to competition with respect to the figures of production, and this local zeal for declaring high figures reached its peak in 1960, when total production of cereals was announced as 275 million tons, apparently an exaggeration of over 100 per cent. It had been thought democratic to bring the masses into the work of compiling statistics; the consequent socialist rivalry seems to have genuinely deceived the regime, as well as its subjects, with subsequent disastrous consequences. There are clear signs that in the Soviet Union, as in older industrial societies, trustworthy statistics are now recognized as something more than a bourgeois luxury; whether the dependency of good decisions on good statistics is now understood in China is not clear.

Technical contributions

Extensive contributions have been made to technique in nearly every division of statistics by agencies attempting to implement efficiently their legislative assignment to collect data. One may mention the methods of calculating life tables; the deseasonalization of economic time series; the theory and practice of index-number calculation, as it has been developed in the United States Bureau of Labor Statistics and in the Dominion Bureau of Statistics in Canada; the classification of occupations, industries, and commodities (Coats 1925). Particularly important for the growth of demography were the technical contributions during the nineteenth century by William Farr and other statisticians of the United Kingdom General Register Office [*see* INDEX NUMBERS; LIFE TABLES; POPULATION; TIME SERIES].

The most striking single example of these contributions is the intimate relation of the U.S. Bureau of the Census to the development of tabulating and computing equipment, from the primitive punch-card devices of the 1890s, built in the Census Bureau itself by Herman Hollerith, to the Univac, built privately with bureau encouragement and financing and technical help from the Bureau of Standards. The Canadian census office also pioneered in this, with some highly original electric and compressed-air tabulators, the result of the ingenuity of Fernand Belisle, a lifelong employee of the Canadian Bureau of Statistics. Both Canadian and United States census offices have in recent years built or stimulated the building of input devices to avoid the keypunching of data, the most tedious part of the processing of large-scale surveys.

Besides having had a part in the development of computers, government statistical agencies have shown great initiative in using them. Such use, whether in an insurance office, an oil refinery, or a government statistical office, requires extensive re-thinking of processes that have developed in the course of decades. Several of the more advanced of the world's statistical offices have drastically reorganized their work in order to exploit electronic computation, with consequences of more extensive cross tabulation, better control of error in processing, and economy. In the United States the demand for machine-readable results has increased as users of statistics have acquired their own computers. The Bureau of the Census has an extensive catalogue of results available on punch cards or electronic tape; this mode of publication is sure to become widespread.

Publication of results

Prompt and full publication is the highest of virtues in government statistics—provided that the data published are accurate as well as relevant. This follows from the place of statistics in a decision-making process: the appropriateness of the decision—for example, to build a factory—will depend on the situation that exists at some future date; and if the statistician is not in a position to count the population of five or 25 years hence, he can at least describe what the situation was up to as recent a moment as possible. On the content of what is published—what cross classifications of distributions, what percentages, what time comparisons, what charts—the judgment of the government statistician becomes better the greater his contact with users of his results. With the multiplicity of governmental and private sources, the need increases for good indexing within any publication, as well as for cross referencing of comparable data in other publications.

Government statistical offices have entered the field of social science in their efforts to interpret their data. This runs from comment on statistical tables that enables the reader to know how the entities counted have been defined, along with measures of sampling and nonsampling error, through calculations distributing not-stated ages and deseasonalizing economic series, to full-scale monographs that have become a regular part of the census, in the United States and Canada going back at least a full generation. India is preparing a set of monographs based on the 1961 census, and Pakistan is planning to do likewise. If one thinks of the continuum, from the collection of raw statistical data to its final use as an ingredient either in scientific investigation or in the making of decisions, then there is room for differences of opinion as to where the role of the government statistical office ends and that of the user begins. The vital minimum is that the government statistician describe all aspects of his collection procedures that can possibly affect the interpretation of the results. It is to be hoped that in some future time no survey will be issued without realistic estimates of the accuracy of its figures, but that time still seems to be far in the future.

Notwithstanding all this, a certain abstemiousness is forced on the official statistician by virtue of his position; he cannot afford to take the sorts of risks in the interpretation of data that newspapermen can take so freely. Public confidence in the accuracy of his figures, and hence their usefulness, would be jeopardized by palpable arbitrariness in judgments expressed in his text. This consideration often drives him to the writing of text that is no more than a gloss on what is obviously revealed in the tables and is perhaps less clear than the figures themselves. On the other hand, the government statistician can argue with justice that interpretation, lively or dull, made without his intimate knowledge of the basis of the figures is likely to be misleading. The answer is that, as a minimum, he give enough detail on his procedures to put the reader in a position to interpret correctly.

Secrecy. The matter of secrecy enters into statistical work in two ways, to which exactly opposite principles apply. In the report made by the individual to a government agency, it is generally considered that the most honest reporting will be secured if a guarantee of confidentiality is provided, giving the supplier assurance that his contribution will not be identified outside the statistical office and that only the statistical aggregates of which it is a part will be made public. The government statistician is endowed with the power to enforce reporting on the part of the persons or corporate bodies to which he addresses his questionnaires; the obverse of this power is the obligation to keep individual returns secret (Dobrovits 1947). In the large number of government surveys for which reporting is not mandatory, the degree of voluntary response may be proportional to the public confidence in provisions for maintaining secrecy.

On the other hand, the aggregate results of every survey ought to be given the widest possible publicity. One of the difficulties of government publication is that the government does not have complete access to the distribution channels of the private book trade; sometimes a solution is possible through private publication, as was done for the monographs on the 1950 census of the United States and as is done in the Netherlands and Germany. The principle of equal access of the public to statistics is important; this is safeguarded by preannounced release times, at which statistics are simultaneously made available to all who are interested. In many countries there is much diffusion of government statistical results through nongovernmental intermediate sources, including trade yearbooks and scientific journals; it is customary to allow republishing without specific permission.

A serious problem arises from the desire of government to keep certain statistical results secret. This was a regrettable necessity in the United States and Canada during World War II in respect, for instance, to detailed foreign trade figures, because the information would have been used by the Axis powers in their submarine campaign against Allied shipping. Aside from such exceptional cases, it is fair to say that there are no instances in which the public as a whole benefits from concealment of statistical reports that provide accurate data, although governments and particular departments within them may indeed benefit at the expense of the public. The discussion of the publication of government statistics merges at this point with the wider question of the free flow of information in the society as a whole.

NATHAN KEYFITZ

[*See also* ELECTIONS, *article on* ELECTORAL SYSTEMS.]

BIBLIOGRAPHY

BAINES, ATHELSTANE 1918 The History and Development of Statistics in Great Britain and Ireland. Pages 365–389 in John Koren (editor), *The History of Statistics*. New York: Macmillan.

BOWMAN, RAYMOND T. 1964 The American Statistical Association and Federal Statistics. *Journal of the American Statistical Association* 59:1–17.

COATS, ROBERT H. 1925 The Classification Problem in Statistics. *International Labor Review* 11:509–525.

CUMMINGS, JOHN 1918 Statistical Work of the Federal Government of the United States. Pages 573–689 in John Koren (editor), *The History of Statistics*. New York: Macmillan.

Demographic Yearbook. → Issued by the United Nations since 1948.

DOBROVITS, ALEXANDRE 1947 Sur le secret en statistique. Volume 3, pages 769–778 in International Statistical Conference, Washington, D.C., *Proceedings*. Calcutta: Eka.

FAURE, FERNAND 1918 The Development and Progress of Statistics in France. Pages 217–329 in John Koren (editor), *The History of Statistics*. New York: Macmillan.

GODFREY, ERNEST H. 1918 The History and Development of Statistics in Canada. Pages 179–198 in John Koren (editor), *The History of Statistics*. New York: Macmillan.

GREENWOOD, MAJOR et al. 1932 Discussion on the Quantity and Quality of Official Statistical Publications. *Journal of the Royal Statistical Society* 95:279–302.

HAUSER, PHILIP M. 1963 Statistics and Society. *Journal of the American Statistical Association* 58:1–12.

HAUSER, PHILIP M.; and LEONARD, WILLIAM R. (editors) (1946) 1956 *Government Statistics for Business Use.* New York: Wiley.

HOLMES, OLIVER W. 1960 "Public Records"—Who Knows What They Are? *American Archivist* 23:3–26.

JULIN, ARMAND 1918 The History and Development of Statistics in Belgium. Pages 125–175 in John Koren (editor), *The History of Statistics*. New York: Macmillan.

KNIBBS, GEORGE H. 1918 The History and Development of the Statistical System of Australia. Pages 55–81 in John Koren (editor), *The History of Statistics*. New York: Macmillan.

KOREN, JOHN (editor) 1918 *The History of Statistics.* New York: Macmillan.

LEONARD, WILLIAM R. 1958 An Outlook Report. *Journal of the American Statistical Association* 53:1–10.

LI, CHOH-MING 1962 *The Statistical System of Communist China.* Berkeley: Univ. of California Press.

LINDER, FORREST E. 1959 World Demographic Data. Pages 321–360 in Philip M. Hauser and Otis Dudley Duncan (editors), *The Study of Population: An Inventory and Appraisal.* Univ. of Chicago Press.

MEITZEN, AUGUST (1886) 1891 *History, Theory, and Technique of Statistics.* Philadelphia: American Academy of Political and Social Science. → First published in German.

MILLS, FREDERICK C.; and LONG, CLARENCE D.   1949   *The Statistical Agencies of the Federal Government.* Washington: Government Printing Office.

MORGENSTERN, OSKAR   (1950) 1963   *On the Accuracy of Economic Observations.* 2d ed. Princeton Univ. Press.

NIXON, JAMES W.   1960   *A History of the International Statistical Institute: 1885–1960.* The Hague: International Statistical Institute.

NORTH, S. N. D.   1918   Seventy-five Years of Progress in Statistics: The Outlook for the Future. Pages 15–49 in John Koren (editor), *The History of Statistics.* New York: Macmillan.

STERN, JOHANNA   1958   [Review of] Th. L. Galland's *Statistik der Beschaeftigten und Arbeitslosen. Journal of the American Statistical Association* 53:1040–1043.

STUART, C. A. V.   1918   The History and Development of Statistics in the Netherlands. Pages 429–444 in John Koren (editor), *The History of Statistics.* New York: Macmillan.

UNITED NATIONS, STATISTICAL OFFICE   1954   *Handbook of Statistical Organization.* Studies in Methods, Series F, No. 6. New York: United Nations.

U.S. BUREAU OF THE BUDGET, OFFICE OF STATISTICAL STANDARDS   (1947) 1963   *Statistical Services of the United States Government.* Rev. ed. Washington: Government Printing Office.

WESTERGAARD, HARALD L.   1932   *Contributions to the History of Statistics.* London: King.

WURZBURGER, EUGENE   1918   The History and Development of Official Statistics in the German Empire. Pages 333–362 in John Koren (editor), *The History of Statistics.* New York: Macmillan.

GRAEBNER, FRITZ

Fritz Graebner (1877–1934), German ethnologist and one of the principal exponents of the culture-historical approach to ethnology, was born in Berlin. The noted botanist Paul Graebner was his brother. Like many German ethnologists at the turn of the century, Graebner started out in another field. He obtained his PH.D. in Berlin in 1901 as a historian, with a dissertation on a topic in medieval history. But as early as 1899, he became a research assistant on the staff of the Royal Museum of Ethnology in Berlin, which was directed by Adolf Bastian. Graebner was assigned to classify the museum's rich holdings of South Seas material in Felix von Luschan's Africa and South Seas department.

Here he worked in close contact with Bernhard Ankermann, the Africanist, and together they developed the method of the Kulturkreis. They collaborated on two lectures that were delivered on November 19, 1904, to the Berlin Gesellschaft für Anthropologie, Ethnologie, und Urgeschichte; these were published in 1905 in the *Zeitschrift für Ethnologie.* The lectures attempted to interpret Oceanian history on the basis of a study of artifacts and an extensive knowledge of the literature, in terms of the geographical diffusion of clusters of cultural traits. It is of course true that Leo Frobenius had already used a similar approach to Africa in his *Ursprung der afrikanischen Kulturen* (1898), but Ankermann's work and Graebner's research on Kulturkreise in Oceania were considerably more thorough and precise.

Graebner plotted the diffusion of individual culture traits cartographically throughout the South Seas; he recognized the linkages that seemed to occur; and he arranged complexes or clusters of traits into Kulturkreise. He then proposed a chronological sequence for the diffusion of the Kreise: the Tasmanian culture, the Old Australian culture, the western Papuan or totem culture, the eastern Papuan or two-class culture, the Melanesian or bow culture, the Polynesian culture, and a few more recent "cultural movements."

In his article "Die melanesische Bogenkultur und ihre Verwandten" (1909*a*), he tried for the first time to establish in a larger region the Kulturkreise he had worked out locally for parts of the Pacific. This marked the beginning of the trend in European ethnology that was called *Kulturkreislehre.* After World War I, Wilhelm Schmidt of Vienna, who had initially had strong disagreements with Graebner (see, for example, 1909*c*), attempted a world-wide application of Graebner's system. Graebner, in his contribution to the volume on anthropology in Hinneberg's anthology, *Die Kultur der Gegenwart* (1923), himself transferred some of his South Seas Kulturkreise to other regions of the globe, although he did so with much greater moderation than did either Father Schmidt or Father Wilhelm Koppers.

In 1906 Graebner left the Berlin Museum, accepting the invitation of Willi Foy, director of the Rautenstrauch-Joest Museum in Cologne, who became one of his most active supporters. In Cologne he published his *Methode der Ethnologie* (1911), a work that explicitly acknowledged a debt to Ernst Bernheim's *Lehrbuch der historischen Methode und der Geschichtsphilosophie* (1889), and thus reestablished his connection with the discipline of history. By now he had at his command great quantities of ethnological material, and he and Foy considered ethnology as essential to a universal history.

The *Methode der Ethnologie* became the cornerstone for the culture-historical school of ethnology. In this work Graebner's principal concern was to work out methodological guidelines for research into culture affinities, although this work also con-

tained an exemplary chapter on critical study of
the original sources and a discussion of the ways
of interpreting ethnological sources. The "criteria
of cultural links" (1911, pp. 104–125) are still
valid. If there are *numerous* homologous elements
of culture in a region of the globe that are *not*
functionally interdependent (criterion of quantity),
and if their *similarity of form* is extensive without
being due to identity of purpose and identity of
material (criterion of form), it must be presumed
that they did not originate independently of one
another but came from the same original source or
are related by borrowing. If these elements of culture belong to many or all cultural spheres (economy, society, religion, art, etc.), they constitute a
Kulturkreis or a "culture complex." If parts of this
complex are widely separated geographically, cultural relationship is more likely if certain elements
that are, as it were, cultural bridges can be located
between them (criterion of continuity). Moreover,
if it can be shown that the separated complexes
are most alike where their areas of distribution are
nearest (criterion of degree of relatedness), cultural relationship and nonindependent origin can
be inferred from this situation as well. Zones of
"leveling" and "draining" of a Kulturkreis, discontinuity of the area, penetration by groups from
another culture complex, and so forth, produce a
sequence of Kulturkreise that subsequently may be
regarded as culture layers.

Graebner never did any field work. When he did
go to Australia at the invitation of the Australian
government, the outbreak of World War I prevented
him from doing research. He was interned and not
released until 1919. Nevertheless he made use of
his time there to do much studying, and he produced a comparison of the myths of Indo-European,
Mongolian, Polynesian, and Hamito–Semitic peoples, "Thor und Maui" (1919/1920), and a study
of Old and New World calendars (1920/1921).
These two works were important preliminary
studies for *Das Weltbild der Primitiven* (1924).
Here Graebner advanced for the first time a broad
theory of history, visualizing an archaic "advanced
culture" that was diffused throughout the Old
World and the New World. Many of his arguments
in support of links between the advanced cultures
of the Old World and the New are still valid. His
theory was wholly independent of the so-called
British school of diffusionism led by Grafton Elliott
Smith and W. J. Perry.

In 1925 Graebner succeeded Foy as director of
the Cologne museum. The following year he was
appointed to an honorary professorship at the Uni-

versity of Cologne. A prolonged illness forced him
to resign in 1928; he returned to Berlin, where he
died in 1934.

                                    HERMANN BAUMANN

[*For the historical context of Graebner's work, see* DIF-
FUSION; HISTORY, *article on* CULTURE HISTORY; *and
the biographies of* BASTIAN *and* FROBENIUS. *For discussion of the subsequent development of Graebner's
ideas, see the biographies of* KOPPERS *and* SCHMIDT.]

WORKS BY GRAEBNER

1905   Kulturkreise und Kulturschichten in Ozeanien. *Zeit-
       schrift für Ethnologie* 37:28–53.
1906   Wanderung und Entwicklung sozialer Systeme in
       Australien. *Globus* 90:181–186, 207–210, 220–224,
       237–241.
1907   STEPHAN, EMIL; and GRAEBNER, FRITZ. *Neu-Meck-
       lenburg (Bismarck-Archipel).* Berlin: Reimer.
1908   Die sozialen Systeme in der Südsee. *Zeitschrift für
       Sozialwissenschaft* 11:663–681, 748–755.
1909a Die melanesische Bogenkultur und ihre Verwand-
       ten. *Anthropos* 4:726–780.
1909b Völkerkunde der Santa-Cruz-Inseln. *Ethnologica* 1:
       71–84.
1909c Zur australischen Religionsgeschichte. *Globus* 96:
       341–344, 362–366, 373–378.
1910   Handel bei Naturvölkern. Volume 1, pages 149–218
       in Karl Andree, *Geographie des Welthandels: Eine
       wirtschaftsgeographische Schilderung der Erde.* 2d ed.
       Vienna: Seidel.
1911   *Methode der Ethnologie.* Heidelberg: Winter.
1913   Amerika und die Südseekulturen. *Ethnologica* 2:
       43–66.
1915/1916 Totemismus als kulturgeschichtliches Problem.
       Anthropos 10/11:248–256.
1919/1920 Thor und Maui. *Anthropos* 14/15:1099–1119.
1920/1921 Alt- und neuweltliche Kalender. *Zeitschrift
       für Ethnologie* 52/53:6–37.
1923   Ethnologie. Pages 435–587 in *Die Kultur der Gegen-
       wart: Ihre Entwicklung und ihre Ziele.* Edited by Paul
       Hinneberg. Part 3, section 5: Anthropologie, by Gus-
       tav Schwalbe. Leipzig: Teubner.
1924   *Das Weltbild der Primitiven.* Munich: Reinhard.

SUPPLEMENTARY BIBLIOGRAPHY

BERNHEIM, ERNST (1889) 1960 *Lehrbuch der histori-
       schen Methode und der Geschichtsphilosophie.* 2 vols.
       Burt Franklin Bibliographical and Reference Series,
       Vol. 21. New York: Franklin.

GRANET, MARCEL

Marcel Granet (1884–1940), pre-eminent French
sociological Sinologist, was born at Luc-en-Diois
and died at Sceaux. He was admitted to the École
Normale Supérieure in 1904 and received the
agrégation d'histoire in 1907. He was named *direc-
teur d'études* at the École Pratique des Hautes
Études in 1913 and *chargé de cours* at the Sorbonne
in 1920, the same year that he received his *doctorat*

ès lettres. In 1926 he became the first director of the Institut des Hautes Études Chinoises of the Sorbonne as well as professor at the École des Langues Orientales of Paris. He received the Croix de Guerre for his services in World War I.

It was his teacher Édouard Chavannes who suggested to Granet that his interest in feudalism might well lead to the study of Sinology. Another teacher of Granet's was Émile Durkheim. The historian Marc Bloch was a friend and fellow student of Granet's at the École Normale, as was also Marcel Mauss, the nephew of Durkheim. Granet married Marie Terrien in 1919. While Granet was studying in China, from 1911 to 1913, the Ch'ing dynasty was replaced by the Republic of China. He visited China once more, after World War I, as a member of a mission.

Granet was a special sort of pioneer in the social sciences—he became a Sinologist in pursuit of more general interests in social phenomena. After an initial thorough grounding in the discipline of history, he was exposed to Durkheim's ideas, and these were decisive in developing his more general sociological interests. Granet was also a pioneer figure in stimulating the interest of non-Sinological social scientists in the Far East—most directly in Chinese society, but also, as a consequence of new attention to comparative studies, in Japanese society.

As a Sinologist, Granet freed himself from the dependence on secondary Chinese materials that had hampered earlier social scientists who studied China. He made it clear that difficult language barriers are no excuse for inferior standards of expertise. Moreover, unlike most orthodox Sinologists of his day, he found "inauthentic" texts no less valuable than authentic ones as evidence of social life. Rather than concentrating largely on the question of the "authenticity" of documents, Granet felt social scientists would do well to examine these documents critically in order to distinguish between ideal and actual patterns in Chinese society.

Granet addressed his efforts at broad interpretations of Chinese life, cutting across historical epochs. Mainly, however, he concentrated on feudal China and the transition to imperial China. As was pointed out by Émile Benoît-Smullyan, in a review that introduced Granet's work to many American sociologists (1936), Granet found Durkheim's "sociologistic epistemology" especially relevant to his work, leading him to important empirical elaborations of Durkheim's analysis. Thus, Granet showed the fundamental differences between Chinese and modern European modes of thought and suggested that those differences stemmed from far-reaching differences in social structure.

For scholars with a general interest in the social sciences, as well as for many scholars who are not Sinologists in the strict sense, Granet's most important contributions are to be found in his two volumes *Chinese Civilization* (1929*a*) and *La pensée chinoise* (1934). Both volumes have excellent introductions by Henri Berr, with carefully chosen titles: "L'originalité de la Chine" and "Mentalité chinoise et psychologie comparée."

Granet's subtitle of *Chinese Civilization* conveys an important distinction: "La vie publique et la vie privée" (the English translation dropped the subtitle). In this book he subdivided his treatment into political history and Chinese society, and these parts in turn contain discussions of traditional history (through the beginning of the imperial era in Han times), the chief data of ancient history, the people of the countryside, the foundation of the chieftainships, the seignioral town, and society at the beginning of the imperial era. Granet used the ancient texts, the legends, dances, and feasts, and what archeological evidence he could find in an attempt to reconstruct the preimperial background and demonstrate its relevance for an understanding of imperial China. Imperial Chinese society represents one of the most elaborate and sophisticated developments in the varied history of mankind: it was perhaps the only society with a large-scale membership, spread over a vast area, which was nevertheless sufficiently stable in its main outlines to endure for some two thousand years. Granet used the available materials to make a careful attempt to reconstruct both the life of the peasants—the vast majority of the people—and the public roles and the domestic lives of the nobles.

The most complex, powerful, and difficult of Granet's contributions is *La pensée chinoise*, and it is this work which still constitutes one of the most important attempts to apply empirically the leads furnished by Durkheim in *Elementary Forms of the Religious Life.* Granet explicitly rejected any interpretation of Chinese thought as mystical or prelogical—any such interpretation, he believed, was "lacking in the humanistic spirit"—and he rested his interpretations of Chinese thought squarely on Durkheim's view that modes of thought are themselves social manifestations and reflect other social facts. Most notably, modes of thought reflect those forms of social organization whose very persistence, Granet held, in some sense proves their value (1934, pp. 27–29). He began his analysis of Chinese thought with an examination of language and writing, and in so doing, he was at once very French and precociously modern. His chapters on the Chinese conceptions of time and space, *yang* and *yin*, numbers, and the Tao are classics, although they are controversial.

Even at the time Granet published his interpretation of China, some scholars felt that his treatment of China as a special instance of social universals led him to overlook or misunderstand many features of Chinese society, and materials discovered since Granet's time necessitate other qualifications of his interpretation. Yet there is general admiration among scholars for the stimulus Granet's work gave to Sinology in particular and to social science more generally. His intellectual descendants do him the honor of challenging his positions within the whole field he opened for them.

MARION J. LEVY, JR.

[For the historical context of Granet's work, see the biographies of BLOCH; DURKHEIM; MAUSS. Also related is the article CHINESE SOCIETY.]

WORKS BY GRANET

(1912) 1953   Coutumes matrimoniales de la Chine antique. Pages 63–94 in Marcel Granet, *Études sociologiques sur la Chine*. Paris: Presses Universitaires de France.

(1912–1933) 1953   *Études sociologiques sur la Chine*. Paris: Presses Universitaires de France.

(1919) 1932   *Festivals and Songs of Ancient China*. London: Routledge. → First published as *Fêtes et chansons anciennes de la Chine*.

(1920a) 1953   La polygynie sororale et le sororat dans la Chine féodale: Étude sur les formes anciennes de la polygamie chinoise. Pages 1–62 in Marcel Granet, *Études sociologiques sur la Chine*. Paris: Presses Universitaires de France.

(1920b) 1953   Quelques particularités de la langue et de la pensée chinoises. Pages 95–155 in Marcel Granet, *Études sociologiques sur la Chine*. Paris: Presses Universitaires de France.

(1921) 1953   La vie et la mort: Croyances et doctrines de l'antiquité chinoise. Pages 203–220 in Marcel Granet, *Études sociologiques sur la Chine*. Paris: Presses Universitaires de France.

(1922a) 1953   Le dépôt de l'enfant sur le sol: Rites anciens et ordalies mythiques. Pages 157–202 in Marcel Granet, *Études sociologiques sur la Chine*. Paris: Presses Universitaires de France.

(1922b) 1953   Le langage de la douleur d'après le rituel funéraire de la Chine classique. Pages 221–242 in Marcel Granet, *Études sociologiques sur la Chine*. Paris: Presses Universitaires de France.

(1922c) 1951   *La religion des Chinois*. 2d ed. Paris: Presses Universitaires de France.

(1925) 1953   Remarques sur le taoïsme ancien. Pages 243–249 in Marcel Granet, *Études sociologiques sur la Chine*. Paris: Presses Universitaires de France.

(1926) 1959   *Danses et légendes de la Chine ancienne*. New ed., 2 vols. Paris: Presses Universitaires de France.

1928   L'expression de la pensée en chinois. *Journal de psychologie normale et pathologique* 25:617–656.

(1929a) 1957   *Chinese Civilization*. London: Routledge. → First published in French.

(1929b) 1953   L'esprit de la religion chinoise. Pages 251–260 in Marcel Granet, *Études sociologiques sur la Chine*. Paris: Presses Universitaires de France.

(1933) 1953   La droite et la gauche en Chine. Pages 261–278 in Marcel Granet, *Études sociologiques sur la Chine*. Paris: Presses Universitaires de France.

(1934) 1950   *La pensée chinoise*. Paris: Michel.

1939   *Catégories matrimoniales et relations de proximité dans la Chine ancienne*. Paris: Alcan.

1952   *La féodalité chinoise*. Instituttet for Sammenlignende Kulturforskning, Oslo, Serie A: Forelesninger, 22. Oslo: Aschehoug.

SUPPLEMENTARY BIBLIOGRAPHY

BENOîT-SMULLYAN, ÉMILE 1936   [A Book Review of] *La pensée chinoise*, by Marcel Granet. *American Sociological Review* 1:487–492.

GRAPHIC PRESENTATION

Graphic presentation represents a highly developed body of techniques for elucidating, interpreting, and analyzing numerical facts by means of points, lines, areas, and other geometric forms and symbols. Graphic techniques are especially valuable in presenting quantitative data in a simple, clear, and effective manner, as well as facilitating comparisons of values, trends, and relationships. They have the additional advantages of succinctness and popular appeal; the comprehensive pictures they provide can bring out hidden facts and relationships and contribute to a more balanced understanding of a problem.

The choice of a particular graphic technique to present a given set of data is a difficult one, and no hard and fast rules can be made to cover all circumstances. There are, however, certain general goals that should always be kept in mind. These include completeness, clarity, and honesty; but there is often conflict between the goals. For instance, completeness demands that all data points be included in a chart, but often this can be done only at some sacrifice of clarity. Such problems can be mitigated by the practice (highly desirable on other grounds as well) of indicating the source of the data from which the chart was constructed so that the reader himself can investigate further. Another problem occurs when it is necessary to break an axis in order to fit all the data in a reasonable space; clarity is then served, but honesty demands that attention be strongly called to the break.

A choice among graphic techniques also depends upon the proposed use to which the chart will be put. As Schmid (1954) has pointed out, graphs that are satisfactory in memoranda for private circulation may be inappropriate for a published book or paper.

In classifying charts and graphs, criteria of purpose, of circumstances of use, of type of comparison, and of form have been used. On the basis of form, charts and graphs may be classified as (1) rectilinear coordinate graphs; (2) semilogarithmic charts; (3) bar and column charts; (4) frequency graphs and related charts; (5) maps; (6) miscellaneous charts, including pie diagrams, scattergrams, fan charts, ranking charts, etc.; (7) pictorial charts; and (8) three-dimensional projection charts.

In graphic presentation, three different basic geometrical forms can be utilized for purposes of comparing magnitudes of coordinate items: (1) linear or one-dimensional, (2) areal or two-dimensional, and (3) cubic or three-dimensional. The simplest and most exact comparisons are those made on a linear basis; comparison of relative sizes of areas is more difficult and of volumes most difficult. Accordingly, where possible, the use of areal and cubic forms should be avoided in graphic presentation.

Rectilinear coordinate graphs.   Perhaps the best known form of graphic presentation, and certainly one of the most frequently used, is the simple arithmetic line chart, one of several types of the *rectilinear* (or *Cartesian*) coordinate graph.

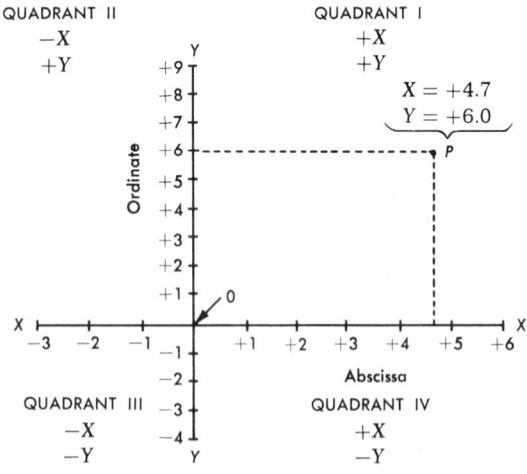

Figure 1 — Basic structural features of a rectangular coordinate graph

The basic form of this type of graph is derived by plotting one or more series of figures on a coordinate surface in which the successive plotting points are joined together in the form of a continuous line, customarily referred to as a "curve." A curve on a graph of this kind is not necessarily smooth and regular but instead may be straight and angular. Figure 1 indicates the basic structural characteristics of a rectilinear coordinate system.

Figure 2 portrays the characteristic features and basic standards of the rectilinear coordinate graph. Many of the essential elements and specifications of the rectilinear coordinate graph are also applicable to other graphic forms.

Semilogarithmic charts.   The semilogarithmic chart is often superior to the arithmetic chart (as used in Figure 1), for the former can show relative changes clearly; hence it is sometimes referred to as a ratio chart. Sometimes the semilogarithmic chart has the merit of representing as nearly straight lines functions that otherwise would be appreciably curved.

The essential feature of the semilogarithmic chart is that one scale is logarithmic and the other arithmetic, so that the chart effectively is a convenient device for plotting log y against x, or log x against y. There is no zero line on the logarithmic scale, since the logarithm of zero is minus infinity. The logarithmic scale consists of one or more sets of rulings calibrated in terms of logarithmic values; each complete set of rulings is referred to as a "deck," "cycle," "bank," or "tier." The rulings for each deck are the same, but the scale values change from one to the other. For example, if one deck runs from 1 to 10, the adjacent deck above will vary from 10 to 100, the third from 100 to 1,000, and so forth. On the other hand, the adjacent deck below the one from 1 to 10 would vary from 0.1 to 1.0. The logarithmic scale can thus be extended upward or downward indefinitely.

In a semilogarithmic chart, relative rate-of-change comparisons can be made readily between different parts of a single series or between two or more series. The relative rate of change of y with respect to x is the slope of y as a function of x, divided by x; equivalently it is the slope of log y except for a constant depending on the logarithmic base. The slope of the logarithmic scale variable is the relative rate of change of the variable. If the slope is steep, the relative rate of change is great. It makes no difference on what part of a semilogarithmic chart a curve is located; the same slope

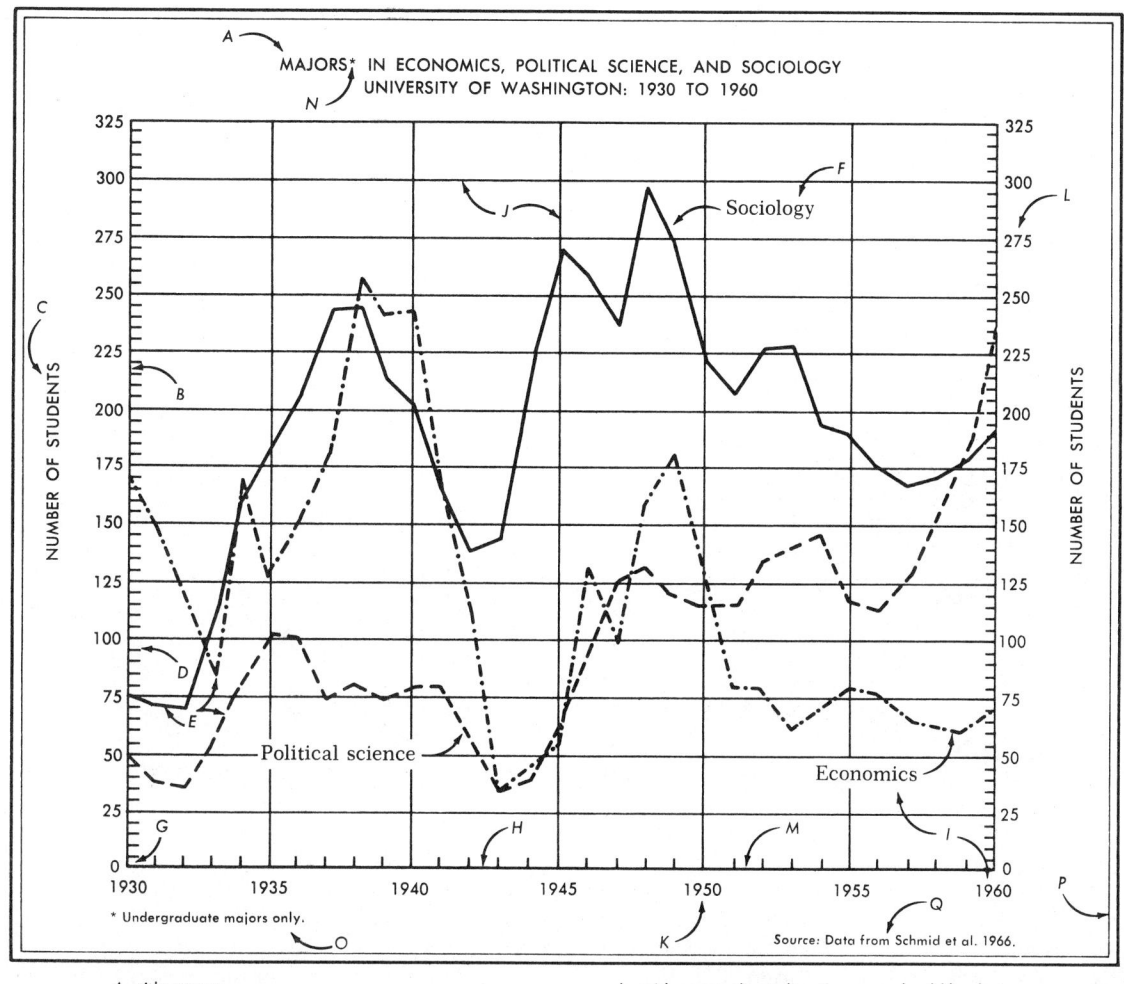

Figure 2 — Essential characteristics and specifications of a rectilinear coordinate graph

A—title at top
B—axis of ordinates, or Y axis
C—scale legend for Y axis
D—scale points
E—curves differentiated (solid, dashed, and dot-dashed)
F—contiguous legends for curves
G—origin
H—zero lines heavier than other coordinate lines
I—lettering arranged horizontally whenever possible

J—grid, or coordinate lines (no more should be shown than are necessary)
K—scale figures for X axis
L—scale figures for Y axis
M—axis of abscissae, or X axis
N—reference symbol
O—explanatory note
P—border (optional)
Q—source

means the same relative rate of change. This is particularly convenient if the two series being compared have very different ranges of values.

This situation is illustrated in Figure 3, where the same data have been plotted on both arithmetic and semilogarithmic grids, placed in juxtaposition. On the arithmetic grid, the relative rate of growth of the city in comparison to that of the entire state cannot be easily determined; by con-

trast, the curves on the semilogarithmic chart portray relative rate of growth clearly and correctly. Note, however, that this clarity is achieved only at the expense of some distortion; careful labeling is imperative to prevent the reader from mistakenly concluding that the absolute growth of Dallas is greater than that of the state as a whole.

Other special graph papers exist, such as double logarithmic, normal, and hyperbolic.

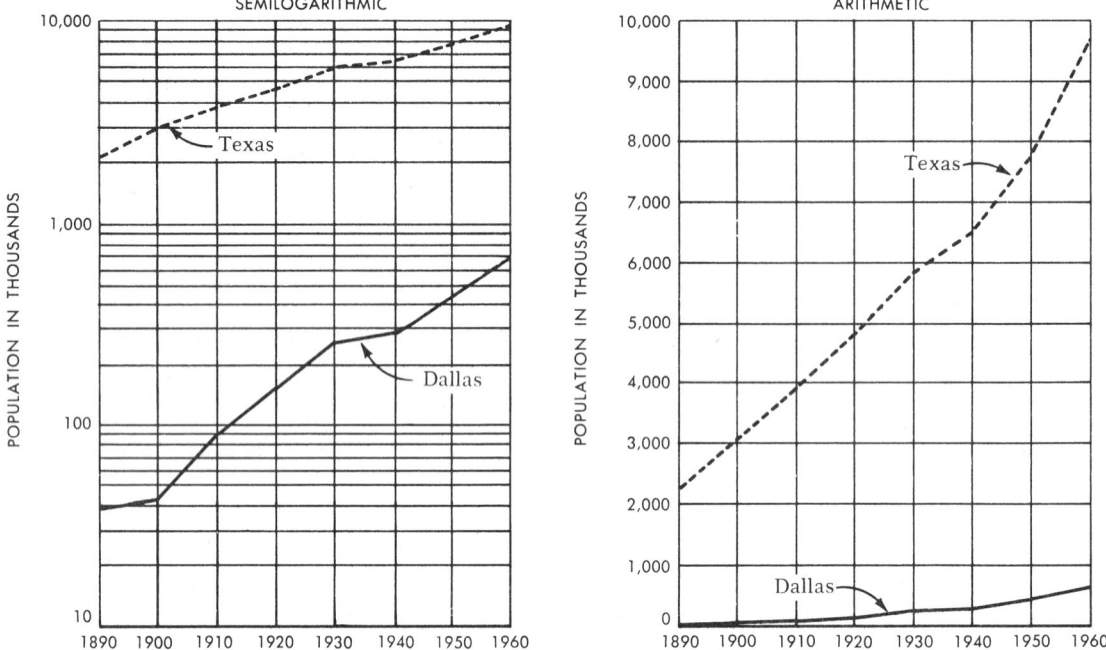

Figure 3 — Comparison* of rectangular coordinate and semilogarithmic graphs

* Comparison clearly demonstrates the superiority of the semilogarithmic graph in portraying relative rates of change.

Source: Data from U.S. Bureau of the Census 1963, pp. 45-19, 45-22.

Bar and column charts. Bar and column charts are simple, flexible, and effective techniques for comparing the size of coordinate values or of parts of a total. The basis of comparison is linear or one-dimensional; the length of each bar or column is proportional to the value portrayed. Bar and column charts are very much alike; they differ mainly in that the bars are arranged horizontally in a bar chart and the columns are arranged vertically in a column chart. In addition, the bar chart is seldom used for depicting time series, whereas the column chart is often used for that purpose.

There are several different kinds of bar and column charts. Four of them are illustrated in Figure 4.

Frequency graphs and related charts. The most common graphic forms for portraying simple frequency distributions are the frequency polygon, the histogram, and the smoothed frequency curve. Frequency graphs are usually drawn on rectilinear coordinates, with the Y axis representing frequencies and the X axis representing the class intervals. The Y axis always begins with zero, and under no circumstances is it broken. The horizontal scale does not have to begin with zero unless, of course, the lower limit of the first class interval

is zero. In laying out a frequency polygon the appropriate frequency of each class customarily is located at the midpoint of the interval, and the plotting points are then connected by straight lines. The typical histogram is constructed by erecting vertical lines at the limits of the class intervals and forming a series of contiguous rectangles or columns. The area of each rectangle represents the respective class frequencies. (If the class intervals are unequal, special care must be taken.) Smoothed frequency curves may be constructed by either mathematical or graphic techniques. The main purpose of smoothing a frequency graph is to remove accidental irregularities resulting mainly from sampling errors; the data from which the smoothed curve was obtained should always be presented as should some indication of the method of smoothing employed.

For some purposes, the cumulative-frequency curve, or ogive, is more useful than the simple frequency graph. In a cumulative-frequency distribution, the frequencies of the successive class intervals are accumulated, beginning at one end of the distribution. If the cumulation process is from the lesser to the greater, it is referred to as a "less than" type of distribution; if from the greater to the lesser, it is known as a "more than" type of distribution. In constructing an ogive, the cumulative frequencies are represented by the vertical axis and the class intervals by the horizontal axis. The cumulated frequencies are plotted either at the lower or upper end of the respective class intervals, depending on whether the cumulation is of the "less than" or "more than" type. A common configuration of the cumulative-frequency curve is that of an elongated S.

Concentration curves. A special kind of graph, related to cumulative frequency graphs, is known as a concentration curve or a Lorenz curve. Such a graph is used to portray the nature of nonuniformity in the distributions of inherently positive quantities like wealth, income, amount of retail sales, etc. The graph shows the proportions of total wealth (to be definite) held by various proportions of the relevant population; one reads from the graph that the least wealthy 10 per cent of the population holds, say, 1 per cent of total wealth, that the most wealthy 5 per cent of the population holds, say, 30 per cent of total wealth, etc. Thus the graph is a curve running through points given

parametrically by cumulative relative frequencies and cumulative relative totals; it is usually presented in square form, with both axes taking values from 0 to 1 (for proportions) or 0 to 100 (for per cents). If wealth, or whatever, is uniformly (equally) distributed in the population, the concentration curve is a straight line, the diagonal of the square from (0,0) to (1,1). The more the concentration curve deviates from the straight line the greater is inequality.

Statistical maps. There are many varieties of maps used in portraying statistical data. They can be grouped under the following basic types: (1) crosshatched or shaded maps; (2) spot or point-symbol maps; (3) isoline maps; (4) maps with one or more types of graphs superimposed, such as the bar, column, line, flow, or pictorial forms (see Figure 7); and (5) a combination of two or more of the preceding types. [*For an overview of map making, see* CARTOGRAPHY.]

Crosshatched maps. The crosshatched or shaded map, characteristically, is used to portray rates and ratios that are based on clearly delineated areal units such as regions, nations, states, coun-

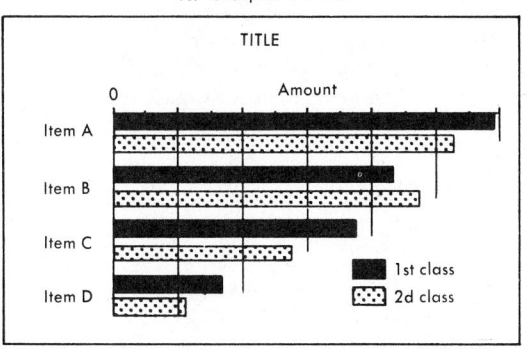

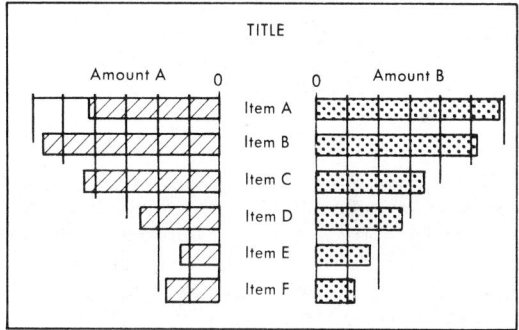

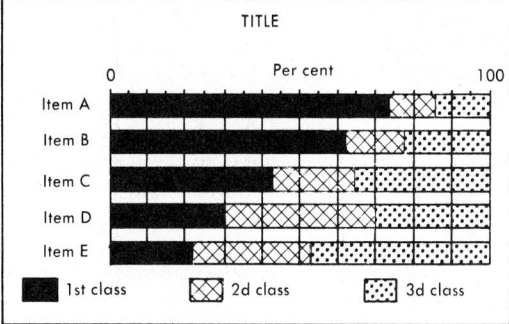

Figure 4 — Four types of bar charts

ties, or census tracts. Value ranges of rates and percentages are represented by a graded series of crosshatchings. Figure 5 is an illustration of a crosshatched map. Since this figure is for illustration only, the medians were computed by the simplest formula, with no attempt made to correct for the fact that most school dropouts occur at the end of a school year.

Spot maps.   In spot or point-symbol maps emphasis is placed on frequencies or absolute amounts rather than on rates or proportions as in the crosshatched map. Although there may be some overlapping, spot maps may be differentiated into five types on the basis of the symbols used. Symbols may stress (1) size, (2) number, (3) density, (4) shading, or (5) form. In the first type of map the size of each symbol is proportional to the frequency or magnitude of the phenomena represented. Symbols may be either two-dimensional or three-dimensional and are normally in the form of circles or spheres rather than rectangles, cubes, or irregular forms. In the second type of spot map the basic criterion is not size but number or frequency of spots or point symbols. The spots are uniform in size, each representing a specific value. The spots are designed and arranged to make them as readily countable as possible. The third type of map is also a multiple-spot variety; but instead of emphasizing countable frequencies, comparative density and distribution are emphasized. Figure 6 is an example of the third type of spot map, in which over-all density patterns are stressed. In the fourth type of spot map the criterion is shading. The size of the symbols is uniform, but the amount of shading is indicative of the magnitude or value represented. The form of the symbol in the fifth type of map represents certain qualities or attributes rather than quantities, as in the previous types. For example, if the dichotomy male–female is to be portrayed on a map, one type of symbol would represent male and another symbol would represent female.

Isoline maps.   There are two fundamental types of isoline (from the Greek *isos*, meaning equal) maps: the isometric map, in which the lines are drawn through points of equal value or intensity, and the isopleth map, in which the lines connect equal rates or ratios for specific areas. The isopleth map is particularly valuable in the social sciences.

Miscellaneous graphic forms.   Although not as basic or as widely used as the graphs and charts discussed in the preceding sections, there are certain other graphic forms that possess advantages for certain problems.

Pie charts.   The pie or sector chart is widely used to portray proportions of an aggregate or total. Given the several proportions of the total, a pie chart is made by dividing a circle into pieces, one for each separate proportion, by boundary radii. Each proportion corresponds to a single slice, or sector, thus formed; and the central angles (equivalently, the circumference arcs, or again the sector areas) are proportional to the magnitudes of the proportions. Frequently, shading or coloring is used to help distinguish the sectors, and of course proper labeling is essential. Although a pie chart can be very effective in simple situations, it becomes difficult to use if there are more than four or five sectors or if one wishes to compare corresponding proportions for several pie charts.

Trilinear charts.   The trilinear chart (or barymetric coordinate system) is used to portray simultaneously three nonnegative variables with a fixed sum. Usually they are percentages and the sum is 100. It is drawn in the form of an equilateral triangle, each side of which is calibrated in equal percentage divisions ranging from 0 to 100.

Scatter diagrams.   The scatter diagram (scattergram) and other types of correlation charts portray in graphic form the degree and type of relationship or covariation between two series of data. The scatter diagram shows a two-way or bivariate frequency distribution. Customarily, arithmetic scales are used in the construction of scatter diagrams, although semilogarithmic or double-logarithmic scales sometimes may be more appropriate.

Pictorial charts.   Pictorial graphs are used mainly because of their popular appeal, although they rarely convey more information than do more conventional graphic forms. In general, there are four basic types of charts in which pictorial symbols are used, distinguished by criteria of purpose and emphasis.

The four types of pictorial charts are (1) charts in which the size of the pictorial symbol is proportional to the values portrayed; (2) pictorial unit graphs, in which each symbol represents a definite and uniform value; (3) cartoon and sketch charts, in which the basic graphic form, such as a curve or bar, is portrayed as a picture; and (4) charts with pictorial embellishments ranging from a single pictorial filler to elaborate and detailed pictorial backgrounds.

Three-dimensional projection charts.   In recent years it has become common practice to portray various kinds of graphs and charts in axonometric, oblique, and perspective projection. Charts in three-dimensional form, with depth and other picturelike qualities, unquestionably possess definite popular appeal.

The design of charts and graphs in three-dimen-

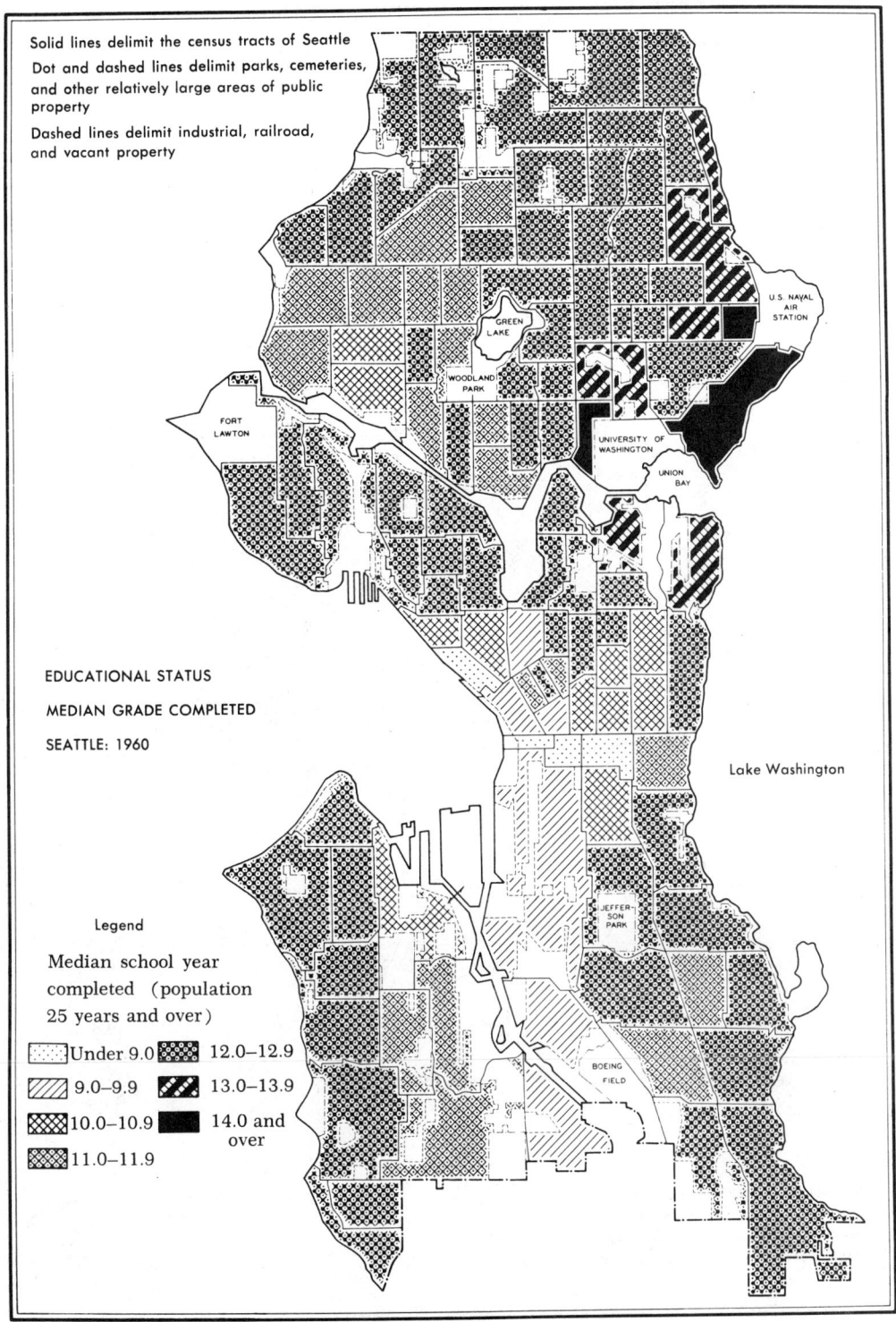

Solid lines delimit the census tracts of Seattle

Dot and dashed lines delimit parks, cemeteries, and other relatively large areas of public property

Dashed lines delimit industrial, railroad, and vacant property

U.S. NAVAL AIR STATION

GREEN LAKE

WOODLAND PARK

FORT LAWTON

UNIVERSITY OF WASHINGTON

UNION BAY

EDUCATIONAL STATUS

MEDIAN GRADE COMPLETED

SEATTLE: 1960

Lake Washington

Legend

Median school year completed (population 25 years and over)

Under 9.0	12.0–12.9
9.0–9.9	13.0–13.9
10.0–10.9	14.0 and over
11.0–11.9	

JEFFER-SON PARK

BOEING FIELD

*Figure 5 — Crosshatched map**

* Note hatching gradation from light to dark. Each type of crosshatching represents a value interval in a series of averages.

Source: Data from U.S. Bureau of the Census 1962, pp. 15–24.

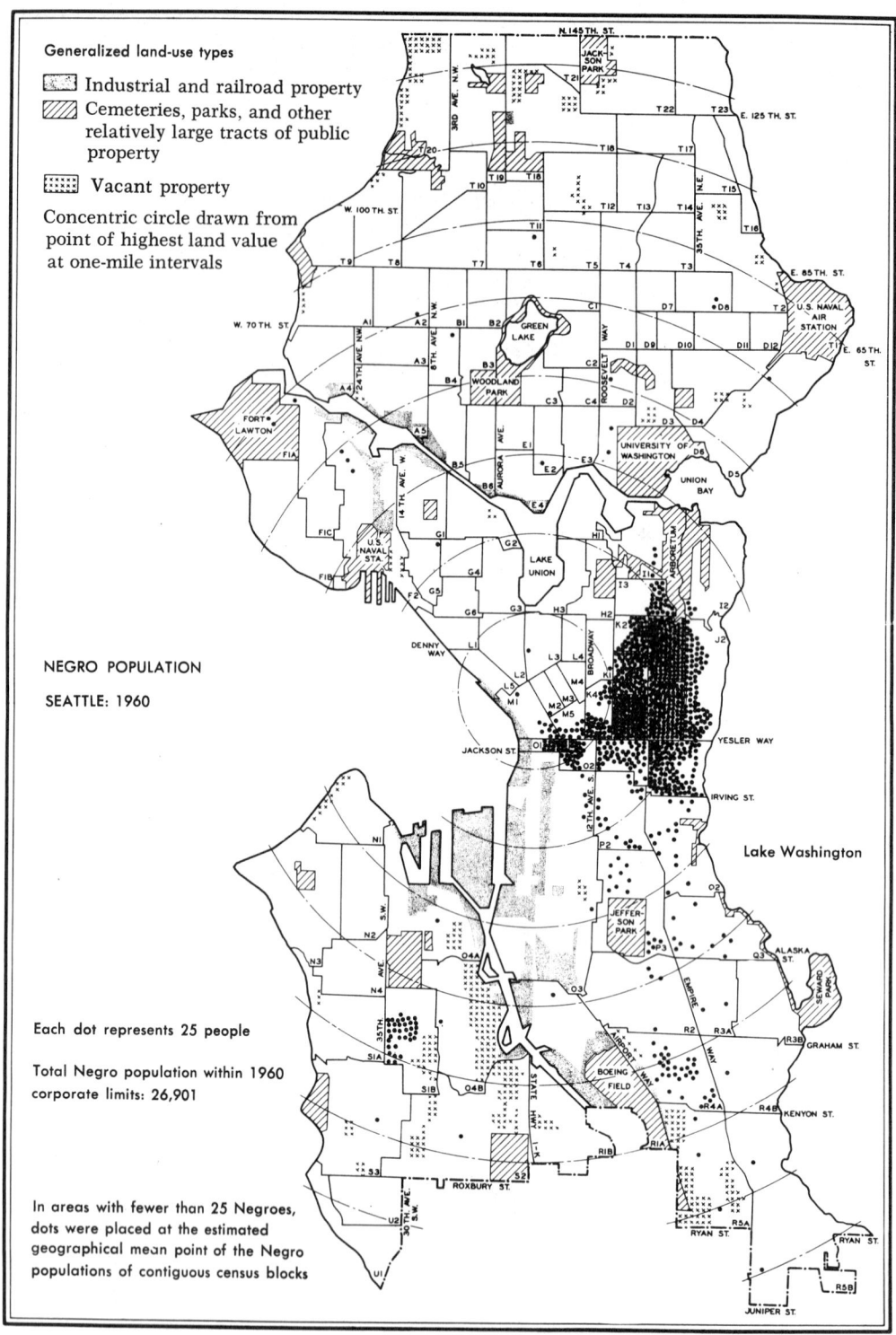

Figure 6 — Spot map*

*This type of spot map is designed to emphasize comparative density and basic distributional patterns. Note also census tracts, concentric circles, and generalized land-use features on base map.

Source: Schmid & McVey 1964, p. 9.

250

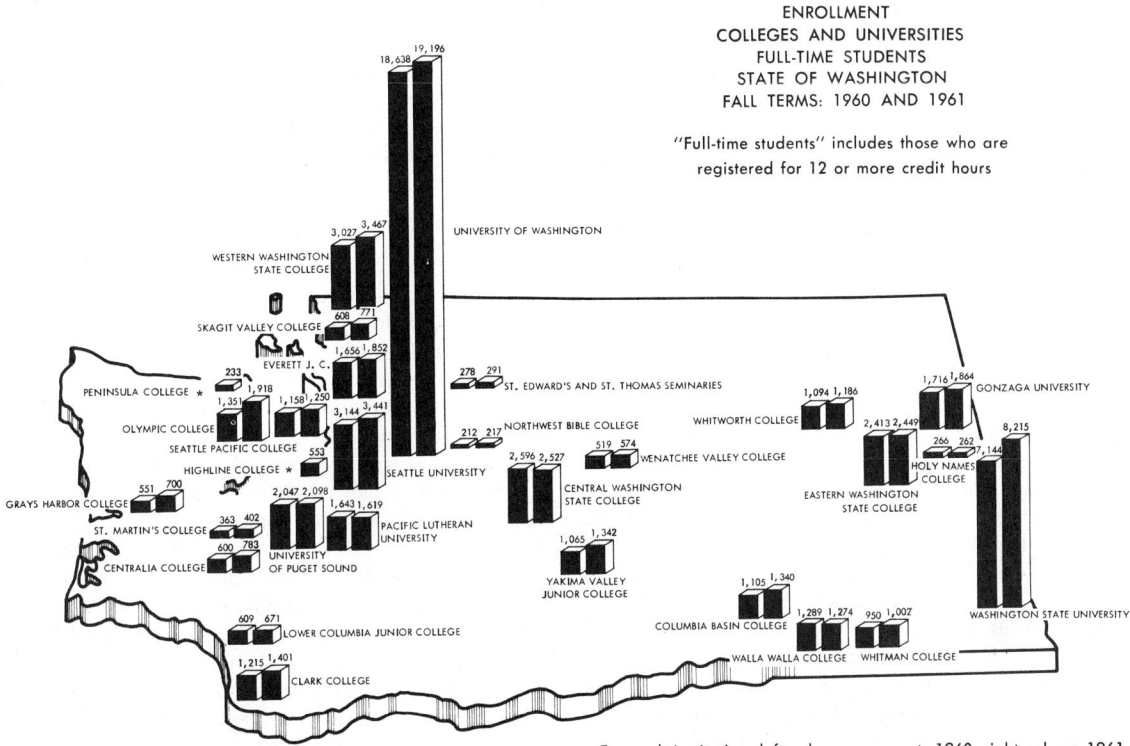

**ENROLLMENT
COLLEGES AND UNIVERSITIES
FULL-TIME STUDENTS
STATE OF WASHINGTON
FALL TERMS: 1960 AND 1961**

"Full-time students" includes those who are
registered for 12 or more credit hours

For each institution, left column represents 1960, right column 1961

* Organized after fall term, 1960.

Figure 7 — Chart in three-dimensional projection[a]

a. Note especially that columns are drawn in oblique projection.

Source: Schmid et al. 1962, p. 9.

sional form should be based on technically acceptable principles of axonometric, oblique, and perspective projection. Axonometric and oblique projections are the most satisfactory for three-dimensional graphs. Although perspective projection is perhaps the most realistic of the three, it possesses serious limitations as a technique in graphic presentation. Charts constructed in perspective projection are generally distorted; they do not portray exact distance, shape, or size. Figure 7 illustrates a map in three-dimensional form.

CALVIN F. SCHMID

[*See also* TABULAR PRESENTATION.]

BIBLIOGRAPHY

REFERENCES ON GRAPHIC PRESENTATION

BRINTON, WILLARD C. 1939 *Graphic Presentation.* New York: Brinton.

FUNKHOUSER, H. G. 1937 Historical Development of the Graphical Representation of Statistical Data. *Osiris* 3:269–404.

HUFF, DARREL; and GEIS, IRVING 1954 *How to Lie With Statistics.* New York: Norton. → Contains a discussion of graphical fallacies. Also published in paperback.

JENKS, G. F.; and BROWN, D. A. 1966 Three-dimensional Map Construction. *Science* 154:857–864.

MODLEY, RUDOLF; and LOWENSTEIN, DYNO 1952 *Pictographs and Graphs: How to Make and Use Them.* New York: Harper.

PÈPE, PAUL 1959 *Présentation des statistiques.* Paris: Dunod.

ROYSTON, ERICA 1956 Studies in the History of Probability and Statistics. III. A Note on the History of the Graphical Representation of Data. *Biometrika* 43:241–247.

SCHMID, CALVIN F. 1954 *Handbook of Graphic Presentation.* New York: Ronald.

SCHMID, CALVIN F. 1956 What Price Pictorial Charts? *Estadistica: Journal of the Inter-American Statistical Institute* 15:12–25.

SCHMID, CALVIN F.; and MacCANNELL, EARLE H. 1955 Basic Problems, Techniques, and Theory of Isopleth Mapping. *Journal of the American Statistical Association* 50:220–239.

SOURCES OF FIGURES AND DATA

SCHMID, CALVIN F.; and McVEY, WAYNE W. JR. 1964 *Growth and Distribution of Minority Races in Seattle, Washington.* Seattle Public Schools.

SCHMID, CALVIN F. et al. 1962 *Enrollment Statistics, Colleges and Universities: State of Washington, Fall Term, 1961.* Seattle: Washington State Census Board.

SCHMID, CALVIN F. et al.   1966   *Studies in Enrollment Trends and Patterns.* Part 1: Regular Academic Year: 1930 to 1964. Seattle: Univ. of Washington.

U.S. BUREAU OF THE CENSUS   1962   *U.S. Censuses of Population and Housing: 1960.* Census Tracts, Final Report PHC (1) 142: Seattle, Wash. Washington: Government Printing Office. → See especially pages 15–34, Table P-1, "General Characteristics of the Population, by Census Tracts: 1960."

U.S. BUREAU OF THE CENSUS   1963   *U.S. Census of Population: 1960.* Vol. 1, Part 45: Texas. Washington: Government Printing Office.

GRAS, N. S. B.

Norman Scott Brien Gras, pioneer business historian, was born in 1884 in Toronto of German and Irish parentage. His father was an unsuccessful general retailer and moved from place to place in search of a living. As a child, Gras had to work as a mill delivery boy and at other lowly jobs, hard beginnings which help to explain him as an adult. Endowed with extraordinary intellectual capacity, he was able to overcome economic difficulties and complete his undergraduate training at the University of Western Ontario. He went on to obtain his PH.D. in economics at Harvard University. His thesis was written under Edwin F. Gay, America's first economic historian, whom Gras himself considered his "intellectual father." From 1912 to 1917 Gras was an assistant professor at Clark College and in 1917/1918 an associate professor at Clark University. From there he went as a full professor to the University of Minnesota and then in 1927 to the Graduate School of Business Administration, Harvard University, where he remained as Isidor Strauss professor of business history until 1950, when he retired. From 1949 to his death in 1956, he was president of the Business History Foundation, Inc., under whose auspices the history of the Standard Oil Company (New Jersey) was being written.

Gras's career falls into two main periods. In the first he devoted himself chiefly to problems in English social and economic history, and he carried on most of his research in England. English scholars appreciated his work, and he was made a member of the Council of the English Economic History Society and eventually, in 1939, a vice-president.

The second period in Gras's career began with his appointment to the faculty of the Harvard Business School. In the 1920s and early 1930s, which constituted his most creative period, Gras had begun to focus on a new intellectual problem: he began to make business the subject of systematic historical research. Similar ideas were then being broached by leading professors at the Harvard Business School, and when the new field was established at that school, Gras's appointment was eminently suitable.

The result of his endeavors was "business history," a new concept to which Gras gave content and which he initially defined broadly. Because he was the first American teacher in this field, it was incumbent on him to collect source material. Since the Harvard Business School used the case method in its teaching, in 1939 Gras and his lifelong associate, Henrietta M. Larson, brought out a *Casebook in American Business History* for use in his classes. Even earlier he had begun to edit a series of company histories, the Harvard Studies in Business History. He wrote two of them himself, one on the First National Bank of Boston (1937) and another on the Harvard Co-operative Society (1942). In and outside of the school, Gras worked incessantly for the recognition of the new field. It is his merit that the use of business records has become common among economic historians.

Shortly after Gras's arrival at Harvard, the *Journal of Economic and Business History* was founded. It was the first American journal to deal with economic history and the first in the world to aim at combining economic history with the new business history. Gras became its highly efficient managing editor. Unfortunately, he pushed his special interest somewhat too hard and came into conflict with the powerful Edwin F. Gay, the editor of the journal. Gay withdrew in 1931, and Gras succeeded him as editor, but his opportunity to mold the journal was short-lived, since financial reasons compelled the ceasing of publication in 1932. The conflict between Gay and Gras was ultimately to isolate Gras from the rest of the American economic historians, since most of them were Gay's former students; worse yet, it produced a separation between business history and the better-developed older field, economic history.

Gras's attempt to publish a synthesis and generalization of the material on business history he had accumulated for more than 15 years was hardly successful. He failed to distinguish between analytical constructs, such as his stages of capitalist development, and the economic reality which they were designed to explain.

After its auspicious beginnings, the development of business history ran into difficulties in the 1930s. Financial trouble in the wake of the depression made it necessary to abandon the original broad concept of "business history" and to concentrate on company histories. Also, Gras was now faced with that resistance which many innovators are bound to meet. Besides these problems beyond Gras's control, his endeavors did suffer from his alienation from his colleagues. The narrowing down of the field, originally forced on Gras, became after a while a matter of his choice, and he came to identify "business history" with the study of the administration and policies of individual enterprises. His work, moreover, was empiricistic. His attempts to stimulate interest in the new area through an appeal to businessmen and his way of gaining access to business records aroused the suspicion of intellectuals and social scientists, because in this period they tended to be hostile toward business. Finally, although Gras was an inspiring teacher and a friend of students, in his later years he seemed unable to deal with his peers on the basis of intellectual give-and-take. He appeared unwilling to cooperate with other scholars who came to the new field of research on business with more refined tools and with related, yet different, goals. By the time of Gras's death the exponents of business history had returned to the broad and fruitful conception of his earlier years and were developing the field as the social and economic history of business.

FRITZ REDLICH

[For discussion of the subsequent development of Gras's ideas, see HISTORY, article on BUSINESS HISTORY.]

WORKS BY GRAS

1915   Evolution of the English Corn Market From the Twelfth to the Eighteenth Century. Harvard Economic Studies, Vol. 13. Cambridge, Mass.: Harvard Univ. Press.

1918   The Early English Customs System: A Documentary Study of the Institutional and Economic History of the Customs From the Thirteenth to the Sixteenth Century. Harvard Economic Studies, Vol. 18. Cambridge, Mass.: Harvard Univ. Press.

1922   An Introduction to Economic History. New York: Harper.

(1925) 1940   A History of Agriculture in Europe and America. 2d ed. New York: Crofts.

1930   Industrial Evolution. Cambridge, Mass.: Harvard Univ. Press.

1930   GRAS, NORMAN S. B.; and GRAS, ETHEL C. The Economic and Social History of an English Village (Crawley, Hampshire) A.D. 909–1928. Harvard Economic Studies, Vol. 34. Cambridge, Mass.: Harvard Univ. Press.

1937   The Massachusetts First National Bank of Boston: 1784–1934. Harvard Studies in Business History, No. 4. Cambridge, Mass.: Harvard Univ. Press.

1939   Business and Capitalism: An Introduction to Business History. New York: Crofts.

1939   GRAS, NORMAN S. B.; and LARSON, HENRIETTA M. Casebook in American Business History. New York: Crofts.

1942   Harvard Co-operative Society Past and Present: 1882–1942. Cambridge, Mass.: Harvard Univ. Press.

1962   Development of Business History up to 1950. Edited by Ethel C. Gras. New York: Lincoln Educational Foundation. → Published posthumously.

GRAUNT, JOHN

John Graunt (1620–1674) is generally regarded as having laid the foundations of demography as a science with the publication of his *Natural and Political Observations Made Upon the Bills of Mortality* (1662a). Graunt began, as many scientists have done, by exercising idle curiosity—"Now having (I know not by what accident) engaged my thoughts upon the *Bills of Mortality* . . ." ([1662a] 1939, p. 3)—and proceeding to "observations, which I happened to make (for I designed them not) . . ." (*ibid.*, p. 5). Characteristically, he did not believe that curiosity should remain idle: "finding some *Truths*, and not commonly-believed Opinions . . . I proceeded further, to consider what benefit the knowledge of the same would bring the World" (*ibid.*, p. 18).

Graunt's application of the statistical method to raw material had two essential elements: (1) *classification* of like with like, so as to break the data down into homogeneous groups, and (2) the *comparison* of those groups in order to recognize significant differentials. Another attribute of Graunt as a statistician was his ability to apply logic to his arithmetic. He never accepted a calculation if it offended his common sense; nor did he accept it without a test, if he had the means of testing it.

As to classification, we may read in Chapter 2 of his *Observations* his very sound remarks about the identification of causes of death, then dependent on the observation of the "ancient matron" searchers (*ibid.*, pp. 27–32). Deaths at advanced ages, he argued, can hardly be safely attributed to one specific cause, and not much worthwhile information can be expected about sudden deaths beyond their suddenness. As to comparison, we find in the same chapter his observation about the stability of proportionate mortality rates for certain causes, and in Chapter 4 (*ibid.*, pp. 45–48) his observation that in plague years, deaths from causes other than plague were inflated to such an extent as to lead to his conclusion that of deaths from plague fully one-fifth were attributed to some other cause (in order to avoid the closure of the plague-infested dwelling and the virtual incarceration of the surviving members of the household). Again in Chapter 3 (*ibid.*, pp. 33–44), we may see how comparison of mortality rates for rickets with mortality rates referring to possible similar names for the same disease led Graunt, after examining the figures, to conclude that rickets was a new disease and not a new name for an old one. (This was probably a wrong conclusion, but Graunt was not a physician and would not have known that medical attention was at that time being drawn to the disease.)

The method of comparison was again employed when Graunt estimated the population of London in Chapter 11 (*ibid.*, pp. 67–70). He used three methods and reconciled them. First, he estimated that a fertile woman had a baby every other year, that fertile women numbered half the married women, and that there were seven other members of a family (husband, 3 children, 3 servants); therefore, the population was 32 times the number of annual births. This gives 384,000. Next he estimated that in certain parishes there were annually three deaths from every 11 families; therefore, the number of deaths (13,000) multiplied by 11/3 yielded 48,000 families, or 384,000 persons. Finally, he observed 54 families per 100 square yards within the walls (12,000 families) and guessed that there were three times as many families outside the walls.

Graunt's most important contribution to demography was his rudimentary life table. Its importance lies not in the table itself, which is indeed defective, but in the novelty of presenting mortality in terms of survivorship. Graunt began with only two observations—the proportion of births surviving to age 6 (.64) and the proportion surviving to age 76 (.01). He then assumed that a constant multiplier is involved in proceeding from the first proportion to the last by decennial intervals of age. He did not make clear how he got his multiplier (or "mean proportion," as he called it), but it was obviously about .6. Michel Ptouka (1938) has put forward the hypothesis that the multiplier was $(64 - 1)/100 = .63$. D. V. Glass has suggested (1950) that Graunt made a second difference interpolation from $l_0 = 100$, $l_6 = 64$, and $l_{76} = 1$. The method and any error in it is not important. (Halley was not to make the correct calculation for another sixty years or so.) So much has been developed from this simple but immensely powerful thought that actuarial criticism would be quite out of place.

Graunt is rarely considered apart from another English scientist of the time, Sir William Petty.

Both were of Hampshire stock; Graunt was born in 1620 and Petty in 1623. They became acquainted in or before 1650. It appears that their relationship was initially that of client and patron (Graunt being Petty's patron; see Greenwood 1941–1943), but the roles were reversed after the fire of London in 1666.

Graunt was the son of a city tradesman and became a haberdasher and a man of substance. Petty, who had sampled the merchant navy, studied mathematics in France, spent a short time in the Royal Navy, returned to the Continent to study anatomy, spent some time in business in London, and went to Oxford in 1649, becoming a doctor of medicine by dispensation. Later he rose to be professor of anatomy and vice-principal of Brasenose. He became a candidate for a Gresham professorship in London and made contact with Graunt. We do not know what interests they shared at that time or whether Graunt (or his father) had any influence in Petty's subsequent appointment as Gresham professor of music. Soon after, Petty (who seems to have had no professional duties) went to Ireland and made a fortune. For many years Graunt remained a prosperous tradesman, but the fire of 1666 destroyed his business. A little later he became a Roman Catholic convert and was apparently not interested in rebuilding his business, for he was soon bankrupt. It was now Petty's turn to be the patron, and Graunt, the client—and apparently not an easy one. Despite Petty's attempts to help him, Graunt's financial troubles were with him until he died in 1674.

Petty's vital statistical work was on a different level from that of Graunt. Petty had inspiration and brilliance, many ideas and a breadth of vision, but he did not pursue his ideas as persistently as Graunt did. It was Petty who proposed a central government statistical office and a system of census taking. He anticipated William Farr in estimating the economic loss due to mortality. Many of his calculations, however, do not stand up to the tests of consistency that Graunt would have applied. It seems to be generally agreed that Graunt made an immeasurably greater contribution to demography.

Essentially, Graunt was a man with an inquiring mind whose ideas laid the foundation of the political arithmetic that we now accept as part of good social organization and government. The Royal Society of London, of which Graunt was elected a fellow, commemorated the tercentenary of the publication of his *Observations* by holding a special series of scientific meetings to which leading demographers in England and other countries contributed papers (Glass 1963). The Institute of Actuaries of England paid its own tribute to Graunt by republishing, in a more modern format but without abridgment or alteration, his original *Observations*.

B. BENJAMIN

[*For the historical context of Graunt's work, see* PUBLIC HEALTH; VITAL STATISTICS; *and the biography of* PETTY. *For discussion of the subsequent development of his ideas, see* LIFE TABLES; MORTALITY; *and the biographies of* KŐRÖSY; LOTKA.]

WORKS BY GRAUNT

(1662a) 1939 *Natural and Political Observations Made Upon the Bills of Mortality*. Edited with an introduction by Walter F. Willcox. Baltimore: Johns Hopkins Press. → See especially Chapter 2, "General Observations Upon the Casualties"; Chapter 3, "Of Particular Casualties"; Chapter 4, "On the Plague"; Chapter 11, "Of the Number of Inhabitants."
(1662b) 1964 *Natural and Political Observations Mentioned in a Following Index, and Made Upon the Bills of Mortality: With Reference to the Government, Religion, Trade, Growth, Ayre, Diseases, and Several Changes of the Said City* [London]. *Journal of the Institute of Actuaries* (London) 90:1–61. → Includes a three-page introduction by B. Benjamin.

SUPPLEMENTARY BIBLIOGRAPHY

GLASS, D. V. 1950 Graunt's Life Table. *Journal of the Institute of Actuaries* (London) 76:60–64.
GLASS, D. V. 1963 John Graunt and His *Natural and Political Observations*. Royal Society of London, *Proceedings* Series B 159:1–38. → Includes six pages of discussion.
GREENWOOD, MAJOR (1941–1943) 1948 *Medical Statistics From Graunt to Farr*. Cambridge Univ. Press. → First published in *Biometrika*.
NEWMAN, JAMES R. 1956 Commentary on an Ingenious Army Captain and on a Generous and Many-sided Man. Volume 3, pages 1416–1419 in James R. Newman (editor), *The World of Mathematics: A Small Library of the Literature of Mathematics From A'h-mosé the Scribe to Albert Einstein*. New York: Simon & Schuster.
PTOUKA, MICHEL 1938 John Graunt, fondateur de la démographie: 1620–1674. Volume 2, pages 61–74 in International Congress for Studies on Population, Paris, 1937, *Congrès international de la population*. Paris: Hermann.
SUTHERLAND, IAN 1963 John Graunt: A Tercentenary Tribute. *Journal of the Royal Statistical Society* Series A 126:537–556.

GREEN, T. H.

Thomas Hill Green (1836–1882), English philosopher, social theorist, and reformer, was born in Birkin, Yorkshire, where his father was rector. He became a fellow of Balliol College, Oxford, in 1860, and professor of moral philosophy in 1878 but died four years later at the age of 45. Green initiated and inspired the British renaissance of Hegelian idealism, which started in Oxford in the 1870s and dominated academic philosophy in Britain until its retreat before the criticisms of Bertrand Russell and G. E. Moore in the early years of the twentieth century.

Green's aim was to demolish the prevailing system of thought that grafted evolutionary ideas onto the stem of traditional empiricism and to lead his contemporaries away from J. S. Mill and Huxley and toward Kant and Hegel. He began with an attack on received views in metaphysics and theory of knowledge, which appeared in an introduction to the works of David Hume (1874). Knowledge, he held, could not be derived by a merely passive mind from a sequence of discrete sensations. Nature is an unalterable scheme of intelligible relations constructed by the mind; this implies an equally unalterable and objective eternal consciousness of which all finite minds are parts. As the constructer of nature, mind cannot be a part or product of it.

The prevailing system of philosophy, which regarded man as a part of nature governed by deterministic laws, ruled out conduct as much as it ruled out knowledge. Green believed will and choice, the rational determinants of action, must instead be distinguished from passive compliance with the promptings of natural desire. In an act of will, a man identifies himself with his ideal self or character, which is part of the eternal consciousness and not of the mechanical order of nature. The moral end is the full realization of one's potentialities, and these can be realized only in a social community. For Green, as for Rousseau and Hegel before him, genuine human personality was an essentially social phenomenon, and it was inconceivable that isolated natural man should be a moral agent. Green was not entirely hostile to Mill's chastened utilitarianism; he shared its rejection of customary rules but conceived the ideal end of conduct as moral perfection, not individual contentment. (For Green's metaphysics and ethics see Green 1883.)

Green's social theory (1882) follows Rousseau and Hegel to some extent in subordinating the individual to the community. The duty of the citizen is to follow the general will for the common good. But for Green the community is not coterminous with the state; he remained in the liberal tradition in asserting the sovereignty of morals over politics. There is some of Hegel's contempt for the individual conscience in Green's well-known view that there can be no unrecognized rights, but he did not say that all true rights were legal ones. The recognizing authority is not the state but the moral consensus of the community. Positive law can be criticized and improved upon in the light of the state's ideal purpose: the moral perfection of men. Since morality presupposes freedom the state cannot serve this end directly, but it can create favorable conditions for it. Green valued democracy as giving men the kind of responsibility that is conducive to moral improvement. Participation in democracy is a duty, not a right; an opportunity for moral development, not a negative emancipation from authority and constraint.

Green's special combination of moral individualism and collectivism, in particular his idea of the state as an indirect agent of moral improvement, led him to favor the intervention of the state to secure the welfare of its citizens (1881). He was opposed to Mill's libertarianism and Spencer's barbarous version of laissez-faire. In his support of the enlargement of the state's responsibilities he anticipated the doctrines of the British Labour party. He became the first Oxford tutor to serve on the city council, where he actively promoted temperance reform and public secondary education. Realistic in his respect for the force of circumstances and the moral sense of the community, Green was no traditionalist. He admired Cromwell (from whom he claimed descent) and shared his republicanism. He was hostile to class distinction, militarism, and patriotic display. The first important English philosopher since Ralph Cudworth to spend his active life in a university, he supported, by precept and example, the involvement of philosophers in the social and political life of their society. The character of Mr. Grey in Mrs. Humphry Ward's novel *Robert Elsmere* is an admiring portrait of Green's nobly serious personality, in which a determined puritanism was at once strengthened and mitigated by decency and practical good sense.

ANTHONY QUINTON

[*For the historical context of Green's work, see the biographies of* HEGEL; MILL; ROUSSEAU. *For discussion of the development of his ideas, see the biographies of* BOSANQUET; FIGGIS; LINDSAY.]

WORKS BY GREEN

(1874) 1906 Introduction to Hume's *Treatise of Human Nature.* Pages 1–371 in Thomas Hill Green, *Works . . .* Volume 1: Philosophical Works. London: Longmans.

(1881) 1906 Lecture on Liberal Legislation and Freedom of Contract. Pages 365–386 in Thomas Hill Green, *Works . . .* Volume 3: Miscellanies and Memoir. London: Longmans.

(1882) 1960 *Lectures on the Principles of Political Obligation.* London: Longmans.

(1883) 1929 *Prolegomena to Ethics.* 5th ed. Oxford: Clarendon.

1906 *Works of Thomas Hill Green.* Edited by R. L. Nettleship. 3 vols. London: Longmans. → Volumes 1–2: *Philosophical Works.* Volume 3: *Miscellanies and Memoir.*

SUPPLEMENTARY BIBLIOGRAPHY

FAIRBROTHER, WILLIAM H. (1896) 1900 *The Philosophy of Thomas Hill Green.* 2d ed. London: Methuen.

MILNE, A. J. M. 1962 *The Social Philosophy of English Idealism.* London: Allen & Unwin.

MUIRHEAD, JOHN HENRY 1908 *The Service of the State: Four Lectures on the Political Teaching of T. H. Green.* London: Murray.

RICHTER, MELVIN 1964 *The Politics of Conscience: T. H. Green and His Age.* Harvard Univ. Press.

RITCHIE, DAVID G. (1887) 1902 The Political Philosophy of Thomas Hill Green. Pages 125–151 in David G. Ritchie, *The Principles of State Interference: Four Essays on the Political Philosophy of Mr. Herbert Spencer, J. S. Mill, and T. H. Green.* London: Sonnenschein. → First published in *Contemporary Review.*

GRIEF

See DEATH; SYMPATHY AND EMPATHY.

GROSS NATIONAL PRODUCT

See NATIONAL INCOME AND PRODUCT ACCOUNTS.

GROSS REPRODUCTION RATE

See FERTILITY.

GROTIUS, HUGO

Huig de Groot (1583–1645), better known by the Latinized version of his name, Hugo Grotius, was born at Delft in the province of Holland. He was carefully educated by his father, whose intellectual interests were both broad and profound, and who imbued in him the characteristic civic pride of the Dutch patriciate.

Grotius was extraordinarily young when his exceptional gifts became apparent. From 1594 to 1597 he studied in the faculty of arts of the University of Leiden, the Protestant university that had been opened in 1575. In 1599 he was called to the bar at The Hague; and in 1607 he received his first public office as *advocaat fiscaal* (deputy attorney general) at the highest law court in the province of Holland. Five years later he was appointed pensionary of Rotterdam, a political office that gave him power not only in the city itself but also in the States (the representative assembly) of the province, where he acted as Rotterdam's representative.

Meanwhile, Grotius' publications established him both as an accomplished neo-Latin poet and dramatist and as an ambitious historian and jurist. As a jurist he wrote a short book *The Freedom of the Seas* (1609)—it was, in fact, just one chapter of the manuscript *De jure praedae* (1604), not published until 1868—in which he tried to prove that no authority is entitled to claim sovereignty over the high seas; although it was aimed at Spanish pretensions, the book also aroused the wrath of James I of England.

In the 1610s Grotius became one of the major supporters of the grand pensionary, Johan van Oldenbarnevelt, who was engaged in a bitter struggle with the stadholder, Prince Maurice of Orange, on two issues: Oldenbarnevelt and Grotius supported the cause of the Arminians and of provincial sovereignty, particularly that of Holland. After their defeat in 1618, Oldenbarnevelt was executed and Grotius sentenced to life imprisonment. Thanks to the resourcefulness of his wife, Grotius escaped to France after three years; he was welcomed by Louis XIII, who paid him a pension, albeit irregularly. From 1621 to 1631 he lived in Paris with his family in relatively poor circumstances. He lived by his pen, expecting all the while that the justice of his cause would lead to his eventual rehabilitation in the Netherlands. In 1631 he made an attempt to re-establish himself there but was forced to leave the following year. In 1634 he accepted the offer of Queen Christina of Sweden to become her ambassador to France, and for ten years he worked in that capacity in Paris, a somewhat eccentric scholar of bourgeois origin among titled professional diplomats.

Diplomacy bored Grotius, and he could not afford to wait long years for his salary to be paid, as could his noble colleagues. He tried to compensate for his inadequacy as a diplomat by working for a goal far above the pettiness of routine politics: the restoration of Christian unity. During his last years, this came to be his major preoccupation. In 1645 he went to Sweden to offer his resignation. He went by way of Holland, where at last he was welcomed with the warmth he had been expecting in vain for two decades. On the journey back from Sweden, where Christina had received him with utmost politeness and with equal politeness accepted his resignation, his ship was driven off course, and he went ashore on the Pomeranian coast. He took the road to Lübeck but did not reach that city: forced to rest in Rostock, he died there from exhaustion.

Grotius' intellectual achievement has a paradoxical character. He won great fame as a poet and dramatist, as a historian, a philologist, a theologian, and, of course, a jurist. But learned discussions about the contributions he made to all these different fields have not come to any conclusion about whether he was essentially a con-

servative who put together in magnificent syntheses opinions previously held by others or an innovator boldly treading new ground. The endless variety of his work, the mixture of precision and suppleness in his thought, and the sheer bulk of his learning make it almost impossible to determine with any certainty the degree of originality of his views.

He was very much a man of the baroque age. His motto, *ruit hora* (time flies), the Latin language in which he wrote most of his books, and his profound awareness of life's antinomies indicate how fully he belonged to the civilization of his time. Yet in the deeply pessimistic early seventeenth century his optimism and rationalism were exceptional and so effortless that they may seem shallow in comparison with the views of such philosophers as Descartes. His theological studies were inspired by deep religious feelings, but they brought him into conflict with Protestants of various denominations and gave both Catholics and, later, deists the erroneous impression that he supported their views. His constant endeavors to heal the breaches in the Christian church caused the most confusing misunderstandings and involved him in acrimonious controversy.

During his imprisonment, from 1618 to 1621, Grotius wrote, in rhyme, *The Truth of the Christian Religion*; it was published in Dutch in 1622, and in 1627 Grotius' own Latin version followed. In this simple book, written for seamen who might be impressed by foreign religions, Grotius explained and lauded the main tenets of Christianity. The book was a great success; it was translated not only into all the major European languages but also into Danish, Irish, Hungarian, and Arabic, and there are 110 known editions of it.

Grotius' masterpiece, *The Law of War and Peace* (1625), was also an immediate and widespread success, if not on the same scale as his little book on Christianity: it has gone through at least 75 editions and has been translated 24 times. In this book he presented his famous doctrine of the just war. War, in his view, is justified as a means of obtaining justice in cases where no law court exists to give a ruling upon the matter under dispute. Most of these cases are, of course, international conflicts, such as the revolt of the United Provinces against Spain. A contestant may take up arms in order to defend his property or his rights, to take possession of what is due to him, or to punish criminal offenses. Thus, war is essentially a lawsuit carried out by armed force because there is no court that can deal with it.

Other concepts are also presented in this large book, which is like a warehouse of opinions, quotations, conflicting doctrines, and debates. Especially noteworthy is Grotius' doctrine of natural law, for it exerted considerable influence, even if it was neither coherent nor strikingly original. Since he considered natural law to be basic to all social organization, international or national, Grotius' initially juridical theory developed into a more general one that analyzed and explained not only the conditions of international justice but every aspect of human society. In other words, his work pertains as much to general sociology as to international law.

Grotius defined the law of nature as "a dictate of right reason, showing the moral necessity or moral baseness of any act according to its agreement or disagreement with rational nature, and indicating that such an act is either commanded or forbidden by the author of nature, God" (1625, pp. 20–21 in a 1949 edition). This does not differ essentially from scholastic conceptions, and it is somewhat misleading to claim, as has often been done, that Grotius made an original contribution by secularizing the medieval interpretation of natural law. For Grotius, just as for the medieval thinkers and the sixteenth-century Spanish lawyers whom he quoted, the law of nature is an objective datum, an absolute norm given for all eternity. It is only later in the century, with Hobbes and other theorists, that the law of nature, identified with the instinct of self-preservation, developed into an essentially individualistic, subjective, and secular concept. Grotius, according to Erik Wolf (Wolf 1939) saw God, nature, and reason as only different names for the metaphysical foundation of life, which to human beings becomes manifest in law. Society is a natural and necessary form of concrete law because man is a social being endowed with reason. Thus, human society is also by definition rational.

These premises served Grotius as starting points for determining the rational quality in social and political life. It was not his purpose to draft a political theory. Various political concepts that seemed essential to his contemporaries were rather indifferently treated by him. Sovereignty, for example, did not mean much to a thinker educated in the corporative, patrician Dutch republic that was slowly emerging when he was young. Yet he transcended his origins by regarding all nations, sovereignties, and even churches as mere elements of the largest possible social entity, the human race in general. Therefore, the societies under examination appeared to him as manifestations of a social and ethical order in which each social element has its place, determined by its own existential principle.

But all of them are embraced by the corporative unity which is humanity—primarily, of course, Christian humanity.

The *Law of War and Peace* is more than a philosophical and sociological monograph. To make it useful to the practical statesman, Grotius endeavored to determine the justifiability of particular actions that are often taken prior to war or in war, according to simple principles laid out by him. Although, for example, Gustavus Adolphus is said to have consulted the book frequently while campaigning in Germany, it is obviously impossible to assess the actual impact of its prescriptions on the conduct of war. But this much is certain: the work exercised a profound influence on the development of international law, and even in the present century it is referred to not only by professional lawyers but also by statesmen. The remarkable mixture of idealistic optimism—for in spite of international chaos, Grotius viewed the ethical content of natural law as a principle that automatically asserts itself, since, in the last analysis, rational and natural behavior are identical—and realism, which sprang from a critical study of history, rendered his concepts and advice applicable to many situations and attractive to many different groups.

E. H. KOSSMANN

[See also INTERNATIONAL LAW and the biography of VATTEL.]

WORKS BY GROTIUS

(1597–1628) 1928–1965 *Briefwisseling van Hugo Grotius.* 4 vols. Edited by P. C. Molhuysen and B. L. Meulenbroek. The Hague: Nijhoff. → Additional volumes are projected.

(1604) 1950 *De jure praedae commentarius: Commentary on the Law of Prize and Booty.* 2 vols. Oxford: Clarendon Press. → The manuscript of 1604 was first published in 1868.

(1609) 1916 *The Freedom of the Seas: Or, the Right Which Belongs to the Dutch to Take Part in the East India Trade.* New York: Oxford Univ. Press. → First published as *Mare liberum.*

(1622) 1823 *The Truth of the Christian Religion.* 16th ed. Corrected and illustrated with notes by Le Clerc. Oxford: Baxter. → First published in Dutch.

(1625) 1962 *The Law of War and Peace: De jure belli ac pacis.* Translated by Francis W. Kelsey, with an introduction by James Brown Scott. Indianapolis, Ind.: Bobbs-Merrill. → An edition was published in 1949 by Black.

1687 *Epistolae quotquot reperiri potuerunt: In quibus praeter hactenus editas, plurimae theologici, iuridici, philologici, historici, et politici argumenti occurrunt.* Amsterdam: Blaeu.

SUPPLEMENTARY BIBLIOGRAPHY

KNIGHT, WILLIAM S. M. 1925 *The Life and Works of Hugo Grotius.* London: Sweet & Maxwell.

MEULEN, JACOB TER; and DIERMANSE, P. J. J. 1950 *Bibliographie des écrits imprimés de Hugo Grotius.* The Hague: Nijhoff.

MEULEN, JACOB TER; and DIERMANSE, P. J. J. 1961 *Bibliographie des écrits sur Hugo Grotius imprimés au XVIIᵉ siècle.* The Hague: Nijhoff.

WOLF, ERIK (1939) 1963 *Grosse Rechtsdenker der deutschen Geistesgeschichte.* 4th ed., rev. & enl. Tübingen: Mohr. → See especially "Hugo Grotius," pages 253–311.

GROUP DYNAMICS

See FIELD THEORY *and the biography of* LEWIN.

GROUPED OBSERVATIONS

See under STATISTICAL ANALYSIS, SPECIAL PROBLEMS OF.

GROUPS

I
THE STUDY OF GROUPS

In social science the study of groups is often called *small-group research.* A "group" is defined as a number of persons, or members, each of whom, while the group is meeting, interacts with every other, or is able to do so, or can at least take personal cognizance of every other. This requirement, which cannot be met for larger social units, such as armies, justifies calling groups "small." Although no investigator has specified the number of members that would make a group "large" rather than "small," the groups actually studied have seldom had more than fifty members. It is, moreover, often difficult to draw the boundaries between groups, as marginal persons may interact with members of two or more groups.

Investigators working within the field of small groups seldom study the behavior of groups as such. More often they study the characteristics of face-to-face interaction among men, of which the behavior of groups considered as units is only a part. Accordingly, the subject should perhaps be called "elementary social behavior" (Homans 1961) rather than "small groups." A group so small that an investigator can observe the behavior of each of its members in some detail is a good setting for the study of this subject, but the group usually remains the setting rather than the object of investigation.

For this reason the problem of defining a group or demarcating its boundaries is seldom of theoretical importance. When the behavior of a group as such is to be studied, its boundaries, in practice, are apt to be quite clear.

History of small-group research

The interest in groups has sprung from two main sources, which may be called psychological and sociological after the disciplinary affiliations of the chief investigators. In psychology the interest perhaps began with studies of social facilitation. From the 1930s on, it was stimulated by the experimental and theoretical work of Kurt Lewin on social influence. Lewin trained a group of students, including R. Lippitt, D. Cartwright, A. Bavelas, and L. Festinger (Cartwright & Zander 1953; compare Lewin 1939–1947). Members of the Tavistock Institute in England largely shared their viewpoint. Although many psychologists in the field were not students of Lewin's, few escaped his influence.

In sociology much of the work of Georg Simmel (1902–1917) lay in the field now called small-group research. But his influence was not direct: indeed, later research had the effect of reviving interest in him. The other early name of importance is that of Charles H. Cooley, who pointed out the influence of certain kinds of groups, such as the family and the children's play group, which he called *primary groups,* in forming the attitudes of men (Cooley 1909).

Simmel and Cooley were intuitive observers and theorists. For empirical investigation, Elton Mayo was to sociology what Lewin was to psychology. The researches carried out in the 1920s in the Hawthorne plant of the Western Electric Company by Mayo and his associates of the Harvard Graduate School of Business Administration were conceived as studies of human relations in industry (Roethlisberger & Dickson 1939). But several of the researches put small industrial groups under close scrutiny and suggested the possible fruitfulness of more general work. E. D. Chapple and C. M. Arensberg (1940), who developed operational measures of face-to-face interaction, were indirectly associated with the Western Electric researches; so were sociologists like W. F. Whyte (1943) and G. C. Homans (1950), who have worked in the small-group field, as well as investigators at the Harvard Business School. Yet there is plenty of such work in sociology that does not stem directly from the school of Mayo.

A third, rather specialized, influence in the 1930s was that of J. L. Moreno (1934) and his associate, H. H. Jennings, who worked at the New

York State Training School for Girls. They contributed interesting empirical findings and, more important, the technique they called the *sociometric test*, which in one form or another is now used by most investigators.

Great Britain, France, and the Scandinavian countries have also made important contributions to the field; in France an early theoretical influence was the "microsociology" of G. Gurvitch (1950).

Methodology

One justification for speaking of psychological and sociological "schools" is that until recently they tended to use somewhat different research designs. True to the traditions of their discipline, the psychologists emphasized experimental and survey methods. They would bring groups, sometimes groups artificially constituted for research purposes, into laboratories where some of the variables affecting the subjects' behavior might be held constant and others experimentally manipulated. They developed quantitative measures of behavior and administered standardized questionnaires; they formulated hypotheses relating the independent, experimentally manipulated variables to the dependent ones; they tested the significance of these hypotheses statistically. They also exploited natural situations that provided some approximation to experimental control—for instance, a set of groups all alike in some respect, such as residents of houses of identical design or groups having identical tasks to perform. The psychologists would correlate statistically the variations along a number of dimensions of behavior occurring naturally in these groups.

Instead of studying several similar groups under more or less controlled conditions, the sociologists were apt to concentrate on single, "real-life" groups. Instead of using systematic quantitative and survey methods, they would use the techniques of anthropological field work and nondirective interviewing, which provided, as they hoped, a richer and more rounded understanding. And instead of testing hypotheses statistically, they would work out a qualitative description of the social structure of the group in question.

It is easy to exaggerate the differences between the psychological and sociological methodologies. Although the Western Electric researches are thought of as belonging to the sociological tradition, the study of the Relay Assembly Test Room employed a more rigorous method of measuring output, gathered a greater body of quantitative data, and made a more elaborate statistical analysis than any other small-group study has ever done

(Whitehead 1938). Today all investigators use in different mixtures much the same battery of techniques. The sociologists are ready to use survey methods in order to provide support for hypotheses first suggested by field work; and the psychologists will admit both that field work is a necessary preliminary to the design of a survey and that it helps the investigator understand what the findings of his survey "mean"—that is, how they are to be explained. Most investigators now think of themselves as social psychologists rather than as either psychologists or sociologists.

Above all, both methodologies lead to the same end. The first business of any science is to state propositions, or hypotheses, about the relations between variables. The psychologists tend to make their propositions explicit and to pretend they were formulated before the data were gathered. The sociologists are more apt to pretend that they studied their groups with open minds, ready for any relationship to appear in the data, and they often leave their propositions implicit in their descriptions of social structure. But their propositions can always be made explicit, and a proposition supported by data remains a finding, whether formulated ex ante facto or ex post facto. Nor is it easy to understand why one should put greater confidence in a proposition tested on a set of groups similar in some controlled respect than in one that can be shown, as many of the findings of field research can be shown, to hold good for a number of otherwise quite dissimilar groups. In any event, no one has ever demonstrated that the findings of, for instance, laboratory research are inconsistent with those of field research, once the very different conditions that obtain for artificial and for "real" groups are taken into account. They are not always taken into sufficient account.

Some leading problems

Within the field of small groups numerous problems call for investigation, and there have been a number of surveys and anthologies of research (Cartwright & Zander 1953; Hare 1962; Hare et al. 1955; Olmsted 1959). Here only the chief questions to which research has sought answers are mentioned.

What determines whether a man changes his behavior or opinion under the influence of others? In particular, what determines whether or not he conforms to the norms of a group? What gives some men power over others?

Small-group research deals with all these questions within the context of a general concern about interpersonal relations, which may often be regarded as stabilized resultants of processes of in-fluence. Accordingly, the researcher in this area, starting with a broad interest in the relations between the behavior and opinions of men and their attitudes toward one another, may come to ask more specific questions. Here the ideas that have come to be called "balance theory" (Heider 1958) should be specially mentioned. What are the conditions of status congruence and distributive justice, and what are the effects on interpersonal relations of failure to meet these conditions? What determines an attitude of "respect" for another, rather than a more relaxed "liking"? What determines embarrassment or a "joking relationship"?

Interpersonal relations combine to form larger social structures; consideration of this elementary social fact raises a new order of problems. How do coalitions form in the smallest social groups, such as triads? How do differences in status build up among the members of a group? What are the determinants of different forms of status system? What are the relations between status, influence, and conformity, or between status, the channels of communication in a group, and its division of labor? What are the determinants of conflict between groups, and what are its effects on social structure within groups? Finally, there is the question of social control: What are the conditions maintaining stability in a social structure?

Many studies have been devoted to questions arising from collaboration among group members in attaining a common goal. Is a group more effective than an individual in solving problems? What are the results of competition as opposed to collaboration? How do the motivation of its members, their interpersonal relations, patterns of communication, and division of labor render a group more or less effective in attaining a goal? Are there any necessary phases a group goes through in solving its problems and reaching its goals? What are the effects of success or failure upon its internal structure? What are the determinants of individual satisfaction with collaborative work?

There are also a number of special questions related to what English-speaking people call *leadership*. A "leader" may be defined as someone whose orders are in fact obeyed by many other persons, especially by the members of a group to which he belongs. What, if any, are the traits of personality that make a man a leader? What are the relations between the values of members and the behavior of the man who emerges as leader of a group? What is the relation between status and leadership, or between leadership informally won and authority formally assigned to a man by a larger organiza-tion of which his group is a part? What makes a leader successful in attaining individual goals or goals assigned to, or adopted by, a group? What are the effects of strong leadership on the other behavior of the leader himself and on the behavior of others toward him?

Many of these questions lend themselves to applied research, which is research designed to provide people with knowledge that might allow them to change social behavior for the better from their point of view. The "better" behavior envisaged has ranged all the way from more productive industrial groups to discussion groups better organized to train the leaders of other discussion groups. In this field, research has been none the worse for being "applied" [*see* LEADERSHIP].

Codification of research findings

The findings, the tested empirical propositions of small-group research, possess the following characteristics. In substance, they are very varied. They are formulated in many different terminologies: almost every investigator makes up one of his own. And they often appear to have no high degree of generality, to be contradictory or to hold good only in special circumstances.

Since, nevertheless, the findings are all concerned with face-to-face social behavior, their chaotic nature in other respects has stimulated a few investigators to the kind of criticism sometimes called *codification* (Homans 1950; 1961; Thibaut & Kelley 1959). When carried out deliberately, which it seldom is, codification goes behind the different names given to the variables entering the findings and asks how these variables were actually measured. When the same or equivalent operations of measurement were used in different investigations, codification gives these variables the same name. By this means it can sometimes show that the same findings have been reached in different investigations and so reduce the number of findings.

When apparently contradictory findings survive such criticism, codification goes on to examine the conditions under which the findings were established, since two findings are not contradictory unless all the circumstances in which each holds good are identical. If one research, for instance, shows that two persons who interact often with each other tend to like each other and another shows that they do not, an examination of the other features of the two researches may reveal that in the latter the two persons were constrained to interact, whereas in the former they were not.

These first steps in codification immediately suggest the next: an effort to reduce the number of independent findings still further by showing that a number of different findings, including contradictory ones, can be derived from the same set of general propositions under specified given conditions. From an assumption, for instance, about the determinants of sociometric choice (expressions of liking), together with the condition, which is approximately true of some groups, that members use the same criteria for choice, it follows both that a few members will receive many more choices than others do—which is an empirical finding—and that highly chosen members will choose one another—which is another empirical finding.

At this point codification begins to organize and unify the findings by explaining them. In any science, what is to be explained is always an empirical proposition of the general form x varies as y. Explanation is the process of showing that the proposition follows logically in a deductive system from more general propositions under specified given conditions, themselves stated in the form of propositions. The more general propositions are more general in the sense that they enter into deductive systems by which other empirical propositions are explained; this is their unifying function. The given conditions are not general propositions, nor does the investigator undertake to explain them; he simply accepts them as matters of fact. A characteristic given condition in small-group research is the physical layout of the room in which a group meets.

To explain a phenomenon is to produce a theory of the phenomenon: a theory is nothing if it is not an explanation. Many investigators, especially psychologists, begin their research reports by formulating a theory from which, they assert, the propositions (hypotheses) they tested were derived. Codification begins by disregarding these theories and looking at the empirical findings themselves. But it must come back in the end to asking how they are to be explained. For this purpose it need not come back to the investigators' own theories. A theory may be fruitful in suggesting hypotheses to be tested without in the long run providing the most general way of explaining the hypotheses [see SCIENTIFIC EXPLANATION].

The uses of theory

The process of codification almost forces the codifier to ask himself what his general theory is. Two main types of general theory have been used, not always explicitly, in small-group research. They may be called sociological and psychological, but here these words refer to the characteristics of their general propositions and not to the academic affiliations of the men who use them, since a sociologist may perfectly well use a psychological theory, and vice versa.

Sociological theory. The sociological type of theory is an offshoot of the "functional" theory with which the name of Talcott Parsons is particularly associated. It is sociological because its general propositions are propositions about social units as such and not about the behavior of individuals. It attempts to state the general conditions under which any social system survives, maintains itself, or remains in equilibrium. From these general conditions it claims to derive the particular features a given social system remaining in equilibrium "must" possess. The empirical findings represent these features.

In small-group research a good example of such a theory is that of R. F. Bales (1950). He argues that if a discussion group is to remain in equilibrium and reach its goal, such as the formulation of a decision, the behavior of the members must collectively display certain characteristics. For instance, the group must pass through certain characteristic phases in discussion, or its members must develop a certain distribution of attitudes of respect and liking for one another. Like other functional theories, Bales's derives the features of individual behavior from the necessities of group equilibrium, and not vice versa [see INTERACTION, *article on* INTERACTION PROCESS ANALYSIS].

The difficulties with functional theories of small groups are those of functional theories in general. No social scientist has ever succeeded in formulating a rigorous statement of the general conditions of social equilibrium. The statements actually used are so vague that nothing definite can be derived from them. Moreover, many social groups do not remain in equilibrium, however it is defined, so that the range of phenomena the theory could explain must at best be limited. Finally, it is not at all clear that another type of theory cannot explain the phenomena, one that lacks the disadvantages of functional theory and possesses the further advantage of explaining findings functional theory cannot cope with. Indeed, functional theorists often find themselves inadvertently using the propositions of the other type of theory.

Psychological theory. Most students of small groups use in explanation, not always explicitly, some form of psychological theory. Psychological theories are so called because their most general propositions are propositions about the behavior of individual men, and not about the conditions of equilibrium in groups. They do not in the least deny that the behavior of men is social. What they do, in effect, deny is (for instance) that the general propositions describing the behavior of men when rewarded by the physical environment are different from those describing their behavior when rewarded by other men, although the analysis may be much more complex in the latter case than in the former. Psychological theories also assume there is no characteristic of a group that cannot be explained by the characteristics of the individuals making it up: in this sense the whole is not greater than the sum of its parts. Finally, psychological theories assume that their propositions hold good for all men, that although, for instance, members of different societies learn to behave in concretely different ways because the present circumstances and past histories of these societies have been different, yet the general characteristics of the learning process remain the same for all men.

Behavioral theory. In particular, some of the most prominent codifiers of small-group research have come to find most satisfactory for the explanation of the phenomena one or another of the psychological theories (called "behavioral" or "learning" theories) first developed by experimental psychologists working with animals. These theories need not be incompatible with other psychological theories, such as psychoanalytic ones, although the terminologies employed may be quite dissimilar.

The chief propositions of behavioral theory are of the following sorts: A man whose activity (some item of "voluntary" behavior) has been rewarded (or "reinforced") is apt to repeat that activity. He will repeat it the more often, the more successful it is in obtaining the reward. He is also more apt to repeat it, the more valuable (reinforcing) the reward is to him, and the value of the reward depends on the degree to which he has been deprived of it. Any activity that allows a man to escape or avoid punishment is also by that fact rewarded. A man usually has more than one activity open to him and more than one reward for these activities. The probability of his emitting one of the activities rather than another depends on the relative value of the alternative rewards and the relative probability of the success of the activities in obtaining them. When a particular stimulus situation (some set of cognitive elements) has also attended an occasion in the past when an activity has been rewarded, the presence of some similar stimulus on a new occasion will render it more probable that the activity will again be emitted. Finally, behavioral psychology states various propositions about emotional behavior, such as that when a man's activity has been regularly rewarded under

particular circumstances and then suddenly ceases to be so, he is apt to become angry, and in anger he is apt to find aggressive behavior rewarding. This is sometimes called the frustration–aggression hypothesis.

Behavior is social when the activities of each of at least two men reward (or punish) the activities of the other. Accordingly, the propositions of behavioral psychology may be used to explain the characteristics of social behavior, which is the real subject of small-group research. The variables whose relations are explained are the relative frequency with which each person emits alternative activities, the values to each of the rewards provided by the other, and the variations of stimuli along various cognitive dimensions, including the stimuli each person presents to the other. Since the value and frequency of the activities each emits affect the value and frequency of the other's activities, the way is at once opened for the explanation of social influence. As the number of persons in interaction increases the analysis obviously becomes very complex, but it can sometimes be handled with the help of simplifying assumptions that may approximate real conditions. Particularly interesting is the situation in which many members of a group set a high value on a scarce reward (scarce in the sense that only a few of the members are able to supply it). In this situation behavioral psychology is able to explain why there should be differences between the members in status and power. It can also begin to explain how a social structure, a stabilized set of social relations, may develop and maintain itself in a group. Indeed, most of the phenomena investigated by small-group research can be explained, at least in a gross way, by the propositions of behavioral psychology [see LEARNING THEORY].

Since this theory envisages social behavior as an exchange between persons of goods (rewards) in different amounts and of different values, it envisages social behavior as a generalized economy, and the specialized and highly developed economics dealing with prices and markets can be used to sharpen its formulations. Alternatively, behavioral psychology can help to explain the propositions of elementary economics, thus contributing to the intellectual unification of social science.

The need for explanatory principles

Too high hopes should not be held out for detailed explanation and prediction. The problem is partly one of getting the necessary information. Among the crucial variables, for instance, is the relative value to individuals of different rewards.

Yet many values are not innate in men but acquired by them in the course of their past experience. If the investigator knows that a man grew up in a particular culture, he may infer correctly that the man has shared the experiences, and hence the values, of other members of that culture. In other cases, the man's values may be quite atypical, the precipitate of idiosyncratic experiences. Without detailed knowledge of the man's past, the investigator, even if he commands the best psychology in the world, may be unable to predict the man's social behavior. Behavioral psychology itself explains why this should be so.

It must also be remembered that any small group, even one artificially formed, is part of a larger institutional structure. The behavior of its members cannot be wholly explained without reference to that structure. Thus a jury is certainly a small group, but one required by law to reach a unanimous decision in secret. So far as its members conform to the legal norms, their conformity affects their other relations. This does not mean that conformity to institutional norms, or even the nature of the norms themselves, cannot be explained by psychological principles. It does mean that institutional norms are always among the given conditions to be used in explaining face-to-face social behavior. Differences in cultural and institutional norms may help explain why apparently similar small-group experiments do not always yield the same results in different societies.

Detailed explanation and prediction also presents a problem of a different kind. The fundamental propositions of behavioral psychology are very general and refer to the behavior of individuals. How is the investigator to show what the resultant, or synthetic, implications of a set of propositions would be when many individuals are interacting in complicated and varying circumstances? Here the best hope lies in the increasing use of high-speed computers, whose virtue is precisely that of working out quickly the detailed implications of general propositions under varied parametric conditions.

Although students of elementary social behavior will take their basic explanatory principles from behavioral psychology, they will get little other help from the behavioral psychologists. Psychologists who have experimented with animals tend, when applying their principles to human behavior, to explain the learning processes of individuals or to jump to the gross features of institutions like religion and government in the larger society. Yet it may well be that in the long run a more convincing link between psychology and sociology will be forged by those who study at the same time the detailed behavior of individuals in interaction and the simpler social structures that emerge therefrom. They may indeed establish the first theoretical organization of the social sciences on a sound basis. This is the continuing justification of small-group research.

GEORGE CASPAR HOMANS

[*Directly related are the entries* COHESION, SOCIAL; INDUSTRIAL RELATIONS, *article on* HUMAN RELATIONS; SOCIOMETRY. *Other relevant material may be found in* FUNCTIONAL ANALYSIS; ROLE; SOCIAL PSYCHOLOGY; STATUS, SOCIAL; *and in the biographies of* COOLEY; LEWIN; MAYO; SIMMEL.]

BIBLIOGRAPHY

BALES, ROBERT F. 1950 *Interaction Process Analysis: A Method for the Study of Small Groups.* Reading, Mass.: Addison-Wesley.

BLAU, PETER (1955) 1963 *The Dynamics of Bureaucracy: A Study of Interpersonal Relations in Two Government Agencies.* Rev. ed. Univ. of Chicago Press.

BLAU, PETER M. 1964 *Exchange and Power in Social Life.* New York: Wiley.

CARTWRIGHT, DORWIN; and ZANDER, ALVIN (editors) (1953) 1960 *Group Dynamics: Research and Theory.* 2d ed. Evanston, Ill.: Row, Peterson.

CHAPPLE, ELIOT D.; and ARENSBERG, CONRAD M. 1940 Measuring Human Relations: An Introduction to the Study of the Interaction of Individuals. *Genetic Psychology Monographs* 22:3-147.

COHEN, ARTHUR R. 1964 *Attitude Change and Social Influence.* New York and London: Basic Books.

COOLEY, CHARLES H. (1909) 1956 *Social Organization: A Study of the Larger Mind.* In Charles H. Cooley, *Two Major Works:* Social Organization *and* Human Nature and the Social Order. Glencoe, Ill.: Free Press. → Each title reprinted with individual title page and pagination. Separate paperback editions were published in 1962 by Schocken.

GOLEMBIEWSKI, ROBERT T. 1962 *The Small Group: An Analysis of Research Concepts and Operations.* Univ. of Chicago Press.

GURVITCH, GEORGES (1950) 1957-1963 *La vocation actuelle de la sociologie.* 2d ed., 2 vols. Paris: Presses Universitaires de France. → Volume 1: *Vers la sociologie différentielle.* Volume 2: *Antécédents et perspectives.*

HARE, A. PAUL 1962 *Handbook of Small Group Research.* New York: Free Press.

HARE, A. PAUL; BORGATTA, E. F.; and BALES, R. F. (1955) 1965 *Small Groups: Studies in Social Interaction.* Rev. ed. New York: Knopf.

HEIDER, FRITZ 1958 *The Psychology of Interpersonal Relations.* New York: Wiley.

HOLLANDER, EDWIN P. 1964 *Leaders, Groups, and Influence.* New York: Oxford Univ. Press.

HOMANS, GEORGE C. 1950 *The Human Group.* New York: Harcourt.

HOMANS, GEORGE C. 1961 *Social Behavior: Its Elementary Forms.* New York: Harcourt.

HOPKINS, TERENCE K. 1964 *The Exercise of Influence in Small Groups.* Totowa, N.J.: Bedminster Press.

JENNINGS, HELEN H. (1943) 1950 *Leadership and Isolation: A Study of Personality in Inter-personal Relations.* 2d ed. New York: Longmans.

Klein, Josephine 1956 *The Study of Groups*. London: Routledge; New York: Humanities.

Lewin, Kurt (1939–1947) 1963 *Field Theory in Social Science: Selected Theoretical Papers*. Edited by Dorwin Cartwright. London: Tavistock.

Moreno, Jacob L. (1934) 1953 *Who Shall Survive? Foundations of Sociometry, Group Psychotherapy and Sociodrama*. Rev. & enl. ed. Beacon, N.Y.: Beacon House.

Olmsted, Michael S. 1959 *The Small Group*. New York: Random House.

Roethlisberger, Fritz J.; and Dickson, William J. (1939) 1961 *Management and the Worker: An Account of a Research Program Conducted by the Western Electric Company, Hawthorne Works, Chicago*. Cambridge, Mass.: Harvard Univ. Press. → A paperback edition was published in 1964 by Wiley.

Shepherd, Clovis R. 1964 *Small Groups: Some Sociological Perspectives*. San Francisco: Chandler.

Simmel, Georg (1902–1917) 1950 *The Sociology of Georg Simmel*. Translated and edited by Kurt H. Wolff. Glencoe, Ill.: Free Press.

Thibaut, John W.; and Kelley, Harold H. 1959 *The Social Psychology of Groups*. New York: Wiley.

Whitehead, Thomas N. 1938 *The Industrial Worker: A Statistical Study of Human Relations in a Group of Manual Workers*. 2 vols. Cambridge, Mass.: Harvard Univ. Press.

Whyte, William F. (1943) 1961 *Street Corner Society: The Social Structure of an Italian Slum*. 2d ed., enl. Univ. of Chicago Press.

II

GROUP BEHAVIOR

Although William James, Charles H. Cooley, and George H. Mead had, at the beginning of the century, stressed the importance of primary groups in the development of individual personality, it was not until the 1930s that the small group became a serious focus of scientific attention. A most remarkable independent development of research interest in small groups by a number of creative people in different social science disciplines occurred during this period. Elton Mayo and his colleagues at the Harvard Business School conducted their famous studies of industrial work groups at Western Electric; Jacob Moreno and Helen H. Jennings developed sociometric methods for investigating group structure; William F. Whyte employed anthropological techniques in the study that led to *Street Corner Society*; and Kurt Lewin, Ronald Lippitt, and Ralph White initiated the experimental study of democratic and authoritarian group leadership. At the same time, Paul Schilder, Samuel Slavson, and Trigant Burrow were doing pioneer work in group therapy.

These early interests and activities collectively seemed to have reached the "critical mass" by the end of World War II, resulting in an explosive and rapidly mushrooming interest in small groups. By 1960, about 2,200 small-group studies had been published, more than 80 per cent of which appeared in the decade 1950–1960. Since 1960, articles have been appearing at the rate of more than 250 per year.

No attempt will be made in this article to present the detailed findings of this enormous outpouring of research. Hare (1962) and McGrath and Altman (1966) provide useful summaries of the literature. Here I shall attempt to provide a framework within which some of the important findings can be integrated. The framework is oriented to such questions as: what is a group? what are the significant ways in which groups differ from one another? what are the effects of such differences?

What is a group? An examination of the different usages of the term "group" suggests that each combines a greater or lesser number of the following distinguishing criteria: two or more persons who (1) have one or more characteristics in common, (2) perceive themselves as forming a distinguishable entity, (3) are aware of the interdependence of some of their goals or interests, and (4) interact with one another in pursuit of their interdependent goals. In addition, some writers, particularly those with sociological backgrounds, indicate that (5) groups endure over a period of time and as a result develop (6) a set of social norms that regulate and guide member interaction and (7) a set of roles, each of which has specific activities, obligations, and rights associated with it. I shall use the term "group" to signify at least the first four of the distinguishing criteria listed above. This usage is consonant with the intuitive notion that a group is an entity that consists of interacting people who are aware of being psychologically bound together in terms of mutually linked interests. A group is thus to be distinguished from an aggregate, class, category, or type, which consist of people who are classified together because of some common characteristic. Also, "group" implies a psychological or perceived bond, not merely an objective linkage, between the members' interests or goals. Moreover, the psychological linkage has some cohesive feature to it—i.e., members of a group see that in some respects they sink or swim together. This latter statement is not meant to deny that divisive and disruptive tendencies may exist within a group; rather, it is meant to indicate that by definition a group does not exist if its cohesive bonds are not strong enough to contain its disunifying influences.

How groups differ. There are endless ways in which groups differ. It is useful to have some simplifying outline that highlights the central characteristics of groups and that permits a proliferation of detail as this becomes necessary. It is well to recognize that an outline abstracts variables from their contexts and their interrelationships, and thus presents them in somewhat distorted form. The outline that follows is guided by—but not limited to—the criteria of groups listed in the preceding section.

(1) Group size: the number of members in a group.

(2) Group composition: the individual characteristics of the members, including their distribution and patterning.

(3) Group structure: the patterning of member characteristics as perceived by the group members.

(4) The existential criteria of groups: the criteria for recognizing a group's existence, members, action, property, etc.

(5) Group cohesiveness: the type and strength of the interests binding the members to the group.

(6) Group task and environment: the task confronting the group, and the environment within which the group functions.

(7) Interactional process: the modes and patterns of interaction between members and with the task environment.

(8) Group culture: the norms, standards, role patterns, traditions, and customs operating within the group.

(9) Group effectiveness: the task performance, the viability of the group, the membership satisfaction, and the change within individual members.

It is useful to recognize that any causal arrow connecting an item with any other item in this outline is likely to be bidirectional rather than unidirectional. Consider group size and group composition. It is evident that increasing the number of members in a group will affect the composition of the group—e.g., the more people there are in a randomly composed group, the more likely it is that the group will contain an individual whose intelligence is above or below any specified level. However, the causal arrow also points in the other direction; if a group is composed of a certain kind of members, its size is likely to be affected. Thus, groups of young children are likely to have fewer members than groups of older children. Of course, the causal path in the direction from group composition to group size is longer and more circuitous than the path in the opposite direction: it weaves from group composition to interactional process to group effectiveness (member satisfaction) to group cohesiveness and arrives finally at group size (presumably a size that permits interactions that are satisfying to the children because they are within

their cognitive capabilities, and hence, the children are motivated to continue the group).

Some findings from the study of groups

I shall employ the outline presented above to organize the discussion of illustrative findings obtained from the study of groups. The studies of groups have been mainly of temporary *ad hoc* laboratory groups, created by the investigator, rather than of ongoing natural groups in their native habitats. Hence, there is no assurance that the research findings are generalizable. However, they do not seem inconsistent with everyday observations. Necessarily, the presentation is oversimplified. It largely ignores the evident fact that the effects of any given variable upon another (e.g., of group size upon interaction patterns) are very much influenced by other factors in the situation (e.g., the nature of the group task).

Group size. Hare (1962) and Thomas and Fink (1963) have reviewed the relevant research literature in some detail. The latter have presented a useful framework for viewing the major effects of variations in size. The schema presented here borrows from theirs. It is helpful to make a distinction between the statistical properties of size and the psychological properties of size. The former are those properties of a group that come from taking a given-sized sample of individuals, according to a given procedure, from a population with certain characteristics. The group is considered as an aggregate, and the psychological properties that arise from the compresence and interaction of its members are disregarded.

The statistical properties of size can be appreciated by observing how variations in size affect some common statistical measures: the sum, the mean, intragroup variability, the probability of the occurrence of any characteristic, the probability of concordance of characteristics, the variability of the statistical properties. Consider the resources (perceptual capacity, memory capacity, information, intellectual capacity, physical strength, skills, money, tools, and so forth) available as size increases. Clearly, the *total* resources, such as the total money in the group, will increase as a linear function of size. However, the *usable* resources will be determined by the task and environment. In certain tasks it does not help the group to have any duplication of a resource (e.g., to have more than one person who knows how to type; to have several mimeographing machines). Hence, the usable resources will often increase at a slower rate than the total resources and often will, beyond a certain point, not increase at all. If this is so, as size increases, the average usable resource per member will decrease. This reasoning explains why, for certain kinds of tasks, group performance as measured by production per group member decreases as size increases, even as total production goes up: not all of the total resources are usable.

As the size of a sample increases, the probability that any given characteristic will appear (that someone will have red hair, that someone will favor vegetarianism) increases. The probability that at least one individual of a group has some given characteristic clearly depends on the frequency of the characteristic in the population from which the group was formed, the size of the group, and the manner of group formation. If the members of the group manifest statistical independence regarding the characteristic, and if the probability, P_i, that any individual has the characteristic is a constant, then the probability that *at least* one member of the group has the characteristic is $1 - (1 - P_i)^N$, where N is group size. Thus, as N increases, the probability increases toward 1. Even for more realistic assumptions about group formation, it is clear that, as group size increases, so does the probability that the group contains at least one individual having any preassigned characteristic. Thus, the larger the size of a group, the more likely it is to have any or all of the following: a very bright person, a very stupid person, a quiet person, a talkative person, a "right-winger," a "left-winger."

Similarly, the probability that *every* member of the group has the given characteristic generally decreases as group size increases, for most reasonable assumptions about group formation. Under the assumptions of independence and constancy, the probability that all group members have the characteristic is P_i^N, which decreases exponentially as N increases. Hence, as the size of a group increases, it is less likely that all individuals will have the same opinion or speak the same language or be equally informed or be equally resourceful. Although heterogeneity is likely to be greater within larger groups, larger groups are less likely to vary from one another in aggregate properties than are smaller groups. (A group of 20 persons is more likely to have the same average IQ as another group the same size than are two groups of three persons.)

Size affects not only the statistical properties of the aggregated resources and other characteristics of the group but also the *opportunity* to satisfy individual wants—for example, the larger the group, the more time, space, supplies, and facilities it will need to enable all individuals in the group to talk and be heard. Thus, if the total amount of time, reward, and space remain constant for a given task environment, the opportunity for individual participation and reward will decrease as the size of the group increases. On the other hand, the number of potential interpersonal relations increases geometrically as size increases. For example, the number of possible dyadic relations in any group increases with size (N) according to the formula: $(N^2 - N)/2$. Since there appears to be a numerical limit to the capacity to establish close associations with others, a smaller proportion of the possible linkages will be formed as size increases.

From our discussion so far, it should be clear that different-sized aggregates of noninteracting individuals should differ predictably. The larger-sized aggregates should have more resources and more handicaps; more good solutions and more bad solutions; more diversity and difference; more demands for the available opportunities; more opportunity for diversified interpersonal contact but less for repeated contact. If the task environment is such that the presence of resources, good solutions, heterogeneity, and so forth, are more important factors than the presence of handicaps, bad solutions, and homogeneity in determining productivity, then larger aggregates should be more productive than smaller aggregates. But groups are not simply aggregates; they are composed of interacting individuals. A group's performance may differ from the performance of a comparable aggregate of individuals because the contributions the individuals make in the group will be affected by the group milieu and because the group will combine or assemble the individual performances in a unique manner.

Audience effects. Social influence on individual thinking may reflect either the effect of working before an audience (such as other group members) or the impact of the contributions being made by the other group members. Research results, generally, indicate that there is increased motivation and increased distraction when a person works on intellectual problems before an audience rather than by himself (Kelley & Thibaut 1954). In addition, there tend to be fewer idiosyncratic thoughts, more moderation in judgments, more common associations, more cautiousness, and a general taking into account of the anticipated reactions of the audience. Over a period of time, adaptation to being observed tends to occur (Deutsch 1949), and hence the "audience effects" tend to decrease. Some research evidence (Atkinson 1964) suggests that once motivation to achieve passes beyond a certain moderate level, further increase in motivation tends to result in less effective performance.

Problem solving and productivity. The preceding discussion of "audience effects" suggests the possibility that as the size of a group increases, the intellectual functioning of its members will deteriorate: they will be "overmotivated," more distracted, and more conventional. But other members of a group do not merely serve as an audience. They also contribute new information and different perspectives; they invoke more aspects of memory and demand greater attention; they provide more material for the individual to think with and about. That is, the contributions of other members may provide new associational starting points, may help the individual to break out of an ineffective set by suggesting new orientations, may fill in gaps or reveal unnoticed errors in the individual's thinking. On the other hand, the contributions of other members may distract, interrupt a chain of thought, blot out an individual's own associations, or confuse him by providing too much material for him to assimilate at one time. The meager relevant research indicates that the contribution of others may be more distracting than useful when the task confronting the individual is one that requires sustained, directed attention to a complex pattern where the relations between sequentially ordered parts must be kept in mind (e.g., in "reasoning" problems). In such a task, individuals working alone will hit upon different approaches (or will symbolize the same approach differently), and once they have taken a few steps on their respective approaches, understanding each other may be difficult without going back to the initial formulation of the approach or until an obvious solution has been reached. Hence, with such a task, the larger the group, the more likely it is that it will interfere with the individual's thinking. On the other hand, when the task is such that the individual is likely to have an initial set that would lead to a clichéd or superficial solution to the problem and would overlook some of its major dimensions, the contributions of other members (starting from different sets, which may also be superficial) may force the individual to go deeper into the problem [*see* PROBLEM SOLVING].

A group solution will depend not only upon the abilities of its members to think within the milieu of the group but also upon the readiness and ability of the members to contribute to the group and upon the way in which their contributions are coordi-nated, assembled, or weighted to produce the resultant group solution. With regard to the readiness and ability of members to contribute, research indicates that the inequality of participation among the various members of a group increases as the size of the group increases (Stephan & Mishler 1952; Bales et al. 1951). These results suggest that individuals who tend to be shy are unlikely to participate actively in larger groups, although they may contribute much in small groups. On the other hand, individuals who tend to be assertive are likely to have a disproportionately large influence in larger groups as compared with smaller groups.

With regard to the coordination, assembling, or weighting of the contributions that individual members make, investigations have found that the difficulty of keeping track of the contributions of the various members, of coordinating and assembling them, will increase as the size of the group increases. For success in resolving this difficulty, larger groups have to devote more of their energy to activities directed toward coordination than do smaller groups. In addition, it is reasonable to hypothesize that such personality factors as self-confidence, assertiveness, and persuasiveness are more likely to play a significant role in determining the individual's impact upon the group solution in larger groups than in smaller groups.

Member satisfaction, also, is affected by the size of the group. Laboratory and field studies both indicate that members of small groups are more likely to feel satisfied with their group, more likely to inhibit expression of disagreement, and less likely to develop cliques and factions. Large groups, on the other hand, are characterized by more absenteeism, more formality, and more internal conflict than are smaller groups.

Group composition. How are the individual members of a group characterized? The answers to this question presuppose that one knows what features of the members may influence the way they interact, interrelate, and function together. There is as yet, however, little systematic knowledge of how group composition—the distribution and patterning of member characteristics—affects group behavior. Nevertheless, it is reasonable to think that a group's behavior will be affected by the distribution and patterning of such member characteristics as abilities, knowledge, resources, attitudes, interests, personality dispositions, age, sex, and social status. The combined characteristics of the members may be considered in terms of their influence upon the group's effectiveness in coping with the task confronting it. Or they may be related to the compatibility of the members with one another, the attraction of the group for various members, the likelihood of the formation of cliques, and so forth.

Effectiveness. With regard to group effectiveness, considerable research supports the common-sense proposition that groups whose members have high abilities, training, or experience are more effective than groups whose members are lacking in these respects (McGrath & Altman 1966). However, it is not simply the average level of abilities that is important, but rather whether the kinds of abilities necessary to carrying out the role requirements set by the group's task exist among the group members and are appropriately distributed. Group composition must be evaluated in reference to the demands confronting the group rather than in a vacuum. Homogeneity of member characteristics is an asset when the various group members are called upon to fulfill the same task functions, but it is a liability when there are varied functions to perform. For example, it is reasonable to assume that a group composed of both "abstract thinkers" and "concrete thinkers" will be more effective in performing in a task requiring both intellectual analysis and action than a group composed exclusively of one or the other type. Hoffman, Harburg, and Maier (1962) report results indicating that groups composed of individuals with dissimilar personalities are more productive than homogeneous groups. Schutz (1958) has theorized that compatibility is likely to be greater when people with different but complementary personality dispositions are paired together (e.g., people who wish to give affection and people who wish to receive it) than when people of similar dispositions are paired together (e.g., two people who wish to dominate). His research indicates that groups composed of members with compatible interpersonal tendencies are more productive than those composed of members with incompatible tendencies.

Patterns of interaction. There is a vast body of research on the effect of the personal and social characteristics of members on the development of attitudes toward the group, interactional patterns within the group, etc. Much of this research is considered in the sociometric literature. In general, research supports the saying, Birds of a feather flock together. People prefer to associate and interact with others who are similar rather than dissimilar to themselves in attitudes, status, background, interests, and so forth. The major exceptions to this generalization occur when similarity enhances competition (e.g., when two suitors are interested in the same girl); personal needs require complementarity rather than similarity (e.g., in heterosexual relations); or task requirements necessitate differentiated functions and statuses.

Individual behavior. There has also been much study of the personality characteristics that affect the performance of members in small groups. Mann (1959), reviewing the literature from 1900 through October 1957, focused on seven personality factors: intelligence, adjustment, extroversion–introversion, dominance, masculinity–femininity, conservatism, and interpersonal sensitivity. He summarized the relations between each of the seven personality variables and each of the following measures of an individual's status and behavior in groups: leadership, popularity, total activity rate, task activity, social–emotional activity, and conformity. His survey indicates that the best single predictor of an individual's behavior in the group is his intelligence. Intelligence and also extroversion and adjustment are positively related to total activity rate, leadership, and popularity in the group. In addition, the more intelligent and better-adjusted members are likely to contribute a relatively larger share of their total activity to building up group solidarity and providing emotional support for other members and a relatively smaller share to being critical or rejecting other members. Dominance is related positively to leadership and negatively to conformity; conservatism, on the other hand, is associated negatively with leadership and correlated positively with conformity. Masculinity and interpersonal sensitivity show positive relationships to leadership and popularity. Mann (1959, p. 266) concludes his review with the caution that the magnitude of the median of the correlations between an aspect of personality and performance is in no case higher than .25, and most of the medians of the correlations are nearer .15.

Group structure. Popular conceptions of group and organizational structure have been very much influenced by organizational charts, developed in the military and other large bureaucracies, that stress lines of formal authority. This is too limited a view. It is more fruitful to think of structure in terms of the way members actually relate to one another. In a sense the term "group structure" is a misnomer; there may be many different "structures" within a group—the work structure, the communication structure, the friendship structure, the power structure, the prestige structure, and so forth.

There is often a correspondence among the positions an individual holds in the different structures, so that an individual who holds a central position in one structure (e.g., the communication structure) is likely to hold a central position in other structures (power, friendship, and prestige). The research of Galtung (1964) in Norway indicates that this is the case for Norwegian society: people who are more central on social variables (income, education, occupation, residence, age, and sex) are also more central in the communication and power structures. In the status-equilibration hypothesis, Benoît-Smullyan (1944) and, later, Homans (1961) have stressed the forces that operate to make for similarity in the positions of an individual in different structures. However, status equilibrium is not always achieved. Research by Adams (1953) with air crews demonstrated that lack of congruence on such status dimensions as age, military rank, education, reputed ability, popularity, combat time, and position importance was related to poor morale, less friendliness, and lack of mutual confidence. Exline and Ziller (1959), working with experimentally created groups, found that groups constructed so as to have incongruent status hierarchies manifested more interpersonal conflict and less productivity than congruent groups.

In addition to research on status congruency, research on group structures has investigated such topics as (1) the effects of different communication structures (Guetzkow 1953); (2) the effects of different leadership structures, for example, leaderless groups versus groups with leaders, and of leadership style (Fiedler 1964); (3) the effects of different residential and propinquity structures (Festinger et al. 1950); (4) the effects of similarity or dissimilarity on various social and personal characteristics, such as age, sex, religious belief, attitudes; (5) the Kafkaesque effects of complex organizational structures, which are dimly perceived and little understood by members; (6) the determinants of sociometric structure, leadership structure, communication structure, etc.; (7) methods of classifying and identifying roles within groups (Bales 1950); and (8) mathematical procedures for characterizing different types of structures and different positions within a structure (Coleman 1964).

The existential criteria of groups. Although a vast body of legal principle and practice has been concerned with the conditions under which a "legal personality," such as a corporation, can come into existence, and with the identifying of those who can act in its name, there has been little social-psychological research that bears upon such related problems as how a group is identified and what determines whether an action of a member is attributed to the group or to him personally. However, drawing upon studies of perceptual organization, it is possible to indicate some general principles concerning the conditions that are conducive to the perception that a collection of individuals or units are part of a system rather than an unorganized aggregate of elements.

As Koffka (1935) pointed out, abrupt discontinuity produces segregating forces between the parts of a visual field that it separates, as well as unifying forces within the separated parts. Further, he indicated that homogeneity tends to produce unifying forces in the visual field. Homogeneity may be based upon (1) the common fate of the elements perceived (they move together); (2) their qualitative or quantitative similarity (they have the same color or the same luminosity); (3) proximity (they occur in spatial or temporal contiguity); (4) a common boundary; (5) past experience or custom that has led to similar responses to the various elements; and (6) set or the expectation that the elements are to be grouped together [see GESTALT THEORY].

It seems evident that processes analogous to these determine whether an individual will perceive a collection of individuals as a social group and whether he will perceive himself to be part of the group. Thus, if an individual perceives that he and some others are strikingly different in certain respects from the remainder of the people in their surroundings; that he and the others tend to be satisfied or dissatisfied at the same time or under similar circumstances; that he and the others have similar attitudes or similar backgrounds; that he and the others live or work in close proximity; that he and the others are associated together in other people's minds or treated similarly by other people —if he perceives any of these patterns, the individual is likely to perceive himself and the others as cooperatively interdependent. I would stress, as does Campbell (1958), the central role of the perception of common fate in determining the consciousness of being joined with others to form a group.

Group cohesiveness. In everyday usage "cohesiveness" refers to the tendency to stick together; its usage in social psychology is much the same. It refers to the linkages that bind the members of a group together. Deutsch (1949; 1962) has stressed that the linkages among members are cohesive, rather than disruptive, when the goals and interests of the members are cooperatively, rather than competitively, interrelated. Various aspects of these linkages have been the focus of research: the nature of the mutually linked goals or interests—such as friendship, work, money; the strength of the mutually linked goals or interests; the degree of linkage, and the availability of other means of obtaining one's goals; the forces operating to restrain members from leaving the group; other interests or memberships that are in opposition to continued membership in the group.

Since group cohesiveness is central to the existence of groups, it is natural that its determinants and also its consequences have been studied extensively (Hare 1962; Collins & Guetzkow 1964; McGrath & Altman 1966). Research findings, over-all, indicate that cohesiveness (as measured by interpersonal congeniality, the desire to remain a member of the group, attitudes toward the group's functioning, or other similar measures) is consistently associated with greater communication between group members, greater readiness of group members to be influenced by the group, more consensus among members on attitudes and beliefs that relate to group functioning, more sense of responsibility toward each other among group members, a greater feeling of personal ease and security within the group by the group members, and so forth. Also, task effectiveness is generally positively correlated with cohesiveness if high accomplishment on the task is valued by the group (some groups restrict performance to achieve their objectives) and if the task is such that its performance is likely to be enhanced by increased group effort. It should be noted that the causal arrow is bidirectional: group cohesiveness not only increases intragroup communication and group success, but group success and intragroup communication increase group cohesiveness [see COHESION, SOCIAL].

Group task and environment. It is self-evident that the task confronting the group and the environment within which the group functions can influence all the other characteristics of a group. Unfortunately, however, the research relating to task and environmental characteristics has been meager, largely because there has not yet been developed any systematic way of characterizing tasks or environments. Nevertheless, certain useful distinctions have been made.

It is possible to characterize many tasks and environments in terms of the type of requirements for success that they impose upon the group. It is apparent that tasks differ in the types and amounts of skills, knowledge, effort, and resources required and in the way these factors have to be interrelated. In other words, the roles within the group, the structure of the group, the size of the group, etc., may vary as a function of the group's task and environment.

Fiedler (1964), for example, has shown that the effectiveness of different types of leaders is very closely related to the structure of the task confronting the group. In both field and laboratory studies, his findings indicate that controlling, authoritarian leaders tend to be most effective either in very favorable or else in relatively unfavorable group-task situations, while the permissive, considerate, democratic leaders are most effective in situations that are intermediate in favorableness. Fiedler indicates that a situation is very favorable when (1) the leader–member relations are positive, (2) the task is clear and well structured, and (3) the leader has well-defined authority and power to reward and punish. Thus, for example, if a leader has good personal relations with his group and the task is routine and his authority well-defined, he is likely to be more effective if he is "directive," rather than democratic and permissive. On the other hand, if the task is novel and unstructured but the situation is otherwise similar, democratic, permissive leadership is likely to be more effective [see LEADERSHIP].

Task structure helps to determine the types and amounts of interaction and communication within a group and also the sequencing and organization of the activities within the group. These, in turn, will often affect the social relations that develop within a group. Much research has supported the proposition (Homans 1950) that people who interact frequently with one another tend to like one another, and vice versa. Thus, tasks that require certain group members to work closely with one another and limit their interaction with other members may, if the task is long-enduring, help to create patterns of friendship that parallel the interactional requirements of the task. Further, the research indicates that if a task places a given individual in a central position because he is able to communicate readily with other members or because he possesses a scarce resource (a skill, specialized information, or a particular tool) that is of critical value to group success, then he is likely to have high status within the group (and high satisfaction with the group).

Tasks differ in the degree to which they permit division of labor and specialization of function. The problem of dividing tasks into subtasks, of sequencing them, and of assigning personnel and resources to them has been of major interest to economists and operations-research analysts, and they have had considerable success in developing rational methods of predicting the effectiveness of different methods of dividing up a task. Here let us note some psychological aspects of the division of labor. Among its possible negative consequences are the loss of one's identification with the over-all group objectives; the loss of a sense of an over-all significance and meaning to one's activities; the development of vested interests in one's specialized activities; the development of specialized languages, values, and modes of thought that interfere with coordination and communication between the various specialized activities. Among the possible positive consequences of specialization is, in addition to increased group productivity and individual economic reward, the greater chance that an individual will be able to find some activity that matches his particular interests and abilities.

Tasks and environments differ not only in their activity and interaction requirements but also in their stressfulness. The term "stress" has been used to refer to a hypothetical state of tension, frustration, or internal conflict induced by such conditions as task difficulty (e.g., a problem without any solution), lack of information about how well the task is being performed, threat of punishment for task failure, danger (e.g., as in combat or survival in the Arctic), intense criticism, time pressure, an unpredictable environment. The results of studies of the effects of such varied conditions are not univocal. The safest generalization seems to be that mild stress often improves group performance and enhances group cohesiveness, while severe stress often has the opposite effects. Optimal stress for a group is presumably higher the more able and cohesive the group is and the more the members see themselves as able and motivated to cope with problems (Deutsch 1959).

Finally, it is relevant to note that environments differ in the probability of reward and the amount of reward they provide for effective group action and also in the manner in which rewards are distributed within a group. Little research has been done on the effects of different "schedules of reinforcement" upon group behavior, yet there is reason to assume that they would influence group performance (Shapiro 1963). On the other hand, a considerable number of research studies (e.g., Deutsch 1949; Raven & Eachus 1963) have demonstrated that whether rewards are distributed cooperatively or competitively within a group may have a striking effect on member behavior. In general, group members who are rewarded cooperatively show more positive response to one another, have greater involvement in the group, are less likely to work at cross-purposes, communicate with one another more effectively, and work more productively together than group members who are rewarded competitively.

Interactional process. The observable transactions between members and their observable transactions with their task environments are lumped together under the term "interactional process." It is, in effect, what goes on in groups. There are many different ways of characterizing what goes on. Most of them focus on one or more of the following aspects of a transaction: *who* communicates or does *what* to or with *whom;* with what *intent* or function; *how, when,* or under what conditions; through what *media* or channels; with what *effects* upon *whom,* as perceived by *whom.* Each of the italicized terms could be elaborated in considerable detail. For example, if one specified the characteristics of the potential communicators and communicatees (the *who* and the *whom*)—their statuses, their personality tendencies, their pre-existing attitudes toward one another—one could predict, to some degree, *who* will talk to *whom* and *how* they will talk. (The demeanor of a subordinate making a critical remark to a superior will be rather different from that of a superior criticizing a subordinate.) Similarly, knowledge of the *conditions* —e.g., what stage in problem solving the group is at—enables one to predict what kinds of content (the *what*) a transaction is likely to have.

The most widely used system for categorizing interactions is the one developed by Bales (1950). It focuses on the *who*-to-*whom*-and-*what* interaction. His system consists of 12 distinct categories of the content of communication: content that (1) shows solidarity, (2) shows tension release, (3) agrees, (4) gives suggestion, (5) gives opinion, (6) gives orientation, (7) asks for orientation, (8) asks for opinion, (9) asks for suggestion, (10) disagrees, (11) shows tension, and (12) shows antagonism. The categories are grouped in various ways. One major grouping is into task categories (subdivided into questions and attempted answers) and social–emotional categories (classified as positive and negative). More recently Stone and his co-workers (1962) have devised a more generalized system of content analysis called the General Inquirer, which employs a computer to code the actual verbal text of group interaction into 164 categories [*see* INTERACTION, *article on* INTERACTION PROCESS ANALYSIS].

Slater (1955) has shown that members who are ranked high as "idea men" by the other members in problem-solving groups initiate interaction more markedly in "attempted answers," while members who are ranked high in likability participate more heavily in the categories grouped as "positive social–emotional." His research has also indicated that often the task leader, or idea man, and the social–emotional leader are not the same person; this specialization of interaction function is more evident if the group exists over a period of time. In other words, as Barnard (1938) had noted earlier, the two major problems confronting groups —adaptation to their task environment and provision of personal satisfaction to the individual members—do not necessarily lead to the same emphases within a group.

Why do people interact? Few theorists have gone beyond the common-sense viewpoint that they do so because it is instrumental to a given end or because it is gratifying in itself. Festinger and his associates (1950), however, have suggested that one of the major instrumental functions of interaction is helping to establish "social reality": the validation of opinions, beliefs, abilities, and emotions in terms of a social consensus. That is, one of the functions of communication within a group is to establish uniform views about reality, so as to provide the members with some confidence in their beliefs and to enable them to coordinate their behavior for effective group action. Thus, group members whose views deviate from those held by the rest of the group will be subject, through communication, to pressures to change their views to conform to those of the rest, or they will be rejected or isolated by the group, so as to eliminate a source of disturbance to the group. Festinger hypothesized that these pressures are greater the more cohesive the group is, the more relevant the belief is to the group, the more discrepant the deviant's viewpoint is, etc. A considerable body of research is consistent with these hypotheses. Festinger has also suggested that communication may function as a substitute for social locomotion—people who would like to be in powerful positions direct their communication toward those who hold such positions. The study by Kelley (1951) of communication in experimentally created hierarchies is consistent with this hypothesis. However, Cohen (1958) suggests that upward communication may be more directly motivated by the desire to receive the benefits that a higher-status person can bestow upon someone of lower status.

Group culture. The members of any group who have had a prolonged experience of interacting with one another tend to develop shared values, expectations, and rules—a normative consensus that helps to regulate interaction between members and between the group and its task environment and that also serves to define the roles of the various members, including their specialized activities, rights, and responsibilities. A normative consensus, or group norm, sets criteria for evaluating the desirability–undesirability, acceptability–unacceptability, of the group members' activities, beliefs, appearance, etc., and for responding with various sanctions, positive or negative, such as reward–punishment, approval–disapproval, to a member's conformity with or violation of the norm [see NORMS].

Norms develop about many things, from the type of pronoun to be used in addressing intimates or strangers to the type of wine one should serve on certain occasions. Yet not everything is regulated. Norms tend to develop mostly in areas that are relevant to the group's functioning, and it seems likely that the more important an area is to the group, the more norms there will be, the more intense will be the sanctions employed to obtain conformity to them, and the smaller will be the range of acceptable behavior. Thus, as Sutherland has shown, the norm of punctuality in appearing at a prearranged time and place is strictly enforced among professional thieves because its violation may endanger an enterprise and lead to arrest (Conwell 1937). Norms are more often developed with regard to overt behavior than private beliefs, not only because the former are usually more important to group functioning but also because beliefs are less controllable, being less observable than behavior. Further, it is apparent that the norms of different types of groups will differ—for example, the norms of a friendship group and those of a work group. It is not uncommon for a person to experience conflict because he belongs to groups that have conflicting norms [see CONFORMITY].

There is an extensive research literature on the determinants of conformity and deviation to group norms (for a summary, see Symposium on Conformity . . . 1961). It is not a great oversimplification to sum up the findings as indicating that conformity appears to be a function of such factors as the person's awareness of the norm, the strength of the norm, the strength of the person's attraction to the group, the likelihood that conformity or deviation will be observable by others, the strength of the sanctions expected for conforming or deviating, personality predisposition (such as dependency, acceptance of authority, self-confidence). Whether a person will conform will depend not only on these factors but also on the strength of the tendency to deviate, which is determined by parallel considerations (e.g., is the tendency to deviate from the norms of one group a tendency to conform to the norms of another group to which the person belongs?).

Groups not only develop norms, which specify the "shoulds" and "should nots"; often they also develop styles, traditions, or customs (and these often become the object of norms), which are the habitual ways of dealing with recurring situations. Thus, a group may develop a unique language (almost every profession and trade develops its own "slang," its own peculiar abbreviations); distinctive garb, insignia, or appearance, to permit ready identification; a distinctive locale for meeting and engaging in its activities; a special style of inducing emotional responsiveness and of expressing emotion (e.g., distinctive dances, ceremonies), etc. Case-study material suggests that groups are most likely to develop idiosyncratic traditions if they are relatively isolated, as a result of geographical or social factors (due to superior or inferior status); if they are in conflict with other groups; or if their task environment is unique.

Anthropologists have, of course, studied and described in considerable detail the customs and traditions of many simple societies. A similar kind of analysis could be made of the development of customs and traditions in experimentally created or naturally formed groups, to investigate some of the determinants of particular kinds of traditions and customs. Unfortunately, little research has been conducted, apart from the pioneering studies of Sherif (1936), Merei (1949), and Rose and Felton (1955).

Group effectiveness. A group's effectiveness may be characterized in such terms as (1) *task performance*—the quality and quantity of the group's outputs, as measured in terms of external criteria; (2) *group viability*—the group's ability to maintain itself as a functioning group under varying conditions; (3) *member satisfaction*—the desire of the members to maintain their membership and to contribute to the group's viability and the attainment of group goals; and (4) *member change*—the change in knowledge, skills, attitudes, adjustment, or personality of the individual members of the group. Although there may be relations between these different types of group effectiveness over the long run, in the short run, however, it is evident that these different types of outcome may vary independently of one another. For example, high member satisfaction may result from or result in high task accomplishment, but high task accomplishment may also occur at the cost of member satisfaction (as when a demanding leader drives the group members on despite their protests).

The bulk of research on group effectiveness has been concerned with the determinants of task performance. This research highlights the importance of the following types of determinants: (1) the strength of the values associated with effective task performance—e.g., the greater the potential rewards for good performance and the more task-oriented the group norms, the more effort the group will be willing to put into the task; (2) the cohesiveness of the group—e.g., the more the members value the group and one another, the more willing they will be to expend effort in compliance with group norms or to achieve group-defined goals; (3) the perceived difficulty of the task—e.g., a task that is perceived to be very easy or virtually impossible is likely to stimulate less effort than a task that is viewed as difficult but attainable; (4) the amount of task-revelant abilities, information, and experience of the group members; (5) the appropriateness of the group structure to the requirements of the task—e.g., how efficient is the particular kind of division of labor for the task? how do the abilities, knowledge, and interests of the role occupants fit the requirements of their roles?; (6) the central role of the group leader and the appropriateness of his leadership style to the task and to the group.

Although there have been many studies of task performance, research in this area has been plagued by the problem of establishing reliable and valid measures of group achievement. There is little evidence to indicate that one group tends to perform reliably or consistently better than another group on a given task. Nor can one predict with much confidence, from a group's performance on one task, how it will do on another similar task. Research investigators in this area have not yet begun to develop any measures of group achievement that have the usefulness of many of the measures of individual achievement.

The determinants of member satisfaction have been studied as extensively as those of task effectiveness (for summaries, see Collins & Guetzkow 1964; McGrath & Altman 1966). In brief, the relevant research indicates that a member's satisfaction is affected by (1) the status of the group—its successfulness, its task achievements, its prestige; (2) the interpersonal relations within the group—the attractiveness of the other group members, their attitude toward him, their attitude toward belonging to the group; (3) the member's role within the group—its prestige, communication centrality, power, significance, interest; (4) the direct rewards and benefits received from membership; (5) the group atmosphere, as determined by such factors as leadership style, group size, group composition; and (6) the nature and desirability of conflicting memberships or activities.

Little research has been done on the determinants of environmental input and of group viability.

There is, however, an extensive literature on member change. Much of the relevant research has been done under the rubric of conformity and deviation (for summaries, see Symposium on Conformity . . . 1961). Also, the growing literature on group psychotherapy (for representative papers, see Rosenbaum & Berger 1963) contains many insightful case discussions, even though the amount of systematic research is still quite small [*see* MENTAL DISORDERS, TREATMENT OF, *article on* GROUP PSYCHOTHERAPY].

In addition, there is a rapidly developing list of publications dealing with human-relations training groups that are concerned with helping people learn how to function more effectively in groups. Here, too, the amount of published research is negligible. Nevertheless, since the stimulus to this approach to human-relations training came from the theoretical writings on re-education and reaction research of Kurt Lewin (1935–1946), much of the literature on training groups is imbued with social science concepts and suggests research. The major ideas of Kurt Lewin that underlie the training-group approach are that the re-education process basically involves the equivalent of a change in culture, and that for the individual to accept a new system of values and beliefs, he must come to value his membership in a group that has these new values and beliefs as a central component of its culture.

MORTON DEUTSCH

[*Other relevant material may be found in* SOCIAL PSYCHOLOGY *and in the biography of* LEWIN.]

BIBLIOGRAPHY

ADAMS, STUART 1953 Status Congruency as a Variable in Small Group Performance. *Social Forces* 32:16–22.

ATKINSON, JOHN W. 1964 *An Introduction to Motivation.* New York: Van Nostrand.

BALES, ROBERT F. 1950 A Set of Categories for the Analysis of Small Group Interaction. *American Sociological Review* 15:257–263.

BALES, ROBERT F. et al. 1951 Channels of Communication in Small Groups. *American Sociological Review* 16:461–468.

BARNARD, CHESTER I. (1938) 1962 *The Functions of the Executive.* Cambridge, Mass.: Harvard Univ. Press.

BENOÎT-SMULLYAN, ÉMILE 1944 Status, Status Types, and Status Interrelations. *American Sociological Review* 9:151–161.

CAMPBELL, DONALD T. 1958 Common Fate, Similarity, and Other Indices of the Status of Aggregates of Persons as Social Entities. *Behavioral Science* 3:14–25.

COHEN, ARTHUR R. 1958 Upward Communication in Experimentally Created Hierarchies. *Human Relations* 11:41–53.

COLEMAN, JAMES S. 1964 *Introduction to Mathematical Sociology.* New York: Free Press.

COLLINS, BARRY E.; and GUETZKOW, HAROLD 1964 *A So-cial Psychology of Group Processes for Decision-making.* New York: Wiley.

CONWELL, CHIC 1937 *The Professional Thief: By a Professional Thief.* Annotated and interpreted by Edwin H. Sutherland. Univ. of Chicago Press. → A paperback edition was published in 1960.

DEUTSCH, MORTON 1949 An Experimental Study of the Effects of Co-operation and Competition Upon Group Process. *Human Relations* 2:199–231.

DEUTSCH, MORTON 1959 Some Factors Affecting Membership Motivation and Achievement Motivation in a Group. *Human Relations* 12:81–95.

DEUTSCH, MORTON 1962 Cooperation and Trust: Some Theoretical Notes. Volume 10, pages 275–319 in *Nebraska Symposium on Motivation,* edited by Marshall R. Jones. Lincoln: Univ. of Nebraska Press.

EXLINE, RALPH V.; and ZILLER, ROBERT C. 1959 Status Congruency and Interpersonal Conflict in Decision-making Groups. *Human Relations* 12:147–162.

FESTINGER, LEON; SCHACHTER, STANLEY; and BACK, KURT (1950) 1963 *Social Pressures in Informal Groups: A Study of Human Factors in Housing.* Stanford Univ. Press.

FIEDLER, FRED E. 1964 A Contingency Model of Leadership Effectiveness. Volume 1, pages 149–190 in *Advances in Experimental Social Psychology.* New York: Academic Press.

GALTUNG, JOHAN 1964 Foreign Policy Opinion as a Function of Social Position. *Journal of Peace Research* 1:206–231.

GUETZKOW, HAROLD (1953) 1960 Differentiation of Roles in Task-oriented Groups. Pages 683–704 in Dorwin Cartwright and Alvin Zander (editors), *Group Dynamics: Research and Theory.* 2d ed. Evanston, Ill.: Row, Peterson.

HARE, ALEXANDER P. 1962 *Handbook of Small Group Research.* New York: Free Press.

HOFFMAN, L. RICHARD; HARBURG, ERNEST; and MAIER, NORMAN R. F. 1962 Differences and Disagreement as Factors in Creative Group Problem Solving. *Journal of Abnormal and Social Psychology* 64:206–214.

HOMANS, GEORGE C. 1950 *The Human Group.* New York: Harcourt.

HOMANS, GEORGE C. 1961 *Social Behavior: Its Elementary Forms.* New York: Harcourt.

KELLEY, HAROLD H. 1951 Communication in Experimentally Created Hierarchies. *Human Relations* 4:39–56.

KELLEY, HAROLD H.; and THIBAUT, JOHN W. 1954 Experimental Studies of Group Problem Solving and Process. Volume 2, pages 735–785 in Gardner Lindzey (editor), *Handbook of Social Psychology.* Cambridge, Mass.: Addison-Wesley.

KOFFKA, KURT 1935 *Principles of Gestalt Psychology.* New York: Harcourt.

LEWIN, KURT (1935–1946) 1948 *Resolving Social Conflicts: Selected Papers on Group Dynamics.* Edited by Gertrud W. Lewin. A publication of the University of Michigan Research Center for Group Dynamics. New York: Harper.

McGRATH, J. E.; and ALTMAN, I. 1966 *Small Group Research: A Synthesis and Critique.* New York: Holt.

MANN, RICHARD D. 1959 A Review of the Relationships Between Personality and Performance in Small Groups. *Psychological Bulletin* 56:241–270.

MEREI, FERENC 1949 Group Leadership and Institutionalization. *Human Relations* 2:23–39.

RAVEN, BERTRAM H.; and EACHUS, H. TODD 1963 Cooperation and Competition in Means-interdependent

Triads. *Journal of Abnormal and Social Psychology* 67:307–316.

ROSE, EDWARD; and FELTON, WILLIAM 1955 Experimental Histories of Culture. *American Sociological Review* 20:383–392.

ROSENBAUM, MAY; and BERGER, MILTON (editors) 1963 *Group Psychotherapy and Group Function.* New York: Basic Books.

SCHUTZ, WILLIAM C. 1958 *FIRO: A Three-dimensional Theory of Interpersonal Behavior.* New York: Holt.

SHAPIRO, DAVID 1963 The Reinforcement of Disagreement in a Small Group. *Behavior Research and Therapy* 1:267–272.

SHERIF, MUZAFER (1936) 1965 *The Psychology of Social Norms.* New York: Octagon.

SLATER, PHILIP E. 1955 Role Differentiation in Small Groups. *American Sociological Review* 20:300–310.

STEPHAN, FREDERICK F.; and MISHLER, ELLIOT G. 1952 The Distribution of Participation in Small Groups: An Exponential Approximation. *American Sociological Review* 17:598–608.

STONE, PHILIP J. et al. 1962 The General Inquirer: A Computer System for Content Analysis and Retrieval Based on the Sentence as a Unit of Information. *Behavioral Science* 7:484–498.

SYMPOSIUM ON CONFORMITY AND DEVIATION, LOUISIANA STATE UNIVERSITY, *1960* 1961 *Conformity and Deviation.* Edited by Irwin A. Berg and Bernard M. Bass. New York: Harper.

THOMAS, EDWIN J.; and FINK, CLINTON F. 1963 Effects of Group Size. *Psychological Bulletin* 60:371–384.

III

GROUP FORMATION

Groups are composed of individuals. But when and how does a collection of individuals become a group? The phrase "group formation" suggests that something is formed. The task here is to trace the appearance of essential properties or characteristics that distinguish a *human* group.

Both for theory and research, it is instructive to adopt the strategy of tracing the formation of informal groups rather than of those instituted formally through blueprints handed down by outside authority (such as a committee or board). Despite the limitation of considering groups formed through the interaction of the membership, the implications are broad. Many social institutions and formal organizations (including governments) had informal beginnings. Informal groups are almost invariably found within stable formal structures such as industrial, commercial, political, educational, religious, military, and recreational organizations. Finally, informal groups possess the *minimal* characteristics essential to any organized association, whether large or small.

Background. The properties characterizing the formation of a group were treated by the nineteenth-century social philosophers for various reasons and with varying emphasis, each using illustrative examples known to him. But the topic was doomed to controversy until data were collected through scientific methods.

In the 1920s, Robert E. Park at the University of Chicago inspired and directed a series of investigations into human groups and their relationships to their settings (for example, Thrasher 1927; Landesco 1929; Shaw 1929; Zorbaugh 1929). Initiated to deal with the problem of homeless and antisocial children, the work of the Soviet educator Makarenko included concrete data on the formation of group properties, which he gradually came to regard as crucial conditions for the effectiveness of his educational efforts (Makarenko 1933; Bowen 1962).

In the 1930s, under the impetus of Elton Mayo of the Harvard Business School, studies in Western Electric's Hawthorne plant revealed the emergence of groups and their impact on the behavior of workers who had initially been placed together in observation rooms for the purpose of studying the effects of varying illumination and rest periods (Roethlisberger & Dickson 1939). J. L. Moreno (1934) and his co-workers began the systematic sociometric mapping of friendship choices among girls in reformatory cottages and children in classrooms. Using the methods of laboratory psychology, Sherif (1936) tested sociological theories dealing with the formation of social norms in situations of ambiguity and instability, demonstrating the subsequent retention of the norms as personal standards when individuals were alone. Lewin and his students (Lewin et al. 1939) initiated experiments varying the manner of adult supervisors of children's clubs. Meanwhile, the failure of "personality" or "intelligence" tests in selecting military leaders led the military in several countries to sponsor studies of what came to be called "leaderless groups" (Gibb 1954; U.S. Office of Strategic Services 1948).

Properties

The definition presented here includes only the minimal properties found essential through extensive surveys of empirical and theoretical literature on groups of all kinds (Sherif & Cantril 1947; Sherif & Sherif 1948).

Definition. A group is a social unit consisting of a number of individuals who stand in status and role relationships to one another that are stabilized in some degree at a given time and who possess a set of values or norms regulating their behavior, at least in matters of consequence to the group.

By this definition, the "groupness" of a group is a matter of degree. A collection of persons forms into a group proportional to (a) the degree of stability of its organization (consisting of roles and status relations) and (*b*) the degree to which its particular set of norms for behavior are shared and binding for the participants. The undefined terms in the definition (role, status, norms) will be specified through research operations with conceptual relationship to the process of group formation.

It should be noted that this definition includes the properties covered in many modern works, while excluding others. Similar specifications are found in Bales (1950), Blau and Scott (1962), Bonner (1959), Cartwright and Zander (1953), Golembiewski (1962), and Hare (1962). The following characteristics, included by some investigators, were omitted here for the reasons specified: *Interaction* and *communication* are not distinctive to group formation but are essential to any kind of human association of consequence. *Shared sentiments, attitudes,* and *behavior patterns* of group members are implied in the normative property; in fact, the extent of sharing is one of the research measures for the degree of group formation at a given time. Many properties of existing groups (for example, *morale, solidarity* or *cohesiveness,* and *loyalty* of members) are dependent upon the conditions of group formation, especially the degree of stability attained.

The properties essential to group formation will aid the reader in evaluating the large body of experimental research on so-called "small groups" conducted in both the United States and Europe since World War II. In summarizing this literature, Golembiewski (1962, p. 47) found that the great majority of these "groups" consisted of strangers exposed briefly in the laboratory to tasks or instructions creating temporary interdependence. Very few studies have allowed a sufficient time span for group properties to form.

Generality of group formation. Beneath the organized forms and routines of societies, the formation and disintegration of groups occur in all walks of life, frequently with important consequences. Informal group formation is well documented within industrial, military, school, prison, and neighborhood settings (see Hare 1962; Sherif & Sherif 1948). In studying the Near North Side of Chicago, Zorbaugh (1929, p. 192) reported group formations in neighborhoods of all socioeconomic ranks with "an enormously important role in the lives of their members": exclusive clubs on the fashionable Gold Coast, intimate groups of nonconformists in artists studios, mutual benefit societies in foreign colonies, gangs in slum areas, and cults and sects in the rooming house district.

The extensive documentation on the generality of group formation also shows the striking dependence of the process on other groups and on the material and ideational features and facilities of the environment. The process of group formation is not insulated by the bounds of the membership. The formation that results is not a closed system. The circumstances bringing individuals together initially, their motives in continuing to interact, the particular organization and norms that develop, and the degree of their stability are inevitably dependent upon environmental circumstances. Included in the environmental circumstances are other groups whose activities and aims impinge favorably or unfavorably upon those of the group in formation.

Four essentials of group formation

The essentials of group formation can be traced, starting with the initial conditions for interaction among individuals. The encounter with another person is the most elementary social situation. Even the mere presence of other persons has consequential effects on behavior and task performance. From the time when individuals are merely together to the time when the properties of a group begin to appear, we see that the consequential effects on behavior begin to assume regularities. As time goes on, these regularities reflect patterns that are the organizational and normative properties of the group. Accordingly, the essentials in the process of group formation are the following: (1) A motivational base conducive to repeated interaction; (2) formation of an organization (structure) consisting of roles and statuses; (3) formation of rules, traditions, values, or norms; and (4) differential effects of the group properties on the attitude and behavior of participants over time.

Motivational base. Any human motive, frustration, problem, or desired goal that an individual cannot handle effectively alone is conducive to his interaction with others who are seen as being in the same plight. The prerequisite for group formation is that persons with motives conducive to initial interaction have the opportunity over a span of time to recognize the concerns they share or reciprocate and to attempt to deal with them in concert.

The common motive or motives faced in the initial stages of interaction may be one or several of those found in any society—for example, hunger, sexual desire, desire for recognition or power in some respect, and fear or anxiety in the face of threat. They may be culturally defined—for example, desire for material possessions or prestige through particular activities, or pursuit of political goals. Here only a few points can be considered:

The common problem, motive, or goal conducive to repeated interactions is necessarily dependent on environmental circumstances, both in its occurrence and in attempts to deal with it. Whatever its nature, the motivational base for group formation invariably affects the activities and tasks engaged in by the group's members and the kinds of personal qualities that become prized by them. When a set of norms takes shape, those most binding are typically related to the motives or problems that initially brought the persons together. One reason why the many controversies over problems of conformity–nonconformity are inconclusive is that many theorists pay scant attention to the relationship between the particular norms of a group and the initial motivational base underlying them.

However, to the degree that group formation achieves a degree of stability over time, new sources of motivation and new goals, arising from the existence of the group itself, are generated among the members. These may even take precedence over those that originally brought the members together. Thus, the hungry person may refrain from eating until he can share with his starving fellows; the politician may spurn an advantageous political bargain out of loyalty to his supporters; the member of a group struggling for equal opportunity and freedom from fear may undergo great deprivation and bodily injury to secure recognition of his group.

Formation of organization or structure.   As individuals interact over a period of time in activities related to the common problems that brought them together, their behavior and their expectations for one another's behavior assume regularities from which a pattern can be constructed. Here we shall define certain features of these regularities that appear to be crucial in any group formation. Heavy reliance will be placed upon findings from three experiments on group formation and relations between groups, each experiment lasting several weeks (summarized in Sherif & Sherif [1948] 1956, chapters 6 and 9; and Sherif 1966), and from more recent studies of naturally formed groups (Sherif & Sherif 1964). In each case the experiments started with unacquainted persons divided into collections of 10–12 as similar as possible in composition. All of these studies were conducted under naturalistic conditions, and data were collected without constant awareness by the individuals that they were being investigated.

The development of organization has been defined in terms of role and status relationships among a number of individuals. *Role* denotes reciprocities in the treatments and expectations of individuals, each for the others. Unlike well-defined occupational or sex roles, definite prescriptions for behavior are lacking when unacquainted persons first meet. Reciprocities among them must be built on the basis of performance in the activities engaged in, the reactions of others to a person, and his reactions to them. The typical finding at early stages of interaction is that individual contributions to task performance differ from one activity to the next (U.S. Office of Strategic Services 1948; Gibb 1954). Thus, observers rating behavior in the different situations find that the degree of participation and prominence of the individuals differs from one task to the next, according to individual differences in skills, abilities, temperament, or physical resources and tools relative to the activities in question.

The single most salient feature of group formation is that over time the various member roles become differentiated, not merely with regard to task performance or personal qualities but according to the evaluation of the roles by the members themselves. Members are accorded differing degrees of prestige and respect by their fellows. The member roles acquire different degrees of relative *power* to initiate and control activities important to all of the individuals in the group.

A member's position (rank) in a developing power structure is his *status* in the group, defined in terms of the relative effectiveness of his actions in initiating activities, making or approving decisions affecting the group, coordinating interaction, and invoking correctives for deviation.

Power, defined as effective initiative, is not identical with influence, in the limited sense that person A affects the actions of person B. Influence of this kind may occur with little or no relation to the effectiveness of person A's actions in the group. Power is implemented by *sanctions*, while influence is not.

Status (rank in power) is not identical with popularity or degree to which the person is liked. In fact, status and popularity may be poorly correlated (see Hare 1962, p. 115; Sherif & Sherif 1964, chapter 6). Nor should status be confused with the use of force or aggression. As Whyte (1943) showed, even in a street corner group whose members valued masculine toughness, the best potential fighter was not necessarily highest in status. Status was rooted in "mutual obligations" incurred among the group members over time and the reliability with which a member lived up to his obligations.

Since it is defined as effective initiative, status in a group is necessarily hierarchical. The highest status represents the leadership role. Especially in societies or situations where social equality is emphasized, the operational leader, defined by observation of his effectiveness over time, may not be openly chosen "leader" by the group's members.

The accompanying figure is a diagram of the stabilization of statuses, based on experimental findings for six groups. At time T_i (the top) the individuals in two collections have first encountered one another. The circles represent the individuals and indicate that, at that time, independent observers do not agree on regularities in the relationships among them from one situation to the next. Instead, their ratings of effective initiative are different in various activities. (See Figure 1.)

Just below, at time T_j, the observers' ratings begin to agree (from one activity to the next and one day to the next) that the highest and lowest

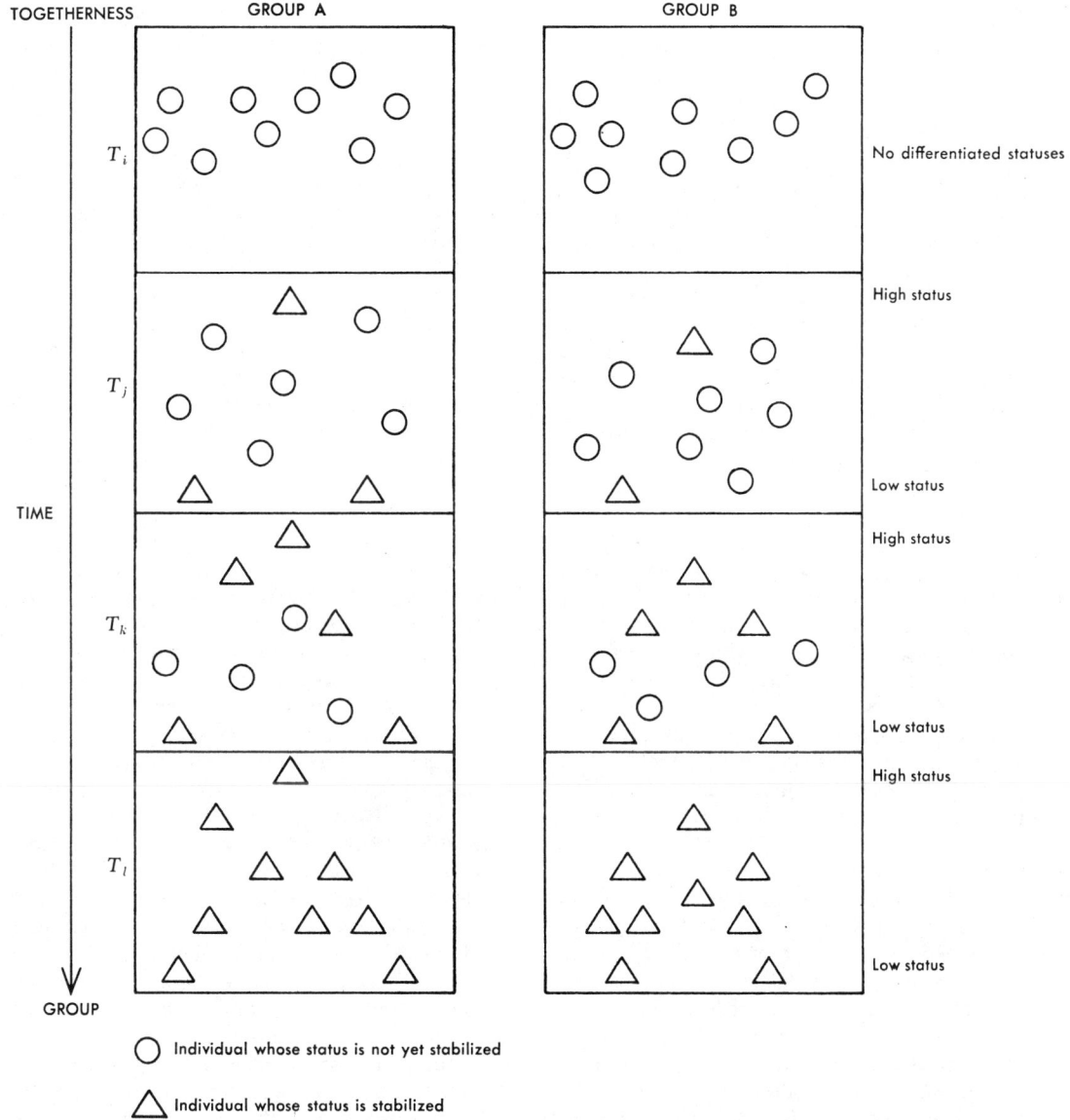

Figure 1 — *Formation of status structure in two groups, from initial togetherness to group stabilization*

Source: Sherif & Sherif 1964.

positions (represented by triangles) are stabilized. Both in the experiments and in real-life groups, the leader position typically stabilizes earlier than other high positions. This does not imply that group formation consists of the "search for a leader." On the contrary, leadership is subject to change. As Hofstätter correctly pointed out (1957, especially p. 24), tracing group organization over time is necessary to clear up many glib formulas propounded without sufficient evidence.

At time T_k in the figure, observers are able to agree on the positions most members occupy, except in the middle of the diagram. Again, this is a typical finding. In part it reflects attempts by those in the middle to improve their standing or to align themselves with those higher in status. At time T_l in the diagram the status relationships are stabilized, all observers agreeing on the status structure, which is also revealed in members' perceptions of it as manifested by sociometric choices obtained from them.

The diagram is intended to be representative. The different patterns of status in the two groups are intended to suggest that there is no predetermined form to the "steepness" or "flatness" of the hierarchy. Group formation represents an ideal occasion to study factors affecting the organization of groups, but little research has been done on this problem.

The rate of stabilization varies. In the experiments, the groups stabilized within about a week of continuous living together. Other investigators have reported the discernible beginnings of group structure among individuals meeting in the same location with similar activities within three to five meetings of a few hours duration (Merei 1949). Environmental events are as important as internal events in affecting the speed of stabilization. The stability of the pattern is sensitive to the introduction of new members, to changes in location and facilities, and to outside threat or emergency.

In particular, the stabilization of group structure is never independent of relationships with other groups. Prolonged competition between groups for mutually incompatible goals is particularly effective in quickly stabilizing a structure. Important intergroup confrontations, especially those resulting in defeat or humiliation, produce changes in the internal organization of a group (Sherif 1966).

The leader of a group, although most powerful, is still a member subject to loss of status. When the group structure is stabilized in some degree for the time, no person within it is free to ignore its regulation. It defines for members the bounds of "we"

or the in-group, as compared to others who are not members. If sufficiently stabilized, the group can continue after a leader's departure with little disruption (see Toki 1935). This persistence of a group structure and the effects of the group even on the leader are clearer in terms of the normative property of group formation.

Formation of group norms. As a group structure takes shape, members come to prefer certain ways of going about their important activities. They may adopt a group name. They set up standards for the ways members should and should not behave among themselves and with outsiders. "Norm" is a general term to refer to such results of interaction which produce regularities among group members.

Unlike the "norm" on an examination or a test, a group norm does not necessarily refer to the average of individual behaviors. It designates what is expected as proper, as moral, or even as ideal. Yet a group norm seldom denotes a single action as the only way to behave. A range for individual variations is permissible in any group. A norm denotes the range of behaviors that members come to deem socially desirable and acceptable (latitude of acceptance) and a range of behaviors condemned as objectionable (latitude of rejection).

A norm implies, therefore, an evaluative scale (measuring rod) defining for individual members a latitude of acceptance and a latitude of rejection, to regulate their behavior in matters of consequence to the group (Sherif et al. 1965). Not all social behavior is regulated by clear-cut norms, particularly when groups are in formation.

How can a group norm be detected? There are at least three objective ways:

(1) By observing similarities and regularities in the behaviors (words and deeds) found among one set of persons but not another set in a similar situation.

(2) By observing correctives (sanctions) for certain behaviors and praise or reward for others. *Reactions to deviations* are among the best evidence of the bounds of acceptable behavior. These may range from disapproval, frowns, and correctives to threats and actual punishment.

(3) By noting the increasing similarity or convergence over time in the behaviors of individuals who initially behaved differently. For example, the entrance of a new member into a group provides an opportunity to detect the existence of its norms.

When groups are in the process of formation, as in the experiments, one of the best indicators of their stability is the degree of consensus among members on the correctness of their norms and the degree to which the latitude of acceptance is binding without direct social pressure or threat of sanctions. Stabilization of the set of norms is indicated when members privately regulate their own behavior within the latitude of acceptance. The person's own conception of how he should behave and how others should act comes to fall within bounds defined by the norms. Especially when the individual has had a part in creating the norms as a group member, they become aspects of his self concept relative to others. He experiences personal guilt or shame if he violates them.

The personal acceptance of group norms during group formation accounts in large measure for the tenacity of tradition once established. Merei (1949) demonstrated this tenacity by permitting play groups to develop procedures and rules and then introducing a new child who was older and had evidenced leadership skills in other situations. In every group the new child quickly found that his superior skills in coordinating play were not effective, for no one paid attention. In every case, the new child was then absorbed into the group, adopting its traditions and rules.

Sherif and Sherif (1964) present evidence that the stringency of norms and resistance to their change varies according to the importance of the norm for the group. Violations in major activities or in dealings with outsiders, exposure of group secrets, or other behavior jeopardizing the maintenance of the group were unerringly responded to by strong sanctions such as expulsion, threat, or physical punishment. Even leaders whose actions exposed the group or its members to humiliation, embarrassment, or danger were chastised.

In less important activities the range of tolerance for individual differences was much wider, particularly for the leader and higher-status members. In matters of daily routine or amusement strictly within the group, leaders were free to innovate and sometimes engaged in behavior that would not have been tolerated in lesser members. In these fairly stable groups, the great bulk of conforming behavior occurred without direct social pressure or threat of sanctions, particularly behavior by members of moderate or high status.

Differential effects on behavior. The formation of a group structure and norms has consequences for the attitudes and behavior of individuals within its fold. These consequences may be referred to as the differential effects of group formation.

Any social situation provides a context for behavior which differs from that in a solitary situation. The context includes the other people present, the activities and tasks undertaken, the physical site and its facilities, and the person's relationship to all of these. Experiments have repeatedly shown the differential effects of various aspects of the social context on behavior as compared to behavior when alone.

The formation of a role system and norms during interaction among persons over time brings about alterations in the relative contribution of the task, activity, setting, and individual reactions. When the persons are at first simply *together*, without stabilized reciprocities, their personal characteristics and skills relative to the tasks and those of other people are important determinants of behavior (Gibb 1954; Hare 1962). As the process of group formation starts taking shape, the developing organizational and normative schemes become more and more binding on members. As a result, over time, the characteristics of the task and location—in short, immediate situational factors—recede in relative importance, and behavior increasingly reflects the person's role in the group, the roles of others, and the emerging norms.

The group formation experiments of Sherif and Sherif ([1948] 1956, chapters 6 and 9) traced the development of a "we-feeling." It was found that sociometric friendship choices became almost exclusively concentrated within the group, even though initial choices before group formation had been given predominantly to persons placed (deliberately) in another group. In one experiment it was shown that estimates made by members of one another's performance became significantly related to the member's status, the relationship being closer when the structure was more stable. Performance by high-status members was overestimated, and that of low-status persons was minimized.

In another experiment the groups formed separately, then competed for a series of mutually exclusive goals. As predicted, norms developed in each group justifying hostility to the other group. The performance by members of the other group in a novel task was estimated to be significantly lower than performance by members of the ingroup, revealing the prejudicial norm in the judgments of individual members (Oklahoma, University . . . 1961).

In proportion to the significance a particular group has in a person's life, his membership in it affects his attitude and behavior. As the group formation stabilizes, his sense of identity becomes tied to being a member of that group, proportional to its scope and importance in his daily living. For this reason the socialization of the person is incompletely described by reference only to his acquisition of formal prescriptions from family, school, and other official institutions. From early childhood through adolescence, groups formed among age-mates exert compelling impact upon the person's conceptions of what is desirable for him, what is acceptable in others, and what is right and wrong (Campbell 1964; Sherif & Sherif 1964). In other words, they become aspects of the individual's own conscience.

Recognition of the consequences for the self concepts and attitudes of participants has led to attempts in various countries to utilize group formation for corrective and therapeutic purposes. The varied outcomes reveal both gaps in the knowledge of group formation and lack of familiarity with the knowledge available on the part of many practitioners (Rosenbaum & Berger 1963, especially pp. 1–32).

The emphasis earlier in this article on the motivational base of group formation and on the importance of environmental alternatives suggests fruitful lines of inquiry. The significance of the motivational base was revealed in a study of group formation among "emotionally disturbed young adolescents of poor prognosis" by Rafferty (1962, p. 263). They interacted rather freely in a wide range of activities for five hours daily, five days a week for nine months. They lacked motivation toward the institution's aim of changing their behavior, and their personal disturbances hindered any kind of stable interpersonal relationships. However, they did unite with incipient group formation in activities reflecting a motivation genuine to them: defiance of the hospital staff in forbidden activities.

This instructive finding raises the issue of predicting or controlling the character of the structure and norms during group formation. Here the importance of the environmental setting and the behavioral alternatives it encourages or permits becomes evident. In the group experiments referred to frequently here, solidary groups devoted to constructive activities were formed simply by placing unacquainted persons in situations of high appeal to them, with facilities and conditions so arranged that coordination of activity was the only way to secure individual satisfaction. Subsequently, conflict and hostility between the groups were produced, followed by their reduction through cooperative efforts by the groups. These effects were achieved merely by varying the facilities available, the other persons present, and other conditions external to both groups. Future research on group formation and its applied implications might profitably focus on the effects of varying the environmental alternatives and facilities available to groups, including other groups and persons, upon the character of the organization and norms that develop.

Conclusions

The material briefly presented above warrants the following conclusions:

Whenever individuals with similar motives, similar frustrations, and similar personal concerns for acceptance, for recognition, and for stabilizing their perception of themselves encounter one another, and when these goal-directed concerns are not effectively dealt with through the established channels of custom and law or the routine of prevailing arrangements of social organization—these individuals then tend to interact among themselves.

Repeated interaction in some common striving is conducive to differentiation of roles or functions to be performed toward the common end. And differentiation of roles and functions among the participating individuals, *over a time span*, is the pattern or formation that can be designated as *the group*. Every such human formation creates its own set of rules or norms to stabilize the regulation of behavior and the attitudes of members within its bounds.

In a natural group, as in any other group, the rules or norms that count and have salience in the eyes of the members are generally the ones that pertain to the existence and perpetuation of the group and to the spheres of activity that are related to the common motivational concerns that were initially conducive to repeated interaction among the individuals in question.

The main properties of the group thus formed are an organization (structure) of roles and statuses and a set of rules or standards (norms) for its activities toward the common ends. The "organization" (which need not be formally recognized) and the set of norms (which need not be formally written in blueprints) define the sense of "we-ness" cherished within the group and upheld by its members in their dealings with outsiders.

In time, the standards or norms shared in the feeling of "we-ness" become personally binding for individual members. The members who are worthy and true make their judgments and justify or condemn events within the sphere related to their "we-ness" in terms of their sense of identification with the group. Proportional to the importance of the group in the lives of its members, the person's self picture, his sense of personal accountability, his loyalty, and the "do's" and "don'ts" of the group become parts of his *conscience*. Hence, group formation has broad implications for the regulation of individual attitude and behavior with and without external sanctions and controls.

MUZAFER SHERIF AND CAROLYN W. SHERIF

[*Directly related are the entries* COHESION, SOCIAL; CONFORMITY; LEADERSHIP. *Other relevant material may be found in* ATTITUDES; FRIENDSHIP; INTERACTION; NORMS; ROLE; SELF CONCEPT; SOCIAL PSYCHOLOGY; SOCIAL STRUCTURE; SOCIALIZATION.]

BIBLIOGRAPHY

BALES, ROBERT F. 1950 *Interaction Process Analysis: A Method for the Study of Small Groups.* Reading, Mass.: Addison-Wesley.

BLAU, PETER M.; and SCOTT, W. RICHARD 1962 *Formal Organizations: A Comparative Approach.* San Francisco: Chandler. → Contains an extensive bibliography.

BONNER, HUBERT 1959 *Group Dynamics: Principles and Applications.* New York: Ronald Press.

BOWEN, JAMES 1962 *Soviet Education: Anton Makarenko and the Years of Experiment.* Madison: Univ. of Wisconsin Press.

CAMPBELL, JOHN D. 1964 Peer Relations in Childhood. Volume 1, pages 289–322 in Martin L. Hoffman and Lois W. Hoffman (editors), *Review of Child Development Research.* New York: Russell Sage Foundation.

CARTWRIGHT, DORWIN; and ZANDER, ALVIN (editors) (1953) 1960 *Group Dynamics: Research and Theory.* 2d ed. Evanston, Ill.: Row, Peterson.

GIBB, CECIL A. 1954 Leadership. Volume 2, pages 877–920 in Gardner Lindzey (editor), *Handbook of Social Psychology.* Cambridge, Mass.: Addison-Wesley.

GOLEMBIEWSKI, ROBERT T. 1962 *The Small Group: An Analysis of Research Concepts and Operations.* Univ. of Chicago Press.

HARE, ALEXANDER P. 1962 *Handbook of Small Group Research.* New York: Free Press.

HOFSTÄTTER, PETER R. 1957 *Gruppendynamik: Die Kritik der Massenpsychologie.* Hamburg (Germany): Rowohlt.

LANDESCO, JOHN 1929 Organized Crime in Chicago. Pages 823–841 in Illinois Association for Criminal Justice, *The Illinois Crime Survey.* Chicago: The Association.

LEWIN, KURT; LIPPITT, R.; and WHITE, R. K. 1939 Patterns of Aggressive Behavior in Experimentally Created "Social Climates." *Journal of Social Psychology* 10:271–299.

MAKARENKO, ANTON S. (1933) 1951 *The Road to Life: An Epic of Education.* 3 vols. Moscow: Foreign Languages Publishing House. → First published as *Pedagogicheskaia poema.*

MEREI, FERENC 1949 Group Leadership and Institutionalization. *Human Relations* 2:23–39.

MORENO, JACOB L. (1934) 1953 *Who Shall Survive? Foundations of Sociometry, Group Psychotherapy and Sociodrama.* Rev. & enl. ed. Beacon, N.Y.: Beacon House.

OKLAHOMA, UNIVERSITY OF, INSTITUTE OF GROUP RELATIONS 1961 *Intergroup Conflict and Cooperation: The Robbers Cave Experiment,* by Muzafer Sherif et al. Norman, Okla.: University Book Exchange.

RAFFERTY, F. T. 1962 Development of a Social Structure in Treatment Institutions. *Journal of Nervous and Mental Disease* 134:263–267.

ROETHLISBERGER, FRITZ J.; and DICKSON, WILLIAM J. (1939) 1961 *Management and the Worker: An Account of a Research Program Conducted by the Western Electric Company, Hawthorne Works, Chicago.* Cambridge, Mass.: Harvard Univ. Press. → A paperback edition was published in 1964 by Wiley.

ROSENBAUM, MAX; and BERGER, M. (editors) 1963 *Group Psychotherapy and Group Function.* New York: Basic Books.

SHAW, CLIFFORD R. 1929 *Delinquency Areas: A Study of the Geographic Distribution of School Truants, Juvenile Delinquents, and Adult Offenders in Chicago.* Univ. of Chicago Press.

SHERIF, CAROLYN W.; SHERIF, M.; and NEBERGALL, R. E. 1965 *Attitude and Attitude Change: The Social Judgment–Involvement Approach.* Philadelphia: Saunders.

SHERIF, MUZAFER (1936) 1965 *The Psychology of Social Norms.* New York: Octagon. → A paperback edition was published in 1966 by Harper.

SHERIF, MUZAFER 1966 *In Common Predicament: Social Psychology of Intergroup Conflict and Cooperation.* Boston: Houghton Mifflin. → A British edition was published by Routledge as *Group Conflict and Cooperation: Their Social Psychology.*

SHERIF, MUZAFER; and CANTRIL, HADLEY 1947 *The Psychology of Ego-involvements, Social Attitudes and Identifications.* New York: Wiley; London: Chapman & Hall.

SHERIF, MUZAFER; and SHERIF, CAROLYN W. (1948) 1956 *An Outline of Social Psychology.* Rev. ed. New York: Harper.

SHERIF, MUZAFER; and SHERIF, CAROLYN W. 1964 *Reference Groups: Exploration Into Conformity and Deviation of Adolescents.* New York: Harper.

THRASHER, FREDERIC (1927) 1963 *The Gang: A Study of 1,313 Gangs in Chicago.* Abridged and with an introduction by James F. Short. Univ. of Chicago Press.

TOKI, K. 1935 The Leader–Follower Structure in the School Class. *Japanese Journal of Psychology* 10:27–56. → A discussion of Toki's article appears on pages 8–10, 604, 608, 613, and 631–635 in *Fundamentals of Social Psychology,* by Eugene L. and Ruth Hartley.

U.S. OFFICE OF STRATEGIC SERVICES, ASSESSMENT STAFF 1948 *The Assessment of Men.* New York: Rinehart.

WHYTE, WILLIAM F. (1943) 1961 *Street Corner Society: The Social Structure of an Italian Slum.* 2d ed., enl. Univ. of Chicago Press.

ZORBAUGH, HARVEY W. 1929 *The Gold Coast and the Slum.* Univ. of Chicago Press.

IV

ROLE STRUCTURE

"Role" refers to a set of "expectations" for interaction between a person who holds one position in a group and another person who holds a reciprocal position. In other words, there can be no "leader" role without a "follower" role. Since the person playing the role has a personality (or self) which he brings to the situation, the behavior of a person in a role will be some combination of the tendencies of his personality and the expectations of his role.

Roles in discussion groups, which are the focus of much of the research on groups, are usually not fixed. Any aspect of an individual's behavior that is initially an expression of his personality can come to be expected by other group members and thus become part of his role. In general, the dimensions of role are the same as the dimensions of interaction and of personality. Roles have a *form* and a *content*, where the form includes the frequency of interaction and the communication network and the content includes task and social–emotional behavior. Within the task area, the expectations refer to problem-solving behavior and within the social–emotional area, according to one recent formulation, to behavior along at least three dimensions: dominance–submission, positive–negative, and joking–serious (Couch 1960; Hare 1962).

Patterns of role differentiation.   Natural groups which have been in existence for some time will probably have a greater degree of role differentiation than laboratory groups (Sherwood & Walker 1960), unless the group organization allows only one leader who is expected to perform all functions. Thus, in some industrial and governmental conference groups a "sharing" of leadership is resisted by the members (Berkowitz 1953). Over the life of a group there may be more differentiation in roles when functional problems of the group become more acute, for example, when the group is under stress or the task is complex (Bales 1953). Similarly, members in cooperative groups are more apt to be differentiated in their functions than members who are competing (Homans 1961, p. 135).

The small military unit or industrial work team is perhaps the best example of the simplest form of role differentiation. In each case one or two members may have clearly defined functions with little overlap in their "expectations," while the remainder of the members play undifferentiated roles of "soldier" or "worker." In discussion groups (and especially in laboratory groups) it is not always clear whether a single person plays one role or many roles, or whether these roles are assumed at the same or at different times.

In some research all members are viewed as specializing in some content area, with those with the highest interaction rates identified as the leaders (Heinicke & Bales 1953; Grusky 1957). In other research some individuals may be described as playing a variety of roles and others none (Davis et al. 1961; Cloyd 1964). In either case the authors are not usually concerned with the rights and duties associated with each role. They rather use the terms "expectations" in the sense that group members can predict or "expect" that a group member will act in a given way on the basis of past performance. There is no sense that the member is "obliged" to act in this way to fulfill a function in the group or that he is entitled to any special privileges for performing this function [*see* ETHICS, *article on* ETHICAL SYSTEMS AND SOCIAL STRUCTURES].

In some research, the evidence that a person is playing a given role is that other members associate a certain set of behavioral characteristics with him; these behavioral characteristics are presented as a cluster without any special rationale concerning their interconnection (Bates & Cloyd 1956; Davis 1961; Cloyd 1964). In other research a person is described as playing a role because he has been nominated as a frequent contributor of some specified type of behavior, for example, giving information or giving opinion (Bales 1958; Borg 1960). An even less functionalist view is taken in research in which some members are described as playing individual or self-oriented roles that presumably are extraneous to the group task (Benne & Sheats 1948). Another variation on the use of the term "role" is for the experimenter to describe someone as playing a role such as "newcomer" (Mills et al. 1957) or "doctor's assistant" (Margolin 1952) without actually assessing the perceptions of the other group members.

Most of the research on small groups has so far not used a definition of role as a set of rights and duties but rather as a description of recurring patterns of behavior. But the former, more limited definition of role still appears to be theoretically useful even though it is not widely used. For instance, in those studies that report the interaction in initially "leaderless" groups, the expectations for the average member are probably most clearly related to the directions given by the experimenter at the beginning of the session. Often, indeed, the experimenter will test to see if the subjects have been as friendly or as competitive as he directed them to be, but he will not refer to these instructions as "role expectations" (Olmsted 1954).

The power of an experimenter's instructions is evident in an experiment in which one member in each of several discussion groups was given more information about the task than the other members. In some of these groups the experimenter announced, "Some of you may have more information than others." In other groups he gave the impression that all members were equally informed. It was observed that group members reacted negatively to the best-informed man unless they had been led to "expect" that he would play a different role (Shaw & Penrod 1962).

Although early research on groups, especially with children, often described "individual" or "self-oriented" roles as if the only role of some individuals was to satisfy their own needs in the group (Benne & Sheats 1948), later formulations by Redl (1942), Bion (1961), and Stock and Thelen (1958) suggest that all roles in the group serve some function. However, some of these roles, particularly the ones that allow members to deal with emotional themes, may not be recognized as part of the "official" group structure. For example, in a training group composed of teachers who were being led by Bion's methods of "interpretive group discussion," the group members persisted, without success, in trying to induce the leader to act as a therapist. Finally six members did not appear at the scheduled group session and a spokesman for the absentees sent in a paper on truancy to be discussed by the remaining members. Thus, by taking the "role" of absent members, some of the group acted out the group's need for flight from the task (Herbert & Trist 1953).

Task versus social–emotional roles. The most common division of roles that has been described in small discussion and work groups, as well as in families viewed as small groups, is specialization in the task and social–emotional areas (Bales & Slater 1955; Bales 1958). This has been shown most clearly in small laboratory groups in which members have a high degree of consensus at the end of a meeting on the relative amount of interaction in each of these areas exhibited by group members. These groups appear to recognize two kinds of role specialists: one an "idea man" who concentrates on the task and plays a more aggressive role; the other a "best-liked" man who concentrates on social–emotional problems of group process and member satisfaction, giving emotional rewards, and playing a more passive role. However, in groups similar to these in which there is less consensus on the status of members, a third type of person appears to be present, one who talks a great deal but who is not well liked or highly rated on his task ability. He has been referred to as a "deviant." In addition, researchers have found a more passive task specialist and a "popular" person (Slater 1955).

The so-called "deviant" who overtalks is probably expressing the group's anxiety about the discussion task. To please the experimenter, the group allows a member to fill the time with "discussion"

even though he may not be the most effective at the task. This tendency to have a high or low interaction rate has often been reported as the first of three factors or dimensions that may be used to describe behavior, the other two being task behavior and sociability (Carter 1954). However, the frequency of interaction should probably be considered an independent dimension because it describes the "form" of interaction and not because it represents a separate area of "content."

In families, the father has been identified as the task specialist, the mother as the social–emotional specialist (Parsons & Bales 1955). A similar dichotomy has been reported among caseworkers in a welfare agency where some colleagues were respected and sought out for consultation on cases and others were attractive because of their sociable companionship (Blau 1962). However, a study of therapy groups reported that the distinction was not evident in this setting, since the "task" of the group was to deal with social–emotional problems (Talland 1957).

When the same individual is required to play the role of both the task and the social–emotional leader, he may find some aspects of the roles incompatible and thus experience "role conflict" (Seeman 1953). Officers in small military units, for example, may be required to consider the personal problems of their men as well as to be task leaders. The second role requires distance, since some assignments must be made without regard to personal feelings, yet the first role requires closeness and intimacy (Hutchins & Fiedler 1960).

The joker. In addition to these two roles, a third role has been identified in some groups which actually has a long history in many cultures. This is the role of the clown or the joker. Just as the English court jester's costume set him apart from the group, so the joker tends to take a somewhat marginal position with regard to the task. He tends to look at things differently, providing both a source of humor and of new ideas. Under the cover of wit he is able to introduce ideas that the group might otherwise find unacceptable.

In its literary form, comedy has been described as "an escape, not from truth but from despair: a narrow escape into faith" (Fry 1960, p. 27). One must be able to grasp the tragic nature of life before one can go on to grasp its comic nature. Thus, the comic person in a play or in a real-life small group is often one who gives special insight into the problem. This is evident from a study of a series of "great-books" discussion groups where the joking role was most highly correlated with the role of providing "fuel" for the discussions in the form of new ideas and opinions (Davis et al. 1961). In a study of laboratory discussion groups the following cluster of behavioral characteristics was identified as composing a role: jokes and makes humorous remarks, is liberal, challenges other's opinions, gets off the subject, is egotistical, is cynical, and interrupts others (Cloyd 1964). Within the dimension of "joking versus task-serious behavior" there may be different styles of wit. Thus, sarcastic wit may be perceived as powerful but unpopular in a group, while clowning wit may be seen as popular but powerless (Goodchilds 1959).

The member.   The fact that simple membership in a group carries with it a set of rights and duties is evident in the group's concern for the "silent member." Although silence may be functional if it means that more able persons are being allowed to solve problems (Homans 1961, p. 136), group members are usually dissatisfied with a member's performance if he does not participate. This dissatisfaction may be reduced if it is made clear at the outset that certain members will not participate at all (Smith 1957). On the other hand the group will be more concerned if a member appears indifferent and neglectful in his role (Rosenthal & Cofer 1948).

Another type of member role that has received some attention in the literature is that of the "newcomer." Group members will have an easier time assimilating the newcomer if they have been told to expect change (Ziller et al. 1961), provided that the newcomer is not seen as too different from other group members (Ziller et al. 1960) and that group members have already had a pleasant time with each other (Heiss 1963). In any event there will probably be a minimal alteration in the role patterns of the old members at first (Mills et al. 1957).

Other roles.   Other roles may be found in groups with special tasks. In therapy groups a "doctor's assistant" may fill the group's need to keep the discussion going when the therapist is playing a rather passive role and a "help-rejecting complainer" may give the group case material to discuss (Frank et al. 1952; Margolin 1952). Somewhat similar to the "doctor's assistant" may be the "feeder-to-leaders" identified in a sociometric study of a home for girls (Jennings 1947). These were girls who would have their ideas accepted after they had been endorsed by highly chosen leaders, although they were not highly chosen themselves [see LEADERSHIP].

The classic study of authoritarian and demo-cratic group atmospheres by Lewin, Lippitt, and White does not focus on role differentiation; however, two types of roles are mentioned in addition to the leaders. In the "democratic" groups the authors describe two boys who are allies of the adult leaders, and in the "autocratic" groups they describe a scapegoat who receives the aggression of the group (White & Lippitt 1960, pp. 160–186). Thrasher (1927) in his study of gangs in Chicago gives a longer list of special roles, to which he gives such names as brains of gang, funny boy, sissy, show-off, and goat. Redl (1942) lists ten types of roles of central persons, which may be grouped into three categories: identification objects, objects of drives, and ego supports.

In addition to roles which may arise naturally in groups, some authors have suggested certain roles which should be introduced if a group is to operate with maximum efficiency. For example, Jenkins (1948) suggests that effective discussion requires attention to such mechanics of operation as awareness of direction, goal, and rate of progress. He proposes that groups appoint a "group productivity observer" who will report at the end of each meeting.

Where role differentiation occurs in a group, individuals accustomed to playing the same roles in other groups will probably continue to play them in the new situation (Strodtbeck & Mann 1956; Davis et al. 1961). In addition, differences in age, sex, social class, and occupation between members will result in role differentiation in small discussion groups even when these differences are not related to the task at hand (Maas 1954; Torrance 1954).

Six roles in discussion groups.   From the review of the literature presented above it is evident that a variety of roles have been identified in discussion groups. The number of roles reported may be small or large depending upon the level of analysis, the task, the group size, and the length of time the members have been together. Although the dichotomy of task versus social–emotional roles is adequate to describe the basic differentiation in some groups, in others there are probably more distinct roles that have been grouped under these two more general headings. A framework for the description of more distinct and independent roles is provided by Couch's (1960) factor analysis of categories of interaction in five-man laboratory discussion groups. He finds that interpersonal behavior can be described by the following independent dimensions: dominance versus submission; positive versus negative; task serious versus joking; influence attempts versus receptivity; and surface acqui-escence versus resistance. If we assume that be-havior at the extremes of each dimension may identify a role, we find a rather good fit with six role patterns identified by Cloyd (1964) without reference to any particular dimensions and with-out actually assigning them names.

At the dominance end of Couch's first factor we find a set of behaviors similar to a cluster identified by Cloyd that includes "aggressive, self-confident, and gets things started." This role might be called the "high talker." At the submissive end of Couch's first factor is Cloyd's cluster of traits: "modest, shy, and ill at ease." This role might be called the "silent member."

In a similar way one could match dimensions and clusters of traits to identify a "supporter" who is friendly and objective, a "critic" who is idealistic and argumentative, a "serious worker" who is de-pendable and constructive, and a "joker" who makes humorous remarks and challenges others' opinions. Cloyd does not provide examples that would fit the last two of Couch's dimensions; how-ever, the last dimension suggests the roles of "con-formist" and "nonconformist."

From this example it will be seen how small group experiments, although independently de-signed by researchers using different concepts, can be said to deal with a recurrent, scientifically identifiable class of phenomena. Indeed, such is the wealth of suggestive findings in this area that the organization of our present knowledge has be-come both an indispensable and a rewarding pre-liminary to future progress.

A. PAUL HARE

[See also INTERACTION, *article on* INTERACTION PROC-ESS ANALYSIS; LEADERSHIP; SOCIOMETRY.]

BIBLIOGRAPHY

Many of the articles listed below are discussed in more detail in Hare 1962, while 11 of them have been reprinted in whole or in part in Hare, Borgatta & Bales 1964. Refer-ences to other introductory texts or readers will be found in the bibliographies to GROUPS, article on THE STUDY OF GROUPS; and SOCIOMETRY. For the layman who has no training in statistics but would like to savor some of the interest and importance of the field, Bion 1961; Homans 1961; and Mills 1957 should prove rewarding.

BALES, ROBERT F. 1953 The Equilibrium Problem in Small Groups. Pages 111–161 in Talcott Parsons et al., *Working Papers in the Theory of Action.* Glencoe, Ill.: Free Press.

BALES, ROBERT F. 1958 Task Roles and Social Roles in Problem-solving Groups. Pages 437–447 in Eleanor E. Maccoby, T. M. Newcomb, and E. L. Hartley (edi-tors), *Readings in Social Psychology.* 3d ed. New York: Holt.

BALES, ROBERT F.; and SLATER, PHILIP 1955 Role Dif-ferentiation in Small Decision-making Groups. Pages 259–306 in Talcott Parsons and Robert F. Bales, *Family, Socialization and Interaction Process.* Glen-coe, Ill.: Free Press.

BATES, ALAN P.; and CLOYD, JERRY S. 1956 Toward the Development of Operations for Defining Group Norms and Member Roles. *Sociometry* 19:26–39.

BENNE, KENNETH D.; and SHEATS, PAUL 1948 Func-tional Roles of Group Members. *Journal of Social Is-sues* 4, no. 2:41–49.

BERKOWITZ, LEONARD 1953 Sharing Leadership in Small Decision-making Groups. *Journal of Abnormal and Social Psychology* 48:231–238.

BION, WILFRED R. 1961 *Experiences in Groups, and Other Papers.* New York: Basic Books. → Seven of these papers were published in *Human Relations* from 1948 to 1951.

BLAU, PETER M. 1962 Patterns of Choice in Interper-sonal Relations. *American Sociological Review* 27:41–55.

BORG, WALTER R. 1960 Prediction of Small Group Role Behavior From Personality Variables. *Journal of Ab-normal and Social Psychology* 60:112–116.

CARTER, LAUNOR F. 1954 Evaluating the Performance of Individuals as Members of Small Groups. *Person-nel Psychology* 7:477–484.

CLOYD, JERRY S. 1964 Patterns of Role Behavior in In-formal Interaction. *Sociometry* 27:161–173.

COUCH, A. S. 1960 Psychological Determinants of Inter-personal Behavior. Ph.D. dissertation, Harvard Univ.

DAVIS, JAMES A. 1961 Compositional Effects, Role Sys-tems, and the Survival of Small Discussion Groups. *Public Opinion Quarterly* 25:575–584.

DAVIS, JAMES A. et al. 1961 *Great Books and Small Groups.* New York: Free Press.

FRANK, JEROME D. et al. 1952 Two Behavior Patterns in Therapeutic Groups and Their Apparent Motivation. *Human Relations* 5:289–317.

FRY, CHRISTOPHER 1950 Comedy. *Adelphi* Third Series 27:27–29.

GOODCHILDS, JACQUELINE D. 1959 Effects of Being Witty on Position in the Social Structure of a Small Group. *Sociometry* 22:261–272.

GRUSKY, OSCAR 1957 A Case for the Theory of Familial Role Differentiation in Small Groups. *Social Forces* 35:209–217.

HARE, A. PAUL 1962 *Handbook of Small Group Re-search.* New York: Free Press.

HARE, A. PAUL; BORGATTA, E. F.; and BALES, R. F. (1955) 1964 *Small Groups: Studies in Social Interaction.* 2d ed. New York: Knopf.

HEINICKE, CHRISTOPHER; and BALES, ROBERT F. (editors) 1953 Developmental Trends in the Structure of Small Groups. *Sociometry* 16:7–38.

HEISS, JEROLD S. 1963 The Dyad Views the Newcomer: A Study of Perception. *Human Relations* 16:241–248.

HERBERT, ELÉONORE L.; and TRIST, E. L. 1953 The In-stitution of an Absent Leader by a Students' Discus-sion Group. *Human Relations* 6:215–248.

HOMANS, GEORGE C. 1961 *Social Behavior: Its Elemen-tary Forms.* New York: Harcourt.

HUTCHINS, EDWIN B.; and FIEDLER, FRED E. 1960 Task-oriented and Quasi-therapeutic Role Functions of the

Leader in Small Military Groups. *Sociometry* 23:393–406.

JENKINS, DAVID H. 1948 Feedback and Group Self-evaluation. *Journal of Social Issues* 4, no. 2:50–60.

JENNINGS, HELEN H. 1947 Leadership and Sociometric Choice. *Sociometry* 10:32–49.

MAAS, HENRY S. 1954 The Role of Member in Clubs of Lower-class and Middle-class Adolescents. *Child Development* 25:241–251.

MARGOLIN, JOSEPH B. 1952 The Use of an Interaction Matrix to Validate Patterns of Group Behavior. *Human Relations* 5:407–416.

MILLS, THEODORE M. et al. 1957 Group Structure and the Newcomer: An Experimental Study of Group Expansion. *Studies in Society* No. 1.

OLMSTED, MICHAEL S. 1954 Orientation and Role in the Small Group. *American Sociological Review* 19:741–751.

PARSONS, TALCOTT; and BALES, ROBERT F. 1955 *Family, Socialization and Interaction Process.* Glencoe, Ill.: Free Press; London: Routledge.

REDL, FRITZ 1942 Group Emotion and Leadership. *Psychiatry* 5:573–596.

ROSENTHAL, DAVID; and COFER, CHARLES N. 1948 The Effect on Group Performance of an Indifferent and Neglectful Attitude Shown by One Group Member. *Journal of Experimental Psychology* 38:568–577.

SEEMAN, MELVIN 1953 Role Conflict and Ambivalence in Leadership. *American Sociological Review* 18:373–380.

SHAW, MARVIN E.; and PENROD, WILLIAM E. JR. 1962 Does More Information Available to a Group Always Improve Group Performance? *Sociometry* 25:377–390.

SHERWOOD, CLARENCE E.; and WALKER, W. S. 1960 Role Differentiation in Real Groups: An Extrapolation of a Laboratory Small-group Research Finding. *Sociology and Social Research* 45:14–17.

SLATER, PHILIP E. 1955 Role Differentiation in Small Groups. *American Sociological Review* 20:300–310.

SMITH, EWART E. 1957 The Effects of Clear and Unclear Role Expectations on Group Productivity and Defensiveness. *Journal of Abnormal and Social Psychology* 55:213–217.

STOCK, DOROTHY; and THELEN, H. A. 1958 *Emotional Dynamics and Group Culture: Experimental Studies of Individual and Group Behavior.* New York Univ. Press.

STRODTBECK, FRED L.; and MANN, RICHARD D. 1956 Sex Role Differentiation in Jury Deliberations. *Sociometry* 19:3–11.

TALLAND, GEORGE A. 1957 Role and Status Structure in Therapy Groups. *Journal of Clinical Psychology* 13:27–33.

THRASHER, FREDERIC M. (1927) 1963 *The Gang: A Study of 1,313 Gangs in Chicago.* Abridged and with an introduction by James F. Short. Univ. of Chicago Press.

TORRANCE, E. P. 1954 Some Consequences of Power Differences on Decision-making in Permanent and Temporary Three-man Groups. Washington State University, *Research Studies* 22:130–140.

WHITE, RALPH K.; and LIPPITT, RONALD 1960 *Autocracy and Democracy: An Experimental Inquiry.* New York: Harper.

ZILLER, ROBERT C.; BEHRINGER, RICHARD D.; and GOODCHILDS, JACQUELINE D. 1960 The Minority Newcomer in Open and Closed Groups. *Journal of Psychology* 50:75–84.

ZILLER, ROBERT C.; BEHRINGER, RICHARD D.; and JANSEN, MATHILDA J. 1961 The Newcomer in Open and Closed Groups. *Journal of Applied Psychology* 45:55–58.

V
GROUP PERFORMANCE

It was a practical interest in group performance which led to the massive literature dealing with experimental studies of groups. The industrial revolution and the growth of the large factory raised such practical questions as: How can groups of workers become more productive? How might the performance of the individual worker be affected by the presence of others? When is a group more effective than the sum of its individual members? Thus, the typical study of group performance will vary some factor and measure differences in quantity, quality, speed (number of units produced per unit time), or efficiency (number of units produced per man per unit time). Some studies might concentrate on homogeneity or similarity of behavior and production of individuals in the group as compared to that of individuals working alone. The original industrial interest spread to other areas, such as military situations, research laboratories, and classrooms, where the problems were often quite different. Reviews of studies of group performance may be found in Hare (1962), Kelley and Thibaut (1954), and Lorge and his associates (1958).

Studies of group performance have been grouped into four major problem areas: (*a*) *group productivity*—e.g., studies of how many relays can be wired by a group in a given period of time, or how many addition problems can be completed; (*b*) *group problem solving*—e.g., studies of the solution of puzzles, construction of a complex design involving thought and planning, creativity in determining unusual uses for everyday implements; (*c*) *group judgment*—e.g., group estimation of the number of parachutes seen in an air photo of military exercises, estimation of number of beans in a jar, judgment of lengths of lines or movement of lights; and (*d*) *group learning and retention*—e.g., group memorizing of a complex story, learning a maze or series of words, military units learning complex strategy as a unit. Although these categories are convenient, it is obvious that a given task will often involve several of the above problems in combination: the group must form some judgments in learning and retention, learning and retention are involved in problem solving, group productivity may be improved through creative problem solving in the reorganization of group operations, etc.

Individual versus group performance. Early observations suggested that workers on production lines would tend to increase their level of activity when working together. Floyd H. Allport (1920) considered such "social facilitation" in terms of classical conditioning. The sounds of tapping from the shoemaker's hammer become conditioned stimuli for the muscular movements which move his hammer. When he works in the presence of others, the tapping sounds from his co-workers serve as additional conditioned stimuli and thus increase further the rate at which the shoemaker pounds his shoes. Allport found, in fact, that subjects given word-association tasks, vowel-cancellation tests, or multiplication tests performed more rapidly when working in the presence of others. This was true even when rivalry was diminished by using instructions and by not permitting knowledge of the scores of others. [*See the biography of* ALLPORT.]

Early studies of problem solving also indicated the superiority of groups over individuals. It was suggested that this resulted from erroneous solutions being rejected in group discussions (Shaw 1932). It would follow that the superiority of the group over individual problem solving would be greater in tasks which permitted a greater variety of responses, with elimination of incorrect solutions being more crucial. Such was, indeed, demonstrated by Thorndike (1938). [*See the biography of* THORNDIKE.]

In one of the few clear-cut experiments on group versus individual learning, subjects were asked to learn lists of nonsense syllables. Some learned cooperatively, in groups of three, and then alone; for others the order was reversed. It appeared that, generally, subjects learned more rapidly in groups and after the group experience could learn better on their own. Some superior subjects, however, did not benefit from the group learning experience (Perlmutter & de Montmollin 1952).

There is evidence that groups can inhibit the behavior of individuals. In an early study most children asked to turn a crank to move a flag to a finish line tended to show "social facilitation" when operating together. However, some operated less effectively when coacting with others. This decrement was attributed to overstimulation (Triplett 1898).

While the studies of individual versus group performance indicated some superiority of group performance, they also suggested limitations on any such conclusions. The problem can be reconsidered in terms of the factors which lead to variations in group performance.

Size of group. In an early study by Moede (1927), a man was given a rope to pull as hard as he could, then a second man was added and given the same instructions, then others, until eight men were pulling, with the strength of pull measured. The first man pulled, on the average, 63 kilograms; the two together pulled 118; three, 160; and eight, 248 kilograms. Clearly the total amount of pull increased with each man, but the work per man was reduced with additional members—each new member reduced the work per man by approximately 10 per cent. This early study of group productivity is a prototype of later research on size of group in group performance. The results of later studies seem to be the same. A study of problem solving in the game "Twenty Questions" found four-person groups asking fewer questions than dyads, but the four-person groups were less efficient (Taylor & Faust 1952). Thomas and Fink, summarizing the literature, say that generally "both quality of performance and group productivity were positively correlated with group size under some conditions, and under no conditions were smaller groups superior. In contrast, measures of speed showed no difference or else favored the smaller groups" (1963, p. 373).

Cohesiveness and morale. In 1927 the Hawthorne plant of the Western Electric Company initiated a series of experiments to raise productivity and morale. A group of female workers engaged in wiring relays was placed in a separate room and, in the tradition of efficiency experts Frederick W. Taylor and Frank B. Gilbreth, changes in working conditions were introduced which were calculated to improve efficiency—changes to piecework production, increased rest periods, hot meals, earlier quitting times, etc.—and with each change productivity increased. However, when all these improvements were removed, productivity rose still higher. It was pointed out that, clearly, the physical factors were not as crucial for increasing productivity as cohesiveness and morale [*see* COHESION, SOCIAL; INDUSTRIAL RELATIONS; *see also* Roethlisberger & Dickson 1939, p. 86].

Later studies in various types of work groups, including railroad maintenance workers, office staffs, and machinery workers, also indicated that productivity increased with attraction to the work group (Michigan, University of . . . 1954, p. 7). Other research indicated similar relationships in military crews (Berkowitz 1956). In a careful experiment, Van Zelst, working in conjunction with the supervisor and foreman of a large construction project, made up some work groups of carpenters and bricklayers according to their personal choices of co-workers and some of members who were not mutually attracted to one another. The former groups showed greater job satisfaction, lower labor and material cost, and lower turnover rates (1952).

There are, however, limitations to any generalization that cohesiveness increases productivity. Mutual friendliness, when it shows itself in high sociability and horseplay, can decrease productivity (Horsfall & Arensberg 1949). Thus, group goals and group norms must also be considered.

Interdependence, cooperation, and competition. Patterns of interdependence can have a great effect on group performance. The individual worker on the production line may be under great pressure to work rapidly either through the "pull" of the man next in line, who is waiting for the next piece, or through the "push" of the preceding worker, whose rapid rate of work leaves work piling up on his successor. In the British coal mines, a change to a "longwall method" of mining led to each shift of workers becoming less aware of other shifts and less aware of the extent to which each was dependent upon the other. Accidents increased because a preceding shift departed without allowing proper safeguards for those that followed. For similar reasons, productivity decreased. A major remedy involved increasing both formal and informal communications between shifts and, through other means, making shifts and workers aware of their interdependence (Trist & Bamforth 1951). Thomas (1957) indicates the importance of considering both interdependence with respect to means and with respect to goals. He found greatest productivity in a group with division of labor where both types of interdependence obtained, though there were signs of greater emotional tension as well.

Early studies indicated that rivalry, or competition, tended to increase rate of performance, though sometimes at the expense of quality (Triplett 1898). However, later studies found more rapid performance among persons who are cooperating.

Part of the answer lies in the extent to which there is also interdependence with respect to means. When each person works on a parallel task, as in the Triplett experiment in which each subject turned his own crank, with speed being the basis of success, then competition will likely be more effective in increasing performance. When each person depends on others for his own movement— for example, three persons raising or lowering corners of a triangular board so as to center carpenter's levels (Raven & Eachus 1963)—then com-

petition will be detrimental. With competition and interdependence of means, each person is concerned about his activity helping others. There is less division of labor, and a person may not wish to give information to a co-worker who might thus be helped to defeat him (Deutsch 1949).

Division of labor and information. While division of labor may be beneficial to a cooperative work group, mutual interdependence also imposes additional pressures on the individual, resulting in greater pressures to produce but also greater tension and greater loss of individuality and craftsmanship. This has been observed in industrial settings. It has been demonstrated that such resulting tensions can be alleviated somewhat, with greater group cohesiveness, greater acceptance of influence from co-workers, and less hostility, through clarifying for the individual the nature of the final product and the ways in which the individual worker's task fits in with that of his co-workers (Raven & Reitsema 1957).

The question arises as to how information should be distributed for maximal group retention. If, for example, a complex military tactic must be learned by a squad, giving all the information to each member would increase learning time and lead to an increased rate of forgetting. On the other hand, giving each person a nonoverlapping portion, while reducing redundancy, increases the possibility of a piece of information being permanently lost if only one member forgets it. Zajonc and Smoke (1959) suggest a mathematical model for dealing with this problem, but extensive empirical testing is still lacking.

Group norms and decisions. In the Hawthorne study, while it was found that group morale contributed to higher productivity, it was also observed that norms developed which prevented production from either exceeding a given level (such a worker would be considered a "rate-buster") or falling below (being a "slacker"). Similarly, the study by Seashore found that increased cohesiveness did not lead to greater productivity but rather to greater homogeneity of performance in a work group (Michigan, University of . . . 1954). It has been demonstrated in experimental situations that a highly cohesive group will not only be better able to influence a member to increase his production but also to decrease it (Schachter et al. 1951).

Lewin suggested that changing the level of productivity of a work group involves a process of "unfreezing" an old norm, then change, and "refreezing" at a new normative level (1951, p. 228). A reduction in productivity, due to a change in methods of production, may lead to establishment of a lower group norm, which will remain long after necessary relearning has taken place. Members who exceed the norm may be subject to strong group pressure to work more slowly. This suggestion led to studies which indicated that involving the work group in the re-evaluation of the job, with establishment through group discussion of an appropriate group standard of production, will ultimately lead to a higher level of production with less tension and higher morale among the workers (Coch & French 1948).

With respect to group judgments, group norms might also have a deleterious effect. Though a group would be more likely to have the combined skills necessary to make a proper judgment, it may sometimes happen that a majority is wrong. In that case, there will be strong pressures for an individual who might otherwise judge correctly to refrain from uttering the correct answer and, instead, to go along with the group. A properly trained leader can sometimes assist a group in group judgment or problem solving through encouraging the expression of minority opinion and bringing out the useful ideas and contributions of members who are otherwise restrained by conformity pressures (Maier & Solem 1952).

Communication networks. An application of principles of topology to group behavior by Alex Bavelas (1950) led to a series of studies of the effects of restriction of communication channels on productivity and morale. In an early study, five-man groups were given a problem of finding which symbols were held in common by all members. The communication possibilities were varied. The most effective group was that in which four members could communicate only with the one "central person," a pattern called a "wheel." A "circle" was least effective, with a "chain" and a "Y" being intermediate. The more involved the person was in the network, the happier he was with the group task. The "circle," while least effective, had the greatest overall morale (Leavitt 1951). The initial findings indicate that restriction of communication leads to greater efficiency. It is suggested that this may be true for the simple problems in which information must be collated to find a correct answer. The restricted pattern of the "wheel" saves the group from spending time on organization for effective problem solving. However, it also lessens flexibility, making for less efficiency when the tasks are changed or become more complex (Guetzkow & Dill 1957). When the problem is complex and involves a number of alternative paths to solution, the less restricted network is more efficient (Shaw 1954).

Personality factors undoubtedly play a role.

Workers high in acceptance of authority will be relatively more efficient in a centralized group structure; those low in acceptance of authority will be more effective in a decentralized structure (Shaw 1959). It might also follow that an increase in intelligence and skills would lead to increased efficiency for the decentralized structure relative to the centralized network.

Leadership and supervision. Clearly, leadership and supervision play a very important part in group performance, since the leader can often affect and control many of the other critical variables discussed above. The style of leadership has been given particular attention in the literature. In a pioneer experiment with groups of boys, it was found that the greatest productivity and morale occurred with a "democratic" leader, who encouraged participation in decisions, gave a clear picture of the group activities and the reasons for his requests, took an active but not overactive role in the group's activities, etc. A "laissez-faire" leader, who allowed complete freedom and assumed no active role, achieved the least productivity. An "authoritarian" leader, who was very active in issuing commands without giving reasons, was effective in raising productivity only insofar as the group was under his immediate surveillance. Morale was lowest in the last case (White & Lippitt 1960). Other studies in industrial settings confirm that productivity and morale are higher with a participatory leader or supervisor who assumes an active role in the group, gives support to his workers, delegates authority, and maintains an optimal degree of supervision (Kahn & Katz 1953). There is evidence that similar group-oriented roles on the part of the teacher may also lead to improved learning.

Characteristics of the leader have also received some attention in relationship to productivity. For example, Fiedler (1958), in investigations in a large variety of settings, has found that productivity is highest in teams where the leader maintains an optimal distance from his team and where he perceives clear differentiation between his best and worst co-workers [*see* LEADERSHIP].

Training and group process. Given a knowledge of factors which contribute toward improved group performance, it should follow that training and education in the application of these principles would be a logical next step. Indeed, there have been many attempts to introduce training for improved group performance—either through training the groups themselves or the leaders and supervisors. It has been demonstrated that a discussion leader who is trained to encourage expression of minority opinions will effect superior problem solving and decision making (Maier 1953; Maier & Solem 1952). It is generally assumed that educators can be taught to improve learning in the classroom.

On the assumption that group ideation can be more productive than individual ideation and that a group may sometimes inhibit the expression of unusual ideas which might be modified so as to be fruitful, Alexander F. Osborn introduced training in what he called "brainstorming." In this problem-solving situation, members are given a problem, such as how to increase the attractiveness of teaching as a profession, and then are asked to give whatever ideas come to mind, no matter how outlandish. Thus, group norms are established to encourage rather than discourage strange suggestions. These are then gradually selected and evaluated, and a unique practical solution may be developed from an initially bizarre suggestion. Though the basis appears sound, one of the few careful evaluative experiments suggests that "brainstorming" inhibits rather than facilitates creative thinking (Taylor et al. 1958). [See CREATIVITY; PROBLEM SOLVING.]

The National Training Laboratories were established at Bethel, Maine, for the purpose of providing summer workshops in interpersonal relations. Educators, military leaders, supervisors in industry, and others participate in programs involving some theory sessions, but largely free interaction in groups, in order to become aware of how they affect others and others affect them. The original program spread widely and may now take place in sessions lasting from a few hours to months. "Sensitivity training" is said to have produced dramatic changes in the effectiveness of organizations. Unfortunately, the problems of evaluating the effectiveness of "sensitivity training" are immense, but the clearest evidence to date of its effectiveness consists of testimonials from members of organizations which have participated and the fact that many such organizations have continued to train their supervisors and employees in this way (Tannenbaum et al. 1961, pp. 233–238).

Another recent approach to training is that developed in the System Development Corporation. In "system training," the working unit (in this case, most work has been done with air defense crews) is considered as a "man–machine system" involving more than the time–motion aspects emphasized in an earlier period and the interpersonal relationships of a later stage. In practice, an air defense crew at its home site is presented with a series of problems which are simulated on the crew's own radar scopes, with detailed flight plans, etc. After the problem, a careful record is available of all relevant interactions, and the crew holds a debriefing session in which members analyze their faults and attempt to make necessary corrections. One goal is to develop greater flexibility in the crew, allowing for rapid changes in task assignment so as to provide for effective adjustment to all sorts of problem situations. Data indicate that there is, indeed, improvement in ability to deal with the simulated problems. It is assumed that such improvement also applies to future problems which the crew might encounter in real life as well (Gagné 1962).

BERTRAM H. RAVEN

[See also FIELD THEORY.]

BIBLIOGRAPHY

ALLPORT, FLOYD H. 1920 The Influence of the Group Upon Association and Thought. *Journal of Experimental Psychology* 3:159–182.

BAVELAS, ALEX 1950 Communication Patterns in Task-oriented Groups. *Journal of the Acoustical Society of America* 22:725–730.

BERKOWITZ, LEONARD 1956 Group Norms Among Bomber Crews: Patterns of Perceived Crew Attitudes, "Actual" Crew Attitudes and Crew Liking Related to Aircrew Effectiveness in Far Eastern Combat. *Sociometry* 19:141–153.

COCH, LESTER; and FRENCH, JOHN R. P. JR. 1948 Overcoming Resistance to Change. *Human Relations* 1:512–532.

DEUTSCH, MORTON 1949 An Experimental Study of the Effects of Co-operation and Competition Upon Group Process. *Human Relations* 2:199–231.

FIEDLER, FRED E. 1958 *Leader Attitudes and Group Effectiveness.* Urbana: Univ. of Illinois Press.

GAGNÉ, ROBERT M. (editor) 1962 *Psychological Principles in System Development.* New York: Holt.

GUETZKOW, HAROLD; and DILL, WILLIAM R. 1957 Factors in the Organizational Development of Task-oriented Groups. *Sociometry* 20:175–204.

HARE, ALEXANDER P. 1962 *Handbook of Small Group Research.* New York: Free Press.

HORSFALL, ALEXANDER B.; and ARENSBERG, C. M. 1949 Teamwork and Productivity in a Shoe Factory. *Human Organization* 8, no. 1:13–25.

KAHN, ROBERT L.; and KATZ, DANIEL 1953 Leadership Practices in Relation to Productivity and Morale. Pages 612–628 in Dorwin Cartwright and Alvin F. Zander (editors), *Group Dynamics: Research and Theory.* Evanston, Ill.: Row, Peterson.

KELLEY, HAROLD H.; and THIBAUT, JOHN W. 1954 Experimental Studies of Group Problem Solving and Process. Volume 2, pages 735–785 in Gardner Lindzey (editor), *Handbook of Social Psychology.* Cambridge, Mass.: Addison-Wesley.

LEAVITT, HAROLD J. 1951 Some Effects of Certain Communication Patterns on Group Performance. *Journal of Abnormal and Social Psychology* 46:38–50.

LEWIN, KURT 1951 *Field Theory in Social Science: Selected Theoretical Papers.* Edited by Dorwin Cartwright. New York: Harper. → A collection of papers first published between 1939 and 1947. A British edition was published in 1963 by Tavistock.

LORGE, IRVING et al. 1958 A Survey of Studies Contrasting the Quality of Group Performance and Individual Performance: 1920–1957. *Psychological Bulletin* 55:337–372.

MAIER, NORMAN R. F. 1953 An Experimental Test of the Effect of Training on Discussion Leadership. *Human Relations* 6:161–173.

MAIER, NORMAN R. F.; and SOLEM, ALLEN R. 1952 The Contribution of a Discussion Leader to the Quality of Group Thinking: The Effective Use of Minority Opinions. *Human Relations* 5:277–288.

MICHIGAN, UNIVERSITY OF, SURVEY RESEARCH CENTER 1954 *Group Cohesiveness in the Industrial Work Group*, by Stanley Seashore. Ann Arbor: Univ. of Michigan Press.

MOEDE, W. 1927 Die Richtlinien der Leitungspsychologie. *Industrielle Psychotechnik* 4:193–209.

PERLMUTTER, HOWARD V.; and DE MONTMOLLIN, GERMAINE 1952 Group Learning of Nonsense Syllables. *Journal of Abnormal and Social Psychology* 47:762–769.

RAVEN, BERTRAM H.; and EACHUS, H. TODD 1963 Cooperation and Competition in Means-interdependent Triads. *Journal of Abnormal and Social Psychology* 67:307–316.

RAVEN, BERTRAM H.; and REITSEMA, JAN 1957 The Effects of Varied Clarity of Group Goal and Group Path Upon the Individual and His Relation to His Group. *Human Relations* 10:29–45.

ROETHLISBERGER, FRITZ J.; and DICKSON, WILLIAM J. (1939) 1961 *Management and the Worker: An Account of a Research Program Conducted by the Western Electric Company, Hawthorne Works, Chicago.* Cambridge, Mass.: Harvard Univ. Press. → A paperback edition was published in 1964 by Wiley.

SCHACHTER, STANLEY et al. 1951 An Experimental Study of Cohesiveness and Productivity. *Human Relations* 4:229–238.

SHAW, MARJORIE E. 1932 A Comparison of Individuals and Small Groups in the Rational Solution of Complex Problems. *American Journal of Psychology* 44:491–504.

SHAW, MARVIN E. 1954 Some Effects of Problem Complexity Upon Problem Solution Efficiency in Different Communication Nets. *Journal of Experimental Psychology* 48:211–217.

SHAW, MARVIN E. 1959 Acceptance of Authority, Group Structure and the Effectiveness of Small Groups. *Journal of Personality* 27:196–210.

TANNENBAUM, ROBERT; WESCHLER, IRVING R.; and MASSARIK, FRED 1961 *Leadership and Organization: A Behavioral Science Approach.* New York: McGraw-Hill.

TAYLOR, DONALD W.; BERRY, PAUL C.; and BLOCK, CLIFFORD H. 1958 Does Group Participation When Using Brain-storming Facilitate or Inhibit Creative Thinking? *Administrative Science Quarterly* 3:23–47.

TAYLOR, DONALD W.; and FAUST, WILLIAM L. 1952 Twenty Questions: Efficiency in Problem Solving as a Function of Size of Group. *Journal of Experimental Psychology* 44:360–368.

THOMAS, EDWIN J. 1957 Effects of Facilitative Role Interdependence on Group Functioning. *Human Relations* 10:347–366.

THOMAS, EDWIN J.; and FINK, CLINTON F. 1963 Effects of Group Size. *Psychological Bulletin* 60:371–384.

THORNDIKE, R. L. 1938 On What Type of Task Will a Group Do Well? *Journal of Abnormal and Social Psychology* 33:409–413.

TRIPLETT, NORMAN 1898 The Dynamogenic Factors in Pacemaking and Competition. *American Journal of Psychology* 9:507–533.

TRIST, E. L.; and BAMFORTH, K. W. 1951 Some Social and Psychological Consequences of the Longwall Method of Coal-getting. *Human Relations* 4:3–38.

VAN ZELST, RAYMOND H. 1952 Validation of a Sociometric Regrouping Procedure. *Journal of Abnormal and Social Psychology* 47:299–301.

WHITE, RALPH K.; and LIPPITT, RONALD 1960 *Autocracy and Democracy: An Experimental Inquiry.* New York: Harper.

ZAJONC, ROBERT B.; and SMOKE, WILLIAM H. 1959 Redundancy in Task Assignments and Group Performance. *Psychometrika* 24:361–369.

GUIDANCE
See COUNSELING PSYCHOLOGY; EDUCATIONAL PSYCHOLOGY; VOCATIONAL INTEREST TESTING.

GUILDS
See GILDS.

GUILT
See MORAL DEVELOPMENT; PSYCHIATRY, *article on* FORENSIC PSYCHIATRY; PSYCHOANALYSIS; PUNISHMENT.

GUMPLOWICZ, LUDWIG

Ludwig Gumplowicz (1838–1909), of Polish-Jewish parentage, was professor of public law at the University of Graz, Austria, from 1875 until his death. He is best known for his pioneer work in establishing sociology as a social science. His contributions to political science and jurisprudence were also important, but they consisted mainly of applications of his sociological generalizations to government and law. A clear and vigorous writer, he was much given to controversy in all three fields.

The sociological system of Gumplowicz was based on a number of fundamental dogmas or principles: (1) social phenomena are governed by universal laws that operate in a completely secular manner, unrelated to religious or moral considerations, and they must be studied by using a thoroughly scientific method; (2) sociology rejects all value judgments; and (3) sociology is the science of the interaction of groups.

Applying these principles to the evolution of society and states, Gumplowicz held that the earliest forms of group life were small, natural, ethnic or blood-kin hordes. These groups were unified by consanguinity and common, rudimentary economic interests; their members lived in sexual promiscuity and relative equality of social position. Solidarity developed in a group through a process of "syngenism," which gradually produces unity in any social group. Out of this earliest form of group life arose, in succession, the matriarchate and the patriarchate, the first types of organized control.

Since the appearance of the matriarchate and the patriarchate, social and political evolution has been a never-ending process of external conflict between groups, in the form of wars, and of internal conflict of interests within groups. The motive in all conquests has been the desire for the material gain that may be obtained by exploiting the labor of the conquered. Material interests, therefore, have furnished the dynamic impulse in social evolution. "So conquest and the satisfaction of needs through the labor of the conquered, essentially the same though differing in form, is the great theme of human history from prehistoric times to the latest plan for a Congo state. . . . It cannot be otherwise since man's material need is the prime motive of his conduct" ([1885] 1963, pp. 203–205).

When the process of conquest and subjugation becomes well developed, the principle of amalgamation supplements syngenism in producing unity in the state, which, as the highest form of social grouping, is the culmination of a long process of conquest and of many adjustments subsequent to conquest. Gumplowicz believed that there is no such thing as indefinite social progress; the historic process is the record of the rise and fall of states and follows an inevitable cyclical course of growth and decline.

In the initial stage of conquest, there were only two social classes, the conquerors and the subjugated. Foreign merchants who moved in produced a third class—the middle class or bourgeoisie. With the development of social and political institutions, the activities of the primary classes of rulers, merchants, and exploited masses created a need for secondary or derived classes, such as priests, professional men, and artisans. These social classes were based on a division of labor which was created and maintained by coercion.

The rise of social classes produced a complex and unending struggle among them to control the policy of the state in order to promote their various special interests. These interests were best advanced through participation in legislation, and social classes found that political parties were the most effective agencies for controlling the legislative process. Whatever form the struggle of classes within the state has taken, it has provided the dynamic core of history ([1877] 1907, pp. 33 ff.).

Paralleling political and economic developments there were various processes of assimilation, such as the adoption of the language, religion, and manners and customs of the conquerors, which tended to produce cultural unity. Finally, through intermarriage, an ethnic unity was achieved. The homogeneous society thus created is the "folk-state" or nation, which is the ultimate outcome of social and political evolution. The tendency throughout history has been for such a folk-state or nation to seek to conquer a neighboring nation, and when it is successful the whole process of subjugation, assimilation, and amalgamation is repeated.

Gumplowicz' sociological system is not simply an application of Darwinian biology to the operation of human society. He was indebted to Darwin for the general idea of a struggle for existence, but he was also indebted to others: to Comte for the determination to analyze social phenomena with scientific rigor, and to Spencer for the idea of universal evolution and the application of the laws of universal evolution to society. His conception of the primordial and ceaseless conflict of races and social groups came from the writings of Count Joseph Arthur de Gobineau and from his own life-long contact with the intense struggles among races and groups in the Austro–Hungarian Empire. He had participated in the Polish revolt of 1863 and had absorbed much of the socialist and anarchist literature of the first half of the nineteenth century: his dogma that the basis of conflict is always the promotion of material self-interest was based chiefly on the stress laid in this literature on the exploitation and expropriation of the masses by the property owners, and to a lesser extent on Marxist writings.

The outstanding contribution of Gumplowicz to sociology was his naturalistic and secular approach to society and social evolution and his conception of social evolution as a process of conflict. The concept of "social process" appeared in the writings of such European sociologists as Franz Oppenheimer and Gustav Ratzenhofer; in America, the works of Gumplowicz and Ratzenhofer were read and digested by Albion Small, founder of the so-called Chicago school of sociology. Small and his disciples, such as Park and Burgess, and other American sociologists, notably Ross and Cooley, carried further the development of the concept of the "social process."

Gumplowicz' contributions to realistic political science were notable. He assembled and developed in a well-integrated and systematic fashion the previously scattered suggestions relative to the social conditioning of political phenomena: that society is a group held together by material interests; that the state is a society organized and controlled by coercion; and that political legislation is a product and reflection of the social process at any given time ([1877] 1907, pp. 33 ff.; [1892] 1902, pp. 49–66). Gumplowicz' well-documented argument that the state has always been founded through wars and conflict cleared away pietistic, idealistic, and metaphysical misconceptions. His argument has won general acceptance, although some sociologists, notably Jacques Novicow, have charged that he neglected the role of pacific and cooperative factors in the origins of states. Gumplowicz' conception of political parties as interest groups has become, perhaps, the most useful truism of dynamic political science and has been adopted and developed by Durkheim, Duguit, Laski, and A. F. Bentley, among others.

Gumplowicz' fundamental assumptions led him to reject the possibility that man can plan his social future and promote his happiness by such social inventions as the welfare state. He even suggested that the practical value of sociology may be to save mankind from wasting time and energy on futile schemes of utopian reform. There is some evidence, however, that Lester Ward was able to convince Gumplowicz to a certain extent that the social sciences may enable man to plan a better future (1905).

Gumplowicz spent most of his professional life as a professor of law. His legal theories were a direct outgrowth of his sociological doctrines, and he is generally regarded as one of the founders of the sociological school of jurisprudence. He saw laws as invariably growing out of the conflict of classes and interests within the state, as social products rather than divine revelations, or as wise and rational human creations, or as derived in some mysterious manner from nature. He believed that there are no natural laws, except in the sense that laws are a result of the nature of man and of the social processes. This precludes the validity of classifying laws as good or bad: laws are not passed to promote justice in any abstract sense but rather to enable the dominant social class or classes to carry out their exploitation ([1892] 1902, pp. 55 ff.). Justice does not determine political and legal rights; rather, these rights are the product of the conflict of interests among social classes:

The premise of "inalienable human rights" rests upon the most unreasonable self-deification of man and overestimation of the value of human life, and upon complete misconception of the only possible basis of the existence of the State. . . . Rights are not founded upon justice. On the contrary, justice is created only by the actual rights as they exist in the state. . . . It is the simple abstraction of political rights, and it stands or falls with them.   ([1885], pp. 180–181, 263 in 1899 edition)

HARRY ELMER BARNES

[*For the historical context of Gumplowicz' work, see* LEGAL SYSTEMS; *and the biographies of* COMTE; DARWIN; GOBINEAU; SPENCER. *For discussion of the subsequent development of his ideas, see* CONFLICT; CONSTITUTIONAL LAW, *article on* CIVIL RIGHTS; LAW, *article on* THE LEGAL SYSTEM; *and the biographies of* BENTLEY; DUGUIT; DURKHEIM; LASKI; OPPENHEIMER; RATZENHOFER; SMALL.]

WORKS BY GUMPLOWICZ

(1877) 1907   *Allgemeines Staatsrecht.* 3d ed. Innsbruck (Austria): Wagner. → First published as *Philosophisches Staatsrecht.*

1881   *Rechtsstaat und Socialismus.* Innsbruck (Austria): Wagner.

1882   *Verwaltungslehre mit besonderer Berücksichtigung des österreichischen Verwaltungsrechts.* Innsbruck (Austria): Wagner.

(1883–1905) 1926–1928   *Ausgewählte Werke.* Edited by F. Oppenheimer, F. Savorgnan, M. Adler, G. Salomon. 4 vols. Innsbruck (Austria): Wagner. → Volume 1: *Geschichte der Staatstheorien,* (1905) 1926. Volume 2: *Grundriss der Soziologie,* (1885) 1926. Volume 3: *Der Rassenkampf,* (1883) 1928. Volume 4: *Soziologische Essays* (1899), *Soziologie und Politik,* (1892) 1928.

(1885) 1963   *The Outlines of Sociology.* Edited with an introduction and notes by Irving L. Horowitz. 2d ed. New York: Paine-Whitman. → First published in German.

1887   *System socyologii.* Warsaw: Orgelbrand.

(1892) 1902   *Die soziologische Staatsidee.* 2d ed. Innsbruck (Austria): Wagner.

1905   An Austrian Appreciation of Lester F. Ward. *American Journal of Sociology* 10:643–653.

1910   *Sozialphilosophie im Umriss.* Innsbruck (Austria): Wagner.

SUPPLEMENTARY BIBLIOGRAPHY

BARNES, HARRY E. 1919   The Struggle of Races and Social Groups as a Factor in the Development of Political and Social Institutions: An Exposition and Critique of the Sociological System of Ludwig Gumplowicz. *Journal of Race Development* 9:394–419.

BEROLZHEIMER, FRITZ (1905) 1912   *The World's Legal Philosophies.* Boston: Boston Book. → First published as *Die Kulturstufen der Rechts- und Wirtschaftsphilosophie.*

KOCHANOWSKI, I. 1909   Ludwig Gumplowicz. *American Journal of Sociology* 15:405–409.

POSNER, STANISLAW 1911   *Ludwik Gumplowicz 1838–1909: Zarys zycia i pracy.* Warsaw: Orgelbrand.

WARD, LESTER F. 1909   Ludwig Gumplowicz. *American Journal of Sociology* 15:410–413.

ZEBROWSKI, BERNHARD 1926   *Ludwig Gumplowicz: Eine Bio-Bibliographie.* Berlin: Prager.

GUTHRIE, EDWIN R.

American psychologist, educator, and philosopher, Edwin Ray Guthrie (1886–1959) was the oldest of five children. He was born in Lincoln, Nebraska, where he spent his boyhood. His mother, Harriet Pickett Guthrie, the daughter of a newspaperman, was an elementary-school teacher before marriage; his father was the son of a minister and the manager of a piano store.

Guthrie had exhibited vivid intellectual interests even as a child. At the University of Nebraska, which he entered in 1903, he majored in mathematics and minored in philosophy. After receiving his A.B. in 1907 he remained at Nebraska for graduate work, majoring in philosophy and minoring in mathematics and psychology. In 1910 he received his A.M. from Nebraska and was made a Harrison Fellow at the University of Pennsylvania, where he received his PH.D. in 1912 with a thesis resolving various paradoxes of Bertrand Russell (1915a).

Professional life. For five years Guthrie taught high-school mathematics, from 1907 to 1910 in Lincoln and from 1912 to 1914 in Philadelphia. He then joined the faculty of the University of Washington, where he remained, except for temporary leaves, for the rest of his life.

At Washington, Guthrie started as instructor in the department of philosophy, then chaired by William Savery. Savery (a student of William James at Harvard) and Guthrie (a student of Edgar A. Singer at Pennsylvania) became lifetime friends. In 1918 Guthrie became assistant professor and in 1919 joined the department of psychology, chaired by Stevenson Smith, who also became Guthrie's close friend. Guthrie was made associate professor in 1925 and professor in 1928.

Guthrie married Helen Macdonald in 1920. With her, he translated Pierre Janet's *Principles of Psychotherapy* (1924) and traveled extensively—especially in France, where Guthrie met Janet, and in England, Italy, and Hungary.

Guthrie was the second winner of the gold medal awarded by the American Psychological Foundation for "outstanding lifetime contributions to psychology." Awarded an honorary LL.D. from the University of Nebraska in 1945, he was elected president of the American Psychological Association in the same year. During World War II, he was chief consultant to the overseas branch of the general staff of the U.S. War Department in 1941 and chief psychologist of the overseas branch of the Office of War Information in 1942. He was dean of the graduate school of the University of Washington from 1943 to 1951 and was honored by a building on the campus being named after him while he was still alive.

Contributions to science

Guthrie's close association with philosophers and his formal training in philosophy at an advanced level had considerable impact on the problems to which he addressed himself and on his resolutions of some of these.

Philosophical clarifications. *The nature of explanation.* Guthrie deemed the question "why" as unprofitable and almost nonsensical—unless by "why" one means "how come," "under what circumstances," or "what next." "Why" in the sense of "for what purpose" carries implicit teleological assumptions perhaps unwarranted and not the most fruitful for understanding.

The most illuminating explanations, Guthrie pointed out, are those which summarize sequences of observable events: Given this set of observable circumstances, what observable subsequent events may be most reasonably expected? Such explanations answer the question "what next" or "how come." An explanation states the general class of which some particular sequence is an instance, nothing more.

Causation and the nature of theory. Seeking "causes," as ordinarily conceived, distracts and confuses us. The usual notion of "cause" implies that there is a force within some set of circumstances which somehow pushes events in a certain direction. Building on the work of David Hume, Guthrie abandoned the usual notion of "cause" and thought instead in terms of sequences of events. Certain events precede other events in time. The earlier events need not be assumed to force the later ones; they simply precede them.

Certain events do precede others with great regularity. Our problem as theorists then becomes one of devising general terms to label these classes of events and to describe these more regular sequences. Theory construction, so conceived, is an inductive process and consists in devising general statements (principles) to summarize as many sequences as possible.

Hedonism. One of the very ancient Greek philosophies (refined by Aristotle and Plato) held that man by his nature is a pleasure-seeking organism. A variation of this turns up in the popular idea that learning occurs only when some satisfaction or need reduction is involved for the learner [see LEARNING, *article on* REINFORCEMENT]. This is a very comforting view. It is heartening to believe that, whenever we learn, at least some of our needs are thereby being met. The view poses difficulties, however, in accounting for the many instances in which learning is followed by distress, and no apparent satisfaction or need reduction. To handle this difficulty, psychologists posited an ever-lengthening list of motives (conscious and unconscious) or drives (primary, secondary, tertiary) or needs, in an attempt to account for seemingly dysfunctional learning.

Guthrie handled the difficulty by abandoning the idea that we learn only what is followed by some need reduction. His approach has economy in the numerosity of presumed "needs" or "drives." It also facilitates understanding of mistakes, learned awkwardnesses, and habitual stupidities—without having to presume a "death instinct," "will to failure," or anything similar—and alerts us to circumstances in which learning may lead to damage or disaster.

The unity of learning. There is, Guthrie suggested, one kind of learning only; the same principles which hold for learning in one instance hold also for learning in all other instances. The apparent diversity of learning does not stem from there being different kinds of learning following different principles but arises instead from differences of other sorts: different kinds of situations, different kinds of responses possible to organisms with different musculatures, and different kinds of stimuli that can become cues for differing species with their differing sense organs and differing neural structures. We need not formulate separate principles for each of the differing situations, differing response types, or differing stimulus sensitivities. The same set of principles may hold for all and be illustrated by all.

New concepts. *Multiple "causation."* At the time when Guthrie wrote, a prevalent way of thinking about the responding organism was in terms of "a" stimulus or "the" CS (conditioned stimulus) for various responses. In contrast, gestalt psychologists (Köhler, Koffka, et al.) were stressing the importance of the totality of the situation. Their emphasis was on the totality as a unit—responses purportedly being evoked by the total situation as a unified, in some ways indivisible, whole.

Guthrie's idea, inspired by both theories, was also different from both. He emphasized multiple stimulation as a more adequate basis for comprehending behavior than either the single stimulus or than the whole situation as merely a unitary totality. He suggested we view any response as a consequence of the interplay and, in a way, the summation of all stimuli impinging on the organism at that moment. He held that the nature of the response made by the responding organism is not a function merely (or even primarily) of the feature most

salient to the observer or experimenter—for example, not a function of "the" conditioned stimulus merely. Neither is the response a function of an unanalyzable total situation. Rather, the total situation can be analyzed into component stimulus patterns and their relationships, the organism's response being predictable from these various components simultaneously considered.

Role of internal stimuli. Throughout the first half of the twentieth century, psychologists primarily emphasized external stimuli, except for those internal stimuli considered under the heading of "drives." In accord with his view that all stimuli acting on the organism should be considered in predicting behavior, Guthrie called attention to the many internal stimuli besides those thought of as drives. He emphasized that proprioceptive stimuli, kinesthetic stimuli, stimuli from visceral responses, stimuli from endocrine states, fatigue states, and chemicothermal conditions, and other internal stimuli all are present too and should be considered for the best understanding of behavior.

He saw no particular advantage in subdividing internal stimuli into two classes: drive-connected stimuli versus others. It appeared to Guthrie that the various internal stimuli and the various external stimuli all act in substantially the same way and are of equal importance when of equal duration and equal intensity. Our difficulty in understanding behavior stems largely from our failure to note enough of the dimensions of the stimulus situation acting upon the organism rather than from a lack of knowledge about an individual's "motives" or "drives."

Movement-produced stimuli. Every time we make any response whatsoever, a wealth of new stimuli is brought into existence: new visual stimuli, new tactual stimuli, new proprioceptive stimuli, sometimes new auditory and olfactory stimuli, and others. This class of stimuli Guthrie called "movement-produced stimuli," emphasizing that our own responses always change the stimulus world we are in.

Conditioning. The work of Bekhterev and Pavlov was immensely stimulating to Guthrie, as it was to other American psychologists [see LEARNING, *article on* CLASSICAL CONDITIONING]. One result of their influence was Guthrie's suggestion concerning the relationship between conditioning and learning. Instead of thinking of the phenomena found in conditioning experiments as arising primarily from a pairing of the so-called CS and US (unconditioned stimulus), Guthrie considered them as arising from the pairing of the CS and some *response* (the unconditioned response [UR] or others)—or more precisely, from the concomitance of various stimuli and some ongoing response. Conditioning so conceived becomes a paradigm of one subclass of the more general class of "learning," and all learning, including that called conditioning, becomes the result of a pairing of new stimuli with ongoing *responses*. In what appears to be Pavlov's only paper published in a United States journal (1932), he restated his original position that it is the pairing of stimuli rather than of stimuli and responses that is critical. Guthrie (1934a) rejected Pavlov's view and the problem remains moot today.

A theory of learning

Guthrie thus created a highly original, parsimonious theory of learned behavior, presenting much of it in *The Psychology of Learning* (1935). Formulations of the basic principles and concepts are given in a paper by Voeks (1950).

Learning, as Guthrie conceived of it, is the process of establishing new stimuli as cues for some specified response. This process occurs in a single trial and is disrupted only through unlearning.

Recency versus postremity. Ebbinghaus, Watson, and others, on the basis of experimental work, stressed that the length of time elapsed since learning is a key dimension in the preservation of learning [see FORGETTING]. Recency was adopted as a crucial factor in the preservation of learning. Sigmund Freud, through his clinical work, came to the conclusion that learning which has occurred early in childhood often is preserved strikingly even when there has been little or no opportunity for further strengthening of that learning. People observing daily life noted that sometimes things recently learned are best preserved, whereas at other times things learned in the distant past seem most intact and reappear after long lapses of time. A hodgepodge of chaotic data accumulated.

Guthrie proposed a new conceptualization and a new principle which reconciles these divergent findings. He suggested that what most other psychologists call a "response" or "behavior" is actually a series of discrete, more-or-less integrated responses. For example, the response labeled "picking up a pencil" involves a large number of separate muscular activities. Similarly, even so simple a "stimulus" as a pencil combines many visual, tactile, and other stimuli. Each component of such a compound stimulus object can be, according to Guthrie, a cue for a separate response and may tend to elicit such a response. The response remaining cued to each component will always be the response most recently made in the presence of that particular component.

When a series of responses is made to a changing series of situations which—while changing—have some components in common, responses are successively attached and detached from the reappearing stimulus components. Again, the response remaining cued to each stimulus component is the response last made to that particular part. Even when the stimulus component and the response occur early in the stimulus series and at a remote time, nonetheless the response remains cued to that component whenever the component has not turned up subsequently.

The role of recency in this theory differs a great deal from the role it plays in the traditional recency principle. According to the latter, as has been mentioned, a given stimulus–response connection tends to grow weaker with elapsed time. But Guthrie held that the cue properties of stimuli cannot be weakened by time alone. So long as the response is the last-made response to the particular stimulus component, the cue properties remain at full strength; as soon as some other response is made contiguously with the perceived stimulus, the original cue property will cease to exist and a new cue property will be at full strength. This sequential regularity has been formulated in the principle of postremity: the last response an organism makes to each component in a particular situation is the response remaining cued to that component—regardless of how long the time since that stimulus occurred.

Thus, Guthrie would argue, the old principle of recency on occasion tends to operate because the more recent the stimuli and the given bit of behavior, the less time there has been for those stimuli to reappear while any other behavior is occurring; and hence the less likelihood there is that some other response can have become cued to those stimuli. However, certain very early stimulus–response connections will tend to be perpetuated (as Freud reported) because the particular stimulus conditions are highly unusual, thus reducing the possibility of their being present while some other new response is being made; hence it becomes likely no new response will be cued to those sets of stimuli.

Removal of stimuli established as cues. The view derived from philosophical hedonism, that we learn only those forms of behavior which are in some way rewarding, was common when Guthrie was writing. Both psychologists and laymen believed that unless a response is reinforced by drive reduction or tension reduction or in some other way satisfies some need, no learning will occur.

Guthrie, however, did not hold that view. He noted that under some circumstances men and animals learn forms of behavior that make matters worse for them, satisfy no need whatsoever, accord with no "motive," and attain no goal. Furthermore, under some circumstances these unwanted habits are preserved.

The necessary and sufficient condition for learning, Guthrie suggested, is the occurrence of a response in the presence of a stimulus not already a cue for that response. Similarly, the necessary and sufficient condition for the preservation of learning is to have the current cues for some response absent whenever incompatible' responses occur. By this theory, a "reward" will preserve learning either when it is itself a cue for the new response or when it closely follows the response and removes the stimulus established as a cue for that response. But *any* state of affairs, including "punishment," will likewise preserve learning equally well, so long as the cue is removed from the organism (or the organism is removed from the cue) immediately after the response is made—i.e., before another response can be made in the presence of the same stimulus, thus canceling the original association. Punishment will disrupt learning when it induces the organism to make a response incompatible with the previously learned response while the original stimulus is yet present. Rewards also will disrupt learning under those circumstances. Degree of "removal from a situation" (or partial removal of the situation from the animal) may enable us to predict learning and its preservation or disruption more fully than do "reward" and "punishment."

One-trial learning. For two thousand years, following Aristotle and his basic assumptions, philosophers, laymen, and behavioral scientists alike have put great faith in frequency of association as a mode of strengthening associations. In our century, Pavlov, Thorndike, and Hull all stressed the desirability or even necessity of repetitive trials to inculcate learning. In contradistinction, Guthrie was much impressed by the experimental work of Köhler and others on "insight" behavior.

Guthrie suggested that frequency of trials as ordinarily conceived may well be a misleading way of thinking about learning and an often futile way of addressing oneself to the practical problems of learning. He offered his revolutionary principle of one-trial learning: Whatever stimuli happen to be acting on the behaving organism become full-strength cues for whatever responses the organism is making at that time. A single occasion on which the specified response occurs concomitantly with various stimuli will establish all those stimuli as full-strength cues for the specified response. Additional trials are useful only for establishing additional stimuli as cues for the specified response.

According to this principle, repetition is often futile and under some circumstances actually worse than no trials at all. Repetition is futile to the degree that the stimuli are the same from one trial to another, that the desired response is not being made in each trial, or that the stimuli one wishes to establish as cues for the response are not those actually present.

Repetition is worse than futile whenever the responses actually being made by the organism are incompatible with the desired response; for under those circumstances more and more stimuli become cues for responses incompatible with the desired responses. This has the dual effect of increasing the number of stimuli which are cues for some undesired response (thus increasing the probability of the undesired response being the one to appear on subsequent occasions) and of decreasing the pool of stimuli which could elicit the desired response.

Frequency has value only to the degree that new stimuli are present from trial to trial and then only when the desired response actually is being made on the various trials. Under these circumstances, additional stimuli become cues for the response each time it occurs. Thus, repeatedly practicing a difficult passage on the piano will be profitable only when correct notes actually are being played in a variety of circumstances, the correct notes thus becoming cued to additional combinations of auditory, muscular, and other stimuli accompanying them or immediately preceding them. What happens otherwise is either nothing or the learning of errors.

Probability of response. The likelihood of any specified response occurring at some particular time is directly proportional to the extent to which the stimulating situation is composed of cues for that response. The greater the number of cues present at some particular time for the response desired, the greater the probability that that response will occur (if the total number of stimuli is the same for the various situations being compared). This principle in the hands of William Estes became the basis of what currently is called "modern statistical learning theory" [*see* MODELS, MATHEMATICAL; *see also* Estes 1950; 1959].

Cross-disciplinary implications

Education. Dewey emphasized that "we learn by doing." Guthrie extended this to "we learn only what we ourselves do." If in classrooms the student watches a teacher skillfully solve problems or engage in intricate feats of cogent reasoning, the student will become an intent observer of the teacher solving problems—but he will not become better at solving problems himself, unless he himself is doing something other than watching. The responses we wish to cue to various stimuli must be made by the individual himself in the presence of those stimuli.

Guthrie's theory of learning leads one also to place considerably less faith in drill. Making the same response over and over again will not further learning unless the circumstances are changed—and only to the extent that the circumstances are changed. Sitting in the same seat in the same room with the same internal stimuli from the same emotional make-up acting upon one while making the same response would add nothing to what was gained by making the response in the presence of those stimuli once.

A further implication is that the circumstances under which one wishes the desired response to be made in the future should be approximated as closely as possible by the present circumstances. The responses made get cued only to those stimuli actually present.

The theory implies too that teachers commonly are too prominent a part of the schoolroom situation. Whenever a learner is making desired responses, the teacher would be wise to be as small a part of the stimulating situation as possible. When the teacher is a large part of the situation, the learner's responses will, of course, be cued to the sight and sound of the teacher (as well as to other stimuli from the teacher); when these stimuli constitute a major part of the total situation, the desired responses are being cued to relatively little else besides the teacher. Hence, in the teacher's subsequent absence, the desired response is less apt to be made than would be the case had the teacher been less prominent.

Many further implications for formal education are presented in a book by Guthrie and Powers (1950).

Psychotherapy. We ask "Why did you do this?" assuming the person acts toward some end. We search for "motives" and speculate on what the person gains by his unwanted behavior. But possibly he gains nothing by it—even in his own eyes.

That could be the crux of his problem: he does not customarily act in accord with his own values or goals. His behavior is largely unaimed.

From Guthrie's theory we should expect that much learned behavior may be unsatisfying even to the person engaged in it. The person does not necessarily direct his behavior toward any goal, conscious or unconscious. He is not necessarily acting in a fashion that meets his basic needs or fulfills his major hopes. He simply is doing what he has been trained to do, making the responses to various stimuli that he last made to those stimuli, responses that in some prior context he had perhaps been forced to make. The responses may meet no need and yet persist.

Instead of assuming that all behavior is goal-directed and meets some need, we should try in psychotherapy to help the person develop more goal-directed behavior and develop behavior consonant with his needs: for example, we should help him to acquire habits of aiming at goals, habits of evaluating his actions, habits of ascertaining *whether* any need is indeed being met by his behavior [see MENTAL DISORDERS, TREATMENT OF, *article on* CLIENT-CENTERED COUNSELING].

Further, in light of Guthrie's theory, instead of concentrating primarily on the circumstances under which the unwanted behavior or feelings occur, we should search also for the circumstances under which the individual currently does make valued responses. The latter offer leads concerning the stimuli which already are cues for valued responses and thereby offer a basis on which to build.

Subsequently, when confronted with unwanted behavior, the appropriate question is not "Why?" but "What are the circumstances eliciting that unwanted response?" and "What stimuli are cues for it?" To get a different response cued to those stimuli, one should not present all at once many of the stimuli that are cues for the unwanted response. (That is, one should not, for example, put the individual back in the original situation.) This would make the unwanted response very likely, according to the probability principle. Rather, we should present only a few of those stimuli that now are cues for the unwanted response while simultaneously presenting many stimuli that are cues for a desired response. When the new response occurs, a few more of the stimuli may be introduced that are cues for the unwanted response. Thus, gradually, we could detach from unwanted behavior more and more of the stimuli formerly cues for unwanted behavior and establish them as new cues for the new response. On this installment plan, unlearning of the old and learning of the new proceeds most efficaciously.

One of the most brilliant and kindly of men, Guthrie has given us a rich heritage through his teaching, articles, and books. He worked with sustained endeavor on an extraordinary array of topics. His writings, remarkably illuminating, thoughtful, and thought-provoking, reflect his high good humor, courage, and great concern for his fellow men.

VIRGINIA VOEKS

[For the historical context of Guthrie's work, see the biographies of BEKHTEREV; KÖHLER; PAVLOV.]

WORKS BY GUTHRIE

1914a   Formal Logic and Logical Form. *Midwest Quarterly* 1:146–155.

1914b   Old Solutions of a New Problem. *Midwest Quarterly* 1:236–241.

1915a   *The Paradoxes of Mr. Russell: With a Brief Account of Their History.* Lancaster, Pa.: New Era Printing.

1915b   Russell's Theory of Types. *Journal of Philosophy, Psychology and Scientific Methods* 12:381–385.

1916   The Field of Logic. *Journal of Philosophy, Psychology and Scientific Methods* 13:152–158.

1921a   SMITH, STEVENSON; and GUTHRIE, EDWIN R. *Chapters in General Psychology.* Seattle: Univ. of Washington Press.

1921b   SMITH, STEVENSON; and GUTHRIE, EDWIN R. *General Psychology in Terms of Behavior.* New York: Appleton.

1922   SMITH, STEVENSON; and GUTHRIE, EDWIN R. Exhibitionism. *Journal of Abnormal and Social Psychology* 17:206–209.

1924   Purpose and Mechanism in Psychology. *Journal of Philosophy* 21:673–682.

1927a   Measuring Student Opinion of Teachers. *School and Society* 25:175–176.

1927b   Measuring Introversion and Extroversion. *Journal of Abnormal and Social Psychology* 22:82–88.

1928a   Psychological Bases of War and Peace. Pages 78–83 in Charles E. Martin and Edith Dobie (editors), *Problems in International Understanding.* Seattle: Univ. of Washington Book Store.

1928b   GUTHRIE, EDWIN R.; and MORRILL, H. The Fusion of Non-musical Intervals. *American Journal of Psychology* 40:624–625.

1930   Conditioning as a Principle of Learning. *Psychological Review* 37:412–428.

1933a   On the Nature of Psychological Explanations. *Psychological Review* 40:124–137.

1933b   Association as a Function of Time Interval. *Psychological Review* 40:355–367.

1934a   Pavlov's Theory of Conditioning. *Psychological Review* 41:199–206.

1934b   Reward and Punishment. *Psychological Review* 41:450–460.

(1935) 1960   *The Psychology of Learning.* Rev. ed. Gloucester, Mass.: Smith.

1936   Thorndike's Concept of "Belonging." *Psychological Bulletin* 33:621 only.

1937a   YACORZINSKI, GEORGE K.; and GUTHRIE, EDWIN R. A Comparative Study of Involuntary and Voluntary Conditioned Responses. *Journal of General Psychology* 16:235–257.

1937b   Tolman on Associative Learning. *Psychological Review* 44:525–528.

(1938) 1962   *The Psychology of Human Conflict: The Clash of Motives Within the Individual.* Gloucester, Mass.: Smith.

1939   The Effect of Outcome on Learning. *Psychological Review* 46:480–485.

1940a   Association and the Law of Effect. *Psychological Review* 47:127–148.

1940b   [A Book Review of] *Organizing and Memorizing: Studies in the Psychology of Learning and Teaching,* (1940) by G. Katona. *Psychological Bulletin* 37:820–823.

1942a   The Principle of Associative Learning. Pages 100–114 in *Philosophical Essays in Honor of Edgar Arthur Singer, Jr.,* edited by F. P. Clark and M. C. Nahm. Philadelphia: Univ. of Pennsylvania Press.

1942b   Conditioning: A Theory of Learning in Terms of Stimulus, Response, and Association. National Society for the Study of Education, *Yearbook* 41, part 2:17–60.

1943   Leadership. Pages 366–384 in National Research Council, *Psychology for the Fighting Man, Prepared for the Fighting Man Himself. . . .* Washington: Infantry Journal. → An unsigned article by Guthrie. A paperback edition was published in the same year by Penguin.

1944   Personality in Terms of Associative Learning. Volume 1, pages 49–68 in Joseph McV. Hunt (editor), *Personality and the Behavior Disorders: A Handbook Based on Experimental and Clinical Research.* New York: Ronald Press.

1945   The Evaluation of Faculty Service. American Association of University Professors, *Bulletin* 31:255–262.

1946a   The Conditioned Response. Pages 100–104 in Philip L. Harriman (editor), *Encyclopedia of Psychology.* New York: Philosophical Library.

1946b   GUTHRIE, EDWIN R.; and HORTON, GEORGE P. *Cats in a Puzzle Box.* New York: Rinehart.

1946c   Psychological Facts and Psychological Theory. *Psychological Bulletin* 43:1–20.

1946d   Recency or Effect? A Reply to V. J. O'Connor. *Harvard Educational Review* 16:286–289.

1949a   The Evaluation of Teaching. *Educational Record* 30:109–115.

1949b   GUTHRIE, EDWIN A.; and EDWARDS, ALLEN L. *Psychology: A First Course in Human Behavior.* New York: Harper.

1950   GUTHRIE, EDWIN R.; and POWERS, FRANCIS F. *Educational Psychology.* New York: Ronald Press.

1959a   *The State University: Its Function and Its Future.* Seattle: Univ. of Washington Press.

1959b   Association by Contiguity. Volume 2, pages 158–195 in Sigmund Koch (editor), *Psychology: A Study of a Science.* New York: McGraw-Hill.

SUPPLEMENTARY BIBLIOGRAPHY

American Psychological Foundation Gold Medal Award 1958. 1958   *American Psychologist* 13:739–740.

CARTER, L. F.   1936   Maze Learning With a Differential Proprioceptive Cue. *Journal of Experimental Psychology* 19:758–762.

ESTES, WILLIAM K.   1950   Toward a Statistical Theory of Learning. *Psychological Review* 57:94–107.

ESTES, WILLIAM K. 1959 The Statistical Approach to Learning Theory. Volume 2, pages 380–491 in Sigmund Koch (editor), *Psychology: A Study of a Science.* New York: McGraw-Hill.

JANET, PIERRE 1924 *Principles of Psychotherapy.* Translated by H. M. and E. R. Guthrie. New York: Macmillan. → Contains lectures delivered at Harvard University.

KIMBLE, GREGORY A.; and KENDALL, JOHN W. JR. 1953 A Comparison of Two Methods of Producing Experimental Extinction. *Journal of Experimental Psychology* 45:87–90. → An experiment testing Guthrie's theory.

OSGOOD, CHARLES E. (1953) 1958 *Method and Theory in Experimental Psychology.* New York: Oxford Univ. Press. → See especially pages 362–372, "Guthrie: A Contiguity Theory."

PAVLOV, I. P. 1932 The Reply of a Physiologist to Psychologists. *Psychological Review* 39:91–127.

SHEFFIELD, FRED D. 1948 Avoidance Training and the Contiguity Principle. *Journal of Comparative and Physiological Psychology* 41:165–177. → An experimental test of Guthrie's theory.

SHEFFIELD, FRED D. 1949 Hilgard's Critique of Guthrie. *Psychological Review* 56:284–291.

SHEFFIELD, FRED D. 1951 The Contiguity Principle in Learning Theory. *Psychological Review* 58:362–367.

SHEFFIELD, VIRGINIA F. 1950 Resistance to Extinction as a Function of the Distribution of Extinction Trials. *Journal of Experimental Psychology* 40:305–313.

VOEKS, VIRGINIA W. 1945 What Fixes the Correct Response? *Psychological Review* 52:49–51.

VOEKS, VIRGINIA W. 1948 Postremity, Recency and Frequency as Bases for Prediction in the Maze Situation. *Journal of Experimental Psychology* 38:495–510.

VOEKS, VIRGINIA W. 1950 Formalization and Clarification of a Theory of Learning. *Journal of Psychology* 30:341–362.

VOEKS, VIRGINIA W. 1955 Gradual Strengthening of S–R Connections or Increasing Number of S–R Connections? *Journal of Psychology* 39:289–299. → An experiment testing Guthrie's theory.

ZEAMAN, DAVID; and RADNER, LOUIS 1953 A Test of the Mechanisms of Learning Proposed by Hull and Guthrie. *Journal of Experimental Psychology* 45:239–244.

H

HABIT

See LEARNING.

HADDON, ALFRED CORT

Alfred Cort Haddon (1855–1940), "the father of Cambridge anthropology," was the son of strictly Nonconformist parents living on the outskirts of London. His father, John, was more successful as a Baptist deacon and Sunday-school teacher than in business, and the printing works that he had inherited produced dwindling profits. Haddon's mother, Caroline Waterman, eked out their scanty income by writing children's books, mostly religious, but, significantly, her best seller was *Look, Listen and Learn*, an introduction to nature study based on walks with her children. Her son dedicated his *Head-hunters* "to my Mother who first taught me to observe."

After a scrappy schooling Haddon entered the family business, "duty and drudgery," as he called it. There, however unwillingly, he learned some useful lessons: careful and exact lettering and drawing, printing technique, proofreading, and business methods. But his whole heart was devoted to the study of plants and animals, and his spare time was spent in collecting, drawing, dissecting, bottling, and noting in his diary everything he could find, from squashed hedgehogs and unwanted kittens to water fleas and animalcula.

"Duty and drudgery" came to an end in 1875, when his father decided that the young scientist was a bungling failure in the office and that he would lose less money by sending him to the university. Haddon was enrolled at Christ's College,

Cambridge. He won a scholarship and did brilliantly in his tripos. He was nominated to the zoological station at Naples and in 1880 was appointed professor of zoology at Dublin.

Haddon's marriage the following year to Fanny Rose was the climax of a college joke that the participants never regretted. He and his friend Holland Rose had arranged to exchange sisters for the May Week festivities of 1877. Rose married Laura Haddon in 1880, and at their wedding Haddon announced his engagement to Fanny Rose.

Armchair science never satisfied him, and in 1888, "tired of lecturing about things I have never seen," he planned his first visit to the Torres Strait, a turning point in his life and in the history of anthropology. His carefully kept journal shows how his interest in coral reefs was gradually eclipsed by interest in the natives. He realized that corals could wait but native culture was disintegrating so rapidly with the impact of civilization that the saving of vanishing data was an urgent need.

When he left the islands, in 1889, he was already planning the Cambridge Anthropological Expedition to the Torres Strait, a landmark in anthropological research. It took him almost ten years to collect the men and the money. He felt a thorough record of native life needed a team of specialists that included not only those equipped to study physical characters, arts and crafts, music, language, religion, and folklore but also, for the first time, a psychologist who might interpret native thought. In the end there were two psychologists, W. H. R. Rivers, a lecturer in the medical school, and his pupil C. S. Myers, who was a musician as well; from the medical school also came William McDougall and C. G. Seligman. All these names

303

later became famous in the social sciences. The team was completed by S. H. Ray, an elementary-school teacher with an uncanny knowledge of Melanesian languages, and Anthony Wilkin, a capable photographer interested in material culture. Their work is enshrined both in the six volumes of the *Reports* (1901–1935) and, more popularly, in *Head-hunters* (1901).

The expedition was a tremendous success, mainly because of Haddon's foresighted organization and the affectionate welcome he received from the islanders. Its members hoped that on its return it would be crowned by some recognition from the university. But Haddon's only reward was a lectureship in ethnology at £50 a year. He had never been interested in money and was used to a frugal life, but with a wife and three children to support he had to augment his meager income by lecturing all over the country and writing articles and reviews at the same time he was writing and editing the *Reports*.

Americans were more appreciative than "poor blind Cambridge," as Haddon's own university was described. G. A. Dorsey of the Field Columbian Museum invited him to lecture at Chicago and elsewhere in 1900, offering twice as much as Cambridge paid him in a year. And when, later, at the invitation of W. Z. Ripley, Haddon gave the Lowell lectures at Boston, he calculated gleefully that he was getting two dollars a minute. He would return to England from these visits enriched and encouraged, only to be depressed again by the apathy and financial anxieties at home. It was not until 1904 that a readership at £200 a year was established, and Haddon assumed this post and undertook all the lecturing it entailed, pursuing his duties with unflagging energy and enthusiasm until his resignation, in 1925.

When Haddon first came to Cambridge, in 1875, the science of anthropology was nonexistent. When he died, in 1940, it had been raised, mainly by his selfless devotion, to an honored position in the university. His influence was due primarily to his personality. He was not a good lecturer, his thoughts dashing ahead of his hesitant speech. He lacked social graces, retaining to the end of his life something of the gaucherie of a schoolboy. At the same time that his Nonconformist conscience never forsook him, he was intolerant of cramping conventions, ignored creeds and sects, and respected only those aspects of religion, civilized or uncivilized, that were heartfelt and genuine. He made friends with high and low. He was a welcome associate of academic dignitaries (although barely polite to the pompous or pretentious) and was always at his best

with those in the humbler ranks—illiterate Irish peasants, fishermen, and his beloved "savages." His students were among his most devoted admirers, and they have maintained his high standards of honest work in the study of mankind.

A. H. QUIGGIN

[*For discussion of the subsequent development of Haddon's work, see* OCEANIAN SOCIETY *and the biographies of* RADCLIFFE-BROWN; RIVERS; SELIGMAN, C. G.]

WORKS BY HADDON

(1895) 1914 *Evolution in Art: As Illustrated by the Life-histories of Designs.* New ed. London: Scott.

(1898) 1908 *The Study of Man.* 2d ed. New York: Putnam.

1901 *Head-hunters: Black, White and Brown.* London: Methuen.

1901–1935 *Reports of the Cambridge Anthropological Expedition to Torres Straits.* 6 vols. Cambridge Univ. Press; New York: Macmillan. → Volume 1: *General Ethnography*, 1935. Volume 2: *Physiology and Psychology*, 2 parts, 1901–1903. Volume 3: *Linguistics*, 1907. Volume 4: *Arts and Crafts*, 1912. Volume 5: *Sociology, Magic and Religion of the Western Islanders*, 1904. Volume 6: *Sociology, Magic and Religion of the Eastern Islanders*, 1908.

(1909) 1929 *Races of Man and Their Distribution.* Rev. ed. Cambridge Univ. Press; New York: Macmillan.

(1911) 1927 *Wanderings of Peoples.* 2d ed. Cambridge Univ. Press.

1936 HUXLEY, JULIAN S.; and HADDON, ALFRED CORT *We Europeans: A Survey of "Racial" Problems.* New York and London: Harper.

1936–1938 HADDON, ALFRED CORT; and HORNELL, JAMES *Canoes of Oceania.* 3 vols. Honolulu, Hawaii: Bishop Museum. → Volume 1: *Canoes of Polynesia, Fiji, and Micronesia*, 1936. Volume 2: *Canoes of Melanesia, Queensland, and New Guinea*, 1938. Volume 3: *Definition of Terms and General Survey of Oceanic Canoe*, 1938.

WORK ABOUT HADDON

QUIGGIN, A. H. 1942 *Haddon the Head-hunter: A Short Sketch of the Life of A. C. Haddon.* Cambridge Univ. Press.

HALBWACHS, MAURICE

Maurice Halbwachs (1877–1945), a sensitive and humane scholar whose works are among the most important in the sociology of the first half of the twentieth century, was arrested by the Gestapo in Paris in July 1944 and died about eight months later in the Buchenwald concentration camp.

Halbwachs was born in Rheims. For three years one of his teachers at the Lycée Henri IV in Paris was Henri Bergson, who influenced him greatly. He completed his studies at the École Normale Supérieure with a well-written book on Leibniz (1907) and participated in the preparation of the *Catalogue des manuscrits leibniziens.* Soon, however, the social sciences attracted his interest. He worked with Simiand, Lévy-Bruhl, and especially Durkheim and helped edit *L'année sociologique.* His dissertation, *La classe ouvrière et les niveaux de vie* (1913*a*), marked the beginning of his extensive studies in social psychology.

This study is characteristic of Halbwachs' work. It reveals his sense for the concrete and his concern for getting down to reality. Only after immersing himself in concrete data did he develop general ideas, working hypotheses, theories, and laws. Moreover, Halbwachs made specific methodological and theoretical contributions in this study. By discovering what the group accepted as the proper order of importance of expenditures, he established a scale of working-class needs. He revealed the primary importance in these choices of the group's representation and of what is consistent with it. Clearly, Halbwachs was here applying Durkheim's theory of collective representations.

This scientific study of the scale of working-class needs was supported by a theory of the worker's position in modern capitalist societies, a theory that now seems questionable at certain points. According to Halbwachs, these societies assign to the working class the task of mastering matter, and since the members of this class are thereby limited to contact with things, they become isolated from the rest of mankind. In their isolation as a group from other groups in society, the solidarity among the members of the working class becomes enhanced, and it is only by virtue of their class consciousness that they remain attached to the larger society at all.

A later work, *L'évolution des besoins dans les classes ouvrières* (1933), applied the principal conclusions of the 1913 thesis to those social groups in the great industrial nations of the West that occupy positions analogous to that of the older working class.

Georges Gurvitch raised some questions about Halbwachs' criteria of social-class membership, but he gave him credit for having been clearly aware of the great complexity of social class phenomena and for having kept his concepts entirely separate from all philosophy of history and all political positions (Gurvitch 1950).

Halbwachs displayed a distinct tendency to explain needs by relative and subjective factors. He admitted that trends of opinion are important factors in defining needs, but he did not consider the extent to which objective elements also enter into the subjective experience of need. For example, a *real* lack of food or clothing is felt by the workers when they compare their standard of living with that of the middle class, or the bourgeoisie.

Halbwachs' influence as a pioneer in research on the definition of needs, as well as on budgets and consumption patterns, has been stressed by P. Chombart de Lauwe in his book *La vie quotidienne des familles ouvrières* (1956). Chombart de Lauwe also points out that Halbwachs was the first to make a genuinely sociological study of the development of workers' budgets.

Halbwachs' study *Les causes du suicide* (1930) extends and refines Durkheim's classic work on the same subject. For Durkheim, religious factors are most important in determining the extent of an individual's integration into a society (and he related a lack of integration to a high rate of suicide). Halbwachs felt that the nature and importance of the religious factor vary with the social and psychological context and that this context, in turn, varies in different countries.

He was interested in the influence of collective memory and tradition on beliefs, and his essay *La topographie légendaire des évangiles en terre sainte* (1941) was a specific study of this influence. Thus, in various periods of history, the appearance attributed to the holy places has changed according to the needs and hopes of the Christian groups describing these places.

In his recent book on social psychology, Jean Stoetzel (1963) shows how Halbwachs influenced the study of memory by distinguishing between individual memory, i.e., the present knowledge of the past, and collective memory and by seeking the patterns governing this collective, or group, memory. Halbwachs' contributions in this area are only now beginning to be appreciated outside France.

During the last years of his life, Halbwachs became increasingly preoccupied with social morphology and demography. He contributed an important article on demographical statistics to the *Encyclopédie française.* He also developed the concept of social morphology that appears in a rudimentary and rather abstract form in Durkheim's work. Halbwachs was frequently able to discern the social and economic structure behind morphological data, especially the influence of social classes. In his *Psychology of Social Class* (1938), he examined motivation among the peasant classes, the bourgeoisie, industrial workers, and the lower middle classes.

It is possible here only to suggest the importance of the results of Halbwachs' studies and the originality of his methods. He invariably looked at reality from many different perspectives. There is no rigidity or dogmatism in any of his work. He culled important elements from several intellectual traditions: he was inspired by Durkheim's vigorous mind and was concerned to use such new scientific approaches as those of American sociology, but he also incorporated Marxist sociology in certain broad orientations of his work.

GEORGES FRIEDMANN

[*For the historical context of Halbwachs' work, see the biographies of* DURKHEIM; LE PLAY; LÉVY-BRUHL; SIMIAND. *For discussion of the subsequent development of Halbwachs' ideas, see* SUICIDE, *article on* SOCIAL ASPECTS.]

WORKS BY HALBWACHS

1907 *Leibniz.* Paris: Delaplane.

1913a *La classe ouvrière et les niveaux de vie: Recherches sur la hiérarchie des besoins dans les sociétés industrielles contemporaines.* Paris: Alcan.

1913b *La théorie de l'homme moyen: Essai sur Quetelet et la statistique morale.* Paris: Alcan.

1930 *Les causes du suicide.* Paris: Alcan.

1933 *L'évolution des besoins dans les classes ouvrières.* Paris: Alcan.

(1938) 1959 *The Psychology of Social Class.* With an Introduction by Georges Friedmann. Glencoe, Ill.: Free Press; London: Heinemann. → First published as *Analyse des mobiles dominants qui orientent l'activité des individus dans la vie sociale.*

1941 *La topographie légendaire des Évangiles en Terre Sainte: Étude de mémoire collective.* Paris: Presses Universitaires de France.

(1949) 1950 *La mémoire collective.* Edited by Jeanne Alexandre. Paris: Presses Universitaires de France. → Published posthumously.

SUPPLEMENTARY BIBLIOGRAPHY

ALEXANDRE, JEANNE 1949 Maurice Halbwachs. *Année sociologique* 3d Series [1940–1948] 1:3–10.

CANGUILHEM, GEORGES 1947 Maurice Halbwachs (1877–1945). Volume 103, pages 229–241 in Strasbourg, Université, Faculté des Lettres, *Mémorial des années: 1939–1945.* Paris: Belles Lettres.

CHOMBART DE LAUWE, PAUL H. 1956 *La vie quotidienne des familles ouvrières: Recherches sur les comportements sociaux de consommation.* Paris: Centre National de la Recherche Scientifique.

GURVITCH, GEORGES (1950) 1957–1963 *La vocation actuelle de la sociologie.* 2d ed., 2 vols. Paris: Presses Universitaires de France. → Volume 1: *Vers la sociologie différentielle.* Volume 2: *Antécédents et perspectives.*

STOETZEL, JEAN 1963 *La psychologie sociale.* Paris: Flammarion.

HALE, HORATIO

Horatio Emmons Hale (1817–1896), American ethnologist, was born at Newport, New Hampshire. His mother was Sarah Josepha Hale, for many years editor of *Godey's Lady's Book.* While Hale was still a student at Harvard, which he entered in 1833, he made a study of the language of an Algonquian-speaking band encamped on the college grounds; he himself set into type and published the results of the study. This early attempt at linguistic research within an ethnological context set the tone for all his later work in the emerging anthropology of the nineteenth century: throughout a long life of periodic, although always enthusiastic, involvement in anthropological research, he continued to stress language as the "true basis of ethnology."

Upon his graduation from Harvard, Hale accepted a position as philologist with a United States expedition to survey and chart areas of the Pacific, under the command of Captain Charles Wilkes. Hale's senior colleague in the scientific corps of this first research expedition sponsored by the United States government was Charles Pickering, who with du Ponceau and Gallatin was a leader among those early nineteenth-century ethnologists who stressed the collection of comparative linguistic data from the human societies recently discovered and constantly threatened by western expansion. When the expedition stopped at the Oregon Territory, toward the end of its four-year voyage in the Pacific, Hale left it to devote more time to the study of the languages of the Indians of the Northwest Territory, after which he returned overland to the East. Hale's contribution to the *Reports of the Expedition* was published in 1846 as Volume 6, *Ethnography and Philology.* Its primary emphasis was upon his collection from the southern Pacific, and although it contained a mass of miscellaneous and often superficial ethnographic observations, Hale's linguistic data, especially those from the Polynesian islands, were carefully recorded and are still useful. It was upon this linguistic evidence that Hale built his theory of Polynesian migrations, which, except for refinements derived from more recent data, is still essentially sound.

After the Wilkes expedition and Gallatin's death in 1849, the linguistic emphasis of American ethnology gave way to the rapid rise of archeological interests. About this time, also, Hale married and moved to Clinton, Ontario, where for the next twenty years he devoted himself to business activities. Yet, he was to resume his ethnological investigations, stimulated by the proximity of the Six Nations Reserve, on the Grand River at Brantford and probably also by a developing friendship with Lewis H. Morgan. Toward the end of the 1860s he began the collection of traditional literature from older informants on the reserve. These form the basis of his most important substantive contributions to the anthropological literature and particularly to that of Iroquoian studies.

His interest in language as the foremost indicator of ethnological status led him to concentrate upon that aspect of Iroquois culture. And it was his continuing concern for language that led Hale in all his work to stress the distinction between race, defined biologically, and language and to stress the superiority of language for establishing the historical (i.e., ethnological) relations of existing groups. More particularly, he defined Tutelo as a Siouan language within the Iroquoian geographical range; he rescued Wyandot Huron from disappearance and demonstrated that it had been the most ancient Iroquoian language; using a technique which anticipated more recent glottochronological methods, he attempted an arrangement of existing Iroquoian languages into a historical sequence; and perhaps most important of all for later ethnological methods, he used the traditional tales of the Iroquois as a source for ethnological data.

In his most significant work, *The Iroquois Book of Rites* (1883a), he summarized much of his work on the Iroquois. Here, using his several approaches, he reconstructed the late prehistory of the Six Nations, with a particular emphasis, drawn from the traditions he had recovered, upon the story of the legendary hero Hiawatha (which he rescued from the romanticism and errors of H. R. Schoolcraft) and the formation of the League of the Iroquois. Hale's published contributions to the ethnological literature are relatively few, but all of them are graced with his intelligence and originality, with his theoretical bent and his humanism.

Hale's greatest contribution to American anthropology, however, lies in his influence upon Franz Boas, much of whose early field work on the Northwest Coast was done under Hale's supervision and direction. Although Boas had spent a productive season among the Northwest Coast Indians in 1886, his subsequent field work in this area during the early 1890s was subsidized by a special committee of the British Association for the Advancement of Science, of which Hale was the driving force. It was Hale who recruited Boas for this work; and although differences of approach to field problems developed, Hale was Boas' constant and enthusiastic supporter. Correspondence between the two men indicates that Hale not only provided Boas with the material support required but was also the source of much in Boas' emerging point of view toward the anthropological enterprise, a point of view which was to form the foundation of American anthropology for half a century. Hale transmitted to Boas the intensity of his feeling for the diversity of culture and language and his distaste for the construction of universal historical systems;

he provided Boas with the technique for the recapture of lost elements of culture through the collection and analysis of myths and legends; he persuaded Boas of the insufficiency of biological criteria for the establishment of a classification of the varieties of man and for the evaluation of his varying capacities; and by his insistence that Boas collect all the data relating to the differences between human groups, Hale laid the foundation in a field approach for the concept of a "general anthropology," which came to be the hallmark of the work of Boas and his followers.

Horatio Hale died in 1896. He was mourned by Boas as "a man who contributed more to our knowledge of the human races than perhaps any other single student." Sufficient praise indeed.

JACOB W. GRUBER

[*For discussion of the subsequent development of Hale's ideas, see* INDIANS, NORTH AMERICAN *and the biography of* BOAS.]

WORKS BY HALE

1846   *Ethnography and Philology: United States Exploring Expedition.* Philadelphia: Lee & Blanchard.
(1883a) 1963   *The Iroquois Book of Rites.* With an introduction by William M. Fenton. Univ. of Toronto Press.
1883b   The Tutelo Tribe and Language. American Philosophical Society, *Proceedings* 21:1–47.
1890   *An International Idiom: A Manual of the Oregon Trade Language, or "Chinook Jargon."* London: Whitaker.
1891   *Language as a Test of the Mental Capacity: Being an Attempt to Demonstrate the True Basis of Anthropology.* Ottawa.
1894   The Fall of Hochelaga: A Study of Popular Tradition. Pages 252–266 in International Congress of Anthropology, Chicago, 1893, *Memoirs.* Chicago: Shulte.

SUPPLEMENTARY BIBLIOGRAPHY

Bibliography of the Royal Society of Canada: Hale, Horatio. 1894   Royal Society of Canada, Ottawa, *Proceedings and Transactions* 12:44–46.
BRINTON, DANIEL G. 1897   Horatio Hale. *American Anthropologist* 10:25–27.
GRUBER, JACOB W. 1967   Horatio Hale and the Development of American Anthropology. American Philosophical Society, *Proceedings* 111:5–37.

HALÉVY, ÉLIE

Élie Halévy (1870–1937), French historian, produced a monumental history of England and also wrote about socialism and other modern political ideas. He was born into a family known for its contributions to the arts. Its founder, a Bavarian cantor, came to Paris at the end of the eighteenth century. He believed in the possibility of combining the moral principles of Judaism with the political program of the French Revolution, which had emancipated his people from their ancient disabilities. This faith found its way into the title of the review *L'Israélite français*, which he founded during the Bourbon restoration. His two sons were soon assimilated into Parisian intellectual and musical circles. Jacques Fromental became a prominent composer, professor at the Conservatory, the first Jewish member and, ultimately, the secretary of the Academy of Fine Arts. His wife was a member of the Rodrigues family. Like so many other Saint-Simonians, members of this family came to be bankers and entrepreneurs during the Second Empire. Fromental's daughter Geneviève married Bizet. She was a friend of Proust and was among his models for the Duchesse de Guermantes.

Léon Halévy, Fromental's brother, succeeded Comte as Saint-Simon's secretary. Léon himself wrote extensively, but he was most notable for having two sons who were elected to the Académie Française. Lucien Anatole Prévost-Paradol, an illegitimate son, was a brilliant essayist and a critic of the Second Empire. His ideas greatly influenced the authors of the Third Republic's constitution. Léon's other son, Ludovic Halévy, was a prolific and successful author as well as a librettist for Offenbach and Bizet. Although brought up as a Catholic, his mother's faith, Ludovic married Louise Breguet, whose Protestant family of artisan inventors had gone from watchmaking to the position of France's leading constructors of precision instruments. Breguets were among the pioneers of telegraphy and aviation.

Ludovic's sons, Élie and Daniel, were raised as Protestants. Their home was the center of a brilliant set, which included their uncle, Marcellin Berthelot, the great chemist, as well as the painter Degas. Both sons were ardent supporters of Dreyfus and helped organize the famous "Manifesto of the Intellectuals." Daniel, who collaborated with Péguy on the *Cahiers de la quinzaine*, later supported Georges Sorel, contributed to the foundation of *L'Humanité* and the *universités populaires* (what the English call workingmen's colleges). His name was prominent for more than half a century as historian, journalist, and editor.

Élie was more ascetic and brilliant, placing first in the national philosophy examination he took before entering the École Normale Supérieure. There philosophy continued to be his main concern, as it was of such life-long friends as Xavier Léon, Alain [E. Chartier], Celestin Bouglé, Léon Brunschvicg, and Dominique Parodi. Committed to a secular and rationalist individualism, passionately concerned to unite theory and practice, Élie Halévy

helped found the *Revue de métaphysique et de morale* and the Société Française de Philosophie, associations he maintained until his death. Like Max Weber and Durkheim, Halévy gained much from participation in a great journal that brought him into contact with the pivotal works and authors of his time. Even after he turned from philosophy to the history of ideas and thence to general history, his analytical method still marked everything he wrote.

In his first book, *La théorie platonicienne des sciences* (1896), Halévy carefully demonstrated Plato's apparent contradictions before establishing their ultimate congruity. This way of proceeding stemmed from Halévy's belief that if "one has the courage to go to the very end of a 'negative dialectic,' he then perceives that such criticism prepares the way for a 'progressive dialectic.' By distinguishing levels, this positive dialectic leads to the discernment of values in terms of a conception of the world and of life that is at once hierarchical and constructive, that not only *founds* and *justifies* but also fulfils the no less essential function of condemning what does not meet its standards" (Brunschvicg 1937, p. 680). Plato served as an example of a thinker who had made his way from criticism of others to positive construction of his own. His standards were rational and self-conscious; he used them to pass judgment on the institutions of his society.

As a historian of ideas, Halévy made extensive use of "negative dialectic" as a means of penetrating to the real, if often contradictory, values and motives underlying a school of thought. In addition, he sought to chart and explain the discrepant actual effects of a doctrine. In *The Growth of Philosophic Radicalism* (1901–1904), Halévy used his method to order the results of his extraordinarily thorough research on Benthamism. Its political and economic aspects could not, he thought, be logically reconciled. In his political theory, Bentham assumed that only by a legislator can conflicts of interest be reconciled in such a way as to secure the greatest good of the greatest number; in his economic theory, he assumed that individual interests are harmonized naturally by some sort of invisible hand. Thus, utilitarianism could produce either faith in bureaucratic paternalism based on legislative intervention or belief in anarchical individualism and laissez-faire. Both conclusions were in fact drawn by Bentham's disciples; both had important effects upon political theory and public policy.

From this model work in intellectual history, Halévy moved to a study of England that owed much to his teaching responsibilities at the École Libre des Sciences Politiques. The school was established after the defeat of 1871 and the Commune. Its founders sought to discover the sources of France's political instability as well as her failure to develop an elite and institutions such as those of England, the pre-eminent example of a nation that combined national power with liberty. Halévy taught two courses at the "Sciences Po" alternately for over forty years: English history and European socialism. The first was the subject, the second the polemical target, of his life's work, *A History of the English People in the Nineteenth Century* (1912–1932). In the first volume, *England in 1815*, he isolated his dominant theoretical concern: "Why [is] it that of all the countries of Europe England has been the most free from revolutions, violent crises, and sudden changes?" (*ibid.*, vol. 1, p. 424). His answer was a sustained effort to demonstrate the inadequacy of Marxism as a monistic theory of historical explanation. But like Max Weber, Halévy respected Marx enough to accept his formulation of the problem: England, the first country to be dominated by the capitalist mode of production, should have been the first to experience a revolution produced by the internal contradictions of that economic system. It did not. What could explain this? Again like Weber, Halévy did not wish simply to replace Marxism by an idealist hypothesis asserting that ideas and beliefs cause events. Rather, he wished to show that this was an instance, and a crucial one, in which religion had exercised a force independent of the means of production. Weber emphasized the effects of religious movements upon economic activity; Halévy, their political consequences.

The decisive difference between British and French development stemmed from indirect and unanticipated consequences of the Methodist revival. In France religion had been identified with an established church, controlled by the same class that dominated the state. Consequently, radicals were forced to attack both institutions simultaneously. But in England, Wesleyanism, rejected by the Church of England, became associated with the Nonconformist tradition of the free churches and contributed to their reinvigoration. Thus, Nonconformity could act as a social control, disposing radicals to think in terms of piecemeal reforms. Because in every class Methodism had made converts who shared its philanthropic values, channels were created for communicating the grievances of the lower classes. Reforms from above moderated injustices unacknowledged by the Continental bourgeoisie.

Working-class leadership was likewise affected. The sects supplied many causes with men from the working class, who had learned organizational techniques and means of influencing opinion from their chapels and classes. Yet the teaching of these same sects imposed internal restraints upon any tendency to resort to violence. Thus, those members of the working class who led their fellows differed from the middle-class and atheist revolutionary elite on the Continent. Orderly change focused on specific measures, and abuses were attacked as violations of Christian morality. These elements of political style were discovered rather than invented by the Independent Labour party.

In seeking in the sociology of religion the explanation for British stability, Halévy did not perform a speculative leap. Before discounting the significance of explanations based on political institutions on the one hand and economic forces on the other, he subjected the evidence for both to the rigorous "negative dialectic" essential to his method. It was only after this that he passed to his own positive theory based on inquiry into "beliefs, emotions, and opinions, as well as [into] the institutions and sects in which these take a form suitable for scientific inquiry" (*ibid.*, vol. 1, p. 383).

This hypothesis remained at the center of the following volumes in Halévy's *History*, although as he approached his own time, he became more narrative and covered subjects essential to general history. *Imperialism and the Rise of Labour* and *The Rule of Democracy*, which took his account up to 1914, are more remarkable for their thoroughness and objectivity than for the analytical and sociological qualities that characterized *England in 1815*.

As his work progressed, Halévy became one of the intellectual symbols of the *entente cordiale*. Sequestered and indefatigable in France, he was more sociable during his frequent visits to England, where he spent several months every year. Accompanied by his wife, who aided him in his research, he mingled freely with politicians of all parties, as well as with his university friends. The Webbs, Bertrand Russell, H. A. L. Fisher, Sir Ernest Barker, G. P. Gooch, and Graham Wallas were among his oldest and best friends. During World War I he voluntarily served in the medical service. When fighting ended, he was offered an important position in the League of Nations Secretariat. This he refused, as he did the offer of a chair at the Sorbonne, so that he could devote himself to the writing of his life work. Although he never accepted any of the French decorations offered him, he was touched by the honorary D.PHIL. awarded him by Oxford. Halévy played an important part in the commission charged with the publication of official French documents on the origins of World War I.

Two other volumes of Halévy's work were not published until after his death. The *Histoire du socialisme européen* (1948) consists largely of students' notes from his lectures. Halévy had planned to write such a book but died before he could do so. More valuable is the collection called *L'ère des tyrannies* (1938). The title address, given in 1936, summed up his views not only of socialism but also of the regimes of Stalin, Hitler, and Mussolini. Halévy was among the first to assert that communism and fascism, as actually practiced, shared crucial characteristics:

In both cases the country is governed by an armed sect, which claims to rule in the interests of the community, and which is able to impose its will because all of its members are inspired by a common faith. (*Ibid.*, p. 226)

On the one side and the other, the same mixture of a proletarian ideology with militarism. Labor camps. Labor front. Battles for this or that. As for the regime itself, it can be defined only as a permanent state of siege under the control of para-military formations united by a common faith. (*Ibid.*, p. 245)

Because such regimes constitute a durable form of rule rather than a temporary expedient, Halévy called them "tyrannies" in preference to "dictatorships." Despite his use of classical terms, he considered such governments to be unprecedented. Their rulers exercised political and intellectual controls never before available. As for their origin, he attributed such tyrannies less to ideas than to certain means adopted by the belligerents during World War I: central economic planning, nationalization, use of union leaders to eliminate strikes, "organization of enthusiasm" by propaganda, and suppression of all opinions judged by the regime as adverse to the national interest.

In *The World Crisis of 1914–1918* (1930), Halévy examined the concepts of "revolution" and "war" to show their interrelation and cumulative effects during that period. Previously, historians had treated these two subjects in isolation from each other. Halévy found the causes of the war and the Russian Revolution not in decisions consciously taken by statesmen but in collective and anonymous forces, such as the beliefs in national self-determination and the reality of class struggle. As in his *History*, he turned to collective sentiments for explanation. He concluded that the waste of lives and resources in twentieth-century wars and revolutions was due to what men thought and believed. Only by transforming their ideas and emotions can international peace be attained, only by substituting compromise for fanaticism can there be an end to violence. No one knew better than Halévy how unlikely it was that such advice would be accepted. He died in 1937, believing that war was inevitable and that it would perpetuate tyranny throughout Europe.

MELVIN RICHTER

[*Directly related are the entries* LIBERALISM; RADICALISM; UTILITARIANISM. *Other relevant material may be found in* ANGLO–AMERICAN SOCIETY; DICTATORSHIP; HISTORY, *article on* SOCIAL HISTORY; *and in the biographies of* BENTHAM; DURKHEIM; MARX; WEBER, MAX.]

WORKS BY HALÉVY

1896 *La théorie platonicienne des sciences.* Paris: Alcan.

(1901–1904) 1952 *The Growth of Philosophic Radicalism.* New ed. London: Faber & Faber. → First published in French.

(1912–1932) 1961 *A History of the English People in the Nineteenth Century.* 6 vols. 2d rev. ed. London: Benn. → Volume 1: *England in 1815.* Volume 2: *The Liberal Awakening, 1815–1830.* Volume 3: *The Triumph of Return, 1830–1841.* Volume 4: *Victorian Years, 1841–1895.* Volume 5: *Imperialism and the Rise of Labour, 1895–1905.* Volume 6: *The Rule of Democracy, 1905–1914.* First published in French.

1930 *The World Crisis of 1914–1918: An Interpretation.* Oxford: Clarendon.

1938 *L'ère des tyrannies.* Paris: Gallimard. → The translations of the extracts in the text were provided by Melvin Richter. A paperback edition was published in 1965 by Doubleday as *The Era of Tyrannies: Essays on Socialism and War.*

1948 *Histoire du socialisme européen.* Paris: Gallimard.

SUPPLEMENTARY BIBLIOGRAPHY

BREBNER, J. BARTLET 1948 Halévy: Diagnostician of Modern Britain. *Thought* 23:101–113.

BRUNSCHVICG, LÉON 1937 Élie Halévy. *Revue de métaphysique et de morale* 44:679–691. → The translation of the extract in the text was provided by Melvin Richter.

[CHARTIER, ÉMILE] 1958 *Correspondance avec Élie et Florence Halévy,* by Alain [pseud.]. Paris: Gallimard.

GILLISPIE, CHARLES C. 1950 The Work of Élie Halévy: A Critical Appreciation. *Journal of Modern History* 22:232–249. → The best criticism and appraisal of Halévy.

HALL, G. STANLEY

G. Stanley Hall (1844–1924), American psychologist and educator, was born in the rural hamlet of Ashfield, Massachusetts. In 1863 he enrolled at Williams College, where he studied with Mark Hopkins. After graduation, although he was without a strong sense of vocation, he enrolled at the Union Theological Seminary in New York City. He spent a year there, more intent on absorbing the various facets of city life than on theological study. He then sought and received from Henry Ward Beecher a loan of $500 for foreign study. He went to Bonn, where he concentrated on philosophy and theology, but afterward, at Berlin, his interests broadened to include physiology, physics, and work in a clinic for mental diseases. He also enjoyed the lighter side of Berlin, its beer gardens and theaters. In 1871, heavily in debt and without a degree, he returned home. Failing to receive an appointment at a midwestern university, he accepted a position as tutor to the children of a New York City banker and remained for more than a year in this post.

A charming, enthusiastic person, Hall had a lively interest in many of the intellectual issues and writers of the day, from associationism to evolutionism, and from John Stuart Mill to Thomas Carlyle. His religious leanings, which had never been strong, disappeared and were replaced by a mild skepticism. University teaching became his professional goal.

He was offered a post at Antioch College, the midwestern outpost of Unitarianism, where for three years he taught English literature, French and German language and literature, and philosophy, as well as serving as librarian, choirmaster, and even occasionally as preacher. He read Wilhelm Wundt's *Principles of Physiological Psychology* when it first appeared and immediately decided to return to Germany to study psychology. But he got only as far as Cambridge, Massachusetts, when an offer of an instructorship in English at Harvard diverted him from his plan. Although the grading of sophomore English themes consumed much of his time, he also carried on research in the Medical School laboratory of Henry P. Bowditch. This physiological research and some study with William James were accepted by the department of philosophy as fulfilling the requirements of a PH.D. degree in psychology. Hall was the first in the United States to receive this degree.

Immediately thereafter he left for Europe. He did work in physiology at Berlin and then went to Leipzig where he was the first of Wundt's many American students. Yet the enthusiasm engendered by his reading of Wundt's work did not survive direct contact: although he attended Wundt's lectures and served as a subject in his psychological experiments, he apparently did not carry on any research of his own.

On returning to Boston he was without a job or even any prospects of one. A providential offer from President Eliot of Harvard to sponsor him in

a series of extension lectures on education saved the day financially and, what is more important, brought him to the attention of Daniel C. Gilman, president of the then recently founded Johns Hopkins University, an institution already celebrated for its pioneer graduate program, organized after the plan of the German universities. In 1882 Hall arrived in Baltimore, and in 1884 he was made professor of psychology and pedagogics.

To further scientific psychology, in 1883 Hall set up a laboratory in a private house adjacent to the campus. The following year he opened the first university psychology laboratory to win formal acceptance in the United States. While at Johns Hopkins he and his students published papers on optical illusions, skin sensitivity, the perception of space, and the time sense. John Dewey completed a dissertation on the psychology of Kant, William Burnham published on memory, and James McKeen Cattell (1890) wrote papers on reaction time and speed of association, as well as his famous "Mental Tests and Measurements," which introduced the term mental test.

Hall had for some time dreamed of the possibility of establishing a journal devoted to psychology. One day a stranger walked into his office and offered him $500 to help found a journal. Although the gift was apparently based on a misunderstanding—the benefactor discontinued his subscription after the second year when he discovered that the journal did not intend to foster psychic research (spiritualism)—it did result in the appearance, in 1887, of the *American Journal of Psychology*, the first psychological journal in this country.

Meanwhile, Hall was preparing to leave for Clark University in Worcester, Massachusetts, to become its first president. The school was being financed by Jonas G. Clark, a wealthy, retired merchant who wished to endow an educational institution in his home town. After what eventually turned out to be too sketchy an understanding with Clark, Hall departed for a tour of European educational centers to inspect possible models for the new university and to find likely prospects for professional appointments (Rush 1948). He had visions of a graduate school modeled on the German universities and perhaps even superior to Johns Hopkins. Research was to be paramount, teaching secondary.

In 1889 Clark University opened its doors with only a few departments staffed and with no pretense at covering all academic fields. Mr. Clark, a reticent man, had different ideas from those of the eager Hall and proved to be secretive about his financial plans for the university. The amount of money he advanced was small, very much smaller than Hall had been led to expect. Hall did not disclose this discrepancy to the faculty, who blamed him for the less than expected equipment, salaries, and assistantships. "Calls" from the University of Chicago, then being founded—and supported by the Rockefeller millions—decimated the Clark faculty. Over the next few years, those who remained made the necessary adjustments, some more money was raised, and toward the end of the century, the bulk of the Clark estate did come to the university. It was divided among the library, the graduate school, and a new undergraduate college. Although Clark's will stipulated that he was to have no connection with the college, Hall continued as president.

Hall, fortunately, had appointed himself professor of psychology and all through these hectic years taught in the graduate school; it was his most brilliant and productive period. From Johns Hopkins he had brought along Edmund C. Sanford to head the laboratory and W. H. Burnham to teach pedagogy, which was interpreted to mean educational psychology and mental hygiene. Adolf Meyer, then with the Worcester State Hospital and destined to become the leading psychiatrist of his day, gave lectures in abnormal psychology.

Hall was an inspiring teacher to a majority of the first generation of American-trained psychologists. By 1893, 11 of 14 and by 1898, 30 of 54 of the PH.D.s granted in psychology were awarded to his students (Harper 1949). Among them were Lewis M. Terman, who developed the Stanford–Binet Scales of Intelligence, Henry H. Goddard, who was a pioneer student of the mentally retarded, and Arnold Gesell, who did so much painstaking research on the mental and physical development of children.

Their work indicated that Hall's own interest had shifted from experimental to developmental psychology, although he continued eloquently to defend laboratory work of all sorts. While at Hopkins he had published a paper entitled "Content of Children's Minds" (1883). With the aid of a questionnaire technique, which he was the first to apply in the United States, he unearthed a variety of information about the thinking of children. He questioned them about such matters as the sense of self, religious experience, fears, and favorite foods. This approach generated great public enthusiasm and before long led to the so-called child study movement. Large numbers of parents and teachers, outside of Hall's personal sway, uncritically and dogmatically used his technique to secure information about children. Hall lost interest in the technique and not long afterward a reaction, both within psychology and from the public itself, set in and the movement disappeared. It did have the salutary effect of bringing to the public some awareness of the importance of child study and, by its very excesses, created a more critical attitude toward research in child psychology (Bradbury 1937).

Hall had a more sustained interest in adolescence. His monumental and influential work, *Adolescence* (1904), contained the most complete statement of his particular theory of recapitulation in development. The individual child was seen as repeating the life history of the race: when a child played at cowboys and Indians, for example, he was seen as behaving at the level of primitive man. In his old age Hall returned to the problem of development and published a volume entitled *Senescence* (1922).

Along with his research, writing, teaching, and administrative duties, Hall was concerned with psychology on the national scene. In July 1892 he called the meeting which resulted in the founding of the American Psychological Association (Dennis & Boring 1952). Almost as a matter of course he was elected its first president. The scientific purpose of this organization was firmly established under his guidance. He founded and edited still other journals: in 1891 the *Pedagogical Seminary* (now the *Journal of Genetic Psychology*), in 1904 the *Journal of Religious Psychology*, and in 1917 the *Journal of Applied Psychology*.

Hall was one of the first Americans to arrange for a hearing of Freud's views and to teach his theories. Indeed, Freud's only visit to the United States was at Hall's invitation to the twentieth anniversary celebration of Clark University in 1909. In view of the suspicion and dislike that the psychoanalytic movement raised at this time, the invitation showed courage on Hall's part.

Hall's administrative–organizational efforts continue to live on: the American Psychological Association that he founded had 24,000 members by 1966; Johns Hopkins and Clark University departments of psychology each went through a series of unsettling experiences but at present are among the strong graduate departments; the journals he founded, in all but one instance, continue to flourish. He was very modern in his stress on development despite the fact that his way of using Haeckel's discredited biogenetic principle has disappeared without a trace. He has had little direct effect upon current intellectual traditions, but his enthusiasms, his broad convictions, and his emphasis on developmental issues were transmitted to his students, many of whose formulations are very much part of the current scene.

ROBERT I. WATSON

[*Other relevant material may be found in* ADOLESCENCE; AGING, *article on* PSYCHOLOGICAL ASPECTS; DEVELOPMENTAL PSYCHOLOGY; INTELLECTUAL DEVELOPMENT; *and in the biographies of* BALDWIN; CATTELL; GESELL; SEASHORE; TERMAN; WUNDT.]

WORKS BY HALL

1883   Content of Children's Minds. *Princeton Review* 11: 249–272.

1904   *Adolescence: Its Psychology and Its Relations to Physiology, Anthropology, Sociology, Sex, Crime, Religion and Education.* New York: Appleton.

1922   *Senescence: The Last Half of Life.* New York: Appleton.

1923   *Life and Confessions of a Psychologist.* New York: Appleton.

Letters of G. Stanley Hall to Jonas Gilman Clark. Edited by N. Orwin Rush. Worcester, Mass.: Clark Univ. Library, 1948.

SUPPLEMENTARY BIBLIOGRAPHY

BRADBURY, DOROTHY E. 1937 The Contribution of the Child Study Movement to Child Psychology. *Psychological Bulletin* 34:21–38.

CATTELL, JAMES MCKEEN 1890 Mental Tests and Measurements. *Mind* 15:373–381.

CATTELL, JAMES MCKEEN 1943 The Founding of the Association and of the Hopkins & Clark Laboratories. *Psychological Review* 50:61–64.

DENNIS, WAYNE; and BORING, EDWIN G. 1952 The Founding of APA. *American Psychologist* 7:95–97.

HARPER, ROBERT S. 1949 Tables of American Doctorates in Psychology. *American Journal of Psychology* 62: 579–587.

WATSON, ROBERT I. 1963 *The Great Psychologists: From Aristotle to Freud.* Philadelphia: Lippincott.

HAMILTON, ALEXANDER

Alexander Hamilton (1757?–1804) was born on the West Indian island of Nevis and therefore lacked the attachment to state or region which characterized many eighteenth-century Americans. His experiences during the American Revolution and the decade of government under the Articles of Confederation reinforced his belief that American greatness must be based on a strong and energetic central government.

In 1777, five years after his arrival in the United States, he was appointed aide-de-camp to General George Washington. Viewing the Revolution from the vantage point of Washington's headquarters, he was deeply concerned about the state rivalries, the weakness of the Continental Congress, and the absence of national sentiment that impeded the American war effort. In the years that followed independence, Hamilton worked steadily to breathe life into the moribund Confederation government. As a delegate to the Continental Congress in 1782–1783, he worked closely with such like-minded nationalists as James Madison to invest the Confederation with powers, in his phrase, "adequate to the exigencies of the Union" (*Papers*, vol. 3, p. 689). Despairing of this effort, he became one of the prime promoters of the Constitutional Convention and served as a delegate from the state of New York.

Political ideas. Hamilton's proposals for a government modeled closely on the British system were unacceptable to most members of the convention, but he labored industriously to have them "tone their Government as high as possible" (*ibid.*, vol. 4, p. 218). Although ultimately "no man's ideas were more remote from the plan" (*ibid.*, vol. 4, p. 253), Hamilton signed the constitution and was one of its most eloquent and persuasive defenders. At the New York State ratifying convention, which met in June 1788, Hamilton combined the gifts of political theorist and practical politician to lead a reluctant New York into the federal fold.

Hamilton's greatest contribution to American political thought was *The Federalist* (1788), a brilliant defense of the convention's work, which he, John Jay, and James Madison wrote to persuade the people of New York to adopt the proposed constitution. Hamilton wrote more than half of the 85 essays. Some of the issues he discussed at length are no longer important (the dangers of a standing army, for example), but his analysis of a viable federalism as a system in which laws operate directly upon individuals rather than upon states, his exposition of the powers of the presidency, and his arguments for the necessity of judicial review in a federal system remain among the most astute comments on American government.

Hamilton was not an original political thinker of the stature of Hobbes, Locke, Montesquieu, Rousseau, or Hegel. His particular genius lay in the bold and imaginative way in which he adapted and applied the ideas of others to the needs of an infant republic. He had read many of the political philosophers of the eighteenth century, among them Adam Smith, David Hume, and Sir William Blackstone, and he was familiar with the work of such European statesmen as William Pitt and Jacques Necker. But he learned the most from his experience in the American Revolution, the Continental Congress, and the New York legislature, namely, that a strong government is necessary to promote national prosperity and safeguard personal liberty. Like other Federalists, Hamilton believed that liberty must be predicated on order and that a just and enduring government must be one of laws and not of men. Far from subscribing to Thomas Jefferson's dictum that that government is best which governs least, he believed that government to be best which, possessing ample powers, uses them energetically to achieve national goals. In any discussion of the state, his favorite word was "energy." As Clinton Rossiter has remarked, to Hamilton "energy was the essence of good government, impotence the sign of bad: here was one obsessive principle of his political science that set him off sharply from the progressives of his time" (1964, p. 163).

The belief that Hamilton favored a government of the rich, the well-born, and the able, and that he despised democracy, has long been a commonplace of American history. That he wished to win over the wealthy to the support of the Union is indisputable; that the purpose of his policies was to enrich any particular class is debatable. The object of his statecraft, as he said, was ". . . a great Federal Republic, closely linked in the pursuit of a common interest, tranquil and prosperous at home, respectable abroad . . ." (*Papers*, vol. 3, p. 106). That he distrusted democracy is also certain. But by democracy he meant a government that is directly responsive to the peoples' whims or moods, as in ancient Athens or in eighteenth-century New England towns. He was, on the other hand, "affectionately attached to the republican theory" (*Works*, vol. 9, p. 533), by which he meant democracy modified by a system of checks and balances such as those imposed by the U.S. constitution.

Economic ideas. By common consent Hamilton is ranked as the most forceful and influential secretary of the treasury in U.S. history. He was appointed to that post on September 11, 1789, and within the brief span of two and a half years (1790–1792) submitted to Congress a number of reports that are among the greatest state papers in U.S. history. The first and most controversial of these papers was the "First Report on the Public Credit" ([1790], 1934, pp. 1–50), in which he called for the payment in full of the foreign and domestic debt contracted by the Confederation government; for the assumption of the debts incurred by the separate states in the prosecution of the War of Independence; and for a system of finance and taxation adequate to meet these new national obligations. Hamilton's report was based on the assumption that national honor, strength, and prosperity are inseparably connected with the estab-

lishment of sound national credit. After six months of acrimonious debate and a famous compromise in which Hamilton gave his support to a site on the Potomac River as the national capital in exchange for the support of his plan by Thomas Jefferson and James Madison, Hamilton's proposals were adopted in only slightly modified form.

In December 1790, six months after the funding and assumption measures became law, Hamilton submitted to Congress a "Report . . . on a National Bank . . ." ([1790] 1934, pp. 51–95), calling for a great quasi-public institution that would provide a uniform circulating medium for the country, increase its "active wealth," and furnish a safe depository for government funds and a source of government loans in time of national need.

The "Report on Manufactures" ([1791] 1934, pp. 175–276), Hamilton's only major report rejected by Congress, was perhaps his most important state paper and certainly the clearest statement of his economic philosophy. Rejecting the laissez-faire economics of Adam Smith as well as the agrarian philosophy of Thomas Jefferson, he called on the federal government to foster and encourage manufactures. The report was based on Hamilton's interpretation of the stage of economic development which the United States had reached and the measures necessary for further economic growth.

Administrative activity. Hamilton's work as secretary of the treasury was not confined to recommendations for the country's financial and industrial growth. His organization and management of the Treasury Department was a model of efficiency and his administrative theory was, in the words of the leading student of the history of public administration in the United States, "the first systematic exposition of public administration, a contribution which stood alone for generations" (White [1948] 1959, p. 127).

Hamilton's role in the Washington administration was not restricted to fiscal policy. He provided congressional leadership, preparing detailed reports for congressional guidance, drafting legislation, defending his conduct of the treasury, and occasionally preparing speeches for political allies. Nor did he refrain from interfering in the management of other departments. His help was welcomed by his friend Henry Knox, the phlegmatic secretary of war, but resented by his political opponent Thomas Jefferson, the secretary of state. Hamilton, in brief, was the chief policy maker as well as the storm center of the administrations of George Washington.

In the perspective of a century and a half, it may well be that Hamilton's most important contribution to American history was his interpretation of the constitution. To him it was not a mere compact among states but a grant of power to the central government. The powers conferred on the federal government were not to be construed narrowly but interpreted so broadly as to allow the exercise of powers adequate to its needs. That the constitution has been sufficiently flexible to endure for so long is due in no small part to Hamilton's role in making it the charter for a strong national state.

JACOB E. COOKE

[*See also the biographies of* JEFFERSON *and* MADISON.]

WORKS BY HAMILTON

(1788) 1961 HAMILTON, ALEXANDER; MADISON, JAMES; and JAY, JOHN *The Federalist*. Edited with introduction and notes by Jacob E. Cooke. Middletown, Conn.: Wesleyan Univ. Press.

(1790–1792) 1934 *Papers on Public Credit, Commerce and Finance*. Edited by Samuel McKee, with an introduction by Harvey Williams. New York: Columbia Univ. Press. → A paperback edition was published in 1957 by Liberal Arts Press. See especially pages 1–50, "First Report on Public Credit," pages 51–95, "Report on a National Bank," and pages 175–276, "Report on Manufactures."

The Papers of Alexander Hamilton. Edited by H. Syrett and Jacob E. Cooke. Vols. 1–11. New York: Columbia Univ. Press, 1961–1966.

The Works of Alexander Hamilton. 2d ed., 12 vols. Edited by Henry Cabot Lodge. New York and London: Putnam, 1904. → The standard edition of Hamilton's writings.

SUPPLEMENTARY BIBLIOGRAPHY

HAMILTON, JOHN C. (1857–1864) 1879 *The Life of Alexander Hamilton: A History of the Republic of the United States as Traced in His Writings and Those of His Contemporaries*. 7 vols. Boston: Houghton Mifflin. → Marred by J. C. Hamilton's reverence for his father's memory, but a storehouse of facts relating to Alexander Hamilton's life and times.

MILLER, JOHN C. 1959 *Alexander Hamilton: Portrait in Paradox*. New York: Harper. → The best one-volume work on Hamilton's life. A paperback edition was published in 1964 as *Alexander Hamilton and the Growth of a New Nation*.

MITCHELL, BROADUS 1957–1962 *Alexander Hamilton*. 2 vols. New York: Macmillan. → Volume 1: *Youth to Maturity: 1755–1788*. Volume 2: *The National Adventure: 1788–1804*. The definitive biography.

ROSSITER, CLINTON L. 1964 *Alexander Hamilton and the Constitution*. New York: Harcourt. → An excellent study of Hamilton's political philosophy.

WHITE, LEONARD DUPEE (1948) 1959 *The Federalists: A Study in Administrative History*. New York: Macmillan. → An account of Hamilton's contributions to administrative theory and practice.

HAMILTON, WALTON H.

Walton Hale Hamilton (1881–1958), economist and lawyer, was born in Madisonville, Tennessee. He was educated at the University of Texas and later taught in the economics department there. He then taught economics at the University of Michigan and the University of Chicago. In 1915 he went to Amherst College and remained at Amherst until 1923. During this period there occurred the celebrated intrafaculty dispute over the resignation of the president of Amherst, Alexander Meiklejohn, who was allegedly compelled to resign because the trustees of Amherst objected to his progressive educational views. Hamilton was the leader of a group among the faculty that protested against what they considered interference by conservative businessmen in the educational policies of the college. Subsequently, the entire group resigned, and Hamilton was immediately appointed to the Brookings School of Economics and Political Science in Washington, D.C. (now the Brookings Institution). He was entirely in sympathy with the liberal economic and political views that prevailed at the Brookings School.

In 1928 Hamilton shifted from teaching economics to teaching law. Although he had no previous legal training, he was selected by Robert Hutchins, then dean of the Yale Law School, as one of a new group of professors who would teach the law as a part of a larger social, political, and economic system. Hamilton remained at Yale for 20 years.

While at Yale, Hamilton also served the federal government. He was one of the brain trusters of Roosevelt's New Deal, and he held important posts in the National Recovery Administration. He worked with the antitrust division of the Department of Justice in connection with the economic problems involved in the administration of the antitrust laws. He served on the staff of the Temporary National Economic Committee, which was appointed by President Roosevelt to study and report on the economic structure of the United States during the depression, especially with regard to the operation of the free competitive market and the sources of its failure to achieve economic equilibrium.

In 1948, Hamilton retired as professor of law at Yale, and at age 67 he began a new career as a practicing lawyer. Joining the newly organized firm of Arnold, Fortas & Porter, he brought to the practice of law and the writing of legal briefs a fresh economic outlook, and he was very successful in actual litigation before courts and administrative bodies.

The dominant theme of Hamilton's academic thought and of his legal arguments was the essential unity of law, economics, political science, and social science. He maintained that all of the social sciences deal with precisely the same problems and that only their points of reference with regard to social phenomena differ. This orientation was most noticeable in Hamilton's contribution to the reform of legal education that was undertaken at Yale.

Hamilton and his colleagues at the Yale Law School, William O. Douglas, Wesley A. Sturges, Charles E. Clark (who succeeded Hutchins as dean), Myres S. McDougal, George H. Dession, Fleming James, Jr., Thurman W. Arnold, and others, criticized the conservative method of legal analysis, epitomized by the Harvard Law School, for its fragmentation of subject matter and its rigid classification and separation of the traditional fields of law—contracts, torts, conflicts of law, etc. Instead, they adopted an entirely new philosophical attitude toward the law, based on the premise that the only laws to have any practical impact on society are the rules of procedure. Procedure, therefore, became the center of the Yale curriculum, and this required a complete reorganization of the so-called substantive law courses.

What was involved here was not a debunking of the law to show that legal principles are simply horses which judges and attorneys ride to get wherever they choose to go; rather, the legal realists at Yale held that reverence for the immutable logic of the substantive law is essential to the maintenance of social institutions. Although the function of this logic is purely symbolic, it has considerable importance in that it is part of the process by which we form images of social institutions. Widely as this approach to the law is accepted today, it was revolutionary when Hamilton and his colleagues first advocated it.

What Hamilton mainly taught at Yale was called "public control of business," which in fact covered a sizable part of public and constitutional law. He had initially tackled law untutored, out of the realization that no one could understand the nation's economy without knowing the legal rules-upon-rules that had made Adam Smith's and Herbert Spencer's theories obsolete, and without an understanding of the ways and workings, the facts and folklore of the U.S. Supreme Court, where so many of the final decisions affecting business, industry, commerce, and agriculture seemed to be made. This concern with the noneconomic factors in economics had as a by-product an important impact on the development of American sociology: Talcott Parsons was a student at Amherst when Hamilton was teaching there; Hamilton's approach aroused his interest in the study of the institutional

bases of economics, which led ultimately to his study of sociology.

Throughout his life Hamilton combined keen observation and commentary on the American political, legal, and economic scene with active participation in the cause of social justice.

THURMAN ARNOLD

[*See also* PUBLIC LAW.]

WORKS BY HAMILTON

(1915) 1925 *Current Economic Problems: A Series of Readings in the Control of Industrial Development.* 3d ed. Univ. of Chicago Press.

1923 HAMILTON, WALTON H.; and MAY, STACY *The Control of Wages.* New York: Doran.

(1925) 1926 HAMILTON, WALTON H.; and WRIGHT, HELEN R. *The Case of Bituminous Coal.* New York: Macmillan.

1932 Institution. Volume 8, pages 84–89 in *Encyclopaedia of the Social Sciences.* New York: Macmillan. → Hamilton contributed 16 other articles to the *Encyclopaedia of the Social Sciences.*

1940 *The Pattern of Competition.* New York: Columbia Univ. Press.

1941 . . . *Patents and Free Enterprise.* U.S. Temporary National Economic Committee, Monograph No. 31. Washington: Government Printing Office.

1957 *The Politics of Industry: Five Lectures Delivered on the William W. Cook Foundation at the University of Michigan, February–March, 1955.* New York: Knopf.

HAMMOND, J. L. and BARBARA

John Lawrence le Breton Hammond (1872–1949) was the son of a Yorkshire clergyman; Lucy Barbara Bradby (1873–1961), the daughter of the headmaster of Haileybury School. Both took greats at Oxford—Barbara with distinction—and it was by standards derived from Greece and Rome that they passed judgment on later times. When they married in 1901 Hammond was already deeply involved in Liberal journalism; he published a study of the political career of Charles James Fox (1903) and for several years edited the *Speaker,* a weekly journal that later became the *Nation.* But from 1907, when he was appointed secretary to the Civil Service Commission, he gave his spare time to collaboration with Barbara. She had become deeply involved in research in public and private archives; it was his role to transmute her findings into vivid and arresting prose. In 1933 Oxford gave recognition to the parity of their contribution by conferring on each an honorary D.LITT.

Their most widely read books, *The Village Labourer* (1911), *The Town Labourer* (1917), and

The Skilled Labourer (1919), treat the period from the accession of George III to the first Reform Act and consist primarily of "a discussion of the lines on which Parliament regulated the lives and fortunes of a class that had no voice in its own destinies" ([1911] 1948, Preface). These were pathbreaking works, and, as is usual with such, it is not difficult to point to errors of fact and emphasis. It is now generally agreed that the enclosure of land was carried out less ruthlessly than they thought. Their use of the report of Sadler's Committee of 1832 on the employment of children was uncritical. Their concentration on the records of the Home Office led them to present the abnormal cases brought to the notice of this department as though they were typical. But few historians would deny that the dismal account of class struggles presented in this trilogy is substantially accurate. In 1923 came their sympathetic, though critical, biography of Lord Shaftesbury (1923), to be followed two years later by an admirable background study, *The Rise of Modern Industry* (1925). In *The Age of the Chartists; 1832–1854* (1930), they extended their inquiries to a later generation in which repeal of the Corn Laws, and the Ten Hours Act of 1847, the Public Health Act of 1848, and other measures reflected a growing sensitivity of the wealthier classes to the needs of the poor and the beginnings of what the Hammonds called "common enjoyment." In none of these works did the authors pay much attention to strictly economic or demographic trends. But, at a time when the "depersonalization of history" has gone quite far enough, it is worthwhile to turn again to books which are emphatically about people and in which moral judgments are freely and forcefully expressed.

Lawrence Hammond was special correspondent of the *Manchester Guardian* at the Paris Peace Conference in 1919 and the Conference on Ireland in 1921. He continued for the rest of his life to contribute articles, reviews, and occasional editorials to the paper and in World War II became a permanent member of its staff. His later books are all biographical. *James Stansfeld: A Victorian Champion of Sex Equality* (1932) was written jointly with Barbara; but *C. P. Scott of the Manchester Guardian* (1934) and *Gladstone and the Irish Nation* (1938)—the greatest, if least known, of his works—are from his pen alone. They show his liberalism, insight, and command of words.

After his death in 1949, Barbara continued to follow her earlier interests: she lived to the age of 88, leaving an almost completed (but as yet unpublished) book on the enclosure of commons in the nineteenth century. The Hammonds were modest about their own achievements and generous toward opponents. Their books had wide popular appeal and, apart from quickening interest in the social life of the past, did much to shape contemporary opinion and policy.

T. S. ASHTON

WORKS BY THE HAMMONDS

1903   HAMMOND, J. L. *Charles James Fox: A Political Study*. London: Methuen.
(1911) 1948   *The Village Labourer*. London: Longmans. → First published as *The Village Labourer; 1760–1832: A Study in the Government of England Before the Reform Bill*.
(1917) 1949   *The Town Labourer; 1760–1832: The New Civilisation*. London: Longmans.
(1919) 1927   *The Skilled Labourer: 1760–1832*. 2d ed. London: Longmans.
(1923) 1924   *Lord Shaftesbury*. 2d ed. New York: Harcourt.
(1925) 1947   *The Rise of Modern Industry*. 7th ed. London: Methuen.
(1930) 1962   *The Age of the Chartists; 1832–1854: A Study of Discontent*. Hamden, Conn.: Shoe String Press.
1932   *James Stansfeld: A Victorian Champion of Sex Equality*. London: Longmans.
1934   HAMMOND, J. L. *C. P. Scott of the Manchester Guardian*. London: Bell.
(1938) 1964   HAMMOND, J. L. *Gladstone and the Irish Nation*. 2d ed. Hamden, Conn.: Shoe String Press.

SUPPLEMENTARY BIBLIOGRAPHY

TAWNEY, RICHARD H. 1960   J. L. Hammond: 1872–1949. British Academy, London, *Proceedings* 46:267–294. → Contains a bibliography of the Hammonds' works on pages 293–294.

HANKINS, FRANK H.

Frank Hamilton Hankins, an American sociologist, devoted special attention to the role of biological factors in human traits and in social behavior. He was born in Wilshire, Ohio, in 1877 and received his bachelor's degree from Baker University in Baldwin, Kansas, in 1901 and his PH.D. from Columbia University in 1908. In 1964 Clark University awarded him an honorary degree. Most of his academic career was spent at Clark, from 1906 to 1907 and again from 1908 to 1922, and at Smith College, from 1922 until 1946.

Hankins was a philosophical realist, toughminded, and rigorously scientific. He was most deeply influenced in philosophy and logic by John Stuart Mill; in his general sociological thinking by Herbert Spencer, Lester F. Ward, William Graham Sumner, and Franklin H. Giddings; and in the quantitative approach to social problems by Adolphe

Quetelet, about whom he wrote his doctoral dissertation, Francis Galton, Karl Pearson, and Henry L. Moore, who in turn had studied under Benini in Italy. To be sure, although Hankins himself was a talented statistician, he was caustically skeptical of the assumptions and methods of the extreme quantitative approach of some of his sociological colleagues: he characterized their work as "merely sinking postholes here and there in the vast field of social phenomena."

He was a strict scientific determinist and conceived all phenomena, personal and social, as undergoing endless change and rearrangement in adjustment to environmental conditions. Thus, a particular personality was for Hankins the product of an individual's genetic constitution and his molding experiences. The self so formed has to express itself, and this self-expression is the sociological equivalent of the traditional metaphysical freedom of the will. By his reason and by the acquisition of scientific methods man can discover causal sequences, not only in the physical world but also in the psychosocial and cultural realms, and he can learn to adjust to these sequences and even to modify or direct them. Yet Hankins had no utopian illusions; he doubted that the social sciences could achieve control of change comparable to that of the physical sciences. Whereas the laws of physical science do not vary with time and place, the causes of cultural sequences differ from one era to another, even in the same society. Cultural phenomena emerge in what are often new causal combinations, and predictability is therefore severely limited. Hankins agreed with Spencer that efforts to control political and economic life more often than not produce unexpected results.

In the realm of social institutions, Hankins' determinism was economic: he saw successive political theories as rationalizations of new class or sectional interests and new religious doctrines as sanctions of new economic modes. He believed that cultural change is the cumulative product of slow alterations in the everyday activities of increasing proportions of the populations—changes in daily routine that carry with them modifications of folkways, mores, techniques, and political policies and that eventuate in new values and new ideologies.

Deeply influenced as he was by the work of Galton and Pearson, Hankins was perennially concerned with the effect of such selective processes as war, celibacy, persecution, urbanization, and education on the quantity and quality of the population, and with the consequences of demographic changes on social life. He regarded population pressure as an important factor in group hostilities,

and he believed uncontrolled differential fertility of the social classes to be dysgenic: modern medicine and hygiene, combined with humanitarian views, made it possible for people with hereditary deficiencies to bear children and so to imperil racial soundness and human well-being. He believed genetically above-average parents are most likely to produce children who are morally superior and capable of greater success in a competitive social order.

Hankins did of course recognize the moral imperative of a humanitarian perspective and rejected any scheme for the ruthless elimination of the unfit. He did not believe that the speedy adoption of positive eugenic measures was likely and therefore favored the active spreading of information about contraception, of facilities that would give the less favored strata of the population access to contraceptive equipment, and of realistic eugenic instruction for all. He doubted on both historical and genetic grounds the validity of the assumption that the number of potential men of genius is constant in any given population at all times. However, further advances in the science of human genetics may conceivably enable man not only to modify human nature in general but also to increase the number of potential geniuses, to discover them early in life, and to develop their powers.

These concerns naturally led Hankins to consider the role of heredity and inborn ability in relation to social leadership and to question the assumptions of egalitarian democracy. He was highly critical of egalitarian doctrine, holding that for "democratic society . . . to continue in a sound, healthy condition, it must concern itself quite as much, if not more, with the hereditary constitution of its people as with efforts at a further equalization of material conditions" (1923, p. 411). Any realistic approach, he thought, must take the form of effective birth control policies, which will, in a quantitative sense, keep the number of people down to a level where their material needs can be supplied and, in the qualitative realm, assure an increase in the number of the superior types required to deal with the increasingly difficult problems of our era. Thus, in order to survive, democracy must both accept hereditary differentiation in ability and, by education and other means, mitigate and undermine hereditary stratification in society. If the channels between the different strata are kept as wide-open as possible, the basic fact of individual differences may be harmonized with democratic ideology.

Hankins was deeply interested in the problem of race and the impact of racial dogmas on political theories. His chapter "Race as a Factor in Political Theory" (1924) remains the most authoritative exposition and appraisal of the subject. In his book, *The Racial Basis of Civilization* (1926a), he took a middle ground between the fervid exponents of racial superiority and racial purity and the followers of Franz Boas and others who contended that there is no real validity in the notion of racial differences and hence, scientifically, no race problem. Hankins believed that all nations and nationalities, although greatly mixed racially through conquest and immigration, ultimately acquire a sense of racial solidarity and pride of both race and culture. He maintained that race crossing is a source of racial soundness and strength and that the historical record shows that periods of high civilization have been preceded by an extensive mingling of racial stocks. While he doubted, in principle, that all racial stocks have the same capacity for cultural achievement, since this would mean that they all had had identical mutational and selective processes, he recognized that actual racial superiority or inferiority cannot be proved or disproved because race mixture is so extensive and cultural environments are so different.

Hankins' place in American sociology is secure. His concern with the problem of population quantity was shared by his professional colleagues, and he stood out among them by stressing the important issue of population quality. His work on the race issue was a sane and valuable contribution. Despite the fact that most of his students were undergraduates, a surprisingly large number of them became professional sociologists as a result of his influence, and some of them, like Howard Odum, Clifford Kirkpatrick, and Franklin Frazier, became well-known in the field. The esteem in which he was held by his fellow sociologists is evident from the fact that he was elected first president of the Eastern Sociological Society in 1930, president of the American Sociological Society in 1938, and president of the Population Association of America in 1945. Hankins' most important editorial contribution in the sociological field was to act, from 1936 to 1937, as the first editor-in-chief of the *American Sociological Review*, the official journal of the American Sociological Society (now Association).

HARRY ELMER BARNES

[*For the historical context of Hankins' work, see* CREATIVITY, *article on* GENIUS AND ABILITY; RACE; *and the biographies of* BENINI; GALTON; GIDDINGS; MILL; MOORE, HENRY L.; PEARSON; SPENCER; SUMNER; WARD, LESTER F.]

WORKS BY HANKINS

1908 *Adolphe Quetelet as Statistician.* New York: Longmans.

1922 Individual Differences and Their Significance for Social Theory. American Sociological Society, *Publications* 17:27–39.

1923 Individual Differences and Democratic Theory. *Political Science Quarterly* 38:388–412.

1924 Race as a Factor in Political Theory. Pages 508–548 in Charles E. Merriam and Harry E. Barnes (editors), *A History of Political Theories: Recent Times.* New York: Macmillan.

1925a Individual Freedom With Some Sociological Implications of Determinism. *Journal of Philosophy* 22: 617–634.

1925b Sociology. Pages 255–332 in Harry E. Barnes (editor), *The History and Prospects of the Social Sciences.* New York: Knopf.

1926a *The Racial Basis of Civilization: A Critique of the Nordic Doctrine.* New York: Knopf.

1926b Humanitarianism in the Light of Biology. *American Review* 4:52–60.

(1927) 1931 Society and Its Biological Equipment. Book 2, part 2, pages 307–394 in Jerome Davis and Harry E. Barnes (editors), *An Introduction to Sociology.* Boston: Heath.

1928a Organic Plasticity Versus Organic Responsiveness in the Development of the Personality. American Sociological Society, *Publications* 22:43–51.

(1928b) 1935 *An Introduction to the Study of Society.* Rev. ed. New York: Macmillan.

1931a Charles Robert Darwin. Volume 5, pages 4–5 in *Encyclopaedia of the Social Sciences.* New York: Macmillan.

1931b Divorce. Volume 5, pages 177–184 in *Encyclopaedia of the Social Sciences.* New York: Macmillan.

1931c The Prospects of the Social Sciences. Pages 27–53 in Edward M. East (editor), *Biology in Human Affairs.* New York: McGraw-Hill.

1933 Is the Differential Fertility of the Social Classes Selective? *Social Forces* 12:33–39.

1935 Quetelet's Average Man in Modern Scientific Research. Institut de Sociologie Solvay, *Revue* 15:577–586.

1936 Sociology and Social Guidance. *American Sociological Review* 1, no. 1:33–37.

1938 Freedom of Speech and Freedom of Teaching. American Association of University Professors, *Bulletin* 24, no. 6:497–508.

1939 Social Science and Social Action. *American Sociological Review* 4:1–15.

1940 Demographic and Biological Contributions to Sociological Principles. Part 4, pages 279–325 in Harry E. Barnes et al. (editors), *Contemporary Social Theory.* New York: Appleton.

1950 Underdeveloped Areas With Special Reference to Population Problems. *International Social Science Bulletin* 2:307–316.

1956 A Forty-year Perspective. *Sociology and Social Research* 40:391–398.

HANSEN, ALVIN

Alvin Hansen's place in the history of economic thought and the importance of his role as an economic adviser are undisputed. By propagating and developing the ideas formulated by Keynes, Hansen did more to effect the Keynesian revolution than any other American economist. His books are widely read in the United States and abroad; his *Guide to Keynes* (1953), for example, was translated into Spanish, Japanese, Italian, French, Hindi, and Korean. Most of his other books have also been widely translated.

Born in 1887 in South Dakota of Scandinavian parentage, Hansen achieved academic eminence despite the handicap of having received his education at small, impoverished Yankton College. For some years he worked as a schoolteacher, principal, and school superintendent. Then he went for graduate training to the University of Wisconsin, where he also began teaching. From Wisconsin he moved to Brown and then to the University of Minnesota before going to Harvard in 1937 as the Lucius N. Littauer professor of political economy. He spent almost twenty years as an economist in Cambridge. After retirement he yielded to demands to serve as a visiting professor at various institutions, including the University of Bombay, Yale, Smith, Vassar, Michigan State, Haverford, and Wesleyan.

Hansen excelled as a teacher. A Harvard seminar in fiscal policy, which he shared with John H. Williams, became one of the most famous in the country. Week after week, for almost twenty years, outstanding scholars and public servants attended this seminar. The gifts of Hansen and Williams were dissimilar but complementary. Williams was a cautious theorist and rather critical of many of Keynes's ideas, but open-minded and far from dogmatic either in criticism or advocacy and acute in analyzing issues. Hansen, too, could be critical, but his dominant attitude was one of enthusiasm for the New Economics. The interplay between Williams' skepticism and Hansen's acceptance provided just the right atmosphere for the exploration and examination of the new ideas. Hansen's zest was contagious: he not only inspired his students; there were few visitors who came away from these seminars uninfluenced. The seminars served as a platform for debates among the participants, whether regular members, other Harvard colleagues, or guests. Faculty members who were too sensitive to indulge in public debates with their peers soon learned to stay away. It is a tribute both to Williams and Hansen that their debates never led to personal differences.

Although Hansen's influence is most effectively conveyed by cataloguing his students, it is not possible here to list the hundreds of students he inspired and the numerous doctoral dissertations he supervised. His former students are members of virtually every distinguished department of economics, for example, the departments at the Massachusetts Institute of Technology, Yale, Harvard, the University of California, Stanford, the University of Chicago, Princeton, and Cambridge, England.

There was a reciprocal exchange of ideas between Hansen and his students. His influence is clearly evident in *An Economic Program for American Democracy* (1938), a prescient document signed by R. V. Gilbert and six other young Harvard and Tufts economists. Hansen, in turn, was influenced by the young economists who wrote the book. At age 50, he had a receptivity to new ideas that was quite remarkable.

It is likely that no American economist of the twentieth century has had more influence on economists in the government than Hansen. As early as 1933–1934 he served as director of research and secretary of the important Committee of Inquiry on National Policy in International Economic Relations. In the years when Cordell Hull's reciprocal trade agreements were first being established, Hansen served as an aide to the State Department; this was a time when economists were rare indeed in the department. A few years later, he was the economic adviser to the prairie provinces before the Canadian Royal Commission on Dominion–Provincial Relations. At the same time, 1937–1938, he became a member of the Advisory Council on Social Security. Again, in 1941–1943, he had the privilege of being the chairman of the United States–Canadian Joint Economic Committee. One of his most important assignments was that of special economic adviser to the Federal Reserve Board, a post which he held from 1940 to 1945.

Before 1933 Hansen had been somewhat of a deflationist and a critic of those who questioned Say's law, which assumes that what is produced will be taken off the market. Keynes was the boldest critic of Say's law: he asserted that investment may not equal the gap between what the economy is capable of producing and what people wish to consume. Hence his great emphasis on investment and the means of stimulating it. In fact, Keynes built a theory of income formation on the basis of a relatively stable consumption function and multiplier.

Hansen was always capable of changing his mind, and in a review of Keynes's *General Theory* (1936) he was generally favorable to Keynes's views. But neither Hansen nor, very likely, any other economist in the United States at that time anticipated the tremendous impact the *General Theory* was to have. (In part, its many obscurities concealed the cogency of its argument.) Hansen appreciated Keynes's intellectual adventurousness:

"We are living in a time when economics stands in danger of a sterile orthodoxy. The book under review warns us once again, in a provocative manner, of the danger of reasoning based on assumptions which no longer fit the facts of economic life . . ." (1936, p. 686). But Hansen was clearly at odds with Keynes on some issues. Keynes had urged a reduction of the rate of interest as a means of stimulating investment, since the amount of investment depends upon the relation of the rate of interest and the marginal efficiency of capital, although his stress on manipulation of the interest rate was not nearly so great in the *General Theory* as it had been in his earlier *Treatise on Money*. Hansen was not as enthusiastic as Keynes about interest rate policy, cautioning that efforts at general monetary control had already revealed the weakness of this method.

Both in the *Treatise on Money* and in the *General Theory*, Keynes had shown an awareness of the need for adequate investment and of the dependence of the amount of investment on the opportunity for investment. Hansen was the principal architect of a theory of stagnation, built on this theme of Keynes and concerned with the circumstances of insufficiency of demand. Hansen agreed with Keynes that the business cycle reflects the variations in the marginal efficiency of capital and that the impact of secular trends is more disrupting than that of the cycle. He wrote in 1938 that "not every period can be characterized as a kind of new industrial revolution. . . . Add to this the wholly new fact of a rapidly approaching cessation of population growth. Let the perennial optimist reflect on the enormous masses of capital that found investment outlets during the nineteenth century for no other reason than that the population of England quadrupled, that of Europe trebled, while that of the United States increased fifteen-fold. For these and other reasons we shall do well to ponder deeply the problem of . . . secular stagnation" (1938a, pp. 477–478).

Time and again, and especially in the 1930s, Hansen returned to the theme of the insufficiency of demand and the method of treating it. One of his great contributions was to establish and popularize the idea that compensatory fiscal policy is the most powerful means of maintaining the right level of aggregate demand. One cause of the unsatisfactory conditions of the 1930s, he believed, was the accumulation of reserves in the Old Age Insurance Fund. This meant that purchasing power was being hoarded. The recovery of the 1930s was, according to Hansen's theory, a consumption recovery generated by a $4,000 million expansion in consumer installment credit and by $14,000 million of federal expenditures for recovery and relief; and it vanished when these two stimuli were played out. Hansen was among the earliest to develop a pump-priming policy to deal with recessions.

In the 1930s Hansen's stagnation theory attracted much attention, but in the prosperous 1940s and 1950s its validity was doubted and even ridiculed. Detractors of the theory did not take into account, however, the extent to which World War II created a pent-up and temporarily sustained demand, which Hansen *had* predicted but which he did not expect to be permanent. By the late 1950s Hansen appeared to be vindicated: demand was insufficient to curb the rise of unemployment that resulted from productivity gains and the inflow of new entrants into the labor market. (This influx rises with improved conditions and requires an even larger increase in output—and consequently an increased demand—to prevent rising unemployment.) And it was the expansion of government, which Hansen had advocated and which his critics had considered absurd, that served to prevent the stagnation that Hansen had warned against. Ironically, the same critics who had denied that the slowing of population growth could depress business were predicting booms for the 1960s as the result of the acceleration of population growth.

In the 1930s Hansen anticipated some of the problems that were to confront the United States in the 1960s (see 1938b, pp. 303–318). Unlike Keynes, he was not inclined to assume that if general demand is adequate, most of our problems will be solved. He found that between 1870 and 1930 the rise in the white-collar group was six times as large as that of other classes and that the gains of the managerial and professional classes had also been large. He related this relative growth to the large amount of unemployment among unskilled workers and concluded that these workers needed more education. He was well aware that although adequacy of demand is crucial, there are some pockets of unemployment that must be treated directly, for example, the mining areas and the textile towns.

Keynes's theory was broadly conceived and left much for others to do. He was not concerned about the consequences of a rising national debt, and Hansen was able to show that the elimination of the national debt would raise more problems than it would solve. Interested in the consumption function, Keynes was aware of the relation of consumption to tax structure; but it was Hansen, in his *State and Local Finance in the National Economy* (Hansen & Perloff 1944), who revealed the perversity of modern state and local tax systems and spelled out the required tax and spending policies for periods of boom and depression. In this book Hansen revealed that a basic inadequacy of fiscal policy in the 1930s was the lack of control over state and local government contributions to total spending. In periods of boom these governments, with their slight dependence on income taxes, were unable to achieve the automatic rise of tax receipts that would help contain the boom, while in a period of depression they aggravated the economic situation and discouraged consumption when they compensated for the declining yield of direct taxes by an increasing recourse to consumption taxes.

Today there is wide acceptance of views that were generally rejected before Keynes's *General Theory* was published—witness the 1964 federal tax cut. Among the innovations in economic thinking that owe much to Hansen's influence are the following: an appreciation of the importance of keeping interest rates low enough vis-à-vis the marginal efficiency of capital to assure adequate investment; an awareness that the level of investment depends not only on interest rates and the marginal efficiency of capital but also on the relation of consumption and income, and that without adequate consumption investment outlets will soon dry up; the concept of an equilibrium in modern economies at a point far below full employment, with full employment only a "limiting point of the whole range of possible positions of equilibrium"; a policy of national debt management that does not only strive to keep interest costs at a minimum but also considers the effects on the economy of issuing securities when rates are low and money is being created to stimulate the private economy. Hansen deserves as much credit for these advances as any American economist. He helped clothe the Keynesian skeleton, and his simple, clear presentation, in the classroom and out, won many adherents to the New Economics.

Hansen did not, however, limit his work to the elaboration of Keynesian economics. He had, for example, much to say about international monetary policy, and he contributed to the creation of the International Monetary Fund. Yet even in this area he was influenced by Keynes (1944), asserting that international disequilibrium prevails even if gold or foreign exchange reserves are not being reduced, so long as the domestic restraints which are used to conserve reserves bring about unemployment. Adequacy of demand is crucial. Hence the need to keep international reserves large enough so that temporary imbalance can be treated, thus leaving enough time to deal with structural change.

As an economic analyst, also, Hansen made significant contributions. Here are but a few examples: (1) The familiar diagram with the marginal cost curve cutting up through the unit cost curve at its bottom seems to have been first presented by Hansen in the 1920s. (2) About 1930, when the Anglo-Saxon literature stressed monetary factors in cycles, Hansen (with D. H. Robertson) was one of the few to stress real fluctuations in exogenous investment opportunities, in the fashion of Marx, Tugan-Baranovskii, Spiethoff, Cassel, Schumpeter, and other Continental writers. (3) Hansen pioneered accelerator–multiplier models, and he and Keynes stressed the importance for investment of steady income growth. (4) He and some of his students were among the independent discoverers of the balanced-budget multiplier theorem. Associated with Hansen in this discovery were such economists as William A. Salant, Paul A. Samuelson, Harold Somers, and Henry C. Wallich, and the theorem was also discovered in Denmark by J. Galting and in the United Kingdom by Keynes and N. Kaldor. (5) Independently of J. K. Galbraith, Hansen emphasized the important social utility at the margin of the public sector as against the private sector.

The diversity and the importance of Hansen's contributions to the theory and application of economics place him among the great economists of recent times.

SEYMOUR E. HARRIS

[*For the historical context of Hansen's work, see the biography of* KEYNES, JOHN MAYNARD. *For discussion of the subsequent development of his ideas, see* FISCAL POLICY.]

WORKS BY HANSEN

1921   *Cycles of Prosperity and Depression in the United States, Great Britain and Germany: A Study of Monthly Data 1902–1908.* University of Wisconsin Studies in the Social Sciences and History, No. 5. Madison: Univ. of Wisconsin Press.

1927   *Business-cycle Theory: Its Development and Present Status.* Boston: Ginn.

1932   *Economic Stabilization in an Unbalanced World.* New York: Harcourt.

1936   Mr. Keynes on Underemployment Equilibrium. *Journal of Political Economy* 44:667–686.

1938a   The Consequences of Reducing Expenditures. Academy of Political Science, *Proceedings* 17:466–478.

1938b   *Full Recovery or Stagnation?* New York: Norton. → See especially pages 303–318 on "Investment Outlets and Secular Stagnation."

1941   *Fiscal Policy and Business Cycles.* New York: Norton.

1944   A Brief Note on "Fundamental Disequilibrium." *Review of Economics and Statistics* 26:182–184.

1944   HANSEN, ALVIN H.; and PERLOFF, HARVEY S. *State and Local Finance in the National Economy.* New York: Norton.

1945 *America's Role in the World Economy.* New York: Norton.

1947 *Economic Policy and Full Employment.* New York and London: McGraw-Hill.

1947 HANSEN, ALVIN H.; and SAMUELSON, PAUL A. *Economic Analysis of Guaranteed Wages.* U.S. Bureau of Labor Statistics, Bulletin No. 907. Washington: Government Printing Office.

1949 *Monetary Theory and Fiscal Policy.* New York: McGraw-Hill.

(1951) 1964 *Business Cycles and National Income.* Enl. ed. New York: Norton.

1953 *A Guide to Keynes.* New York: McGraw-Hill.

1957 *The American Economy.* New York: McGraw-Hill.

1960 *Economic Issues of the 1960s.* New York: McGraw-Hill.

1965 *The Dollar and the International Monetary System.* New York: McGraw-Hill.

SUPPLEMENTARY BIBLIOGRAPHY

An Economic Program for American Democracy, by Seven Harvard and Tufts Economists. 1938 New York: Vanguard.

HARRINGTON, JAMES

James Harrington (1611–1677), English political theorist, was the oldest son and heir of Sir Sapcotes Harrington, a member of an aristocratic family that had risen to eminence under the Tudors. Orphaned at an early age, he enjoyed throughout his life the means to live as he pleased. After a brief stay in Oxford, where he perfected his knowledge of languages, he traveled extensively on the Continent. There he befriended the exiled elector palatine and professed a militant Protestantism. By the time he returned to England in 1635 he was a firm republican. He was, however, also deeply attached to Charles I and remained with him to the end. Torn by such a conflict between personal friendship and political conviction, he took no direct part in the Civil War. After the execution of the king he devoted himself entirely to his studies. The product of his retirement was *The Commonwealth of Oceana,* a constitutional blueprint. Published in 1656 after some opposition by Cromwell, it remained Harrington's only book. All his other writings are explanations of its main points or answers to its critics. His public life was limited to publishing and debating his proposals for a constitution. After the Restoration he was put in prison, where his health, mental as well as physical, was utterly destroyed. He died without ever recovering his mental health.

It was perhaps Harrington's own social position that made him a decidedly aristocratic republican: no society, he felt, can do without the military and political talents of the nobility. The greatest influ-

ence upon his thinking was not personal experience, however, but the works of the "masters of ancient prudence"—Plato's *Laws,* Aristotle's *Politics,* Polybius' *Histories,* and the works of their only heir, Machiavelli. In stark contrast to these sources of wisdom, he saw the "modern prudence" of feudal and absolutist theories as nothing but a series of errors. Among his contemporaries only Hobbes won his grudging approval. For although he despised Hobbes's reasoning "by geometry" and his monarchical ideas, he shared with Hobbes a distaste for religious warfare. Harrington's solution to the problem of religious strife was to establish a state church that would represent "the public conscience" without limiting toleration, leaving theological disputes to the universities.

Political theory, according to Harrington, has to be historical, and he based his own ideas on a theory of historical development. As he saw it, the "Gothick balance," or feudalism, had come to an end. It had never been a stable order, but a tug of war between the nobility and the kings, who had uneasily shared both property and power. In England this order had come to an end when Tudor legislation reduced the nobility and put the balance of property into the hands of the people. This had made the old order impossible and had brought about the Civil War. The same impersonal forces, moreover, were at work in the revolutions in Europe as well, and this linking together of all the upheavals of the age was one of Harrington's most original perceptions.

Government is, in Harrington's view, a superstructure based on property. Ruling requires armies and whoever feeds the soldiers will thereby rule. Hence, if the balance of property is in the hands of the people, stability requires a republican form of government, and stability is the great end of political organization.

Harrington saw his own task as that of revealing to the people of England the necessities of their situation and of suggesting to them the appropriate political institutions. This was "political anatomy," which he considered a science analogous to that of William Harvey. The analogy implies that attention to details, to every artery of the body politic, is necessary, and such was the approach he used. His suggestion for producing the necessary order in England was a bicameral legislature, indirectly elected by all "who lived off their own," by secret ballot, with rotation in office, and a citizen army to defend the new society. Eternal stability was to be ensured by an agrarian law that would permanently limit the amount of property any one person might own. For changes in the balance of ownership of land had always been the source of strife and had caused the decline of ancient and modern republics.

While Harrington's influence upon his contemporaries was limited, he enjoyed a great reputation in eighteenth-century America. Constitution makers have continued to admire him, since he was the very epitome of the constitutional engineer. In recent years his contribution to social history has become the subject of debate. Since Eduard Bernstein, many Marxist historians have regarded Harrington as a precursor of dialectical materialism. They have found evidence in his ideas for the theory that the Civil War in seventeenth-century England was a bourgeois revolution caused by the "rise of the gentry." Against this view, it has been said that the gentry was a declining class, in no sense bourgeois, and that Harrington used his political fantasy to justify its power. All these theories tend to underestimate his passionate classicism. Harrington avowedly looked to the remote past to find guidance for a desirable future. From Polybius he learned that deliberately planned constitutions are more likely to endure than those that develop haphazardly. From him, too, he took the theory of the inevitable cycle of decline that all the "pure," unbalanced forms of government—monarchy, aristocracy, and democracy—must suffer. However, while Polybius thought of these constitutions entirely in terms of divisions of governmental power, Harrington held that they depend upon the distribution, or "balance," of landed property. If stability was his end, no less than Polybius', he did not stop with the latter's theory of a mixed constitution, in which democratic, aristocratic, and monarchical elements are poised in such a way as to prevent any changes in the political order. Instead Harrington proposed his agrarian law as the means of achieving stability: its enactment would permit a "natural" aristocracy to form a deliberative assembly and the people to be represented in a deciding body. This proposal was, indeed, his own contribution to constitutional theory. His ideas of historical change, however, were derivative, as he was perfectly happy to admit—witness his endless tributes to "ancient prudence." The necessity for a return to the classical past both in theory and in practice was not, in his view, a historical inevitability, but the sole means by which England might learn to become stable and powerful.

JUDITH N. SHKLAR

[*For the historical context of Harrington's work, see* CONSTITUTIONS AND CONSTITUTIONALISM; UTOPIANISM; *and the biographies of* ARISTOTLE; HOBBES; MACHIAVELLI; PLATO. *For discussion of the subsequent development of his ideas, see the biography of* BERNSTEIN.]

WORKS BY HARRINGTON

(1656) 1924 *The Commonwealth of Oceana.* Edited by S. B. Liljegren. Heidelberg: Winter.
(1700) 1963 *The Oceana of James Harrington, and His Other Works.* Edited by John Toland. Aalen (Germany): Scientia.
1955 *Political Writings: Representative Selections.* Edited with an introduction by Charles Blitzer. New York: Liberal Arts Press.

SUPPLEMENTARY BIBLIOGRAPHY

BERNSTEIN, EDUARD (1908) 1963 *Cromwell and Communism: Socialism and Democracy in the Great English Revolution.* New York: Kelley. → First published in German.
BLITZER, CHARLES 1960 *An Immortal Commonwealth: The Political Thought of James Harrington.* New Haven: Yale Univ. Press.
DWIGHT, THEODORE W. 1887 James Harrington and His Influence Upon American Political Institutions and Political Thought. *Political Science Quarterly* 2:1–44.
FINK, ZERA S. (1945) 1962 *The Classical Republicans: An Essay in the Recovery of a Pattern of Thought in Seventeenth Century England.* 2d ed. Evanston, Ill.: Northwestern Univ. Press.
GOOCH, GEORGE P.; and LASKI, HAROLD L. (1898) 1954 *English Democratic Ideas in the Seventeenth Century.* Cambridge Univ. Press. → First published as *The History of English Democratic Ideas in the Seventeenth Century,* by George P. Gooch.
GREENLEAF, W. H. 1964 *Order, Empiricism and Politics: Two Traditions of English Political Thought, 1500–1700.* Oxford Univ. Press.
KOEBNER, RICHARD 1927–1928 Die Geschichtslehre James Harringtons. Volume 3, pages 4–21 in *Geist und Gesellschaft: Kurt Breysig zu seinem sechzigsten Geburtstage.* Breslau: Marcus.
MACPHERSON, CRAWFORD B. 1962 *The Political Theory of Possessive Individualism: Hobbes to Locke.* Oxford: Clarendon.
POCOCK, JOHN G. A. 1957 *The Ancient Constitution and the Feudal Law: A Study of English Historical Thought in the Seventeenth Century.* Cambridge Univ. Press.
POLIN, RAYMOND 1952 Économique et politique au XVIIᵉ siècle: L'Oceana de James Harrington. *Revue française de science politique* 2:24–41.
RAAB, FELIX 1964 *The English Face of Machiavelli: A Changing Interpretation, 1500–1700.* With a foreword by Hugh Trevor-Roper. London: Routledge.
RUSSELL SMITH, HUGH F. 1914 *Harrington and His Oceana: A Study of a Seventeenth Century Utopia and Its Influence in America.* Cambridge Univ. Press.
SHKLAR, JUDITH 1959 Ideology Hunting: The Case of James Harrington. *American Political Science Review* 53:662–692.
TAWNEY, RICHARD H. 1941 Harrington's Interpretation of His Age. British Academy, *Proceedings* 27:199–223.
TREVOR-ROPER, H. R. 1953 *The Gentry: 1540–1640.* Economic History Review, Supplement 1. Cambridge Univ. Press.

HARTLEY, DAVID

David Hartley (1705–1757), called the father of British psychology, was indeed the first to use the word "psychology" in its modern sense. He attempted a comprehensive interpretation of psychological phenomena based on the observation of behavior, bearing in mind its physiological substrate. His *Observations on Man: His Frame, His Duty and His Expectations* (1749) sets out a philosophy of human life in terms of a special theory of association. It is as the first comprehensive "associationist" that Hartley is chiefly remembered in histories of philosophy and psychology. But he also deserves study for his general method and his grasp of the special complexities involved in any attempt to elucidate mental processes by reference to physiological mechanisms.

Hartley's theory of association is derived from Locke's *Essay Concerning Human Understanding* (1690) and John Gay's preface to King's *Essay on the Origin of Evil* (King 1702). Parallel to the formulation in terms of the association of ideas and equally important is his physiological theory. This avowedly hypothetical physiology is based on Newton's suggestion that the sensation of seeing comes from "vibrations, being propagated along the solid Fibres of the optic Nerves into the Brain. . . . For because dense Bodies conserve their heat a long time . . . the Vibrations of their parts are of a lasting nature, and therefore may be propagated along solid Fibres of uniform dense Matter to a great distance, for conveying into the Brain the impressions made upon all the Organs of sense" (Newton [1704] 1952, Query 12, p. 345). Hartley was thus among those who denied the view, then commonly held, that the nerve fibers are hollow and allow the transmission of influence by flow of animal spirits. He thought such vibrations might underlie the transmission of all sensory and motor messages to and from the brain and considered how the resulting cerebral activity might represent the whole variety of human experience. He supposed that all coding and decoding of both sensations and ideas take place within the "medullary substance" of the brain—that is, the white matter —and that "Vibratiuncles"—miniature vibrations that correspond to the incoming vibrations of sensation—are generated and persist there, giving rise, by combination and contiguous association, to memory and ideas. He illustrated and tried to test these suppositions against his own observations of human and animal behavior, ranging from "automatic actions" (that is, reflexes) such as respiration and digestion to such "ideas of intellect" as "theopathy."

For this ambitious and possibly premature undertaking, Hartley had good qualifications. Son of a country clergyman, a scholar of Jesus College, Cambridge, he studied classics, mathematics, and divinity, intending to take holy orders. Doctrinal scruples caused him to turn instead to medicine.

While a fellow of Jesus College, he came across Gay's suggestion of the all-pervasive power of association and elaborated on this theme in a brief pamphlet, *Conjecturae quaedam de sensu, motu, et idearum generatione* (1730). All his further work was devoted to the development of the ideas here outlined, and he determined to try physiological and philosophical theory "to give guidance to the art of ethics and customs." Nineteen years elapsed before the publication of his magnum opus. During this time he was occupied with a medical practice among rich and poor, with family life, and with the cultivation of numerous friends. Among his intimates were Stephen Hales, Sir Hans Sloane, William Cheselden, Bishop Butler, and John Byrom. He was elected fellow of the Royal Society in 1743. Always receptive to other people's ideas, he was courageous, if not always discreet, in trying out new ones, and his contemporaries did not take him quite seriously as a philosopher or scientist.

The *Observations* seems to have made little impression at the time of its publication. Joseph Priestley, however, who found the implied necessitarianism congenial, republished the work in 1775, omitting all the physiological parts, which he regarded as valueless speculation. Hartley's theory of association became the major influence on the English empiricist school of the nineteenth century, notably in the psychological works of the Mills and Alexander Bain (Warren 1921; Ribot 1870).

Although there is little in Hartley's work that directly influenced his immediate successors, it still bears examination for its freshness of outlook and catholicity of interest. Hartley wove into his formal argument a mass of material whose relevance to the science of psychology has progressively increased since his day. Parallel to the analysis of consciousness, from primitive sensations to abstract ideas, runs an account of the evolution of behavioral mechanisms, from the simplest "automatic actions" (reflexes) through the "secondarily automatic actions"—that is, basic muscular skills such as walking, whose character Hartley was the first to define and comment on—to the supposed cerebral concomitants of such "mental" skills as thinking. The reflexes, of course, derive from Descartes (1662). Of particular interest is the analysis of the mechanics of habit, which Hartley evidently gained from some lesser known passages in Malebranche's *De la recherche de la vérité* (1674–1675). In his account of the higher mental functions, Hartley revealed the considerable influence of the work of John Wilkins, bishop of Chester, on language (1668). Thus, his theory of memory relies on the "perpetual recurrency of the same impressions, and clusters of impressions" which come to form "the rudiments or elements of memory" in the same way as letters of the alphabet form the rudiments of language (1749, part 1, pp. 374–375). Similarly, his discussion of conjecture and hypothetical thinking draws on the work of Abraham de Moivre (1718) and other contemporary mathematicians who were concerning themselves with the practical aspects of probability theory.

It was from Thomas Willis (1664; 1672) that Hartley gained the knowledge of the anatomy of the brain which brought him close to a post-Darwinian view of the relation of man and animals. "The brute creatures," he wrote, "prove their near relation to us, not only by the general resemblance of the body but by that of the mind also" (1749, part 1, pp. 413–414). Hartley was led, on the basis of the very meager information available, to a primitive doctrine of the localization of cerebral function. This preoccupation passed out of psychology and neurology and, in the form in which he stated it, only reappeared in late nineteenth-century experimental and clinical studies of brain function. Nor had Hartley neglected that other pre-occupation of nineteenth-century medicine, the hysterical disorders.

Hartley's theology, sometimes trite and always constrained by contemporary Biblical interpretations, is nevertheless nodal to his philosophy as a whole. It was his primary concern to provide religion with a natural and scientific basis through a genuinely psychological analysis of religious experience. Hartley regarded the second (and much longer) part of the *Observations*, devoted to man's "Duty and Expectations," as interdependent with the first. He seems to have perceived that his attempt did not wholly succeed, but he pressed the laws of mechanism as far as they would go. "All the evidences for the mechanical nature of body and mind," he wrote, "are so many encouragements to study them faithfully and diligently, since what is mechanical *may* be both understood and remedied" (1749, part 1, p. 267). Later psychologists have increasingly adopted this principle of method, even if some, like Hartley, have remained aware of elements in human consciousness that are resistant to it.

KATHLEEN C. OLDFIELD

[*For the historical context of Hartley's work, see the biography of* LOCKE; *for discussion of the subsequent development of Hartley's ideas, see* NERVOUS SYSTEM, *article on* STRUCTURE AND FUNCTION OF THE BRAIN; STRESS.]

WORKS BY HARTLEY

(1730) 1837 *Conjecturae quaedam de sensu, motu, et idearum generatione.* Pages 143–185 in Samuel Parr (editor), *Metaphysical Tracts by English Philosophers of the Eighteenth Century.* London: Lumley.
(1749) 1834 *Observations on Man: His Frame, His Duty and His Expectations.* 6th ed., corr. & rev. London: Tegg.

SUPPLEMENTARY BIBLIOGRAPHY

DESCARTES, RENÉ 1662 *De homine.* Lugduni Batavorum (now Leiden): Moyardus & Lessen.
KING, WILLIAM (1702) 1732 *An Essay on the Origin of Evil.* Preface by John Gay. 2d ed. London. → First published as *De origine mali.*
LOCKE, JOHN (1690) 1959 *An Essay Concerning Human Understanding.* 2 vols. New York: Dover.
MALEBRANCHE, NICOLAS 1674–1675 *De la recherche de la vérité.* 2 vols. Paris: Pralard.
MOIVRE, ABRAHAM DE (1718) 1756 *The Doctrine of Chances: Or, a Method of Calculating the Probabilities of Events in Play.* 3d ed. London: Millar.
NEWTON, ISAAC (1704) 1952 *Opticks.* New York: Dover.
OLDFIELD, R. C.; and OLDFIELD, KATHLEEN C. 1951 Hartley's *Observations on Man. Annals of Science* 7:371–381.
PRIESTLEY, JOSEPH 1775 *Hartley's Theory of the Human Mind, on the Principle of Association of Ideas.* London: Johnson.
RIBOT, T. (1870) 1873 *English Psychology.* London: King. → First published in French.
WARREN, HOWARD C. 1921 *A History of the Association Psychology.* New York: Scribner.
WILKINS, JOHN 1668 *An Essay Towards a Real Character and a Philosophical Language.* London: Gellibrand.
WILLIS, THOMAS 1664 *De cerebri anatome cui accessit nervorumque descriptio et usus.* London: Roycroft.
WILLIS, THOMAS 1672 *De anima brutorum quae hominis vitalis ac sensitiva est. . . .* Oxford: Shelden.

HAURIOU, MAURICE

Maurice Hauriou (1856–1929), French legal theorist, was born at Ladiville (Charente). He studied law at Bordeaux and, after taking first place in the 1882 competition for *agrégation*, was appointed professor at Toulouse. He taught there for 46 years, until his death.

Hauriou taught the history of law for several years. He then went on to teach administrative law, and it was in this field that he was to make his most lasting contributions. He became deeply interested in sociology—in 1893 he wrote *Les facultés de droit et la sociologie*—but after his most important work in this area, *La science sociale traditionelle* (1896), aroused considerable opposition, he decided, as he wrote to Georges Renard, to present in juridical dress the ideas that he had at first tried to get accepted in sociological dress (Renard 1931). Indeed, this approach is implicit in the commentaries on decisions that he made for the Sirey collection for 37 years, from 1892 to 1929 (1929), and in his *Précis de droit administratif* (1892), which went through 11 editions during his lifetime. But it is primarily in his *Principes de droit public* (1910), his *Précis de droit constitutionnel* (1923), and in his article "La théorie de l'institution et de la fondation" (1925) that his sociophilosophical views may be found.

Hauriou's thought is marked by liberalism, individualism, and attachment to tradition. He was strongly influenced by Bergson and by the doctrine of the Catholic church; he described himself, in the *Principes de droit public*, as a Comtean positivist turned Catholic positivist, that is, as a positivist who will go so far as to utilize the social, moral, and juridical content of Catholic dogma. As a traditionalist, he saw himself restoring the classic doctrines of French public law and defending natural-law conceptions from the menace of the aggressive objectivism of Hans Kelsen.

However, Hauriou was not simply a conservative content to do battle from old positions. He did not regard the substance of law as purely conceptual but saw it as a concrete reality that embodies objective ideas and is subject to their creative influence. In this way he introduced into juridical thinking the sociological data that the normative (objective) method prescribed. Hauriou did not believe that the sociological study of the law meant merely the observation of social facts; instead, he was concerned with discovering how government *de facto* becomes government *de jure* (1892). As he saw it, this transformation occurs as ideas are incorporated into facts, thus creating what G. Gurvitch has called normative facts.

What has become known as the "Hauriou theory of the institution" focuses on this process of the penetration of social reality by ideas and analyzes the way in which ideas order that reality. An institution, by Hauriou's definition, is an "idea of a project, or enterprise, that becomes a reality and persists juridically in a social milieu" (1925, p. 10). An institution is an objective reality, the product of a particular social equilibrium, and the source of legal rules. With this definition Hauriou eliminated all voluntaristic interpretations of the creation of law. He introduced a dynamic factor into the realm of law, for although institutions give stability to the law, this is not a stability that precludes change. The continuity of an institution depends on its constant adaptation to new conditions of social life (1910, pp. 213, 250).

On these bases Hauriou erected a theory of the state. Rejecting the theory of the social contract, he based the origin of the state on the institution: individuals do not delegate power to a governing minority; they assent, *by custom*, to that institution which is the state. While the subject consents only indirectly to the power of the law, he accepts directly the institution to which that power is linked and in whose behalf it is exercised. Furthermore, Hauriou believed that the state exists only in certain civilizations, that the institution of the state is taken seriously only by certain races, and that with certain others it becomes a mere facade behind which traditions of personal power or the organization of clans and clienteles are perpetuated. As he saw it, there are peoples that are incapable of putting into effect the idea of the commonweal (1929).

The state, therefore, is distinct from the nation. It is subject to law only at its own will, and this is why Hauriou, on the political plane, believed firmly in the merits of democracy and, more particularly, of parliamentary democracy. But taking a wide historical perspective, he considered this type of government to be nothing more than a temporary political form. For all its recognized merits, parliamentary democracy is only a stage in an irreversible development that begins with aristocratic monarchies and ends with administrative empires (1929, p. 142). The successive types of government evolve as governmental institutions become nationwide; within the nation, more and more numerous elites are formed, which enter into the machinery of government and transform its operation by their presence.

So far as the functioning of parliamentary democracy in particular is concerned, Hauriou advocated the dominance of the executive over the legislative power. He believed that the best way to maintain the superiority of the executive over the legislative power is to limit the power of the deputies to initiate legislation. In his view, the conciliation of power and liberty is brought about by virtue of order, that order which follows if the people support actions originated by the executive. This support is almost always spontaneous; force enters into the picture only in exceptional cases, to keep refractory minorities within bounds.

Hauriou stressed that the character of the state is determined to a large extent by what he called its social constitution; that is, its socioeconomic structure, the place of citizens within the state, and the rights and liberties of individuals. He was deeply committed to individual liberty as the prerequisite to law that is based on the juridical person and on subjective right, and he believed that individual initiative is the basis of social order (1929, p. vii). However, he did recognize that human fallibility makes the limitation of individualism necessary: liberty must be conditional on rules of morality and social sanctions. On the socioeconomic level, limitations on individual liberty can be achieved by certain modifications in the structure of power: "Freedom of association, decentralization, corporative representation, here are three essential reforms, all three interdependent, which will assure a harmonious separation between the state and positive society, and permit the development of collective intervention in economic conflicts without a monstrous increase in the power of the state" (1896, pp. 392–393).

In the sphere of administrative law, Hauriou succeeded in erecting an extremely solid body of doctrine that is still suggestive, although it has become outmoded by changes in the extent and modes of action of the state. In general, to be sure, his influence was less in his day than that of Duguit, the other master of French public law at the turn of the century. Yet despite certain obscure points, Hauriou's thinking is still provocative, and his work foreshadowed the orientation of those French political scientists who are studying the nature of political institutions in general and of power in particular.

G. BURDEAU

[*See also* ADMINISTRATIVE LAW; STATE; *and the biographies of* DUGUIT *and* KELSEN.]

WORKS BY HAURIOU

(1892) 1933 *Précis de droit administratif et de droit public.* 12th ed. Paris: Sirey.
1893 *Les facultés de droit et la sociologie.* Paris: Thorin.
1896 *Cours de science sociale: La science sociale traditionelle.* Paris: Larose.
(1910) 1916 *Principes de droit public à l'usage des étudiants en license (3ᵉ année) et en doctorat ès-sciences politiques.* 2d ed. Paris: Tenin.
(1923) 1929 *Précis de droit constitutionnel.* 2d ed. Paris: Sirey. → The second edition is particularly recommended.
1925 *La théorie de l'institution et de la fondation.* Pages 1–45 in *La cité moderne et les transformations du droit.* Paris: Bloud & Gay.
(1929) 1931 *La jurisprudence administrative de 1892 à 1929.* 3 vols. Paris: Sirey.

SUPPLEMENTARY BIBLIOGRAPHY

RENARD, GEORGES 1931 La filosofia politica di Maurice Hauriou. Volume 2, pages 195–204 in *Scritti di diritto pubblico in onore di Oreste Ranelletti nel XXXV anno d'insegnamento.* Padua (Italy): Milani.
SFEZ, LUCIEN 1966 *Essai sur la contribution du doyen Hauriou au droit administratif français.* Paris: Librairie Générale de Droit et de Jurisprudence.

HAWTREY, R. G.

Ralph George Hawtrey, English economist, was born in 1879. He was educated at Eton and Trinity College, Cambridge, where he obtained a first-class honors degree in mathematics. After leaving Cambridge he entered the administrative civil service and worked at the Treasury from 1904 until his retirement in 1945. He was knighted in 1956.

Throughout his career he held only two academic (or quasi-academic) appointments: in 1928–1929 he was given special leave by the Treasury to lecture in economics at Harvard University; and after his official retirement he was elected Price professor of international economics at the Royal Institute of International Affairs, a post which he held from 1947 to 1952.

Hawtrey is often wrongly regarded as one of the Cambridge academic economists and is grouped with Pigou, Keynes, Robertson, and other pupils of Marshall. But he acquired his knowledge of economics not at Cambridge (he never attended even one of Marshall's lectures) but at the Treasury, where he came under the stimulating influence of Sir John (later Lord) Bradbury, permanent secretary of the Treasury.

The first of Hawtrey's books, *Good and Bad Trade* (1913), contains the germ of many of his later ideas on monetary theory. He subsequently developed these ideas at greater length and with more precision in such major works as *Currrency and Credit* (1919), *The Art of Central Banking* (1932), and *Capital and Employment* (1937).

Hawtrey was one of the outstanding figures among those British economists who led the way in much of the rethinking of monetary theory after World War I, and he had a considerable influence on the early development of Keynes's thought (Harrod 1951, p. 357). The emphasis he laid on the concept of money as something abstract, though capable of numeration—a unit of account, divorced from any necessary link with a metallic or other substance—made a marked impact on the minds of a generation of economists who had grown up with the traditional nineteenth-century attitude toward the gold standard.

He was one of the English pioneers of the "income" approach; thus, he wrote in *Good and Bad Trade*: "The total effective demand for all commodities per unit of time is the aggregate of all money incomes. The total cost of production of all commodities per unit of time is the aggregate of all money incomes" ([1913] 1962, p. 7). He developed this idea further in his *Currency and Credit* by bringing in, for example, the notion of the income velocity of money, which he defined as the ratio of consumers' outlay to the unspent margin: Consumers' outlay (out of income) includes investment, while the unspent margin is the supply of the means of payment—that is, the excess of the purchasing power people and businesses have acquired over what they have spent.

Hawtrey based his monetary explanation primarily on the argument that credit is inherently unstable because of the working of the banking system and its effect on the holders of stocks in particular. Dealers (merchants, wholesalers, and retailers) occupy a key position in the economy: "[They] are the economic leaders. They take the initiative in production, and the activity of the manufacturers depends on the orders they give" ([1919] 1950, p. 427). Since dealers hold stocks largely with borrowed money, they are peculiarly susceptible to changes in the rate of interest they have to pay for the money they borrow. It is chiefly because of the importance which he attached to the role of dealers that Hawtrey, unlike Keynes and many other economists of recent times, always maintained that the operative instrument for credit regulation is the short-term, not the long-term rate of interest.

While Hawtrey agreed that a low short-term rate may be able to do little to assist an economy to recover from a deep depression, he was convinced that a sufficiently high bank rate (possibly even 10 per cent or higher) can damp down and counteract inflationary forces caused by credit expansion, however strongly they may be working. He recently contended that the 7 per cent bank rate, which operated for six months in 1964–1965, was largely ineffective because it was too low at a time when the long-term rate (the yield on consols) was itself 7 per cent.

His views as to the utility of public works underwent a good deal of modification in the course of time. In his earliest work he contended that "the Government by the very fact of borrowing for this expenditure is withdrawing from the investment market savings which would otherwise be applied to the creation of capital" ([1913] 1962, p. 260). Later he said: "It is not the Government expenditure [on capital works] that gives employment, but the Government borrowing. The borrowing would have the same effect if it were to meet a deficit due to a remission of taxation" (1928, pp. 112–113). The shift in his position is even clearer in the following passage: "Now it is quite true that capital outlay undertaken by the Government may conduce under appropriate conditions to an expansion of general demand. It must be *additional*, that is to say, must not by using up the resources of the investment market, prevent or delay an equal amount of privately initiated capital outlay. It need not necessarily be financed by avowedly inflationary methods; if it merely sets in motion money held idle in balances for want of eligible investments, it will enlarge the flow of money" (1944, p. 95). But he went on to say that business ought never to be allowed to lapse into such a state of depression and

stagnation that government expenditure is the appropriate remedy. If this is allowed to happen, it points to a failure on the part of those who control the banking system to exercise their proper function. He consistently preached the doctrine that the best way to stop depression is to stop the preceding boom; and for this purpose credit regulation can be fully effective.

Hawtrey's position in the ranks of modern monetary theorists does not depend so much upon the validity of his views on the causation and control of the trade cycle as upon the deeper and clearer understanding which he made possible of both the operation of the banking system and the role of money in a modern economy.

His name is associated in the minds of most economists with the doctrine that the trade cycle is essentially a monetary phenomenon, and it should not be overlooked that his writings include a careful analysis of the part played by the period of production and by the widening and deepening of capital in different phases of the cycle.

No account of his work, however short, should omit mention of the contribution Hawtrey made at the International Monetary Conference held at Genoa in April 1922. He was one of the representatives of the British Treasury there, and it was largely through his influence that agreement was reached on the desirability of cooperation between the central banks in the regulation of credit in order to prevent undue fluctuations in the purchasing power of gold. However, the Genoa Resolutions were never put into effect.

When Hawtrey was 82 years of age, he published *The Pound at Home and Abroad* (1961), in which, *inter alia*, he upheld with customary vigor the thesis that the primary causes of the recent difficulties of the British economy were, first, the fixed parity of the sterling exchange with a depreciating dollar, and second, the undervaluation of the pound ever since it was devalued in 1949 from $4.03 to $2.80—in this latter contention his has been a lone voice among British economists. This book also contains his memorandum of evidence submitted to the Radcliffe Committee on the Working of the Monetary System and some trenchant criticisms of parts of the report of that body.

Although Hawtrey adhered in general to the same fundamental tenets throughout his career, he modified their expression so as to take account both of historical developments and of the evolution of contemporary economic thought, and it is by his later books and editions that his work should be assessed.

C. W. GUILLEBAUD

[*See also* BANKING, CENTRAL; BUSINESS CYCLES.]

WORKS BY HAWTREY

(1913) 1962 *Good and Bad Trade: An Inquiry Into the Causes of Trade Fluctuations.* New York: Kelley.

(1919) 1950 *Currency and Credit.* 4th ed. New York and London: Longmans.

1921 *The Exchequer and the Control of Expenditure.* New York: Oxford Univ. Press.

(1923) 1926 *Monetary Reconstruction.* 2d ed. London: Longmans.

1926 *The Economic Problem.* London: Longmans.

(1927) 1947 *The Gold Standard in Theory and Practice.* 5th ed. London: Longmans.

1928 *Trade and Credit.* London and New York: Longmans.

(1930) 1952 *Economic Aspects of Sovereignty.* 2d ed. London and New York: Longmans.

(1931) 1933 *Trade Depression and the Way Out.* New ed. London and New York: Longmans.

(1932) 1962 *The Art of Central Banking.* 2d ed. London: Cass.

(1937) 1952 *Capital and Employment.* 2d ed. London and New York: Longmans. → See especially pages 157–219 on "Keynes' *General Theory of Employment, Interest and Money.*"

(1938) 1962 *A Century of Bank Rate.* 2d ed. London: Cass.

1944 *Economic Destiny.* New York and London: Longmans.

1946a *Economic Rebirth.* London and New York: Longmans.

1946b *Bretton Woods for Better or Worse.* London and New York: Longmans.

1949 *Western European Union: Implications for the United Kingdom.* London: Royal Institute of International Affairs.

1950 *The Balance of Payments and the Standard of Living.* London: Royal Institute of International Affairs.

1954 *Towards the Rescue of Sterling.* London and New York: Longmans.

1955 *Cross Purposes in Wage Policy.* London and New York: Longmans.

1961 *The Pound at Home and Abroad.* London: Longmans. → See especially Chapter 2, "Relative Strength of the Pound and the Dollar"; Chapter 12, "The Undervaluation of the Pound"; and Chapter 14, "The Radcliffe Committee: Aims of Monetary Policy."

SUPPLEMENTARY BIBLIOGRAPHY

ARMITAGE-SMITH, GEORGE (1906) 1935 *Principles and Methods of Taxation.* 11th ed. Revised by R. G. Hawtrey. London: Murray.

HARROD, R. F. 1951 *The Life of John Maynard Keynes.* London: Macmillan. → A paperback edition was published in 1963 by St. Martins.

HEALTH

"Health is a state of complete physical, mental and social well-being and not merely the absence of disease or infirmity," according to the World Health Organization (1946). It will be the purpose of this article to develop some concepts about health and disease, exploring a few implications of the WHO definition in the context of both Western and non-Western medical ideas. First, notions of singular and multiple causation of disease will be contrasted. Second, three types of ideas about health will be defined. Finally, some applications of the health concept to units beyond the human individual will be mentioned.

Disease and its causes

Illness is a disvalued process that impairs the functioning or appearance of a human person and may ultimately lead to death. The definition of health given by the WHO includes *social* as well as physical and mental well-being. This reflects a concern with the person as a member of human groups—an entity certainly not limited to the body of that person. The components of an individual (e.g., blood, body, soul, spirit, shadow, name, etc.) are defined differently from one culture to the next. The death of the organism, however, is a biological constant which is taken into account conceptually in all cultures, and customs prescribe how the disposition of the corpse is to be arranged. Different components of the individual may be thought to depart from the presence of the living at different times, and these various departures are marked by a series of ceremonies (van Gennep [1909] 1960, pp. 146 ff.). Some components, such as the "soul," may be thought never to cease existing entirely but to remain near the living or in some locality specially set aside for its kind.

Disease, then, may involve a temporary or permanent impairment in the functioning of any single component, or of the relationship between components making up the individual. An impairment of a person, furthermore, need not be restricted to a decrease in his ability to function in his ordinary ways: for example, among the Ashanti of West Africa, a congenital birthmark which leads to no discomfort or danger of death can be considered a sufficiently severe fault to disqualify a man from the office of chief. In many cultures, theories of disease will include explanations of congenital defects or imperfections, and the distinction between these and other illnesses may become relevant for further analysis (Polgar 1963).

Explanations of illness are not only useful to reaffirm the values of a social unit or to make death psychologically more tolerable for the next of kin but serve most immediately to indicate courses of preventive and curative action. To effect prevention or cure one should identify a course of events which presumably has produced the impairment. Herein lies the rationale of *diagnosis*, which is one of the three basic elements of all medical systems (the other two being therapy and prophylaxis).

Notions of singular causation. During the last decades of the nineteenth and the early part of the twentieth century, Western medicine was heavily dominated by the notion that most diseases are a result of infection caused by microorganisms. This type of conception—that disease simply results from the entry by a foreign agency into the body of the patient—is paralleled by the ideas found among many tribal people that illness is caused by "object intrusion" or "spirit possession." Walther Riese has drawn attention to this similarity of ideas in stating that "ontologic" etiology (a conception of disease as caused by a monadic "alien-ferment") "in its crudest form . . . identifies these agents, if not the diseases themselves, with demons, in its scientific form, with germs" (Riese 1953, pp. 66–67). He does not imply, of course, that demons and germs are equally valid concepts in an empirical sense.

The emergence of the "doctrine of specific etiology of disease" (Dubos [1959] 1961, p. 90) as the dominant idea in medicine is related to the mechanistic world view prevalent in the late nineteenth century. Far older features of Western thought, such as the grammatical dualism of subject and predicate, the Judeo–Christian and Platonic mind–body dichotomy, and the experimental approach of the alchemists, provided a suitable background for the development of this "doctrine." Of the greatest immediate relevance to it were the discoveries of Pasteur and Koch in the realm of bacteriology. Instead of emphasizing the patient and his total environment, as Western medical traditions had done previously, proponents of this "doctrine" spread the notion that all important infections could be controlled by therapeutic serums and preventive vaccines specific for all microbes (Dubos [1959] 1961, p. 130). Although a number of vaccines and antitoxins had been developed before the turn of the century, it was not until the 1930s that the sulfa drugs were discovered, and it was another decade later that penicillin came to be used. The great decreases in the mortality of children and young adults, which are nowadays often attributed to clinical medicine and the use of specific drugs, actually preceded these discoveries and mostly resulted from better nutrition and the hygienic measures carried out under the leadership of medical reformers, many of whom had even opposed the germ theory of disease (Rosen 1958, pp. 225 ff.; Dubos [1959] 1961, p. 131).

In the contemporary practice of clinical medicine, the inadequate care often received by patients unfortunate enough to suffer from a disability for which no specific etiology can be identified is symptomatic of the legacy of the bacteriological era. Von Mering and Earley (1965) trace the difficulties of such problem patients to, among other factors, the hospital as the main locale for diagnosis and treatment, as well as to the "growth of medicine as a science of tests and measurements rather than an art involving the five senses." These authors find that "the clinic physician and general practitioner share a kind of 'molecular man' orientation which seems to predispose them to be more concerned with the specifics of the presenting complaint, and to look eagerly for major disease in every bed or consulting room" (von Mering & Earley 1965, p. 199; see also Pflanz 1964).

Multicausal conceptions of disease. The recent theoretical developments away from the doctrine of specific etiology are spearheaded by advocates of comprehensive medical care and psychosomatic medicine and by some epidemiologists. All three of these segments of the medical community regard illness as an interaction of many factors and, correspondingly, favor treatment of patients once more as total organisms in a complex setting. One of the foremost modern exponents of this view is the epidemiologist John Gordon, who has shown the interplay of the *host*, the *agent*, and the (physical, biological, and social) *environment* in the spread of a good number of both infectious and noninfectious diseases (see, for example, Gordon 1958). The studies of John Cassel, another noted epidemiologist, on the spectrum of health disorders resulting from independently documented sociocultural processes exemplify a further step away from the one cause–one disease manner of thinking (Cassel 1964). Although writers in the psychosomatic tradition of medicine often use concepts like "stress" or "conflict" as if they were specific causes of illness, the emphasis in this school of thought is on the patient's physical *and* mental well-being, and consideration is often given to his social milieu as well (King 1963). Comprehensive medical care is more than a movement to improve the institutional means by which patients and sometimes families are medically supervised. The theory that underlies these arrangements includes rejection of both the dominant disease orientation of modern Western medicine and the organic–functional dichotomy, and it places a strong emphasis on the patient as a person (Steiger et al. 1962).

Multicausal conceptions of disease are neither new in the Western medical tradition nor unique to it. One main theme in the Hippocratic writings is that disease is to be traced to an imbalance between the person and his external environment; much emphasis is also given to the relationships among different environmental factors, such as exercise and diet, and to the connections between disturbances in an organ and the whole body (Sigerist 1951–1961, vol. 2, pp. 317 ff.; Dubos [1959] 1961, pp. 117 ff.). In non-Western societies there are many multicausal ideas about disease. The distinction between conditions that make persons particularly susceptible and events that precipitate the onset of the disease is particularly common: for example, the Maori of New Zealand see "bad acts" by the patient as predisposing to, and external spirits or objects as the immediate cause of, an illness episode (Newell 1957); in the Middle East, a well-formed male child is identified as especially susceptible to attack by the "evil eye" (Shiloh 1958).

Related to this division between predisposing and precipitating factors is the division between the reasons why a particular person becomes ill at a particular time and the explanation of the way in which it happens. These latter two types of causes may be termed *incidence notions* and *etiological notions* (Polgar 1962, pp. 166 ff.); they also bear some similarity to the Aristotelian efficient and material causes (Riese 1953, pp. 66 ff.). In some non-Western medical systems there are categories for "natural" diseases—usually minor ills such as the digestive problems of infants (Nurge 1958)—which do not require an explanation for the occurrence of the disability in the particular instance and hence do not raise questions about who is "responsible." In urbanized as well as nonurban societies, however, the search for the transgression of the patient himself or the malevolent action of another being (human or supernatural) is a major element of the diagnostic process.

In small tribal or peasant communities, the assignment of responsibility for illness to a relative or neighbor (whose departure from prescribed norms of behavior is pinpointed as a breach of taboo, witchcraft, irresponsibility, or sin) helps to bring latent interpersonal conflicts into the open where they are more easily resolved (Paul 1953; Firth 1959, pp. 135 ff.). Similarly in the Judeo–Christian tradition the attribution of illness to sinful behavior served to reinforce the mores of the society. With increasing secularization, this diagnostic category became less satisfactory, and in scientific medicine it was replaced by "naturalistic" explanations. However, residues of this earlier concept of sin still affect attitudes toward disease; for patients and their families, a physician's diagnosis which fails to blame anyone for the occurrence of the illness also fails to deal with the sense of guilt they often have and leaves them vaguely dissatisfied (Sigerist 1951–1961, vol. 1, p. 157).

Three conceptions of health

If disease is seen as an individual's departure from perfectly well-meshed social or physiological performance, health, by contrast, becomes an *asymptote*—an ideal that can be approached but never attained in actuality. In the WHO definition, the expression "*complete* physical, mental and social well-being" [emphasis added] echoes this type of conception.

Variants of the asymptotic concept. Two main variants of the asymptotic notion about health can be identified. One variant, the harmonious working together of disparate elements, is a dominant theme in the Indo–European tradition, antedating Galen's notion of the "four fluids" and manifest today in the influence of Walter B. Cannon's ideas about homeostasis. The yang and yin of Chinese philosophy also indicate a search for balance, the restoration of which is one of the healer's primary goals (Huard & Wong 1959, pp. 105 ff.). Grand designs of physiological, physical, and metaphysical order —each replicating the elements of the other—are typical of classical times.

The second type of asymptotic conception is a backward-looking romanticism, which has been described by Dubos in his chapter "The Gardens of Eden" ([1959] 1961, pp. 1–25). For Rousseau and his followers, the ills that beset Western society are consequences of the departure from a perfect state of harmony with nature that is entailed in the process of becoming civilized. Freud also accepted the myth of a precursor of modern man who was exempt from the latter's neuroses, since this imaginary "savage" did not inhibit the biological drives toward aggression and sexuality (Riese 1953, pp. 14 ff.). Remnants of ideas about "primitive man's" closeness to "nature" remain today in such medical folklore as the myth of easier parturition among American Indians and the "innate" superiority of their sense organs. When this theme is transposed to the life cycle of individuals, children may be seen romantically (for example, by the poet Wordsworth) as endowed with sensitive understanding which they gradually lose by exposure to the eroding influence of the "civilized" ways of adults.

In operational terms, the asymptotic definition of health is mostly negative; it implies the *absence* of manifest disturbance. While this notion has advantages in focusing attention on the nonexistence of a clear break between the presence or absence of disease, by the same token it makes for difficulties in conducting health surveys and planning for medical facilities (Lewis 1953; U.S. Department of Health . . . 1966).

The elastic concept.   Another set of notions about health centers on the accumulation of resistance to potential danger. This may be termed the *elastic* concept. Examples of health behavior derived from this manner of thinking include restricting the water intake of children to make them hardy, homeopathic medicine, and variolation (of differing empirical value, of course). Adversity is not regarded here as a disruption of some prior or ultimate harmony but rather as an ordinary and expected circumstance for which preparations can and should be made. This manner of regarding health seems to play a substantial part in modern preventive medicine. Another good contemporary example of an application of the elastic view of health is psychoprophylactic training for childbirth, by which women are taught to cope with the hardships of delivery through psychological conditioning together with certain exercises (Bing et al. 1961). Some accumulated resistance potentials can be measured operationally in the scientific laboratory by testing an individual's capacity to produce specific antibodies when challenged by an antigenic substance or his capacity for continued adequate performance of sensory tasks under controlled changes in temperature, humidity, pressure, and other conditions.

The open-ended concept.   The outstanding difficulty with the asymptotic notion of health (which is circumvented by elastic conceptions) is its unattainability. By turning the argument around, one can start with death as a kind of absolute zero and fix no upper limit for human functioning (Bates 1959, p. 59). This may be termed the *open-ended* conception of health. The outstanding example of this ideology is involved in the attempts to formulate a philosophy of "positive mental health." While some concepts used by the writers in this tradition, such as "self-actualization," would fall in the category of asymptotic notions, the criteria of *growth*, *zest*, and *creativity* clearly belong under the open-ended rubric. The theorists of positive mental health share with the authors of the WHO definition and others mentioned above the desire to construct a manner of looking at health which is based "not merely on the absence of disease or infirmity." However, they go beyond the WHO view

of health, and beyond most of preventive medicine generally, in their search for positive goals which are independent of disease (Jahoda 1958). Health promotion in nutrition, for example, aims to prevent deficiency diseases (a goal which is of the "elastic" type) or persuade people to consume recommended daily norms of nutrients (an asymptotic-type idea). By contrast, "zestful living" does not reach an optimum at certain levels of energy expenditure and could even make people occasionally *more* prone to injury or disease.

Modern medical practice

In terms of actual health behavior in urban societies, open-ended conceptions are more likely to be put into practice in national parks, beauty parlors, bathrooms, or athletic studios than in the offices of doctors or psychologists. Physicians may recommend vacations, walks in the "fresh air," or other types of exercise, but this is usually prescribed for incipient illness or problems of overweight rather than for promoting health as such. In non-Western societies one may find practices aimed at increasing supernatural power, physical strength, prosperity, wisdom, virility, or femininity, which are conceptually and behaviorally integrated with actions to prevent or cure disease. In industrialized societies, however, increased specialization results in the separation of medical institutions from the religious, esthetic, recreational, and economic spheres. As mentioned above, the focus of Western medicine narrowed as the doctrine of specific etiology of disease became the dominant view. Thus, health promotion through such customs as taking cold showers, swallowing vitamin pills to "pep you up," giving laxatives routinely to children, taking walks, and the like is seldom transmitted as part of the professional medical system but rather is passed on through relatives, friends, or the mass media.

The attempt of the mental hygienists to develop a new and positive content for the concept of health is further limited by concern for the possibility of their encroachment on other institutions. Brewster Smith (1961, p. 301) has commented on the difficult position of the psychologist who is asked to provide notions of mental health as substitutes for weakened religious values; and Freidson (1961/1962, pp. 125 ff.) has warned about the dangers of bringing questions of nonconformity to moral, legal, or political norms under the umbrella of medicine. In spite of these problems, it may be predicted that scientific medicine will gradually adopt a more open-ended conception of health as the technological tasks of health maintenance in a population with increasing proportions of older people are accomplished and as the relationship between people and their environment once again becomes the central arena of medical concern.

Health beyond the individual

The WHO definition does not specify whether its terms apply only to the health of the individual. In the Greek medical system of the fifth century B.C. and that of some modern Western physicians, as described above, health is seen as an *interaction* between a person and his surroundings. This type of conception is carried even further in the ideas of many non-Western peoples. Margaret Mead (World Federation for Mental Health 1953, pp. 217 ff.) mentions several examples of "continuity" between the well-being of man and of the soil and between the body and "other bodies of the social unit." It is but a short step from a focus on these interrelationships to a consideration of the larger unit itself, without necessarily looking at the individual within it at all times.

As the student in schools of public health is often reminded, his "patient" will usually be a community. Public health is thus not only the name of a medical specialty but also refers to the well-being of various publics (Brockington 1958, pp. 19 ff.). The health of other entities, such as families, societies, the human species, or the entire ecosphere of this planet, has also been discussed.

The resistance potential of a human collectivity to an epidemic of infectious disease cannot be described as the sum or the average of individual immunity: the degree of resistance in different age groups or the spatial dispersion of the population are crucial in estimating the level of "herd immunity" (Gordon 1958). Mental illness is regarded by a number of psychologists and psychiatrists as a pathological state of an entire family. The illness may be discovered through the request for treatment of a single member who acts as the "messenger boy," carrying the information about the trouble to the outside world, although he is neither the only one sick nor necessarily the one most seriously disturbed (Gruenberg 1957). There are also some writers who consider it appropriate to label entire societies (for example, Nazi Germany) as pathological and to wonder if any "healthy adjustment" is possible for individuals living in them (Devereux 1956).

Western medical practitioners almost inevitably put a higher value on prolonging individual life than on the health of the social unit—witness the grotesque situation where catheters, sedatives, exorbitant hospital bills, and oxygen tents prevent a dying man from making a decent and meaningful departure from his relatives. Under different cultural circumstances the reverse evaluation may predominate, as among the Navajo Indians of the southwestern United States, who are more concerned with the well-being of the entire kin group than with the maximum comfort of, say, a congenitally malformed infant (Levy 1962).

For an entire species, health may be regarded as a matter of Darwinian "fitness" for continued survival. Unless a species is approaching death through extinction, however, it may be impossible to diagnose its current degree of fitness. The possibility of using modern medicine to keep alive individuals with genetically inherited diseases and the higher reproductive rate of the impoverished classes have been a focus for alarm by some eugenicists. Whether any real danger of "deterioration" exists for the gene pool of the whole human species is debatable (Medawar 1960); but, of course, conceptions of health which regard the proliferation of a "chosen people" as good and their relative submergence by "heathens" or other out-groups as bad are not a recent development (Haller 1963).

The health of the entire ecological system that exists on the surface of the earth can also be evaluated in terms of the survival potential of "life." Evolution on this planet—inorganic, biological, and social—has in the past moved toward increasing degrees of entropy retardation (Polgar 1961). The catastrophe of nuclear war or the slower but equally irreparable consequences of accelerating population growth are threats to the survival not only of "civilized" man but also of the energy balance of our entire terrestrial ecosystem. According to this view, our future well-being in this world as we know it depends on mankind's acting deliberately to safeguard and to continue accumulating the ordered energy and information that evolution represents.

STEVEN POLGAR

[*See also* ILLNESS; MEDICAL CARE; MENTAL HEALTH; PUBLIC HEALTH. *Other relevant material may be found in the articles on* CREATIVITY; EPIDEMIOLOGY; EUGENICS; PSYCHOSOMATIC ILLNESS; SOCIAL DARWINISM.]

BIBLIOGRAPHY

BATES, MARSTON 1959 The Ecology of Health. Pages 56–77 in Iago Galdston (editor), *Medicine and Anthropology*. New York: International Universities Press. → The health of human individuals and collectivities seen in relation to the rest of living organisms on the planet. A primary source.

BING, ELIZABETH D.; KARMEL, MARJORIE; and TANZ, ALFRED 1961 *A Practical Training Course for the Psychoprophylactic Method of Childbirth.* New York: American Society for Psycho-prophylaxis in Obstetrics.

BROCKINGTON, C. FRASER 1958 *World Health.* Harmondsworth (England): Penguin. → A compendium on diseases and the organizations involved in public health. An excellent basic volume.

CASSEL, JOHN 1964 Social Science Theory as a Source of Hypotheses in Epidemiological Research. *American Journal of Public Health* 54, no. 9:1482–1488.

DEVEREUX, GEORGE 1956 Normal and Abnormal: The Key Problem in Psychiatric Anthropology. Pages 23–48 in Anthropological Society of Washington, *Some Uses of Anthropology: Theoretical and Applied.* Washington: The Society. → Discusses the usefulness of the culture concept, with particular emphasis on the shaman. A unique and illuminating essay.

DUBOS, RENÉ J. (1959) 1961 *Mirage of Health, Utopias, Progress, and Biological Change.* New York: Harper. → A discourse on health and disease—their history, treatment and characteristics—by an eminent biologist. A primary source.

FIRTH, RAYMOND 1959 Acculturation in Relation to Concepts of Health and Disease. Pages 129–165 in Iago Galdston (editor), *Medicine and Anthropology.* New York: International Universities Press. → A fine essay on the sociocultural context of medical practice. A primary source.

FREIDSON, ELIOT 1961/1962 The Sociology of Medicine: A Trend Report and Bibliography. *Current Sociology* 10/11: 123–192. → The best sociological summary.

GENNEP, ARNOLD VAN (1909) 1960 *The Rites of Passage.* London: Routledge; Univ. of Chicago Press. → First published in French. A classic anthropological essay on birth, puberty, marriage, childbirth, and death.

GORDON, JOHN E. 1958 Medical Ecology and the Public Health. *American Journal of the Medical Sciences* 235:337–359. → A summary of Gordon's views, with examples from numerous investigations.

GRUENBERG, ERNEST M. 1957 Socially Shared Psychopathology. Pages 201–225 in *Explorations in Social Psychiatry.* Edited by A. L. Leighton et al. New York: Basic Books.

HALLER, MARK H. 1963 *Eugenics: Hereditarian Attitudes in American Thought.* New Brunswick, N.J.: Rutgers Univ. Press. → History and evaluation of the eugenics movement in the United States.

HUARD, PIERRE A.; and WONG, MING 1959 *La médecine chinoise au cours des siècles.* Paris: Dacosta. → The best contemporary summary of Chinese medicine in a Western language.

JAHODA, MARIE 1958 *Current Concepts of Positive Mental Health.* New York: Basic Books. → A good synopsis of the field.

KING, STANLEY H. 1963 Social Psychological Factors in Illness. Pages 99–121 in *Handbook of Medical Sociology.* Edited by H. E. Freeman et al. Englewood Cliffs, N.J.: Prentice-Hall. → Psychological aspects of doctor-patient relations, as well as of illness.

LEVY, JERROLD E. 1962 Comment on "Health and Human Behavior" by Steven Polgar. *Current Anthropology* 3:186–187.

LEWIS, AUBREY 1953 Health as a Social Concept. *British Journal of Sociology* 4:109–124. → Separates health from social well-being, delineating operational criteria for physical and mental illness in the "asymptotic" tradition.

MEDAWAR, PETER B. 1960 *The Future of Man.* New York: Basic Books; London: Methuen. → An essay on human genetics; grapples with many difficult and fundamental value problems.

MERING, OTTO VON; and EARLEY, L. WILLIAM 1965 Major Changes in the Western Medical Environment: Impact of Changes in Care of Undifferentiated Disorders. *Archives of General Psychiatry* 13:195–201.

NEWELL, KENNETH W. 1957 Medical Development Within a Maori Community. *Health Education Journal* 15:83–90.

NURGE, ETHEL 1958 Etiology of Illness in Guinhangdan. *American Anthropologist* New Series 60:1158–1172.

PAUL, BENJAMIN D. 1953 Mental Disorder and Self-regulating Processes in Culture: A Guatemalan Illustration. Pages 51–68 in Milbank Memorial Fund, *Interrelations Between the Social Environment and Psychiatric Disorders.* Proceedings, No. 29. New York: The Fund. → Describes the sequence of events in serving patients and their significance for treating disturbances in social relationships.

PFLANZ, MANFRED 1964 Der unklare Fall. *Münchener medizinische Wochenschrift* 106:1649–1655. → A discussion of the characteristics of patients, physicians, and medical thought, as these bear on the frequency of undifferentiated diagnoses in medical practice.

POLGAR, STEVEN 1961 Evolution and the Thermodynamic Imperative. *Human Biology* 33:99–109. → A development of four principles in organic and social evolution, from which a value position is derived.

POLGAR, STEVEN 1962 Health and Human Behavior: Areas of Interest Common to the Social and Medical Sciences. *Current Anthropology* 3:159–205. → A charting of the field, with an extensive bibliography.

POLGAR, STEVEN 1963 Health Action in Cross-cultural Perspective. Pages 397–419 in *Handbook of Medical Sociology.* Edited by H. E. Freeman et al. Englewood Cliffs, N.J.: Prentice-Hall. → An essay-review on the values and notions relevant to health, on medical practitioners, and on cross-cultural health programs.

RIESE, WALTHER 1953 *The Conception of Disease: Its History, Its Versions and Its Nature.* New York: Philosophical Library. → Fourteen types of disease conceptions, almost exclusively from the Western tradition.

ROSEN, GEORGE 1958 *A History of Public Health.* New York: MD Publications..

SHILOH, A. 1958 Middle East Culture and Health. *Health Education Journal* 16:232–244.

SIGERIST, HENRY 1951–1961 *A History of Medicine.* 2 vols. New York: Oxford Univ. Press. → Volume 1: *Primitive and Archaic Medicine.* Volume 2: *Early Greek, Hindu, and Persian Medicine.* A lucid, scholarly, and thorough history.

SMITH, M. BREWSTER 1961 "Mental Health" Reconsidered: A Special Case of the Problem of Values in Psychology. *American Psychologist* 16:299–306. → An excellent attempt to cut through the conceptual dilemma in order to arrive at operational guidelines for applied psychology.

STEIGER, W. A. et al. 1962 A Definition of Comprehensive Medicine. *Journal of Health and Human Behavior* 1:83–86.

U.S. DEPARTMENT OF HEALTH, EDUCATION, AND WELFARE, DIVISION OF VITAL STATISTICS 1966 *Conceptual*

Problems in Developing an Index of Health, by Daniel F. Sullivan. Washington: Government Printing Office.

WORLD FEDERATION FOR MENTAL HEALTH (1953) 1955 *Cultural Patterns and Technical Change*. Edited by Margaret Mead. New York: New American Library. → A very useful overview in the form of a collage of case histories and topical discussions.

WORLD HEALTH ORGANIZATION 1946 *Constitution of the World Health Organization*. Geneva: The Organization.

HEARING

Hearing is an especially important avenue by which we gain information about the world around us; one reason is that it plays a primary role in speech communication, a uniquely human activity. Clearly, then, our ability to perceive our environment and therefore to interact with it, both in a physical and verbal or abstract sense, is dependent in large measure upon our sense of hearing [*see* LANGUAGE, *article on* SPEECH PATHOLOGY; PERCEPTION, *article on* SPEECH PERCEPTION].

The study of the auditory system is carried on by a variety of disciplines, including psychology, physics, engineering, mathematics, anatomy, physiology, and chemistry. This article deals primarily with work in psychology, although it will be necessary to refer to other areas for a more complete understanding of certain phenomena. The peripheral hearing mechanism is reviewed from the standpoint of anatomy, hydromechanical action, and electrical activity. The basic subjective correlates of auditory stimuli are discussed, together with current research and theory. In all cases, we are concerned with the normal rather than pathological auditory system.

The peripheral hearing mechanism. When one speaks of the ear, the image that first comes to mind is the flap of cartilaginous tissue, or the *pinna*, fixed to either side of the head. The presumed function of the pinna is to direct sound energy into the ear canal, or *external auditory meatus*. In some animals, such as the cat, the pinna may be directionally oriented independently of the head. For all practical purposes, however, man does not possess this ability. It has been shown that because of the particular shape of man's pinnae, sound arriving at the head is modified differentially depending on its direction of arrival. This may well provide a cue for the localization of a sound source in space.

The external meatus and the eardrum. The external meatus is a tortuous canal about one inch in length, closed at the inner end by the eardrum, or *tympanic membrane*. The meatus forms a passageway through which sound energy may be transmitted to the inner reaches of the ear. The meatus has the general shape of a tube closed at one end; it tends to resonate at a frequency of about 3,000 cycles per second. Because of this resonance the pressure of sound waves at the eardrum, for frequencies in this vicinity, is twenty times greater than that at the pinna. The meatus, therefore, serves as a selective amplification device, and, interestingly enough, it is primarily in this frequency range that our hearing is most sensitive.

The middle ear. The eardrum marks the boundary between the outer and middle ear. At this point variations in sound pressure are changed into mechanical motion, and it is a function of the middle ear to transmit this mechanical motion to the inner ear, where it may excite the auditory nerve. This transmission is affected by three small bones, the *auditory ossicles*, which form a bridge across the middle ear. The ossicles are named for their shapes: the *malleus* (hammer), which is attached to the eardrum; the *incus* (anvil), which is fixed to the malleus; and the *stapes* (stirrup), which articulates with the incus and at the same time fits into an oval opening of the inner ear. The ossicles not only provide simple transmission of vibratory energy but in doing so actually furnish a desirable increase in pressure. The ossicles are held in place by ligaments and may be acted upon by two small muscles, the *tensor tympani* and the *stapedius*. The function of these muscles is not clear, but it has been suggested that their contraction, together with changes in mode of ossicular motion, serves at high levels of stimulation to reduce the effective input to the inner ear.

The inner ear. The "foot plate" of the stapes marks the end of the middle ear and the beginning of the inner ear. The inner ear actually consists of two portions that, although anatomically related, serve essentially independent functions. Here we are concerned only with the *cochlea*, which contains the sensory end organs of hearing. The cochlea, spiral in shape, is encased in bone and contains three nearly parallel, fluid-filled ducts running longitudinally. The middle of the three ducts has as its bottom a rather stiff membrane known as the *basilar membrane*. On this membrane is the *organ of Corti*, within which are the *hair cells*, or the sensory receptors for hearing. The hairs of the hair cells extend a short distance up into a gelatinous plate known as the *tectorial membrane*. When the basilar membrane is displaced transversely, the hairs are moved to the side in a shearing motion and the hair cells are stimulated.

Displacement of the basilar membrane is brought

about by fluid movement induced by the pistonlike action of the stapes in the oval window. Since fluid is essentially noncompressible, its displacement is possible because of the existence of a second opening between the cochlea and the middle ear, the *round window*. When the stapes moves inward, a bulge is produced in the basilar membrane and the round window membrane moves outward. The bulge or local displacement of the basilar membrane is not stationary but moves down the membrane away from the windows. If the movement of the stapes is periodic, such as in response to a pure tone, then the basilar membrane is displaced alternately up and down. Thus, when a pure tone is presented to the ear, a wave travels continuously down the basilar membrane. The amplitude of this wave is not uniform but achieves a maximum value at a particular point along the membrane determined by the stimulus frequency. High frequencies yield maxima near the stapes; lower frequencies produce maxima progressively farther down the membrane.

Electrical potentials.   Many of the mechanical events just described have an electrical counterpart. The *cochlear microphonic*, an electrical potential derived from the cochlea, reflects the displacement of the basilar membrane. The *endocochlear potential* represents static direct current voltages within various portions of the cochlea, whereas the *summating potential* is a slowly changing direct current voltage that occurs in response to a high-intensity stimulus. Also observable is the *action potential*, which is generated by the auditory neurons in the vicinity of the cochlea. Neural potentials reflecting the activity of the hair cells are transmitted by the eighth cranial nerve to the central nervous system.

Psychoacoustics.   Although it is true that one of the principal functions of man's auditory system is the perception of speech, it does not necessarily follow that the exclusive use of speech stimuli is the best way to gain knowledge of our sense of hearing. In the study of hearing, the use of simple stimuli predominates and the common stimulus is the sine wave, or pure tone.

Traditionally, psychophysics has investigated problems in (1) detection of stimuli, (2) detection of differences between stimuli, and (3) relations among stimuli. Psychoacoustics has followed a similar pattern.

Threshold effects.   It has been shown that a number of factors are influential in determining the minimum magnitude (often called intensity or amplitude) of an auditory signal that can be detected. Specifically, absolute thresholds are a function primarily of the frequency and duration of the signal. Under optimum conditions, sound magnitudes so faint as to approach the random movement of air molecules, known as Brownian movement, may be heard; the displacement of the basilar membrane in these cases is a thousand times less than the diameter of a hydrogen atom. Masked thresholds, those obtained in the simultaneous presence of a signal and other stimuli that mask its effect, depend on the frequency and relative magnitude of each stimulus.

In addition, previous auditory stimulation will affect subsequent absolute thresholds. Generally the effect is to lower auditory sensitivity, although in some instances sensitivity may be enhanced. Pertinent factors here include the magnitude, frequency, and duration of the "fatiguing" stimulus as well as the interval between the presentation of the fatiguing and test stimuli.

Differential thresholds.   There are as many studies dealing with the detection of differences between two stimuli as there are ways in which stimuli may be varied. Only a few examples, therefore, will be cited here. With pure tones thresholds for hearing frequency differences become greater as frequency is increased, and smaller as magnitude is increased. Differences as small as one part in a thousand are detectable. Differential thresholds for magnitude depend upon the same parameters, but in a more complex way.

Noise stimuli, those sound waves lacking a periodic structure, may be varied with respect to magnitude, bandwidth, and center frequency, but differential thresholds with noise are generally predictable from the pure tone data.

Signal detection theory.   Recently, there has come into psychophysics, principally by way of psychoacoustics, a new way of thinking about detection data. This new approach makes use of signal detection theory and offers some novel ideas. First, it offers a way to measure sensory aspects of detection independently of decision processes. That is, under ordinary circumstances, the overt response to the signal depends not only upon the functioning of the receptor but on the utility of the response alternatives. If it is extremely important that a signal be detected, under ordinary circumstances a subject is more likely to give a positive response regardless of the activity of the receptor.

Second, it rejects the notion of a threshold; that is, a threshold in the sense that a mechanism exists which is triggered if some critical stimulus level is exceeded. One basis for such rejection is clear from the previous paragraph.

The theory of signal detectability substitutes for the concept of a threshold, the view that detection of a stimulus is a problem in the testing of statistical hypotheses. For example, the testing situation can be so structured that two stimulus conditions exist: the signal is present and the signal is absent. Clearly, there are four alternatives: (1) the listener can accept the hypothesis that the signal was present when, in fact, it was; (2) he can reject this hypothesis under the same conditions; (3) he can accept the hypothesis that the signal was absent when, in fact, it was; (4) he can reject this hypothesis. By making certain assumptions about the characteristics of the stimulus and proceeding under the ideal condition that the observer makes use of all information in the signal, the probabilities associated with these alternatives may be mapped out. It has been shown that an actual observer behaves as if he were performing in this fashion, and his performance may therefore be compared to that ideally obtainable.

Suprathreshold phenomena. With signals that are easily audible, it is generally conceded that there are three primary perceptual dimensions to hearing: pitch, loudness, and quality. Considerable effort has been expended in searching for the stimulus correlates and physiological mechanisms associated with these dimensions.

Pitch and theories of hearing. With a simple pure tone, pitch is usually associated with the frequency of vibration of the stimulus. High frequencies tend to give rise to high pitches. Historically, there have been two general types of theories of hearing: "place" theories and "volley" theories (often called frequency theories).

The most commonly suggested mechanism of pitch is based on a place hypothesis, which holds that the pertinent cue for pitch is the particular *locus of activity* within the nervous system. It seems likely that stimulation of specific neurons or groups of neurons is related to the displacement patterns of the basilar membrane. The chief alternative to the place hypothesis is the volley or rate of neural discharge hypothesis, which holds that the *rate* or *frequency* with which neural discharge occurs within the auditory nerve is the determinant of pitch; the higher the frequency, the higher the pitch. The frequency of neural discharge, in turn, is synchronous with the stimulus frequency.

Any results in which pitch is influenced by any parameter other than frequency is not in accord with the neural discharge hypothesis. Such results include changes in pitch brought about by differences in the magnitude of the stimulus, by masking, fatigue, or auditory pathology. On the other hand, the place hypothesis cannot readily explain how a pitch corresponding to a particular frequency is perceived, when, in fact, little or no energy exists in the stimulus at that frequency. Such a situation exists for several pitch phenomena: the residue, periodicity pitch, time separation pitch, and Huggins' effect.

Loudness. Loudness is related to the magnitude of the stimulus, but not exclusively so. Frequency and duration of the stimulus are secondary factors in determining loudness. The loudness of a stimulus depends upon prior acoustic stimulation in somewhat the same manner that absolute threshold does. Generally, loudness decreases following adaptation, and the pertinent parameters are the same as those that influence threshold shifts.

Quality. Quality, or timbre, is a complex perceptual quantity that appears to be associated with the harmonic structure of the sound wave. The greater the number of audible harmonics, the richer or fuller the sound will appear. The converse also appears to be true. Relatively little work has been done in this area.

Scaling and harmonics. Psychophysical scaling, or the assessment of the relation between the magnitude of the stimulus and the magnitude of the sensation, has been of interest for many years. New methods, whose chief virtues are simplicity and relative freedom from bias, have recently stimulated additional research. Auditory dimensions that have been studied include loudness, pitch, duration, volume, density, and noxiousness.

The principal finding is that in nearly all cases the relation between stimulus and sensation is a power function.

Nonlinear effects. In simple systems in which response magnitude is a nonlinear function of stimulus input, harmonics are generated when the system input is in the form of a simple sinusoid. When the input is two sinusoids, or pure tones, then in addition to harmonics, components exist whose frequency is equal to the sum and the difference of the input frequencies. Such effects are seen when the auditory system is driven at moderate and high intensities. That is, additional tones called aural harmonics and sum and difference tones are perceived corresponding to the predicted frequencies. This seems to indicate that the auditory system behaves in a nonlinear fashion over the upper part of its dynamic range.

Binaural hearing. Under most conditions, stimuli arising from a single sound source are represented somewhat differently at each of the two ears. The auditory system makes use of these subtle differences in such a fashion that we are able to localize the sound in space. The binaural system is especially sensitive to small temporal disparities in the two inputs, being capable of discriminating differences as small as 0.000008 second. Intensity differences at the two ears also play a role in localization.

Although localization effects are the most dramatic event in binaural hearing, other interesting binaural phenomena occur. For example, less energy is required for threshold if both ears, rather than just one ear, are stimulated. Similarly, the same loudness may be achieved binaurally with less energy than it could be monaurally.

Our sense of hearing provides us with information relative to vibratory or acoustic events. This information relates to the magnitude, frequency, duration, complexity, and spatial locus of the event. The peripheral auditory system is an elegantly designed hydromechanical structure. The sensory cells themselves and complexities of their enervation are of considerable importance, but are less well understood. In total, hearing is an extremely versatile sensory process with exquisite sensitivity.

ARNOLD M. SMALL, JR.

[*Other relevant material may be found in* ATTENTION; NERVOUS SYSTEM; PSYCHOPHYSICS; SENSES; *and in the biography of* HELMHOLTZ.]

BIBLIOGRAPHY

CONFERENCE ON THE NEURAL MECHANISMS OF THE AUDITORY AND VESTIBULAR SYSTEMS, BETHESDA, MD., *1959* 1960 *Neural Mechanisms of the Auditory and Vestibular Systems.* Springfield, Ill.: Thomas. → The first 16 chapters deal with the auditory system.

GELDARD, FRANK A. 1953 *The Human Senses.* New York: Wiley.

HARVARD UNIVERSITY, PSYCHO-ACOUSTIC LABORATORY 1955 *Bibliography on Hearing.* Cambridge, Mass.: Harvard Univ. Press. → Contains more than ten thousand titles.

HELMHOLTZ, HERMANN L. F. VON (1862) 1954 *On the Sensations of Tone as a Physiological Basis for the Theory of Music.* New York: Dover. → First published as *Die Lehre von den Tonempfindungen als physiologische Grundlage für die Theorie der Musik.* A classic which in many ways is as important today as when it was written.

JERGER, JAMES (editor) 1963 *Modern Developments in Audiology.* New York: Academic Press. → Especially valuable for its readable review of signal detection theory and its coverage of the effect of acoustic stimulation on subsequent auditory perception.

VON BÉKÉSY, GEORG (1928–1958) 1960 *Experiments in Hearing.* New York: McGraw-Hill. → A compilation of Georg Von Békésy's writings on cochlear mechanics, psychoacoustics, and the ear's conductive processes.

WEVER, ERNEST G. 1949 *Theory of Hearing.* New York: Wiley. → A review of theories of hearing with a special attempt to show the cogency of a volley theory.

WEVER, ERNEST G.; and LAWRENCE, MERLE 1954 *Physiological Acoustics.* Princeton Univ. Press. → Emphasis on the mechanics of the middle ear.

HECKSCHER, ELI

Eli F. Heckscher (1879–1952) was from the beginning of his academic studies at the University of Uppsala (Sweden) both an economist and a historian. A distinctive feature of his life work was his insistence on the importance of both economic theory and statistical evidence to economic history. He first stated this position in his dissertation *Till belysning af järnvägarnas betydelse för Sveriges ekonomiska utveckling* (1907; "The Contribution of the Railroads to Swedish Economic Growth") and later expressed it in the acknowledgment of his debts to Alfred Marshall and William Cunningham, one a theorist and the other a historian.

In 1909 Heckscher became the first professor of economics and statistics at the new business school in Stockholm, and twenty years later a personal chair was created for him as the head of the Stockholm Institute for Economic History.

Heckscher's passionate involvement with the central issues of Swedish economic and social policy throughout the first half of the twentieth century produced a steady flow of pamphlets and articles, and even an incomplete bibliography contains 1,148 items (Ekonomisk-historiska Institutet, Stockholm 1950). As a publicist he was independent of political parties and spoke from a position of laissez-faire liberalism. He considered state intervention proper to few areas other than education and basic social legislation, although he did advocate strong government measures to maintain competition. He was orthodox in monetary and fiscal matters; he championed the restoration of the gold standard in the 1920s and objected to deficit finance in the 1930s.

The application of economics to problems of policy and history was more congenial to Heckscher than the development of pure theory. His most important theoretical contribution, an article entitled "The Effect of Foreign Trade on the Distribution of Income" (1919), was, in fact, provoked by Knut Wicksell's review of a collection of his essays on Swedish economic policy. In this article Heckscher stressed the role of factor endowments in giving rise to comparative advantage. His purpose was to establish that free trade, possibly combined with a policy of redistributive taxation, was preferable to protection, which would give rise to economic loss for the country as a whole. Elaborated by Bertil Ohlin, the argument came to be known as the Heckscher–Ohlin theorem about the tendency, on certain assumptions, for the prices of factors of production to move toward equality as the result of trade in commodities.

In his teaching, articles, and essays, Heckscher roamed the entire span of Western economic history, but he made his main scholarly contributions in two specific fields. His active concern with public affairs led him first to the historical study of economic policy. His *Continental System* (1918), written during World War I concurrently with a study of war economics, remains the classic interpretation of Napoleonic policy, although he has been charged with dismissing too lightly the potential danger to the English economy. It was, however, as the author of the monumental study of *Mercantilism* (1931) that Heckscher secured a lasting international reputation. Conceived as a study of the intellectual history of European economic policy between the Middle Ages and the coming of laissez-faire, this extensive analysis of the objectives and the rationale of mercantilism united strands of earlier appraisals. Like Schmoller and Cunningham, Heckscher regarded the pursuit of power and national unification as the mainspring of mercantilist policy; like Adam Smith he found protectionism and erroneous monetary conceptions to be central and objectionable features of the "mercantile system" of commercial policy.

In spite of his exposure of the intellectual crudeness of mercantilist doctrine and despite his own distrust of regulatory policy, the doctrine emerged in Heckscher's treatment as a comprehensive view of economic life rather than a system of random fallacies. Indeed, since he believed that the concept of "mercantilism" explains the general characteristics of European history at that time, he stressed the uniformity rather than the diversity of national economic policies. Later criticism and controversy arose from Heckscher's emphasis on economic ideas, i.e., his refusal to explain economic policy in terms of particular conditions and interests, which he regarded as of secondary importance compared to the prevailing *conception* of economic facts and relationships.

Heckscher's second field of major achievement was his pathbreaking economic history of Sweden. His magnum opus on *Sveriges ekonomiska historia från Gustav Vasa* (1935–1949) was to remain unfinished; but his shorter history of Swedish economic growth (1941a) constitutes the first survey of its kind. The backwardness of the medieval Swedish economy relative to the European continental countries and the lateness and rapidity of Swedish industrialization were the problems that Heckscher attacked, with a rare attention to both details and the grand design. Although his humanism and erudition led him into every branch of historical inquiry, his scholarly credo stressed the importance of quantifiable evidence. The relatively rich material on Swedish demographic conditions since the early eighteenth century provided him with especially valuable material, but he also studied every aspect of the economy by his creative statistical use of archival sources.

Heckscher's view of Swedish economic history has on several points been revised by later research. (See the appendices to the second Swedish edition of *Svenskt arbete och liv* 1941b.) This does not detract from its significance as a point of departure for any interpretation of the growth of the Swedish economy. Some of Heckscher's statistical analyses —for instance, his studies of the role and prevalence of "natural economy" in fiscal administration and of the structure of Swedish foreign trade in the sixteenth century, and his Malthusian analysis of Swedish population movements in the eighteenth century—have, of course, been modified or replaced. However, such revisions are in the spirit of Heckscher's own achievement and are therefore a tribute to it rather than a rejection.

GÖRAN OHLIN

[*Directly related are the entries* ECONOMIC THOUGHT; *article on* MERCANTILIST THOUGHT; INTERNATIONAL TRADE; *and the biographies of* CUNNINGHAM; MARSHALL; SMITH, ADAM.]

WORKS BY HECKSCHER

1907 *Till belysning af järnvägarnas betydelse för Sveriges ekonomiska utveckling.* Stockholm: Centraltryckeriet.

(1918) 1922 *The Continental System: An Economic Interpretation.* Edited by Harald Westergaard. Oxford: Clarendon Press; New York: Milford. → First published in Swedish.

(1919) 1949 The Effect of Foreign Trade on the Distribution of Income. Pages 272–300 in American Economic Association, *Readings in the Theory of International Trade.* Philadelphia: Blakiston. → First published in Swedish.

(1929) 1953 A Plea for Theory in Economic History. Pages 421–430 in Frederic C. Lane and Jelle C. Riemersma (editors), *Enterprise and Secular Change: Readings in Economic History.* Homewood, Ill.: Irwin.

(1931) 1955 *Mercantilism.* 2 vols., rev. ed. London: Allen & Unwin; New York: Macmillan. → First published in Swedish.

1935–1949 *Sveriges ekonomiska historia från Gustav Vasa.* 4 vols. Stockholm: Bonnier. → Volumes 1–2: *Före frihetstiden.* Volumes 3–4: *Det moderna Sveriges grundläggning.*

(1941*a*) 1954 *An Economic History of Sweden.* Translated by Goran Ohlin, with a supplement by Gunnar Heckscher and a preface by Alexander Gerschenkron. Cambridge, Mass.: Harvard Univ. Press. → First published as *Svenskt arbete och liv.*

(1941*b*) 1957 *Svenskt arbete och liv från medeltiden till nutiden.* 2d ed., rev. & enl. Stockholm. Bonnier. → See especially the appendices to the 1957 edition.

SUPPLEMENTARY BIBLIOGRAPHY

COLEMAN, DONALD C. 1957 Eli Heckscher and the Idea of Mercantilism. *Scandinavian Economic History Review* 5, no. 1:3–25.

EKONOMISK-HISTORISKA INSTITUTET, STOCKHOLM 1950 *Eli F. Heckschers bibliografi: 1897–1949.* Stockholm: The Institute.

GERSCHENKRON, ALEXANDER A. 1954 Preface. In Eli F. Heckscher, *An Economic History of Sweden.* Cambridge, Mass.: Harvard Univ. Press.

HEDGING

See SPECULATION, HEDGING, AND ARBITRAGE.

HEGEL, GEORG WILHELM FRIEDRICH

Georg Wilhelm Friedrich Hegel (1770–1831), who left his deepest mark upon the philosophy of history, is commonly regarded as the representative philosopher of German idealism in the post-Kantian era. To his contemporaries, however, he appeared rather as the continuator of a mode of thought begun by Kant (1724–1804) and amplified by Fichte, Schelling, and the romantic school, which responded to certain logical and metaphysical problems originally raised by the natural sciences. Born in 1770, the year in which Kant inaugurated his professorship at Königsberg with his dissertation *De mundi sensibilis atque intelligibilis forma et principiis* ("The Form and Principles of the Sensible and Intelligible Worlds"), Hegel grew up in the relatively liberal milieu of refugee Protestantism in the south German Duchy of Württemberg. As a student in Tübingen, 1788–1793, he participated in the then widespread enthusiasm for the French Revolution. He was to spend the next seven years in Bern and Frankfurt, tutoring the children of patrician families. During these years he immersed himself in the philosophy of religion, was influenced by his reading of Spinoza, and wrote (but did not publish) some highly critical studies of Christian theology, which remained unknown for over a century. His appointment to a post at the University of Jena in 1801 set him free for systematic teaching in philosophy; and this phase of his activity was crowned by the publication of his first major work, *The Phenomenology of Mind* (1807), completed during the battle of Jena.

The upheaval that followed the triumph of Napoleon over the Prussian army gave Hegel the personal satisfaction of seeing the emperor—that "world-soul on horseback," as he described him—but it also deprived him of his teaching position. After editing a newspaper in Bamberg (Bavaria) for a year, he was appointed rector of a Gymnasium at Nuremberg, a post he held from 1808 to 1816. During these years (which also witnessed his marriage to Marie von Tucher) he completed his second great work, the *Science of Logic* (1812–1816). Appointed to a chair of philosophy at Heidelberg (1816–1818), he there published his *Encyclopedia of Philosophy* (1817), a work which carried into effect a scheme already propounded by him in 1801: that of a tripartite philosophical system embracing a logic, a philosophy of nature, and a philosophy of spirit. The last mentioned formed the basis of the *Philosophy of Right* (1821), the last major work published during his lifetime, which was written during his early years at the University of Berlin, where he taught from 1818 to 1831. By that time he had become famous, and his courses attracted students from all over Germany. The lectures he gave during those years on history, religion, aesthetics, and the history of philosophy were published after his death and helped to spread his fame to a wider public. During these last years he had become a confidant of the Prussian minister of education and something of a conservative, but he retained his theological rationalism and some of his early enthusiasm for the French Revolution and Napoleon. His death in November 1831, during a cholera epidemic, precipitated the dissolution of his school into conflicting liberal and conservative factions.

The extreme complexity of Hegel's thought, and the all-embracing character of his system, along with a certain ambiguity in his political utterances, made it possible for exponents of very different schools to lay claim to his authority; and throughout the remainder of the century his name was a battle cry for opposing parties in philosophy and politics. Contrary to a widespread misconception, Hegel was never in his lifetime associated with German nationalism; he gave guarded support to the Prussian state but remained firmly committed to the principle of equality before the law. His mature political philosophy has affinities with that of Edmund Burke, and even his notorious utterances on the subject of the Prussian monarchy and the loyalty due to its representatives maintain a balance between Hobbesian authoritarianism and conventional Toryism: they are not in the slightest degree "totalitarian" and bear only an indirect relation to the doctrines of those twentieth-century German and Italian ideologists who invoked his authority.

While the philosophy of history (notably in the form it assumed in nineteenth-century Germany) bears Hegel's mark, the impact of Hegelianism on the social sciences is more difficult to assess. Social thought in Hegel's own day was subsumed under political theory. The study of economics was still in its infancy (although Hegel had become acquainted with it during his Frankfurt years), and social theorizing in general turned upon constitutional problems. These indeed had been the subject of Hegel's first publication, in 1798, a critical study of Swiss constitutional developments. His last major work, the *Philosophy of Right*, develops a political philosophy which holds a precarious balance between rationalism and authoritarianism, somewhat in the manner of Fichte, Kant, and the Enlightenment theorists who preceded them. By the 1840s this book had furnished a target for the first major broadside directed by the youthful Marx against Hegel in his *Kritik des Hegelschen Staatsrechts* (1843). In general the theory of civil society is subsumed by Hegel under the theory of the state; the latter is viewed as the embodiment of rationality, as against the conflicts of material interests that make up the daily life of the civil society. Hegel counterposes the rational universality of the whole to the particular desires and strivings of the individuals in a manner reminiscent of Hobbes and contrary to Rousseau, for whom the "general will" springs from the fusion of individual wills. Such a fusion, and with it the notion of a social contract, is denied by Hegel on the grounds that civil society is too anarchic to generate a true consensus. The "actuality of the ethical Idea" is attained in the state, which is "absolutely rational," "mind objectified," "the actuality of concrete freedom" ([1821] 1942, pp. 155–160). Hegel differs from Hobbes in holding that the state is not to be viewed as the guarantor of civil society, but as an end in itself. It is not simply the guardian of personal freedom and property, for in that case loyalty to the state would be optional, whereas according to Hegel it is only as a member of the political realm that the individual has objective reality and an ethical life (*ibid.*, p. 156). This exaltation of the state appears to have been a fruit of Hegel's youthful enthusiasm for the classical *polis*. It led him into what even his contemporaries regarded as an extravagant glorification of the Prussian monarchy; but since it was coupled with conservative distrust of popular movements and indeed of the people, of that part of the body politic "which does not know

what it wants" (*ibid.*, para. 301), Hegel's doctrine cannot be described as totalitarian even by implication. Its nature is traditionalist rather than romantic and belongs to the eighteenth century rather than to the twentieth.

Hegel did, however, repudiate traditional natural law and—by implication—international law. His influence on European (notably German) thinking thus ran counter to the gradual acceptance of liberal doctrines throughout the nineteenth century. The Hegelian view of interstate relations, which entered the consciousness of the German educated classes by way of the Prussian bureaucracy and the educational system it controlled, is Hobbesian and subversive of much that is regarded as fundamental in Anglo–American jurisprudence. On Hegelian principles, contracts between states are not valid, since sovereignty cannot be abrogated by treaty. The test of sovereignty is war, which discloses the truth that nations are not subordinate to law but operate in a Hobbesian "state of nature." War is necessary and may even be regarded as beneficial, since it is the test of a people's willingness to maintain its freedom and independence. It also makes it possible to achieve a degree of social integration which civil society by itself cannot secure (*ibid.*, para. 324). These doctrines became part of the official credo of Bismarckian Germany and may be said to have deepened the ideological gulf between Germany and the West which was first made manifest in the war of 1914–1918. They clearly run parallel to the critique of natural law doctrine implicit in the "pure theory of law" (*reine Rechtslehre*) associated with H. Kelsen and his followers. This influential school of "legal positivism" maintains that the substantive concept of law as the embodiment of prelegal rules of a moral nature is metaphysical and irrelevant to the actual practice of lawmaking (Kelsen 1955; cf. Kelsen 1945). The displacement of the older doctrine by this positivist doctrine, which implicitly sanctions the abrogation of "so-called fundamental liberties," may be regarded as a belated triumph of Hegelianism, although outside central Europe similar ideas were developed without reference to Hegel's philosophy. So far as the U.S.S.R. is concerned, its legal theory may perhaps be described as Hegelian; but there are elements of natural law doctrine both in classical Marxism and in the Russian Populist tradition, and since the late 1950s there has been a tendency to revive them.

Hegel's ideas also reached the social sciences by a different channel: via the philosophy of history, and in particular through the growing influence of

Marxism. The relationship of Marx to Hegel is, however, more complex than appears from the popular notion that Marx merely inverted the Hegelian system by "standing it on its head," i.e., by substituting a supposed "materialist dialectic" for Hegel's idealist one. Marx took over from Hegel the conception of history as the self-creation of man and the idea (first expounded by Hegel in the *Phenomenology*) that the prime motive force of the historical process is human labor, or the practical activity of men in society. Marx did not, however, subscribe to the notion that this process can be reduced to a logical schematization, and his approach to empirical history is more in tune with French materialism than with German idealism. (This part of his work in some respects anticipates modern sociology.) He also repudiated Hegel's political doctrine. The state appears in the Marxian corpus as an arbitrary external power superimposed upon human society; and it is thus a form of "human self-alienation" [*see* ALIENATION]. Hegel's authoritarian political philosophy did have some influence on Ferdinand Lassalle (1825–1864), and through him on German socialism, but was antipathetic to Marx.

The relevance of Hegel's general philosophy to what is often called "historicism" is difficult to assess. The notion (which Whitehead restated and applied to the natural sciences) that the peculiarities of reality are only local and temporary concretions of a process stretching beyond them has been popularized by Marxian writers, but it is not held by them alone. Its conservative counterpart is the doctrine that cultures are to be regarded as "organic wholes" rather than as casual accretions of unrelated features. The Hegelian concept of dialectical change can be, and has been, reformulated as a description of processes whereby social organisms create their own environment and are in turn influenced by it. Hence it has been said that "a philosopher–scientist like Whitehead can restate Hegel's theory, not knowing that it is Hegel's" (Collingwood 1946, p. 128). Although originally intended by Hegel to account for natural processes, the idea of a "dialectical" interrelationship between man and his environment is clearly of general application, and it may be that the long-run significance of Hegel's philosophy for the social sciences will be found to lie in this kind of approach. Hegel is unquestionably the chief originator of what is sometimes called "process thought." His philosophy finds room for the efflorescence of the higher forms of culture and for the values we attach to them by postulating a series of "levels of organization," rising from the lower to the higher through historically conditioned transformations which introduce new qualitative changes. This concept has proved fertile in inducing historians and sociologists to look upon history not as a field governed by immutable "laws" but as a process in which something fresh is created at every moment.

GEORGE LICHTHEIM

[*See also* HISTORY, *article on* THE PHILOSOPHY OF HISTORY; MARXISM; POLITICAL THEORY; *and the biographies of* CROCE; DURKHEIM; GREEN; HOBBES; KANT; KELSEN; MARX; STIRNER.]

WORKS BY HEGEL

(1795–1809) 1961 *On Christianity: Early Theological Writings.* Gloucester, Mass.: Smith. → First published in 1907 as *Hegels theologische Jugendschriften*. Edited by Herman Nohl. A paperback edition was published in 1961 by Harper.

(1799–1831) 1964 *Hegel's Political Writings.* Translated by T. M. Knox, with an introductory essay by Z. A. Pelczynski. Oxford: Clarendon Press. → The first essay, "The German Constitution," was written by Hegel between 1799 and 1802 and left in manuscript until after his death.

(1807) 1961 *The Phenomenology of Mind.* 2d ed., rev. London: Allen & Unwin; New York: Macmillan. → First published as *Phänomenologie des Geistes.*

(1812–1816) 1951 *Hegel's Science of Logic.* 2 vols. London: Allen & Unwin; New York: Macmillan. → First published as *Wissenschaft der Logik.*

(1817) 1959 *Encyclopedia of Philosophy.* New York: Philosophical Library. → First published as *Encyklopädie der philosophischen Wissenschaften im Grundrisse.*

(1821) 1942 *The Philosophy of Right.* Oxford: Clarendon. → First published as *Grundlinien der Philosophie des Rechts.*

(1837) 1956 *The Philosophy of History.* New York: Dover. → First published as *Vorlesungen über die Philosophie der Weltgeschichte.*

Sämtliche Werke. 26 vols. Stuttgart (Germany): Frommann, 1927–1940.

SUPPLEMENTARY BIBLIOGRAPHY

COLLINGWOOD, R. G. 1946 *The Idea of History.* Oxford: Clarendon. → A paperback edition was published in 1956.

FINDLAY, JOHN N. 1958 *Hegel: A Re-examination.* London: Allen & Unwin. → A paperback edition was published in 1962 by Collier.

GURVITCH, GEORGES D. 1962 *Dialectique et sociologie.* Paris: Flammarion.

HABERMAS, JÜRGEN 1963 *Theorie und Praxis.* Neuwied (Germany): Luchterhand.

HYPPOLITE, JEAN 1955 *Études sur Marx et Hegel.* Paris: Rivière.

KELSEN, HANS (1945) 1961 *General Theory of Law and State.* New York: Russell. → First published in German.

KELSEN, HANS 1955 Foundation of Democracy. *Ethics* 66, part 2:1–101.

KRONER, RICHARD (1921–1924) 1961 *Von Kant bis Hegel.* 2d ed., 2 vols. Tübingen (Germany): Mohr.

Löwith, Karl (1941) 1964 *From Hegel to Nietzsche: The Revolution in 19th Cent. Thought.* New York: Holt. → First published in German.

Marcuse, Herbert (1941) 1955 *Reason and Revolution: Hegel and the Rise of Social Theory.* 2d ed. New York: Humanities Press. → A paperback edition was published in 1960 by Beacon.

Marx, Karl (1843) 1953 *Kritik des Hegelschen Staatsrechts.* Pages 20–149 in Karl Marx, *Die Frühschriften.* Stuttgart (Germany): Kroner.

Mure, Geoffrey R. G. (1940) 1948 *An Introduction to Hegel.* Oxford: Clarendon Press.

Stace, Walter T. (1924) 1955 *The Philosophy of Hegel: A Systematic Exposition.* New York: Dover.

HELLER, HERMANN

Hermann Heller (1891–1933), German political scientist, was born at Teschen in Austria. He taught at Kiel, Leipzig, Berlin, and Frankfurt. In 1933, he emigrated and died in Madrid in the same year.

Heller revived political theory in Germany, where it had been emptied of content by both legal positivism and political voluntarism. The central problem of order, Heller taught, is the tension between will and norm, which must not be resolved in favor of either pole. Man's nature is essentially utopian, looking toward what ought to be. What ought to be, however, cannot order human existence without the acts of a public will that in any society makes binding decisions about legal rules and assures their regular enforcement. The modern state is essentially a hierarchically organized unity of will that performs the function of deciding and enforcing positive law within a given territory. In relation to the legal system, the state is sovereign, that is, a supreme will subject to no other will. For the sake of the law, the state must in an emergency maintain itself even against the law. The sovereign will, however, can posit law only within the range of transpositive fundamental principles of law (*Rechtsgrundsätze*), which are either formal (logical) or substantive (ethical) norms.

Heller construed this higher law not as unchanging but as shaped by various historical civilizations. Political theory must explain the state in world-immanent terms but not reduce it to nature. Rather, the state is a part of human culture (defined as facts suffused with meaning). It exists in and through human activities, among which it has reality as a gestalt, a structure retaining its identity in the flow of its changing parts. The proper method of political theory is neither normative nor causal but, rather, sociological. It can never be "value-free" in Max Weber's sense, although it can free itself from bias. An explanation of the state must take into account underlying social entities, for example, historical entities of national culture (*Kultureinheiten*). Human nature, a constant in any political order, must be seen as shaped by history. Man, society, and culture are basic conditions of any state and cannot be artificially produced.

Much of Heller's work dealt with the political crisis of the West. He conceived of it as a collapse of political order stemming from the destruction of political theory by positivism. The antipolitical notion of the automatically self-regulating natural order produced modern legal positivism, which construed the concept of order without the state and apart from any concrete content. As a reaction there arose the twentieth-century cult of sheer force—or the strong man—and the notion of the intrinsic value of a command. Heller blamed this development on the bourgeoisie, which, when it was in power, disavowed its former moral convictions about the necessity of order and embraced positivist legality instead.

Heller was a leading German socialist, although not a follower of Marx, whose materialism and historical messianism he rejected. Socialism was justified, he felt, by the desirability of social homogeneity, of a community of interests and values that alone can form the basis of a democratic state. Class antagonism endangers this community, which can be restored only by including the workers in its economic and cultural benefits. No such community is possible apart from the historically grown unity of common national language, traditions, values, and ways of life. Socialism and the national community are interdependent. Heller's socialism was national although not nationalistic. He favored the unification of Europe as the only way of safeguarding national cultures in an age of superpowers.

Heller's thought was eclectic rather than derived from any one master. Although he rejected the major conclusions of Hegel, Marx, Weber, Dilthey, and Kelsen, he made use of some of the ideas and methods of each to compensate for the biases of the others. The result was not a historical dialectic but a dialectic that synthesized elements which political theorists had often separated. Man consists of both body and soul, society includes physical as well as spiritual meaning, legal order presupposes both norm and will, political theory must use not only causal but also normative analysis, and so forth. It was his ability to hold such tensions in his mind without trying to resolve them for the sake of a unified system that secured Heller's position as one of the strong voices of sanity in an age of political disorder.

GERHART NIEMEYER

[*See also* POLITICAL THEORY; POSITIVISM; STATE; *and the biographies of* AUSTIN; KELSEN.]

WORKS BY HELLER

1921   *Hegel und der nationale Machtstaatsgedanke in Deutschland: Ein Beitrag zur politischen Geistesgeschichte.* Leipzig and Berlin: Teubner.

(1925) 1931   *Sozialismus und Nation.* 2d ed. Berlin: Rowohlt.

1926a   Die Krisis der Staatslehre. *Archiv für Sozialwissenschaft und Sozialpolitik* 55:289–316.

1926b   *Die politischen Ideenkreise der Gegenwart.* Kiel (Germany): Hirt.

1927   *Die Souveränität: Ein Beitrag zur Theorie des Staats- und Völkerrechts.* Leipzig and Berlin: de Gruyter.

(1929) 1931   *Europa und der Fascismus.* 2d ed. Leipzig and Berlin: de Gruyter.

1930   *Rechtsstaat oder Diktatur?* Tübingen (Germany): Mohr.

1934a   Political Science. Volume 12, pages 207–224 in *Encyclopaedia of the Social Sciences.* New York: Macmillan.

1934b   Political Power. Volume 12, pages 300–305 in *Encyclopaedia of the Social Sciences.* New York: Macmillan.

1934c   *Staatslehre.* Leiden (Netherlands): Sijthoff.

HELMHOLTZ, HERMANN VON

From the perspective of posterity, Hermann Ludwig Ferdinand von Helmholtz (1821–1894) made his most significant contributions to the fields of sensory physiology and psychology. In particular, he laid the foundations for the experimental investigation of the sensory processes in audition and vision. His successes resulted from his unusual mathematical and mechanical abilities and from his skill in assembling, sifting, and logically interrelating large quantities of information.

Helmholtz was born in Potsdam, the eldest of five children. The atmosphere of his home, although not scientific, was intellectual. Helmholtz mentioned that he frequently listened to the philosophical discussions between his father, August, a distinguished teacher of languages and philosophy in the Gymnasium, and his colleagues. August Helmholtz was most important in guiding his son's early education. He taught him Greek and Arabic, encouraged him to study poetry, art, and music, and trained him in the writing of expository essays. Even at an early age, however, Helmholtz was attracted more to physics and mathematics than to the humanities. Speaking of his youth, Helmholtz recalled, in 1891, that while the rest of his class in the Gymnasium read Cicero and Vergil, he himself would work out optical and geometrical problems under his desk.

Helmholtz represented a scientific ideal to his contemporaries. He was a man of remarkable talents, universal interests, and indefatigable energy. He published over 200 papers and books making fundamental contributions to the fields of anatomy, medicine, physics, physiology, and psychology. He invented scientific and medical instruments. A contemplative mind led him to consider the philosophic questions raised by developments in science. A sense of social responsibility led him to deplore the gulf separating those trained in the humanities and those trained in the sciences; this gulf he sought to bridge by delivering popular lectures explaining the developments of science to laymen.

For the social sciences, Helmholtz' views on the methodology of science and the theory of knowledge are of most immediate relevance. The method of studying and interpreting biological and psychological phenomena was a crucial issue for the scientists and philosophers of the nineteenth century. Helmholtz was convinced that the same scientific method is appropriate for the analysis of vital and mental phenomena as for the analysis of physical phenomena. However, he did not advocate a reductive materialism. For him, memory and learning are facts, the laws of which can be investigated by experimental procedures, even if they cannot be reduced to known physiological processes (Koenigsberger [1902–1903] 1906, p. 305). Rather, he emphasized that the basic method of all scientific inquiry is to discover facts through systematic experimentation and to go beyond these facts to general laws by analysis and abstraction. His lecture on Goethe (see Helmholtz [1853–1870] 1962, pp. 1–21) contains an interesting presentation of his views. After acknowledging Goethe's insightful contributions on the morphology of the skull and the plant, Helmholtz brought up the matter of Goethe's obstinate animosity to Newton's analysis of color. The difference between them, Helmholtz suggested, lay in their attitudes toward the acquisition and conception of knowledge. Goethe, the artist, believed that direct confrontation with a phenomenon is sufficient to provide an understanding of it. He was "accustomed to look as it were, right into the subject, and to reproduce his intuition. . . . His success [was] proportionate to the vividness of the intuition" (*ibid.,* p. 16). Helmholtz acknowledged that intuitive insight is the source of the creative idea for both the scientist and the artist but insisted that, for the scientist, careful observation and reflection are an initial step sufficient only to suggest a hypothesis. The establishment of scientific truth depends on experimental verification. Moreover, the artist is satisfied simply to describe and hesitates to abstract. "A step into the region of abstract conceptions which must be necessarily taken if we wish to penetrate into the causes of phenomena, scares the poet away" (*ibid.*, p. 16). Goethe objected to Newton's theory of color because it substitutes quantitative measurements of the color-mixing relationships for direct naturalistic observation of colors. Helmholtz correctly described how observational intuition led Goethe badly astray when he asserted that it is absurd for white light to be the result of a fusion of colored lights. On the other hand, Goethe's appeal to experience did reveal important phenomenological facts (the distinction between warm and cold colors, the existence of a psychologically unique red, yellow, green, and blue, and the coupling of the colors red and green and yellow and blue) whose potential physiological significance Helmholtz apparently overlooked. Helmholtz' intellectual attitude was that of the nineteenth-century physicist: it was the source of his acute and penetrating analyses, although it occasionally led him to miss the point.

Work in physics. At the age of 16, Helmholtz announced to his father that he wanted to study physics. His father, however, could not support the cost of an academic course and enrolled him in the Friedrich Wilhelm Medical Institute in Berlin. This institute gave free instruction on the condition that those enrolled later spend some years as surgeons in the Prussian army. In Berlin, Helmholtz came under the influence of Johannes Müller, professor of physiology at the University of Berlin, and Müller's influence is apparent throughout his physiological research. In 1842, at 21, he received his doctorate for a thesis in anatomy confirming Müller's conjecture that the nerve fibers originate in the ganglion cells. Yet Helmholtz was to join Du Bois-Reymond, Brücke, and Virchow, all Müller's students, in a pact to abolish Müller's notion that within the living organism there exists a separate vital force distinct from chemical and physical forces. These men realized that physiology needed to be securely established as a branch of chemistry and physics. Liebig had placed the question of vitalism within the domain of experimental science by transforming the philosophic question into the experimental problem of whether or not the mechanical energy and the heat produced by

an organism result entirely from its own metabolism. Helmholtz realized that this problem is closely connected to the law of the conservation of energy and turned his attention to that law. Joule had already established the equivalence between mechanical work and heat, and Helmholtz sought to extend the principle of the conservation of energy to physiology. He began by investigating the relation between muscular activity and heat. For this purpose he devised the myograph, a device which records the twitching of a muscle, a thermal galvanometer sensitive to temperature changes of $.001°$ centigrade, and a means by which a muscle can be stimulated by electric shocks of short duration. He found that a single muscle contraction can give rise to an increase in temperature of from $.001°$ centigrade to $.005°$ centigrade, showing that the chemical processes in muscle contraction produce heat. Helmholtz then turned to determining the equivalence between the heat produced by an animal and the caloric value of the food taken in. He calculated the amounts of heat given off in various ways and the efficiency of an animal's metabolism and concluded that the total heat given off corresponds to the heat generated by the oxidation of the food consumed. Unknown to Helmholtz, the extension of the law of the conservation of energy from inanimate to animate phenomena had already been suggested by Robert Mayer. Helmholtz next set himself the task of showing the universal application of the conservation of energy principle by theoretically deriving it from more fundamental physical principles. He showed that if all matter consists of particles, and if these interact according to forces acting along the lines joining the particles, and if all forms of energy depend upon the motion and position of the particles, then the conservation of energy must hold. These results he announced in a lecture he gave (at the age of 26) to the Physical Society of Berlin on July 23, 1847.

Work in physiology. Helmholtz' scientific ability now became generally recognized, and with the aid of Alexander von Humboldt, president of the Academy of Sciences in Berlin, he was released from further military service. After a year as a lecturer in anatomy at the Academy of Arts in Berlin, Helmholtz became professor of physiology at Königsberg. He remained in Königsberg from 1849 to 1855.

Nerve impulses. The first important physiological problem to concern Helmholtz after his move to Königsberg was the rate of nerve transmission. Müller had stated that the speed of the nerve impulse is comparable to the speed of light and unmeasurable. Du Bois-Reymond's theory of the polarization of molecules in nervous tissue suggested to Helmholtz that the nerve impulse, although electrical in nature, is not simply an electric current. Helmholtz stimulated nerves near and far from a muscle and measured the time it takes for the muscle to contract. The difference in time divided by the distance between the two points showed that the rate of the neural impulse in the motor nerve of a frog is about 27 meters per second. Helmholtz also devised the reaction time experiment to measure the speed of nerve transmission in humans. An electric shock was given to a point on the skin and the observer was directed to move his hand as quickly as he could. Although variable, the results showed that the rate of transmission of the impulse is between 50 and 60 meters per second. The novelty of these studies provoked opposition from physiologists. In fact, both Müller and von Humboldt refused at first to believe the results and it was only through the continued arguments of Du Bois-Reymond that they were convinced of the correctness of Helmholtz' work.

Optics and visual perception. In 1851 Helmholtz invented the ophthalmoscope, the most celebrated of his inventions. He suggested that the blackness of the pupil results from the fact that the head of an observer looking at the eye of a person blocks the rays of light that would illuminate the retina. The ophthalmoscope is a device that illuminates the retina through the pupil, rendering it visible. In its modern form, constructed by H. Reute in 1852 (M'Kendrick 1899, p. 78), the ophthalmoscope enables one to look at the retina through a small opening in a reflecting plate. In 1852 Helmholtz invented the ophthalmometer, a device for measuring the radii of curvature of the anterior and posterior surfaces of the cornea and the lens. At this time Helmholtz turned to the problem of accommodation. A Dutch physiologist, Cramer, had shown that accommodation consists in an increasing curvature of the lens when the eye changes from a far point to a near point. Helmholtz, unacquainted with the work of Cramer, arrived independently at the same conclusion. Helmholtz' new contribution to the theory of accommodation was his hypothesis about the way in which the curvature of the lens is altered. Using his anatomical knowledge, he suggested that when the fibers of the ciliary muscles contract, the tension of the lens capsule is reduced, and the lens's own elasticity causes the anterior surface of the lens to bulge forward.

From 1851 to 1856 Helmholtz was mainly engaged in research in physiological optics. The result of this work, together with a survey of the germane literature, is presented in his monumental three-volume handbook on physiological optics (Helmholtz 1867). The handbook demonstrates Helmholtz' mastery of the physical, mathematical, and physiological problems involved in vision and visual perception. The worth of the handbook is attested to by its continued scientific pertinence a hundred years later. Volume 1 describes the anatomy and optical properties of the eye. Volume 2 deals with problems of visual sensation. In 1852 Helmholtz undertook to test the laws of color mixture. Newton had failed to distinguish between the mixture of colored lights and of colored pigments. Thomas Young, in his famous paper of 1801, had suggested (in analogy to the mixture of pigments) that red, yellow, and blue are the three primaries from which all colors can be derived by suitable mixtures. But to his surprise, Helmholtz discovered that the combination of yellow and blue lights produces not green, as was supposed, but white. Helmholtz was the first to differentiate clearly between the addition of lights, which produces a color because of the superposition of excitations of different wave lengths stimulating the eye, and the addition of pigments, which produces a color that is a result of the wave lengths reflected by both pigments. Yellow and blue pigments when mixed give green because neither pigment absorbs green light. After clearing up the confusion between light mixtures and pigment mixtures, Helmholtz proceeded to develop a comprehensive theory of color vision. He based his theory on the extension of Müller's law of specific nervous energies to the sense organs and on the assumption that the facts of color matching accurately mirror underlying physiological processes. Just as the difference between the sensations of light and sound depends on the kind of nerve fibers stimulated, so the sensation of color depends on the kind of nerve fiber excited in the eye. The data on color mixture, moreover, indicate that all hues except the most saturated can be obtained by suitable combinations of three primaries: red, green, and violet. Helmholtz made explicit that part of Young's theory which dealt with nerve activity, by postulating that the nerve fibers must respond in varying degrees to all wave lengths. Hue depends on the relative frequencies of the impulses set up in the three types of fibers, brightness on the total excitation of the fibers, and saturation on the amount of white produced by fusion. He also extended the theory to account for color blindness, negative afterimages, and successive contrasts. The Young–Helmholtz theory of color vision is still widely accepted, although certain facts of color blindness and color thresholds pose difficulties for it.

Volume 3 deals with problems of space perception and object perception. Central to Helmholtz' theory of space and object perception is his doctrine of unconscious inference. Helmholtz argued in his inaugural lecture at Königsberg in 1852 that the law of specific nerve energies implies that sensations serve only as the signs of external objects. That is, sensations tell us as much about the real nature of external phenomena as the name of a man tells us about the man. Accordingly, perceptual experience involves a construction on the part of the observer. A problem of great concern for Helmholtz was to determine what in the nature of perceptual experience is innate and what is derived from experience. He asserted that what in the perceptual image can be modified by experience must itself be considered a product of experience ([1867] 1924–1925, vol. 3, p. 13). Applying this criterion, he concluded that the only innate properties are the intensity and the quality of a sensation. Thus, conscious experience consists initially of a mass of sight, sound, taste, and smell sensations, each differentiated only with respect to quality and intensity. How does one come to experience coherent objects ordered in space and time? The answer lies in the distinction between sensation and perception. Perception involves a two-stage process: (1) sensation and (2) unconscious inference. Sensations are the immediate products of stimulating sense organs and associated neural systems. Unconscious inference is a central reasoning-like process which utilizes the information provided by sensation to infer the properties of external objects and events. Thus, perception is not simply an aggregate of sensations. Perception goes beyond the sensations provided by the receptor organs and entails a judgment about the environment. The unconscious judgments in perception are automatic and irresistible. The knowledge gained in perception, based on sensations and the memory of sensations, is a knowledge of acquaintance (*kennen*). In contrast, the conscious judgments in thought are flexible and deliberate, and the knowledge gained, based on concepts, is a knowledge of awareness (*wissen*). For Helmholtz these differences, however, are only superficial. Both the unconscious judgments in perception and the conscious judgments in thought involve the same mental operations and have the same logical status ([1853–1870] 1962, pp. 178–181). The view that perception inherently involves a judgment has played an important role in psychological theory.

Acoustics. In 1855 Helmholtz was appointed professor of anatomy and physiology at Bonn, where he remained until 1858, when he became professor of physiology at Heidelberg. While still immersed in the preparation of his *Physiological Optics* Helmholtz had decided to write a similar work on acoustics. In 1856 he reported the discovery of summation tones. These tones, whose frequencies are the sum of two input frequencies, are generated because of the nonlinear response of structures in the external ear. In 1857 Helmholtz formulated his well-known theory of vowel quality. Differences between vowel sounds arise because the mouth cavity when shaped for different vowels serves as an adjustable resonator which differentially strengthens the harmonic components of the fundamental voice tone. Papers quickly followed on sound production, tone quality, harmony, and the musical scales. In 1862 Helmholtz' classic work, *On the Sensations of Tone*, appeared. This book brings together his many experimental and historical studies in acoustics and music theory. The aim of the work is to provide connecting links between the fields of physical acoustics, physiological acoustics, and music. The most famous of Helmholtz' contributions to audition is his theory of pitch perception. Applying the law of specific nerve energies to the ear, Helmholtz suggested that there exist specific fibers in the inner ear that respond by resonance to the different frequencies. Each fiber excites its own nerve so that the neural impulses transmitted to the brain correspond to the component frequencies of a sound wave. Thus, the resonance theory of pitch provides an explanation of Ohm's law which asserts that it is possible to hear the simple harmonic components into which a complex sound may be analyzed. Although such a simple resonance theory is no longer tenable, experiments have demonstrated that a locus of maximum vibration which changes with sound frequency does occur on the basilar membrane in the way Helmholtz suggested. Helmholtz extended his theory of pitch to provide an account of timbre, dissonance, consonance, and melody. Timbre depends upon the relative intensities of the harmonics present, dissonance on the beats generated when two frequencies affect overlapping segments of the basilar membrane, consonance and melody on the identity of harmonics produced by simultaneous tones or a succession of tones. Helmholtz' views on the musical relationships have been much discussed and criticized but are still relevant today.

Aesthetics. Since his early student days, Helmholtz had been concerned with problems of aesthetic significance. Although science and art differ in their methods, he believed them to be intimately connected because both seek to acquaint us with reality (Koenigsberger [1902–1903] 1906, p. 172). While the scientist expresses truth by means of abstract concepts, the artist expresses truth by means of images. Since art has a cognitive function, the articulation of meanings that cannot be conveyed by words, it must conform to the laws governing human intelligence. The function of the scientist is not, however, to instruct the artist. This is essentially impossible since neither the artist nor the observer is consciously aware of the laws on whose fulfillment beauty depends ([1862] 1954, p. 366). Rather, the function of the scientist is to provide the artist with the information which may aid him in his artistic invention. The artist can succeed in his work only when he is aware of the subtle relations present within a phenomenon and of their effects upon an observer (Koenigsberger [1902–1903] 1906, p. 106). In a lecture on anatomy and sculpture delivered in 1848, Helmholtz considered the methods and benefits of teaching anatomy to artists (*ibid.*, pp. 51–57), and in a lecture on optics and painting, Helmholtz ([1853–1870] 1962, pp. 250–286) discussed the complex problems faced by the painter who seeks to produce an accurate representation of the forms, sizes, distances, and illuminations of objects in a scene. To cope successfully with these problems, the artist must translate rather than copy nature, taking into careful consideration the operation of the sensory system. For Helmholtz the relations between art and science are particularly clear and striking in music. Musical composition depends more on the immediate sensations than is the case with the other arts, like sculpture, in which the object represented has a much greater importance ([1862] 1954, p. 3). Part 3 of the *Sensations of Tone* deals with the agreeableness of different chords, the formation of scales, and the elementary rules of musical composition. Helmholtz cautioned that the history of music shows that the construction of scales and musical composition is by no means determined by the properties of the ear but depends on artistic invention and aesthetic principles which change with time (*ibid.*, p. 235).

Epistemology. Helmholtz' interest in sensory physiology naturally led him to the problems of epistemology. Following the English tradition, he appealed to psychology for an understanding of epistemology. He argued that a knowledge of the sensory mechanisms is necessary for determining the status of objects. In a letter to Carl Ludwig, in 1855, Helmholtz wrote, "I believe that philosophy will only be reinstated when it turns with zeal and energy to the investigation of epistemological processes and of scientific methods. . . . Most essential of all in this critical investigation is the exact knowledge of the processes of sense-perception" (Koenigsberger [1902–1903] 1906, p. 139). Kant had established 12 categories of a priori concepts. These represented the operation of inherent characteristics of the mind, which condition experience and do not arise from experience. Examples of a priori concepts are space and time, the geometrical axioms, and the law of causality. Helmholtz first questioned the correctness of Kant's position concerning the inherent nature of space. He concluded that the experience of an ordered space is not innate but is derived from movements of the eye and body ([1853–1870] 1962, p. 156). Helmholtz' empirical theory of perception led him to an empirical theory of cognition. In 1866 he turned to the epistemology of mathematics. He undertook to show that the geometric axioms are also the products of experience and that they depend upon the notion of congruence, which is based upon mechanical movements and is itself acquired through experience. Thus, the axioms of geometry are not innate but have their origin in an individual's experience with objects and with the space in which he lives. To show that the axioms of Euclidean geometry are not examples of a priori intuitions, Helmholtz independently developed Riemannian non-Euclidean geometry. In 1888 Helmholtz tried to show that the axioms of arithmetic can also be derived from experience. He accepted only the law of causality as a priori and transcendental and asserted that all thought presupposes the law of causation, which is therefore not derivable from experience (Koenigsberger [1902–1903] 1906, p. 142). For example, the law of causation underlies the unconscious inference by which we pass from sensation to perception, since this process assumes the existence of external objects that cause our sensations. Whether the mechanism of unconscious inference is itself innate or is derived from experience, Helmholtz left as an open question (*ibid.*, p. 110).

In 1871 Helmholtz became professor of physics in Berlin. He spent the last years of his life primarily in physical research. He was concerned with experiments in electrodynamics, physical optics, meteorological physics, and the physical significance of the principle of least action. Helmholtz also encouraged Heinrich Hertz, perhaps his most famous student, who verified Maxwell's theory by producing electromagnetic waves. In 1887 the Physical–Technical Institute was founded in Berlin, with Helmholtz as director. In 1893 he visited the Chicago World's Columbian Exposition and toured the United States and Canada. While returning home, he fell down the ship's stairs and suffered a concussion and severe loss of blood. He recovered, but those who saw him reported that he tired easily and found it difficult to work. In July 1894 he suffered a cerebral hemorrhage and died in September of that year.

JACOB BECK

[*See also* HEARING; PERCEPTION, *article on* DEPTH PERCEPTION; PSYCHOPHYSICS; VISION, *especially the article on* COLOR VISION AND COLOR BLINDNESS.]

WORKS BY HELMHOLTZ

(1853–1870) 1962 *Popular Scientific Lectures.* New York: Dover. → First published in German.

(1862) 1954 *On the Sensations of Tone as a Physiological Basis for the Theory of Music.* New York: Dover. → First published as *Die Lehre von den Tonempfindungen als physiologische Grundlage für die Theorie der Musik.*

(1867) 1924–1925 *Helmholtz's Treatise on Physiological Optics.* Edited by James P. C. Southall. 3 vols. New York: The Optical Society of America. → Translated from the third German edition.

SUPPLEMENTARY BIBLIOGRAPHY

BORING, EDWIN G. (1929) 1950 *A History of Experimental Psychology.* 2d ed. New York: Appleton.

KOENIGSBERGER, LEO (1902–1903) 1906 *Hermann von Helmholtz.* Oxford: Clarendon. → First published in German.

M'KENDRICK, JOHN G. 1899 *Hermann Ludwig Ferdinand von Helmholtz.* New York: Longmans.

HENDERSON, L. J.

Lawrence Joseph Henderson (1878–1942), American chemist and sociologist, was born in Lynn, Massachusetts. His father was a ship chandler of Salem, with business interests in the French islands of St. Pierre and Miquelon; and it was there, of all strange places, that Henderson acquired his life-long devotion to the civilization of France.

His regular academic career lay in the field of biological chemistry. He graduated from Harvard College in 1898 and from Harvard Medical School in 1902. There followed two years' work in chemical research at the University of Strasbourg. Henderson then returned to Harvard, rising through the academic ranks to become professor of chemistry. In the light of his later interests in social science, it is significant that his early research was devoted to the mechanisms of neutrality regulation in the animal organism and that in 1908 he achieved a precise mathematical formulation of the acid–base equilibrium. There was much interest in research on problems of physiological equilibrium at Harvard at the time. Henderson had some influence on, and was always interested in, the work on homeostasis carried out by his colleague Walter B. Cannon, professor of physiology (Cannon 1932). Henderson's later research turned to similiar problems in the chemistry of blood. Here his investigations were of fundamental importance, leading, through the work of his students, to such applications as the use of blood plasma to save the lives of the wounded in World War II. He was one of the most original and distinguished biological chemists of his time.

Henderson also kept up an irregular interest in the wider problems suggested by his chemical research, problems in the philosophy of science and the methodology of inquiry into systems of variables in complex relations of mutual dependence. For years he took part in seminars in the philosophy department at Harvard, and in 1911 he offered the first course given there on the history of science. He wrote two general books on the relationships between the organism and its environment and between determinism and teleology: *The Fitness of the Environment* (1913) and *The Order of Nature* (1917). His general question might be put thus: How do nature's efficient causes cooperate with her final ones?

Henderson's interest in sociology came late in his life but was a natural development of what had gone before. About 1926 William M. Wheeler of Harvard, whose study of insect societies led him to read widely in human sociology, suggested to Henderson that he read Pareto's *Sociologie générale* (see Pareto 1916). At once Henderson became an enthusiast. He felt that Pareto's treatment of scientific methodology and equilibrium phenomena was excellent and that Pareto's substantive views on human society made explicit conclusions he himself had arrived at more intuitively. In 1932–1933 Henderson conducted a seminar on Pareto's sociology—the first such seminar in an English-speaking country. One of the products of the seminar was *An Introduction to Pareto* (1934) by Homans and Curtis, the first book on the subject in English. Henderson published his own book, *Pareto's General Sociology* (1935), emphasizing such matters as equilibrium, the social system, the mutual dependence of variables, and the problems of induction and abstraction. Through his book, his seminar, and a later course he offered called "Concrete Sociology," he made these ideas part of the thinking of a number of sociologists present at Harvard at the time, including Talcott Parsons and Robert K. Merton. Henderson was also the first chairman of the Society of Fellows at Harvard, established in 1933, whose members, besides receiving scholarships to study whatever they wished, dined together once a week. Among the early members were C. M. Arensberg, B. F. Skinner, W. F. Whyte, and G. C. Homans. They soon became familiar, through their conversations, with Henderson's views.

One final connection of Henderson with social science should be mentioned. In 1926 he became director of the Fatigue Laboratory of the Harvard Graduate School of Business Administration. In the adjoining office was Elton Mayo, then beginning his researches in the Western Electric Company. The plan was that Henderson should study the physiology of work, while Mayo studied its psychology. Henderson had no direct influence on the conduct of the Western Electric researches, but his ideas became part of the intellectual atmosphere in which the research team—Mayo, T. N. Whitehead, and F. J. Roethlisberger—did their work. Through the Harvard Business School Henderson also came into contact with Chester I. Barnard and encouraged him to write *The Functions of the Executive* (1938). In 1939 Henderson was appointed chairman of the Committee on Work in Industry of the National Research Council, and under his leadership the committee surveyed and evaluated much research in this field, both physiological and sociological (National Research Council 1941).

Henderson never carried out any empirical research in social science, nor did he become widely read in its literature, but his ideas about methodology in the broadest sense of the word were deeply influential at a time and place of more than ordinary significance in the development of sociology.

GEORGE CASPAR HOMANS

[*Other relevant material may be found in the biographies of* BARNARD; CANNON; MAYO; PARETO.]

WORKS BY HENDERSON

1913   *The Fitness of the Environment: An Inquiry Into the Biological Significance of the Properties of Matter.* New York: Macmillan. → A paperback edition was published in 1958 by Beacon.

1917   *The Order of Nature: An Essay.* Cambridge, Mass.: Harvard Univ. Press.

1935   *Pareto's General Sociology: A Physiologist's Interpretation.* Cambridge, Mass.: Harvard Univ. Press.

SUPPLEMENTARY BIBLIOGRAPHY

BARNARD, CHESTER I. (1938) 1962   *The Functions of the Executive.* Cambridge, Mass.: Harvard Univ. Press.

CANNON, WALTER B. (1932) 1963   *The Wisdom of the Body.* Rev. & enl. ed. New York: Norton.

CANNON, WALTER B. 1945   Biographical Memoir of Lawrence Joseph Henderson: 1878–1942. Volume 23, pages 31–58 in National Academy of Sciences, *Biographical Memoirs.* Washington: The Academy.

HOMANS, GEORGE C. 1962   *Sentiments and Activities: Essays in Social Science.* New York: Free Press. → See especially pages 1–49, "Autobiographical Introduction."

HOMANS, GEORGE C.; and BAILEY, ORVILLE T. (1948) 1959   The Society of Fellows, Harvard University, 1933–1947. Pages 1–37 in Clarence C. Brinton (editor), *The Society of Fellows.* Cambridge, Mass.: The Society.

HOMANS, GEORGE C.; and CURTIS, CHARLES P. JR. 1934   *An Introduction to Pareto: His Sociology.* New York: Knopf.

NATIONAL RESEARCH COUNCIL, COMMITTEE ON WORK IN INDUSTRY 1941   *Fatigue of Workers: Its Relation to Industrial Production.* New York: Reinhold.

PARETO, VILFREDO (1916) 1963   *The Mind and Society: A Treatise on General Sociology.* 4 vols. New York: Dover. → First published as *Trattato di sociologia generale* and in 1917 as *Sociologie générale.* Volume 1: *Non-logical Conduct.* Volume 2: *Theory of Residues.* Volume 3: *Theory of Derivations.* Volume 4: *The General Form of Society.*

HERDING

See PASTORALISM.

HEREDITY AND ENVIRONMENT

See ENVIRONMENTALISM; EUGENICS; GENETICS, *especially the article on* GENETICS AND BEHAVIOR; IMPRINTING; INSTINCT.

HERING, EWALD

Ewald Hering (1834–1918) was a sense physiologist who played an important role as a pioneer in the new experimental physiological psychology that got under way as a separate discipline in the 1860s. The founder of this new branch of psychology was, it is said, Wilhelm Wundt, who was Hering's contemporary. Hering's fame was based specifically upon his contributions to the understanding of the phenomena of vision—the psychophysiology both of visual space perception and of color vision. Hering was a nativist; that is to say, he believed that the spatial ordering of points on the retina and the skin is innate, that it is not learned, as the empiricists, led by Hermann von Helmholtz, believed. Hering is, however, best known to posterity for his theory of color vision, a theory that for many years remained the alternative to Helmholtz' theory. Moreover, he designed many beautiful pieces of apparatus to illustrate crucial points in his theories and is more responsible than anyone else for this new psychology's being dubbed "brass-instrument psychology." Indeed, he participated in the new experimental movement in many ways; he was, for instance, one of the first editors of the *Zeitschrift für Psychologie*, the first independent journal of experimental psychology in Germany.

Hering was born in Altgersdorf, a small town south of Berlin. At the age of 19 he went to Leipzig to study medicine; there he was influenced by E. H. Weber, the physiologist who established the law that bears his name, and G. T. Fechner, the founder of psychophysics. The dean of physiologists, Johannes Müller, at Berlin, influenced him from afar, and Hering would have liked to work under him but never did. In 1860 Hering began practicing as a physician and also writing in the field of physiology. He had published the five parts of his treatise on space perception by 1864, a year before Helmholtz published the third volume of a handbook on psychophysiological optics—the part that included what Helmholtz had to say about the perception of space. Thus began a long-continued opposition between Hering and Helmholtz—Hering, the nativist; Helmholtz, the empiricist. Hering was following Johannes Müller, whose thought had been influenced by Kant. Helmholtz, an empiricist, was holding to the tradition of Hermann Lotze and found himself supported by Wundt. Hering's views were taken up presently by Carl Stumpf and later, after the turn of the century, by the gestalt psychologists, who have readily acknowledged their debt to him. There was a bitter and indecorous quarrel between Hering and Helmholtz about the true shape of the visual horopter, the locus of points perceived as single by the two eyes.

Hering's publication on space perception was enough to effect a call to Vienna to succeed the distinguished physiologist Carl Ludwig, who himself went to Leipzig. Five years later Hering was invited to Prague to succeed J. E. Purkinje, another well-known physiologist. At Prague his attention turned to the problems of color. His volume of 1878 presented his theory of color vision and again brought him into conflict with Helmholtz, who held to the three-element theory originally suggested by Thomas Young. Hering argued for three different color substances in the retina, each one capable of two reversible, opposite reactions, giving respec-

tively the colors red or green, yellow or blue, and white or black, and their combinations. Both types of theory were still alive eighty years later. Hering also, in 1879, suggested a theory of the temperature sense that was similar to his color theory, cold and warmth being elicited by a pair of antagonistic reactions in the thermal sense organ.

After 25 years at Prague, Hering was called to Leipzig in 1895, to succeed for a second time the now very famous Ludwig. Here he undertook his more mature work on visual sensation, which came out in four fasciculi from 1905 to 1920, the last published posthumously, for Hering died at Leipzig in 1918, at the close of World War I.

At the turn of the century every undergraduate student of psychology was taught Hering's and Helmholtz' theories of vision. For a while Helmholtz' conception seemed to prevail over Hering's, but subsequently Hering's view of antagonistic biological processes gained plausibility as a result of new research, and both types of theory continued to receive consideration at a sophisticated level. Hering, the nativist, also influenced gestalt psychology and the scientific movement toward phenomenology and existentialism. With respect to phenomenology, Hering himself showed the influence of two of his great predecessors in visual theory—Goethe and Purkinje.

EDWIN G. BORING

[*Directly related are the entries* VISION, *especially the article on* COLOR VISION AND COLOR BLINDNESS; PERCEPTION, *article on* DEPTH PERCEPTION. *Other relevant material may be found in the biographies of* HELMHOLTZ; MÜLLER, JOHANNES; STUMPF.]

WORKS BY HERING

1861–1864   *Beiträge zur Physiologie.* 5 parts. Leipzig: Engelmann.

1868   *Die Lehre vom binocularen Sehen.* Leipzig: Engelmann.

(1872–1875) 1964   *Outlines of a Theory of the Light Sense.* Cambridge, Mass.: Harvard Univ. Press. → First published in German. Contains a biographical note and historical discussion by L. M. Hurvich and D. Jameson, translators.

1879   *Der Raumsinn und die Bewegungen des Auges.* Part 1, pages 343–601 in Ludimar Hermann (editor), *Handbuch der Physiologie.* Volume 3: Physiologie der Sinnesorgane. Leipzig: Vogel. → For an English translation of this essay, see "Spatial Sense and Movements of the Eye" in the *Manual of Physiology of the Sense Organs,* published by the American Academy of Optometry in 1942.

1880   *Der Temperatursinn.* Part 2, pages 415–450 in Ludimar Hermann (editor), *Handbuch der Physiologie.* Volume 3: Physiologie der Sinnesorgane. Leipzig: Vogel.

1931   *Wissenschaftliche Abhandlungen.* 2 vols. Edited by M. Gildemeister. Leipzig: Thieme. → Contains a portrait and a complete bibliography.

WORKS ABOUT HERING

BORING, EDWIN G. (1929) 1950 *A History of Experimental Psychology.* 2d ed. New York: Appleton. → See pages 351–356 and 379.

GARTEN, SIEGFRIED 1918 Ewald Hering zum Gedächtnis. *Pfluger's Archiv für die gesamte Physiologie des Menschen und der Tiere* 172:501–522.

HERSKOVITS, MELVILLE JEAN

Melville Jean Herskovits (1895–1963) was an American anthropologist. Two points are central in understanding his conception of anthropology: first, he was a humanist concerned with the total range of cultural behavior and, second, he believed that the inductive method is the only valid methodology for anthropology. In both he revealed the pervasive influence of Franz Boas, his teacher at Columbia University.

The most complete presentation of Herskovits' views is found in *Man and His Works* (1948), revised and abridged as *Cultural Anthropology* (1955). Culture was the inclusive concept for him, comprehending the behavioral and the ideational, the group and the individual. His humanistic orientation was apparent in his interest in the individual, whom he viewed as an active participant in the shaping of culture. As the individual was important in his view of culture, history was important in his ideas of culture change. Acculturation, reinterpretation, retention, and syncretism are concepts which he helped formulate and each has its historical dimension.

The continuity of past and present was a frequent theme of Herskovits' studies of Africa and of the Negro in the New World. It was his thesis in *The Myth of the Negro Past* (1941) that New World Negroes reveal their west African heritage in motor habits, codes of behavior, social institutions, family organization, religion, language, and art. In opposition, sociologists argued that synchronic factors adequately explain American Negro behavior and that it is unwise to link the Negro so directly to his origins in west Africa [*see the biography of* FRAZIER]. Although the book stimulated interest in Africa among some students of the New World Negro, it did not achieve general attention for almost two decades, when some of the facts about Africa became better understood.

Herskovits' approach to cultural change was theoretical as opposed to practical in its orientation. He was always critical of applied anthropology and, in this as well as in his historical approach, was at variance with much of the work of British anthropology in Africa. His views on these points were summarized in *Acculturation: The Study of Culture Contact* (1938a), which was the subject of a rejoinder by Malinowski (1939) in behalf of functionalism and administration-oriented anthropology that appeared in *Africa.*

Herskovits' opposition to applied anthropology was to a large extent based in cultural relativism. Although he in no sense originated the concept, in *Man and His Works* and in subsequent writing he became one of its most uncompromising spokesmen. He derived relativism from the enculturative experience through which standards of judgment are learned, and from this he concluded that judgmental evaluations of cultures are culture-bound. This, of course, does not abrogate comparison but implies that the bases of comparison are culturally determined and should be made explicit. He insisted that the concept of relativism had relevance to all cultural learning and called attention to the influence of culture on perception. He felt that it was important to distinguish between "absolutes," which vary from culture to culture, and "universals," which are consequences of the human condition; and he concluded, "To say that there is no absolute criterion of value or morals, or even, psychologically, of time or space, does not mean that such criteria, in differing *forms*, do not comprise universals in human culture" (1948, p. 76). Cultural relativism led him to reject the term "primitive," though he had used it extensively, as a pejorative, to indicate a lack of unity of custom, tradition, belief, or institution. He subsequently used "nonliterate," a term which he felt was more neutral and descriptive.

Consistent with his humanistic interests, Herskovits was interested in religion, music, graphic and plastic arts, and folklore, particularly in African cultures. *Dahomean Narrative: A Cross-cultural Analysis* (1958), written with Frances S. Herskovits, who collaborated with him throughout his career, is a detailed group of tales assembled during their first African field trip. It is an important work because it carefully relates the narratives to their cultural matrix and abstracts from them items of comparative theoretical interest. Herskovits was interested in the ways culture influences the arts, as well as the ways the arts validate culture. He used both religious and aesthetic data to document African retentions among New World Negroes.

If Herskovits was often humanistic in his orientation he was not narrowly so, and he did not neglect the social aspects of culture. One of his earliest interests was in the field of economics, and *The Economic Life of Primitive Peoples* (1940) was the first general text in that field. It stressed the importance of the cultural context of economic behavior and the limitations of a conception of economics based exclusively upon experience in Western society. However, he adopted the conventional, "formal" definition of economics, the application of scarce means to given ends, and, in the main, tried to follow the categories of academic economics in ordering his data. This compromise is most apparent in the first chapter of the revised edition, entitled *Economic Anthropology* (1940). While Polanyi and his followers (Polanyi et al. 1957) proposed a more sociological, "substantive" definition of economics, Herskovits, typically, objected that their approach seems to deny the role of individual choice and concluded that "we must not reject Economic Man only to substitute Society as an exclusive formula for understanding economic behavior and as a base-point for analysis" ([1940] 1952, p. 8). Polanyi was even more skeptical than Herskovits about the application of traditional economics to nonliterate behavior. His followers have suggested that the characteristics of markets, money, and surpluses in industrial society are so peculiar that the terms are scarcely applicable in nonliterate societies. While Herskovits saw the difference between the economies of nonliterate and industrial society as being one of degree, followers of Polanyi, like George Dalton, see them as differing in kind. It is worth noting that the field of economic anthropology has developed along the general directions of Herskovits' pioneering efforts. [*See* ECONOMIC ANTHROPOLOGY; EXCHANGE AND DISPLAY; TRADE AND MARKETS; *and the biography of* POLANYI.]

Africa was an early interest of Herskovits; his doctoral thesis was on the cattle complex of east Africa. His culture area mapping (1924; see also Bascom & Herskovits 1959) has been used extensively. Many early American Africanists were trained in the program of African studies that he founded and directed at Northwestern University. As interest in Africa expanded, the African Studies Association was formed with Herskovits as its first president. One of his last books, *The Human Factor in Changing Africa* (1962), is a summary of his encyclopedic knowledge of the continent, his interest in culture change, and his humanistic orientation.

JAMES H. VAUGHAN, JR.

[*For the historical context of Herskovits' work, see the biography of* BOAS; *for discussion of the subsequent development of Herskovits' ideas, see* FOLKLORE; HISTORIOGRAPHY, *article on* AFRICAN HISTORIOGRAPHY; PRIMITIVE ART.]

WORKS BY HERSKOVITS

1924   A Preliminary Consideration of the Culture Areas of Africa. *American Anthropologist* New Series 26: 50–64.

1928   *The American Negro: A Study in Racial Crossing.* New York: Knopf.

(1937) 1964   *Life in a Haitian Valley.* New York: Octagon Books.

(1938*a*) 1958   *Acculturation: The Study of Culture Contact.* Gloucester, Mass.: Smith.

1938*b*   *Dahomey: An Ancient West African Kingdom.* 2 vols. New York: Augustin.

(1940) 1952   *Economic Anthropology: A Study in Comparative Economics.* 2d ed., rev. & enl. New York: Knopf. → First published as *The Economic Life of Primitive Peoples.* A paperback edition was published in 1965 by Norton.

1941   *The Myth of the Negro Past.* New York: Harper. → A paperback edition was published in 1958 by Beacon.

1948   *Man and His Works: The Science of Cultural Anthropology.* New York: Knopf.

1955   *Cultural Anthropology.* New York: Knopf. → An abridged revision of *Man and His Works,* 1948.

1958   HERSKOVITS, MELVILLE J.; and HERSKOVITS, FRANCES S. *Dahomean Narrative: A Cross-cultural Analysis.* Northwestern University African Studies, No. 1. Evanston, Ill.: Northwestern Univ. Press.

(1959) 1962   BASCOM, WILLIAM R.; and HERSKOVITS, MELVILLE J. (editors) *Continuity and Change in African Cultures.* Univ. of Chicago Press. → See especially page 37 in the 1959 edition.

1962   *The Human Factor in Changing Africa.* New York: Knopf.

SUPPLEMENTARY BIBLIOGRAPHY

MALINOWSKI, BRONISLAW   1939   The Present State of Studies in Culture Contact: Some Comments on an American Approach. *Africa* 12:27–47.

MERRIAM, ALAN P.   1964   Melville Jean Herskovits, 1895–1963. *American Anthropologist* New Series 66:83–109. → Includes a bibliography of 479 items by Herskovits, compiled by Anne Moneypenny and Barrie Thorne.

POLANYI, KARL; ARENSBERG, CONRAD M.; and PEARSON, HARRY W. (editors)   1957   *Trade and Market in the Early Empires: Economics in History and Theory.* Glencoe, Ill.: Free Press.

HETTNER, ALFRED

Alfred Hettner (1859–1941) was an important leader in the development of German geography and was particularly influential in defining for geographers generally the scope and methods of their subject.

He was born in Dresden and grew up there in a large family with intellectual and artistic interests. He became interested in geography while he was in secondary school and declared his intention of specializing in that field as soon as he began his university training. He studied at four different German universities and traveled and did field work for four years in South America. After teaching for ten years in Leipzig, he was appointed in 1897 to the newly established chair of geography at Tübingen and then, less than two years later, to the new chair at Heidelberg, which he held until his retirement in 1928.

Although his training and his early work were principally in geomorphology, Hettner, like Ritter and Ratzel, was more interested in human geography. Moreover, he became increasingly involved in establishing a methodology for geography, an enterprise he had initially regarded as auxiliary to work on other problems but which ultimately became a primary aspect of his life's work (1927, p. iii).

The opportunity to present his methodological position came in 1895, when at the age of 36 he founded the *Geographische Zeitschrift*. The new journal was to be devoted to "the advancement of genuine geographical learning," and Hettner opened his introductory article with the questions, "What is geography? What does it seek to accomplish and what is it able to accomplish?" (1895, p. 1). During the following two decades he presented detailed answers to these questions in a series of essays that came to be regarded as classics in geographic methodology (1927). During his career he also published numerous substantive studies in different aspects of systematic geography, which elaborate or illustrate his methodological principles (see his four-volume work in systematic physical geography, *Vergleichende Länderkunde*, 1933–1935; and his three-volume *Allgemeine Geographie des Menschen*, 1947–1957). Important as these studies were, Hettner's principal influence was exerted through the *Geographische Zeitschrift*, over which he maintained close control for forty years (Schmitthenner 1941, p. 453; "Drei autobiographische Skizzen," pp. 22–26).

The concepts of geography that Hettner promoted were not derived by logical deduction from any a priori philosophical position; they were developed empirically from the study of the history of the development of the field since antiquity (1927, pp. 110 ff.). Among geographers he was influenced particularly by Humboldt, Ritter, Kirchhoff, Marthe, and Richthofen ("Drei autobiographische Skizzen"; Hartshorne 1939). His distinctive function was to justify the conclusions drawn from the historical development of geography in terms of the methodology and philosophy of science. His general philosophical viewpoint was based, he said, neither on Kant nor on Comte but on Lange's *Geschichte des Materialismus;* and his scientific methodology, on Wundt's *Logik* (Hettner 1926, p. 306). But in explaining the relation of geography to other fields, Hettner formulated a scheme of the division of the sciences which, as he later learned, had been presented a century earlier by Kant and by Humboldt, also, apparently, independently (Hartshorne 1958).

In examining the historical development of geography, Hettner found that major misunderstandings had arisen through the failure to identify correctly the object of study. Geography is not, as its name suggests, the over-all science of the earth but the study of the earth shell, more commonly called earth surface, as it varies in the character or content of its areal parts. The basic approach is chorological: to describe and interpret the varied character of the earth surface. This areal variation is formed by many diverse elements, which vary from place to place, interrelated in any particular place and interconnected between different places.

If geography is basically chorological, Hettner reasoned, it is not dualistic; rather, in any inhabited area the physical and human features are so intricately interlaced as to form a single subject for study. Geography is, therefore, not to be divided between the natural and the social sciences or defined as the study of relations between natural and human features of the earth surface. It is a unitary discipline, and the reality it studies is composed of heterogeneous but interrelated elements.

Two theoretically different approaches are usefully combined in the study of areas: the approach of regional geography, which analyzes the full complex of features in individual areas, and the approach of general (or systematic, or topical) geography, which compares areas in terms of particular kinds of features. While Hettner regarded the former, the analysis of individual regions, as the "crowning" product of geographic study, he considered comparative systematic studies no less essential. Geography, then, is both nomothetic and idiographic (1927, pp. 217–218, 221–224, 398–404).

Hettner's work helped to produce a marked degree of agreement among German geographers in the early decades of the twentieth century; such agreement does not exist in many other countries. Outside of German-speaking countries Hettner's ideas were not widely known until they were expounded at length in English (Hartshorne 1939). They have since become familiar and influential in many countries. In establishing his basic methodological structure, Hettner did not attempt to build something new; rather, he believed that he "had clearly expressed and methodologically established what was actually present in the development" of geography (1934*b*, p. 382). This may well be the reason why the influence of his work has been so strong and can be expected to endure.

RICHARD HARTSHORNE

[*For the historical context of Hettner's work, see the biographies of* HUMBOLDT; RITTER; WUNDT. *For discussion of the subsequent development of his ideas, see* GEOGRAPHY, *especially the article on* SOCIAL GEOGRAPHY.]

WORKS BY HETTNER

1895 Geographische Forschung und Bildung. *Geographische Zeitschrift* 1:1–19.

1926 [Book Review of] Otto Graf, *Vom Begriff der Geographie. Geographische Zeitschrift* 32:304–306.

1927 *Die Geographie: Ihre Geschichte, ihr Wesen und ihre Methoden.* Breslau: Hirt.

1933–1935 *Vergleichende Länderkunde.* 4 vols. Leipzig: Teubner.

1934*a* Der Begriff der Ganzheit in der Geographie. *Geographische Zeitschrift* 40:141–144.

1934*b* Neue Angriffe auf die heutige Geographie. *Geographische Zeitschrift* 40:341–343, 380–383.

1947–1957 *Allgemeine Geographie des Menschen.* 3 vols. Edited by Heinrich Schmitthenner and E. Plewe. Stuttgart: Kohlhammer. → Published posthumously.

Drei autobiographische Skizzen. Pages 41–80 in *Alfred Hettner, 6.8.1859: Gedenkschrift zum 100. Geburtstag.* Heidelberg (Germany): Keyser, 1960.

SUPPLEMENTARY BIBLIOGRAPHY

Alfred Hettner, 6.8.1859: Gedenkschrift zum 100. Geburtstag. 1960 Heidelberg (Germany): Keyser. → A bibliography of Hettner's works compiled by E. Plewe appears on pages 81–88.

HARTSHORNE, RICHARD (1939) 1964 *The Nature of Geography: A Critical Survey of Current Thought in the Light of the Past.* Lancaster, Pa.: Association of American Geographers.

HARTSHORNE, RICHARD 1958 The Concept of Geography as a Science of Space, From Kant and Humboldt to Hettner. Association of American Geographers, *Annals* 48:97–108.

PFEIFER, GOTTFRIED 1959 Alfred Hettner zum 100. Geburtstag. *Kosmos* 55:351–353.

SCHMITTHENNER, HEINRICH 1941 Alfred Hettner. *Geographische Zeitschrift* 47:441–468.

HILDEBRAND, BRUNO

Bruno Hildebrand (1812–1878), economist and one of the founders of the German historical school, was born in Naumburg (Thuringia), the son of a civil servant. He entered the University of Leipzig as a student of theology but soon shifted to history. He very early joined the liberal–nationalist student movement, and since this affiliation made him the object of police attention, he fled to Breslau to escape harassment; however, he was imprisoned there before being allowed to continue his studies. In 1836 the University of Breslau awarded him his doctorate and shortly afterward the rights of *Dozent*. In 1839 he was promoted to acting professor of history. But Hildebrand's restless and intensely political nature found the scope of historical study too confining; increasingly his interests and his lectures focused on political philosophy and economics.

The most productive decade of Hildebrand's academic career began with his appointment, in 1841, to the chair of *Staatswissenschaften* (government) at the University of Marburg. Here, once again, he clashed with the authorities, especially when as university rector he championed the liberties of students and staff; in 1845 he was relieved of his administrative position, and in 1846 he was charged with *lèse-majesté* and dismissed from his teaching post. Hildebrand was eventually acquitted, but he was not reinstated in his professorship until the 1848 revolution had swept a liberal government into office.

Hildebrand was elected deputy of the Frankfurt National Assembly, where he distinguished himself as an uncompromising protagonist of constitutional government and as an indefatigable member of the parliamentary commission on economic and social affairs. With the triumph of absolutism, however, his cause was doomed. The Diet was abolished, and Hildebrand, as one of the outspoken liberals, was charged with high treason and forced to flee into Switzerland where, in 1851, he was appointed to a chair at the University of Zurich. Hildebrand spent five years in Zurich, active not only as a professor but also as a company director promoting and building a railway. He then moved to the University of Bern and helped establish the first Swiss statistical office at Bern.

In 1861 Hildebrand accepted an invitation extended by the University of Jena and returned to his native Thuringia. In 1863 he started the *Jahrbücher für Nationalökonomie und Statistik*. In the following year he was instrumental in founding the statistical office of the Thuringian states. As its first director, he planned the work of the new bureau in such a way as to link it closely with the research and teaching activities of the university program in economics.

Although Hildebrand was neither a fluent nor an exciting lecturer, good students found him an inspiring teacher, and some of the better economists of the German historical school were products of his "Jena seminar." Because of this impact, Hildebrand's position in the history of German economic thought cannot be assessed in terms of his writings alone.

One of Hildebrand's earliest works, *Die National-ökonomie der Gegenwart und Zukunft* (1848), is also his most important; it is clearly the work of a youthful *homme engagé*. The first chapter is devoted to an evaluation of Adam Smith. Acknowledging the greatness of the Scotsman's contribution, Hildebrand proceeded to criticize the philosophy of natural law and the instinct of self-interest underlying Smith's reasoning. Hildebrand denied the universality that Smith claimed for his theory and asserted that Smith's basic assumptions were ahistorical; inasmuch as they derived from the English scene, they were irrelevant to an understanding of the problems in other eras and other lands. Above all, Hildebrand felt that the premises did not fit the peculiarities of German conditions.

Hildebrand admitted that his view of classical economics had been influenced by Adam Müller. Yet he added that he could accept neither the feudal and medieval notions of the German romantic school nor its reactionary conclusions. Even Friedrich List, though allowed some credit for his insights and for his contributions to the important public debate on international trade policy, was given short shrift by Hildebrand.

Significantly, Hildebrand devoted the largest part of *Die Nationalökonomie der Gegenwart und Zukunft* to a review of socialist literature, in particular to an examination of the recently published *Condition of the Working Class in England* by the then unknown Friedrich Engels. He saw the socialist writers as "up-to-date," with a historical perspective and above all a focus on the predicament of the proletariat in industrial society. At the same time, Hildebrand rejected all socialist values, warning that the socialist society would be the "grave of individualism and civilization," and his stage theory of economic progress was surely intended as a polemic against Marxist socialism. According to Arthur Sommer, Hildebrand's vision of society as advancing from barter to monetary exchange before reaching its highest synthesis in a credit economy was meant as an anticommunist manifesto. In this scheme the fully developed credit economy would give the propertyless wage earner access to capital and thereby resolve one of modern society's most pressing problems without recourse to socialism.

In the last 15 years of his life, Hildebrand turned away from theoretical issues and concentrated on directing statistical studies bearing upon important social problems. He thus anticipated the program of the Verein für Sozialpolitik, which he joined as a charter member in 1873. (He was the only one of the founders of the German historical school to do so.)

Hildebrand failed to develop a coherent system of economics. The source of his failure lies (see Eisermann 1956) in his petty bourgeois parochialism, with all its fears and prejudices regarding the rapidly industrializing world. This was the cause of his fuzzy thinking and of his pathetic efforts to reconcile basically irreconcilable points of view. Fighting, as it were, a two-front battle against the feudal aristocracy on the one hand and the emerging proletariat on the other—while simultaneously concerned about the precariousness of its own economic status—the German middle class was doomed to political impotence. Its intellectual leaders, including Hildebrand, reacted to their conflict by abandoning clarification of the social process in favor of politically innocuous empirical research and social engineering.

HERBERT KISCH

[For the historical context of Hildebrand's work, see ECONOMIC THOUGHT, *article on* THE HISTORICAL SCHOOL; *and the biographies of* MÜLLER, ADAM HEINRICH; SMITH, ADAM.]

WORKS BY HILDEBRAND

(1848) 1922 *Die Nationalökonomie der Gegenwart und Zukunft, und andere gesammelte Schriften.* Jena: Fischer.

1853 *Statistische Mitteilungen über die volkswirtschaftlichen Zustände Kurhessens, nach amtlichen Quellen.* Berlin: Guttentag.

1863 Die gegenwärtige Aufgabe der Wissenschaft der Nationalökonomie. *Jahrbücher für Nationalökonomie und Statistik* 1: 5–25; 137–146.

1864 Natural-, Geld- und Kreditwirtschaft. *Jahrbücher für Nationalökonomie und Statistik* 2: 1–24.

1866a Die wissenschaftliche Aufgabe der Statistik. *Jahrbücher für Nationalökonomie und Statistik* 6: 1–11.

1866b Zur Geschichte der deutschen Wollenindustrie. *Jahrbücher für Nationalökonomie und Statistik* 6: 186–254; 7: 81–153.

1866–1878 THURINGIAN STATES, STATISTISCHES BÜREAU, *Statistik Thüringens: Mitteilungen des statistichen Büreaus vereinigter thüringischer Staaten.* 2 vols. Edited by Bruno Hildebrand. Jena (Germany): Frommann. → Volume 1: *Das Land; Die Bevölkerung,* 1866–1867. Volume 2: *Agrarstatistik,* 1871–1878.

1869 Vergangenheit und Gegenwart der deutschen Leinenindustrie. *Jahrbücher für Nationalökonomie und Statistik* 13: 215–251.

1872 Die Verdienste der Universität Jena um die Fortbildung und das Studium der Staatswissenschaften. *Jahrbücher für Nationalökonomie und Statistik* 18: 1–11.

SUPPLEMENTARY BIBLIOGRAPHY

CONRAD, JOHANNES 1878 Bruno Hildebrand. *Jahrbücher für Nationalökonomie und Statistik* 30: i–xvi.

EISERMANN, GOTTFRIED 1956 *Die Grundlagen des Historismus in der deutschen Nationalökonomie.* Stuttgart (Germany): Enke. → See especially pages 158–188 on Bruno Hildebrand.

FRANZ, GOTTFRIED 1928 *Studien über Bruno Hildebrand.* Kirchhain (Germany): Schroeder.

GRÜNBERG, CARL 1925 Bruno Hildebrand über den kommunistichen Arbeiterbildungsverein in London: Zugleich ein Beitrag zu Hildebrands Biographie. *Archiv für die Geschichte des Sozialismus und der Arbeiterbewegung* 11:445–459.

HILDEBRAND 1880 Volume 12, pages 399–402 in *Allgemeine deutsche Biographie.* Leipzig: Duncker & Humblot.

HOSELITZ, BERT F. 1960 Theories of Stages of Economic Growth. Pages 193–238 in Bert F. Hoselitz et al., *Theories of Economic Growth.* Glencoe, Ill.: Free Press.

KALVERAM, GERTRUD 1933 *Die Theorien von den Wirtschaftsstufen.* Leipzig: Buske. → See especially pages 91–97 on "Die Wirtschaftsstufentheorie von Bruno Hildebrand."

SOMMER, ARTHUR 1948 Über Inhalt, Rahmen und Sinn älterer Stufentheorien (List und Hildebrand). Pages 535–565 in *Synopsis: Festgabe für Alfred Weber, 30.VII.1868–30.VII.1948.* Heidelberg (Germany): Schneider.

HINDUISM

Hindus are found living in many parts of the world, but the vast majority of them (approximately 376.5 million) are concentrated in the Indo–Pakistan subcontinent. Of this population, approximately 366.5 million are in India and ten million in Pakistan. Hindus are also found in the Himalayan states of Nepal (the only contemporary Hindu state), Sikkim, and Bhutan; in Burma, Ceylon, Malaysia, and other countries of southeast Asia; and in east and south Africa, the Caribbean islands, Guyana (British Guiana), Fiji, and the United Kingdom.

The study of Hinduism

The doctrines of Hinduism, unlike those of Christianity and Islam, are not embodied in any one sacred book, nor does Hinduism have a single historical founder. There are not one but innumerable gods, and it is not essential to believe in the existence of God in order to be a Hindu. Hinduism is rich in contradictions, there being no particular beliefs or institutions that are common to all Hindus. Every belief considered basic to Hinduism has been rejected by one Hindu group or another.

A major problem in the study of Hinduism, as in that of any world religion, is to understand the interaction between the theological and popular levels. There is a vast body of sacred literature in Hinduism, including the Vedas, Brāhmaṇas, Upaniṣads, Vedāṅgas, Dharmaśāstras, Nibandhas, Purāṇas, Itihāsas, Darsanas, Āgamas, and Tantras. These texts contain elaborate and abstract philosophies and theologies, mythologies, manuals for the performance of sacrifices and other sacred rites in temples and homes, and codes of conduct for daily life. Generally speaking, until recently Indian and foreign scholars concentrated on the literature, while the description of actual institutions, rites, and beliefs was left to missionaries, travelers, and administrators. It is only in the last twenty years that bibliocentricism has been replaced by a more rounded view of Hinduism and the relation between the texts and actual behavior.

The social scientist's concern for understanding any religion in its social context is likely to be satisfied more for the modern than for the earlier periods of history. Source materials are almost entirely lacking for the study of the history of popular Hinduism; even in the study of the history of literary Hinduism, data are not available for the reconstruction of the social context. For example, the date, provenance, and authorship of texts are not certain. And finally, the student of contemporary Hinduism is faced with the problem that the systematic reconstruction of Indian history, which began with the coming of the British, has brought to light material that has since become an active part of the Hindu religion. In the reinterpretation of Hinduism that has been occurring since the nineteenth century, the philosophical and literary levels have been emphasized, to the neglect of actual institutions, rites, and beliefs.

Hinduism and the social order

Hinduism, lacking a centralized church, is so inextricably entangled with Hindu society that it is very difficult to say where one ends and the other begins. This is particularly true of caste, which according to creation beliefs expressed in the Ṛg Veda has a divine origin. The four *varṇas*, or caste orders, emerged from the limbs of primeval man, who is a victim in the divine sacrifice that produced the cosmos. The *brāhmans* emerged from his mouth, *kṣatriyas* from his arms, the *vaiśyas* from his thighs, and the *śūdras* from his feet. (The untouchables are not mentioned in the hymn.) There are in reality not four but innumerable castes, called *jātis*, each of which claims to belong to one of the four *varṇas*. When the Hindu sacred or legal texts discuss caste, it is mostly *varṇa* that they have in view and very rarely *jāti*.

Certain ideas regarding pollution and purity are cardinal in Hinduism, although there are differences among the various castes in the strictness with which rules deriving from these ideas are adhered to and the degree of elaboration found in behavior governed by them. Intercaste relations are generally defined by ideas of pollution. Normally, each caste is endogamous and complete commensality prevails only within it. Thus, there are many kinds of restrictions between castes—on the free acceptance of food and drink, on intermarriage and sex relations, on touching or going near a member of another caste, etc.—and they are expressed in terms of pollution. This means that failure to observe the rules makes the upper-caste person impure, and he has to perform a purificatory rite, simple or elaborate, according to the seriousness of the violation.

While caste is central, it does not entirely determine Hindu religious behavior. There are other aspects of the social structure that embody religious behavior. The village community and the family also function as cult groups. There are deities—usually goddesses—in every village who, if suitably propitiated, keep out epidemics and drought and look after the villagers. There is an elaborate complex of *rites de passage*, including wedding rituals and funeral rites that may take several days to perform. Calendrical festivals and *vratas*, or ritual austerities carried out for specific periods to attain particular ends (e.g., birth of a son), consume a good part of people's energies, time, and money.

It is important to demarcate those aspects of religious behavior that are affected by caste from those that are not. The relation between sect and caste, in particular, offers a fruitful area for research.

Dominant theological ideas of Hinduism

Hinduism does not have a body of clearly defined dogma, but some theological ideas may be considered basic. And while the many sects and schools have taken different standpoints on theological issues, the issues themselves are common to most. Since the time of the Upaniṣads, which laid the foundations of Hindu philosophical thinking, certain concepts recur again and again. A major issue has been the nature of Brahman (universal soul) and its relation with Ātman (the individual soul). One view is concerned only with this dichotomy, does not posit the existence of God, and considers Brahman as absolute and attributeless. (There was also the Chārvāka school, which was atheistic and hedonistic.) Most other views, however, recognize the existence of God and consider the issue of his relation with Brahman, on the one hand, and Ātman, on the other. The Ātman is considered to be indestructible and passes through an endless migration, or series of incarnations. The character of any incarnation,

human, animal, or superhuman, is influenced by *karma*, the net balance of good and bad deeds in previous births. Goodness or badness is defined by reference to *dharma*. The reward for a saintly life is *mokṣa*, which releases the individual from the chain of births and deaths and brings him into contact with God.

The ideas of *karma*, *dharma*, and *mokṣa* are intimately related to the caste system. The Dharma-sūtra states that if a man does good deeds, he will be reborn in a high caste and well endowed, while if he does sinful acts, he will be reborn in a low caste or even as an animal. *Dharma* is thus identified with the duties of one's caste, and birth in a particular caste becomes an index of the soul's progress toward liberation.

The nature of *mokṣa* and how to achieve it are major issues in Hindu theology. The main ways of achieving *mokṣa* are through knowledge, deeds, and love and devotion toward God. Generally, the way of knowledge requires an individual to renounce the world, including caste and family, and lead the life of an ascetic. This way has been followed by only a few. It was the Bhagavad Gītā that first emphasized the way of works and devotion and thus brought liberation within reach of the "man-in-the-world," including women and the lower castes. The most popular form of devotion, however, is the worship of one's chosen god according to tradition. In the last hundred years the Bhagavad Gītā has been reinterpreted by Indian political leaders, including Gandhi and B. G. Tilak, to provide the basis for a life devoted to altruistic action.

Discussion of these issues by theologians has been in Sanskrit and in the context of ideas developed in logic, metaphysics, astronomy, grammar, literature, law, and other branches of traditional learning. The basic theological positions have, however, reached the common people through myths and stories narrated in local languages. How influential these ideas were and the nature of their relation to strictly local or sectional ideas and beliefs are still subjects for research (see, in this connection, Srinivas 1952, p. 227).

Sanskritic deities. Those deities whose attributes and modes of worship are described in mythological, liturgical, and other texts may be called Sanskritic. The Vedic pantheon reflects the syncretism that resulted from the conquest by nomadic Indo-European Aryans of the ancient urbanized civilizations of the Indus Valley and a continuing contact with the aboriginal tribal peoples of the subcontinent. Most of the deities, major and minor, are nature gods: Indra, the most prominent of all, is the sky god; Agni, the fire god; Varuṇa, the water god; Sūrya, the sun god; and so on. Viṣṇu, who later became a high god, began as only a minor figure, a mere aspect of the sun god. The Vedic god of thunder, Rudra, was at first associated with Śiva, who eventually became the dominant partner. The chief Vedic gods were gradually transformed into the trinity of Brahmā, the creator; Viṣṇu, the protector; and Śiva, the destroyer. Brahmā does not appear in the Vedas but seems to have developed during the period of the Brāhmaṇas. His importance subsequently declined, and nowadays Viṣṇu and Śiva are the two most important gods.

Every major deity in Hinduism has many forms, and around each form there is a myth. Viṣṇu has a number of incarnations, the chief of which are Rāma (man), Krishna (man), Narasiṃha (man-lion), and Varāha (boar). The idea behind the many forms is that God periodically allows himself to be reborn on earth, to overcome evil and restore righteousness. In addition to incarnations, Viṣṇu has one thousand names, according to the Mahābhārata, and many more according to other texts. Rāma and Krishna, originally incarnations of Viṣṇu, became important gods in themselves, each with many forms and names. The idea of incarnation is not associated with Śiva, but he, too, has many names. In addition, each deity or each form of a deity has a wife, who is usually worshiped along with her husband.

Śakti, the personification of the female principle in the creation of the universe, occupies almost as important a place in the Hindu pantheon as Viṣṇu and Śiva. In the Śakti cult a female deity is sometimes worshiped independently of association with a male deity, but when a male deity alone is worshiped, generally he is some form of Śiva rather than of Viṣṇu. Further, Skanda and Ganeśa, the sons of Śiva, and Hanumant, the chief of the monkey army of Rāma, are also popular deities. The birds and animals on which the gods sit are called *vāhanas* ("vehicles") and are worshiped. The sun, moon, stars, fire, mountains, lakes, animals, snakes, trees, and plants continue to be objects of worship. Frequently river deities are anthropomorphized. For example, Ganga, or Ganges, is a form of the goddess Pārvatī, and many smaller rivers are believed to be manifestations of Ganga. The cobra cult in southern India is identified with Skanda. There are also deities symbolizing the synthesis of different deities, such as the three-headed Trimūrti and Dattatreya, representing the unity of Brahmā, Viṣṇu, and Śiva. The union of Śiva and Viṣṇu is expressed in the composite god Harihara; Ardha-

nārīśvara represents an attempt to symbolize the unity of Śiva and Pārvatī.

The henotheistic tendency is important in Hindu mythology and ritual: the deity who is being worshiped is praised above all others. Pantheism prevails, but all deities, from Viṣṇu or Śiva to the lowest village deity, are considered to be manifestations of the same god. These ideas have enabled Hinduism to absorb local cults and deities and even accept all other religions as true.

A Hindu temple embodies the henotheistic idea. There is, accordingly, one principal deity, from whom a temple derives its name and whose image occupies a prominent place in the temple, and there are also a few minor deities, represented by smaller images in different parts of the temple. Thus, in a Śiva temple Śiva would be the principal deity, and Pārvatī, Ganeśa, and the bull Nandi would be minor deities; whereas in a Śakti temple, Śakti would be the principal deity and Śiva would be one of the minor deities. Not all Hindu deities are associated with temples, however. Some of the Vedic deities, such as Varuṇa and Agni, are invoked mostly during sacrifices, while Brahmā and Sūrya seem to have had temples in the past but do not have them nowadays. Some deities (e.g., Ganeśa) have temples only in certain regions.

Sectarianism

Like other religions, Hinduism has given birth to many sects in the course of its history, and it is not always easy to say whether a sect is within the Hindu fold or outside. Buddhism and Jainism had emerged as distinct sects by about the fifth century B.C., and both spread over wide areas, Buddhism, in particular, spreading over almost the entire country. But over the centuries their influence declined, and Buddhism had almost entirely disappeared from the country of its origin by about A.D. 1000. It is only in recent years that large numbers of Untouchables, in particular the Mahar of Maharashtra, became converted to Buddhism in protest against the indignities they were subjected to under the caste system. There is a sizable Jain population in India today, and Jains are very similar to Hindus. Not only are there castes among them, but some trading castes of Gujarāt have Jain and Hindu subdivisions, and marriage occurs across sect lines. Islam has presented a serious challenge to Hinduism. There are about 129.5 million Muslims (nearly 47 million in India and 82.5 million in Pakistan) in the subcontinent. While a small proportion of them came from the Middle East, the majority were converts from among the Hindus. They have a caste system in some ways similar to that of the Hindus, and the converts have retained many Hindu practices —so much so that in the case of some groups it is even now extremely difficult to say whether they are Hindu or Muslim. There are also sects (Kabīrpanthi, Sikhism) and cults that combine both Hindu and Muslim traits. One of them, Sikhism, has claimed to be a distinct religion, but this does not mean that Sikhs do not have anything in common with Hindus. The Sikhs are divided into castes, with even an Untouchable division, and have veneration for Hindu holy places. Until recently, in many families in rural Punjab one son would become a Sikh while the others remained Hindu. Many Hindu castes became Sikhs in an effort to improve their status. The Pirāna sect in Gujarāt and the recent Saibaba cult have both Hindu and Muslim followers. In its later phase the Bhakti movement was influenced by Sufism.

At the present time there are a very large number of sects, a few major and many minor. Each sect has a founder, a cult, a body of doctrine, and a social organization of its own.

In most sects one deity is considered to be supreme and is identified with the supreme Brahman. While Viṣṇu, Śiva, and Śakti are the most important nuclei for the formation of sects, they are not, however, the only nuclei, sects having also arisen around Sūrya, Gaṇeśa, and Dattatreya. It is wrong to speak of a single, homogeneous sect associated with any of these deities. The many Vaiṣṇavite sects, for example, are distinguished from each other, first, by the particular form of Viṣṇu and his consort that they worship; and second, where the same form and consort are worshiped, by differences in the mode of worship and body of theological doctrine; and finally, by their internal organization. There are elaborate rules regarding the making of idols, and there is a systematized iconography. The Śrī-Vaiṣṇavas worship Viṣṇu and his consort Lakṣmī; the Madhvas worship Krishna but not Rādhā; the Nimbarkas, Vallabhacharis, and Chaitanyaites worship both Krishna and Rādhā but differ in several other respects; and the Rāmanandis worship only Rāma and his associates. Comparable differences exist among Śiva and Śakti sects.

Each sect recognizes several minor deities, including its chief deity's spouse, but they rarely include the entire Hindu pantheon. In each sect the founder and the things associated with him are objects of special veneration. Each sect has an elaborate complex of rituals for temple and domestic worship and for life-cycle ceremonies. It has its own specially emphasized festivals and sacrifices and its own identifying word or sentence of great religious potency. A sect mark put on the forehead easily distinguishes a member of one sect from that of another.

The major sects are known for their distinctive philosophical standpoints, as for example, the pure monism of the Smartas, the qualified monism of the Śrī-Vaiṣṇavas, and the dualism of the Madhvas. Minor sects do not have elaborate philosophies, although they do have their own special ideas and beliefs. While the philosophical and ethical position of a sect is important in understanding its religious practices, other elements are influential.

Each sect has not only its own sacred literature, written by its founder and other leaders, but also a selective attitude toward the great texts of Hinduism.

Another major problem in the study of sects is understanding the nature of their relation to asceticism. Sects composed entirely of ascetics represent a bizarre element in Hinduism. The members of these sects go about scantily clothed, smear their bodies with funeral ashes, wear long, matted hair, and perform a number of physical feats. They maintain monasteries (*akhādas*, literally "gymnasiums"), where they are reputed to carry on occult practices, and they also manage temples, which enable them to keep in touch with the masses and recruit members.

Sects composed entirely of householders and those consisting of both ascetics and householders are the most numerous and popular. The ascetics in the latter sects are grouped into different monasteries, each having its own core of hereditary adherents and its corporate property in temples, land, etc. Many ascetics are found to be involved in intersectarian rivalry and politics. When a sect is composed only of householders, the patrilineal descendants of the founder preside over the sect.

There are many small sects, whose membership is confined to a single linguistic region or to a small area within a linguistic region, but the membership of the major sects cuts across language barriers. In the case of a major sect, it is necessary to distinguish between areas with a high concentration of its members and areas with relatively few members. Thus, while the majority of the Madhvas are found in southern India, there are small groups of them in Gujarāt, Uttar Pradesh, Bihār, and Bengal. While the majority of Vallabhacharis are found in Gujarāt and Rājasthān, there are small groups of them all over northern, western, and eastern India. Another noteworthy feature is that, while the majority of the members, temples, and monasteries of a sect may be found in one part of the country, it may have a temple or a monastery in each of the major pilgrim centers in the country. The founder of every major sect traveled about the country, first in search of knowledge, then to win dialectical battles, and finally, to give discourses and recruit followers. Frequently the founder and his followers came from different regions. There were centers of religious learning in different areas, and there was a convergence of schools of learning at each center; finally the centers were woven into networks. Some of these centers, such as Banāras, Vrindāban, and Śrīrangam, enjoyed high prestige, and a scholar's victory in religious disputation may have taken place at the court of the king or at a religious fair.

Normally, membership in a sect, unlike that in a caste, is not hereditary but comes through initiation. And there is hardly any sect that is composed of only one *jāti*. Even the Lingāyat sect of the Kannada region, which is commonly regarded as a caste, is composed of a number of *jātis*, or endogamous units. And even when a whole caste is included in a single sect, membership in the sect is not automatic but by initiation. Sometimes the members of a caste will be distributed among more than one sect, and some may not belong to any sect at all. Some castes in Gujarāt contain not only members of two or three Hindu sects but also Jains. Sometimes the members of a single family have different sectarian affiliations. The rise and fall of various sects over the centuries indicates that religious positions were not always determined by birth.

No sect recruits members from all castes. Untouchables are very rarely admitted into sects including the high castes; even a sect admitting "touchable" castes would cover only a certain span in the caste hierarchy. Generally speaking, Untouchables have produced their own sects. The older sects recruited *brāhmans* and higher non-*brāhmans* but not lower non-*brāhmans*, and there are sects founded by non-*brāhmans* that do not include *brāhmans*. Even though a sect includes members from more than one caste, caste distinctions are not entirely obliterated.

Nonsectarian Hinduism

Nonsectarian Hinduism is found both in towns and villages; it is largely Sanskritic in towns and non-Sanskritic in villages.

Non-Sanskritic Hinduism is, however, an ideal type and has the following characteristics: the deities have non-Sanskritic names and oral myths attached to them; they are represented by unhewn stones or crude images; the modes of worship are local and do not follow any liturgy; offerings include meat and liquor, and the priests, or shamans, as well as the devotees, are generally drawn from the lower castes. All these conditions rarely occur simultaneously, and it is more common for the Sanskritic and non-Sanskritic elements to be mixed in varying proportions. Thus, a deity's name may be a corrupt form of a Sanskritic name or a compound of a Sanskritic and a non-Sanskritic name. Usually village goddesses are regarded as manifestations of Pārvatī, and village gods of Śiva. Such identification makes possible the acquisition of Sanskritic characteristics by non-Sanskritic deities, and it is not unknown for a deity with a single name to be worshiped according to non-Sanskritic modes in one village and Sanskritic modes in another. In one village the deity's image may be housed in a fine temple, while in another it is embedded in the earth at the foot of a tree. Frequently, there are institutionalized links between a village deity and the pilgrim center of the Sanskritic deity with which he is identified.

There are also temples to Sanskritic deities, where *brāhmans* are priests, the offerings vegetarian, and the mode of worship Sanskritic. But on certain occasions, such as the deity's festival, the *brāhman* withdraws and animals are sacrificially decapitated by a non-*brāhman*. The *brāhman* priest re-enters the temple only after purifying it. In temples where non-*brāhmans* are priests, *brāhmans* may propitiate such a deity during an epidemic or other disaster. In exceptional situations a *brāhman* might even make an offering of a fowl to a non-Sanskritic deity through a non-*brāhman* friend.

It is important to note that the attitude of *brāhmans* and other high castes toward non-Sanskritic deities is not fixed and unalterable. There are different types of *brāhmans*, high as well as low, and learned as well as ignorant. (Among the Smarta *brāhmans* of Tamilnad, the priests, Kurukkals, are regarded as lower than other *brāhmans*. In Gujarāt, the priestly Tapodhan *brāhmans* are rated very low indeed.) A learned *brāhman* may have to oblige his powerful non-*brāhman* patrons by manufacturing a myth in Sanskrit for one of their deities. Hindu mythology has grown in this manner (see the Appendix on "The Kāvēri Myth" in Srinivas 1952, pp. 241–246).

A temple is sectarian only when it is part of a sectarian organization. In this sense a large majority of Hindu temples, including some of the biggest, are nonsectarian. Many of these are extremely wealthy, having vast land estates, large amounts of jewelry and precious metals, and also a considerable income from offerings by devotees. They employ many people and have an elaborate and complex body of ritual, calendrical festivals, special *pūjās*, etc. Although nonsectarian, these temples are subject to regional sectarian influences. For example, the modes of worship in nonsectarian temples of Krishna in Gujarāt are influenced by the modes of worship prevalent in Krishna temples of the dominant Vallabhachari sect of the area.

In the majority of temples dedicated to Sanskritic deities, the priests are *brāhmans;* only vegetarian and nonalcoholic offerings are made, and the rituals are conducted according to a liturgical text. Even in some Śiva temples, where priests are Liṅgāyats (southern India) or Gosais (Gujarāt), they perform liturgical rituals and make only vegetarian and nonalcoholic offerings. In many Śakti temples, particularly those influenced by the left-hand Śakti sects, the deity is worshiped according to the Tantric texts and offerings of meat and liquor are made. However, although Sanskritization has had a widespread effect, some temples continue to sacrifice animals and make liquor offerings on certain occasions. In Bengal, Bihār, and Assam blood sacrifice still remains a normal mode of worship.

Nonsectarian Hindus generally worship many deities, although there are some who are devotees of a single deity, sometimes a deity in a particular temple. It is common to see a devout Hindu going on a daily round of the principal temples in a village or in a ward of a city. They observe the festivals of Śiva, Viṣṇu, and others, and they go on pilgrimages to great shrines all over the country.

Hinduism and the polity

Devout Hindus regarded their king as a representative of God on earth. This belief was common to all, including *brāhmans*, who themselves claimed to be gods on earth. The social order, as represented by the caste system, was also believed to be divinely created. The rules of the social and moral order were subsumed under the ethicoreligious concept of *dharma*. In his role as the guardian of *dharma*, the king had to maintain the caste system. This meant that the idea of inequality expressed in the caste system had the king's support and sanction. Different castes had different rights, duties, and privileges, and punishment had to take into account the caste of the offender and that of the victim. The disabilities traditionally imposed on untouchables also had the king's sanction. His powers included the right to promote or demote individual castes, and he was the final court of

appeal in any matter pertaining to caste. This power was so integral to kingship that it was exercised by the Mughal rulers and also by the British in their very early days in India.

It is important to remember that the king had this power, inasmuch as uncritical reliance on the sacred literature conveys the impression that the *brāhmans* were all-powerful and that kings only carried out their decisions. The privileges enjoyed by *brāhmans* and religious personages were in fact conferred on them by the king, and they could be withdrawn. As recently as 1892, in the princely state of Mysore, the government passed an order that all nominations to the headship of monasteries must have the prior approval of the maharaja, and failure to obtain this approval would involve the retraction of grants of land and money made by the state (Smith 1963, pp. 302–303). A *swāmī*, or head of a monastery, is revered, and the maharaja even performs the ritual of washing the feet of some *swāmīs;* but he also has the power to determine who becomes a *swāmī.*

The Hindu king had the same beliefs and values and took part in the same ceremonies as his people, although the manner of his celebrating a festival or his devotion to a particular deity or temple often set the religious style of the kingdom. Temples favored by royalty (e.g., Tirupati, Tanjore, and Madurai) developed into great pilgrimage centers. They were generously endowed with land and jewelry; famous sculptors were invited to lavish their skill on them; and great musicians sang there on certain occasions. The conversion of a prince to a sect was an important event in its history, and a large number of people followed their king into the new faith. And while there is a tradition of tolerance in Hinduism, discrimination against the members of a rival sect was not unknown.

It is clear that no conceptual separation between the state and the church was possible in the Hindu system of ideas. Nor was the need for such a distinction very necessary. First, Hinduism did not possess a powerful, centralized church, with a single pontiff and a hierarchy of officials, which would constitute a potential threat to kingly supremacy. Second, the castewise division of functions confined *brāhmans* to the religious realm, while the *kṣatriyas* had the political realm to themselves. That a separation between the two did not always obtain should not surprise us. In fact, the development of sacrifice during the late Vedic period marked an increase in *brāhman* power and arrogance, and Buddhism and Jainism both appealed to *kṣatriyas* and *vaiśyas*, partly because of their rejection of *brāhman* pretensions (Ghurye 1932, pp. 65, 69, 70, in 1950 edition). Speaking generally, it was not so much the throne that attracted *brāhmans* as the power behind it.

Hinduism has a tradition of tolerance, and Hindu rulers in general seem to have been hospitable to different sects and religions. Hindu tolerance is, however, related to the caste system in several ways. First, each caste has its own style of life, and from childhood onward people accept diversity as a basis for relationship. Second, caste, along with village and extended kin groups, ensured conformity in practice, and a stable society could afford to give its members intellectual freedom. The other source of such freedom was the institution of the holy man, who ritually renounced the world—his relatives even performed funeral rites for him at his initiation into the order—and who could then preach as he wished. Max Weber has rightly said, "The freedom of thought in ancient India was so considerable as to find no parallel in the West before the most recent age" (quoted in Smith 1963, p. 62).

Hindu tolerance of other religions and its hospitality to new ideas provided a favorable soil for the eventual declaration of India as a secular state. There were, however, other tendencies, and certain nineteenth-century attempts (e.g., the Ārya Samāj) to purge Hinduism of its many evils by advocating a return to the Vedas contained frankly revivalist elements. Moreover, Indian nationalism also expressed itself occasionally in the Hindu idiom, and this had the effect of alienating the Muslims. But during British rule there emerged a highly westernized Hindu elite, which, while rooted in the country and its traditions, was committed to independence, democracy, egalitarianism, and secularism. It is this elite that not only declared India a secular state but also attempted wholeheartedly to establish the principle of the equality of man.

Hinduism and economic development. Weber (1921) thought that the Hindu belief in the transmigration of the soul and the related doctrines of *karma* and *dharma*, seen in the context of caste, produced an irrational, otherworldly social ethic that prevented the development of industrial capitalism. Weber's thesis has gained wide popularity, and Hinduism is now believed to be one of the major obstacles in India's economic development. This belief, however, rests on a partial view of Hinduism. Weber himself noted a few elements of a "rational" ethic in Hinduism—the existence of this-worldly asceticism and positive economic motivation among Jains, Liṅgāyats, and Madhvas, and

an occupational ethic among merchants and artisans. There are elements in Hinduism favorable to economic development (Singer et al. 1958; Lambert & Hoselitz 1963). The very ascetics whom Weber considered disseminators of irrational and otherworldly ideas among the masses are often the heads of large and wealthy monasteries and temples, the management of which calls for considerable administrative ability.

Hindu reform and modernization. Hinduism has, in the course of its long history, undergone many and radical changes, and several diverse forces have contributed to making Hinduism what it is today. The establishment of the Pax Britannica released many new forces, affecting Hinduism at every point. The disruption by the British of some of the social institutions of Hinduism, such as caste, untouchability, *satī*, human sacrifice, female infanticide, infant marriage, etc., made it clear to the orthodox that the state could use its power to alter their religious institutions. European missionaries who came to India for evangelical purposes sharply criticized Hinduism, and Hindus were made to realize poignantly that some influential outsiders thought that everything was wrong with their religion. Reformist Hindus—many of whom had attended mission schools—could not help remembering missionary criticisms of their religion, and in creating institutions to bring about changes in their society, they naturally emulated the organizations and work of their critics. From a long-term point of view the most important element in the reinterpretation and reformulation of Hinduism was the emergence of a westernized Indian elite, which eventually took over power from the British and which used that power to introduce fundamental changes, such as the abolition of untouchability, the legalization of intercaste marriage, widow marriage, and divorce, and the enforcement of monogamy. It is this elite that after a century and a half of Western influence declared India to be a secular state. Secularism does not mean that evil social institutions will be allowed to flourish, just as the principle of equality has not prevented the state from giving a variety of special privileges to Scheduled Castes and Tribes for a specific period of time, in order to enable them to catch up with the others.

One of the great reforming leaders of the new elite was Rājā Rām Mohan Roy, who founded a religious society, the Brāhma Samāj, in 1828. A daring religious thinker, scholar, and educator, Rām Mohan Roy was influenced by Vedānta and Islam before he studied Christianity; he was a monotheist and opposed to idolatry. He was an able and courageous controversialist and fought the orthodox *pandits* with arguments they could appreciate. For instance, in his efforts to purge Hinduism of the idolatrous accretions it had acquired over the centuries, he advocated a return to Vedic Hinduism: "Like Luther, who appealed to the Bible as an authority against medieval corruptions, he took his stand on the *Vedas*, the earliest Hindu scriptures, in which he found a form of pure Hinduism, of which the basis was a belief in one God, which was not vitiated by idolatry, and which gave no sanction to distinctions of caste or such practices as suttee" (O'Malley 1941, p. 67). (Dayananda Saraswati, who founded the Ārya Samāj, a religious brotherhood, in 1875, was only following Rām Mohan Roy in his efforts to introduce radical changes in Hinduism by championing a revival of Vedic Hinduism.) Rām Mohan Roy was aware that an appeal to the authority of the Vedas would carry weight with the orthodox *pandits*, and he set the style for a debate that went on for nearly a hundred years between reformists and diehards, both of whom quoted the scriptures in support of their views.

Rām Mohan Roy also discovered that a principle of reason lay at the basis of the classical Indian philosophy of Vedanta, as set forth in the Upaniṣads. "Ram Mohan Roy abandoned the traditionally accepted bases of Hindu religion and Brahminic authority in favor of reason. Hinduism could be justified in its essentials on the ground that it provided a reasoned explanation of reality. Everything from the West could be considered in the same light. There could be assimilation and not merely borrowing at random" (Spear 1961, p. 296). He thus laid the foundation for a reinterpretation of Hinduism freeing it not only from social institutions such as caste and untouchability but also from a welter of beliefs, ideas, myths, and ritual. He did not regard these as the "essence" of Hinduism. The essence was selected portions of the Vedānta, the Bhagavad Gītā, and *bhakti* or devotional literature. Subsequent reformers, such as Vivekānanda, Saraswati, Aurobindo Ghose, Tilak, Gandhi, and Rādhākrishnan, carried on the work of reinterpretation. Over the years the reformers, the greatest of whom was Gandhi, built up a body of public opinion in favor of introducing drastic changes in Hinduism. It was this opinion which later enabled the state to take legislative action against certain Hindu practices that were repugnant to the modern outlook.

The second half of the nineteenth century saw the beginnings of the growth of nationalist sentiment among Hindus, and nascent patriotism drew upon Hindu sentiment and traditions. A concern for the people and the country inevitably meant activism, and the Bhagavad Gītā provided a religious source for political activism and altruism. The *karma marga*, or "path of works," received emphasis at the expense of the other two paths.

Two contrary processes have been gaining strength in modern India. The first one is Sanskritization, a process by which the rites, customs, beliefs, and style of life of the higher castes, and in particular the *brāhmans*, are taken over by the lower groups, including the Untouchables and the tribal peoples. But while the lower groups increasingly Sanskritize their style of life, the higher strata become increasingly westernized. Westernization, like Sanskritization, is a multilayered process, including the acceptance of Western technology, Western political, legal, and social institutions, and Western literature, philosophy, and science. The spread of Sanskritization and westernization across the country and to different structural levels is beginning to produce nationwide uniformities in religion and culture. Everywhere village deities traditionally associated with epidemics of diseases such as plague, smallpox, and cholera seem to be losing ground, while the prestigious Sanskritic deities are becoming more popular. Blood sacrifices and offerings of liquor to deities are also becoming less popular. The horizon of the peasant is widening, and the richer peasants now visit pilgrimage centers several hundred miles away from their villages. Films, radio, textbooks, newspapers, journals, and paperback books are strengthening "regional" and "all-India" Hinduism, at the expense of strictly "local" forms. Life-cycle rituals are becoming abbreviated, while the purely social aspects of such rituals get elaborated; this seems to be particularly true of educated Hindus in towns. In fact, the forms Hinduism is taking among the educated urban Hindus is only beginning to be explored by social scientists (see, for example, Singer 1959). The search for a satisfying philosophy leads many members of this class to become devotees of one or another spiritual leader. Some of these leaders are traditional heads of monasteries, while others are modern figures. Hinduism has in the past depended upon caste, village, joint family, Hindu kings, monasteries, and centers of pilgrimage for its perpetuation. Radical changes have occurred in all of them. Moreover, there has been a growth in secularization, egalitarianism, and rationalism. But new organizations such as the Rāmakrishna Mission, the various hermitages of religious leaders, the Bharatiya Vidya Bhavan, and finally, departments of the central government such as the All-India Radio, and in some states departments supervising temple administration, are reinterpreting Hinduism in a modern direction.

M. N. SRINIVAS AND A. M. SHAH

[*See also* ASIAN SOCIETY, *article on* SOUTH ASIA; CASTE, *especially the article on* THE INDIAN CASTE SYSTEM; POLLUTION.]

BIBLIOGRAPHY

BASHAM, ARTHUR L. (1954) 1963 *The Wonder That Was India: A Study of the History and Culture of the Indian Sub-continent Before the Coming of the Muslims.* New ed., rev. New York: Hawthorn.
Contributions to Indian Sociology (Paris). → Published since 1957 under the editorship of Louis Dumont and D. Pocock.
FARQUHAR, JOHN N. 1920 *An Outline of the Religious Literature of India.* Oxford Univ. Press.
GHURYE, GOVIND S. (1932) 1961 *Caste, Class and Occupation.* 4th ed., rev. Bombay: Popular Book Depot. → First published as *Caste and Race in India.*
GHURYE, GOVIND S. 1953 *Indian Sadhus.* Bombay: Popular Book Depot.
GHURYE, GOVIND S. 1962 *Gods and Men.* Bombay: Popular Book Depot.
HUBERT, HENRI; and MAUSS, MARCEL (1899) 1964 *Sacrifice: Its Nature and Function.* Univ. of Chicago Press. → First published in French.
KANE, P. V. 1930–1962 *History of Dharmaśāstra: Ancient and Mediaeval Religious and Civil Law in India.* Vols. 1–5. Poona: Bhandarkar Oriental Research Institute.
LAMBERT, RICHARD D.; and HOSELITZ, BERT F. (editors) 1963 *The Role of Savings and Wealth in Southern Asia and the West.* Paris: UNESCO.
MARRIOTT, McKIM (editor) 1955 *Village India: Studies in the Little Community.* Univ. of Chicago Press. → Also published as Memoir No. 83 of the American Anthropological Association, which was issued as *American Anthropologist,* Volume 57, No. 3, Part 2, June 1955.
MORGAN, KENNETH W. (editor) 1953 *The Religion of the Hindus.* New York: Ronald Press.
O'MALLEY, LEWIS S. S. (editor) 1941 *Modern India and the West: A Study of the Interaction of Their Civilizations.* Oxford Univ. Press.
SINGER, MILTON (editor) 1959 *Traditional India: Structure and Change.* Philadelphia: American Folklore Society.
SINGER, MILTON et al. 1958 India's Cultural Values and Economic Development: A Discussion. *Economic Development and Cultural Change* 7:1–12.
SMITH, DONALD E. 1963 *India as a Secular State.* Princeton Univ. Press.
SPEAR, PERCIVAL 1961 *India: A Modern History.* Ann Arbor: Univ. of Michigan Press.
SRINIVAS, M. N. 1952 *Religion and Society Among the Coorgs of South India.* Oxford: Clarendon.
SRINIVAS, M. N. 1962 *Caste in Modern India, and Other Essays.* New York: Asia Pub. House.
STEVENSON, MARGARET 1920 *The Rites of the Twiceborn.* London: Milford.
WEBER, MAX (1921) 1958 *The Religion of India: The Sociology of Hinduism and Buddhism.* Translated and edited by Hans H. Gerth and Don Martindale. Glencoe, Ill.: Free Press. → First published as *Hinduismus und Buddhismus,* Volume 2 of *Gesammelte Aufsätze zur Religionssoziologie.*

HINTZE, OTTO

Otto Hintze (1861–1940) spent the first twenty years of his life in his native Prussian province of Pomerania. After studying for two years at the University of Greifswald, he transferred in 1880 to the University of Berlin, where as a student of J. G. Droysen he became deeply imbued with the ethical implications and political principles of the Prussian tradition. He early impressed his teachers at the university with his capacity for relating minutiae to generalizations as well as with his independent, critical judgment (Hartung [1941] 1961, pp. 500–501). At a later point in his studies Hintze became associated with Gustav Schmoller, and this association greatly influenced his development as a professional historian, an influence reflected in his publications during the next decades.

Hintze's first major work was a study of the Prussian silk industry in the eighteenth century. It consisted of two volumes of documents and a third volume that analyzed the effects on the industry of the mercantilist policies of Frederick II. At the completion of this work Hintze, at the age of 34, was given an appointment at the University of Berlin, and thereafter he was rapidly promoted. His position entailed lecturing on constitutional, administrative, and economic history as well as on politics, a rather unusual combination at the time.

As a collaborator of Schmoller's in the publication of the *Acta borussica,* Hintze next turned to the study of Prussian administration from 1740 to 1756. The six volumes of documents published as a result of this work carried an introduction by Hintze (1901) that was a penetrating analysis of this administrative system and of the major political decisions it embodied. Subsequently, Hintze continued to be associated with the *Acta borussica* in a leading capacity, while also becoming editor-in-chief of the *Forschungen zur brandenburgischen und preussischen Geschichte.*

Hintze's writings on Prussian history—a series of essays published at various times between 1896 and 1931 and collected as *Geist und Epochen der preussischen Geschichte* (1896–1931) and his summary volume *Die Hohenzollern und ihr Werk* (1915)—show a high order of critical, scholarly judgment. Although he was an avowed admirer of the Prussian monarchy and an avowed conservative, his approach to Prussian political institutions was objective and comparative. He came to see the Prussian case as a "paradigm for the formations and transformations of the modern state generally" (Hartung [1941] 1961, p. 506). The case of Prussia, as Hintze saw it, illustrates J. R. Seeley's dictum that the degree of internal freedom in a country is inversely proportional to the political and military pressures on its frontiers. More generally, this means that the internal social structure of a country—its class conflicts and constitutional framework—and its international position must be analyzed together. Such an approach shows that Prussia's militarism and monarchical constitution were by-products of her central European location; no attempt to form a nation-state in this area could succeed without the discipline and centralized authority of Prussian institutions (1915, pp. vi–vii). Applying this analysis to other times and places Hintze showed that in the sixteenth and seventeenth centuries the great struggle between France and the Hapsburg empire, together with the impotence of Germany, left countries like Poland in a power vacuum, which greatly facilitated such internal conflicts as those between powerful families and thus militated against the formation of a strong political structure ([1902–1932] 1962, pp. 515–521). Again, in England, early political centralization, together with relative military security, strongly militated against absolutism, bureaucracy, and militarism of the Continental type, so that the modern English state of the eighteenth and nineteenth centuries depended on the ruling agrarian and industrial classes rather than on the crown ([1902–1932] 1962, pp. 362–368).

Hintze's nationalist and monarchist persuasion was severely shaken by Germany's defeat in 1918. That experience brought greater acceptance on his part of democratic tendencies nationally and federative tendencies internationally, although so great a change of view was naturally difficult for a convinced conservative (Oestreich 1964, pp. 21–22). Impaired health forced him to discontinue university teaching, and during the years of the Weimar Republic he was a private scholar and publicist. Hitler's rise to power completely destroyed the world in which he had grown to maturity, and in 1938 Hintze, whose wife was Jewish, resigned from the Prussian Academy of Science. When his collected essays were published shortly after his death in 1940, all his discussions of the work of Jewish authors were excised.

Despite disillusionment and personal adversity, after World War I Hintze turned to a fuller elaboration of his projected comparative, constitutional history. There are indications that he completed a major work in this field but that it was lost during World War II. What remains is a series of essays on administrative history, feudalism, the estate-constitutions of Europe, the world-historical conditions of representative institutions in Western European societies, and Polish constitutional history, as well as brief synopses of his views concerning the major phases of European political history. Taken together, these writings do for the study of political institutions what Max Weber's sociology of religion did for the study of religious beliefs. By comparative analysis they reveal the institutional preconditions that shaped the Western system of constitutional states and the major types of constitutions that emerged within this system.

Hintze's work, which is informed with his wide knowledge of history, has a developmental emphasis that is not evolutionist and a conceptual approach that, like Weber's, brings out the singularity of a historical sequence or configuration by means of strategic contrasts with other civilizations. He had no use for biological analogies in social analysis, since he was much concerned with the role of ideas and political decisions in social change. For him as for Weber, functional relations are the end products of human actions that may produce innovations that are no less genuine because they are conditioned. Although it remained fragmentary, Hintze's work is a major contribution to the comparative analysis of social and political institutions.

REINHARD BENDIX

[For the historical context of Hintze's work, see the biographies of SCHMOLLER; WEBER, MAX.]

WORKS BY HINTZE

(1896–1931) 1943 Geist und Epochen der preussischen Geschichte: Gesammelte Abhandlungen. Leipzig: Koehler & Amelang.

(1897–1930) 1964 Soziologie und Geschichte: Gesammelte Abhandlungen zur Soziologie, Politik und Theorie der Geschichte. 2d ed., enl. Göttingen (Germany): Vandenhoeck & Ruprecht. → A collection of essays first published in book form in 1942 as Zur Theorie der Geschichte.

1901 Einleitende Darstellung der Behördenorganisation und allgemeinen Verwaltung in Preussen beim Regierungsantritt Friedrichs II. Volume 6, Part 1 in Acta borussica: Denkmäler der preussischen Staatsverwaltung im 18. Jahrhundert. Berlin: Parey.

(1902–1932) 1962 Staat und Verfassung: Gesammelte Abhandlungen zur allgemeinen Verfassungsgeschichte. 2d ed., enl. Göttingen (Germany): Vandenhoeck & Ruprecht. → Contains a bibliography of Hintze's writings.

1915 Die Hohenzollern und ihr Werk: Fünfhundert Jahre vaterländischer Geschichte. Berlin: Parey.

SUPPLEMENTARY BIBLIOGRAPHY

HARTUNG, FRITZ (1941) 1961 Otto Hintze. Pages 497–520 in Fritz Hartung, *Staatsbildende Kräfte der Neuzeit: Gesammelte Aufsätze*. Berlin: Duncker & Humblot.

OESTREICH, GERHARD 1964 Otto Hintzes Stellung zur Politikwissenschaft und Soziologie. Pages 7–67 in Otto Hintze, *Soziologie und Geschichte: Gesammelte Abhandlungen zur Soziologie, Politik und Theorie der Geschichte*. Göttingen (Germany): Vandenhoeck & Ruprecht.

HISTORICAL SCHOOL

See under ECONOMIC THOUGHT.

HISTORIOGRAPHY

The articles under this heading deal with the problems and traditions of history writing. A detailed guide to related articles will be found under HISTORY. *For discussions of historians who have contributed to the development of historiography, see the biographies of* ACTON; BEARD; BLOCH; BÜCHER; BURCKHARDT; CROCE; DILTHEY; FEBVRE; FUSTEL DE COULANGES; GIERKE; HALÉVY; HECKSCHER; HINTZE; HUIZINGA; IBN KHALDŪN; KOYRÉ; LAMPRECHT; MACAULAY; MAINE; MAITLAND; MARX; MCILWAIN; MEINECKE; NAMIER; PIRENNE; RANKE; ROBINSON; SARTON; SOMBART; SPENCER; SPENGLER; TAWNEY; TOCQUEVILLE; TOYNBEE; TREITSCHKE; TROELTSCH; TURNER; VICO; WEBER, MAX.

I

THE RHETORIC OF HISTORY

In this article the word "historiography" will be taken to mean the craft of writing history and/or the yield of such writing considered in its rhetorical aspect. The term "history" will be used to describe the study of the past as a systematic discipline. It will not be used to refer to the past as such. Unnecessary ambiguities created by using the term "history" to identify both the past and the systematic study of it have occasionally led to gratuitous confusion. The terms "historiography," "the rhetoric of history," and "history writing" will be used as synonyms. Historiography is different from the collection of historical evidence, the editing of historical sources, the exercise of historical thought and imagination, the criticism of historical writing, and the philosophy of history, but it is related to all of them and overlaps some of them. It is also different from the history of history writing. This distinction must be kept in mind because in recent decades the term "historiography" has increasingly been used to mean the history of history writing—in effect, a branch of intellectual history or a subbranch of the sociology of knowledge. It will not be used in that sense here.

Perhaps the drift of the term "historiography" from its initial moorings of meaning resulted from the neglect of systematic study of the rhetoric of history and from the view, usually implicit rather than explicit, that that rhetoric is not specific to history, or not specific enough to warrant systematic study; for if the rhetoric of history is generic rather than specific, then historiography so defined has no separate identity and merges into general rhetoric. Although many historians have said wise and witty things about the writing of history, none has focused more than intermittent attention on the problems it raises. The casualness with which historians have investigated the structure of historiography, compared with the care and exacting scrutiny to which they subject the nature of data, evidence, and inference in works of history, indicates that in their role as critics they regard the latter as the historians' legitimate central preoccupation and the former as a secondary and independent matter in which excellence, although desirable, is dispensable and without effect on the validity of the finished work.

To test this implied judgment—which is very hard to reconcile with the care and pains which many of the best historians lavish on their own history writing—this article will attempt an analysis of historiography.

The models of history writing that will be dealt with will be those provided in recent times by the better historians in their better moments. "In recent times" because, although the writing of history is old, the *general* professional commitment of historians *always* to write it with the maximum verisimilitude to the past is relatively new—scarcely 150 years old. The focus will be on "the better historians in their better moments" because they should and often do set the standards at which the profession aims. It is the practice of these historians when actually writing history, not their explicit theoretical or quasi-philosophical views, that is of concern here; for it is in their practice of historiography rather than in peripheral excursions into the problems of methodology that they reveal their effective commitments. Although much that follows will apply to all historiography, the article is only incidentally concerned with historical writings intended to codify knowledge of history already available, such as textbooks; primarily it is focused on history writing aimed at extending the bounds of historical knowledge. Since historiography communicates what the historian knows or thinks he knows, a consideration of the historian's way of writing that does not relate it to his way of knowing is doomed to triviality. Finally, as an overarching principle this article will seek to relate the rhetoric of history to the rhetoric of the mathematizing natural sciences, taking physics and chemistry as models, in order to make clear the similarities of historiography to these other ways in which men seek to communicate what they think they know, and its differences from them.

The language of historians

The most cursory comparison of any professional journal of history with an issue of the *Physical Review* will carry the conviction that the rhetoric of history differs grossly from that of physics. Ideally the vocabulary of physics is exact and denotative, and its syntax is mathematical, expressing quantitative relations between entities defined with the minimum ambiguity possible, given the current state of knowledge of the science. Now a part of the distinctive vocabulary of historiography is also denotative and unambiguous—the terms "pipe roll" or "writ of trespass" no less so, for example, than the term "specific gravity," although most if not all of the vocabulary of history that is at once distinctive and unambiguous is likely to refer to universes more constricted in time and space or less homogeneous and uniform than the ones the vocabulary of physics refers to. Moreover, historians often use quantitative data: grain yields per acre, rates of population growth, average rainfall; and sometimes they employ the syntax of mathematics to determine such matters as median income, ratio of cargo weight to number of sailors, range of probable error in equating number of manors owned with gross income from land. Thus, they occasionally mathematize, they often quantify and enumerate, and part of their vocabulary is wholly denotative. When operating in a sector of history writing where they deem rhetorical devices of this sort alone to be appropriate, they assimilate the form of their vocabulary very closely to that of the natural sciences and exercise a like care to decontaminate it of con-

notative and evocative overtones. Yet very few historians consistently write history this way, and scarcely any of that very few would insist that *all* history ought to aim at the rhetoric of the natural sciences as an ideal goal; they do not seek to make the rhetorical form which they find convenient into a prescriptive rule for the entire profession, as they would be obligated to do if they thought that *only* with such a rhetoric could one come close to an account of things past that approaches maximum verisimilitude.

In this respect historians differ notably from many social scientists. Both historians and social scientists claim, as natural scientists do, that by their method of investigation and formulation appropriately applied, they are able to produce cumulative increments to men's knowledge. Both historians and social scientists acknowledge that the form of their rhetoric is not always coincident with that of the natural sciences. But since most social scientists take the rhetoric of the natural sciences as their goal and ideal, they make a major intellectual effort to assimilate their way of writing to that of the natural sciences. In this matter they regard any nonconformity on their part as a deformity, to be either overcome or lamented. In practice, historians rarely see historiographic problems in this light. Far from always seeking the forms of language which will enable them to make historiography into the closest possible replica of the language of the natural sciences, they choose —often unself-consciously, but sometimes well aware of what they are doing—to write in a way that the rhetoric of the sciences forecloses. They deliberately choose a word or a phrase that is imprecise and may turn out to be ambiguous, because of its rich aura of connotation. Without compunction they sacrifice exactness for evocative force. Since the only common purpose to which historians are bound by their calling to commit themselves is to advance understanding of the past, the only possible justification for such a sacrifice is that it serves to increase knowledge of the past, that sometimes an evocative rhetoric is the best means a historian has for formulating and communicating what he knows. Whether or not the historians who in practice follow this rhetorical strategy are fully aware of it, the implication of this strategy is very radical. It entails the claim that historians can produce cumulative increments of knowledge without consistent resort to the rhetoric which scientists have found indispensable for formulating and communicating what they know. Positively it implies that for communicating what the historian knows, a rhetoric more like that employed in the fictive arts than like that employed in the sciences is not only permissible but on occasion indispensable.

Knowing and communicating

To analyze historiography, we must first determine its place in the general process of knowing and communicating. In order to identify and comprehend this general process, we will start with a concrete proposition: Willie Mays knows baseball. To deny this proposition is to fly in the face of the unanimous and considered judgment of several million people who have seen Mays play ball. Alternatively, it is to restrict the meaning of the term "know" so drastically as to impede the flow of discourse and snarl up a channel of communication. For a man who can convince some five million observers out of five million, and his employers to the tune of a salary of $125,000 per year, that he knows has come as close to ironclad demonstration as one can get in matters involving human judgment. To generate this conviction, Mays employs the rhetoric of action, the most common and universal method of demonstrating that one knows. (The author realizes that he is rather stretching the common sense of the term "rhetoric" in the present context.) The adequacy of such demonstration is measured by consistent appropriateness of visible (or perceivable) response. Briefly, Willie Mays shows that he knows by what he does. While he demonstrates almost perfectly *that* he knows, for two reasons he would have great difficulty in saying how he knows what he knows. (1) Since much of what he knows lies in the area of action, he probably knows no way of putting it into words. (2) Much of what he knows, he knows from long experience, and although some of what he knows in this way can be rendered accessible in verbal form, and is known by others in that form, that is not in fact how *he* knows it. If we went further and insisted that he so exactly communicate in words what he knows that others could test its validity by replication, we would clearly be asking the impossible, because he does not know what he knows with some abstraction from himself called his discursive intellect but with his whole person; and in every game he plays, he demonstrates its validity, not by verbal or mathematical formulation but by the unique and unreplicable perfection of his response.

In one area of human knowing, investigation in the natural sciences, however, formal convention has established as a minimal evidence of knowing the ability to state the results in a wholly denotative rhetoric of verbal signs; all consistently appropriate responses are required ulti-

mately to assume this form. This convention has been adopted because scientists set a very high value on generalizability of statement, replicability of experiment, and logical entailment as tests of knowing; and the rhetoric they have chosen enforces entailment and makes generalization and replication possible with maximum efficiency and certainty. Scientists have no doubt adopted this particular rhetorical stratagem because they have found it very useful for eliciting and testing answers to the kinds of questions they habitually ask. Correlatively, however, it prevents them, as scientists, from asking questions that are recalcitrant to formulation in the rhetoric they have chosen, and a fortiori from answering such questions. As a result of this set of circumstances, in the sciences it is by definition meaningless to say that one knows or understands a result, a law, or a hypothesis but cannot state or communicate what one thus claims to understand. If I cannot state the binomial theorem, or the law of inverse squares, or the valence rule, I do not know it, and any claim to the contrary is simply nonsense. In effect, the strategy of the sciences in the codification of their results is to reduce to a minimum in practice and to nothing in theory the gap between cognition and written communication.

The range of knowing, then, extends from what Willie Mays knows about baseball, which we would accept as demonstrated whether or not Mays can put together a single coherent sentence on the subject, to what a physicist knows about the results of investigations in physics, which he can demonstrate only with a denotative vocabulary and a mathematical syntax. The common factor is the capacity of each to render a consistently appropriate response; the difference lies in the nature of the response that is deemed appropriate; and the criterion of appropriateness is efficacy in encompassing the purpose of the activity to which the actor has committed himself.

In this general setting of the relation between knowing and communicating, what is the relation between knowing history and its communication in writing, that is, historiography? In the first place, among professional historians there is a rough consensus about the responses appropriate for writers of history when they set out to communicate what they know. This consensus enables one to speak of "the better historians" with a sense that one's judgment is not merely personal, random, or arbitrary. The consensus is approximately registered by the price a particular historian fetches in the current job market. (Only approximately, however, since a number of items other than the profession's estimate of his history writing go to make his price—his age, his reputed aptitude in face-to-face teaching, his personal qualities, the relation of supply to demand in his special field of interest, and so on.) Second, in writing history, as we have seen, some historians consistently use a vocabulary and a syntax similar to those which are standard in the natural sciences and some do not. There is, however, no significant correlation between the list of those who do so and the list of "better historians." This implies that in historiography, historians do not accept the scientists' conception of what constitutes a consistently appropriate response in the public presentation of the results of scientific investigation. An inquiry of no very pressing sort would reveal that in practice they have refused fully to commit themselves to a scientific rhetoric because they concern themselves with questions and answers which are not wholly tractable to the kind of formulation that scientists aim at, and because they assume in practice a relationship between cognition and communication in history different from that which is currently acceptable in the sciences.

Historians acquire their command of the data that they ultimately deploy in writing history through reading and considering what men have written in the past and about the past and by giving attention to remnants and traces of men's handiwork surviving from the past: buildings, tools, pictures, field systems, tombs, pots—archeological data in the broadest sense. The process of learning starts in a haphazard way with the student's earliest interest in history, and for the professional historian becomes more systematic and more sharply focused in the course of his training. In general, the training of a historian aims at the complementary but sometimes conflicting goals of simultaneously extending the range of his knowledge and of bringing it intensively to bear on some limited constellation of past happenings, in writing about which he is expected to make some contribution to the advancement of historical knowledge.

This process of knowing which goes on throughout the historian's active professional life is not identical with the knowing through experience which enables most men to meet most of the contingencies of their days on earth without continual bafflement, frustration, and disaster; but it is similar to it. It is not identical because in some measure the historian chooses what he will confront, while much of what men know through day-to-day experience comes at them haphazardly by no choice of their own.

Second, the layman's kind of knowledge is in large part acquired through face-to-face confrontation with persons and situations, while the historian's confrontation with men and situations of the past is mainly (in most cases, wholly) indirect, mediated by the surviving documentary and archeological record. Nevertheless, the difference ought not to be exaggerated, for there is considerable overlap. The printing press and more recent media of communication have vastly extended the role of indirect confrontation in day-to-day experiential knowledge. Moreover, in his quest for understanding of the past, the historian relies to a considerable extent on the cautious and qualified analogical application of experiential knowledge which he has accumulated in personal, face-to-face transactions during his own lifetime.

Finally, the difference between face-to-face confrontation and confrontation mediated by the historical record is one of mode but not necessarily of quality, or intensity, or depth, or coherence, or completeness. Any man who reads and meditates on the 12 volumes of the correspondence of Desiderius Erasmus, extending over a span of four decades, plus his massive literary output, may justly argue that in quality, intensity, depth, coherence, and completeness his experiential knowledge of that sixteenth-century intellectual, acquired through mediated confrontation, is more firmly based than the experiential knowledge that any contemporary of Erasmus had of him. Indeed, it is as firmly based as the knowledge available today about any intellectual now living. The similarity between the two kinds of knowledge we have been considering is that for many purposes the consistently appropriate response which indicates their presence is not and need not be verbal, and when verbal, it need not and quite possibly cannot take the form of wholly denotative statement, much less of mathematical formulation. For such purposes it lies closer to the Willie Mays pole of response by effective action than to the scientific pole of response by communicating results in unambiguous statement.

In a large part of his work, the historian has no need at all for such statement or for any coherent verbal statement at all. He is massively engaged in finding out what happened and how it happened. To do these things he must formulate rough hypotheses, often very rough, about what happened and how it happened, and then examine the available record to verify or correct his hypotheses. But at the outset, from an almost limitless range of conceivable hypotheses he must select for investigation the very few that lie somewhere in the target area; he must select only those for which the surviving records hold forth some hope of verification; and he must have a sense of what records among a multitude are likely to provide the evidence he needs. A historian unable to do any of these things would remain an inept novice all his life. Relying on their knowledge of the past, historians successfully do these things day after day, yet most of them would be at a loss to explain their particular choices. They tend to ascribe their general aptitude for making better rather than worse choices to "knowing the ropes" and "having been around a long time in this period." In effect, the knowledge that a historian relies on for a very considerable part of his work is experiential and results from a long and extensive familiarity with the historical record. (There is a legitimate doubt whether much of the foregoing does not apply as readily to the actual work of scientists as to that of historians.) For the historian the link between knowing and communicating is loose and weak; on the basis of his own experience of this looseness, he inclines to give some, if not full, faith and credit to colleagues who claim to know about the past much that they cannot adequately express in writing. Communication through historiography requires historians to put into written words what they know experientially and diffusely about the past, to organize it into coherent and sequential statements in order to make it fully accessible first to themselves and then to others. Their communication with others, the history they end up writing, thus starts four removes from the episodes in the past that concern them. Between the two lie the historical record, the historians' experiential knowledge acquired through their exploration of that record, and their attempts to communicate to themselves what they know.

Through these interposed layers historians, in and by their writing, seek, along with many other things, to enable their readers to follow the movement and to sense the tempo of events; to grasp and do justice to the motives and actions of men; to discern the imperatives that move men to action; and to distinguish those imperatives from the pseudo imperatives that have become mere exercises in pious ejaculation; to recognize the impact on the course of events of an accident, a catastrophe, or a bit of luck; and to be aware of what the participants in a struggle conceived the stakes to be. (This particular set of items which historians sometimes feel called on to communicate through the three layers has purposely been selected because (1) none of them are explanatory in the scientific sense and (2) none can be effectively communicated in a purely scientific rhetoric.) The historian's ability both as an investigator of the past and as a writer of history is measured nega-

tively by the extent to which he lets the layers that intervene between the episode in the past and the reader of his work insulate the reader from the past, positively by the extent to which he is able to make these layers serve as a conductor of knowledge of the past to his readers. Historians give faith and credit to their fellows who protest that they know and yet confess that they cannot communicate what they know, because in some measure every historian is aware how far he has failed in his writing of history to penetrate those layers in his effort to communicate what he knows of the past.

Given this sense of the inadequacy of their use of language to their task, historians would surely welcome as an alternative a wholly denotative universal vocabulary which would narrow to a scarcely discernible crevice the perilous chasm that for them separates cognition from communication and sets them ransacking the whole storehouse of their mother tongue instead of relying on a manageable number of well-designed symbolic structures to overcome it. The fact that no such alternative adequate to communicate what historians know about the past has up to now emerged suggests that the relation between knowing the past and the writing of history is such as to preclude that alternative, that in practice historians believe that the sacrifice of the knowledge of the past which it would entail renders inappropriate the universal imposition in historiography of the denotative rhetoric of scientific discourse.

Of course historians can avoid their rhetorical difficulties (1) by attempting to communicate about the past only that knowledge which can be expressed in a rhetoric nearly like that of the natural sciences or (2) by attempting to know about the past only what can be so communicated. In fact, historians have pursued both these courses. Some historians have taken the first course either because of a special interest in the sorts of historical problems manageable within the confines of a quasi-scientific rhetoric or because their special aptitude for that rhetoric has turned their attention to the sorts of problem with which it can deal. Others have taken the second course either out of allegiance to a conception (or misconception) called scientific history or because by calling their thinking and writing about the past scientific history, they thought they could sanctify their incompetence and dullness.

On the whole, however, historians have not been willing to truncate their knowledge of the past to fit the special aptitudes of a few historians or the misconceptions or painful ineptitude of a number of others. Instead, to make their experiential knowledge of the past accessible to readers who cannot recapitulate the processes by which that knowledge was acquired, they have used almost every device of rhetoric compatible with their commitment to a clear and intelligible presentation of the evidence on which their knowledge is based. That the language they use is frequently evocative and even metaphorical and that much of its vocabulary is not that of scientific demonstration but of the ordinary discourse of educated men, testifies to their conviction—rarely explicit, sometimes not wholly conscious—that these are the appropriate means for bringing their readers into that confrontation with events long past and men long dead which is an indispensable condition of knowing them. To the extent that the historian's rhetoric falls short of communicating what he believes he has discovered about the past, what he thinks he knows does not become generally available and cannot be tested publicly by other historians. To that extent, therefore, there is a loss of potential knowledge of the past. Conversely, to the extent that he succeeds in communicating anything that hitherto he alone has known, there is gain. Therefore, the advancement of historical knowledge depends to a considerable extent on the quality of the historian's rhetoric, on the efficacy of his historiography, and is almost inseparable from it; far from impeding the advancement of historical knowledge, language evocative rather than wholly denotative in intent and character becomes a means and a condition of that advancement.

Modes of explanation

Historiography is the means for communicating in writing what the historian thinks he knows about the past. Efficient and effective communication requires him, in writing history, to array what he knows according to some principle of coherence. The principle of coherence traditionally and still most generally employed by historians is narrative. Usually, but not always, they communicate what they know by telling a story or stories. Despite its venerable antiquity, narrative has recently come under attack as a means for providing coherence in history. The most general ground for attack seems to be the contention that the coherence it provides is nonexplanatory or inadequately explanatory. In this respect it is compared invidiously with the principle of coherence by subsumption under general laws supposedly standard in the rhetoric of the sciences, which is said to provide adequate explanation. If subsumption under general laws is the principle of coherence standard in the sciences, if by the criteria of the sciences it alone provides adequate explanation, and if the provision of adequate explanation is the sole or prime function of the sciences, then clearly narrative does *not* meet the scientific standard of coherence, nor does it provide adequate scientific explanation. It remains to ask, however, why historians should prefer a principle of coherence and criteria of explanatory adequacy borrowed from the rhetoric of the sciences both to narrative, their own traditional principle of coherence, and to the view of the nature and conditions of historical explanation which their use of narrative implies.

The ascription of adequacy to explanations of the general-law type seems to be based on both aesthetic and practical considerations. (1) Elegance, precision, clarity, internal consistency, and structural tidiness—a place for everything and everything in its place—in the domain of knowing: all these are aesthetically attractive concomitants of general-law explanations and are the generator and the justification of the denotative vocabulary and the mathematical syntax at which scientists aim. (2) In many or most cases, such explanations afford scientists the opportunity to replicate the experiment that was offered as evidence of the applicability of the general law, and thus to test the validity either of the law or of its application. (3) The rhetoric of the sciences facilitates the rapid and efficient identification of new problems and problem areas. (4) The expansion of the range and precision of general-law explanations has roughly coincided on the temporal scale with an extraordinary expansion of man's control of vast tracts of his environment over which hitherto he had exercised no control at all. Although by the general-law canon, or indeed by any canon of explanation that has not been in disrepute since Aristotle, such a coincidence taken alone does *not* adequately explain the expansion of control, still nothing succeeds like success, and the aura of prestige acquired by the natural sciences in the past three centuries has rubbed off on the criteria of adequate explanation ascribed to them, especially in the eyes of intellectually insecure social scientists and historians.

No one has ever made clear why the criteria of adequate explanation acceptable to scientists in their work should also be acceptable to historians in theirs, or why adequacy of explanation should be the *sole* criterion of consistently appropriate response for the historian engaged in the work of communicating his knowledge in writing. Adequacy of explanation is clearly relative to that which is to be explained. A guidebook to a city, for example, explains the location of a "point of interest" by designating what streets it is on and nearest to and by indicating the means of access to it from other points by various means of transportation. A real estate survey explains its location by designating the frontage and length of the lot, the street it faces on, and the distance of the lot from the nearest intersecting street. Both explanations are accurate, exact enough for their respective purposes, and therefore adequate; each communicates the knowledge likely to be sought by one particular sort of seeker and thus provides the appropriate response to his questions; neither invokes any general law, nor need it do so; neither is a scientific explanation, nor need it be so. Moreover, the notion that the sole appropriate response of the historian to his commitment to communicate what he knows is something designated "explanation" is wildly arbitrary. It involves either consigning a large part of that response to the domain of irrelevance or so extending the meaning of "explanation" as to render it unrecognizable by scientists, philosophers, ordinary readers, and historians themselves.

Historical narrative. Narrative, which is the rhetorical mode most commonly resorted to by historians, is also their most common mode of explanation. It is not in fact scientific by the criteria just indicated; it cannot be rendered scientific because it is formally not reducible to the general-law type of explanation; and no more than the "explanations where" set forth above need it be scientific in order to be adequate, unless one insists on applying the scientific criteria of adequacy to a nonscientific explanation. Narrative is the most common mode of historical explanation because it is often the kind of explanatory answer solicited by a kind of question that historians very often ask and that is very often asked of them. Two ordinary forms of this question are "How did it come about that . . . ?" and "How did he (or they) happen to . . . ?" For example, "How did it come about that a Labour government took power in England in 1964?" or "How did the New York Giants happen to play in the World Series in 1951?" The following discussion will be organized around a treatment of this second question. The writer has selected it because it leads quickly into so many of the topics of this section and because its evidential base is one on which he is more than ordinarily well informed.

The call for an explanation of how the Giants happened to play in the World Series of 1951 can be so construed as to make it amenable to explanation of the general-law type.

A. *The particular facts*
1. In 1951 the New York Giants were a baseball team in the National League.
2. In 1951, during the official National League baseball season, the New York Giants won more games from the other teams in that league and lost fewer to them than any of the other teams in the league won or lost.

B. *The general law*
Whenever during the official National League season a National League team wins more games and loses fewer than any other team in that league, it plays in the World Series.

The answer perfectly fulfills all the requirements of the general-law type of explanation, including denotative univocal vocabulary and strict deductive entailment. Yet from the point of view of the writer and reader of history, such an answer is patently unsatisfactory. The reason is that in the context of the National League season of 1951, the appropriate response to the question "How did the Giants happen to play in the World Series of 1951?" is the historical *story* of how the Giants came to lead the National League at the end of the official season that year. A general-law explanation cannot tell that story; indeed, it cannot tell any story. It is not built to tell stories. From this very simple instance an important conclusion follows: general law and narrative are not merely alternative but equally valid modes of explanation. In the above instance the general-law explanation does not tell the questioner what he wants to know; for him it is neither a good nor a bad, neither an adequate nor an inadequate, explanation—it is no explanation at all. And conversely, to other questioners asking scientists *and* historians for an "explanation," a response in the form of a story would be quite inappropriate and therefore no explanation at all. The validity of either mode of explanation is determined by the appropriateness and adequacy of its response to a particular question. In effect, the validity of modes of explanation is not something that exists *in vacuo*, but only in relation to what particular inquirers at particular moments seek to know.

In view of the frequent irrelevance of pure general-law explanation to past situations that require the telling of a story, attempts have been made to adapt the general-law type of explanation to narrative. Narrative explanation is usually presented as a series of statements of continuous causal linkages between events such that in the chains of causation (1) each effect is imputed to precedent causes and (2) the imputation implies either the actuality or the possibility of a general law or laws such that, taken with the precedent causes, they entail the effect.

For present purposes it is to our advantage that the official rules of baseball provide us with a vocabulary almost as purely denotative as that of the sciences. In that vocabulary we can produce a narrative explanation of how the New York Giants won the 1951 National League pennant and thus played in the World Series; this explanation conforms to the foregoing model.

National League Standings as of September 30, 1951

	Won	Lost
Brooklyn Dodgers	96	58
New York Giants	96	58

Because of the tie at the end of the regular season Brooklyn and New York were required to play additional games, the first team to win two games to be designated as the National League entry in the World Series.

First additional game, Oct. 1, 1951: final score, New York 3, Brooklyn 1; games won, New York 1, Brooklyn 0.

Second additional game, Oct. 2, 1951: final score, Brooklyn 10, New York 0; games won, New York 1, Brooklyn 1.

Third additional game, Oct. 3, 1951: inning-by-inning score to second half of the ninth inning:

Brooklyn	1	0	0	0	0	0	0	3	0
New York	0	0	0	0	0	0	1	0	

Score to second half of the ninth inning, Brooklyn 4, New York 1. New York at bat.

The first batter singled. The second batter singled. Because the first batter was a reasonably fast runner, he advanced to third base. Because the third batter hit a short fly ball which was caught, he was out. Because the fourth batter doubled, the first batter scored a run, and the second batter advanced to third base, where he was replaced by a substitute runner because he had hurt his leg. The Brooklyn pitcher was replaced because three New York players out of four had made safe hits off his pitching. Because the fifth batter hit a home run the substitute runner, the fourth batter, and the fifth batter scored runs. Because New York scored four runs in the second half of the ninth inning, making the score 5 to 4, they won the game. Because they won two games of the play-off before Brooklyn did, they won more games and lost fewer than any other team in the National League. Because of this they played in the World Series of 1951.

About the preceding narrative explanation a number of highly instructive points are worth noting.

(1) It almost perfectly conforms to the proposed structure of narrative explanation outlined above; that is, it is a series of sentences in which the causal connections between the events mentioned are explicit or clearly implicit, and into which the relevant possible general laws may readily be inserted. Any number of such laws are not merely possible but actually available, e.g., if the two leading teams in the National League have won and lost the same number of games at the end of the regular season, the rules require that they resolve the tie by playing against each other until one of them has won two games.

(2) All the facts as stated are verifiably true and all the causal inferences are valid, and therefore the whole narrative explanation is historically true and accurate in every respect.

(3) Nevertheless, at a number of crucial points it is hard to see how particular effects were strictly entailed by a combination of antecedent causes and general laws. What, for example, is the general law which with the precondition (three hits and one out, among four men at bat) entails the replacement of one pitcher by another? Even if one elaborated further on the boundary conditions— and that can be done—it is difficult to see how general laws can be invoked and a strict entailment made to work here.

(4) It is true that once the substitute Brooklyn pitcher, Ralph Branca, whose mere presence in the game seems not amenable to narrative explanation (see above), released the ball, and once the fifth New York batter, Bobby Thomson, began his swing of the bat, a combination of a few special cases (mainly ballistic) of the general laws of motion with the National League ground rules on home runs suffices strictly to entail that Thomson hit a home run. It is hard, however, to envision the combination of conditions and laws that would strictly entail a decisive precondition of that home run: to wit, that Thomson decided to swing at Branca's pitch in the first place.

(5) Even if these problems of the logic of narrative explanation can be resolved, the account as presented raises a number of difficulties and questions. (a) Why does the explanation begin with the play-off at the end of the regular season? On the face of it, in a regular season that ends in a tie, every game played throughout the season by the tied teams is of equal causal importance and therefore should receive equal treatment. (b) By the same token, why is a fuller account (inning-by-inning score) given of the last game of the official season than of the two previous games, and a still fuller account of the last half of the last inning of the last game?

(6) Most important, the explanation is historio-

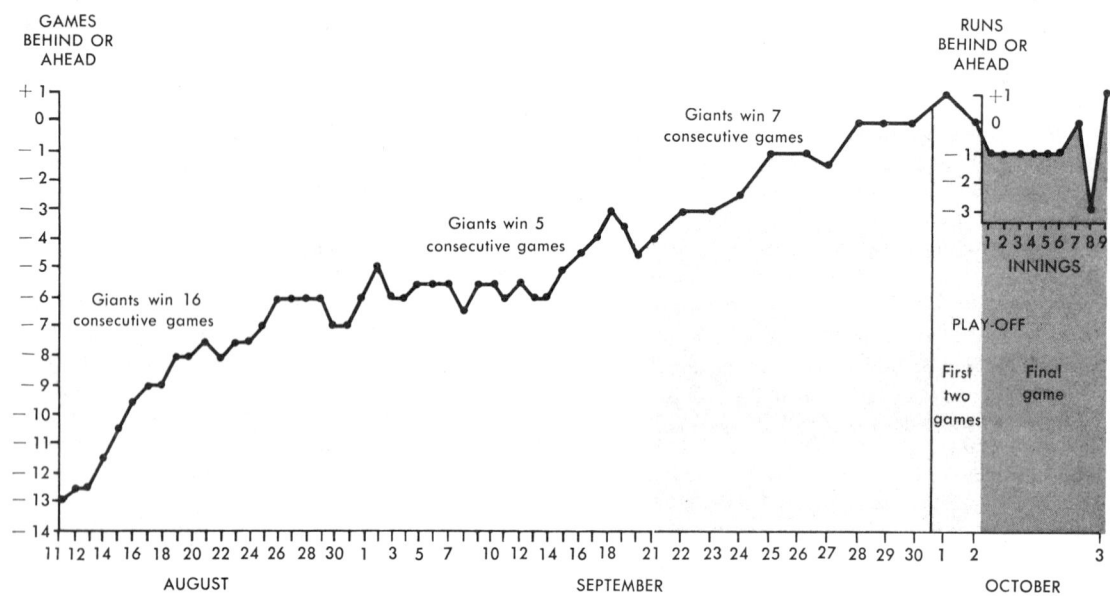

Figure 1 — The positions of the New York Giants in relation to the Brooklyn Dodgers in the 1951 pennant race, with standings shown at end of play on given date

graphically pitiful, and the historian who offered it would immediately lose the historian's moral equivalent of a union card.

Given the problem with which we started, these difficulties go to the heart of the trouble. They make it clear that offering an answer in the form of a narrative explanation which is structurally determined solely by the logic of causal ascription is not an appropriate response to the difficulties or an adequate solution to the problem. Within the bounds of the logic of causal ascription there is no solution for them. That logic cannot justify the shifts in the scale of the story. Yet it is reasonable to suspect that one of the few things which most readers would intuitively regard as appropriate about the above dreary but true narrative response to the question about New York being in the World Series in 1951 would be precisely the successive expansions of the scale of the story. The reason for this is that the appropriate response to the question is not a true narrative explanation determined by the logic of causal ascription but the historical story truest to the past, determined by the rules of historical evidence and the rhetorical rules of historical storytelling. Of this larger context a true narrative explanation is a part, but only a part. If this is so, then the true historical story rightly determined by the rules of historical rhetoric will be preferable to a true narrative explanation because it communicates more knowledge and truth about the past

than such an explanation does. But if that is so, then the rhetoric of history writing, not its logic alone, is implicated in providing increments of knowledge and truth about the past.

Let us continue with the example under examination, keeping in mind the problems of where to start the historical story and on what scale to tell it. Figure 1 describes the relative positions of the two contenders in the National League pennant race of 1951.

The first things to note in Figure 1 are the shifts in scale and the considerations which determined them. The over-all consideration is that of telling a historical story in such a way as to maximize the increment of knowledge and truth communicated. That within a framework identical with the one in which the figure is constructed (the 154-game baseball season) it may be desirable to have no change of scale and not to tell a story at all becomes clear on considering the description of the American League season of 1939 in Figure 2.

Figure 2 is constructed on uniform scales for each axis, plotting the games won by the New York Yankees against the games won by the team in the league that was in second place. That this season calls for no narrative explanation is manifested by the nonconvergence of the lines in Figure 2, which shows (1) that by June 1, the Yankees were seven games ahead, (2) that thereafter the minimum gap between them and their nearest rival was six

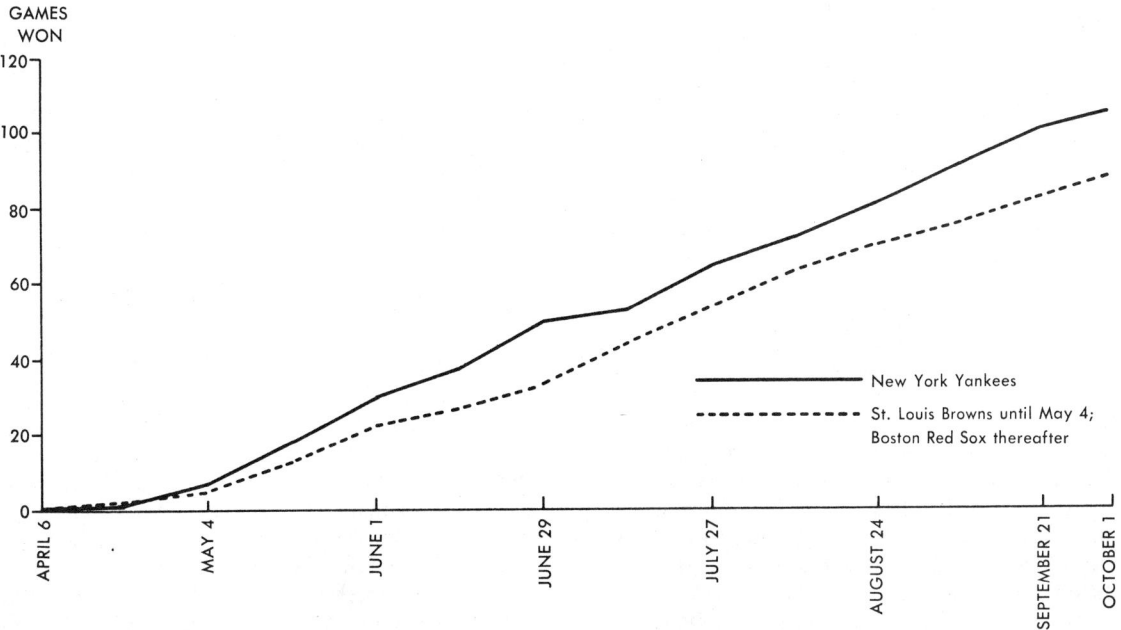

Figure 2 — The positions of the New York Yankees and the second-place American League team in the 1939 baseball season

games, (3) that by the end of the season the Yankees led by 17 games. In short, for more than the latter two-thirds of the season there was never a moment when it even looked like a pennant race, so that on the face of the record, to answer the question "How did the Yankees come to be in the World Series?" with a historical story would be a historiographic error: the even-paced, dull, and trivial chronicle which the effort would yield would itself demonstrate the inappropriateness of such a rhetorical response.

By the same token, the climbing line in Figure 1 indicates that the record of the 1951 National League season calls for a historical story, and that to write about its history without telling such a story is to fail to make the appropriate historiographic response. The data in Figure 1 start at the point where the extended historical story should begin: August 11, 1951, at the end of play. At that point New York was at its maximum distance behind Brooklyn, 13 games; and the next day New York began a series of 16 consecutive wins. For the next extension of the narrative and for the expansion of the scale of the graph, the directive of the record is more ambivalent. The options lie between (1) September 14, when, still six games behind, New York began a series of five consecutive wins which by September 18 moved it to within three

games of Brooklyn and (2) September 21, when, four games behind, New York won the last seven games of the regular season. It had moved into a tie at the end of play September 28, kept the tie by winning the last two games of the regular season, and was again tied at the end of the second game of the play-off. It is to be noted that (1) although there are two options for starting this expansion, there are *only* two serious options, and (2) they have an identical *terminus ad quem*, the point at which the next expansion of scale begins in the final game of the play-off. Either of the above alternative solutions is historiographically correct; *any other* is incorrect. There may be two or more right answers to some historiographic, as to some mathematical, problems. This does not imply or entail that there are no wrong answers. This simple observation and distinction, evident to any mathematics student who has gotten as far as quadratic equations, seems to have escaped most historians.

The expansions of scale, then, are not arbitrary; each can clearly be justified from the historical record on historiographic grounds, and each expansion coincides with a period in telling about which the historical storyteller would extend the dimensions of his story. Three further points must be made.

(1) On the basis of true narrative explanation

determined by the logic of causal connection, it proved impossible to determine where to begin the historical story of the 1951 pennant race or what dimensions to give to any of its parts. Indeed, since causal connection is subject both to infinite regress and to infinite ramification, and since that historical story and any other must have a beginning and finite dimensions of its parts, it is in principle impossible on the basis of the logic of narrative explanation alone to tell a historical story at all. On the other hand, the rhetoric of historical storytelling provided us with the means of recognizing whether there was a historical story to tell, where the story should start, and roughly what the relative dimensions of its parts should be. If this is so, (*a*) in the telling of a historical story, increments of historical knowledge and truth are unattainable on the basis of the logic of narrative explanation alone, for on that basis alone it is impossible so much as to begin such a story; and (*b*) for achieving such increments, insights into the rhetoric of historical storytelling, whether experiential and implicit or discursive and explicit, are indispensable.

(2) The clock and the calendar provide no guidance to the appropriate dimensions of a historical story. Between those dimensions and mere duration, measured in homogeneous scaled increments, there is no congruence. The historical storyteller's time is not clock-and-calendar time; it is historical tempo. The problems involved in reasonably accurate determination of historical tempo have never been systematically studied, although results of the disaster of not studying them strew the historiographic landscape. But two points are clear. (*a*) Disproportions in historical stories induced by failure correctly to appraise historical tempo result in the telling of distorted stories about the past. To that extent they diminish, and correct perception of tempo increases, available knowledge of the past. (*b*) The logic of narrative explanation has nothing to say on the subject of historical tempo; it is a question that can be dealt with only in the area of the rhetoric of historical storytelling. And so once again the communication of increments of knowledge and truth about the past hinges on the correct solution of problems of historiography. (*c*) Correct determinations of historical tempo and the appropriate correlative expansions and contractions of scale in a historical story depend on the examination *in retrospect* of the historical record. That is to say, when the historian tells a historical story, he must not only know something of the outcomes of the events that concern him; he must use what he knows in telling his story.

In the case of writers of history, Gallie's interesting analogy between historical understanding and following a game or story breaks down (1964, pp. 22–50). It applies to consumers of history, the readers, not to its producers, the writers. The readers need not know the outcome of the story; and it is well if, at least, they do not know the writer's construal of the outcome, since not knowing it whets their curiosity and intensifies their engagement and vicarious participation in the story, thus augmenting their knowledge of the past. But unless the writer has the outcome in mind as he writes the story, he will not know how to adapt the proportions of his story to the actual historical tempo, since that is knowable only to one who knows the outcome. For example, the decisive point for transforming the proportions of the historical story of the 1951 pennant race was entirely unobserved, unpredictable, and unpredicted by any contemporary observer. On August 11, at the point of maximum distance between Brooklyn and New York, no one foresaw or could have foreseen that New York was on the point of beginning a 16-game winning streak that transformed the baseball season into a pennant race in which New York was the ultimate victor. Indeed, the perspective of the historical storyteller throughout should be double —that of a contemporary observer and that of one who knows about Bobby Thomson's home run; but it is from the latter perspective, not the former, that the historian can perceive the historical tempo and thus determine the appropriate proportion of the historical story.

Historical analysis. Telling a historical story is not the only way in which a writer of history can increase knowledge of the past, as we have seen in the case of the American League season of 1939. Even to the question "How did it happen that . . .?" it is not always an appropriate response. Yet in the case in point, the response must have a historical character. The structure of Figure 2 suggests that it should take the form of historical analysis; for with its nonconverging lines it indicates that New York was a team so much better than any other in the league that it was beyond effective challenge. Consequently, to increase historical understanding there is nothing to do but analyze that betterness of New York, to seek out its ingredients and render them intelligible to the reader. Here, of course, the abundant surviving statistics of baseball provide a useful historical record to start with—the base-on-balls, strike-out, and earned-run averages of the pitchers; the batting and total base averages, the stolen bases, runs scored, and home runs of the hitters. (Fielding statistics, however, do not provide a satisfactory statistical basis for evaluating defensive performance in baseball.)

If the rhetoric of historical storytelling has received little attention from historians or others, the rhetoric of historical analysis has received none. When considering historical storytelling, the rhetoric of the fictive story offers a useful model; when considering historical analysis, the rhetoric of sciences in which the subject matter is less compatible with universal generalization than in physics might be appropriate. The almost complete lack of any serious concern with the problem may be due to the notion that the sciences have no rhetoric; but if one conceives of rhetoric as the organization of language appropriate to that particular kind of communication which is relevant to a particular activity, then any activity which is committed to verbal communication of its results has a rhetoric.

In recent years, instead of giving serious consideration to the serious problems of historical rhetoric, historians have engaged in considerable, and sometimes somewhat rancorous, discussion of the nonproblem of the relative merits of analysis and narrative in history writing. The discussion is footless because of two false assumptions: (1) that regardless of the character of the historical record, the historian has a wholly free option between analysis and narrative; (2) that these two historiographic modes mutually exclude each other, so that historians in all their work must opt wholly for the one or wholly for the other. With respect to the first assumption, we have seen in the instance of the two baseball seasons that the historical record presents us with constellations of events in which there is no serious option, where in one case to choose analysis, in the other to choose narrative, as the *predominant mode* would be a historiographic error and would prevent the historian from communicating what he knows about the past, and even from knowing it adequately.

In the second place, these modes are not mutually exclusive, and this again is evident with respect to our two "models." Although the mode of writing the history of the 1939 season should be predominantly analytical, still the force of the analysis would be strengthened by the resort to exemplary stories; and this is particularly the case with respect to fielding, in which the New York Yankees indeed excelled but which, because of limitations in the statistical record, lends itself better to anecdotal treatment, that is, to telling short illustrative stories. The case for the use of any analysis at all in the instance of the 1951 season might seem more dubious. The very fact of the tie at the end of the regular season could be taken as fair proof from

Table 1 — Percentage of games won by the New York Giants and the Brooklyn Dodgers in the 1951 baseball season

	New York Giants	Brooklyn Dodgers
Beginning of season to August 11*	54%	66%
August 12 to end of season	84%	60%
Total season (154 games)	62%	62%

* As of August 11 the Giants had played 110 games and the Dodgers 106.

a large sample of 154 games that overall the two teams were so well matched as to make analysis an exercise in futility. Actually, an examination of the record yields a quite different result.

Table 1 shows the percentage of games won out of games played by each team up to August 11, and from August 12 to the end of the regular season. It clearly poses two analytical questions: (*a*) how to account for the marked superiority of Brooklyn in the first hundred-odd games of the season; (*b*) how to explain the overwhelming superiority of New York in the last forty-odd games. For such an undertaking, as we have seen, analysis is the proper historiographic mode. Note that the selection of analysis as the dominant mode for the first seven-tenths of the season does away with the need for telling an inevitably thin story and thus enables the historian to maintain the proportion called for by the demand of historical tempo. One further complication: The analysis would fail to reveal a part of what made the difference, the part, told by Eddie Stanky more than a decade later, about a battered battalion with pulled muscles, bad throwing arms, and cracked bones that still could not lose for winning. And thus, to do the analysis itself justice, the historian would have to afforce it with historical stories about Alvin Dark, Wes Westrum, Sal Maglie, and Stanky's own slides-into-bases that were hard to distinguish from overt assault and battery. Our two examples were themselves carefully selected extreme cases of records that call respectively for analysis and storytelling. In most history writing, the need for a mix of the historiographic modes of storytelling and analysis is even more obvious. The serious historiographic problem is not how to avoid the mix in order to maintain the superiority of one mode over the other, but how to proportion it and how to manage it.

In the foregoing "model" of the pennant race of 1951, the discussion has slipped—the author has intentionally allowed it to slip—insensibly from the problem of narrative explanation to the problems of historical storytelling. In this it has followed the curve, as it were, of historical curiosity itself, both in the reader and in the writer of history. The original question, "How did it come about that . . .?," has become the more amorphous "Tell me (or let me find out) more about. . . ." The demand is no longer merely further *explanation*. A reasonably full explanation is presumably already in hand. That explanation itself has led reader and writer of history alike to shift the ground of their interest. Because of it they have become aware that they have stumbled onto one of the great events in baseball history, the event that culminated in Bobby Thomson's home run—the equivalent (in its sphere) of the defeat of the Armada, the battle of Stalingrad, the Normandy landings. What they want under these circumstances is not more or fuller explanation; what they want is confrontation with the riches of the event itself, a sense of vicarious participation in a great happening, the satisfaction of understanding what those great moments were like for the ordinarily cool Russ Hodges, Giant radio announcer, who, as the ball arched from Thomson's bat into the stands, went berserk and screamed into the microphone, "The Giants win the pennant! *The Giants win the pennant!* THE GIANTS WIN THE PENNANT!" And what those moments were like for those who saw what he saw and for those who heard him. Confrontation and vicarious participation are not historical explanation or explanation of any sort in any ordinary sense of the word. Yet clearly they are sometimes a part, and an indispensable part, of understanding the past as it actually was. Therefore, to argue that they have no place in historiography is at once arbitrary and absurd.

Finally, when the historian needs to bring those who seek to understand the past into confrontation with and vicarious participation in some part of it, he often finds the rhetoric of the sciences wholly inadequate for his purposes. In this sector of historiography it is hard to imagine a response to the proper demand on historians to render an accurate and effective account of the past that would be less appropriate than one couched in scientific rhetoric. In this sector, indeed, to do his work properly, *to tell the truth about the past*, the historian must marshal resources of rhetoric utterly alien to the rhetoric of the sciences in order to render his account forceful, vivid, and lively; to impart to it the emotional and intellectual impact that will render it maximally accessible and maximally intelligible to those who read it.

The analysis of historiography

The attitude of the historical profession to the writing of history has been ambivalent. Compared with the systematic attention historians have given to the techniques of historical investigation, their attention to the problems of historiography has been casual, and in their public judgments of the work of other historians they have tended to regard the rhetoric of history as at best a peripheral concern. On the other hand, some very able historians take far greater pains with their writing than would be warranted if the rhetoric of history were a mere pleasing embellishment not substantially involved in the advancement of the understanding of the past; and the consensus of the profession has ratified their practice by conferring on the most skillful writers of history rewards in prestige and pay that would be exorbitant if the yield of that skill were judged to be merely an amusing but supererogatory display of verbal pyrotechnics.

If the preceding arguments about the inseparability of the communication, and therefore the advancement, of historical knowledge from the rhetoric of history have any merit, then it would seem that a concerted effort to develop useful methods of analyzing historical rhetoric should stand high on the agenda of historians. In fact, however, their general concerns seem to be directed mainly toward two other areas, indeed, toward two nonproblems: (1) generalization and (2) the application of new knowledge in the social sciences to the study of history. The first is a nonproblem because in fact historians generalize and have generalized fruitfully at many levels for at least a couple of centuries, so that to raise at this late date the question of whether they do so or whether they ought to do so seems a little useless. Second, the application to the historical enterprise of any viable new technique for knowing is always desirable and is conditional only on the mastery of the technique and the identification of historical problems to which it can be usefully applied. In this respect the social sciences do not constitute a special case distinct from other techniques. Some historians have found some of the work of the social sciences useful for their particular purposes; others have not; still others have been preoccupied with other legitimate professional concerns. Their resistance to the demand for immediate and universal application to history of quantitative methods and of psychoanalytic insight does not seem to warrant the concern that it elicits from those who regard it as a chronic and possibly fatal disease of the historical profession as a whole. It does not appear to stand much above the level that reasonable professional prudence, sensible and limited skepticism, and resentment of new encroachments on limited resources of time, energy, and ability ordinarily generate.

Indifference to the problems of analyzing historiography, however, is easy to understand. In the first place, such analysis may well turn out to be a sterile exercise. In the second place, the need for analysis is evident only if one accepts the view that such attributes of historiography as accessibility, force, vividness, and depth are not merely decorative but have true noetic value. Although in unselfconscious practice many historians in fact accept this view, it remains submerged because of the counterthrust of an equally unself-conscious and incoherent assent to the ascription of noetic value only to the rhetoric of the sciences, especially to its denotative vocabulary and to its attributes of precision, simplicity, univocality, and so on.

In order to justify presenting the sketchy program for the analysis of historiography which this section will offer, it may be well to indicate the noetic bearing of at least one of the potential and requisite traits of historiography mentioned above —accessibility. In *On the Origin of Species* Charles Darwin says, "Nothing is easier to admit in words than the truths of the universal struggle for life, or more difficult—at least I have found it so—than constantly *to bear this conclusion in mind.*" The rhetorical problem that Darwin here points to is that of accessibility. It is a persistent problem for explanation in the narrative mode. The writer of history needs to be always watchful to see that pertinent previous generalizations, pertinent patterns of action previously identified, and pertinent parts of the story, already told, come to bear for the reader at the places where they are enlightening and revelatory. Even where it is technically accurate, dull history is bad history to the extent to which it is dull. By subjecting all the historian knows to the homogenizing and flattening operations of his own mechanical rhetoric, dull history blurs his findings for himself and for those who read his writing. Those findings then fail to become, or rapidly cease to be part of, the "workable reserve," the readily accessible knowledge, of the writer and reader, which remains concurrently present in their minds as the one composes and the other tries to follow the narrative or analysis. Consequently, in the course of events neither will see a partly ordered and patterned, and therefore partly intelligible, procession of change but a disjointed and arbitrary and therefore unintelligible one—just one damn thing after the other. A reader to whom almost nothing is communicated may reasonably suspect that the writer had almost nothing to communicate; but, as we have seen, because of the gap between knowing and communicating in history, this is not necessarily so. Rather, unintelligible communication is not communication at all; uncommunicated knowing can add no increment to the available body of

knowledge, and frequently the failure to produce such an increment is a failure in historiography, the absence of accessibility.

Accessibility has been treated here as an absolute trait of history writing, and of course it is not so. It is relative not only to the historian's rhetorical capacities but also to the absorptive capacities of the historian's audience, which depend on their prior knowledge. An amount of detail necessary to render what he wishes to communicate accessible to one audience would simply clutter the text for another audience and stultify their imaginations, thus diminishing for that second audience the range of conceptions that the historian wants them to have in mind. The problem that this situation poses for the writer of history is a complex one; it is another of the many places where the rhetoric of the historian intersects and is entwined with the knowledge he communicates and the truth-value of what he has to say. There is not space to treat the matter of accessibility further here, but what is said below on the matter of word lists indicates some of the ramifications of the problem.

The analysis of historiography can conveniently be divided into macroanalysis, microanalysis, and analysis of structure. Macroanalysis is the analysis of an individual piece of history writing as a whole; microanalysis is the analysis of any fragment of historical rhetoric without primary regard to and out of relation to the historiographic whole of which it is a part. Analysis of structure deals with historiographic traits, devices, and practices which are common to all or to a very considerable number of historical works. Hitherto we have keyed our discussion of historiography to the rhetoric of scientific statement and explanation in order to make and keep clear the likenesses and differences between the two. We have suggested, however, that in at least one trait which it requires in order to communicate some of the things the historian knows—its reliance on a connotative and evocative vocabulary—the rhetoric of history is nearer to that of the fictive arts than to that of the natural sciences. So before examining the types of historiographic analysis, it will be appropriate to point out a major difference between historical and fictive rhetoric—the overriding commitment of historians to fidelity to the surviving records of the past

Fidelity to records. The difference between historical and fictive rhetoric blurs slightly at the extreme limits, where, on the one hand, a novelist tells a story which he intends to reflect his conception of historical actualities and, on the other, a historian makes a story of a "typical case" that he imaginatively constructs out of his long experience with the historical record. The blurring itself becomes visible in a comparison of Conrad's *Nostromo* and Oscar Handlin's *The Uprooted*, but so does the difference that is blurred. For the worth of *Nostromo* as a novel would not diminish if the patterns of life Conrad ascribes to Costaguana, the imaginary Latin American republic which provides its setting and the substrate of its characters, were shown to be quite remote from extrinsic actuality. On the other hand, unless the record suggested that the immigrants' emotional response to their move to America was something like what *The Uprooted* imputes to them, the historiographic worth of *The Uprooted* would be nil, regardless of any merits that literary critics might ascribe to Handlin's prose style.

The standard of judgment of a fictive work does not depend on its compatibility with external actuality. The work as such depends for its authenticity or validity only on its relevance to the sector of general human experience which its author intends it to explore, describe, and render accessible. It can be true or false only to itself; and the knowledge which it communicates is independent of any particular in the record of man's past (though not, of course, independent of human experience in general). Or as A. J. Liebling put it, in treating the problems of a newspaperman, "To transmit more than half of what you understand is a hard trick, far beyond the task of the so-called creative artist who if he finds a character in his story awkward can simply change its characteristics. (Even to sex, *vide* Proust and Albertine. Let him try it with General de Gaulle.)"

It is precisely with Charles de Gaulle and his sort that reporters like Liebling and historians often have to deal. The standard of judgment of a historical work is ultimately extrinsic. Its authenticity, validity, and truth depend on the effectiveness with which it communicates knowledge (not misunderstanding) of the actual past congruent with the surviving record. The quality of its rhetoric is to be measured solely by its success in communicating such knowledge.

Macroanalysis. It follows from what has just been said that the unit of macroanalysis in historiography differs from the unit of macroanalysis in fictive studies. In the latter it is the entire particular work—novel or drama, ode or sonnet—considered as a self-contained unit. The macroanalyst can therefore demand of himself an examination of the whole relevant documentation and can reasonably expect those for whom he is writing to have the core element of that documentation (the work under analysis) before them. Ordinarily the macro-

analyst of historiography cannot demand so much of himself, still less expect so much of his readers. For him the relevant documentation is the work itself plus the historical record of the episodes with which the author concerned himself, not merely the part he used but any important part that through errors of omission he failed to use. It is improbable that in most instances the analyst will command the full range of documentation; it is practically impossible under ordinary circumstances to expect the reader of the analysis to have the documentation in front of him.

Despite these limitations, some experiments in detailed macroanalysis seem desirable because only in such analysis does one deal with the actual unit of historiography—the historical work. Whether that work be a long treatise or a short article, its presentation is the means by which by far the largest part of the increments of historical knowledge is communicated. It is also the place where historians meet their worst failures—from the novices who, having researched their subject, have not a notion how to organize it for effective communication to those senior historians who have so completely surrendered to their own ineptitude as to transform verbosity into a criterion of excellence. By selecting a relatively short piece of historical writing based on a record of manageable dimension and reproducing both the piece and the record, it would be possible to perform the sort of detailed macroanalysis in historiography that is a commonplace in the field of literary criticism.

Until a few such analyses are attempted, it is impossible to estimate what gains, if any, in the understanding of historiography may accrue from them; but it is hard to see why the macroanalysis of a historical study would be less fruitful of knowledge than the analysis of, say, *Waiting for Godot*. It is evident that unless such analysis is attempted, some aspects of the writing of history are bound to remain wrapped in mystery. For example, the present writer is a reasonably competent practitioner of history writing, and he has done a reasonable amount. One of the most effective sentences he has ever written in a historical essay is the following: "It was just the right thing for him to do." To understand why that simple declaratory statement composed of flat monosyllables should be effective would depend on a careful macroanalysis of the entire essay of which it is the last sentence.

To the best of the writer's knowledge, up to the present no macroanalysis of any historical work has even been attempted on the scale and in the way above proposed. Only after it has been attempted several times will any estimate of its value be more than an idle guess. In the meantime, the discussion of historical story writing and historical analysis in previous sections of this article points to a very few of the problems—proportion of the story, historical tempo, balance of analysis and narrative—with which macroanalysis would have to concern itself.

Microanalysis.   Although microanalysis is primarily concerned with single small items of historical rhetoric, the radical severance of it from macroanalysis is not practically possible. Some sense of the whole framework remains essential, because only through that sense can one arrive at a judgment on the ultimate efficacy and appropriateness of a given small item of historical writing which is a part of a historiographic whole. "The Army of the Covenant of the Scots with their God marched across the Tweed to rescue their sore beset English brethren" is historiographically sound, if its general context requires at the point of its introduction a quick communication of the spirit in which the Scots took the field in 1644. If the total context is the logistical problems created by the presence of a considerable military force in the agriculturally unproductive north of England in the mid-seventeenth century, however, a less allusive statement, detailing the number of Scots who entered the northern counties and their daily requirement of food and forage, would be rather more appropriate.

For the examination of any single element of historical rhetoric, macroanalysis (although not necessarily on the scale above suggested) is desirable. Only by means of it can one finally judge whether that element is appropriate, for its appropriateness is a function of the *whole* context of which it is a part. Ostensible grotesquerie—Alexander in full plate armor—may be appropriate enough if we see the whole picture, as Panofsky showed in discussing medieval representations of that hero. Because, however, the single historical statement has a dual context—both the work of history in which it is embedded and the actuality of the past to which it refers—it is possible to clarify some of the specific characteristics of the rhetoric of history by microanalysis considered with minimal reference to the total structure of the historical work of which the fragment under microanalysis is a part. In effect, given a five-page account of the battle of Waterloo embedded in a historical work, by referring the account to the historical record, it is usually possible to say within the limits the historian set for the account whether it is historiographically sound at the level of microanalysis. On examining it in connection with the whole work, however, we might alter our judgment on the grounds that in its

macroanalytic context it is disproportionately long or short, that it is dissonant with the rest of the book, or even that it is wholly irrelevant.

Microanalysis of historiography is therefore provisional in the judgments it yields on the material it deals with, but it does at least yield provisional judgments. Here we have space to treat only one hypothetical example of microanalysis. Let us suppose a historian faced with the problem of dealing in two pages with the character and administration of U.S. President Warren G. Harding. One can conceive of his choosing to do it in the style of the late Ring Lardner and with a rhetoric—a vocabulary and syntax—as close to Lardner's as his own sense of historiographic proprieties and that of his editor would permit. Or one can conceive of a characterization the whole tone of which was heavily heroic in vocabulary and syntax—so long as the undertone made it evident that the verbal heroics were mock heroics. What would be wholly inappropriate to a brief characterization of Harding and his entourage would be a rhetoric of intentional, unrelenting, and unremitting solemnity. On the other hand, briefly to characterize Abraham Lincoln in either of the former rhetorical modes would not only be bad taste, it would be bad historiography; and the historian who employed either would promptly be marked by his peers as inept and incompetent. For Lincoln was a serious man (which did not prevent him from being a very humorous one) and a serious historical figure, and any attempt to present him in a short sketch which failed to reflect this fact would to that extent fail to communicate to the reader something he needed to understand about the realities of a part of the past. It would thereby not only fail to advance but perhaps would even diminish his knowledge and understanding of the past, his grasp of part of its meaning, his store of historical truth.

The implications of this excursus on the use of microanalysis of historiography in connection with characterizing actual persons of the past are worth a little further attention, since one of the persistent problems of history writing, calling for microanalysis, is that of characterization. In effect, in many kinds of historical investigation the historian encounters persons in the record of the past. He can disregard them as persons and transform them into, say, numbers; and a demographic historian quite rightly does just this, simply because that is in fact the aspect under which he encounters them. He is like a man trying to get on a full elevator who encounters the persons already aboard merely as "a full elevator." But that is not always, or even often, the way a historian encounters persons in the record of the past. If he encounters them *as persons*, an attempt to avoid characterizing those implicated in an important way in the account he is rendering is a refusal to deal faithfully with the record of the past.

No one whose judgment is worth serious consideration has ever suggested that historians must never characterize people they encounter in the past; and it is at least arguable that the normal rhetoric of history is such that a historian dealing with extensive data on the deeds and words of a person of the past cannot avoid characterizing him, that the only question is whether he characterizes him well or ill, whether he does him justice or injustice. Nor has anyone ever argued that it is desirable or indeed even possible adequately to characterize a man in the wholly denotative rhetoric that is appropriate to scientific discourse. Indeed, the very phrase "do justice," which is quite appropriate to describe the goal of characterizing a man, is itself so massively connotative, so indispensably imprecise, as to render nugatory any hope of accomplishing with a sterilized denotative vocabulary and syntax a mission so vaguely described and imprecisely delimited. And yet it is possible by microanalysis of historical writing to arrive at judgments not merely of "bad" and "good" but also of "false" and "true" (or at least "truer") with respect to the connotative rhetoric which a historian chooses to employ in fulfilling his commitment to do justice to the character of a man. Nor is there any great mystery about this in the case of men concerning whom the historical record is reasonably ample. Considering the rhetorical possibilities as a very broad spectrum and also as a complete spectrum within the bounds of the rhetorical potentialities of the common language structure, there will be areas of that spectrum into which what is known about a particular man cannot be fit without manifest distortion of the record and areas into which it fairly fits, although in both cases there may be several such areas. This was manifestly the case in the instances of Harding and Lincoln dealt with above. But to distort the record is precisely to communicate ignorance rather than knowledge, misunderstanding rather than understanding, falsehood rather than truth.

The only necessary qualification here is that no historian does, and no sensible historian claims to, communicate the whole truth about a man, since there are many things about any man living or dead which no human being, not even the man himself, knows. The full knowledge on which alone a final judgment is possible exists only in the mind of God. The facts remain that in certain reaches of historiography the characterization of men is inescapable, that the rhetoric of such characterization is inescapably nonscientific, and that the knowledge, understanding, and truth communicated by the history of which the characterization is a part will in some measure depend on how well or ill the historian deploys the resources of this inevitably nonscientific rhetoric, on the appropriateness of his response to the demands that the historical record makes on his ability to use nonscientific language in delineating a character. The curious problems that this situation implies deserve further examination.

Analysis of structure. The general analysis of historiography deals with those traits and devices of historical rhetoric which are unique to the writing of history, or, more frequently, with those traits and devices which historians use in a unique way, a way which differentiates them from their use in the sciences or in the fictive arts. In the following treatment of structural analysis of historiography we will focus attention on three devices of the rhetoric of history: (1) the footnote, (2) the quotation in the text, (3) the word list; and we will concentrate on what differentiates the historian's use of these devices from the use scientists make of their homologues in scientific rhetoric.

Footnotes. Historians and scientists both use footnotes, and for one purpose they use them in about the same way: they use them to cite to the "literature" of the subject or problem about which they are writing. Historians, however, also use footnotes in a variety of other ways. One way historians use them and physicists do not is to cite to the historical record, the substrate of evidence on which historians erect their accounts of the past. Citation to that record is the way a historian makes his professional commitment clear in action, as the report on the experiment is the way a physicist makes his commitment clear. In both instances it is a commitment to maximum verisimilitude (which does not mean exact replication in every detail). For the physicist it is maximum verisimilitude to the operations of nature as glimpsed through consideration of the experimental cluster; for the historian, verisimilitude to the happenings of the past as glimpsed through consideration of the surviving record.

The well-nigh universal use of footnotes to the record by historians indicates that they are all still committed to writing about the past, as Ranke put it, *wie es eigentlich gewesen*, as it actually happened. In today's somewhat more sophisticated language, we might say that historians are concerned and committed to offer the best and most likely account of the past that can be sustained by the relevant extrinsic evidence. Let us call this statement about the historian's commitment the "reality" rule.

Historians employ the footnote for a host of residual matters other than citations to the record—lists of names, minor qualifications of assertions made in the text, polemic criticisms of other historians, short statistical tables, suggestions for future historical investigation, and many more. This raises two questions. (1) Amid the apparent chaos of "residual" footnotes, are there any rules at all regulating their use? (2) What is the relation of any rules found to the "reality" rule?

As to the first question, the application of any rule about footnotes requires an act of judgment in each case, and among historians judgment about the uses of residual footnotes differs. It might seem that in matters of judgment, as in those of taste, there is no disputing. But is this so? Let us consider an example.

At Shilbottle, in the case of three separate parcels of meadow, 31, 20 and 14 acres respectively, the first rendered 42s. in 1415–16 and 30s. in 1435–6, the second 28s. in 1420–1 and 23s. in 1435–6, and the third 24s. in 1422–3 and 14s. in 1435–6. At Guyzance 6½ husbandlands each rendered 13s.4d. in 1406–7, but 10s. in 1435–6.

At Chatton and Rennington, on the other hand, the situation was more stable. At Rennington the clear revenues were £17.8s.3d. in 1435–6 and £17 in 1471–2 and at Chatton £40.18s.7d. in 1434–5 and £36.18s.7d in 1472–3. At Chatton the decline was due to a fall in the value of the farm of the park, from £6.13s.4d. to £2.13s.4d. . . .

The above passage is embedded in the *text* of a study of the wealth of a magnate family in the fifteenth and early sixteenth centuries and the effect on that wealth of concurrent changes in the economy, the military apparatus, and the political situation in England. Can anyone suggest that embedding it in the text instead of quarantining it in a footnote was *not* an error of judgment? But to say it was one is to imply a *rule* from which the erroneous judgment was a deviation. Can such a rule, a "law" of historical rhetoric or historiography, be stated? Approximately the rule might go: "Place in footnotes evidence and information which if inserted in the text diminish the impact on the reader of what you, as a historian, aim to convey to him."

So although in the matter of the use of residual footnotes judgment is inescapable, we are not at all confronted with mere arbitrariness but with a reasonably precise rule or law. We may name it the "maximum impact" rule. Inevitably, marginal situa-

tions exist in which historians disagree about how to achieve maximum impact or the success of a particular rhetorical presentation. The existence of such marginal situations, however, does not mean that all situations are marginal and that therefore there is no rule, or that any rule is as good as any other. Lawyers have a saying that hard cases make bad law, but they do not feel impelled thereupon to argue that there are no easy cases and no good law. Because there are some matters both substantive and procedural concerning which they are very uncertain, some historians have fallen victim to the notion that everything about the past and about writing about it is infected with a total uncertainty. Yet this is clearly not so in the case of the residual footnote, where there was no difficulty in finding a rule not heavily infected with uncertainty.

What, then, is the relation of the two rules—the "reality" rule and "maximum impact" rule—to each other? In the example of data that, by the second rule, ought to be withdrawn from the text and consigned to a residual footnote, those data are informative and relevant with respect to the substantive historical argument the historian is presenting, and they are as complete, as explicit, and as exact as possible. But the historian is also committed to conveying to the reader with maximum impact his conception and understanding of the past as it actually happened, the "reality" of the first rule. And paradoxically, this implies that in the interest of conveying historical reality to the reader with maximum impact, the rules of historiography may require a historian to subordinate completeness, explicitness, and exactness to other considerations. If this is so, it indeed separates historiography from the rhetoric of the sciences as currently conceived.

Quotation in the text. Again, although both may quote in the text, there is a major difference here between the historians and the physicists. If physicists could not quote in the text, they would not feel that much was lost with respect to advancement of knowledge of the natural world. If historians could not quote, they would deem it a disastrous impediment to the communication of knowledge about the past. A luxury for physicists, quotation is a necessity for historians, indispensable to historiography.

The kind of quotation that historians deem indispensable is quotation from the record. Again two questions arise. (1) Is there any rule governing quotation from the record? (2) How does that rule relate to the "reality" rule?

Consider a hypothetical case of inept quotation.

Suppose in writing the history of the Civil Rights Act of 1964, a historian were to quote verbatim from the *Congressional Record* the entire debate on the act in both the House and the Senate. The result would be relevant, exact, and accurate—and not only the judgment but the sanity of the historian would fall under serious question. Again the paradox: maximum completeness, accuracy, and exactness are not always essential or even desirable in the historian's work of trying to tell the reader what really happened. Now consider an adept quotation taken from E. Harris Harbison's *The Christian Scholar in the Age of the Reformation*:

Erasmus had absorbed [Lorenzo] Valla's historical perspective, his sense of the historical discontinuity between pagan antiquity and the Christian era . . . a sensitivity to anachronism. On one occasion he ridiculed the absurdity of the practice . . . of using Ciceronian words to describe an utterly different modern world: "Wherever I turn my eyes I see all things changed, I stand before another stage and I behold a different play, nay, even a different world." The world of Cicero (or of Paul) can be understood and even in a sense relived—but only if we recognize that it had its unique existence, once, in a past now dead.   (1956, p. 93)

The function of Harbison's brief but apt quotation from Erasmus is not mere validation or proof of his assertions; he could as well have effected that by citation or quotation in a footnote. By using Erasmus' own words in the text, he sought and won a response not merely of assent but of conviction, not just "Yes," but "Yes, indeed!" Nothing Harbison could have said about Erasmus' sense of history could produce the conviction about it that Erasmus' own assertion of his intense feeling of distance from antiquity produces.

The quotation aims at something in addition to conviction, however. The quotation communicates the historian's own view of what happened in the past by the particular means of confrontation. It says in effect, "In my judgment the most economical way at this point to tell you what I believe Erasmus meant and to convince you that he meant it is to confront you directly with what Erasmus said." This provides us with a third general rule of historiography—an "economy-of-quotation" rule: Quote from the record of the past only when and to the extent that confrontation with that record is the best way to help the reader to an understanding of the past *wie es eigentlich gewesen*. It is evident, however, from the instance of the hypothetical case of the *Congressional Record* that mere confrontation with the *record* of the past is not necessarily the best way to achieve this understanding or even to achieve historical confrontation. Indeed, far from being a clear glass window through which the reader may capture an image of the past, quotation from the record injudiciously used can be a thick opaque wall that cuts him off from it. Granted that confrontation is an appropriate means for a historian to avail himself of in his efforts to convey to the reader an understanding of what actually happened, it then becomes possible to transcend the paradox previously noted. It opens up the possibility that the microscopic means of historiography have to be adapted to its macroscopic ends and that it is part of the task of the writer of history to mediate understanding and confrontation by devices of the rhetoric of history less direct but more compelling, more to the purpose than a simple maximizing of completeness, accuracy, and exactness.

The word list. The word list is a device useful both in the rhetoric of history and in the rhetoric of the sciences. (It is a sequence of words, usually nouns, whose relations as members of a set are often made evident by a sequence of commas and/or semicolons, the conjunction "and," or typographical arrangement in a table.) Consider the following lists:

An inert element will not react or enter into chemical combination with any other element. In order of increasing atomic weight the inert elements are helium (4), neon (20), argon (39), krypton (84), xenon (131), and radon (222).

The average incomes of only three of the learned professions fall into the first quartile of all average incomes. In descending order of quartile and rank, the average incomes of members of the learned professions were as follows: surgeons (1,2), physicians (1,4), dentists (1,7), college professors (2,23), high school teachers (3,41), clergymen (3,47), grade school teachers (3,52).

The first list is scientific; the second, historiographic. They are in many respects similar. In intent the words composing them are wholly denotative. They are not supposed to cast any shadow, to connote or evoke anything. Their arrangement (ascending order, descending order) is dictated entirely by considerations of rational utility. They both implicitly relate to an informational framework equally denotative in intention—the periodic table of all chemical elements, the table of average incomes of the total population classified by profession and trade. Both listings aim to achieve a purpose universal in the rhetoric of the sciences, common but not universal in the rhetoric of history. The scientist always wants the state, process, and set of entities he is dealing with so labeled that the labels unambiguously and unequivocally point to that state, process, and set only. For the scientist's purpose when he is formally communicating what he knows, words need to be free of contamination, of connotation, evocation, and emotive force, as sterile as the apparatus in an operating room. Otherwise he may find the wires of communication snarled and, as a consequence, have to rectify avoidable confusion. In this matter the historian's purpose often coincides exactly with that of the scientist. It is only under the conditions and with a vocabulary of the kind above specified that he can to his own satisfaction transmit some of the kinds of information and understanding that he intends to communicate. Yet even the very close approximation to scientific rhetoric exemplified by the foregoing historiographic word list deviates from the scientific standard in ways that help to differentiate both the problems and the purposes of history from those of the sciences. Consider the question "Is not zinc (65) also an inert element?" To answer this question one can pour hydrochloric acid over zinc. Since one of the yields of this operation is zinc chloride ($ZnCl$), a chemical combination or compound, zinc is not an inert element.

The taxonomic system of chemical elements— the periodic table—is thus free of ambiguity. Suppose, on the other hand, the question were raised whether clergymen and elementary and high school teachers should be included as members of the learned professions when the executives of large corporations are excluded. The question points to doubts about a system of classification that might include store-front preachers and graduates of retrograde teacher-training colleges among members of the learned professions while excluding the products of the better graduate schools of business administration. These doubts thus revolve about the identifying traits of the learned professions and the expediencies involved in the selection of any one set as against alternative sets of traits for classificatory purposes.

In any developed natural science, expediency in the choice of traits for a taxonomic system depends on the "importance" of the traits within the bounds of that science—e.g., in chemistry, valence and atomic weight as against color and taste. And importance is graded by applicability within the framework of generalizations or "scientific laws" that articulate the structure of the science in question and form the basis of its dominant mode of explanation. The dominant mode of historical explanation, narrative, emits no such clear, uniform signal for determining importance, and therefore in historiography the expediencies of alternative

taxonomic systems often remain equivocal and debatable. It is this situation which generates the interminable discussions among historians about whether sixteenth-century monarchies were *really* absolute, whether the Indians in the *encomiendas* in the Spanish colonies were *really* in servitude, whether the owner–operator of a small newsstand is *really* a capitalist. Such discussions seem futile because they purport to deal directly with the actual character of the past, a historical problem, when in fact they are concerned with the relative expediencies of alternative taxonomic devices for communicating knowledge of the past, a historiographic problem. The problem of taxonomy so considered, however, is anything but trivial (1) because classification systems both condition effectiveness of communication and channel the course of historical thinking, and (2) because in the very nature of the rhetoric of history, terms like "capitalist," "absolute," and "learned profession" cannot be rendered wholly denotative to the consumer of history writing. Given the nonscientific values pursued in historiography, a historian using such terms will have to decide, for the purposes of the story or narrative explanation engaging him at the moment, how much time and effort he should expend in separating the connotative values from those terms and how important those connotative values are for advancing the historical understanding of the matter at hand. It is evident, in any case, that the general analysis of historical rhetoric involves a study of problems of taxonomy in history closer than any undertaken up to now.

One further trait of the above historiographic word list needs to be noted: it is either elliptical or meaningless. It acquires meaning only if time and place are specified, whereas no such specification is necessary in the above scientific list. A statement whose formal structure and manifest purpose seem very close to those that characterize the natural sciences illustrates the dominant time–place specificity of the rhetoric of history as against the dominant time–space generality of the rhetoric of the sciences. Thus the analysis of a historical word list reinforces the conclusion that has emerged time and again in the course of this discussion of the rhetoric of history: despite occasional likenesses, historiography is radically unassimilable to the rhetoric of the natural sciences.

This can be even more effectively illustrated by another example of the historiographic use of a list.

The Christian Revival, that intensification of religious sentiment and concern that began long before 1517 and extended long beyond, in its full span had room for Cardinal Ximenes and Girolamo Savonarola; Martin Luther and Ignatius Loyola, the Reformed churches and the Jesuits, John of Leiden and Paul IV, Thomas Cranmer and Edmund Campion and Michael Servetus.

The names constitute a historiographic list, intended to serve a particular purpose of the rhetoric of history. It emits a signal, and what the signal says to all who hear it is: "Draw on the reservoir of your knowledge of the times in which these men lived to give meaning to this list." If that reservoir is altogether empty, then inevitably the list will itself be historiographically empty, meaningless, a mere collection of sounds, just as the sentences about the inert gases are empty of meaning to any who have no notion of what a chemical element or a chemical reaction or atomic weight is. The reason for this similarity is that in the present case both the historiographic rhetoric and the scientific rhetoric presuppose that the reader already possesses a body of precise and exact knowledge of the particular universes to which they refer. The scientific and the second historiographic statement both conform to the "reality" rule; they are meaningless unless there are such elements as helium, neon, and argon; and unless there were such men as Loyola, Cranmer, and Paul IV. Yet the second historiographic list serves a rhetorical function quite different from that served by the scientific list. First, consider the order of the two lists. Given the gases' common trait of inertness, the order of the scientific list indicates the scientist's normal preoccupation with establishing scalable differences of homogeneous traits—in this case, weight. In the historiographical list, on the other hand, no such preoccupation is discernible, yet the arrangement of the names lies at the very heart of the matter.

Note that there are three alternative ways of writing the historiographic list, all of which maintain the essential arrangement, to convey whatever information it contains.

(1) Cardinal Ximenes and Girolamo Savonarola, Martin Luther and Ignatius Loyola, the Reformed churches and the Jesuits, John of Leiden and Paul IV, Thomas Cranmer and Edmund Campion and Michael Servetus.

(2) The pre-Reformation cardinal who reformed the church in Spain, and the pre-Reformation monk who was burned at the stake for his reforming efforts in Florence; the first great figure of the Reformation and the first great figure of the Counter Reformation; the cutting edge of the Protestant attack and the cutting edge of the Catholic counterattack; the most fanatical prophet of the radical Reformation and the most fanatical pope of the era of religious strife; the Protestant martyred by the Catholics, the Catholic martyred by the Protestants, and the martyr who escaped death

at the hands of the Catholics only to receive it at the hands of the Protestants.

(3) Cardinal Ximenes, the pre-Reformation cardinal who reformed the church in Spain, and Girolamo Savonarola, the pre-Reformation monk who was burned at the stake for his reforming efforts in Florence; Luther, the first great figure of the Reformation, and Loyola, the first great figure of the Counter Reformation; the Reformed churches, the cutting edge of the Protestant attack, and the Jesuits, the cutting edge of the Catholic counterattack. . . .

The persons balanced in tension with one another are the same for all three versions of the list, and the arraying is identical in all three. On mathematical principles, a member of any of the lists should be freely substitutable for the corresponding member of either of the other two, but in writing history *this is not so*. Each list must retain its integrity. On what grounds can a historian choose among the three? One might argue that the second list is preferable to the first since it explicates the rationale upon which the persons in the first list were arrayed and that, in point of information about the past, the third is best of all, since it both names the persons and explicates the rationale of their array. Yet a reasonably experienced historian committed to communicating what he understands about the past actually chose the *first* option—the bare list of names with no indication as to his grounds for choosing them or for ordering them as he did. His choice is explicable when related to an earlier observation about the signal emanated by the list: "Draw on the reservoir of your knowledge of the times in which these men lived to give meaning to the list." The writer assumed that most of his readers could and would in fact draw from their particular reservoirs the items of general information in the second and third lists.

The effect of spelling out that information, however, is to emit another kind of rhetorical signal, a stop signal: "Stop drawing on the reservoir of your knowledge. I have already told you how I want you to think about these men." And this stop signal is just what the writer did *not* want the list to emit. The third version of the list is more exact, more overtly informative than the bare names in the first list, and just for that reason it is more empty, less ample. It dams up the informed reader's imagination instead of letting it flow freely, bringing with it the mass of connotation and association that those names have for him. Therefore, to prevent such a blockage the writer chose the first list. In doing so, he made a judgment. He judged (or gambled) that the connotative, evocative list would communicate a fuller meaning than the exact one, that it would more effectively confront the reader with the reality of the Christian revival, and that therefore it was the more appropriate device for advancing the reader's understanding of it. Whether he was correct in his judgment or not is immaterial. In setting forth his findings, a scientist never needs to make such a judgment at all. Scientific rhetoric is purposefully constructed to free him of that need by barring connotative terms and evocative devices. To a scientist the idea that he had to choose between a rhetoric of clarity and precision on the one hand and one of evocative force on the other would be shocking. The idea that the writer of history has to select between mutually exclusive ways of setting forth the same data and that the knowledge of history that he conveys depends in some measure on his judgment in selecting among alternative rhetorical devices is perhaps as disturbing and perplexing. But one is impelled to the latter conclusion by an investigation of the peculiarities of the way writers of history use footnotes, quotations, and word lists.

Codification of historiographic principles

The whole preceding article may be regarded as a prolegomenon to a codification of principles of historiography. Its aim has not been to produce such a codification but (1) to indicate that it might be possible to produce one and (2) to educe a few of the rules that would have place there. It has been concerned time and again to mark the irreducible differences that separate the rhetoric of history from that of the natural sciences because, given the prestige of those sciences and the striking similarity of some of the objectives of history writing and science writing, there is a danger that an attempt to codify the principles of historiography might take the form of a systematic effort to reduce as far as possible those principles to the ones current in the natural sciences. This indeed has already been the outcome of attempts by analytic philosophers from Carl Hempel to Morton White to codify the rules of historiography. The outcome of such an effort would be catastrophic, not because it would be an utter failure but because it would be a partial success. It would succeed in codifying rules about a great deal of what historians write in a way that would relate it closely to what scientists write. It might then be inferred that only the part of the rhetoric of history which can be articulated with that of the sciences is fit for communicating what in the course of

their researches historians learn about the past, or that only that part is amenable to codification. In the foregoing discussion, however, we have already seen that in the writing of history it is often necessary to employ language in ways that scientists quite properly reject for communicating the results of their investigations. Therefore, instead of extending our knowledge of the past, to limit historiography to those statements about the past which can be formulated in the rhetoric of the sciences would sharply constrict it.

The rational procedure in attempting to elicit general rules of historiography would be, rather, to make a series of analyses of the kinds classified and discussed in the previous section, taking as their subject pieces of historical writing which on the basis of a broad consensus of historians have been extraordinarily successful in transmitting what their writers knew about the past. It is impossible, of course, to predict in substance the outcome of such an analytical effort. Because in the section on general analysis we were able to elicit a few sample rules, it may, however, be possible to hazard a conjecture about its form. On the basis of that small sample one might conjecture that a codification of the rules of historiography would resemble a manual of military strategy more than a handbook of physics. It would consist of a number of maxims generally applicable to the solution of recurrent problems in writing history, leaving the identification of his particular problems and application of the maxims to the experience of the trained historian.

The most important professional use of such codification would be precisely in the training of historians. Historians do not lack the ability to discriminate between historiography which badly and inadequately communicates what a historian knows and historiography which communicates it well. Unfortunately, because that ability is now acquired almost wholly through experience rather than through a combination of experience and systematic knowledge, it is rarely and inefficiently transmitted from teacher to pupil. Indeed, the systematic training of historians is almost solely given over to the transmission of competence in the operations they must perform *before* they engage in the activity that defines their craft—the writing of history. Many historians receive the doctoral degree, which is supposed to certify their competence in their craft, without ever being compelled to rewrite anything they have written after having it subjected to rigorous and systematic criticism. The chronic ineptitude that hosts of historians display in their attempts to communicate what they know is a testimonial to the inadequacy of their training in this respect, or to its complete neglect. This ineptitude may suggest the desirability of an attempt to state coherently at least part of what the better historians know experientially about writing history and demonstrate visibly in the consistent appropriateness of their responses to the problems of historiographic statement.

Theoretical implications

The examination of historiography in this article has at various points suggested what becomes quite evident in the treatment of narrative explanation as against historical storytelling and in the section on the analysis of the form of a historical work —that the practices of historians in writing history may have some peculiar and serious implications in that wide area of human concern in which men struggle with the difficult problems of the meaning and nature of knowledge, understanding, and truth. The principal relevant points that have emerged may be summarized as follows.

First, historiography is a rule-bound discipline by means of which historians seek to communicate their knowledge of the past.

Second, the relation of writing history, of its rhetoric, to history itself is quite other than it has traditionally been conceived. Rhetoric is ordinarily deemed icing on the cake of history, but our investigation indicates that it is mixed right into the batter. It affects not merely the outward appearance of history, its delightfulness and seemliness, but its inward character, its essential function—its capacity to convey knowledge of the past as it actually was. And if this is indeed the case, historians must subject historiography, the process of writing history, to an investigation far broader and far more intense than any that they have hitherto conducted.

Third, there is an irreducible divergence between the rhetoric of history and the rhetoric of science; the vocabulary and syntax that constitute the appropriate response of the historian to his data are neither identical with nor identifiable with the vocabulary and syntax that constitute the appropriate response of the scientist to his data. But the historian's goal in his response to the data is to render the best account he can of the past as it really was. Therefore, by his resort to the rhetoric of history, regardless of its divergence from that of the sciences, the historian affirms in practice and action his belief that it is more adequate than the latter as a vehicle to convey the kind of knowledge, understanding, truth, and

meaning that historians achieve. Indeed, instances were discovered in which, in order to transmit an increment of knowledge and meaning, the very rules of historiography demand a rhetoric which sacrifices generality, precision, control, and exactness to evocative force and scope—a choice entirely out of bounds according to the rules of scientific statement. And this implies that in the rhetoric of history itself there are embedded assumptions about the nature of knowing, understanding, meaning, and truth and about the means of augmenting them that are not completely congruent with the corresponding assumptions in the sciences, at least insofar as the philosophy of science has succeeded in identifying them.

Historiography has generated a crisis in the currently dominant Anglo–American school of philosophy, the school that has as its main subgroups logical positivism, the philosophy of science, and language analysis. That it has done so is evident from a cursory examination of the index of one of the more recent works on history writing by an analytical philosopher (Danto 1965). Besides the philosophical magnates, living and dead, tangentially involved in the dialogue—Ayer, Bradley, Dewey, Hume, Kant, Lewis, Peirce, Ryle, Russell, Wittgenstein—the index mentions Agassi, Danto, Donegan, Dray, Gallie, Gardiner, Gellner, Hempel, Mandelbaum, Nagel, Passmore, Popper, Scriven, Walsh, and Watkins, all of whom since 1940 have directly confronted the problems that in their view historiography poses for philosophy; and the list is by no means complete. The close attention that this group of philosophers has directed to history writing is especially significant because of their central preoccupation with the way in which language communicates knowledge, understanding, meaning, and truth. In the broadest sense this large collective enterprise has been trying to define the relationship between the practices of writers of history and the nature of knowledge, understanding, meaning, and truth, especially as revealed in the structure of scientific rhetoric.

The preceding prolegomenon to an inquiry into the rules of the rhetoric of history provides a clue to the character of the crisis (symptomatically marked by the profusion of their output on the subject) with which the writing of history has confronted the analytical philosophers. History has posed for them a very difficult puzzle. Most historians in theory, *all* in practice, treat their subject as if through their current methods and their current rhetoric they were achieving and transmitting increments of knowledge about it. That is to say, they declare that if a piece of historical work is well done and properly set down, readers will know more about the past after they have read it than they did before. And for practical purposes very few people have seriously doubted the propriety of this claim (the few that do, appear to have read very little history). And yet historiography—the forms of statement historians adopt, their rhetoric—does not seem to fit into the sign structure suitable for scientific explanation, the classical rhetoric for communicating increments of knowledge, and most historians have been either indifferent or actively hostile to the notion that in the interest of rendering an account of the past as it actually was, they ought to elaborate and consistently employ such a sign structure. It is with this paradox that so many analytical philosophers have tried to deal systematically since 1940.

The course of this large collective effort is far too complex and has had too many ramifications to be dealt with here in detail. Briefly, the initial supposition (Hempel 1942), set forth above, was (1) that the universal valid model of explanation is that of the natural sciences, (2) that this consists in linking an event to general laws in such a way that the event is entailed by the laws through strict deduction, (3) that any activity of a historian that does not achieve this end does not explain anything, (4) that although in some instances historians can perform the necessary operations, they rarely do so, and therefore (5) that by and large in most of their actual operations historians explain nothing. Twenty-five years of intensive discussion by analytical philosophers has taken off from, and resulted in a number of proposals for modifying, this rigorist position. It seems likely that the dis-ease which some of these modifications manifest is in part the consequence of an often unarticulated sense on the part of analytical philosophers who have read history books that the actual procedures of historians, for knowing, understanding, and giving an account of the past as it actually was, do achieve their explicit or implicit purpose. In the course of bringing about a *partial* confrontation of the general-law theory of explanation with historiography, the analytical philosophers discovered a number of facts about the latter which because of their apparent deviation from the general-law or scientific model caused them perplexity. Among these were (1) that for many purposes of "explanation why," historians do not resort to general laws but to truisms; (2) that when historians are confronted with the question "Why?" their frequent, indeed normal, impulse is not to recite or seek relevant general laws, as a scientist would do, but to tell a story,

and that such a story often seems to provide a satisfying answer to the question "Why?" while a general law does not; (3) that the questions historians are often most heavily engaged in answering are not why-questions at all but what-questions (and also, one might add parenthetically, who-, when-, and where-questions); and (4) that a great deal of the activity of historians can be construed as having explanation as its aim only by so far extending the meanings of explanation current in analytical philosophy as to destroy even the appearance of synonymy and to impose well-nigh unbearable strains even on analogy.

In the process of coping with these problems, the analytical philosophers have produced a series of solutions, not always coherent with each other, of considerable interest to themselves but apparently of very little interest to historians as such. The character of most of these answers (and perhaps the explanation of their lack of interest for historians) may properly be described as "assimilationist." The common characteristics of these assimilationist answers are first to seek out all traits of historiography that can reasonably be identified with or assimilated to the model of scientific explanation by means of general laws; then to make epicyclic modifications of the general-law structure of explanation to accommodate some of the more evident deviations of historiography from its pattern, always holding such modifications to the minimum; and finally wholly to prescind from some of the most evident traits of historiography on the ground that they are irrelevant to the quest for knowledge, understanding, and truth. The last procedure, which for present purposes is of the most importance, is illustrated by a passage in Morton White's *Foundations of Historical Knowledge*, a passage of special interest because among the practitioners of analytical philosophy White alone is also a practitioner of historiography at a very high level of excellence.

The historical narrative, the extended story, is so large and rambling by contrast to the single sentence treated by the logician that any effort to treat it as a repeatable and identifiable pattern of language may give an impression of remoteness and distortion well beyond what might be felt by the historian who finds his causal statements cast in a single syntactical mold. On the other hand, the very qualities of narrative which might lead a historian to think that logical analysis distorts it are those that might inhibit a logician from trying to discern its structure. The complexity and variety of narrative, the fact that one story seems so different in structure from another, may give both the romantically minded historian and the classically minded logician pause. Yet the vast differences that human beings exhibit do not prevent us from X-raying them in an effort to discern the skeletal structure that each of them possesses. . . . History is a literary art as well as a discipline aimed at discovering and ordering truth, and if we neglect some of the narrative's literary qualities in order to clarify certain epistemological problems connected with it, our procedure is like that of the sane roentgenologist, who searches for the skull without denying that the skin exists and without denying that the skin may vary enormously in color, texture, and beauty. (1965, pp. 220–221)

The equation here is at once interesting, dubious, and exemplary of the assimilationist posture above described. Before presenting it, by the addition of a couple of rather large epicycles, White had already assimilated several common traits of historiography as closely as possible to the general-law model of scientific discourse. The quotation announces his intention to do the like with another major trait, the storylike character of much history writing. But he knows this is going to leave him with a very large residue of what historians write still on his hands. This residue consists in part of matters that the analysis of historical rhetoric in this article has called attention to. He disposes of this uncomfortable residue by assigning it to history as "a literary art" rather than history as "a discipline aimed at discovering and ordering truth." In this connection his analogy with roentgenology is not wholly fortunate. For it is at least arguable that the knowledge that history makes accessible is no more fully revealed by the mere skeletal structure of its narrative than the knowledge of the human head is fully exhausted by what an X-ray plate shows about its mere ossature. Just as it may be suggested that while the human head is partly a bony structure and partly (sometimes) a thing of beauty, it is also a number of other things, too, so it is possible to grant that history *is* a literary art while denying that all those aspects of history writing which White consigns to that function and that function alone are actually irrelevant to the function of history as a discipline aimed at discovering and ordering truth. It has been one purpose of the foregoing article to suggest some grounds for such a denial.

The mention of epicycles in the preceding paragraphs provides us with a clue to the dis-ease of analytical philosophy with historiography, a dis-ease so acute that it has become an intellectual disease which may be a prelude to a general and deep intellectual crisis. Epicycles suggest the Ptolemaic system of astronomy, and examination of the ultimate crisis of that system may by analogy help toward an understanding of the current crisis with respect to knowing, understanding, explaining, and truth that the study of historiography has

induced in analytical philosophy. The crisis in the Ptolemaic system came in the sixteenth century, when it was destroyed by the Copernican revolution. For centuries before, it had been normal science. Following the terminology of Thomas Kuhn, it was structured about several paradigms, among which were (1) the earth is at the center of the cosmos; (2) the earth does not move; (3) the orbits of all heavenly bodies are circular; (4) the circular motion of each heavenly body is uniform in rate. These paradigms were invoked to support an area of pre-Copernican science far more extensive than celestial mechanics; and to save this science, the observed deviations of the planets from presumed circular orbits and uniform speeds were dealt with by an ingenious but exceedingly intricate system of epicycles, eccentrics, and equants. The Copernican revolution was initiated by Copernicus' allegation that this system could be greatly simplified by assuming that the earth was not at the center of the cosmos and that it moved around the sun annually and rotated on its own axis daily.

Certain facts about the Copernican revolution are worth noting in the present context. (1) Copernicus' own work by no means provided a wholly satisfactory solution to the difficulties it sought to deal with. (2) Although the third and fourth paradigms of Ptolemaic astronomy—those dealing with the orbit, shape, and speed of the planets—ultimately crumbled under the impact of the revolution Copernicus started, he had no intention of displacing them and in fact held firmly to them. (3) Copernicus' heliocentrism and geomobilism implied the destruction not merely of Ptolemaic celestial mechanics but of other large tracts of the science of his day; what he offered in place of what he destroyed was, however, unsatisfactory. In some matters he offered nothing in place of it, and in others he does not seem to have been aware that he had destroyed it, so that overall for a long time the old normal science provided better explanations of many phenomena than the Copernicans did. (4) For all the above reasons the marginal advantage of the Copernican over the Ptolemaic celestial mechanics was not at all clear, and the conservatism of those who continued to adhere to the older scientific paradigms for a long time is quite intelligible.

Let us now apply this analogy to the crisis that has confronted the analytical philosophers as a result of their explorations of historiography. Until and except for that confrontation, their paradigms—essentially the modes of rhetoric they ascribed to the sciences—provided them with a reasonably satisfactory way of understanding and rendering intelligible the syntactical structure and vocabulary of a language capable of conveying frequent increments of knowledge, meaning, and truth—the language of the natural sciences. From this fact of experience they assumed that all knowing, meaning, and truth can be incorporated into statements in their paradigmatic rhetoric and that nothing that cannot be reduced to that rhetoric can claim a place in the region of knowing, meaning, and truth. During their 25-year confrontation with historiography they have discovered one anomaly after another in the rhetoric of history, place after place where it appears to deviate from the language of the sciences. Their most general response has been to try to save their normal view of the nature of knowing, meaning, understanding, and truth and of the proper rhetoric for communicating them by constructing a complex structure of the logical equivalents of epicycles, eccentrics, and equants in order to assimilate to it as much of the rhetoric of history as possible and thereby save the paradigms which support that structure. This procedure has been less than satisfactory, since it requires them quite arbitrarily and without evidence to assign to many traits of the rhetoric of history an altogether aesthetic rather than a noetic function. This has been especially the case with respect to those aspects of the work of the writer of history which concern themselves with the telling of a historical story and with the disposition and arrangement of his evidence and the choice among alternatives, all connotative rather than purely denotative, for the communication of what he knows. The philosophers have proceeded as they have for the very good reason that to do otherwise would be to raise extremely perplexing questions about the nature of knowing, understanding, meaning, and truth to which, as of now, neither they nor anyone else has any very plausible answers.

One of the aims of this article is to suggest that nevertheless a paradigm shift which would raise such questions may now be desirable and even necessary. The first step would be to assume that the rhetoric of history, including much to which analytical philosophers assign only aesthetic value, constitutes an appropriate response on the part of historians to their commitment to advance the knowledge and understanding of the past as it actually was. There are no better reasons for rejecting this assumption than for making it; logically to reject it or to accept it involves decisions equally arbitrary. It has, however, a certain prima-facie empirical plausibility; it is based on an uninvidious view of the consistent refusal of some of the very best historians dedicated to communi-

cating the truth about the past wholly to adopt the rhetoric of the sciences. To start with this favorable assumption would provide room among the means of knowing for certain rules of historiography concerned with the advancement of knowledge, for which there seems to be no room within the present structure of knowing as the analytical philosophers conceive it.

It would by no means open the way for the sort of intellectual slatternliness that analytical philosophers rightly object to and oppose. On the contrary, it would assist in the introduction of some much-needed conscious intellectual rigor into regions in which rigor has often been sadly lacking or in which its presence has been due to the experience and temperament of particular historians rather than to thoughtfully codified professional standards of performance. But to do all this requires an acknowledgment and acceptance (1) that in some areas of human inquiry the pursuit of truth can be effectively carried on only by means of a rhetoric which diverges from that of the sciences and (2) that this is not wholly due to the peculiarities and perversities of those who pursue the truth in those areas but in part to the very nature of the terrain over which they must pursue it. Once analytical philosophers fully recognize that there may and indeed must be more than one style, one rhetoric, for communicating the things that are both knowable and communicable, and that the problem is not that of reducing all styles to one but of carefully investigating what style is appropriate to the particular problems of communication inherent in a particular kind of knowing, it will be possible to bridge the now ever-widening gaps that separate analytical philosophers, historians, and rhetoricians. They might then join in trying to discover whether a thorough exploration of historiography, the rhetoric of history, can teach them anything worth finding out about knowing, understanding, meaning, and truth.

J. H. HEXTER

[See also SCIENTIFIC EXPLANATION; HISTORY; PERIODIZATION; SCIENCE.]

BIBLIOGRAPHY

This bibliography includes selected works on the history of history writing in the Western world. Extensive bibliographies can also be found in Nevins 1932; Gottschalk 1963.

AGASSI, JOSEPH 1963 Towards an Historiography of Science. History and Theory, Beiheft 2. The Hague: Mouton.

ANTONI, CARLO; and MATTIOLI, RAFFAELE (editors) 1950 Cinquant'anni di vita intellettuale italiana, 1896–1946. 2 vols. Naples (Italy): Edizioni Scientifiche Italiane.

Aron, Raymond (1935) 1957 *German Sociology.* Glencoe, Ill.: Free Press. → First published in French.

Barnes, Harry Elmer (1937) 1962 *A History of Historical Writing.* 2d rev. ed. New York: Dover.

Bellot, H. Hale 1952 *American History and American Historians: A Review of Recent Contributions to the Interpretation of the History of the United States.* Norman: Univ. of Oklahoma Press.

Bowman, Francis J. 1951 *A Handbook of Historians and History Writing.* Dubuque, Iowa: Brown.

Butterfield, Herbert 1955 *Man on His Past: The Study of the History of Historical Scholarship.* Cambridge Univ. Press. → A paperback edition was published by Beacon in 1960.

Collingwood, R. G. 1946 *The Idea of History.* Oxford Univ. Press. → A paperback edition was published in 1956.

Croce, Benedetto (1921) 1947 *Storia della storiografia italiana nel secolo decimonono.* 3d ed. 2 vols. Bari (Italy): Laterza.

Danto, Arthur C. 1965 *Analytical Philosophy of History.* Cambridge Univ. Press.

Diwald, Hellmut 1955 *Das historische Erkennen: Untersuchungen zum Geschichtsrealismus im 19. Jahrhundert.* Leiden (Netherlands): Brill.

Encyclopédie française. Volume 20: Le monde en devenir. 1964 Paris: Société de Gestion de l'Encyclopédie Française.

Engel-Janosi, Friedrich 1944 *The Growth of German Historicism.* Baltimore: Johns Hopkins Press.

Ferguson, Wallace K. 1948 *The Renaissance in Historical Thought: Five Centuries of Interpretation.* Boston: Houghton Mifflin.

Fitzsimons, Matthew A. et al. (editors) 1954 *The Development of Historiography.* Harrisburg, Pa.: Stackpole.

Fueter, Eduard (1911) 1914 *Histoire de l'historiographie moderne.* Paris: Alcan. → First published in German.

Gallie, W. B. 1964 *Philosophy and the Historical Understanding.* London: Chatto & Windus.

Gooch, George P. (1913) 1952 *History and Historians in the Nineteenth Century.* 2d ed. New York: Longmans.

Görlitz, Walter 1949 *Idee und Geschichte: Die Entwicklung des historischen Denkens.* Freiburg (Germany): Badischer Verlag.

Gottschalk, Louis R. (editor) 1963 *Generalization in the Writing of History.* Univ. of Chicago Press.

Harbison, E. Harris 1956 *The Christian Scholar in the Age of the Reformation.* New York: Scribner.

Hempel, Carl G. 1942 The Function of General Laws in History. *Journal of Philosophy* 39:35–48.

Higham, John; Krieger, Leonard; and Gilbert, Felix 1965 *History.* Englewood Cliffs, N.J.: Prentice-Hall.

Histoire et historiens depuis cinquante ans. 2 vols. 1927–1928 Paris: Alcan.

Kesting, Hanno 1959 *Geschichtsphilosophie und Weltbürgerkrieg: Deutungen der Geschichte von der französischen Revolution bis zum Ost–West Konflikt.* Heidelberg (Germany): Winter.

Kraus, Michael 1953 *The Writing of American History.* Norman: Univ. of Oklahoma Press.

Mazour, Anatole (1939) 1958 *Modern Russian Historiography.* 2d ed. Princeton, N.J.: Van Nostrand. → First published as *An Outline of Modern Russian Historiography.*

Nevins, Allan 1932 History and Historiography. Volume 7, pages 357–389 in *Encyclopaedia of the Social Sciences.* New York: Macmillan. → A bibliography appears on pages 389–391.

Passmore, John (editor) 1965 *The Historiography of the History of Philosophy.* History and Theory, Beiheft 5. The Hague: Mouton.

Pocock, J. G. A. 1957 *The Ancient Constitution and the Feudal Law: A Study of English Historical Thought in the Seventeenth Century.* Cambridge Univ. Press.

Rossi, Pietro 1956 *Lo storicismo tedesco contemporaneo.* Turin (Italy): Einaudi.

Sampson, Ronald V. 1956 *Progress in the Age of Reason: The Seventeenth Century to the Present Day.* Cambridge, Mass.: Harvard Univ. Press.

Sanchez Alonso, Benito 1941–1950 *Consejo superior de investigaciones científicas: Historia de la historiografía española.* 3 vols. Madrid.

Srbik, Heinrich von 1950–1951 *Geist und Geschichte vom deutschen Humanismus bis zur Gegenwart.* 2 vols. Munich (Germany): Bruckmann.

Thompson, James W. 1942 *A History of Historical Writing.* 2 vols. New York: Macmillan.

Van Tassel, David 1960 *Recording America's Past: An Interpretation of the Development of Historical Studies in America, 1607–1884.* Univ. of Chicago Press.

Wagner, Fritz 1960 *Moderne Geschichtsschreibung: Ausblick auf eine Philosophie der Geschichtswissenschaft.* Berlin: Duncker & Humblot.

White, Morton G. 1965 *Foundations of Historical Knowledge.* New York: Harper.

Wish, Harvey 1960 *The American Historian: A Social–Intellectual History of the Writing of the American Past.* New York: Oxford Univ. Press.

Ziffer, Bernard 1952 *Poland, History and Historians: Three Bibliographical Essays.* New York: Mid-European Studies Center.

II

AFRICAN HISTORIOGRAPHY

A belief in the continuity of life, a life after death, and a community of interest between the living, the dead, and the generations yet unborn is fundamental to all African religious, social, and political life. Thus, although the serious writing of African history has only just begun, a sense of history and tradition has always been part of the African way of life.

The ancient Egyptians were very conscious of the continuity of life and death. They were conscious not only of the overriding importance of an after-life but also of the continuing relevance of the dead to the living. They prepared the burial chambers and preserved the bodies of the dead with great care. The essence of the Horus myth was that the dead, particularly the kings, continued to influence the life of the living by affecting the annual inundations of the Nile and the germination of crops. A good deal of Egyptian religion revolved around the commemoration of the dead. Impressive monuments were erected, and the priests who ministered in those shrines became very knowledgeable about the traditions and folk-lore of the past.

This fundamental belief in the continuity of life is found among all African peoples. It is an essential element in traditional African historiography. Throughout sub-Saharan Africa one finds the continuing relevance of the dead to the life of the present and of future generations. It is expressed in the belief that each community was founded by an ancestor or a group of ancestors, that whatever the status or possessions of the community, they were owed to the ancestors, and that the ancestors had established for all time the basic charter of life, which could be adapted and modified but which could not be completely changed. The ancestors and the tradition they represented were a living reality. Reverence for the ancestors sometimes became worship. The fear of "what the ancestors would say" was an ever-present consideration and one of the most powerful sanctions in African societies.

Traditions of origins

Each community—family, clan, village, town, or state—however large or small, had an established tradition concerning its origins. The community might split up, migrate, and assimilate new elements, or be conquered by others and absorbed by new immigrants. At each stage of transformation, the tradition was recrystallized to accommodate changed conditions, and a new tradition of origin was formulated by the new community. These traditions became the core of the community's view of history. The very process of tradition-making and acculturation in the community, and of transmitting tradition to succeeding generations, developed a consciousness of history that became widespread in Africa.

These origin traditions did not attempt a historical explanation in the modern European sense of verifiable texts and chronology. They promoted understanding of and a respect for the institutions and practices of the community. They offered explanations of the world as the community conceived of it—the origin of land and sea, man and the other species, the origin of the state, the basis of different laws and customs, the title of the community to the land it held, how and why it differed from its neighbors in the gods it worshipped and the customs it upheld—but the explanations were not so much historical as philosophical, literary, and didactic. Accurate chronology and causation were of little relevance. To a large extent, history was merged with myth and was part of the general philosophy of life. In this way traditional African historiography resembled that of Europe before the scientific revolution split philosophy into its component parts. The making and transmission of tradition was not the work of historians in the modern sense, but of priests and diviners, elders, and wise men in general. Tradition explained not only the relationship between the ancestors of different communities but also the relationship between the existing community, the ancestors, and the gods. It was expressed not only in narrative but also in sacred poetry, in ritual reenactments, and other religious manifestations. Tradition was part of the philosophy of the community, part of its own peculiar way of life. Thus there could be no concept of universal history extending beyond the life of the particular community.

The making and the transmission of tradition varied from place to place. It depended on the size, nature, beliefs, and resources of the particular community. In segmented societies where roles were often not differentiated, it was part of the functions of the clan head as he fulfilled specific political and religious roles. In organized states, however, particularly those with centralized monarchies, such as Benin, Ashanti, or Dahomey, where the political and legal implications of tradition were of everyday importance, the making and transmission of tradition became a controlled and well-regulated specialism.

Oral transmission

The commonest method of transmitting tradition was through stories, fables, and proverbs told by the elders as part of the general education of the young. In those story-telling sessions, after the evening meal in the family compounds or during festivals of the full moon when people stayed up late, traditions telling of the origin of the whole community or of the particular family or clan were related. More recent events that had occurred within remembered history, particularly those of the previous two or three generations, were also talked about.

Traditions were transmitted more formally when there were organized educational institutions such as those connected with puberty rites, initiation into age-grades and secret societies, or during the training or apprenticeship of priests and diviners. The rites by which the king-elect was initiated into the kingship were of particular interest. As the successor to and representative of the ancestors, the king became the custodian of the traditions of the community. One of the most important functions of the rites preceding his coronation, therefore, was to initiate him into the secrets of his ancestors and the traditional lore of his people. More than that, partly as ritual offerings to the ancestors, partly as entertainment and education for the people at large, the traditions of the people were recited publicly: symbolic events from the past were dramatized; the names, genealogies, cognomens, titles, and praise songs of the ancestors were chanted. The new king announced his own title. The title frequently was intended to characterize the expectations of his reign. The praise singers responded, and a new chapter in the people's tradition opened.

Thus the process of transmitting tradition cannot be separated from the process of creating tradition. Tradition was made by those who transmitted it—the village and clan elders, the singers and drummers who assisted at coronations and other public festivals, the officials of age-grades and secret societies who conducted the puberty rites or initiated new members. These persons were appointed sometimes from among eligible members of a single family, sometimes from a wider circle of candidates who had to demonstrate their mastery of past traditions and folklore and their wit at entertaining people and making tradition out of contemporary affairs. In the daily life both of the community and of individuals, tradition was invoked, challenged, modified, and created in the processes of litigation, of settling disputed successions to all types of offices, of recording new events and new situations that resulted when masterful individuals or communities made innovations in the guise of merely fulfilling tradition.

Factual versus literary traditions

It is necessary to distinguish between different types of tradition, or oral tradition, as it is now generally described (Vansina 1961). The first distinction is between traditions of a factual and historical type and those of a literary and philosophical type. Of the more factual type, it is important to distinguish between events of the recent past that can be recalled from the personal experience of grandfathers and fathers and events of the more distant past. The authenticity of these remote traditions is in large part dependent on the special institutions that may have existed for making and transmitting tradition and on how efficiently these institutions functioned. Such factual traditions include formal lists of kings and other office holders, chronicles of each reign, appellations and praise verses (which often included either direct or implied criticism) of each king or other leading chiefs, genealogies, and certain laws or customs.

But even traditions that appear well preserved and factual may turn out on examination to be symbolic; apparent biographical data may represent summaries of the life of the whole community over one or more generations. References to years, generations, and periods may in fact refer to structural and not chronological time.

The more literary types of tradition include proverbs and sayings, songs and lyrics, of which some are general and others peculiar to particular guilds, age-grades and other associations. The more philosophical traditions are enshrined in the sacred chants of different religious organizations and cults, such as the praise verses of the gods, divination poems, funeral dirges, liturgies, and hymns. Finally, one should distinguish between traditions narrated in the words of the speaker and those with set and formal texts.

Ethiopian influence

There have been, of course, other historical traditions in Africa whose influence on African historiography is difficult to evaluate at the present state of our knowledge. One important example is the Ethiopian historical tradition, partly African and partly of Judaeo–Christian inspiration. The supremacy of the Solomonid dynasty, the unity of church and state, and the integrity of the monophysite church were the dynamic historical forces. As in other parts of Africa, in the twelfth century Ethiopia developed a legend that linked the ruling dynasty with the Holy Land. But it was a written tradition, enshrined in the *Book of Kings* that became a major feature of coronation rites. The monasteries recorded the annals of each reign and preserved important texts and charters. Yet the primary interest of Ethiopian intellectual life was theological, not historical; there was little attempt until recent times to analyze and interpret the annals and the chronicles to produce history. Of more relevance to African historiography are the traditions of the Berbers. Like other Africans, the Berbers were very conscious of the continued relevance of the past. In their reaction both to Roman Christianity and Arabian Islam they manifested an attitude of mysticism and dissent combined with the veneration of ancestors. It may be said that this attitude produced hagiography and not critical history, but hagiography itself was a method of enshrining and immortalizing the idealized social and religious virtues of the people. It was, in a sense, the literary expression of respect for the norms and virtues of ancestors, similar to the traditions found in other parts of Africa. The tracing of real genealogy, always of great importance to the Arabs, has remained a marked feature of Muslim Africa, but, in addition, the Berbers introduced veneration of ancestors in the form of tracing spiritual genealogies of Muslim leaders. This was expressed in the *tariqa* chains and the handing down of the *wird* among Muslim Brotherhoods. Initiation into the *tariqa* conferred spiritual knowledge and benefits; this paralleled initiation into traditional African associations, guilds, and cults.

Muslim influence

Muslim influence was important not only in north Africa but also in east Africa, the whole of the Sudan, and even in a few places within the forest areas. In addition to real and spiritual genealogies, Muslim writers produced a number of *tarikhs* and chronicles, especially in the eleventh to the seventeenth centuries. These embodied eyewitness accounts, oral tradition, and evidence from earlier accounts by geographers, travelers and traders. Muslim writers were particularly interested in the spread and influence of Islam and in the religious and the economic life of the main centers of Islam. These factors were singled out of the totality of African life and traditions and given undue emphasis. In important centers of Muslim learning like Timbuktu, Gao, Djenné, Kano, Katsina, and Bornu in the west and central Sudan, or Kilwa, Malindi, and Mombasa in east Africa, traditions of the people were written down, mostly in Arabic but sometimes also in the Arabic transcriptions of the vernacular. The accounts centered on leading personalities of the Muslim community rather than traditional states or clans. Rulers were judged good or bad insofar as they extended or hindered the influence of Islam and the privileges of Muslim scholars.

It is now recognized that the *Prolegomena* of Ibn Khaldūn, the famous Tunisian scholar of the fourteenth century, is one of the world's most important works on historiography. He emphasized the importance of sociology to history. He sought to study the past not only in terms of the actions of individuals but also by an analysis of the laws, customs, and institutions of the different peoples as well as the interaction of state and society. This approach would have provided a basis for synthesizing the many traditions in Africa into a history of the continent, but until recently, his work had little influence. The contemporary medieval world was more interested in the study of theology, law, and rhetoric. Within Africa itself, Islamic scholarship declined and was at its lowest ebb in the eighteenth century. It was in this period that the study of history was revived in Europe, but because

of the abundance of written documentary evidence, European scholars did not adopt the sociological approach of Ibn Khaldūn, but concerned themselves mainly with the decrees, wars, and politics of kings. In the nineteenth century the legal and biographical approach was broadened to take social and economic factors into account, but documentary evidence had become so overwhelmingly important for the European scholar that he tended to equate written documents with history. The absence of documents was thus taken to mean the absence of any events worthy of historical study.

European influence

In the nineteenth century, when European influence intruded into Africa, it did not build on the existing historical traditions but challenged and supplanted them. The European view of documentary history supported the propaganda of the colonial rulers: Africa had no history worthy of record; therefore the history of European traders, missionaries, explorers, conquerors, and rulers constituted the sum total of African history. European history and the history of European expansion began to displace local history and tradition in the education of the African youth, although some attention was given to Arabic and other sources. European historians of the late nineteenth and early twentieth centuries sought to explain the Atlantic slave trade, the European technological supremacy, and the subjugation of Africa not in terms of any historical study of the continent but in terms of racial and psychological prejudices about the inherent inferiority of people with dark skins. Missionary circles even introduced the religious explanation that Africans were the children of Ham and were under Noah's curse to be hewers of wood and drawers of water for their lighter-skinned brethren. African historiography thus became nothing more than a justification of European imperialism.

Africans who became literate in the European languages at first accepted these theories, but because the traditional African historical consciousness remained alive, they soon began to challenge the absurdities of the European historians. Some of them who did not necessarily question the basic European standpoint began, nevertheless, to record the laws, customs, proverbs, sayings, and historical traditions of their own communities. They recorded also the major events of the nineteenth century, especially in the period just preceding the establishment of European rule. Notable among such writers may be mentioned James Africanus Horton of Sierra Leone, Carl C. Reindorf and John M. Sarbah of Ghana, Otomba Payne and Samuel Johnson of Nigeria, and Apolo Kagwa of Uganda. For a long time the work of these men and the material in missionary and government records on specifically African peoples escaped the attention of historians. It was the anthropologists who discovered them, but they were then not interested in history. With a few notable exceptions like Franz Boas and Emil Torday, their primary concern was to describe the quaintness and the peculiarities of "tribes," to justify as well as to facilitate the imposition of colonial rule. Other literate Africans, more conscious and more resentful of the European standpoint, began to protest. But since they were restricted by the axiom that only documentary history is real history, they could only reply with polemics and counter-theories. Uncritical use of the few written sources available, particularly those of the ancient Greek writers on Africa, the Muslim geographers or travelers, and the European traders on the west and east African coasts, laid the foundation of new myths. An example of such a myth is the so-called "Hamitic hypothesis," the view that all light and civilization in sub-Saharan Africa had come from north Africa and the Middle East and that the civilizations of Africa are thus civilizations of the Hamites; another myth regards the influence of the Atlantic slave trade as so all-pervasive that it can explain all major trends in African history since the fifteenth century.

World War I, the Russian Revolution, the rise of the Indian National Congress, the increasing dissatisfaction with the facile theory of European superiority—all these encouraged a new appraisal of the African past. African works of art, looted from Africa and scattered all over Europe and North America, inspired new art forms in Europe. New masterpieces of sculpture and terracotta were discovered, and their African origin became more difficult to deny. Anthropologists became less tied to the colonial regimes, less ethnocentric, and consequently more appreciative of African culture and historical traditions. The International Institute of African Languages and Cultures in London began to publish *Africa*, and the French established the Institut Français d'Afrique Noire in west Africa. The *Journal of Negro History*, in the United States, primarily concerned with the history of the Negro in America, drew attention to the possibilities of African history. Anthropologists like Melville J. Herskovits began to take African culture and its survivals in the New World seriously and to seek understanding of the African past.

The impulse toward a new African historiography came with the movement toward independence, which gathered pace in Africa during and immediately after World War II. This nationalist movement firmly rejected the European appraisal of the African past and demanded a new orientation and improved educational facilities to produce this reappraisal. With the establishment of new universities in Africa, it was inevitable that the teaching of history and the training of African historians would receive special attention. The old theories were maintained at first: besides European history, there were courses only on "European Activities in Africa" and some postgraduate research on British or French policy toward this or that territory at such and such a period. By the late 1940s, however, African research students were insisting that African history must be the history of Africans and not of Europeans in Africa, that local records and historical traditions must be used to supplement European metropolitan archives —in short, oral tradition must be accepted as valid material for historical research. This new approach produced works like *Trade and Politics in the Niger Delta* (Dike 1956) and *The Egba and Their Neighbours* (Biobaku 1957).

Research problems and prospects

No doubt the validity of nonwritten sources for historical research had been pointed out before, but it was new for university departments of history to accept it. Even then not everyone was happy about it. Anthropologists replied cautiously that oral tradition, even when seemingly factual, was not history and could only be interpreted in terms of its function in society and within the particular culture. But this did not destroy its validity as material for history; it only argued for a return to the link between history and sociology advocated in the fourteenth century by Ibn Khaldūn. This interdisciplinary approach has been the most fruitful trend in African historiography in the last decade.

There have been three major developments to promote this interdisciplinary approach. The first has been the creation of special centers or institutes of African studies within which historians, anthropologists, linguists, and archeologists can cooperate, both in research and in the training of future historians. The second consists of specific culture-history projects like the Benin and Yoruba schemes, in which teams of people from different disciplines cooperate under the direction of one person to throw light on the culture history of a particular culture. The third is the formation of associations and the convening of periodic conferences or congresses on African history or African studies in general, bringing experts together from many disciplines to review progress in different fields and bring their joint consideration to bear on specific problems of Africa history. This cooperation has extended beyond the social and humanistic studies; the experimental sciences are also applying the benefit of their techniques to resolving problems in African history.

The interdisciplinary approach has been very fruitful in the collection and evaluation of material for African history. Since the end of the war, many African states have founded national archives. This in turn has stimulated the exploitation of government, missionary, commercial, and private archives in Europe. Materials relevant to African history are now being copied and transferred to archival centers and places of learning in Africa, where they are supplemented by local records in European, Arabic, and other African languages. Similarly, more care is now taken of ancient monuments, and museums of art and crafts are being established. The recording of oral tradition has become a major preoccupation. Evidence from all these sources is cross-checked and supplemented by the study of linguistics and African languages, social anthropology, archeology, and other sciences. Gaps in our knowledge are being filled, and a specific chronology is beginning to emerge. Historians can now attempt a synthesis of the history of the whole continent, particular regions, or of the newly independent states. While insisting on the validity of traditional African historical material, the new African historiography has been able to accept the European concept of continental and universal history.

African historians have also adopted rigorous standards and methodology in the collection of data. Indeed, the emphasis in the last decade has been placed so much upon this scientific methodology that it is a question worth raising whether the proper interpretation and synthesis of the material has not tended to lag behind. While the interdisciplinary approach has been very successful in the collection of data, teams or conferences of experts from different disciplines do not write history. The interdisciplinary approach has alerted the historian to the validity of nonwritten sources; it has not superseded him or relieved him of the necessity to sift the diverse evidence, synthesize, and write history. Moreover, it would appear that the new historiography is still so tied to the universities that the proper functions of history in the new

Africa, to educate and entertain society as a whole, have received little attention. We have still to create a new philosophy of African history to replace that of the old palace historians and singers.

K. O. Dike and J. F. A. Ajayi

[*See also* African society; Historiography, *article on* Islamic historiography; *and the biographies of* Herskovits *and* Ibn Khaldūn.]

BIBLIOGRAPHY

Abraham, D. P. 1961 Maramuca: An Exercise in the Combined Use of Portuguese Records and Oral Tradition. *Journal of African History* 2:211–225.

Ajayi, J. F. A. 1961 The Place of African History and Culture in the Process of Nation-building in Africa South of the Sahara. *Journal of Negro Education* 30: 206–213.

Andrzejewski, Bogumil W.; and Lewis, I. M. 1964 *Somali Poetry: An Introduction.* Oxford: Clarendon.

Biobaku, Saburi O. 1957 *The Egba and Their Neighbours: 1842–1872.* Oxford Univ. Press.

Biobaku, Saburi O. 1963 African Studies in an African University. *Minerva* 1:285–301.

Bradbury, R. E. 1959 Chronological Problems in the Study of Benin History. *Journal of the Historical Society of Nigeria* 1:263–287.

Conference on African History and Archaeology, Third, London, *1961* 1962 Report. *Journal of African History* 3, no. 2.

Dike, Kenneth O. 1953 African History and Self-government. *West Africa* 37:177–178, 225–226, 251.

Dike, Kenneth O. (1956) 1962 *Trade and Politics in the Niger Delta; 1830–1885: An Introduction to the Economic and Political History of Nigeria.* Oxford: Clarendon.

Dike, Kenneth O. 1964 The Study of African History. Pages 55–67 in International Congress of Africanists, First, Accra, 1962, *Proceedings.* London: Longmans.

Evans-Pritchard, E. E. 1961 *Anthropology and History.* Manchester (England) Univ. Press.

International African Seminar, Fourth, Dakar, Senegal, *1961* 1964 *The Historian in Tropical Africa.* Oxford Univ. Press.

Jones, G. I. 1963 European and African Tradition on the Rio Real. *Journal of African History* 4:391–402.

Jordan, A. C. 1957–1960 Towards an African Literature. *Africa South* 1, no. 4:90–98; 2, no. 1:97–105, no. 2:101–104, no. 3:112–115, no. 4:113–118; 3, no. 1:114–117, no. 2:74–79, no. 3:114–117, no. 4:111–115; 4, no. 1:117–121, no. 2:110–113, no. 3:112–116.

Lawrence, A. W. 1961 Some Source Books for West African History. *Journal of African History* 2:227–234.

Lewis, I. M. 1962 Historical Aspects of Genealogies in Northern Somali Social Structure. *Journal of African History* 3:35–48.

McCall, Daniel F. 1964 *Africa in Time-perspective: A Discussion of Historical Reconstruction From Unwritten Sources.* Boston Univ. Press.

Morris, Henry F. 1964 *The Heroic Recitations of the Bahima of Ankole.* Oxford: Clarendon.

Smith, M. G. 1961 Field Histories Among the Hausa. *Journal of African History* 2:87–101.

VANSINA, JAN 1960 *Recording the Oral History of the Bakuba. Journal of African History* 1:45–53, 257–270. → Part 1: "Methods." Part 2: "Results."

VANSINA, JAN (1961) 1964 *The Oral Tradition: A Study in Historical Methodology.* Chicago: Aldine. → First published in French. Contains a comprehensive bibliography on and discussion of the nature and significance of oral traditions.

WHITELEY, W. H. (compiler) 1964 *A Selection of African Prose.* 2 vols. Oxford: Clarendon. → Volume 1: *Traditional Oral Texts.* Volume 2: *Written Prose.*

III
CHINESE HISTORIOGRAPHY

China can claim the oldest continuous historical tradition on earth. The appointment of court historians has been attributed to the Yellow Emperor, one of the legendary founders of a Chinese order. Modern archeology has shown that the court diviners of the Shang kings (1751–1111 B.C., according to Tung Tso-pin) maintained "archives" of their divinations, inscribed on bone and shell; here at the beginning was an association between magico-religious operations and record keeping that was to have long-term effects on the historiographical tradition.

Fragmentary records from the early part of the Chou dynasty (1111–221 B.C.)—principally certain chapters of the *Shu-ching*, or "Classic of History"—reflect a continuing interest in royal genealogy, ritual operations, and political legitimacy. With the gradual emergence of semi-independent states, from the eighth century B.C. on, traditions of recording and compilation developed in several courts. The Warring States period (481–221 B.C.) was China's first great age of systematic thought. Scholars searched the records of the past for examples and precedents to sustain their arguments; this habit of appealing to history figures importantly in all subsequent Chinese thought. Confucius (551–479 B.C.) and his followers laid great stress on the moral content of history, maintaining that the records of the past, if properly studied, would reveal the operation of moral norms in the affairs of men. The *Ch'un-ch'iu* chronicle of the state of Lu, allegedly edited by Confucius to express his judgments, came to be regarded as the prototype of moralistic–normative history.

The unified empire created in 221 B.C. was to be the model for subsequent Chinese political development. The imperial court continued and elaborated earlier traditions of historian-officials who kept records of the actions of the emperor and of events in the realm. These historians were deeply influenced by Confucian orthodoxy of the Han period, with its interest in the moral and didactic

uses of history. In the Former Han dynasty (206 B.C.–A.D. 8) the Grand Historian Ssu-ma Ch'ien, continuing the work of his father, drew on court records, on chronicles and inscriptions from earlier times, and on oral traditions to produce the *Shih-chi*, the first great history of the Chinese ecumene from its shadowy beginnings to about 100 B.C. During the Later Han dynasty (A.D. 25–220) another great court historian, Pan Ku, wrote the first of the "dynastic histories" (*tuan-tai shih*), his *History of the Former Han Dynasty*. These two Han works provided models that were returned to again and again by later historians.

The breakup of the Han empire was followed by a long period of political disunion, from 220 to 589. During much of this period north China, the heartland of Chinese civilization, was under the domination of "barbarian" invaders, while Buddhism gradually became a pervasive force in Chinese thought and life. The early part of this period was the second great age of creative thought—thought that ranged with greater depth and imagination than ever before over the problems of man, society, and the cosmos. This is reflected in historical writings, which became more self-conscious and more critical. Historiography began to achieve its independence. Liu Hsieh (465–522) devoted part of his great treatise on literature to problems of historiography: the need for general principles, criteria for the selection of particulars, standards of credibility, and problems of objectivity and bias. The autonomy of the Chinese historical tradition was strikingly affirmed in this age of Buddhist dominance; Buddhism had slight effects on Chinese historical thinking, and Buddhist historians shaped their works after approved secular models.

The great reunified empire of T'ang (618–906) was notable for its artistic and literary brilliance. History became, for the first time, a standard ingredient of the curriculum for state examinations. The noted T'ang official Tu Yu (735–812) sought to break free of dynastic chronicles and wrote an encyclopedic compilation, the *T'ung-tien*, that may be regarded as the first institutional history of China. In the early T'ang the bureaucratic apparatus for recording events, processing documents, maintaining archives, and writing history was greatly elaborated. At this time imperial commissions replaced individual authors in the compilation of dynastic histories. This marked the inception of a division between official and unofficial historiography that persisted until the end of the imperial order. A severe critic of this change was Liu Chih-chi (661–721), whose "Conspectus of History" (*Shih-t'ung*) is the first major work of historical criticism, signaling the emergence of history as a separate and independent branch of study. In it Liu dealt with such problems as the credibility of evidence, historical style and form, the qualities of historians, the effects of bias and political pressure, and the moral dilemmas of historians.

Toward the end of the T'ang, Confucianism, which had long seemed intellectually anachronistic, began to be revived and modernized. The resulting system of Neo-Confucianism had far-reaching effects on the writing of history. The rationalism of the new system was reflected in lessened attention to supernatural events and interpretations. It fostered, in the centuries that followed, a strong tradition of historical empiricism and critical scholarship. The historical writings of the Neo-Confucianists of the Sung (960–1279) show a new meticulousness in historical inquiry, a disposition to use unofficial sources, a devotion to rational explanation combined with a profound belief in moral dynamics. Perhaps the greatest historian of this age was Ssu-ma Kuang (1019–1086). His *Tzu-chih t'ung-chien* was a history of the Chinese world from 403 B.C. to A.D. 959, arranged in annalistic form. The author drew on an immense variety of works and appended his study of doubtful points (*k'ao-i*) to the completed history. He emphasized in his preface his moral–political purpose: ". . . taking in all that a prince ought to know—everything pertaining to the rise and fall of dynasties and the good and ill fortune of the common people, all good and bad examples that can furnish models and warnings."

The development of printing in the Sung dynasty and the spread of literacy among an enlarged elite meant a great proliferation of private historiography, an expanded reading public, and vastly increased possibilities for preserving historical records. These trends and the dominant Neo-Confucian view of history—most authoritatively expressed by Chu Hsi (1130–1200) in his "epitome" (*kang-mu*) of Ssu-ma Kuang's history—continued through the age of Mongol rule (1279–1368) and the Chinese dynasty of Ming (1368–1644). These centuries are better known for monumental compilations and exhaustive commentaries than for creative historical works. An exception is the second major institutional history of China, the *Wen-hsien t'ung-k'ao,* by Ma Tuan-lin (*c.* 1250–1325).

The shock of the imposition of Manchu rule in 1644 plus a growing impatience with Neo-Confucian orthodoxy as it devolved into pedantry on the one hand and vapid philosophizing on the other provoked a new critical movement of great importance. A new rational empiricism produced new principles of textual criticism and new work in historical geography, epigraphy, archeology, and other fields. Ku Yen-wu (1613–1682) was one of the pioneers in this movement and began the development of the inductive method of research that had far-reaching effects on historical and philological studies. Chao I (1727–1814) wrote of recurrent patterns and forces in Chinese history with unusual acumen. Chang Hsüeh-ch'eng (1738–1801), ignored in his own time, presented an enlarged view of history, a conception of historical synthesis, and ideas about the qualities of a historian that were new to the Chinese tradition. These men and the other historians of this autumnal flowering never—for all their new ideas and rigorous methods—renounced their allegiance to Confucian morality, to the belief that history should be written to illuminate moral truths and thereby to reform the world. When the imperial order and Confucian orthodoxy had collapsed, the methods and skeptical spirit of these men figured largely in the modernization of Chinese historiography.

The Chinese view of history

The usual Chinese term for history, *shih,* has several meanings: writings about the past, one who (usually under official appointment) records events, and, in early times, "astrologer" or "astronomer." The term does not have the second meaning of the English word "history," the past as such. The Chinese conception of history was shaped by certain elements in the Chinese world view. One of these was ethnocentrism, derived from the relative isolation of Chinese civilization. History was primarily concerned with the "Central Kingdom" (*chung-kuo*), with the world (*t'ien-hsia*) in which China was "central." Thus peoples peripheral to China were treated as "barbarians," or peoples to be contained, "chastised," or converted to Chinese culture. Since the Chinese had only fragmentary knowledge of other great civilizations, there was no trace of comparative history, such as one finds in Ibn Khaldūn. A second element is holism, the view that human and natural events are interrelated in a coherent whole; symptoms of dislocation in one order are interpreted as signs of malfunction in the other. Especially in histories written before about A.D. 1000, much attention is given to natural catastrophes, portents, and the like. Yet the force for harmony or dislocation originates in the actions of men, and a rational–secular view of historical causation gradually becomes dominant. A third element is a view of history as a devolution from a golden age: the sage-kings of the distant past had presided over an ideal order; in later times men moved further and further from that ideal. Change was considered desirable if it promised a return to ancient ideals. This gives to all Chinese histories—even those of periods of innovation—a pronouncedly archaistic tone. A fourth element is a cyclical conception of political history; polities, like men, have sequences of birth, youth, maturity, senescence, and death. The habit of holistic thinking led historians to see symptoms of the same cyclical stages in all the spheres of culture: literature, the arts, the ethos of the villages, the customs and habits of the elite. The practice of dating all events by dynasty and era name (*nien-hao*) reinforced the conception of political change as the dominant force in cyclical change.

A fifth element is the view that there is a moral dynamic in the affairs of men; the Confucian sages had specified the principles. History, if properly written, would lay bare the working of those principles in a nexus of events or in an individual life. This belief tended to give a moralistic coloration to all cause-and-effect statements and to reduce biography to exemplary or minatory stereotypes.

Scope and purposes of historiography. From the earliest times the keeping of records and the writing of history were official functions. Every dynasty had its history office. It was staffed by men who had been educated in the standard curriculum and had passed the state examinations. The common experience of all officials included a great deal of history: study of the style and content of the ancient chronicles, memorization of historical sequences, the use of historical allusion and historical precedent in the most routine official communications, the marshaling of historical cases in policy argument. Thus, history was an integral part of training and of official life. This meant that a high percentage of officials at some point in their careers would be assigned for a period to the history office, where they might work at daily record keeping or at one of the several types of compilation periodically ordered by the throne. From the T'ang dynasty (618–906) on, high-ranking officials were appointed to chair or to serve on the commissions in charge of major historical compilations. All works compiled in the history office were presented to the throne for approval. Private historians were usually members of the official class, were largely dependent for their materials on official records, and often felt it politic to present their works to the throne for approval.

Historians of all kinds were thus deeply involved in official life and shared the general concerns of the official class: the maintenance of stability and order through governmental operations and the institutions of social control, the preservation of Confucian orthodoxy and the maintenance of Confucian ethical standards in society, the upholding of inherited standards of excellence in literature and the arts, the defense of the privileged position of the literate gentry against threats from autocratic emperors and upstart power groups.

These interests, working together with the world view discussed above, determined the scope of Chinese history writing. The overriding concern with order produced a concentration of attention on political history and the lessons about stability and change that could be drawn from it. Similarly, the history of institutions was viewed from the capital and from the official viewpoint; thus, for example, the "economic" monographs of the dynastic histories are focused on the regulatory function of government, and the "geographical" monographs are concerned with what we would call administrative geography. Biographies deal less with individual character than with the subjects' official posts and social role; they tend to be grouped according to a common social role or according to certain moral standards that the subjects exemplified, for example, "loyal ministers," "literary men," "virtuous women," "harsh officials," "partisans."

Slight attention was given to all the groups that challenged the literate gentry's power: military leaders, merchants, eunuchs, court favorites, and members of the empresses' families. (The last three were treated when their machinations were adduced as prime causes of dynastic weakness or collapse.) Heterodox religions tended to be given little attention. Although Buddhism dominated Chinese culture for five hundred years or more (from 350 to 850) and was a major force in life and thought in later centuries, references to it in official histories are few; only one monograph in one dynastic history is devoted to Buddhism and religious Taoism. References to these and other heterodoxies are usually pejorative and emphasize their socially disruptive effects. Unsuccessful rebels are given scant attention beyond the account of measures taken to suppress them. Common life and popular culture are seldom given detailed treatment, except when natural calamities created problems of relief and rehabilitation or subversive movements appeared among the oppressed peasantry.

The whole picture of life that appears in the standard histories and official compilations tends to minimize tensions, cultural differences between one region and another, clashes of opinion, and other phenomena that in the modern Western view seem most significant in the development of Chinese civilization. Yet these defects are in part counterbalanced by the sheer volume of the record; it would require 45 million English words to translate the 25 dynastic histories. And from the sixth or seventh century on the dynastic histories can be checked and supplemented by an enormous wealth of published official and private sources: diaries, memoirs, collected papers, essays, poems, collections of inscriptions, stories, travelogues, and miscellanies. Surviving manuscripts, notably those discovered at Tun-huang, provide further raw material and additional checks. The *shih-lu*, or "veritable records," of the last two dynasties have been preserved and provide a daily record of court and government from 1368 to 1912. Thus the modern historian can, by using all these varieties of material, reconstruct substantial segments of the Chinese past.

Historical method. The methods used by Chinese historians fall into two closely related groups. One consists of the methods of recording contemporary happenings, the other of the methods of compiling a coherent account from such records. Court historians were charged with writing up, day by day, the events at court: audiences, rituals, memorials to the throne, imperial edicts, digests of reports received from outside the capital. Private historians would usually record events they witnessed, journeys they took, or the lives of their relatives and friends. The exercise of the recording function, especially at the official level, was a solemn obligation, for the historian had the moral duty to record accurately, without fear or favor, and this usually in a power situation fraught with tensions. Heroic examples of historians who died rather than distort the record were constantly before them.

The second type of method is compilation. Court historians from time to time edited and digested the daily records into chronological accounts of a dynastic period (*kuo-shih*) or of a single reign (*shih-lu*). These accounts in turn formed the basis for the "annals" (*pen-chi*) section of the dynastic history written by the historians of the succeeding dynasty. The bare chronological accounts in the dynastic histories were supplemented with biographies prepared from both official and nonofficial records and with monographs pieced together from official papers dealing with particular topics, for example, imperial edicts on judicial administration, ceremonies, economic and fiscal affairs, etc. The procedure of compilation was to select integral passages from the records and piece them together with words or sentences of transition, usually within a chronological framework. Thus, official histories were compiled rather than written afresh, and the same may be said of most private historiography.

In the whole process of recording and compilation, the historian was circumscribed by a variety of attitudes and conventions, many of which had come down from the distant past. The world view and interests of the Chinese elite limited the historian's horizons, and Confucian morality governed his choices. Moreover, the Chinese attitude of respect for the written word meant that he handled documents from the past with care and circumspection. He did not alter them lightly, and when two accounts of an event were in conflict he generally chose the one that showed greater consistency with his other materials and inserted it integrally into his text. The discussion of discrepancies in evidence appeared rather late in the tradition and was then relegated to separate sections of a history or to separate works.

The chronological arrangement of historical particulars derived naturally from the system of court record keeping. It also had an ancient and authoritative prototype in the "Spring and Autumn Annals" (*Ch'un-ch'iu*), allegedly edited by Confucius. This method of compilation (*pien-nien*) was dominant in the tradition, and even the institutional historians who sought to transcend dynastic chronology arranged the materials in their topical chapters chronologically. The devolutionary view of history precluded the full development of ideas of history-as-process. In general, "befores" and "afters" were thought to indicate to the discerning reader the elements of moral causation that were believed to inhere in any sequence of events.

But the historian was enjoined by tradition to make clear the moral lessons of history. There were certain approved means of doing this. Two of these were methods attributed to Confucius: "appropriate concealment." which meant omission or disguise by euphemism of particulars that might impair the image. of a worthy individual or group, and the selection of terminology in such a way as to apportion moral praise or blame, for example, "succeed to" or "usurp" the throne. More explicit judgments by the historian were to be found in brief comments appended to a section or chapter of his work; there the moral point was made, the lesson drawn. Furthermore. the historian could express degrees of approval and disapproval by his arrangement of material. For instance, in a collection of biographies the lives were grouped according to certain types. The historian's judgment was reflected in the group to which a given biography was assigned and in the position of the group in the collection: the most worthy were placed first; the least worthy came at the end.

Both recording and compilation were subject to verbal and ritual conventions. Drawing up an imperial edict was a solemn and complex task that involved choosing the right references to the classics and the appropriate allusions to historical precedent, the observance of the official taboos in referring to members of the ruling house, choosing the rhetorical flourishes proper to the matter in hand. When the historian used such an edict in compiling a history, he had to understand what it meant and fit it into his narrative with only those minor verbal changes dictated by the lapse of time. There were proper and improper ways of recording all events: the selection of a crown prince, the death of an emperor or empress dowager, the reception of a tributary envoy. The recorder used these conventions, and the subsequent historian reproduced them in his account. To all these formulas were added standardized literary locutions for describing certain types of events: famine in the provinces, incursions along the frontiers, and so forth. Much of Chinese history, particularly official history, is thus cast in standardized ritualistic or literary formulas.

Biography was also subject to formulas. This had two roots in historiographical tradition. One was the dependence of the biographer on funerary writings of all kinds, which presented individual lives in the conventional formulas of filial piety and the cult of ancestors. The other was the conception of the individual life as having an exemplary or minatory purpose; if history was to teach moral lessons, biographies must serve to illustrate virtue and vice in individual lives. The historian–compiler, as we have noted, grouped his biographies and thus tended to stereotype the lives classified according to any one type. Particulars concerning the life of a man that were at variance with the type to which his biography was assigned were sometimes included in other parts of the same history.

The weight of convention was heaviest upon the compilers of dynastic histories and other official works. In general, the historian who recorded or compiled accounts of nonofficial personages (monks, recluses, certain literary figures) or of events of marginal concern to the court (ethnography of certain peoples, popular festivals) enjoyed greater freedom. It was always in the sector of private historiography that innovation occurred: for example, the invention of a new type of "unofficial biography" (*pieh-chuan*) in the Ch'ing dynasty, the development first of the "life chronicle" (*nien-p'u*) and subsequently of the autobiographical life chronicle, the creation of institutional history (which later atrophied under official sponsorship), and the development of local histories (*fang-chih*) given a fresh impetus by Chang Hsüehch'eng and his successors. But if some of the official conventions were less burdensome in such cases as these, the method of compilation, governed as it was by tradition and the world view of the elite, remained very much the same. One of the effects of this is that the reader seldom—except in certain kinds of prefaces—glimpses the personality or point of view of the historian in the objective, factual flow of the prose. Another effect—especially pronounced after the bureaucratization of history —was that nearly all personal and evocative writing was relegated to "nonhistorical" categories: novels, anecdotes, and the like. This deprived the historiographical tradition of the vividness and color found in the early chronicles.

The modernization of historiography

The breakup of the millennial traditions of Chinese historiography occurred gradually in phases paralleling the dissolution of the imperial order of which it had been a part: a period of resistance to the intrusive forces from the West, followed, from about 1860 to 1905, by a phase of attempted compromise and accommodation, followed in turn by a period of increasing acceptance of Western ideas and institutions. The abolition of the examination system in 1905, accompanied by sweeping educational reforms after the models of the Japanese modernizers, ushered in revolutionary changes in the organization of learning. The old academies were swept away and replaced by state-supported schools; the long-gowned man of learning who divided his time between official service and scholarly activities gave way—as scholar and teacher— to the new generation of Western-trained and Japanese-trained professors in the newly established universities and research institutes. History was institutionalized in new careers and in new institutions, where it struggled to re-establish itself as one of the new disciplines among the many transplanted from the West.

The universities were the first of the new institutions for the study of history. They grew from small beginnings under the empire to a nationwide system of state, provincial, and accredited private universities under the Nationalist government (1927–1949). Although the scale was small (only about 25,000 students attended accredited universities in 1930–1931), the universities provided positions for historians engaged in teaching and research and the intellectual forums in which they developed their ideas. The principal institution for advanced research was the Institute of History and Philology, one of the branches of the Academia Sinica established by the government in 1928. The institute supported a variety of research activities aimed at the reorganization of the historical heritage and the application of new methods of analysis. This included an approach to validating historical documents through archeological investigation. Its excavations of the late Shang capital at Anyang revolutionized the study of early Chinese history. National libraries in Peking and Nanking and libraries attached to universities grew in size and were organized along Western lines. After a considerable lapse of time, the Nationalist government took over the archives of the defunct dynasty, and the collection and organization of archival materials were gradually modernized; substantial archival collections were published, notably by the Palace Museum in Peking.

The senior historians who worked within this new framework of institutions were scholars trained under the old order. The younger men—those who wrought the modernization of historiography— were, typically, deeply influenced by Western ideas and in many cases by study in Japan, Europe, or the United States.

The movement for a new history, although it had earlier beginnings, may best be seen in the context of the May Fourth Movement of 1919, which was basically a movement in search of a new Chinese culture adapted to the needs of a modern society. In the intellectual ferment of Peking in the 1920s, ideas and programs were vigorously discussed. Western ideas from Diderot to Dewey (and from Plato to Lenin) found their champions and interpreters. Historians, like other intellectuals, argued the great issues: Why had the Chinese order weakened and fallen victim to Western imperialism? What should be the ingredients of a modern Chinese civilization, and how could this develop in the midst of political chaos and continuing foreign pressures? What elements from the Chinese past could be used as explanations of China's present and as guides to its future? And which of these elements might be worked into the fabric of a new Chinese culture?

Although there were last-ditch defenders of the older scholarly traditions, the net effects of these controversies on historiography were revolutionary. The classics ceased to be regarded as sacred and were rigorously re-examined for authenticity and credibility as historical documents; "heterodox"

works—Taoist, Buddhist, and others—were reappraised for their historical and philosophic content; the vast range of popular stories, novels, dramas, and other works disdained by the older literati as "vulgar" were seriously studied for the light they might shed on China's social past; field-work techniques from the West were put to use in the study of village life, popular cults, and folklore, and the findings were used to further understanding of traditional popular culture. The comparative method was introduced, and the age-old habit of regarding everything Chinese as *sui generis* was broken. The moral–political emphasis of traditional history was challenged from every side, and materials were collected, regrouped, and studied for the light they might shed on social and economic history or the history of material culture and the arts. Archeology, although underfinanced, produced rich new finds and new ways of understanding the life of the past from surviving objects; analytical history based on stated hypotheses replaced the time-honored forms of compilation. Exact citations and footnotes began to replace the ancient method of piecing together passages from earlier works.

The publications of the new historians of the 1920s and early 1930s reflect all these changes. Research societies, with their quarterly bulletins and monograph series, were a typical medium of communication, and their publications reflect the effort to reorganize China's past. Thus, for example, there were new journals of economic history and geography, the journal and the monographs of the Society for Research in the History of Chinese Architecture, journals of Buddhist studies, and numerous journals of general historical studies, many of them the organs of new university departments and institutes. Semipopular magazines and newspaper supplements carried the findings of historians to a wider reading public. The great publishing houses of Shanghai (notably Chung-hwa and the Commercial Press) commissioned new works, organized series on the national past, and reprinted large collections of choice editions of the literary and historical works of the past. Punctuated editions and vernacular translations of classical works made the heritage more accessible to the young. Modern reference works, indexes, and concordances of traditional sources were developed. Despite the social and political instability of these years, the vitality of the new historical scholarship promised well for the future.

These prospects were dimmed, first by the Japanese attack of 1931 and then by the Japanese invasion of north China in the summer of 1937. Centers of learning were destroyed, and faculties and students fled to the southwest, where the universities continued valiantly to function, but in dire poverty and without libraries or other facilities for scholarly research. Despite these hardships, important works of scholarship were published in the years 1937–1945. The return of the universities to north China in 1945 was followed by catastrophic inflation and the onset of civil war. The Nationalist government was increasingly intolerant of dissent, and the atmosphere became steadily more tense and oppressive.

In the deepening crisis of the civil war, historians, like other intellectuals, had to make a choice: to remain in China under the Communist party or to flee with the Nationalists to Taiwan. The great majority remained. After 1949 there were two principal centers of historical studies: the People's Republic of China and the Republic of China on Taiwan.

Historical scholarship in the People's Republic is institutionalized in academic posts at the universities and in several of the institutes of the Academy of Sciences (Chung-kuo K'o-hsüeh Yüan). Voluminous publications of many kinds have appeared since 1949. Large documentary collections have been published, for instance, on the peasant revolts of Chinese history, on China's wars with the Western powers, on the beginnings of capitalism, on economic history, on reform movements. Excellent punctuated editions of traditional works and vernacular translations have been published on a large scale, and many of the important historical studies of the period from 1920 to 1949 have been reprinted, often with few changes other than a new preface. As the ground has been cleared for public construction, archeologists have conducted new excavations; publication has lagged behind discovery, but it is clear that the new finds now being assembled and classified in national and provincial museums will permit the rewriting of much of China's history.

Like other intellectuals, historians in the People's Republic have been subjected to "thought reform," so that their thinking and writing would wholly conform to the dominant orthodoxy. They have been constantly exhorted to perfect their theoretical grasp of Marxism, to use Marxist theories to bring forth a new history that will serve the new order. Each article may bring upon the historian the wrath of a party theorist who finds something in it that does not conform to the party's view of the past and future. The historian enjoys less prestige than the scientist and is far more exposed to ideological pressures. The older generation that came to maturity under the Republic have not maintained their earlier creativity, and Peking critics have complained that after ten years of the "New China" the younger historians are poorly trained in language and Chinese and Western history and that there are no satisfactory textbooks or general histories.

Since 1949 the problems and results of historical study have been laid down by the government and the party according to the doctrines of Marxism–Leninism–Stalinism and Maoism. The historian has been ordered to document and validate, not to explore and question. The long period from 770 B.C., or perhaps from 481 B.C., to 1840 has been authoritatively categorized as "feudal"—a necessary stage in the Marxist evolution of society. The only sustained attention given to this long period has been in the study of peasant rebellions, each of which, as Mao Tse-tung has said, "dealt a blow to the existing feudal regime and more or less furthered the development of the social productive forces." Mao Tse-tung has also prescribed the study of the "sprouts of capitalism," for it is his thesis that China would herself have progressed from "feudalism" to her own "capitalism" if it had not been for the intrusion of foreign imperialism. The discussion of this thesis has produced polemics, but it has also led to the publication of important historical documents and a few usuable monographs. Modern history from 1840 to 1919 is characterized as semifeudal and semicolonial, and much effort has been expended on documenting imperialist aggressions and on attempting to periodize these years in terms of their "contradictions," changes in the "mode of production," and so on. The concentration on universal Marxist determinants has, by depriving China of a distinctive past, come into conflict with the intense nationalism of the People's Republic. Recently there have been efforts to re-examine the key figures of Chinese history rather than to restrict historical emphasis to peasant rebels and impersonal social forces. This is at least a step toward the re-creation of a distinctive Chinese history. In general, however, dogmatic concerns have made sterile the historical studies since 1949; indeed, one noted Peking historian exclaimed in 1957 that they had brought historiography to "the brink of death."

On Taiwan, the government re-established the Academia Sinica, which now has its old Institute of History and Philology and a new Institute of Modern History. National Taiwan University has a history faculty, as do the smaller colleges on the island. Considerable collections of rare books, archeological materials, government archives, and works of art were brought from the mainland.

There has been a steady output of documentary collections, notably on the history of the nineteenth and the early twentieth centuries. Some of the Academia Sinica's earlier serials have been resumed, and the output of historical monographs has been considerable. Yet the historical community on Taiwan is small and impoverished; historians are sensitive to their insularity and the garrison-state atmosphere around them. It is not surprising that no major works of synthesis and interpretation have appeared on Taiwan.

The present is indeed one of the low points in the long history of Chinese historiography. Meanwhile, scholars in Japan, Europe, and the United States—many of them of Chinese birth—are in a position to push forward in an atmosphere of freedom toward new understandings of the Chinese past.

ARTHUR F. WRIGHT

[*See also* CHINESE SOCIETY *and* CHINESE POLITICAL THOUGHT.]

BIBLIOGRAPHY

BEASLEY, WILLIAM G.; and PULLEYBLANK, E. G. (editors) 1961 *Historians of China and Japan.* University of London, School of Oriental and African Studies, Historical Writing on the Peoples of Asia, Vol. 3. London and New York: Oxford Univ. Press.
BIELENSTEIN, HANS 1953 Historiography. Pages 9–81 in Hans Bielenstein, *The Restoration of the Han Dynasty; With Prolegomena on the Historiography of the Hou Han Shu.* Stockholm: No publisher given.
GARDNER, CHARLES S. (1938) 1961 *Chinese Traditional Historiography.* Harvard Historical Monograph No. 11. Cambridge, Mass.: Harvard Univ. Press.
NIVISON, DAVID S. 1966 *The Life and Thought of Chang Hsüeh-ch'eng: 1738–1801.* Stanford Studies in the Civilization of Eastern Asia. Stanford (Calif.) Univ. Press.
WATSON, BURTON D. 1958 *Ssu-ma Ch'ien, Grand Historian of China.* New York: Columbia Univ. Press.
WRIGHT, ARTHUR F. 1963 On the Uses of Generalization in the Study of Chinese History. Pages 36–58 in Louis R. Gottschalk (editor). *Generalization in the Writing of History.* A report of the Committee on Historical Analysis of the Social Science Research Council. Univ. of Chicago Press.

IV
ISLAMIC HISTORIOGRAPHY

Islamic historiography is the historical literature written by adherents of the various branches of the religion of Islam. Although much of it is written in Arabic, a great deal has appeared in other languages employed by Muslims; Persian (beginning with the tenth century) and Turkish (from the sixteenth century onward) were used intensively for the writing of histories. Various minorities living under Muslim domination, especially the Eastern Christian denominations, produced historical works bearing a close resemblance to their Islamic counterparts, but these will not be considered here. On the other hand, the rapidly growing number of historical works written by Muslims in our time must not be excluded, even if the old forms and techniques have been abandoned, together with most of the values that were characteristic of Islamic historiography from medieval times well into the nineteenth century.

Origins and early beginnings. Pre-Islamic Arabs took a keen interest in genealogy and in major events affecting tribal politics, but the memory of the past was transmitted orally. In the Byzantine and Persian territories conquered by the Muslims during the first half of the seventh century, historiographical traditions of long standing were alive, if not exactly flourishing. In these areas, personal contacts between Muslims and learned non-Muslims or converts seem to have set in motion a certain minor impetus toward the creation of Muslim historical writing.

The principal motivation behind the subsequent tremendous development of this historical writing lies in the conception of Islam as a historical religion. The Prophet Muḥammad (ca. 570–632) saw himself as the culmination and fulfillment of a historical process that started with the beginning of the world in time. Through a chain of divinely ordained messengers (principally, the great figures of Judaism and Christianity), of whom he was the last, this process was leading toward a clearly foreseeable end of the world. Moreover, Muḥammad saw himself as a religiosocial reformer fulfilling prophecies and giving directions for the future. Thus, he provided the outline on a vast historical canvas that was left to be filled in and interpreted by the historian. There was another aspect of the awareness of history fostered by the Prophet. Historical precedent, in all its essential manifestations, was very important in the development of Islamic civilization. From the outset, and increasingly so with the passing of time, political, legal, religious, and scholarly institutions, as well as moral ideas and values, were considered as deriving their ultimate authority from the events of early Islam and the actions and behavior of the early Muslims. The historical truth and significance of these events and actions required constant reaffirmation, confirmation, and re-evaluation. This sharpened historical consciousness and was responsible for a great amount of historical research and writing.

Although there is no doubt as to the motivation that made Islamic historiography an inevitability, the mechanisms through which this took place are much harder to trace. The early authorities responsible for the historical information reported in later writings are represented as having transmitted the material orally. This may be true, but it is more likely that there existed a method of oral transmission that was supplemented by unpublished written notes that were the reporters' personal *aide-mémoires*. In fact, there seems to have been no regular procedure for the orderly publication of works written in Arabic until the end of the seventh century. The subsequent introduction of paper, at about 750, or the beginning of the 'Abbâsid dynasty, made possible a literary activity that in the quantity of production was something not seen before in the Mediterranean world. However, it would seem that relatively few works that could be called histories were written, and they almost certainly enjoyed no wide circulation. Earlier Muslim historical works have largely been lost because of the absence of institutions of publication and durable writing materials and also, perhaps, because of the dynastic change that made works written under the Umayyads (660–750) largely unacceptable. 'Urwah b. az-Zubayr (ca. 650–711), a member of the Muslim elite, is credited with the composition of the book *Raids of the Prophets*. In the generation following 'Urwah, al-Zuhrî (ca. 670–740) is said to have written a work on "the genealogy of his people." He also wrote, apparently for his personal use, on the length of the reigns of the caliphs. From the work of a third early authority, Mûsâ b. 'Uqbah (d. 758/759), a brief fragment, not entirely historical in character, has come down to us. The earliest large-scale work that is preserved, although only in later recensions, is the biography of the Prophet (*Sîrah*, "Way of Life") by Ibn Isḥâq (ca. 704–767). It deals with the history of pre-Islamic Arabia and with all the details and events of the Prophet's life. The same author is also credited with a history of the caliphs. From the evidence now at our disposal, we may conclude that by around 700 historical research, focused on the life of Muḥammad, began to serve the political and social needs of the new religion. It also seems certain that most of the formal elements of later historical writing were to some degree already present at that time.

Forms and contents of historical works. The importance of form in literary presentation is particularly noticeable in Islamic historiography, which has, for better or for worse, always remained in bondage to the forms it first developed. Pre-Islamic Arab tradition had already stressed the concrete "factual" element in history, isolated from its environment and as much as possible unmodified by human thought processes. Thus, simple statements, isolated events, superficial, if colorful, characterizations, put next to each other and left without any explicit elaboration of their inner or causal connections, came to determine the basic appearance of Muslim history books. Historical truth, like religious truth, was considered ensured by the unimpeachable character of the succession of men through whom a given item of information was transmitted, the so-called chain of transmitters or *isnâd*. Even if the historian did not mention these chains of authorities for all the individual items he reported (and many historians did not), the concept of each historical fact possessing a great, even absolute, degree of autonomy was strengthened. The effects have been felt throughout all Muslim historical writing, which can be characterized as fundamentally episodic, no matter how long and detailed and skillfully narrated the individual episode.

Annalistic histories. Larger units for organizing the historical material were soon needed to hold together the constantly growing volume of data. They were readily found in the proven principles of dynastic arrangement according to the reigns of successive rulers and in annalistic arrangement according to the years of the era. The era of the *hijrah* was introduced about the year 638, and Muslim historians were fortunate compared to all their predecessors inasmuch as they were able, from the outset, to rely upon a continuous, unambiguous, and generally accepted chronology. The strictly annalistic arrangement was thought particularly suitable to historical presentation. It was also easily combined with other arrangements, such as that according to reigns; and it fitted in well with the fragmented episodic approach and helped to perpetuate it. Systematically practiced, it was rarely interrupted even to the extent of the consecutive reporting of events that extended over several years. It was especially useful in that it facilitated the continuation of standard histories in the form of supplements often called *dhayl* ("tail") or some variant. Such continuations might be independent works containing only new material, or they might repeat the earlier material, shortening the narrative for the older period and becoming more and more detailed as they approach the actual time of writing. Authors then would systematically date events according to the month and the day and list even trivial news. The oldest preserved, at least in part, annalistic histories in Arabic were written by Khalîfah b. Khayyâṭ in the first half of the ninth century and by Ya'qûb b. Sufyân in the second half of the same century. The multi-volume standard work of Muslim annalistic historiography, which decisively influenced its future course, was written by aṭ-Ṭabarî (d. 923).

Biographies. Of the areas of study cultivated by the Muslim historians, the most important was biography. This was due not so much to the often expressed fact that history is the record of man and his actions, but rather to the fact that Muslim historiography, in its early beginnings, was concerned with the story of the life of a great individual, the Prophet Muḥammad, and with the circumstances surrounding the activities of the early Muslims. It then became necessary to scrutinize the lives of all those connected in any way with Muslim law and religion and to learn the dates of their birth and their death, their local affiliations, their teachers and disciples, their moral character, and their works and activities. Depending on the importance attached to a given individual, biographies could at times grow into large volumes while still remaining restricted, by and large, to these topics. The majority of biographies were brief and were entered early, in the form of obituaries of notable persons, into annalistic histories. Biographies dealing with representatives of certain scholarly categories were collected in special works, and biographies of religious scholars constituted the main contents of the large, theologically oriented segment of local historiography.

In order to facilitate reference, biographies were grouped in "classes" (*ṭabaqah*, plural *ṭabaqât*) comprising those who had died in approximately the same period. This somewhat clumsy arrangement served quite well the need of religious scholars to judge the genuineness and reliability of a chain of transmitters. However, as the number of biographees increased, an alphabetical arrangement was instituted. Beginning with the tenth century, alphabetization thus became the preferred method of arrangement in collections of biographies, although the *ṭabaqât* system continued to be used. It must be noted that the merchants, military men, government officials who were not at the same time religious scholars, scholars in the nonreligious disciplines, poets, and so on were originally not the object of any systematic biographical research. Factual information was often plentiful but always scattered. Much of it would have been lost if some later Muslim authors had not put together the scattered information and produced excellent biographical collections dealing with some of these groups, such as the littérateurs treated by Yâqût (d. 1229) in his *Irshâd al-arîb*

ilâ ma'rifat al-adîb, the physicians collected in the great work on the history of medicine by Ibn Abî Uṣaybi'ah (d. 1270), entitled '*Uyûn al-anbâ' fî ṭabaqât al-aṭibbâ'*, or the fine choice of biographies of illustrious men presented by Ibn Khallikân (d. 1282) in his *Wafayât al-a'yân*.

General histories. Political history, restricted to the administrative and military exploits of rulers and statesmen, was the essential raw material for most Muslim historical writing. Monographs on particular events or periods were written in great profusion; in fact, the early ninth-century historians, most of whose works are known to us only by title, wrote copiously on politically significant individual events. Comprehensive world histories, usually traced from the creation of the world or from the coming of Islam to the times of their particular authors, also met with success. They were universal only in the Muslim sense, not admitting more than a rather limited amount of set data from pre-Islamic times and largely insensitive to non-Muslim history, even where it impinged upon Muslim affairs. The assimilation of the Hellenistic heritage, and with it the development of a taste for cultural history, broadened the horizons of historiography. In the late ninth century, political history combined with intellectual history to touch on all the noteworthy and accessible features of the various civilizations then known. This trend produced such outstanding works as the *History* by al-Ya'qûbî and the series of publications by al-Mas'ûdî (d. 945/946), among them the preserved *Murûj adh-dhahab*. It continued to echo weakly in the works of much later periods. Interest in the contemporary or near-contemporary non-Muslim world remained nevertheless subdued. While the scholarly curiosity of historians welcomed "strange" information, they undertook no systematic search for it. Measured against the enormous mass of Muslim historical writing, references to events that took place outside the Muslim world are few indeed. Al-Mas'ûdî, for instance, included a list of the kings of the Franks (see Maqbul Ahmad 1960, pp. 7–10). Embassies from abroad occasionally provided an opening for referring to events on the international scene. Historians of the time of the Crusades were well aware of cultural and political differences, but in their political and military analysis they did not venture beyond the borders of Islam. In central Asia, the singular circumstances created by the Mongol Empire, with its tentacles stretching far outside the old Muslim world, produced the statesman and historian Rashîd-ad-dîn Faḍlallâh (d. 1318). His *General History* (*Jâmi' at-tawârikh*), written in Persian, is probably the first genuine universal history of Islam. The local historiography of cities and regions was also persistently cultivated. It emphasized political and religious history but also included topographical description and antiquarian data. As might be expected, data on social, economic, and financial history are incidental to most historical writing in Islam and, therefore, comparatively scarce. Some annalistic histories give us a rather intimate view of medieval urban life with its crimes, suicides, recurrent inflation, and other social problems.

Historians. For a very large and influential part of its production, Islamic historiography is indebted to scholars trained in the religious studies who earned their living by virtue of this training but whose literary activities included the writing of histories. For example, al-Bukhârî (d. 870), the author of the most authoritative collection of Prophetic traditions, wrote several collections of terse biographies of religious authorities. He entitled each of these works *History*, thus establishing himself in Muslim consciousness as a historian. From the eleventh century on, a great many historians were religious scholars who held positions in the judiciary, in the civilian branch of the political administration, and in the madrasahs (mosque schools), all of them depending on the religious establishment for their livelihood.

Court historians. In Islamic countries, wherever ambitious and powerful rulers were to be found, history was the "royal science" par excellence, which kings, courtiers, and wazirs, as well as the tutors of princes, were expected to master. Caliphs and sultans often ordered officials to set down the history of their reign or dynasty. It may have happened even more frequently that historical works were written for presentation to the ruler in the hope of a reward or preferment. The professional court historian became an established fixture at certain courts. For example, the courts of the later dynasties in Persia and the Ottoman Empire provided a particularly favorable atmosphere for historical studies. However, it would hardly be correct to speak of a clearly defined Muslim court historiography. Regardless of the position and the motivation of these writers, their works as a rule remained individualistic efforts. The personalities of their authors can be glimpsed even through the curtain of flattery and obsequious verbosity that was often extremely dense.

The term "court historian" would also hardly be the appropriate designation for government officials who, because of their proximity to the seats of power where they were able to witness important

events in the making, wrote historical works. Their number was not inconsiderable, and to them we owe some of the best historical works produced in Islam. Late tenth-century historians such as Miskawayh (d. 1030) and Hilâl aṣ-Ṣâbi' (d. 1036) were government officials who not only possessed an inside knowledge of political affairs (the family of aṣ-Ṣâbi' had served in government for generations) but were also accomplished writers and well versed in philosophy and the secular sciences. All of this is reflected in the quality of their works and in their historical insight. The work of 'Imâd-ad-dîn al-Isfahânî (d. 1201) is an outstanding example of historical memoirs written by a high official who consulted documents and diaries. In particular, his *Barq ash-Sha'mî* deserves high praise as representing the apogee of diplomatic historiography in Islam.

Amateur historians. 'Imâd al-Isfahânî and rulers who wrote historical works and memoirs may be called amateur historians. Most of the numerous genealogical works were written privately by men who frequently were members of the only true Muslim nobility, the descendants of 'Alî. In general, quite a few historical works were probably produced as labors of love, out of reverence for the importance of history and in recognition of the need for preserving an adequate historical record.

Professional historians. In exceptional cases, it appears that an author might be paid for writing historical works on the basis of copies sold through booksellers; but in any case, we may safely surmise that this was not sufficient to live on. The professional historian, in the modern sense, could hardly have existed in the medieval Muslim environment. History was not included in the curriculum of the madrasahs, although lectures on historical topics were occasionally given by professors employed and paid for teaching other subjects. However, there were men who spent their lives producing historical works and who came to consider themselves, and to be considered by Muslim tradition, as historians, for example, al-Mas'ûdî and, during the Mamlûk period in Egypt, when interest in history ran high, al-Maqrîzî (d. 1442) and many others like him.

Purpose and methodology of Muslim historiography. Muslim historians were in the habit of introducing their works with statements concerning the purpose of historical writing (for a number of these statements collected by as-Sakhâwî, see Rosenthal 1952, pp. 219 ff.). The ideas expressed in this connection soon became standardized and did not possess any individual ring. This fact itself is significant in that it shows the general and unquestioned acceptance of their validity. These statements expressed the belief that history is useful; it teaches by both negative and positive examples, that is, it teaches everybody how to handle his own affairs in this fleeting world and, most importantly, it teaches political leaders how to govern properly. Furthermore, history is entertaining; it provides amusing, yet thoughtful, relaxation from more exacting intellectual tasks. And history is instructive and edifying as a handmaiden of religion, proving the truth of Islam and the correctness of the view of the world expounded by it. On the surface, this last point may seem to have been raised merely in order to provide the greatly needed excuse for the waste of time assumed to be involved in any occupation with secular subjects. In reality, it touches on the very meaning of historiography as a part of Muslim civilization. Only as an integral component of the religiously determined structure of the world and society could the study of history be meaningful in Islam.

The idea of history as a powerful weapon in political and ideological struggles does not seem to have been entertained openly or commonly by Muslim historians. On occasion, they were conscious of the fact that their work was used to serve the purpose of exalting an individual or of fortifying the political aspirations of a ruling house. In some instances, minutely detailed modern research has been able to uncover concealed political tendencies or a purposeful manipulation of the evidence in historical writings. However, Muslim historians considered themselves as the custodians and transmitters of facts that could not be altered and neither required nor admitted of interpretation. The historian's proper activities were restricted to reporting, shortening, collecting different recensions of, and, perhaps, retelling the information provided by the available sources.

This view largely determined the method of historical research. The historian's main task was setting down what had actually happened, and his main problem was ascertaining the truth of his information, whether it came to him orally or through written sources. Truth was understood, above all, as verification of the presumption that an item of information was derived from someone in a position to know. All history being in a sense contemporary history, personal observation was the real basis of historical knowledge and the best assurance of historical truth. For the rest, the elaborate system developed by scholars of the science of Prophetic traditions, a system for ascertaining the genuineness of these traditions, came to be considered as applicable also to historical research. Of

necessity, written histories were granted evidential authority. Archival research and the study of inscriptions, coins, and similar historical evidence were only sporadically practiced. A full discussion of the methodology of medieval Muslim historiography is preserved in a work written in Arabic by a Persian scholar, Muḥammad b. Ibrâhîm al-Îjî, who wrote in 1381–1382 and whose work is thus the oldest extensive treatise on the subject known so far. On a less theoretical level, comprehensive works on Islamic historiography, its methods, its problems, and its history were composed in Egypt in the following century by al-Kâfiyajî (d. 1474), who wrote in 1463, and, following him, by as-Sakhâwî (d. 1497), who wrote in 1492.

Philosophy and sociology of history. The Islamic historians' own views regarding the meaning of history are implied in their works and spelled out in the methodological writings just mentioned. They were convinced that history was the chosen instrument of God for the gradual improvement of mankind and for man's preparation for the final reckoning at the inevitable end of the world. The coming of Muḥammad and Islam was viewed as the great turning point of world history, at which, for the first time, the purpose of history revealed itself clearly and history became a comprehensible reality. From then on, control of history's progress was within the reach of human beings, if—and that remained the great question—they followed the comprehensive plan for the good life laid down, for both the individual and society, in the religious injunctions of Islam. While there was no automatic sin-and-retribution mechanism operative in history, the rulers at least were judged by their compliance or noncompliance, according to the historian's sources of information, with Islamic moral norms. There were, however, a few exceptional historians who, while not denying the validity of Islamic theology, tried to understand history as a purely human social phenomenon. This approach ran counter to the major premises of the Muslim world view and was, therefore, always slightly suspect. It was hinted at by Miskawsyh when, in his large history entitled *The Experiences of the Nations*, he denied that events caused by the interference of the supernatural in history, such as the events connected with the life of the Prophet, could provide a useful experience for students of history. Eventually, the northwest African Ibn Khaldūn (d. 1406), writing in 1377, constructed a coherent system of the historical process in purely human terms and devoted to its exposition the famous *Muqaddimah* ("Introduction") of his large universal history, *Kitâb al-'Ibar*. He explained human society as depending on material and psychological forces, which were described by him in detail; and he defined history in terms of a cyclic motion (with a slight, but continuous, forward movement) of growth and decay within the various forms of human associations. [*See the biography of* IBN KHALDŪN.]

Contemporary Muslim historiography. The old forms of historical writing have persisted until recent times, especially in the more shielded regions of the Muslim world. At the time of the first true clash of Islam with the modern world, precipitated by Napoleon's Egyptian campaign, it was still possible for an important work of the annalistic type to be produced by a man of genuine historical perception, the Egyptian al-Jabartî (d. 1826?). During the nineteenth century, there were a few Arabic translations of then popular Western historical works. The study of certain aspects of world history not directly affecting the Muslim countries began to attract some limited interest, especially on the educational level. To this day, it can fairly be said that the interest in all non-Islamic history has remained limited, and nothing of first-rate importance appears to have been produced in the field. On the other hand, from the beginning of the twentieth century and increasingly accelerated by the political developments that took place in the wake of World War II, the meaning of history and the practice of historiography as it affects Muslim life has become a major concern everywhere in Muslim countries. Some have contended, for example, that the communal conflict between Muslims and Hindus preceding the partition of India was largely the result of the wrong teaching of history and, therefore, amenable to redirection through the efforts of historians (see S. Nadvi, in Philips 1961, p. 493). Others have held that Muslim history is unable to give any guidance for the solution of present-day problems and remains better forgotten and disregarded.

Popular feeling tends to glorify the study of the great Muslim past as an inexhaustible source for the building of national morale and the strengthening of nationalist aspirations. This use of history is fostered by writers devoting their literary talents to historical themes, writers such as Muḥammad Ḥusayn Haykal and Maḥmûd 'Abbâs al-'Aqqâd. Motion pictures and, to a lesser degree, stage plays effectively exploit historical themes (see Landau 1958, pp. 114 ff., 198 f.). More recently, numerous Muslim historians with Western training in scholarship and methodology have begun to publish, in their various languages, serious and often important historical works as well as biographical, social, and economic studies on past Muslim history.

Archival studies are getting underway—particularly in Turkey, where much of the preserved material is concentrated. The publication of medieval historical texts is being continued at an accelerated pace with the maintenance of, generally speaking, satisfactory standards in editing technique.

The great pre-Islamic past of the Muslim countries inspired different political ideologies and movements based on historical speculation. These had their greatest efflorescence between 1920 and 1945. At present, the excavation, conservation, and study of the archeological remains of the pre-Islamic and the Islamic past are competently cultivated nearly everywhere.

FRANZ ROSENTHAL

[*See also* ISLAM.]

BIBLIOGRAPHY

The bibliography is restricted to works written in west European languages. The most convenient sources of information on contemporary Islamic historiography are Lewis & Holt 1962 *and* Philips 1961; *other works on this subject are* Ayalon 1960; Chejne 1960 *and* 1963; Haddad 1961; Hourani 1962; Inalcik 1953; Key 1954; *and* Von Grunebaum 1962.

GENERAL

ABBOTT, NABIA 1957 *Studies in Arabic Literary Papyri.* Volume 1: Historical Texts. Univ. of Chicago Press.

AYALON, DAVID 1960 The Historian al-Jabartī and His Background. London, University of, School of Oriental and African Studies, *Bulletin* 23:217–249.

BABINGER, FRANZ 1927 *Die Geschichtsschreiber der Osmanen und ihre Werke.* Leipzig: Harrassowitz.

BROCKELMANN, CARL 1937–1949 *Geschichte der arabischen Litteratur.* 5 vols. Leiden (Netherlands): Brill.

CHEJNE, ANWAR G. 1960 The Use of History by Modern Arab Writers. *Middle East Journal* 14:382–396.

CHEJNE, ANWAR G. 1963 Intellectual Revival in the Arab World: An Introduction. *Islamic Studies* (Karachi) 2:413–437.

FISCHEL, WALTER J. 1967 *Ibn Khaldūn in Egypt; His Public Functions and His Historical Research (1382–1406): An Essay in Islamic Historiography.* Berkeley: Univ. of California Press.

GIBB, HAMILTON A. R. 1962 *Studies on the Civilization of Islam.* Boston: Beacon.

HADDAD, GEORGE M. 1961 Modern Arab Historians and World History. *Muslim World* 51:37–43.

HARDY, P. 1960 *Historians of Medieval India: Studies in Indo–Muslim Historical Writing.* London: Luzac.

HOURANI, ALBERT H. 1962 *Arab Thought in the Liberal Age: 1798–1939.* New York: Oxford Univ. Press. → See especially pages 87 and 333 ff.

INALCIK, HALIL 1953 Some Remarks on the Study of History in Islamic Countries. *Middle East Journal* 7:451–455.

KEY, KERIM K. 1954 *An Outline of Modern Turkish Historiography.* Istanbul: Kâğit ve Basĭm Isleri.

LANDAU, JACOB M. 1958 *Studies in the Arab Theater and Cinema.* Philadelphia: Univ. of Pennsylvania Press.

LEWIS, BERNARD; and HOLT, P. M. (editors) 1962 *Historians of the Middle East.* Oxford Univ. Press.

MAQBUL AHMAD, S. (editor) 1960 *Al-Mas'ûdî Millenary Commemoration Volume.* Algiers: Aligarh Univ., Institute of Islamic Studies. → See especially pages 7–10, written by Bernard Lewis.

PHILIPS, CYRIL H. (editor) 1961 *Historians of India, Pakistan and Ceylon.* University of London, School of Oriental and African Studies, Historical Writing on the Peoples of Asia, Vol. 1. New York: Oxford Univ. Press.

ROSENTHAL, FRANZ 1952 *A History of Muslim Historiography.* Leiden: Brill. → Includes translations of the works of al-Kâfiyajî and as-Sakhâwî.

SAUVAGET, JEAN; and CAHEN, CLAUDE (1943) 1965 *Introduction to the History of the Muslim East.* Berkeley and Los Angeles: Univ. of California Press. → First published in French.

STOREY, CHARLES A. 1935–1953 *Persian Literature: A Bio–Bibliographical Survey.* London: Luzac.

VON GRUNEBAUM, GUSTAVE E. (1962) 1964 *Modern Islam: The Search for Cultural Identity.* New York: Vintage.

TRANSLATIONS OF HISTORICAL WORKS

AL-BALÂDHÛRÎ *Il Califfo Mu'âwiya I.* Translated by Olga Pinto and Giorgio Levi Della Vida. Rome: Bardi, 1938. → A translation of a chapter from al-Balâdhûrî's *Ansâb.*

AL-BALÂDHÛRÎ *The Origins of the Islamic State, Being a Translation From the Arabic, Accompanied With Annotations, Geographic and Historical Notes of the* Kitâb futûḥ al-buldân. 2 vols. in 3. Translated by Philip K. Hitti. New York: Columbia Univ. Press, 1927–1958.

AL-SÛLI *Akhbâr ar-Râdî billâh wa'l-Mutaqqî billâh (Histoire de la dynastie abbaside de 322 à 333/934 à 944).* Translated from the Arabic by Marius Canard. Institut d'Études Orientales de la Faculté des Lettres d'Alger, Publications 10, 12. Algiers: Carbonel, 1946–1950.

AṬ-ṬABARÎ *The Reign of al-Mu'taṣim (833–842).* Translated and annotated by Elma Marin. American Oriental Series, Vol. 35. New Haven: American Oriental Society, 1951.

IBN HISHÂM *The Life of Muhammad.* A translation of Ibn Hishâm's adaptation of Ibn Isḥâq's *Sîrat rasûl Allâh,* with introduction and notes by A. Guillaume. London and New York: Oxford Univ. Press, 1955.

IBN KHALDÛN (1375–1382) 1958 *The Muqaddimah: An Introduction to History.* 3 vols. Translated by Franz Rosenthal. New York: Pantheon Books. → Contains a selected bibliography by Walter J. Fischel.

IBN ṢAṢRÂ *A Chronicle of Damascus 1389–1397.* 2 vols. Translated, edited, and annotated by William M. Brinner. Berkeley and Los Angeles: Univ. of California Press, 1963. → Volume 1 is the English translation; Volume 2 is the original Arabic text.

JOVEYNÎ *The History of the World Conqueror.* 2 vols. Translated from the text of Mirza Muhammad Qazvini by John A. Boyle. Cambridge, Mass.: Harvard Univ. Press, 1958. → A translation of *Tâʾrîkh-i-Jahân-gushâ.*

MISKAWSYH *Tajârib al-umam: And Excerpts From Other Historians of His Time.* Edited by H. F. Amedroz. Volumes 1–2 in H. F. Amedroz and David S. Margoliouth, *The Eclipse of the Abbasid Caliphate.* 7 vols. Oxford: Blackwell, 1920–1921. → Volumes 4–5 are the English translation, by D. S. Margoliouth, of Volumes 1–2.

NARSHAKHÎ *The History of Bukhara.* Translated by Richard N. Frye from a Persian abridgment of the Arabic original. Cambridge, Mass.: Mediaeval Academy of America, 1954.

YŪSUF IBN TAGHRĪ-BIRDĪ *History of Egypt: 1382–1469 A.D.* Translated by William Popper. Parts 1–7 and indexes. Berkeley and Los Angeles: Univ. of California Press, 1954–1960. → First published as *an-Nujûm az-zâhirah.*

V

JAPANESE HISTORIOGRAPHY

The Japanese historiographical genius has extended less to the fashioning of grand systems of interpretation than to the assiduous working out of domestic history. Of all national histories outside the Western world, none has been revealed in such precise and abundant detail or in such a variety of interpretive forms as that of Japan. The work of Japanese historians, particularly in the last century, has been both prolific and comprehensive. And while the events of Japanese history have yet to find a prominent place in the main body of world historiography, the reverse condition, whereby Japanese history is treated in world context, has been carried forward in impressive fashion by the Japanese. Today every segment of Japanese history is served by the professional archivist, the scholarly monographer, and the interpretive synthesizer, alive to modern currents of historical philosophy and methodology.

History is one of the most popular academic fields in Japan today. The standard Japanese *Publisher's Annual* for 1964 lists 1,249 single titles under history. Each of Japan's more than 230 universities has its department of history, often in more than one faculty. A recent handbook of historical research lists 75 libraries and archival repositories worthy of general note. The same handbook lists 56 scholarly serials published by national historical associations and 40 by societies of primarily local importance.

While Japan does not have a central national archives, the Historiographical Institute of Tokyo University serves somewhat in this capacity, and in addition, numerous private and government libraries preserve or collect materials on a large scale. Printed archival collections are abundantly available. The Historiographical Institute alone has published over 350 weighty volumes of sources, while the standard reprinting of premodern Japanese histories runs to more than sixty volumes. The aspiring Japanese historian has at his command the product of four generations of modern historical scholarship and a full reference shelf of encyclopedias and dictionaries on every major subject from bibliography to religion. For stimulus to his thinking he may turn to volumes on the meaning of history by notable Japanese historians or to translations of standard works by Croce, Weber, Marx, Toynbee, Freud, or Parsons.

Japanese use of history

History is more than a popular field well served by its specialists; history is, and has been, important to the Japanese people in their persistent search for their own identity and for a sense of order in the world about them. Japanese historians have been eclectic in the theories to which they have subscribed but remarkably consistent in the objectives that they have pursued. Since the eighth century, Japanese historians have looked to history to explain the political and moral order. This search has been served by a variety of world views and historiographical traditions just as it has had to respond to the constantly shifting conditions of Japan's domestic politics and world position. The earliest and most original view of history adopted by the Japanese grew out of an age when Japan existed in comparative isolation from China and the dominant culture of the continent. It conceived of a world with Japan at the center, the proud inheritor of an ideal order built around the imperial house and protected by the native (Shinto) deities. This world view was kept alive into modern times as the Japanese clung to various tokens of their imagined cultural or racial superiority. But Japanese ethnocentrism was seldom free of competition from other, more widely based systems, and by the sixth century both Confucianism and Buddhism were challenging the claims of Shinto.

By medieval times, while not openly admitting the moral superiority of China or India, Japanese historians had taken to explaining causation in political affairs by reference to Confucian conceptions of proper or improper conduct or to Buddhist interpretations of retribution for good and evil. Japan's confrontation with Western civilization was historiographically even more traumatic, for it not only presented Japan with a multiplicity of theories of historical explanation, but also imposed upon her a view of the world order that placed the West at the center of the human drama and made the Judaeo–Christian tradition the driving force in human progress.

Japanese historical writing, reacting to these several pressures, has tended to be assimilative in concept and methodology. In strictly technical terms it has demonstrated a growing sophistication in its capacity to deal with basic facts and causal phenomena. And this cumulative quality of Japanese historiography—its constant increase in historical detachment and critical judgment and its steady improvement in basic techniques—is one of its most impressive over-all features. On the other hand, the search for order and status has proved continually illusive. The questions asked by every Japanese—who are we? what distinguishes us as a people and culture? what is our place in the world order?—remain a source of uncertainty even today; and it is this uncertainty that has kept Japanese historiography oscillating between the extremes of nationalism and universalism.

The Japanese have never been ones to accept a secondary position in the world gracefully. Historiography in modern Japan has kept pace with the national desire to achieve world prominence. History and nation, in fact, have been closely linked. For history has been drawn into the service of the state, either to provide the people with a crucial sense of continuity with their traditional values or as a means of justifying the revolutionary changes endorsed by a government intent upon modern reform. Throughout most of the last century, history has seemed inevitably to teach the lesson of Japan's inferiority to the more enlightened peoples of the West. Only once did the Japanese people appear to have it in their power to turn history in their favor so that their private view of the world could be extended into a universal vision. During the era of continental expansion, the march of Japanese armies seemed on the verge of making truth out of the propagandist's claim that the goal of world history was to draw mankind under the benevolent rule of the Japanese emperor. The discrediting of that claim gave back to the Japanese historian the task of finding a realistic position for Japanese history in an objectively conceived world environment. The task has not been easy.

Early historical writing

Japan's earliest extant histories, the *Kojiki* (A.D. 712; "Record of Ancient Matters") and the *Nihon shoki* (A.D. 720; "Chronicle of Japan"), were both products of the desire of the Japanese ruling house to "clarify the political order" and to produce a national chronicle comparable to those that added luster to the dynasties of China. The *Kojiki* is a narrative of the Japanese people from the "age of the gods" through the establishment of the Yamato hegemony to the end of the reign of Empress Suiko in A.D. 628. The purpose of the work is to display the background of the Yamato house and to document the dependent status of various noble lines. While the sources of the *Kojiki* are obscure, and hence its historiographical conceptions difficult to date, it is safe to assume that it exemplifies the earliest recorded views of the Japanese people regarding themselves and their past. The work is notable for its matter-of-fact treatment of super-natural events, particularly its uncomplicated handling of the relationship between human society and the deities. The *Kojiki* contains no generalized myths of creation and no culture heroes. Nor does it depict the Japanese gods as active agents in the lives of mortals once the world of man was set down upon the Japanese islands. Rather, the story of creation begins with the first male and female deities, proceeds through generations of their offspring, and then by genealogical descent enters the age of man in Japan. In the human political world, power and status derived simply from the circumstances of lineal descent from particular ancestral deities. The imperial family established its claim to sovereignty by virtue of direct descent from Amaterasu, the Sun Goddess.

Because of its limited circulation, the *Kojiki* had little immediate influence on Japanese historians. Not until the eighteenth century, when nationalistic scholars found in its archaic contents the ingredients of an idealized society based on "pure Japanese" values, did it become the revered source of the Japanese view of history. For over a millennium, therefore, it was the *Nihon shoki* that had the reputation of being Japan's first history. The *Nihon shoki* had the advantage of being written in Chinese and being more closely based on Chinese models than was the *Kojiki*; it sought, in other words, to place Japanese history into a world that acknowledged the existence of China as the source of a Confucian world view, although it sought to maintain Japan's independent and competitive position in that world. More historiographically self-conscious than the writers of the *Kojiki*, the *Nihon shoki*'s authors attempted to assign dates to the amorphous events associated with the early generations of the imperial house and thus establish a chronology comparable to that of China. It was from this effort, using the Chinese theory of "great cycles," that the authors arrived at the controversial date 660 B.C. for the ascension of Jimmu, "the first emperor," a date that modern historians more properly place in the third or fourth century A.D.

The *Nihon shoki* and five succeeding official histories that chronicled the events of the imperial court down to 887 are known together as the *Rikkokushi* ("Six National Histories"). Although they constitute an attempt of the Japanese to write history in the Chinese official manner, they differ considerably from their models. The writer of history met in Japan conditions very different from those in China, for the Japanese dynasty had al-ready established itself "in perpetuity," and the historian could have very little to say about its right to rule. As a consequence, the Japanese never fully adopted the premises of the Confucian moral order which made political power contingent on virtue but rather found ways of equating their own highly aristocratic social hierarchy to that of China by the assumption that the moral right to sovereignty followed the line of hereditary succession. In fact, as the Japanese imperial line continued unbroken for century after century, the Japanese began to turn the Confucian order to their advantage and to claim superiority in matters of government over the Chinese, who were constantly rebelling against their emperors.

The writing of official history lost its meaning in Japan once the imperial bureaucracy gave way to the direct rule of aristocratic houses and the emperor was pushed above politics to serve as a sacred legitimizer. By the tenth century the compilation of official annals had given way to the writing of private histories. The *monogatari* (narratives) and *kagami* (mirrors) exemplify a style of history that was as distinctive a product of the aristocratic society of the Heian court as the literary masterpiece, the "Tale of Genji." Written in Japanese, not Chinese, the new histories combined the intimacy of single authorship with the immediacy of narrative writing. The most famous of these, the *Ōkagami* ("Great Mirror"), combined a synthesis of Japanese history up to the eleventh century with an explanation of the rise of the Fujiwara family, which then dominated the court.

The Middle Ages

By the twelfth century Japanese historical works were showing the influence of Buddhist concepts of karma and salvation. The immensely popular epic history of the war between the Minamoto and Taira, *Heike monogatari*, was written and recited chiefly for its didactic message. The writing of history generally passed into the hands of priests, who relied on Buddhist explanations for the rise and fall of family or individual fortunes. Their works were characteristically suffused with a sense of compassion for human suffering, sadness over the transience of life, and concern over the imminence of the age of decay. Works written from the point of view of the Buddhist establishment, therefore, looked at Japan from a viewpoint that played down worldly political orders in the face of the universality of the human condition. Visible power and circumstance were often depicted only to reveal the inevitability of decline. Yet even among the

Buddhists, a voice was raised which claimed Japan to be the center of the Buddhist world. Nichiren (1222–1282) militantly proclaimed Japan to be the land destined to bring the Buddhist faith to perfection.

In terms of domestic history, the rise of the military aristocracy and the creation of the shogunate (headquarters of the military hegemony) in 1192 added new dimensions to the historians' task of interpretation. Historians now had to explain not only the virtue of the imperial house but also the reason for the decline of the civil aristocracy and the ascendancy of military houses. Two noteworthy products of the Middle Ages in Japan deal with these questions at the same time that they show distinct advances in historiographical technique. *Gukanshō* ("Miscellany of Ignorant Views"), written by the priest Fujiwara Jien (1155–1225), explains the balance between civil and military ministers as dependent on the quality of service they provided and on the requirements of the times. Jien, to some extent, therefore, applied Confucian concepts of rulership to the behavior of "imperial advisors." But the *Gukanshō* is particularly noted for being the first example of "purposeful" historical writing in which the author was able not merely to record but to survey, interpret, and explain while exercising personal detachment.

Jinnō shōtōki ("Records of the True Descent of the Divine Emperors") by General Kitabatake Chikafusa (1291–1354) was written to inform the scion of a displaced branch of the imperial family of the true state of political affairs into which he was born. Its great importance to later generations lay in its emotional revival of the theme of Japan's superiority as a nation because of the unique virtue of the unbroken imperial line.

The Tokugawa period

Japan's great age of historical writing prior to modern times came in the peaceful years of the Tokugawa period (1600–1868). Up to this point the writing of history had been the province of relatively few courtiers and priests. With the cessation of civil war in 1600, the Tokugawa house and the territorial lords (the daimyo) gave official encouragement to the pursuit of learning, and history became a major concern of the entire samurai class. The multicentered political order, which included a regenerated imperial court, a shogun with unmatched powers, and stable daimyo administrations in the provinces, provided incentive for the compilation of numerous official histories, while the cultivation of intellectualism led many a private

scholar into the fields of Japanese history and literature.

At the same time, profound changes were affecting the Japanese climate of opinion. The rigorous pursuit of Confucian philosophy among the samurai, not simply as an esoteric pastime, but for practical use in political affairs and the betterment of education, improved the Japanese scholar's mastery of historical technique. More important, it rejected Buddhist mysticism for a more rationalistic view of history. In addition, a new interest in native Japanese studies (e.g., study of the *Kojiki*), which refocused interest upon the imperial house, gave the Japanese the ingredients of a nationalistic revival in scholarship and the confidence to reject in time even the Confucian values that had so long dominated their thinking.

Chief among the historical works of this age were certain products of official patronage and committee authorship. Heading the list of "house histories" was the voluminous *Tokugawa jikki* ("Veritable Annals of the Tokugawa House"), the first part of which was completed in 516 chapters between 1809 and 1849. The primary effort of the Tokugawa house to write a national history so as to legitimize its rule was the *Honchō tsugan* ("Comprehensive Mirror of Japan"), completed in 1670 by the Hayashi family of shogunal Confucian advisors. The text was in Chinese, and, as the title indicates, the form was modeled after Ssu-ma Kuang's famous *Tzu-chih t'ung-chien* (1084; "Comprehensive Mirror for Government").

Destined to become more influential than the *Honchō tsugan* was the *Dai Nihon shi* ("History of Japan"), compiled under the auspices of the Mito branch of the Tokugawa house. It was the first (and only) successful attempt of the Japanese to write according to the full specifications of the Chinese dynastic history style and required the efforts of a large compilation bureau from 1657 to 1906, when the essays were finally complete. But the annals had been made public in 1720, and from that time the work had acquired a reputation for its sentiments of loyalty to the imperial house.

Historiographically more important than the works of group authorship, however, were the writings of two private historians. Arai Hakuseki (1657–1725), a scholar–statesman in the Confucian sense, was a writer of wide versatility. His *Dokushi yoron* ("Commentaries on History") contained an entirely original system of periodization based on the shifting locus of political power. The *Koshi tsū* ("Survey of Ancient History"), in which he called for philological studies to penetrate the Japanese classics and state that the *kami* (gods) were humans and understandable in rational terms, exemplified both the high moral sense of the Confucianist and the growing rationalism with which many Japanese scholars were able to approach historical causation.

Rai Sanyō (1780–1832), less competent as a historian, exemplified the new interest in national studies. His *Nihon gaishi* ("Unofficial History of Japan") continued in the tradition of Kitabatake's emperor-centered historical narrative. More accessible than the Mito *Dai Nihon shi*, it was widely read and everywhere stirred up sentiments of loyalty toward the emperor and pride in the uniqueness of Japan's national structure.

Such works of compilation and interpretation could hardly have been written had it not been for the diligent labor of a large body of archivists and antiquarians during the Tokugawa period. This labor, in fact, laid the foundations of Japan's modern archival repositories. The contemporary Cabinet Library, for example, is heavily dependent upon collections begun under Tokugawa patronage. The program of the Historiographical Institute today is also a continuation of the remarkable work of the blind bibliographer Hanawa Hokiichi (1746–1821) and his son, who scoured the country collecting and collating historical texts, which they published according to a subject classification under the title *Gunsho ruijū* ("Classified Texts").

These highlights of the historiographical story of the Tokugawa period constitute but a small fraction of the total activity of the age. By the eighteenth century, historical studies were no longer limited to a narrow court circle or to individuals patronized by the central military authorities. Nearly all of the more than 250 daimyo promoted the writing of house histories or the collection of local documents. The spread of learning among diverse groups (even outside the ruling class) encouraged variety and specialization. Antiquarians wrote on ancient usages or court ceremonies, philologists studied the meaning of archaic Japanese words, and bibliographers began the task of examining critically Japan's heritage in the field of letters. Adding impetus to the growth of scholarship and the diffusion of ideas was the remarkable expansion of the printing industry, which put much of the output of Tokugawa writers on the market and into the hands of other scholars. The growth of private and official academies, particularly in the great cities of Edo, Osaka, Kyoto, and Nagasaki, led to a lively interchange of ideas.

By the middle of the nineteenth century, when Japan was abruptly thrust into the company of Western powers and her intellectuals were brought face to face with the latest products of science and scholarship from the West, Japan had at her disposal a mature tradition of historical scholarship, based on sound, though antiquated, principles of Chinese methodology and suffused with a growing national self-consciousness. It required only the touch of Western influence to set in motion a complex historiographical revolution. On the one hand, the Japanese were quick to absorb the methods and philosophies of history offered by the West. On the other hand, they comprehended immediately that the West posed a vital threat to their intellectual security and their historical importance as a nation. In the world views of the West, Japan had no recognized place other than among the "uncivilized" peoples.

The Meiji period

The basic revolution in historiography took Japan roughly thirty years, the same period of time required to lay the foundation for the modern Japanese state. Japan's first task was the fairly straightforward one of recapturing in modern scientific form the facts of Japan's past. For several years the government dominated this work of basic compilation. Interest in history ranked high among the Meiji leaders, for they sought justification for the new regime as well as knowledge about past laws and administrative practices to serve as a basis for new legislation. In 1869 an Office for Collection of Historical Materials and Compilation of National History was established by government order. Its director, Shigeno Yasutsugu, was immediately caught in the dilemma of objective versus propagandistic compilation. The projected national history was eventually abandoned after attack from Shintoist scholars, who claimed the work gave insufficient support to the emperor. The collection of materials, however, has been continued to the present. Meanwhile most of the new departments of government were busy collecting records and compiling documentary histories. The most ambitious and currently useful of these transitional works is *Koji ruien* ("Encyclopedia of Ancient Matters"), a monumental encyclopedia in the Chinese manner compiled by the Department of Shrines between 1879 and 1913.

The conflict over interpretation that divided the official historiographers of the early Meiji era reflected the deep problems that Japan faced in the realm of historical ideology. Ranged on one side were the successors to the Shinto revivalist school of the Tokugawa period, who wished to use history to stimulate patriotism and to keep alive the memory of a noble past with which they could proudly confront the rest of the world. For them Rai Sanyō's history remained a model, and between 1876 and 1884 five supplements to this work were printed. Yet just as in the political arena, the traditionalists were attacked by the advocates of "progress" and intellectual freedom. Private historians with more flexible and cosmopolitan views were at work absorbing new Western concepts and rethinking Japan's historical circumstances. Many of them, in fact, saw Japan as half-civilized in contrast to the "enlightened" peoples of the West. Soon translations of such contemporary laissez-faire writers as Mill and Spencer began to circulate in Japan, and the broadly interpretative works of men like Henry Thomas Buckle and François Guizot showed the way to the writing of cultural history. Fukuzawa Yukichi's *Bummei ron no gairyaku* (1875; "A Short Account of the Theory of Civilization") and Taguchi Ukichi's *Nihon kaika shōshi* (1877–1882; "Short History of Japanese Civilization"), based on these models, opened a new era of Japanese historiography that would shift the attention of the historian away from the purely political to encompass the intellectual, artistic, and religious dimensions of Japanese culture and would begin the task of finding a place for Japan in a world view made larger by the addition of the West.

These two streams of historiography, official-nationalistic and private-international, carried on into the 1890s, but not until the government had abandoned direct interference in the writing of history behind an avowed insistence on objectivity and the advocates of patriotic history had turned their attention to the more impressionable field of elementary education. In the realm of scholarship it was expected that history would become an objective science. And for this purpose a German scholar, Ludwig Reiss (1861–1928), had been invited to establish a chair of history at Tokyo University. Under Reiss the German *Geschichtswissenschaft* school was accepted as the basis for historical training at Tokyo. In 1895 the government attached its Historical Bureau to Tokyo University with the aim of compiling the *Dai Nippon shiryō* ("Historical Materials of Japan") along the lines of the German *Monumenta germaniae historica*. Thus the combination of the University of Tokyo professorships and the Historiographical Institute became the hard core of Japan's modern historical profession, from which emanated the dominant academic orthodoxy.

Beginnings of modern historiography

Japanese historiography came of age as a modern discipline during the forty years after 1890. This era was marked by conspicuous success along four main lines: (1) the perfection of a modern historical methodology, (2) the writing of specialized monographic studies on particular institutions and aspects of Japanese civilization, (3) the preparation of general historical surveys, and (4) the publication of reference works and source materials. The outstanding historiographic work of the period was undoubtedly Kuroita Katsumi's *Kokushi no kenkyū* (1908; "Study of Japanese History"). Kuroita, of Tokyo University and schooled in the German historical–scientific tradition, succeeded in formalizing the periodization of Japanese history and in supplying a definitive critique of the standard sources in the field of political history. Simultaneously, Japanese historians began the task of dividing their history both horizontally by periods and vertically by topics into numerous specialties. Monographic studies of political history, foreign relations, legal institutions, economic history, and the history of art, literature, and religion were produced in abundance. By the 1920s the ground had been prepared for the appearance of new and more satisfactory historical surveys, such as *Nihon bunkashi* (1922; "Cultural History of Japan," 12 volumes) and *Sōgō Nihon shi taikei* (1926; "Synthetic Survey of Japanese History," 20 volumes), both works of multiple authorship.

The mid-1920s stand out as a quiet and productive interlude in Japanese historiography, when few fundamental conflicts of interpretation disturbed the academic calm. Although "academic" and "cultural" historians were separated by obvious differences in approach or subject matter, they shared basic premises about the function and aim of history. Both believed essentially in "scientific" methodology, and both were concerned with the task of "discovering" Japan's past in all its political subtleties and cultural richness. They saw Japan as having successfully joined the ranks of the modern powers, so that Japanese history could be viewed as simply another tributary flowing into the mainstream of modern progress. The Japanese were content to study their past descriptively as a subject sufficient to itself and worthy of pride.

But this atmosphere was not to last long. First of all, Japanese historians began of their own accord to look beyond their own history to discover relationships with other histories and to subject their history to new comparative judgments. Nishida Naojirō's brilliant analysis of Japanese culture saw in Japan its "Gothic art," and its "rise of a commercial spirit." Tsuda Sōkichi broke through the taboos that still obscured Japan's early history to reveal Japan's cultural growth as an unfolding of human qualities shared by "all people." Honjō Eijirō, Ono Takeo, and Tsuchiya Takao began the economic interpretation of Japanese history.

The new currents of historical inquiry were sufficiently strong to bring into being a number of new societies dedicated to specific types of history. Up to then the chief association of Japanese historians had been the Shigakkai (Historical Society of Japan), founded at Tokyo University in 1889. Among the new associations, the Keizaishi Kenkyūkai (Society for the Study of Economic History) was organized at Kyoto University in 1929, and the Shakai Keizaishi Gakkai (Social and Economic History Society) was organized in Tokyo in 1931. In 1933 a group of young historians of the Tokyo area, organizing themselves into the Rekishigaku Kenkyūkai (Historical Science Society), began the move toward "progressive" history that was to lead increasingly in the Marxian direction.

By the late 1920s history had again become a pivotal subject for a people who had begun to question the course their country was pursuing both at home and abroad. Social and political problems that followed World War I and were accentuated by the depression now agitated the academic world. Intellectuals saw a growing discrepancy between "government" and "people," between the way things were and the way they ought to be. The fading of the democratic ideal, not only in Japan but in much of Europe, left the Japanese open to the competitive ideals of socialism and national socialism.

During the 1930s, as Japan began her expansion on the continent and drifted toward war in the Pacific, her scholarly world was torn increasingly between the ideas of left and right. Marxist historians rewrote Japanese history as a story of national development from primitive to socialist society. They hotly debated whether or not the Meiji Restoration was a bourgeois revolution and criticized the government of Japan as capitalist and imperialist. Perhaps the most significant contribution of the Marxist school in these years was the series entitled *Nihon shihonshugi hattatsu shi kōza* (1932; "Essays on the History of the Development of Capitalism in Japan"). Marxists eventually came under heavy attack. After the middle 1930s open expression of their views declined, although a strong underground commitment to them continued among Japanese intellectuals and much of the Marxist vocabulary passed into common usage.

By the mid-1930s the tempo of nationalistic writing had accelerated. Incited by government and public opinion, historians lent their energies to propagandistic purposes and the rewriting of national history along messianic lines. Although the higher levels of scholarship were able to maintain a precarious objectivity, by the time of the war Japan's youth was uniformly being taught a brand of history that stressed the old myths of uniqueness and invincibility and claimed as the goal of history the ultimate conquest of the world by the Japanese.

Postwar historiography

After disastrous defeat in war, Japan embarked upon the slow process of economic and spiritual rehabilitation. The very foundations of her history had been challenged: much of her heroic past had been discredited, and the seemingly successful attempt at modernization had ended in failure. Where did Japan now stand in the world? And what of Japan's past was now worthy of remembrance? These questions were put to a generation of scholars strongly disillusioned by their wartime experience. The purging of old-guard scholars brought younger men in large numbers into the universities, while the freedom of expression that the Occupation authorities permitted encouraged a vigorous iconoclasm among all intellectuals. Many of the new scholars were men of strong Marxist conviction whose desire to express themselves had been increased by the long years of silence imposed upon them during the war.

Few subjects were as controversial as history during the first fifteen years after World War II. For history lay both at the heart of the revised system of "education for democracy" and of the Japanese attempt to understand a world divided between two great power blocs and two ideologies. Battles raged over the rewriting of elementary school history textbooks, and lines were drawn between the Marxist-dominated Rekishigaku Kenkyūkai and the still academically oriented Shigakkai.

In the first years after the war, it seemed as though Japanese historians had uniformly and precipitously abandoned the extreme of nationalist history only to take up another extreme of socialist history in which nation and emperor were both totally rejected. The theme of the common man in his struggle against feudalism, absolutism, fascism, and capitalism was played with dramatic eloquence.

Yet by the 1950s, as political and economic conditions began to settle down, historians also began to relax their extreme ideological orientation. In volume of research and publication, historians of the 1950s had begun to surpass their prewar output; new encyclopedias, new survey histories, new works of basic research were published, so that by the end of the decade the entire literature of Japanese history had practically renewed itself. New documentary series that penetrated even more deeply into the details of government or economic activity encouraged research at new levels of refinement and precision. The creation of new universities and research centers served to break up the prewar factions of historians and increase the variety of historical writing.

In the face of such diversity, any simple characterization of the Japanese historiographical scene today is hardly possible. Most of the vast product of the Japanese historian is of a strictly empirical nature and is little affected by problems of bias or interpretation. But there are underlying issues of great consequence. Japanese historians are still troubled by questions of fundamental philosophy. Marxism continues to provide the most widely accepted historical world view. Recent experimentation with various social science methods has offered certain alternatives to Marxism, although nothing like a "complete system." There are followers of Max Weber and of special techniques of statistical data gathering or group research, but these are chiefly techniques, and the Japanese must still grapple with the question of where history is taking them and where Japan fits into the ultimate scheme of things. Increasingly, however, it does appear that the Japanese are gaining the assurance to forgo their ideological preconceptions and engage in a less self-conscious approach to their own history.

JOHN WHITNEY HALL

[*Directly related are the entries* BUDDHISM *and* JAPANESE SOCIETY.]

BIBLIOGRAPHY

BEASLEY, WILLIAM G.; and PULLEYBLANK, E. G. (editors) 1961 *Historians of China and Japan.* New York and London: Oxford Univ. Press. → Contains five essays on Japanese historiography. The first three provide the most complete analysis of premodern historical writing available in English.

COMITÉ JAPONAIS DES SCIENCES HISTORIQUES 1960 *Le Japon au XIe congrès international des sciences his-toriques à Stockholm: L'état actuel et les tendances des études historiques au Japon.* Tokyo: Nippon Gakujutsu Shinkōkai. → Part 1 contains essays by leading Japanese historians on the state of research, latest trends, and major fields of Japanese history. Parts 2 and 3 cover Asian history and European history. Contents are in English; a Japanese language version was also published.

HALL, JOHN W. 1954a Historiography in Japan. Pages 284–304 in Henry S. Hughes (editor), *Teachers of History: Essays in Honor of Laurence Bradford Packard.* Ithaca, N.Y.: Cornell Univ. Press. → A survey of Japanese historical writing from its origins to the time of writing.

HALL, JOHN W. 1954b *Japanese History: A Guide to Japanese Reference and Research Materials.* Ann Arbor: Univ. of Michigan Press. → A bibliographical study of the Japanese treatment of Japanese history. Introductory essays cover basic reference works, historical sources, documentary collections, journals, and secondary works in each major field of study. A total of 1,551 works are annotated.

Iwanami kōza Nihon rekishi (Essays on Japanese History). 1963 Tokyo: Iwanami. → Volume 22 is devoted to essays on Japanese historians. This is the latest of many Japanese works surveying Japanese historical writing.

Nihon shi kenkyū nyūmon (Introduction to the Study of Japanese History). 2 vols. Compiled by Tōyama Shigeki and Satō Shin'ichi. 1954–1962 Tokyo Univ. Press. → Practical handbooks for aspiring Japanese historians, these volumes contain essays on the latest trends in major fields, bibliographical lists, and information on research institutions and libraries.

NIHON SHISŌSHI KENKYŪKAI 1961 *Nihon ni okeru re-kishishishisō no tenkai* (The Development of Japanese Historical Thought). Tokyo: Shibundō. → A collection of fourteen essays on historiography and historical thought in Japan from early times to the present. Contains a chronology and one of the most complete bibliographies of Japanese historiography available.

1963-nen no rekishi gakkai (Historical Studies in 1963). 1964 *Shigaku zasshi* [1964] Annual summary. → Begun in the journal *Shirin*, the series has been kept alive since~1916 and provides an annual summary of the previous year's publication by Japanese historians. The journal *Rekishigaku kenkyū* has published a similar series since 1933.

VI

SOUTH AND SOUTHEAST ASIAN HISTORIOGRAPHY

Historiography in south and southeast Asia, as elsewhere, developed in close relation with the sources of literacy. As literacy came from several sources and at different times, so was history writing similarly varied and differentiated. Most important of such sources before the twentieth century, however, were the many religions which, for at least six centuries, united some parts of the region and divided others. Five of the areas representing different religions and literate experiences may be distinguished for a survey of historiographical traditions.

There has been little in common between popular Hinduism in India and the Theravada Buddhism of Thailand, Cambodia, Burma, and Ceylon. These two areas again have little in common with a third area, the extensive sphere of Islam, with large centers in Pakistan and India and in Muslim societies throughout Malaysia, Indonesia, and the southern Philippines. The fourth and the fifth areas are somewhat peripheral to the rest, that of Vietnam, where a variety of Chinese religion and culture still survives, and that of the largely Christianized society of the Philippines. In each of these areas a different attitude toward the idea of history may be discerned.

Traditional historiography

South Asia.   The earliest literate religion introduced to the preliterate animistic communities of the region was that of the Vedas. The religion was restricted primarily to India and produced its earliest annalistic literature in the Purāṇas. The purāṇic tradition was further extended and other dynastic and regional annals were compiled, but they remained "marked by obscurity, exaggeration, paucity of authentic data and neglect of topography and chronology" (Ghoshal 1961, p. 2) down to the Muslim invasions of the twelfth century. The only exception to this Hindu heritage was a work completed in the middle of the twelfth century, the Rājataraṅgiṇī ("Kashmir Chronicle") by Kalhaṇa. Of Kalhaṇa, Majumdar (1961a, p. 21) says that he "held that the first requisite of a true historian was to keep a detached mind, free from bias and prejudices (and), like a judge, must discard love and hatred while recounting the events of the past . . . ," but Basham (1961a, p. 61) maintains that Kalhaṇa was more concerned "to teach moral lessons."

The great epics, the Mahābhārata and the Rāmāyaṇa, had considerable influence and were used as sources by an independent historical tradition. While they did not lead to the growth of history writing, they were remarkable repositories of stories which were as real and meaningful to most of the peoples of south and southeast Asia as the Homeric epics were to the peoples of Europe. For centuries, they were the nearest thing to history and may be said to have performed the role of history among the peoples who transmitted the stories.

In addition, the two epics, in conjunction with the stories of the Pañcatantra and the Buddhist Jātaka stories, also provided a strong anecdotal and narrative tradition for the Buddhist genealogies and chronicles of Ceylon and mainland southeast Asia. Such Buddhist stories and chronicles ranged from simple eulogies to types of hagiography and were used for moral and spiritual education in the monasteries and at the courts. It took several centuries before the chronicles advanced from recounting the philosophical progress of Gautama Buddha and his disciples to the conscious record of contemporary political and religious events. Eventually, in Ceylon, where the *vaṃsa* tradition (notably, the chronicles known as the Dīpavaṃsa, the Mahāvamsa, and the Cūlavaṃsa) produced several court-sponsored chronicles compiled by learned monks, a kind of history writing appeared. The works were annalistic and anecdotal and mainly written in verse. They were also restricted to court use. There was no tradition of individual authorship, for each chronicle was largely the continuation of a previous one and incorporated materials from earlier chronicles. The success of any set of chronicles was determined more by its literary quality than by its historical accuracy. If a new compilation achieved high literary standards, it might supersede earlier works altogether (Perera 1961; Godakumbura 1961).

Indian historiography was greatly enriched after the Muslim conquests of northern India at the end of the twelfth century. A well-developed tradition of history writing was introduced, and for more than six centuries a branch of Muslim historiography dominated the south Asian scene. The main features of these Muslim writings are common to those of Muslim historiography in Persia, west Asia, and north Africa. They remained bound to the need for orthodox authority and the desire to serve God and the Muslim community. They were also largely directed to teaching moral and religious lessons through descriptions of prophets, caliphs, sultans, and other great men of both religion and government. Furthermore, they were limited to the accounts of the triumphs and disasters of Muslim rulers and kingdoms and barely touched on the peoples of other faiths in India.

Despite these limitations, the Muslim writings provided a historical picture of India not available among any other community in India until recent times. For this reason, at least two of the greatest Indo–Muslim historians may be singled out to illustrate the range and scope of the tradition. The first is Ziauddin Barani, whose work, the *Tarīkh-i Feroz-shāhī*, was completed in 1357. Here, Barani achieved a new consciousness of the value of history. Not only could history strengthen faith, reason, and judgment, give comfort, teach patience, and distinguish between good and evil, but it was also "the necessary foundation of truth" (Hardy 1960, pp. 22–23). Although his awareness of truth was strictly within the framework of Islam, it remains a vital ingredient in distinguishing the best Muslim histories from the many written.

This was also true of the Moghul historian Abul Fazl (1551–1602), whose history of the reign of the emperor Akbar (1556–1605) is regarded as the height of Indo–Muslim historiographical achievements. This work, the *Akbar Namah*, is not free from conventional eulogy and stylistic flourish, but it represents the result of great steps forward in archival collection, document examination, and close analytical research. To this day the section called *Ain-i-Akbari* is regarded as the classic study of the institutions and workings of an empire at the height of its extent and power.

Although all Indo–Muslim writings were determined by extraneous non-Indian concepts of history, they have become part of the Indian (and now also Pakistani) historical heritage and may be seen now as an integral part of traditional south Asian historiography (Hardy 1961; Rashid 1961; Elliot 1867–1877).

Southeast Asia. The Mon–Khmer and Cham peoples of mainland southeast Asia acquired much of the art and architecture of India and left many great historical monuments which are still intact to attest to the richness of the heritage (Coedès [1948] 1964, pp. 35–72). But the earlier Hindu–Buddhist accretions left little impact on the Mon and Cambodian chronicles that came to be written later.

With the spread of Theravada Buddhism after the thirteenth century, the Mons in particular compiled chronicles (Rājāwan, or genealogies of various kinds) which established the tradition of bringing together dynastic information, anecdotes about the kings, and various myths and legends which gave meaning to each reign (Shorto 1961, p. 64). This tradition was strengthened by the Burmese, who brought a keener sense of chronology to the compilations. Although still essentially a derived tradition from Buddhist Ceylon, the later Burmese Yazawin ("Chronicles") of the eighteenth and nineteenth centuries were clearly indigenous writings influenced by local animism and Burmese concepts of kingship and cosmology. As works compiled by learned monks, learned brāhmaṇs, and learned ministers, they provided valuable material for early European works on Burmese history (Htoot 1961; Ohn 1961; Mahā Yāza Win Taw Kyī).

Similarly, the Thai tradition, also developed by learned monks and ministers, was derived from Ceylon, probably through the Mon–Khmer-speaking peoples of the Menam valley. Most of the earlier versions of the Thai chronicles were destroyed when Ayuthia was sacked by the Burmese in 1767.

A notable exception was the *P'ongsawadan*, compiled in 1680, which covered the period 1350–1605. This chronicle form was revived during the late eighteenth century, and many chronicles were written not only for Thailand but also for Burma, Cambodia, and the states of southern Thailand, including the Malay states of Songkhla and Saiburi (Kedah).

The situation was different, however, among the Javanese and Malay peoples. Hindu–Buddhist monuments and inscriptions abound, but there also developed quite independently a native concern with the past and the use of the past as symbol and magic to give power and confirm authority. From the epic poem *Nagara–Kertagama* to the *Pararaton* and the *Babad Tanah Jawi* (fourteenth to seventeenth centuries), the court poets lauded their kings, worked out impressive genealogies, and perfected their verse. These were not works of history, but they were approaching an autonomous tradition in historical awareness. Of particular interest is the framework of Hindu gods, Buddhist identifications, and indigenous beliefs in the first two works and their extension to include Muslim prophets in the *Babad*. The sense of continuity is unmistakable. The desire to link legitimacy and sovereignty to past heroes and their origins is sustained through the centuries. Lacking both an accurate chronology and a secular concern with kings, ministers, subjects, and enemies, the great lists of names of people and places are more like exercises in metrics and incantation than history writing. But as the tradition developed into the nineteenth century, later *Babad* closer to modern histories were produced, notably the *Babad Dipanagara* and the *Sejarah Banten*. In addition, there were lesser historical writings in south Celebes (Sudjatmoko et al. 1965; Berg 1965; Graaf 1965; Noorduyn 1965; Johns 1964).

Far better developed as histories are the writings in Malay, especially the *Sejarah Melayu* and a number of works concerning the Johore and Riau Lingga empires, as well as "rhymed chronicles" like the *Sha'ir Perang Mengkasar* and similar compositions. Malay writing is richer than the Javanese in anecdote and more vivid in the description of men and places. It still lacks chronology but is more accurate about personal relationships. There is less concern with magic than with moral values like loyalty and sincerity, and, as a whole, Malay histories entertain as well as teach. Three outstanding examples of a nascent social history, the *Misa Melayu*, the *Hikayat Abdullah*, and the *Tuhfat-ul Nafis*, appeared in the eighteenth and nineteenth centuries. It is possible to discover a certain amount of outside influence in these works, but they clearly show their continuity with the *Sejarah Melayu* tradition (Bottoms 1959; Amin 1963, pp. 1–46; Teeuw 1964; Josselin de Jong 1964).

Finally, a brief note on the importation of traditional Chinese historiographical forms in the writing of Annamese (Vietnamese) history. In ruling the Tongking region of north Vietnam for a thousand years, the Chinese determined the nature of its historiography. Such traditional works were still being written throughout the nineteenth century and even during the early years of the twentieth century. But, interestingly, these forms are not traceable in those parts of the Indochinese peninsula which fell under the influence of Theravada Buddhism. Similarly, with the Spanish invasion of the Philippines at the end of the sixteenth century, a kind of traditional Roman Catholic historiography was introduced which matched the Malay chronicles of the Sulu Archipelago. This limited European clerical tradition remained dominant in the Philippines until the latter half of the nineteenth century, and vestiges remain even today.

Features of traditional historiography. It has often been noted that the history of south and southeast Asia had little unity of theme until the coming of modern industrial civilization during the last hundred years. The traditional historiography of the region seems to confirm this view. Except for the common lack of chronology in the historical works and the fact that there are so many gaps to be filled in the region's history, there appear to be more major differences than similarities in the types of writings mentioned above. Some of the traditions may have had common origins, but they developed as discrete and autonomous traditions in Ceylon, Burma, Thailand, Java, and the Malay world. Even the Islamic tradition was not homogeneous, and what emerged in northern India was quite different from Muslim historical writings in Acheh, Java, Malacca, Johore, south Celebes, and Sulu. This suggests that there were strong indigenous features in each of the traditions which were peculiar to the different peoples. The subject has now aroused considerable interest, and it is to be expected that more precise analyses of the indigenous cultures will soon appear to help us understand the differences better.

Based on present information, the following list indicates the common features and major differences.

Common features are that (*a*) most of the works are strong in genealogy but weak in chronology and biographical detail; (*b*) the emphasis is on literary style, anecdotal material, and the use of history as moral and religious teaching; (*c*) where they are primarily secular, there is a common central interest in kingship, and the emphasis is placed on orthodox qualities of loyalty and conformity; (*d*) cosmological and astrological considerations tend to exclude causal explanations as well as the idea of progress.

Major differences are that (*a*) religion cut off the Indo–Muslim historians from the Hindu socioeconomic background of Indian history; it cut off the Thais and Cambodians from the east Asian historiographical tradition in its Vietnamese form; and it cut off the Malayo–Javanese world from the Thais and Burmese on the one hand and the Filipinos on the other; (*b*) national rivalry influenced, for example, Burmese and Thai historical writing about each other; (*c*) language differences in India before the use of Persian and in mainland southeast Asia after the decline of Pali were complex; most of the works were not intelligible outside of the country's boundaries; (*d*) royal policies about historical writings varied considerably; Muslim and Malay works were in circulation, while Thai, Burmese, and Vietnamese works were kept mainly for official use.

Two further points about the nature of the early traditional chronicles need to be emphasized. First, modern scholarship has begun to show appreciation of such traditional writings and has applied the techniques of Biblical and Homeric criticism to their study. It is now realized that these chronicles are best understood in the context of the total cultural system in which they were compiled. Second, whether these works may be called "histories" or not, their value as historical documents has now been proved. What is required are finer and more sensitive techniques for obtaining from them the data needed to write the history of south and southeast Asia.

Modern historiography

The growth of modern historiography in Europe coincided with the expansion of European activities in Asia. But as European activities were peripheral to Asian history between the sixteenth and nineteenth centuries and as traditional European attitudes toward the nature and use of history changed very slowly, there was no impact on the historiography of south and southeast Asia during this period. It was only in the latter half of the nineteenth century, when Western science and culture were consciously taught and learned, first in south Asia and then in parts of southeast Asia, that the region became affected by Western historical methods. What was being widely introduced, however, were the traditional techniques of the late eighteenth and early nineteenth centuries, for example, the philological methods of William Jones and the historical writings of James Mill, Mountstuart Elphinstone, and Vincent Smith. There was a time lag in methodological change, and these traditional techniques were still regarded in the early part of the twentieth century as advanced and valid for imitation. The developments toward "scientific" history and the growth of social sciences in Europe and America were hardly noticed until after the end of World War II. Application of Western historiographical techniques to the study of India and Ceylon came first, but the Dutch eventually applied them to Indonesia, and the French, although coming last, were quick to apply them in their thorough study of Indochina.

South Asia. Serious Western scholarship in India dates from William Jones's founding of the Asiatic Society at Calcutta in 1784. The activities of this and similar kinds of societies for Oriental research in Bombay, Madras, Mysore, and Ceylon, together with the growth of learned societies in France and Germany and the creation of university chairs in Europe during the nineteenth century, laid the foundations of modern south Asian historiography.

The most important contributions were initially in the field of Sanskrit philology and in the editing of Vedic and Buddhist texts, but the study of Indian antiquities eventually provided a more scientific basis for dealing with the otherwise intractable materials on ancient India. The pre-Muslim period was the most challenging because there were none of the essentials for the historian—no chronology, no reliable genealogies, no clear identifications of people and places. It was here, too, that the most dramatic discoveries and achievements were recorded. Particularly notable was James Tod's *Annals and Antiquities of Rajast'han*, published from 1829 to 1832, and James Prinsep's epigraphical and numismatic studies published in 1858 under the title *Essays on Indian Antiquities*. Their success led to the setting up of an archeological department in 1862 under Alexander Cunningham; this became in 1902 the famous Indian Archaeological Survey under John Marshall (*Ancient India*, 1953).

In comparison, the traditional European historians were far less successful. Mill, Elphinstone, and Smith, as well as French and German historians of India, were either too ready to show the superiority of Western rule or too uncritical of the available Muslim and non-Muslim material. Their impact was initially greater on European audiences than on Indians. It was not until the establishment of British-type universities in Calcutta, Bombay, Madras (all three in 1857), and elsewhere that formal history teaching introduced the European writings to young Indian scholars. By that time, while historical sciences in Europe had made further progress, Indian scholars like R. G. Bhandarkar were learning the techniques and attitudes of the earlier period well enough to criticize the works of European historians themselves (Philips 1961a; Basham 1961b).

It is only in the twentieth century that south Asian historiography began to respond directly and strongly to Western methodology. It did so in at least two different directions. The first was a more intensive appreciation of Western scientific methods, especially following the brilliant archeological work on the Indus civilization at Mohenjo-daro and Harappa. The second was a nationalistic or antiimperialistic approach, which in its extreme forms produced obscurantist and revivalist historical writings on the one hand and stimulated Marxist and other forms of radical historiography on the other (Majumdar 1961b).

Modern historiography may be said to have begun with the British publication of the *Cambridge History of India*, published in 6 volumes between 1922 and 1932. This aroused considerable interest in India, even among those who resented the dominance of British contributors. It was recognized, however, that in the fields of archeology, epigraphy, and numismatics, the great collections produced by European scholars were indispensable. So also were the collections of documents and the interpretative works on British activities, the politics of the East India Company, and the extension of British power in India. But this was not the case with works that dealt with Indian religion and culture, the Indian response to British rule (for example, the 1857 mutiny and the nationalist movement), and the social and economic changes in India since the beginning of the nineteenth century. It was in these fields that a new generation of scholars first challenged the results of European scholarship. Notable among this generation were R. C. Majumdar, H. C. Raychaudhuri, K. A. A. Nilakanta Sastri, and K. M. Pannikar. Most of them were products of university departments of history, whether in Britain or in India, and many were professional teachers of history. They continued the tradition of forming learned societies to publish scholarly journals and learned to use and appreciate the great libraries and archival collections organized by the states and the government of India (see Nilakanta Sastri 1956; Datta 1957).

Since independence, the work of history writing has continued. Institutions like the Archaeological Survey, the Historical Records Commission, and the Indian History Congress are particularly active. Among the historical publications of academic standing, two are noteworthy: the *Indian Historical Quarterly* and the *Journal of Indian History*. A major enterprise has been the 11-volume series, *History and Culture of the Indian People*, published by the Bharatiya Vidya Bhavan under the general editorship of R. C. Majumdar. Also significant has been the Indian History Congress conference on Asian history in 1961 and the meeting at Delhi in 1965 of the International Congress of Orientalists. These developments reflect the new Indian historical consciousness, which has revealed a considerable acceptance of modern scientific methods of historiography. The most important measure of modern Indian achievements is that there are today trained historians to cover almost every period and type of problem in Indian history. In addition, several of the younger historians have begun to apply the tools of social science to the study of modern history. In this respect, many have turned to new academic disciplines developed in the United States for their methodological assistance.

Less outstanding has been the development of historiography in Pakistan after 1947. Separation from India deprived the new state of the best developed research facilities and the best library and archival collections in the region. The scholars, therefore, had to work under grave disadvantages. They continued to revive the traditions of Islamic historiography, but the most important achievements are the works of those scholars who first made their reputations before separation from India, for example, A. Yusof Ali, Shafa'at Ahmad Khan, and I. H. Qureshi. Although the majority of the scholars feel greater kinship with the historical traditions of Persia and west Asia, they cannot deny their Indian heritage completely. Their struggles with modern historiography, therefore, are part of the progress of history writing in south Asia.

In Ceylon, modern historical attitudes developed later, but standards are high, as may be seen in the publications of the Ceylon Branch of the Royal Asiatic Society and the recent *Ceylon Journal of Historical and Social Studies*.

Finally, the remarkable fact must be noted that the bulk of historical works of significance in south Asia have been written in English. There have been important works published in Bengali, Urdu, and Hindi from the early years of the twentieth century, but so far none are widely known outside of regional schools and universities. It is important to note they all show the influence of modern historical works. There is no reason to doubt that in time more scholarly studies in the Indian languages will reach the high academic standards achieved by works in English.

Southeast Asia. Unlike south Asia, there was no center in southeast Asia where modern scholarship could take root and fan out over the whole region. The manner in which different parts of the region came under European control and the limited resources of the small states prevented a systematic development of modern historiography. For example, the early Portuguese, Spanish, Dutch, and English accounts of the region (sixteenth to eighteenth centuries) had no influence on southeast Asian writings and were really part of the history of European historiography. Even the founding of the famous Bataviaasch Genootschap von Kunsten en Wetenschappen (Batavian Society for the Study of Arts and Sciences) in Jakarta in 1778 and the publication of William Marsden's *History of Sumatra* in 1783 and T. S. Raffles' *History of Java* in 1817 gave little impetus to the study of history. Only in the latter half of the nineteenth century, with the revival of the Bataviaasch Genootschap and with the founding of the Straits Branch of the Royal Asiatic Society in 1878, did serious scholarship begin in Indonesia and Malaysia. In fact, European writings of the nineteenth century were produced while the indigenous traditions of *Babad* and *Sejarah* were still alive, and Western scholars often depended on native chronicles for their material on earlier history. In any case, such European works ran parallel to and were external to the local efforts at historical writing and did not affect the traditional forms and attitudes.

Similarly, among the mainland countries of southeast Asia, the Burmese and the Thais were particularly active at compiling their Yazawin and P'ongsawadan, even as European amateur scholars like Arthur Phayre (*History of Burma*, 1883) and W. A. R. Wood (*A History of Siam*, 1926) were working on their histories and as research journals like the *Journal of the Burma Research Society* and the *Journal of the Siam Society* were being published. Both British scholars, for example, acknowledged their great debt to native scholarship. In Vietnam, traditional Vietnamese historians helped early French scholars attached to the École Française d'Extrême Orient (founded in 1900), whose works were to gain fame for the school's *Bulletin*. Also, the Imperial Archives at Hué preserved their documents in the traditional fashion for some years after the French conquest.

426 HISTORIOGRAPHY: South and Southeast Asian Historiography

The Philippines was a special case where one stage of Western historical scholarship displaced another. Still, Spanish traditional history continued to be written under American rule (after 1898), while scholars from the United States studied Philippine history from Spanish colonial and missionary records. The most valuable of its kind was E. H. Blair and J. A. Robertson's 55-volume work *The Philippine Islands, 1493–1898*, published between 1903 and 1909.

In the nineteenth and first half of the twentieth centuries, there have been three distinct areas of modern southeast Asian historiography. First, ancient history, of which the native peoples had little or no knowledge, was being recovered by the methods of philology, epigraphy, and archeology. Second, colonial history, involving European trade, wars, treaties, and administration, was the special interest of European historians themselves and aroused little interest among local scholars. And third, the "middle period," varying from four to ten centuries before the nineteenth century, was a period of some indigenous historical writing; modern methods can be used to help rearrange, date more accurately, and even reinterpret the writings of this period (Hall 1961).

In contrast to what they did in south Asia, the British, the Dutch, and the French in southeast Asia made no effort to train local historians until the years just before World War II. Except among the Dutch in the twentieth century, history writing was primarily an amateur affair, a by-product of administration and long residence in the country concerned. There were fine scholarly works, in particular by the professionals, for example, N. J. Krom on early Indonesian history and George Coedès on southeast Asian epigraphy before the coming of Islam. R. O. Winstedt's textual work for Malay history and G. H. Luce's great collections of inscriptions for Burmese history were also outstanding. The best work, however, was done in early history; no historians of the colonial period produced works of comparable stature. Furthermore, such colonial history as was written could better be seen as part of European historiography than of southeast Asian historiography.

There were two countries in the region where developments were different—independent Thailand and the Philippines under United States administration. In Thailand, Thai royal patronage was given to the Siam Society, which published a useful journal; and Chulalongkorn University, founded in 1917, taught both traditional and modern history. In the Philippines, missionary universities like Santo Tomás, founded in 1611, taught little secular history but began to introduce modern historical methods into the curriculum by the end of the nineteenth century. In addition, the Americans founded in 1908 a secular university, the University of the Philippines, which taught some modern history from the start, although little work was done on southeast Asian history itself.

Since the end of World War II and particularly following the independence of the Philippines, Burma, Indonesia, and Malaya (now Malaysia), there have been new advances in the historiography of the region. A major landmark was the publication in 1955 of D. G. E. Hall's *A History of Southeast Asia*, which has successfully established that the whole span of history for all of southeast Asia is an intelligible historical unit. Also, a searching debate on the nature of European scholarship on southeast Asia has followed the provocative studies on early Asian trade by J. C. van Leur. As a result, southeast Asia was given a separate place in the series of conferences held in London in 1956 on historical writings on the peoples of Asia (Hall 1961). This stimulated another collection of papers on Indonesian historiography, first sparked by the seminar on national history held in Jogjakarta in 1957 (Singhal 1960; Smail 1961; Benda 1962; Sudjatmoko et al. 1965; cf. Seminar Sedjarah 1958).

The region still faces a long debate about whether national history should form the basis of the new southeast Asian historiography. The struggle for national identity in Burma, Indonesia, and Vietnam has reduced historical research to a trickle in those countries. Only in the Philippines, Malaysia, and Singapore has there been sustained interest in modern research, and these countries have supported international conferences on history to keep this interest alive. A joint effort led to the creation of the International Association of Historians of Asia, which meets every three or four years and shows signs of being an organization primarily for southeast Asian historians.

Features of modern historiography. In the two regions of south and southeast Asia, modern Indian historiography is clearly the most impressive both in volume and in quantity. Pakistan and Ceylon, however, have much in common with Indonesia, Burma, Malaysia, and the Philippines in terms of stage of growth, present and future resources, and trends of scholarship. There is a chance that Ceylon, the Philippines, Malaysia, and Singapore may develop differently because their traditional historiography does not stand in the way of rapid modernization. What is clear is that modern historiography is being confronted by nationalism and may well be subordinated to national needs. The example of India is before the others. National history takes precedence over scientific history, but as long as the means of teaching and using modern academic tools and methods remain, this situation may soon change. Thailand remains the exception. Active historical research is limited, and some work is still being done within the framework of traditional values, but there is no nationalist flavor in the work. Also, a new generation is using modern methods with increasing skill and confidence.

Autonomy of historiographic tradition

History has had a relatively small place in south and southeast Asian traditions. Its main functions had been to strengthen the authority of kings, to teach moral and religious lessons, and possibly also to please and amuse. Exact times and places and the lives of great and lesser men had never been important in themselves. They had to serve the purpose of the historian's audience, which often comprised only the kings, priests, and courtiers of the day. Each historiographical tradition had evolved according to the needs of different audiences and had been either strong or weak depending on whether the institutions which produced the audiences were stable or unstable. As long as the institutions had been able to survive, the historical tradition which supported them also survived.

In south Asia and in the Philippines, the impact of colonial rule was felt over a long period, and this had marked consequences on the indigenous historiographical traditions. Hence, apart from some of the traditions of Muslim historiography, no other tradition has survived. In other parts of southeast Asia, however, Western influence has had only a brief history—in most cases, much less than a hundred years, during which colonial scholars and policy makers did not try to destroy the local traditions. Thus, much of the traditions still survive within the new historiography itself. This is particularly true where nationalist movements have effectively revived the historical works of the past.

But historiography is no longer a static discipline even in the West, and it is undergoing radical changes as new social science disciplines are turning to the study of the past. What is important is not that historiography in south and southeast Asia has still not freed itself completely from traditional attitudes and their limitations. It is that lines of communication have been established between Asian and Western academic institutions, important works have become mutually available, and new disciplines have been introduced and understood. The key concepts have already reached south and southeast Asia: that time and place must be accurate, that knowledge about man's past must be secular and humanistic, and that historical fact and interpretation must always be tested by the best scientific methods.

WANG GUNGWU

[*See also* ASIAN SOCIETY, *articles on* SOUTH ASIA *and* SOUTHEAST ASIA. *Other relevant material may be found in* BUDDHISM *and* ISLAM.]

BIBLIOGRAPHY

AMIN, ENTJI' 1963 *Sja'ir Perang Mengkasar (The Rhymed Chronicle of the Macassar War).* Edited and translated by C. Skinner. Instituut voor Taal- , Land-en Volkenkunde, The Hague, Verhandelingen, Vol. 40. The Hague: Nijhoff.

Ancient India. → Published since 1946. See especially the "Special Jubilee Number," No. 9, 1953.

BASHAM, A. L. 1961a The Kashmir Chronicle. Pages 57–65 in Cyril H. Philips (editor), *Historians of India, Pakistan and Ceylon.* Oxford Univ. Press.

BASHAM, A. L. 1961b Modern Historians of Ancient India. Pages 260–293 in Cyril H. Philips (editor), *Historians of India, Pakistan and Ceylon.* Oxford Univ. Press.

BASTIN, JOHN; and ROOLVINK, R. (editors) 1964 *Malayan and Indonesian Studies: Essays Presented to Sir Richard Winstedt on His Eighty-fifth Birthday.* Oxford: Clarendon.

BENDA, HARRY J. 1962 The Structure of Southeast Asian History: Some Preliminary Observations. *Journal of Southeast Asian History* 3, no. 1:106–138.

BERG, C. C. 1965 The Javanese Picture of the Past. Pages 87–117 in Sudjatmoko et al. (editors), *An Introduction to Indonesian Historiography.* Ithaca, N.Y.: Cornell Univ. Press.

BOTTOMS, J. C. (1959) 1965 Some Malay Historical Sources: A Bibliographical Note. Pages 156–193 in Sudjatmoko et al. (editors), *An Introduction to Indonesian Historiography.* Ithaca, N.Y.: Cornell Univ. Press.

COEDÈS, GEORGE (1948) 1964 *Les états hindouisés d'Indochine et d'Indonésie.* New ed. Paris: Boccard.

DATTA, KALIKINKAR (1957) 1963 *A Survey of Recent Studies on Modern Indian History.* 2d ed. Calcutta: Mukhopadhyay.

ELLIOT, HENRY M. (1867–1877) 1964 *The History of India, as Told by Its Own Historians: The Muhammadan Period; the Posthumous Papers of the Late Sir H. M. Elliot.* Edited and continued by John Dowson. 8 vols. Allahabad (India): Kitab Mahal. → Reprinted with an introduction by Muhammad Habib.

GHOSHAL, U. N. (1944) 1957 *Studies in Indian History and Culture.* Rev. ed. Calcutta: Orient Longmans. → First published as *The Beginnings of Indian Historiography and Other Essays.*

GHOSHAL, U. N. 1961 Presidential Address. Part 1, pages 1–20 in Indian History Congress, *Proceedings of the Twenty-third Session, Aligarh, 1960.* Calcutta.

GODAKUMBURA, C. E. 1961 Historical Writing in Sinhalese. Pages 72–86 in Cyril H. Philips (editor), *Historians of India, Pakistan and Ceylon*. Oxford Univ. Press.

GRAAF, J. J. DE 1965 Later Javanese Sources and Historiography. Pages 119–136 in Sudjatmoko et al. (editors), *An Introduction to Indonesian Historiography*. Ithaca, N.Y.: Cornell Univ. Press.

HALL, DANIEL G. E. (editor) 1961 *Historians of South East Asia*. University of London, School of Oriental and African Studies, Historical Writing on the Peoples of Asia, Vol. 2. Oxford Univ. Press.

HARDY, PETER 1960 *Historians of Medieval India: Studies in Indo–Muslim Historical Writing*. London: Luzac.

HARDY, PETER 1961 Some Studies in Pre-Mughal Muslim Historiography. Pages 115–127 in Cyril H. Philips (editor), *Historians of India, Pakistan and Ceylon*. Oxford Univ. Press.

HTOOT, U TET 1961 The Nature of the Burmese Chronicles. Pages 50–62 in Daniel G. E. Hall (editor), *Historians of South East Asia*. Oxford Univ. Press.

INDIAN HISTORY CONGRESS *Proceedings*. → The first congress was held in 1935.

JOHNS, ANTHONY H. 1964 The Role of Structural Organisation and Myth in Javanese Historiography. *Journal of Asian Studies* 24:91–99.

JOSSELIN DE JONG, P. E. DE 1964 The Character of the *Malay Annals*. Pages 235–241 in John Bastin and R. Roolvink (editors), *Malayan and Indonesian Studies*. Oxford: Clarendon.

MAHĀ YĀZA WIN TAW KYĪ *The Glass Palace Chronicles of the Kings of Burma*. Translated by Pe Maung Tin and G. H. Luce. Oxford Univ. Press, 1923.

MAJUMDAR, R. C. 1961a Ideas of History in Sanskrit Literature. Pages 13–28 in Cyril H. Philips (editor), *Historians of India, Pakistan and Ceylon*. Oxford Univ. Press.

MAJUMDAR, R. C. 1961b Nationalist Historians. Pages 416–428 in Cyril H. Philips (editor), *Historians of India, Pakistan and Ceylon*. Oxford Univ. Press.

NILAKANTA SASTRI, K. A.; and RAMANA, H. S. 1956 *Historical Method in Relation to Indian History*. Madras (India): Viswanathan.

NOORDUYN, J. 1965 Origins of South Celebes Historical Writing. Pages 137–155 in Sudjatmoko et al. (editors), *An Introduction to Indonesian Historiography*. Ithaca, N.Y.: Cornell Univ. Press.

OHN, TIN 1961 Modern Historical Writing in Burmese, 1724–1942. Pages 85–93 in Daniel G. E. Hall (editor), *Historians of South East Asia*. Oxford Univ. Press.

PERERA, L. S. 1961 The Pali Chronicle of Ceylon. Pages 29–43 in Cyril H. Philips (editor), *Historians of India, Pakistan and Ceylon*. Oxford Univ. Press.

PHILIPS, CYRIL H. 1961a James Mill, Mountstuart Elphinstone, and the History of India. Pages 217–229 in Cyril H. Philips (editor), *Historians of India, Pakistan and Ceylon*. Oxford Univ. Press.

PHILIPS, CYRIL H. (editor) 1961b *Historians of India, Pakistan and Ceylon*. University of London, School of Oriental and African Studies, Historical Writing on the Peoples of Asia, Vol. 1. Oxford Univ. Press.

RASHID, ABDUR 1961 The Treatment of History by Muslim Historians in Mughal Official and Biographical Works. Pages 139–151 in Cyril H. Philips (editor), *Historians of India, Pakistan and Ceylon*. Oxford Univ. Press.

SEMINAR SEDJARAH, JOGJAKARTA, INDONESIA, *1957* 1958 *Laporan lengkap atjara I dan II tentang konsepsi filsafat sedjarah nasional dan periodisasi sedjaraj Indonesia*. Jogjakarata (Indonesia): Universitas Gadjah Mada.

SHORTO, H. L. 1961 A Mon Genealogy of Kings: Observations on *The Nidāna Ārambhakathā*. Pages 63–72 in Daniel G. E. Hall (editor), *Historians of South East Asia*. Oxford Univ. Press.

SINGHAL, D. P. 1960 Some Comments on the Western Element in Modern Southeast Asian History. *Journal of Southeast Asian History* 1, no. 2:118–123.

SMAIL, JOHN R. W. 1961 On the Possibility of an Autonomous History of Modern Southeast Asia. *Journal of Southeast Asian History* 2, no. 2:72–102.

SUDJATMOKO et al. (editors) 1965 *An Introduction to Indonesian Historiography*. Ithaca, N.Y.: Cornell Univ. Press. → The author's name is spelled Soedjatmoko on the title page.

TEEUW, A. 1964 *Hikayat Raja-Raja Pasai* and *Sejarah Melayu*. Pages 222–234 in John Bastin and R. Roolvink (editors), *Malayan and Indonesian Studies*. Oxford: Clarendon.

HISTORY

The articles under this heading deal with varying conceptions of the nature of history and its subject matter, as does the article on THE HISTORY OF SCIENCE, *listed under* SCIENCE. *An analysis of what historians do when they write history and discussions of traditions of history writing in different parts of the world will be found under* HISTORIOGRAPHY. *Major related topics are* ARCHEOLOGY; EVOLUTION; KNOWLEDGE, SOCIOLOGY OF; PERIODIZATION; TIME, *article on* SOCIAL ORGANIZATION. *Other relevant material appears in* ECONOMIC THOUGHT; POLITICAL THEORY; RELIGION; SOCIOLOGY, *article on* THE DEVELOPMENT OF SOCIOLOGICAL THOUGHT.

I
THE PHILOSOPHY OF HISTORY

The expression "philosophy of history" has come to refer to two quite distinct types of inquiry.

Traditionally, it has been used to refer to attempts to provide a comprehensive explanation or interpretation of the entire historical process. "Philosophies of history" in this sense have been characteristically concerned with such questions as: "What is the meaning (significance, purpose) of history?" or "What fundamental laws govern historical development and change?" Among the chief exponents of this type of theory may be numbered Vico, Herder, Hegel, Comte, Marx, Buckle, Spengler, and—in our own time—Arnold Toynbee and Pitirim Sorokin. Men like these have been inspired by the belief that history presents problems beyond those that occupy the attention of ordinary practicing historians, whose activities, being largely confined to the investigation of particular areas or sections of the past, fail to satisfy the demand for an intellectually or morally acceptable conception of the course of history "as a whole." By offering accounts of the human past that exhibit it as conforming to certain principles of universal validity, they have sought to meet this demand; at the same time they have often (though not always) claimed that their interpretations may enable us to make predictions or forecasts concerning the future development of society.

The grounds upon which such interpretations have been based, ranging from empirical considerations to notions that are frankly religious or metaphysical, have been various. Nor have they always taken the same form. Marx, for example, portrayed history as following a unilinear pattern in the direction of a particular foreseeable "goal"; Spengler and Toynbee have presented it as conforming to certain regular and recurrent cycles of change; while others, again, have treated it as somehow combining both these features. Common to all, however, has been the assumption that the historical process is more than an agglomeration of events "senselessly" succeeding one another in time: there is an underlying structure or theme waiting to be discovered, in terms of which this apparently arbitrary sequence can be seen to be ultimately meaningful or intelligible.

Even in the nineteenth century, when such speculation was at its peak, there were philosophers and historians—Schopenhauer and Burckhardt, for instance—who challenged its pretensions; and in the twentieth, it has been exposed to a series of logical and methodological criticisms which in their cumulative impact have proved extremely damaging. In any case, projects of this kind must be sharply distinguished from the type of inquiry that will be chiefly considered here, and which is sometimes referred to as "formal" or "critical" philosophy of history. Philosophy of history in this sense has developed comparatively recently, its rise broadly coinciding with the decline of its speculative counterpart. It has for its subject matter not the course of historical events, but rather the nature of history conceived as a specific discipline and branch of knowledge. In other words, it may be said to be concerned with such topics as the purposes of historical inquiry, the ways in which historians describe and classify their material, the manner in which they arrive at and substantiate explanations and hypotheses, the assumptions and principles that underlie their procedures, and the relations between history and other forms of investigation. Thus, while the problems with which it deals are not speculative problems of the sort previously mentioned, neither are they problems of the type to which practicing historians typically address themselves in the course of their work: the questions involved arise from reflection upon historical thinking and reasoning and are primarily of an epistemological or conceptual character.

The autonomy of history

Philosophical concern with the nature of historical understanding originated largely as part of a general protest against the tendency (prevalent among followers of the Enlightenment) to regard the natural sciences as representing the paradigm of all true knowledge. Even to some of the earlier speculative philosophers of history, the view that the categories and modes of interpretation employed so successfully in the investigation of physical nature could be validly extended to human studies appeared far from self-evident; in particular, the writings of both Vico and Hegel can be said to embody an implicit challenge to this opinion. Yet the belief that there are no differences in principle separating history from other disciplines and that the historian should strive as far as possible to apply to his own field the methods established in other areas of inductive inquiry was a persistent one: in the eighteenth century, empiricists like David Hume saw no reason to question it, and in the nineteenth it was to be constantly reaffirmed by a host of positivistically minded theorists. And, insofar as it was maintained, there appeared to be no grounds for supposing that the study of history presented any *special* problems from a philosophical point of view; logically and epistemologically it was on a level with any other form of empirical science.

Dilthey and Croce. The close of the last century, however, witnessed the emergence of a number of thinkers to whom this comfortable assumption no longer seemed acceptable and who raised awkward questions: among the more influential of the writers involved in the new trend were Georg Simmel, Heinrich Rickert, and (above all) Wilhelm Dilthey (see Hodges 1944) in Germany, and the philosopher and historian Benedetto Croce

(1917) in Italy. To summarize what they said would be difficult; they were not lucid expositors of their ideas, and they incorporated into their theories metaphysical conceptions that have lost much of their appeal since they wrote. Nevertheless, they succeeded in focusing attention upon features of the historian's activity that had been overlooked and ignored by many of their predecessors. It was pointed out, for instance, that the historian's aims are ostensibly very different from those characteristic of the natural scientist: historians are not concerned with the discovery of universal laws or theories from which predictions can be derived and which can serve as guides to action in practical or technical contexts; on the contrary, their primary purpose is to determine what happened in the past and why. This necessarily involves a concentration upon the concrete particularity of events that are in themselves unique and unrepeatable. The abstract categories of science ("pseudo-concepts," as Croce called them) are, however, adapted to quite different ends; their proper field of application is the sphere of the universal and unchanging, and they can therefore play no role in history as truly conceived. For the historian is not interested in phenomena regarded as "specimens" or as instances of general truths; as Michael Oakeshott (1933, p. 154) has expressed it, "the moment historical facts are regarded as instances of general laws, history is dismissed."

There is, moreover, a further point of fundamental importance that such critics have wished to emphasize. Both Dilthey and Croce underlined the distinction, considered by them to be crucial, between the respective subject matters of science and history. In crude terms, this may be represented by the familiar dichotomy of "spirit" and "nature"; more specifically, it involves the belief that it is impossible to view the activities of historical agents as mere pieces of observable "behavior," reducible to (or explicable in terms of) purely physical items. It follows that the principles of knowledge and understanding that are appropriate here cannot be those presupposed by scientific interpretations of the world. For the historian it is essential that he should be able to reconstruct "from within" the reasons, purposes, and emotions that motivated the persons with whom he is concerned and that found outward expression in their deeds. Various notions, such as "reliving" and *Einfühlung*," or "empathy," were appealed to in order to characterize this process; but, however described, it was posited as a distinctive feature of historical thinking, sufficient in itself to mark history off from typically scientific modes of inquiry.

Collingwood. The basic contention was perhaps most forcefully and clearly formulated by the English philosopher R. G. Collingwood (1946), who was in his own work deeply influenced by Croce. According to Collingwood, the essential task of the historian is to "rethink" or "re-enact" in his mind the deliberations of historical agents, thereby rendering intelligible the events with which he has to deal in a way that finds no parallel in the physical sciences. This led him to claim, among other things, that the term "cause" has its own meaning in the context of historical narrative, not to be confused with any it may bear elsewhere. Thus, to show what caused a given occurrence in history is not a matter of subsuming it beneath scientific laws or empirical generalizations; rather, it is a question of eliciting its "inner side"—that is to say, the thoughts and reasons that, once uncovered, exhibit what happened as the response of a rational being confronted by a situation requiring a practical solution.

The rise of analytic philosophy

Considerations like the above provided the stimulus to much modern philosophical analysis of history. This has turned very largely on the issue of whether, and if so in what way, historical thought has its own distinctive logic that resists interpretation in scientific terms. In general, controversy has tended to center on two main topics. The first concerns the logical character of the explanations historians give of particular events and developments. The second relates to the epistemological status of historical accounts of the past and to the question of whether they possess an objective validity comparable to that claimed for the results of scientific investigation.

Historical explanation. A major difficulty that tends to beset discussions of historical explanation derives from the variety of forms such explanation can assume. It is tempting to imagine that there is a single model to which all explanations in history ultimately conform; to explain an historical occurrence, it may be suggested, is always to exhibit it as being in some sense the consequence of certain other events or conditions. Yet in practice it is far from clear that the narratives historians provide, rich as they are in interpretative devices, invariably follow this neat pattern. For example, we may be told that a particular happening or circumstance was of a certain type (e.g., it is described as representing a "political revolution" or an "imperialist war"); or that it was part of a general trend ("The struggle was a phase of evolving nationalism."); or that it was significant as indicating changes with wider social implications ("The influence of women at court was a symptom of dynastic decline."). These may all constitute valid ways of increasing or illuminating our understanding of what occurred; they do not, however, appear to do so by providing anything obviously analogous to a causal explanation.

Nevertheless, whatever supplementary methods the historian may use to render the past intelligible, it may still be urged that causality remains the fundamental category of historical understanding. The crucial problem, therefore, is one of elucidating the notion of causal connection in history (Gardiner 1952; Dray 1957). Has this notion some special application in historical contexts, as Collingwood claimed? Or is it susceptible to an interpretation which demonstrates that historical explanations do not, after all, diverge in any essential manner from those characteristically employed in the natural sciences?

The theory of "covering laws." The view that no radical differences divide historical from other kinds of explanation has found its chief defenders among philosophers whose general conception of causality largely derives from Hume. Since there are no "necessary connections" between matters of fact, any claim to the effect that a causal relation holds between certain events must contain a covert reference to a natural regularity or law. In other words, to explain an occurrence is to show that it was bound to occur, given the fulfillment of certain antecedent or initial conditions, and given the existence of some law or laws correlating such conditions with events of the type to which the *explicandum* belongs. According to this account, the historian, along with any other inquirer into causes, cannot avoid appealing to general statements asserting empirically verified uniformities; it is the latter that afford the essential backing or warrant that his explanations require. To point out that his direct concern is with the particular, not the general, is to say something that, though true, does not materially affect the issue. There is no incompatibility between the claim that the historian's object is to explain particular events and the claim that, in doing so, he necessarily commits himself to the acceptance of certain general truths. To accept the second of these contentions is not even to deny that there may be an intelligible sense in which each historical event is "unique" (though here it is worth emphasizing that, if such events were unique in the absolute and unrestricted manner. sometimes suggested, it would be impossible

to say anything about them at all). For all that is required for explanatory purposes is that the occurrence to be explained should resemble other happenings in *certain* respects or aspects—namely, those that permit the application of relevant generalizations or laws. From this point of view there is no difference in principle between the procedures of the historian and the natural scientist; if a chemist or an astronomer wishes to explain a particular phenomenon falling within his field, a similar abstraction is involved.

On the face of it, this theory seems to have much to commend it, agreeably combining conceptual economy with empirical hardheadedness. A closer look may, however, reveal difficulties. In the first place, the theory appears to assume that all causal explanations in history take the form of showing that, given certain initial conditions, a particular event *had* to occur. But this is far from being universally true: the historian's object in citing causes is frequently the more limited one of explaining how a certain historical occurrence was *possible*, not why it was bound to happen; the causes referred to represent the necessary rather than the sufficient conditions of what happened. In itself, this hardly constitutes a conclusive objection; it might, for instance, be replied that the determination of necessary conditions also involves an implicit reference to laws, and that a more complex formulation of the proposed analysis, capable of accommodating this kind of case, could easily be devised. Where the theory is more clearly vulnerable is in its bland assumption that laws of the type it postulates lie ready to hand and that it is these to which historians refer when they offer their explanations. For when attempts are made to specify general statements connecting "causes" and "effects" in the required fashion, the propositions elicited tend to be so vague and indeterminate as to make it hard to see how they could conceivably perform the explanatory function attributed to them. Nor does historical practice appear to bear out the suggested interpretation. Thus it may be argued that a historian, when confronted by the task of explaining what caused a specific event, such as the French Revolution, does not do so by attempting to subsume it beneath putative laws concerning revolutions in general; on the contrary, he proceeds to an analysis of the particular case, showing through detailed inquiry how various connected sequences of factors combined to give rise to the complex phenomenon under examination.

The theory of "continuous series." Appreciation of such points has led some modern writers to oppose to the previous "covering law" conception of historical explanation one that has been called "the model of the continuous series." In the latter view, the historian traces, step by step, the relations between earlier and later phases of historical change, thereby building up an intelligible narrative whose various components can be seen to stand in "intrinsic" or "natural" connections with one another: it is by such careful and particularized investigation, and not by applying universal laws or generalizations, that explanation in history characteristically proceeds. But this account, though plausible in many ways, still leaves a question unanswered. For it may be inquired how we are to understand the individual connections stated to obtain between the events of which the series is composed. To say that they are "intrinsic" or "natural" is surely, if anything, to appeal to the notion of what generally happens or can normally be expected to occur; but is this not to reintroduce the conception of empirical uniformities? It would appear, in other words, that the essential difference between the two interpretative models consists not in the fact that one relies upon the notion of generalizations whereas the other does not, but rather in an (admittedly important) disagreement concerning the kinds of generalizations that are relevant, and the levels of inquiry at which they are employed or presupposed.

The historical point of view

It is perhaps hard to see how any theory of historical explanation could wholly dispense with reference to general statements at some stage of its analysis. What is less clear is whether such general statements have the status and role in history which the use of the term "law," with its predominantly scientific associations, implies. There is something eccentric in the idea that the construction of an historical narrative involves a continuous resort to generalizations concerning human behavior, if by "generalizations" is meant a set of inductively established or experimentally confirmed propositions that can be precisely listed and formulated. It is not merely that words like "insight" and "judgment," together with others that are embedded in the vocabulary of ordinary historical criticism, would seem to have little application to history conceived along such rigorous and tidy lines; the picture further suggests an "external" or "spectatorial" approach to the material that appears to obscure a salient feature of much historical writing and understanding. For it is arguable that in order truly to comprehend the policies or decisions of a particular historical figure or the motives or ideals that inspired some large-scale historical

movement (whether political, intellectual, or artistic), it is necessary to be able to share imaginatively the point of view of the participants; and this in turn requires a firsthand acquaintance with what it is, for example, to appreciate a situation and plan accordingly or to entertain certain hopes, desires, or fears. To speak of historical events as being "naturally" related or as forming an "intelligible" sequence may well be to imply that what happened was such as to fulfill our normal expectations; but it is important to recognize that, in human contexts, what we expect is closely tied to what we find understandable in the light of our own experience as rational purposive agents. It was this consideration, above all others, that earlier thinkers like Collingwood wished to stress when criticizing positivist attempts to assimilate history to natural science. Though often expressed in misleading or exaggerated terms, it is a point that still retains considerable force.

Is objectivity possible?   The claim that the historian stands in an especially intimate relation to his subject matter has sometimes been regarded as indicating a further significant difference between history and the natural sciences. This is the suggestion that the very nature of the historian's task and situation precludes him from achieving in his descriptions and interpretations the kind of objectivity that characterizes scientific work. It is not merely that, as a matter of fact, historians often offer widely dissimilar accounts of the same historical phenomena, even when basing what they say on broadly identical sources; it may be argued that such striking divergences are necessary and inevitable. Thus, suppose it is held—as it was, for instance, by Croce—that historical knowledge essentially involves the "re-creation" of the past by each historian within his own mind; it then becomes difficult to see how any historical account can fail to be to some extent colored and shaped by the individual interests and personality of its author—a conclusion tacitly accepted by Croce himself when he spoke of all history as "contemporary."

Even if such "idealist" theories of historical knowledge are rejected, further independent factors may be adduced that point in the same general direction. It has been maintained, for example, that the fact that the historian is engaged in discussing human beings and their activities, using everyday language to do so, commits him to introducing considerations which would be manifestly out of place in scientific contexts: there can be no such thing as a purely objective or "value-free" historical account, since language that is adapted to the description of what people feel, think, and do necessarily reflects the element of evaluation and appraisal that pervades the whole texture of human life and experience. Again, attention may be drawn to the manner in which all history is necessarily selective. The historian cannot pack into his account everything he knows about the subject he is studying, nor would he be considered a good historian if he tried to do so; the employment of judgments of relevance, of relative importance or triviality, is fundamental to his undertaking. But such judgments are founded upon assumptions and preconceptions of diverse kinds that are inherently disputable and that vary from person to person, society to society, age to age. What is of significance to an historian belonging to one period or milieu may seem unworthy of mention to another whose time and background are different; religious opinions, political beliefs, moral or social ideals, must all, consciously or unconsciously, influence such things as the historian's presentation of his material, his decisions as to what to include or omit, the weight he assigns to particular factors, and even his critical assessment of evidence and sources.

Subjectivity and historical evaluation. A conclusion frequently drawn from all this, both by philosophers and by practicing historians who have reflected on their craft, is that history is infected by some kind of radical and irremediable "subjectivity." Yet the claim in question, together with the arguments used to support it, have tended to be framed in highly general and abstract terms; in consequence, as a number of recent critics have pointed out (see, for instance, Carr 1961), several significant distinctions are in danger of being overlooked. It is a mistake, for instance, to suppose that the selection and presentation of material are always determined by "subjective" convictions and preconceptions of the kind stressed above; they may be, and very often are, dictated in a quite incontestable manner by the particular nature of the problem with which the historian is concerned. Likewise, it is one thing to say that an historian's choice of problem is due to certain personal interests or predilections he may have, and another to argue that these will necessarily affect his manner of solving it; the two have not, however, always been clearly separated. Again, judgments of relative importance may sometimes be made in the light of what has been called the "causal fertility" of events; but the question of whether some specific occurrence was productive of more far-reaching changes than another is an empirical matter, decidable by investigation—it has nothing essen-

tially to do with subjective values or attitudes peculiar to the historian.

Similar possibilities of confusion may arise with regard to the suggestion that the historian's subject matter is such as to render evaluation unavoidable. No doubt it is true that the purposes and doings of historical agents were to a large extent informed by the values and principles (moral or otherwise) to which they subscribed; but this by itself in no way entails that the historian cannot discuss their activities without engaging in such evaluation on his own account. If, on the other hand, it is the historian's use of common language that is held to preclude the possibility of his providing "neutral" descriptions, the precise force of this contention (assuming it to be correct) is open to doubt; what, for example, is to prevent historians from devising a reformed terminology to meet the difficulty?

Remaining problems. Taken together, the above and related points may go some way toward reducing the prima facie persuasiveness of the claim that anything akin to objectivity in the scientific sense is unattainable in history. But the issue remains a curiously intractable one, involving various puzzles and ambiguities into whose complexities it is impossible to enter here. Nor does it stand alone in this respect. The rich field of the critical philosophy of history contains a host of similarly disputed problems, with roots extending into many adjoining areas of inquiry (Gardiner 1959; see also Stern 1956; Meyerhoff 1959; New York University . . . 1963). From this point of view their further investigation does not only concern the future development of the historical studies: it also has an obvious and important bearing upon some of the fundamental methodological questions that, at the present time, confront the neighboring social sciences.

PATRICK GARDINER

[See also Marxist sociology; Positivism; Sociology, *article on* THE DEVELOPMENT OF SOCIOLOGICAL THOUGHT; *and the biographies of* Comte; Croce; Dilthey; Hegel; Hume; Marx; Simmel; Sorokin; Spengler; Vico; Weber, Max.]

BIBLIOGRAPHY

Aron, Raymond (1938) 1961 *Introduction to the Philosophy of History: An Essay on the Limits of Historical Objectivity.* Boston: Beacon. → First published in French.

Berlin, Isaiah 1955 *Historical Inevitability.* London and New York: Oxford Univ. Press.

Cairns, Grace E. 1962 *Philosophies of History: Meeting of East and West in Cycle-pattern Theories of History.* New York: Philosophical Library.

Carr, Edward H. (1961) 1962 *What Is History?* New York: Knopf.

COLLINGWOOD, ROBIN G. 1946 *The Idea of History.* Oxford Univ. Press. → A paperback edition was published in 1956.

CROCE, BENEDETTO (1917) 1960 *History: Its Theory and Practice.* New York: Russell. → First published as *Teoria e storia della storiografia.*

DANTO, ARTHUR C. 1965 *Analytical Philosophy of History.* Cambridge Univ. Press.

DRAY, WILLIAM 1957 *Laws and Explanation in History.* Oxford Univ. Press.

GALLIE, W. B. 1964 *Philosophy and the Historical Understanding.* London: Chatto & Windus.

GARDINER, PATRICK (1952) 1958 *The Nature of Historical Explanation.* Oxford Univ. Press.

GARDINER, PATRICK (editor) 1959 *Theories of History: Readings From Classical and Contemporary Sources.* Glencoe, Ill.: Free Press.

HODGES, HERBERT A. 1944 *Wilhelm Dilthey: An Introduction.* London: Routledge. → Contains extracts from some of Dilthey's principal writings.

KAHLER, ERICH 1964 *Meaning of History.* New York: Braziller.

LÖWITH, KARL (1949) 1950 *Meaning in History: The Theological Implications of the Philosophy of History.* Cambridge Univ. Press. → A paperback edition was published in 1957 by Phoenix.

MANDELBAUM, MAURICE H. 1938 *The Problem of Historical Knowledge: An Answer to Relativism.* New York: Liveright.

MEYERHOFF, HANS (editor) 1959 *The Philosophy of History in Our Time: An Anthology.* Garden City, N.Y.: Doubleday.

NEW YORK UNIVERSITY, INSTITUTE OF PHILOSOPHY, 5th, 1962 1963 *Philosophy and History: A Symposium.* Edited by Sidney Hook. New York Univ. Press.

OAKESHOTT, MICHAEL 1933 *Experience and Its Modes.* Cambridge Univ. Press.

POPPER, KARL R. 1957 *The Poverty of Historicism.* Boston: Beacon.

STERN, FRITZ R. (editor) 1956 *The Varieties of History: From Voltaire to the Present.* New York: Meridian.

WALSH, WILLIAM H. (1951) 1958 *An Introduction to Philosophy of History.* London: Hutchinson. → A paperback edition was published in 1960 by Harper as *The Philosophy of History.*

WHITE, MORTON G. 1965 *Foundations of Historical Knowledge.* New York: Harper.

WINCH, PETER 1958 *The Idea of a Social Science and Its Relation to Philosophy.* London: Routledge; New York: Humanities.

II

HISTORY AND THE SOCIAL SCIENCES

To social scientists, all history is social history, whether historians classify it as social history, political history, economic history, religious history, or history of some other kind. It cannot be said, therefore, that there is a distinct category of historical study which is devoted specifically to the past as the social scientist would deal with it. Rather, a new method of studying history of all kinds is emerging which is intended to satisfy the criteria of the social sciences and which provides or will provide evidence to illuminate the task of the sociologist, the anthropologist, the social psy-

chologist, and so on. The historian working in this way makes use of the theories, categories, and techniques of the social scientist whose work he is trying to parallel. The social scientist, when he turns to accounts of the past for evidence, attempts to master the outlook and methods of the historian. The purpose of the present article is to examine in a summary way the principles which are beginning to govern these activities of historians and social scientists. It must not be supposed, however, that all history is now to be written or ever will be written with the scientific study of society as the end in view. The writing of history is a much more general activity than the systematic study of social relationships. Accounts of the past seem to have been composed in some form or other in every society. In literate societies with a high degree of cultivation, these accounts are rewritten every century or every generation, in some cases every few years, in conflicting versions.

The writing of history is undertaken for many purposes, which themselves would be a legitimate object of a social scientific investigation. These purposes can only be hinted at here. Reconstructions are worked out and interpretations are built up in order to reconcile a national society (or a group of any kind) with its past and with the way in which its present differs from that past. They are needed to make intelligible to every new generation its ordained place in time. They are needed to justify religious beliefs and practices, to provide political rationalizations, to enrich aesthetic and intellectual experience, and merely to satisfy curiosity. Even the simple keeper of the annals of his people or his church does something in all these directions and also does something to ensure, as d'Alembert said in the great *Encyclopédie*, that the achievements of the past shall not be lost to the men of the future.

The successive authors of the *Anglo-Saxon Chronicle* could not possibly have conceived of a science of society or imagined that the work which they produced could give rise to such an enterprise, let alone that it might provide an alternative to it. But since their time and down to our day, historians have advanced all these propositions about the relationship between history and the social sciences. It has been claimed that there is a distinctive historical method which provides its own account of how society works or, perhaps, its own unique attempt to do all that can be done, in view of the fact that the workings of society can never be more than partially established. According to this view, narration and description are the proper methods to be used (for an argument of this kind, see Collingwood 1946). Since no social situation, no past event, can ever be described in full in all its changing aspects, selection of the typical, after as exhaustive a study as possible, has to govern the undertaking. Some claim that the principles of such selection can be scientific principles, but others deny this, on the grounds that the selection can only be intuitive. Thus, the study of history has been seen as the point of origin of the social sciences; or as the rationale of an alternative type of special explanation; or as all that can be advanced, since social science is a chimera. A very different claim has also been put forward. The domain of the historian has been defined as all the social scientific evidence coming from the past. In this way, the phrases "historical science" and "the historical sciences" have come into being.

All the various claims about the relationship between history and the social sciences raise logical, conceptual, and philosophical issues, some of them of great intricacy [see HISTORY, *article on* THE PHILOSOPHY OF HISTORY]. In the present article recourse will be had to an archaic or even obsolete use of the word "history," as an aid to understanding history's present relationship with the social sciences. History will be conceived of here as bearing the very wide meaning it had in the phrase "natural history." Some biological scientists still call themselves naturalists.

Nowadays "natural history" is a way of referring to biology, botany, zoology, and geology, with a distinct implication of their being pursued rather unsystematically by amateurs, as a diversion. Before and during the scientific revolution, however, "natural history" meant all that could be known about nature simply by description, as contrasted with "natural philosophy," which meant that part of nature which could be understood on principle, scientifically, and which was acquired by the systematic use of certain techniques of observation. If we substitute the word "societal" for "natural," the new phrase "societal history" can be used in contrast with the phrase "social science," in rather the same way "natural history" was used in contrast to "natural philosophy" or "natural science." Such a usage recognizes that history is legitimately pursued for many purposes other than the complementing of the social sciences. It avoids the difficulties, already described, which attach to the phrase "social history." It emphasizes that social information which does not yet belong to the analytically formulated and technically cultivated social sciences (and which may never belong there) can nevertheless be apprehended, if not understood, in the historical, narrative, descriptive, intuitive mode.

Societal history, or the "history" of ordinary usage taken in its very widest sense, stands to the social sciences as natural history stands or once stood to the natural sciences. Once this roundabout definition is laid down, it becomes clear that although every form of historical study necessarily belongs to societal history whether or not it would usually be described as social, no form of historical study necessarily belongs to the social sciences. Particular types of historical inquiry may be said to be part of the social sciences, nevertheless, if certain conditions, discussed later in this article, are satisfied. We shall, in fact, distinguish those historical studies intended to advance the social sciences as a particular area of societal history and give them a collective name, "deliberative societal history."

The limitations usually placed upon the simple word "history" will be disregarded in a further way. Archeological evidence is sometimes excluded from history, but it will be included here as part of societal history, as will the material gained by anthropologists and sociologists in direct observation and oral communication. But although societal history is a descriptive undertaking, dealing with a very wide range of sources and with indefinitely extensible information, it has to satisfy the strictly chronological criterion rather more exactly than does natural history. It can deal only with those facts which belong to past time and which are to be understood in one-way temporal succession. Even this limitation becomes tenuous in the case of evidence assembled for the current situation by social scientists, which must all belong to past time, even if it is only the very recent past. But in practice the very near past, as represented by the most recently available social survey data, and so on, is excluded from societal history.

Since their subjects are related in this way, the social scientist and the societal historian are by no means always distinct individuals, any more than are the natural historian and the natural scientist; each individual is more the one than the other— more the sociologist, for example, than the social-structure historian. Some important sociologists (e.g., Max Weber and T. H. Marshall) wrote specifically historical works, and most technical works of the social sciences contain some discussion of a historical character. This is true even of economic theory (see, for example, John Maynard Keynes 1930), while the studies of anthropologists and sociologists sometimes have to present a considerable amount of descriptive and narrative history of the conventional kind. Only theoretical statistical works are likely to be entirely wanting in historical content. There are, moreover, as is well known, books written as history which are rightly regarded as classics of the social sciences (Tocqueville's works are good examples).

Types of societal history

It is possible to delineate five types of historical undertakings, together with their particular functions in the study of society. They are listed here in descending order of significance to the social sciences, and, of course, they overlap to a certain extent.

Social science works. The first type of historical writing of significance to the social scientist belongs to the literature of the social sciences themselves, since it consists of parts of works written by social scientists. Every such work, as has been said, contains narrative–descriptive components, and these belong to societal history. They are of varying length and importance. There are the short historical descriptions and arguments which are found in such books as Gunnar Myrdal's *An American Dilemma* (1944) and in the very long historical citations and discussions which go to make up most of the text of Wittfogel's *Oriental Despotism* (1957). Neither this latter book nor any other book of the same type belongs wholly with societal history, since its object is to illuminate a particular institution in its significance for all societies at all times.

Social structural studies. The second type of historical writing of significance to the social scientist is social structural history. It consists of complete works deliberately undertaken by scholars calling themselves historians, rather than social scientists, that provide comparative historical examples which can be used alongside the comparative geographical examples of anthropologists. Such studies may take various forms: they may be comprehensive surveys of particular societies at certain points in the past, or they may contain records of social change over a particular period. But they will always tend to embrace whole national societies or whole cultural areas, rather than dealing in specified institutions alone. Although they belong with the established tradition of social history, they are undertaken, as far as possible, in conformity with two principles not usually made explicit in traditional works. One is that the evidence shall be assembled and analyzed in accordance with the methods and techniques of all the social sciences. The other is that conclusions shall be presented in a form which can be used in social analysis generally.

An example of an experimental work of this kind, using the method of comparison rather than

of narrative and dealing with the whole social structure rather than with specific institutions, is Laslett's *The World We Have Lost* (1965), which covers English society before and after industrialization and attempts to satisfy the principles just cited. If it is compared with Trevelyan's *English Social History* (1942), the difference between social structural history and traditional social history is brought out. A summary of the principles of this emerging form of historical writing is attempted below.

Areas of social activity. The third type of historical writing of significance to the social scientist consists of studies of the past of some isolable area of social activity. The distinctions between these special historical areas consist, to a large extent, simply of their varying subject matter. But a more interesting and important principle of difference is beginning to appear. Part of the definition of a recognized social science is that it should possess its own particular body of theory and technique, although there are differences between various social sciences in this respect. Historical writing within the area of each social science must attempt to make use of its theory and its technique, and in one conspicuous case, that of economic history, it has certainly begun to do so. Only one other isolable historical area shows signs of a similar evolution, and that is demographic history, using the theory and technique of demography. These are the two social sciences which lend themselves most easily to quantification and mathematical analysis; but it need not be supposed that the less effective tools and devices at the disposal of other social scientists are quite without their effect on historical studies. The history of religion and the history of education, for example, can in principle make use of religious and educational psychology and sociology.

The theory and technique of sociology and psychology can in principle be adapted so as to apply to the history of literature and the fine arts, to the history of social and political thinking, and to the history of mathematics and science. All these historical studies may also come to be illuminated by such techniques as content analysis and the other expedients used by sociologists and psychologists to reach an understanding of beliefs, attitudes, opinions, and ideologies in the contemporary world. (For an example of these expedients, see Lane 1962; and for a highly speculative attempt at psychological and intellectual analysis in past time, see Erikson 1958.) A further historical area may soon show signs of independence, making use, where it can, of the theory and techniques of political sociology. This new subject might tentatively be called the history of political systems, communication, and participation. Although such a subject will inevitably have to grow out of voting studies undertaken historically, there are already signs that even in societies without democratic procedures, past and present political behavior can be fruitfully studied (see, e.g., Vincent 1966). The distinction between this nascent subject and political history of the conventional kind will concern us below.

Nevertheless, these studies are difficult to classify, as can be seen from the example of the history of technology, which certainly belongs as much to economic history as it does to the history of mathematics and science and which may well have its part to play in some other areas as well. These studies, by treating their data and presenting their conclusions in a manner appropriate to their subject, will be of direct use to the social scientist, providing him with comparative historical examples in specialized spheres. Social structural history would ideally represent an amalgamation of all possible studies of this kind, as well as a general framework within which each of them might be pursued.

It is unlikely that many books of this type would actually deal with any one specialized area as a whole, although it is possible that works, especially multivolume collaborative studies, will continue to appear with titles such as "A History of Social and Political Thought." Most of the narrower studies can have two distinct objectives. The first objective is the social analysis of certain features of historically distant situations, with the issues of the social sciences generally in view. An example of this kind of study is Smelser's *Social Change in the Industrial Revolution* (1959). Although a historical monograph, applying theory to a particular topic, the Lancashire cotton factories of the early nineteenth century, it is also intended as a contribution to general social theory. The second objective is to illuminate past events and to revise interpretations of them, with only incidental reference to social analysis of present institutions and attitudes. It is noticeable that the studies carried out so far by the econometric economic historians tend to belong to this second type.

Documentary and preparatory works. The fourth category of historical writing of significance to the social sciences consists of documentary and preparatory works. Studies of this kind have considerable value, especially in the present, developing stage of many of the subjects already described. For example, the discovery and preparation of data for the description of social structure from listings of inhabitants, including familial structure and kinship systems, has been of the first importance for social structural history. The editing and printing of records such as licenses to marry issued by episcopal courts, regular series of documents drawn up in connection with poor relief, and parochial registers containing detailed recordings of baptisms, marriages, and burials all come under this heading and are of great value to demographic as well as social structural history (Wrigley 1966).

Traditional historical studies. The fifth category of historical writing of significance to the social scientist is the residual one and consists of all other historical works, of whatever kind.

Works of traditional history are less likely to be of direct importance to the social scientist than any of those listed in the first four categories. But this does not mean that works which have been or are now being produced in accordance with traditional historical conventions are irrelevant. According to the definition adopted here, they belong to societal history and could have been mentioned as containing documentary and preparatory material. Many of them are, in fact, of great value in the hands of percipient and conscientious social inquirers. Moreover, the realistic and critical historian is often in a position to illuminate the use made of historical evidence by social scientists in a peculiarly effective way. He may even, on entirely historical criteria, demonstrate the inefficacy of explanations used both by his fellow historians and by social scientists. An example of this is the devastating work recently done by Hexter (1961) on the-rise-of-a-class hypotheses. Even if a historical work is composed without any intention of recording or illuminating social change, it may nevertheless do so or it may be shown to have done so by a later critic.

Deliberative societal history

There clearly is a distinction between historical works intended by their authors as contributions to social analysis and those written in indifference to such an aim. Works of the first type constitute the category of deliberative societal history, in contrast with traditional historical studies. Although some of the characteristics of deliberative societal history have been sketched above, the criteria which mark historical work of this kind are not yet clear, distinct, or universally recognized. Nevertheless, it is already obvious that most traditional historical studies could not conform to the required conditions.

In the first place, many historians would be unwilling to recognize deliberative societal history as a description of their work. Some would reject the whole project of social and political science. Their methods belong to the category of tacit knowledge, not only in the understanding of past events but also in the selection of what will interest, inform, or even elevate their readers. Analysis of society and of social situations is by no means absent, even from writing of this kind, but the emphasis is upon description and narration, and the task is regarded as being entirely literary, with, perhaps, philosophical overtones. History, after all, as well as being the companion to the social sciences, is one of the traditional arts, with its own individual muse. Historians who insist that any human experience is unique are understandably skeptical of attempts at formulating general rules for the study of society and social change.

But even if and when it is not done in conscious divergence from the social sciences, most traditional historical study is still accomplished in ignorance of them. It is undertaken without knowledge of the relevant theories, concepts, and techniques. This is the second reason so much writing of this character is of problematic value to the social scientist.

The interests of the general public, rather than of the academic world or of the social scientists, give rise to the third reason that the relationship between traditional historical studies and the social sciences is so indirect and arbitrary. The demand that history shall be "interesting," that it shall tell a relevant, informative story with a moral or a message, has effects on the academic historian as well as on the writers of textbooks, the biographers, and the journalists. Tradition has tended to establish in historical studies specific requirements which have been even more limiting. It is expected that a national society will ordinarily be the unit of historical investigation and of historical narrative. The chronological divisions usually have to be those of the conventional political landmarks, and the events, sentiments, and attitudes to be explained have for the most part to be political, chosen for the importance they have for the reader's sense of citizenship.

These influences continue even when the subject matter is no longer of the traditional political character. Hence, many specialized studies still bear titles such as "The History of American Science in the Colonial Period" or "The History of Japanese Education Under the Tokugawa." It is true that the growing importance of the social sciences in recent years is beginning to remove some of these limitations and that the domination of politics, the state, and the values of citizenship is much less than it used to be. It is also true that

economic history shows signs of transcending these limitations altogether, although it still seems to select topics as much for their polemical, and often political, interest as for their economic significance. Quite apart from traditional historical studies, then, none of the subjects we have classed as deliberative societal history can as yet be said to be under the controlling influence of the social sciences.

Quantitative history. Of all recent developments, it is clear that econometric economic history stands in sharpest contrast to traditional historical pursuits. Its rapid development in recent years makes it necessary to consider the question of the use of quantification in historical studies and its effect on their relationship with the social sciences. Douglass C. North sets out the characteristics of econometric economic history, but even among the economic historians there are some who do not consider it history at all or, at most, call it, in Fritz Redlich's term, quasi history. [See HISTORY, article on ECONOMIC HISTORY.]

The insistence on giving a numerical value to everything in a historical situation which is relevant to the problem in hand is one source of the criticism. This has given the title "cleometrics" to the new pursuit and brings it directly into line with trends in the social sciences. Although this pursuit has been severely criticized, I do not believe that its numerative characteristic makes the subject any the less historical.

Even if the numerical equivalents seem quite unreal to the common-sense observer and introduce a host of uncertainties into the issues which have to be judged, it has to be remembered that all historical judgments are beset with uncertainties of the same logical kind. Attempting to reckon the percentage of the gross national product of the United States made up by the railroads in 1850 is the same kind of undertaking as estimating the amount of influence which the growth of Christianity had on the decline of imperial Rome. Nor does it appear that the counterfactual type of argument used in cleometrics is necessarily a contradiction of the historical outlook and method. Estimating what might have happened if what did happen had not happened is characteristic of much historical argument of a conventional kind, and all that cleometrics does is to argue confessedly in this way, openly estimating the risk of error.

The truly significant point about cleometrics, for traditional historical studies, is that it attempts to do economic analysis on noncontemporaneous subjects. That is why this type of economic history belongs to the social sciences to an extent that no other historical study yet does. It has ceased to be mere societal history and has become social science. Only the recent advances in the theory of economic growth have made such work possible, and it is clear that the more fragmentary the quantifiable evidence, the more sophisticated the necessary theory is likely to be. For most of the other social sciences having equivalents among types of deliberative societal history, no such advanced theory exists or seems likely to be developed, except perhaps in demography. It must be remembered, also, that vast areas of information from the economic past cannot be dealt with by cleometrics and will never become susceptible to such methods.

It seems unlikely, therefore, that the rise of cleometrics is a portent of the future course of the relationship between traditional historical studies and the social sciences. In the foreseeable future only very few historians will be able to call themselves social scientists. Not many more social scientists will, perhaps, be able to apply their theories and practice their techniques on chronologically distant materials. The most important change will come at a more modest level: much more historical writing will surely come under the heading of "deliberative societal history." The elaboration of social structural history will be an important means by which this change will take place.

Social structural history

Two of the characteristics of social structural history have also been made plain: first, it should assemble its evidence and carry out its analysis in accordance with the methods and techniques of the social sciences, and second, it should present its conclusions in a form which can be used in social analysis generally. It has also been suggested that social structural history may dispense with the narrative method, which has in the past been an almost universal feature of historical writing.

Since social description is to be done in wholes, narrative would in any case be a peculiarly difficult form for history written in this way. But although works of this kind will probably tend to consist of contrasts between a "before" and an "after," the dates selected will represent the median years of particular generations, rather than exact moments. The choice of the generations to be described will itself be a matter of importance and, like everything else, will have to be made with the interests of the social sciences generally in mind, as well as being made in accordance with historical criteria.

The social structural historian should begin his descriptions where the anthropologists and the sociologists do, that is, with the size, structure, and functions of the family in the society in question. Then will come the kinship system, then the other relationships, the geographical, the economic, the religious, the intellectual, that go to make up the community. "Community" here is understood in a plural sense, for the local, the tribal, and the regional associations and finally the national community, if indeed all these existed, are all to be included. Only then, and this is in sharp contrast with the practice of the traditional historian, will he concern himself with political institutions and the state itself.

It is clear that historical writing of this character will be faced with a particularly acute form of the problem which affects all historiography, that of summarizing and abbreviating sufficiently to make its account intelligible. Traditional history has a traditional expedient for this purpose: the choosing of significant instances, which are presented as typical. Since the social structural historian is still writing societal *history*, rather than social *science*, he will of course be at liberty to use the same method. But he must be expected to have a much clearer notion of the social theory or theories which make his chosen instances significant, and he will recognize that total description is a chimera, that all he can ever put on paper is a model of the society he is dealing with. The function of theories and the usefulness of models in pursuits of this kind is to order the data, to select and insist upon the regularities, to simplify drastically by approximation.

In the course of time, then, the social structural historian may find himself having to handle whole sets of theories and several different types of models. By this time the theories and models used by economists and demographers should be familiar to him. But his first concern will be to construct a model of his society in the much simpler sense just referred to; perhaps "miniature" would be a better term. He must, at all points in his descriptions, analyses, and comparisons, have the whole of the society in mind as well as a simplified notion of its over-all workings. He may find it useful to think of two separate models, or miniatures, one static and one dynamic, fitting into each other in the way any theory appropriate to a system in the process of change fits into a theory of that system as it is when at rest. He should at all times be aware of the ways in which his chosen models misrepresent the realities he is striving to deal with, and his duty will be to try to improve them. He should be conscious of the haphazard nature of the theories he has to use and aware of the areas in which, like his companions and predecessors among the traditional historians, he has to rely on intuition and guesswork. He may or may not find general theories of social action, like those of Talcott Parsons, useful to him in his difficult and challenging task. The essential point is that he should recognize that his is a theoretical, as well as an empirically descriptive, undertaking.

Social structural history and the other forms of deliberative societal history which have been defined here are not propounded as alternatives to traditional historical writing which should, and ultimately will, replace it. The writing of history has many functions other than providing social scientists with comparative instances and with a continuum in which they can do their work. History will continue to be written for all the many purposes for which it has always been written, regardless of what the social sciences do and how they may develop. All that has been attempted here is a sketch of the somewhat complex relationship between history as traditionally written and the social sciences as they are now pursued. Let it be stressed again that the historian and the social scientist have often been the same person, and this will probably increasingly be the case in the future. But in the writing of social structural history, the differences between the two roles become especially clear. Complicated and difficult as composing history of this kind may be, it presents a challenge which neither the historian nor the social scientist can any longer afford to ignore.

PETER LASLETT

BIBLIOGRAPHY

The Anglo-Saxon Chronicle. Translated with an introduction by G. N. Garmonsway. London: Dent, 1953.

CAHNMAN, WERNER J.; and BOSKOFF, ALVIN (editors) 1964 *Sociology and History: Theory and Research.* New York: Free Press.

COLLINGWOOD, R. G. 1946 *The Idea of History.* Oxford Univ. Press. → A paperback edition was published in 1956.

ERIKSON, ERIK H. (1958) 1962 *Young Man Luther: A Study in Psychoanalysis and History.* Austin Riggs Monograph No. 4. New York: Norton.

FÜRER-HAIMENDORF, CHRISTOPH VON 1955 Culture History and Cultural Development. *Yearbook of Anthropology* 1:149–168.

HEXTER, J. H. 1961 *Reappraisals in History: New Views on History and Society in Early Modern Europe.* Evanston, Ill.: Northwestern Univ. Press. → A paperback edition was published in 1963 by Harper.

History and Social Science. 1965 *International Social Science Journal* 17, no. 4 (entire issue).

KEYNES, JOHN MAYNARD (1930) 1958–1960 *A Treatise on Money.* 2 vols. London: Macmillan. → Volume 1: *The Pure Theory of Money.* Volume 2: *The Applied Theory of Money.*

LANE, ROBERT E. 1962 *Political Ideology: Why the American Common Man Believes What He Does.* New York: Free Press.

LASLETT, PETER 1965 *The World We Have Lost.* London: Methuen.

MYRDAL, GUNNAR (1944) 1962 *An American Dilemma: The Negro Problem and Modern Democracy.* New York: Harper. → A paperback edition was published in 1964 by McGraw-Hill.

REDLICH, FRITZ 1965 "New" and Traditional Approaches to Economic History and Their Interdependence. *Journal of Economic History* 25:480–495.

SMELSER, NEIL J. 1959 *Social Change in the Industrial Revolution.* London: Routledge; Univ. of Chicago Press.

TREVELYAN, GEORGE M. (1942) 1947 *English Social History: A Survey of Six Centuries, Chaucer to Queen Victoria.* London: Longmans.

VINCENT, JOHN 1966 *The Formation of the Liberal Party, 1857–1868.* London: Constable.

WITTFOGEL, KARL A. 1957 *Oriental Despotism: A Comparative Study of Total Power.* New Haven: Yale Univ. Press. → A paperback edition was published in 1963.

WRIGLEY, EDWARD A. (editor) 1966 *An Introduction to English Historical Demography.* London: Weidenfeld.

III
ETHNOHISTORY

Although it has appeared sporadically since the early twentieth century, the term "ethnohistory" was first used systematically in the 1940s by some North American cultural anthropologists, archeologists, and historians, to describe their writings and research on the history of the aborigines of the New World. In more recent years "ethnohistory" has come to mean the historical study of any non-European peoples. Utilizing documentary, oral, and archeological sources and the conceptual framework and insights of cultural and social anthropology, these studies attempt to reconstruct the history of indigenous peoples before and after European contact.

Ethnohistorians combine their "historical" sources with ethnographic field work among the present-day members of the societies whose past they aim to reconstruct. Their goal is to present "rounded" history, which will take into account the social and cultural systems of indigenous peoples; thus, ethnohistorians of North America have paid particular attention to the location and migration of Indian tribes, changing cultural adaptions to environment, demographic history, the exact nature of the relations of particular tribes with Europeans, and the effects which activities such as the fur trade and warfare have had on American Indians ("Symposium on the Concept of Ethnohistory" 1961).

Ethnohistory has led mainly to studies of particular cultural units, equivalent to the field anthropologists' ethnographic accounts. There has been little effort to build a body of generalizations, either through comparison or through the development of concepts or categories of sequences which would make interregional comparison possible. The characteristic approaches and problems of ethnohistory derive from the nature of the indigenous societies being studied, the period, type, and duration of European domination, the kinds of documentation available, and the theoretical orientation of the anthropologists who have studied the region.

Ethnohistory differs from the work of conventional colonial historians in several respects. The ethnohistorian usually has firsthand field experience in the area; this experience increases his knowledge of the indigenous society and how it actually functions or functioned. Thus, his interpretation of documentary evidence is deepened. The ethnohistorian tends to think in systemic, functional terms rather than in terms only of accident and particulars. He tries to use his general knowledge of social and cultural organization and constructs his units in terms of such concepts as "segmentary lineage-based societies," "peasant societies," and "patrimonial societies." The ethnohistorian tries to perceive historical events from the position of the aborigine rather than that of the European administrator, even when he is using the administrator's documents. He is more interested in the impact of colonial policy and practice than in the genesis of these policies in the metropolitan society.

History of the approach

One of the major sources of the field of anthropology was a concern with the history of man in general, the comparative study of societies and institutions, and the reconstructions of the history of particular societies. Voltaire, Gustav Klemm, Sir Henry Maine, J. F. McLennan, J. J. Bachofen, N. D. Fustel de Coulanges, L. H. Morgan, and E. B. Tylor drew heavily on historical materials to establish a comparative science of society and culture. These early anthropologists utilized information about classical civilizations, Hindu India, European barbarians, medieval European institutions, and missionary and traveler accounts of primitive societies. In their broad-ranging and speculative reconstructions of the history of man, they discovered and labeled some of the basic features of primitive and peasant societies. [See the biographies of BACHOFEN; FUSTEL DE COULANGES; McLENNAN; MAINE; MORGAN, L. H.; TYLOR; VOLTAIRE.]

Subsequently, the broad schemes of "evolutionary history" put forward by these early anthropolo-

gists were rejected; however, they did illustrate how documentary material, illuminated by comparative theory, may be used to understand particular sequences of social and cultural change.

At the beginning of the twentieth century the diffusionists, e.g., Ratzel and Graebner, and then the distributionists, e.g., Wissler, Kroeber, and Lowie, denied the possibility of the use of direct historical methods to reconstruct the history of aboriginal societies. Kroeber believed that for the study of "poor dateless primitives . . . we do not possess even one document written before our day" ([1901–1951] 1952, p. 65). Lowie, in his attack on Swanton and Dixon's use of oral traditions and travelers' accounts in their history of North American Indian migrations (Swanton & Dixon 1914), utterly denied "that primitive man is endowed with historical sense or perspective" (Lowie [1917] 1960, p. 206). Lowie believed that the anthropologist's "historical problems can be solved only by the objective methods of comparative ethnology, archeology, linguistics and physical anthropology" (ibid., p. 210).

The American distributionist, or "historical," school was based on the attempt to discover items of culture and society from the "memory culture" of surviving elderly members of American Indian tribes. These social and cultural items or traits— items of material culture and linguistic data—were plotted geographically, in attempts to infer historical or chronological relationships between tribes. The distributionists were not concerned in any detailed fashion with the history of particular tribes. Typical of this approach, Sapir's "Time Perspective in Aboriginal American Culture: A Study in Method," published in 1916, devoted only two pages out of 87 to the use of documents and indigenous oral traditions. Dependence on distribution studies of individual traits or complexes (e.g., the Sun Dance, particular tales and myths) and lack of systematic use of documents and oral histories weakened the work of the American historical school, and they tended to produce timeless descriptions of phenomena on an areal basis or descriptive synchronic accounts of particular memory cultures.

In England in the 1920s Malinowski and Radcliffe-Brown also rejected historically oriented research in anthropology. Both argued that documents for the study of primitive society were unavailable. Radcliffe-Brown contended that the nature of social anthropology and history were antithetical: social anthropologists, as distinguished from ethnologists, were to be concerned with the development of generalizations about the structure of society derived from the comparative study of primitive societies, without reference to their history. Synchronic, or cross-sectional, studies of societies were carefully distinguished from diachronic studies, or studies of societies as they changed through time; the latter could lead only to explanations of uniqueness. Until the 1950s most British social anthropologists kept to Radcliffe-Brown's strictures and avoided diachronic studies. [*See the biographies of* MALINOWSKI; RADCLIFFE-BROWN; SAPIR.]

British and American anthropologists continued to study social and cultural change without reference to historical materials, even when, as in the case of Lucy Mair's study of the Baganda (1934) or Monica Hunter Wilson's of the Pondo (1936), documentary sources were readily available. Gluckman's study of the Zulu political system (1940) and Nadel's *Black Byzantium* (1942) did use historical materials to develop a model of political structures before European incursions. However, these studies are not histories but analytical abstractions from historical sources to illuminate structural principles. The one outstanding exception during this period is E. E. Evans-Pritchard's study of the bedouin of Cyrenaica (1949). In this study Evans-Pritchard analyzed the process by which a lineage-based society developed centralized political roles and institutions. The Sanusi, an order of Muslim religious leaders, had moved into Cyrenaica in the early nineteenth century and provided needed religious and trade functions in the society. Geographically and structurally they located their religious centers at boundaries of existing lineage and tribal territories. Largely through the pressure of Turkish and, subsequently, Italian administrators who tried to rule the bedouin, the heads of the religious order, as the only visible leaders, were impelled into society-wide political roles. Evans-Pritchard used available colonial records and reports, published narratives, oral traditions, and the memories of participants in the events which make up the historical narrative. *The Sanusi of Cyrenaica* is based on Evans-Pritchard's understanding of the operation of an acephalous lineage-based political system, and it is this which gives him the structural principles on which he organized his historical narrative and provides a model for the study of the process of internal structural change in such a society under the impact of foreign rule.

In the United States in the period from 1910 to 1930 a few anthropologists, notably John R. Swanton, in his studies of the Indians of the American southeast (1922; 1946), and Frank G. Speck, working on the tribes of the northeastern United States (1928), used direct historical methods to reconstruct the tribal pasts. For this task they drew on their field work among the remnants of the tribes of the areas and made intensive use of a wide range of documentary materials. [*See the biography of* SWANTON.]

Fittingly, the clearest early examples of systematic ethnohistorical work are found in a volume of studies dedicated to Swanton and published by the Smithsonian Institution in 1940. William Fenton used seventeenth-century and eighteenth-century documents to trace location and movement of Iroquois bands (1940); William Duncan Strong demonstrated that documentary materials could be used with archeological data to provide a continuous record from present into the past of particular sites (1940); Julian Steward's study of Great Basin societies combines ecology, history, archeology, and ethnography and yielded insight into structural and cultural processes (1940). These three studies indicated the ethnohistoric approach that was to become formalized in the 1950s. [*See the biography of* STRONG; ECOLOGY, *especially the article on* CULTURAL ECOLOGY.]

The accumulation of ethnographic data made it clear that early assumptions about the stability of cultures and societies before European contact were false. Anthropologists began to recognize that instead of a precontact situation of stagnation in aboriginal societies, changes of three types had occurred. First, there were small-scale cyclical changes, exemplified by the growth and fission of extended families and lineages. There were also larger cycles of political and cultural expansion as lineages within tribes came to dominate similar units; however, many societies could not develop institutions to contain reassertion of independence of such units, so that large-scale tribal organizations would develop for a time under one or another section of a tribe, only to break apart into smaller units again. The third type of change involved large-scale tribal migrations, leading to greatly changed political, social, and ceremonial orders.

In addition to these internal processes of change, ethnohistorians have demonstrated the indirect effects of outsiders—Europeans and Arabs, for example—on indigenous societies and cultures even before the period of European domination. The slave trade in both east and west Africa, the trans-Sahara trade in west Africa, and the ivory trade in east and central Africa led to major political changes in African societies. The fur trade in North America led to major intertribal warfare, the development of ideas of property, and the emergence of a stratified social system based on differential possession of or access to furs. The introduction of the horse to the Great Plains of North America changed the way of life of many tribes who then bordered the region. In each case the culture and society that anthropologists assumed were static and stable and from which one could measure or describe change were in themselves changing because of outside influences (Ewers 1955; Leacock 1954; Jones 1963; Dike 1956).

The passage of the Indian Claims Act in 1946 by Congress led to a marked rise in ethnohistorical research in the United States. Under the provisions of this act Indian tribes could sue the federal government for recompense for lands taken from them after the Indians had signed treaties protecting their rights. Anthropologists were employed as experts by both Indian tribes and the government, to establish location, extent, and nature of aboriginal control over various territories and the exact nature of treaty obligations. This drew the attention of many ethnographers, who previously had paid little heed to the extensive archival resources of the federal government and the various states in their study of the American Indian. *Ethnohistory,* the principal journal in the field, was founded in 1954 partly to provide an outlet for materials and interest developed by the Indian claims cases.

The expansion of field-work opportunities in Latin America and Asia and the emergence of many states from colonial rule has been a tremendous stimulus to ethnohistorical work since the end of World War II. In many of these areas there are long literary traditions and a wealth of documentary material. In Latin America, for example, certain areas have been covered in historical sources for a four-hundred-year period (for a brief review of the literature, see Adams 1962; Armillas 1960; Gibson 1955). In east and southeast Asia there have been important ethnohistorical studies of kinship and clan structure (Freedman 1958; R. J. Smith 1962), land tenure (T. C. Smith 1959), the recruitment and training of indigenous bureaucracies (Ho 1962; Marsh 1961; Silberman 1964), urban social history and mobility (R. J. Smith 1963), immigrant communities (Skinner 1957), and indigenous political systems (Gullick 1958). Ethnohistorical studies of south Asia and the Middle East are beginning to appear (Cohn 1962*a*; 1962*b*; Polk 1963).

In European studies there has been a long tradition in the study of classical, medieval, and early modern society, enlightened by sociological and anthropological method and concepts. Most of this work has been carried out by social, economic, and legal historians rather than by anthropologists themselves. The ethnohistorical study of classical society has attracted considerable attention (Kluck-hohn 1961). M. I. Finley, on the basis of the *Odyssey,* has written an essay on the culture and social structure of the Greeks of the heroic era; in this he consciously used the ideas of Malinowski, Mauss, and Radcliffe-Brown (Finley 1954). E. R. Dodds, in his analysis of Greek literature, has drawn on some of the concepts of psychoanalytically oriented anthropology (1951). Marc Bloch's great works on feudal society (1939–1940) and the rural structure of medieval France (1931) illustrate the possibilities of an ethnohistory of medieval Europe.

The writing of British social history from the time of Maitland (1897) and Vinogradoff (1905) has been marked by the conscious and unconscious use of social anthropology. Modern subjects that have received sophisticated ethnohistorical treatment include the blood feud of the Franks (Wallace-Hadrill 1959), Anglo-Saxon kinship (Lancaster 1958), and marriage systems of the early modern period (Stone 1965, pp. 589–671; Habakkuk 1950). Although social anthropologists have done considerable field work in European peasant societies, few examples of systematic and careful ethnohistorical work have appeared. An exception is the work of Lawrence Wylie, a student of French literature and civilization, who on the basis of field work among French peasants has been able to show the usefulness of oral traditions and documents for studying the changing value systems of a peasant village (Wylie 1965).

In areas without long written traditions, careful and important ethnohistorical work has begun. The *Journal of African History,* founded in 1960, demonstrates the utilization of official records, recorded African traditions, and Arabic and Coptic materials. The institutional history of the Maori from the eighteenth century is being written (Vayda 1961; Biggs 1960). The *Journal of Pacific History* was recently established as an outlet for the growing ethnohistorical research on the Pacific area.

Sources and methods

Written documents. In his use of written documents, the ethnohistorian initially has the same problem and uses the same techniques as conventional historians. The ethnohistorian who has been trained as an anthropologist and has carried out field work is often highly frustrated when he has to depend on documents. The research problems of the ethnohistorian usually pertain to local history or "subhistorical" problems. He is not concerned with major, well-documented events, which a political historian deals with; very often he wants to know the minutiae of the past, e.g., the kinship connections of shadowy historical figures in an indigenous society, the movement and location of particular lineages at particular times, the symbolic meanings of a coronation ceremony in an African kingdom, the population of an American Indian group in the seventeenth century.

Often it is difficult to identify adequately the individuals and groups the ethnohistorian is concerned with. As an anthropologist, he expects to build inductively, from disparate bits of information, a picture of a functioning system; but he cannot generate his own data by asking people questions and observing their behavior in the context of living experiences. The documents he deals with are rarely written by the people whose social structure or culture he wants to study but are accounts by observers, naïve and biased, who often only half understood what they were recording. If he uses administrative records, not only must he know, as a good historian, who wrote the minutes or the statements of decisions taken and why they wrote them; he must place the data in a broader context of administrative policy. Certain official records, such as tax records, land surveys, and documents from actual legal proceedings, as distinguished from decisions and policies, frequently yield the best data. These materials are less finely filtered through the cultural screen of the administrators. The ethnohistorian must constantly try to understand the categories of the administrator and outside observer, as well as the indigenous classification systems. The interpretation of official or nonofficial documents, of policy statements and other primary data, requires an understanding of the culture and society of colonial administrators. This in itself is difficult, for the gross features of the metropolitan society may be misleading. The ethnohistorian has to know what particular group in the society the administrator came from, whether his values, education, and social and political philosophy differed from the rest of the society, and if so, how. The ethnohistorian must understand the structure of the colonial administration and know the partisanship of the men responsible for the documents he studies. He must understand the relationships between the decision makers in the metropolitan center, the administrators in the colonial center, and the men in the field. He has to know how administrators collected data and information and whom they dealt with and employed from the indigenous society. He must perceive which notions developed about the indigenous society were mistaken, how they affected decisions and observations, and how decisions which may have been based on such misinformation affected the indigenous society. The ethnohistorian's task is to use conventional historical methods but to ask different questions and to keep in mind his concern with the indigenous society (Curtin 1964).

There are, for almost every region, extensive published collections of source material; for example, Thwaites's 73-volume series (Jesuits Letters From Missions 1896–1901) for North America, the collections of Theal (1883) and Brásio (1952–1960) for southeast Africa, and parliamentary papers of Great Britain for India and Africa. The main resources, however, are to be found in the national and regional archives and local administrative and record offices of the area being studied.

In areas such as Uganda, the emirates of northern Nigeria, and the Malay States, where Europeans ruled indirectly and tried to maintain the indigenous political system, documents were produced by members of the society themselves. Political and social development can be traced through the eyes of some of the indigenous peoples.

Oral traditions. In recent years, particularly in the study of the history of African societies, the ethnohistorian and the anthropologist with a historical interest, have demonstrated convincingly how oral tradition can be recorded, collated, checked, and utilized for historical purposes (Abraham 1961; Vansina 1961; M. G. Smith 1961). Oral traditions cover a wide variety of subject matter and can be found in a variety of forms. Societies with centralized political institutions and conquest states have often produced well-developed oral histories, and frequently there are specialists whose concern it is to memorize and transmit these traditions. In the use of this form of oral tradition, great caution is obviously necessary, since the history reflects as much about present social and political structure as it does about the past and is constantly being changed to account for changing situations (Barnes 1951; Cunnison 1951).

Oral history reflects the social units within the society; villages and lineages will have accounts of their past, which perform the specific function of relating groups to each other and which validate or correct local claims and support relationships. The ethnohistorian is often confronted with an extraordinary multiplicity of conflicting accounts of the past, even from the same village (Cohn 1961). Tribal segments, royal lineages, and courts may have well-preserved histories, which function as charters to justify contemporary social structure.

As Vansina (1961) demonstrates, historical narratives are not the only aspect of oral tradition that can be recorded, collated, and utilized; sacred formulas, names, poetry, genealogies, folk tales, myths, and legal precedents are useful to the ethnohistorian. In the interpretation of oral tradition, stress must first be put on the cultural context in which the tradition is found. Vansina defines oral tradition as "testimonies of the past which are deliberately transmitted from mouth to mouth." As he does in the case of written documents, the researcher must always ask what function the tradition performs in the contemporary society. Even material which is demonstrably false can be of great value, as it might incidentally contain historical facts.

Where outsiders have been recording indigenous oral traditions for a long time (as, for example, among the Maori), the relationship between the oral tradition and contemporary political structure can be used to understand not only the past referred to in the tradition but the actual political situation existing at the time the tradition was recorded.

Field work.   Field work is essential to the work of the ethnohistorian. The basic anthropological orientation, which differentiates the ethnohistorian from the conventional colonial historian, is developed through the experience of systematic field observation and the collection of data from living people; the aim of field work is to present a description and analysis of a functioning social system.

Field work, then, is a major part of the ethnohistorian's training; through field work he develops a sensitivity to the structure of a society that is difficult to achieve from study of documentary evidence alone. Ideas relating to historical relationships and processes may actually be tested in the field, where aspects of the society and culture are still in operation. [See FIELD WORK.]

Ethnohistory and anthropology

Thus far diachronic studies have not yielded theoretical formulations. While synchronic studies are useful in enabling the ethnohistorian to infer social processes from documentary evidence, the contribution that diachronic studies will make to theory building or even to the development of descriptive generalizations regarding society and culture is harder to demonstrate. Even in the most rigid synchronic ethnographic study, the ethnographer must deal with the dimension of time. At the very least, he is dealing with three generations and with individuals whose lives have covered a sixty-year period. Invariably the field ethnographer asks questions about the past; he must confront the question of norms and changing norms, accidental social arrangements, and enduring aspects of the social structure.

Through historical study the anthropologist may identify changes within the system which are the result of flux, accident, or cyclical sequences and those which are due to structural realignments. Nadel and others have argued that to know the direction of social structural change, one needs time depth (Nadel 1957, chapter 6; Lévi-Strauss 1949). Thus, for example, careful statistical study frequently shows that there are in some, if not all, societies degrees of latitude or freedom in an individual's choice of residence, whether it be virilocal or uxorilocal, and these choices may be related to other variables. Synchronic studies may account for these relationships, but if we want to account for change, then historical methods for studying a society—primitive, peasant, or industrial—are the prerequisite for the development of adequate theories (Evans-Pritchard 1961; M. G. Smith 1962; Thomas 1963).

Historians and anthropologists

The development of nineteenth-century "scientific history"—the study of the past divorced from the values and passions of the historian's times, the idea that historical facts could be determined and, if chronologically ordered, would speak for themselves—has led, with some notable exceptions, to the historian's consciously eschewing concepts and generalizations that might guide and illuminate his description and analysis of the past. In the twentieth century, though, historians have become increasingly aware that they do use and have to use generalizations if they are to do more than edit texts. H. Stuart Hughes (1960, pp. 25–26) has pointed to at least four levels at which historians generalize. First, they generalize semantically; by using words, such as "nation," "revolution," "development," "trend," and "social class," historians implicitly abstract, generalize, and compare. Second, "conclusions" in the form of a grouping of statements about a man, a period, or a movement are generalizations. Third, schematizations, inherent in such ideas as "urbanization" and "industrialization," by which bits and pieces of historical study are organized in terms of process or structure, are generalizations and are close to the kinds of generalizations social scientists make. Finally, there are the broad, all-inclusive systematizations of history or metahistory, associated with the work of men like Spengler and Toynbee. It is at this fourth level, that is, in the conscious use of concepts regarding process and structure in society and culture, that the social scientist and the historian can best interrelate their study. If the characteristic activity of the historian is the study of the past and if his organizing principle is a time sequence, then he must borrow organizing principles from other disciplines, both the humanities and the social sciences. In major subfields of history, this process of borrowing is explicit, for example, in economic history, where the concepts and methods of economics are consciously used to provide the conceptual framework. Intellectual and social history have borrowed from psychology, sociology, and anthropology.

In the last thirty years there have been several efforts to utilize the anthropologist's approach in the study of history; the anthropology which has proven most congenial to historians is cultural anthropology. The concept of culture as an all-embracing idea covering behavior and values of a particular people at a particular time fits well with historians' predilections. Hughes puts it well when he says: ". . . the approach of the cultural anthropologist so closely resembles that of the historian as frequently to seem identical with it. Like the historical scholar, the student of exotic cultures adopts a highly permissive attitude towards his data; he is perfectly happy in the realm of imprecision and of 'intuitive' procedures; and he tries to grapple with what he regards as the central problems of the societies with which he is concerned" (Hughes 1960, p. 34; see also Ware 1940; Social Science Research Council 1954; Gottschalk 1963). Books such as Ruth Benedict's *Patterns of Culture* (1934) and attempts on the part of anthropologists to do national character studies are taken by historians as models (for example, see Potter 1954) because the approach, rather than the techniques, methods, and concepts, of the cultural anthropologist is useful to historians. With notable exceptions, such as Marc Bloch, historians have not been eager to combine field work with historical research to find still extant in societies traces of previous industrial and agricultural techniques or surviving forms of social organization [*see the biography of* BLOCH].

It is, however, in the study of the preindustrial and modernizing societies of today and of the historical societies that characterized the whole world before the beginning of the nineteenth century that the anthropologist and the historian would appear to need each other.

BERNARD S. COHN

[*See also* ARCHEOLOGY; ETHNOLOGY; HISTORIOGRAPHY.]

BIBLIOGRAPHY

ABRAHAM, D. P. 1961 Maramuca: An Exercise in the Combined Use of Portuguese Records and Oral Tradition. *Journal of African History* 2:211–225.

ADAMS, RICHARD N. 1962 Ethnohistoric Research Methods: Some Latin American Features. *Ethnohistory* 9:179–205.

ARMILLAS, PEDRO 1960 *Program of the History of American Indians.* Part 2: Post Columbian America. Social Science Monographs, No. 8. Washington: Pan American Union, Department of Cultural Affairs, Social Science Section.

BARNES, J. A. (1951) 1961 History in a Changing Society. Pages 318–327 in Simon Ottenberg and Phoebe Ottenberg (editors), *Cultures and Societies of Africa.* New York: Random House.

BELSHAW, CYRIL S. 1957 The Changing Cultures of Oceanic Peoples During the Nineteenth Century. *Journal of World History* 3:647–664.

BENEDICT, RUTH 1934 *Patterns of Culture.* Boston: Houghton Mifflin. → A paperback edition was published in 1961.

BIGGS, BRUCE 1960 *Maori Marriage: An Essay in Reconstruction.* Polynesian Society Maori Monographs, No. 1. Wellington: The Society.

BLOCH, MARC (1931) 1952–1956 *Les caractères originaux de l'histoire rurale française.* 2 vols. New ed. Paris: Colin. → Volume 2, *Supplément établi d'après les travaux de l'auteur (1931–1944)*, was written by Robert Dauvergne.

BLOCH, MARC (1939–1940) 1961 *Feudal Society.* Univ. of Chicago Press. → First published as *La société féodale: La formation des liens de dépendance* and *La société féodale: Les classes et le gouvernement des hommes.*

BRÁSIO, ANTÓNIO D. (editor) 1952–1965 *Monumenta missionaria africana: Africa ocidental.* 10 vols. Lisbon: Agência Geral do Ultramar, Divisão de Publicações e Biblioteca.

COHN, BERNARD S. 1961 The Pasts of an Indian Village. *Comparative Studies in Society and History* 3:241–250.

COHN, BERNARD S. 1962a The British in Benares: A Nineteenth Century Colonial Society. *Comparative Studies in Society and History* 4:169–199.

COHN, BERNARD S. 1962b Political Systems in Eighteenth Century India: The Banaras Region. *Journal of the American Oriental Society* 82:312–320.

CUNNISON, IAN 1951 *History of the Luapula: An Essay on the Historical Notions of a Central African Tribe.* Rhodes–Livingstone Papers, No. 21. Oxford Univ. Press.

CURTIN, PHILIP D. 1964 *The Image of Africa: British Ideas and Action, 1780–1850.* Madison: Univ. of Wisconsin Press.

DIKE, KENNETH O. (1956) 1962 *Trade and Politics in the Niger Delta, 1830–1885: An Introduction to the Economic and Political History of Nigeria.* Oxford: Clarendon.

DODDS, ERIC R. (1951) 1963 *The Greeks and the Irrational.* Berkeley: Univ. of California Press.

EGGAN, FRED 1937 Historical Changes in the Choctaw Kinship System. *American Anthropologist* New Series 39:34–52.

EVANS-PRITCHARD, E. E. (1949) 1954 *The Sanusi of Cyrenaica.* Oxford: Clarendon.

EVANS-PRITCHARD, E. E. (1961) 1963 Anthropology and History. Pages 46–65 in E. E. Evans-Pritchard, *Essays in Social Anthropology.* New York: Free Press. → A lecture delivered at the University of Manchester in 1961.

EWERS, JOHN C. 1955 *The Horse in Blackfoot Culture: With Comparative Material From Other Western*

Tribes. U.S. Bureau of American Ethnology, Bulletin No. 159. Washington: Smithsonian Institution.

FENTON, WILLIAM N. 1940 Problems Arising From the Historic Northeastern Position of the Iroquois. Pages 159–251 in Smithsonian Institution, *Essays in Historical Anthropology of North America in Honor of John R. Swanton.* Smithsonian Miscellaneous Collections, Vol. 100. Washington: The Institution.

FENTON, WILLIAM N. 1951 Locality as a Basic Factor in the Development of Iroquois Social Structure. Pages 35–54 in *Symposium on Local Diversity in Iroquois Culture.* U.S. Bureau of American Ethnology, Bulletin No. 149. Washington: Government Printing Office.

FENTON, WILLIAM N. 1961 Iroquoian Culture History: A General Evaluation. Pages 253–277 in *Symposium on Cherokee and Iroquois Culture.* U.S. Bureau of American Ethnology, Bulletin No. 180. Washington: Government Printing Office.

FINLEY, MOSES I. (1954) 1956 *The World of Odysseus.* Rev. ed. London: Chatto & Windus.

FREEDMAN, MAURICE (1958) 1965 *Lineage Organization in Southeastern China.* London School of Economics Monographs on Social Anthropology, No. 18. New York: Humanities.

GIBSON, CHARLES 1955 The Transformation of the Indian Community in New Spain. *Journal of World History* 2:581–607.

GIBSON, CHARLES 1964 *The Aztecs Under Spanish Rule: A History of the Indians of the Valley of Mexico, 1519–1810.* Stanford Univ. Press.

GLUCKMAN, MAX 1940 The Kingdom of the Zulu of South Africa. Pages 25–55 in Meyer Fortes and E. E. Evans-Pritchard (editors), *African Political Systems.* Oxford Univ. Press.

GOTTSCHALK, LOUIS R. (editor) 1963 *Generalization in the Writing of History.* Univ. of Chicago Press.

GULLICK, J. M. 1958 *Indigenous Political Systems of Western Malaya.* London School of Economics Monographs on Social Anthropology, No. 17. London: Athlone.

HABAKKUK, H. J. 1950 Marriage Settlements in the Eighteenth Century. Royal Historical Society, *Transactions* Fourth Series 32:15–30.

HO, PING-TI 1962 *The Ladder of Success in Imperial China: Aspects of Social Mobility, 1368–1911.* New York: Columbia Univ. Press.

HOMANS, GEORGE C. (1941) 1960 *English Villagers of the Thirteenth Century.* New York: Russell.

HUGHES, H. STUART 1960 The Historian and the Social Scientist. *American Historical Review* 66:20–46.

JESUITS, LETTERS FROM MISSIONS (NORTH AMERICA) (1896–1901) 1959 *The Jesuit Relations and Allied Documents: Travels and Explorations of the Jesuit Missionaries in New France, 1610–1791. . . .* 73 vols. Edited by Reuben G. Thwaites. New York: Pageant.

JONES, G. I. 1963 *The Trading States of the Oil Rivers: A Study of Political Development in Eastern Nigeria.* Oxford Univ. Press.

KLUCKHOHN, CLYDE 1961 *Anthropology and the Classics.* Providence, R.I.: Brown Univ. Press.

KROEBER, A. L. (1901–1951) 1952 *The Nature of Culture.* Univ. of Chicago Press. → See especially pages 63–65 on "History and Science in Anthropology."

LANCASTER, LORRAINE 1958 Kinship in Anglo-Saxon Society. Parts 1 and 2. *British Journal of Sociology* 9:230–250, 359–377.

LEACOCK, ELEANOR 1954 The Montagnais "Hunting Territory" and the Fur Trade. American Anthropological Association, *Memoir* No. 78.

LÉVI-STRAUSS, CLAUDE (1949) 1963 Introduction: History and Anthropology. Pages 1–27 in Claude Lévi-Strauss, *Structural Anthropology.* New York: Basic Books. → First published in French.

LOWIE, ROBERT H. (1917) 1960 Oral Tradition and History. Pages 202–210 in Robert H. Lowie, *Selected Papers in Anthropology.* Edited by Cora DuBois. Berkeley: Univ. of California Press.

MAIR, LUCY P. (1934) 1965 *An African People in the Twentieth Century.* New York: Russell.

MAITLAND, FREDERIC W. 1897 *Domesday Book and Beyond.* Cambridge Univ. Press.

MARSH, ROBERT M. 1961 *The Mandarins: The Circulation of Elites in China, 1600–1900.* New York: Free Press.

MORGAN, LEWIS HENRY 1871 *Systems of Consanguinity and Affinity of the Human Family.* Smithsonian Contributions to Knowledge, Vol. 17, Publication No. 218. Washington: Smithsonian Institution.

NADEL, SIEGFRIED F. 1942 *A Black Byzantium: The Kingdom of Nupe in Nigeria.* Published for the International Institute of African Languages and Cultures. Oxford Univ. Press.

NADEL, SIEGFRIED F. 1957 *The Theory of Social Structure.* London: Cohen & West; Glencoe, Ill.: Free Press. → Published posthumously.

OLIVER, DOUGLAS L. (1951) 1961 *The Pacific Islands.* Rev. ed. Garden City, N.Y.: Doubleday.

POLK, WILLIAM R. 1963 *The Opening of South Lebanon: 1788–1840.* Cambridge, Mass.: Harvard Univ. Press.

POTTER, DAVID M. (1954) 1963 *People of Plenty: Economic Abundance and the American Character.* Univ. of Chicago Press.

ROWE, JOHN H. (1946) 1963 Inca Culture at the Time of the Spanish Conquest. Pages 183–330 in Julian H. Steward (editor), *Handbook of South American Indians.* Volume 2: *The Andean Civilizations.* U.S. Bureau of American Ethnology, Bulletin No. 143. New York: Cooper Square.

SAPIR, EDWARD (1916) 1949 Time Perspective in Aboriginal American Culture: A Study in Method. Pages 389–462 in Edward Sapir, *Selected Writings . . . in Language, Culture and Personality.* Edited by D. Mandelbaum. Berkeley: Univ. of California Press.

SILBERMAN, BERNARD S. 1964 *Ministers of Modernization: Elite Mobility in the Meiji Restoration, 1868–1873.* Tucson: Univ. of Arizona Press.

SKINNER, GEORGE W. 1957 *Chinese Society in Thailand.* Ithaca, N.Y.: Cornell Univ. Press.

SMITH, MICHAEL G. 1960 *Government in Zazzau: 1800–1950.* Oxford Univ. Press.

SMITH, MICHAEL G. 1961 Field Histories Among the Hausa. *Journal of African History* 2:87–101.

SMITH, MICHAEL G. 1962 History and Social Anthropology. *Journal of the Royal Anthropological Institute of Great Britain and Ireland* 92:73–85.

SMITH, ROBERT J. 1962 Stability in Japanese Kinship Terminology: The Historical Evidence. Pages 25–33 in Pacific Science Congress, Tenth, Honolulu, 1961, *Japanese Culture: Its Development and Characteristics.* Edited by Robert J. Smith and Richard K. Beardsley. Chicago: Aldine.

SMITH, ROBERT J. 1963 Aspects of Mobility in Pre-industrial Japanese Cities. *Comparative Studies in Society and History* 5:416–423.

SMITH, THOMAS C. 1959 *The Agrarian Origins of Modern Japan.* Stanford Univ. Press.

SMITHSONIAN INSTITUTION 1940 *Essays in Historical Anthropology of North America in Honor of John R. Swanton.* Smithsonian Miscellaneous Collections, Vol. 100. Washington: The Institution.

SOCIAL SCIENCE RESEARCH COUNCIL, COMMITTEE ON HISTORIOGRAPHY 1954 *The Social Sciences in Historical Study: A Report.* Social Science Research Council, Bulletin No. 64. New York: The Council.

SPECK, FRANK G. 1928 *Territorial Subdivisions and Boundaries of the Wampanoag, Massachusetts and Nauset Indians.* Indian Notes and Monographs, No. 44. New York: Museum of the American Indian, Heye Foundation.

SPICER, EDWARD H. 1962 *Cycles of Conquest.* Tucson: Univ. of Arizona Press.

STEWARD, JULIAN H. 1940 Native Cultures of the Intermontane (Great Basin) Area. Pages 445–502 in Smithsonian Institution, *Essays in Historical Anthropology of North America in Honor of John R. Swanton.* Smithsonian Miscellaneous Collections, Vol. 100. Washington: The Institution.

STONE, LAWRENCE 1965 *The Crisis of the Aristocracy: 1558–1641.* Oxford: Clarendon.

STRONG, WILLIAM D. 1940 From History to Prehistory in the Northern Great Plains. Pages 353–394 in Smithsonian Institution, *Essays in Historical Anthropology of North America in Honor of John R. Swanton.* Smithsonian Miscellaneous Collections, Vol. 100. Washington: The Institution.

SWANTON, JOHN REED 1922 *Early History of the Creek Indians and Their Neighbors.* Smithsonian Institution, Bureau of American Ethnology, Bulletin No. 73. Washington: Government Printing Office.

SWANTON, JOHN REED 1946 *The Indians of the Southeastern United States.* Smithsonian Institution, Bureau of American Ethnology, Bulletin No. 137. Washington: Government Printing Office.

SWANTON, JOHN REED; and DIXON, ROLAND B. 1914 Primitive American History. *American Anthropologist* New Series 16:376–412.

Symposium on the Concept of Ethnohistory. 1961 *Ethnohistory* 8:12–92.

THEAL, GEORGE McC. (editor) (1883) 1964 *Basutoland Records.* Capetown: Struik.

THOMAS, KEITH 1963 History and Anthropology. *Past and Present* 24:3–24.

VANSINA, JAN (1961) 1964 *The Oral Tradition: A Study in Historical Methodology.* Chicago: Aldine. → First published in French.

VAYDA, ANDREW P. 1961 *Maori Warfare.* Maori Monographs, No. 2. Wellington: Polynesian Society.

VINOGRADOFF, PAUL (1905) 1920 *The Growth of the Manor.* 3d ed. New York: Macmillan.

WALLACE-HADRILL, J. M. 1959 The Bloodfeud of the Franks. John Rylands Library, *Bulletin* 41:459–487.

WARE, CAROLINE F. (editor) (1940) 1965 *The Cultural Approach to History.* Port Washington, N.Y.: Kennikat.

WILSON, MONICA [Hunter] (1936) 1961 *Reaction to Conquest: Effects of Contact With Europeans on the Pondo of South Africa.* 2d ed. Oxford Univ. Press. → The first edition was published under the author's maiden name.

WYLIE, LAURENCE 1965 The Life and Death of a Myth. Pages 164–185 in Melford E. Spiro (editor), *Context and Meaning in Cultural Anthropology.* New York: Free Press.

IV
CULTURE HISTORY

Culture history is the subdivision of general history that is concerned with the historical development of nonliterate peoples, present and past. It is almost always practiced by cultural anthropologists, if we include under this designation such specialists as archeologists and anthropological linguists. This definition implies that there is no real difference in principle between the history of the professional historian and the culture historian. Sometimes an attempt is made to distinguish between the two by contrasting the use of written documentary sources as the chief or only kind of evidence admitted by the historian proper with the variety of other, more conjectural methods used by the student of nonliterate cultures. This point of view has occasionally been taken either by historians who wished to resist extension of the field of history through these methods or by "schools" of anthropologists, such as the earlier social functionalists, who admitted the value of "genuine" history based on documentary evidence, while rejecting the "conjectural" culture history of historically minded anthropologists.

It is clear, however, that such a distinction cannot be maintained on principle. As noted in standard handbooks of historiography, the task of historical investigation involves the use of all types of evidence regarding the past. Thus E. Bernheim ([1905] 1926, p. 62) states that all peoples can be subject to historical investigation and that the principles of historical investigation are everywhere the same but that differences in the nature of the evidence require specialized knowledge and training. Thus, ". . . it is in the interest of a scientific division of labor to assign the history of primitives and prehistoric peoples to the ethnologist and archeologist." Besides, even where documentary evidence exists in abundance, as it does from the ancient classical world, nondocumentary techniques, such as archeology and comparative linguistics, have made essential contributions and are used by professional historians. On the other hand, anthropologists have come to realize that they are by no means limited to nondocumentary methods. For many parts of the world there are frequently historical documents that may shed valuable light on cultural changes undergone during the centuries between first contact with the West and professional anthropological field study. In some instances, there may even be indigenous historical records neglected by the historians because the area is outside of the normal purview of their interests. This was the case, for example, with the Islamized peoples of the Sudan.

The aim, then, of culture history, is in no essential respect different from that of conventional history, particularly when the latter is viewed in its most general aspect as not merely political history but as history of all aspects of culture. It may be added that for his primary goal, the understanding of cultural development, the culture historian will need certain noncultural data, such as environmental changes, human racial differentiation as the result of isolating mechanisms paralleling ethnic differentiation, and inferences concerning ancient demographic factors. The differences between culture history and conventional history is then one of degree rather than kind. Since he necessarily relies to a greater extent on nondocumentary sources, the culture historian will be concerned with groups and not individual actors, and the time scale will often be relative rather than absolute. However, with the development of radioactive and other methods of absolute dating, even this latter difference tends to be effaced.

General methodology

All historical investigations proceed by inferences, often very complex, from evidence existing in the present. The relation between the evidence itself and the fact of which it is a trace is of two main logical types: cause and effect, as when an artifact is taken as evidence for the human activity that produces it, or symbol and referent, as in verbal accounts (whether written or oral) in which the evidence is a description of the fact. Traces differ, as will be seen later, in still other respects. Particularly in culture history, where documentary evidence is usually minimal or lacking, the general strategy of the historical enterprise is based on the circumstance that the same event may leave multiple traces, each of which provides independent evidence for the fact.

For example, if at some time in the past one people has borrowed the cultivation of a food plant from another, it will have taken over the genetic varieties utilized by the donors and the same or similar methods of cultivation. They may have borrowed the word for the plant itself or other terminology connected with its cultivation. These aspects are independent, in that some might have been present in the original event without the others and since their present outcomes are distinct, e.g., the genetic plant varieties now utilized, the observable agricultural methods, and one or more words in the present language. Each of these evidences may be said to belong to a different

system, because for its interpretation we must put it into a context of different facts. Thus the data concerning a particular genetic variety of plant are significant in the light of the totality of varieties, their geographical distribution, and the reconstructed genetic history of the species itself in relation to the wild ancestral form. The agricultural methods are part of an ethnologic distribution. The linguistic terminology is part of a language and must be evaluated in terms of appearance or nonappearance in related languages deriving from a linguistic classification itself based on linguistic evidence.

Each of these traces, then, is interpreted in terms of the system to which it belongs. Although the details of method differ for each system, they all have in common the important characteristics of being comparative and involving assumptions regarding diachronic processes.

It has sometimes been felt that certain types of historical inferences involve a comparative method, for example, those based on language or ethnological trait distributions, while archeological artifacts or documents give direct testimony concerning the facts for which they are evidence. There is at best, again, merely a difference of degree of complexity and not of kind. An archeological implement must be compared with other implements with regard to form, function, place, and time before it can be assigned any historical meaning. This is true for written documents, as we are reminded emphatically by the historians Langlois and Seignobos, who state that a document "in respect of which we necessarily are in total ignorance of the author, the place, and the date is good for nothing" ([1898] 1925, p. 87).

Another fundamental set of considerations involved in the construction of such interpretive systems refers to process. By a process is meant a class of similar changes. To draw an example from textual analysis, if the same word appears twice within a few lines of a manuscript that is being copied, a scribe, in looking back through the manuscript, will sometimes mistake the second occurrence for the first and so eliminate the intervening material. Such an error is called haplology and may be called a process. Since manuscripts of all periods, places, and languages are subject to haplological change, like other such processes it may be considered as a class in abstraction from its specific temporal and spatial loci. If two manuscripts share the same haplologies along with other specific changes, one may conclude that they have both been copied from the same version and thus do not furnish independent evidence regarding the original text. By such reasoning, manuscripts may be arranged in a genealogy and their comparative study can lead to the reconstruction of the lost original. In reasoning by means of process, such factors as the frequency with which instances are likely to occur, whether two identical instances will tend to occur independently, and the length of time required for their occurrence are all among the fundamental considerations. For example, another process in manuscript transmission is the interpolation of marginal explanatory glosses into the body of the text. Obviously, it is more likely that a particular haplological error will occur twice independently than that an interpolation involving precisely the same words will occur at all.

Human activities are not the only processes relevant to cultural-historical reconstruction. For example, the patination due to the weathering of artifacts is a process of change and allows us to draw very approximate conclusions regarding age. The point here is that the historical conclusions to which we are led by particular existing evidence is dependent on our assumptions about the processes of change it has undergone since the time it came into existence.

Specific methods

A number of the independent methods mentioned earlier may now be considered in greater detail.

Verbal evidence. All verbal evidence has as its source linguistically formulated descriptions by observers of the original event or events. Whether this primary source is oral or written in its first form makes little or no difference; it is subject to the same possibilities of error through observer bias, inaccuracy, or prevarication. The differences between written and oral sources stem from the mode of subsequent transmission. The advantage of writing is that, because of its semipermanence, it will go through fewer reproductions and will be less changed in the course of such reproductions. Since it will thus be closer to the original report, it will be easier to reconstruct the exact verbal form of the report. The form in which the historian encounters the report is not in itself decisive. Thus, literary sources often contain accounts written down at some time from oral tradition, so that the report has been transmitted orally during the earlier part of its career and in writing later on. The opposite also occurs when literary formulations become the subject of folkloristic transmission.

The critical use of written documents, the chief source of the historian's history, falls under the methodology of history proper and is thus only briefly discussed in the present connection. It is relevant, however, to point out that the culture historian's written documentation is most frequently that of the outside observer, such as the explorer or missionary, rather than the participant. It is therefore subject to errors based rather on the outsider's inability to comprehend the cultural frame of reference of the actors than on bias. Therefore, the inaccuracies are characteristically of a different kind from those of the internally placed participant. Thus, contrary to the latter, the outside observer will not tend to conceal military defeats or the historical illegitimacy of the power exercised by a ruling dynasty.

Anthropologists take as their point of departure the notion of primitive peoples as peoples without written history; but beginning about 1950 it became apparent that the extent and the value of both external and, in certain cases (e.g., west Africa), internal documentary sources had been seriously underestimated. The Indian land claims cases in the United States also led to much documentary research into land occupation and use patterns of the aboriginal period. Such interests led to the development of ethnohistory as a subdiscipline of anthropology [see HISTORY, *article on* ETHNOHISTORY].

The other chief source of verbal reports is oral tradition, which includes not only orally transmitted narrative history but other kinds of spoken material containing historical information, e.g., proverbs and epic poetry. This source is perhaps the most controversial. Thus, G. P. Murdock (1959) discounts it as altogether unreliable, while J. Vansina (1961) makes it the very keystone for his reconstruction of the history of a number of African peoples. As Vansina has pointed out, oral tradition must be used critically, and, indeed, it requires a methodology very similar in principle to that required for the study of documentary sources. More perhaps than any other source, it has been employed uncritically in the past. Oral traditions have been published without indication of the individual, place, or date from which they derive, of facts, if any, regarding the manner of their earlier transmission, and without variant versions. As for manuscripts, it is possible to develop a genealogy of lines of independent transmission and reconstruct the archetype or original version, a method similar in basic respects to that developed by the Finnish school of folklorists for oral literature in general. The time depth and chronological precision of oral traditions are necessarily limited, but within these limitations they can give important and reliable information when treated critically.

Archeology. Among the remaining research methods, which have in common the reasoning from trace as effect to historical cause, archeology is to be distinguished from the rest in that it deals with material objects as evidences of cultural activities of the period in which they were produced rather than with existing cultural phenomena viewed as developments from, and hence evidences for, earlier cultural traits. Thus, subsequent modifications of form, if any, are normally the result of natural forces independent of man. The strength of archeology is the reliability and concreteness of its evidence and the definiteness of its spatial attribution. Its necessary limitations stem from the fact that it is confined to material culture and deductions that can be made therefrom. The set of artifacts found at a particular site and stratigraphic level, sometimes called a *component*, is taken as the material expression of the life of a local community. Often very similar assemblages are found over a continuous area with indications that they all date from roughly the same chronological period. Such a unit, often called a *phase*, may be conjectured to represent some sociocultural unit, such as a tribe. The interpretation of archeological evidences regarding a phase has both cultural and social aspects. From settlement patterns, density of remains, the functions of the artifacts themselves, and evidences regarding contemporary climate, fauna, and flora, the attempt is made to reconstruct the basic technologic and demographic patterns with whatever further, usually less certain, inference can be made regarding other aspects of culture, such as social structure or religion. There has also been an attempt to identify and determine the geographic boundaries of ethnic groups. Contemporary evidence shows that such conclusions are subject to a considerable margin of error, since, on occasion, ethnic groups with highly similar material cultures may differ fundamentally in language and other cultural aspects and constitute politically independent groupings.

The second fundamental aim of archeology is to reconstruct the time–space relationships of the sociocultural entities inferred from material remains. The basic problem is, of course, chronological rather than spatial. Relative dating methods include the stratificational (when in the same site more recent material is superimposed on more ancient), estimates of length of occupation from the nature of the deposits, inferences regarding the rough contemporaneity of sites with similar material, cross-dating from traded objects whose date and provenience is known from documentary sources, and geochronology. Where other methods fail, the evolutionary assumption that simpler types precede more developed has been utilized. Such conclusions are most plausible where we are dealing with mechanical inventions that presuppose other less complex devices that enter into them or where a more efficient device requires the development of some specific and recondite skill, e.g., smelting metal as compared with the utilization of stone. In recent years the development of methods of radioactive dating, such as carbon-14, has revolutionized archeology by providing absolute dates.

Beyond the placing of archeological units in space or time, there are inferences regarding the historical relationship of particular cultural traits, complexes, or cultures as a whole. With the prerequisite of space–time continuity established or reasonably to be conjectured, cultural similarities are interpreted as resulting from such historical processes as geographic migration of a people or by diffusion, in which the traits are borrowed through contact with a neighboring people. Such integral spread or adoption of cultural features is often called genetic. Sometimes however the connection is not genetic, although historical. For example, trade objects may be distributed along recognizable trade routes, which indicate cultural connections, although the objects themselves are not actually produced in all of the sites in which they are found. There are of course cultural resemblances that are nonhistorical in origin and are the result of independent parallel developments. What is to be assumed a similarity will, of course, depend on the definitional criteria adopted. Under more general criteria things will be considered similar that are rejected under narrower criteria. The disputed cases are characteristically those that combine generality of criteria with absence of well-proved space–time continuity, e.g., Egyptian and Mayan pyramids.

A further major contribution of archeology has been to furnish materials from the distant past that complement the documentary history of more recent periods and permit speculation about the long-term "evolutionary" trends of cultural development. Thus, archeology provides support for theories regarding the evolution of technology and systems of economic subsistence. [*See* DOMESTICATION; HUNTING AND GATHERING, *article on* NEW WORLD PREHISTORIC SOCIETIES; URBAN REVOLUTION.]

Trait distribution. Another basic method for reconstructing history that employs cultural materials is the study of the geographical distribution of cultural traits, which reads historical depth into spatially arranged data. In the broadest sense, comparative linguistics is but one example of this approach, but since it is the least controversial, has the most explicitly developed method, and contributes most largely and reliably of all cultural distributional methods, it will be discussed first.

Comparative linguistics.   We may consider that every language is a cultural subsystem, that such subsystems are distributed over geographical space, and that each meaningful item in a language is a cultural trait that involves form ("sound") and function ("meaning"). The first step in comparative linguistics is the classification of language into mutually exclusive families, each consisting of related languages. A family of languages is a set of distinct languages presumed to have arisen from a single earlier language (the so-called protolanguage) through a course of differential changes. In the initial period of such changes, when the differences are still small and mutual intelligibility still obtains, localized variants are called dialects. Dialects, as they diverge more and more in the course of time, cease to be mutually intelligible and rank as separate languages. The languages resulting from such an earlier process are said to have a common origin and form a family of related languages. This process may occur a number of times successively and still give recoverable results. Thus, Proto-Indo-European developed dialects that became the ancestral languages of the various branches of Indo-European, e.g., Celtic, Germanic, Slavic, Indo-Aryan, Italic. Italic, like the others, in turn split into separate languages, e.g., Latin, Oscan, Umbrian, Venetic. Of those, only Latin survived, and it in turn has developed into the modern Romance languages.

The comparative method reconstructs this course of events by classifications, such as the one just briefly sketched. Through the observation and evaluation of resemblances involving sound and meaning and, further, through the regularities inherent in processes of linguistic change, most conspicuously phonetic change, the further step is taken of reconstructing as far as possible, and often in considerable detail, the phonetic system, grammar, and vocabulary of the ancestral language. Only exceptionally, as in the case of Latin as ancestral to the Romance languages, is there independent written evidence regarding this language.

Thus every family of languages at whatever level of classification implies an ancestral language that is capable of at least partial reconstruction. Such an ancestral language implies a community of peo-

ple as its users, a degree of cultural homogeneity, such as is normally found among speakers of the same language at the present time and for past documented history, and a placement within geographical and chronological limits. It is clear that the determination of spatial–temporal location of a sociocultural unit speaking a language whose features have been largely reconstructed and historically related to later or contemporary speech communities is in itself an important cultural-historical datum.

Nonlinguistic inference.   The reconstructed linguistic facts are themselves cultural-historical facts, but what is of wider interest to the culture historian are the nonlinguistic cultural inferences that flow from such linguistic facts, as, for example, words that show the probable acquaintance of the speakers with certain technological items or religious concepts. Such items of protovocabulary are reconstructed word-forms, continued in a sufficient number of later instances to allow us to infer their approximate phonetic shape and meaning and to assign them to the ancestral language. It is a further advantage of the comparative linguistic method that it almost always allows us to distinguish between resemblances among languages that result from continuation of an actual item in modified form (cognates) and resemblances among languages, whether related or not, that result from the borrowing of words from one language by another where the speakers have been in contact. It is also often possible through purely linguistic methods to arrive at conclusions regarding the direction of borrowing.

Accordingly, there are three chief types of inference regarding nonlinguistic cultural phenomena that can be derived from the comparative study of language: those drawn from facts concerning the classification and distribution of languages, those based on protovocabulary, and those based on interlinguistic contacts. From the detailed classification and subclassification of the members of a linguistic family, combined with their present geographical distribution or, where available, from the evidence of documentary history, their past distribution, it is possible to draw probabilistic conclusions regarding the area occupied by the ancestral speech community. From this will also follow certain hypotheses regarding subsequent migrational spread resulting in the distributions found in later historical periods. The fundamental assumption made is that every genetic branch of a linguistic stock, regardless of its present population size or geographical extent, provides, by its location, equal and independent evidence regarding the original center of linguistic distribution. The procedure implicit in this assumption may be called the "center of gravity" method. The best possible guess is the average of positions of each genetic branch. The center of each of these branches that enters into such a calculation may itself require calculation in terms of its subbranches, if any. Thus, if we had no written records to show whether English had originated in the British Isles, North America, South Africa, or Australia, the classification of English as a Germanic language within Indo-European, the fact that its closest relative within Germanic is Frisian, spoken by a small fishing population on the Dutch and German coasts, and the distribution of other subbranches of Germanic in Germany and Scandinavia would point to England as the immediate point of dispersal and to the continent of Europe as the location of ultimate origin. In fact, considering the level of classification represented by dialect variation, since the deepest and most fundamental dialect divisions exist in the British Isles, one can assume that this is the center of dispersal and that the rest of English distribution results from the relatively recent spread of certain older dialects from this center. An important independent check involves an application of the protoword method. Part of the reconstructed vocabulary of the proto-language may reflect the geographical environment of the original area of settlement but must be interpreted in the light of paleoclimatic and pale-ontological knowledge. This method requires considerable caution in its application because of the possibility of parallel semantic changes and because it is often necessary to argue from the negative standpoint of the absence of a given terminology. Both points can be illustrated for a hypothetical example of a language family in which it is impossible to reconstruct an original word for "ocean," thus leading to the conclusion that the protocommunity lived inland. It may either be the case that there was such a word but it has independently been replaced by different terms in each linguistic branch or that it survived but transferred its meaning to "lake" several times independently through movements inland, so that the meaning of the term has been incorrectly reconstructed. The possibility of the reconstruction of a whole set of semantically related terms obviously strengthens such a case greatly.

For reconstructing the time as against the place of the ancestral speech community, the only method of absolute chronology that has been proposed is that of glottochronology (see Hymes 1960). The method is based on the assumption that every language has a basic vocabulary that is composed of certain elements, such as pronouns, low numerals, and parts of the body, and that this basic vocabulary has a relatively low and constant rate of replacement by new forms, whether by internal changes or by borrowing. The rate of replacement is estimated from test cases involving historical documentation with a known chronology, e.g., Latin to French. If we assume random and independent loss for related languages at the same rate as for the test cases, then from the proportion of cognates in the list for any pair of languages the date at which the ancestral language began to diverge can be estimated. The estimate in current use is that in one millennium 14 per cent of the 100-word list is lost. This method has been widely applied but has also suffered severe criticism, both regarding the empirical results obtained in the test cases and the mathematical assumptions. It is, however, quite possible that when subjected to necessary revisions, it will give useful results.

The protoword method also permits inference from reconstructed vocabulary regarding the culture of the ancestral speech community. Thus the essentially village, neolithic nature of the Proto-Indo-European culture is shown by the existence of reconstructed terms for a number of domesticated plants and animals, the words for "plow," "village," etc. Other reconstructible parts of the ancestral vocabulary of Indo-European include the kinship terminology and the names of certain divinities.

Culture contact. The remaining major source of cultural-historical information based on linguistic data is the study of linguistic-contact phenomena. The most important data are furnished by loan words because they frequently have specific cultural content and because the direction of borrowing can be determined in favorable cases. One type of linguistic-contact study is that which concentrates on the contact of one language with another over an extended period. Such an investigation may be considered the linguistic analogue of acculturation studies. It is often possible to distinguish different periods of contact based on the "stratigraphy" of the changes undergone in the borrowing language. An over-all study of this kind will also show the specific aspects of culture in which borrowings are most numerous and fundamental and thus provide important evidence concerning the nature of the culture contact.

Instead of considering the language communities and the nature of their linguistic contacts as the primary interest, we may focus our attention on a specific cultural item. For example, we may examine the linguistic evidence in its bearing on the details of the spread of tobacco. Since a cultural item may be borrowed without the word being borrowed and because the direction of borrowing cannot in every case be discovered, linguistic evidence will not usually provide a complete history of diffusion, but it will furnish many important detailed hypotheses.

The detection of borrowed words may sometimes show that speech communities not now in contact must have been so in the past. Sometimes the contact must have been with an earlier protocommunity. Thus, Finnish has a number of words borrowed from very early Germanic that approximate reconstructed Proto-Germanic forms.

In addition to borrowings, where languages have been in intimate contact with a large bilingual population over a considerable period, there will be a tendency to convergence in the sound system and grammatical structure. Thus, a number of Balkan languages of diverse branches of Indo-European share such features as a postposed definite article (Rumanian, Albanian, Bulgarian), a future formed from an auxiliary "to wish" (Rumanian, Albanian, Serbo-Croatian, Bulgarian, Greek), and other details. These are not borrowings, since, for example, the verb "to wish" is in each case the indigenous word. Thus, areas of mutual linguistic influences can be determined that parallel the notion of culture area in cultural anthropology.

The independent nonlinguistic methods involve the mapping of the distribution of cultural traits. The main conclusions drawn are that highly detailed traits, e.g., specified art motifs, if found in a restricted geographical area, have a common historic origin. The place of origin and process of spread are difficult to recover on purely distributional evidence. One widely accepted principle of inference is that a trait is older in an area in which it is more elaborated and more integrated in the cultures in which it is found or exists in a greater variety of forms, since such developments require time. Another is known as the age–area hypothesis: other things being equal, a more widely distributed trait is older, since such spread requires time.

Reconstructing social systems. One class of methods using nonlinguistic cultural data involves an extension of the comparative linguistic method. The attempt can be made to reconstruct aspects of the culture of the ancestral speech community by a comparison of nonlinguistic traits of the speakers of the languages. This method has met with

limited success in the case of comparative Indo-European mythology. Just as the names of divinities may be reconstructed by linguistic comparisons, so the plots of myths involving the divinities may be compared in order to reconstitute their original forms. Such attempts encounter the difficulty that for nonlinguistic aspects of culture, there is no systematic way to differentiate between resemblances resulting from diffusion and those stemming from common origin. The method developed by Murdock (1949) belongs here. Since only certain changes of type are regarded as possible and since social structure is presumed to be, like language, relatively impervious to external diffusional influences, the comparison of social structures of linguistically related peoples leads to the reconstruction of the type of social structure of the ancestral population and its subsequent changes. Unlike language, where there are thousands of independent vocabulary elements, there are relatively few types of social structure; therefore, the same type of social structure is not probative of historical connection between two peoples. Linguistic comparison is thus a method for reconstructing the social structure of peoples known to be related on other grounds and not primarily a method of discovering historical relationships not otherwise known.

Biological history. The study of certain noncultural phenomena may be coordinated with that of culture history. Thus the genetic history of human populations is clearly relevant to culture history. The isolating mechanisms that produce partly or fully discrete breeding populations are in general congruent with those producing cultural and linguistic isolation. For example, the linguistic distinction of Eskimo–Aleut from the remaining language groups of the indigenous Americas parallels a physical distinction and is the common result of the same isolating factors. There is thus the possibility of mutual corroboration for historical inferences in both areas. For example, the genetic distinctness of the African and Oceanic Negro, which now seems assured on genetic grounds, is in agreement with the linguistic evidence, which is also negative on the same point.

Domestication. A further important noncultural source of cultural-historical conclusions is the study of domesticated plants and animals. Given a genetic classification of species and varieties or races and their relationship to wild forms, the basic principle is one parallel to the center-of-gravity method discussed above in relation to linguistic classification. Thus, the center of origin should be in the same area as the wild forms, and the earlier and more basic genetic differentiations of the domesticated forms should have taken place at earlier centers of cultivation. Here again, the history of plant and animal domestication is in itself important as culture history and provides further independent evidence regarding contacts of people.

The potentialities of the methods outlined here have been only very partially realized. The reasons for this are both theoretical and technical. Since they were applied on a grand scale but based on limited range of evidence and an unsophisticated methodology by the cultural-historical schools of the early twentieth century, in the reaction that followed, interest was focused on structural–funcitional problems to the relative neglect of culture history. Moreover, practical difficulties are raised by the wide variety of methods required that cannot easily, if at all, be controlled by a single specialist. The most noteworthy attempt thus far is that of Murdock's study of Africa (1959), which utilizes evidence from archeology, linguistic classification, social structure, and plant genetics. But even this study does not take into account many further lines of evidence, such as loan words and the distribution of art styles.

JOSEPH H. GREENBERG

[*Directly related are the entries* ARCHEOLOGY; DIFFUSION; ETHNOLOGY; FOLKLORE; LINGUISTICS, *articles on* HISTORICAL LINGUISTICS *and* THE SPEECH COMMUNITY. *Other relevant material may be found in* HISTORIOGRAPHY, *article on* AFRICAN HISTORIOGRAPHY; *and in the biographies of* GRAEBNER; KOPPERS; NORDENSKIÖLD; RATZEL; SCHMIDT.]

BIBLIOGRAPHY

BERNHEIM, ERNEST (1905) 1926 *Einleitung in die Geschichtswissenschaft.* 4th ed. Berlin: Gruyter. → Translation in text provided by Joseph Greenberg.
GREENBERG, JOSEPH H. 1953 Historical Linguistics and Unwritten Languages. Pages 265–286 in A. L. Kroeber (editor), *Anthropology Today.* Univ. of Chicago Press.
HYMES, DELL H. 1960 Lexicostatistics So Far. *Current Anthropology* 1:3–44.
LANGLOIS, CHARLES V.; and SEIGNOBOS, CHARLES (1898) 1925 *Introduction to the Study of History.* London: Duckworth. → First published in French.
MURDOCK, GEORGE P. 1949 *Social Structure.* New York: Macmillan. → A paperback edition was published in 1965 by the Free Press.
MURDOCK, GEORGE P. 1959 *Africa: Its Peoples and Their Culture History.* New York: McGraw-Hill.
SAPIR, EDWARD (1916) 1949 Time Perspective in Aboriginal American Culture: A Study in Method. Pages 389–462 in Edward Sapir, *Selected Writings . . . in Language, Culture and Personality.* Edited by David Mandelbaum. Berkeley: Univ. of California Press.
VANSINA, JAN (1961) 1964 *The Oral Tradition: A Study in Historical Methodology.* Chicago: Aldine. → First published in French.
WILLEY, GORDON R.; and PHILLIPS, PHILIP 1958 *Method and Theory in American Archaeology.* Univ. of Chicago Press.

V
SOCIAL HISTORY

Ideally considered, social history is the study of the structure and process of human action and interaction as they have occurred in sociocultural contexts in the recorded past. In practice, however, it has seldom been conceived in such analytical terms and has by no means always been envisaged in such comprehensive ones. Its investigators, in fact, have been content for the most part to chronicle, recount, and describe. They have been sharply divided, moreover, as to the proper scope of social history. Some have held that it embraces the whole range of life and culture in societies that have existed in historical time. Others have insisted that its concern is most properly confined to a residuum left by the abstraction of the polity, the economy, and large areas of culture, such as religious beliefs and technology. Still others have restricted it more narrowly to a heterogeneous lot of domestic and communal institutions, customs, attitudes, and artifacts. Numerous minor variations of these basic definitions also have been propounded. This diversity of views as to the scope of social history has engendered much confusion concerning the nature of the discipline.

The sources of social history are virtually omnifarious. They include such diverse materials as official reports, legal documents, newspapers, pamphlets, art objects, graffiti, literary works, and artifacts. One important category of materials is personal papers, such as letters, diaries, and journals, which reveal in depth and detail highly intimate areas of human experience. But there are no materials that social history can claim as peculiarly its own—another cause of confusion regarding its nature.

Origins

Ever since Herodotus reported the folkways of the Scythians and Tacitus described the institutions of the Germanic tribes, historians have written accounts that are identifiable as social history of one variety or another. Until the eighteenth century such accounts invariably appeared as insignificant fragments embedded in general works. Then, however, as acute concern with the institutions of the past was created by the growing desire to place the study of man and society on a solid empirical basis, social history emerged as a distinctive genre.

Although Justus Möser is traditionally credited with having been the progenitor of the genre and his *Osnabrückische Geschichte* (1768) is often acclaimed as its first intensive treatment of the commonality of a region, Voltaire was really the primary agent of its emergence. In *The Age of Louis XIV* (1751) he treats French society as a totality. Essaying to present a comprehensive view, he examines numerous facets of its life and culture, such as its wars, finances, administration, science, literature, art, customs, and religion. Moreover, he attempts to identify the ethos that animated the whole. Essentially the same approach is employed in his *Essai sur l'histoire générale et sur les moeurs et l'esprit* (1756), a series of disparate and unconnected discourses in which he surveys "the genius, manners, and customs of the principal nations" that flourished between the time of Charlemagne and the era of Louis XIV. Implicit in both works is the assumption that since mankind effected the transition from the "barbarism" of the Middle Ages to the "enlightenment" of the eighteenth century, the historical process advances by stages.

"Kulturgeschichte" as social history

The pioneer works by Voltaire inaugurated the development of *Kulturgeschichte*, which, although nominally preoccupied with the description and dissection of cultural patterns, is vitally concerned with social types and institutions. Basic among the postulates of *Kulturgeschichte* are the notions that each society, although characterized by multiformity of life and thought, possesses an essential unity, that it is pervaded by a peculiar ethos, and that it inevitably passes, like an organism, through a series of developmental phases. These postulates were strongly supported in the eighteenth century by major ideological currents. One was that congeries of ideas conventionally denominated romanticism, which, as in Johann Gottfried von Herder's *Outlines of a Philosophy of the History of Man* (1784–1791), attributed to each people certain basic psychological peculiarities that, through the operation of a characteristic spirit, produce a unique set of social and cultural forms. Another was the concept of progress, which, as in A. R. J. Turgot's *On the Progress of the Human Mind* (1750) and Condorcet's *Sketch for a Historical Picture of the Progress of the Human Mind* (1795), implied that history is a cumulative process and that each of its stages is a necessary antecedent of the next. These currents of thought were fused in the idealism of Fichte, Schelling, and Hegel, which during the

early nineteenth century provided similar support. As conceived by idealism, history is a plan whose inner logic obliges it to unfold step by step, each step representing a progression, each being an epoch endowed with a distinctive character that penetrates every detail of life.

Buttressed by the influence of this concept, *Kulturgeschichte* developed rapidly. Sometimes it was less dynamic and comprehensive in practice than in theory, epochal and thematic works being no rarity among those that bore its stamp. As a rule, however, it traced societal development over a protracted temporal span. An early, embryonic example of the genre is Henry Hallam's *View of the State of Europe During the Middle Ages* (1818), which includes surveys of social institutions, literature, education, and commerce. More fully endowed with its essential attributes are François Guizot's history of European civilization (1828) and Jules Michelet's universal history (1831), which dilate on ideology and values. With the publication of Jacob Burckhardt's *The Age of Constantine the Great* (1853), a study of the decline of the Roman Empire, the genre reached maturity; with the appearance of his *Civilization of the Renaissance in Italy* (1860), a study of the birth of modernity, it achieved its full fruition.

Burckhardt's treatment of the Italian Renaissance is in many respects an excellent example of the *kulturgeschichtliche* method. Concerned with the development of the cities of northern Italy between the fourteenth and sixteenth centuries, he centers his attention on the cultural configuration that evolved there, tracing the various mutations that it underwent as medieval elements were gradually replaced by modern. Its genesis he attributes to the prevailing illegitimacy of political power. He identifies its ethos as an ineluctable individualism that manifested itself in distinctive patterns of vision, thought, and norms. Closely interwoven with his delineation of these cultural patterns is a detailed survey of the concomitant social order. He explains how the dominant patriciate arose from a fusion of nobility and burghers; he describes the origins, growth, and characteristics of other new groups, such as humanists and artists. His examination of behavioral patterns illuminates a wide variety of interrelated matters, like the frequency of violence, the prevalence of corruption, the liberty accorded women, and the intensity of competition. Similarly enlightening is his depiction of significant social types, such as the despot, the polyhedrous man, and the perfect courtier. In sum, as he charts the phases of a changing society, he effectively portrays its full complexity.

There are other works that, although of lesser stature, are equally representative of *Kulturgeschichte* in its heyday. One of them is Gustav Freytag's enormously popular *Bilder aus der deutschen Vergangenheit* (1859–1867), a detailed and intimate survey of the social and cultural life of the German people from the earliest times to the mid-nineteenth century. Another is Wilhelm Riehl's well-received *Culturstudien aus drei Jahrhunderten* (1859), a miscellany of essays on sociocultural themes. A later example of distinction is Karl Lamprecht's *Deutsche Geschichte* (1891–1909), which traces the course of social and cultural change through a sequence of six periods of German history.

Lamprecht represented a positivistic variety of *Kulturgeschichte*, which, inspired by the progress of natural science, especially the elaboration of the evolutionary hypothesis and the application of the concept of natural selection, rested on the premise that a veritable historical science could be constructed by diligent scholarship, i.e., that the laws governing the historical process could be ascertained. The means of realizing this possibility, it assumed, was the application of the methodology of the social sciences to the whole course of human history. It thus bore a strong affinity to historical sociology, which from Auguste Comte through Herbert Spencer to Franklin Giddings sought to discriminate the principles and successive phases of sociocultural evolution. One of the earliest exponents of this position was Henry T. Buckle, whose *History of Civilization in England* (1857–1861) exerted considerable influence, especially in the United States and Russia. The most important of its later advocates included Lamprecht himself and his disciples Kurt Breysig, who, in *Der Stufen-Bau und die Gesetze der Welt-Geschichte* (1905), presumed to formulate 24 laws of history, and James Harvey Robinson, whose *New History* (1912) pointed the way to the contrivance of similar fabrications. These were the last paladins of *Kulturgeschichte;* the vitality of the genre did not long survive them.

Unschematic social history

Simultaneously with the development of *Kulturgeschichte*, which had begun with Voltaire, there also evolved an unschematic species of social history. Characterized by a virtual absence of concern with sociocultural morphology and dynamics, its objective is essentially the depiction of life in society. It varies widely as to the range of life that it considers, sometimes presenting a societal conspectus, as in Sir Albert Richardson's survey of England under the Georges (1931) and Sir Arthur Bryant's essays on England during the reign of Charles II (1935), and sometimes confining its inquiry to a narrow sector, as in Warwick Wroth's *London Pleasure Gardens of the Eighteenth Century* (1896) and Robert J. Allen's *Clubs of Augustan London* (1933). Social history likewise varies greatly in seriousness of purpose and therefore in scholarly level, as is evident in the considerable qualitative difference between such works as F. Karl Biedermann's sober and solid study of Germany in the eighteenth century (1854–1880) and Max von Boehn's light and airy sketch of England during the same period (1920). Moreover, it varies markedly in degree and character of interpretation; some studies, like Arthur W. Calhoun's history of the family in the United States (1917–1919), are almost wholly devoid of tendentiousness, others, like Ulrich B. Phillips' classic work on slavery in the American South (1918), argue, or at least suggest, a cogent thesis. Diversity, in short, is one of the principal attributes of social history.

Typical of the genre in essentials is Ludwig Friedländer's *Roman Life and Manners Under the Early Empire* (1862–1871), which treats Roman society from the reign of Augustus to the reign of Commodus. Beginning with a panoramic view of the imperial city, its sights and sounds, Friedländer proceeds to survey the court, the various social classes, the diurnal routine, the position of women, the experiences of the traveler, the means of communication, the spectacles, and the proliferation of luxury. Although he also considers art, religion, and philosophy, his primary objective is the recreation of past life, its vivid and realistic portrayal. Those of its aspects that constitute the cardinal features of his tableau are a rather arbitrary selection. They are dealt with in a succession of virtually independent essays whose order follows no particular principle. The essays are almost entirely descriptive; when here and there Friedländer interjects interpretive comments, they are fragmentary, belletristic, and simple: homiletic judgments, comparisons between Roman and later times, general observations on human progress. Another essential characteristic of the essays is their complete disregard of social change and development; they treat two centuries of history as a static unit.

A number of influences contributed to the rise of this unschematic type of social history. Despite a long historiographical ancestry composed of rudimentary prototypes, such as the account of the plague at Athens given by Thucydides, it received its first really significant impetus when the example of Voltaire sanctioned the historical investigation of every aspect of society. Something of the early effect of that example is apparent in the latitude of Arnold Heeren's *Ideen über die Politik, den Verkehr, und den Handel der alten Welt* (1793–1812), which examines agriculture, trade, finances, and manufactures as well as law, constitutional systems, and politics. This new breadth of scope was soon further extended by the inclusion of the ordinary people of the past among the subjects of historical inquiry. Long before the influence of Marx produced a school that made those strata its primary focus, they were extensively treated in studies like John Wade's *History of the Middle and Working Classes* (1833) and James A. St. John's *History of the Manners and Customs of Ancient Greece* (1842). Their inclusion in the historian's purview had a twofold origin, deriving in part from romanticism, which placed strong emphasis on the folk in all its aspects, in part from the social problems created by industrialization and from the resultant quest for panaceas.

No less important than this expansion of scope were the effects of the influence subsequently exerted by other disciplines. As legal and economic history developed into distinctive fields of inquiry, scholars like Sir Henry Maine, Sir Paul Vinogradoff, Sir Frederic Seebohm, and Gustav Schmoller adopted a new approach. Thoroughly convinced of the sterility of studying legal and economic institutions *in vacuo*, they investigated them in relation to the rest of the social structure. The adoption of this practice gradually produced an intensified awareness of the social aspect of all institutions. Moreover, it created a strong tendency to consider social and economic history as closely conjoined and complementary fields, as in such works as Henri Pirenne's *Medieval Cities: Their Origins and the Revival of Trade* (1925) and Henri Sée's *Esquisse d'une histoire économique et sociale de la France* (1929).

But the two disciplines were not conceived to be of equal consequence. As a result of the protracted and pervasive vogue enjoyed by the concept of economic determinism, which found its fullest expression in Marxian historiography, social history was regarded as ancillary to economic history. Only toward the middle of the present century did the conjunction of social and economic history tend to dissolve, as advances in theory and technique gave the latter a new preoccupation with problems of its own.

The Bloch–Febvre movement

While the conjunction of social and economic history was at its closest, a movement was launched that sought to disrupt it. Led by Marc Bloch and Lucien Febvre, the movement represented a convergence of the traditions of *Kulturgeschichte* and unschematic social history. Much of the inspiration that actuated it derived from Émile Durkheim; some may also have come from Max Weber and Ernst Troeltsch, whose practice belied their belief that history and sociology are immiscible (see Troeltsch 1922; McGrew 1958).

The aim of the movement was ambitious. Imbued with the conviction that the comprehension of sociocultural contexts demands they be studied as totalities, it aspired to convert social into societal history. It envisioned such history as a reconstruction of past epochs that would include their entire physical, ideational, and normative milieus and that would be at once more "scientific" and more "human" than the treatment they have usually received, an ideal that bears a strong resemblance to the objective of much recent cultural anthropology. Illustrative of the success with which that ideal could be translated into reality is Marc Bloch's own masterpiece, *Feudal Society* (1939–1940). The principal means that the movement prescribed for the achievement of such success was the creation of a coherent synthesis out of data drawn from sociology, psychology, economics, and geography. But it also ordained that the data to be accorded the most serious consideration were survivals from an earlier time, a variety of evidence whose value was first fully appreciated by Giovanni Battista Vico (1725) and a century later first fully used by Wilhelm Riehl. Assuming that such survivals, whether archeological, cartographical, linguistic, or folkloric, were much more reliable than documentary material, it held that they could provide the basal insight necessary to recreate the past. To give expression to this approach, Bloch and Febvre founded in 1929 the *Annales d'histoire économique et sociale*, which has both perpetuated and diffused the influence of the movement. That influence, which remains strongest in France, where it is at present represented by such scholars as Charles Morazé and Robert Mandrou, has contributed heavily over the decades to the weakening of the traditional position enjoyed by political history.

The dominance of political history

Almost from the inception of both *Kulturgeschichte* and unschematic social history, their practitioners were obliged to strive against the dominance of political history. The completeness of that dominance in the nineteenth century is strikingly reflected in Edward A. Freeman's terse definition of history in general as "past politics" (1886). Its vestiges in the mid-twentieth century may be seen in Geoffrey R. Elton's insistence (1956) that political history provides the best possible framework for the marshaling of historical data.

As long as this dominance subsisted unimpaired, one of its major manifestations was a strong resistance to any broadening of the scope of historical studies and to any deviation from Leopold von Ranke's prescription of their proper concerns, which he held to be factual accretion, not generalization; narration, not analysis; individuals, not groups; notables, not nonentities. This resistance affected the development of social history in significant ways. Beginning with August Böckh's seminal *Die Staatshaushaltung der Athener* (1817), which treats both state and society with about equal thoroughness, it was not unusual for research undertaken in that discipline to appear as a volume, either monographic or comprehensive. But the amount of space allocated to the fruits of such research in works of general narrative history was extremely small. An outstanding case in point is the celebrated third chapter of Thomas B. Macaulay's *History of England* (1849–1861), which serves as a diminutive *mise-en-scène* for a massive political survey. Similarly, only five of the 21 chapters that comprise William E. H. Lecky's great work on eighteenth-century England (1878–1890) are concerned with nonpolitical institutions. An even smaller proportion, 7 out of 55 chapters, exists in G. M. Trevelyan's history of England during the reign of Queen Anne (1930–1934), although the author is known primarily as a social historian. This engrossment of general narrative history by politics constituted a major impediment that the advocates of social history had to overcome in order to advance their discipline. Not until the early twentieth century did they achieve a substantial measure of success. The essence of that success was a marked expansion of the scope of general history. Very frequently, however, the new breadth amounted to no more than a compartmentalized presentation of diverse aspects of society, with political matters still receiving the largest share of attention. Even much later, when the space allotted to such matters had finally been greatly reduced, there were relatively few attempts to achieve the sort of highly fused synthesis advocated by scholars like Marc Bloch and Henri Berr, whose views may be gleaned from Berr's prefatory article to his *Revue de synthèse historique* ("Sur notre programme" 1900).

Underlying this disparity in the attention accorded political and social history was the difference in the prestige enjoyed by the two disciplines. Political history was highly esteemed. Regarded as edifying as well as informative, it was taken seriously; viewed as a custodian of national tradition as well as an inculcator of patriotism, it was considered valuable. In contrast, social history commanded much less respect. Whether *Kulturgeschichte* or the unschematic variety, it was thought of primarily as entertainment that might invoke nostalgia, gratify curiosity, and generate fantasies. As the new disciplines of sociology and anthropology developed, their insistence that society was more important, more fundamental than the state contributed somewhat to the reduction of this differential in prestige. But it survived for a protracted period. Moreover, it created an antagonism between the two disciplines that erupted most forcibly in the years 1888 to 1891, when Eberhard Gothein engaged in heated controversy with Dietrich Schäfer over whether society or the state ought to be the subject of historical research (Gothein 1889; Goldfriedrich 1902). The antagonism has long been extinct; the difference in prestige, although much diminished, continues.

Current trends

Dissatisfaction. Although at present there is little concern regarding the relative prestige of social history, there is much disquiet at its unsatisfactory state. This disquiet is occasioned by its amorphous, invertebrate character, which derives very largely from the absence of a corpus of theory capable of providing concepts and hypotheses; its indeterminate confines, whose nature arises from the persistent disagreement over scope and from the lack of a peculiar type of source material; its insufficiently rigorous discipline, which, tolerant of impressionistic portrayal, imprecise assessment, and ill-supported assertion, stems from its strong humanistic heritage; and its penchant for description and eschewal of analysis, which proceed from the Rankean prescript.

The hostility to sociology. These defects could be remedied to a large extent through an extensive and systematic application of sociological concepts and techniques. But for the most part historians are unwilling to adopt this course, which would effectively transmute social into sociological history. Their unwillingness originates in a deeply rooted hostility to sociology that has existed for a century, except among such deviates as the exponents of positivistic *Kulturgeschichte* and the epigoni of Marc Bloch and Lucien Febvre. That hostility arose out of profound apprehension and prejudice. Historians feared sociology's synoptic pretensions and its putative design to reduce their discipline to the secondary role of fact collection. Moreover, they abhorred its techniques and aspirations as pseudoscientific. Finally, they disdained its achievement as negligible and its subordination of empirical research to the construction of grandiose abstractions as only the philosophy of history in a new guise. The transformation that sociology has undergone since about 1940, when it entered its modern age, has almost entirely dispelled their apprehension and extinguished their disdain; but the strong humanistic bias that inspired their aversion for its concerns, techniques, and objectives continues to foster hostility.

The hostility of sociologists. This hostility has had its counterpart among sociologists. Resentful of the ancient heritage, academic respectability, superior prestige, and large-scale pretensions of history, they long entertained a strong animus against it. Two pretensions in particular contributed to this animus, because they seemed to be in serious conflict with the claims of sociology. One was history's pre-emption of all recorded behavior as its proper sphere; the other was the pedagogic role that it assumed as grand interpreter of human experience. But if history was disliked as a rival discipline, it was also looked upon as an inferior one. Sociologists regarded its data as of dubious validity; they considered its concern with discrete facts as obsessive and its refusal to seek uniformities as unscientific. As sociology's claims to intellectual and institutional legitimacy gained greater recognition, all these attitudes tended to soften; but the residues are substantial.

To explain the origins and persistence of such hostility on both sides, historians and sociologists alike have emphasized that a fundamental antithesis exists between their disciplines. Drawing their principal argument from the neoidealism formulated by Wilhelm Dilthey and Heinrich Rickert toward the end of the nineteenth century, both sides have maintained that history is idiographic, hence concerned with the unique, the singular, the individual, which makes descriptive treatment inevitable; whereas sociology is nomothetic, hence concerned with the recurrent, the repetitive, the regular, which makes generalization and abstraction possible. They have likewise contended that history's perspective is diachronic, since it considers data in temporal sequence, while sociology is synchronic, since it considers data without reference to time. Then, too, they have argued that the techniques of historical research are particularly suitable for investigation of the past, whereas the techniques peculiar to sociology are applicable only to contemporary phenomena.

The rapprochement of history and sociology

On both sides, however, there has long been a spirited minority, which, denying these contentions and repudiating the hostility that underlies them, has resolutely advocated close communion between history and sociology. From time to time during the past half century, its efforts to promote such communion have produced intensive discussion, punctuated by exhortatory and programmatic pronunciamentos. The most recent efforts have received powerful support from the growing sentiment in favor of interdisciplinary exchange in general, which has exalted the mutual advantages to be derived from close cooperation between history and all the social sciences. They have likewise received considerable support from sociologists who have lately become uneasy over the ahistorical orientation of their discipline. That orientation, which was deliberately adopted when sociology was striving for intellectual autonomy and creating a unified system of theory, has been emphatically rejected by the empiricist C. Wright Mills and his followers, who have held a knowledge of the past to be valuable, if not essential, for an understanding of contemporary society and its problems. Much more important is the increasing number of proponents of systematic theory who, captained by scholars like Robert K. Merton and Bernard Barber, have not only strongly recommended the data of history and the course of social change as worthy of investigation but have also energetically encouraged a *rapprochement* between historians and sociologists.

Although such a *rapprochement* remains no more than a possibility, some progress has been made in that direction. As certain relatively simple sociological concepts have gained currency among scholars in general, they have been employed half consciously by historians. Then, too, some scholars in areas like political, intellectual, and religious history have toyed with such concepts, permitting them to serve as stimuli to the imaginative faculty in research as well as in synthesization. Again, still others have adopted them deliberately and applied them directly, albeit in an irregular, immethodical manner. As a result of these practices, recent historiography includes a substantial segment of partially sociologized work. Representative of such work are the writings of Georges Lefebvre, Albert Soboul, and Pierre Goubert.

Sociological history. Few social historians have gone further than this piecemeal, *ad hoc* use of sociological theory. Those few, however, who have employed theory both extensively and systematically have produced genuine sociological history. Their work is well exemplified by Elinor G. Barber's *The Bourgeoisie in Eighteenth Century France* (1955), which forcefully demonstrates the full potentialities of the approach. Utilizing concepts drawn from structural–functional theory, this pioneer study skillfully analyzes the changing position of the middle strata of French society during the decades prior to the revolution of 1789. At the outset, it identifies the prevailing stratificational system as a composite in which caste elements were predominant and open class elements were secondary; accordingly, social mobility was given only limited approval. Then, having carefully examined the composition and internal differentiation of the bourgeoisie, it demonstrates the harassing strains experienced by the socially mobile class, which sought to reconcile a partial abandonment of traditional Catholic values with a partial adoption of modern secular ones, and an acceptance of a hierarchical class structure with a determination to rise. These conflicts, it likewise shows, produced in many of the bourgeoisie a strong ambivalence concerning the choice of an appropriate style of life—guilt, uneasiness, and apprehension attaching them to the traditional pattern of their class, ambition driving them to adopt the pattern of the nobility, whose ranks they sought to enter. Finally, after examining the channels whereby they might ascend to noble status, the study analyzes their plight when such mobility became increasingly difficult to achieve, showing how their frustration intensified the strains created by their conflicting values and how in consequence they were impelled to reject the whole class structure. Thus Elinor Barber, by considering familiar data within a new framework, achieves a superbly articulated interpretation of unusual depth and subtlety and provides an entirely fresh perspective.

Some sociologists, animated by their recently found interest in historical data, have likewise undertaken studies of this type. The possibility of their eventually pre-empting the area of social history is raised anew by such works as Robert N. Bellah's *Tokugawa Religion: The Values of Pre-industrial Japan* (1957), Neil J. Smelser's *Social Change in the Industrial Revolution* (1959), Seymour M. Lipset's *The First New Nation: The United States in Historical and Comparative Perspective* (1963), and Charles Tilly's *The Vendée* (1964). It is this challenge from the outside no less than the current defects within that makes it imperative for social historians to put themselves under the tutelage of sociologists in order to transform their discipline.

J. JEAN HECHT

[*Other relevant material may be found in the biographies of* BLOCH; CONDORCET; FEBVRE; LAMPRECHT; MACAULAY; MILLS; PIRENNE; ROBINSON; SÉE; TURGOT; VOLTAIRE.]

EXAMPLES OF SOCIAL HISTORY

ALLEN, ROBERT J. 1933 *The Clubs of Augustan London.* Cambridge, Mass.: Harvard Univ. Press.

BARBER, ELINOR G. 1955 *The Bourgeoisie in Eighteenth Century France.* Princeton Univ. Press.

BELLAH, ROBERT N. 1957 *Tokugawa Religion: The Values of Pre-industrial Japan.* Glencoe, Ill.: Free Press.

BIEDERMANN, F. KARL 1854–1880 *Deutschland im achtzehnten Jahrhundert.* 2 vols. Leipzig: Weber.

BLOCH, MARC (1939–1940) 1961 *Feudal Society.* Univ. of Chicago Press. → First published as *La société féodale: La formation des liens de dépendance* and *La société féodale: Les classes et le gouvernement des hommes.*

BÖCKH, AUGUST (1817) 1886 *Die Staatshaushaltung der Athener.* 3d ed., 2 vols. Berlin: Reimer.

BOEHN, MAX VON 1920 *England im achtzehnten Jahrhundert.* Berlin: Askanischer Verlag.

BREYSIG, KURT 1905 *Der Stufen-Bau und die Gesetze der Welt-Geschichte.* Berlin: Bondi.

BRYANT, ARTHUR 1935 *The England of Charles II.* London and New York: Longmans.

BUCKLE, HENRY T. (1857–1861) 1913 *The History of Civilization in England.* 2d ed., 2 vols. New York: Hearst.

BURCKHARDT, JACOB (1853) 1949 *The Age of Constantine the Great.* London: Routledge. → First published as *Die Zeit Constantin's des Grossen.*

BURCKHARDT, JACOB (1860) 1958 *The Civilization of the Renaissance in Italy.* New York: Harper. → First published as *Die Cultur der Renaissance in Italien.*

CALHOUN, ARTHUR W. (1917–1919) 1945 *A Social History of the American Family From Colonial Times to the Present.* 3 vols. New York: Barnes & Noble. → A paperback edition was published in 1960.

CONDORCET, MARIE JEAN ANTOINE NICOLAS CARITAT (1795) 1955 *Sketch for a Historical Picture of the Progress of the Human Mind.* New York: Noonday. → First published in French.

ELTON, GEOFFREY R. 1956 *England Under the Tudors.* London: Methuen.

FREYTAG, GUSTAV (1859–1867) 1930 *Bilder aus der deutschen Vergangenheit.* New ed., 3 vols. Berlin: Deutsche Buchgemeinschaft.

FRIEDLÄNDER, LUDWIG (1862–1871) 1908–1913 *Roman Life and Manners Under the Early Empire.* 7th ed., rev. & enl., 4 vols. London: Routledge. → First published as *Darstellungen aus der Sittengeschichte Roms.*

GUIZOT, FRANÇOIS P. (1828) 1896 *General History of Civilization in Europe.* Edited, with critical and supplementary notes, by George Wells Knight. New York: Appleton. → First published in French.

HALLAM, HENRY (1818) 1904 *View of the State of Europe During the Middle Ages.* 2 vols. New York: Appleton.

HEEREN, ARNOLD H. L. (1793–1812) 1824–1826 *Ideen über die Politik, den Verkehr, und den Handel der alten Welt.* 4th ed., 3 vols. Göttingen (Germany): No publisher given.

HERDER, JOHANN GOTTFRIED VON (1784–1791) 1800 *Outlines of a Philosophy of the History of Man.* London: Hansard. → First published in German.

LAMPRECHT, KARL 1891–1909 *Deutsche Geschichte.* 12 vols. Berlin: Gärtner.

LECKY, WILLIAM EDWARD H. (1878–1890) 1892–1893 *A History of England in the Eighteenth Century.* New ed., 7 vols. New York: Appleton.

LIPSET, SEYMOUR M. 1963 *The First New Nation: The United States in Historical and Comparative Perspective.* New York: Basic Books.

MACAULAY, THOMAS B. (1849–1861) 1953 *History of England From the Accession of James II.* 4 vols. New York: Dutton.

MICHELET, JULES (1831) 1962 *Introduction à l'histoire universelle.* Paris: Colin.

MÖSER, JUSTUS (1768) 1819–1824 *Osnabrückische Geschichte.* 3d ed., 3 vols. Berlin: Nicolai.

PHILLIPS, ULRICH B. 1918 *American Negro Slavery: A Survey of the Supply, Employment and Control of Negro Labor as Determined by the Plantation Régime.* New York: Appleton.

PIRENNE, HENRI (1925) 1956 *Medieval Cities: Their Origins and the Revival of Trade.* Garden City, N.Y.: Doubleday. → First published in French.

RICHARDSON, ALBERT E. 1931 *Georgian England: A Survey of Social Life, Trades, Industries and Art From 1700 to 1820.* New York: Scribner; London: Batsford.

RIEHL, WILHELM H. 1859 *Culturstudien aus drei Jahrhunderten.* Stuttgart (Germany): Cotta.

ROBINSON, JAMES HARVEY (1912) 1958 *The New History: Essays Illustrating the Modern Historical Outlook.* Springfield, Mass.: Walden.

ST. JOHN, JAMES A. 1842 *The History of the Manners and Customs of Ancient Greece.* 3 vols. London: Bentley.

SÉE, HENRI 1929 *Esquisse d'une histoire économique et sociale de la France.* Paris: Alcan.

SMELSER, NEIL J. 1959 *Social Change in the Industrial Revolution.* London: Routledge; Univ. of Chicago Press.

TILLY, CHARLES H. 1964 *The Vendée.* Cambridge, Mass.: Harvard Univ. Press.

TREVELYAN, GEORGE M. 1930–1934 *England Under Queen Anne.* 3 vols. London and New York: Longmans.

TURGOT, ANNE ROBERT J. (1750) 1929 *On the Progress of the Human Mind.* Hanover, N.H.: Sociological Press. → Originally a lecture given in Latin at the Sorbonne.

VICO, GIOVANNI B. (1725) 1948 *The New Science.* Ithaca, N.Y.: Cornell Univ. Press. → First published in Italian. A paperback edition was published in 1961 by Doubleday.

VOLTAIRE, FRANÇOIS M. A. (1751) 1962 *The Age of Louis XIV.* New York: Dutton. → First published in French.

VOLTAIRE, FRANÇOIS M. A. (1756) 1835 *Essai sur l'histoire générale et sur les moeurs et l'esprit.* 4 vols. Paris: Treuttel.

WADE, JOHN (1833) 1835 *History of the Middle and Working Classes, With a Popular Exposition of the Economical and Political Principles Which Have Influenced the Past and Present Condition of the Industrious Orders.* 3d ed. London: Wilson.

WROTH, WARWICK 1896 *The London Pleasure Gardens of the Eighteenth Century.* London and New York: Macmillan.

WORKS ABOUT SOCIAL HISTORY

BERGER, BENNETT 1957 Sociology and the Intellectuals: An Analysis of a Stereotype. *Antioch Review* 67:275–290.

BRIGGS, ASA 1962 Sociology and History. Pages 91–98 in Alan T. Welford et al. (editors), *Society: Problems and Methods of Study.* New York: Philosophical Library.

CAHNMAN, WERNER J.; and BOSKOFF, ALVIN (editors) 1964 *Sociology and History: Theory and Research.* New York: Free Press.

COBBAN, ALFRED 1961 History and Sociology. *Historical Studies* 3:1–8.

ELIOT, THOMAS D. 1922 The Use of History for Research in Theoretical Sociology. *American Journal of Sociology* 27:628–636.

FREEMAN, EDWARD A. 1886 *The Methods of Historical Study.* London: Macmillan. → See especially Lecture 1.

GINSBERG, MORRIS 1932 *Studies in Sociology.* London: Methuen.

GOLDFRIEDRICH, JOHANN A. 1902 *Die historische Ideenlehre in Deutschland.* Berlin: Gärtner.

GOTHEIN, EBERHARD 1889 *Die Aufgaben der Kulturgeschichte.* Leipzig: Duncker & Humblot.

HERTZLER, JOYCE O. 1925 The Sociological Uses of History. *American Journal of Sociology* 31:173–198.

HOLLOWAY, S. W. F. 1963 Sociology and History. *History* 48:154–184.

McGREW, R. E. 1958 History and the Social Sciences. *Antioch Review* 18:276–289.

McKINNEY, JOHN C. 1957 Methodology, Procedures, and Techniques in Sociology. Pages 186–235 in Howard Becker and Alvin Boskoff (editors), *Modern Sociological Theory in Continuity and Change.* New York: Dryden.

MANTOUX, PAUL 1903 Histoire et sociologie. *Revue de synthèse historique* 7:121–140.

MERTON, ROBERT K. 1961 Social Conflict Over Styles of Sociological Work. Pages 21–44 in World Congress of Sociology, Fourth, Milan and Stresa, 8–15 September 1959, *Transactions.* Volume 3: Abstracts of Papers and Discussions. Louvain (Belgium): International Sociological Association.

PERKIN, HAROLD J. 1953 What Is Social History? John Rylands Library, Manchester, *Bulletin* 36:56–74.

PERKIN, HAROLD J. 1962 Social History. Pages 51–82 in H. P. R. Finberg (editor), *Approaches to History: A Symposium.* London: Routledge.

Sur notre programme [by Henri Berr]. 1900 *Revue de synthèse historique* 1:1–8.

TROELTSCH, ERNST 1922 *Der Historismus und seine Probleme.* Tübingen (Germany): Mohr.

WOLFF, KURT H. 1959 Sociology and History: Theory and Practice. *American Journal of Sociology* 65:32–38.

VI
INTELLECTUAL HISTORY

The term "intellectual history" is fairly well established in the United States, though the American Historical Association's *Guide to Historical Literature* (1961) uses it sparingly, preferring such rubrics as "cultural history" or "social ideas." There are in common use in the Western world, however, many other terms: history of ideas, *Geistesgeschichte, Ideengeschichte, histoire de la pensée,* and various others. In its widest sense, intellectual history may be said to have as its subject matter whatever record is left of the activities of the human mind. Its most important and most available materials are the products of philosophers, artists, writers, scientists, recorded in their works and in the special histories of specific disciplines—philosophy, literature, religion, the sciences, the arts. But intellectual history is not merely a summary or even a synthesis of such materials; it commonly also attempts to trace and understand the dissemination of the work of cultural leaders—their "ideas"—in a given society; and it also seeks to understand the relation between such ideas on one hand and, on the other, "drives," "interests," and nonintellectual factors generally, in individual and in social psychology. At its narrowest, intellectual history attempts to tell who produced what intellectual or cultural achievement when and how; at its broadest, it can come close to being a kind of retrospective sociology of knowledge, even a retrospective general sociology.

Yet intellectual history is not to be understood as a kind of master history. It takes the products of the human intellect as its source materials; it does not in itself exhaust the possible play of the historian's own intellect on all the diverse materials left by the past. All historical writing, of course, requires from the historian at least minimal attention to the record of man thinking. Especially in modern works in such fields as social and economic history, awareness of the role of ideas is increasing. Usually, however, intellectual history can, if only roughly, be delimited by its major concern with the written or spoken word, and even, to use a term still somewhat suspect among historians, with "theory." There remains then the difficulty of clearly distinguishing between intellectual history and, for example, the history of philosophy, the history of literature, the history of science, and of other branches of culture. It is not quite enough to say that intellectual history is the all-inclusive history of all these. Sometimes an intellectual historian, like Preserved Smith in the two volumes of his *History of Modern Culture* (vol. 1, *Origins of Modern Culture, 1543–1687*; vol. 2, *The Enlightenment, 1687–1776* 1930–1934), left unfinished at his death, does attempt such a difficult all-inclusive task, and some of Smith's topical headings—"The Propaganda of the Enlightenment," "Persecution and Tolerance," "Humanitarianism," "Morals and Manners"—show that he did not limit himself to the discussion of clusters of ideas and their affiliation. But generally the historian of philosophy, for instance, is primarily if not exclusively concerned with explaining to philosophers or to students of philosophy the ideas of other philosophers. He may indeed criticize these ideas, that is, evaluate, praise, blame; he may, though he need not, attempt to find some explanation of these ideas in a given philosopher's personal history and in his total environment; but he may also treat ideas as breeding

ideas in a vacuum—or in a "mind." The intellectual historian, concerned, as he very often is, with the same set of philosophical ideas, must also do some of what the historian of philosophy does; but his main concern must be with what happens to these ideas among ordinary educated people and even among ordinary uneducated people.

Perhaps the point can be made more clearly from the history of science. It is possible to write a history of science, and a very scholarly one, in which the aim of the historian is to record discoveries, inventions, theories; place them in chronological sequence; and even explain their dissemination *among scientists.* Such, in fact, was the whole work of the distinguished historian of science George Sarton. An intellectual historian concerned at all with natural science would certainly have to master much of the foregoing; but he would also have to ask himself what happened to these scientific theories when they passed into circulation among the many. You could write a good history of what the work of Darwin has meant to the science of biology in its present state without a word about what is commonly called "social Darwinism"; but you could not write a good intellectual history of the nineteenth century without very serious attention to social Darwinism. The difference between what the work of Freud means to practicing psychoanalysts, and indeed to psychiatrists who are not orthodox Freudians, and what Freud's work has meant to novelists, playwrights, painters, essayists, and the general public is very great indeed. The intellectual historian will have to deal with all these last, even though for the professional psychoanalyst this *Vulgar-Freudismus* is a shocking perversion of the master's true meaning. Much of this is well treated in Erik Erikson's *Insight and Responsibility* (1964).

This difference, then, between concentrating on, placing emphasis on what ideas mean to the expert, the professional in a given field, and what they mean to the many to whom they somehow do filter down is the basic distinction between the historian of a special intellectual discipline and the historian of ideas.

Some component of intellectual history is to be found in historical writing as far back as the Greeks. Herodotus, when he discussed the religious beliefs of the Egyptians, and Thucydides, when he contrasted the national character of the Athenians and the Spartans, were both writing intellectual history. The vein of philosophical history that attempts to discern what Alfred Kroeber called "configurations of culture growth" was never quite pinched out even in the Middle Ages, as witness the sequence Augustine–Orosius–Otto of Freising, and has widened greatly in our own time. Machiavelli's *Discorsi* has as its major theme an attempt to explain the influence of the religious beliefs of the Romans on their political achievements. With the Enlightenment of the eighteenth century, intellectual history, still unnamed, assumed a prominent place in historiography, if only as "philosophy teaching by example."

The actual designation "intellectual history," or history of ideas or of thought, and its general acceptance as a form of historical writing date from the late nineteenth century and the organization of professional academic history. In the United States the term was made popular by James Harvey Robinson, whose *Mind in the Making* (1921) was a best-selling sketch of Western intellectual history based largely on his famous Columbia University course on "the history of the intellectual classes." In Germany Dilthey was in many ways a precursor of modern intellectual historians, and Max Weber, although formally listed as a sociologist, set the mold for much work in the field. Indeed, his *Protestant Ethic and the Spirit of Capitalism* may be taken as a most representative piece of intellectual history. Among the works of professional historians, Friedrich Meinecke's *Die Entstehung des Historismus* and the Austrian Friedrich Heer's monumental *Europäische Geistesgeschichte* are evidence that the field is solidly established in Germany and Austria.

Professional historians in both France and Great Britain have been more reluctant to write intellectual history, at least under that name. In France historians interested in synthesis, such as Henri Berr and Lucien Febvre, have certainly made contributions to the field; and literary scholars like Paul Hazard, whose *European Mind, 1680–1715* is now standard, have written in the mainstream of intellectual history. British historians like J. B. Bury, R. H. Tawney, and Christopher Dawson have paid full attention to the intellectual element in history, but intellectual history has been written primarily by literary men like Leslie Stephen, whose *History of English Thought in the Eighteenth Century* is a classic. The philosophy of history is represented in Great Britain by H. T. Buckle (*History of Civilization in England*), Charles Collingwood (*The Idea of History*), and Arnold J. Toynbee, whose 12-volume *Study of History*, as summarized in two volumes by D. C. Somervell, has had a very wide audience, especially in the United States. Croce set the pattern for a whole generation of historians in Italy. Croce must be listed first as a philosopher, but almost all his writing as a historian shows the hand of the intellectual historian. Among his many writings in the field, we may note *La Spagna nella vita italiana durante la Rinascenza* and *Storia della età barocca in Italia*.

Among the first few generations of professional historians throughout the Western world, there was considerable resistance to the formal field of intellectual history as not "scientific" enough. As compared with the concreteness of the materials of institutional, economic, and conventional social history, the materials of intellectual history seemed vague and difficult to pin down as part of "real" life. Moreover, what the intellectual historian probably has to call—for want of a better term—the "spirit of the age" or the "climate of opinion" of the late nineteenth century, at least among scholars, tended to minimize, if not to deny, the driving force of "ideas," particularly philosophical ideas or ideals, in human life.

Although traces of this resistance to intellectual history still exist, the subject has now attained academic respectability; indeed, in the United States it has become fashionable. It is proving to be one of the most effective bridges between historians and the practitioners of the social sciences, groups still rather definitely separated by mutual distrust in most Western countries. The problems that the intellectual historian must face, while often essentially philosophical, are increasingly like those confronting the social scientist. The intellectual historian is bound to try to be a thinker rather than a storyteller. Indeed, he hardly has a story to tell. Passage from general sociology and the sociology of knowledge to intellectual history has become both easy and frequent; it is equally easy—some would say too easy—to go from depth psychology to historical writing. It seems likely that many historians for a long time to come will proudly and a bit defensively call themselves humanists and scorn the social sciences; the intellectual historian, however, cannot really practice his craft if he shares this scorn.

Types of intellectual history

No rigorous classification of the kinds of intellectual history is possible. We shall here attempt a rough classification into three types, with the necessary warning that any given work may display some touches of all three.

First, there is intellectual history that tries to establish the "facts" about who wrote what when, in what form it was published, as well as similar facts about what was produced in cultural media other than words, particularly if these other media served for "propaganda." A good example of this kind of intellectual history is afforded by the work of Charles H. Haskins, notably the articles collected as *The Renaissance of the Twelfth Century* (1927) and *Studies in Medieval Culture* (1929). Haskins was an impeccably trained medievalist of the old school who did much work in institutional history. What interested him in intellectual history was chiefly the ways in which Greco-Roman works —the actual manuscripts—survived, were copied, indeed often came back into Western culture via translations into Arabic and thence into medieval Latin. He was certainly not indifferent to the content of the manuscripts he so carefully studied— in fact his very use of the term "Renaissance" in his title involves another level of historical generalization, another kind of intellectual history. Still, his main task was to establish by research in the original sources a straightforward account in the Rankean tradition of *wie es eigentlich gewesen.*

Spadework of a similar kind is, of course, always essential. For the modern intellectual historian there are even many problems of "fact" that must be cleared up before he can go on to other problems—problems such as who wrote certain pseudonymous or anonymous works, problems of clandestine publication, authenticity of memoirs, and the like. In this classification too belongs the effort to establish the facts (sometimes capable of being put statistically) of the dissemination in specific circumstances of certain works and even of the ideas contained in them. Ancillary to this effort is work close to demography, such as the study of the degree of literacy in a given population. In actual practice many of these investigations can hardly be separated from studies of problems in the sociology of knowledge, from simple literary ones of "influence of A on B" to more sophisticated attempts to· analyze the relations between words and deeds. But the establishment of the facts is essential spadework in intellectual as in any other kind of historical writing.

Second, there is the more difficult kind of intellectual history, also concerned rather more with establishing than with evaluating or synthesizing facts, to which American usage in particular tends to apply the term "history of ideas." We are here concerned with what can be called the cartography of ideas or (perhaps) semantics. The school formed around Arthur O. Lovejoy at Johns Hopkins affords a good example of this approach. Lovejoy identified as a "cluster of ideas" such complex and usually very common terms as "nature," "reason," "romantic." His major task was that of analyzing the constituent elements of these clusters of ideas. His *Great Chain of Being* (1936), for example, traces in Western culture the history of one such cluster of ideas, that of a hierarchy of interrelated living beings from barely sentient ones to the highest and best developed. Although other historians have not always matched the scholarly subtlety of Lovejoy and his colleagues—who have found some sixty shades of meaning for the word "nature"— this sort of analysis is an essential part of intellectual history. It can be applied to the work of a given thinker: what did Hobbes, Locke, Rousseau understand, "really mean," by "social contract," or just what did Nietzsche intend the "superman" to be and do? It can also be applied to distinguish between different uses, different emotional effects, of certain words or phrases in given times and places. For this a very neat example is the difference between the effect of the word "federalist" when used in France and in the United States in 1793—or, indeed, when used in New England and in Virginia at the same time.

Both these first two kinds of intellectual history are essential to the third, which is the central concern of intellectual history in our time. Its task may be put with undue simplicity as the study of the relation between what men say and what they do. "Do" has its obvious complexities; but "say" too is mere shorthand for all that goes on in the cerebral cortex, and unless modern psychology is wholly on the wrong track, in less noble parts of the human central nervous system. A very good if rather worn example of this kind of intellectual history is afforded by the old debate over the influence of the Enlightenment on the French Revolution (see Church 1964). One extreme position in this debate, taken for instance by Felix Rocquain in *L'esprit révolutionnaire avant la révolution,* is that hard, specific grievances were all-important in producing the revolution and that the work of the *philosophes* was of little, if any, importance. Rocquain's position has significance for later intellectual historians as a probable reflection of Marxist ideas and is certainly a reflection of the distrust felt by French political radicals in the 1870s for any form of "idealism." The opposite extreme position is commonly taken by conservatives who dislike the French Revolution and who subscribe to one form or another of the conspiracy theory of history. Freemasons, *philosophes,* Illuminati, Jacobins, are variously singled out as the fanatics of the Enlightenment responsible for everything that happened during the revolution. Taine's famous metaphor in his *Origines de la France contemporaine* is typical: if you see a healthy man take up a full glass, drain it, and then fall down foaming at the mouth in convulsions, you know there was a poison in the glass; the man was the Jacobin, the glass contained the ideas of the *philosophes*. In between these extremes the debate, which is by no means ended, shows many variants of interpretation of the nature and extent of the effect of the Enlightenment on what really happened.

The intellectual historian who attempts to judge the nature of the effects of an idea or cluster of ideas on human events is confronted with the old problem of value judgments. It is all very well to use, as we have used above, the metaphor of intellectual history as the "cartography of ideas." But the map maker does not judge, evaluate, criticize, or even comment on the actual piece of the terrestrial globe he is mapping; only the traveler using the map as guide may indeed feel and say "This is lovely" or "This is ugly" as he looks at the landscape. The historian, strive though he may to be like the map maker, can hardly avoid being like the traveler.

To use once more the field of the Enlightenment as an example, intellectual historians have not only varied greatly in their interpretations of what certain eighteenth-century political thinkers meant, but in whether what they meant was productive of good or bad. Rousseau's *Social Contract* is a good focusing point for this problem. One school, represented by Jacob T. Talmon, in his *Rise of Totalitarian Democracy*, finds that Rousseau himself meant the work to set up a sovereign power whose will was absolute and that the effect of the work on political activists like Robespierre and Babeuf was certainly to justify their arbitrary "democratic totalitarianism." An opposite point of view is represented by the distinguished German philosopher Ernst Cassirer, whose *Question of Jean-Jacques Rousseau*, translated with an illuminating introduction by Peter Gay, holds that Rousseau meant the general will to represent a kind of idealized moral imperative and that its real influence has indeed been to promote the democratic and individualistic freedoms.

Types of studies

It must be admitted that into whatever subclassifications intellectual history is broken down, it is a sprawling field, with a very great range of subject matter and treatment. It can be concerned with tracing over a long period a recurring theme of man's thinking. Such "thread" accounts are Lovejoy's above-mentioned *Great Chain of Being* or J. B. Bury's *Idea of Progress*. It can adopt the approach of comparative history, which tries to discern common as well as unique elements in ideas and attitudes expressed at different times and in different places. An interesting and highly controversial instance of this approach is the work in American intellectual history of Richard Hofstadter, who finds common elements, such as belief in the "conspiracy theory" of politics, in groups commonly held to be quite unlike—Populists, Progressives, and McCarthyites. At least as controversial, if not of such timely interest, is Carl Becker's *Heavenly City of the Eighteenth-Century Philosophers*, in which, as the title implies, the author finds significant intellectual attitudes common to medieval Augustinians and the *philosophes* of the Enlightenment.

Histories of utopias—both the writings usually so classified in histories of literature and the actual experiments with group living in communities under the influence of utopian thinking—are obviously subjects for the intellectual historian. Although there is an enormous body of historical and literary writing about utopias, the subject has not had a first-rate general treatment in all its phases, a difficult and challenging task. Many wide topics in intellectual history, however, have had such treatment. This is especially true of the history of Christianity and, indeed, of the history of religion generally. While the historian of formal philosophy can always limit himself to the analysis of ideas in and for themselves, a process which is *not* intellectual history, the historian of religion can hardly avoid taking up the relation between religious beliefs and the behavior of human beings, as well as the history of institutions founded on these beliefs. Much in this field that can be classified as intellectual history has been the work of sociologists, particularly in Germany. Although Harnack is commonly listed as a historian, Troeltsch and Weber are listed as sociologists.

An important problem in intellectual history, that of the cultural generation, has been neglected by historians; it has had its best specific treatment in a short article by Karl Mannheim, "The Problem of Generations" (1928). There are interesting reflections on the problem in Ortega y Gasset, *Man and Crisis* (1933, pp. 30–85 in 1959 edition), a translation of his *En torno a Galileo*.

It would be hard to deny an element of intellectual history to all the interpretative "leads," the suggestive "ideas" in the folk sense of that word, that have enriched historical writing. There are recent examples, such as the Pirenne thesis that the real break between late Roman culture and that of the Middle Ages was not caused by the Germanic invasions of the fifth and sixth centuries but by the Arab invasions several centuries later, followed by the Viking incursions; Marc Bloch's interpretation of French agrarian history in *Les caractères originaux de l'histoire rurale française;* the contrasting conceptions advanced by Tawney and Trevor-Roper on the composition and the role of the "gentry" in early modern England (Tawney's *Religion and the Rise of Capitalism* is an English variation of the work of Max Weber); Braudel's use of leads from human geography in his study of the Mediterranean; Meinecke's clear definition of one kind of historicism; the very familiar Turner thesis of the role of the frontier in American history; and so on down to theses involving apparently very minor concrete details, such as that brought out by Lynn White on the wide-reaching effects of the early medieval invention of the horse collar or that advanced by Walter Webb on the changes in the American great plains made possible by the availability of inexpensive barbed wire.

The task of the intellectual historian is difficult. He must try to get source materials for the opinions and attitudes of at least a sampling of those strata in a given society that he thinks are touched by the ideas he discusses. With the invention of printing and especially with the development of the mass media and, in our own day, opinion polling, he gets almost too much material. For earlier periods he has to scrape together what he can, much helped by what several generations of workers have accumulated under such headings as social history, history of morals, *Sittengeschichte,* and the like. The very great body of what is commonly called "literature" from the Egyptians, Greeks, ancient Chinese, and others down to the present is, of course, a mine of information on the opinions and attitudes of fictional men and women who were not "intellectuals" and who may often have been "typical" of their culture.

Finally, intellectual history has necessarily close relations with some of the social sciences, notably sociology and what is usually called cultural anthropology. The practitioners of cultural anthropology are now venturing increasingly into the study of developed societies with abundant recorded history. For these, and for some of the other social sciences, intellectual history—and, indeed,

other kinds of history—can supplement observation and experimentation by providing materials essential for the understanding of development through time, materials comparable in no mere figure of speech to those that paleontology and historical geology contribute to the earth sciences.

Crane Brinton

[*See also* Science, *article on* the history of science; *and the biographies of* Croce; Dilthey; Febvre; Mannheim; Marx; Meinecke; Robinson; Sarton.]

BIBLIOGRAPHY

American Historical Association 1961 *Guide to Historical Literature.* New York: Macmillan.

Barnes, Harry E. (1937) 1961 *Intellectual and Cultural History of the Western World.* 3d rev. ed., 3 vols. New York: Reynal-Hitchcock. → A paperback edition was published by Dover in 1965.

Brinton, Crane (1958) 1963 *Ideas and Men: The Story of Western Thought.* 2d ed. Englewood Cliffs, N.J.: Prentice-Hall.

Brinton, Crane 1964 *European Intellectual History.* New York: Macmillan. → Contains a selective bibliography.

Church, William F. (editor) 1964 *The Influence of the Enlightenment on the French Revolution: Creative, Disastrous, or Non-existent.* Boston: Heath.

Ekirch, Arthur A. Jr. 1963 *American Intellectual History.* New York: Macmillan.

Erikson, Erik H. 1964 *Insight and Responsibility: Lectures on the Ethical Implications of Psychoanalytic Insight.* New York: Norton.

Haskins, Charles H. (1927) 1957 *The Renaissance of the Twelfth Century.* New York: Meridian.

Haskins, Charles H. (1929) 1958 *Studies in Medieval Culture.* New York: Ungar.

Ideas in Cultural Perspective. Edited by Philip Wiener and Aaron Noland. 1962 New Brunswick, N.J.: Rutgers Univ. Press. → Essays from the *Journal of the History of Ideas* arranged to illustrate problems of method in intellectual history and its various fields.

Lovejoy, Arthur O. (1936) 1961 *The Great Chain of Being: A Study of the History of an Idea.* Cambridge, Mass.: Harvard Univ. Press.

Mannheim, Karl (1928) 1952 The Problem of Generations. Pages 276–320 in Karl Mannheim, *Essays on the Sociology of Knowledge.* New York: Oxford Univ. Press. → First published in German.

Ortega y Gasset, José (1933) 1962 *Man and Crisis.* New York: Norton. → First published as *En torno a Galileo.*

Randall, John H. Jr. (1926) 1940 *The Making of the Modern Mind: A Survey of the Intellectual Background of the Present Age.* Rev. ed. Boston: Houghton Mifflin.

Robinson, James Harvey (1921) 1950 *The Mind in the Making: The Relation of Intelligence to Social Reform.* With an introduction by Stuart Chase. New York: Harper.

Smith, Preserved (1930–1934) 1962 *A History of Modern Culture.* 2 vols. New York: Collier. → Volume 1: *Origins of Modern Culture, 1543–1687.* Volume 2: *The Enlightenment, 1687–1776.*

SOCIAL SCIENCE RESEARCH COUNCIL, COMMITTEE ON HIS-
TORIOGRAPHY 1946 *Theory and Practice in Historical Study.* Bulletin No. 54. New York: The Council.
SOCIAL SCIENCE RESEARCH COUNCIL, COMMITTEE ON HIS-
TORICAL ANALYSIS 1963 *Generalization in the Writing of History.* Edited by Louis R. Gottschalk. Univ.
of Chicago Press.

VII
ECONOMIC HISTORY

Economic history is broadly concerned with the performance of economies in the past. The issues that are relevant to an economic historian range as widely as an interest in the growth, stagnation, or decline of economies; the well-being of individual groups in the economy during the course of economic change; and the interrelationship between economic organization and performance. This last issue necessarily focuses on the institutional structure of the society. As a result, economic history frequently spills over into the allied fields of social and political history. However, the major issues of economic history fall into two rather broad categories—(1) the over-all growth of the economy over time and the determinants of that growth (or stagnation or decline) and (2) the distribution of income within that economy in the course of its growth or decline. The latter concern covers the whole range of issues of the well-being of diverse groups in the society during the course of economic change in the past.

The distinguishing feature of economic history as compared with the discipline of economics itself is its paramount concern with problems of the past rather than of the present. It is distinguishable from general historical inquiry not only by its specialized concern with economic aspects of past societies but also by its appeal to a systematic body of theory as a source of generalization and by the equally systematic use of quantitative methods of organizing evidence.

Recent changes in the discipline. The use of the above characteristics to separate economic history from general historical inquiry reflects a distinct change in the discipline in recent times. In the *Encyclopaedia of the Social Sciences,* John Clapham could describe the discipline as "a branch of general institutional history, a study of the economic aspects of the social institutions of the past" (1931, p. 327). In his article, Clapham made clear that economic theory had a minor role in economic history and "the relationship of economic history to social history is much closer" (1931, p. 329). Essentially, the field was a branch of historical inquiry employing the methods of the historian.

In the intervening years, the discipline has grad-
ually adopted more of the methodology of the social sciences. While this revolution in economic history is far from over, and while today much if not most economic history is still written by scholars trained as historians, the direction of change is unmistakable. The pioneering studies in this transformation include Clapham's emphasis on measurement (1926–1938); Eli Heckscher's plea for an increasing use of economic theory in economic history (Lane & Riemersma 1953); and the studies of the International Committee on Price History (Cole & Crandall 1964), including William Beveridge's work on England (1939), Earl Hamilton's on Spain (1934), N. W. Posthumus' on Holland (1943), and Arthur Cole's on the United States (1938). Occasional efforts to systematically apply principles of economic analysis to problems in economic history were highlighted by T. S. Ashton's work on the English industrial revolution (1948) and Walt W. Rostow's effort to analyze the British economy of the nineteenth century (1948).

In the period since World War II, and particularly since 1950, the professionally trained economist has led the new development of the field. In some instances, such as the work of the Entrepreneurial Center at Harvard, research was inspired by Joseph Schumpeter's emphasis on the creative role of the entrepreneur in economic development (1939). The direction of research under Arthur Cole's leadership of the center was an early (and perhaps premature) attempt to synthesize the social sciences in order to establish a more comprehensive theoretical framework for economic historians (Harvard University . . . 1949). [*See* HISTORY, *article on* BUSINESS HISTORY.]

Three developments have furnished the major stimuli to the redirection of economic history. First there has been the growing interest of economists in the study of economic growth. Since World War II economists have devoted a major share of their attention to attempting to understand the sources of economic development and to account for the widely divergent patterns of economic growth between the high-income countries of the Western world and the low-income countries of the underdeveloped parts of the world. The study of economic development has led economists to isolate important elements and determinants of economic development, even though they do not fit as yet into an over-all general theory. These elements include the problems of adapting and modifying technology from one economy to another having different factor endowments; the importance of investment in human capital; and the study of the development of efficient factor and product markets. The research of the economist on the sources of increased productivity, which underlies economic development, has revolutionary implications for re-examining the way in which economic historians have accounted for development in the past. [*See* AGRICULTURE, *article on* PRODUCTIVITY AND TECHNOLOGY; ECONOMIC GROWTH; PRODUCTIVITY.]

The second source of change has been the growing interest of economists in the more precise testing of their hypotheses. The development of operational propositions which can be tested has become a major concern of economists and is being extended to problems in economic history. This involves the sophisticated use of statistical techniques and methods as well, of course, as the careful use of economic theory. [*See* ECONOMETRICS.]

The third source of change has been the growing volume of quantitative information about the past. This concern with measurement of the performance of economies in the past has been largely the work of economists—or, in recent years, of economic historians trained in economics. The development of national income accounting has contributed significantly to the measurement of the performance of economies in the past. Simon Kuznets has played a pioneering role in both the development of national income accounts and their systematic application to the measurement of the past performance of economies (1956–1963). The pioneering studies in price history have been supplemented in many Western countries. The quantitative studies of the National Bureau of Economic Research in the United States have been paralleled in many other countries. The result is an enormous increase in quantitative information, which provides the economic historian with empirical data that he may put to systematic use in testing his propositions.

Taken together, these three developments have led to a growing reorientation of economic history toward the employment of scientific methodology and the systematic use of quantitative measurement. With these essential tools, the economic historian may be able to provide far greater understanding of the past than he has heretofore done. Therefore this article essentially offers a methodological prescription for the present and the future instead of surveying the past literature of the field. While the illustrations are drawn from American economic history, the underlying principles they illustrate are universally applicable.

Explanation in economic history. The primary objective of the economic historian is explanation. He seeks to understand the way economies have operated or the way the welfare of people in the society has been affected by economic phenomena. In this respect, explanation in economic history does not differ significantly from scientific explanation in the natural and physical sciences. It not only involves the careful unearthing of facts and evidence about the phenomenon to be explained but also requires the application of generalizations to reduce the shapeless mass of evidential information to an orderly explanation. Therefore, explanation in economic history, as in the sciences, involves the statement of the essential background conditions—that is, singular statements of facts which provide the setting for the particular pattern of events to be explained—followed by the application of general principles which will provide the explanation.

The economic historian, then, is concerned with determining the extent to which his explanation fits the empirical evidence he is able to obtain. Ideally, this empirical evidence is quantitative in nature; it may be, however, only a number of qualitative statements to which he assigns particular weights. To the extent that the empirical evidence runs contrary to his generalizations, the economic historian should re-explore the background conditions which he has assumed or modify and develop new generalizations which will be more consistent with the available empirical evidence. This process of give-and-take between the development of generalizations, the specification of background conditions, and the testing of the generalizations against systematic empirical evidence is the way by which the economic historian attempts to provide the explanation of historical phenomena.

The body of theory that the economic historian employs is that of economics. This theory rests upon a number of basic axioms and postulates from which are derived subsidiary propositions that express the general form of the functions used in constructing models. These models represent broad generalizations of economic behavior. [*See* ECONOMICS.] This body of economic theory has emerged in the past two centuries in the course of a continual interchange between the development of generalizations and their testing against empirical evidence. While economic theory provides certain basic models of economic behavior, application of these models to given historical situations requires the specification of the particular functional forms, parameters, or changes in parameters which may not be known to the economic historian. Therefore, the model that he constructs is one in which these forms and shifts of functions must be discovered and specified. The empirical verification of historical models requires the testing of the functional relationships implicitly or explicitly embodied in the explanation in order to see whether the parameters of these equations are consistent with available data.

For example, hypotheses that attribute the failure of the southern United States to industrialize before the Civil War to the small size of southern markets for manufactured goods rest upon assumed shapes of the supply functions of manufacturing industries at that time and can be tested, at least in part, by standard statistical procedures. Likewise, the contention that the discontent of farmers in western Massachusetts in the post-Revolutionary War period was due to the severe burden imposed upon them by a whiskey tax can be tested by measuring the elasticity of the demand for whiskey at that time. This information is needed to determine the incidence of the tax.

Causal explanations implicitly involve counterfactual propositions. That is, they imply that "had conditions been different" the causal sequence inferred in the proposition would not have taken place. A statement that the industrial revolution in Britain was induced by the expansion of population implies the counterfactual proposition that in the absence of this population increase the industrial revolution would not have occurred. A statement that the monopoly practices of the "robber barons" at the end of the nineteenth century significantly lowered the income of workers and farmers implies the counterfactual statement that in the absence of monopoly profits the incomes of farmers and workers would have been significantly higher.

The testing of hypotheses. The testing of explanations in economic history can take several forms. These include examination of (1) the empirical validity of the background conditions; (2) the logical consistency of the model; (3) the empirical validity of functions that relate the background conditions to the conclusions; (4) the empirical validity of the conclusions. The most appropriate point at which to test a given explanation depends on the issues under consideration and the availability of data. Thus, an explanation of the causes of farmer discontent in the late nineteenth century in the United States which asserts that the source of this discontent was the more rapid fall of farm prices than of prices of other goods can be refuted by empirical data showing that farm prices fell no more rapidly than other prices (North 1966). A hypothesis which maintains that slavery would have fallen under its own weight without a civil war rests upon the economic viability of slavery as an institution. It can be refuted by a subsidiary hypothesis if, under testing, the latter shows that slavery was a profitable institution (Meyer & Conrad 1958). It should be noted that a confirmation of the profitability of slavery will refute the earlier hypothesis; but if slavery should prove to have been unprofitable, it still would not prove the institution was nonviable, since Southerners may have wanted to buy and hold slaves for noneconomic reasons.

The economic historian may also be able to test a given counterfactual proposition. Thus, an argument that the railroad was indispensable for U.S. economic development in the nineteenth century could be refuted by testing the counterfactual proposition on which it rests—that is, by showing that the cost of moving goods by the best alternative form of transportation would not have been substantially higher than the cost of moving goods by railroad. Such a test involves the determination of the supply function of rail and nonrail transport services (Fogel 1964). Similarly, the statement that the robber barons significantly lowered the income of farmers and workers by monopoly practices could be refuted if it were shown that the total amount of monopoly profit at that time, if redistributed among farmers and workers, would not have significantly raised their incomes (North 1966)—and under the further assumption that the misallocation of resources under monopoly conditions would not have significantly affected this.

Methodological techniques illustrated. An extended illustration can illuminate the whole process of research and testing and the problems involved. The hypothesis that British imperial policy significantly lowered the income of the American colonists in the period 1763–1775 will serve as the example. This hypothesis implies as a counterfactual statement that in the absence of specific British policies the income of the colonies would have been significantly higher. The information needed to obtain a precise answer to this question is the actual income of the colonists between 1763 and 1775 as against the hypothetical income the colonists would have received during this period in the absence of the British policies (i.e., as an independent country outside British regulation and protection). Since the actual income of the colonists is not known, the problem cannot be attacked directly, but it might be resolved indirectly by measuring the net difference in income that would have occurred had the specific policies been eliminated.

The researcher requires first an intimate knowledge of the structure and characteristics of the colonial economy and the specific aspects of the Navigation Acts and other British imperial policies that impinged upon the colonial economy. It should be noted that even the process of selection of facts as a part of the background conditions involves theorizing, since it is impossible to separate out relevant and important facts from irrelevant ones without a theory concerning the way an economy operates. Thus, when the economic historian discards as relatively unimportant the British restrictions on colonial manufacturing, he does so first because economic theory tells him that any economy characterized by a scarcity of labor and capital relative to land—the situation of the American colonies—will not typically engage in manufacturing because its costs will be higher than those of competing regions. He is furthermore supported in his initial assumption through examination of data on the economy of the United States after independence, which shows that manufacturing did not loom large even when the ex-colonists were free to engage in it. On the other hand, he will be impressed by the fact that tobacco and rice were enumerated (i.e., had to be shipped to England), and the requirement that imports move through Britain probably had a significant effect upon colonial income.

While the general shape of the relevant demand curves would stem from basic economic axioms (i.e., that the demand curves would be negatively sloped), it now becomes necessary to obtain a specific measure of the elasticity of demand and supply for tobacco in order to assess exactly the extent of the burden involved. By getting data on the spread between Virginia and Amsterdam prices of tobacco before and again after the revolution, the economic historian is able to show how the price spread narrowed. However, in order to be able to find out how much more tobacco would have been bought at the lower price that would have prevailed without British restriction, he must know the elasticity of demand. Since the data needed to compute that elasticity are not available, the historian may have recourse to other studies of commodities which appear to have similar characteristics and which give him the assumed elasticity of demand. He must also know how much more tobacco would have been supplied had a higher price prevailed (i.e., he must know the elasticity of supply). Here he may get a proxy by seeing how much the tobacco supply expanded after the revolution in response to a higher price. Alternatively, he might look at the conditions of supply in Virginia and Maryland to see to what extent the supply of inputs of land, labor, and capital was capable of providing more tobacco and whether at the same cost or at rising costs.

The economic historian must examine all other aspects of the colonial economy on which British policy impinged. The intimate knowledge of those facts of the period which theory attests to be relevant will lead him not only to assess individual burdens but also to recognize that there were benefits to being a part of the British imperial system which will have to be calculated in similar fashion. Thus, he will have to measure the extent to which income from shipping was increased by inclusion within the British imperial system. Similarly, he will have to measure the extent to which the colonists would have had to underwrite their own defense in the absence of British protection. He may find that a proxy for these counterfactual conditions can be found in the period from 1785 to 1793, after the colonies became independent. That is, he is assuming that the period 1785–1793 approximates in significant aspects the way the economy would have operated had it been free and independent in the years 1763–1775.

This illustration not only provides a capsule indication of the necessary and essential methods by which the economic historian may do meaningful research, but it also provides some indication of the problems and difficulties involved in his task. Has he really specified and taken into account all of the indispensable conditions? Was he correct in ignoring the Stamp Act as not imposing significant burdens upon the colonists? Are his assumed elasticities of supply and demand the correct ones, or can additional evidence be garnered which would indicate that they were different from those he specified? Were the conditions between 1785 and 1793 really a proxy for those from 1763 to 1775, thereby enabling him properly to employ this period as a proxy to the counterfactual situation? In fact, what he is doing is comparing a condition that existed—that is, income of the colonists between 1763 and 1775—with the hypothetical model of what would have occurred in the absence of British policies. This hypothetical model of a situation that did not in fact exist is essentially a general equilibrium model, and therefore it is essential to his argument and his conclusions that the repercussion effects of those things which he does not take into account or which he argues are of small magnitude are in fact immaterial and would not significantly alter the conclusions he reaches.

Advances in economic theory will lead to reappraisals of the economic past. Like the traditional historian, the present-day economic historian will frequently be guided by his ideological preconceptions in making a choice of issues to be examined; but his testing of the resultant hypotheses should be neutral with respect to current ideological biases and should result in a continuous narrowing of the range of disagreement and an increasing understanding of the past.

It can be seen from the above illustration that the limitations of inquiry in economic history are those imposed by the limitations of existing theory and of available evidence.

The uses and limitations of theory. While economic theory provides generalizations that can be applied to a broad range of issues in economic history, particularly to those dealing with the welfare of groups at particular times in the past, there is no general theory of economic growth to which the economic historian can turn in exploring this major aspect of economic history. While research in the study of economic growth of the past twenty or thirty years casts doubt upon many of the implicit or explicit hypotheses of economic historians, there is still no over-all framework which the economic historian can neatly apply. So, in this field, as in so many other aspects of economic history, the scholar must essentially develop his own theoretical framework. Similarly, where the economic historian wishes to explore the theoretical borderlines between economic and social history, he must rely on the other social science disciplines or develop a framework of his own to explore these relationships. There is no reason, of course, why the economic historian should be limited to received theory in economics. He is free to develop and apply theory of his own. However, caution in such an endeavor is obviously essential. The likelihood that the economic historian who is untrained in the principles of economics can derive theoretical propositions of any significance is very slim indeed. There is as wide a gap between common-sense observations in economics and economic generalizations as there is between common-sense observations in the physical sciences and the general laws of those physical sciences. We would not expect a layman to be able to derive from simple observation of physical properties the general laws of physics; nor can observations of economic phenomena lead an untrained economic historian to develop valid generalizations with respect to economic theory. Economic theory has evolved in the give-and-take between the development of generalizations and their testing over a long enough period of time, and it cannot and should not be ignored in the course of analysis. The economic historian trained in economic theory will be well aware of the pitfalls inherent in economic analysis. Therefore, if he wishes to develop his own theoretical framework, he will take careful account of

the work that has gone on before and the degree to which previous generalizations are supported by available evidence.

The limitations of empirical evidence. Limitations of empirical evidence pose equally serious problems for the economic historian. He is faced with discrete, nonrepetitive, past performance: the artifacts and evidence that remain are his material. Therefore, it is essential that he attempt systematically to develop evidence about the past from this fragmentary information. As indicated above, that which comes closest to providing him with accurate tests is quantitative evidence which precisely defines and isolates the particular phenomena that he wants to measure. Quantitative information in such ideal form seldom exists, and the economic historian is forced to make use of the more fragmentary evidence which has typically survived from the past. Making the most of the evidence requires a knowledge of statistical theory so that he can use to the best effect whatever data are available.

The illustration used above indicates some of the ways the economic historian can employ bits and pieces of quantitative information when the ideal data are not available. In the above case, neither the actual national income of the colonists between 1763 and 1775 nor the hypothetical income in the absence of British policies is known. But the net difference in income can be derived even without the absolute figures. A complete series of prices and quantities for tobacco, rice, and other affected commodities is also not available, but proxies for these can be obtained that provide reasonably good measures for the unknowns with respect to the shape of the relevant demand and supply curves.

The further back in time the economic historian explores, the more inadequate the data are likely to be. However, the quantitative information may be far more abundant than economic historians have heretofore believed, since hypotheses dictate the search for data, and it is only in recent years that self-conscious employment of theory has characterized research in the field. The quantitative information available about the past has usually not been mined because its relevance has not been appreciated. In the absence of quantitative data, the economic historian is forced to fall back on the use of qualitative description embodied in other kinds of information; but it should be noted here that he does not thereby escape the essential rules of statistical inference. That is, it remains imperative that he demand that the qualitative information meet the same rules of statistical sampling and representativeness required in the use of quantitative knowledge. In this respect, Clapham's warning in the article on economic history in the *Encyclopaedia of the Social Sciences* is still timely.

Every economic historian should, however, have acquired what might be called the statistical sense, the habit of asking in relation to any institution, policy, group or movement the question: how large? how long? how often? how representative? The requirement seems obvious; but a good deal of the older politico–institutional economic history was less useful than it might have been through neglect of it. (1931, p. 328)

The writing of economic history. While explanation of the economic past is the ultimate objective of the economic historian, and an awareness of the principles of scientific method is an essential requirement in the pursuit of this objective, characterization of the discipline solely in these terms would give a distorted picture of the field. The traditional craft of the historian—the careful unearthing of evidence and the assessment of its reliability—is fully as important in economic history as it is in general history. The present-day scholar has inherited a rich store of descriptive material and data about the economic past which has been mined and assayed largely by historians. The present-day analytically oriented economic historian who ignores this treasure-trove from the past does so at the risk that he will be unaware of essential background conditions when he constructs his model. It is incumbent upon him not only to be thoroughly versed in the traditional literature in the field but also to be possessed of that fine sense of the detective, which has always been the trademark of the good historian.

Finally, the economic historian is attempting to provide a systematic and integrated explanation of the economic past, and this inevitably involves something more than the development and testing of a single hypothesis. It is a relatively easy task for any well-trained economic historian to test (and typically in recent research to destroy) a specific explanation about the past, but it is well for him to remember that the ultimate objective he seeks is far more difficult—to construct a unified explanation of the economic past. This involves the development of a set of consistent hypotheses together with the essential background conditions, both woven together in the fabric of a narrative. Such a story not only possesses the characteristics of good narrative but also makes clear the essential background conditions and states clearly the hypotheses involved, so that it is consistent with the principles of scientific explanation and so that its

several parts can be tested by other economic historians.

DOUGLASS C. NORTH

[*Directly relevant are the biographies of* CLAPHAM; HECKSCHER; SCHUMPETER. *For discussion of the approaches of some other economic historians, see the biographies of* ASHLEY; BÜCHER; CUNNINGHAM; EHRENBERG; HAMMOND, J. L. AND BARBARA; LEVASSEUR; PIRENNE; POLANYI; ROGERS; SÉE; TAWNEY; UNWIN; USHER; WEBB, SIDNEY AND BEATRICE; WEBER, MAX.]

BIBLIOGRAPHY

GENERAL

ASHTON, T. S. (1948) 1964 *The Industrial Revolution: 1760–1830.* Rev. ed. Oxford Univ. Press.

BEVERIDGE, WILLIAM H. 1939 *Prices and Wages in England From the Twelfth to the Nineteenth Century.* New York and London: Longmans.

CLAPHAM, JOHN H. (1926–1938) 1950–1952 *An Economic History of Modern Britain.* 3 vols. Cambridge Univ. Press. → Volume 1: *The Early Railway Age: 1820–1850.* Volume 2: *Free Trade and Steel: 1850–1886.* Volume 3: *Machines and National Rivalries (1887–1914)* with an epilogue (1914–1929).

CLAPHAM, JOHN H. 1931 "Survey of Development to the Twentieth Century" and "Economic History as a Discipline." Volume 5, pages 315–320 and 327–330 in *Encyclopaedia of the Social Sciences.* New York: Macmillan. → Definitive of earlier views of the discipline; includes a bibliography. These are two parts of the article "Economic History."

COLE, ARTHUR H. 1938 *Wholesale Commodity Prices in the United States: 1700–1861.* 2 vols. Cambridge, Mass.: Harvard Univ. Press.

COLE, ARTHUR H.; and CRANDALL, RUTH 1964 The International Scientific Committee on Price History. *Journal of Economic History* 24:381–388. → A review of the work of the committee and a bibliography.

FOGEL, ROBERT W. 1964 *Railroads and American Economic Growth: Essays in Econometric History.* Baltimore: Johns Hopkins Press.

HAMILTON, EARL J. (1934) 1965 *American Treasure and the Price Revolution in Spain: 1501–1650.* Harvard Economic Studies, Vol. 43. New York: Octagon. Cambridge, Mass.: Harvard Univ. Press.

HARVARD UNIVERSITY, RESEARCH CENTER IN ENTREPRENEURIAL HISTORY 1949 *Change and the Entrepreneur: Postulates and Patterns for Entrepreneurial History.* Edited by Arthur Cole. Cambridge, Mass.: Harvard Univ. Press.

HECKSCHER, ELI F. (1929) 1953 A Plea for Theory in Economic History. Pages 421–430 in Frederic C. Lane and Jelle C. Riemersma (editors), *Enterprise and Secular Change: Readings in Economic History.* Homewood, Ill.: Irwin. → First published in a supplement to the *Economic Journal.*

KUZNETS, SIMON 1956–1963 Quantitative Aspects of the Economic Growth of Nations. Parts 1–8. *Economic Development and Cultural Change* 5, no. 1:5–94, no. 4 (Supplement); 6, no. 4:part 2; 7, no. 3:part 2; 8, no. 4:part 2; 9, no. 4:part 2; 10, no. 2:part 2; 11, no. 2:part 2.

LANE, FREDERIC C.; and RIEMERSMA, JELLE C. (editors) 1953 *Enterprise and Secular Change: Readings in*

Economic History. Homewood, Ill.: Irwin. → Contains a number of useful articles on earlier views of methodology.

MEYER, JOHN R.; and CONRAD, ALFRED H. 1957 Economic Theory, Statistical Inference and Economic History. *Journal of Economic History* 17:524–544.

NORTH, DOUGLASS C. 1966 *Growth and Welfare in the American Past: A New Economic History.* Englewood Cliffs, N.J.: Prentice-Hall.

POSTHUMUS, NICOLAAS W. (1943) 1946 *Inquiry Into the History of Prices in Holland.* Volume 1: Wholesale Prices at the Exchange of Amsterdam, 1585–1914. Leiden (Netherlands): Brill. → First published in Dutch.

ROSTOW, WALT W. 1948 *British Economy of the Nineteenth Century: Essays.* Oxford: Clarendon. → A pioneering effort to apply Keynesian theory to analyzing the British economy in the nineteenth century.

SCHUMPETER, JOSEPH A. 1939 *Business Cycles: A Theoretical, Historical, and Statistical Analysis of the Capitalist Process.* 2 vols. New York and London: McGraw-Hill. → An abridged version was published in 1964.

PHILOSOPHY AND METHODOLOGY

There is an extensive literature in the philosophy of science and the philosophy of history on the methodological problems of writing history. Two of the most lucid as they bear upon explanation in economic history are Hempel 1942 *and* 1962. *See also* Nagel 1952. *For the application of these principles specifically to economic history, a pioneering article is* Meyer & Conrad 1958.

HEMPEL, CARL G. 1942 The Function of General Laws in History. *Journal of Philosophy* 39:35–48.

HEMPEL, CARL G. 1962 Explanation in Science and History. Pages 7–33 in Robert G. Colodny (editor), *Frontiers of Science and Philosophy.* Univ. of Pittsburgh Press.

MEYER, JOHN R.; and CONRAD, ALFRED H. 1958 The Economics of Slavery in the Ante Bellum South. *Journal of Political Economy* 66:95–130.

NAGEL, ERNEST 1952 Some Issues in the Logic of Historical Analysis. *Scientific Monthly* 74:162–169.

STATISTICAL SOURCES

It is impossible to enumerate the large and ever-increasing body of statistical studies now appearing. The most convenient major sources are the statistical abstracts which so far have been done for three countries.

MITCHELL, BRIAN R. 1962 *Abstract of British Historical Statistics.* Cambridge Univ. Press.

U.S. BUREAU OF THE CENSUS 1960 *Historical Statistics of the United States; Colonial Times to 1957: A Statistical Abstract Supplement.* Washington: Government Printing Office.

URQUHART, M. C.; and BUCKLEY, K. A. H. (editors) 1965 *Historical Statistics of Canada.* Cambridge Univ. Press.

VIII
BUSINESS HISTORY

Although business history in the broadest sense encompasses all the activities of businessmen in the past, the academic discipline, as developed by historians, has certain distinguishing characteristics. To date it has been primarily concerned with the written record of decision making by individuals seeking private profit through production of goods and services.

Business history in practice rests basically on one assumption and one derivative from it. The key assumption is that man enjoys a measure of freedom of will and, accordingly, that his individual decisions affect the course of historical events. From that is derived the conviction that human decisions, made with an eye to producing profit, have significantly shaped the stream of economic and social change over a long period of time and in many parts of the world.

In business history, change is regarded as continuous, interacting in character, variable in rate, and open-ended—but always initiated by man. Through a complex of interrelated decision-making processes, businessmen are seen to have contributed, together with other individuals and groups in society, to the generation of changes in their environment, both internal and external to their own institutions.

Certain methodological characteristics of business history follow from the foregoing assumptions and ideas. It emphasizes microeconomic elements in the past more than its parent discipline, economic history, and concentrates more on the process of change and the generation of change. To date, business historians have employed impersonal analysis of economic performance in the past less than those who have utilized the techniques of economists to evaluate trends in quantitative terms or to "fill in" gaps in historical knowledge. In fact, the tools of sociology, anthropology, and psychology are frequently as relevant to the questions business historians ask of data as is economic analysis, particularly with reference to motivation of men and their relation to the society in which they live. Concentration on businessmen as decision makers and as builders or destroyers of institutions, as well as on the ideas and accumulated knowledge affecting the place, timing, and conduct of business activities, has, of course, also differentiated business history from economic history.

The tools employed by the professional business historian depend on his objective and on the approach to the businessman that he selects. Each major approach involves a different context for viewing businessmen and business of the past. Concern with the businessman as an individual in society is the approach of the biographer of a businessman. Viewed in the framework of one or more organizations for the production of profit, with all that this implies for policy formulation and implementation, the businessman is the province of company histories and industry studies. Some students have chosen the functional areas of business development, such as finance, production, and marketing, as the subjects of historical research. Others have emphasized the implements and institutions of business. Still other scholars have concentrated their research on the interaction between businessmen and their environment in terms of its influence on developments both inside and outside the world of business.

These varied approaches indicate that business history embraces many diverse areas of study, accommodates many interests, and calls on numerous disciplines. It therefore attracts researchers from many areas of history, economics, and other scholarly disciplines, as well as those whose qualifications are based on other credentials. In the latter category are amateur historians with business experience and publicists employed to write business history for nonacademic purposes. Although a number of these contributions meet good scholarly standards and many contribute useful information, most significant works in business history are produced by scholars trained in one or more of the traditional disciplines. By no means all of this latter group, however, would claim to be professional business historians. In many instances their forays into the field are one-time expeditions, using the subject matter of business history to explore an area related to their primary interests.

Professional historians both benefit and suffer from the amorphous nature of their field. They have benefited most from outsiders' contributions to such areas as the theory of the firm and have suffered most from the popular identification of their field with histories of firms written by amateurs without scholarly standards. In part, this has been the price of progress, for business history has matured slowly as an academic discipline and until recently has concentrated on the study of business administration through the medium of company histories.

Since professional business historians have been located chiefly in schools of business administration, it is not surprising that the variety of their approaches to research and teaching has been governed in large measure by the applications that could be made of their work in such institutions. As the curricula of schools of business have broadened from functional specialties to such larger preoccupations as the responsibilities of businessmen in society and the challenge of undeveloped and underdeveloped areas to private enterprise, new applications of business history have been found. Some of these coincide with objectives of historians

concerned with all phases of social and economic change. In many business history courses, histories of firms have been supplemented by industry histories, by studies of the leadership styles and personal qualities of businessmen in the past, by analyses of government–business relations viewed in broad perspective, and by increasing concern with the historical problems and lessons of economic growth. Thus the field of business history has been in the process of change since it was first recognized as an academic discipline.

Initial development by Gras at Harvard

Business history began as an area of academic research and teaching at the Graduate School of Business Administration of Harvard University. Dean Wallace B. Donham believed that scholarly histories of "specific situations as they came to businessmen in their communities in the past" were essential in order that those situations might be compared "understandably" with "current conditions" (Redlich 1962, pp. 61–62). Donham had in mind the use of business history for training prospective business administrators, the utilization of the case method, and the comparison of past techniques, decisions, and their implementation with those of the present.

To initiate such teaching, research, and writing, in 1927 Donham chose N. S. B. Gras, a scholar already manifesting an interest in the role of business and businessmen in history. In his classes at the University of Minnesota he had encouraged students to do research in this field and had embarked on assessing business activities in several areas. He was trained in economic theory as well as economic history, and he had read widely in the literature of sociology and social theory.

Given his training and experience, Gras at first visualized business history quite broadly. From his reading in social, political, and economic history he gathered data on the environments in which businessmen had operated, as well as information on the creation and evolution of business instruments and institutions. Gras accepted the concept of capitalism and made the study of the evolution of capitalism one of his major concerns. But neither in the publications of economic theorists and economic historians nor in the works of Marx, Engels, Sombart, and others did he find a satisfactory explanation of the changing character of capitalism over time. While recognizing that environmental factors influenced businessmen to some degree, he rejected economic determinism; he remained convinced that men have enjoyed some freedom of will and that, by choosing courses of action from a range of alternatives, they have changed the course of history.

Accordingly, to understand the process of change in the business sector of society, Gras believed scholars must study and analyze the decisions of men reflected in the policies and practices of firms, the basic units of business systems. In the studies of Richard Ehrenberg (1902–1905) he had examples of how meaningful histories of firms could be written. From such biographies of firms, written and to be written, Gras hoped to be able to learn how capitalism had evolved as a system.

With these ideas in mind, Gras embarked on an ambitious program for the development of business history at the Harvard Business School. With the aid of associates, notably Henrietta M. Larson, he started developing cases for the course he taught. That offering embraced discussion and analysis of activities of businessmen from the European Middle Ages to the twentieth-century United States; lectures on background materials alternated with class discussion of both specific and general situations. At the same time, to encourage publication of the current results of research, Edwin F. Gay, then a professor at Harvard, as editor, and Gras as managing editor, began issuing the *Journal of Economic and Business History* (*JEBH*) in November 1928. Some members of the group also undertook book-length biographies of businessmen and firms.

Soon after the beginning of this program, economic and other factors induced Gras to modify his approach to the new area of study. The financial crisis of 1929 and ensuing depression brought a drastic diminution in supporting funds. The *JEBH* ceased publication in 1932, a year after Gay and Gras disagreed on editorial policies and the latter became sole editor; not until 1938 did the business history group at the Harvard Business School assume responsibility for issuing the *Bulletin of the Business Historical Society*, known as *Business History Review* (*BHR*), a quarterly since 1954, and it was a much less ambitious periodical than the earlier one. Meanwhile, money to underwrite research in depth could be found only in limited amounts, often restricted to study of the families and firms providing the financial support. Simultaneously, the use of the case method in the course, as well as the lack of published information on the decision-making process and the policies of businessmen, fortified Gras's tendency to concentrate on biographies of businessmen and of firms.

In spite of serious difficulties during the 1930s, Gras and his group established the contours of the new field. They, as well as others, published their research findings in both the *JEBH* and the *Bulle-*

tin. In the Harvard Studies in Business History, under the editorship of Gras, appeared books dealing with merchants, an investment banking firm, a commercial bank, and an advertising agency. In 1939 Gras and Larson published the teaching materials assembled for the course—*Casebook in American Business History*—and Gras issued his preliminary synthesis of business history in *Business and Capitalism*.

In little more than ten years Gras had modified his concepts and had put a particular stamp on business history. Instead of realizing his early expectation of studying and writing the history of business within a broad political, social, and economic framework, he gradually came to visualize the field more narrowly. To him, business history became "primarily the study of the administration of business units in the past," administration being in two parts—policy formulation and management or execution of policy (Gras & Larson 1939, p. 3). From such statements, as well as the subject matter of the books published, many observers adopted the idea, unfortunately not yet fully abandoned, that to Gras business history was "company history" and nothing more.

Actually, *Business and Capitalism* indicated that Gras was seeking, through business history, an explanation of the changes in the character of private capitalism over a thousand years. Influenced by Karl Bücher and others, Gras related the evolution of stages in capitalism to changes in business systems, identifying each stage with dominant business types and groups—petty, mercantile, industrial (specializing), financial, and national. When he started writing the book, he did not think all the stages mentioned actually fitted the history of private enterprise in every national economy, but after its publication the idea became more than a tentative hypothesis in his mind. To supplement *Business and Capitalism*, he began writing a multivolume history of industries in the United States, a task never completed. However, Larson published her *Guide to Business History* in 1948, and the Business History Foundation, Inc., an organization chartered in New York by Gras and Larson in 1947 to forward research and writing on the history of business (chiefly on that of large-scale enterprise), is still active.

Subsequent broadening of approaches

Starting with the *Casebook* and *Business and Capitalism* as the bases of courses in other institutions, historians soon began to utilize a variety of approaches to the history of business. Some accepted Gras's ideas generally, but increasingly used his stage theory for comparative purposes and not as a rigid framework for analyzing the history of businessmen and business institutions. Other scholars reacted more critically, explicitly and implicitly, to Grasian thought. Some regarded his stage theory as outmoded; they considered it too rigid and not sufficiently effective as an analytical tool. Others were convinced that his definition of the subject was too narrow; they thought the history of business and businessmen was more than the history of business administration and that Gras gave too little attention to the motivation and environment of businessmen. Many disagreed with the broad generalizations, especially those on the period since 1870, which Gras made on the basis of research by his group and by predecessors among economic and social historians. Still others sought a less positivistic and more theoretical base for analyzing the behavior and achievements of businessmen in history. Almost all were more interested in analyzing the activities of businessmen or in seeking explanations of changes in business than in the history of capitalism as such.

Entrepreneurial studies.   One group of scholars, the most influential, sought understanding of change in the history of business through the concept of entrepreneurship. Arthur H. Cole reviewed the historical changes in that concept in his presidential address to the Economic History Association (1946). A year later, in a paper presented to the same body, Joseph A. Schumpeter built onto the idea of innovation that of the creative entrepreneur as the main force in generating change in business (1947). Jointly the two initiated the Research Center in Entrepreneurial History at Harvard in 1948. Led by Cole, and ably supported by Thomas C. Cochran, Leland H. Jenks, Fritz Redlich, and several others, the group brought together numerous scholars to enunciate their ideas and to discuss historical tools and techniques as well as concepts. Over a ten-year period the center helped to train a number of young historians and published many of the products of discussion and research in *Explorations in Entrepreneurial History*.

Cole has provided his personal interpretation of the significant findings of the center (1959). First, he assessed the relationship of the entrepreneur to his organization, to the process of social conditioning, and to elements important "for the proper functioning of an entrepreneurial flow." Then he turned to analysis of five categories of "entrepreneurial realities" drawn from historical data: the social order, underdeveloped areas, technological change, business organization, and the state. Each of these had three subsegments of illustrative mate-

rial which not only summarized existing substantive knowledge about types of entrepreneurial activity but also presented other historians of business with examples which could be utilized in class, tested by research, and added to as the study of businessmen and their institutions continued.

Even before Cole's synthesis appeared, both older scholars and a new generation of historians of business began to fuse the center's products with those of the Grasian group. Some welcomed the center's analysis of business history in a broad sociological as well as economic context. Many noted with approval that Cole defined entrepreneurship as "the purposeful activity (including an integrated sequence of decisions) of an individual or group of associated individuals, undertaken to initiate, maintain or aggrandize a profit-oriented business unit for the production or distribution of goods and services" (1959, p. 7). That definition, business historians generally thought, embraced both policy formulation, which they now visualized as closely related to Schumpeterian creative entrepreneurship, and management (implementation of policy), which was seemingly included in an "integrated sequence of decisions."

In addition to concepts, ideas, and information adduced by the Gras and Cole groups, business historians have turned to other disciplines for tools and techniques. From writers on economic growth (Hirschman 1958) and on the theory of the firm (Boulding & Spivey 1960), as well as from anthropologists, sociologists, and social psychologists (Hagen 1962), scholars interested in the history of business have borrowed and tested concepts, theories, and research methods. They have been particularly interested in any study dealing with motivation of the businessman and his "need of achievement" (McClelland 1961).

In the 1950s and 1960s research continues to reflect the mixture of approaches noted early in this article. Some scholars focus on a businessman as an individual in society (see, for example, Nevins 1953). There have been numerous semipopular histories of firms (see, for example, Lief 1958; Blochman 1958). In some instances histories of firms written by insiders have been distinguished by thorough research and a comprehensive analysis (see, for example, Beaton 1957).

Studies of firms and industries.   Since 1950 academicians have added significantly to the list of firms that have been studied in detail. Several large firms have submitted to detailed scholarly portraits. In large measure these works exhibit the increased sophistication arising from the fusion of ideas noted earlier. The most distinguished study of the much-examined late medieval period deals with the rise and decline of the Medici Bank (de Roover 1963). In their histories of large firms some students have focused their attention on the response and adjustment of businessmen to changing environment (Cochran 1948). One outstanding study is devoted to grand strategy on a global scale (Wilson 1954). Noteworthy have been the analyses of policy *and* its implementation on the part of firms in the petroleum industry, in particular those sponsored by the Business History Foundation (*History of Standard Oil . . .*, 1955–1956; Larson & Porter 1959). Recent histories of American railroad companies tend to present them broadly as common carriers operating for a profit within an environment experiencing rapid change (Overton 1965). Among studies of financial institutions, several life insurance companies have received detailed attention (Williamson & Smalley 1957). A midwestern historian has provided the best portrayal of a public utility (Miller 1957).

The history of small business has attracted fewer scholars than has that of large-scale enterprise. Only rarely has a small firm been appraised in detail (for one example, see Marburg 1956). More attention has been given to generalizations based on a study of a significant sample of firms within an industry, such as that of metal fabricators in New England (Soltow 1965).

Few historians have attempted histories of entire industries in recent years. Among the few examples are those on rubber (Woodruff 1958) and brewing (Mathias 1959), both within the British economy, and, outstanding in scope and economic analysis, that on the American petroleum industry —the authors having at hand at the inception of the research numerous histories of firms as well as special studies (Williamson & Daum 1959–1963).

Recent trends. A growing number of business historians have centered their interest on what has been labeled "business in history." They seek to understand the interaction between businessmen and business institutions on the one hand and pertinent, influential segments of the environment on the other. They are concerned with analyzing both the process and the results of the process. Most prominent in this area have been studies of government–business relationships, well exemplified by many articles found in the *BHR* (and elsewhere). For example, one author has focused on the roles of business institutions and values in relation to evolving political institutions in Africa, Asia, and Latin America (Robinson 1962). Another has evaluated the relationship of business to the emergence of

the Nazi dictatorship (Schweitzer 1964). A third has assessed the connection between a defensive national economic policy, coupled with a desire for political unity, and Canadian regulation of business (Aitken 1964). A similar but more specific approach to the history of government–business relations is exemplified in a study of the evolution of American petroleum pipelines and related public policy (Johnson 1956).

Comparative studies in business history have become more common in recent years, providing new and meaningful interpretations for business historians. Most noteworthy among studies dealing with early industrialization is the pioneer monograph on managerial techniques of British entrepreneurs (Pollard 1965). One author has analyzed causation and cycles in centralization and decentralization in administration of large-scale enterprise (Chandler 1956; 1959; 1962; 1965). Another has studied evolution of systematic methods for coordinating production flows (Litterer 1961a; 1961b; 1963). Still another can be cited for his evaluation of evolving financial reporting by American corporations within a changing environment (Hawkins 1963). One of the most significant books analyzes the attitudes and ideas of a broad group of railroad executives (Cochran 1953).

Most of these recent articles and books manifest more refined analysis than characterized the written history of business in earlier years, but conceptualization of thought in the field has grown slowly and theoretical works have been few. Fritz Redlich has written more in this area than has anyone else, and his essays dealing with the entrepreneur have now been collected (1964). His contributions range from an analysis of the "daimonic" in business history to categorizations of entrepreneurial types. To date, only one author has attempted to advance a theory of the growth of the firm (Penrose 1959).

No widely accepted synthesis of business history has yet been achieved, even for the United States, the country in which literature on the subject is most voluminous. To be sure, some narrations of national business achievement have been produced (Chamberlain 1963; Walker 1949), and some periods in the history of business have been objectively appraised (Cochran 1957).

In spite of vastly increased study of the history of business and of business in history, scholars still evince a marked lack of interest in numerous important topics. Business failures, labor–management relations, small business, and other likely subjects are receiving little, if any, attention. Moreover, although the preliminary moves mentioned above have been made, attempts to conceptualize and to theorize on the history of business have been few.

Formal courses in business history have been developed slowly but steadily. By the mid-1960s more than three-score universities, colleges, and schools of business in the United States listed courses in the field, but the focus on topics involving business history was their single common denominator; content and emphasis varied widely. Meanwhile, academicians in other countries, notably in the United Kingdom, Holland, West Germany, Australia, and Japan, have inaugurated research and/ or teaching programs in business history, bringing the world total of institutions sponsoring such efforts to more than one hundred. Participants in such activities find continuous additions to their body of information in the *Business History Review, Tradition* (published in West Germany since 1956), *Business Archives and History* (published in Australia since 1956), *Business History* (published in the United Kingdom since 1958), and pertinent articles in many other periodicals.

The broadening of horizons noted in this article has destroyed the exclusiveness of the original small pioneering band of professional historians and to a degree has outmoded the original framework that once gave their study of the subject great unity. The results of this change are still far from clear, and the need for a new synthesis has become increasingly apparent. Nevertheless, the governing assumptions about the nature of economic change and the significance of the businessman in it still hold. The increasingly varied approaches and applications of business history are in the tradition of the evolutionary development that has characterized the field since it was first recognized as an academic discipline.

RALPH W. HIDY

[*See also* ENTREPRENEURSHIP; *and the biographies of* GRAS; SCHUMPETER.]

BIBLIOGRAPHY

AITKEN, HUGH G. J. 1964 Government and Business in Canada: An Interpretation. *Business History Review* 38:4–21.

BEATON, KENDALL 1957 *Enterprise in Oil: A History of Shell in the United States.* New York: Appleton.

BLOCHMAN, LAWRENCE G. 1958 *Doctor Squibb: The Life and Times of a Rugged Idealist.* New York: Simon & Schuster.

BOULDING, KENNETH E.; and SPIVEY, W. ALLEN 1960 *Linear Programming and the Theory of the Firm.* New York: Macmillan.

BRUCHEY, STUART W. 1965 *The Roots of American Economic Growth, 1607–1861: An Essay in Social Causation.* New York: Harper.

CHAMBERLAIN, JOHN 1963 *The Enterprising Americans: A Business History of the United States.* New York: Harper.

CHANDLER, ALFRED D. JR. 1956 Management Decentralization: An Historical Analysis. *Business History Review* 30:111–174.

CHANDLER, ALFRED D. JR. 1959 The Beginnings of "Big Business" in American Industry. *Business History Review* 33:1–31.

CHANDLER, ALFRED D. JR. 1962 *Strategy and Structure: Chapters in the History of the Industrial Enterprise.* Cambridge, Mass.: M.I.T. Press.

CHANDLER, ALFRED D. JR. 1965 The Railroads: Pioneers in Modern Corporate Management. *Business History Review* 39:16–40.

COCHRAN, THOMAS C. 1948 *The Pabst Brewing Company: The History of an American Business.* New York Univ. Press.

COCHRAN, THOMAS C. (1953) 1966 *Railroad Leaders, 1845–1890: The Business Mind in Action.* Cambridge, Mass.: Harvard Univ. Press.

COCHRAN, THOMAS C. 1957 *The American Business System: A Historical Perspective, 1900–1955.* Cambridge, Mass.: Harvard Univ. Press.

COLE, ARTHUR H. 1946 An Approach to the Study of Entrepreneurship: A Tribute to Edwin F. Gay. *Journal of Economic History* 6 (Supplement):1–15.

COLE, ARTHUR H. 1959 *Business Enterprise in Its Social Setting.* Cambridge, Mass.: Harvard Univ. Press.

DE ROOVER, RAYMOND A. 1963 *The Rise and Decline of the Medici Bank, 1397–1494.* Harvard Studies in Business History, No. 21. Cambridge, Mass.: Harvard Univ. Press.

EHRENBERG, RICHARD (1902–1905) 1925 *Grosse Vermögen, ihre Entstehung und ihre Bedeutung.* 2d ed. Jena (Germany): Fischer.

GRAS, N. S. B. 1939 *Business and Capitalism: An Introduction to Business History.* New York: Crofts.

GRAS, N. S. B.; and LARSON, HENRIETTA M. 1939 *Casebook in American Business History.* New York: Crofts.

HAGEN, EVERETT E. (1962) 1964 *On the Theory of Social Change: How Economic Growth Begins.* London: Tavistock.

HAWKINS, DAVID F. 1963 The Development of Modern Financial Reporting Practices Among American Manufacturing Corporations. *Business History Review* 37: 135–168.

HIRSCHMAN, ALBERT O. 1958 *The Strategy of Economic Development.* Yale Studies in Economics, No. 10. New Haven: Yale Univ. Press. → A paperback edition was published in 1962.

History of Standard Oil Company (New Jersey). 2 vols. 1955–1956. New York: Harper. → Volume 1: *Pioneering in Big Business, 1888–1911,* by Ralph W. Hidy and Muriel E. Hidy. Volume 2: *The Resurgent Years, 1912–1927,* by George S. Gibb and Evelyn H. Knowlton.

JOHNSON, ARTHUR M. 1956 *The Development of American Petroleum Pipelines: A Study in Private Enterprise and Public Policy, 1862–1906.* Ithaca, N.Y.: Cornell Univ. Press.

LARSON, HENRIETTA M. 1948 *Guide to Business History: Materials for the Study of American Business History and Suggestions for Their Use.* Harvard Studies in

Business History, No. 12. Cambridge, Mass.: Harvard Univ. Press.

LARSON, HENRIETTA M.; and PORTER, KENNETH W. 1959 *History of Humble Oil & Refining Company: A Study in Industrial Growth*. New York: Harper.

LIEF, ALFRED 1958 *It Floats: The Story of Procter & Gamble*. New York: Rinehart.

LITTERER, JOSEPH A. 1961a Alexander Hamilton Church and the Development of Modern Management. *Business History Review* 35:211–225.

LITTERER, JOSEPH A. 1961b Systematic Management: The Search for Order and Integration. *Business History Review* 35:461–476.

LITTERER, JOSEPH A. 1963 Systematic Management: Design for Organizational Recoupling in American Manufacturing Firms. *Business History Review* 37: 369–391.

McCLELLAND, DAVID C. 1961 *The Achieving Society*. Princeton, N.J.: Van Nostrand.

McDONALD, FORREST 1962 *Insull*. Univ. of Chicago Press.

MARBURG, THEODORE F. 1956 *Small Business in Brass Fabricating: The Smith & Griggs Manufacturing Co. of Waterbury*. New York Univ. Press.

MATHIAS, PETER 1959 *The Brewing Industry in England, 1700–1830*. Cambridge Univ. Press.

MILLER, RAYMOND C. 1957 *Kilowatts at Work: A History of the Detroit Edison Company*. Detroit, Mich.: Wayne State Univ. Press.

MILLER, WILLIAM (editor) 1952 *Men in Business: Essays in the History of Entrepreneurship*. Cambridge, Mass.: Harvard Univ. Press.

NEVINS, ALLAN 1953 *Study in Power: John D. Rockefeller, Industrialist and Philanthropist*. 2 vols. New York: Scribner.

OVERTON, RICHARD C. 1965 *Burlington Route: A History of the Burlington Lines*. New York: Knopf.

PENROSE, EDITH T. 1959 *The Theory of the Growth of the Firm*. New York: Wiley.

POLLARD, SIDNEY 1965 *The Genesis of Modern Management: A Study of the Industrial Revolution in Great Britain*. Cambridge, Mass.: Harvard Univ. Press.

REDLICH, FRITZ 1962 Approaches to Business History. *Business History Review* 36:61–70.

REDLICH, FRITZ 1964 *Der Unternehmer: Wirtschafts- und sozialgeschichtliche Studien*. Göttingen (Germany): Vandenhoeck & Ruprecht.

ROBINSON, RICHARD D. 1962 Interrelationship of Business Enterprise and Political Development. *Business History Review* 36:287–324.

SCHUMPETER, JOSEPH A. 1947 The Creative Response in Economic History. *Journal of Economic History* 7: 149–159.

SCHWEITZER, ARTHUR 1964 Business Policy in a Dictatorship. *Business History Review* 38:413–438.

SOLTOW, JAMES H. 1965 Origins of Small Business Metal Fabricators and Machinery Makers in New England, 1890–1957. American Philosophical Society, *Transactions* New Series 55, part 10.

WALKER, JAMES B. 1949 *The Epic of American Industry*. New York: Harper.

WILLIAMSON, HAROLD F.; and DAUM, ARNOLD R. 1959–1963 *The American Petroleum Industry*. 2 vols. Evanston, Ill.: Northwestern Univ. Press.

WILLIAMSON, HAROLD F.; and SMALLEY, ORANGE A. 1957 *Northwestern Mutual Life: A Century of Trusteeship*. Evanston, Ill.: Northwestern Univ. Press.

WILSON, CHARLES 1954 *The History of Unilever: A Study in Economic Growth and Social Change*. London: Cassell.

WOODRUFF, WILLIAM 1958 *The Rise of the British Rubber Industry During the Nineteenth Century*. Liverpool Univ. Press.

HJÄRNE, HARALD

Harald Hjärne (1848–1922), Swedish historian and political writer, came from a family of the nobility. He studied at Uppsala University, where he became assistant professor of history in 1872 and professor of history in 1889. His historical works fall into three groups. Those written between 1872 and 1876 deal mainly with old Germanic and medieval law and social conditions; those of the 1880s deal with the history of Russia and connections between Russia and Sweden; and those from 1890 on deal with the Reformation and the seventeenth century in Sweden. His numerous political essays and articles exerted an important influence on conservative and right-wing liberal thinking, especially during the 1890s. Hjärne was a member of the second chamber of the Riksdag from 1903 to 1908 and a member of the first chamber from 1912 to 1918.

When Hjärne first emerged as a political writer, around 1875, Swedish politics was characterized by economic controversies about defense and taxation on the one hand and by a blurring of ideological positions on the other. The old conservative view of a society based on the estates had disappeared since the abolition of the four-estates Riksdag in 1865. The conservatives then tended to merge with the successful right-wing liberals, who in turn were becoming more conservative, intent on maintaining their conquests. This synthesis of conservatism and right-wing liberalism characterized most political argument and also colored the philosophical doctrine prevalent at the universities—the political idealism of Christoph Jacob Boström.

Hjärne cast off Boström's philosophy, with its idealization of the four-estate Riksdag and its liberal tendency to assert the rights of the individual and private interests. He also moved away from the national liberalism of his family, replacing this by a conservative philosophy of his own. According to this political philosophy, the functions of the state are purely juridical; on this point Hjärne agreed with classical liberalism and Boström's ideas, but private interests have no place in his system. The only object of the rights granted by the king, as representative of the state, to his subjects is to enable them to fulfill their obligations toward the state. The greater the personal contribution of the individual, the greater the rights to which he is entitled. Representation should be based on these principles and thus be regarded as a means of public administration, not as a tool for private interests. Hjärne himself maintained that his philosophy stemmed entirely from ancient Swedish law and the Swedish constitution under the Vasa kings (1875; 1876). Actually, however, all the essentials came from the German historian and right-wing liberal politician Rudolf von Gneist, whose works on English constitutional history Hjärne encountered early in the 1870s (Gneist 1857–1860). Gneist saw local self-government as the main way of fulfilling personal obligations toward the state, but Hjärne considered military service to be the most important form of such obligations. The great stress on duty in his philosophy reflects his contempt for the kind of haggling about defense and taxation carried on by the economic group interests in the Riksdag.

In the 1880s there arose a partly new, more extreme form of conservatism. Strongly nationalistic, protectionist, and decidedly antidemocratic in outlook, its adherents opposed the growing demands by Norway for equality and greater independence within the Union. At first, Hjärne's work reflected this outlook, but he rejected it after 1890, when its supporters threatened to become too powerful. It was then that he launched his own conservative reform program, "Defense and Reforms." In accordance with his early ideas about the connection between duties and rights he demanded the franchise for all citizens who had completed a year's military service, regardless of their income and property. He repudiated the Conservative party and its aggressive Union policy, calling himself a right-wing liberal. He retained his basic conservative antiparliamentary philosophy, however.

Hjärne's historical works helped to foster the patriotic trend in the cultural life of the 1890s, and at times he himself succumbed to the nationalist ethos. At the same time he sharply criticized the principles of nationalism and race prejudice and supported the stand of England and the United States against Germany (1903; 1908; 1932–1940).

Troubled by the growing threat of war and presumably also by his own lack of success in the Riksdag, around 1908 Hjärne began to develop a strongly antidemocratic outlook, maintaining that defense and foreign policy should take precedence over domestic reforms. As in the 1880s, he again considered Germany to be Sweden's potential ally against the hereditary enemy, Russia. In this belief he anticipated the reactionary trend that once more dominated conservative thought after the liberals came to power in 1911.

Unlike some other conservative thinkers, Hjärne avoided identifying himself with dogmatic policies and fatalistic conceptions about inevitable historical laws, and he was able to accept with equanimity the defeat of Germany and the victory of democracy. Primarily through his program "Defense and Reforms" he was a precursor of the moderate line, which was to inspire most conservative political activity during the following decades.

NILS ELVANDER

WORKS BY HJÄRNE

1875   Våra ståndsriksdagar. *Svensk tidskrift för literatur, politik och ekonomi* [1875]:151–180, 550–569, 701–730.
1876   Skandinavisk laghistoria. *Svensk tidskrift för literatur, politik och ekonomi* [1876]:178–288.
1903   *Blandade spörsmål.* Stockholm: Bonnier.
1908   *Svenskt och främmande.* Stockholm: Geber.
1914   *Från försvarsstriden 1914.* Uppsala: Askerberg.
1932–1940   *Samlade skrifter.* Stockholm: Bonnier. → Volume 1: *Karl XII*, 1932. Volume 2: *Gustaf II Adolf*, 1932. Volume 3: *Moskovitiska rikets uppväxt*, 1933. Volume 4: *Samfundsliy och tankevärld*, 1940.

SUPPLEMENTARY BIBLIOGRAPHY

ELVANDER, NILS 1961 *Harald Hjärne och konservatismen: Konservativ idédebatt i Sverige, 1865–1922.* Stockholm: Almqvist & Wiksell.
GNEIST, RUDOLF (1857–1860) 1871–1884 *Das heutige englische Verfassungs- und Verwaltungsrecht.* 3d ed., 2 vols. Berlin: Springer. → Volume 1: *Das englische Verwaltungsrecht der Gegenwart in Vergleichung mit den deutschen Verwaltungssystemen*, 1883–1884. Volume 2: *Selfgovernment: Communalverfassung und Verwaltungsgerichte in England*, 1871.

HOBBES, THOMAS

Thomas Hobbes (1588–1679), English philosopher and political theorist, was one of the originators of the new mathematico–mechanical view of the world established in the seventeenth century through the interaction of philosophic reflection and natural science. While Descartes was the most influential thinker in the movement which gave rise to modern philosophy, Hobbes was equally representative of it and scarcely less important. During the 1630s Hobbes arrived, independently of Descartes, at the formulation of the mechanical conception of nature; he had also reached, independently not only of Descartes but also of Galileo, the notion of the subjectivity of sensible qualities such as light and color (Brandt 1921). Like

Descartes, Hobbes rejected scholasticism as a philosophy of sterile disputation and held that mathematical reasoning must provide the model of philosophic method. His thought differed from Cartesianism, however, in its thoroughgoing materialism. In Hobbes's view, bodies are the sole existents, and the sole cause of phenomena lies in the diversity of corporeal motions. Even more than corporeality, motion is the governing idea in Hobbes's materialist metaphysics, and he employed it with impressive ingenuity as the universal explanatory principle in his mechanistic account of the world.

Hobbes also made an important contribution to the establishment of psychology as a field of empirical inquiry. His interest in psychology derived from his preoccupation with sensation and imagery. Realizing that mental occurrences—i.e., the phenomena of experience itself—require explanation, he provided one which treated them as material movements in the brain. Thus, sense, according to him, "is but an apparition unto us of that motion, agitation, or alteration, which the object worketh in the brain, or spirits, or some internal substance in the head" ([1640] 1928, p. 4). He left unclear whether imaging is identical with certain minute motions in the brain or a concomitant of them. His analysis of mental phenomena has a reductionist tendency, in that it loses sight of what is distinctively psychological in its description of physical or physiological causes. His account did, nevertheless, adumbrate the possibility of a scientific psychology in which subjects such as sensation, dreaming, and imagery could be investigated by the same methods used in the sciences of nature.

Hobbes's most enduring intellectual achievement is his theory of politics. The first expression of his political interests, however, was historical and classical, rather than philosophical. The son of a Wiltshire clergyman, he began his classical education as a child and was sent to Oxford at 14. Following his departure from the university with the B.A. degree in 1608, he became tutor to the son of William Cavendish, Lord Hardwick, who was later created earl of Devonshire. This was the commencement of a lifelong connection with the Cavendish family, to whose friendship and patronage he owed the support that permitted him to pursue his career as philosopher. In 1629, after many years spent mainly, it would seem, in the study of classical literature, he published his first book, a translation of Thucydides' *History*. Hobbes conceived history's principal business to be the instruction of a governing class in political prudence. For this purpose he thought Thucydides' masterpiece unexcelled. It is highly suggestive that of all the an-

cient historians he should have preferred the writer who is the most naturalistic in his inquiry into the causes of events as well as the most profound analyst of the derangement of political life, and even of the meaning of words, which results from civil strife.

When the Thucydides translation appeared, Hobbes had already turned his attention permanently to philosophy. Until the age of 40 he knew nothing of geometry; but about 1629, according to the curious story related by Aubrey, his contemporary biographer, he came by chance on a copy of Euclid's *Elements*. From the study of Euclid he perceived the demonstrative certainty attainable through geometrical reasoning (Aubrey 1898). He held thenceforth that truth is a matter of the laying down of clear definitions and the correct deduction of all their consequences.

In the 1630s Hobbes visited the Continent several times, where he formed some important intellectual friendships and became *au courant* with the most recent philosophical and scientific developments. His earliest surviving philosophical composition (*A Short Tract on First Principles*), a work framed on strictly deductive lines, dates from this period.

This was the time also when the revolution against the government of Charles I was brewing. The beginning of rebellion in Scotland and England at the close of the 1630s evidently stimulated Hobbes to develop his political doctrines. Thereafter, wrote Aubrey, "for ten yeares together his thoughts were much, or almost altogether, unhinged from the Mathematiques" and intent chiefly on the philosophy of politics (Aubrey [1898] 1957, p. 151). The result was the composition of three works that contain the substance of his political theory: *The Elements of Law* (1640), *De cive* (1642*a*), and *Leviathan* (1651). In addition, Hobbes included observations of great importance in philosophical method and the nature of political philosophy in *Elementorum philosophiae sectio prima: De corpore* (1655). He also wrote two minor works expressive of his political views, both published posthumously: *Behemoth* (1679), an account of the English Civil War, and *A Dialogue . . . of the Common Laws of England* (1681*a*).

Hobbes's approach to political theory reflects the spirit of the contemporary scientific movement. In his view, the state forms one department in a tripartite division of philosophy, the whole of which centers on body. According to this classification, philosophy deals first with body under its simplest and most general aspects; next, with man as a natural body of a particular kind; finally, with the commonwealth as a type of artificial body contrived by reason.

Hobbes claimed to be the founder of politics as a science and boldly compared himself with such great inaugurators as Copernicus, Galileo, and Harvey. The meaning of this self-confident assertion is connected with his conception of method. The mode of proceeding in philosophy, he held, is exclusively by way of cause and effect; hence, to reason philosophically means either to demonstrate the effects of a phenomenon from its known causes or to demonstrate its causes from its known effects. He conceived of cause not as a necessary connection between occurrences verified experimentally but, in a purely intellectualistic–deductive sense, as a hypothetical explanation attained by correct reasoning and consistent with ordinary experience. In the study of natural phenomena, he believed man can attain only to a knowledge of *possible* causes; by contrast, in the study of the commonwealth, an artificial body contrived by human reason, man can establish causes with certainty. Indeed, he went so far as to compare civil philosophy with geometry in this respect. Just as geometry is demonstrable because men themselves define its figures, so "civil philosophy is demonstrable, because we make the commonwealth ourselves" ([1656] 1962, p. 184). More specifically, the definitions of just and unjust, law, covenant, etc., on which the political order rests, derive from human invention and agreement. To found politics as a science would therefore mean to propound definitions from which the generation of the commonwealth and the rules necessary to its being are strictly deducible. This is what Hobbes thought he had accomplished.

Hobbes began his political theory with an analysis of human nature. He portrayed man as a creature of incessant activity who can find no rest in any final end. Within this stream of activity man pursues specific ends. What man desires, he calls good; what causes him fear or aversion, he calls evil. Thus, good and evil possess diverse meanings according to men's purposes. In so describing how men form their notions of good and evil, Hobbes was not endorsing a relativistic conception of moral judgment; indeed, it was a cornerstone of his political theory that men must concur in certain common definitions if they are to achieve what they all evidently want, namely, self-preservation, the condition of any activity whatsoever. Nor did Hobbes blame man for or accuse him of being the self-centered creature he is. He held that political philosophy must take human nature as its datum if it is to show how peace and community can be-come possible to creatures who necessarily refer all things to their own single selves. Hobbes's politics are therefore linked to his psychology. The task he assigned reason is not to conquer or extinguish passion—an impossibility anyway—but to instruct it. Reason will teach passion what it must refrain from and what rules it must accept in order to attain its ends of self-preservation and, beyond that, of well-being and the commodities of civilized life.

It was when Hobbes shifted from man in general and in the abstract to the state of nature, where allowance must be made for the coexistence of *many* men, that he confronted the political problem proper, namely, how to secure peace and order among a multitude. Whether a state of nature ever existed historically was of little importance to Hobbes. For him it represented the hypothetical alternative to the commonwealth and sovereignty and was therefore a condition in which men in the pursuit of their diverse ends are subject to no power other than that which they can casually impose on one another. Hobbes intended to think away civil society in order to picture life in the absence of a coercive political order. What he displayed was a state of endless and oppressive insecurity, a war of all against all, where nothing is anyone's with certainty, in which the notions of just and unjust can have no place, and where each literally has a right to everything.

Amid this very anarchy Hobbes discerned the basis of natural right in man's desire to live. As all men seek their own good, they also naturally shun death, the chief of evils. Reason accordingly dictates, said Hobbes, that men should attempt by all means to preserve themselves. Whatever is done according to reason is "done justly, and with right" ([1642a] 1949, pp. 8–9). Natural right was considered by Hobbes as antecedent to the political order: it is a moral claim logically derived from the premise of all human activity and passion, the wish to live. Thus, when reason teaches that to secure themselves men must renounce the liberty of the state of nature, the route from anarchy to the commonwealth and civilization has been pointed out. Moreover, only reason can demonstrate which means do in fact conduce to that which all men want, and such means alone will be real goods. They will be the norms that men as rational beings must maintain to make their right effective.

The precepts of reason that lead to self-preservation Hobbes called the law of nature. He listed a number of these precepts, of which the most important is that men should seek peace, and as a further deduction from this, that they should relinquish their right to all things, each being content ". . . *with so much liberty against other men, as he would allow other men against himselfe*" ([1651] 1958, p. 100).

Yet in what sense are these precepts laws? Hobbes answered that they are such only if considered as the commands of God. Otherwise they are not properly laws, since they are merely advisive and not externally obligatory. A correct definition would be "Conclusions or Theoremes concerning what conduceth to . . . conservation . . ." (*ibid.*, pp. 122–123). Hence, to Hobbes the law of nature appears to signify little more than the means or conditions which the calculating intellect demonstrates to be necessary to preservation. This constituted a radical departure from the traditional view. In traditional political philosophy, the law of nature was held to be genuine law and to prescribe ethical rules originating in the divine order and binding upon earthly communities. Hobbes, however, was strongly skeptical of this conception and took a different line. He refused to derive the dicta of natural law from the supernatural realm, on the ground that neither God nor revelation can be a subject of knowledge and both are thus beyond the scope of philosophy. He held also that the dicta of natural law are vacuous until positive law defines their meaning. Accordingly, while natural law forbids theft, murder, and adultery, it remains for positive law to determine what actions are to be called by these names. Hobbes strove to remove the ambiguities in the concept of natural law in two ways: by denying that natural law is properly law at all and by deriving its precepts autonomously from the rationally instructed striving of men for self-preservation. In effect, therefore, he rejected the divine order as the basis of moral valuation. For him, values are neither divinely guaranteed nor cosmically underwritten; they are made by man.

The fundamental dictate of the law of nature, then, is that men should seek peace. This entails their renunciation of the right to all things, which is theirs in the state of nature. Yet while reason always obliges men to do this, the conditions have to be established in which they can do so with security. Agreement among themselves to lay down their right is insufficient unless there is also a power to ensure that they adhere to this rational resolution. Thence arises, as a further inference, the commonwealth in which a single will represents the wills of all and possesses the right to coerce those who violate the agreement to which reason compels them. Therefore the ultimate cause of the commonwealth, according to Hobbes, is the foresight of men who perceive that civil society is the sole means of self-preservation and a contented life. Proceeding from this view, Hobbes rejected the Aristotelian doctrine that man is a political animal. He did not deny that man is naturally sociable; but commonwealths, he insisted, are not mere meetings, but true unions to whose contrivance the making of compacts is necessary.

Hobbes explained with elaborate care how the consent of men to government is embodied in contracts or covenants. Like the state of nature, covenant for Hobbes is a necessary hypothesis: it is required to show that the commonwealth is unthinkable except as something to which men consent for the sake of life and civility. It also has the further function of justifying the coercion and punishment imposed by the state. If these are to be more than mere acts of power, they must be traced to a covenant whereby man himself, as a rational being, becomes the author of the punishment his transgressions incur in civil society.

In every commonwealth, Hobbes said, there must be a sovereign power to enforce the covenant to peace that men have made: "Covenants, without the Sword, are but Words, and of no strength to secure a man at all" ([1651] 1958, p. 128). So sovereignty is necessitated by the same sequence of deductions that accounts for civil society. The attributes of the sovereign are the same in any form of government—democracy, aristocracy, or monarchy—and are very comprehensive. The sovereign power is not removable or punishable by its subjects; it is the only judge of what conduces to peace and therefore of what doctrines and opinions may be taught; its will alone makes law and determines the rules of property, of good and evil, of lawful and unlawful actions; it rewards and punishes, commands the armed forces, decides on war and peace. (Hobbes, of course, recognized that in actual fact sovereigns neither exercise all these powers nor do subjects allow that they have the right to do so. This to him, however, was mere illogic: if the sovereign is to keep peace and order, subjects ought to acknowledge all its attributes as inescapable.)

With this rigorous reasoning Hobbes brought the modern doctrine of sovereignty into the world. That doctrine already had a long history when Hobbes wrote: an approach to it appeared both in the work of the sixteenth-century French thinker Jean Bodin and, much earlier, in the writings of the medieval canonists and publicists who upheld the most extreme claims of the papal monarchy. But Hobbes's conception was novel in that he allowed no *legal* limitation on the sovereign power. This was the consequence of his view of law, which was defined for him not by any moral content but solely by its character as the sovereign's command. The sovereign cannot be limited by positive law, because the origin of positive law is the sovereign's will; nor can it be limited by the law of nature, because the law of nature is, properly speaking, not a law.

Yet, since the right of nature—man's claim to self-preservation—is the root from which Hobbes's political doctrine grew, this right results in substantial qualifications upon the absolutist character of his thought. Although, for instance, obedience is a duty in civil society, Hobbes pointed out that the subject retains his liberty to do whatever he cannot be conceived to have renounced or transferred by any covenant. This liberty is, in fact, considerable. The subject is not obliged to obey a command to kill or wound himself and may also refuse to endanger his life by service in war; again, while rebellion is not justifiable, subjects have the right, once it is begun, to continue in their resistance in order to preserve themselves. Most important of all, Hobbes exempted the subject from the obligation to obey a command that ". . . frustrates the End for which the Soveraignty [*sic*] was ordained . . ." ([1651] 1958, p. 167). He thus left to subjects both a vital right of private judgment and a moral vantage point vis-à-vis the sovereign.

Hobbes also stressed that the sovereign has duties toward its subjects. It is obliged, he stated, to make the safety and well-being of the people the rule of its actions. While this is a moral rather than a legal obligation, it is nonetheless real, founded as it is on men's basic purpose in consenting to submit to the commonwealth and sovereignty. A sovereign which acts otherwise "will act against the reasons of peace, that is to say, against the law of nature" ([1642*a*] 1962, p. 167). And safety, Hobbes added, means not only bare preservation but happiness and living delightfully, so far as these are possible. His advice to sovereigns respecting taxation, equal justice, and other matters of government is unexceptionable in its care for the subject's interests. Nor did he fail to point out that the sovereign's disregard of its duty will lead to rebellion as a natural consequence.

It is evident, then, that alongside the absolutist element in Hobbes's thought is a strong tendency toward liberalism. This appeared not only in his account of the subject's rights and the sovereign's duties but also in his progressive theory of punishment, which anticipated Beccaria and Bentham, and in his dislike of religious intolerance and clerical pretensions. Hobbes's liberalism is intrinsic to his conception of natural right, the dominant theme of his politics. Hence there results the paradoxical fact that he established his absolutism on liberal presuppositions. For him the state is not an object of awe and reverence. No sacred mystique veils Leviathan, the "mortal God," created by human association, to which men owe their peace and defense. The commonwealth is the work of men; its utility is its sole justification. It makes men moral and educates them for civility, but does so by their own consent and to advance their own purposes. If Hobbes defended absolutism, it was because he assumed absolutism to be in the general interest. Without this premise, there would be no great difficulty in constructing a liberal system out of the materials provided by his own political philosophy.

Hobbes was one of the most famous thinkers of his time. His writings were widely read, and although he formed no school, he probably exercised a greater and more varied influence upon English political theory than did any contemporary. Of Continental philosophers, Pufendorf and Spinoza, to mention only the foremost, were strongly affected by his ideas. A royalist in sympathy, he emigrated in 1640 and spent the next 11 years in France. He returned to England after the defeat and execution of Charles I, justifying his return with the argument that a subject's obligation ceases when the sovereign can no longer protect him ([1651] 1958, see "Review and Conclusion"). Despite this conduct, Hobbes retained the favor and friendship of Charles II after the Stuart restoration of 1660.

Hobbes's materialism, determinism, and skeptical temper brought upon him a host of attackers. Clerical opponents accused him of heresy and atheism, and in 1683 the University of Oxford condemned a number of his works to the flames. Some of the controversies he waged, such as that with Bishop Bramhall over free will, belong to the great intellectual debates of the age. Even upon his critics Hobbes exerted a powerful influence. He obliged them to lay aside theological and moral conceptions, to meet him on his own ground of strict and severe reasoning, and to deal with issues on their intellectual merits. His remarkable prose style, perfectly expressive of the hard, confident, and probing character of his mind, also contributed not a little to the effect he had upon friend and foe alike. By virtue both of his positive doctrines and of the scope and rigor of his philosophical inquiries, Hobbes was one of the foremost agents in the dissemination of the rationalism that altered the moral and mental climate of Europe in the course of the seventeenth century.

PEREZ ZAGORIN

[See also CONSENSUS; CONSTITUTIONS AND CONSTITUTIONALISM; NATURAL LAW; POWER; SOCIAL CONTRACT; SOVEREIGNTY; UTILITARIANISM; and the biographies of AUSTIN; BACON; BODIN; DESCARTES; DURKHEIM; HARRINGTON; HEGEL; MACHIAVELLI; MANDEVILLE; VICO.]

WORKS BY HOBBES

(1640) 1928 The Elements of Law, Natural & Political. Edited, with a preface and critical notes, by Ferdinand Tönnies, to which are subjoined selected extracts from unprinted mss. of Thomas Hobbes. Cambridge Univ. Press. → Written in 1640; first published in 1650.

(1642a) 1949 De cive or The Citizen. Edited and abridged by Sterling P. Lamprecht. New York: Appleton. → First published as Elementa philosophica de cive.

(1642b) 1962 Philosophical Rudiments Concerning Government and Society. Volume 2 of Thomas Hobbes, The English Works of Thomas Hobbes of Malmesbury. Aalen (Germany): Scientia. → First published as Elementorum philosophiae sectio tertia: De cive.

(1651) 1958 Leviathan: Or, the Matter, Forme and Power of a Commonwealth, Ecclesiasticall and Civil. With an essay by W. G. Pogson Smith. Oxford: Clarendon. → See also the introduction by Michael Oakeshott in the 1946 edition published by Clarendon, and the introduction by A. D. Lindsay in the 1950 edition published by Dutton.

(1655) 1951 Elementorum philosophiae sectio prima: De corpore. Volume 1, pages 1–431 in Thomas Hobbes, . . . Opera philosophica quae Latine scripsit omnia. Aalen (Germany): Scientia.

(1656) 1962 Six Lessons to the Professors of the Mathematics. Volume 7, pages 181–356 in Thomas Hobbes, The English Works of Thomas Hobbes of Malmesbury. Aalen (Germany): Scientia.

(1679) 1962 Behemoth. Volume 6, pages 161–418 in Thomas Hobbes, The English Works of Thomas Hobbes of Malmesbury. Aalen (Germany): Scientia.

(1681a) 1962 A Dialogue Between a Philosopher and a Student of the Common Laws of England. Volume 6, pages 1–160 in Thomas Hobbes, The English Works of Thomas Hobbes of Malmesbury. Aalen (Germany): Scientia. → First published posthumously.

(1681b) 1951 Vita. Volume 1, pages xiii–xxi in Thomas Hobbes, . . . Opera philosophica quae Latine scripsit omnia. Aalen (Germany): Scientia. → First published posthumously.

The English Works of Thomas Hobbes of Malmesbury. Edited by Sir William Molesworth. 11 vols. Aalen (Germany): Scientia, 1962. → A reprint of an 1839–1845 edition.

A Short Tract on First Principles. Appendix 1 in Thomas Hobbes, The Elements of the Law, Natural & Political. Cambridge Univ. Press, 1928. → Previously unpublished.

Thomae Hobbes Malmesburiensis opera philosophica quae Latine scripsit omnia. Edited by Sir William Molesworth. 5 vols. Aalen (Germany): Scientia, 1951. → A reprint of an 1839–1845 edition.

SUPPLEMENTARY BIBLIOGRAPHY

AUBREY, JOHN (1898) 1957 Thomas Hobbes. Pages 147–159 in John Aubrey, Brief Lives. Ann Arbor: Univ. of Michigan Press. → Written between 1669 and 1696.

BORING, EDWIN G. 1942 Sensation and Perception in the History of Experimental Psychology. New York: Appleton.

BOWLE, JOHN 1951 Hobbes and His Critics: A Study in Seventeenth Century Constitutionalism. London: Cape.

BRANDT, FRITHIOF (1921) 1928 Thomas Hobbes' Mechanical Conception of Nature. Copenhagen: Levin & Munksgaard. → First published in Danish.

BROWN, J. M. 1953 A Note on Professor Oakeshott's Introduction to the Leviathan. Political Studies 1:53–64.

BROWN, KEITH C. (editor) 1965 Hobbes Studies. Oxford: Blackwell; Cambridge, Mass.: Harvard Univ. Press.

BROWN, STUART M. (1959) 1965 The Taylor Thesis: Some Objections. Pages 57–71 in Keith C. Brown (editor), Hobbes Studies. Oxford: Blackwell; Cambridge, Mass.: Harvard Univ. Press. → First published in Volume 68 of the Philosophical Review.

GOLDSMITH, M. M. 1966 The Political Philosophy of Hobbes: The Rationale of the Sovereign State. New York: Columbia Univ. Press.

HOOD, FRANCIS C. 1964 The Divine Politics of Thomas Hobbes. Oxford Univ. Press.

KROOK, DOROTHEA 1953 Mr. Brown's Note Annotated. Political Studies 1:216–227.

LAIRD, JOHN 1934 Hobbes. London: Benn.

LEVI, ADOLFO 1929 La filosofia di Tommaso Hobbes. Milan: Società Editrice Dante Alighieri.

ŁUBIEŃSKI, ZBIGNIEW 1932 Die Grundlagen des ethisch-politischen Systems von Hobbes. Munich: Reinhardt.

MACDONALD, HUGH; and HARGREAVES, MARY 1952 Thomas Hobbes: A Bibliography. London: Bibliographical Society.

MACPHERSON, CRAWFORD B. 1962 The Political Theory of Possessive Individualism: Hobbes to Locke. Oxford: Clarendon.

MINTZ, SAMUEL I. 1962 The Hunting of the Leviathan: Seventeenth-century Reactions to the Materialism and Moral Philosophy of Thomas Hobbes. Cambridge Univ. Press. → Also available from University Microfilms.

NAGEL, THOMAS 1959 Hobbes's Concept of Obligation. Philosophical Review 68:68–83.

PETERS, RICHARD S. 1956 Hobbes. Harmondsworth (England): Penguin.

PLAMENATZ, JOHN P. (1957) 1965 Mr. Warrender's Hobbes. Pages 73–87 in Keith C. Brown (editor), Hobbes Studies. Oxford: Blackwell; Cambridge, Mass.: Harvard Univ. Press. → First published in Volume 5 of Political Studies.

POLIN, RAYMOND 1952 Politique et philosophie chez Thomas Hobbes. Paris: Presses Universitaires de France.

ROBERTSON, GEORGE C. (1886) 1901 Hobbes. Edinburgh: Blackwood.

SKINNER, QUENTIN 1966 Thomas Hobbes and His Disciples in France and England. Comparative Studies in Society and History 8:153–167.

STEPHEN, LESLIE (1904) 1928 Hobbes. London: Macmillan.

STRAUSS, LEO (1936) 1961 *The Political Philosophy of Hobbes: Its Basis and Its Genesis.* Translated by E. M. Sinclair. Univ. of Chicago Press. → Written in German but first published in English.

TAYLOR, A. E. (1938) 1965 The Ethical Doctrine of Hobbes. Pages 35–55 in Keith C. Brown (editor), *Hobbes Studies.* Oxford: Blackwell; Cambridge, Mass.: Harvard Univ. Press. → First published in Volume 13 of *Philosophy.*

TÖNNIES, FERDINAND (1896) 1925 *Hobbes Leben und Lehre.* 3d ed. Stuttgart: Fromman.

WARRENDER, HOWARD (1960) 1965 A Reply to Mr. Plamenatz. Pages 89–100 in Keith C. Brown (editor), *Hobbes Studies.* Oxford: Blackwell; Cambridge, Mass.: Harvard Univ. Press. → First published in Volume 8 of *Political Studies.*

WATKINS, J. W. N. 1965 *Hobbes's System of Ideas: A Study in the Political Significance of Philosophical Theories.* London: Hutchinson.

ZAGORIN, PEREZ 1954 *A History of Political Thought in the English Revolution.* London: Routledge.

HOBHOUSE, L. T.

Leonard Trelawny Hobhouse (1864–1929), British sociologist and philosopher, was educated at Oxford. He was appointed fellow of Merton College in 1887 and fellow of Corpus Christi in 1894. Early in his career he showed an active interest in social and political movements: he was secretary of the Free Trade Union from 1903 to 1905 and published several political works, notably *The Labour Movement* (1893), *Democracy and Reaction* (1904), and *Liberalism* (1911a). From 1897 to 1902 he served on the staff of the *Manchester Guardian,* and from 1905 to 1907 he was political editor of the *Tribune* in London.

The main lines of the social philosophy that he was to develop in his later studies can be clearly discerned in these early political writings. This philosophy is based on principles differing fundamentally both from laissez-faire liberalism and from the bureaucratic, or as Hobhouse called it, "official" socialism of the Fabians. It may best be described as social liberalism, and in working it out he presented a cogent and still vitally important analysis of the relations between individual freedom and responsibility and state control.

In 1907 Hobhouse was appointed the first Martin White professor in sociology at the University of London and thereafter devoted himself mainly to his scientific and philosophical pursuits; but he never abandoned his earlier passionate interest in the deeper issues of politics, internal and foreign, as can be seen in his important contributions to the *Manchester Guardian* during World War I and in his work as chairman of trade boards and as arbitrator in various disputes.

The key to Hobhouse's work is to be found in his conception of development. He was profoundly dissatisfied both with Spencer's account of evolution as dependent on the struggle for existence and the survival of the fittest and with the idealist philosophers' metaphysical theory of an absolute mind reaching self-consciousness in the historical process. In his view, a theory of development has to be solidly based on empirical facts. In his early work on logic and epistemology, *The Theory of Knowledge* (1896), he had subjected the dominant idealist view of the nature of thought to a detailed critical analysis and worked out a realistic theory based on a synthesis of empiricism and rationalism. Subsequently he turned to the study of the growth of the mind in the animal world and of the transition to the mind of man. The results were embodied in *Mind in Evolution* (1901).

The publication of *Morals in Evolution* (1906) marked a new epoch in the development of sociology. Hobhouse revealed a grasp of anthropological data, of the history of law, morals, and religion, and of scientific and philosophical thought and laid the foundations of an impressive sociological system. A later work incorporated research on preliterate societies carried out in collaboration with G. C. Wheeler and the present writer and was published in 1915 under the title *The Material Culture and Social Institutions of the Simpler Peoples.*

From 1918 to 1922 Hobhouse published three works devoted to political and ethical theory, and in 1924 there appeared his *Social Development,* in which he presented a restatement of the whole of his sociological work. In this book he gave a fresh analysis of the nature of social development and of the factors making for progress, arrest, or decay. His treatment avoids both the mistakes inherent in the kind of crude evolutionism that has brought the theory of development into disrepute and those that result from the one-sided emphasis on economic factors implicit in many forms of historical materialism. Only the general lines of this methodology are indicated here:

(1) He worked out a social morphology, that is, a classification of types of society and of the forms of social institutions, based on a wide survey of the data of anthropology and history. He was well aware of the difficulties inherent in the comparative method but sought to meet them by penetrating beneath outward resemblances to basic functions.

(2) He attempted to correlate the various aspects of social change with their contribution to

the general advance of the community, as estimated by certain criteria deduced from the general nature of development. They are extension in the scale of organization, growing efficiency in control and direction, and increasing freedom and cooperation in the satisfaction of mutual needs. It should be noted that these criteria are, at this stage of the inquiry, to be taken as ethically neutral: scale and efficiency are clearly so, and even though freedom and mutuality might appear to be ethically tinged, they are defined by Hobhouse in a manner that does not involve any particular ethical theory. Thus, a society is said to be free internally if its component parts can operate with the least loss of energy, without interfering with or obstructing each other. Mutuality depends on the extent to which the parts not only do not obstruct each other but work together so as to maintain the system as a whole.

(3) He put forward a hypothesis that there is a broad correlation between mental development and social development as estimated in the light of the above criteria. To establish this correlation he undertook an elaborate analysis of mental development in (a) the growth of scientific thought, (b) the control of the forces of nature, including human nature, (c) the ethicoreligious sphere, and (d) more briefly, the history of art. It is not suggested that the movements in these various spheres are parallel or that their rate of advance is similar but that, making due allowance for conditions in different periods of time and different parts of the world, they may be taken as a general indication of the growth of the human mind.

(4) Hobhouse then tried to show that there is indeed a broad correlation between mental advance and the development of societies. Thus, in the earlier phases of thought and belief, societies grow in scale and efficiency and in control and direction, although at the cost of mutuality and freedom. Governments tend to be authoritarian in character, and social differentiation rests on subordination. In relatively higher phases this growth in scale and efficiency continues to increase as does subordination. But with the beginning of critical and systematic thought free forms of government arise, and, in theory at any rate, there emerge ideals of a unitary spiritual order. In the ancient world the embodiment of these ideals is still very restricted. In more recent times, in the stage of "experiential reconstruction," when conceptual analysis is combined with empirical verification, there is not only an increase in scale and efficiency but also the beginning of a concrete embodiment of the elements of mutuality and freedom on a world scale; and attempts are made at a genuine synthesis of personal and political freedom with moral universalism. A survey of history thus suggests that there has been, on the whole, correlated growth of mind and civilization.

(5) Hobhouse next argued that the process of development, so far examined by him independently of any ethical commitment, may be shown to be generally in the direction required by his theory of the rational good. This good consists in the harmonious fulfillment of human potentialities, and it is clear that it can be achieved only by the willing cooperation of all mankind. In theory, therefore, ethical and social development have a common end. But although they tend to converge, they do not in fact coincide. For this there are many reasons. Each different society develops, if not wholly independently, yet in its own way and in accord with its own peculiarities and distinguishable internal sources of change. Furthermore, they advance at different rates. As a result, inequalities in economic and political power arise that offer opportunities for exploitation and domination and have been among the root causes of war. Again, development in one direction may bring retrogression in another. Thus, the extension of the area of organization may reduce the chances of conflict but may make it more destructive when it does occur. The parts may develop at the expense of the whole or the changes that they undergo may not be duly balanced, with resulting structural strains and possible collapse. These causes of arrest or decay can easily be illustrated from the history of communities and are readily discerned in the contemporary world. It is in this connection that Hobhouse's analysis may be fruitfully extended in dealing with the problems of our own day. Progress is, in any case, not automatic or unilinear but depends on human thought and will: on the rationality of the mind and its capacity for forming an intelligible conception of a good in which all men can share and for securing an effective will directed to this good. Humanity has not yet reached the stage of self-direction; but reviewing the state of the world in the 1920s, Hobhouse felt justified in concluding, despite serious misgivings, that it contained many essentials of such self-direction and that these were sufficient to indicate the direction of future development.

Hobhouse further strengthened his argument by an examination of the conditions affecting social change: environmental, biological, psychological, and distinctively sociological. The great value of his contributions to sociology does not depend solely on the strength of his main hypothesis; it also lies in the light he threw on various phases in the history of knowledge, religion, and morals and their relation to social change, in the careful way in which he distinguished judgments of fact and of value, and in the skill with which he eventually brought facts and values together in a comprehensive synthesis.

Hobhouse will be remembered not only as a contributor to sociology and to comparative and social psychology but also as a philosopher of great distinction. The fullest exposition of his philosophical theories is to be found in his *Development and Purpose* (1913), which he himself regarded as completing a scheme that had occupied him for 26 years and that had been carried through successive stages in his previous major works. In this book he showed that development proceeds by the liberation of elements originally indifferent to or in conflict with one another and by the building up of structures of varying degrees of plasticity and coherence. The power behind development is mind, essentially a correlating activity, manifested in all orderly structures but most clearly in living organisms, in which mechanical and teleological factors are interwoven. Mind is, in this view, not coextensive with reality but is the principle of orderly growth within it. It is limited by the material it works upon, and its purposes themselves undergo development. His fundamental principle, which he entitled "conditional teleology," is examined both from the point of view of the logical requirements of explanation in dealing with systems undergoing change and from the point of view of its value as an instrument of investigation, especially in the fields of biology and sociology.

MORRIS GINSBERG

[*Directly related are the entries* EVOLUTION, *article on* CULTURAL EVOLUTION; LIBERALISM; SOCIAL DARWINISM; SOCIAL INSTITUTIONS. *Other relevant material may be found in* CONSTITUTIONAL LAW, *article on* CIVIL LIBERTIES; TRIBAL SOCIETY; WAR, *article on* PRIMITIVE WARFARE; *and in the biographies of* BOSANQUET; OGBURN; TOYNBEE.]

WORKS BY HOBHOUSE

(1893) 1912 *The Labour Movement*. 3d ed. New York. Macmillan.
(1896) 1921 *The Theory of Knowledge: A Contribution to Some Problems of Logic and Metaphysics*. 3d ed. London: Methuen.
(1901) 1926 *Mind in Evolution*. 3d ed. London: Macmillan.
(1904) 1909 *Democracy and Reaction*. 2d ed., rev. & enl. London: Allen & Unwin.
(1906) 1951 *Morals in Evolution: A Study in Comparative Ethics*. With a new introduction by Morris Ginsberg. 7th ed. London: Chapman & Hall.
(1911a) 1945 *Liberalism*. Oxford Univ. Press. → A paperback edition was published in 1964.
1911b *Social Evolution and Political Theory*. New York: Columbia Univ. Press.
(1913) 1927 *Development and Purpose: An Essay Towards a Philosophy of Evolution*. New ed., rev. & enl. London: Macmillan.
(1915) 1965 HOBHOUSE, LEONARD T.; WHEELER, GERALD C.; and GINSBERG, MORRIS *The Material Culture and Social Institutions of the Simpler Peoples: An Essay in Correlation*. London: Routledge.
(1918) 1951 *The Metaphysical Theory of the State: A Criticism*. London: Allen & Unwin; New York: Macmillan.
(1921) 1947 *The Rational Good: A Study in the Logic of Practice*. London: Watts.
(1922) 1958 *The Elements of Social Justice*. London: Allen & Unwin.
1924 *Social Development: Its Nature and Conditions*. London: Allen & Unwin.
Sociology and Philosophy: A Centenary Collection of Essays and Articles. Preface by Sir Sydney Caine. Introduction by Morris Ginsberg. Cambridge, Mass.: Harvard Univ. Press; London: Bell, 1966.

SUPPLEMENTARY BIBLIOGRAPHY

BARKER, ERNEST 1929 Leonard Trelawny Hobhouse. British Academy, London, *Proceedings* 15:536–554.
HOBSON, J. A.; and GINSBERG, MORRIS 1931 *L. T. Hobhouse, His Life and Work: With Selected Essays and Articles*. London: Allen & Unwin.

HOBSON, JOHN A.

John Atkinson Hobson (1858–1940) was a British economist. In his appealing autobiography, *Confessions of an Economic Heretic* (1938, p. 15), he described himself as "born and bred in the middle stratum of the middle class of a middle-sized industrial town of the Midlands." The town in question was Derby, and the family derived its income from the *Derbyshire Advertiser*, a Liberal newspaper. The family's resources sufficed to assure Hobson an adequate private income all his life and the chance to pursue a heterodox career free of financial strain. At Oxford he specialized in classics. He also made a close study of Marx, but *Capital* repelled him and he dismissed the dialectical method as frivolous. As a child he broke with formal religion because it failed "to satisfy my elementary sense of reason and of justice in the doctrines of the atonement and of everlasting punishment for unrepentant sinners" (1938, p. 20).

The intellectual influences that impinged on Hobson included Mill's *On Liberty* and *Utilitarianism* and Herbert Spencer's *Study of Sociology*. John Ruskin's message impressed him while he was teaching classics in two successive public schools. Even though Hobson recognized the speculative cast of much of Ruskin's thought, he was attracted by Ruskin's criticism of the conventional economists' tendency to identify economic value with the monetary costs of producing marketable commodities. Ruskin's slogan "there is no wealth but life" animated all of Hobson's writings, especially the two volumes that best express his humanistic conception of economics, *The Industrial System* (1909) and *Work and Wealth* (1914). Thorstein Veblen's criticisms of capitalist waste and capitalist standards of consumption also attracted Hobson. With American institutional economists of the period he shared a basic distrust of marginal economics and a disposition to interpret all aspects of economic activity within the broader framework of ethics and sociology.

Hobson's two enduring contributions to economic thought are connected with the doctrine of oversaving and the theory of imperialism. The possibility, even the probability, of oversaving is the central lesson of his first book, *The Physiology of Industry* (Mummery & Hobson 1889), which he wrote in collaboration with the businessman and mountain climber A. F. Mummery. Hobson directed this first attack at a central proposition of conventional economics—that a society can never save too large a proportion of its income—asserting that excess saving brings about the construction of unneeded capital equipment whose products lack consumer markets. In later works Hobson strengthened his argument with explicit emphasis upon the maldistribution of income, which causes the wealthy to save too large a share of their income and thus generates unemployment and economic depression. Hobson's conception of oversaving differs from contemporary theories in its assumption that saving is actually and necessarily converted into fixed investment. The Keynesian version maintains that an effort to save too much diminishes total spending rather than fixing itself in surplus machines.

Hobson's second major contribution is contained in *Imperialism* (1902). This was an extension of his oversaving theory, but its impetus and a great deal of its historical detail derived from Hobson's experience in South Africa as a correspondent of the *Manchester Guardian* just prior to the Boer War. He explained the revived drive for empire as the result of a search by English capitalists for savings outlets. Lenin borrowed freely of Hobson's doctrine.

Although trenchant as a critic, Hobson was less successful as an inventor of concepts and programs. He never put into acceptable theoretical style his human conception of value or his perception that the money costs of production inadequately measure the human pains of economic output. Nor did he find a completely satisfactory

political vehicle for his ideas. He began as a Liberal and then became a somewhat reluctant member of the Labour party. Never accepting class war as the proper route to a better society, always seeking to enlist portions of the middle class under his banner, Hobson was also skeptical of nationalization as the single remedy for a defective society. Although he was perfectly willing to nationalize industries which suffered from monopoly, inefficiency, or excessive routinization of their operations, he attached at least equal importance to less concentration within private industry, progressive taxation of income and wealth, and the social policies now embodied in the welfare state. Like R. H. Tawney and G. D. H. Cole, he emphasized the quality of consumption and the satisfactions of the worker as elements of a humane society. He took pride in what he called "'the jumble' of politics, ethics, art, religion, which constitutes the setting of my thought" (1938, p. 164).

Orthodox economists admired Hobson little more than he admired them. F. Y. Edgeworth, in an influential review of *The Physiology of Industry*, denied Hobson and Mummery the "undoubted speculative genius" or the "extraordinarily wide learning" that alone might justify such paradoxical conclusions. As a direct consequence of the book, Hobson lost two extension lectureships and won a reputation for heresy that placed him on the fringes of the academic world for the rest of his career. As late as 1954, Schumpeter summed him up in this way: "In economics he was self-taught in a wilful way that made him both able to see aspects that trained economists refused to see and unable to see others that trained economists took for granted" (1954, p. 832, footnote).

Hobson felt himself vindicated, however, when Keynes in *The General Theory of Employment, Interest and Money* (1936) termed the publication of *The Physiology of Industry* "an epoch in economic thought" and credited Hobson with anticipating a good half of Keynes's own theory of underemployment equilibrium. As an anticipator of both Lenin and Keynes, Hobson seems to have a secure place in the history of economic doctrine.

ROBERT LEKACHMAN

[*For the historical context of Hobson's work, see the biographies of* MILL; SPENCER; VEBLEN; *for discussion of the subsequent development of Hobson's ideas, see* CONSUMPTION FUNCTION; IMPERIALISM; *and the biographies of* KEYNES, JOHN MAYNARD; LENIN.]

WORKS BY HOBSON

(1889) 1956 MUMMERY, ALBERT F.; and HOBSON, JOHN A. *The Physiology of Industry: Being an Ex-*

posure of Certain Fallacies in Existing Theories of Economics. New York: Kelley.

(1894) 1949 The Evolution of Modern Capitalism: A Study of Machine Production. Rev. ed. New York: Macmillan.

(1902) 1948 Imperialism: A Study. 3d ed. London: Allen & Unwin.

(1909) 1910 The Industrial System: An Inquiry Into Earned and Unearned Income. New ed., rev. London and New York: Longmans.

(1914) 1933 Work and Wealth: A Human Valuation. Rev. ed. London: Allen & Unwin.

1938 Confessions of an Economic Heretic. New York: Macmillan.

SUPPLEMENTARY BIBLIOGRAPHY

BRAILSFORD, HENRY N. 1948 The Life-work of J. A. Hobson. London: Oxford Univ. Press.

HOMAN, PAUL T. 1928 Contemporary Economic Thought. New York: Harper. → See especially pages 281–374 on "John A. Hobson."

HUTCHISON, TERENCE W. (1953) 1962 A Review of Economic Doctrines: 1870–1929. 2d ed. Oxford: Clarendon. → See especially pages 118–129 on "J. A. Hobson."

KEYNES, JOHN MAYNARD 1936 The General Theory of Employment, Interest and Money. London: Macmillan. → A paperback edition was published in 1965 by Harcourt.

SCHUMPETER, JOSEPH A. (1954) 1960 History of Economic Analysis. Edited by E. B. Schumpeter. New York: Oxford Univ. Press.

HOLMES, OLIVER WENDELL

The career of Oliver Wendell Holmes, Jr., as a judge spanned half a century. Yet quite apart from this long and distinguished service on the highest courts of his state and nation, his pervasive influence as historian and philosopher of the law is bound to assure him a permanent place in American jurisprudence. It is his 30 notable years as an associate justice of the United States Supreme Court, however, that no doubt constitute his special claim to importance and fame as a jurist. In so many ways a true product of New England's intellectual aristocracy, in time he came to capture the popular imagination of the whole country.

His father was Dr. Oliver Wendell Holmes, whose work as poet, essayist, and physician was in itself a significant chapter in the flowering of America's cultural and scientific maturity. The future judge was born in Boston on March 8, 1841, and died in Washington, D.C., on March 6, 1935. In July 1861, shortly after graduating from Harvard College, he enlisted with the Twentieth Massachusetts Volunteers and was mustered out three years later with the rank of captain. Holmes was wounded three times—at Bull's Bluff, at Antietam, and at Marye's Hill, Fredericksburg. Both his philosophy and his rhetoric were destined to reflect his

Civil War experience. That experience may help explain "the inner resolution he felt bound to achieve . . . between skepticism and faith," as Paul A. Freund has phrased it (see the foreword in Frankfurter 1938).

Once out of uniform, Holmes resolved his doubts concerning the choice of a life's calling—philosophy versus law—by enrolling at the Harvard Law School, where he studied between 1864 and 1866. "A man may live greatly in the law as well as elsewhere," he was to say many years later in "The Profession of the Law" (1962, p. 29).

It is significant that almost from the start of his law practice, scholarly interests claimed Holmes's chief attention. As Mark DeWolfe Howe has noted, "the young lawyer's affiliations of mind and sympathy had early shown themselves to be more with the Brahmins than with the merchants of New England" (Howe 1957–1963, vol. 2, p. 2). He served as editor of the American Law Review from 1870 to 1873 and edited the twelfth edition of James Kent's Commentaries on American Law. But it was the publication of his book The Common Law in 1881 that doubtless established his reputation as a legal scholar, leading in the following year to his appointment as Feld professor of law at Harvard and shortly thereafter to his selection as an associate justice of the Massachusetts Supreme Judicial Court. The book is permeated by all of the major strains of thought that have come to be identified with Holmes's outlook and method both as scholar and judge: his deep sense of history, his rejection of the rigidities of legal logic, his aversion to the confusion between law and morals, and his awareness of the psychological roots of judicial decisions. Some of the sentences of the opening paragraph have become famous in themselves:

The life of the law has not been logic: it has been experience. The felt necessities of the time, the prevalent moral and political theories, intuitions of public policy, avowed or unconscious, even the prejudices which judges share with their fellow-men, have had a good deal more to do than the syllogism in determining the rules by which men should be governed. The law embodies the story of a nation's development through many centuries, and it cannot be dealt with as if it contained only the axioms and corollaries of a book of mathematics. ([1881] 1963, p. 7)

Holmes served on the Massachusetts bench for 20 years, 1882 to 1902, the last three as chief justice. Most of his opinions dealt with the traditional concerns of common law litigation—torts, contracts, and crimes—but there were cases in which he had the opportunity to discuss broader issues of public policy and constitutional law. When that happened he usually gave expression to ideas that can also be found in his legal essays; they foreshadowed the dominant themes of his philosophy as a Supreme Court justice. He insisted that the judiciary has but a limited role to play in the process of government and that the judge must allow ample scope to the provisions of constitutions and the discretion of legislators.

It was Holmes's dissenting opinions in labor cases, especially those in which he vindicated the rights to peaceful picketing and the closed shop, that made some circles think of him as a radical. Yet these seemingly pro-labor opinions were the result of his basically conservative slant—what he called "the battle of trade" or the "free struggle for life." If the pursuit of economic advantage was leading businessmen to combine, he saw no reason for keeping workers from cooperating with each other in promoting their interests.

Judging from the correspondence between Henry Cabot Lodge and Theodore Roosevelt, it may have been Holmes's views on the labor problem that induced Roosevelt to name him to the Supreme Court in 1902. Ironically, when Holmes, much to Roosevelt's displeasure, dissented only a year later from the Court's opinion upholding the dissolution of the Northern Securities Company, he invoked the same general economic beliefs implicit in his Massachusetts labor opinions.

Although the number of occasions on which Holmes differed from Supreme Court majorities was comparatively small, he came to be regarded as the "great dissenter" on the Court. It was largely these dissenting opinions that made the public think of him as a liberal judge, not realizing that in private he was opposed to many of the reforms that, as a judge, he was seeking to save (Biddle 1961, p. 68).

Holmes's reputation as a liberal no doubt originated with his celebrated 1905 dissent in *Locher* v. *New York*—an opinion which Roscoe Pound characterized as the "best exposition" of sociological jurisprudence. In eloquent and increasingly sharp language, the justice continued to protest against the tendency of many of his colleagues to annul labor and social welfare laws because they disapproved of the policies these laws embodied. He furnished one of the best clues to the reason why he often dissented on such questions in a case in which a majority of the Supreme Court had struck down an Arizona law forbidding the use of injunctions in labor disputes. "There is nothing I more deprecate," Holmes confessed in 1921, "than the use of the Fourteenth Amendment beyond the absolute compulsion of its words to prevent the making of social experiments that an important part of the community desires, in the insulated chambers afforded by the several States, even though the experiments may seem futile or even noxious to me and to those whose judgment I most respect" (*Truax* v. *Corrigan,* 257 U.S. 312, 344).

There is still another reason for the popular image of Holmes as a liberal dissenter. In a number of free speech cases he voted against the government and spoke out in defense of the individual's right of free expression. But he had also delivered the Court's opinions in several cases upholding convictions under the Espionage Act of 1917, including the conviction of Eugene V. Debs, the militant head of the Socialist party. It was in the first of these wartime cases—*Schenck* v. *United States*—that he set forth his celebrated formula of "clear and present danger." "The question in every case," he wrote, "is whether the words used are used in such circumstances and are of such a nature as to create a clear and present danger that they will bring about the substantive evils that Congress has a right to prevent" (249 U.S. 47, 52, 1919).

When Holmes became convinced—possibly through the influence of his frequent companion in dissent, Justice Louis D. Brandeis—that the objectionable speech or publication was not likely to bring about "a clear and present danger," he did not hesitate to register his disagreement. His opinions in *Abrams* v. *United States* and *Gitlow* v. *New York* (268 U.S. 652, 1925) are perhaps most notable. In the Abrams dissent, Holmes said:

But when men have realized that time has upset many fighting faiths, they may come to believe even more than they believe the very foundations of their own conduct that the ultimate good desired is better reached by free trade in ideas—that the best test of truth is the power of the thought to get itself accepted in the competition of the market, and that truth is the only ground upon which their wishes safely can be carried out. (*Abrams* v. *United States,* 250 U.S. 616, 630, 1919)

What Justice Frankfurter once said about these dissents is a good measure of Holmes's lasting contribution as a constitutional judge: ". . . some of his weightiest utterances are dissenting opinions —but they are dissents that record prophecy and shape history" (*Mr. Justice Holmes* [1916–1930] 1931, p. 116).

SAMUEL J. KONEFSKY

[*For the historical context of Holmes's work, see the biographies of* BRANDEIS; CARDOZO; POUND.]

WORKS BY HOLMES

(1861–1864) 1946 *Touched With Fire: Civil War Letters and Diary of Oliver Wendell Holmes, Jr., 1861–1864.*

Edited by Mark DeWolfe Howe. Cambridge, Mass.: Harvard Univ. Press.

(1861–1932) 1954   *The Mind and Faith of Justice Holmes: His Speeches, Essays, Letters, and Judicial Opinions.* Selected and edited with introduction and commentary by Max Lerner. New York: Modern Library.

(1870–1935) 1936   *Justice Oliver Wendell Holmes: His Book Notices and Uncollected Letters and Papers.* Edited and annotated by Harry C. Shriver, with an introduction by Harlan Fiske Stone. New York: Central.

(1874–1932) 1961   HOLMES, OLIVER WENDELL; and POLLOCK, FREDERICK *Holmes–Pollock Letters: The Correspondence of Mr. Justice Holmes and Sir Frederick Pollock, 1874–1932.* 2d ed., 2 vols. Edited by Mark DeWolfe Howe. Cambridge, Mass.: Belknap Press.

(1881) 1963   *The Common Law.* Cambridge, Mass.: Harvard Univ. Press.

(1883–1902) 1940   *The Judicial Opinions of Oliver Wendell Holmes.* Edited by Harry C. Shriver. Buffalo, N.Y.: Dennis.

(1885–1918) 1952   *Collected Legal Papers.* Edited by Harold J. Laski. New York: Smith.

(1902–1928) 1929   *The Dissenting Opinions of Mr. Justice Holmes.* Edited by Alfred Lief. New York: Vanguard.

(1903–1930) 1931   *Representative Opinions of Mr. Justice Holmes.* Edited by Alfred Lief. New York: Vanguard.

(1903–1935) 1964   HOLMES, OLIVER WENDELL; and EINSTEIN, LEWIS *The Holmes–Einstein Letters: Correspondence of Mr. Justice Holmes and Lewis Einstein. 1903–1935.* Edited by James Bishop Peabody. New York: St. Martins.

(1916–1935) 1953   HOLMES, OLIVER WENDELL; and LASKI, HAROLD J. *Holmes–Laski Letters: The Correspondence of Mr. Justice Holmes and Harold J. Laski, 1916–1935.* Edited by Mark DeWolfe Howe, with a foreword by Felix Frankfurter. 2 vols. Cambridge, Mass.: Harvard Univ. Press.

1948   HOLMES, OLIVER WENDELL; and COHEN, MORRIS R. *Holmes–Cohen Correspondence. Journal of the History of Ideas* 9:3–52.

1962   *Occasional Speeches.* Compiled by Mark DeWolfe Howe. Cambridge, Mass.: Belknap Press.

WORKS ABOUT HOLMES

BENT, SILAS 1932   *Justice Oliver Wendell Holmes: A Biography.* New York: Vanguard.

BIDDLE, FRANCIS B. 1942   *Mr. Justice Holmes.* New York: Scribner.

BIDDLE, FRANCIS B. 1961   *Justice Holmes, Natural Law and the Supreme Court.* New York: Macmillan.

BOWEN, CATHERINE DRINKER 1944   *Yankee From Olympus: Justice Holmes and His Family.* Boston: Little.

FRANKFURTER, FELIX (1938) 1961   *Mr. Justice Holmes and the Supreme Court.* 2d ed. Foreword by Paul A. Freund. Cambridge, Mass.: Belknap Press.

HOWE, MARK DEWOLFE 1957–1963   *Justice Oliver Wendell Holmes.* 2 vols. Cambridge, Mass.: Belknap Press. → Volume 1: *The Shaping Years, 1841–1870.* Volume 2: *The Proving Years, 1870–1882.*

KONEFSKY, SAMUEL J. 1956   *The Legacy of Holmes and Brandeis: A Study in the Influence of Ideas.* New York: Macmillan.

Mr. Justice Holmes: Contributions by Benjamin N. Cardozo, Morris R. Cohen, John Dewey. . . . (1916–1930) 1931   Edited by Felix Frankfurter. New York: Coward-McCann.

HOLT, EDWIN B.

Edwin Bissell Holt (1873–1946) was an American psychologist-philosopher, an erudite scholar, a brilliant and graceful writer, a man of strong likes and dislikes in his opinions and social relations, and a thinker who had more influence than prestige, being more often followed than quoted.

Philosophically Holt was a radical empiricist, building enthusiastically on the foundation laid by his admired teacher William James. By 1908, when Holt had completed his *Concept of Consciousness* (although he did not publish it until 1914), he had accepted James's belief that the unit of nature is not an atom or a sensation, but a relation, and that consciousness is all those relations in which the nervous system makes possible responses of the living organism to particular objects in its environment. To such general views James gave the name "radical empiricism," and in 1910 Holt and five other philosophers laid down a program for what they called the New Realism; this became the title of a book that they published together in 1912. In it Holt's essay on illusion and error made his views clear. In 1915 he published *The Freudian Wish* (1915a), which became his most influential book, in part because it continued the fight against consciousness as Cartesian unextended substance, but chiefly because it fitted into the positivistic and physicalistic trend in psychology, which led from earlier materialistic and objective psychology to the behaviorism that was founded by John B. Watson in 1913. Holt gave behaviorism a philosophical sophistication which Watson was incapable of providing.

Holt's insight into the nature of consciousness connected him not only with behaviorism but also with the emergence of dynamic psychology. Holt took from Freud the word *wish* and employed it as the unit of his realistic monistic psychology, the relation of response that explains mind. To express this dynamic relation Holt in 1931 adopted the term *drive*. Dynamic psychology has now become the psychology of human nature, and its achievements, which are many, represent the success of the protest against the dualism of German introspective psychology, which initiated the experimental movement. Holt played a significant part in this development.

About 1920 Holt began to write *Animal Drive and the Learning Process,* intending it as a revision of William James's classic *Principles of Psychology,* but that task proved impossible even for Holt's brilliance. Instead, more than a decade later *Animal Drive* came out as a psychophysiological text that explicated the importance of radical empiricism for psychology.

Holt was born in Winchester, Massachusetts, went to school in Winchester, entered Amherst College for a year in 1892, and then transferred to Harvard, where he received the A.B. *magna cum laude* in 1896. After a year at Harvard graduate school, he volunteered for the army in the Spanish–American War, coming back to academic life with a virile and picturesque mode of speech that characterized him ever after. There followed a year abroad at the University of Freiburg, an A.M. from Columbia University, and then a PH.D. from Harvard in 1901. At Harvard, William James and Hugo Münsterberg stimulated him most; the latter made Holt first an instructor and then assistant professor, a position Holt held until his resignation in 1918. While Münsterberg lived—he died in 1916—Holt was his adjutant in the laboratory, helping the graduate students with the research that Münsterberg put them on, maintaining the apparatus in apple-pie order, and leading an experimentalist's life, not a philosopher's. However, he did not publish much experimental work of his own. On coming into a considerable inheritance in 1918 he decided to resign from Harvard, sticking to his decision in spite of the offer of a full professorship and the directorship of the psychological laboratory.

For the next eight years Holt lived in many places, reading, discovering that it was too late to revise James's *Principles*, starting to write the book that eventually became *Animal Drive,* and finally publishing it in 1931. Meanwhile, he had gone to Princeton in 1926 to spend ten years as visiting professor, where he taught a much-liked semester-course on social psychology and worked on a second volume of *Animal Drive.* He retired, however, without finishing the work.

EDWIN G. BORING

[*For the historical context of Holt's work, see the biographies of* JAMES *and* MÜNSTERBERG. *For discussion of the subsequent development of his ideas, see* DRIVES *and* MOTIVATION.]

WORKS BY HOLT

1912   The Place of Illusory Experience in a Realistic World. Pages 303–373 in Edwin B. Holt et al., *The New Realism: Cooperative Studies in Philosophy.* New York: Macmillan.

1914   *The Concept of Consciousness.* New York: Macmillan.

1915a   *The Freudian Wish and Its Place in Ethics.* New York: Holt.

1915b   Response and Cognition. *Journal of Philosophy, Psychology and Scientific Methods* 12:365–373; 393–409.

1931   *Animal Drive and the Learning Process.* Vol. 1. New York: Holt.

SUPPLEMENTARY BIBLIOGRAPHY

BORING, EDWIN G.   (1929) 1950   *A History of Experimental Psychology.* 2d ed. New York: Appleton. → See especially pages 645 ff., 661 ff., and 718 ff. on Holt.

CARMICHAEL, LEONARD   1946   Edwin Bissell Holt: 1873–1946. *American Journal of Psychology* 59:478–480.

Edwin Bissell Holt.   1932   Volume 3, pages 238–239 in *Psychological Register.* Worcester, Mass.: Clark Univ. Press; Oxford Univ. Press. → A bibliography of 30 items.

LANGFELD, HERBERT S.   1946   Edwin Bissell Holt: 1873–1946. *Psychological Review* 53:251–258.

HOME RULE

See LOCAL GOVERNMENT.

HOMELESSNESS

Homelessness is a condition of detachment from society characterized by the absence or attenuation of the affiliative bonds that link settled persons to a network of interconnected social structures.

Homelessness takes many forms, depending on the type of detachment involved and the local circumstances. Homeless families and homeless men appear, so far as can be determined, in all large-scale societies. Homeless women and children are relatively rare. Their appearance denotes widespread disorder and instability, such as follow famines and civil wars.

Degrees of homelessness.   Homeless families fall into three general types: permanent wanderers, such as gypsies and carnival performers; wanderers with a fixed base, especially migratory farm workers; and refugees, for whom homelessness is an accident and not a way of life. Homeless men fall into a variety of categories: single men in itinerant occupations, such as peddlers, tinkers, and sailors; migratory laborers; vagrants and beggars; religious mendicants; outlaws and other fugitives; and hoboes and derelicts.

These types suggest that homelessness is a matter of degree, ranging from temporary to permanent and from the loss of a single affiliation to the absence of all affiliations. In general, homelessness is less acute for families than for individuals. The homeless family may have no place in any community, but its members carry a web of roles and obligations with them wherever they go. Some, like the gypsies, develop something like a portable community independent of the surrounding social structure. Others, like the millions of families displaced toward the end of World War II, are rendered homeless without their consent and resume normal affiliations at the first opportunity.

There is even more variation in degree of homelessness among men without families. Some, like the itinerant worker, may preserve multiple affiliations: occupational, religious, political, and so on. They are only as homeless as their mobility forces them to be. Others, like religious mendicants, elect one overriding identification that supplants all of their former roles.

At the extreme point of the scale, the modern skid row man demonstrates the possibility of nearly total detachment from society. The present discussion is focused on this end of the homelessness scale and omits any consideration of the minor degrees of homelessness represented by Bohemians, "beatniks," troubadours, residents in alien societies, and other adventurers whose partial detachment from role obligations is arranged deliberately and with substitute goals in view.

Homelessness as a syndrome.   The common characteristics of homeless populations display a distinct and unmistakable pattern that is roughly applicable to any homeless population though fully descriptive of none. Homeless persons are poor, anomic, inert, and nonresponsible. They command no resources, enjoy no esteem, and assume no burden of reciprocal obligations. Social action, in the usual sense, is almost impossible for them. Lacking organizational statuses and roles, their sphere of activity extends no further than the provision of personal necessities on a meager scale. Their decisions have no implications for others. Only the simplest forms of concerted action are open to them, since homelessness is incompatible with sustained involvement in a complex division of labor.

The observable behavior of the homeless person consists largely of activities that furnish subsistence or enjoyment without incurring responsibilities: mendicancy, petty crime, scavenging, casual conversation, and an incurious attention at spectacles. This quality of social inertness renders him both innocuous and helpless. He is unlikely to engage in major crime or political movements or to protest his own condition forcefully. A certain apathy regarding self-preservation often develops in addition to the collective helplessness. The homeless in great cities and in refugee camps stand and watch their companions assaulted by strangers without offering to interfere and without taking any measures to protect themselves. The combined effect of poor nutrition, exposure of all kinds, neglect of injuries and illness, and insensitivity to emergencies leads to very high rates of morbidity and mortality among homeless persons as compared to the settled population around them.

The homeless versus the settled.   For reasons not entirely understood, the presence of homeless persons often arouses a degree of hostility in the settled population that seems entirely disproportionate. Ancient ballads preserve the image of the gypsy as rapist and kidnapper. Being homeless or vagrant became a felony in England in the fourteenth century and a capital crime under the Tudors; it is still treated as a criminal offense in most American and European cities. These external attitudes and the punitive measures to which they lead further separate the homeless man from his settled neighbor. Homeless populations often occupy an underworld with a special argot, secret signs, and a conventional refusal to communicate with outsiders. Such manifestations may lead romantic observers to imagine an entire clandestine social system, such as the "kingdom of beggars" or the "hobo republic," but on closer view, these fantasies disappear and reveal the homeless as an aggregate of unrelated individuals who share a common situation and some elements of a common culture.

A theory of homelessness.   The Germanic term "home," with its special connotations of warmth, safety, and emotional dependence, has no exact equivalent in other linguistic systems. Aside from its familiar overtones, it expresses the idea of a fixed place of residence shared with a limited number of other persons. In current usage, home does not imply a family (unrelated persons can "make a home" together), a household (a rest home may be much larger), more than moderate fixity (in any given year, more than one in five U.S. families moves to a new home), or exclusivity (a special body of tax law covers taxpayers with two or more homes). Living outside a family, with no permanent address, does not make a priest or a soldier homeless, but the man who occupies the same lodging on skid row for forty uninterrupted years is properly considered homeless. The essence of the concept goes beyond residential arrangements. Homelessness is best visualized as a relationship to society at large and best understood by examining the difference between the settled and the homeless.

A settled, active adult in any society participates simultaneously in several major types of organization. This participation anchors him in the social structure by linkages with near and distant kin, neighbors, compatriots, superiors and subordinates, co-workers, departed ancestors, sacred and supernatural personages, persons with the same special interests, and even those who like to play the same games. Each of these memberships involves duties and privileges, restraints and rights, status and roles. Each requires sustained interaction with particular other persons who enter into the subject's life history and become part of the audience for his socially meaningful acts.

The pattern of these affiliations varies in detail from one time and place to another, but the main outlines remain unchanged. In modernized countries of the twentieth century, the individual's attachment to society seems to be mediated through eight major types of organization: family, school, community, state, production group, occupational union, church, and recreational associations. Taken together, these memberships define who the settled person is, how he schedules his days and his years, and the benefits he may claim from, and the duties he owes to, the social order. Above all, they identify the others who are influenced by him and define the extent of that influence.

The fully homeless man is unaffiliated in all sectors. He is not an active member of any organization and therefore has no enforceable responsibilities toward fellow members, no audience of persons influenced by his actions, no claim on social rewards beyond whatever minimum has been set to avoid the scandal of his starvation, and no duties to fulfill except those imposed as a condition of remaining in the territory. Clearly, this condition will be uncomfortable and sometimes dangerous. On the other hand, it may be attractive to those who reject the cultural goals together with the means of achieving them.

Homelessness as an ideal.   The age of modernization is singularly unsympathetic to the positive values of homelessness. However, in other times and places it has been regarded as a desirable, or at least admirable, way of life.

The exaltation of homelessness as an ideal is a central, recurrent theme of Christianity, reflecting such scriptural teachings as "lay not up for yourself treasures on earth." Poverty, detachment from previous affiliations, and the abandonment of worldly aspirations are the first principles of monasticism. The Christian ethos of vagrancy was most fully developed by St. Francis of Assisi and the several orders of wandering, mendicant friars who followed the Franciscan model.

A parallel theme runs through Muslim history. The "St. Francis of Islam" is Mulai 'Abd al-Qādir al-Jīlāni (1078–1166), the patron of the needy and suffering. From the Muslim viewpoint, the beggar performs a kind of social service by enabling others to attain merit by almsgiving: "As long as Islam flourishes," says one writer, "there will be beggars, for there will always be devout people who will give away all they have, and so become beggars themselves" (Edwards 1912, p. 931).

In addition to friars, hermits, and holy beggars,

Christianity and Islam recognize and honor the pilgrim, who becomes a homeless wanderer temporarily, partly for the spiritual benefit of visiting the sacred shrine and partly to withdraw from settled society. In the Middle Ages pilgrims played a vital part in integrating both the Christian and Muslim worlds. The pilgrim routes to Mecca and Medina, to Rome and Santiago de Compostela, are as crowded today as ever, but the modern pilgrim is more often a religious tourist than a holy vagrant.

The ethos of vagrancy is even more conspicuous in Buddhism. Buddha and his disciples were members of an already ancient order of wandering almsmen, and Buddha charged his disciples to "go forth and wander about for the good of the Many." The *bhikshu-sangha* was (and is) a community of homeless men entered by "going forth from a house to a houseless state." A *bhikshu* is an almsman. "He is differentiated from an ordinary beggar by the sacramental character of his begging. His beggary is not just a means of subsistence, but an outward token that he has renounced the world and all its goods and thrown himself for bare living on the chances of public charity" (Dutt 1962, p. 36).

Similar themes exalting homelessness and attaching a positive value to mendicancy may be discerned in Hinduism, the religion of Zoroaster, and a number of Hellenistic cults. Indeed, approval and abhorrence of religious mendicancy may occur together. One appeal of the world religions may lie precisely in their ability to combine doctrinal elements supporting the performance of status obligations with others that allow the believer to withdraw from the world without penalty.

Modern forms of homelessness

Although the traditional types of homelessness may still be observed on the contemporary scene, they are overshadowed by new forms that arise directly from the dominant processes of the modern era: industrialization, urbanization, decolonization, and the redistribution of political power. The three types to be considered here are refugees, migratory workers, and skid row men.

Refugees.   Involuntary migration has occurred throughout historic times, but the displacements of the twentieth century have been unprecedented in scale, scope, and duration. Refugees are persons who migrate to escape actual or threatened persecution because of their race, religion, political convictions, or for any reasons related to war (Proudfoot 1957, pp. 53, 446). A broader definition of refugees includes any persons compelled to abandon their homes because of events for which they cannot be held responsible (Vernant 1953, p. 3).

The involuntary migration of refugees contrasts sharply with voluntary migration in search of economic opportunities. Voluntary migrants are mostly young adults usually assured of a welcome in the host country and of continued ties with the country of origin. Involuntary migration often affects entire communities, including people of all ages and conditions, uprooted without their consent and set down in a place selected at random, where their numbers increase their helplessness.

The wars and revolutions of the twentieth century have created both temporary and permanent refugees. The temporary refugee may flee from his home in the face of an invading army to return at the first opportunity. The permanent refugee leaves a country where his enemies have come to power with no real hope of eventual return. Sometimes he is resettled after an interval of hardship in a new community among people of his own persuasion. But if no such place is available, he may linger indefinitely in refugee camps, living on a dole. One observer speaks of *Heimatlosenausländer* as "ultimate refugees" and describes their loss of affiliations:

Here you meet men whose environment has ceased to succour them. In their former normal life they had the solace of their homes in times of weariness or perplexity, perhaps even in times of unemployment. They had the consolation of their church in times of spiritual need and of family sadness. They had their trade union and political association in times when work and politics preoccupied them. They had their village inn and folk festivals on high days and holidays. All these props and cushions in life's pilgrimage are taken from them. . . .   (Rees 1960, p. 37)

The large-scale refugee movements of the twentieth century began with the Balkan wars of 1912–1914. World War I displaced several million civilians, most of whom were subsequently relocated. Almost every major disturbance of the interwar period generated a refugee problem, and World War II displaced between 20 and 50 million persons; the exact number is unknown and cannot be accurately estimated. In the postwar period, the displacement of populations continued unabated in Europe, Asia, Africa, the Near East, the islands of the Pacific, the Mediterranean, and the Caribbean. Not without reason has this been called the "century of the homeless man." Most refugees are ultimately resettled, but not without great cost in suffering and dislocation. Meanwhile, the making of refugees continues at a rate that reflects the peculiar and fanatical character of twentieth-century nationalism.

Migratory farm laborers.   Large-scale agriculture often requires large amounts of hand labor for brief seasonal periods. This situation frequently occurs during the transition from a plantation or family farm system with a fixed labor force to a fully mechanized system of cultivation. The transition may extend over several decades, during which the local labor force is incapable of planting and harvesting a crop without outside help. Arranging the appearance of the required number of workers at the right time and place is a perennial problem for the planters. Protecting the workers against exploitation and the natural hazards of migration is a major problem for whatever authorities assume the responsibility.

Seasonal migratory labor is required for such diverse products as coffee, cocoa, rubber, cotton, citrus fruits, wheat, apples, potatoes, and wild rice. The seasonal movement of migratory workers is significant throughout the world, often transmitting a modernizing influence from advanced to backward areas. The preliterate tribesmen brought to the coastal banana plantations of Central America, the Italian peasants cultivating sugar beets in France, the tribal Africans who migrate to cocoa plantations of Ghana, and the Mexican *braceros* picking peaches in Oregon all acquire new ideas and attitudes to carry back with them.

Movements of this kind are often internal as well as international. In the United States in the middle 1960s, for example, Mexicans were admitted annually on a temporary basis under a farm labor program jointly administered by the two countries, and sizable numbers were drawn under other programs from Canada, the British West Indies, Japan, and Puerto Rico. But the stream of migrants is also fed by many internal groups: Indians, mountain whites, Spanish Americans, and southern Negroes. The annual cycle begins in the South and moves steadily northward with the advancing season; some workers follow the wheat harvest all the way from southern Texas to Manitoba.

Migratory laborers vary in degree of homelessness. John Steinbeck's novel, *The Grapes of Wrath*, painted an unforgettable picture of migrant families displaced from their ancestral farms in Oklahoma during the depression and cut loose to drift helplessly from one temporary job to another. Even in times of prosperity, the United States has an estimated one million transients who have no fixed base (Shotwell 1961, p. 34); and there are many others who have home bases to which they return between seasons or when forced back by unemployment.

A migrant work force may be composed of single

men, entire families, or both. Their living and working conditions range from adequate to wretched. Like other homeless persons, migratory workers are prevented from forming or retaining normal affiliations and are subject to disproportionate hostility from their settled neighbors.

Migrancy engenders community resentment, puts in peril such practical aspects of normal family living as regular schooling for children, housing that is sanitary and convenient and conducive to wholesome family relationships, voting privileges, stable income, health and welfare services available to residents. Migrancy reduces to zero the chance to develop the feeling of belonging to a stable community. (Shotwell 1961, pp. 36–37)

The farm laborer occupies a place at the very bottom of the socioeconomic ladder, doing the most work for the lowest wages with less security and opportunity than any other segment of the population.

Solidary organizations among migrant laborers are rare. Attempts to unionize them, when not violently suppressed, have usually failed. However, a loose form of crew organization often develops, whereby a group of individuals or families is represented by a leader who negotiates with employers and arranges transportation and lodging.

The impact of this form of homelessness on individuals is mitigated by its temporary character. The available evidence suggests that most migratory workers return to a settled life at the first opportunity, often in an area they have discovered as migrants.

The skid row man. In proportion to their numbers, skid row men in the United States and comparable homeless men in western Europe have received disproportionate attention from both scientific and literary observers. In a study using 1950 census data, Bogue (1963) identified skid row areas in 41 American cities and estimated their combined homeless population at under 100,000. The individual settlements are correspondingly small. Careful enumerations in the New York Bowery, one of the most conspicuous skid row areas in the world, disclosed less than seven thousand homeless men in 1964 and 1965 (Baker 1965, p. 7).

The name "skid row" (or "skid road") apparently derives from the log skidways on which felled timber was transported in the forests of the Pacific northwest. It came to be applied to the Seattle area where lumbermen wintered and then to similar enclaves in other cities where single homeless men were housed in dormitories and lodging houses, surrounded by facilities that served their special needs.

Most of these enclaves, in their present locations, can be traced back about a century. In recent decades, their populations have been declining, although irregularly; and the migratory workers identified as the principal inhabitants of "hobohemia" after World War I (Anderson 1923) have given way to the practically immobile pensioners, alcoholics, and disadvantaged workers who make up the bulk of the population today.

The interest aroused by skid row may be explained partly by its unique institutions, partly by its high visibility, partly by the resistance of the skid row alcoholic to ameliorative programs, and partly by a life style that deviates dramatically from the success-oriented, family-centered ethos of the surrounding society. The visible facilities are cubicle lodging houses, cheap restaurants and bars, missions, barber colleges, secondhand stores and pawnshops, newspaper reading rooms, sidewalk gatherings, all-night movies and burlesque shows, tattoo parlors, "jungles" near railroad yards, and the "revolving door" of police court and workhouse. In several major cities the original area has been cleared in the course of urban redevelopment, but substitute skid rows have invariably appeared.

Ethnic and occupational characteristics vary somewhat from one skid row to another, but the population is almost exclusively male. Their average age is much higher than that of the general population; a large proportion are past the usual age of retirement (Bogue 1963, pp. 8–10). About a third of the men are heavy drinkers, frequently arrested for drunkenness and apparently addicted to alcohol, although there is some doubt about their being true alcoholics. The remainder are divided between social drinkers, whose need for liquor is apparently controllable, and moderate drinkers or abstainers (Bogue 1963, pp. 90–93). Most report themselves unmarried and without active family ties. Their histories show less than average involvement in family relationships from early childhood on (Pittman & Gordon 1958, pp. 10, 125–138). Their organizational affiliations have often been slight throughout adult life, reflecting a permanent state of social detachment. The typical skid row man has a background of intermittent unskilled or semiskilled employment, with minimal involvement in political, religious, and recreational organizations (Bahr & Langfur 1966).

Morbidity and mortality rates are startlingly high. The risks of contagious disease, infection, exposure, injury, and malnutrition are greater on skid row than in any other urban environment (Bogue 1963, pp. 199–230). Most men live close to the margin of bare subsistence on sporadic earnings, pensions, relief payments, begging, or some combination of these. A few depend on savings or assistance from relatives; a few enjoy regular incomes and remain on skid row by preference (Bogue 1963, pp. 13–17; 46–77).

In addition to the core population, the skid row area provides temporary accommodation for migratory workers and work seekers, eccentrics, and fugitives of various kinds. Some of these men are not strictly homeless, and some homeless men have no contact with skid row. However, the predominant type is unmistakable.

The principal current trends in the status of skid row inhabitants are decreased mobility and a decline of relative income. There is, however, a rising provision of public assistance for them, and experimental programs are being undertaken in the rehabilitation of alcoholics.

THEODORE CAPLOW, HOWARD M. BAHR,
AND DAVID STERNBERG

[*Directly related is the entry* REFUGEES. *Other relevant material may be found in* DRINKING AND ALCOHOLISM, *article on* SOCIAL ASPECTS; MIGRATION.]

BIBLIOGRAPHY

ANDERSON, NELS 1923 *The Hobo: The Sociology of the Homeless Man.* Univ. of Chicago Press.

BAHR, HOWARD M.; and LANGFUR, STEPHEN J. 1966 Social Attachment and Drinking in Skid-row Life Histories. Unpublished report, Columbia Univ., Bureau of Applied Social Research.

BAKER, MICHAEL A. 1965 An Estimate of the Population of Homeless Men in the Bowery Area, New York City, February 28, 1965. Unpublished manuscript, Columbia Univ., Bureau of Applied Social Research.

BOGUE, DONALD J. 1963 *Skid Row in American Cities.* Univ. of Chicago, Community and Family Study Center.

CAPLOW, THEODORE 1940 Transiency as a Cultural Pattern. *American Sociological Review* 5:731–739.

CIRTAUTAS, CLAUDIUS K. 1957 *The Refugee: A Psychological Study.* Boston: Meador.

DUTT, SUKUMAR 1962 *Buddhist Monks and Monasteries of India.* London: Allen & Unwin.

EDWARDS, ALBERT 1912 The Beggars of Mogador. *Outlook* 101:929–936.

GILMORE, HARLAN W. 1940 *The Beggar.* Chapel Hill: Univ. of North Carolina Press.

HOLBORN, LOUISE W. 1960 *The World's Refugees: Everyone's Concern.* Washington: American Association of University Women, Committee on International Relations.

INTERNATIONAL LABOUR REVIEW STAFF 1957 Interterritorial Migrations of Africans South of the Sahara. *International Labour Review* 76:292–310.

MARTIN, NORMAN F. 1957 *Los vagabundos en la Nueva España, siglo XVI.* Mexico City: Editorial Jus.

O'CONNOR, PHILIP 1963 *Vagrancy: Ethos and Actuality.* Baltimore: Penguin.

OREGON, BUREAU OF LABOR 1959 *. . . And Migrant Problems Demand Attention: The Final Report of the 1958–1959 Migrant Farm Labor Studies in Oregon.* Salem: The Bureau.

ORWELL, GEORGE (1933) 1950 *Down and Out in Paris and London.* New York: Harcourt. → Orwell is the pseudonym of Eric Blair.

PITTMAN, DAVID J.; and GORDON, C. WAYNE 1958 *Revolving Door: A Study of the Chronic Police Case Inebriate.* Glencoe, Ill.: Free Press.

POLLITT, DANIEL H.; and LEVINE, SELMA M. 1960 *The Migrant Farm Worker in America: Background Data on the Migrant Worker Situation in the United States Today.* Washington: Government Printing Office.

PROUDFOOT, MALCOLM J. 1957 *European Refugees, 1939–1952: A Study in Forced Population Movement.* London: Faber.

REES, ELFAN 1960 Common Psychological Factors in Refugee Problems Throughout the World. Pages 31–43 in World Federation for Mental Health, *Uprooting and Resettlement.* London: The Federation.

SHOTWELL, LOUISA R. 1961 *The Harvesters: The Story of the Migrant People.* Garden City, N.Y.: Doubleday.

SOLENBERGER, ALICE W. 1911 *One Thousand Homeless Men: A Study of Original Records.* New York: Russell Sage Foundation, Charities Publication Committee.

STOESSINGER, JOHN G. 1956 *The Refugee and the World Community.* Minneapolis: Univ. of Minnesota Press.

STRAUS, ROBERT 1946 Alcohol and the Homeless Man. *Quarterly Journal of Studies on Alcohol* 7:360–404.

SUTHERLAND, EDWIN H.; and LOCKE, HARVEY J. 1936 *Twenty Thousand Homeless Men: A Study of Unemployed Men in the Chicago Shelters.* Philadelphia: Lippincott.

VERNANT, JACQUES 1953 *The Refugee in the Post-war World.* New Haven: Yale Univ. Press.

VEXLIARD, ALEXANDRE 1956 *Introduction à la sociologie du vagabondage.* Paris: Rivière.

WALLACE, SAMUEL E. 1965 *Skid Row as a Way of Life.* Totowa, N.J.: Bedminster.

WOOD, MARGARET M. 1953 *Paths of Loneliness: The Individual Isolated in Modern Society.* New York: Columbia Univ. Press.

HOMEOSTASIS

The concept of homeostasis is widely used, in physiology and psychology, to identify what seems to be a general attribute of living organisms: the tendency to maintain and restore certain steady states or conditions of the organism. An obvious example is that of body temperature, which in the human tends to fluctuate only in a narrow range about the value 98.6° F. When the temperature rises above the normal range, corrective reflexes (perspiration, reduced metabolism, etc.) go into action to restore the steady state. Persistent deviation may initiate other actions (moving into the shade, plunging into water, etc.). If body temperature drops, other corrective actions are observed.

Many bodily steady states follow this pattern. Blood glucose level, blood pH, and osmotic pressure are examples. The key concepts are: an observable steady state that persists over time with minor changes; thresholds above and below this normal range; a sensory input that reports changes in the steady state; and effector mechanisms for restoring the steady state.

When a deviation goes beyond either the upper or the lower threshold, energy is mobilized to restore the steady state to its optimal value. Physiologists have been concerned mainly with the reflexes triggered by such deviations, but psychologists have emphasized those homeostatic actions that are seen in learned behavior. Man will exert considerable energy to protect optimal states. He may take *restorative* action (building a fire when cold) or *forestalling* action (moving south before winter arrives). The simple reflex level and the complex learned response to homeostatic disturbance are often labeled differently: Stagner and Karwoski (1952) called the former "static homeostasis" and the latter "dynamic homeostasis"; Cofer and Appley (1964) used the terms "physiological homeostasis" and "behavioral homeostasis."

The biochemical and reflex defenses function adequately to protect some constancies; if blood osmotic pressure drops too low or vitamin concentration is too high, kidney mechanisms correct the situation. In other cases, the reflex machinery may fail, and learned behavior is activated. There are probably two thresholds in the system, one for reflexive response and another (further from optimum) that initiates voluntary action.

Damaging the biochemical mechanism forces increased reliance on the learned systems of defense. Thyroidectomized rats build nests to protect against heat loss; parathyroidectomy or adrenalectomy leads to increased drinking of solutions containing calcium or sodium. It seems reasonable, therefore, to consider the cerebral cortex as the highest level of a homeostatic protective mechanism.

Heterostasis. The concept of heterostasis must be introduced into any systematic discussion of homeostasis. Action to restore one steady state may disrupt another steady state (perspiration to cool the body upsets the osmotic equilibrium in the blood, triggering thirst). Heterostasis points to a hierarchy of steady states; deviation of an "important" value will initiate action that disrupts one lower in the scale, but the reverse is not true. Thirst dominates over hunger, and the need for oxygen is prepotent over either. Deviations from optimum dominate behavior as a function of their relevance to organismic survival. Oxygen lack can be tolerated for only a few minutes, water lack for a day or two, food lack for many days.

Sensory controls. Homeostasis depends upon a negative feedback loop; disturbance of a steady state initiates sensory cues that trigger responses tending to restore the previous state; and as the sensory input indicates that the optimal value is being approached, the intensity of corrective action diminishes. Each steady state must have built into its control system, in neural or biochemical form, some representation of the tolerable range of values and upper and lower thresholds. However, all such monitoring systems probably report to a central mechanism, giving rise to something like Morgan's (1957) "central motive state," a state of *tension* that elicits dynamic homeostatic responses. Tension is thus an important intervening variable in homeostatic theory.

Some types of stimuli have inherent equilibrium-disturbing or equilibrium-restoring properties. Sweet tastes not only signal reduction of hunger for infants; they also seem to have general tension-reducing value. Pain disturbs equilibrium and raises tension. Soft, warm contact may be a universal tension reducer for mammals (cf. Harlow 1958). This need not imply a one-to-one correspondence between pleasure or "subjective utility" and homeostatic value in a goal object. For example, the organism may make mistakes (saccharin is sought by the organism because it is misperceived as equilibrium restoring); and learning may cause the organism to value objects that are purely symbolic and not in themselves effective either to disturb or to restore steady states [see LEARNING, *article on* REINFORCEMENT].

Imprinting. Imprinting may be a determiner of cue value. When a gosling first hatches, it seems to fixate on the first moving object and endow this with positive valence; the gosling will follow this object and behave as if a steady state were disturbed when the object disappears [see IMPRINTING].

Adaptation level. Adaptation level modifies the sensory controls in homeostatic cycles. As Cannon (1932) pointed out, the "baseline" (herein referred to as optimal value) may shift as a result of experience. Infants learn to adapt to a two-hour, three-hour, or four-hour feeding schedule and become "hungry" at the proper time. If subjected to radio and television noises, they show distress at first but later may seem to enjoy the sound level (Chodorkoff 1960). Europeans find room temperatures comfortable that Americans experience as chilly and disturbing.

Effector processes. The effector mechanisms set off by homeostatic disturbances vary from simple biochemical buffering of the blood stream, through hormonal modifications and autonomic nervous system reflex changes, to complex and elaborate learned responses. As Bernard (1859) noted, homeostasis in its simplest form involves protection of constancies of body fluids. Life escaped from the sea when techniques evolved for carrying the sea (as cell environment) within the organism. He wrote that internal constancies are basic to the free life—free from the limitations of an oceanic environment, free to live on land and in the air.

The more complex activities described above expand this conception markedly. First, the organism may remove itself from disturbing stimuli (avoid heat, seek shade). Second, the organism may restore the constancy of the external environment (air conditioning, stores of food). There seems to be general agreement that these two kinds of responses, while remote from biochemical secretion or mechanical reflexes, qualify as homeostatic in nature. Third, the organism may seek to protect (or restore) symbolic conditions associated with homeostatic success—bank accounts, institutional systems, and the like. There is less agreement that these phenomena belong under the homeostatic rubric, yet it is difficult to find a logical rule by which to exclude them.

Evaluation of homeostatic theory. Critics have objected to homeostatic theory as being too conservative, as implying that motivation is conceived solely as operating to restore pre-existing conditions. In a very narrow sense this criticism is true: unless the essential steady states are restored to their normal range, the organism dies. (It is also true that most people are conservative unless deprived.) In a broader sense, homeostatic theory says that energy is mobilized to take action that will restore and protect these *steady states,* but that the *action* may be novel and inventive. Fire, clothing, and other inventions serve homeostatic uses. The individual, frustrated by inadequate habits, may acquire new ones which will reduce tensions.

The assertion that all energy mobilizations derive from disturbances of steady states does encounter problems. The phenomena of curiosity, manipulative motivation, and sensory deprivation, as well as the sex drive, offer difficulties. Some psychologists have preferred to treat homeostasis as one segment of the topic of motivation. Those who prefer to press for an inclusive view, in which all motivation obeys homeostatic principles, resort to assumptions such as efficient organismic functioning "demanding" a certain level of sensory stimulation, just as it "demands" a certain level of glucose or vitamin B. "Sensory deprivation" may be motivating because the central nervous system has a normal activity level that is disrupted by either an excess or a deficit of external stimulation [*see* PERCEPTION, *article on* PERCEPTUAL DEPRIVATION; STIMULATION DRIVES; *see also* Hebb 1955; Miller 1960].

Aspiration level studies can also be incorporated into this schema. Motivation, in the sense of effort directed toward a specific goal, obeys aspiration principles. An incentive below present attainment levels is ignored; one that is too far above present achievement is perceived as impossible. Effective incentives, therefore, must fall within the "normal range" as a function of adaptation level. Repeated successes lead to a shift upward, failures to a shift downward, in aspiration level. Prior experience determines what will be anticipated [*see* ACHIEVEMENT MOTIVATION].

Homeostatic conception of personality. Personalities can be described by the hierarchy of steady states that are defended, by the cues that disturb these states, and by the techniques utilized to protect and restore equilibriums (Stagner 1961).

Preferred steady states. Some individuals value physical comfort; others, a quiet family life; others, a buzz of activity. Variations in adaptation or aspiration level may be involved. Objects that symbolize internal equilibrium, such as the mother, a house, or a bank account, become values protected in themselves. The self-image, the individual's percept of himself, becomes an object of value. Threats to the self-image (failure, social ridicule, loss of status) provoke blood pressure and glandular changes as well as vigorous action to restore the integrity of the ego.

Sources of disturbance. Some persons manifest phobias and other disturbances that are obviously not realistic. Neurotic aggressions and anxieties fit into this category. Others are disturbed only by realistic threats to physical constancies or to acquired values.

Methods of restoring equilibriums. The individual may rely chiefly upon overt muscular action to protect and restore valued constancies, or he may utilize symbols and fantasy. The whole range of coping and defensive reactions indicates individual differences in ways of maintaining steady states.

Personality defense mechanisms. Sigmund Freud has often been cited as a forerunner of homeostatic theory, although he never discussed negative feedback loops (Fletcher 1942; Walker 1956). His conception of repression, projection, dreams, rationalization, and other mechanisms as devices for protecting the individual against threatened disturbance, or devices for restoring equilibrium, places him in this category [see DEFENSE MECHANISMS].

When anxiety and tension are aroused, infantile ways of restoring equilibrium may be reinstated. Eating, drinking, and sexual contact are primitive devices for reducing tension. Unfortunately, if the steady state that has been disturbed involves a need for other substances, these defenses have only temporary effect; the tension returns promptly. Neurotic behavior, in homeostatic terms, is behavior that diminishes tension without correcting the basic imbalance (Menninger et al. 1963).

One must note that some psychologists take issue vigorously with attempts to conceptualize personality in homeostatic terms. Allport (1955) asserts that man can be understood more by what he is striving for in the future than by what he is seeking to restore of the past.

Homeostasis as a social phenomenon. Cannon (1932) noted that the concept of homeostasis seemed relevant also to social processes. One such implication derives from the process of mutual assistance (Dempsey 1951). There is some evidence (Chodorkoff 1960) that the mother–infant relationship is a true dyadic system, in which each organism can be a cue disturbing the other, and in which the behavior of one may be equilibrium restoring for the other. Most convincing is the fact that social conditions can trigger the same reflexive mechanisms involved in physiological homeostasis (cf. Denenberg et al. 1964; Hoagland 1964). Hoagland, for example, reported that rats reared in overcrowded cages develop glandular disorders and die at earlier ages than less crowded littermates. These animals show distinct evidences of tension and behavioral disturbance. Hoagland also commented that equilibrium develops at a given population density. Below this point, reproduction is usually accelerated; but above the equilibrium value, infertility and early death reduce the population. Thus he is disposed to favor the view that homeostatic functions are true group processes, not merely manifestations of individual disturbance. Allee et al. (1949) have pointed out that ecological balance often shows all the properties ascribed to homeostatic equilibrium.

To apply the concept of homeostasis to even more complex social phenomena, such as the market economy, one must identify the steady state, the factors disrupting this state, the cues indicating disturbance, and the restorative mechanisms. Equilibrium theory in economics seems to meet these requirements. In a specific economic market, for example, clothing, one finds a tendency for the price to stabilize. An increase in consumer demand will upset the existing steady state; information spreads by way of efforts to purchase; producers in the clothing industry scent possibilities for profit and increase output accordingly. Thus there is a feedback loop analogous to that observed in individuals.

Failures of homeostasis. One criticism of homeostatic theory is that humans often do things that disrupt, rather than restore, equilibrium. To some extent this is merely a function of errors in informational input or in guiding action. A young lion who charges his prey from too great a distance is not thereby proved to be disobeying homeostatic principles; he simply has not learned effective responses.

In some cases homeostasis operates inefficiently at the individual level because of inadequate sensory controls. Man is not endowed with receptors sensitive to gamma radiation, so, without warning, he may die of fall-out. If the species survives, mutation may provide such sense organs.

Group phenomena also show catastrophic effects of poor information input. War between nations has frequently come about because the leaders of one nation did not accurately perceive the situation (for example, in 1939 Hitler thought England would not fight over Poland). Disputes between a union and management can be settled more amicably if information flows freely between the two (Muench 1960).

These illustrations do not *prove* that the homeostatic model explains group action; no such logical proof exists at this time. Nevertheless, the homeostatic model has been a fruitful one in pointing to areas for research and in suggesting genotypic unities that cut across phenotypic discontinuities, just as the theory of gravitation cut across events from atoms to galaxies. Consequently, homeostasis has been a healthy influence in psychology and in the other social sciences.

ROSS STAGNER

[*Directly related are the entries* DRIVES; MOTIVATION. *Other relevant material may be found in* CYBERNETICS; STRESS; *and in the biography of* CANNON.]

BIBLIOGRAPHY

An extensive and scholarly discussion of homeostatic theories may be found in Cofer & Appley 1964. *The homeostatic conception of personality is supported in* Stagner

1961, *and the opposing view is well stated in* Allport 1955. *Applications to social groups are proposed in* Cannon 1932 *and* 1941 *and to industry in* Stagner 1956.

ALLEE, W. C. et al.   1949   *Principles of Animal Ecology.* Philadelphia: Saunders.

ALLPORT, GORDON W.   1955   *Becoming: Basic Considerations for a Psychology of Personality.* New Haven: Yale Univ. Press.

BERNARD, CLAUDE   1859   *Leçons sur les propriétés physiologiques et les altérations pathologiques des liquides de l'organisme.* 2 vols. Paris: Baillière.

CANNON, WALTER B.   (1932) 1963   *The Wisdom of the Body.* Rev. & enl. ed. New York: Norton.

CANNON, WALTER B.   1941   The Body Physiologic and the Body Politic. *Science* 93:1–10.

CHODORKOFF, JOAN R.   1960   Infant Development as a Function of Mother–Child Interaction. Ph.D. dissertation, Wayne State Univ.

COFER, C. N.; and APPLEY, M. H.   1964   Homeostatic Concepts and Motivation. Pages 302–365 in C. N. Cofer and M. H. Appley, *Motivation: Theory and Research.* New York: Wiley.

DEMPSEY, EDWARD W.   1951   Homeostasis. Pages 209–235 in S. S. Stevens (editor), *Handbook of Experimental Psychology.* New York: Wiley.

DENENBERG, W. H.; HUDGENS, G. A.; and ZARROW, M. X.   1964   Mice Reared With Rats: Modification of Behavior by Early Experience With Another Species. *Science* 143:380–381.

FLETCHER, JOHN M.   1942   Homeostasis as an Explanatory Principle in Psychology. *Psychological Review* 49:80–87.

HARLOW, HARRY F.   1958   The Nature of Love. *American Psychologist* 13:673–685.

HEBB, DONALD O.   1955   Drives and the C.N.S. (Conceptual Nervous System). *Psychological Review* 62:243–254.

HOAGLAND, HUDSON   1964   Cybernetics of Population Control. *Bulletin of the Atomic Scientists* 20, no. 2: 2–6.

MASLOW, A. H.   1937   The Influence of Familiarization on Preference. *Journal of Experimental Psychology* 21:162–180.

MENNINGER, KARL; MAYMAN, MARTIN; and PRUYSER, PAUL   1963   *The Vital Balance: The Life Processes in Mental Health and Illness.* New York: Viking.

MILLER, JAMES G.   1960   Information Input Overload and Psychopathology. *American Journal of Psychiatry* 116:695–704.

MORGAN, CLIFFORD T.   1957   Physiological Mechanisms of Motivation. Volume 5, pages 1–35 in *Nebraska Symposium on Motivation.* Edited by Marshall R. Jones. Lincoln: Univ. of Nebraska Press.

MUENCH, GEORGE A.   1960   A Clinical Psychologist's Treatment of Labor–Management Conflicts. *Personnel Psychology* 13:165–172.

SOUTHWICK, CHARLES H.   1964   Peromyscus Leucopus: An Interesting Subject for Studies of Socially Induced Stress Responses. *Science* 143:55–56.

STAGNER, ROSS   1956   *Psychology of Industrial Conflict.* New York: Wiley. → See especially pages 89–116, "Motivation: Principles," and pages 117–154, "Motivation: Some Applications."

STAGNER, ROSS   1961   The Nature of Personality Structure. Pages 69–86 in Ross Stagner, *Psychology of Personality.* 3d ed. New York: McGraw-Hill.

STAGNER, ROSS; and KARWOSKI, T. F.   1952   *Psychology.* New York: McGraw-Hill.

WALKER, NIGEL   1956   Freud and Homeostasis. *British Journal for the Philosophy of Science* 7:61–72.

HOMICIDE
See under CRIME.

HOMOSEXUALITY
See under SEXUAL BEHAVIOR.

HONESTY
See MORAL DEVELOPMENT.

HONOR

The notion of honor has several facets. It is a sentiment, a manifestation of this sentiment in conduct, and the evaluation of this conduct by others, that is to say, reputation. It is both internal to the individual and external to him—a matter of his feelings, his behavior, and the treatment that he receives. Many authors have stressed one of these facets at the expense of the others; however, from the point of view of the social sciences it is essential to bear in mind that honor is simultaneously all of these, for both its psychological and social functions relate to the fact that it stands as a mediator between individual aspirations and the judgment of society.

Like the other self-regarding sentiments, honor expresses an evaluation of self in the terms which are used to evaluate others—or as others might be imagined to judge one. It can, therefore, be seen to reflect the values of the group with which a person identifies himself. But honor as a fact, rather than as a sentiment, refers not merely to the judgment of others but to their behavior. The facets of honor may be viewed as related in the following way: honor felt becomes honor claimed, and honor claimed becomes honor paid. The payment of honor involves the expression of respect which is due to a person either by virtue of his role on a particular occasion, as when a guest is honored in accordance with the laws of hospitality, or by virtue of his status or rank, which entitles him to a permanent right to precedence marked by honorific insignia, expressed in modes of address and titles and demonstrated in deference. Honor is also exchanged in mutual recognition: in salutations and the return of invitations and favors.

The same principles that govern the transactions of honor are present in those of dishonor, though in reverse: the withdrawal of respect dishonors, since it implies a rejection of the claim to honor and this inspires the sentiment of shame. To be put to shame is to be denied honor, and it follows that this can only be done to those who have some pretension to it. He who makes no such claim has nothing to lose; he cannot be denied precedence if he prefers to go last. Those who aspire to no honor cannot be humiliated. Honor and dishonor, therefore, provide the currency in which people compete for reputation and the means whereby their appraisal of themselves can be validated and integrated into the social system —or rejected, thus obliging them to revise it. Hence, honor is not only the internalization of the values of society in the individual but the externalization of his self-image in the world.

The sentiment of honor seeks validation, but from what quarter? From God or from the conscience of the person himself? From friends or from kinsmen? From persons in authority or from the crowd? Public opinion, allegedly the arbiter of reputations, arbitrates with anything but a firm hand, since it varies according to the activity and the context. Consensus is not easily established in a complex society; individual views differ, and different groups have different standards. The significance of the acts of public honor and the granting of dignities is, therefore, this: they place the seal of public recognition on reputations that would otherwise stand in doubt and endow them with permanence. It is the function of authority to impose consensus, and it does this with regard to the worth of persons: it converts prestige into status.

Theories of honor have varied greatly as to the relative importance which they accord to different qualities, and this is due to the different social contexts and reference groups from which they derive.

Honor as a moral concept.   Honor is commonly considered by moral philosophers to be a state of the individual conscience and, as such, equivalent to the absence of self-reproach. It relates to intentions rather than to the objective consequences of action, and a man is therefore said to be the only judge of his own honor. If he knows his intentions to be "above reproach," then he is indifferent to the comments of others, who cannot evaluate the quality of his motives. He is committed by his honor to the fulfillment of duties that are recognized as attaching to social roles. The casuists recognized honor as a personal responsibility and admitted the defense of honor as a licit form of self-defense which could excuse actions that would otherwise be sinful. Nevertheless, the churches have always considered that, in the evaluation of his own motives, a man is bound to refer to their authority, which claims for itself the right to define honor in terms of religious virtue.

Somewhat different is the view of honor which derives it from civic virtue, for here it is ratified not by religious doctrine but by the market place. Popular acclaim comes in to qualify, if not to guide, the judgments of the individual conscience, and honor becomes the reputation for virtue. (This was Aristotle's view.) But once the notion of reputation is admitted as a constituent of honor, its value as a purely moral concept faces ambiguities: a potential conflict emerges between the dictates of conscience and the facts of recognition. This is brought to the forefront by those moralists (not by any means confined to churchmen) who have upbraided the code of honor of their day from the standpoint of morality. Public opinion cannot be trusted to confirm even the most modest man's claim to civic virtues or even to accord reputation on that basis at all. It is apt to give its applause to more spectacular qualities and to pay honor to other sorts of excellence. With regard to dishonor, it is yet more capricious, for here its great weapon is ridicule, which seldom employs a moral criterion at all, but destroys reputations on the grounds of a man's pretentiousness, foolishness, or misfortune, not his wickedness. As Molière observed, one would rather be Tartuffe than Orgon. Public opinion, in its sympathy for the successful, betrays the notion of honor as a purely moral concept.

Honor as precedence.   In contrast to the moral view of honor, which relates it to merit—whether religious, civic, or professional—other writers have insisted upon its factual aspect. For example, Hobbes (*Leviathan*, chapter 10) saw no more in honor than the achievement of precedence and the competition for worldly honors. Honor, in his view, is not a matter of sentiment and aspirations (since all men would like to be honored), but one of individual preferment, to the attainment of which virtue is quite irrelevant.

It is, moreover, from this aspect that the word honor derives etymologically: it first applied to grants of land or the privilege of levying taxes ceded by a sovereign to his eminent servants and supporters. Royal favor was, therefore, not only the "fountain of honor," as in the view of many later political theorists, but literally the origin of the word. As might be expected, honor was particularly to be earned through military prowess, and originally, it should be noted, it conceded not only social dignity but economic advantage as well.

Honor in this sense accorded precedence. This, however, is not only conferred by royal statute but derives from social interaction at every level in a society; the claim to honor depends always, in the last resort, upon the ability of the claimant to impose himself. Might is the basis of right to precedence, which goes to the man who is bold enough to enforce his claim, regardless of what may be thought of his merits.

Worldly honor validates itself by an appeal to the facts, submitting always to the reality of power, whether military, political, social, or economic and whether it rests upon the consensus of a community, the favor of superiors, or the control of sanctions. For this reason courage is the *sine qua non* of honor, and cowardice is always its converse. This fact is inherent in its nature and not merely the heritage of a class which once earned its status, or so it claimed, through feats of arms. The mottoes of the nobility (which may serve as a gloss upon their conception of honor) commonly emphasize not only the claim to prestige and status but, above all, the moral quality necessary to win and to retain them; when "all is lost save honor," this at least has been preserved, and while this is so, a return of fortune is always possible. Willingness to stand up to opposition is essential to the acquisition, as to the defense, of honor, regardless of the mode of action that is adopted. No amount of moral justification validates the honor of a coward, even where retaliation to an affront is ruled out on moral grounds; to turn the other cheek is not the same thing as to hide it. Indeed, in terms of the code of honor, turning the other cheek is simply a means of demonstrating contempt. Christian forgiveness cloaks a claim to superiority that cannot but irritate the sensitivities of the forgiven, for it not only implies disdain, it attempts to alter the rules whereby honor is achieved or lost.

However well courage may promote the claims of the courageous, the fact of triumph is ultimately what counts. The distribution of the spoils is the privilege of the victor; where claims to precedence conflict, the decision goes to the big battalions. It is the *fact* of precedence that establishes the *right* to command and the privilege of speaking first or last. In this sense, therefore, honor and leadership imply one another, for both are subject to the reality of power.

Honor as a personal attribute.   Since honor is felt as well as demonstrated, it is allied to the conception of the self in the most intimate ways. It is a state of grace. It is liable to defilement. It is linked to the physical person in terms of the symbolic functions attached to the body: to the blood, the heart, the hand, the head, and the genitalia. Honor is inherited through the "blood," and the shedding of blood has a specially honorific value in transactions of honor—the stains of honor, it was said, could be cleansed only by blood. The heart is the symbol of sincerity, since it is thought of—in the European tradition at least—as the seat of the intentions and therefore the home of the true self, which lies behind all worldly disguises. The right hand is the purveyor of honor: it touches; it shakes or is shaken; it is kissed or waved; it wins honor, for it wields the sword and pulls the trigger. The head is the representation of the self in social life, that by which a man is recognized, that which is placed in effigy on coins, and that which is touched in salute, crowned, covered or uncovered, bowed, or shorn. The private parts are the seat of shame, vulnerable to the public view and represented symbolically in the gestures and verbal expressions of desecration. In their association with the excretory function they are the source of pollution, yet as the means of procreation they are intimately connected with honor, for they signify the extension of the self in time. Sexual purity is, therefore, often regarded as the essence of honor in women, whose feminine status precludes their striving for it by might. The body as a whole is especially associated with honor, since physical contact implies intimacy and makes explicit the honorific relationship with another, whether to express attachment, obeisance, or contempt.

Because honor centers in the physical being, a person's presence bears a particular significance, as Simmel observed when he spoke of a sacred aura surrounding each individual. Whatever occurs in a person's presence obliges him to react in one way or another, positively or negatively, for he cannot hide his cognizance of it: he is inescapably a party to what he witnesses, and his will is thereby committed. This is important because the essence of the social person comprises his will and (as the moralists understood, though in a different context) his intentions. Hence, apologies for an affront normally take the form of denying the intention, thereby making the affront in a sense fortuitous because not willed. The true affront to honor must be intended as such. For the same reason oaths are binding only if freely sworn and, like the rites of the church, are invalid if devoid of good intention. The oath commits the honor of the swearer by guaranteeing his intentions, for it is not dishonoring to deceive another man, only to "break faith"—that is to say, to rescind an established commitment, for this implies cowardice. This is underlined by the mottoes of the aristocracy (so often devoted to the theme of steadfastness), the broken weapons which clutter up their arms, and the defiant invitations to fate to put them to the test.

This emphasis on intention or will marks an essential point: the essence of honor is personal autonomy. All men are bound by certain irrevocable ties, but the man of honor cannot otherwise *be* committed; he can only commit himself. To be forced by whatever circumstance to revoke his intentions once they are committed is to abnegate his personal autonomy. Thus, the concept of honor is tied to precedence, for to command over others enhances it, while obedience restricts it.

Collective honor.   The group possesses collective honor, in which the individual members participate. It affects their honor and is affected by their behavior. The honor of a collectivity is vested in its head and in symbolic representations; flags, crests, coats of arms, badges, uniforms, and all the insignia whereby members of the group are recognized are the objects of a greater or lesser degree of reverence and are treated as though they possess honor in themselves. In the anthropological language of an earlier generation, such objects have *mana*, a concept that also expresses the idea of honor when it is applied to individuals or to parts of their person.

While some types of groups are joined voluntarily and may be left in the same way (or may expel one of their number), membership in other groups is ascribed at birth. In the latter type of group, honor is bound up integrally, for the group defines a person's essential nature. The family (and in some societies the kin group) and the nation are the most fundamental of these collectivities, and thus traitors to their fathers or their sovereigns are the most execrable of all. (Parricide and regicide are sacrilegious but homicide is not.) The family is the repository of personal honor, for honor is hereditary, not merely in its aspect as social status but also with regard to the moral qualities which attach to it. Therefore, the dishonor cast on one member is felt by all.

Male and female honor are clearly differentiated with regard to conduct. A moral division of labor operates within the family, especially in the Latin countries: the aspect of honor as precedence becomes, according to this system of values, the prerogative of the male, while honor as sexual purity is restricted to the female. Hence, sexual conquest enhances the prestige of men; sexual liberty defiles the honor of women. (Congruently, a high value is attached to virginity in unmarried girls.) The defense of female purity, however, is a male responsibility, and men are therefore vulnerable to dishonor not through their own sexual misconduct but through that of their womenfolk—that is to say, members of the same nuclear family, including mother, wife, unmarried sister, and daughter. Hence, sexual insults that impugn the honor of men refer not to them but to their women.

The aspect of honor that is associated with social status descends preferentially in the male line —as hereditary titles, for example—but in its moral aspect a man's honor comes to him primarily from his mother, and further, his sister's honor reflects upon his through their mother. However, if a man inherits his honor in this way, he is, above all, actively responsible for the honor of his wife, and the cuckold (expressed in the Mediterranean by an analogy with the he-goat) is the paragon of dishonor, equal only, if in a different way. to the traitor. It should be noted that the cuckolder is exculpated: though he represents the cuckoo in the analogy on which the word is based, the title is reserved for the man whose marital right is usurped (and the same transposition is performed in the symbolism of the Mediterranean by endowing the wronged husband with the horns). Although the cuckolder may be thought immoral, he bears no stigma of dishonor. Once more dishonor goes to the defeated, and ridicule is visited on the defiled one rather than on the guilty. This code of honor is attenuated to the degree that women are regarded as independent of male authority.

Honor and the sacred.   The connection between honor and the sacred does not derive simply from the ambition of the church to stand as the arbiter of honor, a role that it has never entirely succeeded in achieving in the popular view, but rather from the sacred nature of honor itself, which, as the essence of the social personality and the personal destiny of the individual, stands in a preferential relation to the deity; a man's true self is known only to God, from whom nothing can be hidden and in whose eyes honor is ultimately vindicated. Honor is committed by invoking the sacred, whether in the form of a conditional curse witnessed by the spiritual powers or by implicating any other agency from which honor derives. The appeal to the sacred acts as a guarantee that the swearer will accept his shame under the prescribed circumstances. Hence, even in modern law courts oaths are required. The commitment of honor to the sovereign derives also from the fact that he stands, as divinely authorized ruler, in a preferential relationship to the Deity, a conception that has survived centuries of rebellion and even the passing of the monarchy altogether in many instances. Sacredness attaches to the notion of legitimate rule, regardless of the doctrine in which this is expressed. For this reason republics have tended to conserve the sanctifying rituals of the monarchies they superseded.

Honor and social status

The distribution of honor in communities of equals, whether local groups or specialized institutions, tends to relate to eminence, recognized virtue, and age. However, in a stratified society it accords with social status, and as such, it is more often ascribed by birth than achieved. Thus, medieval society was ranked in terms of honor, from the aristocracy, who had the most—on account of their power, their valor, and their proximity to the king —to those who had none at all, the heretics and the outcasts, those who indulged in infamous occupations or had been convicted of infamy.

Honor is hereditary, as we have seen; the excellence that once brought honor to the forebears is credited to their offspring, even though it may no longer be discernible in their conduct. Titles and property, the honorific and effective forms of hereditary power, endow the social system with continuity in this regard; honor is ascribed. Yet, the supposition of excellence derived from birth is constantly betrayed, and a conflict therefore emerges between the criterion of prestige derived from personal worth and that which looks to social origins. This has provided one of the favorite themes of European literature from the twelfth-century *Poem of the Cid* onward, a theme which is matched in popularity only by its counterpart: the role of money rather than excellence in the acquisition of honor. The ideal unity of honor is apt to fragment when it strikes the facts, and the different bases for according it become opposed to one another.

Moreover, the criteria by which honor is bestowed have greatly varied in time: occupation and religious orthodoxy were once important, although they are no longer. With the evolution from a system of legal status to a class system, economic privileges ceased to be attached to status, and the contrary came to be true. In the modern world the criteria appear to be changing again: titles can no longer be purchased and wealth gives way to fame as the measure of reputation—a fact not unconnected with the development of the communications industry. The theater, which was once a dishonorable occupation, now presents candidates for the British sovereign's Honours List, which also finds a place for jockeys and football players.

The struggle for honor is palliated by a provision that saves society from anarchy. Indeed, this struggle is not only the basis upon which individuals compete but also that on which they cooperate.

Here the notion of steadfastness is crucial, whether it binds together those who recognize their mutual equality or those whose relationship is one of patron and client. The reciprocal demonstrations of favor, which might be called mutual honoring, establish relationships of solidarity. The notion of a community of honorable men replaces the competition for honor; reputation attaches to honesty, and the steadfastness that honor enjoins is seen in financial reliability and contractual faith—the "honoring" of a check or bond displays this sense. Honor then comes to be the guarantor of the credit system. This notion of honor was, in particular, the ideal of the Puritans, who attempted to suppress all its competitive and flamboyant aspects in favor of equating it to conscience (only to see them reemerge triumphant with the Restoration, whose literature pays more tribute to cuckoldry than that of any other period in the English language). The relation of the puritan ethic to capitalism, first stressed by Max Weber and R. H. Tawney, restricts competition to the field of wealth and, while giving financial probity a prime place in the notion of honor, makes financial success the arbiter of prestige. Under such conditions social status inevitably becomes increasingly an economic matter, to the exclusion of all other criteria.

Honor is always bound to wealth and possessions, for they provide an idiom in which to express relationships of relative inequality. Thus, hospitality, charity, and generosity are highly honorific; provided that they derive from free will, they gain honor as expressions of magnanimity. Beneficence transforms economic power into honor. However, honor is thus gained at the potential expense of the recipient. By doing someone a favor you humiliate him unless he may reciprocate. Hence comes the necessity for the return of hospitality and for accepting its return. The Northwest Coast Indians of America carried this principle to its limits in the potlatch, in which the demonstrations of largesse and the destruction of property were performed with the open intention of humiliating a rival. Through the challenge to reciprocate hospitality, they expressed their hostilities and, as they put it, "fought with property."

Honor is the backbone of the system of patronage. He who admits his inferiority and accepts patronage is not dishonored by attaching himself to a superior. On the contrary, his honor is enhanced by participating, through this attachment, in his patron's honor. The honor of a patron is equally enhanced by the possession of clients; he gains prestige in return for the protection that he affords to those who recognize his power. Honor accrues through being paid and is lost through being denied where it is due. By giving it away, you show that you have it; by striving for it, you imply that you need it. This is the meaning of magnanimity.

The struggle for honor takes place, therefore, only where precedence is both of value and in doubt. Competition for it has understandably been more acute in the higher reaches of society, where family pride and also the practical importance of precedence are greatest (this can be clearly seen, for example, in the descriptions of the French aristocracy in the memoirs of the duke of Saint-Simon). It must not, however, be thought that there is no competition for honor in plebeian communities. The agonistic quality of personal and kin-group relations in the villages of the Mediterranean is most striking, especially among pastoralists, whose unstable fortunes urge them to compete. This competition occurs, nonetheless, within a framework of moral values that public opinion upholds. The point of honor, whether among the aristocracies of former times or the modern Greek shepherds or Arab peasants, imposes a code for the distribution of honor that contains conflict within boundaries set by the ethical code of the community.

The point of honor

In the courts of Renaissance Italy there arose a code of behavior which regulated the exchange of honor and the competition for it and whose ultimate sanction was the duel. This code spread, not without changes and adaptations, throughout Europe and America and persisted in many places into the twentieth century. A flow of published works four centuries long defined the modes and pretexts for taking offense, the formalities of challenge and the duel, and the circumstances in which honor could be judged to be lost or redeemed. A veritable jurisprudence of honor was elaborated, which makes explicit certain fundamental characteristics of the concept.

The point of honor, as this code of behavior was called, was confined to the upper class. The honor of a man could not be impugned by someone who was not a social equal—that is, someone with whom he could not compete without loss of dignity. The impudence or the infidelity of an inferior could be punished, but honor was not attained by reacting to the action of an inferior. Thus, honor was impregnable from below. Willingness to enter a duel depended upon the recognition of equality of class (but not of rank).

An affront depends upon being made public, for repute is lost only in the eyes of others. Hence, it was even sometimes maintained that no affront could be given in a purely private conversation. On the other hand, against public ridicule there is no recourse, since an affront must be performed individually to be resented by an individual. The act of resentment is always an individual responsibility; whether or not a man wishes to accept humiliation depends upon his own will. According to the code of honor, an insult could only be resented by the recipient himself, unless he were impeded from doing this because of age, sex, infirmity, or clerical status. Even then it could be resented only by a close kinsman—that is, one who participated in his honor. Briefly, the duel decided quarrels between individuals who competed for precedence and repute in the eyes of a public composed of their social equals. It was even at one time suggested that by destroying the honor of another man one might add to one's own, just as knights once added to their fame by their victories in single combat.

The affront placed honor in jeopardy, a state of threatened desecration from which it could only be saved by the demand for satisfaction. By showing his readiness to fight, a man restored his honor to a state of grace. Honor, however, was indifferent to the result of the duel, which demonstrated only the prowess of the victor and the choice of fate. The form of the act of resentment which constituted a challenge was the *mentita*, "giving the lie." Since deception was not in itself considered dishonorable behavior, it seems anomalous that the accusation of lying constituted the paramount indictment of honor. However, first of all, the accusation constituted a counterinsult and bound the man who delivered the original insult to issue the challenge, thereby permitting his antagonist to gain the choice of weapons. Yet, other than as a tactical device, this form of challenge relates to the obligation to tell the truth: one is under no obligation to tell it to an inferior; one owes it to a superior. (Children are required to tell the truth to adults, who feel no reciprocal duty.) To lie to an equal is an affront, since it represents an attempt to treat him as an inferior. On the other hand, lying could be interpreted as the subterfuge of one who lacked the courage to tell the truth or to act openly. The *mentita*, therefore, committed the response of the accused person, since failure to respond confirmed this implication of cowardice, while honorable response invalidated it at the cost of making manifest the intention to insult.

Failure to react to a slight was open to two conflicting interpretations. Either it implied cowardice and the acceptance of humiliation, which entailed the loss of honor, or it implied contempt, the denial that the author of the slight possessed sufficient honor to affront, that is, a denial of his equality. In the latter case the author, not the victim, of the slight was dishonored. Disregarding a slight could even be treated as magnanimity, on condition that the insulted person possessed the right to forgive or to overlook—that is to say, that he was indeed superior. On the other hand, to pick quarrels over nothing, to exploit the humiliation of others beyond the point that public opinion recognized as legitimate in order to establish precedence, was considered dishonorable, for it spelled lack of magnanimity. It was the court of public opinion that judicated between rival interpretations of the failure to react to a slight; in the last resort, a man was dishonored only at the point where he was forced to realize that he had been, where his shame was brought home to him. Those who possessed impregnable honor could afford not to compete for precedence, but to show those magnanimous qualities which are associated with it in the figurative senses of the words that denote high status: nobility, gentlemanliness, etc. Words which denote low status imply the contrary of magnanimity: meanness, villainy.

Although the point of honor was much criticized from the moral viewpoint, it provided a means of settling disputes. It did not permit the unbridled use of violence. Once satisfaction was accorded, the quarrel could not rightfully be taken up again. In this way it can be contrasted with the moral obligation to seek vengeance in order to redeem honor and with the state of feud that this commonly leads to. The point of honor was, therefore, a pseudolegal institution governing the sphere of social etiquette where the law was either not competent or not welcome.

Honor and the law

The code of honor associated with the duel appeared in history at a time when the state was endeavoring to suppress private violence; dueling was made illegal, as well as condemned by the church, almost from its inception as a formalized mode of settling disputes. Yet, the duel was also, in some ways, a continuation of an earlier tradition. The right of knights to prove their worth in single combat was at one time inherent in the right to bear arms, and jousting provided a festive occasion on which to do so (though it finally developed into a sport). During the Middle Ages the private encounter was also recognized as a form of legal process. The judicial combat allowed for the settlement of disputes by remitting the decision to divine judgment; it was a form of ordeal.

With the development of the legal system and the increased centralization of power, sovereigns aspired to take the settlement of disputes out of the unpredictable hands of the Deity and submit it to the adjudication of courts. The courts, however, are ill-designed to fulfill the requirements of the man of honor, in that, first of all, they oblige him to place his jeopardized honor in the hands of others and thus prevent him from redeeming it for himself—the only way in which this can be done. The legal process involves delay (prejudicial to its state), expense (unwarranted for one who would settle accounts at once and for nothing), and publicity, which aggravates instead of mitigating the affront which is the cause of the dispute. Moreover, honor is not commutable into payment, so the compensation that courts impose offers no valid satisfaction. Finally, the settlement of a dispute in court excludes the possibility of demonstrating personal worth through the display of courage. The law has never, therefore, appealed to adherents to the code of honor, even where it has provided a means of redress against the kind of conduct that constitutes an affront. This it cannot easily do in any case, since it operates according to a different reasoning. Thus, although in all the countries of Europe legislation against dueling was passed repeatedly from the sixteenth century onward, the custom continued, with a large measure of connivance from the judicial authorities, until the twentieth century.

Although all the countries of Europe use the concept of honor in their ceremonial pronouncements, it is explicitly recognized only in the laws of the countries of southern Europe, where honor appears not only as a factor in the cultural background of court proceedings but also as a legal concept. In these countries the legal codes define the jural significance of honor. However, honor relates to conduct as a disculpating factor by making otherwise reprehensible behavior justifiable in terms of the legitimate motive which derives from the sense of honor. The right of a man to defend his honor is far more clearly recognized in the judicial procedures of southern European countries than in Anglo-Saxon law, which generally requires the demonstration of material damage for an affront to be actionable.

The constancy required by honor prefigures the law's demand for regularity; both establish a commitment upon the future. Nevertheless they differ in the way they commit the future, for honor demands fidelity to individuals, law to abstract principles. Therefore, where they exist together, they are liable to conflict, for one relates to persons and is centered in the will; the other aspires to reduce persons to legal categories, which involves attacking the fundamental principle of personal autonomy. The man of honor is a law, but a law unto himself. Wherever the authority of law is questioned or ignored, the code of honor re-emerges to allocate the right to precedence and dictate the principles of conduct: among aristocracies and criminal underworlds, schoolboy and street-corner societies, open frontiers and those closed communities where reigns "the Honorable Society," as the Mafia calls itself.

Honor in literature

As we have seen, the different aspects of honor are liable to come into conflict with each other and to present individuals with an unenviable choice. This was the theme of the Spanish theater of the "Golden Century" in which concern for honor had become exacerbated. The dramatists presented this theme in the form of tragedy in an aristocratic setting while the novelists tended to treat it with comic satire in a plebeian context. Hence, the *teatro de honor* concerns such matters as marital honor, honor as precedence, honor as social status, civic virtue represented by plebeian honor, female purity, fidelity to the king, the duty to redeem honor by vengeance, the difficulty of hiding dishonor, and the power and perfidy of public opinion. The Spanish dramatists were, on the whole, critical of aristocratic honor and sometimes betrayed a reformatory intention, while the satires of the novelists frequently attacked the very notion of honor itself, contrasting it with the real power of money. The greatest and most savage satire on honor is assuredly the *Lazarillo de Tormes*, which antedates Falstaff's famous tirade by nearly half a century.

Every ruling power claims the right to distribute honor; to lay down the principles by which it is to be won is the essence of authority and the process of legitimation. Authority, like honor, is allied both to the sentiments and to the reality of social status and looks both to the possession of force and to popular consent, for authority is, as it were, the judicial aspect of honor, whose transactions and rituals set the seal of legitimacy upon the social order, making its commands appear necessary and right. The king can do no wrong. His word imposes consensus. Yet, if what is done in his name is unpopular, it does not escape criticism. His legitimacy is eventually brought into question. The frailty in authority qualifies its sacredness by exposing it to the danger that a counterconsensus will emerge to brand as infamous the fount of honor. The withdrawal of consent reveals the Achilles' heel of authority; the loss of respect foreshadows delegitimation.

Therefore, the polemics with regard to the nature of honor mirror the social conflicts of their age, for they reflect the interests of different groups and classes striving to impose their evaluations of behavior. The polemics both reflect and promote the struggle between these groups. The facts of power decide the moral arguments. Through its social function as a mediator, honor dictates the modes of allegiance that obtain throughout the social structure, and each particular notion of honor favors a certain faction. Hence, the aristocracy and the church adhered to quite different definitions of honor throughout the history of modern Europe. The new middle classes had a different notion of it, again, as Speier (1935) has pointed out. Different classes differ in their concepts of honor, and the concepts of rural communities differ from those of the city, though not always in accordance with that romanticized image of Arcadia which has stirred the literary imagination ever since Horace. A particular code of honor must be seen against its social background in order to be understood.

Modern urban society accords precedence largely on an economic basis. The independence of women has relieved men to some extent of their responsibility for them and, thus, of their vulnerability through them. The power of the law and the range of its competence have greatly increased, thus eliminating the possibility of winning honor through physical courage, save in certain sports and in war. The power of personal patronage has declined in favor of impersonal and institutional allegiances. The vocabulary of honor has acquired archaic overtones in modern English, yet the principles of honor remain, for they are not, like the particular conceptions in which they are manifested, the product of a given culture at a given time, but universal principles of social action that may be found clothed in the idiom of head-hunting, social refinement, financial acumen, religious purity, or civic merit. Whatever the form the principles of honor may take, they serve to relate the ideal values of a society to its social structure and to reconcile the world as its members would see it with the world as it is.

JULIAN PITT-RIVERS

BIBLIOGRAPHY

ADKINS, ARTHUR W. H. 1960 "Honour" and "Punishment" in the Homeric Poems. London, University of, Institute of Classical Studies, *Bulletin* 7:23–32.

ASHLEY, ROBERT (c. 1600) 1947 *Of Honour.* Edited by Virgil B. Heltzel. San Marino, Calif.: Huntington Library.

BARBER, CHARLES L. 1957 *The Idea of Honour in the English Drama: 1591–1700.* Göteborg (Sweden): Elanders.

Bryson, Frederick R. 1935 *The Point of Honor in Six-teenth-century Italy: An Aspect of the Life of the Gentleman*. New York: Columbia Univ.

Campbell, John K. 1964 *Honour, Family and Patronage: A Study of Institutions and Moral Values in a Greek Mountain Community*. Oxford: Clarendon.

Farès, Bishr 1932 *L'honneur chez les Arabes avant l'Islam: Étude de sociologie*. Paris: Librairie d'Amérique et d'Orient.

Hooker, Timothy 1741 *An Essay on Honour: In Several Letters Lately Published in the* Miscellany. London: No publisher given.

Jones, G. F. 1959 *Honor in German Literature*. Chapel Hill: Univ. of North Carolina Press.

Menéndez Pidal, Ramón 1957 Del honor en el teatro español. Volume 2, pages 357–371 in Ramón Menéndez Pidal, *España y su historia*. Madrid: Ediciones Minotauro.

Montesquieu (1748) 1962 *The Spirit of the Laws*. 2 vols. New York: Hafner. → First published in French.

Peristiany, J. G. 1966 *Honour and Shame: The Values of Mediterranean Society*. Univ. of Chicago Press.

Speier, Hans (1935) 1952 Honor and the Social Structure. Pages 36–52 in Hans Speier, *Social Order and the Risks of War: Papers in Political Sociology*. New York: Stewart.

Thimm, Carl A. 1896 *A Complete Bibliography of Fencing and Duelling, as Practiced by All European Nations From the Middle Ages to the Present Day*. London and New York: Lane.

Wilson, John L. (1838) 1858 *The Code of Honor: Or Rules for the Government of Principal and Seconds in Duelling*. Charleston, S.C.: Phinney.

HOOTON, EARNEST A.

From 1913 until he died in 1954, Earnest Albert Hooton taught anthropology at Harvard. Born in Clemansville, Wisconsin, in 1887, he lived in a succession of small towns in the state, moving from one to another as his father, a Methodist minister, received calls from various churches. His mother, of Scottish origin, remained in his memory as the decisive influence on his childhood.

An unathletic and bookish boy, young Hooton won distinction in school and was class valedictorian at the age of 15, when he graduated from the Manitowoc High School. He was already an instructor in anthropology at Harvard when he married Mary Camp in 1915.

Hooton was trained initially as a classicist at Lawrence College (B.A., 1907) and the University of Wisconsin (M.A., 1908; PH.D., 1911). While a graduate student he was awarded a Rhodes scholarship and spent three years at New College, Oxford. He was strongly influenced by the Oxford anthropologists, particularly R. R. Marett, whom he greatly admired; and it was probably an interlude of study with Sir Arthur Keith, the distinguished British anatomist and student of human evolution, that bent his general interest in anthropology to a special concern with its physical or biological aspect.

Although Hooton never altogether lost his interest in cultural anthropology and for many years taught courses on European prehistory and African ethnology, he did become more and more involved with the problems presented by physical anthropology, the field with which his name is now principally associated.

He was perhaps the first in the United States to offer a systematic coverage of physical anthropology. During his lifetime Hooton's laboratory became the principal center in the United States for training specialists in physical anthropology, and as a result his students were established widely throughout the nation and even abroad. His success as a university lecturer, however, extended far beyond the corps of graduate students who worked closely with him. He possessed a witty, informal style that was extremely attractive and that drew large numbers of undergraduates and others to his courses.

Although it was Hooton's influence as a teacher that was especially noteworthy, it was his scientific and popular writing that made him known to a much wider circle than his professional activity alone could reach. His pungent and graceful style was notably successful in *Up From the Ape* (1931), in which he covered the traditional themes of physical anthropology: human evolution and the development of racial differentiation. In a similar vein he produced *Man's Poor Relations* (1942), which deals with the primate relatives of man; as well as *Apes, Men, and Morons* (1937), *Twilight of Man* (1939a), and *Why Men Behave Like Apes, and Vice Versa* (1940). In "*Young Man, You Are Normal*" (1945) he concerned himself with the dysgenic effects of modern society and the relationship between body build and behavior. These books were written for the general reader and were widely distributed. They did much to introduce the subject matter of physical anthropology to a public unfamiliar with it. But because they were solidly written, several of them were quickly adopted as standard textbooks; *Up From the Ape*, for example, went into a number of editions.

Hooton's scientific writing embraced a wide variety of topics. He wrote on human evolution, developing among other ideas a concept of asymmetry in the morphological evolution of man. Originally intended to account for the discrepancies in that now discredited fossil, the Piltdown skull, the principle of asymmetrical evolution has proven valid and useful. Instead of the widely held belief of that time that all segments of the body had evolved *pari passu*, Hooton envisioned an evolutionary process capable of producing apparent disharmonies by affecting one part more than another. This implied that the adaptive process is selective rather than necessarily general and total. He was a frequent contributor to discussions on the evolution of human dentition, a subject on which he also lectured at the Harvard Dental School.

The classification of human populations and their description was one of Hooton's abiding interests. Much of his work reveals a persistent concern with typology, exploring and refining the methods of analysis as well as the correlates of type. In his first major study, *The Ancient Inhabitants of the Canary Islands*, published in 1925, he had already come to grips with the problem. Influenced by Goring's applications of statistics to the analysis of a sampling of English convicts (1913) and by the voluminous contributions of Pearson to anthropometric data, he enthusiastically adapted these new mathematical tools to a relatively large series of prehistoric Guanche craniums and skeletons. By these statistical procedures he succeeded in identifying a number of coexistent physical types that he then attempted to derive from various related population groups in north Africa. On the basis of such type analyses and supported by archeological evidence he reconstructed a population history of the Canary Islands.

A similar orientation is clearly discernible in *The Indians of Pecos Pueblo* (1930) where, applying similar but more detailed methods of type analysis, he recognized a variety of distinct racial or subracial groups. Based on this typology, which was derived from the study of an Indian population in the Southwest, he reconstructed a tentative aboriginal history of the New World.

His interest in body build led him into the field of applied anthropology, in which he was a pioneer. He published studies on body build for use in designing furniture, and he carried out investigations for the government on other parameters of body build that were intended for guidance in selecting personnel for specialized functions. Later this interest was to involve him in problems of the association of body build with variations in behavior.

The attempt to isolate the various physical types in a random sample of a population was not original with Hooton. His colleague Dixon had embarked on a similar survey, and others had tried the same thing. But Hooton's distinction in this type of research was his far greater sophistication in statistical methods and his use of subjective sortings that were subsequently validated by mathematical tests. Type analysis, however, has not been very fruitful, since it assumes gene behavior that modern genetics does not support. In other words, type analysis implies that the various strains that compose a population somehow survive intact in the mixture of a breeding population; it does not take into account that some of the types defined may be artifacts of the mixture itself rather than survivals of original components.

For the remainder of his research career Hooton was primarily concerned with studies on living populations. During the 1930s he was mainly engaged in a very large-scale survey of the criminal population of the United States. In this study he sought to apply to a major social problem any insights to be derived from a racial and constitutional approach. But unlike the earlier researchers, he was primarily seeking to determine if relationships existed between body type and behavior, and, in this case, if criminal behavior or any of its varieties was linked with racial or physical criteria. His conclusion that such correlations did in fact exist recalled the work of Cesare Lombroso in the nineteenth century, which had long been repudiated. Hooton's investigations, however, were far more sophisticated and were free of the gross errors that had marred Lombroso's work. The reception of Hooton's results, published in *The American Criminal* (1939b) and in *Crime and the Man* (1939c), was negative on the whole. Some critics, in fact, were extremely harsh, attacking him primarily from the conviction that social behavior is determined more significantly by environmental factors than by biological ones. Nevertheless, when reexamined, his results cannot be summarily dismissed on such theoretical grounds. The questions raised by this monumental study have yet to be resolved, and Hooton's service in bringing them forward has not been fully appreciated.

His last researches were a natural outgrowth of the study of body build and crime, for he now turned to a broader application of these same theoretical principles. Using the principle of somatotype he investigated the association of varieties of temperament and behavior with body build in a carefully selected sample of Harvard students. He also followed the same procedures in analyzing large bodies of data derived from military sources. Much of this work has never been published.

Hooton was notable for his warmth and his ready responsiveness to people, his humor, and his acute perception. Among his other gifts he had a remarkable flair for light verse.

HARRY L. SHAPIRO

[*For the historical context of Hooton's work, see* PHYSI-CAL ANTHROPOLOGY *and the biographies of* DIXON; HRDLIČKA; MARETT.]

WORKS BY HOOTON

1925   *The Ancient Inhabitants of the Canary Islands*. Harvard African Studies, Vol. 7. Cambridge, Mass.: Peabody Museum.
1930   *The Indians of Pecos Pueblo: A Study of Their Skeletal Remains*. Phillips Academy, Andover, Mass., Papers of the Southwestern Expedition, No. 4. New Haven: Yale Univ. Press.
(1931) 1947   *Up From the Ape*. Rev. ed. New York: Macmillan.
1937   *Apes, Men, and Morons*. New York: Putnam.
1939a   *Twilight of Man*. New York: Putnam.
1939b   *The American Criminal: An Anthropological Study*. Volume 1: The Native White Criminal of Native Parentage. Cambridge, Mass.: Harvard Univ. Press. → No other volumes were published.
1939c   *Crime and the Man*. Cambridge, Mass.: Harvard Univ. Press.
1940   *Why Men Behave Like Apes, and Vice Versa: Or, Body and Behavior*. Princeton Univ. Press.
1942   *Man's Poor Relations*. Garden City, N.Y.: Doubleday.
1945   *"Young Man, You Are Normal": Findings From a Study of Students*. New York: Putnam.

SUPPLEMENTARY BIBLIOGRAPHY

GORING, CHARLES B.   1913   *The English Convict: A Statistical Study*. London: H.M. Stationery Office.

HORNEY, KAREN

The work of Karen Horney (1885–1952) influenced the course of development of psychoanalysis decisively. Although her revisions of psychoanalytic principles resemble those of Alfred Adler—which has led some to label her as no more than an updated Adlerian—she went well beyond his innovations to formulate a theory of psychopathology that was at once more comprehensive in its scope and more penetrating in its insights. Her ideas, grounded in clinical experience, are almost totally devoid of the dramatic speculation that frequently marked the writings of the man she always acknowledged to be her indispensable forerunner, Sigmund Freud.

Karl Abraham, Freud's student and close adherent, supervised Horney's psychoanalytic training in Berlin. After completing her training in 1915, she spent five years in clinical and outpatient work in Berlin hospitals and 12 years as instructor at the Berlin Psychoanalytic Institute, supplementing her work with private practice. In 1932 Franz Alexander invited her to become associate director of the Chicago Institute for Psychoanalysis; two years later she moved to New York to pursue her own practice. Her dissatisfaction with orthodox psychoanalytic theory is stated most ex-plicitly in *New Ways in Psychoanalysis* (1939). This was such a thoroughgoing critique of the rigidities of Freudian doctrine that it placed her in the forefront of that wing of psychoanalysis which has since become known as the Neo-Freudian movement.

Critique of orthodox Freudianism. Horney took exception to several components of Freud's system. The feature she found most objectionable was the libido theory. She could not accept the notion that an allegedly somatic, yet imperceptible, source of erotic instinctual energy called libido could account not only for individual personality traits and individual behavior but also for the character development of a lifetime. She thought that this theory made most human relationships exclusively sexual relationships; that it explained adult behavior as a mere repetition of the experiences of infancy, to the virtual neglect of the influence of later experiences; that it made fixed and ineradicable instincts the controlling forces of human destiny. Horney deplored the psychic determinism Freud's libido theory inflicted on psychology, as well as the excessive orientation of that psychology toward biology and anatomy. Thus, Freudian, or orthodox, psychoanalysis gave the Oedipus complex a strictly sexual interpretation—that is, the child's relationships with his parents, later transferred to others, are to be understood as symbolic of sexual desires and frustrations—while Horney's clinical experience led her to claim that this did not correspond to the facts of psychopathology. Again, Horney disagreed with the orthodox view that deprived the ego of its directive and discretionary role, reducing it to a sentinel eternally on guard against instinctual excesses and dependent on the id (representing instincts) or the superego (representing conscience) or objective reality for its activation and purpose. Finally, orthodox psychoanalysis considered man to be doomed by the "death instinct" to destructive impulses which must be turned against others if he is to avoid self-destruction; Horney countered that the prevalence of destructiveness or hostility did not prove its instinctual nature and that hostility might be an appropriate reaction to a provoking social environment. These and other of Horney's objections amounted to a revision of accepted psychoanalytic principles and led, in 1941, to her disqualification as training analyst by the New York Psychoanalytic Institute and an abrupt severance from the New York Psychoanalytic Society. Independence, however, brought the opportunity to found the Association for the Advancement of Psychoanalysis, whose very name indicates her insistence on pushing forward the frontiers of the still young science.

Anxiety. Crucial to Horney's thought is the concept of anxiety. Conditions of life in infancy may generate a basic anxiety in which the child feels himself helpless and isolated in the face of a world conceived of as hostile and as jeopardizing his safety and security. The sources of all anxiety are to be found in interpersonal relations, chiefly those encountered in early family life, but at all events those resulting from the culture in which one lives. The unconsciously developed neurotic trends in personality—trends which enable the individual to cope with a demoralizing array of conflicting values presented to him by the patterns of his culture—assume a compulsory character, deflecting him from bringing his real self to maturity and substituting the vain pursuit of fantastic and unrealizable images of himself.

Contemporary Western society's contradictory demands of success (obtaining power) versus love (obtaining affection), of the arousal of desires versus their frustration, and of individual freedom versus the limitations imposed on freedom by reality, produce, as Horney described vividly in all her writings, an almost incredible variety of neurotic behavior patterns. The value given to individualistic achievement makes competition pervasive and leaves a heritage of isolation, fear, insecurity, hostility, and anxiety, which continually undermines self-esteem. The experience of the inadequacy and falsity of love is especially likely to turn healthy affection into neurotic defensive patterns. Clearly, the etiology of neuroses must be referred not to instincts and their vicissitudes, but to interpersonal relations and cultural exigencies. Psychoanalysis must become more a social than a medical science, Horney implied, and so make itself available as a basis for social and economic reform. The writings of her closest colleagues, Harry Stack Sullivan and Erich Fromm, point in the same direction; the three comprised the nucleus of the Neo-Freudian school of psychoanalysis, with Sullivan developing the concept of anxiety and its roots in interpersonal relations and Fromm exploring the deficiencies and incongruities in modern capitalist society that make it what he considers an insane society.

Alienation. The concept of anxiety enabled Horney to connect psychopathology with culture, thereby giving her work the dimension of a social philosophy. The concept of alienation, prominent in her later writings, coupled with that of conflict, strengthened the connection of psychopathology with the inner dimension, the psyche, which some critics hold to be the true, if not the exclusive, concern of psychoanalytic psychology. Alienation refers to a condition in which the individual is divorced from his real self, a condition in which not only his standards and values but also his capacities for judgment, initiative, and self-direction, his very feelings and thoughts, are imputed to a false image of himself which he manufactures unconsciously to allay his basic anxiety. His psychic energies are diverted to the realization of this phantom ideal of himself, which is happily free of conflicting neurotic trends, while his real self comes to be regarded as an indwelling stranger who is to be hated and repressed. An internal numbness to genuine feelings, compounded into a loss of identity, supplants the vital dynamism of psychic development. Concealed from awareness are conflicts among neurotic trends, such as compliance, aggressiveness, and detachment, or the central inner conflict between the idealized image and the real self, whose healthy trend is to strive for its unfettered growth. As Horney's conception of neurosis matured, she saw neurosis not simply as a conflict among neurotic trends but as a process, culminating in alienation, in which these neurotic trends are pitted against healthy ones.

With her unusual insight into psychic malfunctioning, Horney saw that a neurosis, far from being a temporary maladjustment, has a dynamism of its own: it dominates the whole personality and becomes a way of life. The conditions of life in contemporary Western society, as often as not, compel the individual to relinquish his true identity if he is to survive and have any identity at all, to maintain an inferior type of psychic activity rather than undergo a total breakdown. Neurosis, in other words, has become virtually equivalent to "normality," by virtue of social conditions largely beyond individual control. But if mental illness has become a way of life, mental health may be attained not so much by sponsoring a crusade for social reform as by a reintegration of personality that enables each person to rely on his own inner capacities for psychic development. For therapeutic purposes, having satisfactory interpersonal relations in general takes second place to resolving intrapsychic conflicts by intensive self-analysis. Ultimately, psychoanalysis had for Horney more of a clinical than a political application, so that, surprisingly enough, this most outspoken of rebels against the conservatism of orthodox Freudian psychoanalysis in the end accepted its more conventional uses in psychotherapy.

Psychic growth. Implicit in the foregoing is the idea of psychic growth, the postulate that under favorable circumstances—notably interpersonal relations featuring warmth and cordiality—the real self emerges, stabilizes, and develops; that is, the latent potentialities for constructive change in the personality are able to bring about a condition of inner freedom, unity, happiness, and self-direction that for want of a better term may be called normality. In a world where normality is an ambiguous standard, Horney believed that this tendency toward psychic growth provides the most nearly absolute criterion for human values. It is a morality of evolution, as she called it, an evolution of human personality whose *terminus ad quem*, however, can neither be prescribed uniformly for all people nor specified for any single individual. If, as critics charged, psychic growth provides a nebulous standard for ethics and if, as was also charged, it gives psychoanalysis an unwarranted—meaning unwonted—optimistic bias, Horney could retort to the first charge that a preconceived notion of what is good or bad presumes a universality of cultural norms that is contrary to fact, and to the second that clinical experience confirmed repeatedly the existence of a drive toward mental health making possible the liberation of developmental forces in the personality. Without it, psychoanalytic therapy itself could not proceed.

Psychotherapy. Horney was led by both theory and practice to revise the principles of psychoanalytic therapy. A return to mental health involves more than bringing unconscious conflicts to the level of consciousness and more than the removal of overt symptoms, as Freud had thought. Since every neurosis is a disorder of personality, she held, therapy requires the reorganization of personality and the analysis of the entire structure of the neurosis and the current conditions necessitating it. While this idea also stems from the earlier work of Franz Alexander, Horney made it the linchpin of her innovations in therapy. Psychotherapy that proceeded by seeking a direct causal connection between infantile experiences and the present neurosis, on the assumption that the neurosis is an elaborate repetition of early instinctual life, tended to neglect the function performed by anxiety and neurotic trends in the current psychic situation, as well as the ramifications of the neurosis in all facets of the patient's daily life. Horney sought to return the individual to his own spontaneous self-direction and cognizance, free of the grip of neurotic trends and idealized illusions, by developing his emotional self-awareness as well as

by rational or intellectual introspection. The interaction between patient and analyst, known technically as transference, also received a significant modification in Horney's hands. Since it is but one type of interpersonal relation, and since all interpersonal relations involve feelings, the inevitable emotional confrontation of analyst and patient should not be avoided by constructing a façade of professional impersonality, as recommended by Freud, but should be used to obtain a more intimate understanding of the pervasive character of the neurosis. Love, hostility, defiance, pride, self-accusation, and so forth, permeate the analytic session; under the guidance of an alert and sensitive analyst they can be studied intensively and fruitfully. Horney accepted, without appreciable modification, free association and the interpretation of dreams and paraplaxes, the other conventional tools of psychoanalysis.

Feminine psychology. Not the least of Horney's contributions to a revised psychoanalysis was her reappraisal of feminine psychology. Unwilling to accept Freud's opinion of it as an offshoot of masculine psychology, an accidental, inferior, and necessarily warped by-product of women's genital differences from men, Horney argued that Freud had ignored the impact of cultural conditions on the psychic orientation of women. In a predominantly masculine culture women are deprived of considerable conjugal and maternal fulfillment by the undervaluing of love, and consequently they have neurotic problems peculiar to their sex. More than anything else, this protest against Freud's negative attitude toward women and their psychology seems to have been responsible for driving Horney from the Freudian fold and for giving her thought its characteristic turn. If women could and should have lives of their own, once the distorting pressures of culture were relaxed, by the same token other culture-produced neuroses might be eliminated. by reducing cultural pressures.

The goal of mental health and growth during a lifetime of psychic integrity and independence persisted in Horney's thought and received ever more resonant expression in her writings. To the blasé and world-weary generation of the 1920s her affirmation of positive and humanistic values was refreshing. The years of economic hardship and international tension that followed created an audience for her writings that responded to her sympathetic understanding of its plight. She gave a renewed impulse to the psychoanalytic movement and by her rebellion reaffirmed the principle of scientific inquiry free of the confines of dogma. The value of her work will be estimated in terms of the reduction of human suffering and the expansion of human living that it made possible.

MARTIN BIRNBACH

[*For the historical context of Horney's work, see* PSYCHOANALYSIS *and the biographies of* ABRAHAM; ADLER; ALEXANDER; FREUD. *Directly related are* ANXIETY; NEUROSIS; *and the biography of* SULLIVAN.]

WORKS BY HORNEY

1937   *The Neurotic Personality of Our Time.* New York: Norton.

1939   *New Ways in Psychoanalysis.* New York: Norton.

1942   *Self-analysis.* New York: Norton.

1945   *Our Inner Conflicts: A Constructive Theory of Neurosis.* New York: Norton.

1950   *Neurosis and Human Growth.* New York: Norton.

SUPPLEMENTARY BIBLIOGRAPHY

ALEXANDER, FRANZ   1940   *Psychoanalysis Revised. Psychoanalytic Quarterly* 9:1–36.

BIRNBACH, MARTIN   1961   *Neo-Freudian Social Philosophy.* Stanford (Calif.) Univ. Press.

Karen Horney Memorial Issue.   1954   *American Journal of Psychoanalysis* 14:5–133.

PORTNOY, ISIDORE   1951   [Review of] *Neurosis and Human Growth. American Journal of Psychoanalysis* 11:63–71.

ROBBINS, IRVING   1958   An Analysis of Horney's Concept of the Real Self. *Educational Theory* 8:162–168.

THOMPSON, CLARA   (1950) 1957   *Psychoanalysis: Evolution and Development.* New York: Grove.

WEISS, FREDERICK A.   1954   Karen Horney: Her Early Papers. *American Journal of Psychoanalysis* 14:55–64.

HORTICULTURE

See AGRICULTURE.

HOSPITALS

See ILLNESS; MEDICAL CARE; MEDICAL PERSONNEL; MENTAL DISORDERS, TREATMENT OF, *article on* THE THERAPEUTIC COMMUNITY.

HOURS OF WORK

See under LABOR FORCE.

HOUSING

I. SOCIAL ASPECTS   *John Madge*
II. ECONOMIC ASPECTS   *Sherman J. Maisel*

I
SOCIAL ASPECTS

Although it varies according to climatic differences, housing constitutes one of the most universal forms of material culture, being found in all except nomadic societies. Housing also represents an important element in all capital formation and the largest single component in the total building effort of any nation. From a sociological point of view, housing has a major part to play in ensuring continuity of community life.

There is also a close interrelationship between housing and family organization. In all cultures and at all times the type of housing has corresponded in some way to the organization of the family and has in turn sustained and reinforced existing forms of family organization. In many parts of the world, the extended family system is reflected in various clusters of rooms within which there are sections reserved for the basic units. The long house, for example, is found in a variety of cultures, from the Iroquois of North America to the peoples of southeast Asia; while the polygamous family structure still found in many parts of Africa requires a complex of huts, one for the husband and one for each wife and her children, arranged in order of rank.

The home is a ménage for production as well as for consumption and may therefore also reflect features of economic organization; for example, in the eighteenth-century wool centers in England many cottages included an upstairs room in which family members worked, and rural cottages everywhere tend to confuse the housing of humans and of livestock. The greater systematization of modern Western life has eliminated most of this form of provision, at least in urban communities; but new dwellings may still incorporate doctors' offices, artists' studios, or scholars' libraries, and new shops still often include living accommodations for owner or manager.

Control of house building.   Until the nineteenth century there were few specialist builders, and in most cases members of the family unit built their own houses. This is still the case in many parts of the world, with the result that there is a close correspondence between the dwellings built and the way of life of those who build them. However, in more industrialized societies this identity of aim is easily lost. Indeed there are typically three parties to the house-building operation: the builder and his workmen, the owner or entrepreneur who commissions the dwelling, and the family that will in due course occupy it. The situation is further complicated by the fact that in many cases the new development will be associated with the migration of families into towns, a move which in any case requires them to urbanize their way of life and may involve renouncing the extended family or tribal system to which they had previously been accustomed.

Where an entrepreneur or landlord places himself between the occupier and the designer and builder, it is inevitable that the housing type will to some extent be imposed on the occupier. The motives of a landlord can vary considerably; but whatever they may be, his control of the means and nature of house provision is very powerful.

Although public authority housing takes an important and increasing share in the total building effort of most industrialized countries, the share of the private landlord is declining even faster and is being largely replaced by a growth in owner occupancy. Even in the socialist countries of eastern Europe, an important proportion of new house building is being undertaken privately. But the number of custom-built houses in such cases is relatively small, and most owner-occupiers move into houses that were, for all practical purposes, designed without consulting them. If there is a greater correspondence in the private sector between design and family needs, it is because the unsuitable houses prove more difficult to sell and their design is therefore not repeated; such houses, however, will not be destroyed but will merely be passed down to a householder who is less able to pay for what he wants.

Trends in housing standards. In every industrialized and industrializing country in the world there is an acute shortage of urban dwellings, and a substantial proportion of the world's population is living in severely substandard housing: slums that have survived the uncontrolled building of the nineteenth century or shacks that reflect the uncontrolled urbanization of the twentieth century. But in spite of overcrowding and the physical decay of buildings, it is often difficult to demonstrate that bad housing is directly responsible for bad physical health; although bad health is often associated with bad housing, this is because both of these are generally secondary effects of poverty (Schorr 1964, pp. 6–7, 143–145).

Space standards. There is clearer evidence that inadequate space standards can disorganize family life. The current expert consensus in European countries is that the lower limit for mental health is 170 square feet of floor area per person (Chombart de Lauwe 1955; Musil 1962), and the desirable standards established by the American Public Health Association (1950) are twice the above figures. But these represent standards for new construction; and many European and North American families probably have a current space stand-

ard of less than 80 square feet per person, while it is certain that families are to be found in Latin America, Africa, and Asia with less than 20 square feet of floor area per person.

There is also evidence that an equally important criterion is the number of rooms in the dwelling. A careful survey by Loring (1956), using paired groups of "well adapted" and "disorganized" families, showed that significant differences were associated with number of rooms available, floor area, and general surroundings, but not with other supposedly significant factors such as possession of a bath or the physical condition of the dwelling.

In spite of the gigantic backlog of substandard housing, it is expected that new construction will continue to improve its minimum standards of equipment and space. In Britain during the past sixty years, the recommended minimum space standard has increased by about 40 per cent (or 50 square feet per person), and it is believed that the increase may have been greater in most other industrialized societies, which started from a lower base. On the basis of a sustained 3.5 per cent annual growth in productivity, it seems very possible that the minimum standard of new housing will double in the next forty years; even if space standards increase at only half this rate, a standard for new construction of 250 square feet of floor area per person would then be commonplace by the early twenty-first century.

The family and the home

In affluent countries, the rise of general space standards to the level previously reserved for middle-class homes has coincided with, and may have helped to stimulate, the growth of individuation in the home. Whereas in the traditional working-class home family life was lived collectively in the "living-kitchen," today there is more stress on individual privacy and a greater tendency for members of the family to follow their own pursuits. There is a consequent trend toward the use of study-bedrooms and a greater willingness to recognize the distinctive needs of children in the home.

At the same time, new dwellings continue to play a substantial part in bringing about changes in family organization. This is illustrated particularly vividly in the context of urbanization. In eastern Europe, for example, there is a traditional type of peasant cottage consisting essentially of two rooms: the white room, which contains all the most valued family possessions and also acts as a store for grain and other nonperishable food; and the black room, which is used for all normal household purposes and includes niches for sleeping. Comparable arrangements are found in most other rural economies in Europe. Obviously such a subdivision is not appropriate or even possible in a multistory apartment building; the application of urban behavior standards requires more individual privacy, for example, for sleeping, but also requires less space for food storage and for other functions around which the traditional rural home rotates.

The urban wife is increasingly employed outside the home, and the development of substitutes for household tasks—launderettes, partly prepared foods, ironing and mending services—is proceeding rapidly alongside industrialization. Meal-taking is unlikely to disappear from the home, but the habit of taking some meals in company cafeterias and in restaurants is likely to grow. The care of children will probably be increasingly shared between the family and the social and educational agencies, and there may even be an increase in the use of boarding schools (cf. Musil 1962, p. 555). This should not, however, be interpreted as indicating a reduction in the space requirements in the home. It is regarded as important for family cohesion that the child should feel a member of the household even when absent; few authorities anticipate a widespread adoption of the deliberate segregation of parents and children practiced in many Israeli kibbutzim.

It is anticipated that a decreasing proportion of households will contain three generations; if present trends continue, more separate accommodations will be provided for elderly couples and single or widowed old people. There will probably be a concurrent increase in the number of young people living alone or with their peers. The net result of these and other changes will probably be that the proportion of households consisting solely of parents and dependent children will further increase.

The ecology of housing

In preindustrial countries, the majority still live in rural settlements, which have in most cases developed a close internal communication network commensurate with their internal social cohesion. With industrialization and the accompanying urbanization, the traditional close-knit integrated community is increasingly replaced by a pluralistic type of community comprising a number of subcultures, at once interlocking and independent of each other. To a considerable extent the ecology of the community will reflect these divisions among its population.

Invasion and succession. The ecological theories and studies of the early Chicago school were to a large extent concerned with what classes of people occupied different zones of the city (for example, Zorbaugh 1929). Similarly the ecological principles of *invasion* and *succession* were applied by these authors to the successive waves of occupants that passed through old existing stocks of houses. That succession took place at all is a reflection of the durability of houses, which so regularly outlive their original purpose, so that mansions originally built for wealthy families and their servants survive in multiple family occupation or as small hotels and rooming houses.

As has been stated, the main tendency in industrialized countries in the past fifty years has been the convergence in space and other standards of middle- and lower-class houses. Particularly in town centers, the relatively small row houses built for lower-class families three or more generations ago are coming within the size range of the urban middle-class family; and if they survive the hazard of urban renewal they are liable to experience "succession in reverse," reappearing with brightly painted doors as bijou residences for those who can afford to buy out their less affluent lower-class occupants. Even in the United States, with its tendency to tear down and replace, succession is now sometimes a two-way process.

Slums and ghettos. One of the forms of succession that has been most documented and studied, particularly in the United States, has been the process by which immigrants or visible races such as Negroes have been forcibly segregated into slum-ghettos. This has come about because earlier inhabitants have typically first resisted invasion and then fled, leaving the newcomers in possession. Housing for nonwhites and for underprivileged immigrants is generally substandard in space, amenities, and repair; out-of-bounds for mortgage investment or other private financing; overpriced for what it is; and underprovided with public and social services (Abrams 1955, pp. 74–75).

Areas with the above characteristics are not inevitably turned into ghettos. Slums and substandard areas occur in almost all cities of any size, particularly if the population is growing. If obsolescent housing ripe for slum formation does not already exist, shacks are often built on the perimeter of the town to act as a substitute. This type of development is resisted by civic authorities with varying vigor and success.

Urban renewal and relocation. Unlike perimeter shack development, substandard areas are often well located near the city center, and some offer tempting possibilities for urban renewal. The extent to which this situation has been exploited for private gain has varied greatly, but there have been notorious examples in American cities and elsewhere in which whole neighborhoods of underprivileged families have been displaced in favor of luxury apartment buildings, creating even greater pressures on surviving slums. Until comparatively recently the net effect of urban renewal has probably been to increase the amount of segregation; and while, by the mid-1960s (except in countries such as the Republic of South Africa, which retained a philosophy of segregation) there appeared to be a tide toward integration and interracial housing, it seems probable that the general trend toward social stratification and class division is being accentuated.

Whether urban renewal reduces or increases the problem of the slums, it is commonly believed that its net effect is to harm the community spirit of the long-established neighborhoods. Young and Willmott (1957) and Gans (1962) have argued that relocation programs almost inevitably break up the cohesion provided by the kinship network, while Jacobs (1961) has stressed the inhumanity and monotony of many renewal projects. In discussing older neighborhoods, it is necessary to distinguish clearly between those sections containing a fluid, disorganized, and often no-family population, and those sections containing close-knit but poor families, often recent immigrants or otherwise underprivileged.

The success of relocation largely depends on how it is administered. The "melting-pot" theory, based on the idea that slum dwellers can be "reformed" by placing them in a project where they will be influenced by respectable neighbors, can produce a calamitous and quite unnecessary destruction of social cohesion and lead to loneliness, anxiety, and temporary neurosis. For all families that move there is a painful period of adjustment which is only bearable if the move was wanted and if established neighbors are welcoming. It has been shown (for example, by Festinger et al. 1950) that friendships can depend on physical layout and that satisfaction and morale in the neighborhood are maximized if the layout as well as the social climate encourage interaction. European research workers (for example, Kuper 1953) support this thesis but tend to set more store on the need for the individual to be able to select and regulate the extent of his interactions.

Suburban development.   Whatever the density of redevelopment, a normal result of renewal is an increment of pressure on suburban housing. Even without these pressures, improvements in transport and communications are rapidly increasing the range and popularity of the commuter areas around cities [see TRANSPORTATION, *article on* COMMUTATION]. It is in the most urbanized and industrialized countries that the suburban belt is most clearly in evidence. The original "new towns," although planned as communities and occupationally more or less self-sufficient, have so far reflected in a more organized way the same demographic tendencies as have elsewhere led to peripheral suburban development. Their populations are generally to a large extent self-selected and consist mainly of upwardly mobile middle-class families. It has been claimed (for example, by Whyte 1956) that such families have developed a new interactive way of life that leaves little room for permanence or privacy, but more recent studies (Berger 1960; Dobriner 1963) have shown that new communities set up under different circumstances can develop along more traditional working-class lines.

Beyond the city suburbs and the "green belts" there is a still newer wave of community development. This may have started with the quest for exclusiveness of upper-class "exurbanites," but emancipation by automobile has brought whole counties into range, and the sprawl of an even looser suburbanism lacking either physical or social focus is extending every year. This type of development is occurring throughout the Western world in all regions of relatively high density, and it has so far overwhelmed the resistances of even the most assiduous planners. In the more industrialized counties it is becoming difficult to find a genuine rural village. The old types of social activity that generations of country dwellers have gradually built up are largely inappropriate, and the older rural institutions are unable, if not unwilling, to adapt to the new pattern of social demand.

Status attributes of housing

In spite of the convergence of social class characteristics, there are distinctive class differences in ideology and behavior that transcend differences in wealth and can be readily detected by objective comparisons. The two main differences between middle-class and working-class ideologies that are reflected in their homes are the former's greater stress on individualism, which requires a home that gives some scope for privacy and self-expression to every member of the household, and the latter's greater stress on saving and repairing as opposed to spending and discarding, which requires greater provision for storage of possessions. The middle-class home is also used for more or less discreet displays of "conspicuous consumption." These early insights, including those of Veblen (1899) and the

Lynds (1929), were followed by the systematic attempts of Warner and Lunt (1941), Chapin (1947), Guttman (1942), and others to construct a scale of social status. In spite of various anomalies, it is clear that the importance of space and material possessions to the individual family, and the state of repair in which the home is kept, can quite properly be used as one component in the perennial search for an objective index of social class.

There is naturally a general correlation between the type of house and the neighborhood, both because of the tendency toward uniformity of standards in any particular section and also because of the physical fact that adjacent dwellings will often have about the same date of construction. As a general rule, the location of a home is likely to be even more revealing of the social status of a family than the type of house and its contents. In the United States a large number of ecological reports have been prepared since the early 1930s, with the help of the census tract data provided by the Bureau of the Census, showing social class and other related characteristics of cities and city neighborhoods all over the country. Similar information is becoming available in Britain and elsewhere and is being used for sophisticated forms of ecological analysis.

Social policy

On a world view, very great variations are to be found in the extent to which different governments take responsibility for housing their populations. Some intervention is found necessary wherever urbanization is occurring, if only in order to prevent the outbreak of epidemics and other illnesses caused by unsanitary and overcrowded conditions. Furthermore, if the government is promoting industrial development, it will be under pressure to provide, or stimulate the building of, workers' housing within reach of the new plant; the incentive of good housing is an important lever in attracting suitable families into the towns from rural areas. In addition to these motives of enlightened self-interest, governments may also be impelled on grounds of social welfare to make provision for their less privileged citizens, for example, by producing houses for special groups such as old people, by creating new interracial neighborhoods, or by subsidizing the provision of new houses in order to raise housing standards.

Historically, the provision of housing for special groups in industrialized countries has been one of the responsibilities assumed by private charities. As still occasionally happens, the close-knit indus-

trial and professional groups looked after the housing needs of the less privileged of their members' or ex-members' families. Other more general private charities in a great variety of countries have built almshouses and continue to build and maintain housing projects for low-cost rentals. In the nineteenth century money for these purposes was raised in Great Britain from so-called "five per cent philanthropists," who were willing to loan money for a return at less than the current rate of interest so that these projects could be financed.

Subsidized housing. It is only in the last fifty years that the burden of subsidizing the housing of the poor has been partly assumed by the state and the city authorities. Even today there are some industrialized countries in which the public provision of housing is negligible. The outstanding example is the United States, where new public housing represents only 3 or 4 per cent of new permanent starts (U.S. Bureau of the Census, as quoted in Van den Broek 1964), so that the total share of public housing is probably now only 1 or 2 per cent. Some states have even passed legislation containing clauses that effectively prevent any additional provision of public housing (in 1966 the constitutionality of such clauses was being tested in the courts).

In the United States and in other countries with similar policies, very substantial public funds are invested in the housing program; but they are used not as a form of social service but to help citizens to buy their own houses. This policy is intended to benefit those most able to help themselves; the assumption is that the houses thus vacated will become available for poorer families and that a general reshuffling will take place so that virtually all sections of the community may benefit.

In spite of the great divergence in philosophy between this kind of assisted self-help and the welfare-state policies now being implemented over much of the globe, the difference in *practice* has been far less striking. Governments have generally shied away from making direct provision by building new houses for the poorest families. This follows the experience of the private philanthropists that it is unattractively expensive to subsidize new housing to the point at which really poor families can afford the rents.

Even in countries with a relatively low economic growth rate, much of the current demand for housing at any date is from newly married couples and from upwardly (and, in the case of the urban population, outwardly) mobile families, and the provision of new housing is predominantly attuned to their needs. It is only in cities undertaking a vigorous urban renewal and slum-clearance program that a substantial number of really poor families are displaced and forced to seek new homes. Even with generous subsidies many of these underprivileged families find the new rents too high and tend to gravitate back to the remaining slums, thereby further overcrowding these areas.

There is by now a fair understanding in some countries of human needs in housing and also of the means by which these needs can be satisfied. This will have to be extended to other areas and also kept up to date as new housing forms are developed. What is now needed in addition is a fuller knowledge of what conditions are most favorable to satisfactory social organization and, in particular, what types of social planning should accompany the massive relocation and urban renewal programs that we shall have to undertake in the coming years. In other words, the balance of effort should swing from static to dynamic studies, from social investigation toward participation and social action.

JOHN MADGE

[See also PLANNING, SOCIAL, *articles on* REGIONAL AND URBAN PLANNING *and* WELFARE PLANNING; SEGREGATION.]

BIBLIOGRAPHY

ABRAMS, CHARLES 1955 *Forbidden Neighbors: A Study of Prejudice in Housing.* New York: Harper.

AMERICAN PUBLIC HEALTH ASSOCIATION, COMMITTEE ON THE HYGIENE OF HOUSING 1950 *Planning the Home for Occupancy.* Chicago: Public Administration Service.

BERGER, BENNETT M. 1960 *Working-class Suburb: A Study of Auto Workers in Suburbia.* Berkeley: Univ. of California Press.

CHAPIN, FRANCIS S. (1947) 1955 *Experimental Designs in Sociological Research.* Rev. ed. New York: Harper.

CHOMBART DE LAUWE, P. H. 1955 Le logement, le ménage et l'espace familial. *Informations sociales* 9:956–980.

DOBRINER, WILLIAM M. 1963 *Class in Suburbia.* Englewood Cliffs, N.J.: Prentice-Hall.

FESTINGER, LEON; SCHACHTER, STANLEY; and BACK, KURT (1950) 1963 *Social Pressures in Informal Groups: A Study of Human Factors in Housing.* Stanford Univ. Press.

GANS, HERBERT J. 1962 *The Urban Villagers: Group and Class in the Life of Italian-Americans.* New York: Free Press.

GUTTMAN, LOUIS 1942 A Revision of Chapin's Social Status Scale. *American Sociological Review* 7:362–369.

JACOBS, JANE 1961 *The Death and Life of Great American Cities.* New York: Random House. → A paperback edition was published in 1962 by Random House and by Cape.

KUPER, LEO (editor) 1953 *Living in Towns.* London: Cresset.

LORING, WILLIAM C. JR. 1956 Housing Characteristics and Social Disorganization. *Social Problems* 3:160–168.

LYND, ROBERT S.; and LYND, HELEN M. (1929) 1930 *Middletown.* New York: Harcourt. → A paperback edition was published in 1959.

MUSIL, JIŘI 1962 The Sociological Approach in Planning Workers' Housing: The Experience of Czechoslovakia. *International Labour Review* 86:545–566.

SCHORR, ALVIN L. 1964 *Slums and Social Insecurity.* London: Nelson.

VAN DEN BROEK, J. H. (editor) 1964 *Habitation.* 3 vols. Amsterdam: Elsevier.

VEBLEN, THORSTEIN (1899) 1953 *The Theory of the Leisure Class: An Economic Study of Institutions.* Rev. ed. New York: New American Library. → A paperback edition was published in 1959.

WARNER, W. LLOYD; and LUNT, PAUL S. 1941 *The Social Life of a Modern Community.* New Haven: Yale Univ. Press.

WHYTE, WILLIAM H. JR. 1956 *The Organization Man.* New York: Simon & Schuster. → A paperback edition was published in 1957 by Doubleday.

YOUNG, MICHAEL; and WILLMOTT, PETER 1957 *Family and Kinship in East London.* Institute of Community Studies, Report No. 1. London: Routledge; Glencoe, Ill.: Free Press. → A paperback edition was published in 1963 by Penguin.

ZORBAUGH, HARVEY W. 1929 *The Gold Coast and the Slum.* Univ. of Chicago Press.

II
ECONOMIC ASPECTS

Economic problems, analyses, and policies concerning housing differ considerably between the various types of national economies. Dissimilar needs and suggested solutions appear among developed as compared to emerging economies. The market structure, whether planned, quasi-planned, or more laissez-faire, also strongly influences the manner in which problems arise.

Economists have approached the housing question from three rather disparate points of view: that of real investment, consumption, and technology. Most analysis has been concerned with construction and housing as investment problems. Major interest has focused on the fact that construction is a large, significant industry with one of the greatest year-to-year variances. This literature has dealt with fluctuations and possible cycles. However, other investment questions such as exploring optimum rates of construction in relation to a country's existing and planned expansion of capital and present and expected levels of consumption have received more attention in recent years.

For over one hundred years, housing has also played a prominent role in the theory of consumption and social reform. Housing takes a large share of consumption budgets. Individual standards of living are heavily influenced by the level of housing and the amount paid for it. Criticisms of the housing level achieved are common, and economists have sought the reasons why better standards of housing do not prevail.

Other economic problems arise with respect to the methods of production. Housing techniques have developed over thousands of years, but many feel that their rate of improvement has lagged behind other fields. Studies of production have attempted to find the economic rationale for existing techniques while searching for methods to improve the production process.

New investment in housing. Table 1 shows the relative importance of construction and housing in different economies. Total construction expenditures range from 3.5 to about 15 per cent of the gross national product (GNP) and from 40 to 70 per cent of gross fixed investment. Depending on the economy, housing production varies from 2 to 5 per cent of the GNP. In each case, the magnitude of housing production is sufficiently large for its movements to cause related repercussions throughout the economy. The impact is heightened because construction in general, and particularly housing construction, is among the most volatile of all major industries. Housing fluctuations have had large amplitudes. In the United States, for example, the value of housing production in 1933 was less than 13 per cent of its value in 1929. In the post-World War II period, while economies experienced relative general stability, housing remained extremely unstable.

Economists have debated whether the fluctuation pattern of building differs basically from that of the rest of the economy. The evidence is not clear-cut, but most observers note that long swings or cycles of 18 to 20 years appear to mark the indexes of building construction in both the United States and the United Kingdom. Some of the literature on the subject attaches the name of "the building or construction cycle" to these observed movements. Abramovitz (1962) holds that since the Civil War there has been a succession of long swings in aggregate construction activity, consisting of upsurges followed by either protracted declines or pronounced retardations, in which all the major sectors of the industry have usually if not invariably participated.

Causes of fluctuations. Many have attempted to describe the special factors which could make housing fluctuations differ from the rest of the economy. As in other areas of cycle theory, some have tried to derive simple, constant models for all past movements; the majority of theories, however, are eclectic. They hold that while housing fluctuations do take a unique form because of the nature of the industry, the proximate cause or causes of past movements differ.

The theories ascribe unique demand, supply, and market interactions to the housing market. Uniqueness arises from special demand factors, the size and durability of houses, the few times the average family enters the market and the family's relative ignorance, the importance of credit in facilitating construction and purchases, the entrepreneurs' small size and lack of capital, and the difficulties of market adjustment.

A high percentage of construction is that required to house or service net additions to households. An expanding population, either through natural growth as births exceed deaths or through migration, requires more dwellings. Another important demographic force is the splitting of extended families into separate households. Young couples may seek their own homes earlier in life rather than share units with their parents. The

Table 1 — Patterns of investment, 1960

	GNP (millions of dollars)	GROSS FIXED INVESTMENT (As per cent of GNP)	TOTAL CONSTRUCTION AS PER CENT OF:		DWELLING CONSTRUCTION AS PER CENT OF:	
			GNP	Gross fixed investment	GNP	Gross fixed investment
Argentina	9,444.1	20.9	7.8	37.6	*	*
Canada	37,046.6	22.7	14.9	65.6	4.0	17.7
Chile	4,892.2	8.7	3.6	41.2	*	*
Germany (F.R.G.)	67,708.2	24.0	12.0	50.2	5.4	22.4
Japan	38,845.0	31.4	*	*	2.3	7.4
Kenya	630.0	18.4	10.3	55.8	3.0	16.4
South Africa	7,433.5	20.7	11.8	57.2	*	*
Sweden	12,287.0	21.9	14.1	64.5	5.0	22.8
United Kingdom	71,068.8	16.1	7.9	48.7	3.0	18.6
United States	504,404.0	16.4	10.9	66.6	4.5	27.4

* Not available.

Source: *Year Book of National Accounts Statistics: 1962.* Copyright, United Nations (1963). Reproduced by permission.

number of single individuals, particularly widows, maintaining their own homes may rise.

In the past, waves of household additions appear to have resulted from variations in migration and from an uneven age distribution in the population. Even within given population structures the rate of family formation has varied significantly as a result of both social and economic forces.

The need to replace existing units is another demand factor. Net replacements have ranged from zero to a third or more of total demand. Several theories posit a replacement cycle. Required replacements could fluctuate as an echo of bunched dwelling construction in the past. However, replacement cycles are not evident in the data. Since the housing stock has been expanding rapidly, the percéntage of the stock old enough to require replacement is minor. The useful life of dwellings is extremely long. Few buildings require replacement on merely physical grounds; most replacement takes place because the location is needed for other uses. Replacements appear more closely related to the size of the stock and to economic conditions than to the age and quality of existing units.

Over periods such as a decade, most of the demand for new construction is directly related to the number of net additions to the households in a locality, plus the net number of units demolished, replaced, or removed. Movements in unoccupied units (vacancies) are significant in short periods, but their importance diminishes the longer the time span examined.

The short-run movements in demand have causes similar to those of fluctuations in other spheres. Movements in employment, in assets (particularly equities of existing dwellings), in prices, costs, and in credit all change the demand for new units. Insofar as these variables move with business conditions, the resulting housing fluctuations resemble those of other spheres.

There are also logical reasons to expect that construction will at times fluctuate in a pattern differing from the remainder of the economy. Many authors place particular emphasis on credit. Because of size and cost of buildings, construction is highly dependent on the existence and terms of debt financing. Movements in credit availability, the required down payment, the period of amortization, and the interest rate can force individual owners and builders in and out of the market. Credit terms may move separately from other economic variables. The length of lag between the movements of credit terms and their impact in the construction market differs from that of other industries. Many writers believe that the post-World War II experience in both the United States and western Europe gave evidence that credit did cause special fluctuations.

Housing demand has two dimensions: one consists of the number of separate dwellings required; the second measures the amount spent per dwelling. This latter amount varies with the size, quality, and features included in a house. Economic variables appear to have a much larger impact on the amount spent per dwelling than they have on the number of dwellings demanded.

When the demand for the services of dwellings shifts, still larger fluctuations occur in required new investment. This creates greater amplitude in the movements of building. The acceleration principle is at work: a 2 per cent increase in the desire for housing may cause new construction demand to double, while in response to a similar decrease new construction might fall almost to zero. [See INVESTMENT, *article on* THE AGGREGATE INVESTMENT FUNCTION.]

Other reaction differences arise because of peculiar factors in the market and the real estate industry. Supply adjusts slowly. Because of lack of information much building, particularly of apartment houses, may occur even after an excess of supply exists. The "gestation period" for large structures is long. Apparent increases in demand can easily be multiplied through high expectations, easy credit, and the large number of small firms. Furthermore, builders or promoters who sell to others can often make a profit simply through the building process, even if the completed unit is unneeded.

When the new excess supply reaches the market, vacancies result. As these build up new construction is slowed down. If a demand drop occurs with vacancies already high, as happened after 1929, the disruption of the market is heightened. Since the number of units required has a low price elasticity, no fall in prices is sufficient to fill the vacant space.

Stabilization policies. Because the industry's structure makes large-scale fluctuations probable, interest has attached to governmental policies which might dampen some cycles. Suggested policies have included better market information, credit controls, varying subsidies, and direct governmental action either to remove old units from the stock or to purchase new ones.

Stabilization programs may attempt to increase the long-run basic demand or to concentrate more demand in particular periods. Attempts to offset short-run movements are difficult. Forecasting problems, the complicated lag situation, and a slow reaction time all make it extremely difficult to inject the stabilizing demand into the market at the necessary times.

Other investment problems. Developed countries have studied housing because of its fluctuations. In developing economies, housing investment has been looked at primarily as a major drain on limited funds. Industrialization and urbanization go hand in hand; individuals and families leave the farm village to work in the city, where they must be housed. Each industrial job requires additional investment in the urban infrastructure. Analysts cannot consider merely the direct investment requirements and the payoff for a transfer of employment from farm to factory. They must take into account many additional costs, of which housing is a major item. Investments in housing tend to be expensive and slow. In developing economies, slums and urban growth are virtually synonymous. Decisions as to how to meet these additional needs are difficult and complex. Significant social costs result when investment is channeled to housing rather than to seemingly more productive spheres. On the other hand, slums and housing shortages create social costs which may in turn reduce the productive effort.

Within developed economies, major debates have occurred as to the proper amount of investment to be allocated to housing when the economy is at full employment. Some feel that housing needs were given too low a priority as western Europe attempted to fight inflation in the post-World War II period. New housing space was rationed during a period when other parts of the economy were booming.

Consumption of housing. Housing standards vary greatly from country to country, and even wider ranges of consumption standards exist within countries. Almost everywhere some people live in shacks while others occupy mansions. Large numbers of families would occupy both more and higher-quality space if either their incomes were increased or the costs of housing lowered. The problem of why adequate housing is not made available to all income groups has received considerable analysis, but no generally accepted answers are available (Grigsby 1963).

Table 2 shows the percentage of expenditures going to rent. It shows large variations; the average spent on rent varies from 1 to nearly 15 per cent among the countries listed. Within individual countries the highest percentage spent is commonly double or triple the lowest.

Considerable effort has been expended on the analysis of these variations. The reasons for some

Table 2 — Percentage of household consumption expenditures spent on rent

		AVERAGE (MEAN) PER CENT SPENT ON RENT	RANGE OF PER CENT SPENT ON RENT
British Guiana	1955–1956	2.9	0.6 to 5.9
France	1956–1957	5.2	4.3 to 6.4
India	1950–1951	1.1	0.5 to 1.7
Nigeria	1953–1955	10.0	9.5 to 10.6
Philippines	1956–1957	9.1	6.8 to 16.5
South Africa	1955	14.6	11.2 to 16.5
Sweden	1958	11.6	9.6 to 13.5
United Arab Republic	1958	12.4	10.5 to 17.0
United Kingdom	1959	10.3	5.9 to 15.6
United States	1950	11.9	9.5 to 17.9

Source: Compendium of Social Statistics: 1963.

differences are evident. One area's rents may appear to exceed others purely because of definitions—what is included in rent and the services furnished vary. The relative level of housing costs, frequently based on differences in climate and standards, will be important. Tastes in housing are also extremely broad, so that what is demanded and paid for will differ. Within a given country, factors influencing family expenditures are known to be numerous. Maisel and Winnick (1960) report results similar to those of many other studies. Tenure (rental or ownership) and the type of credit available for ownership cause significant expenditure variations. Among a given tenure group, income is the most important variable. The cross-section income elasticity of housing appears to fall around .5 and .6.

Family demographic features are also important. The type of head, the age of head, and race are all related to differences in tenure and in expenditures within tenure groups. Other factors which influence housing demanded and received include education, occupation, and the location of the family by size and type of community.

Use of subsidies. Many value judgments have been made that people underspend for housing. The level of housing purchased in a free market by many groups of the population is held to be below a desirable standard based on concepts of national health and welfare. It is argued that since housing of good quality is an expensive item, low-income families can purchase or rent sound dwellings only at the expense of other budget items. Since their income is inadequate for all wants, they tend to sacrifice the quality of housing. Compared to sacrifices of food, clothing, or other items, poorer housing can more easily be accepted.

In almost all countries the problem of inadequate housing has been met through subsidies. These tend to take the form of direct housing subsidies rather than general income subsidies which could be spent as the low-income family desired. Among existing types of subsidies are public ownership of dwellings with rents charged at less than costs, rent payments, government payment of part of the costs of construction, and government subsidies in the form of easier or cheaper credit.

The use of housing subsidies rather than income subsidies would appear to be based on the assumption that the housing market is special. It is feared that general income subsidies would be dissipated through higher rents with only minor improvements in the quality or quantity of housing. It is argued that unless the government uses its expenditures to assure an increased supply of adequate housing, the money will be wasted. Various reasons for such possible poor results are cited. Improper transmission of information in the housing market is one. The market structure may be such that unless the quality is controlled through the form of the subsidy most of the increased supply will be poor. Furthermore, if subsidies are general the recipients might choose to continue to live in housing deemed unsatisfactory by those favoring the subsidies.

Low-income housing programs have frequently been teamed with those for slum clearance. It is argued that the normal market cannot clear slums unless governmental powers are utilized. The external economies and diseconomies are such that a few property owners could frustrate the will of the majority by threatening or attempting to gather most of the joint values for themselves. Tying a housing subsidy program to slum clearance is not a necessary condition, but it simplifies the process. Joint programs make replacement units available for some of the displaced households.

Effects of rent controls. In many periods of housing shortages, rent controls have been adopted. Arguments for controls depend primarily on concepts of a fair distribution of income. Additional housing can be brought into the market only slowly, or, in periods of war or disaster, not at all. Since the price elasticity of household formation appears to be low, even rapidly rising rents would not have much impact on the number of dwellings demanded. Higher rents would have to be met from already inadequate budgets. These higher rents would increase the income of landlords, who are assumed to be among the wealthier classes. Rent controls are also used because they

are comparatively simple to administer. Potential capital gains on dwellings can be limited. Whether or not it is economically sound, the ability to contain one area of prices has obvious practical advantages.

Most arguments against rent controls consider difficulties that arise if controls are extended beyond immediate emergencies. It is claimed that controls halt market adjustments. They artificially raise demand because of lower prices, while they hold down supply since higher returns cannot be earned. Also over longer periods, the redistribution effects tend to alter. Instead of tenants being favored over landlords, old tenants are favored over new and some industries over others. The costs of operating in an artificial market rise with time, while the economic advantages fall.

Production of housing. The types of houses produced vary widely. The United States and England mix single-family units and larger apartments, with most emphasis given to single-family units. In Europe a higher percentage of apartments is produced. In many other areas small, simply constructed individual units predominate.

In most countries, however, the housing industry has roughly similar characteristics. Entry is simple, and the number of firms is large. The amount of overhead and of mechanical equipment required is low. The rate of technological innovation is slow, and labor tends to be skilled in specific crafts. Difficulties arise in training and in planning the progression of jobs. People compare housing to other industries and usually conclude that it is unprogressive or backward.

In many countries popular comment seems to attribute the difficulties of the industry to a "devil theory." Progress is thought to be blocked by some entrenched group, be it builders, labor, financial institutions, bureaucratic government, or others. The few economic studies of the housing industry (Maisel 1953; Kelly 1959) place much greater emphasis on its structure as a normal response to the unique problems of building dwellings.

Houses are primarily assembled and attached to individual plots of land. Land costs are significant, and each lot is unique. The joining of the land and building is complex and expensive. The buildings are large, heavy, bulky, and durable. A great deal of the expense in housing construction results simply from moving materials from point to point rather than from fabrication. In the assembly process, many different skills must be used because the variety of materials and finishes is great.

The industry produces a wide variety of custom-made products. Its demand is fickle and fluctuates widely; builders must be prepared to expand and contract production rapidly. Flexibility is possible through drawing on the labor and materials available in the much broader area of total construction; however, such flexibility tends to be at the expense of specialization and large-scale automated production.

Probably the rate of innovation has been somewhat greater than is commonly believed. On the other hand, it has certainly been slower than in most highly industrialized parts of the economy. It is virtually impossible to separate the structure of the industry and the uniqueness of the product and market from the rate of change. Many different types of control, of management, and of labor exist in various countries; nevertheless, no country or form of organization has developed a vastly different product or obviously more efficient techniques.

There is some indication that because of the industry's fragmented structure, research expenditures and results are less than elsewhere. Firms work on their own product but pay little attention to the process as a whole. No firm controls enough of the final product to make an over-all point of view worthwhile. While there appear to be potential external economies, governments have done small amounts of research; and their efforts and results thus far are minor.

Many observers conclude that any major changes in structure and technique will depend upon the discovery of new materials and vastly different methods of production. As long as houses continue to be built approximately as they were in the past, changes can only be gradual. No single part of the structure, or individual material, or task is important enough for a saving in its cost to be truly significant. More rapid progress appears to require the elimination of whole groups of materials and functions.

SHERMAN J. MAISEL

BIBLIOGRAPHY

ABRAMOVITZ, MOSES 1962 Long Swings in Economic Growth in the United States. Pages 46–48 in National Bureau of Economic Research, *Annual Report, Forty-second.* New York: The Bureau.

BEYER, GLENN H. 1958 *Housing: A Factual Analysis.* New York: Macmillan. → Contains a bibliography.

BURNS, ARTHUR F. 1935 Long Cycles in Residential Construction. Pages 63–104 in *Economic Essays in Honor of Wesley Clair Mitchell.* New York: Columbia Univ. Press.

CALIFORNIA, UNIVERSITY OF, LOS ANGELES, REAL ESTATE RESEARCH PROGRAM 1966 *Essays in Urban Land Economics in Honor of the Sixty-fifth Birthday of Leo Grebler.* Los Angeles: The University.

COLUMBIA UNIVERSITY, INSTITUTE FOR URBAN LAND USE AND HOUSING STUDIES 1953 *Housing Market Analysis: A Study of Theory and Methods,* by Chester Rapkin, Louis Winnick, and David M. Blank. Washington: U.S. Housing and Home Finance Agency, Office of the Administration, Division of Housing Research.

Compendium of Social Statistics: 1963. 1963 United Nations, Statistical Office, *Statistical Papers,* Series K. No. 2. New York: United Nations.

GREBLER, LEO; BLANK, DAVID M.; and WINNICK, LOUIS 1956 *Capital Formation in Residential Real Estate.* Princeton Univ. Press.

GREBLER, LEO; and MAISEL, SHERMAN J. 1963 Determinants of Residential Construction: Research Study Four. Pages 475–620 in Commission on Money and Credit, *Impacts of Monetary Policy.* Englewood Cliffs, N.J.: Prentice-Hall. → Contains a bibliography on fluctuations.

GRIGSBY, WILLIAM G. 1963 *Housing Markets and Public Policy.* Philadelphia: Univ. of Pennsylvania Press. → Contains a bibliography.

KELLY, BURNHAM 1959 *Design and the Production of Houses.* New York: McGraw-Hill.

MAISEL, SHERMAN J. 1953 *Housebuilding in Transition.* Berkeley: Univ. of California Press.

MAISEL, SHERMAN J. 1963 A Theory of Fluctuations in Residential Construction Starts. *American Economic Review* 53:359–383.

MAISEL, SHERMAN J.; and WINNICK, LOUIS 1960 Family Housing Expenditures: Elusive Laws and Intrusive Variances. Volume 1, pages 359–435 in Conference on Consumption and Saving, University of Pennsylvania, 1959, *Proceedings.* Philadelphia: Univ. of Pennsylvania Press.

RATCLIFF, RICHARD U. 1949 *Urban Land Economics.* New York: McGraw-Hill.

TWENTIETH CENTURY FUND, HOUSING COMMITTEE 1944 *American Housing, Problems and Prospects: The Factual Findings,* by Miles L. Colean. New York: The Fund.

WINNICK, LOUIS 1958 *Rental Housing Opportunities for Private Investment.* New York: McGraw-Hill.

Yearbook of National Accounts Statistics: 1962. 1963 New York: United Nations Statistical Office, Department of Economic and Social Affairs.

HOVLAND, CARL I.

Carl I. Hovland (1912–1961), American pioneer in communications research, began his career as an experimental psychologist working on classical problems of conditioning and human learning. By the age of 30, when he turned to the newly developing field of research on attitude change, he had already become one of the most eminent psychologists of his generation.

The most important of Hovland's early research studies were focused on the generalization of conditioned responses. During the 1930s, he also made significant discoveries concerning factors that influence reminiscence effects in human memory functioning, the efficiency of alternative methods of rote-learning, and the modes of resolution of motor conflicts. From 1942 until his untimely death from cancer in 1961, Hovland devoted the major part of his time to careful investigations of the effects of social communication, using research designs and analytic methods derived from the more highly developed fields of experimental psychology. It is primarily for his contributions in this area that he is regarded as one of the foremost social scientists of the twentieth century. Wilbur Schramm (1963, p. 5), in reviewing communications research in the United States, refers to the work that came out of Hovland's research program at Yale University between 1950 and 1961 as "the largest single contribution . . . [to this field] any man has made." The Distinguished Scientific Contribution Award was presented to Hovland by the American Psychological Association, in 1957, "for his original and provocative contributions to the scientific study of persuasive communications and the modification of beliefs and attitudes." The citation states further:

. . . Combining a sensitive use of controlled experimentation with penetrating logical analysis, he has done much to isolate the major factors at work when an individual is confronted with the complex informational input of a persuasive argument. By judicious use of psychological theory, he has been able to relate this area of social psychology to basic investigations of the higher mental processes. His work has been of central importance in advancing attitude research from the early stage of merely demonstrating that changes can be produced to the point of making predictions about when and where they will occur. His work has provided a convincing demonstration of the values of a sustained and integrated program of research.   (American Psychological Association 1958, p. 158)

Formative years.   A native of Chicago, Hovland attended nearby Northwestern University, where he devoted himself to acquiring as thorough a background as possible in mathematics, physics, and biology, as well as in experimental psychology. After obtaining his M.A. degree in 1933, he completed his graduate studies in psychology at Yale University. He remained affiliated with Yale throughout his entire academic career, starting as an instructor in 1936 (immediately after receiving his PH.D. degree), attaining the rank of professor of psychology in 1945 and the chair of Sterling professor two years later.

As a graduate student and junior faculty member during the prewar years at Yale, Hovland participated in the stimulating intellectual environment of the Yale Institute of Human Relations, which helped to shape his interests and approach to the study of human behavior. Of particular importance in Hovland's training was the influence of the great American psychologist Clark L. Hull. Using a rigorous empirical approach in conjunction with analytic theory construction, Hull was highly successful during the late 1930s in organizing and stimulating talented young psychologists at Yale to carry out research on significant problems of motivation and learning. After serving as Hull's research assistant for several years, Hovland became a coinvestigator in the series of studies on human learning, which led to his being a coauthor of the well-known book by Hull and his collaborators, *Mathematico–Deductive Theory of Rote Learning* (1940). Although not sharing Hull's predilection for far-reaching theoretical formulations, Hovland acquired an extraordinary degree of methodological sophistication, both from Hull himself and from other specialists whom Hull had recruited to participate in his research program. Of equal importance was the optimistic vision he acquired that led him to extend the analytic approach of experimental psychology to other research areas in the human sciences—particularly those suffering from a dearth of dependable generalizations in the midst of an abundance of vague theoretical speculations.

After he had received his PH.D. in 1936, Hovland's outlook and approach to social science research continued to be fostered by collaboration with the staff of Yale's Institute of Human Relations, which was at the height of its influence during the late 1930s and early 1940s. Outstanding social scientists from all over the world were brought together and given ample time and resources to pursue the inquiries of their choice. Hopes ran high that this would make for rapid cross-fertilization among traditionally isolated fields and lead to vital new breakthroughs, comparable to those emerging from interdisciplinary developments in the physical and biological sciences. Among the outstanding personalities with whom Hovland came in contact were Dusser de Barenne, Mark May, Walter Miles, Edward Sapir, and Robert Yerkes.

Although the senior members of the institute rarely achieved their high aspirations for interdisciplinary advances, the intellectual ferment created among the research assistants and junior staff members of Hovland's generation did produce unexpected gains. Coming from different social science disciplines, these well-trained young men began to influence each other as they examined the implications of generalizations that purported to account for complex aspects of human behavior. Among Hovland's contemporaries at the institute were John Dollard, Leonard Doob, Clellan S. Ford,

Neal Miller, O. Hobart Mowrer, George P. Murdock, Robert R. Sears, and John W. M. Whiting. With these men he formed bonds of personal friendship and often participated with them in lively seminars. One well-known product was the collaborative Yale volume *Frustration and Aggression* (Dollard et al. 1939). Several members of this group, together with Donald Marquis, Ernest R. Hilgard, and Kenneth W. Spence, who were also at Yale during the early 1940s, played an important role in the development of learning theory.

Following the lead of Hull, the Yale group attempted to formulate unambiguous behavioral laws concerning the conditions under which habits are strengthened and weakened. These laws were then used as a basis for explaining complex social phenomena, such as the displacement of hostility from the family to outsiders, observed by specialists in such diverse fields as anthropology, psychoanalysis, and social psychology. Hovland contributed to the work of this group not so much by suggesting comprehensive theoretical insights as by focusing on rigorous analysis of empirical evidence. His originality took the form of discovering new functional relationships by working closely with the available findings, noting inconsistencies and reversals that others might be inclined to overlook, and then proceeding to unravel the puzzles by ingeniously testing a series of alternative explanations with a new set of data. These qualities also characterized his later work on communication effects.

Research on mass communication.   In 1942 Hovland took a leave of absence from Yale in order to serve as a research expert on morale problems for the United States government. He became chief psychologist and director of experimental studies in the research branch of the information and education division of the War Department. In this role, he worked closely with two eminent sociologists, Samuel Stouffer, who was then the research director of the research branch, and Leonard C. Cottrell, senior social analyst in the same organization. For four years Hovland participated in the planning of a series of large-scale investigations on social psychological factors in military morale; the empirical findings from these studies were subsequently incorporated into the *American Soldier* volumes by Stouffer and his collaborators.

Hovland's main role in the military research organization, however, was to conduct psychological experiments on the effectiveness of training and information programs, including the series of "Why We Fight" films that were intended to influence the motivation of men in the American armed forces. In his own experimental section of the research branch, Hovland assembled a group of six psychology graduate students, who worked with him on these studies for several years: John Finan, Irving L. Janis, Arthur A. Lumsdaine, Nathan Maccoby, Fred D. Sheffield, and M. Brewster Smith. Although partly oriented toward meeting the practical needs of the military services, the studies conducted by Hovland and his group embodied a research approach that led to major advances on many basic problems in social psychology.

Following the pattern of his earlier work at Yale, Hovland set up investigations designed to test hypotheses concerning the conditions under which mass communications are effective and to explore fully the implications of all the relevant data. But instead of confining the research to restricted laboratory settings, the mainstay of experimental social psychology up to that time, Hovland took advantage of the unique opportunities afforded by his military research mission. He and his group investigated the effects of different types of communication on "live" issues by conducting experimental studies with equated groups of soldiers at U.S. Army training centers. One of the most widely cited of these pioneering communications experiments involved testing the effects of a one-sided versus a two-sided presentation of a controversial issue. The results contradicted some of the well-publicized contentions of Nazi propaganda strategists who claimed that to be successful a communication should never mention the opposing side of an argument. Among men initially hostile to the point of view fostered by a communication (and particularly those familiar with cogent opposing arguments), it was found to be more effective to include mention of the opposing arguments than to give a strictly one-sided presentation.

Many of the investigations by Hovland and his group provide systematic data bearing on the sources of audience resistance to persuasive efforts and call attention to factors that help to overcome such resistance. These wartime studies formed the basis for a book entitled *Experiments on Mass Communication* by Hovland, Lumsdaine, and Sheffield (1949), which was published as part of the same series as the *American Soldier* volumes, jointly sponsored by the U.S. War Department and the Social Science Research Council.

The Yale communication studies.   After the war Hovland returned to Yale University as chairman of the department of psychology and was awarded a Sterling professorship. Having recruited for his department several members of his wartime research team, Hovland continued to devote his energies to systematic research on communication effects. With the support of the Rockefeller Foundation, he organized and directed the Yale studies in attitude and communication, which enabled a large number of junior faculty members and graduate students to participate in collaborative research on a variety of communication problems of their own choice.

The main purpose of the research project was to explore systematically the factors that influence the effectiveness of social communications. Hovland himself continued to take a leading role as an active research worker, and his own experiments set a high standard as models of analytic precision. Among his best-known studies are those elucidating the influence of the communicator's prestige and the ways that prestige effects disappear with the passage of time. Following a lead obtained from the wartime research reported in *Experiments on Mass Communication*, Hovland and his collaborators showed that when a persuasive message is presented by an untrustworthy source it tends to be discounted by the audience, so that immediately after exposure there is little or no attitude change; but then, after several weeks, the source is no longer associated with the issue in the minds of the audience and positive attitude changes appear (Hovland & Weiss 1951). This delayed or "sleeper" effect was shown to vanish, as predicted, when after several weeks the unacceptable communicator was "reinstated" by reminding the audience about who had presented the earlier persuasive material (Kelman & Hovland 1953).

For more than fifteen years Hovland systematically investigated factors that determine the effectiveness of persuasive communications, including studies of different sequential arrangements of arguments, the retention of arguments and conclusions, and judgmental processes that enter into attitude change. While pursuing his own research, Hovland continually encouraged his associates on the Yale project to select other variables in line with their own research interests, such as the influence of group affiliation, role playing, emotional appeals, and personality predispositions. The major research findings of the first five years of the communications research project, together with theoretical analyses of the problems under investigation, were summarized in a volume entitled *Communication and Persuasion* by Hovland, Janis, and Kelley (1953). This volume was followed during the next eight years by a series of four multi-authored monographs on more specific topics: *The Order of Presentation in Persuasion* (Hovland et al. 1957); *Personality and Persuasibility* (Janis, Hovland et al. 1959); *Attitude Organization and Change* (1960b); and *Social Judgment* (Sherif & Hovland 1961). The series of works by Hovland and his co-workers, according to Nathan Maccoby (1963), furnishes the empirical core of "the new scientific rhetoric," the body of psychological knowledge accumulated from objective description and analysis of the processes of persuasion.

Research on thought processes.   In the last decade of his life Hovland's research on verbal concepts and judgment led him into an intensive analysis of symbolic processes. Once again he played a pioneering role in developing a new field of research—computer simulation of human thought processes. His first major contribution in this field was a "communication analysis" of concept learning (1952) which showed how a newly developed mathematical theory could be applied to computer simulation of the ways in which people form new concepts. His general method of analyzing concept learning and his notational system were soon adopted by many other research workers who were conducting experiments on human learning and cognitive processes.

Several years after Hovland's pioneering paper, there were some breakthroughs in the programming of digital computers, which Hovland immediately applied in constructing a computer simulation model of the steps a person goes through as he thinks out the solution of problems requiring the attainment of a new concept. Supported by generous research grants from the Ford Foundation and the Bell Telephone Laboratories, Hovland and his collaborators began devising a series of experiments in order to obtain some of the missing information needed for an adequate theory to account for human acquisition of complex concepts through experience. One of the main findings, reported in a paper by Hunt and Hovland (1960), was that most human learners readily make use of information about *conjunctive* concepts (for example, all members of the given class share two characteristics, A and B) but tend to ignore information pointing to *disjunctive* concepts (for example, all members of the given class possess either characteristic A or B). Accordingly, Hovland developed a computer model of concept formation in which a hierarchy of responses was programmed in such a way that the conjunctive concepts would be the first type tried out and disjunctive concepts would be scanned only after other approaches consistently failed. In a highly influential paper entitled "Computer Simulation of Thinking" (1960a), Hovland pointed out the potential advantages of making use of new developments in mathematics and computer technology for advancing the human sciences. Many research workers are now implementing the mixed research strategy he recommended, combining experimental studies of human thinking with the development of computer programs that simulate human psychological processes.

Other contributions. Hovland's influence on the methodology of social science research was consistently directed toward integrating seemingly divergent lines of research. One of his best-known papers deals with the problems of reconciling conflicting results derived from experimental and survey studies of attitude change (1959). He pointed out that one gets the impression from survey research that very few people are affected by mass communications, whereas experiments on opinion change show that from one-third to one-half of the audience is influenced by a single exposure to a persuasive message. This apparent divergence can be accounted for by a number of well-known factors that are often overlooked, such as the use of captive audiences and remote or unfamiliar issues in experimental studies, in contrast to the audience's self-selective exposure and high ego-involvement in the issues typically studied by survey research. Hovland's recommendation was that the two research approaches should be used conjointly, "combining their virtues so that we may develop a social psychology of communication with the conceptual breadth provided by correlational study of process and with the rigorous but more delimited methodology of the experiment" (1959, p. 17).

At a memorial session of the New England Psychological Association, held a year after Hovland's premature death, his former students and associates recalled his "uncanny ability to integrate and focus knowledge" and "to discern the central aspects of a problem" while at the same time fulfilling his leadership role in a "gentle and supportive" way. As Herbert Kelman put it, he was "the world's most non-authoritarian leader." Indeed, Hovland welcomed diverse theoretical viewpoints and encouraged those working with him to try out new research strategies. His incisive comments stimulated his co-workers and students to make their studies as rigorous as possible and to pursue fully the substantive inferences that could be drawn from the data. This type of direction, combined with the atmosphere of freedom of inquiry which he consistently fostered, nurtured the talents of the many younger psychologists whose names appear as coauthors of his books and articles, most of whom have subsequently become leading figures in American social psychology.

Not the least of Hovland's contributions was the public service he rendered in the role of a "statesman of the social sciences." As one of the few psychologists of his generation elected to the National Academy of Sciences, Hovland was invited to be a committee member or consultant to the Rockefeller Foundation, the Ford Foundation, the Russell Sage Foundation, the Bell Telephone Laboratories, the Social Science Research Council, the National Research Council, the Research Development Board, the Fund for Adult Education, and a number of other private national research organizations, as well as to some of the social research agencies of the U.S. government. Hovland fulfilled his consultant role by consistently working to improve the standards and quality of research in psychology and related fields.

Perhaps the most comprehensive statement of the scope of Hovland's substantive contributions to social science research is contained in the citation of the Warren medal, awarded by the Society of Experimental Psychologists in the last year of his life: "For his systematic analyses . . . [in] four areas of research—verbal learning, conditioning, concept formation and attitude change."

IRVING L. JANIS

[*Directly related are the entries* ATTITUDES, *article on* ATTITUDE CHANGE; PERSUASION; SOCIAL PSYCHOLOGY; SUGGESTION. *Other relevant material may be found in* COMMUNICATION, MASS; *and in the biographies of* HULL; SAPIR; STOUFFER; YERKES.]

WORKS BY HOVLAND

1937a   The Generalization of Conditioned Responses: 1. The Sensory Generalization of Conditioned Responses With Varying Frequencies of Tone. *Journal of General Psychology* 17:125–148.

1937b   The Generalization of Conditioned Responses: 2. The Sensory Generalization of Conditioned Responses With Varying Intensities of Tone. *Journal of Genetic Psychology* 51:279–291.

1937c   The Generalization of Conditioned Responses: 3. Extinction, Spontaneous Recovery, and Disinhibition of Conditioned and of Generalized Responses. *Journal of Experimental Psychology* 21:47–62.

1937d   The Generalization of Conditioned Responses: 4. The Effects of Varying Amounts of Reinforcement Upon the Degree of Generalization of Conditioned Responses. *Journal of Experimental Psychology* 21:261–276.

1938   HOVLAND, CARL I.; and SEARS, ROBERT R. Experiments on Motor Conflict: 1. Types of Conflict and Their Modes of Resolution. *Journal of Experimental Psychology* 23:477–493.

1940   HOVLAND, CARL I.; and SEARS, ROBERT R. Minor Studies of Aggression: 6. Correlation of Lynchings With Economic Indices. *Journal of Psychology* 9:301–310.

1940   *Mathematico–Deductive Theory of Rote Learning.* New Haven: Yale Univ. Press. → By Carl I. Hovland, C. L. Hull, R. T. Ross, M. Hall, D. T. Perkins, and F. B. Fitch.

1940   SEARS, ROBERT R.; HOVLAND, CARL I.; and MILLER, NEAL E. Minor Studies of Aggression: 1. Measurement of Aggressive Behavior. *Journal of Psychology* 9:275–295.

1949 HOVLAND, CARL I.; LUMSDAINE, ARTHUR A.; and SHEFFIELD, FREDERICK D. *Experiments on Mass Communication.* Studies in Social Psychology in World War II, Vol. 3. Princeton Univ. Press; Oxford Univ. Press.

1951 Human Learning and Retention. Pages 613–689 in S. S. Stevens (editor), *Handbook of Experimental Psychology.* New York: Wiley.

(1951) 1954 HOVLAND, CARL I; and WEISS, WALTER The Influence of Source Credibility on Communication Effectiveness. Pages 337–347 in Society for the Psychological Study of Social Issues, *Public Opinion and Propaganda.* New York: Dryden. → First published in Volume 15 of *Public Opinion Quarterly.*

1952 A "Communication Analysis" of Concept Learning. *Psychological Review* 59:461–472.

1952 HOVLAND, CARL I.; and MANDELL, WALLACE An Experimental Comparison of Conclusion-drawing by the Communicator and by the Audience. *Journal of Abnormal and Social Psychology* 47:581–588.

1953 HOVLAND, CARL I.; JANIS, IRVING L.; and KELLEY, HAROLD H. *Communication and Persuasion: Psychological Studies of Opinion Change.* New Haven: Yale Univ. Press.

1953 HOVLAND, CARL I.; and WEISS, WALTER Transmission of Information Concerning Concepts Through Positive and Negative Instances. *Journal of Experimental Psychology* 45:175–182.

1953 KELMAN, HERBERT C.; and HOVLAND, CARL I. "Reinstatement" of the Communicator in Delayed Measurement of Opinion Change. *Journal of Abnormal and Social Psychology* 48:327–335.

1954 Effects of the Mass Media of Communication. Volume 2, pages 1062–1103 in Gardner Lindzey (editor), *Handbook of Social Psychology.* Cambridge, Mass.: Addison-Wesley.

1955 KELLEY, H. H.; HOVLAND, CARL I.; SCHWARTZ, M.; and ABELSON, R. P. The Influence of Judges' Attitudes in Three Methods of Attitude Scaling. *Journal of Social Psychology* 42:147–158.

1956 KURTZ, KENNETH H.; and HOVLAND, CARL I. Concept Learning With Differing Sequences of Instances. *Journal of Experimental Psychology* 51:239–243.

1957 HOVLAND, CARL I. et al. *The Order of Presentation in Persuasion.* New Haven: Yale Univ. Press. → Coauthors are W. Mandell, E. H. Campbell, T. Brock, A. S. Luchins, A. R. Cohen, W. J. McGuire, I. L. Janis, R. L. Feierabend, and N. H. Anderson.

1959 Reconciling Conflicting Results Derived From Experimental and Survey Studies of Attitude Change. *American Psychologist* 14:8–17.

1959 JANIS, IRVING L.; HOVLAND, CARL I. et al. *Personality and Persuasibility.* New Haven: Yale Univ. Press. → Coauthors are P. B. Field, H. Linton, E. Graham, A. R. Cohen, D. Rife, R. P. Abelson, G. S. Lesser, and B. T. King.

1959 MORRISETT, LLOYD N.; and HOVLAND, CARL I. A Comparison of Three Varieties of Training in Human Problem Solving. *Journal of Experimental Psychology* 58:52–55.

1960a Computer Simulation of Thinking. *American Psychologist* 15:687–693.

1960 HOVLAND, CARL I.; and HUNT, EARL B. Computer Simulation of Concept Attainment. *Behavioral Science* 5:265–267.

1960b *Attitude Organization and Change.* Yale Studies in Attitude and Communication, Vol. 3. New Haven: Yale Univ. Press. → By Carl I. Hovland, M. J. Rosenberg, W. J. McGuire, J. W. Brehm, and R. P. Abelson.

1960 HUNT, EARL B.; and HOVLAND, CARL I. Order of Consideration of Different Types of Concepts. *Journal of Experimental Psychology* 59:220–225.

1961 HUNT, EARL B.; and HOVLAND, CARL I. Programming a Model of Human Concept Formation. Pages 145–155 in Western Joint Computer Conference, Los Angeles, 1961, *Proceedings.* Los Angeles: The Conference.

1961 SHERIF, MUZAFER; and HOVLAND, CARL I. *Social Judgment: Assimilation and Contrast Effects in Communication and Attitude Change.* Yale Studies in Attitude and Communication, Vol. 4. New Haven: Yale Univ. Press.

SUPPLEMENTARY BIBLIOGRAPHY

AMERICAN PSYCHOLOGICAL ASSOCIATION 1958 Distinguished Scientific Contribution Awards, 1957. *American Psychologist* 13:155–168.

COHEN, ARTHUR R. 1964 *Attitude Change and Social Influence.* New York: Basic Books.

DOLLARD, JOHN et al. 1939 *Frustration and Aggression.* New Haven: Yale Univ. Press. → A paperback edition was published in 1961. Coauthors are L. W. Doob, N. E. Miller, O. H. Mowrer, and R. R. Sears.

JANIS, IRVING L.; and SMITH, M. BREWSTER 1965 Effects of Education and Persuasion on National and International Images. Pages 188–235 in H. C. Kelman (editor), *International Behavior.* New York: Holt.

MACCOBY, NATHAN 1963 The New "Scientific" Rhetoric. Pages 41–53 in Wilbur Schramm (editor), *The Science of Human Communication.* New York: Basic Books.

SCHRAMM, WILBUR 1963 Communication Research in the United States. Pages 1–16 in Wilbur Schramm (editor), *The Science of Human Communication.* New York: Basic Books.

HRDLIČKA, ALEŠ

Aleš Hrdlička (1869–1943), a leading American physical anthropologist, was born in Humpolec, Bohemia (now Czechoslovakia), the oldest of seven children of Maximilian and Caroline Hrdlička. In 1882 he immigrated with his father to New York City where he first worked in a cigar factory while learning English in night schools. Later he attended the Eclectic Medical College in New York City, from which he graduated in 1892 at the head of his class. To improve his medical standing he then attended the New York Homeopathic Medical College and Hospital, also in New York City, graduating in 1894, and again topping his class. He immediately began interning in the State Homeopathic Hospital for the Insane at Middletown, New York. In 1896, after accepting a research position in the Pathological Institute of the New York State Hospitals, he went to Paris where, among other things, he studied anthropology under Léonce Manouvrier.

Hrdlička's program at the institute brought him

into contact with F. W. Putnam of the department of anthropology of the American Museum of Natural History. This connection led to an invitation to accompany the explorer and author Carl Lumholtz on a trip to Mexico in 1898. The resulting experience with American Indians was a turning point in Hrdlička's career; when the Pathological Institute closed in 1899, he turned his attention entirely to anthropology. From that time until the end of 1902, he participated in the Hyde expeditions of the American Museum to the Southwest and to Mexico.

In 1903 Hrdlička accepted an invitation from William H. Holmes to become assistant curator in charge of a new division of physical anthropology of the United States National Museum in Washington. In 1910 he was made curator, which position he held until his retirement in 1942.

One of Hrdlička's first acts as assistant curator was to arrange for the transfer to the National Museum of human skeletal material found at archeological sites which the Smithsonian Institution had deposited at the Army Medical Museum. He then devoted his energies to extending the geographical, chronological, and racial coverage of the collection. At the same time he continued his studies of living peoples. The extent of these activities can best be seen in the record of his travels: 1905—southern Arizona and New Mexico (Apache and Pima); 1906—Florida; 1909—Egypt and Europe; 1910—South America and Mexico; 1912—Europe, Siberia, and Mongolia; 1913—Peru; 1915—Minnesota and Missouri (Chippewa and Sioux); 1916—Florida; 1917—New England, Virginia, and Tennessee (Old Americans); 1918—Florida; 1920—Japan, Korea, China, and Hawaii; 1922—Brazil and Europe; 1923—Europe; 1925—Europe, India, southeast Asia, Australia, and South Africa; 1926–1938—Alaska and Commander Islands (Eskimo and Aleut); 1939—Europe and Siberia.

Ultimately Hrdlička accumulated for the museum one of the world's largest skeletal collections. By studying this material he was able to publish a large number of scientific reports, including catalogues of crania and monographs on the antiquity of man in America and on the most ancient skeletal remains from the Old World. He also published several reports on living American Indians, two books on the American white population (1925; 1931), and a book on anthropometry.

Hrdlička influenced anthropology through the *American Journal of Physical Anthropology*, which he founded in 1918 and edited until 1942, and through the American Association of Physical Anthropologists, which he founded in 1929, serving as president in 1930–1931. In these roles, unfortunately, he tried too much to control and dominate the thinking in the field.

Hrdlička also gave much of his time to general scientific organizations and international congresses. He was largely responsible for the organization of the 19th International Congress of Americanists held in Washington in 1919. He was elected a member of the American Philosophical Society in 1918 and of the National Academy of Sciences in 1921. In 1922 he received an honorary SC.D. from the University of Prague, in 1926 the same degree from the University of Brno, and in 1927 the Huxley Memorial Medal from the Royal Anthropological Institute of Great Britain and Ireland.

On his way to Europe in 1939 Hrdlička suffered a heart attack but, after a month in a hospital in England, continued on to Siberia. He died of a subsequent heart attack in Washington.

T. D. STEWART

[*For the historical context of Hrdlička's work, see* PHYSICAL ANTHROPOLOGY.]

WORKS BY HRDLIČKA

(1920) 1952 *Practical Anthropometry*. Edited by T. D. Stewart. Philadelphia: Wistar Institute of Anatomy and Biology. → First published as *Anthropometry*.
1925 *The Old Americans*. Baltimore: Williams & Wilkins.
1931 *Children Who Run on All Fours, and Other Animal-like Behaviors in the Human Child*. New York: McGraw-Hill.

WORKS ABOUT HRDLIČKA

Dr. Aleš Hrdlička: Zivotopisný nástin. 1929 *Anthropologie* (Prague) 7:6–61.
SCHULTZ, ADOLPH H. 1945 Biographical Memoir of Aleš Hrdlička: 1869–1943. Volume 23, pages 305–338 in National Academy of Sciences, *Biographical Memoirs*. Washington: The Academy. → Contains a bibliography on pages 319–338.
STEWART, T. D. 1940 The Life and Writings of Dr. Aleš Hrdlička. *American Journal of Physical Anthropology* 26:3–40.
STEWART, T. D. 1964 Aleš Hrdlička: Pioneer American Physical Anthropologist. Pages 505–509 in Czechoslovak Society of Arts and Sciences in America, *The Czechoslovak Contribution to World Culture*. The Hague: Mouton.

HUIZINGA, JOHAN

Johan Huizinga (1872–1945), the Dutch cultural historian, was born in Groningen and died at De Steeg, a village outside Arnhem. His family combined the deep piety of a long line of Baptist ministers with a scientific devotion to factual truth, exemplified by Huizinga's father, a doctor and professor of physiology at Groningen. Although in his mature years Huizinga subscribed to no religious confession, he was a lifelong believer; his nonconformist background was partly responsible for his toleration, his respect for the privacy of others, his strong ethical stoicism, and his moderation in political (even in historical) issues. His respect for factual integrity is everywhere apparent in his work and became the basis for his attack upon totalitarianism.

After studying Dutch language and literature at Groningen and taking his degree in 1896 in comparative philology (on a Sanskrit subject), Huizinga began teaching history to high school students in Haarlem. Here he did the research for his first— and only archival—historical work, a study of the rise of Haarlem (1905–1906). Through his mentor, the historian Petrus Johannes Blok, Huizinga was appointed professor of history at Groningen in 1905: his inaugural lecture, "Het aesthetische bestanddeel van geschiedkundige voorstellingen" (1905; "The Aesthetic Element in Historical Presentation"), gave promise of his use of literature and the visual arts to interpret history. Until his appointment as professor of history at Leiden, however, the harvest of this approach remained only a promise.

It was in his Leiden years, from 1915 until his death, that Huizinga's special talents were revealed. His youthful interest in *fin-de-siècle* literature (French, English, and Dutch) and his knowledge of Flemish "primitive" and modern painting provided him with a fresh view of the social significance of aesthetic forms. *The Waning of the Middle Ages* (1919), his masterpiece, is a study of the forms of life of fifteenth-century France and Burgundy, based upon his critical reading of aesthetic and philological sources normally overlooked by the working historian. Huizinga attempted to do for the late medieval North what his acknowledged master, Jacob Burckhardt, had done for the Italian Renaissance.

In 1918 Huizinga published "Mensch en menigte in Amerika" ("Man and Mass in America"), an extrapolation from American materials worked up to introduce his Leiden students to American history—itself an event of considerable cultural importance. After several studies of Renaissance history (1920; 1924), he published "De taak der cultuurgeschiedenis" ("The Task of Cultural History") in 1929. It was a description and prescription for his students and other historians, in which he plainly advocated subsuming to history other "philological" disciplines—the law, philosophy, histories of music, literature, and the fine arts—as

well as pillaging from the social sciences conceptualizations to facilitate both the setting of historical questions and the organization of historical answers.

Except for his study of Haarlem, Huizinga made no great contributions to political or economic history; unlike Burckhardt, he did not seem to regard even the state as a work of art. Huizinga was primarily interested in "intellectual" history, the history of the literate classes; but he was further interested in every aspect of "social" history, the forms through which men in the past conducted their lives. From texts normally regarded as nonhistorical, Huizinga produced evidence for forms of collective and private life of past periods and places. Like an archeologist, he excavated life "as it really was." His methodological writings from this period emphasize the usefulness to historians of the insights and methods of sociology and anthropology.

Although Huizinga never collected quantitative data for his own research, he nonetheless respected conclusions about social and cultural habits based on quantitative analysis. His own preference for the work of Max Weber and Ernst Troeltsch, among sociologists, and for Marcel Mauss, among anthropologists, was the result of his admiration of the hypotheses they framed and their use of hypotheses in the analysis of various data. His own comparable work is his study of seventeenth-century Dutch culture (1932), the best epitome of that complex period ever written; there he advanced the thesis that Dutch Calvinism was not of primary importance in the formation of Golden Age culture. *The Waning of the Middle Ages* and *Homo ludens* (1938) extrapolate cultural manifestations from surrounding historical data in order to draw up, more schematically than is usual in historical writing, the structure of, in the first instance, northern European society in the fifteenth century and, in the second, the functions and variations of play, playing, and games in human culture as a whole. Huizinga was much interested in the historical work of the group headed by Lucien Febvre and Marc Bloch, to be found in the periodical *Annales d'histoire économique et sociale*, with its self-conscious use of social materials and sociological method. However, despite this sociological emphasis, Huizinga reacted unfavorably to the work of Freud and seems to have made almost no use of Marxian ideas throughout his work.

From 1935 on, Huizinga's principal work was not historical, although it was certainly cultural, or moral–sociological. In that year, only two years after Hitler's *coup*, he published *In the Shadow of*

Tomorrow: A Diagnosis of the Spiritual Distemper of Our Time, a highly polemical study of contemporary mass culture. Although his critics attacked his disgust with the cheapness of the radio and of yellow journalism as reactionary, Huizinga regarded these as signs of a general loss of value far more seriously manifest in the political, social, and moral behavior of contemporary totalitarianism. Ten years later, his posthumous *Geschonden wereld: Een beschouwing over de kansen op herstel van onze beschaving* (1945; "World in Ruins: A Consideration of the Chances of Rebuilding Our Civilization") was published, both a sequel and a corrective to *In the Shadow of Tomorrow*. Like de Tocqueville (really, even more than Burckhardt, Huizinga's model) in *Democracy in America*, Huizinga was conservative in his insistence upon conscientious individual responsibility and optimistic in his conviction that by individual recommitment a collective responsible world could be reconstructed.

Homo ludens, Huizinga's most extraordinary and original book, is a study of the "play-element" in culture—occidental, oriental, primitive, ancient, and modern. He considered all sorts of playing, from children's games to the dialectic of philosophy and of the law courts. By no means a history book—its lesson is psychosociological or even metasocial rather than historical—*Homo ludens* is nonetheless the book of a historian who relates each specific form of such an activity as play to the temporal and local culture of which it is a part.

A generation earlier, Huizinga might have become a literary and artistic critic; a generation later, he might have become a sociologist. As it was, he practiced cultural history as if "high" culture and "sociological" or "anthropological" culture were mutually dependent. Although he preferred the man to the mass, the individual to the crowd, he saw the task of the cultural historian to be the interpretation of societies, or groups made up of individuals. Huizinga's work has made it difficult for historians to ignore the signs of nonpolitical social forms within which human beings have always lived their lives.

ROSALIE L. COLIE

[*For the historical context of Huizinga's work, see* HISTORY, *articles on* INTELLECTUAL HISTORY *and* SOCIAL HISTORY; *and the biographies of* BURCKHARDT; MAUSS; TOCQUEVILLE; TROELTSCH; WEBER, MAX.]

WORKS BY HUIZINGA

(1905) 1952   Het aesthetische bestanddeel van geschiedkundige voorstellingen. Volume 7, pages 3–28 in Johan Huizinga, *Verzamelde werken*. Haarlem: Tjeenk Willink.

(1905–1906) 1948   De opkomst van Haarlem. Volume 1, pages 203–364 in Johan Huizinga, *Verzamelde werken*. Haarlem: Tjeenk Willink.

(1918) 1950   Mensch en menigte in Amerika: Vier essays over moderne beschavingsgeschiedenis. Volume 5, pages 249–417 in Johan Huizinga, *Verzamelde werken*. Haarlem: Tjeenk Willink.

(1919) 1924   *The Waning of the Middle Ages: A Study in the Forms of Life, Thought and Art in France and the Netherlands in the 14th and 15th Centuries.* London: Arnolds. → First published in Dutch. A paperback edition was published in 1954 by Doubleday.

(1920) 1949   Renaissancestudiën I: Het probleem. Volume 4, pages 231–275 in Johan Huizinga, *Verzamelde werken*. Haarlem: Tjeenk Willink.

(1924) 1952   *Erasmus of Rotterdam.* 3d ed. London: Phaidon. → First published in Dutch.

(1929) 1952   De taak der cultuurgeschiedenis. Volume 7, pages 35–94 in Johan Huizinga, *Verzamelde werken*. Haarlem: Tjeenk Willink.

1932   *Holländische Kultur des siebzehnten Jahrhunderts: Ihre sozialen Grundlagen und nationale Eigenart.* Jena (Germany): Diedrichs.

(1935) 1936   *In the Shadow of Tomorrow: A Diagnosis of the Spiritual Distemper of Our Time.* London: Heinemann; New York: Norton. → First published in Dutch.

(1938) 1949   *Homo ludens: A Study of the Play-element in Culture.* London: Routledge. → First published in Dutch. A paperback edition was published in 1955 by Beacon.

1942   *Im Bann der Geschichte: Betrachtungen und Darstellungen.* Basel and Amsterdam: Pantheon.

1945   *Geschonden wereld: Een beschouwing over de kansen op herstel van onze beschaving.* Haarlem: Tjeenk Willink.

1947   *Mein Weg zur Geschichte.* Basel: Benno Schwabe.

Verzamelde werken. 9 vols. Haarlem: Tjeenk Willink, 1948–1953. → Volume 1: *Oud-Indie; Nederland*, 1948. Volume 2: *Nederland*, 1948. Volumes 3–5: *Cultuurgeschiedenis*, 1949–1950. Volume 6: *Biografie*, 1951. Volume 7: *Geschiedwetenschap; Hedendaagsche cultuur*, 1952. Volume 8: *Universiteit: Wetenschap en kunst*, 1952. Volume 9: *Bibliographie en registers*, 1953.

SUPPLEMENTARY BIBLIOGRAPHY

COLIE, R. L.   1964   Johan Huizinga and the Task of Cultural History. *American Historical Review* 63:607–630.

GEYL, PIETER   (1946) 1962   De betekenis van Huizinga. Pages 122–127 in Pieter Geyl, *Nederlandse figuren I*. Amsterdam: Wereld-Bibliotheek.

GEYL, PIETER   1961   *Huizinga als aanklager van zijn tijd.* Amsterdam: North-Holland Publishing.

KAEGI, WERNER   1946   Johan Huizinga zum Gedächtnis. Volume 2, pages 7–42 in Werner Kaegi, *Historische Meditationen*. Zurich: Fretz & Wasmuth.

KAMERBEEK, J.   1954   Huizinga en de beweging van tachtig. *Tijdschrift voor geschiedenis* 67:145–164.

ROMEIN, JAN M.   1950   Huizinga als historicus. Pages 212–253 in Jan Romein, *Tussen vrees en vrijheid: vijftien historische verhandelingen*. Amsterdam: Querido.

VALKENBURG, CHRISTIAAN T. VAN   1946   *J. Huizinga: Zijn leven en zijn persoonlijkheid.* Amsterdam: Pantheon.

HULL, CLARK L.

Clark L. Hull (1884–1952) was the most influential figure in the experimental psychology of learning during the decades immediately preceding and following World War II [see LEARNING; LEARNING THEORY]. This was not because his researches were unusually definitive or his theory universally accepted. If there was a single cause, it was that Hull presented his theoretical ideas with a degree of rigor and analytical detail then unfamiliar in psychology. A substantial proportion of the research in learning in this era was formulated in terms of Hull's theory, whether designed to sustain or to disprove it, and virtually all such research at least acknowledged a relationship to Hullian conceptions. Although Hull's theory contained some ambiguities and inconsistencies, it set a challenging level of explicitness that contributed in an important way to the developing image of psychology as a science.

Hull's ideas drew on many sources. Darwin had proposed the principle of natural selection that formed a rationale for much of Hull's theory. Many of the phenomena of conditioning that Hull described and some of the theoretical constructs that he espoused had been discussed by Pavlov. Freud had asserted the central role of motivation in behavior, a position Hull increasingly adopted. Watson had established the behavioristic departure from earlier introspectionism; Hull followed in the less radical, neobehavioristic tradition. Thorndike's law of effect, asserting the important role of reinforcement in learning, was central to Hull's major theorizing. Tolman had described the place of the intervening variable in behavior theory and had drawn the critical distinction between learning and performance, which Hull later formalized. Not only was Hull indebted to these predecessors, but he was unusually careful also to acknowledge the important contributions of his colleagues, notably Neal E. Miller and Kenneth W. Spence, in developing his approach.

To this potpourri of influences, Hull added integration and purpose. He made more explicit the ideas of these and other men and in so doing added a wealth of his own conceptual innovations. He believed that controlled studies of simple learning situations would reveal a core set of principles of behavior and that these could then be applied to the more complex conditions of individual and group behavior. If successful, this program, he felt, would have inestimable value for understanding, predicting, and, where appropriate, controlling behavior.

Hull was born in a log cabin on a farm in New York State in 1884. His education, which began in a rural school, was interrupted by a job as a mining engineer and an attack of poliomyelitis that made the use of a cane necessary thereafter. He was 34 when he received a PH.D. from the University of Wisconsin. Early in life, Hull began a series of personal notebooks in which he recorded a variety of facts, ideas, and reflections, hoping to preserve the thoughts of his youth for later, less creative years. These "idea books" show an early sense of destiny and a developing obsession with urgency. They also contain many detailed analyses of his theory-in-the-making which illustrate his conviction that the explicit, formal statement of an idea is most likely to reveal its weaknesses. As he said in *Principles of Behavior*, "It is believed that a clear formulation, even if later found incorrect, will ultimately lead more quickly and easily to a correct formulation than will a pussyfooting statement which might be more difficult to convict of falsity" (1943, p. 398). Hull was uncompromising in his expectation of speed, effort, and punctuality from his associates and intolerant of slipshod thinking by his students. He was generous both with personal attention and professional credit to all who worked with him. He consciously avoided vindictive arguments, to which some of the reviews of his work could easily have led, but accepted, indeed welcomed, considered criticism.

Hull's early scientific activities are noteworthy in themselves. Continuing at the University of Wisconsin after obtaining his degree, Hull worked in the area of the measurement and prediction of achievement. His first major work, *Aptitude Testing* (1928), reveals his principal concern—the problems of validation of tests. To reduce computational time and errors, Hull designed an automatic correlation machine, a beautifully complex unit that, as he said in his autobiography, "really worked," and that illustrates his unusual talent for gadgetry. He then became interested in hypnosis and conducted a series of experimental studies, published in his second major work, *Hypnosis and Suggestibility* (1933), that brought scientific rigor to this often quasi-scientific area. Hull moved to the Institute of Human Relations at Yale University in 1929 and there, at the age of 45, started to formalize a mechanistic theory of behavior. He was to make his major contribution to psychology in this area. [See ACHIEVEMENT TESTING; APTITUDE TESTING; HYPNOSIS; SUGGESTION.]

The institute housed a vigorous group of workers of varying ages, fields, and persuasions, all dedicated to the concept of a science of behavior.

Nevertheless, it was 11 years before Hull and several colleagues formalized a set of learning principles in *Mathematico–Deductive Theory of Rote Learning* (1940), a work less well known than it deserves to be, probably because of its use of the language of formal logic and mathematics. Three years later a more general and readable statement of the fundamental principles appeared in Hull's third and most influential major work, *Principles of Behavior* (1943). Another nine years passed before Hull's *A Behavior System* (1952a) described selected examples of more complex individual behavior in terms of his theoretical principles. This last work was published posthumously; the intended application to social and cultural problems remained to be written at the time of Hull's death in 1952.

Reinforcement theory of learning. Hull's theory can be characterized as a mechanistic stimulus–response conception of behavior. Learning, Hull believed, consists in the bonding together of some stimulus event (a light, a tone, a maze) with some response of the organism (salivating, running, turning). Behavior in general is describable in terms of hierarchies and constellations of such connections. Hull did not, however, deny the reality of ideas, knowledge, and purpose; indeed, he accepted these as obvious descriptive properties of molar behavior. He argued, rather, that these are not the basic units of behavior and that they are understandable in terms of more fundamental stimulus–response events. He introduced, therefore, the notion of the fractional, anticipatory goal response, which assumes that a portion of the reinforcing event at the end of a behavior chain can have an effect at the beginning of the chain. This response, or more properly, its response-produced stimulus, serves to guide overt behavior, as if purposefully, toward the goal. Whatever the complexity of behavior apparent to direct inspection, it could be reduced to simpler principles by the further discovery of response mechanisms, often hypothetical internal responses with no other function than to provide the organism with guiding stimuli.

Principles of Behavior provides the epitome of a reinforcement theory of learning: the formation of stimulus–response connections is assumed to depend on a subsequent reinforcing state of affairs, and the degree to which the connection is strengthened depends upon the quantitative properties of the reinforcement. That is to say, learning occurs only if the response is rewarded, and the larger and more immediate the reward, the better the learning. Recognizing the possible circularity of this theory in the absence of an independent definition of re-inforcement, Hull proposed the drive reduction hypothesis [*see* DRIVES]. He assumed that a hungry rat learns to run through a maze because the turning responses at the choice-points are reinforced by the eventual reduction in hunger drive occasioned by eating in the goal box. Furthermore, since choice-points near the goal are followed most quickly by this reinforcement, Hull correctly inferred that errors would be eliminated in backward fashion, the appropriate responses at the beginning of the maze being learned last. These two explicit postulates—that learning occurs only if responses are reinforced and that reinforcement occurs only if a drive is reduced—generated a substantial proportion of the research of Hull and his colleagues.

Habit and drive. The stimulus–response connection, which Hull called habit strength and symbolized $_sH_R$, is itself not the sole determinant of behavior. In order to appear in overt performance, habits must be energized by drive. This latter construct, symbolized D, is related to presumed biological and survival needs of the organism and species (hunger, thirst, pain, sex) and is assumed to combine multiplicatively with habit to determine excitatory potential ($_sE_R$), which in turn determines performance. This equation—$_sE_R = {_sH_R} \times D$—formalizes the distinction between learning and performance and inextricably entangles learning with motivation. When elaborated and expanded, the formulation became a powerful source of hypotheses.

The proper use of this equation requires a sophisticated understanding of both habit and drive. Consider first $_sH_R$. The actual stimulus to which a response is attached is not the distal event as it occurs in the environment or even the proximal event as it occurs on the receptor. Rather, it is a trace of this latter event, which, according to Hull, decays over time. Moreover, because stimuli are never exactly identical, Hull further hypothesized that habit learned to one stimulus generalizes some habit strength to other similar stimuli. The postulates of the stimulus trace and habit generalization illustrate the way Hull derived behavioral phenomena.

Pavlov had shown that if the sound of a bell regularly occurs, say, ten seconds before food is delivered to a hungry dog, the salivation that had occurred only after the food was in the dog's mouth becomes anticipatory, i.e., begins to occur when the bell sounds and before the food arrives. Hull's theoretical interpretation is that the bell initiates a stimulus trace in the nervous system of the dog which immediately begins to decay, but which is present in some unique intensity ten seconds later when the food is delivered. Since the food elicits salivation as an unlearned reflex, and since it also provides reinforcement by reducing hunger, the appropriate conditions are present for the formation of a habit connection between the ten-second trace of the bell and salivation. Now, because earlier traces of a bell are similar to the ten-second trace of that same bell, the habit being formed to the latter will generalize to the former. Hence, the dog salivates anticipatorily as a result of generalization. By making explicit quantitative assumptions about the shape of the stimulus trace function and the degree of generalization between different traces, one can make detailed derivations about the expected latency of salivation at different stages of training and the importance of the time interval separating the ringing of the bell and the presentation of the food.

Hull also expanded the construct of drive. Perhaps his most important elaboration is the concept of the association of any particular intensity of any particular drive (e.g., a rat deprived of food for 24 hours) and a characteristic drive stimulus which differs to some extent from that produced by other drives (e.g., deprivation of water) or other intensities of the same drive (e.g., 12 hours of food deprivation). Hence, although Hull's conception of drive is that of a general energizer—hunger can as well motivate a response learned under thirst— drives do have a directing function, because each drive stimulus will tend to become selectively attached to those responses most likely to reduce it. Thus, a rat in a maze can learn to turn right when hungry and left when thirsty even though, as motivators, these drives act indiscriminately on all habits.

Given the fact that there is experimental extinction—the weakening and disappearance of responses when reinforcement is terminated—Hull was faced with two theoretical alternatives. One was the assumption that $_sH_R$ itself is weakened by nonreinforcement. However, there were a variety of reasons for believing that learning is a relatively permanent process, not the least of which is the dramatic evidence of memory Hull had obtained using hypnosis. Hence, Hull followed Pavlov in assuming that experimental extinction does not represent the loss of habit, but rather the accumulation of inhibition. Excitatory potential is reduced by inhibition resulting from nonreinforcement; the dog does not forget how to salivate to the bell; instead, learning is inhibited if food no longer follows the bell.

The system was completed by relating excitatory potential to performance. One common response measure is the probability that a response will occur on any presentation of a stimulus. To adapt this measure to his theory, Hull borrowed the notion of a threshold from physiology and assumed that excitatory potential is subject to oscillation from moment to moment according to an essentially random distribution. A response will occur only if $_sE_R$ is above threshold at the moment and, if this is so, the speed and amplitude of response will depend directly upon the momentary value of excitatory potential.

One of the persistent problems that Hull faced in developing his theory was that the intervening variables such as habit and drive are inherently unobservable by direct inspection and hence cannot be measured. Since the theory is cast in quantitative terms, Hull's derivations typically consist of illustrative examples, with arbitrary values for the important variables. He foresaw the importance of quantifying these variables in units that might be applied to the wide range of situations to which the theory was intended to apply. Toward this end, Hull undertook a meticulous series of studies employing the Thurstone scaling technique to quantify habit and drive. Hull valued this work greatly, in keeping with his belief that mathematics is a fundamental tool of behavioral as well as physical science.

Stimulus dynamism and incentive motivation. Almost as soon as *Principles of Behavior* was published, major modifications of its theory began. One unsolved problem was the role of stimulus intensity; Hull became convinced that not only do drive stimuli have energizing and directing functions, but that all stimuli have dynamogenic as well as cue properties. Furthermore, the rapid changes in an animal's response after a change in the amount of reward suggested that reinforcement is a motivational variable as well as a learning variable. A new equation for excitatory potential therefore appeared. It included the concepts of stimulus dynamism based on the intensity of the eliciting stimulus, and of incentive motivation based on the amount and time of delay of reward as additional motivational factors multiplying habit. According to this new conception, a dog salivates more to a strong than a weak bell not because he has learned to salivate better, but because the stronger stimulus energizes a more vigorous response. A rat runs a maze faster for a larger reward than for a smaller not because he has learned the maze better, but because the larger reward provides more incentive to run. Motivational factors thus began to dominate Hull's learning theory, although he clung to the assumption that some reinforcement is required for the accretion of habit strength.

Discrimination learning. All these hypotheses were generated on the basis of data obtained in relatively simple learning situations. The logic of Hull's program, it will be recalled, is that these principles will be applicable, when properly interpreted and possibly expanded, to more complex situations as well.

In *A Behavior System*, Hull described the following case, among others: If an organism is confronted with two stimuli differing, let us say, in brightness, and is consistently rewarded if he chooses one of these, he will learn to behave adaptively; he will learn to discriminate between the stimuli and consistently to choose the rewarded alternative. In Hullian language, choice between responses is somehow based on excitatory potential. The simplest hypothesis is that if several responses are in competition the one that has the largest excitatory potential will occur. With the choice measure specified in this way, discrimination learning follows readily from the theory.

It is first noted that the excitatory potential of the positive stimulus will be increased by the reinforcement following responses to it. Although generalization will produce some excitatory potential for the nonreinforced stimulus, this will be reduced by the inhibition developed whenever response is made to it. Thus, continued training will lead to a gradual separation of the excitatory potentials of the two stimuli and hence a developing preference for the reinforced one. A number of additional and more detailed implications also follow. For example, the discrimination should be easier the more different the two stimuli are, since there will be less generalization between them and more rapid separation of their excitatory potentials. As is true of most useful theories, this analysis has more implications than appear at first glance, many of which have been derived by Spence (1960) from his related theory and tested with tolerably good results.

Assessment of Hull's theory. Hull correctly foresaw that the details of his theory were tentative and likely to require revision as relevant data were collected. His principal lasting contribution lies more in his extensive illustration of an approach to behavior theory than in the specific theory itself. This approach leans heavily upon the availability of empirical data, since it involves the postulation of intervening variables or empirical constructs which are intended to summarize the existing data and to generalize upon them for predicting new data. For example, it is known that rats run a maze to water faster the longer they have been previously deprived of water. The intervening variable approach assumes that deprivation of water affects the organism by producing thirst that potentiates the response. It is important to note the two essential criteria of an adequately formulated intervening variable: it must be anchored to some independent variable such as deprivation, and it must also be anchored to some dependent variable such as response speed.

Hull believed that intervening variables actually exist in the neurophysiological structure of the organism, and many of his postulates are couched in physiological-sounding terms. Some critics may therefore incorrectly assume that the usefulness of the theory is dependent upon the adequacy of such physiological speculations. But Hull intended only to stress the ultimate reducibility of molar behavioral events to more predictable molecular physiological events and to suggest possible rather than specific avenues toward such reduction. For example, he felt that his concept of drive might be related to endocrine and chemical mechanisms, and if this were true, an important link would be established between psychology and physiology. But such a result would be a bonus; the value of the approach is assessed by its ability to predict behavioral facts and not by its physiological validity.

The construct "thirst" integrates a wider set of findings than the single one that longer water deprivation leads to faster running. The same independent variable (deprivation of water) also affects behavior in a number of other ways—the amount the rat will drink, the vigor with which he will operate a manipulandum, the intensity of electric shock he will tolerate in order to obtain water, etc. Furthermore, a number of operations other than the withholding of water can be found to produce the same pattern of behavioral consequences (responses)—feeding dry or salty food, injecting drugs into the rat's brain, etc. All of these empirical relationships are tied together by the single notion of thirst. A quite similar constellation of findings appears with deprivation of food, and the construct "drive" integrates at a more abstract level the energizing and directing functions common to hunger, thirst, and other needs.

The postulation of the combination rule that drive multiplies habit permits novel predictions. For example, since the choice between two alternatives depends upon the difference between their excitatory potentials, rats will learn a maze faster under high than under low drive. This is because the developing differential in habit, resulting from the reinforcement of only one alternative, will be amplified in proportion to the prevailing level of drive. When such implications are tested and the results fail to conform to prediction, the theory necessarily is modified.

The extension of the simple principles to more complex situations follows a similar progression. For example, when it is observed that a previously neutral stimulus paired temporally with a noxious stimulus takes on some of the properties ascribed to drive, the richness of the theory can be drawn upon to develop the concept of learned drive. The principles of learning should describe the way drives are acquired, and the principles of performance should describe the way such acquired drives affect behavior. Dollard and Miller (1950) have carefully extended the application of the basic principles along these lines, and they have applied the resulting theory to psychotherapy.

Hull assumed further that these same principles could be applied to still more molar social and economic situations. This might require some additional principles not apparent in the simple situations from which the theory sprang. A boy and a girl on a date are reacting in accordance with their drives and habits just as much as a rat in a maze; the drives include a variety of social pressures toward conformity, approval, and morality, and the habits involve fine discriminations of the cues provided by the other person. Hull believed that the reduction of such situations to his theoretical conception was in principle possible, and certainly could not be proved impossible a priori.

Hull's program, even as far as he carried it, was certainly not flawless, and it led psychologists to overestimate the imminent attainment of a general behavior theory. Hull tended to oversell the program, to offer more than could be delivered, to be willing to guess at systematic behavioral facts in order to construct the framework of a theory. Partly as a reaction to this, subsequent workers have tended to have more modest goals, to build miniature models, or to delve in detail into circumscribed aspects of the larger problem. When and where behavior theory on the grand scale will again be promoted cannot be predicted. Hull, for one, was confident that it could be achieved, that it would be achieved, and that his work would provide a useful stepping stone to the goal. His last book concludes with this hope:

And finally, the crowning achievement of all will be the creation of a really quantitative system of social behavior. . . . It seems incredible that nature would create one set of primary sensory-motor laws for the mediation of individual behavior and another set for the mediation of group behavior. Presumably, then, the laws which are derived for social behavior will be based for the most part on the same postulates as those which form the basis of individual behavior. If this turns out to be true, we are even now an appreciable distance on our way toward the ultimate goal of integrating the individual-social sciences with the group-social sciences. (1952a, pp. 355–356)

FRANK A. LOGAN

[See also the biographies of THORNDIKE and TOLMAN.]

WORKS BY HULL

1928 *Aptitude Testing.* New York: World.

1933 *Hypnosis and Suggestibility: An Experimental Approach.* New York: Appleton.

1940 *Mathematico–Deductive Theory of Rote Learning: A Study in Scientific Methodology,* by Clark L. Hull et al. New Haven: Yale Univ. Press; Oxford Univ. Press.

1943 *Principles of Behavior: An Introduction to Behavior Theory.* New York: Appleton.

1952a *A Behavior System: An Introduction to Behavior Theory Concerning the Individual Organism.* New Haven: Yale Univ. Press.

1952b Autobiography. Volume 4, pages 143–162 in *A History of Psychology in Autobiography.* Worcester, Mass.: Clark Univ. Press.

1962 Psychology of the Scientist: 4. Passages From the "Idea Books" of Clark L. Hull. *Perceptual and Motor Skills* 15:807–882. → Published posthumously.

SUPPLEMENTARY BIBLIOGRAPHY

BEACH, FRANK A. 1959 Clark Leonard Hull: May 24, 1884–May 10, 1952. Volume 33, pages 124–146 in National Academy of Sciences, *Biographical Memoirs.* Washington: Government Printing Office.

DOLLARD, JOHN; and MILLER, NEAL E. 1950 *Personality and Psychotherapy: An Analysis in Terms of Learning, Thinking and Culture.* New York: McGraw-Hill.

HILGARD, ERNEST R. (1948) 1956 *Theories of Learning.* 2d ed. New York: Appleton.

HOVLAND, CARL I. 1952 Clark Leonard Hull: 1884–1952. *Psychological Review* 59:347–350.

KOCH, SIGMUND 1954 Clark L. Hull. Pages 1–176 in *Modern Learning Theory: A Critical Analysis of Five Examples,* by William K. Estes et al. New York: Appleton.

LOGAN, FRANK 1959 The Hull–Spence Approach. Volume 2, pages 293–358 in Sigmund Koch (editor), *Psychology: A Study of a Science.* New York: McGraw-Hill.

SPENCE, KENNETH W. 1951 Theoretical Interpretations of Learning. Pages 690–729 in Stanley S. Stevens (editor), *Handbook of Experimental Psychology.* New York: Wiley.

SPENCE, KENNETH W. 1960 *Behavior Theory and Learning: Selected Papers.* Englewood Cliffs, N.J.: Prentice-Hall.

HUMAN CAPITAL
See CAPITAL, HUMAN.

HUMAN ECOLOGY
See under ECOLOGY.

HUMAN FACTORS ENGINEERING
See ENGINEERING PSYCHOLOGY.

HUMAN GEOGRAPHY

See GEOGRAPHY, *article on* SOCIAL GEOGRAPHY.

HUMAN RELATIONS IN INDUSTRY

See under INDUSTRIAL RELATIONS; *see also the biography of* MAYO.

HUMAN RIGHTS

The subject of this article is the international concern with human rights. The article cannot, however, concentrate exclusively on the activities of international organizations and on conferences which purport to promote respect for human rights. The instruments, institutions, and operations of the international organizations of our day have roots in the philosophical, constitutional, and legal developments of many nations spread over many centuries. The work on the international plane has in its turn had considerable influence on constitutional, legal, and political developments within nation-states, not least on the written law of many of the states of Asia, Africa, and the Caribbean which have recently acceded to independence.

Origins and basic concepts

The expression "human rights," as a term of art, is of recent origin. Even in its French-inspired form "rights of man" (*droits de l'homme*), it goes back only to the last decades of the eighteenth century. The idea, however, of the law, or the lawgiver, defining and protecting the legal rights of men—mainly the mutual rights of the members of the community—is very old indeed. It would, perhaps, be somewhat farfetched to look for elements of the protection of human rights in the Code of the Babylonian king Hammurabi (about 2130 to 2088 B.C.), the most ancient code of law at present known. The sanctions which it provides in trying to protect worthy human-rights objectives (such as the administration of justice, marriage, and the family) are so disproportionately cruel that it is preferable to disregard this legislator in our context. However, as Rudolph von Jhering pointed out a century ago, the law of ancient republican Rome guaranteed to the Roman citizen (not to the foreigner or to the slave) the right to take part in the government of his country by participating in the exercise of the power of legislation, in the administration of criminal justice, in electing public officials, and even in having a share in the police power (Jhering 1852–1878).

An eminent American scholar has said (Yntema 1958) that the concepts of the Roman civil law, which were formulated by the Roman juridical genius in order to render justice in the mutual relations of individual men, are in essence a practical definition of the rights of man and a reasonable and authoritative criterion to which those who seek justice and protection of the inherent dignity of the human person can appeal. This holds true, in Yntema's view, of the Roman law as it was applied on the continent of Europe and of the common law of the Anglo-Saxon countries. The common law and the civil law, so different in their institutions and techniques and, at the same time, so similar in their criteria of what is fair, offer an objective yardstick for judging conduct in terms of individual rights and freedoms. These systems have, of course, also tolerated institutions and practices which are inconsistent with the modern conception of a public order protecting human dignity. Nevertheless, through many centuries communities have existed where at least part of what are now considered to be fundamental human rights were well protected by elaborate and refined bodies of law.

In England of the seventeenth century battles were fought against the nonobservance of the ancient rights of Englishmen. Out of these struggles there came two great documents: the Petition of Right of 1628 and the Bill of Rights of 1689. These did not purport to define the basic human rights of all mankind. They were intended to give relief for specific grievances by limiting the power of the king and by strengthening the power of Parliament and of the courts. Their ideas and even their texts are, however, reflected in the work of the American and French revolutionaries of the eighteenth century: in the immortal passages of the American Declaration of Independence, in the Virginia bill of rights of 1776, in the French Declaration of the Rights of Man and of the Citizen, and in the American bill of rights.

In the course of the nineteenth and twentieth centuries, the example set by the United States and France of adopting bills of rights or otherwise embodying such rights in their constitutions, was followed on the entire continent of Europe, and the movement spread to the Americas, Asia, and Africa, but until very recently Britain and the British dominions and possessions remained aloof from this movement.

The Russian Revolution of 1917, while following the American–French precedent in the form of its pronouncements, gave it a fundamentally different substance. The difference lies not in the emphasis on economic and social rights in addition to the traditional political and civil rights. Such provisions are also found in other constitutions, for example, in the Mexican constitution of 1917, in the Weimar constitution of Germany of 1919, and in the constitution of the Republic of Spain of 1931. The difference between the Soviet pronouncements and their Western predecessors lies in the complete transformation of the meaning of political and civil rights.

This basic difference in concepts becomes clear when one compares the provisions of the American bill of rights with the corresponding provisions of the first Soviet constitution. The first amendment to the American constitution provides, among other things, that Congress shall make no law abridging the freedom of speech or of the press; the Russian constitution of 1918 "for the purpose of securing freedom of expression to the toiling masses," abolishes all dependence of the press upon capital, and turns over to the working people and the poorest peasantry "all technical and material means for the publication of newspapers, pamphlets, books," etc. The American constitution prohibits abridgment of the right of the people peaceably to assemble, while the Lenin constitution, in order to ensure complete freedom of assembly to the working class and to the poorest peasantry, offers "all premises convenient for public gatherings together with lighting, heating, and furniture."

The Soviet constitution of 1936, while changing the wording, has, by and large, maintained this general approach. The Western constitutional ideas were designed to prevent interference with fundamental rights mainly, though not exclusively, by the public authorities. The Soviet concept does not treat of this aspect at all. It promises to make available technical facilities; it does not promise freedom in the choice of the purposes for which they will be used. In trying to draw conclusions from the existence in so many legal systems of catalogues of rights, one must keep in mind these differences in the basic concepts.

Human rights and international law

Attempts to seek a foundation for the rights of the individual in the law of nations go back to an early stage in the history of international law. The work of the Spanish theologian–lawyer Francisco de Vitoria—born 1480, died 1546—is perhaps the first attempt to use legal reasoning, moral principle, and political courage in support of a cause which we might consider as involving human rights as well as international law. He lectured about "the Indians recently discovered" and pleaded for their rights vis-à-vis the Spanish conquerors. The greatest figures in the literature of international law in the seventeenth and eighteenth centuries exercised a powerful influence on the growth of the concept of the inalienable rights of man. In 1950 Sir Hersch Lauterpacht characterized the close connection between human rights and international law by saying that "the law of nations, in itself conceivable only as being above the legal order of sovereign States, is not only a law governing their mutual relations but is also, upon final analysis, the universal law of humanity in which the individual human being as the ultimate unit of all law rises sovereign over the limited province of the State" (p. 120).

In the field of action, as distinct from scholarship, the international concern with human rights has manifested itself in two different ways: by so-called "humanitarian intervention" and by the adoption of international treaties.

In traditional international law it was assumed that a state had the authority to treat its own nationals as it saw fit. When, however, the ill-treatment by a state of its own population was of such an intensity that it shocked the conscience of mankind, other states, usually the great powers of the period, took it upon themselves to threaten, or even to use, force in order to come to the rescue of the oppressed population. While resort to this type of action was not infrequent, the doctrine underlying it has never become a generally recognized part of international law because of the abuse inherent in the concept of "humanitarian intervention."

The protection of oppressed or endangered groups by international treaty started in the seventeenth and eighteenth centuries in matters of religious liberty. In the course of the nineteenth century the international treaty was used also to protect ethnic and racial groups and to combat the slave trade and slavery; in the twentieth century it has been used to improve labor conditions, to arrange for the supervision of the administration of mandated territories, and to provide under the supervision of the League of Nations for certain rights of racial, religious, or linguistic minorities in a number of states, mainly in central and eastern Europe.

The United Nations and human rights

Not until the world had passed through the tragic events of World War II and had witnessed the barbarous acts committed by the totalitarian regimes of that period was the universal organization of the international community, the United Nations, charged with some responsibilities in the matter of human rights, and its members pledged themselves to take action for the achievement of universal respect for and observance of human rights and fundamental freedoms for all.

The San Francisco Charter of 1945 through which the peoples of the United Nations reaffirmed their faith in "fundamental human rights" did not define these rights. The charter has made it abundantly clear, however, that one particular activity at least is repugnant to it: discrimination on the grounds of race, sex, language, or religion.

Nor has the charter established specific international machinery for the enforcement of its human-rights provisions, except for arrangements under the trusteeship system. But it has created organs of general and wide competence—the General Assembly, the Security Council, and the Economic and Social Council—and it has laid the foundations for the establishment of an unlimited number of subsidiary bodies, including commissions in the field of human rights.

The General Assembly, and to some extent also the Economic and Social Council, have not hesitated to use their general powers of investigation and recommendation to take action of varying character and intensity in such situations as violations of religious or political freedom in eastern Europe, race conflict in South Africa, forced labor in various parts of the world, infringement of trade union freedom, practices violating the human dignity of women in less developed communities, the status of Buddhists in South Vietnam, and many others. The fight against colonialism has been one of the characteristics of the international scene in the post-World War II world. Rightly or wrongly, the majority of governments have, to a large extent, identified the struggle against colonial domination with the struggle for human rights.

International bill of rights. Since the United Nations Charter had not defined human rights and had not created special international institutions for their enforcement, it was widely assumed in 1945 that this would soon be done in an "International bill of rights." In 1947–1948 it was decided that this "bill" would consist of two or more documents: a declaration, a covenant, and "measures of implementation." In 1948 the General Assembly proclaimed in a resolution the first part of this bill of rights as the Universal Declaration of Human Rights. The drafting of the other parts of the bill has not yet been completed; according to later decisions, they are to consist of two covenants, one on civil and political rights, the other on economic, social, and cultural rights, with provision for international supervision of their implementation. (By the end of 1963 all the general and substantive provisions of the two covenants had been approved

on the General Assembly level, while—as of 1965 —the international procedural arrangements have still to be agreed upon.)

The declaration of 1948 is the only world-wide official document where the human rights of which the charter speaks are set forth. Its range is very wide. It proclaims not only the traditional political and civil rights and freedoms of its national predecessors but also "economic, social and cultural rights." The declaration has, to some extent, filled the gap created by the delay in completing the covenants and acquired a status different from and more important than the one which was originally intended for it. It has been used by the United Nations, by other international organizations and conferences, and by governments as a yardstick to measure the compliance by governments with the obligations deriving from the charter in matters of human rights. It has penetrated into international conventions, national constitutions, and legislation, and even, in isolated cases, into court proceedings.

The technique of developing international standards by proclaiming instruments of the declaration type has been frequently used, the most potent post-1948 example being the Declaration on the Granting of Independence to Colonial Countries and Peoples, of 1960. Additional human-rights declarations were also adopted: the Declaration of the Rights of the Child, in 1959, and the United Nations Declaration on the Elimination of All Forms of Racial Discrimination, in 1963. In other fields examples are the declarations on Permanent Sovereignty Over Natural Resources, 1962, and on Legal Principles Governing the Activities of States in the Exploration and Use of Outer Space, 1963. Many more are in various stages of drafting and preparation.

Conventions on specific human-rights subjects. While the work of drafting the comprehensive covenants on human rights has been going on, the United Nations and its specialized agencies have produced a considerable body of treaty law on the subject of human rights by adopting and putting into force conventions on more limited subjects. Important examples are the Freedom of Association and Protection of the Right to Organize Convention, 1948; the Genocide Convention, 1948; the Convention on the Political Rights of Women, 1952; the Conventions on the Status of Refugees, 1951, and of Stateless Persons, 1954; the Conventions on the Reduction of Statelessness, 1961, and on the Nationality of Married Women, 1957; the Supplementary Convention on the Abolition of Slavery, 1956, and the Convention on the Abolition of Forced Labor, 1957; the Discrimination (Employment and Occupation) Convention, 1958, and the Convention against Discrimination in Education, 1960; the Convention on Consent to Marriage, Minimum Age for Marriage and Registration of Marriages, 1962; and the International Convention on the Elimination of All Forms of Racial Discrimination, 1965.

Regional arrangements.   In the years during which the United Nations has been slowly working its way toward the completion of the world-wide covenants, much more rapid progress was achieved in western Europe. Under the auspices of the Council of Europe, the European Convention of Human Rights of 1950 came into being, supplemented by protocols of 1952 and 1963 and by the European Social Charter of 1961. By the convention, the 15 European states which are parties to it have undertaken to secure to everyone within their jurisdiction the rights which it defines—most of the traditional political and civil rights. The convention established two new organs to ensure the observance of the engagements undertaken by the parties: the European Commission on Human Rights and the European Court of Human Rights.

The existence of the court is significant primarily as a symbol. Its jurisdiction is very narrowly circumscribed. It was established in 1959, and by the beginning of 1965 only two cases had gone before it. The commission, however, has played an important and effective part. Ten of the European states (not including the United Kingdom and France, the latter not being a party to the convention at all) have accepted the right of individuals to petition the commission and to claim to be the victims of a violation of the convention by one of the parties. It has been the commission's examination of petitions, and especially the examination of their admissibility, which offered the commission the opportunity to build up an impressive body of case law. And although in the overwhelming majority of cases the commission has had to reject the petition, its work has transformed the abstract idea of the international protection of human rights into a concrete, tangible, day-to-day task. This operation has laid bare the formidable problems and pitfalls inherent in so novel an experiment.

For many years, the Organization of American States has tried to establish inter-American institutions for the promotion of respect for human rights. In 1948 the "American Declaration of the Rights and Duties of Man" was proclaimed at Bogotá; conventions on political and civil rights of women and on territorial and diplomatic asylum were signed in 1948 and 1954 respectively. An Inter-American Convention on Human Rights providing for the establishment of a commission and a court of human rights, on the European model, was drafted by the Inter-American Council of Jurists in 1959. At the beginning of 1965 final action on the draft had not yet been taken by the political organs.

Program of practical action.   The effectiveness and desirability of the international treaty as an instrument for the promotion of human rights was challenged early in the history of the United Nations. The most weighty challenge came in 1953 when U.S. Secretary of State John Foster Dulles stated that the new Eisenhower administration did not believe in "treaty coercion" and did not favor "formal undertakings" as the proper and most effective way to achieve throughout the world the goals of human liberty. As a consequence the United States declared its intention not to become a party to any covenant on human rights or to sign human-rights conventions of a more limited scope. As we have seen, the majority of governments has continued to hold that multilateral conventions have their place among the endeavors to give effect to the human-rights provisions of the charter. Those governments consented, however, to a new program proposed by the United States, provided it was adopted in addition to treaties and not instead of them.

Thus, in 1955–1956 the United Nations started a series of new activities: (1) periodic (triennial) reporting by states on developments; (2) studies of specific rights or groups of rights; and (3) advisory services in the field of human rights. A great number of governments have participated in the reporting procedure in the first three triennial cycles; the Commission on Human Rights has, however, not yet arrived at a final policy about the use to be made of the reports. The first of the studies was a world-wide inquiry and investigation into the status of the right to be free from arbitrary arrest, detention, and exile. The most fruitful branch of the program of advisory services has been the convening of mostly regional conferences (called seminars) to exchange views and experiences on important and topical problems, such as the protection of human rights in criminal law and procedure, the role of the police in the protection of human rights, or the status of women in family law. It was a series of seminars on judicial and other remedies against the illegal exercise or abuse of administrative authority which made the institution of the "ombudsman" known outside the Scandinavian countries and led to its acceptance in at least two other countries (England and New Zealand) and to its consideration elsewhere (Canada and some United States jurisdictions). One such regional conference, held in Kabul, Afghanistan, in 1964, was devoted to "human rights in developing countries," a basic problem which deserves more detailed discussion (Seminar . . . 1964).

Human rights in developing countries

Observance of human rights poses problems everywhere, and no country's record, be it highly industrialized or economically underdeveloped, is faultless. In most of the countries which have acceded to independence only recently the problems are aggravated. Many of these countries have implacable enemies: poverty, ignorance, disease, and inertia. Western commentators have tended to underestimate the importance of illiteracy and ignorance, particularly in unsophisticated rural societies (De Smith 1964, p. 237). At the Kabul conference it was agreed that there could be no meaningful exercise of many human rights in a country where economic resources were scarce and the bulk of the population lived on the margin of subsistence. It was argued that in such matters as the development of the whole economy and the improvement of health, education, and housing, the state needed the necessary powers to implement its plans even though, meanwhile, the rights of individuals or groups might be temporarily curtailed. Some speakers wondered, however, whether the governments of some developing countries did not show an excessive concern for the internal and external security of the state and apply unnecessary restrictions on human rights.

Developing countries experience difficulties not only in regard to economic and social rights, the enjoyment of which clearly presupposes a certain economic standard, but also in regard to the "classical" civil and political rights. A basic prerequisite of the right to a fair trial is the existence of an adequate number of well-trained lawyers, and "crash programs" for their training were recommended at the Kabul conference. The scarcity of competent and efficient public officials is also an obstacle to progress in the human-rights field. Another specific problem of the underdeveloped world arises in the very sensitive area of "labor mobilization." In some countries, it was alleged at the conference, it is not yet possible to rely exclusively upon systems of voluntary labor to satisfy the basic needs of the nation. Recourse has sometimes to be had to certain forms of labor mobilization involving the compulsory removal of people to areas other than those of their residences. It was claimed, however, that such national labor services should be distinguished from the practices of forced labor which were forbidden by international conventions (see also Cowen 1964).

Neither the human-rights provisions of the United Nations Charter and the Universal Declaration of Human Rights nor the other treaties and declarations mentioned above have brought about the millennium. It is therefore not the purpose of this article to convey the idea that the rights set forth in these instruments are, in fact, respected and observed throughout the world. In 1952, in 1957, and, again, in 1962 the General Assembly of the United Nations reiterated that notwithstanding the obligations arising from the charter and notwithstanding the Universal Declaration of Human Rights, violations of human rights continue to occur in various parts of the world, and that notwithstanding some progress the situation in many parts of the world was unsatisfactory.

The task of making the protection of human rights general, permanent, and effective still lies ahead. This should not lead us, however, to belittle the progress that has been achieved on the international and national levels since World War II. Whatever the technical position might be in particular instances, and however difficult it might often be to achieve redress through international or national remedies, the traditional concept, that the way a state treats those subject to its power and jurisdiction is within its unfettered discretion, is a thing of the past. A vast but asymmetrical structure of international obligations has been built, some vague, some precise; and injunctions and exhortations have been issued, some authoritative, others less so. The fate of the individual may still in fact be at the mercy of his state, but it is also a matter of continuing and increasing international concern.

EGON SCHWELB

[See also INTERNATIONAL CRIMES. Other relevant material may be found in CONSTITUTIONAL LAW, articles on CIVIL LIBERTIES and CIVIL RIGHTS; INTERNATIONAL LAW; INTERNATIONAL ORGANIZATION.]

BIBLIOGRAPHY

BOUTMY, ÉMILE (1902) 1907 La déclaration des droits de l'homme et du citoyen et M. Jellinek. Pages 119–182 in Émile Boutmy, Études politiques. Paris: Colin. → First published in Volume 17 of the Annales des sciences politiques.

CASSIN, RENÉ 1952 La déclaration universelle et la mise en oeuvre des droits de l'homme. The Hague, Academy of International Law, Recueil des cours, 1951 79:237–367.

COWEN, DENIS V. 1964 Human Rights in Contemporary Africa. Natural Law Forum 9:1–24.

DE SMITH, STANLEY A. 1964 *The New Commonwealth and Its Constitutions*. London: Stevens.

FRIEDRICH, CARL J. 1963 Rights, Liberties, Freedoms: A Reappraisal. *American Political Science Review* 57: 841–854.

GANJI, MANOUCHEHR 1962 *International Protection of Human Rights*. Geneva: Droz.

GOLSONG, HERIBERT 1958 *Das Rechtsschutzsystem der europäischen Menschenrechtskonvention*. Karlsruhe (Germany): Müller.

GURADZE, HEINZ 1956 *Der Stand der Menschenrechte im Völkerrecht*. Göttingen (Germany): Schwartz.

HAMBURGER, ERNEST 1960 Droits de l'homme et relations internationales. The Hague, Academy of International Law, *Recueil des cours, 1959*. 97:293–429.

HOLCOMBE, ARTHUR N. 1948 *Human Rights in the Modern World*. New York Univ. Press; Oxford Univ. Press.

JELLINEK, GEORG (1898) 1901 *The Declaration of the Rights of Man and of Citizens: A Contribution to Modern Constitutional History*. New York: Holt. → First published in German. A third German edition was published in 1919 by Duncker and Humblot.

JHERING, RUDOLPH VON (1852–1878) 1906–1923 *Geist des römischen Rechts auf den verschiedenen Stufen seiner Entwicklung*. 6th ed., 3 vols. Leipzig: Breitkopf & Härtel.

LAUTERPACHT, HERSCH 1945 *An International Bill of the Rights of Man*. New York: Columbia Univ. Press.

LAUTERPACHT, HERSCH 1950 *International Law and Human Rights*. New York: Praeger.

LIN, MOU-SHÊNG 1963 The Human Rights Program. *Annual Review of United Nations Affairs* [1961/1962]: 102–136.

McDOUGAL, MYRES S.; and BEBR, GERHARD 1964 Human Rights in the United Nations. *American Journal of International Law* 58:603–641.

ROBERTSON, ARTHUR H. 1963 *Human Rights in Europe*. Dobbs Ferry, N.Y.: Oceana; Manchester (England) Univ. Press.

SCHWELB, EGON 1960 International Conventions on Human Rights. *International and Comparative Law Quarterly* 9:654–675.

SCHWELB, EGON 1964 *Human Rights and the International Community: The Roots and Growth of the Universal Declaration of Human Rights, 1948–1963*. Chicago: Quadrangle Books.

SEMINAR ON HUMAN RIGHTS IN DEVELOPING COUNTRIES, KABUL 1964 *Seminar on Human Rights in Developing Countries, Kabul, Afghanistan*. New York: United Nations. → Organized by the United Nations in cooperation with the government of Afghanistan.

UNITED NATIONS, GENERAL ASSEMBLY *Official Records*. → Published since 1946. Contains resolutions adopted by the General Assembly, first to twentieth sessions.

U.S. CONGRESS, SENATE, COMMITTEE ON FOREIGN RELATIONS 1955 *Review of the United Nations Charter: A Collection of Documents*. 83rd Congress, 2d Session. Senate Document No. 87. Washington: Government Printing Office. → See especially pages 263 and 295.

VASAK, KAREL 1964 *La convention européenne des droits de l'homme*. Paris: Librairie Générale de Droit et de Jurisprudence.

Yearbook on Human Rights. → Published by the United Nations since 1946.

Yearbook of the European Convention on Human Rights— The European Commission and European Court of Human Rights. → Published since 1955. From 1955– 1957 published as *Documents and Decisions of the European Commission of Human Rights*, prepared by the Directorate of Human Rights of the Council of Europe.

YNTEMA, HESSEL E. 1958 Le droit comparé et l'humanisme. *Revue internationale de droit comparé* 10:693– 700.

HUMBOLDT, ALEXANDER VON

Alexander von Humboldt (1769–1859), the most famous German of his time, was celebrated as a geographer, explorer, and naturalist; he was less well known for his valuable contributions to the development of the social sciences. He came from a Pomeranian family that had been lately ennobled. After the early death of his father, a major in the Prussian Army, his bourgeois mother ceased to keep up the family's connections with the court; instead, she employed excellent private tutors to set her two sons on the road traveled by the bourgeois elite—the sciences. Humboldt studied at Frankfurt on the Oder, Göttingen, Hamburg, and Freiberg (in Saxony). C. W. Dohm, Karl Ludwig Willdenow, and Georg Forster, his principal teachers, awakened his interest in political and botanical geography and in exploration. In his youth he also associated with Goethe, Schiller, and many other writers.

With this background he was exceedingly well prepared for his first voyage of exploration, which took place between 1799 and 1804. He was accompanied on this voyage by Aimé Bonpland, the French physician and botanist. Humboldt explored the territories of what are now Venezuela, Cuba, Colombia, Ecuador, Peru, and Mexico, sailed up the Casiquiare and determined its longitude and latitude, climbed Mount Chimborazo to the height of 17,900 feet, and suggested various improvements in mining technology and other aspects of the economy to the Spanish colonial authorities.

After a visit to the United States, where he met not only various scientists in Philadelphia but also President Thomas Jefferson, he returned to Europe. He then settled in Paris, where he proceeded to evaluate the results of his expedition and to prepare for a new project of exploration in Asia. This latter expedition did not take place until 1829, after he had spent two years in Berlin.

The preparation, execution, and evaluation of Humboldt's expeditions were exemplary and won him world fame. The 23 volumes of his travel descriptions (1805–1834) are the most comprehensive ever published by a private individual. He collaborated with German, French, and British scholars to produce the last major achievement of the republic of letters of the eighteenth century and so combined in characteristic fashion the *idée encyclopédique* with his belief in the division of labor among specialists.

Humboldt early rejected the purely utilitarian point of view in science, stressing instead the value of research for the sake of knowledge. This permitted him to give unbiased consideration to social scientific problems. In the field of anthropology, for example, he was able to appreciate without prejudice the culture of the Indian tribes of South America, since he did not believe in higher or lower races but rather in the unity of mankind and its destiny of liberty. In his celebrated *Political Essay on the Kingdom of New Spain* (1811–1812), he laid the foundations of modern regional geography on the basis of physical geography, using Mexico as his example. His portrait of colonial rule is based on statistical evidence, for Humboldt managed to gain access to the jealously guarded Spanish colonial archives. Both for the social sciences and for geography this early description of Mexico is still a useful source book.

Humboldt convincingly refuted Friedrich List's theory of economic stages. Whereas List conceived of the transition from hunters and gatherers to shepherds and peasants in terms of the development of material capital under Old World conditions, Humboldt demonstrated that in America agriculture must have evolved from gathering, without the intermediate stage of pastoral life, since no large domesticable animals had existed in the New World.

Political scientists should appreciate that Humboldt was one of the first Europeans to predict a great future for the United States. Publication of his travels also gave intellectual aid and moral support to the South American wars of independence.

Humboldt's efforts in the field of demography are of enduring value. He introduced the examination of the quotient of extremes into population statistics, thus making it possible to supplement the abstract figure of population density by citing the low quotient in countries uniformly densely (or sparsely) settled and the high quotient in countries unevenly settled. He also made allowance for population dynamics, furnishing birth and mortality rates for Mexico. These figures were long unavailable for such regions.

Humboldt's old age was devoted to completion of his *Cosmos: A Sketch of a Physical Description of the Universe* (1845–1858), in which he expanded his geographical thinking into a more general "description of the world in physical terms." His great prestige in Germany did much to shift attention from predominantly philological studies to the natural sciences.

HANNO BECK

[*See also* GEOGRAPHY *and* POPULATION, *article on* THE FIELD OF DEMOGRAPHY.]

WORKS BY HUMBOLDT

1805–1834   *Voyage de Humboldt et Bonpland.* 23 vols. Paris: Schoell. → Often cited by the title of Part 1: *Voyage aux régions équinoxiales du nouveau continent.* Complete sets are rare and vary in arrangement and collation.

(1811–1812) 1811–1822   *Political Essay on the Kingdom of New Spain.* 4 vols. London: Longmans. → First published in French.

1843   *Asie centrale: Recherches sur les chaînes de montagnes et la climatologie comparée.* 3 vols. Paris: Gide.

(1845–1858) 1850–1859   *Cosmos: A Sketch of a Physical Description of the Universe.* 5 vols. New York: Harper. → First published in German.

1959   *Gespräche.* Edited by Hanno Beck. Berlin: Akademie-Verlag.

SUPPLEMENTARY BIBLIOGRAPHY

AKADEMIE DER WISSENSCHAFTEN, BERLIN   1959   *Alexander von Humboldt, 14.9.1769–6.5.1859: Gedenkschrift zur 100. Wiederkehr seines Todestages.* Berlin: Akademie-Verlag.

BECK, HANNO   1959–1961   *Alexander von Humboldt.* 2 vols. Wiesbaden (Germany): Steiner. → Volume 1: *Von der Bildungsreise zur Forschungsreise: 1769–1804.* Volume 2: *Vom Reisewerk zum "Kosmos": 1804–1859.*

BRUHNS, KARL   1872   *Alexander von Humboldt: Eine wissenschaftliche Biographie.* 3 vols. Leipzig (Germany): Brockhaus.

HUME, DAVID

David Hume was one of the most distinguished writers of the eighteenth century. Although he was only partly appreciated in his own period, with the passage of time his stature has grown, and his writings have attracted increasing attention from students in many disciplines.

Born in Scotland in 1711, Hume died in 1776, the year of the publication of Adam Smith's *Wealth of Nations.* His major work, *A Treatise of Human Nature* (1739–1740), lies in the field of philosophy. But the range of Hume's writings is vast. In a large number of essays (which in 1758 were incorporated into a volume entitled *Essays Moral, Political and Literary*) Hume dealt with the fields of economics, politics, and aesthetics, as well as with much that would now be regarded as sociological material. Hume was also a historian. His interest in history is reflected in many of his writings, and in the later years of his life he published (1754–1762), in serial volumes, a *History of England* that was a pioneering work in the area.

Owing to the subsequent compartmentalization of the fields that Hume explored, students of his thought have tended to treat his work in a compartmentalized fashion. This is difficult to avoid, since Hume dealt with a large variety of problems, and their analysis often requires specialized training. An unfortunate consequence of this, however, has been the tendency to overlook the important unifying elements in Hume's thought. Philosophers have argued that in turning to the essays, Hume was abandoning philosophy—allegedly because of the poor reception accorded his *Treatise*, and because of his passion for literary fame. Economists, on the other hand, have generally treated Hume's economic essays (which first appeared in 1752 under the title *Political Discourses*) as a substantially self-contained segment of his thought, bearing little or no relation to his philosophy.

Hume, however, made it clear that he intended his philosophy to serve as the "capital or center" of all the "moral" (i.e., psychological and social) sciences, or as the center of a general science of human experience ([1739–1740] 1958, p. xix). And as is evident from the prefatory "Advertisement" to the *Treatise*, he hoped, if the *Treatise* met with success, to incorporate a study of the various "moral sciences" into a subsequent edition of this work. Many of Hume's essays thus display relations to the substance of the *Treatise;* and this is clearly the case in his treatment of economics. Hume was pre-eminently, and notably more so than his close friend Adam Smith, the philosopher–economist of the eighteenth century.

A brief sketch of Hume's general system of thought will help clarify the relation between his philosophy and his economic thought. The "capital or center" of Hume's system consists of the "principles of human nature," those qualities and relations pertaining to the human understanding and human passions that Hume believed to be irreducible and common to all mankind. Discussed in Books I and II of the *Treatise*, these principles constitute the analytical phase of Hume's thought. The second and synthetic phase of Hume's thought consists of laws of human behavior in which Hume sought to show that various aspects of man's behavior are products of environmental forces operating on "human nature." The framing of these general uniformities is Hume's concern in his study of the various "moral sciences." An emphasis on psychology is thus a major distinctive characteristic of Hume's treatment of these sciences.

Hume's interest in history is likewise of major importance in his thought. This interest emerged early in Hume's life and was integral to his approach to experience. As a philosophical empiricist, Hume repeatedly stressed the importance of the study of history for achieving understanding of human experience, pointing out that history constitutes the exclusive source of our "experiments" concerning human nature and human behavior (*ibid.*, p. xxiii). Moreover, as both "moral scientist" and historian, Hume, by employing his principles of human nature, sought to frame historical laws of behavior, or laws that may explain basic transformations in human behavior. This approach he termed "natural history" (the word "natural" here denoting the "usual" or "probable"). Representing an attempt at "scientific history," this differs from conventional historiography, with its stress on unique particulars, which predominates in Hume's own *History of England*. Historical generalizations, reflecting the "natural history" approach, interlace much of Hume's work. And within the context of his economic writings the method of "natural history" is of central importance. Its role becomes fully apparent when Hume's economic thought is considered at three different levels of analysis: his economic psychology, political economy, and economic philosophy.

Before turning to this, however, it is well to consider one other aspect of Hume's thought: his treatment of the methodology of science, which, as one of the most important of Hume's contributions, is likewise relevant to his economic thought. Hume considered this question in Book I of the *Treatise*, where he was concerned with the basis of our "beliefs" concerning empirical events. His position represents an attack on the rationalist acceptance of a "necessary connection" between such events. As Hume argued, all beliefs concerning matters of fact are reducible to associations of ideas that are separable from each other. All causal relations take this form. We thus can "conceive any object to be non-existent this moment, and existent the next, without conjoining to it the distinct idea of a cause or productive principle." What is conceivable, moreover, is possible. And the demonstrability of a "necessary connection" requires that the opposite be shown to be impossible. Hence, "necessary connection" between matters of fact (unlike the logical relations between propositions, where validity depends wholly on the principle of noncontradiction) cannot be demonstrated (*ibid.*, pp. 79–80).

On what, then, are our beliefs in matters of fact based? All that Hume could find here was a psychological process. More specifically, we come to "believe," say, that a causal relation exists between two events because, as a result of our repeated observation of their contiguity and reoccurrence (their "constant conjunction"), the mind—simply through a nonrational associative mechanism—so firmly links the two that the occurrence of one leads us to expect its usual attendant (*ibid.,* p. 96). For Hume, "belief" is, in a word, a "habit." The implication of this for "science" is clear: since we have no a priori justification for beliefs in empirical events, the only way we can enlarge our understanding of experience is through further investigation with a view to establishing additional "constant conjunctions." It must be recognized, however, that the notion of the uniformity of nature itself, or the view that the future will resemble the past, is based on faith.

Hume's observations on the prospects for discovering uniformities in the "moral sciences" are also noteworthy. Although he believed that history had already provided an adequate basis for framing "principles of human nature" ([1739–1779] vol. 4, p. 69 in 1898 edition), he was acutely aware of the wide historical variability of human behavior and the difficulty, especially in view of the range and complexity of human passions, of specifying how man would respond to changing circumstance (*ibid.,* vol. 3, p. 163; [1739–1740] 1958, p. 131). With considerable caution, he sought to discriminate between different areas of human behavior in terms of their tractability to scientific treatment. It is very difficult, he pointed out, to discover uniformities in aspects of behavior which are peculiar to small numbers of individuals, since in such cases the passions involved are delicate and subtle and are often affected by imperceptible influences ([1739–1779] vol. 3, p. 175 in 1898 edition). It is difficult, also, to establish reliable generalizations in the field of "politics" (*ibid.,* vol. 3, pp. 156–157). Since mass behavior, on the other hand, is frequently governed by passions that are "gross" and "stubborn," reliable uniformities may be found here. Its dependence upon such "gross" passions as avarice, for example, would make it easier to account for the "rise and progress of commerce" than for the growth of "learning" (*ibid.,* vol. 3, p. 176). Significantly, it is with a justification of the use of generalization in economics (which he contrasted with the chance-ridden field of foreign diplomacy) that Hume introduced his economic essays ([1752–1758] 1955, pp. 3–4).

With a view to the central role of psychology and history, let us turn now to the substance of Hume's economic thought and consider first his economic psychology, which links his economic thought to the "capital or center" of all the "moral sciences,"

as developed in the *Treatise.* Here the analysis takes the form of a natural history of the "rise and progress of commerce" in which Hume sought to explain the economic growth of his own general period in terms of the impact of changing historical circumstance on human passions. In the economic essays these passions are regarded as "causes of labour." Because the analysis stems directly from Hume's general treatment of human nature, it is notably multidimensional and is considerably more complex than the economic psychology typical of Hume's own period. Beyond considering the importance of the desire for consumption pleasures as an incentive to economic activity, Hume called attention to the role played by the desire for "action" as well as a desire for "liveliness" (a state of lively passion that is common to the experience both of consumption pleasures and interesting activity). In turn, the desire for "gain," joined to the desire for action, is treated in large part as a desire for the trophies of success in the "economic game." All these motives are integral to the "rise and progress of commerce," the initial stimulus to which is found in the opening of foreign trade and whose self-perpetuating character is traced to the growth of new habits of industry (*ibid.,* chapter 2; Rotwein 1955).

Political economy, the second level of Hume's economic thought, comprises the main portion of his economic essays. Here, where Hume was concerned with specific aspects of market relations, he dealt with several of the principal controversial questions of his period: monetary theory, interest theory, the issue of free trade, the shifting and incidence of taxes, and fiscal policy. At this level the role of the natural history of the "rise and progress of commerce" is seen in Hume's critical evaluation of the doctrines of his period; for his analysis is predominantly concerned with one question: Are prevailing beliefs regarding market relations acceptable when considered in the light of economic growth and the psychological and other factors involved in the growth process?

A brief summary of several of the major aspects of Hume's political economy will serve to make clear the general importance of this perspective. One of the most frequently emphasized of Hume's contributions to later classical doctrine is his analysis of the quantity theory–specie flow mechanism. Here Hume sought to show that there is no ground for the mercantilist fear that without trade restrictions a nation will lose its money supply. The quantity theory–specie flow doctrine is thus introduced to show that it is ultimately a nation's level of economic development that determines the quantity of money it can attract and retain. "I should as soon dread, that all our springs and rivers should be exhausted, as that money should abandon a kingdom where there are people and industry" ([1752*b*] 1955, p. 61). Hume's interest theory—in its emphasis on the importance of real capital (as against the mercantilist stress on the quantity of money)—also anticipated the classical position. But, more fundamentally, Hume was concerned to show that the availability of real capital is itself determined by the impact of the growth of industry on economic motivation. And here he made use of all the "causes of labour" introduced in his economic psychology. In an industrially advancing economy, he argued, there is increasing opportunity for "action" in the form of "lucrative employment." This induces frugality both by providing an alternative to pleasure seeking (the preoccupation of the idle landowner in an agrarian economy) as a mode of gratifying the desire for liveliness, and by intensifying the desire for gain, or the desire to accumulate the tokens of economic success. As the income of the industrious class grows, along with its contribution to output, there is thus a substantial increase in the supply of real savings, and the interest rate inevitably falls ([1752–1758] 1955, pp. 53–54).

In his treatment of the issue of trade restrictions, Hume recognized that free trade increases real income (at any given level of economic development) by bringing about a more efficient allocation of resources (*ibid.,* pp. 66, 75, 79)—the argument Adam Smith was later to elaborate more fully and systematically. Growth considerations, however, occupy the center of Hume's analysis: meeting the mercantilist argument for trade restrictions on its own ground, he sought to show that, far from inhibiting the economic growth of other countries, one nation's economic growth commonly contributes to the development of its neighbors. An expansion of industry abroad, he emphasized, yields new technology that the home country can emulate, and since such an expansion increases foreign income, it also increases the foreign demand for home exports. In his detailed treatment of the growth of foreign industry that competes directly with domestic output, Hume stressed the stimulating effects of foreign competition on the spirit of industry at home: he argued, for example, that such competitive pressure encourages a nation to divert unemployed resources to new uses and, further, that the resulting diversification will minimize the impact on employment of any subsequent fluctuations of demand in particular markets (*ibid.,* pp. 78–81).

In some respects Hume's doctrine is a complex of classical elements and elements exhibiting an affinity to the mercantilist position (with inconsistencies between the two remaining unresolved). But this complex can itself be traced mainly to Hume's interest in stressing the importance of developmental considerations. For example, Hume generally employed the quantity theory of money to show that it is economic growth rather than the quantity of money that is of basic significance to a nation. But with a view to growth considerations he was also led to argue that gradual changes in the money supply (as against large absolute quantities of money as such) are desirable. By repeatedly stimulating employment in the short run, such changes, he contended, will in the long run enhance the spirit of industry itself (*ibid.,* pp. 37–40). Similarly, although on quantity theory grounds Hume argued that money has no effect on interest rates, he also acknowledged that if it affects economic growth, a long-run increase in the money supply will lower interest rates (*ibid.,* p. 59).

Hume's economic philosophy—the third level of his economic thought—is contained in his essay "Of Refinement in the Arts." Here, Hume presented a moral justification for a commercial and industrial society and, as a basis for judgment, invoked the utilitarian ethic, which he had earlier elaborated and extensively defended in Book III of the *Treatise* and in his *Inquiry Concerning the Principles of Morals* (1751). On this level of Hume's economic thought the perspective of "natural history" played an especially important role. In this context, where Hume considered the relation between economic growth and the happiness of the individual, the "causes of labour" (the desires for "pleasure," "action," and "liveliness") are treated as "ends" whose attainment is furthered by the development of industry ([1752–1758] 1955, pp. 21–22). His analysis here, both in its detail and in its adoption of a pluralistic position on human happiness, bears a direct relation to his earlier series of essays on the "good life" entitled "The Epicurean," "The Stoic," "The Platonist," and "The Sceptic." Among all ends, Hume placed the greatest emphasis on "action" (the response to challenge); and a reading of "The Stoic" makes clear that, when treating this end most broadly, Hume had in mind the value that is now generally stressed in justifying a free society—the striving for self-fulfillment (Rotwein 1955, pp. xcv–xcix).

Hume also considered the influence of economic development on the intellectual, cultural, moral, and political life of society; with regard to politics, he argued (in a passage Adam Smith was later to cite for its central importance and originality) that the growth of political liberty itself is traceable to the economic decentralization and individualism brought about by the development of commerce ([1752–1758] 1955, pp. 28–29). Making all allowances for gaps in Hume's knowledge of medieval society (with which he compared an industrial society) and for other shortcomings in his argument, his analysis—in its statement of the case for a liberal social order—deserves recognition as an early classic.

Compared to the *Wealth of Nations*, Hume's treatment of economics is brief. Hume, moreover, gave relatively little attention to the questions of value and distribution which absorbed much of Smith's analysis, and which were to become the dominant interest of the classical and neoclassical economists. In its theoretical treatment of psychological and historical influences, Hume's analysis, however, is both more comprehensive and more penetrating than Smith's, although Smith was more concerned with such influences than the generality of the later classical economists.

Since Hume's time, however, others have given these influences a prominent place in their work. The "historical" and "institutional" economists are cases in point. Other important themes that occur in Hume's work are to be found in contemporary economic literature. Most conspicuous is the revived interest in economic growth and in the cultural forces associated with this process, a product of the concern with underdeveloped economies. Also, interest in the question of full employment has led to a consideration of the psychology underlying aggregate behavior, while the shift in emphasis from impersonal markets to the role of individual units or collective entities (including business organizations and trade unions) and to the area of imperfect competition generally has likewise directed attention to a variety of psychological considerations not ordinarily stressed in "orthodox" economic analysis. In view of the rapidity of institutional change in recent decades, it is not surprising that the very question of the desirability of alternative institutional "systems" and the consequent normative and historical analysis of institutions should now be receiving increasing attention.

In various ways, these streams of thought differ from Hume's approach. Nonetheless, owing to Hume's remarkable capacity to treat important issues with a view to relevant psychological and historical factors, much of his economic thought still retains its freshness. In the standard literature it has long been the practice to give Hume relatively little attention (as one of a group of "predecessors" of Smith), although over the years several major technical aspects of his work have received general recognition. Hume's contribution can be fully appreciated, however, only when the body of his economic analysis as a whole is related to the context of broad and systematic social inquiry in which it was developed.

EUGENE ROTWEIN

[*Other relevant material may be found in* ECONOMIC GROWTH; HISTORY, *article on* THE PHILOSOPHY OF HISTORY; MONEY; UTILITARIANISM; *and in the biographies of* MANDEVILLE; RICARDO; SMITH, ADAM; TURGOT.]

WORKS BY HUME

(1739–1740) 1958 *A Treatise of Human Nature.* Edited by L. A. Selby-Bigge. Oxford: Clarendon. → Reprinted from the original edition; contains an analytical index.

(1739–1779) 1964 *The Philosophical Works.* 4 vols. Aalen (Germany): Scientia Verlag. → Volumes 1 and 2 are reprints of the 1886 edition, Volumes 3 and 4 reprinted from the 1882 edition.

(1741–1742) 1912 *Essays Moral, Political and Literary.* 2 vols. Edited by T. H. Green and T. H. Grose. New York and London: Longmans. → First published as *Essays Moral and Political* and changed to the above title in the 1758 edition.

(1751) 1957 *An Inquiry Concerning the Principles of Morals.* New York: Liberal Arts Press.

1752a *Political Discourses.* Edinburgh: Fleming.

(1752b) 1955 Of the Balance of Trade. Pages 60–77 in David Hume, *Writings on Economics.* Edited by Eugene Rotwein. London: Nelson; Madison: Univ. of Wisconsin Press.

(1752–1758) 1955 *Writings on Economics.* Edited by Eugene Rotwein. London: Nelson; Madison: Univ. of Wisconsin Press. → Also contains correspondence from 1749–1776.

(1754–1762) 1894 *The History of England.* 3 vols. London: Routledge.

WORKS ABOUT HUME

JESSOP, THOMAS E. 1938 *A Bibliography of David Hume and of Scottish Philosophy From Francis Hutcheson to Lord Balfour.* London and Hull: Brown.

MOSSNER, ERNEST C. 1954 *The Life of David Hume.* Austin: Univ. of Texas Press.

ROTWEIN, EUGENE 1955 Introduction. In David Hume, *Writings on Economics.* London: Nelson; Madison: Univ. of Wisconsin Press.

SCHATZ, ALBERT 1902 *L'oeuvre économique de David Hume.* Paris: Rousseau.

SMITH, NORMAN K. 1949 *The Philosophy of David Hume: A Critical Study of Its Origins and Central Doctrines.* London: Macmillan.

STEWART, JOHN B. 1963 *The Moral and Political Philosophy of David Hume.* New York: Columbia Univ. Press.